# Risk Management Association

# ANNUAL STATEMENT STUDIES

## FINANCIAL RATIO BENCHMARKS

**Volume II**

## 2024 2025

# RMA
Annual Statement Studies®
Copyright, Ordering, Licensing, and Use of Data Information

All of the information contained herein is obtained from sources believed to be accurate and reliable.

ALL REPRESENTATIONS CONTAINED HEREIN ARE BELIEVED BY RMA TO BE AS ACCURATE AS THE DATA AND METHODOLOGIES WILL ALLOW. HOWEVER, BECAUSE OF THE POSSIBILITIES OF HUMAN AND MECHANICAL ERROR, AS WELL AS UNFORESEEN FACTORS BEYOND RMA'S CONTROL, THE INFORMATION IN THIS BOOK IS PROVIDED "AS IS" WITHOUT WARRANTY OF ANY KIND. RMA MAKES NO REPRESENTATIONS OR WARRANTIES EXPRESS OR IMPLIED TO A SUBSCRIBER OR LICENSEE OR ANY OTHER PERSON OR ENTITY AS TO THE ACCURACY, TIMELINESS, COMPLETENESS, MERCHANTABILITY OR FITNESS FOR ANY PARTICULAR PURPOSE OF ANY OF THE INFORMATION CONTAINED IN THIS BOOK. MOREOVER, INFORMATION IS SUPPLIED WITHOUT WARRANTY ON THE UNDERSTANDING THAT ANY PERSON WHO ACTS UPON IT OR OTHERWISE CHANGES POSITION IN RELIANCE THEREON DOES SO ENTIRELY AT SUCH PERSON'S OWN RISK.

This Annual Statement Studies® book and information is not intended to provide loan advice or recommendations of any kind. The information contained herein is intended for educational, informational, and research purposes only. Accordingly, RMA does not offer any advice regarding the suitability of any loan, of any debtor or of any other business determination related to the information contained in this Annual Statement Studies® book. You use this book and information at your own risk, and RMA assumes no responsibility or liability for any advice or other guidance that you may take from this book or the information contained therein. Prior to making any business decisions, you should conduct all necessary due diligence as may be appropriate under the circumstances, and RMA assumes no responsibility or liability for any business decisions, including but not limited to loan decisions, or other services rendered by you based upon the Statement Studies® data or results obtained therefrom.

---

The Annual Statement Studies®:
*Financial Ratio Benchmarks*, 2024-2025
is a copyrighted product of RMA.
All rights reserved.
No part of this product may be copied, reproduced, replicated, disseminated, or distributed in any form or by any means, electronic or mechanical, without the express written permission of RMA.

---

To **obtain permission** to copy, quote, reproduce, replicate, disseminate, or distribute the Statement Studies® data/material please fax or email a brief letter stating who you are and how you intend to use the Statement Studies® data to: Statement Studies Information Products at fax number 215-446-4101 or via email to estatementstudies@rmahq.org. Depending on the requested use, RMA may require a license agreement and royalty fee.

A **License Agreement is required** if you wish to use or incorporate any portion of the data, in whole or in part in other products that will in turn be sold to others, such as in software oriented or derived products, scholarly publications, or training materials.

To **purchase** a copy, or additional copies, of the Statement Studies® data in book or online format, contact RMA's Customer Relations at 1-800-677-7621. Regional data presented in the same fashion as you see in this book is only available in eStatement Studies.

If you have a **question regarding the data** please reference the detailed explanatory notes provided in the Introduction section of the enclosed product. If you are unable to find the answer to your question, please contact us by e-mail at: estatementstudies@rmahq.org. Be sure to include your detailed question along with your telephone number, fax number, and email address.

The Risk Management Association
2005 Market Street, 36th Floor
Philadelphia, PA 19103
© 2024 by RMA
ISBN# 978-1-57070-365-2

# TABLE OF CONTENTS

Information on Copyright, Ordering, Licensing, and use of Data ... iii
List of Participating Institutions ... vi
Introduction to Statement Studies and Organization of Content ... viii
Definition of Ratios ... x
Explanation of Noncontractor Balance Sheet and Income Data ... xix
Explanation of Contractor—Percentage-of-Completion Basis of Accounting ... xx
IDP Sample Report ... xxiii
NAICS Codes Appearing in the Statement Studies ... 27
Full Descriptions of Industries Appearing in the Statement Studies ... 31

| | Description Index | Data Set Begins On |
|---|---|---|
| Agriculture, Forestry, Fishing and Hunting | 31 | 85 |
| Mining | 32 | 125 |
| Utilities | 33 | 141 |
| Construction—General Industries Format* | 33 | 157 |
| Manufacturing | 36 | 219 |
| Wholesale Trade | 50 | 587 |
| Retail Trade | 54 | 715 |
| Transportation and Warehousing | 57 | 797 |
| Information | 60 | 863 |
| Finance and Insurance | 61 | 893 |
| Real Estate and Rental and Leasing | 63 | 939 |
| Professional, Scientific and Technical Services | 64 | 983 |
| Management of Companies and Enterprises | 68 | 1059 |
| Administrative and Support and Waste Management and Remediation Services | 68 | 1065 |
| Educational Services | 71 | 1129 |
| Health Care and Social Assistance | 72 | 1149 |
| Arts, Entertainment and Recreation | 76 | 1225 |
| Accommodation and Food Services | 77 | 1257 |
| Other Services (Except Public Administration) | 78 | 1285 |
| Public Administration | 81 | 1345 |
| Construction—Percentage of Completion Basis of Accounting* | 82 | 1369 |

Supplemental Information:

Text—Key Word Index of Industries Appearing in the Statement Studies ... I
Construction Financial Management Association Data ... VII
RMA's Credit & Lending Dictionary ... XVII

*General Industries Format means that a valid construction NAICS was assigned to the subject companies contained in the sample; however, the financial statements were prepared using a general or traditional manufacturing or service industries presentation of results versus using a percentage-of-completion method of accounting. Industries found in the percentage-of-completion presentation follow the presentation used by RMA in the past.

## About Risk Management Association (RMA)

Founded in 1914, the Risk Management Association is a not-for-profit, member-driven professional association whose sole purpose is to advance the use of sound risk management principles in the financial services industry, including the farm credit sector. RMA promotes an enterprise approach to risk management that focuses on credit risk, market risk, and operational risk. Headquartered in Philadelphia, Pennsylvania, RMA has 1,600 institutional members that include banks of all sizes as well as nonbank financial institutions. They are represented in the Association by 35,000 individuals located throughout North America, Europe, Australia, and Asia/Pacific.

Guided by RMA's mission of advancing sound risk management principles, RMA brings financial institutions high-quality, cost-effective model risk management services delivered by a team of industry practitioners with more than 25 advanced degrees.

## RMA ACKNOWLEDGES AND THANKS THE FOLLOWING INSTITUTIONS, CONTRIBUTORS TO THE 2024 STATEMENT STUDIES DATA SUBMISSION PROGRAM.

**ARKANSAS**
Legacy National Bank

**CALIFORNIA**
Banc of California
Pinnacle Bank

**CONNECTICUT**
Dime Bank
Jewett City Savings Bank

**FLORIDA**
Axiom Bank National Association
Community Bank NA
EverBank

**HAWAII**
American Savings Bank

**IDAHO**
Washington Trust Bank

**ILLINOIS**
First Merchants Bank

**INDIANA**
1st Source Bank
First Merchants Bank

**IOWA**
MidWestOne Bank
Northwest Bank
The Security National Bank of Sioux City

**KANSAS**
Emprise Bank
Fidelity Bank, N.A.
Vintage Bank Kansas

**KENTUCKY**
Community Trust Bank, Inc.

**LOUISIANA**
b1Bank
Hancock Whitney Bank

**MAINE**
Bangor Savings Bank

**MARYLAND**
Harford Bank

**MASSACHUSETTS**
BankFive
Community Bank, N.A.
Eastern Bank
Enterprise Bank & Trust Co.
Pittsfield Cooperative Bank

**MICHIGAN**
Comerica Bank
Commercial Bank
First Merchants Bank
First National Bank of Michigan
First State Bank
Huron Community Bank
Mercantile Bank

**MINNESOTA**
Bremer Bank, NA
Community Resource Bank
First Minnetonka City Bank
Minnwest Bank
New Market Bank
Scale Bank

**MISSISSIPPI**
Cadence Bank
Hancock Whitney Bank
The Peoples Bank, Boloxi

**MISSOURI**
Academy Bank

**MONTANA**
First Interstate Bank

**NEBRASKA**
Union Bank and Trust

**NEW HAMPSHIRE**
Community Bank, N.A.

**NEW JERSEY**
The First National Bank of Elmer

**NEW YORK**
Community Bank, N.A.
Lake Shore Savings Bank
M&T Bank
NBT Bank, NA
The Adirondack Trust Company
TSB

**NORTH CAROLINA**
First Citizens Bank
HomeTrust Bank
Truist Financial Corporation

**NORTH DAKOTA**
Bell State Bank & Trust

**OHIO**
Community Bank NA
Fifth Third Bank
First Merchants Bank
First National Bank
Huntington National Bank

**OKLAHOMA**
First United Bank & Trust
Oklahoma Fidelity Bank, N.A.

**OREGON**
Bank of the Pacific
Washington Trust Bank

**PENNSYLVANIA**
1st SUMMIT BANK
Community Bank
Community Bank, N.A.
First Columbia Bank & Trust Co.
Fulton Bank
PNC Bank, National Association
QNB Bank
Somerset Trust Company
Washington Financial Bank

**RHODE ISLAND**
Citizens Financial Group
The Washington Trust Company

**SOUTH CAROLINA**
Southern First Bank
United Community

**SOUTH DAKOTA**
First PREMIER Bank
The First National Bank in Sioux Falls

**TENNESSEE**
First Horizon Bank
Pinnacle Bank

**TEXAS**
American Bank of Commerce
American National Bank of Texas
Frost Bank
Independent Financial
Southside Bank
Woodforest National Bank

**UTAH**
Cache Valley Bank

**VERMONT**
Union Bank

**VIRGINIA**
Atlantic Union Bank
First Community Bank
TowneBank
United Bank
Virginia National Bank

**WASHINGTON**
1st Security Bank of Washington
Bank of the Pacific
Banner Bank
HomeStreet Bank
Mountain Pacific Bank
Washington Trust Bank

**WEST VIRGINIA**
Wesbanco Bank Wheeling

**WISCONSIN**
Associated Bank N.A.
Bank Five Nine
Johnson Financial Group

# Introduction to Annual Statement Studies: Financial Ratio Benchmarks, 2024-2025 and General Organization of Content

The notes below will explain the presentation of *Annual Statement Studies: Financial Ratio Benchmarks*, describe how the book is organized, and answer most of your questions.

**The Quality You Expect from RMA:** RMA is the most respected source of objective, unbiased information on issues of importance to credit risk professionals. In its 105th year, RMA's *Annual Statement Studies®* has been the industry standard for comparison financial data. Material contained in today's *Annual Statement Studies* was first published in the March 1919 issue of the *Federal Reserve Bulletin*. In the days before computers, the *Annual Statement Studies* data was recorded in pencil on yellow ledger paper! Today, it features data for over 645 industries derived <u>directly</u> from more than 182,000 statements of financial institutions' borrowers and prospects.

- **Data That Comes Straight from Original Sources:** The more than 182,000 statements used to produce the composites presented here come directly from RMA member institutions and represent the financials from their commercial customers and prospects. RMA does not know the names of the individual entities. In fact, to ensure confidentiality, company names are removed before the data is even delivered to RMA. The raw data making up each composite is not available to any third party.

- **Data Presented in Common Size:** *Annual Statement Studies: Financial Ratio Benchmarks* contains composite financial data. Balance sheet and income statement information is shown in common size format, with each item a percentage of total assets and sales. RMA computes common size statements for each individual statement in an industry group, then aggregates and averages all the figures. In some cases, because of computer rounding, the figures to the right of the decimal point do not balance exactly with the totals shown. A minus sign beside the value indicates credits and losses.

- **Includes the Most Widely Used Ratios:** Nineteen of the most widely used ratios in the financial services industry accompany the balance sheet information, including various types of liquidity, coverage, leverage, and operating ratios.

- **Organized by the NAICS for Ease of Use:** This edition is organized according to the 2022 North American Industry Classification System (NAICS), a product of the U.S. Office of Management and Budget. At the top of each page of data, you will find the NAICS. Please note, the NAICS catalog is revised every FIVE years, in which industries may change code, description, or may be removed completely, while other industries may be added. For more information on the NAICS, visit the RMA site or: https://www.census.gov/naics/

- **Twenty Sections Outline Major Types of Businesses:** To provide further delineation, the book is divided into 20 sections outlining major lines of businesses. If you know the NAICS number you are looking for, use the NAICS-page guide provided in the front of this book. In general, the book is arranged in ascending NAICS numerical order. For your convenience, full descriptions of each NAICS are presented in this book. In addition, you will find a text-based index near the end of the book.

- **If You Do Not Know the NAICS Code You Are Looking for…** If you do not know the precise industry NAICS you are looking for, contact the Census Bureau at 1-888-75NAICS or naics@census.gov. Describe the activity of the establishment for which you need an industry code and you will receive a reply. Another source to help you assign the correct NAICS industry name and number can be found at https://www.census.gov/naics/ .

- **Can't Find the Industry You Want?** There are a number of reasons you may not find the industry you are looking for (i.e., you know you need industry xxxxxx but it is not in the product). Many times we have information on an industry, but it is not published because the sample size was too small or there were significant questions concerning the data. (For an industry to be displayed in the *Annual Statement Studies: Financial Ratio Benchmarks*, there must be at least 30 valid statements submitted to RMA.) In other instances, we simply do not have the data. Generally, most of what we receive is published.

- **Composite Data Not Shown?** When there are fewer than 10 financial statements in a particular asset or sales size category, the composite data is not shown because a sample this small is not considered representative and could be misleading. However, all the data for that industry is shown in the All Sizes column. The total number of statements for each size category is shown in bold print at the top of each column. In addition, the number of statements used in a ratio array will differ from the number of statements in a sample because certain elements of data may not be present in all financial statements. In these cases, the number of statements used is shown in parentheses to the left of the array.

- **Presentation of the Data on Each Page-Spread:** For all non-contracting spread statements, the data for a particular industry appears on both the left and right pages. The heading Current Data Sorted by Assets is in the five columns on the left side. The center section of the double-page presentation contains the Comparative Historical Data, with the All Sizes column for the current year shown under the heading 4/1/23-3/31/24. Comparable data from past editions of the *Annual Statement Studies: Financial Ratio Benchmarks* also appears in this section. Current Data Sorted by Sales is displayed in the five columns to the far right.

- **Companies with Less than $250 Million in Total Assets:** In our presentation, we used companies having less than $250 million in total assets—except in the case of contractors who use the percentage-of-completion method of accounting. *The section for contractors using the percentage-of-completion method of accounting contains data only sorted by revenue.* There is no upper limit placed on revenue size for any industry. Its information is found on only one page.

- **Page Headers:** The information shown at the top of each page includes the following: 1) the identity of the industry group; 2) its North American Industry Classification System (NAICS); 3) a breakdown by size categories of the types of financial statements reported; 4) the number of statements in each category; 5) the dates of the statements used; and 6) the size categories. For instance, 16 (4/1-9/30/23) means that 16 statements with fiscal dates between April 1 and September 30, 2023, make up part of the sample.

- **Page Footers:** At the bottom of each page, we have included the sum of the sales (or revenues) and total assets for all the financial statements in each size category. This data allows recasting of the common size statements into dollar amounts. To do this, divide the number at the bottom of the page by the number of statements in that size category. Then multiply the result by the percentages in the common size statement. Please note: The dollar amounts will be an approximation because RMA computes the balance sheet and income statement percentages for each individual statement in an industry group, then aggregates and averages all the figures.

- **Our Thanks to CFMA:** RMA appreciates the cooperation of the Construction Financial Management Association in permitting us to reproduce excerpts from its *Construction Industry Annual Financial Survey*. This data complements the RMA contractor industry data. For more details on this data, please visit www.cfma.org.

- **Recommended for Use as General Guidelines:** RMA recommends you use *Annual Statement Studies: Financial Ratio Benchmarks* data only as general guidelines and not as absolute industry norms. There are several reasons why the data may not be fully representative of a given industry:

    1. **Data Not Random** — The financial statements used in the *Annual Statement Studies: Financial Ratio Benchmarks* are not selected by any random or statistically reliable method. RMA member banks voluntarily submit the raw data they have available each year with no limitation on company size.

    2. **Categorized by Primary Product Only** — Many companies have varied product lines; however, the *Annual Statement Studies: Financial Ratio Benchmarks* categorizes them by their primary product NAICS number only.

    3. **Small Samples** — Some of the industry samples are small in relation to the total number of firms for a given industry. A relatively small sample can increase the chances that some composites do not fully represent an industry.

    4. **Extreme Statements** — An extreme or outlier statement can occasionally be present in a sample, causing a disproportionate influence on the industry composite. This is particularly true in a relatively small sample.

    5. **Operational Differences** — Companies within the same industry may differ in their method of operations, which in turn can directly influence their financial statements. Since they are included in the sample, these statements can significantly affect the composite calculations.

    6. **Additional Considerations** — There are other considerations that can result in variations among different companies engaged in the same general line of business. These include different labor markets, geographical location, different accounting methods, quality of products handled, sources and methods of financing, lease classification held by a lessee or lessor, and terms of sale.

    For these reasons, RMA does not recommend using the *Annual Statement Studies: Financial Ratio Benchmarks* figures as absolute norms for a given industry. Rather, you should use the figures only as general guidelines and as a supplement to the other methods of financial analysis. RMA makes no claim regarding how representative the figures printed in this book are.

# DEFINITION OF RATIOS
## Introduction

On each data page, below the common size balance sheet and income statement information, you will find a series of ratios computed from the financial statement data.

*Here is how these figures are calculated for any given ratio:*

1. The ratio is computed for each financial statement in the sample.

2. These values are arrayed (listed) in an order from the strongest to the weakest. In interpreting ratios, the "strongest" or "best" value is not always the largest numerical value, nor is the "weakest" always the lowest numerical value. (For certain ratios, there may be differing opinions as to what constitutes a strong or a weak value. RMA follows general banking guidelines consistent with sound credit practice to resolve this problem.)

3. The array of values is divided into four groups of equal size. The description of each ratio appearing in the *Statement Studies* provides details regarding the arraying of the values.

### What Are Quartiles?

Each ratio has three points, or "cutoff values," that divide an array of values into four equal-sized groups called quartiles, as shown below. The quartiles include the upper quartile, upper-middle quartile, lower-middle quartile, and the lower quartile. The upper quartile is the cutoff value where one-quarter of the array of ratios falls between it and the strongest ratio. The median is the midpoint—that is, the middle cutoff value where half of the array falls above it and half below it. The lower quartile is the point where one-quarter of the array falls between it and the weakest ratio. In many cases, the average of two values is used to arrive at the quartile value. You will find the median and quartile values on all *Statement Studies* data pages in the order indicated in the chart below.

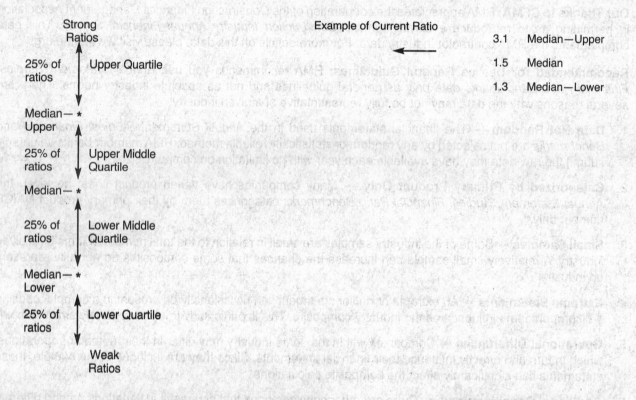

### Why Use Medians/Quartiles Instead of the Average?

There are several reasons why medians and quartiles are used instead of an average. Medians and quartiles eliminate the influence of an "outlier" (an extremely high or low value compared to the rest of the values). They also more accurately reflect the ranges of ratio values than a straight averaging method would.

It is important to understand that the spread (range) between the upper and lower quartiles represents the middle 50% of all the companies in a sample. Therefore, ratio values greater than the upper quartile or less than the lower quartile may begin to approach "unusual" values.

## Nonconventional Values:

For some ratio values, you will occasionally see an entry that is other than a conventional number. These entries are defined as follows:

(1) <u>UND</u> — This stands for "undefined," the result of the denominator in a ratio calculation approaching zero.

(2) <u>NM</u> — This may occasionally appear as a quartile or median for the ratios sales/working capital, debt/worth, and fixed/worth. It stands for "no meaning" in cases where the dispersion is so small that any interpretation is meaningless.

(3) <u>999.8</u> — When a ratio value equals 1,000 or more, it also becomes an "unusual" value and is given the "999.8" designation. This is considered to be a close enough approximation to the actual unusually large value.

## Linear versus Nonlinear Ratios:

An array that is ordered in ascending sequence or in descending sequence is linear. An array that deviates from true ascending or true descending when its values change from positive to negative (low to high positive, followed by high to low negative) is non-linear.

A specific example of a nonlinear ratio would be the Sales/Working Capital ratio. In other words, when the Sales/Working Capital ratio is positive, then the top quartile would be represented by the *lowest positive* ratio. However, if the ratio is negative, the top quartile will be represented by the *highest negative* ratio! In a nonlinear array such as this, the median could be either positive or negative because it is whatever the middle value is in the particular array of numbers.

### Nonlinear Ratios
Sales/Working Capital
Fixed/Worth
Debt/Worth

### Linear Ratios
Current Ratio
Quick Ratio
Sales Receivables
Days' Receivables
Cost of Sales/Inventory
Days' Inventory
Cost of Sales/Payables
Days' Payables
EBIT/Interest
Net Profit + Deprec, Depletion, Amort/Current Maturities Long-Term Debt
% Profits Before Taxes/Tangible Net Worth
% Profits Before Taxes/Total Assets
Sales/Net Fixed Assets
Sales/Total Assets
% Depreciation, Depletion, Amortization/Sales
% Officers', Directors', Owners' Compensation/Sales

## Important Notes on Ratios:

*Turnover Ratios* — For certain ratios (sales/receivables, cost of sales/inventory, cost of sales/payables) you will see two numbers, one in **BOLD** and one in regular type. These ratios are generally called turnover ratios. The number in **BOLD** represents **the number of days** and the number in regular type is **the number of times**. Please see the definition of sales/receivables on the following pages for a more complete description of the two types of calculations and what each means.

*Inventory Presentations* — **Inventory presentations** are based on fiscal year-end point-in-time balances, not averages. In addition, our data capture does not permit us to know what method of inventory accounting (LIFO or FIFO, for instance) was used.

The following ratios contained in the *Statement Studies* are grouped into five principal categories: liquidity, coverage, leverage, operating, and specific expense items.

# LIQUIDITY RATIOS

Liquidity is a measure of the quality and adequacy of current assets to meet current obligations as they come due. In other words, can a firm quickly convert its assets to cash — without a loss in value — in order to meet its immediate and short-term obligations? For firms such as utilities that can readily and accurately predict their cash inflows, liquidity is not nearly as critical as it is for firms like airlines or manufacturing businesses that can have wide fluctuations in demand and revenue streams. These ratios provide a level of comfort to lenders in case of liquidation.

## 1. Current Ratio

**How to Calculate:** Divide total current assets by total current liabilities.

$$\frac{\text{Total Current Assets}}{\text{Total Current Liabilities}}$$

**How to Interpret:** This ratio is a rough indication of a firm's ability to service its current obligations. Generally, the higher the current ratio, the greater the "cushion" between current obligations and a firm's ability to pay them. While a stronger ratio shows that the numbers for current assets exceed those for current liabilities, the composition and quality of current assets are critical factors in the analysis of an individual firm's liquidity.

The ratio values are arrayed from the highest positive to the lowest positive.

## 2. Quick Ratio

**How to Calculate:** Add cash and equivalents to trade receivables. Then, divide by total current liabilities.

$$\frac{\text{Cash \& Equivalents + Trade Receivables (net)}}{\text{Total Current Liabilities}}$$

**How to Interpret:** Also known as the "acid test" ratio, this is a stricter, more conservative measure of liquidity than the current ratio. This ratio reflects the degree to which a company's current liabilities are covered by its most liquid current assets, the kind of assets that can be converted quickly to cash and at amounts close to book value. Inventory and other less liquid current assets are removed from the calculation. Generally, if the ratio produces a value that's less than 1 to 1, it implies a "dependency" on inventory or other "less" current assets to liquidate short-term debt.

The ratio values are arrayed from the highest positive to the lowest positive.

## 3. Sales/Receivables

**How to Calculate:** Divide net sales by trade receivables.

$$\frac{\text{Net Sales}}{\text{Trade Receivables (net)}}$$

*Please note* — In the contractor section, both accounts receivable-progress billings and accounts receivable-current retention are included in the receivables figure used in calculating the revenues/receivables and receivables/payables ratios.

**How to Interpret:** This ratio measures the number of times trade receivables turn over during the year. The higher the turnover of receivables, the shorter the time between sale and cash collection.

> For example, a company with sales of $720,000 and receivables of $120,000 would have a sales/receivables ratio of 6.0. This means receivables turn over six times a year. If a company's receivables appear to be turning more slowly than the rest of the industry, further research is needed and the quality of the receivables should be examined closely.

*Cautions* — A problem with this ratio is that it compares one day's receivables, shown at statement date, to total annual sales and does not take into consideration seasonal fluctuations. An additional problem in interpretation may arise when there is a large proportion of cash sales to total sales.

When the receivables figure is zero, the quotient will be undefined (UND) and represents the best possible ratio. The ratio values are therefore arrayed starting with undefined (UND) and then from the numerically highest value to the numerically lowest value. The only time a zero will appear in the array is when the sales figure is low and the quotient rounds off to zero. By definition, this ratio cannot be negative.

### 4. Days' Receivables

The sales/receivables ratio will have a figure printed in bold type directly to the left of the array. This figure is the days' receivables.

**How to Calculate the Days' Receivables:** Divide the sales/receivables ratio into 365 (the number of days in one year).

$$\frac{365}{\text{Sales/Receivable ratio}}$$

**How to Interpret the Days' Receivables:** This figure expresses the average number of days that receivables are outstanding. Generally, the greater the number of days outstanding, the greater the probability of delinquencies in accounts receivable. A comparison of a company's daily receivables may indicate the extent of a company's control over credit and collections.

*Please note* — You should take into consideration the terms offered by a company to its customers because these may differ from terms within the industry.

*For example*, using the sales/receivable ratio calculated above, 365 ÷ 6 = 61 (i.e., the average receivable is collected in 61 days).

### 5. Cost of Sales/Inventory

**How to Calculate:** Divide cost of sales by inventory.

$$\frac{\text{Cost of Sales}}{\text{Inventory}}$$

**How to Interpret:** This ratio measures the number of times inventory is turned over during the year.

*High Inventory Turnover* — On the positive side, high inventory turnover can indicate greater liquidity or superior merchandising. Conversely, it can indicate a shortage of needed inventory for sales.

*Low Inventory Turnover* — Low inventory turnover can indicate poor liquidity, possible overstocking, or obsolescence. On the positive side, it could indicate a planned inventory buildup in the case of material shortages.

*Cautions* — A problem with this ratio is that it compares one day's inventory to cost of goods sold and does not take seasonal fluctuations into account. When the inventory figure is zero, the quotient will be undefined (UND) and represents the best possible ratio. The ratio values are arrayed starting with undefined (UND) and then from the numerically highest value to the numerically lowest value. The only time a zero will appear in the array is when the figure for cost of sales is very low and the quotient rounds off to zero.

*Please note* — For service industries, the cost of sales is included in operating expenses. In addition, please note that the data collection process does not differentiate the method of inventory valuation.

### 6. Days' Inventory

The days' inventory is the figure printed in bold directly to the left of the cost of sales/inventory ratio.

**How to Calculate the Days' Inventory:** Divide the cost of sales/inventory ratio into 365 (the number of days in one year).

$$\frac{365}{\text{Cost of Sales/Inventory ratio}}$$

**How to Interpret:** Dividing the inventory turnover ratio into 365 days yields the average length of time units are in inventory.

## 7. Cost of Sales/Payables

**How to Calculate:** Divide cost of sales by trade payables.

$$\frac{\text{Cost of Sales}}{\text{Trade Payables}}$$

*Please note* — In the contractor section, both accounts payable-trade and accounts payable-retention are included in the payables figure used in calculating the cost of revenues/payables and receivables/payables ratios.

**How to Interpret:** This ratio measures the number of times trade payables turn over during the year. The higher the turnover of payables, the shorter the time between purchase and payment. If a company's payables appear to be turning more slowly than the industry, then the company may be experiencing cash shortages, disputing invoices with suppliers, enjoying extended terms, or deliberately expanding its trade credit. The ratio comparison of company to industry suggests the existence of these or other possible causes. If a firm buys on 30-day terms, it is reasonable to expect this ratio to turn over in approximately 30 days.

*Cautions* — A problem with this ratio is that it compares one day's payables to cost of goods sold and does not take seasonal fluctuations into account. When the payables figure is zero, the quotient will be undefined (UND) and represents the best possible ratio. The ratio values are arrayed starting with undefined (UND) and then from the numerically highest to the numerically lowest value. The only time a zero will appear in the array is when the figure for cost of sales is very low and the quotient rounds off to zero.

## 8. Days' Payables

The days' payables is the figure printed in bold type directly to the left of the cost of sales/payables ratio.

**How to Calculate the Days' Payables:** Divide the cost of sales/payables ratio into 365 (the number of days in one year).

$$\frac{365}{\text{Cost of Sales/Payables ratio}}$$

**How to Interpret:** Division of the payables turnover ratio into 365 days yields the average length of time trade debt is outstanding.

## 9. Sales/Working Capital

**How to Calculate:** Divide net sales by net working capital (current assets less current liabilities equals net working capital).

$$\frac{\text{Net Sales}}{\text{Net Working Capital}}$$

**How to Interpret:** Because it reflects the ability to finance current operations, working capital is a measure of the margin of protection for current creditors. When you relate the level of sales resulting from operations to the underlying working capital, you can measure how efficiently working capital is being used.

*Low ratio* (close to zero) — A low ratio may indicate an inefficient use of working capital.

*High ratio* (high positive or high negative) — A very high ratio often signifies overtrading, which is a vulnerable position for creditors.

*Please note* — The sales/working capital ratio is a nonlinear array. In other words, it is an array that is NOT ordered from highest positive to highest negative as is the case for linear arrays. The ratio values are arrayed from the lowest positive to the highest positive, to undefined (UND), and then from the highest negative to the lowest negative. If working capital is zero, the quotient is undefined (UND).

If the sales/working capital ratio is positive, then the top quartile would be represented by the lowest positive ratio. However, if the ratio is negative, the top quartile will be represented by the highest negative ratio! In a nonlinear array such as the sales/working capital ratio, the median could be either positive or negative because it is whatever the middle value is in the particular array of numbers.

*Cautions* — When analyzing this ratio, you need to focus on working capital, not on the sales figure. Although sales cannot be negative, working capital can be. If you have a large, positive working capital number, the ratio will be small *and* positive — which is good. Because negative working capital is bad, if you have a large, negative working capital number, the sales/working capital ratio will be small *and* negative — which is NOT good. Therefore, the lowest positive ratio is the best and the lowest negative ratio is the worst. If working capital is a small negative number, the ratio will be large, which is the best of the negatives.

## COVERAGE RATIOS

Coverage ratios measure a firm's ability to service its debt. In other words, how well does the flow of a company's funds cover its short-term financial obligations? In contrast to liquidity ratios that focus on the possibility of liquidation, coverage ratios seek to provide lenders a comfort level based on the belief the firm will remain a viable enterprise.

### 1. Earnings Before Interest and Taxes (EBIT)/Interest

**How to Calculate:** Divide earnings (profit) before annual interest expense and taxes by annual interest expense.

$$\frac{\text{Earnings Before Interest \& Taxes}}{\text{Annual Interest Expense}}$$

**How to Interpret:** This ratio measures a firm's ability to meet interest payments. A high ratio may indicate that a borrower can easily meet the interest obligations of a loan. This ratio also indicates a firm's capacity to take on additional debt.

*Please note* — Only statements reporting annual interest expense were used in the calculation of this ratio. The ratio values are arrayed from the highest positive to the lowest positive and then from the lowest negative to the highest negative.

### 2. Net Profit + Depreciation, Depletion, Amortization/Current Maturities Long-Term Debt

**How to Calculate:** Add net profit to depreciation, depletion, and amortization expenses. Then, divide by the current portion of long-term debt.

$$\frac{\text{Net Profit + Depreciation, Depletion, Amortization Expenses}}{\text{Current Portion of Long-Term Debt}}$$

**How to Interpret:** This ratio reflects how well cash flow from operations covers current maturities. Because cash flow is the primary source of debt retirement, the ratio measures a firm's ability to service principal repayment and take on additional debt. Even though it is a mistake to believe all cash flow is available for debt service, this ratio is still a valid measure of the ability to service long-term debt.

*Please note* — Only data for corporations with the following items was used:

(1) Profit or loss after taxes (positive, negative, or zero).

(2) A positive figure for depreciation/depletion/amortization expenses.

(3) A positive figure for current maturities of long-term debt.

Ratio values are arrayed from the highest to the lowest positive and then from the lowest to the highest negative.

## LEVERAGE RATIOS

How much protection do a company's assets provide for the debt held by its creditors? Highly leveraged firms are companies with heavy debt in relation to their net worth. These firms are more vulnerable to business downturns than those with lower debt-to-worth positions. While leverage ratios help measure this vulnerability, keep in mind that these ratios vary greatly depending on the requirements of particular industry groups.

## 1. Fixed/Worth

**How to Calculate:** Divide fixed assets (net of accumulated depreciation) by tangible net worth (net worth minus intangibles).

$$\frac{\text{Net Fixed Assets}}{\text{Tangible Net Worth}}$$

**How to Interpret:** This ratio measures the extent to which owner's equity (capital) has been invested in plant and equipment (fixed assets). A lower ratio indicates a proportionately smaller investment in fixed assets in relation to net worth and a better "cushion" for creditors in case of liquidation. Similarly, a higher ratio would indicate the opposite situation. The presence of a substantial number of fixed assets that are leased — and not appearing on the balance sheet — may result in a deceptively lower ratio.

Fixed assets may be zero, in which case the quotient is zero. If tangible net worth is zero, the quotient is undefined (UND). If tangible net worth is negative, the quotient is negative.

*Please note* — Like the sales/working capital ratio discussed above, this fixed/worth ratio is a nonlinear array. In other words, it is an array that is NOT ordered from highest positive to highest negative as a linear array would be. The ratio values are arrayed from the lowest positive to the highest positive, to undefined (UND), and then from the highest negative to the lowest negative.

If the Fixed/Worth ratio is positive, then the top quartile would be represented by the lowest positive ratio. However, if the ratio is negative, the top quartile will be represented by the highest negative ratio! In a nonlinear array such as this, the median could be either positive or negative because it is whatever the middle value is in the particular array of numbers.

## 2. Debt/Worth

**How to Calculate:** Divide total liabilities by tangible net worth.

$$\frac{\text{Total Liabilities}}{\text{Tangible Net Worth}}$$

**How to Interpret:** This ratio expresses the relationship between capital contributed by creditors and that contributed by owners. Basically, it shows how much protection the owners are providing creditors. The higher the ratio, the greater the risk being assumed by creditors. A lower ratio generally indicates greater long-term financial safety. Unlike a highly leveraged firm, a firm with a low debt/worth ratio usually has greater flexibility to borrow in the future.

Tangible net worth may be zero, in which case the ratio is undefined (UND). Tangible net worth may also be negative, which results in the quotient being negative. The ratio values are arrayed from the lowest to highest positive, to undefined, and then from the highest to lowest negative.

*Please note* — Like the sales/working capital ratio discussed above, this debt/worth ratio is a nonlinear array. In other words, it is an array that is NOT ordered from highest positive to highest negative as a linear array would be. The ratio values are arrayed from the lowest positive to the highest positive, to undefined (UND), and then from the highest negative to the lowest negative.

If the debt/worth ratio is positive, then the top quartile would be represented by the *lowest positive* ratio. However, if the ratio is negative, the top quartile will be represented by the *highest negative* ratio! In a nonlinear array such as this, the median could be either positive or negative because it is whatever the middle value is in the particular array of numbers.

## OPERATING RATIOS

Operating ratios are designed to assist in the evaluation of management performance.

### 1. % Profits Before Taxes/Tangible Net Worth

**How to Calculate:** Divide profit before taxes by tangible net worth. Then, multiply by 100.

$$\frac{\text{Profit Before Taxes}}{\text{Tangible Net Worth}} \times 100$$

**How to Interpret:** This ratio expresses the rate of return on tangible capital employed. While it can serve as an indicator of management performance, you should always use it in conjunction with other ratios. Normally associated with effective management, a high return could actually point to an undercapitalized firm. Conversely, a low return that's usually viewed as an indicator of inefficient management performance could actually reflect a highly capitalized, conservatively operated business.

This ratio has been multiplied by 100 because it is shown as a percentage.

Profit before taxes may be zero, in which case the ratio is zero. Profits before taxes may be negative, resulting in negative quotients. Firms with negative tangible net worth have been omitted from the ratio arrays. Negative ratios will therefore only result in the case of negative profit before taxes. If the tangible net worth is zero, the quotient is undefined (UND). If there are fewer than 10 ratios for a particular size class, the result is not shown. The ratio values are arrayed starting with undefined (UND), then from the highest to the lowest positive values, and finally from the lowest to the highest negative values.

### 2. % Profits Before Taxes/Total Assets

**How to Calculate:** Divide profit before taxes by total assets and multiply by 100.

$$\frac{\text{Profit Before Taxes}}{\text{Total Assets}} \times 100$$

**How to Interpret:** This ratio expresses the pre-tax return on total assets and measures the effectiveness of management in employing the resources available to it. If a specific ratio varies considerably from the ranges found in this book, the analyst will need to examine the makeup of the assets and take a closer look at the earnings figure. A heavily depreciated plant and a large amount of intangible assets or unusual income or expense items will cause distortions of this ratio.

This ratio has been multiplied by 100 since it is shown as a percentage. If profit before taxes is zero, the quotient is zero. If profit before taxes is negative, the quotient is negative. These ratio values are arrayed from the highest to the lowest positive and then from the lowest to the highest negative.

### 3. Sales/Net Fixed Assets

**How to Calculate:** Divide net sales by net fixed assets (net of accumulated depreciation).

$$\frac{\text{Net Sales}}{\text{Net Fixed Assets}}$$

**How to Interpret:** This ratio is a measure of the productive use of a firm's fixed assets. Largely depreciated fixed assets or a labor-intensive operation may cause a distortion of this ratio.

If the net fixed figure is zero, the quotient is undefined (UND). The only time a zero will appear in the array will be when the net sales figure is low and the quotient rounds off to zero. These ratio values cannot be negative.

They are arrayed from undefined (UND) and then from the highest to the lowest positive values.

### 4. Sales/Total Assets

**How to Calculate:** Divide net sales by total assets.

$$\frac{\text{Net Sales}}{\text{Total Assets}}$$

**How to Interpret:** This ratio is a general measure of a firm's ability to generate sales in relation to total assets. It should be used only to compare firms within specific industry groups and in conjunction with other operating ratios to determine the effective employment of assets.

The only time a zero will appear in the array will be when the net sales figure is low and the quotient rounds off to zero. The ratio values cannot be negative. They are arrayed from the highest to the lowest positive values.

# EXPENSE TO SALES RATIOS

The following two ratios relate specific expense items to net sales and express this relationship as a percentage. Comparisons are convenient because the item, net sales, is used as a constant. Variations in these ratios are most pronounced between capital- and labor-intensive industries.

### 1. % Depreciation, Depletion, Amortization/Sales

**How to Calculate:** Divide annual depreciation, amortization, and depletion expenses by net sales and multiply by 100.

$$\frac{\text{Depreciation, Amortization, Depletion Expenses}}{\text{Net Sales}} \times 100$$

### 2. % Officers', Directors', Owners' Compensation/Sales

**How to Calculate:** Divide annual officers', directors', owners' compensation by net sales and multiply by 100. Include total salaries, bonuses, commissions, and other monetary remuneration to all officers, directors, and/or owners of the firm during the year covered by the statement. This includes drawings of partners and proprietors.

$$\frac{\text{Officers', Directors', Owners' Compensation}}{\text{Net Sales}} \times 100$$

Only statements showing a positive figure for each of the expense categories shown above were used. The ratios are arrayed from the lowest to highest positive values.

# Explanation of Noncontractor Balance Sheet and Income Data

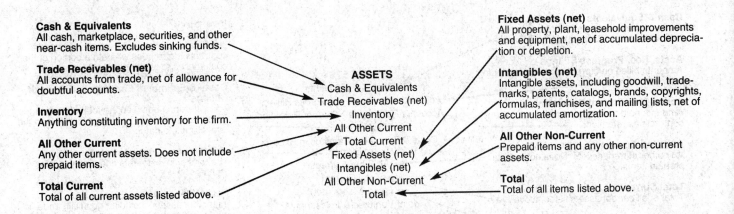

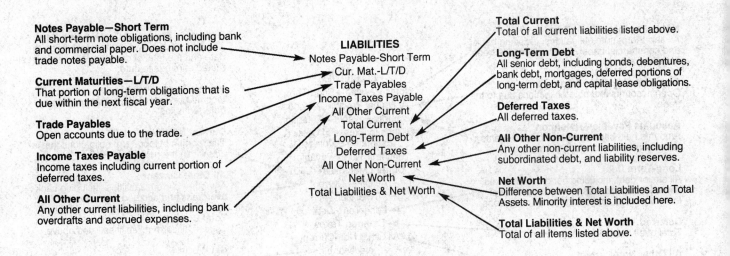

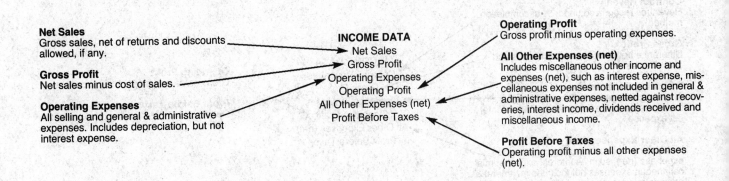

# Explanation of Contractor Percentage-of-Completion Basis of Accounting Balance Sheet and Income Data

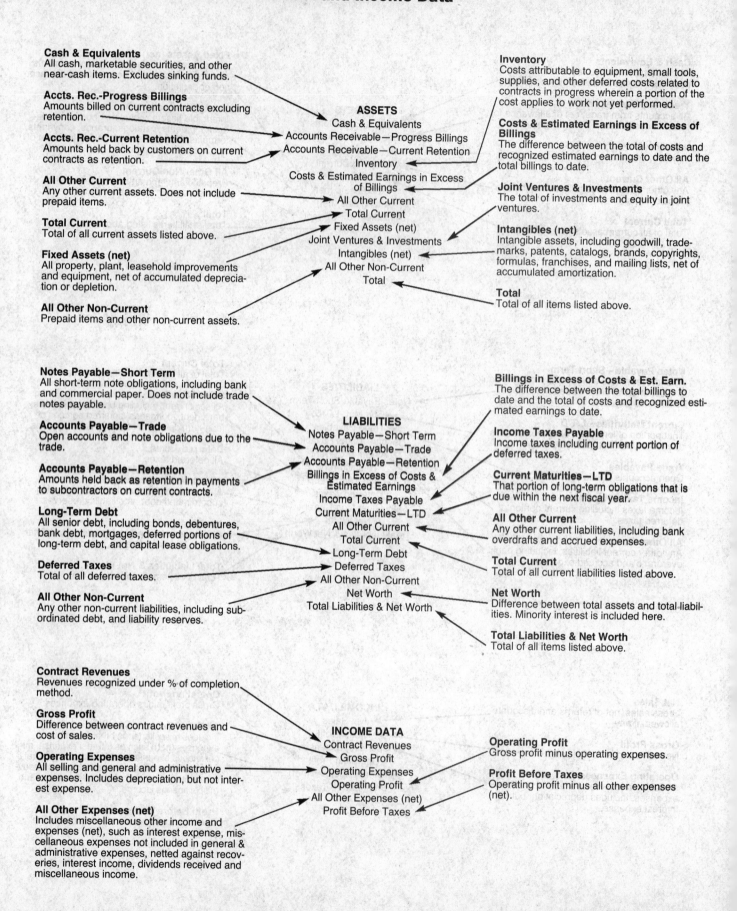

**For further analysis, please refer to *Industry Default Probabilities and Cash Flow Measures***

If you think *Financial Ratio Benchmarks* is a valuable resource, wait until you see its companion study. Now in its twenty-third year and bigger than ever, *Industry Default Probabilities and Cash Flow Measures* is a major expansion of our *Annual Statement Studies*. These benchmarks add substantial value to the critical analysis of cash flow for private companies.

The latest edition of *Industry Default Probabilities and Cash Flow Measures* includes many new industries, stronger statements, five years of historical data sorted by assets and sales. In short, it is more like our traditional *Statement Studies*.

*Industry Default Probabilities and Cash Flow Measures* includes:
- Cash flow measures on a common-size percentage scale. Ratios include:
  - Cash from Trading
  - Cash after Operations
  - Net Cash after Operations
  - Cash after Debt Amortization
  - Debt Service P&I Coverage
  - Interest Coverage (Operating Cash)
- Change in position, normalized, year over year, for eight financial statement line items. Ratios include:
  - Change in Inventory
  - Total Current Assets (TCA)
  - Total Assets (TA)
  - Retained Earnings (RE)
  - Net Sales (NS)
  - Cost of Goods Sold (CGS)
  - Profit before Interest & Taxes (PBIT)
  - Depreciation/Depletion/Amortization (DDA)
- Trend data available for the past five years.
- Other ratios:
  - Sustainable Growth Rate
  - Funded Debt/EBITDA
- Data arrayed by asset and sales size.

**Access to the Industry Default Probabilities and Cash Flow Measures is only available in the eStatement Studies online database. A copy of a sample report can be found on the next page. For more information on how to upgrade to eStatement Studies, please see the inside back cover, or contact us at 1-800-677-7621.**

# INDUSTRY DEFAULT PROBABILITIES AND CASH FLOW MEASURES SAMPLE REPORT

## AGRICULTURE—Soybean Farming  NAICS 111110

| Current Data Sorted by Assets | | | | | | | Comparative Historical Data | |
|---|---|---|---|---|---|---|---|---|
| | 2 | 1<br>3<br>2 | 4<br>3 | 1 | 1 | **Type of Statement**<br>Unqualified<br>Reviewed<br>Compiled<br>Tax Returns<br>Other | 10<br>5<br>5<br>25<br>33 | 20<br>19<br>12<br>30<br>52 |
| 6<br>2 | 2<br>8<br>5 | 1<br>6<br>9 | 1<br>3 | | | | 4/1/13-<br>3/31/14 | 4/1/14-<br>3/31/15 |
| 0-500M<br>8 | 7 (4/1-9/30/17)<br>500M-2MM<br>17 | 2-10MM<br>20 | 53 (10/1/17-3/31/18)<br>10-50MM<br>11 | 50-100MM<br>3 | 100-250MM<br>1 | Assets Size<br>Number of Statements | ALL<br>78 | ALL<br>133 |
| % | % | % | % | % | % | | % | % |

| | | | | | | | | |
|---|---|---|---|---|---|---|---|---|
| % | % | % | % | % | % | **CASH FLOW MEASURES** | % | % |
| | | | | | | Cash from<br>Trading/Sales | | |
| | 17.2<br>6.5<br>-16.9 | 38.9<br>19.3<br>3.9 | 25.1<br>9.7<br>-1.7 | | | Cash after<br>Operations/Sales | (76) 25.3<br>10.5<br>4.8 | 26.4<br>10.0<br>3.2 |
| | 16.7<br>5.3<br>-.3 | 28.1<br>15.0<br>2.6 | 23.8<br>9.0<br>2.1 | | | Net Cash after<br>Operations/Sales | (76) 25.8<br>10.7<br>5.3 | 26.3<br>11.7<br>3.9 |
| (16) | 12.6<br>5.7<br>-3.0 | 5.6<br>.9<br>-11.2 | 4.9<br>-2.2<br>-6.7 | | | Net Cash after Debt<br>Amortization/Sales | (76) 12.5<br>4.1<br>-2.3 | 8.7<br>2.2<br>-2.6 |
| (14) | 14.7<br>9.6<br>-.2 | 2.4<br>1.3 (16)<br>.1 | 29.3<br>2.2 (10)<br>.0 | | | Debt Service<br>P&I Coverage | (68) 7.1<br>2.8 (120)<br>.8 | 6.0<br>2.4<br>1.1 |
| (13) | 51.9<br>8.3<br>-3.3 | 22.1<br>5.7 (16)<br>.5 | 59.6<br>16.3 (10)<br>2.2 | | | Interest Coverage<br>(Operating Cash) | (66) 18.4<br>5.1 (118)<br>1.3 | 24.1<br>7.0<br>2.5 |
| | | 48.0<br>-.5 (10)<br>-17.4 | | | | Δ Inventory | (43) 31.5<br>6.0 (66)<br>-6.6 | 22.9<br>4.1<br>-5.9 |
| | 28.6<br>2.8<br>-35.1 | 31.7<br>10.5<br>-20.4 | 4.9<br>-6.2<br>-26.1 | | | Δ Total Current Assets | 47.0<br>14.1<br>-13.4 | 49.4<br>9.1<br>-12.6 |
| | 36.3<br>3.1<br>-5.8 | 20.8<br>3.1<br>-7.7 | 8.3<br>-1.9<br>-5.7 | | | Δ Total Assets | 26.9<br>6.1<br>-3.5 | 24.1<br>4.9<br>-3.7 |
| (15) | 111.1<br>10.8<br>-72.0 | 32.9<br>4.2 (19)<br>-38.7 | 6.6<br>-15.0<br>-91.3 | | | Δ Retained Earnings | (76) 82.3<br>17.1 (131)<br>-.8 | 36.6<br>10.1<br>-4.3 |
| | 34.7<br>-2.5<br>-11.7 | 13.8<br>6.9<br>.3 | 16.5<br>5.4<br>-7.8 | | | Δ Net Sales | 27.9<br>10.0<br>-2.3 | 23.3<br>3.2<br>-6.3 |
| | | | | | | Δ Cost of Goods Sold | | |
| (16) | 96.1<br>.7<br>-44.8 | 88.0<br>13.6<br>-34.1 | 73.5<br>-7.4<br>-47.6 | | | Δ Profit before<br>Int. & Taxes | 120.8<br>35.5 (131)<br>-18.0 | 82.7<br>14.9<br>-35.3 |
| (12) | 67.7<br>-21.3<br>-81.6 | 12.6<br>2.3 (18)<br>-15.8 | 100.7<br>7.7<br>-31.1 | | | Δ Depr./Depl./Amort. | (69) 11.3<br>-4.7 (118)<br>-33.6 | 21.1<br>.0<br>-16.3 |
| | | | | | | **RATIOS** | | |
| | 64.9<br>.0<br>-39.7 | 50.4<br>17.7<br>-.2 | 12.5<br>-.1<br>-11.5 | | | Sustainable<br>Growth Rate | (77) 16.1<br>.1 (131)<br>-17.7 | 26.3<br>5.6<br>-7.9 |
| | .0<br>1.0<br>3.4 | .6<br>1.4<br>8.3 | .5<br>8.2<br>15.4 | | | Funded Debt/EBITDA | .5<br>2.1<br>5.9 | .6<br>2.2<br>7.6 |
| 9580M<br>2078M | 42882M<br>21645M | 289548M<br>95307M | 468863M<br>207335M | 141379M<br>218849M | 56029M<br>105246M | Net Sales ($)<br>Total Assets ($) | 1170146M<br>874532M | 3006125M<br>1601154M |

M = $ thousand    MM = $ million

© RMA 2018

## AGRICULTURE—Soybean Farming  NAICS 111110

| Comparative Historical Data | | | Type of Statement | Current Data Sorted by Sales | | | | | |
|---|---|---|---|---|---|---|---|---|---|
| 14 | 6 | 7 | Unqualified | | 1 | | | | 5 |
| 13 | 5 | 8 | Reviewed | 1 | 1 | | 3 | 2 | 2 |
| 9 | 8 | 3 | Compiled | | 1 | 1 | | 1 | |
| 31 | 23 | 21 | Tax Returns | 5 | 12 | 2 | 2 | 4 | 5 |
| 50 | 40 | 21 | Other | 5 | 4 | | 4 | | |
| 4/1/15- | 4/1/16- | 4/1/17- | | | 7 (4/1-9/30/17) | | 53 (10/1/17-3/31/18) | | |
| 3/31/16 | 3/31/17 | 3/31/18 | | 0-1MM | 1-3MM | 3-5MM | 5-10MM | 10-25MM | 25MM & OVER |
| ALL | ALL | ALL | Sales Size | | | | | | |
| 117 | 82 | 60 | Number of Statements | 10 | 19 | 4 | 8 | 7 | 12 |
| % | % | % | | % | % | % | % | % | % |

| | | | | | | | | | | | | | |
|---|---|---|---|---|---|---|---|---|---|---|---|---|---|
| | % | | % | | % | **CASH FLOW MEASURES** | % | | % | % | % | % | % |
| | | | | | | Cash from Trading/Sales | | | | | | | |
| | 25.2 | | 18.7 | | 22.0 | Cash after | 98.9 | | 22.7 | | | | 9.8 |
| | 10.0 | | 5.0 | | 6.7 | Operations/Sales | 19.0 | | 18.9 | | | | 6.3 |
| | 3.6 | | -2.1 | | -1.9 | | -15.4 | | 3.6 | | | | 1.9 |
| | 24.1 | | 18.4 | | 20.4 | Net Cash after | 90.5 | | 27.2 | | | | 9.6 |
| (116) | 10.0 | | 5.8 | | 7.5 | Operations/Sales | 1.0 | | 17.1 | | | | 7.1 |
| | 4.5 | | .0 | | 1.1 | | -19.1 | | 4.9 | | | | 1.9 |
| | 14.5 | | 5.7 | | 8.8 | Net Cash after Debt | 3.0 | | 11.8 | | | | 3.7 |
| (116) | 2.7 | (81) | .7 | (59) | .0 | Amortization/Sales | -15.4 | | 8.8 | | | | -1.0 |
| | -3.5 | | -6.0 | | -6.7 | | -65.5 | | -2.6 | | | | -5.4 |
| | 8.9 | | 8.9 | | 11.9 | Debt Service | | | 13.4 | | | | 13.1 |
| (95) | 2.6 | (70) | 1.9 | (50) | 1.7 | P&I Coverage | (16) | | 7.4 | | | (11) | 2.4 |
| | .7 | | .0 | | .0 | | | | .5 | | | | .6 |
| | 21.5 | | 22.4 | | 23.9 | Interest Coverage | | | 42.8 | | | | 30.4 |
| (90) | 6.0 | (64) | 5.8 | (49) | 5.1 | (Operating Cash) | (15) | | 10.9 | | | (11) | 13.1 |
| | 2.2 | | .0 | | .0 | | | | 1.8 | | | | 1.2 |
| | 13.8 | | 25.6 | | 38.4 | Δ Inventory | | | | | | | |
| (49) | .0 | (42) | -1.0 | (27) | 1.6 | | | | | | | | |
| | -17.5 | | -19.5 | | -15.4 | | | | | | | | |
| | 47.1 | | 38.8 | | 23.3 | | -15.8 | | 39.4 | | | | 11.7 |
| | 4.4 | | 3.7 | | 2.1 | Δ Total Current Assets | -49.2 | | 13.7 | | | | .5 |
| | -15.0 | | -17.3 | | -25.0 | | -80.4 | | -26.1 | | | | -10.4 |
| | 27.3 | | 16.8 | | 21.0 | | 34.7 | | 33.9 | | | | 9.3 |
| | 3.3 | | -.4 | | 2.4 | Δ Total Assets | -7.1 | | 8.3 | | | | -2.8 |
| | -4.0 | | -9.0 | | -7.7 | | -61.7 | | -5.6 | | | | -5.5 |
| | 45.7 | | 44.3 | | 35.5 | | 28.5 | | 135.5 | | | | 5.6 |
| (112) | 8.3 | (80) | 4.1 | (57) | 4.5 | Δ Retained Earnings | 11.8 | (16) | 10.6 | | | | -12.3 |
| | -9.3 | | -24.5 | | -39.5 | | -52.3 | | -.3 | | | | -51.2 |
| | 17.7 | | 19.2 | | 14.5 | | 7.8 | | 49.8 | | | | 30.1 |
| | .2 | | 4.5 | | 6.0 | Δ Net Sales | -.6 | | 11.8 | | | | 9.7 |
| | -14.7 | | -9.5 | | -4.9 | | -30.2 | | -3.1 | | | | -.8 |
| | | | | | | Δ Cost of Goods Sold | | | | | | | |
| | 90.4 | | 85.5 | | 101.7 | Δ Profit before | 101.4 | | 188.1 | | | | 55.8 |
| (116) | 11.9 | | 12.0 | (59) | 6.5 | Int. & Taxes | 15.5 | (18) | 30.3 | | | | -25.6 |
| | -44.7 | | -46.3 | | -44.8 | | -72.9 | | -10.1 | | | | -68.9 |
| | 29.4 | | 28.5 | | 36.4 | | | | 30.6 | | | | 43.8 |
| (89) | .0 | (70) | -5.6 | (49) | .0 | Δ Depr./Depl./Amort. | (16) | | -15.8 | | | (16) | 21.4 |
| | -34.0 | | -55.5 | | -26.8 | | | | -37.5 | | | | -17.1 |
| | | | | | | **RATIOS** | | | | | | | |
| | 24.5 | | 19.8 | | 27.4 | Sustainable | 4.5 | | 42.7 | | | | 22.3 |
| | 6.5 | (81) | 1.4 | | .3 | Growth Rate | -.9 | | 2.2 | | | | .6 |
| | -7.0 | | -7.0 | | -13.8 | | -32.4 | | -24.5 | | | | -17.0 |
| | .3 | | .3 | | .3 | | 2.7 | | .2 | | | | .5 |
| | 2.4 | | 2.1 | | 2.3 | Funded Debt/EBITDA | 9.0 | | 1.0 | | | | 1.9 |
| | 6.7 | | 10.5 | | 9.1 | | NM | | 2.8 | | | | 10.2 |
| | 2343689M | | 1692251M | | 1006281M | Net Sales ($) | 5415M | | 34506M | 17030M | 56384M | 130791M | 764155M |
| | 1662679M | | 922447M | | 650460M | Total Assets ($) | 24514M | | 51377M | 12629M | 44608M | 123974M | 393158M |

© RMA 2018    M = $ thousand    MM = $ million

# RETAIL TRADE

# RETAIL—New Car Dealers  NAICS 441110

## Current Data Sorted by Assets | Comparative Historical Data

| 0-500M | 500M-2MM | 2-10MM | 10-50MM | 50-100MM | 100-250MM | Type of Statement | 4/1/19-3/31/20 ALL | 4/1/20-3/31/21 ALL |
|---|---|---|---|---|---|---|---|---|
| 1 | | | 4 | 15 | 5 | 6 | Unqualified | 51 | 37 |
| 1 | | | 4 | 48 | 13 | 6 | Reviewed | 184 | 74 |
| | | | 3 | 13 | 3 | 2 | Compiled | 32 | 23 |
| 2 | | 1 | 24 | 69 | 4 | 1 | Tax Returns | 130 | 75 |
| | 3 | 135 (4/1-9/30/23) | 208 | 743 | 129 | 57 | Other | 2647 | 973 |
| | | | | 1,230 (10/1/23-3/31/24) | | | | | |
| 4 | 4 | 243 | 888 | 154 | 72 | NUMBER OF STATEMENTS | 3044 | 1182 |
| % | % | % | % | % | % | **ASSETS** | % | % |
| | | 17.3 | 19.8 | 19.4 | 19.4 | Cash & Equivalents | 14.0 | 17.9 |
| | | 6.0 | 5.8 | 5.3 | 5.9 | Trade Receivables (net) | 5.2 | 6.2 |
| | | 57.5 | 45.6 | 38.1 | 31.4 | Inventory | 58.1 | 51.4 |
| | | 2.2 | 1.7 | 2.0 | 1.7 | All Other Current | 2.2 | 2.7 |
| | | 83.0 | 73.0 | 64.8 | 58.5 | Total Current | 79.4 | 78.2 |
| | | 7.9 | 11.3 | 14.8 | 19.9 | Fixed Assets (net) | 9.3 | 10.2 |
| | | 2.7 | 4.5 | 5.6 | 7.6 | Intangibles (net) | 5.1 | 4.8 |
| | | 6.3 | 11.2 | 14.9 | 14.1 | All Other Non-Current | 6.2 | 6.8 |
| | | 100.0 | 100.0 | 100.0 | 100.0 | Total | 100.0 | 100.0 |
| | | | | | | **LIABILITIES** | | |
| | | 36.0 | 34.4 | 27.4 | 25.7 | Notes Payable-Short Term | 44.3 | 40.7 |
| | | 1.9 | 1.1 | .8 | 2.2 | Cur. Mat.-L.T.D. | .9 | 1.7 |
| | | 4.4 | 4.7 | 5.9 | 3.7 | Trade Payables | 12.0 | 5.8 |
| | | .4 | .1 | .2 | .2 | Income Taxes Payable | .1 | .1 |
| | | 12.9 | 10.0 | 10.9 | 8.6 | All Other Current | 9.6 | 10.7 |
| | | 55.6 | 50.3 | 45.3 | 40.3 | Total Current | 66.8 | 59.1 |
| | | 6.3 | 7.6 | 10.5 | 17.4 | Long-Term Debt | 6.4 | 9.3 |
| | | .0 | .2 | .2 | .3 | Deferred Taxes | .1 | .1 |
| | | 6.7 | 4.4 | 5.5 | 6.2 | All Other Non-Current | 2.7 | 4.4 |
| | | 31.3 | 37.5 | 38.6 | 35.8 | Net Worth | 24.0 | 27.1 |
| | | 100.0 | 100.0 | 100.0 | 100.0 | Total Liabilties & Net Worth | 100.0 | 100.0 |
| | | | | | | **INCOME DATA** | | |
| | | 100.0 | 100.0 | 100.0 | 100.0 | Net Sales | 100.0 | 100.0 |
| | | 12.6 | 12.2 | 12.2 | 15.8 | Gross Profit | 10.2 | 11.4 |
| | | 12.4 | 11.0 | 10.1 | 12.7 | Operating Expenses | 10.5 | 11.2 |
| | | .1 | 1.1 | 2.1 | 3.1 | Operating Profit | -.3 | .2 |
| | | -2.0 | -2.4 | -2.3 | -1.8 | All Other Expenses (net) | -1.6 | -2.2 |
| | | 2.1 | 3.5 | 4.4 | 4.9 | Profit Before Taxes | 1.3 | 2.4 |
| | | | | | | **RATIOS** | | |
| | | 2.0 | 1.8 | 1.7 | 1.8 | | 1.3 | 1.6 |
| | | 1.4 | 1.4 | 1.4 | 1.4 | Current | 1.2 | 1.3 |
| | | 1.2 | 1.2 | 1.2 | 1.2 | | 1.1 | 1.2 |
| | | .7 | .8 | .8 | 1.0 | | .4 | .6 |
| | | .3 | (886) .5 | .5 | .6 | Quick (3041) | .3 | .4 |
| | | .2 | .3 | .3 | .4 | | .2 | .3 |
| | 2 | 220.3 | 3 135.8 | 3 110.0 | 3 121.0 | | 2 169.8 | 3 141.2 |
| | 4 | 104.0 | 5 79.0 | 5 69.5 | 5 68.6 | Sales/Receivables | 4 82.3 | 5 67.6 |
| | 7 | 53.5 | 7 49.1 | 10 37.0 | 9 41.3 | | 8 47.0 | 9 39.5 |
| | 44 | 8.3 | 37 9.8 | 38 9.6 | 34 10.6 | | 60 6.1 | 50 7.3 |
| | 61 | 6.0 | 53 6.9 | 55 6.6 | 49 7.5 | Cost of Sales/Inventory | 76 4.8 | 63 5.8 |
| | 89 | 4.1 | 73 5.0 | 73 5.0 | 72 5.1 | | 96 3.8 | 81 4.5 |
| | 2 | 231.5 | 2 214.0 | 2 197.3 | 3 140.1 | | 2 203.0 | 2 201.5 |
| | 3 | 134.6 | 3 122.4 | 4 93.8 | 4 86.9 | Cost of Sales/Payables | 4 103.3 | 4 102.5 |
| | 5 | 68.0 | 5 68.2 | 7 51.8 | 8 45.5 | | 9 42.6 | 7 54.7 |
| | | 9.0 | 10.2 | 9.6 | 8.8 | | 15.2 | 11.4 |
| | | 16.5 | 16.6 | 15.9 | 14.2 | Sales/Working Capital | 26.8 | 18.3 |
| | | 32.4 | 32.6 | 32.9 | 28.5 | | 64.1 | 32.0 |
| | | 13.9 | 33.6 | 28.0 | 32.5 | | 13.8 | 17.0 |
| | (144) | 4.3 | (536) 9.6 | (113) 10.3 | (58) 12.8 | EBIT/Interest (1937) | 4.0 | (948) 6.6 |
| | | 1.3 | 3.5 | 3.9 | 5.2 | | 1.5 | 3.0 |
| | | | 24.8 | 8.9 | | Net Profit + Depr., Dep., | 10.3 | 13.7 |
| | | (32) 8.9 | (11) 2.3 | | Amort./Cur. Mat. L/T/D | (85) 4.7 | (44) 5.1 |
| | | 3.7 | 1.1 | | | 2.0 | 1.2 |
| | | .1 | .1 | .1 | .2 | | .1 | .1 |
| | | .2 | .2 | .4 | .6 | Fixed/Worth | .3 | .3 |
| | | .5 | .6 | 1.0 | 1.8 | | 1.1 | 1.1 |
| | | 1.1 | 1.0 | 1.1 | 1.2 | | 2.3 | 1.8 |
| | | 2.4 | 2.1 | 1.9 | 2.0 | Debt/Worth | 4.4 | 3.3 |
| | | 6.2 | 4.0 | 4.0 | 4.7 | | 10.5 | 8.3 |
| | | 41.8 | 61.2 | 52.8 | 53.0 | % Profit Before Taxes/Tangible | 42.6 | 60.2 |
| | (220) | 19.7 | (852) 35.4 | (144) 34.4 | (65) 28.0 | Net Worth (2712) | 21.7 | (1063) 34.2 |
| | | 4.7 | 18.1 | 17.6 | 20.9 | | 6.6 | 16.3 |
| | | 13.2 | 19.6 | 17.6 | 15.2 | % Profit Before Taxes/Total | 7.9 | 12.6 |
| | | 7.1 | 11.5 | 10.9 | 10.7 | Assets | 4.0 | 7.5 |
| | | 1.0 | 5.2 | 5.4 | 6.1 | | .8 | 3.5 |
| | | 278.1 | 142.3 | 82.2 | 45.9 | | 162.9 | 148.5 |
| | | 89.6 | 57.5 | 26.0 | 14.0 | Sales/Net Fixed Assets | 66.2 | 60.7 |
| | | 36.6 | 21.3 | 13.1 | 8.0 | | 24.3 | 23.0 |
| | | 4.9 | 4.3 | 3.6 | 3.1 | | 3.8 | 4.0 |
| | | 3.8 | 3.5 | 2.8 | 2.6 | Sales/Total Assets | 3.1 | 3.3 |
| | | 2.9 | 2.7 | 1.9 | 1.7 | | 2.4 | 2.6 |
| | | .1 | .1 | .2 | .2 | | .1 | .1 |
| | (182) | .2 | (804) .2 | (148) .3 | (66) .3 | % Depr., Dep., Amort./Sales (2633) | .2 | (997) .2 |
| | | .4 | .4 | .5 | .6 | | .4 | .5 |
| | | .2 | .2 | .1 | .0 | | .2 | .2 |
| | (134) | .6 | (534) .4 | (91) .4 | (39) .2 | % Officers', Directors' (1720) | .4 | (618) .5 |
| | | 1.1 | 1.4 | | .5 | Owners' Comp/Sales | .6 | .9 |
| 3421M | 63186M | 6423842M | 73593927M | 29909716M | 28120296M | Net Sales ($) | 243263000M | 92005749M |
| 714M | 4339M | 1609231M | 21042709M | 10423662M | 11161985M | Total Assets ($) | 84565243M | 30287922M |

© RMA 2024    M = $ thousand    MM = $ million
See Pages viii through xx for Explanation of Ratios and Data

# RETAIL—New Car Dealers  NAICS 441110

## Comparative Historical Data | Current Data Sorted by Sales

| Comparative Historical Data ||| Type of Statement | Current Data Sorted by Sales ||||||
|---|---|---|---|---|---|---|---|---|---|
| 17 | 19 | 31 | Unqualified | 1 | | | 1 | 3 | 26 |
| 58 | 84 | 72 | Reviewed | 1 | | | | 5 | 71 |
| 17 | 18 | 21 | Compiled | | | | 2 | 11 | 16 |
| 81 | 80 | 99 | Tax Returns | | | | 14 | 114 | 86 |
| 889 | 1154 | 1142 | Other | 3 | 3 | 6 | 14 | 114 | 1002 |
| 4/1/21-3/31/22 ALL | 4/1/22-3/31/23 ALL | 4/1/23-3/31/24 ALL | | 135 (4/1-9/30/23) ||| 1,230 (10/1/23-3/31/24) |||
| 1062 | 1355 | 1365 | NUMBER OF STATEMENTS | 0-1MM | 1-3MM | 3-5MM | 5-10MM | 10-25MM | 25MM & OVER |
| | | | | 5 | 3 | 6 | 17 | 133 | 1201 |
| % | % | % | ASSETS | % | % | % | % | % | % |
| 24.2 | 23.3 | 19.3 | Cash & Equivalents | | | | 11.5 | 17.0 | 19.7 |
| 6.9 | 6.2 | 5.9 | Trade Receivables (net) | | | | 3.9 | 5.2 | 5.9 |
| 38.7 | 40.0 | 46.0 | Inventory | | | | 54.7 | 56.5 | 45.0 |
| 2.2 | 2.1 | 1.9 | All Other Current | | | | 3.9 | 2.7 | 1.7 |
| 72.0 | 71.5 | 73.1 | Total Current | | | | 73.9 | 81.5 | 72.3 |
| 13.6 | 11.8 | 11.5 | Fixed Assets (net) | | | | 12.2 | 7.0 | 11.9 |
| 3.9 | 5.4 | 4.5 | Intangibles (net) | | | | 2.4 | 3.5 | 4.6 |
| 10.5 | 11.3 | 10.9 | All Other Non-Current | | | | 11.4 | 8.0 | 11.2 |
| 100.0 | 100.0 | 100.0 | Total | | | | 100.0 | 100.0 | 100.0 |
| | | | LIABILITIES | | | | | | |
| 24.0 | 27.0 | 33.3 | Notes Payable-Short Term | | | | 30.2 | 36.3 | 33.2 |
| 2.0 | 1.2 | 1.3 | Cur. Mat.-L.T.D. | | | | 1.0 | 1.2 | 1.3 |
| 4.9 | 4.9 | 4.8 | Trade Payables | | | | 2.4 | 5.9 | 4.7 |
| .1 | .2 | .2 | Income Taxes Payable | | | | 3.9 | .1 | .1 |
| 12.1 | 10.9 | 10.7 | All Other Current | | | | 5.2 | 12.9 | 10.4 |
| 43.1 | 44.3 | 50.2 | Total Current | | | | 42.8 | 56.3 | 49.7 |
| 11.1 | 8.7 | 8.2 | Long-Term Debt | | | | 9.3 | 7.7 | 8.1 |
| .2 | .2 | .2 | Deferred Taxes | | | | .0 | .0 | .1 |
| 4.8 | 4.5 | 5.0 | All Other Non-Current | | | | 12.4 | 8.0 | 4.6 |
| 40.9 | 42.3 | 36.4 | Net Worth | | | | 35.5 | 28.0 | 37.4 |
| 100.0 | 100.0 | 100.0 | Total Liabilities & Net Worth | | | | 100.0 | 100.0 | 100.0 |
| | | | INCOME DATA | | | | | | |
| 100.0 | 100.0 | 100.0 | Net Sales | | | | 100.0 | 100.0 | 100.0 |
| 13.2 | 14.3 | 12.5 | Gross Profit | | | | 16.4 | 12.2 | 12.2 |
| 10.7 | 11.6 | 11.3 | Operating Expenses | | | | 17.1 | 13.1 | 10.9 |
| 2.5 | 2.7 | 1.2 | Operating Profit | | | | -.7 | -.9 | 1.4 |
| -2.4 | -2.1 | -2.2 | All Other Expenses (net) | | | | -1.1 | -2.0 | -2.3 |
| 5.0 | 4.7 | 3.4 | Profit Before Taxes | | | | .3 | 1.1 | 3.7 |
| | | | RATIOS | | | | | | |
| 2.2 | 2.1 | 1.8 | | | | | 3.0 | 1.7 | 1.8 |
| 1.7 | 1.6 | 1.4 | Current | | | | 1.7 | 1.4 | 1.4 |
| 1.4 | 1.3 | 1.2 | | | | | 1.2 | 1.2 | 1.2 |
| 1.2 | 1.1 | .8 | | | | | 1.2 | .6 | .8 |
| (1060) .7 | (1352) .7 | (1363) .5 | Quick | | | | .4 | .3 (1199) | .5 |
| .4 | .4 | .3 | | | | | .2 | .2 | .3 |
| 2 147.0 | 2 168.0 | 3 139.9 | | | | | 1 300.7 | 2 200.3 | 3 136.9 |
| 4 82.5 | 4 88.9 | 5 79.1 | Sales/Receivables | | | | 4 89.4 | 4 94.4 | 5 78.0 |
| 7 50.3 | 7 49.9 | 8 47.6 | | | | | 9 39.0 | 8 47.9 | 8 48.5 |
| 23 15.9 | 28 13.0 | 38 9.5 | | | | | 83 4.4 | 58 6.3 | 36 10.0 |
| 33 11.0 | 41 9.0 | 54 6.7 | Cost of Sales/Inventory | | | | 91 4.0 | 81 4.5 | 51 7.1 |
| 49 7.4 | 59 6.2 | 74 4.9 | | | | | 166 2.2 | 111 3.3 | 70 5.2 |
| 2 196.3 | 2 197.1 | 2 213.6 | | | | | 2 147.5 | 2 175.9 | 2 214.5 |
| 3 115.9 | 3 105.8 | 3 116.6 | Cost of Sales/Payables | | | | 4 82.5 | 4 90.7 | 3 121.6 |
| 5 66.6 | 6 62.2 | 6 64.0 | | | | | 11 34.0 | 8 47.9 | 5 69.1 |
| 10.8 | 10.1 | 9.9 | | | | | 2.9 | 7.3 | 10.2 |
| 15.8 | 15.9 | 16.4 | Sales/Working Capital | | | | 9.7 | 11.6 | 16.9 |
| 25.3 | 27.0 | 31.9 | | | | | 15.7 | 21.9 | 32.9 |
| 74.5 | 57.6 | 29.2 | | | | | | 7.4 | 33.1 |
| (751) 27.5 | (877) 20.1 | (853) 8.7 | EBIT/Interest | | | | (82) 2.4 | (754) 9.8 |
| 12.0 | 8.1 | 3.2 | | | | | | .6 | 3.7 |
| 17.0 | 29.0 | 23.4 | Net Profit + Depr., Dep., | | | | | | 24.0 |
| (37) 10.2 | (54) 7.0 | (56) 6.7 | Amort./Cur. Mat. L/T/D | | | | | (51) 7.2 |
| 4.9 | 3.0 | 2.7 | | | | | | | 3.0 |
| .1 | .1 | .1 | | | | | .1 | .0 | .1 |
| .2 | .2 | .2 | Fixed/Worth | | | | .4 | .2 | .2 |
| .7 | .6 | .7 | | | | | 9.6 | .5 | .7 |
| .8 | .8 | 1.1 | | | | | .6 | 1.5 | 1.0 |
| 1.5 | 1.6 | 2.1 | Debt/Worth | | | | 3.6 | 2.5 | 2.1 |
| 3.2 | 2.9 | 4.2 | | | | | 38.7 | 6.2 | 4.0 |
| 86.7 | 74.1 | 56.0 | | | | | 23.0 | 27.3 | 59.9 |
| (1009) 56.4 | (1287) 43.5 | (1288) 32.3 | % Profit Before Taxes/Tangible Net Worth | | (14) 1.6 | (118) 13.7 | (1146) 34.6 |
| 35.6 | 27.2 | 16.1 | | | | | -21.2 | -4.0 | 18.4 |
| 29.7 | 26.1 | 18.1 | | | | | 7.5 | 8.7 | 19.4 |
| 20.5 | 16.0 | 10.4 | % Profit Before Taxes/Total Assets | | | | -1.6 | 3.0 | 11.5 |
| 13.4 | 9.7 | 4.5 | | | | | -4.5 | -2.4 | 5.6 |
| 155.4 | 171.4 | 141.2 | | | | | 244.6 | 225.1 | 135.0 |
| 64.4 | 58.8 | 54.7 | Sales/Net Fixed Assets | | | | 22.8 | 70.9 | 53.8 |
| 20.2 | 20.9 | 19.4 | | | | | 7.4 | 26.2 | 19.0 |
| 5.6 | 4.9 | 4.3 | | | | | 3.3 | 3.8 | 4.3 |
| 4.4 | 3.8 | 3.4 | Sales/Total Assets | | | | 1.5 | 2.8 | 3.5 |
| 3.2 | 2.9 | 2.6 | | | | | 1.2 | 2.1 | 2.7 |
| .1 | .1 | .1 | | | | | .1 | .1 | .1 |
| (879) .2 | (1145) .2 | (1202) .2 | % Depr., Dep., Amort./Sales | | (12) .4 | (101) .2 | (1085) .2 |
| .4 | .4 | .4 | | | | | .8 | .5 | .4 |
| .2 | .2 | .2 | % Officers', Directors' | | | | | .2 | .2 |
| (638) .4 | (818) .5 | (799) .4 | Owners' Comp/Sales | | | | (73) .6 | (717) .4 |
| 1.1 | 1.0 | .9 | | | | | | 1.0 | .8 |
| 105339448M | 138326026M | 138114388M | Net Sales ($) | 2031M | 8240M | 25322M | 119723M | 2437033M | 135522039M |
| 26927227M | 38919978M | 44242640M | Total Assets ($) | 10499M | 4463M | 55127M | 80680M | 1069858M | 43022013M |

M = $ thousand  MM = $ million
See Pages viii through xx for Explanation of Ratios and Data

© RMA 2024

# RETAIL—Used Car Dealers  NAICS 441120

## Current Data Sorted by Assets

| 0-500M | 500M-2MM | 2-10MM | 10-50MM | 50-100MM | 100-250MM | | Type of Statement | | Comparative Historical Data | | | |
|---|---|---|---|---|---|---|---|---|---|---|---|---|
| | | | 1 | | 4 | | Unqualified | | 15 | | 9 | |
| | | 2 | 5 | 1 | 1 | | Reviewed | | 22 | | 19 | |
| | 1 | 13 | 4 | | | | Compiled | | 22 | | 18 | |
| 11 | 32 | 37 | 5 | | 1 | | Tax Returns | | 129 | | 94 | |
| 11 | 38 | 80 | 35 | 7 | 3 | | Other | | 168 | | 147 | |
| | 20 (4/1-9/30/23) | | 278 (10/1/23-3/31/24) | | | | | | 4/1/19-3/31/20 | | 4/1/20-3/31/21 | |
| 22 | 72 | 137 | 49 | 9 | 9 | | NUMBER OF STATEMENTS | | 356 ALL | | 287 ALL | |
| % | % | % | % | % | % | | ASSETS | | % | | % | |
| 10.6 | 12.0 | 10.3 | 9.4 | | | | Cash & Equivalents | | 10.2 | | 13.7 | |
| 1.8 | 7.7 | 8.0 | 15.6 | | | | Trade Receivables (net) | | 11.5 | | 11.6 | |
| 60.4 | 59.1 | 64.9 | 55.7 | | | | Inventory | | 62.6 | | 58.5 | |
| 2.0 | 1.5 | 3.1 | 3.4 | | | | All Other Current | | 1.6 | | 2.5 | |
| 74.7 | 80.4 | 86.3 | 84.2 | | | | Total Current | | 85.8 | | 86.3 | |
| 16.4 | 10.5 | 8.6 | 8.5 | | | | Fixed Assets (net) | | 9.2 | | 7.8 | |
| .8 | 1.4 | 1.0 | 1.2 | | | | Intangibles (net) | | 1.4 | | 2.1 | |
| 8.1 | 7.7 | 4.0 | 6.1 | | | | All Other Non-Current | | 3.6 | | 3.8 | |
| 100.0 | 100.0 | 100.0 | 100.0 | | | | Total | | 100.0 | | 100.0 | |
| | | | | | | | LIABILITIES | | | | | |
| 30.9 | 23.9 | 31.5 | 30.2 | | | | Notes Payable-Short Term | | 39.9 | | 31.5 | |
| 11.9 | 1.2 | 2.9 | 2.7 | | | | Cur. Mat.-L.T.D. | | 2.1 | | 3.2 | |
| 8.1 | 5.0 | 4.9 | 6.8 | | | | Trade Payables | | 5.6 | | 5.6 | |
| .0 | .0 | .1 | .2 | | | | Income Taxes Payable | | .1 | | .1 | |
| 10.5 | 11.3 | 11.9 | 9.2 | | | | All Other Current | | 12.7 | | 12.1 | |
| 61.3 | 41.3 | 51.3 | 49.0 | | | | Total Current | | 60.5 | | 52.4 | |
| 11.3 | 20.5 | 9.8 | 6.0 | | | | Long-Term Debt | | 9.3 | | 11.5 | |
| .0 | .0 | .0 | .0 | | | | Deferred Taxes | | .0 | | .0 | |
| 16.3 | 4.7 | 7.3 | 6.9 | | | | All Other Non-Current | | 7.8 | | 5.3 | |
| 11.2 | 33.5 | 31.7 | 38.0 | | | | Net Worth | | 22.4 | | 30.7 | |
| 100.0 | 100.0 | 100.0 | 100.0 | | | | Total Liabilities & Net Worth | | 100.0 | | 100.0 | |
| | | | | | | | INCOME DATA | | | | | |
| 100.0 | 100.0 | 100.0 | 100.0 | | | | Net Sales | | 100.0 | | 100.0 | |
| 29.3 | 24.5 | 15.3 | 15.5 | | | | Gross Profit | | 16.5 | | 19.5 | |
| 25.3 | 18.6 | 12.9 | 12.6 | | | | Operating Expenses | | 14.9 | | 17.0 | |
| 4.0 | 5.8 | 2.4 | 2.9 | | | | Operating Profit | | 1.6 | | 2.5 | |
| .4 | .8 | .9 | .4 | | | | All Other Expenses (net) | | .2 | | -.2 | |
| 3.6 | 5.1 | 1.5 | 2.4 | | | | Profit Before Taxes | | 1.4 | | 2.7 | |
| | | | | | | | RATIOS | | | | | |
| 9.3 | 7.3 | 3.0 | 3.2 | | | | | | 2.1 | | 3.0 | |
| 1.7 | 1.8 | 1.6 | 1.6 | | | | Current | | 1.3 | | 1.6 | |
| 1.0 | 1.1 | 1.2 | 1.2 | | | | | | 1.1 | | 1.2 | |
| 2.2 | 2.5 | .9 | 1.2 | | | | | | .7 | | 1.1 | |
| .2 | (71) .3 | .3 | .4 | | | | Quick | | .3 | (286) | .4 | |
| .1 | .1 | .1 | .1 | | | | | | .1 | | .2 | |
| 0 UND | 0 UND | 0 UND | 2 192.5 | | | | | | 0 999.8 | | 0 UND | |
| 0 UND | 0 UND | 2 158.5 | 7 53.2 | | | | Sales/Receivables | | 3 117.7 | | 3 143.1 | |
| 0 UND | 5 72.8 | 7 51.8 | 22 16.3 | | | | | | 9 38.5 | | 11 33.8 | |
| 25 14.6 | 41 9.0 | 49 7.4 | 48 7.6 | | | | | | 45 8.1 | | 50 7.3 | |
| 58 6.3 | 63 5.8 | 74 4.9 | 61 6.0 | | | | Cost of Sales/Inventory | | 70 5.2 | | 70 5.2 | |
| 140 2.6 | 122 3.0 | 114 3.2 | 104 3.5 | | | | | | 94 3.9 | | 99 3.7 | |
| 0 UND | 0 UND | 0 999.8 | 1 334.2 | | | | | | 0 UND | | 0 UND | |
| 0 UND | 0 UND | 2 218.3 | 4 85.0 | | | | Cost of Sales/Payables | | 2 175.5 | | 2 212.0 | |
| 1 607.7 | 3 113.2 | 6 62.4 | 9 40.5 | | | | | | 8 47.4 | | 8 44.7 | |
| 7.9 | 4.4 | 5.7 | 4.7 | | | | | | 7.0 | | 5.4 | |
| 17.1 | 13.1 | 11.7 | 11.4 | | | | Sales/Working Capital | | 18.7 | | 11.6 | |
| NM | 49.4 | 30.8 | 31.7 | | | | | | 59.8 | | 24.5 | |
| 14.8 | 10.5 | 6.8 | 11.6 | | | | | | 5.1 | | 11.6 | |
| (18) 2.9 | (55) 2.6 | (119) 1.8 | (41) 2.8 | | | | EBIT/Interest | (307) | 2.3 | (248) | 4.1 | |
| -2.4 | .9 | .8 | 1.3 | | | | | | 1.1 | | 1.9 | |
| | | | | | | | Net Profit + Depr., Dep., Amort./Cur. Mat. L/T/D | | 17.5 | | | |
| | | | | | | | | (15) | 2.4 | | | |
| | | | | | | | | | .1 | | | |
| .0 | .0 | .0 | .0 | | | | | | .0 | | .0 | |
| .1 | .1 | .1 | .1 | | | | Fixed/Worth | | .2 | | .1 | |
| 15.5 | 1.0 | .8 | .4 | | | | | | 1.1 | | .5 | |
| 1.3 | .7 | 1.0 | .9 | | | | | | 1.6 | | 1.0 | |
| 7.5 | 2.3 | 2.3 | 1.9 | | | | Debt/Worth | | 3.9 | | 2.5 | |
| -6.3 | 25.9 | 10.4 | 5.2 | | | | | | 13.4 | | 7.1 | |
| 42.5 | 50.2 | 42.3 | 42.7 | | | | | | 48.4 | | 59.6 | |
| (14) 20.4 | (57) 18.8 | (118) 13.2 | (47) 17.8 | | | | % Profit Before Taxes/Tangible Net Worth | (304) | 22.5 | (254) | 30.5 | |
| -6.8 | 2.6 | 3.9 | 3.7 | | | | | | 4.8 | | 10.5 | |
| 24.9 | 17.5 | 12.2 | 14.4 | | | | | | 11.1 | | 16.3 | |
| 7.3 | 7.6 | 4.1 | 5.0 | | | | % Profit Before Taxes/Total Assets | | 4.4 | | 8.0 | |
| -3.1 | .4 | -.8 | .6 | | | | | | .3 | | 2.7 | |
| UND | 999.8 | 594.0 | 346.4 | | | | | | 842.8 | | 681.0 | |
| 310.9 | 162.3 | 112.6 | 113.2 | | | | Sales/Net Fixed Assets | | 121.3 | | 137.6 | |
| 15.5 | 31.6 | 32.1 | 33.7 | | | | | | 39.3 | | 36.8 | |
| 8.3 | 6.2 | 4.9 | 5.2 | | | | | | 5.7 | | 5.1 | |
| 4.3 | 3.8 | 3.6 | 4.2 | | | | Sales/Total Assets | | 3.9 | | 3.7 | |
| 2.1 | 2.1 | 2.4 | 1.6 | | | | | | 2.6 | | 2.4 | |
| | .1 | .1 | .0 | | | | | | .1 | | .1 | |
| (26) | (68) .2 | (29) .2 | .1 | | | | % Depr., Dep., Amort./Sales | (208) | .2 | (158) | .2 | |
| | .5 | .4 | .2 | | | | | | .4 | | .5 | |
| 2.2 | .9 | .5 | .3 | | | | | | .4 | | .5 | |
| (10) 6.9 | (39) 1.6 | (69) 1.0 | (25) .7 | | | | % Officers', Directors' Owners' Comp/Sales | (169) | 1.1 | (149) | 1.0 | |
| 11.3 | 4.0 | 1.7 | 1.1 | | | | | | 2.1 | | 2.1 | |
| 36377M | 433164M | 2675008M | 2984221M | 637350M | 15022355M | | Net Sales ($) | | 9637214M | | 7895478M | |
| 6712M | 90940M | 672076M | 844318M | 579855M | 1592424M | | Total Assets ($) | | 3323244M | | 2856493M | |

© RMA 2024

M = $ thousand    MM = $ million
See Pages viii through xx for Explanation of Ratios and Data

# RETAIL—Used Car Dealers  NAICS 441120

## Comparative Historical Data | Current Data Sorted by Sales

| Comparative Historical Data | | | | Type of Statement | Current Data Sorted by Sales | | | | | |
|---|---|---|---|---|---|---|---|---|---|---|
| 9 | 11 | 11 | | Unqualified | | | 2 | | | 9 |
| 14 | 11 | 9 | | Reviewed | | | | 1 | 3 | 5 |
| 17 | 23 | 18 | | Compiled | | 2 | | 1 | 8 | 7 |
| 109 | 114 | 86 | | Tax Returns | 9 | 13 | 6 | 24 | 20 | 14 |
| 165 | 196 | 174 | | Other | 9 | 15 | 11 | 29 | 50 | 60 |
| 4/1/21-3/31/22 | 4/1/22-3/31/23 | 4/1/23-3/31/24 | | | 20 (4/1-9/30/23) | | | 278 (10/1/23-3/31/24) | | |
| ALL | ALL | ALL | | | 0-1MM | 1-3MM | 3-5MM | 5-10MM | 10-25MM | 25MM & OVER |
| 314 | 355 | 298 | | NUMBER OF STATEMENTS | 18 | 30 | 19 | 55 | 81 | 95 |
| % | % | % | | ASSETS | % | % | % | % | % | % |
| 15.1 | 14.4 | 10.5 | | Cash & Equivalents | 10.0 | 12.2 | 12.7 | 12.8 | 8.5 | 10.1 |
| 12.5 | 12.7 | 11.1 | | Trade Receivables (net) | 11.2 | 8.3 | 8.7 | 6.8 | 10.0 | 16.0 |
| 55.4 | 55.9 | 59.1 | | Inventory | 37.4 | 55.0 | 50.2 | 65.0 | 66.9 | 56.3 |
| 2.6 | 3.3 | 2.9 | | All Other Current | 7.8 | 1.3 | 4.0 | 1.0 | 1.7 | 4.3 |
| 85.6 | 86.3 | 83.7 | | Total Current | 66.4 | 76.9 | 75.6 | 85.7 | 87.2 | 86.7 |
| 8.0 | 8.3 | 9.4 | | Fixed Assets (net) | 24.2 | 11.6 | 12.2 | 10.1 | 7.4 | 6.7 |
| 1.1 | 1.4 | 1.2 | | Intangibles (net) | 1.0 | 3.1 | .2 | .9 | 1.1 | 1.0 |
| 5.3 | 4.1 | 5.7 | | All Other Non-Current | 8.4 | 8.5 | 12.0 | 3.3 | 4.3 | 5.6 |
| 100.0 | 100.0 | 100.0 | | Total | 100.0 | 100.0 | 100.0 | 100.0 | 100.0 | 100.0 |
| | | | | LIABILITIES | | | | | | |
| 29.8 | 27.5 | 29.1 | | Notes Payable-Short Term | 19.2 | 25.4 | 9.5 | 24.4 | 36.4 | 32.4 |
| 2.3 | 2.4 | 3.3 | | Cur. Mat.-L.T.D. | 12.3 | 2.8 | .4 | .8 | 2.9 | 3.9 |
| 6.2 | 5.6 | 5.7 | | Trade Payables | 6.0 | 5.0 | 1.1 | 6.4 | 5.6 | 6.5 |
| .1 | .2 | .1 | | Income Taxes Payable | .0 | .0 | .0 | .1 | .0 | .1 |
| 10.8 | 11.0 | 11.6 | | All Other Current | 14.3 | 8.1 | 14.8 | 14.3 | 9.3 | 11.9 |
| 49.3 | 46.7 | 49.7 | | Total Current | 51.8 | 41.2 | 25.9 | 46.0 | 54.4 | 54.9 |
| 12.5 | 14.3 | 12.2 | | Long-Term Debt | 17.8 | 20.2 | 15.1 | 13.9 | 10.9 | 8.3 |
| .0 | .0 | .0 | | Deferred Taxes | .0 | .0 | .0 | .0 | .0 | .0 |
| 7.0 | 6.2 | 7.0 | | All Other Non-Current | 14.7 | 8.2 | 12.6 | 1.6 | 8.5 | 5.9 |
| 31.2 | 32.7 | 31.1 | | Net Worth | 15.8 | 30.4 | 46.4 | 38.5 | 26.3 | 30.9 |
| 100.0 | 100.0 | 100.0 | | Total Liabilities & Net Worth | 100.0 | 100.0 | 100.0 | 100.0 | 100.0 | 100.0 |
| | | | | INCOME DATA | | | | | | |
| 100.0 | 100.0 | 100.0 | | Net Sales | 100.0 | 100.0 | 100.0 | 100.0 | 100.0 | 100.0 |
| 20.4 | 18.1 | 19.7 | | Gross Profit | 44.5 | 32.8 | 25.9 | 16.9 | 14.8 | 15.3 |
| 15.8 | 15.2 | 15.9 | | Operating Expenses | 38.4 | 23.5 | 24.7 | 12.9 | 12.2 | 12.5 |
| 4.6 | 2.8 | 3.7 | | Operating Profit | 6.1 | 9.3 | 1.2 | 4.0 | 2.7 | 2.8 |
| -.3 | -.1 | .9 | | All Other Expenses (net) | -.8 | .8 | .2 | 1.4 | 1.0 | .9 |
| 4.9 | 3.0 | 2.9 | | Profit Before Taxes | 6.9 | 8.5 | 1.0 | 2.5 | 1.7 | 1.9 |
| | | | | RATIOS | | | | | | |
| 3.1 | 4.3 | 4.0 | | | 13.4 | 7.5 | 9.1 | 9.7 | 2.5 | 2.3 |
| 1.6 | 1.7 | 1.6 | | Current | 2.0 | 2.3 | 3.3 | 1.5 | 1.5 | 1.4 |
| 1.3 | 1.3 | 1.2 | | | 1.0 | 1.3 | 1.5 | 1.1 | 1.2 | 1.2 |
| 1.2 | 1.3 | 1.1 | | | 4.4 | 2.0 | 3.7 | 1.2 | .8 | 1.1 |
| .5 (354) | .5 (297) | .3 | | Quick | .8 (29) | .2 | .7 | .3 | .3 | .3 |
| .2 | .2 | .1 | | | .1 | .1 | .2 | .1 | .1 | .2 |
| 0 UND | 0 UND | 0 UND | | | 0 UND | 0 UND | 0 UND | 0 UND | 1 313.7 | |
| 2 199.1 | 3 124.5 | 2 172.4 | | Sales/Receivables | 0 UND | 0 UND | 0 UND | 0 999.8 | 3 132.6 | 5 69.9 |
| 10 38.4 | 11 34.1 | 9 40.8 | | | 7 50.2 | 9 38.8 | 2 146.5 | 5 69.8 | 9 39.4 | 13 28.1 |
| 40 9.2 | 41 8.9 | 45 8.1 | | | 0 UND | 91 4.0 | 40 9.1 | 49 7.4 | 47 7.7 | 43 8.4 |
| 59 6.2 | 63 5.8 | 70 5.2 | | Cost of Sales/Inventory | 99 3.7 | 135 2.7 | 72 5.1 | 73 5.0 | 85 4.3 | 57 6.4 |
| 79 4.6 | 94 3.9 | 114 3.2 | | | 215 1.7 | 203 1.8 | 118 3.1 | 101 3.6 | 118 3.1 | 73 5.0 |
| 0 UND | 0 UND | 0 UND | | | 0 UND | 0 UND | 0 UND | 0 UND | 0 875.5 | 1 358.0 |
| 1 250.0 | 3 141.0 | 2 233.1 | | Cost of Sales/Payables | 0 UND | 0 UND | 0 UND | 1 560.7 | 2 187.4 | 4 96.7 |
| 6 56.4 | 7 54.6 | 6 56.7 | | | 3 140.3 | 2 206.6 | 5 70.6 | 6 56.9 | 6 64.2 | 9 38.9 |
| 5.8 | 5.1 | 4.9 | | | 3.6 | 1.6 | 3.8 | 4.7 | 6.4 | 6.1 |
| 12.7 | 11.6 | 11.3 | | Sales/Working Capital | 23.1 | 3.6 | 6.0 | 11.3 | 11.6 | 13.0 |
| 27.7 | 24.4 | 36.6 | | | NM | 14.8 | 37.3 | 48.0 | 33.3 | 41.4 |
| 17.0 | 10.8 | 8.9 | | | 7.0 | 11.3 | 24.0 | 6.9 | 4.7 | 10.7 |
| 7.4 (305) | 4.0 (250) | 2.2 | | EBIT/Interest | 2.7 (13) | 1.8 (21) | 6.6 (15) | 2.0 (43) | 1.8 (76) | 2.6 (82) |
| (257) 3.5 | 1.6 | 1.0 | | | -3.9 | .8 | .9 | .9 | .8 | 1.4 |
| | | | | Net Profit + Depr., Dep., Amort./Cur. Mat. L/T/D | | | | | | |
| .0 | .0 | .0 | | | .0 | .0 | .0 | .0 | .0 | .0 |
| .1 | .1 | .1 | | Fixed/Worth | .5 | .1 | .1 | .0 | .2 | .1 |
| .5 | .5 | .7 | | | 12.0 | 4.9 | .5 | .4 | 1.4 | .5 |
| 1.0 | 1.1 | 1.0 | | | .7 | .9 | .4 | .4 | 1.1 | 1.4 |
| 2.2 | 2.3 | 2.7 | | Debt/Worth | 4.9 | 3.1 | 1.2 | 2.2 | 3.2 | 2.8 |
| 5.7 | 5.7 | 10.3 | | | -6.2 | -28.5 | 2.1 | 11.6 | 16.3 | 5.4 |
| 86.7 | 60.2 | 43.7 | | % Profit Before Taxes/Tangible Net Worth | 57.9 | 48.5 | 30.1 | 42.1 | 43.7 | 47.4 |
| 46.1 (325) | 25.8 (253) | 16.7 | | | 16.9 (12) | 18.8 (21) | 11.7 (17) | 15.6 (49) | 11.7 (67) | 20.5 (87) |
| (287) 25.4 | 8.7 | 3.9 | | | -19.4 | 3.9 | 1.0 | 2.6 | 2.3 | 4.7 |
| 25.4 | 16.1 | 14.1 | | % Profit Before Taxes/Total Assets | 24.9 | 17.0 | 15.8 | 15.4 | 12.5 | 14.1 |
| 14.5 | 7.7 | 4.6 | | | 7.0 | 4.2 | 5.6 | 4.6 | 3.8 | 5.1 |
| 6.6 | 2.1 | .2 | | | -5.9 | 1.0 | 1.1 | .2 | -.9 | .8 |
| 999.8 | 999.8 | 686.8 | | Sales/Net Fixed Assets | 253.8 | UND | 999.8 | 999.8 | 639.8 | 371.0 |
| 182.8 | 150.7 | 113.2 | | | 26.2 | 137.0 | 128.9 | 191.0 | 133.0 | 97.2 |
| 39.7 | 37.0 | 30.5 | | | 3.7 | 14.8 | 11.5 | 50.3 | 30.9 | 43.4 |
| 5.8 | 5.5 | 5.3 | | Sales/Total Assets | 3.9 | 2.7 | 4.9 | 5.0 | 5.4 | 5.9 |
| 4.2 | 3.8 | 3.7 | | | 1.4 | 1.5 | 2.8 | 3.8 | 3.4 | 4.6 |
| 2.7 | 2.4 | 1.9 | | | .7 | 1.0 | 1.9 | 2.9 | 2.3 | 2.6 |
| .1 | .1 | .1 | | % Depr., Dep., Amort./Sales | .1 | .4 | | .1 | .1 | .1 |
| .2 (177) | .2 (145) | .2 | | | (11) .4 | | (22) | (41) .2 | (59) .1 | |
| (148) .4 | .5 | .4 | | | | 2.9 | | .4 | .4 | .3 |
| .5 | .4 | .6 | | % Officers', Directors', Owners' Comp/Sales | 1.8 | 1.5 | | .8 | .5 | .3 |
| 1.0 (174) | 1.0 (146) | 1.2 | | | (16) 3.2 | (12) 2.7 | (28) 1.4 | (37) 1.0 | (47) .7 | |
| (150) 2.3 | 1.8 | 2.5 | | | | 6.3 | 3.8 | 2.7 | 1.6 | 1.1 |
| 9566005M | 12524638M | 21788475M | | Net Sales ($) | 11040M | 53304M | 78287M | 392776M | 1290043M | 19963025M |
| 3458149M | 4054102M | 3786325M | | Total Assets ($) | 11831M | 39212M | 37232M | 129996M | 513841M | 3054213M |

© RMA 2024

M = $ thousand    MM = $ million

See Pages viii through xx for Explanation of Ratios and Data

# RETAIL—Recreational Vehicle Dealers  NAICS 441210

## Current Data Sorted by Assets

| | | | | | | Type of Statement | | |
|---|---|---|---|---|---|---|---|---|
| 1 | 1 | 11 | 4 | 4 | 1 | Unqualified | | |
| | 6 | 34 | 26 | 3 | | Reviewed | | |
| 2 | 16 | 67 | 8 | 3 | | Compiled | | |
| 1 | 36 | 304 | 18 | 2 | | Tax Returns | | |
| | | | 215 | 22 | 17 | Other | | |
| | 265 (4/1-9/30/23) | | 537 (10/1/23-3/31/24) | | | | | |
| 0-500M | 500M-2MM | 2-10MM | 10-50MM | 50-100MM | 100-250MM | | | |

## Comparative Historical Data

| | | | |
|---|---|---|---|
| | 9 | | 6 |
| | 34 | | 4 |
| | 35 | | 13 |
| | 40 | | 19 |
| | 181 | | 33 |
| | 4/1/19-3/31/20 ALL | | 4/1/20-3/31/21 ALL |

| 0-500M | 500M-2MM | 2-10MM | 10-50MM | 50-100MM | 100-250MM | | Hist 1 | Hist 2 |
|---|---|---|---|---|---|---|---|---|
| 4 | 59 | 416 | 271 | 34 | 18 | NUMBER OF STATEMENTS | 299 | 75 |
| % | % | % | % | % | % | ASSETS | % | % |
| | 12.9 | 11.7 | 10.8 | 11.1 | 10.8 | Cash & Equivalents | 12.5 | 27.0 |
| | 2.1 | 2.3 | 3.0 | 2.9 | 2.8 | Trade Receivables (net) | 3.4 | 4.9 |
| | 69.4 | 73.7 | 70.0 | 61.6 | 60.5 | Inventory | 70.1 | 51.5 |
| | .6 | 1.3 | 2.0 | 2.6 | 8.5 | All Other Current | 1.6 | 1.6 |
| | 85.0 | 89.0 | 85.8 | 78.1 | 82.7 | Total Current | 87.6 | 85.0 |
| | 12.3 | 7.3 | 7.1 | 7.5 | 9.7 | Fixed Assets (net) | 8.2 | 10.2 |
| | 2.0 | 2.0 | 3.0 | 5.5 | 3.6 | Intangibles (net) | 2.7 | 2.7 |
| | .7 | 1.8 | 4.1 | 8.8 | 4.0 | All Other Non-Current | 1.6 | 2.0 |
| | 100.0 | 100.0 | 100.0 | 100.0 | 100.0 | Total | 100.0 | 100.0 |
| | | | | | | LIABILITIES | | |
| | 8.7 | 4.8 | 12.5 | 21.1 | 18.9 | Notes Payable-Short Term | 49.8 | 28.4 |
| | 1.0 | .4 | .4 | .2 | .2 | Cur. Mat.-L.T.D. | 1.0 | 1.6 |
| | 41.1 | 52.3 | 42.5 | 31.6 | 22.2 | Trade Payables | 4.7 | 7.1 |
| | .0 | .1 | .1 | .0 | .4 | Income Taxes Payable | .1 | .1 |
| | 3.9 | 4.1 | 4.8 | 4.7 | 7.2 | All Other Current | 6.0 | 8.4 |
| | 54.8 | 61.7 | 60.2 | 57.6 | 48.8 | Total Current | 61.5 | 45.5 |
| | 6.4 | 4.6 | 2.8 | 2.1 | 7.2 | Long-Term Debt | 6.1 | 13.3 |
| | .0 | .1 | .0 | .0 | .6 | Deferred Taxes | .1 | .0 |
| | 3.4 | 3.2 | 4.6 | 8.2 | 9.9 | All Other Non-Current | 3.8 | 3.0 |
| | 35.4 | 30.4 | 32.4 | 32.1 | 33.5 | Net Worth | 28.6 | 38.2 |
| | 100.0 | 100.0 | 100.0 | 100.0 | 100.0 | Total Liabilties & Net Worth | 100.0 | 100.0 |
| | | | | | | INCOME DATA | | |
| | 100.0 | 100.0 | 100.0 | 100.0 | 100.0 | Net Sales | 100.0 | 100.0 |
| | 24.5 | 21.8 | 20.3 | 20.6 | 20.9 | Gross Profit | 21.0 | 26.1 |
| | 22.7 | 19.8 | 16.9 | 16.1 | 15.6 | Operating Expenses | 17.3 | 19.7 |
| | 1.9 | 2.0 | 3.3 | 4.5 | 5.3 | Operating Profit | 3.6 | 6.4 |
| | 2.3 | 2.4 | 1.5 | 1.4 | 2.5 | All Other Expenses (net) | .9 | -.4 |
| | -.4 | -.4 | 1.9 | 3.1 | 2.8 | Profit Before Taxes | 2.8 | 6.9 |
| | | | | | | RATIOS | | |
| | 2.2 | 1.7 | 1.7 | 1.5 | 2.2 | | 1.6 | 3.6 |
| | 1.4 | 1.4 | 1.3 | 1.3 | 1.7 | Current | 1.3 | 1.8 |
| | 1.1 | 1.2 | 1.2 | 1.2 | 1.4 | | 1.2 | 1.4 |
| | .6 | .4 | .3 | .4 | .3 | | .4 | 1.6 |
| | .2 | .2 | .2 | .2 | .3 | Quick | .2 | .6 |
| | .1 | .1 | .1 | .1 | .2 | | .1 | .3 |
| 0 UND | 0 999.8 | 1 361.7 | 2 187.4 | 3 118.2 | | | 1 607.5 | 0 999.8 |
| 1 554.7 | 2 161.2 | 3 109.5 | 5 69.8 | 5 73.7 | | Sales/Receivables | 2 166.9 | 2 176.1 |
| 4 89.4 | 6 61.1 | 7 50.8 | 8 44.0 | 9 42.1 | | | 6 64.3 | 7 52.6 |
| 91 4.0 | 130 2.8 | 130 2.8 | 146 2.5 | 126 2.9 | | | 107 3.4 | 50 7.3 |
| 126 2.9 | 174 2.1 | 166 2.2 | 152 2.4 | 152 2.4 | | Cost of Sales/Inventory | 140 2.6 | 78 4.7 |
| 243 1.5 | 228 1.6 | 203 1.8 | 166 2.2 | 192 1.9 | | | 174 2.1 | 114 3.2 |
| 13 28.5 | 81 4.5 | 12 31.6 | 6 57.9 | 5 80.4 | | | 1 345.5 | 1 324.8 |
| 74 4.9 | 130 2.8 | 122 3.0 | 114 3.2 | 14 25.6 | | Cost of Sales/Payables | 3 112.7 | 4 81.7 |
| 114 3.2 | 182 2.0 | 166 2.2 | 146 2.5 | 146 2.5 | | | 9 42.4 | 10 38.2 |
| | 3.5 | 4.8 | 5.7 | 6.2 | 2.9 | | 6.2 | 4.6 |
| | 9.6 | 7.5 | 8.5 | 9.5 | 5.2 | Sales/Working Capital | 10.8 | 8.5 |
| | 28.8 | 15.1 | 15.2 | 13.5 | 11.6 | | 16.9 | 14.7 |
| | 2.7 | 2.4 | 3.7 | 2.7 | 5.6 | | 5.4 | 18.2 |
| (58) | 1.1 (406) | 1.1 (267) | 1.7 (33) | 2.1 | 3.0 | EBIT/Interest | (291) 2.9 | (72) 10.4 |
| | -.6 | .0 | .7 | | 1.3 | .8 | 1.5 | 3.7 |
| | | 3.0 | 15.5 | | | | 23.8 | |
| | (18) .2 | (12) 7.9 | | | | Net Profit + Depr., Dep., Amort./Cur. Mat. L/T/D | (15) 7.8 | |
| | -3.3 | 4.7 | | | | | .9 | |
| | .1 | .0 | .1 | .1 | .1 | | .1 | .1 |
| | .3 | .1 | .2 | .2 | .5 | Fixed/Worth | .2 | .2 |
| | 1.0 | .4 | .4 | .4 | 1.3 | | .6 | .4 |
| | .7 | 1.4 | 1.4 | 1.8 | 1.2 | | 1.7 | .9 |
| | 2.5 | 2.6 | 2.7 | 2.6 | 2.2 | Debt/Worth | 3.1 | 1.7 |
| | 7.0 | 5.9 | 4.6 | 4.7 | 12.4 | | 5.6 | 4.1 |
| | 17.9 | 17.9 | 25.4 | 23.8 | 27.8 | | 47.8 | 97.5 |
| (54) | 6.4 (386) | 2.8 (261) | 12.1 | 12.9 (16) | 18.9 | % Profit Before Taxes/Tangible Net Worth | (281) 25.5 | (71) 60.4 |
| | -20.5 | -21.0 | -6.4 | 3.7 | 9.7 | | 10.1 | 25.8 |
| | 7.0 | 5.3 | 9.4 | 5.6 | 12.1 | | 11.4 | 29.7 |
| | .4 | .5 | 3.3 | 3.8 | 6.9 | % Profit Before Taxes/Total Assets | 5.9 | 17.7 |
| | -8.6 | -5.6 | -1.7 | .7 | -1.0 | | 2.2 | 8.9 |
| | 169.4 | 172.6 | 139.2 | 160.6 | 46.5 | | 190.7 | 146.9 |
| | 23.5 | 57.3 | 51.8 | 47.6 | 31.4 | Sales/Net Fixed Assets | 60.7 | 70.0 |
| | 9.8 | 18.9 | 21.8 | 13.2 | 15.9 | | 28.4 | 26.2 |
| | 3.2 | 2.5 | 2.3 | 2.0 | 2.0 | | 2.9 | 4.2 |
| | 2.5 | 2.0 | 1.9 | 1.8 | 1.9 | Sales/Total Assets | 2.3 | 3.1 |
| | 1.3 | 1.5 | 1.6 | 1.5 | 1.4 | | 1.9 | 2.4 |
| | .2 | .2 | .1 | .1 | .2 | | .2 | .2 |
| (36) | .4 (239) | .5 (204) | .3 (32) | .2 | .3 | % Depr., Dep., Amort./Sales | (204) .4 | (45) .3 |
| | 1.0 | .9 | .6 | .8 | .7 | | .6 | .6 |
| | 1.2 | .8 | .3 | | .3 | | .6 | .8 |
| (31) | 2.3 (215) | 1.4 (133) | .6 (17) | | .5 | % Officers', Directors' Owners' Comp/Sales | (166) 1.1 | (41) 1.3 |
| | 4.7 | 2.3 | 1.2 | | 1.0 | | 2.0 | 2.6 |
| 5730M | 225792M | 4625940M | 11185002M | 4502730M | 5369087M | Net Sales ($) | 13723924M | 5110013M |
| 613M | 86608M | 2287039M | 5574596M | 2532706M | 2862165M | Total Assets ($) | 5986080M | 1554971M |

M = $ thousand    MM = $ million
See Pages viii through xx for Explanation of Ratios and Data

© RMA 2024

# RETAIL—Recreational Vehicle Dealers NAICS 441210

## Comparative Historical Data

| | | | | | | | Type of Statement | | | | | | | |
|---|---|---|---|---|---|---|---|---|---|---|---|---|---|---|
| | 2 | | 2 | | 9 | | Unqualified | | | | | | 1 | 8 |
| | 7 | | 30 | | 42 | | Reviewed | 1 | | 1 | 2 | 3 | 11 | 24 |
| | 10 | | 18 | | 51 | | Compiled | | | 8 | 4 | 7 | 24 | 8 |
| | 20 | | 25 | | 105 | | Tax Returns | | | 10 | 11 | 27 | 40 | 17 |
| | 133 | | 187 | | 595 | | Other | 4 | | 20 | 36 | 129 | 207 | 199 |
| | 4/1/21-3/31/22 ALL | | 4/1/22-3/31/23 ALL | | 4/1/23-3/31/24 ALL | | | | | 265 (4/1-9/30/23) | | | 537 (10/1/23-3/31/24) | |
| | | | | | | | | 0-1MM | | 1-3MM | 3-5MM | 5-10MM | 10-25MM | 25MM & OVER |
| | 172 | | 262 | | 802 | NUMBER OF STATEMENTS | | 5 | | 39 | 53 | 166 | 283 | 256 |
| | % | | % | | % | **ASSETS** | | % | | % | % | % | % | % |
| | 21.0 | | 15.5 | | 11.5 | Cash & Equivalents | | | | 10.9 | 14.6 | 10.4 | 12.6 | 10.6 |
| | 4.3 | | 2.6 | | 2.6 | Trade Receivables (net) | | | | 1.9 | 2.0 | 2.4 | 2.4 | 3.2 |
| | 56.1 | | 64.4 | | 71.2 | Inventory | | | | 72.6 | 68.4 | 73.1 | 71.8 | 69.7 |
| | 2.2 | | 2.2 | | 1.7 | All Other Current | | | | 1.6 | .6 | 1.3 | 1.7 | 2.2 |
| | 83.7 | | 84.7 | | 87.0 | Total Current | | | | 87.0 | 85.6 | 87.2 | 88.4 | 85.6 |
| | 10.9 | | 9.1 | | 7.6 | Fixed Assets (net) | | | | 10.2 | 11.5 | 8.9 | 6.2 | 7.1 |
| | 1.5 | | 2.6 | | 2.5 | Intangibles (net) | | | | 2.2 | 2.3 | 2.1 | 2.9 | 2.5 |
| | 3.9 | | 3.5 | | 2.8 | All Other Non-Current | | | | .6 | .5 | 1.7 | 2.5 | 4.8 |
| | 100.0 | | 100.0 | | 100.0 | Total | | | | 100.0 | 100.0 | 100.0 | 100.0 | 100.0 |
| | | | | | | **LIABILITIES** | | | | | | | | |
| | 14.4 | | 25.0 | | 8.8 | Notes Payable-Short Term | | | | 6.6 | 5.9 | 3.7 | 7.9 | 14.0 |
| | .6 | | .6 | | .4 | Cur. Mat.-L.T.D. | | | | 1.3 | .5 | .4 | .4 | .2 |
| | 25.6 | | 25.2 | | 46.3 | Trade Payables | | | | 39.5 | 46.9 | 54.1 | 48.0 | 40.8 |
| | .1 | | .2 | | .1 | Income Taxes Payable | | | | .0 | .0 | .1 | .1 | .1 |
| | 7.0 | | 5.6 | | 4.6 | All Other Current | | | | 5.4 | 2.9 | 4.1 | 4.8 | 4.5 |
| | 47.8 | | 56.5 | | 60.2 | Total Current | | | | 52.8 | 56.3 | 62.3 | 61.2 | 59.6 |
| | 8.8 | | 6.3 | | 4.1 | Long-Term Debt | | | | 8.4 | 3.6 | 4.7 | 3.9 | 3.1 |
| | .0 | | .1 | | .1 | Deferred Taxes | | | | .0 | .0 | .1 | .1 | .0 |
| | 4.5 | | 2.8 | | 4.0 | All Other Non-Current | | | | 2.7 | 4.1 | 4.4 | 2.9 | 5.1 |
| | 38.8 | | 34.4 | | 31.6 | Net Worth | | | | 36.1 | 36.0 | 28.5 | 31.8 | 32.1 |
| | 100.0 | | 100.0 | | 100.0 | Total Liabilties & Net Worth | | | | 100.0 | 100.0 | 100.0 | 100.0 | 100.0 |
| | | | | | | **INCOME DATA** | | | | | | | | |
| | 100.0 | | 100.0 | | 100.0 | Net Sales | | | | 100.0 | 100.0 | 100.0 | 100.0 | 100.0 |
| | 25.7 | | 23.9 | | 21.4 | Gross Profit | | | | 26.4 | 22.9 | 22.8 | 21.2 | 19.4 |
| | 17.1 | | 17.7 | | 18.8 | Operating Expenses | | | | 25.5 | 20.5 | 21.3 | 18.6 | 15.8 |
| | 8.6 | | 6.2 | | 2.6 | Operating Profit | | | | .8 | 2.4 | 1.5 | 2.6 | 3.6 |
| | -.2 | | .7 | | 2.0 | All Other Expenses (net) | | | | 3.2 | 3.2 | 2.5 | 1.8 | 1.5 |
| | 8.9 | | 5.6 | | .6 | Profit Before Taxes | | | | -2.4 | -.8 | -1.0 | .9 | 2.1 |
| | | | | | | **RATIOS** | | | | | | | | |
| | 2.6 | | 1.8 | | 1.7 | | | | | 2.3 | 1.8 | 1.6 | 1.7 | 1.7 |
| | 1.7 | | 1.4 | | 1.4 | Current | | | | 1.5 | 1.5 | 1.3 | 1.4 | 1.3 |
| | 1.3 | | 1.2 | | 1.2 | | | | | 1.2 | 1.2 | 1.2 | 1.2 | 1.2 |
| | 1.0 | | .6 | | .4 | | | | | .6 | .5 | .4 | .4 | .3 |
| | .5 | | .3 | | .2 | Quick | | | | .2 | .2 | .2 | .2 | .2 |
| | .2 | | .1 | | .1 | | | | | .1 | .1 | .1 | .1 | .1 |
| | | | | | | | | 0 UND | | 0 999.8 | 0 UND | 1 666.0 | 1 250.8 | |
| 0 | 746.4 | 0 | 999.8 | 1 | 681.2 | Sales/Receivables | | 1 316.7 | | 2 183.0 | 2 154.4 | 2 168.8 | 4 97.0 | |
| 3 | 111.4 | 1 | 251.2 | 3 | 125.9 | | | 13 27.3 | | 5 79.3 | 7 53.4 | 6 63.3 | 7 50.1 | |
| 7 | 49.0 | 5 | 77.4 | 7 | 55.9 | | | | | | | | | |
| 69 | 5.3 | 114 | 3.2 | 126 | 2.9 | | | 192 1.9 | | 122 3.0 | 126 2.9 | 126 2.9 | 126 2.9 | |
| 91 | 4.0 | 152 | 2.4 | 166 | 2.2 | Cost of Sales/Inventory | | 332 1.1 | | 215 1.7 | 182 2.0 | 166 2.2 | 152 2.4 | |
| 122 | 3.0 | 203 | 1.8 | 215 | 1.7 | | | 456 .8 | | 281 1.3 | 228 1.6 | 215 1.7 | 182 2.0 | |
| 4 | 97.2 | 3 | 120.4 | 51 | 7.2 | | | 4 91.9 | | 73 5.0 | 81 4.5 | 66 5.5 | 10 36.6 | |
| 30 | 12.1 | 10 | 34.8 | 122 | 3.0 | Cost of Sales/Payables | | 130 2.8 | | 122 3.0 | 135 2.7 | 122 3.0 | 111 3.3 | |
| 78 | 4.7 | 130 | 2.8 | 174 | 2.1 | | | 332 1.1 | | 228 1.6 | 192 1.9 | 166 2.2 | 146 2.5 | |
| | 5.8 | | 5.1 | | 5.0 | | | | | 2.1 | 4.3 | 5.3 | 4.8 | 5.8 |
| | 8.3 | | 8.9 | | 8.2 | Sales/Working Capital | | | | 3.5 | 7.0 | 9.1 | 7.8 | 9.4 |
| | 16.5 | | 15.9 | | 15.9 | | | | | 11.6 | 11.7 | 19.0 | 14.4 | 15.9 |
| | 37.0 | | 13.9 | | 2.9 | | | | | 2.0 | 2.3 | 2.0 | 2.8 | 3.4 |
| (164) | 18.8 | (241) | 6.7 | (785) | 1.3 | EBIT/Interest | | (37) .5 | | (52) 1.0 | (164) .8 | (275) 1.3 | (253) 2.0 | |
| | 9.5 | | 2.7 | | .3 | | | -1.0 | | .2 | -.4 | .5 | .8 | |
| | | | | | 10.1 | Net Profit + Depr., Dep., | | | | | | | 24.5 | 24.4 |
| | | | (39) | | 3.7 | Amort./Cur. Mat. L/T/D | | | | | | (11) 2.7 | (15) 8.4 | |
| | | | | | -.2 | | | | | | | | -2.8 | 5.6 |
| | .1 | | .1 | | .1 | | | | | .1 | .1 | .0 | .0 | .1 |
| | .2 | | .2 | | .2 | Fixed/Worth | | | | .2 | .3 | .2 | .1 | .2 |
| | .5 | | .5 | | .5 | | | | | 2.0 | .4 | .6 | .4 | .4 |
| | .8 | | 1.2 | | 1.4 | | | | | .6 | 1.1 | 1.7 | 1.3 | 1.5 |
| | 1.8 | | 2.3 | | 2.6 | Debt/Worth | | | | 2.5 | 2.6 | 3.2 | 2.3 | 2.8 |
| | 4.1 | | 4.3 | | 5.3 | | | | | 6.6 | 4.3 | 7.7 | 4.9 | 4.8 |
| | 109.6 | | 68.1 | | 21.8 | | | | | 13.9 | 10.6 | 17.7 | 21.2 | 26.0 |
| (164) | 70.8 | (247) | 39.5 | (753) | 6.9 | % Profit Before Taxes/Tangible Net Worth | | (34) -2.4 | | (49) 3.1 | (154) -.2 | (264) 6.8 | (250) 13.6 | |
| | 41.9 | | 19.6 | | -13.5 | | | -18.5 | | -26.4 | -35.2 | -10.8 | -3.7 | |
| | 34.5 | | 18.5 | | 6.8 | | | | | 1.8 | 4.9 | 5.2 | 6.9 | 9.1 |
| | 25.9 | | 12.0 | | 1.6 | % Profit Before Taxes/Total Assets | | | | -1.9 | .0 | -1.0 | 1.8 | 4.0 |
| | 16.6 | | 4.9 | | -3.6 | | | | | -6.7 | -4.9 | -8.1 | -3.5 | -.9 |
| | 119.6 | | 140.5 | | 155.4 | | | | | 81.1 | 96.6 | 194.9 | 210.6 | 123.5 |
| | 47.9 | | 49.6 | | 52.6 | Sales/Net Fixed Assets | | | | 15.8 | 15.9 | 54.0 | 64.3 | 50.0 |
| | 23.1 | | 17.0 | | 17.3 | | | | | 5.3 | 10.3 | 15.3 | 25.0 | 22.0 |
| | 3.5 | | 2.7 | | 2.4 | | | | | 1.5 | 2.5 | 2.5 | 2.5 | 2.4 |
| | 2.9 | | 2.0 | | 1.9 | Sales/Total Assets | | | | 1.1 | 1.7 | 1.9 | 2.0 | 2.0 |
| | 2.3 | | 1.6 | | 1.5 | | | | | .9 | 1.2 | 1.4 | 1.6 | 1.7 |
| | .1 | | .1 | | .1 | | | | | .3 | .2 | .2 | .1 | .1 |
| (115) | .3 | (179) | .3 | (531) | .4 | % Depr., Dep., Amort./Sales | | (22) .7 | | (36) .5 | (98) .6 | (159) .3 | (211) .3 | |
| | .6 | | .7 | | .8 | | | 1.8 | | 1.3 | 1.1 | .7 | .6 | |
| | .4 | | .5 | | .5 | | | | | 2.3 | 1.3 | .9 | .7 | .2 |
| (86) | 1.2 | (131) | 1.0 | (404) | 1.1 | % Officers', Directors' Owners' Comp/Sales | | (20) 4.9 | | (18) 1.7 | (88) 1.6 | (150) 1.2 | (127) .5 | |
| | 2.5 | | 2.1 | | 2.0 | | | 9.3 | | 2.8 | 2.5 | 1.9 | 1.0 | |
| | 10621408M | | 13048152M | | 25914281M | Net Sales ($) | | 2520M | | 77381M | 219359M | 1265998M | 4450789M | 19898234M |
| | 3737997M | | 6109529M | | 13343727M | Total Assets ($) | | 2852M | | 73885M | 152913M | 763859M | 2313559M | 10036659M |

M = $ thousand  MM = $ million
See Pages viii through xx for Explanation of Ratios and Data

© RMA 2024

## RETAIL—Boat Dealers  NAICS 441222

### Current Data Sorted by Assets

| | | | | | | | Type of Statement | | |
|---|---|---|---|---|---|---|---|---|---|
| | | | | 7 | 4 | 5 | Unqualified | | |
| | 1 | 20 | 43 | 6 | 1 | Reviewed | | |
| | 2 | 64 | 25 | 3 | | Compiled | | |
| 3 | 17 | 143 | 55 | 1 | | Tax Returns | | |
| 8 | 53 | 591 | 418 | 35 | 4 | Other | | |
| | 454 (4/1-9/30/23) | | 1,055 (10/1/23-3/31/24) | | | | | | |
| 0-500M | 500M-2MM | 2-10MM | 10-50MM | 50-100MM | 100-250MM | | | | |
| 11 | 73 | 818 | 548 | 49 | 10 | NUMBER OF STATEMENTS | | |

### Comparative Historical Data

| | | |
|---|---|---|
| 2 | 1 | |
| 15 | 8 | |
| 28 | 8 | |
| 35 | 17 | |
| 102 | 44 | |
| 4/1/19- | 4/1/20- | |
| 3/31/20 | 3/31/21 | |
| ALL | ALL | |
| 182 | 78 | |

| % | % | % | % | % | % | ASSETS | % | % |
|---|---|---|---|---|---|---|---|---|
| 37.2 | 11.2 | 10.3 | 8.7 | 7.2 | 4.5 | Cash & Equivalents | 10.2 | 23.2 |
| 10.2 | 3.9 | 2.0 | 2.5 | 4.0 | 5.2 | Trade Receivables (net) | 4.9 | 4.8 |
| 22.2 | 55.9 | 73.3 | 70.7 | 58.8 | 53.2 | Inventory | 64.5 | 51.3 |
| 1.2 | 3.5 | 1.8 | 2.9 | 2.7 | 3.3 | All Other Current | 1.7 | 2.0 |
| 70.8 | 74.5 | 87.4 | 84.8 | 72.6 | 66.2 | Total Current | 81.3 | 81.4 |
| 20.9 | 16.9 | 8.3 | 9.3 | 15.0 | 16.1 | Fixed Assets (net) | 13.4 | 14.2 |
| 3.9 | 4.6 | 2.2 | 3.1 | 3.7 | 13.9 | Intangibles (net) | 1.6 | 1.5 |
| 4.4 | 4.0 | 2.1 | 2.8 | 8.7 | 3.8 | All Other Non-Current | 3.6 | 2.9 |
| 100.0 | 100.0 | 100.0 | 100.0 | 100.0 | 100.0 | Total | 100.0 | 100.0 |
| | | | | | | **LIABILITIES** | | |
| 23.2 | 6.6 | 3.3 | 3.1 | 2.3 | 5.9 | Notes Payable-Short Term | | |
| .1 | 1.5 | .4 | .4 | 1.0 | 1.9 | Cur. Mat.-L.T.D. | 32.3 | 22.9 |
| 15.7 | 35.9 | 53.5 | 51.6 | 43.8 | 30.6 | Trade Payables | 1.6 | 4.5 |
| .0 | .1 | .1 | .1 | .0 | .0 | Income Taxes Payable | 7.1 | 6.8 |
| 23.8 | 7.1 | 3.6 | 4.3 | 6.3 | 7.6 | All Other Current | .1 | .2 |
| 62.8 | 51.2 | 60.8 | 59.5 | 53.4 | 46.1 | Total Current | 11.6 | 13.9 |
| 68.5 | 13.3 | 7.2 | 6.3 | 6.8 | 19.9 | Long-Term Debt | 52.8 | 48.3 |
| .0 | .0 | .0 | .0 | .3 | .2 | Deferred Taxes | 13.2 | 13.9 |
| 9.0 | 11.7 | 3.9 | 3.6 | 8.6 | 6.0 | All Other Non-Current | .0 | .0 |
| -40.4 | 23.7 | 28.1 | 30.6 | 30.9 | 27.7 | Net Worth | 5.7 | 6.0 |
| 100.0 | 100.0 | 100.0 | 100.0 | 100.0 | 100.0 | Total Liabilities & Net Worth | 28.3 | 31.8 |
| | | | | | | | 100.0 | 100.0 |
| | | | | | | **INCOME DATA** | | |
| 100.0 | 100.0 | 100.0 | 100.0 | 100.0 | 100.0 | Net Sales | 100.0 | 100.0 |
| 36.9 | 33.2 | 25.4 | 23.5 | 26.7 | 27.0 | Gross Profit | 27.3 | 24.8 |
| 32.5 | 28.3 | 20.4 | 18.7 | 21.1 | 21.5 | Operating Expenses | 22.8 | 20.2 |
| 4.5 | 4.9 | 4.9 | 4.8 | 5.6 | 5.4 | Operating Profit | 4.5 | 4.6 |
| 2.3 | .7 | 1.4 | 1.2 | 1.4 | 1.5 | All Other Expenses (net) | 1.2 | -.4 |
| 2.2 | 4.2 | 3.5 | 3.6 | 4.2 | 3.9 | Profit Before Taxes | 3.3 | 5.0 |
| | | | | | | **RATIOS** | | |
| 5.4 | 2.1 | 1.7 | 1.7 | 1.5 | 2.2 | | 2.3 | 2.6 |
| 1.4 | 1.5 | 1.4 | 1.4 | 1.3 | 1.3 | Current | 1.4 | 1.6 |
| .9 | 1.2 | 1.2 | 1.2 | 1.2 | 1.1 | | 1.2 | 1.3 |
| 5.4 | .5 | .3 | .3 | .3 | .4 | | .5 | 1.2 |
| .8 | .2 | .1 | .1 | .1 | .1 | Quick | .2 | .5 |
| .1 | .1 | .1 | .1 | .0 | .1 | | .1 | .2 |
| 0 UND | 0 UND | 0 UND | 1 585.2 | 2 164.0 | 3 105.6 | | 1 724.4 | 0 UND |
| 0 UND | 1 399.2 | 1 289.2 | 3 118.7 | 7 53.5 | 6 56.6 | Sales/Receivables | 3 139.1 | 1 279.6 |
| 0 UND | 9 39.8 | 5 71.5 | 7 52.9 | 16 22.4 | 17 22.0 | | 11 34.5 | 7 51.9 |
| 0 UND | 74 4.9 | 159 2.3 | 166 2.2 | 203 1.8 | 107 3.4 | | 118 3.1 | 49 7.5 |
| 10 37.9 | 146 2.5 | 215 1.7 | 215 1.7 | 243 1.5 | 159 2.3 | Cost of Sales/Inventory | 174 2.1 | 89 4.1 |
| 20 18.3 | 243 1.5 | 304 1.2 | 281 1.3 | 332 1.1 | 261 1.4 | | 228 1.6 | 130 2.8 |
| 0 UND | 26 14.1 | 101 3.6 | 107 3.4 | 135 2.7 | 16 22.6 | | 1 309.1 | 0 999.8 |
| 0 UND | 74 4.9 | 159 2.3 | 166 2.2 | 174 2.1 | 50 7.3 | Cost of Sales/Payables | 5 76.9 | 4 103.6 |
| 7 53.3 | 174 2.1 | 228 1.6 | 228 1.6 | 243 1.5 | 215 1.7 | | 17 21.0 | 13 28.2 |
| 19.0 | 5.1 | 4.6 | 4.6 | 5.6 | 6.1 | | 4.5 | 5.3 |
| 64.3 | 8.7 | 7.2 | 7.1 | 6.9 | 10.8 | Sales/Working Capital | 9.0 | 9.0 |
| -291.0 | 35.0 | 12.3 | 11.1 | 10.1 | 37.2 | | 20.2 | 17.3 |
| | 6.5 | 6.3 | 7.0 | 6.3 | | | 6.3 | 16.5 |
| (68) | 3.3 | (793) 2.6 | (537) 3.0 | 3.8 | | EBIT/Interest | (168) 3.4 | (74) 5.5 |
| | 1.5 | 1.2 | 1.2 | 1.5 | | | 1.4 | 2.5 |
| | | 17.9 | 17.5 | 24.7 | | | 11.4 | |
| | (38) 7.7 | (36) 7.8 | (12) 7.7 | | Net Profit + Depr., Dep., Amort./Cur. Mat. L/T/D | (12) 6.6 | |
| | | 2.2 | 4.8 | 5.1 | | | 1.0 | |
| .1 | .1 | .1 | .1 | .2 | .5 | | .0 | .1 |
| 1.0 | .4 | .2 | .2 | .4 | 1.5 | Fixed/Worth | .2 | .3 |
| -1.2 | 7.8 | .6 | .7 | 1.1 | NM | | 1.3 | .9 |
| 1.4 | 1.0 | 1.5 | 1.4 | 1.5 | 2.1 | | 1.3 | 1.1 |
| 8.9 | 3.6 | 3.1 | 2.7 | 3.0 | 5.4 | Debt/Worth | 2.9 | 2.1 |
| -2.9 | 452.5 | 7.2 | 6.1 | 7.7 | NM | | 7.3 | 6.0 |
| | 59.7 | 40.6 | 39.9 | 42.0 | | | 39.8 | 75.0 |
| (56) | 24.4 | (740) 18.2 | (500) 21.9 | (48) 19.3 | | % Profit Before Taxes/Tangible Net Worth | (162) 23.1 | (69) 42.4 |
| | 9.1 | 5.4 | 7.9 | 5.1 | | | 8.7 | 13.3 |
| 28.6 | 15.7 | 10.7 | 11.6 | 8.5 | 13.8 | | 11.2 | 21.5 |
| .0 | 8.7 | 4.4 | 5.6 | 5.1 | 4.3 | % Profit Before Taxes/Total Assets | 5.4 | 11.6 |
| -11.6 | 1.8 | .7 | 1.1 | 1.4 | 1.3 | | 1.0 | 4.0 |
| 493.2 | 178.8 | 154.5 | 109.3 | 35.2 | 15.3 | | 254.9 | 143.9 |
| 24.6 | 27.5 | 46.3 | 34.0 | 15.0 | 13.2 | Sales/Net Fixed Assets | 55.1 | 68.7 |
| 11.9 | 8.8 | 15.9 | 12.5 | 3.8 | 5.7 | | 11.1 | 14.3 |
| 15.6 | 2.8 | 2.1 | 1.9 | 1.4 | 2.0 | | 2.6 | 3.7 |
| 9.3 | 1.9 | 1.6 | 1.6 | 1.1 | 1.7 | Sales/Total Assets | 1.9 | 2.8 |
| 3.2 | 1.5 | 1.3 | 1.2 | 1.0 | 1.3 | | 1.4 | 2.3 |
| | .3 | .2 | .3 | .7 | | | .2 | .2 |
| (42) | .9 | (465) .6 | (364) .6 | (41) 1.1 | | % Depr., Dep., Amort./Sales | (110) .5 | (56) .5 |
| | 3.9 | 1.3 | 1.3 | 1.8 | | | 1.5 | 1.1 |
| | 1.6 | .9 | .5 | .4 | | | .9 | .7 |
| (30) | 2.7 | (421) 1.6 | (297) 1.0 | (10) .8 | | % Officers', Directors' Owners' Comp/Sales | (80) 1.6 | (39) 1.6 |
| | 4.8 | 2.5 | 1.4 | | | | 2.9 | 4.2 |
| 18047M | 233201M | 8287305M | 16396822M | 4405921M | 2358821M | Net Sales ($) | 2801744M | 2239308M |
| 2526M | 96748M | 4624617M | 10009355M | 3409291M | 1467914M | Total Assets ($) | 1625728M | 708921M |

© RMA 2024

M = $ thousand    MM = $ million
See Pages viii through xx for Explanation of Ratios and Data

# RETAIL—Boat Dealers  NAICS 441222

## Comparative Historical Data | Current Data Sorted by Sales

| Comparative Historical Data | | | Type of Statement | Current Data Sorted by Sales | | | | | |
|---|---|---|---|---|---|---|---|---|---|
| 1 | 3 | 16 | Unqualified | | 1 | 2 | 10 | 1 17 | 15 41 |
| 14 | 26 | 71 | Reviewed | | 7 | 13 | 24 | 30 | 20 |
| 11 | 16 | 94 | Compiled | | 12 | 20 | 57 | 105 | 23 |
| 19 | 40 | 219 | Tax Returns | 2 | 64 | 85 | 264 | 459 | 231 |
| 154 | 196 | 1109 | Other | 6 | 454 (4/1-9/30/23) | | | 1,055 (10/1/23-3/31/24) | |
| 4/1/21- 3/31/22 ALL | 4/1/22- 3/31/23 ALL | 4/1/23- 3/31/24 ALL | | 0-1MM | 1-3MM | 3-5MM | 5-10MM | 10-25MM | 25MM & OVER |
| 199 | 281 | 1509 | NUMBER OF STATEMENTS | 8 | 84 | 120 | 355 | 612 | 330 |
| % | % | % | ASSETS | % | % | % | % | % | % |
| 18.4 | 13.5 | 9.8 | Cash & Equivalents | | 10.9 | 9.8 | 9.1 | 10.2 | 9.2 |
| 4.2 | 2.9 | 2.4 | Trade Receivables (net) | | 4.6 | 2.7 | 1.8 | 1.9 | 3.3 |
| 51.1 | 60.8 | 70.5 | Inventory | | 58.6 | 67.2 | 74.5 | 72.7 | 67.6 |
| 3.3 | 3.7 | 2.3 | All Other Current | | 3.2 | 1.7 | 1.9 | 2.2 | 3.0 |
| 77.0 | 80.9 | 85.1 | Total Current | | 77.3 | 81.4 | 87.3 | 87.1 | 83.1 |
| 15.2 | 10.7 | 9.5 | Fixed Assets (net) | | 16.1 | 13.8 | 7.8 | 8.0 | 10.4 |
| 2.4 | 1.5 | 2.8 | Intangibles (net) | | 4.3 | 2.9 | 1.8 | 2.8 | 3.0 |
| 5.4 | 6.9 | 2.7 | All Other Non-Current | | 2.3 | 1.8 | 3.0 | 2.1 | 3.6 |
| 100.0 | 100.0 | 100.0 | Total | | 100.0 | 100.0 | 100.0 | 100.0 | 100.0 |
| | | | LIABILITIES | | | | | | |
| 9.7 | 13.3 | 3.5 | Notes Payable-Short Term | | 7.0 | 4.4 | 3.4 | 3.3 | 2.7 |
| .8 | 1.2 | .5 | Cur. Mat.-L.T.D. | | 1.1 | .7 | .5 | .2 | .6 |
| 25.0 | 30.5 | 51.2 | Trade Payables | | 38.1 | 50.5 | 55.8 | 53.0 | 47.1 |
| .1 | .0 | .1 | Income Taxes Payable | | .1 | .0 | .1 | .1 | .1 |
| 11.1 | 9.6 | 4.3 | All Other Current | | 9.7 | 3.3 | 3.4 | 3.5 | 5.8 |
| 46.7 | 54.6 | 59.5 | Total Current | | 55.9 | 58.8 | 63.2 | 60.0 | 56.2 |
| 10.3 | 6.9 | 7.7 | Long-Term Debt | | 19.8 | 11.3 | 7.2 | 6.5 | 5.9 |
| .1 | .0 | .0 | Deferred Taxes | | .0 | .0 | .0 | .0 | .2 |
| 4.9 | 3.3 | 4.3 | All Other Non-Current | | 9.5 | 6.4 | 3.6 | 3.3 | 4.8 |
| 37.9 | 35.1 | 28.4 | Net Worth | | 14.8 | 23.5 | 26.0 | 30.1 | 32.9 |
| 100.0 | 100.0 | 100.0 | Total Liabilities & Net Worth | | 100.0 | 100.0 | 100.0 | 100.0 | 100.0 |
| | | | INCOME DATA | | | | | | |
| 100.0 | 100.0 | 100.0 | Net Sales | | 100.0 | 100.0 | 100.0 | 100.0 | 100.0 |
| 25.5 | 27.1 | 25.2 | Gross Profit | | 35.4 | 30.1 | 24.9 | 23.6 | 23.2 |
| 19.0 | 20.1 | 20.3 | Operating Expenses | | 29.2 | 24.8 | 20.8 | 18.7 | 17.9 |
| 6.5 | 7.0 | 4.9 | Operating Profit | | 6.2 | 5.3 | 4.1 | 4.9 | 5.3 |
| -.1 | -.2 | 1.3 | All Other Expenses (net) | | 2.1 | 1.7 | 1.4 | 1.3 | .7 |
| 6.7 | 7.3 | 3.6 | Profit Before Taxes | | 4.0 | 3.6 | 2.7 | 3.6 | 4.5 |
| | | | RATIOS | | | | | | |
| 2.4 | 2.0 | 1.7 | | | 2.0 | 1.8 | 1.6 | 1.7 | 1.8 |
| 1.7 | 1.4 | 1.4 | Current | | 1.4 | 1.3 | 1.3 | 1.4 | 1.4 |
| 1.3 | 1.2 | 1.2 | | | 1.1 | 1.1 | 1.2 | 1.2 | 1.2 |
| .9 | .5 | .3 | | | .6 | .4 | .3 | .3 | .4 |
| (198) .4 | .2 | .1 | Quick | | .2 | .2 | .1 | .1 | .1 |
| .2 | .1 | .1 | | | .1 | .1 | .0 | .1 | .1 |
| 0 999.8 | 0 UND | 0 999.8 | | 0 UND | 0 UND | 0 UND | 0 999.8 | 1 311.5 | |
| 2 184.4 | 2 169.2 | 2 180.6 | Sales/Receivables | 3 120.7 | 2 168.6 | 1 294.2 | 2 236.8 | 4 92.0 | |
| 7 55.7 | 8 44.7 | 6 57.2 | | 15 25.0 | 9 42.8 | 5 71.8 | 5 72.6 | 7 49.7 | |
| 61 6.0 | 111 3.3 | 159 2.3 | | 146 2.5 | 203 1.8 | 182 2.0 | 152 2.4 | 135 2.7 | |
| 87 4.2 | 159 2.3 | 215 1.7 | Cost of Sales/Inventory | 304 1.2 | 281 1.3 | 261 1.4 | 215 1.7 | 192 1.9 | |
| 122 3.0 | 228 1.6 | 304 1.2 | | 406 .9 | 365 1.0 | 332 1.1 | 281 1.3 | 228 1.6 | |
| 5 69.3 | 6 64.4 | 99 3.7 | | 29 12.7 | 126 2.9 | 130 2.8 | 99 3.7 | 73 5.0 | |
| 35 10.4 | 73 5.0 | 159 2.3 | Cost of Sales/Payables | 174 2.1 | 215 1.7 | 192 1.9 | 159 2.3 | 130 2.8 | |
| 72 5.1 | 146 2.5 | 228 1.6 | | 365 1.0 | 281 1.3 | 243 1.5 | 215 1.7 | 182 2.0 | |
| 5.8 | 4.6 | 4.7 | | | 3.5 | 3.9 | 4.4 | 4.8 | 5.4 |
| 9.3 | 8.1 | 7.3 | Sales/Working Capital | | 7.2 | 6.0 | 7.3 | 7.3 | 7.7 |
| 15.0 | 14.6 | 12.3 | | | 26.9 | 16.4 | 12.1 | 11.6 | 13.2 |
| 48.1 | 34.6 | 6.5 | | 6.0 | 4.4 | 4.7 | 7.3 | 8.8 | |
| (182) 17.1 | (264) 14.8 | (1464) 2.8 | EBIT/Interest | (75) 2.2 | (116) 2.2 | (343) 2.0 | (600) 2.9 | (322) 4.6 | |
| 5.5 | 5.4 | 1.2 | | 1.3 | 1.0 | .9 | 1.2 | 2.0 | |
| | | 17.9 | Net Profit + Depr., Dep., | | 17.9 | 16.2 | 28.3 | 18.3 | |
| | (91) 7.8 | Amort./Cur. Mat. L/T/D | | (11) 2.7 | (12) 5.3 | (23) 10.2 | (42) 8.2 | | |
| | | 3.5 | | | 1.5 | 1.5 | 6.7 | 4.6 | |
| .1 | .1 | .1 | | .1 | .1 | .1 | .0 | .1 | |
| .3 | .2 | .2 | Fixed/Worth | .8 | .4 | .2 | .1 | .2 | |
| .7 | .5 | .7 | | 5.0 | 2.8 | .7 | .5 | .7 | |
| .7 | 1.0 | 1.4 | | 1.4 | 1.7 | 1.7 | 1.4 | 1.3 | |
| 1.5 | 1.9 | 2.9 | Debt/Worth | 5.8 | 4.1 | 3.6 | 2.8 | 2.4 | |
| 4.2 | 4.7 | 7.1 | | -47.9 | 14.4 | 8.4 | 5.6 | 4.5 | |
| 69.6 | 64.2 | 40.6 | % Profit Before Taxes/Tangible | 60.8 | 41.1 | 32.4 | 38.8 | 48.9 | |
| (174) 45.7 | (265) 43.5 | (1358) 19.9 | Net Worth | (61) 19.0 | (97) 18.5 | (323) 13.8 | (566) 19.8 | (305) 28.9 | |
| 26.4 | 19.7 | 6.4 | | 7.2 | 5.8 | .9 | 6.5 | 14.5 | |
| 28.5 | 23.3 | 11.3 | | 10.7 | 8.6 | 8.4 | 11.5 | 14.3 | |
| 18.0 | 13.2 | 5.0 | % Profit Before Taxes/Total Assets | 3.2 | 3.9 | 3.3 | 5.0 | 8.1 | |
| 8.4 | 6.5 | .8 | | .4 | .1 | -.1 | .9 | 3.1 | |
| 89.6 | 87.2 | 125.7 | | 87.6 | 90.8 | 149.8 | 153.6 | 84.9 | |
| 29.1 | 31.8 | 38.4 | Sales/Net Fixed Assets | 21.6 | 21.7 | 38.9 | 53.3 | 28.3 | |
| 12.3 | 12.9 | 13.5 | | 7.1 | 7.6 | 16.8 | 15.3 | 12.2 | |
| 3.4 | 2.4 | 2.1 | | 1.9 | 1.7 | 1.9 | 2.1 | 2.4 | |
| 2.8 | 1.9 | 1.6 | Sales/Total Assets | 1.3 | 1.3 | 1.5 | 1.7 | 1.8 | |
| 2.1 | 1.5 | 1.2 | | .9 | 1.0 | 1.2 | 1.3 | 1.4 | |
| .2 | .2 | .3 | | .3 | .2 | .2 | .2 | .3 | |
| (94) .5 | (158) .5 | (927) .6 | % Depr., Dep., Amort./Sales | (47) .8 | (76) .8 | (199) .6 | (355) .5 | (244) .6 | |
| 1.1 | 1.1 | 1.4 | | 3.1 | 2.1 | 1.5 | 1.3 | 1.2 | |
| .6 | .6 | .7 | % Officers', Directors' | 2.2 | 1.7 | 1.0 | .7 | .4 | |
| (81) 1.4 | (119) 1.2 | (762) 1.3 | Owners' Comp/Sales | (31) 3.3 | (49) 2.6 | (180) 1.7 | (343) 1.2 | (158) .7 | |
| 2.9 | 2.5 | 2.4 | | 5.3 | 4.2 | 2.7 | 2.0 | 1.3 | |
| 4609565M | 7365981M | 31700117M | Net Sales ($) | 5506M | 184491M | 481257M | 2630517M | 10009587M | 18388759M |
| 1827035M | 4212528M | 19610451M | Total Assets ($) | 6009M | 173524M | 391382M | 1885080M | 6268391M | 10886065M |

M = $ thousand  MM = $ million
See Pages viii through xx for Explanation of Ratios and Data

© RMA 2024

# RETAIL—Motorcycle, ATV, and All Other Motor Vehicle Dealers  NAICS 441227

## Current Data Sorted by Assets

| | | | | | | Type of Statement | | |
|---|---|---|---|---|---|---|---|---|
| | | 2 | 13 | 3 | 11 | Unqualified | | |
| | 4 | 59 | 64 | 8 | 1 | Reviewed | | |
| | 10 | 116 | 40 | 4 | | Compiled | | |
| 3 | 18 | 153 | 68 | 3 | | Tax Returns | | |
| 12 | 81 | 848 | 499 | 54 | 23 | Other | | |
| | 658 (4/1-9/30/23) | | 1,439 (10/1/23-3/31/24) | | | | | |
| 0-500M | 500M-2MM | 2-10MM | 10-50MM | 50-100MM | 100-250MM | | | |
| 15 | 113 | 1178 | 684 | 72 | 35 | NUMBER OF STATEMENTS | | |
| % | % | % | % | % | % | ASSETS | | |
| 31.5 | 15.1 | 10.6 | 9.4 | 9.3 | 10.0 | Cash & Equivalents | | |
| .3 | 3.7 | 3.9 | 4.5 | 7.0 | 8.0 | Trade Receivables (net) | | |
| 21.0 | 60.0 | 71.8 | 67.0 | 57.6 | 40.9 | Inventory | | |
| 3.1 | 3.1 | 1.9 | 2.6 | 3.3 | 3.4 | All Other Current | | |
| 55.9 | 81.9 | 88.2 | 83.4 | 77.2 | 62.4 | Total Current | | |
| 37.6 | 12.5 | 6.5 | 8.2 | 12.2 | 19.1 | Fixed Assets (net) | | |
| 5.3 | 4.0 | 3.6 | 4.9 | 6.7 | 9.5 | Intangibles (net) | | |
| 1.2 | 1.6 | 1.7 | 3.4 | 4.0 | 9.0 | All Other Non-Current | | |
| 100.0 | 100.0 | 100.0 | 100.0 | 100.0 | 100.0 | Total | | |
| | | | | | | LIABILITIES | | |
| 4.8 | 3.9 | 3.8 | 3.8 | 5.7 | 3.7 | Notes Payable-Short Term | | |
| 5.7 | 2.1 | .3 | .6 | 1.8 | 1.9 | Cur. Mat.-L.T.D. | | |
| 5.0 | 41.7 | 53.9 | 48.1 | 40.0 | 25.7 | Trade Payables | | |
| .0 | .2 | .1 | .1 | .3 | .1 | Income Taxes Payable | | |
| 5.9 | 11.0 | 4.5 | 5.0 | 7.5 | 7.7 | All Other Current | | |
| 21.4 | 58.9 | 62.7 | 57.6 | 55.3 | 39.0 | Total Current | | |
| 25.9 | 10.4 | 4.8 | 5.1 | 8.3 | 12.4 | Long-Term Debt | | |
| .0 | .0 | .1 | .1 | .1 | 1.2 | Deferred Taxes | | |
| 10.1 | 6.8 | 4.1 | 4.9 | 6.2 | 10.0 | All Other Non-Current | | |
| 42.6 | 23.9 | 28.3 | 32.4 | 30.0 | 37.5 | Net Worth | | |
| 100.0 | 100.0 | 100.0 | 100.0 | 100.0 | 100.0 | Total Liabilities & Net Worth | | |
| | | | | | | INCOME DATA | | |
| 100.0 | 100.0 | 100.0 | 100.0 | 100.0 | 100.0 | Net Sales | | |
| 58.6 | 30.2 | 22.1 | 21.7 | 22.7 | 23.8 | Gross Profit | | |
| 46.8 | 27.7 | 18.1 | 16.8 | 18.0 | 19.2 | Operating Expenses | | |
| 11.7 | 2.5 | 4.0 | 4.9 | 4.7 | 4.6 | Operating Profit | | |
| 2.0 | .9 | .9 | .7 | .6 | .5 | All Other Expenses (net) | | |
| 9.7 | 1.6 | 3.1 | 4.2 | 4.1 | 4.1 | Profit Before Taxes | | |
| | | | | | | RATIOS | | |
| 9.7 | 2.0 | 1.7 | 1.7 | 1.6 | 2.6 | | | |
| 3.7 | 1.5 | 1.4 | 1.4 | 1.3 | 1.5 | Current | | |
| 1.1 | 1.1 | 1.2 | 1.2 | 1.2 | 1.2 | | | |
| 9.7 | .5 | .4 | .4 | .5 | 1.2 | | | |
| 1.9 | .2 | .2 | .2 | .2 | .5 | Quick | | |
| .4 | .1 | .1 | .1 | .1 | .1 | | | |
| 0 UND | 0 UND | 1 319.0 | 3 111.9 | 4 82.4 | 8 47.2 | | | |
| 0 UND | 1 368.6 | 4 92.1 | 7 62.5 | 12 29.6 | | Sales/Receivables | | |
| 1 490.0 | 6 65.5 | 8 43.9 | 10 37.2 | 17 21.8 | 19 19.0 | | | |
| 0 UND | 78 4.7 | 122 3.0 | 126 2.9 | 111 3.3 | 74 4.9 | | | |
| 13 28.0 | 130 2.8 | 159 2.3 | 159 2.3 | 152 2.4 | 135 2.7 | Cost of Sales/Inventory | | |
| 159 2.3 | 203 1.8 | 215 1.7 | 203 1.8 | 174 2.1 | 174 2.1 | | | |
| 0 UND | 21 17.0 | 85 4.3 | 74 4.9 | 51 7.1 | 19 18.9 | | | |
| 0 UND | 99 3.7 | 126 2.9 | 118 3.1 | 126 2.9 | 59 6.2 | Cost of Sales/Payables | | |
| 39 9.3 | 146 2.5 | 174 2.1 | 159 2.3 | 152 2.4 | 135 2.7 | | | |
| 5.6 | 5.4 | 5.8 | 5.4 | 6.9 | 5.7 | | | |
| 6.7 | 10.1 | 8.9 | 8.1 | 9.2 | 8.5 | Sales/Working Capital | | |
| 124.3 | 24.3 | 14.6 | 14.7 | 15.3 | 28.6 | | | |
| 8.8 | 9.7 | 9.4 | 11.3 | 16.3 | 28.8 | | | |
| (14) 3.6 | (102) 2.8 | (1124) 3.9 | (665) 4.9 | (65) 4.1 | 7.0 | EBIT/Interest | | |
| .1 | -.2 | 1.2 | 1.8 | 1.8 | 2.7 | | | |
| | | 24.6 | 29.7 | 29.3 | | | | |
| | (71) 5.8 | (66) 7.9 | (18) 8.6 | | Net Profit + Depr., Dep., Amort./Cur. Mat. L/T/D | | | |
| | | 2.3 | 3.8 | 3.4 | | | | |
| .0 | .0 | .0 | .1 | .2 | .4 | | | |
| .9 | .2 | .2 | .2 | .4 | .7 | Fixed/Worth | | |
| 14.8 | 2.0 | .5 | .5 | 1.8 | 4.6 | | | |
| .3 | 1.2 | 1.6 | 1.4 | 1.7 | 1.0 | | | |
| 1.9 | 3.4 | 3.0 | 2.7 | 3.5 | 1.9 | Debt/Worth | | |
| 15.6 | 222.1 | 7.0 | 6.3 | 9.4 | 40.4 | | | |
| 63.5 | 57.4 | 49.9 | 50.8 | 49.5 | 53.7 | | | |
| (12) 24.6 | (88) 24.1 | (1054) 26.2 | (658) 30.3 | (59) 31.5 | (27) 23.9 | % Profit Before Taxes/Tangible Net Worth | | |
| -6.2 | 5.6 | 6.0 | 13.8 | 18.2 | 11.7 | | | |
| 29.0 | 14.2 | 13.0 | 13.3 | 14.2 | 11.4 | | | |
| 6.5 | 4.6 | 6.1 | 8.2 | 8.1 | 7.7 | % Profit Before Taxes/Total Assets | | |
| -2.8 | -4.1 | .7 | 3.3 | 1.2 | 2.2 | | | |
| 490.0 | 267.2 | 188.6 | 111.2 | 45.4 | 25.4 | | | |
| 13.3 | 63.1 | 64.8 | 42.7 | 23.6 | 14.7 | Sales/Net Fixed Assets | | |
| 2.2 | 15.6 | 25.8 | 20.9 | 13.4 | 6.6 | | | |
| 4.8 | 2.9 | 2.6 | 2.4 | 2.2 | 2.1 | | | |
| 1.8 | 2.1 | 2.1 | 1.9 | 1.8 | 1.5 | Sales/Total Assets | | |
| 1.4 | 1.6 | 1.6 | 1.5 | 1.4 | 1.3 | | | |
| | .2 | .2 | .2 | .3 | .3 | | | |
| (58) | .3 | (681) .4 | (509) .4 | (67) .7 | (32) .7 | % Depr., Dep., Amort./Sales | | |
| | .8 | .8 | .8 | 1.3 | 1.4 | | | |
| | 1.4 | .6 | .4 | .1 | | | | |
| (37) | 2.2 | (499) 1.2 | (298) .7 | (22) .7 | | % Officers', Directors', Owners' Comp/Sales | | |
| | 3.5 | 3.0 | 1.4 | 1.7 | | | | |
| 21994M | 382209M | 13824944M | 25553231M | 9856428M | 10675902M | Net Sales ($) | | |
| 5343M | 156596M | 6449489M | 12554442M | 5059266M | 5772999M | Total Assets ($) | | |

## Comparative Historical Data

| | | | | Type of Statement |
|---|---|---|---|---|
| | 12 | | 12 | Unqualified |
| | 31 | | 20 | Reviewed |
| | 39 | | 16 | Compiled |
| | 89 | | 25 | Tax Returns |
| | 238 | | 122 | Other |
| | 4/1/19-3/31/20 ALL | | 4/1/20-3/31/21 ALL | |
| | 409 | | 195 | NUMBER OF STATEMENTS |
| | % | | % | ASSETS |
| | 9.9 | | 18.8 | Cash & Equivalents |
| | 7.2 | | 6.8 | Trade Receivables (net) |
| | 56.8 | | 48.1 | Inventory |
| | 2.1 | | 2.5 | All Other Current |
| | 76.0 | | 76.3 | Total Current |
| | 13.3 | | 13.3 | Fixed Assets (net) |
| | 5.3 | | 5.7 | Intangibles (net) |
| | 5.4 | | 4.8 | All Other Non-Current |
| | 100.0 | | 100.0 | Total |
| | | | | LIABILITIES |
| | 30.9 | | 21.6 | Notes Payable-Short Term |
| | 3.0 | | 3.3 | Cur. Mat.-L.T.D. |
| | 11.3 | | 10.2 | Trade Payables |
| | .1 | | .1 | Income Taxes Payable |
| | 11.0 | | 12.0 | All Other Current |
| | 56.2 | | 47.3 | Total Current |
| | 12.3 | | 15.6 | Long-Term Debt |
| | .0 | | .1 | Deferred Taxes |
| | 4.5 | | 5.2 | All Other Non-Current |
| | 26.9 | | 31.8 | Net Worth |
| | 100.0 | | 100.0 | Total Liabilities & Net Worth |
| | | | | INCOME DATA |
| | 100.0 | | 100.0 | Net Sales |
| | 23.8 | | 23.6 | Gross Profit |
| | 20.6 | | 19.8 | Operating Expenses |
| | 3.2 | | 3.8 | Operating Profit |
| | .7 | | -.6 | All Other Expenses (net) |
| | 2.5 | | 4.5 | Profit Before Taxes |
| | | | | RATIOS |
| | 1.8 | | 2.5 | |
| | 1.3 | | 1.5 | Current |
| | 1.1 | | 1.2 | |
| | .5 | | 1.1 | |
| | .2 | | .5 | Quick |
| | .1 | | .2 | |
| 2 | 194.5 | 1 | 313.4 | |
| 6 | 58.0 | 6 | 65.3 | Sales/Receivables |
| 13 | 27.1 | 14 | 26.8 | |
| 79 | 4.6 | 60 | 6.1 | |
| 114 | 3.2 | 85 | 4.3 | Cost of Sales/Inventory |
| 166 | 2.2 | 114 | 3.2 | |
| 4 | 90.1 | 4 | 91.9 | |
| 9 | 39.6 | 10 | 36.9 | Cost of Sales/Payables |
| 22 | 16.7 | 21 | 17.7 | |
| | 6.9 | | 5.6 | |
| | 14.6 | | 11.3 | Sales/Working Capital |
| | 47.7 | | 23.5 | |
| | 8.2 | | 17.7 | |
| (371) | 3.1 | (175) | 5.4 | EBIT/Interest |
| | 1.4 | | 2.7 | |
| | 14.3 | | 10.2 | |
| (25) | 2.0 | (17) | 2.3 | Net Profit + Depr., Dep., Amort./Cur. Mat. L/T/D |
| | .6 | | 1.4 | |
| | .1 | | .1 | |
| | .4 | | .3 | Fixed/Worth |
| | 1.8 | | 1.2 | |
| | 1.3 | | 1.1 | |
| | 3.3 | | 2.4 | Debt/Worth |
| | 15.8 | | 9.1 | |
| | 44.8 | | 67.4 | |
| (344) | 22.3 | (161) | 33.6 | % Profit Before Taxes/Tangible Net Worth |
| | 7.1 | | 11.9 | |
| | 11.1 | | 19.1 | |
| | 4.5 | | 8.9 | % Profit Before Taxes/Total Assets |
| | .9 | | 3.4 | |
| | 125.3 | | 112.2 | |
| | 44.2 | | 38.6 | Sales/Net Fixed Assets |
| | 13.7 | | 12.8 | |
| | 3.0 | | 3.4 | |
| | 2.3 | | 2.6 | Sales/Total Assets |
| | 1.7 | | 1.9 | |
| | .2 | | .3 | |
| (275) | .5 | (129) | .7 | % Depr., Dep., Amort./Sales |
| | 1.0 | | 1.7 | |
| | .7 | | .7 | |
| (163) | 1.2 | (63) | 1.3 | % Officers', Directors', Owners' Comp/Sales |
| | 2.5 | | 2.5 | |
| | 16875407M | | 6812436M | Net Sales ($) |
| | 7686187M | | 3107111M | Total Assets ($) |

M = $ thousand   MM = $ million
See Pages viii through xx for Explanation of Ratios and Data

© RMA 2024

# RETAIL—Motorcycle, ATV, and All Other Motor Vehicle Dealers  NAICS 441227

## Comparative Historical Data | Current Data Sorted by Sales

| Comparative Historical Data | | | | Type of Statement | Current Data Sorted by Sales | | | | | |
|---|---|---|---|---|---|---|---|---|---|---|
| 9 | 13 | 29 | | Unqualified | | 2 | 3 | 30 | 3 50 | 26 51 |
| 26 | 37 | 136 | | Reviewed | 2 | 7 | 19 | 41 | 68 | 33 |
| 15 | 28 | 170 | | Compiled | 4 | 6 | 13 | 55 | 113 | 54 |
| 37 | 54 | 245 | | Tax Returns | 20 | 55 | 93 | 328 | 593 | 428 |
| 124 | 306 | 1517 | | Other | | | | | | |
| 4/1/21-3/31/22 ALL | 4/1/22-3/31/23 ALL | 4/1/23-3/31/24 ALL | | | 658 (4/1-9/30/23) | | | 1,439 (10/1/23-3/31/24) | | |
| | | | | | 0-1MM | 1-3MM | 3-5MM | 5-10MM | 10-25MM | 25MM & OVER |
| 211 | 438 | 2097 | NUMBER OF STATEMENTS | | 26 | 70 | 128 | 454 | 827 | 592 |
| % | % | % | ASSETS | | % | % | % | % | % | % |
| 21.7 | 14.3 | 10.5 | | Cash & Equivalents | 16.6 | 11.8 | 11.5 | 9.7 | 11.2 | 9.6 |
| 7.2 | 5.0 | 4.2 | | Trade Receivables (net) | 3.1 | 3.4 | 5.5 | 3.3 | 4.0 | 5.2 |
| 45.5 | 55.7 | 68.2 | | Inventory | 33.5 | 56.9 | 66.8 | 72.9 | 69.6 | 65.9 |
| 2.3 | 3.1 | 2.3 | | All Other Current | 1.2 | 4.7 | 2.8 | 1.9 | 2.1 | 2.6 |
| 76.7 | 78.2 | 85.3 | | Total Current | 54.3 | 76.7 | 86.5 | 87.8 | 86.8 | 83.2 |
| 12.7 | 11.6 | 8.0 | | Fixed Assets (net) | 34.7 | 13.9 | 9.6 | 6.8 | 6.4 | 9.0 |
| 5.7 | 5.4 | 4.3 | | Intangibles (net) | 7.8 | 7.2 | 2.3 | 3.5 | 4.6 | 4.3 |
| 4.9 | 4.8 | 2.5 | | All Other Non-Current | 3.2 | 2.1 | 1.6 | 1.9 | 2.2 | 3.5 |
| 100.0 | 100.0 | 100.0 | | Total | 100.0 | 100.0 | 100.0 | 100.0 | 100.0 | 100.0 |
| | | | LIABILITIES | | | | | | | |
| 16.4 | 13.9 | 3.9 | | Notes Payable-Short Term | 4.5 | 4.3 | 3.4 | 4.1 | 3.8 | 3.8 |
| 3.3 | 1.0 | .6 | | Cur. Mat.-L.T.D. | 8.5 | 1.2 | .5 | .5 | .4 | .8 |
| 10.2 | 23.2 | 50.0 | | Trade Payables | 20.7 | 41.5 | 49.0 | 54.9 | 51.8 | 46.4 |
| .3 | .2 | .1 | | Income Taxes Payable | .0 | .2 | .2 | .1 | .1 | .1 |
| 10.2 | 8.5 | 5.2 | | All Other Current | 4.6 | 17.4 | 6.1 | 4.8 | 4.1 | 5.5 |
| 40.4 | 46.8 | 59.9 | | Total Current | 38.2 | 64.4 | 59.1 | 64.3 | 60.2 | 56.6 |
| 11.6 | 9.6 | 5.6 | | Long-Term Debt | 26.4 | 8.1 | 7.6 | 5.7 | 4.6 | 5.4 |
| .1 | .0 | .1 | | Deferred Taxes | 1.8 | .0 | .0 | .0 | .0 | .2 |
| 2.9 | 4.5 | 4.7 | | All Other Non-Current | 8.9 | 6.6 | 7.6 | 3.9 | 4.2 | 5.0 |
| 45.1 | 39.0 | 29.7 | | Net Worth | 24.8 | 20.8 | 25.7 | 26.0 | 31.0 | 32.8 |
| 100.0 | 100.0 | 100.0 | | Total Liabilities & Net Worth | 100.0 | 100.0 | 100.0 | 100.0 | 100.0 | 100.0 |
| | | | INCOME DATA | | | | | | | |
| 100.0 | 100.0 | 100.0 | | Net Sales | 100.0 | 100.0 | 100.0 | 100.0 | 100.0 | 100.0 |
| 24.5 | 25.5 | 22.7 | | Gross Profit | 58.6 | 30.2 | 24.9 | 22.4 | 21.9 | 21.2 |
| 19.2 | 19.7 | 18.4 | | Operating Expenses | 52.3 | 30.2 | 22.2 | 18.8 | 17.1 | 16.2 |
| 5.3 | 5.8 | 4.3 | | Operating Profit | 6.3 | -.1 | 2.8 | 3.6 | 4.8 | 5.0 |
| -1.2 | -.1 | .8 | | All Other Expenses (net) | 2.3 | 1.6 | 1.4 | 1.1 | .7 | .5 |
| 6.5 | 5.9 | 3.5 | | Profit Before Taxes | 3.9 | -1.6 | 1.4 | 2.5 | 4.0 | 4.5 |
| | | | RATIOS | | | | | | | |
| 2.9 | 2.2 | 1.7 | | Current | 4.2 | 1.7 | 1.9 | 1.6 | 1.7 | 1.8 |
| 1.9 | 1.6 | 1.4 | | | 2.0 | 1.3 | 1.5 | 1.3 | 1.4 | 1.4 |
| 1.4 | 1.3 | 1.2 | | | .5 | 1.1 | 1.2 | 1.1 | 1.2 | 1.2 |
| 1.3 | .7 | .4 | | Quick | 1.6 | .5 | .4 | .3 | .4 | .4 |
| (210) .7 | (437) .3 | .2 | | | .4 | .2 | .2 | .1 | .2 | .2 |
| .3 | .2 | .1 | | | .1 | .1 | .1 | .1 | .1 | .1 |
| 1 275.5 | 1 282.4 | 2 223.0 | | Sales/Receivables | 0 UND | 0 UND | 0 UND | 0 870.4 | 2 203.6 | 3 105.6 |
| 4 82.9 | 4 87.6 | 5 76.4 | | | 1 372.2 | 4 92.6 | 4 95.7 | 3 113.5 | 5 79.3 | 6 60.6 |
| 13 27.3 | 10 36.2 | 9 39.3 | | | 32 11.3 | 13 27.1 | 14 25.3 | 9 42.8 | 8 43.4 | 10 34.8 |
| 47 7.8 | 81 4.5 | 122 3.0 | | Cost of Sales/Inventory | 0 UND | 111 3.3 | 140 2.6 | 140 2.6 | 122 3.0 | 107 3.4 |
| 68 5.4 | 118 3.1 | 159 2.3 | | | 89 4.1 | 203 1.8 | 203 1.8 | 182 2.0 | 152 2.4 | 140 2.6 |
| 94 3.9 | 159 2.3 | 215 1.7 | | | 456 .8 | 406 .9 | 281 1.3 | 261 1.4 | 192 1.9 | 174 2.1 |
| 5 74.1 | 7 52.4 | 76 4.8 | | Cost of Sales/Payables | 0 UND | 46 7.9 | 99 3.7 | 96 3.8 | 79 4.6 | 64 5.7 |
| 10 35.1 | 26 13.9 | 118 3.1 | | | 21 17.8 | 159 2.3 | 140 2.6 | 146 2.5 | 118 3.1 | 101 3.6 |
| 19 18.8 | 89 4.1 | 166 2.2 | | | 243 1.5 | 304 1.2 | 228 1.6 | 203 1.8 | 152 2.4 | 135 2.7 |
| 5.3 | 5.0 | 5.7 | | Sales/Working Capital | 2.3 | 3.6 | 3.9 | 5.5 | 5.9 | 6.0 |
| 9.1 | 8.5 | 8.7 | | | 6.2 | 7.8 | 6.5 | 8.9 | 8.7 | 8.9 |
| 18.3 | 14.6 | 15.0 | | | -2.9 | 65.0 | 13.3 | 16.4 | 13.7 | 15.2 |
| 55.7 | 39.6 | 10.5 | | EBIT/Interest | 7.3 | 8.3 | 4.9 | 6.6 | 10.8 | 14.3 |
| (176) 18.8 | (381) 13.2 | (2005) 4.3 | | | (23) 1.0 | (61) 1.6 | (120) 1.9 | (433) 2.7 | (801) 4.9 | (567) 6.2 |
| 7.3 | 5.1 | 1.5 | | | -.5 | -2.1 | -.5 | .9 | 1.9 | 2.9 |
| 42.5 | 43.5 | 24.6 | | Net Profit + Depr., Dep., Amort./Cur. Mat. L/T/D | | | | 6.2 | 36.4 | 31.9 |
| (21) 5.1 | (23) 10.1 | (167) 6.6 | | | | | (36) 2.7 | (49) 8.5 | (70) 11.2 |
| 1.1 | 3.5 | 2.9 | | | | | | .6 | 3.9 | 4.3 |
| .1 | .1 | .1 | | Fixed/Worth | .0 | .0 | .0 | .1 | .0 | .1 |
| .2 | .3 | .2 | | | 1.9 | .4 | .3 | .2 | .1 | .2 |
| .6 | .7 | .6 | | | -1.1 | 6.6 | 1.4 | .7 | .5 | .6 |
| .7 | .9 | 1.5 | | Debt/Worth | .6 | 1.4 | 1.7 | 1.8 | 1.5 | 1.3 |
| 1.3 | 1.9 | 2.9 | | | 6.4 | 4.9 | 3.1 | 3.7 | 2.7 | 2.5 |
| 3.2 | 4.4 | 7.1 | | | -9.3 | -804.7 | 15.7 | 11.4 | 6.2 | 5.5 |
| 79.7 | 65.5 | 50.6 | | % Profit Before Taxes/Tangible Net Worth | 63.5 | 45.9 | 31.2 | 44.0 | 52.6 | 53.9 |
| (196) 41.8 | (409) 36.7 | (1898) 27.7 | | | (16) 1.7 | (52) 11.6 | (106) 12.6 | (399) 16.8 | (764) 30.8 | (561) 33.9 |
| 24.2 | 19.4 | 9.1 | | | -6.6 | -2.3 | -1.8 | .4 | 12.3 | 19.6 |
| 27.6 | 19.2 | 13.2 | | % Profit Before Taxes/Total Assets | 15.7 | 7.6 | 7.8 | 8.9 | 13.9 | 15.2 |
| 15.8 | 12.1 | 7.0 | | | -.1 | .7 | 3.0 | 3.4 | 8.3 | 9.7 |
| 8.5 | 5.6 | 1.3 | | | -7.4 | -8.6 | -2.5 | -.3 | 2.4 | 4.2 |
| 113.4 | 83.1 | 146.5 | | Sales/Net Fixed Assets | 256.0 | 117.2 | 143.0 | 137.4 | 194.2 | 107.6 |
| 44.3 | 35.9 | 52.3 | | | 5.7 | 24.6 | 35.2 | 58.7 | 64.8 | 40.4 |
| 19.9 | 14.5 | 21.1 | | | 1.6 | 6.8 | 13.1 | 19.8 | 27.1 | 20.8 |
| 3.9 | 2.9 | 2.5 | | Sales/Total Assets | 1.6 | 2.1 | 2.1 | 2.3 | 2.6 | 2.7 |
| 3.1 | 2.3 | 2.0 | | | 1.1 | 1.5 | 1.6 | 1.8 | 2.1 | 2.1 |
| 2.1 | 1.7 | 1.6 | | | .5 | .8 | 1.2 | 1.4 | 1.7 | 1.7 |
| .3 | .2 | .2 | | % Depr., Dep., Amort./Sales | .5 | .2 | .2 | .2 | .2 | .2 |
| (140) .5 | (267) .5 | (1351) .5 | | | (12) 6.6 | (33) .7 | (80) .5 | (252) .6 | (501) .4 | (473) .4 |
| 1.0 | .9 | .9 | | | 20.8 | 1.9 | 1.7 | 1.0 | .7 | .8 |
| .6 | .6 | 1.0 | | % Officers', Directors' Owners' Comp/Sales | 1.4 | 1.4 | .8 | .5 | .3 | |
| (76) 1.2 | (154) 1.2 | (867) 1.0 | | | (12) 2.0 | (45) 2.2 | (177) 1.2 | (363) 1.1 | (264) .6 | |
| 2.2 | 2.6 | 1.9 | | | 3.0 | 3.6 | 2.2 | 1.9 | 1.1 | |
| 9419822M | 15213825M | 60314708M | | Net Sales ($) | 16815M | 150021M | 521926M | 3453751M | 13487885M | 42684310M |
| 3448622M | 6689663M | 29998135M | | Total Assets ($) | 31340M | 139332M | 348614M | 2037013M | 6795755M | 20646081M |

© RMA 2024  M = $ thousand   MM = $ million
See Pages viii through xx for Explanation of Ratios and Data

# RETAIL—Automotive Parts and Accessories Retailers NAICS 441330

## Current Data Sorted by Assets

| | | | | | | Type of Statement | | |
|---|---|---|---|---|---|---|---|---|
| | | 1 | 3 | 2 | 1 | Unqualified | 12 | 7 |
| 3 | | 3 | 8 | 3 | | Reviewed | 14 | 10 |
| 8 | 14 | 9 | 4 | | | Compiled | 14 | 16 |
| 7 | 15 | 17 | 5 | | | Tax Returns | 62 | 54 |
| | 22 (4/1-9/30/23) | 35 | 31 | 5 | 3 | Other | 114 | 83 |
| 0-500M | 500M-2MM | 2-10MM | 10-50MM | 50-100MM | 100-250MM | | 4/1/19-3/31/20 ALL | 4/1/20-3/31/21 ALL |
| 18 | 29 | 65 | 51 | 10 | 4 | NUMBER OF STATEMENTS | 216 | 170 |
| % | % | % | % | % | % | ASSETS | % | % |
| 44.4 | 22.9 | 15.9 | 6.3 | 4.3 | | Cash & Equivalents | 12.5 | 19.4 |
| 5.7 | 6.7 | 12.2 | 12.3 | 9.2 | | Trade Receivables (net) | 14.0 | 10.2 |
| 15.0 | 43.2 | 45.4 | 48.0 | 48.8 | | Inventory | 42.7 | 40.6 |
| 5.0 | 2.3 | 4.1 | 4.2 | 1.9 | | All Other Current | 1.8 | 1.8 |
| 70.1 | 75.0 | 77.5 | 70.8 | 64.3 | | Total Current | 71.0 | 72.1 |
| 15.0 | 14.3 | 15.4 | 13.9 | 16.5 | | Fixed Assets (net) | 17.3 | 16.8 |
| 7.1 | 5.2 | 2.3 | 4.8 | 6.3 | | Intangibles (net) | 4.9 | 6.7 |
| 7.7 | 5.4 | 4.9 | 10.5 | 12.9 | | All Other Non-Current | 6.7 | 4.5 |
| 100.0 | 100.0 | 100.0 | 100.0 | 100.0 | | Total | 100.0 | 100.0 |
| | | | | | | LIABILITIES | | |
| 18.0 | 6.4 | 6.8 | 9.4 | 16.7 | | Notes Payable-Short Term | 11.8 | 9.1 |
| 1.0 | 3.0 | 1.9 | 3.4 | 5.2 | | Cur. Mat.-L.T.D. | 3.3 | 2.9 |
| 4.3 | 25.3 | 16.4 | 16.3 | 12.3 | | Trade Payables | 16.4 | 12.9 |
| .0 | .1 | .2 | .1 | .2 | | Income Taxes Payable | .1 | .1 |
| 32.6 | 10.7 | 8.2 | 12.7 | 7.7 | | All Other Current | 12.6 | 13.5 |
| 56.0 | 45.5 | 33.5 | 42.0 | 42.0 | | Total Current | 44.2 | 38.6 |
| 14.4 | 15.7 | 21.7 | 11.0 | 11.9 | | Long-Term Debt | 20.2 | 26.6 |
| .0 | .0 | .0 | .1 | .3 | | Deferred Taxes | .1 | .1 |
| 4.0 | 11.6 | 3.7 | 10.4 | 8.3 | | All Other Non-Current | 6.3 | 5.5 |
| 25.7 | 27.2 | 41.1 | 36.4 | 37.5 | | Net Worth | 29.3 | 29.3 |
| 100.0 | 100.0 | 100.0 | 100.0 | 100.0 | | Total Liabilities & Net Worth | 100.0 | 100.0 |
| | | | | | | INCOME DATA | | |
| 100.0 | 100.0 | 100.0 | 100.0 | 100.0 | | Net Sales | 100.0 | 100.0 |
| 47.0 | 42.4 | 39.0 | 37.0 | 36.7 | | Gross Profit | 34.8 | 40.3 |
| 38.5 | 36.4 | 33.2 | 33.5 | 31.6 | | Operating Expenses | 31.0 | 36.3 |
| 8.5 | 6.0 | 5.7 | 3.5 | 5.1 | | Operating Profit | 3.8 | 4.0 |
| .4 | -.2 | .2 | 1.7 | .7 | | All Other Expenses (net) | .5 | -.7 |
| 8.1 | 6.2 | 5.5 | 1.8 | 4.4 | | Profit Before Taxes | 3.3 | 4.6 |
| | | | | | | RATIOS | | |
| 20.6 | 8.4 | 4.5 | 3.1 | 2.0 | | | 3.4 | 4.6 |
| 4.7 | 2.4 | 3.1 | 1.8 | 1.4 | Current | 1.8 | 2.5 |
| 1.4 | .9 | 1.5 | 1.3 | 1.2 | | 1.2 | 1.3 |
| 16.2 | 1.5 | 1.7 | .9 | .6 | | | 1.4 | 1.9 |
| 2.9 | .5 | .8 | .6 | .3 | Quick | .6 | .8 |
| .5 | .3 | .4 | .2 | .1 | | .3 | .4 |
| 0 UND | 0 UND | 2 150.1 | 7 53.9 | 7 53.1 | | | 4 102.5 | 2 237.0 |
| 0 UND | 4 86.0 | 16 23.0 | 23 15.8 | 21 17.4 | | Sales/Receivables | 16 23.2 | 11 32.2 |
| 5 71.0 | 23 15.8 | 30 12.3 | 35 10.4 | 26 13.8 | | | 29 12.5 | 23 15.7 |
| 0 UND | 22 16.3 | 42 8.6 | 89 4.1 | 69 5.3 | | | 33 11.1 | 48 7.6 |
| 0 UND | 107 3.4 | 118 3.1 | 182 2.0 | 146 2.5 | | Cost of Sales/Inventory | 79 4.6 | 101 3.6 |
| 29 12.6 | 243 1.5 | 228 1.6 | 243 1.5 | 243 1.5 | | | 159 2.3 | 192 1.9 |
| 0 UND | 5 70.7 | 13 28.4 | 23 16.1 | 16 22.3 | | | 9 38.8 | 2 147.1 |
| 0 UND | 31 11.9 | 31 11.6 | 45 8.2 | 40 9.1 | | Cost of Sales/Payables | 23 15.8 | 24 15.4 |
| 6 62.7 | 89 4.1 | 63 5.8 | 76 4.8 | 70 5.2 | | | 46 8.0 | 49 7.5 |
| 5.2 | 3.2 | 3.1 | 3.5 | 5.6 | | | 4.2 | 3.1 |
| 8.7 | 10.3 | 5.5 | 7.1 | 6.8 | Sales/Working Capital | 10.0 | 5.7 |
| 49.2 | -52.0 | 12.7 | 11.5 | 21.0 | | 33.9 | 22.0 |
| 77.0 | 19.1 | 31.5 | 12.9 | 6.1 | | | 16.0 | 23.4 |
| (11) 16.8 | (18) 4.8 | (55) 7.0 | (46) 3.2 | 5.2 | EBIT/Interest | (173) 3.9 | (138) 4.9 |
| 1.2 | 1.0 | 2.6 | .9 | 3.0 | | 1.1 | 1.0 |
| | | | 11.5 | | | | 9.3 | 7.2 |
| | | (13) | 2.0 | | | Net Profit + Depr., Dep., Amort./Cur. Mat. L/T/D | (22) 3.4 | (23) 2.6 |
| | | | .6 | | | | 1.1 | .7 |
| .0 | .1 | .1 | .2 | .3 | | | .1 | .1 |
| .3 | .7 | .2 | .3 | .6 | Fixed/Worth | .4 | .4 |
| .7 | -.5 | .8 | .8 | .8 | | 2.7 | 3.9 |
| .1 | .7 | .5 | .9 | 1.2 | | | .7 | .8 |
| .9 | 2.0 | 1.8 | 2.0 | 2.0 | Debt/Worth | 2.0 | 2.0 |
| 5.4 | -23.1 | 5.0 | 5.9 | 2.8 | | 13.4 | 17.0 |
| 143.8 | 69.4 | 50.5 | 43.2 | | | | 58.0 | 58.2 |
| (16) 74.6 | (20) 33.2 | (57) 28.8 | (45) 22.1 | | | % Profit Before Taxes/Tangible Net Worth | (175) 21.6 | (135) 24.5 |
| 25.5 | 12.9 | 17.4 | 6.3 | | | | 5.7 | 3.0 |
| 75.1 | 24.7 | 19.2 | 13.8 | 12.8 | | | 21.4 | 22.2 |
| 37.5 | 13.5 | 12.4 | 4.8 | 8.0 | | % Profit Before Taxes/Total Assets | 6.9 | 7.6 |
| 5.1 | 3.8 | 5.1 | .5 | 2.7 | | | .7 | .0 |
| UND | 815.8 | 149.4 | 51.6 | 29.5 | | | 106.7 | 80.8 |
| 66.3 | 72.4 | 32.0 | 19.8 | 15.3 | | Sales/Net Fixed Assets | 32.0 | 24.0 |
| 17.0 | 11.7 | 10.5 | 7.9 | 5.9 | | | 11.0 | 11.1 |
| 9.8 | 4.9 | 3.4 | 2.4 | 2.7 | | | 4.2 | 3.3 |
| 4.5 | 2.3 | 2.4 | 1.7 | 1.6 | Sales/Total Assets | 2.5 | 2.2 |
| 3.3 | 1.5 | 1.6 | 1.2 | 1.4 | | 1.8 | 1.5 |
| | .3 | .5 | .5 | .6 | | | .6 | .8 |
| | (12) .6 | (37) .9 | (42) .9 | 1.1 | % Depr., Dep., Amort./Sales | (136) 1.2 | (106) 1.3 |
| | 1.2 | 1.8 | 1.6 | 1.9 | | 2.0 | 2.4 |
| 4.7 | 1.6 | 1.0 | .5 | | | | 1.7 | 1.2 |
| (12) 8.0 | (15) 3.5 | (39) 1.7 | (11) 1.1 | | | % Officers', Directors' Owners' Comp/Sales | (91) 3.1 | (74) 2.6 |
| 13.0 | 6.3 | 2.8 | 1.6 | | | | 6.2 | 4.7 |
| 25920M | 118840M | 806975M | 2105548M | 1335566M | 1313489M | Net Sales ($) | 5573087M | 4298960M |
| 4492M | 33125M | 289809M | 1252983M | 641883M | 727007M | Total Assets ($) | 2763961M | 2217024M |

© RMA 2024

M = $ thousand    MM = $ million
See Pages viii through xx for Explanation of Ratios and Data

# RETAIL—Automotive Parts and Accessories Retailers  NAICS 441330

## Comparative Historical Data | Current Data Sorted by Sales

| | | | | | Type of Statement | | | | | | |
|---|---|---|---|---|---|---|---|---|---|---|---|
| | 10 | | 10 | 7 | Unqualified | | 1 | | 4 | 4 | 7 |
| | 6 | | 7 | 14 | Reviewed | | 1 | | 9 | 5 | 9 |
| | 9 | | 9 | 16 | Compiled | 2 | 14 | 1 | 7 | 7 | 4 |
| | 40 | | 46 | 44 | Tax Returns | 3 | 12 | 3 | 10 | 7 | 8 |
| | 87 | | 99 | 96 | Other | 4 | 12 | 12 | 10 | 24 | 34 |
| | 4/1/21-3/31/22 ALL | | 4/1/22-3/31/23 ALL | 4/1/23-3/31/24 ALL | | | 22 (4/1-9/30/23) | | 155 (10/1/23-3/31/24) | | |
| | | | | | | 0-1MM | 1-3MM | 3-5MM | 5-10MM | 10-25MM | 25MM & OVER |
| | 152 | | 171 | 177 | NUMBER OF STATEMENTS | 9 | 27 | 16 | 23 | 40 | 62 |
| | % | | % | % | ASSETS | % | % | % | % | % | % |
| | 16.2 | | 14.3 | 16.3 | Cash & Equivalents | | 25.4 | 18.9 | 23.5 | 13.7 | 8.4 |
| | 10.9 | | 11.2 | 10.5 | Trade Receivables (net) | | 7.7 | 7.1 | 10.2 | 13.3 | 12.0 |
| | 41.9 | | 44.4 | 42.9 | Inventory | | 26.6 | 45.1 | 42.5 | 47.6 | 46.8 |
| | 3.6 | | 2.5 | 4.0 | All Other Current | | 4.3 | 3.3 | 4.5 | 3.6 | 4.7 |
| | 72.6 | | 72.4 | 73.7 | Total Current | | 64.0 | 74.4 | 80.6 | 78.1 | 71.9 |
| | 17.5 | | 15.2 | 14.6 | Fixed Assets (net) | | 20.0 | 12.8 | 13.8 | 13.0 | 14.1 |
| | 4.8 | | 4.4 | 4.2 | Intangibles (net) | | 7.0 | 8.2 | 1.7 | 1.6 | 5.3 |
| | 5.2 | | 8.0 | 7.5 | All Other Non-Current | | 9.0 | 4.6 | 3.9 | 7.3 | 8.7 |
| | 100.0 | | 100.0 | 100.0 | Total | | 100.0 | 100.0 | 100.0 | 100.0 | 100.0 |
| | | | | | LIABILITIES | | | | | | |
| | 9.0 | | 10.2 | 9.3 | Notes Payable-Short Term | | 11.5 | 10.9 | 5.4 | 7.6 | 10.5 |
| | 2.5 | | 2.0 | 2.6 | Cur. Mat.-L.T.D. | | 2.3 | 3.2 | 2.2 | 1.7 | 3.5 |
| | 13.7 | | 17.0 | 16.4 | Trade Payables | | 8.9 | 24.4 | 22.2 | 17.5 | 16.6 |
| | .1 | | .1 | .1 | Income Taxes Payable | | .1 | .1 | .1 | .2 | .1 |
| | 10.3 | | 12.5 | 12.4 | All Other Current | | 9.1 | 38.3 | 5.8 | 4.7 | 14.3 |
| | 35.6 | | 41.8 | 40.8 | Total Current | | 31.7 | 76.9 | 35.7 | 31.7 | 45.0 |
| | 19.1 | | 18.0 | 16.1 | Long-Term Debt | | 22.1 | 14.7 | 17.2 | 21.9 | 10.1 |
| | .0 | | .1 | .1 | Deferred Taxes | | .0 | .0 | .0 | .0 | .2 |
| | 4.6 | | 4.7 | 7.6 | All Other Non-Current | | 5.2 | 8.0 | 5.3 | 6.5 | 8.9 |
| | 40.7 | | 35.4 | 35.4 | Net Worth | | 41.0 | .4 | 41.8 | 39.9 | 35.8 |
| | 100.0 | | 100.0 | 100.0 | Total Liabilities & Net Worth | | 100.0 | 100.0 | 100.0 | 100.0 | 100.0 |
| | | | | | INCOME DATA | | | | | | |
| | 100.0 | | 100.0 | 100.0 | Net Sales | | 100.0 | 100.0 | 100.0 | 100.0 | 100.0 |
| | 38.0 | | 37.1 | 39.6 | Gross Profit | | 50.2 | 39.2 | 38.6 | 38.6 | 35.4 |
| | 32.0 | | 31.8 | 34.2 | Operating Expenses | | 43.5 | 35.2 | 33.8 | 33.5 | 31.1 |
| | 6.0 | | 5.3 | 5.3 | Operating Profit | | 6.7 | 4.0 | 4.8 | 5.2 | 4.3 |
| | -.8 | | -.3 | .6 | All Other Expenses (net) | | .1 | -.1 | .6 | .5 | 1.2 |
| | 6.8 | | 5.6 | 4.7 | Profit Before Taxes | | 6.6 | 4.1 | 4.2 | 4.6 | 3.1 |
| | | | | | RATIOS | | | | | | |
| | 4.8 | | 3.7 | 4.0 | | | 8.5 | 6.2 | 3.9 | 4.2 | 2.8 |
| | 2.5 | | 2.0 | 2.2 | Current | | 3.3 | 2.8 | 2.3 | 3.1 | 1.7 |
| | 1.4 | | 1.4 | 1.3 | | | 1.2 | .9 | 1.6 | 1.7 | 1.2 |
| | 2.0 | | 1.2 | 1.4 | | | 5.1 | 1.4 | 1.6 | 1.4 | .8 |
| | .9 | (170) | .7 | .7 | Quick | | 1.4 | .4 | .8 | .9 | .5 |
| | .3 | | .3 | .3 | | | .3 | .1 | .5 | .4 | .2 |
| 3 | 139.5 | 4 | 83.5 | 2 171.2 | | 0 UND | 0 999.4 | 2 214.3 | 6 65.4 | 5 68.4 | |
| 15 | 24.2 | 17 | 21.3 | 16 23.3 | Sales/Receivables | 9 41.2 | 13 41.0 | 13 27.1 | 16 22.6 | 20 18.3 | |
| 26 | 13.9 | 27 | 13.4 | 29 12.5 | | 32 11.3 | 22 16.9 | 33 11.2 | 28 13.1 | 30 12.1 | |
| 43 | 8.4 | 47 | 7.7 | 39 9.4 | | 0 UND | 22 16.7 | 33 11.0 | 46 7.9 | 69 5.3 | |
| 96 | 3.8 | 101 | 3.6 | 122 3.0 | Cost of Sales/Inventory | 74 4.9 | 91 4.0 | 118 3.1 | 130 2.8 | 159 2.3 | |
| 182 | 2.0 | 203 | 1.8 | 228 1.6 | | 192 1.9 | 228 1.6 | 182 2.0 | 215 1.7 | 228 1.6 | |
| 8 | 43.7 | 11 | 32.4 | 10 36.2 | | 0 UND | 0 UND | 20 18.3 | 19 18.8 | 19 19.7 | |
| 24 | 15.4 | 31 | 11.9 | 31 11.6 | Cost of Sales/Payables | 13 27.1 | 37 9.9 | 31 11.9 | 37 9.8 | 37 9.9 | |
| 49 | 7.5 | 54 | 6.8 | 66 5.5 | | 66 5.5 | 66 5.5 | 76 4.8 | 63 5.8 | 70 5.2 | |
| | 3.4 | | 4.0 | 3.6 | | | 3.4 | 4.4 | 3.1 | 3.6 | 3.9 |
| | 7.0 | | 8.2 | 6.5 | Sales/Working Capital | | 9.5 | 8.8 | 5.8 | 5.3 | 7.3 |
| | 18.2 | | 19.6 | 18.4 | | | 42.8 | -19.3 | 15.5 | 7.7 | 17.3 |
| | 36.0 | | 40.8 | 19.6 | | | 19.0 | 19.7 | 24.6 | 40.6 | 12.9 |
| (127) | 14.6 | (149) | 9.3 | (144) 5.1 | EBIT/Interest | (19) 5.5 | (11) 3.4 | (18) 6.7 | (36) 6.6 | (55) 3.7 | |
| | 4.9 | | 2.4 | 2.0 | | | 2.6 | .1 | 3.0 | 2.3 | 1.7 |
| | 99.5 | | 15.3 | 7.0 | Net Profit + Depr., Dep., | | | | | | 7.2 |
| (14) | 8.4 | (17) | 6.3 | (20) 2.3 | Amort./Cur. Mat. L/T/D | | | | | (15) 2.0 | |
| | 3.0 | | .5 | 1.1 | | | | | | | 1.0 |
| | .1 | | .1 | .1 | | | .1 | .1 | .0 | .1 | .2 |
| | .3 | | .3 | .3 | Fixed/Worth | | .4 | .7 | .2 | .3 | .4 |
| | .8 | | 1.0 | 1.1 | | | 3.2 | -1.5 | .9 | .7 | .8 |
| | .4 | | .6 | .7 | | | .4 | .5 | .7 | .6 | 1.1 |
| | 1.3 | | 1.5 | 1.9 | Debt/Worth | | 1.8 | 5.0 | 1.3 | 1.7 | 2.3 |
| | 3.9 | | 4.7 | 5.8 | | | 4.6 | -23.7 | 5.7 | 4.0 | 6.3 |
| | 66.7 | | 62.8 | 54.9 | % Profit Before Taxes/Tangible | | 69.7 | | 65.1 | 57.1 | 44.3 |
| (135) | 31.7 | (146) | 26.9 | (151) 26.7 | Net Worth | (23) 29.1 | | (20) 28.7 | (37) 30.3 | (54) 24.2 | |
| | 16.1 | | 9.0 | 12.6 | | | 10.2 | | 19.1 | 14.5 | 7.3 |
| | 27.3 | | 22.0 | 18.8 | % Profit Before Taxes/Total | | 23.0 | 22.5 | 22.7 | 19.2 | 16.7 |
| | 14.1 | | 10.6 | 10.0 | Assets | | 10.5 | 12.2 | 11.1 | 10.1 | 7.4 |
| | 5.6 | | 2.7 | 2.9 | | | 6.0 | -1.6 | 6.1 | 4.5 | 1.8 |
| | 71.9 | | 145.1 | 94.3 | | | 199.4 | 355.8 | 311.5 | 92.1 | 76.6 |
| | 25.4 | | 28.6 | 26.6 | Sales/Net Fixed Assets | | 25.4 | 30.3 | 36.7 | 33.4 | 21.6 |
| | 10.4 | | 12.9 | 11.2 | | | 9.3 | 13.3 | 8.2 | 10.5 | 13.0 |
| | 3.9 | | 3.5 | 3.4 | | | 4.1 | 5.0 | 3.6 | 3.5 | 2.8 |
| | 2.4 | | 2.3 | 2.2 | Sales/Total Assets | | 1.9 | 2.1 | 2.5 | 2.4 | 1.8 |
| | 1.6 | | 1.6 | 1.5 | | | 1.2 | 1.6 | 1.8 | 1.6 | 1.3 |
| | .6 | | .5 | .5 | | | .4 | | .6 | .5 | .4 |
| (94) | 1.2 | (106) | 1.0 | (114) .9 | % Depr., Dep., Amort./Sales | (12) 1.2 | | (14) .9 | (21) .8 | (54) .9 | |
| | 2.5 | | 2.4 | 1.5 | | | 2.0 | | 1.4 | 1.4 | 1.5 |
| | 1.1 | | 1.1 | 1.1 | % Officers', Directors' | | 3.9 | | 1.2 | .7 | .5 |
| (60) | 3.0 | (77) | 2.2 | (79) 2.1 | Owners' Comp/Sales | (17) 5.6 | | (16) 2.0 | (18) 1.2 | (14) 1.0 | |
| | 5.1 | | 4.4 | 4.5 | | | 10.6 | | 2.5 | 1.6 | 2.7 |
| | 3790923M | | 4512183M | 5706338M | Net Sales ($) | 7243M | 51296M | 59846M | 153089M | 629606M | 4805258M |
| | 2095210M | | 2389318M | 2949299M | Total Assets ($) | 3714M | 28784M | 25349M | 70937M | 311774M | 2508741M |

M = $ thousand     MM = $ million
See Pages viii through xx for Explanation of Ratios and Data

© RMA 2024

# RETAIL—Tire Dealers  NAICS 441340

## Current Data Sorted by Assets | Comparative Historical Data

| | | | | | | Type of Statement | | |
|---|---|---|---|---|---|---|---|---|
| | | | 1 | 2 | | Unqualified | 3 | 4 |
| | | 1 | 3 | 4 | 2 | Reviewed | 38 | 8 |
| | 1 | 3 | 6 | 1 | 1 | Compiled | 10 | 12 |
| 6 | 4 | 7 | 5 | | | Tax Returns | 23 | 23 |
| 5 | 14 | 16 | 11 | 5 | 9 | Other | 61 | 54 |
| | 15 (4/1-9/30/23) | | 92 (10/1/23-3/31/24) | | | | 4/1/19-3/31/20 | 4/1/20-3/31/21 |
| 0-500M | 500M-2MM | 2-10MM | 10-50MM | 50-100MM | 100-250MM | | ALL | ALL |
| 11 | 19 | 27 | 26 | 12 | 12 | **NUMBER OF STATEMENTS** | 135 | 101 |
| % | % | % | % | % | % | **ASSETS** | % | % |
| 37.5 | 40.2 | 15.0 | 9.8 | 5.2 | 7.8 | Cash & Equivalents | 10.5 | 22.8 |
| .0 | 7.2 | 9.9 | 15.7 | 10.9 | 16.3 | Trade Receivables (net) | 14.4 | 11.2 |
| 28.6 | 17.6 | 38.0 | 46.1 | 33.5 | 31.7 | Inventory | 39.0 | 35.5 |
| 1.5 | 3.4 | 4.0 | 5.3 | 1.4 | .6 | All Other Current | 2.8 | 1.6 |
| 67.6 | 68.5 | 66.9 | 76.9 | 51.0 | 56.3 | Total Current | 66.6 | 71.1 |
| 22.2 | 19.2 | 17.5 | 14.3 | 31.4 | 20.6 | Fixed Assets (net) | 22.0 | 18.9 |
| 4.3 | 7.5 | .6 | 2.1 | 1.5 | 7.2 | Intangibles (net) | 3.9 | 3.3 |
| 5.9 | 4.8 | 15.0 | 6.7 | 16.1 | 15.8 | All Other Non-Current | 7.4 | 6.7 |
| 100.0 | 100.0 | 100.0 | 100.0 | 100.0 | 100.0 | Total | 100.0 | 100.0 |
| | | | | | | **LIABILITIES** | | |
| 5.7 | 3.6 | 5.6 | 5.6 | 4.4 | 4.5 | Notes Payable-Short Term | 11.2 | 5.9 |
| 3.0 | 1.5 | 1.1 | 1.2 | 2.3 | 4.6 | Cur. Mat.-L.T.D. | 2.8 | 2.2 |
| 5.4 | 15.7 | 21.4 | 25.4 | 14.5 | 25.7 | Trade Payables | 25.3 | 20.3 |
| .0 | 1.5 | .3 | .1 | .0 | .0 | Income Taxes Payable | .1 | .2 |
| 6.3 | 7.9 | 5.0 | 10.1 | 6.3 | 7.7 | All Other Current | 12.2 | 9.8 |
| 20.5 | 30.2 | 33.4 | 42.5 | 27.5 | 42.5 | Total Current | 51.7 | 38.4 |
| 41.3 | 14.0 | 13.8 | 11.1 | 17.8 | 21.8 | Long-Term Debt | 14.0 | 19.9 |
| .0 | .0 | .2 | .4 | .5 | .0 | Deferred Taxes | .2 | .2 |
| 3.1 | 6.0 | 5.5 | 6.7 | 17.7 | 13.1 | All Other Non-Current | 3.0 | 9.2 |
| 35.1 | 49.8 | 47.0 | 39.3 | 36.6 | 22.6 | Net Worth | 31.2 | 32.2 |
| 100.0 | 100.0 | 100.0 | 100.0 | 100.0 | 100.0 | Total Liabilities & Net Worth | 100.0 | 100.0 |
| | | | | | | **INCOME DATA** | | |
| 100.0 | 100.0 | 100.0 | 100.0 | 100.0 | 100.0 | Net Sales | 100.0 | 100.0 |
| 49.1 | 52.6 | 41.7 | 30.0 | 29.6 | 29.3 | Gross Profit | 37.1 | 38.6 |
| 43.2 | 41.7 | 38.9 | 27.1 | 28.2 | 28.4 | Operating Expenses | 34.6 | 35.2 |
| 5.9 | 10.9 | 2.8 | 3.0 | 1.4 | .9 | Operating Profit | 2.6 | 3.4 |
| .2 | .1 | -1.1 | .0 | -.2 | 1.0 | All Other Expenses (net) | .1 | -1.1 |
| 5.7 | 10.7 | 3.9 | 3.0 | 1.6 | -.1 | Profit Before Taxes | 2.5 | 4.5 |
| | | | | | | **RATIOS** | | |
| 27.5 | 4.6 | 3.4 | 2.9 | 2.2 | 1.8 | | 2.2 | 3.0 |
| 4.3 | 3.0 | 1.9 | 1.9 | 2.0 | 1.3 | Current | 1.5 | 1.9 |
| 2.6 | 1.6 | 1.3 | 1.3 | 1.3 | 1.1 | | 1.0 | 1.3 |
| 8.5 | 4.2 | 1.0 | 1.0 | .8 | .8 | | .9 | 1.8 |
| 1.7 | 1.8 | .7 | .6 | .5 | .4 | Quick | .4 | .9 |
| 1.0 | .8 | .3 | .3 | .3 | .3 | | .3 | .4 |
| 0 UND | 0 UND | 2 219.7 | 8 45.2 | 14 26.3 | 15 24.9 | | 6 63.4 | 2 187.0 |
| 0 UND | 1 458.7 | 12 29.2 | 21 17.3 | 18 19.8 | 21 17.8 | Sales/Receivables | 15 24.6 | 10 36.0 |
| 0 UND | 8 47.2 | 22 16.3 | 27 13.3 | 22 16.5 | 31 11.9 | | 25 14.8 | 22 16.6 |
| 14 26.6 | 18 19.8 | 57 6.4 | 55 6.6 | 65 5.6 | 54 6.7 | | 36 10.2 | 31 11.9 |
| 27 13.4 | 27 13.3 | 66 5.5 | 78 4.7 | 87 4.2 | 85 4.3 | Cost of Sales/Inventory | 72 5.1 | 63 5.8 |
| 135 2.7 | 70 5.2 | 152 2.4 | 111 3.3 | 111 3.3 | 101 3.6 | | 99 3.7 | 91 4.0 |
| 0 UND | 0 UND | 14 25.5 | 21 17.8 | 30 12.1 | 36 10.1 | | 22 16.5 | 16 22.3 |
| 0 UND | 15 23.7 | 43 8.5 | 32 11.4 | 43 8.5 | 52 7.0 | Cost of Sales/Payables | 41 9.0 | 31 11.8 |
| 14 26.3 | 46 8.0 | 61 6.0 | 69 5.3 | 49 7.5 | 76 4.8 | | 62 5.9 | 54 6.7 |
| 4.1 | 4.4 | 4.4 | 5.0 | 6.6 | 7.4 | | 8.3 | 5.9 |
| 15.6 | 10.3 | 9.8 | 7.5 | 8.9 | 16.4 | Sales/Working Capital | 15.8 | 10.1 |
| 36.9 | 20.3 | 19.6 | 34.2 | 13.7 | 41.7 | | 111.5 | 23.2 |
| | 88.9 | 31.0 | 30.3 | 10.7 | 5.4 | | 13.0 | 29.9 |
| | (10) 10.5 | (22) 7.5 | (23) 6.1 | 3.8 | (11) .1 | EBIT/Interest | (113) 4.6 | (81) 10.4 |
| | 3.3 | 1.2 | 2.9 | 1.2 | -1.6 | | 2.0 | 4.3 |
| | | | | | | Net Profit + Depr., Dep., Amort./Cur. Mat. L/T/D | 9.0 | 14.6 |
| | | | | | | | (25) 4.6 | (13) 4.4 |
| | | | | | | | 2.3 | 3.0 |
| .0 | .1 | .1 | .1 | .3 | .2 | | .2 | .1 |
| .3 | .6 | .4 | .4 | .5 | 1.2 | Fixed/Worth | .5 | .5 |
| .9 | 1.3 | .7 | 1.0 | 2.2 | 3.1 | | 1.6 | 1.2 |
| .1 | .4 | .6 | .6 | .7 | 2.2 | | .7 | .8 |
| .6 | 1.1 | 1.0 | 2.5 | 2.0 | 5.2 | Debt/Worth | 1.9 | 1.7 |
| 1.3 | 1.7 | 3.1 | 5.6 | 4.4 | 14.7 | | 5.0 | 3.6 |
| | 119.3 | 28.6 | 36.6 | 18.5 | 23.5 | % Profit Before Taxes/Tangible Net Worth | 31.5 | 52.7 |
| | (16) 51.1 | (26) 22.8 | (25) 20.1 | (11) 8.1 | (11) -9.1 | | (112) 18.7 | (87) 25.2 |
| | 41.3 | 7.8 | 13.7 | 1.9 | -21.5 | | 7.9 | 13.6 |
| 52.6 | 71.0 | 16.0 | 12.9 | 6.4 | 7.2 | | 12.2 | 19.8 |
| 9.2 | 32.2 | 6.1 | 6.4 | 3.3 | -.9 | % Profit Before Taxes/Total Assets | 6.6 | 9.0 |
| -13.5 | 14.1 | .2 | 3.0 | .2 | -3.8 | | 2.4 | 3.9 |
| 999.8 | 157.4 | 81.0 | 142.3 | 17.7 | 37.9 | | 40.5 | 65.7 |
| 45.1 | 40.1 | 15.8 | 17.6 | 12.2 | 25.2 | Sales/Net Fixed Assets | 23.1 | 26.0 |
| 15.9 | 5.7 | 7.5 | 12.6 | 3.6 | 10.2 | | 12.4 | 11.8 |
| 10.3 | 6.2 | 3.3 | 3.6 | 2.8 | 2.9 | | 4.2 | 4.5 |
| 7.6 | 3.4 | 2.5 | 3.0 | 2.1 | 2.3 | Sales/Total Assets | 3.3 | 3.3 |
| 2.0 | 2.1 | 1.8 | 2.1 | 1.2 | 1.5 | | 2.4 | 2.3 |
| | .3 | .4 | .6 | 1.1 | .5 | | .8 | .6 |
| (12) | 1.0 | (17) 1.5 | (20) 1.3 | 1.5 | (11) .9 | % Depr., Dep., Amort./Sales | (107) 1.2 | (65) 1.2 |
| | 2.4 | 1.9 | 1.8 | 2.2 | 1.7 | | 1.9 | 1.9 |
| | | 1.5 | | | | | 1.0 | .8 |
| | (11) | 2.0 | | | | % Officers', Directors' Owners' Comp/Sales | (42) 3.8 | (39) 2.1 |
| | | 2.3 | | | | | 5.9 | 6.7 |
| 18592M | 61396M | 338796M | 2386898M | 1623616M | 4088151M | Net Sales ($) | 7175861M | 5456016M |
| 3003M | 18094M | 127655M | 673418M | 837655M | 1867927M | Total Assets ($) | 2867741M | 2075430M |

© RMA 2024    M = $ thousand    MM = $ million
See Pages viii through xx for Explanation of Ratios and Data

RETAIL—Tire Dealers  NAICS 441340

| Comparative Historical Data | | | | | Current Data Sorted by Sales | | | | | |
|---|---|---|---|---|---|---|---|---|---|---|
| 3 | 6 | 3 | Type of Statement | | | | 1 | 1 | 2 | |
| 14 | 10 | 10 | Unqualified | | | | 1 | 1 | 9 | |
| 8 | 13 | 12 | Reviewed | | | 1 | 1 | 1 | 9 | |
| 18 | 12 | 22 | Compiled | | 1 | 3 | 3 | 4 | 5 | |
| 51 | 54 | 60 | Tax Returns | 4 | 3 | 11 | 7 | 9 | 24 | |
| 4/1/21-3/31/22 ALL | 4/1/22-3/31/23 ALL | 4/1/23-3/31/24 ALL | Other | 4 | 5 | 15 (4/1-9/30/23) | 92 (10/1/23-3/31/24) | | | |
| | | | | 0-1MM | 1-3MM | 3-5MM | 5-10MM | 10-25MM | 25MM & OVER | |
| 94 | 95 | 107 | NUMBER OF STATEMENTS | 8 | 9 | 14 | 12 | 15 | 49 | |
| % | % | % | ASSETS | % | % | % | % | % | % | |
| 19.4 | 16.3 | 18.6 | Cash & Equivalents | | | 44.8 | 20.0 | 17.0 | 8.6 | |
| 12.2 | 14.6 | 10.7 | Trade Receivables (net) | | | 7.1 | 13.9 | 6.8 | 14.8 | |
| 34.3 | 37.9 | 34.2 | Inventory | | | 27.8 | 31.1 | 37.0 | 40.9 | |
| 2.6 | 2.9 | 3.3 | All Other Current | | | 5.0 | 2.2 | 5.5 | 2.0 | |
| 68.5 | 71.7 | 66.7 | Total Current | | | 84.7 | 67.2 | 66.2 | 66.2 | |
| 19.4 | 16.8 | 19.4 | Fixed Assets (net) | | | 13.4 | 13.4 | 21.0 | 19.2 | |
| 5.4 | 3.7 | 3.4 | Intangibles (net) | | | 1.1 | .0 | .5 | 3.4 | |
| 6.8 | 7.8 | 10.4 | All Other Non-Current | | | .8 | 19.4 | 12.3 | 11.1 | |
| 100.0 | 100.0 | 100.0 | Total | | | 100.0 | 100.0 | 100.0 | 100.0 | |
| | | | LIABILITIES | | | | | | | |
| 6.4 | 7.1 | 5.0 | Notes Payable-Short Term | | | 5.1 | 8.1 | 3.7 | 5.1 | |
| 1.7 | 1.3 | 1.9 | Cur. Mat.-L.T.D. | | | .1 | .4 | 1.6 | 2.3 | |
| 19.0 | 26.2 | 19.4 | Trade Payables | | | 22.2 | 20.8 | 19.6 | 23.2 | |
| .1 | .4 | .4 | Income Taxes Payable | | | 1.4 | .1 | .5 | .1 | |
| 10.2 | 7.5 | 7.3 | All Other Current | | | 7.7 | 5.5 | 5.3 | 8.9 | |
| 37.3 | 42.5 | 34.1 | Total Current | | | 36.5 | 34.9 | 30.7 | 39.6 | |
| 15.7 | 10.4 | 17.4 | Long-Term Debt | | | 2.5 | 6.2 | 18.2 | 15.2 | |
| .4 | .3 | .2 | Deferred Taxes | | | .0 | .5 | .0 | .3 | |
| 7.4 | 5.5 | 7.8 | All Other Non-Current | | | 2.6 | 6.0 | 8.9 | 9.9 | |
| 39.1 | 41.3 | 40.5 | Net Worth | | | 58.4 | 52.4 | 42.2 | 35.0 | |
| 100.0 | 100.0 | 100.0 | Total Liabilities & Net Worth | | | 100.0 | 100.0 | 100.0 | 100.0 | |
| | | | INCOME DATA | | | | | | | |
| 100.0 | 100.0 | 100.0 | Net Sales | | | 100.0 | 100.0 | 100.0 | 100.0 | |
| 39.4 | 36.2 | 38.8 | Gross Profit | | | 46.2 | 42.2 | 42.6 | 29.6 | |
| 34.4 | 32.2 | 34.6 | Operating Expenses | | | 37.2 | 39.4 | 40.5 | 27.4 | |
| 5.0 | 4.0 | 4.2 | Operating Profit | | | 9.1 | 2.8 | 2.1 | 2.2 | |
| -.9 | -.7 | -.2 | All Other Expenses (net) | | | -.9 | -1.6 | -1.4 | .2 | |
| 5.9 | 4.7 | 4.4 | Profit Before Taxes | | | 10.0 | 4.4 | 3.5 | 1.9 | |
| | | | RATIOS | | | | | | | |
| 3.2 | 2.6 | 3.5 | | | | 7.8 | 6.6 | 3.1 | 2.5 | |
| 1.8 | 1.8 | 2.0 | Current | | | 3.1 | 1.5 | 2.0 | 1.7 | |
| 1.4 | 1.3 | 1.3 | | | | 1.5 | 1.2 | 1.4 | 1.3 | |
| 1.7 | 1.3 | 1.7 | | | | 5.0 | 3.1 | 1.0 | .8 | |
| .8 | .6 | .8 | Quick | | | 1.9 | .9 | .8 | .5 | |
| .5 | .3 | .3 | | | | 1.0 | .4 | .5 | .3 | |
| 1  249.9 | 6  62.4 | 1  458.7 | | 0  UND | 6  65.4 | 1  686.9 | 12  29.6 | | | |
| 14  26.9 | 18  20.5 | 13  27.2 | Sales/Receivables | 1  638.7 | 22  16.7 | 8  46.9 | 19  18.9 | | | |
| 25  14.5 | 29  12.4 | 23  15.9 | | 9  39.0 | 25  14.4 | 13  27.1 | 25  14.6 | | | |
| 40  9.1 | 47  7.8 | 40  9.1 | | 18  20.2 | 24  15.2 | 49  7.4 | 63  5.8 | | | |
| 68  5.4 | 78  4.7 | 69  5.3 | Cost of Sales/Inventory | 27  13.4 | 78  4.7 | 65  5.6 | 81  4.5 | | | |
| 96  3.8 | 114  3.2 | 101  3.6 | | 49  7.5 | 107  3.4 | 99  3.7 | 111  3.3 | | | |
| 15  23.7 | 24  14.9 | 14  25.7 | | 0  UND | 15  23.8 | 14  25.5 | 26  14.3 | | | |
| 38  9.7 | 45  8.2 | 34  10.7 | Cost of Sales/Payables | 14  25.2 | 49  7.5 | 34  10.7 | 41  9.0 | | | |
| 60  6.1 | 63  5.8 | 54  6.7 | | 48  7.6 | 81  4.5 | 57  6.4 | 58  6.3 | | | |
| 5.8 | 5.7 | 5.0 | | | | 4.2 | 4.5 | 5.0 | 5.6 | |
| 9.6 | 10.2 | 10.3 | Sales/Working Capital | | | 10.0 | 11.4 | 9.4 | 10.3 | |
| 23.7 | 21.4 | 20.0 | | | | 18.4 | 25.0 | 17.9 | 25.5 | |
| 78.7 | 29.0 | 24.8 | | | | 51.1 | 7.5 | 21.1 | | |
| (74)  21.9 | (75)  11.0 | (82)  4.9 | EBIT/Interest | | (10) 19.3 | (12) 4.1 | (45) 3.8 | | | |
| 7.3 | 5.3 | 1.2 | | | | 1.2 | -.6 | 1.4 | | |
| | | | | | | | | | 5.6 | |
| 12.2 | 11.5 | 6.0 | Net Profit + Depr., Dep., | | | | | (16) 2.5 | | |
| (21) 7.4 | (24) 4.8 | (17) 2.6 | Amort./Cur. Mat. L/T/D | | | | | .3 | | |
| 4.8 | 2.3 | .3 | | | | | | | | |
| .2 | .1 | .1 | | | | .0 | .1 | .2 | .2 | |
| .5 | .4 | .4 | Fixed/Worth | | | .1 | .2 | .5 | .5 | |
| 1.1 | .8 | 1.1 | | | | .8 | .5 | .8 | 1.5 | |
| .7 | .6 | .6 | | | | .2 | .3 | .6 | .8 | |
| 1.6 | 1.4 | 1.3 | Debt/Worth | | | .5 | 1.0 | 1.0 | 2.4 | |
| 3.9 | 3.5 | 5.3 | | | | 1.3 | 1.7 | 6.2 | 5.7 | |
| 59.1 | 43.2 | 41.3 | | | | 117.8 | 40.4 | 28.6 | 25.9 | |
| (83) 35.0 | (86) 25.3 | (98) 22.0 | % Profit Before Taxes/Tangible Net Worth | | (13) 49.0 | 19.2 | (14) 24.0 | (46) 16.7 | | |
| 21.7 | 16.3 | 6.6 | | | | 40.4 | 2.9 | 10.7 | 4.3 | |
| 24.4 | 19.2 | 18.2 | | | | 75.5 | 19.4 | 16.0 | 8.8 | |
| 13.2 | 10.6 | 6.7 | % Profit Before Taxes/Total Assets | | | 43.0 | 8.0 | 8.8 | 5.0 | |
| 6.8 | 4.9 | .8 | | | | 11.5 | .7 | -1.4 | .4 | |
| 42.1 | 53.8 | 71.4 | | | | 658.6 | 91.1 | 71.4 | 44.4 | |
| 24.1 | 21.7 | 17.9 | Sales/Net Fixed Assets | | | 64.0 | 24.6 | 9.2 | 17.0 | |
| 11.0 | 10.5 | 9.2 | | | | 31.6 | 13.0 | 6.4 | 12.0 | |
| 3.8 | 3.9 | 3.6 | | | | 6.4 | 3.3 | 3.8 | 3.1 | |
| 2.9 | 2.9 | 2.8 | Sales/Total Assets | | | 3.9 | 2.4 | 3.1 | 2.7 | |
| 2.1 | 1.9 | 1.8 | | | | 2.5 | 2.0 | 1.8 | 1.8 | |
| .6 | .7 | .6 | | | | | | .3 | .7 | |
| (67) 1.3 | (67) 1.3 | (78) 1.3 | % Depr., Dep., Amort./Sales | | | | | (11) 1.0 | (41) 1.3 | |
| 1.9 | 1.9 | 1.9 | | | | | | 2.1 | 1.8 | |
| 1.3 | 1.3 | .7 | | | | | | | .5 | |
| (34) 2.0 | (26) 2.5 | (31) 2.0 | % Officers', Directors', Owners' Comp/Sales | | | | | (10) .7 | | |
| 5.5 | 5.8 | 3.4 | | | | | | | 1.8 | |
| 5291300M | 6783714M | 8517449M | Net Sales ($) | 4927M | 17278M | 52557M | 94787M | 256855M | 8091045M | |
| 1944836M | 2974164M | 3527752M | Total Assets ($) | 5251M | 6394M | 15954M | 38430M | 107492M | 3354231M | |

© RMA 2024  
M = $ thousand  MM = $ million  
See Pages viii through xx for Explanation of Ratios and Data

# RETAIL—Home Centers  NAICS 444110

## Current Data Sorted by Assets | Comparative Historical Data

| | | | | | | Type of Statement | | |
|---|---|---|---|---|---|---|---|---|
| | | | 2 | | 2 | Unqualified | 13 | 6 |
| | | 4 | 7 | 2 | | Reviewed | 13 | 11 |
| | 1 | 4 | 2 | | | Compiled | 8 | 6 |
| | 2 | 4 | 1 | | | Tax Returns | 8 | 5 |
| | 8 | 17 | 12 | 3 | 5 | Other | 47 | 46 |
| 0-500M | 6 (4/1-9/30/23) | | 70 (10/1/23-3/31/24) | | | | 4/1/19-3/31/20 | 4/1/20-3/31/21 |
| | 500M-2MM | 2-10MM | 10-50MM | 50-100MM | 100-250MM | NUMBER OF STATEMENTS | ALL | ALL |
| | 11 | 29 | 24 | 5 | 7 | | 89 | 74 |
| % | % | % | % | % | % | ASSETS | % | % |
| | 13.1 | 15.8 | 18.5 | | | Cash & Equivalents | 8.8 | 15.7 |
| D | 15.5 | 17.6 | 19.5 | | | Trade Receivables (net) | 17.3 | 20.2 |
| A | 42.5 | 39.4 | 31.8 | | | Inventory | 37.8 | 37.9 |
| T | 9.4 | 2.7 | 2.3 | | | All Other Current | 1.3 | 1.4 |
| A | 80.5 | 75.5 | 72.1 | | | Total Current | 65.1 | 75.1 |
| | 15.4 | 12.7 | 16.9 | | | Fixed Assets (net) | 24.9 | 16.8 |
| N | 1.4 | 1.3 | 2.2 | | | Intangibles (net) | 2.5 | 2.4 |
| O | 2.7 | 10.5 | 8.7 | | | All Other Non-Current | 7.5 | 5.6 |
| T | 100.0 | 100.0 | 100.0 | | | Total | 100.0 | 100.0 |
| | | | | | | LIABILITIES | | |
| A | 12.2 | 2.4 | 1.8 | | | Notes Payable-Short Term | 10.9 | 7.9 |
| V | .5 | 2.0 | 1.2 | | | Cur. Mat.-L.T.D. | 2.1 | 3.4 |
| A | 8.5 | 10.3 | 11.3 | | | Trade Payables | 12.4 | 13.6 |
| I | .0 | .0 | .0 | | | Income Taxes Payable | .0 | .1 |
| L | 8.0 | 11.7 | 14.5 | | | All Other Current | 9.5 | 11.4 |
| A | 29.3 | 26.3 | 28.8 | | | Total Current | 35.0 | 36.4 |
| B | 10.2 | 7.8 | 8.1 | | | Long-Term Debt | 14.4 | 11.7 |
| L | .0 | .0 | .0 | | | Deferred Taxes | .2 | .1 |
| E | 19.2 | 8.5 | 3.4 | | | All Other Non-Current | 4.3 | 6.6 |
| | 41.3 | 57.4 | 59.6 | | | Net Worth | 46.1 | 45.2 |
| | 100.0 | 100.0 | 100.0 | | | Total Liabilities & Net Worth | 100.0 | 100.0 |
| | | | | | | INCOME DATA | | |
| | 100.0 | 100.0 | 100.0 | | | Net Sales | 100.0 | 100.0 |
| | 35.5 | 31.8 | 31.7 | | | Gross Profit | 32.0 | 30.7 |
| | 32.0 | 26.7 | 25.5 | | | Operating Expenses | 28.5 | 26.1 |
| | 3.5 | 5.1 | 6.2 | | | Operating Profit | 3.5 | 4.6 |
| | .0 | -.5 | -.6 | | | All Other Expenses (net) | .3 | -.4 |
| | 3.5 | 5.5 | 6.8 | | | Profit Before Taxes | 3.2 | 5.0 |
| | | | | | | RATIOS | | |
| | 10.8 | 5.2 | 5.8 | | | | 3.4 | 3.4 |
| | 5.2 | 3.5 | 3.1 | | | Current | 2.0 | 2.2 |
| | 1.3 | 1.9 | 1.6 | | | | 1.3 | 1.5 |
| | 2.2 | 2.9 | 3.0 | | | | 1.3 | 1.6 |
| | 1.4 | 1.0 | 1.1 | | | Quick | .8 | 1.0 |
| | .7 | .6 | .8 | | | | .4 | .6 |
| 0 | UND | 9 42.6 | 15 24.3 | | | | 10 37.3 | 13 27.9 |
| 7 | 56.0 | 17 21.1 | 26 13.8 | | | Sales/Receivables | 24 15.2 | 27 13.6 |
| 27 | 13.5 | 27 13.6 | 38 9.7 | | | | 37 9.8 | 41 8.8 |
| 27 | 13.3 | 49 7.4 | 34 10.7 | | | | 45 8.1 | 51 7.1 |
| 50 | 7.3 | 85 4.3 | 57 6.4 | | | Cost of Sales/Inventory | 72 5.1 | 69 5.3 |
| 182 | 2.0 | 104 3.5 | 91 4.0 | | | | 99 3.7 | 111 3.3 |
| 0 | UND | 11 34.5 | 9 40.8 | | | | 14 26.0 | 14 25.2 |
| 0 | UND | 15 24.6 | 16 22.2 | | | Cost of Sales/Payables | 20 18.5 | 21 17.5 |
| 24 | 15.3 | 32 11.3 | 28 12.9 | | | | 30 12.1 | 36 10.1 |
| | 2.5 | 3.7 | 3.2 | | | | 4.9 | 4.7 |
| | 7.1 | 5.3 | 5.4 | | | Sales/Working Capital | 8.0 | 6.3 |
| | 22.1 | 8.8 | 9.1 | | | | 24.4 | 10.8 |
| | | 38.3 | 29.7 | | | | 14.3 | 60.7 |
| | (20) | 13.6 | (16) 23.9 | | | EBIT/Interest | (76) 5.0 | (64) 14.3 |
| | | 5.2 | 10.2 | | | | 1.7 | 6.2 |
| | | | | | | | 5.5 | 5.5 |
| | | | | | | Net Profit + Depr., Dep., Amort./Cur. Mat. L/T/D | (21) 2.3 | (21) 3.0 |
| | | | | | | | 1.5 | .7 |
| | .0 | .0 | .1 | | | | .2 | .1 |
| | .3 | .2 | .3 | | | Fixed/Worth | .6 | .3 |
| | -17.5 | .4 | .6 | | | | .9 | .6 |
| | .1 | .3 | .2 | | | | .6 | .5 |
| | .6 | .9 | .6 | | | Debt/Worth | 1.1 | 1.0 |
| | -50.4 | 1.7 | 1.7 | | | | 2.3 | 1.9 |
| | | 32.6 | 41.2 | | | | 36.6 | 44.0 |
| | | 22.2 | 28.5 | | | % Profit Before Taxes/Tangible Net Worth | (84) 15.8 | (69) 28.3 |
| | | 11.1 | 16.0 | | | | 4.6 | 15.7 |
| | 37.0 | 19.7 | 22.7 | | | | 14.6 | 21.0 |
| | 8.2 | 12.3 | 16.3 | | | % Profit Before Taxes/Total Assets | 6.9 | 12.9 |
| | 4.8 | 6.1 | 6.5 | | | | 1.7 | 7.1 |
| | 105.8 | 79.0 | 47.0 | | | | 24.0 | 35.6 |
| | 26.2 | 23.7 | 19.4 | | | Sales/Net Fixed Assets | 13.2 | 17.6 |
| | 13.8 | 13.2 | 8.7 | | | | 6.5 | 10.4 |
| | 4.7 | 2.9 | 3.3 | | | | 3.3 | 3.3 |
| | 3.8 | 2.6 | 2.5 | | | Sales/Total Assets | 2.6 | 2.7 |
| | 2.1 | 2.1 | 1.8 | | | | 2.0 | 2.1 |
| | | .6 | .5 | | | | .7 | .8 |
| | (24) | .8 | (20) .9 | | | % Depr., Dep., Amort./Sales | (69) 1.2 | (58) 1.2 |
| | | 1.4 | 1.2 | | | | 1.7 | 1.6 |
| | | 1.0 | | | | | .9 | 1.2 |
| | (14) | 1.9 | | | | % Officers', Directors' Owners' Comp/Sales | (33) 2.2 | (24) 2.1 |
| | | 7.9 | | | | | 3.3 | 3.6 |
| 44474M | 382400M | 1660080M | 691740M | 1990125M | | Net Sales ($) | 4518575M | 3185643M |
| 13111M | 138213M | 666811M | 331305M | 1130529M | | Total Assets ($) | 2275873M | 1307565M |

M = $ thousand    MM = $ million
See Pages viii through xx for Explanation of Ratios and Data

© RMA 2024

# RETAIL—Home Centers  NAICS 444110

## Comparative Historical Data / Current Data Sorted by Sales

| | | | | | Type of Statement | | | | | | |
|---|---|---|---|---|---|---|---|---|---|---|---|
| | 2 | | 5 | 4 | Unqualified | | | | | 4 | 4 |
| | 6 | | 8 | 13 | Reviewed | | | | | 1 | 9 |
| | 11 | | 8 | 7 | Compiled | | | | 3 | 1 | 3 |
| | 21 | | 10 | 7 | Tax Returns | | 2 | | 3 | 1 | 1 |
| | 35 | | 50 | 45 | Other | 1 | 3 | 5 | 8 | 9 | 19 |
| | 4/1/21- | | 4/1/22- | 4/1/23- | | | 6 (4/1-9/30/23) | | | 70 (10/1/23-3/31/24) | |
| | 3/31/22 | | 3/31/23 | 3/31/24 | | 0-1MM | 1-3MM | 3-5MM | 5-10MM | 10-25MM | 25MM & OVER |
| | ALL | | ALL | ALL | NUMBER OF STATEMENTS | | | | | | |
| | 75 | | 81 | 76 | | 1 | 5 | 5 | 14 | 15 | 36 |
| | % | | % | % | ASSETS | % | % | % | % | % | % |
| | 14.0 | | 13.8 | 15.3 | Cash & Equivalents | | | | 18.5 | 18.4 | 14.2 |
| | 17.5 | | 16.2 | 16.6 | Trade Receivables (net) | | | | 20.9 | 23.7 | 15.7 |
| | 41.5 | | 38.0 | 35.8 | Inventory | | | | 26.2 | 37.8 | 32.9 |
| | 1.5 | | 3.9 | 3.5 | All Other Current | | | | 10.7 | .9 | 1.3 |
| | 74.5 | | 71.9 | 71.1 | Total Current | | | | 76.3 | 80.9 | 64.1 |
| | 14.4 | | 14.3 | 16.0 | Fixed Assets (net) | | | | 12.3 | 13.7 | 19.7 |
| | 2.2 | | 2.2 | 3.7 | Intangibles (net) | | | | 1.4 | 1.3 | 6.2 |
| | 8.9 | | 11.5 | 9.1 | All Other Non-Current | | | | 10.0 | 4.1 | 10.0 |
| | 100.0 | | 100.0 | 100.0 | Total | | | | 100.0 | 100.0 | 100.0 |
| | | | | | LIABILITIES | | | | | | |
| | 6.0 | | 3.9 | 4.0 | Notes Payable-Short Term | | | | 2.3 | 3.9 | 3.1 |
| | 2.3 | | 1.9 | 1.5 | Cur. Mat.-L.T.D. | | | | 1.2 | 2.1 | 1.7 |
| | 10.8 | | 12.3 | 10.5 | Trade Payables | | | | 9.0 | 13.3 | 12.5 |
| | .1 | | .2 | .0 | Income Taxes Payable | | | | .0 | .0 | .0 |
| | 8.7 | | 10.5 | 12.5 | All Other Current | | | | 10.3 | 15.5 | 13.1 |
| | 27.8 | | 28.8 | 28.6 | Total Current | | | | 22.9 | 34.9 | 30.3 |
| | 10.2 | | 12.2 | 11.2 | Long-Term Debt | | | | 10.2 | 8.4 | 14.9 |
| | .2 | | .1 | .1 | Deferred Taxes | | | | .0 | .0 | .2 |
| | 7.1 | | 3.4 | 8.9 | All Other Non-Current | | | | 12.4 | 6.7 | 6.0 |
| | 54.7 | | 55.6 | 51.2 | Net Worth | | | | 54.5 | 50.0 | 48.6 |
| | 100.0 | | 100.0 | 100.0 | Total Liabilities & Net Worth | | | | 100.0 | 100.0 | 100.0 |
| | | | | | INCOME DATA | | | | | | |
| | 100.0 | | 100.0 | 100.0 | Net Sales | | | | 100.0 | 100.0 | 100.0 |
| | 30.1 | | 31.5 | 33.3 | Gross Profit | | | | 31.2 | 31.2 | 33.5 |
| | 24.6 | | 24.8 | 27.8 | Operating Expenses | | | | 24.2 | 26.3 | 27.8 |
| | 5.5 | | 6.7 | 5.4 | Operating Profit | | | | 7.0 | 4.9 | 5.8 |
| | -1.7 | | -.1 | -.3 | All Other Expenses (net) | | | | -.4 | .0 | -.2 |
| | 7.2 | | 6.8 | 5.7 | Profit Before Taxes | | | | 7.3 | 4.9 | 5.9 |
| | | | | | RATIOS | | | | | | |
| | 5.6 | | 5.6 | 5.3 | | | | | 12.7 | 3.9 | 3.7 |
| | 2.8 | | 3.1 | 3.0 | Current | | | | 4.8 | 3.3 | 2.2 |
| | 2.0 | | 1.8 | 1.8 | | | | | 2.4 | 1.7 | 1.4 |
| | 2.8 | | 2.5 | 2.3 | | | | | 8.5 | 2.3 | 1.9 |
| | 1.1 | | 1.2 | 1.1 | Quick | | | | 2.4 | 1.1 | .9 |
| | .7 | | .7 | .6 | | | | | .8 | .6 | .4 |
| 6 | 65.6 | 5 | 73.5 | 8 | 43.9 | Sales/Receivables | | | 5 | 71.2 | 18 | 20.2 | 9 | 38.8 |
| 21 | 17.0 | 17 | 21.3 | 21 | 17.1 | | | | 16 | 22.3 | 25 | 14.4 | 24 | 15.5 |
| 42 | 8.7 | 35 | 10.5 | 30 | 12.1 | | | | 31 | 11.6 | 41 | 8.8 | 32 | 11.5 |
| 49 | 7.5 | 46 | 7.9 | 41 | 9.0 | Cost of Sales/Inventory | | | 9 | 39.5 | 48 | 7.6 | 41 | 8.9 |
| 83 | 4.4 | 73 | 5.0 | 81 | 4.5 | | | | 46 | 7.9 | 81 | 4.5 | 76 | 4.8 |
| 107 | 3.4 | 104 | 3.5 | 111 | 3.3 | | | | 87 | 4.2 | 89 | 4.1 | 99 | 3.7 |
| 11 | 34.0 | 9 | 41.3 | 9 | 41.7 | Cost of Sales/Payables | | | 0 | UND | 15 | 24.6 | 13 | 27.3 |
| 20 | 18.0 | 18 | 20.1 | 17 | 21.2 | | | | 11 | 34.5 | 27 | 13.6 | 22 | 16.5 |
| 30 | 12.3 | 29 | 12.5 | 31 | 11.8 | | | | 22 | 16.3 | 38 | 9.6 | 33 | 11.0 |
| | 3.7 | | 3.7 | 3.7 | Sales/Working Capital | | | | 2.9 | 4.7 | 4.5 |
| | 5.4 | | 5.6 | 5.8 | | | | | 4.5 | 6.1 | 7.3 |
| | 8.1 | | 9.7 | 9.2 | | | | | 6.6 | 9.1 | 15.2 |
| | 71.2 | | 63.5 | 31.3 | EBIT/Interest | | | | | 53.8 | 29.6 |
| (59) | 30.2 | (66) | 24.1 | (55) | 15.1 | | | | | (12) | 11.6 | (29) | 17.9 |
| | 10.1 | | 8.4 | 4.9 | | | | | | 3.2 | 6.1 |
| | 15.4 | | 27.1 | 35.4 | Net Profit + Depr., Dep., | | | | | | 32.6 |
| (19) | 6.5 | (13) | 10.0 | (15) | 4.3 | Amort./Cur. Mat. L/T/D | | | | | (10) | 4.0 |
| | 2.6 | | 2.2 | 2.1 | | | | | | | 2.6 |
| | .1 | | .1 | .1 | Fixed/Worth | | | | .0 | .1 | .2 |
| | .2 | | .2 | .3 | | | | | .1 | .3 | .4 |
| | .5 | | .5 | .6 | | | | | .7 | .5 | 1.1 |
| | .3 | | .3 | .3 | Debt/Worth | | | | .1 | .4 | .4 |
| | .8 | | .8 | .9 | | | | | .5 | 1.1 | 1.0 |
| | 1.5 | | 1.5 | 2.3 | | | | | 3.6 | 2.1 | 2.5 |
| | 53.8 | | 44.1 | 41.1 | % Profit Before Taxes/Tangible | | | | 40.5 | 53.0 | 41.1 |
| (72) | 35.6 | (76) | 32.6 | (70) | 25.2 | Net Worth | | | (12) | 23.5 | 21.1 | (33) | 31.5 |
| | 17.3 | | 20.9 | 13.3 | | | | | 12.4 | 10.7 | 15.8 |
| | 28.4 | | 24.6 | 19.9 | % Profit Before Taxes/Total | | | | 22.7 | 24.0 | 19.6 |
| | 18.4 | | 18.4 | 12.3 | Assets | | | | 12.7 | 10.3 | 13.6 |
| | 10.0 | | 9.9 | 6.1 | | | | | 8.5 | 4.0 | 6.3 |
| | 81.2 | | 143.6 | 49.0 | Sales/Net Fixed Assets | | | | 117.9 | 49.2 | 34.4 |
| | 21.8 | | 24.8 | 16.0 | | | | | 44.1 | 23.7 | 13.2 |
| | 11.7 | | 10.9 | 9.4 | | | | | 14.8 | 13.0 | 7.2 |
| | 3.3 | | 3.3 | 3.1 | Sales/Total Assets | | | | 3.9 | 2.9 | 3.1 |
| | 2.7 | | 2.6 | 2.5 | | | | | 2.5 | 2.8 | 2.4 |
| | 2.1 | | 2.0 | 1.8 | | | | | 1.5 | 2.3 | 1.6 |
| | .8 | | .4 | .5 | % Depr., Dep., Amort./Sales | | | | .2 | .6 | .9 |
| (58) | 1.2 | (61) | .8 | (59) | .9 | | | | (10) | .6 | (12) | 1.0 | (27) | 1.1 |
| | 1.6 | | 1.2 | 1.3 | | | | | .8 | 1.5 | 1.3 |
| | 1.1 | | 1.1 | .7 | % Officers', Directors', | | | | | | |
| (35) | 2.1 | (29) | 1.5 | (23) | 1.3 | Owners' Comp/Sales | | | | | |
| | 3.8 | | 3.6 | 4.1 | | | | | | | |
| | 2929760M | | 3854554M | 4768819M | Net Sales ($) | 251M | 11093M | 21351M | 104705M | 247102M | 4384317M |
| | 1344913M | | 1731492M | 2279969M | Total Assets ($) | 1300M | 4585M | 10664M | 49559M | 93470M | 2120391M |

© RMA 2024  M = $ thousand   MM = $ million
See Pages viii through xx for Explanation of Ratios and Data

# RETAIL—Hardware Retailers  NAICS 444140

## Current Data Sorted by Assets | Comparative Historical Data

| | | | | | | Type of Statement | | | | |
|---|---|---|---|---|---|---|---|---|---|---|
| | | | 2 | 3 | 1 | Unqualified | | 13 | | 4 |
| | | 2 | 6 | 1 | 1 | Reviewed | | 10 | | 3 |
| | 2 | 7 | 3 | 1 | | Compiled | | 28 | | 11 |
| 1 | 20 | 15 | | | | Tax Returns | | 53 | | 31 |
| 9 | 31 | 29 | 7 | 2 | 3 | Other | | 95 | | 53 |
| | 9 (4/1-9/30/23) | | 137 (10/1/23-3/31/24) | | | | | 4/1/19-3/31/20 ALL | | 4/1/20-3/31/21 ALL |
| 0-500M | 500M-2MM | 2-10MM | 10-50MM | 50-100MM | 100-250MM | NUMBER OF STATEMENTS | | 199 | | 102 |
| 10 | 53 | 53 | 18 | 7 | 5 | | | | | |
| % | % | % | % | % | % | ASSETS | | % | | % |
| 14.7 | 14.5 | 15.3 | 13.9 | | | Cash & Equivalents | | 9.1 | | 16.5 |
| 3.6 | 7.2 | 7.9 | 9.2 | | | Trade Receivables (net) | | 9.0 | | 9.7 |
| 60.3 | 50.3 | 41.3 | 39.5 | | | Inventory | | 49.5 | | 46.1 |
| .0 | 3.2 | 5.3 | 7.8 | | | All Other Current | | 2.2 | | 1.3 |
| 78.5 | 75.2 | 69.8 | 70.4 | | | Total Current | | 69.7 | | 73.6 |
| 14.5 | 11.7 | 16.2 | 11.8 | | | Fixed Assets (net) | | 17.2 | | 11.8 |
| 1.7 | 3.5 | 2.7 | 1.5 | | | Intangibles (net) | | 2.8 | | 4.5 |
| 5.2 | 9.6 | 11.2 | 16.3 | | | All Other Non-Current | | 10.3 | | 10.0 |
| 100.0 | 100.0 | 100.0 | 100.0 | | | Total | | 100.0 | | 100.0 |
| | | | | | | **LIABILITIES** | | | | |
| 1.2 | 1.8 | 3.1 | .8 | | | Notes Payable-Short Term | | 8.0 | | 6.2 |
| 2.5 | 2.4 | 1.5 | 1.4 | | | Cur. Mat.-L.T.D. | | 2.2 | | 1.9 |
| 13.1 | 5.4 | 10.8 | 8.8 | | | Trade Payables | | 10.7 | | 12.9 |
| .0 | .0 | .0 | .1 | | | Income Taxes Payable | | .1 | | .2 |
| 10.4 | 6.9 | 6.5 | 7.7 | | | All Other Current | | 6.5 | | 7.9 |
| 27.2 | 16.5 | 22.0 | 18.8 | | | Total Current | | 27.5 | | 29.0 |
| 22.1 | 19.9 | 24.2 | 10.2 | | | Long-Term Debt | | 18.6 | | 18.1 |
| .0 | .0 | .0 | .3 | | | Deferred Taxes | | .1 | | .0 |
| 26.5 | 9.2 | 5.0 | 9.0 | | | All Other Non-Current | | 9.7 | | 6.5 |
| 24.1 | 54.4 | 48.8 | 61.6 | | | Net Worth | | 44.0 | | 46.3 |
| 100.0 | 100.0 | 100.0 | 100.0 | | | Total Liabilities & Net Worth | | 100.0 | | 100.0 |
| | | | | | | **INCOME DATA** | | | | |
| 100.0 | 100.0 | 100.0 | 100.0 | | | Net Sales | | 100.0 | | 100.0 |
| 42.6 | 39.7 | 37.2 | 38.0 | | | Gross Profit | | 37.4 | | 36.3 |
| 44.3 | 34.9 | 31.4 | 32.5 | | | Operating Expenses | | 33.1 | | 30.3 |
| -1.7 | 4.7 | 5.8 | 5.5 | | | Operating Profit | | 4.3 | | 6.0 |
| .1 | -.9 | -1.0 | -1.1 | | | All Other Expenses (net) | | -.1 | | -1.2 |
| -1.8 | 5.6 | 6.7 | 6.6 | | | Profit Before Taxes | | 4.3 | | 7.2 |
| | | | | | | **RATIOS** | | | | |
| 7.9 | 10.3 | 7.2 | 7.0 | | | | | 6.0 | | 6.1 |
| 3.0 | 5.3 | 4.3 | 4.9 | | Current | | | 3.3 | | 3.2 |
| 1.9 | 3.5 | 2.2 | 2.6 | | | | | 1.7 | | 1.8 |
| 3.6 | 3.7 | 2.6 | 2.6 | | | | | 1.6 | | 1.7 |
| .7 | 1.1 | 1.0 | 1.3 | | Quick | | (197) | .7 | | 1.0 |
| .3 | .4 | .4 | .4 | | | | | .2 | | .5 |
| 0 UND | 2 231.5 | 2 216.0 | 4 92.8 | | | | 3 | 133.3 | 3 | 124.0 |
| 0 UND | 7 49.7 | 5 75.3 | 9 41.2 | | Sales/Receivables | | 8 | 45.7 | 7 | 55.9 |
| 10 37.1 | 19 19.6 | 23 15.7 | 34 10.8 | | | | 17 | 21.0 | 19 | 19.2 |
| 64 5.7 | 94 3.9 | 89 4.1 | 76 4.8 | | | | 99 | 3.7 | 81 | 4.5 |
| 85 4.3 | 146 2.5 | 111 3.3 | 135 2.7 | | Cost of Sales/Inventory | | 140 | 2.6 | 118 | 3.1 |
| 122 3.0 | 203 1.8 | 166 2.2 | 182 2.0 | | | | 192 | 1.9 | 166 | 2.2 |
| 0 UND | 2 224.5 | 4 93.5 | 10 35.0 | | | | 8 | 44.4 | 10 | 36.1 |
| 14 26.8 | 14 26.5 | 18 20.8 | 18 19.8 | | Cost of Sales/Payables | | 19 | 19.5 | 22 | 16.9 |
| 31 11.7 | 20 18.5 | 28 13.0 | 30 12.1 | | | | 33 | 10.9 | 38 | 9.7 |
| 8.4 | 2.6 | 3.2 | 2.6 | | | | | 3.4 | | 3.2 |
| 11.2 | 3.8 | 4.3 | 3.3 | | Sales/Working Capital | | | 5.0 | | 5.1 |
| 15.0 | 5.6 | 5.8 | 5.9 | | | | | 9.3 | | 8.6 |
| | 42.1 | 12.3 | 98.1 | | | | | 19.6 | | 57.8 |
| (37) | 6.2 | (38) 5.4 | (16) 20.1 | | EBIT/Interest | | (174) | 5.8 | (92) | 11.3 |
| | 1.1 | 1.5 | 11.6 | | | | | 2.0 | | 5.7 |
| | | | | | | Net Profit + Depr., Dep., | | | 5.8 | | 6.7 |
| | | | | | | Amort./Cur. Mat. L/T/D | | (24) | 3.4 | (13) | 6.1 |
| | | | | | | | | 2.0 | | 2.6 |
| .0 | .0 | .0 | .1 | | | | | .1 | | .1 |
| .2 | .2 | .2 | .2 | | Fixed/Worth | | | .3 | | .2 |
| NM | 1.1 | 1.2 | .3 | | | | | 1.1 | | .5 |
| .4 | .2 | .2 | .4 | | | | | .4 | | .4 |
| 1.0 | .5 | .7 | .7 | | Debt/Worth | | | 1.1 | | 1.0 |
| -5.8 | 3.8 | 3.7 | 1.2 | | | | | 3.6 | | 2.7 |
| | 47.0 | 33.0 | 31.6 | | % Profit Before Taxes/Tangible | | | 36.4 | | 55.8 |
| (45) | 26.3 | (46) 18.0 | 16.9 | | Net Worth | | (181) | 17.2 | (90) | 36.0 |
| | 10.6 | 8.1 | 11.6 | | | | | 7.2 | | 15.7 |
| 8.8 | 26.5 | 18.6 | 19.7 | | | | | 15.3 | | 24.3 |
| -1.8 | 15.7 | 9.3 | 10.0 | | % Profit Before Taxes/Total Assets | | | 8.1 | | 15.3 |
| -44.3 | 1.4 | 4.3 | 6.4 | | | | | 2.2 | | 6.7 |
| UND | 80.0 | 84.5 | 51.3 | | | | | 66.3 | | 85.5 |
| 63.6 | 24.9 | 17.3 | 17.7 | | Sales/Net Fixed Assets | | | 18.6 | | 28.5 |
| 21.5 | 11.4 | 7.7 | 9.6 | | | | | 6.6 | | 11.8 |
| 6.9 | 2.8 | 2.7 | 2.3 | | | | | 2.9 | | 2.8 |
| 5.9 | 2.2 | 2.0 | 1.8 | | Sales/Total Assets | | | 2.1 | | 2.2 |
| 3.9 | 1.8 | 1.4 | 1.3 | | | | | 1.5 | | 1.8 |
| | .4 | .5 | .5 | | | | | .6 | | .5 |
| (31) | .9 | (39) .9 | (13) .8 | | % Depr., Dep., Amort./Sales | | (130) | 1.2 | (65) | 1.2 |
| | 1.3 | 1.6 | 1.2 | | | | | 2.0 | | 1.8 |
| | 1.9 | .9 | | | | | | 1.6 | | 1.8 |
| (20) | 3.5 | (26) 1.5 | | | % Officers', Directors' | | (85) | 2.5 | (54) | 2.8 |
| | 4.6 | 2.6 | | | Owners' Comp/Sales | | | 5.5 | | 4.4 |
| 13480M | 159802M | 509508M | 738076M | 629479M | 1466049M | Net Sales ($) | | 4539889M | | 1900600M |
| 2575M | 71840M | 255082M | 371733M | 451354M | 748356M | Total Assets ($) | | 2417046M | | 854872M |

M = $ thousand   MM = $ million
See Pages viii through xx for Explanation of Ratios and Data

© RMA 2024

# RETAIL—Hardware Retailers  NAICS 444140

## Comparative Historical Data | Current Data Sorted by Sales

| | | | | Type of Statement | | | | | | |
|---|---|---|---|---|---|---|---|---|---|---|
| 2 | | 4 | 6 | Unqualified | | | | 1 | 3 | 6 |
| 4 | | 8 | 10 | Reviewed | | | 1 | 1 | 6 | 6 |
| 23 | | 17 | 13 | Compiled | | 1 | 13 | 1 | 6 | 4 |
| 48 | | 52 | 36 | Tax Returns | | 10 | 12 | 9 | 3 | 1 |
| 53 | | 84 | 81 | Other | 7 | 26 | | 15 | 12 | 9 |
| 4/1/21-3/31/22 ALL | | 4/1/22-3/31/23 ALL | 4/1/23-3/31/24 ALL | | | 9 (4/1-9/30/23) | | | 137 (10/1/23-3/31/24) | |
| | | | | | 0-1MM | 1-3MM | 3-5MM | 5-10MM | 10-25MM | 25MM & OVER |
| 130 | | 165 | 146 | NUMBER OF STATEMENTS | 7 | 37 | 26 | 26 | 24 | 26 |
| % | | % | % | ASSETS | % | % | % | % | % | % |
| 14.5 | | 12.6 | 13.8 | Cash & Equivalents | 12.8 | 14.9 | 16.5 | 16.0 | 9.0 | |
| 8.7 | | 7.8 | 7.7 | Trade Receivables (net) | 5.0 | 6.6 | 9.8 | 6.9 | 11.8 | |
| 47.8 | | 47.4 | 45.0 | Inventory | 54.0 | 45.3 | 39.5 | 38.2 | 39.1 | |
| 2.9 | | 4.2 | 4.1 | All Other Current | 3.5 | 1.9 | 5.5 | 8.3 | 3.2 | |
| 73.9 | | 71.9 | 70.6 | Total Current | 75.3 | 68.8 | 71.3 | 69.4 | 63.1 | |
| 12.6 | | 12.7 | 15.1 | Fixed Assets (net) | 14.4 | 13.5 | 13.0 | 16.4 | 19.7 | |
| 3.5 | | 5.3 | 3.2 | Intangibles (net) | 3.5 | 3.1 | 3.2 | 2.0 | 3.6 | |
| 10.1 | | 10.1 | 11.1 | All Other Non-Current | 6.7 | 14.6 | 12.6 | 12.2 | 13.6 | |
| 100.0 | | 100.0 | 100.0 | Total | 100.0 | 100.0 | 100.0 | 100.0 | 100.0 | |
| | | | | **LIABILITIES** | | | | | | |
| 5.3 | | 3.7 | 2.9 | Notes Payable-Short Term | 1.6 | 1.4 | 1.7 | 5.0 | 6.0 | |
| 1.1 | | 2.3 | 2.0 | Cur. Mat.-L.T.D. | 2.2 | 3.2 | 1.2 | 1.6 | 2.2 | |
| 9.9 | | 8.6 | 8.5 | Trade Payables | 11.4 | 4.7 | 5.7 | 10.3 | 10.0 | |
| .2 | | .1 | .0 | Income Taxes Payable | .1 | .0 | .0 | .1 | .0 | |
| 5.9 | | 8.3 | 7.2 | All Other Current | 7.1 | 5.0 | 7.5 | 7.4 | 8.0 | |
| 22.4 | | 23.1 | 20.7 | Total Current | 22.3 | 14.3 | 16.1 | 24.3 | 26.2 | |
| 15.7 | | 18.0 | 20.2 | Long-Term Debt | 31.1 | 10.6 | 27.5 | 18.3 | 12.4 | |
| .1 | | .1 | .1 | Deferred Taxes | .0 | .0 | .0 | .1 | .2 | |
| 8.0 | | 7.9 | 9.2 | All Other Non-Current | 8.0 | 7.4 | 4.2 | 5.6 | 11.5 | |
| 53.8 | | 50.9 | 49.9 | Net Worth | 38.6 | 67.8 | 52.2 | 51.7 | 49.7 | |
| 100.0 | | 100.0 | 100.0 | Total Liabilities & Net Worth | 100.0 | 100.0 | 100.0 | 100.0 | 100.0 | |
| | | | | **INCOME DATA** | | | | | | |
| 100.0 | | 100.0 | 100.0 | Net Sales | 100.0 | 100.0 | 100.0 | 100.0 | 100.0 | |
| 37.8 | | 38.3 | 38.8 | Gross Profit | 40.7 | 39.7 | 38.2 | 37.0 | 38.0 | |
| 31.0 | | 32.9 | 34.0 | Operating Expenses | 38.2 | 34.7 | 29.4 | 32.5 | 32.8 | |
| 6.8 | | 5.4 | 4.8 | Operating Profit | 2.5 | 5.0 | 8.8 | 4.5 | 5.1 | |
| -2.1 | | -.9 | -.8 | All Other Expenses (net) | -.6 | -2.0 | -.6 | -.5 | -.5 | |
| 8.9 | | 6.3 | 5.6 | Profit Before Taxes | 3.1 | 7.1 | 9.4 | 5.1 | 5.7 | |
| | | | | **RATIOS** | | | | | | |
| 8.0 | | 6.9 | 7.2 | Current | 9.2 | 13.9 | 7.4 | 6.0 | 3.9 | |
| 4.4 | | 3.5 | 4.2 | | 4.0 | 5.7 | 5.2 | 3.8 | 2.5 | |
| 2.6 | | 2.1 | 2.4 | | 2.4 | 3.6 | 3.4 | 2.1 | 1.5 | |
| 2.5 | | 1.8 | 2.5 | Quick | 2.6 | 5.0 | 4.0 | 2.0 | 1.8 | |
| 1.1 | | .9 | 1.0 | | .9 | 2.1 | 1.0 | .9 | .6 | |
| .6 | | .4 | .4 | | .3 | .2 | .5 | .5 | .2 | |

### Turnover Ratios

| | | | | | | | | | | | | | |
|---|---|---|---|---|---|---|---|---|---|---|---|---|---|
| 3 | 140.9 | 2 | 153.0 | 2 | 230.2 | Sales/Receivables | 0 | UND | 1 | 600.9 | 0 | UND | 3 | 107.5 | 7 | 53.9 |
| 6 | 60.1 | 7 | 50.3 | 8 | 47.2 | | 4 | 95.9 | 2 | 148.4 | 14 | 26.4 | 7 | 52.2 | 17 | 21.0 |
| 14 | 25.7 | 21 | 17.3 | 21 | 17.6 | | 14 | 26.6 | 20 | 18.5 | 26 | 14.0 | 18 | 19.9 | 32 | 11.4 |
| 87 | 4.2 | 89 | 4.1 | 87 | 4.2 | Cost of Sales/Inventory | 91 | 4.0 | 101 | 3.6 | 73 | 5.0 | 85 | 4.3 | 70 | 5.2 |
| 126 | 2.9 | 135 | 2.7 | 130 | 2.8 | | 135 | 2.7 | 146 | 2.5 | 107 | 3.4 | 104 | 3.5 | 114 | 3.2 |
| 182 | 2.0 | 203 | 1.8 | 174 | 2.1 | | 215 | 1.7 | 174 | 2.1 | 140 | 2.6 | 159 | 2.3 | 192 | 1.9 |
| 10 | 37.5 | 8 | 45.3 | 4 | 82.5 | Cost of Sales/Payables | 3 | 130.4 | 1 | 398.5 | 0 | UND | 14 | 26.9 | 15 | 24.6 |
| 21 | 17.7 | 20 | 18.6 | 17 | 22.0 | | 16 | 22.3 | 11 | 32.5 | 13 | 28.1 | 24 | 15.2 | 23 | 15.7 |
| 33 | 11.1 | 31 | 11.6 | 27 | 13.5 | | 22 | 16.4 | 20 | 18.0 | 21 | 17.8 | 29 | 12.4 | 36 | 10.1 |

### Other Ratios

| | | | | | | | | | |
|---|---|---|---|---|---|---|---|---|---|
| 3.0 | 3.0 | 2.9 | Sales/Working Capital | 2.7 | 2.7 | 3.3 | 2.6 | 4.0 | |
| 4.2 | 4.5 | 4.4 | | 5.0 | 3.8 | 4.2 | 4.3 | 6.3 | |
| 6.8 | 7.4 | 7.2 | | 8.7 | 5.6 | 5.5 | 7.7 | 9.1 | |
| 89.3 | 40.5 | 25.1 | EBIT/Interest | 21.2 | 50.5 | 26.9 | 12.3 | 20.4 | |
| (102) 29.0 | (123) 12.0 | (106) 6.4 | | (26) 1.8 | (16) 17.3 | (15) 11.9 | (22) 6.4 | (24) 11.3 | |
| 11.9 | 3.5 | 1.7 | | -2.0 | 3.6 | 2.2 | -.2 | 3.3 | |
| 16.7 | 16.7 | 25.8 | Net Profit + Depr., Dep., Amort./Cur. Mat. L/T/D | | | | | | |
| (10) 10.8 | (13) 3.7 | (16) 6.0 | | | | | | | |
| 3.6 | 1.7 | 3.2 | | | | | | | |
| .1 | .0 | .1 | Fixed/Worth | .1 | .0 | .0 | .1 | .2 | |
| .2 | .2 | .3 | | .4 | .1 | .2 | .3 | .3 | |
| .5 | .6 | 1.1 | | NM | .8 | .5 | .9 | .9 | |
| .3 | .3 | .3 | Debt/Worth | .4 | .1 | .1 | .3 | .5 | |
| .7 | .8 | .7 | | 1.4 | .3 | .6 | .7 | 1.3 | |
| 2.3 | 2.9 | 3.5 | | NM | .9 | 3.2 | 2.0 | 2.3 | |
| 55.3 | 43.3 | 37.5 | % Profit Before Taxes/Tangible Net Worth | 46.5 | 36.3 | 42.6 | 32.1 | 33.0 | |
| (121) 38.4 | (142) 22.2 | (128) 19.7 | | (28) 24.5 | (24) 22.4 | (23) 20.5 | (22) 15.9 | 19.2 | |
| 20.0 | 9.6 | 8.0 | | -2.0 | 11.4 | 12.4 | 3.6 | 13.7 | |
| 29.5 | 23.2 | 20.1 | % Profit Before Taxes/Total Assets | 22.2 | 21.0 | 32.6 | 13.8 | 13.6 | |
| 19.6 | 10.8 | 9.5 | | 5.2 | 14.5 | 15.7 | 6.9 | 9.2 | |
| 10.1 | 3.1 | 1.5 | | -4.7 | 7.9 | 7.4 | -1.0 | 5.3 | |
| 75.5 | 113.1 | 68.8 | Sales/Net Fixed Assets | 67.6 | 93.3 | 97.5 | 60.3 | 29.7 | |
| 24.1 | 25.6 | 19.9 | | 24.3 | 28.5 | 36.8 | 20.2 | 10.8 | |
| 11.9 | 11.4 | 8.4 | | 11.4 | 9.4 | 8.4 | 5.8 | 6.3 | |
| 2.8 | 2.7 | 2.7 | Sales/Total Assets | 3.8 | 2.4 | 3.0 | 2.6 | 2.5 | |
| 2.2 | 2.1 | 2.0 | | 2.5 | 2.1 | 2.0 | 2.1 | 1.9 | |
| 1.7 | 1.5 | 1.5 | | 1.5 | 1.6 | 1.6 | 1.3 | 1.7 | |
| .5 | .4 | .5 | % Depr., Dep., Amort./Sales | .4 | .7 | .4 | .5 | .7 | |
| (94) .9 | (108) .8 | (95) .9 | | (23) .9 | (18) 1.1 | (17) .7 | (18) .8 | (18) 1.4 | |
| 1.6 | 1.3 | 1.7 | | 1.9 | 1.7 | 1.5 | 1.3 | 2.4 | |
| 1.4 | 1.2 | .9 | % Officers', Directors' Owners' Comp/Sales | 2.4 | .9 | .8 | | | |
| (60) 2.7 | (81) 2.1 | (53) 2.1 | | (10) 3.5 | (12) 2.2 | (13) 1.5 | (10) 1.6 | | | |
| 3.7 | 3.7 | 3.6 | | 5.3 | 4.4 | 3.2 | 2.2 | | | |
| 3200448M | 2800848M | 3516394M | Net Sales ($) | 5099M | 87451M | 97300M | 193251M | 344954M | 2788339M |
| 1345540M | 1557637M | 1900940M | Total Assets ($) | 4083M | 43720M | 50689M | 98565M | 190221M | 1513662M |

© RMA 2024
M = $ thousand   MM = $ million
See Pages viii through xx for Explanation of Ratios and Data

# RETAIL—Other Building Material Dealers  NAICS 444180

## Current Data Sorted by Assets | Comparative Historical Data

| | | | | | | Type of Statement | | |
|---|---|---|---|---|---|---|---|---|
| | | | 10 | 4 | 4 | Unqualified | 17 | 10 |
| 2 | 3 | 17 | 26 | 4 | | Reviewed | 63 | 25 |
| | 1 | 13 | 10 | | | Compiled | 39 | 19 |
| 5 | 28 | 28 | 7 | 1 | | Tax Returns | 96 | 35 |
| 6 | 23 | 60 | 42 | 12 | 5 | Other | 159 | 129 |
| | 47 (4/1-9/30/23) | | 264 (10/1/23-3/31/24) | | | | 4/1/19-3/31/20 | 4/1/20-3/31/21 |
| 0-500M | 500M-2MM | 2-10MM | 10-50MM | 50-100MM | 100-250MM | | ALL | ALL |
| 13 | 55 | 118 | 95 | 21 | 9 | NUMBER OF STATEMENTS | 374 | 218 |
| % | % | % | % | % | % | ASSETS | % | % |
| 28.7 | 18.6 | 16.4 | 16.8 | 17.4 | | Cash & Equivalents | 12.5 | 19.2 |
| 18.9 | 20.5 | 20.8 | 24.8 | 20.7 | | Trade Receivables (net) | 25.4 | 22.2 |
| 34.1 | 29.7 | 34.0 | 25.8 | 17.2 | | Inventory | 31.2 | 29.5 |
| .0 | 1.9 | 3.9 | 3.6 | 6.2 | | All Other Current | 2.2 | 2.3 |
| 81.6 | 70.6 | 75.1 | 70.9 | 61.6 | | Total Current | 71.3 | 73.3 |
| 14.5 | 10.4 | 13.1 | 18.9 | 16.3 | | Fixed Assets (net) | 17.8 | 16.1 |
| .0 | 10.2 | 3.9 | 2.4 | 11.6 | | Intangibles (net) | 4.5 | 4.9 |
| 3.4 | 8.7 | 7.8 | 7.7 | 10.6 | | All Other Non-Current | 6.4 | 5.7 |
| 100.0 | 100.0 | 100.0 | 100.0 | 100.0 | | Total | 100.0 | 100.0 |
| | | | | | | LIABILITIES | | |
| 4.9 | 5.0 | 4.2 | 3.7 | 3.5 | | Notes Payable-Short Term | 8.2 | 8.6 |
| .6 | 1.8 | 1.4 | 1.9 | 2.5 | | Cur. Mat.-L.T.D. | 2.3 | 1.9 |
| 14.6 | 13.0 | 14.9 | 11.6 | 10.9 | | Trade Payables | 16.5 | 13.1 |
| .0 | .1 | .1 | .2 | .1 | | Income Taxes Payable | .1 | .2 |
| 6.0 | 18.6 | 12.7 | 10.9 | 12.8 | | All Other Current | 10.5 | 11.7 |
| 26.1 | 38.5 | 33.2 | 28.3 | 29.7 | | Total Current | 37.5 | 35.5 |
| 46.7 | 17.8 | 10.4 | 11.0 | 14.0 | | Long-Term Debt | 15.6 | 13.9 |
| .0 | .0 | .2 | .1 | .2 | | Deferred Taxes | .1 | .3 |
| .0 | 3.2 | 4.8 | 5.3 | 9.9 | | All Other Non-Current | 4.6 | 6.2 |
| 26.8 | 40.6 | 51.4 | 55.3 | 46.2 | | Net Worth | 42.1 | 44.1 |
| 100.0 | 100.0 | 100.0 | 100.0 | 100.0 | | Total Liabilities & Net Worth | 100.0 | 100.0 |
| | | | | | | INCOME DATA | | |
| 100.0 | 100.0 | 100.0 | 100.0 | 100.0 | | Net Sales | 100.0 | 100.0 |
| 42.6 | 34.4 | 33.1 | 28.3 | 34.5 | | Gross Profit | 31.5 | 31.6 |
| 30.9 | 30.3 | 25.8 | 22.3 | 24.0 | | Operating Expenses | 26.5 | 25.1 |
| 11.6 | 4.1 | 7.3 | 6.0 | 10.4 | | Operating Profit | 5.0 | 6.5 |
| 1.5 | -.1 | -.1 | -.3 | 1.6 | | All Other Expenses (net) | .4 | -.9 |
| 10.1 | 4.2 | 7.4 | 6.3 | 8.9 | | Profit Before Taxes | 4.6 | 7.4 |
| | | | | | | RATIOS | | |
| 8.7 | 5.4 | 4.6 | 4.6 | 4.1 | | | 3.9 | 4.4 |
| 6.1 | 2.5 | 2.6 | 2.7 | 1.9 | | Current | 2.2 | 2.6 |
| 2.1 | 1.4 | 1.6 | 1.8 | 1.4 | | | 1.4 | 1.5 |
| 7.0 | 2.3 | 2.4 | 2.6 | 2.7 | | | 2.1 | 2.6 |
| 1.2 | 1.3 | 1.2 | 1.4 | 1.3 | | Quick | 1.1 | 1.4 |
| .7 | .6 | .6 | .9 | .6 | | | .6 | .6 |
| 0 UND | 5 77.6 | 17 21.7 | 21 17.0 | 25 14.5 | | | 19 19.7 | 15 25.1 |
| 14 26.0 | 20 18.5 | 24 15.1 | 30 12.2 | 31 11.7 | | Sales/Receivables | 32 11.3 | 28 13.0 |
| 29 12.4 | 30 12.1 | 36 10.0 | 38 9.6 | 49 7.4 | | | 44 8.3 | 42 8.7 |
| 4 87.4 | 3 107.8 | 35 10.4 | 32 11.3 | 29 12.6 | | | 29 12.7 | 32 11.4 |
| 44 8.3 | 39 9.3 | 68 5.4 | 51 7.1 | 40 9.1 | | Cost of Sales/Inventory | 56 6.5 | 55 6.6 |
| 83 4.4 | 96 3.8 | 111 3.3 | 73 5.0 | 62 5.9 | | | 87 4.2 | 85 4.3 |
| 6 57.6 | 5 78.0 | 9 40.6 | 12 30.6 | 12 30.8 | | | 12 29.8 | 11 33.2 |
| 20 18.7 | 17 20.9 | 20 18.0 | 19 19.6 | 20 18.7 | | Cost of Sales/Payables | 21 17.0 | 21 17.1 |
| 38 9.7 | 35 10.4 | 40 9.1 | 27 13.3 | 29 12.7 | | | 43 8.5 | 33 10.9 |
| 4.9 | 5.2 | 4.2 | 4.0 | 4.1 | | | 4.8 | 4.4 |
| 8.8 | 10.2 | 6.0 | 5.7 | 8.2 | | Sales/Working Capital | 8.0 | 6.6 |
| 17.9 | 32.4 | 11.4 | 10.3 | 11.4 | | | 19.7 | 14.0 |
| | 68.6 | 46.6 | 50.0 | 54.3 | | | 27.5 | 48.3 |
| | (41) 8.9 | (95) 13.8 | (77) 16.5 | (18) 30.2 | | EBIT/Interest | (323) 9.9 | (170) 15.0 |
| | 2.6 | 3.0 | 5.2 | 7.4 | | | 2.6 | 4.9 |
| | | 15.8 | 21.2 | | | | 18.6 | 21.7 |
| | (13) 6.3 | (24) 9.1 | | | | Net Profit + Depr., Dep., Amort./Cur. Mat. L/T/D | (55) 4.8 | (23) 5.6 |
| | | 4.3 | 3.1 | | | | 2.1 | 1.9 |
| .0 | .0 | .1 | .1 | .1 | | | .1 | .1 |
| .1 | .2 | .2 | .2 | .3 | | Fixed/Worth | .3 | .3 |
| .5 | 1.5 | .6 | .5 | NM | | | 1.0 | .9 |
| .3 | .3 | .3 | .4 | .5 | | | .4 | .4 |
| .5 | 1.4 | .7 | .8 | .9 | | Debt/Worth | 1.3 | 1.0 |
| NM | 58.9 | 2.5 | 1.4 | NM | | | 3.9 | 3.7 |
| 69.7 | 94.8 | 44.3 | 36.9 | 64.4 | | | 46.0 | 60.3 |
| (10) 45.4 | (42) 32.3 | (107) 30.0 | (89) 26.3 | (16) 33.7 | | % Profit Before Taxes/Tangible Net Worth | (333) 22.8 | (190) 35.9 |
| -1.0 | 5.4 | 18.3 | 13.5 | 22.9 | | | 9.1 | 17.0 |
| 45.5 | 36.6 | 24.3 | 22.3 | 24.8 | | | 19.5 | 27.6 |
| 29.3 | 12.9 | 14.8 | 12.4 | 20.1 | | % Profit Before Taxes/Total Assets | 10.4 | 16.0 |
| 6.7 | 1.7 | 6.1 | 7.9 | 14.1 | | | 3.1 | 6.9 |
| UND | 340.0 | 112.0 | 43.5 | 40.2 | | | 72.5 | 88.3 |
| 223.8 | 53.0 | 32.2 | 17.9 | 16.5 | | Sales/Net Fixed Assets | 26.7 | 24.9 |
| 15.4 | 21.9 | 16.0 | 8.7 | 9.3 | | | 10.4 | 10.3 |
| 5.7 | 5.0 | 3.4 | 3.3 | 3.1 | | | 3.8 | 3.6 |
| 4.0 | 3.5 | 2.7 | 2.5 | 2.0 | | Sales/Total Assets | 2.9 | 2.6 |
| 2.8 | 2.5 | 1.9 | 1.9 | 1.3 | | | 2.0 | 1.8 |
| | .3 | .6 | .5 | .5 | | | .5 | .5 |
| | (24) .7 | (68) 1.2 | (78) 1.0 | (18) .9 | | % Depr., Dep., Amort./Sales | (269) 1.1 | (138) 1.1 |
| | 1.9 | 1.9 | 1.4 | 1.7 | | | 1.7 | 1.6 |
| | 1.2 | 1.2 | .6 | | | | 1.2 | 1.1 |
| | (24) 2.7 | (59) 2.1 | (31) 1.2 | | | % Officers', Directors' Owners' Comp/Sales | (162) 2.2 | (88) 2.1 |
| | 5.9 | 3.5 | 3.3 | | | | 4.4 | 4.0 |
| 16507M | 266410M | 1767966M | 5546306M | 3304493M | 2441958M | Net Sales ($) | 15754733M | 6252896M |
| 3538M | 67375M | 653569M | 2093025M | 1585695M | 1326717M | Total Assets ($) | 6287762M | 2869466M |

© RMA 2024

M = $ thousand    MM = $ million
See Pages viii through xx for Explanation of Ratios and Data

# RETAIL—Other Building Material Dealers NAICS 444180

| Comparative Historical Data ||| Type of Statement | Current Data Sorted by Sales |||||||||||
|---|---|---|---|---|---|---|---|---|---|---|---|---|---|
| 9 | 11 | 18 | Unqualified | | | 1 | | 3 | | 1 | | 17 | |
| 39 | 56 | 52 | Reviewed | 1 | 2 | | 1 | | 3 | | 15 | | 30 |
| 25 | 22 | 24 | Compiled | | | 1 | | 3 | | 12 | | 8 | |
| 67 | 80 | 69 | Tax Returns | | 10 | 16 | 16 | | 16 | | 9 | | |
| 150 | 171 | 148 | Other | 2 | 13 | 9 | 18 | | 45 | | 59 | | |
| 4/1/21- | 4/1/22- | 4/1/23- | | 4 | | | | | | | | | |
| 3/31/22 | 3/31/23 | 3/31/24 | | | 47 (4/1-9/30/23) ||| 264 (10/1/23-3/31/24) ||||
| ALL | ALL | ALL | | 0-1MM | 1-3MM | 3-5MM | 5-10MM | 10-25MM | 25MM & OVER |
| 290 | 340 | 311 | NUMBER OF STATEMENTS | 7 | 26 | 26 | 40 | 89 | 123 |
| % | % | % | **ASSETS** | % | % | % | % | % | % |
| 15.4 | 17.2 | 17.5 | Cash & Equivalents | 18.0 | 21.7 | 17.3 | 16.1 | 16.8 | |
| 22.6 | 22.6 | 21.7 | Trade Receivables (net) | 11.9 | 20.6 | 17.7 | 22.4 | 25.3 | |
| 33.1 | 30.8 | 29.3 | Inventory | 35.1 | 23.3 | 31.9 | 32.6 | 26.1 | |
| 2.9 | 3.3 | 3.4 | All Other Current | .3 | 2.4 | 6.3 | 3.5 | 3.5 | |
| 74.0 | 73.9 | 71.9 | Total Current | 65.3 | 67.9 | 73.2 | 74.6 | 71.6 | |
| 15.9 | 15.7 | 14.9 | Fixed Assets (net) | 12.0 | 11.6 | 13.6 | 15.5 | 16.1 | |
| 4.5 | 4.0 | 4.9 | Intangibles (net) | 7.4 | 13.4 | 6.5 | 2.6 | 4.0 | |
| 5.5 | 6.4 | 8.2 | All Other Non-Current | 15.4 | 7.0 | 6.7 | 7.3 | 8.3 | |
| 100.0 | 100.0 | 100.0 | Total | 100.0 | 100.0 | 100.0 | 100.0 | 100.0 | |
| | | | **LIABILITIES** | | | | | | |
| 6.0 | 5.9 | 4.1 | Notes Payable-Short Term | 2.1 | 4.1 | 6.0 | 4.1 | 3.7 | |
| 1.6 | 2.0 | 1.7 | Cur. Mat.-L.T.D. | 1.5 | 2.3 | 1.6 | 1.1 | 2.1 | |
| 14.5 | 15.0 | 13.1 | Trade Payables | 10.4 | 11.7 | 16.8 | 14.1 | 12.3 | |
| .3 | .2 | .1 | Income Taxes Payable | .1 | .0 | .0 | .1 | .2 | |
| 15.8 | 13.0 | 12.7 | All Other Current | 8.8 | 26.0 | 10.4 | 12.4 | 12.1 | |
| 38.1 | 36.1 | 31.7 | Total Current | 23.0 | 44.1 | 34.9 | 31.7 | 30.4 | |
| 15.1 | 14.7 | 13.6 | Long-Term Debt | 25.5 | 22.0 | 12.8 | 11.3 | 9.7 | |
| .2 | .2 | .1 | Deferred Taxes | .0 | .0 | .2 | .2 | .1 | |
| 6.5 | 4.5 | 4.8 | All Other Non-Current | 2.4 | 6.7 | 2.0 | 6.5 | 4.9 | |
| 40.1 | 44.5 | 49.8 | Net Worth | 49.2 | 27.2 | 50.2 | 50.4 | 54.9 | |
| 100.0 | 100.0 | 100.0 | Total Liabilities & Net Worth | 100.0 | 100.0 | 100.0 | 100.0 | 100.0 | |
| | | | **INCOME DATA** | | | | | | |
| 100.0 | 100.0 | 100.0 | Net Sales | 100.0 | 100.0 | 100.0 | 100.0 | 100.0 | |
| 30.6 | 30.7 | 32.2 | Gross Profit | 39.6 | 38.2 | 34.1 | 31.0 | 28.7 | |
| 24.1 | 24.2 | 25.4 | Operating Expenses | 33.2 | 32.4 | 26.0 | 25.1 | 22.2 | |
| 6.4 | 6.5 | 6.7 | Operating Profit | 6.4 | 5.8 | 8.1 | 5.9 | 6.5 | |
| -.7 | -.1 | .0 | All Other Expenses (net) | .4 | .2 | -.4 | .3 | -.2 | |
| 7.1 | 6.6 | 6.7 | Profit Before Taxes | 6.0 | 5.6 | 8.5 | 5.6 | 6.7 | |
| | | | **RATIOS** | | | | | | |
| 4.4 | 4.3 | 5.1 | | 7.4 | 5.7 | 5.2 | 4.8 | 4.0 | |
| 2.3 | 2.5 | 2.7 | Current | 4.6 | 2.4 | 2.7 | 2.6 | 2.5 | |
| 1.5 | 1.5 | 1.6 | | 1.5 | 1.2 | 1.4 | 1.6 | 1.7 | |
| 2.3 | 2.3 | 2.6 | | 4.9 | 3.0 | 2.4 | 2.6 | 2.4 | |
| 1.2 | 1.2 | 1.3 | Quick | 1.1 | 1.2 | 1.2 | 1.2 | 1.4 | |
| .6 | .7 | .7 | | .6 | .4 | .7 | .6 | .9 | |
| 15  24.8 | 11  32.6 | 17  22.0 | | 0  UND | 9  40.4 | 13  27.2 | 17  21.7 | 20  18.0 | |
| 30  12.0 | 26  14.0 | 26  14.1 | Sales/Receivables | 13  28.3 | 22  16.3 | 20  18.6 | 26  14.1 | 29  12.5 | |
| 44  8.3 | 40  9.2 | 36  10.1 | | 26  14.0 | 33  11.1 | 33  11.1 | 38  9.5 | 38  9.5 | |
| 33  10.9 | 27  13.3 | 27  13.5 | | 26  14.1 | 10  36.5 | 35  10.3 | 31  11.7 | 31  11.9 | |
| 61  6.0 | 53  6.9 | 51  7.1 | Cost of Sales/Inventory | 78  4.7 | 24  15.1 | 51  7.1 | 58  6.3 | 50  7.3 | |
| 104  3.5 | 81  4.5 | 87  4.2 | | 118  3.1 | 99  3.7 | 96  3.8 | 99  3.7 | 70  6.2 | |
| 11  32.1 | 9  39.4 | 10  36.3 | | 0  UND | 7  55.2 | 5  75.1 | 11  34.4 | 12  29.9 | |
| 21  17.7 | 20  18.6 | 19  19.1 | Cost of Sales/Payables | 16  22.2 | 19  19.6 | 17  21.2 | 22  16.8 | 19  19.1 | |
| 37  9.8 | 36  10.2 | 31  11.6 | | 34  10.7 | 35  10.4 | 38  9.6 | 43  8.5 | 27  13.4 | |
| 4.2 | 4.4 | 4.2 | | 3.8 | 3.3 | 4.6 | 4.1 | 4.5 | |
| 6.8 | 7.0 | 6.7 | Sales/Working Capital | 6.5 | 9.0 | 6.1 | 5.8 | 7.3 | |
| 14.1 | 13.6 | 12.9 | | 13.9 | 49.4 | 14.2 | 14.0 | 10.5 | |
| 77.8 | 59.4 | 48.9 | | 10.4 | 68.6 | 90.5 | 57.7 | 43.7 | |
| (240)  20.2 | (284)  19.2 | (246)  13.8 | EBIT/Interest | (17)  2.6 | (21)  9.5 | (30)  28.0 | (75)  13.8 | (99)  16.8 | |
| 5.7 | 6.2 | 4.1 | | 1.1 | 2.9 | 8.0 | 3.4 | 5.5 | |
| 37.7 | 26.7 | 17.3 | Net Profit + Depr., Dep., | | | | 17.7 | 16.7 | |
| (38)  8.6 | (51)  9.9 | (40)  6.9 | Amort./Cur. Mat. L/T/D | | | (15)  7.2 | (23)  7.3 | | |
| 5.0 | 4.2 | 3.3 | | | | | 3.5 | 3.2 | |
| .1 | .1 | .1 | | .0 | .0 | .0 | .1 | .1 | |
| .3 | .3 | .2 | Fixed/Worth | .1 | .4 | .2 | .2 | .2 | |
| .7 | .7 | .6 | | .5 | -.7 | .8 | .6 | .5 | |
| .5 | .4 | .3 | | .2 | .4 | .3 | .3 | .4 | |
| 1.0 | .9 | .8 | Debt/Worth | 1.1 | 5.7 | .6 | .8 | .8 | |
| 2.6 | 2.6 | 2.4 | | 3.3 | -5.2 | 4.0 | 2.2 | 1.5 | |
| 60.6 | 59.2 | 45.5 | | 45.1 | 113.6 | 67.7 | 44.4 | 41.3 | |
| (260)  38.7 | (298)  35.7 | (273)  28.9 | % Profit Before Taxes/Tangible Net Worth | (21)  9.7 | (16)  52.1 | (35)  34.5 | (81)  26.1 | (114)  29.3 | |
| 19.1 | 17.3 | 14.5 | | .6 | 17.2 | 18.6 | 13.1 | 17.2 | |
| 27.4 | 30.0 | 24.5 | | 18.0 | 24.4 | 33.8 | 21.3 | 24.1 | |
| 17.6 | 17.5 | 14.6 | % Profit Before Taxes/Total Assets | 5.6 | 13.4 | 21.5 | 12.1 | 16.1 | |
| 7.5 | 7.4 | 6.4 | | .4 | 5.1 | 8.6 | 4.2 | 8.5 | |
| 82.1 | 100.5 | 86.9 | | 464.9 | 256.0 | 211.7 | 81.8 | 51.9 | |
| 28.6 | 27.4 | 26.1 | Sales/Net Fixed Assets | 31.3 | 54.0 | 41.4 | 24.5 | 20.3 | |
| 12.1 | 11.4 | 12.2 | | 19.9 | 19.5 | 7.7 | 15.1 | 10.3 | |
| 3.6 | 3.9 | 3.5 | | 4.2 | 3.7 | 4.2 | 3.3 | 3.5 | |
| 2.7 | 2.9 | 2.7 | Sales/Total Assets | 2.5 | 3.1 | 2.8 | 2.6 | 2.9 | |
| 1.9 | 2.1 | 1.9 | | 1.7 | 2.2 | 1.8 | 1.9 | 2.0 | |
| .5 | .4 | .5 | | .5 | .2 | .5 | .8 | .4 | |
| (193)  .9 | (223)  .9 | (203)  1.0 | % Depr., Dep., Amort./Sales | (10)  1.6 | (14)  .5 | (20)  1.1 | (56)  1.4 | (99)  .9 | |
| 1.8 | 1.6 | 1.7 | | 2.8 | 1.2 | 2.3 | 2.1 | 1.2 | |
| 1.1 | 1.0 | 1.1 | | | 1.6 | 1.5 | 1.2 | .5 | |
| (120)  2.2 | (122)  1.9 | (123)  2.0 | % Officers', Directors' Owners' Comp/Sales | (16)  3.0 | (19)  2.1 | (43)  1.7 | (35)  1.1 | | |
| 3.9 | 3.5 | 3.9 | | 5.6 | 3.2 | 3.5 | 2.1 | | |
| 10029416M | 15033078M | 13343640M | Net Sales ($) | 3867M | 56728M | 103597M | 299714M | 1450990M | 11428744M |
| 4354039M | 6290367M | 5729919M | Total Assets ($) | 1616M | 27808M | 40561M | 134780M | 715467M | 4809687M |

M = $ thousand    MM = $ million
See Pages viii through xx for Explanation of Ratios and Data

© RMA 2024

# RETAIL—Outdoor Power Equipment Retailers  NAICS 444230

## Current Data Sorted by Assets

| | | | | | | | Type of Statement | | |
|---|---|---|---|---|---|---|---|---|---|
| | | | | 10 | 16 | 14 | Unqualified | 3 | 1 |
| | | 1 | 16 | 42 | 13 | 2 | Reviewed | 9 | 3 |
| | | 45 | 84 | 27 | 1 | 1 | Compiled | 4 | 4 |
| | 11 | 37 | 81 | 7 | | | Tax Returns | 15 | 15 |
| | 29 | 176 | 249 | 91 | 22 | 10 | Other | 39 | 18 |
| | | 161 (4/1-9/30/23) | | 824 (10/1/23-3/31/24) | | | | 4/1/19-3/31/20 | 4/1/20-3/31/21 |
| | 0-500M | 500M-2MM | 2-10MM | 10-50MM | 50-100MM | 100-250MM | | ALL | ALL |
| | 40 | 259 | 430 | 177 | 52 | 27 | NUMBER OF STATEMENTS | 70 | 41 |
| | % | % | % | % | % | % | ASSETS | % | % |
| | 14.5 | 10.9 | 10.0 | 6.7 | 4.7 | 5.1 | Cash & Equivalents | 9.2 | 15.9 |
| | 2.4 | 4.1 | 4.9 | 6.4 | 8.5 | 8.4 | Trade Receivables (net) | 6.5 | 7.3 |
| | 44.7 | 68.4 | 70.0 | 67.9 | 57.9 | 57.7 | Inventory | 65.8 | 55.1 |
| | 4.8 | .6 | .6 | .9 | .7 | 1.0 | All Other Current | 1.3 | 1.3 |
| | 66.4 | 83.9 | 85.4 | 81.9 | 71.9 | 72.2 | Total Current | 82.7 | 79.5 |
| | 27.4 | 11.3 | 9.4 | 10.3 | 13.6 | 17.0 | Fixed Assets (net) | 12.1 | 13.8 |
| | 5.3 | 4.3 | 4.4 | 4.9 | 8.1 | 6.8 | Intangibles (net) | 2.4 | 4.3 |
| | 1.0 | .5 | .7 | 3.0 | 6.3 | 4.1 | All Other Non-Current | 2.7 | 2.3 |
| | 100.0 | 100.0 | 100.0 | 100.0 | 100.0 | 100.0 | Total | 100.0 | 100.0 |
| | | | | | | | LIABILITIES | | |
| | 20.2 | 3.2 | 3.4 | 6.8 | 8.7 | 8.2 | Notes Payable-Short Term | 26.9 | 14.1 |
| | 4.1 | 1.7 | 1.3 | 1.3 | 1.3 | 2.1 | Cur. Mat.-L.T.D. | 1.9 | 2.4 |
| | 28.3 | 46.9 | 47.5 | 44.9 | 36.3 | 33.3 | Trade Payables | 14.2 | 18.3 |
| | .0 | .0 | .1 | .1 | .1 | .0 | Income Taxes Payable | .1 | .1 |
| | 7.5 | 4.1 | 3.5 | 4.8 | 5.5 | 6.9 | All Other Current | 7.3 | 5.1 |
| | 60.1 | 56.0 | 55.7 | 57.8 | 51.8 | 50.6 | Total Current | 50.4 | 40.0 |
| | 49.1 | 12.1 | 7.9 | 6.3 | 9.2 | 17.0 | Long-Term Debt | 10.5 | 18.6 |
| | .0 | .0 | .0 | .1 | .2 | .1 | Deferred Taxes | .1 | .1 |
| | 11.3 | 5.5 | 4.5 | 5.1 | 8.1 | 6.0 | All Other Non-Current | 6.9 | 5.2 |
| | -20.6 | 26.4 | 31.9 | 30.7 | 30.7 | 26.4 | Net Worth | 32.1 | 36.1 |
| | 100.0 | 100.0 | 100.0 | 100.0 | 100.0 | 100.0 | Total Liabilities & Net Worth | 100.0 | 100.0 |
| | | | | | | | INCOME DATA | | |
| | 100.0 | 100.0 | 100.0 | 100.0 | 100.0 | 100.0 | Net Sales | 100.0 | 100.0 |
| | 35.0 | 29.7 | 27.2 | 23.2 | 24.3 | 21.2 | Gross Profit | 26.6 | 28.1 |
| | 34.1 | 26.0 | 23.3 | 18.7 | 19.8 | 15.5 | Operating Expenses | 22.5 | 24.6 |
| | .9 | 3.8 | 4.0 | 4.6 | 4.5 | 5.7 | Operating Profit | 4.1 | 3.5 |
| | .4 | .5 | .5 | .5 | .5 | 1.0 | All Other Expenses (net) | .3 | -.5 |
| | .5 | 3.2 | 3.5 | 4.1 | 3.9 | 4.7 | Profit Before Taxes | 3.8 | 4.0 |
| | | | | | | | RATIOS | | |
| | 3.0 | 2.0 | 2.0 | 1.6 | 1.8 | 1.8 | | 2.3 | 3.7 |
| | 1.3 | 1.4 | 1.5 | 1.4 | 1.5 | 1.3 | Current | 1.5 | 1.8 |
| | 1.0 | 1.1 | 1.2 | 1.2 | 1.2 | 1.2 | | 1.2 | 1.4 |
| | 1.0 | .5 | .5 | .3 | .6 | .4 | | .5 | 1.4 |
| | .2 | .2 | .2 | .2 | .2 | .2 | Quick | .2 | .6 |
| | .1 | .1 | .1 | .1 | .1 | .1 | | .1 | .2 |
| 0 | UND | 0 UND | 2 225.2 | 4 88.7 | 6 58.6 | 5 78.0 | | 3 137.9 | 1 246.9 |
| 0 | UND | 3 116.3 | 6 60.3 | 9 40.2 | 14 25.7 | 12 30.7 | Sales/Receivables | 6 56.5 | 5 68.4 |
| 2 | 224.4 | 7 48.7 | 13 27.1 | 18 20.5 | 26 14.0 | 32 11.3 | | 16 22.7 | 15 23.9 |
| 0 | UND | 114 3.2 | 146 2.5 | 146 2.5 | 122 3.0 | 122 3.0 | | 101 3.6 | 63 5.8 |
| 45 | 8.1 | 182 2.0 | 203 1.8 | 182 2.0 | 166 2.2 | 146 2.5 | Cost of Sales/Inventory | 159 2.3 | 130 2.8 |
| 107 | 3.4 | 281 1.3 | 281 1.3 | 261 1.4 | 203 1.8 | 203 1.8 | | 203 1.8 | 166 2.2 |
| 0 | UND | 52 7.0 | 81 4.5 | 81 4.5 | 42 8.6 | 51 7.2 | | 4 86.6 | 4 84.7 |
| 15 | 24.3 | 122 3.0 | 135 2.7 | 122 3.0 | 114 3.2 | 89 4.1 | Cost of Sales/Payables | 14 25.4 | 21 17.6 |
| 51 | 7.2 | 203 1.8 | 203 1.8 | 192 1.9 | 166 2.2 | 118 3.1 | | 45 8.1 | 68 5.4 |
| | 11.0 | 4.6 | 4.1 | 5.5 | 5.8 | 5.2 | | 4.3 | 4.6 |
| | 32.1 | 7.9 | 6.3 | 7.9 | 7.7 | 10.3 | Sales/Working Capital | 8.4 | 6.2 |
| | -154.8 | 20.9 | 11.5 | 12.7 | 13.7 | 18.2 | | 16.6 | 9.8 |
| | 10.8 | 30.7 | 15.2 | 12.6 | 17.7 | 12.3 | | 11.3 | 14.2 |
| (27) | 1.9 | (210) 4.2 | (379) 4.4 | (172) 5.2 | (50) 5.7 | 6.0 | EBIT/Interest | (63) 6.2 | (38) 7.6 |
| | .6 | .3 | 1.4 | 2.2 | 2.1 | 2.4 | | 2.0 | 3.3 |
| | | | 13.2 | 12.5 | 15.1 | | Net Profit + Depr., Dep., | | |
| | | (50) 5.8 | (46) 6.6 | (21) 7.4 | | Amort./Cur. Mat. L/T/D | | |
| | | | 2.2 | 2.8 | 3.5 | | | | |
| | .0 | .0 | .1 | .1 | .3 | .2 | | .1 | .1 |
| | 3.1 | .3 | .2 | .3 | .4 | .8 | Fixed/Worth | .3 | .4 |
| | -1.0 | 2.1 | .8 | .6 | 1.1 | 1.9 | | .7 | .6 |
| | 1.6 | 1.3 | 1.2 | 1.8 | 1.6 | 2.3 | | 1.2 | 1.1 |
| | -62.4 | 3.3 | 2.7 | 3.0 | 3.3 | 3.5 | Debt/Worth | 2.2 | 2.1 |
| | -3.8 | 15.4 | 7.3 | 5.5 | 13.1 | 7.3 | | 5.1 | 3.9 |
| | 93.0 | 60.8 | 40.3 | 39.0 | 39.2 | 65.7 | % Profit Before Taxes/Tangible | 42.3 | 43.2 |
| (18) | 27.9 | (209) 24.4 | (386) 19.6 | (168) 23.2 | (46) 22.2 | (25) 29.5 | Net Worth | (66) 19.6 | (38) 22.8 |
| | 8.3 | 3.9 | 4.6 | 9.0 | 14.5 | 24.2 | | 6.7 | 8.8 |
| | 28.3 | 14.8 | 11.4 | 9.7 | 10.7 | 12.5 | % Profit Before Taxes/Total | 12.2 | 15.7 |
| | 4.1 | 5.0 | 4.9 | 5.7 | 5.8 | 7.5 | Assets | 6.9 | 8.5 |
| | -2.4 | -.5 | 1.1 | 2.0 | 2.8 | 3.6 | | 1.7 | 3.1 |
| | 343.9 | 207.8 | 100.0 | 68.6 | 37.6 | 32.2 | | 98.2 | 177.6 |
| | 41.9 | 44.1 | 36.3 | 27.6 | 17.4 | 17.0 | Sales/Net Fixed Assets | 38.4 | 25.1 |
| | 12.9 | 12.8 | 14.6 | 10.1 | 7.1 | 4.5 | | 13.4 | 10.7 |
| | 7.8 | 2.8 | 2.2 | 2.2 | 1.9 | 2.3 | | 2.8 | 3.1 |
| | 4.1 | 1.9 | 1.7 | 1.7 | 1.7 | 1.7 | Sales/Total Assets | 2.2 | 2.4 |
| | 3.1 | 1.5 | 1.3 | 1.3 | 1.4 | 1.2 | | 1.5 | 1.8 |
| | .3 | .3 | .3 | .4 | .6 | .5 | | .5 | .5 |
| (18) | .8 | (116) .7 | (251) .7 | (136) .8 | (44) .9 | (21) .8 | % Depr., Dep., Amort./Sales | (47) .7 | (20) .9 |
| | 2.4 | 1.6 | 1.3 | 1.5 | 1.5 | 1.3 | | 1.4 | 1.5 |
| | 1.6 | | 1.0 | .5 | | | | 1.0 | .9 |
| (10) | 2.5 | (97) 3.0 | (184) 2.0 | (63) .9 | | | % Officers', Directors' | (30) 2.6 | (16) 1.5 |
| | 10.7 | 4.9 | 3.1 | 1.5 | | | Owners' Comp/Sales | 4.4 | 2.9 |
| | 55301M | 727808M | 3581983M | 6580009M | 6264505M | 7558447M | Net Sales ($) | 2994818M | 980986M |
| | 10628M | 331979M | 1938218M | 3660153M | 3740651M | 4236158M | Total Assets ($) | 1512761M | 406682M |

© RMA 2024   M = $ thousand   MM = $ million
See Pages viii through xx for Explanation of Ratios and Data

# RETAIL—Outdoor Power Equipment Retailers  NAICS 444230

## Comparative Historical Data / Current Data Sorted by Sales

| | | | | | | | | | | | | |
|---|---|---|---|---|---|---|---|---|---|---|---|---|
| | | | | **Type of Statement** | | | | | 2 | 38 | | |
| 5 | | 6 | 40 | Unqualified | | | 4 | 8 | 13 | 49 | | |
| 3 | | 9 | 74 | Reviewed | 4 | 28 | 27 | 49 | 38 | 12 | | |
| 5 | | 6 | 158 | Compiled | 7 | 35 | 30 | 35 | 22 | 7 | | |
| 14 | | 16 | 136 | Tax Returns | 28 | 136 | 98 | 121 | 103 | 91 | | |
| 21 | | 63 | 577 | Other | | | | | | | | |
| 4/1/21-3/31/22 ALL | | 4/1/22-3/31/23 ALL | 4/1/23-3/31/24 ALL | | | 161 (4/1-9/30/23) | | | 824 (10/1/23-3/31/24) | | | |
| 48 | | 100 | 985 | **NUMBER OF STATEMENTS** | 0-1MM 39 | 1-3MM 199 | 3-5MM 159 | 5-10MM 213 | 10-25MM 178 | 25MM & OVER 197 | | |
| % | | % | % | **ASSETS** | % | % | % | % | % | % | | |
| 16.7 | | 11.9 | 9.4 | Cash & Equivalents | 9.1 | 9.3 | 12.0 | 11.3 | 8.0 | 6.8 | | |
| 7.0 | | 8.2 | 5.2 | Trade Receivables (net) | 2.5 | 3.4 | 4.3 | 4.9 | 6.1 | 7.6 | | |
| 48.3 | | 55.6 | 67.2 | Inventory | 55.2 | 68.6 | 68.8 | 67.3 | 71.7 | 62.5 | | |
| 1.4 | | 1.3 | .8 | All Other Current | 1.3 | .9 | .7 | .7 | .7 | 1.0 | | |
| 73.4 | | 77.0 | 82.6 | Total Current | 68.1 | 82.1 | 85.7 | 84.2 | 86.5 | 78.0 | | |
| 17.0 | | 14.8 | 11.2 | Fixed Assets (net) | 24.3 | 13.4 | 8.9 | 10.1 | 7.9 | 12.4 | | |
| 4.5 | | 3.5 | 4.8 | Intangibles (net) | 6.2 | 3.9 | 5.1 | 4.8 | 4.2 | 5.6 | | |
| 5.2 | | 4.8 | 1.4 | All Other Non-Current | 1.3 | .5 | .3 | .9 | 1.4 | 4.0 | | |
| 100.0 | | 100.0 | 100.0 | Total | 100.0 | 100.0 | 100.0 | 100.0 | 100.0 | 100.0 | | |
| | | | | **LIABILITIES** | | | | | | | | |
| 12.1 | | 16.3 | 5.1 | Notes Payable-Short Term | 7.4 | 3.7 | 4.7 | 4.4 | 4.6 | 7.4 | | |
| 2.3 | | 1.5 | 1.5 | Cur. Mat.-L.T.D. | 4.8 | 1.6 | 1.5 | 1.5 | 1.1 | 1.4 | | |
| 20.3 | | 20.4 | 45.1 | Trade Payables | 26.6 | 49.6 | 49.9 | 42.9 | 49.4 | 38.8 | | |
| .2 | | .0 | .1 | Income Taxes Payable | .0 | .0 | .0 | .1 | .1 | .1 | | |
| 6.5 | | 7.1 | 4.2 | All Other Current | 5.9 | 3.7 | 3.2 | 4.1 | 4.1 | 5.6 | | |
| 41.4 | | 45.3 | 56.0 | Total Current | 44.7 | 58.5 | 59.3 | 53.1 | 59.3 | 53.3 | | |
| 16.9 | | 16.1 | 10.7 | Long-Term Debt | 44.5 | 15.0 | 7.5 | 9.1 | 6.1 | 8.2 | | |
| .0 | | .0 | .0 | Deferred Taxes | .0 | .0 | .0 | .0 | .0 | .0 | | |
| 1.7 | | 4.0 | 5.4 | All Other Non-Current | 5.7 | 6.3 | 3.8 | 4.5 | 5.6 | 6.5 | | |
| 39.9 | | 34.6 | 27.9 | Net Worth | 5.1 | 20.2 | 29.5 | 33.3 | 29.1 | 31.8 | | |
| 100.0 | | 100.0 | 100.0 | Total Liabilities & Net Worth | 100.0 | 100.0 | 100.0 | 100.0 | 100.0 | 100.0 | | |
| | | | | **INCOME DATA** | | | | | | | | |
| 100.0 | | 100.0 | 100.0 | Net Sales | 100.0 | 100.0 | 100.0 | 100.0 | 100.0 | 100.0 | | |
| 27.2 | | 29.2 | 27.2 | Gross Profit | 38.8 | 30.0 | 28.7 | 26.4 | 25.5 | 23.0 | | |
| 23.1 | | 24.0 | 23.2 | Operating Expenses | 37.3 | 26.0 | 25.1 | 22.6 | 21.1 | 18.6 | | |
| 4.0 | | 5.2 | 4.0 | Operating Profit | 1.6 | 4.0 | 3.6 | 3.8 | 4.4 | 4.5 | | |
| -1.2 | | .2 | .5 | All Other Expenses (net) | 1.5 | .7 | .3 | .4 | .5 | .5 | | |
| 5.2 | | 5.0 | 3.4 | Profit Before Taxes | .1 | 3.3 | 3.3 | 3.4 | 3.9 | 4.0 | | |
| | | | | **RATIOS** | | | | | | | | |
| 2.4 | | 2.4 | 1.9 | | 2.2 | 1.9 | 2.0 | 2.0 | 1.7 | 1.8 | | |
| 1.7 | | 1.6 | 1.4 | Current | 1.5 | 1.4 | 1.5 | 1.5 | 1.4 | 1.4 | | |
| 1.4 | | 1.3 | 1.2 | | 1.1 | 1.1 | 1.2 | 1.2 | 1.2 | 1.2 | | |
| .9 | | .8 | .5 | | .5 | .5 | .5 | .5 | .4 | .4 | | |
| .5 | | .4 | .2 | Quick | .2 | .1 | .2 | .2 | .2 | .2 | | |
| .3 | | .2 | .1 | | .1 | .1 | .1 | .1 | .1 | .1 | | |
| 2 | 181.5 | 2 187.3 | 2 242.4 | | 0 UND | 0 UND | 1 424.1 | 1 252.8 | 2 170.8 | 5 77.6 | | |
| 5 | 67.4 | 6 59.0 | 6 62.8 | Sales/Receivables | 1 244.3 | 3 126.8 | 5 78.9 | 6 61.2 | 7 53.6 | 11 33.2 | | |
| 15 | 24.2 | 18 20.4 | 13 27.2 | | 12 31.3 | 8 44.3 | 10 38.0 | 12 29.5 | 17 21.3 | 22 16.6 | | |
| 62 | 5.9 | 73 5.0 | 130 2.8 | | 54 6.8 | 140 2.6 | 140 2.6 | 126 2.9 | 146 2.5 | 118 3.1 | | |
| 94 | 3.9 | 140 2.6 | 182 2.0 | Cost of Sales/Inventory | 243 1.5 | 228 1.6 | 182 2.0 | 174 2.1 | 192 1.9 | 166 2.2 | | |
| 122 | 3.0 | 192 1.9 | 261 1.4 | | 456 .8 | 304 1.2 | 261 1.4 | 261 1.4 | 261 1.4 | 192 1.9 | | |
| 8 | 46.2 | 10 36.0 | 63 5.8 | | 2 242.0 | 54 6.7 | 69 5.3 | 62 5.9 | 81 4.5 | 50 7.3 | | |
| 37 | 9.9 | 29 12.6 | 118 3.1 | Cost of Sales/Payables | 66 5.5 | 159 2.3 | 126 2.9 | 111 3.3 | 130 2.8 | 99 3.7 | | |
| 73 | 5.0 | 89 4.1 | 192 1.9 | | 243 1.5 | 261 1.4 | 215 1.7 | 166 2.2 | 192 1.9 | 140 2.6 | | |
| | 5.8 | 4.3 | 4.7 | | 2.0 | 4.2 | 4.3 | 4.3 | 5.2 | 5.4 | | |
| | 8.8 | 7.1 | 7.3 | Sales/Working Capital | 5.3 | 7.6 | 7.4 | 6.6 | 7.4 | 8.2 | | |
| | 12.3 | 14.2 | 15.1 | | 45.2 | 31.0 | 18.0 | 11.7 | 13.0 | 13.8 | | |
| | 36.1 | 27.1 | 16.1 | | 17.9 | 14.0 | 31.8 | 17.3 | 13.7 | 15.9 | | |
| (40) | 13.9 | (83) 9.5 | (865) 4.5 | EBIT/Interest | (27) .5 | (168) 3.4 | (128) 6.0 | (183) 4.5 | (168) 4.5 | (191) 6.3 | | |
| | 5.9 | 1.6 | 1.4 | | -2.8 | .2 | 1.1 | 1.3 | 2.0 | 2.5 | | |
| | | 21.8 | 11.7 | Net Profit + Depr., Dep., | | | | 11.3 | 10.7 | 15.4 | | |
| | | (10) 6.9 | (124) 6.3 | Amort./Cur. Mat. L/T/D | | | (28) 5.1 | (29) 6.2 | (54) 7.7 | | | |
| | | 1.9 | 2.5 | | | | | 2.3 | 3.0 | 3.5 | | |
| | .1 | .1 | .1 | | .0 | .1 | .0 | .1 | .1 | .2 | | |
| | .4 | .3 | .3 | Fixed/Worth | .4 | .4 | .2 | .2 | .2 | .4 | | |
| | .8 | .9 | 1.1 | | -2.8 | 5.2 | .8 | .8 | .6 | .9 | | |
| | .9 | 1.1 | 1.4 | | 1.3 | 1.5 | 1.2 | 1.1 | 1.6 | 1.6 | | |
| | 1.5 | 2.1 | 3.1 | Debt/Worth | 6.7 | 4.5 | 2.9 | 2.5 | 3.5 | 3.0 | | |
| | 3.3 | 6.7 | 8.9 | | -7.4 | 78.3 | 8.7 | 6.8 | 6.4 | 5.7 | | |
| | 53.5 | 61.8 | 44.4 | | 81.6 | 57.5 | 45.7 | 39.9 | 42.6 | 41.7 | | |
| (45) | 30.6 | (90) 26.6 | (852) 22.4 | % Profit Before Taxes/Tangible Net Worth | (23) 33.3 | (152) 24.1 | (141) 20.5 | (186) 16.2 | (164) 24.6 | (186) 24.7 | | |
| | 19.0 | 13.7 | 7.2 | | .0 | 4.4 | 2.9 | 3.8 | 10.5 | 13.9 | | |
| | 20.0 | 15.8 | 11.5 | | 24.0 | 11.1 | 11.9 | 11.5 | 11.4 | 11.2 | | |
| | 13.4 | 9.4 | 5.3 | % Profit Before Taxes/Total Assets | .7 | 3.8 | 4.6 | 5.4 | 5.6 | 6.4 | | |
| | 7.6 | 2.2 | 1.1 | | -11.4 | -1.4 | .4 | 1.2 | 2.0 | 2.7 | | |
| | 50.8 | 72.1 | 100.0 | | 320.0 | 139.3 | 197.8 | 92.8 | 109.6 | 57.4 | | |
| | 23.6 | 27.3 | 33.3 | Sales/Net Fixed Assets | 13.0 | 36.6 | 44.1 | 34.7 | 42.6 | 24.7 | | |
| | 10.9 | 8.5 | 12.3 | | 3.3 | 8.0 | 17.9 | 14.3 | 17.1 | 10.2 | | |
| | 3.2 | 2.6 | 2.3 | | 3.0 | 2.3 | 2.5 | 2.4 | 2.4 | 2.3 | | |
| | 2.4 | 2.0 | 1.8 | Sales/Total Assets | 1.2 | 1.6 | 1.8 | 1.9 | 1.9 | 1.9 | | |
| | 2.0 | 1.4 | 1.4 | | .9 | 1.2 | 1.5 | 1.4 | 1.5 | 1.5 | | |
| | .5 | .6 | .4 | | .4 | .4 | .2 | .4 | .3 | .5 | | |
| (31) | 1.0 | (56) 1.0 | (586) .7 | % Depr., Dep., Amort./Sales | (14) 1.0 | (103) 1.0 | (71) .7 | (136) .7 | (100) .6 | (162) .8 | | |
| | 1.6 | 2.4 | 1.4 | | 6.7 | 1.9 | 1.1 | 1.3 | 1.4 | 1.4 | | |
| | .8 | .7 | .9 | | | 2.1 | 1.1 | 1.1 | .6 | .4 | | |
| (21) | 1.5 | (33) 2.3 | (367) 2.0 | % Officers', Directors' Owners' Comp/Sales | (65) 3.6 | (70) 2.3 | (97) 2.1 | (74) 1.1 | (55) .7 | | | |
| | 2.9 | 4.7 | 3.5 | | | 5.8 | 3.4 | 3.5 | 2.1 | 1.3 | | |
| 3568791M | | 4133610M | 24768053M | Net Sales ($) | 25803M | 413362M | 630350M | 1459469M | 2806199M | 19432870M | | |
| 1000135M | | 2040190M | 13917787M | Total Assets ($) | 22501M | 292659M | 355321M | 835071M | 1609882M | 10802353M | | |

© RMA 2024  
M = $ thousand    MM = $ million  
See Pages viii through xx for Explanation of Ratios and Data

# RETAIL—Nursery, Garden Center, and Farm Supply Retailers  NAICS 444240

## Current Data Sorted by Assets

| | | | | | | Type of Statement | |
|---|---|---|---|---|---|---|---|
| | | | 3 | 1 | 3 | Unqualified | |
| | 3 | | 4 | 11 | | Reviewed | |
| 6 | 4 | 3 | 2 | 3 | 1 | Compiled | |
| 4 | 14 | 4 | 26 | 12 | 6 | Tax Returns | |
| | | 24 (4/1-9/30/23) | | 84 (10/1/23-3/31/24) | 4 | Other | |
| 0-500M | 500M-2MM | 2-10MM | 10-50MM | 50-100MM | 100-250MM | | |
| 10 | 21 | 35 | 27 | 8 | 7 | NUMBER OF STATEMENTS | |

| % | % | % | % | % | % | | |
|---|---|---|---|---|---|---|---|
| | | | | | | **ASSETS** | |
| 30.5 | 14.8 | 12.4 | 13.5 | | | Cash & Equivalents | |
| 4.8 | 13.8 | 10.6 | 12.7 | | | Trade Receivables (net) | |
| 23.3 | 28.2 | 42.0 | 36.5 | | | Inventory | |
| 2.3 | 2.0 | .8 | 2.0 | | | All Other Current | |
| 60.8 | 58.9 | 65.7 | 64.7 | | | Total Current | |
| 28.6 | 34.3 | 20.4 | 26.9 | | | Fixed Assets (net) | |
| 5.3 | 1.0 | 4.6 | 2.3 | | | Intangibles (net) | |
| 5.3 | 5.8 | 9.2 | 6.1 | | | All Other Non-Current | |
| 100.0 | 100.0 | 100.0 | 100.0 | | | Total | |
| | | | | | | **LIABILITIES** | |
| 9.7 | 6.8 | 5.6 | 8.2 | | | Notes Payable-Short Term | |
| .7 | 2.5 | 1.5 | 2.2 | | | Cur. Mat.-L.T.D. | |
| 6.8 | 11.6 | 14.7 | 10.0 | | | Trade Payables | |
| .1 | .2 | .1 | .1 | | | Income Taxes Payable | |
| 13.5 | 7.3 | 6.5 | 7.7 | | | All Other Current | |
| 30.8 | 28.3 | 28.5 | 28.2 | | | Total Current | |
| 26.7 | 24.7 | 16.0 | 15.3 | | | Long-Term Debt | |
| .0 | .0 | .1 | .1 | | | Deferred Taxes | |
| 22.4 | 3.5 | 1.5 | 4.3 | | | All Other Non-Current | |
| 20.1 | 43.5 | 53.9 | 52.2 | | | Net Worth | |
| 100.0 | 100.0 | 100.0 | 100.0 | | | Total Liabilities & Net Worth | |
| | | | | | | **INCOME DATA** | |
| 100.0 | 100.0 | 100.0 | 100.0 | | | Net Sales | |
| 52.9 | 46.9 | 38.7 | 31.8 | | | Gross Profit | |
| 48.4 | 42.0 | 30.8 | 27.1 | | | Operating Expenses | |
| 4.6 | 4.9 | 7.9 | 4.7 | | | Operating Profit | |
| .1 | .3 | .1 | -.4 | | | All Other Expenses (net) | |
| 4.4 | 4.5 | 7.8 | 5.1 | | | Profit Before Taxes | |
| | | | | | | **RATIOS** | |
| 6.3 | 7.0 | 8.5 | 5.8 | | | | |
| 2.4 | 2.1 | 2.3 | 2.4 | | | Current | |
| 1.4 | 1.2 | 1.5 | 1.3 | | | | |
| 3.2 | 3.2 | 2.2 | 3.0 | | | | |
| 1.4 | .9 | 1.0 | 1.2 | | | Quick | |
| .4 | .4 | .3 | .2 | | | | |

## Comparative Historical Data

| | | | |
|---|---|---|---|
| 7 | | 9 | |
| 16 | | 8 | |
| 23 | | 7 | |
| 39 | | 28 | |
| 114 | | 52 | |
| 4/1/19- | | 4/1/20- | |
| 3/31/20 | | 3/31/21 | |
| ALL | | ALL | |
| 199 | | 104 | |
| % | | % | |
| 11.3 | | 20.9 | |
| 11.0 | | 9.2 | |
| 38.2 | | 31.5 | |
| 2.8 | | 1.7 | |
| 63.4 | | 63.2 | |
| 27.6 | | 27.0 | |
| 2.7 | | 2.6 | |
| 6.3 | | 7.1 | |
| 100.0 | | 100.0 | |
| | | | |
| 11.3 | | 7.5 | |
| 2.9 | | 3.0 | |
| 15.4 | | 8.7 | |
| .0 | | .3 | |
| 9.2 | | 10.5 | |
| 38.8 | | 30.0 | |
| 24.3 | | 24.7 | |
| .1 | | .3 | |
| 6.5 | | 4.7 | |
| 30.2 | | 40.3 | |
| 100.0 | | 100.0 | |
| | | | |
| 100.0 | | 100.0 | |
| 37.2 | | 40.2 | |
| 32.5 | | 32.4 | |
| 4.6 | | 7.8 | |
| .8 | | -.7 | |
| 3.8 | | 8.5 | |
| | | | |
| 3.0 | | 3.8 | |
| 1.6 | | 2.2 | |
| 1.2 | | 1.6 | |
| 1.4 | | 2.4 | |
| .5 | | 1.1 | |
| .2 | | | |

| | | | | | | | | | | | | |
|---|---|---|---|---|---|---|---|---|---|---|---|---|
| 0 | UND | 1 | 648.5 | 4 | 103.6 | 6 | 59.7 | | | | | |
| 2 | 223.2 | 5 | 70.1 | 8 | 48.2 | 18 | 20.1 | Sales/Receivables | 2 | 220.4 | 1 | 386.7 |
| 10 | 35.1 | 16 | 23.4 | 24 | 14.9 | 38 | 9.5 | | 8 | 46.2 | 9 | 38.9 |
| | | | | | | | | | 26 | 14.0 | 18 | 20.4 |
| 0 | UND | 19 | 19.5 | 55 | 6.6 | 41 | 8.8 | | 35 | 10.3 | 35 | 10.3 |
| 47 | 7.7 | 59 | 6.2 | 101 | 3.6 | 96 | 3.8 | Cost of Sales/Inventory | 76 | 4.8 | 57 | 6.4 |
| 69 | 5.3 | 107 | 3.4 | 174 | 2.1 | 281 | 1.3 | | 159 | 2.3 | 111 | 3.3 |
| 0 | UND | 0 | UND | 4 | 103.2 | 10 | 35.8 | | 6 | 62.7 | 3 | 109.1 |
| 0 | UND | 15 | 23.8 | 22 | 16.6 | 37 | 9.8 | Cost of Sales/Payables | 26 | 14.1 | 17 | 21.1 |
| 16 | 22.5 | 40 | 9.1 | 45 | 8.1 | 48 | 7.6 | | 46 | 7.9 | 36 | 10.1 |
| | 6.7 | | 5.4 | | 4.1 | | 3.1 | | | 5.4 | | 5.0 |
| | 12.7 | | 9.0 | | 5.6 | | 4.7 | Sales/Working Capital | | 12.2 | | 8.4 |
| | NM | | 37.9 | | 13.0 | | 23.1 | | | 36.4 | | 13.9 |
| | | | 35.4 | | 129.1 | | 25.9 | | | 15.9 | | 34.8 |
| | (18) | | 3.3 | (28) | 8.4 | (23) | 3.3 | EBIT/Interest | (180) | 5.6 | (87) | 15.8 |
| | | | 1.7 | | 2.2 | | 1.7 | | | 1.9 | | 5.8 |
| | | | | | | | | Net Profit + Depr., Dep., | | 11.8 | | 11.2 |
| | | | | | | | | Amort./Cur. Mat. L/T/D | (26) | 4.3 | (19) | 6.0 |
| | | | | | | | | | | 1.5 | | 2.2 |
| | .2 | | .1 | | .0 | | .2 | | | .2 | | .2 |
| | .5 | | .5 | | .3 | | .4 | Fixed/Worth | | .8 | | .6 |
| | -2.8 | | 5.2 | | .9 | | 1.5 | | | 2.7 | | 1.3 |
| | .5 | | .5 | | .4 | | .3 | | | .8 | | .6 |
| | 6.7 | | .8 | | .9 | | 1.2 | Debt/Worth | | 1.9 | | 1.3 |
| | -7.1 | | 4.8 | | 2.0 | | 2.6 | | | 7.7 | | 3.6 |
| | | | 42.1 | | 51.7 | | 29.1 | | | 51.4 | | 83.4 |
| | (18) | | 17.5 | (33) | 26.2 | | 13.8 | % Profit Before Taxes/Tangible Net Worth | (166) | 20.9 | (96) | 47.4 |
| | | | 3.8 | | 6.3 | | 3.6 | | | 6.9 | | 17.5 |
| | 43.7 | | 21.1 | | 27.9 | | 11.8 | | | 17.3 | | 32.9 |
| | 15.3 | | 10.7 | | 10.9 | | 5.7 | % Profit Before Taxes/Total Assets | | 7.6 | | 16.4 |
| | -2.8 | | 1.8 | | 2.5 | | 1.8 | | | 2.5 | | 8.7 |
| | 110.9 | | 162.6 | | 180.1 | | 16.5 | | | 37.4 | | 40.1 |
| | 21.0 | | 11.0 | | 22.9 | | 6.4 | Sales/Net Fixed Assets | | 11.9 | | 12.1 |
| | 8.8 | | 3.5 | | 6.4 | | 3.4 | | | 5.9 | | 5.1 |
| | 7.8 | | 4.1 | | 2.7 | | 2.1 | | | 3.6 | | 3.7 |
| | 4.0 | | 2.8 | | 2.3 | | 1.7 | Sales/Total Assets | | 2.5 | | 2.4 |
| | 2.6 | | 1.8 | | 1.4 | | 1.0 | | | 1.6 | | 1.7 |
| | | | | | .8 | | 1.1 | | | .8 | | .9 |
| | | | (14) | | 1.9 | (24) | 2.0 | % Depr., Dep., Amort./Sales | (142) | 1.4 | (81) | 1.7 |
| | | | | | 3.4 | | 5.1 | | | 2.8 | | 3.4 |
| | | | | | 1.1 | | | | | 1.6 | | 1.4 |
| | | | (12) | | 1.4 | | | % Officers', Directors' Owners' Comp/Sales | (69) | 2.3 | (44) | 3.1 |
| | | | | | 3.4 | | | | | 4.6 | | 6.0 |
| 17148M | 75450M | 405501M | 1110881M | 956004M | 2326446M | Net Sales ($) | 4686067M | 3800258M |
| 3288M | 23742M | 171857M | 677058M | 618281M | 1263429M | Total Assets ($) | 2338941M | 1879547M |

© RMA 2024  M = $ thousand   MM = $ million
See Pages viii through xx for Explanation of Ratios and Data

# RETAIL—Nursery, Garden Center, and Farm Supply Retailers  NAICS 444240

## Comparative Historical Data | Current Data Sorted by Sales

| Comparative Historical Data | | | | Type of Statement | | Current Data Sorted by Sales | | | | |
|---|---|---|---|---|---|---|---|---|---|---|
| 3 | 3 | 5 | | Unqualified | | | | | 3 | 5 |
| 13 | 11 | 14 | | Reviewed | | | | | 3 | 11 |
| 9 | 9 | 10 | | Compiled | | 1 | 2 | 3 | 3 | 1 |
| 16 | 29 | 13 | | Tax Returns | 3 | 5 | 3 | 1 | 1 | 1 |
| 47 | 54 | 66 | | Other | 5 | 5 | 8 | 15 | 13 | 20 |
| 4/1/21-3/31/22 ALL | 4/1/22-3/31/23 ALL | 4/1/23-3/31/24 ALL | | | 24 (4/1-9/30/23) | | | 84 (10/1/23-3/31/24) | | |
| | | | | | 0-1MM | 1-3MM | 3-5MM | 5-10MM | 10-25MM | 25MM & OVER |
| 88 | 106 | 108 | | NUMBER OF STATEMENTS | 8 | 11 | 13 | 19 | 19 | 38 |
| % | % | % | | ASSETS | % | % | % | % | % | % |
| 19.3 | 14.5 | 14.0 | | Cash & Equivalents | | 24.0 | 13.4 | 9.2 | 13.3 | 12.6 |
| 10.8 | 11.7 | 10.5 | | Trade Receivables (net) | | 6.4 | 13.2 | 7.6 | 19.6 | 8.9 |
| 30.4 | 39.3 | 34.1 | | Inventory | | 24.5 | 33.5 | 47.7 | 36.8 | 32.5 |
| 3.3 | 2.7 | 1.6 | | All Other Current | | .1 | 2.5 | .9 | 1.8 | 2.0 |
| 63.7 | 68.3 | 60.2 | | Total Current | | 55.0 | 62.7 | 65.4 | 71.5 | 55.9 |
| 28.3 | 24.2 | 26.7 | | Fixed Assets (net) | | 32.1 | 25.3 | 17.8 | 24.7 | 26.6 |
| 2.5 | 1.0 | 3.3 | | Intangibles (net) | | 5.0 | 5.4 | 3.3 | 1.4 | 3.2 |
| 5.5 | 6.5 | 9.7 | | All Other Non-Current | | 7.9 | 6.6 | 13.5 | 2.4 | 14.2 |
| 100.0 | 100.0 | 100.0 | | Total | | 100.0 | 100.0 | 100.0 | 100.0 | 100.0 |
| | | | | LIABILITIES | | | | | | |
| 5.4 | 7.4 | 6.7 | | Notes Payable-Short Term | | 4.0 | 10.6 | 8.0 | 6.7 | 5.8 |
| 2.1 | 2.4 | 2.2 | | Cur. Mat.-L.T.D. | | 2.5 | 1.3 | 1.2 | 2.7 | 2.8 |
| 9.7 | 12.2 | 11.5 | | Trade Payables | | 8.8 | 15.7 | 12.3 | 14.0 | 10.2 |
| .2 | .2 | .1 | | Income Taxes Payable | | .0 | .3 | .0 | .1 | .1 |
| 9.7 | 11.3 | 8.4 | | All Other Current | | 10.7 | 3.4 | 3.2 | 6.4 | 11.7 |
| 27.1 | 33.4 | 29.0 | | Total Current | | 26.1 | 31.3 | 24.8 | 29.9 | 30.5 |
| 17.7 | 18.1 | 17.7 | | Long-Term Debt | | 36.3 | 28.9 | 12.2 | 14.9 | 11.7 |
| .4 | .1 | .1 | | Deferred Taxes | | .0 | .0 | .0 | .3 | .1 |
| 5.4 | 8.0 | 7.5 | | All Other Non-Current | | 15.8 | 5.6 | 1.3 | 1.6 | 11.9 |
| 49.4 | 40.5 | 45.8 | | Net Worth | | 21.7 | 34.2 | 61.7 | 53.4 | 45.8 |
| 100.0 | 100.0 | 100.0 | | Total Liabilities & Net Worth | | 100.0 | 100.0 | 100.0 | 100.0 | 100.0 |
| | | | | INCOME DATA | | | | | | |
| 100.0 | 100.0 | 100.0 | | Net Sales | | 100.0 | 100.0 | 100.0 | 100.0 | 100.0 |
| 38.1 | 40.2 | 39.8 | | Gross Profit | | 51.0 | 43.2 | 38.0 | 32.0 | 35.7 |
| 31.0 | 35.9 | 34.0 | | Operating Expenses | | 47.0 | 36.9 | 29.7 | 28.6 | 29.7 |
| 7.1 | 4.3 | 5.8 | | Operating Profit | | 4.0 | 6.4 | 8.2 | 3.4 | 6.0 |
| -.9 | -.2 | .1 | | All Other Expenses (net) | | .3 | .9 | .2 | -.5 | -.1 |
| 8.0 | 4.5 | 5.7 | | Profit Before Taxes | | 3.8 | 5.5 | 8.0 | 3.9 | 6.1 |
| | | | | RATIOS | | | | | | |
| 7.1 | 3.8 | 4.9 | | | | 4.0 | 5.5 | 9.3 | 10.4 | 3.2 |
| 2.8 | 2.3 | 2.1 | | Current | | 1.8 | 2.4 | 2.6 | 2.6 | 1.7 |
| 1.4 | 1.5 | 1.3 | | | | 1.3 | 1.2 | 2.0 | 1.4 | 1.2 |
| 2.9 | 1.7 | 2.4 | | | | 2.5 | 2.2 | 5.3 | 6.9 | 1.3 |
| 1.4 | .9 | .8 | | Quick | | 1.2 | .9 | .7 | 1.1 | .6 |
| .5 | .3 | .3 | | | | .2 | .4 | .2 | .5 | .2 |
| 0  770.7 | 2  152.6 | 3  117.1 | | | 0  UND | 0  UND | 1  316.9 | 6  59.7 | 5  70.6 | |
| 7  51.1 | 11  33.1 | 8  43.8 | | Sales/Receivables | 2  178.4 | 5  70.1 | 7  55.5 | 18  20.2 | 15  25.1 | |
| 21  17.6 | 23  16.0 | 24  15.1 | | | 9  41.3 | 18  20.2 | 23  15.6 | 30  12.0 | 29  12.7 | |
| 35  10.5 | 45  8.1 | 41  8.9 | | | 39  9.3 | 16  23.4 | 55  6.6 | 29  12.6 | 49  7.5 | |
| 55  6.6 | 85  4.3 | 83  4.4 | | Cost of Sales/Inventory | 58  6.3 | 101  3.6 | 122  3.0 | 89  4.1 | 99  3.7 | |
| 96  3.8 | 152  2.4 | 152  2.4 | | | 63  5.8 | 192  1.9 | 174  2.1 | 166  2.2 | 152  2.4 | |
| 2  215.9 | 8  47.3 | 6  61.0 | | | 0  UND | 1  526.8 | 1  419.7 | 6  63.5 | 21  17.4 | |
| 17  21.6 | 23  16.1 | 23  15.9 | | Cost of Sales/Payables | 8  48.4 | 25  14.7 | 18  20.0 | 33  10.9 | 33  10.9 | |
| 30  12.0 | 39  9.4 | 45  8.1 | | | 33  11.0 | 58  6.3 | 45  8.2 | 48  7.6 | 42  8.7 | |
| 4.8 | 5.0 | 4.6 | | | | 6.6 | 5.3 | 4.3 | 3.9 | 4.6 |
| 8.2 | 8.1 | 7.6 | | Sales/Working Capital | | 11.0 | 5.9 | 5.4 | 6.6 | 8.8 |
| 15.0 | 12.8 | 25.9 | | | | 42.4 | 22.7 | 9.0 | 13.1 | 31.3 |
| 53.4 | 35.6 | 33.7 | | | | 36.7 | 330.2 | 31.7 | 23.9 | |
| (75) 21.2 | (89) 11.1 | (90) 6.5 | | EBIT/Interest | (11) 6.3 | (15) 33.6 | (14) 7.9 | (34) 5.7 | | |
| 8.0 | 1.6 | 2.2 | | | | 1.4 | 2.3 | 1.6 | 1.8 | |
| 32.2 | 5.7 | 10.3 | | Net Profit + Depr., Dep., | | | | | | 16.6 |
| (15) 10.2 | (11) 3.1 | (11) 2.6 | | Amort./Cur. Mat. L/T/D | | | | | (10) 3.2 | |
| 3.8 | .8 | 1.6 | | | | | | | | 2.0 |
| .2 | .2 | .1 | | | | .0 | .3 | .0 | .1 | .3 |
| .5 | .4 | .4 | | Fixed/Worth | | .7 | .5 | .2 | .4 | .6 |
| 1.1 | 1.3 | 1.3 | | | | -2.2 | 4.9 | .4 | 1.1 | 1.2 |
| .3 | .5 | .6 | | | | .6 | .9 | .1 | .3 | .7 |
| 1.2 | 1.1 | 1.2 | | Debt/Worth | | 5.4 | 1.5 | .7 | 1.3 | 1.3 |
| 2.6 | 3.5 | 3.7 | | | | -3.4 | 12.1 | 1.0 | 1.7 | 2.8 |
| 66.7 | 44.1 | 40.2 | | % Profit Before Taxes/Tangible | | 46.1 | 48.7 | 42.4 | 30.6 | |
| (80) 31.5 | (91) 22.0 | (98) 18.3 | | Net Worth | (11) 26.4 | (18) 28.2 | 24.4 | (37) 17.1 | | |
| 21.8 | 10.2 | 6.3 | | | | -.7 | 7.7 | 5.7 | 6.7 | |
| 29.8 | 22.7 | 19.7 | | % Profit Before Taxes/Total | | 11.9 | 32.6 | 27.9 | 21.2 | 13.6 |
| 18.5 | 10.4 | 8.4 | | Assets | | 6.8 | 12.2 | 16.0 | 10.5 | 5.7 |
| 9.0 | 2.0 | 2.4 | | | | .2 | .3 | 4.6 | 2.4 | 2.0 |
| 26.6 | 46.6 | 39.4 | | | | 223.3 | 49.7 | 999.8 | 139.4 | 11.3 |
| 12.3 | 12.5 | 9.6 | | Sales/Net Fixed Assets | | 9.5 | 17.1 | 26.6 | 9.6 | 7.2 |
| 5.2 | 6.5 | 4.5 | | | | 4.3 | 5.6 | 11.1 | 3.9 | 4.3 |
| 3.5 | 4.0 | 2.9 | | | | 5.4 | 4.2 | 2.7 | 2.9 | 2.3 |
| 2.8 | 2.5 | 2.1 | | Sales/Total Assets | | 3.1 | 2.8 | 2.3 | 2.1 | 1.7 |
| 2.0 | 1.9 | 1.5 | | | | 1.9 | 1.8 | 1.4 | 1.2 | 1.2 |
| 1.0 | .7 | 1.0 | | | | | | | 1.4 | 1.0 |
| (59) 1.9 | (65) 1.7 | (63) 2.3 | | % Depr., Dep., Amort./Sales | | | | | (11) 1.9 | (32) 2.3 |
| 4.5 | 2.7 | 4.1 | | | | | | | 3.1 | 3.7 |
| 1.3 | 1.1 | 1.2 | | % Officers', Directors' | | | | | | |
| (33) 2.0 | (39) 2.7 | (30) 2.8 | | Owners' Comp/Sales | | | | | | |
| 4.8 | 5.5 | 5.3 | | | | | | | | |
| 2134793M | 3538609M | 4891430M | | Net Sales ($) | 6587M | 22932M | 53325M | 142490M | 310613M | 4355483M |
| 960560M | 1664518M | 2757655M | | Total Assets ($) | 3554M | 10297M | 25498M | 70996M | 170272M | 2477038M |

© RMA 2024  M = $ thousand    MM = $ million
See Pages viii through xx for Explanation of Ratios and Data

# RETAIL—Supermarkets and Other Grocery Retailers (except Convenience Retailers) NAICS 445110

## Current Data Sorted by Assets

| | | | | | | Type of Statement | Comparative Historical Data | |
|---|---|---|---|---|---|---|---|---|
| | 1 | | 6 | 3 | 10 | Unqualified | 24 | 17 |
| | 3 | 8 | 19 | 5 | | Reviewed | 28 | 14 |
| 18 | 51 | 11 | 7 | | 1 | Compiled | 39 | 26 |
| 6 | 62 | 32 | 3 | 11 | 16 | Tax Returns | 72 | 49 |
| | 63 (4/1-9/30/23) | 61 | 45 | | | Other | 245 | 176 |
| 0-500M | 500M-2MM | 2-10MM | 10-50MM | 50-100MM | 100-250MM | | 4/1/19-3/31/20 ALL | 4/1/20-3/31/21 ALL |
| 24 | 117 | 112 | 80 | 19 | 27 | NUMBER OF STATEMENTS | 408 | 282 |
| % | % | % | % | % | % | ASSETS | % | % |
| 24.3 | 24.0 | 24.6 | 19.6 | 14.2 | 13.8 | Cash & Equivalents | 16.6 | 27.3 |
| 2.2 | .9 | 2.9 | 3.2 | 4.1 | 3.2 | Trade Receivables (net) | 3.1 | 2.9 |
| 46.2 | 39.4 | 24.2 | 17.7 | 15.4 | 16.0 | Inventory | 27.1 | 25.2 |
| .7 | 4.6 | 4.4 | 4.2 | 1.2 | 6.3 | All Other Current | 2.9 | 2.9 |
| 73.4 | 68.9 | 56.0 | 44.7 | 34.9 | 39.3 | Total Current | 49.6 | 58.3 |
| 12.9 | 18.3 | 21.7 | 31.1 | 34.8 | 29.8 | Fixed Assets (net) | 32.4 | 26.6 |
| 6.1 | 5.1 | 6.0 | 7.6 | 7.5 | 1.2 | Intangibles (net) | 6.1 | 6.2 |
| 7.6 | 7.6 | 16.3 | 16.6 | 22.8 | 29.8 | All Other Non-Current | 11.9 | 8.9 |
| 100.0 | 100.0 | 100.0 | 100.0 | 100.0 | 100.0 | Total | 100.0 | 100.0 |
| | | | | | | LIABILITIES | | |
| 10.2 | 2.1 | .7 | 2.3 | 2.4 | 1.1 | Notes Payable-Short Term | 3.4 | 3.1 |
| .5 | .9 | 1.8 | 2.6 | 4.0 | 1.7 | Cur. Mat.-L.T.D. | 2.9 | 2.8 |
| 18.6 | 16.6 | 14.1 | 12.2 | 14.9 | 9.1 | Trade Payables | 17.7 | 15.1 |
| 1.3 | .2 | .1 | .1 | .1 | .2 | Income Taxes Payable | .1 | .2 |
| 50.4 | 13.9 | 9.8 | 8.3 | 7.4 | 9.7 | All Other Current | 12.2 | 12.6 |
| 81.0 | 33.9 | 26.5 | 25.4 | 28.8 | 21.7 | Total Current | 36.3 | 33.8 |
| 8.7 | 20.0 | 16.8 | 17.4 | 18.0 | 13.8 | Long-Term Debt | 20.0 | 20.9 |
| .0 | .0 | .0 | .1 | .6 | .9 | Deferred Taxes | .2 | .2 |
| 3.7 | 5.3 | 6.2 | 11.3 | 17.9 | 25.9 | All Other Non-Current | 8.4 | 5.4 |
| 6.6 | 40.8 | 50.5 | 45.8 | 34.8 | 37.7 | Net Worth | 35.1 | 39.8 |
| 100.0 | 100.0 | 100.0 | 100.0 | 100.0 | 100.0 | Total Liabilties & Net Worth | 100.0 | 100.0 |
| | | | | | | INCOME DATA | | |
| 100.0 | 100.0 | 100.0 | 100.0 | 100.0 | 100.0 | Net Sales | 100.0 | 100.0 |
| 30.8 | 30.7 | 28.5 | 31.3 | 31.1 | 29.2 | Gross Profit | 29.0 | 29.7 |
| 26.3 | 27.0 | 24.6 | 27.7 | 27.2 | 27.1 | Operating Expenses | 26.9 | 25.5 |
| 4.5 | 3.7 | 3.9 | 3.7 | 3.9 | 2.1 | Operating Profit | 2.1 | 4.2 |
| .1 | -.1 | -.8 | -.3 | -.3 | -.3 | All Other Expenses (net) | -.4 | -.7 |
| 4.5 | 3.8 | 4.7 | 4.0 | 4.2 | 2.5 | Profit Before Taxes | 2.5 | 4.8 |
| | | | | | | RATIOS | | |
| 7.2 | 6.7 | 4.7 | 3.0 | 2.4 | 2.8 | | 2.9 | 3.9 |
| 2.1 | 2.4 | 2.6 | 2.0 | 1.1 | 1.7 | Current | 1.6 | 1.9 |
| .6 | 1.4 | 1.4 | 1.2 | .7 | 1.2 | | 1.0 | 1.2 |
| 2.7 | 2.9 | 2.3 | 1.6 | 1.2 | 1.1 | | 1.3 | 2.2 |
| 1.0 | .9 | 1.1 | .8 | .5 | .8 | Quick | .5 | 1.0 |
| .1 | .2 | .4 | .4 | .3 | .4 | | .2 | .4 |
| 0 UND | 0 UND | 0 UND | 0 999.8 | 1 292.7 | 1 297.1 | | 0 UND | 0 UND |
| 0 UND | 0 UND | 0 999.8 | 1 386.8 | 3 127.2 | 2 165.2 | Sales/Receivables | 1 403.9 | 1 638.0 |
| 0 UND | 0 UND | 1 265.9 | 3 116.9 | 6 64.2 | 4 98.5 | | 3 107.2 | 3 113.1 |
| 10 35.8 | 16 22.2 | 15 23.7 | 20 18.3 | 20 18.0 | 17 20.9 | | 18 20.5 | 16 22.4 |
| 23 16.2 | 27 13.6 | 23 15.9 | 25 14.6 | 23 15.8 | 26 14.2 | Cost of Sales/Inventory | 24 15.0 | 24 15.3 |
| 56 6.5 | 40 9.2 | 32 11.3 | 33 10.9 | 30 12.3 | 37 9.9 | | 35 10.4 | 31 11.6 |
| 0 UND | 3 122.4 | 11 32.0 | 16 23.0 | 13 27.7 | | | 8 43.1 | 8 48.3 |
| 2 241.1 | 6 64.7 | 11 34.4 | 19 19.3 | 24 15.4 | 19 19.3 | Cost of Sales/Payables | 15 23.9 | 15 25.1 |
| 8 45.3 | 18 20.2 | 21 17.8 | 26 14.1 | 30 12.2 | 23 16.0 | | 24 15.3 | 21 17.7 |
| 10.8 | 9.1 | 8.9 | 9.3 | 14.0 | 9.7 | | 13.4 | 9.7 |
| 42.3 | 17.2 | 14.7 | 20.6 | 171.8 | 19.1 | Sales/Working Capital | 31.0 | 19.8 |
| -27.1 | 52.9 | 50.3 | 56.4 | -32.6 | 62.7 | | -435.9 | 72.8 |
| 44.4 | 33.0 | 76.0 | 31.9 | 61.3 | 37.1 | | 21.9 | 70.9 |
| (11) 20.2 | (63) 7.6 | (79) 23.3 | (65) 9.3 | (18) 8.7 | (25) 10.6 | EBIT/Interest | (306) 5.3 | (222) 23.8 |
| 1.3 | 1.0 | 3.8 | 2.4 | 1.5 | 2.6 | | 1.7 | 7.5 |
| | | | 11.0 | 4.4 | 12.2 | | 7.1 | 17.0 |
| | | | (26) 4.1 | (11) 2.6 | (13) 3.4 | Net Profit + Depr., Dep., Amort./Cur. Mat. L/T/D | (51) 3.2 | (34) 8.8 |
| | | | 1.5 | 2.1 | 1.3 | | 1.7 | 1.8 |
| .1 | .0 | .1 | .3 | .8 | .5 | | .3 | .2 |
| .3 | .3 | .3 | .8 | 1.5 | .7 | Fixed/Worth | .9 | .7 |
| -2.1 | 1.2 | 1.2 | 1.8 | 4.5 | .9 | | 2.9 | 2.0 |
| .2 | .3 | .3 | .6 | 1.2 | 1.3 | | .5 | .5 |
| 1.4 | .9 | .7 | 1.3 | 2.6 | 1.9 | Debt/Worth | 1.5 | 1.2 |
| -4.1 | 8.9 | 2.3 | 4.3 | 12.5 | 3.8 | | 6.6 | 4.6 |
| 410.9 | 77.6 | 73.1 | 40.6 | 61.9 | 23.8 | | 50.2 | 89.6 |
| (16) 47.9 | (96) 34.6 | (102) 36.5 | (70) 21.0 | (18) 25.2 | (26) 11.4 | % Profit Before Taxes/Tangible Net Worth | (338) 22.1 | (241) 54.2 |
| 20.6 | 12.7 | 13.5 | 10.6 | 12.1 | 4.8 | | 7.8 | 27.0 |
| 63.2 | 40.1 | 36.3 | 18.2 | 13.1 | 6.5 | | 17.9 | 39.5 |
| 20.7 | 20.2 | 17.3 | 8.7 | 8.1 | 3.7 | % Profit Before Taxes/Total Assets | 7.7 | 21.5 |
| 4.0 | 4.3 | 5.4 | 3.1 | 3.6 | .9 | | 2.1 | 9.5 |
| 627.6 | 697.7 | 121.4 | 38.2 | 16.2 | 16.6 | | 45.9 | 63.6 |
| 126.7 | 74.9 | 43.4 | 13.1 | 12.2 | 8.8 | Sales/Net Fixed Assets | 17.3 | 23.9 |
| 60.4 | 20.8 | 13.2 | 6.5 | 5.7 | 6.5 | | 8.3 | 10.0 |
| 15.4 | 10.4 | 7.2 | 4.1 | 3.6 | 3.1 | | 6.7 | 6.5 |
| 10.3 | 6.8 | 4.8 | 3.0 | 3.0 | 2.5 | Sales/Total Assets | 4.5 | 4.8 |
| 6.1 | 4.0 | 2.8 | 2.1 | 2.3 | 2.0 | | 3.2 | 3.3 |
| .2 | .2 | .3 | .6 | .9 | .7 | | .6 | .5 |
| (11) .4 | (54) .7 | (76) .7 | (68) 1.0 | 1.3 | (23) 1.4 | % Depr., Dep., Amort./Sales | (289) 1.1 | (199) .9 |
| 1.1 | 1.5 | 1.5 | 1.4 | 1.9 | 1.7 | | 1.7 | 1.5 |
| 1.5 | .8 | | | | | | .6 | .5 |
| (16) 2.9 | (40) 1.6 | (38) .8 | (12) 1.5 | | | % Officers', Directors' Owners' Comp/Sales | (130) 1.1 | (82) 1.1 |
| 5.2 | 2.2 | 1.7 | 4.2 | | | | 2.2 | 2.7 |
| 65375M | 1012405M | 2467194M | 6212857M | 4308576M | 13676026M | Net Sales ($) | 46984928M | 27283114M |
| 6367M | 136803M | 481671M | 1783567M | 1348003M | 4307045M | Total Assets ($) | 10139562M | 5757885M |

M = $ thousand    MM = $ million
See Pages viii through xx for Explanation of Ratios and Data

© RMA 2024

# RETAIL—Supermarkets and Other Grocery Retailers (except Convenience Retailers) NAICS 445110

## Comparative Historical Data | Current Data Sorted by Sales

| | | | | Type of Statement | | | | | | | |
|---|---|---|---|---|---|---|---|---|---|---|---|
| | 19 | 25 | 20 | Unqualified | | | 1 | | | | 19 |
| | 13 | 33 | 32 | Reviewed | | | 1 | 1 | 5 | | 25 |
| | 20 | 24 | 21 | Compiled | | | | 2 | 7 | | 12 |
| | 58 | 102 | 105 | Tax Returns | 3 | 13 | 15 | 24 | 39 | | 11 |
| | 171 | 240 | 201 | Other | 4 | 12 | 10 | 43 | 44 | | 88 |
| | 4/1/21- | 4/1/22- | 4/1/23- | | | | 63 (4/1-9/30/23) | | 316 (10/1/23-3/31/24) | | |
| | 3/31/22 | 3/31/23 | 3/31/24 | | | | | | | | |
| | ALL | ALL | ALL | | 0-1MM | 1-3MM | 3-5MM | 5-10MM | 10-25MM | | 25MM & OVER |
| | 281 | 424 | 379 | NUMBER OF STATEMENTS | 7 | 25 | 27 | 70 | 95 | | 155 |
| | % | % | % | ASSETS | % | % | % | % | % | | % |
| | 27.3 | 24.1 | 22.0 | Cash & Equivalents | 17.1 | 21.7 | 26.5 | 24.0 | 19.7 | | |
| | 2.7 | 2.9 | 2.4 | Trade Receivables (net) | .4 | .7 | .8 | 2.3 | 3.5 | | |
| | 24.9 | 25.3 | 27.9 | Inventory | 37.3 | 36.4 | 30.4 | 30.1 | 21.5 | | |
| | 2.9 | 4.1 | 4.2 | All Other Current | 3.9 | 4.5 | 7.8 | 3.7 | 3.0 | | |
| | 57.8 | 56.4 | 56.5 | Total Current | 58.7 | 63.2 | 65.5 | 60.0 | 47.7 | | |
| | 26.2 | 26.5 | 23.3 | Fixed Assets (net) | 20.4 | 20.6 | 20.3 | 19.3 | 28.2 | | |
| | 5.2 | 5.9 | 5.8 | Intangibles (net) | 13.5 | 6.2 | 5.9 | 4.6 | 5.4 | | |
| | 10.8 | 11.3 | 14.4 | All Other Non-Current | 7.4 | 9.9 | 8.3 | 16.0 | 18.6 | | |
| | 100.0 | 100.0 | 100.0 | Total | 100.0 | 100.0 | 100.0 | 100.0 | 100.0 | | |
| | | | | LIABILITIES | | | | | | | |
| | 2.6 | 2.4 | 2.2 | Notes Payable-Short Term | 9.8 | 1.9 | 2.5 | 1.0 | 1.7 | | |
| | 2.4 | 1.9 | 1.7 | Cur. Mat.-L.T.D. | 1.3 | .3 | 1.2 | 1.9 | 2.4 | | |
| | 14.4 | 15.5 | 14.5 | Trade Payables | 7.4 | 13.2 | 14.8 | 14.5 | 15.4 | | |
| | .1 | .2 | .2 | Income Taxes Payable | .1 | 1.1 | .3 | .1 | .1 | | |
| | 9.6 | 10.4 | 13.2 | All Other Current | 38.8 | 28.6 | 11.3 | 12.0 | 8.3 | | |
| | 29.2 | 30.4 | 31.8 | Total Current | 57.4 | 45.1 | 29.6 | 29.6 | 27.9 | | |
| | 18.1 | 20.8 | 17.2 | Long-Term Debt | 21.9 | 20.0 | 16.9 | 19.4 | 15.4 | | |
| | .2 | .1 | .1 | Deferred Taxes | .0 | .0 | .0 | .0 | .3 | | |
| | 7.4 | 7.3 | 8.9 | All Other Non-Current | 3.7 | 7.1 | 7.5 | 6.9 | 12.2 | | |
| | 45.0 | 41.3 | 42.0 | Net Worth | 16.9 | 27.8 | 45.9 | 44.1 | 44.3 | | |
| | 100.0 | 100.0 | 100.0 | Total Liabilities & Net Worth | 100.0 | 100.0 | 100.0 | 100.0 | 100.0 | | |
| | | | | INCOME DATA | | | | | | | |
| | 100.0 | 100.0 | 100.0 | Net Sales | 100.0 | 100.0 | 100.0 | 100.0 | 100.0 | | |
| | 28.4 | 28.7 | 30.1 | Gross Profit | 30.1 | 33.3 | 31.3 | 27.9 | 29.7 | | |
| | 24.7 | 24.8 | 26.4 | Operating Expenses | 29.5 | 31.5 | 26.1 | 24.1 | 26.5 | | |
| | 3.8 | 3.9 | 3.7 | Operating Profit | .6 | 1.8 | 5.2 | 3.8 | 3.3 | | |
| | -1.1 | -.4 | -.4 | All Other Expenses (net) | .4 | -.8 | -.5 | -.5 | -.4 | | |
| | 4.9 | 4.3 | 4.1 | Profit Before Taxes | .2 | 2.5 | 5.7 | 4.3 | 3.7 | | |
| | | | | RATIOS | | | | | | | |
| | 3.8 | 3.5 | 4.2 | | 6.6 | 24.2 | 5.8 | 4.3 | 2.8 | | |
| | 2.2 | 2.1 | 2.2 | Current | 2.4 | 6.7 | 2.6 | 2.1 | 1.9 | | |
| | 1.3 | 1.2 | 1.2 | | .6 | 1.8 | 1.3 | 1.2 | 1.2 | | |
| | 2.1 | 1.9 | 2.1 | | 3.0 | 3.6 | 2.5 | 2.3 | 1.6 | | |
| (280) | 1.1 | (422) .9 | .9 | Quick | .8 | 1.2 | 1.0 | .9 | .8 | | |
| | .5 | .4 | .3 | | .1 | .7 | .2 | .3 | .4 | | |
| 0 | UND | 0 UND | 0 UND | | 0 UND | 0 UND | 0 UND | 0 UND | 0 UND | 0 | 999.8 |
| 0 | 820.9 | 0 999.8 | 0 999.8 | Sales/Receivables | 0 UND | 0 UND | 0 UND | 0 UND | 0 UND | 1 | 292.7 |
| 3 | 144.5 | 3 142.4 | 2 201.2 | | 0 UND | 0 UND | 0 999.8 | 1 497.0 | 3 | 104.4 |
| 16 | 22.7 | 16 22.8 | 17 22.0 | | 12 29.5 | 25 14.8 | 17 21.5 | 15 24.8 | 18 | 20.7 |
| 23 | 16.2 | 23 15.7 | 25 14.7 | Cost of Sales/Inventory | 28 13.0 | 40 9.2 | 28 12.9 | 22 16.9 | 24 | 15.2 |
| 30 | 12.0 | 32 11.3 | 35 10.3 | | 60 6.1 | 60 6.1 | 41 8.8 | 29 12.6 | 33 | 11.2 |
| 6 | 61.6 | 6 64.9 | 2 168.3 | | 0 UND | 0 UND | 0 UND | 0 999.8 | 10 | 37.7 |
| 14 | 25.2 | 14 26.8 | 12 30.5 | Cost of Sales/Payables | 0 934.0 | 1 331.8 | 9 42.8 | 9 40.1 | 20 | 20.3 |
| 20 | 18.4 | 23 15.7 | 23 16.0 | | 27 13.6 | 16 23.3 | 23 15.7 | 18 20.2 | 25 | 14.5 |
| | 11.1 | 11.1 | 9.3 | | 7.3 | 7.6 | 6.9 | 10.8 | 12.2 | | |
| | 18.5 | 20.1 | 17.4 | Sales/Working Capital | 15.7 | 12.6 | 15.5 | 21.3 | 23.3 | | |
| | 49.1 | 77.2 | 62.7 | | -29.5 | 20.3 | 47.3 | 89.1 | 68.6 | | |
| | 68.8 | 42.8 | 47.7 | | 11.0 | 20.3 | 56.4 | 65.0 | 47.7 | | |
| (214) | 24.3 | (294) 14.9 | (261) 11.0 | EBIT/Interest | (11) 3.1 | (15) 7.5 | (42) 10.5 | (63) 22.2 | (126) | 11.0 |
| | 6.9 | 4.7 | 2.4 | | -5.5 | 1.0 | 2.5 | 1.8 | 3.5 | | |
| | 17.0 | 12.4 | 9.0 | Net Profit + Depr., Dep., | | | | | 9.0 | | |
| (26) | 6.0 | (55) 5.1 | (56) 3.6 | Amort./Cur. Mat. L/T/D | | | | (48) | 3.5 | | |
| | 3.5 | 2.7 | 1.8 | | | | | | 2.1 | | |
| | .2 | .2 | .1 | | .0 | .2 | .1 | .0 | .3 | | |
| | .8 | .6 | .5 | Fixed/Worth | .5 | .5 | .3 | .2 | .7 | | |
| | 1.4 | 1.9 | 1.6 | | -5.0 | -.8 | 1.8 | 1.0 | 1.5 | | |
| | .4 | .5 | .4 | | .3 | .2 | .3 | .3 | .6 | | |
| | 1.0 | 1.2 | 1.1 | Debt/Worth | 1.6 | .9 | .8 | .8 | 1.3 | | |
| | 3.0 | 5.5 | 4.7 | | -6.9 | -3.9 | 7.5 | 3.0 | 3.8 | | |
| | 72.5 | 77.3 | 64.5 | % Profit Before Taxes/Tangible | 57.5 | 62.0 | 65.5 | 86.9 | 52.9 | | |
| (244) | 40.4 | (370) 36.6 | (328) 26.9 | Net Worth | (17) 24.5 | (20) 37.8 | (58) 39.6 | (84) 29.7 | (142) | 22.7 |
| | 20.8 | 19.0 | 11.5 | | 12.4 | 6.8 | 15.1 | 12.8 | 10.6 | | |
| | 34.0 | 29.4 | 32.5 | % Profit Before Taxes/Total | 17.7 | 29.0 | 43.0 | 40.6 | 18.7 | | |
| | 19.5 | 13.8 | 12.6 | Assets | 7.4 | 13.6 | 24.0 | 16.7 | 9.1 | | |
| | 8.6 | 6.0 | 3.6 | | 2.1 | .0 | 5.8 | 4.0 | 3.6 | | |
| | 81.0 | 87.1 | 121.6 | | 458.4 | 83.8 | 167.9 | 394.3 | 41.4 | | |
| | 24.0 | 23.7 | 32.7 | Sales/Net Fixed Assets | 59.7 | 35.6 | 51.2 | 82.9 | 15.4 | | |
| | 9.6 | 9.1 | 10.7 | | 12.2 | 14.1 | 13.0 | 20.9 | 8.1 | | |
| | 7.1 | 7.1 | 7.9 | | 8.5 | 7.8 | 8.3 | 10.2 | 6.2 | | |
| | 4.7 | 4.3 | 4.4 | Sales/Total Assets | 4.5 | 4.4 | 5.3 | 6.2 | 3.4 | | |
| | 3.1 | 2.8 | 2.6 | | 2.4 | 2.7 | 2.8 | 3.4 | 2.4 | | |
| | .5 | .5 | .5 | | .3 | .4 | .2 | .3 | .6 | | |
| (203) | .9 | (289) 1.0 | (251) .9 | % Depr., Dep., Amort./Sales | (12) .6 | (16) .8 | (34) .5 | (55) .7 | (131) | 1.0 |
| | 1.5 | 1.6 | 1.6 | | 2.5 | 1.6 | 1.8 | 1.4 | 1.7 | | |
| | .6 | .6 | .6 | | 1.9 | 1.3 | .9 | .5 | .3 | | |
| (93) | 1.4 | (135) 1.4 | (111) 1.3 | % Officers', Directors' Owners' Comp/Sales | (10) 3.2 | (13) 1.9 | (24) 1.9 | (35) .9 | (27) | .6 |
| | 2.6 | 2.1 | 2.2 | | 6.2 | 3.6 | 3.6 | 1.7 | 1.5 | | |
| | 21879961M | 30307417M | 27742433M | Net Sales ($) | 6138M | 48360M | 110828M | 509197M | 1488739M | | 25579171M |
| | 5220365M | 8707858M | 8063456M | Total Assets ($) | 3355M | 16411M | 30423M | 166067M | 347661M | | 7499539M |

© RMA 2024  
M = $ thousand   MM = $ million  
See Pages viii through xx for Explanation of Ratios and Data

# RETAIL—Convenience Retailers  NAICS 445131

## Current Data Sorted by Assets | Comparative Historical Data

| | | | | | | | Type of Statement | | |
|---|---|---|---|---|---|---|---|---|---|
| | 1 | | | 1 | 1 | 1 | Unqualified | 2 | 5 |
| | | 3 | 2 | 1 | | | Reviewed | 7 | 2 |
| | | 20 | | | | | Compiled | 3 | 2 |
| 26 | 20 | | 8 | 4 | 2 | | Tax Returns | 66 | 48 |
| 17 | 9 (4/1-9/30/23) | 20 | 98 (10/1/23-3/31/24) | | | | Other | 45 | 53 |
| | | | | | | | | 4/1/19-3/31/20 | 4/1/20-3/31/21 |
| 0-500M | 500M-2MM | 2-10MM | 10-50MM | 50-100MM | 100-250MM | | NUMBER OF STATEMENTS | ALL | ALL |
| 44 | 43 | 10 | 6 | 3 | 1 | | | 123 | 110 |
| % | % | % | % | % | % | | ASSETS | % | % |
| 25.1 | 20.9 | 15.1 | | | | | Cash & Equivalents | 14.0 | 22.0 |
| .1 | 1.7 | 2.9 | | | | | Trade Receivables (net) | 3.8 | 2.7 |
| 42.5 | 24.1 | 12.1 | | | | | Inventory | 28.3 | 27.5 |
| .7 | 4.8 | 3.6 | | | | | All Other Current | 1.6 | 1.7 |
| 68.4 | 51.5 | 33.6 | | | | | Total Current | 47.7 | 53.9 |
| 17.6 | 29.6 | 43.9 | | | | | Fixed Assets (net) | 37.3 | 28.5 |
| 8.2 | 8.1 | 14.4 | | | | | Intangibles (net) | 9.6 | 10.2 |
| 5.7 | 10.7 | 8.1 | | | | | All Other Non-Current | 5.4 | 7.4 |
| 100.0 | 100.0 | 100.0 | | | | | Total | 100.0 | 100.0 |
| | | | | | | | LIABILITIES | | |
| 5.0 | .7 | .3 | | | | | Notes Payable-Short Term | 3.0 | 2.6 |
| 1.3 | .9 | 2.1 | | | | | Cur. Mat.-L.T.D. | 1.5 | 1.6 |
| 10.2 | 6.5 | 7.3 | | | | | Trade Payables | 9.8 | 11.4 |
| .0 | .1 | .0 | | | | | Income Taxes Payable | .1 | .0 |
| 13.3 | 12.4 | 5.9 | | | | | All Other Current | 13.0 | 8.3 |
| 29.8 | 20.5 | 15.6 | | | | | Total Current | 27.4 | 24.0 |
| 10.1 | 26.9 | 33.9 | | | | | Long-Term Debt | 26.7 | 22.9 |
| .0 | .0 | .0 | | | | | Deferred Taxes | .1 | .0 |
| 8.0 | 13.3 | 5.2 | | | | | All Other Non-Current | 12.6 | 18.2 |
| 52.0 | 39.3 | 45.3 | | | | | Net Worth | 33.1 | 34.9 |
| 100.0 | 100.0 | 100.0 | | | | | Total Liabilties & Net Worth | 100.0 | 100.0 |
| | | | | | | | INCOME DATA | | |
| 100.0 | 100.0 | 100.0 | | | | | Net Sales | 100.0 | 100.0 |
| 24.8 | 22.8 | 27.0 | | | | | Gross Profit | 21.8 | 21.6 |
| 22.2 | 17.7 | 20.2 | | | | | Operating Expenses | 19.4 | 17.9 |
| 2.7 | 5.1 | 6.8 | | | | | Operating Profit | 2.4 | 3.7 |
| -1.2 | -.5 | .3 | | | | | All Other Expenses (net) | -.6 | -.7 |
| 3.8 | 5.6 | 6.5 | | | | | Profit Before Taxes | 2.9 | 4.4 |
| | | | | | | | RATIOS | | |
| 14.7 | 18.0 | 14.5 | | | | | | 6.0 | 5.6 |
| 6.2 | 3.9 | 4.2 | | | | | Current | 1.9 | 2.5 |
| 1.5 | 1.7 | 1.2 | | | | | | 1.0 | 1.5 |
| 5.7 | 8.5 | 7.6 | | | | | | 1.7 | 2.9 |
| (43) 1.3 | (42) 1.2 | 3.1 | | | | | Quick | (122) .6 | (109) 1.0 |
| .3 | .4 | .7 | | | | | | .2 | .4 |
| 0 UND | 0 UND | 0 UND | | | | | | 0 UND | 0 UND |
| 0 UND | 0 UND | 1 266.2 | | | | | Sales/Receivables | 0 UND | 0 UND |
| 0 UND | 0 999.8 | 7 50.3 | | | | | | 2 171.2 | 2 170.3 |
| 11 32.6 | 8 44.7 | 7 54.1 | | | | | | 9 39.1 | 9 40.2 |
| 18 20.3 | 20 18.1 | 8 43.8 | | | | | Cost of Sales/Inventory | 16 22.8 | 15 24.3 |
| 53 6.9 | 37 9.9 | 21 17.6 | | | | | | 29 12.4 | 22 16.3 |
| 0 UND | 0 UND | 0 UND | | | | | | 0 UND | 0 UND |
| 0 UND | 0 UND | 0 UND | | | | | Cost of Sales/Payables | 4 87.1 | 6 62.2 |
| 6 57.7 | 7 55.0 | 7 49.9 | | | | | | 13 28.5 | 13 28.4 |
| 9.6 | 6.4 | 7.4 | | | | | | 17.0 | 11.9 |
| 30.0 | 18.2 | 17.9 | | | | | Sales/Working Capital | 39.3 | 21.3 |
| 67.1 | 33.5 | NM | | | | | | -902.7 | 67.1 |
| 95.0 | 16.3 | | | | | | | 14.0 | 18.9 |
| (10) 14.0 | (25) 5.8 | | | | | | EBIT/Interest | (80) 6.0 | (57) 9.0 |
| 4.4 | 1.9 | | | | | | | 1.7 | 3.7 |
| | | | | | | | Net Profit + Depr., Dep., Amort./Cur. Mat. L/T/D | | |
| .0 | .3 | .6 | | | | | | .2 | .1 |
| .2 | 1.0 | 1.1 | | | | | Fixed/Worth | .9 | .7 |
| .7 | 6.8 | 5.5 | | | | | | 14.0 | 2.0 |
| .1 | .5 | .8 | | | | | | .4 | .6 |
| .7 | 2.2 | 2.1 | | | | | Debt/Worth | 1.7 | 1.4 |
| 3.7 | 104.2 | 6.0 | | | | | | 252.0 | 10.7 |
| 102.2 | 129.0 | | | | | | | 87.5 | 185.6 |
| (37) 54.5 | (34) 70.0 | | | | | | % Profit Before Taxes/Tangible Net Worth | (94) 31.0 | (89) 52.2 |
| 19.5 | 35.2 | | | | | | | 14.6 | 22.5 |
| 58.2 | 42.3 | 33.9 | | | | | | 26.0 | 41.7 |
| 25.5 | 21.8 | 13.2 | | | | | % Profit Before Taxes/Total Assets | 10.2 | 17.6 |
| 6.3 | 5.7 | 4.4 | | | | | | 3.1 | 6.1 |
| 343.2 | 106.3 | 64.3 | | | | | | 152.4 | 228.3 |
| 71.0 | 13.9 | 10.2 | | | | | Sales/Net Fixed Assets | 21.1 | 32.5 |
| 37.8 | 7.3 | 2.9 | | | | | | 5.7 | 7.3 |
| 18.6 | 8.7 | 6.9 | | | | | | 10.4 | 10.7 |
| 8.5 | 4.0 | 2.5 | | | | | Sales/Total Assets | 6.0 | 5.6 |
| 4.1 | 2.3 | 1.6 | | | | | | 3.0 | 2.3 |
| .2 | .5 | | | | | | | .6 | .5 |
| (17) .7 | (25) 1.2 | | | | | | % Depr., Dep., Amort./Sales | (74) 1.6 | (60) 1.0 |
| 1.5 | 2.0 | | | | | | | 2.5 | 1.7 |
| 1.4 | .6 | | | | | | | .7 | .7 |
| (15) 2.2 | (20) 1.2 | | | | | | % Officers', Directors' Owners' Comp/Sales | (54) 1.6 | (55) 1.2 |
| 5.0 | 2.5 | | | | | | | 2.7 | 2.4 |
| 129773M | 271860M | 166724M | 1050976M | 396664M | 433796M | | Net Sales ($) | 12960761M | 5996700M |
| 12734M | 40877M | 39829M | 148052M | 210680M | 154815M | | Total Assets ($) | 1618033M | 1413847M |

© RMA 2024

M = $ thousand   MM = $ million
See Pages viii through xx for Explanation of Ratios and Data

# RETAIL—Convenience Retailers  NAICS 445131

## Comparative Historical Data / Current Data Sorted by Sales

| Comparative Historical Data | | | | | Current Data Sorted by Sales | | | | | |
|---|---|---|---|---|---|---|---|---|---|---|
| 3 | 2 | 4 | | Type of Statement | | 1 | | | | 3 |
| 5 | 2 | 1 | | Unqualified | | | | | | 1 |
| 3 | 4 | 5 | | Reviewed | | 1 | | 2 | 2 | |
| 42 | 43 | 46 | | Compiled | 9 | 22 | 5 | 7 | 2 | 1 |
| 49 | 56 | 51 | | Tax Returns | 1 | 14 | 5 | 18 | 2 | 8 |
| 4/1/21- | 4/1/22- | 4/1/23- | | Other | | | | | | |
| 3/31/22 | 3/31/23 | 3/31/24 | | | 9 (4/1-9/30/23) | | | 98 (10/1/23-3/31/24) | | |
| ALL | ALL | ALL | | | 0-1MM | 1-3MM | 3-5MM | 5-10MM | 10-25MM | 25MM & OVER |
| 102 | 107 | 107 | | NUMBER OF STATEMENTS | 10 | 38 | 10 | 27 | 9 | 13 |
| % | % | % | | ASSETS | % | % | % | % | % | % |
| 24.1 | 20.9 | 21.0 | | Cash & Equivalents | 17.9 | 21.6 | 29.5 | 18.3 | | 14.0 |
| 2.2 | 4.0 | 1.6 | | Trade Receivables (net) | .0 | 1.1 | .0 | 1.7 | | 5.8 |
| 27.3 | 30.5 | 30.1 | | Inventory | 38.6 | 32.6 | 32.4 | 30.2 | | 23.2 |
| 1.7 | 2.7 | 3.1 | | All Other Current | .0 | .6 | 5.8 | 6.1 | | 4.1 |
| 55.3 | 58.1 | 55.8 | | Total Current | 56.5 | 55.9 | 67.6 | 56.2 | | 47.0 |
| 31.1 | 27.3 | 27.0 | | Fixed Assets (net) | 22.0 | 25.2 | 21.2 | 27.4 | | 36.7 |
| 6.6 | 7.1 | 8.7 | | Intangibles (net) | 19.7 | 9.0 | 6.1 | 7.3 | | 5.7 |
| 6.9 | 7.6 | 8.5 | | All Other Non-Current | 1.6 | 9.9 | 5.1 | 9.0 | | 10.6 |
| 100.0 | 100.0 | 100.0 | | Total | 100.0 | 100.0 | 100.0 | 100.0 | | 100.0 |
| | | | | LIABILITIES | | | | | | |
| 4.9 | 3.8 | 2.7 | | Notes Payable-Short Term | .0 | 5.1 | 5.1 | .3 | | 2.9 |
| 1.0 | 1.9 | 1.2 | | Cur. Mat.-L.T.D. | .0 | 2.3 | .0 | 1.0 | | .9 |
| 9.8 | 9.8 | 8.6 | | Trade Payables | 2.1 | 4.3 | 15.4 | 9.6 | | 19.0 |
| .5 | .0 | .1 | | Income Taxes Payable | .0 | .0 | .2 | .1 | | .0 |
| 8.5 | 8.2 | 11.6 | | All Other Current | 32.4 | 8.0 | 13.5 | 9.8 | | 10.6 |
| 24.8 | 23.7 | 24.1 | | Total Current | 34.5 | 19.7 | 34.2 | 20.8 | | 33.4 |
| 27.3 | 24.0 | 20.0 | | Long-Term Debt | 16.3 | 25.1 | 15.2 | 17.7 | | 15.7 |
| .1 | .0 | .1 | | Deferred Taxes | .0 | .0 | .0 | .0 | | .0 |
| 10.7 | 8.8 | 10.0 | | All Other Non-Current | 4.9 | 11.1 | 19.5 | 10.7 | | 9.0 |
| 37.2 | 43.5 | 45.7 | | Net Worth | 44.1 | 44.1 | 31.2 | 50.8 | | 40.9 |
| 100.0 | 100.0 | 100.0 | | Total Liabilties & Net Worth | 100.0 | 100.0 | 100.0 | 100.0 | | 100.0 |
| | | | | INCOME DATA | | | | | | |
| 100.0 | 100.0 | 100.0 | | Net Sales | 100.0 | 100.0 | 100.0 | 100.0 | | 100.0 |
| 21.9 | 19.6 | 23.6 | | Gross Profit | 33.9 | 25.9 | 19.9 | 21.9 | | 17.8 |
| 18.7 | 18.3 | 19.8 | | Operating Expenses | 33.3 | 21.0 | 15.6 | 17.4 | | 17.0 |
| 3.2 | 1.3 | 3.8 | | Operating Profit | .6 | 4.8 | 4.3 | 4.4 | | .8 |
| -1.1 | -1.6 | -.7 | | All Other Expenses (net) | -.2 | -1.7 | 1.0 | -.4 | | .0 |
| 4.3 | 2.9 | 4.5 | | Profit Before Taxes | .8 | 6.5 | 3.3 | 4.8 | | .8 |
| | | | | RATIOS | | | | | | |
| 8.8 | 9.0 | 13.3 | | | 18.7 | 16.3 | 23.6 | 14.8 | | 2.7 |
| 2.9 | 3.3 | 3.9 | | Current | 7.5 | 5.9 | 4.1 | 4.5 | | 1.4 |
| 1.5 | 1.6 | 1.4 | | | .8 | 1.7 | 1.1 | 1.7 | | 1.0 |
| 3.0 | 3.3 | 5.7 | | | | 8.5 | 9.7 | 4.0 | | 1.1 |
| 1.1 | 1.3 | 1.3 | | Quick | | 1.3 | 2.0 | 1.2 | | .5 |
| .5 | .6 | .4 | | | | .5 | .3 | .4 | | .4 |
| (101) | (106) | (105) | | | | | | (26) | | |
| 0 UND | 0 UND | 0 UND | | | 0 UND | 0 UND | 0 UND | 0 UND | | 0 861.3 |
| 0 UND | 0 UND | 0 UND | | Sales/Receivables | 0 UND | 0 UND | 0 UND | 0 UND | | 0 151.8 |
| 1 286.0 | 2 180.8 | 0 999.8 | | | 0 UND | 0 UND | 0 UND | 1 297.6 | | 7 50.4 |
| 8 44.2 | 7 50.0 | 9 40.8 | | | 33 11.1 | 17 21.3 | 9 41.4 | 8 44.7 | | 7 52.2 |
| 12 30.2 | 13 28.8 | 17 21.2 | | Cost of Sales/Inventory | 58 6.3 | 29 12.8 | 12 31.5 | 11 34.7 | | 13 28.4 |
| 24 15.5 | 24 15.0 | 35 10.4 | | | 146 2.5 | 72 5.1 | 17 21.5 | 20 18.1 | | 19 19.0 |
| 0 UND | 0 UND | 0 UND | | | 0 UND | 0 UND | 0 UND | 0 UND | | 7 53.9 |
| 3 129.1 | 2 232.3 | 0 UND | | Cost of Sales/Payables | 0 UND | 0 UND | 0 UND | 0 999.8 | | 9 42.4 |
| 10 37.4 | 9 42.3 | 8 44.9 | | | 8 45.7 | 3 142.9 | 9 40.9 | 9 40.7 | | 15 24.2 |
| 8.7 | 12.3 | 7.7 | | | 4.0 | 5.4 | 10.6 | 13.4 | | 27.9 |
| 28.7 | 26.6 | 21.4 | | Sales/Working Capital | 14.0 | 11.4 | 22.1 | 29.6 | | 93.4 |
| 55.1 | 55.6 | 60.8 | | | -10.9 | 34.6 | NM | 47.0 | | -999.8 |
| 26.8 | 26.3 | 18.5 | | | | 17.3 | | 34.6 | | |
| 8.4 | 8.7 | 5.8 | | EBIT/Interest | | 4.9 | | 7.0 | | |
| 4.8 | 2.5 | 1.6 | | | | 1.1 | | 3.2 | | |
| (57) | (58) | (50) | | | (16) | | | (14) | | |
| | | | | Net Profit + Depr., Dep., Amort./Cur. Mat. L/T/D | | | | | | |
| .1 | .1 | .1 | | | .1 | .0 | .1 | .2 | | .7 |
| .8 | .5 | .6 | | Fixed/Worth | .5 | .5 | 1.0 | .5 | | 1.0 |
| 4.1 | 4.4 | 2.9 | | | -1.4 | 2.7 | NM | 2.8 | | 9.9 |
| .3 | .3 | .2 | | | .1 | .2 | .6 | .3 | | .7 |
| 1.5 | 1.2 | 1.4 | | Debt/Worth | 2.3 | 1.7 | 1.5 | 1.1 | | 1.1 |
| 9.6 | 6.8 | 7.6 | | | -3.4 | 9.5 | NM | 4.1 | | 15.8 |
| 162.4 | 114.8 | 102.7 | | % Profit Before Taxes/Tangible | | 100.7 | | 121.2 | | 23.3 |
| 54.3 | 56.1 | 50.4 | | Net Worth | | 41.6 | | 75.5 | | 9.5 |
| 20.4 | 17.7 | 18.4 | | | | 17.4 | | 44.1 | | -14.6 |
| (86) | (92) | (89) | | | (30) | | (25) | | (11) | |
| 44.5 | 53.3 | 42.3 | | % Profit Before Taxes/Total | 17.0 | 37.4 | 38.3 | 58.9 | | 15.7 |
| 18.3 | 21.6 | 18.9 | | Assets | 4.0 | 17.4 | 29.0 | 24.9 | | 7.5 |
| 6.8 | 5.4 | 5.3 | | | -7.1 | 2.7 | 18.8 | 13.2 | | -1.8 |
| 166.5 | 193.1 | 152.7 | | | 60.9 | UND | 491.5 | 214.3 | | 53.5 |
| 29.7 | 47.5 | 44.9 | | Sales/Net Fixed Assets | 19.9 | 31.5 | 88.5 | 52.2 | | 16.5 |
| 6.0 | 12.1 | 8.9 | | | 7.7 | 7.0 | 45.1 | 13.9 | | 8.9 |
| 12.2 | 13.7 | 11.8 | | | 4.5 | 6.9 | 19.3 | 19.2 | | 14.5 |
| 5.3 | 7.0 | 4.8 | | Sales/Total Assets | 2.4 | 3.7 | 8.5 | 8.7 | | 5.9 |
| 3.3 | 3.4 | 2.6 | | | 1.1 | 2.4 | 6.4 | 3.7 | | 2.4 |
| .6 | .3 | .5 | | | | .3 | | | | |
| .9 | .6 | 1.0 | | % Depr., Dep., Amort./Sales | | .9 | | | | |
| 1.5 | 1.4 | 1.9 | | | | 1.3 | | | | |
| (55) | (57) | (54) | | | | (22) | | | | |
| .5 | .6 | .7 | | % Officers', Directors' | | 1.3 | | | | |
| 1.3 | 1.4 | 1.9 | | Owners' Comp/Sales | | 2.1 | | | | |
| 2.4 | 2.3 | 2.9 | | | | 2.8 | | | | |
| (36) | (39) | (40) | | | | (17) | | | | |
| 11892631M | 3393265M | 2449793M | | Net Sales ($) | 5236M | 68712M | 38756M | 194245M | 107852M | 2034992M |
| 1665821M | 956603M | 606987M | | Total Assets ($) | 2658M | 21618M | 4765M | 41092M | 16161M | 520693M |

M = $ thousand    MM = $ million
See Pages viii through xx for Explanation of Ratios and Data

© RMA 2024

# RETAIL—Meat Retailers  NAICS 445240

## Current Data Sorted by Assets | Comparative Historical Data

| | | | | | | Type of Statement | | | | |
|---|---|---|---|---|---|---|---|---|---|---|
| | | | | | | Unqualified | | | 1 | |
| 1 | 3 | 2 | | | | Reviewed | | | 4 | 2 |
| 3 | 5 | 3 | | | | Compiled | | | 12 | 8 |
| 4 | | | | | 2 | Tax Returns | | | 19 | 10 |
| 0-500M | 3 (4/1-9/30/23) 500M-2MM | 2-10MM | 22 (10/1/23-3/31/24) 10-50MM | 50-100MM | 100-250MM | Other | | | 4/1/19-3/31/20 | 4/1/20-3/31/21 |
| 8 | 8 | 7 | | | 2 | NUMBER OF STATEMENTS | | | ALL 36 | ALL 20 |
| % | % | % | % | % | % | | | | % | % |

| | | | | | | ASSETS | | | | |
|---|---|---|---|---|---|---|---|---|---|---|
| | | | DATA | DATA | | Cash & Equivalents | | | 20.3 | 26.5 |
| | | | | | | Trade Receivables (net) | | | 10.0 | 2.4 |
| | | | NOT | NOT | | Inventory | | | 20.9 | 16.0 |
| | | | | | | All Other Current | | | 8.6 | 6.0 |
| | | | AVAILABLE | AVAILABLE | | Total Current | | | 59.7 | 51.0 |
| | | | | | | Fixed Assets (net) | | | 23.6 | 31.3 |
| | | | | | | Intangibles (net) | | | 8.4 | 9.5 |
| | | | | | | All Other Non-Current | | | 8.3 | 8.2 |
| | | | | | | Total | | | 100.0 | 100.0 |

| | LIABILITIES | | |
|---|---|---|---|
| Notes Payable-Short Term | | 8.3 | 4.0 |
| Cur. Mat.-L.T.D. | | 5.2 | 1.2 |
| Trade Payables | | 15.3 | 9.0 |
| Income Taxes Payable | | .0 | .0 |
| All Other Current | | 20.3 | 17.1 |
| Total Current | | 49.1 | 31.3 |
| Long-Term Debt | | 14.5 | 20.8 |
| Deferred Taxes | | .0 | .3 |
| All Other Non-Current | | 2.9 | 2.7 |
| Net Worth | | 33.5 | 44.9 |
| Total Liabilities & Net Worth | | 100.0 | 100.0 |

| INCOME DATA | | | |
|---|---|---|---|
| Net Sales | | 100.0 | 100.0 |
| Gross Profit | | 36.3 | 37.1 |
| Operating Expenses | | 31.4 | 31.9 |
| Operating Profit | | 4.8 | 5.2 |
| All Other Expenses (net) | | .9 | -.8 |
| Profit Before Taxes | | 3.9 | 6.0 |

| RATIOS | | | | | |
|---|---|---|---|---|---|
| Current | | | 2.5 | | 5.2 |
| | | | 1.4 | | 2.0 |
| | | | .9 | | .7 |
| Quick | | | 1.5 | | 2.6 |
| | | | .6 | | 1.2 |
| | | | .3 | | .5 |
| Sales/Receivables | 0 | | 839.3 | 0 | UND |
| | 3 | | 117.2 | 0 | 999.8 |
| | 8 | | 44.8 | 4 | 92.4 |
| Cost of Sales/Inventory | 9 | | 40.0 | 6 | 58.5 |
| | 22 | | 16.8 | 17 | 22.0 |
| | 33 | | 10.9 | 28 | 12.9 |
| Cost of Sales/Payables | 2 | | 155.4 | 0 | UND |
| | 14 | | 26.0 | 8 | 47.1 |
| | 29 | | 12.5 | 24 | 15.2 |
| Sales/Working Capital | | | 13.9 | | 8.7 |
| | | | 52.4 | | 20.9 |
| | | | -99.6 | | -53.3 |
| EBIT/Interest | | | 34.0 | | 62.7 |
| | (30) | | 13.5 | (15) | 24.9 |
| | | | 3.4 | | 4.5 |
| Net Profit + Depr., Dep., Amort./Cur. Mat. L/T/D | | | | | |
| Fixed/Worth | | | .1 | | .3 |
| | | | .9 | | .8 |
| | | | 12.5 | | 6.3 |
| Debt/Worth | | | .3 | | .4 |
| | | | 2.7 | | 2.7 |
| | | | NM | | 29.5 |
| % Profit Before Taxes/Tangible Net Worth | | | 70.7 | | 281.6 |
| | (27) | | 34.7 | (18) | 60.8 |
| | | | 7.7 | | 19.5 |
| % Profit Before Taxes/Total Assets | | | 26.3 | | 51.2 |
| | | | 14.0 | | 19.1 |
| | | | 1.9 | | 7.9 |
| Sales/Net Fixed Assets | | | 126.3 | | 107.1 |
| | | | 31.7 | | 15.9 |
| | | | 10.6 | | 6.8 |
| Sales/Total Assets | | | 7.2 | | 7.6 |
| | | | 5.6 | | 3.8 |
| | | | 3.2 | | 2.3 |
| % Depr., Dep., Amort./Sales | | | .3 | | .3 |
| | (19) | | 1.1 | (10) | 1.1 |
| | | | 1.6 | | 3.0 |
| % Officers', Directors' Owners' Comp/Sales | | | 1.4 | | 2.8 |
| | (16) | | 4.0 | (14) | 3.9 |
| | | | 6.4 | | 6.2 |

| 15961M | 37908M | 183948M | | 1859863M | | Net Sales ($) | | | 1267723M | 652699M |
| 2033M | 9199M | 31948M | | 324190M | | Total Assets ($) | | | 427850M | 300782M |

© RMA 2024   M = $ thousand   MM = $ million
See Pages viii through xx for Explanation of Ratios and Data

# RETAIL—Meat Retailers  NAICS 445240

## Comparative Historical Data | Current Data Sorted by Sales

| | | | | Type of Statement | | | | | | |
|---|---|---|---|---|---|---|---|---|---|---|
| | 1 | 1 | | Unqualified | | | | | | |
| | | | | Reviewed | | 1 | | | 1 | |
| | 3 | 2 | 3 | Compiled | | 3 | | | 3 | |
| | 10 | 11 | 8 | Tax Returns | 2 | 6 | | 3 | | 3 |
| | 13 | 21 | 14 | Other | 1 | 3 (4/1-9/30/23) | 1 | 22 (10/1/23-3/31/24) | | |
| | 4/1/21-3/31/22 | 4/1/22-3/31/23 | 4/1/23-3/31/24 | | 0-1MM | 1-3MM | 3-5MM | 5-10MM | 10-25MM | 25MM & OVER |
| | ALL | ALL | ALL | | | | | | | |
| | 27 | 35 | 25 | NUMBER OF STATEMENTS | 3 | 10 | 1 | 3 | 4 | 4 |
| | % | % | % | ASSETS | % | % | % | % | % | % |
| | 21.8 | 20.6 | 14.8 | Cash & Equivalents | | 12.9 | | | | |
| | 7.7 | 9.5 | 6.1 | Trade Receivables (net) | | .8 | | | | |
| | 19.9 | 23.0 | 21.0 | Inventory | | 17.7 | | | | |
| | 5.1 | 5.7 | 11.8 | All Other Current | | 20.7 | | | | |
| | 54.6 | 58.8 | 53.7 | Total Current | | 52.0 | | | | |
| | 32.4 | 26.0 | 29.8 | Fixed Assets (net) | | 37.8 | | | | |
| | 9.7 | 8.1 | 11.3 | Intangibles (net) | | 5.6 | | | | |
| | 3.3 | 7.1 | 5.2 | All Other Non-Current | | 4.7 | | | | |
| | 100.0 | 100.0 | 100.0 | Total | | 100.0 | | | | |
| | | | | LIABILITIES | | | | | | |
| | 4.1 | 11.2 | 4.0 | Notes Payable-Short Term | | 6.9 | | | | |
| | 2.0 | 1.7 | 3.1 | Cur. Mat.-L.T.D. | | .5 | | | | |
| | 11.4 | 15.7 | 6.1 | Trade Payables | | 2.2 | | | | |
| | .1 | .1 | .2 | Income Taxes Payable | | .0 | | | | |
| | 11.9 | 28.3 | 15.9 | All Other Current | | 16.3 | | | | |
| | 29.5 | 57.0 | 29.2 | Total Current | | 26.0 | | | | |
| | 32.6 | 22.6 | 26.3 | Long-Term Debt | | 26.3 | | | | |
| | .1 | .0 | .0 | Deferred Taxes | | .0 | | | | |
| | 3.7 | 7.5 | 4.8 | All Other Non-Current | | 4.7 | | | | |
| | 34.1 | 12.8 | 39.7 | Net Worth | | 43.0 | | | | |
| | 100.0 | 100.0 | 100.0 | Total Liabilities & Net Worth | | 100.0 | | | | |
| | | | | INCOME DATA | | | | | | |
| | 100.0 | 100.0 | 100.0 | Net Sales | | 100.0 | | | | |
| | 33.7 | 38.7 | 38.4 | Gross Profit | | 48.6 | | | | |
| | 30.5 | 36.5 | 36.6 | Operating Expenses | | 44.7 | | | | |
| | 3.2 | 2.2 | 1.8 | Operating Profit | | 3.8 | | | | |
| | .0 | .9 | -.3 | All Other Expenses (net) | | -.5 | | | | |
| | 3.2 | 1.3 | 2.1 | Profit Before Taxes | | 4.3 | | | | |
| | | | | RATIOS | | | | | | |
| | 4.4 | 4.1 | 5.3 | | | 8.0 | | | | |
| | 2.3 | 1.9 | 2.2 | Current | | 2.6 | | | | |
| | 1.2 | .7 | .9 | | | .9 | | | | |
| | 2.7 | 2.0 | 2.9 | | | | | | | |
| | 1.2 | .7 | (24) .9 | Quick | | | | | | |
| | .7 | .2 | .3 | | | | | | | |
| 0 | UND | 0 UND | 0 UND | | 0 | UND | | | | |
| 2 | 204.3 | 0 841.2 | 0 UND | Sales/Receivables | 0 | UND | | | | |
| 11 | 32.3 | 15 25.0 | 7 55.2 | | 0 | UND | | | | |
| 7 | 53.9 | 6 63.2 | 10 37.5 | | 0 | UND | | | | |
| 16 | 23.5 | 19 19.2 | 18 20.8 | Cost of Sales/Inventory | 19 | 19.6 | | | | |
| 25 | 14.5 | 38 9.7 | 30 12.1 | | 33 | 10.9 | | | | |
| 0 | UND | 0 UND | 0 UND | | 0 | UND | | | | |
| 7 | 49.0 | 8 45.0 | 0 UND | Cost of Sales/Payables | 0 | UND | | | | |
| 20 | 18.4 | 28 13.0 | 13 27.1 | | 9 | 41.8 | | | | |
| | 10.2 | 11.4 | 10.9 | | | 9.1 | | | | |
| | 17.8 | 28.9 | 24.7 | Sales/Working Capital | | 23.7 | | | | |
| | 61.1 | -16.9 | -293.6 | | | -414.0 | | | | |
| | 27.4 | 28.4 | 42.9 | | | | | | | |
| (19) | 9.1 | (23) 5.6 | (17) 3.7 | EBIT/Interest | | | | | | |
| | 1.8 | 2.1 | .7 | | | | | | | |
| | | | | Net Profit + Depr., Dep., Amort./Cur. Mat. L/T/D | | | | | | |
| | .3 | .0 | .1 | | | .0 | | | | |
| | .9 | .7 | .7 | Fixed/Worth | | 1.9 | | | | |
| | 31.0 | -182.7 | NM | | | NM | | | | |
| | .5 | .8 | .3 | | | .2 | | | | |
| | 1.2 | 2.8 | 1.1 | Debt/Worth | | 1.7 | | | | |
| | 285.0 | -4.4 | -10.8 | | | NM | | | | |
| | 55.0 | 60.5 | 115.6 | % Profit Before Taxes/Tangible Net Worth | | | | | | |
| (21) | 24.2 | (23) 24.2 | (18) 22.9 | | | | | | | |
| | 10.0 | 7.9 | 3.5 | | | | | | | |
| | 20.0 | 25.1 | 45.5 | % Profit Before Taxes/Total Assets | | 33.7 | | | | |
| | 11.7 | 6.0 | 8.8 | | | 9.2 | | | | |
| | 3.9 | -2.6 | -1.0 | | | -.4 | | | | |
| | 48.8 | 767.9 | 271.2 | | | UND | | | | |
| | 21.6 | 43.5 | 21.0 | Sales/Net Fixed Assets | | 14.4 | | | | |
| | 7.6 | 8.7 | 4.5 | | | 2.9 | | | | |
| | 7.2 | 9.0 | 7.8 | | | 7.1 | | | | |
| | 4.0 | 5.5 | 4.3 | Sales/Total Assets | | 3.6 | | | | |
| | 2.5 | 3.1 | 1.7 | | | 1.4 | | | | |
| | .4 | .3 | .3 | | | | | | | |
| (15) | .7 | (13) 1.0 | (13) 1.6 | % Depr., Dep., Amort./Sales | | | | | | |
| | 1.8 | 2.6 | 3.4 | | | | | | | |
| | 1.6 | | .7 | % Officers', Directors' Owners' Comp/Sales | | | | | | |
| (14) | 2.7 | | (12) 1.8 | | | | | | | |
| | 4.4 | | 2.7 | | | | | | | |
| | 828931M | 1369076M | 2097680M | Net Sales ($) | 995M | 19357M | 4523M | 19966M | 81869M | 1970970M |
| | 297316M | 338291M | 367370M | Total Assets ($) | 1986M | 6902M | 135M | 7107M | 13944M | 337296M |

© RMA 2024   M = $ thousand   MM = $ million
See Pages viii through xx for Explanation of Ratios and Data

# RETAIL—Baked Goods Retailers  NAICS 445291

## Current Data Sorted by Assets

| | | | | | | Type of Statement | | |
|---|---|---|---|---|---|---|---|---|
| | | | | 1 | | Unqualified | | |
| | | | 1 | 1 | | Reviewed | | |
| 1 | | 2 | 1 | | 1 | Compiled | | |
| 11 | 10 | 2 | 2 | | | Tax Returns | | |
| 6 | 6 | 4 | 4 | 5 | | Other | | |
| | 2 (4/1-9/30/23) | | 48 (10/1/23-3/31/24) | | | | | |
| 0-500M | 500M-2MM | 2-10MM | 10-50MM | 50-100MM | 100-250MM | | | |
| 18 | 16 | 8 | 7 | 1 | | NUMBER OF STATEMENTS | | |
| % | % | % | % | % | % | ASSETS | | |
| 34.8 | 17.1 | | | | | Cash & Equivalents | | |
| .0 | .0 | | | | | Trade Receivables (net) | | |
| 3.2 | 2.7 | | | | D | Inventory | | |
| 1.3 | 3.4 | | | | A | All Other Current | | |
| 39.3 | 23.3 | | | | T | Total Current | | |
| 40.8 | 41.0 | | | | A | Fixed Assets (net) | | |
| 12.3 | 18.9 | | | | | Intangibles (net) | | |
| 7.7 | 16.8 | | | | N | All Other Non-Current | | |
| 100.0 | 100.0 | | | | O | Total | | |
| | | | | | T | LIABILITIES | | |
| 9.1 | 7.4 | | | | | Notes Payable-Short Term | | |
| 7.1 | 8.9 | | | | A | Cur. Mat.-L.T.D. | | |
| 5.9 | 1.1 | | | | V | Trade Payables | | |
| .0 | .0 | | | | A | Income Taxes Payable | | |
| 27.9 | 21.1 | | | | I | All Other Current | | |
| 49.9 | 38.5 | | | | L | Total Current | | |
| 73.4 | 21.7 | | | | A | Long-Term Debt | | |
| .0 | .0 | | | | B | Deferred Taxes | | |
| 8.2 | 4.5 | | | | L | All Other Non-Current | | |
| -31.5 | 35.3 | | | | E | Net Worth | | |
| 100.0 | 100.0 | | | | | Total Liabilties & Net Worth | | |
| | | | | | | INCOME DATA | | |
| 100.0 | 100.0 | | | | | Net Sales | | |
| 63.0 | 56.8 | | | | | Gross Profit | | |
| 56.3 | 50.6 | | | | | Operating Expenses | | |
| 6.6 | 6.2 | | | | | Operating Profit | | |
| 1.2 | -.3 | | | | | All Other Expenses (net) | | |
| 5.5 | 6.5 | | | | | Profit Before Taxes | | |

## Comparative Historical Data

| | | | |
|---|---|---|---|
| | | | 1 |
| | | 2 | 1 |
| | | 2 | 5 |
| | | 15 | 7 |
| | | 12 | 16 |
| | | 4/1/19-3/31/20 | 4/1/20-3/31/21 |
| | | ALL | ALL |
| | | 31 | 30 |
| | | % | % |
| Cash & Equivalents | | 19.4 | 29.7 |
| Trade Receivables (net) | | 9.7 | 1.0 |
| Inventory | | 6.5 | 3.0 |
| All Other Current | | 3.5 | 9.3 |
| Total Current | | 39.1 | 43.0 |
| Fixed Assets (net) | | 36.3 | 30.8 |
| Intangibles (net) | | 8.6 | 17.1 |
| All Other Non-Current | | 15.9 | 9.1 |
| Total | | 100.0 | 100.0 |
| Notes Payable-Short Term | | 5.1 | 3.2 |
| Cur. Mat.-L.T.D. | | 3.7 | 4.9 |
| Trade Payables | | 6.3 | 4.9 |
| Income Taxes Payable | | .4 | .1 |
| All Other Current | | 7.2 | 16.2 |
| Total Current | | 22.7 | 29.3 |
| Long-Term Debt | | 24.2 | 61.3 |
| Deferred Taxes | | .0 | .0 |
| All Other Non-Current | | 7.5 | 2.0 |
| Net Worth | | 45.6 | 7.4 |
| Total Liabilties & Net Worth | | 100.0 | 100.0 |
| Net Sales | | 100.0 | 100.0 |
| Gross Profit | | 58.3 | 58.7 |
| Operating Expenses | | 49.0 | 52.3 |
| Operating Profit | | 9.3 | 6.5 |
| All Other Expenses (net) | | 1.6 | -.1 |
| Profit Before Taxes | | 7.7 | 6.6 |

## RATIOS

| | | | | | | | | | | |
|---|---|---|---|---|---|---|---|---|---|---|
| 4.5 | | 1.2 | | | | | | Current | 3.7 | 5.5 |
| 1.0 | | .6 | | | | | | | 2.4 | 1.6 |
| .3 | | .3 | | | | | | | 1.2 | 1.1 |
| 3.3 | | .9 | | | | | | Quick | 2.8 | 4.9 |
| 1.0 | | .6 | | | | | | | 1.7 | 1.2 |
| .2 | | .2 | | | | | | | .6 | .7 |
| 0 | UND | 0 | UND | | | | | Sales/Receivables | 0 | UND | 0 | UND |
| 0 | UND | 0 | UND | | | | | | 2 | 226.7 | 0 | UND |
| 0 | UND | 0 | UND | | | | | | 20 | 18.2 | 0 | UND |
| 0 | UND | 0 | UND | | | | | Cost of Sales/Inventory | 2 | 147.0 | 1 | 531.2 |
| 0 | UND | 5 | 71.0 | | | | | | 7 | 52.8 | 3 | 133.7 |
| 5 | 73.4 | 9 | 38.6 | | | | | | 34 | 10.6 | 10 | 36.5 |
| 0 | UND | 0 | UND | | | | | Cost of Sales/Payables | 0 | UND | 0 | UND |
| 0 | UND | 6 | 65.9 | | | | | | 6 | 60.2 | 12 | 31.2 |
| 8 | 46.8 | 8 | 45.6 | | | | | | 26 | 14.1 | 21 | 17.6 |
| 9.1 | | 43.1 | | | | | | Sales/Working Capital | 8.7 | 7.1 |
| UND | | -31.7 | | | | | | | 14.9 | 19.1 |
| -19.2 | | -7.7 | | | | | | | 90.9 | 250.0 |
| 12.5 | | | | | | | | EBIT/Interest | 32.7 | 21.9 |
| (12) 5.3 | | | | | | | | | (23) 5.0 | (19) 4.2 |
| 2.0 | | | | | | | | | 1.5 | .0 |
| | | | | | | | | Net Profit + Depr., Dep., Amort./Cur. Mat. L/T/D | | |
| .4 | | .8 | | | | | | Fixed/Worth | .4 | .5 |
| -28.9 | | 2.1 | | | | | | | .7 | 2.0 |
| -.3 | | -2.0 | | | | | | | 10.5 | -17.1 |
| 1.4 | | .6 | | | | | | Debt/Worth | .3 | .8 |
| -7.2 | | 3.9 | | | | | | | 1.2 | 4.7 |
| -2.1 | | -5.8 | | | | | | | 17.3 | -3.6 |
| | | 156.8 | | | | | | % Profit Before Taxes/Tangible Net Worth | 120.6 | 271.4 |
| | (10) | 60.2 | | | | | | | (26) 55.1 | (19) 99.5 |
| | | 25.7 | | | | | | | 22.0 | 30.1 |
| 133.3 | | 66.6 | | | | | | % Profit Before Taxes/Total Assets | 47.8 | 38.3 |
| 29.1 | | 13.8 | | | | | | | 18.3 | 15.6 |
| -4.6 | | 5.5 | | | | | | | 6.1 | 1.2 |
| UND | | 14.1 | | | | | | Sales/Net Fixed Assets | 37.9 | 15.8 |
| 30.3 | | 6.0 | | | | | | | 11.8 | 9.1 |
| 5.8 | | 4.1 | | | | | | | 5.9 | 5.5 |
| 18.5 | | 4.0 | | | | | | Sales/Total Assets | 4.9 | 3.5 |
| 4.6 | | 1.9 | | | | | | | 3.4 | 2.0 |
| 2.8 | | 1.3 | | | | | | | 1.4 | 1.4 |
| | | 1.3 | | | | | | % Depr., Dep., Amort./Sales | 1.4 | 1.6 |
| | (10) | 2.0 | | | | | | | (24) 2.5 | (17) 3.0 |
| | | 3.2 | | | | | | | 3.8 | 5.6 |
| | | | | | | | | % Officers', Directors' Owners' Comp/Sales | 3.1 | |
| | | | | | | | | | (13) 5.3 | |
| | | | | | | | | | 6.4 | |
| 15466M | 40065M | 62220M | 147041M | 59574M | | Net Sales ($) | 313520M | 98237M |
| 3078M | 15714M | 30826M | 124942M | 74502M | | Total Assets ($) | 256633M | 54590M |

© RMA 2024

M = $ thousand    MM = $ million
See Pages viii through xx for Explanation of Ratios and Data

# RETAIL—Baked Goods Retailers  NAICS 445291

## Comparative Historical Data | Current Data Sorted by Sales

| Comparative Historical Data | | | | | Current Data Sorted by Sales | | | | | |
|---|---|---|---|---|---|---|---|---|---|---|
| 1 | 2 | 1 | **Type of Statement** | | | | | 1 | | |
| | 1 | 2 | Unqualified | | | | | 1 | 1 | |
| | 4 | 3 | Reviewed | | 1 | | 1 | 1 | 1 | 1 |
| 12 | 16 | 23 | Compiled | 8 | 10 | 2 | 2 | 2 | 1 | |
| 7 | 12 | 21 | Tax Returns | 5 | 6 | 3 | 3 | 3 | 3 | 2 |
| 4/1/21- | 4/1/22- | 4/1/23- | Other | | 2 (4/1-9/30/23) | | 48 (10/1/23-3/31/24) | | | |
| 3/31/22 | 3/31/23 | 3/31/24 | | | | | | | | |
| ALL | ALL | ALL | | 0-1MM | 1-3MM | 3-5MM | 5-10MM | 10-25MM | 25MM & OVER | |
| 21 | 35 | 50 | **NUMBER OF STATEMENTS** | 13 | 17 | 5 | 5 | 7 | 3 | |
| % | % | % | **ASSETS** | % | % | % | % | % | % | |
| 45.5 | 28.6 | 21.3 | Cash & Equivalents | 34.9 | 23.7 | | | | | |
| 5.0 | 4.8 | 1.9 | Trade Receivables (net) | .0 | .0 | | | | | |
| 3.5 | 6.4 | 4.5 | Inventory | 2.7 | 2.9 | | | | | |
| 2.3 | 3.8 | 1.7 | All Other Current | 2.9 | 2.4 | | | | | |
| 56.4 | 43.4 | 29.4 | Total Current | 40.5 | 29.0 | | | | | |
| 28.7 | 33.2 | 41.4 | Fixed Assets (net) | 48.7 | 32.3 | | | | | |
| 11.5 | 13.0 | 15.9 | Intangibles (net) | 7.3 | 23.1 | | | | | |
| 3.4 | 10.2 | 13.4 | All Other Non-Current | 3.5 | 15.6 | | | | | |
| 100.0 | 100.0 | 100.0 | Total | 100.0 | 100.0 | | | | | |
| | | | **LIABILITIES** | | | | | | | |
| 3.5 | 2.3 | 6.4 | Notes Payable-Short Term | 19.1 | 2.0 | | | | | |
| 8.7 | 8.4 | 6.2 | Cur. Mat.-L.T.D. | 1.5 | 7.2 | | | | | |
| 6.0 | 5.5 | 4.5 | Trade Payables | .5 | 6.6 | | | | | |
| .0 | .1 | .0 | Income Taxes Payable | .0 | .0 | | | | | |
| 12.0 | 16.8 | 18.5 | All Other Current | 19.3 | 31.6 | | | | | |
| 30.1 | 32.9 | 35.6 | Total Current | 40.4 | 47.3 | | | | | |
| 31.6 | 26.4 | 44.3 | Long-Term Debt | 93.2 | 15.3 | | | | | |
| .0 | .0 | .0 | Deferred Taxes | .0 | .0 | | | | | |
| 5.2 | 9.4 | 7.5 | All Other Non-Current | .0 | 12.9 | | | | | |
| 33.1 | 31.3 | 12.6 | Net Worth | -33.6 | 24.5 | | | | | |
| 100.0 | 100.0 | 100.0 | Total Liabilities & Net Worth | 100.0 | 100.0 | | | | | |
| | | | **INCOME DATA** | | | | | | | |
| 100.0 | 100.0 | 100.0 | Net Sales | 100.0 | 100.0 | | | | | |
| 54.2 | 49.6 | 54.8 | Gross Profit | 62.1 | 62.3 | | | | | |
| 39.9 | 44.2 | 49.0 | Operating Expenses | 56.8 | 53.1 | | | | | |
| 14.3 | 5.4 | 5.8 | Operating Profit | 5.3 | 9.2 | | | | | |
| -2.3 | -.1 | .4 | All Other Expenses (net) | 3.3 | -1.6 | | | | | |
| 16.6 | 5.5 | 5.4 | Profit Before Taxes | 2.0 | 10.8 | | | | | |
| | | | **RATIOS** | | | | | | | |
| 8.5 | 3.2 | 3.2 | | 7.8 | 1.5 | | | | | |
| 1.8 | 1.9 | 1.0 | Current | 1.1 | .8 | | | | | |
| 1.3 | .9 | .4 | | .2 | .4 | | | | | |
| 7.2 | 2.7 | 2.3 | | 3.2 | 1.3 | | | | | |
| 1.8 | 1.4 | .8 | Quick | 1.0 | .6 | | | | | |
| .8 | .6 | .3 | | .2 | .2 | | | | | |
| 0 UND | 0 UND | 0 UND | | 0 UND | 0 UND | | | | | |
| 0 UND | 0 UND | 0 UND | Sales/Receivables | 0 UND | 0 UND | | | | | |
| 1 312.7 | 9 42.1 | 0 UND | | 0 UND | 0 UND | | | | | |
| 1 543.8 | 0 UND | 0 UND | | 0 UND | 0 UND | | | | | |
| 5 71.1 | 3 130.8 | 4 92.6 | Cost of Sales/Inventory | 0 UND | 4 91.8 | | | | | |
| 13 28.1 | 14 26.8 | 9 39.7 | | 6 58.0 | 9 39.6 | | | | | |
| 0 UND | 0 UND | 0 UND | | 0 UND | 0 UND | | | | | |
| 3 141.3 | 6 59.1 | 6 65.9 | Cost of Sales/Payables | 0 UND | 8 48.1 | | | | | |
| 18 20.3 | 19 19.1 | 12 31.4 | | 0 UND | 10 38.4 | | | | | |
| 6.2 | 7.3 | 23.4 | | 5.9 | 39.2 | | | | | |
| 11.6 | 34.6 | UND | Sales/Working Capital | 41.7 | -65.5 | | | | | |
| 52.2 | -53.2 | -16.3 | | -17.5 | -13.5 | | | | | |
| 38.3 | 51.2 | 12.5 | | | | | | | | |
| (13) 15.6 | (26) 10.2 | (36) 6.4 | EBIT/Interest | | | | | | | |
| 5.3 | 1.2 | 1.5 | | | | | | | | |
| | | | Net Profit + Depr., Dep., Amort./Cur. Mat. L/T/D | | | | | | | |
| .2 | .2 | .8 | | .5 | .6 | | | | | |
| .9 | 1.0 | 2.5 | Fixed/Worth | -128.0 | 2.3 | | | | | |
| 2.0 | 4.4 | -1.2 | | -3.2 | -.5 | | | | | |
| .4 | .5 | .8 | | 1.4 | .4 | | | | | |
| 1.9 | 1.6 | 20.9 | Debt/Worth | -8.8 | 5.6 | | | | | |
| 29.0 | 17.2 | -4.5 | | -4.3 | -2.2 | | | | | |
| 190.3 | 75.7 | 114.4 | | 264.0 | | | | | | |
| (17) 87.5 | (27) 34.4 | (28) 40.0 | % Profit Before Taxes/Tangible Net Worth | (10) 97.0 | | | | | | |
| 27.1 | 6.3 | 12.2 | | 33.0 | | | | | | |
| 73.8 | 30.0 | 49.8 | | 36.1 | 88.5 | | | | | | |
| 40.0 | 9.9 | 11.7 | % Profit Before Taxes/Total Assets | 12.4 | 32.9 | | | | | |
| 14.7 | -1.4 | 2.1 | | -45.3 | 13.6 | | | | | |
| 46.7 | 121.7 | 28.7 | | UND | 32.7 | | | | | |
| 16.1 | 8.1 | 6.3 | Sales/Net Fixed Assets | 5.9 | 14.8 | | | | | |
| 4.9 | 4.5 | 3.6 | | 2.0 | 6.0 | | | | | |
| 5.0 | 4.1 | 4.5 | | 6.6 | 9.7 | | | | | |
| 2.8 | 2.4 | 2.1 | Sales/Total Assets | 3.2 | 3.3 | | | | | |
| 1.6 | 1.7 | 1.3 | | 1.4 | 1.4 | | | | | |
| .4 | 1.4 | 1.2 | | | .9 | | | | | |
| (15) 1.3 | (20) 2.0 | (31) 2.2 | % Depr., Dep., Amort./Sales | (11) | 1.9 | | | | | |
| 1.7 | 3.3 | 4.4 | | | 2.3 | | | | | |
| 2.7 | 2.7 | .9 | | | | | | | | |
| (11) 3.6 | (13) 4.8 | (17) 2.1 | % Officers', Directors' Owners' Comp/Sales | | | | | | | |
| 7.2 | 7.0 | 4.7 | | | | | | | | |
| 150510M | 540729M | 324366M | Net Sales ($) | 6691M | 28036M | 18534M | 35753M | 115989M | 119363M | |
| 101225M | 456075M | 249062M | Total Assets ($) | 3237M | 11054M | 11130M | 13311M | 79495M | 130835M | |

© RMA 2024   M = $ thousand   MM = $ million
See Pages viii through xx for Explanation of Ratios and Data

# RETAIL—All Other Specialty Food Retailers  NAICS 445298

## Current Data Sorted by Assets | Comparative Historical Data

| | | | | | | | Type of Statement | | | | |
|---|---|---|---|---|---|---|---|---|---|---|---|
| | | | 1 | | 1 | 1 | Unqualified | | 3 | | 2 |
| | | | 1 | | 1 | | Reviewed | | 4 | | 2 |
| | | 4 | 3 | | | | Compiled | | 7 | | 5 |
| 14 | | 7 | 6 | 1 | | | Tax Returns | | 46 | | 36 |
| 8 | | 16 | 20 | 17 | 6 | | Other | | 46 | | 42 |
| | 9 (4/1-9/30/23) | | | 98 (10/1/23-3/31/24) | | | | | 4/1/19-3/31/20 | | 4/1/20-3/31/21 |
| 0-500M | 500M-2MM | 2-10MM | 10-50MM | 50-100MM | 100-250MM | | | | ALL | | ALL |
| 22 | 27 | 31 | 18 | 8 | 1 | | NUMBER OF STATEMENTS | | 106 | | 87 |
| % | % | % | % | % | % | | ASSETS | | % | | % |
| 23.8 | 32.4 | 12.3 | 9.0 | | | | Cash & Equivalents | | 18.0 | | 28.4 |
| 1.5 | 7.5 | 8.7 | 10.4 | | | | Trade Receivables (net) | | 4.5 | | 4.5 |
| 16.2 | 16.7 | 18.6 | 21.6 | | | | Inventory | | 16.7 | | 13.5 |
| .8 | 1.2 | 7.4 | 4.1 | | | | All Other Current | | 2.1 | | 2.2 |
| 42.3 | 57.8 | 47.1 | 45.1 | | | | Total Current | | 41.3 | | 48.5 |
| 24.4 | 29.4 | 38.3 | 19.5 | | | | Fixed Assets (net) | | 39.8 | | 30.3 |
| 23.1 | 7.9 | 5.3 | 14.4 | | | | Intangibles (net) | | 9.7 | | 14.0 |
| 10.1 | 5.0 | 9.3 | 21.0 | | | | All Other Non-Current | | 9.3 | | 7.2 |
| 100.0 | 100.0 | 100.0 | 100.0 | | | | Total | | 100.0 | | 100.0 |
| | | | | | | | LIABILITIES | | | | |
| 14.4 | 4.5 | 7.1 | 4.6 | | | | Notes Payable-Short Term | | 6.2 | | 9.0 |
| 2.3 | 3.0 | 1.0 | .8 | | | | Cur. Mat.-L.T.D. | | 5.2 | | 1.9 |
| 5.4 | 9.7 | 10.4 | 17.3 | | | | Trade Payables | | 12.3 | | 9.6 |
| .1 | .0 | .3 | .0 | | | | Income Taxes Payable | | .3 | | .3 |
| 17.7 | 8.9 | 11.4 | 16.6 | | | | All Other Current | | 15.0 | | 10.1 |
| 39.9 | 26.1 | 30.2 | 39.3 | | | | Total Current | | 39.0 | | 30.8 |
| 20.4 | 23.4 | 23.5 | 11.5 | | | | Long-Term Debt | | 24.7 | | 33.3 |
| .0 | .0 | .0 | .1 | | | | Deferred Taxes | | .2 | | .0 |
| 11.6 | 11.8 | 5.1 | 17.3 | | | | All Other Non-Current | | 10.2 | | 8.9 |
| 28.1 | 38.6 | 41.1 | 31.8 | | | | Net Worth | | 25.9 | | 27.0 |
| 100.0 | 100.0 | 100.0 | 100.0 | | | | Total Liabilities & Net Worth | | 100.0 | | 100.0 |
| | | | | | | | INCOME DATA | | | | |
| 100.0 | 100.0 | 100.0 | 100.0 | | | | Net Sales | | 100.0 | | 100.0 |
| 55.6 | 52.8 | 42.3 | 34.7 | | | | Gross Profit | | 50.2 | | 48.8 |
| 47.5 | 42.4 | 37.0 | 30.0 | | | | Operating Expenses | | 44.7 | | 44.8 |
| 8.1 | 10.4 | 5.3 | 4.7 | | | | Operating Profit | | 5.4 | | 4.1 |
| 1.7 | 1.0 | .7 | -.9 | | | | All Other Expenses (net) | | .6 | | -.6 |
| 6.4 | 9.5 | 4.6 | 5.6 | | | | Profit Before Taxes | | 4.8 | | 4.6 |
| | | | | | | | RATIOS | | | | |
| 2.6 | 11.9 | 3.5 | 2.7 | | | | | | 3.6 | | 4.7 |
| 1.2 | 2.2 | 1.6 | 1.9 | | | | Current | | 1.5 | | 2.0 |
| .7 | 1.0 | .8 | .9 | | | | | | .6 | | 1.1 |
| 2.2 | 5.2 | 2.1 | 1.1 | | | | | | 2.1 | | 3.2 |
| .7 | 2.0 | (30) 1.0 | .8 | | | | Quick | (105) | .8 | | 1.6 |
| .4 | .5 | .3 | .3 | | | | | | .3 | | .6 |
| 0 UND | 0 UND | 1 545.5 | 1 667.0 | | | | | 0 | UND | 0 | UND |
| 0 UND | 2 201.3 | 4 82.1 | 11 32.9 | | | | Sales/Receivables | 0 | 999.8 | 0 | UND |
| 0 UND | 8 46.5 | 17 21.9 | 29 12.4 | | | | | 4 | 91.7 | 3 | 106.6 |
| 0 UND | 4 96.8 | 8 48.1 | 34 10.8 | | | | | 8 | 47.1 | 5 | 78.1 |
| 12 29.6 | 21 17.0 | 25 14.7 | 53 6.9 | | | | Cost of Sales/Inventory | 18 | 20.1 | 11 | 32.8 |
| 58 6.3 | 57 6.4 | 72 5.1 | 65 5.6 | | | | | 41 | 8.9 | 39 | 9.3 |
| 0 UND | 0 UND | 3 106.0 | 12 29.9 | | | | | 0 | UND | 0 | UND |
| 0 UND | 8 47.0 | 17 21.2 | 28 13.0 | | | | Cost of Sales/Payables | 13 | 29.1 | 10 | 37.6 |
| 13 28.6 | 35 10.5 | 33 11.1 | 49 7.5 | | | | | 33 | 11.2 | 27 | 13.5 |
| 31.7 | 5.5 | 10.8 | 7.5 | | | | | | 14.0 | | 8.6 |
| 102.7 | 11.3 | 18.9 | 16.2 | | | | Sales/Working Capital | | 43.6 | | 17.4 |
| -39.9 | -788.0 | -46.6 | -59.5 | | | | | | -21.6 | | 130.7 |
| 66.0 | 27.1 | 11.2 | 41.4 | | | | | | 9.7 | | 39.7 |
| (11) 13.4 | (17) 10.2 | (26) 3.7 | (15) 7.1 | | | | EBIT/Interest | (70) | 3.9 | (65) | 7.0 |
| .9 | .5 | .3 | .7 | | | | | | .2 | | 1.4 |
| | | | | | | | Net Profit + Depr., Dep., Amort./Cur. Mat. L/T/D | | | | |
| .0 | .0 | .4 | .2 | | | | | | .6 | | .2 |
| 1.6 | .6 | 1.1 | .5 | | | | Fixed/Worth | | 1.1 | | 1.3 |
| -1.3 | -4.0 | 2.3 | NM | | | | | | -8.7 | | -9.6 |
| .6 | .4 | .4 | .9 | | | | | | .3 | | .9 |
| 4.8 | 1.1 | 1.4 | 3.0 | | | | Debt/Worth | | 2.3 | | 2.7 |
| -3.6 | -6.9 | 3.0 | NM | | | | | | -11.5 | | -7.2 |
| 299.9 | 59.5 | 52.1 | 71.9 | | | | | | 74.5 | | 131.1 |
| (14) 122.9 | (20) 21.3 | (26) 17.3 | (14) 44.1 | | | | % Profit Before Taxes/Tangible Net Worth | (73) | 27.5 | (58) | 58.7 |
| 48.8 | -10.9 | 1.8 | 21.2 | | | | | | 14.8 | | 26.4 |
| 43.0 | 40.5 | 21.4 | 28.3 | | | | | | 36.6 | | 45.3 |
| 26.6 | 17.3 | 6.8 | 9.4 | | | | % Profit Before Taxes/Total Assets | | 10.6 | | 22.4 |
| -13.4 | -1.6 | .2 | -2.4 | | | | | | -.6 | | .3 |
| UND | 121.8 | 24.0 | 45.2 | | | | | | 32.7 | | 70.3 |
| 46.1 | 14.2 | 9.9 | 18.0 | | | | Sales/Net Fixed Assets | | 13.4 | | 12.9 |
| 8.2 | 5.7 | 2.3 | 9.6 | | | | | | 4.8 | | 4.5 |
| 5.0 | 4.8 | 4.3 | 3.4 | | | | | | 7.8 | | 5.8 |
| 3.8 | 2.3 | 2.9 | 2.2 | | | | Sales/Total Assets | | 4.3 | | 3.0 |
| 2.4 | 1.4 | 1.8 | 1.1 | | | | | | 1.8 | | 1.8 |
| | .8 | 1.0 | .4 | | | | | | .9 | | .8 |
| | (11) 2.2 | (19) 1.4 | (14) .9 | | | | % Depr., Dep., Amort./Sales | (79) | 1.5 | (53) | 1.6 |
| | 4.9 | 3.9 | 1.7 | | | | | | 3.3 | | 3.9 |
| | 2.0 | 1.5 | | | | | | | 2.2 | | 1.9 |
| (10) | 3.2 | (10) 2.0 | | | | | % Officers', Directors' Owners' Comp/Sales | (42) | 3.9 | (40) | 3.5 |
| | 4.2 | 4.4 | | | | | | | 5.9 | | 6.2 |
| 21409M | 76896M | 445847M | 1033121M | 1211785M | 200406M | | Net Sales ($) | | 1503809M | | 1169854M |
| 5528M | 27688M | 156921M | 418790M | 598248M | 203954M | | Total Assets ($) | | 754919M | | 484276M |

© RMA 2024   M = $ thousand   MM = $ million
See Pages viii through xx for Explanation of Ratios and Data

# RETAIL—All Other Specialty Food Retailers NAICS 445298

## Comparative Historical Data | Current Data Sorted by Sales

| | | | | | | | | | | | |
|---|---|---|---|---|---|---|---|---|---|---|---|
| | | | | **Type of Statement** | | | | | 1 | 2 | |
| 4 | 5 | 3 | | Unqualified | | | | 1 | 1 | 1 | |
| 2 | 4 | 2 | | Reviewed | 2 | 2 | | 2 | 1 | 1 | |
| 11 | 10 | 8 | | Compiled | 8 | 11 | 2 | 1 | 4 | 1 | |
| 31 | 32 | 27 | | Tax Returns | 6 | 11 | 7 | 1 | 10 | 22 | |
| 44 | 56 | 67 | | Other | | | | | | | |
| 4/1/21-3/31/22 | 4/1/22-3/31/23 | 4/1/23-3/31/24 | | | | 9 (4/1-9/30/23) | | 98 (10/1/23-3/31/24) | | | |
| ALL | ALL | ALL | | | 0-1MM | 1-3MM | 3-5MM | 5-10MM | 10-25MM | 25MM & OVER | |
| 92 | 107 | 107 | | **NUMBER OF STATEMENTS** | 16 | 24 | 9 | 15 | 16 | 27 | |
| % | % | % | | **ASSETS** | % | % | % | % | % | % | |
| 25.0 | 24.4 | 19.5 | | Cash & Equivalents | 20.8 | 30.5 | | 11.7 | 13.7 | 14.0 | |
| 3.1 | 6.8 | 6.8 | | Trade Receivables (net) | 1.6 | 6.9 | | 4.7 | 10.7 | 9.8 | |
| 13.7 | 18.7 | 17.5 | | Inventory | 15.3 | 14.9 | | 23.8 | 18.3 | 21.2 | |
| 2.3 | 5.8 | 3.8 | | All Other Current | .4 | 1.1 | | 5.9 | 9.7 | 4.6 | |
| 44.1 | 55.7 | 47.6 | | Total Current | 38.1 | 53.3 | | 46.1 | 52.4 | 49.6 | |
| 36.1 | 27.7 | 27.7 | | Fixed Assets (net) | 32.1 | 23.8 | | 36.2 | 22.5 | 19.3 | |
| 12.6 | 8.3 | 13.1 | | Intangibles (net) | 16.1 | 17.0 | | 6.6 | 15.8 | 12.6 | |
| 7.2 | 8.3 | 11.5 | | All Other Non-Current | 13.7 | 5.8 | | 11.1 | 9.4 | 18.5 | |
| 100.0 | 100.0 | 100.0 | | Total | 100.0 | 100.0 | | 100.0 | 100.0 | 100.0 | |
| | | | | **LIABILITIES** | | | | | | | |
| 3.2 | 4.8 | 7.2 | | Notes Payable-Short Term | 16.1 | 6.8 | | 8.8 | 5.1 | 4.3 | |
| 2.6 | 1.9 | 1.7 | | Cur. Mat.-L.T.D. | 2.8 | 1.3 | | 2.7 | .1 | 1.0 | |
| 8.4 | 12.6 | 10.2 | | Trade Payables | 3.4 | 9.5 | | 3.3 | 12.3 | 16.1 | |
| .1 | .1 | .1 | | Income Taxes Payable | .2 | .0 | | .1 | .1 | .3 | |
| 13.0 | 11.7 | 12.7 | | All Other Current | 18.8 | 12.2 | | 3.9 | 24.2 | 10.1 | |
| 27.2 | 31.0 | 31.9 | | Total Current | 41.3 | 29.8 | | 18.8 | 41.8 | 31.9 | |
| 31.0 | 26.3 | 19.6 | | Long-Term Debt | 18.2 | 20.9 | | 26.8 | 17.8 | 11.5 | |
| .1 | .2 | .0 | | Deferred Taxes | .0 | .0 | | .0 | .0 | .1 | |
| 8.1 | 13.9 | 11.7 | | All Other Non-Current | 20.3 | 6.1 | | 2.7 | 10.4 | 16.7 | |
| 33.6 | 28.5 | 36.8 | | Net Worth | 20.3 | 43.3 | | 51.7 | 30.1 | 39.8 | |
| 100.0 | 100.0 | 100.0 | | Total Liabilities & Net Worth | 100.0 | 100.0 | | 100.0 | 100.0 | 100.0 | |
| | | | | **INCOME DATA** | | | | | | | |
| 100.0 | 100.0 | 100.0 | | Net Sales | 100.0 | 100.0 | | 100.0 | 100.0 | 100.0 | |
| 49.1 | 48.1 | 46.3 | | Gross Profit | 57.9 | 54.4 | | 44.7 | 42.7 | 33.3 | |
| 41.7 | 43.4 | 39.4 | | Operating Expenses | 48.0 | 42.1 | | 41.4 | 37.4 | 29.6 | |
| 7.5 | 4.7 | 7.0 | | Operating Profit | 9.9 | 12.3 | | 3.3 | 5.4 | 3.8 | |
| -1.7 | -.5 | .7 | | All Other Expenses (net) | 3.4 | 1.0 | | -1.3 | 1.3 | .4 | |
| 9.1 | 5.2 | 6.2 | | Profit Before Taxes | 6.6 | 11.3 | | 4.6 | 4.1 | 3.4 | |
| | | | | **RATIOS** | | | | | | | |
| 5.7 | 5.6 | 3.1 | | | 2.8 | 5.4 | | 5.6 | 3.8 | 2.7 | |
| 2.3 | 2.3 | 1.8 | | Current | 1.0 | 2.0 | | 2.2 | 1.5 | 1.9 | |
| .8 | 1.2 | .9 | | | .7 | .9 | | 1.1 | .8 | 1.1 | |
| 3.4 | 3.9 | 2.1 | | | 2.8 | 4.5 | | 3.4 | 1.9 | 1.3 | |
| 1.2 | 1.3 | (106) .9 | | Quick | .5 | 1.3 | (14) | 1.3 | .9 | .8 | |
| .5 | .4 | .4 | | | .3 | .5 | | .3 | .3 | .4 | |
| 0 UND | 0 UND | 0 UND | | | 0 UND | 0 UND | | 0 999.8 | 1 248.5 | 2 191.1 | |
| 0 UND | 1 256.0 | 3 142.9 | | Sales/Receivables | 0 UND | 0 UND | | 4 82.1 | 10 36.6 | 8 46.0 | |
| 5 79.3 | 14 25.6 | 13 28.5 | | | 0 UND | 7 50.1 | | 11 33.7 | 26 13.9 | 20 18.2 | |
| 2 181.3 | 5 79.8 | 6 59.3 | | | 0 UND | 5 74.3 | 13 27.6 | 7 50.6 | 24 15.5 | | |
| 14 25.6 | 24 15.3 | 29 12.8 | | Cost of Sales/Inventory | 4 95.8 | 18 20.6 | 43 8.4 | 26 13.8 | 39 9.4 | | |
| 43 8.4 | 70 5.2 | 59 6.2 | | | 107 3.4 | 57 6.4 | 83 4.4 | 74 4.9 | 54 6.7 | | |
| 0 UND | 0 UND | 0 UND | | | 0 UND | 0 UND | | 0 999.8 | 15 24.3 | 15 24.4 | |
| 8 44.7 | 11 34.2 | 15 24.4 | | Cost of Sales/Payables | 0 UND | 8 46.2 | | 6 56.8 | 27 13.4 | 21 17.1 | |
| 25 14.6 | 29 12.8 | 37 9.9 | | | 0 UND | 36 10.1 | | 22 16.5 | 49 7.4 | 38 9.5 | |
| 6.4 | 5.4 | 7.8 | | | 33.2 | 7.0 | | 7.8 | 7.5 | 7.6 | |
| 22.5 | 13.9 | 18.8 | | Sales/Working Capital | NM | 18.3 | | 13.6 | 10.4 | 11.5 | |
| -102.0 | 84.0 | -113.1 | | | -31.6 | -293.2 | | 313.6 | -33.7 | 206.0 | |
| 57.8 | 29.1 | 29.3 | | | | 45.7 | | 12.5 | 34.1 | 45.5 | |
| (75) 14.0 | (76) 7.3 | (75) 5.0 | | EBIT/Interest | (13) | 3.2 | (12) | 3.8 | (12) 4.0 | (23) 5.6 | |
| 2.4 | .6 | .0 | | | | 1.0 | | 2.4 | -1.0 | -.9 | |
| | | | | Net Profit + Depr., Dep., Amort./Cur. Mat. L/T/D | | | | | | | |
| .4 | .2 | .2 | | | 1.0 | .0 | | .1 | .2 | .4 | |
| 1.5 | .8 | 1.0 | | Fixed/Worth | 2.0 | .3 | | 1.0 | .9 | .6 | |
| -20.8 | UND | 4.6 | | | -.7 | 8.5 | | 2.2 | -1.1 | 2.4 | |
| .4 | .4 | .6 | | | .6 | .4 | | .3 | .9 | .6 | |
| 2.2 | 1.6 | 2.3 | | Debt/Worth | 10.2 | 1.5 | | 1.3 | 2.6 | 3.4 | |
| -28.9 | -10.6 | 55.0 | | | -3.4 | 17.0 | | 2.5 | -4.3 | 5.3 | |
| 119.0 | 57.4 | 77.2 | | % Profit Before Taxes/Tangible Net Worth | 283.1 | 78.1 | | 36.4 | | 89.3 | |
| (66) 54.3 | (78) 30.1 | (82) 37.3 | | | (10) 122.9 | (19) 46.2 | | (14) 16.0 | (24) | 39.4 | |
| 32.4 | 11.3 | 1.9 | | | 48.3 | 1.8 | | 5.8 | | -35.4 | |
| 47.1 | 26.5 | 33.2 | | % Profit Before Taxes/Total Assets | 33.3 | 41.2 | | 20.5 | 22.0 | 27.9 | |
| 27.3 | 12.4 | 9.3 | | | 21.0 | 16.2 | | 6.8 | 4.9 | 9.5 | |
| 8.9 | .8 | -2.6 | | | -15.5 | .2 | | 3.6 | -5.2 | -6.4 | |
| 35.1 | 52.3 | 59.9 | | | 72.7 | UND | | 27.0 | 35.6 | 57.5 | |
| 14.9 | 16.0 | 14.6 | | Sales/Net Fixed Assets | 11.0 | 37.7 | | 8.2 | 15.7 | 18.2 | |
| 4.5 | 6.0 | 6.1 | | | 4.2 | 5.9 | | 2.2 | 9.3 | 11.5 | |
| 4.6 | 4.9 | 4.4 | | | 3.9 | 4.4 | | 4.1 | 4.3 | 4.5 | |
| 2.9 | 3.1 | 2.6 | | Sales/Total Assets | 2.5 | 2.4 | | 2.9 | 2.6 | 2.6 | |
| 1.7 | 1.8 | 1.5 | | | 1.5 | 1.3 | | 1.2 | 1.3 | 1.6 | |
| .9 | .7 | .9 | | | | | | | | .5 | |
| (63) 2.2 | (63) 1.5 | (55) 1.8 | | % Depr., Dep., Amort./Sales | | | | | (22) | 1.1 | |
| 3.3 | 2.7 | 4.1 | | | | | | | | 3.4 | |
| 1.3 | 1.1 | 1.8 | | % Officers', Directors' Owners' Comp/Sales | | | | | | | |
| (45) 2.7 | (40) 2.7 | (28) 3.2 | | | | | | | | | |
| 5.9 | 7.3 | 5.4 | | | | | | | | | |
| 1161481M | 2448747M | 2989464M | | Net Sales ($) | 8085M | 42718M | 31349M | 115352M | 241306M | 2550654M | |
| 517390M | 978887M | 1411129M | | Total Assets ($) | 5189M | 23240M | 13707M | 64147M | 159433M | 1145413M | |

© RMA 2024  M = $ thousand  MM = $ million
See Pages viii through xx for Explanation of Ratios and Data

# RETAIL—Beer, Wine, and Liquor Retailers  NAICS 445320

## Current Data Sorted by Assets | Comparative Historical Data

| | | | | | | | Type of Statement | | |
|---|---|---|---|---|---|---|---|---|---|
| | | 1 | 1 | 3 | | | Unqualified | 10 | 8 |
| | 1 | 1 | 3 | 3 | 1 | 1 | Reviewed | 8 | 5 |
| 1 | 2 | 2 | 3 | 3 | | | Compiled | 10 | 6 |
| 23 | 46 | 46 | 16 | 1 | | | Tax Returns | 76 | 89 |
| 15 | 26 | 26 | 17 | 6 | 1 | 2 | Other | 65 | 68 |
| | 17 (4/1-9/30/23) | | | 156 (10/1/23-3/31/24) | | | | 4/1/19-3/31/20 | 4/1/20-3/31/21 |
| 0-500M | 500M-2MM | 2-10MM | 10-50MM | 50-100MM | 100-250MM | | | ALL | ALL |
| 39 | 76 | 40 | 13 | 2 | 3 | | NUMBER OF STATEMENTS | 169 | 176 |
| % | % | % | % | % | % | | **ASSETS** | % | % |
| 15.0 | 13.7 | 15.4 | 9.0 | | | | Cash & Equivalents | 14.2 | 21.2 |
| .1 | 1.7 | 2.6 | 3.5 | | | | Trade Receivables (net) | 1.9 | 1.6 |
| 57.8 | 43.3 | 36.8 | 46.6 | | | | Inventory | 46.4 | 41.4 |
| .1 | 3.7 | 3.2 | 3.8 | | | | All Other Current | 2.2 | 1.9 |
| 73.0 | 62.5 | 58.1 | 62.9 | | | | Total Current | 64.6 | 66.1 |
| 8.5 | 12.1 | 19.1 | 22.3 | | | | Fixed Assets (net) | 17.8 | 16.0 |
| 15.7 | 21.0 | 18.4 | 2.5 | | | | Intangibles (net) | 13.3 | 14.6 |
| 2.9 | 4.5 | 4.4 | 12.3 | | | | All Other Non-Current | 4.3 | 3.3 |
| 100.0 | 100.0 | 100.0 | 100.0 | | | | Total | 100.0 | 100.0 |
| | | | | | | | **LIABILITIES** | | |
| 6.6 | 1.8 | 5.0 | 10.7 | | | | Notes Payable-Short Term | 8.0 | 4.0 |
| 5.0 | 2.0 | 2.0 | 3.2 | | | | Cur. Mat.-L.T.D. | 1.7 | 1.5 |
| 5.2 | 8.9 | 9.9 | 13.8 | | | | Trade Payables | 14.8 | 13.7 |
| .0 | .1 | .0 | .2 | | | | Income Taxes Payable | .2 | .1 |
| 13.2 | 11.6 | 12.7 | 8.9 | | | | All Other Current | 9.7 | 8.5 |
| 30.0 | 24.4 | 29.7 | 36.9 | | | | Total Current | 34.4 | 27.8 |
| 35.5 | 18.0 | 33.5 | 15.4 | | | | Long-Term Debt | 22.2 | 19.5 |
| .0 | .0 | .0 | .4 | | | | Deferred Taxes | .0 | .0 |
| 14.0 | 7.2 | 5.8 | 13.8 | | | | All Other Non-Current | 6.5 | 7.6 |
| 20.5 | 50.4 | 30.9 | 33.5 | | | | Net Worth | 36.9 | 45.1 |
| 100.0 | 100.0 | 100.0 | 100.0 | | | | Total Liabilities & Net Worth | 100.0 | 100.0 |
| | | | | | | | **INCOME DATA** | | |
| 100.0 | 100.0 | 100.0 | 100.0 | | | | Net Sales | 100.0 | 100.0 |
| 31.1 | 26.4 | 28.2 | 27.2 | | | | Gross Profit | 24.2 | 25.6 |
| 27.0 | 21.3 | 24.1 | 20.2 | | | | Operating Expenses | 21.1 | 19.9 |
| 4.2 | 5.1 | 4.2 | 7.0 | | | | Operating Profit | 3.2 | 5.7 |
| -.3 | -.2 | 1.6 | 1.8 | | | | All Other Expenses (net) | .2 | -.1 |
| 4.5 | 5.3 | 2.5 | 5.3 | | | | Profit Before Taxes | 3.0 | 5.8 |
| | | | | | | | **RATIOS** | | |
| 15.5 | 15.0 | 5.1 | 3.1 | | | | | 4.4 | 6.8 |
| 6.6 | 4.0 | 2.4 | 1.7 | | | | Current | 2.1 | 2.8 |
| 1.3 | 1.7 | 1.3 | 1.2 | | | | | 1.2 | 1.4 |
| 5.5 | 2.3 | 1.6 | .9 | | | | | 1.2 | 2.2 |
| .6 | .5 | .5 | .3 | | | | Quick | .4 | .8 |
| .1 | .2 | .1 | .1 | | | | | .1 | .4 |
| 0 UND | 0 UND | 0 UND | 0 UND | | | | | 0 UND | 0 UND |
| 0 UND | 0 UND | 0 UND | 1 309.5 | | | | Sales/Receivables | 0 UND | 0 UND |
| 0 UND | 0 UND | 3 112.7 | 9 41.9 | | | | | 1 332.6 | 0 999.8 |
| 37 9.9 | 46 8.0 | 38 9.5 | 60 6.1 | | | | | 33 11.0 | 37 9.8 |
| 65 5.6 | 73 5.0 | 74 4.9 | 89 4.1 | | | | Cost of Sales/Inventory | 58 6.3 | 56 6.5 |
| 140 2.6 | 96 3.8 | 130 2.8 | 126 2.9 | | | | | 96 3.8 | 83 4.4 |
| 0 UND | 0 UND | 0 UND | 12 31.1 | | | | | 0 UND | 0 UND |
| 0 UND | 0 UND | 16 23.0 | 19 18.8 | | | | Cost of Sales/Payables | 17 21.2 | 13 28.4 |
| 9 39.4 | 21 17.5 | 40 9.1 | 46 7.9 | | | | | 33 11.1 | 34 10.8 |
| 4.3 | 4.3 | 4.4 | 3.8 | | | | | 6.8 | 5.6 |
| 11.8 | 7.7 | 8.1 | 12.8 | | | | Sales/Working Capital | 13.0 | 10.3 |
| 25.8 | 24.0 | 39.2 | 40.8 | | | | | 38.4 | 20.2 |
| 16.1 | 26.3 | 9.7 | 34.4 | | | | | 20.3 | 36.5 |
| (20) 7.8 | (43) 12.5 | (36) 2.4 | (12) 3.8 | | | | EBIT/Interest | (120) 4.4 | (114) 10.4 |
| -1.7 | 3.6 | .7 | 1.8 | | | | | 1.7 | 3.0 |
| | | | | | | | Net Profit + Depr., Dep., Amort./Cur. Mat. L/T/D | | |
| .0 | .0 | .0 | .3 | | | | | .0 | .0 |
| .1 | .2 | .5 | .7 | | | | Fixed/Worth | .3 | .3 |
| .6 | 2.3 | 7.9 | 1.0 | | | | | 7.4 | 1.5 |
| .1 | .3 | 1.1 | 1.4 | | | | | .4 | .5 |
| 3.3 | 1.5 | 3.8 | 2.8 | | | | Debt/Worth | 1.9 | 1.5 |
| -3.4 | NM | -4.2 | 4.4 | | | | | -12.5 | 12.1 |
| 67.9 | 71.2 | 62.7 | 50.8 | | | | | 57.5 | 83.2 |
| (24) 24.5 | (57) 33.9 | (28) 38.5 | (12) 29.8 | | | | % Profit Before Taxes/Tangible Net Worth | (121) 20.3 | (135) 46.7 |
| -.2 | 16.0 | 5.4 | 14.2 | | | | | 7.2 | 21.2 |
| 55.7 | 25.0 | 16.2 | 12.7 | | | | | 17.6 | 30.8 |
| 14.5 | 13.5 | 6.3 | 8.7 | | | | % Profit Before Taxes/Total Assets | 7.6 | 16.4 |
| -3.5 | 5.1 | -.3 | 1.8 | | | | | 1.3 | 5.8 |
| UND | 650.8 | 638.5 | 47.6 | | | | | 301.3 | 212.9 |
| 310.3 | 68.6 | 39.8 | 15.0 | | | | Sales/Net Fixed Assets | 45.3 | 55.0 |
| 32.9 | 19.0 | 4.3 | 4.2 | | | | | 10.7 | 14.4 |
| 6.6 | 4.4 | 3.7 | 3.4 | | | | | 5.9 | 4.7 |
| 3.7 | 2.9 | 2.1 | 2.0 | | | | Sales/Total Assets | 3.0 | 3.3 |
| 2.6 | 1.8 | 1.1 | 1.4 | | | | | 2.1 | 2.3 |
| .2 | .4 | .3 | .5 | | | | | .3 | .2 |
| (10) 1.0 | (37) .8 | (25) 1.3 | (11) .8 | | | | % Depr., Dep., Amort./Sales | (98) .7 | (102) .6 |
| 2.4 | 1.7 | 3.6 | 1.1 | | | | | 1.8 | 1.4 |
| 1.8 | 1.3 | .8 | | | | | | 1.3 | .9 |
| (17) 2.3 | (33) 2.4 | (22) 1.1 | | | | | % Officers', Directors' Owners' Comp/Sales | (68) 2.1 | (79) 2.0 |
| 6.1 | 3.8 | 1.9 | | | | | | 2.9 | 3.7 |
| 51154M | 254806M | 441875M | 559674M | 202515M | 1121230M | | Net Sales ($) | 5894295M | 2838712M |
| 10803M | 82039M | 177717M | 242688M | 125756M | 422414M | | Total Assets ($) | 1555798M | 1004612M |

© RMA 2024

M = $ thousand  MM = $ million
See Pages viii through xx for Explanation of Ratios and Data

# RETAIL—Beer, Wine, and Liquor Retailers  NAICS 445320

| Comparative Historical Data ||| | Current Data Sorted by Sales ||||||
|---|---|---|---|---|---|---|---|---|---|
| | | | **Type of Statement** | | | | | | |
| 7 | 7 | 7 | Unqualified | | | 2 | | 1 | 4 |
| 5 | 10 | 7 | Reviewed | | 2 | | 1 | 3 | 2 |
| 5 | 5 | 7 | Compiled | 1 | 2 | | 2 | 2 | 1 |
| 57 | 57 | 85 | Tax Returns | 11 | 38 | 20 | 8 | 6 | 2 |
| 54 | 69 | 67 | Other | 10 | 24 | 9 | 9 | 9 | 9 |
| 4/1/21-3/31/22 ALL | 4/1/22-3/31/23 ALL | 4/1/23-3/31/24 ALL | | 17 (4/1-9/30/23) || | 156 (10/1/23-3/31/24) |||
| | | | | 0-1MM | 1-3MM | 3-5MM | 5-10MM | 10-25MM | 25MM & OVER |
| 128 | 148 | 173 | NUMBER OF STATEMENTS | 22 | 66 | 31 | 18 | 18 | 18 |
| % | % | % | **ASSETS** | % | % | % | % | % | % |
| 18.1 | 16.3 | 13.9 | Cash & Equivalents | 12.3 | 12.8 | 13.8 | 12.0 | 26.1 | 9.6 |
| 1.7 | 1.8 | 1.7 | Trade Receivables (net) | .1 | .5 | 1.0 | 9.1 | 2.0 | 1.4 |
| 45.3 | 46.6 | 45.3 | Inventory | 53.4 | 44.2 | 45.6 | 39.0 | 37.8 | 52.3 |
| 2.3 | 2.8 | 2.7 | All Other Current | .4 | 1.5 | 3.0 | 12.4 | 1.4 | .7 |
| 67.3 | 67.5 | 63.5 | Total Current | 66.2 | 59.0 | 63.4 | 72.5 | 67.3 | 64.0 |
| 15.4 | 14.7 | 14.1 | Fixed Assets (net) | 10.8 | 14.2 | 11.3 | 10.3 | 20.8 | 19.3 |
| 11.9 | 10.2 | 17.5 | Intangibles (net) | 21.7 | 22.1 | 20.1 | 11.8 | 9.1 | 5.5 |
| 5.4 | 7.6 | 4.9 | All Other Non-Current | 1.3 | 4.6 | 5.2 | 5.3 | 2.8 | 11.1 |
| 100.0 | 100.0 | 100.0 | Total | 100.0 | 100.0 | 100.0 | 100.0 | 100.0 | 100.0 |
| | | | **LIABILITIES** | | | | | | |
| 4.4 | 7.0 | 4.3 | Notes Payable-Short Term | 11.4 | 1.4 | 3.8 | 2.0 | 2.6 | 10.9 |
| 1.1 | 1.4 | 2.8 | Cur. Mat.-L.T.D. | 3.2 | 3.2 | 3.4 | 1.4 | .7 | 3.0 |
| 13.8 | 12.6 | 8.6 | Trade Payables | 2.2 | 4.1 | 12.6 | 17.1 | 14.6 | 11.6 |
| .1 | .2 | .1 | Income Taxes Payable | .0 | .0 | .0 | .4 | .0 | .2 |
| 10.3 | 9.4 | 12.0 | All Other Current | 18.6 | 11.3 | 14.4 | 10.5 | 5.8 | 10.2 |
| 29.7 | 30.6 | 27.8 | Total Current | 35.4 | 20.0 | 34.3 | 31.6 | 23.7 | 35.9 |
| 21.8 | 18.8 | 25.8 | Long-Term Debt | 15.9 | 31.9 | 26.8 | 21.0 | 27.5 | 17.1 |
| .0 | .0 | .0 | Deferred Taxes | .0 | .0 | .0 | .0 | .4 | .0 |
| 6.2 | 9.1 | 8.7 | All Other Non-Current | 21.1 | 6.7 | 6.1 | 11.2 | 4.5 | 7.4 |
| 42.3 | 41.6 | 37.7 | Net Worth | 27.6 | 41.4 | 32.8 | 36.2 | 44.0 | 39.6 |
| 100.0 | 100.0 | 100.0 | Total Liabilties & Net Worth | 100.0 | 100.0 | 100.0 | 100.0 | 100.0 | 100.0 |
| | | | **INCOME DATA** | | | | | | |
| 100.0 | 100.0 | 100.0 | Net Sales | 100.0 | 100.0 | 100.0 | 100.0 | 100.0 | 100.0 |
| 25.8 | 27.9 | 27.9 | Gross Profit | 34.9 | 27.5 | 26.9 | 30.1 | 22.7 | 25.7 |
| 20.7 | 22.7 | 23.1 | Operating Expenses | 33.7 | 21.9 | 22.3 | 23.4 | 18.3 | 20.7 |
| 5.2 | 5.2 | 4.8 | Operating Profit | 1.2 | 5.5 | 4.6 | 6.6 | 4.4 | 5.0 |
| -.3 | -.5 | .4 | All Other Expenses (net) | -.1 | -.1 | .8 | .7 | .6 | 1.3 |
| 5.5 | 5.7 | 4.4 | Profit Before Taxes | 1.3 | 5.6 | 3.8 | 6.0 | 3.8 | 3.7 |
| | | | **RATIOS** | | | | | | |
| 9.5 | 8.6 | 8.8 | | 27.1 | 20.1 | 3.9 | 3.8 | 8.4 | 2.4 |
| 2.6 | 2.5 | 2.9 | Current | 6.5 | 6.4 | 1.9 | 2.7 | 3.3 | 1.7 |
| 1.4 | 1.3 | 1.4 | | .9 | 1.7 | .9 | 1.8 | 1.7 | 1.3 |
| 2.2 | 1.7 | 2.1 | | 4.1 | 3.3 | .6 | 1.3 | 4.4 | .5 |
| .7 | .4 | .5 | Quick | .6 | 1.1 | .4 | .6 | 1.1 | .2 |
| .2 | .2 | .2 | | .1 | .2 | .1 | .2 | .5 | .1 |
| 0 UND | 0 UND | 0 UND | | 0 UND | 0 UND | 0 UND | 0 UND | 0 UND | 0 UND |
| 0 UND | 0 UND | 0 UND | Sales/Receivables | 0 UND | 0 UND | 0 UND | 1 673.2 | 0 UND | 0 999.8 |
| 1 358.6 | 1 335.8 | 0 999.8 | | 0 UND | 0 UND | 2 158.2 | 6 62.8 | 2 233.7 | 5 75.9 |
| 38 9.6 | 45 8.2 | 44 8.3 | | 65 5.6 | 38 9.5 | 44 8.3 | 27 13.7 | 28 13.0 | 64 5.7 |
| 63 5.8 | 76 4.8 | 74 4.9 | Cost of Sales/Inventory | 130 2.8 | 74 4.9 | 70 5.2 | 51 7.1 | 51 7.1 | 87 4.2 |
| 94 3.9 | 111 3.3 | 118 3.1 | | 243 1.5 | 111 3.3 | 118 3.1 | 91 4.0 | 99 3.7 | 107 3.4 |
| 0 UND | 0 UND | 0 UND | | 0 UND | 0 UND | 0 UND | 1 383.9 | 9 39.4 | |
| 10 38.2 | 14 25.4 | 2 155.1 | Cost of Sales/Payables | 0 UND | 0 UND | 2 167.1 | 21 17.1 | 14 26.6 | 18 20.7 |
| 33 11.0 | 34 10.8 | 23 15.8 | | 4 88.1 | 8 44.9 | 38 9.5 | 39 9.3 | 42 8.7 | 26 14.3 |
| 4.6 | 4.8 | 4.3 | | 3.1 | 4.0 | 4.4 | 3.6 | 5.4 | 7.4 |
| 9.0 | 8.4 | 8.7 | Sales/Working Capital | 6.6 | 6.7 | 14.8 | 8.4 | 7.5 | 12.0 |
| 20.7 | 24.8 | 25.2 | | -7.1 | 23.3 | -49.4 | 14.0 | 15.2 | 17.9 |
| 33.0 | 20.4 | 17.5 | | | 16.9 | 22.5 | 25.5 | 15.8 | 34.0 |
| (78) 9.8 | (89) 7.9 | (116) 5.2 | EBIT/Interest | (40) 6.0 | (24) 6.0 | (12) 11.6 | (14) 4.4 | (17) 4.2 | |
| 2.5 | 2.2 | 1.5 | | | 1.5 | 1.6 | 2.5 | 2.1 | 1.5 |
| | | | Net Profit + Depr., Dep., Amort./Cur. Mat. L/T/D | | | | | | |
| .0 | .0 | .0 | | .0 | .0 | .1 | .0 | .0 | .2 |
| .3 | .3 | .2 | Fixed/Worth | .1 | .2 | .5 | .3 | .1 | .5 |
| 1.4 | 1.7 | 2.6 | | UND | .8 | -1.4 | NM | 3.3 | 1.0 |
| .6 | .4 | .4 | | .2 | .2 | .9 | .5 | .5 | .9 |
| 1.9 | 1.5 | 2.3 | Debt/Worth | UND | 1.1 | 7.1 | 2.1 | 3.3 | 1.9 |
| 15.0 | 28.6 | -12.5 | | -2.0 | -34.3 | -3.3 | -11.5 | 7.1 | 4.2 |
| 79.0 | 71.9 | 63.5 | | 32.0 | 63.1 | 133.6 | 86.6 | 67.9 | 67.3 |
| (100) 40.2 | (117) 37.0 | (125) 32.3 | % Profit Before Taxes/Tangible Net Worth | (12) 19.1 | (48) 27.2 | (18) 41.5 | (13) 55.2 | 48.3 | (16) 23.9 |
| 15.4 | 12.7 | 11.7 | | -35.1 | 14.7 | 9.1 | 26.3 | 17.6 | 3.3 |
| 25.2 | 26.0 | 24.2 | | 15.6 | 28.0 | 22.9 | 39.8 | 22.6 | 21.5 |
| 15.9 | 13.1 | 9.2 | % Profit Before Taxes/Total Assets | .2 | 11.9 | 8.3 | 15.4 | 9.2 | 7.9 |
| 5.3 | 2.4 | 1.5 | | -6.7 | 4.1 | .7 | 3.7 | 6.8 | 1.2 |
| 479.2 | 424.7 | 659.3 | | UND | 879.2 | 305.3 | 688.1 | 880.8 | 71.4 |
| 50.1 | 46.7 | 54.6 | Sales/Net Fixed Assets | 116.4 | 71.9 | 59.8 | 68.3 | 80.5 | 17.8 |
| 9.7 | 13.9 | 15.5 | | 16.6 | 14.3 | 20.1 | 31.2 | 6.3 | 8.0 |
| 4.4 | 4.4 | 4.3 | | 3.1 | 4.3 | 4.1 | 5.8 | 4.5 | 4.1 |
| 3.1 | 3.0 | 2.7 | Sales/Total Assets | 2.0 | 2.9 | 2.6 | 4.5 | 3.2 | 2.6 |
| 2.0 | 2.0 | 1.7 | | .8 | 1.6 | 1.4 | 2.1 | 2.3 | 1.8 |
| .3 | .3 | .4 | | | .7 | .2 | .1 | .2 | .6 |
| (69) .6 | (80) .8 | (87) .8 | % Depr., Dep., Amort./Sales | (25) 1.3 | (18) .6 | (11) .5 | (13) .8 | (13) .8 | |
| 1.9 | 1.7 | 2.0 | | | 2.7 | | 1.8 | 2.4 | 1.0 |
| .9 | .9 | 1.1 | | | 1.7 | 1.1 | | .8 | |
| (48) 1.8 | (50) 2.4 | (72) 1.9 | % Officers', Directors' Owners' Comp/Sales | (32) 2.4 | (11) 1.6 | | (11) 1.0 | | |
| 2.9 | 4.0 | 3.9 | | | 4.1 | 3.2 | | 1.8 | |
| 3631370M | 3158631M | 2631254M | Net Sales ($) | 13355M | 135272M | 114913M | 126040M | 294625M | 1947049M |
| 1117855M | 1200756M | 1061417M | Total Assets ($) | 9993M | 67965M | 49942M | 50854M | 119424M | 763239M |

© RMA 2024    M = $ thousand    MM = $ million
See Pages viii through xx for Explanation of Ratios and Data

# RETAIL—Furniture Retailers  NAICS 449110

## Current Data Sorted by Assets | Comparative Historical Data

| | | | | | | | Type of Statement | | |
|---|---|---|---|---|---|---|---|---|---|
| | | | 2 | 2 | 7 | 7 | Unqualified | 19 | 14 |
| 1 | 1 | 11 | 6 | 2 | | | Reviewed | 23 | 15 |
| 1 | 2 | 16 | 6 | | 2 | | Compiled | 38 | 23 |
| 8 | 16 | 21 | 4 | | | | Tax Returns | 83 | 55 |
| 4 | 20 | 39 | 45 | 16 | 12 | | Other | 150 | 112 |
| | 51 (4/1-9/30/23) | | 200 (10/1/23-3/31/24) | | | | | 4/1/19-3/31/20 | 4/1/20-3/31/21 |
| 0-500M | 500M-2MM | 2-10MM | 10-50MM | 50-100MM | 100-250MM | | NUMBER OF STATEMENTS | ALL | ALL |
| 14 | 39 | 89 | 63 | 25 | 21 | | | 313 | 219 |
| % | % | % | % | % | % | | ASSETS | % | % |
| 34.4 | 20.0 | 16.0 | 14.5 | 7.5 | 9.0 | | Cash & Equivalents | 12.9 | 26.7 |
| 2.8 | 3.9 | 10.7 | 7.7 | 15.1 | 5.9 | | Trade Receivables (net) | 9.6 | 9.8 |
| 48.3 | 48.4 | 39.2 | 34.8 | 25.2 | 23.4 | | Inventory | 43.3 | 39.8 |
| 4.2 | 2.9 | 2.3 | 3.5 | 3.6 | 4.6 | | All Other Current | 3.2 | 2.2 |
| 89.7 | 75.2 | 68.2 | 60.4 | 51.5 | 42.9 | | Total Current | 69.0 | 78.6 |
| 9.7 | 13.1 | 17.1 | 24.8 | 26.9 | 28.0 | | Fixed Assets (net) | 22.1 | 12.9 |
| .0 | 3.7 | 5.8 | 4.2 | 6.1 | 1.5 | | Intangibles (net) | 2.6 | 3.6 |
| .6 | 8.0 | 8.9 | 10.6 | 15.5 | 27.6 | | All Other Non-Current | 6.4 | 4.9 |
| 100.0 | 100.0 | 100.0 | 100.0 | 100.0 | 100.0 | | Total | 100.0 | 100.0 |
| | | | | | | | LIABILITIES | | |
| 5.0 | 7.4 | 4.6 | 2.9 | 2.0 | 2.1 | | Notes Payable-Short Term | 6.4 | 4.5 |
| 6.8 | 1.3 | 2.1 | 2.7 | 3.5 | .9 | | Cur. Mat.-L.T.D. | 2.0 | 1.5 |
| 6.9 | 8.9 | 8.7 | 7.1 | 8.8 | 7.0 | | Trade Payables | 14.8 | 11.7 |
| .7 | .2 | .2 | .2 | .1 | .0 | | Income Taxes Payable | .1 | .3 |
| 28.3 | 15.1 | 21.1 | 18.7 | 17.5 | 13.4 | | All Other Current | 20.2 | 24.5 |
| 47.7 | 33.0 | 36.6 | 31.6 | 31.9 | 23.4 | | Total Current | 43.6 | 42.6 |
| 21.3 | 13.9 | 17.0 | 16.5 | 25.3 | 18.1 | | Long-Term Debt | 15.1 | 12.1 |
| .0 | .0 | .0 | .0 | .0 | .0 | | Deferred Taxes | .0 | .0 |
| 8.9 | 3.2 | 3.7 | 11.1 | 13.1 | 30.3 | | All Other Non-Current | 7.0 | 7.1 |
| 22.2 | 49.9 | 42.7 | 40.7 | 29.7 | 28.2 | | Net Worth | 34.3 | 38.2 |
| 100.0 | 100.0 | 100.0 | 100.0 | 100.0 | 100.0 | | Total Liabilities & Net Worth | 100.0 | 100.0 |
| | | | | | | | INCOME DATA | | |
| 100.0 | 100.0 | 100.0 | 100.0 | 100.0 | 100.0 | | Net Sales | 100.0 | 100.0 |
| 36.1 | 49.1 | 45.1 | 46.0 | 46.4 | 48.7 | | Gross Profit | 44.9 | 43.1 |
| 32.3 | 45.2 | 40.8 | 41.3 | 43.0 | 44.5 | | Operating Expenses | 40.5 | 38.5 |
| 3.8 | 3.8 | 4.3 | 4.7 | 3.4 | 4.2 | | Operating Profit | 4.4 | 4.7 |
| .5 | -.6 | .0 | .1 | .3 | -.1 | | All Other Expenses (net) | .3 | -.8 |
| 3.3 | 4.4 | 4.3 | 4.5 | 3.1 | 4.2 | | Profit Before Taxes | 4.1 | 5.4 |
| | | | | | | | RATIOS | | |
| 7.0 | 5.1 | 3.5 | 2.6 | 1.9 | 3.0 | | | 2.8 | 3.4 |
| 3.4 | 2.4 | 2.0 | 1.9 | 1.6 | 1.8 | | Current | 1.7 | 1.9 |
| 1.0 | 1.5 | 1.2 | 1.5 | 1.3 | 1.0 | | | 1.1 | 1.3 |
| 2.5 | 1.4 | 1.3 | 1.2 | 1.0 | 1.0 | | | 1.1 | 1.6 |
| 1.2 | (38) .8 | .7 | .5 | .5 | .7 | | Quick | (311) .5 | .8 |
| .3 | .3 | .3 | .2 | .2 | .2 | | | .2 | .5 |
| 0 UND | 0 UND | 0 794.9 | 0 999.8 | 1 359.9 | 0 802.6 | | | 0 UND | 0 UND |
| 0 UND | 1 650.3 | 5 73.6 | 2 155.6 | 3 116.1 | 3 110.3 | | Sales/Receivables | 3 134.9 | 3 127.6 |
| 0 UND | 7 49.4 | 26 14.3 | 19 19.2 | 36 10.1 | 8 46.6 | | | 14 25.9 | 20 18.7 |
| 7 56.0 | 65 5.6 | 73 5.0 | 91 4.0 | 78 4.7 | 87 4.2 | | | 58 6.3 | 73 5.0 |
| 57 6.4 | 130 2.8 | 140 2.6 | 126 2.9 | 101 3.6 | 122 3.0 | | Cost of Sales/Inventory | 114 3.2 | 111 3.3 |
| 96 3.8 | 192 1.9 | 192 1.9 | 182 2.0 | 140 2.6 | 166 2.2 | | | 166 2.2 | 166 2.2 |
| 0 UND | 0 UND | 8 46.9 | 11 33.6 | 22 16.3 | 26 14.3 | | | 14 25.2 | 14 26.3 |
| 0 UND | 10 36.8 | 26 14.0 | 21 17.1 | 31 11.6 | 33 11.0 | | Cost of Sales/Payables | 28 13.1 | 26 14.0 |
| 15 25.0 | 29 12.8 | 41 8.9 | 35 10.5 | 36 10.1 | 48 7.6 | | | 48 7.6 | 43 8.4 |
| 5.0 | 3.4 | 3.9 | 4.1 | 6.8 | 4.0 | | | 5.0 | 3.9 |
| 11.1 | 5.7 | 6.6 | 7.1 | 10.8 | 10.0 | | Sales/Working Capital | 10.4 | 6.7 |
| UND | 11.8 | 20.4 | 12.8 | 18.2 | NM | | | 38.1 | 15.4 |
| | 44.7 | 29.7 | 23.4 | 28.5 | 90.4 | | | 20.7 | 60.0 |
| (20) | 4.9 | (68) 6.6 | (52) 7.5 | (24) 5.2 | (18) 5.9 | | EBIT/Interest | (251) 5.7 | (167) 12.7 |
| | .3 | 1.3 | 2.5 | 2.5 | 1.1 | | | 2.1 | 2.5 |
| | | | 57.0 | | 4.5 | | | 6.9 | 9.6 |
| | | (11) 9.3 | (10) 2.8 | | | | Net Profit + Depr., Dep., Amort./Cur. Mat. L/T/D | (33) 2.6 | (18) 5.7 |
| | | | .4 | | 1.9 | | | 1.1 | 2.7 |
| .0 | .0 | .1 | .1 | .5 | .5 | | | .1 | .1 |
| .0 | .1 | .2 | .5 | 1.3 | .9 | | Fixed/Worth | .5 | .3 |
| .3 | .6 | 1.3 | 1.3 | 3.3 | 2.6 | | | 1.9 | 1.0 |
| .3 | .3 | .6 | .6 | 1.8 | 1.3 | | | .6 | .7 |
| .8 | .8 | 1.8 | 1.4 | 2.6 | 3.6 | | Debt/Worth | 1.5 | 1.5 |
| -4.3 | 2.6 | 4.5 | 4.5 | 9.1 | 9.6 | | | 7.7 | 4.2 |
| 171.5 | 42.1 | 45.1 | 36.0 | 35.1 | 67.0 | | | 50.0 | 56.9 |
| (10) 24.4 | (35) 13.2 | (79) 20.1 | (59) 17.0 | (21) 21.3 | (18) 21.5 | | % Profit Before Taxes/Tangible Net Worth | (267) 21.4 | (194) 29.2 |
| -4.6 | 6.7 | 4.5 | 8.2 | 15.4 | 2.6 | | | 6.6 | 9.7 |
| 53.6 | 19.0 | 18.5 | 12.5 | 8.8 | 11.0 | | | 16.2 | 23.6 |
| 17.6 | 7.2 | 5.8 | 7.0 | 5.9 | 8.5 | | % Profit Before Taxes/Total Assets | 7.6 | 11.0 |
| -4.0 | 4.5 | 1.0 | 2.5 | 3.6 | 1.3 | | | 1.8 | 2.1 |
| UND | 471.6 | 83.7 | 45.9 | 15.6 | 17.9 | | | 72.8 | 106.0 |
| UND | 69.4 | 33.7 | 11.0 | 9.9 | 8.3 | | Sales/Net Fixed Assets | 19.7 | 36.4 |
| 53.0 | 15.1 | 10.2 | 4.6 | 3.0 | 3.4 | | | 7.3 | 12.8 |
| 16.3 | 3.4 | 2.7 | 2.6 | 2.6 | 1.7 | | | 3.8 | 3.2 |
| 5.2 | 2.5 | 2.1 | 1.7 | 1.7 | 1.3 | | Sales/Total Assets | 2.6 | 2.4 |
| 3.1 | 1.8 | 1.4 | 1.2 | 1.2 | 1.0 | | | 1.6 | 1.6 |
| | .3 | .4 | .5 | .4 | 1.0 | | | .4 | .4 |
| (16) | .8 | (64) .8 | (53) .9 | (24) 1.1 | (20) 1.3 | | % Depr., Dep., Amort./Sales | (231) .9 | (140) .8 |
| | 2.5 | 1.1 | 1.6 | 1.9 | 2.0 | | | 1.5 | 1.5 |
| | 2.7 | | .4 | | | | | 1.1 | 1.1 |
| (20) | 4.9 | (41) 2.4 | (14) 1.2 | | | | % Officers', Directors', Owners' Comp/Sales | (118) 2.6 | (94) 2.5 |
| | 8.1 | 4.0 | 1.8 | | | | | 5.2 | 5.7 |
| 19643M | 132385M | 990802M | 2823479M | 3427953M | 4082364M | | Net Sales ($) | 11401694M | 7299987M |
| 3111M | 46839M | 457679M | 1533816M | 1821263M | 3061334M | | Total Assets ($) | 5108510M | 3502200M |

© RMA 2024  M = $ thousand  MM = $ million
See Pages viii through xx for Explanation of Ratios and Data

# RETAIL—Furniture Retailers  NAICS 449110

## Comparative Historical Data | Current Data Sorted by Sales

| | | | Type of Statement | | | | | | |
|---|---|---|---|---|---|---|---|---|---|
| 8 | 13 | 18 | Unqualified | | 1 | | | 1 | 16 |
| 18 | 21 | 21 | Reviewed | | 3 | 2 | 4 | 4 | 8 |
| 18 | 28 | 27 | Compiled | | 3 | 5 | 6 | 8 | 5 |
| 56 | 51 | 49 | Tax Returns | 4 | 16 | 8 | 9 | 9 | 3 |
| 124 | 149 | 136 | Other | 2 | 15 | 8 | 15 | 29 | 67 |
| 4/1/21-3/31/22 ALL | 4/1/22-3/31/23 ALL | 4/1/23-3/31/24 ALL | | | 51 (4/1-9/30/23) | | | 200 (10/1/23-3/31/24) | |
| | | | | 0-1MM | 1-3MM | 3-5MM | 5-10MM | 10-25MM | 25MM & OVER |
| 224 | 262 | 251 | NUMBER OF STATEMENTS | 6 | 38 | 23 | 34 | 51 | 99 |
| % | % | % | ASSETS | % | % | % | % | % | % |
| 23.8 | 15.9 | 15.8 | Cash & Equivalents | | 23.5 | 13.9 | 15.6 | 16.2 | 12.3 |
| 9.6 | 8.4 | 8.5 | Trade Receivables (net) | | 4.0 | 7.0 | 8.8 | 10.1 | 10.1 |
| 40.6 | 43.8 | 37.3 | Inventory | | 41.1 | 43.1 | 47.1 | 38.6 | 30.4 |
| 2.4 | 4.0 | 3.1 | All Other Current | | 1.9 | 1.5 | 1.4 | 3.0 | 3.8 |
| 76.3 | 72.2 | 64.8 | Total Current | | 70.5 | 65.5 | 73.0 | 67.8 | 56.6 |
| 15.1 | 17.8 | 19.9 | Fixed Assets (net) | | 18.8 | 17.7 | 12.9 | 19.3 | 24.1 |
| 3.4 | 2.6 | 4.4 | Intangibles (net) | | 3.7 | 14.3 | 3.7 | 2.1 | 4.1 |
| 5.2 | 7.4 | 11.0 | All Other Non-Current | | 7.0 | 2.5 | 10.5 | 10.8 | 15.2 |
| 100.0 | 100.0 | 100.0 | Total | | 100.0 | 100.0 | 100.0 | 100.0 | 100.0 |
| | | | LIABILITIES | | | | | | |
| 5.0 | 4.9 | 4.2 | Notes Payable-Short Term | | 5.9 | 4.3 | 7.7 | 4.0 | 2.6 |
| 1.3 | 1.7 | 2.4 | Cur. Mat.-L.T.D. | | 3.1 | 3.5 | 1.5 | 2.3 | 2.5 |
| 10.3 | 9.6 | 8.1 | Trade Payables | | 7.5 | 9.9 | 7.4 | 8.8 | 8.1 |
| .2 | .2 | .2 | Income Taxes Payable | | .4 | .2 | .2 | .1 | .2 |
| 23.7 | 20.8 | 19.0 | All Other Current | | 16.0 | 18.5 | 18.9 | 21.0 | 19.3 |
| 40.4 | 37.1 | 33.8 | Total Current | | 32.8 | 36.4 | 35.7 | 36.2 | 32.5 |
| 13.5 | 15.3 | 17.5 | Long-Term Debt | | 23.0 | 25.9 | 11.2 | 17.3 | 16.8 |
| .0 | .1 | .0 | Deferred Taxes | | .0 | .0 | .0 | .1 | .0 |
| 6.4 | 8.1 | 8.9 | All Other Non-Current | | 2.3 | 7.8 | 3.0 | 6.3 | 15.4 |
| 39.7 | 39.5 | 39.7 | Net Worth | | 41.8 | 29.9 | 50.1 | 40.2 | 35.3 |
| 100.0 | 100.0 | 100.0 | Total Liabilities & Net Worth | | 100.0 | 100.0 | 100.0 | 100.0 | 100.0 |
| | | | INCOME DATA | | | | | | |
| 100.0 | 100.0 | 100.0 | Net Sales | | 100.0 | 100.0 | 100.0 | 100.0 | 100.0 |
| 44.9 | 44.9 | 45.9 | Gross Profit | | 47.5 | 46.6 | 46.4 | 44.7 | 46.1 |
| 38.0 | 38.6 | 41.7 | Operating Expenses | | 43.9 | 41.2 | 42.5 | 40.8 | 41.6 |
| 6.9 | 6.2 | 4.2 | Operating Profit | | 3.6 | 5.4 | 3.8 | 3.9 | 4.5 |
| -1.3 | .0 | .0 | All Other Expenses (net) | | .9 | .2 | -.7 | -.6 | .1 |
| 8.3 | 6.3 | 4.2 | Profit Before Taxes | | 2.7 | 5.2 | 4.5 | 4.5 | 4.4 |
| | | | RATIOS | | | | | | |
| 3.6 | 3.6 | 3.1 | | | 5.2 | 2.8 | 3.5 | 3.3 | 2.6 |
| 1.9 | 2.1 | 2.0 | Current | | 2.6 | 2.2 | 2.6 | 2.0 | 1.6 |
| 1.3 | 1.4 | 1.3 | | | 1.2 | 1.4 | 1.4 | 1.2 | 1.3 |
| 1.4 | 1.3 | 1.3 | | | 2.4 | 1.2 | 1.6 | 1.3 | 1.0 |
| .8 | .6 (250) | .7 | Quick | | .8 | .7 | .7 | .6 | .5 |
| .4 | .2 | .3 | | | .3 | .2 | .2 | .3 | .2 |
| 0 UND | 0 UND | 0 999.8 | | 0 UND | 0 UND | 0 UND | 1 394.3 | 0 999.8 | |
| 2 158.9 | 3 135.9 | 2 150.3 | Sales/Receivables | 0 UND | 2 241.8 | 4 91.5 | 7 48.8 | 2 166.6 | |
| 18 20.4 | 11 34.3 | 16 23.1 | | 5 74.9 | 9 39.2 | 20 18.3 | 25 14.6 | 21 17.8 | |
| 66 5.5 | 83 4.4 | 72 5.1 | | 57 6.4 | 72 5.1 | 79 4.6 | 83 4.4 | 79 4.6 | |
| 107 3.4 | 122 3.0 | 122 3.0 | Cost of Sales/Inventory | 135 2.7 | 130 2.8 | 152 2.4 | 122 3.0 | 118 3.1 | |
| 159 2.3 | 192 1.9 | 174 2.1 | | 228 1.6 | 228 1.6 | 243 1.5 | 182 2.0 | 152 2.4 | |
| 9 39.9 | 10 38.4 | 8 44.9 | | 0 UND | 16 23.1 | 8 43.1 | 7 49.8 | 17 21.7 | |
| 21 17.8 | 23 15.6 | 23 15.7 | Cost of Sales/Payables | 4 81.2 | 30 12.2 | 23 15.7 | 21 17.2 | 26 13.9 | |
| 38 9.6 | 35 10.4 | 36 10.0 | | 20 18.2 | 42 8.6 | 39 9.4 | 37 9.8 | 36 10.0 | |
| 4.5 | 4.2 | 4.1 | | | 2.8 | 4.1 | 3.8 | 3.8 | 5.8 |
| 7.6 | 6.8 | 7.2 | Sales/Working Capital | | 7.2 | 5.1 | 5.6 | 5.9 | 9.6 |
| 16.2 | 16.8 | 17.7 | | | 122.1 | 18.9 | 13.5 | 17.7 | 19.9 |
| 94.5 | 74.7 | 30.3 | | | 7.3 | 11.6 | 61.1 | 24.2 | 35.1 |
| (159) 25.4 | (196) 16.4 | (186) 6.3 | EBIT/Interest | (19) 1.2 | (18) 2.8 | (24) 12.8 | (40) 8.4 | (84) 7.5 | |
| 6.9 | 4.1 | 1.9 | | -1.1 | -.5 | 2.3 | 2.2 | 2.5 | |
| 25.4 | 13.4 | 13.8 | Net Profit + Depr., Dep., | | | | | | 10.8 |
| (17) 8.5 | (33) 4.9 | (34) 3.8 | Amort./Cur. Mat. L/T/D | | | | | (25) 3.6 | |
| 3.6 | 1.1 | .9 | | | | | | .9 | |
| .1 | .0 | .1 | | | .0 | .0 | .0 | .1 | .2 |
| .3 | .3 | .4 | Fixed/Worth | | .2 | .2 | .2 | .3 | .7 |
| 1.0 | .9 | 1.5 | | | 1.8 | 240.6 | .8 | 1.2 | 1.8 |
| .6 | .6 | .6 | | | .3 | .9 | .4 | .7 | .9 |
| 1.4 | 1.4 | 1.7 | Debt/Worth | | .8 | 1.7 | 1.1 | 1.8 | 2.2 |
| 4.0 | 3.9 | 4.8 | | | 4.2 | -42.5 | 3.3 | 4.5 | 5.4 |
| 80.4 | 50.2 | 42.7 | % Profit Before Taxes/Tangible | | 30.0 | 63.4 | 39.2 | 31.2 | 49.0 |
| (199) 47.0 | (231) 30.6 | (222) 19.6 | Net Worth | (31) 10.5 | (17) 33.8 | (32) 17.0 | (47) 18.1 | (89) 21.6 | |
| 23.8 | 14.2 | 6.4 | | -.9 | 6.2 | 4.6 | 5.1 | 12.1 | |
| 31.2 | 22.1 | 13.1 | % Profit Before Taxes/Total | | 17.6 | 19.7 | 19.0 | 12.5 | 11.8 |
| 18.7 | 12.8 | 6.7 | Assets | | 6.5 | 6.4 | 8.5 | 6.2 | 6.9 |
| 9.7 | 4.0 | 2.0 | | | -1.3 | .2 | 1.1 | 2.5 | 3.0 |
| 99.6 | 116.5 | 99.1 | | | 999.8 | 199.5 | 111.3 | 83.5 | 33.0 |
| 28.7 | 24.0 | 21.2 | Sales/Net Fixed Assets | | 61.6 | 55.7 | 45.0 | 21.2 | 11.2 |
| 11.0 | 7.4 | 5.9 | | | 7.3 | 6.2 | 15.1 | 5.9 | 3.8 |
| 3.4 | 3.1 | 2.8 | | | 3.4 | 2.5 | 3.2 | 2.8 | 2.8 |
| 2.4 | 2.3 | 2.0 | Sales/Total Assets | | 2.0 | 1.8 | 2.4 | 2.1 | 1.8 |
| 1.7 | 1.6 | 1.3 | | | 1.2 | 1.1 | 1.3 | 1.4 | 1.3 |
| .3 | .5 | .4 | | | .4 | .3 | .4 | .4 | .6 |
| (136) .8 | (176) .8 | (180) .9 | % Depr., Dep., Amort./Sales | (20) .9 | (13) 1.0 | (20) .6 | (40) .9 | (86) 1.0 | |
| 1.4 | 1.3 | 1.6 | | | 2.6 | 3.0 | 1.0 | 1.2 | 1.7 |
| 1.3 | 1.1 | .9 | | | 3.1 | | | 1.3 | .4 |
| (85) 3.0 | (86) 2.7 | (87) 2.4 | % Officers', Directors' Owners' Comp/Sales | (19) 4.7 | (18) 2.3 | (23) 1.7 | (15) .5 | | |
| 4.3 | 4.8 | 5.0 | | | 8.4 | | 4.0 | 2.8 | 1.4 |
| 7993455M | 12164767M | 11476626M | Net Sales ($) | 3808M | 78846M | 88660M | 237270M | 827032M | 10241010M |
| 3602215M | 6392809M | 6924042M | Total Assets ($) | 1365M | 49910M | 57136M | 137227M | 448788M | 6229616M |

© RMA 2024  
M = $ thousand    MM = $ million  
See Pages viii through xx for Explanation of Ratios and Data

# RETAIL—Floor Covering Retailers NAICS 449121

## Current Data Sorted by Assets | Comparative Historical Data

| | | | | | | | Type of Statement | | | | |
|---|---|---|---|---|---|---|---|---|---|---|---|
| | | | | 2 | 1 | | Unqualified | | 3 | | 3 |
| | 1 | 4 | | 5 | | | Reviewed | | 9 | | 3 |
| | 2 | 2 | | 1 | | | Compiled | | 7 | | 3 |
| 3 | 5 | 9 | | 2 | | | Tax Returns | | 40 | | 25 |
| 5 | 12 | 33 | | 12 | 3 | 3 | Other | | 59 | | 68 |
| | 7 (4/1-9/30/23) | | | 98 (10/1/23-3/31/24) | | | | | 4/1/19-3/31/20 | | 4/1/20-3/31/21 |
| 0-500M | 500M-2MM | 2-10MM | | 10-50MM | 50-100MM | 100-250MM | | | ALL | | ALL |
| 8 | 20 | 48 | | 22 | 4 | 3 | NUMBER OF STATEMENTS | | 118 | | 102 |
| % | % | % | | % | % | % | ASSETS | | % | | % |
| | 23.0 | 15.7 | | 16.9 | | | Cash & Equivalents | | 12.9 | | 22.7 |
| | 18.0 | 23.0 | | 22.2 | | | Trade Receivables (net) | | 25.0 | | 22.5 |
| | 33.2 | 34.5 | | 30.0 | | | Inventory | | 33.9 | | 30.0 |
| | 1.6 | 3.2 | | 6.9 | | | All Other Current | | 2.7 | | 1.9 |
| | 75.7 | 76.4 | | 76.0 | | | Total Current | | 74.5 | | 77.0 |
| | 12.8 | 12.4 | | 14.0 | | | Fixed Assets (net) | | 14.6 | | 12.9 |
| | 2.4 | 2.7 | | 4.0 | | | Intangibles (net) | | 3.9 | | 5.6 |
| | 9.0 | 8.5 | | 6.0 | | | All Other Non-Current | | 6.9 | | 4.5 |
| | 100.0 | 100.0 | | 100.0 | | | Total | | 100.0 | | 100.0 |
| | | | | | | | LIABILITIES | | | | |
| | 8.1 | 2.8 | | 3.8 | | | Notes Payable-Short Term | | 8.4 | | 6.3 |
| | .7 | 1.9 | | 1.7 | | | Cur. Mat.-L.T.D. | | 1.9 | | 2.8 |
| | 13.7 | 13.0 | | 12.8 | | | Trade Payables | | 20.5 | | 15.0 |
| | .3 | .0 | | .1 | | | Income Taxes Payable | | .2 | | .6 |
| | 20.8 | 15.7 | | 23.4 | | | All Other Current | | 21.1 | | 19.3 |
| | 43.5 | 33.4 | | 41.8 | | | Total Current | | 52.2 | | 43.8 |
| | 14.0 | 10.1 | | 11.3 | | | Long-Term Debt | | 14.4 | | 15.5 |
| | .0 | .0 | | .0 | | | Deferred Taxes | | .1 | | .1 |
| | 2.7 | 2.5 | | 6.1 | | | All Other Non-Current | | 5.2 | | 5.4 |
| | 39.8 | 53.9 | | 40.8 | | | Net Worth | | 28.2 | | 35.2 |
| | 100.0 | 100.0 | | 100.0 | | | Total Liabilties & Net Worth | | 100.0 | | 100.0 |
| | | | | | | | INCOME DATA | | | | |
| | 100.0 | 100.0 | | 100.0 | | | Net Sales | | 100.0 | | 100.0 |
| | 37.4 | 33.1 | | 30.0 | | | Gross Profit | | 35.1 | | 35.5 |
| | 32.1 | 28.3 | | 24.5 | | | Operating Expenses | | 31.2 | | 31.1 |
| | 5.3 | 4.8 | | 5.5 | | | Operating Profit | | 4.0 | | 4.4 |
| | .4 | -.1 | | .1 | | | All Other Expenses (net) | | .1 | | -.9 |
| | 4.9 | 4.9 | | 5.5 | | | Profit Before Taxes | | 3.9 | | 5.4 |
| | | | | | | | RATIOS | | | | |
| | 2.7 | 3.9 | | 3.4 | | | | | 3.0 | | 3.0 |
| | 2.1 | 2.6 | | 1.9 | | | Current | | 1.5 | | 1.9 |
| | 1.5 | 1.6 | | 1.0 | | | | | 1.0 | | 1.2 |
| | 2.1 | 2.3 | | 1.5 | | | | | 1.4 | | 2.0 |
| | .8 | 1.0 | | .9 | | | Quick | | .7 | | 1.0 |
| | .4 | .5 | | .4 | | | | | .3 | | .6 |
| 5 | 75.8 | 3 | 117.9 | 21 | 17.8 | | | 6 | 60.5 | 7 | 54.6 |
| 11 | 32.0 | 26 | 13.9 | 29 | 12.5 | | Sales/Receivables | 19 | 19.0 | 21 | 17.0 |
| 29 | 12.7 | 49 | 7.4 | 49 | 7.5 | | | 33 | 10.9 | 39 | 9.3 |
| 13 | 27.5 | 35 | 10.4 | 30 | 12.3 | | | 18 | 20.6 | 26 | 14.2 |
| 52 | 7.0 | 56 | 6.5 | 76 | 4.8 | | Cost of Sales/Inventory | 43 | 8.4 | 45 | 8.1 |
| 101 | 3.6 | 122 | 3.0 | 104 | 3.5 | | | 83 | 4.4 | 83 | 4.4 |
| 11 | 32.7 | 12 | 29.7 | 16 | 23.5 | | | 12 | 29.9 | 12 | 30.4 |
| 19 | 19.2 | 22 | 16.9 | 24 | 15.0 | | Cost of Sales/Payables | 23 | 15.9 | 23 | 16.0 |
| 33 | 11.0 | 39 | 9.3 | 40 | 9.1 | | | 40 | 9.2 | 37 | 9.8 |
| | 6.2 | 3.9 | | 3.8 | | | | | 7.1 | | 5.4 |
| | 8.0 | 6.8 | | 6.1 | | | Sales/Working Capital | | 16.2 | | 9.0 |
| | 18.8 | 9.0 | | 71.8 | | | | | 141.7 | | 30.4 |
| | 81.6 | 55.7 | | 61.6 | | | | | 27.5 | | 65.9 |
| | (15) 11.8 | (31) 14.1 | | (20) 17.0 | | | EBIT/Interest | (88) | 6.5 | (76) | 12.6 |
| | 1.1 | 3.8 | | 3.3 | | | | | 2.1 | | 2.5 |
| | | | | | | | Net Profit + Depr., Dep., | | 14.3 | | |
| | | | | | | | Amort./Cur. Mat. L/T/D | (10) | 2.5 | | |
| | | | | | | | | | 1.3 | | |
| | .2 | .0 | | .0 | | | | | .1 | | .1 |
| | .3 | .1 | | .3 | | | Fixed/Worth | | .4 | | .3 |
| | 1.1 | .3 | | .9 | | | | | 6.2 | | 1.4 |
| | .6 | .3 | | .7 | | | | | .7 | | .7 |
| | 1.8 | .9 | | 1.1 | | | Debt/Worth | | 2.2 | | 2.1 |
| | 5.6 | 2.0 | | 4.7 | | | | | 288.6 | | 6.2 |
| | 58.8 | 48.8 | | 45.0 | | | % Profit Before Taxes/Tangible | | 61.3 | | 83.2 |
| | (18) 22.2 | 27.7 | | (20) 22.2 | | | Net Worth | (90) | 28.9 | (88) | 39.3 |
| | 6.6 | 6.2 | | 11.0 | | | | | 12.5 | | 14.4 |
| | 35.2 | 21.5 | | 17.6 | | | % Profit Before Taxes/Total | | 22.6 | | 26.7 |
| | 11.3 | 10.3 | | 11.5 | | | Assets | | 9.4 | | 13.3 |
| | 2.8 | 3.1 | | 4.6 | | | | | 2.6 | | 3.4 |
| | 128.6 | 169.3 | | 81.5 | | | | | 112.4 | | 129.5 |
| | 33.5 | 60.3 | | 46.5 | | | Sales/Net Fixed Assets | | 53.5 | | 48.4 |
| | 17.9 | 15.2 | | 12.6 | | | | | 19.7 | | 18.1 |
| | 4.3 | 3.3 | | 3.0 | | | | | 5.2 | | 4.2 |
| | 3.5 | 2.7 | | 2.4 | | | Sales/Total Assets | | 3.6 | | 2.9 |
| | 2.9 | 1.9 | | 1.8 | | | | | 2.6 | | 2.1 |
| | | .3 | | .4 | | | | | .5 | | .2 |
| | (31) | .5 | (19) | .9 | | | % Depr., Dep., Amort./Sales | (70) | .8 | (64) | .6 |
| | | 1.1 | | 1.2 | | | | | 1.3 | | 1.2 |
| | | .7 | | | | | | | 1.8 | | 1.2 |
| | (21) | 1.7 | | | | | % Officers', Directors' Owners' Comp/Sales | (62) | 3.1 | (50) | 3.1 |
| | | 3.9 | | | | | | | 5.7 | | 5.4 |
| 17858M | 93491M | 652667M | | 980827M | 617948M | 838402M | Net Sales ($) | | 2191951M | | 1791132M |
| 1796M | 25316M | 236339M | | 417121M | 229524M | 377767M | Total Assets ($) | | 721708M | | 719063M |

© RMA 2024  M = $ thousand  MM = $ million
See Pages viii through xx for Explanation of Ratios and Data

RETAIL—Floor Covering Retailers NAICS 449121

## Comparative Historical Data / Current Data Sorted by Sales

| Comparative Historical Data | | | | | Current Data Sorted by Sales | | | | | |
|---|---|---|---|---|---|---|---|---|---|---|
| | | | | **Type of Statement** | | | | | | |
| | | 5 | 3 | Unqualified | | | | 1 | | 3 |
| 5 | 9 | 10 | Reviewed | | 1 | | 1 | 5 | 3 |
| 5 | 9 | 5 | Compiled | | 1 | | 1 | 3 | |
| 25 | 30 | 19 | Tax Returns | | 3 | 5 | 4 | 1 | 5 |
| 58 | 65 | 68 | Other | 1 | 4 | 8 | 16 | 21 | 18 |
| 4/1/21-3/31/22 ALL | 4/1/22-3/31/23 ALL | 4/1/23-3/31/24 ALL | | 7 (4/1-9/30/23) | | | 98 (10/1/23-3/31/24) | | | |
| | | | | 0-1MM | 1-3MM | 3-5MM | 5-10MM | 10-25MM | 25MM & OVER |
| 93 | 118 | 105 | **NUMBER OF STATEMENTS** | 2 | 9 | 13 | 22 | 30 | 29 |
| % | % | % | **ASSETS** | % | % | % | % | % | % |
| 19.4 | 18.6 | 16.8 | Cash & Equivalents | | | 16.0 | 16.0 | 22.7 | 12.2 |
| 25.4 | 22.9 | 21.5 | Trade Receivables (net) | | | 24.1 | 16.1 | 25.5 | 24.4 |
| 29.1 | 30.4 | 31.7 | Inventory | | | 32.0 | 33.3 | 31.2 | 29.9 |
| 2.8 | 3.2 | 4.4 | All Other Current | | | 1.4 | 3.8 | 3.1 | 6.4 |
| 76.7 | 75.1 | 74.5 | Total Current | | | 73.6 | 69.2 | 82.5 | 72.9 |
| 13.5 | 12.6 | 15.0 | Fixed Assets (net) | | | 15.3 | 15.5 | 8.3 | 19.6 |
| 3.6 | 4.9 | 2.8 | Intangibles (net) | | | 2.4 | 4.0 | 2.3 | 2.7 |
| 6.2 | 7.4 | 7.8 | All Other Non-Current | | | 8.8 | 11.2 | 7.0 | 4.9 |
| 100.0 | 100.0 | 100.0 | Total | | | 100.0 | 100.0 | 100.0 | 100.0 |
| | | | **LIABILITIES** | | | | | | |
| 5.2 | 5.5 | 5.7 | Notes Payable-Short Term | | | 6.2 | 3.1 | 3.8 | 4.5 |
| 1.5 | 1.1 | 2.3 | Cur. Mat.-L.T.D. | | | 2.4 | 3.6 | .8 | 2.1 |
| 16.3 | 15.7 | 13.1 | Trade Payables | | | 15.8 | 11.7 | 11.6 | 15.4 |
| .6 | .2 | .1 | Income Taxes Payable | | | .3 | .0 | .0 | .1 |
| 20.0 | 16.8 | 17.9 | All Other Current | | | 12.6 | 13.9 | 22.6 | 20.1 |
| 43.6 | 39.3 | 39.1 | Total Current | | | 37.2 | 32.4 | 38.7 | 42.2 |
| 22.3 | 12.7 | 16.6 | Long-Term Debt | | | 16.3 | 15.3 | 7.1 | 13.7 |
| .0 | .0 | .1 | Deferred Taxes | | | .0 | .1 | .0 | .3 |
| 3.4 | 5.9 | 4.2 | All Other Non-Current | | | 5.8 | 2.6 | 2.2 | 5.6 |
| 30.7 | 42.0 | 40.0 | Net Worth | | | 40.6 | 49.6 | 52.0 | 38.1 |
| 100.0 | 100.0 | 100.0 | Total Liabilities & Net Worth | | | 100.0 | 100.0 | 100.0 | 100.0 |
| | | | **INCOME DATA** | | | | | | |
| 100.0 | 100.0 | 100.0 | Net Sales | | | 100.0 | 100.0 | 100.0 | 100.0 |
| 35.0 | 33.0 | 33.8 | Gross Profit | | | 40.3 | 33.5 | 31.3 | 30.4 |
| 28.8 | 27.8 | 28.8 | Operating Expenses | | | 34.7 | 29.8 | 25.1 | 26.0 |
| 6.2 | 5.2 | 5.1 | Operating Profit | | | 5.6 | 3.7 | 6.2 | 4.5 |
| -1.2 | -.4 | .1 | All Other Expenses (net) | | | .2 | .4 | -.2 | .0 |
| 7.4 | 5.6 | 5.0 | Profit Before Taxes | | | 5.3 | 3.3 | 6.5 | 4.5 |
| | | | **RATIOS** | | | | | | |
| 2.6 | 3.1 | 3.3 | | | | 2.9 | 4.6 | 3.7 | 3.2 |
| 1.9 | 2.2 | 2.2 | Current | | | 2.5 | 2.6 | 2.4 | 1.7 |
| 1.3 | 1.4 | 1.4 | | | | 1.5 | 1.3 | 1.6 | 1.2 |
| 1.6 | 2.0 | 2.1 | | | | 2.4 | 2.6 | 2.4 | 1.2 |
| 1.0 | .9 | .8 | Quick | | | .9 | .8 | 1.2 | .7 |
| .6 | .4 | .4 | | | | .6 | .3 | .6 | .5 |
| 6  61.8 | 4  94.4 | 6  61.4 | | 7  49.5 | 3  142.8 | 5  79.3 | 21  17.1 | | |
| 24  15.0 | 24  15.1 | 26  14.3 | Sales/Receivables | 15  23.6 | 16  23.1 | 36  10.2 | 29  12.7 | | |
| 41  9.0 | 46  8.0 | 46  8.0 | | 45  8.2 | 41  8.8 | 64  5.7 | 41  8.9 | | |
| 21  17.6 | 11  33.4 | 24  15.4 | | 13  27.2 | 15  24.6 | 30  12.2 | 32  11.4 | | |
| 43  8.4 | 44  8.3 | 54  6.8 | Cost of Sales/Inventory | 54  6.7 | 62  5.9 | 54  6.7 | 54  6.8 | | |
| 89  4.1 | 96  3.8 | 104  3.5 | | 114  3.2 | 135  2.7 | 122  3.0 | 81  4.5 | | |
| 14  26.6 | 12  30.9 | 13  27.8 | | 16  23.2 | 8  43.5 | 12  30.5 | 16  22.9 | | |
| 24  15.3 | 21  17.4 | 22  16.7 | Cost of Sales/Payables | 30  12.0 | 18  19.9 | 21  17.5 | 24  15.3 | | |
| 34  10.6 | 38  9.7 | 37  9.9 | | 36  10.2 | 42  8.6 | 35  10.4 | 41  9.0 | | |
| 4.9 | 4.6 | 4.8 | | | | 5.6 | 3.6 | 3.9 | 5.7 |
| 9.8 | 7.8 | 7.5 | Sales/Working Capital | | | 7.5 | 6.8 | 6.3 | 11.9 |
| 22.1 | 22.0 | 18.3 | | | | 16.7 | 30.8 | 8.8 | 38.8 |
| 106.2 | 74.5 | 53.9 | | | | 43.4 | 76.3 | 129.1 | 47.3 |
| (69) 26.1 | (80) 17.3 | (81) 14.1 | EBIT/Interest | (10) 5.6 | (15) 14.1 | (20) 28.9 | (26) 15.5 | | |
| 5.0 | 3.8 | 3.2 | | | | -1.1 | 4.0 | 3.9 | 2.6 |
| | | 310.5 | 16.4 | Net Profit + Depr., Dep., | | | | | |
| | (10) 45.6 | (14) 3.1 | Amort./Cur. Mat. L/T/D | | | | | | |
| | 21.4 | .5 | | | | | | | |
| .1 | .0 | .0 | | | | .2 | .1 | .0 | .1 |
| .2 | .2 | .2 | Fixed/Worth | | | .3 | .2 | .1 | .3 |
| .7 | .7 | .8 | | | | 1.8 | .5 | .3 | 1.6 |
| .7 | .5 | .5 | | | | .5 | .4 | .4 | .7 |
| 1.5 | 1.3 | 1.3 | Debt/Worth | | | 1.9 | 1.2 | 1.0 | 2.7 |
| 3.6 | 4.3 | 3.5 | | | | 12.1 | 2.8 | 1.8 | 4.5 |
| 80.9 | 59.3 | 52.2 | % Profit Before Taxes/Tangible | | | 61.5 | 51.6 | 48.8 | 49.8 |
| (78) 46.7 | (99) 33.2 | (96) 26.3 | Net Worth | (12) 13.3 | 22.4 | (28) 25.4 | (27) 28.7 | | |
| 23.5 | 14.2 | 9.2 | | | | -4.3 | 7.8 | 10.8 | 10.6 |
| 35.6 | 26.1 | 22.4 | % Profit Before Taxes/Total | | | 39.6 | 13.7 | 24.1 | 20.6 |
| 20.0 | 12.8 | 11.3 | Assets | | | 9.2 | 8.2 | 14.3 | 12.1 |
| 7.1 | 3.8 | 3.4 | | | | -1.4 | 2.7 | 3.9 | 4.3 |
| 148.8 | 134.4 | 137.4 | | | | 125.5 | 96.5 | 176.9 | 83.7 |
| 52.9 | 53.5 | 44.0 | Sales/Net Fixed Assets | | | 33.2 | 33.7 | 75.9 | 25.0 |
| 17.9 | 17.2 | 12.9 | | | | 14.1 | 12.2 | 36.4 | 7.9 |
| 4.7 | 4.5 | 3.5 | | | | 4.5 | 3.3 | 3.3 | 3.3 |
| 2.9 | 3.0 | 2.8 | Sales/Total Assets | | | 3.1 | 2.7 | 2.6 | 2.4 |
| 2.2 | 2.0 | 2.1 | | | | 2.0 | 1.8 | 1.9 | 2.1 |
| .3 | .3 | .3 | | | | | | .2 | .3 |
| (57) .6 | (70) .5 | (71) .5 | % Depr., Dep., Amort./Sales | | | | | (24) .4 | (25) .5 |
| 1.2 | 1.1 | 1.2 | | | | | | 1.1 | 1.2 |
| 1.2 | 1.3 | 1.0 | % Officers', Directors' | | | | | .7 | |
| (43) 3.3 | (47) 3.0 | (36) 2.4 | Owners' Comp/Sales | | | | | (12) 1.5 | |
| 6.2 | 4.4 | 5.0 | | | | | | 2.5 | |
| 2342827M | 3602439M | 3201193M | Net Sales ($) | 477M | 19289M | 49801M | 157857M | 480524M | 2493245M |
| 987631M | 1689790M | 1287863M | Total Assets ($) | 159M | 5543M | 16679M | 63431M | 213720M | 988331M |

© RMA 2024  M = $ thousand  MM = $ million
See Pages viii through xx for Explanation of Ratios and Data

# RETAIL—All Other Home Furnishings Retailers  NAICS 449129

## Current Data Sorted by Assets | Comparative Historical Data

| | | | | | | | Type of Statement | | |
|---|---|---|---|---|---|---|---|---|---|
| | | | 1 | 2 | 1 | | Unqualified | 7 | 1 |
| | | 1 | 1 | 3 | | | Reviewed | 3 | 3 |
| | | 1 | 5 | 2 | | | Compiled | 8 | 1 |
| 2 | 8 | 5 | 4 | 2 | | | Tax Returns | 30 | 18 |
| 5 | 6 | 4 | 9 | 9 | 2 | 3 | Other | 54 | 34 |
| | | 8 (4/1-9/30/23) | | 57 (10/1/23-3/31/24) | | | | 4/1/19-3/31/20 | 4/1/20-3/31/21 |
| 0-500M | 500M-2MM | 2-10MM | 10-50MM | 50-100MM | 100-250MM | | | ALL | ALL |
| 7 | 14 | 20 | 18 | 3 | 3 | | NUMBER OF STATEMENTS | 102 | 57 |
| % | % | % | % | % | % | | ASSETS | % | % |
| | 16.2 | 23.5 | 15.1 | | | | Cash & Equivalents | 17.1 | 25.1 |
| | 11.2 | 11.7 | 12.7 | | | | Trade Receivables (net) | 8.2 | 11.1 |
| | 37.6 | 33.2 | 38.3 | | | | Inventory | 44.3 | 37.5 |
| | .9 | 5.3 | 7.2 | | | | All Other Current | 3.6 | 1.2 |
| | 65.8 | 73.6 | 73.4 | | | | Total Current | 73.2 | 74.9 |
| | 21.8 | 16.1 | 15.0 | | | | Fixed Assets (net) | 15.2 | 13.5 |
| | 11.9 | 3.1 | 4.6 | | | | Intangibles (net) | 6.4 | 5.1 |
| | .5 | 7.2 | 7.0 | | | | All Other Non-Current | 5.3 | 6.5 |
| | 100.0 | 100.0 | 100.0 | | | | Total | 100.0 | 100.0 |
| | | | | | | | LIABILITIES | | |
| | 3.4 | 4.5 | 10.2 | | | | Notes Payable-Short Term | 9.9 | 11.9 |
| | .2 | .6 | 5.2 | | | | Cur. Mat.-L.T.D. | 2.1 | 1.1 |
| | 10.9 | 12.3 | 11.6 | | | | Trade Payables | 16.2 | 11.9 |
| | .2 | .8 | .1 | | | | Income Taxes Payable | .1 | .1 |
| | 15.3 | 21.6 | 13.8 | | | | All Other Current | 16.2 | 17.8 |
| | 29.9 | 39.9 | 41.0 | | | | Total Current | 44.4 | 42.7 |
| | 23.1 | 13.8 | 14.9 | | | | Long-Term Debt | 18.4 | 13.5 |
| | .0 | .0 | .0 | | | | Deferred Taxes | .1 | .0 |
| | 7.2 | 4.4 | 7.2 | | | | All Other Non-Current | 7.6 | 7.1 |
| | 39.7 | 41.9 | 37.0 | | | | Net Worth | 29.5 | 36.7 |
| | 100.0 | 100.0 | 100.0 | | | | Total Liabilities & Net Worth | 100.0 | 100.0 |
| | | | | | | | INCOME DATA | | |
| | 100.0 | 100.0 | 100.0 | | | | Net Sales | 100.0 | 100.0 |
| | 42.1 | 44.7 | 38.9 | | | | Gross Profit | 45.3 | 43.2 |
| | 39.2 | 33.0 | 35.1 | | | | Operating Expenses | 41.2 | 35.9 |
| | 2.9 | 11.7 | 3.8 | | | | Operating Profit | 4.1 | 7.4 |
| | .3 | .6 | .9 | | | | All Other Expenses (net) | 1.2 | -.2 |
| | 2.5 | 11.1 | 2.9 | | | | Profit Before Taxes | 2.9 | 7.6 |
| | | | | | | | RATIOS | | |
| | 7.4 | 3.3 | 3.7 | | | | | 3.4 | 5.1 |
| | 2.2 | 2.4 | 2.2 | | | | Current | 2.0 | 1.8 |
| | 1.7 | 1.3 | 1.4 | | | | | 1.1 | 1.2 |
| | 2.4 | 1.6 | 1.6 | | | | | 1.4 | 2.6 |
| | 1.1 | .9 | .8 | | | | Quick  (101) | .6 | .8 |
| | .6 | .3 | .5 | | | | | .2 | .4 |
| 0 | UND | 1 | 248.0 | 0 | 911.0 | | | 0  UND | 0  UND |
| 0 | UND | 14 | 26.2 | 16 | 22.8 | | Sales/Receivables | 3  142.5 | 4  85.9 |
| 23 | 16.2 | 33 | 11.1 | 54 | 6.8 | | | 18  20.8 | 24  15.4 |
| 40 | 9.1 | 32 | 11.5 | 66 | 5.5 | | | 58  6.3 | 42  8.7 |
| 70 | 5.2 | 76 | 4.8 | 111 | 3.3 | | Cost of Sales/Inventory | 104  3.5 | 87  4.2 |
| 174 | 2.1 | 174 | 2.1 | 203 | 1.8 | | | 192  1.9 | 135  2.7 |
| 6 | 58.7 | 7 | 52.0 | 10 | 35.4 | | | 10  35.2 | 4  100.9 |
| 15 | 25.1 | 25 | 14.6 | 20 | 17.9 | | Cost of Sales/Payables | 33  11.1 | 23  15.7 |
| 50 | 7.3 | 57 | 6.4 | 39 | 9.4 | | | 53  6.9 | 49  7.5 |
| | 4.7 | 3.0 | 2.6 | | | | | 4.9 | 4.5 |
| | 9.1 | 7.1 | 5.4 | | | | Sales/Working Capital | 8.0 | 8.7 |
| | 15.1 | 16.4 | 11.8 | | | | | 69.8 | 33.8 |
| | 47.0 | 47.4 | 20.7 | | | | | 14.4 | 28.3 |
| (10) | 7.4 | (16) 12.6 | (14) 2.9 | | | | EBIT/Interest | (81) 5.9 | (42) 7.0 |
| | 1.1 | 3.7 | -1.5 | | | | | 1.5 | 3.6 |
| | | | | | | | Net Profit + Depr., Dep., Amort./Cur. Mat. L/T/D | | |
| | .2 | .0 | .1 | | | | | .1 | .0 |
| | .7 | .1 | .4 | | | | Fixed/Worth | .5 | .3 |
| | NM | 1.2 | 1.6 | | | | | 4.6 | 1.0 |
| | 1.0 | .7 | .8 | | | | | .6 | .6 |
| | 1.9 | 1.6 | 1.8 | | | | Debt/Worth | 2.2 | 2.1 |
| | NM | 3.7 | 7.3 | | | | | 14.9 | 6.2 |
| | 42.8 | 95.2 | 39.0 | | | | | 54.3 | 141.2 |
| | (11) 21.3 | (19) 50.4 | (16) 13.4 | | | | % Profit Before Taxes/Tangible Net Worth | (80) 29.8 | (51) 46.8 |
| | -6.2 | 23.2 | 1.2 | | | | | 5.1 | 17.2 |
| | 15.8 | 32.0 | 17.6 | | | | | 20.9 | 31.3 |
| | 3.5 | 13.9 | 5.0 | | | | % Profit Before Taxes/Total Assets | 6.7 | 12.8 |
| | -6.3 | 4.6 | -3.1 | | | | | .3 | 5.4 |
| | 132.1 | 119.1 | 123.9 | | | | | 90.6 | 142.1 |
| | 31.2 | 46.2 | 28.2 | | | | Sales/Net Fixed Assets | 27.1 | 26.4 |
| | 6.8 | 19.5 | 5.7 | | | | | 11.0 | 14.5 |
| | 3.4 | 2.8 | 2.2 | | | | | 3.6 | 3.6 |
| | 2.3 | 2.0 | 1.5 | | | | Sales/Total Assets | 2.5 | 2.4 |
| | 1.8 | 1.2 | 1.2 | | | | | 1.7 | 1.8 |
| | | .4 | .4 | | | | | .4 | .5 |
| | | (10) .6 | (13) .8 | | | | % Depr., Dep., Amort./Sales | (63) .6 | (32) .9 |
| | | 1.2 | 1.9 | | | | | 1.3 | 1.5 |
| | | | | | | | | 1.8 | 2.9 |
| | | | | | | | % Officers', Directors' Owners' Comp/Sales | (40) 3.9 | (17) 6.0 |
| | | | | | | | | 6.9 | 11.8 |
| 6856M | 35360M | 195823M | 886435M | 437392M | 940887M | | Net Sales ($) | 3228983M | 1363219M |
| 1485M | 13601M | 91725M | 429729M | 220281M | 483148M | | Total Assets ($) | 1494967M | 716179M |

M = $ thousand    MM = $ million
See Pages viii through xx for Explanation of Ratios and Data

© RMA 2024

# RETAIL—All Other Home Furnishings Retailers  NAICS 449129

| Comparative Historical Data ||| Type of Statement | Current Data Sorted by Sales ||||||
|---|---|---|---|---|---|---|---|---|---|
| 3 | 6 | 4 | Unqualified | | | | | 2 | 2 |
| 1 | 4 | 4 | Reviewed | | | | 1 | 1 | 2 |
| 3 | 6 | 7 | Compiled | | | 1 | 2 | 2 | 2 |
| 20 | 18 | 16 | Tax Returns | 2 | 4 | 5 | 2 | 2 | 1 |
| 38 | 44 | 34 | Other | 4 | 8 | 1 | 5 | 5 | 11 |
| 4/1/21-3/31/22 ALL | 4/1/22-3/31/23 ALL | 4/1/23-3/31/24 ALL | | 0-1MM | 1-3MM (4/1-9/30/23) | 3-5MM | 5-10MM | 10-25MM (10/1/23-3/31/24) | 25MM & OVER |
| 65 | 78 | 65 | NUMBER OF STATEMENTS | 6 | 12 | 7 | 10 | 12 | 18 |
| % | % | % | ASSETS | % | % | % | % | % | % |
| 19.7 | 15.9 | 17.9 | Cash & Equivalents | 21.0 | 21.5 | | 20.2 | 15.9 | |
| 16.8 | 13.0 | 12.3 | Trade Receivables (net) | 9.7 | 21.7 | | 10.5 | 11.3 | |
| 37.0 | 40.5 | 34.7 | Inventory | 33.5 | 28.7 | | 43.2 | 35.5 | |
| 1.9 | 4.0 | 4.8 | All Other Current | 2.3 | 1.5 | | 3.4 | 6.8 | |
| 75.5 | 73.3 | 69.7 | Total Current | 66.5 | 73.3 | | 77.3 | 69.5 | |
| 12.3 | 15.2 | 16.6 | Fixed Assets (net) | 6.0 | 16.6 | | 15.2 | 14.2 | |
| 4.5 | 2.1 | 5.4 | Intangibles (net) | 12.3 | 6.1 | | 3.6 | 4.4 | |
| 7.7 | 9.4 | 8.4 | All Other Non-Current | 15.2 | 4.0 | | 3.9 | 11.9 | |
| 100.0 | 100.0 | 100.0 | Total | 100.0 | 100.0 | | 100.0 | 100.0 | 100.0 |
| | | | LIABILITIES | | | | | | |
| 5.4 | 9.0 | 9.4 | Notes Payable-Short Term | 18.7 | 1.7 | | 5.6 | 10.8 | |
| 1.1 | 2.7 | 1.8 | Cur. Mat.-L.T.D. | .2 | .8 | | 4.2 | 3.1 | |
| 9.5 | 14.4 | 11.4 | Trade Payables | 8.4 | 15.8 | | 10.5 | 13.0 | |
| .6 | .4 | .4 | Income Taxes Payable | .0 | 1.4 | | .2 | .3 | |
| 26.4 | 17.6 | 16.0 | All Other Current | 20.3 | 14.5 | | 18.9 | 18.2 | |
| 43.1 | 44.2 | 39.0 | Total Current | 47.5 | 34.2 | | 39.5 | 45.3 | |
| 19.4 | 21.9 | 17.1 | Long-Term Debt | 18.0 | 13.9 | | 15.0 | 16.2 | |
| .0 | .1 | .0 | Deferred Taxes | .0 | .0 | | .0 | .0 | |
| 3.7 | 3.6 | 6.7 | All Other Non-Current | 8.6 | 4.9 | | 4.8 | 8.8 | |
| 33.9 | 30.2 | 37.2 | Net Worth | 25.9 | 47.0 | | 40.8 | 29.7 | |
| 100.0 | 100.0 | 100.0 | Total Liabilties & Net Worth | 100.0 | 100.0 | | 100.0 | 100.0 | |
| | | | INCOME DATA | | | | | | |
| 100.0 | 100.0 | 100.0 | Net Sales | 100.0 | 100.0 | | 100.0 | 100.0 | |
| 46.1 | 43.3 | 42.9 | Gross Profit | 49.8 | 42.8 | | 42.3 | 39.8 | |
| 37.4 | 35.1 | 36.9 | Operating Expenses | 42.0 | 34.0 | | 38.4 | 34.5 | |
| 8.7 | 8.2 | 6.0 | Operating Profit | 7.8 | 8.7 | | 3.9 | 5.3 | |
| -1.1 | -.1 | 1.0 | All Other Expenses (net) | .7 | -.6 | | 1.1 | 1.9 | |
| 9.8 | 8.3 | 5.0 | Profit Before Taxes | 7.0 | 9.3 | | 2.8 | 3.4 | |
| | | | RATIOS | | | | | | |
| 4.3 | 3.0 | 3.7 | | 7.0 | 3.6 | | 3.7 | 2.8 | |
| 2.0 | 1.8 | 2.1 | Current | 2.0 | 2.2 | | 2.2 | 1.7 | |
| 1.2 | 1.2 | 1.2 | | 1.0 | 1.4 | | 1.3 | 1.2 | |
| 1.8 | 1.6 | 1.7 | | 2.9 | 2.6 | | 1.5 | 1.4 | |
| (64) 1.0 | .6 | .9 | Quick | .9 | 1.0 | | 1.0 | .6 | |
| .4 | .2 | .4 | | .3 | .5 | | .4 | .3 | |
| 0 999.8 | 0 999.8 | 0 999.8 | | 0 UND | 20 18.0 | | 6 65.6 | 1 594.1 | |
| 9 38.7 | 7 54.9 | 10 36.2 | Sales/Receivables | 0 UND | 39 9.4 | | 18 20.5 | 6 57.5 | |
| 34 10.8 | 32 11.3 | 34 10.6 | | 17 21.4 | 53 6.9 | | 39 9.4 | 51 7.2 | |
| 54 6.8 | 46 8.0 | 40 9.1 | | 0 UND | 42 8.7 | | 64 5.7 | 66 5.5 | |
| 114 3.2 | 111 3.3 | 78 4.7 | Cost of Sales/Inventory | 51 7.1 | 76 4.8 | | 135 2.7 | 96 3.8 | |
| 203 1.8 | 215 1.7 | 174 2.1 | | 159 2.3 | 174 2.1 | | 261 1.4 | 159 2.3 | |
| 6 64.7 | 11 32.6 | 10 37.8 | | 0 757.5 | 20 18.4 | | 9 40.4 | 13 28.5 | |
| 24 15.4 | 33 11.2 | 22 16.6 | Cost of Sales/Payables | 10 37.8 | 41 8.8 | | 24 14.9 | 22 16.9 | |
| 51 7.2 | 58 6.3 | 51 7.2 | | 47 7.8 | 107 3.4 | | 48 7.6 | 41 8.9 | |
| 3.6 | 4.0 | 3.3 | | 5.1 | 3.1 | | 2.9 | 5.0 | |
| 6.7 | 7.9 | 7.4 | Sales/Working Capital | 18.8 | 6.0 | | 5.1 | 7.6 | |
| 21.0 | 21.3 | 19.1 | | NM | 14.9 | | 21.5 | 28.9 | |
| 71.4 | 43.5 | 29.7 | | | | | | | 32.0 |
| (43) 21.8 | (57) 9.6 | (49) 5.7 | EBIT/Interest | | | | | (16) 3.0 | |
| 5.8 | 2.3 | 1.1 | | | | | | | .1 |
| | | | Net Profit + Depr., Dep., Amort./Cur. Mat. L/T/D | | | | | | |
| .1 | .0 | .1 | | .0 | .0 | | .0 | .1 | |
| .2 | .3 | .3 | Fixed/Worth | 1.0 | .2 | | .1 | .4 | |
| 1.2 | 1.0 | 1.9 | | -.1 | 1.8 | | .9 | 1.4 | |
| 1.0 | .7 | .8 | | .5 | .4 | | .7 | 1.0 | |
| 1.9 | 2.0 | 1.9 | Debt/Worth | 4.7 | 1.8 | | 2.0 | 1.8 | |
| 5.4 | 5.0 | 5.3 | | -3.5 | 2.4 | | 9.9 | 5.9 | |
| 105.3 | 77.9 | 55.1 | % Profit Before Taxes/Tangible Net Worth | | | | 85.5 | 45.1 | |
| (56) 59.6 | (71) 35.9 | (56) 27.3 | | | 13.1 | | (15) 27.5 | | |
| 33.8 | 4.9 | 4.4 | | | | | | 1.2 | 12.4 |
| 35.6 | 34.9 | 25.0 | % Profit Before Taxes/Total Assets | 47.9 | 26.2 | | 13.5 | 28.8 | |
| 22.7 | 14.1 | 8.3 | | 11.2 | 13.6 | | 4.2 | 7.7 | |
| 10.5 | 3.7 | .5 | | -5.2 | 4.5 | | .7 | -3.8 | |
| 140.9 | 116.9 | 107.8 | Sales/Net Fixed Assets | UND | 83.9 | | 999.8 | 56.3 | |
| 33.6 | 33.9 | 34.2 | | 105.5 | 38.8 | | 36.5 | 31.4 | |
| 12.9 | 12.3 | 8.3 | | 30.8 | 13.3 | | 4.1 | 8.5 | |
| 3.2 | 3.2 | 3.1 | Sales/Total Assets | 6.7 | 2.3 | | 3.0 | 3.9 | |
| 2.2 | 2.2 | 2.0 | | 2.3 | 2.0 | | 1.5 | 1.9 | |
| 1.6 | 1.6 | 1.4 | | 1.6 | 1.2 | | 1.3 | 1.5 | |
| .5 | .5 | .4 | | | | | | | .6 |
| (35) .7 | (48) .9 | (36) .8 | % Depr., Dep., Amort./Sales | | | | | (14) 1.0 | |
| 1.3 | 1.7 | 2.0 | | | | | | | 2.0 |
| 1.6 | 1.8 | 1.5 | % Officers', Directors' Owners' Comp/Sales | | | | | | |
| (24) 3.1 | (26) 4.9 | (20) 3.6 | | | | | | | |
| 5.5 | 7.8 | 5.3 | | | | | | | |
| 1815855M | 3847695M | 2502753M | Net Sales ($) | 3892M | 22312M | 26236M | 65723M | 216945M | 2167645M |
| 927417M | 1923978M | 1239969M | Total Assets ($) | 4938M | 11710M | 12836M | 40132M | 134741M | 1035612M |

© RMA 2024  M = $ thousand   MM = $ million
See Pages viii through xx for Explanation of Ratios and Data

# RETAIL—Electronics and Appliance Retailers  NAICS 449210

## Current Data Sorted by Assets | Comparative Historical Data

| Type of Statement | | | | | | | | |
|---|---|---|---|---|---|---|---|---|
| | | | | 1 | 3 | 5 | | |
| | | | 2 | 9 | 3 | 1 | 9 | 16 |
| | | 4 | 9 | 4 | | | 19 | 7 |
| 4 | | 6 | 16 | 2 | | | 21 | 14 |
| 7 | | 5 | 43 | 56 | 22 | 8 | 51 | 20 |
| | 72 (4/1-9/30/23) | | | 138 (10/1/23-3/31/24) | | | 117 | 63 |
| | | | | | | | 4/1/19- | 4/1/20- |
| | | | | | | | 3/31/20 | 3/31/21 |
| 0-500M | 500M-2MM | 2-10MM | 10-50MM | 50-100MM | 100-250MM | | ALL | ALL |

| | | | | | | | NUMBER OF STATEMENTS | | |
|---|---|---|---|---|---|---|---|---|---|
| 11 | 15 | 70 | 72 | 28 | 14 | | 217 | 120 |
| % | % | % | % | % | % | ASSETS | % | % |
| 22.5 | 16.9 | 17.4 | 16.9 | 18.7 | 16.2 | Cash & Equivalents | 17.1 | 24.9 |
| 19.4 | 9.4 | 9.8 | 14.2 | 11.3 | 10.5 | Trade Receivables (net) | 16.0 | 12.0 |
| 35.9 | 33.4 | 58.0 | 49.6 | 46.5 | 32.6 | Inventory | 38.4 | 28.9 |
| 6.3 | 1.8 | 1.4 | 2.5 | 4.9 | 1.9 | All Other Current | 2.9 | 5.7 |
| 84.1 | 61.5 | 86.6 | 83.1 | 81.4 | 61.1 | Total Current | 74.4 | 71.5 |
| 3.3 | 24.1 | 7.6 | 9.1 | 9.4 | 12.1 | Fixed Assets (net) | 13.2 | 10.8 |
| 4.5 | 2.1 | 1.8 | 1.7 | .4 | 6.7 | Intangibles (net) | 5.3 | 8.8 |
| 8.1 | 12.2 | 4.0 | 6.2 | 8.8 | 20.1 | All Other Non-Current | 7.1 | 9.0 |
| 100.0 | 100.0 | 100.0 | 100.0 | 100.0 | 100.0 | Total | 100.0 | 100.0 |
| | | | | | | LIABILITIES | | |
| 26.1 | 3.7 | 6.9 | 4.2 | .2 | 3.1 | Notes Payable-Short Term | 10.3 | 8.0 |
| 4.4 | 3.0 | .6 | .8 | .5 | .2 | Cur. Mat.-L.T.D. | 1.6 | 2.3 |
| 19.9 | 15.7 | 26.3 | 28.0 | 13.8 | 8.6 | Trade Payables | 18.7 | 12.9 |
| .6 | .0 | .1 | .1 | .3 | .1 | Income Taxes Payable | .1 | .2 |
| 17.9 | 22.5 | 20.1 | 17.0 | 13.4 | 10.0 | All Other Current | 19.2 | 20.1 |
| 69.0 | 44.9 | 54.0 | 50.1 | 28.2 | 22.0 | Total Current | 49.9 | 43.6 |
| 33.8 | 33.4 | 8.3 | 6.8 | 2.7 | 7.8 | Long-Term Debt | 12.2 | 16.3 |
| .0 | .0 | .3 | .1 | .1 | .0 | Deferred Taxes | .1 | .2 |
| 10.2 | 2.4 | 4.2 | 4.9 | 13.5 | 17.5 | All Other Non-Current | 4.5 | 6.3 |
| -13.1 | 19.3 | 33.2 | 38.1 | 55.5 | 52.7 | Net Worth | 33.2 | 33.6 |
| 100.0 | 100.0 | 100.0 | 100.0 | 100.0 | 100.0 | Total Liabilities & Net Worth | 100.0 | 100.0 |
| | | | | | | INCOME DATA | | |
| 100.0 | 100.0 | 100.0 | 100.0 | 100.0 | 100.0 | Net Sales | 100.0 | 100.0 |
| 39.6 | 35.7 | 32.3 | 28.3 | 31.3 | 35.9 | Gross Profit | 34.0 | 39.6 |
| 37.0 | 35.3 | 30.4 | 25.9 | 27.0 | 31.9 | Operating Expenses | 30.0 | 33.6 |
| 2.6 | .4 | 1.9 | 2.3 | 4.3 | 4.0 | Operating Profit | 4.0 | 5.9 |
| .2 | 1.1 | -.2 | -.1 | -.4 | -.7 | All Other Expenses (net) | .1 | .0 |
| 2.5 | -.8 | 2.1 | 2.4 | 4.7 | 4.7 | Profit Before Taxes | 3.9 | 6.0 |
| | | | | | | RATIOS | | |
| 2.0 | 2.7 | 2.7 | 2.5 | 4.1 | 7.7 | | 2.7 | 3.0 |
| 1.4 | 1.3 | 1.8 | 1.6 | 3.2 | 4.6 | Current | 1.6 | 1.7 |
| .8 | .8 | 1.3 | 1.3 | 2.0 | 2.7 | | 1.1 | 1.2 |
| .9 | 1.1 | 1.0 | 1.0 | 1.6 | 5.6 | | 1.4 | 2.0 |
| .5 | .7 | .5 | .5 | .9 | 1.1 | Quick | .7 | .9 |
| .2 | .3 | .2 | .3 | .5 | .6 | | .3 | .4 |
| 0 UND | 0 758.7 | 2 240.8 | 8 43.7 | 9 41.7 | 9 41.5 | | 4 103.1 | 2 210.6 |
| 5 72.3 | 4 99.1 | 6 62.1 | 14 25.5 | 13 27.4 | 11 34.2 | Sales/Receivables | 11 34.5 | 11 32.1 |
| 21 17.5 | 17 22.1 | 17 20.9 | 22 16.7 | 28 13.0 | 29 12.5 | | 27 13.7 | 24 14.9 |
| 4 91.6 | 25 14.7 | 74 4.9 | 68 5.4 | 81 4.5 | 43 8.5 | | 24 15.5 | 10 34.8 |
| 25 14.8 | 54 6.8 | 101 3.6 | 96 3.8 | 101 3.6 | 89 4.1 | Cost of Sales/Inventory | 63 5.8 | 60 6.1 |
| 74 4.9 | 96 3.8 | 140 2.6 | 122 3.0 | 122 3.0 | 118 3.1 | | 107 3.4 | 89 4.1 |
| 0 UND | 3 134.2 | 16 22.9 | 25 14.7 | 17 21.6 | 2 150.3 | | 8 46.0 | 7 50.4 |
| 4 100.4 | 18 20.8 | 40 9.2 | 49 7.5 | 30 12.0 | 18 20.0 | Cost of Sales/Payables | 26 13.8 | 24 14.9 |
| 30 12.3 | 62 5.9 | 63 5.8 | 66 5.5 | 38 9.5 | 31 11.7 | | 47 7.8 | 45 8.1 |
| 11.3 | 6.1 | 4.9 | 4.4 | 3.2 | 3.5 | | 6.3 | 4.8 |
| 46.5 | 26.3 | 7.1 | 9.8 | 5.5 | 4.2 | Sales/Working Capital | 13.4 | 10.5 |
| -67.2 | -36.6 | 24.0 | 19.3 | 6.5 | 5.8 | | 54.1 | 20.6 |
| | 3.9 | 101.6 | 131.0 | 999.8 | 60.5 | | 14.9 | 39.3 |
| (13) 2.6 | (51) 8.4 | (62) 11.3 | (14) 289.9 | (10) 19.0 | EBIT/Interest | (166) 6.3 | (91) 9.3 |
| | -2.2 | .3 | 1.3 | 9.9 | 6.2 | | 1.7 | 1.5 |
| | | | | | | Net Profit + Depr., Dep., | 8.4 | 3.4 |
| | | | | | | Amort./Cur. Mat. L/T/D | (18) 2.8 | (12) 1.5 |
| | | | | | | | 1.1 | .7 |
| .0 | .0 | .0 | .1 | .1 | .0 | | .1 | .1 |
| .0 | .9 | .1 | .1 | .1 | .3 | Fixed/Worth | .3 | .3 |
| 1.1 | -1.2 | .9 | .3 | .3 | .4 | | 1.4 | 2.8 |
| 1.0 | .8 | .7 | .8 | .4 | .5 | | .7 | .6 |
| 11.1 | 2.9 | 2.0 | 1.6 | .7 | 1.0 | Debt/Worth | 2.5 | 2.0 |
| -2.1 | -6.9 | 5.8 | 3.5 | 1.6 | 1.7 | | 9.3 | 53.4 |
| | | 47.1 | 36.4 | 31.9 | 18.8 | % Profit Before Taxes/Tangible | 73.6 | 80.5 |
| | (60) 19.0 | (69) 16.4 | 24.6 | (12) 15.8 | Net Worth | (184) 28.7 | (92) 37.9 |
| | | 1.6 | 1.0 | 11.3 | 3.3 | | 6.1 | 16.4 |
| 33.9 | 16.9 | 16.2 | 13.2 | 17.8 | 15.2 | % Profit Before Taxes/Total | 19.8 | 25.9 |
| 18.5 | 6.8 | 6.1 | 6.2 | 13.2 | 8.1 | Assets | 9.3 | 12.9 |
| 1.7 | -2.3 | -.3 | .4 | 4.1 | .5 | | 2.2 | 4.1 |
| UND | 131.3 | 252.2 | 192.9 | 124.1 | 127.8 | | 146.6 | 144.1 |
| UND | 15.2 | 80.3 | 57.9 | 63.8 | 21.9 | Sales/Net Fixed Assets | 52.1 | 53.2 |
| 161.7 | 3.7 | 38.9 | 17.3 | 15.1 | 8.3 | | 18.7 | 20.9 |
| 13.5 | 3.9 | 3.8 | 3.5 | 3.3 | 2.2 | | 5.5 | 3.8 |
| 7.3 | 3.0 | 2.9 | 2.5 | 2.1 | 1.8 | Sales/Total Assets | 3.3 | 2.6 |
| 2.6 | 1.6 | 2.3 | 1.9 | 1.7 | 1.5 | | 2.2 | 1.8 |
| | .4 | .2 | .1 | .3 | .3 | | .3 | .3 |
| (11) 1.0 | (48) .4 | (53) .4 | (27) .4 | (13) .6 | % Depr., Dep., Amort./Sales | (150) .7 | (75) .5 |
| | 3.7 | .6 | .7 | .9 | 1.1 | | 1.4 | 1.6 |
| | | .6 | .3 | | | % Officers', Directors' | 1.3 | 1.2 |
| | (41) 1.4 | (28) .7 | | | Owners' Comp/Sales | (77) 2.4 | (37) 2.6 |
| | | 3.5 | 1.4 | | | | 4.2 | 5.5 |
| 27212M | 57405M | 1173267M | 4495167M | 5106557M | 4337643M | Net Sales ($) | 10602437M | 7260070M |
| 3289M | 19055M | 345117M | 1781277M | 2099712M | 2143177M | Total Assets ($) | 3676485M | 3305345M |

M = $ thousand    MM = $ million
See Pages viii through xx for Explanation of Ratios and Data

© RMA 2024

## RETAIL—Electronics and Appliance Retailers  NAICS 449210

### Comparative Historical Data / Current Data Sorted by Sales

| Comparative Historical Data | | | | | | | Current Data Sorted by Sales | | | | | |
|---|---|---|---|---|---|---|---|---|---|---|---|---|
| | | | | | | Type of Statement | | | | | | |
| | 13 | | 9 | | 9 | Unqualified | | | | 1 | 2 | 9 |
| | 10 | | 15 | | 15 | Reviewed | | | | 3 | 6 | 12 |
| | 5 | | 8 | | 17 | Compiled | | | 1 | 8 | 6 | 7 |
| | 27 | | 37 | | 28 | Tax Returns | 1 | 5 | 4 | 11 | 6 | 4 |
| | 50 | | 92 | | 141 | Other | 3 | 6 | 1 | 11 | 42 | 78 |
| | 4/1/21-3/31/22 ALL | | 4/1/22-3/31/23 ALL | | 4/1/23-3/31/24 ALL | | 72 (4/1-9/30/23) | | | 138 (10/1/23-3/31/24) | | |
| | | | | | | | 0-1MM | 1-3MM | 3-5MM | 5-10MM | 10-25MM | 25MM & OVER |
| | 105 | | 161 | | 210 | NUMBER OF STATEMENTS | 4 | 11 | 6 | 23 | 56 | 110 |
| | % | | % | | % | ASSETS | % | % | % | % | % | % |
| | 22.4 | | 19.4 | | 17.5 | Cash & Equivalents | | 16.9 | | 22.3 | 15.6 | 16.8 |
| | 14.1 | | 13.4 | | 12.0 | Trade Receivables (net) | | 6.6 | | 13.2 | 9.1 | 13.2 |
| | 37.1 | | 40.1 | | 49.0 | Inventory | | 22.3 | | 50.7 | 57.9 | 47.6 |
| | 3.3 | | 3.0 | | 2.6 | All Other Current | | 6.8 | | 1.6 | 1.2 | 3.2 |
| | 76.9 | | 75.8 | | 81.1 | Total Current | | 52.6 | | 87.8 | 83.7 | 80.8 |
| | 11.4 | | 12.2 | | 9.6 | Fixed Assets (net) | | 29.2 | | 6.2 | 8.9 | 9.0 |
| | 5.0 | | 4.5 | | 2.1 | Intangibles (net) | | 5.1 | | 2.0 | 1.6 | 2.1 |
| | 6.6 | | 7.4 | | 7.2 | All Other Non-Current | | 13.1 | | 4.0 | 5.8 | 8.2 |
| | 100.0 | | 100.0 | | 100.0 | Total | | 100.0 | | 100.0 | 100.0 | 100.0 |
| | | | | | | LIABILITIES | | | | | | |
| | 7.5 | | 5.0 | | 5.6 | Notes Payable-Short Term | | 8.2 | | 9.8 | 4.7 | 3.9 |
| | 1.1 | | 1.5 | | 1.0 | Cur. Mat.-L.T.D. | | 4.0 | | .9 | .9 | .5 |
| | 12.5 | | 16.4 | | 23.0 | Trade Payables | | 14.4 | | 9.6 | 29.8 | 22.6 |
| | .1 | | .2 | | .2 | Income Taxes Payable | | .0 | | .0 | .2 | .1 |
| | 18.5 | | 19.1 | | 17.5 | All Other Current | | 14.2 | | 18.0 | 24.2 | 13.7 |
| | 39.7 | | 42.3 | | 47.2 | Total Current | | 40.8 | | 38.3 | 59.8 | 40.8 |
| | 13.5 | | 14.2 | | 10.2 | Long-Term Debt | | 61.9 | | 6.7 | 7.4 | 6.2 |
| | .0 | | .1 | | .2 | Deferred Taxes | | .0 | | .0 | .4 | .1 |
| | 6.1 | | 5.6 | | 6.7 | All Other Non-Current | | .1 | | 2.5 | 3.0 | 8.8 |
| | 40.7 | | 37.8 | | 35.7 | Net Worth | | -2.8 | | 52.5 | 29.4 | 44.2 |
| | 100.0 | | 100.0 | | 100.0 | Total Liabilities & Net Worth | | 100.0 | | 100.0 | 100.0 | 100.0 |
| | | | | | | INCOME DATA | | | | | | |
| | 100.0 | | 100.0 | | 100.0 | Net Sales | | 100.0 | | 100.0 | 100.0 | 100.0 |
| | 38.6 | | 36.6 | | 31.7 | Gross Profit | | 39.6 | | 36.2 | 31.2 | 29.5 |
| | 31.8 | | 30.7 | | 29.2 | Operating Expenses | | 40.2 | | 33.4 | 30.1 | 26.0 |
| | 6.8 | | 5.9 | | 2.4 | Operating Profit | | -.7 | | 2.9 | 1.1 | 3.4 |
| | -.9 | | -.2 | | -.1 | All Other Expenses (net) | | 2.0 | | .0 | -.2 | -.2 |
| | 7.7 | | 6.1 | | 2.5 | Profit Before Taxes | | -2.6 | | 2.8 | 1.3 | 3.7 |
| | | | | | | RATIOS | | | | | | |
| | 3.3 | | 3.3 | | 3.1 | | | 2.7 | | 7.8 | 2.5 | 3.4 |
| | 1.9 | | 1.8 | | 1.8 | Current | | 1.1 | | 2.2 | 1.7 | 2.0 |
| | 1.4 | | 1.3 | | 1.3 | | | .7 | | 1.6 | 1.1 | 1.5 |
| | 1.5 | | 1.4 | | 1.2 | | | 1.1 | | 2.5 | .7 | 1.2 |
| | .9 | | .8 | | .6 | Quick | | .7 | | 1.1 | .4 | .7 |
| | .5 | | .4 | | .3 | | | .3 | | .3 | .2 | .3 |
| 1 | 727.1 | 3 | 116.4 | 5 | 73.0 | | 0 | UND | 0 | UND | 3 129.1 | 8 43.7 |
| 8 | 43.2 | 11 | 32.0 | 10 | 35.2 | Sales/Receivables | 2 | 223.3 | 5 | 72.3 | 7 53.3 | 13 28.2 |
| 33 | 11.0 | 28 | 12.9 | 21 | 17.5 | | 17 | 22.1 | 21 | 17.3 | 17 22.0 | 22 16.4 |
| 19 | 19.7 | 42 | 8.6 | 66 | 5.5 | | 27 | 13.5 | 54 | 6.8 | 76 4.8 | 66 5.5 |
| 73 | 5.0 | 85 | 4.3 | 96 | 3.8 | Cost of Sales/Inventory | 46 | 8.0 | 107 | 3.4 | 101 3.6 | 91 4.0 |
| 107 | 3.4 | 135 | 2.7 | 126 | 2.9 | | 96 | 3.8 | 140 | 2.6 | 135 2.7 | 122 3.0 |
| 2 | 177.6 | 9 | 42.1 | 17 | 22.1 | | 0 | UND | 4 | 92.5 | 24 15.1 | 18 20.0 |
| 18 | 20.4 | 25 | 14.6 | 34 | 10.6 | Cost of Sales/Payables | 28 | 13.2 | 14 | 26.0 | 54 6.8 | 33 11.2 |
| 38 | 9.5 | 47 | 7.7 | 59 | 6.2 | | 66 | 5.5 | 37 | 9.9 | 76 4.8 | 51 7.1 |
| | 5.3 | | 4.7 | | 4.5 | | | 5.0 | | 3.6 | 5.2 | 4.1 |
| | 8.6 | | 7.9 | | 7.4 | Sales/Working Capital | | 44.4 | | 5.6 | 8.1 | 6.6 |
| | 19.1 | | 19.7 | | 20.3 | | | -24.3 | | 17.6 | 35.0 | 11.4 |
| | 74.3 | | 106.3 | | 100.6 | | | 3.2 | | 16.5 | 145.0 | 169.0 |
| (74) | 19.0 | (123) | 17.2 | (157) | 10.3 | EBIT/Interest | (10) | 2.3 | (15) | 4.7 | (43) 11.5 | (82) 14.8 |
| | 9.2 | | 3.2 | | 1.4 | | | -4.5 | | .2 | .5 | 2.7 |
| | | | 31.2 | | 84.6 | Net Profit + Depr., Dep., | | | | | | 95.7 |
| | | (15) | 4.0 | (16) | 8.6 | Amort./Cur. Mat. L/T/D | | | | | (11) | 5.9 |
| | | | .8 | | .0 | | | | | | | -1.8 |
| | .1 | | .0 | | .0 | | | .4 | | .0 | .1 | .0 |
| | .2 | | .2 | | .1 | Fixed/Worth | | .9 | | .0 | .1 | .1 |
| | .6 | | .6 | | .4 | | | -.9 | | .2 | .9 | .3 |
| | .7 | | .7 | | .6 | | | .8 | | .2 | .7 | .5 |
| | 1.7 | | 1.8 | | 1.6 | Debt/Worth | | UND | | 1.1 | 2.0 | 1.4 |
| | 3.8 | | 3.8 | | 4.5 | | | -2.7 | | 2.9 | 9.2 | 3.3 |
| | 96.9 | | 64.0 | | 34.2 | % Profit Before Taxes/Tangible | | 26.0 | | | 33.3 | 37.3 |
| (95) | 43.0 | (140) | 33.3 | (184) | 18.2 | Net Worth | (22) | 17.0 | (46) | 12.3 | (106) | 19.0 |
| | 19.8 | | 12.8 | | 2.9 | | | -5.0 | | | .7 | 7.8 |
| | 33.5 | | 21.8 | | 16.2 | % Profit Before Taxes/Total | | 12.4 | | 18.1 | 11.1 | 16.6 |
| | 16.9 | | 11.9 | | 6.8 | Assets | | 6.8 | | 7.6 | 5.1 | 9.1 |
| | 7.8 | | 3.4 | | .7 | | | -5.4 | | -.5 | -.6 | 2.8 |
| | 174.3 | | 181.5 | | 202.3 | | | 32.9 | | 999.8 | 198.7 | 180.5 |
| | 52.1 | | 39.9 | | 65.5 | Sales/Net Fixed Assets | | 11.6 | | 93.2 | 70.9 | 63.8 |
| | 23.0 | | 11.5 | | 17.1 | | | 2.9 | | 35.4 | 38.7 | 15.1 |
| | 4.0 | | 3.4 | | 3.7 | | | 3.2 | | 3.9 | 3.7 | 3.8 |
| | 2.9 | | 2.6 | | 2.6 | Sales/Total Assets | | 1.9 | | 2.7 | 2.9 | 2.5 |
| | 1.9 | | 1.6 | | 1.9 | | | 1.4 | | 1.8 | 2.1 | 1.8 |
| | .2 | | .2 | | .2 | | | | | .1 | .2 | .2 |
| (65) | .6 | (98) | .5 | (154) | .4 | % Depr., Dep., Amort./Sales | | | (12) | .5 | (44) .4 | (86) .4 |
| | 1.3 | | 1.1 | | .8 | | | | | 1.5 | .5 | .9 |
| | | | .9 | | .5 | | | | | 2.0 | .7 | .2 |
| (34) | 2.5 | (72) | 2.4 | (86) | 1.2 | % Officers', Directors' Owners' Comp/Sales | | | (10) | 3.1 | (28) 1.4 | (38) .5 |
| | 5.4 | | 4.6 | | 3.1 | | | | | 5.1 | 3.7 | 1.0 |
| | 3766174M | | 10572913M | | 15197251M | Net Sales ($) | 2139M | 21222M | 24995M | 162399M | 945098M | 14041398M |
| | 1861497M | | 4291795M | | 6391627M | Total Assets ($) | 650M | 10839M | 11682M | 63101M | 419586M | 5885769M |

© RMA 2024  M = $ thousand  MM = $ million
See Pages viii through xx for Explanation of Ratios and Data

# RETAIL—All Other General Merchandise Retailers  NAICS 455219

## Current Data Sorted by Assets / Comparative Historical Data

| | | | | | | | | | |
|---|---|---|---|---|---|---|---|---|---|
| | | | | 1 | 2 | 2 | **Type of Statement** | | |
| | 1 | | | 3 | | 1 | Unqualified | 5 | 4 |
| | | | 3 | | | | Reviewed | 2 | |
| 1 | 8 | 3 | | 19 | 2 | | Compiled | 3 | 4 |
| 6 | 7 | 21 | | | 8 | | Tax Returns | 15 | 6 |
| | 22 (4/1-9/30/23) | | | 66 (10/1/23-3/31/24) | | 5 | Other | 36 | 16 |
| 0-500M | 500M-2MM | 2-10MM | 10-50MM | 50-100MM | 100-250MM | | | 4/1/19-3/31/20 ALL | 4/1/20-3/31/21 ALL |
| 7 | 16 | 24 | 23 | 10 | 8 | | **NUMBER OF STATEMENTS** | 61 | 30 |
| % | % | % | % | % | % | | **ASSETS** | % | % |
| | 17.5 | 8.5 | 13.2 | 2.8 | | | Cash & Equivalents | 11.6 | 18.4 |
| | 6.2 | 5.8 | 5.8 | 8.3 | | | Trade Receivables (net) | 7.1 | 7.2 |
| | 49.9 | 60.4 | 48.6 | 60.5 | | | Inventory | 54.3 | 42.5 |
| | .8 | 2.7 | 7.4 | 5.4 | | | All Other Current | 1.6 | 2.0 |
| | 74.4 | 77.4 | 75.0 | 76.9 | | | Total Current | 74.5 | 70.1 |
| | 14.5 | 14.0 | 14.0 | 15.3 | | | Fixed Assets (net) | 17.0 | 20.8 |
| | 9.0 | 1.6 | 2.3 | 1.3 | | | Intangibles (net) | 2.1 | 3.5 |
| | 2.0 | 7.0 | 8.7 | 6.5 | | | All Other Non-Current | 6.4 | 5.7 |
| | 100.0 | 100.0 | 100.0 | 100.0 | | | Total | 100.0 | 100.0 |
| | | | | | | | **LIABILITIES** | | |
| | 9.6 | 6.0 | 5.2 | 9.6 | | | Notes Payable-Short Term | 15.8 | 8.5 |
| | 1.4 | 1.1 | 3.6 | 3.8 | | | Cur. Mat.-L.T.D. | 1.7 | 1.5 |
| | 19.7 | 35.1 | 11.3 | 12.6 | | | Trade Payables | 16.4 | 12.7 |
| | .7 | .0 | .0 | .2 | | | Income Taxes Payable | .2 | |
| | 12.5 | 12.2 | 9.3 | 7.9 | | | All Other Current | 12.1 | 9.5 |
| | 43.9 | 54.5 | 29.3 | 34.1 | | | Total Current | 46.2 | 32.2 |
| | 30.9 | 6.9 | 12.5 | 25.1 | | | Long-Term Debt | 14.0 | 21.1 |
| | .0 | .0 | .0 | .0 | | | Deferred Taxes | .0 | .1 |
| | 1.9 | 13.1 | 15.3 | 7.1 | | | All Other Non-Current | 6.6 | 20.0 |
| | 23.3 | 25.6 | 42.9 | 33.6 | | | Net Worth | 33.1 | 26.6 |
| | 100.0 | 100.0 | 100.0 | 100.0 | | | Total Liabilities & Net Worth | 100.0 | 100.0 |
| | | | | | | | **INCOME DATA** | | |
| | 100.0 | 100.0 | 100.0 | 100.0 | | | Net Sales | 100.0 | 100.0 |
| | 41.9 | 31.9 | 37.6 | 42.0 | | | Gross Profit | 39.4 | 41.2 |
| | 37.5 | 29.1 | 33.3 | 38.4 | | | Operating Expenses | 35.1 | 34.0 |
| | 4.4 | 2.7 | 4.3 | 3.6 | | | Operating Profit | 4.3 | 7.1 |
| | 1.2 | .0 | .4 | -1.1 | | | All Other Expenses (net) | .4 | -.5 |
| | 3.2 | 2.7 | 3.8 | 4.7 | | | Profit Before Taxes | 3.9 | 7.6 |
| | | | | | | | **RATIOS** | | |
| | 5.6 | 4.1 | 5.9 | 4.2 | | | | 3.7 | 4.5 |
| | 2.2 | 1.3 | 3.4 | 2.8 | | | Current | 1.8 | 2.5 |
| | 1.1 | 1.1 | 1.5 | 1.7 | | | | 1.3 | 1.6 |
| | 1.1 | .7 | 1.3 | .5 | | | | .8 | 1.5 |
| | .7 | .2 | .6 | .1 | | | Quick | .4 | .6 |
| | .1 | .1 | .2 | .0 | | | | .1 | .2 |
| 0 | UND | 0 | 999.8 | 3 | 110.6 | 0 | UND | 0 | UND | 0 | UND |
| 0 | UND | 3 | 124.7 | 5 | 79.5 | 1 | 441.4 | Sales/Receivables | 1 | 395.1 | 1 | 368.9 |
| 11 | 32.0 | 9 | 39.6 | 12 | 31.4 | 3 | 138.2 | | 10 | 37.3 | 5 | 72.0 |
| 21 | 17.3 | 81 | 4.5 | 104 | 3.5 | 62 | 5.9 | | 66 | 5.5 | 26 | 13.8 |
| 63 | 5.8 | 126 | 2.9 | 146 | 2.5 | 118 | 3.1 | Cost of Sales/Inventory | 107 | 3.4 | 104 | 3.5 |
| 203 | 1.8 | 243 | 1.5 | 215 | 1.7 | 456 | .8 | | 182 | 2.0 | 182 | 2.0 |
| 0 | UND | 15 | 24.0 | 15 | 25.0 | 17 | 21.9 | | 4 | 96.5 | 9 | 42.3 |
| 24 | 15.1 | 57 | 6.4 | 27 | 13.5 | 30 | 12.1 | Cost of Sales/Payables | 24 | 14.9 | 22 | 16.4 |
| 49 | 7.5 | 135 | 2.7 | 43 | 8.5 | 38 | 9.7 | | 41 | 8.9 | 29 | 12.8 |
| | 3.8 | 4.6 | 2.2 | 2.5 | | | | 4.8 | 3.3 |
| | 8.4 | 11.9 | 4.6 | 5.2 | | | Sales/Working Capital | 10.5 | 7.6 |
| | 31.5 | 37.0 | 9.7 | 11.8 | | | | 30.8 | 22.0 |
| | 8.0 | 19.4 | 77.2 | | | | | 16.5 | 32.6 |
| | (13) 3.9 | (22) 2.5 | (22) 6.1 | | | | EBIT/Interest | (52) 6.0 | (26) 16.7 |
| | -1.0 | -5.0 | 1.1 | | | | | 1.8 | 5.7 |
| | | | | | | | Net Profit + Depr., Dep., Amort./Cur. Mat. L/T/D | | |
| | .0 | .2 | .1 | .1 | | | | .1 | .1 |
| | .4 | .5 | .2 | .2 | | | Fixed/Worth | .4 | .3 |
| | 8.1 | 1.9 | .9 | .9 | | | | 1.2 | 1.8 |
| | 1.3 | .5 | .3 | .3 | | | | .6 | .4 |
| | 2.9 | 4.0 | 1.8 | 1.1 | | | Debt/Worth | 1.3 | 1.4 |
| | 64.0 | 12.4 | 3.8 | 5.1 | | | | 8.5 | 7.0 |
| | 110.4 | 50.3 | 32.8 | | | | | 71.1 | 66.3 |
| | (13) 34.4 | (21) 6.1 | (21) 13.3 | | | | % Profit Before Taxes/Tangible Net Worth | (51) 24.2 | (24) 48.4 |
| | -1.9 | -35.9 | 8.8 | | | | | 6.6 | 15.8 |
| | 25.8 | 12.2 | 9.9 | 17.6 | | | | 21.6 | 38.8 |
| | 7.7 | 1.6 | 7.6 | 5.5 | | | % Profit Before Taxes/Total Assets | 8.5 | 20.8 |
| | -6.1 | -11.9 | 1.2 | .7 | | | | 1.7 | 5.4 |
| | UND | 108.7 | 65.2 | 64.3 | | | | 99.0 | 71.3 |
| | 97.2 | 32.7 | 22.6 | 41.2 | | | Sales/Net Fixed Assets | 23.6 | 24.0 |
| | 11.4 | 10.0 | 9.0 | 15.6 | | | | 12.1 | 9.3 |
| | 4.9 | 3.4 | 3.1 | 3.2 | | | | 4.3 | 3.9 |
| | 2.7 | 2.4 | 1.8 | 2.0 | | | Sales/Total Assets | 3.1 | 2.9 |
| | 1.2 | 1.5 | 1.3 | 1.6 | | | | 1.9 | 1.7 |
| | | .6 | .3 | | | | | .6 | .6 |
| | | (18) 1.1 | (20) .9 | | | | % Depr., Dep., Amort./Sales | (43) .9 | (19) 1.2 |
| | | 1.7 | 1.2 | | | | | 1.5 | 2.1 |
| | | | | | | | % Officers', Directors' Owners' Comp/Sales | 1.3 | |
| | | | | | | | | (18) 2.4 | |
| | | | | | | | | 5.8 | |
| 8973M | 68020M | 259469M | 1862816M | 1547034M | 2886600M | | Net Sales ($) | 3895628M | 2974734M |
| 2525M | 21256M | 105836M | 854553M | 644164M | 1204898M | | Total Assets ($) | 1374080M | 737880M |

M = $ thousand    MM = $ million
See Pages viii through xx for Explanation of Ratios and Data

© RMA 2024

# RETAIL—All Other General Merchandise Retailers  NAICS 455219

| Comparative Historical Data ||| | Current Data Sorted by Sales |||||||
|---|---|---|---|---|---|---|---|---|---|---|
| | | | **Type of Statement** | | | | | | 1 | 4 |
| 4 | 4 | 5 | Unqualified | | | | | | | 4 |
| 2 | 3 | 5 | Reviewed | 1 | | | | | | |
| 1 | 1 | | Compiled | | | | | | | |
| 8 | 6 | 12 | Tax Returns | 1 | 4 | 3 | 2 | 2 | | |
| 15 | 30 | 66 | Other | 4 | 5 | 4 | 9 | 11 | 33 | |
| 4/1/21-3/31/22 ALL | 4/1/22-3/31/23 ALL | 4/1/23-3/31/24 ALL | | 22 (4/1-9/30/23) ||| 66 (10/1/23-3/31/24) ||||
| | | | | 0-1MM | 1-3MM | 3-5MM | 5-10MM | 10-25MM | 25MM & OVER ||
| 30 | 44 | 88 | NUMBER OF STATEMENTS | 6 | 9 | 7 | 11 | 14 | 41 |
| % | % | % | ASSETS | % | % | % | % | % | % |
| 23.3 | 17.6 | 12.0 | Cash & Equivalents | | | | 5.9 | 9.4 | 11.6 |
| 10.6 | 6.1 | 8.4 | Trade Receivables (net) | | | | 7.5 | 8.2 | 7.6 |
| 42.7 | 42.3 | 50.8 | Inventory | | | | 54.8 | 63.3 | 48.9 |
| 4.9 | 4.4 | 4.3 | All Other Current | | | | 1.9 | 3.0 | 6.6 |
| 81.6 | 70.4 | 75.5 | Total Current | | | | 70.1 | 84.0 | 74.7 |
| 10.8 | 15.7 | 13.6 | Fixed Assets (net) | | | | 22.9 | 9.1 | 14.1 |
| .7 | 7.1 | 4.8 | Intangibles (net) | | | | .8 | 1.7 | 3.5 |
| 6.9 | 6.8 | 6.1 | All Other Non-Current | | | | 6.2 | 5.3 | 7.6 |
| 100.0 | 100.0 | 100.0 | Total | | | | 100.0 | 100.0 | 100.0 |
| | | | **LIABILITIES** | | | | | | |
| 7.2 | 7.6 | 7.9 | Notes Payable-Short Term | | | | 2.5 | 12.4 | 5.5 |
| .8 | 2.0 | 2.3 | Cur. Mat.-L.T.D. | | | | .7 | .7 | 3.6 |
| 11.2 | 15.8 | 20.0 | Trade Payables | | | | 33.4 | 40.7 | 12.6 |
| .4 | .6 | .3 | Income Taxes Payable | | | | .3 | .0 | .0 |
| 12.0 | 9.1 | 11.5 | All Other Current | | | | 12.9 | 10.1 | 9.6 |
| 31.5 | 35.0 | 42.0 | Total Current | | | | 49.8 | 63.9 | 31.4 |
| 15.5 | 18.6 | 19.0 | Long-Term Debt | | | | 15.0 | 5.9 | 17.8 |
| .0 | .1 | .0 | Deferred Taxes | | | | .0 | .0 | .0 |
| 8.2 | 6.5 | 10.4 | All Other Non-Current | | | | 21.6 | 1.8 | 12.9 |
| 44.8 | 39.8 | 28.5 | Net Worth | | | | 13.6 | 28.5 | 37.9 |
| 100.0 | 100.0 | 100.0 | Total Liabilties & Net Worth | | | | 100.0 | 100.0 | 100.0 |
| | | | **INCOME DATA** | | | | | | |
| 100.0 | 100.0 | 100.0 | Net Sales | | | | 100.0 | 100.0 | 100.0 |
| 44.3 | 45.7 | 37.8 | Gross Profit | | | | 35.9 | 25.5 | 39.0 |
| 35.3 | 37.0 | 33.8 | Operating Expenses | | | | 31.2 | 26.6 | 35.8 |
| 9.0 | 8.6 | 3.9 | Operating Profit | | | | 4.7 | -1.1 | 3.2 |
| -.8 | .5 | .3 | All Other Expenses (net) | | | | -.3 | .0 | .1 |
| 9.9 | 8.2 | 3.6 | Profit Before Taxes | | | | 4.9 | -1.1 | 3.1 |
| | | | **RATIOS** | | | | | | |
| 5.1 | 4.2 | 4.5 | | | | | 5.8 | 4.3 | 4.5 |
| 3.4 | 1.9 | 2.0 | Current | | | | 1.4 | 1.2 | 3.1 |
| 1.6 | 1.4 | 1.2 | | | | | 1.2 | 1.0 | 1.6 |
| 2.6 | 1.7 | 1.1 | | | | | 1.2 | .7 | 1.3 |
| 1.4 | .7 | .5 | Quick | | | | .2 | .3 | .5 |
| .4 | .2 | .1 | | | | | .0 | .1 | .1 |
| 0 UND | 0 UND | 0 956.8 | | | | | 0 999.8 | 1 572.9 | 1 333.9 |
| 3 128.5 | 3 138.8 | 4 94.4 | Sales/Receivables | | | | 4 86.2 | 4 85.8 | 4 94.8 |
| 19 18.9 | 15 25.1 | 11 33.9 | | | | | 15 23.7 | 9 38.5 | 10 36.0 |
| 41 9.0 | 51 7.1 | 54 6.8 | | | | | 34 10.7 | 66 5.5 | 65 5.6 |
| 89 4.1 | 107 3.4 | 122 3.0 | Cost of Sales/Inventory | | | | 228 1.6 | 107 3.4 | 130 2.8 |
| 159 2.3 | 192 1.9 | 215 1.7 | | | | | 261 1.4 | 130 2.8 | 203 1.8 |
| 3 130.6 | 9 42.8 | 12 30.5 | | | | | 14 25.6 | 15 24.4 | 15 24.5 |
| 18 20.7 | 33 11.2 | 29 12.8 | Cost of Sales/Payables | | | | 33 10.9 | 39 9.3 | 27 13.5 |
| 35 10.5 | 57 6.4 | 59 6.2 | | | | | 159 2.3 | 96 3.8 | 41 8.8 |
| 3.3 | 3.4 | 3.8 | | | | | 3.3 | 5.7 | 2.5 |
| 5.5 | 10.2 | 6.9 | Sales/Working Capital | | | | 11.4 | 26.1 | 5.5 |
| 14.6 | 22.3 | 18.7 | | | | | 14.5 | NM | 10.7 |
| 128.3 | 32.5 | 16.6 | | | | | | 12.2 | 56.2 |
| (23) 24.1 | (37) 14.1 | (75) 4.7 | EBIT/Interest | | | | (13) 3.0 | (36) 6.3 | |
| 7.1 | 3.8 | .1 | | | | | -11.4 | 1.1 | |
| | | | Net Profit + Depr., Dep., Amort./Cur. Mat. L/T/D | | | | | | |
| .0 | .1 | .1 | | | | | .4 | .2 | .1 |
| .1 | .3 | .3 | Fixed/Worth | | | | .5 | .4 | .2 |
| .3 | 2.3 | 1.8 | | | | | 4.2 | 2.2 | 1.1 |
| .2 | .5 | .7 | | | | | .9 | .3 | .3 |
| .7 | 1.6 | 2.3 | Debt/Worth | | | | 2.7 | 9.6 | 1.4 |
| 1.8 | 17.4 | 13.0 | | | | | 5.4 | 18.7 | 3.9 |
| 74.1 | 112.0 | 45.3 | % Profit Before Taxes/Tangible Net Worth | | | | | 55.8 | 23.5 |
| (27) 41.5 | (37) 30.7 | (73) 16.4 | | | | | (12) 7.1 | (35) 15.0 | |
| 24.9 | 17.9 | 1.9 | | | | | -181.9 | 5.1 | |
| 48.8 | 27.4 | 13.1 | | | | | 32.1 | 9.6 | 11.1 |
| 26.5 | 13.3 | 7.0 | % Profit Before Taxes/Total Assets | | | | 8.4 | 1.8 | 7.6 |
| 10.0 | 6.0 | -1.5 | | | | | .5 | -15.0 | 1.0 |
| 228.8 | 100.2 | 110.7 | | | | | 18.5 | 112.3 | 73.0 |
| 52.4 | 30.4 | 41.7 | Sales/Net Fixed Assets | | | | 14.2 | 82.4 | 39.4 |
| 20.5 | 8.6 | 10.2 | | | | | 9.9 | 37.0 | 9.9 |
| 4.4 | 3.6 | 3.4 | | | | | 3.1 | 4.1 | 3.1 |
| 2.6 | 2.4 | 2.2 | Sales/Total Assets | | | | 1.6 | 3.0 | 1.9 |
| 2.1 | 1.3 | 1.4 | | | | | 1.1 | 2.4 | 1.4 |
| .3 | .4 | .5 | | | | | | | .4 |
| (17) .4 | (30) .7 | (61) 1.0 | % Depr., Dep., Amort./Sales | | | | | (32) .8 | |
| 1.3 | 1.9 | 1.6 | | | | | | | 1.2 |
| 1.4 | 2.1 | 1.0 | | | | | | | |
| (12) 3.6 | (11) 3.7 | (26) 1.7 | % Officers', Directors' Owners' Comp/Sales | | | | | | |
| 7.2 | 5.7 | 5.7 | | | | | | | |
| 3153330M | 3731436M | 6632912M | Net Sales ($) | 3457M | 17313M | 26818M | 71751M | 208879M | 6304694M |
| 878578M | 1642178M | 2833232M | Total Assets ($) | 3139M | 13462M | 11290M | 40067M | 71082M | 2694192M |

M = $ thousand    MM = $ million
See Pages viii through xx for Explanation of Ratios and Data

© RMA 2024

# RETAIL—Pharmacies and Drug Retailers  NAICS 456110

## Current Data Sorted by Assets | Comparative Historical Data

| | | | | | | | Type of Statement | | |
|---|---|---|---|---|---|---|---|---|---|
| | | 2 | | 2 | 1 | 2 | Unqualified | 5 | 7 |
| | | | 2 | 1 | 3 | 1 | Reviewed | 5 | 2 |
| | | 6 | 10 | 1 | | | Compiled | 24 | 11 |
| | 9 | 22 | 13 | 1 | | | Tax Returns | 75 | 52 |
| | 19 | 34 | 29 | 26 | 4 | 6 | Other | 122 | 101 |
| | | 24 (4/1-9/30/23) | | 170 (10/1/23-3/31/24) | | | | 4/1/19-3/31/20 | 4/1/20-3/31/21 |
| | 0-500M | 500M-2MM | 2-10MM | 10-50MM | 50-100MM | 100-250MM | | ALL | ALL |
| | 28 | 64 | 54 | 31 | 8 | 9 | NUMBER OF STATEMENTS | 231 | 173 |
| | % | % | % | % | % | % | **ASSETS** | % | % |
| | 23.8 | 20.9 | 21.3 | 21.1 | | | Cash & Equivalents | 17.0 | 23.5 |
| | 17.6 | 19.1 | 23.3 | 28.5 | | | Trade Receivables (net) | 24.9 | 18.2 |
| | 26.4 | 21.5 | 15.9 | 11.7 | | | Inventory | 26.3 | 23.0 |
| | 2.9 | 3.5 | 2.1 | 4.3 | | | All Other Current | 1.7 | 2.1 |
| | 70.7 | 65.1 | 62.6 | 65.6 | | | Total Current | 69.9 | 66.8 |
| | 16.1 | 10.1 | 8.4 | 10.1 | | | Fixed Assets (net) | 13.1 | 10.4 |
| | 1.4 | 13.8 | 14.7 | 12.2 | | | Intangibles (net) | 9.7 | 16.0 |
| | 11.7 | 11.1 | 14.2 | 12.1 | | | All Other Non-Current | 7.3 | 6.9 |
| | 100.0 | 100.0 | 100.0 | 100.0 | | | Total | 100.0 | 100.0 |
| | | | | | | | **LIABILITIES** | | |
| | 7.5 | 8.5 | 6.2 | 2.5 | | | Notes Payable-Short Term | 11.7 | 12.1 |
| | 6.8 | 2.0 | 2.4 | 1.5 | | | Cur. Mat.-L.T.D. | 2.9 | 2.9 |
| | 36.2 | 17.8 | 21.5 | 27.0 | | | Trade Payables | 26.0 | 21.0 |
| | .0 | .1 | .0 | .0 | | | Income Taxes Payable | .1 | .0 |
| | 22.3 | 10.1 | 6.0 | 15.1 | | | All Other Current | 10.7 | 9.9 |
| | 72.8 | 38.5 | 36.1 | 46.2 | | | Total Current | 51.3 | 45.9 |
| | 38.1 | 23.8 | 21.6 | 13.6 | | | Long-Term Debt | 19.0 | 25.3 |
| | .0 | .0 | .0 | .0 | | | Deferred Taxes | .0 | .0 |
| | 19.7 | 4.0 | 3.4 | 6.5 | | | All Other Non-Current | 6.7 | 7.5 |
| | -30.6 | 33.6 | 38.9 | 33.7 | | | Net Worth | 23.0 | 21.2 |
| | 100.0 | 100.0 | 100.0 | 100.0 | | | Total Liabilities & Net Worth | 100.0 | 100.0 |
| | | | | | | | **INCOME DATA** | | |
| | 100.0 | 100.0 | 100.0 | 100.0 | | | Net Sales | 100.0 | 100.0 |
| | 25.4 | 30.9 | 30.6 | 32.0 | | | Gross Profit | 26.8 | 29.7 |
| | 20.4 | 25.0 | 22.3 | 23.5 | | | Operating Expenses | 23.5 | 26.3 |
| | 5.0 | 5.9 | 8.2 | 8.5 | | | Operating Profit | 3.3 | 3.4 |
| | 2.9 | 1.8 | .5 | .5 | | | All Other Expenses (net) | .3 | -.2 |
| | 2.1 | 4.1 | 7.8 | 8.0 | | | Profit Before Taxes | 3.0 | 3.6 |
| | | | | | | | **RATIOS** | | |
| | 2.4 | 5.1 | 3.2 | 2.6 | | | | 2.9 | 3.6 |
| | 1.2 | 2.3 | 1.9 | 1.6 | | | Current | 1.5 | 1.6 |
| | .4 | 1.1 | 1.3 | 1.0 | | | | 1.0 | 1.1 |
| | 1.5 | 3.7 | 2.5 | 1.8 | | | | 1.6 | 2.1 |
| | .8 (63) | 1.2 | 1.3 | 1.2 | | | Quick | .9 (172) | 1.0 |
| | .3 | .6 | .7 | .7 | | | | .5 | .5 |
| | 0 UND | 0 966.3 | 1 273.6 | 15 23.6 | | | | 2 146.1 | 0 UND |
| | 1 453.9 | 9 42.6 | 19 18.9 | 23 15.7 | | | Sales/Receivables | 16 22.6 | 13 28.1 |
| | 18 20.8 | 22 16.9 | 33 11.2 | 32 11.4 | | | | 28 12.9 | 26 14.0 |
| | 4 103.0 | 9 40.1 | 11 34.6 | 9 42.9 | | | | 11 33.9 | 13 29.0 |
| | 11 32.5 | 18 19.9 | 19 19.2 | 14 27.0 | | | Cost of Sales/Inventory | 21 17.2 | 24 14.9 |
| | 17 20.9 | 30 12.0 | 31 11.7 | 23 16.0 | | | | 38 9.7 | 39 9.4 |
| | 0 UND | 0 UND | 5 72.7 | 20 18.6 | | | | 7 51.0 | 4 82.4 |
| | 6 62.4 | 8 46.8 | 20 18.4 | 33 11.2 | | | Cost of Sales/Payables | 18 19.9 | 18 19.9 |
| | 25 14.4 | 26 13.9 | 37 9.8 | 38 9.7 | | | | 36 10.0 | 33 11.1 |
| | 19.0 | 10.9 | 9.3 | 7.5 | | | | 12.4 | 9.3 |
| | 511.8 | 24.5 | 15.5 | 17.8 | | | Sales/Working Capital | 26.7 | 19.5 |
| | -24.0 | 179.8 | 44.0 | 467.5 | | | | UND | 211.5 |
| | 21.2 | 43.3 | 37.4 | 91.5 | | | | 27.1 | 45.6 |
| (12) | 9.8 | (46) 9.7 | (39) 6.3 | (25) 9.2 | | | EBIT/Interest | (177) 7.0 | (127) 7.2 |
| | 1.5 | 1.9 | 2.9 | 3.6 | | | | .4 | 1.0 |
| | | | | | | | Net Profit + Depr., Dep., Amort./Cur. Mat. L/T/D | | 56.3 |
| | | | | | | | | (11) | 4.6 |
| | | | | | | | | | .9 |
| | .0 | .0 | .0 | .1 | | | | .1 | .1 |
| | 1.7 | .3 | .3 | .3 | | | Fixed/Worth | .5 | .4 |
| | -.2 | NM | 5.9 | 2.1 | | | | -2.5 | -.7 |
| | 1.2 | .4 | .8 | 1.4 | | | | 1.0 | 1.0 |
| | -18.9 | 1.9 | 2.4 | 1.9 | | | Debt/Worth | 3.2 | 7.4 |
| | -3.4 | -4.2 | 924.0 | 25.5 | | | | -14.5 | -5.1 |
| | 133.3 | 106.6 | 99.6 | 131.3 | | | | 129.1 | 132.1 |
| (13) | 96.4 | (42) 50.7 | (42) 65.6 | (26) 76.3 | | | % Profit Before Taxes/Tangible Net Worth | (164) 46.0 | (100) 57.1 |
| | 37.3 | 16.8 | 24.7 | 41.5 | | | | 11.8 | 17.6 |
| | 56.9 | 37.3 | 24.6 | 34.1 | | | | 32.6 | 33.1 |
| | 25.6 | 17.1 | 14.4 | 18.6 | | | % Profit Before Taxes/Total Assets | 10.5 | 12.5 |
| | -12.0 | 1.8 | 7.9 | 9.5 | | | | -.2 | .7 |
| | 714.5 | 999.8 | 849.5 | 201.2 | | | | 300.3 | 492.6 |
| | 194.9 | 102.4 | 69.9 | 51.4 | | | Sales/Net Fixed Assets | 73.9 | 74.4 |
| | 62.4 | 51.8 | 30.2 | 20.9 | | | | 25.9 | 25.9 |
| | 14.7 | 8.3 | 5.7 | 5.7 | | | | 7.8 | 6.6 |
| | 10.4 | 6.1 | 3.6 | 4.2 | | | Sales/Total Assets | 5.0 | 4.5 |
| | 7.3 | 4.5 | 2.2 | 2.4 | | | | 3.6 | 2.9 |
| | .0 | .1 | .2 | .1 | | | | .2 | .2 |
| (14) | .3 | (28) .3 | (29) .7 | (21) .5 | | | % Depr., Dep., Amort./Sales | (133) .5 | (95) .5 |
| | .7 | .8 | 1.2 | 2.5 | | | | 1.0 | 1.2 |
| | | | 1.2 | 1.3 | | | | | |
| | | (32) 2.6 | (20) 1.8 | | | | % Officers', Directors' Owners' Comp/Sales | 1.1 | 1.4 |
| | | 4.1 | 3.2 | | | | | (90) 2.8 | (69) 2.7 |
| | | | | | | | | 4.5 | 5.9 |
| | 93710M | 387754M | 908065M | 2790411M | 1490039M | 2991603M | Net Sales ($) | 9544407M | 7749346M |
| | 8723M | 61683M | 240277M | 676132M | 579233M | 1208086M | Total Assets ($) | 2495662M | 2202624M |

© RMA 2024   M = $ thousand   MM = $ million
See Pages viii through xx for Explanation of Ratios and Data

# RETAIL—Pharmacies and Drug Retailers NAICS 456110

| Comparative Historical Data | | | | Current Data Sorted by Sales | | | | | |
|---|---|---|---|---|---|---|---|---|---|
| | | | **Type of Statement** | | | | | | |
| 10 | 12 | 7 | Unqualified | | 1 | | 1 | | 5 |
| 5 | 2 | 7 | Reviewed | | | | | 2 | 5 |
| 15 | 10 | 17 | Compiled | | 1 | | 6 | 7 | 3 |
| 46 | 58 | 45 | Tax Returns | 2 | 3 | 12 | 18 | 7 | 3 |
| 90 | 144 | 118 | Other | 1 | 16 | 19 | 21 | 23 | 38 |
| 4/1/21-3/31/22 | 4/1/22-3/31/23 | 4/1/23-3/31/24 | | 24 (4/1-9/30/23) | | | 170 (10/1/23-3/31/24) | | |
| ALL | ALL | ALL | | 0-1MM | 1-3MM | 3-5MM | 5-10MM | 10-25MM | 25MM & OVER |
| 166 | 226 | 194 | **NUMBER OF STATEMENTS** | 3 | 21 | 31 | 46 | 39 | 54 |
| % | % | % | **ASSETS** | % | % | % | % | % | % |
| 20.6 | 19.7 | 20.1 | Cash & Equivalents | 16.8 | 20.8 | 25.4 | 20.2 | 16.3 | |
| 22.6 | 22.3 | 22.5 | Trade Receivables (net) | | 19.4 | 18.7 | 15.4 | 23.2 | 32.5 |
| 24.4 | 20.3 | 18.4 | Inventory | 20.5 | 25.3 | 17.2 | 19.5 | 13.7 | |
| 2.4 | 4.3 | 3.0 | All Other Current | 4.5 | 1.9 | 2.8 | 4.2 | 2.5 | |
| 69.9 | 66.6 | 64.0 | Total Current | 61.3 | 66.8 | 60.8 | 67.2 | 65.1 | |
| 10.3 | 10.2 | 10.5 | Fixed Assets (net) | 19.8 | 9.2 | 7.9 | 6.2 | 10.5 | |
| 12.9 | 12.6 | 12.9 | Intangibles (net) | 8.8 | 11.9 | 16.6 | 13.1 | 12.5 | |
| 6.9 | 10.6 | 12.6 | All Other Non-Current | 10.0 | 12.1 | 14.7 | 13.5 | 12.0 | |
| 100.0 | 100.0 | 100.0 | Total | 100.0 | 100.0 | 100.0 | 100.0 | 100.0 | |
| | | | **LIABILITIES** | | | | | | |
| 9.3 | 7.7 | 6.4 | Notes Payable-Short Term | 10.8 | 3.5 | 7.3 | 7.0 | 3.2 | |
| 2.8 | 2.6 | 2.9 | Cur. Mat.-L.T.D. | 1.2 | 8.0 | 1.6 | 2.2 | 2.5 | |
| 20.3 | 17.4 | 23.5 | Trade Payables | 25.6 | 25.8 | 15.9 | 22.8 | 29.6 | |
| .0 | .1 | .1 | Income Taxes Payable | .3 | .0 | .0 | .0 | .0 | |
| 10.5 | 14.1 | 11.9 | All Other Current | 13.3 | 8.7 | 14.1 | 8.1 | 12.4 | |
| 43.0 | 41.8 | 44.7 | Total Current | 51.1 | 46.1 | 38.8 | 40.0 | 47.8 | |
| 23.9 | 23.1 | 22.9 | Long-Term Debt | 26.0 | 41.7 | 29.7 | 15.9 | 11.4 | |
| .0 | .0 | .0 | Deferred Taxes | .0 | .0 | .0 | .1 | .0 | |
| 4.4 | 5.3 | 7.2 | All Other Non-Current | 19.8 | 6.4 | 3.1 | 4.3 | 6.9 | |
| 28.8 | 29.7 | 25.2 | Net Worth | 2.9 | 5.9 | 28.4 | 39.6 | 34.0 | |
| 100.0 | 100.0 | 100.0 | Total Liabilities & Net Worth | 100.0 | 100.0 | 100.0 | 100.0 | 100.0 | |
| | | | **INCOME DATA** | | | | | | |
| 100.0 | 100.0 | 100.0 | Net Sales | 100.0 | 100.0 | 100.0 | 100.0 | 100.0 | |
| 27.7 | 29.9 | 30.5 | Gross Profit | 34.7 | 27.3 | 31.9 | 31.7 | 28.7 | |
| 24.0 | 24.3 | 23.7 | Operating Expenses | 28.8 | 19.3 | 24.9 | 24.0 | 22.4 | |
| 3.7 | 5.6 | 6.7 | Operating Profit | 5.9 | 8.0 | 7.0 | 7.7 | 6.3 | |
| -.4 | -.2 | 1.4 | All Other Expenses (net) | 1.9 | 4.1 | 1.1 | .4 | .8 | |
| 4.1 | 5.8 | 5.3 | Profit Before Taxes | 4.1 | 3.9 | 5.9 | 7.3 | 5.5 | |
| | | | **RATIOS** | | | | | | |
| 3.4 | 3.8 | 3.2 | | 3.8 | 7.7 | 4.2 | 3.2 | 2.1 | |
| 1.9 | 2.0 | 1.7 | Current | 2.3 | 2.3 | 1.8 | 2.1 | 1.4 | |
| 1.2 | 1.1 | 1.0 | | .7 | 1.1 | 1.0 | 1.2 | 1.0 | |
| 2.1 | 2.5 | 2.2 | | 2.8 | 4.1 | 3.0 | 2.6 | 1.5 | |
| (165) 1.2 | (193) 1.2 | 1.1 | Quick | (20) 1.3 | 1.1 | 1.1 | 1.2 | 1.1 | |
| .7 | .6 | .6 | | .3 | .6 | .6 | .7 | .6 | |
| 0 910.7 | 0 999.8 | 1 626.0 | | 0 812.9 | 0 UND | 0 UND | 1 329.8 | 16 22.5 | |
| 16 23.3 | 16 22.5 | 15 23.6 | Sales/Receivables | 14 26.6 | 8 47.3 | 7 49.8 | 14 25.4 | 22 16.3 | |
| 27 13.4 | 30 12.3 | 27 13.4 | | 29 12.6 | 19 19.4 | 23 15.6 | 37 9.8 | 33 11.1 | |
| 13 28.4 | 10 35.5 | 9 40.7 | | 10 35.8 | 7 52.6 | 7 53.1 | 11 34.4 | 9 42.1 | |
| 22 16.3 | 21 17.6 | 17 21.0 | Cost of Sales/Inventory | 20 18.3 | 16 22.3 | 15 24.4 | 17 21.1 | 18 20.0 | |
| 35 10.3 | 36 10.2 | 30 12.3 | | 42 8.6 | 30 12.2 | 29 12.5 | 27 13.4 | 32 11.3 | |
| 8 45.2 | 0 UND | 3 127.9 | | 0 UND | 2 212.6 | 0 UND | 7 54.0 | 23 15.9 | |
| 18 20.7 | 15 24.1 | 20 18.2 | Cost of Sales/Payables | 13 27.4 | 7 49.2 | 5 78.7 | 24 14.9 | 33 11.0 | |
| 32 11.5 | 29 12.5 | 36 10.1 | | 31 11.6 | 26 13.9 | 26 14.2 | 37 9.8 | 46 8.0 | |
| 9.4 | 8.7 | 10.5 | | 9.3 | 10.8 | 11.6 | 9.1 | 10.1 | |
| 15.6 | 15.1 | 21.3 | Sales/Working Capital | 19.6 | 30.6 | 25.2 | 16.5 | 19.9 | |
| 49.7 | 61.0 | NM | | -39.7 | 106.2 | -305.2 | 79.0 | 590.5 | |
| 31.2 | 47.0 | 39.1 | | 23.3 | 20.0 | 26.7 | 74.0 | 61.3 | |
| (115) 10.4 | (165) 9.5 | (137) 9.2 | EBIT/Interest | (12) 15.2 | (19) 8.5 | (30) 7.5 | (29) 9.5 | (44) 10.3 | |
| 1.5 | 2.1 | 2.8 | | 4.0 | 1.6 | 2.7 | 2.9 | 4.4 | |
| | | 29.6 | Net Profit + Depr., Dep., | | | | | | |
| | (16) | 4.3 | Amort./Cur. Mat. L/T/D | | | | | | |
| | | 1.6 | | | | | | | |
| .1 | .0 | .0 | | .1 | .0 | .0 | .0 | .2 | |
| .3 | .2 | .3 | Fixed/Worth | 1.6 | .3 | .3 | .2 | .4 | |
| -8.6 | -3.1 | -2.6 | | -.8 | -1.0 | -1.0 | 1.7 | 2.5 | |
| .8 | .5 | .8 | | .4 | .3 | 1.0 | .5 | 1.5 | |
| 2.9 | 2.5 | 2.8 | Debt/Worth | -7.8 | 3.0 | 7.3 | 2.1 | 2.8 | |
| -9.4 | -11.2 | -5.8 | | -3.4 | -3.3 | -4.2 | -12.2 | 15.7 | |
| 105.6 | 105.4 | 111.4 | | 104.6 | 168.1 | 162.7 | 115.3 | 104.7 | |
| (113) 50.7 | (155) 43.7 | (133) 62.1 | % Profit Before Taxes/Tangible Net Worth | (10) 72.5 | (20) 52.7 | (27) 62.5 | (29) 56.2 | (45) 68.0 | |
| 15.6 | 14.5 | 30.2 | | 31.5 | 6.8 | 31.2 | 22.1 | 35.3 | |
| 33.1 | 31.4 | 34.2 | | 27.7 | 51.3 | 33.7 | 58.0 | 25.6 | |
| 13.0 | 13.0 | 16.9 | % Profit Before Taxes/Total Assets | 17.3 | 16.1 | 19.2 | 14.6 | 13.9 | |
| 2.6 | 2.7 | 5.2 | | 6.9 | 1.7 | 5.4 | 4.1 | 7.1 | |
| 414.3 | 358.8 | 533.7 | | 252.3 | UND | 858.8 | 999.8 | 192.8 | |
| 98.4 | 89.8 | 86.2 | Sales/Net Fixed Assets | 49.2 | 132.2 | 129.1 | 107.7 | 45.1 | |
| 32.1 | 30.5 | 30.1 | | 10.1 | 62.9 | 48.0 | 48.6 | 20.8 | |
| 7.8 | 6.6 | 7.5 | | 8.4 | 9.3 | 8.6 | 7.1 | 5.7 | |
| 4.8 | 4.4 | 5.0 | Sales/Total Assets | 4.2 | 6.3 | 5.7 | 5.0 | 3.7 | |
| 3.2 | 2.6 | 2.7 | | 2.2 | 4.6 | 2.6 | 2.7 | 2.4 | |
| .1 | .1 | .1 | | .0 | .1 | .1 | .1 | .2 | |
| (94) .4 | (118) .4 | (105) .5 | % Depr., Dep., Amort./Sales | (10) .7 | (16) .4 | (21) .3 | (20) .5 | (36) .6 | |
| 1.1 | 1.1 | 1.1 | | 1.8 | .8 | 1.2 | .8 | 1.5 | |
| 1.0 | 1.3 | 1.0 | | | 2.0 | 1.2 | 1.3 | .4 | |
| (65) 2.4 | (68) 2.4 | (67) 2.6 | % Officers', Directors', Owners' Comp/Sales | (12) 2.6 | (21) 2.7 | (14) 2.5 | (12) .8 | | |
| 4.4 | 4.4 | 4.2 | | | 4.4 | 4.6 | 3.5 | 2.3 | |
| 10722044M | 9150202M | 8661582M | Net Sales ($) | 2167M | 45070M | 126584M | 329220M | 616587M | 7541954M |
| 2685844M | 2745543M | 2774134M | Total Assets ($) | 1042M | 11294M | 22537M | 86998M | 347604M | 2304659M |

M = $ thousand    MM = $ million
See Pages viii through xx for Explanation of Ratios and Data

© RMA 2024

# RETAIL—Cosmetics, Beauty Supplies, and Perfume Retailers  NAICS 456120

## Current Data Sorted by Assets | Comparative Historical Data

| | | | | | | | Type of Statement | | |
|---|---|---|---|---|---|---|---|---|---|
| | | | 1 | 1 | | | Unqualified | 4 | 1 |
| | | 1 | 2 | | | | Reviewed | 3 | |
| 2 | | 2 | 1 | | | | Compiled | 3 | 2 |
| 4 | 7 | 14 | 15 | 2 | 3 | | Tax Returns | 13 | 23 |
| | 5 | | 1 | | | | Other | 30 | 28 |
| | 6 (4/1-9/30/23) | | 55 (10/1/23-3/31/24) | | | | | 4/1/19- | 4/1/20- |
| 0-500M | 500M-2MM | 2-10MM | 10-50MM | 50-100MM | 100-250MM | | | 3/31/20 | 3/31/21 |
| 6 | 12 | 17 | 20 | 3 | 3 | | NUMBER OF STATEMENTS | ALL 53 | ALL 54 |
| % | % | % | % | % | % | | ASSETS | % | % |
| | 20.3 | 26.0 | 15.1 | | | | Cash & Equivalents | 14.8 | 21.9 |
| | 4.1 | 12.8 | 16.7 | | | | Trade Receivables (net) | 12.7 | 7.0 |
| | 48.0 | 47.0 | 31.9 | | | | Inventory | 39.7 | 49.6 |
| | 10.8 | 1.0 | 9.3 | | | | All Other Current | 4.3 | 2.7 |
| | 83.2 | 86.9 | 73.0 | | | | Total Current | 71.5 | 81.1 |
| | 4.7 | 3.5 | 12.3 | | | | Fixed Assets (net) | 8.1 | 11.2 |
| | 10.3 | 5.2 | 11.1 | | | | Intangibles (net) | 14.2 | 4.2 |
| | 1.7 | 4.5 | 3.6 | | | | All Other Non-Current | 6.2 | 3.6 |
| | 100.0 | 100.0 | 100.0 | | | | Total | 100.0 | 100.0 |
| | | | | | | | LIABILITIES | | |
| | 11.0 | 24.5 | 6.9 | | | | Notes Payable-Short Term | 7.2 | 6.8 |
| | 5.0 | 1.7 | 1.9 | | | | Cur. Mat.-L.T.D. | 1.6 | 1.4 |
| | 5.9 | 17.4 | 10.5 | | | | Trade Payables | 12.6 | 10.8 |
| | .0 | .0 | .4 | | | | Income Taxes Payable | .0 | .3 |
| | 9.5 | 6.5 | 9.1 | | | | All Other Current | 11.0 | 13.3 |
| | 31.3 | 50.1 | 28.8 | | | | Total Current | 32.4 | 32.5 |
| | 26.3 | 14.0 | 16.0 | | | | Long-Term Debt | 13.5 | 16.1 |
| | .0 | .0 | .4 | | | | Deferred Taxes | .0 | .0 |
| | 15.5 | 5.1 | 5.2 | | | | All Other Non-Current | 13.2 | 14.0 |
| | 26.8 | 30.8 | 49.6 | | | | Net Worth | 40.9 | 37.4 |
| | 100.0 | 100.0 | 100.0 | | | | Total Liabilities & Net Worth | 100.0 | 100.0 |
| | | | | | | | INCOME DATA | | |
| | 100.0 | 100.0 | 100.0 | | | | Net Sales | 100.0 | 100.0 |
| | 48.1 | 40.3 | 59.9 | | | | Gross Profit | 48.4 | 47.2 |
| | 47.8 | 31.0 | 51.7 | | | | Operating Expenses | 40.1 | 40.0 |
| | .3 | 9.4 | 8.1 | | | | Operating Profit | 8.3 | 7.3 |
| | .6 | 1.8 | 1.8 | | | | All Other Expenses (net) | .9 | .9 |
| | -.3 | 7.6 | 6.3 | | | | Profit Before Taxes | 7.3 | 6.4 |
| | | | | | | | RATIOS | | |
| | 20.4 | 4.0 | 4.3 | | | | | 5.1 | 6.2 |
| | 4.9 | 2.6 | 2.8 | | | Current | | 2.4 | 2.8 |
| | 1.6 | 1.3 | 1.7 | | | | | 1.3 | 1.6 |
| | 4.7 | 2.0 | 1.7 | | | | | 1.7 | 2.7 |
| | .7 | .7 | 1.1 | | | Quick | | .9 | .7 |
| | .4 | .5 | .5 | | | | | .3 | .4 |
| 0 | UND | 0 | UND | 6 | 64.2 | | | 0 UND | 0 UND |
| 0 | UND | 5 | 75.4 | 41 | 9.0 | | Sales/Receivables | 9 39.0 | 0 UND |
| 3 | 127.9 | 35 | 10.3 | 54 | 6.8 | | | 44 8.3 | 7 54.1 |
| 16 | 23.3 | 54 | 6.8 | 101 | 3.6 | | | 68 5.4 | 79 4.6 |
| 126 | 2.9 | 94 | 3.9 | 146 | 2.5 | | Cost of Sales/Inventory | 114 3.2 | 122 3.0 |
| 228 | 1.6 | 166 | 2.2 | 332 | 1.1 | | | 203 1.8 | 215 1.7 |
| 0 | UND | 20 | 18.6 | 26 | 13.9 | | | 11 33.9 | 0 UND |
| 0 | UND | 25 | 14.4 | 51 | 7.2 | | Cost of Sales/Payables | 30 12.0 | 17 21.0 |
| 24 | 15.2 | 59 | 6.2 | 79 | 4.6 | | | 65 5.6 | 48 7.6 |
| | | 2.0 | 5.3 | 2.9 | | | | 3.2 | 3.3 |
| | | 5.8 | 6.8 | 4.8 | | | Sales/Working Capital | 6.5 | 5.8 |
| | | 14.5 | 13.7 | 6.6 | | | | 23.4 | 11.1 |
| | | | 45.0 | 42.7 | | | | 33.4 | 37.4 |
| | | (15) | 5.9 | (16) 3.1 | | | EBIT/Interest | (30) 4.4 | (29) 9.3 |
| | | | 2.4 | .5 | | | | 1.4 | 1.1 |
| | | | | | | | Net Profit + Depr., Dep., Amort./Cur. Mat. L/T/D | | |
| | .1 | .0 | .0 | | | | | .0 | .0 |
| | .1 | .1 | .1 | | | Fixed/Worth | | .1 | .2 |
| | NM | 1.0 | 4.1 | | | | | .6 | .5 |
| | .2 | .5 | .3 | | | | | .6 | .6 |
| | 2.0 | 2.6 | .9 | | | Debt/Worth | | 1.3 | 1.6 |
| | -2.4 | 5.5 | 7.0 | | | | | 31.4 | 5.3 |
| | | 75.2 | 59.1 | | | | | 54.2 | 97.0 |
| | | (14) 41.7 | (16) 18.5 | | | | % Profit Before Taxes/Tangible Net Worth | (42) 38.2 | (47) 44.8 |
| | | 11.0 | -6.2 | | | | | 9.2 | 10.3 |
| | 21.7 | 29.8 | 25.2 | | | | | 24.5 | 30.7 |
| | 13.0 | 12.7 | 4.5 | | | % Profit Before Taxes/Total Assets | | 13.5 | 13.3 |
| | -.2 | 7.6 | -2.3 | | | | | 2.5 | 2.7 |
| | 350.2 | 796.3 | 426.2 | | | | | 999.8 | 566.4 |
| | 85.6 | 193.6 | 62.0 | | | Sales/Net Fixed Assets | | 68.8 | 41.0 |
| | 35.1 | 44.4 | 17.0 | | | | | 15.7 | 17.0 |
| | 4.9 | 3.9 | 2.4 | | | | | 3.4 | 3.9 |
| | 3.0 | 2.9 | 2.1 | | | Sales/Total Assets | | 2.0 | 2.1 |
| | 1.6 | 2.2 | 1.3 | | | | | 1.3 | 1.6 |
| | | | .2 | | | | | .2 | .3 |
| | | (13) 1.1 | | | | | % Depr., Dep., Amort./Sales | (22) .6 | (27) .7 |
| | | 2.3 | | | | | | 1.5 | 1.4 |
| | | | | | | | % Officers', Directors' Owners' Comp/Sales | 2.1 | 2.1 |
| | | | | | | | | (19) 4.6 | (23) 5.3 |
| | | | | | | | | 13.6 | 9.4 |
| 10878M | 55871M | 226840M | 875418M | 280944M | 1162977M | | Net Sales ($) | 2165025M | 1636472M |
| 1641M | 15290M | 79920M | 445769M | 226294M | 509932M | | Total Assets ($) | 1570599M | 924586M |

© RMA 2024   M = $ thousand   MM = $ million
See Pages viii through xx for Explanation of Ratios and Data

# RETAIL—Cosmetics, Beauty Supplies, and Perfume Retailers  NAICS 456120

## Comparative Historical Data | Current Data Sorted by Sales

| Comparative Historical Data | | | | | | | Current Data Sorted by Sales | | | | | |
|---|---|---|---|---|---|---|---|---|---|---|---|---|
| | | | | | | Type of Statement | | | | | | |
| | 2 | | 2 | | 2 | Unqualified | | | | | 1 | 2 |
| | 5 | | 7 | | 3 | Reviewed | | | | | 2 | 2 |
| | 1 | | 4 | | 5 | Compiled | 2 | | 1 | 3 | | 1 |
| | 8 | | 17 | | 8 | Tax Returns | | 4 | | 7 | 13 | 16 |
| | 31 | | 49 | | 43 | Other | | 5 | 2 | | | |
| | 4/1/21-3/31/22 ALL | | 4/1/22-3/31/23 ALL | | 4/1/23-3/31/24 ALL | | 6 (4/1-9/30/23) | | | 55 (10/1/23-3/31/24) | | |
| | | | | | | | 0-1MM | 1-3MM | 3-5MM | 5-10MM | 10-25MM | 25MM & OVER |
| | 47 | | 79 | | 61 | **NUMBER OF STATEMENTS** | 2 | 9 | 3 | 10 | 16 | 21 |
| | % | | % | | % | **ASSETS** | % | % | % | % | % | % |
| | 19.3 | | 19.6 | | 19.5 | Cash & Equivalents | | | | 35.2 | 17.8 | 15.1 |
| | 9.7 | | 13.3 | | 11.5 | Trade Receivables (net) | | | | 9.0 | 12.7 | 13.4 |
| | 33.9 | | 39.1 | | 38.0 | Inventory | | | | 39.1 | 37.0 | 33.4 |
| | 6.2 | | 3.8 | | 5.9 | All Other Current | | | | 1.4 | 8.3 | 6.9 |
| | 69.1 | | 75.8 | | 74.9 | Total Current | | | | 84.7 | 75.8 | 68.8 |
| | 14.3 | | 14.7 | | 10.2 | Fixed Assets (net) | | | | 2.8 | 13.5 | 9.7 |
| | 8.4 | | 6.3 | | 8.9 | Intangibles (net) | | | | 8.5 | 6.5 | 12.3 |
| | 8.2 | | 3.2 | | 6.0 | All Other Non-Current | | | | 4.0 | 4.3 | 9.2 |
| | 100.0 | | 100.0 | | 100.0 | Total | | | | 100.0 | 100.0 | 100.0 |
| | | | | | | **LIABILITIES** | | | | | | |
| | 9.8 | | 11.5 | | 12.6 | Notes Payable-Short Term | | | | 16.7 | 16.5 | 6.2 |
| | 1.8 | | 2.9 | | 2.8 | Cur. Mat.-L.T.D. | | | | 5.8 | 3.0 | 1.4 |
| | 10.5 | | 21.9 | | 11.5 | Trade Payables | | | | 11.7 | 12.6 | 13.0 |
| | .9 | | .1 | | .1 | Income Taxes Payable | | | | .0 | .0 | .4 |
| | 12.5 | | 13.3 | | 11.9 | All Other Current | | | | 10.6 | 7.6 | 13.0 |
| | 35.5 | | 49.6 | | 39.0 | Total Current | | | | 44.9 | 39.8 | 33.9 |
| | 23.2 | | 21.8 | | 27.9 | Long-Term Debt | | | | 8.3 | 17.7 | 38.3 |
| | .0 | | .0 | | .1 | Deferred Taxes | | | | .0 | .0 | .4 |
| | 7.5 | | 10.1 | | 9.2 | All Other Non-Current | | | | 13.6 | 2.8 | 10.8 |
| | 33.8 | | 18.4 | | 23.7 | Net Worth | | | | 33.1 | 39.8 | 16.6 |
| | 100.0 | | 100.0 | | 100.0 | Total Liabilities & Net Worth | | | | 100.0 | 100.0 | 100.0 |
| | | | | | | **INCOME DATA** | | | | | | |
| | 100.0 | | 100.0 | | 100.0 | Net Sales | | | | 100.0 | 100.0 | 100.0 |
| | 48.6 | | 49.1 | | 50.0 | Gross Profit | | | | 50.2 | 46.6 | 57.0 |
| | 40.4 | | 44.4 | | 43.1 | Operating Expenses | | | | 46.2 | 38.8 | 47.9 |
| | 8.3 | | 4.7 | | 6.9 | Operating Profit | | | | 3.9 | 7.8 | 9.1 |
| | -1.4 | | 1.8 | | 1.9 | All Other Expenses (net) | | | | .6 | 1.8 | 2.9 |
| | 9.7 | | 2.9 | | 5.1 | Profit Before Taxes | | | | 3.3 | 6.0 | 6.3 |
| | | | | | | **RATIOS** | | | | | | |
| | 4.7 | | 2.9 | | 4.9 | | | | | 6.4 | 2.8 | 3.5 |
| | 2.3 | | 1.6 | | 2.7 | Current | | | | 1.9 | 2.2 | 1.9 |
| | 1.2 | | 1.0 | | 1.4 | | | | | 1.3 | 1.1 | 1.3 |
| | 1.7 | | 1.3 | | 2.3 | | | | | 3.1 | 1.0 | 1.6 |
| | .8 | | .6 | | .8 | Quick | | | | 1.0 | .7 | .8 |
| | .3 | | .3 | | .4 | | | | | .6 | .2 | .3 |
| 0 | UND | 0 | UND | 0 | UND | | 0 | UND | | 0 | UND | 4 | 87.3 |
| 4 | 86.8 | 9 | 42.3 | 5 | 75.4 | Sales/Receivables | 2 | 228.1 | | 8 | 44.9 | 12 | 29.8 |
| 23 | 15.9 | 40 | 9.1 | 43 | 8.4 | | 11 | 33.5 | | 51 | 7.1 | 46 | 8.0 |
| 49 | 7.4 | 51 | 7.2 | 59 | 6.2 | | 47 | 7.7 | | 57 | 6.4 | 76 | 4.8 |
| 89 | 4.1 | 104 | 3.5 | 118 | 3.1 | Cost of Sales/Inventory | 104 | 3.5 | | 96 | 3.8 | 126 | 2.9 |
| 135 | 2.7 | 182 | 2.0 | 192 | 1.9 | | 130 | 2.8 | | 152 | 2.4 | 243 | 1.5 |
| 0 | UND | 5 | 78.0 | 2 | 219.8 | | 9 | 40.9 | | 20 | 18.6 | 34 | 10.7 |
| 23 | 15.8 | 30 | 12.1 | 27 | 13.5 | Cost of Sales/Payables | 23 | 15.9 | | 26 | 14.2 | 60 | 6.1 |
| 46 | 7.9 | 83 | 4.4 | 62 | 5.9 | | 43 | 8.4 | | 59 | 6.2 | 76 | 4.8 |
| | 5.0 | | 4.9 | | 3.2 | | | | | 3.7 | 4.0 | 4.1 |
| | 6.5 | | 10.1 | | 6.4 | Sales/Working Capital | | | | 9.4 | 7.0 | 6.4 |
| | 34.9 | | 868.0 | | 18.8 | | | | | NM | 63.6 | 20.5 |
| | 55.1 | | 26.0 | | 29.9 | | | | | | 15.2 | 45.5 |
| (33) | 13.1 | (53) | 4.6 | (49) | 5.2 | EBIT/Interest | | | | (12) | 1.9 | (20) | 6.1 |
| | 6.0 | | -2.6 | | 1.2 | | | | | | .7 | 1.3 |
| | | | 99.0 | | | Net Profit + Depr., Dep., | | | | | | |
| | | (10) | 5.0 | | | Amort./Cur. Mat. L/T/D | | | | | | |
| | | | .5 | | | | | | | | | |
| | .0 | | .0 | | .0 | | | | | .0 | .1 | .0 |
| | .2 | | .2 | | .2 | Fixed/Worth | | | | .1 | .1 | .4 |
| | 2.2 | | 1.9 | | 4.3 | | | | | -.1 | 1.4 | -1.5 |
| | .8 | | 1.0 | | .5 | | | | | .2 | .6 | .5 |
| | 2.0 | | 3.0 | | 1.7 | Debt/Worth | | | | 2.1 | 3.0 | 2.3 |
| | 9.5 | | 40.7 | | NM | | | | | -4.6 | 6.4 | -34.4 |
| | 125.1 | | 85.6 | | 66.7 | | | | | | 92.1 | 63.8 |
| (41) | 56.9 | (62) | 22.7 | (46) | 22.9 | % Profit Before Taxes/Tangible Net Worth | | | | (14) | 31.9 | (15) | 25.5 |
| | 19.5 | | -3.8 | | 1.7 | | | | | | .5 | 1.9 |
| | 47.3 | | 28.8 | | 25.4 | | | | | 38.7 | 23.6 | 24.8 |
| | 20.2 | | 8.6 | | 9.3 | % Profit Before Taxes/Total Assets | | | | 19.7 | 9.3 | 6.1 |
| | 9.7 | | -1.8 | | .5 | | | | | 4.7 | .3 | .5 |
| | 265.5 | | 809.2 | | 361.7 | | | | | 585.8 | 277.8 | 469.7 |
| | 40.3 | | 70.1 | | 66.9 | Sales/Net Fixed Assets | | | | 208.3 | 44.4 | 58.8 |
| | 9.0 | | 9.5 | | 21.8 | | | | | 110.5 | 17.0 | 18.8 |
| | 4.0 | | 4.1 | | 3.5 | | | | | 4.6 | 4.2 | 2.7 |
| | 2.2 | | 2.7 | | 2.3 | Sales/Total Assets | | | | 3.3 | 2.2 | 2.2 |
| | 1.5 | | 1.6 | | 1.7 | | | | | 2.8 | 1.4 | 1.9 |
| | .4 | | .1 | | .3 | | | | | | | .2 |
| (27) | .9 | (38) | .6 | (34) | .6 | % Depr., Dep., Amort./Sales | | | | | (13) | .9 |
| | 1.4 | | 2.3 | | 1.2 | | | | | | | 1.3 |
| | 1.4 | | 2.8 | | 1.0 | | | | | | | |
| (11) | 6.0 | (24) | 7.2 | (20) | 4.5 | % Officers', Directors', Owners' Comp/Sales | | | | | | |
| | 8.4 | | 12.9 | | 13.1 | | | | | | | |
| | 828571M | | 3345129M | | 2612928M | Net Sales ($) | 938M | 17798M | 11650M | 73655M | 259081M | 2249806M |
| | 385673M | | 1344127M | | 1278846M | Total Assets ($) | 578M | 7645M | 6111M | 28649M | 141780M | 1094083M |

© RMA 2024   M = $ thousand    MM = $ million
See Pages viii through xx for Explanation of Ratios and Data

# RETAIL—Food (Health) Supplement Retailers  NAICS 456191

## Current Data Sorted by Assets | Comparative Historical Data

| | | | | | | Type of Statement | | |
|---|---|---|---|---|---|---|---|---|
| | | 2 | 1 | 1 | 1 | Unqualified | 1 | 1 |
| | | 2 | | | | Reviewed | 2 | 2 |
| | 4 | 4 | | | | Compiled | 4 | 1 |
| 3 | 5 | | 9 | | | Tax Returns | 11 | 4 |
| | 6 (4/1-9/30/23) | 8 | 37 (10/1/23-3/31/24) | 2 | 1 | Other | 25 | 14 |
| 0-500M | 500M-2MM | 2-10MM | 10-50MM | 50-100MM | 100-250MM | | 4/1/19-3/31/20 ALL | 4/1/20-3/31/21 ALL |
| 3 | 9 | 16 | 10 | 3 | 2 | NUMBER OF STATEMENTS | 43 | 22 |
| % | % | % | % | % | % | ASSETS | % | % |
| | | 14.7 | 13.8 | | | Cash & Equivalents | 19.8 | 24.9 |
| | | 9.3 | 12.5 | | | Trade Receivables (net) | 11.5 | 11.4 |
| | | 37.8 | 27.5 | | | Inventory | 31.7 | 32.7 |
| | | 6.2 | 7.0 | | | All Other Current | 2.3 | 3.7 |
| | | 68.0 | 60.8 | | | Total Current | 65.3 | 72.7 |
| | | 15.3 | 8.7 | | | Fixed Assets (net) | 14.5 | 15.1 |
| | | 9.7 | 11.8 | | | Intangibles (net) | 10.5 | 9.6 |
| | | 7.0 | 18.7 | | | All Other Non-Current | 9.8 | 2.6 |
| | | 100.0 | 100.0 | | | Total | 100.0 | 100.0 |
| | | | | | | LIABILITIES | | |
| | | 9.4 | 2.0 | | | Notes Payable-Short Term | 9.0 | 4.4 |
| | | 2.6 | 3.3 | | | Cur. Mat.-L.T.D. | 3.0 | 3.3 |
| | | 19.8 | 19.1 | | | Trade Payables | 16.1 | 18.1 |
| | | .1 | .6 | | | Income Taxes Payable | .1 | .0 |
| | | 3.9 | 12.4 | | | All Other Current | 20.7 | 28.0 |
| | | 35.8 | 37.5 | | | Total Current | 48.9 | 53.7 |
| | | 21.2 | 7.7 | | | Long-Term Debt | 16.1 | 28.6 |
| | | .0 | .0 | | | Deferred Taxes | .3 | .0 |
| | | 8.3 | 18.7 | | | All Other Non-Current | 5.5 | 3.6 |
| | | 34.7 | 36.1 | | | Net Worth | 29.2 | 14.1 |
| | | 100.0 | 100.0 | | | Total Liabilities & Net Worth | 100.0 | 100.0 |
| | | | | | | INCOME DATA | | |
| | | 100.0 | 100.0 | | | Net Sales | 100.0 | 100.0 |
| | | 54.1 | 55.5 | | | Gross Profit | 47.8 | 45.5 |
| | | 48.3 | 50.2 | | | Operating Expenses | 44.6 | 42.7 |
| | | 5.8 | 5.4 | | | Operating Profit | 3.2 | 2.9 |
| | | 1.8 | -1.1 | | | All Other Expenses (net) | 1.1 | -1.1 |
| | | 4.0 | 6.5 | | | Profit Before Taxes | 2.1 | 4.0 |
| | | | | | | RATIOS | | |
| | | 5.5 | 5.7 | | | | 3.8 | 5.3 |
| | | 1.6 | 1.4 | | | Current | 1.5 | 1.9 |
| | | 1.1 | 1.0 | | | | 1.0 | 1.2 |
| | | 2.2 | 1.1 | | | | 1.5 | 1.9 |
| | | .7 | .7 | | | Quick | .7 | 1.2 |
| | | .3 | .3 | | | | .3 | .3 |
| | | 2  188.9 | 1  399.1 | | | | 0  UND | 0  UND |
| | | 6  56.8 | 11  34.7 | | | Sales/Receivables | 4  84.4 | 2  162.7 |
| | | 19  18.9 | 29  12.8 | | | | 23  15.8 | 30  12.0 |
| | | 40  9.2 | 62  5.9 | | | | 29  12.5 | 22  16.5 |
| | | 73  5.0 | 152  2.4 | | | Cost of Sales/Inventory | 87  4.2 | 60  6.1 |
| | | 166  2.2 | 182  2.0 | | | | 114  3.2 | 152  2.4 |
| | | 17  21.4 | 23  16.0 | | | | 5  78.8 | 2  162.3 |
| | | 38  9.6 | 51  7.1 | | | Cost of Sales/Payables | 35  10.3 | 31  11.9 |
| | | 58  6.3 | 89  4.1 | | | | 72  5.1 | 49  7.5 |
| | | 6.1 | 4.2 | | | | 6.9 | 5.1 |
| | | 15.5 | 22.9 | | | Sales/Working Capital | 12.2 | 7.5 |
| | | 66.3 | NM | | | | 187.2 | NM |
| | | 16.0 | | | | | 14.0 | 47.3 |
| | (14) | 4.6 | | | | EBIT/Interest | (33) 5.6 | (15) 26.9 |
| | | .8 | | | | | 1.1 | 3.4 |
| | | | | | | Net Profit + Depr., Dep., Amort./Cur. Mat. L/T/D | | |
| | | .0 | .0 | | | | .0 | .1 |
| | | .5 | .4 | | | Fixed/Worth | .2 | .5 |
| | | -4.0 | -1.3 | | | | 1.0 | -.3 |
| | | .5 | 1.0 | | | | .6 | .8 |
| | | 6.1 | 7.4 | | | Debt/Worth | 1.6 | 1.6 |
| | | -13.6 | -9.4 | | | | 60.7 | -2.7 |
| | | 101.4 | | | | | 54.7 | 81.9 |
| | (11) | 48.1 | | | | % Profit Before Taxes/Tangible Net Worth | (34) 24.1 | (15) 32.2 |
| | | 17.3 | | | | | 2.7 | 8.2 |
| | | 18.3 | 15.6 | | | | 19.0 | 36.7 |
| | | 14.0 | 13.0 | | | % Profit Before Taxes/Total Assets | 8.2 | 13.3 |
| | | .7 | .2 | | | | .6 | 1.0 |
| | | 999.8 | 607.4 | | | | 296.9 | 324.5 |
| | | 134.8 | 152.9 | | | Sales/Net Fixed Assets | 51.1 | 39.2 |
| | | 7.7 | 38.1 | | | | 13.9 | 12.2 |
| | | 5.1 | 2.8 | | | | 5.0 | 6.7 |
| | | 3.1 | 2.2 | | | Sales/Total Assets | 3.0 | 2.7 |
| | | 1.9 | 1.2 | | | | 1.7 | 1.6 |
| | | | | | | | .4 | .3 |
| | | | | | | % Depr., Dep., Amort./Sales | (20) .9 | (12) .7 |
| | | | | | | | 1.6 | 2.9 |
| | | | | | | | 1.8 | |
| | | | | | | % Officers', Directors' Owners' Comp/Sales | (12) 5.4 | |
| | | | | | | | 10.5 | |
| 1350M | 39451M | 285087M | 478855M | 560579M | 199901M | Net Sales ($) | 1320472M | 1405924M |
| 340M | 10242M | 85764M | 217566M | 195347M | 227610M | Total Assets ($) | 435895M | 434245M |

© RMA 2024  M = $ thousand  MM = $ million
See Pages viii through xx for Explanation of Ratios and Data

# RETAIL—Food (Health) Supplement Retailers  NAICS 456191

## Comparative Historical Data / Current Data Sorted by Sales

| Comparative Historical Data | | | Type of Statement | Current Data Sorted by Sales | | | | | |
|---|---|---|---|---|---|---|---|---|---|
| 2 | 7 | 3 | Unqualified | | | | | | 3 |
| 2 | 3 | 2 | Reviewed | | | | 1 | | 1 |
| 1 | | 2 | Compiled | | | | | 1 | 1 |
| 2 | 11 | 8 | Tax Returns | | | | 3 | 2 | 2 |
| 18 | 36 | 28 | Other | 2 | 1 | | 5 | 6 | 11 |
| 4/1/21-3/31/22 ALL | 4/1/22-3/31/23 ALL | 4/1/23-3/31/24 ALL | | 3 | 3 | 6 (4/1-9/30/23) | 37 (10/1/23-3/31/24) | | |
| | | | | 0-1MM | 1-3MM | 3-5MM | 5-10MM | 10-25MM | 25MM & OVER |
| 25 | 57 | 43 | NUMBER OF STATEMENTS | 5 | 4 | | 9 | 9 | 16 |
| % | % | % | ASSETS | % | % | % | % | % | % |
| 16.3 | 19.8 | 15.9 | Cash & Equivalents | | | | | | 10.4 |
| 8.3 | 9.7 | 10.5 | Trade Receivables (net) | | | | | | 12.6 |
| 39.8 | 31.5 | 32.6 | Inventory | | | DATA | | | 36.6 |
| 2.9 | 6.1 | 8.6 | All Other Current | | | NOT | | | 4.2 |
| 67.4 | 67.1 | 67.6 | Total Current | | | AVAILABLE | | | 63.8 |
| 15.8 | 14.8 | 11.9 | Fixed Assets (net) | | | | | | 15.7 |
| 11.5 | 11.3 | 11.5 | Intangibles (net) | | | | | | 10.8 |
| 5.3 | 6.7 | 9.0 | All Other Non-Current | | | | | | 9.7 |
| 100.0 | 100.0 | 100.0 | Total | | | | | | 100.0 |
| | | | LIABILITIES | | | | | | |
| 6.3 | 7.1 | 8.2 | Notes Payable-Short Term | | | | | | 6.3 |
| 3.9 | 1.4 | 2.3 | Cur. Mat.-L.T.D. | | | | | | 2.7 |
| 21.9 | 12.2 | 18.3 | Trade Payables | | | | | | 25.8 |
| .0 | .2 | .3 | Income Taxes Payable | | | | | | .4 |
| 21.6 | 15.3 | 9.8 | All Other Current | | | | | | 5.6 |
| 53.7 | 36.2 | 38.8 | Total Current | | | | | | 40.9 |
| 24.1 | 20.3 | 21.3 | Long-Term Debt | | | | | | 10.7 |
| .5 | .4 | .0 | Deferred Taxes | | | | | | .0 |
| 5.5 | 4.0 | 9.5 | All Other Non-Current | | | | | | 11.0 |
| 16.1 | 39.1 | 30.3 | Net Worth | | | | | | 37.4 |
| 100.0 | 100.0 | 100.0 | Total Liabilities & Net Worth | | | | | | 100.0 |
| | | | INCOME DATA | | | | | | |
| 100.0 | 100.0 | 100.0 | Net Sales | | | | | | 100.0 |
| 52.1 | 51.3 | 53.3 | Gross Profit | | | | | | 40.2 |
| 47.1 | 43.2 | 46.5 | Operating Expenses | | | | | | 34.6 |
| 5.0 | 8.0 | 6.8 | Operating Profit | | | | | | 5.6 |
| -.9 | .3 | .9 | All Other Expenses (net) | | | | | | .5 |
| 5.9 | 7.7 | 6.0 | Profit Before Taxes | | | | | | 5.1 |
| | | | RATIOS | | | | | | |
| 3.9 | 4.1 | 5.5 | | | | | | | 4.0 |
| 2.1 | 2.0 | 1.7 | Current | | | | | | 1.5 |
| 1.3 | 1.3 | 1.1 | | | | | | | 1.0 |
| 1.7 | 1.7 | 2.0 | | | | | | | 1.2 |
| .8 | .8 | .7 | Quick | | | | | | .5 |
| .3 | .3 | .3 | | | | | | | .2 |
| 0  883.2 | 0  UND | 0  999.8 | | | | | | | 2  202.8 |
| 12  31.4 | 5  76.7 | 10  37.6 | Sales/Receivables | | | | | | 13  27.9 |
| 36  10.0 | 24  15.1 | 21  17.6 | | | | | | | 30  12.0 |
| 57  6.4 | 33  10.9 | 44  8.3 | | | | | | | 50  7.3 |
| 152  2.4 | 91  4.0 | 85  4.3 | Cost of Sales/Inventory | | | | | | 78  4.7 |
| 182  2.0 | 166  2.2 | 166  2.2 | | | | | | | 166  2.2 |
| 2  186.8 | 12  30.7 | 10  38.1 | | | | | | | 26  14.0 |
| 36  10.1 | 25  14.5 | 36  10.2 | Cost of Sales/Payables | | | | | | 38  9.7 |
| 59  6.2 | 41  8.8 | 62  5.9 | | | | | | | 87  4.2 |
| 4.3 | 4.3 | 3.5 | | | | | | | 3.7 |
| 6.5 | 8.9 | 13.8 | Sales/Working Capital | | | | | | 23.1 |
| 29.7 | 36.4 | 183.1 | | | | | | | 350.4 |
| 25.0 | 53.4 | 17.6 | | | | | | | 13.6 |
| (19)  7.2 | (40)  7.9 | (33)  3.8 | EBIT/Interest | | | | | | (12)  5.2 |
| 3.8 | 1.4 | .4 | | | | | | | 3.5 |
| | | | Net Profit + Depr., Dep., Amort./Cur. Mat. L/T/D | | | | | | |
| .1 | .0 | .0 | | | | | | | .0 |
| .6 | .3 | .5 | Fixed/Worth | | | | | | .7 |
| -.8 | 2.1 | -3.0 | | | | | | | 1.9 |
| .6 | .7 | .6 | | | | | | | 1.0 |
| 6.5 | 1.6 | 1.8 | Debt/Worth | | | | | | 3.3 |
| -3.2 | 381.1 | -16.3 | | | | | | | NM |
| 65.9 | 160.5 | 96.0 | % Profit Before Taxes/Tangible Net Worth | | | | | | 64.7 |
| (13)  19.7 | (44)  56.3 | (30)  42.8 | | | | | | | (12)  29.4 |
| 1.3 | 24.9 | 14.6 | | | | | | | 10.8 |
| 26.0 | 32.5 | 26.1 | % Profit Before Taxes/Total Assets | | | | | | 16.0 |
| 9.4 | 13.7 | 13.5 | | | | | | | 11.4 |
| 1.1 | 1.8 | .7 | | | | | | | 3.6 |
| 66.2 | 492.9 | 851.2 | | | | | | | 962.7 |
| 22.3 | 34.6 | 68.6 | Sales/Net Fixed Assets | | | | | | 57.4 |
| 9.5 | 10.2 | 12.6 | | | | | | | 10.7 |
| 3.5 | 5.0 | 4.0 | | | | | | | 4.2 |
| 2.2 | 2.3 | 2.8 | Sales/Total Assets | | | | | | 2.8 |
| 1.8 | 1.5 | 1.3 | | | | | | | 1.2 |
| 1.3 | .4 | .5 | | | | | | | |
| (12)  1.8 | (35)  1.1 | (16)  2.1 | % Depr., Dep., Amort./Sales | | | | | | |
| 3.4 | 1.9 | 4.1 | | | | | | | |
| | | .9 | 1.1 | % Officers', Directors' Owners' Comp/Sales | | | | | |
| | (19)  4.6 | (11)  2.8 | | | | | | | |
| | | 7.9 | 5.6 | | | | | | |
| 992617M | 3089235M | 1565223M | Net Sales ($) | 2769M | 10521M | | 65706M | 177720M | 1308507M |
| 520327M | 1478342M | 736869M | Total Assets ($) | 2183M | 3430M | | 37946M | 85669M | 607641M |

© RMA 2024  M = $ thousand  MM = $ million
See Pages viii through xx for Explanation of Ratios and Data

# RETAIL—All Other Health and Personal Care Retailers  NAICS 456199

## Current Data Sorted by Assets | Comparative Historical Data

| | | | | | | | Type of Statement | | | | |
|---|---|---|---|---|---|---|---|---|---|---|---|
| | | | | 1 | 1 | | Unqualified | | 1 | | |
| | 1 | | | 1 | | | Reviewed | | 4 | | 2 |
| | 5 | | 4 | 5 | | | Compiled | | 5 | | 1 |
| 1 | 5 | 4 | 5 | 6 | 1 | | Tax Returns | | 10 | | 10 |
| 0-500M | 3 (4/1-9/30/23) 500M-2MM | 2-10MM | 10-50MM | 28 (10/1/23-3/31/24) 50-100MM | 100-250MM | | Other | | 31 4/1/19- 3/31/20 ALL | | 20 4/1/20- 3/31/21 ALL |
| 1 | 11 | 9 | 8 | 1 | 1 | | NUMBER OF STATEMENTS | | 50 | | 34 |
| % | % | % | % | % | % | | ASSETS | | % | | % |
| | 20.3 | | | | | | Cash & Equivalents | | 13.8 | | 22.8 |
| | 26.8 | | | | | | Trade Receivables (net) | | 21.8 | | 15.5 |
| | 22.4 | | | | | | Inventory | | 18.9 | | 28.5 |
| | 1.5 | | | | | | All Other Current | | 5.4 | | .7 |
| | 71.1 | | | | | | Total Current | | 59.9 | | 67.5 |
| | 12.6 | | | | | | Fixed Assets (net) | | 18.9 | | 12.5 |
| | 3.4 | | | | | | Intangibles (net) | | 6.5 | | 8.8 |
| | 12.9 | | | | | | All Other Non-Current | | 14.6 | | 11.3 |
| | 100.0 | | | | | | Total | | 100.0 | | 100.0 |
| | | | | | | | LIABILITIES | | | | |
| | 8.4 | | | | | | Notes Payable-Short Term | | 12.1 | | 7.4 |
| | 2.5 | | | | | | Cur. Mat.-L.T.D. | | 2.2 | | 5.6 |
| | 9.3 | | | | | | Trade Payables | | 18.1 | | 14.0 |
| | .0 | | | | | | Income Taxes Payable | | .0 | | .1 |
| | 8.1 | | | | | | All Other Current | | 12.8 | | 15.3 |
| | 28.3 | | | | | | Total Current | | 45.2 | | 42.4 |
| | 16.6 | | | | | | Long-Term Debt | | 16.7 | | 33.1 |
| | .0 | | | | | | Deferred Taxes | | .2 | | .3 |
| | 12.6 | | | | | | All Other Non-Current | | 7.3 | | 10.4 |
| | 42.4 | | | | | | Net Worth | | 30.7 | | 13.9 |
| | 100.0 | | | | | | Total Liabilties & Net Worth | | 100.0 | | 100.0 |
| | | | | | | | INCOME DATA | | | | |
| | 100.0 | | | | | | Net Sales | | 100.0 | | 100.0 |
| | 50.4 | | | | | | Gross Profit | | 52.3 | | 52.0 |
| | 44.5 | | | | | | Operating Expenses | | 45.3 | | 45.9 |
| | 5.9 | | | | | | Operating Profit | | 7.0 | | 6.1 |
| | .2 | | | | | | All Other Expenses (net) | | .9 | | -.2 |
| | 5.8 | | | | | | Profit Before Taxes | | 6.0 | | 6.3 |
| | | | | | | | RATIOS | | | | |
| | 6.3 | | | | | | | | 2.5 | | 4.0 |
| | 2.8 | | | | | | Current | | 1.4 | | 1.9 |
| | 1.5 | | | | | | | | .9 | | 1.0 |
| | 3.5 | | | | | | | | 1.5 | | 2.7 |
| | 2.0 | | | | | | Quick | | .7 | | 1.1 |
| | 1.1 | | | | | | | | .4 | | .5 |
| 0 | UND | | | | | | | 2 | 222.3 | 0 | UND |
| 16 | 22.8 | | | | | | Sales/Receivables | 30 | 12.0 | 8 | 46.1 |
| 47 | 7.7 | | | | | | | 55 | 6.6 | 36 | 10.2 |
| 0 | UND | | | | | | | 19 | 19.1 | 27 | 13.7 |
| 24 | 15.0 | | | | | | Cost of Sales/Inventory | 43 | 8.5 | 59 | 6.2 |
| 74 | 4.9 | | | | | | | 70 | 5.2 | 174 | 2.1 |
| 0 | UND | | | | | | | 15 | 25.0 | 0 | UND |
| 14 | 25.8 | | | | | | Cost of Sales/Payables | 52 | 7.0 | 22 | 16.6 |
| 44 | 8.3 | | | | | | | 85 | 4.3 | 55 | 6.6 |
| | 3.1 | | | | | | | | 7.3 | | 4.2 |
| | 11.2 | | | | | | Sales/Working Capital | | 19.4 | | 15.4 |
| | 36.1 | | | | | | | | -44.1 | | 76.1 |
| | | | | | | | | | 25.2 | | 32.5 |
| | | | | | | | EBIT/Interest | (40) | 9.2 | (27) | 8.5 |
| | | | | | | | | | 1.9 | | 1.8 |
| | | | | | | | Net Profit + Depr., Dep., Amort./Cur. Mat. L/T/D | | | | |
| | .0 | | | | | | | | .1 | | .0 |
| | .1 | | | | | | Fixed/Worth | | .7 | | .2 |
| | 1.0 | | | | | | | | 2.8 | | -1.1 |
| | .4 | | | | | | | | .5 | | .6 |
| | 1.8 | | | | | | Debt/Worth | | 2.2 | | 2.9 |
| | 2.7 | | | | | | | | 28.1 | | -5.6 |
| | | | | | | | | | 86.8 | | 102.1 |
| | | | | | | | % Profit Before Taxes/Tangible Net Worth | (39) | 38.9 | (22) | 53.5 |
| | | | | | | | | | 9.6 | | 29.4 |
| | 48.4 | | | | | | | | 31.4 | | 28.5 |
| | 6.3 | | | | | | % Profit Before Taxes/Total Assets | | 11.9 | | 13.5 |
| | .7 | | | | | | | | 2.7 | | 1.6 |
| | 344.4 | | | | | | | | 71.3 | | 322.6 |
| | 110.8 | | | | | | Sales/Net Fixed Assets | | 27.7 | | 38.6 |
| | 52.9 | | | | | | | | 8.6 | | 16.3 |
| | 7.2 | | | | | | | | 4.3 | | 4.6 |
| | 3.0 | | | | | | Sales/Total Assets | | 2.5 | | 2.6 |
| | 2.0 | | | | | | | | 1.7 | | 1.6 |
| | | | | | | | | | .3 | | .2 |
| | | | | | | | % Depr., Dep., Amort./Sales | (28) | 1.8 | (19) | 1.0 |
| | | | | | | | | | 4.0 | | 2.1 |
| | | | | | | | | | .9 | | 1.8 |
| | | | | | | | % Officers', Directors' Owners' Comp/Sales | (20) | 2.4 | (11) | 2.5 |
| | | | | | | | | | 6.1 | | 8.1 |
| 1934M | 58318M | 155219M | 347112M | 49007M | 177004M | | Net Sales ($) | | 1917758M | | 883862M |
| 368M | 12740M | 46177M | 207420M | 89681M | 136195M | | Total Assets ($) | | 701664M | | 573443M |

© RMA 2024          M = $ thousand    MM = $ million
See Pages viii through xx for Explanation of Ratios and Data

# RETAIL—All Other Health and Personal Care Retailers  NAICS 456199

**Page 769**

## Comparative Historical Data / Current Data Sorted by Sales

| Comparative Historical Data | | | | | Current Data Sorted by Sales | | | | | |
|---|---|---|---|---|---|---|---|---|---|---|
| 3 | | 2 | | Type of Statement | | | | | | 2 |
| | | 1 | | Unqualified | | | | | 1 | 1 |
| | 2 | 1 | | Reviewed | | | | | 2 | |
| 9 | 2 | 10 | | Compiled | 4 | 1 | 3 | 1 | 2 | 8 |
| 20 | 19 | 17 | | Tax Returns | 3 | | 1 | 2 | 5 | |
| 4/1/21- | 4/1/22- | 4/1/23- | | Other | | | | | | |
| 3/31/22 | 3/31/23 | 3/31/24 | | | 3 (4/1-9/30/23) | | | 28 (10/1/23-3/31/24) | | |
| ALL | ALL | ALL | | | 0-1MM | 1-3MM | 3-5MM | 5-10MM | 10-25MM | 25MM & OVER |
| 32 | 23 | 31 | | NUMBER OF STATEMENTS | 7 | 1 | 4 | 8 | | 11 |
| % | % | % | | **ASSETS** | % | % | % | % | % | % |
| 29.3 | 16.3 | 16.9 | | Cash & Equivalents | | | | | | 10.7 |
| 13.0 | 17.0 | 27.9 | | Trade Receivables (net) | D | | | | | 30.6 |
| 18.8 | 30.0 | 24.9 | | Inventory | A | | | | | 18.3 |
| .8 | 2.5 | 2.1 | | All Other Current | T | | | | | 2.6 |
| 61.9 | 65.8 | 71.9 | | Total Current | A | | | | | 62.2 |
| 15.7 | 18.1 | 13.5 | | Fixed Assets (net) | | | | | | 20.7 |
| 12.1 | 7.9 | 2.4 | | Intangibles (net) | N | | | | | 1.6 |
| 10.3 | 8.3 | 12.3 | | All Other Non-Current | O | | | | | 15.4 |
| 100.0 | 100.0 | 100.0 | | Total | T | | | | | 100.0 |
| | | | | **LIABILITIES** | A | | | | | |
| 3.3 | 5.3 | 5.4 | | Notes Payable-Short Term | V | | | | | 4.0 |
| 1.4 | 3.3 | 3.3 | | Cur. Mat.-L.T.D. | A | | | | | 3.9 |
| 12.7 | 18.9 | 15.9 | | Trade Payables | I | | | | | 19.5 |
| .1 | .0 | .0 | | Income Taxes Payable | L | | | | | .0 |
| 8.3 | 7.7 | 12.3 | | All Other Current | A | | | | | 10.0 |
| 25.8 | 35.2 | 36.8 | | Total Current | B | | | | | 37.4 |
| 23.5 | 32.8 | 17.7 | | Long-Term Debt | L | | | | | 12.0 |
| .0 | .0 | .0 | | Deferred Taxes | E | | | | | .0 |
| 4.7 | 7.3 | 6.6 | | All Other Non-Current | | | | | | 4.3 |
| 46.0 | 24.6 | 38.8 | | Net Worth | | | | | | 46.4 |
| 100.0 | 100.0 | 100.0 | | Total Liabilities & Net Worth | | | | | | 100.0 |
| | | | | **INCOME DATA** | | | | | | |
| 100.0 | 100.0 | 100.0 | | Net Sales | | | | | | 100.0 |
| 55.2 | 50.2 | 51.8 | | Gross Profit | | | | | | 53.4 |
| 46.7 | 44.4 | 43.7 | | Operating Expenses | | | | | | 41.8 |
| 8.5 | 5.8 | 8.1 | | Operating Profit | | | | | | 11.6 |
| -.2 | 1.7 | 1.0 | | All Other Expenses (net) | | | | | | 1.9 |
| 8.7 | 4.1 | 7.0 | | Profit Before Taxes | | | | | | 9.7 |
| | | | | **RATIOS** | | | | | | |
| 4.9 | 3.4 | 4.0 | | Current | | | | | | 3.3 |
| 2.3 | 1.6 | 2.6 | | | | | | | | 1.3 |
| 1.5 | 1.3 | 1.2 | | | | | | | | .9 |
| 3.3 | 1.6 | 2.7 | | Quick | | | | | | 2.7 |
| 1.5 | .8 | 1.2 | | | | | | | | 1.1 |
| .8 | .6 | .7 | | | | | | | | .4 |
| 0  UND | 0  UND | 5  78.6 | | Sales/Receivables | | | | | 41 | 8.9 |
| 17  21.1 | 20  18.2 | 42  8.6 | | | | | | | 53 | 6.9 |
| 39  9.3 | 60  6.1 | 74  4.9 | | | | | | | 72 | 5.1 |
| 12  29.6 | 28  13.1 | 21  17.8 | | Cost of Sales/Inventory | | | | | 21 | 17.8 |
| 33  11.1 | 73  5.0 | 47  7.8 | | | | | | | 47 | 7.8 |
| 85  4.3 | 130  2.8 | 101  3.6 | | | | | | | 96 | 3.8 |
| 4  91.5 | 7  54.2 | 27  13.3 | | Cost of Sales/Payables | | | | | 35 | 10.3 |
| 31  11.8 | 46  7.9 | 38  9.5 | | | | | | | 61 | 6.0 |
| 78  4.7 | 74  4.9 | 61  6.0 | | | | | | | 70 | 5.2 |
| 4.4 | 4.5 | 4.3 | | Sales/Working Capital | | | | | | 5.0 |
| 10.9 | 10.3 | 11.1 | | | | | | | | 16.1 |
| 15.3 | 23.5 | 36.1 | | | | | | | | -156.9 |
| 82.9 | 21.0 | 60.7 | | EBIT/Interest | | | | | | |
| (22)  9.8 | (15)  5.9 | (22)  12.0 | | | | | | | | |
| 1.2 | -1.3 | 1.6 | | | | | | | | |
| | | | | Net Profit + Depr., Dep., Amort./Cur. Mat. L/T/D | | | | | | |
| .0 | .0 | .0 | | Fixed/Worth | | | | | | .0 |
| .3 | .3 | .2 | | | | | | | | .3 |
| .9 | 2.8 | 1.0 | | | | | | | | .5 |
| .4 | .9 | .4 | | Debt/Worth | | | | | | .3 |
| 1.0 | 2.4 | 1.8 | | | | | | | | 1.7 |
| 12.3 | 4.8 | 7.4 | | | | | | | | 4.7 |
| 60.0 | 69.4 | 49.6 | | % Profit Before Taxes/Tangible Net Worth | | | | | | 51.6 |
| (26)  43.7 | (18)  31.6 | (26)  37.0 | | | | | | | | 40.2 |
| 8.0 | 5.7 | 6.1 | | | | | | | | 31.7 |
| 37.9 | 27.8 | 30.9 | | % Profit Before Taxes/Total Assets | | | | | | 30.9 |
| 14.1 | 8.4 | 17.2 | | | | | | | | 26.8 |
| 1.0 | -4.7 | 1.9 | | | | | | | | 10.8 |
| 796.4 | 526.4 | 283.1 | | Sales/Net Fixed Assets | | | | | | 272.7 |
| 36.6 | 36.9 | 67.7 | | | | | | | | 27.8 |
| 11.9 | 9.3 | 23.3 | | | | | | | | 4.5 |
| 3.4 | 3.9 | 4.2 | | Sales/Total Assets | | | | | | 4.1 |
| 2.3 | 3.0 | 2.7 | | | | | | | | 1.7 |
| 1.3 | 1.1 | 1.5 | | | | | | | | 1.3 |
| .4 | | .3 | | % Depr., Dep., Amort./Sales | | | | | | |
| (16)  1.0 | | (17)  .9 | | | | | | | | |
| 3.2 | | 1.8 | | | | | | | | |
| | | | | % Officers', Directors' Owners' Comp/Sales | | | | | | |
| 1041569M | 935172M | 788594M | | Net Sales ($) | 12632M | 3642M | 28403M | 111942M | | 631975M |
| 797908M | 490079M | 492581M | | Total Assets ($) | 6277M | 1330M | 6889M | 50702M | | 427383M |

M = $ thousand    MM = $ million
See Pages viii through xx for Explanation of Ratios and Data

© RMA 2024

# RETAIL—Gasoline Stations with Convenience Stores  NAICS 457110

## Current Data Sorted by Assets / Comparative Historical Data

| 0-500M | 500M-2MM | 2-10MM | 10-50MM | 50-100MM | 100-250MM | Type of Statement | | 4/1/19-3/31/20 ALL | | 4/1/20-3/31/21 ALL |
|---|---|---|---|---|---|---|---|---|---|---|
| 2 | 3 | 2 | 9 | 8 | 11 | Unqualified | | 46 | | 26 |
| 1 | 1 | 5 | 21 | 9 | 2 | Reviewed | | 45 | | 28 |
| 13 | 17 | 7 | 9 | 1 | 1 | Compiled | | 60 | | 47 |
| 51 | 42 | 23 | 2 | | | Tax Returns | | 215 | | 158 |
| 34 | 62 | 92 | 58 | 17 | 26 | Other | | 312 | | 259 |
| | 63 (4/1-9/30/23) | | 465 (10/1/23-3/31/24) | | | | | | | |
| 100 | 125 | 129 | 99 | 35 | 40 | NUMBER OF STATEMENTS | | 678 | | 518 |
| % | % | % | % | % | % | ASSETS | | % | | % |
| 28.0 | 22.7 | 13.8 | 14.2 | 14.9 | 10.2 | Cash & Equivalents | | 16.3 | | 21.7 |
| 1.8 | 1.8 | 3.4 | 7.0 | 3.5 | 6.0 | Trade Receivables (net) | | 4.3 | | 3.7 |
| 42.3 | 14.5 | 11.0 | 10.4 | 9.0 | 9.8 | Inventory | | 19.0 | | 16.2 |
| 2.5 | 2.2 | 5.6 | 3.0 | 1.1 | 2.6 | All Other Current | | 2.4 | | 2.2 |
| 74.5 | 41.2 | 33.8 | 34.5 | 28.5 | 28.6 | Total Current | | 42.0 | | 43.8 |
| 13.0 | 36.5 | 47.9 | 49.4 | 57.8 | 54.0 | Fixed Assets (net) | | 44.5 | | 41.6 |
| 8.4 | 11.3 | 6.0 | 4.6 | 5.2 | 5.6 | Intangibles (net) | | 6.3 | | 7.9 |
| 4.1 | 10.9 | 12.3 | 11.5 | 8.5 | 11.8 | All Other Non-Current | | 7.2 | | 6.7 |
| 100.0 | 100.0 | 100.0 | 100.0 | 100.0 | 100.0 | Total | | 100.0 | | 100.0 |
| | | | | | | LIABILITIES | | | | |
| 2.2 | .9 | 1.2 | .9 | .5 | .6 | Notes Payable-Short Term | | 2.3 | | 3.5 |
| 1.5 | 2.3 | 2.1 | 5.5 | 3.1 | 2.5 | Cur. Mat.-L.T.D. | | 2.5 | | 2.7 |
| 7.2 | 4.6 | 4.8 | 10.9 | 8.6 | 9.5 | Trade Payables | | 10.9 | | 8.8 |
| .3 | .2 | .1 | .1 | .1 | .1 | Income Taxes Payable | | .3 | | .4 |
| 23.8 | 10.7 | 7.6 | 6.2 | 5.5 | 7.3 | All Other Current | | 10.0 | | 6.0 |
| 35.0 | 18.6 | 15.7 | 23.5 | 17.7 | 20.0 | Total Current | | 25.9 | | 21.4 |
| 18.5 | 40.4 | 50.3 | 28.6 | 38.6 | 33.5 | Long-Term Debt | | 32.7 | | 39.0 |
| .0 | .0 | .0 | .8 | .5 | .2 | Deferred Taxes | | .2 | | .2 |
| 9.7 | 8.2 | 3.8 | 6.5 | 4.7 | 5.9 | All Other Non-Current | | 7.5 | | 8.1 |
| 36.8 | 32.7 | 30.1 | 40.5 | 38.6 | 40.4 | Net Worth | | 33.7 | | 31.4 |
| 100.0 | 100.0 | 100.0 | 100.0 | 100.0 | 100.0 | Total Liabilites & Net Worth | | 100.0 | | 100.0 |
| | | | | | | INCOME DATA | | | | |
| 100.0 | 100.0 | 100.0 | 100.0 | 100.0 | 100.0 | Net Sales | | 100.0 | | 100.0 |
| 18.8 | 19.6 | 18.7 | 17.7 | 18.2 | 20.1 | Gross Profit | | 18.0 | | 20.4 |
| 17.5 | 15.1 | 13.6 | 14.6 | 15.6 | 14.8 | Operating Expenses | | 15.4 | | 16.5 |
| 1.3 | 4.4 | 5.1 | 3.1 | 2.7 | 5.3 | Operating Profit | | 2.6 | | 3.9 |
| -1.6 | -.3 | .5 | .1 | .1 | 1.5 | All Other Expenses (net) | | -.1 | | -.4 |
| 2.9 | 4.8 | 4.7 | 3.0 | 2.5 | 3.7 | Profit Before Taxes | | 2.7 | | 4.3 |
| | | | | | | RATIOS | | | | |
| 15.3 | 14.4 | 5.8 | 2.3 | 2.3 | 2.1 | | | 3.8 | | 5.7 |
| 5.9 | 3.9 | 2.5 | 1.6 | 1.4 | 1.2 | Current | | 1.8 | | 2.5 |
| 1.7 | 1.7 | 1.3 | .9 | 1.1 | .9 | | | 1.0 | | 1.3 |
| 4.8 | 8.0 | 2.8 | 1.6 | 1.6 | 1.5 | | | 2.0 | | 3.6 |
| 1.3 | 1.8 | 1.1 | .8 | .8 | .7 | Quick | | .8 | | 1.4 |
| .4 | .6 | .4 | .4 | .5 | .4 | | (677) | .3 | (516) | .6 |
| 0 UND | 0 UND | 0 UND | 1 486.4 | 1 478.8 | 2 181.5 | | 0 | UND | 0 | UND |
| 0 UND | 0 UND | 0 UND | 4 103.6 | 2 150.9 | 5 81.0 | Sales/Receivables | 0 | 993.8 | 0 | 999.8 |
| 0 UND | 0 938.3 | 2 160.0 | 7 56.0 | 5 80.9 | 10 38.0 | | 3 | 110.1 | 4 | 103.2 |
| 8 46.0 | 6 59.0 | 6 56.9 | 6 60.8 | 8 48.4 | 5 67.7 | | 6 | 60.1 | 8 | 45.1 |
| 13 28.6 | 10 35.4 | 10 37.9 | 9 40.4 | 11 34.5 | 9 42.4 | Cost of Sales/Inventory | 10 | 36.3 | 12 | 29.9 |
| 21 17.7 | 19 19.4 | 15 24.3 | 15 24.2 | 16 23.5 | 13 28.9 | | 16 | 23.3 | 20 | 18.5 |
| 0 UND | 0 UND | 0 UND | 4 102.7 | 6 62.4 | 6 60.7 | | 0 | 999.8 | 0 | UND |
| 0 UND | 1 372.0 | 3 117.3 | 10 37.3 | 10 37.3 | 11 32.0 | Cost of Sales/Payables | 5 | 71.5 | 5 | 66.5 |
| 3 124.7 | 5 76.2 | 8 47.5 | 14 25.6 | 14 25.2 | 16 22.7 | | 11 | 32.3 | 11 | 32.1 |
| 15.6 | 12.1 | 12.6 | 18.3 | 19.9 | 19.3 | | | 20.0 | | 11.3 |
| 27.9 | 24.3 | 26.0 | 38.2 | 38.9 | 95.8 | Sales/Working Capital | | 44.4 | | 21.6 |
| 64.2 | 63.8 | 119.0 | -317.9 | 372.6 | -163.2 | | | -999.8 | | 73.4 |
| 18.5 | 15.5 | 9.2 | 11.0 | 22.8 | 10.6 | | | 12.8 | | 16.8 |
| (35) 5.7 | (88) 5.8 | (100) 3.6 | (85) 4.5 | (34) 4.8 | (32) 4.7 | EBIT/Interest | (520) | 4.8 | (388) | 6.3 |
| 2.0 | 2.6 | 2.1 | 2.2 | 2.1 | 2.2 | | | 2.1 | | 2.9 |
| | | | 4.9 | | | | | 8.1 | | 7.8 |
| | | (28) 3.3 | | | | Net Profit + Depr., Dep., Amort./Cur. Mat. L/T/D | (56) | 3.7 | (42) | 3.5 |
| | | 1.8 | | | | | | 2.2 | | 2.4 |
| .0 | .2 | .7 | .6 | .7 | .9 | | | .4 | | .4 |
| .1 | 1.6 | 2.2 | 1.4 | 1.6 | 1.8 | Fixed/Worth | | 1.5 | | 1.6 |
| 1.1 | UND | 8.6 | 4.0 | 4.3 | 3.6 | | | 5.4 | | 6.9 |
| .1 | .6 | .9 | .7 | .7 | .8 | | | .7 | | .9 |
| 1.1 | 1.7 | 3.2 | 1.8 | 1.7 | 2.3 | Debt/Worth | | 2.0 | | 2.3 |
| 7.8 | UND | 15.4 | 4.7 | 5.2 | 4.4 | | | 10.9 | | 16.9 |
| 144.1 | 95.8 | 77.7 | 34.7 | 27.1 | 37.7 | % Profit Before Taxes/Tangible Net Worth | | 63.1 | | 92.2 |
| (82) 71.5 | (95) 54.7 | (106) 44.1 | (88) 20.0 | (31) 20.6 | (39) 24.0 | | (548) | 28.6 | (409) | 39.7 |
| 22.3 | 24.1 | 19.8 | 7.6 | 8.4 | 15.5 | | | 10.6 | | 18.4 |
| 76.2 | 41.1 | 19.8 | 13.9 | 9.6 | 13.0 | % Profit Before Taxes/Total Assets | | 23.7 | | 25.4 |
| 28.4 | 15.8 | 9.7 | 8.3 | 5.7 | 8.5 | | | 9.6 | | 12.8 |
| 9.0 | 6.9 | 4.5 | 1.7 | 3.5 | 3.8 | | | 3.2 | | 5.9 |
| UND | 146.1 | 25.3 | 20.1 | 10.5 | 10.4 | | | 66.7 | | 77.1 |
| 510.8 | 16.1 | 6.1 | 7.5 | 5.8 | 5.3 | Sales/Net Fixed Assets | | 11.1 | | 8.9 |
| 55.7 | 5.3 | 2.7 | 3.0 | 3.1 | 3.0 | | | 4.4 | | 3.7 |
| 21.3 | 8.0 | 5.2 | 5.5 | 4.6 | 5.9 | | | 10.2 | | 7.3 |
| 12.9 | 4.9 | 3.0 | 3.8 | 3.0 | 2.9 | Sales/Total Assets | | 5.0 | | 3.8 |
| 8.1 | 2.6 | 1.7 | 1.9 | 2.0 | 2.3 | | | 2.9 | | 2.2 |
| .2 | .4 | .4 | .8 | .9 | .7 | | | .6 | | .6 |
| (34) .5 | (75) .9 | (76) 1.0 | (88) 1.2 | 1.4 | (26) 1.5 | % Depr., Dep., Amort./Sales | (479) | 1.2 | (347) | 1.4 |
| 1.1 | 1.9 | 2.9 | 2.0 | 2.5 | 2.0 | | | 1.8 | | 2.5 |
| .8 | .5 | .3 | .1 | | | | | .5 | | .5 |
| (40) 1.4 | (47) 1.2 | (37) .5 | (14) .3 | | | % Officers', Directors' Owners' Comp/Sales | (225) | .9 | (177) | 1.1 |
| 2.6 | 2.0 | 1.2 | .8 | | | | | 1.9 | | 2.0 |
| 369350M | 833692M | 2298542M | 10362474M | 9191651M | 32999580M | Net Sales ($) | | 63871326M | | 31381126M |
| 25557M | 144809M | 541468M | 2454369M | 2656190M | 6375222M | Total Assets ($) | | 13176126M | | 9848703M |

© RMA 2024  
M = $ thousand   MM = $ million  
See Pages viii through xx for Explanation of Ratios and Data

# RETAIL—Gasoline Stations with Convenience Stores  NAICS 457110

## Comparative Historical Data | Current Data Sorted by Sales

| | | | Type of Statement | | | | | | |
|---|---|---|---|---|---|---|---|---|---|
| 25 | 30 | 35 | Unqualified | 1 | 3 | | 1 | 3 | 27 |
| 32 | 45 | 38 | Reviewed | | 1 | 3 | 3 | 3 | 31 |
| 52 | 45 | 48 | Compiled | | | 10 | 9 | 12 | 6 | 11 |
| 174 | 183 | 118 | Tax Returns | 6 | 34 | 32 | 23 | 14 | 9 |
| 285 | 270 | 289 | Other | 6 | 26 | 29 | 67 | 45 | 116 |
| 4/1/21-3/31/22 ALL | 4/1/22-3/31/23 ALL | 4/1/23-3/31/24 ALL | | 63 (4/1-9/30/23) | | | 465 (10/1/23-3/31/24) | | |
| | | | | 0-1MM | 1-3MM | 3-5MM | 5-10MM | 10-25MM | 25MM & OVER |
| 568 | 573 | 528 | NUMBER OF STATEMENTS | 13 | 74 | 70 | 106 | 71 | 194 |
| % | % | % | **ASSETS** | % | % | % | % | % | % |
| 21.9 | 20.7 | 18.5 | Cash & Equivalents | 14.5 | 23.1 | 19.7 | 19.4 | 20.1 | 15.4 |
| 3.8 | 3.3 | 3.6 | Trade Receivables (net) | 1.5 | .7 | 2.1 | 1.9 | 3.3 | 6.4 |
| 17.7 | 17.7 | 17.4 | Inventory | 27.2 | 26.9 | 24.9 | 16.8 | 11.8 | 12.9 |
| 2.7 | 3.8 | 3.2 | All Other Current | .5 | 2.6 | 2.4 | 3.7 | 4.0 | 3.3 |
| 46.1 | 45.4 | 42.7 | Total Current | 43.8 | 53.2 | 49.0 | 41.8 | 39.1 | 38.1 |
| 39.1 | 40.4 | 40.0 | Fixed Assets (net) | 40.9 | 31.0 | 32.2 | 38.0 | 42.0 | 46.6 |
| 6.8 | 6.3 | 7.3 | Intangibles (net) | 10.2 | 10.3 | 7.7 | 9.8 | 6.7 | 4.8 |
| 7.9 | 7.9 | 10.0 | All Other Non-Current | 5.2 | 5.5 | 11.1 | 10.5 | 12.2 | 10.5 |
| 100.0 | 100.0 | 100.0 | Total | 100.0 | 100.0 | 100.0 | 100.0 | 100.0 | 100.0 |
| | | | **LIABILITIES** | | | | | | |
| 1.5 | 1.5 | 1.2 | Notes Payable-Short Term | 2.1 | .4 | 2.4 | 1.5 | 1.2 | .8 |
| 2.4 | 1.6 | 2.7 | Cur. Mat.-L.T.D. | .6 | 2.0 | 1.6 | 1.7 | 3.6 | 3.8 |
| 8.1 | 7.7 | 7.0 | Trade Payables | 3.3 | 2.5 | 4.8 | 5.2 | 6.6 | 10.8 |
| .3 | .2 | .2 | Income Taxes Payable | .0 | .2 | .3 | .2 | .0 | .1 |
| 8.2 | 7.2 | 11.0 | All Other Current | 12.2 | 21.7 | 10.3 | 11.4 | 7.0 | 8.3 |
| 20.5 | 18.2 | 22.0 | Total Current | 18.2 | 26.7 | 19.5 | 20.0 | 18.4 | 23.8 |
| 34.9 | 35.1 | 35.8 | Long-Term Debt | 34.9 | 30.3 | 33.4 | 45.4 | 49.2 | 28.8 |
| .2 | .2 | .2 | Deferred Taxes | .0 | .0 | .0 | .0 | .0 | .5 |
| 7.4 | 7.0 | 6.7 | All Other Non-Current | 3.1 | 11.5 | 5.6 | 7.6 | 7.6 | 4.7 |
| 37.1 | 39.4 | 35.3 | Net Worth | 43.9 | 31.4 | 41.6 | 27.1 | 24.9 | 42.2 |
| 100.0 | 100.0 | 100.0 | Total Liabilities & Net Worth | 100.0 | 100.0 | 100.0 | 100.0 | 100.0 | 100.0 |
| | | | **INCOME DATA** | | | | | | |
| 100.0 | 100.0 | 100.0 | Net Sales | 100.0 | 100.0 | 100.0 | 100.0 | 100.0 | 100.0 |
| 18.1 | 18.0 | 18.8 | Gross Profit | 26.9 | 24.1 | 17.9 | 17.9 | 19.3 | 16.9 |
| 14.5 | 14.5 | 15.1 | Operating Expenses | 24.5 | 21.4 | 13.1 | 13.2 | 13.8 | 14.3 |
| 3.7 | 3.5 | 3.7 | Operating Profit | 2.3 | 2.7 | 4.8 | 4.7 | 5.5 | 2.6 |
| -.8 | -.5 | -.1 | All Other Expenses (net) | .0 | -2.0 | .4 | .1 | .7 | .0 |
| 4.5 | 4.0 | 3.8 | Profit Before Taxes | 2.3 | 4.7 | 4.5 | 4.5 | 4.8 | 2.6 |
| | | | **RATIOS** | | | | | | |
| 6.9 | 8.0 | 6.4 | | 20.6 | 16.7 | 13.6 | 9.5 | 4.3 | 2.5 |
| 2.6 | 2.9 | 2.3 | Current | 9.3 | 5.8 | 4.2 | 3.0 | 2.1 | 1.6 |
| 1.3 | 1.5 | 1.2 | | 1.0 | 2.0 | 1.4 | 1.5 | 1.2 | 1.0 |
| 3.9 | 3.8 | 2.9 | | 6.8 | 7.4 | 4.8 | 4.6 | 3.4 | 1.6 |
| (566) 1.4 | (571) 1.5 | 1.1 | Quick | .7 | 1.4 | 1.2 | 1.3 | 1.3 | .9 |
| .6 | .7 | .4 | | .0 | .5 | .5 | .5 | .3 | .4 |
| 0 UND | 0 UND | 0 UND | | 0 UND | 0 UND | 0 UND | 0 UND | 0 UND | 1 477.9 |
| 0 999.8 | 0 UND | 0 999.8 | Sales/Receivables | 0 UND | 0 UND | 0 UND | 0 UND | 0 UND | 3 115.9 |
| 3 118.3 | 3 140.8 | 3 109.1 | | 0 UND | 0 UND | 0 999.8 | 1 368.1 | 2 148.2 | 6 62.9 |
| 6 56.6 | 6 64.7 | 6 57.4 | | 24 15.4 | 12 30.3 | 7 51.0 | 6 58.7 | 5 81.0 | 6 60.0 |
| 11 34.4 | 9 40.3 | 10 35.5 | Cost of Sales/Inventory | 52 7.0 | 18 19.8 | 12 30.5 | 9 39.3 | 7 53.8 | 10 37.5 |
| 17 22.0 | 15 24.7 | 17 21.9 | | 62 5.9 | 29 12.6 | 18 20.5 | 13 29.0 | 10 37.1 | 15 25.1 |
| 0 UND | 0 UND | 0 UND | | 0 UND | 0 UND | 0 UND | 0 UND | 1 333.4 | 4 102.8 |
| 4 85.0 | 4 93.5 | 3 107.0 | Cost of Sales/Payables | 0 UND | 0 UND | 0 UND | 2 228.6 | 5 74.9 | 9 39.2 |
| 11 34.4 | 9 40.5 | 10 38.0 | | 0 UND | 2 222.2 | 3 113.3 | 5 69.7 | 9 40.6 | 14 26.9 |
| 13.1 | 13.0 | 14.5 | | 5.9 | 10.5 | 12.9 | 14.6 | 13.3 | 18.7 |
| 24.0 | 25.9 | 29.8 | Sales/Working Capital | 11.5 | 18.6 | 27.2 | 33.8 | 36.1 | 38.9 |
| 78.5 | 61.9 | 159.0 | | NM | 30.9 | 63.0 | 98.4 | 192.7 | -546.3 |
| 23.0 | 20.9 | 12.3 | | | 15.3 | 9.7 | 12.6 | 11.8 | 16.1 |
| (399) 9.0 | (405) 7.8 | (374) 4.6 | EBIT/Interest | (41) 4.3 | (36) 3.9 | (78) 5.5 | (55) 3.9 | (157) 4.8 |
| 4.3 | 3.4 | 2.3 | | | 1.4 | 1.9 | 2.5 | 2.4 | 2.2 |
| 8.9 | 9.0 | 9.5 | Net Profit + Depr., Dep., | | | | | | 10.6 |
| (41) 4.8 | (46) 4.7 | (47) 3.8 | Amort./Cur. Mat. L/T/D | | | | | (41) 4.0 |
| 2.9 | 2.4 | 2.4 | | | | | | | 2.6 |
| .3 | .2 | .2 | | .2 | .0 | .0 | .2 | .4 | .6 |
| 1.2 | 1.1 | 1.4 | Fixed/Worth | 1.2 | .9 | .7 | 1.6 | 1.9 | 1.4 |
| 5.7 | 4.6 | 5.4 | | 6.5 | 6.3 | 7.0 | 12.1 | 18.5 | 3.3 |
| .6 | .5 | .6 | | .3 | .4 | .4 | .9 | .7 | .6 |
| 2.0 | 1.7 | 1.9 | Debt/Worth | 2.5 | 1.5 | 1.6 | 2.4 | 3.4 | 1.7 |
| 11.4 | 7.7 | 8.5 | | 7.4 | 100.3 | 14.8 | 43.6 | 863.5 | 4.7 |
| 95.7 | 77.1 | 75.9 | % Profit Before Taxes/Tangible | 85.0 | 77.7 | 112.0 | 120.1 | 94.0 | 38.0 |
| (474) 40.7 | (482) 36.9 | (441) 34.4 | Net Worth | (12) 18.2 | (57) 41.1 | (57) 67.7 | (82) 61.8 | (55) 51.7 | (178) 21.3 |
| 21.5 | 18.2 | 15.6 | | 7.7 | 14.0 | 22.9 | 30.1 | 27.6 | 10.3 |
| 26.5 | 26.9 | 26.2 | % Profit Before Taxes/Total | 8.3 | 42.8 | 45.5 | 32.0 | 28.5 | 14.2 |
| 14.7 | 13.6 | 10.8 | Assets | 6.1 | 10.9 | 15.9 | 16.1 | 13.1 | 8.5 |
| 7.9 | 6.3 | 4.9 | | .6 | 4.8 | 5.9 | 8.5 | 5.5 | 2.9 |
| 83.9 | 87.2 | 119.9 | | UND | 945.6 | 999.8 | 155.7 | 65.1 | 24.5 |
| 13.2 | 12.7 | 10.6 | Sales/Net Fixed Assets | 6.3 | 50.1 | 38.6 | 14.5 | 10.2 | 8.5 |
| 4.6 | 4.8 | 4.0 | | 2.6 | 3.6 | 3.7 | 4.3 | 4.3 | 4.0 |
| 8.6 | 8.8 | 8.8 | | 4.5 | 10.4 | 14.1 | 9.8 | 7.5 | 7.3 |
| 4.3 | 4.8 | 4.2 | Sales/Total Assets | 3.1 | 5.3 | 6.1 | 4.6 | 3.9 | 4.1 |
| 2.6 | 2.7 | 2.4 | | 1.3 | 1.9 | 2.4 | 2.4 | 2.5 | 2.5 |
| .5 | .5 | .5 | | | .7 | .4 | .4 | .3 | .6 |
| (356) 1.1 | (364) 1.0 | (334) 1.1 | % Depr., Dep., Amort./Sales | (39) 1.5 | (26) .9 | (51) .9 | (48) 1.0 | (162) 1.1 |
| 1.9 | 1.7 | 2.2 | | | 3.7 | 1.6 | 2.2 | 3.1 | 1.9 |
| .5 | .5 | .4 | | | .9 | 1.0 | .5 | .3 | .1 |
| (208) 1.0 | (215) .9 | (145) 1.0 | % Officers', Directors' Owners' Comp/Sales | (27) 1.8 | (25) 1.4 | (39) 1.0 | (23) .5 | (28) .3 |
| 1.7 | 1.6 | 1.8 | | | 3.3 | 1.8 | 1.6 | .7 | .8 |
| 43448786M | 58132557M | 56055289M | Net Sales ($) | 10306M | 153301M | 284209M | 748623M | 1055130M | 53803720M |
| 10169151M | 12786272M | 12197615M | Total Assets ($) | 5887M | 52788M | 84912M | 225310M | 558039M | 11270679M |

© RMA 2024  M = $ thousand    MM = $ million
See Pages viii through xx for Explanation of Ratios and Data

# RETAIL—Other Gasoline Stations  NAICS 457120

**Current Data Sorted by Assets** / **Comparative Historical Data**

| 0-500M | 500M-2MM | 2-10MM | 10-50MM | 50-100MM | 100-250MM | Type of Statement | ALL 4/1/19-3/31/20 | ALL 4/1/20-3/31/21 |
|---|---|---|---|---|---|---|---|---|
|  |  | 1 | 3 | 2 | 2 | Unqualified | 4 | 2 |
|  | 1 | 1 | 3 | 1 |  | Reviewed | 7 |  |
| 1 | 1 | 1 |  |  | 1 | Compiled | 6 | 4 |
| 1 | 3 | 3 | 5 | 1 | 2 | Tax Returns | 11 | 8 |
| 1 | 3 | 5 |  |  |  | Other | 24 | 19 |
| **3** | **7** | **10** | **8** | **4** | **5** | **NUMBER OF STATEMENTS** | **52** | **33** |
| % | % | % | % | % | % | **ASSETS** | % | % |
|  |  | 18.8 |  |  |  | Cash & Equivalents | 17.2 | 27.5 |
|  |  | 5.2 |  |  |  | Trade Receivables (net) | 9.1 | 5.0 |
|  |  | 9.4 |  |  |  | Inventory | 12.9 | 14.2 |
|  |  | 7.8 |  |  |  | All Other Current | 1.5 | 2.4 |
|  |  | 41.2 |  |  |  | Total Current | 40.7 | 49.1 |
|  |  | 37.8 |  |  |  | Fixed Assets (net) | 43.4 | 32.8 |
|  |  | 7.5 |  |  |  | Intangibles (net) | 4.9 | 10.8 |
|  |  | 13.5 |  |  |  | All Other Non-Current | 11.0 | 7.2 |
|  |  | 100.0 |  |  |  | Total | 100.0 | 100.0 |
|  |  |  |  |  |  | **LIABILITIES** |  |  |
|  |  | 5.7 |  |  |  | Notes Payable-Short Term | 2.1 | 4.6 |
|  |  | 1.2 |  |  |  | Cur. Mat.-L.T.D. | 1.8 | 2.8 |
|  |  | 10.0 |  |  |  | Trade Payables | 9.4 | 7.2 |
|  |  | .0 |  |  |  | Income Taxes Payable | .5 | .4 |
|  |  | 1.8 |  |  |  | All Other Current | 3.7 | 6.6 |
|  |  | 18.6 |  |  |  | Total Current | 17.4 | 21.6 |
|  |  | 39.3 |  |  |  | Long-Term Debt | 34.5 | 25.4 |
|  |  | 1.0 |  |  |  | Deferred Taxes | .3 | .1 |
|  |  | 1.2 |  |  |  | All Other Non-Current | 7.7 | 11.7 |
|  |  | 39.9 |  |  |  | Net Worth | 40.1 | 41.1 |
|  |  | 100.0 |  |  |  | Total Liabilties & Net Worth | 100.0 | 100.0 |
|  |  |  |  |  |  | **INCOME DATA** |  |  |
|  |  | 100.0 |  |  |  | Net Sales | 100.0 | 100.0 |
|  |  | 19.5 |  |  |  | Gross Profit | 17.4 | 20.8 |
|  |  | 11.5 |  |  |  | Operating Expenses | 15.0 | 16.7 |
|  |  | 8.0 |  |  |  | Operating Profit | 2.4 | 4.1 |
|  |  | .6 |  |  |  | All Other Expenses (net) | -.2 | -.4 |
|  |  | 7.4 |  |  |  | Profit Before Taxes | 2.5 | 4.5 |
|  |  |  |  |  |  | **RATIOS** |  |  |
|  |  | 6.7 |  |  |  |  | 3.9 | 5.0 |
|  |  | 3.6 |  |  |  | Current | 2.4 | 2.1 |
|  |  | 1.9 |  |  |  |  | 1.2 | 1.4 |
|  |  | 3.3 |  |  |  |  | 2.7 | 3.3 |
|  |  | 2.5 |  |  |  | Quick | 1.4 | 1.4 |
|  |  | 1.0 |  |  |  |  | .8 | .6 |
|  |  | 0  UND |  |  |  |  | 0  999.8 | 0  UND |
|  |  | 1  557.9 |  |  |  | Sales/Receivables | 3  120.0 | 3  143.3 |
|  |  | 11  32.8 |  |  |  |  | 10  36.4 | 7  55.8 |
|  |  | 4  89.2 |  |  |  |  | 3  120.1 | 8  44.7 |
|  |  | 9  42.3 |  |  |  | Cost of Sales/Inventory | 7  53.6 | 13  27.6 |
|  |  | 14  26.4 |  |  |  |  | 12  29.3 | 20  18.6 |
|  |  | 2  172.4 |  |  |  |  | 2  185.5 | 0  UND |
|  |  | 9  42.1 |  |  |  | Cost of Sales/Payables | 7  55.6 | 6  65.6 |
|  |  | 36  10.2 |  |  |  |  | 12  29.5 | 11  32.6 |
|  |  | 5.6 |  |  |  |  | 14.1 | 10.5 |
|  |  | 12.6 |  |  |  | Sales/Working Capital | 27.8 | 15.9 |
|  |  | 35.0 |  |  |  |  | 97.2 | 59.6 |
|  |  |  |  |  |  |  | 8.0 | 12.3 |
|  |  |  |  |  |  | EBIT/Interest | (38) 3.5 | (23) 5.3 |
|  |  |  |  |  |  |  | 1.9 | 2.2 |
|  |  |  |  |  |  | Net Profit + Depr., Dep., Amort./Cur. Mat. L/T/D |  |  |
|  |  | .3 |  |  |  |  | .4 | .2 |
|  |  | .8 |  |  |  | Fixed/Worth | 1.2 | 1.0 |
|  |  | 3.2 |  |  |  |  | 4.2 | 3.7 |
|  |  | .4 |  |  |  |  | .4 | .6 |
|  |  | 1.4 |  |  |  | Debt/Worth | 2.0 | 1.5 |
|  |  | 59.9 |  |  |  |  | 5.9 | 9.4 |
|  |  |  |  |  |  |  | 55.1 | 53.2 |
|  |  |  |  |  |  | % Profit Before Taxes/Tangible Net Worth | (47) 26.5 | (27) 31.0 |
|  |  |  |  |  |  |  | 8.5 | 14.2 |
|  |  | 28.7 |  |  |  |  | 20.3 | 19.7 |
|  |  | 7.4 |  |  |  | % Profit Before Taxes/Total Assets | 8.9 | 9.6 |
|  |  | 2.0 |  |  |  |  | 3.4 | 4.8 |
|  |  | 39.3 |  |  |  |  | 37.6 | 154.6 |
|  |  | 6.4 |  |  |  | Sales/Net Fixed Assets | 10.2 | 13.2 |
|  |  | 2.4 |  |  |  |  | 3.8 | 4.1 |
|  |  | 4.1 |  |  |  |  | 8.0 | 6.2 |
|  |  | 2.4 |  |  |  | Sales/Total Assets | 4.3 | 3.8 |
|  |  | 1.5 |  |  |  |  | 1.9 | 1.7 |
|  |  |  |  |  |  |  | .7 | .6 |
|  |  |  |  |  |  | % Depr., Dep., Amort./Sales | (39) 1.3 | (18) 1.2 |
|  |  |  |  |  |  |  | 2.0 | 2.2 |
|  |  |  |  |  |  |  | .7 | .7 |
|  |  |  |  |  |  | % Officers', Directors' Owners' Comp/Sales | (16) 1.2 | (10) 1.0 |
|  |  |  |  |  |  |  | 2.5 | 3.0 |
| 15040M | 48694M | 182626M | 735188M | 1802605M | 3058002M | Net Sales ($) | 6413740M | 1796596M |
| 689M | 6942M | 53225M | 173302M | 228127M | 952456M | Total Assets ($) | 1752955M | 623516M |

M = $ thousand   MM = $ million
See Pages viii through xx for Explanation of Ratios and Data

© RMA 2024

## RETAIL—Other Gasoline Stations  NAICS 457120

### Comparative Historical Data | Current Data Sorted by Sales

| | | | | Type of Statement | | | | | | |
|---|---|---|---|---|---|---|---|---|---|---|
| 1 | 2 | 3 | | Unqualified | | | | | 1 | 3 |
| 6 | 4 | 7 | | Reviewed | | | | | | 6 |
| 3 | 1 | 3 | | Compiled | | | 1 | 2 | | |
| 7 | 10 | 7 | | Tax Returns | | 1 | 1 | 2 | 2 | 1 |
| 16 | 19 | 17 | | Other | | | 5 | 3 | 2 | 7 |
| 4/1/21- | 4/1/22- | 4/1/23- | | | | 5 (4/1-9/30/23) | | 32 (10/1/23-3/31/24) | | |
| 3/31/22 | 3/31/23 | 3/31/24 | | | 0-1MM | 1-3MM | 3-5MM | 5-10MM | 10-25MM | 25MM & OVER |
| ALL | ALL | ALL | | | | | | | | |
| 33 | 36 | 37 | | NUMBER OF STATEMENTS | | 1 | 7 | 7 | 5 | 17 |
| % | % | % | | ASSETS | % | % | % | % | % | % |
| 17.7 | 16.6 | 17.3 | | Cash & Equivalents | | | | | | 11.9 |
| 10.5 | 8.2 | 7.4 | | Trade Receivables (net) | DATA | | | | | 14.1 |
| 13.2 | 16.8 | 11.0 | | Inventory | | | | | | 5.9 |
| 4.3 | 4.4 | 6.5 | | All Other Current | NOT | | | | | 8.8 |
| 45.7 | 45.9 | 42.1 | | Total Current | | | | | | 40.7 |
| 31.2 | 26.1 | 34.4 | | Fixed Assets (net) | AVAILABLE | | | | | 37.0 |
| 8.7 | 10.0 | 9.9 | | Intangibles (net) | | | | | | 3.3 |
| 14.7 | 17.9 | 13.6 | | All Other Non-Current | | | | | | 19.0 |
| 100.0 | 100.0 | 100.0 | | Total | | | | | | 100.0 |
| | | | | LIABILITIES | | | | | | |
| 1.2 | 3.7 | 3.3 | | Notes Payable-Short Term | | | | | | 3.9 |
| 2.5 | 1.3 | 2.0 | | Cur. Mat.-L.T.D. | | | | | | 2.9 |
| 10.4 | 9.3 | 8.4 | | Trade Payables | | | | | | 11.1 |
| 1.1 | .1 | .2 | | Income Taxes Payable | | | | | | .0 |
| 8.4 | 17.6 | 20.3 | | All Other Current | | | | | | 12.3 |
| 23.8 | 32.0 | 34.2 | | Total Current | | | | | | 30.2 |
| 32.6 | 31.6 | 28.2 | | Long-Term Debt | | | | | | 23.2 |
| .8 | .4 | .3 | | Deferred Taxes | | | | | | .0 |
| 14.4 | 6.7 | 7.5 | | All Other Non-Current | | | | | | 11.7 |
| 28.5 | 29.3 | 29.9 | | Net Worth | | | | | | 34.8 |
| 100.0 | 100.0 | 100.0 | | Total Liabilities & Net Worth | | | | | | 100.0 |
| | | | | INCOME DATA | | | | | | |
| 100.0 | 100.0 | 100.0 | | Net Sales | | | | | | 100.0 |
| 19.9 | 18.7 | 18.5 | | Gross Profit | | | | | | 15.6 |
| 18.6 | 13.9 | 14.3 | | Operating Expenses | | | | | | 13.6 |
| 1.3 | 4.9 | 4.3 | | Operating Profit | | | | | | 2.0 |
| -1.7 | .0 | -.3 | | All Other Expenses (net) | | | | | | -1.3 |
| 3.0 | 4.9 | 4.5 | | Profit Before Taxes | | | | | | 3.2 |
| | | | | RATIOS | | | | | | |
| 3.8 | 5.9 | 4.8 | | | | | | | | 2.1 |
| 1.8 | 2.2 | 2.0 | | Current | | | | | | 1.2 |
| 1.3 | 1.3 | .9 | | | | | | | | .8 |
| 1.8 | 3.0 | 2.9 | | | | | | | | 1.4 |
| 1.2 | 1.5 | 1.3 | | Quick | | | | | | .9 |
| .6 | .5 | .5 | | | | | | | | .5 |
| 0 UND | 0 UND | 0 UND | | | | | | | | 2 148.5 |
| 2 183.3 | 1 397.3 | 2 147.8 | | Sales/Receivables | | | | | | 3 112.0 |
| 11 32.3 | 8 44.9 | 7 52.8 | | | | | | | | 13 28.5 |
| 6 63.5 | 5 79.9 | 6 66.1 | | | | | | | | 4 94.5 |
| 10 37.6 | 8 48.3 | 7 49.9 | | Cost of Sales/Inventory | | | | | | 6 56.4 |
| 14 25.3 | 20 18.1 | 12 29.3 | | | | | | | | 8 45.5 |
| 3 126.3 | 0 UND | 2 192.9 | | | | | | | | 4 92.8 |
| 9 40.8 | 6 64.1 | 6 58.9 | | Cost of Sales/Payables | | | | | | 8 43.6 |
| 12 29.4 | 9 41.4 | 16 23.3 | | | | | | | | 17 21.4 |
| 14.8 | 15.1 | 11.4 | | | | | | | | 14.2 |
| 24.0 | 30.2 | 26.2 | | Sales/Working Capital | | | | | | 72.4 |
| 100.3 | 74.8 | -245.0 | | | | | | | | -154.7 |
| 9.4 | 24.5 | 21.7 | | | | | | | | 37.6 |
| (22) 5.3 | (26) 6.9 | (27) 5.6 | | EBIT/Interest | | | | | | (16) 7.6 |
| .8 | 2.5 | 1.9 | | | | | | | | 2.4 |
| | | | | Net Profit + Depr., Dep., Amort./Cur. Mat. L/T/D | | | | | | |
| .4 | .1 | .3 | | | | | | | | .4 |
| 1.5 | .4 | 1.0 | | Fixed/Worth | | | | | | 1.7 |
| NM | 3.7 | 4.1 | | | | | | | | 6.2 |
| .9 | 1.1 | .5 | | | | | | | | .8 |
| 2.8 | 3.0 | 1.6 | | Debt/Worth | | | | | | 2.6 |
| -52.9 | 18.5 | 18.4 | | | | | | | | 18.4 |
| 55.6 | 165.8 | 52.3 | | | | | | | | 59.3 |
| (24) 36.1 | (31) 58.7 | (31) 22.3 | | % Profit Before Taxes/Tangible Net Worth | | | | | | (15) 36.4 |
| 9.7 | 24.0 | 13.0 | | | | | | | | 13.0 |
| 17.7 | 24.0 | 18.6 | | | | | | | | 18.3 |
| 9.2 | 11.2 | 9.3 | | % Profit Before Taxes/Total Assets | | | | | | 11.2 |
| 1.0 | 7.0 | 2.7 | | | | | | | | 3.1 |
| 154.9 | 682.1 | 59.3 | | | | | | | | 44.6 |
| 19.5 | 44.4 | 14.8 | | Sales/Net Fixed Assets | | | | | | 14.8 |
| 6.4 | 9.7 | 4.8 | | | | | | | | 5.5 |
| 7.1 | 11.7 | 7.4 | | | | | | | | 7.4 |
| 4.2 | 5.9 | 4.7 | | Sales/Total Assets | | | | | | 5.0 |
| 2.3 | 2.6 | 2.1 | | | | | | | | 3.0 |
| .4 | .2 | .5 | | | | | | | | .4 |
| (19) 1.0 | (20) .7 | (23) 1.1 | | % Depr., Dep., Amort./Sales | | | | | | (14) .6 |
| 2.5 | 1.8 | 2.6 | | | | | | | | 2.0 |
| .5 | .5 | .2 | | | | | | | | |
| (12) 1.3 | (14) .9 | (11) 1.0 | | % Officers', Directors' Owners' Comp/Sales | | | | | | |
| 2.6 | 1.8 | 1.8 | | | | | | | | |
| 3055041M | 9094377M | 5842155M | | Net Sales ($) | 2831M | 26796M | 51851M | 66760M | 5693917M | |
| 1330718M | 1530549M | 1414741M | | Total Assets ($) | 624M | 19042M | 12732M | 53453M | 1328890M | |

M = $ thousand  MM = $ million
See Pages viii through xx for Explanation of Ratios and Data

© RMA 2024

# RETAIL—Fuel Dealers  NAICS 457210

## Current Data Sorted by Assets | Comparative Historical Data

| | | | | | | | Type of Statement | | |
|---|---|---|---|---|---|---|---|---|---|
| | | | | 5 | 5 | 4 | Unqualified | 18 | 10 |
| | | 11 | | 20 | 1 | 1 | Reviewed | 31 | 19 |
| | | 8 | | 2 | | | Compiled | 22 | 7 |
| 1 | 9 | 5 | | 3 | | | Tax Returns | 30 | 18 |
| 3 | 3 | 12 | | 18 | 7 | 6 | Other | 57 | 51 |
| | | 39 (4/1-9/30/23) | | 85 (10/1/23-3/31/24) | | | | 4/1/19-3/31/20 | 4/1/20-3/31/21 |
| 0-500M | 500M-2MM | 2-10MM | 10-50MM | 50-100MM | 100-250MM | | NUMBER OF STATEMENTS | ALL | ALL |
| 4 | 12 | 36 | 48 | 13 | 11 | | | 158 | 105 |
| % | % | % | % | % | % | | ASSETS | % | % |
| | 31.0 | 23.3 | 20.1 | 4.2 | 6.8 | | Cash & Equivalents | 18.0 | 24.6 |
| | 12.1 | 20.1 | 18.8 | 15.8 | 16.3 | | Trade Receivables (net) | 20.3 | 16.8 |
| | 6.9 | 12.1 | 8.8 | 11.6 | 8.5 | | Inventory | 11.2 | 10.4 |
| | 10.6 | 2.1 | 3.3 | 13.6 | 4.9 | | All Other Current | 2.5 | 2.9 |
| | 60.6 | 57.6 | 51.1 | 45.2 | 36.5 | | Total Current | 52.1 | 54.7 |
| | 32.1 | 31.9 | 31.4 | 36.3 | 34.6 | | Fixed Assets (net) | 30.6 | 32.1 |
| | 1.8 | 1.6 | 6.0 | 9.7 | 19.8 | | Intangibles (net) | 7.4 | 5.8 |
| | 5.5 | 8.9 | 11.6 | 8.8 | 9.2 | | All Other Non-Current | 9.9 | 7.4 |
| | 100.0 | 100.0 | 100.0 | 100.0 | 100.0 | | Total | 100.0 | 100.0 |
| | | | | | | | LIABILITIES | | |
| | 7.3 | 2.1 | 3.0 | 2.4 | 3.6 | | Notes Payable-Short Term | 6.9 | 5.7 |
| | .8 | 2.8 | 2.4 | 2.6 | 1.6 | | Cur. Mat.-L.T.D. | 4.5 | 2.9 |
| | 14.0 | 14.9 | 13.8 | 9.7 | 11.4 | | Trade Payables | 12.1 | 12.1 |
| | .0 | .0 | .2 | .0 | .3 | | Income Taxes Payable | .2 | .0 |
| | 5.6 | 18.3 | 13.7 | 18.6 | 12.1 | | All Other Current | 12.1 | 13.4 |
| | 27.6 | 38.1 | 33.2 | 33.3 | 28.9 | | Total Current | 35.8 | 34.0 |
| | 24.6 | 16.5 | 12.1 | 25.0 | 22.1 | | Long-Term Debt | 17.6 | 18.0 |
| | .0 | .0 | .9 | .0 | .8 | | Deferred Taxes | .8 | .6 |
| | 9.0 | 3.9 | 4.5 | 6.6 | 9.9 | | All Other Non-Current | 7.8 | 7.5 |
| | 38.7 | 41.6 | 49.3 | 35.1 | 38.3 | | Net Worth | 38.0 | 39.9 |
| | 100.0 | 100.0 | 100.0 | 100.0 | 100.0 | | Total Liabilities & Net Worth | 100.0 | 100.0 |
| | | | | | | | INCOME DATA | | |
| | 100.0 | 100.0 | 100.0 | 100.0 | 100.0 | | Net Sales | 100.0 | 100.0 |
| | 24.7 | 23.1 | 27.0 | 16.9 | 24.2 | | Gross Profit | 26.7 | 34.0 |
| | 20.8 | 21.6 | 21.8 | 14.1 | 20.6 | | Operating Expenses | 22.9 | 29.2 |
| | 3.9 | 1.5 | 5.2 | 2.8 | 3.5 | | Operating Profit | 3.8 | 4.8 |
| | .5 | -.1 | -.7 | -.2 | 3.2 | | All Other Expenses (net) | .0 | -.6 |
| | 3.5 | 1.6 | 5.9 | 3.1 | .4 | | Profit Before Taxes | 3.8 | 5.4 |
| | | | | | | | RATIOS | | |
| | 4.2 | 3.0 | 2.6 | 1.9 | 1.5 | | | 2.4 | 3.1 |
| | 2.6 | 1.7 | 1.5 | 1.3 | 1.1 | | Current | 1.6 | 1.7 |
| | 1.3 | 1.1 | 1.0 | .7 | .9 | | | 1.0 | 1.0 |
| | 3.9 | 2.6 | 1.7 | 1.1 | 1.0 | | | 2.0 | 2.2 |
| | 1.6 | 1.2 | 1.2 | .6 | .7 | | Quick | 1.1 | 1.3 |
| | .8 | .6 | .6 | .3 | .4 | | | .6 | .7 |
| 0 | UND | 8 | 45.4 | 10 | 36.1 | 2 | 186.2 | 6 | 57.5 | | 8 | 44.8 | 7 | 49.0 |
| 3 | 128.6 | 16 | 23.3 | 19 | 19.6 | 10 | 37.8 | 30 | 12.0 | Sales/Receivables | 19 | 19.2 | 19 | 19.0 |
| 20 | 18.4 | 25 | 14.6 | 25 | 14.8 | 21 | 17.7 | 36 | 10.1 | | 28 | 12.9 | 28 | 12.9 |
| 0 | UND | 2 | 152.7 | 3 | 105.0 | 2 | 234.3 | 6 | 61.5 | | 6 | 65.9 | 5 | 69.8 |
| 4 | 85.6 | 10 | 34.8 | 12 | 31.6 | 7 | 52.4 | 10 | 37.0 | Cost of Sales/Inventory | 12 | 30.5 | 14 | 26.7 |
| 19 | 19.2 | 31 | 11.7 | 29 | 12.4 | 11 | 34.7 | 19 | 19.3 | | 28 | 13.2 | 36 | 10.1 |
| 4 | 90.0 | 8 | 48.0 | 9 | 39.7 | 4 | 88.9 | 11 | 34.3 | | 8 | 46.8 | 9 | 42.8 |
| 11 | 33.4 | 12 | 30.6 | 14 | 25.3 | 8 | 44.6 | 12 | 31.0 | Cost of Sales/Payables | 12 | 29.4 | 18 | 20.2 |
| 14 | 25.8 | 25 | 14.5 | 26 | 14.2 | 12 | 31.4 | 30 | 12.0 | | 22 | 16.4 | 32 | 11.3 |
| | 8.2 | 12.7 | 7.6 | 19.7 | 25.2 | | | 9.2 | 6.8 |
| | 32.0 | 25.9 | 24.8 | 76.5 | 69.2 | | Sales/Working Capital | 23.1 | 16.1 |
| | 87.8 | 95.5 | NM | -48.9 | -35.6 | | | -255.8 | NM |
| | 18.5 | 14.8 | 40.5 | 14.5 | 8.2 | | | 21.1 | 31.8 |
| (10) | 7.1 | (32) | 8.0 | (44) | 14.9 | (12) | 7.1 | 1.7 | EBIT/Interest | (143) | 7.3 | (90) | 12.0 |
| | 2.7 | 5.4 | 7.6 | 2.9 | .7 | | | 2.7 | 3.3 |
| | | | 13.3 | | | | | 5.5 | 8.1 |
| | | (18) | 6.4 | | | | Net Profit + Depr., Dep., Amort./Cur. Mat. L/T/D | (32) | 2.6 | (16) | 2.9 |
| | | | 2.5 | | | | | 1.4 | 1.8 |
| | .1 | .2 | .3 | .7 | .5 | | | .3 | .4 |
| | 1.4 | .8 | .7 | 1.0 | 1.8 | | Fixed/Worth | .8 | .9 |
| | NM | 2.0 | 1.0 | NM | -1.9 | | | 2.8 | 2.1 |
| | .3 | .6 | .6 | 1.0 | 1.4 | | | .6 | .7 |
| | 1.4 | 1.4 | 1.2 | 1.7 | 2.9 | | Debt/Worth | 1.7 | 1.4 |
| | NM | 2.9 | 2.4 | NM | -4.2 | | | 5.3 | 5.1 |
| | | 45.1 | 47.6 | 34.5 | | | | 50.0 | 61.9 |
| | (34) | 22.2 | (45) | 31.2 | (10) | 27.5 | % Profit Before Taxes/Tangible Net Worth | (135) | 24.2 | (90) | 33.1 |
| | | 6.0 | 16.3 | 13.0 | | | | 12.2 | 15.0 |
| | 23.8 | 15.3 | 19.3 | 12.7 | 9.4 | | | 16.7 | 24.8 |
| | 15.9 | 8.2 | 11.9 | 8.4 | 1.1 | | % Profit Before Taxes/Total Assets | 10.7 | 13.0 |
| | 6.4 | 3.0 | 6.5 | 4.0 | -1.0 | | | 3.4 | 4.3 |
| | 808.3 | 75.9 | 44.7 | 37.6 | 34.2 | | | 39.2 | 31.7 |
| | 46.9 | 15.3 | 9.4 | 11.9 | 6.3 | | Sales/Net Fixed Assets | 13.1 | 10.4 |
| | 6.1 | 6.3 | 5.4 | 6.5 | 2.0 | | | 5.6 | 4.4 |
| | 12.9 | 7.3 | 6.1 | 8.8 | 5.6 | | | 5.4 | 4.6 |
| | 5.0 | 3.2 | 2.5 | 4.6 | 2.9 | | Sales/Total Assets | 3.4 | 2.7 |
| | 3.5 | 2.5 | 1.9 | 2.7 | .7 | | | 2.4 | 2.0 |
| | | .6 | .9 | .6 | | | | 1.2 | 1.2 |
| | (31) | 2.1 | (40) | 1.8 | (12) | 1.6 | % Depr., Dep., Amort./Sales | (115) | 2.1 | (71) | 2.5 |
| | | 3.2 | 3.5 | 4.8 | | | | 3.2 | 4.9 |
| | | .5 | .9 | | | | | .9 | 1.0 |
| | (18) | 1.7 | (18) | 1.9 | | | % Officers', Directors' Owners' Comp/Sales | (65) | 1.9 | (43) | 3.1 |
| | | 3.3 | 2.7 | | | | | 3.7 | 5.7 |
| 7673M | 111090M | 929001M | 5520972M | 5461589M | 7728901M | | Net Sales ($) | 8830417M | 5501040M |
| 1104M | 15581M | 197409M | 1121713M | 979498M | 1712766M | | Total Assets ($) | 3099075M | 2065734M |

© RMA 2024

M = $ thousand    MM = $ million
See Pages viii through xx for Explanation of Ratios and Data

# RETAIL—Fuel Dealers NAICS 457210

## Comparative Historical Data / Current Data Sorted by Sales

| | | | | Type of Statement | | | | | | |
|---|---|---|---|---|---|---|---|---|---|---|
| | 7 | 14 | 14 | Unqualified | | | | 1 | 1 | 13 |
| | 26 | 35 | 33 | Reviewed | | | | 1 | 9 | 23 |
| | 15 | 9 | 10 | Compiled | | | | 2 | 2 | 6 |
| | 20 | 11 | 18 | Tax Returns | | | | 4 | 6 | 4 |
| | 43 | 57 | 49 | Other | | 1 | 3 | 5 | 10 | 30 |
| | 4/1/21-3/31/22 | 4/1/22-3/31/23 | 4/1/23-3/31/24 | | | 39 (4/1-9/30/23) | | | 85 (10/1/23-3/31/24) | |
| | ALL | ALL | ALL | | 0-1MM | 1-3MM | 3-5MM | 5-10MM | 10-25MM | 25MM & OVER |
| | 111 | 126 | 124 | NUMBER OF STATEMENTS | | 5 | 3 | 12 | 28 | 76 |
| | % | % | % | ASSETS | % | % | % | % | % | % |
| | 18.3 | 15.9 | 19.6 | Cash & Equivalents | D | | | 30.6 | 18.5 | 17.7 |
| | 21.2 | 21.8 | 17.9 | Trade Receivables (net) | A | | | 12.0 | 13.2 | 21.3 |
| | 11.4 | 13.2 | 9.8 | Inventory | T | | | 7.6 | 10.2 | 10.0 |
| | 2.9 | 3.1 | 4.9 | All Other Current | A | | | 9.2 | 5.3 | 4.4 |
| | 53.8 | 53.9 | 52.2 | Total Current | | | | 59.4 | 47.2 | 53.5 |
| | 33.1 | 32.5 | 32.4 | Fixed Assets (net) | N | | | 31.1 | 40.7 | 28.4 |
| | 4.3 | 5.4 | 5.7 | Intangibles (net) | O | | | .3 | 2.5 | 8.1 |
| | 8.8 | 8.3 | 9.6 | All Other Non-Current | T | | | 9.3 | 9.6 | 10.1 |
| | 100.0 | 100.0 | 100.0 | Total | | | | 100.0 | 100.0 | 100.0 |
| | | | | LIABILITIES | A | | | | | |
| | 5.2 | 7.2 | 3.0 | Notes Payable-Short Term | V | | | .5 | 4.7 | 2.9 |
| | 3.0 | 3.3 | 2.2 | Cur. Mat.-L.T.D. | A | | | .5 | 3.1 | 2.3 |
| | 12.7 | 14.2 | 13.3 | Trade Payables | I | | | 7.4 | 10.5 | 15.7 |
| | .5 | .1 | .1 | Income Taxes Payable | L | | | .1 | .0 | .2 |
| | 13.7 | 12.4 | 14.9 | All Other Current | A | | | 22.3 | 16.7 | 13.1 |
| | 35.1 | 37.2 | 33.6 | Total Current | B | | | 30.8 | 35.1 | 34.2 |
| | 16.9 | 15.4 | 17.2 | Long-Term Debt | L | | | 10.5 | 23.6 | 14.9 |
| | .5 | .5 | .4 | Deferred Taxes | E | | | .0 | .7 | .4 |
| | 2.8 | 2.9 | 6.5 | All Other Non-Current | | | | 2.2 | 1.2 | 6.8 |
| | 44.7 | 44.0 | 42.3 | Net Worth | | | | 56.5 | 39.4 | 43.7 |
| | 100.0 | 100.0 | 100.0 | Total Liabilities & Net Worth | | | | 100.0 | 100.0 | 100.0 |
| | | | | INCOME DATA | | | | | | |
| | 100.0 | 100.0 | 100.0 | Net Sales | | | | 100.0 | 100.0 | 100.0 |
| | 28.0 | 21.8 | 24.3 | Gross Profit | | | | 30.4 | 28.2 | 20.7 |
| | 24.8 | 18.2 | 20.5 | Operating Expenses | | | | 23.9 | 24.9 | 17.7 |
| | 3.2 | 3.6 | 3.8 | Operating Profit | | | | 6.5 | 3.3 | 3.0 |
| | -1.3 | -.8 | .0 | All Other Expenses (net) | | | | -.3 | -.2 | .1 |
| | 4.6 | 4.4 | 3.8 | Profit Before Taxes | | | | 6.8 | 3.5 | 2.9 |
| | | | | RATIOS | | | | | | |
| | 2.5 | 2.4 | 2.6 | | | | | 8.4 | 1.9 | 2.1 |
| | 1.6 | 1.5 | 1.5 | Current | | | | 4.0 | 1.4 | 1.4 |
| | 1.0 | .9 | 1.0 | | | | | 2.3 | .9 | 1.0 |
| | 1.8 | 1.7 | 2.0 | | | | | 7.3 | 1.7 | 1.6 |
| | 1.1 | .9 | 1.1 | Quick | | | | 2.8 | .9 | 1.1 |
| | .6 | .6 | .6 | | | | | 1.0 | .5 | .5 |
| 12 | 31.6 | 8 47.2 | 6 58.0 | | 8 | 43.3 | 7 | 55.0 | 6 | 57.2 |
| 21 | 17.5 | 18 20.1 | 16 23.5 | Sales/Receivables | 25 | 14.7 | 16 | 22.3 | 14 | 25.2 |
| 31 | 11.8 | 29 12.7 | 25 14.8 | | 33 | 11.0 | 25 | 14.6 | 23 | 15.8 |
| 5 | 69.2 | 3 105.1 | 2 170.2 | | 0 | UND | 3 | 117.3 | 2 | 153.9 |
| 17 | 22.1 | 12 29.7 | 10 37.9 | Cost of Sales/Inventory | 10 | 36.5 | 13 | 27.3 | 8 | 43.5 |
| 30 | 12.1 | 29 12.4 | 25 14.8 | | 29 | 12.8 | 37 | 9.8 | 19 | 19.7 |
| 8 | 44.4 | 8 47.7 | 8 47.1 | | 8 | 45.0 | 9 | 38.6 | 8 | 46.0 |
| 15 | 25.0 | 14 26.6 | 12 31.3 | Cost of Sales/Payables | 13 | 28.0 | 16 | 22.9 | 11 | 32.8 |
| 27 | 13.7 | 21 17.5 | 22 16.4 | | 21 | 17.7 | 34 | 10.6 | 19 | 19.0 |
| | 9.2 | 12.2 | 11.1 | | | | | 3.3 | 9.4 | 17.9 |
| | 20.0 | 35.5 | 31.4 | Sales/Working Capital | | | | 5.8 | 32.1 | 34.9 |
| | 999.8 | -188.8 | 262.9 | | | | | 13.0 | -72.8 | 839.4 |
| | 29.6 | 30.8 | 21.1 | | | | | | 21.5 | 18.9 |
| (98) | 13.0 | (102) 11.4 | (112) 8.8 | EBIT/Interest | | | | (27) 8.2 | (70) | 8.5 |
| | 4.1 | 4.7 | 3.9 | | | | | | 2.8 | 4.1 |
| | 13.7 | 27.6 | 13.9 | | | | | | | 16.7 |
| (18) | 3.0 | (27) 3.6 | (29) 5.9 | Net Profit + Depr., Dep., Amort./Cur. Mat. L/T/D | | | | | (24) | 6.1 |
| | 1.7 | 2.4 | 2.4 | | | | | | | 2.7 |
| | .4 | .2 | .3 | | | | | .0 | .7 | .3 |
| | .8 | .9 | .8 | Fixed/Worth | | | | .5 | 1.2 | .8 |
| | 1.7 | 2.1 | 2.0 | | | | | 1.3 | 2.7 | 1.6 |
| | .7 | .5 | .6 | | | | | .1 | .7 | .8 |
| | 1.3 | 1.4 | 1.4 | Debt/Worth | | | | .3 | 1.9 | 1.4 |
| | 3.0 | 3.2 | 4.1 | | | | | 1.5 | 4.9 | 3.6 |
| | 59.5 | 57.8 | 44.7 | % Profit Before Taxes/Tangible Net Worth | | | | 40.7 | 45.1 | 45.1 |
| (105) | 34.9 | (112) 33.8 | (107) 28.2 | | (11) | 30.9 | (26) | 23.3 | (66) | 28.5 |
| | 17.7 | 14.5 | 12.1 | | | 6.1 | | 6.4 | | 13.0 |
| | 20.9 | 24.6 | 18.4 | % Profit Before Taxes/Total Assets | | | | 22.8 | 16.7 | 13.9 |
| | 12.6 | 10.6 | 9.7 | | | | | 12.2 | 11.0 | 9.5 |
| | 5.2 | 5.2 | 4.2 | | | | | 4.9 | 2.5 | 4.1 |
| | 35.3 | 49.9 | 53.1 | Sales/Net Fixed Assets | | | | 249.9 | 36.2 | 56.5 |
| | 12.5 | 15.3 | 12.7 | | | | | 12.4 | 8.0 | 16.4 |
| | 5.9 | 6.1 | 5.7 | | | | | 2.1 | 3.0 | 6.9 |
| | 5.3 | 7.1 | 7.0 | Sales/Total Assets | | | | 3.9 | 4.5 | 8.8 |
| | 3.2 | 4.0 | 3.3 | | | | | 2.8 | 2.5 | 4.6 |
| | 2.1 | 2.5 | 2.1 | | | | | 1.2 | 1.8 | 2.4 |
| | .9 | .6 | .7 | | | | | | 1.4 | .6 |
| (84) | 2.3 | (89) 1.7 | (96) 1.8 | % Depr., Dep., Amort./Sales | | | | (25) | 2.3 | (60) 1.1 |
| | 3.4 | 3.2 | 3.3 | | | | | | 3.7 | 2.8 |
| | .8 | .6 | .6 | | | | | | .6 | .5 |
| (54) | 1.4 | (45) 1.3 | (46) 1.7 | % Officers', Directors' Owners' Comp/Sales | | | | (15) | 1.5 | (23) 1.8 |
| | 4.6 | 3.3 | 3.0 | | | | | | 2.4 | 3.1 |
| | 7816465M | 19166371M | 19759226M | Net Sales ($) | | 10664M | 11485M | 91296M | 478898M | 19166883M |
| | 2153643M | 3475653M | 4028071M | Total Assets ($) | | 2395M | 4020M | 62630M | 213060M | 3745966M |

M = $ thousand MM = $ million

© RMA 2024 See Pages viii through xx for Explanation of Ratios and Data

# RETAIL—Clothing and Clothing Accessories Retailers  NAICS 458110

## Current Data Sorted by Assets | Comparative Historical Data

| | | | | | | Type of Statement | | |
|---|---|---|---|---|---|---|---|---|
| 1 | | | | 12 | 5 | Unqualified | 16 | 14 |
| | 1 | 10 | 16 | 6 | 2 | Reviewed | 14 | 10 |
| 1 | 2 | 6 | 2 | | | Compiled | 15 | 6 |
| 14 | 16 | 4 | 2 | | | Tax Returns | 81 | 42 |
| 35 | 30 | 42 | 44 | 6 | 15 | Other | 138 | 113 |
| | 40 (4/1-9/30/23) | | 232 (10/1/23-3/31/24) | | | | 4/1/19-3/31/20 | 4/1/20-3/31/21 |
| 0-500M | 500M-2MM | 2-10MM | 10-50MM | 50-100MM | 100-250MM | | ALL | ALL |
| 51 | 49 | 62 | 76 | 12 | 22 | NUMBER OF STATEMENTS | 264 | 185 |
| % | % | % | % | % | % | ASSETS | % | % |
| 22.8 | 24.1 | 17.1 | 16.8 | 7.2 | 12.0 | Cash & Equivalents | 17.9 | 25.4 |
| 4.2 | 5.7 | 10.5 | 6.3 | 7.1 | 4.7 | Trade Receivables (net) | 5.6 | 7.6 |
| 39.0 | 39.2 | 39.0 | 38.6 | 38.9 | 25.1 | Inventory | 43.7 | 36.3 |
| 11.6 | 4.0 | 2.3 | 4.5 | 2.8 | 3.4 | All Other Current | 3.2 | 2.7 |
| 77.6 | 73.0 | 68.8 | 66.2 | 56.0 | 45.2 | Total Current | 70.3 | 72.0 |
| 10.5 | 11.1 | 16.5 | 12.7 | 18.0 | 21.9 | Fixed Assets (net) | 17.9 | 14.4 |
| 5.7 | 4.3 | 4.6 | 5.6 | 7.2 | 14.2 | Intangibles (net) | 5.6 | 6.1 |
| 6.2 | 11.6 | 10.1 | 15.6 | 18.8 | 18.7 | All Other Non-Current | 6.3 | 7.4 |
| 100.0 | 100.0 | 100.0 | 100.0 | 100.0 | 100.0 | Total | 100.0 | 100.0 |
| | | | | | | LIABILITIES | | |
| 16.2 | 12.7 | 8.0 | 8.5 | 9.2 | 6.8 | Notes Payable-Short Term | 12.7 | 8.7 |
| .4 | 1.5 | 2.4 | 2.2 | 5.9 | 3.8 | Cur. Mat.-L.T.D. | 2.3 | 2.1 |
| 17.1 | 7.9 | 15.9 | 15.5 | 17.4 | 7.6 | Trade Payables | 15.7 | 12.0 |
| .2 | 1.0 | .1 | .2 | .1 | .1 | Income Taxes Payable | .2 | .1 |
| 19.5 | 10.9 | 10.2 | 14.6 | 13.6 | 9.5 | All Other Current | 12.3 | 12.8 |
| 53.4 | 33.9 | 36.6 | 41.0 | 46.2 | 27.8 | Total Current | 43.3 | 35.8 |
| 34.0 | 24.8 | 17.8 | 12.5 | 19.5 | 19.3 | Long-Term Debt | 13.5 | 19.9 |
| .0 | .0 | .1 | .0 | .0 | .0 | Deferred Taxes | .0 | .1 |
| 9.3 | 5.0 | 3.9 | 13.5 | 10.7 | 9.6 | All Other Non-Current | 9.2 | 11.0 |
| 3.1 | 36.3 | 41.6 | 32.9 | 23.6 | 43.2 | Net Worth | 34.0 | 33.4 |
| 100.0 | 100.0 | 100.0 | 100.0 | 100.0 | 100.0 | Total Liabilities & Net Worth | 100.0 | 100.0 |
| | | | | | | INCOME DATA | | |
| 100.0 | 100.0 | 100.0 | 100.0 | 100.0 | 100.0 | Net Sales | 100.0 | 100.0 |
| 50.7 | 53.4 | 49.2 | 49.6 | 49.6 | 52.4 | Gross Profit | 48.9 | 49.2 |
| 42.5 | 41.7 | 41.3 | 44.9 | 46.8 | 44.2 | Operating Expenses | 44.5 | 45.3 |
| 8.2 | 11.7 | 7.8 | 4.7 | 2.8 | 8.2 | Operating Profit | 4.4 | 4.0 |
| .5 | .7 | 1.3 | -.2 | 1.3 | -.3 | All Other Expenses (net) | 1.0 | -.7 |
| 7.8 | 11.0 | 6.5 | 4.9 | 1.5 | 8.5 | Profit Before Taxes | 3.5 | 4.7 |
| | | | | | | RATIOS | | |
| 6.3 | 18.4 | 4.5 | 2.7 | 1.6 | 3.0 | | 4.0 | 5.0 |
| 2.0 | 4.4 | 2.3 | 1.7 | 1.2 | 1.5 | Current | 1.9 | 2.2 |
| 1.1 | 1.7 | 1.2 | 1.1 | .9 | 1.1 | | 1.1 | 1.3 |
| 2.9 | 5.1 | 1.9 | 1.0 | .5 | 1.5 | | 1.3 | 2.2 |
| (50) .9 | 1.5 | .8 | .6 | .3 | .6 | Quick | (263) .4 | (184) .9 |
| .2 | .3 | .3 | .3 | .1 | .1 | | .2 | .4 |
| 0 UND | 0 UND | 0 UND | 0 UND | 1 260.9 | 1 302.1 | | 0 UND | 0 UND |
| 0 UND | 0 UND | 5 79.8 | 2 238.5 | 4 77.8 | 4 95.4 | Sales/Receivables | 1 429.2 | 1 362.2 |
| 0 UND | 1 418.9 | 14 26.4 | 13 28.8 | 25 14.4 | 23 15.7 | | 9 40.4 | 14 25.7 |
| 0 UND | 5 72.5 | 54 6.7 | 83 4.4 | 126 2.9 | 118 3.1 | | 64 5.7 | 59 6.2 |
| 69 5.3 | 99 3.7 | 122 3.0 | 126 2.9 | 152 2.4 | 174 2.1 | Cost of Sales/Inventory | 130 2.8 | 107 3.4 |
| 203 1.8 | 203 1.8 | 215 1.7 | 215 1.7 | 192 1.9 | 243 1.5 | | 215 1.7 | 192 1.9 |
| 0 UND | 0 UND | 7 55.5 | 24 15.1 | 36 10.1 | 22 16.3 | | 8 43.1 | 7 55.7 |
| 0 UND | 4 81.3 | 30 12.2 | 46 7.9 | 59 6.2 | 51 7.2 | Cost of Sales/Payables | 31 11.7 | 24 15.5 |
| 16 22.4 | 34 10.8 | 60 6.1 | 74 4.9 | 89 4.1 | 85 4.3 | | 64 5.7 | 56 6.5 |
| 5.0 | 2.6 | 3.1 | 4.8 | 9.3 | 2.4 | | 4.8 | 3.4 |
| 10.0 | 4.7 | 5.6 | 7.0 | 106.9 | 7.1 | Sales/Working Capital | 9.3 | 6.5 |
| 81.7 | 11.5 | 20.4 | 39.5 | -24.4 | NM | | 43.3 | 18.8 |
| 14.7 | 52.2 | 30.7 | 32.8 | 19.2 | 50.6 | | 18.8 | 20.8 |
| (28) 7.8 | (34) 5.4 | (50) 5.5 | (60) 7.6 | (10) 2.7 | (21) 14.5 | EBIT/Interest | (213) 4.5 | (141) 6.4 |
| 3.3 | 1.9 | 1.7 | .4 | .3 | 1.1 | | -.1 | -.2 |
| | | | 51.5 | | | Net Profit + Depr., Dep., | | 64.6 70.9 |
| | | (13) 3.8 | | | | Amort./Cur. Mat. L/T/D | (20) 6.2 (13) 4.1 |
| | | | .7 | | | | 1.0 | .9 |
| .0 | .0 | .0 | .1 | .2 | .2 | | .1 | .0 |
| .2 | .1 | .2 | .2 | 1.0 | .8 | Fixed/Worth | .3 | .2 |
| 1.4 | 1.2 | 1.0 | 1.5 | NM | 1.5 | | 2.1 | 1.8 |
| .6 | .2 | .4 | .6 | 2.0 | .8 | | .5 | .5 |
| 3.2 | 1.8 | 1.3 | 1.8 | 5.7 | 2.0 | Debt/Worth | 1.8 | 1.7 |
| -10.6 | 7.7 | 6.7 | 6.3 | NM | 10.5 | | 10.2 | 11.9 |
| 165.3 | 115.8 | 63.4 | 53.4 | | 54.6 | % Profit Before Taxes/Tangible | 54.6 | 59.5 |
| (37) 87.6 | (42) 56.1 | (53) 23.1 | (65) 24.5 | | (18) 22.8 | Net Worth | (210) 23.0 | (147) 24.1 |
| 11.3 | 7.1 | 4.7 | 6.4 | | 6.9 | | 4.0 | 1.0 |
| 51.3 | 45.6 | 19.9 | 19.2 | 13.4 | 15.9 | % Profit Before Taxes/Total | 19.4 | 21.7 |
| 21.7 | 18.6 | 10.2 | 9.2 | 4.6 | 8.6 | Assets | 8.7 | 7.2 |
| 3.3 | 3.4 | 1.4 | .6 | 1.2 | .1 | | -.3 | -3.1 |
| UND | UND | 129.0 | 123.8 | 71.9 | 14.6 | | 117.9 | 174.8 |
| 84.5 | 104.6 | 27.6 | 28.3 | 21.2 | 6.4 | Sales/Net Fixed Assets | 23.0 | 29.6 |
| 22.4 | 19.5 | 9.6 | 12.9 | 4.1 | 3.5 | | 10.0 | 10.1 |
| 6.4 | 3.8 | 3.0 | 2.9 | 2.2 | 1.3 | | 3.7 | 3.1 |
| 3.3 | 2.3 | 2.2 | 2.0 | 1.8 | 1.1 | Sales/Total Assets | 2.5 | 2.1 |
| 2.3 | 1.7 | 1.3 | 1.3 | 1.2 | .9 | | 1.7 | 1.3 |
| .1 | .1 | .1 | .1 | .2 | .4 .7 | | .4 | .4 |
| (14) .7 | (21) .7 | (28) .5 | (59) .7 | (11) 1.5 | (20) 1.8 | % Depr., Dep., Amort./Sales | (163) 1.0 | (107) 1.0 |
| 1.8 | 1.1 | 1.5 | 1.2 | 3.1 | 3.3 | | 2.2 | 2.5 |
| 3.2 | 3.7 | 1.3 | .8 | | | % Officers', Directors' | 1.5 | 2.2 |
| (19) 5.4 | (19) 4.7 | (20) 2.0 | (11) 1.3 | | | Owners' Comp/Sales | (95) 3.9 | (64) 4.3 |
| 11.0 | 9.4 | 5.0 | 4.5 | | | | 7.5 | 7.9 |
| 53651M | 170756M | 652025M | 4304854M | 1613067M | 3731943M | Net Sales ($) | 14248131M | 5817179M |
| 12602M | 54221M | 273459M | 1928401M | 897348M | 3333891M | Total Assets ($) | 6905019M | 3129395M |

M = $ thousand  MM = $ million
See Pages viii through xx for Explanation of Ratios and Data

© RMA 2024

# RETAIL—Clothing and Clothing Accessories Retailers  NAICS 458110

## Comparative Historical Data | Current Data Sorted by Sales

| | | | | | | | | | | |
|---|---|---|---|---|---|---|---|---|---|---|
| 16 | 21 | 24 | **Type of Statement** | | | | | 1 | 22 | |
| 8 | 22 | 29 | Unqualified | 1 | | | | 7 | 17 | |
| 7 | 8 | 11 | Reviewed | | 2 | 3 | | 1 | 1 | |
| 48 | 56 | 36 | Compiled | | 3 | 5 | | 3 | 2 | |
| 114 | 140 | 172 | Tax Returns | | 18 | 1 | 3 | | 61 | |
| 4/1/21- | 4/1/22- | 4/1/23- | Other | 7 | 34 | 3 | 3 | 3 | | |
| 3/31/22 | 3/31/23 | 3/31/24 | | 27 | | 11 | 18 | 21 | | |
| ALL | ALL | ALL | | | 40 (4/1-9/30/23) | | 232 (10/1/23-3/31/24) | | | |
| 193 | 247 | 272 | | 0-1MM | 1-3MM | 3-5MM | 5-10MM | 10-25MM | 25MM & OVER | |
| | | | **NUMBER OF STATEMENTS** | 35 | 55 | 17 | 29 | 33 | 103 | |
| % | % | % | **ASSETS** | % | % | % | % | % | % | |
| 29.4 | 20.5 | 18.5 | Cash & Equivalents | 24.1 | 19.6 | 22.4 | 22.9 | 16.2 | 14.9 | |
| 7.0 | 6.6 | 6.7 | Trade Receivables (net) | 1.3 | 4.0 | 18.3 | 5.2 | 9.9 | 7.3 | |
| 38.0 | 43.7 | 37.8 | Inventory | 43.3 | 35.9 | 32.6 | 38.5 | 39.4 | 37.0 | |
| 2.5 | 3.3 | 5.1 | All Other Current | .4 | 12.8 | .5 | 3.1 | 4.4 | 4.0 | |
| 76.9 | 74.1 | 68.0 | Total Current | 69.1 | 72.3 | 73.9 | 69.8 | 69.9 | 63.2 | |
| 10.6 | 11.9 | 13.8 | Fixed Assets (net) | 13.3 | 13.3 | 8.7 | 16.8 | 14.3 | 14.2 | |
| 5.9 | 5.3 | 5.9 | Intangibles (net) | 8.1 | 5.2 | 1.3 | 5.1 | 6.9 | 6.2 | |
| 6.6 | 8.7 | 12.2 | All Other Non-Current | 9.4 | 9.2 | 16.1 | 8.3 | 8.8 | 16.4 | |
| 100.0 | 100.0 | 100.0 | Total | 100.0 | 100.0 | 100.0 | 100.0 | 100.0 | 100.0 | |
| | | | **LIABILITIES** | | | | | | | |
| 9.3 | 8.5 | 10.5 | Notes Payable-Short Term | 16.3 | 9.5 | 8.0 | 3.1 | 18.2 | 9.0 | |
| 1.8 | 2.0 | 2.1 | Cur. Mat.-L.T.D. | .5 | 1.1 | 1.5 | 1.4 | 2.9 | 3.1 | |
| 11.4 | 12.5 | 14.0 | Trade Payables | 5.5 | 12.0 | 28.3 | 9.9 | 20.1 | 14.7 | |
| .2 | .2 | .3 | Income Taxes Payable | .2 | .1 | .1 | .0 | 1.5 | .2 | |
| 12.1 | 12.3 | 13.4 | All Other Current | 15.8 | 10.5 | 14.6 | 9.4 | 18.4 | 13.5 | |
| 34.8 | 35.5 | 40.2 | Total Current | 38.3 | 33.1 | 52.5 | 23.9 | 61.1 | 40.6 | |
| 17.4 | 15.1 | 20.8 | Long-Term Debt | 30.4 | 30.8 | 30.2 | 18.3 | 13.1 | 13.8 | |
| .1 | .1 | .0 | Deferred Taxes | .0 | .0 | .0 | .1 | .0 | .0 | |
| 7.5 | 8.1 | 8.6 | All Other Non-Current | 3.8 | 3.1 | 29.4 | 4.7 | 5.0 | 11.9 | |
| 40.2 | 41.3 | 30.3 | Net Worth | 27.4 | 33.0 | -12.0 | 52.9 | 20.8 | 33.6 | |
| 100.0 | 100.0 | 100.0 | Total Liabilities & Net Worth | 100.0 | 100.0 | 100.0 | 100.0 | 100.0 | 100.0 | |
| | | | **INCOME DATA** | | | | | | | |
| 100.0 | 100.0 | 100.0 | Net Sales | 100.0 | 100.0 | 100.0 | 100.0 | 100.0 | 100.0 | |
| 51.1 | 48.6 | 50.6 | Gross Profit | 54.5 | 53.1 | 47.1 | 52.2 | 46.8 | 49.3 | |
| 41.6 | 41.6 | 43.1 | Operating Expenses | 44.5 | 40.4 | 41.3 | 44.6 | 43.0 | 43.9 | |
| 9.5 | 7.0 | 7.5 | Operating Profit | 10.1 | 12.7 | 5.8 | 7.6 | 3.7 | 5.4 | |
| -1.7 | .3 | .5 | All Other Expenses (net) | .9 | 1.2 | .9 | .2 | 1.0 | -.1 | |
| 11.2 | 6.7 | 7.0 | Profit Before Taxes | 9.2 | 11.5 | 4.8 | 7.4 | 2.7 | 5.6 | |
| | | | **RATIOS** | | | | | | | |
| 5.6 | 5.1 | 4.7 | | 8.5 | 7.4 | 18.0 | 10.4 | 2.4 | 2.5 | |
| 2.8 | 2.5 | 2.1 | Current | 3.3 | 3.3 | 2.9 | 3.4 | 1.6 | 1.6 | |
| 1.5 | 1.4 | 1.2 | | 1.3 | 1.6 | .8 | 1.5 | .9 | 1.1 | |
| 2.8 | 2.0 | 1.8 | | 3.0 | 2.8 | 5.9 | 4.2 | 1.2 | 1.0 | |
| 1.3 | .8 | (271) .7 | Quick | 1.0 | (54) 1.1 | 1.5 | 1.3 | .5 | .5 | |
| .5 | .3 | .2 | | .3 | .2 | .2 | .5 | .1 | .2 | |
| 0 UND | 0 UND | 0 UND | | 0 UND | 0 UND | 0 UND | 0 UND | 0 999.8 | 0 999.8 | |
| 1 570.1 | 1 576.1 | 1 601.5 | Sales/Receivables | 0 UND | 0 UND | 1 636.6 | 2 178.1 | 3 117.7 | 3 112.8 | |
| 11 32.8 | 11 32.1 | 10 36.1 | | 0 UND | 0 999.8 | 19 18.9 | 12 29.3 | 20 18.6 | 15 24.1 | |
| 65 5.6 | 79 4.6 | 61 6.0 | | 0 UND | 5 79.1 | 4 102.2 | 74 4.9 | 38 9.5 | 83 4.4 | |
| 118 3.1 | 122 3.0 | 122 3.0 | Cost of Sales/Inventory | 126 2.9 | 118 3.1 | 41 8.8 | 140 2.6 | 99 3.7 | 130 2.8 | |
| 203 1.8 | 215 1.7 | 215 1.7 | | 304 1.2 | 281 1.3 | 152 2.4 | 203 1.8 | 192 1.9 | 215 1.7 | |
| 2 222.2 | 3 110.3 | 2 202.1 | | 0 UND | 0 UND | 0 UND | 5 77.7 | 15 24.1 | 24 15.4 | |
| 26 14.0 | 25 14.7 | 29 12.5 | Cost of Sales/Payables | 0 UND | 4 81.8 | 15 24.1 | 31 11.6 | 49 7.5 | 46 7.9 | |
| 59 6.2 | 58 6.3 | 63 5.8 | | 26 14.2 | 33 10.9 | 61 6.0 | 56 6.5 | 69 5.3 | 76 4.8 | |
| 3.2 | 3.5 | 3.8 | | 2.7 | 2.7 | 3.2 | 2.7 | 5.9 | 4.8 | |
| 5.4 | 6.4 | 6.8 | Sales/Working Capital | 5.7 | 5.6 | 5.8 | 4.8 | 9.1 | 9.0 | |
| 11.0 | 15.2 | 37.4 | | 27.0 | 28.8 | -43.1 | 10.6 | -82.1 | 42.7 | |
| 77.9 | 46.0 | 29.2 | | 9.3 | 18.2 | 33.2 | 92.7 | 29.4 | 33.8 | |
| (138) 21.1 | (175) 9.5 | (203) 6.7 | EBIT/Interest | (19) 5.0 | (36) 7.2 | (12) 3.4 | (23) 12.5 | (28) 5.2 | (85) 11.2 | |
| 2.9 | 2.1 | 1.5 | | 2.3 | 2.3 | -1.0 | 3.9 | .4 | .9 | |
| 28.0 | 16.5 | 17.7 | Net Profit + Depr., Dep., | | | | | | 27.8 | |
| (11) 5.7 | (20) 6.0 | (28) 5.0 | Amort./Cur. Mat. L/T/D | | | | | | (22) 5.0 | |
| 1.8 | 3.0 | 1.1 | | | | | | | 1.0 | |
| .0 | .0 | .0 | | .0 | .0 | .0 | .1 | .0 | .1 | |
| .2 | .2 | .2 | Fixed/Worth | .3 | .1 | .0 | .2 | .5 | .3 | |
| .8 | .8 | 1.3 | | 15.9 | .4 | 1.9 | .9 | NM | 1.4 | |
| .5 | .4 | .6 | | .3 | .3 | 1.1 | .2 | .7 | .7 | |
| 1.4 | 1.1 | 1.8 | Debt/Worth | 1.9 | 1.5 | 2.7 | 1.0 | 1.7 | 2.1 | |
| 6.8 | 8.4 | 9.1 | | -23.1 | 8.5 | -7.5 | 3.7 | -22.9 | 7.4 | |
| 105.8 | 66.6 | 76.6 | % Profit Before Taxes/Tangible | 116.6 | 126.6 | 123.5 | 66.0 | 52.7 | 60.0 | |
| (163) 64.0 | (200) 31.5 | (224) 32.2 | Net Worth | (26) 47.6 | (46) 44.0 | (11) 84.7 | (28) 35.1 | (24) 16.3 | (89) 29.0 | |
| 22.6 | 13.3 | 6.5 | | 6.0 | 8.6 | 22.6 | 2.9 | 3.3 | 11.2 | |
| 43.0 | 27.6 | 24.4 | % Profit Before Taxes/Total | 46.5 | 45.3 | 32.7 | 26.7 | 16.6 | 17.7 | |
| 21.8 | 13.5 | 11.7 | Assets | 13.7 | 17.3 | 15.2 | 11.7 | 4.5 | 9.6 | |
| 8.3 | 2.9 | 1.5 | | 1.5 | 4.3 | -9.9 | 1.7 | 1.0 | .4 | |
| 190.3 | 215.3 | 229.1 | | UND | UND | UND | 73.3 | 227.6 | 79.5 | |
| 48.8 | 47.7 | 33.5 | Sales/Net Fixed Assets | 41.0 | 92.7 | UND | 21.0 | 23.8 | 23.6 | |
| 17.0 | 14.2 | 11.7 | | 10.1 | 22.3 | 18.2 | 7.2 | 12.4 | 7.4 | |
| 3.3 | 3.3 | 3.3 | | 3.6 | 3.6 | 5.2 | 2.8 | 4.8 | 2.8 | |
| 2.2 | 2.2 | 2.2 | Sales/Total Assets | 2.3 | 2.4 | 2.6 | 2.1 | 2.8 | 1.9 | |
| 1.6 | 1.5 | 1.4 | | 1.2 | 1.6 | 1.7 | 1.5 | 1.8 | 1.4 | |
| .5 | .4 | .2 | | | .2 | | .1 | .1 | .3 | |
| (98) 1.0 | (139) .8 | (153) .8 | % Depr., Dep., Amort./Sales | (21) .7 | | (16) .5 | (18) .4 | (65) .8 | | |
| 1.8 | 1.6 | 1.5 | | | 1.2 | | 1.1 | 1.8 | 1.7 | |
| 2.0 | 2.3 | 1.3 | | 3.2 | 4.0 | | 1.0 | 1.2 | .9 | |
| (71) 4.3 | (78) 3.7 | (72) 4.1 | % Officers', Directors' Owners' Comp/Sales | (11) 6.2 | (24) 5.4 | (10) 1.6 | (11) 1.4 | (13) 1.3 | | |
| 8.6 | 6.9 | 7.5 | | 17.4 | 9.6 | | 6.2 | 2.2 | 7.2 | |
| 6642112M | 7808558M | 10526296M | Net Sales ($) | 19165M | 105924M | 65638M | 211647M | 568991M | 9554931M | |
| 3344320M | 4159935M | 6499922M | Total Assets ($) | 14870M | 60338M | 27242M | 126442M | 277251M | 5993779M | |

© RMA 2024  M = $ thousand  MM = $ million
See Pages viii through xx for Explanation of Ratios and Data

# RETAIL—Shoe Retailers NAICS 458210

## Current Data Sorted by Assets | Comparative Historical Data

| 0-500M | 500M-2MM | 2-10MM | 10-50MM | 50-100MM | 100-250MM | Type of Statement | | 4/1/19-3/31/20 ALL | 4/1/20-3/31/21 ALL |
|---|---|---|---|---|---|---|---|---|---|
| | | | | | | Unqualified | | 1 | |
| | | | 1 | | | Reviewed | | 3 | |
| | | 1 | 1 | | 3 | Compiled | | 3 | 1 |
| 3 | 1 | 7 | 5 | | | Tax Returns | | 15 | 13 |
| 2 | | 3 (4/1-9/30/23) | 3 | 4 (10/1/23-3/31/24) | 1 | Other | | 29 | 10 |
| | | | 30 (10/1/23-3/31/24) | | | | | | |
| 5 | 8 | 10 | 6 | 4 | | NUMBER OF STATEMENTS | | 51 | 24 |
| % | % | % | % | % | % | ASSETS | | % | % |
| | | 14.5 | | | | Cash & Equivalents | | 10.8 | 22.7 |
| | | 7.4 | | | | Trade Receivables (net) | | 6.5 | 2.8 |
| | | 57.3 | | DATA | | Inventory | | 51.4 | 56.2 |
| | | 8.4 | | NOT | | All Other Current | | 3.3 | 1.6 |
| | | 87.7 | | AVAILABLE | | Total Current | | 72.1 | 83.3 |
| | | 6.8 | | | | Fixed Assets (net) | | 10.9 | 10.8 |
| | | 1.7 | | | | Intangibles (net) | | 6.1 | 3.1 |
| | | 3.9 | | | | All Other Non-Current | | 10.9 | 2.9 |
| | | 100.0 | | | | Total | | 100.0 | 100.0 |
| | | | | | | LIABILITIES | | | |
| | | 3.2 | | | | Notes Payable-Short Term | | 6.7 | 10.9 |
| | | 2.1 | | | | Cur. Mat.-L.T.D. | | 1.5 | .3 |
| | | 18.7 | | | | Trade Payables | | 23.0 | 23.9 |
| | | .0 | | | | Income Taxes Payable | | .2 | .1 |
| | | 8.3 | | | | All Other Current | | 12.6 | 9.6 |
| | | 32.3 | | | | Total Current | | 44.0 | 44.9 |
| | | 10.6 | | | | Long-Term Debt | | 14.0 | 17.4 |
| | | .0 | | | | Deferred Taxes | | .0 | .0 |
| | | 1.5 | | | | All Other Non-Current | | 6.0 | 26.6 |
| | | 55.7 | | | | Net Worth | | 36.0 | 11.1 |
| | | 100.0 | | | | Total Liabilities & Net Worth | | 100.0 | 100.0 |
| | | | | | | INCOME DATA | | | |
| | | 100.0 | | | | Net Sales | | 100.0 | 100.0 |
| | | 41.4 | | | | Gross Profit | | 44.7 | 43.5 |
| | | 38.2 | | | | Operating Expenses | | 39.1 | 47.3 |
| | | 3.2 | | | | Operating Profit | | 5.6 | -3.8 |
| | | .0 | | | | All Other Expenses (net) | | .9 | -1.1 |
| | | 3.2 | | | | Profit Before Taxes | | 4.7 | -2.7 |
| | | | | | | RATIOS | | | |
| | | 4.3 | | | | | | 3.4 | 3.6 |
| | | 2.5 | | | | Current | | 2.1 | 1.9 |
| | | 1.9 | | | | | | 1.1 | 1.2 |
| | | 1.9 | | | | | | .9 | 1.2 |
| | | .6 | | | | Quick | | .3 | .4 |
| | | .1 | | | | | | .1 | .3 |
| | | 0 UND | | | | | | 0 UND | 0 UND |
| | | 0 752.7 | | | | Sales/Receivables | | 0 UND | 0 UND |
| | | 12 31.3 | | | | | | 5 78.4 | 3 128.1 |
| | | 54 6.8 | | | | | | 96 3.8 | 72 5.1 |
| | | 152 2.4 | | | | Cost of Sales/Inventory | | 130 2.8 | 130 2.8 |
| | | 174 2.1 | | | | | | 228 1.6 | 304 1.2 |
| | | 26 14.0 | | | | | | 1 317.7 | 0 UND |
| | | 33 11.1 | | | | Cost of Sales/Payables | | 45 8.2 | 43 8.4 |
| | | 53 6.9 | | | | | | 70 5.2 | 107 3.4 |
| | | 3.2 | | | | | | 5.1 | 3.1 |
| | | 5.7 | | | | Sales/Working Capital | | 7.7 | 8.5 |
| | | 9.9 | | | | | | 27.8 | 23.6 |
| | | | | | | | | 13.0 | 5.4 |
| | | | | | | EBIT/Interest | (43) | 4.7 | (19) -3.1 |
| | | | | | | | | 1.3 | -12.5 |
| | | | | | | Net Profit + Depr., Dep., Amort./Cur. Mat. L/T/D | | | |
| | | .0 | | | | | | .0 | .0 |
| | | .1 | | | | Fixed/Worth | | .2 | .3 |
| | | .1 | | | | | | .6 | .7 |
| | | .3 | | | | | | .5 | .8 |
| | | 1.0 | | | | Debt/Worth | | 1.7 | 2.0 |
| | | 1.9 | | | | | | 7.4 | 32.2 |
| | | 31.3 | | | | | | 56.8 | 77.0 |
| | | 9.1 | | | | % Profit Before Taxes/Tangible Net Worth | (44) | 21.7 | (19) 13.8 |
| | | -8.0 | | | | | | 4.8 | -21.1 |
| | | 19.5 | | | | | | 18.4 | 16.9 |
| | | 4.4 | | | | % Profit Before Taxes/Total Assets | | 8.6 | 1.1 |
| | | -3.2 | | | | | | 2.1 | -17.8 |
| | | 203.1 | | | | | | 311.3 | 270.3 |
| | | 112.8 | | | | Sales/Net Fixed Assets | | 33.7 | 36.4 |
| | | 37.5 | | | | | | 17.7 | 15.6 |
| | | 3.8 | | | | | | 3.8 | 3.9 |
| | | 2.8 | | | | Sales/Total Assets | | 2.2 | 2.5 |
| | | 2.1 | | | | | | 1.6 | 1.3 |
| | | | | | | | | .5 | .5 |
| | | | | | | % Depr., Dep., Amort./Sales | (31) | .9 | (13) 1.0 |
| | | | | | | | | 1.6 | 1.4 |
| | | | | | | | | 2.5 | 1.9 |
| | | | | | | % Officers', Directors' Owners' Comp/Sales | (17) | 3.9 | (15) 4.5 |
| | | | | | | | | 5.1 | 8.4 |
| 14429M | 25376M | 163732M | 316710M | | 835620M | Net Sales ($) | | 1535741M | 262175M |
| 1651M | 9382M | 58063M | 151667M | | 568125M | Total Assets ($) | | 847746M | 206199M |

M = $ thousand    MM = $ million
See Pages viii through xx for Explanation of Ratios and Data

© RMA 2024

# RETAIL—Shoe Retailers  NAICS 458210

## Comparative Historical Data | Current Data Sorted by Sales

| Comparative Historical Data | | | | | | Current Data Sorted by Sales | | | | | |
|---|---|---|---|---|---|---|---|---|---|---|---|
| 4 | | 4 | | 4 | | | | | | 1 | 3 |
| 2 | | 2 | | 2 | | | | | | 1 | 1 |
|   | | 1 | | 1 | | | | | | | 1 |
| 5 | | 10 | | 9 | Type of Statement | | | | | | 1 |
| 12 | | 21 | | 17 | Unqualified / Reviewed / Compiled / Tax Returns / Other | 2 | 5 | 1 | 2 | 3 | 5 |
| 4/1/21-3/31/22 ALL | | 4/1/22-3/31/23 ALL | | 4/1/23-3/31/24 ALL | | 0-1MM | 1-3MM | 3 (4/1-9/30/23) 3-5MM | 5-10MM | 30 (10/1/23-3/31/24) 10-25MM | 25MM & OVER |
| 23 | | 38 | | 33 | NUMBER OF STATEMENTS | 2 | 5 | 4 | 3 | 8 | 11 |
| % | | % | | % | ASSETS | % | % | % | % | % | % |
| 27.9 | | 14.5 | | 13.1 | Cash & Equivalents | | | | | | 13.3 |
| 4.8 | | 3.3 | | 4.3 | Trade Receivables (net) | | | | | | 3.1 |
| 49.6 | | 48.4 | | 52.5 | Inventory | | | | | | 40.4 |
| 3.1 | | 4.7 | | 3.1 | All Other Current | | | | | | .9 |
| 85.4 | | 70.9 | | 73.1 | Total Current | | | | | | 57.7 |
| 9.0 | | 17.1 | | 9.4 | Fixed Assets (net) | | | | | | 20.8 |
| 2.5 | | 3.3 | | 2.4 | Intangibles (net) | | | | | | 5.8 |
| 3.1 | | 8.8 | | 15.1 | All Other Non-Current | | | | | | 15.7 |
| 100.0 | | 100.0 | | 100.0 | Total | | | | | | 100.0 |
| | | | | | LIABILITIES | | | | | | |
| 5.1 | | 8.8 | | 7.8 | Notes Payable-Short Term | | | | | | 10.3 |
| .5 | | 2.1 | | 1.6 | Cur. Mat.-L.T.D. | | | | | | 2.1 |
| 23.8 | | 14.3 | | 13.7 | Trade Payables | | | | | | 12.4 |
| .1 | | .0 | | .1 | Income Taxes Payable | | | | | | .0 |
| 12.8 | | 29.9 | | 10.0 | All Other Current | | | | | | 6.7 |
| 42.3 | | 55.2 | | 33.1 | Total Current | | | | | | 31.5 |
| 16.3 | | 14.4 | | 12.1 | Long-Term Debt | | | | | | 15.1 |
| .0 | | .1 | | .1 | Deferred Taxes | | | | | | .3 |
| 6.4 | | 8.0 | | 7.4 | All Other Non-Current | | | | | | 8.2 |
| 34.9 | | 22.4 | | 47.3 | Net Worth | | | | | | 45.0 |
| 100.0 | | 100.0 | | 100.0 | Total Liabilities & Net Worth | | | | | | 100.0 |
| | | | | | INCOME DATA | | | | | | |
| 100.0 | | 100.0 | | 100.0 | Net Sales | | | | | | 100.0 |
| 47.3 | | 47.2 | | 40.4 | Gross Profit | | | | | | 41.1 |
| 39.5 | | 43.2 | | 36.1 | Operating Expenses | | | | | | 37.8 |
| 7.8 | | 4.0 | | 4.3 | Operating Profit | | | | | | 3.3 |
| -2.0 | | -.2 | | -.1 | All Other Expenses (net) | | | | | | .1 |
| 9.8 | | 4.2 | | 4.4 | Profit Before Taxes | | | | | | 3.2 |
| | | | | | RATIOS | | | | | | |
| 6.3 | | 3.7 | | 6.8 | | | | | | | 2.5 |
| 2.4 | | 1.8 | | 2.6 | Current | | | | | | 1.6 |
| 1.4 | | 1.1 | | 1.5 | | | | | | | 1.3 |
| 2.9 | | 1.0 | | 1.5 | | | | | | | 1.1 |
| .9 | | .5 | | .6 | Quick | | | | | | .5 |
| .4 | | .2 | | .1 | | | | | | | .1 |
| 0 | UND | 0 | UND | 0 | UND | | | | | 0 | UND |
| 0 | 999.8 | 1 | 363.4 | 0 | 999.8  Sales/Receivables | | | | | 0 | UND |
| 7 | 52.7 | 5 | 78.6 | 9 | 39.2 | | | | | 4 | 91.3 |
| 83 | 4.4 | 122 | 3.0 | 89 | 4.1 | | | | | 73 | 5.0 |
| 122 | 3.0 | 174 | 2.1 | 140 | 2.6  Cost of Sales/Inventory | | | | | 122 | 3.0 |
| 192 | 1.9 | 261 | 1.4 | 215 | 1.7 | | | | | 215 | 1.7 |
| 18 | 20.7 | 14 | 26.8 | 5 | 66.9 | | | | | 15 | 24.5 |
| 38 | 9.6 | 47 | 7.8 | 27 | 13.4  Cost of Sales/Payables | | | | | 35 | 10.5 |
| 91 | 4.0 | 68 | 5.4 | 46 | 8.0 | | | | | 53 | 6.9 |
| 3.4 | | 3.4 | | 4.4 | | | | | | | 6.9 |
| 6.3 | | 6.7 | | 6.1 | Sales/Working Capital | | | | | | 10.9 |
| 10.6 | | 59.5 | | 14.6 | | | | | | | 15.5 |
| 98.4 | | 39.7 | | 62.2 | | | | | | | 27.9 |
| (17) | 25.6 | (28) | 9.8 | (22) | 8.7  EBIT/Interest | | | | | | 3.9 |
| 5.9 | | 5.0 | | 1.3 | | | | | | | .7 |
| | | | | | Net Profit + Depr., Dep., Amort./Cur. Mat. L/T/D | | | | | | |
| .0 | | .0 | | .0 | | | | | | | .4 |
| .2 | | .4 | | .1 | Fixed/Worth | | | | | | .7 |
| .9 | | NM | | .6 | | | | | | | .9 |
| .5 | | .4 | | .3 | | | | | | | .7 |
| 1.5 | | 1.8 | | 1.1 | Debt/Worth | | | | | | 1.2 |
| 14.1 | | NM | | 3.4 | | | | | | | 4.2 |
| 106.1 | | 41.1 | | 40.0 | | | | | | | 39.2 |
| (20) | 57.4 | (29) | 28.7 | (31) | 17.1  % Profit Before Taxes/Tangible Net Worth | | | | | | 17.1 |
| 31.3 | | 13.3 | | 7.7 | | | | | | | -2.1 |
| 43.3 | | 16.2 | | 22.5 | | | | | | | 10.8 |
| 21.6 | | 7.8 | | 5.7 | % Profit Before Taxes/Total Assets | | | | | | 4.8 |
| 9.0 | | -.3 | | 2.3 | | | | | | | -.4 |
| 118.5 | | 113.6 | | 184.7 | | | | | | | 30.1 |
| 33.9 | | 24.8 | | 59.0 | Sales/Net Fixed Assets | | | | | | 10.2 |
| 22.3 | | 7.5 | | 18.7 | | | | | | | 7.5 |
| 3.5 | | 2.6 | | 3.5 | | | | | | | 2.5 |
| 2.3 | | 1.7 | | 2.5 | Sales/Total Assets | | | | | | 1.9 |
| 1.8 | | 1.4 | | 1.7 | | | | | | | 1.4 |
| .4 | | .6 | | .4 | | | | | | | .7 |
| (15) | .7 | (24) | 1.2 | (19) | .7  % Depr., Dep., Amort./Sales | | | | | (10) | 1.1 |
| 1.4 | | 2.6 | | 1.1 | | | | | | | 2.4 |
| 3.2 | | 2.5 | | 2.1 | % Officers', Directors' Owners' Comp/Sales | | | | | | |
| (11) | 4.6 | (14) | 3.5 | (17) | 3.8 | | | | | | |
| 6.7 | | 4.6 | | 5.8 | | | | | | | |
| 854433M | | 1499893M | | 1355867M | Net Sales ($) | 775M | 8076M | 13991M | 20965M | 123588M | 1188472M |
| 424450M | | 850173M | | 788888M | Total Assets ($) | 427M | 3822M | 4684M | 11070M | 50955M | 717930M |

© RMA 2024  
M = $ thousand   MM = $ million  
See Pages viii through xx for Explanation of Ratios and Data

# RETAIL—Jewelry Retailers  NAICS 458310

## Current Data Sorted by Assets | Comparative Historical Data

| Type of Statement | | | | | | | | | |
|---|---|---|---|---|---|---|---|---|---|
| | | | 2 | 2 | 4 | Unqualified | | 6 | 2 |
| | | 1 | 8 | | | Reviewed | | 14 | 6 |
| | | 8 | 4 | 1 | | Compiled | | 20 | 9 |
| 4 | 9 | 10 | 4 | | | Tax Returns | | 33 | 21 |
| 2 | 5 | 23 | 15 | 2 | 4 | Other | | 73 | 55 |
| | 21 (4/1-9/30/23) | | 87 (10/1/23-3/31/24) | | | | | 4/1/19-3/31/20 | 4/1/20-3/31/21 |
| 0-500M | 500M-2MM | 2-10MM | 10-50MM | 50-100MM | 100-250MM | NUMBER OF STATEMENTS | | 146 ALL | 93 ALL |
| 6 | 14 | 42 | 33 | 5 | 8 | | | | |
| % | % | % | % | % | % | **ASSETS** | | % | % |
| | 14.7 | 15.8 | 15.6 | | | Cash & Equivalents | | 12.6 | 20.0 |
| | 3.1 | 2.4 | 1.9 | | | Trade Receivables (net) | | 4.3 | 3.7 |
| | 64.8 | 59.0 | 57.9 | | | Inventory | | 63.2 | 56.2 |
| | .8 | 1.8 | 3.0 | | | All Other Current | | 1.4 | 3.0 |
| | 83.5 | 79.0 | 78.5 | | | Total Current | | 81.5 | 82.8 |
| | 8.1 | 11.1 | 11.1 | | | Fixed Assets (net) | | 10.0 | 9.2 |
| | 1.1 | 3.1 | 1.5 | | | Intangibles (net) | | 2.7 | 3.8 |
| | 7.3 | 6.8 | 9.0 | | | All Other Non-Current | | 5.8 | 4.2 |
| | 100.0 | 100.0 | 100.0 | | | Total | | 100.0 | 100.0 |
| | | | | | | **LIABILITIES** | | | |
| | 5.7 | 6.0 | 4.6 | | | Notes Payable-Short Term | | 10.1 | 5.8 |
| | 1.2 | 1.2 | .7 | | | Cur. Mat.-L.T.D. | | 1.7 | 1.8 |
| | 14.8 | 12.6 | 12.2 | | | Trade Payables | | 19.1 | 13.3 |
| | .0 | .0 | .0 | | | Income Taxes Payable | | .1 | .2 |
| | 7.0 | 12.4 | 8.6 | | | All Other Current | | 12.9 | 18.7 |
| | 28.7 | 32.2 | 26.0 | | | Total Current | | 43.9 | 39.7 |
| | 10.0 | 10.5 | 11.6 | | | Long-Term Debt | | 11.4 | 11.9 |
| | .0 | .0 | .1 | | | Deferred Taxes | | .1 | .1 |
| | 1.6 | 4.8 | 2.5 | | | All Other Non-Current | | 4.6 | 5.7 |
| | 59.8 | 52.4 | 59.8 | | | Net Worth | | 40.1 | 42.4 |
| | 100.0 | 100.0 | 100.0 | | | Total Liabilties & Net Worth | | 100.0 | 100.0 |
| | | | | | | **INCOME DATA** | | | |
| | 100.0 | 100.0 | 100.0 | | | Net Sales | | 100.0 | 100.0 |
| | 47.3 | 41.1 | 37.0 | | | Gross Profit | | 40.6 | 39.7 |
| | 38.7 | 33.9 | 27.1 | | | Operating Expenses | | 35.3 | 34.4 |
| | 8.7 | 7.3 | 9.9 | | | Operating Profit | | 5.3 | 5.3 |
| | .9 | .1 | .0 | | | All Other Expenses (net) | | .9 | -.3 |
| | 7.8 | 7.2 | 9.9 | | | Profit Before Taxes | | 4.5 | 5.6 |
| | | | | | | **RATIOS** | | | |
| | 12.5 | 4.4 | 5.7 | | | | | 3.4 | 4.9 |
| | 4.3 | 2.4 | 3.7 | | Current | | | 2.0 | 2.6 |
| | 1.6 | 1.6 | 2.1 | | | | | 1.4 | 1.9 |
| | 2.5 | 1.6 | 1.2 | | | | | .8 | 1.3 |
| | .6 | .4 | .5 | | Quick | | | .3 (92) | .7 |
| | .3 | .2 | .1 | | | | | .1 | .3 |
| 0 UND | 0 UND | 1 340.1 | | | | | 0 UND | 0 UND | |
| 0 UND | 1 595.5 | 3 128.8 | | | | Sales/Receivables | 3 129.0 | 2 174.9 | |
| 4 86.7 | 4 90.0 | 6 61.9 | | | | | 11 32.6 | 9 42.4 | |
| 146 2.5 | 166 2.2 | 122 3.0 | | | | | 146 2.5 | 140 2.6 | |
| 215 1.7 | 203 1.8 | 182 2.0 | | | | Cost of Sales/Inventory | 261 1.4 | 203 1.8 | |
| 365 1.0 | 332 1.1 | 304 1.2 | | | | | 365 1.0 | 281 1.3 | |
| 0 UND | 17 21.7 | 23 15.8 | | | | | 33 11.1 | 16 23.5 | |
| 32 11.5 | 45 8.2 | 43 8.4 | | | | Cost of Sales/Payables | 54 6.8 | 43 8.5 | |
| 72 5.1 | 76 4.8 | 76 4.8 | | | | | 94 3.9 | 73 5.0 | |
| | 1.9 | 3.0 | 2.4 | | | | | 2.5 | 2.4 |
| | 3.6 | 3.8 | 3.0 | | Sales/Working Capital | | | 4.7 | 3.5 |
| | 9.9 | 5.9 | 4.4 | | | | | 9.0 | 6.1 |
| | 141.5 | 45.2 | 32.8 | | | | | 10.7 | 25.6 |
| (12) | 11.9 | (34) 8.9 | (24) 10.4 | | | EBIT/Interest | (126) 4.3 | (72) 11.8 | |
| | 3.0 | 1.2 | 4.4 | | | | | 1.7 | 2.3 |
| | | | | | | Net Profit + Depr., Dep., Amort./Cur. Mat. L/T/D | | 6.5 | |
| | | | | | | | (17) | 3.0 | |
| | | | | | | | | 1.0 | |
| | .0 | .0 | .0 | | | | | .1 | .0 |
| | .0 | .1 | .1 | | Fixed/Worth | | | .2 | .1 |
| | .3 | .4 | .3 | | | | | .6 | .4 |
| | .1 | .5 | .3 | | | | | .7 | .5 |
| | .7 | .8 | .7 | | Debt/Worth | | | 1.4 | 1.2 |
| | 2.3 | 2.2 | 1.5 | | | | | 3.3 | 3.3 |
| | 52.7 | 33.3 | 40.4 | | | | | 27.3 | 44.5 |
| | 25.5 | (39) 22.1 | 20.9 | | % Profit Before Taxes/Tangible Net Worth | (130) 13.9 | (84) 25.3 | | |
| | 8.6 | 4.3 | 13.5 | | | | | 2.9 | 8.0 |
| | 38.9 | 17.9 | 24.3 | | | | | 12.3 | 19.4 |
| | 18.0 | 11.2 | 12.8 | | % Profit Before Taxes/Total Assets | | | 6.3 | 10.6 |
| | 3.8 | 2.0 | 6.5 | | | | | 1.6 | 1.4 |
| | UND | 89.5 | 79.3 | | | | | 66.5 | 142.6 |
| | 157.6 | 31.8 | 22.9 | | Sales/Net Fixed Assets | | | 24.2 | 30.3 |
| | 12.1 | 9.8 | 10.3 | | | | | 11.3 | 12.8 |
| | 2.9 | 2.3 | 1.9 | | | | | 2.3 | 2.4 |
| | 2.2 | 1.7 | 1.5 | | Sales/Total Assets | | | 1.6 | 1.6 |
| | 1.5 | 1.3 | 1.1 | | | | | 1.2 | 1.3 |
| | | .4 | .3 | | | | | .4 | .4 |
| | (27) | .9 | (23) .4 | | % Depr., Dep., Amort./Sales | (101) .8 | (61) .8 | | |
| | | 1.4 | .9 | | | | | 1.5 | 1.6 |
| | | 1.4 | | | | | | 2.5 | 2.6 |
| | (28) | 3.3 | | | % Officers', Directors' Owners' Comp/Sales | (66) 4.8 | (42) 4.6 | | |
| | | 5.2 | | | | | | 7.6 | 6.8 |
| 4317M | 56404M | 419077M | 1163112M | 398541M | 1531178M | Net Sales ($) | | 3515675M | 2416782M |
| 1194M | 17509M | 220821M | 713723M | 292721M | 1210210M | Total Assets ($) | | 2268836M | 1682895M |

© RMA 2024     M = $ thousand     MM = $ million
See Pages viii through xx for Explanation of Ratios and Data

RETAIL—Jewelry Retailers  NAICS 458310

## Comparative Historical Data / Current Data Sorted by Sales

| Comparative Historical Data | | | Type of Statement | Current Data Sorted by Sales | | | | | |
|---|---|---|---|---|---|---|---|---|---|
| 5 | 2 | 8 | Unqualified | | | | | 6 | 8 |
| 11 | 11 | 9 | Reviewed | | | | | 6 | 3 |
| 14 | 11 | 13 | Compiled | | | 3 | 2 | 6 | 2 |
| 20 | 29 | 27 | Tax Returns | 3 | 8 | 1 | 6 | 7 | 2 |
| 48 | 55 | 51 | Other | 2 | 9 | 2 | 7 | 12 | 19 |
| 4/1/21-3/31/22 | 4/1/22-3/31/23 | 4/1/23-3/31/24 | | | 21 (4/1-9/30/23) | | 87 (10/1/23-3/31/24) | | |
| ALL | ALL | ALL | | 0-1MM | 1-3MM | 3-5MM | 5-10MM | 10-25MM | 25MM & OVER |
| 98 | 108 | 108 | NUMBER OF STATEMENTS | 5 | 17 | 6 | 15 | 31 | 34 |
| % | % | % | ASSETS | % | % | % | % | % | % |
| 17.2 | 16.2 | 16.2 | Cash & Equivalents | | 15.7 | | 16.4 | 16.2 | 13.2 |
| 4.2 | 3.7 | 3.2 | Trade Receivables (net) | | 3.4 | | 3.5 | 1.9 | 4.9 |
| 59.2 | 60.2 | 57.1 | Inventory | | 65.3 | | 57.7 | 56.0 | 53.5 |
| 2.5 | 1.9 | 2.0 | All Other Current | | 1.4 | | 3.7 | 1.8 | 2.3 |
| 83.1 | 81.9 | 78.4 | Total Current | | 85.9 | | 81.2 | 75.9 | 73.9 |
| 9.5 | 9.1 | 12.0 | Fixed Assets (net) | | 7.0 | | 9.2 | 12.6 | 15.8 |
| 2.1 | 1.2 | 2.0 | Intangibles (net) | | 2.8 | | 1.5 | 2.1 | 2.3 |
| 5.4 | 7.9 | 7.6 | All Other Non-Current | | 4.3 | | 8.1 | 9.3 | 8.0 |
| 100.0 | 100.0 | 100.0 | Total | | 100.0 | | 100.0 | 100.0 | 100.0 |
| | | | LIABILITIES | | | | | | |
| 4.7 | 5.0 | 5.0 | Notes Payable-Short Term | | 8.5 | | 6.9 | 4.6 | 3.4 |
| 2.8 | .8 | 2.0 | Cur. Mat.-L.T.D. | | 2.2 | | 1.8 | .7 | 3.8 |
| 13.9 | 12.0 | 13.2 | Trade Payables | | 8.6 | | 13.0 | 13.5 | 14.4 |
| .2 | .1 | .0 | Income Taxes Payable | | .0 | | .0 | .0 | .0 |
| 13.7 | 11.6 | 10.6 | All Other Current | | 7.8 | | 16.9 | 9.3 | 9.6 |
| 35.3 | 29.6 | 30.8 | Total Current | | 27.1 | | 38.7 | 28.2 | 31.2 |
| 10.2 | 12.1 | 17.0 | Long-Term Debt | | 18.1 | | 9.5 | 8.3 | 13.2 |
| .1 | .1 | .1 | Deferred Taxes | | .0 | | .0 | .1 | .2 |
| 4.0 | 5.3 | 4.0 | All Other Non-Current | | 5.2 | | 4.9 | 2.8 | 4.6 |
| 50.4 | 53.0 | 48.2 | Net Worth | | 49.7 | | 46.9 | 60.6 | 50.7 |
| 100.0 | 100.0 | 100.0 | Total Liabilities & Net Worth | | 100.0 | | 100.0 | 100.0 | 100.0 |
| | | | INCOME DATA | | | | | | |
| 100.0 | 100.0 | 100.0 | Net Sales | | 100.0 | | 100.0 | 100.0 | 100.0 |
| 41.8 | 42.2 | 41.7 | Gross Profit | | 45.6 | | 50.3 | 32.0 | 43.4 |
| 31.1 | 32.6 | 33.8 | Operating Expenses | | 37.7 | | 45.1 | 23.9 | 34.5 |
| 10.7 | 9.6 | 8.0 | Operating Profit | | 7.9 | | 5.3 | 8.1 | 8.9 |
| -1.0 | -.4 | .2 | All Other Expenses (net) | | 1.1 | | .5 | .0 | -.1 |
| 11.7 | 9.9 | 7.8 | Profit Before Taxes | | 6.8 | | 4.7 | 8.2 | 9.0 |
| | | | RATIOS | | | | | | |
| 4.3 | 5.2 | 5.6 | | | 6.0 | | 3.5 | 5.7 | 5.7 |
| 2.3 | 3.4 | 2.7 | Current | | 3.3 | | 2.3 | 2.5 | 2.4 |
| 1.8 | 2.0 | 1.7 | | | 2.0 | | 1.3 | 1.9 | 1.8 |
| 1.3 | 1.5 | 1.3 | | | 1.7 | | .8 | 2.1 | 1.0 |
| .6 | .6 | .6 | Quick | | .6 | | .4 | .5 | .6 |
| .2 | .2 | .2 | | | .4 | | .1 | .2 | .2 |
| 0 UND | 0 UND | 0 UND | | | 0 UND | | 0 UND | 0 UND | 1 563.8 |
| 1 398.8 | 1 325.0 | 2 228.9 | Sales/Receivables | | 1 420.2 | | 1 866.7 | 3 123.4 | 3 123.4 |
| 9 42.1 | 7 51.1 | 5 68.1 | | | 6 65.2 | | 5 77.4 | 4 86.3 | 9 40.8 |
| 122 3.0 | 122 3.0 | 146 2.5 | | 146 2.5 | | 174 2.1 | 114 3.2 | 126 2.9 | |
| 203 1.8 | 215 1.7 | 203 1.8 | Cost of Sales/Inventory | 243 1.5 | | 203 1.8 | 182 2.0 | 215 1.7 | |
| 304 1.2 | 304 1.2 | 304 1.2 | | 456 .8 | | 281 1.3 | 215 1.7 | 304 1.2 | |
| 16 22.4 | 11 33.6 | 15 23.8 | | | 0 UND | 15 23.6 | 13 28.0 | 37 9.9 | |
| 34 10.7 | 32 11.4 | 45 8.2 | Cost of Sales/Payables | | 34 10.7 | 40 9.1 | 38 9.7 | 60 6.1 | |
| 72 5.1 | 57 6.4 | 79 4.6 | | | 73 5.0 | 76 4.8 | 53 6.9 | 85 4.3 | |
| 2.5 | 2.3 | 2.6 | | | 1.6 | | 3.0 | 2.9 | 2.3 |
| 3.8 | 3.2 | 3.7 | Sales/Working Capital | | 3.5 | | 5.8 | 3.8 | 3.3 |
| 7.1 | 5.5 | 6.0 | | | 4.7 | | 10.4 | 4.9 | 6.1 |
| 63.0 | 62.7 | 36.8 | | | 15.7 | | 51.5 | 91.5 | 18.8 |
| (75) 25.5 | (81) 24.3 | (86) 9.2 | EBIT/Interest | (15) 5.0 | | (12) 8.9 | (27) 17.4 | (24) 10.4 | |
| 9.5 | 7.4 | 3.5 | | | .0 | | -2.7 | 3.8 | 4.7 |
| | | 14.5 | Net Profit + Depr., Dep., | | | | | | |
| | (11) 2.6 | | Amort./Cur. Mat. L/T/D | | | | | | |
| | | -1.9 | | | | | | | |
| .0 | .0 | .0 | | | .0 | | .0 | .0 | .1 |
| .1 | .1 | .1 | Fixed/Worth | | .1 | | .1 | .1 | .3 |
| .4 | .3 | .4 | | | .3 | | .5 | .3 | .8 |
| .4 | .4 | .3 | | | .3 | | .4 | .3 | .3 |
| 1.0 | .9 | .9 | Debt/Worth | | 1.0 | | 1.7 | .7 | 1.1 |
| 2.5 | 1.6 | 2.1 | | | 3.5 | | 3.7 | 1.6 | 2.0 |
| 78.0 | 52.6 | 38.7 | % Profit Before Taxes/Tangible | | 38.6 | | 45.0 | 35.6 | 42.0 |
| (94) 36.7 | (104) 29.9 | (102) 21.5 | Net Worth | (15) 16.2 | | 26.4 | 22.6 | (31) 20.9 | |
| 25.4 | 16.6 | 10.4 | | | -17.4 | | 4.3 | 13.1 | 11.9 |
| 27.6 | 27.4 | 21.2 | % Profit Before Taxes/Total | | 20.3 | | 17.5 | 24.7 | 20.1 |
| 19.3 | 15.6 | 11.9 | Assets | | 12.0 | | 10.5 | 12.8 | 11.7 |
| 13.1 | 7.5 | 4.6 | | | -.7 | | 2.1 | 5.8 | 5.5 |
| 127.5 | 118.1 | 116.7 | | | UND | | 205.5 | 79.9 | 29.1 |
| 29.4 | 30.1 | 27.4 | Sales/Net Fixed Assets | | 109.8 | | 33.9 | 33.7 | 14.4 |
| 14.2 | 15.0 | 9.2 | | | 11.9 | | 13.6 | 10.0 | 6.9 |
| 2.6 | 2.4 | 2.3 | | | 2.5 | | 2.5 | 2.2 | 2.0 |
| 1.7 | 1.8 | 1.7 | Sales/Total Assets | | 1.5 | | 2.0 | 1.7 | 1.5 |
| 1.2 | 1.3 | 1.3 | | | 1.1 | | 1.6 | 1.4 | 1.0 |
| .3 | .4 | .3 | | | | | | .2 | .4 |
| (65) .7 | (68) .6 | (68) .6 | % Depr., Dep., Amort./Sales | | | | (24) .5 | (25) .7 | |
| 1.7 | 1.3 | 1.4 | | | | | | 1.2 | 1.8 |
| 1.5 | 2.5 | 1.5 | | | 3.6 | | 2.7 | 1.4 | |
| (40) 3.3 | (51) 3.6 | (51) 3.2 | % Officers', Directors' Owners' Comp/Sales | (11) 7.8 | | (12) 3.3 | (17) 2.6 | | |
| 4.9 | 7.5 | 6.6 | | | 16.2 | | 7.5 | 4.2 | |
| 3892358M | 3394362M | 3572629M | Net Sales ($) | 3097M | 36308M | 24795M | 106849M | 519123M | 2882457M |
| 2330064M | 1982002M | 2456178M | Total Assets ($) | 795M | 29960M | 24103M | 52263M | 322825M | 2026232M |

M = $ thousand   MM = $ million
See Pages viii through xx for Explanation of Ratios and Data

© RMA 2024

## RETAIL—Sporting Goods Retailers  NAICS 459110

### Current Data Sorted by Assets / Comparative Historical Data

| | | | | | | Type of Statement | | |
|---|---|---|---|---|---|---|---|---|
| | | | 3 | 2 | 3 | Unqualified | 2 | 3 |
| 1 | 2 | 5 | 8 | 1 | | Reviewed | 9 | 6 |
| 9 | 14 | 9 | 2 | | | Compiled | 15 | 12 |
| 8 | 19 | 18 | 2 | | 4 | Tax Returns | 82 | 36 |
| | | 40 | | 5 | | Other | 85 | 74 |
| | 26 (4/1-9/30/23) | | 142 (10/1/23-3/31/24) | | | | 4/1/19-3/31/20 | 4/1/20-3/31/21 |
| 0-500M | 500M-2MM | 2-10MM | 10-50MM | 50-100MM | 100-250MM | | ALL | ALL |
| 18 | 35 | 72 | 28 | 8 | 7 | NUMBER OF STATEMENTS | 193 | 131 |
| % | % | % | % | % | % | ASSETS | % | % |
| 21.9 | 18.7 | 16.0 | 13.7 | | | Cash & Equivalents | 11.3 | 22.9 |
| 1.1 | 2.9 | 4.8 | 6.3 | | | Trade Receivables (net) | 4.1 | 4.7 |
| 45.2 | 56.0 | 52.4 | 47.3 | | | Inventory | 59.1 | 49.1 |
| 3.5 | 5.8 | 1.8 | 1.5 | | | All Other Current | 1.1 | 2.3 |
| 71.7 | 83.5 | 75.0 | 68.7 | | | Total Current | 75.6 | 79.1 |
| 15.7 | 10.2 | 14.6 | 17.1 | | | Fixed Assets (net) | 14.7 | 10.8 |
| 7.3 | 2.5 | 3.9 | 2.8 | | | Intangibles (net) | 3.7 | 5.7 |
| 5.3 | 3.9 | 6.6 | 11.3 | | | All Other Non-Current | 6.0 | 4.4 |
| 100.0 | 100.0 | 100.0 | 100.0 | | | Total | 100.0 | 100.0 |
| | | | | | | LIABILITIES | | |
| 25.7 | 8.6 | 5.5 | 6.2 | | | Notes Payable-Short Term | 13.3 | 7.8 |
| .6 | 1.1 | .9 | 1.3 | | | Cur. Mat.-L.T.D. | 1.6 | .9 |
| 11.8 | 17.9 | 17.8 | 18.8 | | | Trade Payables | 24.4 | 18.0 |
| 1.3 | .2 | .1 | .1 | | | Income Taxes Payable | .1 | .3 |
| 16.3 | 7.9 | 10.4 | 11.0 | | | All Other Current | 13.8 | 14.2 |
| 55.7 | 35.6 | 34.7 | 37.5 | | | Total Current | 53.3 | 41.2 |
| 76.9 | 23.0 | 12.7 | 12.4 | | | Long-Term Debt | 14.9 | 15.7 |
| .0 | .0 | .1 | .1 | | | Deferred Taxes | .1 | .1 |
| 3.9 | 2.6 | 3.3 | 9.6 | | | All Other Non-Current | 11.6 | 5.9 |
| -36.5 | 38.7 | 49.2 | 40.5 | | | Net Worth | 20.1 | 37.2 |
| 100.0 | 100.0 | 100.0 | 100.0 | | | Total Liabilities & Net Worth | 100.0 | 100.0 |
| | | | | | | INCOME DATA | | |
| 100.0 | 100.0 | 100.0 | 100.0 | | | Net Sales | 100.0 | 100.0 |
| 44.3 | 43.8 | 40.2 | 37.2 | | | Gross Profit | 41.3 | 39.6 |
| 42.9 | 39.1 | 36.6 | 34.3 | | | Operating Expenses | 36.8 | 32.7 |
| 1.4 | 4.7 | 3.6 | 3.0 | | | Operating Profit | 4.5 | 6.9 |
| 1.5 | 1.0 | .3 | -.3 | | | All Other Expenses (net) | 1.0 | -.6 |
| -.1 | 3.6 | 3.3 | 3.3 | | | Profit Before Taxes | 3.5 | 7.5 |
| | | | | | | RATIOS | | |
| 11.0 | 5.9 | 6.4 | 3.3 | | | | 2.9 | 3.4 |
| 3.0 | 2.8 | 2.3 | 2.0 | | | Current | 1.6 | 2.0 |
| .9 | 1.6 | 1.3 | 1.5 | | | | 1.2 | 1.5 |
| 4.3 | 1.3 | 1.8 | 1.4 | | | | .6 | 1.5 |
| .8 | .5 | .7 | .4 | | | Quick | (192) .2 | .6 |
| .1 | .2 | .2 | .2 | | | | .1 | .3 |
| 0 UND | 0 UND | 0 UND | 1 501.8 | | | | 0 UND | 0 UND |
| 0 UND | 0 UND | 2 211.3 | 3 109.3 | | | Sales/Receivables | 0 999.8 | 0 989.0 |
| 0 UND | 4 95.5 | 10 37.6 | 10 37.4 | | | | 4 96.0 | 5 66.7 |
| 0 UND | 85 4.3 | 114 3.2 | 89 4.1 | | | | 94 3.9 | 74 4.9 |
| 118 3.1 | 146 2.5 | 146 2.5 | 146 2.5 | | | Cost of Sales/Inventory | 159 2.3 | 114 3.2 |
| 182 2.0 | 228 1.6 | 228 1.6 | 215 1.7 | | | | 228 1.6 | 166 2.2 |
| 0 UND | 8 44.5 | 14 26.4 | 26 14.3 | | | | 21 17.4 | 10 36.7 |
| 0 UND | 35 10.5 | 41 9.0 | 41 8.8 | | | Cost of Sales/Payables | 50 7.3 | 36 10.0 |
| 42 8.6 | 66 5.5 | 68 5.4 | 70 5.2 | | | | 85 4.3 | 63 5.8 |
| 3.0 | 2.7 | 2.6 | 3.1 | | | | 4.7 | 4.2 |
| 19.3 | 5.1 | 5.0 | 5.4 | | | Sales/Working Capital | 8.8 | 7.0 |
| -34.7 | 8.7 | 12.1 | 11.3 | | | | 30.0 | 12.3 |
| 22.0 | 23.4 | 18.9 | 59.4 | | | | 10.9 | 62.7 |
| (15) 4.3 | (27) 6.2 | (56) 6.5 | (26) 7.5 | | | EBIT/Interest | (157) 3.8 | (106) 18.8 |
| -2.8 | 2.2 | .3 | 3.0 | | | | .6 | 4.7 |
| | | | | | | Net Profit + Depr., Dep., Amort./Cur. Mat. L/T/D | 6.0 | |
| | | | | | | | (12) 2.0 | |
| | | | | | | | -.7 | |
| .0 | .0 | .0 | .1 | | | | .1 | .0 |
| .7 | .2 | .2 | .2 | | | Fixed/Worth | .4 | .2 |
| -.3 | .9 | .7 | 1.2 | | | | 8.5 | .8 |
| .7 | .4 | .3 | .5 | | | | .9 | .6 |
| NM | 1.0 | 1.0 | 1.6 | | | Debt/Worth | 2.5 | 1.4 |
| -2.2 | 3.2 | 4.7 | 2.6 | | | | -181.2 | 5.1 |
| | 52.2 | 29.4 | 42.1 | | | % Profit Before Taxes/Tangible Net Worth | 44.0 | 85.3 |
| (29) | 26.8 | (62) 12.6 | (25) 19.5 | | | | (144) 16.1 | (107) 50.7 |
| | 5.7 | .1 | 9.7 | | | | 1.0 | 23.3 |
| 26.9 | 24.0 | 11.2 | 14.4 | | | % Profit Before Taxes/Total Assets | 14.5 | 32.9 |
| 7.0 | 11.2 | 6.6 | 10.3 | | | | 6.2 | 17.7 |
| -19.2 | -.9 | -2.2 | 3.1 | | | | -.7 | 6.7 |
| UND | 765.1 | 85.6 | 59.4 | | | | 107.3 | 259.3 |
| 27.4 | 49.6 | 27.6 | 19.4 | | | Sales/Net Fixed Assets | 35.6 | 47.0 |
| 11.5 | 19.1 | 10.3 | 9.0 | | | | 11.9 | 17.6 |
| 5.7 | 3.5 | 2.8 | 2.2 | | | | 3.6 | 3.5 |
| 2.8 | 2.5 | 1.8 | 1.9 | | | Sales/Total Assets | 2.4 | 2.8 |
| 1.9 | 1.6 | 1.3 | 1.5 | | | | 1.6 | 1.8 |
| .1 | .1 | .4 | .3 | | | | .3 | .3 |
| (11) .9 | (20) .5 | (52) 1.0 | (26) .6 | | | % Depr., Dep., Amort./Sales | (133) .8 | (76) .8 |
| 3.7 | 1.9 | 2.5 | 1.2 | | | | 1.5 | 1.4 |
| | 1.4 | 1.4 | | | | % Officers', Directors' Owners' Comp/Sales | 1.8 | 1.6 |
| | (18) 2.9 | (36) 2.1 | | | | | (95) 3.1 | (64) 3.1 |
| | 4.7 | 3.9 | | | | | 5.5 | 6.2 |
| 20937M | 127381M | 823098M | 1401351M | 914861M | 1618785M | Net Sales ($) | 3376006M | 1725106M |
| 4651M | 42132M | 377046M | 709279M | 647507M | 1205625M | Total Assets ($) | 1947335M | 895715M |

© RMA 2024    M = $ thousand    MM = $ million
See Pages viii through xx for Explanation of Ratios and Data

# RETAIL—Sporting Goods Retailers NAICS 459110

## Comparative Historical Data | | Current Data Sorted by Sales

| Comparative Historical Data ||| Type of Statement | Current Data Sorted by Sales |||||||
|---|---|---|---|---|---|---|---|---|---|
| 3 | 6 | 8 | Unqualified | | | | 3 | 3 | 8 |
| 9 | 12 | 14 | Reviewed | | | | 8 | 1 | 8 |
| 9 | 13 | 14 | Compiled | 1 | 1 | 1 | 8 | 8 | 2 |
| 47 | 49 | 43 | Tax Returns | 6 | 11 | 5 | 8 | 8 | 5 |
| 77 | 99 | 89 | Other | 9 | 11 | 12 | 20 | 16 | 21 |
| 4/1/21-3/31/22 ALL | 4/1/22-3/31/23 ALL | 4/1/23-3/31/24 ALL | | 0-1MM | 26 (4/1-9/30/23) 1-3MM | 3-5MM | 142 (10/1/23-3/31/24) 5-10MM | 10-25MM | 25MM & OVER |
| 145 | 179 | 168 | NUMBER OF STATEMENTS | 16 | 23 | 18 | 39 | 28 | 44 |
| % | % | % | ASSETS | % | % | % | % | % | % |
| 22.1 | 15.7 | 16.1 | Cash & Equivalents | 21.0 | 13.2 | 12.8 | 19.7 | 18.2 | 12.8 |
| 5.0 | 5.1 | 4.2 | Trade Receivables (net) | 2.5 | 1.7 | 2.4 | 4.4 | 7.0 | 4.9 |
| 48.2 | 54.5 | 50.3 | Inventory | 42.6 | 58.7 | 58.1 | 49.8 | 50.9 | 45.6 |
| 2.9 | 2.3 | 2.9 | All Other Current | 3.9 | 2.0 | 9.1 | 2.3 | 1.2 | 2.0 |
| 78.1 | 77.6 | 73.5 | Total Current | 70.0 | 75.6 | 82.4 | 76.1 | 77.3 | 65.3 |
| 10.6 | 12.8 | 15.4 | Fixed Assets (net) | 20.8 | 13.1 | 14.3 | 12.8 | 15.1 | 17.6 |
| 6.4 | 4.5 | 4.0 | Intangibles (net) | 4.5 | 5.7 | 1.1 | 4.8 | 3.0 | 4.0 |
| 4.9 | 5.0 | 7.1 | All Other Non-Current | 4.7 | 5.6 | 2.1 | 6.3 | 4.7 | 13.2 |
| 100.0 | 100.0 | 100.0 | Total | 100.0 | 100.0 | 100.0 | 100.0 | 100.0 | 100.0 |
| | | | LIABILITIES | | | | | | |
| 6.8 | 10.7 | 8.4 | Notes Payable-Short Term | 27.6 | 6.0 | 18.6 | 3.4 | 2.3 | 6.7 |
| 1.1 | 1.2 | 1.1 | Cur. Mat.-L.T.D. | .8 | 1.3 | .9 | .7 | 1.3 | 1.5 |
| 15.5 | 17.2 | 17.2 | Trade Payables | 11.5 | 14.7 | 15.6 | 14.8 | 22.1 | 20.3 |
| .4 | .3 | .2 | Income Taxes Payable | 1.6 | .2 | .0 | .1 | .0 | .1 |
| 12.8 | 10.4 | 10.6 | All Other Current | 10.9 | 10.4 | 7.1 | 10.2 | 11.3 | 12.0 |
| 36.5 | 39.8 | 37.6 | Total Current | 52.5 | 32.6 | 42.2 | 29.3 | 37.0 | 40.5 |
| 14.7 | 13.4 | 22.3 | Long-Term Debt | 76.3 | 32.4 | 21.7 | 9.4 | 16.2 | 12.9 |
| .1 | .0 | .1 | Deferred Taxes | .0 | .0 | .1 | .1 | .0 | .1 |
| 4.7 | 4.7 | 4.9 | All Other Non-Current | 3.4 | 3.2 | 1.8 | 6.1 | 5.3 | 6.2 |
| 44.0 | 42.1 | 35.2 | Net Worth | -32.1 | 31.8 | 34.2 | 55.1 | 41.5 | 40.2 |
| 100.0 | 100.0 | 100.0 | Total Liabilities & Net Worth | 100.0 | 100.0 | 100.0 | 100.0 | 100.0 | 100.0 |
| | | | INCOME DATA | | | | | | |
| 100.0 | 100.0 | 100.0 | Net Sales | 100.0 | 100.0 | 100.0 | 100.0 | 100.0 | 100.0 |
| 41.6 | 38.9 | 40.1 | Gross Profit | 46.0 | 45.5 | 45.5 | 37.9 | 40.2 | 35.0 |
| 32.2 | 33.8 | 36.6 | Operating Expenses | 42.7 | 38.4 | 44.7 | 33.8 | 38.3 | 31.7 |
| 9.4 | 5.1 | 3.5 | Operating Profit | 3.3 | 7.1 | .8 | 4.1 | 1.9 | 3.3 |
| -.9 | .1 | .5 | All Other Expenses (net) | 1.8 | 1.3 | 1.6 | .2 | -1.0 | .4 |
| 10.3 | 5.0 | 3.0 | Profit Before Taxes | 1.6 | 5.8 | -.8 | 3.9 | 2.9 | 2.9 |
| | | | RATIOS | | | | | | |
| 4.7 | 3.7 | 5.9 | | 14.8 | 4.3 | 6.8 | 7.2 | 4.8 | 3.0 |
| 2.4 | 2.0 | 2.2 | Current | 6.7 | 3.0 | 2.5 | 2.4 | 2.1 | 1.7 |
| 1.5 | 1.3 | 1.3 | | 1.0 | 1.6 | 1.2 | 1.6 | 1.3 | 1.2 |
| 2.0 | 1.0 | 1.5 | | 5.0 | 1.3 | 1.2 | 1.8 | 1.4 | 1.3 |
| .7 (178) | .4 | .5 | Quick | 1.3 | .4 | .3 | .8 | .7 | .3 |
| .3 | .1 | .2 | | .1 | .2 | .1 | .3 | .2 | .1 |
| 0 UND | 0 UND | 0 UND | | 0 UND | 0 UND | 0 UND | 0 UND | 0 999.8 | 0 UND |
| 0 907.9 | 1 468.8 | 1 562.2 | Sales/Receivables | 0 UND | 0 UND | 0 777.3 | 2 198.3 | 2 149.7 | 3 109.3 |
| 4 82.4 | 6 61.1 | 7 49.1 | | 0 UND | 0 796.3 | 5 74.9 | 8 44.3 | 12 29.3 | 9 41.0 |
| 70 5.2 | 99 3.7 | 89 4.1 | | 3 116.5 | 107 3.4 | 87 4.2 | 114 3.2 | 83 4.4 | 87 4.2 |
| 126 2.9 | 146 2.5 | 146 2.5 | Cost of Sales/Inventory | 159 2.3 | 215 1.7 | 146 2.5 | 159 2.3 | 135 2.7 | 140 2.6 |
| 182 2.0 | 228 1.6 | 228 1.6 | | 281 1.3 | 456 .8 | 332 1.1 | 228 1.6 | 182 2.0 | 174 2.1 |
| 11 33.4 | 14 26.6 | 11 33.2 | | 0 UND | 0 UND | 10 35.3 | 15 24.7 | 20 18.3 | 27 13.5 |
| 33 11.1 | 37 9.9 | 38 9.5 | Cost of Sales/Payables | 0 UND | 41 8.9 | 30 12.1 | 35 10.5 | 44 8.3 | 45 8.2 |
| 66 5.5 | 74 4.9 | 65 5.6 | | 34 10.8 | 91 4.0 | 61 6.0 | 63 5.8 | 72 5.1 | 72 5.1 |
| 3.6 | 3.7 | 2.9 | | 1.6 | 2.4 | 3.9 | 1.9 | 3.6 | 5.1 |
| 6.2 | 6.4 | 5.5 | Sales/Working Capital | 4.2 | 3.5 | 5.8 | 4.6 | 6.1 | 8.0 |
| 11.5 | 13.0 | 15.9 | | NM | 8.7 | 16.4 | 9.1 | 18.7 | 24.5 |
| 94.1 | 34.4 | 21.4 | | 20.8 | 15.1 | 20.9 | 21.1 | 22.5 | 36.3 |
| (109) 30.7 | (139) 7.8 | (137) 5.5 | EBIT/Interest | (14) 3.1 | (18) 4.9 | (13) 7.1 | (26) 8.3 | (26) 2.9 | (40) 7.1 |
| | 7.0 | 2.1 | 1.1 | | -1.9 | 2.0 | 1.7 | 2.5 | -4.9 | 7.1 |
| | | 17.4 | Net Profit + Depr., Dep., | | | | | | 19.2 |
| | (18) | 2.9 | Amort./Cur. Mat. L/T/D | | | | | (10) | 2.7 |
| | | 1.1 | | | | | | | 1.1 |
| .0 | .0 | .1 | | .1 | .0 | .1 | .0 | .0 | .1 |
| .2 | .2 | .3 | Fixed/Worth | 1.2 | .2 | .2 | .1 | .4 | .4 |
| .6 | 1.0 | 1.4 | | -.4 | .9 | 2.4 | .8 | .7 | 1.7 |
| .4 | .5 | .4 | | .8 | .5 | .2 | .2 | .5 | .5 |
| 1.3 | 1.4 | 1.4 | Debt/Worth | 4.6 | 1.6 | 1.3 | .8 | 1.7 | 1.6 |
| 4.1 | 6.4 | 5.7 | | -2.5 | 5.4 | NM | 2.7 | 6.2 | 7.8 |
| 95.5 | 53.9 | 37.1 | % Profit Before Taxes/Tangible | | 63.2 | 43.6 | 36.5 | 27.7 | 31.8 |
| (129) 54.8 | (159) 30.3 | (139) 19.3 | Net Worth | | (19) 22.0 | (14) 21.4 | (34) 13.0 | (24) 16.1 | (39) 19.3 |
| 32.0 | 11.7 | 5.2 | | | 7.5 | -5.6 | 4.5 | -5.0 | 6.0 |
| 36.6 | 22.3 | 14.5 | % Profit Before Taxes/Total | 16.2 | 24.0 | 19.7 | 13.3 | 15.1 | 13.6 |
| 23.9 | 10.7 | 7.4 | Assets | 2.6 | 10.9 | 8.6 | 8.6 | 4.2 | 7.7 |
| 8.3 | 2.5 | -1.1 | | -15.7 | 1.9 | -8.3 | 1.0 | -4.0 | 1.1 |
| 149.5 | 248.2 | 102.9 | | 150.3 | 236.5 | 290.1 | 119.5 | 99.4 | 59.4 |
| 45.8 | 41.0 | 26.8 | Sales/Net Fixed Assets | 13.1 | 46.4 | 27.7 | 38.6 | 27.6 | 17.2 |
| 15.7 | 10.8 | 9.0 | | 7.9 | 10.5 | 15.5 | 12.2 | 12.1 | 5.8 |
| 3.2 | 2.9 | 2.9 | | 4.0 | 2.6 | 3.2 | 2.5 | 3.1 | 2.7 |
| 2.4 | 2.2 | 2.0 | Sales/Total Assets | 2.2 | 1.9 | 2.6 | 1.6 | 2.5 | 1.9 |
| 1.7 | 1.4 | 1.3 | | 1.0 | 1.1 | 1.3 | 1.2 | 1.8 | 1.5 |
| .3 | .3 | .3 | | .4 | .1 | .4 | .2 | .4 | .3 |
| (80) .9 | (94) .8 | (121) .8 | % Depr., Dep., Amort./Sales | (10) 1.4 | (14) 1.2 | (10) .7 | (27) .7 | (21) 1.3 | (39) .6 |
| 1.8 | 2.0 | 2.1 | | 3.9 | 3.6 | 2.7 | 1.5 | 2.6 | 1.2 |
| 2.0 | 1.5 | 1.4 | % Officers', Directors' | | 2.0 | | 1.6 | 1.0 | |
| (63) 3.6 | (70) 2.3 | (67) 2.3 | Owners' Comp/Sales | | (13) 3.1 | | (19) 2.6 | (17) 1.5 | |
| 5.7 | 4.0 | 4.3 | | | 5.0 | | 3.9 | 3.4 | |
| 3535481M | 4669028M | 4906413M | Net Sales ($) | 10329M | 42073M | 70619M | 272637M | 453659M | 4057096M |
| 1921918M | 2629229M | 2986240M | Total Assets ($) | 6758M | 27251M | 36334M | 173972M | 198735M | 2543190M |

M = $ thousand    MM = $ million
See Pages viii through xx for Explanation of Ratios and Data

© RMA 2024

# RETAIL—Musical Instrument and Supplies Retailers  NAICS 459140

## Current Data Sorted by Assets | Comparative Historical Data

| 0-500M | 500M-2MM | 2-10MM | 10-50MM | 50-100MM | 100-250MM | Type of Statement | | 4/1/19-3/31/20 ALL | | 4/1/20-3/31/21 ALL |
|---|---|---|---|---|---|---|---|---|---|---|
| 1 | 1 | 1 | 3 | 1 | | Unqualified | | 3 | | 6 |
| | 3 | 2 | 2 | | | Reviewed | | 5 | | 2 |
| | | 3 | 1 | | | Compiled | | 13 | | 5 |
| 2 | 3 | 9 | 8 | 4 | | Tax Returns | | 29 | | 21 |
| | 12 (4/1-9/30/23) | | 29 (10/1/23-3/31/24) | | | Other | | | | |
| 3 | 7 | 12 | 14 | 5 | | **NUMBER OF STATEMENTS** | | 50 | | 34 |
| % | % | % | % | % | % | **ASSETS** | | % | | % |
| | | 13.8 | 4.8 | | | Cash & Equivalents | | 12.7 | | 10.7 |
| | | 9.2 | 21.7 | | | Trade Receivables (net) | | 11.2 | | 14.3 |
| | | 61.5 | 34.8 | | | Inventory | | 50.9 | | 44.1 |
| | | 2.0 | 3.8 | | | All Other Current | | 2.0 | | 5.5 |
| | | 86.4 | 65.1 | | | Total Current | | 76.8 | | 74.6 |
| | | 10.2 | 20.6 | DATA | | Fixed Assets (net) | | 17.6 | | 16.4 |
| | | .3 | 1.5 | NOT | | Intangibles (net) | | 2.2 | | .5 |
| | | 3.1 | 12.8 | AVAILABLE | | All Other Non-Current | | 3.4 | | 8.5 |
| | | 100.0 | 100.0 | | | Total | | 100.0 | | 100.0 |
| | | | | | | **LIABILITIES** | | | | |
| | | 2.7 | 16.8 | | | Notes Payable-Short Term | | 9.5 | | 17.1 |
| | | .4 | 3.1 | | | Cur. Mat.-L.T.D. | | 3.1 | | 2.8 |
| | | 25.8 | 12.4 | | | Trade Payables | | 18.0 | | 8.9 |
| | | .1 | .0 | | | Income Taxes Payable | | .0 | | .0 |
| | | 17.5 | 7.2 | | | All Other Current | | 12.6 | | 17.4 |
| | | 46.4 | 39.5 | | | Total Current | | 43.2 | | 46.1 |
| | | 22.0 | 12.0 | | | Long-Term Debt | | 12.7 | | 20.8 |
| | | .1 | .0 | | | Deferred Taxes | | .3 | | .7 |
| | | 7.9 | 13.8 | | | All Other Non-Current | | 10.5 | | 9.6 |
| | | 23.5 | 34.7 | | | Net Worth | | 33.2 | | 22.8 |
| | | 100.0 | 100.0 | | | Total Liabilities & Net Worth | | 100.0 | | 100.0 |
| | | | | | | **INCOME DATA** | | | | |
| | | 100.0 | 100.0 | | | Net Sales | | 100.0 | | 100.0 |
| | | 41.9 | 50.5 | | | Gross Profit | | 46.5 | | 48.5 |
| | | 39.8 | 45.8 | | | Operating Expenses | | 43.1 | | 48.2 |
| | | 2.1 | 4.7 | | | Operating Profit | | 3.4 | | .3 |
| | | 1.6 | .3 | | | All Other Expenses (net) | | -.2 | | -1.5 |
| | | .5 | 4.4 | | | Profit Before Taxes | | 3.6 | | 1.8 |
| | | | | | | **RATIOS** | | | | |
| | | 3.6 | 2.8 | | | | | 4.7 | | 4.0 |
| | | 1.8 | 1.5 | | | Current | | 1.9 | | 2.6 |
| | | 1.5 | 1.1 | | | | | 1.2 | | 1.5 |
| | | 1.5 | 1.4 | | | | | 1.7 | | 1.4 |
| | | .4 | .5 | | | Quick | | .6 | | .7 |
| | | .2 | .2 | | | | | .2 | | .4 |
| | | 4  92.5 | 20  17.9 | | | | 1 | 501.7 | 5 | 76.6 |
| | | 10  36.4 | 48  7.6 | | | Sales/Receivables | 7 | 53.9 | 18 | 20.6 |
| | | 34  10.8 | 159  2.3 | | | | 26 | 14.2 | 57 | 6.4 |
| | | 192  1.9 | 174  2.1 | | | | 91 | 4.0 | 104 | 3.5 |
| | | 261  1.4 | 281  1.3 | | | Cost of Sales/Inventory | 174 | 2.1 | 203 | 1.8 |
| | | 365  1.0 | 365  1.0 | | | | 261 | 1.4 | 406 | .9 |
| | | 26  13.9 | 33  10.9 | | | | 4 | 92.0 | 21 | 17.8 |
| | | 111  3.3 | 89  4.1 | | | Cost of Sales/Payables | 28 | 13.1 | 29 | 12.5 |
| | | 174  2.1 | 114  3.2 | | | | 61 | 6.0 | 50 | 7.3 |
| | | 2.2 | 2.3 | | | | | 2.4 | | 2.0 |
| | | 6.9 | 5.5 | | | Sales/Working Capital | | 6.5 | | 3.8 |
| | | 8.3 | 10.3 | | | | | 23.4 | | 8.8 |
| | | 1.9 | 8.1 | | | | | 8.7 | | 16.0 |
| | | 1.4 | 3.3 | | | EBIT/Interest | (42) | 2.9 | (31) | 3.4 |
| | | -1.0 | 1.6 | | | | | 1.0 | | -.1 |
| | | | | | | Net Profit + Depr., Dep., Amort./Cur. Mat. L/T/D | | | | |
| | | .1 | .2 | | | | | .1 | | .1 |
| | | .7 | .6 | | | Fixed/Worth | | .3 | | .3 |
| | | 1.7 | 1.6 | | | | | 1.4 | | .8 |
| | | 1.2 | .9 | | | | | .7 | | .5 |
| | | 7.8 | 3.3 | | | Debt/Worth | | 1.9 | | 1.4 |
| | | 12.8 | 5.3 | | | | | 6.3 | | 4.3 |
| | | 30.1 | 24.9 | | | | | 40.4 | | 37.5 |
| | | 7.7 | (13) 18.4 | | | % Profit Before Taxes/Tangible Net Worth | (46) | 16.8 | (30) | 12.8 |
| | | -50.6 | 5.6 | | | | | .3 | | -2.8 |
| | | 4.8 | 8.0 | | | | | 13.1 | | 16.0 |
| | | 1.1 | 3.7 | | | % Profit Before Taxes/Total Assets | | 5.4 | | 4.1 |
| | | -6.5 | .8 | | | | | .0 | | -2.3 |
| | | 38.1 | 18.3 | | | | | 88.6 | | 70.9 |
| | | 16.7 | 6.8 | | | Sales/Net Fixed Assets | | 24.3 | | 25.7 |
| | | 10.6 | 2.3 | | | | | 7.6 | | 5.9 |
| | | 2.2 | 1.7 | | | | | 3.4 | | 2.7 |
| | | 1.7 | .9 | | | Sales/Total Assets | | 2.1 | | 1.5 |
| | | 1.1 | .7 | | | | | 1.3 | | 1.0 |
| | | | .7 | | | | | .4 | | .7 |
| | | 1.5 | | | | % Depr., Dep., Amort./Sales | (33) | 1.2 | (20) | 1.9 |
| | | | 8.4 | | | | | 3.7 | | 3.3 |
| | | | | | | | | 2.6 | | 1.2 |
| | | | | | | % Officers', Directors', Owners' Comp/Sales | (28) | 4.4 | (18) | 2.8 |
| | | | | | | | | 7.8 | | 6.2 |
| 2484M | 19418M | 131283M | 381524M | 346372M | | Net Sales ($) | | 921982M | | 367591M |
| 852M | 9121M | 60874M | 376458M | 279759M | | Total Assets ($) | | 396161M | | 278859M |

© RMA 2024    M = $ thousand    MM = $ million
See Pages viii through xx for Explanation of Ratios and Data

# RETAIL—Musical Instrument and Supplies Retailers  NAICS 459140

## Comparative Historical Data | Current Data Sorted by Sales

| Comparative Historical Data | | | | | | Current Data Sorted by Sales | | | | | |
|---|---|---|---|---|---|---|---|---|---|---|---|
| | | | | | Type of Statement | | | | | | |
| | 4 | | 10 | | 2 Unqualified | 2 | | | 1 | 2 | 2 |
| | 2 | | 7 | | 5 Reviewed | | 2 | | | 2 | 1 |
| | 7 | | 4 | | 5 Compiled | 1 | 1 | | 2 | | |
| | 14 | | 14 | | 25 Tax Returns | | 2 | 4 | 1 | 7 | 10 |
| | 18 | | | | Other | 1 | | | | | |
| | 4/1/21- | | 4/1/22- | | 4/1/23- | | 12 (4/1-9/30/23) | | 29 (10/1/23-3/31/24) | | |
| | 3/31/22 | | 3/31/23 | | 3/31/24 | 0-1MM | 1-3MM | 3-5MM | 5-10MM | 10-25MM | 25MM & OVER |
| | ALL | | ALL | | ALL | | | | | | |
| | 31 | | 35 | | 41 | 4 | 5 | 4 | 4 | 11 | 13 |

### ASSETS
| % | | % | | % | | % | % | % | % | % | % |
|---|---|---|---|---|---|---|---|---|---|---|---|
| 18.3 | | 11.5 | | 11.6 | Cash & Equivalents | | | | | 8.5 | 9.0 |
| 13.2 | | 16.3 | | 14.7 | Trade Receivables (net) | | | | | 12.3 | 20.1 |
| 45.5 | | 47.3 | | 44.9 | Inventory | | | | | 50.7 | 34.6 |
| 3.2 | | 2.4 | | 2.9 | All Other Current | | | | | 2.0 | 4.7 |
| 80.2 | | 77.5 | | 74.1 | Total Current | | | | | 73.6 | 68.4 |
| 12.5 | | 12.7 | | 15.6 | Fixed Assets (net) | | | | | 19.0 | 17.3 |
| .6 | | 2.7 | | 2.8 | Intangibles (net) | | | | | .7 | 2.3 |
| 6.8 | | 7.1 | | 7.5 | All Other Non-Current | | | | | 6.7 | 12.0 |
| 100.0 | | 100.0 | | 100.0 | Total | | | | | 100.0 | 100.0 |

### LIABILITIES
| | | | | | | | | | | | |
|---|---|---|---|---|---|---|---|---|---|---|---|
| 12.4 | | 8.6 | | 9.5 | Notes Payable-Short Term | | | | | 9.9 | 17.0 |
| 2.4 | | 2.1 | | 2.0 | Cur. Mat.-L.T.D. | | | | | 2.8 | 1.0 |
| 13.5 | | 16.1 | | 15.1 | Trade Payables | | | | | 22.5 | 15.7 |
| .0 | | .1 | | .0 | Income Taxes Payable | | | | | .0 | .1 |
| 6.7 | | 9.0 | | 10.5 | All Other Current | | | | | 8.6 | 8.4 |
| 34.9 | | 35.9 | | 37.2 | Total Current | | | | | 43.8 | 42.2 |
| 12.4 | | 8.3 | | 17.3 | Long-Term Debt | | | | | 17.2 | 12.6 |
| .7 | | .4 | | .0 | Deferred Taxes | | | | | .0 | .0 |
| 12.5 | | 11.6 | | 9.0 | All Other Non-Current | | | | | 11.8 | 5.7 |
| 39.6 | | 43.9 | | 36.5 | Net Worth | | | | | 27.3 | 39.5 |
| 100.0 | | 100.0 | | 100.0 | Total Liabilities & Net Worth | | | | | 100.0 | 100.0 |

### INCOME DATA
| | | | | | | | | | | | |
|---|---|---|---|---|---|---|---|---|---|---|---|
| 100.0 | | 100.0 | | 100.0 | Net Sales | | | | | 100.0 | 100.0 |
| 45.5 | | 43.6 | | 46.5 | Gross Profit | | | | | 51.7 | 44.5 |
| 42.3 | | 39.8 | | 41.7 | Operating Expenses | | | | | 47.8 | 39.2 |
| 3.1 | | 3.9 | | 4.9 | Operating Profit | | | | | 3.9 | 5.3 |
| -4.4 | | -.6 | | .4 | All Other Expenses (net) | | | | | 1.6 | -.5 |
| 7.6 | | 4.5 | | 4.5 | Profit Before Taxes | | | | | 2.3 | 5.8 |

### RATIOS
| | | | | | | | | | | | |
|---|---|---|---|---|---|---|---|---|---|---|---|
| 6.0 | | 3.9 | | 3.9 | Current | | | | | 2.2 | 2.8 |
| 2.5 | | 2.3 | | 2.2 | | | | | | 1.5 | 1.3 |
| 1.8 | | 1.6 | | 1.3 | | | | | | 1.4 | 1.2 |
| 3.3 | | 1.5 | | 1.5 | Quick | | | | | .9 | 1.1 |
| .8 | | .9 | | .7 | | | | | | .3 | .6 |
| .4 | | .3 | | .3 | | | | | | .2 | .4 |
| 3 | 120.9 | 4 | 87.6 | 6 | 59.3 | Sales/Receivables | | | 5 | 68.1 | 21 | 17.8 |
| 18 | 20.2 | 24 | 15.5 | 20 | 17.9 | | | | 10 | 35.5 | 37 | 9.9 |
| 55 | 6.6 | 68 | 5.4 | 81 | 4.5 | | | | 87 | 4.2 | 166 | 2.2 |
| 107 | 3.4 | 87 | 4.2 | 135 | 2.7 | Cost of Sales/Inventory | | | 203 | 1.8 | 96 | 3.8 |
| 215 | 1.7 | 174 | 2.1 | 243 | 1.5 | | | | 261 | 1.4 | 332 | 1.1 |
| 281 | 1.3 | 304 | 1.2 | 332 | 1.1 | | | | 281 | 1.3 | 365 | 1.0 |
| 15 | 24.7 | 24 | 15.5 | 25 | 14.5 | Cost of Sales/Payables | | | 17 | 22.0 | 31 | 11.8 |
| 48 | 7.6 | 42 | 8.6 | 51 | 7.1 | | | | 60 | 6.1 | 91 | 4.0 |
| 65 | 5.6 | 78 | 4.7 | 122 | 3.0 | | | | 182 | 2.0 | 215 | 1.7 |
| 1.9 | | 2.0 | | 2.8 | Sales/Working Capital | | | | | 2.6 | 4.2 |
| 3.2 | | 3.9 | | 4.8 | | | | | | 7.5 | 6.7 |
| 5.8 | | 9.5 | | 8.5 | | | | | | 11.5 | 8.5 |
| | 18.8 | | 23.1 | | 10.6 | EBIT/Interest | | | | 4.4 | | 32.8 |
| (25) | 6.9 | (28) | 5.4 | (37) | 2.0 | | | | | 1.6 | (12) | 3.8 |
| | 2.9 | | 1.1 | | 1.4 | | | | | .4 | | 2.0 |
| | | | | | Net Profit + Depr., Dep., Amort./Cur. Mat. L/T/D | | | | | | |
| | .0 | | .1 | | .1 | Fixed/Worth | | | | | .2 | .1 |
| | .3 | | .2 | | .6 | | | | | | 1.0 | .4 |
| | .5 | | .5 | | 1.6 | | | | | | 1.8 | 1.5 |
| | .4 | | .5 | | .5 | Debt/Worth | | | | | 1.4 | .7 |
| | 1.2 | | 1.2 | | 3.6 | | | | | | 6.7 | 3.6 |
| | 2.7 | | 2.9 | | 8.4 | | | | | | 13.5 | 4.5 |
| | 29.7 | | 30.5 | | 24.8 | % Profit Before Taxes/Tangible Net Worth | | | | | 28.6 | 23.4 |
| (28) | 17.6 | (31) | 14.6 | (38) | 16.9 | | | | | (10) 5.6 | 19.9 |
| | 9.3 | | 2.8 | | 2.0 | | | | | | -38.8 | 17.8 |
| | 17.3 | | 14.1 | | 9.7 | % Profit Before Taxes/Total Assets | | | | | 6.3 | 12.6 |
| | 8.7 | | 4.1 | | 3.7 | | | | | | 1.0 | 4.4 |
| | 5.2 | | .5 | | .5 | | | | | | -3.9 | 3.7 |
| | 100.0 | | 80.8 | | 30.0 | Sales/Net Fixed Assets | | | | | 20.8 | 24.8 |
| | 26.4 | | 22.8 | | 13.6 | | | | | | 15.4 | 8.2 |
| | 7.6 | | 8.4 | | 7.1 | | | | | | 5.3 | 2.2 |
| | 2.0 | | 2.6 | | 2.2 | Sales/Total Assets | | | | | 2.1 | 1.8 |
| | 1.5 | | 1.4 | | 1.6 | | | | | | 1.8 | .9 |
| | 1.2 | | 1.0 | | .9 | | | | | | 1.0 | .6 |
| | .5 | | .3 | | .9 | % Depr., Dep., Amort./Sales | | | | | .9 | .7 |
| (20) | 1.6 | (27) | 1.0 | (33) | 1.5 | | | | | (10) 1.1 | 1.5 |
| | 5.5 | | 4.3 | | 1.8 | | | | | | 8.4 | 1.7 |
| | 2.0 | | 1.1 | | 2.0 | % Officers', Directors', Owners' Comp/Sales | | | | | | |
| (14) | 4.2 | (14) | 2.2 | (19) | 2.9 | | | | | | | |
| | 5.7 | | 5.6 | | 4.0 | | | | | | | |
| | 251837M | | 528548M | | 881081M | Net Sales ($) | 3291M | 10402M | 16024M | 28121M | 163756M | 659487M |
| | 185087M | | 334737M | | 727064M | Total Assets ($) | 1420M | 8992M | 9180M | 27794M | 116218M | 563460M |

M = $ thousand    MM = $ million
See Pages viii through xx for Explanation of Ratios and Data
© RMA 2024

# RETAIL—Office Supplies and Stationery Retailers  NAICS 459410

## Current Data Sorted by Assets

| | | | | | | Type of Statement | | |
|---|---|---|---|---|---|---|---|---|
| | | | | | | Unqualified | | |
| | | 2 | | 1 | | Reviewed | | |
| 2 | 2 | 1 | 4 | | | Compiled | | |
| | 1 | 3 | 1 | | | Tax Returns | | |
| | 3 | 3 (4/1-9/30/23) | 6 | 3 | 1 | Other | | |
| 0-500M | 500M-2MM | 2-10MM | 10-50MM | 50-100MM | 100-250MM | | | |
| 2 | 6 | 11 | 21 (10/1/23-3/31/24) 4 | | 1 | | | |
| % | % | % | % | % | % | NUMBER OF STATEMENTS | | |

## Comparative Historical Data

| | | |
|---|---|---|
| 4 | 2 | |
| 2 | | |
| 5 | 3 | |
| 9 | 4 | |
| 27 | 17 | |
| 4/1/19-3/31/20 | 4/1/20-3/31/21 | |
| ALL | ALL | |
| 47 | 26 | |

| | 2-10MM | 10-50MM | | ASSETS | ALL (4/1/19-3/31/20) | ALL (4/1/20-3/31/21) |
|---|---|---|---|---|---|---|
| | % | % | | | % | % |
| | 12.1 | | D | Cash & Equivalents | 11.5 | 20.5 |
| | 25.6 | | A | Trade Receivables (net) | 29.6 | 27.9 |
| | 16.9 | | T | Inventory | 22.3 | 12.2 |
| | 8.5 | | A | All Other Current | 3.3 | 4.6 |
| | 63.2 | | | Total Current | 66.8 | 65.2 |
| | 23.7 | | N | Fixed Assets (net) | 15.7 | 12.3 |
| | 5.8 | | O | Intangibles (net) | 11.2 | 17.9 |
| | 7.2 | | T | All Other Non-Current | 6.3 | 4.6 |
| | 100.0 | | | Total | 100.0 | 100.0 |
| | | | A | **LIABILITIES** | | |
| | 5.2 | | V | Notes Payable-Short Term | 11.3 | 15.4 |
| | 2.5 | | A | Cur. Mat.-L.T.D. | 4.2 | 3.3 |
| | 13.3 | | I | Trade Payables | 19.9 | 19.5 |
| | .0 | | L | Income Taxes Payable | .0 | .0 |
| | 8.3 | | A | All Other Current | 14.6 | 12.2 |
| | 29.3 | | B | Total Current | 50.0 | 50.4 |
| | 24.7 | | L | Long-Term Debt | 20.5 | 27.2 |
| | .0 | | E | Deferred Taxes | .2 | .2 |
| | 4.7 | | | All Other Non-Current | 3.2 | 5.4 |
| | 41.3 | | | Net Worth | 26.0 | 16.8 |
| | 100.0 | | | Total Liabilities & Net Worth | 100.0 | 100.0 |
| | | | | **INCOME DATA** | | |
| | 100.0 | | | Net Sales | 100.0 | 100.0 |
| | 38.2 | | | Gross Profit | 41.3 | 40.8 |
| | 34.7 | | | Operating Expenses | 35.9 | 36.8 |
| | 3.6 | | | Operating Profit | 5.4 | 4.1 |
| | .0 | | | All Other Expenses (net) | .5 | -1.2 |
| | 3.6 | | | Profit Before Taxes | 4.8 | 5.3 |
| | | | | **RATIOS** | | |
| | 2.9 | | | | 2.6 | 3.1 |
| | 2.8 | | | Current | 1.5 | 1.7 |
| | 1.5 | | | | 1.2 | 1.0 |
| | 2.4 | | | | 1.4 | 2.0 |
| | 1.2 | | | Quick | (46) .9 | 1.2 |
| | .6 | | | | .6 | .8 |
| 20 | 18.4 | | | | 21  17.6 | 16  22.7 |
| 31 | 11.6 | | | Sales/Receivables | 29  12.7 | 30  12.3 |
| 38 | 9.7 | | | | 39  9.4 | 43  8.5 |
| 3 | 129.4 | | | | 6  56.4 | 4  84.7 |
| 29 | 12.4 | | | Cost of Sales/Inventory | 38  9.7 | 19  19.5 |
| 33 | 10.9 | | | | 118  3.1 | 45  8.2 |
| 9 | 42.3 | | | | 13  27.4 | 4  94.5 |
| 21 | 17.2 | | | Cost of Sales/Payables | 23  16.0 | 19  18.8 |
| 51 | 7.2 | | | | 40  9.2 | 40  9.2 |
| | 6.3 | | | | 6.6 | 5.6 |
| | 7.5 | | | Sales/Working Capital | 11.6 | 12.7 |
| | 11.1 | | | | 40.7 | NM |
| | | | | | 35.7 | 22.5 |
| | | | | EBIT/Interest | (43) 6.0 | (23) 5.4 |
| | | | | | 1.5 | 1.4 |
| | | | | Net Profit + Depr., Dep., Amort./Cur. Mat. L/T/D | | |
| | .1 | | | | .1 | .1 |
| | .3 | | | Fixed/Worth | .5 | .5 |
| | 3.5 | | | | 1.7 | NM |
| | .3 | | | | .8 | 1.4 |
| | 2.5 | | | Debt/Worth | 1.8 | 3.6 |
| | 6.8 | | | | 7.3 | -2.8 |
| | | | | | 67.9 | 131.9 |
| | | | | % Profit Before Taxes/Tangible Net Worth | (40) 33.1 | (18) 77.1 |
| | | | | | 7.6 | 14.6 |
| | 16.9 | | | | 21.5 | 37.0 |
| | 5.3 | | | % Profit Before Taxes/Total Assets | 9.9 | 14.5 |
| | -4.8 | | | | 1.1 | 1.8 |
| | 81.5 | | | | 141.8 | 149.8 |
| | 37.6 | | | Sales/Net Fixed Assets | 43.2 | 34.3 |
| | 19.0 | | | | 9.6 | 16.2 |
| | 3.8 | | | | 5.3 | 4.8 |
| | 3.2 | | | Sales/Total Assets | 3.8 | 3.1 |
| | 2.3 | | | | 1.6 | 1.7 |
| | | | | | .4 | .1 |
| | | | | % Depr., Dep., Amort./Sales | (23) .8 | (13) .8 |
| | | | | | 1.1 | 3.4 |
| | | | | | 1.6 | 1.3 |
| | | | | % Officers', Directors', Owners' Comp/Sales | (21) 3.2 | (12) 3.0 |
| | | | | | 5.6 | 7.2 |
| 1673M | 29421M | 138248M | 171405M | | 130136M | Net Sales ($) | 1325887M | 896863M |
| 602M | 6946M | 51470M | 94985M | | 187010M | Total Assets ($) | 883230M | 573337M |

M = $ thousand    MM = $ million
See Pages viii through xx for Explanation of Ratios and Data

© RMA 2024

# RETAIL—Office Supplies and Stationery Retailers NAICS 459410

## Comparative Historical Data

| | | | Type of Statement | | | | | | |
|---|---|---|---|---|---|---|---|---|---|
| 1 | 2 | | Unqualified | | | | 2 | 2 | 1 |
| 1 | 2 | 5 | Reviewed | | | 1 | 1 | | |
| 3 | 2 | 2 | Compiled | | | | 2 | | |
| 3 | 7 | 4 | Tax Returns | 1 | 1 | | | 3 | 3 |
| 15 | 12 | 13 | Other | | | 3 | 21 | | |
| 4/1/21-3/31/22 ALL | 4/1/22-3/31/23 ALL | 4/1/23-3/31/24 ALL | | 0-1MM | 1-3MM | 3 (4/1-9/30/23) 3-5MM | 21 (10/1/23-3/31/24) 5-10MM | 10-25MM | 25MM & OVER |
| 23 | 25 | 24 | NUMBER OF STATEMENTS | 1 | 2 | 3 | 9 | 5 | 4 |
| % | % | % | ASSETS | % | % | % | % | % | % |
| 22.2 | 16.5 | 10.1 | Cash & Equivalents | | | | | | |
| 25.2 | 18.1 | 24.5 | Trade Receivables (net) | | | | | | |
| 21.9 | 25.1 | 22.2 | Inventory | | | | | | |
| 1.9 | 3.6 | 9.3 | All Other Current | | | | | | |
| 71.2 | 63.2 | 66.2 | Total Current | | | | | | |
| 16.4 | 12.9 | 16.5 | Fixed Assets (net) | | | | | | |
| 8.1 | 12.7 | 9.4 | Intangibles (net) | | | | | | |
| 4.2 | 11.1 | 7.9 | All Other Non-Current | | | | | | |
| 100.0 | 100.0 | 100.0 | Total | | | | | | |
| | | | **LIABILITIES** | | | | | | |
| 5.1 | 6.4 | 6.2 | Notes Payable-Short Term | | | | | | |
| 1.9 | 3.7 | 3.5 | Cur. Mat.-L.T.D. | | | | | | |
| 14.6 | 9.7 | 11.8 | Trade Payables | | | | | | |
| .0 | .1 | .0 | Income Taxes Payable | | | | | | |
| 8.4 | 12.9 | 7.0 | All Other Current | | | | | | |
| 29.9 | 32.8 | 28.5 | Total Current | | | | | | |
| 12.9 | 27.2 | 27.1 | Long-Term Debt | | | | | | |
| .0 | .2 | .2 | Deferred Taxes | | | | | | |
| 10.7 | 4.2 | 5.5 | All Other Non-Current | | | | | | |
| 46.5 | 35.6 | 38.8 | Net Worth | | | | | | |
| 100.0 | 100.0 | 100.0 | Total Liabilities & Net Worth | | | | | | |
| | | | **INCOME DATA** | | | | | | |
| 100.0 | 100.0 | 100.0 | Net Sales | | | | | | |
| 40.6 | 36.5 | 37.7 | Gross Profit | | | | | | |
| 34.4 | 32.1 | 34.3 | Operating Expenses | | | | | | |
| 6.1 | 4.5 | 3.5 | Operating Profit | | | | | | |
| -1.8 | -.3 | .3 | All Other Expenses (net) | | | | | | |
| 8.0 | 4.7 | 3.2 | Profit Before Taxes | | | | | | |
| | | | **RATIOS** | | | | | | |
| 4.9 | 5.4 | 2.9 | | | | | | | |
| 2.8 | 2.1 | 2.7 | Current | | | | | | |
| 2.0 | 1.3 | 1.6 | | | | | | | |
| 3.6 | 2.7 | 1.9 | | | | | | | |
| 1.6 | 1.2 | 1.3 | Quick | | | | | | |
| 1.2 | .4 | .6 | | | | | | | |
| 14  25.3 | 3  115.0 | 19  19.5 | | | | | | | |
| 31  11.7 | 23  15.7 | 30  12.0 | Sales/Receivables | | | | | | |
| 45  8.2 | 39  9.3 | 40  9.1 | | | | | | | |
| 8  44.5 | 15  24.2 | 20  17.9 | | | | | | | |
| 49  7.5 | 37  9.9 | 31  11.7 | Cost of Sales/Inventory | | | | | | |
| 89  4.1 | 87  4.2 | 91  4.0 | | | | | | | |
| 13  27.9 | 2  197.3 | 9  41.1 | | | | | | | |
| 23  15.9 | 21  17.0 | 21  17.3 | Cost of Sales/Payables | | | | | | |
| 41  8.8 | 34  10.6 | 43  8.4 | | | | | | | |
| 3.4 | 4.3 | 5.7 | | | | | | | |
| 6.3 | 7.6 | 7.1 | Sales/Working Capital | | | | | | |
| 12.8 | 22.8 | 10.2 | | | | | | | |
| 70.7 | 52.4 | 4.6 | | | | | | | |
| (20) 24.9 | (22) 5.5 | (20) 1.2 | EBIT/Interest | | | | | | |
| 5.0 | 2.6 | -2.0 | | | | | | | |
| | | | Net Profit + Depr., Dep., Amort./Cur. Mat. L/T/D | | | | | | |
| .0 | .0 | .1 | | | | | | | |
| .3 | .3 | .3 | Fixed/Worth | | | | | | |
| 1.0 | NM | .9 | | | | | | | |
| .7 | .6 | .6 | | | | | | | |
| 1.0 | 1.6 | 2.4 | Debt/Worth | | | | | | |
| 2.7 | NM | 6.6 | | | | | | | |
| 83.7 | 55.1 | 36.6 | | | | | | | |
| (22) 57.6 | (19) 27.6 | (20) 10.7 | % Profit Before Taxes/Tangible Net Worth | | | | | | |
| 11.9 | 14.3 | -7.9 | | | | | | | |
| 33.9 | 20.5 | 13.3 | | | | | | | |
| 19.7 | 10.1 | 2.7 | % Profit Before Taxes/Total Assets | | | | | | |
| 5.8 | 3.5 | -5.3 | | | | | | | |
| 199.7 | 246.0 | 115.1 | | | | | | | |
| 41.0 | 31.7 | 38.9 | Sales/Net Fixed Assets | | | | | | |
| 10.0 | 11.9 | 12.9 | | | | | | | |
| 4.1 | 4.3 | 4.0 | | | | | | | |
| 2.4 | 2.9 | 3.0 | Sales/Total Assets | | | | | | |
| 1.9 | 1.5 | 1.9 | | | | | | | |
| .6 | .8 | .4 | | | | | | | |
| (13) .8 | (12) 1.3 | (17) 1.5 | % Depr., Dep., Amort./Sales | | | | | | |
| 1.8 | 3.3 | 2.1 | | | | | | | |
| 2.5 | .8 | .5 | | | | | | | |
| (10) 6.2 | (13) 2.4 | (10) 2.6 | % Officers', Directors' Owners' Comp/Sales | | | | | | |
| 9.9 | 7.4 | 5.3 | | | | | | | |
| 325805M | 460225M | 470883M | Net Sales ($) | 308M | 3459M | 11569M | 68757M | 93795M | 292995M |
| 126536M | 311471M | 341013M | Total Assets ($) | 107M | 1180M | 7243M | 30896M | 32612M | 268975M |

M = $ thousand    MM = $ million
See Pages viii through xx for Explanation of Ratios and Data

© RMA 2024

# RETAIL—Gift, Novelty, and Souvenir Retailers  NAICS 459420

## Current Data Sorted by Assets | Comparative Historical Data

| | | | | | | Type of Statement | | |
|---|---|---|---|---|---|---|---|---|
| | | | | | | Unqualified | 3 | |
| | | 3 | 1 | 4 | 1 | Reviewed | 4 | 1 |
| 6 | 8 | 1 | 1 | | | Compiled | 7 | 5 |
| 10 | 6 | 14 | 12 | 5 | 6 | Tax Returns | 22 | 20 |
| | 11 (4/1-9/30/23) | | 67 (10/1/23-3/31/24) | | | Other | 41 | 27 |
| 0-500M | 500M-2MM | 2-10MM | 10-50MM | 50-100MM | 100-250MM | | 4/1/19-3/31/20 | 4/1/20-3/31/21 |
| 16 | 17 | 16 | 17 | 6 | 6 | NUMBER OF STATEMENTS | ALL 77 | ALL 53 |
| % | % | % | % | % | % | ASSETS | % | % |
| 40.6 | 23.0 | 22.1 | 20.1 | | | Cash & Equivalents | 21.2 | 27.7 |
| 5.3 | 6.6 | 5.5 | 11.9 | | | Trade Receivables (net) | 7.5 | 6.3 |
| 36.5 | 32.3 | 26.5 | 18.9 | | | Inventory | 44.3 | 42.5 |
| .9 | 14.1 | 4.0 | 1.9 | | | All Other Current | 2.3 | .7 |
| 83.3 | 75.9 | 58.2 | 52.7 | | | Total Current | 75.3 | 77.2 |
| 11.7 | 17.3 | 22.3 | 21.0 | | | Fixed Assets (net) | 14.2 | 11.6 |
| 1.1 | 1.4 | 8.0 | 14.0 | | | Intangibles (net) | 4.7 | 5.2 |
| 3.9 | 5.3 | 11.5 | 12.2 | | | All Other Non-Current | 5.9 | 6.0 |
| 100.0 | 100.0 | 100.0 | 100.0 | | | Total | 100.0 | 100.0 |
| | | | | | | LIABILITIES | | |
| 3.4 | 6.4 | 5.8 | 4.6 | | | Notes Payable-Short Term | 8.9 | 14.9 |
| 8.4 | 1.5 | 1.6 | 2.0 | | | Cur. Mat.-L.T.D. | 1.6 | 2.0 |
| 8.4 | 12.8 | 5.9 | 8.9 | | | Trade Payables | 12.6 | 11.1 |
| .0 | .8 | .3 | .0 | | | Income Taxes Payable | .1 | .1 |
| 6.3 | 9.4 | 13.3 | 10.4 | | | All Other Current | 13.9 | 9.1 |
| 26.4 | 30.8 | 26.8 | 25.9 | | | Total Current | 37.1 | 37.2 |
| 68.4 | 29.0 | 11.3 | 16.4 | | | Long-Term Debt | 6.9 | 15.4 |
| .0 | .0 | .0 | .0 | | | Deferred Taxes | .0 | .4 |
| 20.6 | .0 | 3.5 | 7.9 | | | All Other Non-Current | 4.2 | 4.8 |
| -15.4 | 40.2 | 58.5 | 49.9 | | | Net Worth | 51.7 | 42.2 |
| 100.0 | 100.0 | 100.0 | 100.0 | | | Total Liabilities & Net Worth | 100.0 | 100.0 |
| | | | | | | INCOME DATA | | |
| 100.0 | 100.0 | 100.0 | 100.0 | | | Net Sales | 100.0 | 100.0 |
| 49.5 | 59.4 | 58.5 | 50.6 | | | Gross Profit | 50.5 | 51.0 |
| 40.6 | 52.2 | 47.5 | 42.0 | | | Operating Expenses | 44.3 | 43.6 |
| 8.9 | 7.2 | 11.1 | 8.5 | | | Operating Profit | 6.1 | 7.4 |
| .0 | .6 | .3 | -.1 | | | All Other Expenses (net) | .0 | -.4 |
| 8.9 | 6.6 | 10.7 | 8.6 | | | Profit Before Taxes | 6.2 | 7.8 |
| | | | | | | RATIOS | | |
| 16.9 | 9.9 | 5.0 | 3.9 | | | | 5.0 | 5.6 |
| 4.7 | 2.6 | 3.0 | 1.9 | | | Current | 2.6 | 3.0 |
| 1.6 | 1.6 | 1.1 | 1.2 | | | | 1.7 | 1.4 |
| 7.7 | 2.2 | 2.4 | 2.4 | | | | 2.1 | 2.6 |
| 2.4 | .7 | 1.2 | 1.4 | | | Quick | 1.0 | .9 |
| .8 | .3 | .3 | .3 | | | | .3 | .3 |
| 0 UND | 0 UND | 0 UND | 0 UND | | | | 0 UND | 0 UND |
| 0 UND | 1 311.0 | 1 564.0 | 4 90.1 | | | Sales/Receivables | 0 UND | 0 UND |
| 0 UND | 6 57.8 | 19 19.5 | 38 9.5 | | | | 4 104.0 | 14 25.6 |
| 25 14.5 | 38 9.6 | 6 65.5 | 35 10.5 | | | | 60 6.1 | 54 6.7 |
| 45 8.1 | 68 5.4 | 76 4.8 | 70 5.2 | | | Cost of Sales/Inventory | 114 3.2 | 122 3.0 |
| 118 3.1 | 135 2.7 | 182 2.0 | 152 2.4 | | | | 166 2.2 | 281 1.3 |
| 0 UND | 0 UND | 0 UND | 5 70.5 | | | | 1 325.7 | 6 66.0 |
| 0 UND | 14 26.9 | 2 211.2 | 21 17.3 | | | Cost of Sales/Payables | 26 14.2 | 17 21.0 |
| 19 19.5 | 55 6.6 | 27 13.3 | 49 7.4 | | | | 45 8.1 | 66 5.5 |
| 4.5 | 3.3 | 3.6 | 3.2 | | | | 4.8 | 2.6 |
| 7.6 | 7.7 | 8.7 | 9.1 | | | Sales/Working Capital | 6.7 | 5.0 |
| 27.8 | 23.8 | 38.2 | 34.9 | | | | 14.7 | 10.6 |
| 39.9 | 38.8 | 101.3 | 50.9 | | | | 42.3 | 17.2 |
| (12) 12.1 | (14) 8.9 | (14) 25.1 | (16) 17.1 | | | EBIT/Interest | (59) 11.4 | (36) 4.1 |
| 3.4 | .8 | 4.0 | 2.7 | | | | 1.4 | .4 |
| | | | | | | Net Profit + Depr., Dep., Amort./Cur. Mat. L/T/D | | |
| .0 | .0 | .1 | .1 | | | | .1 | .0 |
| .1 | .2 | .4 | .5 | | | Fixed/Worth | .2 | .2 |
| .8 | 2.3 | 1.3 | 1.4 | | | | .6 | 1.1 |
| .6 | .5 | .2 | .4 | | | | .3 | .3 |
| 3.0 | .9 | .6 | 1.0 | | | Debt/Worth | .7 | 1.0 |
| -5.9 | 40.8 | 3.6 | 4.9 | | | | 1.8 | 11.3 |
| 209.2 | 111.3 | 47.3 | 30.4 | | | % Profit Before Taxes/Tangible Net Worth | 70.0 | 70.2 |
| (11) 153.5 | (14) 40.5 | (14) 29.5 | (14) 18.6 | | | | (68) 26.8 | (43) 19.7 |
| 25.9 | .6 | 8.8 | 9.6 | | | | 3.6 | 3.9 |
| 99.9 | 53.7 | 36.8 | 16.5 | | | % Profit Before Taxes/Total Assets | 44.5 | 30.2 |
| 40.6 | 32.1 | 19.4 | 8.0 | | | | 17.9 | 10.3 |
| 7.4 | .6 | 6.2 | 3.7 | | | | 2.0 | .6 |
| UND | 577.7 | 113.0 | 23.4 | | | Sales/Net Fixed Assets | 123.8 | 159.6 |
| 62.4 | 22.3 | 29.0 | 12.1 | | | | 37.0 | 44.5 |
| 28.8 | 10.8 | 5.7 | 3.7 | | | | 15.7 | 12.4 |
| 8.0 | 5.2 | 3.7 | 2.0 | | | | 4.5 | 3.0 |
| 4.2 | 3.3 | 2.1 | 1.6 | | | Sales/Total Assets | 3.0 | 2.0 |
| 2.6 | 1.5 | 1.1 | .8 | | | | 2.1 | 1.4 |
| | | .1 | .7 | | | | .3 | .3 |
| | (10) | .5 | 1.2 | | | % Depr., Dep., Amort./Sales | (55) .7 | (29) .9 |
| | | 1.0 | 2.9 | | | | 1.3 | 2.2 |
| | 1.8 | | | | | | 1.9 | 2.4 |
| | (12) 3.8 | | | | | % Officers', Directors' Owners' Comp/Sales | (37) 3.7 | (26) 5.7 |
| | 14.7 | | | | | | 7.0 | 9.3 |
| 20778M | 58846M | 170116M | 628093M | 857109M | 1579897M | Net Sales ($) | 783284M | 1287294M |
| 4166M | 17992M | 71512M | 368383M | 445507M | 1022957M | Total Assets ($) | 355269M | 612239M |

M = $ thousand   MM = $ million
See Pages viii through xx for Explanation of Ratios and Data

© RMA 2024

# RETAIL—Gift, Novelty, and Souvenir Retailers  NAICS 459420

## Comparative Historical Data | Current Data Sorted by Sales

| | | | | Type of Statement | | | | | | |
|---|---|---|---|---|---|---|---|---|---|---|
| 2 | 2 | | | Unqualified | | | | 2 | 1 | 3 |
| 4 | 5 | 6 | | Reviewed | | | | | | 1 |
| 3 | 7 | 4 | | Compiled | 1 | 2 | | 3 | | |
| 15 | 16 | 15 | | Tax Returns | 3 | 6 | 3 | 3 | 6 | 19 |
| 25 | 34 | 53 | | Other | 5 | 6 | 7 | 5 | 11 | |
| 4/1/21-3/31/22 ALL | 4/1/22-3/31/23 ALL | 4/1/23-3/31/24 ALL | | | | 11 (4/1-9/30/23) | | 67 (10/1/23-3/31/24) | | |
| | | | | | 0-1MM | 1-3MM | 3-5MM | 5-10MM | 10-25MM | 25MM & OVER |
| 49 | 64 | 78 | | NUMBER OF STATEMENTS | 9 | 14 | 10 | 10 | 12 | 23 |
| % | % | % | | ASSETS | % | % | % | % | % | % |
| 30.0 | 21.8 | 24.0 | | Cash & Equivalents | 33.1 | 17.2 | 16.1 | 19.8 | 19.7 | |
| 9.3 | 8.6 | 6.9 | | Trade Receivables (net) | 8.5 | 8.3 | 1.4 | 13.3 | 6.7 | |
| 34.5 | 38.7 | 27.9 | | Inventory | 31.4 | 32.8 | 25.3 | 21.3 | 24.8 | |
| 2.7 | 3.6 | 4.9 | | All Other Current | 4.7 | 8.5 | 3.2 | 3.6 | 2.9 | |
| 76.5 | 72.8 | 63.7 | | Total Current | 77.7 | 66.8 | 46.0 | 58.0 | 54.0 | |
| 13.5 | 9.3 | 19.1 | | Fixed Assets (net) | 18.6 | 25.4 | 20.9 | 25.1 | 18.9 | |
| 4.3 | 5.2 | 9.4 | | Intangibles (net) | 2.0 | 1.6 | 17.3 | 10.8 | 16.6 | |
| 5.6 | 12.8 | 7.8 | | All Other Non-Current | 1.7 | 6.2 | 15.7 | 6.2 | 10.4 | |
| 100.0 | 100.0 | 100.0 | | Total | 100.0 | 100.0 | 100.0 | 100.0 | 100.0 | |
| | | | | LIABILITIES | | | | | | |
| 6.8 | 7.8 | 5.0 | | Notes Payable-Short Term | 6.7 | 3.3 | 5.1 | 6.8 | 4.1 | |
| 2.9 | 1.1 | 3.2 | | Cur. Mat.-L.T.D. | 4.9 | 9.3 | 2.6 | 1.4 | 1.9 | |
| 10.2 | 10.1 | 8.9 | | Trade Payables | 10.7 | 5.1 | 13.2 | 10.7 | 9.2 | |
| .1 | .1 | .3 | | Income Taxes Payable | .3 | 1.0 | .0 | .0 | .1 | |
| 6.1 | 10.8 | 10.2 | | All Other Current | 10.0 | 8.1 | 12.7 | 10.9 | 12.7 | |
| 26.2 | 29.8 | 27.6 | | Total Current | 32.6 | 26.8 | 33.6 | 29.8 | 28.1 | |
| 28.7 | 14.7 | 31.5 | | Long-Term Debt | 42.6 | 70.3 | 22.1 | 9.8 | 25.2 | |
| .0 | .0 | .0 | | Deferred Taxes | .0 | .0 | .0 | .0 | .1 | |
| 4.2 | 8.3 | 7.3 | | All Other Non-Current | 1.9 | .0 | 2.3 | 5.1 | 6.7 | |
| 40.9 | 47.2 | 33.6 | | Net Worth | 23.0 | 2.9 | 42.0 | 55.3 | 40.0 | |
| 100.0 | 100.0 | 100.0 | | Total Liabilities & Net Worth | 100.0 | 100.0 | 100.0 | 100.0 | 100.0 | |
| | | | | INCOME DATA | | | | | | |
| 100.0 | 100.0 | 100.0 | | Net Sales | 100.0 | 100.0 | 100.0 | 100.0 | 100.0 | |
| 48.3 | 49.5 | 54.2 | | Gross Profit | 56.1 | 56.1 | 58.3 | 50.7 | 53.0 | |
| 37.7 | 42.7 | 45.8 | | Operating Expenses | 46.3 | 46.5 | 43.8 | 40.8 | 47.9 | |
| 10.6 | 6.8 | 8.4 | | Operating Profit | 9.9 | 9.6 | 14.5 | 9.9 | 5.1 | |
| -1.0 | -.1 | .4 | | All Other Expenses (net) | 1.0 | .5 | -.1 | .3 | .5 | |
| 11.6 | 6.8 | 8.0 | | Profit Before Taxes | 8.9 | 9.1 | 14.5 | 9.6 | 4.6 | |
| | | | | RATIOS | | | | | | |
| 11.5 | 7.6 | 4.7 | | | 9.5 | 11.9 | 4.4 | 3.3 | 3.8 | |
| 3.5 | 2.8 | 2.4 | | Current | 2.3 | 3.3 | 1.3 | 2.2 | 1.9 | |
| 1.7 | 1.4 | 1.1 | | | 1.4 | 1.0 | .5 | 1.2 | .9 | |
| 5.4 | 2.6 | 2.6 | | | 3.3 | 4.3 | 1.0 | 2.0 | 2.4 | |
| 1.9 | .9 | 1.1 | | Quick | 1.3 | 1.5 | .4 | 1.2 | .8 | |
| .8 | .3 | .4 | | | .7 | .4 | .3 | .2 | .3 | |
| 0 UND | 0 UND | 0 UND | | | 0 UND | 0 UND | 0 UND | 0 UND | 1 322.2 | |
| 0 UND | 1 292.5 | 1 283.9 | | Sales/Receivables | 0 UND | 3 104.3 | 0 UND | 1 564.0 | 4 90.1 | |
| 12 29.9 | 15 23.9 | 10 37.7 | | | 6 56.4 | 19 19.4 | 3 139.2 | 20 18.3 | 30 12.2 | |
| 34 10.6 | 51 7.1 | 37 9.8 | | | 22 16.3 | 17 21.4 | 0 UND | 20 18.1 | 56 6.5 | |
| 85 4.3 | 122 3.0 | 73 5.0 | | Cost of Sales/Inventory | 49 7.4 | 39 9.3 | 76 4.8 | 72 5.1 | 89 4.1 | |
| 174 2.1 | 174 2.1 | 146 2.5 | | | 174 2.1 | 83 4.4 | 182 2.0 | 135 2.7 | 182 2.0 | |
| 2 188.8 | 0 UND | 0 UND | | | 0 UND | 0 UND | 0 UND | 4 100.5 | 19 19.1 | |
| 16 22.9 | 23 16.1 | 15 24.6 | | Cost of Sales/Payables | 4 83.0 | 0 UND | 8 45.7 | 21 17.1 | 35 10.4 | |
| 39 9.4 | 41 8.9 | 43 8.5 | | | 68 5.4 | 5 72.3 | 46 7.9 | 40 9.2 | 54 6.7 | |
| 3.1 | 2.9 | 4.1 | | | 5.2 | 5.4 | 10.0 | 7.4 | 2.5 | |
| 5.9 | 5.4 | 8.7 | | Sales/Working Capital | 6.8 | 8.4 | 36.0 | 9.2 | 8.6 | |
| 12.3 | 12.6 | 39.5 | | | 71.6 | NM | -11.7 | 23.6 | -108.2 | |
| 61.9 | 21.2 | 36.0 | | | 44.5 | | 58.2 | 82.7 | 23.2 | |
| (32) 12.9 | (40) 5.9 | (68) 8.6 | | EBIT/Interest | (12) 14.6 | | 20.7 | (10) 30.4 | (22) 5.7 | |
| 3.7 | 2.1 | 2.4 | | | 2.1 | | 8.7 | 3.8 | .4 | |
| | | | | Net Profit + Depr., Dep., Amort./Cur. Mat. L/T/D | | | | | | |
| .0 | .0 | .1 | | | .0 | .0 | .3 | .2 | .2 | |
| .2 | .2 | .5 | | Fixed/Worth | .4 | .8 | 1.9 | .5 | .6 | |
| 1.0 | .6 | 2.9 | | | 1.4 | NM | -.7 | 1.0 | -1.4 | |
| .4 | .3 | .5 | | | .4 | .4 | .4 | .3 | .5 | |
| 1.5 | 1.2 | 1.4 | | Debt/Worth | 1.1 | 1.2 | 3.8 | .8 | 3.4 | |
| 12.2 | 3.3 | NM | | | NM | NM | -4.0 | 3.8 | -4.4 | |
| 105.1 | 65.3 | 75.9 | | % Profit Before Taxes/Tangible Net Worth | 209.2 | | | 63.1 | 27.8 | |
| (39) 61.7 | (55) 37.1 | (59) 25.9 | | | (11) 65.6 | | | 33.9 | (15) 19.3 | |
| 23.9 | 12.4 | 11.4 | | | 11.5 | | | 11.3 | 11.0 | |
| 51.0 | 31.8 | 37.4 | | % Profit Before Taxes/Total Assets | 96.2 | 60.5 | 54.6 | 36.8 | 16.5 | |
| 16.5 | 11.9 | 12.0 | | | 16.5 | 33.1 | 33.9 | 10.1 | 5.9 | |
| 7.7 | 4.1 | 3.8 | | | 2.3 | 5.6 | 9.9 | 6.6 | -2.2 | |
| 832.7 | 231.2 | 90.1 | | Sales/Net Fixed Assets | UND | 357.3 | 90.1 | 35.2 | 23.8 | |
| 60.0 | 38.9 | 22.2 | | | 31.9 | 47.1 | 13.3 | 15.0 | 11.0 | |
| 14.3 | 14.7 | 6.6 | | | 11.8 | 3.8 | 8.4 | 2.9 | 5.6 | |
| 3.9 | 3.5 | 4.2 | | Sales/Total Assets | 5.9 | 5.3 | 5.2 | 3.7 | 2.3 | |
| 2.6 | 2.2 | 2.1 | | | 3.1 | 3.5 | 2.2 | 2.2 | 1.6 | |
| 1.4 | 1.4 | 1.4 | | | 1.7 | 1.9 | 1.0 | .9 | 1.3 | |
| .3 | .4 | .5 | | | | | | .1 | .9 | |
| (26) .8 | (41) .8 | (46) .9 | | % Depr., Dep., Amort./Sales | | | | (11) .8 | (17) 1.3 | |
| 2.1 | 1.5 | 1.7 | | | | | | .9 | 2.1 | |
| 1.5 | .9 | 2.1 | | % Officers', Directors', Owners' Comp/Sales | | | | | | |
| (19) 5.2 | (23) 3.9 | (28) 3.9 | | | | | | | | |
| 10.7 | 11.2 | 11.0 | | | | | | | | |
| 1160647M | 2228705M | 3314839M | | Net Sales ($) | 4961M | 25206M | 39052M | 61218M | 190250M | 2994152M |
| 550808M | 1211325M | 1930517M | | Total Assets ($) | 3402M | 9818M | 19255M | 39788M | 123763M | 1734491M |

M = $ thousand   MM = $ million
See Pages viii through xx for Explanation of Ratios and Data
© RMA 2024

# RETAIL—Used Merchandise Retailers  NAICS 459510

## Current Data Sorted by Assets | Comparative Historical Data

| | | | | | | Type of Statement | | |
|---|---|---|---|---|---|---|---|---|
| | | | 1 | 1 | 1 | Unqualified | 7 | 2 |
| | | | | 2 | | Reviewed | 1 | 2 |
| | 2 | 1 | 2 | | | Compiled | 8 | 1 |
| 2 | 2 | 2 | | 1 | | Tax Returns | 11 | 10 |
| 5 | 2 | 8 | 6 | 5 | 1 | Other | 37 | 26 |
| 0-500M | 4 (4/1-9/30/23) 500M-2MM | 2-10MM | 38 (10/1/23-3/31/24) 10-50MM | 50-100MM | 100-250MM | | 4/1/19-3/31/20 ALL | 4/1/20-3/31/21 ALL |
| 7 | 6 | 11 | 8 | 8 | 2 | NUMBER OF STATEMENTS | 64 | 41 |
| % | % | % | % | % | % | ASSETS | % | % |
| | | 21.7 | | | | Cash & Equivalents | 16.5 | 25.3 |
| | | 16.1 | | | | Trade Receivables (net) | 9.8 | 10.3 |
| | | 39.3 | | | | Inventory | 27.9 | 22.4 |
| | | 7.3 | | | | All Other Current | 5.3 | 4.6 |
| | | 84.4 | | | | Total Current | 59.4 | 62.6 |
| | | 5.8 | | | | Fixed Assets (net) | 20.4 | 24.2 |
| | | 5.5 | | | | Intangibles (net) | 2.0 | 6.2 |
| | | 4.2 | | | | All Other Non-Current | 18.2 | 7.0 |
| | | 100.0 | | | | Total | 100.0 | 100.0 |
| | | | | | | LIABILITIES | | |
| | | 9.5 | | | | Notes Payable-Short Term | 7.1 | 3.6 |
| | | .9 | | | | Cur. Mat.-L.T.D. | 2.1 | 1.9 |
| | | 2.9 | | | | Trade Payables | 6.9 | 4.1 |
| | | .2 | | | | Income Taxes Payable | .0 | .1 |
| | | 10.8 | | | | All Other Current | 15.8 | 12.7 |
| | | 24.3 | | | | Total Current | 31.8 | 22.5 |
| | | 11.8 | | | | Long-Term Debt | 13.8 | 19.1 |
| | | .0 | | | | Deferred Taxes | .2 | .2 |
| | | 10.9 | | | | All Other Non-Current | 6.0 | 7.5 |
| | | 52.9 | | | | Net Worth | 48.1 | 50.7 |
| | | 100.0 | | | | Total Liabilities & Net Worth | 100.0 | 100.0 |
| | | | | | | INCOME DATA | | |
| | | 100.0 | | | | Net Sales | 100.0 | 100.0 |
| | | 52.1 | | | | Gross Profit | 56.9 | 53.2 |
| | | 48.2 | | | | Operating Expenses | 50.3 | 47.3 |
| | | 3.9 | | | | Operating Profit | 6.6 | 5.9 |
| | | 1.4 | | | | All Other Expenses (net) | .9 | -.5 |
| | | 2.6 | | | | Profit Before Taxes | 5.7 | 6.4 |
| | | | | | | RATIOS | | |
| | | 5.2 | | | | | 8.8 | 8.1 |
| | | 4.4 | | | | Current | 2.1 | 4.5 |
| | | 2.3 | | | | | 1.0 | 2.3 |
| | | 3.0 | | | | | 2.5 | 5.2 |
| | | 1.2 | | | | Quick | .9 | 2.2 |
| | | .6 | | | | | .4 | 1.0 |
| | 0 | UND | | | | | 0 UND | 0 UND |
| | 43 | 8.4 | | | | Sales/Receivables | 0 849.1 | 4 87.5 |
| | 135 | 2.7 | | | | | 16 22.3 | 34 10.8 |
| | 63 | 5.8 | | | | | 13 28.7 | 22 16.5 |
| | 182 | 2.0 | | | | Cost of Sales/Inventory | 45 8.1 | 89 4.1 |
| | 281 | 1.3 | | | | | 118 3.1 | 159 2.3 |
| | 0 | 999.8 | | | | | 0 UND | 0 UND |
| | 4 | 88.1 | | | | Cost of Sales/Payables | 6 63.3 | 3 131.6 |
| | 59 | 6.2 | | | | | 30 12.2 | 45 8.1 |
| | | 2.2 | | | | | 4.5 | 2.9 |
| | | 2.9 | | | | Sales/Working Capital | 12.9 | 5.0 |
| | | 5.8 | | | | | 211.7 | 11.8 |
| | | 16.3 | | | | | 34.7 | 30.2 |
| | (10) | 1.9 | | | | EBIT/Interest | (41) 5.3 | (32) 10.0 |
| | | -1.5 | | | | | .4 | 2.1 |
| | | | | | | Net Profit + Depr., Dep., Amort./Cur. Mat. L/T/D | | |
| | | .0 | | | | | .0 | .1 |
| | | .1 | | | | Fixed/Worth | .2 | .3 |
| | | .2 | | | | | 1.0 | 1.5 |
| | | .4 | | | | | .2 | .2 |
| | | 1.1 | | | | Debt/Worth | .6 | .7 |
| | | 1.5 | | | | | 5.6 | 4.3 |
| | | 41.0 | | | | | 68.6 | 49.4 |
| | (10) | 14.5 | | | | % Profit Before Taxes/Tangible Net Worth | (51) 25.0 | (36) 18.4 |
| | | -9.5 | | | | | 9.6 | 2.3 |
| | | 19.2 | | | | | 31.3 | 25.6 |
| | | 5.2 | | | | % Profit Before Taxes/Total Assets | 11.4 | 11.4 |
| | | -5.4 | | | | | 2.3 | 1.2 |
| | | 115.5 | | | | | 143.7 | 78.8 |
| | | 20.9 | | | | Sales/Net Fixed Assets | 26.3 | 13.8 |
| | | 16.2 | | | | | 12.6 | 5.0 |
| | | 4.3 | | | | | 4.3 | 3.1 |
| | | 1.7 | | | | Sales/Total Assets | 2.7 | 1.7 |
| | | .8 | | | | | 1.3 | 1.2 |
| | | | | | | % Depr., Dep., Amort./Sales | .5 | .9 |
| | | | | | | | (37) .8 | (21) 1.8 |
| | | | | | | | 2.0 | 3.0 |
| | | | | | | % Officers', Directors' Owners' Comp/Sales | 3.0 | 2.0 |
| | | | | | | | (16) 5.9 | (10) 4.3 |
| | | | | | | | 15.8 | 7.0 |
| 14983M | 15706M | 137720M | 933498M | 824736M | 598994M | Net Sales ($) | 1353990M | 1282548M |
| 1769M | 5568M | 64061M | 175277M | 536259M | 378232M | Total Assets ($) | 688410M | 959547M |

M = $ thousand    MM = $ million
See Pages viii through xx for Explanation of Ratios and Data

© RMA 2024

# RETAIL—Used Merchandise Retailers  NAICS 459510

## Comparative Historical Data | Current Data Sorted by Sales

| | | | | | | | Type of Statement | | | | | | |
|---|---|---|---|---|---|---|---|---|---|---|---|---|---|
| | 2 | | 6 | | 3 | | Unqualified | | | | | 1 | 2 |
| | 2 | | 2 | | 2 | | Reviewed | | | | | 1 | 1 |
| | 2 | | | | 3 | | Compiled | | | | 2 | | |
| | 11 | | 11 | | 7 | | Tax Returns | 1 | 2 | | 2 | 2 | 1 |
| | 25 | | 21 | | 27 | | Other | 4 | 3 | | 4 | 5 | 11 |
| | 4/1/21-3/31/22 | | 4/1/22-3/31/23 | | 4/1/23-3/31/24 | | | 4 (4/1-9/30/23) | | | 38 (10/1/23-3/31/24) | | |
| | ALL | | ALL | | ALL | | | 0-1MM | 1-3MM | 3-5MM | 5-10MM | 10-25MM | 25MM & OVER |
| | 42 | | 40 | | 42 | | NUMBER OF STATEMENTS | 6 | 6 | | 6 | 9 | 15 |
| | % | | % | | % | | ASSETS | % | % | % | % | % | % |
| | 20.5 | | 18.1 | | 22.6 | | Cash & Equivalents | | | | | | 32.7 |
| | 7.8 | | 6.6 | | 10.5 | | Trade Receivables (net) | | | | | | 5.6 |
| | 28.4 | | 33.9 | | 32.5 | | Inventory | | | | | | 28.6 |
| | 7.3 | | 5.2 | | 5.0 | | All Other Current | | | | | | 2.2 |
| | 64.0 | | 63.7 | | 70.6 | | Total Current | | | | | | 69.1 |
| | 19.0 | | 21.4 | | 16.2 | | Fixed Assets (net) | | | | | | 13.9 |
| | 5.4 | | 2.9 | | 4.4 | | Intangibles (net) | | | DATA NOT AVAILABLE | | | 6.0 |
| | 11.5 | | 12.0 | | 8.8 | | All Other Non-Current | | | | | | 11.0 |
| | 100.0 | | 100.0 | | 100.0 | | Total | | | | | | 100.0 |
| | | | | | | | LIABILITIES | | | | | | |
| | 3.8 | | 3.4 | | 6.6 | | Notes Payable-Short Term | | | | | | 5.4 |
| | 2.8 | | 4.1 | | 2.5 | | Cur. Mat.-L.T.D. | | | | | | 5.3 |
| | 5.4 | | 5.6 | | 6.9 | | Trade Payables | | | | | | 8.8 |
| | .0 | | .0 | | .1 | | Income Taxes Payable | | | | | | .1 |
| | 17.4 | | 8.9 | | 12.1 | | All Other Current | | | | | | 12.6 |
| | 29.5 | | 21.9 | | 28.2 | | Total Current | | | | | | 32.2 |
| | 28.5 | | 16.1 | | 11.4 | | Long-Term Debt | | | | | | 15.9 |
| | .2 | | .2 | | .4 | | Deferred Taxes | | | | | | .0 |
| | 6.1 | | 3.9 | | 6.1 | | All Other Non-Current | | | | | | 3.6 |
| | 35.7 | | 57.9 | | 53.9 | | Net Worth | | | | | | 48.3 |
| | 100.0 | | 100.0 | | 100.0 | | Total Liabilities & Net Worth | | | | | | 100.0 |
| | | | | | | | INCOME DATA | | | | | | |
| | 100.0 | | 100.0 | | 100.0 | | Net Sales | | | | | | 100.0 |
| | 54.3 | | 50.8 | | 49.1 | | Gross Profit | | | | | | 48.7 |
| | 46.1 | | 44.0 | | 42.1 | | Operating Expenses | | | | | | 42.3 |
| | 8.1 | | 6.8 | | 7.1 | | Operating Profit | | | | | | 6.3 |
| | -.8 | | -.3 | | .9 | | All Other Expenses (net) | | | | | | 1.5 |
| | 9.0 | | 7.1 | | 6.2 | | Profit Before Taxes | | | | | | 4.9 |
| | | | | | | | RATIOS | | | | | | |
| | 7.2 | | 6.8 | | 5.4 | | | | | | | | 10.9 |
| | 3.8 | | 3.0 | | 2.9 | | Current | | | | | | 2.3 |
| | 2.0 | | 2.2 | | 1.8 | | | | | | | | .9 |
| | 3.4 | | 2.4 | | 3.0 | | | | | | | | 10.8 |
| | 1.6 | | 1.4 | | 1.3 | | Quick | | | | | | 1.1 |
| | .5 | | .7 | | .6 | | | | | | | | .3 |
| 0 | UND | 0 | UND | 0 | UND | | | | | | | 0 | 791.4 |
| 5 | 80.3 | 5 | 74.5 | 3 | 123.6 | | Sales/Receivables | | | | | 4 | 85.0 |
| 17 | 21.1 | 18 | 19.8 | 51 | 7.1 | | | | | | | 10 | 36.6 |
| 25 | 14.4 | 27 | 13.5 | 17 | 21.5 | | | | | | | 5 | 68.8 |
| 118 | 3.1 | 111 | 3.3 | 85 | 4.3 | | Cost of Sales/Inventory | | | | | 70 | 5.2 |
| 203 | 1.8 | 174 | 2.1 | 261 | 1.4 | | | | | | | 140 | 2.6 |
| 1 | 301.5 | 1 | 431.9 | 1 | 247.8 | | | | | | | 2 | 234.2 |
| 12 | 31.1 | 14 | 26.1 | 6 | 57.0 | | Cost of Sales/Payables | | | | | 22 | 16.3 |
| 29 | 12.6 | 34 | 10.6 | 39 | 9.3 | | | | | | | 47 | 7.7 |
| | 3.3 | | 2.9 | | 2.5 | | | | | | | | 5.5 |
| | 4.8 | | 4.7 | | 5.7 | | Sales/Working Capital | | | | | | 12.7 |
| | 12.6 | | 10.7 | | 16.1 | | | | | | | | -34.0 |
| | 56.6 | | 58.0 | | 18.6 | | | | | | | | 90.8 |
| (38) | 18.3 | (33) | 15.2 | (33) | 6.3 | | EBIT/Interest | | | | | (12) | 5.5 |
| | 3.4 | | 3.2 | | -.9 | | | | | | | | -6.7 |
| | | | | | | | Net Profit + Depr., Dep., Amort./Cur. Mat. L/T/D | | | | | | |
| | .1 | | .0 | | .1 | | | | | | | | .1 |
| | .3 | | .2 | | .2 | | Fixed/Worth | | | | | | .4 |
| | 1.4 | | .6 | | .8 | | | | | | | | 2.8 |
| | .3 | | .3 | | .3 | | | | | | | | .1 |
| | .8 | | .6 | | .7 | | Debt/Worth | | | | | | 1.0 |
| | 6.0 | | 1.6 | | 2.4 | | | | | | | | 17.8 |
| | 59.0 | | 57.4 | | 47.1 | | | | | | | | 55.7 |
| (33) | 33.6 | (38) | 30.8 | (38) | 24.0 | | % Profit Before Taxes/Tangible Net Worth | | | | | (13) | 26.4 |
| | 13.0 | | 5.6 | | .5 | | | | | | | | -63.3 |
| | 37.2 | | 31.7 | | 28.6 | | | | | | | | 32.1 |
| | 17.7 | | 12.2 | | 13.9 | | % Profit Before Taxes/Total Assets | | | | | | 16.1 |
| | 5.1 | | 3.4 | | -3.1 | | | | | | | | -8.8 |
| | 118.5 | | 104.7 | | 125.4 | | | | | | | | 86.0 |
| | 14.7 | | 18.2 | | 19.6 | | Sales/Net Fixed Assets | | | | | | 14.1 |
| | 5.8 | | 8.2 | | 7.5 | | | | | | | | 8.5 |
| | 3.0 | | 3.3 | | 4.9 | | | | | | | | 4.5 |
| | 1.8 | | 2.1 | | 2.0 | | Sales/Total Assets | | | | | | 2.4 |
| | 1.1 | | 1.3 | | 1.0 | | | | | | | | 1.4 |
| | .6 | | .2 | | .8 | | | | | | | | |
| (25) | 1.6 | (27) | .8 | (26) | 1.1 | | % Depr., Dep., Amort./Sales | | | | | | |
| | 2.7 | | 2.1 | | 2.6 | | | | | | | | |
| | 1.1 | | 2.6 | | 1.3 | | | | | | | | |
| (13) | 1.9 | (13) | 4.8 | (16) | 4.1 | | % Officers', Directors' Owners' Comp/Sales | | | | | | |
| | 9.0 | | 8.7 | | 8.1 | | | | | | | | |
| | 1159745M | | 1555143M | | 2525637M | | Net Sales ($) | 4119M | 11218M | | 44686M | 147219M | 2318395M |
| | 845604M | | 835526M | | 1161166M | | Total Assets ($) | 2140M | 13835M | | 21476M | 231847M | 891868M |

M = $ thousand   MM = $ million
See Pages viii through xx for Explanation of Ratios and Data

© RMA 2024

## RETAIL—Pet and Pet Supplies Retailers  NAICS 459910

### Current Data Sorted by Assets / Comparative Historical Data

| | | | | | | | Type of Statement | | | | |
|---|---|---|---|---|---|---|---|---|---|---|---|
| | | | 2 | 2 | 1 | | Unqualified | | 2 | 3 | |
| | | 2 | 1 | | | | Reviewed | | | 1 | |
| 3 | 5 | 4 | | | | | Compiled | | 2 | 1 | |
| 6 | 7 | 5 | 6 | | 2 | | Tax Returns | | 12 | 6 | |
| | 4 (4/1-9/30/23) | | 42 (10/1/23-3/31/24) | | | | Other | | 33 | 28 | |
| 0-500M | 500M-2MM | 2-10MM | 10-50MM | 50-100MM | 100-250MM | | | | 4/1/19-3/31/20 | 4/1/20-3/31/21 | |
| 9 | 12 | 11 | 9 | 2 | 3 | | NUMBER OF STATEMENTS | | ALL 49 | ALL 39 | |
| % | % | % | % | % | % | | ASSETS | | % | % | |
| | 19.1 | 17.1 | | | | | Cash & Equivalents | | 14.8 | 19.1 | |
| | 6.9 | 9.9 | | | | | Trade Receivables (net) | | 7.1 | 9.1 | |
| | 29.0 | 35.2 | | | | | Inventory | | 37.5 | 31.5 | |
| | .2 | 2.8 | | | | | All Other Current | | 2.2 | 1.8 | |
| | 55.3 | 65.1 | | | | | Total Current | | 61.6 | 61.5 | |
| | 35.2 | 16.2 | | | | | Fixed Assets (net) | | 26.7 | 20.4 | |
| | 4.1 | 16.3 | | | | | Intangibles (net) | | 3.8 | 13.6 | |
| | 5.4 | 2.5 | | | | | All Other Non-Current | | 7.9 | 4.5 | |
| | 100.0 | 100.0 | | | | | Total | | 100.0 | 100.0 | |
| | | | | | | | LIABILITIES | | | | |
| | 6.6 | 3.2 | | | | | Notes Payable-Short Term | | 8.9 | 5.4 | |
| | 1.9 | 3.6 | | | | | Cur. Mat.-L.T.D. | | 1.9 | 2.1 | |
| | 5.3 | 12.0 | | | | | Trade Payables | | 11.3 | 9.4 | |
| | .1 | .0 | | | | | Income Taxes Payable | | .0 | .0 | |
| | 8.4 | 7.7 | | | | | All Other Current | | 9.5 | 14.6 | |
| | 22.3 | 26.4 | | | | | Total Current | | 31.7 | 31.4 | |
| | 32.1 | 25.6 | | | | | Long-Term Debt | | 17.3 | 24.0 | |
| | .0 | .0 | | | | | Deferred Taxes | | .2 | .0 | |
| | 1.8 | 2.6 | | | | | All Other Non-Current | | 18.9 | 6.6 | |
| | 43.8 | 45.4 | | | | | Net Worth | | 31.9 | 38.0 | |
| | 100.0 | 100.0 | | | | | Total Liabilities & Net Worth | | 100.0 | 100.0 | |
| | | | | | | | INCOME DATA | | | | |
| | 100.0 | 100.0 | | | | | Net Sales | | 100.0 | 100.0 | |
| | 51.7 | 47.0 | | | | | Gross Profit | | 38.9 | 44.0 | |
| | 51.2 | 41.0 | | | | | Operating Expenses | | 32.9 | 38.5 | |
| | .5 | 6.0 | | | | | Operating Profit | | 6.0 | 5.4 | |
| | -1.3 | 1.1 | | | | | All Other Expenses (net) | | 1.8 | -.1 | |
| | 1.8 | 4.9 | | | | | Profit Before Taxes | | 4.3 | 5.5 | |
| | | | | | | | RATIOS | | | | |
| | 7.2 | 8.7 | | | | | | | 5.3 | 5.6 | |
| | 3.2 | 1.9 | | | | | Current | | 2.4 | 2.7 | |
| | 2.0 | 1.4 | | | | | | | 1.4 | 1.4 | |
| | 2.3 | 3.8 | | | | | | | 1.7 | 3.3 | |
| | 1.4 | 1.0 | | | | | Quick | (48) | .6 | 1.3 | |
| | .4 | .3 | | | | | | | .2 | .4 | |
| 0 | UND | 0 | UND | | | | | 0 | UND | 0 | UND |
| 4 | 82.7 | 4 | 101.8 | | | | Sales/Receivables | 1 | 262.8 | 3 | 132.8 |
| 11 | 31.9 | 13 | 27.8 | | | | | 13 | 27.6 | 26 | 14.1 |
| 24 | 15.4 | 32 | 11.4 | | | | | 34 | 10.8 | 53 | 6.9 |
| 55 | 6.6 | 72 | 5.1 | | | | Cost of Sales/Inventory | 61 | 6.0 | 69 | 5.3 |
| 114 | 3.2 | 99 | 3.7 | | | | | 104 | 3.5 | 111 | 3.3 |
| 0 | UND | 2 | 231.7 | | | | | 0 | UND | 6 | 61.6 |
| 4 | 98.1 | 18 | 19.8 | | | | Cost of Sales/Payables | 18 | 20.2 | 20 | 18.6 |
| 11 | 33.4 | 54 | 6.7 | | | | | 29 | 12.5 | 33 | 10.9 |
| | 6.0 | 5.2 | | | | | | | 6.7 | 4.1 | |
| | 10.9 | 8.5 | | | | | Sales/Working Capital | | 12.4 | 7.3 | |
| | 17.1 | 17.2 | | | | | | | 26.5 | 16.1 | |
| | 41.5 | 14.8 | | | | | | | 15.2 | 29.8 | |
| (10) | 5.0 | (10) | 9.4 | | | | EBIT/Interest | (36) | 7.1 | (31) | 5.5 |
| | -.7 | 3.3 | | | | | | | 1.1 | -.5 | |
| | | | | | | | Net Profit + Depr., Dep., Amort./Cur. Mat. L/T/D | | | | |
| | .1 | .1 | | | | | | | .1 | .2 | |
| | 1.2 | .4 | | | | | Fixed/Worth | | .6 | 1.0 | |
| | NM | 2.7 | | | | | | | 2.0 | -1.9 | |
| | .2 | .6 | | | | | | | .6 | .6 | |
| | 2.1 | 2.3 | | | | | Debt/Worth | | 1.5 | 2.8 | |
| | NM | 8.7 | | | | | | | 16.8 | -8.9 | |
| | | | | | | | % Profit Before Taxes/Tangible Net Worth | | 57.8 | 92.6 | |
| | | | | | | | | (38) | 30.9 | (26) | 42.2 |
| | | | | | | | | | 11.4 | 7.6 | |
| | 21.3 | 16.4 | | | | | | | 22.4 | 27.4 | |
| | 9.3 | 16.0 | | | | | % Profit Before Taxes/Total Assets | | 12.6 | 14.4 | |
| | -9.4 | 4.9 | | | | | | | -1.1 | -3.4 | |
| | 373.2 | 139.0 | | | | | | | 158.7 | 96.8 | |
| | 6.8 | 42.9 | | | | | Sales/Net Fixed Assets | | 14.6 | 15.1 | |
| | 3.9 | 15.4 | | | | | | | 6.3 | 8.9 | |
| | 4.6 | 3.8 | | | | | | | 5.7 | 3.6 | |
| | 2.9 | 3.2 | | | | | Sales/Total Assets | | 3.2 | 2.9 | |
| | 2.2 | 2.1 | | | | | | | 2.0 | 1.8 | |
| | .2 | | | | | | | | .3 | .5 | |
| (10) | .9 | | | | | | % Depr., Dep., Amort./Sales | (29) | 1.0 | (26) | 1.6 |
| | 3.1 | | | | | | | | 2.0 | 2.4 | |
| | | | | | | | % Officers', Directors' Owners' Comp/Sales | | 1.0 | | |
| | | | | | | | | (17) | 3.4 | | |
| | | | | | | | | | 8.5 | | |
| 16997M | 50539M | 146477M | 525255M | 271502M | 1284509M | | Net Sales ($) | | 924873M | 1421472M | |
| 2942M | 13203M | 45283M | 212378M | 126340M | 441326M | | Total Assets ($) | | 380104M | 669357M | |

© RMA 2024   M = $ thousand   MM = $ million
See Pages viii through xx for Explanation of Ratios and Data

# RETAIL—Pet and Pet Supplies Retailers  NAICS 459910

| Comparative Historical Data | | | | Current Data Sorted by Sales | | | | | |
|---|---|---|---|---|---|---|---|---|---|
| 1 | 5 | 5 | Type of Statement | | | | | | 5 |
| | 1 | | Unqualified | | | | | 1 | 1 |
| 2 | 2 | 3 | Reviewed | | | | 1 | 3 | 1 |
| 12 | 17 | 12 | Compiled | | 5 | 3 | 5 | 3 | 8 |
| 22 | 30 | 26 | Tax Returns | 4 | 4 | 3 | 42 | 3 | |
| 4/1/21- | 4/1/22- | 4/1/23- | Other | | 4 (4/1-9/30/23) | | 42 (10/1/23-3/31/24) | | |
| 3/31/22 | 3/31/23 | 3/31/24 | | 0-1MM | 1-3MM | 3-5MM | 5-10MM | 10-25MM | 25MM & OVER |
| ALL | ALL | ALL | | | | | | | |
| 37 | 55 | 46 | NUMBER OF STATEMENTS | 4 | | 6 | 5 | 7 | 15 |
| % | % | % | **ASSETS** | % | % | % | % | % | % |
| 23.3 | 16.4 | 15.5 | Cash & Equivalents | | | | | | 15.1 |
| 4.6 | 5.8 | 7.9 | Trade Receivables (net) | | | | | | 10.0 |
| 34.4 | 32.4 | 32.6 | Inventory | | | | | | 28.6 |
| 1.6 | 2.6 | 2.3 | All Other Current | | | | | | 3.0 |
| 63.9 | 57.1 | 58.2 | Total Current | | | | | | 56.7 |
| 19.3 | 23.5 | 22.4 | Fixed Assets (net) | | | | | | 21.9 |
| 9.6 | 8.6 | 12.4 | Intangibles (net) | | | | | | 9.0 |
| 7.2 | 10.8 | 7.0 | All Other Non-Current | | | | | | 12.4 |
| 100.0 | 100.0 | 100.0 | Total | | | | | | 100.0 |
| | | | **LIABILITIES** | | | | | | |
| 10.9 | 11.1 | 6.5 | Notes Payable-Short Term | | | | | | 7.9 |
| 1.6 | 2.7 | 2.0 | Cur. Mat.-L.T.D. | | | | | | 2.1 |
| 11.8 | 9.4 | 11.4 | Trade Payables | | | | | | 13.4 |
| .3 | .1 | .1 | Income Taxes Payable | | | | | | .0 |
| 10.3 | 9.8 | 7.6 | All Other Current | | | | | | 11.3 |
| 34.9 | 33.1 | 27.5 | Total Current | | | | | | 34.7 |
| 28.8 | 35.8 | 23.4 | Long-Term Debt | | | | | | 16.2 |
| .0 | .1 | .0 | Deferred Taxes | | | | | | .1 |
| 7.2 | 4.7 | 9.3 | All Other Non-Current | | | | | | 16.8 |
| 29.1 | 26.3 | 39.8 | Net Worth | | | | | | 32.3 |
| 100.0 | 100.0 | 100.0 | Total Liabilities & Net Worth | | | | | | 100.0 |
| | | | **INCOME DATA** | | | | | | |
| 100.0 | 100.0 | 100.0 | Net Sales | | | | | | 100.0 |
| 49.2 | 43.8 | 44.5 | Gross Profit | | | | | | 38.6 |
| 42.1 | 41.5 | 42.9 | Operating Expenses | | | | | | 39.3 |
| 7.1 | 2.3 | 1.6 | Operating Profit | | | | | | -.7 |
| -.2 | .1 | -.5 | All Other Expenses (net) | | | | | | .0 |
| 7.3 | 2.2 | 2.1 | Profit Before Taxes | | | | | | -.6 |
| | | | **RATIOS** | | | | | | |
| 6.0 | 3.4 | 4.1 | | | | | | | 2.0 |
| 2.3 | 1.8 | 2.0 | Current | | | | | | 1.5 |
| 1.5 | 1.3 | 1.4 | | | | | | | 1.4 |
| 3.0 | 1.7 | 1.8 | | | | | | | 1.1 |
| 1.1 | .4 | .7 | Quick | | | | | | .6 |
| .3 | .3 | .4 | | | | | | | .5 |
| 0 UND | 0 UND | 0 UND | | | | | | 0 | 999.8 |
| 0 914.8 | 2 205.6 | 2 175.6 | Sales/Receivables | | | | | 5 | 73.3 |
| 5 74.9 | 9 39.4 | 12 30.1 | | | | | | 20 | 18.7 |
| 20 18.5 | 43 8.5 | 42 8.6 | | | | | | 45 | 8.2 |
| 60 6.1 | 73 5.0 | 63 5.8 | Cost of Sales/Inventory | | | | | 63 | 5.8 |
| 85 4.3 | 99 3.7 | 94 3.9 | | | | | | 99 | 3.7 |
| 0 UND | 1 293.5 | 3 114.4 | | | | | | 20 | 18.4 |
| 13 27.5 | 19 19.1 | 16 22.2 | Cost of Sales/Payables | | | | | 33 | 11.2 |
| 31 11.6 | 34 10.7 | 36 10.0 | | | | | | 39 | 9.3 |
| 5.8 | 7.2 | 7.6 | | | | | | | 8.7 |
| 11.2 | 13.0 | 13.4 | Sales/Working Capital | | | | | | 13.2 |
| 24.7 | 25.1 | 17.7 | | | | | | | 18.2 |
| 23.3 | 27.5 | 10.3 | | | | | | | 3.9 |
| (27) 5.9 | (44) 5.0 | (36) 3.7 | EBIT/Interest | | | | | (13) | 2.5 |
| 2.1 | -.5 | -.3 | | | | | | | -3.8 |
| | | | Net Profit + Depr., Dep., Amort./Cur. Mat. L/T/D | | | | | | |
| .0 | .3 | .1 | | | | | | | .5 |
| .6 | .6 | .7 | Fixed/Worth | | | | | | .9 |
| -3.6 | -1.8 | 2.8 | | | | | | | 1.3 |
| .5 | .5 | .8 | | | | | | | 1.6 |
| 1.8 | 2.4 | 2.5 | Debt/Worth | | | | | | 3.1 |
| -6.1 | -7.8 | 11.0 | | | | | | | 4.2 |
| 102.1 | 51.8 | 56.4 | | | | | | | 19.2 |
| (25) 50.8 | (38) 23.4 | (36) 15.4 | % Profit Before Taxes/Tangible Net Worth | | | | | (14) | 4.9 |
| 19.6 | 6.8 | -2.9 | | | | | | | -29.5 |
| 40.1 | 19.0 | 16.3 | | | | | | | 4.7 |
| 14.1 | 8.0 | 4.7 | % Profit Before Taxes/Total Assets | | | | | | .8 |
| 7.6 | -1.2 | -3.1 | | | | | | | -6.4 |
| 649.9 | 71.3 | 187.7 | | | | | | | 24.3 |
| 66.1 | 16.4 | 23.6 | Sales/Net Fixed Assets | | | | | | 10.7 |
| 8.4 | 5.8 | 6.8 | | | | | | | 7.3 |
| 5.6 | 4.7 | 4.5 | | | | | | | 2.9 |
| 3.5 | 2.8 | 3.0 | Sales/Total Assets | | | | | | 2.4 |
| 1.4 | 1.7 | 2.2 | | | | | | | 1.9 |
| .7 | .5 | .5 | | | | | | | 1.0 |
| (18) 1.4 | (35) 1.1 | (33) 1.1 | % Depr., Dep., Amort./Sales | | | | | (13) | 1.8 |
| 4.9 | 1.7 | 2.1 | | | | | | | 2.1 |
| | 2.1 | | | | | | | | |
| | (12) 5.4 | | % Officers', Directors' Owners' Comp/Sales | | | | | | |
| | 6.4 | | | | | | | | |
| 1049362M | 3024913M | 2295279M | Net Sales ($) | 2606M | 16712M | 23902M | 30806M | 114769M | 2106484M |
| 649962M | 1743830M | 841472M | Total Assets ($) | 1161M | 7204M | 6271M | 9764M | 32766M | 784306M |

M = $ thousand    MM = $ million
See Pages viii through xx for Explanation of Ratios and Data

© RMA 2024

# RETAIL—All Other Miscellaneous Retailers NAICS 459999

## Current Data Sorted by Assets / Comparative Historical Data

| | | | | | | | Type of Statement | | |
|---|---|---|---|---|---|---|---|---|---|
| | | | 1 | 6 | 4 | 9 | Unqualified | 35 | 24 |
| | | | 3 | 12 | 1 | | Reviewed | 39 | 14 |
| | | 5 | 6 | 7 | | | Compiled | 41 | 22 |
| | 13 | 31 | 26 | 7 | 1 | | Tax Returns | 179 | 120 |
| | 33 | 51 | 84 | 69 | 12 | 12 | Other | 367 | 260 |
| | | 46 (4/1-9/30/23) | | 347 (10/1/23-3/31/24) | | | | 4/1/19- | 4/1/20- |
| | | | | | | | | 3/31/20 | 3/31/21 |
| | 0-500M | 500M-2MM | 2-10MM | 10-50MM | 50-100MM | 100-250MM | | ALL | ALL |
| | 46 | 87 | 120 | 101 | 18 | 21 | NUMBER OF STATEMENTS | 661 | 440 |
| | % | % | % | % | % | % | ASSETS | % | % |
| | 30.6 | 28.4 | 19.9 | 12.0 | 14.7 | 12.8 | Cash & Equivalents | 16.7 | 24.3 |
| | 8.4 | 10.7 | 14.5 | 11.5 | 8.0 | 8.0 | Trade Receivables (net) | 12.4 | 11.5 |
| | 27.6 | 27.4 | 39.9 | 39.6 | 26.1 | 31.1 | Inventory | 38.8 | 34.2 |
| | 2.3 | 3.9 | 3.1 | 6.1 | 9.9 | 2.9 | All Other Current | 3.2 | 4.3 |
| | 69.0 | 70.4 | 77.3 | 69.2 | 58.7 | 54.8 | Total Current | 71.1 | 74.4 |
| | 11.5 | 14.5 | 9.9 | 14.1 | 20.7 | 17.5 | Fixed Assets (net) | 14.8 | 12.9 |
| | 13.0 | 6.6 | 4.3 | 5.1 | 11.8 | 15.8 | Intangibles (net) | 7.4 | 6.6 |
| | 6.5 | 8.5 | 8.5 | 11.7 | 8.8 | 11.9 | All Other Non-Current | 6.7 | 6.1 |
| | 100.0 | 100.0 | 100.0 | 100.0 | 100.0 | 100.0 | Total | 100.0 | 100.0 |
| | | | | | | | LIABILITIES | | |
| | 19.8 | 8.3 | 6.8 | 9.2 | 9.4 | 7.0 | Notes Payable-Short Term | 12.6 | 12.5 |
| | 3.3 | 1.6 | 2.0 | 1.6 | 2.9 | 12.5 | Cur. Mat.-L.T.D. | 3.2 | 2.3 |
| | 19.0 | 7.6 | 16.5 | 16.5 | 9.7 | 13.1 | Trade Payables | 16.4 | 12.7 |
| | .1 | .1 | .1 | .1 | .0 | .2 | Income Taxes Payable | .1 | .3 |
| | 18.0 | 13.3 | 15.1 | 14.7 | 17.4 | 16.7 | All Other Current | 15.3 | 16.7 |
| | 60.2 | 31.0 | 40.5 | 42.1 | 39.5 | 49.4 | Total Current | 47.6 | 44.4 |
| | 22.3 | 22.8 | 12.6 | 14.7 | 17.0 | 9.7 | Long-Term Debt | 15.2 | 19.0 |
| | .0 | .0 | .1 | .2 | .6 | .3 | Deferred Taxes | .1 | .1 |
| | 11.4 | 7.7 | 3.3 | 7.4 | 12.1 | 9.6 | All Other Non-Current | 7.7 | 9.5 |
| | 6.1 | 38.5 | 43.5 | 35.5 | 30.7 | 31.0 | Net Worth | 29.4 | 26.9 |
| | 100.0 | 100.0 | 100.0 | 100.0 | 100.0 | 100.0 | Total Liabilities & Net Worth | 100.0 | 100.0 |
| | | | | | | | INCOME DATA | | |
| | 100.0 | 100.0 | 100.0 | 100.0 | 100.0 | 100.0 | Net Sales | 100.0 | 100.0 |
| | 53.8 | 45.5 | 40.9 | 41.5 | 40.3 | 42.9 | Gross Profit | 42.3 | 42.5 |
| | 42.8 | 38.6 | 34.0 | 36.3 | 33.7 | 37.9 | Operating Expenses | 36.4 | 35.4 |
| | 11.0 | 6.9 | 6.9 | 5.3 | 6.6 | 5.0 | Operating Profit | 5.9 | 7.1 |
| | 2.3 | .2 | .1 | .2 | .2 | .9 | All Other Expenses (net) | .8 | .1 |
| | 8.7 | 6.7 | 6.8 | 5.1 | 6.4 | 4.0 | Profit Before Taxes | 5.1 | 7.0 |
| | | | | | | | RATIOS | | |
| | 5.0 | 9.6 | 3.7 | 2.8 | 2.3 | 2.2 | | 3.3 | 4.2 |
| | 1.9 | 3.0 | 2.2 | 1.7 | 1.6 | 1.0 | Current | 1.7 | 2.1 |
| | .8 | 1.6 | 1.3 | 1.2 | 1.0 | .7 | | 1.1 | 1.3 |
| | 2.4 | 4.3 | 1.7 | 1.0 | 1.5 | 1.3 | | 1.5 | 2.0 |
| | .7 | 1.4 | .9 | .6 | .5 | .3 | Quick | .6 | .9 |
| | .3 | .6 | .4 | .2 | .2 | .1 | | .2 | .4 |
| 0 | UND | 0 | UND | 0 | 764.1 | 1 | 379.1 | 1 | 351.4 | 2 | 151.7 | | 0 | 999.8 | 0 | UND |
| 0 | UND | 0 | UND | 7 | 50.1 | 7 | 53.3 | 7 | 49.0 | 10 | 38.0 | Sales/Receivables | 6 | 66.0 | 6 | 59.3 |
| 7 | 49.9 | 16 | 23.0 | 32 | 11.5 | 20 | 18.5 | 24 | 15.0 | 29 | 12.6 | | 24 | 15.5 | 27 | 13.7 |
| 0 | UND | 5 | 81.0 | 27 | 13.7 | 45 | 8.2 | 38 | 9.7 | 68 | 5.4 | | 28 | 12.9 | 23 | 15.6 |
| 13 | 28.8 | 36 | 10.1 | 91 | 4.0 | 91 | 4.0 | 118 | 3.1 | 87 | 4.2 | Cost of Sales/Inventory | 72 | 5.1 | 62 | 5.9 |
| 114 | 3.2 | 81 | 4.5 | 159 | 2.3 | 192 | 1.9 | 152 | 2.4 | 140 | 2.6 | | 130 | 2.8 | 122 | 3.0 |
| 0 | UND | 0 | UND | 3 | 120.7 | 16 | 22.9 | 10 | 35.5 | 18 | 20.5 | | 6 | 65.6 | 0 | 999.8 |
| 0 | UND | 0 | UND | 24 | 15.0 | 31 | 11.8 | 24 | 15.1 | 31 | 11.6 | Cost of Sales/Payables | 21 | 17.1 | 18 | 19.8 |
| 22 | 16.3 | 13 | 28.6 | 48 | 7.6 | 58 | 6.3 | 56 | 6.5 | 61 | 6.0 | | 46 | 7.9 | 42 | 8.7 |
| | 5.5 | 4.2 | 4.2 | 5.0 | 4.0 | 5.1 | | 5.7 | 4.6 |
| | 38.3 | 10.1 | 8.3 | 8.6 | 7.4 | 83.5 | Sales/Working Capital | 11.6 | 9.2 |
| | -44.7 | 24.9 | 21.0 | 23.4 | NM | -10.0 | | 99.4 | 30.9 |
| | 16.7 | 29.1 | 29.9 | 33.0 | 37.2 | 40.8 | | 24.7 | 46.6 |
| (32) | 7.2 | (62) | 8.9 | (88) | 9.7 | (83) | 6.4 | (15) | 5.5 | | 7.5 | EBIT/Interest | (517) | 6.1 | (341) | 11.7 |
| | .5 | -.1 | 2.6 | -.3 | 1.8 | -.4 | | 1.9 | 3.2 |
| | | | | 47.8 | | | | 10.4 | 39.2 |
| | | | (10) | 6.1 | | | Net Profit + Depr., Dep., Amort./Cur. Mat. L/T/D | (50) | 2.8 | (32) | 7.6 |
| | | | | .2 | | | | .5 | 3.0 |
| | .0 | .0 | .0 | .1 | .3 | .4 | | .0 | .0 |
| | .1 | .1 | .1 | .3 | 1.5 | 1.0 | Fixed/Worth | .3 | .2 |
| | 1.8 | .8 | .5 | 1.0 | -10.4 | -1.0 | | 2.2 | 1.3 |
| | .5 | .5 | .4 | .8 | .9 | .8 | | .6 | .6 |
| | 3.8 | 1.4 | 1.1 | 1.9 | 6.2 | 3.9 | Debt/Worth | 1.9 | 1.6 |
| | -6.4 | 9.5 | 3.6 | 3.4 | -43.5 | -6.1 | | 16.2 | 7.8 |
| | 163.5 | 79.8 | 77.4 | 47.1 | 152.9 | 51.3 | | 74.8 | 95.4 |
| (32) | 94.1 | (72) | 41.2 | (106) | 32.3 | (88) | 22.4 | (13) | 37.5 | (14) | 28.7 | % Profit Before Taxes/Tangible Net Worth | (519) | 34.3 | (348) | 51.7 |
| | 11.1 | 16.5 | 10.1 | 3.4 | 16.1 | 12.3 | | 11.5 | 19.8 |
| | 83.4 | 32.8 | 34.2 | 18.5 | 17.2 | 18.9 | | 28.2 | 39.8 |
| | 27.2 | 16.9 | 15.6 | 10.0 | 9.0 | 4.9 | % Profit Before Taxes/Total Assets | 11.3 | 17.1 |
| | -2.0 | 1.5 | 3.4 | .3 | 1.7 | -3.1 | | 2.5 | 4.3 |
| | UND | 999.8 | 587.2 | 137.0 | 26.2 | 51.8 | | 296.2 | 444.4 |
| | 226.1 | 131.5 | 133.2 | 31.4 | 14.6 | 10.7 | Sales/Net Fixed Assets | 46.9 | 55.4 |
| | 25.9 | 17.1 | 19.1 | 12.6 | 7.0 | 7.4 | | 13.3 | 15.9 |
| | 7.4 | 6.3 | 4.3 | 3.5 | 2.4 | 2.3 | | 4.8 | 4.7 |
| | 4.2 | 3.3 | 2.9 | 2.6 | 1.5 | 1.9 | Sales/Total Assets | 3.1 | 2.8 |
| | 2.2 | 2.0 | 1.9 | 1.6 | 1.0 | 1.7 | | 1.9 | 1.8 |
| | .2 | .3 | .1 | .3 | .7 | | | .3 | .4 |
| (16) | .9 | (34) | .7 | (58) | .5 | (71) | .9 | (16) | 1.3 | | | % Depr., Dep., Amort./Sales | (368) | .8 | (229) | .8 |
| | 1.9 | 1.9 | 1.3 | 1.7 | 3.1 | | | 2.0 | 2.1 |
| | 4.2 | 1.6 | 1.0 | .6 | | | | 1.2 | 1.3 |
| (24) | 8.9 | (44) | 3.3 | (44) | 2.0 | (30) | 1.2 | | | | % Officers', Directors', Owners' Comp/Sales | (247) | 2.2 | (178) | 2.7 |
| | 12.4 | 7.6 | 3.3 | 1.9 | | | | 5.1 | 5.8 |
| | 88439M | 474548M | 1955901M | 6533074M | 2175056M | 6855679M | Net Sales ($) | 30229460M | 15419045M |
| | 11679M | 97926M | 576561M | 2218114M | 1318139M | 3197072M | Total Assets ($) | 12872348M | 6335307M |

M = $ thousand  MM = $ million
See Pages viii through xx for Explanation of Ratios and Data

© RMA 2024

# RETAIL—All Other Miscellaneous Retailers  NAICS 459999

| Comparative Historical Data ||| | Current Data Sorted by Sales ||||||
|---|---|---|---|---|---|---|---|---|---|
| 18 | 34 | 20 | Type of Statement | | | | | 2 | 18 |
| 20 | 29 | 16 | Unqualified | | | | 1 | 4 | 11 |
| 16 | 17 | 18 | Reviewed | | 1 | 1 | 5 | 5 | 6 |
| 140 | 131 | 78 | Compiled | 11 | 13 | 10 | 18 | 16 | 10 |
| 256 | 288 | 261 | Tax Returns | 25 | 35 | 14 | 40 | 51 | 96 |
| 4/1/21-3/31/22 | 4/1/22-3/31/23 | 4/1/23-3/31/24 | Other | 46 (4/1-9/30/23) ||| 347 (10/1/23-3/31/24) |||
| ALL | ALL | ALL | | 0-1MM | 1-3MM | 3-5MM | 5-10MM | 10-25MM | 25MM & OVER |
| 450 | 499 | 393 | NUMBER OF STATEMENTS | 36 | 49 | 25 | 64 | 78 | 141 |
| % | % | % | ASSETS | % | % | % | % | % | % |
| 22.8 | 19.7 | 20.4 | Cash & Equivalents | 25.2 | 26.1 | 20.4 | 26.5 | 20.5 | 14.3 |
| 12.5 | 13.4 | 11.5 | Trade Receivables (net) | 6.2 | 10.0 | 15.8 | 15.6 | 10.5 | 11.3 |
| 35.2 | 36.5 | 34.5 | Inventory | 28.1 | 29.5 | 24.0 | 33.4 | 38.9 | 37.9 |
| 4.7 | 4.4 | 4.3 | All Other Current | 1.9 | 2.6 | 6.1 | 4.3 | 2.1 | 6.3 |
| 75.2 | 74.1 | 70.7 | Total Current | 61.4 | 68.1 | 66.4 | 79.8 | 72.0 | 69.8 |
| 11.6 | 12.1 | 13.1 | Fixed Assets (net) | 15.6 | 13.8 | 20.0 | 8.3 | 11.8 | 13.8 |
| 6.6 | 6.0 | 7.0 | Intangibles (net) | 15.6 | 10.7 | 2.7 | 3.7 | 4.9 | 6.8 |
| 6.5 | 7.9 | 9.3 | All Other Non-Current | 7.3 | 7.3 | 10.9 | 8.1 | 11.3 | 9.6 |
| 100.0 | 100.0 | 100.0 | Total | 100.0 | 100.0 | 100.0 | 100.0 | 100.0 | 100.0 |
| | | | LIABILITIES | | | | | | |
| 10.5 | 10.1 | 9.4 | Notes Payable-Short Term | 7.7 | 20.1 | 7.4 | 6.7 | 8.4 | 8.2 |
| 2.3 | 1.9 | 2.6 | Cur. Mat.-L.T.D. | 3.5 | 2.2 | 1.1 | 2.1 | 1.9 | 3.3 |
| 15.2 | 14.5 | 14.3 | Trade Payables | 16.4 | 10.2 | 9.5 | 13.3 | 14.5 | 16.5 |
| .3 | .2 | .1 | Income Taxes Payable | .1 | .3 | .0 | .0 | .0 | .2 |
| 13.2 | 14.4 | 15.1 | All Other Current | 13.9 | 14.0 | 14.7 | 18.0 | 12.4 | 16.2 |
| 41.4 | 41.1 | 41.5 | Total Current | 41.6 | 46.7 | 32.6 | 40.1 | 37.3 | 44.3 |
| 14.4 | 17.3 | 16.6 | Long-Term Debt | 28.5 | 27.7 | 22.7 | 12.5 | 13.5 | 12.2 |
| .1 | .1 | .1 | Deferred Taxes | .0 | .0 | .0 | .1 | .2 | .2 |
| 5.6 | 7.0 | 7.0 | All Other Non-Current | 9.9 | 5.7 | 15.6 | 3.3 | 5.1 | 7.9 |
| 38.5 | 34.5 | 34.7 | Net Worth | 20.1 | 20.0 | 29.1 | 44.0 | 43.8 | 35.3 |
| 100.0 | 100.0 | 100.0 | Total Liabilities & Net Worth | 100.0 | 100.0 | 100.0 | 100.0 | 100.0 | 100.0 |
| | | | INCOME DATA | | | | | | |
| 100.0 | 100.0 | 100.0 | Net Sales | 100.0 | 100.0 | 100.0 | 100.0 | 100.0 | 100.0 |
| 42.5 | 41.4 | 43.7 | Gross Profit | 54.7 | 54.9 | 39.5 | 40.7 | 42.1 | 40.0 |
| 34.4 | 34.8 | 36.8 | Operating Expenses | 43.9 | 42.9 | 33.8 | 34.7 | 35.5 | 35.1 |
| 8.1 | 6.6 | 6.9 | Operating Profit | 10.7 | 12.1 | 5.7 | 6.0 | 6.6 | 4.8 |
| -.7 | .4 | .5 | All Other Expenses (net) | 2.1 | 1.4 | .3 | -.2 | .0 | .3 |
| 8.8 | 6.2 | 6.4 | Profit Before Taxes | 8.6 | 10.6 | 5.3 | 6.2 | 6.5 | 4.6 |
| | | | RATIOS | | | | | | |
| 4.4 | 4.4 | 3.8 | | 6.1 | 4.8 | 9.7 | 4.0 | 3.7 | 2.6 |
| 2.1 | 2.0 | 2.1 | Current | 2.2 | 2.1 | 3.4 | 2.3 | 2.3 | 1.7 |
| 1.3 | 1.2 | 1.2 | | 1.1 | .9 | 1.5 | 1.4 | 1.3 | 1.1 |
| 2.2 | 1.9 | 1.8 | | 3.8 | 2.2 | 4.8 | 2.5 | 1.8 | 1.1 |
| .9 | .8 | .8 | Quick | .8 | .7 | 1.5 | 1.0 | .7 | .6 |
| .4 | .3 | .3 | | .4 | .3 | .7 | .6 | .4 | .2 |
| 0 UND | 0 UND | 0 UND | | 0 UND | 0 UND | 0 UND | 0 UND | 0 UND | 1 289.9 |
| 5 71.4 | 6 57.8 | 5 81.0 | Sales/Receivables | 0 UND | 0 UND | 4 100.3 | 8 46.6 | 5 80.9 | 6 59.0 |
| 22 16.7 | 29 12.7 | 22 16.5 | | 7 51.0 | 20 18.6 | 39 9.4 | 42 8.6 | 26 14.3 | 18 19.9 |
| 21 17.6 | 20 18.2 | 21 17.6 | | 0 UND | 0 UND | 13 27.7 | 10 37.1 | 38 9.6 | 35 10.5 |
| 70 5.2 | 70 5.2 | 73 5.0 | Cost of Sales/Inventory | 81 4.5 | 55 6.6 | 49 7.4 | 57 6.4 | 87 4.2 | 83 4.4 |
| 130 2.8 | 146 2.5 | 146 2.5 | | 228 1.6 | 166 2.2 | 130 2.8 | 140 2.6 | 174 2.1 | 140 2.6 |
| 0 999.8 | 1 261.5 | 0 914.7 | | 0 UND | 0 UND | 0 UND | 0 UND | 3 115.1 | 11 34.5 |
| 18 20.6 | 20 18.5 | 18 20.4 | Cost of Sales/Payables | 0 UND | 0 915.0 | 8 46.4 | 14 25.6 | 21 17.7 | 28 13.1 |
| 41 9.0 | 43 8.5 | 42 8.6 | | 19 18.8 | 27 13.3 | 31 11.6 | 42 8.6 | 48 7.6 | 47 7.8 |
| 4.8 | 4.5 | 4.7 | | 3.0 | 3.6 | 3.0 | 4.4 | 4.5 | 6.0 |
| 9.2 | 9.3 | 9.3 | Sales/Working Capital | 6.8 | 9.1 | 8.3 | 7.4 | 9.0 | 12.2 |
| 23.2 | 33.2 | 46.2 | | 471.3 | -26.2 | 24.7 | 19.6 | 20.4 | 81.0 |
| 67.4 | 37.1 | 29.7 | | 12.5 | 24.1 | 22.1 | 45.3 | 29.7 | 39.1 |
| (329) 19.0 | (381) 10.8 | (301) 7.5 | EBIT/Interest | (25) 3.9 | (38) 7.9 | (17) 3.0 | (46) 9.0 | (61) 9.7 | (114) 7.6 |
| 5.3 | 2.5 | 1.2 | | .1 | 1.3 | -.9 | 1.2 | 1.1 | 1.6 |
| 33.6 | 13.5 | 23.1 | | | | | | | 36.0 |
| (22) 11.0 | (40) 3.6 | (25) 4.3 | Net Profit + Depr., Dep., Amort./Cur. Mat. L/T/D | | | | | (19) 5.4 | 5.4 |
| 3.9 | .8 | .3 | | | | | | | .9 |
| .0 | .0 | .0 | | .0 | .0 | .0 | .0 | .0 | .1 |
| .1 | .2 | .2 | Fixed/Worth | .3 | .1 | .4 | .0 | .1 | .3 |
| .9 | 1.0 | 1.0 | | 3.4 | 2.5 | 1.8 | .3 | .5 | 1.7 |
| .5 | .6 | .6 | | .7 | .4 | .7 | .5 | .5 | .8 |
| 1.5 | 1.7 | 1.5 | Debt/Worth | 4.4 | 2.3 | 1.6 | 1.2 | .9 | 1.9 |
| 6.6 | 13.2 | 8.4 | | -8.6 | -8.4 | 7.5 | 3.2 | 3.0 | 9.7 |
| 100.4 | 84.7 | 76.3 | | 176.4 | 95.7 | 78.3 | 63.0 | 64.2 | 62.8 |
| (377) 55.4 | (400) 40.5 | (325) 32.7 | % Profit Before Taxes/Tangible Net Worth | (26) 92.2 | (34) 39.6 | (21) 38.6 | (57) 33.0 | (72) 31.1 | (115) 28.4 |
| 23.8 | 15.3 | 10.3 | | 4.3 | 12.8 | 15.8 | 8.1 | 10.0 | 12.2 |
| 38.9 | 29.6 | 30.8 | | 45.9 | 40.3 | 28.3 | 35.0 | 29.6 | 23.9 |
| 20.1 | 13.8 | 12.8 | % Profit Before Taxes/Total Assets | 14.2 | 20.8 | 11.0 | 14.3 | 14.4 | 10.9 |
| 8.3 | 3.1 | 1.4 | | -2.3 | 1.1 | -2.3 | 2.6 | 3.2 | 1.6 |
| 999.8 | 851.4 | 494.1 | | UND | UND | 255.2 | 999.8 | 367.0 | 166.3 |
| 85.9 | 74.4 | 59.8 | Sales/Net Fixed Assets | 55.6 | 132.9 | 108.5 | 160.0 | 60.9 | 36.2 |
| 18.2 | 18.1 | 14.1 | | 12.1 | 15.6 | 6.4 | 32.4 | 13.4 | 12.4 |
| 4.7 | 4.5 | 4.4 | | 4.3 | 4.2 | 4.5 | 5.1 | 4.7 | 4.2 |
| 3.0 | 3.0 | 2.8 | Sales/Total Assets | 1.6 | 2.7 | 2.4 | 3.0 | 2.9 | 2.9 |
| 2.0 | 1.8 | 1.7 | | .9 | 1.9 | 1.9 | 1.9 | 1.6 | 1.8 |
| .2 | .3 | .3 | | .6 | .3 | .3 | .2 | .2 | .3 |
| (202) .7 | (234) .8 | (203) .8 | % Depr., Dep., Amort./Sales | (14) 1.0 | (19) 1.9 | (12) .6 | (25) .7 | (42) .8 | (91) .7 |
| 1.7 | 1.9 | 1.7 | | 2.4 | 2.7 | 2.3 | 1.1 | 1.9 | 1.4 |
| 1.4 | 1.2 | 1.2 | | 5.1 | 3.0 | 2.0 | 2.1 | 1.5 | .4 |
| (172) 2.7 | (194) 2.4 | (144) 2.3 | % Officers', Directors' Owners' Comp/Sales | (16) 9.5 | (26) 5.4 | (10) 3.3 | (25) 3.0 | (34) 1.5 | (33) 1.0 |
| 5.6 | 5.8 | 5.7 | | 12.4 | 10.5 | 6.8 | 5.0 | 2.9 | 1.5 |
| 18453696M | 23137269M | 18082697M | Net Sales ($) | 19755M | 97039M | 98210M | 491327M | 1272332M | 16104034M |
| 6978185M | 8937327M | 7419491M | Total Assets ($) | 12868M | 47460M | 44533M | 240925M | 578603M | 6495102M |

© RMA 2024  
M = $ thousand  MM = $ million  
See Pages viii through xx for Explanation of Ratios and Data

# TRANSPORTATION AND WAREHOUSING

# TRANSPORTATION—Scheduled Passenger Air Transportation  NAICS 481111

## Current Data Sorted by Assets | Comparative Historical Data

| 0-500M | 5 (4/1-9/30/23) 500M-2MM | 2-10MM | 20 (10/1/23-3/31/24) 10-50MM | 50-100MM | 100-250MM | | Type of Statement | | 4/1/19-3/31/20 ALL | 4/1/20-3/31/21 ALL |
|---|---|---|---|---|---|---|---|---|---|---|
| | | | | | | | Unqualified | | 9 | 1 |
| | | | 2 | | | | Reviewed | | 2 | 2 |
| | 1 | | 1 | 2 | 3 | | Compiled | | | 4 |
| | | | 2 | | | | Tax Returns | | 6 | 2 |
| | | 4 | 5 | | 5 | | Other | | 14 | 13 |
| | 1 | 4 | 10 | 2 | 8 | | NUMBER OF STATEMENTS | | 31 | 22 |
| % | % | % | % | % | % | | ASSETS | | % | % |
| | | | 12.0 | | | | Cash & Equivalents | | 15.7 | 34.3 |
| D | | | 13.0 | | | | Trade Receivables (net) | | 7.7 | 9.6 |
| A | | | 6.4 | | | | Inventory | | 7.3 | 4.8 |
| T | | | 3.0 | | | | All Other Current | | 4.4 | 4.3 |
| A | | | 34.4 | | | | Total Current | | 35.1 | 53.0 |
| | | | 43.2 | | | | Fixed Assets (net) | | 53.1 | 36.8 |
| N | | | 13.1 | | | | Intangibles (net) | | 4.8 | 5.0 |
| O | | | 9.4 | | | | All Other Non-Current | | 7.0 | 5.2 |
| T | | | 100.0 | | | | Total | | 100.0 | 100.0 |
| | | | | | | | LIABILITIES | | | |
| A | | | 2.0 | | | | Notes Payable-Short Term | | 1.7 | 2.8 |
| V | | | 3.7 | | | | Cur. Mat.-L.T.D. | | 10.1 | 5.3 |
| A | | | 10.9 | | | | Trade Payables | | 9.0 | 7.4 |
| I | | | .1 | | | | Income Taxes Payable | | .2 | .2 |
| L | | | 6.1 | | | | All Other Current | | 14.8 | 18.8 |
| A | | | 22.8 | | | | Total Current | | 35.8 | 34.4 |
| B | | | 28.4 | | | | Long-Term Debt | | 61.2 | 39.4 |
| L | | | .6 | | | | Deferred Taxes | | .9 | .5 |
| E | | | 28.6 | | | | All Other Non-Current | | 3.3 | 11.2 |
| | | | 19.7 | | | | Net Worth | | -1.3 | 14.5 |
| | | | 100.0 | | | | Total Liabilties & Net Worth | | 100.0 | 100.0 |
| | | | | | | | INCOME DATA | | | |
| | | | 100.0 | | | | Net Sales | | 100.0 | 100.0 |
| | | | | | | | Gross Profit | | | |
| | | | 95.3 | | | | Operating Expenses | | 91.6 | 93.2 |
| | | | 4.7 | | | | Operating Profit | | 8.4 | 6.8 |
| | | | .4 | | | | All Other Expenses (net) | | 3.2 | -.8 |
| | | | 4.3 | | | | Profit Before Taxes | | 5.2 | 7.6 |
| | | | | | | | RATIOS | | | |
| | | | 5.0 | | | | | | 3.0 | 3.4 |
| | | | 1.4 | | | | Current | | 1.0 | 2.5 |
| | | | .9 | | | | | | .5 | 1.5 |
| | | | 3.7 | | | | | | 2.2 | 2.7 |
| | | | 1.1 | | | | Quick | | .6 | 1.8 |
| | | | .3 | | | | | | .3 | .8 |
| | | 11 | 34.7 | | | | | 3 | 114.3 | 0 UND |
| | | 27 | 13.3 | | | | Sales/Receivables | 18 | 20.6 | 6 56.6 |
| | | 58 | 6.3 | | | | | 36 | 10.2 | 43 8.5 |
| | | | | | | | Cost of Sales/Inventory | | | |
| | | | | | | | Cost of Sales/Payables | | | |
| | | | 4.2 | | | | | | 5.5 | 3.5 |
| | | | 17.2 | | | | Sales/Working Capital | | 215.6 | 7.9 |
| | | | -260.0 | | | | | | -7.7 | 13.9 |
| | | | | | | | | | 9.8 | 10.6 |
| | | | | | | | EBIT/Interest | (28) | 3.4 | (19) 7.3 |
| | | | | | | | | | .1 | -3.3 |
| | | | | | | | Net Profit + Depr., Dep., Amort./Cur. Mat. L/T/D | | | |
| | | | 1.2 | | | | | | 1.0 | .5 |
| | | | 2.4 | | | | Fixed/Worth | | 4.2 | 1.7 |
| | | | NM | | | | | | -4.1 | -2.0 |
| | | | 1.5 | | | | | | .8 | .7 |
| | | | 2.5 | | | | Debt/Worth | | 4.5 | 2.5 |
| | | | NM | | | | | | -5.9 | -5.7 |
| | | | | | | | | | 70.0 | 59.9 |
| | | | | | | | % Profit Before Taxes/Tangible Net Worth | (22) | 35.3 | (14) 21.3 |
| | | | | | | | | | 3.3 | -8.5 |
| | | | 14.3 | | | | | | 14.9 | 33.0 |
| | | | 7.2 | | | | % Profit Before Taxes/Total Assets | | 8.2 | 12.4 |
| | | | -2.5 | | | | | | -1.2 | -8.7 |
| | | | 45.1 | | | | | | 5.2 | 26.7 |
| | | | 3.0 | | | | Sales/Net Fixed Assets | | 2.0 | 5.4 |
| | | | 1.2 | | | | | | 1.3 | 1.5 |
| | | | 2.0 | | | | | | 1.7 | 3.9 |
| | | | 1.4 | | | | Sales/Total Assets | | 1.3 | 1.8 |
| | | | .7 | | | | | | .9 | .8 |
| | | | | | | | | | 3.4 | 1.5 |
| | | | | | | | % Depr., Dep., Amort./Sales | (20) | 6.7 | (14) 8.1 |
| | | | | | | | | | 12.5 | 10.2 |
| | | | | | | | % Officers', Directors' Owners' Comp/Sales | | | |
| | 23474M | 48206M | 370629M | 299381M | 1175591M | | Net Sales ($) | | 2105176M | 1050700M |
| | 1248M | 15117M | 231162M | 144248M | 1402585M | | Total Assets ($) | | 1311191M | 726347M |

© RMA 2024   M = $ thousand   MM = $ million
See Pages viii through xx for Explanation of Ratios and Data

## TRANSPORTATION—Scheduled Passenger Air Transportation  NAICS 481111

### Comparative Historical Data / Current Data Sorted by Sales

| | | | | Type of Statement | | | | | | |
|---|---|---|---|---|---|---|---|---|---|---|
| | 4 | 7 | 7 | Unqualified | | | | | 1 | 7 |
| | 3 | 2 | 1 | Reviewed | | | | 1 | | |
| | 2 | 2 | | Compiled | | | | 4 | 1 | 1 |
| | 3 | 9 | 3 | Tax Returns | | | 1 | | | 8 |
| | 13 | 19 | 14 | Other | | 1 | | | | |
| | 4/1/21-3/31/22 ALL | 4/1/22-3/31/23 ALL | 4/1/23-3/31/24 ALL | | 0-1MM | 5 (4/1-9/30/23) 1-3MM | 3-5MM | 20 (10/1/23-3/31/24) 5-10MM | 10-25MM | 25MM & OVER |
| | 25 | 39 | 25 | NUMBER OF STATEMENTS | | 1 | | 5 | 3 | 16 |
| | % | % | % | **ASSETS** | % | % | % | % | % | % |
| | 21.5 | 17.9 | 19.7 | Cash & Equivalents | D | D | | | | 20.7 |
| | 12.8 | 12.2 | 9.7 | Trade Receivables (net) | A | A | | | | 8.4 |
| | 6.1 | 4.7 | 5.8 | Inventory | T | T | | | | 4.0 |
| | 3.0 | 4.2 | 2.2 | All Other Current | A | A | | | | 2.9 |
| | 43.4 | 39.1 | 37.4 | Total Current | | | | | | 35.9 |
| | 41.3 | 38.9 | 42.2 | Fixed Assets (net) | N | N | | | | 40.2 |
| | 10.9 | 9.5 | 8.4 | Intangibles (net) | O | O | | | | 7.3 |
| | 4.4 | 12.5 | 12.0 | All Other Non-Current | T | T | | | | 16.6 |
| | 100.0 | 100.0 | 100.0 | Total | | | | | | 100.0 |
| | | | | **LIABILITIES** | A | A | | | | |
| | 4.7 | 6.5 | 2.8 | Notes Payable-Short Term | V | V | | | | 1.5 |
| | 2.7 | 3.5 | 4.3 | Cur. Mat.-L.T.D. | A | A | | | | 4.7 |
| | 12.5 | 5.8 | 7.9 | Trade Payables | I | I | | | | 9.2 |
| | .5 | .4 | .2 | Income Taxes Payable | L | L | | | | .3 |
| | 10.4 | 10.9 | 13.4 | All Other Current | A | A | | | | 13.2 |
| | 30.9 | 27.1 | 28.6 | Total Current | B | B | | | | 28.8 |
| | 46.1 | 29.3 | 28.5 | Long-Term Debt | L | L | | | | 30.2 |
| | 1.0 | .6 | 1.4 | Deferred Taxes | E | E | | | | 1.8 |
| | 11.7 | 15.4 | 18.1 | All Other Non-Current | | | | | | 17.6 |
| | 10.3 | 27.6 | 23.4 | Net Worth | | | | | | 21.5 |
| | 100.0 | 100.0 | 100.0 | Total Liabilities & Net Worth | | | | | | 100.0 |
| | | | | **INCOME DATA** | | | | | | |
| | 100.0 | 100.0 | 100.0 | Net Sales | | | | | | 100.0 |
| | | | | Gross Profit | | | | | | |
| | 90.9 | 94.1 | 96.5 | Operating Expenses | | | | | | 97.5 |
| | 9.1 | 5.9 | 3.5 | Operating Profit | | | | | | 2.5 |
| | 1.1 | .4 | .9 | All Other Expenses (net) | | | | | | 1.5 |
| | 8.0 | 5.5 | 2.6 | Profit Before Taxes | | | | | | .9 |
| | | | | **RATIOS** | | | | | | |
| | 4.1 | 4.2 | 2.4 | | | | | | | 1.9 |
| | 2.7 | 2.4 | 1.4 | Current | | | | | | 1.3 |
| | 1.1 | 1.0 | .6 | | | | | | | .6 |
| | 2.7 | 3.4 | 2.2 | | | | | | | 1.7 |
| | 1.7 | 1.5 | 1.0 | Quick | | | | | | .9 |
| | .9 | .5 | .4 | | | | | | | .4 |
| 7 | 50.9 | 8  43.7 | 9  42.7 | | | | | | 8 | 43.4 |
| 33 | 10.9 | 23  15.8 | 18  20.3 | Sales/Receivables | | | | | 17 | 22.1 |
| 47 | 7.8 | 59  6.2 | 46  8.0 | | | | | | 26 | 14.2 |
| | | | | Cost of Sales/Inventory | | | | | | |
| | | | | Cost of Sales/Payables | | | | | | |
| | 3.2 | 4.4 | 8.7 | | | | | | | 8.9 |
| | 6.9 | 8.9 | 31.8 | Sales/Working Capital | | | | | | 31.8 |
| | 31.3 | -128.2 | -7.3 | | | | | | | -8.2 |
| | 24.7 | 8.5 | 9.0 | | | | | | | 3.3 |
| (23) | 9.1 | (35) 3.8 | (21) 1.4 | EBIT/Interest | | | | | (13) | 1.1 |
| | -.6 | .9 | -1.0 | | | | | | | -1.0 |
| | | | | Net Profit + Depr., Dep., Amort./Cur. Mat. L/T/D | | | | | | |
| | .8 | .7 | .9 | | | | | | | 1.2 |
| | 1.3 | 1.6 | 2.2 | Fixed/Worth | | | | | | 2.2 |
| | -8.5 | -87.7 | NM | | | | | | | 13.9 |
| | .8 | .6 | 1.6 | | | | | | | 1.6 |
| | 1.8 | 2.4 | 2.5 | Debt/Worth | | | | | | 2.6 |
| | -19.2 | -170.4 | NM | | | | | | | 94.8 |
| | 54.3 | 52.8 | 38.6 | % Profit Before Taxes/Tangible Net Worth | | | | | | 50.3 |
| (18) | 32.9 | (28) 15.5 | (19) 16.0 | | | | | | (13) | 2.9 |
| | 5.6 | -4.4 | -15.0 | | | | | | | -14.0 |
| | 23.0 | 13.5 | 12.4 | % Profit Before Taxes/Total Assets | | | | | | 12.2 |
| | 8.4 | 8.2 | 3.6 | | | | | | | 2.1 |
| | -2.8 | -.2 | -5.0 | | | | | | | -5.2 |
| | 15.3 | 14.0 | 22.9 | | | | | | | 23.6 |
| | 2.3 | 3.3 | 2.4 | Sales/Net Fixed Assets | | | | | | 2.5 |
| | .9 | 1.2 | 1.2 | | | | | | | 1.4 |
| | 2.0 | 2.6 | 2.1 | | | | | | | 2.2 |
| | 1.1 | 1.1 | 1.1 | Sales/Total Assets | | | | | | 1.1 |
| | .6 | .5 | .7 | | | | | | | .9 |
| | 3.9 | 2.1 | 3.0 | | | | | | | |
| (18) | 7.6 | (28) 5.0 | (16) 6.2 | % Depr., Dep., Amort./Sales | | | | | | |
| | 10.2 | 9.1 | 7.7 | | | | | | | |
| | | | 1.1 | | | | | | | |
| | | (10) 3.4 | | % Officers', Directors' Owners' Comp/Sales | | | | | | |
| | | | 6.2 | | | | | | | |
| | 1488361M | 2007230M | 1917281M | Net Sales ($) | | | 4013M | 40183M | 52874M | 1820211M |
| | 1365064M | 2043980M | 1794360M | Total Assets ($) | | | 6038M | 58166M | 22234M | 1707922M |

© RMA 2024   M = $ thousand   MM = $ million
See Pages viii through xx for Explanation of Ratios and Data

# TRANSPORTATION—Nonscheduled Chartered Passenger Air Transportation  NAICS 481211

## Current Data Sorted by Assets | Comparative Historical Data

| | | | | | | Type of Statement | | |
|---|---|---|---|---|---|---|---|---|
| | | | 1 | 1 | 1 | Unqualified | 5 | 3 |
| | | | 3 | 1 | 1 | Reviewed | 3 | 4 |
| | | 5 | 1 | | | Compiled | 1 | 1 |
| 1 | 2 | 9 | 13 | 4 | 2 | Tax Returns | 9 | 1 |
| 0-500M | 6 (4/1-9/30/23) 500M-2MM | 2-10MM | 40 (10/1/23-3/31/24) 10-50MM | 50-100MM | 100-250MM | Other | 30 4/1/19- 3/31/20 ALL | 20 4/1/20- 3/31/21 ALL |
| 1 | 2 | 14 | 19 | 6 | 4 | NUMBER OF STATEMENTS | 48 | 29 |
| % | % | % | % | % | % | ASSETS | % | % |
| | | 20.3 | 13.8 | | | Cash & Equivalents | 12.9 | 18.7 |
| | | 23.4 | 12.5 | | | Trade Receivables (net) | 20.3 | 9.9 |
| | | 4.2 | 7.7 | | | Inventory | 1.9 | 2.4 |
| | | 5.8 | 3.7 | | | All Other Current | 6.2 | 5.2 |
| | | 53.6 | 37.7 | | | Total Current | 41.4 | 36.1 |
| | | 24.3 | 40.0 | | | Fixed Assets (net) | 48.0 | 46.1 |
| | | .4 | 3.9 | | | Intangibles (net) | 6.0 | 7.8 |
| | | 21.7 | 18.4 | | | All Other Non-Current | 4.6 | 10.0 |
| | | 100.0 | 100.0 | | | Total | 100.0 | 100.0 |
| | | | | | | LIABILITIES | | |
| | | 12.7 | 6.0 | | | Notes Payable-Short Term | 9.6 | 2.6 |
| | | 6.1 | 3.2 | | | Cur. Mat.-L.T.D. | 5.0 | 6.4 |
| | | 20.0 | 6.2 | | | Trade Payables | 12.6 | 6.2 |
| | | .0 | .0 | | | Income Taxes Payable | .2 | .3 |
| | | 16.0 | 17.6 | | | All Other Current | 12.2 | 11.4 |
| | | 54.7 | 33.0 | | | Total Current | 39.6 | 26.8 |
| | | 46.0 | 15.7 | | | Long-Term Debt | 30.7 | 46.2 |
| | | .2 | .1 | | | Deferred Taxes | .8 | .6 |
| | | .7 | 5.8 | | | All Other Non-Current | 9.9 | 14.7 |
| | | -1.6 | 45.4 | | | Net Worth | 19.0 | 11.7 |
| | | 100.0 | 100.0 | | | Total Liabilties & Net Worth | 100.0 | 100.0 |
| | | | | | | INCOME DATA | | |
| | | 100.0 | 100.0 | | | Net Sales | 100.0 | 100.0 |
| | | | | | | Gross Profit | | |
| | | 96.8 | 95.8 | | | Operating Expenses | 86.2 | 92.8 |
| | | 3.2 | 4.2 | | | Operating Profit | 13.8 | 7.2 |
| | | 2.2 | 1.0 | | | All Other Expenses (net) | 6.5 | 1.9 |
| | | 1.0 | 3.2 | | | Profit Before Taxes | 7.3 | 5.2 |
| | | | | | | RATIOS | | |
| | | 2.9 | 2.2 | | | | 2.1 | 3.4 |
| | | 1.4 | 1.7 | | | Current | 1.1 | 1.1 |
| | | .4 | .7 | | | | .5 | .6 |
| | | 2.3 | 2.1 | | | | 1.8 | 2.4 |
| | | 1.2 | 1.4 | | | Quick | .8 | .8 |
| | | .4 | .3 | | | | .3 | .3 |
| | | 7  49.5 | 15  24.9 | | | | 0  UND | 5  66.7 |
| | | 27  13.4 | 22  16.7 | | | Sales/Receivables | 20  18.7 | 14  25.9 |
| | | 78  4.7 | 34  10.6 | | | | 49  7.4 | 31  11.8 |
| | | | | | | Cost of Sales/Inventory | | |
| | | | | | | Cost of Sales/Payables | | |
| | | 3.7 | 11.1 | | | | 7.3 | 3.8 |
| | | 36.4 | 16.1 | | | Sales/Working Capital | 35.7 | 41.7 |
| | | -6.3 | -7.4 | | | | -6.8 | -12.6 |
| | | 6.5 | 6.7 | | | | 6.8 | 8.8 |
| | | (10) 1.8 | 1.3 | | | EBIT/Interest | (35) 3.6 | (25) 3.3 |
| | | -.9 | -6.3 | | | | .3 | .9 |
| | | | | | | Net Profit + Depr., Dep., Amort./Cur. Mat. L/T/D | | |
| | | .0 | .6 | | | | .7 | .7 |
| | | .5 | 1.0 | | | Fixed/Worth | 2.3 | 2.6 |
| | | -4.7 | 2.0 | | | | -37.1 | NM |
| | | 1.3 | .3 | | | | .8 | 1.3 |
| | | 3.5 | 1.7 | | | Debt/Worth | 2.5 | 4.8 |
| | | -14.1 | 2.9 | | | | -10.0 | NM |
| | | 58.5 | 21.3 | | | | 41.9 | 76.9 |
| | | (10) 21.9 | (18) 1.6 | | | % Profit Before Taxes/Tangible Net Worth | (32) 19.4 | (22) 19.5 |
| | | 1.0 | -10.7 | | | | 4.7 | -2.5 |
| | | 21.2 | 7.7 | | | | 12.0 | 15.1 |
| | | 3.6 | 1.0 | | | % Profit Before Taxes/Total Assets | 4.1 | 2.8 |
| | | -3.6 | -4.8 | | | | -.6 | -2.4 |
| | | 999.8 | 10.4 | | | | 42.6 | 14.1 |
| | | 95.5 | 5.1 | | | Sales/Net Fixed Assets | 3.1 | 4.0 |
| | | 2.5 | 2.3 | | | | .7 | .6 |
| | | 7.8 | 2.5 | | | | 3.2 | 2.3 |
| | | 1.9 | 2.0 | | | Sales/Total Assets | 1.4 | .9 |
| | | .6 | .8 | | | | .4 | .4 |
| | | | 1.3 | | | | 2.2 | 2.3 |
| | | (16) | 3.8 | | | % Depr., Dep., Amort./Sales | (30) 6.1 | (22) 6.0 |
| | | | 7.0 | | | | 13.6 | 15.5 |
| | | | | | | | .8 | |
| | | | | | | % Officers', Directors' Owners' Comp/Sales | (10) 1.5 | |
| | | | | | | | 8.9 | |
| 212M | 1625M | 253632M | 844061M | 516005M | 835988M | Net Sales ($) | 1691433M | 1406546M |
| 82M | 1840M | 79228M | 505069M | 406486M | 641423M | Total Assets ($) | 1463312M | 1329568M |

© RMA 2024  M = $ thousand  MM = $ million
See Pages viii through xx for Explanation of Ratios and Data

## TRANSPORTATION—Nonscheduled Chartered Passenger Air Transportation  NAICS 481211

### Comparative Historical Data | Current Data Sorted by Sales

| | | | Type of Statement | | | | | | |
|---|---|---|---|---|---|---|---|---|---|
| 4 | 4 | 3 | Unqualified | | | | | | 3 |
| 3 | 8 | 5 | Reviewed | | | | | 2 | 3 |
| 1 | 1 | 1 | Compiled | | | | 1 | | |
| 2 | 5 | 6 | Tax Returns | | 2 | 1 | | 1 | 2 |
| 29 | 23 | 31 | Other | 2 | 2 | 1 | 3 | 6 | 17 |
| 4/1/21-3/31/22 ALL | 4/1/22-3/31/23 ALL | 4/1/23-3/31/24 ALL | | 0-1MM | 6 (4/1-9/30/23) 1-3MM | 3-5MM | 40 (10/1/23-3/31/24) 5-10MM | 10-25MM | 25MM & OVER |
| 39 | 41 | 46 | **NUMBER OF STATEMENTS** | 2 | 4 | 2 | 4 | 9 | 25 |
| % | % | % | **ASSETS** | % | % | % | % | % | % |
| 25.0 | 23.5 | 16.8 | Cash & Equivalents | | | | | | 17.9 |
| 12.8 | 10.4 | 17.2 | Trade Receivables (net) | | | | | | 17.7 |
| 2.7 | 2.3 | 5.1 | Inventory | | | | | | 3.4 |
| 3.2 | 6.5 | 6.3 | All Other Current | | | | | | 6.6 |
| 43.7 | 42.6 | 45.3 | Total Current | | | | | | 45.6 |
| 33.2 | 35.1 | 33.8 | Fixed Assets (net) | | | | | | 33.9 |
| 10.4 | 6.1 | 2.3 | Intangibles (net) | | | | | | 4.1 |
| 12.7 | 16.1 | 18.6 | All Other Non-Current | | | | | | 16.4 |
| 100.0 | 100.0 | 100.0 | Total | | | | | | 100.0 |
| | | | **LIABILITIES** | | | | | | |
| 3.8 | 3.8 | 6.8 | Notes Payable-Short Term | | | | | | 4.0 |
| 3.3 | 4.7 | 6.3 | Cur. Mat.-L.T.D. | | | | | | 5.9 |
| 17.5 | 10.6 | 11.0 | Trade Payables | | | | | | 9.9 |
| .1 | .1 | .1 | Income Taxes Payable | | | | | | .2 |
| 18.5 | 19.3 | 16.9 | All Other Current | | | | | | 20.5 |
| 43.2 | 38.5 | 41.1 | Total Current | | | | | | 40.4 |
| 44.7 | 38.5 | 40.3 | Long-Term Debt | | | | | | 32.0 |
| .2 | .6 | .1 | Deferred Taxes | | | | | | .3 |
| 7.2 | 10.8 | 5.9 | All Other Non-Current | | | | | | 5.9 |
| 4.6 | 11.6 | 12.5 | Net Worth | | | | | | 21.4 |
| 100.0 | 100.0 | 100.0 | Total Liabilities & Net Worth | | | | | | 100.0 |
| | | | **INCOME DATA** | | | | | | |
| 100.0 | 100.0 | 100.0 | Net Sales | | | | | | 100.0 |
| | | | Gross Profit | | | | | | |
| 93.5 | 91.4 | 92.4 | Operating Expenses | | | | | | 93.8 |
| 6.5 | 8.6 | 7.6 | Operating Profit | | | | | | 6.2 |
| -1.1 | 1.0 | 2.4 | All Other Expenses (net) | | | | | | 1.2 |
| 7.6 | 7.6 | 5.2 | Profit Before Taxes | | | | | | 5.0 |
| | | | **RATIOS** | | | | | | |
| 3.5 | 3.0 | 2.3 | | | | | | | 2.3 |
| 1.3 | 1.4 | 1.5 | Current | | | | | | 1.7 |
| .7 | .6 | .7 | | | | | | | .9 |
| 3.4 | 2.1 | 2.2 | | | | | | | 2.2 |
| 1.1 | .9 | 1.3 | Quick | | | | | | 1.2 |
| .6 | .4 | .4 | | | | | | | .4 |
| 7   50.1 | 3   130.4 | 5   75.3 | | | | | | | 4   95.2 |
| 24  14.9 | 17  21.8 | 25  14.8 | Sales/Receivables | | | | | | 25  14.5 |
| 41  8.8 | 30  12.2 | 37  9.9 | | | | | | | 35  10.5 |
| | | | Cost of Sales/Inventory | | | | | | |
| | | | Cost of Sales/Payables | | | | | | |
| 5.5 | 5.9 | 6.0 | | | | | | | 10.3 |
| 16.7 | 33.8 | 17.2 | Sales/Working Capital | | | | | | 16.1 |
| -12.3 | -9.5 | -15.3 | | | | | | | NM |
| 30.9 | 32.0 | 6.5 | | | | | | | 7.8 |
| (31) 5.8 | (33) 5.6 | (40) 2.1 | EBIT/Interest | | | | | | (23) 1.4 |
| 2.3 | 1.1 | -1.4 | | | | | | | -6.3 |
| | | 2.8 | | | | | | | |
| | (11) | 1.1 | Net Profit + Depr., Dep., Amort./Cur. Mat. L/T/D | | | | | | |
| | | .5 | | | | | | | |
| .4 | .5 | .4 | | | | | | | .7 |
| 1.2 | 1.4 | 1.1 | Fixed/Worth | | | | | | 1.3 |
| 7.7 | 11.3 | 8.4 | | | | | | | 4.9 |
| 1.7 | 1.7 | 1.0 | | | | | | | .9 |
| 3.2 | 2.9 | 2.8 | Debt/Worth | | | | | | 3.1 |
| -6.0 | 22.1 | 24.8 | | | | | | | 20.5 |
| 90.6 | 77.0 | 48.9 | | | | | | | 59.5 |
| (28) 52.1 | (34) 42.3 | (38) 10.0 | % Profit Before Taxes/Tangible Net Worth | | | | | | (22) 6.3 |
| 10.4 | 9.1 | -8.6 | | | | | | | -10.7 |
| 24.5 | 25.2 | 10.0 | | | | | | | 12.0 |
| 11.9 | 6.1 | 3.6 | % Profit Before Taxes/Total Assets | | | | | | 4.9 |
| 4.1 | 1.2 | -2.8 | | | | | | | -3.5 |
| 82.2 | 34.7 | 74.9 | | | | | | | 10.5 |
| 8.4 | 6.9 | 8.3 | Sales/Net Fixed Assets | | | | | | 6.1 |
| 1.4 | 2.2 | 2.4 | | | | | | | 2.8 |
| 3.4 | 2.7 | 2.5 | | | | | | | 2.7 |
| 1.3 | 1.7 | 1.5 | Sales/Total Assets | | | | | | 2.1 |
| .8 | .9 | .8 | | | | | | | 1.1 |
| 1.3 | .9 | .8 | | | | | | | .7 |
| (22) 3.7 | (25) 2.2 | (31) 2.8 | % Depr., Dep., Amort./Sales | | | | | | (20) 2.4 |
| 9.3 | 7.2 | 8.0 | | | | | | | 4.3 |
| | | | % Officers', Directors', Owners' Comp/Sales | | | | | | |
| 2233716M | 1713548M | 2451523M | Net Sales ($) | 248M | 6906M | 8491M | 33742M | 130263M | 2271873M |
| 1754518M | 1130937M | 1634128M | Total Assets ($) | 739M | 19324M | 9376M | 40857M | 178507M | 1385325M |

© RMA 2024  
M = $ thousand    MM = $ million  
See Pages viii through xx for Explanation of Ratios and Data

# TRANSPORTATION—Other Nonscheduled Air Transportation  NAICS 481219

## Current Data Sorted by Assets | Comparative Historical Data

| | | | | | | | Type of Statement | | | | |
|---|---|---|---|---|---|---|---|---|---|---|---|
| | | | | 2 | | 1 | Unqualified | | 3 | | 2 |
| | | | | 1 | | | Reviewed | | 5 | | 3 |
| | | | 1 | 1 | | | Compiled | | 1 | | |
| | | | 1 | | | | Tax Returns | | 7 | | 4 |
| 1 | 2 | | 7 | 10 | 3 | 5 | Other | | 23 | | 23 |
| | 6 (4/1-9/30/23) | | | 29 (10/1/23-3/31/24) | | | | | 4/1/19- | | 4/1/20- |
| 0-500M | 500M-2MM | 2-10MM | 10-50MM | | 50-100MM | 100-250MM | | | 3/31/20 | | 3/31/21 |
| 1 | 2 | 9 | 14 | | 3 | 6 | NUMBER OF STATEMENTS | | ALL 39 | | ALL 32 |
| % | % | % | % | | % | % | **ASSETS** | | % | | % |
| | | | 17.8 | | | | Cash & Equivalents | | 16.4 | | 27.0 |
| | | | 14.7 | | | | Trade Receivables (net) | | 13.4 | | 13.9 |
| | | | 6.4 | | | | Inventory | | 8.7 | | 2.0 |
| | | | 2.6 | | | | All Other Current | | 2.1 | | 2.0 |
| | | | 41.5 | | | | Total Current | | 40.7 | | 44.9 |
| | | | 47.0 | | | | Fixed Assets (net) | | 46.7 | | 43.3 |
| | | | 1.0 | | | | Intangibles (net) | | 4.5 | | 1.8 |
| | | | 10.6 | | | | All Other Non-Current | | 8.1 | | 10.0 |
| | | | 100.0 | | | | Total | | 100.0 | | 100.0 |
| | | | | | | | **LIABILITIES** | | | | |
| | | | 1.0 | | | | Notes Payable-Short Term | | 5.0 | | .5 |
| | | | 3.9 | | | | Cur. Mat.-L.T.D. | | 5.9 | | 6.6 |
| | | | 9.8 | | | | Trade Payables | | 11.4 | | 7.0 |
| | | | .0 | | | | Income Taxes Payable | | .1 | | .1 |
| | | | 15.0 | | | | All Other Current | | 14.1 | | 29.3 |
| | | | 29.7 | | | | Total Current | | 36.4 | | 43.5 |
| | | | 24.8 | | | | Long-Term Debt | | 36.6 | | 46.6 |
| | | | .5 | | | | Deferred Taxes | | .9 | | 1.1 |
| | | | 7.9 | | | | All Other Non-Current | | 12.9 | | 10.2 |
| | | | 37.0 | | | | Net Worth | | 13.2 | | -1.4 |
| | | | 100.0 | | | | Total Liabilities & Net Worth | | 100.0 | | 100.0 |
| | | | | | | | **INCOME DATA** | | | | |
| | | | 100.0 | | | | Net Sales | | 100.0 | | 100.0 |
| | | | | | | | Gross Profit | | | | |
| | | | 91.5 | | | | Operating Expenses | | 94.5 | | 82.9 |
| | | | 8.5 | | | | Operating Profit | | 5.5 | | 17.1 |
| | | | 7.9 | | | | All Other Expenses (net) | | 2.8 | | -.4 |
| | | | .6 | | | | Profit Before Taxes | | 2.7 | | 17.5 |
| | | | | | | | **RATIOS** | | | | |
| | | | 7.7 | | | | | | 2.0 | | 3.6 |
| | | | 1.8 | | | | Current | | 1.2 | | 1.6 |
| | | | .6 | | | | | | .7 | | 1.0 |
| | | | 4.8 | | | | | | 1.5 | | 3.5 |
| | | | 1.3 | | | | Quick | | .9 | | 1.6 |
| | | | .4 | | | | | | .5 | | .7 |
| | | | 0 | UND | | | | 5 | 73.0 | 0 | UND |
| | | | 21 | 17.5 | | | Sales/Receivables | 29 | 12.8 | 18 | 20.8 |
| | | | 38 | 9.5 | | | | 46 | 7.9 | 42 | 8.7 |
| | | | | | | | Cost of Sales/Inventory | | | | |
| | | | | | | | Cost of Sales/Payables | | | | |
| | | | 3.9 | | | | | | 4.5 | | 4.7 |
| | | | 14.7 | | | | Sales/Working Capital | | 20.5 | | 13.6 |
| | | | -12.7 | | | | | | -19.3 | | NM |
| | | | 8.0 | | | | | | 4.3 | | 16.6 |
| | | (10) | 2.1 | | | | EBIT/Interest | (32) | 1.2 | (24) | 7.8 |
| | | | -14.9 | | | | | | -3.5 | | 3.8 |
| | | | | | | | Net Profit + Depr., Dep., Amort./Cur. Mat. L/T/D | | | | |
| | | | .3 | | | | | | .6 | | .8 |
| | | | 1.5 | | | | Fixed/Worth | | 1.9 | | 2.1 |
| | | | NM | | | | | | -12.1 | | -1.8 |
| | | | .4 | | | | | | .7 | | 1.3 |
| | | | 1.7 | | | | Debt/Worth | | 4.7 | | 2.7 |
| | | | NM | | | | | | -6.1 | | -8.3 |
| | | | 21.9 | | | | | | 37.7 | | 70.5 |
| | | (11) | 12.5 | | | | % Profit Before Taxes/Tangible Net Worth | (28) | 13.9 | (22) | 40.2 |
| | | | -6.3 | | | | | | -14.1 | | 14.3 |
| | | | 13.4 | | | | | | 12.4 | | 35.0 |
| | | | 2.8 | | | | % Profit Before Taxes/Total Assets | | 2.4 | | 11.7 |
| | | | -5.8 | | | | | | -14.7 | | 3.9 |
| | | | 18.1 | | | | | | 10.5 | | 25.4 |
| | | | 3.4 | | | | Sales/Net Fixed Assets | | 3.0 | | 3.2 |
| | | | 1.0 | | | | | | .7 | | .6 |
| | | | 2.6 | | | | | | 2.6 | | 2.8 |
| | | | 1.3 | | | | Sales/Total Assets | | 1.2 | | 1.4 |
| | | | .5 | | | | | | .6 | | .5 |
| | | | | | | | | | 1.6 | | 2.1 |
| | | | | | | | % Depr., Dep., Amort./Sales | (31) | 6.3 | (20) | 7.2 |
| | | | | | | | | | 12.8 | | 14.6 |
| | | | | | | | % Officers', Directors' Owners' Comp/Sales | | | | |
| 1452M | 8107M | 80748M | 551912M | | 176505M | 602999M | Net Sales ($) | | 1020264M | | 741686M |
| 339M | 3678M | 48294M | 363015M | | 216853M | 1162590M | Total Assets ($) | | 847450M | | 840035M |

M = $ thousand    MM = $ million
See Pages viii through xx for Explanation of Ratios and Data

© RMA 2024

# TRANSPORTATION—Other Nonscheduled Air Transportation  NAICS 481219

## Comparative Historical Data | Current Data Sorted by Sales

| Comparative Historical Data | | | | | | | | | | | | | Current Data Sorted by Sales | | | | | | | |
|---|---|---|---|---|---|---|---|---|---|---|---|---|---|---|---|---|---|---|---|---|
| | 2 | | 4 | | 3 | **Type of Statement** | | | | | | | | | | | | | | 3 |
| | 3 | | 3 | | 1 | Unqualified | | | | | | | | | | | | | | 1 |
| | 3 | | 2 | | 2 | Reviewed | | | | | | | | | | | | | | 1 |
| | 5 | | 5 | | 1 | Compiled | | | | | | | | | | | | | | |
| | 18 | | 28 | | 28 | Tax Returns | | | | | 1 | | | | 1 | | | | | 14 |
| | 4/1/21-3/31/22 ALL | | 4/1/22-3/31/23 ALL | | 4/1/23-3/31/24 ALL | Other | | | | 5 6 (4/1-9/30/23) | | 3 | | 3 29 (10/1/23-3/31/24) | | 3 | | | | |
| | | | | | | | | 0-1MM | | 1-3MM | | 3-5MM | | 5-10MM | | 10-25MM | | | | 25MM & OVER |
| | 31 | | 42 | | 35 | **NUMBER OF STATEMENTS** | | 1 | | 5 | | 3 | | 4 | | 3 | | | | 19 |
| | % | | % | | % | **ASSETS** | | % | | % | | % | | % | | % | | | | % |
| | 18.1 | | 19.5 | | 19.4 | Cash & Equivalents | | | | | | | | | | | | | | 22.0 |
| | 12.6 | | 10.6 | | 9.5 | Trade Receivables (net) | | | | | | | | | | | | | | 14.0 |
| | 4.4 | | 6.3 | | 7.6 | Inventory | | | | | | | | | | | | | | 6.6 |
| | 4.8 | | 1.4 | | 2.9 | All Other Current | | | | | | | | | | | | | | 4.8 |
| | 40.0 | | 37.8 | | 39.4 | Total Current | | | | | | | | | | | | | | 47.4 |
| | 48.7 | | 44.0 | | 45.9 | Fixed Assets (net) | | | | | | | | | | | | | | 36.8 |
| | 3.7 | | 7.9 | | 3.4 | Intangibles (net) | | | | | | | | | | | | | | 4.9 |
| | 7.6 | | 10.3 | | 11.3 | All Other Non-Current | | | | | | | | | | | | | | 10.9 |
| | 100.0 | | 100.0 | | 100.0 | Total | | | | | | | | | | | | | | 100.0 |
| | | | | | | **LIABILITIES** | | | | | | | | | | | | | | |
| | 3.4 | | 6.1 | | 4.6 | Notes Payable-Short Term | | | | | | | | | | | | | | 2.3 |
| | 4.4 | | 3.7 | | 4.4 | Cur. Mat.-L.T.D. | | | | | | | | | | | | | | 2.7 |
| | 10.8 | | 4.7 | | 5.8 | Trade Payables | | | | | | | | | | | | | | 8.7 |
| | .0 | | .0 | | .0 | Income Taxes Payable | | | | | | | | | | | | | | .0 |
| | 7.7 | | 7.5 | | 9.8 | All Other Current | | | | | | | | | | | | | | 15.1 |
| | 26.4 | | 22.1 | | 24.6 | Total Current | | | | | | | | | | | | | | 28.9 |
| | 43.1 | | 40.2 | | 43.8 | Long-Term Debt | | | | | | | | | | | | | | 18.8 |
| | 1.2 | | 1.1 | | 1.2 | Deferred Taxes | | | | | | | | | | | | | | 2.2 |
| | 6.0 | | 7.5 | | 6.0 | All Other Non-Current | | | | | | | | | | | | | | 7.6 |
| | 23.3 | | 29.2 | | 24.3 | Net Worth | | | | | | | | | | | | | | 42.5 |
| | 100.0 | | 100.0 | | 100.0 | Total Liabilities & Net Worth | | | | | | | | | | | | | | 100.0 |
| | | | | | | **INCOME DATA** | | | | | | | | | | | | | | |
| | 100.0 | | 100.0 | | 100.0 | Net Sales | | | | | | | | | | | | | | 100.0 |
| | | | | | | Gross Profit | | | | | | | | | | | | | | |
| | 90.0 | | 89.4 | | 87.3 | Operating Expenses | | | | | | | | | | | | | | 89.2 |
| | 10.0 | | 10.6 | | 12.7 | Operating Profit | | | | | | | | | | | | | | 10.8 |
| | -1.0 | | 3.2 | | 5.4 | All Other Expenses (net) | | | | | | | | | | | | | | 3.3 |
| | 11.0 | | 7.5 | | 7.3 | Profit Before Taxes | | | | | | | | | | | | | | 7.5 |
| | | | | | | **RATIOS** | | | | | | | | | | | | | | |
| | 4.7 | | 5.1 | | 6.3 | Current | | | | | | | | | | | | | | 6.3 |
| | 1.7 | | 2.3 | | 1.8 | | | | | | | | | | | | | | | 2.0 |
| | 1.2 | | .9 | | .9 | | | | | | | | | | | | | | | 1.3 |
| | 4.3 | | 3.6 | | 4.0 | Quick | | | | | | | | | | | | | | 5.9 |
| | 1.4 | | 1.5 | | 1.3 | | | | | | | | | | | | | | | 1.3 |
| | .5 | | .7 | | .5 | | | | | | | | | | | | | | | .7 |
| 2 | 190.7 | 1 | 657.8 | 3 | 133.5 | Sales/Receivables | | | | | | | | | | | | 14 | | 26.4 |
| 18 | 19.9 | 27 | 13.4 | 20 | 18.3 | | | | | | | | | | | | | 26 | | 13.9 |
| 54 | 6.8 | 49 | 7.5 | 29 | 12.4 | | | | | | | | | | | | | 35 | | 10.4 |
| | | | | | | Cost of Sales/Inventory | | | | | | | | | | | | | | |
| | | | | | | Cost of Sales/Payables | | | | | | | | | | | | | | |
| | 3.8 | | 4.8 | | 2.7 | Sales/Working Capital | | | | | | | | | | | | | | 2.1 |
| | 8.0 | | 10.7 | | 11.1 | | | | | | | | | | | | | | | 6.2 |
| | 27.3 | | -274.4 | | -19.6 | | | | | | | | | | | | | | | 41.8 |
| | 9.6 | | 15.0 | | 12.3 | EBIT/Interest | | | | | | | | | | | | | | 38.8 |
| (25) | 6.8 | (34) | 3.4 | (28) | 2.6 | | | | | | | | | | | | | (16) | | 1.8 |
| | .9 | | -1.1 | | .6 | | | | | | | | | | | | | | | .6 |
| | | | | | | Net Profit + Depr., Dep., Amort./Cur. Mat. L/T/D | | | | | | | | | | | | | | |
| | .7 | | .7 | | .3 | Fixed/Worth | | | | | | | | | | | | | | .3 |
| | 1.7 | | 1.8 | | 1.6 | | | | | | | | | | | | | | | 2.1 |
| | 3.3 | | 7.6 | | 3.1 | | | | | | | | | | | | | | | 3.1 |
| | .9 | | 1.0 | | .4 | Debt/Worth | | | | | | | | | | | | | | .3 |
| | 1.8 | | 2.7 | | 2.1 | | | | | | | | | | | | | | | 1.7 |
| | 5.1 | | 15.4 | | 60.2 | | | | | | | | | | | | | | | 5.0 |
| | 54.8 | | 88.4 | | 63.9 | % Profit Before Taxes/Tangible Net Worth | | | | | | | | | | | | | | 27.7 |
| (26) | 23.9 | (34) | 21.0 | (27) | 18.9 | | | | | | | | | | | | | (15) | | 14.3 |
| | 5.9 | | 3.1 | | 1.4 | | | | | | | | | | | | | | | .0 |
| | 16.7 | | 20.6 | | 27.4 | % Profit Before Taxes/Total Assets | | | | | | | | | | | | | | 25.7 |
| | 9.3 | | 5.3 | | 5.4 | | | | | | | | | | | | | | | 4.7 |
| | .4 | | -1.7 | | -1.0 | | | | | | | | | | | | | | | .0 |
| | 9.3 | | 10.8 | | 10.0 | Sales/Net Fixed Assets | | | | | | | | | | | | | | 10.0 |
| | 2.0 | | 3.5 | | 2.3 | | | | | | | | | | | | | | | 2.9 |
| | 1.2 | | 1.1 | | 1.3 | | | | | | | | | | | | | | | 1.3 |
| | 1.8 | | 2.1 | | 1.8 | Sales/Total Assets | | | | | | | | | | | | | | 2.5 |
| | 1.0 | | 1.4 | | 1.0 | | | | | | | | | | | | | | | 1.1 |
| | .8 | | .5 | | .5 | | | | | | | | | | | | | | | .7 |
| | 4.1 | | 2.1 | | 1.3 | % Depr., Dep., Amort./Sales | | | | | | | | | | | | | | .3 |
| (24) | 7.1 | (24) | 7.5 | (19) | 7.8 | | | | | | | | | | | | | (12) | | 3.0 |
| | 11.2 | | 12.1 | | 10.3 | | | | | | | | | | | | | | | 9.9 |
| | | | | | | % Officers', Directors', Owners' Comp/Sales | | | | | | | | | | | | | | |
| | 698230M | | 1923446M | | 1421723M | Net Sales ($) | | 263M | | 9735M | | 12495M | | 27198M | | 58398M | | | | 1313634M |
| | 734912M | | 2114942M | | 1794769M | Total Assets ($) | | 3304M | | 31220M | | 10772M | | 51029M | | 61135M | | | | 1637309M |

M = $ thousand   MM = $ million
See Pages viii through xx for Explanation of Ratios and Data
© RMA 2024

# TRANSPORTATION—Deep Sea Freight Transportation  NAICS 483111

## Current Data Sorted by Assets

| 0-500M | 500M-2MM | 2-10MM | 10-50MM | 50-100MM | 100-250MM | | Comparative Historical Data | |
|---|---|---|---|---|---|---|---|---|
| | | | 1 | | 4 | Type of Statement | | |
| | | | | | 2 | Unqualified | 6 | 4 |
| | 1 | | | 1 | | Reviewed | 1 | |
| | 2 | 5 | 7 | 5 | 8 | Compiled | 1 | 2 |
| | 11 (4/1-9/30/23) | | 25 (10/1/23-3/31/24) | | | Tax Returns | 2 | 1 |
| | | | | | | Other | 19 | 15 |
| | | | | | | | 4/1/19- | 4/1/20- |
| | | | | | | | 3/31/20 | 3/31/21 |
| | | | | | | | ALL | ALL |
| | 3 | 5 | 8 | 6 | 14 | NUMBER OF STATEMENTS | 29 | 22 |
| | % | % | % | % | % | ASSETS | % | % |
| | | | | | 11.5 | Cash & Equivalents | 12.7 | 9.6 |
| D | | | | | 15.4 | Trade Receivables (net) | 14.9 | 19.3 |
| A | | | | | 1.0 | Inventory | 3.4 | .3 |
| T | | | | | .8 | All Other Current | 6.9 | 1.5 |
| A | | | | | 28.8 | Total Current | 38.0 | 30.7 |
| | | | | | 61.2 | Fixed Assets (net) | 41.1 | 57.1 |
| N | | | | | 1.0 | Intangibles (net) | 4.1 | 2.8 |
| O | | | | | 9.0 | All Other Non-Current | 16.8 | 9.4 |
| T | | | | | 100.0 | Total | 100.0 | 100.0 |
| | | | | | | LIABILITIES | | |
| A | | | | | 2.3 | Notes Payable-Short Term | 1.5 | .4 |
| V | | | | | 3.3 | Cur. Mat.-L.T.D. | 3.4 | 6.2 |
| A | | | | | 4.6 | Trade Payables | 11.0 | 10.0 |
| I | | | | | .2 | Income Taxes Payable | .0 | .0 |
| L | | | | | 9.2 | All Other Current | 13.8 | 9.3 |
| A | | | | | 19.5 | Total Current | 29.6 | 26.0 |
| B | | | | | 27.5 | Long-Term Debt | 19.9 | 29.1 |
| L | | | | | .4 | Deferred Taxes | 1.0 | .3 |
| E | | | | | 2.2 | All Other Non-Current | 5.2 | 1.3 |
| | | | | | 50.3 | Net Worth | 44.3 | 43.3 |
| | | | | | 100.0 | Total Liabilities & Net Worth | 100.0 | 100.0 |
| | | | | | | INCOME DATA | | |
| | | | | | 100.0 | Net Sales | 100.0 | 100.0 |
| | | | | | | Gross Profit | | |
| | | | | | 70.9 | Operating Expenses | 83.4 | 85.4 |
| | | | | | 29.1 | Operating Profit | 16.6 | 14.6 |
| | | | | | 8.2 | All Other Expenses (net) | 4.1 | 3.3 |
| | | | | | 20.9 | Profit Before Taxes | 12.5 | 11.3 |
| | | | | | | RATIOS | | |
| | | | | | 4.0 | | 2.9 | 1.8 |
| | | | | | 1.2 | Current | 1.4 | 1.0 |
| | | | | | .9 | | .8 | .5 |
| | | | | | 3.9 | | 2.5 | 1.5 |
| | | | | | 1.1 | Quick | 1.1 | .9 |
| | | | | | .7 | | .5 | .5 |
| | | | | 2 | 175.9 | | 9  38.9 | 0  UND |
| | | | | 33 | 11.2 | Sales/Receivables | 32  11.3 | 48  7.6 |
| | | | | 66 | 5.5 | | 59  6.2 | 64  5.7 |
| | | | | | | Cost of Sales/Inventory | | |
| | | | | | | Cost of Sales/Payables | | |
| | | | | | 3.6 | | 4.3 | 5.1 |
| | | | | | 11.1 | Sales/Working Capital | 14.9 | 28.4 |
| | | | | | -23.6 | | -17.0 | -3.7 |
| | | | | | 7.5 | | 11.3 | 8.1 |
| | | | | (11) | 5.5 | EBIT/Interest | (19) 3.8 | (16) 3.0 |
| | | | | | 2.5 | | 2.2 | .7 |
| | | | | | | Net Profit + Depr., Dep., Amort./Cur. Mat. L/T/D | | |
| | | | | | .8 | | .0 | .3 |
| | | | | | 1.3 | Fixed/Worth | 1.1 | 1.5 |
| | | | | | 2.0 | | 1.9 | 2.0 |
| | | | | | .4 | | .5 | .7 |
| | | | | | .9 | Debt/Worth | 1.4 | 1.4 |
| | | | | | 2.3 | | 2.7 | 2.8 |
| | | | | | 45.3 | | 41.9 | 37.5 |
| | | | | | 15.6 | % Profit Before Taxes/Tangible Net Worth | (26) 16.6 | 13.8 |
| | | | | | 4.5 | | 7.5 | .8 |
| | | | | | 17.7 | | 17.0 | 9.9 |
| | | | | | 5.3 | % Profit Before Taxes/Total Assets | 7.5 | 4.7 |
| | | | | | 2.4 | | 2.8 | .3 |
| | | | | | 7.6 | | 304.7 | 14.1 |
| | | | | | .5 | Sales/Net Fixed Assets | 3.8 | .6 |
| | | | | | .2 | | .5 | .3 |
| | | | | | 1.1 | | 2.6 | 1.0 |
| | | | | | .4 | Sales/Total Assets | .7 | .4 |
| | | | | | .1 | | .3 | .2 |
| | | | | | 1.6 | | .4 | 2.3 |
| | | | | | 10.0 | % Depr., Dep., Amort./Sales | (19) 7.1 | (16) 10.4 |
| | | | | | 17.2 | | 14.8 | 19.2 |
| | | | | | | % Officers', Directors' Owners' Comp/Sales | | |
| | 4043M | 15190M | 89408M | 461444M | 1905587M | Net Sales ($) | 1712381M | 1089929M |
| | 3211M | 25024M | 243966M | 481910M | 2423927M | Total Assets ($) | 1541027M | 2072045M |

M = $ thousand   MM = $ million
See Pages viii through xx for Explanation of Ratios and Data

© RMA 2024

# TRANSPORTATION—Deep Sea Freight Transportation  NAICS 483111

## Comparative Historical Data / Current Data Sorted by Sales

| | | | | | Type of Statement | | | | | | |
|---|---|---|---|---|---|---|---|---|---|---|---|
| | | 2 | | 5 | Unqualified | | | | | 2 | 3 |
| | 3 | 2 | | 2 | Reviewed | | | | | 1 | 1 |
| | 2 | 1 | | 2 | Compiled | 1 | | | | 1 | |
| | 21 | 17 | | 27 | Tax Returns | 1 | 3 | 3 | 3 | 5 | 12 |
| | 4/1/21-3/31/22 ALL | 4/1/22-3/31/23 ALL | | 4/1/23-3/31/24 ALL | Other | 0-1MM | 11 (4/1-9/30/23) 1-3MM | 3-5MM | 25 (10/1/23-3/31/24) 5-10MM | 10-25MM | 25MM & OVER |
| | 26 | 22 | | 36 | NUMBER OF STATEMENTS | 2 | 3 | 3 | 3 | 9 | 16 |
| | % | % | | % | ASSETS | % | % | % | % | % | % |
| | 11.5 | 10.9 | | 12.7 | Cash & Equivalents | | | | | | 12.4 |
| | 6.1 | 10.5 | | 9.6 | Trade Receivables (net) | | | | | | 16.2 |
| | .2 | .6 | | .9 | Inventory | | | | | | 1.4 |
| | 1.1 | 2.2 | | .9 | All Other Current | | | | | | 1.1 |
| | 18.9 | 24.3 | | 24.2 | Total Current | | | | | | 31.1 |
| | 70.5 | 65.5 | | 67.6 | Fixed Assets (net) | | | | | | 56.2 |
| | .5 | .3 | | 1.6 | Intangibles (net) | | | | | | 3.3 |
| | 10.1 | 9.9 | | 6.5 | All Other Non-Current | | | | | | 9.5 |
| | 100.0 | 100.0 | | 100.0 | Total | | | | | | 100.0 |
| | | | | | LIABILITIES | | | | | | |
| | 2.0 | .0 | | 1.3 | Notes Payable-Short Term | | | | | | 2.9 |
| | 5.6 | 6.9 | | 6.1 | Cur. Mat.-L.T.D. | | | | | | 4.9 |
| | 3.5 | 4.6 | | 5.7 | Trade Payables | | | | | | 6.3 |
| | .0 | .1 | | .1 | Income Taxes Payable | | | | | | .2 |
| | 2.2 | 9.3 | | 6.5 | All Other Current | | | | | | 8.6 |
| | 13.2 | 20.9 | | 19.8 | Total Current | | | | | | 22.8 |
| | 30.2 | 30.3 | | 31.5 | Long-Term Debt | | | | | | 26.1 |
| | .3 | .0 | | .8 | Deferred Taxes | | | | | | .9 |
| | 1.3 | .7 | | 4.2 | All Other Non-Current | | | | | | 4.0 |
| | 55.1 | 48.0 | | 43.7 | Net Worth | | | | | | 46.1 |
| | 100.0 | 100.0 | | 100.0 | Total Liabilities & Net Worth | | | | | | 100.0 |
| | | | | | INCOME DATA | | | | | | |
| | 100.0 | 100.0 | | 100.0 | Net Sales | | | | | | 100.0 |
| | 74.9 | 68.8 | | 69.2 | Gross Profit / Operating Expenses | | | | | | 74.6 |
| | 25.1 | 31.2 | | 30.8 | Operating Profit | | | | | | 25.4 |
| | 7.7 | 5.3 | | 7.3 | All Other Expenses (net) | | | | | | 4.1 |
| | 17.5 | 25.9 | | 23.4 | Profit Before Taxes | | | | | | 21.3 |
| | | | | | RATIOS | | | | | | |
| | 3.0 | 2.1 | | 2.3 | | | | | | | 3.3 |
| | 1.0 | 1.0 | | 1.1 | Current | | | | | | 1.3 |
| | .5 | .7 | | .7 | | | | | | | .9 |
| | 2.7 | 1.4 | | 2.2 | | | | | | | 3.2 |
| | .9 | .8 | | 1.0 | Quick | | | | | | 1.1 |
| | .5 | .6 | | .6 | | | | | | | .8 |
| 0 | UND | 0 | UND | 0 | 925.4 | Sales/Receivables | | | | | 14 | 26.6 |
| 24 | 15.0 | 9 | 42.3 | 12 | 30.3 | | | | | | 33 | 11.2 |
| 54 | 6.8 | 28 | 12.9 | 37 | 9.9 | | | | | | 55 | 6.6 |
| | | | | | Cost of Sales/Inventory | | | | | | |
| | | | | | Cost of Sales/Payables | | | | | | |
| | 3.8 | 8.1 | | 4.9 | | | | | | | 4.6 |
| | NM | NM | | 21.3 | Sales/Working Capital | | | | | | 13.8 |
| | -5.5 | -7.8 | | -15.2 | | | | | | | -62.3 |
| | 10.5 | 11.8 | | 7.5 | | | | | | | 7.5 |
| (22) | 3.4 | (19) | 8.3 | (30) | 5.5 | EBIT/Interest | | | | | (15) | 5.5 |
| | 1.5 | 2.8 | | 2.4 | | | | | | | 2.5 |
| | | | | | Net Profit + Depr., Dep., Amort./Cur. Mat. L/T/D | | | | | | |
| | .8 | .8 | | 1.3 | | | | | | | .9 |
| | 1.6 | 1.7 | | 1.7 | Fixed/Worth | | | | | | 1.4 |
| | 2.0 | 2.2 | | 2.1 | | | | | | | 2.2 |
| | .4 | .7 | | .6 | | | | | | | .5 |
| | .9 | 1.0 | | 1.2 | Debt/Worth | | | | | | 1.5 |
| | 1.2 | 2.0 | | 2.5 | | | | | | | 2.5 |
| | 27.1 | 44.0 | | 47.0 | % Profit Before Taxes/Tangible Net Worth | | | | | | 55.6 |
| | 10.7 | 16.0 | (34) | 24.4 | | | | | | | (15) | 23.4 |
| | 1.8 | 8.7 | | 5.4 | | | | | | | 13.0 |
| | 14.3 | 20.3 | | 18.1 | % Profit Before Taxes/Total Assets | | | | | | 17.8 |
| | 5.0 | 8.8 | | 7.7 | | | | | | | 9.9 |
| | 1.2 | 2.6 | | 2.7 | | | | | | | 4.7 |
| | 2.2 | 6.7 | | 1.2 | | | | | | | 9.0 |
| | .3 | .4 | | .5 | Sales/Net Fixed Assets | | | | | | .7 |
| | .3 | .2 | | .4 | | | | | | | .4 |
| | .6 | .9 | | .6 | | | | | | | 1.1 |
| | .3 | .4 | | .4 | Sales/Total Assets | | | | | | .5 |
| | .2 | .2 | | .3 | | | | | | | .4 |
| | 4.5 | 8.6 | | 6.0 | | | | | | | 1.6 |
| (19) | 13.7 | (16) | 12.3 | (28) | 11.9 | % Depr., Dep., Amort./Sales | | | | | (13) | 8.2 |
| | 22.2 | 22.1 | | 22.8 | | | | | | | 13.6 |
| | | | | | % Officers', Directors' Owners' Comp/Sales | | | | | | |
| | 892340M | 1327005M | | 2475672M | Net Sales ($) | 1158M | 6575M | 11500M | 25404M | 136302M | 2294733M |
| | 2438597M | 1541113M | | 3178038M | Total Assets ($) | 2285M | 7315M | 18635M | 79019M | 790945M | 2279839M |

© RMA 2024  
M = $ thousand    MM = $ million  
See Pages viii through xx for Explanation of Ratios and Data

# TRANSPORTATION—Inland Water Freight Transportation  NAICS 483211

## Current Data Sorted by Assets | Comparative Historical Data

| | | | | | | Type of Statement | | |
|---|---|---|---|---|---|---|---|---|
| | | | 2 | 2 | 1 | Unqualified | 7 | 5 |
| | | 1 | 4 | | 2 | Reviewed | 6 | 3 |
| 3 | | 3 | 1 | 1 | | Compiled | 7 | 2 |
| | 1 | | 1 | | | Tax Returns | 6 | 2 |
| 3 | 3 | 10 | 11 | 5 | 4 | Other | 57 | 29 |
| 0-500M | 8 (4/1-9/30/23) 500M-2MM | 2-10MM | 50 (10/1/23-3/31/24) 10-50MM | 50-100MM | 100-250MM | | 4/1/19-3/31/20 ALL | 4/1/20-3/31/21 ALL |
| 6 | 4 | 14 | 19 | 8 | 7 | NUMBER OF STATEMENTS | 83 | 41 |
| % | % | % | % | % | % | ASSETS | % | % |
| | | 17.8 | 7.3 | | | Cash & Equivalents | 9.3 | 19.4 |
| | | 11.4 | 9.2 | | | Trade Receivables (net) | 11.8 | 10.6 |
| | | 5.6 | 2.0 | | | Inventory | 1.0 | 1.1 |
| | | 1.4 | 2.5 | | | All Other Current | 2.8 | 3.6 |
| | | 36.3 | 20.9 | | | Total Current | 25.0 | 34.7 |
| | | 35.9 | 67.6 | | | Fixed Assets (net) | 63.9 | 57.2 |
| | | 14.4 | .5 | | | Intangibles (net) | 2.4 | 2.1 |
| | | 13.4 | 11.0 | | | All Other Non-Current | 8.8 | 6.1 |
| | | 100.0 | 100.0 | | | Total | 100.0 | 100.0 |
| | | | | | | LIABILITIES | | |
| | | 2.3 | 4.9 | | | Notes Payable-Short Term | 6.0 | 7.4 |
| | | 3.6 | 3.2 | | | Cur. Mat.-L.T.D. | 3.4 | 3.7 |
| | | 8.4 | 3.6 | | | Trade Payables | 6.5 | 5.7 |
| | | .0 | .8 | | | Income Taxes Payable | .3 | .1 |
| | | 10.5 | 7.3 | | | All Other Current | 8.1 | 6.8 |
| | | 24.9 | 19.7 | | | Total Current | 24.3 | 23.6 |
| | | 26.2 | 35.7 | | | Long-Term Debt | 38.2 | 38.9 |
| | | .0 | .1 | | | Deferred Taxes | .6 | .4 |
| | | 11.2 | 1.5 | | | All Other Non-Current | 8.6 | 2.1 |
| | | 37.7 | 42.9 | | | Net Worth | 28.3 | 35.1 |
| | | 100.0 | 100.0 | | | Total Liabilties & Net Worth | 100.0 | 100.0 |
| | | | | | | INCOME DATA | | |
| | | 100.0 | 100.0 | | | Net Sales | 100.0 | 100.0 |
| | | | | | | Gross Profit | | |
| | | 80.8 | 78.8 | | | Operating Expenses | 78.0 | 72.3 |
| | | 19.2 | 21.2 | | | Operating Profit | 22.0 | 27.7 |
| | | 9.2 | 4.7 | | | All Other Expenses (net) | 4.7 | 4.3 |
| | | 10.0 | 16.5 | | | Profit Before Taxes | 17.3 | 23.4 |
| | | | | | | RATIOS | | |
| | | 9.0 | 2.4 | | | | 2.9 | 4.5 |
| | | 1.2 | 1.3 | | | Current | 1.4 | 1.8 |
| | | .7 | .8 | | | | .7 | .9 |
| | | 8.5 | 2.1 | | | | 2.3 | 4.2 |
| | | 1.2 | 1.2 | | | Quick | 1.1 | 1.7 |
| | | .3 | .6 | | | | .5 | .5 |
| | | 0 UND | 18 20.2 | | | | 13 27.6 | 9 41.1 |
| | | 9 40.5 | 41 8.9 | | | Sales/Receivables | 33 11.2 | 33 11.0 |
| | | 26 13.8 | 70 5.2 | | | | 43 8.5 | 47 7.8 |
| | | | | | | Cost of Sales/Inventory | | |
| | | | | | | Cost of Sales/Payables | | |
| | | 5.2 | 5.4 | | | | 5.1 | 5.2 |
| | | 32.1 | 12.0 | | | Sales/Working Capital | 13.8 | 10.4 |
| | | -25.1 | -10.9 | | | | -15.6 | NM |
| | | 9.2 | 8.9 | | | | 12.7 | 13.7 |
| | (11) | 3.9 | (14) 5.9 | | | EBIT/Interest | (67) 4.3 | (30) 5.1 |
| | | .6 | 1.0 | | | | 2.1 | 1.1 |
| | | | | | | Net Profit + Depr., Dep., Amort./Cur. Mat. L/T/D | | |
| | | .0 | .9 | | | | .9 | .6 |
| | | 1.0 | 1.7 | | | Fixed/Worth | 1.9 | 1.4 |
| | | NM | 2.1 | | | | 3.8 | 2.9 |
| | | .5 | .6 | | | | .6 | .5 |
| | | 5.1 | 1.2 | | | Debt/Worth | 1.5 | 1.2 |
| | | -5.2 | 2.9 | | | | 4.7 | 3.2 |
| | | | 17.6 | | | | 26.2 | 61.0 |
| | | (17) | 16.3 | | | % Profit Before Taxes/Tangible Net Worth | (71) 13.5 | (35) 20.4 |
| | | | 9.5 | | | | 6.2 | 8.7 |
| | | 19.6 | 9.4 | | | | 13.5 | 24.2 |
| | | 2.7 | 6.4 | | | % Profit Before Taxes/Total Assets | 6.1 | 7.1 |
| | | -.3 | 1.6 | | | | 1.4 | 1.0 |
| | | 491.4 | 1.6 | | | | 3.1 | 7.8 |
| | | 6.6 | 1.0 | | | Sales/Net Fixed Assets | 1.3 | 1.2 |
| | | 2.3 | .2 | | | | .5 | .5 |
| | | 3.0 | 1.1 | | | | 1.6 | 1.7 |
| | | 1.3 | .7 | | | Sales/Total Assets | .9 | .9 |
| | | .2 | .2 | | | | .4 | .4 |
| | | | 6.4 | | | | 4.7 | 2.6 |
| | | (17) | 10.6 | | | % Depr., Dep., Amort./Sales | (63) 7.7 | (31) 8.5 |
| | | | 25.3 | | | | 14.5 | 19.2 |
| | | | | | | % Officers', Directors' Owners' Comp/Sales | | |
| 5775M | 27830M | 114953M | 496393M | 704721M | 822999M | Net Sales ($) | 3237120M | 1344936M |
| 1391M | 5016M | 66871M | 544985M | 605298M | 984935M | Total Assets ($) | 5450714M | 2049163M |

M = $ thousand    MM = $ million
See Pages viii through xx for Explanation of Ratios and Data

© RMA 2024

# TRANSPORTATION—Inland Water Freight Transportation  NAICS 483211

## Comparative Historical Data | Current Data Sorted by Sales

| Comparative Historical Data ||| Type of Statement | Current Data Sorted by Sales ||||||
|---|---|---|---|---|---|---|---|---|---|
| 6 | 8 | 5 | Unqualified | | | | | 1 | 4 |
| 3 | 4 | 7 | Reviewed | | | | | 2 | 5 |
| 6 | 2 | 8 | Compiled | 1 | 4 | 2 | | 1 | |
| 4 | 1 | 2 | Tax Returns | | | 1 | 3 | | 1 |
| 26 | 35 | 36 | Other | 8 | 2 | 5 | | 8 | 10 |
| 4/1/21-3/31/22 ALL | 4/1/22-3/31/23 ALL | 4/1/23-3/31/24 ALL | | 0-1MM | 8 (4/1-9/30/23) 1-3MM | 3-5MM | 50 (10/1/23-3/31/24) 5-10MM | 10-25MM | 25MM & OVER |
| 45 | 50 | 58 | NUMBER OF STATEMENTS | 9 | 6 | 8 | 3 | 12 | 20 |
| % | % | % | ASSETS | % | % | % | % | % | % |
| 16.0 | 13.0 | 15.8 | Cash & Equivalents | | | | | 13.7 | 10.0 |
| 10.0 | 13.7 | 10.0 | Trade Receivables (net) | | | | | 15.2 | 14.0 |
| 1.1 | 1.1 | 3.1 | Inventory | | | | | .2 | 3.1 |
| 2.4 | 6.3 | 3.0 | All Other Current | | | | | 3.4 | 2.2 |
| 29.4 | 34.1 | 31.9 | Total Current | | | | | 32.5 | 29.2 |
| 58.6 | 53.4 | 50.5 | Fixed Assets (net) | | | | | 43.9 | 55.0 |
| 1.1 | 1.7 | 3.9 | Intangibles (net) | | | | | 11.9 | .8 |
| 10.8 | 10.8 | 13.7 | All Other Non-Current | | | | | 11.7 | 14.9 |
| 100.0 | 100.0 | 100.0 | Total | | | | | 100.0 | 100.0 |
| | | | LIABILITIES | | | | | | |
| 4.7 | 4.2 | 5.1 | Notes Payable-Short Term | | | | | 12.2 | 4.8 |
| 5.0 | 5.2 | 4.1 | Cur. Mat.-L.T.D. | | | | | 4.8 | 3.2 |
| 5.6 | 5.6 | 5.4 | Trade Payables | | | | | 9.0 | 6.2 |
| .3 | .4 | .3 | Income Taxes Payable | | | | | .0 | .8 |
| 3.6 | 6.4 | 17.9 | All Other Current | | | | | 2.5 | 10.3 |
| 19.3 | 21.8 | 32.7 | Total Current | | | | | 28.5 | 25.3 |
| 51.1 | 25.6 | 33.2 | Long-Term Debt | | | | | 29.0 | 23.3 |
| .3 | .9 | .4 | Deferred Taxes | | | | | .2 | 1.1 |
| 7.9 | 19.2 | 15.0 | All Other Non-Current | | | | | 14.5 | 19.2 |
| 21.4 | 32.4 | 18.7 | Net Worth | | | | | 27.8 | 31.2 |
| 100.0 | 100.0 | 100.0 | Total Liabilities & Net Worth | | | | | 100.0 | 100.0 |
| | | | INCOME DATA | | | | | | |
| 100.0 | 100.0 | 100.0 | Net Sales | | | | | 100.0 | 100.0 |
| | | | Gross Profit | | | | | | |
| 83.6 | 78.8 | 79.5 | Operating Expenses | | | | | 95.4 | 87.7 |
| 16.4 | 21.2 | 20.5 | Operating Profit | | | | | 4.6 | 12.3 |
| 2.0 | 1.9 | 4.9 | All Other Expenses (net) | | | | | -.8 | 1.2 |
| 14.4 | 19.3 | 15.6 | Profit Before Taxes | | | | | 5.4 | 11.2 |
| | | | RATIOS | | | | | | |
| 4.2 | 3.5 | 4.4 | | | | | | 2.3 | 2.8 |
| 2.0 | 1.7 | 1.3 | Current | | | | | 1.6 | 1.3 |
| .9 | .9 | .8 | | | | | | 1.0 | .8 |
| 3.7 | 3.0 | 3.2 | | | | | | 2.0 | 2.5 |
| 1.5 | 1.3 | 1.2 | Quick | | | | | 1.5 | 1.1 |
| .8 | .7 | .5 | | | | | | .7 | .5 |
| 0 UND | 21 17.0 | 0 UND | | | | | | 4 91.9 | 33 11.0 |
| 29 12.4 | 36 10.0 | 35 10.3 | Sales/Receivables | | | | | 23 15.9 | 41 8.9 |
| 51 7.2 | 62 5.9 | 49 7.4 | | | | | | 63 5.8 | 49 7.4 |
| | | | Cost of Sales/Inventory | | | | | | |
| | | | Cost of Sales/Payables | | | | | | |
| 3.9 | 5.2 | 4.7 | | | | | | 5.9 | 7.1 |
| 8.3 | 11.1 | 21.5 | Sales/Working Capital | | | | | 17.3 | 27.3 |
| -41.6 | -28.2 | -18.7 | | | | | | NM | -259.6 |
| 14.7 | 28.8 | 10.3 | | | | | | 9.2 | 16.4 |
| (31) 5.7 | (40) 6.4 | (41) 4.0 | EBIT/Interest | | | | | (11) 1.3 | (15) 4.0 |
| 1.7 | 2.5 | .8 | | | | | | -1.8 | 1.3 |
| | | | Net Profit + Depr., Dep., Amort./Cur. Mat. L/T/D | | | | | | |
| .7 | .6 | .5 | | | | | | .8 | .7 |
| 1.5 | 1.3 | 1.4 | Fixed/Worth | | | | | 1.5 | 1.4 |
| 5.3 | 2.2 | 4.3 | | | | | | -5.1 | 5.2 |
| .4 | .4 | .6 | | | | | | .6 | .5 |
| 1.0 | 1.1 | 1.1 | Debt/Worth | | | | | 5.1 | 1.1 |
| 7.0 | 3.4 | -28.1 | | | | | | -7.8 | NM |
| 44.1 | 28.2 | 19.9 | % Profit Before Taxes/Tangible Net Worth | | | | | | 15.1 |
| (36) 13.2 | (41) 13.6 | (42) 13.9 | | | | | | (15) 9.9 | |
| 5.6 | 6.3 | 6.5 | | | | | | | 6.7 |
| 14.5 | 15.3 | 13.2 | % Profit Before Taxes/Total Assets | | | | | 12.8 | 10.0 |
| 7.2 | 7.6 | 6.1 | | | | | | 3.0 | 5.1 |
| .9 | 2.4 | .0 | | | | | | -4.6 | 1.6 |
| 4.9 | 5.9 | 7.8 | | | | | | 258.7 | 5.4 |
| 1.7 | 1.7 | 1.8 | Sales/Net Fixed Assets | | | | | 2.9 | 1.5 |
| .6 | .8 | .5 | | | | | | 1.0 | 1.0 |
| 1.6 | 1.8 | 2.4 | | | | | | 3.1 | 1.8 |
| 1.0 | 1.0 | 1.0 | Sales/Total Assets | | | | | 1.8 | 1.0 |
| .4 | .5 | .3 | | | | | | .6 | .8 |
| 3.7 | 3.2 | 2.7 | | | | | | | 2.6 |
| (37) 7.9 | (37) 6.9 | (45) 7.7 | % Depr., Dep., Amort./Sales | | | | | (18) 7.3 | |
| 17.8 | 11.1 | 15.0 | | | | | | | 10.7 |
| | | | % Officers', Directors' Owners' Comp/Sales | | | | | | |
| 1492453M | 2787327M | 2172671M | Net Sales ($) | 3897M | 13466M | 31343M | 21923M | 206839M | 1895203M |
| 1898529M | 2802719M | 2208496M | Total Assets ($) | 17046M | 31455M | 284281M | 61964M | 172361M | 1641389M |

© RMA 2024  
M = $ thousand   MM = $ million  
See Pages viii through xx for Explanation of Ratios and Data

# TRANSPORTATION—General Freight Trucking, Local NAICS 484110

## Current Data Sorted by Assets | Comparative Historical Data

| | | | | | | | Type of Statement | | |
|---|---|---|---|---|---|---|---|---|---|
| | | | 1 | 10 | 6 | 12 | Unqualified | 16 | 14 |
| | 1 | | 15 | 30 | 12 | 5 | Reviewed | 80 | 33 |
| 1 | 8 | | 26 | 15 | 4 | | Compiled | 71 | 42 |
| 5 | 47 | | 25 | 4 | 1 | | Tax Returns | 167 | 93 |
| 35 | 100 | | 164 | 100 | 29 | 26 | Other | 473 | 283 |
| 40 | 88 (4/1-9/30/23) | | | 634 (10/1/23-3/31/24) | | | | 4/1/19- 3/31/20 ALL | 4/1/20- 3/31/21 ALL |
| 0-500M | 500M-2MM | | 2-10MM | 10-50MM | 50-100MM | 100-250MM | | | |
| 81 | 156 | | 231 | 159 | 52 | 43 | **NUMBER OF STATEMENTS** | 807 | 465 |
| % | % | | % | % | % | % | **ASSETS** | % | % |
| 27.5 | 21.6 | | 15.5 | 12.0 | 11.9 | 7.3 | Cash & Equivalents | 13.1 | 21.2 |
| 11.7 | 18.7 | | 24.2 | 20.1 | 15.7 | 19.3 | Trade Receivables (net) | 23.0 | 22.1 |
| 1.1 | 1.9 | | 1.0 | 1.3 | 1.2 | 1.5 | Inventory | 2.5 | 1.6 |
| 5.3 | 4.3 | | 4.0 | 4.3 | 3.3 | 2.6 | All Other Current | 4.3 | 3.1 |
| 45.6 | 46.5 | | 44.8 | 37.6 | 32.0 | 30.7 | Total Current | 42.9 | 48.0 |
| 35.9 | 34.6 | | 41.4 | 45.5 | 51.0 | 45.2 | Fixed Assets (net) | 43.8 | 39.2 |
| 6.4 | 5.2 | | 4.2 | 5.3 | 4.4 | 5.5 | Intangibles (net) | 4.9 | 4.9 |
| 12.1 | 13.8 | | 9.6 | 11.6 | 12.6 | 18.5 | All Other Non-Current | 8.4 | 7.9 |
| 100.0 | 100.0 | | 100.0 | 100.0 | 100.0 | 100.0 | Total | 100.0 | 100.0 |
| | | | | | | | **LIABILITIES** | | |
| 21.3 | 4.9 | | 4.1 | 4.0 | 2.3 | 2.3 | Notes Payable-Short Term | 7.5 | 8.9 |
| 4.5 | 4.2 | | 4.9 | 8.0 | 9.2 | 8.2 | Cur. Mat.-L.T.D. | 7.2 | 7.0 |
| 14.6 | 8.0 | | 8.1 | 6.5 | 3.6 | 6.1 | Trade Payables | 7.7 | 7.8 |
| .9 | .3 | | .1 | .1 | .1 | .3 | Income Taxes Payable | .1 | .1 |
| 25.4 | 10.2 | | 8.3 | 9.4 | 9.3 | 6.1 | All Other Current | 10.3 | 9.2 |
| 66.7 | 27.5 | | 25.4 | 28.1 | 24.4 | 23.0 | Total Current | 32.8 | 32.9 |
| 48.9 | 38.4 | | 30.9 | 28.6 | 31.9 | 30.9 | Long-Term Debt | 33.3 | 36.2 |
| .1 | .0 | | .3 | .4 | .2 | 1.2 | Deferred Taxes | .4 | .3 |
| 9.7 | 7.5 | | 3.6 | 4.2 | 7.5 | 5.3 | All Other Non-Current | 6.1 | 5.2 |
| -25.4 | 26.5 | | 39.9 | 38.6 | 36.0 | 39.5 | Net Worth | 27.3 | 25.4 |
| 100.0 | 100.0 | | 100.0 | 100.0 | 100.0 | 100.0 | Total Liabilities & Net Worth | 100.0 | 100.0 |
| | | | | | | | **INCOME DATA** | | |
| 100.0 | 100.0 | | 100.0 | 100.0 | 100.0 | 100.0 | Net Sales | 100.0 | 100.0 |
| | | | | | | | Gross Profit | | |
| 93.2 | 92.7 | | 90.8 | 94.4 | 95.0 | 93.0 | Operating Expenses | 93.0 | 91.9 |
| 6.8 | 7.3 | | 9.2 | 5.6 | 5.0 | 7.0 | Operating Profit | 7.0 | 8.1 |
| 1.5 | 1.3 | | .8 | .5 | .6 | 1.3 | All Other Expenses (net) | 1.1 | -.3 |
| 5.3 | 6.0 | | 8.4 | 5.1 | 4.4 | 5.8 | Profit Before Taxes | 5.9 | 8.4 |
| | | | | | | | **RATIOS** | | |
| 3.5 | 5.9 | | 4.5 | 2.2 | 2.0 | 1.5 | | 2.7 | 3.4 |
| .9 | 1.8 | | 2.1 | 1.2 | 1.2 | 1.1 | Current | 1.4 | 1.5 |
| .3 | .8 | | 1.0 | .8 | .9 | .7 | | .8 | .9 |
| 3.3 | 5.4 | | 3.8 | 2.0 | 1.5 | 1.3 | | 2.3 | 3.0 |
| .7 | 1.5 | | 1.8 | 1.0 | 1.1 | .8 | Quick | (806) 1.2 | (464) 1.4 |
| .2 | .6 | | .9 | .6 | .7 | .6 | | .6 | .8 |
| 0 UND | 0 UND | | 11 33.2 | 20 18.6 | 29 12.4 | 33 11.0 | | 5 77.2 | 0 UND |
| 0 UND | 7 55.7 | | 28 13.1 | 34 10.6 | 38 9.6 | 39 9.4 | Sales/Receivables | 29 12.6 | 28 13.1 |
| 13 29.1 | 31 11.9 | | 41 8.8 | 46 8.0 | 45 8.2 | 49 7.5 | | 42 8.6 | 45 8.1 |
| | | | | | | | Cost of Sales/Inventory | | |
| | | | | | | | Cost of Sales/Payables | | |
| 24.1 | 8.5 | | 6.5 | 8.6 | 9.4 | 9.0 | | 9.6 | 7.3 |
| -184.9 | 26.4 | | 15.5 | 32.0 | 26.7 | 75.7 | Sales/Working Capital | 29.6 | 18.5 |
| -16.8 | -68.0 | | 999.8 | -27.6 | -59.4 | -19.7 | | -33.3 | -189.6 |
| 14.4 | 14.4 | | 18.6 | 9.3 | 12.5 | 8.7 | | 12.6 | 17.6 |
| (55) 3.7 | (126) 4.4 | (195) | 7.0 | (141) 4.2 | (51) 3.8 | (41) 3.4 | EBIT/Interest | (698) 4.6 | (374) 6.6 |
| .7 | -.5 | | 1.3 | 1.6 | 1.0 | 1.5 | | 1.4 | 2.0 |
| | | | 4.8 | 3.5 | 2.6 | | | 4.7 | 3.1 |
| | | (19) | 2.6 | (43) 1.8 | (19) 1.5 | | Net Profit + Depr., Dep., Amort./Cur. Mat. L/T/D | (114) 1.9 | (45) 2.0 |
| | | | 1.2 | 1.3 | 1.2 | | | 1.3 | 1.3 |
| .0 | .2 | | .3 | .7 | .8 | .6 | | .5 | .3 |
| 1.8 | 1.0 | | 1.1 | 1.5 | 1.9 | 1.4 | Fixed/Worth | 1.5 | 1.2 |
| -2.1 | UND | | 2.6 | 2.9 | 3.1 | 2.8 | | 6.5 | 5.3 |
| .7 | .5 | | .6 | .8 | 1.3 | .8 | | .8 | .8 |
| 5.8 | 1.6 | | 1.4 | 1.7 | 1.8 | 2.1 | Debt/Worth | 2.1 | 2.1 |
| -2.6 | -345.8 | | 6.5 | 4.5 | 4.0 | 4.5 | | 12.0 | 15.7 |
| 110.3 | 77.3 | | 58.2 | 40.5 | 30.6 | 28.8 | | 59.1 | 75.7 |
| (47) 40.1 | (116) 33.5 | (199) | 25.9 | (142) 20.9 | (49) 16.3 | (40) 13.6 | % Profit Before Taxes/Tangible Net Worth | (648) 23.5 | (366) 34.8 |
| 1.6 | 6.3 | | 4.1 | 5.8 | 1.4 | 9.5 | | 7.9 | 10.8 |
| 58.9 | 31.7 | | 23.8 | 14.8 | 10.2 | 8.4 | | 20.6 | 27.3 |
| 19.4 | 11.7 | | 9.6 | 8.3 | 5.9 | 5.4 | % Profit Before Taxes/Total Assets | 7.7 | 12.5 |
| -2.5 | -2.4 | | 1.2 | 1.5 | .2 | 1.6 | | 1.5 | 2.8 |
| UND | 78.4 | | 32.1 | 11.3 | 4.0 | 5.2 | | 30.5 | 45.7 |
| 30.8 | 16.4 | | 6.7 | 3.6 | 2.4 | 2.2 | Sales/Net Fixed Assets | 5.9 | 7.2 |
| 6.8 | 4.9 | | 2.9 | 2.1 | 1.7 | 1.5 | | 2.5 | 2.7 |
| 11.5 | 5.4 | | 4.2 | 2.6 | 1.6 | 1.6 | | 4.5 | 4.3 |
| 6.4 | 3.4 | | 2.4 | 1.7 | 1.4 | 1.1 | Sales/Total Assets | 2.4 | 2.4 |
| 2.9 | 2.1 | | 1.5 | 1.2 | 1.1 | .9 | | 1.4 | 1.4 |
| 1.2 | 1.7 | | 1.1 | 2.6 | 2.9 | .2 | | 1.6 | 1.9 |
| (29) 7.0 | (72) 4.0 | (137) | 4.9 | (133) 5.8 | (41) 6.3 | (15) 3.8 | % Depr., Dep., Amort./Sales | (528) 5.5 | (261) 6.1 |
| 14.9 | 9.5 | | 9.8 | 9.9 | 9.6 | 7.5 | | 10.4 | 11.6 |
| 1.3 | 1.3 | | .8 | .6 | | | | 1.0 | 1.0 |
| (22) 2.5 | (60) 3.0 | (75) | 1.6 | (34) 1.1 | | | % Officers', Directors' Owners' Comp/Sales | (249) 2.1 | (145) 2.6 |
| 6.6 | 5.2 | | 3.3 | 2.7 | | | | 4.1 | 5.3 |
| 180250M | 796841M | | 3233801M | 7988158M | 5393491M | 10375521M | Net Sales ($) | 22943312M | 12793668M |
| 19483M | 177465M | | 1169083M | 3738122M | 3576902M | 6515181M | Total Assets ($) | 10624145M | 6699831M |

© RMA 2024

M = $ thousand  MM = $ million
See Pages viii through xx for Explanation of Ratios and Data

# TRANSPORTATION—General Freight Trucking, Local  NAICS 484110

## Comparative Historical Data | Current Data Sorted by Sales

| | | | | | | Type of Statement | | | | | | |
|---|---|---|---|---|---|---|---|---|---|---|---|---|
| 27 | | 35 | | 29 | | Unqualified | | | | 1 | 2 | 26 |
| 47 | | 66 | | 64 | | Reviewed | 2 | 1 | 2 | 3 | 12 | 44 |
| 49 | | 53 | | 58 | | Compiled | 4 | 5 | 4 | 8 | 21 | 16 |
| 100 | | 144 | | 112 | | Tax Returns | 17 | 33 | 17 | 25 | 14 | 6 |
| 295 | | 456 | | 459 | | Other | 42 | 43 | 42 | 73 | 108 | 151 |
| 4/1/21-3/31/22 ALL | | 4/1/22-3/31/23 ALL | | 4/1/23-3/31/24 ALL | | | | 88 (4/1-9/30/23) | | | 634 (10/1/23-3/31/24) | |
| | | | | | | | 0-1MM | 1-3MM | 3-5MM | 5-10MM | 10-25MM | 25MM & OVER |
| 518 | | 754 | | 722 | | NUMBER OF STATEMENTS | 65 | 82 | 65 | 110 | 157 | 243 |
| % | | % | | % | | ASSETS | % | % | % | % | % | % |
| 19.2 | | 20.0 | | 16.6 | | Cash & Equivalents | 20.0 | 22.2 | 22.4 | 18.4 | 17.0 | 11.2 |
| 22.4 | | 20.6 | | 19.8 | | Trade Receivables (net) | 10.1 | 10.8 | 17.1 | 22.0 | 23.1 | 23.1 |
| 1.4 | | 1.5 | | 1.3 | | Inventory | 2.3 | 2.4 | .6 | 1.6 | .4 | 1.4 |
| 4.4 | | 4.9 | | 4.1 | | All Other Current | 3.7 | 5.5 | 3.3 | 4.0 | 4.7 | 3.7 |
| 47.4 | | 47.0 | | 41.9 | | Total Current | 36.2 | 40.9 | 43.4 | 45.9 | 45.2 | 39.4 |
| 39.2 | | 39.0 | | 41.1 | | Fixed Assets (net) | 55.9 | 43.1 | 34.9 | 33.9 | 38.5 | 43.1 |
| 4.7 | | 4.2 | | 5.0 | | Intangibles (net) | 2.7 | 4.8 | 5.8 | 7.5 | 3.8 | 5.1 |
| 8.7 | | 9.8 | | 12.0 | | All Other Non-Current | 5.4 | 11.1 | 15.9 | 12.7 | 12.5 | 12.3 |
| 100.0 | | 100.0 | | 100.0 | | Total | 100.0 | 100.0 | 100.0 | 100.0 | 100.0 | 100.0 |
| | | | | | | LIABILITIES | | | | | | |
| 5.9 | | 4.9 | | 5.9 | | Notes Payable-Short Term | 14.2 | 8.1 | 4.9 | 7.0 | 4.3 | 3.9 |
| 6.5 | | 6.6 | | 5.9 | | Cur. Mat.-L.T.D. | 5.8 | 3.7 | 4.5 | 4.9 | 5.2 | 7.9 |
| 7.1 | | 7.1 | | 8.0 | | Trade Payables | 7.0 | 11.3 | 4.8 | 8.7 | 8.1 | 7.6 |
| .1 | | .2 | | .2 | | Income Taxes Payable | 1.0 | .0 | .6 | .1 | .1 | .1 |
| 11.2 | | 10.0 | | 10.8 | | All Other Current | 19.0 | 8.8 | 14.3 | 9.3 | 10.1 | 9.5 |
| 30.8 | | 28.8 | | 30.9 | | Total Current | 47.0 | 32.0 | 29.1 | 30.1 | 27.9 | 29.0 |
| 32.8 | | 35.3 | | 34.1 | | Long-Term Debt | 38.8 | 47.6 | 48.2 | 30.8 | 31.8 | 27.5 |
| .5 | | .3 | | .3 | | Deferred Taxes | .1 | .1 | .0 | .1 | .2 | .5 |
| 3.2 | | 3.6 | | 5.6 | | All Other Non-Current | 8.6 | 9.1 | 7.1 | 3.4 | 4.8 | 4.8 |
| 32.7 | | 32.0 | | 29.1 | | Net Worth | 5.4 | 11.3 | 15.5 | 35.6 | 35.3 | 38.2 |
| 100.0 | | 100.0 | | 100.0 | | Total Liabilities & Net Worth | 100.0 | 100.0 | 100.0 | 100.0 | 100.0 | 100.0 |
| | | | | | | INCOME DATA | | | | | | |
| 100.0 | | 100.0 | | 100.0 | | Net Sales | 100.0 | 100.0 | 100.0 | 100.0 | 100.0 | 100.0 |
| | | | | | | Gross Profit | | | | | | |
| 93.0 | | 91.8 | | 92.7 | | Operating Expenses | 76.0 | 90.1 | 93.9 | 95.4 | 94.4 | 95.4 |
| 7.0 | | 8.2 | | 7.3 | | Operating Profit | 24.0 | 9.9 | 6.1 | 4.6 | 5.6 | 4.6 |
| -1.1 | | .2 | | .9 | | All Other Expenses (net) | 6.1 | 2.2 | .0 | -.3 | .4 | .3 |
| 8.1 | | 7.9 | | 6.4 | | Profit Before Taxes | 17.9 | 7.7 | 6.1 | 4.9 | 5.1 | 4.3 |
| | | | | | | RATIOS | | | | | | |
| 3.5 | | 3.5 | | 3.3 | | | 3.8 | 5.3 | 6.3 | 4.9 | 3.5 | 2.0 |
| 1.7 | | 1.7 | | 1.5 | | Current | .8 | 1.8 | 1.8 | 2.1 | 1.8 | 1.2 |
| 1.0 | | 1.0 | | .8 | | | .2 | .8 | .7 | .8 | 1.0 | .8 |
| 3.1 | | 3.0 | | 2.9 | | | 3.2 | 4.7 | 5.7 | 4.3 | 3.1 | 1.8 |
| (517) 1.4 | | 1.5 | | 1.2 | | Quick | .7 | 1.3 | 1.8 | 1.8 | 1.6 | 1.1 |
| .8 | | .8 | | .6 | | | .2 | .6 | .7 | .6 | .8 | .6 |
| 0 999.8 | | 1 377.0 | | 4 94.4 | | | 0 UND | 0 UND | 0 UND | 6 60.4 | 8 45.0 | 27 13.7 |
| 29 12.6 | | 26 14.1 | | 27 13.6 | | Sales/Receivables | 0 UND | 0 UND | 11 33.2 | 25 14.5 | 28 12.9 | 35 10.3 |
| 47 7.8 | | 41 9.0 | | 41 9.0 | | | 25 14.4 | 21 17.3 | 29 12.7 | 42 8.7 | 42 8.6 | 43 8.4 |
| | | | | | | Cost of Sales/Inventory | | | | | | |
| | | | | | | Cost of Sales/Payables | | | | | | |
| 7.5 | | 8.1 | | 8.0 | | | 5.6 | 6.8 | 9.9 | 7.4 | 7.1 | 9.9 |
| 19.4 | | 17.9 | | 25.7 | | Sales/Working Capital | -149.0 | 30.7 | 25.5 | 15.9 | 20.7 | 33.2 |
| -245.4 | | 999.8 | | -40.7 | | | -5.3 | -62.7 | -64.4 | -59.3 | -342.3 | -34.2 |
| 27.6 | | 27.4 | | 13.5 | | | 8.3 | 13.1 | 18.6 | 18.6 | 18.0 | 11.4 |
| (440) 10.2 | | (632) 9.7 | | (609) 4.7 | | EBIT/Interest | (43) 3.8 | (62) 3.1 | (53) 2.2 | (93) 6.7 | (132) 6.7 | (226) 4.0 |
| 3.9 | | 3.3 | | 1.2 | | | 1.8 | -1.6 | -1.5 | 1.0 | 1.6 | 1.5 |
| 5.6 | | 5.3 | | 4.8 | | Net Profit + Depr., Dep., | | | | | 3.3 | 4.8 |
| (53) 2.5 | | (93) 2.8 | | (90) 1.9 | | Amort./Cur. Mat. L/T/D | | | | (14) 1.9 | (65) 2.0 | |
| 1.4 | | 1.7 | | 1.2 | | | | | | | 1.5 | 1.2 |
| .4 | | .3 | | .4 | | | .6 | .3 | .3 | .2 | .4 | .6 |
| 1.1 | | 1.0 | | 1.3 | | Fixed/Worth | 2.3 | 1.2 | 1.3 | 1.0 | 1.2 | 1.4 |
| 2.8 | | 3.1 | | 3.6 | | | UND | NM | -4.9 | 4.5 | 2.8 | 2.6 |
| .7 | | .7 | | .7 | | | .9 | .5 | .7 | .5 | .6 | .9 |
| 1.7 | | 1.5 | | 1.7 | | Debt/Worth | 2.3 | 2.9 | 1.7 | 1.5 | 1.6 | 1.8 |
| 5.1 | | 5.5 | | 8.4 | | | -88.2 | -18.6 | -5.9 | 19.2 | 7.4 | 4.4 |
| 78.7 | | 75.6 | | 56.6 | | % Profit Before Taxes/Tangible | 63.1 | 91.5 | 69.6 | 58.9 | 56.7 | 41.7 |
| (438) 45.7 | | (641) 40.2 | | (593) 22.9 | | Net Worth | (47) 28.7 | (59) 32.3 | (46) 26.2 | (88) 29.5 | (131) 24.5 | (222) 19.0 |
| 17.9 | | 19.0 | | 5.5 | | | 4.8 | 5.9 | .6 | 5.8 | 5.8 | 5.6 |
| 30.4 | | 30.5 | | 23.0 | | % Profit Before Taxes/Total | 28.1 | 29.8 | 30.8 | 29.3 | 24.4 | 14.7 |
| 15.8 | | 14.1 | | 8.5 | | Assets | 10.3 | 12.6 | 8.2 | 8.6 | 11.0 | 7.3 |
| 6.4 | | 4.8 | | .7 | | | .8 | -4.1 | -2.2 | .8 | 1.3 | 1.3 |
| 44.2 | | 44.5 | | 38.9 | | | 19.7 | 39.8 | 78.2 | 77.9 | 62.8 | 17.1 |
| 6.5 | | 7.5 | | 6.3 | | Sales/Net Fixed Assets | 3.0 | 8.6 | 14.6 | 9.8 | 7.5 | 3.8 |
| 2.7 | | 3.0 | | 2.5 | | | .4 | 3.2 | 2.8 | 4.1 | 3.3 | 2.1 |
| 4.4 | | 4.6 | | 4.4 | | | 3.3 | 5.0 | 5.5 | 4.4 | 5.1 | 3.2 |
| 2.6 | | 2.6 | | 2.3 | | Sales/Total Assets | 1.5 | 2.9 | 3.0 | 2.9 | 2.6 | 1.7 |
| 1.4 | | 1.6 | | 1.4 | | | .3 | 1.6 | 1.6 | 1.8 | 1.5 | 1.2 |
| 2.3 | | 1.7 | | 2.0 | | | 6.1 | 2.4 | 1.7 | 2.0 | 1.8 | 1.8 |
| (321) 5.6 | | (448) 4.5 | | (427) 5.3 | | % Depr., Dep., Amort./Sales | (34) 14.4 | (39) 7.0 | (29) 3.6 | (56) 5.3 | (94) 4.6 | (175) 5.0 |
| 9.6 | | 8.5 | | 9.8 | | | 27.1 | 12.6 | 14.1 | 8.4 | 8.8 | 8.5 |
| .9 | | .9 | | .9 | | % Officers', Directors' | 3.2 | 1.3 | 1.4 | 1.4 | .9 | .4 |
| (151) 2.0 | | (231) 2.2 | | (200) 1.7 | | Owners' Comp/Sales | (10) 6.7 | (30) 3.7 | (25) 3.4 | (45) 2.3 | (42) 1.4 | (48) .9 |
| 4.1 | | 4.6 | | 3.9 | | | 12.1 | 6.7 | 5.0 | 3.3 | 3.0 | 1.5 |
| 20044325M | | 32506419M | | 27968062M | | Net Sales ($) | 33253M | 156341M | 244909M | 834261M | 2529095M | 24170203M |
| 8487330M | | 14045458M | | 15196236M | | Total Assets ($) | 71819M | 130058M | 115074M | 365700M | 1221898M | 13291687M |

© RMA 2024   M = $ thousand   MM = $ million
See Pages viii through xx for Explanation of Ratios and Data

# TRANSPORTATION—General Freight Trucking, Long-Distance, Truckload NAICS 484121

## Current Data Sorted by Assets

| | | | | | | | Type of Statement | | Comparative Historical Data | |
|---|---|---|---|---|---|---|---|---|---|---|
| | | 1 | 1 | 24 | 14 | 29 | Unqualified | | 66 | 52 |
| | | | 26 | 93 | 29 | 12 | Reviewed | | 162 | 93 |
| 1 | 4 | 37 | 52 | 10 | 1 | Compiled | | 139 | 88 |
| 28 | 33 | 47 | 13 | 1 | | Tax Returns | | 159 | 92 |
| 31 | 67 | 178 | 181 | 69 | 70 | Other | | 650 | 395 |
| | 158 (4/1-9/30/23) | | 894 (10/1/23-3/31/24) | | | | | 4/1/19-3/31/20 ALL | 4/1/20-3/31/21 ALL |
| 0-500M | 500M-2MM | 2-10MM | 10-50MM | 50-100MM | 100-250MM | NUMBER OF STATEMENTS | | | |
| 60 | 105 | 289 | 363 | 123 | 112 | | | 1176 | 720 |
| % | % | % | % | % | % | **ASSETS** | | % | % |
| 31.2 | 24.7 | 15.2 | 11.4 | 10.1 | 6.2 | Cash & Equivalents | | 11.6 | 16.8 |
| 12.4 | 21.1 | 21.8 | 16.7 | 15.8 | 14.5 | Trade Receivables (net) | | 21.9 | 20.7 |
| 1.9 | 1.2 | 2.6 | 1.0 | 1.2 | 1.4 | Inventory | | 1.5 | .9 |
| 5.7 | 7.7 | 5.4 | 4.4 | 3.1 | 3.8 | All Other Current | | 4.0 | 3.8 |
| 51.2 | 54.7 | 45.0 | 33.4 | 30.2 | 25.9 | Total Current | | 39.0 | 42.3 |
| 37.0 | 28.1 | 38.2 | 51.5 | 50.6 | 56.3 | Fixed Assets (net) | | 48.8 | 46.7 |
| 2.4 | 6.3 | 5.1 | 3.4 | 6.8 | 5.6 | Intangibles (net) | | 5.0 | 4.0 |
| 9.4 | 10.9 | 11.6 | 11.6 | 12.4 | 12.2 | All Other Non-Current | | 7.2 | 7.0 |
| 100.0 | 100.0 | 100.0 | 100.0 | 100.0 | 100.0 | Total | | 100.0 | 100.0 |
| | | | | | | **LIABILITIES** | | | |
| 11.3 | 3.7 | 4.3 | 2.7 | 1.4 | 3.0 | Notes Payable-Short Term | | 5.9 | 5.6 |
| 10.6 | 6.8 | 6.1 | 10.1 | 9.2 | 9.8 | Cur. Mat.-L.T.D. | | 9.8 | 10.1 |
| 5.4 | 7.1 | 7.1 | 5.2 | 4.8 | 4.1 | Trade Payables | | 7.9 | 7.2 |
| .1 | .1 | .1 | .1 | .0 | .1 | Income Taxes Payable | | .1 | .1 |
| 14.9 | 12.9 | 10.8 | 6.3 | 8.6 | 7.5 | All Other Current | | 9.5 | 8.8 |
| 42.3 | 30.6 | 28.4 | 24.5 | 24.1 | 24.6 | Total Current | | 33.1 | 31.9 |
| 35.3 | 31.8 | 31.4 | 30.3 | 27.8 | 31.5 | Long-Term Debt | | 32.0 | 36.0 |
| .0 | .0 | .2 | .6 | 1.2 | 1.3 | Deferred Taxes | | .9 | .9 |
| 12.2 | 6.0 | 4.3 | 3.9 | 5.4 | 6.2 | All Other Non-Current | | 5.4 | 3.5 |
| 10.3 | 31.7 | 35.7 | 40.7 | 41.6 | 36.5 | Net Worth | | 28.7 | 27.7 |
| 100.0 | 100.0 | 100.0 | 100.0 | 100.0 | 100.0 | Total Liabilities & Net Worth | | 100.0 | 100.0 |
| | | | | | | **INCOME DATA** | | | |
| 100.0 | 100.0 | 100.0 | 100.0 | 100.0 | 100.0 | Net Sales | | 100.0 | 100.0 |
| | | | | | | Gross Profit | | | |
| 95.7 | 98.1 | 94.6 | 94.5 | 94.7 | 94.3 | Operating Expenses | | 94.0 | 92.6 |
| 4.3 | 1.9 | 5.4 | 5.5 | 5.3 | 5.7 | Operating Profit | | 6.0 | 7.4 |
| -.2 | -.2 | 1.0 | .7 | .3 | 1.0 | All Other Expenses (net) | | .9 | .3 |
| 4.5 | 2.1 | 4.4 | 4.8 | 5.0 | 4.6 | Profit Before Taxes | | 5.1 | 7.1 |
| | | | | | | **RATIOS** | | | |
| 5.1 | 4.9 | 4.0 | 2.2 | 1.9 | 1.6 | | | 2.1 | 2.5 |
| 1.4 | 2.2 | 1.7 | 1.2 | 1.2 | 1.0 | Current | | 1.3 | 1.3 |
| .3 | .8 | .9 | .8 | .8 | .7 | | | .7 | .9 |
| 3.7 | 3.8 | 3.1 | 1.9 | 1.6 | 1.2 | | | 1.8 | 2.3 |
| 1.2 | 1.8 | (288) 1.4 | 1.0 | 1.0 | .8 | Quick | | 1.0 | 1.2 |
| .3 | .7 | .7 | .6 | .6 | .6 | | | .6 | .7 |
| 0 UND | 0 UND | 5 76.8 | 21 17.0 | 29 12.8 | 30 12.3 | | | 17 21.1 | 12 29.8 |
| 0 UND | 7 51.2 | 26 13.8 | 32 11.3 | 35 10.5 | 35 10.3 | Sales/Receivables | | 32 11.4 | 33 11.2 |
| 0 UND | 28 13.1 | 38 9.7 | 41 8.8 | 45 8.1 | 42 8.6 | | | 41 8.8 | 44 8.3 |
| | | | | | | Cost of Sales/Inventory | | | |
| | | | | | | Cost of Sales/Payables | | | |
| 10.9 | 9.9 | 8.5 | 8.3 | 9.4 | 14.6 | | | 11.9 | 8.8 |
| 112.9 | 22.5 | 16.7 | 30.3 | 28.0 | NM | Sales/Working Capital | | 38.9 | 24.6 |
| -18.5 | -63.4 | -78.6 | -26.2 | -26.0 | -20.8 | | | -24.0 | -45.0 |
| 14.4 | 14.7 | 13.8 | 9.5 | 10.1 | 7.5 | | | 9.4 | 11.9 |
| (40) 4.6 | (78) 3.4 | (246) 3.5 | (341) 3.5 | (115) 4.2 | (110) 4.6 | EBIT/Interest | | (1066) 3.8 | (630) 5.0 |
| -.6 | -.8 | -.1 | 1.0 | 1.6 | 1.0 | | | 1.6 | 2.1 |
| | | 3.9 | 2.6 | 2.8 | | | | 2.5 | 3.7 |
| | (30) 1.6 | (84) 1.6 | (33) 1.9 | Net Profit + Depr., Dep., | | (232) 1.6 | (104) 2.0 |
| | | .7 | 1.1 | 1.1 | | Amort./Cur. Mat. L/T/D | | 1.1 | 1.3 |
| .0 | .0 | .3 | .8 | 1.0 | 1.1 | | | .8 | .8 |
| 1.3 | .4 | 1.1 | 1.5 | 1.6 | 1.8 | Fixed/Worth | | 1.7 | 1.8 |
| UND | 21.8 | 4.0 | 2.8 | 2.8 | 3.5 | | | 4.8 | 4.7 |
| .6 | .5 | .6 | .8 | .9 | 1.1 | | | .9 | .9 |
| 3.1 | 2.0 | 1.9 | 1.8 | 1.8 | 2.1 | Debt/Worth | | 2.2 | 2.4 |
| -7.1 | -9.9 | 6.5 | 3.5 | 3.5 | 4.6 | | | 7.4 | 8.0 |
| 94.3 | 69.2 | 50.1 | 31.9 | 33.0 | 26.5 | | | 43.9 | 64.7 |
| (42) 51.6 | (76) 36.0 | (246) 17.8 | (343) 14.8 | (116) 17.7 | (104) 15.1 | % Profit Before Taxes/Tangible Net Worth | | (992) 20.3 | (599) 27.2 |
| -.4 | 4.6 | 1.0 | 1.6 | 6.8 | .8 | | | 6.6 | 11.1 |
| 40.4 | 23.3 | 19.3 | 12.1 | 10.3 | 10.3 | | | 14.3 | 19.0 |
| 26.1 | 10.3 | 6.6 | 5.7 | 6.7 | 5.3 | % Profit Before Taxes/Total Assets | | 6.6 | 8.5 |
| -6.3 | -2.8 | -.5 | .1 | 1.6 | .2 | | | 1.5 | 2.6 |
| UND | 712.1 | 39.2 | 6.0 | 4.2 | 3.3 | | | 14.9 | 14.1 |
| 28.6 | 46.7 | 8.1 | 3.0 | 2.6 | 2.1 | Sales/Net Fixed Assets | | 4.1 | 3.8 |
| 4.5 | 7.1 | 3.3 | 1.8 | 1.7 | 1.6 | | | 2.1 | 2.0 |
| 11.8 | 7.8 | 4.4 | 2.2 | 1.8 | 1.5 | | | 3.7 | 3.4 |
| 5.1 | 4.0 | 2.6 | 1.6 | 1.3 | 1.2 | Sales/Total Assets | | 2.1 | 2.0 |
| 2.5 | 2.4 | 1.5 | 1.1 | 1.0 | 1.0 | | | 1.3 | 1.3 |
| 1.7 | .5 | 1.0 | 4.2 | 3.8 | 1.3 | | | 2.6 | 3.1 |
| (22) 6.4 | (44) 3.5 | (189) 5.2 | (318) 8.0 | (89) 6.6 | (21) 4.1 | % Depr., Dep., Amort./Sales | | (837) 6.2 | (480) 7.2 |
| 11.8 | 9.7 | 10.3 | 12.4 | 9.5 | 5.6 | | | 10.9 | 11.5 |
| 1.0 | 1.0 | .5 | .6 | 1.0 | | | | .7 | .8 |
| (27) 4.1 | (43) 1.9 | (89) 1.4 | (63) 1.0 | (15) 2.1 | | % Officers', Directors', Owners' Comp/Sales | | (305) 1.7 | (174) 2.0 |
| 9.6 | 3.6 | 3.2 | 1.9 | 6.9 | | | | 4.6 | 4.8 |
| 177336M | 682342M | 4433486M | 15746463M | 13294639M | 25690968M | Net Sales ($) | | 65576392M | 36646271M |
| 14241M | 125666M | 1474623M | 8995215M | 8829674M | 17727482M | Total Assets ($) | | 34429445M | 20669485M |

M = $ thousand  MM = $ million
See Pages viii through xx for Explanation of Ratios and Data

© RMA 2024

# TRANSPORTATION—General Freight Trucking, Long-Distance, Truckload  NAICS 484121

## Comparative Historical Data | Current Data Sorted by Sales

| Comparative Historical Data | | | | Type of Statement | Current Data Sorted by Sales | | | | | |
|---|---|---|---|---|---|---|---|---|---|---|
| 60 | 70 | 69 | | Unqualified | | | 1 | 1 | 3 | 64 |
| 117 | 145 | 160 | | Reviewed | | 2 | 3 | 10 | 29 | 116 |
| 98 | 135 | 105 | | Compiled | 2 | 4 | 4 | 11 | 37 | 47 |
| 117 | 136 | 122 | | Tax Returns | 19 | 16 | 15 | 26 | 35 | 11 |
| 465 | 609 | 596 | | Other | 27 | 33 | 36 | 65 | 129 | 306 |
| 4/1/21-3/31/22 ALL | 4/1/22-3/31/23 ALL | 4/1/23-3/31/24 ALL | | | 158 (4/1-9/30/23) | | | 894 (10/1/23-3/31/24) | | |
| | | | | | 0-1MM | 1-3MM | 3-5MM | 5-10MM | 10-25MM | 25MM & OVER |
| 857 | 1095 | 1052 | | NUMBER OF STATEMENTS | 48 | 55 | 59 | 113 | 233 | 544 |
| % | % | % | | ASSETS | % | % | % | % | % | % |
| 18.3 | 16.2 | 14.2 | | Cash & Equivalents | 16.1 | 21.1 | 20.3 | 18.2 | 15.4 | 11.3 |
| 20.8 | 19.7 | 17.9 | | Trade Receivables (net) | 5.6 | 16.1 | 15.6 | 18.7 | 18.1 | 19.2 |
| 1.2 | 1.0 | 1.6 | | Inventory | 1.3 | .9 | 2.7 | 4.7 | 1.0 | 1.2 |
| 4.5 | 5.4 | 4.9 | | All Other Current | 4.9 | 4.4 | 10.5 | 4.7 | 5.0 | 4.3 |
| 44.8 | 42.3 | 38.6 | | Total Current | 27.9 | 42.5 | 49.0 | 46.3 | 39.5 | 36.0 |
| 45.0 | 43.3 | 45.1 | | Fixed Assets (net) | 59.4 | 44.1 | 29.8 | 41.2 | 42.4 | 47.6 |
| 3.0 | 4.0 | 4.7 | | Intangibles (net) | 3.0 | 4.3 | 8.4 | 2.5 | 5.3 | 4.7 |
| 7.2 | 10.5 | 11.6 | | All Other Non-Current | 9.7 | 9.1 | 12.8 | 10.1 | 12.7 | 11.7 |
| 100.0 | 100.0 | 100.0 | | Total | 100.0 | 100.0 | 100.0 | 100.0 | 100.0 | 100.0 |
| | | | | LIABILITIES | | | | | | |
| 3.7 | 3.7 | 3.6 | | Notes Payable-Short Term | 5.5 | 2.8 | 3.2 | 5.5 | 4.6 | 2.8 |
| 8.9 | 8.6 | 8.6 | | Cur. Mat.-L.T.D. | 9.4 | 10.1 | 6.4 | 9.1 | 7.2 | 9.1 |
| 7.3 | 7.1 | 5.8 | | Trade Payables | 4.2 | 4.6 | 5.3 | 5.3 | 5.9 | 6.1 |
| .2 | .2 | .1 | | Income Taxes Payable | .1 | .1 | 0 | .1 | .2 | .1 |
| 9.7 | 7.7 | 9.1 | | All Other Current | 12.5 | 12.1 | 8.8 | 10.9 | 8.8 | 8.2 |
| 29.8 | 27.3 | 27.2 | | Total Current | 31.7 | 29.7 | 23.7 | 30.8 | 26.6 | 26.3 |
| 32.3 | 32.8 | 30.9 | | Long-Term Debt | 35.7 | 41.6 | 29.9 | 38.7 | 30.7 | 27.9 |
| .8 | .6 | .5 | | Deferred Taxes | .0 | .0 | .2 | .1 | .3 | .9 |
| 3.4 | 3.4 | 5.1 | | All Other Non-Current | 7.3 | 8.2 | 8.7 | 5.5 | 3.9 | 4.7 |
| 33.7 | 35.9 | 36.3 | | Net Worth | 25.3 | 20.5 | 37.6 | 24.9 | 38.6 | 40.2 |
| 100.0 | 100.0 | 100.0 | | Total Liabilities & Net Worth | 100.0 | 100.0 | 100.0 | 100.0 | 100.0 | 100.0 |
| | | | | INCOME DATA | | | | | | |
| 100.0 | 100.0 | 100.0 | | Net Sales | 100.0 | 100.0 | 100.0 | 100.0 | 100.0 | 100.0 |
| | | | | Gross Profit | | | | | | |
| 90.9 | 91.8 | 95.0 | | Operating Expenses | 86.0 | 91.4 | 94.3 | 94.2 | 96.5 | 95.7 |
| 9.1 | 8.2 | 5.0 | | Operating Profit | 14.0 | 8.6 | 5.7 | 5.8 | 3.5 | 4.3 |
| -.6 | .1 | .6 | | All Other Expenses (net) | 8.0 | 2.2 | .5 | .2 | -.3 | .3 |
| 9.7 | 8.2 | 4.4 | | Profit Before Taxes | 6.1 | 6.4 | 5.2 | 5.6 | 3.8 | 4.0 |
| | | | | RATIOS | | | | | | |
| 2.9 | 3.0 | 2.7 | | | 3.5 | 6.3 | 11.3 | 3.7 | 3.5 | 2.1 |
| 1.6 | 1.7 | 1.3 | | Current | .9 | 1.6 | 2.2 | 1.6 | 1.5 | 1.2 |
| 1.0 | .9 | .8 | | | .2 | .4 | .9 | .7 | .7 | .8 |
| 2.6 | 2.5 | 2.2 | | | 2.0 | 4.4 | 3.9 | 2.8 | 2.9 | 1.8 |
| 1.4 (1093) | 1.3 (1051) | 1.1 | | Quick | .8 | .9 | 1.3 (112) | 1.3 | 1.3 | 1.0 |
| .8 | .7 | .6 | | | .1 | .3 | .4 | .6 | .6 | .6 |
| 10  36.2 | 6  56.4 | 12  31.3 | | | 0  UND | 0  UND | 0  UND | 0  UND | 7  55.9 | 26  14.3 |
| 33  11.0 | 29  12.7 | 30  12.0 | | Sales/Receivables | 0  UND | 0  UND | 6  58.1 | 24  15.2 | 29  12.5 | 33  11.0 |
| 45  8.1 | 41  8.9 | 40  9.1 | | | 12  31.2 | 39  9.4 | 35  10.3 | 38  9.5 | 38  9.5 | 42  8.7 |
| | | | | Cost of Sales/Inventory | | | | | | |
| | | | | Cost of Sales/Payables | | | | | | |
| 7.9 | 8.3 | 9.3 | | | 5.6 | 6.3 | 4.6 | 10.1 | 10.0 | 9.7 |
| 18.5 | 17.3 | 27.9 | | Sales/Working Capital | -64.8 | 25.7 | 14.8 | 20.8 | 24.4 | 30.5 |
| -200.6 | -114.0 | -30.0 | | | -4.9 | -12.0 | -142.9 | -39.7 | -42.3 | -34.1 |
| 20.6 | 21.5 | 10.4 | | | 11.9 | 8.3 | 19.7 | 11.6 | 10.4 | 9.6 |
| (762) 9.9 | (955) 8.6 | (930) 3.9 | | EBIT/Interest | (29) 4.2 | (41) 2.9 | (50) 6.3 | (96) 4.2 | (205) 3.0 | (509) 4.2 |
| 4.3 | 3.6 | .9 | | | -.7 | .1 | 1.6 | .2 | .0 | 1.3 |
| 5.4 | 4.0 | 2.8 | | | | | | | 4.6 | 2.8 |
| (121) 2.8 | (151) 2.2 | (154) 1.6 | | Net Profit + Depr., Dep., Amort./Cur. Mat. L/T/D | | | | (31) 1.4 | (112) 1.8 |
| 1.8 | 1.5 | 1.0 | | | | | | | .9 | 1.1 |
| .6 | .5 | .5 | | | 1.2 | .1 | .0 | .2 | .5 | .8 |
| 1.3 | 1.2 | 1.4 | | Fixed/Worth | 2.7 | 3.0 | .4 | 1.3 | 1.2 | 1.5 |
| 2.8 | 2.8 | 3.2 | | | 21.2 | -4.2 | 3.3 | 4.5 | 3.1 | 2.7 |
| .8 | .8 | .8 | | | .9 | .7 | .5 | .7 | .6 | .9 |
| 1.7 | 1.6 | 1.9 | | Debt/Worth | 3.4 | 4.7 | 1.6 | 2.1 | 1.7 | 1.8 |
| 4.3 | 4.7 | 4.7 | | | 21.4 | -7.8 | 4.9 | 24.1 | 4.4 | 3.5 |
| 82.1 | 64.7 | 39.6 | | | 63.0 | 54.5 | 62.9 | 69.5 | 39.5 | 32.6 |
| (754) 41.6 | (965) 33.7 | (927) 17.1 | | % Profit Before Taxes/Tangible Net Worth | (40) 28.3 | (36) 22.0 | (48) 27.3 | (89) 24.6 | (204) 12.9 | (510) 16.5 |
| 18.7 | 17.3 | 2.5 | | | -2.3 | 2.8 | 8.5 | 4.2 | .3 | 3.5 |
| 27.7 | 23.5 | 14.4 | | | 33.0 | 26.0 | 21.7 | 21.7 | 15.8 | 11.9 |
| 14.8 | 12.9 | 6.2 | | % Profit Before Taxes/Total Assets | 4.6 | 6.6 | 11.6 | 7.9 | 4.1 | 6.0 |
| 6.7 | 5.5 | .1 | | | -.8 | -.5 | 4.7 | -1.6 | -1.8 | 1.0 |
| 15.6 | 20.8 | 16.4 | | | 8.3 | 93.8 | 999.8 | 39.5 | 21.8 | 7.7 |
| 4.4 | 4.8 | 4.0 | | Sales/Net Fixed Assets | 2.5 | 4.7 | 24.0 | 7.1 | 5.5 | 3.2 |
| 2.3 | 2.4 | 2.1 | | | .5 | 1.6 | 2.8 | 2.8 | 2.4 | 2.0 |
| 3.7 | 3.7 | 3.1 | | | 2.8 | 3.7 | 4.0 | 4.7 | 4.2 | 2.5 |
| 2.1 | 2.1 | 1.8 | | Sales/Total Assets | 1.4 | 1.7 | 2.5 | 2.3 | 2.1 | 1.6 |
| 1.4 | 1.3 | 1.2 | | | .2 | .8 | 1.1 | 1.4 | 1.3 | 1.2 |
| 2.1 | 2.5 | 2.8 | | | 5.5 | 6.4 | 3.0 | 2.5 | 2.4 | 2.5 |
| (563) 5.5 | (698) 5.9 | (683) 6.6 | | % Depr., Dep., Amort./Sales | (28) 18.2 | (26) 10.0 | (24) 9.4 | (67) 7.8 | (167) 6.9 | (371) 5.9 |
| 10.3 | 10.1 | 11.1 | | | 32.6 | 37.1 | 15.7 | 14.7 | 11.1 | 9.9 |
| .6 | .6 | .7 | | | 4.1 | 1.5 | 1.9 | 1.0 | .6 | .4 |
| (222) 1.6 | (257) 1.7 | (243) 1.4 | | % Officers', Directors' Owners' Comp/Sales | (15) 9.6 | (18) 2.6 | (21) 3.3 | (30) 2.0 | (77) 1.1 | (82) 1.0 |
| | | | | | 14.3 | 5.9 | 4.5 | 4.4 | 2.1 | 2.3 |
| 56124797M | 66171050M | 60025234M | | Net Sales ($) | 21802M | 112587M | 238191M | 834052M | 3822293M | 54996309M |
| 28552905M | 34563296M | 37166901M | | Total Assets ($) | 76470M | 126028M | 196874M | 624480M | 2255010M | 33888039M |

© RMA 2024    M = $ thousand    MM = $ million
See Pages viii through xx for Explanation of Ratios and Data

## TRANSPORTATION—General Freight Trucking, Long-Distance, Less Than Truckload  NAICS 484122

### Current Data Sorted by Assets | Comparative Historical Data

| | | | | | | | Type of Statement | | |
|---|---|---|---|---|---|---|---|---|---|
| | | | | 2 | 2 | 3 | Unqualified | 8 | 9 |
| | | | 1 | 5 | 1 | 2 | Reviewed | 14 | 10 |
| | | 2 | 2 | 1 | | | Compiled | 7 | 4 |
| | 3 | 1 | | 2 | | | Tax Returns | 12 | 4 |
| 3 | 4 | 3 | 14 | 14 | 9 | 10 | Other | 65 | 38 |
| 4 | 9 (4/1-9/30/23) | | | 72 (10/1/23-3/31/24) | | | | 4/1/19-3/31/20 | 4/1/20-3/31/21 |
| 0-500M | 500M-2MM | 2-10MM | 10-50MM | 50-100MM | 100-250MM | | | ALL | ALL |
| 7 | 6 | 17 | 24 | 12 | 15 | | NUMBER OF STATEMENTS | 106 | 65 |
| % | % | % | % | % | % | | ASSETS | % | % |
| | | | 19.3 | 10.3 | 8.6 | 5.4 | Cash & Equivalents | 7.5 | 13.0 |
| | | | 29.6 | 26.8 | 22.3 | 14.0 | Trade Receivables (net) | 22.5 | 24.7 |
| | | | .7 | .5 | .7 | 2.2 | Inventory | .4 | .6 |
| | | | 6.6 | 3.0 | 6.7 | 2.6 | All Other Current | 4.3 | 3.2 |
| | | | 56.3 | 40.5 | 38.3 | 24.2 | Total Current | 34.6 | 41.4 |
| | | | 32.0 | 44.5 | 47.6 | 50.8 | Fixed Assets (net) | 52.9 | 49.2 |
| | | | 6.7 | 3.0 | 1.7 | 9.1 | Intangibles (net) | 2.6 | 3.8 |
| | | | 5.0 | 12.0 | 12.3 | 15.8 | All Other Non-Current | 9.9 | 5.6 |
| | | | 100.0 | 100.0 | 100.0 | 100.0 | Total | 100.0 | 100.0 |
| | | | | | | | LIABILITIES | | |
| | | | 2.2 | 2.5 | .1 | 2.4 | Notes Payable-Short Term | 4.8 | 3.5 |
| | | | 5.7 | 6.9 | 9.6 | 8.6 | Cur. Mat.-L.T.D. | 9.1 | 8.0 |
| | | | 7.0 | 3.7 | 6.2 | 5.9 | Trade Payables | 8.8 | 10.2 |
| | | | .0 | .1 | .3 | .0 | Income Taxes Payable | .0 | .2 |
| | | | 7.4 | 6.6 | 9.8 | 8.1 | All Other Current | 8.1 | 7.0 |
| | | | 22.3 | 19.8 | 26.0 | 25.1 | Total Current | 30.9 | 28.8 |
| | | | 31.2 | 25.0 | 23.2 | 32.5 | Long-Term Debt | 31.6 | 32.3 |
| | | | .2 | .8 | 1.8 | 1.8 | Deferred Taxes | 1.4 | 1.5 |
| | | | 3.0 | 3.5 | 8.0 | 9.9 | All Other Non-Current | 3.1 | 5.1 |
| | | | 43.3 | 50.8 | 40.9 | 30.7 | Net Worth | 33.0 | 32.2 |
| | | | 100.0 | 100.0 | 100.0 | 100.0 | Total Liabilities & Net Worth | 100.0 | 100.0 |
| | | | | | | | INCOME DATA | | |
| | | | 100.0 | 100.0 | 100.0 | 100.0 | Net Sales | 100.0 | 100.0 |
| | | | | | | | Gross Profit | | |
| | | | 96.0 | 95.0 | 96.2 | 96.8 | Operating Expenses | 94.0 | 93.1 |
| | | | 4.0 | 5.0 | 3.8 | 3.2 | Operating Profit | 6.0 | 6.9 |
| | | | -1.0 | .3 | -.2 | 1.0 | All Other Expenses (net) | 1.3 | -.1 |
| | | | 5.0 | 4.8 | 4.0 | 2.1 | Profit Before Taxes | 4.7 | 7.0 |
| | | | | | | | RATIOS | | |
| | | | 7.1 | 2.9 | 1.9 | 1.3 | | 2.1 | 2.1 |
| | | | 2.7 | 2.1 | 1.4 | 1.0 | Current | 1.2 | 1.6 |
| | | | 1.9 | 1.2 | 1.0 | .6 | | .7 | 1.0 |
| | | | 4.5 | 2.9 | 1.5 | 1.1 | | 1.6 | 1.9 |
| | | | 2.0 | 1.9 | 1.1 | .8 | Quick | .9 | 1.5 |
| | | | 1.7 | 1.1 | .8 | .6 | | .5 | .8 |
| | | 11 | 33.4 | 34  10.7 | 31  11.6 | 31  11.6 | | 16  22.6 | 29  12.8 |
| | | 30 | 12.0 | 44   8.3 | 37   9.9 | 38   9.5 | Sales/Receivables | 33  11.1 | 40   9.1 |
| | | 39 |  9.4 | 52   7.0 | 41   8.8 | 45   8.2 | | 42   8.6 | 47   7.7 |
| | | | | | | | Cost of Sales/Inventory | | |
| | | | | | | | Cost of Sales/Payables | | |
| | | | 5.9 | 7.1 | 9.8 | 24.4 | | 13.5 | 7.7 |
| | | | 12.4 | 14.0 | 22.7 | 999.8 | Sales/Working Capital | 60.1 | 17.6 |
| | | | 22.4 | 32.6 | NM | -11.2 | | -20.5 | NM |
| | | | 67.3 | 9.9 | 15.1 | 14.8 | | 7.4 | 15.1 |
| | | (14) | 11.3 | (23)  5.5 | 4.6 | 2.9 | EBIT/Interest | (91)  3.7 | (58)  4.1 |
| | | | -1.3 | .6 | 2.4 | .4 | | 1.6 | 1.2 |
| | | | | | | | Net Profit + Depr., Dep., | 4.0 | 9.8 |
| | | | | | | | Amort./Cur. Mat. L/T/D | (14)  1.7 | (12)  1.6 |
| | | | | | | | | 1.0 | .9 |
| | | | .1 | .5 | .7 | 1.1 | | 1.0 | .9 |
| | | | .6 | .9 | 1.4 | 2.6 | Fixed/Worth | 1.7 | 1.6 |
| | | | 1.3 | 1.7 | 2.3 | 6.4 | | 5.1 | 4.4 |
| | | | .5 | .4 | 1.2 | 2.3 | | .8 | 1.1 |
| | | | .8 | 1.2 | 1.6 | 3.3 | Debt/Worth | 2.0 | 2.2 |
| | | | 2.2 | 2.3 | 2.7 | 9.2 | | 8.3 | 7.1 |
| | | | 56.7 | 20.1 | 29.0 | 34.7 | | 31.3 | 70.1 |
| | | (15) | 21.6 | (23)  9.0 | 21.1 | (13)  18.4 | % Profit Before Taxes/Tangible Net Worth | (89)  13.0 | (58)  23.1 |
| | | | 4.4 | -8.2 | 4.6 | 8.3 | | 2.8 | 5.5 |
| | | | 20.5 | 12.8 | 13.1 | 8.8 | | 9.7 | 17.3 |
| | | | 12.4 | 5.3 | 6.0 | 4.0 | % Profit Before Taxes/Total Assets | 5.5 | 5.4 |
| | | | -6.0 | -1.4 | 1.5 | -1.8 | | 1.1 | .7 |
| | | | 242.4 | 12.4 | 6.1 | 5.1 | | 12.5 | 9.2 |
| | | | 10.3 | 3.2 | 4.2 | 2.2 | Sales/Net Fixed Assets | 3.5 | 3.6 |
| | | | 5.1 | 1.8 | 2.5 | 1.9 | | 1.8 | 1.9 |
| | | | 5.5 | 3.2 | 2.4 | 1.5 | | 4.6 | 3.3 |
| | | | 3.4 | 1.4 | 2.2 | 1.3 | Sales/Total Assets | 2.0 | 1.8 |
| | | | 2.0 | 1.1 | 1.4 | 1.0 | | 1.3 | 1.3 |
| | | | | 2.5 | 1.5 | | | | 2.3 | 2.7 |
| | | | (20) | 6.4 | (10)  4.5 | | % Depr., Dep., Amort./Sales | (80)  6.6 | (51)  7.1 |
| | | | | 10.5 | 8.3 | | | 10.7 | 11.1 |
| | | | | 1.3 | | | | .6 | .4 |
| | | | (10) | 1.9 | | | % Officers', Directors' Owners' Comp/Sales | (27)  1.1 | (15)  1.1 |
| | | | | 2.6 | | | | 4.2 | 2.9 |
| 3422M | 38732M | 327399M | 1394197M | 1793209M | 3563528M | | Net Sales ($) | 5008043M | 4281958M |
| 1691M | 5915M | 81569M | 588425M | 817053M | 2575110M | | Total Assets ($) | 2542012M | 2493906M |

© RMA 2024  M = $ thousand  MM = $ million  
See Pages viii through xx for Explanation of Ratios and Data

# TRANSPORTATION—General Freight Trucking, Long-Distance, Less Than Truckload  NAICS 484122

## Comparative Historical Data / Current Data Sorted by Sales

| | | | | Type of Statement | | | | | | |
|---|---|---|---|---|---|---|---|---|---|---|
| | 2 | 7 | 7 | Unqualified | | | | | 3 | 7 |
| | 3 | 9 | 9 | Reviewed | | | | | 2 | 6 |
| | 4 | 10 | 5 | Compiled | 1 | | | 1 | 2 | 1 |
| | 12 | 8 | 6 | Tax Returns | 3 | | 4 | | 1 | 2 |
| | 53 | 73 | 54 | Other | 3 | 9 (4/1-9/30/23) | 4 | 3 | 11 | 31 |
| | 4/1/21-3/31/22 ALL | 4/1/22-3/31/23 ALL | 4/1/23-3/31/24 ALL | | 0-1MM | 1-3MM | 3-5MM | 5-10MM | 10-25MM | 25MM & OVER |
| | 74 | 107 | 81 | NUMBER OF STATEMENTS | 7 | 2 | 4 | 4 | 17 | 47 |
| | % | % | % | ASSETS | % | % | % | % | % | % |
| | 14.0 | 16.6 | 15.7 | Cash & Equivalents | | | | | 18.5 | 9.4 |
| | 22.9 | 20.3 | 23.0 | Trade Receivables (net) | | | | | 33.6 | 23.0 |
| | .8 | .7 | .9 | Inventory | | | | | .8 | 1.1 |
| | 2.0 | 3.2 | 4.1 | All Other Current | | | | | 6.7 | 4.0 |
| | 39.7 | 40.9 | 43.7 | Total Current | | | | | 59.7 | 37.5 |
| | 48.8 | 45.8 | 42.0 | Fixed Assets (net) | | | | | 26.7 | 44.6 |
| | 4.7 | 5.2 | 4.2 | Intangibles (net) | | | | | 6.7 | 4.6 |
| | 6.7 | 8.1 | 10.0 | All Other Non-Current | | | | | 6.9 | 13.4 |
| | 100.0 | 100.0 | 100.0 | Total | | | | | 100.0 | 100.0 |
| | | | | LIABILITIES | | | | | | |
| | 5.2 | 3.8 | 2.1 | Notes Payable-Short Term | | | | | 2.3 | 2.0 |
| | 8.3 | 7.2 | 8.1 | Cur. Mat.-L.T.D. | | | | | 12.3 | 7.5 |
| | 7.6 | 6.7 | 6.6 | Trade Payables | | | | | 5.7 | 5.7 |
| | .1 | .0 | .1 | Income Taxes Payable | | | | | .1 | .1 |
| | 4.3 | 7.4 | 8.1 | All Other Current | | | | | 10.2 | 8.2 |
| | 25.5 | 25.1 | 24.9 | Total Current | | | | | 30.7 | 23.5 |
| | 36.0 | 32.7 | 36.9 | Long-Term Debt | | | | | 48.6 | 23.8 |
| | .9 | .9 | .9 | Deferred Taxes | | | | | .3 | 1.4 |
| | 3.8 | 2.6 | 6.0 | All Other Non-Current | | | | | 3.0 | 7.0 |
| | 33.7 | 38.7 | 31.3 | Net Worth | | | | | 17.4 | 44.2 |
| | 100.0 | 100.0 | 100.0 | Total Liabilities & Net Worth | | | | | 100.0 | 100.0 |
| | | | | INCOME DATA | | | | | | |
| | 100.0 | 100.0 | 100.0 | Net Sales | | | | | 100.0 | 100.0 |
| | | | | Gross Profit | | | | | | |
| | 90.7 | 88.5 | 94.9 | Operating Expenses | | | | | 98.8 | 96.6 |
| | 9.3 | 11.5 | 5.1 | Operating Profit | | | | | 1.2 | 3.4 |
| | .5 | 1.1 | .0 | All Other Expenses (net) | | | | | .0 | .1 |
| | 8.8 | 10.4 | 5.0 | Profit Before Taxes | | | | | 1.2 | 3.3 |
| | | | | RATIOS | | | | | | |
| | 3.0 | 2.7 | 2.9 | | | | | | 3.0 | 2.5 |
| | 1.7 | 1.6 | 1.8 | Current | | | | | 1.9 | 1.4 |
| | 1.0 | .9 | 1.0 | | | | | | 1.5 | 1.0 |
| | 2.7 | 2.4 | 2.8 | | | | | | 2.8 | 2.0 |
| | 1.5 | 1.4 | 1.4 | Quick | | | | | 1.8 | 1.2 |
| | .9 | .7 | .9 | | | | | | 1.2 | .8 |
| 8 | 46.3 | 18 | 20.3 | 25 | 14.7 | | | | 26 | 14.2 | 31 | 11.6 |
| 40 | 9.1 | 31 | 11.7 | 36 | 10.0 | Sales/Receivables | | | | 34 | 10.7 | 39 | 9.3 |
| 46 | 8.0 | 38 | 9.6 | 45 | 8.2 | | | | 43 | 8.4 | 46 | 8.0 |
| | | | | Cost of Sales/Inventory | | | | | | |
| | | | | Cost of Sales/Payables | | | | | | |
| | 7.7 | 8.9 | 7.8 | | | | | | 6.8 | 10.1 |
| | 17.6 | 20.7 | 19.8 | Sales/Working Capital | | | | | 15.1 | 24.4 |
| | NM | -83.0 | 844.1 | | | | | | 31.7 | 999.8 |
| | 21.9 | 27.6 | 14.8 | | | | | | 10.1 | 15.0 |
| (64) | 9.6 | (83) | 8.5 | (71) | 5.4 | EBIT/Interest | | | (14) | 2.4 | (46) | 5.7 |
| | 2.9 | 2.7 | 1.1 | | | | | | -3.4 | 2.0 |
| | 7.2 | 14.8 | 4.5 | Net Profit + Depr., Dep., | | | | | | 6.9 |
| (10) | 2.8 | (19) | 3.4 | (17) | 1.5 | Amort./Cur. Mat. L/T/D | | | | | | (13) | 1.6 |
| | 1.3 | 2.0 | .7 | | | | | | | .8 |
| | .7 | .5 | .6 | | | | | | .1 | .7 |
| | 1.6 | 1.3 | 1.2 | Fixed/Worth | | | | | .6 | 1.2 |
| | 3.5 | 3.5 | 2.6 | | | | | | 1.5 | 2.6 |
| | .7 | .6 | .6 | | | | | | .7 | .6 |
| | 2.2 | 1.4 | 1.3 | Debt/Worth | | | | | 1.2 | 1.8 |
| | 8.6 | 4.4 | 3.4 | | | | | | 2.7 | 3.3 |
| | 78.7 | 61.8 | 34.9 | % Profit Before Taxes/Tangible | | | | | 34.8 | 31.0 |
| (63) | 39.5 | (94) | 40.0 | (70) | 17.9 | Net Worth | | | (15) | 10.6 | (45) | 15.9 |
| | 19.5 | 16.4 | 4.3 | | | | | | -18.5 | 4.5 |
| | 28.3 | 29.0 | 14.1 | % Profit Before Taxes/Total | | | | | 12.8 | 10.9 |
| | 15.1 | 15.1 | 6.0 | Assets | | | | | 1.7 | 5.3 |
| | 3.0 | 4.8 | .6 | | | | | | -13.7 | 1.2 |
| | 13.6 | 17.9 | 34.6 | | | | | | 242.4 | 6.2 |
| | 4.5 | 4.9 | 4.2 | Sales/Net Fixed Assets | | | | | 34.5 | 3.6 |
| | 2.2 | 2.3 | 2.1 | | | | | | 6.9 | 2.1 |
| | 2.8 | 4.1 | 3.5 | | | | | | 5.6 | 2.4 |
| | 2.1 | 1.9 | 1.8 | Sales/Total Assets | | | | | 3.6 | 1.6 |
| | 1.3 | 1.3 | 1.2 | | | | | | 2.4 | 1.2 |
| | 2.0 | .9 | 1.3 | | | | | | 1.0 | 1.4 |
| (52) | 5.6 | (70) | 4.8 | (46) | 4.3 | % Depr., Dep., Amort./Sales | | | (10) | 3.7 | (33) | 4.4 |
| | 9.0 | 8.4 | 9.3 | | | | | | 10.0 | 8.5 |
| | .7 | .8 | .9 | % Officers', Directors' | | | | | | 1.0 |
| (22) | 2.6 | (28) | 1.1 | (23) | 1.7 | Owners' Comp/Sales | | | | | | (12) | 1.9 |
| | 9.8 | 2.0 | 2.6 | | | | | | | 9.0 |
| | 4410319M | 8832190M | 7120487M | Net Sales ($) | 2362M | 2950M | 16269M | 28787M | 299234M | 6770885M |
| | 2334850M | 4645416M | 4069763M | Total Assets ($) | 1878M | 2725M | 7586M | 36630M | 108259M | 3912685M |

© RMA 2024    M = $ thousand    MM = $ million
See Pages viii through xx for Explanation of Ratios and Data

## TRANSPORTATION—Used Household and Office Goods Moving  NAICS 484210

### Current Data Sorted by Assets / Comparative Historical Data

| | | | | | | | Type of Statement | | |
|---|---|---|---|---|---|---|---|---|---|
| | | | | 1 | | | Unqualified | 4 | 2 |
| | | | 14 | 10 | 1 | 3 | Reviewed | 14 | 5 |
| | 1 | | 17 | 3 | | 1 | Compiled | 37 | 26 |
| 5 | 10 | 1 | 6 | 2 | 3 | | Tax Returns | 26 | 14 |
| 4 | 20 | 35 | 20 | 3 | 2 | | Other | 94 | 46 |
| 9 | 16 (4/1-9/30/23) | | 158 (10/1/23-3/31/24) | | | | | 4/1/19-3/31/20 | 4/1/20-3/31/21 |
| 0-500M | 500M-2MM | 2-10MM | 10-50MM | 50-100MM | 100-250MM | | | ALL | ALL |
| 19 | 32 | 72 | 37 | 8 | 6 | | NUMBER OF STATEMENTS | 175 | 93 |
| % | % | % | % | % | % | | ASSETS | % | % |
| 41.6 | 20.1 | 14.7 | 12.4 | | | | Cash & Equivalents | 16.0 | 24.6 |
| 8.8 | 28.7 | 28.7 | 26.7 | | | | Trade Receivables (net) | 28.7 | 30.2 |
| 2.5 | .2 | 1.0 | 1.3 | | | | Inventory | .9 | .6 |
| 1.7 | 8.1 | 5.4 | 6.1 | | | | All Other Current | 4.1 | 3.5 |
| 54.7 | 57.1 | 49.8 | 46.5 | | | | Total Current | 49.6 | 58.9 |
| 13.1 | 23.3 | 33.2 | 31.3 | | | | Fixed Assets (net) | 34.0 | 25.0 |
| 10.2 | 6.1 | 6.4 | 5.2 | | | | Intangibles (net) | 5.0 | 6.2 |
| 22.0 | 13.6 | 10.6 | 17.0 | | | | All Other Non-Current | 11.3 | 9.9 |
| 100.0 | 100.0 | 100.0 | 100.0 | | | | Total | 100.0 | 100.0 |
| | | | | | | | LIABILITIES | | |
| 26.8 | 9.8 | 4.8 | 1.9 | | | | Notes Payable-Short Term | 6.5 | 3.8 |
| 9.5 | 4.8 | 5.6 | 4.7 | | | | Cur. Mat.-L.T.D. | 8.8 | 7.7 |
| 12.1 | 12.8 | 7.3 | 7.6 | | | | Trade Payables | 9.8 | 7.1 |
| .0 | .0 | .1 | .0 | | | | Income Taxes Payable | .1 | .0 |
| 15.2 | 23.9 | 16.6 | 11.8 | | | | All Other Current | 13.4 | 20.3 |
| 63.7 | 51.3 | 34.4 | 26.1 | | | | Total Current | 38.6 | 38.8 |
| 33.6 | 19.6 | 21.3 | 17.6 | | | | Long-Term Debt | 27.4 | 27.6 |
| .1 | .0 | .2 | .1 | | | | Deferred Taxes | .2 | .2 |
| 2.3 | 2.4 | 7.0 | 11.6 | | | | All Other Non-Current | 2.6 | 4.7 |
| .4 | 26.8 | 37.1 | 44.6 | | | | Net Worth | 31.3 | 28.7 |
| 100.0 | 100.0 | 100.0 | 100.0 | | | | Total Liabilties & Net Worth | 100.0 | 100.0 |
| | | | | | | | INCOME DATA | | |
| 100.0 | 100.0 | 100.0 | 100.0 | | | | Net Sales | 100.0 | 100.0 |
| | | | | | | | Gross Profit | | |
| 96.6 | 95.8 | 94.9 | 95.5 | | | | Operating Expenses | 92.6 | 95.7 |
| 3.4 | 4.2 | 5.1 | 4.5 | | | | Operating Profit | 7.4 | 4.3 |
| .3 | .7 | 1.9 | 1.2 | | | | All Other Expenses (net) | 1.6 | -1.9 |
| 3.1 | 3.6 | 3.2 | 3.3 | | | | Profit Before Taxes | 5.8 | 6.2 |
| | | | | | | | RATIOS | | |
| 2.1 | 4.2 | 3.6 | 3.3 | | | | | 2.5 | 2.9 |
| 1.1 | 1.4 | 1.5 | 1.6 | | | | Current | 1.5 | 1.8 |
| .6 | .6 | 1.0 | 1.0 | | | | | .8 | 1.2 |
| 2.1 | 3.4 | 3.0 | 3.0 | | | | | 2.2 | 2.6 |
| 1.0 | 1.1 | 1.4 | 1.5 | | | | Quick | 1.3 (92) | 1.6 |
| .6 | .5 | .8 | .9 | | | | | .7 | 1.0 |
| 0 UND | 1 296.8 | 18 20.3 | 30 12.2 | | | | | 10 38.1 | 23 15.8 |
| 0 UND | 19 19.1 | 39 9.3 | 45 8.2 | | | | Sales/Receivables | 36 10.0 | 36 10.0 |
| 8 43.3 | 42 8.6 | 56 6.5 | 66 5.5 | | | | | 59 6.2 | 54 6.8 |
| | | | | | | | Cost of Sales/Inventory | | |
| | | | | | | | Cost of Sales/Payables | | |
| 25.2 | 11.0 | 5.8 | 4.9 | | | | | 8.7 | 6.9 |
| 123.8 | 45.5 | 14.7 | 14.6 | | | | Sales/Working Capital | 19.8 | 12.3 |
| -58.4 | -16.0 | -438.6 | NM | | | | | -31.8 | 43.4 |
| | 24.0 | 15.1 | 16.2 | | | | | 11.8 | 21.1 |
| (27) | 4.3 (64) | 2.4 (28) | 2.0 | | | | EBIT/Interest | (141) 5.0 | (77) 10.0 |
| | -3.8 | -1.6 | -.7 | | | | | 1.5 | 2.9 |
| | | 3.4 | 7.1 | | | | | 4.5 | 12.6 |
| | (20) 1.1 | (16) 1.7 | | | | | Net Profit + Depr., Dep., Amort./Cur. Mat. L/T/D | (36) 2.1 | (22) 5.2 |
| | | .4 | .0 | | | | | 1.0 | 2.7 |
| .0 | .3 | .3 | .4 | | | | | .3 | .2 |
| .2 | .7 | .9 | .7 | | | | Fixed/Worth | .7 | .5 |
| 3.4 | -1.5 | 1.9 | 1.7 | | | | | 3.1 | 2.1 |
| .9 | .2 | .7 | .7 | | | | | .7 | .8 |
| 3.9 | 1.3 | 1.8 | 1.8 | | | | Debt/Worth | 1.5 | 1.5 |
| -25.7 | -7.0 | 4.0 | 4.1 | | | | | 5.5 | NM |
| 381.4 | 55.9 | 27.5 | 23.6 | | | | | 41.9 | 51.0 |
| (14) 37.0 | (23) 19.8 | (61) 7.5 | (36) 8.5 | | | | % Profit Before Taxes/Tangible Net Worth | (141) 18.2 | (70) 23.2 |
| -1.7 | 2.3 | -5.7 | -8.3 | | | | | 4.9 | 8.9 |
| 81.1 | 33.8 | 12.3 | 9.0 | | | | | 20.3 | 23.9 |
| 12.1 | 12.3 | 2.5 | 2.3 | | | | % Profit Before Taxes/Total Assets | 6.5 | 9.5 |
| -1.8 | -5.7 | -3.5 | -1.7 | | | | | 1.1 | 2.7 |
| UND | 49.5 | 19.9 | 15.8 | | | | | 28.8 | 38.3 |
| 254.2 | 19.4 | 9.9 | 6.8 | | | | Sales/Net Fixed Assets | 12.8 | 19.1 |
| 24.7 | 12.8 | 4.4 | 4.6 | | | | | 4.6 | 5.8 |
| 14.6 | 6.0 | 3.3 | 2.6 | | | | | 4.3 | 4.2 |
| 9.7 | 4.4 | 2.6 | 1.6 | | | | Sales/Total Assets | 2.8 | 3.0 |
| 5.0 | 2.9 | 1.8 | 1.0 | | | | | 1.8 | 1.8 |
| | 1.3 | 1.4 | 1.3 | | | | | 1.4 | 1.0 |
| | (15) 1.6 | (59) 2.1 | (33) 2.3 | | | | % Depr., Dep., Amort./Sales | (137) 2.4 | (73) 2.0 |
| | 2.6 | 4.1 | 4.6 | | | | | 4.5 | 4.0 |
| | 2.5 | 2.5 | | | | | | 1.8 | 2.0 |
| | (12) 3.1 | (13) 2.9 | | | | | % Officers', Directors' Owners' Comp/Sales | (49) 5.4 | (23) 4.7 |
| | 3.5 | 6.1 | | | | | | 9.8 | 9.5 |
| 49069M | 170251M | 887839M | 1401971M | 971633M | 3708599M | | Net Sales ($) | 4896758M | 1535323M |
| 4451M | 36107M | 354386M | 734398M | 631798M | 882597M | | Total Assets ($) | 2132665M | 796625M |

© RMA 2024    M = $ thousand    MM = $ million
See Pages viii through xx for Explanation of Ratios and Data

# TRANSPORTATION—Used Household and Office Goods Moving  NAICS 484210

| Comparative Historical Data | | | | Current Data Sorted by Sales | | | | | | |
|---|---|---|---|---|---|---|---|---|---|---|
| | | | Type of Statement | | | | | | | |
| 4 | 4 | 7 | Unqualified | | | | | 1 | 6 | |
| 11 | 14 | 27 | Reviewed | | 1 | 1 | 5 | 15 | 5 | |
| 29 | 34 | 38 | Compiled | 3 | 3 | 7 | 12 | 8 | 5 | |
| 20 | 22 | 13 | Tax Returns | 2 | 6 | | 3 | 2 | | |
| 52 | 67 | 89 | Other | 8 | 8 | 9 | 12 | 30 | 22 | |
| 4/1/21-3/31/22 | 4/1/22-3/31/23 | 4/1/23-3/31/24 | | 16 (4/1-9/30/23) | | | 158 (10/1/23-3/31/24) | | | |
| ALL | ALL | ALL | | 0-1MM | 1-3MM | 3-5MM | 5-10MM | 10-25MM | 25MM & OVER | |
| 116 | 141 | 174 | NUMBER OF STATEMENTS | 13 | 18 | 17 | 32 | 56 | 38 | |
| % | % | % | ASSETS | % | % | % | % | % | % | |
| 23.9 | 20.7 | 17.6 | Cash & Equivalents | 17.9 | 33.4 | 16.2 | 20.4 | 16.8 | 9.4 | |
| 28.4 | 26.9 | 25.9 | Trade Receivables (net) | 11.4 | 6.4 | 32.1 | 24.3 | 31.7 | 30.3 | |
| .4 | .4 | 1.0 | Inventory | .0 | .0 | .2 | .5 | 2.0 | 1.2 | |
| 4.1 | 5.9 | 6.2 | All Other Current | 3.7 | 4.4 | 6.0 | 6.0 | 7.5 | 6.3 | |
| 56.8 | 53.8 | 50.8 | Total Current | 33.0 | 44.2 | 54.6 | 51.2 | 58.0 | 47.2 | |
| 26.0 | 28.4 | 29.1 | Fixed Assets (net) | 44.2 | 21.9 | 17.5 | 35.6 | 25.2 | 32.8 | |
| 6.4 | 5.4 | 6.1 | Intangibles (net) | 11.6 | 15.5 | 3.3 | 5.0 | 3.4 | 6.0 | |
| 10.8 | 12.4 | 14.0 | All Other Non-Current | 11.0 | 18.4 | 24.6 | 8.2 | 13.3 | 14.1 | |
| 100.0 | 100.0 | 100.0 | Total | 100.0 | 100.0 | 100.0 | 100.0 | 100.0 | 100.0 | |
| | | | LIABILITIES | | | | | | | |
| 1.9 | 5.6 | 7.3 | Notes Payable-Short Term | 12.8 | 15.3 | 13.5 | 10.4 | 3.5 | 2.0 | |
| 7.1 | 8.1 | 5.5 | Cur. Mat.-L.T.D. | 3.6 | 7.9 | 8.6 | 4.9 | 4.9 | 4.8 | |
| 8.0 | 8.1 | 9.2 | Trade Payables | .3 | 12.8 | 11.3 | 6.3 | 9.6 | 11.3 | |
| .1 | .1 | .1 | Income Taxes Payable | .0 | .1 | .0 | .0 | .1 | .0 | |
| 18.0 | 14.4 | 16.5 | All Other Current | 22.1 | 9.1 | 32.3 | 15.9 | 16.0 | 12.3 | |
| 35.1 | 36.2 | 38.5 | Total Current | 38.9 | 45.2 | 65.6 | 37.6 | 34.2 | 30.4 | |
| 21.3 | 24.6 | 21.2 | Long-Term Debt | 27.9 | 44.9 | 23.6 | 18.5 | 14.9 | 18.2 | |
| .2 | .2 | .1 | Deferred Taxes | .1 | .0 | .0 | .3 | .1 | .2 | |
| 4.7 | 3.1 | 7.0 | All Other Non-Current | 3.6 | 4.0 | .9 | 6.1 | 9.8 | 9.0 | |
| 38.7 | 35.9 | 33.1 | Net Worth | 29.6 | 5.9 | 9.9 | 37.5 | 41.0 | 42.2 | |
| 100.0 | 100.0 | 100.0 | Total Liabilities & Net Worth | 100.0 | 100.0 | 100.0 | 100.0 | 100.0 | 100.0 | |
| | | | INCOME DATA | | | | | | | |
| 100.0 | 100.0 | 100.0 | Net Sales | 100.0 | 100.0 | 100.0 | 100.0 | 100.0 | 100.0 | |
| | | | Gross Profit | | | | | | | |
| 92.0 | 92.3 | 95.4 | Operating Expenses | 72.9 | 92.4 | 102.0 | 97.2 | 96.7 | 98.1 | |
| 8.0 | 7.7 | 4.6 | Operating Profit | 27.1 | 7.6 | -2.0 | 2.8 | 3.3 | 1.9 | |
| -.9 | .8 | 1.3 | All Other Expenses (net) | 8.8 | 2.6 | -.4 | .3 | 1.1 | -.1 | |
| 8.9 | 6.9 | 3.3 | Profit Before Taxes | 18.3 | 4.9 | -1.6 | 2.5 | 2.2 | 1.9 | |
| | | | RATIOS | | | | | | | |
| 4.3 | 3.2 | 3.1 | | 3.7 | 2.1 | 4.1 | 4.1 | 3.9 | 2.1 | |
| 2.1 | 1.6 | 1.5 | Current | 1.2 | 1.3 | .6 | 1.5 | 1.7 | 1.5 | |
| 1.2 | 1.1 | .9 | | .2 | .7 | .4 | 1.0 | 1.1 | 1.2 | |
| 3.9 | 3.1 | 2.7 | | 3.1 | 2.1 | 3.7 | 2.8 | 3.1 | 1.9 | |
| 1.9 | 1.5 | 1.3 | Quick | 1.0 | 1.2 | .6 | 1.2 | 1.5 | 1.4 | |
| 1.1 | .8 | .8 | | .2 | .7 | .3 | .9 | .9 | .9 | |
| 4  88.7 | 3  142.1 | 9  39.5 | | 0  UND | 0  UND | 3  125.8 | 17  21.6 | 23  16.2 | 32  11.4 | |
| 39  9.4 | 36  10.1 | 33  10.9 | Sales/Receivables | 0  UND | 0  UND | 34  10.8 | 32  11.5 | 47  7.8 | 43  8.5 | |
| 59  6.2 | 55  6.6 | 54  6.7 | | 22  16.3 | 9  41.8 | 49  7.5 | 54  6.7 | 70  5.2 | 61  6.0 | |
| | | | Cost of Sales/Inventory | | | | | | | |
| | | | Cost of Sales/Payables | | | | | | | |
| 6.3 | 6.9 | 7.3 | | 4.4 | 20.5 | 10.2 | 8.0 | 5.8 | 8.9 | |
| 11.3 | 16.9 | 21.7 | Sales/Working Capital | 32.3 | 107.3 | -24.1 | 20.5 | 12.5 | 18.0 | |
| 31.3 | 79.8 | -116.1 | | -1.0 | -73.4 | -7.4 | NM | 111.3 | 47.9 | |
| | 38.4 | 29.3 | 15.9 | | 153.5 | 21.9 | 12.7 | 17.6 | 16.0 | |
| (91) 12.4 | (105) 9.6 | (141) 2.7 | EBIT/Interest | (11) .2 | (16) 2.4 | (29) 1.5 | (46) 3.2 | (31) 2.7 | | |
| 4.1 | 2.4 | -.8 | | | -2.9 | -7.0 | -2.3 | .3 | -.8 | |
| 12.2 | 2.9 | 3.7 | | | | | 5.8 | 3.3 | | |
| (24) 4.1 | (25) 1.8 | (40) 1.3 | Net Profit + Depr., Dep., Amort./Cur. Mat. L/T/D | | | | (18) 1.7 | (12) 1.6 | | |
| .7 | .8 | .4 | | | | | .5 | .3 | | |
| .2 | .2 | .3 | | .3 | .0 | .2 | .5 | .2 | .5 | |
| .5 | .7 | .7 | Fixed/Worth | 1.6 | .4 | .9 | .9 | .6 | .7 | |
| 1.5 | 2.5 | 2.2 | | NM | NM | -.3 | 1.6 | 1.0 | 1.9 | |
| .5 | .5 | .8 | | .9 | .9 | .4 | .7 | .6 | 1.1 | |
| 1.2 | 1.6 | 1.8 | Debt/Worth | 3.9 | 3.1 | 1.9 | 1.7 | 1.4 | 1.7 | |
| 3.4 | 5.8 | 4.9 | | NM | -20.0 | -2.9 | 4.2 | 3.7 | 2.6 | |
| 82.9 | 61.2 | 32.5 | % Profit Before Taxes/Tangible Net Worth | 24.8 | 281.0 | | 35.1 | 27.0 | 23.9 | |
| (99) 37.2 | (117) 24.6 | (148) 13.2 | | (10) 18.4 | (13) 7.7 | | (29) 3.8 | (51) 11.9 | (36) 13.3 | |
| 7.6 | 9.7 | -3.3 | | 5.0 | -7.6 | | -8.4 | -6.1 | 1.8 | |
| 40.3 | 25.3 | 15.1 | % Profit Before Taxes/Total Assets | 16.0 | 73.4 | 20.5 | 13.8 | 15.4 | 10.2 | |
| 13.1 | 9.7 | 4.5 | | 5.1 | 1.5 | 12.1 | 1.2 | 4.9 | 4.5 | |
| 2.6 | 1.8 | -1.9 | | -1.3 | -2.5 | -9.7 | -3.2 | -1.7 | -.7 | |
| 33.5 | 33.4 | 23.2 | | 19.6 | UND | 53.9 | 20.2 | 24.9 | 18.0 | |
| 16.7 | 14.6 | 11.4 | Sales/Net Fixed Assets | 1.6 | 91.9 | 21.1 | 11.3 | 10.7 | 6.6 | |
| 9.5 | 6.0 | 5.0 | | .3 | 10.1 | 12.0 | 3.4 | 6.2 | 4.1 | |
| 4.4 | 4.5 | 4.4 | | 1.3 | 12.7 | 6.3 | 4.4 | 3.5 | 3.6 | |
| 3.0 | 2.9 | 2.7 | Sales/Total Assets | .4 | 5.2 | 4.1 | 3.1 | 2.6 | 2.2 | |
| 2.0 | 1.7 | 1.5 | | .2 | 2.6 | 2.9 | 1.5 | 1.8 | 1.4 | |
| 1.1 | 1.2 | 1.4 | | | | | 1.4 | 1.4 | 1.1 | |
| (85) 2.0 | (97) 2.3 | (124) 2.1 | % Depr., Dep., Amort./Sales | | | | (24) 1.7 | (45) 2.1 | (31) 1.7 | |
| 3.5 | 4.0 | 4.2 | | | | | 3.0 | 3.8 | 4.2 | |
| 1.7 | 2.0 | 2.3 | % Officers', Directors' Owners' Comp/Sales | | | | 2.4 | 1.5 | | |
| (33) 4.5 | (40) 3.5 | (37) 3.1 | | | | | (11) 2.7 | (10) 2.8 | | |
| 8.2 | 7.8 | 4.5 | | | | | 3.1 | 8.8 | | |
| 4402067M | 3609687M | 7189362M | Net Sales ($) | 6865M | 33759M | 69237M | 250031M | 879267M | 5950203M | |
| 1212221M | 1660561M | 2643737M | Total Assets ($) | 18478M | 29352M | 22843M | 119829M | 435539M | 2017696M | |

© RMA 2024   M = $ thousand   MM = $ million
See Pages viii through xx for Explanation of Ratios and Data

# TRANSPORTATION—Specialized Freight (except Used Goods) Trucking, Local  NAICS 484220

## Current Data Sorted by Assets | Comparative Historical Data

| | | | | | | | Type of Statement | | | |
|---|---|---|---|---|---|---|---|---|---|---|
| | | | | 5 | 7 | 4 | Unqualified | | 13 | 13 |
| | | | 8 | 17 | 4 | 1 | Reviewed | | 32 | 21 |
| | | 1 | 10 | 4 | | | Compiled | | 27 | 17 |
| 5 | 22 | 22 | 9 | 1 | | | Tax Returns | | 60 | 29 |
| 9 | 25 | 25 | 55 | 43 | 13 | 5 | Other | | 132 | 88 |
| | 45 (4/1-9/30/23) | | | 203 (10/1/23-3/31/24) | | | | | 4/1/19-3/31/20 | 4/1/20-3/31/21 |
| 0-500M | 500M-2MM | 2-10MM | 10-50MM | 50-100MM | 100-250MM | | NUMBER OF STATEMENTS | | ALL | ALL |
| 14 | 48 | 82 | 70 | 24 | 10 | | | | 264 | 168 |
| % | % | % | % | % | % | | ASSETS | | % | % |
| 36.9 | 20.9 | 16.6 | 14.2 | 9.0 | 3.4 | | Cash & Equivalents | | 14.2 | 21.4 |
| 21.8 | 20.5 | 22.8 | 18.1 | 25.1 | 12.0 | | Trade Receivables (net) | | 18.5 | 16.6 |
| 1.3 | 1.3 | 1.6 | 1.6 | .7 | 5.6 | | Inventory | | 1.6 | 1.4 |
| 1.8 | 3.3 | 3.5 | 4.0 | 4.5 | .7 | | All Other Current | | 3.2 | 3.7 |
| 61.8 | 46.0 | 44.6 | 37.9 | 39.3 | 21.7 | | Total Current | | 37.5 | 43.0 |
| 20.8 | 42.3 | 39.8 | 50.1 | 51.5 | 56.3 | | Fixed Assets (net) | | 50.8 | 41.6 |
| 10.8 | 3.9 | 3.0 | 3.8 | .9 | 10.7 | | Intangibles (net) | | 3.5 | 5.9 |
| 6.6 | 7.8 | 12.7 | 8.2 | 8.3 | 11.2 | | All Other Non-Current | | 8.1 | 9.5 |
| 100.0 | 100.0 | 100.0 | 100.0 | 100.0 | 100.0 | | Total | | 100.0 | 100.0 |
| | | | | | | | LIABILITIES | | | |
| 4.5 | 3.6 | 3.8 | 1.6 | 8.6 | 2.2 | | Notes Payable-Short Term | | 7.3 | 9.3 |
| 8.1 | 7.1 | 7.5 | 9.2 | 10.7 | 10.3 | | Cur. Mat.-L.T.D. | | 8.8 | 10.1 |
| 12.0 | 7.7 | 8.8 | 7.3 | 7.8 | 5.8 | | Trade Payables | | 7.6 | 5.8 |
| .0 | .1 | .0 | .0 | .0 | .0 | | Income Taxes Payable | | .1 | .2 |
| 12.8 | 9.1 | 7.4 | 9.1 | 14.5 | 4.6 | | All Other Current | | 8.7 | 10.6 |
| 37.4 | 27.5 | 27.4 | 27.1 | 41.6 | 22.9 | | Total Current | | 32.4 | 36.0 |
| 64.5 | 47.0 | 35.0 | 26.5 | 31.5 | 37.4 | | Long-Term Debt | | 39.4 | 36.1 |
| .0 | .1 | .3 | .3 | .8 | .4 | | Deferred Taxes | | .4 | .3 |
| .3 | 2.9 | 2.9 | 4.5 | 9.1 | 7.5 | | All Other Non-Current | | 5.4 | 5.1 |
| -2.2 | 22.5 | 34.4 | 41.5 | 16.9 | 31.8 | | Net Worth | | 22.4 | 22.5 |
| 100.0 | 100.0 | 100.0 | 100.0 | 100.0 | 100.0 | | Total Liabilities & Net Worth | | 100.0 | 100.0 |
| | | | | | | | INCOME DATA | | | |
| 100.0 | 100.0 | 100.0 | 100.0 | 100.0 | 100.0 | | Net Sales | | 100.0 | 100.0 |
| | | | | | | | Gross Profit | | | |
| 100.9 | 88.5 | 91.0 | 94.3 | 92.3 | 95.6 | | Operating Expenses | | 93.8 | 95.3 |
| -.9 | 11.5 | 9.0 | 5.7 | 7.7 | 4.4 | | Operating Profit | | 6.2 | 4.7 |
| .2 | 2.0 | .8 | -.7 | 2.0 | 2.0 | | All Other Expenses (net) | | 1.0 | -1.4 |
| -1.1 | 9.4 | 8.1 | 6.4 | 5.6 | 2.4 | | Profit Before Taxes | | 5.2 | 6.0 |
| | | | | | | | RATIOS | | | |
| 7.2 | 4.2 | 5.7 | 2.2 | 1.7 | 2.2 | | | | 2.5 | 3.1 |
| 2.2 | 1.8 | 1.8 | 1.4 | 1.0 | .9 | | Current | | 1.3 | 1.6 |
| .7 | .8 | .8 | 1.1 | .7 | .6 | | | | .7 | .7 |
| 6.0 | 4.1 | 4.1 | 1.9 | 1.4 | 1.5 | | | | 2.2 | 2.7 |
| 2.2 | 1.6 | 1.7 | 1.2 | .9 | .7 | | Quick | | 1.2 | 1.3 |
| .6 | .8 | .7 | .8 | .6 | .3 | | | | .5 | .5 |
| 0  UND | 0  UND | 12  31.5 | 22  16.4 | 21  17.6 | 21  17.1 | | | 7 | 49.2 | 2  242.3 |
| 8  46.8 | 12  29.4 | 29  12.5 | 31  11.7 | 43  8.4 | 33  11.0 | | Sales/Receivables | 25 | 14.4 | 24  14.9 |
| 21  17.3 | 38  9.7 | 45  8.1 | 41  8.8 | 59  6.2 | 47  7.8 | | | 40 | 9.1 | 45  8.1 |
| | | | | | | | Cost of Sales/Inventory | | | |
| | | | | | | | Cost of Sales/Payables | | | |
| 11.0 | 6.5 | 7.0 | 8.8 | 12.5 | 10.2 | | | | 11.1 | 6.6 |
| 34.9 | 28.1 | 18.2 | 18.0 | -138.3 | -47.0 | | Sales/Working Capital | | 33.5 | 16.8 |
| -67.6 | -37.6 | -49.0 | 52.6 | -11.3 | -12.6 | | | | -20.7 | -26.8 |
| | 9.7 | 24.5 | 14.5 | 13.0 | 4.0 | | | | 10.7 | 14.6 |
| (36) | 2.9 | (72)  7.7 | (67)  7.0 | 3.4 | 1.9 | | EBIT/Interest | (234) | 4.0 | (142)  6.3 |
| | .4 | 2.2 | 2.1 | 1.5 | .7 | | | | .9 | 1.0 |
| | | | 3.9 | 7.5 | | | Net Profit + Depr., Dep., | | 3.9 | 3.1 |
| | | (20)  2.7 | (12)  2.5 | | | | Amort./Cur. Mat. L/T/D | (44) | 1.8 | (25)  1.4 |
| | | | 1.7 | 1.0 | | | | | .9 | .6 |
| .0 | .2 | .5 | .8 | 1.0 | 1.5 | | | | .8 | .6 |
| .5 | .8 | 1.2 | 1.1 | 2.7 | 3.1 | | Fixed/Worth | | 1.6 | 1.5 |
| -2.9 | 6.3 | 4.3 | 2.0 | 7.0 | 8.1 | | | | 11.1 | 14.2 |
| .8 | .4 | .6 | .6 | 1.4 | 1.6 | | | | .8 | .9 |
| UND | 1.4 | 1.4 | 1.4 | 2.9 | 4.4 | | Debt/Worth | | 2.6 | 2.3 |
| -2.3 | 27.0 | 11.8 | 2.7 | 10.4 | 10.7 | | | | 19.5 | -51.7 |
| | 57.2 | 67.1 | 38.2 | 46.9 | | | % Profit Before Taxes/Tangible | | 51.4 | 63.9 |
| | (37)  22.5 | (68)  35.0 | (65)  19.0 | (20)  26.0 | | | Net Worth | (207) | 21.7 | (125)  25.1 |
| | | 1.3 | 15.8 | 6.8 | 8.7 | | | | 8.8 | 4.8 |
| 60.4 | 30.0 | 22.5 | 17.7 | 13.1 | 6.2 | | % Profit Before Taxes/Total | | 16.9 | 24.3 |
| 4.4 | 4.2 | 14.1 | 9.4 | 6.7 | 1.9 | | Assets | | 6.9 | 10.6 |
| -36.7 | -1.0 | 2.5 | 3.0 | 1.7 | -.9 | | | | .0 | -.1 |
| UND | 121.8 | 19.7 | 6.1 | 12.5 | 4.7 | | | | 12.4 | 23.6 |
| 93.9 | 6.2 | 6.7 | 3.7 | 2.3 | 2.3 | | Sales/Net Fixed Assets | | 4.3 | 5.5 |
| 9.1 | 2.9 | 3.0 | 2.3 | 1.6 | 1.6 | | | | 2.3 | 2.3 |
| 12.2 | 5.4 | 4.2 | 2.4 | 2.7 | 1.9 | | | | 4.0 | 4.3 |
| 6.8 | 2.8 | 2.3 | 1.8 | 1.3 | 1.4 | | Sales/Total Assets | | 2.1 | 2.1 |
| 3.7 | 1.0 | 1.4 | 1.4 | 1.1 | .9 | | | | 1.4 | 1.3 |
| | 3.2 | 2.2 | 3.8 | 3.0 | | | | | 3.6 | 3.6 |
| | (21)  12.1 | (43)  7.2 | (60)  7.4 | (19)  6.1 | | | % Depr., Dep., Amort./Sales | (190) | 6.6 | (105)  7.1 |
| | 21.1 | 9.9 | 9.7 | 7.4 | | | | | 10.8 | 12.9 |
| | 1.3 | .7 | .6 | | | | | | 1.3 | 1.4 |
| | (14)  2.4 | (24)  1.1 | (15)  .8 | | | | % Officers', Directors' Owners' Comp/Sales | (81) | 2.7 | (54)  3.1 |
| | 4.5 | 1.8 | 2.8 | | | | | | 5.6 | 4.7 |
| 31188M | 220647M | 1032587M | 3711113M | 3260575M | 1963884M | | Net Sales ($) | | 7436726M | 3666397M |
| 3806M | 58604M | 385894M | 1813102M | 1657130M | 1385753M | | Total Assets ($) | | 3801418M | 2035043M |

M = $ thousand    MM = $ million
See Pages viii through xx for Explanation of Ratios and Data

© RMA 2024

# TRANSPORTATION—Specialized Freight (except Used Goods) Trucking, Local   NAICS 484220

## Comparative Historical Data | Current Data Sorted by Sales

| Comparative Historical Data ||| Type of Statement | Current Data Sorted by Sales ||||||
|---|---|---|---|---|---|---|---|---|---|
| 13 | 13 | 16 | Unqualified | | | | | 1 | 15 |
| 16 | 30 | 30 | Reviewed | | 1 | 1 | 1 | 7 | 20 |
| 17 | 18 | 15 | Compiled | | 1 | 1 | 3 | 5 | 5 |
| 30 | 45 | 37 | Tax Returns | 1 | 1 | 5 | 5 | 8 | 4 |
| 102 | 146 | 150 | Other | 3 | 12 | 9 | 5 | 8 | 55 |
| 4/1/21-3/31/22 | 4/1/22-3/31/23 | 4/1/23-3/31/24 | | 11 | 13 | 9 | 32 | 30 | 55 |
| ALL | ALL | ALL | | 45 (4/1-9/30/23) ||| 203 (10/1/23-3/31/24) |||
| | | | | 0-1MM | 1-3MM | 3-5MM | 5-10MM | 10-25MM | 25MM & OVER |
| 178 | 252 | 248 | **NUMBER OF STATEMENTS** | 15 | 27 | 15 | 41 | 51 | 99 |
| % | % | % | **ASSETS** | % | % | % | % | % | % |
| 20.4 | 16.8 | 16.6 | Cash & Equivalents | 10.9 | 21.7 | 25.3 | 20.1 | 15.7 | 13.8 |
| 18.2 | 21.0 | 20.8 | Trade Receivables (net) | 7.1 | 19.4 | 25.3 | 18.9 | 20.8 | 23.2 |
| 1.5 | 1.2 | 1.6 | Inventory | 1.3 | .1 | .5 | 1.8 | 1.8 | 2.1 |
| 3.5 | 4.1 | 3.5 | All Other Current | .9 | 5.8 | 2.4 | 3.7 | 2.3 | 3.9 |
| 43.7 | 43.1 | 42.5 | Total Current | 20.2 | 47.0 | 53.5 | 44.5 | 40.6 | 43.1 |
| 45.3 | 44.7 | 43.9 | Fixed Assets (net) | 68.1 | 38.4 | 28.9 | 40.6 | 44.7 | 45.0 |
| 2.4 | 2.7 | 4.0 | Intangibles (net) | 9.2 | 3.8 | 8.0 | 3.0 | 2.5 | 3.7 |
| 8.7 | 9.5 | 9.6 | All Other Non-Current | 2.6 | 10.7 | 9.6 | 11.9 | 12.2 | 8.2 |
| 100.0 | 100.0 | 100.0 | Total | 100.0 | 100.0 | 100.0 | 100.0 | 100.0 | 100.0 |
| | | | **LIABILITIES** | | | | | | |
| 4.2 | 4.2 | 3.6 | Notes Payable-Short Term | 6.8 | 2.4 | 6.5 | 1.4 | 3.4 | 4.0 |
| 8.1 | 7.1 | 8.3 | Cur. Mat.-L.T.D. | 3.3 | 7.4 | 5.7 | 6.8 | 9.7 | 9.7 |
| 6.7 | 8.3 | 8.1 | Trade Payables | 5.4 | 6.0 | 9.0 | 6.6 | 11.1 | 8.1 |
| .1 | .1 | .0 | Income Taxes Payable | .0 | .0 | .0 | .0 | .1 | .0 |
| 8.4 | 10.0 | 9.1 | All Other Current | 6.3 | 15.7 | 7.0 | 8.4 | 5.3 | 10.2 |
| 27.6 | 29.7 | 29.1 | Total Current | 21.8 | 31.4 | 28.2 | 23.1 | 29.6 | 32.0 |
| 36.4 | 32.4 | 36.3 | Long-Term Debt | 56.7 | 45.2 | 36.7 | 38.9 | 35.5 | 30.2 |
| .4 | .4 | .3 | Deferred Taxes | .0 | .1 | .3 | .2 | .4 | .4 |
| 4.3 | 3.7 | 4.0 | All Other Non-Current | 1.1 | 2.5 | 2.9 | 2.1 | 5.2 | 5.2 |
| 31.4 | 33.9 | 30.2 | Net Worth | 20.4 | 20.7 | 31.9 | 35.6 | 29.4 | 32.3 |
| 100.0 | 100.0 | 100.0 | Total Liabilties & Net Worth | 100.0 | 100.0 | 100.0 | 100.0 | 100.0 | 100.0 |
| | | | **INCOME DATA** | | | | | | |
| 100.0 | 100.0 | 100.0 | Net Sales | 100.0 | 100.0 | 100.0 | 100.0 | 100.0 | 100.0 |
| 95.6 | 92.2 | 92.3 | Gross Profit | | | | | | |
| | | | Operating Expenses | 66.1 | 94.6 | 91.3 | 93.0 | 94.6 | 94.4 |
| 4.4 | 7.8 | 7.7 | Operating Profit | 33.9 | 5.4 | 8.7 | 7.0 | 5.4 | 5.6 |
| -1.1 | -.1 | .8 | All Other Expenses (net) | 11.7 | .4 | -.5 | -.1 | -.4 | .4 |
| 5.5 | 7.9 | 6.9 | Profit Before Taxes | 22.2 | 5.0 | 9.1 | 7.1 | 5.8 | 5.2 |
| | | | **RATIOS** | | | | | | |
| 3.3 | 3.2 | 2.8 | | 2.3 | 7.3 | 9.1 | 8.2 | 2.1 | 2.2 |
| 1.7 | 1.8 | 1.5 | Current | 1.0 | 1.7 | 3.1 | 3.0 | 1.4 | 1.4 |
| .9 | .9 | .8 | | .6 | .7 | .9 | .8 | .9 | .9 |
| 3.0 | 2.9 | 2.5 | | 2.3 | 5.7 | 7.2 | 8.2 | 1.9 | 1.9 |
| (177) 1.5 | 1.5 | 1.3 | Quick | 1.0 | 1.7 | 2.6 | 2.0 | 1.1 | 1.2 |
| .7 | .7 | .7 | | .2 | .7 | .9 | .6 | .8 | .8 |
| 0  732.3 | 12  31.1 | 13  28.2 | | 0  UND | 2  239.4 | 6  65.9 | 4  83.3 | 13  28.0 | 21  17.4 |
| 24  14.9 | 29  12.5 | 29  12.5 | Sales/Receivables | 0  UND | 21  17.5 | 37  9.9 | 29  12.8 | 27  13.4 | 33  11.0 |
| 41  8.9 | 47  7.8 | 43  8.5 | | 31  11.8 | 45  8.1 | 51  7.2 | 41  8.9 | 38  9.6 | 44  8.3 |
| | | | Cost of Sales/Inventory | | | | | | |
| | | | Cost of Sales/Payables | | | | | | |
| 7.3 | 7.2 | 8.6 | | 9.3 | 5.8 | 5.8 | 6.8 | 11.6 | 9.0 |
| 18.8 | 16.1 | 21.4 | Sales/Working Capital | 468.0 | 13.9 | 26.4 | 13.4 | 25.8 | 21.1 |
| -60.1 | -84.6 | -43.7 | | -3.3 | -35.0 | -40.8 | -29.4 | -78.1 | -54.2 |
| 20.7 | 23.4 | 15.4 | | 25.9 | 6.1 | 27.5 | 21.4 | 17.5 | 14.5 |
| (151) 7.4 | (218) 10.1 | (217) 5.4 | EBIT/Interest | (10) 5.0 | (18) 2.3 | (12) 11.9 | (36) 6.2 | (46) 6.2 | (95) 4.6 |
| 1.2 | 2.2 | 1.7 | | .0 | -3.0 | 5.3 | .9 | 3.3 | 1.8 |
| 6.0 | 4.1 | 4.3 | Net Profit + Depr., Dep., | | | | | | 5.3 |
| (19) 2.9 | (40) 2.7 | (41) 2.5 | Amort./Cur. Mat. L/T/D | | | | | (31) | 2.8 |
| 1.9 | 1.8 | 1.4 | | | | | | | 1.7 |
| .5 | .6 | .6 | | 1.8 | .1 | .0 | .3 | .6 | .7 |
| 1.2 | 1.1 | 1.2 | Fixed/Worth | 6.6 | .9 | .7 | .8 | 1.2 | 1.3 |
| 3.5 | 2.4 | 4.3 | | UND | 2.8 | 1.5 | 8.0 | 2.6 | 4.1 |
| .6 | .6 | .6 | | 1.2 | .3 | .3 | .4 | .6 | .8 |
| 1.6 | 1.4 | 1.6 | Debt/Worth | 5.6 | 1.6 | 1.5 | .9 | 1.4 | 1.7 |
| 7.2 | 5.3 | 8.4 | | UND | -11.7 | 3.2 | 15.6 | 11.3 | 4.7 |
| 51.9 | 62.4 | 47.1 | | 74.4 | 46.9 | 71.6 | 55.3 | 58.1 | 39.6 |
| (152) 26.5 | (219) 33.5 | (207) 26.5 | % Profit Before Taxes/Tangible Net Worth | (12) 31.1 | (19) 22.5 | (13) 26.5 | (33) 29.0 | (43) 33.9 | (87) 19.3 |
| 4.8 | 12.8 | 6.9 | | 4.7 | -1.4 | 2.3 | 7.8 | 13.0 | 4.8 |
| 22.7 | 23.7 | 20.2 | | 14.7 | 30.7 | 28.9 | 22.5 | 20.2 | 18.4 |
| 9.8 | 12.7 | 9.0 | % Profit Before Taxes/Total Assets | 1.9 | 4.4 | 13.9 | 9.0 | 10.7 | 7.1 |
| .1 | 3.3 | 1.2 | | .0 | -7.2 | 4.3 | -.6 | 2.6 | 1.6 |
| 14.9 | 12.6 | 13.8 | | 3.7 | 38.4 | 617.4 | 17.7 | 18.3 | 10.1 |
| 5.7 | 4.8 | 4.6 | Sales/Net Fixed Assets | .4 | 5.9 | 23.9 | 7.2 | 3.9 | 4.0 |
| 2.4 | 2.6 | 2.5 | | .1 | 3.0 | 2.2 | 3.5 | 2.4 | 2.6 |
| 3.8 | 3.9 | 3.7 | | 1.0 | 3.9 | 8.6 | 4.3 | 4.6 | 2.9 |
| 2.2 | 2.1 | 2.0 | Sales/Total Assets | .3 | 2.1 | 3.0 | 2.0 | 2.5 | 1.8 |
| 1.4 | 1.4 | 1.3 | | .1 | 1.3 | 1.1 | 1.4 | 1.4 | 1.4 |
| 3.3 | 3.8 | 2.7 | | | 3.5 | | 1.8 | 2.7 | 2.6 |
| (102) 6.8 | (161) 6.8 | (150) 6.9 | % Depr., Dep., Amort./Sales | | (13) 8.6 | | (19) 7.5 | (35) 7.3 | (71) 6.1 |
| 11.6 | 9.8 | 10.1 | | | 16.2 | | 11.9 | 9.4 | 8.7 |
| 1.1 | .6 | .7 | | | | | | .7 | .6 |
| (50) 2.2 | (82) 1.6 | (59) 1.3 | % Officers', Directors' Owners' Comp/Sales | | | | (18) .9 | (18) 1.0 |
| 5.4 | 3.5 | 2.8 | | | | | | 1.5 | 3.0 |
| 5800463M | 8189122M | 10219994M | Net Sales ($) | 5573M | 52438M | 61178M | 305510M | 816837M | 8978458M |
| 2915704M | 4532257M | 5304289M | Total Assets ($) | 17206M | 30160M | 29323M | 147097M | 432001M | 4648502M |

© RMA 2024   M = $ thousand   MM = $ million
See Pages viii through xx for Explanation of Ratios and Data

# TRANSPORTATION—Specialized Freight (except Used Goods) Trucking, Long-Distance  NAICS 484230

## Current Data Sorted by Assets | Comparative Historical Data

| | | | | | | | Type of Statement | | |
|---|---|---|---|---|---|---|---|---|---|
| | | | 3 | 4 | 8 | 14 | Unqualified | 29 | 17 |
| | | | 6 | 12 | 1 | 3 | Reviewed | 31 | 10 |
| | | | 6 | 11 | | 1 | Compiled | 16 | 12 |
| 6 | 4 | | 5 | | | | Tax Returns | 32 | 15 |
| 5 | 8 | | 19 | 39 | 14 | 23 | Other | 157 | 89 |
| | 38 (4/1-9/30/23) | | | 154 (10/1/23-3/31/24) | | | | 4/1/19- | 4/1/20- |
| | | | | | | | | 3/31/20 | 3/31/21 |
| 0-500M | 500M-2MM | 2-10MM | 10-50MM | 50-100MM | 100-250MM | | | ALL | ALL |
| 11 | 12 | 39 | 66 | 23 | 41 | NUMBER OF STATEMENTS | 265 | 143 |
| % | % | % | % | % | % | ASSETS | % | % |
| 36.4 | 30.8 | 15.5 | 14.8 | 9.4 | 4.9 | Cash & Equivalents | 9.7 | 17.1 |
| 27.8 | 37.4 | 29.2 | 19.0 | 16.2 | 13.1 | Trade Receivables (net) | 23.0 | 21.5 |
| .0 | .0 | 1.1 | 1.3 | 1.5 | 4.1 | Inventory | 1.4 | 1.5 |
| 6.1 | 1.7 | 3.8 | 3.8 | 4.9 | 1.5 | All Other Current | 3.9 | 3.8 |
| 70.3 | 69.9 | 49.7 | 38.9 | 31.9 | 23.6 | Total Current | 38.0 | 43.9 |
| 23.1 | 26.8 | 37.3 | 47.5 | 50.9 | 63.7 | Fixed Assets (net) | 49.2 | 45.1 |
| 1.2 | .3 | 1.7 | 2.0 | 1.0 | 4.1 | Intangibles (net) | 4.8 | 4.2 |
| 5.4 | 3.0 | 11.4 | 11.6 | 16.1 | 8.6 | All Other Non-Current | 8.0 | 6.9 |
| 100.0 | 100.0 | 100.0 | 100.0 | 100.0 | 100.0 | Total | 100.0 | 100.0 |
| | | | | | | LIABILITIES | | |
| 20.4 | 11.8 | 4.9 | 2.2 | 1.9 | 4.8 | Notes Payable-Short Term | 7.6 | 5.7 |
| .7 | 2.0 | 4.1 | 10.6 | 6.9 | 10.5 | Cur. Mat.-L.T.D. | 10.6 | 8.3 |
| 7.0 | 7.9 | 15.6 | 5.4 | 6.4 | 4.3 | Trade Payables | 7.8 | 6.9 |
| .0 | .0 | .0 | .2 | .3 | .0 | Income Taxes Payable | .3 | .2 |
| 9.7 | 10.8 | 7.8 | 5.8 | 11.5 | 5.5 | All Other Current | 8.4 | 7.5 |
| 37.8 | 32.6 | 32.5 | 24.2 | 26.9 | 25.2 | Total Current | 34.7 | 28.6 |
| 48.2 | 26.3 | 25.8 | 28.4 | 29.6 | 38.2 | Long-Term Debt | 33.1 | 35.9 |
| .0 | .0 | .1 | .4 | 1.6 | 1.6 | Deferred Taxes | .8 | .8 |
| .7 | .3 | 4.6 | 3.1 | 7.4 | 3.6 | All Other Non-Current | 4.7 | 1.9 |
| 13.3 | 40.7 | 37.0 | 43.8 | 34.6 | 31.3 | Net Worth | 26.7 | 32.8 |
| 100.0 | 100.0 | 100.0 | 100.0 | 100.0 | 100.0 | Total Liabilities & Net Worth | 100.0 | 100.0 |
| | | | | | | INCOME DATA | | |
| 100.0 | 100.0 | 100.0 | 100.0 | 100.0 | 100.0 | Net Sales | 100.0 | 100.0 |
| | | | | | | Gross Profit | | |
| 87.9 | 90.8 | 94.7 | 92.8 | 91.8 | 95.0 | Operating Expenses | 93.8 | 94.2 |
| 12.1 | 9.2 | 5.3 | 7.2 | 8.2 | 5.0 | Operating Profit | 6.2 | 5.8 |
| -.3 | -1.0 | .3 | .8 | 1.3 | 1.2 | All Other Expenses (net) | 1.1 | .4 |
| 12.4 | 10.2 | 4.9 | 6.4 | 6.9 | 3.8 | Profit Before Taxes | 5.0 | 5.3 |
| | | | | | | RATIOS | | |
| 6.3 | 12.1 | 4.0 | 2.5 | 1.7 | 1.3 | | 2.1 | 2.9 |
| 2.0 | 3.4 | 1.5 | 1.4 | 1.2 | .9 | Current | 1.2 | 1.7 |
| 1.0 | 1.7 | 1.0 | 1.0 | .9 | .8 | | .7 | 1.0 |
| 4.9 | 11.8 | 3.9 | 2.2 | 1.4 | 1.1 | | 1.8 | 2.6 |
| 2.0 | 3.3 | 1.5 | 1.3 | 1.0 | .7 | Quick | 1.0 | 1.4 |
| .9 | 1.7 | .8 | .7 | .7 | .5 | | .6 | .8 |
| 0 UND | 1 292.6 | 19 19.4 | 25 14.8 | 21 17.7 | 29 12.5 | | 21 17.8 | 22 16.6 |
| 15 25.1 | 36 10.0 | 31 11.8 | 33 11.1 | 29 12.5 | 37 9.8 | Sales/Receivables | 33 10.9 | 36 10.2 |
| 29 12.4 | 78 4.7 | 41 8.8 | 42 8.6 | 38 9.5 | 47 7.8 | | 43 8.4 | 46 8.0 |
| | | | | | | Cost of Sales/Inventory | | |
| | | | | | | Cost of Sales/Payables | | |
| 10.8 | 4.3 | 10.2 | 6.7 | 12.5 | 28.0 | | 11.4 | 7.7 |
| 32.5 | 8.4 | 20.5 | 20.4 | 42.7 | -82.4 | Sales/Working Capital | 54.3 | 15.0 |
| 860.0 | 49.6 | -788.0 | NM | -36.6 | -25.6 | | -21.2 | 195.6 |
| | 40.9 | 16.4 | 10.5 | 12.2 | 6.5 | | 9.2 | 10.8 |
| (11) 7.0 | (32) 4.3 | (62) 6.0 | (22) 6.0 | 2.9 | EBIT/Interest | (249) 3.9 | (128) 4.7 |
| | 2.3 | .6 | 2.4 | 1.6 | .5 | | 1.1 | 1.7 |
| | | | 2.2 | | | | 4.3 | 3.8 |
| | | (17) 1.4 | | | Net Profit + Depr., Dep., | (55) 1.7 | (28) 2.0 |
| | | | 1.0 | | | Amort./Cur. Mat. L/T/D | 1.0 | 1.1 |
| .0 | .0 | .4 | .5 | .9 | 1.3 | | .8 | .8 |
| 1.0 | .4 | 1.3 | 1.1 | 1.4 | 2.1 | Fixed/Worth | 1.6 | 1.4 |
| -1.6 | 1.1 | 3.1 | 2.2 | 2.9 | 4.6 | | 3.8 | 4.3 |
| .5 | .3 | .6 | .6 | 1.1 | 1.4 | | 1.0 | .9 |
| 2.2 | .6 | 1.9 | 1.4 | 2.4 | 2.0 | Debt/Worth | 2.1 | 1.9 |
| -4.4 | 4.0 | 8.0 | 2.3 | 4.4 | 4.9 | | 5.8 | 6.9 |
| | 104.4 | 57.3 | 48.0 | 36.0 | 32.2 | % Profit Before Taxes/Tangible | 42.6 | 40.1 |
| (11) 64.0 | (35) 19.7 | (62) 16.0 | 17.3 | (37) 11.6 | Net Worth | (225) 19.0 | (120) 17.9 |
| | 4.1 | 10.3 | 8.9 | 4.8 | -1.7 | | 6.6 | 6.2 |
| 109.9 | 57.4 | 25.9 | 16.6 | 15.2 | 10.0 | % Profit Before Taxes/Total | 13.7 | 16.3 |
| 42.8 | 23.6 | 8.7 | 8.2 | 6.2 | 5.2 | Assets | 6.4 | 7.3 |
| 5.0 | 2.7 | 1.2 | 3.7 | 1.3 | -1.7 | | .7 | 1.8 |
| UND | UND | 40.0 | 7.7 | 13.4 | 2.7 | | 13.6 | 14.0 |
| 235.9 | 48.8 | 7.7 | 3.3 | 3.1 | 1.9 | Sales/Net Fixed Assets | 3.7 | 3.6 |
| 4.8 | 3.5 | 3.7 | 2.4 | 1.8 | 1.4 | | 2.0 | 1.9 |
| 27.0 | 6.6 | 4.8 | 2.8 | 2.6 | 1.5 | | 3.2 | 3.2 |
| 7.8 | 4.5 | 3.2 | 1.9 | 1.5 | 1.2 | Sales/Total Assets | 2.0 | 1.8 |
| 2.2 | 1.7 | 2.0 | 1.3 | 1.1 | .9 | | 1.3 | 1.2 |
| | | 1.4 | 4.1 | 2.3 | | | 3.1 | 2.2 |
| | (27) 3.0 | (58) 7.1 | (14) 5.0 | | % Depr., Dep., Amort./Sales | (191) 6.9 | (88) 6.5 |
| | | 6.7 | 10.6 | 8.0 | | | 10.5 | 11.2 |
| | | .6 | | | | | .9 | 1.1 |
| | (18) 1.9 | | | | % Officers', Directors' | (59) 1.9 | (32) 2.2 |
| | | 3.0 | | | | Owners' Comp/Sales | 3.8 | 4.6 |
| 54359M | 88256M | 911553M | 3168726M | 3609912M | 7666967M | Net Sales ($) | 15712535M | 8748264M |
| 2696M | 13974M | 221891M | 1663327M | 1755200M | 5956251M | Total Assets ($) | 8742009M | 5707767M |

M = $ thousand    MM = $ million
See Pages viii through xx for Explanation of Ratios and Data

© RMA 2024

# TRANSPORTATION—Specialized Freight (except Used Goods) Trucking, Long-Distance   NAICS 484230

## Comparative Historical Data | Current Data Sorted by Sales

| Comparative Historical Data | | | Type of Statement | Current Data Sorted by Sales | | | | | |
|---|---|---|---|---|---|---|---|---|---|
| 18 | 36 | 29 | Unqualified | | | | 1 | | 28 |
| 21 | 25 | 22 | Reviewed | | | | 1 | 6 | 15 |
| 14 | 21 | 18 | Compiled | | | | 4 | 2 | 11 |
| 14 | 15 | 15 | Tax Returns | 2 | 4 | 4 | 2 | 3 | |
| 89 | 102 | 108 | Other | 4 | 4 | | 14 | 16 | 70 |
| 4/1/21-3/31/22 ALL | 4/1/22-3/31/23 ALL | 4/1/23-3/31/24 ALL | | 38 (4/1-9/30/23) | | | 154 (10/1/23-3/31/24) | | |
| | | | | 0-1MM | 1-3MM | 3-5MM | 5-10MM | 10-25MM | 25MM & OVER |
| 156 | 199 | 192 | NUMBER OF STATEMENTS | 6 | 9 | 4 | 22 | 27 | 124 |
| % | % | % | ASSETS | % | % | % | % | % | % |
| 15.0 | 13.7 | 14.4 | Cash & Equivalents | | | | 18.7 | 20.4 | 11.9 |
| 25.8 | 22.4 | 21.1 | Trade Receivables (net) | | | | 23.9 | 21.1 | 19.7 |
| 1.2 | 1.7 | 1.7 | Inventory | | | | .6 | 1.0 | 2.4 |
| 3.7 | 4.3 | 3.4 | All Other Current | | | | 2.5 | 4.8 | 3.6 |
| 45.7 | 42.2 | 40.7 | Total Current | | | | 45.6 | 47.3 | 37.6 |
| 45.8 | 47.6 | 46.6 | Fixed Assets (net) | | | | 47.9 | 40.3 | 48.6 |
| 2.0 | 1.8 | 2.1 | Intangibles (net) | | | | 2.1 | 1.0 | 2.6 |
| 6.5 | 8.3 | 10.6 | All Other Non-Current | | | | 4.3 | 11.3 | 11.3 |
| 100.0 | 100.0 | 100.0 | Total | | | | 100.0 | 100.0 | 100.0 |
| | | | LIABILITIES | | | | | | |
| 3.7 | 3.9 | 4.9 | Notes Payable-Short Term | | | | 6.0 | 10.5 | 3.0 |
| 8.8 | 9.1 | 7.7 | Cur. Mat.-L.T.D. | | | | 5.7 | 5.8 | 9.0 |
| 9.9 | 6.8 | 7.6 | Trade Payables | | | | 8.5 | 4.3 | 8.6 |
| .1 | .1 | .1 | Income Taxes Payable | | | | .0 | .0 | .1 |
| 7.8 | 8.0 | 7.4 | All Other Current | | | | 6.5 | 4.9 | 8.2 |
| 30.4 | 27.9 | 27.7 | Total Current | | | | 26.7 | 25.4 | 28.9 |
| 32.3 | 31.7 | 31.1 | Long-Term Debt | | | | 42.1 | 30.4 | 28.2 |
| .7 | .6 | .7 | Deferred Taxes | | | | .0 | .1 | 1.0 |
| 4.4 | 3.2 | 3.7 | All Other Non-Current | | | | 1.0 | 3.7 | 4.4 |
| 32.2 | 36.6 | 36.7 | Net Worth | | | | 30.2 | 40.4 | 37.4 |
| 100.0 | 100.0 | 100.0 | Total Liabilities & Net Worth | | | | 100.0 | 100.0 | 100.0 |
| | | | INCOME DATA | | | | | | |
| 100.0 | 100.0 | 100.0 | Net Sales | | | | 100.0 | 100.0 | 100.0 |
| | | | Gross Profit | | | | | | |
| 92.7 | 90.9 | 93.1 | Operating Expenses | | | | 93.5 | 92.6 | 94.9 |
| 7.3 | 9.1 | 6.9 | Operating Profit | | | | 6.5 | 7.4 | 5.1 |
| -.5 | .5 | .7 | All Other Expenses (net) | | | | 2.8 | .0 | .4 |
| 7.7 | 8.6 | 6.2 | Profit Before Taxes | | | | 3.7 | 7.4 | 4.6 |
| | | | RATIOS | | | | | | |
| 2.6 | 2.2 | 2.5 | | | | | 4.5 | 4.7 | 1.8 |
| 1.6 | 1.5 | 1.3 | Current | | | | 1.4 | 2.2 | 1.3 |
| 1.0 | 1.0 | .9 | | | | | .8 | 1.1 | .9 |
| 2.5 | 2.0 | 2.1 | | | | | 4.5 | 4.5 | 1.5 |
| 1.4 | 1.2 | 1.2 | Quick | | | | 1.4 | 1.9 | 1.1 |
| .9 | .8 | .7 | | | | | .6 | .9 | .7 |
| 25  14.7 | 23  16.2 | 24  15.4 | | 0  UND | | | 23  15.8 | 27  13.6 | |
| 37  9.9 | 34  10.7 | 32  11.3 | Sales/Receivables | 30  12.1 | | | 32  11.4 | 33  11.1 | |
| 49  7.4 | 46  7.9 | 41  8.8 | | 38  9.5 | | | 44  8.3 | 42  8.7 | |
| | | | Cost of Sales/Inventory | | | | | | |
| | | | Cost of Sales/Payables | | | | | | |
| 7.3 | 8.1 | 10.0 | | | | | 8.5 | 6.0 | 12.6 |
| 15.0 | 17.7 | 30.0 | Sales/Working Capital | | | | 27.5 | 14.4 | 36.1 |
| UND | 476.7 | -56.9 | | | | | -44.3 | 399.8 | -42.9 |
| 17.1 | 20.7 | 10.4 | | | | | 9.7 | 25.1 | 9.1 |
| (136) 8.2 | (181) 7.3 | (176) 4.8 | EBIT/Interest | (17) | | | 4.1 | (115) 7.2 | 4.6 |
| 3.3 | 3.6 | 1.5 | | | | | .3 | 2.3 | 1.2 |
| 6.3 | 5.7 | 2.7 | | | | | | | 2.6 |
| (38) 2.9 | (41) 2.5 | (28) 1.7 | Net Profit + Depr., Dep., Amort./Cur. Mat. L/T/D | | | | | (25) 1.7 | |
| 1.5 | 1.3 | 1.1 | | | | | | | 1.1 |
| .6 | .6 | .6 | | | | | .4 | .5 | .8 |
| 1.3 | 1.2 | 1.4 | Fixed/Worth | | | | 1.7 | .9 | 1.4 |
| 2.8 | 2.3 | 2.7 | | | | | 6.8 | 1.9 | 2.6 |
| .8 | .7 | .8 | | | | | .6 | .5 | 1.0 |
| 1.6 | 1.4 | 1.7 | Debt/Worth | | | | 2.2 | 1.4 | 1.7 |
| 4.3 | 3.2 | 3.8 | | | | | 7.0 | 3.3 | 3.3 |
| 62.0 | 56.1 | 47.5 | | | | | 39.9 | 56.3 | 43.9 |
| (139) 37.6 | (180) 32.8 | (175) 17.8 | % Profit Before Taxes/Tangible Net Worth | (19) 17.5 | | (24) 19.2 | (116) 17.6 | | |
| 14.6 | 16.8 | 6.2 | | | | | 3.9 | 10.1 | 5.7 |
| 24.1 | 21.3 | 16.3 | | | | | 33.2 | 31.9 | 14.5 |
| 12.9 | 12.0 | 7.1 | % Profit Before Taxes/Total Assets | | | | 7.7 | 14.1 | 6.5 |
| 4.3 | 5.9 | 1.5 | | | | | .4 | 2.8 | 1.1 |
| 11.0 | 8.1 | 12.4 | | | | | 108.8 | 13.2 | 8.0 |
| 3.9 | 3.8 | 3.7 | Sales/Net Fixed Assets | | | | 5.5 | 5.2 | 3.3 |
| 2.1 | 2.3 | 2.0 | | | | | 2.6 | 2.5 | 1.8 |
| 3.1 | 2.9 | 2.8 | | | | | 4.4 | 3.4 | 2.4 |
| 1.9 | 1.8 | 1.9 | Sales/Total Assets | | | | 2.8 | 2.0 | 1.7 |
| 1.2 | 1.3 | 1.2 | | | | | 1.7 | 1.3 | 1.2 |
| 3.2 | 3.4 | 2.3 | | | | | 2.4 | 1.8 | 2.3 |
| (106) 6.5 | (138) 6.0 | (113) 4.9 | % Depr., Dep., Amort./Sales | (14) | | (21) | 5.6 | 5.3 | (69) 4.4 |
| 11.8 | 9.1 | 9.3 | | | | | 49.4 | 8.4 | 8.0 |
| .5 | .5 | .6 | | | | | | | .5 |
| (36) 1.4 | (45) 1.1 | (37) 1.7 | % Officers', Directors' Owners' Comp/Sales | | | | | (20) | 1.4 |
| 3.7 | 4.1 | 2.8 | | | | | | | 2.7 |
| 9653504M | 15035249M | 15499773M | Net Sales ($) | 2457M | 16970M | 15819M | 161570M | 477318M | 14825639M |
| 5821254M | 8517443M | 9613339M | Total Assets ($) | 2233M | 54976M | 2968M | 174924M | 244269M | 9133969M |

© RMA 2024   M = $ thousand   MM = $ million
See Pages viii through xx for Explanation of Ratios and Data

# TRANSPORTATION—School and Employee Bus Transportation  NAICS 485410

## Current Data Sorted by Assets | Comparative Historical Data

| | | | | | | | Type of Statement | | |
|---|---|---|---|---|---|---|---|---|---|
| | | | 2 | 4 | | 5 | Unqualified | 7 | 5 |
| | | | 3 | 11 | | | Reviewed | 18 | 4 |
| | | | 2 | 1 | | | Compiled | 9 | 4 |
| | 4 | 3 | 4 | | | | Tax Returns | 22 | 9 |
| | | 2 | 4 | 8 | 1 | 3 | Other | 48 | 26 |
| | | 19 (4/1-9/30/23) | | 38 (10/1/23-3/31/24) | | | | 4/1/19-3/31/20 | 4/1/20-3/31/21 |
| | 0-500M | 500M-2MM | 2-10MM | 10-50MM | 50-100MM | 100-250MM | NUMBER OF STATEMENTS | ALL 104 | ALL 48 |
| | 4 | 5 | 15 | 24 | 1 | 8 | | | |
| | % | % | % | % | % | % | ASSETS | % | % |
| | | | 23.1 | 10.0 | | | Cash & Equivalents | 10.5 | 19.7 |
| | | | 7.8 | 15.6 | | | Trade Receivables (net) | 10.8 | 7.5 |
| | | | 1.0 | 13.0 | | | Inventory | 3.9 | 6.3 |
| | | | 4.1 | 3.1 | | | All Other Current | 1.7 | 1.1 |
| | | | 36.0 | 41.7 | | | Total Current | 27.0 | 34.5 |
| | | | 42.7 | 46.3 | | | Fixed Assets (net) | 56.7 | 52.9 |
| | | | 6.8 | 2.3 | | | Intangibles (net) | 5.9 | 5.3 |
| | | | 14.6 | 9.7 | | | All Other Non-Current | 10.3 | 7.2 |
| | | | 100.0 | 100.0 | | | Total | 100.0 | 100.0 |
| | | | | | | | LIABILITIES | | |
| | | | 8.9 | 2.2 | | | Notes Payable-Short Term | 7.0 | 7.6 |
| | | | 6.2 | 6.3 | | | Cur. Mat.-L.T.D. | 10.7 | 10.2 |
| | | | 1.7 | 7.6 | | | Trade Payables | 4.5 | 1.8 |
| | | | .1 | .3 | | | Income Taxes Payable | .2 | .2 |
| | | | 6.7 | 7.2 | | | All Other Current | 8.4 | 8.3 |
| | | | 23.7 | 23.6 | | | Total Current | 30.8 | 28.1 |
| | | | 25.5 | 24.6 | | | Long-Term Debt | 39.2 | 40.9 |
| | | | .0 | 1.1 | | | Deferred Taxes | 1.1 | .8 |
| | | | .4 | 6.9 | | | All Other Non-Current | 6.1 | 7.0 |
| | | | 50.4 | 43.8 | | | Net Worth | 22.8 | 23.2 |
| | | | 100.0 | 100.0 | | | Total Liabilties & Net Worth | 100.0 | 100.0 |
| | | | | | | | INCOME DATA | | |
| | | | 100.0 | 100.0 | | | Net Sales | 100.0 | 100.0 |
| | | | | | | | Gross Profit | | |
| | | | 82.4 | 92.4 | | | Operating Expenses | 92.9 | 94.7 |
| | | | 17.6 | 7.6 | | | Operating Profit | 7.1 | 5.3 |
| | | | -.5 | .2 | | | All Other Expenses (net) | 1.4 | -.6 |
| | | | 18.1 | 7.4 | | | Profit Before Taxes | 5.7 | 6.0 |
| | | | | | | | RATIOS | | |
| | | | 8.5 | 3.2 | | | | 1.5 | 3.1 |
| | | | 1.9 | 1.9 | | | Current | .9 | 1.2 |
| | | | 1.0 | 1.3 | | | | .5 | .6 |
| | | | 7.9 | 3.0 | | | | 1.3 | 2.4 |
| | | | 1.9 | 1.5 | | | Quick | .7 | 1.0 |
| | | | .5 | .7 | | | | .3 | .4 |
| | | | 3  115.3 | 18  20.5 | | | | 5  66.5 | 0  879.6 |
| | | | 13  27.8 | 41  8.9 | | | Sales/Receivables | 17  20.9 | 9  38.7 |
| | | | 22  16.7 | 63  5.8 | | | | 36  10.0 | 37  9.9 |
| | | | | | | | Cost of Sales/Inventory | | |
| | | | | | | | Cost of Sales/Payables | | |
| | | | 4.0 | 5.1 | | | | 16.3 | 6.1 |
| | | | 8.6 | 10.1 | | | Sales/Working Capital | -61.2 | 20.2 |
| | | | -115.3 | 13.7 | | | | -10.9 | -22.2 |
| | | | 20.3 | 16.4 | | | | 7.9 | 8.7 |
| | | | 5.3 | 3.6 | | | EBIT/Interest | (100) 3.1 | (45) 3.3 |
| | | | 1.8 | 2.6 | | | | 1.6 | .8 |
| | | | | | | | Net Profit + Depr., Dep., Amort./Cur. Mat. L/T/D | 2.1 | |
| | | | | | | | | (27) 1.2 | |
| | | | | | | | | 1.0 | |
| | | | .6 | .4 | | | | 1.1 | 1.0 |
| | | | .9 | 1.2 | | | Fixed/Worth | 2.2 | 2.1 |
| | | | 1.2 | 1.9 | | | | 12.2 | 12.4 |
| | | | .4 | .6 | | | | 1.2 | .9 |
| | | | .7 | 1.5 | | | Debt/Worth | 2.7 | 2.3 |
| | | | 4.4 | 2.3 | | | | 52.5 | 15.0 |
| | | | 34.9 | 34.7 | | | % Profit Before Taxes/Tangible Net Worth | 41.3 | 39.4 |
| | | (13) | 21.8 | (23) 15.0 | | | | (81) 16.4 | (41) 19.4 |
| | | | 4.6 | 10.3 | | | | 6.0 | -1.3 |
| | | | 20.0 | 16.1 | | | % Profit Before Taxes/Total Assets | 15.9 | 15.4 |
| | | | 13.9 | 6.7 | | | | 5.3 | 5.7 |
| | | | 2.8 | 4.1 | | | | 1.4 | -.9 |
| | | | 5.0 | 9.7 | | | | 5.3 | 8.8 |
| | | | 3.3 | 2.4 | | | Sales/Net Fixed Assets | 2.3 | 2.5 |
| | | | .9 | 1.3 | | | | 1.5 | 1.0 |
| | | | 1.9 | 2.4 | | | | 2.3 | 2.2 |
| | | | 1.4 | 1.2 | | | Sales/Total Assets | 1.5 | 1.1 |
| | | | .5 | .9 | | | | 1.0 | .8 |
| | | | 5.7 | 1.7 | | | | 6.5 | 7.3 |
| | | (13) | 11.0 | (23) 5.9 | | | % Depr., Dep., Amort./Sales | (81) 10.9 | (33) 11.0 |
| | | | 15.2 | 13.6 | | | | 15.0 | 16.1 |
| | | | | | | | % Officers', Directors' Owners' Comp/Sales | 2.1 | 2.2 |
| | | | | | | | | (33) 4.4 | (21) 5.2 |
| | | | | | | | | 8.1 | 10.4 |
| | 3835M | 19343M | 90713M | 1122728M | 69101M | 1279856M | Net Sales ($) | 3023361M | 1443420M |
| | 1029M | 6083M | 59909M | 670208M | 75348M | 1226121M | Total Assets ($) | 2368950M | 1165547M |

© RMA 2024  M = $ thousand   MM = $ million
See Pages viii through xx for Explanation of Ratios and Data

# TRANSPORTATION—School and Employee Bus Transportation  NAICS 485410

## Comparative Historical Data | Current Data Sorted by Sales

| Comparative Historical Data | | | Type of Statement | Current Data Sorted by Sales | | | | | |
|---|---|---|---|---|---|---|---|---|---|
| 2 | 3 | 11 | Unqualified | 2 | | | 1 | 1 | 8 |
| 4 | 10 | 14 | Reviewed | | | | | 2 | 4 |
| 1 | 4 | 3 | Compiled | | | | 1 | 1 | 1 |
| 12 | 11 | 11 | Tax Returns | 3 | 3 | 1 | 2 | 2 | |
| 28 | 18 | 18 | Other | 1 | 3 | | 2 | 1 | 11 |
| 4/1/21-3/31/22 ALL | 4/1/22-3/31/23 ALL | 4/1/23-3/31/24 ALL | | 19 (4/1-9/30/23) | | | 38 (10/1/23-3/31/24) | | |
| | | | | 0-1MM | 1-3MM | 3-5MM | 5-10MM | 10-25MM | 25MM & OVER |
| 47 | 46 | 57 | NUMBER OF STATEMENTS | 6 | 6 | 1 | 7 | 13 | 24 |
| % | % | % | ASSETS | % | % | % | % | % | % |
| 18.9 | 17.6 | 16.9 | Cash & Equivalents | | | | | 19.1 | 6.7 |
| 8.5 | 15.0 | 12.7 | Trade Receivables (net) | | | | | 11.8 | 18.2 |
| 5.6 | 1.5 | 7.7 | Inventory | | | | | .6 | 17.4 |
| 1.6 | 2.8 | 2.6 | All Other Current | | | | | 6.9 | 2.1 |
| 34.6 | 37.0 | 40.0 | Total Current | | | | | 38.3 | 44.4 |
| 52.8 | 47.4 | 45.1 | Fixed Assets (net) | | | | | 47.6 | 43.7 |
| 5.4 | 4.8 | 3.9 | Intangibles (net) | | | | | 3.2 | 2.2 |
| 7.2 | 10.8 | 11.0 | All Other Non-Current | | | | | 10.8 | 9.7 |
| 100.0 | 100.0 | 100.0 | Total | | | | | 100.0 | 100.0 |
| | | | LIABILITIES | | | | | | |
| 5.6 | 4.1 | 7.2 | Notes Payable-Short Term | | | | | 1.0 | 7.2 |
| 9.0 | 9.8 | 9.0 | Cur. Mat.-L.T.D. | | | | | 8.2 | 5.8 |
| 3.3 | 3.1 | 4.9 | Trade Payables | | | | | 1.3 | 9.1 |
| .2 | .0 | .2 | Income Taxes Payable | | | | | .4 | .2 |
| 4.8 | 5.8 | 6.4 | All Other Current | | | | | 4.9 | 8.3 |
| 22.9 | 22.8 | 27.6 | Total Current | | | | | 15.8 | 30.5 |
| 47.7 | 28.6 | 32.2 | Long-Term Debt | | | | | 22.5 | 22.6 |
| .4 | .1 | .4 | Deferred Taxes | | | | | 1.7 | .1 |
| 9.0 | 3.6 | 4.9 | All Other Non-Current | | | | | 2.5 | 8.7 |
| 20.0 | 44.9 | 34.8 | Net Worth | | | | | 57.5 | 38.0 |
| 100.0 | 100.0 | 100.0 | Total Liabilities & Net Worth | | | | | 100.0 | 100.0 |
| | | | INCOME DATA | | | | | | |
| 100.0 | 100.0 | 100.0 | Net Sales | | | | | 100.0 | 100.0 |
| | | | Gross Profit | | | | | | |
| 93.1 | 93.2 | 90.3 | Operating Expenses | | | | | 93.9 | 93.8 |
| 6.9 | 6.8 | 9.7 | Operating Profit | | | | | 6.1 | 6.2 |
| -1.8 | -.1 | .0 | All Other Expenses (net) | | | | | -.8 | 1.1 |
| 8.6 | 6.8 | 9.7 | Profit Before Taxes | | | | | 6.9 | 5.1 |
| | | | RATIOS | | | | | | |
| 3.1 | 3.2 | 3.5 | | | | | | 3.7 | 2.4 |
| 1.5 | 1.8 | 1.7 | Current | | | | | 2.3 | 1.4 |
| .8 | 1.0 | 1.1 | | | | | | 1.4 | 1.1 |
| 3.1 | 3.0 | 3.2 | | | | | | 3.2 | 1.8 |
| 1.3 | 1.4 | 1.4 | Quick | | | | | 1.5 | 1.0 |
| .6 | .9 | .5 | | | | | | 1.1 | .5 |
| 0  UND | 10  37.9 | 6  57.7 | | | | | 8  45.3 | 26  13.8 | |
| 8  48.4 | 33  11.0 | 26  14.1 | Sales/Receivables | | | | 33  11.2 | 51  7.1 | |
| 36  10.1 | 52  7.0 | 60  6.1 | | | | | 42  8.7 | 65  5.6 | |
| | | | Cost of Sales/Inventory | | | | | | |
| | | | Cost of Sales/Payables | | | | | | |
| 5.5 | 5.2 | 5.4 | | | | | | 4.1 | 7.8 |
| 13.2 | 13.0 | 10.8 | Sales/Working Capital | | | | | 5.5 | 10.9 |
| -33.7 | -189.4 | 73.6 | | | | | | 21.3 | 22.4 |
| 11.8 | 18.3 | 16.1 | | | | | | 30.6 | 11.3 |
| (45)  6.5 | (43)  7.1 | 3.2 | EBIT/Interest | | | | | 5.6 | 3.0 |
| 2.3 | 1.2 | 1.9 | | | | | | 1.9 | 2.3 |
| | | 8.7 | Net Profit + Depr., Dep., | | | | | | |
| | (17) | 5.0 | Amort./Cur. Mat. L/T/D | | | | | | |
| | | 2.8 | | | | | | | |
| .9 | .6 | .7 | | | | | | .7 | .5 |
| 3.4 | 1.2 | 1.1 | Fixed/Worth | | | | | 1.1 | 1.1 |
| -70.3 | 2.8 | 2.1 | | | | | | 1.3 | 1.9 |
| 1.0 | .7 | .6 | | | | | | .5 | 1.0 |
| 3.3 | 1.2 | 1.3 | Debt/Worth | | | | | .7 | 1.9 |
| -100.5 | 2.8 | 2.8 | | | | | | 1.0 | 2.3 |
| 64.7 | 34.4 | 37.8 | % Profit Before Taxes/Tangible | | | | | 27.6 | 32.9 |
| (35)  30.3 | (40)  19.0 | (50)  16.2 | Net Worth | | | | | 9.8  (23) | 15.0 |
| 6.6 | 10.2 | 7.3 | | | | | | 5.0 | 10.2 |
| 21.1 | 14.0 | 18.6 | % Profit Before Taxes/Total | | | | | 19.0 | 9.9 |
| 14.6 | 9.1 | 5.1 | Assets | | | | | 5.1 | 4.5 |
| 2.3 | .1 | 2.5 | | | | | | 1.9 | 3.6 |
| 6.5 | 6.0 | 8.0 | | | | | | 10.4 | 9.7 |
| 2.4 | 3.1 | 2.7 | Sales/Net Fixed Assets | | | | | 3.3 | 2.4 |
| 1.4 | 1.8 | 1.8 | | | | | | 1.4 | 1.9 |
| 2.2 | 2.0 | 2.2 | | | | | | 2.0 | 2.3 |
| 1.3 | 1.4 | 1.3 | Sales/Total Assets | | | | | 1.2 | 1.2 |
| .9 | 1.1 | .9 | | | | | | .9 | .9 |
| 7.0 | 6.2 | 3.0 | | | | | | 5.4 | .4 |
| (36)  11.8 | (33)  9.2 | (46)  8.2 | % Depr., Dep., Amort./Sales | | | | | (11)  11.1  (18) | 5.4 |
| 20.3 | 13.5 | 13.8 | | | | | | 14.3 | 8.4 |
| 1.4 | 3.3 | 1.3 | % Officers', Directors' | | | | | | |
| (23)  3.2 | (15)  5.1 | (16)  2.1 | Owners' Comp/Sales | | | | | | |
| 11.8 | 6.6 | 3.6 | | | | | | | |
| 824163M | 1294637M | 2585576M | Net Sales ($) | 4311M | 10743M | 3126M | 48198M | 205617M | 2313581M |
| 760298M | 1086889M | 2038698M | Total Assets ($) | 7760M | 7997M | 1653M | 30193M | 168564M | 1822531M |

© RMA 2024    M = $ thousand    MM = $ million
See Pages viii through xx for Explanation of Ratios and Data

# TRANSPORTATION—Charter Bus Industry  NAICS 485510

## Current Data Sorted by Assets | Comparative Historical Data

| | | | | | | | Type of Statement | | | | |
|---|---|---|---|---|---|---|---|---|---|---|---|
| | | | 2 | 1 | | | Unqualified | | 4 | | 2 |
| | | | 4 | 1 | | | Reviewed | | 12 | | 3 |
| | | 2 | 1 | 1 | | | Compiled | | 14 | | 2 |
| | 2 | 4 | 2 | | | | Tax Returns | | 13 | | 5 |
| 3 | 8 | 18 | 22 | 4 | 1 | | Other | | 117 | | 27 |
| | 20 (4/1-9/30/23) | | 56 (10/1/23-3/31/24) | | | | | | 4/1/19-3/31/20 | | 4/1/20-3/31/21 |
| 0-500M | 500M-2MM | 2-10MM | 10-50MM | 50-100MM | 100-250MM | | | | ALL | | ALL |
| 3 | 10 | 24 | 31 | 7 | 1 | | NUMBER OF STATEMENTS | | 160 | | 39 |
| % | % | % | % | % | % | | ASSETS | | % | | % |
| | 47.1 | 20.8 | 20.1 | | | | Cash & Equivalents | | 9.4 | | 21.2 |
| | 5.3 | 6.4 | 6.7 | | | | Trade Receivables (net) | | 8.1 | | 8.4 |
| | .4 | 2.2 | 1.4 | | | | Inventory | | 1.5 | | 1.5 |
| | .9 | 4.0 | 2.7 | | | | All Other Current | | 4.3 | | 4.5 |
| | 53.6 | 33.3 | 30.9 | | | | Total Current | | 23.2 | | 35.6 |
| | 36.3 | 53.9 | 58.3 | | | | Fixed Assets (net) | | 63.5 | | 56.5 |
| | 5.0 | 3.4 | 2.7 | | | | Intangibles (net) | | 5.8 | | 2.6 |
| | 5.2 | 9.4 | 8.1 | | | | All Other Non-Current | | 7.5 | | 5.2 |
| | 100.0 | 100.0 | 100.0 | | | | Total | | 100.0 | | 100.0 |
| | | | | | | | LIABILITIES | | | | |
| | .6 | 3.8 | .8 | | | | Notes Payable-Short Term | | 4.2 | | 4.3 |
| | 9.7 | 8.9 | 8.1 | | | | Cur. Mat.-L.T.D. | | 11.7 | | 14.5 |
| | 2.3 | 2.0 | 2.1 | | | | Trade Payables | | 3.0 | | 2.3 |
| | .1 | .0 | .1 | | | | Income Taxes Payable | | .1 | | .0 |
| | 5.6 | 9.1 | 6.5 | | | | All Other Current | | 10.4 | | 16.8 |
| | 18.3 | 23.9 | 17.6 | | | | Total Current | | 29.4 | | 37.9 |
| | 63.3 | 66.9 | 34.1 | | | | Long-Term Debt | | 47.0 | | 39.0 |
| | .0 | .0 | .9 | | | | Deferred Taxes | | .9 | | 1.2 |
| | 8.5 | 2.4 | 4.8 | | | | All Other Non-Current | | 5.1 | | 7.6 |
| | 9.9 | 6.8 | 42.6 | | | | Net Worth | | 17.8 | | 14.2 |
| | 100.0 | 100.0 | 100.0 | | | | Total Liabilities & Net Worth | | 100.0 | | 100.0 |
| | | | | | | | INCOME DATA | | | | |
| | 100.0 | 100.0 | 100.0 | | | | Net Sales | | 100.0 | | 100.0 |
| | | | | | | | Gross Profit | | | | |
| | 91.1 | 88.0 | 81.7 | | | | Operating Expenses | | 91.8 | | 97.6 |
| | 8.9 | 12.0 | 18.3 | | | | Operating Profit | | 8.2 | | 2.4 |
| | .1 | .9 | 1.5 | | | | All Other Expenses (net) | | 3.0 | | 6.1 |
| | 8.8 | 11.2 | 16.8 | | | | Profit Before Taxes | | 5.3 | | -3.7 |
| | | | | | | | RATIOS | | | | |
| | 9.9 | 2.4 | 3.5 | | | | | | 1.5 | | 3.6 |
| | 3.4 | 1.1 | 1.7 | | | Current | | | .8 | | 1.3 |
| | 1.1 | .3 | .9 | | | | | | .4 | | .6 |
| | 9.4 | 2.0 | 3.3 | | | | | | 1.3 | | 3.5 |
| | 3.4 | 1.0 | 1.3 | | | Quick | | | .5 | | 1.0 |
| | 1.0 | .3 | .6 | | | | | | .2 | | .3 |
| | 0 UND | 0 UND | 9 39.5 | | | | | 2 | 182.2 | 4 | 99.1 |
| | 0 UND | 10 37.1 | 23 15.7 | | | Sales/Receivables | | 16 | 23.2 | 15 | 24.3 |
| | 4 89.0 | 24 15.4 | 38 9.5 | | | | | 31 | 11.9 | 31 | 11.6 |
| | | | | | | | Cost of Sales/Inventory | | | | |
| | | | | | | | Cost of Sales/Payables | | | | |
| | 3.6 | 5.3 | 3.1 | | | | | | 19.8 | | 4.4 |
| | 8.3 | 28.5 | 8.5 | | | Sales/Working Capital | | | -34.5 | | 15.0 |
| | NM | -11.1 | -48.1 | | | | | | -7.3 | | -6.9 |
| | | 8.9 | 12.8 | | | | | | 5.9 | | 4.2 |
| | | 3.6 (28) | 5.4 | | | EBIT/Interest | | (147) | 2.2 | (30) | -.6 |
| | | 1.0 | 3.0 | | | | | | .6 | | -4.0 |
| | | | | | | | Net Profit + Depr., Dep., | | | 2.0 | | 1.4 |
| | | | | | | | Amort./Cur. Mat. L/T/D | | (37) | 1.3 | (12) | .7 |
| | | | | | | | | | | .9 | | .3 |
| | .4 | 2.3 | 1.1 | | | | | | 1.7 | | 1.1 |
| | NM | 8.7 | 1.5 | | | Fixed/Worth | | | 3.3 | | 2.0 |
| | -.4 | -2.3 | 2.3 | | | | | | NM | | 7.5 |
| | 1.0 | 2.5 | .7 | | | | | | 1.4 | | 1.4 |
| | NM | 14.0 | 1.2 | | | Debt/Worth | | | 3.6 | | 2.9 |
| | -3.0 | -5.0 | 2.7 | | | | | | -949.5 | | 8.5 |
| | | 120.0 | 41.2 | | | | | | 41.8 | | 18.0 |
| | (14) | 30.4 (28) | 21.6 | | | % Profit Before Taxes/Tangible | | (119) | 13.7 | (31) | -1.8 |
| | | 10.9 | 10.6 | | | Net Worth | | | .9 | | -37.7 |
| | 43.2 | 26.7 | 16.2 | | | | | | 11.0 | | 5.7 |
| | 23.2 | 10.1 | 9.7 | | | % Profit Before Taxes/Total | | | 3.8 | | -3.0 |
| | 1.1 | -.1 | 2.8 | | | Assets | | | -.6 | | -11.1 |
| | 64.1 | 10.4 | 2.5 | | | | | | 4.1 | | 5.1 |
| | 12.6 | 2.1 | 1.8 | | | Sales/Net Fixed Assets | | | 1.6 | | 1.2 |
| | 5.1 | 1.5 | .9 | | | | | | .9 | | .7 |
| | 6.2 | 1.9 | 1.4 | | | | | | 2.4 | | 1.7 |
| | 3.2 | 1.4 | 1.0 | | | Sales/Total Assets | | | 1.1 | | .8 |
| | 1.9 | .8 | .7 | | | | | | .8 | | .4 |
| | | 7.4 | 7.2 | | | | | | 6.5 | | 7.2 |
| | (15) | 10.2 (27) | 9.2 | | | % Depr., Dep., Amort./Sales | | (128) | 11.3 | (32) | 13.3 |
| | | 20.3 | 12.0 | | | | | | 15.4 | | 24.3 |
| | | 1.0 | | | | | | | 1.2 | | |
| | (12) | 1.9 | | | | % Officers', Directors' | | (34) | 2.9 | | |
| | | 3.1 | | | | Owners' Comp/Sales | | | 4.7 | | |
| 2462M | 37050M | 191871M | 692222M | 462010M | 46758M | | Net Sales ($) | | 3675537M | | 1066057M |
| 681M | 10894M | 133169M | 712683M | 523451M | 217710M | | Total Assets ($) | | 3359788M | | 1249796M |

© RMA 2024

M = $ thousand    MM = $ million
See Pages viii through xx for Explanation of Ratios and Data

# TRANSPORTATION—Charter Bus Industry  NAICS 485510

## Comparative Historical Data | Current Data Sorted by Sales

| Comparative Historical Data | | | | | Current Data Sorted by Sales | | | | | |
|---|---|---|---|---|---|---|---|---|---|---|
| | | | Type of Statement | | | | | | | |
| 2 | 3 | 3 | Unqualified | | | | | 1 | 2 | |
| 2 | 7 | 5 | Reviewed | | | | | 2 | 3 | |
| 3 | 6 | 4 | Compiled | 1 | | | | 2 | 1 | |
| 4 | 10 | 8 | Tax Returns | 2 | | 3 | | 2 | 1 | |
| 21 | 44 | 56 | Other | 2 | 7 | 5 | 15 | 12 | 15 | |
| 4/1/21-3/31/22 ALL | 4/1/22-3/31/23 ALL | 4/1/23-3/31/24 ALL | | | 20 (4/1-9/30/23) | | | 56 (10/1/23-3/31/24) | | |
| | | | | 0-1MM | 1-3MM | 3-5MM | 5-10MM | 10-25MM | 25MM & OVER |
| 32 | 70 | 76 | NUMBER OF STATEMENTS | 2 | 10 | 5 | 18 | 19 | 22 |
| % | % | % | ASSETS | % | % | % | % | % | % |
| 25.1 | 20.2 | 22.8 | Cash & Equivalents | | 26.9 | | 26.4 | 16.5 | 19.3 |
| 4.7 | 9.7 | 6.8 | Trade Receivables (net) | | 5.4 | | 4.9 | 8.0 | 6.6 |
| .9 | 1.4 | 2.5 | Inventory | | .4 | | .8 | 3.1 | 5.0 |
| 1.9 | 4.2 | 3.5 | All Other Current | | .1 | | 2.6 | 5.5 | 2.2 |
| 32.5 | 35.5 | 35.7 | Total Current | | 32.7 | | 34.7 | 33.1 | 33.1 |
| 57.0 | 52.7 | 52.1 | Fixed Assets (net) | | 52.1 | | 55.0 | 54.7 | 54.3 |
| 3.5 | 3.2 | 3.8 | Intangibles (net) | | 8.3 | | .6 | 1.6 | 5.4 |
| 6.9 | 8.5 | 8.5 | All Other Non-Current | | 6.9 | | 9.7 | 10.5 | 7.3 |
| 100.0 | 100.0 | 100.0 | Total | | 100.0 | | 100.0 | 100.0 | 100.0 |
| | | | LIABILITIES | | | | | | |
| 2.7 | 1.8 | 2.5 | Notes Payable-Short Term | | 1.8 | | 4.2 | .6 | 3.7 |
| 11.5 | 7.7 | 8.7 | Cur. Mat.-L.T.D. | | 11.1 | | 9.1 | 8.4 | 7.4 |
| 3.4 | 3.4 | 2.0 | Trade Payables | | 2.4 | | 1.2 | 3.2 | 2.1 |
| .0 | .6 | .0 | Income Taxes Payable | | .1 | | .0 | .1 | .0 |
| 2.7 | 7.3 | 10.7 | All Other Current | | 12.3 | | 10.4 | 5.0 | 9.2 |
| 20.3 | 20.8 | 24.1 | Total Current | | 27.7 | | 24.9 | 17.3 | 22.5 |
| 65.5 | 52.3 | 51.7 | Long-Term Debt | | 57.4 | | 55.9 | 50.8 | 38.5 |
| 1.4 | 1.0 | .6 | Deferred Taxes | | .0 | | .0 | 1.0 | 1.1 |
| 9.0 | 4.4 | 5.8 | All Other Non-Current | | 9.1 | | 3.7 | 3.7 | 4.5 |
| 3.9 | 21.5 | 17.9 | Net Worth | | 5.8 | | 15.5 | 27.1 | 33.4 |
| 100.0 | 100.0 | 100.0 | Total Liabilities & Net Worth | | 100.0 | | 100.0 | 100.0 | 100.0 |
| | | | INCOME DATA | | | | | | |
| 100.0 | 100.0 | 100.0 | Net Sales | | 100.0 | | 100.0 | 100.0 | 100.0 |
| | | | Gross Profit | | | | | | |
| 87.0 | 88.9 | 86.4 | Operating Expenses | | 80.0 | | 88.5 | 89.3 | 84.5 |
| 13.0 | 11.1 | 13.6 | Operating Profit | | 20.0 | | 11.5 | 10.7 | 15.5 |
| .2 | -.2 | 1.8 | All Other Expenses (net) | | 6.0 | | .1 | -.4 | 3.2 |
| 12.8 | 11.3 | 11.8 | Profit Before Taxes | | 14.0 | | 11.4 | 11.0 | 12.4 |
| | | | RATIOS | | | | | | |
| 2.5 | 4.6 | 3.0 | | | 14.9 | | 2.6 | 3.5 | 2.7 |
| 1.4 | 1.8 | 1.4 | Current | | 2.5 | | 1.6 | 1.7 | 1.4 |
| .8 | 1.0 | .6 | | | .2 | | 1.0 | .5 | .7 |
| 2.5 | 4.3 | 2.5 | | | 14.5 | | 2.2 | 1.9 | 2.6 |
| 1.2 | 1.6 | 1.2 | Quick | | 2.5 | | 1.6 | 1.2 | 1.1 |
| .7 | .7 | .4 | | | .2 | | .7 | .5 | .3 |
| 1   254.7 | 4   92.7 | 0   UND | | 0   UND | | 0   UND | 0   UND | 10   37.1 | |
| 16   22.8 | 21  17.0 | 14  25.2 | Sales/Receivables | 0   UND | | 9   38.9 | 23  16.2 | 23  16.1 | |
| 45  8.1 | 34  10.7 | 26  13.9 | | 16  22.6 | | 22  16.9 | 36  10.1 | 40  9.1 | |
| | | | Cost of Sales/Inventory | | | | | | |
| | | | Cost of Sales/Payables | | | | | | |
| 2.9 | 4.9 | 4.3 | | | 4.7 | | 4.7 | 4.0 | 3.1 |
| 9.3 | 12.7 | 14.7 | Sales/Working Capital | | NM | | 16.5 | 11.0 | 16.1 |
| -20.2 | 999.8 | -18.9 | | | -4.0 | | -173.8 | -17.8 | -20.7 |
| 12.4 | 15.3 | 11.3 | | | 11.6 | | 10.1 | 11.2 | |
| (27)  4.1 | (64)  7.4 | (71)  3.9 | EBIT/Interest | | 3.3 | | 3.9 | (19)  3.7 | |
| .1 | 2.0 | 1.5 | | | 1.2 | | 2.8 | 1.5 | |
| | 4.1 | 2.6 | | | | | | | |
| (11)  2.0 | (11)  1.7 | Net Profit + Depr., Dep., | | | | | | | |
| 1.3 | 1.1 | Amort./Cur. Mat. L/T/D | | | | | | | |
| 1.4 | 1.2 | 1.2 | | | 1.2 | | 1.6 | 1.1 | 1.2 |
| 3.0 | 2.4 | 2.3 | Fixed/Worth | | 34.6 | | 3.2 | 1.7 | 2.1 |
| -9.2 | -7.8 | -5.4 | | | -.9 | | -6.0 | 6.0 | NM |
| 1.4 | 1.0 | 1.1 | | | .9 | | 1.7 | 1.1 | .9 |
| 3.3 | 3.5 | 2.8 | Debt/Worth | | 38.3 | | 8.2 | 1.5 | 2.3 |
| -9.4 | -27.6 | -13.6 | | | -2.9 | | -15.8 | 6.1 | NM |
| 57.3 | 106.5 | 48.6 | % Profit Before Taxes/Tangible | | 165.8 | | 49.2 | 39.6 | |
| (21)  31.9 | (51)  36.3 | (53)  26.0 | Net Worth | (13)  38.7 | | (15)  19.7 | (17)  26.0 | | |
| 1.3 | 15.7 | 11.0 | | | 20.1 | | 10.3 | 5.8 | |
| 23.1 | 25.9 | 23.0 | % Profit Before Taxes/Total | | 28.4 | | 21.8 | 22.8 | 16.7 |
| 4.4 | 14.0 | 8.4 | Assets | | 9.9 | | 7.6 | 9.9 | 6.4 |
| -4.6 | 3.4 | 1.6 | | | -.8 | | .6 | 5.6 | .8 |
| 2.5 | 8.5 | 7.6 | | | 14.9 | | 7.1 | 5.5 | 2.6 |
| 1.3 | 2.3 | 2.1 | Sales/Net Fixed Assets | | 2.0 | | 2.1 | 1.9 | 1.8 |
| .6 | 1.3 | 1.0 | | | .7 | | 1.5 | 1.2 | .9 |
| 1.0 | 2.2 | 1.9 | | | 3.3 | | 1.7 | 2.0 | 1.5 |
| .7 | 1.3 | 1.2 | Sales/Total Assets | | 1.0 | | 1.3 | 1.1 | 1.2 |
| .5 | .9 | .7 | | | .5 | | .8 | .8 | .6 |
| 6.4 | 3.6 | 6.9 | | | | | 2.8 | 8.4 | 7.0 |
| (21)  12.9 | (45)  8.9 | (53)  9.2 | % Depr., Dep., Amort./Sales | | (15)  8.0 | | (13)  9.2 | (18)  9.4 | |
| 17.7 | 12.2 | 16.5 | | | | | 17.3 | 14.1 | 13.7 |
| | .5 | .9 | % Officers', Directors' | | | | | | |
| (21)  1.5 | (27)  1.7 | Owners' Comp/Sales | | | | | | | |
| | 3.2 | 3.1 | | | | | | | |
| 767033M | 1614526M | 1432373M | Net Sales ($) | 1181M | 20602M | 20638M | 126696M | 291591M | 971665M |
| 1308712M | 1477410M | 1598588M | Total Assets ($) | 394M | 50041M | 16028M | 104601M | 255047M | 1172477M |

© RMA 2024  M = $ thousand  MM = $ million
See Pages viii through xx for Explanation of Ratios and Data

# TRANSPORTATION—All Other Transit and Ground Passenger Transportation   NAICS 485999

**Current Data Sorted by Assets** | **Comparative Historical Data**

| | | | | | | Type of Statement | | |
|---|---|---|---|---|---|---|---|---|
| | | 1 | 1 | 2 | | Unqualified | 8 | 4 |
| | | | | 1 | 1 | Reviewed | 3 | 2 |
| | | 3 | | | | Compiled | 1 | 5 |
| 2 | 3 | 1 | | | | Tax Returns | 8 | 2 |
| 6 | 3 | 10 | 6 | | 1 | Other | 26 | 11 |
| | 4 (4/1-9/30/23) | | 37 (10/1/23-3/31/24) | | | | 4/1/19-3/31/20 ALL | 4/1/20-3/31/21 ALL |
| 0-500M | 500M-2MM | 2-10MM | 10-50MM | 50-100MM | 100-250MM | | | |
| 9 | 6 | 15 | 9 | | 2 | **NUMBER OF STATEMENTS** | 46 | 24 |
| % | % | % | % | % | % | **ASSETS** | % | % |
| | | 29.8 | | | | Cash & Equivalents | 15.9 | 23.0 |
| | | 19.1 | | | | Trade Receivables (net) | 17.0 | 17.9 |
| | | .1 | D | | | Inventory | .5 | 1.6 |
| | | 2.0 | A | | | All Other Current | 6.1 | 6.0 |
| | | 51.0 | T | | | Total Current | 39.5 | 48.5 |
| | | 24.6 | A | | | Fixed Assets (net) | 43.1 | 41.9 |
| | | 5.0 | | | | Intangibles (net) | 8.7 | 5.6 |
| | | 19.3 | N | | | All Other Non-Current | 8.7 | 4.0 |
| | | 100.0 | O | | | Total | 100.0 | 100.0 |
| | | | T | | | **LIABILITIES** | | |
| | | 4.9 | | | | Notes Payable-Short Term | 9.0 | 5.2 |
| | | 4.6 | A | | | Cur. Mat.-L.T.D. | 9.1 | 4.2 |
| | | 2.9 | V | | | Trade Payables | 4.6 | 9.8 |
| | | .0 | A | | | Income Taxes Payable | .2 | .7 |
| | | 6.8 | I | | | All Other Current | 14.4 | 9.2 |
| | | 19.2 | L | | | Total Current | 37.5 | 29.2 |
| | | 31.3 | A | | | Long-Term Debt | 48.1 | 31.9 |
| | | .0 | B | | | Deferred Taxes | .8 | .5 |
| | | 1.5 | L | | | All Other Non-Current | 1.3 | 1.0 |
| | | 48.0 | E | | | Net Worth | 12.3 | 37.4 |
| | | 100.0 | | | | Total Liabilities & Net Worth | 100.0 | 100.0 |
| | | | | | | **INCOME DATA** | | |
| | | 100.0 | | | | Net Sales | 100.0 | 100.0 |
| | | | | | | Gross Profit | | |
| | | 91.7 | | | | Operating Expenses | 94.2 | 86.9 |
| | | 8.3 | | | | Operating Profit | 5.8 | 13.1 |
| | | -1.1 | | | | All Other Expenses (net) | 1.6 | 2.4 |
| | | 9.5 | | | | Profit Before Taxes | 4.1 | 10.7 |
| | | | | | | **RATIOS** | | |
| | | 4.9 | | | | | 2.0 | 2.6 |
| | | 2.6 | | | | Current | 1.3 | 1.7 |
| | | 1.6 | | | | | .7 | 1.0 |
| | | 4.8 | | | | | 1.8 | 2.5 |
| | | 2.6 | | | | Quick | 1.1 | 1.5 |
| | | 1.6 | | | | | .4 | .7 |
| | 4 | 94.0 | | | | | 10  36.3 | 0  UND |
| | 23 | 15.8 | | | | Sales/Receivables | 29  12.7 | 25  14.8 |
| | 43 | 8.5 | | | | | 47  7.8 | 47  7.7 |
| | | | | | | Cost of Sales/Inventory | | |
| | | | | | | Cost of Sales/Payables | | |
| | | 6.2 | | | | | 10.0 | 6.4 |
| | | 7.5 | | | | Sales/Working Capital | 41.9 | 11.3 |
| | | 16.8 | | | | | -15.4 | NM |
| | | 50.7 | | | | | 14.3 | 13.4 |
| | (12) | 12.0 | | | | EBIT/Interest | (41)  3.5 | (20)  4.1 |
| | | 5.0 | | | | | 1.1 | 1.1 |
| | | | | | | Net Profit + Depr., Dep., Amort./Cur. Mat. L/T/D | | |
| | | .1 | | | | | .7 | .4 |
| | | .6 | | | | Fixed/Worth | 2.7 | 1.2 |
| | | 1.1 | | | | | -12.8 | 3.4 |
| | | .2 | | | | | .9 | 1.1 |
| | | 1.1 | | | | Debt/Worth | 3.5 | 2.2 |
| | | 8.5 | | | | | -7.2 | 4.8 |
| | | 61.4 | | | | | 79.8 | 61.0 |
| | (13) | 38.1 | | | | % Profit Before Taxes/Tangible Net Worth | (31)  37.3 | (21)  14.9 |
| | | 9.5 | | | | | 1.2 | 8.2 |
| | | 43.3 | | | | | 18.2 | 12.0 |
| | | 17.5 | | | | % Profit Before Taxes/Total Assets | 8.6 | 6.5 |
| | | .7 | | | | | -.7 | 1.3 |
| | | 344.1 | | | | | 12.3 | 26.3 |
| | | 13.7 | | | | Sales/Net Fixed Assets | 5.3 | 5.6 |
| | | 4.1 | | | | | 1.9 | 1.1 |
| | | 3.9 | | | | | 3.8 | 3.4 |
| | | 2.4 | | | | Sales/Total Assets | 1.9 | 1.7 |
| | | 1.6 | | | | | .9 | .6 |
| | | | | | | | 4.2 | 1.5 |
| | | | | | | % Depr., Dep., Amort./Sales | (28)  7.5 | (14)  7.4 |
| | | | | | | | 11.3 | 10.1 |
| | | | | | | | | 1.5 |
| | | | | | | % Officers', Directors' Owners' Comp/Sales | (13)  4.7 | |
| | | | | | | | | 9.2 |
| 13389M | 45029M | 188826M | 413319M | | 720983M | Net Sales ($) | 1497397M | 805459M |
| 1215M | 8563M | 78029M | 236346M | | 452783M | Total Assets ($) | 883835M | 566647M |

M = $ thousand    MM = $ million
See Pages viii through xx for Explanation of Ratios and Data

© RMA 2024

## TRANSPORTATION—All Other Transit and Ground Passenger Transportation  NAICS 485999

### Comparative Historical Data / Current Data Sorted by Sales

| Comparative Historical Data | | | Type of Statement | Current Data Sorted by Sales | | | | | |
|---|---|---|---|---|---|---|---|---|---|
| 4 | 5 | 4 | Unqualified | 1 | | | 1 | 1 | 1 |
| | 2 | 2 | Reviewed | | | | | 1 | 1 |
| 4 | 3 | 3 | Compiled | | | 1 | | 2 | |
| 2 | 13 | 6 | Tax Returns | | | | 1 | 2 | |
| 13 | 23 | 26 | Other | 2 | 1 | | 1 | 10 | 5 |
| 4/1/21-3/31/22 ALL | 4/1/22-3/31/23 ALL | 4/1/23-3/31/24 ALL | | 4 (4/1-9/30/23) | | | | 37 (10/1/23-3/31/24) | |
| | | | | 0-1MM | 1-3MM | 3-5MM | 5-10MM | 10-25MM | 25MM & OVER |
| 23 | 46 | 41 | NUMBER OF STATEMENTS | 7 | 5 | 3 | 3 | 16 | 7 |
| % | % | % | ASSETS | % | % | % | % | % | % |
| 28.2 | 22.8 | 27.0 | Cash & Equivalents | | | | | 39.3 | |
| 19.9 | 12.1 | 12.8 | Trade Receivables (net) | | | | | 15.7 | |
| .3 | 2.7 | .2 | Inventory | | | | | .1 | |
| 2.8 | 6.2 | 2.2 | All Other Current | | | | | 3.1 | |
| 51.2 | 43.8 | 42.1 | Total Current | | | | | 58.3 | |
| 35.3 | 32.0 | 31.9 | Fixed Assets (net) | | | | | 25.7 | |
| 2.9 | 6.7 | 3.6 | Intangibles (net) | | | | | 4.5 | |
| 10.7 | 17.5 | 22.2 | All Other Non-Current | | | | | 11.5 | |
| 100.0 | 100.0 | 100.0 | Total | | | | | 100.0 | |
| | | | LIABILITIES | | | | | | |
| 2.8 | 5.2 | 5.3 | Notes Payable-Short Term | | | | | 4.8 | |
| 8.7 | 5.3 | 3.8 | Cur. Mat.-L.T.D. | | | | | 3.6 | |
| 5.8 | 5.4 | 3.9 | Trade Payables | | | | | 3.1 | |
| .0 | .0 | .0 | Income Taxes Payable | | | | | .0 | |
| 14.7 | 13.9 | 17.3 | All Other Current | | | | | 7.5 | |
| 32.0 | 29.7 | 30.3 | Total Current | | | | | 19.0 | |
| 33.6 | 29.7 | 31.6 | Long-Term Debt | | | | | 19.8 | |
| .5 | .5 | .0 | Deferred Taxes | | | | | .0 | |
| 20.0 | 16.1 | 3.1 | All Other Non-Current | | | | | 4.6 | |
| 13.9 | 24.1 | 35.1 | Net Worth | | | | | 56.6 | |
| 100.0 | 100.0 | 100.0 | Total Liabilities & Net Worth | | | | | 100.0 | |
| | | | INCOME DATA | | | | | | |
| 100.0 | 100.0 | 100.0 | Net Sales | | | | | 100.0 | |
| | | | Gross Profit | | | | | | |
| 92.8 | 88.2 | 87.4 | Operating Expenses | | | | | 92.4 | |
| 7.2 | 11.8 | 12.6 | Operating Profit | | | | | 7.6 | |
| 2.1 | 1.0 | .5 | All Other Expenses (net) | | | | | -.4 | |
| 5.2 | 10.8 | 12.1 | Profit Before Taxes | | | | | 8.1 | |
| | | | RATIOS | | | | | | |
| 3.9 | 3.7 | 3.8 | | | | | | 15.3 | |
| 2.2 | 1.6 | 1.9 | Current | | | | | 2.5 | |
| .7 | .8 | 1.0 | | | | | | 1.6 | |
| 3.9 | 3.4 | 3.7 | | | | | | 14.8 | |
| 2.1 | 1.4 | 1.7 | Quick | | | | | 2.2 | |
| .6 | .5 | .8 | | | | | | 1.4 | |
| 9  41.7 | 0  UND | 0  964.1 | | | | | | 0  991.0 | |
| 27  13.5 | 17  21.5 | 19  18.8 | Sales/Receivables | | | | | 17  21.5 | |
| 51  7.2 | 41  8.9 | 38  9.5 | | | | | | 40  9.1 | |
| | | | Cost of Sales/Inventory | | | | | | |
| | | | Cost of Sales/Payables | | | | | | |
| 5.7 | 5.2 | 7.1 | | | | | | 6.2 | |
| 12.6 | 24.1 | 16.4 | Sales/Working Capital | | | | | 11.0 | |
| -20.4 | -28.8 | UND | | | | | | 17.3 | |
| 76.8 | 15.0 | 18.6 | | | | | | 60.6 | |
| (20) 9.3 | (35) 6.2 | (32) 10.9 | EBIT/Interest | | | | | (11) 13.8 | |
| 2.5 | 2.0 | 2.6 | | | | | | 3.8 | |
| | | | Net Profit + Depr., Dep., Amort./Cur. Mat. L/T/D | | | | | | |
| .4 | .2 | .3 | | | | | | .0 | |
| 2.0 | .9 | .9 | Fixed/Worth | | | | | .6 | |
| 12.9 | 4.5 | 11.5 | | | | | | 1.4 | |
| 1.1 | .8 | .3 | | | | | | .1 | |
| 4.6 | 2.7 | 1.1 | Debt/Worth | | | | | .8 | |
| 24.6 | -22.5 | 22.9 | | | | | | 3.2 | |
| 100.5 | 91.0 | 72.9 | | | | | | 71.5 | |
| (20) 56.8 | (33) 46.2 | (34) 46.1 | % Profit Before Taxes/Tangible Net Worth | | | | | (14) 41.8 | |
| -3.2 | 6.4 | 20.1 | | | | | | 20.1 | |
| 41.5 | 33.8 | 44.1 | | | | | | 53.1 | |
| 7.6 | 10.8 | 14.6 | % Profit Before Taxes/Total Assets | | | | | 26.1 | |
| 1.0 | 2.1 | 2.5 | | | | | | 8.6 | |
| 29.1 | 49.1 | 44.3 | | | | | | 999.8 | |
| 9.7 | 11.7 | 8.0 | Sales/Net Fixed Assets | | | | | 13.8 | |
| 2.7 | 2.4 | 2.9 | | | | | | 4.5 | |
| 3.8 | 3.5 | 3.7 | | | | | | 4.5 | |
| 2.9 | 1.9 | 2.1 | Sales/Total Assets | | | | | 2.9 | |
| 1.1 | 1.1 | 1.6 | | | | | | 1.8 | |
| .4 | 1.3 | 1.6 | | | | | | | |
| (11) 11.0 | (21) 6.1 | (13) 3.7 | % Depr., Dep., Amort./Sales | | | | | | |
| 15.4 | 8.8 | 8.1 | | | | | | | |
| | 2.2 | .8 | | | | | | | |
| | (10) 4.8 | (11) 2.0 | % Officers', Directors' Owners' Comp/Sales | | | | | | |
| | 7.1 | 3.6 | | | | | | | |
| 649072M | 1069124M | 1381546M | Net Sales ($) | 1383M | 10938M | 13335M | 24470M | 271689M | 1059731M |
| 328014M | 778645M | 776936M | Total Assets ($) | 898M | 6529M | 12174M | 18453M | 113877M | 625005M |

© RMA 2024   M = $ thousand   MM = $ million
See Pages viii through xx for Explanation of Ratios and Data

## TRANSPORTATION—Other Airport Operations  NAICS 488119

### Current Data Sorted by Assets / Comparative Historical Data

| | | | | | | Type of Statement | | |
|---|---|---|---|---|---|---|---|---|
| | | | 2 | | | Unqualified | 10 | 4 |
| | | | 2 | 1 | | Reviewed | 3 | 1 |
| | | 1 | | | | Compiled | 1 | 1 |
| 1 | 1 | 9 | 7 | 4 | 3 | Tax Returns | 4 | 2 |
| 2 | 5 (4/1-9/30/23) | | 28 (10/1/23-3/31/24) | | | Other | 24 | 21 |
| 0-500M | 500M-2MM | 2-10MM | 10-50MM | 50-100MM | 100-250MM | | 4/1/19-3/31/20 ALL | 4/1/20-3/31/21 ALL |
| 3 | 1 | 10 | 11 | 5 | 3 | NUMBER OF STATEMENTS | 42 | 29 |
| % | % | % | % | % | % | ASSETS | % | % |
| | | 24.4 | 12.3 | | | Cash & Equivalents | 14.2 | 11.8 |
| | | 11.2 | 9.4 | | | Trade Receivables (net) | 13.0 | 5.1 |
| | | 7.3 | 14.1 | | | Inventory | 7.1 | 2.0 |
| | | 2.2 | 1.8 | | | All Other Current | 3.5 | 2.9 |
| | | 45.1 | 37.6 | | | Total Current | 37.8 | 21.8 |
| | | 42.0 | 51.3 | | | Fixed Assets (net) | 49.4 | 62.5 |
| | | 9.1 | 7.2 | | | Intangibles (net) | 6.9 | 9.2 |
| | | 3.8 | 3.8 | | | All Other Non-Current | 5.8 | 6.5 |
| | | 100.0 | 100.0 | | | Total | 100.0 | 100.0 |
| | | | | | | LIABILITIES | | |
| | | .2 | 3.2 | | | Notes Payable-Short Term | 5.1 | 6.8 |
| | | 1.3 | 1.8 | | | Cur. Mat.-L.T.D. | 4.3 | 2.9 |
| | | 10.0 | 5.7 | | | Trade Payables | 7.4 | 4.0 |
| | | .0 | .1 | | | Income Taxes Payable | .1 | .1 |
| | | 6.2 | 8.8 | | | All Other Current | 8.5 | 4.5 |
| | | 17.8 | 19.7 | | | Total Current | 25.4 | 18.3 |
| | | 44.7 | 31.9 | | | Long-Term Debt | 30.0 | 36.8 |
| | | .0 | .0 | | | Deferred Taxes | .7 | .3 |
| | | 8.2 | 6.8 | | | All Other Non-Current | 7.2 | 6.8 |
| | | 29.2 | 41.6 | | | Net Worth | 36.7 | 37.8 |
| | | 100.0 | 100.0 | | | Total Liabilities & Net Worth | 100.0 | 100.0 |
| | | | | | | INCOME DATA | | |
| | | 100.0 | 100.0 | | | Net Sales | 100.0 | 100.0 |
| | | | | | | Gross Profit | | |
| | | 85.2 | 91.1 | | | Operating Expenses | 93.5 | 87.3 |
| | | 14.8 | 8.9 | | | Operating Profit | 6.5 | 12.7 |
| | | 3.2 | 2.7 | | | All Other Expenses (net) | 4.3 | 7.4 |
| | | 11.6 | 6.1 | | | Profit Before Taxes | 2.2 | 5.2 |
| | | | | | | RATIOS | | |
| | | 7.5 | 2.0 | | | | 2.3 | 4.1 |
| | | 2.5 | 1.5 | | | Current | 1.7 | 1.3 |
| | | 1.1 | 1.2 | | | | .8 | .7 |
| | | 5.6 | 1.7 | | | | 1.7 | 2.4 |
| | | 2.1 | .6 | | | Quick | 1.1 | 1.0 |
| | | .8 | .4 | | | | .6 | .5 |
| | 0 | UND | 7 | 51.1 | | | 5 | 77.7 | 0 | UND |
| | 10 | 36.7 | 11 | 31.9 | | Sales/Receivables | 18 | 20.5 | 11 | 33.2 |
| | 32 | 11.4 | 32 | 11.4 | | | 32 | 11.4 | 27 | 13.5 |
| | | | | | | Cost of Sales/Inventory | | |
| | | | | | | Cost of Sales/Payables | | |
| | | 3.6 | 6.8 | | | | 4.4 | 3.7 |
| | | 14.4 | 8.5 | | | Sales/Working Capital | 10.1 | 19.7 |
| | | NM | 15.6 | | | | -50.5 | -9.6 |
| | | | 7.3 | | | | 6.9 | 7.4 |
| | | (10) | 2.6 | | | EBIT/Interest | (39) 3.3 | (22) 1.7 |
| | | | -1.0 | | | | .7 | -.3 |
| | | | | | | Net Profit + Depr., Dep., Amort./Cur. Mat. L/T/D | 4.6 | |
| | | | | | | | (15) 3.4 | |
| | | | | | | | 1.7 | |
| | | .3 | .1 | | | | .6 | 1.2 |
| | | 1.9 | 1.3 | | | Fixed/Worth | 1.4 | 2.5 |
| | | NM | 3.0 | | | | 3.6 | 5.1 |
| | | 1.0 | .8 | | | | .7 | .6 |
| | | 2.0 | 2.1 | | | Debt/Worth | 1.8 | 3.2 |
| | | NM | 4.0 | | | | 4.3 | 7.2 |
| | | | 39.3 | | | | 33.3 | 38.5 |
| | | | 19.9 | | | % Profit Before Taxes/Tangible Net Worth | (35) 22.1 | (27) 13.4 |
| | | | -2.0 | | | | .5 | -2.3 |
| | | 33.8 | 7.8 | | | | 15.1 | 9.4 |
| | | 3.8 | 5.7 | | | % Profit Before Taxes/Total Assets | 4.2 | 2.7 |
| | | -3.7 | -1.1 | | | | -.7 | -1.4 |
| | | 31.7 | 122.5 | | | | 8.9 | 2.0 |
| | | 3.9 | .8 | | | Sales/Net Fixed Assets | 3.8 | .8 |
| | | 1.6 | .3 | | | | 1.0 | .2 |
| | | 3.2 | 2.0 | | | | 2.6 | 1.2 |
| | | 1.2 | .5 | | | Sales/Total Assets | 1.3 | .6 |
| | | .6 | .3 | | | | .6 | .2 |
| | | | | | | | 1.9 | 5.5 |
| | | | | | | % Depr., Dep., Amort./Sales | (37) 5.4 | (25) 9.9 |
| | | | | | | | 8.9 | 19.0 |
| | | | | | | % Officers', Directors' Owners' Comp/Sales | | |
| 9540M | 2598M | 79263M | 321181M | 154917M | 441765M | Net Sales ($) | 2061350M | 846873M |
| 572M | 1409M | 46844M | 262249M | 378896M | 571893M | Total Assets ($) | 1579170M | 827545M |

M = $ thousand     MM = $ million

© RMA 2024

## TRANSPORTATION—Other Airport Operations  NAICS 488119

### Comparative Historical Data / Current Data Sorted by Sales

| | | | | | Type of Statement | | | | | | |
|---|---|---|---|---|---|---|---|---|---|---|---|
| | 3 | | 6 | 2 | Unqualified | | | | | 1 | 1 |
| | 2 | | 5 | 3 | Reviewed | | | | 1 | 1 | 1 |
| | | | 2 | | Compiled | | | | | | |
| | 1 | | 8 | 3 | Tax Returns | 1 | 2 | | | | |
| | 20 | | 35 | 25 | Other | | 5 | 2 | 6 | 4 | 8 |
| | 4/1/21- | | 4/1/22- | 4/1/23- | | | 5 (4/1-9/30/23) | | 28 (10/1/23-3/31/24) | | |
| | 3/31/22 | | 3/31/23 | 3/31/24 | | 0-1MM | 1-3MM | 3-5MM | 5-10MM | 10-25MM | 25MM & OVER |
| | ALL | | ALL | ALL | NUMBER OF STATEMENTS | | | | | | |
| | 26 | | 56 | 33 | | 1 | 7 | 3 | 6 | 6 | 10 |
| | % | | % | % | ASSETS | % | % | % | % | % | % |
| | 14.5 | | 14.7 | 18.7 | Cash & Equivalents | | | | | | 14.8 |
| | 4.8 | | 9.5 | 8.4 | Trade Receivables (net) | | | | | | 12.7 |
| | 8.4 | | 9.4 | 7.2 | Inventory | | | | | | 9.7 |
| | 7.6 | | 5.3 | 6.2 | All Other Current | | | | | | 2.6 |
| | 35.4 | | 38.9 | 40.5 | Total Current | | | | | | 39.9 |
| | 51.2 | | 48.2 | 48.1 | Fixed Assets (net) | | | | | | 40.7 |
| | 5.9 | | 3.4 | 5.4 | Intangibles (net) | | | | | | 8.0 |
| | 7.6 | | 9.5 | 6.0 | All Other Non-Current | | | | | | 11.4 |
| | 100.0 | | 100.0 | 100.0 | Total | | | | | | 100.0 |
| | | | | | LIABILITIES | | | | | | |
| | 5.0 | | 4.2 | 4.0 | Notes Payable-Short Term | | | | | | 4.2 |
| | 2.4 | | 2.8 | 2.0 | Cur. Mat.-L.T.D. | | | | | | 3.7 |
| | 6.8 | | 5.1 | 9.9 | Trade Payables | | | | | | 7.2 |
| | .0 | | .0 | .2 | Income Taxes Payable | | | | | | .2 |
| | 8.1 | | 10.4 | 16.0 | All Other Current | | | | | | 10.6 |
| | 22.3 | | 22.6 | 32.2 | Total Current | | | | | | 26.0 |
| | 32.6 | | 31.2 | 38.5 | Long-Term Debt | | | | | | 29.7 |
| | .0 | | .2 | .1 | Deferred Taxes | | | | | | .5 |
| | 3.9 | | 8.2 | 7.0 | All Other Non-Current | | | | | | 7.7 |
| | 41.3 | | 37.8 | 22.3 | Net Worth | | | | | | 36.2 |
| | 100.0 | | 100.0 | 100.0 | Total Liabilties & Net Worth | | | | | | 100.0 |
| | | | | | INCOME DATA | | | | | | |
| | 100.0 | | 100.0 | 100.0 | Net Sales | | | | | | 100.0 |
| | | | | | Gross Profit | | | | | | |
| | 90.9 | | 89.0 | 89.9 | Operating Expenses | | | | | | 94.3 |
| | 9.1 | | 11.0 | 10.1 | Operating Profit | | | | | | 5.7 |
| | .1 | | 2.3 | 2.3 | All Other Expenses (net) | | | | | | 1.6 |
| | 8.9 | | 8.6 | 7.7 | Profit Before Taxes | | | | | | 4.1 |
| | | | | | RATIOS | | | | | | |
| | 2.5 | | 4.5 | 3.4 | | | | | | | 2.0 |
| | 1.7 | | 1.9 | 1.6 | Current | | | | | | 1.3 |
| | 1.1 | | 1.0 | .7 | | | | | | | .5 |
| | 1.8 | | 3.1 | 2.1 | | | | | | | 1.7 |
| | .9 | | 1.2 | .8 | Quick | | | | | | .6 |
| | .3 | | .5 | .4 | | | | | | | .3 |
| 1 | 444.7 | 2 | 190.1 | 1 355.6 | | | | | | 6 | 61.4 |
| 10 | 35.3 | 17 | 22.0 | 11 33.6 | Sales/Receivables | | | | | 24 | 14.9 |
| 19 | 19.4 | 34 | 10.8 | 29 12.6 | | | | | | 42 | 8.6 |
| | | | | | Cost of Sales/Inventory | | | | | | |
| | | | | | Cost of Sales/Payables | | | | | | |
| | 4.8 | | 3.7 | 5.4 | | | | | | | 6.5 |
| | 12.3 | | 8.4 | 15.0 | Sales/Working Capital | | | | | | 24.2 |
| | 26.1 | | NM | -33.3 | | | | | | | -8.8 |
| | 41.4 | | 13.5 | 6.5 | | | | | | | |
| (23) | 4.0 | (44) | 3.9 | (28) 1.8 | EBIT/Interest | | | | | | |
| | .8 | | -.9 | -.5 | | | | | | | |
| | | | | | Net Profit + Depr., Dep., Amort./Cur. Mat. L/T/D | | | | | | |
| | .9 | | .6 | .3 | | | | | | | .1 |
| | 1.7 | | 1.4 | 2.6 | Fixed/Worth | | | | | | 1.5 |
| | NM | | 5.0 | 10.2 | | | | | | | NM |
| | .6 | | .6 | 1.0 | | | | | | | 1.1 |
| | 1.9 | | 1.7 | 2.1 | Debt/Worth | | | | | | 3.2 |
| | NM | | 15.3 | 14.6 | | | | | | | NM |
| | 63.0 | | 38.8 | 39.3 | % Profit Before Taxes/Tangible Net Worth | | | | | | |
| (20) | 22.2 | (47) | 16.9 | (27) 11.3 | | | | | | | |
| | .4 | | .0 | -.1 | | | | | | | |
| | 26.2 | | 18.5 | 12.1 | % Profit Before Taxes/Total Assets | | | | | | 17.9 |
| | 6.4 | | 5.9 | 4.9 | | | | | | | 2.4 |
| | .4 | | -.4 | -.5 | | | | | | | -1.0 |
| | 9.4 | | 13.2 | 31.3 | | | | | | | 125.5 |
| | 2.0 | | 2.7 | 2.1 | Sales/Net Fixed Assets | | | | | | 5.4 |
| | .3 | | .7 | .5 | | | | | | | .8 |
| | 2.0 | | 1.9 | 2.4 | | | | | | | 2.4 |
| | .8 | | 1.0 | .9 | Sales/Total Assets | | | | | | .9 |
| | .3 | | .6 | .4 | | | | | | | .4 |
| | 2.5 | | 2.0 | 1.1 | | | | | | | |
| (20) | 5.1 | (38) | 4.7 | (16) 2.9 | % Depr., Dep., Amort./Sales | | | | | | |
| | 11.6 | | 10.0 | 6.3 | | | | | | | |
| | | | | | % Officers', Directors' Owners' Comp/Sales | | | | | | |
| | 693539M | | 1717610M | 1009264M | Net Sales ($) | 743M | 16317M | 12706M | 49620M | 107572M | 822306M |
| | 684319M | | 1888775M | 1261863M | Total Assets ($) | 2285M | 107550M | 40677M | 41515M | 155664M | 914172M |

© RMA 2024  M = $ thousand  MM = $ million
See Pages viii through xx for Explanation of Ratios and Data

# TRANSPORTATION—Other Support Activities for Air Transportation  NAICS 488190

## Current Data Sorted by Assets | Comparative Historical Data

| | | | | | | | | | | |
|---|---|---|---|---|---|---|---|---|---|---|
| | | | | 2 | 2 | 8 | **Type of Statement** | | | |
| 1 | | 2 | 6 | 1 | | Unqualified | 12 | 3 | | |
| | 1 | 3 | 2 | | | Reviewed | 6 | 2 | | |
| | 4 | 6 | 1 | | | Compiled | 4 | 1 | | |
| 5 | 9 | 23 | 15 | 9 | 5 | Tax Returns | 7 | 7 | | |
| | 13 (4/1-9/30/23) | | 92 (10/1/23-3/31/24) | | | Other | 54 | 34 | | |
| 0-500M | 500M-2MM | 2-10MM | 10-50MM | 50-100MM | 100-250MM | | 4/1/19-3/31/20 ALL | 4/1/20-3/31/21 ALL | | |
| 6 | 14 | 34 | 26 | 12 | 13 | **NUMBER OF STATEMENTS** | 83 | 47 | | |
| % | % | % | % | % | % | **ASSETS** | % | % | | |
| | 43.8 | 18.2 | 11.9 | 10.8 | 5.7 | Cash & Equivalents | 13.5 | 19.2 | | |
| | 11.4 | 14.7 | 20.2 | 22.9 | 26.8 | Trade Receivables (net) | 20.2 | 19.1 | | |
| | 13.9 | 17.3 | 15.3 | 37.2 | 12.3 | Inventory | 17.2 | 20.4 | | |
| | 2.5 | 5.9 | 3.4 | 1.9 | 6.2 | All Other Current | 3.9 | 4.1 | | |
| | 71.5 | 56.0 | 50.8 | 72.8 | 51.0 | Total Current | 54.8 | 62.9 | | |
| | 9.3 | 22.1 | 33.8 | 14.1 | 25.2 | Fixed Assets (net) | 26.6 | 22.8 | | |
| | .5 | 8.6 | 8.7 | 4.2 | 17.7 | Intangibles (net) | 7.8 | 6.0 | | |
| | 18.7 | 13.3 | 6.8 | 8.9 | 6.1 | All Other Non-Current | 10.8 | 8.4 | | |
| | 100.0 | 100.0 | 100.0 | 100.0 | 100.0 | Total | 100.0 | 100.0 | | |
| | | | | | | **LIABILITIES** | | | | |
| | 3.3 | 8.9 | 8.7 | 14.0 | 6.8 | Notes Payable-Short Term | 7.0 | 9.3 | | |
| | 6.3 | 2.1 | 2.5 | 3.9 | 4.1 | Cur. Mat.-L.T.D. | 3.9 | 2.2 | | |
| | 4.1 | 6.8 | 7.5 | 8.9 | 7.5 | Trade Payables | 10.5 | 9.4 | | |
| | .0 | .0 | .1 | .0 | .0 | Income Taxes Payable | .1 | .1 | | |
| | 16.3 | 8.2 | 8.6 | 14.0 | 13.0 | All Other Current | 14.1 | 15.0 | | |
| | 30.0 | 26.1 | 27.5 | 40.7 | 31.3 | Total Current | 35.6 | 36.0 | | |
| | 24.6 | 19.7 | 23.6 | 11.6 | 28.1 | Long-Term Debt | 24.7 | 28.9 | | |
| | .0 | .1 | .7 | .0 | .2 | Deferred Taxes | .4 | .1 | | |
| | .7 | 6.8 | 7.8 | 4.0 | 7.6 | All Other Non-Current | 3.7 | 5.7 | | |
| | 44.7 | 47.3 | 40.5 | 43.6 | 32.9 | Net Worth | 35.6 | 29.3 | | |
| | 100.0 | 100.0 | 100.0 | 100.0 | 100.0 | Total Liabilities & Net Worth | 100.0 | 100.0 | | |
| | | | | | | **INCOME DATA** | | | | |
| | 100.0 | 100.0 | 100.0 | 100.0 | 100.0 | Net Sales | 100.0 | 100.0 | | |
| | | | | | | Gross Profit | | | | |
| | 75.6 | 84.9 | 91.2 | 89.0 | 92.5 | Operating Expenses | 90.7 | 95.9 | | |
| | 24.4 | 15.1 | 8.8 | 11.0 | 7.5 | Operating Profit | 9.3 | 4.1 | | |
| | -.3 | 2.0 | .5 | 1.3 | 2.1 | All Other Expenses (net) | 2.6 | .3 | | |
| | 24.6 | 13.2 | 8.3 | 9.7 | 5.4 | Profit Before Taxes | 6.7 | 3.8 | | |
| | | | | | | **RATIOS** | | | | |
| | 7.1 | 4.6 | 3.1 | 2.0 | 2.9 | | 2.7 | 3.5 | | |
| | 3.2 | 2.3 | 2.0 | 1.8 | 1.8 | Current | 1.7 | 2.3 | | |
| | 1.4 | 1.5 | 1.0 | 1.5 | 1.1 | | 1.1 | 1.2 | | |
| | 6.5 | 3.7 | 2.5 | 1.0 | 1.7 | | 1.8 | 2.5 | | |
| | 1.9 | 1.2 | 1.0 | .6 | 1.0 | Quick | 1.0 | 1.2 | | |
| | 1.3 | .5 | .5 | .5 | .6 | | .6 | .6 | | |
| 0 UND | 12 30.5 | 13 27.1 | 31 11.7 | 38 9.6 | | | 19 19.3 | 16 22.5 | | |
| 2 161.1 | 24 15.2 | 35 10.4 | 49 7.5 | 47 7.7 | | Sales/Receivables | 40 9.2 | 36 10.2 | | |
| 12 30.3 | 61 6.0 | 69 5.3 | 79 4.6 | 54 6.8 | | | 59 6.2 | 49 7.4 | | |
| | | | | | | Cost of Sales/Inventory | | | | |
| | | | | | | Cost of Sales/Payables | | | | |
| | 3.6 | 3.0 | 3.9 | 3.9 | 5.0 | | 4.4 | 4.4 | | |
| | 9.8 | 4.5 | 5.8 | 4.8 | 10.4 | Sales/Working Capital | 7.7 | 7.4 | | |
| | 19.6 | 14.1 | NM | 5.7 | 34.6 | | 58.0 | 47.8 | | |
| | 231.9 | 13.5 | 22.7 | | 6.4 | | 10.5 | 11.9 | | |
| (10) 20.7 | (24) 7.2 | (24) 5.7 | | (12) 4.2 | | EBIT/Interest | (73) 4.9 | (43) 3.4 | | |
| | 9.2 | 2.5 | 3.2 | | 2.2 | | 1.8 | .0 | | |
| | | | | | | Net Profit + Depr., Dep., | 4.5 | | | |
| | | | | | | Amort./Cur. Mat. L/T/D | (14) 2.0 | | | |
| | | | | | | | .5 | | | |
| | .0 | .1 | .2 | .1 | .7 | | .2 | .2 | | |
| | .1 | .3 | 1.2 | .2 | 2.7 | Fixed/Worth | .8 | .5 | | |
| | .3 | 1.1 | 2.9 | .9 | NM | | 3.9 | 10.6 | | |
| | .2 | .6 | 1.0 | .9 | 2.3 | | .8 | .6 | | |
| | .9 | 1.7 | 1.7 | 1.2 | 4.9 | Debt/Worth | 1.6 | 2.0 | | |
| | 3.7 | 3.8 | 4.1 | 2.4 | NM | | 8.6 | -23.7 | | |
| | 120.7 | 54.7 | 48.6 | 53.6 | 89.4 | | 46.6 | 84.2 | | |
| (13) 76.8 | (32) 36.5 | (23) 38.5 | 31.0 | (10) 39.9 | | % Profit Before Taxes/Tangible Net Worth | (68) 23.2 | (35) 25.3 | | |
| | 48.8 | 10.3 | 13.3 | 26.4 | 20.0 | | 11.1 | 3.6 | | |
| | 63.5 | 24.0 | 16.7 | 19.0 | 11.4 | | 16.7 | 24.3 | | |
| | 53.5 | 12.4 | 9.7 | 14.0 | 6.4 | % Profit Before Taxes/Total Assets | 7.9 | 4.1 | | |
| | 24.2 | 4.5 | 5.3 | 8.5 | 3.6 | | 2.0 | -.6 | | |
| | UND | 71.0 | 47.0 | 43.8 | 14.9 | | 56.6 | 123.5 | | |
| | 101.6 | 8.9 | 6.1 | 17.3 | 8.2 | Sales/Net Fixed Assets | 11.6 | 12.8 | | |
| | 21.5 | 4.1 | 1.8 | 5.6 | 3.4 | | 2.9 | 4.4 | | |
| | 5.4 | 2.0 | 2.0 | 1.7 | 1.8 | | 2.9 | 3.6 | | |
| | 3.1 | 1.4 | 1.4 | 1.3 | 1.4 | Sales/Total Assets | 1.6 | 2.0 | | |
| | 1.3 | 1.0 | 1.0 | 1.1 | 1.1 | | .9 | 1.1 | | |
| | | .7 | .8 | | .6 | | .5 | .7 | | |
| | (22) 2.2 | (18) 2.1 | | (10) 1.7 | | % Depr., Dep., Amort./Sales | (58) 2.1 | (28) 2.1 | | |
| | | 6.4 | 7.9 | | 2.8 | | 4.3 | 3.2 | | |
| | | 3.4 | | | | | .7 | 1.3 | | |
| | (11) 3.7 | | | | | % Officers', Directors' Owners' Comp/Sales | (17) 1.7 | (13) 5.5 | | |
| | | 10.2 | | | | | 3.8 | 10.9 | | |
| 4266M | 61966M | 290718M | 1017185M | 1117585M | 4493320M | Net Sales ($) | 5974796M | 1866507M | | |
| 1502M | 17758M | 183990M | 725322M | 729330M | 2064558M | Total Assets ($) | 3129980M | 1227201M | | |

M = $ thousand    MM = $ million
See Pages viii through xx for Explanation of Ratios and Data

© RMA 2024

# TRANSPORTATION—Other Support Activities for Air Transportation  NAICS 488190

## Comparative Historical Data / Current Data Sorted by Sales

| | | | | | Type of Statement | | | | | | |
|---|---|---|---|---|---|---|---|---|---|---|---|
| | | 5 | | 4 | 12 | Unqualified | | | | 1 | 11 |
| | | 3 | | 9 | 10 | Reviewed | | | 1 | 4 | 5 |
| | | 1 | | 5 | 6 | Compiled | | | 2 | 1 | 2 |
| | | 6 | | 7 | 11 | Tax Returns | | | 1 | 4 | 2 |
| | | 30 | | 44 | 66 | Other | 3 | 1 | 4 | 2 | 25 |
| | | 4/1/21-3/31/22 ALL | | 4/1/22-3/31/23 ALL | 4/1/23-3/31/24 ALL | | 4 | 6 | 15 | 12 | |
| | | | | | | | | 13 (4/1-9/30/23) | | 92 (10/1/23-3/31/24) | |
| | | | | | | | 0-1MM | 1-3MM | 3-5MM | 5-10MM | 10-25MM | 25MM & OVER |
| | | 45 | | 69 | 105 | NUMBER OF STATEMENTS | 7 | 10 | 5 | 20 | 20 | 43 |
| | | % | | % | % | ASSETS | % | % | % | % | % | % |
| | | 16.6 | | 23.2 | 18.0 | Cash & Equivalents | | 36.5 | | 22.5 | 13.6 | 11.0 |
| | | 20.5 | | 13.4 | 18.7 | Trade Receivables (net) | | 15.0 | | 15.5 | 17.8 | 23.6 |
| | | 14.8 | | 12.4 | 17.3 | Inventory | | 10.5 | | 11.5 | 19.2 | 21.4 |
| | | 3.9 | | 5.3 | 4.2 | All Other Current | | .2 | | 10.0 | 2.0 | 4.3 |
| | | 55.8 | | 54.3 | 58.2 | Total Current | | 62.2 | | 59.5 | 52.5 | 60.2 |
| | | 28.3 | | 32.2 | 23.0 | Fixed Assets (net) | | 18.3 | | 13.2 | 33.4 | 22.1 |
| | | 7.0 | | 5.4 | 8.4 | Intangibles (net) | | 9.7 | | 9.1 | 4.6 | 10.3 |
| | | 8.8 | | 8.1 | 10.4 | All Other Non-Current | | 9.8 | | 18.3 | 9.5 | 7.3 |
| | | 100.0 | | 100.0 | 100.0 | Total | | 100.0 | | 100.0 | 100.0 | 100.0 |
| | | | | | | LIABILITIES | | | | | | |
| | | 12.9 | | 4.7 | 8.5 | Notes Payable-Short Term | | 8.2 | | 3.5 | 15.9 | 8.8 |
| | | 3.1 | | 2.1 | 3.1 | Cur. Mat.-L.T.D. | | 1.3 | | 4.9 | 2.8 | 3.2 |
| | | 9.6 | | 7.2 | 6.7 | Trade Payables | | 3.7 | | 5.0 | 7.8 | 8.5 |
| | | .1 | | .1 | .0 | Income Taxes Payable | | .0 | | .0 | .2 | .0 |
| | | 11.3 | | 16.3 | 13.0 | All Other Current | | 23.9 | | 9.6 | 8.0 | 12.1 |
| | | 36.9 | | 30.3 | 31.4 | Total Current | | 37.2 | | 23.1 | 34.7 | 32.5 |
| | | 20.9 | | 21.9 | 22.7 | Long-Term Debt | | 15.2 | | 19.9 | 21.8 | 20.0 |
| | | .1 | | .3 | .2 | Deferred Taxes | | .0 | | 1.0 | 1.8 | .1 |
| | | 8.2 | | 6.8 | 5.7 | All Other Non-Current | | 7.8 | | 4.4 | 3.6 | 7.9 |
| | | 33.8 | | 40.6 | 40.1 | Net Worth | | 39.8 | | 52.6 | 39.0 | 39.5 |
| | | 100.0 | | 100.0 | 100.0 | Total Liabilities & Net Worth | | 100.0 | | 100.0 | 100.0 | 100.0 |
| | | | | | | INCOME DATA | | | | | | |
| | | 100.0 | | 100.0 | 100.0 | Net Sales | | 100.0 | | 100.0 | 100.0 | 100.0 |
| | | | | | | Gross Profit | | | | | | |
| | | 91.7 | | 90.2 | 86.7 | Operating Expenses | | 83.2 | | 91.1 | 90.5 | 91.7 |
| | | 8.3 | | 9.8 | 13.3 | Operating Profit | | 16.8 | | 8.9 | 9.5 | 8.3 |
| | | -1.7 | | -.8 | 1.6 | All Other Expenses (net) | | 1.3 | | .3 | 1.0 | 1.0 |
| | | 10.0 | | 10.6 | 11.7 | Profit Before Taxes | | 15.5 | | 8.5 | 8.4 | 7.3 |
| | | | | | | RATIOS | | | | | | |
| | | 3.9 | | 4.3 | 3.5 | | | 13.4 | | 4.8 | 2.6 | 2.8 |
| | | 1.7 | | 2.4 | 2.0 | Current | | 3.3 | | 3.4 | 1.5 | 1.8 |
| | | 1.2 | | 1.1 | 1.2 | | | 1.0 | | 2.1 | .9 | 1.3 |
| | | 2.6 | | 3.4 | 2.5 | | | 10.9 | | 3.9 | 1.0 | 2.1 |
| | | 1.2 | | 1.4 | 1.0 | Quick | | 1.3 | | 1.9 | .8 | 1.0 |
| | | .7 | | .5 | .6 | | | .8 | | 1.3 | .4 | .6 |
| 17 | 22.1 | 4 | 92.9 | 10 | 35.5 | | 0 | UND | 2 | 169.7 | 14 | 25.2 | 23 | 15.9 |
| 38 | 9.5 | 24 | 15.1 | 31 | 11.8 | Sales/Receivables | 9 | 42.8 | 15 | 24.6 | 33 | 11.1 | 46 | 8.0 |
| 61 | 6.0 | 44 | 8.3 | 61 | 6.0 | | 31 | 11.9 | 50 | 7.3 | 62 | 5.9 | 64 | 5.7 |
| | | | | | | Cost of Sales/Inventory | | | | | | |
| | | | | | | Cost of Sales/Payables | | | | | | |
| | | 2.6 | | 3.1 | 3.5 | | | 3.2 | | 3.3 | 4.2 | 4.0 |
| | | 8.1 | | 7.3 | 5.7 | Sales/Working Capital | | 10.4 | | 5.3 | 10.7 | 5.6 |
| | | 29.8 | | 118.0 | 20.1 | | | NM | | 10.5 | -77.2 | 11.0 |
| | | 31.5 | | 26.7 | 19.0 | | | 47.5 | | 12.5 | 9.0 |
| (38) | 8.1 | (51) | 8.1 | (81) | 6.2 | EBIT/Interest | (14) | 12.1 | (19) | 6.1 | (37) | 5.0 |
| | | 2.2 | | 2.5 | 3.0 | | | 1.0 | | 2.3 | 3.1 |
| | | | | | 6.0 | Net Profit + Depr., Dep., | | | | | 6.0 |
| | | | | (15) | 3.9 | Amort./Cur. Mat. L/T/D | | | | | (11) | 4.4 |
| | | | | | 1.7 | | | | | | 1.9 |
| | | .3 | | .1 | .1 | | | .1 | | .0 | .2 | .1 |
| | | .8 | | .8 | .4 | Fixed/Worth | | .3 | | .2 | 1.0 | .5 |
| | | 3.3 | | 2.9 | 2.3 | | | 1.4 | | .4 | 1.7 | 2.9 |
| | | .6 | | .5 | .9 | | | .5 | | .4 | 1.0 | 1.0 |
| | | 1.8 | | 1.6 | 1.9 | Debt/Worth | | 4.9 | | .9 | 1.5 | 2.6 |
| | | 7.1 | | 4.4 | 5.5 | | | NM | | 2.3 | 7.5 | 4.9 |
| | | 68.0 | | 89.2 | 69.9 | % Profit Before Taxes/Tangible | | | | 99.1 | 48.1 | 52.3 |
| (35) | 42.5 | (60) | 23.4 | (93) | 39.8 | Net Worth | | | (19) | 43.2 | (18) | 27.1 | (39) | 33.4 |
| | | 12.6 | | 9.5 | 21.2 | | | | | 11.0 | 6.5 | 20.8 |
| | | 26.8 | | 20.7 | 22.6 | % Profit Before Taxes/Total | | 65.0 | | 31.7 | 19.9 | 15.3 |
| | | 13.1 | | 8.8 | 12.3 | Assets | | 16.8 | | 22.2 | 10.8 | 9.2 |
| | | 2.4 | | 2.4 | 5.1 | | | 5.8 | | 3.8 | .4 | 5.3 |
| | | 61.1 | | 49.2 | 89.6 | | | UND | | 900.4 | 22.5 | 36.9 |
| | | 11.8 | | 7.7 | 9.4 | Sales/Net Fixed Assets | | 23.2 | | 23.3 | 5.5 | 9.0 |
| | | 3.5 | | 2.1 | 3.9 | | | 4.0 | | 5.5 | 3.0 | 3.8 |
| | | 2.4 | | 2.4 | 2.2 | | | 2.8 | | 3.2 | 2.0 | 2.0 |
| | | 1.4 | | 1.4 | 1.5 | Sales/Total Assets | | 1.8 | | 1.9 | 1.6 | 1.4 |
| | | 1.0 | | .9 | 1.1 | | | .8 | | 1.1 | 1.3 | 1.0 |
| | | .6 | | .9 | .7 | | | | | .7 | .6 | .6 |
| (28) | 1.2 | (47) | 2.3 | (61) | 1.9 | % Depr., Dep., Amort./Sales | | | (11) | 2.7 | (15) | 2.1 | (31) | 1.7 |
| | | 4.3 | | 6.7 | 4.0 | | | | | 6.4 | 4.4 | 2.8 |
| | | | | 2.1 | 3.3 | % Officers', Directors' | | | | 2.5 | | |
| | | | (15) | 3.4 | (20) | 3.9 | Owners' Comp/Sales | | | (10) | 3.4 | | |
| | | | | 11.1 | 7.0 | | | | | 5.5 | | |
| | | 2656515M | | 3214931M | 6985040M | Net Sales ($) | 2804M | 17504M | 20159M | 146155M | 302920M | 6495498M |
| | | 1606807M | | 2081819M | 3722460M | Total Assets ($) | 7542M | 13438M | 9064M | 85119M | 211747M | 3395550M |

© RMA 2024  M = $ thousand  MM = $ million
See Pages viii through xx for Explanation of Ratios and Data

# TRANSPORTATION—Support Activities for Rail Transportation  NAICS 488210

## Current Data Sorted by Assets

| | | | | | | Type of Statement |
|---|---|---|---|---|---|---|
| | | | 2 | 3 | 2 | Unqualified |
| | | 1 | 2 | | | Reviewed |
| | 2 | 2 | 2 | | | Compiled |
| 1 | 4 | 2 | 9 | 3 | 6 | Tax Returns |
| 1 | 3 | 2 | 39 (10/1/23-3/31/24) | | | Other |
| | 6 (4/1-9/30/23) | | | | | |
| 0-500M | 500M-2MM | 2-10MM | 10-50MM | 50-100MM | 100-250MM | |
| 2 | 9 | 7 | 13 | 6 | 8 | NUMBER OF STATEMENTS |
| % | % | % | % | % | % | |

### Comparative Historical Data

| | |
|---|---|
| 4 | 2 |
| 1 | 2 |
| 4 | 2 |
| 3 | 3 |
| 31 | 22 |
| 4/1/19-3/31/20 ALL | 4/1/20-3/31/21 ALL |
| 43 | 31 |
| % | % |

## ASSETS

| Current | | Historical |
|---|---|---|
| 12.7 — Cash & Equivalents | | 15.7 / 17.8 |
| 30.2 — Trade Receivables (net) | | 18.9 / 24.9 |
| 3.7 — Inventory | | 6.3 / 5.8 |
| 13.4 — All Other Current | | 5.5 / 2.2 |
| 60.1 — Total Current | | 46.5 / 50.7 |
| 35.4 — Fixed Assets (net) | | 36.7 / 34.5 |
| .6 — Intangibles (net) | | 5.6 / 10.1 |
| 4.0 — All Other Non-Current | | 11.2 / 4.7 |
| 100.0 — Total | | 100.0 / 100.0 |

## LIABILITIES

| | |
|---|---|
| 3.5 — Notes Payable-Short Term | 5.5 / 7.0 |
| 7.2 — Cur. Mat.-L.T.D. | 5.4 / 6.2 |
| 6.8 — Trade Payables | 10.6 / 10.1 |
| .1 — Income Taxes Payable | .1 / .3 |
| 16.6 — All Other Current | 11.8 / 10.1 |
| 34.3 — Total Current | 33.4 / 33.7 |
| 19.8 — Long-Term Debt | 32.3 / 20.0 |
| .9 — Deferred Taxes | 1.0 / .0 |
| 9.7 — All Other Non-Current | 5.5 / 4.7 |
| 35.4 — Net Worth | 27.7 / 41.6 |
| 100.0 — Total Liabilities & Net Worth | 100.0 / 100.0 |

## INCOME DATA

| | |
|---|---|
| 100.0 — Net Sales | 100.0 / 100.0 |
| — Gross Profit | |
| 94.8 — Operating Expenses | 85.0 / 93.8 |
| 5.2 — Operating Profit | 15.0 / 6.2 |
| -.8 — All Other Expenses (net) | 1.9 / -1.0 |
| 6.0 — Profit Before Taxes | 13.1 / 7.1 |

## RATIOS

| Current Data | Ratio | Historical |
|---|---|---|
| 3.5 / 2.0 / 1.2 | Current | 2.6 / 1.4 / .7 — 2.9 / 1.3 / .8 |
| 2.4 / 1.2 / .9 | Quick | 2.2 / 1.1 / .4 — 2.4 / 1.1 / .7 |
| 36  10.2 / 43  8.4 / 57  6.4 | Sales/Receivables | 23 15.7 / 33 11.0 / 55 6.6 — 19 18.8 / 33 11.1 / 54 6.7 |
| | Cost of Sales/Inventory | |
| | Cost of Sales/Payables | |
| 4.0 / 7.9 / 35.5 | Sales/Working Capital | 3.0 / 18.7 / -13.8 — 8.4 / 20.0 / -43.5 |
| 17.5 / (12) 7.1 / 2.3 | EBIT/Interest | (37) 45.8 / 8.3 / 2.7 — (26) 60.3 / 16.6 / -1.3 |
| | Net Profit + Depr., Dep., Amort./Cur. Mat. L/T/D | |
| .3 / .6 / 5.0 | Fixed/Worth | .2 / 1.0 / 4.9 — .2 / 1.0 / 3.6 |
| .5 / 2.3 / 6.0 | Debt/Worth | .5 / 3.3 / 48.2 — .5 / 1.4 / 9.3 |
| 32.2 / (11) 29.6 / 15.0 | % Profit Before Taxes/Tangible Net Worth | (34) 114.0 / 40.9 / 11.4 — (26) 68.3 / 40.9 / 9.6 |
| 18.0 / 9.7 / 3.0 | % Profit Before Taxes/Total Assets | 26.8 / 13.0 / 1.1 — 24.3 / 9.7 / -3.9 |
| 40.0 / 4.4 / 2.6 | Sales/Net Fixed Assets | 31.2 / 6.1 / 1.9 — 24.3 / 7.2 / 2.0 |
| 3.5 / 2.2 / 1.0 | Sales/Total Assets | 2.7 / 1.8 / .8 — 5.5 / 1.6 / 1.1 |
| 1.3 / (12) 7.6 / 16.8 | % Depr., Dep., Amort./Sales | (29) 2.2 / 3.7 / 10.5 — (22) 1.9 / 7.7 / 10.1 |
| | % Officers', Directors' Owners' Comp/Sales | |

| 1239M | 40980M | 128680M | 787028M | 556054M | 1837567M | Net Sales ($) | 1378637M | 1461985M |
| 566M | 8614M | 38780M | 324815M | 357334M | 1455695M | Total Assets ($) | 1044124M | 870821M |

© RMA 2024  
M = $ thousand  MM = $ million  
See Pages viii through xx for Explanation of Ratios and Data

# TRANSPORTATION—Support Activities for Rail Transportation  NAICS 488210

## Comparative Historical Data | Current Data Sorted by Sales

| | | | | | | Type of Statement | | | | | | | |
|---|---|---|---|---|---|---|---|---|---|---|---|---|---|
| | | 4 | | 11 | | 7 | Unqualified | | 1 | | 1 | | 5 |
| | | 5 | | 3 | | 3 | Reviewed | | | | | | 2 |
| | | | | 5 | | 4 | Compiled | | | | | 4 | |
| | | 1 | | 2 | | 7 | Tax Returns | 3 | 2 | | 1 | 1 | 1 |
| | | 20 | | 30 | | 24 | Other | 1 | 1 | 1 | 1 | 3 | 17 |
| | | 4/1/21-3/31/22 | | 4/1/22-3/31/23 | | 4/1/23-3/31/24 | | | 6 (4/1-9/30/23) | | | 39 (10/1/23-3/31/24) | |
| | | ALL | | ALL | | ALL | | 0-1MM | 1-3MM | 3-5MM | 5-10MM | 10-25MM | 25MM & OVER |
| | | 30 | | 51 | | 45 | NUMBER OF STATEMENTS | 4 | 4 | 1 | 2 | 9 | 25 |
| | | % | | % | | % | ASSETS | % | % | % | % | % | % |
| | | 16.9 | | 16.9 | | 15.1 | Cash & Equivalents | | | | | | 10.9 |
| | | 23.2 | | 25.6 | | 23.6 | Trade Receivables (net) | | | | | | 25.7 |
| | | 6.7 | | 7.1 | | 7.5 | Inventory | | | | | | 9.4 |
| | | 4.0 | | 6.1 | | 6.4 | All Other Current | | | | | | 6.3 |
| | | 50.8 | | 55.6 | | 52.6 | Total Current | | | | | | 52.2 |
| | | 35.1 | | 30.4 | | 31.7 | Fixed Assets (net) | | | | | | 33.7 |
| | | 5.5 | | 6.9 | | 6.3 | Intangibles (net) | | | | | | 9.6 |
| | | 8.6 | | 7.0 | | 9.5 | All Other Non-Current | | | | | | 4.4 |
| | | 100.0 | | 100.0 | | 100.0 | Total | | | | | | 100.0 |
| | | | | | | | LIABILITIES | | | | | | |
| | | 2.6 | | 6.7 | | 5.9 | Notes Payable-Short Term | | | | | | 4.3 |
| | | 5.2 | | 11.0 | | 4.1 | Cur. Mat.-L.T.D. | | | | | | 4.7 |
| | | 8.7 | | 11.2 | | 10.5 | Trade Payables | | | | | | 8.4 |
| | | .2 | | .1 | | .0 | Income Taxes Payable | | | | | | .1 |
| | | 12.1 | | 9.7 | | 11.0 | All Other Current | | | | | | 11.4 |
| | | 28.8 | | 38.7 | | 31.6 | Total Current | | | | | | 28.9 |
| | | 34.1 | | 19.8 | | 23.6 | Long-Term Debt | | | | | | 20.6 |
| | | .7 | | .8 | | .6 | Deferred Taxes | | | | | | .5 |
| | | 3.3 | | 5.2 | | 10.2 | All Other Non-Current | | | | | | 5.6 |
| | | 33.1 | | 35.5 | | 34.0 | Net Worth | | | | | | 44.3 |
| | | 100.0 | | 100.0 | | 100.0 | Total Liabilities & Net Worth | | | | | | 100.0 |
| | | | | | | | INCOME DATA | | | | | | |
| | | 100.0 | | 100.0 | | 100.0 | Net Sales | | | | | | 100.0 |
| | | | | | | | Gross Profit | | | | | | |
| | | 88.0 | | 90.9 | | 88.5 | Operating Expenses | | | | | | 92.9 |
| | | 12.0 | | 9.1 | | 11.5 | Operating Profit | | | | | | 7.1 |
| | | -.7 | | 2.0 | | .9 | All Other Expenses (net) | | | | | | .7 |
| | | 12.7 | | 7.1 | | 10.6 | Profit Before Taxes | | | | | | 6.4 |
| | | | | | | | RATIOS | | | | | | |
| | | 2.9 | | 3.1 | | 3.4 | | | | | | | 3.3 |
| | | 1.8 | | 1.7 | | 1.8 | Current | | | | | | 1.7 |
| | | 1.1 | | 1.1 | | 1.2 | | | | | | | 1.3 |
| | | 2.0 | | 1.9 | | 2.3 | | | | | | | 1.9 |
| | | 1.2 | | 1.2 | | 1.1 | Quick | | | | | | 1.1 |
| | | .8 | | .7 | | .7 | | | | | | | .8 |
| 37 | 9.9 | 18 | 20.1 | 24 | 15.1 | | | | | | 36 | 10.1 |
| 43 | 8.5 | 43 | 8.4 | 39 | 9.4 | Sales/Receivables | | | | | 45 | 8.2 |
| 64 | 5.7 | 61 | 6.0 | 57 | 6.4 | | | | | | 64 | 5.7 |
| | | | | | | Cost of Sales/Inventory | | | | | | |
| | | | | | | Cost of Sales/Payables | | | | | | |
| | | 5.9 | | 4.6 | | 5.1 | | | | | | | 6.0 |
| | | 13.8 | | 8.6 | | 8.0 | Sales/Working Capital | | | | | | 8.0 |
| | | 40.6 | | 41.7 | | 35.5 | | | | | | | 28.8 |
| | | 25.5 | | 21.0 | | 14.6 | | | | | | | 12.2 |
| (26) | 10.8 | (46) | 7.0 | (42) | 5.6 | EBIT/Interest | | | | | | 5.4 |
| | | 3.7 | | 2.6 | | 1.6 | | | | | | | 1.7 |
| | | | | | | | Net Profit + Depr., Dep., Amort./Cur. Mat. L/T/D | | | | | | |
| | | .4 | | .2 | | .2 | | | | | | | .2 |
| | | 1.0 | | .9 | | 1.0 | Fixed/Worth | | | | | | 1.1 |
| | | 4.5 | | 2.7 | | 3.0 | | | | | | | 2.2 |
| | | .5 | | 1.0 | | .6 | | | | | | | .6 |
| | | 1.9 | | 1.5 | | 1.9 | Debt/Worth | | | | | | 1.4 |
| | | 61.7 | | 14.2 | | 7.3 | | | | | | | 4.5 |
| | | 49.7 | | 74.4 | | 32.5 | | | | | | | 30.3 |
| (24) | 16.0 | (41) | 33.8 | (37) | 21.0 | % Profit Before Taxes/Tangible Net Worth | | | | | (21) | 17.3 |
| | | 5.9 | | 13.4 | | 5.9 | | | | | | | 3.3 |
| | | 23.8 | | 22.1 | | 17.6 | | | | | | | 13.6 |
| | | 10.7 | | 10.5 | | 7.8 | % Profit Before Taxes/Total Assets | | | | | | 6.5 |
| | | 3.6 | | 1.7 | | 1.1 | | | | | | | 1.3 |
| | | 13.0 | | 65.5 | | 61.0 | | | | | | | 62.4 |
| | | 5.4 | | 7.0 | | 8.1 | Sales/Net Fixed Assets | | | | | | 4.3 |
| | | 2.1 | | 3.1 | | 2.3 | | | | | | | 1.7 |
| | | 3.2 | | 3.9 | | 3.7 | | | | | | | 3.9 |
| | | 1.5 | | 1.9 | | 2.2 | Sales/Total Assets | | | | | | 1.9 |
| | | .6 | | 1.0 | | .8 | | | | | | | .8 |
| | | 2.1 | | .8 | | .8 | | | | | | | .8 |
| (24) | 4.4 | (32) | 3.0 | (35) | 2.2 | % Depr., Dep., Amort./Sales | | | | | (20) | 3.8 |
| | | 9.6 | | 6.2 | | 9.2 | | | | | | | 9.6 |
| | | | | | | | % Officers', Directors' Owners' Comp/Sales | | | | | | |
| | | 1516636M | | 4109550M | | 3351548M | Net Sales ($) | 2529M | 6660M | 4193M | 14770M | 125094M | 3198302M |
| | | 1176753M | | 2281430M | | 2185804M | Total Assets ($) | 2180M | 20363M | 693M | 50625M | 53411M | 2058532M |

© RMA 2024    M = $ thousand    MM = $ million
See Pages viii through xx for Explanation of Ratios and Data

# TRANSPORTATION—Port and Harbor Operations  NAICS 488310

## Current Data Sorted by Assets

| | | | | | | Type of Statement | |
|---|---|---|---|---|---|---|---|
| | 2 | 1 | 1 | 2 | 4 | Unqualified | |
| | 1 | | | | | Reviewed | |
| 1 | 1 | 1 | 1 | | | Compiled | |
| 1 | 4 | | 5 | 3 | 1 | 2 | Tax Returns |
| | 4 (4/1-9/30/23) | | | 28 (10/1/23-3/31/24) | | Other | |
| 0-500M | 500M-2MM | 2-10MM | 10-50MM | 50-100MM | 100-250MM | | |
| 2 | 8 | 7 | 6 | 3 | 6 | NUMBER OF STATEMENTS | |
| % | % | % | % | % | % | ASSETS | |

## Comparative Historical Data

| | |
|---|---|
| 7 | 5 |
| 2 | 1 |
| 2 | 1 |
| 2 | |
| 15 | 4 |
| 4/1/19- | 4/1/20- |
| 3/31/20 | 3/31/21 |
| ALL | ALL |
| 28 | 11 |
| % | % |

| | 4/1/19-3/31/20 ALL | 4/1/20-3/31/21 ALL |
|---|---|---|
| **ASSETS** | | |
| Cash & Equivalents | 12.5 | 12.1 |
| Trade Receivables (net) | 14.7 | 4.7 |
| Inventory | 1.3 | .1 |
| All Other Current | 2.7 | 1.2 |
| Total Current | 31.2 | 18.2 |
| Fixed Assets (net) | 56.7 | 75.0 |
| Intangibles (net) | 5.8 | .5 |
| All Other Non-Current | 6.2 | 6.3 |
| Total | 100.0 | 100.0 |
| **LIABILITIES** | | |
| Notes Payable-Short Term | .6 | 3.0 |
| Cur. Mat.-L.T.D. | 4.8 | 4.3 |
| Trade Payables | 3.6 | 2.1 |
| Income Taxes Payable | .1 | .0 |
| All Other Current | 8.3 | 4.6 |
| Total Current | 17.5 | 13.9 |
| Long-Term Debt | 25.5 | 39.9 |
| Deferred Taxes | 1.3 | .4 |
| All Other Non-Current | 4.1 | 1.2 |
| Net Worth | 51.6 | 44.5 |
| Total Liabilities & Net Worth | 100.0 | 100.0 |
| **INCOME DATA** | | |
| Net Sales | 100.0 | 100.0 |
| Gross Profit | | |
| Operating Expenses | 86.0 | 73.9 |
| Operating Profit | 14.0 | 26.1 |
| All Other Expenses (net) | 2.6 | 2.6 |
| Profit Before Taxes | 11.5 | 23.4 |
| **RATIOS** | | |
| Current | 3.9 | 6.3 |
| | 2.1 | 1.8 |
| | 1.1 | .8 |
| Quick | 3.6 | 5.8 |
| | 1.5 | 1.3 |
| | .8 | .8 |
| Sales/Receivables | 29  12.8 | 0  UND |
| | 36  10.0 | 16  22.8 |
| | 47  7.7 | 46  7.9 |
| Cost of Sales/Inventory | | |
| Cost of Sales/Payables | | |
| Sales/Working Capital | 5.5 | 6.2 |
| | 10.6 | 13.2 |
| | 38.8 | -14.1 |
| EBIT/Interest | 24.8 | 9.5 |
| | (25)  5.0 | (10)  7.1 |
| | 1.7 | 3.3 |
| Net Profit + Depr., Dep., Amort./Cur. Mat. L/T/D | | |
| Fixed/Worth | .7 | .9 |
| | 1.2 | 2.0 |
| | 2.1 | 4.8 |
| Debt/Worth | .4 | .4 |
| | 1.2 | 1.4 |
| | 2.6 | 5.3 |
| % Profit Before Taxes/Tangible Net Worth | 39.4 | 177.2 |
| | 10.6 | (10)  19.6 |
| | -4.3 | 2.9 |
| % Profit Before Taxes/Total Assets | 13.6 | 28.0 |
| | 4.7 | 12.6 |
| | -.4 | 3.3 |
| Sales/Net Fixed Assets | 5.3 | 3.5 |
| | 1.4 | .9 |
| | .5 | .4 |
| Sales/Total Assets | 2.3 | 1.7 |
| | .8 | .7 |
| | .4 | .3 |
| % Depr., Dep., Amort./Sales | 3.5 | |
| | (23)  12.4 | |
| | 26.0 | |
| % Officers', Directors' Owners' Comp/Sales | | |

| 1492M | 38294M | 82707M | 457824M | 525042M | 982632M | Net Sales ($) | 1825664M | 260061M |
| 579M | 9929M | 42562M | 183678M | 180916M | 1213161M | Total Assets ($) | 1934123M | 460704M |

© RMA 2024  
M = $ thousand   MM = $ million  
See Pages viii through xx for Explanation of Ratios and Data

## TRANSPORTATION—Port and Harbor Operations   NAICS 488310

| Comparative Historical Data ||| Type of Statement | Current Data Sorted by Sales |||||||
|---|---|---|---|---|---|---|---|---|---|
| 7 | 8 | 10 | Unqualified | | 2 | | 1 | 1 | 6 |
| 2 | 1 | 1 | Reviewed | | | | | | 1 |
| 2 | | 1 | Compiled | 1 | | | | | |
| 3 | | 4 | Tax Returns | 1 | 2 | 1 | 3 | 2 | |
| 7 | 6 | 16 | Other | 1 | | 4 | | | 6 |
| 4/1/21-3/31/22 | 4/1/22-3/31/23 | 4/1/23-3/31/24 | | | 4 (4/1-9/30/23) ||| 28 (10/1/23-3/31/24) |||
| ALL | ALL | ALL | | 0-1MM | 1-3MM | 3-5MM | 5-10MM | 10-25MM | 25MM & OVER |
| 21 | 15 | 32 | NUMBER OF STATEMENTS | 3 | 4 | 5 | 4 | 3 | 13 |
| % | % | % | ASSETS | % | % | % | % | % | % |
| 14.8 | 13.5 | 18.6 | Cash & Equivalents | | | | | | 7.9 |
| 9.3 | 10.0 | 13.7 | Trade Receivables (net) | | | | | | 20.3 |
| 1.9 | .2 | 9.9 | Inventory | | | | | | 3.2 |
| 1.1 | 1.2 | 4.3 | All Other Current | | | | | | 7.2 |
| 27.0 | 24.9 | 46.5 | Total Current | | | | | | 38.6 |
| 60.7 | 53.5 | 36.2 | Fixed Assets (net) | | | | | | 39.6 |
| 2.6 | 10.5 | 3.7 | Intangibles (net) | | | | | | 8.0 |
| 9.6 | 11.1 | 13.5 | All Other Non-Current | | | | | | 13.8 |
| 100.0 | 100.0 | 100.0 | Total | | | | | | 100.0 |
| | | | LIABILITIES | | | | | | |
| 2.7 | .1 | 7.6 | Notes Payable-Short Term | | | | | | 5.6 |
| 3.1 | 3.2 | 1.7 | Cur. Mat.-L.T.D. | | | | | | 2.6 |
| 2.6 | 4.2 | 5.9 | Trade Payables | | | | | | 4.6 |
| .0 | .0 | .3 | Income Taxes Payable | | | | | | .1 |
| 12.0 | 4.2 | 10.5 | All Other Current | | | | | | 17.4 |
| 20.4 | 11.7 | 26.0 | Total Current | | | | | | 30.4 |
| 29.9 | 17.7 | 14.2 | Long-Term Debt | | | | | | 17.1 |
| .3 | .6 | .1 | Deferred Taxes | | | | | | .3 |
| 2.1 | 8.3 | 5.4 | All Other Non-Current | | | | | | 8.0 |
| 47.2 | 61.6 | 54.2 | Net Worth | | | | | | 44.3 |
| 100.0 | 100.0 | 100.0 | Total Liabilities & Net Worth | | | | | | 100.0 |
| | | | INCOME DATA | | | | | | |
| 100.0 | 100.0 | 100.0 | Net Sales | | | | | | 100.0 |
| | | | Gross Profit | | | | | | 86.6 |
| 75.1 | 79.3 | 88.0 | Operating Expenses | | | | | | 13.4 |
| 24.9 | 20.7 | 12.0 | Operating Profit | | | | | | 1.5 |
| 6.1 | 4.2 | .6 | All Other Expenses (net) | | | | | | 11.9 |
| 18.8 | 16.5 | 11.4 | Profit Before Taxes | | | | | | |
| | | | RATIOS | | | | | | |
| 2.7 | 9.7 | 4.6 | | | | | | | 1.7 |
| 1.3 | 2.8 | 1.7 | Current | | | | | | 1.5 |
| .8 | 1.3 | 1.1 | | | | | | | .6 |
| 2.4 | 9.6 | 3.0 | | | | | | | 1.4 |
| 1.1 | 2.6 | 1.4 | Quick | | | | | | 1.2 |
| .8 | 1.2 | .5 | | | | | | | .4 |
| 16  22.3 | 22  16.3 | 0  UND | | | | | | 30 | 12.3 |
| 34  10.7 | 39  9.3 | 33  11.1 | Sales/Receivables | | | | | | 34  10.8 |
| 51  7.2 | 78  4.7 | 51  7.2 | | | | | | 44 | 8.3 |
| | | | Cost of Sales/Inventory | | | | | | |
| | | | Cost of Sales/Payables | | | | | | |
| 3.6 | .8 | 4.4 | | | | | | | 8.6 |
| 26.3 | 8.1 | 12.4 | Sales/Working Capital | | | | | | 17.3 |
| -39.8 | 13.5 | 153.1 | | | | | | | -11.2 |
| 15.7 | 46.7 | 41.6 | | | | | | | 55.3 |
| (18) 5.7 | (13) 13.7 | (26) 6.1 | EBIT/Interest | | | | | | 4.4 |
| 3.4 | 6.4 | 2.3 | | | | | | | 2.6 |
| | | | Net Profit + Depr., Dep., Amort./Cur. Mat. L/T/D | | | | | | |
| .9 | .8 | .2 | | | | | | | .3 |
| 1.4 | .9 | .9 | Fixed/Worth | | | | | | 1.2 |
| 2.5 | 1.5 | 1.5 | | | | | | | 1.7 |
| .5 | .2 | .3 | | | | | | | 1.0 |
| 1.2 | .7 | 1.0 | Debt/Worth | | | | | | 1.1 |
| 2.1 | 1.9 | 2.1 | | | | | | | 2.8 |
| 38.0 | 27.6 | 46.0 | % Profit Before Taxes/Tangible Net Worth | | | | | | 72.4 |
| (20) 13.0 | (14) 16.8 | (31) 16.0 | | | | | | (12) | 15.9 |
| 3.9 | 5.3 | -1.6 | | | | | | | 4.2 |
| 16.9 | 15.9 | 22.8 | % Profit Before Taxes/Total Assets | | | | | | 36.1 |
| 6.0 | 8.0 | 8.6 | | | | | | | 5.5 |
| 2.8 | 3.2 | .0 | | | | | | | 2.3 |
| 5.2 | 4.3 | 18.0 | | | | | | | 27.8 |
| 1.6 | 1.4 | 6.3 | Sales/Net Fixed Assets | | | | | | 6.4 |
| .3 | .2 | 1.7 | | | | | | | .9 |
| 2.5 | 1.2 | 3.4 | | | | | | | 5.3 |
| 1.2 | .6 | 1.5 | Sales/Total Assets | | | | | | 1.4 |
| .2 | .2 | .7 | | | | | | | .6 |
| 2.5 | 4.5 | .9 | | | | | | | |
| (17) 8.0 | (11) 7.2 | (24) 2.7 | % Depr., Dep., Amort./Sales | | | | | | |
| 16.5 | 38.2 | 8.6 | | | | | | | |
| | | | % Officers', Directors' Owners' Comp/Sales | | | | | | |
| 728165M | 659869M | 2087991M | Net Sales ($) | 2233M | 9178M | 19728M | 26239M | 48392M | 1982221M |
| 1151496M | 1043878M | 1630825M | Total Assets ($) | 1936M | 18358M | 17538M | 19403M | 71835M | 1501755M |

© RMA 2024  M = $ thousand   MM = $ million
See Pages viii through xx for Explanation of Ratios and Data

# TRANSPORTATION—Marine Cargo Handling  NAICS 488320

## Current Data Sorted by Assets | Comparative Historical Data

| Type of Statement | | |
|---|---|---|
| Unqualified | 6 | 5 |
| Reviewed | 3 | 4 |
| Compiled | 2 | |
| Tax Returns | | |
| Other | 31 | 19 |

| 0-500M | 500M-2MM | 2-10MM | 10-50MM | 50-100MM | 100-250MM | | 4/1/19-3/31/20 ALL | 4/1/20-3/31/21 ALL |
|---|---|---|---|---|---|---|---|---|
| | 1 | 3 | 7 (4/1-9/30/23) 8 | 7 | 6 | | | |
| | | | 34 (10/1/23-3/31/24) | | | | | |
| | 1 | 6 | 12 | 12 | 10 | NUMBER OF STATEMENTS | 42 | 30 |
| % | % | % | % | % | % | **ASSETS** | % | % |
| | | | 17.6 | 7.3 | 13.3 | Cash & Equivalents | 13.4 | 20.0 |
| | | | 27.8 | 20.0 | 11.2 | Trade Receivables (net) | 19.3 | 20.1 |
| | | | .5 | 1.7 | 1.5 | Inventory | 1.0 | 1.1 |
| | | | 6.3 | 3.3 | 4.4 | All Other Current | 3.3 | 3.9 |
| | | | 52.2 | 32.3 | 30.4 | Total Current | 37.0 | 45.1 |
| | | | 31.5 | 59.1 | 60.7 | Fixed Assets (net) | 51.0 | 45.5 |
| DATA NOT AVAILABLE | | | 4.3 | .6 | 5.3 | Intangibles (net) | 4.0 | 2.4 |
| | | | 12.0 | 7.9 | 3.6 | All Other Non-Current | 7.9 | 7.0 |
| | | | 100.0 | 100.0 | 100.0 | Total | 100.0 | 100.0 |
| | | | | | | **LIABILITIES** | | |
| | | | .7 | .9 | .7 | Notes Payable-Short Term | 4.3 | 5.6 |
| | | | .9 | 3.1 | 2.2 | Cur. Mat.-L.T.D. | 5.6 | 4.3 |
| | | | 13.4 | 4.3 | 3.0 | Trade Payables | 6.2 | 7.7 |
| | | | .4 | .0 | .1 | Income Taxes Payable | .1 | .1 |
| | | | 16.3 | 8.1 | 8.4 | All Other Current | 8.4 | 12.5 |
| | | | 31.7 | 16.5 | 14.4 | Total Current | 24.5 | 30.2 |
| | | | 8.7 | 18.7 | 37.6 | Long-Term Debt | 19.2 | 16.9 |
| | | | .0 | 1.3 | .0 | Deferred Taxes | .6 | .9 |
| | | | 8.4 | 5.3 | 2.3 | All Other Non-Current | 5.8 | 4.1 |
| | | | 51.2 | 58.1 | 45.7 | Net Worth | 50.0 | 47.8 |
| | | | 100.0 | 100.0 | 100.0 | Total Liabilities & Net Worth | 100.0 | 100.0 |
| | | | | | | **INCOME DATA** | | |
| | | | 100.0 | 100.0 | 100.0 | Net Sales | 100.0 | 100.0 |
| | | | | | | Gross Profit | | |
| | | | 85.8 | 92.3 | 84.9 | Operating Expenses | 89.9 | 88.3 |
| | | | 14.2 | 7.7 | 15.1 | Operating Profit | 10.1 | 11.7 |
| | | | .2 | 2.2 | 1.3 | All Other Expenses (net) | 3.7 | 3.2 |
| | | | 14.0 | 5.4 | 13.8 | Profit Before Taxes | 6.5 | 8.5 |
| | | | | | | **RATIOS** | | |
| | | | 3.1 | 2.3 | 3.7 | | 2.6 | 2.6 |
| | | | 2.0 | 1.5 | 1.7 | Current | 1.4 | 1.4 |
| | | | 1.1 | 1.3 | 1.1 | | .6 | 1.0 |
| | | | 2.7 | 2.1 | 3.5 | | 2.0 | 2.5 |
| | | | 1.7 | 1.2 | 1.2 | Quick | 1.3 | 1.3 |
| | | | .9 | .7 | .7 | | .6 | .8 |
| | | 23 | 16.0 | 35 10.3 | 29 12.5 | | 29 12.5 | 25 14.4 |
| | | 34 | 10.8 | 45 8.2 | 46 8.0 | Sales/Receivables | 42 8.7 | 40 9.1 |
| | | 40 | 9.1 | 66 5.5 | 55 6.6 | | 58 6.3 | 53 6.9 |
| | | | | | | Cost of Sales/Inventory | | |
| | | | | | | Cost of Sales/Payables | | |
| | | | 4.1 | 7.2 | 3.4 | | 5.1 | 4.1 |
| | | | 17.1 | 10.7 | 9.2 | Sales/Working Capital | 13.7 | 12.1 |
| | | | 112.2 | 16.2 | NM | | -14.7 | -687.5 |
| | | | 14.8 | | | | 42.6 | 88.4 |
| | | | 4.3 | | | EBIT/Interest | (34) 4.9 | (25) 5.0 |
| | | | -1.0 | | | | 1.0 | .9 |
| | | | | | | Net Profit + Depr., Dep., | 10.7 | |
| | | | | | | Amort./Cur. Mat. L/T/D | (12) 4.2 | |
| | | | | | | | 1.4 | |
| | | | .2 | .7 | .7 | | .5 | .3 |
| | | | .5 | 1.2 | 1.7 | Fixed/Worth | 1.1 | .9 |
| | | | 1.5 | 1.5 | 4.5 | | 2.2 | 2.0 |
| | | | .4 | .5 | .6 | | .4 | .4 |
| | | | .9 | .7 | 1.4 | Debt/Worth | 1.1 | 1.0 |
| | | | 3.1 | 1.2 | 4.2 | | 2.3 | 3.2 |
| | | | 72.0 | 20.7 | 45.8 | | 42.4 | 43.0 |
| | | (11) | 33.5 | 7.9 | 29.0 | % Profit Before Taxes/Tangible Net Worth | (39) 17.2 | (28) 16.9 |
| | | | 13.2 | -2.4 | -2.6 | | 1.7 | 4.0 |
| | | | 34.9 | 10.6 | 20.5 | | 18.7 | 16.0 |
| | | | 15.8 | 4.7 | 10.0 | % Profit Before Taxes/Total Assets | 6.5 | 6.4 |
| | | | 7.3 | -1.5 | -.6 | | -.2 | 1.2 |
| | | | 49.0 | 3.6 | 4.1 | | 8.7 | 15.0 |
| | | | 20.3 | 1.2 | .9 | Sales/Net Fixed Assets | 3.2 | 3.3 |
| | | | 1.5 | .8 | .4 | | .7 | .8 |
| | | | 3.6 | 1.8 | 1.2 | | 2.2 | 2.7 |
| | | | 2.0 | .9 | .6 | Sales/Total Assets | 1.3 | 1.2 |
| | | | .8 | .5 | .4 | | .5 | .5 |
| | | | .4 | 1.9 | | | 2.0 | 1.8 |
| | | (10) | 1.1 | 8.2 | | % Depr., Dep., Amort./Sales | (37) 6.1 | (25) 3.9 |
| | | | 4.8 | 11.0 | | | 15.0 | 13.8 |
| | | | | | | % Officers', Directors' Owners' Comp/Sales | | |
| | 666M | 50952M | 631606M | 1174832M | 1249955M | Net Sales ($) | 2336183M | 1180003M |
| | 1014M | 34754M | 271771M | 875299M | 1534489M | Total Assets ($) | 2275874M | 1129398M |

M = $ thousand  MM = $ million
See Pages viii through xx for Explanation of Ratios and Data

© RMA 2024

# TRANSPORTATION—Marine Cargo Handling  NAICS 488320

## Comparative Historical Data | Current Data Sorted by Sales

| Comparative Historical Data | | | Type of Statement | Current Data Sorted by Sales | | | | | |
|---|---|---|---|---|---|---|---|---|---|
| 8 | 13 | 10 | Unqualified | | 1 | | 1 | | 9 |
| 3 | 5 | 5 | Reviewed | | | | 1 | | 3 |
|  | 2 | 1 | Compiled | | 1 | | | | |
|  | 2 |  | Tax Returns | | | | | | |
| 23 | 19 | 25 | Other | 1 | 7 (4/1-9/30/23) | | 34 (10/1/23-3/31/24) | | 18 |
| 4/1/21-3/31/22 ALL | 4/1/22-3/31/23 ALL | 4/1/23-3/31/24 ALL | | 0-1MM | 1-3MM | 3-5MM | 5-10MM | 10-25MM | 25MM & OVER |
| 34 | 41 | 41 | NUMBER OF STATEMENTS | 1 |  | 3 | 2 | 5 | 30 |
| % | % | % | **ASSETS** | % | % | % | % | % | % |
| 18.7 | 11.8 | 11.5 | Cash & Equivalents | | | | | | 12.3 |
| 22.1 | 19.3 | 18.8 | Trade Receivables (net) | | D | | | | 22.2 |
| 2.0 | 2.5 | 1.0 | Inventory | | A | | | | 1.3 |
| 4.1 | 3.2 | 4.2 | All Other Current | | T | | | | 5.1 |
| 46.9 | 36.7 | 35.6 | Total Current | | A | | | | 40.8 |
| 44.0 | 47.6 | 52.0 | Fixed Assets (net) | | | | | | 46.8 |
| .9 | 3.3 | 2.9 | Intangibles (net) | | N | | | | 3.7 |
| 8.2 | 12.5 | 9.5 | All Other Non-Current | | O | | | | 8.7 |
| 100.0 | 100.0 | 100.0 | Total | | T | | | | 100.0 |
| | | | **LIABILITIES** | | A | | | | |
| 2.8 | 4.0 | .7 | Notes Payable-Short Term | | V | | | | .8 |
| 3.4 | 2.5 | 2.1 | Cur. Mat.-L.T.D. | | A | | | | 1.9 |
| 8.8 | 8.1 | 6.7 | Trade Payables | | I | | | | 7.7 |
| .3 | .1 | .2 | Income Taxes Payable | | L | | | | .1 |
| 12.9 | 7.8 | 10.6 | All Other Current | | A | | | | 11.5 |
| 28.2 | 22.6 | 20.3 | Total Current | | B | | | | 22.0 |
| 19.2 | 23.8 | 22.8 | Long-Term Debt | | L | | | | 19.1 |
| .4 | .5 | .8 | Deferred Taxes | | E | | | | .5 |
| 2.9 | 7.3 | 4.9 | All Other Non-Current | | | | | | 6.2 |
| 49.4 | 45.9 | 51.2 | Net Worth | | | | | | 52.3 |
| 100.0 | 100.0 | 100.0 | Total Liabilities & Net Worth | | | | | | 100.0 |
| | | | **INCOME DATA** | | | | | | |
| 100.0 | 100.0 | 100.0 | Net Sales | | | | | | 100.0 |
| 89.0 | 85.7 | 86.4 | Gross Profit | | | | | | 89.2 |
| 11.0 | 14.3 | 13.6 | Operating Expenses | | | | | | 10.8 |
| -1.5 | 1.8 | 1.4 | Operating Profit | | | | | | .8 |
| 12.5 | 12.5 | 12.3 | All Other Expenses (net) | | | | | | 10.0 |
| | | | Profit Before Taxes | | | | | | |
| | | | **RATIOS** | | | | | | |
| 2.4 | 3.3 | 2.3 | | | | | | | 2.7 |
| 1.6 | 1.7 | 1.8 | Current | | | | | | 1.9 |
| 1.1 | 1.2 | 1.1 | | | | | | | 1.2 |
| 2.4 | 3.1 | 2.2 | | | | | | | 2.5 |
| 1.3 | 1.6 | 1.3 | Quick | | | | | | 1.2 |
| .8 | .6 | .7 | | | | | | | .8 |
| 34  10.7 | 36  10.2 | 29  12.5 | | | | | | 31 | 11.7 |
| 57  6.4 | 42  8.6 | 37  9.9 | Sales/Receivables | | | | | 42 | 8.6 |
| 72  5.1 | 62  5.9 | 52  7.0 | | | | | | 55 | 6.6 |
| | | | Cost of Sales/Inventory | | | | | | |
| | | | Cost of Sales/Payables | | | | | | |
| 4.4 | 4.6 | 6.3 | | | | | | | 5.5 |
| 8.5 | 8.7 | 12.7 | Sales/Working Capital | | | | | | 10.7 |
| NM | 29.2 | 32.8 | | | | | | | 24.7 |
| 23.4 | 32.8 | 35.3 | | | | | | | 60.8 |
| (30) 16.5 | (35) 10.1 | (35) 8.1 | EBIT/Interest | | | | | (25) | 7.8 |
| 4.6 | 2.0 | 1.2 | | | | | | | .5 |
| | | | Net Profit + Depr., Dep., Amort./Cur. Mat. L/T/D | | | | | | |
| .3 | .3 | .4 | | | | | | | .4 |
| .8 | .8 | 1.0 | Fixed/Worth | | | | | | .9 |
| 1.6 | 2.3 | 1.9 | | | | | | | 1.7 |
| .4 | .4 | .5 | | | | | | | .4 |
| 1.1 | 1.1 | .9 | Debt/Worth | | | | | | .8 |
| 2.2 | 3.0 | 1.8 | | | | | | | 2.1 |
| 60.6 | 46.4 | 42.7 | | | | | | | 48.9 |
| 16.8 | (38) 23.3 | (39) 17.4 | % Profit Before Taxes/Tangible Net Worth | | | | | (29) | 20.4 |
| 9.8 | 10.5 | .7 | | | | | | | -1.1 |
| 18.5 | 20.4 | 21.7 | | | | | | | 25.4 |
| 10.2 | 9.5 | 9.4 | % Profit Before Taxes/Total Assets | | | | | | 9.3 |
| 5.0 | 2.9 | .8 | | | | | | | -.1 |
| 13.9 | 10.1 | 7.9 | | | | | | | 19.9 |
| 4.3 | 2.0 | 2.5 | Sales/Net Fixed Assets | | | | | | 3.2 |
| .7 | .7 | .7 | | | | | | | .9 |
| 2.3 | 1.9 | 2.0 | | | | | | | 2.4 |
| 1.0 | .8 | .9 | Sales/Total Assets | | | | | | 1.0 |
| .5 | .5 | .6 | | | | | | | .6 |
| 2.0 | 1.8 | 1.5 | | | | | | | 1.1 |
| (28) 3.7 | (37) 5.0 | (38) 4.6 | % Depr., Dep., Amort./Sales | | | | | (28) | 3.7 |
| 11.6 | 8.6 | 10.1 | | | | | | | 9.7 |
| | | | % Officers', Directors' Owners' Comp/Sales | | | | | | |
| 2492878M | 2785143M | 3108011M | Net Sales ($) | 666M | 11712M | | 19494M | 83380M | 2992759M |
| 2089699M | 2474515M | 2717327M | Total Assets ($) | 1014M | 15705M | | 35067M | 107247M | 2558294M |

M = $ thousand    MM = $ million
See Pages viii through xx for Explanation of Ratios and Data

© RMA 2024

# TRANSPORTATION—Navigational Services to Shipping  NAICS 488330

## Current Data Sorted by Assets | Comparative Historical Data

| 0-500M | 500M-2MM | 2-10MM | 10-50MM | 50-100MM | 100-250MM | Type of Statement | | 4/1/19-3/31/20 ALL | 4/1/20-3/31/21 ALL |
|---|---|---|---|---|---|---|---|---|---|
| | | 1 | 7 | 1 | 1 | Unqualified | | 6 | 8 |
| | | 1 | 2 | 1 | | Reviewed | | 4 | 2 |
| 1 | 5 | 1 | | 1 | | Compiled | | 1 | 1 |
| 2 | 2 | 9 | 14 | 4 | 2 | Tax Returns | | 5 | |
| | 8 (4/1-9/30/23) | | 47 (10/1/23-3/31/24) | | | Other | | 28 | 12 |
| 3 | 7 | 12 | 23 | 7 | 3 | NUMBER OF STATEMENTS | | 44 | 23 |
| % | % | % | % | % | % | | | % | % |
| | | 28.1 | 13.7 | | | Cash & Equivalents | | 14.0 | 16.5 |
| | | 20.9 | 15.3 | | | Trade Receivables (net) | | 16.3 | 11.5 |
| | | .3 | 1.1 | | | Inventory | | 1.0 | .3 |
| | | 2.4 | 3.9 | | | All Other Current | | 2.8 | 1.3 |
| | | 51.7 | 33.9 | | | Total Current | | 34.1 | 29.7 |
| | | 40.0 | 49.1 | | | Fixed Assets (net) | | 55.7 | 58.0 |
| | | 1.5 | 6.4 | | | Intangibles (net) | | 1.4 | 1.7 |
| | | 6.8 | 10.5 | | | All Other Non-Current | | 8.9 | 10.6 |
| | | 100.0 | 100.0 | | | Total | | 100.0 | 100.0 |
| | | | | | | **LIABILITIES** | | | |
| | | 8.1 | 2.2 | | | Notes Payable-Short Term | | 4.1 | 6.5 |
| | | 3.1 | 5.3 | | | Cur. Mat.-L.T.D. | | 4.4 | 3.3 |
| | | 3.7 | 3.9 | | | Trade Payables | | 4.4 | 4.4 |
| | | .0 | .0 | | | Income Taxes Payable | | .0 | .0 |
| | | 7.1 | 6.8 | | | All Other Current | | 10.6 | 5.4 |
| | | 22.1 | 18.1 | | | Total Current | | 23.5 | 19.6 |
| | | 33.9 | 31.3 | | | Long-Term Debt | | 29.0 | 36.5 |
| | | .0 | 1.4 | | | Deferred Taxes | | .3 | .0 |
| | | 5.1 | 6.8 | | | All Other Non-Current | | 7.1 | 3.8 |
| | | 38.8 | 42.4 | | | Net Worth | | 40.1 | 40.1 |
| | | 100.0 | 100.0 | | | Total Liabilties & Net Worth | | 100.0 | 100.0 |
| | | | | | | **INCOME DATA** | | | |
| | | 100.0 | 100.0 | | | Net Sales | | 100.0 | 100.0 |
| | | | | | | Gross Profit | | | |
| | | 84.9 | 76.8 | | | Operating Expenses | | 83.1 | 81.7 |
| | | 15.1 | 23.2 | | | Operating Profit | | 16.9 | 18.3 |
| | | 6.0 | 3.4 | | | All Other Expenses (net) | | 1.5 | 4.9 |
| | | 9.1 | 19.8 | | | Profit Before Taxes | | 15.4 | 13.4 |
| | | | | | | **RATIOS** | | | |
| | | 7.3 | 3.1 | | | | | 2.6 | 4.0 |
| | | 4.3 | 1.7 | | | Current | | 1.5 | 1.3 |
| | | 1.4 | 1.1 | | | | | .9 | .9 |
| | | 7.0 | 2.4 | | | | | 2.2 | 3.2 |
| | | 3.7 | 1.5 | | | Quick | | 1.4 | 1.2 |
| | | 1.4 | 1.0 | | | | | .8 | .8 |
| | | 0 UND | 29 12.4 | | | | 19 | 19.4 | 2 206.3 |
| | | 38 9.5 | 40 9.1 | | | Sales/Receivables | 40 | 9.1 | 32 11.3 |
| | | 59 6.2 | 55 6.6 | | | | 48 | 7.6 | 54 6.7 |
| | | | | | | Cost of Sales/Inventory | | | |
| | | | | | | Cost of Sales/Payables | | | |
| | | 3.9 | 5.4 | | | | | 6.5 | 6.1 |
| | | 5.7 | 7.6 | | | Sales/Working Capital | | 17.2 | 17.0 |
| | | 50.1 | 46.6 | | | | | -64.7 | -38.3 |
| | | | 61.2 | | | | | 16.8 | 35.2 |
| | | (21) | 4.4 | | | EBIT/Interest | (38) | 4.1 | (21) 6.3 |
| | | | 3.2 | | | | | 1.7 | .7 |
| | | | | | | Net Profit + Depr., Dep., Amort./Cur. Mat. L/T/D | | | |
| | | .1 | .9 | | | | | .8 | .9 |
| | | 1.7 | 1.4 | | | Fixed/Worth | | 1.4 | 1.6 |
| | | 13.2 | 6.3 | | | | | 3.5 | 3.3 |
| | | .2 | .6 | | | | | .6 | 1.0 |
| | | 2.0 | 1.6 | | | Debt/Worth | | 1.1 | 1.3 |
| | | 14.6 | 12.7 | | | | | 3.6 | 2.7 |
| | | 61.9 | 195.8 | | | | | 45.1 | 54.8 |
| | | (11) 14.6 | (21) 54.9 | | | % Profit Before Taxes/Tangible Net Worth | (40) | 19.4 | (21) 21.9 |
| | | -18.5 | 8.2 | | | | | 1.5 | -1.7 |
| | | 58.3 | 33.0 | | | | | 23.4 | 26.2 |
| | | 7.8 | 11.8 | | | % Profit Before Taxes/Total Assets | | 9.1 | 7.4 |
| | | -3.4 | 2.3 | | | | | 1.3 | -1.6 |
| | | 298.8 | 4.1 | | | | | 5.9 | 3.1 |
| | | 5.9 | 2.0 | | | Sales/Net Fixed Assets | | 2.1 | 1.5 |
| | | 1.9 | 1.7 | | | | | 1.0 | .7 |
| | | 2.8 | 1.5 | | | | | 2.2 | 1.8 |
| | | 1.7 | 1.2 | | | Sales/Total Assets | | 1.2 | .8 |
| | | .7 | .7 | | | | | .7 | .5 |
| | | | 1.2 | | | | | 2.5 | 3.2 |
| | | (22) | 4.4 | | | % Depr., Dep., Amort./Sales | (35) | 5.9 | (16) 5.2 |
| | | | 8.9 | | | | | 11.4 | 11.4 |
| | | | | | | % Officers', Directors' Owners' Comp/Sales | | | |
| 1763M | 34315M | 142382M | 714945M | 504813M | 312874M | Net Sales ($) | | 2293900M | 1410063M |
| 634M | 7012M | 77218M | 560280M | 559722M | 480169M | Total Assets ($) | | 2220569M | 1713090M |

M = $ thousand    MM = $ million
See Pages viii through xx for Explanation of Ratios and Data

© RMA 2024

# TRANSPORTATION—Navigational Services to Shipping  NAICS 488330

## Comparative Historical Data | Current Data Sorted by Sales

| | | | | Type of Statement | | | | | | |
|---|---|---|---|---|---|---|---|---|---|---|
| | 8 | 9 | 10 | Unqualified | | | | | 3 | 7 |
| | 4 | 5 | 4 | Reviewed | | | | | 2 | 2 |
| | | | 1 | Compiled | | | | | | 1 |
| | 1 | | 7 | Tax Returns | 2 | 1 | 1 | 3 | | |
| | 23 | 30 | 33 | Other | 4 | 2 | 1 | 2 | 13 | 11 |
| | 4/1/21- | 4/1/22- | 4/1/23- | | | 8 (4/1-9/30/23) | | | 47 (10/1/23-3/31/24) | |
| | 3/31/22 | 3/31/23 | 3/31/24 | | 0-1MM | 1-3MM | 3-5MM | 5-10MM | 10-25MM | 25MM & OVER |
| | ALL | ALL | ALL | | | | | | | |
| | 36 | 44 | 55 | NUMBER OF STATEMENTS | 6 | 3 | 2 | 5 | 18 | 21 |
| | % | % | % | ASSETS | % | % | % | % | % | % |
| | 14.2 | 15.4 | 19.8 | Cash & Equivalents | | | | | 17.8 | 12.5 |
| | 16.8 | 15.1 | 14.6 | Trade Receivables (net) | | | | | 14.3 | 17.2 |
| | 2.8 | .5 | .6 | Inventory | | | | | .9 | .7 |
| | 1.7 | 2.3 | 2.8 | All Other Current | | | | | 4.2 | 2.8 |
| | 35.5 | 33.3 | 37.8 | Total Current | | | | | 37.3 | 33.2 |
| | 48.2 | 47.7 | 46.2 | Fixed Assets (net) | | | | | 46.2 | 49.4 |
| | 2.3 | 4.3 | 3.5 | Intangibles (net) | | | | | 6.3 | 3.4 |
| | 14.0 | 14.8 | 12.5 | All Other Non-Current | | | | | 10.3 | 13.9 |
| | 100.0 | 100.0 | 100.0 | Total | | | | | 100.0 | 100.0 |
| | | | | LIABILITIES | | | | | | |
| | 5.4 | 3.3 | 5.8 | Notes Payable-Short Term | | | | | .4 | 3.6 |
| | 3.9 | 3.4 | 3.6 | Cur. Mat.-L.T.D. | | | | | 5.3 | 3.5 |
| | 5.3 | 6.2 | 3.0 | Trade Payables | | | | | 2.4 | 4.2 |
| | .0 | .0 | .0 | Income Taxes Payable | | | | | .0 | .0 |
| | 7.2 | 11.1 | 8.4 | All Other Current | | | | | 3.8 | 9.0 |
| | 21.8 | 24.2 | 20.8 | Total Current | | | | | 11.8 | 20.3 |
| | 32.5 | 35.6 | 29.6 | Long-Term Debt | | | | | 43.8 | 19.3 |
| | .5 | .3 | .8 | Deferred Taxes | | | | | 1.0 | .7 |
| | 4.1 | 5.9 | 7.3 | All Other Non-Current | | | | | 10.3 | 5.2 |
| | 41.1 | 34.0 | 41.6 | Net Worth | | | | | 33.0 | 54.5 |
| | 100.0 | 100.0 | 100.0 | Total Liabilities & Net Worth | | | | | 100.0 | 100.0 |
| | | | | INCOME DATA | | | | | | |
| | 100.0 | 100.0 | 100.0 | Net Sales | | | | | 100.0 | 100.0 |
| | 73.6 | 78.3 | 80.0 | Gross Profit | | | | | 82.3 | 73.7 |
| | 26.4 | 21.7 | 20.0 | Operating Expenses | | | | | 17.7 | 26.3 |
| | 3.1 | 4.6 | 3.3 | Operating Profit | | | | | .7 | 2.5 |
| | 23.3 | 17.1 | 16.7 | All Other Expenses (net) | | | | | 17.0 | 23.8 |
| | | | | Profit Before Taxes | | | | | | |
| | | | | RATIOS | | | | | | |
| | 3.2 | 3.3 | 3.4 | | | | | | 6.2 | 2.4 |
| | 1.7 | 1.4 | 2.1 | Current | | | | | 3.1 | 1.7 |
| | 1.1 | .8 | 1.1 | | | | | | 1.5 | 1.2 |
| | 2.8 | 3.2 | 3.4 | | | | | | 6.0 | 2.4 |
| | 1.4 | 1.3 | 1.9 | Quick | | | | | 2.5 | 1.3 |
| | 1.0 | .7 | .9 | | | | | | 1.4 | .9 |
| 17 | 21.4 | 9  42.4 | 0  UND | | | | | | 26  14.2 | 30  12.3 |
| 33 | 11.0 | 33  11.0 | 38  9.6 | Sales/Receivables | | | | | 42  8.6 | 43  8.5 |
| 58 | 6.3 | 58  6.3 | 50  7.3 | | | | | | 56  6.5 | 54  6.7 |
| | | | | Cost of Sales/Inventory | | | | | | |
| | | | | Cost of Sales/Payables | | | | | | |
| | 5.0 | 6.6 | 5.6 | | | | | | 3.8 | 6.2 |
| | 7.8 | 15.7 | 9.6 | Sales/Working Capital | | | | | 5.9 | 11.8 |
| | 59.5 | -19.8 | 62.9 | | | | | | 11.4 | 39.4 |
| | 66.5 | 87.8 | 36.2 | | | | | | 8.8 | 104.7 |
| (28) | 13.5 | (37) 13.6 | (47) 6.1 | EBIT/Interest | | | | | (15) 4.4 | 14.7 |
| | 5.2 | 2.3 | 2.2 | | | | | | 2.9 | 2.5 |
| | | | | Net Profit + Depr., Dep., Amort./Cur. Mat. L/T/D | | | | | | |
| | .7 | .6 | .6 | | | | | | 1.1 | .7 |
| | 1.0 | 1.2 | 1.4 | Fixed/Worth | | | | | 1.7 | .9 |
| | 3.4 | 3.8 | 4.8 | | | | | | 9.9 | 2.6 |
| | .4 | .6 | .4 | | | | | | .7 | .4 |
| | .8 | 1.5 | 1.7 | Debt/Worth | | | | | 2.4 | .7 |
| | 4.8 | 7.8 | 9.0 | | | | | | 17.9 | 2.9 |
| | 164.6 | 74.0 | 90.5 | | | | | | 152.0 | 152.8 |
| (31) | 32.7 | (39) 36.7 | (49) 28.2 | % Profit Before Taxes/Tangible Net Worth | | | | | (16) 58.4 | (20) 24.0 |
| | 14.0 | 6.3 | .4 | | | | | | 13.2 | 4.0 |
| | 54.1 | 28.8 | 34.4 | | | | | | 31.2 | 78.5 |
| | 13.7 | 7.5 | 9.5 | % Profit Before Taxes/Total Assets | | | | | 14.7 | 9.1 |
| | 3.8 | .0 | .5 | | | | | | 3.8 | 2.0 |
| | 4.2 | 5.5 | 6.3 | | | | | | 3.6 | 5.1 |
| | 2.1 | 2.2 | 2.4 | Sales/Net Fixed Assets | | | | | 2.5 | 2.2 |
| | 1.2 | .9 | 1.3 | | | | | | 1.8 | 1.3 |
| | 1.7 | 2.1 | 2.2 | | | | | | 1.6 | 2.1 |
| | 1.0 | 1.0 | 1.2 | Sales/Total Assets | | | | | 1.3 | 1.2 |
| | .6 | .5 | .7 | | | | | | .7 | .7 |
| | 2.8 | 2.8 | 1.6 | | | | | | 1.7 | 1.7 |
| (29) | 6.4 | (33) 6.4 | (43) 6.2 | % Depr., Dep., Amort./Sales | | | | | (16) 4.6 | (20) 6.3 |
| | 9.7 | 13.8 | 10.4 | | | | | | 8.4 | 9.0 |
| | | | .8 | | | | | | | |
| | | (10) | 2.7 | % Officers', Directors' Owners' Comp/Sales | | | | | | |
| | | | 19.7 | | | | | | | |
| | 1679682M | 1938117M | 1711092M | Net Sales ($) | 2795M | 4632M | 7943M | 43357M | 296434M | 1355931M |
| | 1784260M | 1957680M | 1685035M | Total Assets ($) | 8156M | 14323M | 3960M | 10938M | 305864M | 1341794M |

© RMA 2024  M = $ thousand  MM = $ million
See Pages viii through xx for Explanation of Ratios and Data

# TRANSPORTATION—Other Support Activities for Water Transportation  NAICS 488390

## Current Data Sorted by Assets / Comparative Historical Data

| | 0-500M | 500M-2MM | 2-10MM | 10-50MM | 50-100MM | 100-250MM | | 4/1/19-3/31/20 ALL | 4/1/20-3/31/21 ALL |
|---|---|---|---|---|---|---|---|---|---|
| **Type of Statement** | | | | | | | | | |
| Unqualified | 4 | 1 | 2 | 1 | 1 | 1 | | 4 | 1 |
| Reviewed | 3 | 1 | 1 | 1 | 1 | | | 2 | 4 |
| Compiled | | | | 1 | | | | 1 | 1 |
| Tax Returns | | | | 2 | 2 | 1 | | 5 | 1 |
| Other | | 1 (4/1-9/30/23) | | 23 (10/1/23-3/31/24) | | | | 17 | 12 |
| NUMBER OF STATEMENTS | 7 | 2 | 3 | 5 | 4 | 3 | | 29 | 19 |
| | % | % | % | % | % | % | | % | % |
| **ASSETS** | | | | | | | | | |
| Cash & Equivalents | | | | | | | | 15.0 | 12.3 |
| Trade Receivables (net) | | | | | | | | 19.2 | 23.3 |
| Inventory | | | | | | | | 1.0 | 2.9 |
| All Other Current | | | | | | | | 2.6 | 3.6 |
| Total Current | | | | | | | | 37.8 | 42.2 |
| Fixed Assets (net) | | | | | | | | 44.9 | 47.9 |
| Intangibles (net) | | | | | | | | 4.5 | 6.2 |
| All Other Non-Current | | | | | | | | 12.8 | 3.7 |
| Total | | | | | | | | 100.0 | 100.0 |
| **LIABILITIES** | | | | | | | | | |
| Notes Payable-Short Term | | | | | | | | 3.0 | 5.9 |
| Cur. Mat.-L.T.D. | | | | | | | | 3.7 | 3.3 |
| Trade Payables | | | | | | | | 9.1 | 6.2 |
| Income Taxes Payable | | | | | | | | .2 | .1 |
| All Other Current | | | | | | | | 10.2 | 9.8 |
| Total Current | | | | | | | | 26.3 | 25.3 |
| Long-Term Debt | | | | | | | | 37.1 | 29.6 |
| Deferred Taxes | | | | | | | | .8 | .6 |
| All Other Non-Current | | | | | | | | 17.8 | 5.0 |
| Net Worth | | | | | | | | 18.1 | 39.4 |
| Total Liabilities & Net Worth | | | | | | | | 100.0 | 100.0 |
| **INCOME DATA** | | | | | | | | | |
| Net Sales | | | | | | | | 100.0 | 100.0 |
| Gross Profit | | | | | | | | | |
| Operating Expenses | | | | | | | | 81.6 | 88.9 |
| Operating Profit | | | | | | | | 18.4 | 11.1 |
| All Other Expenses (net) | | | | | | | | 3.5 | 2.8 |
| Profit Before Taxes | | | | | | | | 14.9 | 8.3 |
| **RATIOS** | | | | | | | | | |
| Current | | | | | | | | 3.4 | 3.7 |
| | | | | | | | | 1.2 | 1.3 |
| | | | | | | | | .8 | .7 |
| Quick | | | | | | | | 3.2 | 2.7 |
| | | | | | | | | 1.1 | 1.1 |
| | | | | | | | | .6 | .5 |
| Sales/Receivables | | | | | | | 16 | 22.3 | 33  11.1 |
| | | | | | | | 35 | 10.5 | 53  6.9 |
| | | | | | | | 50 | 7.3 | 78  4.7 |
| Cost of Sales/Inventory | | | | | | | | | |
| Cost of Sales/Payables | | | | | | | | | |
| Sales/Working Capital | | | | | | | | 8.0 | 3.5 |
| | | | | | | | | 18.8 | 15.4 |
| | | | | | | | | -17.1 | -11.8 |
| EBIT/Interest | | | | | | | | 21.2 | 27.9 |
| | | | | | | (22) | | 6.6 | (18) 5.2 |
| | | | | | | | | 2.8 | 1.5 |
| Net Profit + Depr., Dep., Amort./Cur. Mat. L/T/D | | | | | | | | | |
| Fixed/Worth | | | | | | | | .3 | .3 |
| | | | | | | | | 1.5 | 1.8 |
| | | | | | | | | NM | 6.1 |
| Debt/Worth | | | | | | | | .5 | .4 |
| | | | | | | | | 1.2 | 2.0 |
| | | | | | | | | NM | 5.5 |
| % Profit Before Taxes/Tangible Net Worth | | | | | | | | 62.5 | 55.9 |
| | | | | | | (22) | | 13.3 | (16) 16.8 |
| | | | | | | | | 6.5 | 4.8 |
| % Profit Before Taxes/Total Assets | | | | | | | | 37.7 | 19.4 |
| | | | | | | | | 6.7 | 5.0 |
| | | | | | | | | 1.9 | 1.9 |
| Sales/Net Fixed Assets | | | | | | | | 10.7 | 4.7 |
| | | | | | | | | 2.1 | 1.5 |
| | | | | | | | | .9 | 1.0 |
| Sales/Total Assets | | | | | | | | 2.5 | 1.6 |
| | | | | | | | | .8 | .7 |
| | | | | | | | | .5 | .6 |
| % Depr., Dep., Amort./Sales | | | | | | | | 5.0 | .5 |
| | | | | | | (19) | | 11.8 | (14) 4.2 |
| | | | | | | | | 15.5 | 13.5 |
| % Officers', Directors' Owners' Comp/Sales | | | | | | | | | |
| Net Sales ($) | 3058M | 8118M | 38229M | 212693M | 241021M | 331595M | | 788862M | 499027M |
| Total Assets ($) | 1021M | 1617M | 15472M | 164815M | 262122M | 454465M | | 956276M | 775850M |

M = $ thousand   MM = $ million

# TRANSPORTATION—Other Support Activities for Water Transportation    NAICS 488390

## Comparative Historical Data / Current Data Sorted by Sales

| | | | | Type of Statement | | | | | | |
|---|---|---|---|---|---|---|---|---|---|---|
| | 2 | 3 | 3 | Unqualified | | | | | | 3 |
| | 5 | 6 | 3 | Reviewed | | | | | | 3 |
| | | | 1 | Compiled | | | | | | 1 |
| | 1 | 3 | 7 | Tax Returns | 4 | 1 | | 1 | 1 | |
| | 10 | 7 | 10 | Other | 2 | 2 | | 3 | 3 | 3 |
| | 4/1/21-3/31/22 | 4/1/22-3/31/23 | 4/1/23-3/31/24 | | | 1 (4/1-9/30/23) | | 23 (10/1/23-3/31/24) | | |
| | ALL | ALL | ALL | | 0-1MM | 1-3MM | 3-5MM | 5-10MM | 10-25MM | 25MM & OVER |
| NUMBER OF STATEMENTS | 18 | 19 | 24 | | 6 | 3 | 1 | 1 | 4 | 10 |
| | % | % | % | ASSETS | % | % | % | % | % | % |
| | 10.1 | 28.6 | 27.6 | Cash & Equivalents | | | | | | 6.2 |
| | 21.0 | 12.5 | 11.0 | Trade Receivables (net) | | | D | | | 15.2 |
| | 5.3 | 5.7 | 6.2 | Inventory | | | A | | | 9.4 |
| | 8.0 | 3.3 | 3.3 | All Other Current | | | T | | | 6.6 |
| | 44.4 | 50.1 | 48.1 | Total Current | | | A | | | 37.5 |
| | 46.2 | 37.5 | 34.9 | Fixed Assets (net) | | | | | | 53.0 |
| | 4.0 | 5.1 | 1.0 | Intangibles (net) | | | N | | | 1.4 |
| | 5.5 | 7.2 | 16.3 | All Other Non-Current | | | O | | | 8.0 |
| | 100.0 | 100.0 | 100.0 | Total | | | T | | | 100.0 |
| | | | | LIABILITIES | | | | | | |
| | 4.1 | 4.3 | 2.8 | Notes Payable-Short Term | | | A | | | 6.1 |
| | 6.0 | 4.8 | 4.0 | Cur. Mat.-L.T.D. | | | V | | | 5.9 |
| | 9.2 | 7.3 | 4.6 | Trade Payables | | | A | | | 8.4 |
| | .0 | .0 | .0 | Income Taxes Payable | | | I | | | .0 |
| | 11.1 | 13.5 | 9.7 | All Other Current | | | L | | | 7.8 |
| | 30.5 | 29.9 | 21.1 | Total Current | | | A | | | 28.2 |
| | 40.1 | 27.7 | 29.4 | Long-Term Debt | | | B | | | 42.5 |
| | .4 | 1.4 | .4 | Deferred Taxes | | | L | | | .9 |
| | 8.9 | 4.6 | 5.7 | All Other Non-Current | | | E | | | 4.3 |
| | 20.1 | 36.5 | 43.5 | Net Worth | | | | | | 24.0 |
| | 100.0 | 100.0 | 100.0 | Total Liabilities & Net Worth | | | | | | 100.0 |
| | | | | INCOME DATA | | | | | | |
| | 100.0 | 100.0 | 100.0 | Net Sales | | | | | | 100.0 |
| | | | | Gross Profit | | | | | | |
| | 85.0 | 77.5 | 85.5 | Operating Expenses | | | | | | 84.6 |
| | 15.0 | 22.5 | 14.5 | Operating Profit | | | | | | 15.4 |
| | 3.0 | 9.4 | 1.5 | All Other Expenses (net) | | | | | | 1.1 |
| | 12.0 | 13.0 | 13.0 | Profit Before Taxes | | | | | | 14.2 |
| | | | | RATIOS | | | | | | |
| | 3.6 | 3.1 | 5.5 | | | | | | | 2.8 |
| | 1.4 | 1.4 | 2.6 | Current | | | | | | 1.0 |
| | .5 | 1.1 | 1.0 | | | | | | | .7 |
| | 2.5 | 2.4 | 5.4 | | | | | | | 2.1 |
| | .7 | 1.3 | 1.9 | Quick | | | | | | .6 |
| | .5 | .7 | .5 | | | | | | | .2 |
| 27 | 13.5 | 0 | 999.8 | 0 | UND | | | | 16 | 23.3 |
| 41 | 8.8 | 19 | 18.8 | 19 | 19.4 | Sales/Receivables | | | 30 | 12.1 |
| 59 | 6.2 | 73 | 5.0 | 48 | 7.6 | | | | 62 | 5.9 |
| | | | | Cost of Sales/Inventory | | | | | | |
| | | | | Cost of Sales/Payables | | | | | | |
| | 4.0 | 3.6 | 3.8 | | | | | | | 3.8 |
| | 13.4 | 11.1 | 8.9 | Sales/Working Capital | | | | | | NM |
| | -8.5 | 39.0 | NM | | | | | | | -11.4 |
| | 24.0 | 31.8 | 7.9 | | | | | | | 11.0 |
| (17) | 9.2 | (16) | 13.2 | (18) | 4.2 | EBIT/Interest | | | | 5.4 |
| | 4.2 | | 5.2 | | .9 | | | | | 2.2 |
| | | | | Net Profit + Depr., Dep., Amort./Cur. Mat. L/T/D | | | | | | |
| | .7 | .0 | .1 | | | | | | | .7 |
| | 1.4 | 1.0 | .7 | Fixed/Worth | | | | | | 2.4 |
| | 9.3 | 5.8 | 3.8 | | | | | | | 5.3 |
| | .8 | .6 | .3 | | | | | | | .7 |
| | 2.2 | 2.0 | 1.2 | Debt/Worth | | | | | | 4.0 |
| | 9.1 | 8.4 | 5.4 | | | | | | | 5.9 |
| | 80.5 | 88.7 | 47.8 | % Profit Before Taxes/Tangible Net Worth | | | | | | |
| (15) | 31.3 | (16) | 55.0 | (23) | 21.8 | | | | | |
| | 17.8 | 14.4 | .0 | | | | | | | |
| | 25.7 | 32.8 | 27.5 | % Profit Before Taxes/Total Assets | | | | | | 15.3 |
| | 12.3 | 16.9 | 7.0 | | | | | | | 6.5 |
| | 7.0 | 4.5 | .7 | | | | | | | 3.8 |
| | 33.7 | 326.2 | 66.4 | Sales/Net Fixed Assets | | | | | | 6.3 |
| | 3.7 | 3.8 | 7.0 | | | | | | | 1.4 |
| | 1.3 | 1.9 | 1.3 | | | | | | | .7 |
| | 2.6 | 2.5 | 2.7 | Sales/Total Assets | | | | | | 1.4 |
| | 1.2 | 1.5 | 1.3 | | | | | | | .9 |
| | .6 | .4 | .9 | | | | | | | .6 |
| | 2.7 | 2.9 | 2.7 | % Depr., Dep., Amort./Sales | | | | | | 2.5 |
| (14) | 6.5 | (10) | 8.3 | (15) | 6.9 | | | | | 6.7 |
| | 10.5 | 13.1 | 11.2 | | | | | | | 10.1 |
| | | | | % Officers', Directors' Owners' Comp/Sales | | | | | | |
| Net Sales ($) | 517224M | 466641M | 834714M | | 1740M | 5951M | | 5951M | 76775M | 744297M |
| Total Assets ($) | 673576M | 795784M | 899512M | | 801M | 3853M | | 836M | 81565M | 812457M |

© RMA 2024                                        M = $ thousand      MM = $ million
See Pages viii through xx for Explanation of Ratios and Data

## TRANSPORTATION—Motor Vehicle Towing  NAICS 488410

**Current Data Sorted by Assets** | **Comparative Historical Data**

| 0-500M | 500M-2MM | 2-10MM | 10-50MM | 50-100MM | 100-250MM | | 4/1/19-3/31/20 ALL | 4/1/20-3/31/21 ALL |
|---|---|---|---|---|---|---|---|---|
| 4 | 3 | 2 | | 1 | | Type of Statement — Unqualified | 3 | 1 |
| 7 | 17 | 9 | 3 | | | Reviewed | 4 | 2 |
| | 19 | 16 | 1 | | | Compiled | 11 | 8 |
| | 13 (4/1-9/30/23) | | 5 | | | Tax Returns | 41 | 26 |
| | | | 77 (10/1/23-3/31/24) | | 1 | Other | 48 | 29 |
| 11 | 39 | 29 | 9 | 2 | 2 | **NUMBER OF STATEMENTS** | 107 | 66 |
| % | % | % | % | % | % | **ASSETS** | % | % |
| 43.2 | 28.9 | 21.1 | | | | Cash & Equivalents | 20.9 | 29.4 |
| .9 | 7.2 | 5.0 | | | | Trade Receivables (net) | 11.3 | 10.8 |
| .0 | 1.4 | 8.7 | | | | Inventory | 2.1 | 3.0 |
| .3 | 7.1 | 1.4 | DATA NOT AVAILABLE | | | All Other Current | 4.3 | 2.0 |
| 44.4 | 44.7 | 36.3 | | | | Total Current | 38.6 | 45.2 |
| 47.9 | 43.1 | 48.2 | | | | Fixed Assets (net) | 46.2 | 40.5 |
| 2.1 | 6.6 | 6.8 | | | | Intangibles (net) | 6.3 | 8.3 |
| 5.6 | 5.6 | 8.8 | | | | All Other Non-Current | 8.9 | 6.0 |
| 100.0 | 100.0 | 100.0 | | | | Total | 100.0 | 100.0 |
| | | | | | | **LIABILITIES** | | |
| 3.8 | 3.2 | 1.4 | | | | Notes Payable-Short Term | 8.1 | 5.2 |
| 11.9 | 7.4 | 6.9 | | | | Cur. Mat.-L.T.D. | 8.2 | 7.7 |
| 3.0 | 2.6 | 7.5 | | | | Trade Payables | 5.1 | 2.9 |
| .0 | .1 | .1 | | | | Income Taxes Payable | .2 | .2 |
| 14.2 | 8.0 | 5.4 | | | | All Other Current | 9.4 | 10.1 |
| 33.0 | 21.3 | 21.4 | | | | Total Current | 31.0 | 26.2 |
| 68.4 | 69.3 | 50.8 | | | | Long-Term Debt | 52.2 | 55.8 |
| .0 | .0 | .0 | | | | Deferred Taxes | .6 | .3 |
| 1.5 | 2.9 | 3.7 | | | | All Other Non-Current | 9.0 | 5.4 |
| -2.8 | 6.5 | 24.1 | | | | Net Worth | 7.2 | 12.4 |
| 100.0 | 100.0 | 100.0 | | | | Total Liabilities & Net Worth | 100.0 | 100.0 |
| | | | | | | **INCOME DATA** | | |
| 100.0 | 100.0 | 100.0 | | | | Net Sales | 100.0 | 100.0 |
| | | | | | | Gross Profit | | |
| 70.7 | 94.6 | 90.3 | | | | Operating Expenses | 92.0 | 93.8 |
| 29.3 | 5.4 | 9.7 | | | | Operating Profit | 8.0 | 6.2 |
| 14.0 | -1.4 | .2 | | | | All Other Expenses (net) | .9 | -1.9 |
| 15.4 | 6.8 | 9.5 | | | | Profit Before Taxes | 7.1 | 8.1 |
| | | | | | | **RATIOS** | | |
| 6.0 | 3.9 | 3.0 | | | | | 5.5 | 7.9 |
| 1.0 | 2.1 | 1.5 | | | | Current | 1.6 | 1.9 |
| .4 | 1.4 | .7 | | | | | .7 | 1.1 |
| 6.0 | 3.7 | 2.3 | | | | | 4.2 | 7.3 |
| 1.0 | 1.7 | 1.2 | | | | Quick | 1.3 | 1.7 |
| .4 | .5 | .3 | | | | | .5 | .8 |
| 0 UND | 0 UND | 0 UND | | | | | 0 UND | 0 UND |
| 0 UND | 0 UND | 0 UND | | | | Sales/Receivables | 11  33.9 | 15  23.8 |
| 0 UND | 16  22.9 | 14  25.4 | | | | | 26  13.8 | 28  13.2 |
| | | | | | | Cost of Sales/Inventory | | |
| | | | | | | Cost of Sales/Payables | | |
| 21.3 | 6.7 | 7.4 | | | | | 10.1 | 5.6 |
| 433.0 | 12.3 | 24.0 | | | | Sales/Working Capital | 29.5 | 10.4 |
| -18.6 | 235.3 | -46.4 | | | | | -43.2 | UND |
| | 10.6 | 15.2 | | | | | 11.1 | 15.5 |
| (31) | 5.1 | (25) 2.0 | | | | EBIT/Interest | (91) 3.0 | (58) 5.8 |
| | .5 | .0 | | | | | 1.0 | 1.3 |
| | | | | | | Net Profit + Depr., Dep., Amort./Cur. Mat. L/T/D | | |
| .2 | .6 | .8 | | | | | .6 | .6 |
| 39.4 | 3.0 | 2.5 | | | | Fixed/Worth | 2.2 | 1.6 |
| -3.3 | -2.4 | -4.8 | | | | | -7.0 | -41.3 |
| .1 | .8 | 1.0 | | | | | 1.5 | 1.0 |
| 38.8 | 4.4 | 13.3 | | | | Debt/Worth | 3.6 | 2.5 |
| -4.3 | -4.4 | -9.6 | | | | | -8.7 | -9.4 |
| | 87.7 | 101.5 | | | | | 71.6 | 67.1 |
| (24) | 36.1 | (18) 33.7 | | | | % Profit Before Taxes/Tangible Net Worth | (68) 32.4 | (46) 34.0 |
| | 8.4 | 2.2 | | | | | 10.1 | 17.1 |
| 141.0 | 33.6 | 24.5 | | | | | 26.6 | 27.1 |
| 36.5 | 17.1 | 5.6 | | | | % Profit Before Taxes/Total Assets | 9.0 | 13.1 |
| 7.2 | .0 | -.2 | | | | | 1.2 | 1.5 |
| UND | 18.1 | 14.4 | | | | | 22.0 | 19.4 |
| 25.4 | 9.0 | 3.4 | | | | Sales/Net Fixed Assets | 6.2 | 5.7 |
| 4.4 | 3.9 | 2.3 | | | | | 2.7 | 2.2 |
| 13.0 | 4.0 | 2.8 | | | | | 5.1 | 3.8 |
| 5.5 | 2.6 | 1.7 | | | | Sales/Total Assets | 2.5 | 1.8 |
| 1.9 | 2.0 | 1.0 | | | | | 1.3 | 1.1 |
| | 2.7 | 3.3 | | | | | 4.6 | 1.6 |
| (19) | 5.2 | (18) 6.9 | | | | % Depr., Dep., Amort./Sales | (62) 8.1 | (37) 6.5 |
| | 8.6 | 16.8 | | | | | 11.3 | 12.6 |
| | 3.7 | | | | | | 2.2 | 2.7 |
| (16) | 4.5 | | | | | % Officers', Directors' Owners' Comp/Sales | (41) 3.1 | (33) 5.2 |
| | 8.2 | | | | | | 4.3 | 8.8 |
| 16393M | 125282M | 265993M | 206927M | | 194180M | Net Sales ($) | 806571M | 1353501M |
| 3184M | 40015M | 130373M | 148285M | | 379325M | Total Assets ($) | 520345M | 606238M |

© RMA 2024   M = $ thousand   MM = $ million
See Pages viii through xx for Explanation of Ratios and Data

# TRANSPORTATION—Motor Vehicle Towing  NAICS 488410

## Comparative Historical Data | Current Data Sorted by Sales

| | | | | Type of Statement | | | | | | |
|---|---|---|---|---|---|---|---|---|---|---|
| | 2 | 2 | 1 | Unqualified | | 2 | | | | |
| | 7 | 5 | 2 | Reviewed | | 3 | 2 | 2 | 1 | |
| | 21 | 43 | 8 | Compiled | 3 | 11 | 5 | 3 | | |
| | 63 | 61 | 31 | Tax Returns | | 16 | 8 | 3 | 3 | 1 |
| | 4/1/21- | 4/1/22- | 48 | Other | 4 | | 9 | 7 | 7 | 5 |
| | 3/31/22 | 3/31/23 | 4/1/23- | | 13 (4/1-9/30/23) | | 77 (10/1/23-3/31/24) | | | |
| | ALL | ALL | 3/31/24 | | 0-1MM | 1-3MM | 3-5MM | 5-10MM | 10-25MM | 25MM & OVER |
| | | | ALL | | | | | | | |
| | 93 | 111 | 90 | NUMBER OF STATEMENTS | 7 | 30 | 17 | 14 | 15 | 7 |
| | % | % | % | ASSETS | % | % | % | % | % | % |
| | 28.3 | 26.8 | 26.9 | Cash & Equivalents | | 30.9 | 31.3 | 18.1 | 22.1 | |
| | 6.0 | 8.6 | 5.6 | Trade Receivables (net) | | 4.6 | 7.5 | 5.7 | 6.9 | |
| | 2.4 | 2.1 | 3.7 | Inventory | | .9 | 1.8 | 8.7 | 2.9 | |
| | 3.8 | 4.6 | 4.0 | All Other Current | | 5.6 | 4.5 | 3.5 | 1.2 | |
| | 40.4 | 42.1 | 40.2 | Total Current | | 42.0 | 45.1 | 36.0 | 33.1 | |
| | 48.0 | 41.5 | 46.2 | Fixed Assets (net) | | 45.3 | 40.2 | 49.2 | 51.4 | |
| | 5.7 | 6.5 | 6.7 | Intangibles (net) | | 6.5 | 5.1 | 7.1 | 7.4 | |
| | 5.9 | 10.0 | 7.0 | All Other Non-Current | | 6.2 | 9.7 | 7.6 | 8.0 | |
| | 100.0 | 100.0 | 100.0 | Total | | 100.0 | 100.0 | 100.0 | 100.0 | |
| | | | | LIABILITIES | | | | | | |
| | 3.9 | 5.2 | 2.3 | Notes Payable-Short Term | | 2.1 | 4.1 | 1.8 | .6 | |
| | 10.3 | 8.3 | 7.7 | Cur. Mat.-L.T.D. | | 6.5 | 12.0 | 7.1 | 10.2 | |
| | 2.0 | 3.5 | 4.2 | Trade Payables | | 3.3 | 3.7 | 3.4 | 4.1 | |
| | .3 | .1 | .1 | Income Taxes Payable | | .1 | .0 | .2 | .0 | |
| | 7.0 | 9.1 | 7.4 | All Other Current | | 5.5 | 8.8 | 4.7 | 2.8 | |
| | 23.6 | 26.1 | 21.8 | Total Current | | 17.5 | 28.6 | 17.2 | 17.6 | |
| | 47.8 | 45.6 | 58.2 | Long-Term Debt | | 63.2 | 80.4 | 53.4 | 56.0 | |
| | .2 | .1 | .1 | Deferred Taxes | | .0 | .0 | .0 | .0 | |
| | 2.7 | 3.2 | 3.4 | All Other Non-Current | | 6.7 | 1.7 | .7 | 3.0 | |
| | 25.7 | 25.0 | 16.6 | Net Worth | | 12.7 | -10.8 | 28.7 | 23.3 | |
| | 100.0 | 100.0 | 100.0 | Total Liabilities & Net Worth | | 100.0 | 100.0 | 100.0 | 100.0 | |
| | | | | INCOME DATA | | | | | | |
| | 100.0 | 100.0 | 100.0 | Net Sales | | 100.0 | 100.0 | 100.0 | 100.0 | |
| | | | | Gross Profit | | | | | | |
| | 87.6 | 88.4 | 89.9 | Operating Expenses | | 92.2 | 90.4 | 95.5 | 93.0 | |
| | 12.4 | 11.6 | 10.1 | Operating Profit | | 7.8 | 9.6 | 4.5 | 7.0 | |
| | -1.2 | 1.6 | 1.5 | All Other Expenses (net) | | -1.1 | -1.4 | .8 | .8 | |
| | 13.5 | 10.0 | 8.5 | Profit Before Taxes | | 8.9 | 10.9 | 3.7 | 6.2 | |
| | | | | RATIOS | | | | | | |
| | 5.7 | 5.3 | 3.7 | | | 5.9 | 3.3 | 4.7 | 2.7 | |
| | 2.7 | 2.1 | 1.9 | Current | | 2.3 | 1.9 | 1.8 | 2.1 | |
| | 1.0 | 1.0 | .9 | | | .9 | 1.1 | .5 | 1.2 | |
| | 5.1 | 4.5 | 3.1 | | | 5.6 | 2.5 | 3.0 | 2.7 | |
| | 2.3 | 1.7 | 1.6 | Quick | | 2.0 | 1.7 | 1.4 | 1.8 | |
| | .8 | .7 | .5 | | | .5 | 1.1 | .4 | .9 | |
| | 0 UND | 0 UND | 0 UND | | 0 UND | 0 UND | 0 UND | 0 UND | 0 UND | |
| | 1 604.0 | 0 841.1 | 0 UND | Sales/Receivables | | 0 UND | 0 UND | 8 44.4 | 7 52.4 | |
| | 19 19.2 | 26 14.3 | 16 22.9 | | 4 94.4 | 3 117.1 | 18 19.9 | 26 13.9 | | |
| | | | | Cost of Sales/Inventory | | | | | | |
| | | | | Cost of Sales/Payables | | | | | | |
| | 4.4 | 6.0 | 6.9 | | | 6.3 | 8.6 | 8.6 | 6.7 | |
| | 10.5 | 16.1 | 19.4 | Sales/Working Capital | | 13.6 | 18.6 | 28.7 | 11.7 | |
| | NM | -478.9 | -114.9 | | | -777.5 | NM | -18.3 | 67.0 | |
| | 28.4 | 24.2 | 11.0 | | | 10.6 | 12.3 | 30.1 | 14.6 | |
| (73) | 8.4 | (85) 8.4 | (71) 4.5 | EBIT/Interest | (23) 5.6 | (12) 6.7 | (13) 2.3 | 1.5 | | |
| | 3.3 | 1.7 | .9 | | | .5 | 1.5 | .2 | .5 | |
| | | | | Net Profit + Depr., Dep., Amort./Cur. Mat. L/T/D | | | | | | |
| | .9 | .3 | .6 | | | .5 | .5 | .9 | 1.0 | |
| | 1.9 | 1.5 | 2.5 | Fixed/Worth | | 8.9 | 1.6 | 2.4 | 2.2 | |
| | -9.6 | 8.5 | -4.6 | | | -4.0 | -4.5 | -4.6 | -2.0 | |
| | .7 | .8 | .7 | | | .7 | .8 | .3 | .7 | |
| | 2.0 | 2.2 | 4.1 | Debt/Worth | | 17.9 | 2.9 | 8.9 | 1.7 | |
| | -12.0 | UND | -8.6 | | | -5.6 | -6.1 | -8.6 | -4.3 | |
| | 81.8 | 103.8 | 100.3 | % Profit Before Taxes/Tangible Net Worth | | 240.0 | 97.6 | | | |
| (64) | 50.8 | (84) 51.4 | (58) 37.6 | | (18) 66.6 | (12) 56.0 | | | | |
| | 21.6 | 16.9 | 8.9 | | | 6.2 | 27.7 | | | |
| | 37.4 | 33.2 | 31.7 | % Profit Before Taxes/Total Assets | | 33.6 | 53.8 | 17.1 | 21.9 | |
| | 23.1 | 17.8 | 11.4 | | | 21.3 | 24.9 | 6.1 | 4.9 | |
| | 6.3 | 2.7 | .6 | | | .0 | 7.4 | -2.2 | -1.6 | |
| | 11.9 | 21.7 | 16.8 | Sales/Net Fixed Assets | | 18.6 | 30.3 | 13.5 | 12.4 | |
| | 4.2 | 4.5 | 5.7 | | | 7.2 | 8.6 | 3.2 | 4.8 | |
| | 1.9 | 2.4 | 2.5 | | | 2.5 | 3.6 | 2.5 | 2.0 | |
| | 2.9 | 3.5 | 3.7 | Sales/Total Assets | | 4.0 | 5.7 | 2.9 | 3.1 | |
| | 1.8 | 2.1 | 2.4 | | | 2.5 | 3.4 | 2.1 | 2.0 | |
| | 1.0 | 1.4 | 1.4 | | | 1.7 | 2.3 | 1.2 | 1.4 | |
| | 4.3 | 4.5 | 3.4 | | | 4.3 | | | 5.5 | |
| (45) | 7.5 | (50) 8.3 | (52) 6.5 | % Depr., Dep., Amort./Sales | (15) 6.1 | | (11) 9.3 | | | |
| | 12.5 | 12.5 | 10.7 | | | 9.7 | | | 14.3 | |
| | 2.3 | 2.0 | 2.9 | % Officers', Directors' Owners' Comp/Sales | | 4.0 | | | | |
| (36) | 3.4 | (41) 4.2 | (30) 4.4 | | (12) 4.7 | | | | | |
| | 5.9 | 6.2 | 9.1 | | | 12.5 | | | | |
| | 708436M | 1125817M | 808775M | Net Sales ($) | 2946M | 60223M | 64594M | 92485M | 212386M | 376141M |
| | 573129M | 883650M | 701182M | Total Assets ($) | 9253M | 31428M | 24712M | 53719M | 128297M | 453773M |

M = $ thousand    MM = $ million
See Pages viii through xx for Explanation of Ratios and Data
© RMA 2024

# TRANSPORTATION—Other Support Activities for Road Transportation  NAICS 488490

**Current Data Sorted by Assets** | **Comparative Historical Data**

| 0-500M | 500M-2MM | 2-10MM | 10-50MM | 50-100MM | 100-250MM | Type of Statement | 4/1/19-3/31/20 ALL | 4/1/20-3/31/21 ALL |
|---|---|---|---|---|---|---|---|---|
| | | 1 | 1 | | 1 | Unqualified | 7 | 5 |
| | | 1 | 3 | | 1 | Reviewed | 3 | 1 |
| 1 | | 1 | 1 | | | Compiled | 6 | 1 |
| 6 | 5 | 5 | | 1 | | Tax Returns | 13 | 16 |
| | | 8 | 4 | 2 | 8 | Other | 30 | 20 |
| | 5 (4/1-9/30/23) | | 47 (10/1/23-3/31/24) | | | | | |
| 7 | 8 | 15 | 9 | 3 | 10 | NUMBER OF STATEMENTS | 59 | 43 |
| % | % | % | % | % | % | ASSETS | % | % |
| | | 9.5 | | | 25.7 | Cash & Equivalents | 15.2 | 22.9 |
| | | 19.2 | | | 13.0 | Trade Receivables (net) | 21.7 | 16.0 |
| | | 9.1 | | | 8.4 | Inventory | 3.2 | 5.8 |
| | | 11.1 | | | 5.9 | All Other Current | 5.6 | 3.2 |
| | | 48.9 | | | 52.9 | Total Current | 45.7 | 47.8 |
| | | 42.8 | | | 33.1 | Fixed Assets (net) | 37.9 | 40.7 |
| | | 5.6 | | | 9.9 | Intangibles (net) | 6.1 | 8.3 |
| | | 2.7 | | | 4.0 | All Other Non-Current | 10.4 | 3.2 |
| | | 100.0 | | | 100.0 | Total | 100.0 | 100.0 |
| | | | | | | **LIABILITIES** | | |
| | | 3.1 | | | 7.5 | Notes Payable-Short Term | 8.9 | 12.0 |
| | | 6.9 | | | 3.9 | Cur. Mat.-L.T.D. | 6.7 | 5.5 |
| | | 9.6 | | | 6.9 | Trade Payables | 10.4 | 13.1 |
| | | .0 | | | .0 | Income Taxes Payable | .3 | .3 |
| | | 4.2 | | | 13.7 | All Other Current | 8.2 | 6.8 |
| | | 23.9 | | | 32.0 | Total Current | 34.5 | 37.6 |
| | | 32.5 | | | 33.2 | Long-Term Debt | 21.9 | 29.9 |
| | | .0 | | | .0 | Deferred Taxes | .6 | .4 |
| | | 8.6 | | | 6.0 | All Other Non-Current | 3.7 | 7.2 |
| | | 35.1 | | | 28.8 | Net Worth | 39.3 | 24.9 |
| | | 100.0 | | | 100.0 | Total Liabilities & Net Worth | 100.0 | 100.0 |
| | | | | | | **INCOME DATA** | | |
| | | 100.0 | | | 100.0 | Net Sales | 100.0 | 100.0 |
| | | | | | | Gross Profit | | |
| | | 88.3 | | | 81.3 | Operating Expenses | 91.5 | 91.3 |
| | | 11.7 | | | 18.7 | Operating Profit | 8.5 | 8.7 |
| | | .2 | | | 4.5 | All Other Expenses (net) | 1.4 | .9 |
| | | 11.5 | | | 14.2 | Profit Before Taxes | 7.1 | 7.8 |
| | | | | | | **RATIOS** | | |
| | | 5.9 | | | 2.5 | | 2.3 | 2.5 |
| | | 3.2 | | | 1.7 | Current | 1.2 | 1.5 |
| | | 1.1 | | | 1.2 | | .7 | .8 |
| | | 3.5 | | | 2.3 | | 1.6 | 2.0 |
| | | 1.5 | | | 1.3 | Quick | 1.0 | 1.1 |
| | | .6 | | | 1.0 | | .5 | .5 |
| | | 1  250.7 | | | 6  64.3 | | 1  367.6 | 3  126.2 |
| | | 17  21.1 | | | 35  10.4 | Sales/Receivables | 31  11.7 | 29  12.6 |
| | | 29  12.6 | | | 122  3.0 | | 47  7.7 | 44  8.3 |
| | | | | | | Cost of Sales/Inventory | | |
| | | | | | | Cost of Sales/Payables | | |
| | | 7.0 | | | 1.7 | | 7.6 | 5.7 |
| | | 14.0 | | | 4.7 | Sales/Working Capital | 40.5 | 12.3 |
| | | 131.4 | | | 18.0 | | -26.3 | -36.3 |
| | | 35.8 | | | | | 16.0 | 44.5 |
| | (14) | 5.4 | | | | EBIT/Interest | (51) 6.6 | (34) 5.7 |
| | | 2.1 | | | | | 2.6 | .0 |
| | | | | | | Net Profit + Depr., Dep., Amort./Cur. Mat. L/T/D | 6.6 | |
| | | | | | | | (16) 2.0 | |
| | | | | | | | 1.4 | |
| | | .1 | | | .6 | | .2 | .6 |
| | | 1.1 | | | 3.2 | Fixed/Worth | 1.2 | 1.6 |
| | | 2.1 | | | -.2 | | 5.2 | 12.2 |
| | | .4 | | | 1.2 | | .9 | 1.1 |
| | | .8 | | | 4.5 | Debt/Worth | 1.7 | 3.3 |
| | | 14.5 | | | -3.6 | | 9.1 | 17.3 |
| | | 48.0 | | | | | 109.4 | 179.4 |
| | (13) | 31.9 | | | | % Profit Before Taxes/Tangible Net Worth | (52) 35.9 | (34) 51.9 |
| | | 4.0 | | | | | 14.1 | 13.0 |
| | | 30.7 | | | 26.3 | | 30.3 | 32.6 |
| | | 10.0 | | | 9.7 | % Profit Before Taxes/Total Assets | 9.9 | 14.8 |
| | | 2.0 | | | -.7 | | 3.8 | -.5 |
| | | 124.5 | | | 10.1 | | 45.4 | 30.1 |
| | | 9.0 | | | 3.9 | Sales/Net Fixed Assets | 7.5 | 4.2 |
| | | 1.4 | | | 2.4 | | 3.0 | 1.8 |
| | | 5.4 | | | 1.6 | | 4.2 | 3.3 |
| | | 2.9 | | | .9 | Sales/Total Assets | 2.4 | 1.6 |
| | | 1.0 | | | .3 | | 1.3 | .9 |
| | | | | | | % Depr., Dep., Amort./Sales | 1.7 | 2.1 |
| | | | | | | | (37) 3.5 | (26) 6.0 |
| | | | | | | | 7.8 | 10.0 |
| | | | | | | % Officers', Directors' Owners' Comp/Sales | 2.3 | |
| | | | | | | | (13) 4.7 | |
| | | | | | | | 14.5 | |
| 11099M | 47296M | 267249M | 368359M | 331217M | 2182539M | Net Sales ($) | 2400632M | 909985M |
| 1924M | 9283M | 70423M | 171339M | 231259M | 1649045M | Total Assets ($) | 1637159M | 928876M |

© RMA 2024

M = $ thousand    MM = $ million
See Pages viii through xx for Explanation of Ratios and Data

# TRANSPORTATION—Other Support Activities for Road Transportation  NAICS 488490

## Comparative Historical Data | Current Data Sorted by Sales

| Comparative Historical Data | | | Type of Statement | Current Data Sorted by Sales | | | | | |
|---|---|---|---|---|---|---|---|---|---|
| 4 | 2 | 2 | Unqualified | | 1 | | | 1 | 1 |
| 2 | 1 | 6 | Reviewed | | 1 | | | 1 | 4 |
| 1 | 2 | 3 | Compiled | | | | 1 | | 1 |
| 8 | 22 | 16 | Tax Returns | 1 | 4 | 3 | 2 | 3 | |
| 21 | 32 | 25 | Other | 4 | 5 | | 1 | 4 | 15 |
| 4/1/21-3/31/22 ALL | 4/1/22-3/31/23 ALL | 4/1/23-3/31/24 ALL | | 5 (4/1-9/30/23) | | | 47 (10/1/23-3/31/24) | | |
| | | | | 0-1MM | 1-3MM | 3-5MM | 5-10MM | 10-25MM | 25MM & OVER |
| 36 | 59 | 52 | NUMBER OF STATEMENTS | 5 | 10 | 3 | 4 | 9 | 21 |
| % | % | % | **ASSETS** | % | % | % | % | % | % |
| 22.2 | 22.8 | 23.9 | Cash & Equivalents | | 18.2 | | | | 21.5 |
| 21.3 | 15.7 | 14.8 | Trade Receivables (net) | | 4.8 | | | | 19.3 |
| 4.6 | 7.1 | 12.1 | Inventory | | 9.4 | | | | 18.0 |
| 3.5 | 7.6 | 4.7 | All Other Current | | .8 | | | | 6.6 |
| 51.6 | 53.3 | 55.5 | Total Current | | 33.3 | | | | 65.3 |
| 33.1 | 27.4 | 33.0 | Fixed Assets (net) | | 54.5 | | | | 22.3 |
| 7.5 | 9.5 | 5.5 | Intangibles (net) | | 2.3 | | | | 7.3 |
| 7.8 | 9.9 | 6.0 | All Other Non-Current | | 9.9 | | | | 5.1 |
| 100.0 | 100.0 | 100.0 | Total | | 100.0 | | | | 100.0 |
| | | | **LIABILITIES** | | | | | | |
| 10.5 | 7.0 | 6.6 | Notes Payable-Short Term | | 10.5 | | | | 10.2 |
| 2.9 | 3.1 | 4.3 | Cur. Mat.-L.T.D. | | 3.0 | | | | 5.0 |
| 5.9 | 6.5 | 8.4 | Trade Payables | | .7 | | | | 6.9 |
| .0 | .1 | .1 | Income Taxes Payable | | .4 | | | | .1 |
| 10.2 | 20.2 | 10.3 | All Other Current | | 8.3 | | | | 13.3 |
| 29.4 | 36.9 | 29.7 | Total Current | | 23.0 | | | | 35.6 |
| 23.5 | 31.3 | 29.0 | Long-Term Debt | | 17.7 | | | | 26.3 |
| .3 | .2 | .0 | Deferred Taxes | | .0 | | | | .0 |
| 4.8 | 4.4 | 7.8 | All Other Non-Current | | 9.0 | | | | 4.8 |
| 42.0 | 27.2 | 33.5 | Net Worth | | 50.3 | | | | 33.4 |
| 100.0 | 100.0 | 100.0 | Total Liabilities & Net Worth | | 100.0 | | | | 100.0 |
| | | | **INCOME DATA** | | | | | | |
| 100.0 | 100.0 | 100.0 | Net Sales | | 100.0 | | | | 100.0 |
| | | | Gross Profit | | | | | | |
| 88.6 | 86.9 | 88.2 | Operating Expenses | | 71.8 | | | | 92.9 |
| 11.4 | 13.1 | 11.8 | Operating Profit | | 28.2 | | | | 7.1 |
| -1.1 | 3.2 | 1.3 | All Other Expenses (net) | | 2.9 | | | | 1.2 |
| 12.5 | 9.9 | 10.5 | Profit Before Taxes | | 25.3 | | | | 5.9 |
| | | | **RATIOS** | | | | | | |
| 4.0 | 4.9 | 5.9 | | | 6.1 | | | | 3.4 |
| 2.0 | 1.9 | 2.2 | Current | | 1.4 | | | | 1.9 |
| 1.1 | 1.0 | 1.2 | | | .5 | | | | 1.2 |
| 3.9 | 3.0 | 4.3 | | | 6.0 | | | | 2.5 |
| 1.8 | 1.5 | 1.7 | Quick | | 1.4 | | | | 1.2 |
| 1.1 | .5 | .6 | | | .2 | | | | .6 |
| 4  89.8 | 0  UND | 0  UND | | 0  UND | | | | 11  34.4 | |
| 33  11.1 | 15  24.1 | 17  22.1 | Sales/Receivables | 0  UND | | | | 29  12.4 | |
| 63  5.8 | 51  7.2 | 34  10.7 | | 0  755.7 | | | | 43  8.4 | |
| | | | Cost of Sales/Inventory | | | | | | |
| | | | Cost of Sales/Payables | | | | | | |
| 5.8 | 4.9 | 3.5 | | | 5.8 | | | | 2.9 |
| 15.1 | 9.1 | 9.3 | Sales/Working Capital | | 18.6 | | | | 14.8 |
| 55.2 | -390.0 | 41.8 | | | -6.9 | | | | 23.0 |
| 49.4 | 30.1 | 19.0 | | | | | | | 19.5 |
| (29) 24.5 | (47) 8.7 | (43) 6.4 | EBIT/Interest | | | | | (20) | 9.0 |
| 2.5 | 1.7 | .7 | | | | | | | 1.3 |
| | | | Net Profit + Depr., Dep., Amort./Cur. Mat. L/T/D | | | | | | |
| .4 | .1 | .3 | | | .2 | | | | .5 |
| 1.2 | .9 | 1.1 | Fixed/Worth | | 1.2 | | | | 1.2 |
| 2.5 | 5.4 | 5.4 | | | 27.8 | | | | 15.8 |
| .4 | .7 | .4 | | | .2 | | | | .8 |
| 1.2 | 2.0 | 1.7 | Debt/Worth | | .7 | | | | 3.6 |
| 5.9 | 57.0 | 70.2 | | | 254.9 | | | | 52.6 |
| 95.8 | 86.6 | 92.6 | | | | | | | 105.1 |
| (32) 48.3 | (46) 37.9 | (42) 42.3 | % Profit Before Taxes/Tangible Net Worth | | | | | (17) | 67.5 |
| 18.8 | 8.2 | 9.3 | | | | | | | 31.1 |
| 38.5 | 36.8 | 32.6 | | | 39.0 | | | | 28.6 |
| 22.5 | 10.8 | 9.9 | % Profit Before Taxes/Total Assets | | 19.0 | | | | 9.7 |
| 9.9 | 1.9 | 1.7 | | | 1.3 | | | | 2.6 |
| 33.3 | 122.6 | 87.6 | | | 269.4 | | | | 44.7 |
| 8.9 | 13.4 | 8.3 | Sales/Net Fixed Assets | | 1.3 | | | | 8.1 |
| 3.3 | 4.3 | 2.6 | | | .3 | | | | 3.9 |
| 3.3 | 4.0 | 4.1 | | | 2.9 | | | | 5.4 |
| 1.9 | 2.5 | 2.1 | Sales/Total Assets | | 1.1 | | | | 1.7 |
| 1.3 | 1.0 | 1.1 | | | .2 | | | | 1.2 |
| .8 | 1.5 | 1.5 | | | | | | | .9 |
| (26) 3.7 | (31) 5.0 | (26) 4.1 | % Depr., Dep., Amort./Sales | | | | | (12) | 2.4 |
| 11.5 | 10.8 | 8.3 | | | | | | | 7.7 |
| | 1.8 | 1.4 | % Officers', Directors' Owners' Comp/Sales | | | | | | |
| | (18) 4.1 | (13) 4.0 | | | | | | | |
| | 9.9 | 7.2 | | | | | | | |
| 900026M | 1723127M | 3207759M | Net Sales ($) | 2892M | 18489M | 11329M | 32351M | 138210M | 3004488M |
| 676304M | 1150717M | 2133273M | Total Assets ($) | 1531M | 46919M | 4236M | 17046M | 207516M | 1856025M |

M = $ thousand    MM = $ million
See Pages viii through xx for Explanation of Ratios and Data
© RMA 2024

# TRANSPORTATION—Freight Transportation Arrangement  NAICS 488510

## Current Data Sorted by Assets / Comparative Historical Data

| | | | | | | | | | |
|---|---|---|---|---|---|---|---|---|---|
| | | | | 9 | 9 | 5 | **Type of Statement** | | |
| 1 | 1 | 14 | 18 | 6 | 2 | | Unqualified | 28 | 13 |
| | 3 | 18 | 9 | 2 | | | Reviewed | 41 | 27 |
| 12 | 19 | 21 | 3 | | | | Compiled | 36 | 21 |
| 15 | 31 | 79 | 85 | 29 | 24 | | Tax Returns | 44 | 31 |
| | 43 (4/1-9/30/23) | | 372 (10/1/23-3/31/24) | | | | Other | 252 | 176 |
| | | | | | | | | 4/1/19-3/31/20 | 4/1/20-3/31/21 |
| 0-500M | 500M-2MM | 2-10MM | 10-50MM | 50-100MM | 100-250MM | | | ALL | ALL |
| 28 | 54 | 132 | 124 | 46 | 31 | | **NUMBER OF STATEMENTS** | 401 | 268 |
| % | % | % | % | % | % | | **ASSETS** | % | % |
| 45.0 | 23.1 | 18.9 | 15.7 | 15.9 | 10.6 | | Cash & Equivalents | 13.8 | 20.0 |
| 21.3 | 32.6 | 43.2 | 37.5 | 35.0 | 26.5 | | Trade Receivables (net) | 44.0 | 40.5 |
| .0 | .1 | 1.4 | 1.4 | .4 | 3.2 | | Inventory | 2.7 | 1.5 |
| 5.7 | 5.4 | 4.1 | 4.6 | 5.5 | 6.4 | | All Other Current | 5.5 | 5.8 |
| 71.9 | 61.2 | 67.8 | 59.2 | 56.8 | 46.7 | | Total Current | 66.1 | 67.8 |
| 17.1 | 22.2 | 18.4 | 24.2 | 25.0 | 20.8 | | Fixed Assets (net) | 19.9 | 19.1 |
| 5.7 | 7.3 | 4.4 | 5.0 | 6.0 | 15.8 | | Intangibles (net) | 5.6 | 5.3 |
| 5.4 | 9.4 | 9.4 | 11.7 | 12.2 | 16.7 | | All Other Non-Current | 8.4 | 7.9 |
| 100.0 | 100.0 | 100.0 | 100.0 | 100.0 | 100.0 | | Total | 100.0 | 100.0 |
| | | | | | | | **LIABILITIES** | | |
| 6.3 | 11.3 | 4.7 | 4.3 | 3.0 | 3.4 | | Notes Payable-Short Term | 9.4 | 8.2 |
| 6.0 | 1.3 | 1.9 | 2.8 | 4.9 | 4.4 | | Cur. Mat.-L.T.D. | 3.1 | 3.9 |
| 12.3 | 22.0 | 22.5 | 22.0 | 19.6 | 13.8 | | Trade Payables | 28.1 | 23.8 |
| .1 | .1 | .1 | .2 | .3 | .1 | | Income Taxes Payable | .1 | .1 |
| 20.4 | 13.1 | 11.8 | 11.4 | 11.7 | 15.5 | | All Other Current | 13.1 | 13.7 |
| 45.1 | 47.8 | 41.0 | 40.6 | 39.5 | 37.2 | | Total Current | 53.8 | 49.7 |
| 42.4 | 21.0 | 13.4 | 16.6 | 17.7 | 21.1 | | Long-Term Debt | 14.4 | 18.8 |
| .0 | .0 | .1 | .1 | .5 | .5 | | Deferred Taxes | .3 | .2 |
| 4.7 | 6.3 | 4.6 | 6.3 | 6.7 | 6.7 | | All Other Non-Current | 4.0 | 3.9 |
| 7.8 | 25.0 | 40.9 | 36.4 | 35.7 | 34.6 | | Net Worth | 27.4 | 27.3 |
| 100.0 | 100.0 | 100.0 | 100.0 | 100.0 | 100.0 | | Total Liabilties & Net Worth | 100.0 | 100.0 |
| | | | | | | | **INCOME DATA** | | |
| 100.0 | 100.0 | 100.0 | 100.0 | 100.0 | 100.0 | | Net Sales | 100.0 | 100.0 |
| | | | | | | | Gross Profit | | |
| 93.3 | 93.6 | 95.6 | 93.6 | 94.6 | 94.1 | | Operating Expenses | 94.5 | 93.6 |
| 6.7 | 6.4 | 4.4 | 6.4 | 5.4 | 5.9 | | Operating Profit | 5.5 | 6.4 |
| .2 | .7 | .1 | 1.0 | .3 | 1.6 | | All Other Expenses (net) | .6 | .5 |
| 6.5 | 5.7 | 4.3 | 5.4 | 5.2 | 4.3 | | Profit Before Taxes | 5.0 | 5.9 |
| | | | | | | | **RATIOS** | | |
| 8.3 | 3.3 | 3.4 | 2.5 | 2.1 | 2.0 | | | 2.1 | 2.4 |
| 1.9 | 1.4 | 1.6 | 1.4 | 1.4 | 1.5 | | Current | 1.3 | 1.4 |
| .9 | .8 | 1.1 | .9 | .9 | 1.0 | | | .9 | 1.0 |
| 8.3 | 3.3 | 3.1 | 2.1 | 1.9 | 1.4 | | | 1.9 | 2.2 |
| 1.5 | 1.3 | 1.5 | 1.3 | 1.3 | 1.2 | | Quick | 1.2 | 1.3 |
| .6 | .7 | 1.0 | .8 | .9 | .7 | | | .7 | .8 |
| 0 UND | 0 UND | 22 16.5 | 31 11.7 | 35 10.5 | 35 10.3 | | | 25 14.6 | 22 16.7 |
| 0 UND | 21 17.5 | 34 10.7 | 39 9.3 | 43 8.4 | 42 8.7 | | Sales/Receivables | 36 10.0 | 39 9.4 |
| 21 17.8 | 41 8.8 | 52 7.0 | 54 6.8 | 65 5.6 | 62 5.9 | | | 51 7.1 | 53 6.9 |
| | | | | | | | Cost of Sales/Inventory | | |
| | | | | | | | Cost of Sales/Payables | | |
| 15.5 | 10.2 | 8.6 | 7.2 | 7.9 | 5.8 | | | 11.7 | 8.9 |
| 40.9 | 40.3 | 17.3 | 18.5 | 14.9 | 20.7 | | Sales/Working Capital | 29.5 | 21.8 |
| -889.7 | -76.6 | 68.8 | -170.5 | -67.3 | 168.5 | | | -75.0 | 746.6 |
| 40.8 | 60.4 | 50.9 | 32.4 | 57.7 | 14.2 | | | 33.6 | 34.2 |
| (17) 21.2 | (36) 9.3 | (102) 9.9 | (97) 8.2 | (43) 7.3 | (29) 2.9 | | EBIT/Interest | (305) 7.1 | (195) 8.8 |
| -6.2 | .3 | 2.8 | 2.1 | 1.0 | .5 | | | 1.8 | 2.3 |
| | | | 9.6 | 18.9 | | | | 10.2 | 13.3 |
| | | (22) 2.2 | (18) 3.6 | | | | Net Profit + Depr., Dep., Amort./Cur. Mat. L/T/D | (45) 3.6 | (41) 3.2 |
| | | | .3 | 1.2 | | | | .8 | 1.4 |
| .0 | .0 | .0 | .1 | .2 | .1 | | | .0 | .0 |
| .0 | .4 | .2 | .5 | .8 | .7 | | Fixed/Worth | .4 | .4 |
| UND | -4.6 | 1.2 | 2.4 | 2.0 | 6.9 | | | 2.9 | 2.4 |
| .4 | .7 | .7 | 1.2 | 1.0 | 1.2 | | | 1.0 | 1.0 |
| 3.5 | 2.7 | 1.6 | 2.0 | 1.9 | 2.5 | | Debt/Worth | 2.7 | 2.7 |
| -3.5 | -5.1 | 4.7 | 5.3 | 6.4 | 34.6 | | | 13.3 | 16.6 |
| 400.0 | 90.6 | 68.9 | 57.2 | 47.9 | 51.8 | | % Profit Before Taxes/Tangible Net Worth | 77.0 | 77.6 |
| (18) 70.3 | (37) 40.4 | (119) 24.3 | (114) 27.9 | (40) 33.3 | (24) 23.4 | | | (324) 33.3 | (216) 36.0 |
| 27.8 | 14.3 | 5.1 | 7.1 | 7.1 | 3.8 | | | 13.7 | 15.5 |
| 63.5 | 43.0 | 19.3 | 21.6 | 14.1 | 10.0 | | % Profit Before Taxes/Total Assets | 23.0 | 23.1 |
| 20.6 | 13.9 | 9.3 | 9.0 | 8.8 | 3.4 | | | 9.2 | 9.4 |
| -10.9 | 1.2 | 1.0 | 2.4 | .5 | -1.6 | | | 2.4 | 2.4 |
| UND | UND | 517.3 | 167.4 | 50.3 | 61.5 | | | 381.9 | 491.9 |
| UND | 79.5 | 105.0 | 24.4 | 15.9 | 16.1 | | Sales/Net Fixed Assets | 63.6 | 59.7 |
| 36.5 | 15.3 | 13.7 | 4.7 | 3.3 | 4.0 | | | 10.3 | 7.7 |
| 16.2 | 9.1 | 6.1 | 4.8 | 4.1 | 3.2 | | | 7.1 | 5.6 |
| 8.5 | 5.5 | 3.9 | 2.7 | 2.1 | 1.7 | | Sales/Total Assets | 4.2 | 3.6 |
| 6.0 | 2.6 | 2.2 | 1.6 | 1.4 | 1.0 | | | 2.1 | 1.8 |
| | 1.0 | .1 | .2 | .4 | .9 | | | .2 | .1 |
| | (19) 2.5 | (74) .3 | (93) .8 | (40) .7 | (15) 1.6 | | % Depr., Dep., Amort./Sales | (264) .5 | (168) .6 |
| | 11.3 | 1.9 | 4.3 | 3.8 | 3.5 | | | 2.8 | 2.9 |
| | 1.1 | .7 | .3 | | | | | .8 | .8 |
| | (20) 2.2 | (45) 1.3 | (19) .8 | | | | % Officers', Directors' Owners' Comp/Sales | (93) 1.9 | (68) 1.7 |
| | 5.1 | 3.1 | 2.3 | | | | | 3.8 | 3.2 |
| 101094M | 408449M | 2946948M | 8201656M | 9250525M | 11359006M | | Net Sales ($) | 26690289M | 15817542M |
| 7376M | 60243M | 691141M | 2709493M | 3426475M | 5184191M | | Total Assets ($) | 8918845M | 6961589M |

M = $ thousand    MM = $ million
See Pages viii through xx for Explanation of Ratios and Data

© RMA 2024

# TRANSPORTATION—Freight Transportation Arrangement NAICS 488510

| Comparative Historical Data ||| Type of Statement | Current Data Sorted by Sales |||||||
|---|---|---|---|---|---|---|---|---|---|
| 16 | 33 | 23 | Unqualified | | | | 2 | 9 | 23 |
| 25 | 38 | 42 | Reviewed | | 1 | | 2 | 7 | 30 |
| 12 | 36 | 32 | Compiled | 1 | | 3 | 2 | 7 | 19 |
| 40 | 69 | 55 | Tax Returns | 7 | 4 | 8 | 11 | 15 | 10 |
| 162 | 260 | 263 | Other | 6 | 21 | 14 | 22 | 55 | 145 |
| 4/1/21-3/31/22 | 4/1/22-3/31/23 | 4/1/23-3/31/24 | | 43 (4/1-9/30/23) ||| 372 (10/1/23-3/31/24) |||
| ALL | ALL | ALL | | 0-1MM | 1-3MM | 3-5MM | 5-10MM | 10-25MM | 25MM & OVER |
| 255 | 436 | 415 | NUMBER OF STATEMENTS | 14 | 26 | 25 | 37 | 86 | 227 |
| % | % | % | ASSETS | % | % | % | % | % | % |
| 17.8 | 21.6 | 19.3 | Cash & Equivalents | 41.6 | 24.2 | 25.3 | 25.8 | 17.3 | 16.4 |
| 42.5 | 36.2 | 36.5 | Trade Receivables (net) | 10.1 | 21.5 | 21.6 | 37.8 | 39.2 | 40.3 |
| .9 | 1.0 | 1.2 | Inventory | .0 | .2 | .0 | 1.1 | 1.7 | 1.3 |
| 6.3 | 6.0 | 4.9 | All Other Current | 3.8 | 4.0 | 2.8 | 4.7 | 5.9 | 4.9 |
| 67.6 | 64.8 | 61.8 | Total Current | 55.5 | 49.8 | 49.6 | 69.3 | 64.1 | 62.8 |
| 17.3 | 19.7 | 21.4 | Fixed Assets (net) | 38.9 | 32.4 | 25.7 | 19.5 | 20.5 | 19.3 |
| 6.2 | 6.8 | 6.1 | Intangibles (net) | .2 | 7.6 | 12.4 | 3.8 | 4.5 | 6.5 |
| 8.9 | 8.8 | 10.7 | All Other Non-Current | 5.5 | 10.1 | 12.2 | 7.4 | 10.8 | 11.3 |
| 100.0 | 100.0 | 100.0 | Total | 100.0 | 100.0 | 100.0 | 100.0 | 100.0 | 100.0 |
| | | | LIABILITIES | | | | | | |
| 6.0 | 5.4 | 5.2 | Notes Payable-Short Term | .4 | 5.1 | 10.7 | 6.6 | 5.5 | 4.7 |
| 2.9 | 2.8 | 2.9 | Cur. Mat.-L.T.D. | .6 | 2.9 | .8 | 2.3 | 3.7 | 3.1 |
| 26.4 | 19.1 | 20.6 | Trade Payables | 10.3 | 14.0 | 14.8 | 24.3 | 19.7 | 22.4 |
| .1 | .2 | .1 | Income Taxes Payable | .0 | .2 | .0 | .0 | .1 | .2 |
| 13.1 | 11.5 | 12.7 | All Other Current | 24.7 | 13.7 | 10.8 | 11.1 | 9.9 | 13.4 |
| 48.7 | 38.9 | 41.6 | Total Current | 35.9 | 35.9 | 37.1 | 44.3 | 38.8 | 43.7 |
| 17.1 | 19.1 | 18.4 | Long-Term Debt | 28.8 | 38.0 | 16.2 | 21.1 | 21.2 | 14.2 |
| .2 | .1 | .1 | Deferred Taxes | .0 | .0 | .0 | .1 | .1 | .2 |
| 3.3 | 5.5 | 5.7 | All Other Non-Current | 2.2 | 12.2 | 2.6 | 4.3 | 5.0 | 6.0 |
| 30.8 | 36.3 | 34.2 | Net Worth | 33.2 | 13.9 | 44.1 | 30.2 | 34.8 | 36.0 |
| 100.0 | 100.0 | 100.0 | Total Liabilties & Net Worth | 100.0 | 100.0 | 100.0 | 100.0 | 100.0 | 100.0 |
| | | | INCOME DATA | | | | | | |
| 100.0 | 100.0 | 100.0 | Net Sales | 100.0 | 100.0 | 100.0 | 100.0 | 100.0 | 100.0 |
| | | | Gross Profit | | | | | | |
| 93.8 | 91.8 | 94.4 | Operating Expenses | 80.9 | 91.3 | 89.8 | 96.7 | 95.7 | 95.2 |
| 6.2 | 8.2 | 5.6 | Operating Profit | 19.1 | 8.7 | 10.2 | 3.3 | 4.3 | 4.8 |
| -.4 | .6 | .6 | All Other Expenses (net) | 7.7 | 2.3 | 1.3 | .0 | -.7 | .4 |
| 6.6 | 7.6 | 5.1 | Profit Before Taxes | 11.4 | 6.4 | 8.9 | 3.3 | 5.0 | 4.4 |
| | | | RATIOS | | | | | | |
| 2.2 | 3.1 | 2.8 | | 5.3 | 3.8 | 7.3 | 5.0 | 3.5 | 2.1 |
| 1.4 | 1.7 | 1.5 | Current | 1.5 | 1.5 | 1.3 | 1.5 | 1.7 | 1.5 |
| 1.0 | 1.1 | 1.0 | | .5 | .6 | .7 | .9 | 1.2 | 1.0 |
| 2.0 | 2.8 | 2.5 | | 5.3 | 3.8 | 7.3 | 4.6 | 2.9 | 1.9 |
| 1.3 | (435) 1.5 | 1.3 | Quick | 1.3 | 1.2 | 1.3 | 1.5 | 1.5 | 1.3 |
| .8 | 1.0 | .9 | | .1 | .6 | .7 | .9 | 1.1 | .9 |
| 24 15.5 | 16 22.7 | 21 17.6 | | 0 UND | 0 UND | 0 UND | 12 30.5 | 19 19.3 | 31 11.8 |
| 40 9.2 | 33 11.0 | 37 9.9 | Sales/Receivables | 0 UND | 24 15.4 | 3 117.7 | 34 10.6 | 29 12.5 | 39 9.3 |
| 59 6.2 | 49 7.5 | 52 7.0 | | 1 244.9 | 47 7.7 | 47 7.8 | 70 5.2 | 46 8.0 | 54 6.8 |
| | | | Cost of Sales/Inventory | | | | | | |
| | | | Cost of Sales/Payables | | | | | | |
| 11.3 | 8.3 | 8.5 | | 2.5 | 7.9 | 10.2 | 4.3 | 9.1 | 8.6 |
| 22.9 | 19.2 | 20.9 | Sales/Working Capital | 25.1 | 36.1 | 39.1 | 32.4 | 17.8 | 19.0 |
| 185.1 | 96.9 | -857.6 | | -7.5 | -13.5 | -16.7 | -77.0 | 60.7 | -999.8 |
| 58.7 | 60.4 | 41.8 | | 45.3 | 28.6 | 55.7 | 43.8 | 43.0 | |
| (194) 16.0 | (300) 17.3 | (324) 7.8 | EBIT/Interest | (16) 4.9 | (17) 2.9 | (26) 8.5 | (71) 10.9 | (190) 7.5 | |
| 4.6 | 4.0 | 1.6 | | | -10.8 | -15.6 | .5 | 3.4 | 1.7 |
| 16.0 | 11.8 | 13.1 | Net Profit + Depr., Dep., | | | | | | 14.5 |
| (21) 6.6 | (54) 4.4 | (50) 2.7 | Amort./Cur. Mat. L/T/D | | | | | (45) 2.7 | |
| 2.4 | 1.5 | 1.1 | | | | | | | 1.1 |
| .0 | .0 | .1 | | .0 | .0 | .1 | .0 | .0 | .1 |
| .2 | .3 | .3 | Fixed/Worth | .6 | .5 | .4 | .1 | .2 | .4 |
| 2.1 | 1.7 | 2.3 | | 6.6 | -10.0 | 10.7 | 2.7 | 1.6 | 2.0 |
| .9 | .6 | .9 | | .2 | .9 | .2 | .7 | .7 | 1.1 |
| 2.6 | 2.1 | 1.9 | Debt/Worth | 2.5 | 2.5 | 2.5 | 1.9 | 1.6 | 2.0 |
| 7.8 | 6.9 | 8.1 | | UND | -3.7 | NM | 11.5 | 6.3 | 6.3 |
| 104.1 | 100.0 | 66.1 | | 29.7 | 70.3 | 128.2 | 65.6 | 74.0 | 56.3 |
| (212) 59.9 | (373) 55.2 | (352) 29.6 | % Profit Before Taxes/Tangible Net Worth | (11) 18.1 | (17) 40.4 | (19) 46.4 | (29) 19.1 | (76) 34.5 | (200) 29.7 |
| 27.3 | 28.8 | 7.2 | | 3.4 | 13.7 | -18.4 | -9.2 | 10.2 | 7.9 |
| 29.3 | 34.6 | 20.9 | | 21.1 | 21.5 | 52.5 | 19.9 | 24.4 | 19.2 |
| 13.8 | 17.5 | 9.5 | % Profit Before Taxes/Total Assets | 3.5 | 9.1 | 9.0 | 5.7 | 11.6 | 9.1 |
| 7.0 | 7.1 | 1.0 | | -.4 | -13.8 | -3.1 | -7.3 | 2.1 | 1.7 |
| 736.5 | 623.8 | 311.8 | | UND | UND | 184.9 | 999.8 | 999.8 | 183.5 |
| 90.6 | 66.0 | 51.2 | Sales/Net Fixed Assets | 10.6 | 21.9 | 28.0 | 65.6 | 84.6 | 46.7 |
| 10.8 | 10.5 | 9.3 | | .2 | 1.9 | 9.4 | 14.9 | 8.9 | 9.3 |
| 6.1 | 6.8 | 5.9 | | 6.8 | 6.3 | 7.3 | 6.7 | 5.4 | 5.4 |
| 3.8 | 4.1 | 3.4 | Sales/Total Assets | 1.1 | 2.5 | 3.1 | 3.2 | 4.0 | 3.5 |
| 2.1 | 2.0 | 1.7 | | .2 | 1.0 | 1.8 | 1.6 | 1.8 | 1.8 |
| .2 | .1 | .2 | | .5 | .1 | .3 | .2 | | |
| (150) .6 | (249) .6 | (246) .7 | % Depr., Dep., Amort./Sales | (12) 1.5 | (15) .8 | (42) 1.1 | (164) .5 | | |
| 2.8 | 3.3 | 3.6 | | 2.5 | 3.3 | 3.9 | 3.2 | | |
| .7 | .8 | .8 | | 2.2 | 1.0 | .8 | .5 | | |
| (54) 1.5 | (108) 1.6 | (94) 1.4 | % Officers', Directors' Owners' Comp/Sales | (10) 2.4 | (13) 2.2 | (27) 1.2 | (38) 1.1 | | |
| 3.6 | 3.3 | 3.6 | | 6.3 | 6.4 | 2.5 | 2.0 | | |
| 19733020M | 29225136M | 32267678M | Net Sales ($) | 6904M | 51985M | 98265M | 278112M | 1444198M | 30388214M |
| 6818029M | 9964590M | 12078919M | Total Assets ($) | 13780M | 58915M | 83811M | 124234M | 562509M | 11235670M |

M = $ thousand    MM = $ million
See Pages viii through xx for Explanation of Ratios and Data

© RMA 2024

# TRANSPORTATION—Packing and Crating  NAICS 488991

## Current Data Sorted by Assets

| | | | | | | Type of Statement | |
|---|---|---|---|---|---|---|---|
| | | | | | | Unqualified | |
| | | | | 2 | | Reviewed | |
| | | 1 | 2 | 1 | | Compiled | |
| 4 | 1 | 3 | 1 | 3 | 1 | Tax Returns | |
| | 1 | 17 | 6 | | | Other | |
| | 9 (4/1-9/30/23) | | 32 (10/1/23-3/31/24) | | | | |
| 0-500M | 500M-2MM | 2-10MM | 10-50MM | 50-100MM | 100-250MM | NUMBER OF STATEMENTS | |
| 4 | 2 | 20 | 9 | 4 | 2 | | |
| % | % | % | % | % | % | ASSETS | |
| | | 22.4 | | | | Cash & Equivalents | |
| | | 19.3 | | | | Trade Receivables (net) | |
| | | 10.3 | | | | Inventory | |
| | | 2.3 | | | | All Other Current | |
| | | 54.2 | | | | Total Current | |
| | | 22.9 | | | | Fixed Assets (net) | |
| | | 13.1 | | | | Intangibles (net) | |
| | | 9.8 | | | | All Other Non-Current | |
| | | 100.0 | | | | Total | |
| | | | | | | **LIABILITIES** | |
| | | 3.4 | | | | Notes Payable-Short Term | |
| | | 1.8 | | | | Cur. Mat.-L.T.D. | |
| | | 9.9 | | | | Trade Payables | |
| | | .0 | | | | Income Taxes Payable | |
| | | 5.9 | | | | All Other Current | |
| | | 21.0 | | | | Total Current | |
| | | 9.2 | | | | Long-Term Debt | |
| | | .0 | | | | Deferred Taxes | |
| | | 3.6 | | | | All Other Non-Current | |
| | | 66.2 | | | | Net Worth | |
| | | 100.0 | | | | Total Liabilities & Net Worth | |
| | | | | | | **INCOME DATA** | |
| | | 100.0 | | | | Net Sales | |
| | | | | | | Gross Profit | |
| | | 95.0 | | | | Operating Expenses | |
| | | 5.0 | | | | Operating Profit | |
| | | -.6 | | | | All Other Expenses (net) | |
| | | 5.6 | | | | Profit Before Taxes | |
| | | | | | | **RATIOS** | |
| | | 7.6 | | | | | |
| | | 3.7 | | | | Current | |
| | | 2.0 | | | | | |
| | | 6.1 | | | | | |
| | | 3.1 | | | | Quick | |
| | | 1.3 | | | | | |
| | | 10   37.5 | | | | | |
| | | 25   14.5 | | | | Sales/Receivables | |
| | | 47   7.7 | | | | | |
| | | | | | | Cost of Sales/Inventory | |
| | | | | | | Cost of Sales/Payables | |
| | | 4.9 | | | | | |
| | | 6.0 | | | | Sales/Working Capital | |
| | | 25.9 | | | | | |
| | | 167.2 | | | | | |
| | | (16)  29.1 | | | | EBIT/Interest | |
| | | 3.4 | | | | | |
| | | | | | | Net Profit + Depr., Dep., Amort./Cur. Mat. L/T/D | |
| | | .1 | | | | | |
| | | .3 | | | | Fixed/Worth | |
| | | .8 | | | | | |
| | | .2 | | | | | |
| | | .6 | | | | Debt/Worth | |
| | | 1.2 | | | | | |
| | | 57.3 | | | | | |
| | | (18)  33.6 | | | | % Profit Before Taxes/Tangible Net Worth | |
| | | 13.5 | | | | | |
| | | 32.7 | | | | | |
| | | 14.8 | | | | % Profit Before Taxes/Total Assets | |
| | | 6.2 | | | | | |
| | | 109.8 | | | | | |
| | | 17.6 | | | | Sales/Net Fixed Assets | |
| | | 5.2 | | | | | |
| | | 3.5 | | | | | |
| | | 2.3 | | | | Sales/Total Assets | |
| | | 1.7 | | | | | |
| | | .5 | | | | | |
| | | (13)  1.7 | | | | % Depr., Dep., Amort./Sales | |
| | | 4.9 | | | | | |
| | | | | | | % Officers', Directors' Owners' Comp/Sales | |
| 4571M | 2833M | 279661M | 514522M | 650892M | 611548M | Net Sales ($) | |
| 830M | 1485M | 109341M | 229690M | 266423M | 246928M | Total Assets ($) | |

## Comparative Historical Data

| | | | |
|---|---|---|---|
| | | | 2 |
| | 4 | | 3 |
| | 2 | | 1 |
| | 5 | | |
| | 22 | | 10 |
| | 4/1/19- | | 4/1/20- |
| | 3/31/20 | | 3/31/21 |
| | ALL | | ALL |
| NUMBER OF STATEMENTS | 33 | | 16 |
| | % | | % |
| **ASSETS** | | | |
| Cash & Equivalents | 10.0 | | 11.9 |
| Trade Receivables (net) | 28.5 | | 23.0 |
| Inventory | 9.5 | | 9.5 |
| All Other Current | 6.4 | | 1.6 |
| Total Current | 54.3 | | 46.0 |
| Fixed Assets (net) | 30.5 | | 31.1 |
| Intangibles (net) | 7.3 | | 12.7 |
| All Other Non-Current | 7.9 | | 10.1 |
| Total | 100.0 | | 100.0 |
| **LIABILITIES** | | | |
| Notes Payable-Short Term | 9.1 | | 12.1 |
| Cur. Mat.-L.T.D. | 3.3 | | 5.3 |
| Trade Payables | 11.0 | | 15.4 |
| Income Taxes Payable | .0 | | .0 |
| All Other Current | 13.6 | | 15.0 |
| Total Current | 37.0 | | 47.8 |
| Long-Term Debt | 26.6 | | 19.2 |
| Deferred Taxes | .2 | | .1 |
| All Other Non-Current | 2.5 | | 10.0 |
| Net Worth | 33.7 | | 22.9 |
| Total Liabilities & Net Worth | 100.0 | | 100.0 |
| **INCOME DATA** | | | |
| Net Sales | 100.0 | | 100.0 |
| Gross Profit | | | |
| Operating Expenses | 91.4 | | 95.8 |
| Operating Profit | 8.6 | | 4.2 |
| All Other Expenses (net) | 1.4 | | 1.0 |
| Profit Before Taxes | 7.2 | | 3.2 |
| **RATIOS** | | | |
| Current | 3.9 | | 2.1 |
| | 1.4 | | 1.2 |
| | .9 | | .7 |
| Quick | 2.4 | | 2.0 |
| | 1.1 | | .9 |
| | .6 | | .4 |
| Sales/Receivables | 28  13.0 | 24 | 15.2 |
| | 45  8.2 | 35 | 10.4 |
| | 60  6.1 | 45 | 8.2 |
| Sales/Working Capital | 5.7 | | 14.1 |
| | 17.6 | | 35.7 |
| | NM | | -12.1 |
| EBIT/Interest | 26.3 | | 15.5 |
| | (26)  4.2 | (13) | 2.0 |
| | 1.5 | | -.1 |
| Fixed/Worth | .2 | | .5 |
| | 1.3 | | 6.3 |
| | UND | | -1.0 |
| Debt/Worth | .5 | | .8 |
| | 1.8 | | 12.6 |
| | UND | | -4.6 |
| % Profit Before Taxes/Tangible Net Worth | 73.9 | | |
| | (26)  47.9 | | |
| | 16.1 | | |
| % Profit Before Taxes/Total Assets | 34.3 | | 19.3 |
| | 10.7 | | 5.0 |
| | 2.5 | | -.6 |
| Sales/Net Fixed Assets | 42.1 | | 14.7 |
| | 8.7 | | 6.7 |
| | 4.9 | | 4.5 |
| Sales/Total Assets | 4.1 | | 3.2 |
| | 2.5 | | 1.8 |
| | 1.3 | | 1.5 |
| % Depr., Dep., Amort./Sales | 1.2 | | 2.1 |
| | (26)  2.4 | (15) | 3.4 |
| | 5.3 | | 5.7 |
| Net Sales ($) | 1442373M | | 633677M |
| Total Assets ($) | 841140M | | 336736M |

M = $ thousand   MM = $ million
See Pages viii through xx for Explanation of Ratios and Data

© RMA 2024

# TRANSPORTATION—Packing and Crating  NAICS 488991

## Comparative Historical Data | Current Data Sorted by Sales

| Comparative Historical Data | | | | | Current Data Sorted by Sales | | | | | |
|---|---|---|---|---|---|---|---|---|---|---|
| 3 | 2 | | | Type of Statement | | | | | | 3 |
| 2 | 4 | 3 | | Unqualified | | | | | | 2 |
| | 4 | 2 | | Reviewed | | 4 | | 1 | 1 | 1 |
| 5 | 4 | 8 | | Compiled | 1 | 1 | | 5 | 11 | 11 |
| 14 | 24 | 28 | | Tax Returns | | | | | | |
| 4/1/21- | 4/1/22- | 4/1/23- | | Other | 9 (4/1-9/30/23) | | 32 (10/1/23-3/31/24) | | | |
| 3/31/22 | 3/31/23 | 3/31/24 | | | 0-1MM | 1-3MM | 3-5MM | 5-10MM | 10-25MM | 25MM & OVER |
| ALL | ALL | ALL | | | | | | | | |
| 24 | 38 | 41 | | NUMBER OF STATEMENTS | 1 | 5 | | 6 | 12 | 17 |
| % | % | % | | ASSETS | % | % | | % | % | % |
| 16.0 | 16.2 | 23.1 | | Cash & Equivalents | | | D | | 19.3 | 20.0 |
| 29.6 | 29.4 | 21.8 | | Trade Receivables (net) | | | A | | 22.0 | 24.0 |
| 8.7 | 9.3 | 11.0 | | Inventory | | | T | | 2.9 | 13.0 |
| 3.0 | 4.6 | 1.5 | | All Other Current | | | A | | 2.5 | 1.3 |
| 57.4 | 59.5 | 57.4 | | Total Current | | | | | 46.7 | 58.3 |
| 29.3 | 26.5 | 21.9 | | Fixed Assets (net) | | | N | | 34.4 | 21.4 |
| 6.7 | 5.6 | 9.3 | | Intangibles (net) | | | O | | 6.6 | 4.3 |
| 6.6 | 8.4 | 11.5 | | All Other Non-Current | | | T | | 12.3 | 16.0 |
| 100.0 | 100.0 | 100.0 | | Total | | | | | 100.0 | 100.0 |
| | | | | LIABILITIES | | | A | | | |
| 10.2 | 3.0 | 2.9 | | Notes Payable-Short Term | | | V | | .5 | 1.8 |
| 3.1 | 3.1 | 1.6 | | Cur. Mat.-L.T.D. | | | A | | 2.9 | 1.3 |
| 11.4 | 13.7 | 9.4 | | Trade Payables | | | I | | 6.4 | 10.7 |
| .1 | .0 | .0 | | Income Taxes Payable | | | L | | .0 | .0 |
| 11.1 | 10.3 | 10.8 | | All Other Current | | | A | | 3.6 | 13.3 |
| 35.9 | 30.1 | 24.6 | | Total Current | | | B | | 13.3 | 27.1 |
| 15.7 | 15.7 | 11.4 | | Long-Term Debt | | | L | | 18.5 | 10.8 |
| .4 | .0 | .0 | | Deferred Taxes | | | E | | .0 | .0 |
| 5.7 | 1.5 | 4.6 | | All Other Non-Current | | | | | 4.5 | 6.7 |
| 42.2 | 52.7 | 59.3 | | Net Worth | | | | | 63.7 | 55.5 |
| 100.0 | 100.0 | 100.0 | | Total Liabilties & Net Worth | | | | | 100.0 | 100.0 |
| | | | | INCOME DATA | | | | | | |
| 100.0 | 100.0 | 100.0 | | Net Sales | | | | | 100.0 | 100.0 |
| | | | | Gross Profit | | | | | | |
| 88.4 | 92.9 | 94.7 | | Operating Expenses | | | | | 92.4 | 94.3 |
| 11.6 | 7.1 | 5.3 | | Operating Profit | | | | | 7.6 | 5.7 |
| .0 | -1.1 | -.2 | | All Other Expenses (net) | | | | | -.4 | -.3 |
| 11.6 | 8.1 | 5.6 | | Profit Before Taxes | | | | | 8.0 | 6.0 |
| | | | | RATIOS | | | | | | |
| 3.6 | 4.4 | 5.7 | | | | | | | 11.5 | 4.9 |
| 2.0 | 2.2 | 3.3 | | Current | | | | | 4.3 | 2.3 |
| .7 | 1.6 | 1.4 | | | | | | | 2.9 | 1.1 |
| 2.9 | 4.4 | 5.4 | | | | | | | 11.1 | 3.5 |
| 1.2 | 1.6 | 2.5 | | Quick | | | | | 4.1 | 1.6 |
| .6 | 1.1 | 1.1 | | | | | | | 2.6 | .9 |
| 13  28.4 | 27  13.7 | 12  29.3 | | | | | | 10  37.4 | 26  14.2 | |
| 30  12.3 | 46  8.0 | 32  11.5 | | Sales/Receivables | | | | 37  9.9 | 38  9.5 | |
| 49  7.5 | 66  5.5 | 46  7.9 | | | | | | 59  6.2 | 48  7.6 | |
| | | | | Cost of Sales/Inventory | | | | | | |
| | | | | Cost of Sales/Payables | | | | | | |
| 6.2 | 6.1 | 5.1 | | | | | | | 5.2 | 5.3 |
| 15.5 | 8.8 | 6.2 | | Sales/Working Capital | | | | | 5.9 | 13.8 |
| -46.0 | 23.3 | 34.5 | | | | | | | 11.8 | NM |
| 24.0 | 77.3 | 138.6 | | | | | | | | 293.3 |
| (18)  5.2 | (32)  18.0 | (33)  12.0 | | EBIT/Interest | | | | | (15)  36.8 | |
| 2.9 | 5.6 | 2.9 | | | | | | | | 3.8 |
| | | | | Net Profit + Depr., Dep., Amort./Cur. Mat. L/T/D | | | | | | |
| .1 | .1 | .1 | | | | | | | .2 | .1 |
| 1.0 | .3 | .3 | | Fixed/Worth | | | | | .5 | .3 |
| 7.9 | 1.0 | .8 | | | | | | | 1.7 | .6 |
| .4 | .4 | .3 | | | | | | | .2 | .3 |
| 1.4 | .8 | .6 | | Debt/Worth | | | | | .6 | .6 |
| 8.4 | 1.7 | 2.6 | | | | | | | 1.2 | 2.6 |
| 95.3 | 57.5 | 61.3 | | | | | | | 54.0 | 58.9 |
| (19)  59.5 | (34)  27.8 | (38)  33.6 | | % Profit Before Taxes/Tangible Net Worth | | | | (11)  31.4 | (16)  39.3 | |
| 51.4 | 15.4 | 12.8 | | | | | | | 13.6 | 13.3 |
| 43.1 | 23.8 | 30.0 | | | | | | | 32.7 | 30.0 |
| 19.6 | 13.5 | 10.9 | | % Profit Before Taxes/Total Assets | | | | | 10.5 | 14.4 |
| 7.0 | 5.5 | 2.4 | | | | | | | 6.1 | 3.8 |
| 100.5 | 31.1 | 127.5 | | | | | | | 57.6 | 50.7 |
| 19.2 | 14.3 | 18.6 | | Sales/Net Fixed Assets | | | | | 9.0 | 16.1 |
| 6.2 | 6.6 | 6.1 | | | | | | | 3.2 | 6.4 |
| 5.0 | 3.9 | 3.6 | | | | | | | 3.4 | 3.8 |
| 2.8 | 2.5 | 2.4 | | Sales/Total Assets | | | | | 2.2 | 3.0 |
| 1.4 | 1.4 | 1.7 | | | | | | | 1.7 | 2.0 |
| .4 | .6 | .5 | | | | | | | | .3 |
| (15)  1.7 | (29)  1.7 | (25)  1.1 | | % Depr., Dep., Amort./Sales | | | | | (11)  .6 | |
| 5.8 | 3.5 | 4.5 | | | | | | | | 3.2 |
| | 1.6 | .6 | | | | | | | | |
| | (13)  3.9 | (14)  2.7 | | % Officers', Directors' Owners' Comp/Sales | | | | | | |
| | 9.4 | 4.1 | | | | | | | | |
| 882867M | 1836381M | 2064027M | | Net Sales ($) | 175M | 7229M | | 40808M | 167061M | 1848754M |
| 279879M | 953125M | 854697M | | Total Assets ($) | 87M | 2228M | | 24767M | 85509M | 742106M |

© RMA 2024  
M = $ thousand    MM = $ million  
See Pages viii through xx for Explanation of Ratios and Data

# TRANSPORTATION—All Other Support Activities for Transportation  NAICS 488999

## Current Data Sorted by Assets | Comparative Historical Data

| | | | | | | Type of Statement | | |
|---|---|---|---|---|---|---|---|---|
| | | | 1 | | 1 | Unqualified | 3 | 3 |
| | | 1 | 6 | 1 | | Reviewed | 10 | 5 |
| | 1 | 2 | 1 | 3 | | Compiled | 11 | 4 |
| 1 | 5 | 4 | 3 | | | Tax Returns | 11 | 7 |
| 4 | 9 | 28 | 16 | 8 | 2 | Other | 57 | 37 |
| 4 | 6 (4/1-9/30/23) | | 99 (10/1/23-3/31/24) | | | | 4/1/19-3/31/20 | 4/1/20-3/31/21 |
| 0-500M | 500M-2MM | 2-10MM | 10-50MM | 50-100MM | 100-250MM | | ALL | ALL |
| 9 | 15 | 36 | 30 | 12 | 3 | NUMBER OF STATEMENTS | 92 | 56 |
| % | % | % | % | % | % | ASSETS | % | % |
| | 15.5 | 14.2 | 13.2 | 4.9 | | Cash & Equivalents | 15.2 | 27.8 |
| | 37.5 | 25.1 | 21.1 | 15.0 | | Trade Receivables (net) | 28.7 | 26.4 |
| | 2.2 | 5.3 | 6.0 | 1.0 | | Inventory | 2.3 | .8 |
| | 1.8 | 6.5 | 6.1 | 4.0 | | All Other Current | 3.7 | 5.8 |
| | 57.1 | 51.1 | 46.4 | 24.8 | | Total Current | 49.9 | 60.7 |
| | 32.7 | 31.5 | 38.1 | 48.6 | | Fixed Assets (net) | 36.9 | 25.8 |
| | 7.8 | 9.6 | 2.1 | 2.7 | | Intangibles (net) | 7.5 | 7.6 |
| | 2.4 | 7.8 | 13.4 | 23.8 | | All Other Non-Current | 5.7 | 5.9 |
| | 100.0 | 100.0 | 100.0 | 100.0 | | Total | 100.0 | 100.0 |
| | | | | | | LIABILITIES | | |
| | 12.5 | 3.2 | 6.3 | 2.3 | | Notes Payable-Short Term | 8.8 | 12.5 |
| | 3.5 | 4.7 | 6.2 | 8.3 | | Cur. Mat.-L.T.D. | 6.0 | 7.7 |
| | 16.4 | 11.6 | 8.8 | 4.5 | | Trade Payables | 14.5 | 8.1 |
| | .0 | .1 | .2 | .0 | | Income Taxes Payable | .1 | .1 |
| | 9.6 | 5.1 | 7.0 | 6.8 | | All Other Current | 8.4 | 21.0 |
| | 41.9 | 24.7 | 28.4 | 22.0 | | Total Current | 37.7 | 49.5 |
| | 46.0 | 31.0 | 26.4 | 38.9 | | Long-Term Debt | 30.9 | 29.0 |
| | .0 | .0 | .4 | .8 | | Deferred Taxes | .3 | .0 |
| | .0 | 6.0 | 5.6 | 11.7 | | All Other Non-Current | 4.8 | 6.6 |
| | 12.0 | 38.3 | 39.2 | 26.6 | | Net Worth | 26.3 | 14.9 |
| | 100.0 | 100.0 | 100.0 | 100.0 | | Total Liabilties & Net Worth | 100.0 | 100.0 |
| | | | | | | INCOME DATA | | |
| | 100.0 | 100.0 | 100.0 | 100.0 | | Net Sales | 100.0 | 100.0 |
| | | | | | | Gross Profit | | |
| | 93.1 | 89.4 | 90.0 | 97.1 | | Operating Expenses | 93.7 | 91.8 |
| | 6.9 | 10.6 | 10.0 | 2.9 | | Operating Profit | 6.3 | 8.2 |
| | -.6 | 1.2 | 1.1 | 1.5 | | All Other Expenses (net) | 1.0 | .9 |
| | 7.5 | 9.5 | 8.8 | 1.4 | | Profit Before Taxes | 5.4 | 7.3 |
| | | | | | | RATIOS | | |
| | 2.8 | 12.0 | 4.5 | 1.3 | | | 2.7 | 3.1 |
| | 1.6 | 2.0 | 1.8 | 1.1 | | Current | 1.2 | 1.4 |
| | .6 | 1.3 | 1.0 | .8 | | | .7 | 1.0 |
| | 2.8 | 9.1 | 2.8 | 1.1 | | | 2.2 | 2.5 |
| | 1.6 | 1.8 | 1.2 | .9 | | Quick | 1.1 | 1.3 |
| | .4 | .8 | .5 | .7 | | | .7 | .6 |
| 0 | UND | 0 | UND | 13 | 28.8 | 37 | 9.9 | | | 13 | 27.4 | 6 | 61.7 |
| 22 | 16.6 | 29 | 12.7 | 25 | 14.6 | 46 | 8.0 | Sales/Receivables | 34 | 10.8 | 38 | 9.5 |
| 41 | 9.0 | 53 | 6.9 | 39 | 9.4 | 62 | 5.9 | | 44 | 8.3 | 61 | 6.0 |
| | | | | | | Cost of Sales/Inventory | | |
| | | | | | | Cost of Sales/Payables | | |
| | 14.9 | 4.4 | 4.8 | 17.7 | | | 10.3 | 6.8 |
| | 34.3 | 13.5 | 19.9 | 44.3 | | Sales/Working Capital | 44.1 | 15.5 |
| | -52.6 | 47.1 | NM | -34.7 | | | -25.4 | NM |
| | 63.6 | 29.8 | 15.1 | 6.4 | | | 14.9 | 25.4 |
| (12) | 7.6 | (25) 9.0 | (25) 5.7 | 1.6 | | EBIT/Interest | (79) 4.2 | (46) 6.5 |
| | -.3 | 2.1 | 1.4 | 1.2 | | | 1.2 | 2.3 |
| | | | | | | | 2.8 | 5.4 |
| | | | | | | Net Profit + Depr., Dep., Amort./Cur. Mat. L/T/D | (18) 1.4 | (11) 1.5 |
| | | | | | | | .9 | .8 |
| | .0 | .0 | .1 | .7 | | | .4 | .1 |
| | .5 | .4 | 1.1 | 2.1 | | Fixed/Worth | 1.7 | 1.1 |
| | -1.0 | 5.6 | 3.6 | 28.3 | | | 7.3 | 44.7 |
| | .7 | .7 | .6 | 1.9 | | | .7 | 1.0 |
| | 1.8 | 1.9 | 2.2 | 2.0 | | Debt/Worth | 3.3 | 2.5 |
| | -2.6 | 20.6 | 5.4 | 37.4 | | | 15.3 | -28.2 |
| | 104.5 | 116.6 | 77.1 | 71.7 | | % Profit Before Taxes/Tangible Net Worth | 64.5 | 60.1 |
| (10) | 47.3 | (29) 39.2 | 29.2 | (11) 11.1 | | | (72) 22.4 | (41) 38.3 |
| | 10.9 | 17.2 | 5.3 | 1.5 | | | 7.1 | 10.8 |
| | 37.0 | 35.5 | 22.4 | 4.8 | | % Profit Before Taxes/Total Assets | 14.8 | 21.3 |
| | 18.0 | 16.2 | 7.8 | 1.9 | | | 6.9 | 10.0 |
| | -4.7 | 5.2 | .9 | .6 | | | .8 | 1.0 |
| | UND | 223.2 | 45.7 | 7.0 | | | 52.9 | 109.7 |
| | 33.8 | 11.1 | 4.7 | 2.0 | | Sales/Net Fixed Assets | 7.6 | 19.6 |
| | 5.0 | 4.1 | 3.0 | 1.5 | | | 2.6 | 3.7 |
| | 10.5 | 4.3 | 2.7 | 1.5 | | | 5.3 | 4.5 |
| | 4.1 | 2.8 | 1.8 | 1.2 | | Sales/Total Assets | 2.6 | 2.2 |
| | 3.4 | 1.4 | 1.3 | .9 | | | 1.4 | 1.2 |
| | | .9 | .6 | | | | 1.0 | .6 |
| | (19) | 3.8 | (26) 4.4 | | | % Depr., Dep., Amort./Sales | (61) 3.6 | (32) 3.3 |
| | | 6.6 | 8.4 | | | | 8.8 | 9.9 |
| | | .5 | | | | | .6 | |
| | (12) | 1.3 | | | | % Officers', Directors' Owners' Comp/Sales | (19) 1.6 | |
| | | 3.2 | | | | | 2.9 | |
| 13829M | 107695M | 551868M | 1789715M | 1155381M | 1662207M | Net Sales ($) | 3563656M | 3193469M |
| 2378M | 17841M | 155039M | 680002M | 867663M | 623165M | Total Assets ($) | 1659011M | 1590571M |

© RMA 2024  M = $ thousand  MM = $ million
See Pages viii through xx for Explanation of Ratios and Data

# TRANSPORTATION—All Other Support Activities for Transportation  NAICS 488999

| Comparative Historical Data ||| Type of Statement | Current Data Sorted by Sales ||||||
|---|---|---|---|---|---|---|---|---|---|
| 2 | 10 | 7 | Unqualified | | | | | 1 | 6 |
| 5 | 12 | 10 | Reviewed | | 1 | | 1 | | 8 |
| 4 | 3 | 5 | Compiled | 1 | 1 | 2 | 1 | | 1 |
| 27 | 9 | 16 | Tax Returns | 3 | 3 | 1 | 3 | 3 | 3 |
|   | 59 | 67 | Other | 4 | 6 | 3 | 11 | 20 | 23 |
| 4/1/21- | 4/1/22- | 4/1/23- | | | 6 (4/1-9/30/23) ||| 99 (10/1/23-3/31/24) |||
| 3/31/22 | 3/31/23 | 3/31/24 | | | | | | | |
| ALL | ALL | ALL | | 0-1MM | 1-3MM | 3-5MM | 5-10MM | 10-25MM | 25MM & OVER |
| 38 | 93 | 105 | NUMBER OF STATEMENTS | 7 | 11 | 6 | 16 | 24 | 41 |
| % | % | % | ASSETS | % | % | % | % | % | % |
| 18.4 | 20.1 | 15.7 | Cash & Equivalents | 27.9 | 16.3 | | 12.5 | 11.9 | |
| 34.8 | 25.4 | 24.4 | Trade Receivables (net) | 24.7 | 23.5 | | 36.5 | 23.0 | |
| 1.3 | 3.1 | 4.0 | Inventory | .2 | 8.3 | | 4.9 | 3.3 | |
| 8.9 | 8.7 | 5.1 | All Other Current | 7.0 | 5.9 | | 6.5 | 4.2 | |
| 63.3 | 57.3 | 49.2 | Total Current | 59.9 | 53.9 | | 60.4 | 42.3 | |
| 28.2 | 31.4 | 34.4 | Fixed Assets (net) | 32.9 | 27.3 | | 28.3 | 37.6 | |
| 1.2 | 4.8 | 6.1 | Intangibles (net) | 3.8 | 6.8 | | 3.7 | 5.8 | |
| 7.3 | 6.5 | 10.3 | All Other Non-Current | 3.4 | 12.0 | | 7.6 | 14.3 | |
| 100.0 | 100.0 | 100.0 | Total | 100.0 | 100.0 | | 100.0 | 100.0 | |
| | | | LIABILITIES | | | | | | |
| 4.7 | 5.5 | 5.9 | Notes Payable-Short Term | 13.8 | 9.4 | | 3.0 | 3.8 | |
| 3.1 | 4.0 | 5.7 | Cur. Mat.-L.T.D. | 6.6 | 4.5 | | 2.6 | 8.2 | |
| 16.8 | 10.0 | 10.8 | Trade Payables | 7.4 | 7.6 | | 17.5 | 11.6 | |
| .1 | .0 | .1 | Income Taxes Payable | .0 | .3 | | .0 | .1 | |
| 9.1 | 14.3 | 7.5 | All Other Current | 4.9 | 8.3 | | 4.7 | 8.4 | |
| 33.9 | 33.8 | 30.0 | Total Current | 32.8 | 30.1 | | 27.8 | 32.1 | |
| 30.2 | 25.1 | 33.7 | Long-Term Debt | 61.3 | 28.0 | | 26.8 | 28.9 | |
| .4 | .4 | .2 | Deferred Taxes | .0 | .0 | | .5 | .3 | |
| 4.0 | 6.6 | 5.9 | All Other Non-Current | 3.2 | 5.3 | | 4.3 | 7.2 | |
| 31.5 | 34.1 | 30.1 | Net Worth | 2.8 | 36.6 | | 40.6 | 31.4 | |
| 100.0 | 100.0 | 100.0 | Total Liabilities & Net Worth | 100.0 | 100.0 | | 100.0 | 100.0 | |
| | | | INCOME DATA | | | | | | |
| 100.0 | 100.0 | 100.0 | Net Sales | 100.0 | 100.0 | | 100.0 | 100.0 | |
| | | | Gross Profit | | | | | | |
| 84.8 | 90.0 | 91.5 | Operating Expenses | 91.1 | 92.9 | | 94.4 | 92.7 | |
| 15.2 | 10.0 | 8.5 | Operating Profit | 8.9 | 7.1 | | 5.6 | 7.3 | |
| -.8 | 1.3 | .9 | All Other Expenses (net) | 3.1 | -.7 | | -.5 | 1.0 | |
| 16.0 | 8.7 | 7.6 | Profit Before Taxes | 5.7 | 7.9 | | 6.1 | 6.4 | |
| | | | RATIOS | | | | | | |
| 5.1 | 2.8 | 4.3 | | 16.6 | 8.5 | | 8.0 | 2.2 | |
| 2.0 | 1.6 | 1.7 | Current | 3.5 | 2.9 | | 2.1 | 1.2 | |
| 1.1 | 1.0 | 1.0 | | 1.2 | 1.6 | | 1.7 | .9 | |
| 2.7 | 2.5 | 3.4 | | 16.0 | 5.1 | | 7.3 | 1.9 | |
| 1.6 | 1.5 | 1.5 | Quick | 3.4 | 1.7 | | 1.8 | 1.0 | |
| 1.0 | .8 | .7 | | 1.0 | .5 | | 1.3 | .7 | |
| 15   24.6 | 10   38.4 | 7   48.9 | | 0   UND | 5   69.3 | | 14   25.6 | 15   24.9 | |
| 41   8.9 | 29   12.5 | 26   14.0 | Sales/Receivables | 29   12.6 | 20   18.7 | | 34   10.6 | 33   11.1 | |
| 57   6.4 | 47   7.7 | 49   7.4 | | 58   6.3 | 46   8.0 | | 53   6.9 | 49   7.5 | |
| | | | Cost of Sales/Inventory | | | | | | |
| | | | Cost of Sales/Payables | | | | | | |
| 4.8 | 6.7 | 7.3 | | 1.9 | 4.3 | | 4.9 | 12.8 | |
| 17.0 | 18.0 | 20.4 | Sales/Working Capital | 13.7 | 12.2 | | 12.8 | 26.5 | |
| 105.5 | 96.0 | UND | | 69.3 | 23.3 | | 40.7 | -86.0 | |
| 68.2 | 24.0 | 15.4 | | | 40.6 | | 25.3 | 10.3 | |
| (27) 9.4 | (70) 6.4 | (80) 5.8 | EBIT/Interest | (12) 7.0 | (19) 9.0 | | (36) 5.3 | | |
| 5.9 | 3.1 | 1.3 | | .8 | 2.2 | | | 1.3 | |
| | 30.8 | 13.6 | Net Profit + Depr., Dep., | | | | | | 16.1 |
| (19) 3.0 | (16) 1.8 | Amort./Cur. Mat. L/T/D | | | | | (14) 1.5 | | |
| 1.4 | 1.3 | | | | | | | 1.2 | |
| .0 | .1 | .1 | | .0 | .0 | | .0 | .2 | |
| .5 | .8 | .9 | Fixed/Worth | .3 | .5 | | .3 | 1.4 | |
| 2.3 | 4.3 | 5.3 | | -.9 | 2.3 | | 13.0 | 3.8 | |
| .5 | .9 | .8 | | .4 | .7 | | .5 | 1.3 | |
| 1.8 | 1.9 | 2.3 | Debt/Worth | 5.4 | 1.3 | | 1.4 | 2.3 | |
| 4.7 | 5.9 | 14.4 | | -2.2 | 4.3 | | 14.3 | 7.4 | |
| | | | | | 104.5 | | 98.2 | 80.4 | |
| 90.5 | 84.2 | 81.5 | % Profit Before Taxes/Tangible | | | | | | |
| (35) 52.2 | (80) 44.3 | (89) 32.8 | Net Worth | (14) 34.1 | (20) 42.0 | | (39) 28.7 | | |
| 27.9 | 17.4 | 7.6 | | 17.4 | 7.7 | | 6.8 | | |
| 40.1 | 36.7 | 27.7 | % Profit Before Taxes/Total | 29.2 | 36.5 | | 32.1 | 21.5 | |
| 20.6 | 13.2 | 8.4 | Assets | 7.8 | 16.5 | | 10.9 | 5.6 | |
| 8.8 | 3.6 | 1.4 | | -.4 | 8.8 | | 4.3 | 1.5 | |
| 293.4 | 140.4 | 171.6 | | 206.7 | 263.5 | | 882.1 | 33.4 | |
| 16.5 | 11.9 | 8.0 | Sales/Net Fixed Assets | 9.5 | 23.5 | | 16.4 | 5.5 | |
| 2.9 | 3.6 | 3.6 | | 4.3 | 4.7 | | 4.1 | 2.4 | |
| 4.8 | 6.2 | 4.3 | | 5.3 | 5.0 | | 5.7 | 3.8 | |
| 2.3 | 2.1 | 2.2 | Sales/Total Assets | 2.1 | 2.9 | | 3.4 | 1.9 | |
| 1.2 | 1.2 | 1.3 | | .8 | 1.4 | | 1.7 | 1.3 | |
| .8 | 1.0 | 1.0 | | | | | 1.6 | .6 | |
| (25) 2.6 | (56) 3.5 | (65) 4.6 | % Depr., Dep., Amort./Sales | | | | (12) 5.8 | (33) 2.8 | |
| 6.3 | 8.0 | 9.3 | | | | | 12.2 | 9.0 | |
| | | .4 | % Officers', Directors' | | | | | | |
| | (25) 1.8 | Owners' Comp/Sales | | | | | | | |
| | | 5.0 | | | | | | | |
| 1519216M | 3621682M | 5280695M | Net Sales ($) | 3757M | 24180M | 24986M | 105925M | 399248M | 4722599M |
| 829204M | 1770186M | 2346088M | Total Assets ($) | 8178M | 27378M | 14075M | 64953M | 221419M | 2010085M |

© RMA 2024  
M = $ thousand   MM = $ million  
See Pages viii through xx for Explanation of Ratios and Data

# TRANSPORTATION—Couriers and Express Delivery Services  NAICS 492110

## Current Data Sorted by Assets | Comparative Historical Data

| 0-500M | 500M-2MM | 2-10MM | 10-50MM | 50-100MM | 100-250MM | | Type of Statement | | 4/1/19-3/31/20 ALL | | 4/1/20-3/31/21 ALL |
|---|---|---|---|---|---|---|---|---|---|---|---|
| 2 | | | | | | | Unqualified | | 4 | | 4 |
| | 1 | | | | | | Reviewed | | 8 | | 2 |
| | | 1 | | | | | Compiled | | 3 | | 2 |
| 3 | 3 | 4 | | | | | Tax Returns | | 18 | | 5 |
| 7 | 11 | 11 | 6 | 2 | 2 | | Other | | 21 | | 25 |
| | 4 (4/1-9/30/23) | | 51 (10/1/23-3/31/24) | | | | | | | | |
| 12 | 15 | 16 | 7 | 3 | 2 | | NUMBER OF STATEMENTS | | 54 | | 38 |
| % | % | % | % | % | % | | ASSETS | | % | | % |
| 35.2 | 20.3 | 26.0 | | | | | Cash & Equivalents | | 19.3 | | 20.0 |
| 15.2 | 28.3 | 23.6 | | | | | Trade Receivables (net) | | 22.9 | | 22.6 |
| .0 | .0 | .0 | | | | | Inventory | | .7 | | .1 |
| 5.0 | 2.3 | 12.5 | | | | | All Other Current | | 3.2 | | 1.4 |
| 55.4 | 50.9 | 62.1 | | | | | Total Current | | 46.0 | | 44.1 |
| 30.3 | 26.1 | 29.9 | | | | | Fixed Assets (net) | | 25.8 | | 25.1 |
| 5.2 | 7.6 | 5.3 | | | | | Intangibles (net) | | 18.4 | | 22.0 |
| 9.2 | 15.3 | 2.7 | | | | | All Other Non-Current | | 9.8 | | 8.8 |
| 100.0 | 100.0 | 100.0 | | | | | Total | | 100.0 | | 100.0 |
| | | | | | | | LIABILITIES | | | | |
| 2.6 | 7.2 | .9 | | | | | Notes Payable-Short Term | | 9.8 | | 17.6 |
| 4.7 | .1 | 1.6 | | | | | Cur. Mat.-L.T.D. | | 3.4 | | 5.5 |
| 1.1 | 22.0 | 4.3 | | | | | Trade Payables | | 8.5 | | 7.0 |
| 1.1 | .6 | .0 | | | | | Income Taxes Payable | | .4 | | .1 |
| 37.8 | 22.9 | 6.8 | | | | | All Other Current | | 7.6 | | 8.4 |
| 47.2 | 52.9 | 13.6 | | | | | Total Current | | 29.8 | | 38.6 |
| 35.1 | 15.5 | 37.4 | | | | | Long-Term Debt | | 30.2 | | 49.6 |
| .0 | .0 | .0 | | | | | Deferred Taxes | | .3 | | .0 |
| .0 | 5.3 | .1 | | | | | All Other Non-Current | | 8.1 | | 3.9 |
| 17.6 | 26.3 | 48.9 | | | | | Net Worth | | 31.5 | | 7.9 |
| 100.0 | 100.0 | 100.0 | | | | | Total Liabilities & Net Worth | | 100.0 | | 100.0 |
| | | | | | | | INCOME DATA | | | | |
| 100.0 | 100.0 | 100.0 | | | | | Net Sales | | 100.0 | | 100.0 |
| | | | | | | | Gross Profit | | | | |
| 80.3 | 88.3 | 91.0 | | | | | Operating Expenses | | 92.0 | | 95.2 |
| 19.7 | 11.7 | 9.0 | | | | | Operating Profit | | 8.0 | | 4.8 |
| .6 | 1.1 | 3.5 | | | | | All Other Expenses (net) | | 2.3 | | .3 |
| 19.1 | 10.6 | 5.5 | | | | | Profit Before Taxes | | 5.8 | | 4.5 |
| | | | | | | | RATIOS | | | | |
| 2.4 | 4.4 | 9.2 | | | | | | | 5.4 | | 3.9 |
| .9 | 1.3 | 5.7 | | | | | Current | | 1.9 | | 1.7 |
| .6 | .5 | 2.5 | | | | | | | .8 | | .8 |
| 2.4 | 4.4 | 6.9 | | | | | | | 5.3 | | 3.9 |
| .9 | 1.2 | 4.2 | | | | | Quick | | 1.7 | | 1.5 |
| .6 | .5 | 1.9 | | | | | | | .7 | | .8 |
| 0 UND | 0 UND | 1 425.4 | | | | | | | 0 UND | | 0 UND |
| 0 UND | 36 10.1 | 27 13.7 | | | | | Sales/Receivables | | 30 12.2 | | 30 12.3 |
| 0 UND | 50 7.3 | 38 9.6 | | | | | | | 37 9.8 | | 46 8.0 |
| | | | | | | | Cost of Sales/Inventory | | | | |
| | | | | | | | Cost of Sales/Payables | | | | |
| 27.5 | 7.3 | 2.5 | | | | | | | 8.9 | | 10.1 |
| -874.4 | 48.4 | 7.4 | | | | | Sales/Working Capital | | 18.3 | | 20.4 |
| -38.3 | -12.0 | 10.0 | | | | | | | -37.9 | | -46.0 |
| | | 16.1 | | | | | | | 17.6 | | 28.9 |
| | (12) | 7.8 | | | | | EBIT/Interest | (39) | 5.4 | (33) | 4.9 |
| | | 1.1 | | | | | | | .5 | | 1.1 |
| | | | | | | | Net Profit + Depr., Dep., Amort./Cur. Mat. L/T/D | | | | |
| .0 | .0 | .1 | | | | | | | .2 | | .2 |
| 2.1 | 1.0 | .6 | | | | | Fixed/Worth | | 2.0 | | -22.7 |
| UND | -27.8 | 20.3 | | | | | | | -1.5 | | -.8 |
| .7 | .8 | .4 | | | | | | | .7 | | 1.5 |
| UND | 1.4 | .7 | | | | | Debt/Worth | | 6.5 | | -24.2 |
| -7.9 | -30.0 | 21.3 | | | | | | | -5.2 | | -2.8 |
| | 77.5 | 31.1 | | | | | | | 68.2 | | 110.1 |
| (11) | 62.1 | (13) 17.1 | | | | | % Profit Before Taxes/Tangible Net Worth | (31) | 32.7 | (17) | 44.2 |
| | 21.7 | 2.1 | | | | | | | 17.0 | | 25.3 |
| 135.3 | 40.6 | 20.1 | | | | | | | 33.5 | | 17.9 |
| 65.5 | 9.5 | 8.9 | | | | | % Profit Before Taxes/Total Assets | | 11.4 | | 10.7 |
| 11.2 | 4.6 | .3 | | | | | | | 1.4 | | .6 |
| UND | 999.8 | 70.8 | | | | | | | 97.9 | | 92.3 |
| 108.9 | 20.9 | 6.7 | | | | | Sales/Net Fixed Assets | | 34.8 | | 33.1 |
| 6.3 | 6.9 | 4.4 | | | | | | | 7.4 | | 5.6 |
| 14.9 | 5.6 | 3.6 | | | | | | | 5.2 | | 4.3 |
| 6.5 | 2.2 | 2.2 | | | | | Sales/Total Assets | | 3.2 | | 2.5 |
| 3.1 | 1.8 | 1.1 | | | | | | | 1.8 | | 1.4 |
| | | | | | | | | | .3 | | 1.0 |
| | | | | | | | % Depr., Dep., Amort./Sales | (27) | 1.1 | (15) | 1.8 |
| | | | | | | | | | 3.1 | | 7.4 |
| | | | | | | | | | 2.6 | | 1.7 |
| | | | | | | | % Officers', Directors' Owners' Comp/Sales | (20) | 4.9 | (16) | 2.6 |
| | | | | | | | | | 7.9 | | 4.7 |
| 44005M | 66280M | 192011M | 659278M | 390311M | 800919M | | Net Sales ($) | | 2031489M | | 1185455M |
| 3127M | 18097M | 83478M | 204696M | 231909M | 249464M | | Total Assets ($) | | 1075071M | | 815516M |

© RMA 2024

M = $ thousand   MM = $ million
See Pages viii through xx for Explanation of Ratios and Data

# TRANSPORTATION—Couriers and Express Delivery Services  NAICS 492110

| Comparative Historical Data | | | | Current Data Sorted by Sales | | | | | |
|---|---|---|---|---|---|---|---|---|---|
| | | | Type of Statement | | | | | | |
| 3 | 8 | 2 | Unqualified | | | 1 | 1 | | 2 |
| 3 | 2 | 3 | Reviewed | | | | | 1 | |
| 1 | 2 | 1 | Compiled | | | | 1 | 1 | |
| 7 | 10 | 10 | Tax Returns | 1 | 1 | 1 | 6 | 1 | 11 |
| 26 | 30 | 39 | Other | 7 | 6 | 3 | 7 | 5 | |
| 4/1/21-3/31/22 ALL | 4/1/22-3/31/23 ALL | 4/1/23-3/31/24 ALL | | 0-1MM | 4 (4/1-9/30/23) 1-3MM | 3-5MM | 51 (10/1/23-3/31/24) 5-10MM | 10-25MM | 25MM & OVER |
| 40 | 52 | 55 | NUMBER OF STATEMENTS | 8 | 8 | 5 | 14 | 7 | 13 |
| % | % | % | ASSETS | % | % | % | % | % | % |
| 19.8 | 19.1 | 22.8 | Cash & Equivalents | | | | 31.5 | | 14.2 |
| 26.4 | 23.8 | 24.6 | Trade Receivables (net) | | | | 29.0 | | 27.9 |
| .9 | .4 | .1 | Inventory | | | | .1 | | .2 |
| 4.4 | 7.6 | 6.0 | All Other Current | | | | 5.7 | | 3.3 |
| 51.5 | 50.9 | 53.5 | Total Current | | | | 66.3 | | 45.5 |
| 28.5 | 19.2 | 26.5 | Fixed Assets (net) | | | | 25.4 | | 19.4 |
| 14.8 | 16.9 | 10.7 | Intangibles (net) | | | | 5.4 | | 25.2 |
| 5.2 | 13.0 | 9.4 | All Other Non-Current | | | | 2.8 | | 9.8 |
| 100.0 | 100.0 | 100.0 | Total | | | | 100.0 | | 100.0 |
| | | | LIABILITIES | | | | | | |
| 6.7 | 3.9 | 3.7 | Notes Payable-Short Term | | | | .8 | | 3.6 |
| 3.1 | 6.9 | 2.3 | Cur. Mat.-L.T.D. | | | | 4.1 | | 3.4 |
| 22.4 | 9.3 | 10.2 | Trade Payables | | | | 7.1 | | 9.9 |
| .6 | .2 | .4 | Income Taxes Payable | | | | .1 | | .1 |
| 13.0 | 10.7 | 19.3 | All Other Current | | | | 13.2 | | 12.0 |
| 45.7 | 31.0 | 35.9 | Total Current | | | | 25.2 | | 28.9 |
| 36.0 | 35.1 | 28.6 | Long-Term Debt | | | | 41.9 | | 26.3 |
| .1 | .2 | .0 | Deferred Taxes | | | | .0 | | .1 |
| 1.6 | 6.3 | 4.1 | All Other Non-Current | | | | .0 | | 11.0 |
| 16.5 | 27.4 | 31.4 | Net Worth | | | | 32.9 | | 33.7 |
| 100.0 | 100.0 | 100.0 | Total Liabilities & Net Worth | | | | 100.0 | | 100.0 |
| | | | INCOME DATA | | | | | | |
| 100.0 | 100.0 | 100.0 | Net Sales | | | | 100.0 | | 100.0 |
| | | | Gross Profit | | | | | | |
| 95.5 | 93.0 | 89.6 | Operating Expenses | | | | 95.4 | | 96.4 |
| 4.5 | 7.0 | 10.4 | Operating Profit | | | | 4.6 | | 3.6 |
| .4 | .8 | 1.8 | All Other Expenses (net) | | | | -.4 | | 1.5 |
| 4.1 | 6.1 | 8.7 | Profit Before Taxes | | | | 4.9 | | 2.2 |
| | | | RATIOS | | | | | | |
| 2.7 | 7.8 | 4.5 | | | | | 7.4 | | 2.4 |
| 1.4 | 1.9 | 1.9 | Current | | | | 3.4 | | 1.9 |
| .7 | 1.1 | .9 | | | | | 1.9 | | 1.0 |
| 2.2 | 4.0 | 4.4 | | | | | 6.2 | | 2.3 |
| 1.3 | 1.7 | 1.7 | Quick | | | | 2.7 | | 1.5 |
| .7 | 1.0 | .9 | | | | | 1.5 | | .9 |
| 0 UND | 0 UND | 0 UND | | | | | 0 UND | 26 | 14.3 |
| 28 13.0 | 33 11.2 | 29 12.8 | Sales/Receivables | | | | 29 12.8 | 35 | 10.3 |
| 43 8.5 | 44 8.3 | 45 8.2 | | | | | 46 7.9 | 44 | 8.3 |
| | | | Cost of Sales/Inventory | | | | | | |
| | | | Cost of Sales/Payables | | | | | | |
| 9.9 | 6.6 | 7.2 | | | | | 1.8 | | 8.0 |
| 22.1 | 16.3 | 13.8 | Sales/Working Capital | | | | 8.8 | | 13.8 |
| -24.8 | 93.8 | -43.9 | | | | | 18.6 | | NM |
| 65.4 | 45.1 | 13.2 | | | | | 12.6 | | 10.4 |
| (35) 7.2 | (45) 5.0 | (38) 5.4 | EBIT/Interest | | | | (11) 7.7 | (10) | 1.6 |
| 1.3 | -.2 | .9 | | | | | .3 | | -.1 |
| | | | Net Profit + Depr., Dep., Amort./Cur. Mat. L/T/D | | | | | | |
| .3 | .2 | .1 | | | | | .0 | | .7 |
| 2.9 | 2.8 | 1.3 | Fixed/Worth | | | | .2 | | 3.2 |
| -1.7 | -1.0 | -2.0 | | | | | -1.9 | | -.3 |
| .8 | 1.0 | .7 | | | | | .5 | | 1.8 |
| 4.4 | 8.0 | 2.3 | Debt/Worth | | | | .8 | | 4.9 |
| -3.5 | -5.0 | -7.1 | | | | | -3.8 | | -3.5 |
| 116.9 | 165.3 | 77.8 | | | | | | | |
| (25) 40.5 | (32) 68.3 | (38) 31.1 | % Profit Before Taxes/Tangible Net Worth | | | | | | |
| 16.8 | 19.3 | 16.7 | | | | | | | |
| 46.4 | 29.7 | 36.1 | | | | | 23.9 | | 18.0 |
| 10.1 | 9.7 | 9.9 | % Profit Before Taxes/Total Assets | | | | 8.9 | | 9.8 |
| 2.3 | -1.1 | .4 | | | | | -4.0 | | -4.2 |
| 98.6 | 160.4 | 230.3 | | | | | UND | | 70.3 |
| 18.5 | 24.5 | 20.9 | Sales/Net Fixed Assets | | | | 15.8 | | 31.3 |
| 5.8 | 7.6 | 5.3 | | | | | 4.8 | | 9.7 |
| 5.7 | 4.7 | 5.6 | | | | | 8.0 | | 4.2 |
| 3.5 | 3.1 | 2.8 | Sales/Total Assets | | | | 2.2 | | 3.5 |
| 1.4 | 1.3 | 1.8 | | | | | .8 | | 1.6 |
| .5 | .5 | .6 | | | | | | | |
| (27) 3.3 | (25) 1.8 | (21) 1.9 | % Depr., Dep., Amort./Sales | | | | | | |
| 7.9 | 6.0 | 5.3 | | | | | | | |
| 2.4 | 1.3 | 1.5 | | | | | | | |
| (13) 2.9 | (15) 3.6 | (11) 2.1 | % Officers', Directors', Owners' Comp/Sales | | | | | | |
| 5.6 | 7.3 | 8.4 | | | | | | | |
| 1966763M | 1971837M | 2152804M | Net Sales ($) | 3074M | 14001M | 17946M | 95740M | 119891M | 1902152M |
| 589740M | 677597M | 790771M | Total Assets ($) | 8239M | 5803M | 6397M | 55210M | 30457M | 684665M |

© RMA 2024  
M = $ thousand   MM = $ million  
See Pages viii through xx for Explanation of Ratios and Data

# TRANSPORTATION—Local Messengers and Local Delivery  NAICS 492210

## Current Data Sorted by Assets

| 0-500M | 500M-2MM | 2-10MM | 10-50MM | 50-100MM | 100-250MM | | Type of Statement | | Comparative Historical Data | |
|---|---|---|---|---|---|---|---|---|---|---|
| | 5 | 2 | | 1 | | | Unqualified | | 3 | |
| | 8 | 1 | | | | | Reviewed | | 2 | |
| | 3 (4/1-9/30/23) | 4 | 1 | | | | Compiled | | 2 | |
| | | 4 | 19 (10/1/23-3/31/24) | | | | Tax Returns | | 4 | 2 |
| | | | | | | | Other | | 14 | 7 |
| | | | | | | | | | 4/1/19-3/31/20 | 4/1/20-3/31/21 |
| | 13 | 7 | 1 | 1 | | NUMBER OF STATEMENTS | | ALL 25 | ALL 9 |
| % | % | % | % | % | % | ASSETS | | % | % |
| | 27.2 | | | | | Cash & Equivalents | | 14.0 | |
| | 20.2 | | | | | Trade Receivables (net) | | 29.1 | |
| D | .0 | | | | D | Inventory | | 3.4 | |
| A | 12.4 | | | | A | All Other Current | | 2.8 | |
| T | 59.8 | | | | T | Total Current | | 49.2 | |
| A | 12.1 | | | | A | Fixed Assets (net) | | 24.0 | |
| | 22.9 | | | | | Intangibles (net) | | 19.5 | |
| N | 5.2 | | | | N | All Other Non-Current | | 7.3 | |
| O | 100.0 | | | | O | Total | | 100.0 | |
| T | | | | | T | LIABILITIES | | | |
| | 5.0 | | | | | Notes Payable-Short Term | | 26.6 | |
| A | 1.1 | | | | A | Cur. Mat.-L.T.D. | | 3.5 | |
| V | 3.8 | | | | V | Trade Payables | | 13.6 | |
| A | .1 | | | | A | Income Taxes Payable | | .0 | |
| I | 26.4 | | | | I | All Other Current | | 21.5 | |
| L | 36.4 | | | | L | Total Current | | 65.2 | |
| A | 26.8 | | | | A | Long-Term Debt | | 26.7 | |
| B | .0 | | | | B | Deferred Taxes | | .0 | |
| L | 4.3 | | | | L | All Other Non-Current | | 5.8 | |
| E | 32.5 | | | | E | Net Worth | | 2.3 | |
| | 100.0 | | | | | Total Liabilities & Net Worth | | 100.0 | |
| | | | | | | INCOME DATA | | | |
| | 100.0 | | | | | Net Sales | | 100.0 | |
| | 91.6 | | | | | Gross Profit | | | |
| | 8.4 | | | | | Operating Expenses | | 94.1 | |
| | .7 | | | | | Operating Profit | | 5.9 | |
| | 7.7 | | | | | All Other Expenses (net) | | 1.2 | |
| | | | | | | Profit Before Taxes | | 4.7 | |
| | | | | | | RATIOS | | | |
| | 7.3 | | | | | | | 1.6 | |
| | 2.0 | | | | | Current | | 1.2 | |
| | .9 | | | | | | | .6 | |
| | 7.2 | | | | | | | 1.4 | |
| | 2.0 | | | | | Quick | | 1.1 | |
| | .7 | | | | | | | .6 | |
| 0 | UND | | | | | | 0 | UND | |
| 0 | UND | | | | | Sales/Receivables | 16 | 23.1 | |
| 29 | 12.6 | | | | | | 39 | 9.4 | |
| | | | | | | Cost of Sales/Inventory | | | |
| | | | | | | Cost of Sales/Payables | | | |
| | 9.2 | | | | | | | 20.2 | |
| | 18.1 | | | | | Sales/Working Capital | | 100.6 | |
| | NM | | | | | | | -29.5 | |
| | 182.7 | | | | | | | 20.1 | |
| (10) | 11.8 | | | | | EBIT/Interest | (22) | 5.6 | |
| | 2.5 | | | | | | | 2.3 | |
| | | | | | | Net Profit + Depr., Dep., Amort./Cur. Mat. L/T/D | | | |
| | .0 | | | | | | | .3 | |
| | .4 | | | | | Fixed/Worth | | 1.2 | |
| | -.3 | | | | | | | -.4 | |
| | .5 | | | | | | | 1.7 | |
| | 1.0 | | | | | Debt/Worth | | 4.9 | |
| | -2.4 | | | | | | | -2.2 | |
| | | | | | | | | 324.5 | |
| | | | | | | % Profit Before Taxes/Tangible Net Worth | (16) | 61.1 | |
| | | | | | | | | 34.4 | |
| | 71.9 | | | | | | | 20.3 | |
| | 21.5 | | | | | % Profit Before Taxes/Total Assets | | 12.8 | |
| | 8.4 | | | | | | | 6.6 | |
| | UND | | | | | | | 157.1 | |
| | 61.6 | | | | | Sales/Net Fixed Assets | | 36.5 | |
| | 20.4 | | | | | | | 5.1 | |
| | 6.1 | | | | | | | 6.7 | |
| | 4.9 | | | | | Sales/Total Assets | | 3.5 | |
| | 2.5 | | | | | | | 1.6 | |
| | | | | | | | | .1 | |
| | | | | | | % Depr., Dep., Amort./Sales | (13) | 3.2 | |
| | | | | | | | | 6.6 | |
| | | | | | | % Officers', Directors' Owners' Comp/Sales | | | |
| | 74772M | 82479M | 99675M | 104093M | | Net Sales ($) | | 1184505M | 20667M |
| | 15693M | 27857M | 38644M | 55977M | | Total Assets ($) | | 347140M | 5861M |

M = $ thousand    MM = $ million
See Pages viii through xx for Explanation of Ratios and Data

© RMA 2024

## TRANSPORTATION—Local Messengers and Local Delivery NAICS 492210

### Comparative Historical Data | Current Data Sorted by Sales

| Comparative Historical Data ||| Type of Statement | Current Data Sorted by Sales ||||||
|---|---|---|---|---|---|---|---|---|---|
| 2 | 1 | 3 | Unqualified | | | | 2 | 2 | |
| 3 | 9 | 6 | Reviewed | | | | 7 | 3 | 1 |
| 10 | 18 | 13 | Compiled | 3 | 1 | 2 | 19 (10/1/23-3/31/24) | | |
| 4/1/21-3/31/22 | 4/1/22-3/31/23 | 4/1/23-3/31/24 | Tax Returns | 3 (4/1-9/30/23) | 1 | | | | |
| ALL | ALL | ALL | Other | 0-1MM | 1-3MM | 3-5MM | 5-10MM | 10-25MM | 25MM & OVER |
| 15 | 28 | 22 | NUMBER OF STATEMENTS | 4 | 2 | 9 | 5 | 2 | |
| % | % | % | | % | % | % | % | % | % |
| | | | **ASSETS** | | | | | | |
| 25.2 | 32.3 | 22.8 | Cash & Equivalents | D | | | | | |
| 24.4 | 18.9 | 24.5 | Trade Receivables (net) | A | | | | | |
| 3.1 | 1.0 | .3 | Inventory | T | | | | | |
| 6.1 | 7.4 | 8.7 | All Other Current | A | | | | | |
| 58.8 | 59.6 | 56.3 | Total Current | | | | | | |
| 26.0 | 15.8 | 13.7 | Fixed Assets (net) | N | | | | | |
| 6.9 | 10.2 | 20.4 | Intangibles (net) | O | | | | | |
| 8.3 | 14.4 | 9.6 | All Other Non-Current | T | | | | | |
| 100.0 | 100.0 | 100.0 | Total | | | | | | |
| | | | **LIABILITIES** | A | | | | | |
| 4.4 | 8.0 | 6.0 | Notes Payable-Short Term | V | | | | | |
| 8.6 | 4.9 | 1.7 | Cur. Mat.-L.T.D. | A | | | | | |
| 7.3 | 8.7 | 3.4 | Trade Payables | I | | | | | |
| .0 | .1 | .1 | Income Taxes Payable | L | | | | | |
| 44.1 | 16.0 | 21.8 | All Other Current | A | | | | | |
| 64.4 | 37.7 | 32.9 | Total Current | B | | | | | |
| 41.7 | 21.7 | 22.3 | Long-Term Debt | L | | | | | |
| .0 | .0 | .0 | Deferred Taxes | E | | | | | |
| 20.6 | 4.7 | 3.2 | All Other Non-Current | | | | | | |
| -26.7 | 36.0 | 41.6 | Net Worth | | | | | | |
| 100.0 | 100.0 | 100.0 | Total Liabilities & Net Worth | | | | | | |
| | | | **INCOME DATA** | | | | | | |
| 100.0 | 100.0 | 100.0 | Net Sales | | | | | | |
| | | | Gross Profit | | | | | | |
| 97.4 | 93.3 | 92.6 | Operating Expenses | | | | | | |
| 2.6 | 6.7 | 7.4 | Operating Profit | | | | | | |
| -1.6 | -.6 | .6 | All Other Expenses (net) | | | | | | |
| 4.2 | 7.4 | 6.8 | Profit Before Taxes | | | | | | |
| | | | **RATIOS** | | | | | | |
| 4.8 | 6.7 | 6.4 | | | | | | | |
| 1.6 | 2.8 | 1.8 | Current | | | | | | |
| .7 | .9 | 1.0 | | | | | | | |
| 4.7 | 5.6 | 6.3 | | | | | | | |
| 1.6 | 2.4 | 1.8 | Quick | | | | | | |
| .5 | .6 | .9 | | | | | | | |
| 0 UND | 0 UND | 0 UND | | | | | | | |
| 13 28.7 | 18 20.3 | 27 13.5 | Sales/Receivables | | | | | | |
| 38 9.6 | 37 9.8 | 37 9.9 | | | | | | | |
| | | | Cost of Sales/Inventory | | | | | | |
| | | | Cost of Sales/Payables | | | | | | |
| 8.4 | 7.3 | 8.2 | | | | | | | |
| 28.8 | 23.2 | 27.7 | Sales/Working Capital | | | | | | |
| -34.6 | -106.1 | NM | | | | | | | |
| 94.3 | 74.0 | 27.5 | | | | | | | |
| (14) 7.9 | (22) 11.4 | (16) 3.2 | EBIT/Interest | | | | | | |
| 1.6 | 3.9 | .1 | | | | | | | |
| | | | Net Profit + Depr., Dep., Amort./Cur. Mat. L/T/D | | | | | | |
| .4 | .0 | .0 | | | | | | | |
| 10.9 | .4 | .4 | Fixed/Worth | | | | | | |
| -1.7 | 8.9 | -1.1 | | | | | | | |
| 1.2 | .4 | .5 | | | | | | | |
| -162.2 | 1.3 | 1.0 | Debt/Worth | | | | | | |
| -3.3 | 112.3 | -6.2 | | | | | | | |
| | 139.4 | 124.1 | | | | | | | |
| (22) | 86.6 | (14) 48.8 | % Profit Before Taxes/Tangible Net Worth | | | | | | |
| | 10.5 | 31.5 | | | | | | | |
| 48.4 | 66.2 | 48.4 | | | | | | | |
| 11.2 | 23.3 | 15.5 | % Profit Before Taxes/Total Assets | | | | | | |
| 2.2 | 3.3 | 5.2 | | | | | | | |
| 254.5 | 388.9 | 274.7 | | | | | | | |
| 32.4 | 62.1 | 48.6 | Sales/Net Fixed Assets | | | | | | |
| 5.5 | 12.9 | 13.0 | | | | | | | |
| 6.3 | 7.1 | 5.0 | | | | | | | |
| 4.5 | 4.5 | 3.2 | Sales/Total Assets | | | | | | |
| 2.9 | 2.2 | 2.5 | | | | | | | |
| | .1 | .2 | | | | | | | |
| (11) | 1.1 | (11) 2.3 | % Depr., Dep., Amort./Sales | | | | | | |
| | 6.0 | 5.5 | | | | | | | |
| | 2.3 | | | | | | | | |
| (11) | 5.1 | | % Officers', Directors' Owners' Comp/Sales | | | | | | |
| | 14.1 | | | | | | | | |
| 366573M | 426203M | 361019M | Net Sales ($) | 8120M | 7000M | | 70205M | 719 | |
| 75993M | 175079M | 138171M | Total Assets ($) | 4204M | 1367M | | 17786M | 201 | |

M = $ thousand    MM = $ million
See Pages viii through xx for Explanation of Ratios and Data

© RMA 2024

# TRANSPORTATION—General Warehousing and Storage  NAICS 493110

## Current Data Sorted by Assets | Comparative Historical Data

| | | | | | | | Type of Statement | | | | |
|---|---|---|---|---|---|---|---|---|---|---|---|
| | | | 2 | 6 | 8 | 4 | Unqualified | | 11 | | 9 |
| | | 2 | 3 | 18 | 7 | 6 | Reviewed | | 33 | | 18 |
| | | 8 | 8 | 2 | 2 | | Compiled | | 21 | | 11 |
| 5 | | 8 | 8 | 4 | | 1 | Tax Returns | | 53 | | 20 |
| 6 | | 17 | 36 | 40 | 19 | 14 | Other | | 140 | | 78 |
| | | 30 (4/1-9/30/23) | | 196 (10/1/23-3/31/24) | | | | | 4/1/19- 3/31/20 | | 4/1/20- 3/31/21 |
| 0-500M | 500M-2MM | 2-10MM | 10-50MM | 50-100MM | 100-250MM | | | | ALL | | ALL |
| 11 | 27 | 57 | 70 | 36 | 25 | | NUMBER OF STATEMENTS | | 258 | | 136 |
| % | % | % | % | % | % | | ASSETS | | % | | % |
| 37.5 | 20.0 | 13.5 | 11.9 | 8.9 | 5.1 | | Cash & Equivalents | | 12.2 | | 17.7 |
| 14.3 | 16.9 | 18.8 | 18.0 | 17.8 | 9.8 | | Trade Receivables (net) | | 21.9 | | 21.8 |
| .3 | 3.1 | .6 | 3.0 | 5.0 | .9 | | Inventory | | 2.4 | | 3.8 |
| 4.3 | 6.2 | 6.3 | 4.4 | 2.3 | 1.2 | | All Other Current | | 3.4 | | 4.4 |
| .5 | 46.2 | 39.2 | 37.4 | 34.0 | 17.0 | | Total Current | | 40.0 | | 47.7 |
| .8 | 42.1 | 39.5 | 38.3 | 39.7 | 42.3 | | Fixed Assets (net) | | 42.8 | | 36.3 |
| .9 | 8.1 | 3.5 | 7.1 | 6.8 | 17.6 | | Intangibles (net) | | 5.5 | | 6.5 |
| | 3.6 | 17.8 | 17.2 | 19.5 | 23.2 | | All Other Non-Current | | 11.8 | | 9.4 |
| | 100.0 | 100.0 | 100.0 | 100.0 | 100.0 | | Total | | 100.0 | | 100.0 |
| | | | | | | | LIABILITIES | | | | |
| | 3.1 | 4.0 | 2.4 | 4.4 | 1.4 | | Notes Payable-Short Term | | 6.1 | | 3.5 |
| | 1.9 | 2.6 | 3.7 | 4.9 | 6.7 | | Cur. Mat.-L.T.D. | | 4.2 | | 3.5 |
| | 6.4 | 7.3 | 5.1 | 6.9 | 3.8 | | Trade Payables | | 9.1 | | 9.6 |
| | .3 | .2 | .1 | .0 | .1 | | Income Taxes Payable | | .2 | | .1 |
| | 13.4 | 12.7 | 13.0 | 9.0 | 8.1 | | All Other Current | | 10.5 | | 10.9 |
| | 25.1 | 26.8 | 24.3 | 25.2 | 20.1 | | Total Current | | 30.0 | | 27.6 |
| | 31.7 | 29.5 | 28.9 | 25.7 | 32.7 | | Long-Term Debt | | 30.7 | | 28.2 |
| | .0 | .0 | .4 | .5 | .7 | | Deferred Taxes | | .3 | | .3 |
| | 5.3 | 4.0 | 11.7 | 15.8 | 17.6 | | All Other Non-Current | | 6.9 | | 5.1 |
| | 37.9 | 39.6 | 34.7 | 32.9 | 28.8 | | Net Worth | | 32.1 | | 38.8 |
| | 100.0 | 100.0 | 100.0 | 100.0 | 100.0 | | Total Liabilities & Net Worth | | 100.0 | | 100.0 |
| | | | | | | | INCOME DATA | | | | |
| | 100.0 | 100.0 | 100.0 | 100.0 | 100.0 | | Net Sales | | 100.0 | | 100.0 |
| | 79.6 | 77.5 | 82.8 | 90.4 | 87.9 | | Gross Profit | | | | |
| | 20.4 | 22.5 | 17.2 | 9.6 | 12.1 | | Operating Expenses | | 84.9 | | 85.8 |
| | 4.7 | 7.4 | 6.7 | 1.0 | 3.6 | | Operating Profit | | 15.1 | | 14.2 |
| | 15.7 | 15.1 | 10.5 | 8.6 | 8.5 | | All Other Expenses (net) | | 4.5 | | 1.9 |
| | | | | | | | Profit Before Taxes | | 10.6 | | 12.3 |
| | | | | | | | RATIOS | | | | |
| | 3.9 | 4.6 | 2.7 | 1.7 | 1.3 | | | | 2.9 | | 4.0 |
| | 1.1 | 2.1 | 1.5 | 1.3 | .9 | | Current | | 1.4 | | 1.9 |
| | .9 | .7 | .7 | 1.0 | .6 | | | | .7 | | 1.1 |
| | | 4.2 | 2.1 | 1.4 | 1.1 | | | | 2.6 | | 3.5 |
| | | 1.8 | 1.2 | 1.1 | .7 | | Quick | | 1.2 | | 1.7 |
| | | .5 | .5 | .6 | .4 | | | | .6 | | .9 |
| | | 0 | UND | 21 | 17.3 | 29 | 12.8 | 34 | 10.8 | | | 5 | 70.6 | 7 | 50.2 |
| | | 30 | 12.1 | 41 | 9.0 | 39 | 9.4 | 40 | 9.2 | | Sales/Receivables | | 34 | 10.8 | 37 | 9.8 |
| | | 53 | 6.9 | 54 | 6.7 | 66 | 5.5 | 63 | 5.8 | | | 50 | 7.3 | 51 | 7.1 |
| | | | | | | | Cost of Sales/Inventory | | | | |
| | | | | | | | Cost of Sales/Payables | | | | |
| | | 3.8 | 5.1 | 6.9 | 18.3 | | | | 7.1 | | 4.9 |
| | | 7.3 | 13.9 | 16.4 | -39.0 | | Sales/Working Capital | | 23.9 | | 11.0 |
| | | -10.1 | -7.7 | 318.3 | -6.8 | | | | -17.2 | | 60.4 |
| | | 56.3 | 25.7 | 22.4 | 6.5 | | | | 15.3 | | 23.0 |
| | (44) | 11.0 | (52) | 5.5 | (31) | 7.7 | (23) | 3.3 | | EBIT/Interest | (186) | 5.3 | (102) | 11.2 |
| | | 3.3 | 2.6 | 2.1 | .7 | | | | 1.9 | | 3.0 |
| | | | 6.8 | 7.6 | | | | | 7.6 | | 10.8 |
| | | (17) | 3.2 | (12) | 1.3 | | Net Profit + Depr., Dep., | (43) | 3.4 | (20) | 6.8 |
| | | | 1.1 | 1.1 | | | Amort./Cur. Mat. L/T/D | | 1.4 | | 3.0 |
| | .1 | .3 | .6 | 1.3 | | | | .4 | | .3 |
| | .9 | 1.4 | 1.3 | 3.7 | | | Fixed/Worth | | 1.4 | | 1.1 |
| | 2.9 | 6.5 | 3.9 | -4.7 | | | | 5.1 | | 3.7 |
| | .5 | 1.0 | 1.3 | 2.4 | | | | .6 | | .7 |
| | | 3.5 | 3.2 | 5.7 | | | Debt/Worth | | 2.3 | | 1.6 |
| | | 11.9 | 6.7 | -7.4 | | | | 8.3 | | 8.9 |
| | | 54.7 | 49.0 | 29.5 | | | % Profit Before Taxes/Tangible | | 53.7 | | 67.3 |
| | (59) | 25.3 | (30) | 22.1 | (16) | 15.1 | | Net Worth | (215) | 23.0 | (112) | 31.9 |
| | | 7.9 | 14.6 | 6.4 | | | | | 7.5 | | 12.6 |
| | | 17.8 | 13.6 | 7.9 | | | % Profit Before Taxes/Total | | 18.2 | | 22.7 |
| | | 10.5 | 6.3 | 3.8 | | | Assets | | 7.8 | | 10.9 |
| | | 2.8 | 2.6 | -1.4 | | | | | 2.1 | | 4.3 |
| | | 17.9 | 11.4 | 5.9 | | | | | 21.1 | | 28.5 |
| | | 4.3 | 6.1 | 1.5 | | | Sales/Net Fixed Assets | | 6.2 | | 6.7 |
| | | 1.0 | 1.3 | .6 | | | | | 1.0 | | 1.6 |
| | | | 1.8 | .9 | | | | | 3.3 | | 3.0 |
| | | | 1.1 | .6 | | | Sales/Total Assets | | 1.8 | | 1.7 |
| | | | .7 | .4 | | | | | .6 | | .7 |
| | | | 1.7 | 3.8 | | | | | 1.7 | | 1.6 |
| | | (32) | 3.1 | (15) | 7.5 | | % Depr., Dep., Amort./Sales | (198) | 3.8 | (95) | 2.9 |
| | | | 6.3 | 11.0 | | | | | 8.8 | | 6.7 |
| | | | | | | | % Officers', Directors' | | 1.5 | | 2.4 |
| | | | | | | | Owners' Comp/Sales | (58) | 3.4 | (24) | 5.0 |
| | | | | | | | | | 7.1 | | 9.2 |
| | | | | 1495M | 3015256M | | Net Sales ($) | | 7011385M | | 3318277M |
| | | | | 176M | 4138654M | | Total Assets ($) | | 4607070M | | 2276196M |

M = $ thousand    MM = $ million
See Pages viii through xx for Explanation of Ratios and Data

# TRANSPORTATION—General Warehousing and Storage  NAICS 493110

## Comparative Historical Data | Current Data Sorted by Sales

| | | | | Type of Statement | | | | | | |
|---|---|---|---|---|---|---|---|---|---|---|
| 12 | 16 | 20 | | Unqualified | 1 | 1 | | 1 | 2 | 15 |
| 21 | 23 | 34 | | Reviewed | | 1 | 2 | 3 | 8 | 20 |
| 13 | 17 | 14 | | Compiled | 2 | 2 | 1 | 3 | 4 | 2 |
| 29 | 40 | 26 | | Tax Returns | 8 | 8 | 4 | 1 | 3 | 2 |
| 102 | 118 | 132 | | Other | 19 | 13 | 12 | 15 | 20 | 53 |
| 4/1/21-3/31/22 ALL | 4/1/22-3/31/23 ALL | 4/1/23-3/31/24 ALL | | | 30 (4/1-9/30/23) | | | 196 (10/1/23-3/31/24) | | |
| | | | | | 0-1MM | 1-3MM | 3-5MM | 5-10MM | 10-25MM | 25MM & OVER |
| 177 | 214 | 226 | | NUMBER OF STATEMENTS | 30 | 25 | 19 | 23 | 37 | 92 |
| % | % | % | | ASSETS | % | % | % | % | % | % |
| 16.0 | 17.7 | 13.3 | | Cash & Equivalents | 12.7 | 18.4 | 15.0 | 13.7 | 15.4 | 10.7 |
| 21.7 | 21.4 | 17.0 | | Trade Receivables (net) | 4.3 | 4.3 | 17.4 | 24.7 | 17.8 | 22.2 |
| 2.6 | 2.5 | 2.4 | | Inventory | .1 | .7 | .3 | 1.9 | 4.0 | 3.5 |
| 3.0 | 4.0 | 4.4 | | All Other Current | 2.9 | 4.2 | 8.2 | 6.9 | 2.9 | 4.1 |
| 43.3 | 45.6 | 37.0 | | Total Current | 20.0 | 27.7 | 40.9 | 47.3 | 40.1 | 40.5 |
| 38.3 | 34.7 | 39.3 | | Fixed Assets (net) | 69.1 | 49.5 | 31.9 | 33.4 | 34.1 | 31.7 |
| 7.8 | 5.6 | 7.6 | | Intangibles (net) | 5.2 | 1.8 | 16.0 | 7.3 | 7.4 | 8.4 |
| 10.6 | 14.0 | 16.1 | | All Other Non-Current | 5.7 | 21.0 | 11.2 | 12.0 | 18.4 | 19.4 |
| 100.0 | 100.0 | 100.0 | | Total | 100.0 | 100.0 | 100.0 | 100.0 | 100.0 | 100.0 |
| | | | | LIABILITIES | | | | | | |
| 4.7 | 4.6 | 3.2 | | Notes Payable-Short Term | .3 | .3 | 11.9 | 4.8 | 1.5 | 3.5 |
| 3.1 | 3.9 | 3.5 | | Cur. Mat.-L.T.D. | 2.1 | 1.2 | 3.0 | 2.2 | 3.5 | 5.1 |
| 8.0 | 7.2 | 5.8 | | Trade Payables | 1.0 | 1.7 | 4.4 | 11.6 | 5.6 | 7.4 |
| .1 | .1 | .1 | | Income Taxes Payable | .0 | .0 | .4 | .1 | .2 | .1 |
| 8.7 | 10.4 | 13.0 | | All Other Current | 11.8 | 19.5 | 18.7 | 12.3 | 8.0 | 12.6 |
| 24.5 | 26.1 | 25.7 | | Total Current | 15.2 | 22.8 | 38.4 | 31.0 | 18.8 | 28.7 |
| 36.8 | 29.3 | 29.7 | | Long-Term Debt | 54.4 | 45.0 | 37.7 | 19.7 | 20.7 | 22.1 |
| .3 | .3 | .3 | | Deferred Taxes | .0 | .0 | .0 | .2 | .4 | .4 |
| 6.5 | 7.3 | 9.7 | | All Other Non-Current | 3.0 | 3.4 | 2.6 | 6.9 | 10.3 | 15.6 |
| 32.0 | 37.0 | 34.5 | | Net Worth | 27.4 | 28.8 | 21.4 | 42.1 | 49.8 | 33.1 |
| 100.0 | 100.0 | 100.0 | | Total Liabilities & Net Worth | 100.0 | 100.0 | 100.0 | 100.0 | 100.0 | 100.0 |
| | | | | INCOME DATA | | | | | | |
| 100.0 | 100.0 | 100.0 | | Net Sales | 100.0 | 100.0 | 100.0 | 100.0 | 100.0 | 100.0 |
| | | | | Gross Profit | | | | | | |
| 81.5 | 83.9 | 83.3 | | Operating Expenses | 58.9 | 74.3 | 81.9 | 89.6 | 84.5 | 92.0 |
| 18.5 | 16.1 | 16.7 | | Operating Profit | 41.1 | 25.7 | 18.1 | 10.4 | 15.5 | 8.0 |
| 3.2 | 3.4 | 5.1 | | All Other Expenses (net) | 19.4 | 9.9 | 8.2 | 1.4 | .5 | 1.3 |
| 15.3 | 12.8 | 11.5 | | Profit Before Taxes | 21.7 | 15.7 | 9.9 | 9.0 | 14.9 | 6.7 |
| | | | | RATIOS | | | | | | |
| 4.2 | 5.5 | 3.3 | | | 10.3 | 7.2 | 4.7 | 3.4 | 4.6 | 2.0 |
| 1.9 | 1.8 | 1.5 | | Current | 1.5 | 2.5 | 1.7 | 1.6 | 1.6 | 1.4 |
| 1.1 | 1.0 | .7 | | | .3 | .5 | .2 | .7 | 1.0 | .8 |
| 3.8 | 4.2 | 2.7 | | | 10.3 | 6.2 | 2.8 | 3.3 | 4.1 | 1.6 |
| 1.7 | 1.5 | 1.2 | | Quick | 1.0 | 2.2 | .8 | 1.3 | 1.4 | 1.1 |
| 1.0 | .8 | .6 | | | .3 | .3 | .2 | .4 | .5 | .7 |
| 0  853.5 | 15  24.9 | 6  63.0 | | | 0  UND | 0  UND | 14  26.7 | 13  29.1 | 15  23.7 | 34  10.7 |
| 35  10.4 | 37  9.8 | 35  10.3 | | Sales/Receivables | 0  UND | 1  602.0 | 26  13.9 | 42  8.7 | 40  9.1 | 43  8.5 |
| 53  6.9 | 54  6.7 | 54  6.8 | | | 4  90.7 | 27  13.6 | 49  7.4 | 54  6.8 | 55  6.6 | 63  5.8 |
| | | | | Cost of Sales/Inventory | | | | | | |
| | | | | Cost of Sales/Payables | | | | | | |
| 4.8 | 4.5 | 5.4 | | | 2.1 | 2.4 | 4.0 | 7.1 | 5.4 | 7.5 |
| 10.0 | 11.1 | 14.0 | | Sales/Working Capital | UND | 3.7 | 10.0 | 14.1 | 13.1 | 16.4 |
| 102.9 | NM | -12.2 | | | -4.6 | -3.2 | -3.5 | -7.9 | 91.2 | -31.0 |
| 33.3 | 39.0 | 25.8 | | | 6.1 | 24.6 | 21.6 | 37.7 | 41.7 | 25.4 |
| (136)  8.6 | (166)  13.2 | (175)  5.9 | | EBIT/Interest | (17)  3.3 | (15)  3.7 | (14)  3.1 | (19)  12.7 | (29)  14.8 | (81)  6.4 |
| 2.4 | 3.7 | 2.4 | | | 2.1 | 1.0 | 2.0 | 1.4 | 4.1 | 2.5 |
| 9.1 | 11.0 | 7.1 | | Net Profit + Depr., Dep., | | | | | | 7.5 |
| (24)  2.7 | (35)  6.4 | (42)  2.1 | | Amort./Cur. Mat. L/T/D | | | | | (26)  1.8 | |
| 1.1 | 2.8 | 1.0 | | | | | | | | 1.0 |
| .3 | .2 | .3 | | | 1.3 | .3 | .5 | .1 | .1 | .3 |
| 1.3 | .8 | 1.3 | | Fixed/Worth | 4.0 | 1.6 | 5.5 | .8 | .8 | 1.0 |
| 7.5 | 3.0 | 5.5 | | | -19.2 | 9.1 | -.6 | 4.1 | 3.4 | 3.1 |
| .7 | .6 | .7 | | | .7 | .6 | .6 | .6 | .4 | 1.4 |
| 2.6 | 1.5 | 3.1 | | Debt/Worth | 3.2 | 3.7 | 10.6 | 1.2 | 1.0 | 3.1 |
| 19.8 | 7.1 | 11.9 | | | -28.4 | -21.8 | -4.4 | 9.7 | 5.0 | 6.9 |
| 76.4 | 66.7 | 56.3 | | % Profit Before Taxes/Tangible | 36.2 | 23.5 | 127.5 | 81.1 | 60.6 | 56.3 |
| (143)  33.0 | (182)  33.1 | (181)  27.6 | | Net Worth | (22)  18.2 | (17)  11.5 | (11)  45.5 | (21)  30.8 | (32)  33.9 | (78)  29.7 |
| 17.5 | 13.4 | 10.6 | | | 4.0 | 3.4 | -1.2 | 10.9 | 18.1 | 14.0 |
| 23.4 | 25.0 | 18.1 | | % Profit Before Taxes/Total | 11.3 | 13.0 | 29.8 | 29.5 | 28.4 | 16.2 |
| 10.7 | 13.1 | 7.8 | | Assets | 5.6 | 4.7 | 5.9 | 6.4 | 14.3 | 9.4 |
| 3.8 | 3.7 | 2.4 | | | .2 | .2 | 1.1 | 1.0 | 6.5 | 2.6 |
| 27.4 | 36.6 | 17.6 | | | 1.5 | 7.3 | 25.6 | 93.0 | 31.6 | 15.3 |
| 7.2 | 7.5 | 4.7 | | Sales/Net Fixed Assets | .2 | 1.0 | 4.6 | 11.5 | 6.6 | 7.2 |
| 1.0 | 1.5 | .9 | | | .1 | .2 | .8 | 1.3 | 1.0 | 1.9 |
| 3.1 | 3.0 | 2.1 | | | .6 | .9 | 2.6 | 3.6 | 2.6 | 2.1 |
| 1.7 | 1.7 | 1.0 | | Sales/Total Assets | .2 | .5 | 1.5 | 2.1 | 1.3 | 1.3 |
| .6 | .7 | .5 | | | .1 | .1 | .4 | .8 | .7 | .7 |
| 1.8 | 1.6 | 1.7 | | | 7.3 | 3.5 | 2.1 | .4 | 1.1 | 1.2 |
| (127)  4.1 | (151)  3.8 | (173)  3.7 | | % Depr., Dep., Amort./Sales | (22)  19.0 | (22)  13.9 | (13)  5.2 | (17)  1.9 | (28)  4.1 | (71)  2.5 |
| 10.8 | 9.0 | 10.1 | | | 28.3 | 32.9 | 19.3 | 6.2 | 7.2 | 5.0 |
| 1.2 | 1.9 | 1.6 | | % Officers', Directors', | | | | | | |
| (31)  3.1 | (39)  3.8 | (34)  3.6 | | Owners' Comp/Sales | | | | | | |
| 8.5 | 7.8 | 8.6 | | | | | | | | |
| 5335824M | 6622414M | 8997879M | | Net Sales ($) | 13744M | 48666M | 76119M | 170648M | 624692M | 8064010M |
| 3363204M | 5122131M | 8503926M | | Total Assets ($) | 91425M | 227084M | 156110M | 209994M | 837115M | 6982198M |

© RMA 2024   M = $ thousand   MM = $ million
See Pages viii through xx for Explanation of Ratios and Data

# TRANSPORTATION—Refrigerated Warehousing and Storage  NAICS 493120

## Current Data Sorted by Assets

| | | | | | | Type of Statement |
|---|---|---|---|---|---|---|
| | | 1 | 4 | 1 | 3 | Unqualified |
| 1 | | 1 | 3 | 2 | 1 | Reviewed |
| 1 | 2 | 1 | 2 | 1 | | Compiled |
| | 3 | 3 | | 1 | | Tax Returns |
| 1 | | 11 | 10 | 3 | 3 | Other |
| 0-500M | 5 (4/1-9/30/23) 500M-2MM | 2-10MM | 53 (10/1/23-3/31/24) 10-50MM | 50-100MM | 100-250MM | |
| 2 | 6 | 16 | 19 | 8 | 7 | NUMBER OF STATEMENTS |
| % | % | % | % | % | % | ASSETS |
| | | 19.0 | 16.2 | | | Cash & Equivalents |
| | | 20.9 | 13.5 | | | Trade Receivables (net) |
| | | 1.5 | 1.1 | | | Inventory |
| | | 2.1 | 1.9 | | | All Other Current |
| | | 43.5 | 32.7 | | | Total Current |
| | | 37.6 | 57.4 | | | Fixed Assets (net) |
| | | 5.0 | 3.3 | | | Intangibles (net) |
| | | 13.9 | 6.6 | | | All Other Non-Current |
| | | 100.0 | 100.0 | | | Total |
| | | | | | | LIABILITIES |
| | | 1.5 | 2.2 | | | Notes Payable-Short Term |
| | | 2.6 | 2.3 | | | Cur. Mat.-L.T.D. |
| | | 10.7 | 5.4 | | | Trade Payables |
| | | .0 | .0 | | | Income Taxes Payable |
| | | 10.9 | 2.2 | | | All Other Current |
| | | 25.8 | 12.1 | | | Total Current |
| | | 28.1 | 35.0 | | | Long-Term Debt |
| | | .3 | .7 | | | Deferred Taxes |
| | | .2 | 7.1 | | | All Other Non-Current |
| | | 45.6 | 45.1 | | | Net Worth |
| | | 100.0 | 100.0 | | | Total Liabilities & Net Worth |
| | | | | | | INCOME DATA |
| | | 100.0 | 100.0 | | | Net Sales |
| | | | | | | Gross Profit |
| | | 85.3 | 82.4 | | | Operating Expenses |
| | | 14.7 | 17.6 | | | Operating Profit |
| | | 1.2 | 2.3 | | | All Other Expenses (net) |
| | | 13.5 | 15.3 | | | Profit Before Taxes |
| | | | | | | RATIOS |
| | | 5.8 | 6.0 | | | |
| | | 2.2 | 2.1 | | | Current |
| | | .8 | 1.5 | | | |
| | | 5.8 | 5.9 | | | |
| | | 2.1 | 1.9 | | | Quick |
| | | .6 | 1.4 | | | |
| | 22 | 16.9 | 34 10.8 | | | |
| | 26 | 14.3 | 46 8.0 | | | Sales/Receivables |
| | 36 | 10.0 | 63 5.8 | | | |
| | | | | | | Cost of Sales/Inventory |
| | | | | | | Cost of Sales/Payables |
| | | 5.5 | 3.4 | | | |
| | | 9.7 | 5.3 | | | Sales/Working Capital |
| | | NM | 18.7 | | | |
| | | 66.4 | 14.9 | | | |
| | (11) | 42.0 | (18) 5.9 | | | EBIT/Interest |
| | | 4.6 | 2.8 | | | |
| | | | | | | Net Profit + Depr., Dep., Amort./Cur. Mat. L/T/D |
| | | .3 | .6 | | | |
| | | .8 | 1.6 | | | Fixed/Worth |
| | | 1.4 | 3.6 | | | |
| | | .2 | .5 | | | |
| | | .6 | 1.2 | | | Debt/Worth |
| | | 5.7 | 3.9 | | | |
| | | 72.4 | 38.7 | | | |
| | (14) | 38.9 | (17) 23.3 | | | % Profit Before Taxes/Tangible Net Worth |
| | | 15.1 | 13.5 | | | |
| | | 40.6 | 19.5 | | | |
| | | 22.6 | 9.3 | | | % Profit Before Taxes/Total Assets |
| | | 8.4 | 5.2 | | | |
| | | 47.5 | 3.9 | | | |
| | | 5.6 | 1.1 | | | Sales/Net Fixed Assets |
| | | 2.7 | .5 | | | |
| | | 3.8 | 1.1 | | | |
| | | 2.0 | .8 | | | Sales/Total Assets |
| | | 1.4 | .5 | | | |
| | | 2.4 | 4.3 | | | |
| | (10) | 3.9 | (18) 7.2 | | | % Depr., Dep., Amort./Sales |
| | | 7.4 | 10.6 | | | |
| | | | | | | % Officers', Directors' Owners' Comp/Sales |
| 1322M | 27285M | 232577M | 548739M | 406345M | 455051M | Net Sales ($) |
| 255M | 8306M | 85270M | 521058M | 557062M | 1140802M | Total Assets ($) |

## Comparative Historical Data

| Type of Statement | | |
|---|---|---|
| Unqualified | 5 | 5 |
| Reviewed | 6 | 1 |
| Compiled | 11 | 2 |
| Tax Returns | 2 | 5 |
| Other | 58 | 30 |
| | 4/1/19-3/31/20 ALL | 4/1/20-3/31/21 ALL |
| NUMBER OF STATEMENTS | 82 | 43 |
| ASSETS | % | % |
| Cash & Equivalents | 12.6 | 15.0 |
| Trade Receivables (net) | 17.7 | 20.8 |
| Inventory | 4.3 | 5.6 |
| All Other Current | 1.9 | 2.4 |
| Total Current | 36.5 | 43.8 |
| Fixed Assets (net) | 54.3 | 46.8 |
| Intangibles (net) | 5.4 | 4.1 |
| All Other Non-Current | 3.8 | 5.3 |
| Total | 100.0 | 100.0 |
| Notes Payable-Short Term | 7.9 | 8.3 |
| Cur. Mat.-L.T.D. | 4.7 | 2.5 |
| Trade Payables | 5.6 | 8.1 |
| Income Taxes Payable | .1 | .0 |
| All Other Current | 7.2 | 7.2 |
| Total Current | 25.5 | 26.1 |
| Long-Term Debt | 40.7 | 32.3 |
| Deferred Taxes | .2 | .1 |
| All Other Non-Current | 6.4 | 8.1 |
| Net Worth | 27.3 | 33.3 |
| Total Liabilities & Net Worth | 100.0 | 100.0 |
| Net Sales | 100.0 | 100.0 |
| Operating Expenses | 84.4 | 86.7 |
| Operating Profit | 15.6 | 13.3 |
| All Other Expenses (net) | 6.3 | 6.4 |
| Profit Before Taxes | 9.3 | 6.8 |
| Current | 2.9 | 6.6 |
| | 1.7 | 1.4 |
| | .9 | 1.0 |
| Quick | 2.9 | 6.6 |
| | 1.5 | 1.2 |
| | .5 | .7 |
| Sales/Receivables | 18  20.3 | 23  15.7 |
| | 33  10.9 | 36  10.2 |
| | 45  8.1 | 62  5.9 |
| Sales/Working Capital | 4.8 | 4.7 |
| | 13.8 | 8.7 |
| | -29.9 | 28.0 |
| EBIT/Interest | 13.5 | 27.3 |
| | (65) 3.4 | (30) 6.2 |
| | .9 | .8 |
| Fixed/Worth | .6 | .6 |
| | 1.9 | 1.1 |
| | -47.8 | 15.3 |
| Debt/Worth | .8 | .5 |
| | 2.6 | 1.9 |
| | -65.1 | 23.0 |
| % Profit Before Taxes/Tangible Net Worth | 65.0 | 73.1 |
| | (61) 24.2 | (37) 19.1 |
| | 7.8 | .5 |
| % Profit Before Taxes/Total Assets | 16.2 | 19.1 |
| | 7.9 | 3.9 |
| | .4 | -.8 |
| Sales/Net Fixed Assets | 9.9 | 15.3 |
| | 1.8 | 2.6 |
| | .5 | .6 |
| Sales/Total Assets | 2.6 | 3.1 |
| | 1.0 | 1.3 |
| | .4 | .4 |
| % Depr., Dep., Amort./Sales | 3.1 | 2.2 |
| | (67) 8.1 | (33) 7.4 |
| | 13.8 | 13.5 |
| % Officers', Directors' Owners' Comp/Sales | 1.1 | |
| | (21) 4.0 | |
| | 7.8 | |
| Net Sales ($) | 1526866M | 474372M |
| Total Assets ($) | 1733836M | 734543M |

M = $ thousand    MM = $ million
See Pages viii through xx for Explanation of Ratios and Data

© RMA 2024

## TRANSPORTATION—Refrigerated Warehousing and Storage   NAICS 493120

| Comparative Historical Data ||| Type of Statement | Current Data Sorted by Sales ||||||
|---|---|---|---|---|---|---|---|---|---|
| 7 | 6 | 8 | Unqualified | | | | 1 | 1 | 6 |
| 3 | 10 | 8 | Reviewed | | 2 | | 1 | 2 | 3 |
| 2 | 4 | 5 | Compiled | | | | | 4 | 4 |
| 7 | 5 | 6 | Tax Returns | 1 | | | 1 | 1 | 1 |
| 26 | 40 | 31 | Other | | 3 | 4 | 3 | 13 | 8 |
| 4/1/21-3/31/22 ALL | 4/1/22-3/31/23 ALL | 4/1/23-3/31/24 ALL | | 5 (4/1-9/30/23) || | 53 (10/1/23-3/31/24) ||
| | | | | 0-1MM | 1-3MM | 3-5MM | 5-10MM | 10-25MM | 25MM & OVER |
| 45 | 65 | 58 | NUMBER OF STATEMENTS | 1 | 5 | 5 | 5 | 20 | 22 |
| % | % | % | ASSETS | % | % | % | % | % | % |
| 16.4 | 15.4 | 16.8 | Cash & Equivalents | | | | | 21.8 | 12.6 |
| 20.5 | 14.8 | 13.9 | Trade Receivables (net) | | | | | 15.2 | 14.7 |
| 1.8 | 3.7 | 2.6 | Inventory | | | | | .4 | 4.5 |
| 8.9 | 2.2 | 1.9 | All Other Current | | | | | 1.9 | 2.2 |
| 47.5 | 36.1 | 35.3 | Total Current | | | | | 39.1 | 34.0 |
| 42.5 | 45.3 | 50.1 | Fixed Assets (net) | | | | | 52.4 | 49.2 |
| 3.9 | 7.3 | 4.0 | Intangibles (net) | | | | | .4 | 1.7 |
| 6.1 | 11.3 | 10.6 | All Other Non-Current | | | | | 8.1 | 15.1 |
| 100.0 | 100.0 | 100.0 | Total | | | | | 100.0 | 100.0 |
| | | | LIABILITIES | | | | | | |
| 2.1 | 2.2 | 2.4 | Notes Payable-Short Term | | | | | 1.1 | 4.2 |
| 2.1 | 2.5 | 2.7 | Cur. Mat.-L.T.D. | | | | | 2.0 | 3.2 |
| 5.7 | 6.5 | 7.8 | Trade Payables | | | | | 6.8 | 6.9 |
| .1 | .1 | .1 | Income Taxes Payable | | | | | .0 | .1 |
| 8.8 | 6.6 | 7.8 | All Other Current | | | | | 4.7 | 8.7 |
| 18.8 | 17.8 | 20.7 | Total Current | | | | | 14.6 | 23.1 |
| 43.9 | 32.9 | 31.9 | Long-Term Debt | | | | | 22.5 | 37.0 |
| .5 | .2 | .3 | Deferred Taxes | | | | | .7 | .2 |
| 12.0 | 9.7 | 5.9 | All Other Non-Current | | | | | 4.8 | 8.4 |
| 24.9 | 39.3 | 41.1 | Net Worth | | | | | 57.4 | 31.4 |
| 100.0 | 100.0 | 100.0 | Total Liabilities & Net Worth | | | | | 100.0 | 100.0 |
| | | | INCOME DATA | | | | | | |
| 100.0 | 100.0 | 100.0 | Net Sales | | | | | 100.0 | 100.0 |
| | | | Gross Profit | | | | | | |
| 82.3 | 84.8 | 85.8 | Operating Expenses | | | | | 85.3 | 92.0 |
| 17.7 | 15.2 | 14.2 | Operating Profit | | | | | 14.7 | 8.0 |
| 4.3 | 3.7 | 2.9 | All Other Expenses (net) | | | | | 1.0 | 3.7 |
| 13.5 | 11.5 | 11.3 | Profit Before Taxes | | | | | 13.7 | 4.3 |
| | | | RATIOS | | | | | | |
| 4.7 | 4.0 | 4.8 | | | | | | 6.9 | 3.0 |
| 2.3 | 2.2 | 2.0 | Current | | | | | 3.0 | 1.8 |
| 1.1 | 1.1 | .9 | | | | | | 1.5 | .7 |
| 4.2 | 3.4 | 4.6 | | | | | | 6.7 | 2.2 |
| 1.8 | 1.8 | 1.8 | Quick | | | | | 2.8 | 1.4 |
| .7 | .8 | .6 | | | | | | 1.0 | .5 |
| 30  12.3 | 21  17.8 | 24  15.2 | | | | | 20  18.1 | 24  15.0 |
| 43  8.4 | 35  10.4 | 34  10.8 | Sales/Receivables | | | | | 35  10.3 | 39  9.4 |
| 50  7.3 | 47  7.8 | 47  7.8 | | | | | 46  8.0 | 54  6.8 |
| | | | Cost of Sales/Inventory | | | | | | |
| | | | Cost of Sales/Payables | | | | | | |
| 3.9 | 4.4 | 4.5 | | | | | | 4.3 | 3.6 |
| 7.1 | 8.3 | 9.6 | Sales/Working Capital | | | | | 6.2 | 10.3 |
| NM | 59.9 | -49.0 | | | | | | 24.0 | -31.6 |
| 12.1 | 26.7 | 22.5 | | | | | | 77.1 | 11.9 |
| (29)  4.2 | (50)  7.3 | (47)  4.6 | EBIT/Interest | | | | (14)  9.8 | (21)  2.9 |
| 1.7 | 1.9 | 1.3 | | | | | | 3.2 | -.4 |
| | 4.5 | 12.4 | Net Profit + Depr., Dep., | | | | | | |
| | (15)  3.2 | (11)  4.8 | Amort./Cur. Mat. L/T/D | | | | | | |
| | 2.2 | 1.7 | | | | | | | |
| .2 | .4 | .5 | | | | | | .4 | .8 |
| 1.2 | 1.1 | 1.3 | Fixed/Worth | | | | | .9 | 1.5 |
| 44.3 | 5.2 | 3.6 | | | | | | 2.3 | 9.5 |
| .4 | .4 | .4 | | | | | | .2 | .8 |
| 1.6 | 1.5 | 1.1 | Debt/Worth | | | | | .5 | 1.9 |
| 76.0 | 6.9 | 6.8 | | | | | | 3.1 | 13.2 |
| 63.4 | 54.8 | 51.8 | % Profit Before Taxes/Tangible | | | | | 56.0 | 36.9 |
| (35)  29.2 | (52)  22.7 | (48)  23.4 | Net Worth | | | | (19)  28.6 | (18)  16.7 |
| 17.5 | 7.2 | 13.8 | | | | | | 16.9 | -7.0 |
| 28.7 | 22.8 | 22.8 | % Profit Before Taxes/Total | | | | | 35.7 | 14.7 |
| 14.8 | 10.2 | 9.8 | Assets | | | | | 16.2 | 6.7 |
| 2.6 | 1.3 | 2.2 | | | | | | 6.5 | -1.2 |
| 21.0 | 14.7 | 13.7 | | | | | | 11.9 | 15.1 |
| 4.3 | 2.6 | 2.0 | Sales/Net Fixed Assets | | | | | 3.9 | 1.4 |
| .9 | .9 | .7 | | | | | | 1.0 | .6 |
| 2.5 | 2.3 | 2.0 | | | | | | 3.1 | 1.6 |
| .9 | .9 | 1.0 | Sales/Total Assets | | | | | 1.6 | .7 |
| .6 | .4 | .5 | | | | | | .8 | .4 |
| 1.7 | 1.7 | 3.6 | | | | | | 3.6 | 3.0 |
| (34)  5.7 | (49)  5.9 | (48)  7.2 | % Depr., Dep., Amort./Sales | | | | (17)  6.2 | (19)  7.2 |
| 13.9 | 11.8 | 10.8 | | | | | | 8.8 | 16.8 |
| .8 | .6 | 1.2 | % Officers', Directors' | | | | | | |
| (10)  1.9 | (14)  1.9 | (15)  3.6 | Owners' Comp/Sales | | | | | | |
| 7.1 | 4.4 | 5.3 | | | | | | | |
| 1000565M | 1740295M | 1671319M | Net Sales ($) | 9M | 10469M | 18537M | 35459M | 321380M | 1285465M |
| 1130965M | 1917187M | 2312753M | Total Assets ($) | 39M | 7278M | 11060M | 127424M | 300343M | 1866609M |

M = $ thousand   MM = $ million
See Pages viii through xx for Explanation of Ratios and Data
© RMA 2024

# TRANSPORTATION—Farm Product Warehousing and Storage  NAICS 493130

## Current Data Sorted by Assets | Comparative Historical Data

| | 0-500M | 500M-2MM | 2-10MM | 10-50MM | 50-100MM | 100-250MM | Type of Statement | 4/1/19-3/31/20 ALL | 4/1/20-3/31/21 ALL |
|---|---|---|---|---|---|---|---|---|---|
| | | 1 | 1 | 2 | 2 | 1 | Unqualified | 9 | 5 |
| | 1 | | 3 | 3 | 1 | | Reviewed | 10 | 3 |
| | | 1 | | | | | Compiled | 1 | 3 |
| | 1 | 2 | 2 | 3 | 1 | 1 | Tax Returns | 2 | 4 |
| | | 12 (4/1-9/30/23) | | 13 (10/1/23-3/31/24) | | | Other | 17 | 15 |
| | 1 | 4 | 6 | 8 | 4 | 2 | NUMBER OF STATEMENTS | 39 | 30 |
| | % | % | % | % | % | % | **ASSETS** | % | % |
| | | | | | | | Cash & Equivalents | 7.3 | 10.1 |
| | | | | | | | Trade Receivables (net) | 14.8 | 11.6 |
| | | | | | | | Inventory | 22.3 | 18.2 |
| | | | | | | | All Other Current | 6.3 | 6.6 |
| | | | | | | | Total Current | 50.7 | 46.4 |
| | | | | | | | Fixed Assets (net) | 35.3 | 43.0 |
| | | | | | | | Intangibles (net) | 1.2 | .4 |
| | | | | | | | All Other Non-Current | 12.8 | 10.2 |
| | | | | | | | Total | 100.0 | 100.0 |
| | | | | | | | **LIABILITIES** | | |
| | | | | | | | Notes Payable-Short Term | 11.8 | 11.5 |
| | | | | | | | Cur. Mat.-L.T.D. | 1.8 | 2.1 |
| | | | | | | | Trade Payables | 16.5 | 9.9 |
| | | | | | | | Income Taxes Payable | .0 | .0 |
| | | | | | | | All Other Current | 8.0 | 13.4 |
| | | | | | | | Total Current | 38.2 | 37.0 |
| | | | | | | | Long-Term Debt | 10.9 | 14.8 |
| | | | | | | | Deferred Taxes | .4 | .1 |
| | | | | | | | All Other Non-Current | 2.9 | 3.6 |
| | | | | | | | Net Worth | 47.6 | 44.5 |
| | | | | | | | Total Liabilities & Net Worth | 100.0 | 100.0 |
| | | | | | | | **INCOME DATA** | | |
| | | | | | | | Net Sales | 100.0 | 100.0 |
| | | | | | | | Gross Profit | | |
| | | | | | | | Operating Expenses | 94.1 | 89.5 |
| | | | | | | | Operating Profit | 5.9 | 10.5 |
| | | | | | | | All Other Expenses (net) | .7 | 2.3 |
| | | | | | | | Profit Before Taxes | 5.3 | 8.2 |
| | | | | | | | **RATIOS** | | |
| | | | | | | | Current | 1.6 | 3.1 |
| | | | | | | | | 1.4 | 1.4 |
| | | | | | | | | 1.0 | .9 |
| | | | | | | | Quick | .9 | 2.2 |
| | | | | | | | | .6 | .6 |
| | | | | | | | | .4 | .3 |
| | | | | | | | Sales/Receivables | 16  22.5 | 0  UND |
| | | | | | | | | 31  11.9 | 20  18.1 |
| | | | | | | | | 48  7.6 | 42  8.7 |
| | | | | | | | Cost of Sales/Inventory | | |
| | | | | | | | Cost of Sales/Payables | | |
| | | | | | | | Sales/Working Capital | 8.5 | 4.2 |
| | | | | | | | | 11.0 | 8.9 |
| | | | | | | | | 183.7 | -57.6 |
| | | | | | | | EBIT/Interest | 10.5 | 19.9 |
| | | | | | | | | (34) 2.0 | (24) 6.5 |
| | | | | | | | | .9 | 3.8 |
| | | | | | | | Net Profit + Depr., Dep., Amort./Cur. Mat. L/T/D | | |
| | | | | | | | Fixed/Worth | .4 | .6 |
| | | | | | | | | .7 | .9 |
| | | | | | | | | 1.2 | 2.0 |
| | | | | | | | Debt/Worth | .4 | .6 |
| | | | | | | | | 1.1 | 1.2 |
| | | | | | | | | 2.1 | 3.0 |
| | | | | | | | % Profit Before Taxes/Tangible Net Worth | 22.1 | 23.1 |
| | | | | | | | | (36) 4.3 | 9.0 |
| | | | | | | | | -1.0 | 1.5 |
| | | | | | | | % Profit Before Taxes/Total Assets | 6.7 | 10.8 |
| | | | | | | | | 2.4 | 3.8 |
| | | | | | | | | .0 | .4 |
| | | | | | | | Sales/Net Fixed Assets | 10.7 | 9.4 |
| | | | | | | | | 5.3 | 3.5 |
| | | | | | | | | 2.1 | .2 |
| | | | | | | | Sales/Total Assets | 2.2 | 2.0 |
| | | | | | | | | 1.5 | 1.3 |
| | | | | | | | | .7 | .1 |
| | | | | | | | % Depr., Dep., Amort./Sales | 1.3 | 1.3 |
| | | | | | | | | (37) 2.1 | (24) 2.2 |
| | | | | | | | | 4.9 | 8.6 |
| | | | | | | | % Officers', Directors' Owners' Comp/Sales | | |
| | 113M | 4133M | 50410M | 408090M | 499168M | 1307338M | Net Sales ($) | 1336551M | 1642022M |
| | 17M | 4075M | 29188M | 184251M | 350190M | 347255M | Total Assets ($) | 960177M | 1030887M |

M = $ thousand    MM = $ million
See Pages viii through xx for Explanation of Ratios and Data

© RMA 2024

## TRANSPORTATION—Farm Product Warehousing and Storage  NAICS 493130

### Comparative Historical Data | Current Data Sorted by Sales

| | | | | | | | | | | | | | | | |
|---|---|---|---|---|---|---|---|---|---|---|---|---|---|---|---|
| | 9 | | 10 | | 6 | **Type of Statement** | | | | | | 1 | | 5 | |
| | 7 | | 8 | | 8 | Unqualified | | | 2 | | 2 | 1 | | 3 | |
| | | | | 1 | | Reviewed | | | | | | | | | |
| | 1 | | | | 2 | Compiled | 2 | | | | | | | | |
| | 14 | | 10 | | 9 | Tax Returns | 1 | 1 | | 1 | | 3 | | 3 | |
| | 4/1/21-3/31/22 | | 4/1/22-3/31/23 | | 4/1/23-3/31/24 | Other | | 12 (4/1-9/30/23) | | | | 13 (10/1/23-3/31/24) | | | |
| | ALL | | ALL | | ALL | | 0-1MM | 1-3MM | | 3-5MM | 5-10MM | 10-25MM | | 25MM & OVER | |
| | 31 | | 29 | | 25 | **NUMBER OF STATEMENTS** | 3 | 3 | | 1 | 2 | 5 | | 11 | |
| | % | | % | | % | **ASSETS** | % | % | | % | % | % | | % | |
| | 10.7 | | 8.7 | | 13.2 | Cash & Equivalents | | | | | | | | 5.6 | |
| | 13.3 | | 17.2 | | 13.0 | Trade Receivables (net) | | | | | | | | 13.7 | |
| | 24.2 | | 23.2 | | 21.8 | Inventory | | | | | | | | 33.4 | |
| | 8.2 | | 11.3 | | 6.5 | All Other Current | | | | | | | | 4.1 | |
| | 56.4 | | 60.4 | | 54.4 | Total Current | | | | | | | | 56.8 | |
| | 34.5 | | 29.1 | | 30.9 | Fixed Assets (net) | | | | | | | | 24.3 | |
| | .3 | | .9 | | .1 | Intangibles (net) | | | | | | | | .2 | |
| | 8.8 | | 9.6 | | 14.6 | All Other Non-Current | | | | | | | | 18.7 | |
| | 100.0 | | 100.0 | | 100.0 | Total | | | | | | | | 100.0 | |
| | | | | | | **LIABILITIES** | | | | | | | | | |
| | 11.8 | | 13.4 | | 5.9 | Notes Payable-Short Term | | | | | | | | 5.8 | |
| | 1.9 | | .6 | | 1.5 | Cur. Mat.-L.T.D. | | | | | | | | .9 | |
| | 13.7 | | 19.3 | | 19.8 | Trade Payables | | | | | | | | 28.0 | |
| | .0 | | .0 | | .1 | Income Taxes Payable | | | | | | | | .0 | |
| | 9.6 | | 9.6 | | 6.7 | All Other Current | | | | | | | | 5.2 | |
| | 37.1 | | 42.9 | | 34.0 | Total Current | | | | | | | | 39.9 | |
| | 11.8 | | 6.5 | | 7.7 | Long-Term Debt | | | | | | | | 7.4 | |
| | .3 | | .1 | | .1 | Deferred Taxes | | | | | | | | .3 | |
| | 2.6 | | 9.0 | | 5.8 | All Other Non-Current | | | | | | | | 9.3 | |
| | 48.3 | | 41.4 | | 52.3 | Net Worth | | | | | | | | 43.1 | |
| | 100.0 | | 100.0 | | 100.0 | Total Liabilities & Net Worth | | | | | | | | 100.0 | |
| | | | | | | **INCOME DATA** | | | | | | | | | |
| | 100.0 | | 100.0 | | 100.0 | Net Sales | | | | | | | | 100.0 | |
| | | | | | | Gross Profit | | | | | | | | 97.9 | |
| | 91.7 | | 96.4 | | 92.5 | Operating Expenses | | | | | | | | 2.1 | |
| | 8.3 | | 3.6 | | 7.5 | Operating Profit | | | | | | | | -.2 | |
| | -1.1 | | -.6 | | .7 | All Other Expenses (net) | | | | | | | | 2.3 | |
| | 9.4 | | 4.2 | | 6.9 | Profit Before Taxes | | | | | | | | | |
| | | | | | | **RATIOS** | | | | | | | | | |
| | 2.7 | | 2.0 | | 2.7 | | | | | | | | | 1.8 | |
| | 1.4 | | 1.6 | | 1.6 | Current | | | | | | | | 1.4 | |
| | 1.2 | | 1.1 | | 1.1 | | | | | | | | | 1.1 | |
| | 1.5 | | 1.5 | | 1.4 | | | | | | | | | .8 | |
| | .7 | | .5 | | .6 | Quick | | | | | | | | .5 | |
| | .2 | | .3 | | .4 | | | | | | | | | .2 | |
| | 8 | 46.8 | 8 | 48.6 | 4 | 83.2 | | | | | | | 5 | 80.2 | |
| | 18 | 20.2 | 22 | 16.9 | 20 | 18.4 | Sales/Receivables | | | | | | 20 | 18.4 | |
| | 38 | 9.7 | 33 | 11.1 | 46 | 8.0 | | | | | | | 41 | 9.0 | |
| | | | | | | | Cost of Sales/Inventory | | | | | | | | |
| | | | | | | | Cost of Sales/Payables | | | | | | | | |
| | 3.9 | | 7.5 | | 6.6 | | | | | | | | | 9.4 | |
| | 11.0 | | 12.6 | | 9.4 | Sales/Working Capital | | | | | | | | 18.6 | |
| | 22.7 | | 55.3 | | 59.3 | | | | | | | | | 95.6 | |
| | | 41.4 | | 17.2 | | 14.1 | | | | | | | | 14.8 | |
| | (27) | 7.0 | (26) | 6.4 | (19) | 5.3 | EBIT/Interest | | | | | | (10) | 5.6 | |
| | | 2.8 | | 1.4 | | 2.6 | | | | | | | | 3.9 | |
| | | | | | | 31.6 | Net Profit + Depr., Dep., | | | | | | | | |
| | | | | (10) | 8.0 | Amort./Cur. Mat. L/T/D | | | | | | | | | |
| | | | | | | 2.7 | | | | | | | | | |
| | .4 | | .3 | | .2 | | | | | | | | | .3 | |
| | .7 | | .6 | | .5 | Fixed/Worth | | | | | | | | .5 | |
| | .9 | | 1.1 | | .9 | | | | | | | | | 1.0 | |
| | .4 | | .7 | | .3 | | | | | | | | | .8 | |
| | 1.1 | | 1.2 | | .8 | Debt/Worth | | | | | | | | 1.4 | |
| | 2.0 | | 2.6 | | 2.2 | | | | | | | | | 2.2 | |
| | | 31.5 | | 24.5 | | 23.9 | % Profit Before Taxes/Tangible | | | | | | | 18.9 | |
| | (29) | 12.8 | (27) | 15.5 | (24) | 13.5 | Net Worth | | | | | | | 13.7 | |
| | | 4.0 | | 6.0 | | 3.7 | | | | | | | | 10.6 | |
| | 14.9 | | 9.9 | | 12.1 | % Profit Before Taxes/Total | | | | | | | | 6.9 | |
| | 5.2 | | 6.7 | | 6.7 | Assets | | | | | | | | 5.4 | |
| | 2.4 | | 1.9 | | 1.3 | | | | | | | | | 2.7 | |
| | 16.3 | | 19.3 | | 18.1 | | | | | | | | | 19.5 | |
| | 6.5 | | 9.7 | | 6.6 | Sales/Net Fixed Assets | | | | | | | | 16.1 | |
| | 2.7 | | 3.9 | | 2.5 | | | | | | | | | 4.5 | |
| | 2.5 | | 3.1 | | 3.1 | | | | | | | | | 4.3 | |
| | 1.9 | | 2.3 | | 1.4 | Sales/Total Assets | | | | | | | | 2.6 | |
| | 1.1 | | 1.1 | | .9 | | | | | | | | | 1.4 | |
| | | .8 | | .5 | | .8 | | | | | | | | | .7 | |
| | (29) | 1.4 | (27) | 1.1 | (21) | 1.5 | % Depr., Dep., Amort./Sales | | | | | | | .8 | |
| | | 4.3 | | 2.1 | | 4.7 | | | | | | | | 1.6 | |
| | | | | | | | % Officers', Directors' Owners' Comp/Sales | | | | | | | | |
| | 3042684M | | 3992142M | | 2269252M | Net Sales ($) | 1417M | 5121M | | 3713M | 13972M | 73536M | | 2171493M | |
| | 1289379M | | 1411458M | | 914976M | Total Assets ($) | 1873M | 5472M | | 2153M | 12937M | 199343M | | 693198M | |

M = $ thousand    MM = $ million
See Pages viii through xx for Explanation of Ratios and Data

© RMA 2024

# TRANSPORTATION—Other Warehousing and Storage  NAICS 493190

## Current Data Sorted by Assets | Comparative Historical Data

| | | | | | | Type of Statement | | |
|---|---|---|---|---|---|---|---|---|
| | | 1 | | 1 | 1 | Unqualified | 4 | 1 |
| | | 1 | 1 | 1 | 1 | Reviewed | 4 | 2 |
| | 1 | 1 | 1 | | | Compiled | 4 | 2 |
| 1 | 1 | 1 | | | | Tax Returns | 8 | 3 |
| 3 | 2 | 7 | 9 | 1 | | Other | 25 | 9 |
| | 7 (4/1-9/30/23) | | 28 (10/1/23-3/31/24) | | | | 4/1/19-3/31/20 | 4/1/20-3/31/21 |
| 0-500M | 500M-2MM | 2-10MM | 10-50MM | 50-100MM | 100-250MM | | ALL | ALL |
| 4 | 4 | 11 | 11 | 3 | 2 | NUMBER OF STATEMENTS | 45 | 17 |
| % | % | % | % | % | % | ASSETS | % | % |
| | | 10.5 | 18.2 | | | Cash & Equivalents | 12.8 | 12.5 |
| | | 19.1 | 22.3 | | | Trade Receivables (net) | 14.3 | 16.5 |
| | | 6.0 | 3.1 | | | Inventory | 3.9 | 4.4 |
| | | 3.0 | 2.2 | | | All Other Current | 1.6 | 7.5 |
| | | 38.5 | 45.7 | | | Total Current | 32.6 | 40.9 |
| | | 41.7 | 27.2 | | | Fixed Assets (net) | 47.5 | 42.8 |
| | | 2.7 | 3.6 | | | Intangibles (net) | 8.3 | 10.1 |
| | | 17.1 | 23.6 | | | All Other Non-Current | 11.6 | 6.2 |
| | | 100.0 | 100.0 | | | Total | 100.0 | 100.0 |
| | | | | | | LIABILITIES | | |
| | | 6.5 | 2.7 | | | Notes Payable-Short Term | 3.2 | 2.5 |
| | | 4.5 | 1.7 | | | Cur. Mat.-L.T.D. | 5.1 | 2.2 |
| | | 6.5 | 9.8 | | | Trade Payables | 4.7 | 6.3 |
| | | .0 | .0 | | | Income Taxes Payable | .4 | .0 |
| | | 2.4 | 13.5 | | | All Other Current | 7.6 | 9.0 |
| | | 19.9 | 27.8 | | | Total Current | 21.0 | 20.1 |
| | | 31.9 | 14.4 | | | Long-Term Debt | 35.3 | 43.1 |
| | | .0 | .5 | | | Deferred Taxes | .1 | .1 |
| | | .9 | 15.8 | | | All Other Non-Current | 8.7 | 2.1 |
| | | 47.3 | 41.5 | | | Net Worth | 34.9 | 34.7 |
| | | 100.0 | 100.0 | | | Total Liabilities & Net Worth | 100.0 | 100.0 |
| | | | | | | INCOME DATA | | |
| | | 100.0 | 100.0 | | | Net Sales | 100.0 | 100.0 |
| | | | | | | Gross Profit | | |
| | | 84.8 | 92.6 | | | Operating Expenses | 82.1 | 83.4 |
| | | 15.2 | 7.4 | | | Operating Profit | 17.9 | 16.6 |
| | | .9 | .7 | | | All Other Expenses (net) | 3.6 | 9.1 |
| | | 14.3 | 6.7 | | | Profit Before Taxes | 14.3 | 7.6 |
| | | | | | | RATIOS | | |
| | | 8.2 | 4.3 | | | | 4.0 | 3.5 |
| | | 1.6 | 2.1 | | | Current | 1.6 | 1.6 |
| | | 1.1 | .9 | | | | .9 | 1.1 |
| | | 4.6 | 4.3 | | | | 3.2 | 3.4 |
| | | 1.5 | 1.3 | | | Quick | 1.5 | 1.3 |
| | | .4 | .7 | | | | .8 | .9 |
| | 1 | 670.1 | 32  11.3 | | | | 1  331.7 | 0  UND |
| | 11 | 33.0 | 49  7.4 | | | Sales/Receivables | 34  10.6 | 34  10.7 |
| | 43 | 8.4 | 62  5.9 | | | | 55  6.6 | 63  5.8 |
| | | | | | | Cost of Sales/Inventory | | |
| | | | | | | Cost of Sales/Payables | | |
| | | 6.7 | 3.1 | | | | 6.0 | 4.1 |
| | | 12.7 | 7.1 | | | Sales/Working Capital | 13.0 | 8.4 |
| | | 37.8 | -31.9 | | | | -61.7 | 37.4 |
| | | 21.6 | 61.1 | | | | 26.0 | 27.5 |
| | | (10) 7.3 | 4.3 | | | EBIT/Interest | (36) 4.7 | (11) 10.4 |
| | | 1.4 | 2.4 | | | | 1.8 | 1.5 |
| | | | | | | Net Profit + Depr., Dep., Amort./Cur. Mat. L/T/D | | |
| | | .1 | .1 | | | | .4 | .1 |
| | | .8 | .6 | | | Fixed/Worth | 1.5 | 1.2 |
| | | 2.6 | 1.1 | | | | 9.4 | NM |
| | | .5 | .6 | | | | .4 | .7 |
| | | 1.3 | 1.2 | | | Debt/Worth | 1.4 | 1.4 |
| | | 4.7 | 3.2 | | | | 11.5 | NM |
| | | 78.9 | 74.7 | | | | 48.5 | 51.7 |
| | | (10) 41.9 | (10) 36.8 | | | % Profit Before Taxes/Tangible Net Worth | (35) 21.7 | (13) 36.0 |
| | | 4.0 | 9.2 | | | | 9.8 | 12.5 |
| | | 29.4 | 28.9 | | | | 18.5 | 22.1 |
| | | 12.8 | 6.1 | | | % Profit Before Taxes/Total Assets | 8.7 | 8.9 |
| | | .9 | 1.5 | | | | 3.8 | 1.6 |
| | | 21.0 | 36.4 | | | | 12.6 | 62.7 |
| | | 4.1 | 4.9 | | | Sales/Net Fixed Assets | 2.9 | 2.6 |
| | | 1.0 | 2.8 | | | | .6 | .5 |
| | | 3.4 | 1.8 | | | | 2.3 | 2.4 |
| | | 1.4 | 1.3 | | | Sales/Total Assets | 1.2 | .8 |
| | | .5 | 1.1 | | | | .5 | .2 |
| | | | 1.0 | | | | 1.7 | 1.0 |
| | | | 3.8 | | | % Depr., Dep., Amort./Sales | (38) 5.5 | (13) 10.5 |
| | | | 6.7 | | | | 10.6 | 16.9 |
| | | | | | | % Officers', Directors' Owners' Comp/Sales | | |
| 4244M | 23118M | 116357M | 425831M | 65275M | 527241M | Net Sales ($) | 891254M | 324453M |
| 1367M | 4888M | 62965M | 277498M | 179186M | 272135M | Total Assets ($) | 856921M | 395935M |

© RMA 2024

M = $ thousand     MM = $ million
See Pages viii through xx for Explanation of Ratios and Data

## TRANSPORTATION—Other Warehousing and Storage  NAICS 493190

### Comparative Historical Data | Current Data Sorted by Sales

| Comparative Historical Data | | | | Type of Statement | Current Data Sorted by Sales | | | | | |
|---|---|---|---|---|---|---|---|---|---|---|
| 3 | 2 | 3 | | Unqualified | | | | | 1 | 2 |
| 2 | 4 | 4 | | Reviewed | | | | | 2 | 2 |
| 2 | 1 | 3 | | Compiled | | | 1 | | 2 | |
| 3 | 5 | 3 | | Tax Returns | | | | | 1 | |
| 16 | 22 | 22 | | Other | 1 | 1 | | 1 | 1 | 7 |
| 4/1/21-3/31/22 ALL | 4/1/22-3/31/23 ALL | 4/1/23-3/31/24 ALL | | | 3 | 3 | 1 | 3 | 28 (10/1/23-3/31/24) | |
| | | | | | 7 (4/1-9/30/23) | | | | | |
| | | | | | 0-1MM | 1-3MM | 3-5MM | 5-10MM | 10-25MM | 25MM & OVER |
| 26 | 34 | 35 | | NUMBER OF STATEMENTS | 4 | 4 | 2 | 3 | 11 | 11 |
| % | % | % | | ASSETS | % | % | % | % | % | % |
| 14.4 | 13.5 | 15.2 | | Cash & Equivalents | | | | | 21.7 | 9.0 |
| 13.9 | 17.7 | 21.7 | | Trade Receivables (net) | | | | | 23.5 | 22.9 |
| 3.7 | 1.7 | 7.6 | | Inventory | | | | | 12.8 | 3.3 |
| 6.2 | 2.3 | 2.2 | | All Other Current | | | | | .5 | 3.6 |
| 38.2 | 35.3 | 46.8 | | Total Current | | | | | 58.4 | 38.8 |
| 48.6 | 42.9 | 31.1 | | Fixed Assets (net) | | | | | 25.7 | 24.9 |
| 7.9 | 5.4 | 2.9 | | Intangibles (net) | | | | | 4.5 | 3.4 |
| 5.3 | 16.4 | 19.2 | | All Other Non-Current | | | | | 11.4 | 32.8 |
| 100.0 | 100.0 | 100.0 | | Total | | | | | 100.0 | 100.0 |
| | | | | LIABILITIES | | | | | | |
| 5.8 | 2.4 | 5.9 | | Notes Payable-Short Term | | | | | 4.9 | 5.2 |
| 2.7 | 2.6 | 3.0 | | Cur. Mat.-L.T.D. | | | | | 3.2 | 3.2 |
| 3.0 | 5.5 | 7.0 | | Trade Payables | | | | | 6.8 | 10.8 |
| .0 | .0 | .0 | | Income Taxes Payable | | | | | .0 | .1 |
| 8.5 | 9.5 | 10.5 | | All Other Current | | | | | 9.2 | 11.0 |
| 19.9 | 20.0 | 26.4 | | Total Current | | | | | 24.1 | 30.3 |
| 38.5 | 38.3 | 25.3 | | Long-Term Debt | | | | | 18.2 | 11.9 |
| .6 | .5 | .2 | | Deferred Taxes | | | | | .2 | .3 |
| 2.0 | 3.1 | 11.8 | | All Other Non-Current | | | | | 9.4 | 24.9 |
| 39.0 | 38.2 | 36.4 | | Net Worth | | | | | 48.1 | 32.7 |
| 100.0 | 100.0 | 100.0 | | Total Liabilities & Net Worth | | | | | 100.0 | 100.0 |
| | | | | INCOME DATA | | | | | | |
| 100.0 | 100.0 | 100.0 | | Net Sales | | | | | 100.0 | 100.0 |
| | | | | Gross Profit | | | | | | |
| 80.1 | 81.9 | 87.6 | | Operating Expenses | | | | | 91.7 | 93.7 |
| 19.9 | 18.1 | 12.4 | | Operating Profit | | | | | 8.3 | 6.3 |
| 4.0 | 4.7 | 2.1 | | All Other Expenses (net) | | | | | .7 | .7 |
| 15.9 | 13.4 | 10.3 | | Profit Before Taxes | | | | | 7.6 | 5.6 |
| | | | | RATIOS | | | | | | |
| 4.5 | 2.8 | 7.8 | | | | | | | 13.5 | 2.1 |
| 1.8 | 1.8 | 1.5 | | Current | | | | | 4.0 | 1.1 |
| 1.4 | 1.0 | .9 | | | | | | | 1.2 | .9 |
| 4.0 | 2.8 | 4.3 | | | | | | | 6.2 | 1.3 |
| 1.5 | 1.2 | 1.1 | | Quick | | | | | 4.0 | 1.0 |
| .9 | .8 | .7 | | | | | | | .9 | .7 |
| 1   391.5 | 0   UND | 11   33.0 | | | | | | | 15   24.0 | 25   14.6 |
| 38   9.7 | 32   11.4 | 34   10.6 | | Sales/Receivables | | | | | 43   8.4 | 49   7.4 |
| 52   7.0 | 64   5.7 | 57   6.4 | | | | | | | 64   5.7 | 58   6.3 |
| | | | | Cost of Sales/Inventory | | | | | | |
| | | | | Cost of Sales/Payables | | | | | | |
| 3.2 | 5.7 | 6.6 | | | | | | | 2.5 | 7.1 |
| 5.1 | 14.9 | 15.8 | | Sales/Working Capital | | | | | 9.1 | 80.4 |
| 19.6 | NM | -39.0 | | | | | | | 21.9 | -31.9 |
|   53.0 |   56.8 |   41.6 | | | | | | |   52.4 | 47.0 |
| (23) 4.8 | (29) 7.3 | (32) 11.1 | | EBIT/Interest | | | | | (10) 7.3 | 8.4 |
|   1.9 |   2.1 |   2.5 | | | | | | |   .9 | 2.4 |
| | | | | Net Profit + Depr., Dep., Amort./Cur. Mat. L/T/D | | | | | | |
| .6 | .3 | .1 | | | | | | | .1 | .1 |
| 1.3 | 1.2 | .9 | | Fixed/Worth | | | | | .5 | .9 |
| 11.1 | 12.5 | 2.6 | | | | | | | 1.1 | 1.6 |
| .6 | .5 | .6 | | | | | | | .3 | 1.2 |
| 2.1 | 1.7 | 2.1 | | Debt/Worth | | | | | .7 | 2.6 |
| 11.1 | 16.8 | 6.9 | | | | | | | 4.7 | 5.7 |
|   62.3 |   67.9 |   61.3 | | % Profit Before Taxes/Tangible Net Worth | | | | |   59.5 | 74.7 |
| (21) 26.0 | (28) 40.4 | (30) 36.8 | | | | | | | (10) 31.9 | (10) 40.7 |
|   7.3 |   7.5 |   7.4 | | | | | | |   5.1 | 8.3 |
| 31.7 | 30.7 | 28.9 | | % Profit Before Taxes/Total Assets | | | | | 28.9 | 22.3 |
| 8.8 | 6.9 | 6.9 | | | | | | | 6.0 | 6.1 |
| 2.5 | 2.7 | 1.5 | | | | | | | .6 | 1.2 |
| 8.3 | 10.3 | 36.4 | | | | | | | 87.2 | 36.4 |
| 1.9 | 4.0 | 7.1 | | Sales/Net Fixed Assets | | | | | 5.6 | 12.0 |
| .5 | .7 | 2.4 | | | | | | | 2.4 | 4.1 |
| 2.1 | 2.3 | 3.4 | | | | | | | 3.4 | 3.5 |
| .9 | 1.2 | 1.4 | | Sales/Total Assets | | | | | 1.4 | 1.7 |
| .4 | .4 | .6 | | | | | | | 1.1 | 1.0 |
|   2.6 |   2.8 |   1.5 | | % Depr., Dep., Amort./Sales | | | | | | 1.0 |
| (21) 7.1 | (26) 6.0 | (27) 2.9 | | | | | | | | 2.2 |
|   14.4 |   12.7 |   6.8 | | | | | | | | 4.1 |
| | | | | % Officers', Directors' Owners' Comp/Sales | | | | | | |
| 739981M | 786962M | 1162066M | | Net Sales ($) | 3170M | 5578M | 8151M | 22682M | 159135M | 963350M |
| 609481M | 722800M | 798039M | | Total Assets ($) | 2317M | 10073M | 2072M | 70224M | 161452M | 551901M |

M = $ thousand   MM = $ million
See Pages viii through xx for Explanation of Ratios and Data

© RMA 2024

# INFORMATION

# INFORMATION—Motion Picture and Video Production  NAICS 512110

## Current Data Sorted by Assets | Comparative Historical Data

| | | | | | | Type of Statement | | |
|---|---|---|---|---|---|---|---|---|
| | | 1 | 1 | 3 | 3 | Unqualified | 13 | 3 |
| | | 2 | 1 | | | Reviewed | 3 | |
| | | 3 | 2 | | 1 | Compiled | 4 | 4 |
| 4 | 5 | 1 | | | | Tax Returns | 9 | 10 |
| 6 | 7 | 13 | 15 | 2 | 7 | Other | 61 | 27 |
| | 14 (4/1-9/30/23) | | 63 (10/1/23-3/31/24) | | | | 4/1/19-3/31/20 | 4/1/20-3/31/21 |
| 0-500M | 500M-2MM | 2-10MM | 10-50MM | 50-100MM | 100-250MM | | ALL | ALL |
| 10 | 12 | 20 | 19 | 5 | 11 | NUMBER OF STATEMENTS | 90 | 44 |
| % | % | % | % | % | % | ASSETS | % | % |
| 33.8 | 22.1 | 27.8 | 24.7 | | 10.6 | Cash & Equivalents | 23.6 | 36.3 |
| 12.5 | 10.1 | 22.1 | 23.3 | | 16.0 | Trade Receivables (net) | 19.0 | 20.8 |
| .0 | .0 | .1 | .7 | | 6.0 | Inventory | .7 | .7 |
| 7.2 | 14.8 | 3.2 | 6.6 | | 6.4 | All Other Current | 5.1 | 7.9 |
| 53.5 | 47.0 | 53.3 | 55.3 | | 39.1 | Total Current | 48.3 | 65.7 |
| 16.8 | 31.1 | 26.4 | 19.9 | | 18.2 | Fixed Assets (net) | 24.4 | 19.9 |
| 3.9 | .3 | 8.7 | 18.7 | | 22.1 | Intangibles (net) | 9.8 | 6.9 |
| 25.8 | 21.6 | 11.5 | 6.1 | | 20.7 | All Other Non-Current | 17.4 | 7.5 |
| 100.0 | 100.0 | 100.0 | 100.0 | | 100.0 | Total | 100.0 | 100.0 |
| | | | | | | LIABILITIES | | |
| 13.2 | 4.5 | 8.8 | 3.9 | | 8.0 | Notes Payable-Short Term | 8.3 | 15.4 |
| 1.8 | 4.7 | 5.1 | 4.7 | | 1.5 | Cur. Mat.-L.T.D. | 1.9 | 3.3 |
| .0 | 10.2 | 6.2 | 13.0 | | 2.7 | Trade Payables | 6.4 | 10.1 |
| .0 | .0 | .0 | .0 | | .0 | Income Taxes Payable | .1 | 1.0 |
| 28.1 | 44.6 | 11.3 | 18.2 | | 16.0 | All Other Current | 15.4 | 21.1 |
| 43.1 | 64.0 | 31.4 | 39.8 | | 28.3 | Total Current | 32.1 | 50.9 |
| 6.3 | 30.4 | 26.5 | 10.6 | | 20.5 | Long-Term Debt | 28.0 | 23.9 |
| .0 | .0 | .0 | .0 | | .2 | Deferred Taxes | .2 | .2 |
| 4.7 | 15.5 | 16.3 | 11.0 | | 21.8 | All Other Non-Current | 13.0 | 6.0 |
| 46.0 | -9.9 | 25.8 | 38.6 | | 29.2 | Net Worth | 26.6 | 19.0 |
| 100.0 | 100.0 | 100.0 | 100.0 | | 100.0 | Total Liabilities & Net Worth | 100.0 | 100.0 |
| | | | | | | INCOME DATA | | |
| 100.0 | 100.0 | 100.0 | 100.0 | | 100.0 | Net Sales | 100.0 | 100.0 |
| | | | | | | Gross Profit | | |
| 80.8 | 89.6 | 95.1 | 96.9 | | 83.1 | Operating Expenses | 85.7 | 91.5 |
| 19.2 | 10.4 | 4.9 | 3.1 | | 16.9 | Operating Profit | 14.3 | 8.5 |
| 2.4 | -1.0 | 1.8 | 3.5 | | 5.6 | All Other Expenses (net) | 4.2 | 1.2 |
| 16.8 | 11.4 | 3.1 | -.4 | | 11.3 | Profit Before Taxes | 10.1 | 7.3 |
| | | | | | | RATIOS | | |
| 19.4 | 3.5 | 2.9 | 2.5 | | 2.7 | | 6.3 | 4.7 |
| .9 | 2.3 | 2.0 | 1.8 | | 1.2 | Current | 1.8 | 1.9 |
| .5 | .4 | .9 | .9 | | 1.1 | | .9 | .9 |
| 19.4 | 3.0 | 2.7 | 2.5 | | 1.8 | | 6.3 | 4.3 |
| .9 | 1.3 | 1.8 | 1.5 | | 1.1 | Quick | 1.7 | 1.6 |
| .2 | .4 | .7 | .8 | | 1.0 | | .8 | .6 |
| 0 | UND | 0 | UND | 7 | 55.6 | 21 | 17.8 | 6 | 61.5 | | 0 | UND | 0 | UND |
| 0 | UND | 5 | 77.9 | 30 | 12.2 | 45 | 8.1 | 63 | 5.8 | Sales/Receivables | 32 | 11.5 | 23 | 16.0 |
| 33 | 11.2 | 18 | 20.2 | 63 | 5.8 | 70 | 5.2 | 140 | 2.6 | | 59 | 6.2 | 63 | 5.8 |
| | | | | | | Cost of Sales/Inventory | | |
| | | | | | | Cost of Sales/Payables | | |
| 12.7 | 4.7 | 5.7 | 4.5 | | 4.6 | | 3.3 | 4.4 |
| -516.7 | 13.3 | 12.3 | 8.9 | | 15.2 | Sales/Working Capital | 11.5 | 6.6 |
| -9.6 | -66.5 | -34.9 | -21.4 | | 44.1 | | -112.0 | -101.2 |
| | | 11.8 | 32.2 | | 7.1 | | 26.2 | 70.7 |
| | (16) | 4.1 | (13) | -1.1 | 2.5 | EBIT/Interest | (68) 6.4 | (29) 5.5 |
| | | -3.3 | -4.1 | | -.3 | | 1.3 | -6.8 |
| | | | | | | Net Profit + Depr., Dep., Amort./Cur. Mat. L/T/D | | |
| .0 | .1 | .2 | .1 | | .0 | | .0 | .1 |
| .3 | .7 | .7 | 1.0 | | 1.5 | Fixed/Worth | .5 | .5 |
| -3.1 | 1.3 | NM | 1.4 | | 2.7 | | 1.8 | NM |
| .1 | .7 | .3 | .9 | | 1.0 | | .3 | .4 |
| 1.8 | 1.5 | .9 | 3.1 | | 3.2 | Debt/Worth | 2.2 | 1.7 |
| -11.8 | NM | -3.0 | -24.8 | | -33.5 | | 27.3 | NM |
| | | 21.1 | 34.5 | | | % Profit Before Taxes/Tangible Net Worth | 79.6 | 76.5 |
| | (14) | 6.8 | (14) | 4.5 | | | (70) 35.8 | (33) 47.7 |
| | | -1.8 | -107.0 | | | | 4.2 | -4.9 |
| 142.5 | 22.8 | 21.5 | 12.5 | | 9.6 | % Profit Before Taxes/Total Assets | 35.7 | 35.6 |
| 66.2 | 15.0 | 4.1 | 2.4 | | 3.0 | | 8.5 | 12.4 |
| 3.4 | -26.0 | -5.1 | -8.4 | | -1.8 | | .5 | -5.4 |
| UND | 78.4 | 55.5 | 138.3 | | 792.8 | | 99.3 | 136.3 |
| 22.9 | 22.6 | 18.6 | 20.1 | | 53.7 | Sales/Net Fixed Assets | 18.5 | 18.7 |
| 9.8 | 2.3 | 3.9 | 6.6 | | 1.6 | | 5.3 | 8.0 |
| 9.9 | 6.8 | 3.2 | 3.0 | | .8 | | 3.4 | 3.0 |
| 2.8 | 3.5 | 2.2 | 2.0 | | .5 | Sales/Total Assets | 1.8 | 2.0 |
| 2.0 | .9 | 1.3 | .9 | | .4 | | .7 | 1.2 |
| | | .9 | .5 | | | | 1.3 | 1.0 |
| | (12) | 2.0 | (10) | 2.5 | | % Depr., Dep., Amort./Sales | (41) 2.3 | (26) 2.7 |
| | | 12.5 | 9.8 | | | | 6.0 | 9.2 |
| | | | | | | | 4.1 | 4.4 |
| | | | | | | % Officers', Directors' Owners' Comp/Sales | (21) 6.8 | (13) 10.6 |
| | | | | | | | 12.5 | 14.8 |
| 13963M | 38166M | 262993M | 973253M | 390287M | 1225765M | Net Sales ($) | 2742817M | 890932M |
| 2341M | 10071M | 100150M | 473535M | 370679M | 1846247M | Total Assets ($) | 3449506M | 655229M |

© RMA 2024  M = $ thousand  MM = $ million
See Pages viii through xx for Explanation of Ratios and Data

# INFORMATION—Motion Picture and Video Production  NAICS 512110

**Comparative Historical Data** | **Current Data Sorted by Sales**

| Comparative Historical Data ||| Type of Statement | Current Data Sorted by Sales ||||||
|---|---|---|---|---|---|---|---|---|---|
| 4 | 8 | 8 | Unqualified | | 1 | | | | 7 |
| 1 | 3 | 3 | Reviewed | | | | 1 | 1 | 1 |
| 4 | 8 | 6 | Compiled | | | 2 | 3 | | 1 |
| 8 | 11 | 10 | Tax Returns | 3 | 4 | | 2 | 1 | |
| 36 | 61 | 50 | Other | 7 | 3 | 4 | 6 | 3 | 27 |
| 4/1/21-3/31/22 ALL | 4/1/22-3/31/23 ALL | 4/1/23-3/31/24 ALL | | 14 (4/1-9/30/23) ||| 63 (10/1/23-3/31/24) |||
| | | | | 0-1MM | 1-3MM | 3-5MM | 5-10MM | 10-25MM | 25MM & OVER |
| 53 | 91 | 77 | NUMBER OF STATEMENTS | 10 | 8 | 6 | 12 | 5 | 36 |
| % | % | % | ASSETS | % | % | % | % | % | % |
| 28.9 | 27.0 | 23.0 | Cash & Equivalents | 9.7 | | | 37.6 | | 19.4 |
| 16.2 | 17.9 | 19.2 | Trade Receivables (net) | 3.0 | | | 13.7 | | 26.1 |
| 1.4 | 3.2 | 1.1 | Inventory | .0 | | | .0 | | 2.3 |
| 3.9 | 4.9 | 6.8 | All Other Current | 15.9 | | | 8.9 | | 6.5 |
| 50.3 | 53.1 | 50.1 | Total Current | 28.5 | | | 60.1 | | 54.3 |
| 26.9 | 20.3 | 21.7 | Fixed Assets (net) | 31.1 | | | 15.1 | | 15.1 |
| 11.6 | 12.2 | 12.7 | Intangibles (net) | 3.9 | | | 14.0 | | 17.5 |
| 11.2 | 14.5 | 15.5 | All Other Non-Current | 36.5 | | | 10.8 | | 13.1 |
| 100.0 | 100.0 | 100.0 | Total | 100.0 | | | 100.0 | | 100.0 |
| | | | LIABILITIES | | | | | | |
| 6.9 | 4.3 | 7.2 | Notes Payable-Short Term | 7.5 | | | 9.4 | | 5.9 |
| 2.3 | 4.0 | 3.9 | Cur. Mat.-L.T.D. | 1.3 | | | 6.5 | | 3.5 |
| 5.9 | 5.8 | 7.3 | Trade Payables | 1.6 | | | 9.6 | | 9.1 |
| .1 | .0 | .0 | Income Taxes Payable | .0 | | | .0 | | .0 |
| 13.4 | 14.4 | 21.6 | All Other Current | 21.2 | | | 48.3 | | 20.3 |
| 28.6 | 28.5 | 39.9 | Total Current | 31.6 | | | 73.8 | | 38.8 |
| 21.2 | 27.6 | 18.7 | Long-Term Debt | 21.6 | | | 29.2 | | 11.9 |
| .1 | .0 | .0 | Deferred Taxes | .0 | | | .0 | | .1 |
| 10.1 | 9.9 | 13.5 | All Other Non-Current | 1.2 | | | 15.6 | | 19.6 |
| 39.9 | 34.0 | 27.8 | Net Worth | 45.5 | | | -18.7 | | 29.6 |
| 100.0 | 100.0 | 100.0 | Total Liabilities & Net Worth | 100.0 | | | 100.0 | | 100.0 |
| | | | INCOME DATA | | | | | | |
| 100.0 | 100.0 | 100.0 | Net Sales | 100.0 | | | 100.0 | | 100.0 |
| | | | Gross Profit | | | | | | |
| 91.4 | 90.1 | 90.9 | Operating Expenses | 79.4 | | | 102.2 | | 93.3 |
| 8.6 | 9.9 | 9.1 | Operating Profit | 20.6 | | | -2.2 | | 6.7 |
| -1.4 | 2.5 | 2.4 | All Other Expenses (net) | 3.2 | | | .0 | | 3.4 |
| 9.9 | 7.4 | 6.7 | Profit Before Taxes | 17.5 | | | -2.1 | | 3.3 |
| | | | RATIOS | | | | | | |
| 3.8 | 7.1 | 2.9 | | 2.6 | | | 5.4 | | 2.5 |
| 2.1 | 2.0 | 1.6 | Current | .7 | | | 1.9 | | 1.5 |
| 1.1 | 1.1 | .8 | | .2 | | | .9 | | 1.0 |
| 3.4 | 4.2 | 2.5 | | 2.2 | | | 5.2 | | 2.0 |
| 2.0 | 1.6 | 1.4 | Quick | .5 | | | 1.4 | | 1.3 |
| 1.0 | .8 | .6 | | .1 | | | .4 | | .8 |
| 0 UND | 2  242.5 | 5  80.7 | | 0 UND | | | 5  79.2 | 22  16.7 | |
| 23  16.2 | 34  10.8 | 30  12.0 | Sales/Receivables | 0 UND | | | 16  23.2 | 54  6.7 | |
| 50  7.3 | 63  5.8 | 66  5.5 | | 0 UND | | | 68  5.4 | 96  3.8 | |
| | | | Cost of Sales/Inventory | | | | | | |
| | | | Cost of Sales/Payables | | | | | | |
| 5.2 | 4.2 | 5.3 | | 3.8 | | | 2.1 | | 5.3 |
| 8.5 | 8.9 | 13.7 | Sales/Working Capital | -12.1 | | | 16.8 | | 10.8 |
| 60.5 | 58.2 | -24.2 | | -5.5 | | | -269.9 | | NM |
| 30.6 | 23.5 | 10.1 | | | | | | | 17.3 |
| (34)  9.5 | (57)  8.9 | (59)  2.6 | EBIT/Interest | | | | | (30)  2.0 | |
| 3.4 | -.7 | -1.1 | | | | | | | -1.1 |
| | | | Net Profit + Depr., Dep., Amort./Cur. Mat. L/T/D | | | | | | |
| .0 | .0 | .1 | | .2 | | | .0 | | .1 |
| .7 | .5 | .6 | Fixed/Worth | 1.0 | | | .4 | | .6 |
| 1.8 | 3.1 | 1.8 | | NM | | | NM | | 1.8 |
| .4 | .7 | .8 | | .2 | | | .4 | | .9 |
| 1.4 | 1.8 | 2.1 | Debt/Worth | 1.3 | | | 7.8 | | 3.0 |
| 5.5 | UND | -19.0 | | NM | | | -2.1 | | NM |
| 95.4 | 68.0 | 50.7 | | | | | | | 34.8 |
| (44)  56.1 | (69)  36.0 | (56)  14.6 | % Profit Before Taxes/Tangible Net Worth | | | | | (27)  14.5 | |
| 21.6 | 7.9 | -.9 | | | | | | | -9.2 |
| 33.0 | 25.3 | 21.2 | % Profit Before Taxes/Total Assets | 39.1 | | | 18.6 | | 15.4 |
| 15.6 | 10.5 | 4.2 | | 8.0 | | | -.8 | | 2.7 |
| 5.7 | .2 | -2.9 | | 2.9 | | | -18.9 | | -3.6 |
| 478.1 | 223.3 | 94.8 | | 137.4 | | | UND | | 141.3 |
| 15.0 | 26.6 | 21.6 | Sales/Net Fixed Assets | 7.2 | | | 22.6 | | 51.7 |
| 3.2 | 6.9 | 6.7 | | 2.0 | | | 11.3 | | 7.5 |
| 3.3 | 2.8 | 3.2 | | 2.3 | | | 9.0 | | 2.9 |
| 1.9 | 1.6 | 2.0 | Sales/Total Assets | .9 | | | 2.2 | | 1.8 |
| .9 | .8 | .8 | | .3 | | | 1.3 | | .8 |
| .5 | 1.1 | .6 | | | | | | | .5 |
| (19)  1.2 | (39)  1.9 | (31)  2.0 | % Depr., Dep., Amort./Sales | | | | | (16)  1.3 | |
| 3.6 | 4.3 | 9.4 | | | | | | | 5.7 |
| 3.8 | 1.6 | 1.7 | % Officers', Directors' Owners' Comp/Sales | | | | | | |
| (12)  11.4 | (24)  5.4 | (14)  6.6 | | | | | | | |
| 15.1 | 11.8 | 14.6 | | | | | | | |
| 1426217M | 2732763M | 2904427M | Net Sales ($) | 4869M | 15453M | 24081M | 88645M | 64659M | 2706720M |
| 1283152M | 3403588M | 2803023M | Total Assets ($) | 6692M | 8275M | 29303M | 59143M | 37189M | 2662421M |

© RMA 2024  M = $ thousand  MM = $ million
See Pages viii through xx for Explanation of Ratios and Data

# INFORMATION—Motion Picture Theaters (except Drive-Ins) NAICS 512131

## Current Data Sorted by Assets

| 0-500M | 500M-2MM | 2-10MM | 10-50MM | 50-100MM | 100-250MM | | Comparative Historical Data | |
|---|---|---|---|---|---|---|---|---|
| 2 | 3 | | 1 | | 4 | Type of Statement | | |
| | 6 | | 3 | | 1 | Unqualified | 8 | |
| | | | 1 | | | Reviewed | 6 | |
| 2 | 3 | | 1 | 2 | | Compiled | 3 | 1 |
| | 6 (4/1-9/30/23) | 6 | 32 (10/1/23-3/31/24) | | 3 | Tax Returns | 8 | 19 |
| | | | | | | Other | 47 | 4/1/20- |
| | | | | | | | 4/1/19- | 3/31/21 |
| | | | | | | | 3/31/20 | ALL |
| 2 | 9 | 8 | 9 | 2 | 8 | NUMBER OF STATEMENTS | 72 | 20 |
| % | % | % | % | % | % | ASSETS | % | % |
| | | | | | | Cash & Equivalents | 11.0 | 11.9 |
| | | | | | | Trade Receivables (net) | 1.1 | 5.8 |
| | | | | | | Inventory | .9 | .9 |
| | | | | | | All Other Current | .7 | .9 |
| | | | | | | Total Current | 13.8 | 19.6 |
| | | | | | | Fixed Assets (net) | 71.9 | 69.0 |
| | | | | | | Intangibles (net) | 6.0 | 7.7 |
| | | | | | | All Other Non-Current | 8.3 | 3.8 |
| | | | | | | Total | 100.0 | 100.0 |
| | | | | | | LIABILITIES | | |
| | | | | | | Notes Payable-Short Term | 2.2 | 1.4 |
| | | | | | | Cur. Mat.-L.T.D. | 4.7 | 4.0 |
| | | | | | | Trade Payables | 7.3 | 5.3 |
| | | | | | | Income Taxes Payable | .0 | .0 |
| | | | | | | All Other Current | 8.1 | 10.4 |
| | | | | | | Total Current | 22.3 | 21.2 |
| | | | | | | Long-Term Debt | 41.6 | 55.9 |
| | | | | | | Deferred Taxes | .0 | .0 |
| | | | | | | All Other Non-Current | 9.2 | 6.3 |
| | | | | | | Net Worth | 26.9 | 16.6 |
| | | | | | | Total Liabilities & Net Worth | 100.0 | 100.0 |
| | | | | | | INCOME DATA | | |
| | | | | | | Net Sales | 100.0 | 100.0 |
| | | | | | | Gross Profit | | |
| | | | | | | Operating Expenses | 93.0 | 103.9 |
| | | | | | | Operating Profit | 7.0 | -3.9 |
| | | | | | | All Other Expenses (net) | 3.8 | 7.3 |
| | | | | | | Profit Before Taxes | 3.2 | -11.2 |
| | | | | | | RATIOS | | |
| | | | | | | Current | 1.1 | 1.2 |
| | | | | | | | .8 | .8 |
| | | | | | | | .3 | .5 |
| | | | | | | Quick | 1.1 | 1.2 |
| | | | | | | | .6 | .7 |
| | | | | | | | .3 | .3 |
| | | | | | | Sales/Receivables | 0 UND | 0 UND |
| | | | | | | | 1 535.3 | 1 359.2 |
| | | | | | | | 4 94.1 | 14 26.8 |
| | | | | | | Cost of Sales/Inventory | | |
| | | | | | | Cost of Sales/Payables | | |
| | | | | | | Sales/Working Capital | 75.7 | 15.2 |
| | | | | | | | -56.0 | -20.0 |
| | | | | | | | -7.4 | -5.3 |
| | | | | | | EBIT/Interest | 7.0 | 4.1 |
| | | | | | | | (58) 2.0 | (17) -2.6 |
| | | | | | | | .4 | -7.5 |
| | | | | | | Net Profit + Depr., Dep., Amort./Cur. Mat. L/T/D | | |
| | | | | | | Fixed/Worth | 1.4 | 1.6 |
| | | | | | | | 2.7 | 5.8 |
| | | | | | | | 94.8 | -7.4 |
| | | | | | | Debt/Worth | 1.1 | 1.2 |
| | | | | | | | 2.4 | 5.4 |
| | | | | | | | 100.7 | -9.1 |
| | | | | | | % Profit Before Taxes/Tangible Net Worth | 30.9 | 20.4 |
| | | | | | | | (55) 8.8 | (14) -3.9 |
| | | | | | | | -5.8 | -26.5 |
| | | | | | | % Profit Before Taxes/Total Assets | 12.3 | 5.6 |
| | | | | | | | 2.5 | -4.6 |
| | | | | | | | -2.7 | -18.0 |
| | | | | | | Sales/Net Fixed Assets | 2.7 | 2.1 |
| | | | | | | | 1.4 | .6 |
| | | | | | | | .6 | .3 |
| | | | | | | Sales/Total Assets | 1.8 | 1.1 |
| | | | | | | | 1.0 | .5 |
| | | | | | | | .5 | .3 |
| | | | | | | % Depr., Dep., Amort./Sales | 2.8 | 7.8 |
| | | | | | | | (63) 7.3 | (15) 13.7 |
| | | | | | | | 10.5 | 25.6 |
| | | | | | | % Officers', Directors' Owners' Comp/Sales | 1.4 | |
| | | | | | | | (14) 1.7 | |
| | | | | | | | 2.6 | |
| 1505M | 20056M | 20816M | 146050M | 167833M | 655819M | Net Sales ($) | 2449051M | 331370M |
| 312M | 11863M | 39958M | 215861M | 140209M | 1303617M | Total Assets ($) | 2436158M | 672788M |

© RMA 2024  M = $ thousand   MM = $ million
See Pages viii through xx for Explanation of Ratios and Data

# INFORMATION—Motion Picture Theaters (except Drive-Ins) NAICS 512131

## Comparative Historical Data | Current Data Sorted by Sales

| | | | Type of Statement | | | | | | |
|---|---|---|---|---|---|---|---|---|---|
| 2 | 3 | 7 | Unqualified | | 1 | 1 | 1 | | 4 |
| 2 | 5 | 4 | Reviewed | | | | | 1 | 3 |
| | 1 | 1 | Compiled | | | | 1 | | |
| | 5 | 6 | Tax Returns | 2 | 3 | | 1 | | |
| 13 | 25 | 20 | Other | 1 | 7 | 5 | 1 | | 6 |
| 4/1/21-3/31/22 ALL | 4/1/22-3/31/23 ALL | 4/1/23-3/31/24 ALL | | 6 (4/1-9/30/23) | | | 32 (10/1/23-3/31/24) | | |
| | | | | 0-1MM | 1-3MM | 3-5MM | 5-10MM | 10-25MM | 25MM & OVER |
| 17 | 39 | 38 | NUMBER OF STATEMENTS | 4 | 11 | 6 | 3 | 1 | 13 |
| % | % | % | **ASSETS** | % | % | % | % | % | % |
| 33.1 | 25.5 | 19.1 | Cash & Equivalents | | 22.4 | | | | 11.6 |
| 1.9 | 1.9 | 2.1 | Trade Receivables (net) | | .8 | | | | 1.1 |
| .5 | .8 | .5 | Inventory | | .5 | | | | .6 |
| 2.4 | 3.0 | 4.4 | All Other Current | | 9.3 | | | | .9 |
| 37.9 | 31.1 | 26.2 | Total Current | | 33.1 | | | | 14.3 |
| 52.2 | 51.3 | 57.8 | Fixed Assets (net) | | 53.6 | | | | 64.4 |
| .3 | 2.3 | 2.3 | Intangibles (net) | | 2.6 | | | | 3.4 |
| 9.7 | 15.3 | 13.7 | All Other Non-Current | | 10.7 | | | | 17.9 |
| 100.0 | 100.0 | 100.0 | Total | | 100.0 | | | | 100.0 |
| | | | **LIABILITIES** | | | | | | |
| .7 | 3.5 | .7 | Notes Payable-Short Term | | 2.5 | | | | .0 |
| 4.2 | 4.5 | 5.1 | Cur. Mat.-L.T.D. | | 4.1 | | | | 9.5 |
| 3.1 | 4.0 | 4.2 | Trade Payables | | 5.4 | | | | 3.8 |
| .0 | .0 | .0 | Income Taxes Payable | | .2 | | | | .0 |
| 7.9 | 25.4 | 10.3 | All Other Current | | 19.3 | | | | 10.2 |
| 15.9 | 37.4 | 20.4 | Total Current | | 31.5 | | | | 23.6 |
| 44.6 | 36.3 | 41.4 | Long-Term Debt | | 40.0 | | | | 34.8 |
| .7 | .0 | .0 | Deferred Taxes | | .0 | | | | .0 |
| 14.3 | 12.1 | 26.9 | All Other Non-Current | | 30.1 | | | | 26.7 |
| 24.6 | 14.1 | 11.3 | Net Worth | | -1.5 | | | | 14.9 |
| 100.0 | 100.0 | 100.0 | Total Liabilities & Net Worth | | 100.0 | | | | 100.0 |
| | | | **INCOME DATA** | | | | | | |
| 100.0 | 100.0 | 100.0 | Net Sales | | 100.0 | | | | 100.0 |
| | | | Gross Profit | | | | | | |
| 96.8 | 98.3 | 96.6 | Operating Expenses | | 97.3 | | | | 97.8 |
| 3.2 | 1.7 | 3.4 | Operating Profit | | 2.7 | | | | 2.2 |
| 4.9 | 3.5 | 3.7 | All Other Expenses (net) | | 5.3 | | | | 2.9 |
| -1.7 | -1.8 | -.3 | Profit Before Taxes | | -2.6 | | | | -.8 |
| | | | **RATIOS** | | | | | | |
| 9.5 | 2.7 | 4.6 | | | 2.8 | | | | 1.2 |
| 2.8 | 1.4 | 1.4 | Current | | 1.7 | | | | .9 |
| 1.6 | .4 | .7 | | | .2 | | | | .5 |
| 8.6 | 2.5 | 2.7 | | | 2.4 | | | | 1.1 |
| 2.7 | 1.3 | 1.1 | Quick | | .3 | | | | .8 |
| 1.5 | .3 | .3 | | | .1 | | | | .4 |
| 0 UND | 0 UND | 0 UND | | | 0 UND | | | | 0 UND |
| 1 356.5 | 1 247.4 | 0 804.3 | Sales/Receivables | | 0 UND | | | | 7 50.3 |
| 8 45.5 | 7 53.0 | 8 47.6 | | | 9 41.4 | | | | 8 44.1 |
| | | | Cost of Sales/Inventory | | | | | | |
| | | | Cost of Sales/Payables | | | | | | |
| 1.2 | 3.6 | 3.7 | | | 3.5 | | | | 27.3 |
| 1.5 | 10.4 | 18.0 | Sales/Working Capital | | 18.9 | | | | -95.3 |
| 4.3 | -5.7 | -15.5 | | | -5.7 | | | | -7.7 |
| 3.1 | 3.8 | 2.9 | | | | | | | 1.9 |
| (12) .7 | (32) -.2 | (33) .4 | EBIT/Interest | | | | | | .4 |
| -17.9 | -4.3 | -1.2 | | | | | | | -1.2 |
| | | | Net Profit + Depr., Dep., Amort./Cur. Mat. L/T/D | | | | | | |
| .5 | .8 | 1.2 | | | .9 | | | | 2.0 |
| 2.8 | 2.0 | 3.9 | Fixed/Worth | | -10.7 | | | | 4.4 |
| 8.7 | -20.1 | -3.1 | | | -1.0 | | | | NM |
| 1.4 | .7 | 1.2 | | | .5 | | | | 2.3 |
| 3.4 | 4.1 | 4.1 | Debt/Worth | | -17.7 | | | | 4.1 |
| 9.4 | -18.3 | -7.9 | | | -2.6 | | | | NM |
| 36.3 | 29.9 | 23.1 | % Profit Before Taxes/Tangible Net Worth | | | | | | 35.0 |
| (14) -5.1 | (28) 4.7 | (27) 3.4 | | | | | | (10) | 6.3 |
| -33.6 | -11.6 | -22.6 | | | | | | | -20.7 |
| 5.7 | 6.6 | 5.3 | % Profit Before Taxes/Total Assets | | 9.5 | | | | 3.3 |
| -1.8 | -2.0 | -1.2 | | | -6.9 | | | | -.8 |
| -13.3 | -11.0 | -8.0 | | | -15.7 | | | | -6.4 |
| 2.2 | 4.2 | 3.2 | | | 19.3 | | | | 2.6 |
| .9 | 1.3 | 1.0 | Sales/Net Fixed Assets | | 1.3 | | | | 1.1 |
| .4 | .7 | .5 | | | .8 | | | | .5 |
| .5 | 1.6 | 1.2 | | | 2.9 | | | | 1.1 |
| .4 | .6 | .7 | Sales/Total Assets | | .8 | | | | .6 |
| .3 | .5 | .4 | | | .6 | | | | .4 |
| 4.9 | 4.1 | 5.3 | | | | | | | 5.2 |
| (15) 7.8 | (31) 6.5 | (29) 7.3 | % Depr., Dep., Amort./Sales | | | | | (11) | 7.0 |
| 14.4 | 12.1 | 10.1 | | | | | | | 9.5 |
| | | | % Officers', Directors' Owners' Comp/Sales | | | | | | |
| 221037M | 1095117M | 1012079M | Net Sales ($) | 2186M | 22595M | 22971M | 18907M | 24564M | 920856M |
| 384026M | 1670270M | 1711820M | Total Assets ($) | 7518M | 40536M | 58200M | 29678M | 32769M | 1543119M |

© RMA 2024  M = $ thousand   MM = $ million
See Pages viii through xx for Explanation of Ratios and Data

# INFORMATION—Music Publishers  NAICS 512230

## Current Data Sorted by Assets

| | | | | | | | Comparative Historical Data | |
|---|---|---|---|---|---|---|---|---|
| | | | | | | **Type of Statement** | | |
| | | | 1 | 3 | 2 | Unqualified | | |
| | | | | | 1 | Reviewed | | 2 |
| | 1 | | | | | Compiled | | |
| | 1 | 3 | 4 | 5 | 7 | Tax Returns | 2 | |
| | 5 (4/1-9/30/23) | | 23 (10/1/23-3/31/24) | | | Other | 6 | 5 |
| 0-500M | 500M-2MM | 2-10MM | 10-50MM | 50-100MM | 100-250MM | | 4/1/19-3/31/20 ALL | 4/1/20-3/31/21 ALL |
| % | % | % | % | % | % | **NUMBER OF STATEMENTS** | 8 | 7 |
| | 2 | 3 | 5 | 8 | 10 | **ASSETS** | % | % |
| | | | | | 8.0 | Cash & Equivalents | | |
| | | | | | 4.2 | Trade Receivables (net) | | |
| | | | | | 2.8 | Inventory | | |
| D | | | | | 3.3 | All Other Current | | |
| A | | | | | 18.3 | Total Current | | |
| T | | | | | 2.3 | Fixed Assets (net) | | |
| A | | | | | 58.3 | Intangibles (net) | | |
| | | | | | 21.0 | All Other Non-Current | | |
| N | | | | | 100.0 | Total | | |
| O | | | | | | **LIABILITIES** | | |
| T | | | | | 5.8 | Notes Payable-Short Term | | |
| | | | | | .8 | Cur. Mat.-L.T.D. | | |
| A | | | | | 5.6 | Trade Payables | | |
| V | | | | | .0 | Income Taxes Payable | | |
| A | | | | | 6.6 | All Other Current | | |
| I | | | | | 18.8 | Total Current | | |
| L | | | | | 57.7 | Long-Term Debt | | |
| A | | | | | .0 | Deferred Taxes | | |
| B | | | | | 4.5 | All Other Non-Current | | |
| L | | | | | 19.0 | Net Worth | | |
| E | | | | | 100.0 | Total Liabilities & Net Worth | | |
| | | | | | | **INCOME DATA** | | |
| | | | | | 100.0 | Net Sales | | |
| | | | | | | Gross Profit | | |
| | | | | | 61.2 | Operating Expenses | | |
| | | | | | 38.8 | Operating Profit | | |
| | | | | | 25.2 | All Other Expenses (net) | | |
| | | | | | 13.6 | Profit Before Taxes | | |
| | | | | | | **RATIOS** | | |
| | | | | | 4.4 | | | |
| | | | | | 1.9 | Current | | |
| | | | | | 1.1 | | | |
| | | | | | 4.4 | | | |
| | | | | | 1.2 | Quick | | |
| | | | | | .7 | | | |
| | | | | 0 | UND | | | |
| | | | | 13 | 27.9 | Sales/Receivables | | |
| | | | | 76 | 4.8 | | | |
| | | | | | | Cost of Sales/Inventory | | |
| | | | | | | Cost of Sales/Payables | | |
| | | | | | 2.7 | | | |
| | | | | | 4.9 | Sales/Working Capital | | |
| | | | | | 32.5 | | | |
| | | | | | | EBIT/Interest | | |
| | | | | | | Net Profit + Depr., Dep., Amort./Cur. Mat. L/T/D | | |
| | | | | | .0 | | | |
| | | | | | .0 | Fixed/Worth | | |
| | | | | | NM | | | |
| | | | | | 2.2 | | | |
| | | | | | -1.3 | Debt/Worth | | |
| | | | | | -1.1 | | | |
| | | | | | | % Profit Before Taxes/Tangible Net Worth | | |
| | | | | | 5.8 | | | |
| | | | | | .6 | % Profit Before Taxes/Total Assets | | |
| | | | | | -1.2 | | | |
| | | | | | UND | | | |
| | | | | | UND | Sales/Net Fixed Assets | | |
| | | | | | 11.2 | | | |
| | | | | | .5 | | | |
| | | | | | .1 | Sales/Total Assets | | |
| | | | | | .1 | | | |
| | | | | | | % Depr., Dep., Amort./Sales | | |
| | | | | | | % Officers', Directors' Owners' Comp/Sales | | |
| | 4750M | 16644M | 138893M | 109588M | 670028M | Net Sales ($) | 369912M | 366470M |
| | 2945M | 21115M | 140312M | 643678M | 1735446M | Total Assets ($) | 682307M | 559922M |

M = $ thousand    MM = $ million
See Pages viii through xx for Explanation of Ratios and Data

© RMA 2024

# INFORMATION—Music Publishers  NAICS 512230

## Comparative Historical Data | Current Data Sorted by Sales

| Comparative Historical Data | | | Type of Statement | Current Data Sorted by Sales | | | | | |
|---|---|---|---|---|---|---|---|---|---|
| 3 | 5 | 6 | Unqualified | | | 1 | 1 | 3 | 1 |
| | 1 | 1 | Reviewed | | | | | 1 | |
| 1 | | 1 | Compiled | | | | | | |
| | | | Tax Returns | | | | | | |
| 9 | 24 | 20 | Other | 1 | 1 | 3 | 3 | 5 | 7 |
| 4/1/21- | 4/1/22- | 4/1/23- | | | 5 (4/1-9/30/23) | | 23 (10/1/23-3/31/24) | | |
| 3/31/22 | 3/31/23 | 3/31/24 | | 0-1MM | 1-3MM | 3-5MM | 5-10MM | 10-25MM | 25MM & OVER |
| ALL | ALL | ALL | | | | | | | |
| 13 | 30 | 28 | NUMBER OF STATEMENTS | 1 | 2 | 4 | 4 | 9 | 8 |
| % | % | % | ASSETS | % | % | % | % | % | % |
| 14.3 | 13.8 | 13.5 | Cash & Equivalents | | | | | | |
| 6.6 | 4.1 | 4.7 | Trade Receivables (net) | | | | | | |
| 7.2 | .9 | 2.8 | Inventory | | | | | | |
| 3.1 | 5.5 | 6.9 | All Other Current | | | | | | |
| 31.2 | 24.4 | 27.8 | Total Current | | | | | | |
| .7 | 5.1 | 5.3 | Fixed Assets (net) | | | | | | |
| 60.1 | 62.6 | 53.4 | Intangibles (net) | | | | | | |
| 8.0 | 7.9 | 13.6 | All Other Non-Current | | | | | | |
| 100.0 | 100.0 | 100.0 | Total | | | | | | |
| | | | LIABILITIES | | | | | | |
| 1.3 | 3.0 | 2.3 | Notes Payable-Short Term | | | | | | |
| 1.6 | .9 | 3.2 | Cur. Mat.-L.T.D. | | | | | | |
| 4.3 | 4.6 | 8.8 | Trade Payables | | | | | | |
| .2 | .0 | .0 | Income Taxes Payable | | | | | | |
| 12.3 | 5.4 | 8.8 | All Other Current | | | | | | |
| 19.7 | 13.8 | 23.1 | Total Current | | | | | | |
| 39.5 | 41.3 | 56.7 | Long-Term Debt | | | | | | |
| .0 | .0 | .0 | Deferred Taxes | | | | | | |
| 8.9 | 3.9 | 3.4 | All Other Non-Current | | | | | | |
| 32.0 | 41.0 | 16.8 | Net Worth | | | | | | |
| 100.0 | 100.0 | 100.0 | Total Liabilities & Net Worth | | | | | | |
| | | | INCOME DATA | | | | | | |
| 100.0 | 100.0 | 100.0 | Net Sales | | | | | | |
| | | | Gross Profit | | | | | | |
| 68.6 | 64.4 | 69.7 | Operating Expenses | | | | | | |
| 31.4 | 35.6 | 30.3 | Operating Profit | | | | | | |
| 8.4 | 22.9 | 16.8 | All Other Expenses (net) | | | | | | |
| 23.1 | 12.7 | 13.5 | Profit Before Taxes | | | | | | |
| | | | RATIOS | | | | | | |
| 6.5 | 5.1 | 2.4 | | | | | | | |
| 2.1 | 2.0 | 1.3 | Current | | | | | | |
| .6 | 1.4 | 1.0 | | | | | | | |
| 6.5 | 4.9 | 2.4 | | | | | | | |
| 1.0 | 2.0 | .9 | Quick | | | | | | |
| .6 | .7 | .5 | | | | | | | |
| 7   52.7 | 0   UND | 0   UND | | | | | | | |
| 44   8.3 | 32  11.5 | 7   54.9 | Sales/Receivables | | | | | | |
| 182  2.0 | 118  3.1 | 76  4.8 | | | | | | | |
| | | | Cost of Sales/Inventory | | | | | | |
| | | | Cost of Sales/Payables | | | | | | |
| 1.1 | 1.5 | 2.8 | | | | | | | |
| 3.9 | 2.9 | 7.3 | Sales/Working Capital | | | | | | |
| -4.6 | 8.6 | 169.5 | | | | | | | |
| | 13.3 | 6.8 | | | | | | | |
| (13) | 3.2 | (13) 4.1 | EBIT/Interest | | | | | | |
| | -.6 | 1.5 | | | | | | | |
| | | | Net Profit + Depr., Dep., Amort./Cur. Mat. L/T/D | | | | | | |
| .0 | .0 | .0 | | | | | | | |
| .0 | .0 | .0 | Fixed/Worth | | | | | | |
| .2 | .2 | NM | | | | | | | |
| 17.9 | 122.2 | 14.8 | | | | | | | |
| -1.2 | -1.3 | -2.1 | Debt/Worth | | | | | | |
| -1.1 | -1.1 | -1.1 | | | | | | | |
| | | | % Profit Before Taxes/Tangible Net Worth | | | | | | |
| 13.3 | 6.0 | 7.4 | | | | | | | |
| 4.8 | .7 | 2.6 | % Profit Before Taxes/Total Assets | | | | | | |
| -.1 | -1.6 | -1.1 | | | | | | | |
| UND | UND | UND | | | | | | | |
| UND | UND | UND | Sales/Net Fixed Assets | | | | | | |
| 68.6 | 35.9 | 25.4 | | | | | | | |
| 1.3 | .6 | 1.0 | | | | | | | |
| .2 | .1 | .2 | Sales/Total Assets | | | | | | |
| .0 | .1 | .1 | | | | | | | |
| | | | % Depr., Dep., Amort./Sales | | | | | | |
| | | | % Officers', Directors', Owners' Comp/Sales | | | | | | |
| 690193M | 683182M | 939903M | Net Sales ($) | 457M | 4750M | 17601M | 25648M | 134484M | 756963M |
| 1441797M | 3255831M | 2543496M | Total Assets ($) | 6661M | 2945M | 157266M | 356653M | 1260893M | 759078M |

© RMA 2024  
M = $ thousand    MM = $ million  
See Pages viii through xx for Explanation of Ratios and Data

# INFORMATION—Book Publishers  NAICS 513130

## Current Data Sorted by Assets / Comparative Historical Data

| 0-500M | 500M-2MM | 2-10MM | 10-50MM | 50-100MM | 100-250MM | Type of Statement | | | |
|---|---|---|---|---|---|---|---|---|---|
| | | | | | | Unqualified | | 10 | 1 |
| | | | | 1 | 2 | Reviewed | | 4 | 4 |
| | | | 1 | 5 | | Compiled | | 1 | |
| | | | 5 | 1 | | Tax Returns | | 2 | |
| | 1 | 8 | 1 | | 1 | Other | | 28 | 25 |
| | 8 (4/1-9/30/23) | | 7 | 5 | | | | 4/1/19- | 4/1/20- |
| | | | 29 (10/1/23-3/31/24) | | | | | 3/31/20 | 3/31/21 |
| | | | | | | | | ALL | ALL |
| | 1 | 9 | 14 | 10 | 3 | NUMBER OF STATEMENTS | | 45 | 30 |
| % | % | % | % | % | % | ASSETS | | % | % |
| | | | 25.1 | 13.2 | | Cash & Equivalents | | 15.4 | 15.0 |
| | | | 16.7 | 17.7 | | Trade Receivables (net) | | 20.8 | 19.8 |
| | | | 18.8 | 12.0 | | Inventory | | 19.5 | 25.7 |
| | | | 2.2 | 4.3 | | All Other Current | | 5.7 | 2.8 |
| | | | 62.9 | 47.2 | | Total Current | | 61.4 | 63.4 |
| | | | 4.7 | 16.5 | | Fixed Assets (net) | | 14.4 | 12.9 |
| | | | 18.5 | 28.2 | | Intangibles (net) | | 12.0 | 16.1 |
| | | | 13.9 | 8.0 | | All Other Non-Current | | 12.2 | 7.6 |
| | | | 100.0 | 100.0 | | Total | | 100.0 | 100.0 |
| | | | | | | LIABILITIES | | | |
| | | | 4.6 | 2.1 | | Notes Payable-Short Term | | 8.2 | 2.8 |
| | | | 2.2 | 1.9 | | Cur. Mat.-L.T.D. | | 1.7 | 1.5 |
| | | | 6.3 | 6.6 | | Trade Payables | | 11.1 | 10.4 |
| | | | .0 | .0 | | Income Taxes Payable | | .1 | .2 |
| | | | 21.5 | 17.1 | | All Other Current | | 24.0 | 18.9 |
| | | | 34.6 | 27.7 | | Total Current | | 45.0 | 33.8 |
| | | | 6.6 | 16.7 | | Long-Term Debt | | 10.9 | 6.3 |
| | | | .0 | .5 | | Deferred Taxes | | .3 | .5 |
| | | | 5.5 | 3.7 | | All Other Non-Current | | 5.3 | 10.7 |
| | | | 53.2 | 51.4 | | Net Worth | | 38.4 | 48.7 |
| | | | 100.0 | 100.0 | | Total Liabilities & Net Worth | | 100.0 | 100.0 |
| | | | | | | INCOME DATA | | | |
| | | | 100.0 | 100.0 | | Net Sales | | 100.0 | 100.0 |
| | | | 61.0 | 58.2 | | Gross Profit | | 56.3 | 57.4 |
| | | | 53.0 | 47.7 | | Operating Expenses | | 48.8 | 53.4 |
| | | | 8.0 | 10.5 | | Operating Profit | | 7.5 | 4.0 |
| | | | .0 | 2.1 | | All Other Expenses (net) | | .9 | 1.6 |
| | | | 8.0 | 8.4 | | Profit Before Taxes | | 6.6 | 2.4 |
| | | | | | | RATIOS | | | |
| | | | 5.6 | 2.5 | | | | 2.7 | 3.5 |
| | | | 2.5 | 1.4 | | Current | | 1.6 | 1.8 |
| | | | 1.0 | 1.2 | | | | .9 | 1.1 |
| | | | 3.9 | 1.5 | | | | 1.8 | 2.5 |
| | | | 1.7 | .9 | | Quick | | 1.0 | .9 |
| | | | .4 | .7 | | | | .5 | .5 |
| | | 33 | 11.0 | 28 | 13.2 | | 26 | 13.9 | 27 | 13.3 |
| | | 50 | 7.3 | 64 | 5.7 | Sales/Receivables | 50 | 7.3 | 58 | 6.3 |
| | | 74 | 4.9 | 104 | 3.5 | | 79 | 4.6 | 79 | 4.6 |
| | | 69 | 5.3 | 3 | 137.4 | | 34 | 10.6 | 76 | 4.8 |
| | | 152 | 2.4 | 140 | 2.6 | Cost of Sales/Inventory | 122 | 3.0 | 118 | 3.1 |
| | | 261 | 1.4 | 166 | 2.2 | | 192 | 1.9 | 228 | 1.6 |
| | | 21 | 17.8 | 16 | 22.5 | | 19 | 19.7 | 21 | 17.6 |
| | | 33 | 11.0 | 54 | 6.7 | Cost of Sales/Payables | 51 | 7.2 | 55 | 6.6 |
| | | 83 | 4.4 | 73 | 5.0 | | 107 | 3.4 | 91 | 4.0 |
| | | | 1.8 | 3.8 | | | | 3.0 | 2.4 |
| | | | 4.1 | 8.8 | | Sales/Working Capital | | 8.0 | 5.5 |
| | | | NM | 31.2 | | | | -53.9 | 21.0 |
| | | | 27.4 | | | | | 30.5 | 36.0 |
| | | | (10) 8.7 | | | EBIT/Interest | (34) | 6.0 | (20) | 5.7 |
| | | | 2.2 | | | | | 1.3 | -1.7 |
| | | | | | | Net Profit + Depr., Dep., Amort./Cur. Mat. L/T/D | | | |
| | | | .0 | .2 | | | | .1 | .1 |
| | | | .1 | .5 | | Fixed/Worth | | .3 | .2 |
| | | | -.8 | 1.7 | | | | 1.5 | 1.2 |
| | | | .3 | .6 | | | | .6 | .9 |
| | | | 1.6 | 4.2 | | Debt/Worth | | 1.0 | 1.5 |
| | | | -11.7 | NM | | | | 63.9 | 6.7 |
| | | | 29.1 | | | | | 38.2 | 32.2 |
| | | | (10) 16.2 | | | % Profit Before Taxes/Tangible Net Worth | (35) | 14.5 | (24) | 14.7 |
| | | | 10.1 | | | | | 2.5 | -10.7 |
| | | | 13.4 | 22.3 | | | | 15.4 | 11.4 |
| | | | 9.0 | 7.2 | | % Profit Before Taxes/Total Assets | | 5.8 | 6.3 |
| | | | 3.8 | 1.3 | | | | .4 | -2.4 |
| | | | 101.7 | 22.3 | | | | 138.5 | 108.1 |
| | | | 52.1 | 15.4 | | Sales/Net Fixed Assets | | 19.3 | 33.4 |
| | | | 14.6 | 5.0 | | | | 6.0 | 6.8 |
| | | | 1.5 | 1.2 | | | | 1.9 | 1.6 |
| | | | 1.0 | 1.1 | | Sales/Total Assets | | 1.4 | 1.2 |
| | | | .9 | .8 | | | | .9 | .8 |
| | | | | | | | | 1.1 | 1.0 |
| | | | | | | % Depr., Dep., Amort./Sales | (24) | 2.0 | (18) | 1.5 |
| | | | | | | | | 4.0 | 6.2 |
| | | | | | | % Officers', Directors' Owners' Comp/Sales | | | |
| | 4764M | 125933M | 356395M | 694283M | 511809M | Net Sales ($) | | 1685208M | 1216194M |
| | 1996M | 60735M | 317903M | 685858M | 443158M | Total Assets ($) | | 1747904M | 1085233M |

M = $ thousand     MM = $ million
See Pages viii through xx for Explanation of Ratios and Data

© RMA 2024

# INFORMATION—Book Publishers  NAICS 513130

## Comparative Historical Data | Current Data Sorted by Sales

| Comparative Historical Data ||| Type of Statement | Current Data Sorted by Sales |||||||
|---|---|---|---|---|---|---|---|---|---|
| 2 | 5 | 8 | Unqualified | | | | | 1 | 7 |
| 1 | 3 | 6 | Reviewed | | | | | 1 | 1 |
| 1 | 1 | | Compiled | | | | 4 | | |
| 4 | 5 | 1 | Tax Returns | | | | 1 | | |
| 14 | 17 | 22 | Other | | | 3 | | 29 | 10 |
| 4/1/21-3/31/22 | 4/1/22-3/31/23 | 4/1/23-3/31/24 | | 8 (4/1-9/30/23) | | 1 | | 29 (10/1/23-3/31/24) | |
| ALL | ALL | ALL | | 0-1MM | 1-3MM | 3-5MM | 5-10MM | 10-25MM | 25MM & OVER |
| 22 | 31 | 37 | NUMBER OF STATEMENTS | | | 1 | 5 | 13 | 18 |
| % | % | % | ASSETS | % | % | % | % | % | % |
| 21.7 | 18.7 | 17.5 | Cash & Equivalents | | | | | 16.5 | 23.1 |
| 19.3 | 16.4 | 18.1 | Trade Receivables (net) | D | D | | | 13.6 | 20.3 |
| 27.8 | 27.9 | 20.4 | Inventory | A | A | | | 19.1 | 14.9 |
| 3.3 | 4.4 | 3.1 | All Other Current | T | T | | | 4.2 | 3.3 |
| 72.2 | 67.4 | 59.1 | Total Current | A | A | | | 53.3 | 61.6 |
| 9.1 | 10.3 | 8.6 | Fixed Assets (net) | | | | | 9.3 | 10.7 |
| 6.8 | 13.3 | 18.8 | Intangibles (net) | N | N | | | 21.6 | 18.0 |
| 11.9 | 9.1 | 13.5 | All Other Non-Current | O | O | | | 15.7 | 9.7 |
| 100.0 | 100.0 | 100.0 | Total | T | T | | | 100.0 | 100.0 |
| | | | LIABILITIES | A | A | | | | |
| 11.4 | 3.1 | 6.2 | Notes Payable-Short Term | V | V | | | 3.1 | 3.0 |
| 2.8 | 1.7 | 2.4 | Cur. Mat.-L.T.D. | A | A | | | 4.3 | 1.1 |
| 10.3 | 9.3 | 11.2 | Trade Payables | I | I | | | 8.6 | 9.1 |
| .2 | .0 | .0 | Income Taxes Payable | L | L | | | .0 | .0 |
| 15.8 | 16.3 | 24.6 | All Other Current | A | A | | | 31.1 | 20.1 |
| 40.5 | 30.5 | 44.5 | Total Current | B | B | | | 47.2 | 33.4 |
| 6.8 | 9.2 | 13.3 | Long-Term Debt | L | L | | | 21.7 | 10.9 |
| .0 | .0 | .2 | Deferred Taxes | E | E | | | .0 | .3 |
| 11.6 | 5.6 | 7.4 | All Other Non-Current | | | | | 1.8 | 6.9 |
| 41.1 | 54.7 | 34.6 | Net Worth | | | | | 29.3 | 48.6 |
| 100.0 | 100.0 | 100.0 | Total Liabilities & Net Worth | | | | | 100.0 | 100.0 |
| | | | INCOME DATA | | | | | | |
| 100.0 | 100.0 | 100.0 | Net Sales | | | | | 100.0 | 100.0 |
| 55.4 | 55.1 | 55.5 | Gross Profit | | | | | 58.0 | 58.1 |
| 49.5 | 48.0 | 48.0 | Operating Expenses | | | | | 50.9 | 49.0 |
| 5.8 | 7.1 | 7.5 | Operating Profit | | | | | 7.1 | 9.2 |
| -3.0 | 1.3 | 2.1 | All Other Expenses (net) | | | | | .9 | .7 |
| 8.9 | 5.8 | 5.3 | Profit Before Taxes | | | | | 6.2 | 8.5 |
| | | | RATIOS | | | | | | |
| 3.7 | 3.8 | 3.7 | | | | | | 4.6 | 4.2 |
| 2.1 | 2.3 | 1.5 | Current | | | | | 1.5 | 1.5 |
| 1.3 | 1.6 | .9 | | | | | | .3 | 1.2 |
| 2.4 | 2.7 | 2.5 | | | | | | 3.1 | 2.6 |
| 1.4 | 1.4 | .8 | Quick | | | | | .7 | 1.0 |
| .6 | .6 | .4 | | | | | | .3 | .7 |
| 16  22.4 | 26  13.8 | 26  14.0 | | | | | | 0  UND | 33  11.1 |
| 40  9.1 | 49  7.4 | 51  7.1 | Sales/Receivables | | | | | 43  8.5 | 73  5.0 |
| 64  5.7 | 79  4.6 | 76  4.8 | | | | | | 56  6.5 | 89  4.1 |
| 66  5.5 | 87  4.2 | 59  6.2 | | | | | | 0  UND | 46  7.9 |
| 126  2.9 | 152  2.4 | 140  2.6 | Cost of Sales/Inventory | | | | | 159  2.3 | 146  2.5 |
| 243  1.5 | 203  1.8 | 215  1.7 | | | | | | 261  1.4 | 166  2.2 |
| 14  25.5 | 34  10.6 | 24  15.1 | | | | | | 13  28.7 | 30  12.0 |
| 28  12.9 | 49  7.4 | 54  6.7 | Cost of Sales/Payables | | | | | 27  13.7 | 56  6.5 |
| 79  4.6 | 78  4.7 | 85  4.3 | | | | | | 87  4.2 | 83  4.4 |
| 3.1 | 2.1 | 2.2 | | | | | | 2.1 | 2.0 |
| 4.3 | 4.4 | 6.9 | Sales/Working Capital | | | | | 6.3 | 5.8 |
| 44.1 | 6.3 | NM | | | | | | -4.5 | 18.9 |
| 107.1 | 32.8 | 24.7 | | | | | | 45.0 | 24.8 |
| (18) 25.9 | (22) 13.3 | (29) 3.9 | EBIT/Interest | | | | | (11) 11.3 | (12) 3.5 |
| 12.0 | .0 | .2 | | | | | | 3.9 | 1.3 |
| | | | Net Profit + Depr., Dep., Amort./Cur. Mat. L/T/D | | | | | | |
| .0 | .0 | .0 | | | | | | .0 | .0 |
| .1 | .1 | .2 | Fixed/Worth | | | | | .1 | .3 |
| .5 | .3 | 1.5 | | | | | | NM | 1.7 |
| .6 | .5 | .4 | | | | | | .4 | .4 |
| 1.0 | 1.0 | 2.8 | Debt/Worth | | | | | 2.4 | 1.9 |
| 10.2 | 2.7 | -10.9 | | | | | | NM | NM |
| 76.7 | 32.7 | 35.1 | | | | | | 41.4 | 40.4 |
| (18) 32.4 | (28) 13.5 | (27) 17.5 | % Profit Before Taxes/Tangible Net Worth | | | | | (10) 25.2 | (14) 20.3 |
| 20.3 | -2.6 | 3.8 | | | | | | 10.6 | 9.8 |
| 30.3 | 13.4 | 13.8 | | | | | | 14.7 | 21.5 |
| 14.9 | 6.7 | 6.0 | % Profit Before Taxes/Total Assets | | | | | 6.0 | 10.0 |
| 5.7 | -1.2 | 1.4 | | | | | | 3.6 | 2.0 |
| 613.2 | 706.8 | 121.7 | | | | | | 109.7 | 50.9 |
| 43.2 | 21.2 | 38.3 | Sales/Net Fixed Assets | | | | | 51.3 | 18.2 |
| 11.5 | 7.5 | 12.3 | | | | | | 8.8 | 13.4 |
| 2.7 | 1.7 | 1.7 | | | | | | 2.0 | 1.2 |
| 1.5 | 1.2 | 1.2 | Sales/Total Assets | | | | | 1.4 | 1.1 |
| 1.3 | 1.0 | 1.0 | | | | | | 1.0 | .9 |
| .7 | .9 | .4 | | | | | | .3 | .9 |
| (12) 1.3 | (17) 2.1 | (23) 1.2 | % Depr., Dep., Amort./Sales | | | | | (10) .9 | (11) 1.4 |
| 2.0 | 5.8 | 4.4 | | | | | | 2.6 | 5.8 |
| | | | % Officers', Directors' Owners' Comp/Sales | | | | | | |
| 710595M | 1363902M | 1693184M | Net Sales ($) | | | 4764M | 43101M | 246201M | 1399118M |
| 494857M | 1201245M | 1509650M | Total Assets ($) | | | 1996M | 32746M | 172707M | 1302201M |

M = $ thousand    MM = $ million
See Pages viii through xx for Explanation of Ratios and Data

© RMA 2024

# INFORMATION—Software Publishers  NAICS 513210

## Current Data Sorted by Assets | Comparative Historical Data

| | | | | | | Type of Statement | | |
|---|---|---|---|---|---|---|---|---|
| | | 2 | 12 | 5 | 7 | Unqualified | 32 | 22 |
| | | 1 | 3 | | | Reviewed | 4 | 3 |
| | | 2 | 2 | | 1 | Compiled | 3 | 2 |
| 1 | 2 | 2 | 1 | 1 | | Tax Returns | 13 | 4 |
| 5 | 2 | 21 | 53 | 25 | 34 | Other | 261 | 125 |
| 0-500M | 28 (4/1-9/30/23) 500M-2MM | 2-10MM | 154 (10/1/23-3/31/24) 10-50MM | 50-100MM | 100-250MM | | 4/1/19-3/31/20 ALL | 4/1/20-3/31/21 ALL |
| 6 | 4 | 28 | 71 | 31 | 42 | **NUMBER OF STATEMENTS** | 313 | 156 |
| % | % | % | % | % | % | **ASSETS** | % | % |
| | | 24.2 | 24.5 | 18.5 | 17.0 | Cash & Equivalents | 20.5 | 26.8 |
| | | 31.3 | 20.3 | 14.3 | 10.3 | Trade Receivables (net) | 20.5 | 20.5 |
| | | 2.1 | 3.1 | .0 | 1.1 | Inventory | .8 | 1.0 |
| | | 10.0 | 8.3 | 6.0 | 9.8 | All Other Current | 6.6 | 5.0 |
| | | 67.5 | 56.3 | 38.8 | 38.2 | Total Current | 48.4 | 53.2 |
| | | 17.3 | 7.6 | 4.9 | 3.6 | Fixed Assets (net) | 8.2 | 7.9 |
| | | 7.4 | 27.5 | 37.8 | 46.0 | Intangibles (net) | 34.4 | 28.2 |
| | | 7.8 | 8.6 | 18.5 | 12.2 | All Other Non-Current | 9.0 | 10.7 |
| | | 100.0 | 100.0 | 100.0 | 100.0 | Total | 100.0 | 100.0 |
| | | | | | | **LIABILITIES** | | |
| | | 8.7 | 4.8 | 2.3 | .7 | Notes Payable-Short Term | 3.6 | 3.4 |
| | | 1.5 | 3.1 | 1.1 | 2.5 | Cur. Mat.-L.T.D. | 2.7 | 2.8 |
| | | 13.0 | 7.9 | 4.3 | 2.9 | Trade Payables | 7.6 | 6.1 |
| | | .0 | .6 | .0 | .1 | Income Taxes Payable | .6 | .7 |
| | | 29.2 | 34.0 | 31.9 | 29.6 | All Other Current | 33.1 | 33.2 |
| | | 52.4 | 50.5 | 39.7 | 35.7 | Total Current | 47.5 | 46.1 |
| | | 19.6 | 24.6 | 27.6 | 38.3 | Long-Term Debt | 30.6 | 28.3 |
| | | .0 | .2 | .3 | .4 | Deferred Taxes | .3 | .2 |
| | | 15.9 | 8.0 | 6.1 | 6.7 | All Other Non-Current | 13.0 | 9.6 |
| | | 12.1 | 16.7 | 26.4 | 18.9 | Net Worth | 8.7 | 15.8 |
| | | 100.0 | 100.0 | 100.0 | 100.0 | Total Liabilities & Net Worth | 100.0 | 100.0 |
| | | | | | | **INCOME DATA** | | |
| | | 100.0 | 100.0 | 100.0 | 100.0 | Net Sales | 100.0 | 100.0 |
| | | | | | | Gross Profit | | |
| | | 93.6 | 103.3 | 104.3 | 104.8 | Operating Expenses | 99.2 | 95.3 |
| | | 6.4 | -3.3 | -4.3 | -4.8 | Operating Profit | .8 | 4.7 |
| | | 2.3 | 2.6 | 6.0 | 8.2 | All Other Expenses (net) | 4.9 | 3.7 |
| | | 4.1 | -6.0 | -10.3 | -13.1 | Profit Before Taxes | -4.2 | 1.0 |
| | | | | | | **RATIOS** | | |
| | | 3.4 | 3.0 | 1.6 | 1.8 | | 2.1 | 2.0 |
| | | 1.4 | 1.2 | 1.0 | 1.0 | Current | 1.1 | 1.1 |
| | | 1.0 | .6 | .6 | .6 | | .6 | .7 |
| | | 2.6 | 1.9 | 1.2 | 1.2 | | 1.7 | 1.8 |
| | | 1.1 | 1.0 | .9 | .6 | Quick | .9 | 1.0 |
| | | .6 | .5 | .4 | .4 | | .5 | .6 |
| | 11 | 34.5 | 22 16.9 | 43 8.4 | 36 10.0 | | 31 11.7 | 32 11.5 |
| | 34 | 10.6 | 40 9.1 | 65 5.6 | 62 5.9 | Sales/Receivables | 52 7.0 | 56 6.5 |
| | 70 | 5.2 | 74 4.9 | 85 4.3 | 78 4.7 | | 76 4.8 | 83 4.4 |
| | | | | | | Cost of Sales/Inventory | | |
| | | | | | | Cost of Sales/Payables | | |
| | | 5.0 | 4.1 | 7.4 | 4.5 | | 5.3 | 4.4 |
| | | 14.4 | 21.3 | 90.7 | -42.9 | Sales/Working Capital | 41.3 | 36.6 |
| | | -118.8 | -5.3 | -3.0 | -4.4 | | -5.3 | -6.9 |
| | | 33.3 | 25.5 | 5.1 | 2.9 | | 7.4 | 22.5 |
| | (16) | 2.4 | (54) .4 | (23) -1.3 | (32) -1.0 | EBIT/Interest | (234) -.4 | (116) 2.4 |
| | | -3.7 | -7.5 | -5.1 | -2.8 | | -4.4 | -2.6 |
| | | | | | | Net Profit + Depr., Dep., Amort./Cur. Mat. L/T/D | 21.8 | 12.6 |
| | | | | | | | (25) 6.9 | (12) 5.1 |
| | | | | | | | .2 | .5 |
| | | .0 | .0 | .0 | .0 | | .1 | .1 |
| | | .6 | .4 | 1.1 | NM | Fixed/Worth | -1.1 | -41.5 |
| | | -1.4 | -.1 | .0 | -.1 | | .0 | .0 |
| | | .5 | 1.3 | 1.0 | 31.6 | | 1.9 | 1.7 |
| | | 6.5 | 15.2 | -66.9 | -2.4 | Debt/Worth | -4.0 | -6.9 |
| | | -6.2 | -2.2 | -1.4 | -1.3 | | -1.6 | -1.9 |
| | | 118.6 | 70.6 | 35.0 | 93.4 | % Profit Before Taxes/Tangible Net Worth | 77.6 | 95.9 |
| | (18) | 52.3 | (38) 25.2 | (14) 3.8 | (12) 15.1 | | (129) 30.6 | (70) 50.5 |
| | | 18.5 | 1.1 | -25.0 | -21.8 | | 2.5 | 3.2 |
| | | 21.1 | 16.1 | 4.1 | 4.0 | % Profit Before Taxes/Total Assets | 11.4 | 18.0 |
| | | 5.6 | .2 | -7.5 | -7.1 | | -1.6 | 2.9 |
| | | -4.6 | -20.3 | -15.8 | -15.2 | | -13.8 | -11.5 |
| | | UND | 172.5 | 199.5 | 155.7 | Sales/Net Fixed Assets | 101.5 | 128.4 |
| | | 101.7 | 80.0 | 69.0 | 40.9 | | 43.4 | 53.0 |
| | | 6.9 | 19.2 | 27.6 | 14.0 | | 15.5 | 16.6 |
| | | 3.8 | 2.1 | .9 | .8 | Sales/Total Assets | 1.9 | 1.7 |
| | | 2.4 | 1.2 | .6 | .5 | | 1.0 | 1.1 |
| | | 1.6 | .8 | .3 | .3 | | .5 | .6 |
| | | .9 | .2 | | | % Depr., Dep., Amort./Sales | .4 | .5 |
| | (11) | 1.1 | (30) 1.0 | | | | (129) 1.1 | (56) 1.3 |
| | | 5.2 | 3.1 | | | | 3.1 | 2.7 |
| | | | | | | % Officers', Directors', Owners' Comp/Sales | .5 | 1.9 |
| | | | | | | | (20) 3.9 | (10) 5.5 |
| | | | | | | | 11.7 | 20.4 |
| 3214M | 9416M | 368881M | 3250840M | 1774413M | 4583710M | Net Sales ($) | 15536868M | 8084515M |
| 832M | 3402M | 140371M | 2007870M | 2324977M | 7118388M | Total Assets ($) | 18157877M | 9378760M |

M = $ thousand    MM = $ million
See Pages viii through xx for Explanation of Ratios and Data

© RMA 2024

# INFORMATION—Software Publishers  NAICS 513210

## Comparative Historical Data | Current Data Sorted by Sales

| Comparative Historical Data | | | Type of Statement | Current Data Sorted by Sales | | | | | |
|---|---|---|---|---|---|---|---|---|---|
| 18 | 22 | 26 | Unqualified | | | | | 4 | 22 |
| 3 | 7 | 4 | Reviewed | | | | 1 | 3 | 3 |
| 5 | 6 | 5 | Compiled | | | | | 3 | 2 |
| 5 | 6 | 7 | Tax Returns | 1 | 1 | 2 | | 1 | 2 |
| 109 | 132 | 140 | Other | 6 | 4 | 1 | 7 | 30 | 92 |
| 4/1/21-3/31/22 ALL | 4/1/22-3/31/23 ALL | 4/1/23-3/31/24 ALL | | 28 (4/1-9/30/23) | | | 154 (10/1/23-3/31/24) | | |
| | | | | 0-1MM | 1-3MM | 3-5MM | 5-10MM | 10-25MM | 25MM & OVER |
| 140 | 173 | 182 | NUMBER OF STATEMENTS | 7 | 5 | 3 | 8 | 38 | 121 |
| % | % | % | ASSETS | % | % | % | % | % | % |
| 25.0 | 26.9 | 24.5 | Cash & Equivalents | | | | | 23.3 | 21.1 |
| 17.4 | 21.2 | 18.0 | Trade Receivables (net) | | | | | 20.5 | 18.2 |
| 1.6 | 1.5 | 1.8 | Inventory | | | | | .5 | 2.5 |
| 4.5 | 6.6 | 8.1 | All Other Current | | | | | 11.5 | 7.0 |
| 48.5 | 56.2 | 52.4 | Total Current | | | | | 55.8 | 48.9 |
| 8.8 | 6.1 | 7.6 | Fixed Assets (net) | | | | | 6.2 | 6.3 |
| 34.5 | 27.4 | 29.0 | Intangibles (net) | | | | | 28.1 | 32.9 |
| 8.2 | 10.3 | 11.0 | All Other Non-Current | | | | | 9.8 | 12.0 |
| 100.0 | 100.0 | 100.0 | Total | | | | | 100.0 | 100.0 |
| | | | LIABILITIES | | | | | | |
| 3.6 | 2.7 | 4.1 | Notes Payable-Short Term | | | | | 7.7 | 3.2 |
| 1.2 | 1.7 | 2.2 | Cur. Mat.-L.T.D. | | | | | 1.2 | 2.8 |
| 6.3 | 6.7 | 6.7 | Trade Payables | | | | | 5.8 | 6.7 |
| .3 | .9 | .3 | Income Taxes Payable | | | | | .1 | .2 |
| 29.0 | 29.2 | 32.5 | All Other Current | | | | | 32.3 | 33.5 |
| 40.5 | 41.2 | 45.8 | Total Current | | | | | 47.1 | 46.6 |
| 32.2 | 23.2 | 26.9 | Long-Term Debt | | | | | 16.2 | 31.6 |
| .2 | .3 | .2 | Deferred Taxes | | | | | .3 | .2 |
| 11.4 | 9.2 | 8.2 | All Other Non-Current | | | | | 10.0 | 7.1 |
| 15.7 | 26.1 | 18.9 | Net Worth | | | | | 26.4 | 14.5 |
| 100.0 | 100.0 | 100.0 | Total Liabilities & Net Worth | | | | | 100.0 | 100.0 |
| | | | INCOME DATA | | | | | | |
| 100.0 | 100.0 | 100.0 | Net Sales | | | | | 100.0 | 100.0 |
| | | | Gross Profit | | | | | | |
| 100.5 | 101.5 | 101.5 | Operating Expenses | | | | | 105.3 | 102.8 |
| -.5 | -1.5 | -1.5 | Operating Profit | | | | | -5.3 | -2.8 |
| 3.4 | 3.4 | 4.4 | All Other Expenses (net) | | | | | 2.5 | 5.3 |
| -3.9 | -4.9 | -5.9 | Profit Before Taxes | | | | | -7.8 | -8.1 |
| | | | RATIOS | | | | | | |
| 2.2 | 2.3 | 2.4 | | | | | | 2.7 | 2.3 |
| 1.2 | 1.3 | 1.1 | Current | | | | | 1.1 | 1.1 |
| .7 | .7 | .6 | | | | | | .7 | .6 |
| 2.0 | 2.1 | 1.9 | | | | | | 2.1 | 1.6 |
| 1.1 | 1.1 | .9 | Quick | | | | | .8 | .9 |
| .5 | .6 | .5 | | | | | | .4 | .5 |
| 26  13.9 | 31  11.8 | 23  16.0 | | | | | 18  19.8 | 34  10.8 | |
| 45  8.2 | 54  6.7 | 46  8.0 | Sales/Receivables | | | | 38  9.6 | 56  6.5 | |
| 81  4.5 | 87  4.2 | 76  4.8 | | | | | 70  5.2 | 76  4.8 | |
| | | | Cost of Sales/Inventory | | | | | | |
| | | | Cost of Sales/Payables | | | | | | |
| 4.7 | 3.7 | 4.7 | | | | | | 4.9 | 4.8 |
| 18.0 | 13.4 | 27.8 | Sales/Working Capital | | | | | 45.4 | 32.6 |
| -4.8 | -7.6 | -6.5 | | | | | | -6.0 | -4.9 |
| 15.6 | 14.8 | 16.9 | | | | | | 12.9 | 14.8 |
| (96)  -.2 | (111)  -.4 | (130)  -.2 | EBIT/Interest | | | | (26)  -2.5 | (90)  -.3 | |
| -4.5 | -6.6 | -4.6 | | | | | | -10.5 | -3.9 |
| | | 15.6 | 7.9 | Net Profit + Depr., Dep., Amort./Cur. Mat. L/T/D | | | | | 8.4 |
| | (10)  3.2 | (11)  1.9 | | | | | | (10)  4.0 | |
| | -10.2 | .1 | | | | | | | -1.3 |
| .0 | .0 | .0 | | | | | | .0 | .0 |
| 1.4 | .4 | .5 | Fixed/Worth | | | | | .4 | .6 |
| .0 | -.1 | -.1 | | | | | | -.2 | -.1 |
| 1.4 | 1.0 | 1.4 | | | | | | 1.7 | 1.6 |
| -3.8 | 11.2 | -74.3 | Debt/Worth | | | | | NM | -6.0 |
| -1.5 | -2.0 | -1.9 | | | | | | -2.8 | -1.5 |
| 95.4 | 71.3 | 85.9 | % Profit Before Taxes/Tangible Net Worth | | | | | 67.1 | 85.8 |
| (60)  40.6 | (95)  21.3 | (89)  29.8 | | | | | (19)  22.0 | (55)  30.9 | |
| -2.9 | -10.7 | .8 | | | | | | -51.9 | 1.3 |
| 15.7 | 12.7 | 12.5 | % Profit Before Taxes/Total Assets | | | | | 13.2 | 9.2 |
| -1.3 | .2 | -1.1 | | | | | | -5.5 | -3.8 |
| -12.8 | -11.6 | -16.2 | | | | | | -16.8 | -17.0 |
| 151.8 | 286.7 | 223.8 | Sales/Net Fixed Assets | | | | | UND | 171.8 |
| 66.7 | 66.3 | 77.1 | | | | | | 88.6 | 62.2 |
| 24.8 | 20.7 | 18.6 | | | | | | 26.6 | 17.0 |
| 1.6 | 2.0 | 2.0 | Sales/Total Assets | | | | | 2.6 | 1.8 |
| .8 | 1.0 | 1.0 | | | | | | 1.0 | 1.0 |
| .4 | .5 | .6 | | | | | | .6 | .5 |
| .4 | .3 | .3 | % Depr., Dep., Amort./Sales | | | | | .9 | .3 |
| (47)  1.2 | (59)  .7 | (61)  1.4 | | | | | (11)  2.6 | (43)  1.4 | |
| 4.4 | 2.0 | 3.7 | | | | | | 5.2 | 3.6 |
| | 1.6 | 1.2 | % Officers', Directors' Owners' Comp/Sales | | | | | | |
| | (12)  2.5 | (13)  2.2 | | | | | | | |
| | | 13.7 | | | | | | | 11.2 |
| 5982932M | 8394587M | 9990474M | Net Sales ($) | 2460M | 8348M | 12224M | 62385M | 665401M | 9239656M |
| 8258241M | 11171275M | 11595840M | Total Assets ($) | 5845M | 5015M | 10554M | 85158M | 762686M | 10726582M |

M = $ thousand   MM = $ million
See Pages viii through xx for Explanation of Ratios and Data

© RMA 2024

# INFORMATION—Radio Broadcasting Stations  NAICS 516110

## Current Data Sorted by Assets / Comparative Historical Data

| 0-500M | 500M-2MM | 2-10MM | 10-50MM | 50-100MM | 100-250MM | Type of Statement | 4/1/19-3/31/20 ALL | 4/1/20-3/31/21 ALL |
|---|---|---|---|---|---|---|---|---|
| | | 3 | 1 | | 1 | Unqualified | 8 | 7 |
| | | 3 | 1 | | | Reviewed | 1 | 1 |
| | | 3 | | | | Compiled | 1 | |
| | | 2 | | | | Tax Returns | 9 | 4 |
| | | 5 | 8 | 4 | 3 | Other | 27 | 14 |
| 10 (4/1-9/30/23) | | | 21 (10/1/23-3/31/24) | | | | | |
| | | 13 | 10 | 4 | 4 | **NUMBER OF STATEMENTS** | 46 | 26 |
| % | % | % | % | % | % | **ASSETS** | % | % |
| D | D | 10.8 | 12.5 | | | Cash & Equivalents | 7.9 | 18.3 |
| A | A | 18.2 | 4.6 | | | Trade Receivables (net) | 10.6 | 11.1 |
| T | T | .0 | .0 | | | Inventory | .5 | 1.9 |
| A | A | .8 | 1.5 | | | All Other Current | 1.9 | 5.9 |
| | | 29.8 | 18.7 | | | Total Current | 20.8 | 37.3 |
| N | N | 19.8 | 23.1 | | | Fixed Assets (net) | 25.3 | 18.5 |
| O | O | 46.2 | 40.0 | | | Intangibles (net) | 42.4 | 33.1 |
| T | T | 4.3 | 18.2 | | | All Other Non-Current | 11.5 | 11.1 |
| | | 100.0 | 100.0 | | | Total | 100.0 | 100.0 |
| A | A | | | | | **LIABILITIES** | | |
| V | V | 5.6 | .6 | | | Notes Payable-Short Term | 5.7 | 5.9 |
| A | A | 9.0 | 5.1 | | | Cur. Mat.-L.T.D. | 3.6 | 3.5 |
| I | I | 5.1 | 2.1 | | | Trade Payables | 4.7 | 2.2 |
| L | L | .0 | .0 | | | Income Taxes Payable | .0 | .0 |
| A | A | 4.1 | 2.8 | | | All Other Current | 5.8 | 13.7 |
| B | B | 23.8 | 10.5 | | | Total Current | 19.9 | 25.3 |
| L | L | 35.6 | 13.7 | | | Long-Term Debt | 31.4 | 22.9 |
| E | E | .0 | .0 | | | Deferred Taxes | .7 | .5 |
| | | .3 | 19.0 | | | All Other Non-Current | 8.6 | 29.4 |
| | | 40.4 | 56.8 | | | Net Worth | 39.4 | 21.9 |
| | | 100.0 | 100.0 | | | Total Liabilities & Net Worth | 100.0 | 100.0 |
| | | | | | | **INCOME DATA** | | |
| | | 100.0 | 100.0 | | | Net Sales | 100.0 | 100.0 |
| | | | | | | Gross Profit | | |
| | | 93.9 | 86.0 | | | Operating Expenses | 92.8 | 94.3 |
| | | 6.1 | 14.0 | | | Operating Profit | 7.2 | 5.7 |
| | | 3.9 | 3.1 | | | All Other Expenses (net) | 3.1 | 1.6 |
| | | 2.2 | 10.9 | | | Profit Before Taxes | 4.1 | 4.0 |
| | | | | | | **RATIOS** | | |
| | | 2.1 | 8.2 | | | | 2.3 | 4.2 |
| | | 1.1 | 2.0 | | | Current | 1.2 | 2.1 |
| | | .8 | .6 | | | | .7 | 1.3 |
| | | 2.1 | 7.4 | | | | 2.0 | 3.1 |
| | | 1.1 | 1.8 | | | Quick | 1.2 | 1.8 |
| | | .8 | .5 | | | | .6 | 1.2 |
| | | 53  6.9 | 2  177.6 | | | | 18  19.8 | 24  14.9 |
| | | 55  6.6 | 12  31.0 | | | Sales/Receivables | 46  7.9 | 43  8.5 |
| | | 70  5.2 | 49  7.5 | | | | 63  5.8 | 64  5.7 |
| | | | | | | Cost of Sales/Inventory | | |
| | | | | | | Cost of Sales/Payables | | |
| | | 6.9 | 3.2 | | | | 7.3 | 2.1 |
| | | 53.7 | 7.2 | | | Sales/Working Capital | 23.2 | 7.1 |
| | | -501.3 | -8.8 | | | | -37.8 | 13.8 |
| | | 8.0 | | | | | 9.4 | 24.0 |
| | | (12) 1.9 | | | | EBIT/Interest | (41) 2.3 | (22) 1.1 |
| | | -2.7 | | | | | .5 | -2.8 |
| | | | | | | Net Profit + Depr., Dep., Amort./Cur. Mat. L/T/D | | |
| | | NM | .7 | | | | .4 | .1 |
| | | -1.5 | .9 | | | Fixed/Worth | 3.0 | .9 |
| | | -.8 | -.6 | | | | -1.1 | -.7 |
| | | NM | .5 | | | | .7 | .3 |
| | | -4.4 | .9 | | | Debt/Worth | NM | 3.5 |
| | | -2.8 | -2.8 | | | | -2.0 | -1.7 |
| | | | | | | % Profit Before Taxes/Tangible Net Worth | 60.8 | 47.9 |
| | | | | | | | (23) 12.5 | (14) 8.9 |
| | | | | | | | 1.8 | -5.9 |
| | | 19.4 | 9.9 | | | | 9.9 | 10.2 |
| | | .4 | 4.2 | | | % Profit Before Taxes/Total Assets | 2.8 | 1.2 |
| | | -8.9 | .5 | | | | -1.2 | -6.9 |
| | | 11.1 | 4.8 | | | | 9.0 | 16.7 |
| | | 4.4 | 3.5 | | | Sales/Net Fixed Assets | 4.1 | 6.8 |
| | | 2.8 | 1.2 | | | | 2.0 | 2.4 |
| | | 1.2 | .9 | | | | 1.1 | 1.1 |
| | | 1.0 | .6 | | | Sales/Total Assets | .6 | .8 |
| | | .8 | .3 | | | | .4 | .4 |
| | | 2.5 | | | | | 2.1 | 1.3 |
| | | (11) 6.3 | | | | % Depr., Dep., Amort./Sales | (34) 4.9 | (15) 5.9 |
| | | 7.3 | | | | | 6.8 | 7.1 |
| | | | | | | % Officers', Directors' Owners' Comp/Sales | | |
| | | 63774M | 135543M | 92062M | 287882M | Net Sales ($) | 473284M | 320905M |
| | | 63451M | 228322M | 278951M | 683235M | Total Assets ($) | 885569M | 627472M |

M = $ thousand    MM = $ million
See Pages viii through xx for Explanation of Ratios and Data

© RMA 2024

# INFORMATION—Radio Broadcasting Stations  NAICS 516110

## Comparative Historical Data | Current Data Sorted by Sales

| | | | | | | | Type of Statement | | | | | | |
|---|---|---|---|---|---|---|---|---|---|---|---|---|---|
| | | 4 | | 5 | | 2 | Unqualified | | | | 1 | | 1 |
| | | | | 2 | | 4 | Reviewed | | | 2 | 1 | | 1 |
| | | 1 | | | | 3 | Compiled | | | 3 | | | |
| | | 3 | | 5 | | 2 | Tax Returns | | 2 | | | | |
| | | 11 | | 13 | | 20 | Other | | 3 | | 4 | 8 | 5 |
| | | 4/1/21- | | 4/1/22- | | 4/1/23- | | | 10 (4/1-9/30/23) | | 21 (10/1/23-3/31/24) | | |
| | | 3/31/22 | | 3/31/23 | | 3/31/24 | | 0-1MM | 1-3MM | 3-5MM | 5-10MM | 10-25MM | 25MM & |
| | | ALL | | ALL | | ALL | | | | | | | |
| | | 19 | | 25 | | 31 | NUMBER OF STATEMENTS | | 5 | 5 | 6 | 8 | 7 |
| | | % | | % | | % | ASSETS | % | % | % | % | % | % |
| | | 14.5 | | 12.4 | | 10.5 | Cash & Equivalents | D | | | | | |
| | | 10.8 | | 7.2 | | 10.6 | Trade Receivables (net) | A | | | | | |
| | | .0 | | .0 | | .0 | Inventory | T | | | | | |
| | | 1.7 | | 6.1 | | 1.6 | All Other Current | A | | | | | |
| | | 27.1 | | 25.7 | | 22.7 | Total Current | | | | | | |
| | | 19.2 | | 20.7 | | 19.8 | Fixed Assets (net) | N | | | | | |
| | | 39.5 | | 34.4 | | 45.3 | Intangibles (net) | O | | | | | |
| | | 14.3 | | 19.3 | | 12.2 | All Other Non-Current | T | | | | | |
| | | 100.0 | | 100.0 | | 100.0 | Total | | | | | | |
| | | | | | | | LIABILITIES | A | | | | | |
| | | 5.4 | | 16.6 | | 2.6 | Notes Payable-Short Term | V | | | | | |
| | | 3.8 | | 3.4 | | 6.0 | Cur. Mat.-L.T.D. | A | | | | | |
| | | 3.3 | | 2.4 | | 3.4 | Trade Payables | I | | | | | |
| | | .0 | | .0 | | .0 | Income Taxes Payable | L | | | | | |
| | | 7.9 | | 5.4 | | 3.7 | All Other Current | A | | | | | |
| | | 20.4 | | 27.8 | | 15.6 | Total Current | B | | | | | |
| | | 24.7 | | 27.0 | | 23.4 | Long-Term Debt | L | | | | | |
| | | .5 | | .4 | | .4 | Deferred Taxes | E | | | | | |
| | | 10.0 | | 4.1 | | 7.1 | All Other Non-Current | | | | | | |
| | | 44.3 | | 40.7 | | 53.6 | Net Worth | | | | | | |
| | | 100.0 | | 100.0 | | 100.0 | Total Liabilties & Net Worth | | | | | | |
| | | | | | | | INCOME DATA | | | | | | |
| | | 100.0 | | 100.0 | | 100.0 | Net Sales | | | | | | |
| | | | | | | | Gross Profit | | | | | | |
| | | 89.5 | | 87.3 | | 90.7 | Operating Expenses | | | | | | |
| | | 10.5 | | 12.7 | | 9.3 | Operating Profit | | | | | | |
| | | -.9 | | 3.8 | | 3.0 | All Other Expenses (net) | | | | | | |
| | | 11.5 | | 8.9 | | 6.3 | Profit Before Taxes | | | | | | |
| | | | | | | | RATIOS | | | | | | |
| | | 3.8 | | 3.2 | | 3.1 | | | | | | | |
| | | 2.2 | | 1.3 | | 1.3 | Current | | | | | | |
| | | .8 | | .6 | | 1.0 | | | | | | | |
| | | 3.8 | | 3.1 | | 2.6 | | | | | | | |
| | | 2.0 | | 1.3 | | 1.3 | Quick | | | | | | |
| | | .8 | | .2 | | 1.0 | | | | | | | |
| 29 | 12.4 | 2 | 224.7 | 38 | 9.7 | | | | | | | | |
| 51 | 7.2 | 47 | 7.8 | 54 | 6.8 | Sales/Receivables | | | | | | | |
| 58 | 6.3 | 59 | 6.2 | 60 | 6.1 | | | | | | | | |
| | | | | | | | Cost of Sales/Inventory | | | | | | |
| | | | | | | | Cost of Sales/Payables | | | | | | |
| | | 2.1 | | 4.2 | | 4.1 | | | | | | | |
| | | 5.3 | | 13.7 | | 15.9 | Sales/Working Capital | | | | | | |
| | | -23.6 | | -5.5 | | -993.3 | | | | | | | |
| | | 13.7 | | 4.6 | | 9.7 | | | | | | | |
| (15) | 2.9 | (19) | 2.8 | (26) | 4.5 | EBIT/Interest | | | | | | | |
| | | 1.9 | | -1.0 | | -.9 | | | | | | | |
| | | | | | | | Net Profit + Depr., Dep., Amort./Cur. Mat. L/T/D | | | | | | |
| | | .2 | | .4 | | .8 | | | | | | | |
| | | 1.3 | | 106.9 | | 6.3 | Fixed/Worth | | | | | | |
| | | -.6 | | -1.4 | | -.8 | | | | | | | |
| | | .1 | | .8 | | .8 | | | | | | | |
| | | -23.8 | | 304.3 | | 16.1 | Debt/Worth | | | | | | |
| | | -2.5 | | -4.3 | | -3.2 | | | | | | | |
| | | | | 54.1 | | 49.0 | % Profit Before Taxes/Tangible Net Worth | | | | | | |
| | | (13) | 9.1 | (16) | 9.1 | | | | | | | | |
| | | | | -.2 | | -17.7 | | | | | | | | |
| | | 12.9 | | 6.2 | | 8.1 | | | | | | | |
| | | 5.2 | | 2.5 | | 3.5 | % Profit Before Taxes/Total Assets | | | | | | |
| | | 2.1 | | -2.4 | | -3.8 | | | | | | | |
| | | 10.6 | | 5.5 | | 7.3 | | | | | | | |
| | | 4.2 | | 3.0 | | 3.6 | Sales/Net Fixed Assets | | | | | | |
| | | 2.2 | | 2.1 | | 2.5 | | | | | | | |
| | | 1.1 | | .9 | | 1.0 | | | | | | | |
| | | .6 | | .6 | | .6 | Sales/Total Assets | | | | | | |
| | | .4 | | .4 | | .4 | | | | | | | |
| | | 2.1 | | 2.5 | | 2.9 | | | | | | | |
| (16) | 5.5 | (20) | 3.8 | (24) | 4.7 | % Depr., Dep., Amort./Sales | | | | | | | |
| | | 8.9 | | 9.1 | | 6.7 | | | | | | | |
| | | | | | | | % Officers', Directors' Owners' Comp/Sales | | | | | | |
| | | 232006M | | 377744M | | 579261M | Net Sales ($) | | 12402M | 20424M | 44 | | |
| | | 491247M | | 808157M | | 1253959M | Total Assets ($) | | 31238M | 18105M | 76 | | |

© RMA 2024  
M = $ thousand   MM = $ million  
See Pages viii through xx for Explanation of Ratios and Data

# INFORMATION—Television Broadcasting Stations  NAICS 516120

## Current Data Sorted by Assets | Comparative Historical Data

| | | | | | | Type of Statement | | |
|---|---|---|---|---|---|---|---|---|
| | 1 | 1 | 2 | 3 | 5 | Unqualified | 10 | 7 |
| | | | | | | Reviewed | | |
| | | 1 | 2 | | | Compiled | 1 | 1 |
| | | | | | | Tax Returns | 5 | |
| | 1 | 5 | 6 | 11 | 2 | Other | 19 | 18 |
| | 14 (4/1-9/30/23) | | 26 (10/1/23-3/31/24) | | | | 4/1/19- | 4/1/20- |
| 0-500M | 500M-2MM | 2-10MM | 10-50MM | 50-100MM | 100-250MM | | 3/31/20 | 3/31/21 |
| | | | | | | | ALL | ALL |
| | 2 | 7 | 10 | 14 | 7 | NUMBER OF STATEMENTS | 35 | 26 |
| % | % | % | % | % | % | ASSETS | % | % |
| | | | 19.3 | 3.7 | | Cash & Equivalents | 14.9 | 20.9 |
| | | | 11.4 | 8.3 | | Trade Receivables (net) | 11.0 | 9.9 |
| D | | | .1 | .1 | | Inventory | .0 | .9 |
| A | | | 7.0 | 9.7 | | All Other Current | 4.4 | 4.8 |
| T | | | 37.8 | 21.8 | | Total Current | 30.4 | 36.5 |
| A | | | 23.0 | 40.8 | | Fixed Assets (net) | 27.6 | 31.9 |
| | | | 32.4 | 12.9 | | Intangibles (net) | 26.5 | 23.1 |
| N | | | 6.8 | 24.5 | | All Other Non-Current | 15.6 | 8.5 |
| O | | | 100.0 | 100.0 | | Total | 100.0 | 100.0 |
| T | | | | | | LIABILITIES | | |
| | | | .3 | .2 | | Notes Payable-Short Term | 1.3 | .7 |
| A | | | 9.1 | 2.2 | | Cur. Mat.-L.T.D. | 4.5 | 2.8 |
| V | | | 5.7 | 4.5 | | Trade Payables | 3.3 | 3.1 |
| A | | | .1 | .0 | | Income Taxes Payable | .0 | .0 |
| I | | | 4.7 | 5.8 | | All Other Current | 11.1 | 9.8 |
| L | | | 19.8 | 12.7 | | Total Current | 20.2 | 16.4 |
| A | | | 22.1 | 38.6 | | Long-Term Debt | 23.3 | 26.1 |
| B | | | .1 | .2 | | Deferred Taxes | .4 | .8 |
| L | | | 19.1 | 2.8 | | All Other Non-Current | 8.8 | 4.2 |
| E | | | 39.0 | 45.7 | | Net Worth | 47.3 | 52.5 |
| | | | 100.0 | 100.0 | | Total Liabilities & Net Worth | 100.0 | 100.0 |
| | | | | | | INCOME DATA | | |
| | | | 100.0 | 100.0 | | Net Sales | 100.0 | 100.0 |
| | | | | | | Gross Profit | | |
| | | | 95.3 | 87.2 | | Operating Expenses | 87.0 | 87.8 |
| | | | 4.7 | 12.8 | | Operating Profit | 13.0 | 12.2 |
| | | | 2.1 | 1.9 | | All Other Expenses (net) | 1.3 | -.6 |
| | | | 2.6 | 10.9 | | Profit Before Taxes | 11.7 | 12.8 |
| | | | | | | RATIOS | | |
| | | | 5.0 | 2.3 | | | 3.2 | 6.1 |
| | | | 1.3 | 1.5 | | Current | 1.6 | 1.6 |
| | | | .6 | .8 | | | .9 | .9 |
| | | | 4.1 | 1.4 | | | 1.9 | 5.3 |
| | | | 1.0 | .8 | | Quick | 1.4 | 1.5 |
| | | | .6 | .5 | | | .8 | .7 |
| | | | 18  20.8 | 1  406.9 | | | 12  29.3 | 9  38.9 |
| | | | 53  6.9 | 9  40.0 | | Sales/Receivables | 38  9.6 | 34  10.7 |
| | | | 83  4.4 | 55  6.6 | | | 60  6.1 | 59  6.2 |
| | | | | | | Cost of Sales/Inventory | | |
| | | | | | | Cost of Sales/Payables | | |
| | | | 2.3 | 6.2 | | | 4.4 | 2.1 |
| | | | NM | 15.4 | | Sales/Working Capital | 9.3 | 8.8 |
| | | | -5.7 | -123.4 | | | -49.4 | -123.0 |
| | | | 13.2 | 18.3 | | | 24.3 | 23.2 |
| | | | .0  (12) | 4.3 | | EBIT/Interest | (31)  5.6 | (20)  6.1 |
| | | | -2.0 | 2.8 | | | 2.2 | 2.5 |
| | | | | | | Net Profit + Depr., Dep., Amort./Cur. Mat. L/T/D | | |
| | | | .2 | .3 | | | .4 | .4 |
| | | | 77.3 | 1.0 | | Fixed/Worth | .9 | .9 |
| | | | -.5 | -265.8 | | | -.4 | -.9 |
| | | | .8 | .2 | | | .2 | .3 |
| | | | 242.1 | 1.2 | | Debt/Worth | 1.7 | .8 |
| | | | -1.9 | -307.6 | | | -2.9 | -3.3 |
| | | | | 18.6 | | | 57.9 | 51.7 |
| | | | (10) | 9.0 | | % Profit Before Taxes/Tangible Net Worth | (25)  15.3 | (19)  17.6 |
| | | | | 3.8 | | | 2.9 | 3.2 |
| | | | 6.0 | 6.5 | | | 16.9 | 17.7 |
| | | | .0 | 3.9 | | % Profit Before Taxes/Total Assets | 8.1 | 8.0 |
| | | | -6.1 | 2.2 | | | 1.4 | 3.6 |
| | | | 7.9 | 4.6 | | | 22.6 | 7.3 |
| | | | 4.7 | 2.1 | | Sales/Net Fixed Assets | 3.1 | 2.5 |
| | | | 2.3 | .5 | | | 1.9 | 1.3 |
| | | | 1.0 | 1.3 | | | 1.2 | 1.0 |
| | | | .6 | .5 | | Sales/Total Assets | .8 | .7 |
| | | | .4 | .4 | | | .5 | .3 |
| | | | | 5.3 | | | 3.1 | 3.6 |
| | | | (12) | 6.4 | | % Depr., Dep., Amort./Sales | (26)  6.6 | (22)  6.8 |
| | | | | 13.3 | | | 8.3 | 13.0 |
| | | | | | | % Officers', Directors' Owners' Comp/Sales | | |
| | 1881M | 40280M | 198249M | 761935M | 813085M | Net Sales ($) | 1555840M | 922017M |
| | 2345M | 31991M | 269155M | 980537M | 1280888M | Total Assets ($) | 1752967M | 1086341M |

M = $ thousand    MM = $ million
See Pages viii through xx for Explanation of Ratios and Data

# INFORMATION—Television Broadcasting Stations  NAICS 516120

| Comparative Historical Data | | | | | | | Current Data Sorted by Sales | | | | | |
|---|---|---|---|---|---|---|---|---|---|---|---|---|
| | | | | | | Type of Statement | | | | | | |
| | 5 | | 11 | | 12 | Unqualified | 1 | | 2 | | 3 | 6 |
| | | | | 1 | | Reviewed | | | | | | |
| | 2 | | 5 | | 3 | Compiled | | | | 1 | 1 | 1 |
| | 1 | | | | | Tax Returns | | | | | | |
| | 16 | | 30 | | 25 | Other | 1 | | 2 | 2 | 8 | 10 |
| | 4/1/21-3/31/22 | | 4/1/22-3/31/23 | | 4/1/23-3/31/24 | | 0-1MM | 14 (4/1-9/30/23) 1-3MM | 3-5MM | 26 (10/1/23-3/31/24) 5-10MM | 10-25MM | 25MM & OVER |
| | ALL | | ALL | | ALL | | | | | | | |
| | 24 | | 47 | | 40 | NUMBER OF STATEMENTS | 2 | 2 | 4 | 3 | 12 | 17 |
| | % | | % | | % | **ASSETS** | % | % | % | % | % | % |
| | 22.7 | | 22.1 | | 15.9 | Cash & Equivalents | | | | | 16.6 | 14.6 |
| | 12.4 | | 12.5 | | 9.9 | Trade Receivables (net) | | | | | 9.0 | 12.6 |
| | .3 | | 2.7 | | .0 | Inventory | | | | | .0 | .1 |
| | 4.2 | | 8.4 | | 6.7 | All Other Current | | | | | 5.2 | 10.4 |
| | 39.5 | | 45.7 | | 32.6 | Total Current | | | | | 30.8 | 37.6 |
| | 25.4 | | 21.6 | | 27.0 | Fixed Assets (net) | | | | | 33.6 | 19.1 |
| | 18.3 | | 18.9 | | 20.1 | Intangibles (net) | | | | | 22.9 | 12.7 |
| | 16.7 | | 13.8 | | 20.3 | All Other Non-Current | | | | | 12.7 | 30.6 |
| | 100.0 | | 100.0 | | 100.0 | Total | | | | | 100.0 | 100.0 |
| | | | | | | **LIABILITIES** | | | | | | |
| | 1.8 | | .2 | | .2 | Notes Payable-Short Term | | | | | .3 | .2 |
| | 3.2 | | 4.9 | | 10.8 | Cur. Mat.-L.T.D. | | | | | 6.9 | 16.0 |
| | 6.5 | | 6.3 | | 5.9 | Trade Payables | | | | | 4.4 | 5.9 |
| | .0 | | .0 | | .0 | Income Taxes Payable | | | | | .1 | .0 |
| | 9.6 | | 9.3 | | 5.5 | All Other Current | | | | | 3.7 | 6.9 |
| | 21.1 | | 20.6 | | 22.4 | Total Current | | | | | 15.3 | 29.1 |
| | 24.9 | | 32.6 | | 33.4 | Long-Term Debt | | | | | 34.8 | 23.7 |
| | .1 | | .7 | | .3 | Deferred Taxes | | | | | .0 | .1 |
| | 10.4 | | 18.2 | | 13.0 | All Other Non-Current | | | | | 13.0 | 11.5 |
| | 43.5 | | 27.8 | | 30.9 | Net Worth | | | | | 36.8 | 35.6 |
| | 100.0 | | 100.0 | | 100.0 | Total Liabilities & Net Worth | | | | | 100.0 | 100.0 |
| | | | | | | **INCOME DATA** | | | | | | |
| | 100.0 | | 100.0 | | 100.0 | Net Sales | | | | | 100.0 | 100.0 |
| | | | | | | Gross Profit | | | | | | |
| | 82.4 | | 85.8 | | 89.0 | Operating Expenses | | | | | 89.0 | 86.8 |
| | 17.6 | | 14.2 | | 11.0 | Operating Profit | | | | | 11.0 | 13.2 |
| | -1.4 | | 2.7 | | 3.2 | All Other Expenses (net) | | | | | 4.2 | .5 |
| | 19.0 | | 11.4 | | 7.8 | Profit Before Taxes | | | | | 6.8 | 12.7 |
| | | | | | | **RATIOS** | | | | | | |
| | 4.3 | | 4.6 | | 4.1 | | | | | | 4.6 | 3.5 |
| | 2.1 | | 2.1 | | 1.5 | Current | | | | | 1.4 | 1.5 |
| | 1.2 | | 1.4 | | .8 | | | | | | .6 | 1.2 |
| | 3.9 | | 4.0 | | 3.1 | | | | | | 3.7 | 2.6 |
| | 1.8 | | 1.5 | | 1.2 | Quick | | | | | 1.2 | 1.1 |
| | 1.0 | | 1.1 | | .5 | | | | | | .5 | .5 |
| 7 | 54.2 | 17 | 22.1 | 6 | 60.6 | | | | | 0 | 859.7 | 6 56.5 |
| 29 | 12.8 | 33 | 11.0 | 31 | 11.7 | Sales/Receivables | | | | 20 | 18.3 | 48 7.6 |
| 65 | 5.6 | 65 | 5.6 | 68 | 5.4 | | | | | 63 | 5.8 | 72 5.1 |
| | | | | | | Cost of Sales/Inventory | | | | | | |
| | | | | | | Cost of Sales/Payables | | | | | | |
| | 2.7 | | 2.2 | | 4.5 | | | | | | 4.5 | 2.8 |
| | 7.0 | | 6.1 | | 13.2 | Sales/Working Capital | | | | | NM | 14.2 |
| | 22.4 | | 14.8 | | -12.2 | | | | | | -8.0 | 40.4 |
| | 72.1 | | 19.8 | | 18.3 | | | | | | | 25.6 |
| (17) | 12.0 | (40) | 6.0 | (31) | 3.5 | EBIT/Interest | | | | | (15) 16.2 |
| | 4.4 | | 1.2 | | -.3 | | | | | | | 3.7 |
| | | | | 13.0 | | Net Profit + Depr., Dep., | | | | | | |
| | | (10) | 3.2 | | | Amort./Cur. Mat. L/T/D | | | | | | |
| | | | 1.4 | | | | | | | | | |
| | .2 | | .3 | | .3 | | | | | | .2 | .2 |
| | 1.1 | | 1.1 | | 1.9 | Fixed/Worth | | | | | NM | .4 |
| | -1.4 | | -.6 | | -1.1 | | | | | | -1.9 | 5.6 |
| | .3 | | .3 | | .3 | | | | | | .2 | .3 |
| | 1.5 | | 3.3 | | 5.2 | Debt/Worth | | | | | NM | .9 |
| | -4.6 | | -4.6 | | -3.4 | | | | | | -3.3 | 17.5 |
| | 56.2 | | 63.0 | | 13.5 | % Profit Before Taxes/Tangible | | | | | | 20.4 |
| (16) | 28.3 | (27) | 18.2 | (24) | 5.7 | Net Worth | | | | | | (14) 11.6 |
| | 9.2 | | -.9 | | -1.9 | | | | | | | 3.8 |
| | 27.0 | | 20.4 | | 8.5 | % Profit Before Taxes/Total | | | | | 6.7 | 17.5 |
| | 16.1 | | 6.3 | | 3.0 | Assets | | | | | 2.9 | 6.0 |
| | 7.4 | | -.7 | | -1.9 | | | | | | -4.5 | 2.5 |
| | 21.8 | | 26.0 | | 8.1 | | | | | | 11.7 | 12.9 |
| | 4.0 | | 8.1 | | 4.1 | Sales/Net Fixed Assets | | | | | 3.6 | 5.1 |
| | 2.4 | | 2.2 | | 2.0 | | | | | | .8 | 2.5 |
| | 1.5 | | 1.5 | | 1.3 | | | | | | .9 | 1.5 |
| | .8 | | .9 | | .6 | Sales/Total Assets | | | | | .5 | .8 |
| | .5 | | .6 | | .4 | | | | | | .4 | .5 |
| | 3.3 | | 2.1 | | 3.7 | | | | | | 5.9 | 2.4 |
| (19) | 6.5 | (34) | 6.0 | (34) | 6.4 | % Depr., Dep., Amort./Sales | | | | (11) | 10.5 | (13) 5.1 |
| | 9.8 | | 10.9 | | 13.0 | | | | | | 13.8 | 6.1 |
| | | | | | | % Officers', Directors' Owners' Comp/Sales | | | | | | |
| | 981188M | | 2573874M | | 1815430M | Net Sales ($) | 1548M | 2403M | 16837M | 20448M | 208167M | 1566027M |
| | 1129558M | | 2628828M | | 2564916M | Total Assets ($) | 4004M | 9310M | 63787M | 70097M | 542194M | 1875524M |

© RMA 2024          M = $ thousand     MM = $ million
See Pages viii through xx for Explanation of Ratios and Data

# INFORMATION—Media Streaming Distribution Services, Social Networks, and Other Media Networks and Content Providers NAICS 516210

## Current Data Sorted by Assets | Comparative Historical Data

| | | | | | | Type of Statement | | |
|---|---|---|---|---|---|---|---|---|
| | | 1 | | 1 | 4 | Unqualified | 6 | 6 |
| | | | 1 | | 1 | Reviewed | 2 | 3 |
| | | | 1 | | | Compiled | | |
| 2 | | 1 | 1 | | | Tax Returns | 1 | 1 |
| | 2 | 3 | 1 | | 2 | Other | 1 | 1 |
| | 9 (4/1-9/30/23) | 8 | 5 | 25 (10/1/23-3/31/24) | | | 27 | 15 |
| 0-500M | 500M-2MM | 2-10MM | 10-50MM | 50-100MM | 100-250MM | | 4/1/19-3/31/20 ALL | 4/1/20-3/31/21 ALL |
| 2 | 2 | 13 | 8 | 2 | 7 | NUMBER OF STATEMENTS | 37 | 25 |
| % | % | % | % | % | % | ASSETS | % | % |
| | | 16.8 | | | | Cash & Equivalents | 13.5 | 16.7 |
| | | 13.7 | | | | Trade Receivables (net) | 17.5 | 9.7 |
| | | 5.3 | | | | Inventory | 2.4 | 4.4 |
| | | 2.3 | | | | All Other Current | 3.9 | 10.1 |
| | | 38.2 | | | | Total Current | 37.3 | 41.0 |
| | | 28.3 | | | | Fixed Assets (net) | 33.2 | 36.1 |
| | | 22.9 | | | | Intangibles (net) | 18.4 | 13.2 |
| | | 10.6 | | | | All Other Non-Current | 11.1 | 9.7 |
| | | 100.0 | | | | Total | 100.0 | 100.0 |
| | | | | | | LIABILITIES | | |
| | | 3.6 | | | | Notes Payable-Short Term | 2.6 | 1.5 |
| | | 1.5 | | | | Cur. Mat.-L.T.D. | 5.0 | 2.9 |
| | | 2.7 | | | | Trade Payables | 5.7 | 5.6 |
| | | 1.2 | | | | Income Taxes Payable | .1 | .0 |
| | | 10.8 | | | | All Other Current | 9.4 | 16.8 |
| | | 19.7 | | | | Total Current | 22.9 | 26.9 |
| | | 14.6 | | | | Long-Term Debt | 29.1 | 23.3 |
| | | .0 | | | | Deferred Taxes | 1.1 | 1.0 |
| | | 8.1 | | | | All Other Non-Current | 5.1 | 8.9 |
| | | 57.5 | | | | Net Worth | 41.8 | 39.8 |
| | | 100.0 | | | | Total Liabilties & Net Worth | 100.0 | 100.0 |
| | | | | | | INCOME DATA | | |
| | | 100.0 | | | | Net Sales | 100.0 | 100.0 |
| | | | | | | Gross Profit | | |
| | | 90.6 | | | | Operating Expenses | 85.4 | 88.5 |
| | | 9.4 | | | | Operating Profit | 14.6 | 11.5 |
| | | 1.0 | | | | All Other Expenses (net) | 3.3 | -.6 |
| | | 8.5 | | | | Profit Before Taxes | 11.3 | 12.1 |
| | | | | | | RATIOS | | |
| | | 5.5 | | | | | 3.0 | 3.5 |
| | | 1.7 | | | | Current | 1.8 | 1.6 |
| | | .5 | | | | | 1.1 | 1.3 |
| | | 3.8 | | | | | 2.9 | 2.9 |
| | | 1.3 | | | | Quick | 1.6 | 1.4 |
| | | .4 | | | | | .7 | .6 |
| | 0 | UND | | | | | 14 26.8 | 8 48.4 |
| | 40 | 9.1 | | | | Sales/Receivables | 41 9.0 | 21 17.6 |
| | 51 | 7.2 | | | | | 64 5.7 | 40 9.1 |
| | | | | | | Cost of Sales/Inventory | | |
| | | | | | | Cost of Sales/Payables | | |
| | | 3.3 | | | | | | 4.4 | 3.6 |
| | | 6.1 | | | | Sales/Working Capital | 8.1 | 8.7 |
| | | -24.2 | | | | | NM | 45.5 |
| | | 18.9 | | | | | 14.1 | 23.4 |
| | (11) | 2.9 | | | | EBIT/Interest | (30) 4.8 | (18) 10.1 |
| | | -4.1 | | | | | .7 | 5.4 |
| | | | | | | Net Profit + Depr., Dep., Amort./Cur. Mat. L/T/D | | |
| | | .1 | | | | | .3 | .4 |
| | | .5 | | | | Fixed/Worth | 1.0 | 1.2 |
| | | 6.8 | | | | | 6.8 | 3.1 |
| | | .2 | | | | | .5 | .4 |
| | | 2.1 | | | | Debt/Worth | 1.0 | 1.5 |
| | | 10.0 | | | | | 11.8 | 5.2 |
| | | 103.7 | | | | | 62.5 | 61.4 |
| | (11) | 26.5 | | | | % Profit Before Taxes/Tangible Net Worth | (31) 17.9 | (21) 30.4 |
| | | -4.3 | | | | | 4.3 | 7.6 |
| | | 19.3 | | | | | 14.1 | 19.8 |
| | | 3.9 | | | | % Profit Before Taxes/Total Assets | 5.6 | 12.0 |
| | | -3.9 | | | | | .1 | 2.7 |
| | | 40.3 | | | | | 10.6 | 14.8 |
| | | 3.1 | | | | Sales/Net Fixed Assets | 5.4 | 2.8 |
| | | 1.4 | | | | | 1.8 | 1.1 |
| | | 1.4 | | | | | 2.0 | 2.3 |
| | | 1.1 | | | | Sales/Total Assets | .8 | 1.0 |
| | | .5 | | | | | .6 | .6 |
| | | 1.2 | | | | | 1.7 | 1.8 |
| | (10) | 2.8 | | | | % Depr., Dep., Amort./Sales | (21) 2.3 | (14) 3.1 |
| | | 15.6 | | | | | 8.1 | 12.4 |
| | | | | | | % Officers', Directors' Owners' Comp/Sales | | |
| 4768M | 5652M | 74782M | 281886M | 107513M | 920612M | Net Sales ($) | 2559686M | 1662201M |
| 422M | 2015M | 69440M | 151221M | 141029M | 1101950M | Total Assets ($) | 1921320M | 1558272M |

© RMA 2024

M = $ thousand  MM = $ million
See Pages viii through xx for Explanation of Ratios and Data

# INFORMATION—Media Streaming Distribution Services, Social Networks, and Other Media Networks and Content Providers  NAICS 516210

## Comparative Historical Data / Current Data Sorted by Sales

| | | | | Type of Statement | | | | | | |
|---|---|---|---|---|---|---|---|---|---|---|
| 6 | 7 | 6 | | Unqualified | | 1 | | | | 5 |
| | 6 | 2 | | Reviewed | | | | | 1 | 1 |
| 2 | 4 | 2 | | Compiled | | | | 1 | 1 | |
| | 1 | 6 | | Tax Returns | | | | | | 1 |
| 18 | 23 | 18 | | Other | | 2 | 3 | 1 | 2 | 6 |
| 4/1/21- | 4/1/22- | 4/1/23- | | | 1 | 5 | 3 | 1 | | |
| 3/31/22 | 3/31/23 | 3/31/24 | | | | 9 (4/1-9/30/23) | | | 25 (10/1/23-3/31/24) | |
| ALL | ALL | ALL | | | 0-1MM | 1-3MM | 3-5MM | 5-10MM | 10-25MM | 25MM & OVER |
| 26 | 41 | 34 | | NUMBER OF STATEMENTS | 1 | 8 | 6 | 2 | 4 | 13 |
| % | % | % | | ASSETS | % | % | % | % | % | % |
| 26.1 | 24.6 | 19.4 | | Cash & Equivalents | | | | | | 22.4 |
| 10.5 | 11.4 | 14.0 | | Trade Receivables (net) | | | | | | 15.6 |
| .8 | 3.2 | 2.6 | | Inventory | | | | | | 1.3 |
| 5.2 | 3.4 | 3.4 | | All Other Current | | | | | | 6.3 |
| 42.6 | 42.5 | 39.3 | | Total Current | | | | | | 45.6 |
| 29.9 | 23.7 | 22.0 | | Fixed Assets (net) | | | | | | 17.0 |
| 11.4 | 21.4 | 25.4 | | Intangibles (net) | | | | | | 26.5 |
| 16.1 | 12.4 | 13.3 | | All Other Non-Current | | | | | | 10.9 |
| 100.0 | 100.0 | 100.0 | | Total | | | | | | 100.0 |
| | | | | LIABILITIES | | | | | | |
| 2.0 | 1.6 | 3.2 | | Notes Payable-Short Term | | | | | | 1.9 |
| 6.4 | 3.8 | 4.2 | | Cur. Mat.-L.T.D. | | | | | | 4.5 |
| 4.0 | 7.2 | 5.7 | | Trade Payables | | | | | | 10.5 |
| .0 | .0 | .5 | | Income Taxes Payable | | | | | | .0 |
| 9.8 | 14.4 | 12.7 | | All Other Current | | | | | | 13.2 |
| 22.2 | 27.1 | 26.3 | | Total Current | | | | | | 30.1 |
| 50.6 | 33.7 | 30.8 | | Long-Term Debt | | | | | | 46.2 |
| 2.3 | .0 | 1.2 | | Deferred Taxes | | | | | | 3.2 |
| 11.8 | 8.5 | 6.1 | | All Other Non-Current | | | | | | 7.2 |
| 13.1 | 30.7 | 35.6 | | Net Worth | | | | | | 13.3 |
| 100.0 | 100.0 | 100.0 | | Total Liabilities & Net Worth | | | | | | 100.0 |
| | | | | INCOME DATA | | | | | | |
| 100.0 | 100.0 | 100.0 | | Net Sales | | | | | | 100.0 |
| | | | | Gross Profit | | | | | | |
| 76.3 | 89.8 | 85.3 | | Operating Expenses | | | | | | 84.1 |
| 23.7 | 10.2 | 14.7 | | Operating Profit | | | | | | 15.9 |
| 1.2 | .4 | 2.2 | | All Other Expenses (net) | | | | | | 3.7 |
| 22.5 | 9.8 | 12.5 | | Profit Before Taxes | | | | | | 12.2 |
| | | | | RATIOS | | | | | | |
| 4.7 | 3.8 | 2.5 | | | | | | | | 2.2 |
| 1.8 | 1.7 | 1.5 | | Current | | | | | | 1.5 |
| 1.0 | .9 | .6 | | | | | | | | .6 |
| 3.0 | 3.6 | 2.4 | | | | | | | | 2.2 |
| 1.6 | 1.4 | 1.2 | | Quick | | | | | | .7 |
| .7 | .7 | .4 | | | | | | | | .4 |
| 0  UND | 11  34.2 | 1  337.8 | | | | | | | 17 | 21.0 |
| 16  22.6 | 30  12.1 | 29  12.6 | | Sales/Receivables | | | | | 36 | 10.2 |
| 57  6.4 | 55  6.6 | 50  7.3 | | | | | | | 58 | 6.3 |
| | | | | Cost of Sales/Inventory | | | | | | |
| | | | | Cost of Sales/Payables | | | | | | |
| 3.5 | 3.7 | 3.3 | | | | | | | | 3.2 |
| 8.3 | 11.8 | 11.8 | | Sales/Working Capital | | | | | | 13.1 |
| UND | -32.6 | -17.5 | | | | | | | | -6.3 |
| 80.7 | 19.0 | 7.5 | | | | | | | | 5.7 |
| (20) 18.1 | (34) 4.4 | (26) 2.4 | | EBIT/Interest | | | | | (10) | 2.4 |
| 3.8 | .9 | -.4 | | | | | | | | -.7 |
| | | | | Net Profit + Depr., Dep., Amort./Cur. Mat. L/T/D | | | | | | |
| .2 | .2 | .2 | | | | | | | | .3 |
| .7 | 1.3 | 1.1 | | Fixed/Worth | | | | | | -.5 |
| UND | -1.7 | -.5 | | | | | | | | -.2 |
| .4 | .6 | .6 | | | | | | | | .9 |
| .7 | 3.2 | 2.2 | | Debt/Worth | | | | | | -5.3 |
| UND | -4.0 | -2.9 | | | | | | | | -2.1 |
| 66.3 | 84.0 | 104.0 | | | | | | | | |
| (21) 36.8 | (25) 22.3 | (20) 22.1 | | % Profit Before Taxes/Tangible Net Worth | | | | | | |
| 14.3 | 5.2 | -.5 | | | | | | | | |
| 36.4 | 21.8 | 28.2 | | | | | | | | 47.0 |
| 16.1 | 11.9 | 5.1 | | % Profit Before Taxes/Total Assets | | | | | | 5.5 |
| 5.7 | .7 | -1.4 | | | | | | | | 1.1 |
| 13.8 | 26.4 | 44.7 | | | | | | | | 31.0 |
| 5.5 | 7.0 | 18.2 | | Sales/Net Fixed Assets | | | | | | 19.2 |
| 1.5 | 2.1 | 1.5 | | | | | | | | 1.4 |
| 1.7 | 1.6 | 2.3 | | | | | | | | 2.1 |
| 1.1 | 1.1 | 1.1 | | Sales/Total Assets | | | | | | .9 |
| .5 | .7 | .5 | | | | | | | | .4 |
| 1.0 | 1.2 | 1.1 | | | | | | | | 2.1 |
| (18) 2.3 | (27) 4.1 | (23) 4.0 | | % Depr., Dep., Amort./Sales | | | | | | |
| 6.7 | 8.6 | 15.9 | | | | | | | | |
| | | | | % Officers', Directors' Owners' Comp/Sales | | | | | | |
| 2152819M | 2571187M | 1395213M | | Net Sales ($) | 540M | 18707M | 22577M | 15439M | 65512M | 1272438M |
| 1891502M | 1951799M | 1466077M | | Total Assets ($) | 10179M | 32183M | 25514M | 8655M | 46360M | 1343186M |

M = $ thousand    MM = $ million
See Pages viii through xx for Explanation of Ratios and Data

© RMA 2024

# INFORMATION—Wired Telecommunications Carriers  NAICS 517111

## Current Data Sorted by Assets

| | | | | | | | Type of Statement | | | | |
|---|---|---|---|---|---|---|---|---|---|---|---|
| | | | 2 | 7 | 6 | 8 | Unqualified | | 27 | | 12 |
| | | | 1 | 4 | 2 | | Reviewed | | 3 | | 1 |
| | | | 1 | 1 | | | Compiled | | 2 | | 3 |
| 2 | | | 1 | | | | Tax Returns | | 9 | | 1 |
| 7 | | 3 | 5 | 10 | 11 | 13 | Other | | 55 | | 50 |
| | 15 (4/1-9/30/23) | | | 69 (10/1/23-3/31/24) | | | | | 4/1/19-3/31/20 | | 4/1/20-3/31/21 |
| 0-500M | 500M-2MM | 2-10MM | 10-50MM | 50-100MM | 100-250MM | | | | ALL | | ALL |
| 9 | 3 | 10 | 22 | 19 | 21 | | NUMBER OF STATEMENTS | | 96 | | 67 |
| % | % | % | % | % | % | | ASSETS | | % | | % |
| | | 20.9 | 13.9 | 7.5 | 6.6 | | Cash & Equivalents | | 14.1 | | 17.5 |
| | | 16.8 | 5.8 | 9.2 | 4.8 | | Trade Receivables (net) | | 13.2 | | 13.9 |
| | | 18.2 | 3.2 | 4.1 | 2.9 | | Inventory | | 4.9 | | 4.0 |
| | | 7.5 | 3.6 | 1.4 | 3.8 | | All Other Current | | 3.2 | | 2.5 |
| | | 63.4 | 26.6 | 22.3 | 18.0 | | Total Current | | 35.4 | | 38.0 |
| | | 16.6 | 54.6 | 49.3 | 70.7 | | Fixed Assets (net) | | 45.3 | | 38.8 |
| | | 5.4 | 3.6 | 13.3 | 6.8 | | Intangibles (net) | | 9.1 | | 9.1 |
| | | 14.6 | 15.2 | 15.1 | 4.5 | | All Other Non-Current | | 10.3 | | 14.1 |
| | | 100.0 | 100.0 | 100.0 | 100.0 | | Total | | 100.0 | | 100.0 |
| | | | | | | | LIABILITIES | | | | |
| | | 4.4 | 1.0 | 2.1 | 1.1 | | Notes Payable-Short Term | | 4.3 | | 6.5 |
| | | 1.8 | 2.3 | 4.0 | 5.1 | | Cur. Mat.-L.T.D. | | 5.0 | | 4.3 |
| | | 14.3 | 4.6 | 5.6 | 4.1 | | Trade Payables | | 8.2 | | 5.4 |
| | | .0 | .0 | .1 | .2 | | Income Taxes Payable | | .1 | | .2 |
| | | 19.8 | 6.1 | 10.9 | 7.1 | | All Other Current | | 12.2 | | 9.6 |
| | | 40.3 | 14.0 | 22.6 | 17.6 | | Total Current | | 29.8 | | 26.0 |
| | | 11.2 | 22.7 | 32.7 | 30.0 | | Long-Term Debt | | 23.5 | | 30.2 |
| | | .0 | 2.6 | 1.4 | 1.7 | | Deferred Taxes | | 1.4 | | 2.1 |
| | | 4.1 | 6.8 | 9.2 | 19.0 | | All Other Non-Current | | 6.0 | | 4.9 |
| | | 44.4 | 53.9 | 34.1 | 31.7 | | Net Worth | | 39.2 | | 36.8 |
| | | 100.0 | 100.0 | 100.0 | 100.0 | | Total Liabilties & Net Worth | | 100.0 | | 100.0 |
| | | | | | | | INCOME DATA | | | | |
| | | 100.0 | 100.0 | 100.0 | 100.0 | | Net Sales | | 100.0 | | 100.0 |
| | | | | | | | Gross Profit | | | | |
| | | 95.0 | 87.1 | 88.0 | 81.3 | | Operating Expenses | | 90.0 | | 87.4 |
| | | 5.0 | 12.9 | 12.0 | 18.7 | | Operating Profit | | 10.0 | | 12.6 |
| | | -.1 | 1.5 | 1.2 | 8.7 | | All Other Expenses (net) | | 1.3 | | 2.0 |
| | | 5.2 | 11.5 | 10.8 | 10.0 | | Profit Before Taxes | | 8.7 | | 10.6 |
| | | | | | | | RATIOS | | | | |
| | | 3.9 | 3.9 | 2.7 | 2.1 | | | | 2.6 | | 3.0 |
| | | 1.5 | 1.7 | 1.0 | 1.4 | | Current | | 1.3 | | 1.6 |
| | | 1.0 | .8 | .6 | .5 | | | | .8 | | .9 |
| | | 3.6 | 2.8 | 2.6 | 1.5 | | | | 1.8 | | 2.8 |
| | | .9 | 1.3 | .9 | .6 | | Quick | | 1.0 | | 1.2 |
| | | .2 | .6 | .5 | .2 | | | | .6 | | .6 |
| | 11 | 34.5 | 9 42.6 | 21 17.3 | 5 70.1 | | | 15 | 24.8 | 15 | 23.7 |
| | 39 | 9.4 | 24 14.9 | 36 10.1 | 21 17.3 | | Sales/Receivables | 25 | 14.6 | 26 | 14.2 |
| | 61 | 6.0 | 42 8.6 | 45 8.2 | 46 8.0 | | | 49 | 7.4 | 61 | 6.0 |
| | | | | | | | Cost of Sales/Inventory | | | | |
| | | | | | | | Cost of Sales/Payables | | | | |
| | | 3.6 | 2.5 | 3.7 | 3.1 | | | | 4.9 | | 4.3 |
| | | 24.4 | 7.3 | -165.1 | 9.0 | | Sales/Working Capital | | 15.3 | | 10.1 |
| | | -75.0 | -38.9 | -11.3 | -3.0 | | | | -23.4 | | -23.6 |
| | | | 14.5 | 8.2 | 6.3 | | | | 15.4 | | 17.4 |
| | | | (19) 4.8 | (17) 5.7 | (17) 2.8 | | EBIT/Interest | (79) | 6.0 | (58) | 7.0 |
| | | | 2.7 | .9 | 1.4 | | | | 2.2 | | 2.2 |
| | | | | | | | Net Profit + Depr., Dep., | | 9.9 | | 7.5 |
| | | | | | | | Amort./Cur. Mat. L/T/D | (29) | 4.6 | (14) | 5.0 |
| | | | | | | | | | 2.3 | | 1.8 |
| | | .1 | .5 | .9 | 1.3 | | | | .6 | | .4 |
| | | .5 | 1.1 | 3.7 | 2.1 | | Fixed/Worth | | 1.2 | | 1.1 |
| | | NM | 2.8 | -1.7 | 4.1 | | | | 4.8 | | 4.1 |
| | | .4 | .3 | .6 | 1.0 | | | | .5 | | .5 |
| | | 1.3 | .7 | 7.2 | 1.6 | | Debt/Worth | | 1.2 | | 1.4 |
| | | NM | 2.1 | -6.5 | 3.6 | | | | 8.1 | | 3.9 |
| | | | 23.2 | 36.1 | 12.7 | | % Profit Before Taxes/Tangible | | 45.0 | | 37.9 |
| | | | (21) 10.5 | (14) 12.1 | (18) 6.1 | | Net Worth | (77) | 18.5 | (56) | 16.7 |
| | | | 4.5 | 5.9 | -.7 | | | | 6.3 | | 4.8 |
| | | 21.3 | 9.1 | 11.0 | 5.5 | | % Profit Before Taxes/Total | | 16.4 | | 17.3 |
| | | 11.5 | 4.1 | 5.3 | 2.3 | | Assets | | 8.0 | | 7.0 |
| | | 3.5 | .4 | .6 | -.4 | | | | 1.4 | | 2.1 |
| | | 49.8 | 2.2 | 6.8 | .6 | | | | 19.7 | | 14.6 |
| | | 12.3 | 1.0 | 1.0 | .4 | | Sales/Net Fixed Assets | | 2.1 | | 2.8 |
| | | 4.4 | .6 | .5 | .3 | | | | .8 | | .6 |
| | | 2.9 | .8 | 1.2 | .5 | | | | 2.0 | | 1.7 |
| | | 1.9 | .5 | .7 | .3 | | Sales/Total Assets | | .9 | | .8 |
| | | 1.0 | .3 | .3 | .2 | | | | .5 | | .4 |
| | | | 10.4 | 3.7 | 19.8 | | | | 3.0 | | 2.6 |
| | | | 14.2 | (14) 15.0 | (12) 24.9 | | % Depr., Dep., Amort./Sales | (68) | 13.0 | (46) | 10.7 |
| | | | 20.9 | 19.3 | 28.5 | | | | 19.8 | | 18.2 |
| | | | | | | | % Officers', Directors' | | 1.7 | | |
| | | | | | | | Owners' Comp/Sales | (15) | 3.5 | | |
| | | | | | | | | | 7.3 | | |
| 18591M | 9236M | 145723M | 347637M | 1135648M | 1836352M | | Net Sales ($) | | 4176839M | | 2685735M |
| 1686M | 3550M | 71129M | 588482M | 1337366M | 3629626M | | Total Assets ($) | | 4052734M | | 3188182M |

© RMA 2024

M = $ thousand   MM = $ million
See Pages viii through xx for Explanation of Ratios and Data

## INFORMATION—Wired Telecommunications Carriers  NAICS 517111

| Comparative Historical Data ||| Type of Statement | Current Data Sorted by Sales ||||||
|---|---|---|---|---|---|---|---|---|---|
| 14 | 24 | 23 | Unqualified | | 1 | | 2 | 9 | 11 |
| 2 | 3 | 7 | Reviewed | | | | 2 | 3 | 2 |
|  | 2 | 2 | Compiled | | | | 1 | 1 | |
|  | 5 | 3 | Tax Returns | | | 2 | | | 1 |
| 24 | 44 | 49 | Other | 6 | 3 | | 3 | 11 | 22 |
| 4/1/21-3/31/22 | 4/1/22-3/31/23 | 4/1/23-3/31/24 | | | 15 (4/1-9/30/23) | | 69 (10/1/23-3/31/24) | | |
| ALL | ALL | ALL | | 0-1MM | 1-3MM | 3-5MM | 5-10MM | 10-25MM | 25MM & OVER |
| 40 | 78 | 84 | NUMBER OF STATEMENTS | 6 | 5 | 4 | 9 | 24 | 36 |
| % | % | % | ASSETS | % | % | % | % | % | % |
| 10.2 | 14.4 | 13.0 | Cash & Equivalents | | | | | 14.1 | 9.3 |
| 7.8 | 9.7 | 8.7 | Trade Receivables (net) | | | | | 7.7 | 8.3 |
| 2.2 | 6.3 | 5.2 | Inventory | | | | | 6.9 | 5.5 |
| 2.4 | 3.1 | 5.5 | All Other Current | | | | | 4.8 | 3.6 |
| 22.6 | 33.5 | 32.5 | Total Current | | | | | 33.5 | 26.6 |
| 54.6 | 45.9 | 49.2 | Fixed Assets (net) | | | | | 47.9 | 53.4 |
| 10.2 | 8.3 | 7.3 | Intangibles (net) | | | | | 3.5 | 11.6 |
| 12.6 | 12.3 | 11.1 | All Other Non-Current | | | | | 15.2 | 8.4 |
| 100.0 | 100.0 | 100.0 | Total | | | | | 100.0 | 100.0 |
| | | | LIABILITIES | | | | | | |
| 4.6 | 4.0 | 4.8 | Notes Payable-Short Term | | | | | 2.3 | 1.4 |
| 2.9 | 2.9 | 3.1 | Cur. Mat.-L.T.D. | | | | | 1.9 | 4.7 |
| 5.8 | 7.1 | 6.4 | Trade Payables | | | | | 4.6 | 6.6 |
| .0 | .0 | .1 | Income Taxes Payable | | | | | .0 | .1 |
| 8.6 | 10.0 | 10.1 | All Other Current | | | | | 13.3 | 10.1 |
| 22.0 | 24.1 | 24.5 | Total Current | | | | | 22.2 | 22.9 |
| 29.9 | 29.2 | 24.1 | Long-Term Debt | | | | | 16.9 | 32.2 |
| 2.0 | 1.2 | 1.4 | Deferred Taxes | | | | | 1.9 | 1.4 |
| 8.5 | 8.5 | 10.5 | All Other Non-Current | | | | | 9.4 | 12.8 |
| 37.6 | 36.9 | 39.4 | Net Worth | | | | | 49.6 | 30.7 |
| 100.0 | 100.0 | 100.0 | Total Liabilities & Net Worth | | | | | 100.0 | 100.0 |
| | | | INCOME DATA | | | | | | |
| 100.0 | 100.0 | 100.0 | Net Sales | | | | | 100.0 | 100.0 |
| | | | Gross Profit | | | | | | |
| 87.7 | 86.4 | 86.7 | Operating Expenses | | | | | 88.8 | 85.0 |
| 12.3 | 13.6 | 13.3 | Operating Profit | | | | | 11.2 | 15.0 |
| .3 | 2.6 | 2.9 | All Other Expenses (net) | | | | | .2 | 5.8 |
| 12.0 | 11.0 | 10.3 | Profit Before Taxes | | | | | 11.1 | 9.2 |
| | | | RATIOS | | | | | | |
| 2.0 | 2.7 | 3.3 | | | | | | 3.9 | 2.4 |
| 1.4 | 1.5 | 1.4 | Current | | | | | 1.7 | 1.2 |
| .7 | .7 | .7 | | | | | | 1.0 | .6 |
| 1.8 | 2.2 | 2.3 | | | | | | 2.7 | 1.4 |
| 1.2 | .9 | .9 | Quick | | | | | 1.4 | .6 |
| .4 | .4 | .5 | | | | | | .6 | .3 |
| 10  35.1 | 9  42.1 | 9  41.9 | | | | | | 13  27.6 | 11  34.2 |
| 23  16.2 | 26  14.1 | 24  15.5 | Sales/Receivables | | | | | 22  16.3 | 31  11.7 |
| 38  9.5 | 43  8.4 | 43  8.5 | | | | | | 68  5.4 | 43  8.4 |
| | | | Cost of Sales/Inventory | | | | | | |
| | | | Cost of Sales/Payables | | | | | | |
| 4.5 | 4.2 | 3.5 | | | | | | 2.4 | 4.0 |
| 15.1 | 11.9 | 12.2 | Sales/Working Capital | | | | | 6.1 | 47.1 |
| -14.1 | -13.6 | -13.7 | | | | | | NM | -8.1 |
| 18.3 | 29.5 | 10.1 | | | | | | 16.1 | 8.5 |
| (34) 4.2 | (69) 6.4 | (68) 4.4 | EBIT/Interest | | | | | (21) 7.0 | (30) 4.0 |
| 1.7 | 2.3 | 1.6 | | | | | | 2.7 | 1.4 |
| 7.3 | 6.8 | 6.8 | Net Profit + Depr., Dep., | | | | | | |
| (12) 5.2 | (21) 4.9 | (19) 3.8 | Amort./Cur. Mat. L/T/D | | | | | | |
| 2.4 | 2.2 | 1.6 | | | | | | | |
| .9 | .6 | .8 | | | | | | .5 | 1.0 |
| 1.7 | 1.5 | 1.4 | Fixed/Worth | | | | | 1.0 | 2.3 |
| 8.2 | 5.2 | 6.1 | | | | | | 2.7 | 19.4 |
| .6 | .5 | .6 | | | | | | .3 | .8 |
| 2.2 | 1.6 | 1.6 | Debt/Worth | | | | | .9 | 2.1 |
| 8.2 | 6.4 | 8.9 | | | | | | 6.1 | 27.4 |
| 30.4 | 31.7 | 27.0 | % Profit Before Taxes/Tangible | | | | | 16.2 | 34.9 |
| (32) 14.4 | (63) 13.5 | (69) 10.8 | Net Worth | | | | | (22) 9.2 | (28) 10.7 |
| 5.7 | 5.1 | 4.4 | | | | | | 3.1 | 4.8 |
| 13.3 | 14.9 | 12.9 | % Profit Before Taxes/Total | | | | | 9.5 | 14.0 |
| 4.0 | 7.1 | 4.8 | Assets | | | | | 4.0 | 4.5 |
| 1.1 | 2.0 | .0 | | | | | | .3 | -.1 |
| 4.3 | 11.9 | 6.6 | | | | | | 5.0 | 6.6 |
| .9 | 1.5 | 1.3 | Sales/Net Fixed Assets | | | | | 1.0 | .9 |
| .5 | .6 | .5 | | | | | | .5 | .4 |
| .9 | 1.3 | 1.5 | | | | | | 1.3 | 1.2 |
| .4 | .8 | .6 | Sales/Total Assets | | | | | .5 | .6 |
| .3 | .3 | .3 | | | | | | .3 | .3 |
| 6.7 | 2.6 | 4.2 | | | | | | 11.0 | 2.3 |
| (33) 17.0 | (56) 13.6 | (59) 14.8 | % Depr., Dep., Amort./Sales | | | | | (23) 15.1 | (21) 15.5 |
| 21.7 | 20.4 | 20.5 | | | | | | 20.5 | 22.4 |
| | 1.2 | | % Officers', Directors' | | | | | | |
| | (11) 4.2 | | Owners' Comp/Sales | | | | | | |
| | | 5.9 | | | | | | | |
| 1129048M | 2762819M | 3493187M | Net Sales ($) | 3274M | 9532M | 15654M | 69892M | 410524M | 2984311M |
| 2070118M | 4263374M | 5631839M | Total Assets ($) | 933M | 58699M | 34465M | 163951M | 965248M | 4408543M |

© RMA 2024  
M = $ thousand  MM = $ million  
See Pages viii through xx for Explanation of Ratios and Data

# INFORMATION—Wireless Telecommunications Carriers (except Satellite) NAICS 517112

## Current Data Sorted by Assets | Comparative Historical Data

| | | | | | | Type of Statement | | |
|---|---|---|---|---|---|---|---|---|
| | | | 1 | 4 | 4 | Unqualified | 11 | 2 |
| | 1 | | 2 | 1 | | Reviewed | 1 | 1 |
| | 1 | 1 | | | | Compiled | 1 | 2 |
| | 1 | 1 | 2 | | | Tax Returns | 6 | 2 |
| 1 | 5 (4/1-9/30/23) | | 10 | 9 | 7 | Other | 40 | 29 |
| 0-500M | 500M-2MM | 2-10MM | 42 (10/1/23-3/31/24) 10-50MM | 50-100MM | 100-250MM | | 4/1/19-3/31/20 ALL | 4/1/20-3/31/21 ALL |
| 1 | 4 | 4 | 13 | 14 | 11 | NUMBER OF STATEMENTS | 59 | 36 |
| % | % | % | % | % | % | ASSETS | % | % |
| | | | 22.1 | 18.3 | 3.4 | Cash & Equivalents | 16.5 | 21.4 |
| | | | 10.6 | 14.5 | 12.3 | Trade Receivables (net) | 14.8 | 16.6 |
| | | | 5.3 | 8.0 | 6.3 | Inventory | 7.3 | 11.1 |
| | | | 5.1 | 2.9 | 13.5 | All Other Current | 3.9 | 4.4 |
| | | | 43.1 | 43.7 | 35.4 | Total Current | 42.6 | 53.3 |
| | | | 34.8 | 15.0 | 27.3 | Fixed Assets (net) | 35.5 | 28.9 |
| | | | 10.3 | 23.9 | 25.6 | Intangibles (net) | 11.5 | 11.1 |
| | | | 11.9 | 17.4 | 11.7 | All Other Non-Current | 10.4 | 6.7 |
| | | | 100.0 | 100.0 | 100.0 | Total | 100.0 | 100.0 |
| | | | | | | LIABILITIES | | |
| | | | 7.3 | 7.7 | 6.8 | Notes Payable-Short Term | 2.8 | 4.7 |
| | | | 2.9 | 6.0 | 2.0 | Cur. Mat.-L.T.D. | 4.3 | 2.4 |
| | | | 14.1 | 8.4 | 7.2 | Trade Payables | 12.6 | 13.2 |
| | | | .4 | .0 | .0 | Income Taxes Payable | .1 | .1 |
| | | | 16.2 | 9.9 | 7.7 | All Other Current | 8.7 | 26.1 |
| | | | 40.8 | 32.1 | 23.7 | Total Current | 28.5 | 46.4 |
| | | | 16.1 | 25.4 | 29.6 | Long-Term Debt | 26.7 | 16.2 |
| | | | .6 | .0 | .0 | Deferred Taxes | .5 | .5 |
| | | | 4.7 | 12.3 | .9 | All Other Non-Current | 5.9 | 5.5 |
| | | | 37.8 | 30.3 | 45.8 | Net Worth | 38.4 | 31.4 |
| | | | 100.0 | 100.0 | 100.0 | Total Liabilties & Net Worth | 100.0 | 100.0 |
| | | | | | | INCOME DATA | | |
| | | | 100.0 | 100.0 | 100.0 | Net Sales | 100.0 | 100.0 |
| | | | | | | Gross Profit | | |
| | | | 90.0 | 83.3 | 93.8 | Operating Expenses | 87.0 | 88.5 |
| | | | 10.0 | 16.7 | 6.2 | Operating Profit | 13.0 | 11.5 |
| | | | 2.0 | 2.4 | 3.4 | All Other Expenses (net) | 4.1 | 4.7 |
| | | | 8.0 | 14.3 | 2.8 | Profit Before Taxes | 8.9 | 6.8 |
| | | | | | | RATIOS | | |
| | | | 1.5 | 1.7 | 4.0 | | 2.7 | 3.7 |
| | | | .7 | 1.2 | 1.2 | Current | 1.6 | 1.6 |
| | | | .5 | .9 | 1.0 | | .9 | 1.0 |
| | | | 1.4 | 1.4 | 1.8 | | 2.2 | 3.3 |
| | | | .6 | .9 | .6 | Quick | 1.2 | 1.3 |
| | | | .2 | .5 | .5 | | .5 | .6 |
| | | 3 | 107.0 | 19 | 18.9 | 14 | 25.9 | | 11 | 34.3 | 8 | 46.8 |
| | | 20 | 17.9 | 34 | 10.7 | 34 | 10.7 | Sales/Receivables | 23 | 15.7 | 28 | 13.0 |
| | | 33 | 11.1 | 40 | 9.2 | 46 | 8.0 | | 42 | 8.7 | 62 | 5.9 |
| | | | | | | Cost of Sales/Inventory | | |
| | | | | | | Cost of Sales/Payables | | |
| | | | 21.8 | 10.7 | 3.3 | | 4.3 | 2.6 |
| | | | -13.2 | 29.4 | 30.7 | Sales/Working Capital | 14.0 | 10.3 |
| | | | -5.4 | -101.8 | -129.7 | | -73.3 | NM |
| | | | 45.6 | 33.3 | | | 26.3 | 29.1 |
| | | (11) | 5.9 | (12) | 15.8 | | EBIT/Interest | (47) | 10.5 | (23) | 6.3 |
| | | | 1.8 | .6 | | | 2.7 | 2.5 |
| | | | | | | Net Profit + Depr., Dep., Amort./Cur. Mat. L/T/D | | 4.3 |
| | | | | | | | (10) | 2.7 |
| | | | | | | | | 2.1 |
| | | | .2 | .1 | .1 | | .2 | .1 |
| | | | 1.0 | 1.8 | 1.0 | Fixed/Worth | .9 | 1.0 |
| | | | 12.6 | -.3 | 108.9 | | 2.5 | 3.9 |
| | | | .7 | 2.0 | .5 | | .6 | .6 |
| | | | 2.0 | 3.1 | 3.6 | Debt/Worth | 1.2 | 1.8 |
| | | | 32.0 | -3.7 | 114.2 | | 8.4 | 13.2 |
| | | | 35.6 | | | | 56.4 | 78.5 |
| | | (11) | 13.5 | | | % Profit Before Taxes/Tangible Net Worth | (47) | 30.1 | (29) | 38.8 |
| | | | 4.7 | | | | 7.0 | 8.3 |
| | | | 17.2 | 23.7 | 13.2 | | 23.8 | 23.1 |
| | | | 5.2 | 13.1 | 4.4 | % Profit Before Taxes/Total Assets | 10.9 | 8.7 |
| | | | 1.4 | -1.0 | -.7 | | 1.9 | 2.2 |
| | | | 35.7 | 98.5 | 40.7 | | 38.7 | 31.8 |
| | | | 5.9 | 25.7 | 4.5 | Sales/Net Fixed Assets | 4.1 | 8.5 |
| | | | .7 | 6.3 | .9 | | 1.0 | 1.6 |
| | | | 2.0 | 2.5 | 1.8 | | 2.5 | 2.9 |
| | | | 1.5 | 1.6 | .7 | Sales/Total Assets | 1.3 | 1.4 |
| | | | .5 | 1.0 | .4 | | .7 | .6 |
| | | | 1.0 | | | | 2.6 | 2.7 |
| | | (11) | 4.8 | | | % Depr., Dep., Amort./Sales | (35) | 7.7 | (18) | 8.5 |
| | | | 19.3 | | | | 16.7 | 13.1 |
| | | | | | | % Officers', Directors' Owners' Comp/Sales | | |
| 69M | 33250M | 73966M | 673134M | 1764195M | 1639672M | Net Sales ($) | 2718372M | 2007326M |
| 174M | 4541M | 17892M | 380983M | 1030083M | 1620669M | Total Assets ($) | 2860459M | 1704279M |

© RMA 2024

M = $ thousand    MM = $ million
See Pages viii through xx for Explanation of Ratios and Data

# INFORMATION—Wireless Telecommunications Carriers (except Satellite) NAICS 517112

## Comparative Historical Data | Current Data Sorted by Sales

| Comparative Historical Data | | | | | Current Data Sorted by Sales | | | | | | |
|---|---|---|---|---|---|---|---|---|---|---|---|
| | | | | **Type of Statement** | | | | | | | |
| | 8 | 8 | 9 | Unqualified | | | | | 1 | 8 | |
| | 4 | 4 | 5 | Reviewed | 1 | | 1 | 1 | 1 | 1 | |
| | 1 | 1 | 1 | Compiled | | | | 1 | | | |
| | 6 | 4 | 2 | Tax Returns | | | | | 2 | | |
| | 20 | 28 | 30 | Other | 1 | | 3 | 3 | 4 | 22 | |
| | 4/1/21- | 4/1/22- | 4/1/23- | | | 5 (4/1-9/30/23) | | 42 (10/1/23-3/31/24) | | | |
| | 3/31/22 | 3/31/23 | 3/31/24 | | 0-1MM | 1-3MM | 3-5MM | 5-10MM | 10-25MM | 25MM & OVER | |
| | ALL | ALL | ALL | | | | | | | | |
| | 39 | 45 | 47 | **NUMBER OF STATEMENTS** | 2 | | 1 | 5 | 8 | 31 | |
| | % | % | % | **ASSETS** | % | % | % | % | % | % | |
| | 24.5 | 14.6 | 16.1 | Cash & Equivalents | | | | | | 16.3 | |
| | 11.3 | 19.0 | 14.8 | Trade Receivables (net) | | | | | | 15.9 | |
| | 7.9 | 11.5 | 8.1 | Inventory | | | | | | 7.8 | |
| | 3.3 | 4.5 | 5.8 | All Other Current | | D | | | | 7.6 | |
| | 47.1 | 49.6 | 44.8 | Total Current | | A | | | | 47.5 | |
| | 26.1 | 27.5 | 25.2 | Fixed Assets (net) | | T | | | | 16.9 | |
| | 20.6 | 11.2 | 16.8 | Intangibles (net) | | A | | | | 21.2 | |
| | 6.2 | 11.7 | 13.2 | All Other Non-Current | | | | | | 14.4 | |
| | 100.0 | 100.0 | 100.0 | Total | | N | | | | 100.0 | |
| | | | | **LIABILITIES** | | O | | | | | |
| | 2.7 | 3.0 | 7.3 | Notes Payable-Short Term | | T | | | | 7.6 | |
| | 5.5 | 3.4 | 3.2 | Cur. Mat.-L.T.D. | | | | | | 3.7 | |
| | 10.9 | 13.6 | 8.5 | Trade Payables | | A | | | | 11.7 | |
| | .1 | .2 | .1 | Income Taxes Payable | | V | | | | .0 | |
| | 11.9 | 9.5 | 11.0 | All Other Current | | A | | | | 11.5 | |
| | 31.2 | 29.7 | 30.1 | Total Current | | I | | | | 34.5 | |
| | 26.2 | 21.7 | 20.4 | Long-Term Debt | | L | | | | 23.1 | |
| | .5 | .3 | .2 | Deferred Taxes | | A | | | | .1 | |
| | 2.5 | 4.1 | 6.6 | All Other Non-Current | | B | | | | 4.7 | |
| | 39.6 | 44.1 | 42.7 | Net Worth | | L | | | | 37.6 | |
| | 100.0 | 100.0 | 100.0 | Total Liabilities & Net Worth | | E | | | | 100.0 | |
| | | | | **INCOME DATA** | | | | | | | |
| | 100.0 | 100.0 | 100.0 | Net Sales | | | | | | 100.0 | |
| | 87.7 | 88.7 | 88.1 | Gross Profit | | | | | | 90.0 | |
| | 12.3 | 11.3 | 11.9 | Operating Expenses | | | | | | 10.0 | |
| | -.1 | 3.6 | 1.8 | Operating Profit | | | | | | 1.9 | |
| | 12.4 | 7.7 | 10.1 | All Other Expenses (net) | | | | | | 8.1 | |
| | | | | Profit Before Taxes | | | | | | | |
| | | | | **RATIOS** | | | | | | | |
| | 3.7 | 4.6 | 3.3 | | | | | | | 2.0 | |
| | 1.9 | 1.9 | 1.2 | Current | | | | | | 1.2 | |
| | .9 | .9 | .8 | | | | | | | .9 | |
| | 3.1 | 3.6 | 1.8 | | | | | | | 1.6 | |
| | 1.5 | 1.4 | .9 | Quick | | | | | | .9 | |
| | .5 | .6 | .5 | | | | | | | .5 | |
| 2 | 179.4 | 9 | 39.1 | 14 | 26.8 | Sales/Receivables | | | | 18 | 19.9 |
| 16 | 23.2 | 40 | 9.2 | 27 | 13.3 | | | | | 34 | 10.7 |
| 42 | 8.6 | 59 | 6.2 | 40 | 9.1 | | | | | 41 | 8.9 |
| | | | | Cost of Sales/Inventory | | | | | | | |
| | | | | Cost of Sales/Payables | | | | | | | |
| | 4.1 | 3.9 | 7.0 | | | | | | | 7.1 | |
| | 9.5 | 10.9 | 37.5 | Sales/Working Capital | | | | | | 30.7 | |
| | -133.7 | -37.9 | -62.0 | | | | | | | -115.0 | |
| | 33.0 | 38.4 | 44.1 | | | | | | | 38.7 | |
| (33) | 17.2 | (36) | 24.2 | (36) | 13.3 | EBIT/Interest | | | | (27) | 12.8 |
| | 5.8 | 4.2 | 1.4 | | | | | | | .9 | |
| | | | | Net Profit + Depr., Dep., Amort./Cur. Mat. L/T/D | | | | | | | |
| | .2 | .1 | .1 | | | | | | | .1 | |
| | 1.3 | .5 | 1.0 | Fixed/Worth | | | | | | 1.0 | |
| | -7.1 | 3.7 | 10.6 | | | | | | | -.7 | |
| | .7 | .4 | .7 | | | | | | | .9 | |
| | 1.3 | 1.4 | 2.4 | Debt/Worth | | | | | | 3.5 | |
| | -8.5 | 14.9 | 33.6 | | | | | | | -4.8 | |
| | 78.6 | 63.9 | 87.0 | % Profit Before Taxes/Tangible Net Worth | | | | | | 93.9 | |
| (27) | 37.3 | (36) | 39.0 | (38) | 36.2 | | | | | (23) | 37.5 |
| | 6.9 | 8.4 | 7.2 | | | | | | | 7.5 | |
| | 34.7 | 27.8 | 21.5 | % Profit Before Taxes/Total Assets | | | | | | 19.9 | |
| | 16.1 | 12.1 | 11.3 | | | | | | | 11.5 | |
| | 4.0 | 2.9 | 1.8 | | | | | | | .2 | |
| | 82.2 | 70.0 | 73.3 | Sales/Net Fixed Assets | | | | | | 121.2 | |
| | 9.5 | 10.0 | 9.3 | | | | | | | 15.2 | |
| | 1.9 | 2.0 | 1.9 | | | | | | | 4.5 | |
| | 2.9 | 2.9 | 2.9 | Sales/Total Assets | | | | | | 2.7 | |
| | 1.6 | 1.5 | 1.5 | | | | | | | 1.7 | |
| | .7 | .8 | .6 | | | | | | | .9 | |
| | 2.1 | .7 | .5 | | | | | | | .2 | |
| (26) | 6.2 | (25) | 5.7 | (31) | 2.6 | % Depr., Dep., Amort./Sales | | | | (17) | 2.0 |
| | 14.1 | 12.1 | 11.6 | | | | | | | 8.3 | |
| | .4 | | .8 | % Officers', Directors' Owners' Comp/Sales | | | | | | | |
| (13) | .9 | (10) | 1.2 | | | | | | | | |
| | 6.4 | | 2.7 | | | | | | | | |
| | 2127853M | 2005206M | 4184286M | Net Sales ($) | 611M | | 3624M | 32918M | 135523M | 4011610M | |
| | 1724801M | 1871300M | 3054342M | Total Assets ($) | 1039M | | 2907M | 106894M | 154405M | 2789097M | |

M = $ thousand    MM = $ million
See Pages viii through xx for Explanation of Ratios and Data

© RMA 2024

# INFORMATION—Telecommunications Resellers  NAICS 517121

## Current Data Sorted by Assets

| | | | | | | Type of Statement | | | | |
|---|---|---|---|---|---|---|---|---|---|---|
| | | | | | 1 | Unqualified | | | | |
| | | 1 | | 1 | | Reviewed | | | | |
| | | | | 1 | | Compiled | | | | |
| | 3 | | | | 1 | Tax Returns | | | | |
| 1 | 5 | 1 | 2 | 4 | 4 | Other | | | | |
| | 10 (4/1-9/30/23) | | | 21 (10/1/23-3/31/24) | | | | | | |
| 0-500M | 500M-2MM | 2-10MM | 10-50MM | 50-100MM | 100-250MM | | | | | |
| 1 | 8 | 4 | 6 | 3 | 9 | NUMBER OF STATEMENTS | | | | |

## Comparative Historical Data

| | | |
|---|---|---|
| Unqualified | 8 | 7 |
| Reviewed | 4 | 1 |
| Compiled | 4 | 1 |
| Tax Returns | 5 | 2 |
| Other | 29 | 26 |
| | 4/1/19- | 4/1/20- |
| | 3/31/20 | 3/31/21 |
| | ALL | ALL |
| NUMBER OF STATEMENTS | 50 | 37 |

| | 0-500M % | 500M-2MM % | 2-10MM % | 10-50MM % | 50-100MM % | 100-250MM % | | ALL % | ALL % |
|---|---|---|---|---|---|---|---|---|---|
| | | | | | | | **ASSETS** | | |
| | | | | | | | Cash & Equivalents | 15.7 | 15.9 |
| | | | | | | | Trade Receivables (net) | 21.7 | 23.5 |
| | | | | | | | Inventory | 7.5 | 4.5 |
| | | | | | | | All Other Current | 8.7 | 7.1 |
| | | | | | | | Total Current | 53.7 | 51.0 |
| | | | | | | | Fixed Assets (net) | 29.0 | 26.0 |
| | | | | | | | Intangibles (net) | 7.3 | 17.4 |
| | | | | | | | All Other Non-Current | 10.0 | 5.6 |
| | | | | | | | Total | 100.0 | 100.0 |
| | | | | | | | **LIABILITIES** | | |
| | | | | | | | Notes Payable-Short Term | 8.4 | 6.8 |
| | | | | | | | Cur. Mat.-L.T.D. | 4.8 | 3.3 |
| | | | | | | | Trade Payables | 16.0 | 14.4 |
| | | | | | | | Income Taxes Payable | .1 | .1 |
| | | | | | | | All Other Current | 15.0 | 17.5 |
| | | | | | | | Total Current | 44.4 | 42.2 |
| | | | | | | | Long-Term Debt | 26.2 | 26.3 |
| | | | | | | | Deferred Taxes | 1.2 | 1.3 |
| | | | | | | | All Other Non-Current | 6.8 | 4.6 |
| | | | | | | | Net Worth | 21.6 | 25.7 |
| | | | | | | | Total Liabilities & Net Worth | 100.0 | 100.0 |
| | | | | | | | **INCOME DATA** | | |
| | | | | | | | Net Sales | 100.0 | 100.0 |
| | | | | | | | Gross Profit | | |
| | | | | | | | Operating Expenses | 93.0 | 96.3 |
| | | | | | | | Operating Profit | 7.0 | 3.7 |
| | | | | | | | All Other Expenses (net) | 1.5 | -.1 |
| | | | | | | | Profit Before Taxes | 5.6 | 3.8 |
| | | | | | | | **RATIOS** | | |
| | | | | | | | Current | 2.5 | 2.2 |
| | | | | | | | | 1.2 | 1.2 |
| | | | | | | | | .8 | .7 |
| | | | | | | | Quick | 1.6 | 1.4 |
| | | | | | | | | .8 | .9 |
| | | | | | | | | .6 | .5 |
| | | | | | | | Sales/Receivables | 10  35.8 | 16  23.1 |
| | | | | | | | | 28  12.9 | 34  10.6 |
| | | | | | | | | 59  6.2 | 58  6.3 |
| | | | | | | | Cost of Sales/Inventory | | |
| | | | | | | | Cost of Sales/Payables | | |
| | | | | | | | Sales/Working Capital | 7.1 | 6.6 |
| | | | | | | | | 25.0 | 36.0 |
| | | | | | | | | -36.5 | -14.7 |
| | | | | | | | EBIT/Interest | 16.2 | 6.6 |
| | | | | | | | | (37)  4.4 | (30)  3.8 |
| | | | | | | | | -.5 | -2.4 |
| | | | | | | | Net Profit + Depr., Dep., Amort./Cur. Mat. L/T/D | 9.4 | |
| | | | | | | | | (16)  3.3 | |
| | | | | | | | | 1.9 | |
| | | | | | | | Fixed/Worth | .2 | .5 |
| | | | | | | | | .8 | 1.9 |
| | | | | | | | | -3.7 | -.8 |
| | | | | | | | Debt/Worth | .6 | 1.2 |
| | | | | | | | | 2.7 | 3.3 |
| | | | | | | | | -32.7 | -3.8 |
| | | | | | | | % Profit Before Taxes/Tangible Net Worth | 56.6 | 65.7 |
| | | | | | | | | (35)  27.7 | (21)  13.3 |
| | | | | | | | | 9.4 | 3.8 |
| | | | | | | | % Profit Before Taxes/Total Assets | 17.0 | 9.9 |
| | | | | | | | | 8.0 | 4.6 |
| | | | | | | | | 2.9 | -6.7 |
| | | | | | | | Sales/Net Fixed Assets | 55.6 | 90.3 |
| | | | | | | | | 13.8 | 19.4 |
| | | | | | | | | 2.0 | 1.7 |
| | | | | | | | Sales/Total Assets | 3.7 | 3.1 |
| | | | | | | | | 1.8 | 1.9 |
| | | | | | | | | .8 | .7 |
| | | | | | | | % Depr., Dep., Amort./Sales | .7 | 1.8 |
| | | | | | | | | (36)  2.1 | (17)  3.7 |
| | | | | | | | | 14.6 | 17.2 |
| | | | | | | | % Officers', Directors' Owners' Comp/Sales | | |
| 438M | 72230M | 110757M | 299146M | 473141M | 1784455M | Net Sales ($) | 2605667M | 3169583M |
| 182M | 9709M | 26411M | 99853M | 208582M | 1544161M | Total Assets ($) | 1831032M | 2355501M |

© RMA 2024

M = $ thousand  MM = $ million
See Pages viii through xx for Explanation of Ratios and Data

# INFORMATION—Telecommunications Resellers  NAICS 517121

## Comparative Historical Data | Current Data Sorted by Sales

| Comparative Historical Data | | | | | Type of Statement | | Current Data Sorted by Sales | | | | |
|---|---|---|---|---|---|---|---|---|---|---|---|
| | 5 | | 8 | 5 | Unqualified | | | | | 1 | 4 |
| | 2 | | 2 | 1 | Reviewed | | | | | | 1 |
| | 2 | | | 2 | Compiled | | | | | | 2 |
| | 4 | | 1 | 4 | Tax Returns | | | 1 | 1 | 2 | |
| | 15 | | 24 | 19 | Other | 1 | 2 | 1 | 1 | 3 | 12 |
| | 4/1/21-3/31/22 ALL | | 4/1/22-3/31/23 ALL | 4/1/23-3/31/24 ALL | | 0-1MM | 10 (4/1-9/30/23) 1-3MM | 3-5MM | 21 (10/1/23-3/31/24) 5-10MM | 10-25MM | 25MM & OVER |
| | 28 | | 35 | 31 | NUMBER OF STATEMENTS | 1 | 2 | | 1 | 6 | 19 |
| | % | | % | % | ASSETS | % | % | % | % | % | % |
| | 24.9 | | 23.1 | 18.3 | Cash & Equivalents | | | | | | 13.9 |
| | 19.1 | | 17.7 | 24.6 | Trade Receivables (net) | | | | | | 26.3 |
| | 4.9 | | 7.2 | 8.7 | Inventory | | | | | | 9.0 |
| | 5.3 | | 4.5 | 5.4 | All Other Current | | | | | | 7.3 |
| | 54.2 | | 52.5 | 57.0 | Total Current | | | | | | 56.5 |
| | 24.3 | | 25.4 | 16.2 | Fixed Assets (net) | | | | | | 17.0 |
| | 14.0 | | 14.1 | 16.9 | Intangibles (net) | | | | | | 14.7 |
| | 7.5 | | 8.1 | 9.8 | All Other Non-Current | | | | | | 11.8 |
| | 100.0 | | 100.0 | 100.0 | Total | | | | | | 100.0 |
| | | | | | LIABILITIES | | | | | | |
| | 2.0 | | 3.2 | 3.8 | Notes Payable-Short Term | | | | | | 3.4 |
| | 6.6 | | 2.8 | 2.9 | Cur. Mat.-L.T.D. | | | | | | 2.4 |
| | 10.2 | | 12.9 | 19.7 | Trade Payables | | | | | | 21.7 |
| | .6 | | .1 | .3 | Income Taxes Payable | | | | | | .5 |
| | 12.8 | | 12.0 | 18.3 | All Other Current | | | | | | 16.4 |
| | 32.1 | | 31.0 | 45.0 | Total Current | | | | | | 44.4 |
| | 22.6 | | 25.2 | 30.0 | Long-Term Debt | | | | | | 27.9 |
| | 2.1 | | .4 | .5 | Deferred Taxes | | | | | | .9 |
| | 5.0 | | 10.1 | 17.8 | All Other Non-Current | | | | | | 21.2 |
| | 38.2 | | 33.3 | 6.6 | Net Worth | | | | | | 5.5 |
| | 100.0 | | 100.0 | 100.0 | Total Liabilities & Net Worth | | | | | | 100.0 |
| | | | | | INCOME DATA | | | | | | |
| | 100.0 | | 100.0 | 100.0 | Net Sales | | | | | | 100.0 |
| | | | | | Gross Profit | | | | | | |
| | 90.7 | | 92.8 | 96.6 | Operating Expenses | | | | | | 94.5 |
| | 9.3 | | 7.2 | 3.4 | Operating Profit | | | | | | 5.5 |
| | -.9 | | 1.0 | .8 | All Other Expenses (net) | | | | | | 1.2 |
| | 10.3 | | 6.2 | 2.6 | Profit Before Taxes | | | | | | 4.2 |
| | | | | | RATIOS | | | | | | |
| | 2.9 | | 2.4 | 1.7 | | | | | | | 1.7 |
| | 1.6 | | 1.5 | 1.3 | Current | | | | | | 1.5 |
| | 1.1 | | 1.0 | 1.0 | | | | | | | 1.0 |
| | 2.8 | | 2.3 | 1.4 | | | | | | | 1.4 |
| | 1.2 | | .9 | .9 | Quick | | | | | | .9 |
| | .6 | | .5 | .6 | | | | | | | .6 |
| 15 | 24.3 | 11 | 32.3 | 19 19.7 | | | | | | 30 | 12.0 |
| 28 | 13.0 | 19 | 19.1 | 35 10.3 | Sales/Receivables | | | | | 38 | 9.6 |
| 41 | 8.8 | 36 | 10.1 | 58 6.3 | | | | | | 73 | 5.0 |
| | | | | | Cost of Sales/Inventory | | | | | | |
| | | | | | Cost of Sales/Payables | | | | | | |
| | 4.6 | | 6.0 | 8.2 | | | | | | | 5.3 |
| | 12.5 | | 13.6 | 39.8 | Sales/Working Capital | | | | | | 14.9 |
| | 118.0 | | 207.5 | -110.6 | | | | | | | -110.6 |
| | 32.7 | | 9.8 | 20.3 | | | | | | | 22.8 |
| (25) | 11.8 | (24) | 2.7 | (26) 5.4 | EBIT/Interest | | | | | (16) | 4.1 |
| | 3.4 | | .7 | 1.9 | | | | | | | 1.8 |
| | | | | | Net Profit + Depr., Dep., Amort./Cur. Mat. L/T/D | | | | | | |
| | .1 | | .0 | .1 | | | | | | | .3 |
| | .5 | | 1.1 | .7 | Fixed/Worth | | | | | | .7 |
| | 5.1 | | -1.8 | -.4 | | | | | | | -.4 |
| | .8 | | .7 | 1.3 | | | | | | | 1.3 |
| | 2.8 | | 2.3 | 9.6 | Debt/Worth | | | | | | 7.7 |
| | 46.1 | | -11.4 | -3.2 | | | | | | | -3.9 |
| | 78.2 | | 64.3 | 49.5 | % Profit Before Taxes/Tangible Net Worth | | | | | | 42.6 |
| (22) | 31.2 | (25) | 19.9 | (16) 26.2 | | | | | | (12) | 26.2 |
| | 9.4 | | 5.6 | 1.9 | | | | | | | 1.9 |
| | 33.1 | | 22.4 | 22.0 | % Profit Before Taxes/Total Assets | | | | | | 16.2 |
| | 9.4 | | 6.8 | 8.2 | | | | | | | 3.5 |
| | 3.1 | | -.5 | 1.1 | | | | | | | 1.1 |
| | 184.2 | | 276.0 | 999.8 | | | | | | | 55.3 |
| | 15.0 | | 25.7 | 29.6 | Sales/Net Fixed Assets | | | | | | 11.9 |
| | 1.8 | | 1.4 | 8.4 | | | | | | | 5.7 |
| | 4.6 | | 4.8 | 3.9 | | | | | | | 3.7 |
| | 1.5 | | 1.7 | 2.3 | Sales/Total Assets | | | | | | 1.6 |
| | .5 | | .6 | 1.3 | | | | | | | 1.0 |
| | .6 | | .2 | .4 | | | | | | | .3 |
| (18) | 4.9 | (21) | 2.2 | (13) 1.5 | % Depr., Dep., Amort./Sales | | | | | (10) | 1.6 |
| | 14.9 | | 18.3 | 5.2 | | | | | | | 5.0 |
| | | | | | % Officers', Directors' Owners' Comp/Sales | | | | | | |
| | 1229710M | | 3796441M | 2740167M | Net Sales ($) | 438M | 3567M | 3726M | 11398M | 105655M | 2615383M |
| | 1330810M | | 1879351M | 1888898M | Total Assets ($) | 182M | 2339M | 1065M | 2997M | 33680M | 1848635M |

© RMA 2024   M = $ thousand   MM = $ million
See Pages viii through xx for Explanation of Ratios and Data

# INFORMATION—All Other Telecommunications NAICS 517810

| Current Data Sorted by Assets | | | | | | | Comparative Historical Data | |
|---|---|---|---|---|---|---|---|---|
| | | | 1 | 4 | 4 | 4 | **Type of Statement** | |
| | | | 2 | 5 | | | Unqualified | 16 12 |
| | | 1 | | | | 1 | Reviewed | 5 1 |
| | | 2 | 4 | 3 | | | Compiled | 3 1 |
| 1 | 12 (4/1-9/30/23) | 6 | 10 | 14 | 7 | 9 | Tax Returns | 8 2 |
| | | | | 66 (10/1/23-3/31/24) | | | Other | 52 39 |
| 0-500M | 500M-2MM | 2-10MM | 10-50MM | 50-100MM | 100-250MM | | | 4/1/19-3/31/20 ALL | 4/1/20-3/31/21 ALL |
| 1 | 9 | 17 | 26 | 11 | 14 | | NUMBER OF STATEMENTS | 84 | 55 |
| % | % | % | % | % | % | | **ASSETS** | % | % |
| | | 17.8 | 15.9 | 4.8 | 6.0 | | Cash & Equivalents | 15.2 | 22.3 |
| | | 28.3 | 25.8 | 18.8 | 9.7 | | Trade Receivables (net) | 27.6 | 20.4 |
| | | 15.2 | 6.7 | 6.3 | 6.8 | | Inventory | 4.4 | 3.7 |
| | | 4.3 | 6.3 | 6.1 | 8.4 | | All Other Current | 6.5 | 6.5 |
| | | 65.6 | 54.7 | 36.0 | 31.0 | | Total Current | 53.7 | 52.9 |
| | | 14.3 | 22.6 | 26.6 | 41.7 | | Fixed Assets (net) | 19.9 | 19.2 |
| | | 7.7 | 9.2 | 25.9 | 12.1 | | Intangibles (net) | 14.8 | 20.6 |
| | | 12.4 | 13.5 | 11.5 | 15.3 | | All Other Non-Current | 11.6 | 7.3 |
| | | 100.0 | 100.0 | 100.0 | 100.0 | | Total | 100.0 | 100.0 |
| | | | | | | | **LIABILITIES** | | |
| | | 8.2 | 1.5 | 8.2 | 3.7 | | Notes Payable-Short Term | 7.7 | 6.6 |
| | | 4.9 | 1.7 | 5.1 | 8.5 | | Cur. Mat.-L.T.D. | 3.7 | 2.8 |
| | | 24.6 | 14.7 | 7.1 | 3.5 | | Trade Payables | 14.4 | 8.1 |
| | | .0 | .2 | 1.2 | .0 | | Income Taxes Payable | .2 | .2 |
| | | 7.9 | 27.2 | 13.8 | 13.5 | | All Other Current | 15.5 | 21.4 |
| | | 45.6 | 45.2 | 35.3 | 29.2 | | Total Current | 41.5 | 39.1 |
| | | 23.2 | 14.5 | 35.0 | 53.7 | | Long-Term Debt | 18.9 | 29.7 |
| | | .0 | .2 | .4 | .3 | | Deferred Taxes | .3 | .3 |
| | | 6.2 | 10.9 | 46.9 | 8.4 | | All Other Non-Current | 6.3 | 5.8 |
| | | 25.0 | 29.2 | -17.6 | 8.4 | | Net Worth | 33.0 | 25.1 |
| | | 100.0 | 100.0 | 100.0 | 100.0 | | Total Liabilities & Net Worth | 100.0 | 100.0 |
| | | | | | | | **INCOME DATA** | | |
| | | 100.0 | 100.0 | 100.0 | 100.0 | | Net Sales | 100.0 | 100.0 |
| | | | | | | | Gross Profit | | |
| | | 95.7 | 93.1 | 88.0 | 87.2 | | Operating Expenses | 89.5 | 87.5 |
| | | 4.3 | 6.9 | 12.0 | 12.8 | | Operating Profit | 10.5 | 12.5 |
| | | 1.6 | 3.7 | 7.5 | 9.2 | | All Other Expenses (net) | 2.4 | 1.3 |
| | | 2.6 | 3.2 | 4.4 | 3.6 | | Profit Before Taxes | 8.1 | 11.3 |
| | | | | | | | **RATIOS** | | |
| | | 5.0 | 2.7 | 2.0 | 2.8 | | | 2.4 | 2.8 |
| | | 1.9 | 1.9 | 1.3 | 1.4 | | Current | 1.4 | 1.6 |
| | | 1.3 | .8 | .8 | 1.0 | | | .9 | 1.2 |
| | | 3.1 | 2.4 | 1.4 | 1.5 | | | 1.8 | 2.6 |
| | | 1.4 | 1.5 | .8 | .8 | | Quick | 1.1 | 1.5 |
| | | .5 | .4 | .5 | .1 | | | .6 | .7 |
| | | 22 16.8 | 14 26.1 | 34 10.7 | 14 27.0 | | | 17 21.8 | 9 41.8 |
| | | 40 9.2 | 44 8.3 | 45 8.2 | 24 15.2 | | Sales/Receivables | 38 9.5 | 37 9.8 |
| | | 72 5.1 | 70 5.2 | 73 5.0 | 65 5.6 | | | 65 5.6 | 61 6.0 |
| | | | | | | | Cost of Sales/Inventory | | |
| | | | | | | | Cost of Sales/Payables | | |
| | | 4.2 | 4.3 | 6.3 | 3.3 | | | 6.6 | 5.4 |
| | | 11.6 | 9.0 | 21.5 | 8.2 | | Sales/Working Capital | 18.3 | 11.3 |
| | | 29.0 | -29.1 | -13.5 | NM | | | -29.8 | 45.6 |
| | | 62.8 | 50.8 | 7.1 | 7.5 | | | 19.4 | 25.2 |
| | | (15) 8.4 | (18) 5.7 | (10) 3.6 | (11) 2.7 | | EBIT/Interest | (70) 7.1 | (41) 11.4 |
| | | -6.6 | 2.6 | 1.0 | .9 | | | 1.5 | 2.1 |
| | | | | | | | Net Profit + Depr., Dep., | 6.9 | 5.9 |
| | | | | | | | Amort./Cur. Mat. L/T/D | (14) 4.7 | (11) 3.3 |
| | | | | | | | | 3.7 | 2.4 |
| | | .0 | .1 | .6 | .2 | | | .1 | .3 |
| | | .3 | .5 | 1.5 | 1.0 | | Fixed/Worth | .8 | 1.8 |
| | | .9 | 2.3 | -.1 | 2.6 | | | -2.1 | -1.2 |
| | | .9 | .5 | 2.1 | 1.1 | | | .7 | 1.2 |
| | | 1.9 | 1.6 | 4.5 | 1.7 | | Debt/Worth | 2.4 | 9.1 |
| | | 5.0 | 9.3 | -1.5 | NM | | | -7.8 | -3.5 |
| | | 68.0 | 46.9 | | 21.3 | | | 77.1 | 132.8 |
| | | (14) 35.3 | (22) 30.7 | (11) 7.5 | | | % Profit Before Taxes/Tangible Net Worth | (57) 36.7 | (33) 59.9 |
| | | -14.7 | 9.3 | | -.7 | | | 12.5 | 22.4 |
| | | 27.6 | 19.8 | 12.9 | 5.9 | | % Profit Before Taxes/Total Assets | 21.5 | 38.0 |
| | | 9.1 | 12.7 | 10.0 | 3.0 | | | 8.9 | 14.5 |
| | | -9.0 | 1.6 | .2 | -1.4 | | | 4.4 | 4.4 |
| | | 459.3 | 45.1 | 17.9 | 30.0 | | | 157.0 | 106.8 |
| | | 44.4 | 13.5 | 7.4 | 5.3 | | Sales/Net Fixed Assets | 27.6 | 25.5 |
| | | 6.7 | 3.6 | 3.4 | .4 | | | 5.5 | 6.6 |
| | | 3.7 | 2.6 | 1.8 | 1.3 | | | 3.2 | 2.9 |
| | | 2.3 | 2.2 | 1.6 | .5 | | Sales/Total Assets | 1.9 | 2.1 |
| | | 1.8 | 1.5 | .7 | .3 | | | .9 | .9 |
| | | | .8 | | | | | .7 | .8 |
| | | (21) 2.6 | | | | | % Depr., Dep., Amort./Sales | (48) 2.2 | (26) 1.7 |
| | | 6.0 | | | | | | 6.7 | 12.1 |
| | | | | | | | | 1.7 | |
| | | | | | | | % Officers', Directors' Owners' Comp/Sales | (18) 3.5 | |
| | | | | | | | | 8.0 | |
| 4676M | 85689M | 195880M | 1113475M | 1031821M | 1870261M | | Net Sales ($) | 3660351M | 3010180M |
| 314M | 11036M | 79665M | 553486M | 797180M | 2448238M | | Total Assets ($) | 3046624M | 2564754M |

M = $ thousand   MM = $ million
See Pages viii through xx for Explanation of Ratios and Data

© RMA 2024

# INFORMATION—All Other Telecommunications   NAICS 517810

## Comparative Historical Data / Current Data Sorted by Sales

| | | | | | Type of Statement | | | | | | |
|---|---|---|---|---|---|---|---|---|---|---|---|
| | 17 | | 15 | 13 | Unqualified | | | | | 2 | 11 |
| | 2 | | 2 | 7 | Reviewed | | | 1 | 2 | 2 | 4 |
| | 3 | | 1 | 2 | Compiled | | | | | | 1 |
| | 2 | | 6 | 9 | Tax Returns | | | 1 | 2 | 4 | 3 |
| | 28 | | 54 | 47 | Other | | 3 | 4 | 4 | 10 | 26 |
| | 4/1/21-3/31/22 | | 4/1/22-3/31/23 | 4/1/23-3/31/24 | | | 12 (4/1-9/30/23) | | | 66 (10/1/23-3/31/24) | |
| | ALL | | ALL | ALL | | 0-1MM | 1-3MM | 3-5MM | 5-10MM | 10-25MM | 25MM & OVER |
| | 52 | | 78 | 78 | NUMBER OF STATEMENTS | 3 | 5 | 7 | 18 | 45 | |
| | % | | % | % | ASSETS | % | % | % | % | % | % |
| | 19.6 | | 16.5 | 17.5 | Cash & Equivalents | | | | | 27.9 | 10.9 |
| | 16.1 | | 20.9 | 21.4 | Trade Receivables (net) | | | | | 25.6 | 20.2 |
| | 4.5 | | 7.0 | 9.0 | Inventory | DATA NOT AVAILABLE | | | | 11.9 | 7.4 |
| | 8.6 | | 6.2 | 5.4 | All Other Current | | | | | 4.0 | 7.6 |
| | 48.8 | | 50.6 | 53.4 | Total Current | | | | | 69.4 | 46.1 |
| | 31.1 | | 25.7 | 22.6 | Fixed Assets (net) | | | | | 14.2 | 26.4 |
| | 12.3 | | 13.7 | 11.1 | Intangibles (net) | | | | | 8.1 | 13.3 |
| | 7.7 | | 10.1 | 12.9 | All Other Non-Current | | | | | 8.2 | 14.2 |
| | 100.0 | | 100.0 | 100.0 | Total | | | | | 100.0 | 100.0 |
| | | | | | LIABILITIES | | | | | | |
| | 3.6 | | 5.5 | 5.0 | Notes Payable-Short Term | | | | | 8.4 | 4.0 |
| | 2.1 | | 2.6 | 4.2 | Cur. Mat.-L.T.D. | | | | | 4.8 | 4.8 |
| | 7.5 | | 9.1 | 13.8 | Trade Payables | | | | | 23.2 | 10.7 |
| | .0 | | .3 | .2 | Income Taxes Payable | | | | | .0 | .4 |
| | 11.8 | | 13.5 | 16.6 | All Other Current | | | | | 9.5 | 22.9 |
| | 25.0 | | 31.0 | 39.9 | Total Current | | | | | 45.8 | 42.8 |
| | 25.7 | | 23.1 | 26.0 | Long-Term Debt | | | | | 14.2 | 29.8 |
| | .8 | | .4 | .2 | Deferred Taxes | | | | | .3 | .2 |
| | 13.5 | | 8.7 | 13.1 | All Other Non-Current | | | | | 2.1 | 19.9 |
| | 35.1 | | 36.8 | 20.8 | Net Worth | | | | | 37.7 | 7.3 |
| | 100.0 | | 100.0 | 100.0 | Total Liabilities & Net Worth | | | | | 100.0 | 100.0 |
| | | | | | INCOME DATA | | | | | | |
| | 100.0 | | 100.0 | 100.0 | Net Sales | | | | | 100.0 | 100.0 |
| | | | | | Gross Profit | | | | | | |
| | 89.3 | | 87.3 | 91.2 | Operating Expenses | | | | | 93.2 | 91.5 |
| | 10.7 | | 12.7 | 8.8 | Operating Profit | | | | | 6.8 | 8.5 |
| | .5 | | 2.7 | 4.3 | All Other Expenses (net) | | | | | 1.1 | 4.8 |
| | 10.1 | | 10.0 | 4.5 | Profit Before Taxes | | | | | 5.8 | 3.8 |
| | | | | | RATIOS | | | | | | |
| | 3.7 | | 3.6 | 3.1 | | | | | | 5.4 | 2.4 |
| | 2.3 | | 1.9 | 1.8 | Current | | | | | 2.3 | 1.4 |
| | 1.4 | | 1.1 | 1.1 | | | | | | 1.4 | .8 |
| | 2.5 | | 2.8 | 2.2 | | | | | | 5.2 | 1.9 |
| | 1.6 | | 1.2 | 1.3 | Quick | | | | | 1.7 | .9 |
| | .8 | | .7 | .6 | | | | | | 1.0 | .4 |
| 12 | 29.9 | 16 | 23.1 | 13 | 27.2 | | | | | 0 UND | 13 28.4 |
| 30 | 12.2 | 39 | 9.4 | 38 | 9.7 | Sales/Receivables | | | | 28 12.9 | 39 9.3 |
| 55 | 6.6 | 60 | 6.1 | 65 | 5.6 | | | | | 74 4.9 | 65 5.6 |
| | | | | | Cost of Sales/Inventory | | | | | | |
| | | | | | Cost of Sales/Payables | | | | | | |
| | 3.7 | | 4.8 | 4.4 | | | | | | 3.9 | 5.4 |
| | 7.4 | | 9.1 | 10.9 | Sales/Working Capital | | | | | 13.4 | 11.2 |
| | 16.6 | | 35.0 | 87.2 | | | | | | 35.6 | -17.7 |
| | 42.2 | | 69.9 | 34.7 | | | | | | 83.4 | 9.0 |
| (47) | 13.2 | (65) | 7.8 | (61) | 5.6 | EBIT/Interest | | | (14) | 52.4 | (37) 3.2 |
| | 3.3 | | 1.8 | 1.3 | | | | | | -2.7 | 1.3 |
| | 29.0 | | 18.4 | | Net Profit + Depr., Dep., | | | | | | |
| (10) | 5.0 | (14) | 3.8 | | Amort./Cur. Mat. L/T/D | | | | | | |
| | 2.6 | | 1.9 | | | | | | | | |
| | .2 | | .1 | .1 | | | | | | .0 | .2 |
| | .9 | | .9 | .5 | Fixed/Worth | | | | | .2 | .9 |
| | 3.7 | | 2.4 | 1.7 | | | | | | .7 | 2.7 |
| | .7 | | .5 | .6 | | | | | | .4 | .8 |
| | 2.0 | | 1.5 | 1.9 | Debt/Worth | | | | | 1.7 | 2.2 |
| | 7.3 | | -52.4 | 8.5 | | | | | | 3.8 | NM |
| | 75.9 | | 76.4 | 64.6 | | | | | | 125.1 | 44.2 |
| (42) | 32.2 | (58) | 38.6 | (62) | 31.4 | % Profit Before Taxes/Tangible Net Worth | | | (16) | 65.3 | (34) 26.0 |
| | 12.7 | | 8.4 | 6.6 | | | | | | 15.3 | 7.7 |
| | 22.2 | | 29.0 | 19.9 | | | | | | 46.0 | 17.4 |
| | 11.0 | | 10.7 | 8.3 | % Profit Before Taxes/Total Assets | | | | | 26.5 | 5.6 |
| | 4.6 | | 2.1 | .2 | | | | | | 1.1 | .5 |
| | 58.9 | | 94.5 | 103.6 | | | | | | 992.7 | 27.5 |
| | 7.8 | | 13.4 | 17.2 | Sales/Net Fixed Assets | | | | | 65.1 | 11.9 |
| | 1.1 | | 2.5 | 4.3 | | | | | | 10.5 | 3.6 |
| | 2.5 | | 3.0 | 3.0 | | | | | | 9.5 | 2.4 |
| | 1.7 | | 1.8 | 2.0 | Sales/Total Assets | | | | | 3.3 | 1.8 |
| | .6 | | .9 | 1.1 | | | | | | 1.8 | .8 |
| | 2.2 | | 1.7 | 1.2 | | | | | | | .9 |
| (31) | 3.8 | (43) | 3.4 | (45) | 2.6 | % Depr., Dep., Amort./Sales | | | | | (31) 2.6 |
| | 18.6 | | 11.7 | 6.7 | | | | | | | 6.1 |
| | | | .8 | .8 | % Officers', Directors' Owners' Comp/Sales | | | | | | |
| | | (13) | 2.3 | (13) | 2.2 | | | | | | | |
| | | | 5.2 | 4.2 | | | | | | | |
| | 2893853M | | 4201817M | 4301802M | Net Sales ($) | | 5929M | 21094M | 48322M | 282365M | 3944092M |
| | 2638758M | | 3808838M | 3889919M | Total Assets ($) | | 26181M | 134820M | 32210M | 111982M | 3584726M |

© RMA 2024    M = $ thousand   MM = $ million
See Pages viii through xx for Explanation of Ratios and Data

# INFORMATION—Computing Infrastructure Providers, Data Processing, Web Hosting, and Related Services  NAICS 518210

## Current Data Sorted by Assets | Comparative Historical Data

| | | | | | | | Type of Statement | | |
|---|---|---|---|---|---|---|---|---|---|
| | | | 4 | 11 | 5 | 5 | Unqualified | 30 | 14 |
| | 1 | | 4 | 5 | 1 | | Reviewed | 7 | 8 |
| | | | 1 | 1 | | | Compiled | 3 | 4 |
| 2 | 3 | | 1 | 1 | | | Tax Returns | 16 | 7 |
| 6 | 15 | | 39 | 34 | 20 | 12 | Other | 113 | 87 |
| | | 28 (4/1-9/30/23) | | 143 (10/1/23-3/31/24) | | | | 4/1/19- | 4/1/20- |
| 0-500M | 500M-2MM | 2-10MM | 10-50MM | 50-100MM | 100-250MM | | | 3/31/20 | 3/31/21 |
| | | | | | | | | ALL | ALL |
| 8 | 19 | 49 | 52 | 26 | 17 | | NUMBER OF STATEMENTS | 169 | 120 |
| % | % | % | % | % | % | | ASSETS | % | % |
| | 21.2 | 19.7 | 15.7 | 9.2 | 12.1 | | Cash & Equivalents | 22.5 | 27.4 |
| | 33.2 | 32.7 | 23.9 | 17.3 | 12.3 | | Trade Receivables (net) | 22.0 | 23.3 |
| | 1.4 | 2.3 | 2.6 | 1.7 | 2.3 | | Inventory | 2.1 | 2.6 |
| | .7 | 4.7 | 7.7 | 6.6 | 7.4 | | All Other Current | 5.0 | 3.4 |
| | 56.4 | 59.4 | 49.9 | 34.7 | 34.1 | | Total Current | 51.6 | 56.7 |
| | 24.4 | 17.9 | 16.6 | 16.5 | 23.8 | | Fixed Assets (net) | 26.0 | 20.9 |
| | 5.7 | 10.2 | 14.8 | 37.0 | 26.6 | | Intangibles (net) | 14.1 | 12.3 |
| | 13.5 | 12.5 | 18.7 | 11.8 | 15.5 | | All Other Non-Current | 8.2 | 10.2 |
| | 100.0 | 100.0 | 100.0 | 100.0 | 100.0 | | Total | 100.0 | 100.0 |
| | | | | | | | LIABILITIES | | |
| | 14.6 | 6.1 | 4.1 | 3.2 | 1.3 | | Notes Payable-Short Term | 7.6 | 8.2 |
| | 2.3 | 3.1 | 2.5 | 1.6 | 1.1 | | Cur. Mat.-L.T.D. | 2.9 | 3.7 |
| | 6.6 | 14.4 | 9.9 | 7.0 | 7.1 | | Trade Payables | 9.1 | 8.6 |
| | .1 | .0 | .1 | .7 | .2 | | Income Taxes Payable | .2 | .4 |
| | 6.0 | 13.4 | 18.5 | 14.0 | 25.4 | | All Other Current | 16.7 | 20.0 |
| | 29.7 | 37.0 | 35.1 | 26.5 | 35.1 | | Total Current | 36.5 | 40.8 |
| | 34.2 | 19.1 | 15.3 | 37.8 | 25.6 | | Long-Term Debt | 24.1 | 25.4 |
| | .3 | .0 | .1 | .1 | .6 | | Deferred Taxes | .3 | .3 |
| | .6 | 8.6 | 8.5 | 5.0 | 18.0 | | All Other Non-Current | 7.5 | 7.3 |
| | 35.2 | 35.2 | 41.0 | 30.6 | 20.7 | | Net Worth | 31.6 | 26.2 |
| | 100.0 | 100.0 | 100.0 | 100.0 | 100.0 | | Total Liabilties & Net Worth | 100.0 | 100.0 |
| | | | | | | | INCOME DATA | | |
| | 100.0 | 100.0 | 100.0 | 100.0 | 100.0 | | Net Sales | 100.0 | 100.0 |
| | | | | | | | Gross Profit | | |
| | 87.6 | 88.2 | 88.5 | 88.7 | 95.9 | | Operating Expenses | 89.7 | 90.7 |
| | 12.4 | 11.8 | 11.5 | 11.3 | 4.1 | | Operating Profit | 10.3 | 9.3 |
| | 4.0 | 5.2 | 2.2 | 9.5 | 4.1 | | All Other Expenses (net) | 3.3 | 2.7 |
| | 8.4 | 6.6 | 9.3 | 1.8 | .0 | | Profit Before Taxes | 6.9 | 6.6 |
| | | | | | | | RATIOS | | |
| | 4.7 | 2.7 | 3.1 | 1.8 | 1.7 | | | 2.6 | 3.2 |
| | 1.7 | 1.4 | 1.7 | 1.2 | 1.0 | | Current | 1.4 | 1.7 |
| | 1.1 | .8 | .9 | 1.0 | .7 | | | .9 | 1.0 |
| | 4.7 | 2.7 | 2.5 | 1.7 | 1.3 | | | 2.1 | 2.8 |
| | 1.7 | 1.3 | 1.4 | 1.1 | .6 | | Quick | 1.2 | 1.4 |
| | 1.1 | .5 | .6 | .8 | .5 | | | .6 | .8 |
| 8 | 47.0 | 10 | 34.8 | 27 | 13.5 | 49 | 7.5 | 15 | 24.7 | | | 10 | 36.2 | 14 | 26.8 |
| 42 | 8.7 | 38 | 9.5 | 45 | 8.1 | 62 | 5.9 | 28 | 13.0 | | Sales/Receivables | 39 | 9.3 | 41 | 9.0 |
| 79 | 4.6 | 68 | 5.4 | 76 | 4.8 | 74 | 4.9 | 59 | 6.2 | | | 63 | 5.8 | 68 | 5.4 |
| | | | | | | | Cost of Sales/Inventory | | |
| | | | | | | | Cost of Sales/Payables | | |
| | 5.0 | 4.5 | 3.6 | 6.8 | 8.1 | | | 5.5 | 4.2 |
| | 9.6 | 19.5 | 9.2 | 17.8 | -428.9 | | Sales/Working Capital | 15.7 | 10.3 |
| | 177.2 | -28.2 | -26.4 | 88.3 | -10.3 | | | -45.5 | NM |
| | 43.0 | 121.9 | 50.2 | 4.1 | 10.3 | | | 26.3 | 23.4 |
| (16) | 15.8 | (40) 10.0 | (42) 11.8 | (21) 1.8 | (15) .7 | | EBIT/Interest | (124) 5.7 | (80) 7.8 |
| | 1.0 | .9 | 1.0 | .0 | -8.4 | | | 1.0 | .1 |
| | | | | | | | Net Profit + Depr., Dep., | 6.0 | |
| | | | | | | | Amort./Cur. Mat. L/T/D | (24) 2.6 | |
| | | | | | | | | .9 | |
| | .0 | .0 | .0 | .2 | .6 | | | .1 | .0 |
| | .2 | .2 | .3 | 2.8 | 3.3 | | Fixed/Worth | .9 | .5 |
| | 2.8 | 5.7 | 5.1 | .0 | -.4 | | | 7.9 | NM |
| | .5 | .6 | .6 | 2.1 | 1.3 | | | .7 | .7 |
| | 1.8 | 2.3 | 2.5 | 17.5 | 9.6 | | Debt/Worth | 2.6 | 2.3 |
| | 6.0 | NM | NM | -1.4 | -2.8 | | | 60.8 | -11.3 |
| | 140.9 | 52.2 | 65.2 | 49.8 | | | % Profit Before Taxes/Tangible | 80.8 | 73.9 |
| (17) | 42.0 | (37) 27.7 | (39) 29.3 | (15) 25.8 | | | Net Worth | (128) 30.8 | (87) 26.7 |
| | 7.5 | 8.9 | 3.7 | 8.3 | | | | 8.8 | 8.7 |
| | 43.5 | 19.6 | 17.6 | 6.7 | 13.5 | | % Profit Before Taxes/Total | 28.2 | 20.5 |
| | 16.6 | 6.6 | 9.3 | 2.2 | -.7 | | Assets | 8.9 | 9.8 |
| | .3 | 1.4 | -.4 | -2.2 | -11.4 | | | .6 | .7 |
| | 281.7 | 418.2 | 172.2 | 105.0 | 33.4 | | | 100.1 | 177.5 |
| | 61.7 | 137.5 | 35.7 | 57.5 | 9.3 | | Sales/Net Fixed Assets | 15.4 | 24.3 |
| | 6.8 | 10.3 | 4.3 | 25.4 | 3.1 | | | 3.6 | 3.9 |
| | 3.8 | 3.7 | 2.4 | 1.5 | 1.7 | | | 3.3 | 3.1 |
| | 2.5 | 2.0 | 1.4 | .6 | 1.1 | | Sales/Total Assets | 1.8 | 1.7 |
| | .9 | 1.0 | .6 | .3 | .7 | | | .8 | .9 |
| | | .2 | .3 | .3 | | | | 1.0 | .4 |
| | (18) 1.0 | (33) .9 | (10) 1.6 | | | % Depr., Dep., Amort./Sales | (95) 3.0 | (59) 1.9 |
| | | 14.2 | 3.8 | 9.9 | | | | 8.1 | 5.3 |
| | | | | | | | % Officers', Directors', | 2.0 | 2.5 |
| | | | | | | | Owners' Comp/Sales | (23) 4.4 | (16) 4.4 |
| | | | | | | | | 10.6 | 9.2 |
| 18918M | 63954M | 543036M | 2974664M | 1999481M | 3047921M | | Net Sales ($) | 5748481M | 4765221M |
| 1712M | 22449M | 238780M | 1370665M | 1970887M | 2578320M | | Total Assets ($) | 5385890M | 4269770M |

© RMA 2024

M = $ thousand    MM = $ million
See Pages viii through xx for Explanation of Ratios and Data

## INFORMATION—Computing Infrastructure Providers, Data Processing, Web Hosting, and Related Services  NAICS 518210

### Comparative Historical Data | Current Data Sorted by Sales

| | | | | | | Type of Statement | | | | | | |
|---|---|---|---|---|---|---|---|---|---|---|---|---|
| | | 18 | | 22 | 25 | Unqualified | | 1 | 1 | 8 | 16 |
| | | 7 | | 12 | 11 | Reviewed | | 1 | 1 | 3 | 6 |
| | | 3 | | 3 | 2 | Compiled | | | | 1 | 1 |
| | | 10 | | 17 | 7 | Tax Returns | 1 | 1 | 2 | 3 | |
| | | 67 | | 104 | 126 | Other | 11 | 12 | 14 | 11 | 36 | 42 |
| | | 4/1/21-3/31/22 ALL | | 4/1/22-3/31/23 ALL | 4/1/23-3/31/24 ALL | | 28 (4/1-9/30/23) | | | 143 (10/1/23-3/31/24) | | |
| | | | | | | | 0-1MM | 1-3MM | 3-5MM | 5-10MM | 10-25MM | 25MM & OVER |
| | | 105 | | 158 | 171 | NUMBER OF STATEMENTS | 12 | 14 | 15 | 14 | 51 | 65 |
| | | % | | % | % | ASSETS | % | % | % | % | % | % |
| | | 28.8 | | 26.4 | 17.9 | Cash & Equivalents | 9.1 | 28.3 | 23.5 | 27.6 | 16.2 | 15.2 |
| | | 21.2 | | 24.1 | 24.7 | Trade Receivables (net) | 4.2 | 20.5 | 25.1 | 20.7 | 31.5 | 24.8 |
| | | 2.5 | | 2.2 | 2.1 | Inventory | .3 | 6.4 | 1.7 | 1.3 | .4 | 3.0 |
| | | 4.1 | | 5.1 | 5.6 | All Other Current | .2 | .5 | 1.8 | 3.1 | 5.0 | 9.6 |
| | | 56.6 | | 57.8 | 50.2 | Total Current | 13.8 | 55.7 | 52.2 | 52.7 | 53.1 | 52.6 |
| | | 18.1 | | 16.2 | 18.0 | Fixed Assets (net) | 49.8 | 7.4 | 35.0 | 24.8 | 12.8 | 13.2 |
| | | 12.4 | | 12.0 | 17.3 | Intangibles (net) | 13.0 | 13.9 | 5.6 | 9.3 | 23.5 | 18.3 |
| | | 13.0 | | 14.0 | 14.5 | All Other Non-Current | 23.5 | 23.1 | 7.3 | 13.2 | 10.5 | 15.9 |
| | | 100.0 | | 100.0 | 100.0 | Total | 100.0 | 100.0 | 100.0 | 100.0 | 100.0 | 100.0 |
| | | | | | | LIABILITIES | | | | | | |
| | | 4.1 | | 7.8 | 7.0 | Notes Payable-Short Term | 3.3 | 32.4 | 6.2 | 6.8 | 5.8 | 3.4 |
| | | 3.4 | | 2.3 | 2.3 | Cur. Mat.-L.T.D. | 3.0 | .9 | 3.6 | 3.1 | 2.4 | 1.9 |
| | | 8.3 | | 10.1 | 9.7 | Trade Payables | 1.5 | 1.1 | 4.4 | 4.7 | 14.6 | 11.4 |
| | | .4 | | .1 | .2 | Income Taxes Payable | .0 | .1 | .0 | .0 | .0 | .4 |
| | | 19.8 | | 19.0 | 16.5 | All Other Current | 7.9 | 9.7 | 16.5 | 14.4 | 12.5 | 23.3 |
| | | 36.0 | | 39.3 | 35.6 | Total Current | 15.7 | 44.1 | 30.6 | 29.0 | 35.2 | 40.4 |
| | | 20.2 | | 20.9 | 22.5 | Long-Term Debt | 38.6 | 20.6 | 37.6 | 35.1 | 15.7 | 19.1 |
| | | .8 | | .2 | .2 | Deferred Taxes | .0 | .4 | .0 | .0 | .0 | .3 |
| | | 11.5 | | 8.6 | 8.2 | All Other Non-Current | 8.4 | 1.6 | .8 | 6.6 | 8.7 | 11.3 |
| | | 31.5 | | 31.0 | 33.5 | Net Worth | 37.3 | 33.2 | 30.9 | 29.2 | 40.4 | 29.0 |
| | | 100.0 | | 100.0 | 100.0 | Total Liabilities & Net Worth | 100.0 | 100.0 | 100.0 | 100.0 | 100.0 | 100.0 |
| | | | | | | INCOME DATA | | | | | | |
| | | 100.0 | | 100.0 | 100.0 | Net Sales | 100.0 | 100.0 | 100.0 | 100.0 | 100.0 | 100.0 |
| | | | | | | Gross Profit | | | | | | |
| | | 88.3 | | 92.1 | 89.4 | Operating Expenses | 71.7 | 77.3 | 93.7 | 86.0 | 92.3 | 92.8 |
| | | 11.7 | | 7.9 | 10.6 | Operating Profit | 28.3 | 22.7 | 6.3 | 14.0 | 7.7 | 7.2 |
| | | -.2 | | 1.9 | 4.5 | All Other Expenses (net) | 18.2 | 2.3 | 5.3 | 4.3 | 4.2 | 2.5 |
| | | 12.0 | | 6.1 | 6.1 | Profit Before Taxes | 10.1 | 20.4 | 1.0 | 9.7 | 3.5 | 4.7 |
| | | | | | | RATIOS | | | | | | |
| | | 3.4 | | 3.2 | 2.9 | | 2.9 | 3.6 | 7.0 | 7.4 | 2.8 | 2.0 |
| | | 1.7 | | 1.6 | 1.4 | Current | .7 | 1.6 | 1.6 | 2.0 | 1.5 | 1.3 |
| | | 1.0 | | .9 | .9 | | .2 | 1.1 | .8 | .4 | 1.0 | .9 |
| | | 3.1 | | 2.9 | 2.4 | | 2.6 | 3.6 | 7.0 | 6.4 | 2.5 | 1.8 |
| | | 1.3 | | 1.4 | 1.3 | Quick | .7 | 1.4 | 1.6 | 2.0 | 1.4 | 1.1 |
| | | .7 | | .7 | .6 | | .2 | .7 | .7 | .2 | .7 | .6 |
| 20 | | 18.1 | 16 | 22.5 | 12 | 30.2 | 0 UND | 0 UND | 10 36.0 | 0 UND | 24 15.5 | 25 14.4 |
| 39 | | 9.3 | 42 | 8.6 | 44 | 8.3 | Sales/Receivables | 0 UND | 44 8.3 | 30 12.1 | 17 22.1 | 50 7.3 | 51 7.1 |
| 65 | | 5.6 | 66 | 5.5 | 70 | 5.2 | | 43 8.5 | 83 4.4 | 52 7.0 | 72 5.1 | 74 4.9 | 65 5.6 |
| | | | | | | Cost of Sales/Inventory | | | | | | |
| | | | | | | Cost of Sales/Payables | | | | | | |
| | | 3.8 | | 4.3 | 5.0 | | 6.5 | 3.0 | 3.3 | 3.5 | 5.9 | 6.1 |
| | | 9.6 | | 11.1 | 17.2 | Sales/Working Capital | -4.1 | 7.3 | 6.8 | 10.9 | 19.0 | 18.9 |
| | | NM | | -48.9 | -48.9 | | -1.3 | NM | -55.3 | -6.8 | 122.2 | -57.8 |
| | | 89.2 | | 42.7 | 39.3 | | | 250.0 | 17.5 | 157.0 | 69.7 | 43.7 |
| (80) | | 16.2 | (114) | 6.4 | (139) | 5.3 | EBIT/Interest | (11) 12.3 | (11) .0 | (12) 12.5 | (44) 6.0 | (56) 5.4 |
| | | 2.3 | | .3 | .4 | | | 5.0 | -25.7 | 1.0 | .5 | .2 |
| | | 8.8 | | 9.7 | 22.1 | | | | | | | |
| (15) | | 3.8 | (21) | 5.0 | (12) | 3.8 | Net Profit + Depr., Dep., Amort./Cur. Mat. L/T/D | | | | | |
| | | 1.9 | | 1.5 | 1.8 | | | | | | | |
| | | .1 | | .0 | .0 | | .0 | .0 | .4 | .0 | .0 | .0 |
| | | .5 | | .3 | .4 | Fixed/Worth | 2.5 | .1 | 2.5 | .3 | .3 | .4 |
| | | 6.2 | | 22.9 | -4.0 | | NM | NM | -1.2 | -1.4 | -3.3 | NM |
| | | .5 | | .5 | .7 | | .6 | .7 | .3 | .4 | .6 | .9 |
| | | 1.7 | | 2.2 | 3.0 | Debt/Worth | 3.9 | 2.1 | 2.1 | 1.5 | 4.0 | 3.5 |
| | | NM | | -165.8 | -6.2 | | -6.4 | -3.9 | -7.3 | -2.8 | -5.3 | -11.2 |
| | | 89.9 | | 62.3 | 61.9 | | | 78.1 | 38.3 | | 52.6 | 65.5 |
| (79) | | 42.4 | (116) | 25.6 | (119) | 27.2 | % Profit Before Taxes/Tangible Net Worth | (10) 27.2 | (10) 7.2 | (35) 27.7 | (47) 29.3 |
| | | 9.1 | | 5.4 | 3.9 | | | 10.2 | -15.0 | | 8.6 | 2.7 |
| | | 34.6 | | 24.7 | 19.2 | | 4.0 | 67.8 | 11.0 | 48.7 | 15.8 | 18.9 |
| | | 13.0 | | 6.9 | 6.3 | % Profit Before Taxes/Total Assets | 1.3 | 17.9 | -1.0 | 8.0 | 6.3 | 8.4 |
| | | 2.4 | | -1.3 | -1.1 | | -.4 | 7.2 | -20.8 | 3.1 | -.6 | -1.6 |
| | | 110.5 | | 222.3 | 239.4 | | 232.9 | UND | 114.5 | 564.8 | 405.2 | 176.9 |
| | | 22.0 | | 51.3 | 61.7 | Sales/Net Fixed Assets | .4 | 81.3 | 12.7 | 75.5 | 103.7 | 46.9 |
| | | 5.9 | | 8.1 | 6.1 | | .2 | 5.5 | .9 | 5.4 | 24.1 | 10.0 |
| | | 3.1 | | 3.2 | 2.8 | | .6 | 9.2 | 2.8 | 3.8 | 3.7 | 2.5 |
| | | 1.6 | | 1.8 | 1.6 | Sales/Total Assets | .2 | 1.8 | 1.3 | 1.4 | 1.7 | 1.8 |
| | | .8 | | 1.0 | .7 | | .1 | .8 | .6 | .8 | .9 | .9 |
| | | .7 | | .3 | .3 | | | | | | .3 | .2 |
| (59) | | 2.9 | (76) | 1.3 | (76) | 1.6 | % Depr., Dep., Amort./Sales | | | | (22) 1.8 | (31) .6 |
| | | 6.2 | | 4.6 | 5.5 | | | | | | 4.3 | 1.7 |
| | | 1.6 | | 1.4 | 2.5 | | | | | | | |
| (18) | | 3.8 | (24) | 4.6 | (13) | 4.5 | % Officers', Directors', Owners' Comp/Sales | | | | | |
| | | 10.3 | | 8.3 | 13.9 | | | | | | | |
| | | 6060762M | | 8165045M | 8647974M | Net Sales ($) | 4432M | 29814M | 57561M | 98399M | 880590M | 7577178M |
| | | 4731302M | | 5746437M | 6182813M | Total Assets ($) | 39376M | 62979M | 88034M | 121755M | 1078689M | 4791980M |

© RMA 2024  M = $ thousand   MM = $ million

# INFORMATION—Web Search Portals and All Other Information Services  NAICS 519290

## Current Data Sorted by Assets | Comparative Historical Data

| 0-500M | 500M-2MM | 2-10MM | 10-50MM | 50-100MM | 100-250MM | | Type of Statement | 4/1/19-3/31/20 ALL | 4/1/20-3/31/21 ALL |
|---|---|---|---|---|---|---|---|---|---|
| | 1 | 1 | 1 | 2 | 4 | | Unqualified | 12 | 6 |
| | | | 1 | | | | Reviewed | 4 | 1 |
| 1 | | | | | | | Compiled | 1 | 1 |
| 3 | | 7 | 1 | 1 | | | Tax Returns | 15 | 13 |
| | 4 (4/1-9/30/23) | | 5 | 4 | 7 | | Other | 60 | 36 |
| 4 | 1 | 9 | 8 | 6 | 11 | | NUMBER OF STATEMENTS | 92 | 57 |
| % | % | % | % | % | % | | ASSETS | % | % |
| | | | | | 20.0 | | Cash & Equivalents | 26.8 | 29.3 |
| | | | | | 16.4 | | Trade Receivables (net) | 24.8 | 24.4 |
| | | | | | .0 | | Inventory | 1.6 | .7 |
| | | | | | 4.8 | | All Other Current | 4.6 | 3.9 |
| | | | | | 41.1 | | Total Current | 57.8 | 58.3 |
| | | | | | 6.0 | | Fixed Assets (net) | 18.6 | 14.6 |
| | | | | | 44.3 | | Intangibles (net) | 13.5 | 19.1 |
| | | | | | 8.6 | | All Other Non-Current | 10.1 | 8.0 |
| | | | | | 100.0 | | Total | 100.0 | 100.0 |
| | | | | | | | LIABILITIES | | |
| | | | | | 1.3 | | Notes Payable-Short Term | 9.7 | 12.6 |
| | | | | | 13.2 | | Cur. Mat.-L.T.D. | 3.4 | 2.0 |
| | | | | | 5.4 | | Trade Payables | 10.0 | 10.0 |
| | | | | | .1 | | Income Taxes Payable | .5 | .2 |
| | | | | | 19.0 | | All Other Current | 23.6 | 18.0 |
| | | | | | 39.0 | | Total Current | 47.2 | 42.7 |
| | | | | | 32.7 | | Long-Term Debt | 22.2 | 21.0 |
| | | | | | 1.3 | | Deferred Taxes | .2 | .2 |
| | | | | | 4.0 | | All Other Non-Current | 8.8 | 9.5 |
| | | | | | 23.0 | | Net Worth | 21.6 | 26.6 |
| | | | | | 100.0 | | Total Liabilities & Net Worth | 100.0 | 100.0 |
| | | | | | | | INCOME DATA | | |
| | | | | | 100.0 | | Net Sales | 100.0 | 100.0 |
| | | | | | | | Gross Profit | | |
| | | | | | 99.0 | | Operating Expenses | 91.5 | 87.1 |
| | | | | | 1.0 | | Operating Profit | 8.5 | 12.9 |
| | | | | | 7.0 | | All Other Expenses (net) | 1.4 | 1.0 |
| | | | | | -6.0 | | Profit Before Taxes | 7.1 | 11.9 |
| | | | | | | | RATIOS | | |
| | | | | | 2.5 | | | 4.0 | 4.7 |
| | | | | | 1.3 | | Current | 1.8 | 1.7 |
| | | | | | .5 | | | .7 | .9 |
| | | | | | 2.1 | | | 3.5 | 4.7 |
| | | | | | 1.2 | | Quick | 1.6 | 1.5 |
| | | | | | .5 | | | .6 | .9 |
| | | | | 33 | 11.2 | | | 1  260.1 | 3  125.1 |
| | | | | 57 | 6.4 | | Sales/Receivables | 35  10.5 | 26  13.9 |
| | | | | 118 | 3.1 | | | 66  5.5 | 54  6.8 |
| | | | | | | | Cost of Sales/Inventory | | |
| | | | | | | | Cost of Sales/Payables | | |
| | | | | | 3.4 | | | 4.8 | 3.8 |
| | | | | | 7.2 | | Sales/Working Capital | 17.4 | 9.4 |
| | | | | | -3.0 | | | -19.3 | -49.4 |
| | | | | | | | | 29.0 | 95.6 |
| | | | | | | | EBIT/Interest | (63) 7.5 | (36) 28.7 |
| | | | | | | | | .7 | 3.9 |
| | | | | | | | Net Profit + Depr., Dep., Amort./Cur. Mat. L/T/D | | |
| | | | | | .0 | | | .1 | .0 |
| | | | | | .4 | | Fixed/Worth | .6 | .1 |
| | | | | | .0 | | | -.5 | -1.4 |
| | | | | | 1.3 | | | .5 | .8 |
| | | | | | -2.3 | | Debt/Worth | 3.1 | 3.0 |
| | | | | | -1.5 | | | -3.3 | -2.5 |
| | | | | | | | % Profit Before Taxes/Tangible Net Worth | 125.1 | 135.0 |
| | | | | | | | | (60) 56.6 | (35) 92.6 |
| | | | | | | | | 9.9 | 30.7 |
| | | | | | 11.3 | | % Profit Before Taxes/Total Assets | 46.2 | 56.3 |
| | | | | | 2.5 | | | 14.6 | 19.0 |
| | | | | | -16.3 | | | .2 | 4.6 |
| | | | | | 204.7 | | | 206.6 | 999.8 |
| | | | | | 72.2 | | Sales/Net Fixed Assets | 35.7 | 89.9 |
| | | | | | 7.7 | | | 9.9 | 24.2 |
| | | | | | 1.0 | | | 4.4 | 4.5 |
| | | | | | .7 | | Sales/Total Assets | 2.4 | 2.1 |
| | | | | | .6 | | | 1.2 | 1.2 |
| | | | | | | | | .9 | .5 |
| | | | | | | | % Depr., Dep., Amort./Sales | (44) 2.2 | (21) 1.8 |
| | | | | | | | | 4.7 | 5.5 |
| | | | | | | | | 2.0 | 3.9 |
| | | | | | | | % Officers', Directors', Owners' Comp/Sales | (22) 3.9 | (15) 7.5 |
| | | | | | | | | 9.3 | 11.5 |
| 4314M | 8424M | 144180M | 236883M | 771919M | 1466111M | | Net Sales ($) | 3734168M | 1484853M |
| 798M | 1344M | 53932M | 160752M | 458205M | 1901461M | | Total Assets ($) | 2639546M | 1268369M |

© RMA 2024  
M = $ thousand   MM = $ million  
See Pages viii through xx for Explanation of Ratios and Data

# INFORMATION—Web Search Portals and All Other Information Services  NAICS 519290

## Comparative Historical Data | Current Data Sorted by Sales

| | | | | | | Type of Statement | | | | | | | |
|---|---|---|---|---|---|---|---|---|---|---|---|---|---|
| | | 8 | | 6 | | 8 | Unqualified | | | | 1 | 1 | 7 |
| | | 2 | | 3 | | 2 | Reviewed | | | | | | |
| | | 2 | | 3 | | | Compiled | | | | | | |
| | | 5 | | 3 | | 3 | Tax Returns | | 1 | | 1 | | 1 |
| | | 36 | | 34 | | 26 | Other | 1 | 2 | | 35 | 6 | 15 |
| | | 4/1/21-3/31/22 ALL | | 4/1/22-3/31/23 ALL | | 4/1/23-3/31/24 ALL | | 0-1MM | 4 (4/1-9/30/23) 1-3MM | 3-5MM | (10/1/23-3/31/24) 5-10MM | 10-25MM | 25MM & OVER |
| | | 53 | | 49 | | 39 | NUMBER OF STATEMENTS | 1 | 3 | | 4 | 8 | 23 |
| | | % | | % | | % | ASSETS | % | % | % | % | % | % |
| | | 24.4 | | 24.5 | | 20.1 | Cash & Equivalents | | | | | | 19.0 |
| | | 23.7 | | 32.2 | | 24.0 | Trade Receivables (net) | | | | | | 26.7 |
| | | 2.5 | | 1.5 | | 4.1 | Inventory | | | D | | | 2.6 |
| | | 4.4 | | 7.7 | | 7.3 | All Other Current | | | A | | | 4.5 |
| | | 55.1 | | 65.9 | | 55.5 | Total Current | | | T | | | 52.8 |
| | | 15.8 | | 7.0 | | 11.2 | Fixed Assets (net) | | | A | | | 8.5 |
| | | 21.8 | | 16.6 | | 24.1 | Intangibles (net) | | | | | | 27.1 |
| | | 7.4 | | 10.6 | | 9.2 | All Other Non-Current | | | N | | | 11.7 |
| | | 100.0 | | 100.0 | | 100.0 | Total | | | O | | | 100.0 |
| | | | | | | | LIABILITIES | | | T | | | |
| | | 7.2 | | 13.9 | | 7.5 | Notes Payable-Short Term | | | | | | 3.4 |
| | | 1.4 | | 1.8 | | 5.9 | Cur. Mat.-L.T.D. | | | A | | | 7.9 |
| | | 8.8 | | 15.2 | | 12.1 | Trade Payables | | | V | | | 14.2 |
| | | .1 | | .0 | | .0 | Income Taxes Payable | | | A | | | .0 |
| | | 25.7 | | 25.2 | | 21.3 | All Other Current | | | I | | | 22.5 |
| | | 43.3 | | 56.1 | | 46.8 | Total Current | | | L | | | 48.2 |
| | | 19.5 | | 25.9 | | 26.6 | Long-Term Debt | | | A | | | 19.7 |
| | | .0 | | .1 | | .4 | Deferred Taxes | | | B | | | .6 |
| | | 13.1 | | 14.2 | | 18.9 | All Other Non-Current | | | L | | | 4.7 |
| | | 24.2 | | 3.7 | | 7.3 | Net Worth | | | E | | | 26.8 |
| | | 100.0 | | 100.0 | | 100.0 | Total Liabilites & Net Worth | | | | | | 100.0 |
| | | | | | | | INCOME DATA | | | | | | |
| | | 100.0 | | 100.0 | | 100.0 | Net Sales | | | | | | 100.0 |
| | | | | | | | Gross Profit | | | | | | 97.6 |
| | | 88.9 | | 93.8 | | 94.1 | Operating Expenses | | | | | | 2.4 |
| | | 11.1 | | 6.2 | | 5.9 | Operating Profit | | | | | | |
| | | .8 | | 1.5 | | 3.0 | All Other Expenses (net) | | | | | | 3.9 |
| | | 10.2 | | 4.7 | | 2.9 | Profit Before Taxes | | | | | | -1.4 |
| | | | | | | | RATIOS | | | | | | |
| | | 3.1 | | 3.0 | | 2.4 | | | | | | | 2.4 |
| | | 1.7 | | 1.4 | | 1.2 | Current | | | | | | 1.2 |
| | | .8 | | .9 | | .7 | | | | | | | .7 |
| | | 2.9 | | 2.9 | | 1.8 | | | | | | | 1.9 |
| | | 1.6 | | 1.3 | | 1.0 | Quick | | | | | | 1.1 |
| | | .6 | | .6 | | .5 | | | | | | | .6 |
| 5 | | 67.8 | 15 | 25.1 | 23 | 16.0 | | | | | | 38 | 9.7 |
| 29 | | 12.5 | 49 | 7.5 | 41 | 8.8 | Sales/Receivables | | | | | 56 | 6.5 |
| 58 | | 6.3 | 73 | 5.0 | 70 | 5.2 | | | | | | 85 | 4.3 |
| | | | | | | | Cost of Sales/Inventory | | | | | | |
| | | | | | | | Cost of Sales/Payables | | | | | | |
| | | 5.0 | | 4.7 | | 6.4 | | | | | | | 6.4 |
| | | 11.1 | | 15.1 | | 15.4 | Sales/Working Capital | | | | | | 12.6 |
| | | -36.4 | | -45.6 | | -14.3 | | | | | | | -12.5 |
| | | 83.0 | | 91.0 | | 15.5 | | | | | | | 14.8 |
| (33) | | 27.8 | (35) | 15.0 | (33) | 3.7 | EBIT/Interest | | | | | (18) | 2.0 |
| | | 3.6 | | -.5 | | 1.8 | | | | | | | -1.0 |
| | | | | | | | Net Profit + Depr., Dep., Amort./Cur. Mat. L/T/D | | | | | | |
| | | .0 | | .0 | | .0 | | | | | | | .0 |
| | | .4 | | .2 | | .6 | Fixed/Worth | | | | | | .4 |
| | | -.2 | | -.1 | | -.1 | | | | | | | -.3 |
| | | .6 | | 1.2 | | 1.5 | | | | | | | 1.1 |
| | | 1.8 | | 9.2 | | -18.9 | Debt/Worth | | | | | | 9.3 |
| | | -2.1 | | -2.7 | | -2.3 | | | | | | | -2.3 |
| | | 115.2 | | 109.3 | | 63.5 | % Profit Before Taxes/Tangible Net Worth | | | | | | 61.5 |
| (33) | | 51.0 | (26) | 55.0 | (19) | 29.6 | | | | | | (12) | 24.6 |
| | | 8.1 | | 7.3 | | 4.9 | | | | | | | -5.9 |
| | | 50.6 | | 39.8 | | 25.8 | % Profit Before Taxes/Total Assets | | | | | | 18.1 |
| | | 19.3 | | 15.6 | | 7.9 | | | | | | | 2.6 |
| | | 3.4 | | -2.0 | | .1 | | | | | | | -11.9 |
| | | 307.4 | | 942.5 | | 383.9 | | | | | | | 204.7 |
| | | 54.9 | | 90.4 | | 67.8 | Sales/Net Fixed Assets | | | | | | 67.3 |
| | | 11.8 | | 32.8 | | 9.2 | | | | | | | 9.1 |
| | | 3.9 | | 3.9 | | 2.7 | | | | | | | 2.1 |
| | | 1.8 | | 2.1 | | 1.5 | Sales/Total Assets | | | | | | 1.0 |
| | | .9 | | 1.2 | | .8 | | | | | | | .7 |
| | | .5 | | .3 | | .3 | | | | | | | |
| (21) | | 1.8 | (11) | 1.2 | (11) | .7 | % Depr., Dep., Amort./Sales | | | | | | |
| | | 6.2 | | 1.4 | | 7.6 | | | | | | | |
| | | 2.9 | | | | | | | | | | | |
| (11) | | 3.8 | | | | | % Officers', Directors' Owners' Comp/Sales | | | | | | |
| | | 11.1 | | | | | | | | | | | |
| | | 2966891M | | 2885903M | | 2631831M | Net Sales ($) | 638M | 3676M | | 26756M | 132463M | 2468298M |
| | | 1640398M | | 2158970M | | 2576492M | Total Assets ($) | 35M | 763M | | 16870M | 89502M | 2469322M |

© RMA 2024                    M = $ thousand    MM = $ million
See Pages viii through xx for Explanation of Ratios and Data

# FINANCE AND INSURANCE

# FINANCE—Sales Financing  NAICS 522220

## Current Data Sorted by Assets | Comparative Historical Data

| | | | | | | Type of Statement | | | | |
|---|---|---|---|---|---|---|---|---|---|---|
| | | 1 | 4 | 20 | 14 | 21 | Unqualified | | 44 | 35 |
| | | 1 | 6 | 6 | 2 | 1 | Reviewed | | 10 | 8 |
| | | | 2 | 2 | | | Compiled | | 6 | 7 |
| | 1 | 1 | 5 | 2 | | | Tax Returns | | 16 | 8 |
| | 2 | 9 | 19 | 29 | 11 | 9 | Other | | 75 | 69 |
| | | 18 (4/1-9/30/23) | | 150 (10/1/23-3/31/24) | | | | | 4/1/19-3/31/20 | 4/1/20-3/31/21 |
| | 0-500M | 500M-2MM | 2-10MM | 10-50MM | 50-100MM | 100-250MM | | | ALL | ALL |
| | 3 | 12 | 36 | 59 | 27 | 31 | NUMBER OF STATEMENTS | | 151 | 127 |
| | % | % | % | % | % | % | ASSETS | | % | % |
| | | 20.7 | 6.5 | 5.4 | 3.0 | 3.3 | Cash & Equivalents | | 7.0 | 10.8 |
| | | 29.1 | 38.3 | 42.1 | 57.1 | 51.0 | Trade Receivables (net) | | 51.0 | 44.3 |
| | | 6.4 | 1.6 | 4.3 | .7 | 3.7 | Inventory | | 3.6 | 4.5 |
| | | 12.4 | 13.9 | 7.7 | 4.9 | 4.3 | All Other Current | | 7.4 | 7.8 |
| | | 68.6 | 60.3 | 59.4 | 65.7 | 62.4 | Total Current | | 69.0 | 67.3 |
| | | 19.1 | 17.9 | 12.5 | 7.9 | 8.9 | Fixed Assets (net) | | 10.0 | 13.2 |
| | | .0 | .8 | .8 | 4.0 | 3.2 | Intangibles (net) | | 1.3 | 2.6 |
| | | 12.3 | 21.0 | 27.3 | 22.4 | 25.5 | All Other Non-Current | | 19.7 | 16.9 |
| | | 100.0 | 100.0 | 100.0 | 100.0 | 100.0 | Total | | 100.0 | 100.0 |
| | | | | | | | LIABILITIES | | | |
| | 14.6 | 19.1 | 27.0 | 24.9 | 34.5 | | Notes Payable-Short Term | | 26.2 | 24.2 |
| | 5.8 | 4.3 | 8.3 | 5.9 | 7.4 | | Cur. Mat.-L.T.D. | | 4.7 | 4.3 |
| | 5.7 | 1.6 | 2.1 | 1.5 | 3.3 | | Trade Payables | | 2.2 | 2.0 |
| | 1.4 | .1 | .0 | .1 | .1 | | Income Taxes Payable | | .1 | .2 |
| | 22.1 | 11.6 | 7.1 | 5.1 | 4.0 | | All Other Current | | 9.2 | 10.7 |
| | 49.6 | 36.7 | 44.5 | 37.5 | 49.4 | | Total Current | | 42.3 | 41.4 |
| | 8.8 | 17.0 | 22.0 | 33.8 | 20.4 | | Long-Term Debt | | 19.2 | 20.6 |
| | .0 | .1 | .1 | .1 | .2 | | Deferred Taxes | | .2 | .3 |
| | 26.5 | 17.9 | 8.0 | 4.5 | 9.0 | | All Other Non-Current | | 10.1 | 13.2 |
| | 15.1 | 28.3 | 25.3 | 24.2 | 21.1 | | Net Worth | | 28.1 | 24.5 |
| | 100.0 | 100.0 | 100.0 | 100.0 | 100.0 | | Total Liabilities & Net Worth | | 100.0 | 100.0 |
| | | | | | | | INCOME DATA | | | |
| | 100.0 | | 100.0 | 100.0 | 100.0 | 100.0 | Net Sales | | 100.0 | 100.0 |
| | | | | | | | Gross Profit | | | |
| | 91.7 | 71.8 | 68.0 | 67.3 | 73.9 | | Operating Expenses | | 66.6 | 71.7 |
| | 8.3 | 28.2 | 32.0 | 32.7 | 26.1 | | Operating Profit | | 33.4 | 28.3 |
| | 4.8 | 11.9 | 16.7 | 18.6 | 16.2 | | All Other Expenses (net) | | 13.9 | 10.4 |
| | 3.5 | 16.2 | 15.3 | 14.1 | 9.9 | | Profit Before Taxes | | 19.5 | 17.9 |
| | | | | | | | RATIOS | | | |
| | | 12.0 | 5.4 | 2.0 | 3.1 | 1.7 | | | 2.6 | 2.9 |
| | | 1.7 | 2.0 | 1.2 | 1.5 | 1.3 | Current | | 1.5 | 1.5 |
| | | .6 | .7 | .5 | 1.2 | 1.1 | | | 1.2 | 1.1 |
| | | 9.5 | 3.3 | 1.5 | 1.8 | 1.6 | | | 2.1 | 2.3 |
| | | .7 | 1.4 | 1.0 | 1.2 | 1.2 | Quick | | 1.3 | 1.3 |
| | | .3 | .4 | .2 | .9 | .5 | | | .6 | .5 |
| | 0 | UND | 0 | UND | 1 | 459.3 | 5 | 79.9 | 4 | 93.3 | | 16 | 22.7 | 6 | 58.6 |
| | 19 | 19.4 | 73 | 5.0 | 215 | 1.7 | 730 | .5 | 332 | 1.1 | Sales/Receivables | 406 | .9 | 182 | 2.0 |
| | 228 | 1.6 | 1217 | .3 | 1217 | .3 | 1825 | .2 | 1217 | .3 | | 1217 | .3 | 912 | .4 |
| | | | | | | | Cost of Sales/Inventory | | | |
| | | | | | | | Cost of Sales/Payables | | | |
| | | .6 | .4 | .9 | .4 | 1.1 | | | .6 | .7 |
| | | 5.6 | 2.8 | 3.6 | 1.0 | 3.2 | Sales/Working Capital | | 1.7 | 2.3 |
| | | -24.0 | -8.7 | -2.9 | 3.9 | 25.6 | | | 10.3 | 25.9 |
| | | | 8.9 | 3.7 | 3.9 | 2.1 | | | 9.3 | 8.8 |
| | | (26) | 4.3 | (32) | 2.4 | (11) | 2.0 | (17) | 1.5 | EBIT/Interest | (89) | 3.0 | (86) | 3.7 |
| | | | 1.3 | 1.5 | .2 | 1.2 | | | 1.9 | 1.7 |
| | | | | | | | Net Profit + Depr., Dep., Amort./Cur. Mat. L/T/D | | | |
| | .0 | .0 | .0 | .0 | .0 | | Fixed/Worth | | .0 | .0 |
| | .3 | .0 | .0 | .0 | .1 | | | | .0 | .0 |
| | NM | 1.5 | .2 | .0 | .4 | | | | .3 | .4 |
| | .3 | .6 | 1.5 | 2.5 | 2.6 | | Debt/Worth | | 1.4 | 1.6 |
| | 3.9 | 2.9 | 3.2 | 4.0 | 5.7 | | | | 3.2 | 3.5 |
| | NM | 16.1 | 6.0 | 5.9 | 10.5 | | | | 8.9 | 7.6 |
| | | 40.4 | 25.7 | 26.7 | 23.8 | | | | 37.8 | 39.2 |
| | (32) | 9.7 | (56) | 15.4 | (25) | 13.9 | (30) | 14.8 | % Profit Before Taxes/Tangible Net Worth | (138) | 17.6 | (115) | 22.1 |
| | | 5.1 | 5.6 | 6.3 | 7.1 | | | | 6.9 | 7.1 |
| | 11.0 | 8.0 | 5.7 | 6.3 | 3.8 | | % Profit Before Taxes/Total Assets | | 8.5 | 12.1 |
| | .8 | 3.6 | 3.8 | 2.4 | 2.2 | | | | 4.4 | 4.6 |
| | -7.8 | .2 | 1.1 | 1.0 | .7 | | | | 1.4 | 1.2 |
| | UND | UND | 376.8 | 324.4 | 92.4 | | | | 989.4 | 999.8 |
| | 203.3 | 103.1 | 63.1 | 58.2 | 30.6 | | Sales/Net Fixed Assets | | 70.4 | 48.2 |
| | 3.2 | 1.8 | 13.0 | 14.9 | 9.9 | | | | 12.4 | 7.3 |
| | 1.2 | .5 | .6 | .4 | .6 | | | | .5 | .9 |
| | .6 | .3 | .3 | .2 | .3 | | Sales/Total Assets | | .3 | .3 |
| | .5 | .1 | .2 | .1 | .1 | | | | .1 | .2 |
| | | .2 | .3 | .2 | .2 | | | | .3 | .4 |
| | (20) | 5.9 | (35) | .5 | (18) | .6 | (20) | .5 | % Depr., Dep., Amort./Sales | (76) | .8 | (65) | .7 |
| | | 48.4 | 4.7 | 7.2 | 1.5 | | | | 1.9 | 7.4 |
| | | 4.1 | .8 | | | | | | 2.0 | .8 |
| | (10) | 7.0 | (10) | 4.0 | | | % Officers', Directors' Owners' Comp/Sales | (26) | 7.2 | (16) | 3.1 |
| | | 9.5 | 8.1 | | | | | | 16.1 | 11.8 |
| | 2368M | 45431M | 101076M | 1504810M | 598875M | 3048112M | Net Sales ($) | | 3684534M | 3623202M |
| | 909M | 14637M | 218865M | 1715149M | 1945962M | 5504799M | Total Assets ($) | | 7091373M | 5756561M |

M = $ thousand    MM = $ million
See Pages viii through xx for Explanation of Ratios and Data

© RMA 2024

# FINANCE—Sales Financing  NAICS 522220

## Comparative Historical Data

| | | | | | | | Current Data Sorted by Sales | | | | | |
|---|---|---|---|---|---|---|---|---|---|---|---|---|
| 46 | | 47 | | 60 | | Type of Statement | | | | | | |
| 46 | | 47 | | 60 | | Unqualified | 1 | 3 | 5 | 10 | 17 | 24 |
| 14 | | 10 | | 16 | | Reviewed | 4 | 4 | 1 | 2 | 2 | 3 |
| 5 | | 5 | | 4 | | Compiled | 1 | | 1 | | 1 | 1 |
| 13 | | 17 | | 9 | | Tax Returns | | | | | | 1 |
| 73 | | 79 | | 79 | | Other | 4 | 4 | | | | 14 |
| 4/1/21-3/31/22 ALL | | 4/1/22-3/31/23 ALL | | 4/1/23-3/31/24 ALL | | | 13 | 16 | 8 | 16 | 12 | 14 |
| | | | | | | | 0-1MM | 18 (4/1-9/30/23) 1-3MM | 3-5MM | 5-10MM | 150 (10/1/23-3/31/24) 10-25MM | 25MM & OVER |
| 151 | | 158 | | 168 | | NUMBER OF STATEMENTS | 23 | 27 | 15 | 28 | 32 | 43 |
| % | | % | | % | | ASSETS | % | % | % | % | % | % |
| 12.6 | | 8.5 | | 6.3 | | Cash & Equivalents | 9.2 | 7.7 | 4.3 | 2.8 | 3.2 | 9.0 |
| 41.4 | | 46.7 | | 43.8 | | Trade Receivables (net) | 33.8 | 39.6 | 29.4 | 46.3 | 58.1 | 44.4 |
| 3.3 | | 2.9 | | 3.1 | | Inventory | .6 | .0 | .1 | .5 | 5.2 | 7.6 |
| 7.1 | | 6.2 | | 8.1 | | All Other Current | 18.6 | 15.1 | 9.4 | 1.3 | 5.1 | 4.6 |
| 64.4 | | 64.4 | | 61.3 | | Total Current | 62.1 | 62.4 | 43.2 | 50.9 | 71.6 | 65.5 |
| 12.5 | | 14.8 | | 13.2 | | Fixed Assets (net) | 19.7 | 12.4 | 18.3 | 11.8 | 3.8 | 16.3 |
| 2.6 | | 1.1 | | 1.7 | | Intangibles (net) | .4 | .4 | .5 | 2.5 | .3 | 4.2 |
| 20.4 | | 19.6 | | 23.8 | | All Other Non-Current | 17.9 | 24.8 | 38.0 | 34.8 | 24.3 | 14.0 |
| 100.0 | | 100.0 | | 100.0 | | Total | 100.0 | 100.0 | 100.0 | 100.0 | 100.0 | 100.0 |
| | | | | | | LIABILITIES | | | | | | |
| 28.6 | | 25.1 | | 25.2 | | Notes Payable-Short Term | 19.6 | 21.7 | 20.0 | 24.1 | 27.1 | 31.5 |
| 4.4 | | 7.8 | | 6.7 | | Cur. Mat.-L.T.D. | 4.4 | 8.9 | 8.5 | 8.0 | 5.9 | 5.7 |
| 1.9 | | 2.8 | | 2.4 | | Trade Payables | .5 | .5 | 1.4 | 1.9 | 3.5 | 4.3 |
| .0 | | .1 | | .2 | | Income Taxes Payable | .8 | .1 | .0 | .0 | .2 | .1 |
| 8.6 | | 6.3 | | 8.3 | | All Other Current | 15.7 | 7.3 | 7.7 | 4.3 | 7.2 | 8.6 |
| 43.5 | | 42.0 | | 42.7 | | Total Current | 40.9 | 38.5 | 37.6 | 38.3 | 43.8 | 50.0 |
| 18.9 | | 23.9 | | 23.3 | | Long-Term Debt | 23.8 | 18.9 | 31.2 | 24.4 | 17.9 | 26.5 |
| .0 | | .0 | | .1 | | Deferred Taxes | .0 | .1 | .0 | .1 | .1 | .2 |
| 10.6 | | 7.3 | | 10.9 | | All Other Non-Current | 15.6 | 18.8 | 6.9 | 7.5 | 12.9 | 5.7 |
| 27.0 | | 26.8 | | 23.0 | | Net Worth | 19.7 | 23.7 | 24.3 | 29.7 | 25.4 | 17.6 |
| 100.0 | | 100.0 | | 100.0 | | Total Liabilities & Net Worth | 100.0 | 100.0 | 100.0 | 100.0 | 100.0 | 100.0 |
| | | | | | | INCOME DATA | | | | | | |
| 100.0 | | 100.0 | | 100.0 | | Net Sales | 100.0 | 100.0 | 100.0 | 100.0 | 100.0 | 100.0 |
| | | | | | | Gross Profit | | | | | | |
| 67.2 | | 66.5 | | 71.6 | | Operating Expenses | 69.9 | 64.3 | 62.1 | 66.0 | 70.2 | 85.0 |
| 32.8 | | 33.5 | | 28.4 | | Operating Profit | 30.1 | 35.7 | 37.9 | 34.0 | 29.8 | 15.0 |
| 9.4 | | 11.1 | | 14.8 | | All Other Expenses (net) | 15.2 | 15.7 | 25.4 | 16.4 | 15.4 | 8.7 |
| 23.4 | | 22.4 | | 13.7 | | Profit Before Taxes | 14.9 | 20.0 | 12.5 | 17.6 | 14.4 | 6.3 |
| | | | | | | RATIOS | | | | | | |
| 2.6 | | 3.3 | | 3.1 | | Current | 11.4 | 3.6 | 1.4 | 2.3 | 4.5 | 1.9 |
| 1.5 | | 1.4 | | 1.4 | | | 2.7 | 1.5 | 1.0 | 1.2 | 1.4 | 1.4 |
| 1.0 | | 1.0 | | .8 | | | .4 | 1.0 | .2 | .7 | .9 | 1.1 |
| 2.2 | | 2.6 | | 2.1 | | Quick | 3.9 | 2.5 | 1.2 | 1.9 | 3.1 | 1.8 |
| 1.3 | | 1.3 | | 1.2 | | | .7 | 1.4 | .8 | 1.1 | 1.3 | 1.1 |
| .5 | | .6 | | .4 | | | .2 | .3 | .1 | .6 | .8 | .3 |
| 2 162.3 | | 4 99.9 | | 1 412.1 | | Sales/Receivables | 0 UND | 0 UND | 0 UND | 0 UND | 15 23.9 | 5 79.9 |
| 140 2.6 | | 281 1.3 | | 203 1.8 | | | 99 3.7 | 130 2.8 | 46 8.0 | 730 .5 | 608 .6 | 140 2.6 |
| 912 .4 | | 1217 .3 | | 1217 .3 | | | 1217 .3 | 1217 .3 | 1217 .3 | 1825 .2 | 1217 .3 | 608 .6 |
| | | | | | | Cost of Sales/Inventory | | | | | | |
| | | | | | | Cost of Sales/Payables | | | | | | |
| .6 | | .5 | | .7 | | Sales/Working Capital | .2 | .6 | .9 | .8 | .5 | 1.7 |
| 2.2 | | 2.5 | | 2.9 | | | 1.6 | 2.0 | 146.4 | 1.9 | 1.3 | 4.0 |
| -620.5 | | 79.4 | | -15.2 | | | -1.5 | -35.1 | -5.0 | -4.2 | -65.5 | 37.0 |
| 9.3 | | 8.5 | | 4.5 | | EBIT/Interest | 5.2 | 8.9 | | 11.2 | 5.7 | 2.6 |
| (118) 4.0 | | (110) 3.7 | | (96) 2.2 | | | (14) 3.6 | (14) 2.3 | (13) 2.8 | (17) 2.3 | (33) 1.8 | |
| 1.9 | | 2.3 | | 1.2 | | | -.7 | 1.3 | | 2.1 | .1 | 1.3 |
| | | 15.6 | | 9.1 | | Net Profit + Depr., Dep., | | | | | | |
| | | (10) 1.3 | | (14) 1.2 | | Amort./Cur. Mat. L/T/D | | | | | | |
| | | .1 | | .1 | | | | | | | | |
| .0 | | .0 | | .0 | | Fixed/Worth | .0 | .0 | .0 | .0 | .0 | .0 |
| .0 | | .0 | | .0 | | | .0 | .0 | .0 | .0 | .0 | .1 |
| .3 | | .3 | | .5 | | | 15.3 | .8 | .0 | .1 | .1 | .7 |
| 1.4 | | 1.4 | | 1.8 | | Debt/Worth | .3 | 1.4 | 2.0 | 1.4 | 2.0 | 2.1 |
| 3.2 | | 2.7 | | 3.7 | | | 4.6 | 2.6 | 4.0 | 3.9 | 3.5 | 4.0 |
| 7.2 | | 5.9 | | 8.1 | | | 999.8 | 5.7 | 7.4 | 6.1 | 5.9 | 10.5 |
| 48.4 | | 32.0 | | 26.5 | | % Profit Before Taxes/Tangible Net Worth | 24.2 | 37.4 | 15.6 | 36.9 | 22.9 | 28.2 |
| (143) 26.4 | | (153) 18.4 | | (153) 13.8 | | | (18) 6.9 | (24) 12.7 | (13) 9.3 | 14.8 | (31) 13.9 | (39) 19.1 |
| 12.2 | | 8.8 | | 5.4 | | | -4.0 | 6.7 | 2.7 | 5.7 | 2.4 | 9.7 |
| 12.5 | | 8.3 | | 5.8 | | % Profit Before Taxes/Total Assets | 5.7 | 7.4 | 4.5 | 5.9 | 5.3 | 6.3 |
| 6.0 | | 5.3 | | 3.2 | | | .5 | 3.9 | 1.1 | 3.8 | 3.4 | 3.1 |
| 1.9 | | 2.2 | | .7 | | | -2.1 | 2.1 | .2 | 1.5 | .4 | 1.0 |
| UND | | 999.8 | | 359.1 | | Sales/Net Fixed Assets | UND | UND | 367.8 | UND | 100.4 | 89.5 |
| 88.9 | | 48.9 | | 53.3 | | | 185.2 | 115.9 | 97.6 | 254.9 | 34.8 | 29.4 |
| 17.1 | | 8.9 | | 10.2 | | | 1.2 | 2.3 | 18.8 | 21.7 | 13.0 | 7.7 |
| .7 | | .6 | | .5 | | Sales/Total Assets | .5 | .4 | .4 | .3 | .5 | 1.4 |
| .3 | | .3 | | .3 | | | .1 | .3 | .2 | .2 | .3 | .6 |
| .2 | | .2 | | .1 | | | .1 | .2 | .1 | .1 | .1 | .3 |
| .3 | | .3 | | .3 | | % Depr., Dep., Amort./Sales | | .2 | | .3 | .3 | .2 |
| (75) 1.0 | | (83) .7 | | (97) .7 | | | (15) 5.0 | | (16) .5 | (19) .9 | (30) .5 | |
| 9.8 | | 3.1 | | 8.6 | | | | 29.3 | | 21.6 | 6.1 | 1.7 |
| 2.7 | | 4.5 | | 3.1 | | % Officers', Directors', Owners' Comp/Sales | | | | | | |
| (24) 6.0 | | (26) 7.2 | | (21) 5.5 | | | | | | | | |
| 10.3 | | 12.5 | | 7.5 | | | | | | | | |
| 4306110M | | 4319483M | | 5300672M | | Net Sales ($) | 13144M | 54581M | 55112M | 198670M | 484885M | 4494280M |
| 7267595M | | 8349064M | | 9400321M | | Total Assets ($) | 87957M | 262497M | 412117M | 1160108M | 2230532M | 5247110M |

© RMA 2024

M = $ thousand   MM = $ million
See Pages viii through xx for Explanation of Ratios and Data

# FINANCE—Consumer Lending NAICS 522291

## Current Data Sorted by Assets

| | | | | | | Type of Statement | | Comparative Historical Data | |
|---|---|---|---|---|---|---|---|---|---|
| | | 2 | 14 | 11 | 9 | Unqualified | | 23 | 17 |
| | | 1 | 2 | 2 | | Reviewed | | 4 | 4 |
| | | 1 | 1 | | | Compiled | | 2 | 3 |
| | | 2 | 1 | | 1 | Tax Returns | | 11 | 6 |
| | 3 | 7 | 10 | 5 | 6 | Other | | 40 | 25 |
| 0-500M | 10 (4/1-9/30/23) | | 68 (10/1/23-3/31/24) | | | | | 4/1/19-3/31/20 ALL | 4/1/20-3/31/21 ALL |
| | 500M-2MM | 2-10MM | 10-50MM | 50-100MM | 100-250MM | NUMBER OF STATEMENTS | | 80 | 55 |
| | 5 | 11 | 28 | 18 | 16 | | | | |
| % | % | % | % | % | % | **ASSETS** | | % | % |
| | | 10.4 | 6.8 | 5.2 | 16.7 | Cash & Equivalents | | 13.1 | 10.0 |
| **D** | | 65.7 | 76.8 | 52.4 | 53.6 | Trade Receivables (net) | | 57.6 | 59.6 |
| **A** | | .0 | 2.7 | 1.4 | 1.7 | Inventory | | .8 | .1 |
| **T** | | .7 | 1.8 | 9.7 | 9.5 | All Other Current | | 6.7 | 6.1 |
| **A** | | 76.7 | 88.0 | 68.6 | 81.5 | Total Current | | 78.2 | 75.8 |
| | | 10.8 | 2.8 | 11.2 | 3.3 | Fixed Assets (net) | | 5.3 | 5.8 |
| **N** | | .9 | 1.8 | 6.3 | 3.4 | Intangibles (net) | | 2.2 | 1.4 |
| **O** | | 11.5 | 7.5 | 13.9 | 11.8 | All Other Non-Current | | 14.3 | 17.0 |
| **T** | | 100.0 | 100.0 | 100.0 | 100.0 | Total | | 100.0 | 100.0 |
| | | | | | | **LIABILITIES** | | | |
| **A** | | 22.1 | 40.4 | 40.2 | 35.5 | Notes Payable-Short Term | | 25.0 | 23.8 |
| **V** | | .5 | .6 | 2.1 | 5.7 | Cur. Mat.-L.T.D. | | 2.2 | 2.2 |
| **A** | | .5 | 3.4 | 1.3 | 1.6 | Trade Payables | | 4.0 | 3.1 |
| **I** | | .0 | .0 | .0 | .1 | Income Taxes Payable | | .1 | .0 |
| **L** | | 12.2 | 4.9 | 4.1 | 7.1 | All Other Current | | 8.0 | 5.5 |
| **A** | | 35.3 | 49.3 | 47.7 | 50.1 | Total Current | | 39.3 | 34.6 |
| **B** | | 15.6 | 10.4 | 8.3 | 14.9 | Long-Term Debt | | 19.2 | 16.8 |
| **L** | | .0 | .0 | .0 | .0 | Deferred Taxes | | .1 | .0 |
| **E** | | 11.7 | 5.8 | 9.7 | 12.2 | All Other Non-Current | | 6.5 | 5.6 |
| | | 37.4 | 34.5 | 34.3 | 22.8 | Net Worth | | 34.9 | 42.9 |
| | | 100.0 | 100.0 | 100.0 | 100.0 | Total Liabilties & Net Worth | | 100.0 | 100.0 |
| | | | | | | **INCOME DATA** | | | |
| | | 100.0 | 100.0 | 100.0 | 100.0 | Net Sales | | 100.0 | 100.0 |
| | | | | | | Gross Profit | | | |
| | | 57.6 | 64.5 | 66.1 | 59.5 | Operating Expenses | | 73.8 | 66.0 |
| | | 42.4 | 35.5 | 33.9 | 40.5 | Operating Profit | | 26.2 | 34.0 |
| | | 19.2 | 18.4 | 26.8 | 29.7 | All Other Expenses (net) | | 11.1 | 10.5 |
| | | 23.1 | 17.2 | 7.1 | 10.7 | Profit Before Taxes | | 15.1 | 23.5 |
| | | | | | | **RATIOS** | | | |
| | | 22.4 | 3.9 | 2.6 | 3.4 | | | 4.1 | 5.5 |
| | | 3.6 | 1.6 | 1.5 | 1.4 | Current | | 1.9 | 2.4 |
| | | 1.4 | 1.3 | 1.0 | 1.3 | | | 1.3 | 1.4 |
| | | 22.4 | 3.9 | 2.4 | 2.7 | | | 3.2 | 5.2 |
| | | 3.6 | 1.6 | 1.3 | 1.3 | Quick | | 1.7 | 2.2 |
| | | 1.3 | 1.2 | .2 | 1.1 | | | 1.2 | 1.4 |
| | 49 | 7.4 | 608 | .6 | 0 UND | 1 257.8 | Sales/Receivables | 63 5.8 | 40 9.2 |
| | 608 | .6 | 1217 | .3 | 332 1.1 | 608 .6 | | 730 .5 | 608 .6 |
| | 1825 | .2 | 1825 | .2 | 1217 .3 | 1825 .2 | | 1217 .3 | 1217 .3 |
| | | | | | | Cost of Sales/Inventory | | | |
| | | | | | | Cost of Sales/Payables | | | |
| | | .2 | .3 | .5 | .4 | | | .5 | .4 |
| | | .6 | .8 | 1.9 | .9 | Sales/Working Capital | | 1.2 | .9 |
| | | 6.8 | 1.1 | 37.6 | 2.8 | | | 3.9 | 2.3 |
| | | | 3.8 | 28.6 | | | | 5.0 | 9.1 |
| | | (16) | 2.1 | (10) 2.0 | | EBIT/Interest | (58) | 3.0 | (41) 3.5 |
| | | | 1.1 | 1.4 | | | | 1.6 | 1.8 |
| | | | | | | Net Profit + Depr., Dep., Amort./Cur. Mat. L/T/D | | | |
| | | .0 | .0 | .0 | .0 | | | .0 | .0 |
| | | .0 | .0 | .0 | .0 | Fixed/Worth | | .0 | .0 |
| | | .5 | .1 | .7 | .2 | | | .2 | .1 |
| | | .4 | 1.1 | 1.1 | 2.6 | | | 1.0 | .6 |
| | | 2.1 | 1.9 | 2.5 | 7.1 | Debt/Worth | | 2.2 | 1.5 |
| | | 8.9 | 4.7 | 5.5 | 9.7 | | | 6.5 | 4.4 |
| | | 59.9 | 22.6 | 13.4 | 25.2 | % Profit Before Taxes/Tangible Net Worth | | 32.6 | 28.2 |
| | (10) | 27.9 | (26) 10.9 | (16) 8.0 | 12.7 | | (76) | 17.1 | (54) 14.8 |
| | | 10.6 | 2.7 | 4.7 | -1.4 | | | 5.0 | 6.8 |
| | | 13.4 | 6.1 | 4.5 | 5.0 | % Profit Before Taxes/Total Assets | | 8.4 | 11.5 |
| | | 6.8 | 2.9 | 2.6 | 2.9 | | | 4.0 | 4.8 |
| | | 2.4 | .7 | .8 | -.1 | | | 1.0 | 2.0 |
| | | UND | UND | UND | UND | | | 419.6 | 555.7 |
| | | 881.0 | 56.7 | 56.6 | 114.2 | Sales/Net Fixed Assets | | 44.7 | 64.8 |
| | | 3.7 | 15.5 | 11.0 | 12.4 | | | 11.5 | 18.2 |
| | | 1.0 | .4 | .5 | .6 | | | .8 | .5 |
| | | .2 | .2 | .3 | .2 | Sales/Total Assets | | .4 | .3 |
| | | .1 | .1 | .2 | .1 | | | .2 | .2 |
| | | | .4 | .4 | .2 | | | .3 | .4 |
| | | (13) | .6 | (10) .6 | (11) .9 | % Depr., Dep., Amort./Sales | (51) | 1.1 | (28) .8 |
| | | | .9 | 2.9 | 2.6 | | | 2.2 | 1.5 |
| | | | | | | | | 2.1 | |
| | | | | | | % Officers', Directors' Owners' Comp/Sales | (12) | 7.0 | |
| | | | | | | | | 12.6 | |
| | 11961M | 36279M | 219128M | 481371M | 1146452M | Net Sales ($) | | 2156779M | 883527M |
| | 6731M | 69900M | 690041M | 1180195M | 2815883M | Total Assets ($) | | 3856614M | 2554111M |

M = $ thousand   MM = $ million
See Pages viii through xx for Explanation of Ratios and Data

© RMA 2024

# FINANCE—Consumer Lending NAICS 522291

## Comparative Historical Data | Current Data Sorted by Sales

| Comparative Historical Data | | | Type of Statement | Current Data Sorted by Sales | | | | | |
|---|---|---|---|---|---|---|---|---|---|
| 28 | 29 | 36 | Unqualified | 2 | 4 | 3 | 7 | 11 | 9 |
| | 7 | 5 | Reviewed | | 1 | 1 | | 2 | 1 |
| 4 | 1 | 2 | Compiled | | | 1 | 1 | | |
| 1 | 8 | 4 | Tax Returns | | | | 1 | 2 | |
| 17 | 32 | 31 | Other | 5 | 7 | | 3 | 5 | 7 |
| 4/1/21-3/31/22 ALL | 4/1/22-3/31/23 ALL | 4/1/23-3/31/24 ALL | | 0-1MM | 1-3MM | 3-5MM | 5-10MM | 10-25MM | 25MM & OVER |
| | | | | | 10 (4/1-9/30/23) | | | 68 (10/1/23-3/31/24) | |
| 50 | 77 | 78 | **NUMBER OF STATEMENTS** | 7 | 14 | 9 | 13 | 18 | 17 |
| % | % | % | **ASSETS** | % | % | % | % | % | % |
| 10.8 | 10.2 | 10.7 | Cash & Equivalents | 8.9 | 9.3 | | 14.6 | 6.7 | |
| 53.7 | 51.0 | 60.2 | Trade Receivables (net) | 66.6 | 67.2 | | 60.1 | 56.4 | |
| .6 | 1.7 | 1.6 | Inventory | | 5.3 | | .0 | .4 | 2.3 |
| 5.9 | 9.8 | 6.3 | All Other Current | 2.6 | 8.0 | | 7.4 | 6.3 | |
| 70.9 | 72.5 | 78.9 | Total Current | 83.4 | 84.4 | | 82.5 | 71.7 | |
| 6.9 | 8.5 | 7.1 | Fixed Assets (net) | 5.3 | 6.4 | | 3.1 | 13.3 | |
| 6.6 | 2.4 | 3.3 | Intangibles (net) | .3 | 7.4 | | .1 | 7.4 | |
| 15.6 | 16.5 | 10.7 | All Other Non-Current | 11.0 | 1.9 | | 14.3 | 7.5 | |
| 100.0 | 100.0 | 100.0 | Total | 100.0 | 100.0 | | 100.0 | 100.0 | 100.0 |
| | | | **LIABILITIES** | | | | | | |
| 36.5 | 29.0 | 34.3 | Notes Payable-Short Term | 26.3 | | | 48.1 | 35.6 | 32.7 |
| 2.2 | 2.8 | 2.1 | Cur. Mat.-L.T.D. | .0 | | | .4 | 5.4 | 2.8 |
| 1.8 | 1.4 | 2.1 | Trade Payables | .6 | | | 5.1 | 1.5 | 2.4 |
| .0 | .1 | .0 | Income Taxes Payable | .0 | | | .1 | .0 | .1 |
| 7.8 | 11.3 | 6.6 | All Other Current | 6.4 | | | 9.6 | 8.4 | 5.7 |
| 48.3 | 44.6 | 45.1 | Total Current | 33.3 | | | 63.3 | 51.0 | 43.6 |
| 12.6 | 17.5 | 14.8 | Long-Term Debt | 14.3 | | | 10.4 | 7.1 | 12.6 |
| .0 | .0 | .0 | Deferred Taxes | .0 | | | .0 | .0 | .0 |
| 4.5 | 4.8 | 8.5 | All Other Non-Current | 6.1 | | | 4.5 | 11.1 | 9.9 |
| 34.6 | 33.0 | 31.6 | Net Worth | 46.2 | | | 21.7 | 30.8 | 33.8 |
| 100.0 | 100.0 | 100.0 | Total Liabilities & Net Worth | 100.0 | | | 100.0 | 100.0 | 100.0 |
| | | | **INCOME DATA** | | | | | | |
| 100.0 | 100.0 | 100.0 | Net Sales | 100.0 | | | 100.0 | 100.0 | 100.0 |
| | | | Gross Profit | | | | | | |
| 69.5 | 68.3 | 63.2 | Operating Expenses | 60.2 | | | 68.3 | 63.5 | 73.6 |
| 30.5 | 31.7 | 36.8 | Operating Profit | 39.8 | | | 31.7 | 36.5 | 26.4 |
| 6.1 | 10.4 | 22.0 | All Other Expenses (net) | 21.1 | | | 20.1 | 25.1 | 16.0 |
| 24.4 | 21.3 | 14.8 | Profit Before Taxes | 18.7 | | | 11.7 | 11.5 | 10.4 |
| | | | **RATIOS** | | | | | | |
| 2.2 | 4.4 | 4.0 | | 9.6 | | | 2.5 | 2.6 | 3.7 |
| 1.5 | 1.5 | 1.6 | Current | 3.7 | | | 1.4 | 1.5 | 1.4 |
| 1.2 | 1.1 | 1.3 | | 1.5 | | | 1.0 | 1.2 | 1.3 |
| 1.9 | 3.4 | 3.8 | | 9.6 | | | 2.4 | 2.4 | 3.3 |
| 1.4 | 1.4 | 1.4 | Quick | 3.7 | | | 1.3 | 1.4 | 1.4 |
| .9 | .7 | 1.2 | | 1.4 | | | .6 | 1.2 | 1.2 |
| 4  83.8 | 3  115.6 | 152  2.4 | | 406  .9 | 12  31.5 | 26  14.0 | 146  2.5 | | |
| 608  .6 | 456  .8 | 912  .4 | Sales/Receivables | 1825  .2 | 912  .4 | 912  .4 | 281  1.3 | | |
| 1217  .3 | 1217  .3 | 1825  .2 | | 1825  .2 | 1825  .2 | 1217  .3 | 521  .7 | | |
| | | | Cost of Sales/Inventory | | | | | | |
| | | | Cost of Sales/Payables | | | | | | |
| .7 | .5 | .3 | | .2 | | | .5 | .4 | 1.4 |
| 2.0 | 1.5 | .8 | Sales/Working Capital | .5 | | | 1.0 | .8 | 2.4 |
| 39.4 | 12.2 | 3.3 | | .8 | | | NM | 4.9 | 4.3 |
| 8.2 | 5.0 | 4.4 | | | | | 4.3 | 2.1 | |
| (43) 4.9 | (59) 3.2 | (42) 2.1 | EBIT/Interest | | | | (11) 3.1 | (12) 1.5 | |
| 2.5 | 2.3 | 1.3 | | | | | 2.1 | 1.2 | |
| | | | Net Profit + Depr., Dep., Amort./Cur. Mat. L/T/D | | | | | | |
| .0 | .0 | .0 | | .0 | | | .0 | .0 | .0 |
| .0 | .0 | .0 | Fixed/Worth | .0 | | | .0 | .1 | .1 |
| .2 | .3 | .1 | | .0 | | | .1 | .2 | 1.1 |
| 1.3 | 1.3 | 1.1 | | .4 | | | 1.6 | 1.0 | 1.8 |
| 2.0 | 2.0 | 2.7 | Debt/Worth | 1.3 | | | 3.1 | 2.1 | 3.3 |
| 5.4 | 4.6 | 8.1 | | 3.3 | | | 562.5 | 6.9 | 8.1 |
| 50.1 | 27.9 | 31.3 | % Profit Before Taxes/Tangible Net Worth | 26.8 | | | 30.3 | 25.4 | 42.1 |
| (46) 22.1 | (71) 16.7 | (72) 10.8 | | 10.1 | (11) | | 9.7 | (16) 10.3 | 19.1 |
| 12.4 | 8.1 | 3.5 | | 1.3 | | | 4.6 | 6.6 | -1.1 |
| 12.2 | 7.7 | 6.3 | % Profit Before Taxes/Total Assets | 7.6 | | | 5.3 | 6.9 | 5.9 |
| 6.3 | 5.3 | 3.2 | | 1.7 | | | 2.6 | 4.0 | 3.3 |
| 2.7 | 2.7 | .7 | | .6 | | | .6 | .5 | -.2 |
| 138.9 | UND | UND | Sales/Net Fixed Assets | UND | | | UND | 152.1 | 125.2 |
| 49.7 | 78.4 | 103.3 | | UND | | | 189.6 | 29.8 | 16.1 |
| 16.5 | 9.5 | 13.7 | | 20.3 | | | 17.6 | 13.9 | 5.9 |
| .6 | .6 | .5 | Sales/Total Assets | .2 | | | .8 | .4 | 1.0 |
| .3 | .3 | .2 | | .2 | | | .3 | .3 | .6 |
| .2 | .1 | .1 | | .1 | | | .1 | .2 | .3 |
| .4 | .3 | .3 | % Depr., Dep., Amort./Sales | | | | | .4 | .3 |
| (31) .7 | (38) .5 | (39) .6 | | | | | (14) .5 | (12) .8 | |
| 1.4 | 1.7 | 1.4 | | | | | 1.0 | 3.6 | |
| | | | % Officers', Directors' Owners' Comp/Sales | | | | | | |
| 1292529M | 1721866M | 1895191M | Net Sales ($) | 3748M | 25719M | 35680M | 107509M | 297275M | 1425260M |
| 2817660M | 4000888M | 4762750M | Total Assets ($) | 28560M | 188015M | 329898M | 651202M | 1372317M | 2192758M |

© RMA 2024  
M = $ thousand  MM = $ million  
See Pages viii through xx for Explanation of Ratios and Data

# FINANCE—Real Estate Credit  NAICS 522292

## Current Data Sorted by Assets | Comparative Historical Data

| Type of Statement | | | | | | | |
|---|---|---|---|---|---|---|---|
| | 1 | 28 | 55 | 47 | 45 | Unqualified | 207 | 51 |
| | | 2 | 1 | 1 | | Reviewed | 4 | 4 |
| | 1 | | 2 | | | Compiled | 4 | 4 |
| 2 | 2 | 1 | | 2 | 1 | Tax Returns | 9 | 1 |
| | 13 | 57 | 94 | 38 | 43 | Other | 72 | 7 |
| | | | | | | | | 68 |

| 0-500M | 500M-2MM | 2-10MM | 10-50MM | 50-100MM | 100-250MM | | 4/1/19-3/31/20 ALL | 4/1/20-3/31/21 ALL |
|---|---|---|---|---|---|---|---|---|
| 38 (4/1-9/30/23) | | | 398 (10/1/23-3/31/24) | | | | | |
| 2 | 17 | 88 | 152 | 88 | 89 | NUMBER OF STATEMENTS | 296 | 131 |
| % | % | % | % | % | % | ASSETS | % | % |
| | 44.8 | 35.2 | 20.7 | 13.6 | 13.1 | Cash & Equivalents | 14.0 | 16.0 |
| | 1.1 | 9.0 | 7.7 | 10.4 | 14.3 | Trade Receivables (net) | 13.5 | 28.5 |
| | 10.6 | 23.2 | 41.5 | 40.1 | 34.6 | Inventory | 36.3 | 6.9 |
| | 1.3 | 11.4 | 10.3 | 7.8 | 8.1 | All Other Current | 14.7 | 20.4 |
| | 57.8 | 78.9 | 80.2 | 71.8 | 70.2 | Total Current | 78.4 | 71.8 |
| | 20.1 | 7.6 | 2.3 | 1.9 | 1.3 | Fixed Assets (net) | 3.0 | 3.5 |
| | 7.7 | 1.1 | 2.2 | 1.2 | .9 | Intangibles (net) | 1.4 | 2.9 |
| | 14.4 | 12.5 | 15.2 | 25.1 | 27.5 | All Other Non-Current | 17.2 | 21.8 |
| | 100.0 | 100.0 | 100.0 | 100.0 | 100.0 | Total | 100.0 | 100.0 |
| | | | | | | LIABILITIES | | |
| | 13.7 | 31.3 | 44.1 | 46.8 | 42.8 | Notes Payable-Short Term | 50.6 | 26.3 |
| | 1.4 | 1.9 | .8 | .8 | 1.3 | Cur. Mat.-L.T.D. | 1.3 | 1.2 |
| | 1.5 | 1.7 | 2.0 | 1.7 | 1.6 | Trade Payables | 5.2 | 7.9 |
| | .0 | .0 | .0 | .0 | .1 | Income Taxes Payable | .1 | .0 |
| | 8.1 | 3.9 | 5.7 | 4.7 | 8.2 | All Other Current | 7.2 | 8.6 |
| | 24.7 | 38.8 | 52.6 | 54.0 | 54.0 | Total Current | 64.3 | 43.9 |
| | 7.4 | 7.5 | 5.5 | 6.4 | 8.9 | Long-Term Debt | 9.2 | 21.0 |
| | .0 | .0 | .0 | .0 | .2 | Deferred Taxes | .1 | .0 |
| | 2.5 | 1.8 | 2.2 | 1.9 | 1.9 | All Other Non-Current | 1.4 | 2.6 |
| | 65.4 | 51.9 | 39.7 | 37.7 | 34.9 | Net Worth | 25.1 | 32.5 |
| | 100.0 | 100.0 | 100.0 | 100.0 | 100.0 | Total Liabilities & Net Worth | 100.0 | 100.0 |
| | | | | | | INCOME DATA | | |
| | 100.0 | 100.0 | 100.0 | 100.0 | 100.0 | Net Sales | 100.0 | 100.0 |
| | | | | | | Gross Profit | | |
| | 83.6 | 90.7 | 93.3 | 82.2 | 80.9 | Operating Expenses | 74.4 | 55.4 |
| | 16.4 | 9.3 | 6.7 | 17.8 | 19.1 | Operating Profit | 25.6 | 44.6 |
| | 2.8 | 8.1 | 6.8 | 14.0 | 12.5 | All Other Expenses (net) | 8.4 | 9.4 |
| | 13.7 | 1.2 | -.1 | 3.8 | 6.6 | Profit Before Taxes | 17.2 | 35.2 |
| | | | | | | RATIOS | | |
| | 6.6 | 3.3 | 2.0 | 1.7 | 2.0 | | 1.4 | 3.8 |
| | 3.9 | 1.9 | 1.3 | 1.3 | 1.2 | Current | 1.2 | 1.4 |
| | 1.5 | 1.3 | 1.2 | 1.1 | 1.1 | | 1.1 | 1.1 |
| | 4.2 | 2.6 | .9 | 1.0 | 1.2 | | 1.1 | 3.4 |
| | 3.1 | (87) 1.0 | .4 | .3 | .3 | Quick | .2 | 1.0 |
| | 1.0 | .4 | .2 | .2 | .2 | | .1 | .2 |
| 0 | UND | 0 UND | 0 UND | 3 109.0 | 2 194.2 | | 0 UND | 0 UND |
| 0 | UND | 2 164.4 | 4 83.5 | 14 26.3 | 21 17.5 | Sales/Receivables | 5 76.2 | 15 24.9 |
| 5 | 67.3 | 36 10.2 | 18 20.3 | 37 9.9 | 62 5.9 | | 36 10.1 | 521 .7 |
| | | | | | | Cost of Sales/Inventory | | |
| | | | | | | Cost of Sales/Payables | | |
| | .9 | .5 | .9 | 1.0 | 1.0 | | 2.0 | .7 |
| | 2.2 | 1.0 | 2.1 | 2.6 | 2.5 | Sales/Working Capital | 3.7 | 2.5 |
| | 9.8 | 3.2 | 4.5 | 6.2 | 8.3 | | 7.9 | 5.9 |
| | | 2.4 | 2.0 | 1.6 | 4.6 | | 5.6 | 20.6 |
| | (52) .5 | (112) .7 | (61) .7 | (64) 1.0 | EBIT/Interest | (209) 3.4 | (70) 11.2 |
| | | -1.6 | -.7 | -.2 | -.3 | | 2.1 | 6.7 |
| | | | | | | Net Profit + Depr., Dep., Amort./Cur. Mat. L/T/D | 79.5 | |
| | | | | | | | (16) 40.5 | |
| | | | | | | | 8.0 | |
| | .0 | .0 | .0 | .0 | .0 | | .0 | .0 |
| | .0 | .0 | .0 | .0 | .0 | Fixed/Worth | .0 | .0 |
| | .5 | .1 | .1 | .1 | .1 | | .1 | .1 |
| | .2 | .5 | 1.0 | 1.0 | 1.2 | | 2.1 | 1.3 |
| | .3 | .9 | 1.9 | 2.1 | 2.6 | Debt/Worth | 4.5 | 3.2 |
| | 1.5 | 2.0 | 3.4 | 4.3 | 4.6 | | 7.5 | 6.1 |
| | 24.0 | 9.7 | 8.0 | 7.1 | 8.6 | | 51.5 | 102.2 |
| (16) | 14.4 | (87) .1 | (151) -3.8 | (87) -2.0 | (88) .5 | % Profit Before Taxes/Tangible Net Worth | (291) 27.2 | (128) 53.0 |
| | -6.5 | -9.0 | -20.9 | -8.3 | -20.2 | | 10.1 | 13.8 |
| | 16.2 | 4.7 | 3.0 | 1.9 | 3.5 | | 8.8 | 25.3 |
| | 5.9 | .1 | -1.1 | -.3 | .1 | % Profit Before Taxes/Total Assets | 5.3 | 10.9 |
| | -4.2 | -5.5 | -6.1 | -3.7 | -4.2 | | 2.2 | 4.0 |
| | UND | UND | 237.0 | 352.2 | 304.1 | | 193.1 | 999.8 |
| | 150.8 | 43.4 | 72.6 | 97.4 | 79.1 | Sales/Net Fixed Assets | 80.2 | 132.8 |
| | 3.4 | 7.6 | 23.8 | 35.1 | 26.0 | | 25.7 | 28.8 |
| | 1.5 | .6 | .6 | .5 | .4 | | .6 | .7 |
| | 1.0 | .3 | .5 | .3 | .3 | Sales/Total Assets | .4 | .4 |
| | .3 | .2 | .3 | .2 | .1 | | .2 | .1 |
| | | .8 | .2 | .3 | .3 | | .2 | .1 |
| | (32) 1.2 | (92) .6 | (48) .5 | (48) .7 | % Depr., Dep., Amort./Sales | (206) .4 | (73) .3 |
| | | 2.0 | 1.1 | .9 | 1.3 | | 1.0 | .8 |
| | | | | | | | 2.5 | 3.0 |
| | | | | | | % Officers', Directors' Owners' Comp/Sales | (16) 6.0 | (15) 8.5 |
| | | | | | | | 10.4 | 21.0 |
| 1093M | 18354M | 218715M | 2140543M | 2285338M | 4530832M | Net Sales ($) | 7688019M | 4513025M |
| 934M | 22430M | 486027M | 4233437M | 6325724M | 14694703M | Total Assets ($) | 19135195M | 9521783M |

© RMA 2024   M = $ thousand   MM = $ million
See Pages viii through xx for Explanation of Ratios and Data

# FINANCE—Real Estate Credit  NAICS 522292

| Comparative Historical Data ||| | Current Data Sorted by Sales ||||||
|---|---|---|---|---|---|---|---|---|---|
| 79 | 120 | 176 | Type of Statement / Unqualified | 3 | 20 | 16 | 20 | 59 | 58 |
| 2 | 4 | 4 | Reviewed | 2 |  | 1 |  | 1 | |
| 3 | 7 | 4 | Compiled |  | 2 |  |  | 2 | |
| 6 | 10 | 7 | Tax Returns |  | 1 |  | 1 | 1 | |
| 146 | 303 | 245 | Other | 25 | 47 | 14 | 30 | 66 | 63 |
| 4/1/21- | 4/1/22- | 4/1/23- |  |  | 38 (4/1-9/30/23) ||| 398 (10/1/23-3/31/24) |||
| 3/31/22 | 3/31/23 | 3/31/24 |  | 0-1MM | 1-3MM | 3-5MM | 5-10MM | 10-25MM | 25MM & OVER |
| ALL | ALL | ALL | NUMBER OF STATEMENTS |  |  |  |  |  | |
| 236 | 444 | 436 |  | 34 | 70 | 31 | 51 | 129 | 121 |
| % | % | % | **ASSETS** | % | % | % | % | % | % |
| 21.8 | 25.3 | 21.8 | Cash & Equivalents | 30.3 | 35.5 | 28.9 | 19.2 | 18.1 | 14.7 |
| 20.2 | 12.6 | 9.6 | Trade Receivables (net) | 12.2 | 11.5 | 1.7 | 9.1 | 11.0 | 8.4 |
| 8.6 | 26.3 | 34.7 | Inventory | 5.9 | 21.3 | 28.0 | 28.9 | 39.9 | 49.3 |
| 26.4 | 9.5 | 9.2 | All Other Current | 9.5 | 9.1 | 12.6 | 19.6 | 7.0 | 6.2 |
| 77.0 | 73.7 | 75.3 | Total Current | 57.9 | 77.4 | 71.3 | 76.8 | 75.9 | 78.6 |
| 4.5 | 5.2 | 3.9 | Fixed Assets (net) | 16.4 | 6.2 | 4.4 | 1.9 | 1.8 | 2.0 |
| 1.5 | 2.0 | 1.7 | Intangibles (net) | 5.8 | .5 | .0 | 2.3 | 1.7 | 1.6 |
| 17.0 | 19.2 | 19.1 | All Other Non-Current | 19.9 | 15.9 | 24.3 | 19.0 | 20.5 | 17.8 |
| 100.0 | 100.0 | 100.0 | Total | 100.0 | 100.0 | 100.0 | 100.0 | 100.0 | 100.0 |
|  |  |  | **LIABILITIES** |  |  |  |  |  | |
| 35.5 | 35.8 | 40.4 | Notes Payable-Short Term | 22.1 | 26.8 | 36.0 | 39.7 | 42.5 | 52.6 |
| 2.8 | 1.0 | 1.1 | Cur. Mat.-L.T.D. | .7 | 2.7 | .5 | 2.2 | 1.1 | .1 |
| 6.0 | 2.2 | 1.8 | Trade Payables | .9 | 1.3 | 1.1 | 1.7 | 1.9 | 2.3 |
| .1 | .0 | .0 | Income Taxes Payable | .0 | .0 | .0 | .0 | .0 | .1 |
| 5.5 | 6.1 | 5.7 | All Other Current | 3.5 | 5.1 | 3.2 | 6.6 | 5.7 | 7.0 |
| 49.8 | 45.1 | 49.1 | Total Current | 27.1 | 36.0 | 40.8 | 50.2 | 51.2 | 62.2 |
| 12.9 | 8.5 | 6.9 | Long-Term Debt | 13.6 | 9.2 | 3.4 | 6.7 | 7.4 | 4.0 |
| .0 | .1 | .1 | Deferred Taxes | .0 | .0 | .0 | .0 | .0 | .2 |
| 2.0 | 1.4 | 2.0 | All Other Non-Current | 2.1 | 1.6 | .8 | 2.6 | 1.9 | 2.4 |
| 35.2 | 44.9 | 42.0 | Net Worth | 57.2 | 53.3 | 55.0 | 40.5 | 39.4 | 31.2 |
| 100.0 | 100.0 | 100.0 | Total Liabilities & Net Worth | 100.0 | 100.0 | 100.0 | 100.0 | 100.0 | 100.0 |
|  |  |  | **INCOME DATA** |  |  |  |  |  | |
| 100.0 | 100.0 | 100.0 | Net Sales | 100.0 | 100.0 | 100.0 | 100.0 | 100.0 | 100.0 |
|  |  |  | Gross Profit |  |  |  |  |  | |
| 66.5 | 83.9 | 87.7 | Operating Expenses | 73.6 | 86.4 | 87.1 | 81.4 | 88.0 | 94.9 |
| 33.5 | 16.1 | 12.3 | Operating Profit | 26.4 | 13.6 | 12.9 | 18.6 | 12.0 | 5.1 |
| 5.4 | 7.0 | 9.5 | All Other Expenses (net) | 13.9 | 9.7 | 6.3 | 11.1 | 9.4 | 8.4 |
| 28.1 | 9.1 | 2.8 | Profit Before Taxes | 12.5 | 3.9 | 6.6 | 7.5 | 2.6 | -3.3 |
|  |  |  | **RATIOS** |  |  |  |  |  | |
| 1.9 | 2.6 | 2.5 |  | 9.5 | 3.8 | 2.7 | 2.3 | 2.1 | 1.4 |
| 1.4 | 1.5 | 1.4 | Current | 2.9 | 2.0 | 1.7 | 1.5 | 1.3 | 1.2 |
| 1.2 | 1.2 | 1.2 |  | 1.2 | 1.4 | 1.3 | 1.2 | 1.2 | 1.1 |
| 1.5 | 1.8 | 1.5 |  | 6.3 | 3.0 | 1.3 | 1.1 | 1.0 | .5 |
| .6 | .7 (435) | .5 | Quick | 1.8 (69) | 1.5 | .6 | .5 | .4 | .2 |
| .3 | .3 | .2 |  | .4 | .4 | .4 | .2 | .2 | .1 |
| 0 UND | 0 UND | 0 UND |  | 0 UND | 0 UND | 0 UND | 0 UND | 0 999.8 | 5 80.7 |
| 6 61.0 | 5 68.7 | 7 49.2 | Sales/Receivables | 3 133.7 | 1 356.2 | 5 74.6 | 6 65.1 | 7 48.9 | 15 24.8 |
| 182 2.0 | 36 10.2 | 31 11.7 |  | 47 7.8 | 39 9.4 | 19 18.8 | 20 18.7 | 34 10.6 | 37 9.8 |
|  |  |  | Cost of Sales/Inventory |  |  |  |  |  | |
|  |  |  | Cost of Sales/Payables |  |  |  |  |  | |
| 1.4 | .9 | .8 |  | .3 | .5 | .9 | .9 | .9 | 1.8 |
| 3.4 | 2.1 | 2.1 | Sales/Working Capital | .7 | .9 | 1.4 | 1.8 | 2.1 | 3.1 |
| 6.1 | 6.2 | 5.1 |  | 7.2 | 2.5 | 4.8 | 3.3 | 4.5 | 7.1 |
| 15.1 | 5.3 | 2.6 |  | 7.3 | 2.0 | 5.0 | 6.4 | 3.7 | 1.5 |
| (123) 7.9 | (291) 1.7 | (297) .7 | EBIT/Interest | (11) 3.9 | (41) .3 | (23) .8 | (32) 1.6 | (93) .7 | (97) .5 |
| 4.3 | -.8 | -.7 |  | -1.6 | -2.3 | -.5 | -.2 | -.6 | -.6 |
|  | 15.6 | 10.0 | Net Profit + Depr., Dep., |  |  |  |  |  | |
| (19) | 1.1 (21) | .0 | Amort./Cur. Mat. L/T/D |  |  |  |  |  | |
|  | -17.7 | -9.0 |  |  |  |  |  |  | |
| .0 | .0 | .0 |  | .0 | .0 | .0 | .0 | .0 | .0 |
| .0 | .0 | .0 | Fixed/Worth | .0 | .0 | .0 | .0 | .0 | .0 |
| .1 | .1 | .1 |  | .3 | .1 | .1 | .1 | .1 | .1 |
| 1.3 | .6 | .8 |  | .2 | .3 | .5 | .7 | 1.1 | 1.7 |
| 2.3 | 1.5 | 1.9 | Debt/Worth | .8 | .8 | .9 | 1.8 | 1.9 | 2.8 |
| 4.0 | 2.9 | 3.5 |  | 2.6 | 2.1 | 1.7 | 4.9 | 3.2 | 4.6 |
| 82.7 | 15.3 | 9.0 |  | 10.8 | 11.6 | 9.0 | 10.5 | 9.8 | 4.2 |
| (235) 38.8 | (435) 4.0 | (431) .0 | % Profit Before Taxes/Tangible | (33) 2.6 | 1.7 | .0 | 1.3 | (128) -1.4 | (118) -6.7 |
| 11.6 | -8.3 | -15.4 | Net Worth | -4.5 | -5.3 | -8.7 | -17.9 | -16.6 | -28.8 |
| 22.4 | 6.4 | 4.0 |  | 5.3 | 5.5 | 5.5 | 4.7 | 3.7 | 1.1 |
| 10.0 | 1.6 | .0 | % Profit Before Taxes/Total | 1.8 | .5 | .0 | .4 | -.1 | -1.8 |
| 4.1 | -4.0 | -5.1 | Assets | -3.6 | -3.7 | -5.4 | -3.8 | -5.2 | -6.0 |
| 999.8 | 999.8 | 368.6 |  | UND | UND | 999.8 | 554.2 | 364.3 | 165.8 |
| 177.0 | 75.4 | 72.7 | Sales/Net Fixed Assets | 93.5 | 57.7 | 90.0 | 67.0 | 83.6 | 72.8 |
| 34.3 | 18.9 | 20.2 |  | 2.0 | 7.5 | 7.3 | 19.3 | 26.7 | 33.9 |
| 1.0 | .8 | .6 |  | .3 | .6 | .6 | .5 | .6 | .6 |
| .6 | .5 | .4 | Sales/Total Assets | .2 | .3 | .4 | .3 | .4 | .4 |
| .2 | .2 | .2 |  | .1 | .2 | .3 | .1 | .2 | .3 |
| .1 | .2 | .3 |  | 1.9 | .7 | .3 | .2 | .3 | .3 |
| (96) .3 | (198) .5 | (226) .7 | % Depr., Dep., Amort./Sales | (10) 5.1 | (22) 1.1 | (14) 1.0 | (29) .6 | (79) .6 | (72) .6 |
| .6 | 1.1 | 1.3 |  | 19.7 | 1.3 | 2.7 | 1.3 | 1.0 | 1.0 |
| 2.3 | 2.5 | 1.2 |  |  |  |  |  |  | |
| (14) 6.1 | (27) 5.7 | (26) 5.5 | % Officers', Directors' Owners' Comp/Sales |  |  |  |  |  | |
| 9.9 |  21.5 | 18.5 |  |  |  |  |  |  | |
| 6319591M | 8340762M | 9194875M | Net Sales ($) | 21494M | 140024M | 124574M | 367214M | 2103966M | 6437603M |
| 12515871M | 19612795M | 25763255M | Total Assets ($) | 171810M | 634782M | 487360M | 2001917M | 7647483M | 14819903M |

M = $ thousand    MM = $ million
See Pages viii through xx for Explanation of Ratios and Data

© RMA 2024

# FINANCE—International, Secondary Market, and All Other Nondepository Credit Intermediation  NAICS 522299

## Current Data Sorted by Assets | Comparative Historical Data

| 0-500M | 500M-2MM | 2-10MM | 10-50MM | 50-100MM | 100-250MM | Type of Statement | 4/1/19-3/31/20 ALL | 4/1/20-3/31/21 ALL |
|---|---|---|---|---|---|---|---|---|
|  | 1 | 10 | 39 | 19 | 37 | Unqualified | 71 | 54 |
|  |  | 1 | 3 |  |  | Reviewed | 11 | 7 |
|  |  | 1 | 2 | 2 |  | Compiled | 9 | 1 |
|  | 3 | 5 | 1 | 1 | 1 | Tax Returns | 20 | 15 |
| 3 | 6 | 15 | 53 | 16 | 34 | Other | 159 | 109 |
|  | 59 (4/1-9/30/23) |  | 194 (10/1/23-3/31/24) |  |  | NUMBER OF STATEMENTS |  |  |
| 3 | 10 | 32 | 98 | 38 | 72 |  | 270 | 186 |
| % | % | % | % | % | % | ASSETS | % | % |
|  | 17.7 | 12.1 | 13.0 | 10.5 | 8.3 | Cash & Equivalents | 9.9 | 11.1 |
|  | 19.1 | 44.4 | 45.2 | 51.5 | 35.1 | Trade Receivables (net) | 49.1 | 43.3 |
|  | 19.3 | 3.3 | 1.7 | .3 | 1.0 | Inventory | 3.1 | 3.2 |
|  | 18.3 | 14.2 | 7.7 | 8.9 | 8.4 | All Other Current | 7.9 | 8.9 |
|  | 74.3 | 74.0 | 67.7 | 71.1 | 52.7 | Total Current | 70.0 | 66.5 |
|  | 1.0 | 4.4 | 5.9 | 2.1 | 2.0 | Fixed Assets (net) | 5.1 | 6.3 |
|  | 8.6 | .7 | 2.2 | .6 | 5.2 | Intangibles (net) | 3.3 | 1.2 |
|  | 16.2 | 20.9 | 24.3 | 26.2 | 40.0 | All Other Non-Current | 21.5 | 26.0 |
|  | 100.0 | 100.0 | 100.0 | 100.0 | 100.0 | Total | 100.0 | 100.0 |
|  |  |  |  |  |  | LIABILITIES |  |  |
|  | 10.2 | 13.4 | 17.8 | 24.7 | 20.9 | Notes Payable-Short Term | 21.0 | 19.9 |
|  | .0 | .9 | 3.6 | 7.5 | 2.4 | Cur. Mat.-L.T.D. | 2.8 | 3.9 |
|  | 2.3 | 3.5 | 1.7 | 2.8 | 1.2 | Trade Payables | 3.1 | 1.9 |
|  | .1 | .1 | .0 | .0 | .1 | Income Taxes Payable | .1 | .1 |
|  | 4.2 | 11.4 | 8.0 | 4.5 | 4.3 | All Other Current | 7.9 | 7.1 |
|  | 16.9 | 29.3 | 31.1 | 39.5 | 29.0 | Total Current | 34.9 | 32.9 |
|  | 5.7 | 15.0 | 22.2 | 20.8 | 30.4 | Long-Term Debt | 21.0 | 26.3 |
|  | .0 | .0 | .0 | .0 | .2 | Deferred Taxes | .1 | .0 |
|  | 9.0 | 8.7 | 7.4 | 7.2 | 5.8 | All Other Non-Current | 6.6 | 6.6 |
|  | 68.4 | 47.1 | 39.3 | 32.6 | 34.5 | Net Worth | 37.5 | 34.2 |
|  | 100.0 | 100.0 | 100.0 | 100.0 | 100.0 | Total Liabilties & Net Worth | 100.0 | 100.0 |
|  |  |  |  |  |  | INCOME DATA |  |  |
|  | 100.0 | 100.0 | 100.0 | 100.0 | 100.0 | Net Sales | 100.0 | 100.0 |
|  | 93.0 | 68.9 | 64.8 | 53.6 | 52.0 | Gross Profit |  |  |
|  | 7.0 | 31.1 | 35.2 | 46.4 | 48.0 | Operating Expenses | 67.6 | 61.3 |
|  | 3.9 | 9.7 | 14.7 | 21.9 | 22.7 | Operating Profit | 32.4 | 38.7 |
|  | 3.1 | 21.4 | 20.5 | 24.5 | 25.3 | All Other Expenses (net) | 10.8 | 14.0 |
|  |  |  |  |  |  | Profit Before Taxes | 21.7 | 24.8 |
|  |  |  |  |  |  | RATIOS |  |  |
|  | 38.9 | 15.8 | 12.4 | 4.5 | 7.3 |  | 6.8 | 7.7 |
|  | 5.7 | 3.2 | 2.4 | 1.6 | 1.9 | Current | 1.9 | 2.1 |
|  | 2.1 | 1.6 | 1.3 | 1.3 | 1.3 |  | 1.3 | 1.3 |
|  | 7.7 | 4.7 | 7.5 | 3.8 | 4.9 |  | 5.1 | 5.7 |
|  | 3.4 | 1.6 | 1.9 | 1.5 | 1.8 | Quick | 1.6 | 1.8 |
|  | 1.1 | 1.0 | 1.2 | 1.1 | 1.1 |  | 1.1 | 1.2 |
| 0 | UND | 8 | 43.9 | 20 | 18.4 | 73 | 5.0 | 4 | 89.6 |  |  |  |  |
| 15 | 24.2 | 94 | 3.9 | 406 | .9 | 730 | .5 | 215 | 1.7 | Sales/Receivables | 17 | 21.3 | 13 | 27.4 |
| 64 | 5.7 | 1217 | .3 | 1217 | .3 | 1217 | .3 | 1217 | .3 |  | 332 | 1.1 | 228 | 1.6 |
|  |  |  |  |  |  |  | 1825 | .2 | 1825 | .2 |

| | | | | | | Cost of Sales/Inventory | | |
| | | | | | | Cost of Sales/Payables | | |

| | .7 | .3 | .4 | .4 | .4 | | .4 | .4 |
| | 2.6 | 1.1 | .8 | .7 | .7 | Sales/Working Capital | .9 | .8 |
| | 9.6 | 4.7 | 1.8 | 1.6 | 7.8 | | 3.6 | 2.9 |

|  |  |  | 10.8 |  | 5.5 |  | 5.7 |  | 4.7 |  | 7.4 |  | 6.1 |
|  |  | (19) | 4.6 | (56) | 3.5 | (20) | 2.2 | (29) | 3.5 | EBIT/Interest | (146) | 3.0 | (104) | 3.1 |
|  |  |  | 2.5 |  | 1.6 |  | 1.6 |  | 1.5 |  | 1.8 |  | 2.2 |

| | | | | | | Net Profit + Depr., Dep., Amort./Cur. Mat. L/T/D | | |

| | .0 | .0 | .0 | .0 | .0 | | .0 | .0 |
| | .0 | .0 | .0 | .0 | .0 | Fixed/Worth | .0 | .0 |
| | .0 | .0 | .2 | .1 | .0 | | .1 | .1 |

| | .1 | .3 | .8 | 1.2 | 1.4 | | .9 | 1.1 |
| | .3 | 1.5 | 1.7 | 2.0 | 2.2 | Debt/Worth | 2.3 | 2.3 |
| | 1.2 | 3.6 | 3.5 | 3.7 | 4.1 | | 5.1 | 4.4 |

|  |  |  | 37.5 |  | 25.1 |  | 24.9 |  | 17.5 |  | 30.8 |  | 30.5 |
|  |  |  | 15.1 | (92) | 11.3 | (36) | 15.5 | (66) | 9.8 | % Profit Before Taxes/Tangible Net Worth | (252) | 16.2 | (179) | 14.9 |
|  |  |  | 5.1 |  | 3.2 |  | 7.9 |  | 5.2 |  | 5.2 |  | 6.3 |

| | 9.6 | 10.0 | 8.6 | 7.2 | 5.6 | | 7.8 | 7.1 |
| | 2.5 | 4.0 | 3.8 | 4.5 | 3.2 | % Profit Before Taxes/Total Assets | 4.3 | 3.6 |
| | -2.2 | 2.1 | 1.2 | 1.9 | 1.2 | | 1.5 | 2.0 |

| | UND | UND | UND | UND | UND | | UND | UND |
| | UND | 630.7 | 95.2 | 114.4 | 164.7 | Sales/Net Fixed Assets | 144.3 | 163.5 |
| | 229.0 | 25.8 | 9.7 | 10.7 | 21.6 | | 14.4 | 13.8 |

| | 3.7 | .8 | .4 | .3 | .2 | | .5 | .3 |
| | 1.2 | .4 | .2 | .2 | .1 | Sales/Total Assets | .2 | .2 |
| | .6 | .2 | .1 | .1 | .1 | | .1 | .1 |

|  |  |  | .4 |  | .4 |  | .2 |  | .1 |  | .3 |  | .5 |
|  |  | (14) | 1.0 | (49) | 1.4 | (21) | .6 | (36) | .5 | % Depr., Dep., Amort./Sales | (128) | .8 | (85) | 1.0 |
|  |  |  | 1.6 |  | 3.5 |  | 1.5 |  | 1.0 |  | 2.1 |  | 2.0 |

|  |  |  |  |  |  |  |  |  |  | % Officers', Directors' Owners' Comp/Sales | | 1.5 | | 4.6 |
|  |  |  |  |  |  |  |  |  |  |  | (28) | 5.2 | (19) | 12.8 |
|  |  |  |  |  |  |  |  |  |  |  |  | 17.3 |  | 22.2 |

| 4818M | 21521M | 145216M | 914895M | 721865M | 3272741M | Net Sales ($) | 6144882M | 2440869M |
| 1117M | 10124M | 181230M | 2665168M | 2807976M | 11689747M | Total Assets ($) | 15005861M | 9457471M |

M = $ thousand   MM = $ million
See Pages viii through xx for Explanation of Ratios and Data

© RMA 2024

# FINANCE—International, Secondary Market, and All Other Nondepository Credit Intermediation  NAICS 522299

## Comparative Historical Data / Current Data Sorted by Sales

| Comparative Historical Data | | | | | Current Data Sorted by Sales | | | | | |
|---|---|---|---|---|---|---|---|---|---|---|
| | | | Type of Statement | | | | | | | |
| 48 | 76 | 106 | Unqualified | 2 | 13 | 12 | 24 | 35 | 20 | |
| 5 | 11 | 4 | Reviewed | | 1 | 2 | | 1 | | |
| 8 | 8 | 5 | Compiled | 1 | | 2 | 1 | 1 | | |
| 10 | 11 | 11 | Tax Returns | 3 | 2 | 2 | 1 | 1 | 2 | |
| 121 | 104 | 127 | Other | 7 | 21 | 12 | 32 | 30 | 25 | |
| 4/1/21-3/31/22 ALL | 4/1/22-3/31/23 ALL | 4/1/23-3/31/24 ALL | | 59 (4/1-9/30/23) | | | 194 (10/1/23-3/31/24) | | | |
| | | | | 0-1MM | 1-3MM | 3-5MM | 5-10MM | 10-25MM | 25MM & OVER |
| 192 | 210 | 253 | NUMBER OF STATEMENTS | 13 | 37 | 30 | 58 | 68 | 47 |
| % | % | % | ASSETS | % | % | % | % | % | % |
| 13.6 | 14.2 | 11.6 | Cash & Equivalents | 22.8 | 10.7 | 16.3 | 9.7 | 10.1 | 10.9 |
| 43.9 | 38.9 | 41.6 | Trade Receivables (net) | 23.1 | 38.7 | 27.6 | 46.8 | 44.2 | 47.8 |
| 3.1 | 3.6 | 2.3 | Inventory | 3.3 | 6.5 | 4.3 | .4 | .0 | 3.0 |
| 8.6 | 11.5 | 9.3 | All Other Current | 22.3 | 9.2 | 12.6 | 6.9 | 6.9 | 10.0 |
| 69.3 | 68.2 | 64.8 | Total Current | 71.5 | 65.1 | 60.7 | 63.8 | 61.1 | 71.8 |
| 4.6 | 5.0 | 4.2 | Fixed Assets (net) | 17.4 | 3.3 | 3.5 | 4.1 | 2.2 | 4.6 |
| 2.8 | 3.4 | 2.9 | Intangibles (net) | .5 | 1.4 | 1.0 | 1.3 | .8 | 10.8 |
| 23.4 | 23.4 | 28.2 | All Other Non-Current | 10.6 | 30.2 | 34.8 | 30.8 | 35.8 | 12.8 |
| 100.0 | 100.0 | 100.0 | Total | 100.0 | 100.0 | 100.0 | 100.0 | 100.0 | 100.0 |
| | | | LIABILITIES | | | | | | |
| 22.2 | 18.1 | 18.7 | Notes Payable-Short Term | 12.6 | 13.5 | 12.5 | 17.3 | 19.9 | 28.3 |
| 2.8 | 3.3 | 3.4 | Cur. Mat.-L.T.D. | 2.4 | 2.7 | 2.1 | 2.3 | 4.9 | 4.3 |
| 1.7 | 2.6 | 2.0 | Trade Payables | .4 | .8 | 2.9 | 2.4 | 1.5 | 3.0 |
| .0 | .0 | .1 | Income Taxes Payable | .0 | .1 | .2 | .0 | .0 | .2 |
| 6.9 | 7.6 | 6.7 | All Other Current | 6.5 | 8.1 | 7.4 | 6.6 | 5.9 | 6.6 |
| 33.8 | 31.6 | 30.9 | Total Current | 22.0 | 25.2 | 25.1 | 28.5 | 32.3 | 42.3 |
| 25.8 | 22.7 | 24.3 | Long-Term Debt | 14.8 | 26.3 | 21.4 | 29.7 | 25.5 | 18.9 |
| .0 | .1 | .1 | Deferred Taxes | .0 | .0 | .0 | .0 | .0 | .4 |
| 6.1 | 6.4 | 7.1 | All Other Non-Current | 4.1 | 10.7 | 12.1 | 6.6 | 5.9 | 4.1 |
| 34.3 | 39.2 | 37.7 | Net Worth | 59.1 | 37.8 | 41.3 | 35.3 | 36.3 | 34.3 |
| 100.0 | 100.0 | 100.0 | Total Liabilities & Net Worth | 100.0 | 100.0 | 100.0 | 100.0 | 100.0 | 100.0 |
| | | | INCOME DATA | | | | | | |
| 100.0 | 100.0 | 100.0 | Net Sales | 100.0 | 100.0 | 100.0 | 100.0 | 100.0 | 100.0 |
| | | | Gross Profit | | | | | | |
| 61.0 | 59.8 | 61.5 | Operating Expenses | 67.3 | 57.6 | 68.1 | 61.4 | 52.0 | 72.6 |
| 39.0 | 40.2 | 38.5 | Operating Profit | 32.7 | 42.4 | 31.9 | 38.6 | 48.0 | 27.4 |
| 11.3 | 12.9 | 16.9 | All Other Expenses (net) | 13.6 | 20.6 | 11.0 | 16.2 | 20.9 | 13.6 |
| 27.7 | 27.3 | 21.6 | Profit Before Taxes | 19.2 | 21.7 | 20.9 | 22.3 | 27.2 | 13.9 |
| | | | RATIOS | | | | | | |
| 9.4 | 9.1 | 7.6 | Current | 26.6 | 11.3 | 14.1 | 8.6 | 5.4 | 3.7 |
| 2.0 | 2.1 | 2.2 | | 5.8 | 3.0 | 2.7 | 2.2 | 2.1 | 1.6 |
| 1.3 | 1.4 | 1.3 | | 2.5 | 1.3 | 1.5 | 1.3 | 1.3 | 1.1 |
| 6.2 | 6.2 | 5.1 | Quick | 14.7 | 6.0 | 8.4 | 7.6 | 4.3 | 2.7 |
| 1.7 | 1.7 | 1.8 | | 2.8 | 1.7 | 2.1 | 1.9 | 1.9 | 1.5 |
| 1.1 | 1.1 | 1.1 | | 1.0 | 1.1 | .8 | 1.3 | 1.3 | 1.0 |
| 4   90.6 | 5   80.0 | 14   27.0 | Sales/Receivables | 0   UND | 0   UND | 0   UND | 27   13.4 | 26   14.0 | 22   16.9 |
| 243   1.5 | 114   3.2 | 228   1.6 | | 14   25.4 | 166   2.2 | 27   13.6 | 608   .6 | 365   1.0 | 261   1.4 |
| 1825   .2 | 1217   .3 | 1217   .3 | | 1217   .3 | 1825   .2 | 730   .5 | 1217   .3 | 1217   .3 | 912   .4 |
| | | | Cost of Sales/Inventory | | | | | | |
| | | | Cost of Sales/Payables | | | | | | |
| .4 | .3 | .4 | Sales/Working Capital | .2 | .3 | .4 | .4 | .4 | .7 |
| .8 | .9 | .8 | | .3 | 1.0 | .7 | .7 | .8 | 1.9 |
| 3.1 | 4.0 | 3.6 | | .7 | 3.0 | 11.1 | 1.1 | 2.8 | 16.6 |
| 9.8 | 7.4 | 5.5 | EBIT/Interest | | 22.6 | 5.1 | 5.4 | 5.5 | 4.4 |
| (124) 4.9 | (116) 4.8 | (132) 3.5 | | (14) 6.1 | (19) 3.6 | (29) 3.6 | (31) 3.3 | (33) 1.9 |
| 2.7 | 2.7 | 1.6 | | | 2.2 | 2.5 | 1.6 | 1.8 | 1.4 |
| | 56.9 | 2.8 | Net Profit + Depr., Dep., Amort./Cur. Mat. L/T/D | | | | | | |
| (12) 12.6 | (13) 2.1 | | | | | | | | |
| .6 | .3 | | | | | | | | |
| .0 | .0 | .0 | Fixed/Worth | .0 | .0 | .0 | .0 | .0 | .0 |
| .0 | .0 | .0 | | .0 | .0 | .0 | .0 | .0 | .0 |
| .1 | .1 | .1 | | .4 | .0 | .1 | .0 | .1 | 1.0 |
| 1.0 | .9 | .9 | Debt/Worth | .1 | .3 | .7 | 1.3 | 1.1 | 1.4 |
| 2.6 | 1.9 | 1.9 | | .3 | 1.8 | 2.1 | 2.0 | 2.1 | 1.9 |
| 8.2 | 4.5 | 3.8 | | 4.2 | 5.4 | 3.5 | 3.2 | 3.5 | 34.6 |
| 38.4 | 30.1 | 21.8 | % Profit Before Taxes/Tangible Net Worth | 14.1 | 20.4 | 29.4 | 22.2 | 24.8 | 23.6 |
| (176) 19.2 | (198) 17.7 | (236) 12.1 | | (12) 4.4 | (36) 9.2 | 11.3 | (57) 13.0 | (64) 13.7 | (37) 13.9 |
| 8.1 | 7.2 | 4.9 | | .2 | 2.4 | 7.9 | 4.8 | 6.6 | 5.3 |
| 9.2 | 9.9 | 7.3 | % Profit Before Taxes/Total Assets | 4.4 | 5.8 | 10.9 | 7.7 | 6.3 | 9.4 |
| 5.3 | 4.7 | 3.8 | | 2.9 | 2.1 | 4.1 | 3.8 | 4.4 | 3.4 |
| 1.6 | 2.1 | 1.3 | | .4 | .9 | 1.9 | 1.1 | 2.4 | 1.2 |
| UND | UND | UND | Sales/Net Fixed Assets | UND | UND | UND | UND | UND | 999.8 |
| 234.8 | 86.8 | 151.7 | | UND | UND | 73.1 | 168.1 | 166.2 | 117.8 |
| 22.5 | 11.7 | 18.8 | | 2.0 | 32.2 | 10.6 | 18.2 | 22.6 | 18.9 |
| .3 | .4 | .4 | Sales/Total Assets | .3 | .4 | .4 | .3 | .3 | .9 |
| .2 | .2 | .2 | | .1 | .2 | .2 | .2 | .2 | .3 |
| .1 | .1 | .1 | | .1 | .1 | .1 | .1 | .1 | .2 |
| .3 | .3 | .3 | % Depr., Dep., Amort./Sales | | .3 | .4 | .4 | .2 | .1 |
| (86) .8 | (101) .9 | (122) .7 | | (13) 1.4 | (19) 1.4 | (24) .5 | (33) .8 | (30) .5 |
| 1.6 | 1.8 | 1.8 | | | 3.1 | 2.8 | 1.5 | 1.9 | 1.6 |
| 6.2 | 1.2 | 2.8 | % Officers', Directors' Owners' Comp/Sales | | | | 1.2 | | |
| (16) 14.3 | (25) 8.2 | (27) 12.5 | | | | | (11) 4.2 | | |
| 31.1 | 16.7 | 19.6 | | | | | 38.8 | | |
| 3871594M | 2969398M | 5081056M | Net Sales ($) | 5574M | 70034M | 115880M | 454649M | 1061587M | 3373332M |
| 10574961M | 12441100M | 17355362M | Total Assets ($) | 42110M | 584580M | 638703M | 3172569M | 6810158M | 6107242M |

M = $ thousand    MM = $ million
See Pages viii through xx for Explanation of Ratios and Data

© RMA 2024

# FINANCE—Mortgage and Nonmortgage Loan Brokers  NAICS 522310

| Current Data Sorted by Assets | | | | | | | Comparative Historical Data | |
|---|---|---|---|---|---|---|---|---|
| 1 | | 5 | 31 | 16 | 12 | Type of Statement Unqualified | 80 | 68 |
|   |   |   | 1  |    |    | Reviewed | 4 | 6 |
|   |   |   |    |    |    | Compiled | 7 | 6 |
| 1 | 1 | 2 | 1  |    |    | Tax Returns | 10 | 8 |
| 3 | 3 | 9 | 33 | 21 | 12 | Other | 80 | 71 |
| 0-500M | 12 (4/1-9/30/23) 500M-2MM | 2-10MM | 140 (10/1/23-3/31/24) 10-50MM | 50-100MM | 100-250MM | | 4/1/19- 3/31/20 ALL | 4/1/20- 3/31/21 ALL |
| 5 | 4 | 16 | 66 | 37 | 24 | NUMBER OF STATEMENTS | 181 | 159 |
| % | % | % | % | % | % | ASSETS | % | % |
|   |   | 26.3 | 22.1 | 14.3 | 16.4 | Cash & Equivalents | 23.2 | 22.5 |
|   |   | 11.7 | 4.6 | 2.8 | 4.6 | Trade Receivables (net) | 11.9 | 11.6 |
|   |   | 11.4 | 5.3 | 9.9 | 13.5 | Inventory | | |
|   |   | 19.2 | 49.5 | 53.8 | 48.7 | All Other Current | 33.7 | 23.8 |
|   |   | 68.6 | 81.5 | 80.8 | 83.1 | Total Current | 10.7 | 28.0 |
|   |   |      |      |      |      |                  | 79.5 | 85.9 |
|   |   | 11.8 | 5.4 | 2.5 | 1.1 | Fixed Assets (net) | 7.9 | 6.1 |
|   |   | 4.0 | 1.5 | .7 | 2.4 | Intangibles (net) | 1.6 | 1.0 |
|   |   | 15.7 | 11.6 | 16.0 | 13.3 | All Other Non-Current | 11.0 | 7.0 |
|   |   | 100.0 | 100.0 | 100.0 | 100.0 | Total | 100.0 | 100.0 |
|   |   |      |      |      |      | LIABILITIES | | |
|   |   | 30.5 | 23.8 | 17.6 | 25.8 | Notes Payable-Short Term | 46.0 | 37.9 |
|   |   | .5 | .5 | .3 | 3.6 | Cur. Mat.-L.T.D. | 2.0 | .7 |
|   |   | 3.8 | 3.4 | 2.5 | 2.3 | Trade Payables | 3.0 | 3.1 |
|   |   | .0 | .1 | .0 | .0 | Income Taxes Payable | .1 | .3 |
|   |   | 5.8 | 29.5 | 41.4 | 37.2 | All Other Current | 8.5 | 20.7 |
|   |   | 40.5 | 57.3 | 61.8 | 69.0 | Total Current | 59.7 | 62.7 |
|   |   | 7.3 | 4.8 | 5.0 | 2.7 | Long-Term Debt | 6.3 | 8.2 |
|   |   | .0 | .0 | .0 | .2 | Deferred Taxes | .1 | .2 |
|   |   | 6.1 | 2.5 | 1.4 | 3.4 | All Other Non-Current | 1.8 | 2.0 |
|   |   | 46.0 | 35.3 | 31.8 | 24.7 | Net Worth | 32.2 | 26.9 |
|   |   | 100.0 | 100.0 | 100.0 | 100.0 | Total Liabilities & Net Worth | 100.0 | 100.0 |
|   |   |      |      |      |      | INCOME DATA | | |
|   |   | 100.0 | 100.0 | 100.0 | 100.0 | Net Sales | 100.0 | 100.0 |
|   |   |      |      |      |      | Gross Profit | | |
|   |   | 85.7 | 91.7 | 94.0 | 93.7 | Operating Expenses | 79.2 | 68.4 |
|   |   | 14.3 | 8.3 | 6.0 | 6.3 | Operating Profit | 20.8 | 31.6 |
|   |   | 4.3 | 6.8 | 8.4 | 7.2 | All Other Expenses (net) | 3.6 | 2.8 |
|   |   | 9.9 | 1.5 | -2.4 | -.9 | Profit Before Taxes | 17.2 | 28.8 |
|   |   |      |      |      |      | RATIOS | | |
|   |   | 2.6 | 1.7 | 1.5 | 1.4 | | 1.7 | 1.6 |
|   |   | 1.7 | 1.3 | 1.3 | 1.2 | Current | 1.2 | 1.2 |
|   |   | 1.2 | 1.2 | 1.1 | 1.1 | | 1.1 | 1.1 |
|   |   | 2.5 | .8 | .5 | .5 | | 1.3 | 1.2 |
|   |   | .7 | .3 | .2 | .2 | Quick | .3 | .3 |
|   |   | .3 | .2 | .1 | .1 | | .1 | .1 |
|   |   | 0 UND | 0 UND | 0 UND | 0 UND | | 0 UND | 0 UND |
|   |   | 6 59.9 | 2 183.8 | 9 41.9 | 15 24.4 | Sales/Receivables | 2 202.7 | 4 85.9 |
|   |   | 38 9.7 | 6 61.1 | 31 11.7 | 41 9.0 | | 18 20.7 | 19 19.6 |
|   |   |      |      |      |      | Cost of Sales/Inventory | | |
|   |   |      |      |      |      | Cost of Sales/Payables | | |
|   |   | .5 | 1.5 | 1.3 | 1.3 | | 2.2 | 2.3 |
|   |   | 2.7 | 2.8 | 2.7 | 2.9 | Sales/Working Capital | 4.6 | 3.7 |
|   |   | 5.7 | 5.3 | 4.5 | 9.7 | | 10.8 | 7.3 |
|   |   | 4.0 | 1.9 | 1.5 | 1.7 | | 12.3 | 21.9 |
|   | (12) | 1.3 | (45) .7 | (25) .3 | (19) .2 | EBIT/Interest | (87) 4.1 | (90) 11.2 |
|   |   | -1.8 | -1.1 | -.3 | -.5 | | 2.3 | 7.3 |
|   |   |      |      |      |      | Net Profit + Depr., Dep., Amort./Cur. Mat. L/T/D | | |
|   |   | .0 | .0 | .0 | .0 | | .0 | .0 |
|   |   | .0 | .1 | .0 | .0 | Fixed/Worth | .0 | .0 |
|   |   | .3 | .3 | .1 | .1 | | .2 | .1 |
|   |   | .5 | 1.2 | 1.4 | 2.3 | | 1.6 | 2.1 |
|   |   | 1.2 | 2.0 | 2.2 | 4.0 | Debt/Worth | 3.3 | 4.2 |
|   |   | 3.8 | 4.2 | 4.5 | 8.9 | | 6.4 | 6.1 |
|   |   | 34.0 | 17.0 | 5.4 | 8.4 | | 76.9 | 115.6 |
|   |   | 3.0 | -3.4 | -9.0 | (23) -10.2 | % Profit Before Taxes/Tangible Net Worth | (180) 39.8 | (154) 77.6 |
|   |   | -.6 | -18.5 | -24.5 | -36.7 | | 16.4 | 44.8 |
|   |   | 8.4 | 5.0 | 1.1 | 1.5 | | 14.8 | 24.6 |
|   |   | .9 | -1.1 | -3.5 | -2.9 | % Profit Before Taxes/Total Assets | 7.6 | 14.6 |
|   |   | -.6 | -6.8 | -5.4 | -6.0 | | 3.5 | 7.5 |
|   |   | UND | 112.6 | 330.0 | 351.2 | | 259.0 | 408.6 |
|   |   | 37.6 | 38.2 | 45.6 | 72.0 | Sales/Net Fixed Assets | 73.3 | 99.7 |
|   |   | 3.0 | 8.6 | 13.7 | 22.3 | | 24.7 | 29.1 |
|   |   | .8 | .6 | .6 | .6 | | 1.2 | .8 |
|   |   | .5 | .5 | .4 | .3 | Sales/Total Assets | .5 | .5 |
|   |   | .2 | .4 | .2 | .3 | | .4 | .4 |
|   |   |   | .3 | .3 | .6 | | .2 | .1 |
|   |   | (35) | .6 (13) | .5 (13) | .8 | % Depr., Dep., Amort./Sales | (90) .3 | (88) .3 |
|   |   |   | 1.1 | 1.8 | 1.1 | | 1.0 | .7 |
|   |   |      |      |      |      | | 4.1 | 1.9 |
|   |   |      |      |      |      | % Officers', Directors' Owners' Comp/Sales | (31) 10.9 | (21) 5.7 |
|   |   |      |      |      |      | | 17.8 | 14.1 |
| 4531M | 8633M | 46257M | 1025303M | 1085202M | 1468426M | Net Sales ($) | 3799751M | 4921430M |
| 985M | 4493M | 81933M | 1833174M | 2518160M | 4007759M | Total Assets ($) | 6470587M | 8635894M |

© RMA 2024    M = $ thousand    MM = $ million
See Pages viii through xx for Explanation of Ratios and Data

# FINANCE—Mortgage and Nonmortgage Loan Brokers  NAICS 522310

| Comparative Historical Data ||| Type of Statement | Current Data Sorted by Sales ||||||
|---|---|---|---|---|---|---|---|---|---|
| 49 | 69 | 65 | Unqualified | 1 | 3 | 1 | 10 | 29 | 21 |
| 3 | 3 | 1 | Reviewed |  |  |  |  | 1 |  |
| 2 | 2 |  | Compiled |  |  |  |  |  |  |
| 2 | 8 | 5 | Tax Returns | 2 | 1 | 1 |  | 1 |  |
| 61 | 75 | 81 | Other | 5 | 6 | 6 | 13 | 23 | 28 |
| 4/1/21-3/31/22 | 4/1/22-3/31/23 | 4/1/23-3/31/24 |  |  | 12 (4/1-9/30/23) ||| 140 (10/1/23-3/31/24) |||
| ALL | ALL | ALL |  | 0-1MM | 1-3MM | 3-5MM | 5-10MM | 10-25MM | 25MM & OVER |
| 117 | 157 | 152 | **NUMBER OF STATEMENTS** | 8 | 10 | 8 | 23 | 54 | 49 |
| % | % | % | **ASSETS** | % | % | % | % | % | % |
| 27.2 | 24.0 | 21.8 | Cash & Equivalents |  | 31.1 |  | 18.8 | 21.8 | 15.9 |
| 9.2 | 6.7 | 5.1 | Trade Receivables (net) |  | 16.5 |  | 6.9 | 1.2 | 4.4 |
| 9.2 | 8.4 | 8.6 | Inventory |  | .0 |  | 6.9 | 5.6 | 12.1 |
| 39.0 | 33.0 | 44.9 | All Other Current |  | 18.4 |  | 49.8 | 51.2 | 52.9 |
| 84.6 | 72.2 | 80.3 | Total Current |  | 66.1 |  | 82.4 | 79.8 | 85.4 |
| 3.7 | 7.3 | 5.0 | Fixed Assets (net) |  | 11.3 |  | 9.2 | 3.6 | 2.5 |
| .8 | 2.9 | 1.9 | Intangibles (net) |  | 3.2 |  | 1.3 | 1.3 | 1.6 |
| 10.9 | 17.7 | 12.8 | All Other Non-Current |  | 19.5 |  | 7.1 | 15.3 | -10.4 |
| 100.0 | 100.0 | 100.0 | Total |  | 100.0 |  | 100.0 | 100.0 | 100.0 |
|  |  |  | **LIABILITIES** |  |  |  |  |  |  |
| 20.1 | 20.7 | 22.2 | Notes Payable-Short Term |  | 11.5 |  | 30.4 | 22.1 | 20.3 |
| 1.2 | 1.5 | 1.0 | Cur. Mat.-L.T.D. |  | .7 |  | .3 | .4 | 2.2 |
| 4.0 | 3.7 | 4.4 | Trade Payables |  | 19.9 |  | 2.9 | 2.5 | 2.6 |
| .0 | .0 | .0 | Income Taxes Payable |  | .0 |  | .0 | .1 | .0 |
| 30.7 | 23.5 | 30.9 | All Other Current |  | 19.6 |  | 18.1 | 32.2 | 44.8 |
| 56.0 | 49.4 | 58.6 | Total Current |  | 51.7 |  | 51.6 | 57.3 | 70.0 |
| 5.5 | 7.2 | 5.1 | Long-Term Debt |  | 12.4 |  | 7.3 | 5.2 | 1.3 |
| .1 | .0 | .1 | Deferred Taxes |  | .0 |  | .0 | .0 | .1 |
| .9 | 3.1 | 4.0 | All Other Non-Current |  | 10.1 |  | 3.5 | 1.4 | 2.7 |
| 37.4 | 40.2 | 32.2 | Net Worth |  | 25.7 |  | 37.6 | 36.1 | 25.9 |
| 100.0 | 100.0 | 100.0 | Total Liabilities & Net Worth |  | 100.0 |  | 100.0 | 100.0 | 100.0 |
|  |  |  | **INCOME DATA** |  |  |  |  |  |  |
| 100.0 | 100.0 | 100.0 | Net Sales |  | 100.0 |  | 100.0 | 100.0 | 100.0 |
|  |  |  | Gross Profit |  |  |  |  |  |  |
| 72.5 | 92.4 | 91.6 | Operating Expenses |  | 81.1 |  | 80.8 | 96.2 | 97.1 |
| 27.5 | 7.6 | 8.4 | Operating Profit |  | 18.9 |  | 19.2 | 3.8 | 2.9 |
| 4.0 | 2.9 | 6.7 | All Other Expenses (net) |  | 9.8 |  | 6.4 | 6.6 | 7.0 |
| 23.5 | 4.8 | 1.6 | Profit Before Taxes |  | 9.1 |  | 12.8 | -2.8 | -4.1 |
|  |  |  | **RATIOS** |  |  |  |  |  |  |
| 2.1 | 1.9 | 1.7 |  |  | 2.2 |  | 2.1 | 1.7 | 1.3 |
| 1.3 | 1.4 | 1.3 | Current |  | 1.3 |  | 1.6 | 1.3 | 1.2 |
| 1.2 | 1.1 | 1.1 |  |  | .6 |  | 1.2 | 1.2 | 1.1 |
| 1.4 | 1.1 | .7 |  |  | 1.8 |  | .8 | .6 | .5 |
| .4 | .5 | .3 | Quick |  | .7 |  | .5 | .3 | .2 |
| .2 | .2 | .2 |  |  | .3 |  | .2 | .2 | .1 |
| 0 UND | 0 UND | 0 UND |  | 0 UND |  | 0 UND | 0 UND | 1 252.5 ||
| 3 135.8 | 3 124.2 | 4 98.5 | Sales/Receivables | 0 UND |  | 2 159.9 | 2 178.4 | 12 30.1 ||
| 12 29.9 | 20 18.5 | 21 17.0 |  | 35 10.4 |  | 17 21.1 | 7 51.7 | 33 11.2 ||
|  |  |  | Cost of Sales/Inventory |  |  |  |  |  |  |
|  |  |  | Cost of Sales/Payables |  |  |  |  |  |  |
| 1.9 | 1.5 | 1.3 |  |  | 2.6 |  | .6 | 1.2 | 2.1 |
| 3.3 | 3.3 | 2.8 | Sales/Working Capital |  | 6.1 |  | 1.9 | 2.3 | 3.6 |
| 6.4 | 9.9 | 6.1 |  |  | -6.0 |  | 3.0 | 5.4 | 7.9 |
| 11.6 | 4.5 | 1.8 |  |  |  |  | 8.2 | 1.7 | 1.5 |
| (94) 6.7 | (116) 1.2 | (106) .4 | EBIT/Interest |  | (17) 1.3 | (35) | .3 | (38) .3 ||
| 3.1 | -1.0 | -.6 |  |  |  |  | -.2 | -1.0 | -.4 |
|  |  | 13.5 |  |  |  |  |  |  |  |
|  | (10) | 1.8 | Net Profit + Depr., Dep., Amort./Cur. Mat. L/T/D |  |  |  |  |  |  |
|  |  | -19.7 |  |  |  |  |  |  |  |
| .0 | .0 | .0 |  |  | .0 |  | .0 | .0 | .0 |
| .0 | .0 | .0 | Fixed/Worth |  | .0 |  | .0 | .0 | .1 |
| .1 | .2 | .2 |  |  | .6 |  | .4 | .1 | .2 |
| 1.2 | 1.0 | 1.2 |  |  | .9 |  | .7 | 1.3 | 2.0 |
| 2.2 | 1.8 | 2.3 | Debt/Worth |  | 2.3 |  | 1.5 | 1.8 | 3.7 |
| 3.5 | 3.7 | 4.4 |  |  | 6.9 |  | 5.4 | 3.4 | 5.8 |
| 87.9 | 20.0 | 12.4 |  |  |  |  | 39.1 | 7.0 | 4.1 |
| 49.4 | (152) 3.8 | (148) -1.9 | % Profit Before Taxes/Tangible Net Worth |  | 8.4 |  | -6.9 | (48) -10.2 ||
| 19.2 | -15.8 | -20.9 |  |  | -6.8 |  | -21.2 | -35.8 ||
| 25.1 | 6.9 | 3.7 |  |  | 9.8 |  | 10.9 | 2.9 | 1.3 |
| 15.7 | 1.2 | -1.1 | % Profit Before Taxes/Total Assets |  | 4.1 |  | .9 | -1.8 | -3.5 |
| 6.8 | -4.7 | -5.7 |  |  | -6.5 |  | -2.9 | -7.2 | -6.4 |
| 313.3 | 136.0 | 258.3 |  | UND |  | 135.1 | 122.3 | 257.3 ||
| 111.1 | 33.2 | 43.3 | Sales/Net Fixed Assets |  | 67.4 |  | 33.6 | 40.7 | 59.3 |
| 28.1 | 9.7 | 12.5 |  |  | 2.1 |  | 3.5 | 14.1 | 14.3 |
| 1.0 | .9 | .6 |  |  | 2.9 |  | .5 | .6 | .6 |
| .7 | .6 | .5 | Sales/Total Assets |  | .5 |  | .4 | .5 | .6 |
| .5 | .3 | .3 |  |  | .3 |  | .1 | .3 | .4 |
| .1 | .3 | .3 |  |  |  |  | .3 | .3 | .4 |
| (80) .2 | (92) .6 | (72) .6 | % Depr., Dep., Amort./Sales |  |  | (10) | .5 | (27) .6 | (23) .7 |
| .6 | 1.3 | 1.3 |  |  |  |  | 1.4 | 1.2 | 1.4 |
| 4.0 | 4.1 | 3.4 |  |  |  |  |  |  |  |
| (10) 14.6 | (16) 9.5 | (13) 5.2 | % Officers', Directors' Owners' Comp/Sales |  |  |  |  |  |  |
| 24.1 | 20.9 | 13.3 |  |  |  |  |  |  |  |
| 4832365M | 3393454M | 3638352M | Net Sales ($) | 4040M | 17201M | 31084M | 155577M | 868506M | 2561944M |
| 7271238M | 6750398M | 8446504M | Total Assets ($) | 19747M | 43301M | 81325M | 668332M | 2220292M | 5413507M |

© RMA 2024    M = $ thousand    MM = $ million
See Pages viii through xx for Explanation of Ratios and Data

# FINANCE—Financial Transactions Processing, Reserve, and Clearinghouse Activities  NAICS 522320

## Current Data Sorted by Assets | Comparative Historical Data

| | | | | | | Type of Statement | | |
|---|---|---|---|---|---|---|---|---|
| | 1 | 2 | 8 | 4 | 8 | Unqualified | 13 | 23 |
| | | 1 | 1 | | | Reviewed | 2 | |
| | | 2 | 1 | | | Compiled | 5 | 2 |
| 1 | 4 | 2 | 2 | | | Tax Returns | 8 | 5 |
| 3 | 12 | 18 | 25 | 7 | 11 | Other | 65 | 49 |
| | 13 (4/1-9/30/23) | | 97 (10/1/23-3/31/24) | | | | 4/1/19-3/31/20 | 4/1/20-3/31/21 |
| 0-500M | 500M-2MM | 2-10MM | 10-50MM | 50-100MM | 100-250MM | | ALL | ALL |
| 5 | 16 | 24 | 35 | 11 | 19 | NUMBER OF STATEMENTS | 93 | 79 |
| % | % | % | % | % | % | ASSETS | % | % |
| | 41.9 | 40.1 | 21.0 | 26.9 | 17.9 | Cash & Equivalents | 34.9 | 35.6 |
| | 17.4 | 13.9 | 19.7 | 17.0 | 14.4 | Trade Receivables (net) | 15.4 | 17.8 |
| | 2.9 | 5.4 | .5 | 5.7 | .1 | Inventory | 1.9 | 1.8 |
| | 5.4 | 7.5 | 9.1 | 9.0 | 15.6 | All Other Current | 9.0 | 5.5 |
| | 67.6 | 66.9 | 50.3 | 58.6 | 47.9 | Total Current | 61.2 | 60.8 |
| | 13.5 | 15.3 | 19.8 | 8.2 | 4.0 | Fixed Assets (net) | 14.7 | 10.0 |
| | 10.4 | 4.0 | 9.5 | 24.4 | 34.4 | Intangibles (net) | 16.1 | 18.3 |
| | 8.6 | 13.8 | 20.4 | 8.8 | 13.8 | All Other Non-Current | 8.0 | 10.9 |
| | 100.0 | 100.0 | 100.0 | 100.0 | 100.0 | Total | 100.0 | 100.0 |
| | | | | | | LIABILITIES | | |
| | 14.1 | 7.7 | 4.2 | 1.2 | 7.2 | Notes Payable-Short Term | 5.0 | 5.1 |
| | .8 | 2.4 | 3.4 | 1.9 | .8 | Cur. Mat.-L.T.D. | 3.2 | 3.1 |
| | 7.8 | 9.0 | 11.2 | 18.6 | 8.5 | Trade Payables | 10.5 | 10.0 |
| | .0 | .1 | 1.4 | .1 | .0 | Income Taxes Payable | .2 | .3 |
| | 1.0 | 18.9 | 23.8 | 15.0 | 38.8 | All Other Current | 20.5 | 25.2 |
| | 23.7 | 38.1 | 43.8 | 36.9 | 55.4 | Total Current | 39.4 | 43.7 |
| | 11.7 | 34.1 | 13.0 | 67.2 | 13.2 | Long-Term Debt | 28.5 | 30.4 |
| | .0 | .0 | .2 | .6 | .6 | Deferred Taxes | .3 | .4 |
| | 6.4 | 9.9 | 3.5 | 9.7 | 6.6 | All Other Non-Current | 5.4 | 5.2 |
| | 58.1 | 17.9 | 39.4 | -14.4 | 24.2 | Net Worth | 26.4 | 20.4 |
| | 100.0 | 100.0 | 100.0 | 100.0 | 100.0 | Total Liabilties & Net Worth | 100.0 | 100.0 |
| | | | | | | INCOME DATA | | |
| | 100.0 | 100.0 | 100.0 | 100.0 | 100.0 | Net Sales | 100.0 | 100.0 |
| | | | | | | Gross Profit | | |
| | 82.4 | 94.2 | 87.8 | 85.0 | 97.4 | Operating Expenses | 88.2 | 87.1 |
| | 17.6 | 5.8 | 12.2 | 15.0 | 2.6 | Operating Profit | 11.8 | 12.9 |
| | 2.6 | 2.0 | 3.3 | 9.1 | 5.5 | All Other Expenses (net) | 3.5 | 1.8 |
| | 15.0 | 3.8 | 8.9 | 5.8 | -2.9 | Profit Before Taxes | 8.3 | 11.1 |
| | | | | | | RATIOS | | |
| | 8.0 | 3.6 | 2.9 | 2.2 | 1.1 | | 2.8 | 3.5 |
| | 2.2 | 1.6 | 1.3 | 1.5 | .9 | Current | 1.8 | 1.3 |
| | 1.6 | 1.2 | .8 | .9 | .4 | | 1.1 | 1.0 |
| | 8.0 | 2.6 | 2.7 | 2.1 | 1.0 | | 2.5 | 2.6 |
| | 2.0 | 1.5 | 1.3 | 1.4 | .5 | Quick | 1.4 | 1.3 |
| | 1.0 | 1.1 | .3 | .6 | .3 | | .9 | .8 |
| | 0  UND | 0  999.8 | 16  22.8 | 5  79.6 | 18  19.8 | | 1  305.3 | 5  72.6 |
| | 1  547.4 | 6  63.7 | 31  11.7 | 39  9.3 | 53  6.9 | Sales/Receivables | 24  15.1 | 27  13.3 |
| | 43  8.5 | 30  12.0 | 91  4.0 | 54  6.8 | 99  3.7 | | 48  7.6 | 62  5.9 |
| | | | | | | Cost of Sales/Inventory | | |
| | | | | | | Cost of Sales/Payables | | |
| | 4.3 | 3.2 | 5.2 | 3.3 | 5.1 | | 4.2 | 4.4 |
| | 6.4 | 14.5 | 10.8 | 7.1 | -27.7 | Sales/Working Capital | 8.6 | 7.8 |
| | 62.6 | 42.5 | -15.4 | -17.7 | -6.4 | | 32.9 | -289.6 |
| | 16.6 | 10.8 | 52.0 | | 12.7 | | 25.0 | 17.0 |
| (12) | 4.5 | (17) 4.0 | (20) 7.7 | | (18) -.3 | EBIT/Interest | (68) 5.8 | (52) 2.8 |
| | 1.7 | .5 | .9 | | -2.3 | | 1.0 | .4 |
| | | | | | | Net Profit + Depr., Dep., Amort./Cur. Mat. L/T/D | 15.8 | |
| | | | | | | | (12) 5.4 | |
| | | | | | | | -.4 | |
| | .0 | .0 | .2 | .1 | .3 | | .1 | .0 |
| | .1 | .3 | .5 | .3 | -1.6 | Fixed/Worth | .5 | .3 |
| | 1.0 | 1.7 | 3.4 | -.1 | -.1 | | NM | -5.3 |
| | .1 | .6 | .8 | 1.7 | 9.4 | | .8 | 1.1 |
| | .9 | 1.8 | 2.0 | 4.8 | -53.6 | Debt/Worth | 3.0 | 5.2 |
| | 21.5 | 40.5 | 32.0 | -2.0 | -2.2 | | NM | -6.6 |
| | 152.4 | 41.5 | 57.0 | | | | 97.3 | 107.4 |
| (13) | 76.6 | (19) 12.8 | (27) 18.1 | | | % Profit Before Taxes/Tangible Net Worth | (70) 52.2 | (55) 41.6 |
| | 16.5 | .6 | -1.6 | | | | 9.6 | 5.7 |
| | 33.9 | 15.9 | 18.4 | 8.7 | 8.5 | | 35.5 | 23.6 |
| | 15.1 | 5.7 | 7.2 | 4.4 | -.2 | % Profit Before Taxes/Total Assets | 13.7 | 6.6 |
| | 2.7 | -4.0 | -.4 | -.1 | -11.5 | | .4 | -.5 |
| | UND | 768.1 | 68.1 | 36.1 | 77.1 | | 61.2 | 132.4 |
| | 62.1 | 21.5 | 13.8 | 16.8 | 28.3 | Sales/Net Fixed Assets | 24.4 | 35.9 |
| | 6.8 | 14.4 | 6.0 | 7.4 | 9.8 | | 9.0 | 12.1 |
| | 5.7 | 4.1 | 2.1 | 1.2 | 1.1 | | 2.9 | 2.8 |
| | 3.0 | 2.4 | 1.1 | 1.1 | .8 | Sales/Total Assets | 1.5 | 1.3 |
| | .9 | 1.2 | .5 | .6 | .5 | | .9 | .6 |
| | | .3 | .9 | | | | .8 | .5 |
| | (10) | 1.5 | (19) 2.0 | | | % Depr., Dep., Amort./Sales | (57) 2.3 | (36) 1.4 |
| | | 2.2 | 4.4 | | | | 4.3 | 4.0 |
| | | | | | | % Officers', Directors' Owners' Comp/Sales | 2.4 | 1.5 |
| | | | | | | | (18) 5.9 | (12) 3.8 |
| | | | | | | | 10.5 | 13.3 |
| 8092M | 167218M | 345306M | 1405931M | 824087M | 2396163M | Net Sales ($) | 6026869M | 4179662M |
| 1334M | 17640M | 111178M | 918042M | 759606M | 3135196M | Total Assets ($) | 4785397M | 3990294M |

M = $ thousand    MM = $ million
See Pages viii through xx for Explanation of Ratios and Data

© RMA 2024

# FINANCE—Financial Transactions Processing, Reserve, and Clearinghouse Activities  NAICS 522320

## Comparative Historical Data | | Current Data Sorted by Sales

| Comparative Historical Data | | | | | Current Data Sorted by Sales | | | | | |
|---|---|---|---|---|---|---|---|---|---|---|
| 16 | 18 | 23 | | Type of Statement | | 1 | | 1 | 3 | 18 |
| | 2 | 1 | | Unqualified | | | | | 1 | |
| 2 | 3 | 7 | | Reviewed | | | 2 | 1 | 1 | 1 |
| 3 | 11 | 7 | | Compiled | 2 | 2 | | 1 | 1 | |
| 52 | 75 | 76 | | Tax Returns | 3 | 9 | 8 | 11 | 16 | 29 |
| 4/1/21-3/31/22 | 4/1/22-3/31/23 | 4/1/23-3/31/24 | | Other | | 13 (4/1-9/30/23) | | 97 (10/1/23-3/31/24) | | |
| ALL | ALL | ALL | | | 0-1MM | 1-3MM | 3-5MM | 5-10MM | 10-25MM | 25MM & OVER |
| 73 | 109 | 110 | | NUMBER OF STATEMENTS | 5 | 12 | 10 | 13 | 22 | 48 |
| % | % | % | | ASSETS | % | % | % | % | % | % |
| 37.3 | 37.3 | 29.4 | | Cash & Equivalents | | 39.4 | 53.5 | 20.3 | 24.1 | 25.7 |
| 13.6 | 12.3 | 16.4 | | Trade Receivables (net) | | 6.6 | 6.6 | 27.5 | 18.1 | 17.3 |
| 3.5 | 2.7 | 2.8 | | Inventory | | 2.7 | 7.8 | 7.3 | 1.4 | 1.5 |
| 11.8 | 12.0 | 8.9 | | All Other Current | | 3.5 | 8.8 | 5.9 | 10.9 | 11.1 |
| 66.3 | 64.3 | 57.5 | | Total Current | | 52.2 | 76.6 | 61.0 | 54.4 | 55.6 |
| 6.7 | 9.6 | 13.3 | | Fixed Assets (net) | | 31.2 | 6.3 | 6.5 | 17.6 | 10.6 |
| 19.3 | 15.5 | 13.8 | | Intangibles (net) | | 5.4 | 6.3 | 11.1 | 7.4 | 21.0 |
| 7.6 | 10.6 | 15.5 | | All Other Non-Current | | 11.1 | 10.7 | 21.5 | 20.6 | 12.9 |
| 100.0 | 100.0 | 100.0 | | Total | | 100.0 | 100.0 | 100.0 | 100.0 | 100.0 |
| | | | | LIABILITIES | | | | | | |
| 7.1 | 5.8 | 8.0 | | Notes Payable-Short Term | | 5.0 | 21.5 | 9.9 | 3.9 | 5.2 |
| 1.8 | 3.1 | 2.0 | | Cur. Mat.-L.T.D. | | .9 | .0 | 5.6 | 3.3 | 1.4 |
| 12.9 | 7.3 | 10.1 | | Trade Payables | | 9.6 | 4.4 | 7.2 | 5.1 | 15.5 |
| .2 | .3 | .5 | | Income Taxes Payable | | .0 | .0 | .1 | 2.2 | .1 |
| 22.9 | 22.9 | 20.5 | | All Other Current | | 7.4 | 14.9 | 5.8 | 31.4 | 25.9 |
| 44.9 | 39.4 | 41.1 | | Total Current | | 22.9 | 40.8 | 28.5 | 45.8 | 48.2 |
| 21.3 | 18.9 | 24.2 | | Long-Term Debt | | 22.8 | 15.4 | 39.7 | 18.9 | 23.9 |
| .2 | .2 | .2 | | Deferred Taxes | | .0 | .8 | .0 | .2 | .3 |
| 8.4 | 10.2 | 6.8 | | All Other Non-Current | | 11.2 | 9.5 | 3.4 | 8.0 | 6.0 |
| 25.2 | 31.4 | 27.7 | | Net Worth | | 43.1 | 33.6 | 28.3 | 27.2 | 21.7 |
| 100.0 | 100.0 | 100.0 | | Total Liabilities & Net Worth | | 100.0 | 100.0 | 100.0 | 100.0 | 100.0 |
| | | | | INCOME DATA | | | | | | |
| 100.0 | 100.0 | 100.0 | | Net Sales | | 100.0 | 100.0 | 100.0 | 100.0 | 100.0 |
| 87.1 | 88.4 | 89.1 | | Gross Profit | | | | | | |
| 12.9 | 11.6 | 10.9 | | Operating Expenses | | 87.8 | 78.0 | 88.0 | 92.8 | 92.9 |
| 2.2 | 2.8 | 3.9 | | Operating Profit | | 12.2 | 22.0 | 12.0 | 7.2 | 7.1 |
| 10.8 | 8.8 | 7.0 | | All Other Expenses (net) | | 6.3 | 1.8 | 4.9 | 1.3 | 3.9 |
| | | | | Profit Before Taxes | | 5.9 | 20.2 | 7.1 | 5.8 | 3.1 |
| | | | | RATIOS | | | | | | |
| 3.9 | 4.5 | 2.9 | | | | 22.7 | 13.0 | 6.2 | 2.4 | 1.9 |
| 1.5 | 1.9 | 1.4 | | Current | | 5.6 | 2.0 | 2.4 | 1.5 | 1.1 |
| 1.1 | 1.0 | .9 | | | | 1.1 | 1.0 | 1.2 | .8 | .8 |
| 2.7 | 3.8 | 2.4 | | | | 14.9 | 5.0 | 6.2 | 2.1 | 1.5 |
| 1.1 | 1.4 | 1.2 | | Quick | | 5.4 | 1.8 | 1.7 | 1.1 | .9 |
| .7 | .6 | .5 | | | | .9 | .9 | .9 | .3 | .4 |
| 2  198.2 | 0  UND | 1  353.9 | | | 0  UND | 0  UND | 4  89.8 | 22  16.9 | 11  34.5 | |
| 24  15.4 | 18  20.2 | 26  13.8 | | Sales/Receivables | 2  196.1 | 0  UND | 45  8.2 | 30  12.0 | 31  11.7 | |
| 54  6.8 | 47  7.8 | 50  7.3 | | | 31  11.7 | 2  188.9 | 59  6.2 | 43  8.5 | 64  5.7 | |
| | | | | Cost of Sales/Inventory | | | | | | |
| | | | | Cost of Sales/Payables | | | | | | |
| 3.5 | 3.0 | 5.0 | | | | 4.1 | 3.4 | 1.5 | 4.8 | 6.2 |
| 6.5 | 8.8 | 12.8 | | Sales/Working Capital | | 8.9 | 6.4 | 7.0 | 10.3 | 27.3 |
| 48.1 | 648.4 | -38.1 | | | | 33.0 | NM | 28.5 | -34.8 | -12.5 |
| 32.0 | 39.5 | 15.2 | | | | 21.1 | | 15.2 | | 17.5 |
| (59) 7.6 | (81) 6.1 | (75) 4.1 | | EBIT/Interest | | (10) 4.4 | (15) 1.6 | (33) 2.8 | | |
| 1.5 | 1.0 | .1 | | | | .8 | | -.7 | | -1.6 |
| | | | | Net Profit + Depr., Dep., Amort./Cur. Mat. L/T/D | | | | | | |
| .0 | .0 | .0 | | | | .0 | .0 | .0 | .1 | .2 |
| .3 | .2 | .4 | | Fixed/Worth | | .3 | .0 | .2 | .5 | .5 |
| -.1 | 1.2 | -6.5 | | | | 1.8 | NM | NM | -3.2 | -.6 |
| .7 | .4 | .8 | | | | .2 | .1 | .2 | .6 | 1.3 |
| 5.7 | 3.1 | 3.2 | | Debt/Worth | | 1.4 | 10.8 | .9 | 2.2 | 7.2 |
| -3.0 | -42.7 | -6.8 | | | | 35.3 | -5.4 | NM | -6.8 | -5.4 |
| 99.2 | 70.1 | 65.6 | | % Profit Before Taxes/Tangible Net Worth | | 45.7 | 26.5 | 41.0 | 67.3 | |
| (50) 48.7 | (78) 34.5 | (77) 25.9 | | | (10) 5.7 | (10) 15.2 | (15) 2.5 | (32) 31.6 | | |
| 20.5 | 4.6 | 2.1 | | | | -.1 | -4.2 | -13.6 | 11.0 | |
| 25.6 | 27.8 | 17.0 | | % Profit Before Taxes/Total Assets | | 22.9 | 109.5 | 15.2 | 17.1 | 15.6 |
| 9.0 | 10.5 | 5.7 | | | | 3.8 | 15.1 | 8.9 | 3.7 | 5.2 |
| 1.4 | .2 | -.4 | | | | .6 | 5.5 | -3.7 | -3.3 | -1.6 |
| 192.0 | 316.1 | 192.2 | | | | UND | UND | 524.4 | 37.3 | 74.8 |
| 44.7 | 57.4 | 23.3 | | Sales/Net Fixed Assets | | 18.7 | 169.2 | 56.6 | 15.4 | 24.3 |
| 25.2 | 16.2 | 8.4 | | | | 1.3 | 18.4 | 16.2 | 6.4 | 9.2 |
| 1.9 | 2.4 | 3.0 | | | | 3.9 | 6.0 | 3.2 | 3.8 | 2.3 |
| 1.1 | 1.1 | 1.2 | | Sales/Total Assets | | 1.1 | 3.0 | 1.3 | 1.2 | 1.2 |
| .6 | .6 | .7 | | | | .7 | 1.1 | .5 | .7 | .8 |
| .4 | .4 | .4 | | | | | | | .7 | .8 |
| (19) 2.0 | (41) 1.4 | (48) 1.8 | | % Depr., Dep., Amort./Sales | | | | (15) 1.9 | (22) 1.3 | |
| 4.7 | 2.7 | 3.4 | | | | | | | 3.0 | 3.5 |
| .7 | 2.7 | 2.1 | | % Officers', Directors' Owners' Comp/Sales | | | | | | |
| (12) 6.6 | (17) 9.6 | (15) 5.5 | | | | | | | | |
| 13.9 | | 14.4 | | | | | | | | |
| 3948784M | 4448998M | 5146797M | | Net Sales ($) | 2410M | 21181M | 39650M | 98475M | 412954M | 4572127M |
| 4557046M | 4592297M | 4942996M | | Total Assets ($) | 3504M | 45096M | 52086M | 146239M | 421264M | 4274807M |

© RMA 2024  
M = $ thousand    MM = $ million  
See Pages viii through xx for Explanation of Ratios and Data

# FINANCE—Other Activities Related to Credit Intermediation NAICS 522390

**Current Data Sorted by Assets** | **Comparative Historical Data**

| 0-500M | 500M-2MM | 2-10MM | 10-50MM | 50-100MM | 100-250MM | | ALL 4/1/19-3/31/20 | ALL 4/1/20-3/31/21 |
|---|---|---|---|---|---|---|---|---|
|  |  |  | 1 |  |  | **Type of Statement** |  |  |
|  |  |  |  |  |  | Unqualified | 21 | 15 |
|  |  |  | 4 |  |  | Reviewed | 1 |  |
|  |  |  | 2 |  |  | Compiled | 1 | 1 |
|  |  |  |  | 3 | 3 | Tax Returns | 6 | 1 |
|  | 1 | 1 | 11 | 5 | 5 | Other | 16 | 17 |
| 1 | 2 | 3 | 33 |  |  |  |  |  |
|  | 9 (4/1-9/30/23) |  | (10/1/23-3/31/24) |  |  |  |  |  |
| 1 | 3 | 5 | 17 | 8 | 8 | **NUMBER OF STATEMENTS** | 45 | 34 |
| % | % | % | % | % | % | **ASSETS** | % | % |
|  |  |  | 23.2 |  |  | Cash & Equivalents | 23.2 | 26.6 |
|  |  |  | 38.3 |  |  | Trade Receivables (net) | 28.3 | 22.7 |
|  |  |  | .8 |  |  | Inventory | 4.5 | 1.1 |
|  |  |  | 8.4 |  |  | All Other Current | 12.8 | 9.5 |
|  |  |  | 70.7 |  |  | Total Current | 68.8 | 59.8 |
|  |  |  | 5.2 |  |  | Fixed Assets (net) | 6.0 | 13.5 |
|  |  |  | 3.3 |  |  | Intangibles (net) | 7.3 | 4.9 |
|  |  |  | 20.8 |  |  | All Other Non-Current | 17.9 | 21.8 |
|  |  |  | 100.0 |  |  | Total | 100.0 | 100.0 |
|  |  |  |  |  |  | **LIABILITIES** |  |  |
|  |  |  | 10.5 |  |  | Notes Payable-Short Term | 15.9 | 13.4 |
|  |  |  | 4.5 |  |  | Cur. Mat.-L.T.D. | 5.1 | 1.9 |
|  |  |  | 5.6 |  |  | Trade Payables | 8.3 | 5.6 |
|  |  |  | .0 |  |  | Income Taxes Payable | .2 | .2 |
|  |  |  | 7.3 |  |  | All Other Current | 14.5 | 16.7 |
|  |  |  | 27.9 |  |  | Total Current | 44.1 | 37.8 |
|  |  |  | 15.8 |  |  | Long-Term Debt | 9.1 | 15.6 |
|  |  |  | .0 |  |  | Deferred Taxes | .2 | .1 |
|  |  |  | 4.1 |  |  | All Other Non-Current | 5.4 | 5.5 |
|  |  |  | 52.2 |  |  | Net Worth | 41.3 | 40.9 |
|  |  |  | 100.0 |  |  | Total Liabilities & Net Worth | 100.0 | 100.0 |
|  |  |  |  |  |  | **INCOME DATA** |  |  |
|  |  |  | 100.0 |  |  | Net Sales | 100.0 | 100.0 |
|  |  |  |  |  |  | Gross Profit |  |  |
|  |  |  | 74.3 |  |  | Operating Expenses | 78.4 | 72.9 |
|  |  |  | 25.7 |  |  | Operating Profit | 21.6 | 27.1 |
|  |  |  | 8.5 |  |  | All Other Expenses (net) | 6.0 | 3.5 |
|  |  |  | 17.2 |  |  | Profit Before Taxes | 15.6 | 23.6 |
|  |  |  |  |  |  | **RATIOS** |  |  |
|  |  |  | 9.5 |  |  |  | 2.5 | 3.0 |
|  |  |  | 2.1 |  |  | Current | 1.6 | 1.8 |
|  |  |  | 1.5 |  |  |  | 1.2 | 1.0 |
|  |  |  | 9.2 |  |  |  | 2.4 | 2.6 |
|  |  |  | 2.0 |  |  | Quick | 1.4 | 1.5 |
|  |  |  | 1.3 |  |  |  | .6 | .7 |
|  |  | 16 | 23.1 |  |  |  | 18 20.0 | 0 UND |
|  |  | 114 | 3.2 |  |  | Sales/Receivables | 42 8.7 | 27 13.4 |
|  |  | 912 | .4 |  |  |  | 140 2.6 | 192 1.9 |
|  |  |  |  |  |  | Cost of Sales/Inventory |  |  |
|  |  |  |  |  |  | Cost of Sales/Payables |  |  |
|  |  |  | .5 |  |  |  | 1.7 | 1.2 |
|  |  |  | 1.3 |  |  | Sales/Working Capital | 5.4 | 6.0 |
|  |  |  | 3.1 |  |  |  | 11.7 | -51.0 |
|  |  |  |  |  |  |  | 45.2 | 45.6 |
|  |  |  |  |  |  | EBIT/Interest | (27) 8.7 | (26) 13.8 |
|  |  |  |  |  |  |  | 2.0 | 4.2 |
|  |  |  |  |  |  | Net Profit + Depr., Dep., Amort./Cur. Mat. L/T/D |  |  |
|  |  |  | .0 |  |  |  | .0 | .0 |
|  |  |  | .0 |  |  | Fixed/Worth | .1 | .1 |
|  |  |  | .3 |  |  |  | .2 | .3 |
|  |  |  | .2 |  |  |  | .7 | .8 |
|  |  |  | 1.0 |  |  | Debt/Worth | 2.2 | 1.6 |
|  |  |  | 2.9 |  |  |  | 7.6 | 3.4 |
|  |  |  | 13.6 |  |  |  | 57.4 | 46.1 |
|  |  | (16) | 5.8 |  |  | % Profit Before Taxes/Tangible Net Worth | (42) 32.0 | (33) 23.5 |
|  |  |  | 4.2 |  |  |  | 10.6 | 7.4 |
|  |  |  | 6.4 |  |  |  | 22.4 | 17.5 |
|  |  |  | 3.0 |  |  | % Profit Before Taxes/Total Assets | 6.5 | 6.4 |
|  |  |  | .5 |  |  |  | 2.7 | 3.2 |
|  |  |  | 332.4 |  |  |  | 153.9 | 93.4 |
|  |  |  | 46.8 |  |  | Sales/Net Fixed Assets | 38.5 | 20.7 |
|  |  |  | 9.2 |  |  |  | 15.5 | 8.3 |
|  |  |  | 1.1 |  |  |  | 2.0 | 1.8 |
|  |  |  | .6 |  |  | Sales/Total Assets | 1.0 | .6 |
|  |  |  | .1 |  |  |  | .3 | .1 |
|  |  |  | .3 |  |  |  | .4 | .4 |
|  |  | (10) | .9 |  |  | % Depr., Dep., Amort./Sales | (30) .8 | (26) .7 |
|  |  |  | 2.4 |  |  |  | 1.6 | 1.7 |
|  |  |  |  |  |  |  |  | 4.3 |
|  |  |  |  |  |  | % Officers', Directors' Owners' Comp/Sales | (10) 11.1 |  |
|  |  |  |  |  |  |  | 20.0 |  |
| 1145M | 20641M | 13422M | 290373M | 629283M | 390931M | Net Sales ($) | 1557188M | 1549859M |
| 395M | 2307M | 23894M | 467547M | 559339M | 1174942M | Total Assets ($) | 1994982M | 1586086M |

© RMA 2024

M = $ thousand    MM = $ million
See Pages viii through xx for Explanation of Ratios and Data

# FINANCE—Other Activities Related to Credit Intermediation  NAICS 522390

## Comparative Historical Data / Current Data Sorted by Sales

| Comparative Historical Data | | | Type of Statement | Current Data Sorted by Sales | | | | | |
|---|---|---|---|---|---|---|---|---|---|
| 5 | 14 | 11 | Unqualified | | 2 | | 3 | 4 | 2 |
| 2 | 1 | 2 | Reviewed | 1 | 1 | | | | |
| 2 | 2 | | Compiled | | | | | | |
| 3 | 1 | 2 | Tax Returns | 1 | | | 1 | | |
| 13 | 16 | 27 | Other | 4 | | 1 | 5 | 4 | 13 |
| 4/1/21- | 4/1/22- | 4/1/23- | | | 9 (4/1-9/30/23) | | 33 (10/1/23-3/31/24) | | |
| 3/31/22 | 3/31/23 | 3/31/24 | | 0-1MM | 1-3MM | 3-5MM | 5-10MM | 10-25MM | 25MM & OVER |
| ALL | ALL | ALL | NUMBER OF STATEMENTS | | | | | | |
| 25 | 34 | 42 | | 2 | 7 | 1 | 9 | 8 | 15 |
| % | % | % | ASSETS | % | % | % | % | % | % |
| 24.2 | 36.6 | 21.9 | Cash & Equivalents | | | | | | 19.5 |
| 23.4 | 15.8 | 26.1 | Trade Receivables (net) | | | | | | 27.0 |
| 2.8 | 1.8 | .3 | Inventory | | | | | | .0 |
| 11.8 | 6.7 | 9.8 | All Other Current | | | | | | 6.1 |
| 62.1 | 61.0 | 58.1 | Total Current | | | | | | 52.6 |
| 12.8 | 10.8 | 4.2 | Fixed Assets (net) | | | | | | 6.0 |
| 8.7 | 9.0 | 7.4 | Intangibles (net) | | | | | | 13.8 |
| 16.3 | 19.2 | 30.3 | All Other Non-Current | | | | | | 27.7 |
| 100.0 | 100.0 | 100.0 | Total | | | | | | 100.0 |
| | | | LIABILITIES | | | | | | |
| 14.4 | 11.7 | 7.9 | Notes Payable-Short Term | | | | | | .1 |
| 4.0 | 1.6 | 5.6 | Cur. Mat.-L.T.D. | | | | | | 10.7 |
| 4.4 | 7.4 | 4.3 | Trade Payables | | | | | | 5.8 |
| .0 | .1 | .1 | Income Taxes Payable | | | | | | .1 |
| 8.3 | 18.6 | 12.1 | All Other Current | | | | | | 19.2 |
| 31.2 | 39.3 | 30.0 | Total Current | | | | | | 35.9 |
| 11.7 | 19.7 | 19.4 | Long-Term Debt | | | | | | 17.7 |
| .1 | .5 | .4 | Deferred Taxes | | | | | | 1.1 |
| 9.3 | 18.3 | 5.4 | All Other Non-Current | | | | | | 3.7 |
| 47.7 | 22.1 | 44.8 | Net Worth | | | | | | 41.5 |
| 100.0 | 100.0 | 100.0 | Total Liabilities & Net Worth | | | | | | 100.0 |
| | | | INCOME DATA | | | | | | |
| 100.0 | 100.0 | 100.0 | Net Sales | | | | | | 100.0 |
| 58.2 | 76.0 | 73.5 | Gross Profit | | | | | | 98.3 |
| 41.8 | 24.0 | 26.5 | Operating Expenses | | | | | | 1.7 |
| 4.7 | 4.3 | 6.6 | Operating Profit | | | | | | 3.9 |
| 37.2 | 19.7 | 19.9 | All Other Expenses (net) | | | | | | -2.2 |
| | | | Profit Before Taxes | | | | | | |
| | | | RATIOS | | | | | | |
| 6.6 | 8.3 | 5.9 | | | | | | | 7.6 |
| 1.6 | 2.0 | 2.0 | Current | | | | | | 1.4 |
| 1.1 | 1.0 | 1.3 | | | | | | | .8 |
| 4.4 | 8.0 | 5.2 | | | | | | | 7.6 |
| 1.2 | 1.7 | 1.8 | Quick | | | | | | 1.2 |
| .5 | .6 | 1.0 | | | | | | | .6 |
| 5  77.7 | 0  UND | 12  31.5 | | | | | | 29 | 12.4 |
| 17  20.9 | 31  11.7 | 47  7.7 | Sales/Receivables | | | | | 68 | 5.4 |
| 281  1.3 | 72  5.1 | 243  1.5 | | | | | | 114 | 3.2 |
| | | | Cost of Sales/Inventory | | | | | | |
| | | | Cost of Sales/Payables | | | | | | |
| 1.1 | .8 | .9 | | | | | | | 3.0 |
| 3.8 | 3.3 | 3.0 | Sales/Working Capital | | | | | | 13.8 |
| NM | -585.9 | 16.8 | | | | | | | -6.2 |
| 102.4 | 11.1 | 33.5 | | | | | | | 83.7 |
| (17) 17.2 | (20) 4.4 | (28) 6.1 | EBIT/Interest | | | | | (10) | 17.8 |
| 5.8 | 2.0 | 1.2 | | | | | | | -.8 |
| | | | Net Profit + Depr., Dep., Amort./Cur. Mat. L/T/D | | | | | | |
| .0 | .0 | .0 | | | | | | | .1 |
| .0 | .2 | .1 | Fixed/Worth | | | | | | .2 |
| 1.3 | 3.0 | .5 | | | | | | | -.1 |
| .6 | .5 | .3 | | | | | | | .2 |
| 1.4 | 1.9 | 1.1 | Debt/Worth | | | | | | 3.1 |
| 5.6 | 17.8 | 5.1 | | | | | | | -15.5 |
| 70.8 | 60.6 | 28.7 | | | | | | | 42.1 |
| (23) 37.5 | (28) 13.3 | (35) 7.8 | % Profit Before Taxes/Tangible Net Worth | | | | | (11) | 7.2 |
| 21.9 | 3.3 | 4.5 | | | | | | | -34.8 |
| 32.3 | 18.0 | 11.2 | | | | | | | 16.3 |
| 12.6 | 4.8 | 4.6 | % Profit Before Taxes/Total Assets | | | | | | .3 |
| 5.6 | .3 | .2 | | | | | | | -7.9 |
| 109.0 | 133.0 | UND | | | | | | | 71.4 |
| 34.1 | 21.7 | 91.1 | Sales/Net Fixed Assets | | | | | | 29.8 |
| 8.7 | 4.9 | 19.4 | | | | | | | 8.4 |
| 1.9 | 1.8 | 1.0 | | | | | | | 1.3 |
| .7 | .6 | .5 | Sales/Total Assets | | | | | | .8 |
| .2 | .2 | .2 | | | | | | | .4 |
| .3 | .4 | .4 | | | | | | | |
| (18) .5 | (23) 1.5 | (20) .9 | % Depr., Dep., Amort./Sales | | | | | | |
| 2.5 | 4.9 | 2.0 | | | | | | | |
| | | | % Officers', Directors', Owners' Comp/Sales | | | | | | |
| 1211969M | 960421M | 1345795M | Net Sales ($) | 1589M | 12220M | 4196M | 64388M | 129937M | 1133465M |
| 1064590M | 1643245M | 2228424M | Total Assets ($) | 16256M | 64637M | 38328M | 341385M | 463546M | 1304272M |

© RMA 2024    M = $ thousand    MM = $ million
See Pages viii through xx for Explanation of Ratios and Data

## FINANCE—Investment Banking and Securities Intermediation NAICS 523150

### Current Data Sorted by Assets | Comparative Historical Data

| | | | | | | Type of Statement | | |
|---|---|---|---|---|---|---|---|---|
| 2 | | 3 | 7 | | 2 | Unqualified | 19 | 10 |
| | 1 | 1 | | | | Reviewed | | 1 |
| | | 2 | | | | Compiled | 2 | 3 |
| | 1 | 1 | | 1 | | Tax Returns | 22 | 8 |
| 3 | 6 | 7 | 3 | 4 | 3 | Other | 39 | 29 |
| 0-500M | 10 (4/1-9/30/23) 500M-2MM | 2-10MM | 37 (10/1/23-3/31/24) 10-50MM | 50-100MM | 100-250MM | | 4/1/19-3/31/20 ALL | 4/1/20-3/31/21 ALL |
| 5 | 8 | 14 | 10 | 5 | 5 | NUMBER OF STATEMENTS | 82 | 51 |
| % | % | % | % | % | % | ASSETS | % | % |
| | | 43.0 | 46.0 | | | Cash & Equivalents | 37.8 | 39.0 |
| | | 15.6 | 20.4 | | | Trade Receivables (net) | 13.9 | 15.2 |
| | | .0 | .2 | | | Inventory | 1.0 | 3.3 |
| | | 13.9 | 14.9 | | | All Other Current | 12.8 | 6.7 |
| | | 72.5 | 81.5 | | | Total Current | 65.5 | 64.3 |
| | | 10.4 | 2.6 | | | Fixed Assets (net) | 12.0 | 9.1 |
| | | 3.0 | 6.4 | | | Intangibles (net) | 6.9 | 9.5 |
| | | 14.1 | 9.6 | | | All Other Non-Current | 15.6 | 17.1 |
| | | 100.0 | 100.0 | | | Total | 100.0 | 100.0 |
| | | | | | | LIABILITIES | | |
| | | 5.1 | .3 | | | Notes Payable-Short Term | 14.9 | 5.2 |
| | | 1.6 | 1.1 | | | Cur. Mat.-L.T.D. | 1.6 | 1.5 |
| | | 5.5 | 12.4 | | | Trade Payables | 8.9 | 7.0 |
| | | .1 | .2 | | | Income Taxes Payable | .2 | .3 |
| | | 10.9 | 23.0 | | | All Other Current | 25.4 | 17.6 |
| | | 23.2 | 37.0 | | | Total Current | 50.9 | 31.6 |
| | | 7.1 | 2.0 | | | Long-Term Debt | 15.4 | 10.5 |
| | | .0 | .0 | | | Deferred Taxes | .0 | .0 |
| | | 7.0 | 12.9 | | | All Other Non-Current | 18.4 | 8.0 |
| | | 62.7 | 48.1 | | | Net Worth | 15.4 | 49.9 |
| | | 100.0 | 100.0 | | | Total Liabilities & Net Worth | 100.0 | 100.0 |
| | | | | | | INCOME DATA | | |
| | | 100.0 | 100.0 | | | Net Sales | 100.0 | 100.0 |
| | | | | | | Gross Profit | | |
| | | 77.7 | 83.2 | | | Operating Expenses | 77.3 | 80.5 |
| | | 22.3 | 16.8 | | | Operating Profit | 22.7 | 19.5 |
| | | 5.7 | -.1 | | | All Other Expenses (net) | 1.7 | 2.3 |
| | | 16.6 | 16.9 | | | Profit Before Taxes | 21.0 | 17.2 |
| | | | | | | RATIOS | | |
| | | 20.8 | 11.9 | | | | 4.0 | 4.5 |
| | | 4.5 | 2.2 | | | Current | 1.8 | 2.5 |
| | | 1.4 | 1.2 | | | | 1.1 | 1.3 |
| | | 20.8 | 11.6 | | | | 3.1 | 4.1 |
| | | 4.5 | 1.7 | | | Quick | 1.5 | 2.0 |
| | | .5 | 1.0 | | | | .6 | 1.0 |
| | 0 | UND | 0 | UND | | | 0 UND | 0 UND |
| | 11 | 34.5 | 39 | 9.4 | | Sales/Receivables | 4 97.3 | 13 27.7 |
| | 52 | 7.0 | 107 | 3.4 | | | 41 8.8 | 49 7.5 |
| | | | | | | Cost of Sales/Inventory | | |
| | | | | | | Cost of Sales/Payables | | |
| | | 1.5 | .5 | | | | 2.5 | 2.5 |
| | | 4.1 | 2.8 | | | Sales/Working Capital | 7.8 | 5.1 |
| | | 9.1 | 11.1 | | | | 98.1 | 29.7 |
| | | | | | | | 48.1 | 116.2 |
| | | | | | | EBIT/Interest | (48) 7.9 | (30) 16.5 |
| | | | | | | | 1.7 | 2.3 |
| | | | | | | Net Profit + Depr., Dep., Amort./Cur. Mat. L/T/D | | |
| | | .0 | .0 | | | | .0 | .0 |
| | | .0 | .0 | | | Fixed/Worth | .1 | .1 |
| | | .4 | NM | | | | .6 | .3 |
| | | .1 | .4 | | | | .5 | .3 |
| | | .5 | 1.7 | | | Debt/Worth | 1.5 | 1.3 |
| | | 2.1 | NM | | | | 5.3 | 3.7 |
| | | 52.3 | | | | | 90.4 | 112.5 |
| | | 20.7 | | | | % Profit Before Taxes/Tangible Net Worth | (69) 31.5 | (46) 23.5 |
| | | -.8 | | | | | 12.5 | 8.6 |
| | | 29.6 | 44.7 | | | | 54.7 | 50.2 |
| | | 12.7 | 15.2 | | | % Profit Before Taxes/Total Assets | 13.4 | 11.4 |
| | | -.6 | 6.3 | | | | 4.5 | 2.1 |
| | | UND | UND | | | | UND | 816.3 |
| | | 118.7 | 157.6 | | | Sales/Net Fixed Assets | 82.7 | 69.5 |
| | | 12.6 | 24.4 | | | | 21.8 | 17.3 |
| | | 2.1 | 1.8 | | | | 4.7 | 3.6 |
| | | 1.3 | 1.2 | | | Sales/Total Assets | 1.6 | 1.7 |
| | | .9 | .5 | | | | .7 | .6 |
| | | | | | | | .3 | .2 |
| | | | | | | % Depr., Dep., Amort./Sales | (37) .6 | (24) .6 |
| | | | | | | | 3.0 | 2.9 |
| | | | | | | | 3.7 | 3.1 |
| | | | | | | % Officers', Directors' Owners' Comp/Sales | (22) 9.2 | (14) 12.2 |
| | | | | | | | 15.7 | 22.8 |
| 5820M | 31983M | 130852M | 263221M | 691142M | 531925M | Net Sales ($) | 2354769M | 1697634M |
| 1089M | 10160M | 82813M | 227967M | 334982M | 890268M | Total Assets ($) | 1962196M | 1476157M |

M = $ thousand  MM = $ million
See Pages viii through xx for Explanation of Ratios and Data

© RMA 2024

# FINANCE—Investment Banking and Securities Intermediation  NAICS 523150

## Comparative Historical Data | Current Data Sorted by Sales

| Comparative Historical Data | | | | Type of Statement | Current Data Sorted by Sales | | | | | |
|---|---|---|---|---|---|---|---|---|---|---|
| 5 | 15 | 14 | | Unqualified | 1 | 2 | | 3 | 2 | 6 |
| 2 | 2 | 2 | | Reviewed | | | | 2 | | |
| 1 | 3 | 2 | | Compiled | | | | 2 | | |
| 9 | 8 | 3 | | Tax Returns | | | 1 | | | 1 |
| 28 | 20 | 26 | | Other | 1 | 5 | 3 | 7 | | 10 |
| 4/1/21- | 4/1/22- | 4/1/23- | | | 10 (4/1-9/30/23) | | | 37 (10/1/23-3/31/24) | | |
| 3/31/22 | 3/31/23 | 3/31/24 | | | 0-1MM | 1-3MM | 3-5MM | 5-10MM | 10-25MM | 25MM & OVER |
| ALL | ALL | ALL | | | | | | | | |
| 45 | 48 | 47 | | **NUMBER OF STATEMENTS** | 3 | 7 | 4 | 14 | 2 | 17 |
| % | % | % | | **ASSETS** | % | % | % | % | % | % |
| 41.7 | 37.1 | 36.8 | | Cash & Equivalents | | | | 41.2 | | 36.6 |
| 9.3 | 14.6 | 12.9 | | Trade Receivables (net) | | | | 19.5 | | 13.0 |
| 2.7 | 1.6 | 3.4 | | Inventory | | | | .0 | | 9.3 |
| 9.2 | 6.4 | 12.2 | | All Other Current | | | | 8.6 | | 7.6 |
| 62.9 | 59.6 | 65.2 | | Total Current | | | | 69.3 | | 66.4 |
| 12.4 | 12.7 | 11.0 | | Fixed Assets (net) | | | | 11.3 | | 2.6 |
| 10.6 | 6.5 | 7.6 | | Intangibles (net) | | | | 7.3 | | 13.3 |
| 14.1 | 21.1 | 16.2 | | All Other Non-Current | | | | 12.1 | | 17.6 |
| 100.0 | 100.0 | 100.0 | | Total | | | | 100.0 | | 100.0 |
| | | | | **LIABILITIES** | | | | | | |
| 5.1 | 3.6 | 4.2 | | Notes Payable-Short Term | | | | 3.3 | | 4.3 |
| 2.0 | 3.1 | 2.1 | | Cur. Mat.-L.T.D. | | | | 4.6 | | .9 |
| 5.1 | 6.6 | 9.7 | | Trade Payables | | | | 15.8 | | 8.4 |
| .1 | .1 | .1 | | Income Taxes Payable | | | | .1 | | .2 |
| 26.4 | 13.0 | 18.4 | | All Other Current | | | | 26.2 | | 17.3 |
| 38.8 | 26.4 | 34.4 | | Total Current | | | | 50.1 | | 31.0 |
| 34.5 | 30.9 | 19.3 | | Long-Term Debt | | | | 35.4 | | 12.3 |
| .0 | .1 | .2 | | Deferred Taxes | | | | .0 | | .5 |
| 12.8 | 10.6 | 10.7 | | All Other Non-Current | | | | 5.3 | | 12.1 |
| 13.8 | 31.9 | 35.4 | | Net Worth | | | | 9.2 | | 44.1 |
| 100.0 | 100.0 | 100.0 | | Total Liabilities & Net Worth | | | | 100.0 | | 100.0 |
| | | | | **INCOME DATA** | | | | | | |
| 100.0 | 100.0 | 100.0 | | Net Sales | | | | 100.0 | | 100.0 |
| | | | | Gross Profit | | | | | | |
| 70.6 | 82.1 | 80.5 | | Operating Expenses | | | | 87.0 | | 78.2 |
| 29.4 | 17.9 | 19.5 | | Operating Profit | | | | 13.0 | | 21.8 |
| 3.4 | 3.5 | 3.1 | | All Other Expenses (net) | | | | 5.8 | | 2.0 |
| 26.0 | 14.4 | 16.4 | | Profit Before Taxes | | | | 7.2 | | 19.8 |
| | | | | **RATIOS** | | | | | | |
| 4.1 | 4.4 | 6.0 | | | | | | 20.8 | | 4.9 |
| 2.1 | 2.8 | 2.5 | | Current | | | | 3.7 | | 2.3 |
| 1.3 | 1.4 | 1.2 | | | | | | .9 | | 1.4 |
| 3.6 | 4.0 | 4.9 | | | | | | 20.8 | | 3.8 |
| 1.7 | 2.7 | 2.0 | | Quick | | | | 3.7 | | 2.0 |
| 1.0 | 1.1 | .6 | | | | | | .4 | | .9 |
| 0 UND | 0 UND | 0 UND | | | | | | 0 UND | 13 | 27.8 |
| 0 999.8 | 17 22.1 | 17 21.0 | | Sales/Receivables | | | | 12 30.0 | 26 | 13.8 |
| 35 10.4 | 52 7.0 | 36 10.1 | | | | | | 53 6.9 | 37 | 9.9 |
| | | | | Cost of Sales/Inventory | | | | | | |
| | | | | Cost of Sales/Payables | | | | | | |
| 2.1 | 2.6 | 1.7 | | | | | | 1.7 | | 2.7 |
| 6.0 | 7.2 | 4.4 | | Sales/Working Capital | | | | 5.0 | | 3.9 |
| 12.9 | 20.6 | 11.8 | | | | | | NM | | 9.5 |
| 116.2 | 149.7 | 49.1 | | | | | | | | |
| (23) 20.9 | (24) 16.8 | (18) 23.4 | | EBIT/Interest | | | | | | |
| 2.7 | 7.1 | 3.8 | | | | | | | | |
| | | | | Net Profit + Depr., Dep., Amort./Cur. Mat. L/T/D | | | | | | |
| .0 | .0 | .0 | | | | | | .0 | | .0 |
| .1 | .1 | .0 | | Fixed/Worth | | | | .1 | | .0 |
| 3.4 | 1.0 | .4 | | | | | | NM | | .2 |
| .5 | .3 | .3 | | | | | | .1 | | .5 |
| 1.8 | .9 | 1.2 | | Debt/Worth | | | | .9 | | 1.2 |
| -3.5 | 5.4 | 3.3 | | | | | | NM | | 4.0 |
| 93.1 | 137.8 | 79.7 | | | | | | 19.1 | | 79.8 |
| (33) 26.4 | (41) 29.9 | (40) 21.6 | | % Profit Before Taxes/Tangible Net Worth | | | (11) | 5.8 | (14) | 31.7 |
| 15.5 | 10.7 | 6.0 | | | | | | -1.2 | | 15.1 |
| 67.1 | 52.7 | 33.0 | | | | | | 17.1 | | 41.3 |
| 17.1 | 11.7 | 11.5 | | % Profit Before Taxes/Total Assets | | | | 3.1 | | 19.0 |
| 5.7 | .5 | 1.9 | | | | | | -1.8 | | 7.1 |
| UND | UND | 999.8 | | | | | | UND | | 543.1 |
| 51.6 | 91.0 | 93.0 | | Sales/Net Fixed Assets | | | | 54.4 | | 99.1 |
| 15.6 | 16.5 | 27.3 | | | | | | 14.1 | | 31.3 |
| 3.1 | 3.6 | 2.5 | | | | | | 2.4 | | 2.3 |
| 1.2 | 1.6 | 1.5 | | Sales/Total Assets | | | | 1.4 | | 1.3 |
| .3 | .7 | .8 | | | | | | 1.1 | | .8 |
| .2 | .2 | .1 | | | | | | | | .0 |
| (22) 1.0 | (25) .7 | (23) .2 | | % Depr., Dep., Amort./Sales | | | | | (10) | .1 |
| 3.7 | 4.7 | .9 | | | | | | | | .7 |
| 3.3 | 2.6 | 3.7 | | | | | | | | |
| (12) 14.7 | (12) 10.1 | (13) 15.7 | | % Officers', Directors' Owners' Comp/Sales | | | | | | |
| 18.4 | 17.0 | 26.5 | | | | | | | | |
| 1985181M | 1766116M | 1654943M | | Net Sales ($) | 1175M | 14043M | 13478M | 100414M | 31935M | 1493898M |
| 1728060M | 1478117M | 1547279M | | Total Assets ($) | 1137M | 43793M | 17672M | 81572M | 32874M | 1370231M |

© RMA 2024   M = $ thousand   MM = $ million
See Pages viii through xx for Explanation of Ratios and Data

## FINANCE—Miscellaneous Intermediation  NAICS 523910

| Current Data Sorted by Assets | | | | | | | Comparative Historical Data | |
|---|---|---|---|---|---|---|---|---|
| | | | | | | **Type of Statement** | | |
| | | | 2 | 4 | 3 | 10 | Unqualified | 16 | 8 |
| | | | | 2 | | | Reviewed | 4 | 2 |
| | | 3 | | | | | Compiled | 3 | 3 |
| | 1 | 8 | 13 | 2 | | | Tax Returns | 9 | 13 |
| | 10 | 17 | 18 | 30 | 3 | 8 | Other | 74 | 62 |
| | | 10 (4/1-9/30/23) | | 124 (10/1/23-3/31/24) | | | | 4/1/19-3/31/20 ALL | 4/1/20-3/31/21 ALL |
| | 0-500M | 500M-2MM | 2-10MM | 10-50MM | 50-100MM | 100-250MM | | | |
| | 11 | 28 | 33 | 38 | 6 | 18 | **NUMBER OF STATEMENTS** | 106 | 88 |
| | % | % | % | % | % | % | **ASSETS** | % | % |
| | 44.6 | 19.9 | 8.3 | 15.8 | | 19.5 | Cash & Equivalents | 16.8 | 13.2 |
| | 15.9 | 6.0 | 13.7 | 12.5 | | 16.1 | Trade Receivables (net) | 17.9 | 14.1 |
| | 3.7 | 4.2 | 1.7 | 3.5 | | 6.0 | Inventory | 3.8 | 2.3 |
| | 7.3 | 17.6 | 1.4 | 8.7 | | 5.7 | All Other Current | 7.0 | 5.6 |
| | 71.5 | 47.8 | 25.2 | 40.4 | | 47.4 | Total Current | 45.6 | 35.2 |
| | 12.2 | 37.0 | 48.0 | 25.0 | | 21.7 | Fixed Assets (net) | 21.8 | 27.2 |
| | 1.9 | 2.7 | 6.0 | 4.7 | | 10.3 | Intangibles (net) | 8.4 | 7.6 |
| | 14.4 | 12.5 | 20.8 | 29.9 | | 20.6 | All Other Non-Current | 24.2 | 30.0 |
| | 100.0 | 100.0 | 100.0 | 100.0 | | 100.0 | Total | 100.0 | 100.0 |
| | | | | | | | **LIABILITIES** | | |
| | 12.3 | 20.5 | 9.7 | 11.8 | | 11.3 | Notes Payable-Short Term | 11.4 | 8.8 |
| | 15.8 | 4.8 | 1.2 | .9 | | 1.9 | Cur. Mat.-L.T.D. | 4.1 | 6.2 |
| | 1.2 | 2.5 | 4.0 | 6.6 | | 5.2 | Trade Payables | 4.4 | 6.0 |
| | .0 | .0 | .1 | .0 | | .4 | Income Taxes Payable | .2 | .1 |
| | 39.0 | 16.6 | 9.3 | 7.8 | | 5.0 | All Other Current | 10.7 | 8.0 |
| | 68.4 | 44.4 | 24.4 | 27.1 | | 23.8 | Total Current | 30.8 | 29.1 |
| | 22.0 | 26.0 | 40.0 | 23.4 | | 29.4 | Long-Term Debt | 23.3 | 34.0 |
| | .0 | .0 | .0 | .0 | | .5 | Deferred Taxes | .2 | .1 |
| | 4.1 | 10.1 | 7.3 | 10.4 | | 3.3 | All Other Non-Current | 6.3 | 4.4 |
| | 5.6 | 19.5 | 28.2 | 39.2 | | 43.0 | Net Worth | 39.4 | 32.5 |
| | 100.0 | 100.0 | 100.0 | 100.0 | | 100.0 | Total Liabilities & Net Worth | 100.0 | 100.0 |
| | | | | | | | **INCOME DATA** | | |
| | 100.0 | 100.0 | 100.0 | 100.0 | | 100.0 | Net Sales | 100.0 | 100.0 |
| | | | | | | | Gross Profit | | |
| | 78.2 | 69.2 | 62.4 | 61.7 | | 60.1 | Operating Expenses | 65.5 | 65.2 |
| | 21.8 | 30.8 | 37.6 | 38.3 | | 39.9 | Operating Profit | 34.5 | 34.8 |
| | 3.4 | 12.1 | 9.8 | 17.2 | | 13.0 | All Other Expenses (net) | 10.9 | 11.1 |
| | 18.4 | 18.7 | 27.8 | 21.1 | | 26.9 | Profit Before Taxes | 23.6 | 23.7 |
| | | | | | | | **RATIOS** | | |
| | 11.5 | 4.8 | 4.9 | 4.3 | | 5.4 | | 5.3 | 5.0 |
| | 2.6 | 1.1 | 1.7 | 1.9 | | 1.7 | Current | 1.4 | 1.7 |
| | .7 | .5 | .4 | .7 | | 1.2 | | .7 | .5 |
| | 10.7 | 1.5 | 3.3 | 2.9 | | 5.0 | | 4.4 | 3.2 |
| | 2.4 | .6 | 1.7 | 1.3 | | 1.2 | Quick | 1.0 | 1.2 |
| | .7 | .2 | .4 | .4 | | .5 | | .4 | .3 |
| | 0 UND | 0 UND | 0 UND | 0 UND | 24 15.5 | | | 0 UND | 0 UND |
| | 2 190.7 | 0 UND | 0 UND | 20 17.9 | 39 9.3 | | Sales/Receivables | 5 77.1 | 1 527.4 |
| | 53 6.9 | 5 79.2 | 47 7.7 | 130 2.8 | 64 5.7 | | | 55 6.6 | 33 11.1 |
| | | | | | | | Cost of Sales/Inventory | | |
| | | | | | | | Cost of Sales/Payables | | |
| | 10.7 | 5.1 | 3.3 | 1.5 | | 1.6 | | 2.5 | 2.2 |
| | 15.4 | 89.8 | 18.0 | 4.6 | | 3.5 | Sales/Working Capital | 9.1 | 9.1 |
| | -16.8 | -5.2 | -12.9 | -16.7 | | 20.6 | | -13.3 | -6.4 |
| | | 70.8 | 30.2 | 25.3 | | 12.4 | | 13.2 | 11.7 |
| | (15) | 8.3 (24) | 5.9 (22) | 13.4 | (14) | 4.3 | EBIT/Interest | (65) 4.7 | (49) 3.4 |
| | | 1.9 | 2.0 | 5.3 | | 1.0 | | 2.2 | .9 |
| | | | | | | | Net Profit + Depr., Dep., Amort./Cur. Mat. L/T/D | | |
| | .0 | .0 | .0 | .0 | | .0 | | .0 | .0 |
| | .0 | 1.3 | 1.7 | .2 | | .0 | Fixed/Worth | .1 | .3 |
| | .3 | -4.8 | 22.5 | 1.5 | | 2.0 | | 2.0 | 3.5 |
| | .2 | .9 | 1.0 | .6 | | .3 | | .4 | .4 |
| | 1.3 | 3.2 | 2.8 | 1.6 | | 1.8 | Debt/Worth | 2.2 | 3.0 |
| | -1.9 | -8.3 | NM | 5.0 | | 4.3 | | 191.7 | 48.9 |
| | | 366.5 | 88.1 | 42.2 | | 37.1 | | 65.4 | 50.5 |
| | (18) | 55.9 (25) | 36.3 (34) | 18.8 | (15) | 20.6 | % Profit Before Taxes/Tangible Net Worth | (81) 20.3 | (68) 14.2 |
| | | 20.0 | 5.8 | 2.0 | | 2.9 | | 1.9 | 3.3 |
| | 205.5 | 50.9 | 33.7 | 22.1 | | 16.8 | | 26.3 | 12.7 |
| | 58.3 | 8.8 | 7.0 | 7.7 | | 11.0 | % Profit Before Taxes/Total Assets | 7.2 | 4.3 |
| | -11.6 | .3 | 2.0 | .4 | | -.1 | | 1.3 | .7 |
| | UND | 371.0 | UND | 789.4 | | UND | | UND | UND |
| | UND | 20.1 | 1.5 | 6.5 | | 74.1 | Sales/Net Fixed Assets | 75.3 | 24.9 |
| | 19.3 | .2 | .2 | .9 | | .9 | | 5.1 | .8 |
| | 12.7 | 5.7 | 1.9 | 1.3 | | .7 | | 2.0 | 1.5 |
| | 7.1 | .8 | .5 | .4 | | .6 | Sales/Total Assets | .5 | .3 |
| | 3.5 | .1 | .1 | .1 | | .2 | | .1 | .1 |
| | | .8 | 1.9 | .8 | | .8 | | .7 | 2.3 |
| | (13) | 12.1 (16) | 11.1 (16) | 6.4 | (10) | 7.3 | % Depr., Dep., Amort./Sales | (41) 2.3 | (38) 6.5 |
| | | 39.8 | 17.5 | 15.3 | | 8.2 | | 16.4 | 16.7 |
| | | | | | | | | 2.7 | |
| | | | | | | | % Officers', Directors' Owners' Comp/Sales | (21) 7.0 | |
| | | | | | | | | 27.7 | |
| | 19089M | 101455M | 150558M | 704020M | 200849M | 1658398M | Net Sales ($) | 2841723M | 1586520M |
| | 2708M | 32611M | 135621M | 949124M | 403002M | 2698445M | Total Assets ($) | 3693889M | 3004101M |

M = $ thousand   MM = $ million
See Pages viii through xx for Explanation of Ratios and Data

© RMA 2024

## FINANCE—Miscellaneous Intermediation  NAICS 523910

### Comparative Historical Data / Current Data Sorted by Sales

| | | | | Type of Statement | | | | | | |
|---|---|---|---|---|---|---|---|---|---|---|
| 6 | 14 | 19 | | Unqualified | 1 | 1 | 2 | 3 | 4 | 8 |
| 2 | 3 | 2 | | Reviewed | | | | 1 | | 1 |
| 2 | 3 | 3 | | Compiled | | | | | | |
| 9 | 15 | 24 | | Tax Returns | 1 | 2 | | | | |
| 33 | 80 | 86 | | Other | 17 | 3 | 1 | 1 | 1 | 1 |
| | | | | | 16 | 14 | 12 | 12 | 13 | 19 |
| 4/1/21-3/31/22 | 4/1/22-3/31/23 | 4/1/23-3/31/24 | | | 10 (4/1-9/30/23) | | | 124 (10/1/23-3/31/24) | | |
| ALL | ALL | ALL | | | 0-1MM | 1-3MM | 3-5MM | 5-10MM | 10-25MM | 25MM & OVER |
| 52 | 115 | 134 | | NUMBER OF STATEMENTS | 35 | 20 | 15 | 17 | 18 | 29 |
| % | % | % | | ASSETS | % | % | % | % | % | % |
| 26.5 | 19.7 | 17.9 | | Cash & Equivalents | 12.1 | 15.5 | 27.9 | 14.7 | 16.2 | 24.3 |
| 12.1 | 11.8 | 11.7 | | Trade Receivables (net) | 8.5 | 7.5 | 15.0 | 7.1 | 18.1 | 15.3 |
| 2.7 | 2.5 | 3.6 | | Inventory | 1.0 | 1.8 | .0 | 5.3 | 6.4 | 6.9 |
| 7.6 | 8.5 | 8.5 | | All Other Current | 4.3 | 11.5 | 1.8 | 11.2 | 7.0 | 14.1 |
| 48.8 | 42.6 | 41.6 | | Total Current | 25.9 | 36.3 | 44.7 | 38.3 | 47.7 | 60.7 |
| 14.8 | 27.7 | 30.6 | | Fixed Assets (net) | 57.1 | 38.9 | 12.8 | 21.0 | 18.3 | 15.2 |
| 7.2 | 6.0 | 5.4 | | Intangibles (net) | .3 | 3.5 | 3.0 | 4.3 | 14.2 | 9.4 |
| 29.2 | 23.7 | 22.4 | | All Other Non-Current | 16.6 | 21.2 | 39.5 | 36.4 | 19.8 | 14.7 |
| 100.0 | 100.0 | 100.0 | | Total | 100.0 | 100.0 | 100.0 | 100.0 | 100.0 | 100.0 |
| | | | | LIABILITIES | | | | | | |
| 14.3 | 12.5 | 13.0 | | Notes Payable-Short Term | 10.4 | 6.7 | 27.9 | 10.4 | 28.5 | 4.6 |
| 3.1 | 2.7 | 3.1 | | Cur. Mat.-L.T.D. | 8.5 | 1.8 | .7 | .8 | 1.1 | 1.3 |
| 4.3 | 3.3 | 4.3 | | Trade Payables | .5 | .7 | 1.8 | 9.8 | 4.1 | 9.4 |
| .1 | .2 | .1 | | Income Taxes Payable | .0 | .2 | .0 | .0 | .0 | .3 |
| 10.6 | 11.0 | 12.7 | | All Other Current | 9.7 | 17.0 | 9.3 | 12.4 | 14.3 | 14.3 |
| 32.4 | 29.8 | 33.2 | | Total Current | 29.1 | 26.4 | 39.7 | 33.4 | 48.0 | 29.9 |
| 19.2 | 29.8 | 29.0 | | Long-Term Debt | 39.6 | 45.0 | 14.9 | 26.4 | 16.8 | 21.5 |
| .0 | .1 | .1 | | Deferred Taxes | .0 | .0 | .1 | .0 | .0 | .3 |
| 11.6 | 8.2 | 7.8 | | All Other Non-Current | 4.7 | 13.7 | 7.5 | 11.7 | 7.9 | 5.1 |
| 36.8 | 32.2 | 30.0 | | Net Worth | 26.6 | 14.9 | 37.8 | 28.4 | 27.3 | 43.2 |
| 100.0 | 100.0 | 100.0 | | Total Liabilities & Net Worth | 100.0 | 100.0 | 100.0 | 100.0 | 100.0 | 100.0 |
| | | | | INCOME DATA | | | | | | |
| 100.0 | 100.0 | 100.0 | | Net Sales | 100.0 | 100.0 | 100.0 | 100.0 | 100.0 | 100.0 |
| | | | | Gross Profit | | | | | | |
| 65.7 | 61.0 | 63.9 | | Operating Expenses | 60.0 | 51.0 | 56.0 | 70.6 | 73.2 | 71.7 |
| 34.3 | 39.0 | 36.1 | | Operating Profit | 40.0 | 49.0 | 44.0 | 29.4 | 26.8 | 28.3 |
| 4.4 | 11.0 | 13.2 | | All Other Expenses (net) | 17.4 | 21.3 | 17.2 | 11.3 | 9.0 | 4.2 |
| 29.9 | 28.0 | 22.9 | | Profit Before Taxes | 22.6 | 27.7 | 26.7 | 18.1 | 17.8 | 24.1 |
| | | | | RATIOS | | | | | | |
| 8.2 | 4.5 | 4.9 | | | 5.5 | 7.0 | 7.5 | 2.6 | 4.7 | 4.0 |
| 2.7 | 1.7 | 1.5 | | Current | 2.0 | 1.4 | 1.3 | 1.0 | 1.2 | 2.0 |
| 1.1 | .7 | .6 | | | .5 | .3 | .2 | .5 | .5 | 1.5 |
| 5.5 | 3.4 | 3.1 | | | 5.0 | 2.3 | 6.5 | 1.4 | 2.9 | 3.4 |
| 1.8 | 1.2 | 1.1 | | Quick | 1.3 | 1.1 | 1.3 | .9 | .9 | 1.1 |
| .7 | .4 | .4 | | | .2 | .3 | .2 | .4 | .2 | .6 |
| 0  UND | 0  UND | 0  UND | | | 0  UND | 0  UND | 0  UND | 0  UND | 0  UND | 9  41.1 |
| 1  464.8 | 0  UND | 6  57.0 | | Sales/Receivables | 0  UND | 0  UND | 7  51.0 | 1  259.6 | 16  23.2 | 31  11.9 |
| 31  11.9 | 31  11.8 | 45  8.1 | | | 44  8.3 | 32  11.5 | 281  1.3 | 24  15.2 | 46  7.9 | 47  7.8 |
| | | | | Cost of Sales/Inventory | | | | | | |
| | | | | Cost of Sales/Payables | | | | | | |
| 1.1 | 2.0 | 2.6 | | | 1.8 | .6 | 2.2 | 9.2 | 4.5 | 2.0 |
| 5.6 | 7.2 | 10.7 | | Sales/Working Capital | 18.0 | 8.8 | 15.4 | 243.3 | 21.7 | 4.1 |
| 30.6 | -13.9 | -13.6 | | | -3.3 | -20.6 | -.8 | -13.0 | -8.5 | 6.4 |
| 32.4 | 15.9 | 30.0 | | | 5.9 | 12.7 | | 58.5 | 57.2 | 33.5 |
| (33)  10.4 | (67)  6.3 | (82)  6.6 | | EBIT/Interest | (17)  3.1 | (11)  6.7 | | (12)  14.3 | (12)  33.2 | (22)  6.6 |
| 4.0 | 2.4 | 1.9 | | | .2 | 1.9 | | 1.9 | 9.0 | 1.9 |
| | | | | Net Profit + Depr., Dep., Amort./Cur. Mat. L/T/D | | | | | | |
| .0 | .0 | .0 | | | .0 | .0 | .0 | .0 | .0 | .0 |
| .0 | .3 | .3 | | Fixed/Worth | 2.0 | .4 | .0 | .6 | .2 | .1 |
| .7 | 7.5 | 3.9 | | | 5.3 | 30.9 | .3 | NM | -1.4 | 1.4 |
| .4 | .5 | .6 | | | .5 | 1.9 | .7 | .4 | .7 | .5 |
| 1.7 | 2.1 | 2.0 | | Debt/Worth | 1.8 | 4.5 | 1.7 | 2.3 | 3.4 | 1.2 |
| 7.8 | 113.8 | 24.6 | | | 14.5 | NM | 4.5 | -9.9 | -5.5 | 3.9 |
| 67.7 | 50.8 | 83.4 | | % Profit Before Taxes/Tangible Net Worth | 36.3 | 186.0 | 180.1 | 57.9 | 278.4 | 78.3 |
| (42)  24.2 | (89)  23.5 | (104)  24.7 | | | (27)  15.9 | (15)  4.3 | (14)  62.5 | (11)  24.4 | (12)  45.8 | (25)  39.0 |
| 7.6 | 7.6 | 7.2 | | | 2.8 | 1.0 | 16.8 | 14.2 | 10.5 | 20.8 |
| 25.1 | 20.4 | 24.9 | | % Profit Before Taxes/Total Assets | 10.3 | 27.9 | 61.2 | 38.6 | 57.9 | 30.2 |
| 10.6 | 7.0 | 8.3 | | | 3.9 | 3.3 | 9.8 | 8.1 | 22.2 | 16.4 |
| 2.4 | 1.7 | .6 | | | -.3 | .1 | 4.5 | -.7 | .9 | 9.2 |
| UND | UND | UND | | Sales/Net Fixed Assets | 75.3 | UND | UND | UND | UND | 870.7 |
| 122.3 | 32.4 | 22.2 | | | .2 | 7.7 | UND | 70.9 | 41.6 | 113.2 |
| 8.4 | .8 | .6 | | | .1 | .4 | 20.5 | 2.1 | 4.1 | 6.2 |
| 2.1 | 1.7 | 2.1 | | | .5 | .9 | 2.7 | 5.6 | 6.1 | 1.5 |
| .6 | .3 | .6 | | Sales/Total Assets | .1 | .2 | .8 | 1.6 | 1.7 | .8 |
| .1 | .1 | .1 | | | .1 | .1 | .2 | .3 | .4 | .6 |
| .2 | .7 | .8 | | | 12.0 | | | | | .1 |
| (23)  1.1 | (50)  6.0 | (58)  7.9 | | % Depr., Dep., Amort./Sales | (18)  18.2 | | | | (17)  .8 | |
| 9.6 | 19.2 | 17.2 | | | 41.2 | | | | | 7.3 |
| | | .9 | | % Officers', Directors' Owners' Comp/Sales | | | | | | |
| | (12)  4.8 | | | | | | | | | |
| | | 17.6 | | | | | | | | |
| 896578M | 2316871M | 2834369M | | Net Sales ($) | 13456M | 35010M | 57000M | 121538M | 256196M | 2351169M |
| 1832276M | 3622927M | 4221511M | | Total Assets ($) | 77299M | 267191M | 165799M | 281067M | 540001M | 2890154M |

© RMA 2024    M = $ thousand   MM = $ million
See Pages viii through xx for Explanation of Ratios and Data

## FINANCE—Portfolio Management and Investment Advice  NAICS 523940

### Current Data Sorted by Assets | Comparative Historical Data

| 0-500M | 500M-2MM | 2-10MM | 10-50MM | 50-100MM | 100-250MM | Type of Statement | 4/1/19-3/31/20 ALL | 4/1/20-3/31/21 ALL |
|---|---|---|---|---|---|---|---|---|
| 1 | | 8 | 22 | 12 | 19 | Unqualified | 46 | 38 |
| | | 1 | 1 | 2 | | Reviewed | 3 | 7 |
| 1 | 2 | 2 | 1 | | | Compiled | 13 | 10 |
| 7 | 17 | 7 | | | | Tax Returns | 40 | 24 |
| 27 | 33 | 47 | 37 | 26 | 20 | Other | 185 | 165 |
| | 27 (4/1-9/30/23) | | 266 (10/1/23-3/31/24) | | | | | |
| 36 | 52 | 65 | 61 | 40 | 39 | **NUMBER OF STATEMENTS** | 287 | 244 |
| % | % | % | % | % | % | **ASSETS** | % | % |
| 53.7 | 30.1 | 21.0 | 27.9 | 21.1 | 19.4 | Cash & Equivalents | 28.9 | 32.3 |
| 4.7 | 7.0 | 12.0 | 16.4 | 12.7 | 6.6 | Trade Receivables (net) | 11.6 | 11.9 |
| 2.6 | .7 | .2 | 2.6 | 1.7 | 1.2 | Inventory | .8 | .7 |
| 1.9 | 4.8 | 4.9 | 7.7 | 10.7 | 6.9 | All Other Current | 6.9 | 4.4 |
| 63.0 | 42.6 | 38.1 | 54.6 | 46.2 | 34.2 | Total Current | 48.3 | 49.3 |
| 10.8 | 16.1 | 14.4 | 10.2 | 10.5 | 10.2 | Fixed Assets (net) | 13.7 | 14.0 |
| 14.2 | 28.0 | 22.1 | 14.0 | 14.8 | 10.7 | Intangibles (net) | 16.1 | 18.5 |
| 12.1 | 13.3 | 25.4 | 21.2 | 28.5 | 44.9 | All Other Non-Current | 22.0 | 18.2 |
| 100.0 | 100.0 | 100.0 | 100.0 | 100.0 | 100.0 | Total | 100.0 | 100.0 |
| | | | | | | **LIABILITIES** | | |
| 16.9 | 8.7 | 4.2 | 5.5 | 2.7 | 5.6 | Notes Payable-Short Term | 10.9 | 9.3 |
| 3.8 | 5.0 | 2.9 | 2.4 | 2.1 | 2.5 | Cur. Mat.-L.T.D. | 3.1 | 2.9 |
| 5.0 | 2.4 | 2.2 | 5.2 | 7.4 | 2.4 | Trade Payables | 4.7 | 4.0 |
| .2 | .1 | .2 | .3 | .0 | .0 | Income Taxes Payable | .3 | .1 |
| 17.9 | 16.2 | 14.6 | 15.1 | 11.7 | 9.9 | All Other Current | 16.0 | 15.4 |
| 43.8 | 32.4 | 24.2 | 28.5 | 23.9 | 20.4 | Total Current | 34.9 | 31.7 |
| 30.8 | 32.3 | 38.8 | 16.5 | 25.7 | 21.3 | Long-Term Debt | 26.1 | 27.7 |
| .0 | .4 | .0 | .1 | .0 | .8 | Deferred Taxes | .2 | .2 |
| 5.8 | 13.3 | 5.9 | 9.4 | 9.5 | 7.3 | All Other Non-Current | 10.6 | 8.5 |
| 19.6 | 21.5 | 31.1 | 45.4 | 40.9 | 50.3 | Net Worth | 28.1 | 31.9 |
| 100.0 | 100.0 | 100.0 | 100.0 | 100.0 | 100.0 | Total Liabilities & Net Worth | 100.0 | 100.0 |
| | | | | | | **INCOME DATA** | | |
| 100.0 | 100.0 | 100.0 | 100.0 | 100.0 | 100.0 | Net Sales | 100.0 | 100.0 |
| | | | | | | Gross Profit | | |
| 73.3 | 69.8 | 71.5 | 76.8 | 74.2 | 61.4 | Operating Expenses | 74.7 | 67.8 |
| 26.7 | 30.2 | 28.5 | 23.2 | 25.8 | 38.6 | Operating Profit | 25.3 | 32.2 |
| -.1 | 3.5 | 5.3 | 3.1 | 3.5 | 7.1 | All Other Expenses (net) | 4.3 | 5.7 |
| 26.8 | 26.7 | 23.1 | 20.0 | 22.2 | 31.5 | Profit Before Taxes | 21.0 | 26.5 |
| | | | | | | **RATIOS** | | |
| 7.4 | 3.2 | 8.3 | 3.2 | 4.5 | 3.4 | | 4.4 | 4.6 |
| 2.0 | 1.7 | 1.9 | 2.1 | 1.7 | 1.3 | Current | 1.9 | 1.9 |
| .8 | .7 | .7 | 1.2 | 1.0 | .7 | | .8 | .9 |
| | | | | | | | | |
| 5.6 | 3.2 | 6.8 | 2.7 | 2.7 | 2.2 | | 3.9 | 4.2 |
| 1.6 | 1.6 | 1.6 | 1.8 | 1.2 | 1.0 | Quick (286) | 1.5 | 1.5 |
| .5 | .4 | .6 | .8 | .5 | .5 | | .6 | .7 |
| 0 UND | 0 UND | 0 UND | 0 999.8 | 0 UND | 0 UND | | 0 UND | 0 UND |
| 0 UND | 0 UND | 0 UND | 28 13.2 | 26 13.9 | 22 16.4 | Sales/Receivables  3 111.3 | 0 UND |
| 0 UND | 0 UND | 18 20.8 | 72 5.1 | 68 5.4 | 50 7.3 | 39 9.3 | 29 12.5 |
| | | | | | | Cost of Sales/Inventory | | |
| | | | | | | Cost of Sales/Payables | | |
| 13.0 | 7.5 | 5.0 | 3.2 | 2.9 | 2.4 | | 3.7 | 3.7 |
| 72.2 | 23.2 | 15.9 | 6.2 | 8.8 | 15.8 | Sales/Working Capital | 14.2 | 11.2 |
| -52.7 | -80.5 | -23.4 | 15.3 | NM | -8.9 | | -51.6 | -160.2 |
| 483.5 | 37.7 | 67.2 | 65.2 | 237.5 | 18.2 | | 64.3 | 49.3 |
| (16) 70.5 | (31) 16.4 | (43) 17.8 | (42) 15.1 | (30) 13.2 | (24) 9.6 | EBIT/Interest (178) | 12.2 (138) | 13.4 |
| 9.6 | 7.8 | 3.6 | 4.4 | 3.1 | 2.9 | | 3.7 | 4.4 |
| | | | | | | Net Profit + Depr., Dep., Amort./Cur. Mat. L/T/D | 8.4 (23) 3.5 | 2.1 |
| .0 | .0 | .0 | .0 | .0 | .0 | | .0 | .0 |
| .0 | .1 | .1 | .1 | .2 | .0 | Fixed/Worth | .1 | .1 |
| .3 | 4.3 | 2.2 | 1.4 | -4.9 | 2.4 | | 3.0 | 2.0 |
| .2 | .6 | .6 | .5 | .3 | .2 | | .5 | .4 |
| 2.4 | 4.5 | 4.7 | 1.7 | 1.7 | 1.2 | Debt/Worth | 2.1 | 2.0 |
| -5.4 | -1.6 | -2.5 | 9.8 | -21.0 | -125.8 | | -6.6 | -9.6 |
| 829.9 | 521.4 | 180.7 | 86.6 | 102.0 | 20.7 | % Profit Before Taxes/Tangible Net Worth | 180.3 | 202.3 |
| (25) 284.9 | (30) 103.3 | (38) 42.2 | (49) 28.6 | (29) 33.8 | (29) 7.3 | (198) 36.1 (170) | 41.0 |
| 123.5 | 31.4 | 15.4 | 11.1 | 7.7 | 3.6 | | 8.0 | 8.4 |
| 360.9 | 121.4 | 53.9 | 45.6 | 40.1 | 18.8 | % Profit Before Taxes/Total Assets | 64.9 | 65.7 |
| 211.3 | 33.8 | 22.3 | 13.4 | 9.3 | 5.7 | | 15.4 | 19.7 |
| 50.4 | 11.0 | 4.3 | 3.9 | 2.4 | 1.9 | | 3.8 | 4.0 |
| UND | UND | 999.8 | 305.3 | 811.8 | UND | | 999.8 | UND |
| 767.7 | 174.7 | 212.7 | 49.6 | 49.4 | 68.7 | Sales/Net Fixed Assets | 87.7 | 194.3 |
| 79.7 | 26.6 | 31.9 | 17.8 | 10.7 | 7.0 | | 20.4 | 23.1 |
| 15.9 | 6.3 | 3.1 | 2.0 | 1.7 | 1.0 | | 4.4 | 4.0 |
| 9.7 | 3.0 | 1.6 | 1.2 | 1.1 | .4 | Sales/Total Assets | 1.8 | 1.5 |
| 5.4 | 1.4 | .7 | .6 | .5 | .1 | | .6 | .4 |
| | .1 | .3 | .3 | .2 | .9 | | .4 | .3 |
| (17) .6 | (25) .4 | (37) .8 | (23) .8 | (17) 1.4 | | % Depr., Dep., Amort./Sales (144) .9 (85) | .9 |
| | 1.4 | 1.6 | 1.9 | 1.9 | 4.1 | | 2.6 | 2.8 |
| 14.0 | 11.5 | 11.3 | 1.4 | | | | 7.3 | 8.3 |
| (17) 24.8 | (23) 18.7 | (15) 17.4 | (13) 10.4 | | | % Officers', Directors' Owners' Comp/Sales (64) 15.3 (70) | 16.1 |
| 30.1 | 23.9 | 27.7 | 15.8 | | | | 25.5 | 26.3 |
| 78497M | 268698M | 858132M | 2254361M | 3252988M | 3979465M | Net Sales ($) | 10742034M | 4816581M |
| 8119M | 59589M | 322564M | 1537271M | 2838846M | 5853361M | Total Assets ($) | 8659745M | 5545832M |

© RMA 2024    M = $ thousand    MM = $ million
See Pages viii through xx for Explanation of Ratios and Data

# FINANCE—Portfolio Management and Investment Advice  NAICS 523940

## Comparative Historical Data | Current Data Sorted by Sales

| Comparative Historical Data | | | | Type of Statement | Current Data Sorted by Sales | | | | | |
|---|---|---|---|---|---|---|---|---|---|---|
| 33 | | 55 | 62 | Unqualified | 1 | 4 | 2 | 5 | 15 | 35 |
| 10 | | 4 | 4 | Reviewed | | | | 1 | | 3 |
| 10 | | 5 | 6 | Compiled | | | 3 | 1 | 1 | 1 |
| 41 | | 39 | 31 | Tax Returns | 3 | 14 | 6 | 5 | 3 | |
| 166 | | 212 | 190 | Other | 29 | 24 | 25 | 22 | 30 | 60 |
| 4/1/21-3/31/22 | | 4/1/22-3/31/23 | 4/1/23-3/31/24 | | 27 (4/1-9/30/23) | | | 266 (10/1/23-3/31/24) | | |
| ALL | | ALL | ALL | | 0-1MM | 1-3MM | 3-5MM | 5-10MM | 10-25MM | 25MM & OVER |
| 260 | | 315 | 293 | NUMBER OF STATEMENTS | 33 | 45 | 33 | 34 | 49 | 99 |
| % | | % | % | ASSETS | % | % | % | % | % | % |
| 35.7 | | 30.7 | 27.8 | Cash & Equivalents | 24.3 | 34.8 | 33.6 | 31.1 | 22.9 | 25.3 |
| 9.7 | | 9.1 | 10.5 | Trade Receivables (net) | 3.1 | 3.1 | 5.7 | 9.9 | 15.4 | 15.8 |
| .6 | | .5 | 1.4 | Inventory | .0 | 2.1 | 1.2 | .5 | 3.2 | 1.1 |
| 5.0 | | 7.0 | 6.2 | All Other Current | 3.6 | 2.3 | 6.9 | 4.4 | 5.6 | 9.4 |
| 51.0 | | 47.3 | 46.0 | Total Current | 31.0 | 42.3 | 47.3 | 45.9 | 47.2 | 51.6 |
| 13.9 | | 14.1 | 12.3 | Fixed Assets (net) | 38.1 | 11.6 | 6.9 | 4.9 | 9.4 | 9.8 |
| 17.5 | | 17.7 | 18.0 | Intangibles (net) | 19.3 | 31.7 | 24.2 | 17.4 | 4.7 | 16.0 |
| 17.6 | | 21.0 | 23.7 | All Other Non-Current | 11.6 | 14.3 | 21.6 | 31.9 | 38.7 | 22.6 |
| 100.0 | | 100.0 | 100.0 | Total | 100.0 | 100.0 | 100.0 | 100.0 | 100.0 | 100.0 |
| | | | | LIABILITIES | | | | | | |
| 8.1 | | 7.3 | 6.8 | Notes Payable-Short Term | 9.1 | 8.6 | 14.6 | 3.2 | 6.4 | 4.1 |
| 3.0 | | 2.7 | 3.1 | Cur. Mat.-L.T.D. | 1.5 | 5.1 | 2.7 | 4.5 | 2.1 | 3.0 |
| 2.8 | | 3.3 | 4.0 | Trade Payables | 3.8 | 1.9 | 2.0 | 3.6 | 3.9 | 5.7 |
| .3 | | .5 | .2 | Income Taxes Payable | .2 | .0 | .0 | .1 | .5 | .1 |
| 17.5 | | 16.5 | 14.4 | All Other Current | 9.7 | 5.2 | 19.4 | 7.8 | 19.4 | 18.2 |
| 31.7 | | 30.4 | 28.4 | Total Current | 24.3 | 20.8 | 38.6 | 19.2 | 32.3 | 31.1 |
| 29.5 | | 25.0 | 27.9 | Long-Term Debt | 47.6 | 35.1 | 21.0 | 30.8 | 17.5 | 24.5 |
| .1 | | .2 | .2 | Deferred Taxes | .0 | .0 | .1 | .6 | .2 | .2 |
| 6.8 | | 5.2 | 8.6 | All Other Non-Current | 2.8 | 7.4 | 12.2 | 3.0 | 11.3 | 10.6 |
| 31.8 | | 39.2 | 34.9 | Net Worth | 25.3 | 36.8 | 28.1 | 46.4 | 38.6 | 33.6 |
| 100.0 | | 100.0 | 100.0 | Total Liabilities & Net Worth | 100.0 | 100.0 | 100.0 | 100.0 | 100.0 | 100.0 |
| | | | | INCOME DATA | | | | | | |
| 100.0 | | 100.0 | 100.0 | Net Sales | 100.0 | 100.0 | 100.0 | 100.0 | 100.0 | 100.0 |
| | | | | Gross Profit | | | | | | |
| 67.2 | | 68.4 | 71.6 | Operating Expenses | 57.0 | 66.9 | 75.4 | 71.7 | 72.1 | 77.0 |
| 32.8 | | 31.6 | 28.4 | Operating Profit | 43.0 | 33.1 | 24.6 | 28.3 | 27.9 | 23.0 |
| 2.4 | | 3.7 | 3.9 | All Other Expenses (net) | 9.3 | 6.9 | 1.6 | 5.4 | 3.0 | 1.3 |
| 30.4 | | 27.9 | 24.6 | Profit Before Taxes | 33.8 | 26.2 | 23.0 | 22.9 | 24.9 | 21.7 |
| | | | | RATIOS | | | | | | |
| 7.3 | | 5.5 | 4.2 | | 5.4 | 11.9 | 7.0 | 9.4 | 3.4 | 2.9 |
| 2.3 | | 1.8 | 1.8 | Current | 1.7 | 1.9 | 1.6 | 2.2 | 1.5 | 1.8 |
| 1.0 | | .8 | .8 | | .4 | .7 | .6 | 1.1 | .8 | 1.1 |
| 6.7 | | 4.6 | 3.3 | | 5.4 | 11.9 | 4.6 | 9.2 | 2.9 | 2.1 |
| (259) 2.1 | | (314) 1.5 | 1.5 | Quick | 1.7 | 1.6 | 1.3 | 1.8 | 1.5 | 1.4 |
| .9 | | .6 | .6 | | .3 | .5 | .3 | .8 | .4 | .7 |
| 0 UND | | 0 UND | 0 UND | | 0 UND | 0 UND | 0 UND | 0 UND | 1 619.2 | |
| 0 UND | | 0 UND | 0 UND | Sales/Receivables | 0 UND | 0 UND | 0 UND | 0 UND | 7 52.3 | 27 13.4 |
| 26 14.3 | | 24 14.9 | 37 9.9 | | 0 UND | 0 UND | 5 77.1 | 28 13.1 | 69 5.3 | 54 6.8 |
| | | | | Cost of Sales/Inventory | | | | | | |
| | | | | Cost of Sales/Payables | | | | | | |
| 3.7 | | 3.9 | 4.5 | | 3.6 | 6.3 | 10.5 | 4.5 | 3.7 | 4.4 |
| 11.7 | | 14.4 | 14.0 | Sales/Working Capital | 24.0 | 14.6 | 77.3 | 11.2 | 14.7 | 10.2 |
| 436.8 | | -70.2 | -57.2 | | -4.3 | -56.8 | -21.2 | NM | -30.7 | 41.9 |
| | | 90.0 | 99.8 | 59.0 | | 14.6 | 50.0 | 58.8 | 33.2 | 79.3 | 76.3 |
| (166) 18.0 | | (179) 18.3 | (186) 15.8 | EBIT/Interest | (12) 7.3 | (29) 14.3 | (23) 18.6 | (23) 9.7 | (29) 25.4 | (70) 15.9 |
| 6.0 | | 6.1 | 4.7 | | 5.0 | 3.4 | 3.0 | 4.4 | 6.7 | 4.7 |
| 11.5 | | 12.4 | 18.9 | | | | | | | 20.4 |
| (11) 2.4 | | (16) 4.0 | (25) 6.3 | Net Profit + Depr., Dep., Amort./Cur. Mat. L/T/D | | | | | | (22) 6.7 |
| 1.0 | | 1.6 | 1.5 | | | | | | | 1.6 |
| .0 | | .0 | .0 | | .0 | .0 | .0 | .0 | .0 | .0 |
| .1 | | .1 | .1 | Fixed/Worth | .6 | .0 | .1 | .0 | .1 | .4 |
| 2.3 | | 1.7 | 2.3 | | 3.5 | 1.0 | NM | .1 | .8 | -1.8 |
| .4 | | .4 | .4 | | .8 | .1 | .2 | .4 | .4 | .7 |
| 2.0 | | 1.7 | 1.9 | Debt/Worth | 2.7 | 1.6 | 10.1 | .7 | .8 | 2.2 |
| -5.2 | | -15.4 | -6.9 | | -3.5 | -1.7 | -1.7 | NM | 7.4 | -13.2 |
| 247.9 | | 225.1 | 185.4 | | 71.4 | 283.8 | 598.3 | 337.3 | 93.7 | 153.9 |
| (180) 82.0 | | (233) 77.7 | (200) 43.1 | % Profit Before Taxes/Tangible Net Worth | (23) 18.1 | (25) 97.6 | (18) 140.3 | (26) 25.1 | (41) 14.1 | (67) 76.1 |
| 18.5 | | 17.1 | 10.2 | | 10.6 | 1.2 | 9.5 | 6.0 | 7.3 | 27.9 |
| 96.9 | | 90.2 | 66.7 | | 29.1 | 106.0 | 318.6 | 55.7 | 53.4 | 54.8 |
| 36.9 | | 27.6 | 22.3 | % Profit Before Taxes/Total Assets | 10.0 | 30.5 | 53.1 | 21.8 | 9.3 | 28.0 |
| 8.1 | | 5.9 | 4.3 | | 3.3 | 1.2 | 4.9 | 6.4 | 2.8 | 8.0 |
| UND | | UND | UND | | UND | UND | UND | UND | UND | 182.5 |
| 121.2 | | 100.5 | 112.5 | Sales/Net Fixed Assets | 32.9 | 851.5 | 253.2 | 999.8 | 104.3 | 41.5 |
| 19.4 | | 18.6 | 22.5 | | .2 | 44.5 | 50.8 | 127.9 | 27.5 | 11.2 |
| 3.7 | | 3.6 | 3.3 | | 2.4 | 5.4 | 9.8 | 3.8 | 3.7 | 2.7 |
| 1.8 | | 1.6 | 1.6 | Sales/Total Assets | .2 | 1.9 | 3.2 | 1.6 | 1.1 | 1.7 |
| .5 | | .6 | .6 | | .1 | .5 | .9 | .6 | .2 | 1.0 |
| .4 | | .3 | .3 | | | | | .1 | .3 | .2 |
| (99) 1.2 | | (111) .9 | (123) .8 | % Depr., Dep., Amort./Sales | | | (12) .2 | (22) .7 | (67) .8 | |
| 3.6 | | 2.6 | 1.9 | | | | | 1.0 | 1.2 | 1.9 |
| 7.7 | | 6.8 | 9.7 | | | 11.4 | 5.0 | | | 1.8 |
| (81) 15.1 | | (83) 12.8 | (78) 16.9 | % Officers', Directors' Owners' Comp/Sales | | (21) 17.4 | (14) 20.6 | | (20) 7.9 | |
| 26.7 | | 26.5 | 24.9 | | | 26.7 | 28.1 | | | 18.5 |
| 7083508M | | 9124260M | 10692141M | Net Sales ($) | 16367M | 88195M | 132142M | 238409M | 838846M | 9378182M |
| 7172664M | | 8368152M | 10619750M | Total Assets ($) | 71822M | 513240M | 453873M | 735766M | 2363992M | 6481057M |

© RMA 2024  M = $ thousand   MM = $ million
See Pages viii through xx for Explanation of Ratios and Data

# FINANCE—Trust, Fiduciary, and Custody Activities  NAICS 523991

## Current Data Sorted by Assets / Comparative Historical Data

| | | | | | | Type of Statement | | |
|---|---|---|---|---|---|---|---|---|
| | | 1 | 2 | | 2 | Unqualified | 10 | 11 |
| | | | 1 | | | Reviewed | 1 | 1 |
| | | 1 | 1 | | | Compiled | | |
| 1 | 3 | | | | | Tax Returns | 3 | 3 |
| 1 | 2 | 9 | 6 | 3 | 2 | Other | 23 | 8 |
| 0-500M | 4 (4/1-9/30/23) 500M-2MM | 2-10MM | 34 (10/1/23-3/31/24) 10-50MM | 50-100MM | 100-250MM | | 4/1/19-3/31/20 ALL | 4/1/20-3/31/21 ALL |
| 2 | 6 | 12 | 11 | 3 | 4 | NUMBER OF STATEMENTS | 37 | 23 |
| % | % | % | % | % | % | **ASSETS** | % | % |
| | | 35.4 | 22.3 | | | Cash & Equivalents | 38.9 | 36.9 |
| | | 14.0 | 13.1 | | | Trade Receivables (net) | 14.6 | 13.8 |
| | | 6.1 | .0 | | | Inventory | 1.2 | 3.1 |
| | | 5.7 | 12.2 | | | All Other Current | 3.4 | 2.9 |
| | | 61.2 | 47.7 | | | Total Current | 58.1 | 56.7 |
| | | 4.6 | 19.4 | | | Fixed Assets (net) | 14.9 | 19.9 |
| | | 8.5 | .2 | | | Intangibles (net) | 6.6 | 6.3 |
| | | 25.7 | 32.7 | | | All Other Non-Current | 20.4 | 17.1 |
| | | 100.0 | 100.0 | | | Total | 100.0 | 100.0 |
| | | | | | | **LIABILITIES** | | |
| | | 1.8 | 4.0 | | | Notes Payable-Short Term | 1.4 | 15.2 |
| | | 1.2 | 1.7 | | | Cur. Mat.-L.T.D. | 1.7 | 2.3 |
| | | 4.0 | 3.5 | | | Trade Payables | 7.2 | 5.7 |
| | | 1.3 | .1 | | | Income Taxes Payable | .4 | .0 |
| | | 3.9 | 6.8 | | | All Other Current | 15.0 | 20.1 |
| | | 12.3 | 16.1 | | | Total Current | 25.7 | 43.4 |
| | | 2.0 | 15.4 | | | Long-Term Debt | 7.2 | 19.6 |
| | | .0 | .0 | | | Deferred Taxes | .8 | .0 |
| | | 5.5 | 8.8 | | | All Other Non-Current | 6.1 | 6.5 |
| | | 80.2 | 59.7 | | | Net Worth | 60.3 | 30.6 |
| | | 100.0 | 100.0 | | | Total Liabilties & Net Worth | 100.0 | 100.0 |
| | | | | | | **INCOME DATA** | | |
| | | 100.0 | 100.0 | | | Net Sales | 100.0 | 100.0 |
| | | | | | | Gross Profit | | |
| | | 67.2 | 72.3 | | | Operating Expenses | 78.7 | 69.0 |
| | | 32.8 | 27.7 | | | Operating Profit | 21.3 | 31.0 |
| | | .2 | 6.2 | | | All Other Expenses (net) | .7 | 3.5 |
| | | 32.6 | 21.5 | | | Profit Before Taxes | 20.5 | 27.5 |
| | | | | | | **RATIOS** | | |
| | | 25.7 | 6.1 | | | | 4.7 | 4.3 |
| | | 4.9 | 3.5 | | | Current | 3.0 | 2.6 |
| | | 3.7 | 1.2 | | | | 1.9 | 1.1 |
| | | 10.3 | 5.0 | | | | 4.6 | 4.3 |
| | | 4.8 | 3.1 | | | Quick | 2.5 | 1.7 |
| | | 2.9 | 1.2 | | | | 1.6 | 1.0 |
| | | 0 UND | 9 42.2 | | | | 0 UND | 0 UND |
| | | 7 50.9 | 29 12.6 | | | Sales/Receivables | 19 19.4 | 19 18.8 |
| | | 47 7.7 | 56 6.5 | | | | 49 7.4 | 70 5.2 |
| | | | | | | Cost of Sales/Inventory | | |
| | | | | | | Cost of Sales/Payables | | |
| | | .4 | 1.7 | | | | | |
| | | 1.5 | 8.4 | | | Sales/Working Capital | 2.6 | 2.4 |
| | | 6.0 | 26.4 | | | | 4.9 | 3.9 |
| | | | | | | | 13.7 | 63.9 |
| | | | | | | | 66.0 | |
| | | | | | | EBIT/Interest | (13) 19.9 | |
| | | | | | | | 12.3 | |
| | | | | | | Net Profit + Depr., Dep., Amort./Cur. Mat. L/T/D | | |
| | | .0 | .0 | | | | .0 | .0 |
| | | .0 | .1 | | | Fixed/Worth | .1 | .2 |
| | | .1 | .8 | | | | .6 | 2.3 |
| | | .0 | .1 | | | | .3 | .4 |
| | | .3 | .8 | | | Debt/Worth | .6 | 1.6 |
| | | .5 | 1.5 | | | | 1.5 | 4.6 |
| | | 48.5 | 130.9 | | | | 47.3 | 70.6 |
| | | 23.5 | 38.5 | | | % Profit Before Taxes/Tangible Net Worth | (33) 28.0 | (19) 31.8 |
| | | 11.6 | 2.2 | | | | 10.2 | 17.9 |
| | | 33.1 | 82.4 | | | | 29.2 | 58.3 |
| | | 17.2 | 19.1 | | | % Profit Before Taxes/Total Assets | 17.7 | 22.0 |
| | | 7.9 | .7 | | | | 5.4 | 6.1 |
| | | UND | UND | | | | UND | UND |
| | | 89.9 | 20.2 | | | Sales/Net Fixed Assets | 23.3 | 25.4 |
| | | 11.5 | 4.4 | | | | 4.9 | 5.4 |
| | | 1.6 | 3.5 | | | | 2.4 | 2.4 |
| | | .8 | 1.1 | | | Sales/Total Assets | 1.1 | 1.2 |
| | | .2 | .2 | | | | .5 | .3 |
| | | | | | | | .6 | .9 |
| | | | | | | % Depr., Dep., Amort./Sales | (21) 1.6 | (13) 1.2 |
| | | | | | | | 2.6 | 3.0 |
| | | | | | | % Officers', Directors' Owners' Comp/Sales | | |
| 1504M | 17684M | 78164M | 600549M | 112064M | 392642M | Net Sales ($) | 2175165M | 747821M |
| 365M | 8145M | 71304M | 330993M | 173273M | 645270M | Total Assets ($) | 1799915M | 944515M |

© RMA 2024

M = $ thousand   MM = $ million
See Pages viii through xx for Explanation of Ratios and Data

# FINANCE—Trust, Fiduciary, and Custody Activities  NAICS 523991

| Comparative Historical Data | | | | Current Data Sorted by Sales | | | | | |
|---|---|---|---|---|---|---|---|---|---|
| | | | **Type of Statement** | | | | | | |
| 8 | 8 | 8 | Unqualified | 1 | | 1 | 2 | 4 | |
| 2 | | 1 | Reviewed | | | | 1 | 1 | |
| | 1 | 2 | Compiled | | | 1 | | 1 | |
| 2 | 1 | 4 | Tax Returns | | | 1 | 1 | | |
| 10 | 9 | 23 | Other | 3 | 3 | 3 | 1 | 4 | 6 |
| 4/1/21-3/31/22 ALL | 4/1/22-3/31/23 ALL | 4/1/23-3/31/24 ALL | | 6 (4/1-9/30/23) | | | 34 (10/1/23-3/31/24) | | |
| | | | | 0-1MM | 1-3MM | 3-5MM | 5-10MM | 10-25MM | 25MM & OVER |
| 22 | 19 | 38 | **NUMBER OF STATEMENTS** | 9 | 4 | 3 | 4 | 6 | 12 |
| % | % | % | **ASSETS** | % | % | % | % | % | % |
| 24.8 | 36.0 | 32.8 | Cash & Equivalents | | | | | | 24.2 |
| 9.8 | 13.3 | 11.0 | Trade Receivables (net) | | | | | | 14.2 |
| 1.5 | 2.7 | 4.1 | Inventory | | | | | | 6.8 |
| 4.2 | 8.2 | 5.9 | All Other Current | | | | | | 5.5 |
| 40.3 | 60.2 | 53.8 | Total Current | | | | | | 50.7 |
| 25.7 | 12.0 | 13.3 | Fixed Assets (net) | | | | | | 18.8 |
| 10.2 | 8.6 | 8.2 | Intangibles (net) | | | | | | 8.8 |
| 23.8 | 19.2 | 24.7 | All Other Non-Current | | | | | | 21.7 |
| 100.0 | 100.0 | 100.0 | Total | | | | | | 100.0 |
| | | | **LIABILITIES** | | | | | | |
| .7 | 2.7 | 2.0 | Notes Payable-Short Term | | | | | | .2 |
| 1.8 | 1.2 | 1.5 | Cur. Mat.-L.T.D. | | | | | | 2.3 |
| 5.0 | 3.8 | 3.5 | Trade Payables | | | | | | 5.1 |
| .0 | .1 | .6 | Income Taxes Payable | | | | | | 1.3 |
| 10.6 | 28.2 | 7.9 | All Other Current | | | | | | 9.6 |
| 18.1 | 36.0 | 15.4 | Total Current | | | | | | 18.6 |
| 21.3 | 6.9 | 8.5 | Long-Term Debt | | | | | | 14.4 |
| .1 | .0 | .0 | Deferred Taxes | | | | | | .0 |
| 4.0 | 3.6 | 6.7 | All Other Non-Current | | | | | | 7.4 |
| 56.5 | 53.5 | 69.3 | Net Worth | | | | | | 59.6 |
| 100.0 | 100.0 | 100.0 | Total Liabilties & Net Worth | | | | | | 100.0 |
| | | | **INCOME DATA** | | | | | | |
| 100.0 | 100.0 | 100.0 | Net Sales | | | | | | 100.0 |
| | | | Gross Profit | | | | | | 74.8 |
| 80.5 | 66.6 | 66.0 | Operating Expenses | | | | | | 25.2 |
| 19.5 | 33.4 | 34.0 | Operating Profit | | | | | | 1.7 |
| 1.1 | 4.1 | 1.9 | All Other Expenses (net) | | | | | | 23.5 |
| 18.4 | 29.3 | 32.1 | Profit Before Taxes | | | | | | |
| | | | **RATIOS** | | | | | | |
| 15.2 | 5.1 | 11.3 | | | | | | | 6.1 |
| 2.0 | 2.3 | 3.6 | Current | | | | | | 2.7 |
| 1.5 | 1.1 | 1.6 | | | | | | | 1.4 |
| 11.8 | 4.9 | 8.0 | | | | | | | 4.4 |
| 1.8 | 1.8 | 3.2 | Quick | | | | | | 2.1 |
| 1.1 | .9 | 1.5 | | | | | | | 1.3 |
| 0 UND | 0 999.8 | 0 UND | | | | | | 10 | 36.0 |
| 8 47.4 | 21 17.8 | 14 26.8 | Sales/Receivables | | | | | 34 | 10.6 |
| 62 5.9 | 53 6.9 | 41 8.8 | | | | | | 53 | 6.9 |
| | | | Cost of Sales/Inventory | | | | | | |
| | | | Cost of Sales/Payables | | | | | | |
| 2.3 | 2.1 | .8 | | | | | | | 2.8 |
| 4.0 | 9.5 | 3.8 | Sales/Working Capital | | | | | | 8.9 |
| 10.4 | 62.6 | 23.4 | | | | | | | 21.2 |
| 16.1 | | 346.6 | | | | | | | |
| (15) 6.0 | | (17) 59.5 | EBIT/Interest | | | | | | |
| .8 | | 3.5 | | | | | | | |
| | | | Net Profit + Depr., Dep., Amort./Cur. Mat. L/T/D | | | | | | |
| .0 | .0 | .0 | | | | | | | .0 |
| .2 | .1 | .1 | Fixed/Worth | | | | | | .1 |
| 2.1 | 1.0 | .2 | | | | | | | 1.0 |
| .3 | .2 | .1 | | | | | | | .2 |
| 1.0 | .6 | .4 | Debt/Worth | | | | | | 1.1 |
| 2.9 | 5.2 | 1.5 | | | | | | | 2.2 |
| 64.8 | 80.1 | 98.1 | % Profit Before Taxes/Tangible Net Worth | | | | | | 236.7 |
| (19) 12.2 | (17) 35.8 | (37) 25.1 | | | | | | | 77.9 |
| -1.6 | 6.3 | 11.3 | | | | | | | 15.1 |
| 37.5 | 44.1 | 56.0 | % Profit Before Taxes/Total Assets | | | | | | 79.1 |
| 9.1 | 21.5 | 15.8 | | | | | | | 23.4 |
| -.7 | 2.0 | 6.6 | | | | | | | 9.2 |
| 195.9 | UND | UND | Sales/Net Fixed Assets | | | | | | 777.7 |
| 12.5 | 39.4 | 36.2 | | | | | | | 12.2 |
| .9 | 9.2 | 6.1 | | | | | | | 5.3 |
| 1.7 | 2.2 | 2.5 | Sales/Total Assets | | | | | | 3.3 |
| 1.0 | 1.3 | .8 | | | | | | | 1.3 |
| .2 | .6 | .2 | | | | | | | .7 |
| .8 | .4 | .4 | % Depr., Dep., Amort./Sales | | | | | | |
| (10) 2.0 | (10) 1.6 | (15) 1.7 | | | | | | | |
| 21.9 | 4.0 | 3.9 | | | | | | | |
| | | | % Officers', Directors' Owners' Comp/Sales | | | | | | |
| 767714M | 957837M | 1202607M | Net Sales ($) | 6208M | 5901M | 10835M | 26118M | 90980M | 1062565M |
| 946126M | 611578M | 1229350M | Total Assets ($) | 61092M | 16890M | 71305M | 55394M | 185557M | 839112M |

M = $ thousand   MM = $ million
See Pages viii through xx for Explanation of Ratios and Data

© RMA 2024

# FINANCE—Miscellaneous Financial Investment Activities  NAICS 523999

## Current Data Sorted by Assets | Comparative Historical Data

| | | | | | | | Type of Statement | | |
|---|---|---|---|---|---|---|---|---|---|
| | | | 1 | 5 | 1 | 10 | Unqualified | 12 | 4 |
| | | | | 2 | | | Reviewed | 3 | 2 |
| 3 | 4 | 7 | 1 | 1 | | | Compiled | 6 | 2 |
| 2 | 8 | 19 | 25 | 11 | 11 | | Tax Returns | 17 | 6 |
| | 6 (4/1-9/30/23) | | 104 (10/1/23-3/31/24) | | | | Other | 63 | 54 |
| 0-500M | 500M-2MM | 2-10MM | 10-50MM | 50-100MM | 100-250MM | | | 4/1/19-3/31/20 ALL | 4/1/20-3/31/21 ALL |
| 5 | 12 | 27 | 33 | 12 | 21 | | NUMBER OF STATEMENTS | 101 | 68 |
| % | % | % | % | % | % | | ASSETS | % | % |
| | 39.4 | 30.2 | 25.4 | 17.1 | 13.5 | | Cash & Equivalents | 22.0 | 28.9 |
| | 7.5 | 15.5 | 10.3 | 3.8 | 13.4 | | Trade Receivables (net) | 10.0 | 5.4 |
| | .2 | 2.1 | .2 | .0 | 2.0 | | Inventory | 2.4 | .7 |
| | 4.3 | 8.8 | 9.0 | 5.6 | 7.3 | | All Other Current | 7.5 | 5.3 |
| | 51.4 | 56.6 | 44.9 | 26.6 | 36.1 | | Total Current | 41.8 | 40.3 |
| | 16.9 | 10.3 | 10.4 | 9.1 | 7.7 | | Fixed Assets (net) | 16.5 | 19.7 |
| | 14.4 | 14.5 | 6.6 | .6 | 4.8 | | Intangibles (net) | 11.7 | 11.3 |
| | 17.3 | 18.5 | 38.1 | 63.7 | 51.3 | | All Other Non-Current | 30.0 | 28.7 |
| | 100.0 | 100.0 | 100.0 | 100.0 | 100.0 | | Total | 100.0 | 100.0 |
| | | | | | | | LIABILITIES | | |
| | 18.0 | 4.5 | 7.0 | 2.1 | 5.9 | | Notes Payable-Short Term | 10.2 | 14.6 |
| | .2 | 1.0 | 1.7 | 1.9 | 3.0 | | Cur. Mat.-L.T.D. | 1.2 | 2.8 |
| | 3.0 | 3.6 | 3.4 | 1.5 | 1.6 | | Trade Payables | 2.4 | 2.2 |
| | .1 | .0 | .0 | .0 | .3 | | Income Taxes Payable | .2 | .2 |
| | 13.5 | 18.1 | 9.2 | 4.3 | 6.2 | | All Other Current | 9.3 | 13.8 |
| | 34.9 | 27.2 | 21.4 | 9.8 | 17.1 | | Total Current | 23.3 | 33.6 |
| | 31.6 | 11.1 | 14.4 | 25.1 | 30.4 | | Long-Term Debt | 33.7 | 21.6 |
| | .0 | .0 | .1 | .0 | .1 | | Deferred Taxes | .0 | .1 |
| | 3.5 | 4.9 | 8.0 | 6.4 | 2.0 | | All Other Non-Current | 5.7 | 9.5 |
| | 30.0 | 56.8 | 56.2 | 58.7 | 50.4 | | Net Worth | 37.3 | 35.2 |
| | 100.0 | 100.0 | 100.0 | 100.0 | 100.0 | | Total Liabilities & Net Worth | 100.0 | 100.0 |
| | | | | | | | INCOME DATA | | |
| | 100.0 | 100.0 | 100.0 | 100.0 | 100.0 | | Net Sales | 100.0 | 100.0 |
| | | | | | | | Gross Profit | | |
| | 64.1 | 74.4 | 56.3 | 35.3 | 51.3 | | Operating Expenses | 58.9 | 57.4 |
| | 35.9 | 25.6 | 43.7 | 64.7 | 48.7 | | Operating Profit | 41.1 | 42.6 |
| | 7.6 | -.3 | 13.4 | 15.1 | 12.7 | | All Other Expenses (net) | 11.1 | 4.3 |
| | 28.3 | 25.9 | 30.4 | 49.6 | 36.0 | | Profit Before Taxes | 30.1 | 38.3 |
| | | | | | | | RATIOS | | |
| | 10.4 | 4.4 | 6.1 | 752.9 | 3.8 | | | 7.0 | 6.1 |
| | 3.2 | 1.1 | 2.2 | 1.1 | 2.0 | | Current | 2.2 | 1.9 |
| | .5 | .7 | 1.1 | .6 | .7 | | | 1.1 | .7 |
| | 10.4 | 2.7 | 4.8 | 752.9 | 3.3 | | | 6.5 | 5.3 |
| | 3.2 | 1.0 | 1.7 | .9 | 1.2 | | Quick | 1.7 (67) | 1.8 |
| | .5 | .4 | .2 | .1 | .3 | | | .7 | .5 |
| 0 UND | 0 UND | 0 UND | 0 UND | 0 UND | | | | 0 UND | 0 UND |
| 0 UND | 0 UND | 13 27.7 | 0 999.8 | 0 UND | 18 20.2 | | Sales/Receivables | 1 450.5 | 0 UND |
| 0 UND | 0 UND | 42 8.7 | 15 24.5 | 0 UND | 66 5.5 | | | 32 11.3 | 11 33.7 |
| | | | | | | | Cost of Sales/Inventory | | |
| | | | | | | | Cost of Sales/Payables | | |
| | 5.2 | 4.0 | .5 | .9 | .5 | | | 1.6 | .7 |
| | 27.4 | 19.7 | 5.0 | NM | 3.6 | | Sales/Working Capital | 6.3 | 7.3 |
| | NM | -27.4 | NM | -7.5 | -44.9 | | | 162.7 | -16.7 |
| | | 151.4 | 73.2 | | 30.8 | | | 36.9 | 36.5 |
| | (18) | 21.5 (16) | 10.8 | (15) | 7.6 | | EBIT/Interest | (61) 8.5 (42) | 6.5 |
| | | 7.2 | 4.4 | | 3.6 | | | 3.8 | 2.2 |
| | | | | | | | Net Profit + Depr., Dep., Amort./Cur. Mat. L/T/D | | |
| | .0 | .0 | .0 | .0 | .0 | | | .0 | .0 |
| | .0 | .0 | .0 | .0 | .0 | | Fixed/Worth | .0 | .2 |
| | 4.3 | .8 | .3 | .1 | .3 | | | 1.4 | 27.8 |
| | .2 | .3 | .3 | .0 | .3 | | | .2 | .2 |
| | 1.3 | .7 | .9 | .3 | 1.3 | | Debt/Worth | 1.0 | 1.1 |
| | 10.4 | 3.6 | 2.5 | 2.7 | 2.3 | | | 15.0 | UND |
| | 529.6 | 98.0 | 41.7 | 11.2 | 21.4 | | % Profit Before Taxes/Tangible Net Worth | 62.3 | 66.2 |
| (10) | 118.3 (22) | 49.2 (31) | 25.1 (11) | 8.1 (20) | 15.1 | | | (79) 19.4 (52) | 13.2 |
| | 45.4 | 15.1 | 6.7 | 5.1 | 11.2 | | | 2.0 | 3.1 |
| | 175.0 | 53.8 | 21.9 | 7.1 | 13.5 | | % Profit Before Taxes/Total Assets | 30.6 | 31.9 |
| | 65.0 | 31.7 | 10.9 | 4.8 | 5.5 | | | 7.5 | 9.3 |
| | 19.8 | 9.8 | 3.7 | 2.5 | 2.4 | | | 1.4 | 1.3 |
| | UND | UND | UND | UND | UND | | | UND | UND |
| | 508.1 | 91.7 | 104.8 | UND | 29.7 | | Sales/Net Fixed Assets | 76.7 | 44.0 |
| | 21.8 | 28.2 | 21.7 | 92.7 | 5.3 | | | 6.4 | 2.7 |
| | 9.8 | 3.8 | 1.2 | .3 | .7 | | | 1.6 | 2.3 |
| | 4.2 | 2.1 | .4 | .1 | .1 | | Sales/Total Assets | .4 | .2 |
| | 1.9 | .6 | .1 | .1 | .1 | | | .1 | .1 |
| | | | .3 | | .4 | | | .4 | .8 |
| | | (14) | 1.1 | (10) | 1.1 | | % Depr., Dep., Amort./Sales | (42) 2.5 (23) | 3.2 |
| | | | 3.0 | | 2.4 | | | 13.9 | 15.5 |
| | | | | | | | | 2.4 | 1.9 |
| | | | | | | | % Officers', Directors' Owners' Comp/Sales | (12) 12.6 (10) | 12.1 |
| | | | | | | | | 22.2 | 31.2 |
| 26484M | 69861M | 231027M | 957983M | 385698M | 1668761M | | Net Sales ($) | 2348421M | 774458M |
| 1161M | 13762M | 134235M | 891847M | 839902M | 3538826M | | Total Assets ($) | 4513935M | 2757107M |

M = $ thousand    MM = $ million
See Pages viii through xx for Explanation of Ratios and Data

© RMA 2024

# FINANCE—Miscellaneous Financial Investment Activities  NAICS 523999

## Comparative Historical Data | Current Data Sorted by Sales

| Comparative Historical Data ||| Type of Statement | Current Data Sorted by Sales ||||||
|---|---|---|---|---|---|---|---|---|---|
| 10 | 10 | 17 | Unqualified |  |  |  | 3 | 8 | 6 |
| 1 | 5 |  | Reviewed |  |  |  |  |  | 1 |
| 3 | 1 | 2 | Compiled |  | 1 |  |  |  |  |
| 5 | 19 | 15 | Tax Returns |  | 6 |  | 5 | 2 |  |
| 44 | 85 | 76 | Other | 2 | 11 | 8 | 18 | 19 | 16 |
| 4/1/21-3/31/22 ALL | 4/1/22-3/31/23 ALL | 4/1/23-3/31/24 ALL |  | 4 | 6 (4/1-9/30/23) | 8 | 104 (10/1/23-3/31/24) |  |  |
|  |  |  |  | 0-1MM | 1-3MM | 3-5MM | 5-10MM | 10-25MM | 25MM & OVER |
| 63 | 120 | 110 | NUMBER OF STATEMENTS | 6 | 18 | 8 | 26 | 29 | 23 |
| % | % | % | **ASSETS** | % | % | % | % | % | % |
| 25.0 | 22.3 | 25.8 | Cash & Equivalents | 24.3 | 23.7 |  | 23.7 | 18.1 | 34.1 |
| 12.6 | 11.4 | 10.7 | Trade Receivables (net) |  | 11.6 |  | 12.2 | 10.5 | 13.9 |
| .5 | 3.3 | 1.4 | Inventory |  | .0 |  | .8 | 1.4 | 2.1 |
| 10.0 | 9.6 | 7.3 | All Other Current |  | 3.2 |  | 2.1 | 11.4 | 5.3 |
| 48.1 | 46.7 | 45.2 | Total Current |  | 39.1 |  | 38.8 | 41.3 | 55.4 |
| 9.8 | 16.2 | 10.7 | Fixed Assets (net) |  | 17.7 |  | 5.1 | 6.0 | 11.0 |
| 6.6 | 9.8 | 8.6 | Intangibles (net) |  | 14.9 |  | 13.6 | 3.5 | 9.4 |
| 35.5 | 27.3 | 35.5 | All Other Non-Current |  | 28.3 |  | 42.5 | 49.2 | 24.2 |
| 100.0 | 100.0 | 100.0 | Total |  | 100.0 |  | 100.0 | 100.0 | 100.0 |
|  |  |  | **LIABILITIES** |  |  |  |  |  |  |
| 10.4 | 14.4 | 7.0 | Notes Payable-Short Term |  | 10.6 |  | 5.6 | 10.8 | .7 |
| 2.4 | 1.3 | 1.6 | Cur. Mat.-L.T.D. |  | .5 |  | 1.8 | .9 | 3.7 |
| 3.2 | 7.8 | 2.8 | Trade Payables |  | .7 |  | 2.8 | 2.4 | 5.7 |
| .5 | .0 | .1 | Income Taxes Payable |  | .2 |  | .0 | .1 | .0 |
| 9.2 | 11.4 | 10.5 | All Other Current |  | 2.3 |  | 10.7 | 16.8 | 11.2 |
| 25.7 | 35.0 | 21.9 | Total Current |  | 14.3 |  | 21.0 | 31.1 | 21.3 |
| 28.5 | 26.8 | 19.7 | Long-Term Debt |  | 18.9 |  | 18.6 | 14.5 | 24.6 |
| .0 | .1 | .0 | Deferred Taxes |  | .1 |  | .0 | .1 | .1 |
| 4.3 | 6.8 | 5.1 | All Other Non-Current |  | 7.6 |  | 7.0 | 2.0 | 5.2 |
| 41.4 | 31.4 | 53.3 | Net Worth |  | 59.1 |  | 53.3 | 52.4 | 48.8 |
| 100.0 | 100.0 | 100.0 | Total Liabilities & Net Worth |  | 100.0 |  | 100.0 | 100.0 | 100.0 |
|  |  |  | **INCOME DATA** |  |  |  |  |  |  |
| 100.0 | 100.0 | 100.0 | Net Sales |  | 100.0 |  | 100.0 | 100.0 | 100.0 |
| 55.1 | 65.2 | 58.3 | Gross Profit |  | 42.3 |  | 60.1 | 57.6 | 77.6 |
| 44.9 | 34.8 | 41.7 | Operating Expenses |  | 57.7 |  | 39.9 | 42.4 | 22.4 |
| 7.8 | 8.6 | 8.8 | Operating Profit |  | 10.5 |  | 7.6 | 13.2 | 1.0 |
| 37.1 | 26.2 | 32.9 | All Other Expenses (net) |  |  |  |  |  |  |
|  |  |  | Profit Before Taxes |  | 47.2 |  | 32.3 | 29.2 | 21.3 |
|  |  |  | **RATIOS** |  |  |  |  |  |  |
| 8.6 | 3.7 | 5.7 |  |  | 8.7 |  | 8.2 | 3.5 | 4.8 |
| 2.4 | 1.4 | 1.9 | Current |  | 1.6 |  | 1.8 | 1.0 | 2.8 |
| 1.0 | .6 | .8 |  |  | .8 |  | .6 | .4 | 1.6 |
| 8.2 | 2.7 | 4.4 |  |  | 8.7 |  | 8.0 | 2.4 | 4.6 |
| 2.2 | 1.1 | 1.4 | Quick |  | 1.6 |  | 1.2 | .9 | 2.4 |
| .7 | .3 | .4 |  |  | .7 |  | .2 | .2 | 1.3 |
| 0 UND | 0 UND | 0 UND |  | 0 UND | 0 UND | 0 UND | 0 UND | 0 UND |  |
| 0 999.8 | 0 999.8 | 0 UND | Sales/Receivables | 0 UND | 0 UND | 0 UND | 0 999.8 | 9 41.9 |  |
| 35 10.3 | 42 8.7 | 26 14.0 |  | 21 17.1 |  | 28 13.1 | 42 8.6 | 42 8.6 |  |
|  |  |  | Cost of Sales/Inventory |  |  |  |  |  |  |
|  |  |  | Cost of Sales/Payables |  |  |  |  |  |  |
| .7 | 2.8 | 1.7 |  |  | .3 |  | 3.7 | 3.0 | 2.0 |
| 4.5 | 12.8 | 9.1 | Sales/Working Capital |  | 4.4 |  | 29.4 | 200.7 | 7.4 |
| 59.9 | -18.9 | -29.2 |  |  | -17.1 |  | -27.0 | -8.5 | 18.0 |
| 53.6 | 27.1 | 81.9 |  |  | 108.0 |  | 275.0 | 64.9 | 57.7 |
| (38) 8.7 | (67) 7.0 | (60) 13.6 | EBIT/Interest | (10) 5.1 | (16) 47.0 | (15) 19.5 | (16) 8.9 |  |  |
| 2.7 | 1.7 | 5.3 |  |  | 3.0 |  | 10.6 | 6.7 | 4.6 |
|  |  |  | Net Profit + Depr., Dep., Amort./Cur. Mat. L/T/D |  |  |  |  |  |  |
| .0 | .0 | .0 |  |  | .0 |  | .0 | .0 | .0 |
| .0 | .0 | .0 | Fixed/Worth |  | .0 |  | .0 | .0 | .1 |
| .4 | 1.5 | .4 |  |  | 1.0 |  | .2 | .1 | .7 |
| .3 | .6 | .2 |  |  | .2 |  | .2 | .2 | .3 |
| 1.3 | 2.7 | .8 | Debt/Worth |  | .8 |  | .7 | .8 | 1.3 |
| 4.5 | 13.9 | 2.6 |  |  | 2.3 |  | 3.6 | 2.4 | 2.5 |
| 71.4 | 81.1 | 75.7 |  |  | 74.0 |  | 93.7 | 41.7 | 90.9 |
| (54) 20.5 | (99) 20.9 | (99) 21.0 | % Profit Before Taxes/Tangible Net Worth | (16) 13.1 | (23) 47.9 | (27) 14.1 | (19) 32.4 |  |  |
| 7.0 | 4.4 | 9.1 |  |  | 2.1 |  | 10.9 | 5.1 | 21.0 |
| 32.3 | 29.1 | 45.6 |  |  | 33.4 |  | 52.3 | 32.9 | 48.1 |
| 8.1 | 6.6 | 13.0 | % Profit Before Taxes/Total Assets |  | 6.5 |  | 30.6 | 10.8 | 14.0 |
| 1.8 | 1.0 | 4.1 |  |  | 1.9 |  | 10.0 | 2.4 | 7.7 |
| UND | UND | UND |  |  | UND |  | UND | UND | 460.2 |
| 264.2 | 109.3 | 108.2 | Sales/Net Fixed Assets |  | UND |  | UND | 69.7 | 65.3 |
| 17.3 | 10.4 | 20.3 |  |  | 17.0 |  | 52.2 | 29.9 | 11.0 |
| 1.3 | 2.9 | 3.1 |  |  | .9 |  | 3.8 | 3.1 | 4.0 |
| .5 | .8 | .6 | Sales/Total Assets |  | .1 |  | 1.8 | .6 | 1.5 |
| .1 | .1 | .1 |  |  | .1 |  | .2 | .1 | .7 |
|  |  |  |  |  |  |  |  | .2 | 1.1 |
| (23) .5 | (47) 3.1 | (37) 1.2 | % Depr., Dep., Amort./Sales |  |  |  | (11) .5 | (11) 2.0 |  |
| 8.1 | 8.8 | 4.4 |  |  |  |  |  | 1.2 | 2.5 |
|  | 1.7 | 3.2 |  |  |  |  |  |  |  |
| (15) 4.9 | (14) 10.4 |  | % Officers', Directors', Owners' Comp/Sales |  |  |  |  |  |  |
|  | 18.9 | 18.0 |  |  |  |  |  |  |  |
| 1412996M | 3569519M | 3339814M | Net Sales ($) | 2254M | 34832M | 35471M | 190316M | 442249M | 2634692M |
| 2460944M | 4769809M | 5419733M | Total Assets ($) | 21058M | 505172M | 274370M | 698629M | 1942624M | 1977880M |

M = $ thousand     MM = $ million
See Pages viii through xx for Explanation of Ratios and Data
© RMA 2024

## Current Data Sorted by Assets / Comparative Historical Data

| 0-500M | 500M-2MM | 2-10MM | 10-50MM | 50-100MM | 100-250MM | Type of Statement | 4/1/19-3/31/20 ALL | 4/1/20-3/31/21 ALL |
|---|---|---|---|---|---|---|---|---|
| | | 2 | 7 | 2 | 6 | Unqualified | 9 | 10 |
| | | | | | | Reviewed | 1 | 2 |
| | | | | | | Compiled | | |
| | 2 | | | | | Tax Returns | 6 | 1 |
| | 2 | 2 | 1 | 6 | 10 | Other | 18 | 15 |
| | 8 (4/1-9/30/23) | | 32 (10/1/23-3/31/24) | | | | | |
| | 4 | 4 | 8 | 8 | 16 | NUMBER OF STATEMENTS | 34 | 28 |
| % | % | % | % | % | % | **ASSETS** | % | % |
| DATA NOT AVAILABLE | | | | | 42.4 | Cash & Equivalents | 46.2 | 40.5 |
| | | | | | 13.4 | Trade Receivables (net) | 10.3 | 10.9 |
| | | | | | .1 | Inventory | .1 | .6 |
| | | | | | 7.6 | All Other Current | 5.8 | 10.6 |
| | | | | | 63.5 | Total Current | 62.5 | 62.6 |
| | | | | | 7.2 | Fixed Assets (net) | 10.9 | 9.3 |
| | | | | | 2.9 | Intangibles (net) | 5.9 | 11.5 |
| | | | | | 26.3 | All Other Non-Current | 20.8 | 16.7 |
| | | | | | 100.0 | Total | 100.0 | 100.0 |
| | | | | | | **LIABILITIES** | | |
| | | | | | .2 | Notes Payable-Short Term | 1.5 | 4.1 |
| | | | | | .5 | Cur. Mat.-L.T.D. | .2 | 1.4 |
| | | | | | 12.1 | Trade Payables | 7.9 | 12.3 |
| | | | | | .4 | Income Taxes Payable | .5 | .1 |
| | | | | | 23.5 | All Other Current | 33.2 | 24.7 |
| | | | | | 36.8 | Total Current | 43.4 | 42.6 |
| | | | | | 2.0 | Long-Term Debt | 2.2 | 5.5 |
| | | | | | .1 | Deferred Taxes | .6 | 1.4 |
| | | | | | 3.2 | All Other Non-Current | 5.6 | 4.1 |
| | | | | | 57.9 | Net Worth | 48.3 | 46.4 |
| | | | | | 100.0 | Total Liabilities & Net Worth | 100.0 | 100.0 |
| | | | | | | **INCOME DATA** | | |
| | | | | | 100.0 | Net Sales | 100.0 | 100.0 |
| | | | | | | Gross Profit | | |
| | | | | | 98.8 | Operating Expenses | 94.3 | 95.1 |
| | | | | | 1.2 | Operating Profit | 5.7 | 4.9 |
| | | | | | -2.1 | All Other Expenses (net) | -1.3 | -.2 |
| | | | | | 3.3 | Profit Before Taxes | 7.0 | 5.2 |
| | | | | | | **RATIOS** | | |
| | | | | | 2.4 | | 2.3 | 2.6 |
| | | | | | 1.6 | Current | 1.5 | 1.5 |
| | | | | | 1.3 | | 1.1 | 1.0 |
| | | | | | 2.0 | | 2.3 | 2.2 |
| | | | | | 1.4 | Quick | 1.4 | 1.4 |
| | | | | | 1.1 | | .8 | .7 |
| | | | | | 7 55.0 | | 2 237.4 | 0 UND |
| | | | | | 17 20.9 | Sales/Receivables | 10 37.1 | 6 60.7 |
| | | | | | 44 8.3 | | 22 16.5 | 32 11.3 |
| | | | | | | Cost of Sales/Inventory | | |
| | | | | | | Cost of Sales/Payables | | |
| | | | | | 3.7 | | 5.4 | 7.0 |
| | | | | | 11.8 | Sales/Working Capital | 14.0 | 16.3 |
| | | | | | 32.0 | | 114.3 | NM |
| | | | | | | | 37.5 | 68.1 |
| | | | | | | EBIT/Interest | (12) 9.0 | (13) 21.8 |
| | | | | | | | .7 | 9.2 |
| | | | | | | Net Profit + Depr., Dep., Amort./Cur. Mat. L/T/D | | |
| | | | | | .0 | | .0 | .0 |
| | | | | | .1 | Fixed/Worth | .1 | .2 |
| | | | | | .2 | | .8 | 1.3 |
| | | | | | .4 | | .4 | .4 |
| | | | | | .9 | Debt/Worth | 1.2 | 1.5 |
| | | | | | 1.5 | | 2.2 | 5.8 |
| | | | | | 27.9 | | 20.0 | 29.2 |
| | | | | | 11.2 | % Profit Before Taxes/Tangible Net Worth | (31) 8.6 | (22) 18.4 |
| | | | | | .9 | | .4 | 6.5 |
| | | | | | 13.0 | | 12.1 | 23.7 |
| | | | | | 5.9 | % Profit Before Taxes/Total Assets | 4.8 | 8.8 |
| | | | | | .8 | | .2 | 4.5 |
| | | | | | 594.8 | | UND | 617.5 |
| | | | | | 67.3 | Sales/Net Fixed Assets | 74.0 | 50.4 |
| | | | | | 17.4 | | 27.0 | 19.2 |
| | | | | | 3.3 | | 3.7 | 5.1 |
| | | | | | 2.2 | Sales/Total Assets | 2.9 | 2.6 |
| | | | | | 1.1 | | 2.0 | 1.1 |
| | | | | | .1 | | .1 | .3 |
| | | | | | (12) .2 | % Depr., Dep., Amort./Sales | (23) .3 | (20) .6 |
| | | | | | .8 | | 1.1 | 1.2 |
| | | | | | | % Officers', Directors' Owners' Comp/Sales | | |
| | 5876M | 230135M | 530888M | 1001513M | 5555675M | Net Sales ($) | 6483934M | 2896895M |
| | 3878M | 25931M | 245973M | 628627M | 2433804M | Total Assets ($) | 2302808M | 1467360M |

M = $ thousand MM = $ million

See Pages viii through xx for Explanation of Ratios and Data

## FINANCE—Direct Health and Medical Insurance Carriers  NAICS 524114

### Comparative Historical Data | Current Data Sorted by Sales

| | | | Type of Statement | | | | | | |
|---|---|---|---|---|---|---|---|---|---|
| 10 | 13 | 17 | Unqualified | | | 1 | | 2 | 14 |
| 1 | 1 | | Reviewed | | | | | | |
| 1 | | | Compiled | | | | | | |
| | 2 | 2 | Tax Returns | | | | | 1 | 18 |
| 19 | 14 | 21 | Other | 1 | 1 | | | | |
| 4/1/21- | 4/1/22- | 4/1/23- | | 2 | 8 (4/1-9/30/23) | | 32 (10/1/23-3/31/24) | | |
| 3/31/22 | 3/31/23 | 3/31/24 | | 0-1MM | 1-3MM | 3-5MM | 5-10MM | 10-25MM | 25MM & OVER |
| ALL | ALL | ALL | | | | | | | |
| 31 | 30 | 40 | NUMBER OF STATEMENTS | 3 | 1 | 1 | | 3 | 32 |
| % | % | % | ASSETS | % | % | % | | % | % |
| 34.6 | 38.1 | 44.1 | Cash & Equivalents | | | | | | 44.2 |
| 13.0 | 12.1 | 14.3 | Trade Receivables (net) | | | | D | | 15.4 |
| .8 | .0 | .9 | Inventory | | | | A | | 1.1 |
| 8.5 | 8.1 | 5.5 | All Other Current | | | | T | | 6.5 |
| 56.9 | 58.4 | 64.8 | Total Current | | | | A | | 67.2 |
| 14.7 | 11.9 | 12.6 | Fixed Assets (net) | | | | | | 9.3 |
| 3.8 | 4.5 | 3.3 | Intangibles (net) | | | | N | | 3.4 |
| 24.6 | 25.2 | 19.2 | All Other Non-Current | | | | O | | 20.1 |
| 100.0 | 100.0 | 100.0 | Total | | | | T | | 100.0 |
| | | | LIABILITIES | | | | A | | |
| .3 | .9 | 1.2 | Notes Payable-Short Term | | | | V | | 1.3 |
| .4 | .5 | 1.1 | Cur. Mat.-L.T.D. | | | | A | | .5 |
| 8.6 | 11.6 | 10.1 | Trade Payables | | | | I | | 12.1 |
| .2 | .5 | .2 | Income Taxes Payable | | | | L | | .2 |
| 20.8 | 21.9 | 27.9 | All Other Current | | | | A | | 24.0 |
| 30.3 | 35.4 | 40.5 | Total Current | | | | B | | 38.1 |
| 9.8 | 4.0 | 3.6 | Long-Term Debt | | | | L | | 3.3 |
| .1 | .3 | .3 | Deferred Taxes | | | | E | | .3 |
| 3.4 | 4.3 | 3.7 | All Other Non-Current | | | | | | 4.4 |
| 56.4 | 56.1 | 51.9 | Net Worth | | | | | | 53.8 |
| 100.0 | 100.0 | 100.0 | Total Liabilities & Net Worth | | | | | | 100.0 |
| | | | INCOME DATA | | | | | | |
| 100.0 | 100.0 | 100.0 | Net Sales | | | | | | 100.0 |
| | | | Gross Profit | | | | | | |
| 98.8 | 98.1 | 97.4 | Operating Expenses | | | | | | 99.6 |
| 1.2 | 1.9 | 2.6 | Operating Profit | | | | | | .4 |
| -1.2 | .9 | -.4 | All Other Expenses (net) | | | | | | -.8 |
| 2.3 | 1.0 | 3.0 | Profit Before Taxes | | | | | | 1.2 |
| | | | RATIOS | | | | | | |
| 4.3 | 4.0 | 3.0 | | | | | | | 3.0 |
| 1.8 | 1.6 | 1.6 | Current | | | | | | 1.8 |
| 1.2 | .9 | 1.1 | | | | | | | 1.3 |
| 4.3 | 3.4 | 2.9 | | | | | | | 2.9 |
| 1.4 | 1.4 | 1.4 | Quick | | | | | | 1.5 |
| .8 | .6 | 1.0 | | | | | | | 1.1 |
| 3  121.0 | 5  77.9 | 6  57.5 | | | | | | 7 | 51.3 |
| 14  25.2 | 18  20.7 | 17  21.0 | Sales/Receivables | | | | | 18 | 20.8 |
| 33  11.0 | 34  10.6 | 49  7.5 | | | | | | 51 | 7.2 |
| | | | Cost of Sales/Inventory | | | | | | |
| | | | Cost of Sales/Payables | | | | | | |
| 2.7 | 3.7 | 3.1 | | | | | | | 3.1 |
| 9.4 | 9.6 | 9.2 | Sales/Working Capital | | | | | | 7.2 |
| 31.2 | -44.9 | 39.5 | | | | | | | 32.0 |
| 100.9 | 52.8 | 39.9 | | | | | | | 45.9 |
| (15) 6.4 | (15) 13.6 | (15) 14.8 | EBIT/Interest | | | | | (10) | 16.5 |
| -8.5 | -23.6 | 2.6 | | | | | | | 7.2 |
| | | | Net Profit + Depr., Dep., Amort./Cur. Mat. L/T/D | | | | | | |
| .0 | .0 | .0 | | | | | | | .0 |
| .2 | .2 | .1 | Fixed/Worth | | | | | | .1 |
| .5 | .5 | .3 | | | | | | | .2 |
| .3 | .4 | .5 | | | | | | | .5 |
| .5 | .7 | 1.0 | Debt/Worth | | | | | | .9 |
| 1.2 | 2.0 | 1.9 | | | | | | | 1.8 |
| 30.6 | 30.4 | 18.7 | | | | | | | 18.5 |
| (29) 7.3 | (29) 6.4 | 9.7 | % Profit Before Taxes/Tangible Net Worth | | | | | | 10.4 |
| -.5 | -9.9 | -.1 | | | | | | | 1.4 |
| 11.1 | 10.0 | 10.0 | | | | | | | 10.0 |
| 4.7 | 3.9 | 4.6 | % Profit Before Taxes/Total Assets | | | | | | 5.2 |
| -.6 | -4.6 | -.1 | | | | | | | .6 |
| 75.2 | 133.0 | 633.1 | | | | | | | 240.0 |
| 31.1 | 31.6 | 50.1 | Sales/Net Fixed Assets | | | | | | 42.7 |
| 11.1 | 11.3 | 16.8 | | | | | | | 16.9 |
| 3.9 | 3.7 | 3.2 | | | | | | | 3.2 |
| 1.7 | 2.1 | 1.9 | Sales/Total Assets | | | | | | 2.1 |
| .8 | 1.2 | 1.1 | | | | | | | 1.1 |
| .4 | .2 | .1 | | | | | | | .1 |
| (24) .7 | (23) .5 | (27) .4 | % Depr., Dep., Amort./Sales | | | | | (23) | .4 |
| 1.5 | .9 | 1.4 | | | | | | | 1.0 |
| | | | % Officers', Directors' Owners' Comp/Sales | | | | | | |
| 4994607M | 4523837M | 7324087M | Net Sales ($) | 1241M | 2853M | 4635M | | 64449M | 7250909M |
| 2886263M | 2116264M | 3338213M | Total Assets ($) | 2743M | 2072M | 1135M | | 89184M | 3243079M |

© RMA 2024  
M = $ thousand  MM = $ million  
See Pages viii through xx for Explanation of Ratios and Data

# FINANCE—Direct Property and Casualty Insurance Carriers  NAICS 524126

## Current Data Sorted by Assets / Comparative Historical Data

| 0-500M | 500M-2MM | 2-10MM | 10-50MM | 50-100MM | 100-250MM | Type of Statement | | 4/1/19-3/31/20 ALL | | 4/1/20-3/31/21 ALL |
|---|---|---|---|---|---|---|---|---|---|---|
| 1 | 1 | | 6 | 1 | 7 | Unqualified | | 10 | | 13 |
| | | | 1 | | | Reviewed | | | | 1 |
| | | | 5 | | | Compiled | | | | |
| 1 | 1 | 5 | 38 | 6 | 11 | Tax Returns | | 3 | | 1 |
| | 7 (4/1-9/30/23) | | (10/1/23-3/31/24) | | | Other | | 23 | | 14 |
| 2 | 1 | 5 | 12 | 7 | 18 | **NUMBER OF STATEMENTS** | | 36 | | 29 |
| % | % | % | % | % | % | **ASSETS** | | % | | % |
| | | | 38.5 | | 47.7 | Cash & Equivalents | | 57.9 | | 59.2 |
| | | | 13.0 | | 12.2 | Trade Receivables (net) | | 7.6 | | 8.8 |
| | | | .0 | | .0 | Inventory | | .0 | | .1 |
| | | | 4.4 | | 13.1 | All Other Current | | 2.5 | | 7.9 |
| | | | 55.9 | | 73.1 | Total Current | | 68.0 | | 76.0 |
| | | | 1.7 | | 1.1 | Fixed Assets (net) | | 4.7 | | 5.0 |
| | | | 7.2 | | 4.1 | Intangibles (net) | | 11.1 | | 4.4 |
| | | | 35.2 | | 21.8 | All Other Non-Current | | 16.2 | | 14.5 |
| | | | 100.0 | | 100.0 | Total | | 100.0 | | 100.0 |
| | | | | | | **LIABILITIES** | | | | |
| | | | 3.5 | | 2.4 | Notes Payable-Short Term | | .3 | | 2.5 |
| | | | .4 | | .3 | Cur. Mat.-L.T.D. | | 1.3 | | 1.1 |
| | | | 10.7 | | 7.6 | Trade Payables | | 4.8 | | 8.3 |
| | | | .0 | | .1 | Income Taxes Payable | | .4 | | .2 |
| | | | 26.3 | | 42.4 | All Other Current | | 32.5 | | 30.8 |
| | | | 40.7 | | 52.8 | Total Current | | 39.3 | | 42.9 |
| | | | 11.4 | | 4.0 | Long-Term Debt | | 5.4 | | 5.9 |
| | | | .0 | | .1 | Deferred Taxes | | .1 | | .0 |
| | | | 9.4 | | 8.7 | All Other Non-Current | | 7.7 | | 11.6 |
| | | | 38.4 | | 34.4 | Net Worth | | 47.5 | | 39.6 |
| | | | 100.0 | | 100.0 | Total Liabilities & Net Worth | | 100.0 | | 100.0 |
| | | | | | | **INCOME DATA** | | | | |
| | | | 100.0 | | 100.0 | Net Sales | | 100.0 | | 100.0 |
| | | | | | | Gross Profit | | | | |
| | | | 98.4 | | 100.5 | Operating Expenses | | 86.7 | | 87.9 |
| | | | 1.6 | | -.5 | Operating Profit | | 13.3 | | 12.1 |
| | | | -.1 | | -4.9 | All Other Expenses (net) | | -1.4 | | -3.0 |
| | | | 1.7 | | 4.4 | Profit Before Taxes | | 14.6 | | 15.1 |
| | | | | | | **RATIOS** | | | | |
| | | | 2.0 | | 2.6 | | | 2.6 | | 3.5 |
| | | | 1.6 | | 1.3 | Current | | 1.8 | | 1.7 |
| | | | 1.1 | | 1.1 | | | 1.3 | | 1.4 |
| | | | 2.0 | | 1.8 | | | 2.6 | | 3.5 |
| | | | 1.4 | | 1.1 | Quick | | 1.7 | | 1.6 |
| | | | .7 | | .7 | | | 1.3 | | 1.0 |
| | | | 7   49.9 | | 0   UND | | 0 | UND | 0 | UND |
| | | | 33  11.0 | | 81  4.5 | Sales/Receivables | 5 | 75.0 | 21 | 17.6 |
| | | | 261 1.4 | | 192 1.9 | | 62 | 5.9 | 56 | 6.5 |
| | | | | | | Cost of Sales/Inventory | | | | |
| | | | | | | Cost of Sales/Payables | | | | |
| | | | .8 | | .9 | | | 1.0 | | .8 |
| | | | 2.7 | | 4.3 | Sales/Working Capital | | 2.3 | | 1.8 |
| | | | 527.1 | | NM | | | 7.2 | | 3.3 |
| | | | | | | | | 149.3 | | |
| | | | | | | EBIT/Interest | (11) | 28.8 | | |
| | | | | | | | | 10.9 | | |
| | | | | | | Net Profit + Depr., Dep., Amort./Cur. Mat. L/T/D | | | | |
| | | | .0 | | .0 | | | .0 | | .0 |
| | | | .0 | | .0 | Fixed/Worth | | .0 | | .0 |
| | | | .1 | | .1 | | | .1 | | .2 |
| | | | .7 | | .6 | | | .7 | | .8 |
| | | | 1.2 | | 3.3 | Debt/Worth | | 1.4 | | 1.7 |
| | | | 12.3 | | 7.6 | | | 3.0 | | 5.3 |
| | | | 4.2 | | 20.3 | | | 20.8 | | 22.4 |
| | | | (10) 1.7 | | (15) 5.0 | % Profit Before Taxes/Tangible Net Worth | (33) | 11.9 | (27) | 13.2 |
| | | | -22.6 | | -6.7 | | | -.1 | | 6.4 |
| | | | 1.9 | | 6.2 | | | 10.9 | | 7.8 |
| | | | 1.2 | | 1.3 | % Profit Before Taxes/Total Assets | | 5.0 | | 4.9 |
| | | | -10.5 | | -2.5 | | | .6 | | 2.7 |
| | | | UND | | UND | | | UND | | UND |
| | | | UND | | 657.1 | Sales/Net Fixed Assets | | 354.9 | | 29.1 |
| | | | 20.7 | | 37.1 | | | 26.0 | | 10.5 |
| | | | .9 | | .8 | | | .7 | | .7 |
| | | | .5 | | .3 | Sales/Total Assets | | .5 | | .4 |
| | | | .2 | | .2 | | | .3 | | .2 |
| | | | | | | | | .2 | | .7 |
| | | | | | | % Depr., Dep., Amort./Sales | (13) | 1.0 | (13) | 1.4 |
| | | | | | | | | 2.2 | | 2.4 |
| | | | | | | % Officers', Directors' Owners' Comp/Sales | | | | |
| 429M | 2900M | 23837M | 169976M | 203170M | 1610144M | Net Sales ($) | | 1142234M | | 820276M |
| 64M | 1960M | 28824M | 333499M | 510034M | 3009661M | Total Assets ($) | | 2238281M | | 1623761M |

© RMA 2024   M = $ thousand   MM = $ million
See Pages viii through xx for Explanation of Ratios and Data

# FINANCE—Direct Property and Casualty Insurance Carriers  NAICS 524126

## Comparative Historical Data | Current Data Sorted by Sales

| | | | | Type of Statement | | | | | | |
|---|---|---|---|---|---|---|---|---|---|---|
| 8 | 10 | 14 | | Unqualified | 1 | 1 | | 5 | 7 | |
| 1 | 1 | 3 | | Reviewed | | | | | | |
| | 1 | | | Compiled | | | | | | |
| 19 | 23 | 28 | | Tax Returns | 1 | 1 | | 6 | 4 | 1 |
| 4/1/21- | 4/1/22- | 4/1/23- | | Other | 1 | 2 | | | | 15 |
| 3/31/22 | 3/31/23 | 3/31/24 | | | | 7 (4/1-9/30/23) | | 38 (10/1/23-3/31/24) | | |
| ALL | ALL | ALL | | | 0-1MM | 1-3MM | 3-5MM | 5-10MM | 10-25MM | 25MM & OVER |
| 28 | 35 | 45 | NUMBER OF STATEMENTS | 3 | 4 | | 6 | 9 | 23 | |
| % | % | % | ASSETS | % | % | % | % | % | % | |
| 54.2 | 54.7 | 48.5 | Cash & Equivalents | | | | | | 46.2 | |
| 3.8 | 8.9 | 13.9 | Trade Receivables (net) | | | | | | 15.5 | |
| .0 | .0 | .0 | Inventory | | | | | | .0 | |
| 3.0 | 5.7 | 7.7 | All Other Current | | | | | | 10.9 | |
| 61.0 | 69.4 | 70.1 | Total Current | | DATA NOT AVAILABLE | | | | 72.6 | |
| 8.5 | 4.9 | 1.4 | Fixed Assets (net) | | | | | | 1.0 | |
| 9.9 | 8.4 | 6.9 | Intangibles (net) | | | | | | 5.0 | |
| 20.6 | 17.3 | 21.6 | All Other Non-Current | | | | | | 21.4 | |
| 100.0 | 100.0 | 100.0 | Total | | | | | | 100.0 | |
| | | | LIABILITIES | | | | | | | |
| 2.3 | 2.2 | 2.5 | Notes Payable-Short Term | | | | | | 3.1 | |
| .2 | .5 | .7 | Cur. Mat.-L.T.D. | | | | | | .4 | |
| 7.0 | 9.7 | 9.8 | Trade Payables | | | | | | 6.6 | |
| .3 | .3 | .4 | Income Taxes Payable | | | | | | .1 | |
| 24.0 | 25.1 | 33.4 | All Other Current | | | | | | 47.4 | |
| 33.8 | 37.8 | 46.9 | Total Current | | | | | | 57.6 | |
| 20.8 | 16.3 | 6.0 | Long-Term Debt | | | | | | 7.8 | |
| .0 | .0 | .0 | Deferred Taxes | | | | | | .1 | |
| 10.2 | 11.5 | 7.9 | All Other Non-Current | | | | | | 7.3 | |
| 35.2 | 34.4 | 39.2 | Net Worth | | | | | | 27.3 | |
| 100.0 | 100.0 | 100.0 | Total Liabilities & Net Worth | | | | | | 100.0 | |
| | | | INCOME DATA | | | | | | | |
| 100.0 | 100.0 | 100.0 | Net Sales | | | | | | 100.0 | |
| | | | Gross Profit | | | | | | | |
| 86.8 | 87.9 | 97.4 | Operating Expenses | | | | | | 102.7 | |
| 13.2 | 12.1 | 2.6 | Operating Profit | | | | | | -2.7 | |
| -2.8 | 1.2 | -2.9 | All Other Expenses (net) | | | | | | -3.3 | |
| 16.1 | 10.9 | 5.5 | Profit Before Taxes | | | | | | .6 | |
| | | | RATIOS | | | | | | | |
| 2.8 | 4.2 | 2.4 | | | | | | | 1.8 | |
| 2.1 | 2.0 | 1.5 | Current | | | | | | 1.2 | |
| 1.4 | 1.1 | 1.0 | | | | | | | .8 | |
| 2.7 | 4.1 | 2.2 | | | | | | | 1.5 | |
| 1.7 | 1.7 | 1.2 | Quick | | | | | | 1.0 | |
| 1.1 | 1.1 | .8 | | | | | | | .7 | |
| 0 UND | 0 UND | 6 56.5 | | | | | | 12 | 30.4 | |
| 0 UND | 16 23.4 | 38 9.6 | Sales/Receivables | | | | | 76 | 4.8 | |
| 39 9.3 | 76 4.8 | 192 1.9 | | | | | | 228 | 1.6 | |
| | | | Cost of Sales/Inventory | | | | | | | |
| | | | Cost of Sales/Payables | | | | | | | |
| 1.1 | .8 | .8 | | | | | | | 1.1 | |
| 3.9 | 2.9 | 3.7 | Sales/Working Capital | | | | | | 5.1 | |
| 44.8 | 13.8 | UND | | | | | | | -12.6 | |
| 94.0 | 125.8 | 63.8 | | | | | | | | |
| (11) 28.9 | (14) 46.7 | (17) 11.1 | EBIT/Interest | | | | | | | |
| 9.1 | 8.5 | -17.0 | | | | | | | | |
| | | | Net Profit + Depr., Dep., Amort./Cur. Mat. L/T/D | | | | | | | |
| .0 | .0 | .0 | | | | | | | .0 | |
| .1 | .0 | .0 | Fixed/Worth | | | | | | .0 | |
| 1.9 | .1 | .1 | | | | | | | .2 | |
| .6 | .6 | .6 | | | | | | | 1.3 | |
| 1.3 | 1.7 | 1.6 | Debt/Worth | | | | | | 3.8 | |
| 4.2 | 6.8 | 8.0 | | | | | | | 8.8 | |
| 41.8 | 42.2 | 25.0 | | | | | | | 20.4 | |
| (23) 7.3 | (28) 5.5 | (38) 3.5 | % Profit Before Taxes/Tangible Net Worth | | | | | (18) | 3.8 | |
| -1.3 | -3.4 | -9.0 | | | | | | | -14.3 | |
| 17.3 | 14.4 | 7.1 | | | | | | | 7.5 | |
| 5.4 | 4.6 | 1.1 | % Profit Before Taxes/Total Assets | | | | | | .1 | |
| 1.0 | .1 | -3.7 | | | | | | | -6.9 | |
| UND | UND | UND | | | | | | | UND | |
| 27.3 | 90.0 | 435.0 | Sales/Net Fixed Assets | | | | | | 317.8 | |
| 11.1 | 26.7 | 34.8 | | | | | | | 37.7 | |
| 1.4 | 1.3 | .9 | | | | | | | .9 | |
| .6 | .5 | .5 | Sales/Total Assets | | | | | | .6 | |
| .3 | .3 | .2 | | | | | | | .3 | |
| | .3 | .3 | | | | | | | | |
| (11) | .4 | (11) .5 | % Depr., Dep., Amort./Sales | | | | | | | |
| | 1.5 | 1.4 | | | | | | | | |
| | | | % Officers', Directors' Owners' Comp/Sales | | | | | | | |
| 1099986M | 1566638M | 2010456M | Net Sales ($) | 756M | 8681M | | 43049M | 152916M | 1805054M | |
| 2020709M | 2649975M | 3884042M | Total Assets ($) | 15528M | 55638M | | 100736M | 488230M | 3223910M | |

© RMA 2024  M = $ thousand   MM = $ million  
See Pages viii through xx for Explanation of Ratios and Data

# FINANCE—Other Direct Insurance (except Life, Health, and Medical) Carriers   NAICS 524128

## Current Data Sorted by Assets | Comparative Historical Data

| | | | | | | Type of Statement | | |
|---|---|---|---|---|---|---|---|---|
| | | | 2 | 2 | 1 | Unqualified | 11 | 4 |
| | | 1 | 1 | | | Reviewed | | |
| | | 1 | 1 | | | Compiled | | |
| | | 1 | 1 | | | Tax Returns | 1 | 1 |
| 1 | 2 | 4 | 7 | 1 | 3 | Other | 15 | 6 |
| | 4 (4/1-9/30/23) | | 23 (10/1/23-3/31/24) | | | | 4/1/19- | 4/1/20- |
| 0-500M | 500M-2MM | 2-10MM | 10-50MM | 50-100MM | 100-250MM | | 3/31/20 | 3/31/21 |
| | | | | | | | ALL | ALL |
| 1 | 2 | 7 | 10 | 3 | 4 | NUMBER OF STATEMENTS | 27 | 11 |
| % | % | % | % | % | % | ASSETS | % | % |
| | | | 55.1 | | | Cash & Equivalents | 47.6 | 62.3 |
| | | | 14.1 | | | Trade Receivables (net) | 7.2 | 6.0 |
| | | | .0 | | | Inventory | 1.0 | .0 |
| | | | 2.4 | | | All Other Current | 13.0 | 11.7 |
| | | | 71.6 | | | Total Current | 68.9 | 80.0 |
| | | | 3.2 | | | Fixed Assets (net) | 9.6 | 4.4 |
| | | | 11.0 | | | Intangibles (net) | 3.9 | 6.8 |
| | | | 14.3 | | | All Other Non-Current | 17.6 | 8.8 |
| | | | 100.0 | | | Total | 100.0 | 100.0 |
| | | | | | | LIABILITIES | | |
| | | | 8.6 | | | Notes Payable-Short Term | 3.1 | 12.5 |
| | | | .2 | | | Cur. Mat.-L.T.D. | 4.3 | 8.5 |
| | | | 2.0 | | | Trade Payables | 4.8 | 6.9 |
| | | | 1.2 | | | Income Taxes Payable | .8 | .7 |
| | | | 32.7 | | | All Other Current | 29.4 | 25.5 |
| | | | 44.7 | | | Total Current | 42.4 | 54.1 |
| | | | 5.5 | | | Long-Term Debt | 8.1 | 13.7 |
| | | | .0 | | | Deferred Taxes | .3 | .0 |
| | | | 14.5 | | | All Other Non-Current | 20.5 | 2.2 |
| | | | 35.3 | | | Net Worth | 28.7 | 30.0 |
| | | | 100.0 | | | Total Liabilities & Net Worth | 100.0 | 100.0 |
| | | | | | | INCOME DATA | | |
| | | | 100.0 | | | Net Sales | 100.0 | 100.0 |
| | | | | | | Gross Profit | | |
| | | | 84.3 | | | Operating Expenses | 85.8 | 81.4 |
| | | | 15.7 | | | Operating Profit | 14.2 | 18.6 |
| | | | -.9 | | | All Other Expenses (net) | -1.4 | -2.2 |
| | | | 16.6 | | | Profit Before Taxes | 15.7 | 20.8 |
| | | | | | | RATIOS | | |
| | | | 10.0 | | | | 3.6 | 2.9 |
| | | | 1.9 | | | Current | 1.7 | 1.8 |
| | | | .9 | | | | 1.0 | 1.1 |
| | | | 8.3 | | | | 2.4 | 2.9 |
| | | | 1.8 | | | Quick | 1.6 | 1.4 |
| | | | .9 | | | | .9 | .6 |
| | | | 0 UND | | | | 3 119.4 | 0 UND |
| | | | 21 17.4 | | | Sales/Receivables | 16 23.3 | 1 703.7 |
| | | | 52 7.0 | | | | 42 8.7 | 104 3.5 |
| | | | | | | Cost of Sales/Inventory | | |
| | | | | | | Cost of Sales/Payables | | |
| | | | 1.0 | | | | | .8 | .8 |
| | | | 5.4 | | | Sales/Working Capital | 3.8 | 1.6 |
| | | | -27.7 | | | | -376.0 | 59.9 |
| | | | | | | EBIT/Interest | 139.3 | |
| | | | | | | | (12) 24.3 | |
| | | | | | | | 6.3 | |
| | | | | | | Net Profit + Depr., Dep., Amort./Cur. Mat. L/T/D | | |
| | | | .0 | | | | .0 | .0 |
| | | | .0 | | | Fixed/Worth | .0 | .0 |
| | | | -271.3 | | | | .4 | .2 |
| | | | .6 | | | | .7 | .7 |
| | | | 14.4 | | | Debt/Worth | 1.9 | 1.2 |
| | | | -71.0 | | | | 12.5 | 12.0 |
| | | | | | | % Profit Before Taxes/Tangible Net Worth | 78.9 | |
| | | | | | | | (24) 13.7 | |
| | | | | | | | 3.6 | |
| | | | 23.5 | | | | 19.3 | 42.0 |
| | | | 4.4 | | | % Profit Before Taxes/Total Assets | 5.4 | 10.1 |
| | | | -.7 | | | | 1.6 | 3.3 |
| | | | UND | | | | UND | UND |
| | | | 288.7 | | | Sales/Net Fixed Assets | 999.8 | UND |
| | | | 19.0 | | | | 21.6 | 54.8 |
| | | | 3.4 | | | | 1.5 | 3.4 |
| | | | .7 | | | Sales/Total Assets | 1.1 | .7 |
| | | | .3 | | | | .3 | .3 |
| | | | | | | % Depr., Dep., Amort./Sales | | |
| | | | | | | % Officers', Directors' Owners' Comp/Sales | | |
| 573M | 6881M | 40578M | 392558M | 190575M | 308655M | Net Sales ($) | 753102M | 926763M |
| 327M | 3401M | 36145M | 270117M | 255347M | 528802M | Total Assets ($) | 1337245M | 601108M |

M = $ thousand    MM = $ million
See Pages viii through xx for Explanation of Ratios and Data

© RMA 2024

# FINANCE—Other Direct Insurance (except Life, Health, and Medical) Carriers   NAICS 524128

## Comparative Historical Data | Current Data Sorted by Sales

| | | | | Type of Statement | | | | | | |
|---|---|---|---|---|---|---|---|---|---|---|
| 3 | 4 | 5 | | Unqualified | | | 1 | 1 | | 4 |
| | | 2 | | Reviewed | | 1 | | | 1 | |
| 1 | 1 | 1 | | Compiled | | | | | | |
| | | 1 | | Tax Returns | | 1 | | | | |
| 10 | 11 | 18 | | Other | 3 | 2 | 1 | 2 | 4 | 6 |
| 4/1/21- | 4/1/22- | 4/1/23- | | | | 4 (4/1-9/30/23) | | 23 (10/1/23-3/31/24) | | |
| 3/31/22 | 3/31/23 | 3/31/24 | | | 0-1MM | 1-3MM | 3-5MM | 5-10MM | 10-25MM | 25MM & OVER |
| ALL | ALL | ALL | | NUMBER OF STATEMENTS | | | | | | |
| 14 | 16 | 27 | | | 3 | 3 | 2 | 4 | 5 | 10 |
| % | % | % | | ASSETS | % | % | % | % | % | % |
| 40.5 | 65.5 | 57.1 | | Cash & Equivalents | | | | | | 50.3 |
| 8.9 | 9.4 | 9.4 | | Trade Receivables (net) | | | | | | 10.8 |
| .0 | .0 | .4 | | Inventory | | | | | | 1.2 |
| 8.3 | 1.5 | 1.8 | | All Other Current | | | | | | 1.4 |
| 57.7 | 76.4 | 68.8 | | Total Current | | | | | | 63.7 |
| 7.6 | 5.6 | 3.4 | | Fixed Assets (net) | | | | | | 6.2 |
| 12.8 | 5.7 | 10.2 | | Intangibles (net) | | | | | | 4.9 |
| 21.9 | 12.3 | 17.6 | | All Other Non-Current | | | | | | 25.2 |
| 100.0 | 100.0 | 100.0 | | Total | | | | | | 100.0 |
| | | | | LIABILITIES | | | | | | |
| 5.4 | 1.2 | 3.3 | | Notes Payable-Short Term | | | | | | 6.7 |
| 4.9 | 5.2 | 2.2 | | Cur. Mat.-L.T.D. | | | | | | 4.6 |
| 15.5 | 7.5 | 7.1 | | Trade Payables | | | | | | 4.2 |
| .1 | .4 | .4 | | Income Taxes Payable | | | | | | .0 |
| 42.1 | 36.4 | 35.4 | | All Other Current | | | | | | 31.9 |
| 68.0 | 50.7 | 48.5 | | Total Current | | | | | | 47.5 |
| 21.0 | 7.2 | 6.8 | | Long-Term Debt | | | | | | 1.9 |
| .0 | 1.3 | .1 | | Deferred Taxes | | | | | | .3 |
| 4.8 | 2.7 | 11.2 | | All Other Non-Current | | | | | | 20.6 |
| 6.1 | 38.1 | 33.4 | | Net Worth | | | | | | 29.7 |
| 100.0 | 100.0 | 100.0 | | Total Liabilties & Net Worth | | | | | | 100.0 |
| | | | | INCOME DATA | | | | | | |
| 100.0 | 100.0 | 100.0 | | Net Sales | | | | | | 100.0 |
| | | | | Gross Profit | | | | | | |
| 92.7 | 79.9 | 81.1 | | Operating Expenses | | | | | | 94.3 |
| 7.3 | 20.1 | 18.9 | | Operating Profit | | | | | | 5.7 |
| 1.1 | 15.9 | 5.0 | | All Other Expenses (net) | | | | | | -2.0 |
| 6.1 | 4.2 | 13.9 | | Profit Before Taxes | | | | | | 7.7 |
| | | | | RATIOS | | | | | | |
| 1.5 | 2.7 | 3.3 | | | | | | | | 2.5 |
| .9 | 2.0 | 1.6 | | Current | | | | | | 1.5 |
| .7 | 1.0 | .9 | | | | | | | | .9 |
| 1.4 | 2.7 | 3.3 | | | | | | | | 2.5 |
| .9 | 1.9 | 1.6 | | Quick | | | | | | 1.3 |
| .3 | 1.0 | .9 | | | | | | | | .9 |
| 1   580.5 | 0   UND | 0   UND | | | | | | | | 0   UND |
| 10   38.0 | 0   UND | 12   31.4 | | Sales/Receivables | | | | | | 1   636.9 |
| 182   2.0 | 52   7.0 | 51   7.2 | | | | | | | | 59   6.2 |
| | | | | Cost of Sales/Inventory | | | | | | |
| | | | | Cost of Sales/Payables | | | | | | |
| 7.1 | .9 | 1.8 | | | | | | | | 1.9 |
| NM | 3.7 | 8.8 | | Sales/Working Capital | | | | | | 11.1 |
| -4.7 | NM | -26.3 | | | | | | | | -31.1 |
| 374.8 | | 57.9 | | | | | | | | |
| (10)  3.1 | (10)  3.2 | | | EBIT/Interest | | | | | | |
| -7.8 | | -2.5 | | | | | | | | |
| | | | | Net Profit + Depr., Dep., Amort./Cur. Mat. L/T/D | | | | | | |
| .0 | .0 | .0 | | | | | | | | .0 |
| .0 | .0 | .0 | | Fixed/Worth | | | | | | .3 |
| -.3 | 1.2 | .3 | | | | | | | | -1.3 |
| .8 | .6 | 1.1 | | | | | | | | .5 |
| 10.5 | 1.0 | 5.4 | | Debt/Worth | | | | | | 16.4 |
| -1.8 | 5.7 | -89.3 | | | | | | | | -77.4 |
| | 29.0 | 36.4 | | % Profit Before Taxes/Tangible Net Worth | | | | | | |
| (13)  4.0 | (19)  8.3 | | | | | | | | | |
| | -3.3 | -16.9 | | | | | | | | |
| 18.5 | 15.8 | 12.2 | | % Profit Before Taxes/Total Assets | | | | | | 15.4 |
| 2.8 | 2.7 | 4.8 | | | | | | | | 5.6 |
| -12.3 | -.8 | -1.2 | | | | | | | | 3.8 |
| 368.7 | UND | UND | | | | | | | | 583.8 |
| 59.8 | 226.5 | 336.6 | | Sales/Net Fixed Assets | | | | | | 86.5 |
| 26.8 | 21.2 | 21.5 | | | | | | | | 13.5 |
| 2.0 | 2.0 | 1.8 | | | | | | | | 3.4 |
| 1.1 | 1.0 | .8 | | Sales/Total Assets | | | | | | 1.0 |
| .3 | .3 | .3 | | | | | | | | .6 |
| | | | | % Depr., Dep., Amort./Sales | | | | | | |
| | | | | % Officers', Directors' Owners' Comp/Sales | | | | | | |
| 321078M | 597812M | 939820M | | Net Sales ($) | 1761M | 6716M | 8099M | 27780M | 69399M | 826065M |
| 579492M | 779557M | 1094139M | | Total Assets ($) | 34439M | 12265M | 6066M | 79841M | 150812M | 810716M |

M = $ thousand   MM = $ million
See Pages viii through xx for Explanation of Ratios and Data

© RMA 2024

# FINANCE—Reinsurance Carriers  NAICS 524130

| Current Data Sorted by Assets | | | | | | | | Comparative Historical Data | |
|---|---|---|---|---|---|---|---|---|---|
| | 1 | 4 | 4 | 4 | 5 | | Type of Statement | | |
| | | | | | | | Unqualified | 9 | 7 |
| | | | | | | | Reviewed | | |
| | | | | | | | Compiled | | |
| | | 1 | | | | | Tax Returns | | 1 |
| 2 | 1 | 5 | 5 | | | | Other | 21 | 9 |
| | 9 (4/1-9/30/23) | 2-10MM | 23 (10/1/23-3/31/24) | | | | | 4/1/19- | 4/1/20- |
| 0-500M | 500M-2MM | | 10-50MM | 50-100MM | 100-250MM | | | 3/31/20 | 3/31/21 |
| | | | | | | | | ALL | ALL |
| 2 | 2 | 10 | 9 | 4 | 5 | | NUMBER OF STATEMENTS | 30 | 17 |
| % | % | % | % | % | % | | ASSETS | % | % |
| | | 66.7 | | | | | Cash & Equivalents | 53.6 | 51.6 |
| | | 4.5 | | | | | Trade Receivables (net) | 7.9 | 10.1 |
| | | .0 | | | | | Inventory | .0 | .0 |
| | | 11.0 | | | | | All Other Current | 15.3 | 18.9 |
| | | 82.2 | | | | | Total Current | 76.7 | 80.6 |
| | | .0 | | | | | Fixed Assets (net) | .5 | .0 |
| | | 11.7 | | | | | Intangibles (net) | .2 | .9 |
| | | 6.0 | | | | | All Other Non-Current | 22.6 | 18.4 |
| | | 100.0 | | | | | Total | 100.0 | 100.0 |
| | | | | | | | LIABILITIES | | |
| | | .0 | | | | | Notes Payable-Short Term | 3.9 | 5.8 |
| | | 45.5 | | | | | Cur. Mat.-L.T.D. | 28.9 | 24.5 |
| | | 5.2 | | | | | Trade Payables | 7.8 | 4.8 |
| | | .2 | | | | | Income Taxes Payable | 2.9 | .8 |
| | | 5.3 | | | | | All Other Current | 14.3 | 16.9 |
| | | 56.3 | | | | | Total Current | 57.8 | 52.7 |
| | | .0 | | | | | Long-Term Debt | .3 | .8 |
| | | .0 | | | | | Deferred Taxes | .0 | .0 |
| | | 5.2 | | | | | All Other Non-Current | 7.1 | 11.7 |
| | | 38.5 | | | | | Net Worth | 34.9 | 34.8 |
| | | 100.0 | | | | | Total Liabilities & Net Worth | 100.0 | 100.0 |
| | | | | | | | INCOME DATA | | |
| | | 100.0 | | | | | Net Sales | 100.0 | 100.0 |
| | | | | | | | Gross Profit | | |
| | | 84.8 | | | | | Operating Expenses | 83.7 | 80.6 |
| | | 15.2 | | | | | Operating Profit | 16.3 | 19.4 |
| | | -1.0 | | | | | All Other Expenses (net) | -3.6 | -3.0 |
| | | 16.2 | | | | | Profit Before Taxes | 19.9 | 22.3 |
| | | | | | | | RATIOS | | |
| | | 2.5 | | | | | | 2.2 | 2.2 |
| | | 1.4 | | | | | Current | 1.3 | 1.3 |
| | | 1.1 | | | | | | .9 | 1.1 |
| | | 2.5 | | | | | | 2.0 | 2.1 |
| | | 1.4 | | | | | Quick | 1.1 | 1.2 |
| | | .9 | | | | | | .5 | .8 |
| | | 0    UND | | | | | | 0    UND | 0    UND |
| | | 0    UND | | | | | Sales/Receivables | 0    UND | 9    40.5 |
| | | 35   10.4 | | | | | | 51   7.1 | 101  3.6 |
| | | | | | | | Cost of Sales/Inventory | | |
| | | | | | | | Cost of Sales/Payables | | |
| | | 2.0 | | | | | | .8 | 1.1 |
| | | 5.4 | | | | | Sales/Working Capital | 2.3 | 2.3 |
| | | NM | | | | | | -7.6 | 10.5 |
| | | | | | | | EBIT/Interest | | |
| | | | | | | | Net Profit + Depr., Dep., Amort./Cur. Mat. L/T/D | | |
| | | .0 | | | | | | .0 | .0 |
| | | .0 | | | | | Fixed/Worth | .0 | .0 |
| | | .0 | | | | | | .0 | .0 |
| | | 1.2 | | | | | | 1.3 | 1.2 |
| | | 2.5 | | | | | Debt/Worth | 2.7 | 2.6 |
| | | 5.1 | | | | | | 5.4 | 5.1 |
| | | | | | | | % Profit Before Taxes/Tangible Net Worth | 38.0 | 49.9 |
| | | | | | | | | 19.4 | 38.1 |
| | | | | | | | | 9.9 | 18.8 |
| | | 40.3 | | | | | | 8.9 | 19.5 |
| | | 15.7 | | | | | % Profit Before Taxes/Total Assets | 4.7 | 9.1 |
| | | -1.0 | | | | | | .7 | 4.0 |
| | | UND | | | | | | UND | UND |
| | | UND | | | | | Sales/Net Fixed Assets | UND | UND |
| | | UND | | | | | | UND | UND |
| | | 1.8 | | | | | | .5 | 1.0 |
| | | 1.3 | | | | | Sales/Total Assets | .4 | .5 |
| | | .5 | | | | | | .3 | .3 |
| | | | | | | | % Depr., Dep., Amort./Sales | | |
| | | | | | | | % Officers', Directors' Owners' Comp/Sales | | |
| 1381M | 1180M | 74989M | 115660M | 72430M | 294929M | | Net Sales ($) | 299925M | 197670M |
| 469M | 1280M | 60921M | 245531M | 257962M | 636109M | | Total Assets ($) | 992877M | 575070M |

© RMA 2024          M = $ thousand    MM = $ million
See Pages viii through xx for Explanation of Ratios and Data

# FINANCE—Reinsurance Carriers  NAICS 524130

## Comparative Historical Data

| | | | Type of Statement | | | Current Data Sorted by Sales | | | | |
|---|---|---|---|---|---|---|---|---|---|---|
| 1 | 18 | 18 | Unqualified | | | | | | | |
| | | | Reviewed | | | | | | | |
| | | | Compiled | | 1 | | | | | |
| 2 | | | Tax Returns | | 2 | | | | | |
| 2 | 12 | 1 | Other | 2 | 2 | 4 | 2 | 1 | | |
| 4/1/21- | 4/1/22- | 13 | | | 9 (4/1-9/30/23) | | | 23 (10/1/23-3/31/24) | | |
| 3/31/22 | 3/31/23 | 4/1/23- | | 0-1MM | 1-3MM | 3-5MM | 5-10MM | 10-25MM | 25MM & OVER | |
| ALL | ALL | 3/31/24 | | | | | | | | |
| | | ALL | | | | | | | | |
| 5 | 30 | 32 | NUMBER OF STATEMENTS | 3 | 2 | 5 | 8 | 7 | 7 | |
| % | % | % | ASSETS | % | % | % | % | % | % | |
| | 70.0 | 63.6 | Cash & Equivalents | | | | | | | |
| | 3.2 | 6.5 | Trade Receivables (net) | | | | | | | |
| | .0 | .0 | Inventory | | | | | | | |
| | 15.4 | 10.0 | All Other Current | | | | | | | |
| | 88.6 | 80.0 | Total Current | | | | | | | |
| | .0 | .1 | Fixed Assets (net) | | | | | | | |
| | .0 | 4.8 | Intangibles (net) | | | | | | | |
| | 11.4 | 15.1 | All Other Non-Current | | | | | | | |
| | 100.0 | 100.0 | Total | | | | | | | |
| | | | LIABILITIES | | | | | | | |
| | 4.4 | 4.8 | Notes Payable-Short Term | | | | | | | |
| | 44.5 | 31.3 | Cur. Mat.-L.T.D. | | | | | | | |
| | 1.1 | 2.6 | Trade Payables | | | | | | | |
| | .1 | .4 | Income Taxes Payable | | | | | | | |
| | 13.7 | 23.8 | All Other Current | | | | | | | |
| | 63.8 | 62.9 | Total Current | | | | | | | |
| | .0 | .1 | Long-Term Debt | | | | | | | |
| | .0 | .0 | Deferred Taxes | | | | | | | |
| | 1.1 | 2.3 | All Other Non-Current | | | | | | | |
| | 35.2 | 34.6 | Net Worth | | | | | | | |
| | 100.0 | 100.0 | Total Liabilities & Net Worth | | | | | | | |
| | | | INCOME DATA | | | | | | | |
| | 100.0 | 100.0 | Net Sales | | | | | | | |
| | | | Gross Profit | | | | | | | |
| | 78.0 | 83.4 | Operating Expenses | | | | | | | |
| | 22.0 | 16.6 | Operating Profit | | | | | | | |
| | 7.3 | -1.4 | All Other Expenses (net) | | | | | | | |
| | 14.7 | 18.0 | Profit Before Taxes | | | | | | | |
| | | | RATIOS | | | | | | | |
| | 1.9 | 1.8 | | | | | | | | |
| | 1.4 | 1.3 | Current | | | | | | | |
| | 1.0 | .9 | | | | | | | | |
| | 1.6 | 1.7 | | | | | | | | |
| | 1.2 | 1.2 | Quick | | | | | | | |
| | .8 | .8 | | | | | | | | |
| 0 | UND | 0 | UND | | | | | | | |
| 0 | UND | 0 | UND | Sales/Receivables | | | | | | |
| 18 | 20.4 | 27 | 13.7 | | | | | | | |
| | | | Cost of Sales/Inventory | | | | | | | |
| | | | Cost of Sales/Payables | | | | | | | |
| | .9 | 1.3 | | | | | | | | |
| | 1.6 | 2.7 | Sales/Working Capital | | | | | | | |
| | NM | -118.5 | | | | | | | | |
| | | | EBIT/Interest | | | | | | | |
| | | | Net Profit + Depr., Dep., Amort./Cur. Mat. L/T/D | | | | | | | |
| | .0 | .0 | | | | | | | | |
| | .0 | .0 | Fixed/Worth | | | | | | | |
| | .0 | .0 | | | | | | | | |
| | 1.1 | 1.2 | | | | | | | | |
| | 2.0 | 2.5 | Debt/Worth | | | | | | | |
| | 4.1 | 4.8 | | | | | | | | |
| | 54.7 | 57.3 | | | | | | | | |
| | 17.4 | (30) 17.9 | % Profit Before Taxes/Tangible Net Worth | | | | | | | |
| | -7.6 | 9.2 | | | | | | | | |
| | 18.6 | 18.2 | | | | | | | | |
| | 5.0 | 6.2 | % Profit Before Taxes/Total Assets | | | | | | | |
| | -2.6 | 2.7 | | | | | | | | |
| | UND | UND | | | | | | | | |
| | UND | UND | Sales/Net Fixed Assets | | | | | | | |
| | UND | UND | | | | | | | | |
| | .7 | .9 | | | | | | | | |
| | .4 | .5 | Sales/Total Assets | | | | | | | |
| | .3 | .4 | | | | | | | | |
| | | | % Depr., Dep., Amort./Sales | | | | | | | |
| | | | % Officers', Directors' Owners' Comp/Sales | | | | | | | |
| 58880M | 462359M | 560569M | Net Sales ($) | 1498M | 2700M | 21598M | 51693M | 132731M | 350349M | |
| 97076M | 1344162M | 1202272M | Total Assets ($) | 1623M | 4897M | 33714M | 87252M | 381164M | 693622M | |

© RMA 2024  M = $ thousand  MM = $ million
See Pages viii through xx for Explanation of Ratios and Data

## FINANCE—Insurance Agencies and Brokerages  NAICS 524210

### Current Data Sorted by Assets | Comparative Historical Data

| | | | | | | Type of Statement | | |
|---|---|---|---|---|---|---|---|---|
| 1 | 3 | 5 | 10 | 6 | 7 | Unqualified | 36 | 31 |
|  | 1 | 5 | 9 |  | 2 | Reviewed | 19 | 17 |
| 2 | 3 | 6 | 3 |  | 9 | Compiled | 28 | 19 |
| 32 | 20 | 15 | 4 |  |  | Tax Returns | 172 | 121 |
| 28 | 42 | 51 | 50 | 16 | 13 | Other | 237 | 184 |
|  | 35 (4/1-9/30/23) | | 299 (10/1/23-3/31/24) | | | | 4/1/19-3/31/20 ALL | 4/1/20-3/31/21 ALL |
| 0-500M | 500M-2MM | 2-10MM | 10-50MM | 50-100MM | 100-250MM | | | |
| 63 | 69 | 82 | 76 | 22 | 22 | **NUMBER OF STATEMENTS** | 492 | 372 |
| % | % | % | % | % | % | **ASSETS** | % | % |
| 53.0 | 28.4 | 39.6 | 30.2 | 35.4 | 19.3 | Cash & Equivalents | 32.5 | 39.3 |
| 1.4 | 12.0 | 10.3 | 13.6 | 11.1 | 19.7 | Trade Receivables (net) | 10.9 | 9.3 |
| .0 | .2 | .0 | 1.7 | .1 | .0 | Inventory | .1 | .2 |
| 2.5 | 3.8 | 4.2 | 12.9 | 5.2 | 4.7 | All Other Current | 5.0 | 4.3 |
| 56.9 | 44.4 | 54.1 | 58.4 | 51.7 | 43.6 | Total Current | 48.5 | 53.2 |
| 17.0 | 22.5 | 10.8 | 6.6 | 11.8 | 8.8 | Fixed Assets (net) | 13.7 | 12.6 |
| 15.8 | 19.6 | 19.5 | 15.1 | 11.2 | 17.3 | Intangibles (net) | 23.2 | 22.1 |
| 10.4 | 13.4 | 15.6 | 19.9 | 25.3 | 30.2 | All Other Non-Current | 14.5 | 12.1 |
| 100.0 | 100.0 | 100.0 | 100.0 | 100.0 | 100.0 | Total | 100.0 | 100.0 |
| | | | | | | **LIABILITIES** | | |
| 12.0 | 19.1 | 3.1 | 3.0 | 1.0 | 3.4 | Notes Payable-Short Term | 9.1 | 13.6 |
| 3.0 | 2.6 | 3.7 | 2.8 | 11.5 | 1.4 | Cur. Mat.-L.T.D. | 2.8 | 3.9 |
| .8 | 8.5 | 15.2 | 16.2 | 7.6 | 12.9 | Trade Payables | 11.7 | 10.8 |
| .2 | .0 | .1 | .2 | .4 | .5 | Income Taxes Payable | .1 | .1 |
| 35.2 | 12.3 | 14.9 | 20.3 | 20.3 | 15.6 | All Other Current | 17.9 | 15.9 |
| 51.1 | 42.5 | 37.1 | 42.5 | 40.7 | 33.9 | Total Current | 41.7 | 44.3 |
| 23.5 | 35.1 | 19.2 | 18.7 | 41.4 | 24.5 | Long-Term Debt | 27.8 | 26.6 |
| .1 | .0 | .0 | .1 | .9 | .2 | Deferred Taxes | .1 | .1 |
| 11.1 | 3.0 | 5.0 | 8.3 | 9.6 | 5.9 | All Other Non-Current | 5.3 | 7.8 |
| 14.3 | 19.4 | 38.8 | 30.3 | 7.3 | 35.5 | Net Worth | 25.1 | 21.2 |
| 100.0 | 100.0 | 100.0 | 100.0 | 100.0 | 100.0 | Total Liabilities & Net Worth | 100.0 | 100.0 |
| | | | | | | **INCOME DATA** | | |
| 100.0 | 100.0 | 100.0 | 100.0 | 100.0 | 100.0 | Net Sales | 100.0 | 100.0 |
| | | | | | | Gross Profit | | |
| 78.3 | 78.5 | 81.2 | 81.5 | 80.5 | 74.7 | Operating Expenses | 81.2 | 82.4 |
| 21.7 | 21.5 | 18.8 | 18.5 | 19.5 | 25.3 | Operating Profit | 18.8 | 17.6 |
| 1.2 | 5.4 | .8 | 1.6 | 3.3 | 2.6 | All Other Expenses (net) | 2.4 | .5 |
| 20.5 | 16.1 | 17.9 | 16.9 | 16.3 | 22.7 | Profit Before Taxes | 16.4 | 17.1 |
| | | | | | | **RATIOS** | | |
| 6.5 | 5.9 | 2.6 | 2.3 | 2.4 | 2.4 | | 2.4 | 3.2 |
| 1.7 | 1.4 | 1.4 | 1.3 | 1.2 | 1.2 | Current | 1.3 | 1.4 |
| .6 | .6 | .8 | 1.0 | .7 | .8 | | .7 | .9 |
| 6.5 | 5.8 | 2.5 | 1.9 | 2.3 | 2.3 | | 2.2 | 3.0 |
| 1.7 | 1.4 | 1.3 | 1.1 | 1.1 | 1.1 | Quick | 1.1 | 1.3 |
| .4 | .5 | .6 | .7 | .3 | .7 | | .5 | .9 |
| 0 UND | 0 UND | 0 UND | 0 UND | 0 UND | 13  28.9 | | 0 UND | 0 UND |
| 0 UND | 0 UND | 4  83.5 | 25  14.6 | 12  31.0 | 70  5.2 | Sales/Receivables | 0 UND | 0 UND |
| 0 UND | 18  20.6 | 26  14.0 | 54  6.8 | 46  8.0 | 159  2.3 | | 34  10.7 | 34  10.7 |
| | | | | | | Cost of Sales/Inventory | | |
| | | | | | | Cost of Sales/Payables | | |
| 9.6 | 5.8 | 5.3 | 3.6 | 3.2 | 3.6 | | 7.6 | 4.8 |
| 53.2 | 26.1 | 10.5 | 9.8 | 13.2 | 14.6 | Sales/Working Capital | 23.5 | 15.2 |
| -23.7 | -21.8 | -14.1 | 232.2 | -14.3 | -23.4 | | -28.6 | -39.5 |
| 72.4 | 53.0 | 118.7 | 160.8 | 6.9 | 27.7 | | 41.6 | 50.9 |
| (32) 16.8 | (45) 8.9 | (58) 21.7 | (44) 17.4 | (10) 3.9 | (16) 10.8 | EBIT/Interest | (328) 11.0 | (234) 12.0 |
| 7.0 | 2.3 | 7.1 | 6.6 | 2.6 | 6.0 | | 3.8 | 2.9 |
| | | | | | | Net Profit + Depr., Dep., | 9.8 | 22.3 |
| | | | | | | Amort./Cur. Mat. L/T/D | (25) 3.1 | (18) 2.6 |
| | | | | | | | 1.7 | 1.1 |
| .0 | .0 | .0 | .0 | .0 | .0 | | .0 | .0 |
| .5 | .6 | .1 | .1 | .0 | .1 | Fixed/Worth | .3 | .4 |
| -2.2 | -3.5 | NM | 3.1 | 1.9 | NM | | -7.1 | -1.2 |
| .2 | .5 | .8 | 1.3 | .8 | .6 | | 1.0 | 1.2 |
| 1.4 | 3.4 | 2.3 | 2.7 | 3.2 | 4.0 | Debt/Worth | 5.1 | 7.0 |
| -5.7 | -3.6 | -10.9 | NM | -2.3 | -6.2 | | -3.2 | -2.8 |
| 397.4 | 163.2 | 107.3 | 90.1 | 49.7 | 41.4 | | 295.1 | 237.5 |
| (40) 167.2 | (42) 46.4 | (57) 56.0 | (57) 42.5 | (16) 33.5 | (15) 28.9 | % Profit Before Taxes/Tangible Net Worth | (318) 68.1 | (230) 78.8 |
| 85.1 | 2.7 | 25.0 | 16.1 | 3.1 | 12.6 | | 20.0 | 23.1 |
| 189.5 | 46.5 | 35.6 | 23.0 | 23.9 | 22.2 | | 58.8 | 51.7 |
| 84.4 | 15.8 | 18.8 | 12.0 | 10.5 | 11.5 | % Profit Before Taxes/Total Assets | 17.0 | 19.4 |
| 24.2 | 1.2 | 9.2 | 5.4 | 2.4 | 5.2 | | 4.8 | 5.0 |
| UND | 604.9 | 657.7 | 551.3 | UND | 999.8 | | 728.8 | 736.1 |
| 78.0 | 56.3 | 61.8 | 66.7 | 124.5 | 48.1 | Sales/Net Fixed Assets | 55.3 | 61.0 |
| 16.8 | 9.8 | 16.8 | 25.4 | 14.3 | 8.0 | | 14.5 | 16.6 |
| 10.7 | 4.6 | 2.5 | 1.8 | 1.5 | 1.4 | | 4.0 | 3.4 |
| 6.3 | 1.8 | 1.3 | 1.1 | .9 | .6 | Sales/Total Assets | 1.6 | 1.6 |
| 2.5 | .9 | .7 | .6 | .5 | .4 | | .7 | .8 |
| .3 | .1 | .4 | .4 | .1 | 1.2 | | .5 | .4 |
| (15) .7 | (24) .8 | (33) .8 | (42) .8 | (11) .4 | (11) 3.5 | % Depr., Dep., Amort./Sales | (196) 1.5 | (150) 1.3 |
| 4.1 | 5.0 | 2.0 | 1.8 | 4.9 | 3.8 | | 3.4 | 3.5 |
| 6.5 | 4.3 | 3.2 | .9 | | | | 5.9 | 7.6 |
| (32) 15.1 | (24) 9.4 | (32) 6.4 | (16) 4.5 | | | % Officers', Directors' Owners' Comp/Sales | (215) 10.4 | (153) 14.0 |
| 24.3 | 17.3 | 10.3 | 9.6 | | | | 16.2 | 21.1 |
| 64764M | 256589M | 805486M | 2645209M | 1434471M | 2855695M | Net Sales ($) | 11966100M | 6909822M |
| 11412M | 81238M | 409192M | 1954953M | 1485519M | 3379305M | Total Assets ($) | 9630159M | 6705293M |

© RMA 2024    M = $ thousand    MM = $ million
See Pages viii through xx for Explanation of Ratios and Data

# FINANCE—Insurance Agencies and Brokerages  NAICS 524210

## Comparative Historical Data | Current Data Sorted by Sales

| Comparative Historical Data | | | | Type of Statement | Current Data Sorted by Sales | | | | | |
|---|---|---|---|---|---|---|---|---|---|---|
| 26 | 29 | 32 | | Unqualified | 1 | 4 | 5 | 7 | 15 | |
| 11 | 15 | 17 | | Reviewed | | | 3 | 3 | 5 | 6 |
| 14 | 19 | 14 | | Compiled | | 3 | 2 | 6 | | 3 |
| 93 | 96 | 71 | | Tax Returns | 29 | 23 | 3 | 7 | 8 | 1 |
| 177 | 191 | 200 | | Other | 36 | 29 | 27 | 22 | 27 | 59 |
| 4/1/21- | 4/1/22- | 4/1/23- | | | 35 (4/1-9/30/23) | | 299 (10/1/23-3/31/24) | | | |
| 3/31/22 | 3/31/23 | 3/31/24 | | | 0-1MM | 1-3MM | 3-5MM | 5-10MM | 10-25MM | 25MM & OVER |
| ALL | ALL | ALL | | NUMBER OF STATEMENTS | 66 | 59 | 35 | 43 | 47 | 84 |
| 321 | 350 | 334 | | | | | | | | |
| % | % | % | | ASSETS | % | % | % | % | % | % |
| 39.6 | 37.5 | 36.0 | | Cash & Equivalents | 39.4 | 34.4 | 39.7 | 31.2 | 41.3 | 32.6 |
| 8.7 | 11.6 | 10.4 | | Trade Receivables (net) | 2.7 | 7.2 | 10.0 | 12.8 | 15.8 | 14.6 |
| .1 | .3 | .4 | | Inventory | .0 | .0 | .4 | .0 | .0 | 1.6 |
| 4.3 | 4.7 | 5.9 | | All Other Current | 2.2 | 3.4 | 6.0 | 11.5 | 4.4 | 8.4 |
| 52.7 | 54.1 | 52.8 | | Total Current | 44.4 | 44.9 | 56.0 | 55.5 | 61.5 | 57.2 |
| 11.4 | 11.7 | 13.4 | | Fixed Assets (net) | 27.2 | 13.7 | 8.8 | 8.7 | 8.2 | 9.4 |
| 23.1 | 20.5 | 17.1 | | Intangibles (net) | 17.6 | 23.1 | 19.6 | 17.1 | 15.1 | 12.7 |
| 12.8 | 13.7 | 16.8 | | All Other Non-Current | 10.9 | 18.2 | 15.6 | 18.7 | 15.2 | 20.7 |
| 100.0 | 100.0 | 100.0 | | Total | 100.0 | 100.0 | 100.0 | 100.0 | 100.0 | 100.0 |
| | | | | LIABILITIES | | | | | | |
| 6.9 | 4.8 | 8.0 | | Notes Payable-Short Term | 10.0 | 5.9 | 18.4 | 4.3 | 16.0 | .8 |
| 3.0 | 3.6 | 3.5 | | Cur. Mat.-L.T.D. | 5.2 | 3.6 | 4.3 | 3.7 | 1.6 | 2.7 |
| 10.5 | 12.2 | 10.7 | | Trade Payables | .3 | 6.3 | 8.4 | 17.4 | 20.0 | 14.1 |
| .1 | .3 | .2 | | Income Taxes Payable | .2 | .0 | .0 | .2 | .3 | .3 |
| 18.4 | 16.6 | 19.8 | | All Other Current | 25.4 | 16.1 | 18.8 | 17.4 | 13.0 | 23.4 |
| 39.0 | 37.4 | 42.1 | | Total Current | 41.1 | 31.9 | 49.9 | 43.0 | 50.8 | 41.4 |
| 25.3 | 24.1 | 25.0 | | Long-Term Debt | 38.3 | 30.4 | 13.6 | 19.5 | 11.5 | 25.8 |
| .1 | .1 | .1 | | Deferred Taxes | .1 | .0 | .0 | .0 | .1 | .3 |
| 4.5 | 4.3 | 6.8 | | All Other Non-Current | 3.3 | 9.5 | 1.1 | 7.0 | 8.3 | 9.3 |
| 31.0 | 34.1 | 25.9 | | Net Worth | 17.3 | 28.1 | 35.4 | 30.4 | 29.2 | 23.1 |
| 100.0 | 100.0 | 100.0 | | Total Liabilities & Net Worth | 100.0 | 100.0 | 100.0 | 100.0 | 100.0 | 100.0 |
| | | | | INCOME DATA | | | | | | |
| 100.0 | 100.0 | 100.0 | | Net Sales | 100.0 | 100.0 | 100.0 | 100.0 | 100.0 | 100.0 |
| | | | | Gross Profit | | | | | | |
| 81.4 | 83.2 | 79.7 | | Operating Expenses | 71.1 | 78.2 | 80.5 | 80.1 | 84.7 | 84.1 |
| 18.6 | 16.8 | 20.3 | | Operating Profit | 28.9 | 21.8 | 19.5 | 19.9 | 15.3 | 15.9 |
| .5 | 1.9 | 2.3 | | All Other Expenses (net) | 7.5 | 2.1 | 1.2 | 1.0 | -.5 | 1.1 |
| 18.1 | 14.9 | 18.0 | | Profit Before Taxes | 21.4 | 19.7 | 18.3 | 18.9 | 15.8 | 14.8 |
| | | | | RATIOS | | | | | | |
| 4.1 | 4.1 | 3.5 | | | 5.3 | 5.2 | 2.6 | 2.5 | 2.9 | 2.7 |
| 1.5 | 1.4 | 1.4 | | Current | 1.2 | 1.7 | 1.2 | 1.4 | 1.3 | 1.4 |
| .9 | .9 | .8 | | | .5 | .5 | .6 | .8 | .9 | 1.0 |
| 3.8 | 3.5 | 2.8 | | | 5.3 | 4.8 | 2.6 | 2.3 | 2.6 | 2.3 |
| 1.3 | 1.3 | 1.2 | | Quick | 1.0 | 1.4 | 1.1 | 1.4 | 1.3 | 1.2 |
| .8 | .8 | .6 | | | .4 | .4 | .4 | .7 | .7 | .8 |
| 0 UND | 0 UND | 0 UND | | | 0 UND | 0 UND | 0 UND | 0 UND | 4 89.9 | 2 191.6 |
| 0 UND | 1 280.6 | 1 267.1 | | Sales/Receivables | 0 UND | 0 UND | 0 UND | 7 52.1 | 18 20.8 | 25 14.4 |
| 24 15.2 | 38 9.6 | 31 11.8 | | | 0 UND | 15 23.6 | 32 11.5 | 34 10.8 | 54 6.8 | 61 6.0 |
| | | | | Cost of Sales/Inventory | | | | | | |
| | | | | Cost of Sales/Payables | | | | | | |
| 5.9 | 5.0 | 4.8 | | | 5.4 | 4.1 | 6.0 | 3.5 | 4.4 | 4.4 |
| 13.8 | 15.1 | 15.6 | | Sales/Working Capital | 74.1 | 12.7 | 22.5 | 13.0 | 10.2 | 11.5 |
| -70.8 | -62.0 | -23.6 | | | -11.5 | -14.7 | -17.1 | -22.6 | -29.3 | 254.0 |
| 71.6 | 91.5 | 69.5 | | | 29.9 | 65.6 | 45.8 | 98.5 | 382.1 | 44.9 |
| (190) 14.4 | (198) 15.8 | (205) 13.9 | | EBIT/Interest | (30) 7.1 | (44) 16.1 | (20) 14.3 | (33) 12.9 | (29) 67.6 | (49) 10.3 |
| 4.3 | 4.4 | 5.1 | | | 3.6 | 4.6 | 5.7 | 5.5 | 13.3 | 4.7 |
| 21.4 | 24.4 | 12.3 | | Net Profit + Depr., Dep., | | | | | | 12.3 |
| (14) 4.5 | (19) 5.6 | (19) 2.8 | | Amort./Cur. Mat. L/T/D | | | | | (11) 2.4 | |
| 1.0 | 2.0 | 1.4 | | | | | | | | 1.4 |
| .0 | .0 | .0 | | | .0 | .0 | .0 | .0 | .0 | .0 |
| .2 | .1 | .2 | | Fixed/Worth | 1.4 | .4 | .1 | .1 | .1 | .2 |
| 17.6 | 3.2 | UND | | | -5.1 | -.4 | .8 | 1.3 | -1.3 | 2.1 |
| .7 | .7 | .6 | | | .3 | .5 | 1.3 | .6 | .7 | .8 |
| 4.0 | 2.8 | 2.6 | | Debt/Worth | 4.0 | 2.4 | 2.7 | 1.9 | 2.3 | 2.8 |
| -3.4 | -8.6 | -7.8 | | | -4.1 | -3.5 | 66.0 | -12.1 | -15.5 | -18.4 |
| 209.0 | 155.9 | 138.6 | | % Profit Before Taxes/Tangible | 327.1 | 187.4 | 162.3 | 117.3 | 80.7 | 93.1 |
| (211) 82.9 | (250) 50.7 | (227) 54.8 | | Net Worth | (40) 90.5 | (37) 66.0 | (27) 97.3 | (30) 51.9 | (32) 53.6 | (61) 41.4 |
| 26.3 | 11.2 | 20.0 | | | 13.4 | 30.8 | 19.8 | 22.6 | 11.3 | 18.2 |
| 58.5 | 43.6 | 44.6 | | % Profit Before Taxes/Total | 105.8 | 47.4 | 52.9 | 31.9 | 44.4 | 27.9 |
| 20.9 | 14.5 | 17.6 | | Assets | 25.2 | 21.2 | 16.6 | 15.6 | 15.5 | 14.6 |
| 6.8 | 4.3 | 5.8 | | | 3.5 | 9.0 | 5.4 | 6.2 | 6.5 | 5.1 |
| UND | UND | 999.8 | | | UND | 999.8 | 988.3 | UND | 532.1 | 312.9 |
| 71.9 | 74.4 | 66.2 | | Sales/Net Fixed Assets | 35.1 | 62.9 | 48.8 | 111.0 | 67.3 | 68.4 |
| 22.2 | 16.6 | 16.2 | | | 9.3 | 10.8 | 22.8 | 20.8 | 30.1 | 16.0 |
| 4.3 | 3.1 | 3.6 | | | 6.8 | 3.4 | 4.3 | 4.8 | 3.0 | 2.4 |
| 1.7 | 1.5 | 1.5 | | Sales/Total Assets | 2.2 | 1.5 | 1.5 | 1.6 | 1.5 | 1.4 |
| .8 | .7 | .8 | | | .4 | .7 | .5 | .8 | 1.0 | .8 |
| .5 | .5 | .3 | | | 1.3 | .2 | .1 | .4 | .4 | .3 |
| (108) 1.3 | (134) 1.2 | (136) .9 | | % Depr., Dep., Amort./Sales | (18) 8.3 | (16) .8 | (13) .6 | (17) 1.3 | (22) .8 | (50) .8 |
| 3.5 | 4.5 | 2.7 | | | 20.0 | 3.7 | 1.6 | 1.6 | 1.4 | 2.7 |
| 3.7 | 4.8 | 3.6 | | % Officers', Directors' | 7.8 | 5.2 | 4.0 | 2.5 | 1.7 | |
| (123) 9.3 | (124) 11.6 | (106) 7.6 | | Owners' Comp/Sales | (24) 15.9 | (29) 10.4 | (13) 6.0 | (14) 5.8 | (18) 3.5 | |
| 19.9 | 17.6 | 15.7 | | | 25.2 | 16.2 | 14.6 | 10.8 | 8.3 | |
| 6378880M | 8607499M | 8062214M | | Net Sales ($) | 31911M | 114198M | 139032M | 307725M | 755258M | 6714090M |
| 5344401M | 7289408M | 7321619M | | Total Assets ($) | 147259M | 121290M | 271409M | 343357M | 814914M | 5623390M |

© RMA 2024  M = $ thousand  MM = $ million
See Pages viii through xx for Explanation of Ratios and Data

# FINANCE—Pharmacy Benefit Management and Other Third Party Administration of Insurance and Pension Funds  NAICS 524292

## Current Data Sorted by Assets | Comparative Historical Data

| | | | | | | Type of Statement | | |
|---|---|---|---|---|---|---|---|---|
| 1 | | 2 | 5 | 2 | 3 | Unqualified | 17 | 9 |
| | | 1 | 3 | | | Reviewed | 3 | 1 |
| | | 1 | | | | Compiled | 2 | 1 |
| | 2 | 1 | | | | Tax Returns | 7 | 6 |
| 2 | 3 | 10 | 6 | 3 | 4 | Other | 26 | 19 |
| 0-500M | 500M-2MM | 10 (4/1-9/30/23) 2-10MM | 41 (10/1/23-3/31/24) 10-50MM | 50-100MM | 100-250MM | | 4/1/19-3/31/20 ALL | 4/1/20-3/31/21 ALL |
| 3 | 7 | 15 | 14 | 5 | 7 | NUMBER OF STATEMENTS | 55 | 36 |
| % | % | % | % | % | % | ASSETS | % | % |
| | | 39.7 | 27.7 | | | Cash & Equivalents | 34.9 | 28.8 |
| | | 22.3 | 18.5 | | | Trade Receivables (net) | 19.7 | 18.4 |
| | | 1.3 | .0 | | | Inventory | .1 | .0 |
| | | 9.7 | 10.4 | | | All Other Current | 8.0 | 4.7 |
| | | 73.0 | 56.7 | | | Total Current | 62.8 | 51.8 |
| | | 6.4 | 5.1 | | | Fixed Assets (net) | 12.3 | 14.2 |
| | | 11.5 | 19.1 | | | Intangibles (net) | 9.4 | 17.1 |
| | | 9.1 | 19.1 | | | All Other Non-Current | 15.5 | 16.9 |
| | | 100.0 | 100.0 | | | Total | 100.0 | 100.0 |
| | | | | | | LIABILITIES | | |
| | | 3.7 | 1.7 | | | Notes Payable-Short Term | 4.8 | 5.2 |
| | | .4 | 1.4 | | | Cur. Mat.-L.T.D. | 1.6 | 1.5 |
| | | 14.1 | 15.4 | | | Trade Payables | 12.1 | 14.7 |
| | | .1 | .0 | | | Income Taxes Payable | .5 | .0 |
| | | 17.7 | 20.5 | | | All Other Current | 25.3 | 31.4 |
| | | 35.9 | 39.1 | | | Total Current | 44.4 | 52.9 |
| | | 6.8 | 11.9 | | | Long-Term Debt | 10.2 | 16.4 |
| | | .1 | .8 | | | Deferred Taxes | .3 | .5 |
| | | 2.9 | 6.4 | | | All Other Non-Current | 3.7 | 6.0 |
| | | 54.3 | 41.7 | | | Net Worth | 41.3 | 24.2 |
| | | 100.0 | 100.0 | | | Total Liabilties & Net Worth | 100.0 | 100.0 |
| | | | | | | INCOME DATA | | |
| | | 100.0 | 100.0 | | | Net Sales | 100.0 | 100.0 |
| | | | | | | Gross Profit | | |
| | | 84.1 | 95.0 | | | Operating Expenses | 84.1 | 89.8 |
| | | 15.9 | 5.0 | | | Operating Profit | 15.9 | 10.2 |
| | | .4 | 1.4 | | | All Other Expenses (net) | .9 | 1.0 |
| | | 15.5 | 3.6 | | | Profit Before Taxes | 15.0 | 9.1 |
| | | | | | | RATIOS | | |
| | | 20.6 | 3.1 | | | | 2.3 | 2.2 |
| | | 1.7 | 1.2 | | | Current | 1.7 | 1.0 |
| | | 1.1 | 1.0 | | | | .9 | .8 |
| | | 20.6 | 2.7 | | | | 2.0 | 1.9 |
| | | 1.7 | 1.0 | | | Quick | 1.4 | .9 |
| | | 1.0 | .7 | | | | .8 | .6 |
| | 1 | 364.5 | 0 UND | | | | 0 UND | 0 UND |
| | 15 | 24.3 | 13 28.3 | | | Sales/Receivables | 23 15.7 | 20 18.4 |
| | 49 | 7.4 | 45 8.1 | | | | 43 8.5 | 44 8.3 |
| | | | | | | Cost of Sales/Inventory | | |
| | | | | | | Cost of Sales/Payables | | |
| | | 3.1 | 5.1 | | | | 4.4 | 12.2 |
| | | 8.2 | 35.1 | | | Sales/Working Capital | 14.9 | -442.0 |
| | | 107.6 | NM | | | | -33.8 | -20.1 |
| | | | | | | | 32.8 | 59.3 |
| | | | | | | EBIT/Interest | (25) 11.3 | (20) 5.5 |
| | | | | | | | 3.1 | .6 |
| | | | | | | Net Profit + Depr., Dep., Amort./Cur. Mat. L/T/D | | |
| | | .0 | .0 | | | | .0 | .1 |
| | | .1 | .2 | | | Fixed/Worth | .1 | .6 |
| | | .7 | NM | | | | 3.4 | -7.9 |
| | | .1 | .6 | | | | .5 | .8 |
| | | 1.4 | 2.9 | | | Debt/Worth | 1.5 | 3.6 |
| | | 10.6 | NM | | | | 17.5 | -4.1 |
| | | 88.4 | 75.3 | | | | 83.4 | 154.2 |
| | (12) | 49.8 | (11) 4.5 | | | % Profit Before Taxes/Tangible Net Worth | (45) 25.6 | (23) 37.7 |
| | | 14.7 | -.2 | | | | 10.1 | 21.1 |
| | | 68.6 | 11.5 | | | | 28.3 | 47.8 |
| | | 18.0 | .8 | | | % Profit Before Taxes/Total Assets | 11.1 | 11.3 |
| | | 7.8 | -1.3 | | | | 3.8 | 2.9 |
| | | 999.8 | UND | | | | 380.8 | 225.6 |
| | | 102.9 | 86.4 | | | Sales/Net Fixed Assets | 70.7 | 45.8 |
| | | 27.7 | 19.3 | | | | 18.7 | 14.9 |
| | | 3.8 | 2.5 | | | | 3.7 | 4.8 |
| | | 2.8 | 1.3 | | | Sales/Total Assets | 1.9 | 2.5 |
| | | .7 | .9 | | | | .6 | .9 |
| | | | | | | | .6 | .6 |
| | | | | | | % Depr., Dep., Amort./Sales | (32) 1.1 | (18) 1.2 |
| | | | | | | | 2.7 | 2.4 |
| | | | | | | % Officers', Directors' Owners' Comp/Sales | | |
| 1456M | 47005M | 144186M | 801350M | 464546M | 1279373M | Net Sales ($) | 3072171M | 1316117M |
| 336M | 6960M | 69343M | 353207M | 336617M | 1008063M | Total Assets ($) | 1867813M | 1005264M |

© RMA 2024  M = $ thousand  MM = $ million
See Pages viii through xx for Explanation of Ratios and Data

# FINANCE—Pharmacy Benefit Management and Other Third Party Administration of Insurance and Pension Funds    NAICS 524292

## Comparative Historical Data | Current Data Sorted by Sales

| Comparative Historical Data | | | | | Type of Statement | Current Data Sorted by Sales | | | | | |
|---|---|---|---|---|---|---|---|---|---|---|---|
| | 9 | | 15 | 15 | Unqualified | 2 | | 2 | 1 | 3 | 7 |
| | 1 | | 2 | 4 | Reviewed | | | | | 2 | 2 |
| | | | 2 | 1 | Compiled | | | | 1 | | |
| | 1 | | 4 | 3 | Tax Returns | | | 2 | | 1 | |
| | 18 | | 30 | 28 | Other | 2 | | 2 | 4 | 5 | 13 |
| | 4/1/21- | | 4/1/22- | 4/1/23- | | | 10 (4/1-9/30/23) | | | 41 (10/1/23-3/31/24) | |
| | 3/31/22 | | 3/31/23 | 3/31/24 | | 0-1MM | 1-3MM | 3-5MM | 5-10MM | 10-25MM | 25MM & OVER |
| | ALL | | ALL | ALL | | | | | | | |
| | 29 | | 53 | 51 | NUMBER OF STATEMENTS | 4 | | 6 | 6 | 11 | 22 |
| | % | | % | % | ASSETS | % | % | % | % | % | % |
| | 24.0 | | 29.3 | 28.8 | Cash & Equivalents | | | | | 41.2 | 20.3 |
| | 19.2 | | 19.5 | 22.6 | Trade Receivables (net) | | | | | 27.1 | 16.3 |
| | .0 | | .4 | .4 | Inventory | | | | | .0 | .0 |
| | 6.1 | | 12.4 | 10.4 | All Other Current | | | | | 1.8 | 12.5 |
| | 49.3 | | 61.6 | 62.3 | Total Current | | | | | 70.1 | 49.1 |
| | 6.3 | | 10.5 | 7.8 | Fixed Assets (net) | | | | | 13.3 | 5.1 |
| | 27.0 | | 11.6 | 13.5 | Intangibles (net) | | | | | 6.6 | 21.8 |
| | 17.5 | | 16.3 | 16.4 | All Other Non-Current | | | | | 10.1 | 24.0 |
| | 100.0 | | 100.0 | 100.0 | Total | | | | | 100.0 | 100.0 |
| | | | | | LIABILITIES | | | | | | |
| | 4.1 | | 5.7 | 4.8 | Notes Payable-Short Term | | | | | 6.8 | 5.6 |
| | 1.2 | | 3.2 | 1.3 | Cur. Mat.-L.T.D. | | | | | 1.0 | 1.4 |
| | 9.0 | | 8.5 | 17.8 | Trade Payables | | | | | 15.7 | 16.6 |
| | .1 | | .0 | .0 | Income Taxes Payable | | | | | .0 | .0 |
| | 25.3 | | 27.4 | 24.7 | All Other Current | | | | | 23.0 | 24.5 |
| | 39.6 | | 44.9 | 48.6 | Total Current | | | | | 46.5 | 48.1 |
| | 14.9 | | 11.9 | 15.2 | Long-Term Debt | | | | | 7.1 | 16.2 |
| | .6 | | .3 | .3 | Deferred Taxes | | | | | 1.2 | .0 |
| | 11.3 | | 6.3 | 5.9 | All Other Non-Current | | | | | 3.0 | 8.2 |
| | 33.6 | | 36.6 | 30.0 | Net Worth | | | | | 42.2 | 27.5 |
| | 100.0 | | 100.0 | 100.0 | Total Liabilties & Net Worth | | | | | 100.0 | 100.0 |
| | | | | | INCOME DATA | | | | | | |
| | 100.0 | | 100.0 | 100.0 | Net Sales | | | | | 100.0 | 100.0 |
| | | | | | Gross Profit | | | | | | |
| | 93.9 | | 91.7 | 89.1 | Operating Expenses | | | | | 91.2 | 92.2 |
| | 6.1 | | 8.3 | 10.9 | Operating Profit | | | | | 8.8 | 7.8 |
| | 2.7 | | 1.5 | 1.5 | All Other Expenses (net) | | | | | -.3 | 3.0 |
| | 3.4 | | 6.8 | 9.4 | Profit Before Taxes | | | | | 9.1 | 4.8 |
| | | | | | RATIOS | | | | | | |
| | 5.6 | | 3.8 | 2.6 | | | | | | 5.6 | 1.6 |
| | 1.1 | | 1.4 | 1.3 | Current | | | | | 1.5 | 1.1 |
| | .8 | | 1.0 | .8 | | | | | | 1.0 | .8 |
| | 5.2 | | 2.9 | 2.5 | | | | | | 4.7 | 1.1 |
| | .9 | | 1.1 | 1.1 | Quick | | | | | 1.5 | .8 |
| | .6 | | .7 | .7 | | | | | | 1.0 | .4 |
| 12 | 31.4 | 1 | 506.3 | 2  148.8 | | | | | | 1  425.7 | 11  34.6 |
| 31 | 11.7 | 27 | 13.3 | 23  16.1 | Sales/Receivables | | | | | 15  24.3 | 35  10.3 |
| 51 | 7.1 | 57 | 6.4 | 54  6.7 | | | | | | 57  6.4 | 56  6.5 |
| | | | | | Cost of Sales/Inventory | | | | | | |
| | | | | | Cost of Sales/Payables | | | | | | |
| | 10.5 | | 4.9 | 5.5 | | | | | | 3.5 | 10.7 |
| | 49.6 | | 15.1 | 17.5 | Sales/Working Capital | | | | | 10.4 | 54.4 |
| | -30.3 | | 251.9 | -33.2 | | | | | | 334.8 | -10.7 |
| | 12.3 | | 30.9 | 49.3 | | | | | | | 5.4 |
| (17) | 2.0 | (30) | 6.6 | (33)  5.2 | EBIT/Interest | | | | | (16) | 1.7 |
| | -1.4 | | .3 | 1.4 | | | | | | | .0 |
| | | | | | Net Profit + Depr., Dep., Amort./Cur. Mat. L/T/D | | | | | | |
| | .1 | | .0 | .0 | | | | | | .0 | .0 |
| | .5 | | .3 | .2 | Fixed/Worth | | | | | .3 | .5 |
| | -.1 | | 3.3 | 1.7 | | | | | | 1.1 | -.4 |
| | .5 | | .6 | 1.1 | | | | | | .4 | 1.8 |
| | 9.1 | | 2.0 | 3.3 | Debt/Worth | | | | | 1.3 | 7.9 |
| | -1.9 | | 25.8 | -27.8 | | | | | | 3.7 | -6.6 |
| | 125.0 | | 82.8 | 113.3 | % Profit Before Taxes/Tangible Net Worth | | | | | | 127.5 |
| (17) | 27.5 | (42) | 27.4 | (38)  40.4 | | | | | | (14) | 34.4 |
| | 15.5 | | 5.7 | 8.5 | | | | | | | 5.3 |
| | 22.3 | | 21.0 | 33.1 | % Profit Before Taxes/Total Assets | | | | | 68.6 | 14.4 |
| | 9.4 | | 6.0 | 6.6 | | | | | | 18.0 | 1.3 |
| | -1.6 | | 1.5 | .5 | | | | | | 2.5 | -.5 |
| | 239.7 | | 467.7 | 882.5 | | | | | | 120.1 | 489.3 |
| | 63.5 | | 70.6 | 102.9 | Sales/Net Fixed Assets | | | | | 27.7 | 49.5 |
| | 27.5 | | 16.6 | 16.5 | | | | | | 8.8 | 15.6 |
| | 3.8 | | 3.6 | 3.6 | | | | | | 5.0 | 2.5 |
| | 1.2 | | 2.4 | 2.1 | Sales/Total Assets | | | | | 2.8 | 1.3 |
| | .7 | | .8 | .9 | | | | | | 2.2 | .9 |
| | | | .3 | .5 | | | | | | | |
| | | (24) | .7 | (22)  1.9 | % Depr., Dep., Amort./Sales | | | | | | |
| | | | | 3.5 | | | | | | | |
| | | | | | % Officers', Directors' Owners' Comp/Sales | | | | | | |
| | 1593306M | | 4497100M | 2737916M | Net Sales ($) | 1859M | 3808M | 24028M | 43707M | 167045M | 2497469M |
| | 1257078M | | 2455878M | 1774526M | Total Assets ($) | 16805M | 1327M | 22467M | 18272M | 65311M | 1650344M |

M = $ thousand    MM = $ million
See Pages viii through xx for Explanation of Ratios and Data

© RMA 2024

# FINANCE—All Other Insurance Related Activities  NAICS 524298

## Current Data Sorted by Assets | Comparative Historical Data

| | | | | | | | Type of Statement | | |
|---|---|---|---|---|---|---|---|---|---|
| | | | 1 | | | 7 | Unqualified | 12 | 7 |
| | | | 5 | 1 | | | Reviewed | 3 | 1 |
| | | 1 | 2 | 1 | | | Compiled | 3 | 2 |
| 4 | 1 | 2 | 3 | | | | Tax Returns | 13 | 10 |
| 2 | 5 | 5 | 5 | | 7 | 6 | Other | 34 | 20 |
| | | 10 (4/1-9/30/23) | | 54 (10/1/23-3/31/24) | | | | 4/1/19-3/31/20 | 4/1/20-3/31/21 |
| 0-500M | 500M-2MM | 2-10MM | 10-50MM | 50-100MM | 100-250MM | | | ALL | ALL |
| 6 | 6 | 11 | 19 | 9 | 13 | | NUMBER OF STATEMENTS | 65 | 40 |
| % | % | % | % | % | % | | ASSETS | % | % |
| | | 50.9 | 25.9 | | 19.6 | | Cash & Equivalents | 30.7 | 52.1 |
| | | 20.5 | 27.7 | | 17.0 | | Trade Receivables (net) | 19.8 | 12.4 |
| | | .0 | .0 | | .0 | | Inventory | .1 | .0 |
| | | 3.1 | 10.6 | | 16.1 | | All Other Current | 5.7 | 5.5 |
| | | 74.5 | 64.2 | | 52.7 | | Total Current | 56.3 | 70.0 |
| | | 1.1 | 8.3 | | 8.6 | | Fixed Assets (net) | 10.1 | 7.8 |
| | | 4.8 | 14.0 | | 18.3 | | Intangibles (net) | 11.8 | 13.2 |
| | | 19.6 | 13.5 | | 20.4 | | All Other Non-Current | 21.8 | 9.0 |
| | | 100.0 | 100.0 | | 100.0 | | Total | 100.0 | 100.0 |
| | | | | | | | LIABILITIES | | |
| | | 15.1 | 5.5 | | .0 | | Notes Payable-Short Term | 8.1 | 6.9 |
| | | .0 | .8 | | .8 | | Cur. Mat.-L.T.D. | 3.6 | 3.9 |
| | | 9.8 | 13.2 | | 17.9 | | Trade Payables | 10.3 | 3.8 |
| | | .0 | .4 | | 5.0 | | Income Taxes Payable | .0 | .0 |
| | | 26.5 | 20.9 | | 52.8 | | All Other Current | 33.7 | 24.0 |
| | | 51.4 | 40.8 | | 76.6 | | Total Current | 55.7 | 38.6 |
| | | 2.8 | 13.8 | | 24.2 | | Long-Term Debt | 10.0 | 16.1 |
| | | .0 | .2 | | .0 | | Deferred Taxes | .2 | .0 |
| | | 4.4 | 6.0 | | 4.8 | | All Other Non-Current | 9.5 | 11.3 |
| | | 41.4 | 39.2 | | -5.6 | | Net Worth | 24.6 | 34.2 |
| | | 100.0 | 100.0 | | 100.0 | | Total Liabilities & Net Worth | 100.0 | 100.0 |
| | | | | | | | INCOME DATA | | |
| | | 100.0 | 100.0 | | 100.0 | | Net Sales | 100.0 | 100.0 |
| | | | | | | | Gross Profit | | |
| | | 92.6 | 82.5 | | 89.1 | | Operating Expenses | 83.5 | 82.7 |
| | | 7.4 | 17.5 | | 10.9 | | Operating Profit | 16.5 | 17.3 |
| | | -1.5 | 1.4 | | -.9 | | All Other Expenses (net) | .9 | -.6 |
| | | 8.9 | 16.1 | | 11.7 | | Profit Before Taxes | 15.6 | 17.8 |
| | | | | | | | RATIOS | | |
| | | 2.0 | 2.7 | | 1.0 | | | 3.1 | 4.8 |
| | | 1.4 | 1.6 | | .7 | | Current | 1.2 | 2.0 |
| | | 1.0 | 1.0 | | .5 | | | .7 | 1.2 |
| | | 2.0 | 2.2 | | .8 | | | 2.7 | 4.4 |
| | | 1.3 | 1.1 | | .4 | | Quick | 1.1 | 1.6 |
| | | 1.0 | .7 | | .3 | | | .5 | 1.1 |
| | | 11  33.9 | 23  15.7 | | 0  UND | | | 0  UND | 0  UND |
| | | 18  19.9 | 42  8.7 | | 29  12.6 | | Sales/Receivables | 20  18.5 | 9  40.1 |
| | | 38  9.6 | 72  5.1 | | 152  2.4 | | | 68  5.4 | 38  9.6 |
| | | | | | | | Cost of Sales/Inventory | | |
| | | | | | | | Cost of Sales/Payables | | |
| | | 3.0 | 3.0 | | -27.0 | | | 4.3 | 4.1 |
| | | 9.3 | 17.3 | | -2.2 | | Sales/Working Capital | 13.2 | 10.7 |
| | | 29.6 | -219.3 | | -1.5 | | | -17.4 | 28.0 |
| | | | 31.6 | | 17.7 | | | 64.4 | 163.3 |
| | | (11) | 22.0 | | (12)  4.3 | | EBIT/Interest | (42)  26.9 | (23)  80.7 |
| | | | 2.7 | | 2.4 | | | 1.6 | 1.4 |
| | | | | | | | Net Profit + Depr., Dep., Amort./Cur. Mat. L/T/D | | |
| | | .0 | .0 | | 1.5 | | | .0 | .0 |
| | | .0 | .4 | | -1.9 | | Fixed/Worth | .1 | .1 |
| | | .0 | 26.4 | | .0 | | | 1.5 | NM |
| | | .7 | .5 | | NM | | | .5 | .6 |
| | | 1.6 | 7.6 | | -8.9 | | Debt/Worth | 2.5 | 3.7 |
| | | 4.3 | 196.1 | | -2.2 | | | -21.6 | -8.5 |
| | | 100.0 | 316.8 | | | | | 143.5 | 669.5 |
| | | 38.3 | (16)  52.5 | | | | % Profit Before Taxes/Tangible Net Worth | (47)  36.1 | (29)  141.2 |
| | | -5.2 | 14.4 | | | | | 9.3 | 36.6 |
| | | 20.3 | 23.6 | | 12.0 | | | 43.8 | 93.7 |
| | | 15.7 | 12.0 | | 5.5 | | % Profit Before Taxes/Total Assets | 10.7 | 35.9 |
| | | -2.0 | 3.4 | | 2.0 | | | .5 | 5.5 |
| | | UND | 384.2 | | 150.1 | | | 310.3 | 964.3 |
| | | 892.5 | 29.3 | | 71.7 | | Sales/Net Fixed Assets | 55.3 | 95.2 |
| | | 85.4 | 16.5 | | 11.9 | | | 23.0 | 25.3 |
| | | 5.2 | 2.4 | | 1.3 | | | 4.0 | 11.2 |
| | | 2.5 | 1.6 | | .7 | | Sales/Total Assets | 1.1 | 2.3 |
| | | .5 | .6 | | .5 | | | .4 | .8 |
| | | | .6 | | | | | .4 | .4 |
| | | | (12)  1.3 | | | | % Depr., Dep., Amort./Sales | (29)  1.1 | (13)  .9 |
| | | | 4.1 | | | | | 1.6 | 2.3 |
| | | | | | | | | 3.4 | 4.5 |
| | | | | | | | % Officers', Directors' Owners' Comp/Sales | (14)  5.5 | (12)  11.7 |
| | | | | | | | | 20.7 | 20.8 |
| 9584M | 26111M | 117292M | 664286M | 630601M | 2447271M | | Net Sales ($) | 2125787M | 1215991M |
| 1031M | 8618M | 46333M | 417479M | 627202M | 2203745M | | Total Assets ($) | 1928819M | 900221M |

M = $ thousand    MM = $ million
See Pages viii through xx for Explanation of Ratios and Data

© RMA 2024

# FINANCE—All Other Insurance Related Activities  NAICS 524298

## Comparative Historical Data | Current Data Sorted by Sales

| | | | | | Type of Statement | | | | | | |
|---|---|---|---|---|---|---|---|---|---|---|---|
| | 7 | | 7 | 14 | Unqualified | | | | 1 | 1 | 12 |
| | 2 | | 3 | 1 | Reviewed | | | | | | 1 |
| | 2 | | 4 | 4 | Compiled | | | 2 | | | 2 |
| | 5 | | 8 | 8 | Tax Returns | 2 | 3 | 1 | 1 | 1 | |
| | 21 | | 28 | 37 | Other | 3 | 4 | 3 | 5 | 5 | 19 |
| | 4/1/21-3/31/22 ALL | | 4/1/22-3/31/23 ALL | 4/1/23-3/31/24 ALL | | 0-1MM | 10 (4/1-9/30/23) 1-3MM | 3-5MM | 54 (10/1/23-3/31/24) 5-10MM | 10-25MM | 25MM & OVER |
| | 37 | | 50 | 64 | NUMBER OF STATEMENTS | 5 | 7 | 4 | 7 | 7 | 34 |
| | % | | % | % | ASSETS | % | % | % | % | % | % |
| | 37.2 | | 30.8 | 32.5 | Cash & Equivalents | | | | | | 22.9 |
| | 17.4 | | 16.7 | 20.3 | Trade Receivables (net) | | | | | | 22.7 |
| | 2.7 | | 1.5 | .8 | Inventory | | | | | | 1.4 |
| | 5.3 | | 4.7 | 7.4 | All Other Current | | | | | | 12.3 |
| | 62.6 | | 53.7 | 61.0 | Total Current | | | | | | 59.3 |
| | 4.3 | | 10.8 | 7.3 | Fixed Assets (net) | | | | | | 8.2 |
| | 19.3 | | 14.1 | 15.1 | Intangibles (net) | | | | | | 14.4 |
| | 13.8 | | 21.4 | 16.5 | All Other Non-Current | | | | | | 18.0 |
| | 100.0 | | 100.0 | 100.0 | Total | | | | | | 100.0 |
| | | | | | LIABILITIES | | | | | | |
| | 6.8 | | 7.4 | 16.1 | Notes Payable-Short Term | | | | | | 2.3 |
| | 8.7 | | 2.4 | .8 | Cur. Mat.-L.T.D. | | | | | | 1.2 |
| | 4.6 | | 5.5 | 13.5 | Trade Payables | | | | | | 14.9 |
| | .1 | | .1 | 1.1 | Income Taxes Payable | | | | | | 2.1 |
| | 28.5 | | 24.6 | 24.9 | All Other Current | | | | | | 35.4 |
| | 48.7 | | 40.0 | 56.3 | Total Current | | | | | | 55.8 |
| | 16.0 | | 16.3 | 15.7 | Long-Term Debt | | | | | | 18.4 |
| | .1 | | .0 | .1 | Deferred Taxes | | | | | | .1 |
| | 3.8 | | 6.7 | 4.6 | All Other Non-Current | | | | | | 4.3 |
| | 31.3 | | 37.0 | 23.3 | Net Worth | | | | | | 21.4 |
| | 100.0 | | 100.0 | 100.0 | Total Liabilities & Net Worth | | | | | | 100.0 |
| | | | | | INCOME DATA | | | | | | |
| | 100.0 | | 100.0 | 100.0 | Net Sales | | | | | | 100.0 |
| | 84.6 | | 83.6 | 86.4 | Gross Profit | | | | | | 87.7 |
| | 15.4 | | 16.4 | 13.6 | Operating Expenses | | | | | | 12.3 |
| | -.5 | | 3.7 | 2.1 | Operating Profit | | | | | | 1.5 |
| | 15.8 | | 12.7 | 11.5 | All Other Expenses (net) | | | | | | 10.8 |
| | | | | | Profit Before Taxes | | | | | | |
| | | | | | RATIOS | | | | | | |
| | 2.7 | | 2.4 | 2.2 | | | | | | | 2.0 |
| | 1.5 | | 1.3 | 1.2 | Current | | | | | | 1.0 |
| | .7 | | .7 | .8 | | | | | | | .7 |
| | 2.7 | | 2.1 | 1.9 | | | | | | | 1.6 |
| | 1.1 | | 1.1 | 1.2 | Quick | | | | | | .8 |
| | .6 | | .6 | .5 | | | | | | | .4 |
| 0 | UND | 0 | UND | 2 224.6 | | | | | | 21 | 17.4 |
| 33 | 11.0 | 4 | 93.4 | 31 11.8 | Sales/Receivables | | | | | 40 | 9.1 |
| 83 | 4.4 | 45 | 8.2 | 73 5.0 | | | | | | 73 | 5.0 |
| | | | | | Cost of Sales/Inventory | | | | | | |
| | | | | | Cost of Sales/Payables | | | | | | |
| | 2.1 | | 4.6 | 3.3 | | | | | | | 5.6 |
| | 13.5 | | 14.8 | 26.3 | Sales/Working Capital | | | | | | -227.6 |
| | -13.1 | | -23.0 | -20.6 | | | | | | | -5.3 |
| | 39.3 | | 43.7 | 30.2 | | | | | | | 30.5 |
| (24) | 8.2 | (33) | 8.4 | (40) 5.6 | EBIT/Interest | | | | | (26) | 9.8 |
| | 2.9 | | 1.8 | 2.1 | | | | | | | 2.9 |
| | | | | | Net Profit + Depr., Dep., Amort./Cur. Mat. L/T/D | | | | | | |
| | .0 | | .0 | .0 | | | | | | | .0 |
| | .2 | | .1 | .1 | Fixed/Worth | | | | | | 1.5 |
| | -.3 | | 1.7 | -3.9 | | | | | | | -.3 |
| | .6 | | .8 | 1.0 | | | | | | | 1.3 |
| | 4.2 | | 1.4 | 3.6 | Debt/Worth | | | | | | 22.1 |
| | -4.4 | | NM | -18.1 | | | | | | | -3.4 |
| | 150.4 | | 120.2 | 117.6 | | | | | | | 251.8 |
| (24) | 35.5 | (38) | 14.9 | (45) 38.3 | % Profit Before Taxes/Tangible Net Worth | | | | | (20) | 52.5 |
| | 14.7 | | 1.0 | 4.6 | | | | | | | 9.6 |
| | 30.0 | | 27.2 | 20.0 | | | | | | | 20.1 |
| | 13.2 | | 9.9 | 6.8 | % Profit Before Taxes/Total Assets | | | | | | 8.2 |
| | 5.0 | | 1.4 | 1.6 | | | | | | | 2.1 |
| | UND | | UND | UND | | | | | | | 440.3 |
| | 106.3 | | 104.6 | 86.5 | Sales/Net Fixed Assets | | | | | | 79.0 |
| | 27.8 | | 24.0 | 20.9 | | | | | | | 15.7 |
| | 2.4 | | 4.3 | 3.6 | | | | | | | 2.4 |
| | .9 | | 1.3 | 1.4 | Sales/Total Assets | | | | | | 1.4 |
| | .4 | | .4 | .5 | | | | | | | .6 |
| | .3 | | .3 | .6 | | | | | | | .6 |
| (13) | .5 | (22) | .6 | (25) .9 | % Depr., Dep., Amort./Sales | | | | | (18) | .9 |
| | 2.1 | | 2.5 | 2.7 | | | | | | | 2.0 |
| | | | 4.1 | 1.1 | % Officers', Directors' Owners' Comp/Sales | | | | | | |
| | | (14) | 7.8 | (12) 5.3 | | | | | | | |
| | | | 13.8 | 14.3 | | | | | | | |
| | 1313291M | | 1513915M | 3895145M | Net Sales ($) | 3041M | 13627M | 16139M | 55796M | 103942M | 3702600M |
| | 994821M | | 1121347M | 3304408M | Total Assets ($) | 1350M | 24631M | 48204M | 107681M | 203186M | 2919356M |

M = $ thousand   MM = $ million
See Pages viii through xx for Explanation of Ratios and Data

© RMA 2024

# FINANCE—Open-End Investment Funds  NAICS 525910

## Current Data Sorted by Assets

| 0-500M | 5 (4/1-9/30/23) 500M-2MM | 2-10MM | 24 (10/1/23-3/31/24) 10-50MM | 50-100MM | 100-250MM | Type of Statement | Comparative Historical Data | |
|---|---|---|---|---|---|---|---|---|
| | | | 6 | 4 | 3 | Unqualified | 5 | 3 |
| | | | 1 | | | Reviewed | | |
| | | 5 | 5 | 2 | 3 | Compiled | 2 | 1 |
| | | | | | | Tax Returns | 2 | |
| | | | | | | Other | 20 | 25 |
| | | | | | | | 4/1/19- | 4/1/20- |
| | | | | | | | 3/31/20 | 3/31/21 |
| | | 5 | 12 | 6 | 6 | NUMBER OF STATEMENTS | ALL 29 | ALL 29 |
| % | % | % | % | % | % | **ASSETS** | % | % |
| D | D | | 28.8 | | | Cash & Equivalents | 20.7 | 16.1 |
| A | A | | 6.0 | | | Trade Receivables (net) | 8.9 | 12.9 |
| T | T | | .0 | | | Inventory | 3.5 | 2.6 |
| A | A | | 2.4 | | | All Other Current | 5.1 | 6.5 |
| | | | 37.2 | | | Total Current | 38.2 | 38.2 |
| N | N | | 11.3 | | | Fixed Assets (net) | 13.9 | 11.6 |
| O | O | | 13.6 | | | Intangibles (net) | 10.2 | 2.7 |
| T | T | | 38.0 | | | All Other Non-Current | 37.7 | 47.5 |
| | | | 100.0 | | | Total | 100.0 | 100.0 |
| A | A | | | | | **LIABILITIES** | | |
| V | V | | 1.6 | | | Notes Payable-Short Term | 7.5 | 9.6 |
| A | A | | 2.0 | | | Cur. Mat.-L.T.D. | .3 | .4 |
| I | I | | 2.3 | | | Trade Payables | 2.0 | 4.8 |
| L | L | | .0 | | | Income Taxes Payable | .0 | .1 |
| A | A | | 12.2 | | | All Other Current | 17.9 | 8.6 |
| B | B | | 18.2 | | | Total Current | 27.8 | 23.5 |
| L | L | | 15.4 | | | Long-Term Debt | 18.5 | 19.9 |
| E | E | | .0 | | | Deferred Taxes | .0 | .7 |
| | | | 3.7 | | | All Other Non-Current | 6.0 | 5.7 |
| | | | 62.7 | | | Net Worth | 47.7 | 50.2 |
| | | | 100.0 | | | Total Liabilities & Net Worth | 100.0 | 100.0 |
| | | | | | | **INCOME DATA** | | |
| | | | 100.0 | | | Net Sales | 100.0 | 100.0 |
| | | | | | | Gross Profit | | |
| | | | 57.9 | | | Operating Expenses | 65.2 | 60.6 |
| | | | 42.1 | | | Operating Profit | 34.8 | 39.4 |
| | | | 19.2 | | | All Other Expenses (net) | 12.1 | 10.2 |
| | | | 22.9 | | | Profit Before Taxes | 22.7 | 29.2 |
| | | | | | | **RATIOS** | | |
| | | | 9.0 | | | | 9.4 | 8.8 |
| | | | 2.4 | | | Current | 2.0 | 1.3 |
| | | | .9 | | | | .3 | .9 |
| | | | 3.2 | | | | 4.4 | 8.7 |
| | | | 2.0 | | | Quick | 1.2 | .9 |
| | | | .8 | | | | .3 | .5 |
| | | | 0 UND | | | | 0 UND | 0 UND |
| | | | 17 22.0 | | | Sales/Receivables | 0 UND | 0 UND |
| | | | 49 7.5 | | | | 13 28.1 | 21 17.7 |
| | | | | | | Cost of Sales/Inventory | | |
| | | | | | | Cost of Sales/Payables | | |
| | | | 1.5 | | | | 1.7 | 1.4 |
| | | | 4.3 | | | Sales/Working Capital | 8.9 | 15.0 |
| | | | -40.4 | | | | -5.1 | -105.9 |
| | | | | | | | 78.0 | 14.2 |
| | | | | | | EBIT/Interest | (15) 4.7 | (17) 2.9 |
| | | | | | | | .8 | -1.9 |
| | | | | | | Net Profit + Depr., Dep., Amort./Cur. Mat. L/T/D | | |
| | | | .0 | | | | .0 | .0 |
| | | | .0 | | | Fixed/Worth | .0 | .0 |
| | | | .7 | | | | .5 | .7 |
| | | | .0 | | | | .2 | .2 |
| | | | .2 | | | Debt/Worth | .9 | .5 |
| | | | 8.8 | | | | 11.5 | 8.4 |
| | | | 57.8 | | | | 40.0 | 22.7 |
| | | | (10) 6.6 | | | % Profit Before Taxes/Tangible Net Worth | (23) 7.5 | (24) 7.9 |
| | | | .9 | | | | -10.1 | .4 |
| | | | 7.0 | | | | 21.1 | 13.5 |
| | | | 6.0 | | | % Profit Before Taxes/Total Assets | 1.4 | 5.0 |
| | | | 1.4 | | | | -1.4 | -.3 |
| | | | UND | | | | UND | UND |
| | | | 382.1 | | | Sales/Net Fixed Assets | 136.4 | 291.7 |
| | | | 10.6 | | | | 22.3 | 14.9 |
| | | | 1.3 | | | | 1.8 | 1.8 |
| | | | .2 | | | Sales/Total Assets | .3 | .2 |
| | | | .1 | | | | .1 | .1 |
| | | | | | | | .2 | .3 |
| | | | | | | % Depr., Dep., Amort./Sales | (15) .4 | (11) .8 |
| | | | | | | | 4.2 | 7.9 |
| | | | | | | % Officers', Directors' Owners' Comp/Sales | | |
| | | 35123M | 144177M | 28084M | 369245M | Net Sales ($) | 909823M | 308013M |
| | | 22138M | 276717M | 517899M | 1097870M | Total Assets ($) | 1188996M | 1387841M |

M = $ thousand    MM = $ million
See Pages viii through xx for Explanation of Ratios and Data

© RMA 2024

# FINANCE—Open-End Investment Funds  NAICS 525910

| Comparative Historical Data | | | | Current Data Sorted by Sales | | | | | |
|---|---|---|---|---|---|---|---|---|---|
| 2 | 7 | 13 | **Type of Statement** <br> Unqualified <br> Reviewed <br> Compiled <br> Tax Returns <br> Other | 2 | 2 | 4 | 2 | 2 | 1 |
| 1 | 2 <br> 1 | 1 | | | | | | | |
| 14 <br> 4/1/21- <br> 3/31/22 <br> ALL | 18 <br> 4/1/22- <br> 3/31/23 <br> ALL | 15 <br> 4/1/23- <br> 3/31/24 <br> ALL | | | 1 <br> 1 <br> 5 (4/1-9/30/23) | 2 | 5 <br> 24 (10/1/23-3/31/24) | 2 | 5 |
| | | | | 0-1MM | 1-3MM | 3-5MM | 5-10MM | 10-25MM | 25MM & OVER |
| 17 | 28 | 29 | **NUMBER OF STATEMENTS** | 2 | 4 | 6 | 7 | 4 | 6 |
| % | % | % | **ASSETS** | % | % | % | % | % | % |
| 19.2 | 22.9 | 35.5 | Cash & Equivalents | | | | | | |
| 15.7 | 6.9 | 6.6 | Trade Receivables (net) | | | | | | |
| 2.0 | .0 | .0 | Inventory | | | | | | |
| 8.6 | 15.9 | 2.1 | All Other Current | | | | | | |
| 45.5 | 45.8 | 44.2 | Total Current | | | | | | |
| 18.7 | 14.2 | 11.6 | Fixed Assets (net) | | | | | | |
| 2.7 | 6.6 | 6.8 | Intangibles (net) | | | | | | |
| 33.1 | 33.4 | 37.4 | All Other Non-Current | | | | | | |
| 100.0 | 100.0 | 100.0 | Total | | | | | | |
| | | | **LIABILITIES** | | | | | | |
| 3.8 | 7.6 | 5.0 | Notes Payable-Short Term | | | | | | |
| .9 | 1.5 | 1.6 | Cur. Mat.-L.T.D. | | | | | | |
| 1.4 | .9 | 2.6 | Trade Payables | | | | | | |
| .0 | 15.8 | .0 | Income Taxes Payable | | | | | | |
| 10.1 | 6.7 | 7.3 | All Other Current | | | | | | |
| 16.2 | 32.5 | 16.6 | Total Current | | | | | | |
| 20.2 | 20.6 | 16.7 | Long-Term Debt | | | | | | |
| .0 | .3 | .0 | Deferred Taxes | | | | | | |
| 6.9 | 4.8 | 3.3 | All Other Non-Current | | | | | | |
| 56.7 | 41.7 | 63.4 | Net Worth | | | | | | |
| 100.0 | 100.0 | 100.0 | Total Liabilties & Net Worth | | | | | | |
| | | | **INCOME DATA** | | | | | | |
| 100.0 | 100.0 | 100.0 | Net Sales | | | | | | |
| | | | Gross Profit | | | | | | |
| 45.8 | 52.4 | 56.9 | Operating Expenses | | | | | | |
| 54.2 | 47.6 | 43.1 | Operating Profit | | | | | | |
| 5.7 | 7.7 | 15.1 | All Other Expenses (net) | | | | | | |
| 48.5 | 39.9 | 28.1 | Profit Before Taxes | | | | | | |
| | | | **RATIOS** | | | | | | |
| 18.5 | 12.0 | 44.2 | | | | | | | |
| 2.9 | 2.9 | 2.3 | Current | | | | | | |
| 1.0 | 1.2 | .6 | | | | | | | |
| 8.5 | 9.9 | 44.2 | | | | | | | |
| 2.6 | 2.5 | 2.0 | Quick | | | | | | |
| .9 | .3 | .4 | | | | | | | |
| 0 UND | 0 UND | 0 UND | | | | | | | |
| 3  130.5 | 0  999.8 | 6  61.9 | Sales/Receivables | | | | | | |
| 72  5.1 | 40  9.2 | 62  5.9 | | | | | | | |
| | | | Cost of Sales/Inventory | | | | | | |
| | | | Cost of Sales/Payables | | | | | | |
| .7 | .5 | .2 | | | | | | | |
| 2.1 | 5.3 | 4.2 | Sales/Working Capital | | | | | | |
| NM | 16.0 | -9.1 | | | | | | | |
| | | 163.2 | | | | | | | |
| | 94.9 | 5.5 | EBIT/Interest | | | | | | |
| (11) 9.9 | (15) | 1.9 | | | | | | | |
| | 3.0 | | | | | | | | |
| | | | Net Profit + Depr., Dep., <br> Amort./Cur. Mat. L/T/D | | | | | | |
| .0 | .0 | .0 | | | | | | | |
| .2 | .0 | .0 | Fixed/Worth | | | | | | |
| .9 | .5 | .4 | | | | | | | |
| .1 | .1 | .0 | | | | | | | |
| .3 | .9 | .2 | Debt/Worth | | | | | | |
| 3.4 | 6.0 | 3.0 | | | | | | | |
| 24.9 | 123.0 | 45.9 | | | | | | | |
| (15) 13.3 | (24) 6.9 | (25) 5.8 | % Profit Before Taxes/Tangible <br> Net Worth | | | | | | |
| 5.2 | 2.5 | 2.4 | | | | | | | |
| 24.8 | 24.3 | 8.5 | | | | | | | |
| 12.1 | 4.2 | 5.3 | % Profit Before Taxes/Total <br> Assets | | | | | | |
| 4.5 | 1.9 | 1.7 | | | | | | | |
| UND | UND | UND | | | | | | | |
| 43.6 | UND | UND | Sales/Net Fixed Assets | | | | | | |
| 1.7 | 32.8 | 7.3 | | | | | | | |
| .9 | .8 | 1.5 | | | | | | | |
| .2 | .1 | .1 | Sales/Total Assets | | | | | | |
| .1 | .1 | .1 | | | | | | | |
| | | | % Depr., Dep., Amort./Sales | | | | | | |
| | | | % Officers', Directors' <br> Owners' Comp/Sales | | | | | | |
| 361467M | 298000M | 576629M | Net Sales ($) | 1420M | 6136M | 23011M | 52881M | 60631M | 432550M |
| 1229871M | 1815190M | 1914624M | Total Assets ($) | 101817M | 60056M | 343429M | 332534M | 629528M | 447260M |

© RMA 2024  M = $ thousand  MM = $ million
See Pages viii through xx for Explanation of Ratios and Data

# FINANCE—Trusts, Estates, and Agency Accounts  NAICS 525920

## Current Data Sorted by Assets | Comparative Historical Data

| | | | | | | Type of Statement | | |
|---|---|---|---|---|---|---|---|---|
| | | | | | | Unqualified | | |
| | | | | 1 | | Reviewed | 1 | |
| | | | 1 | 1 | | Compiled | 2 | 2 |
| | | | 3 | 1 | 1 | Tax Returns | 1 | 3 |
| 1 | 1 | 1 | 8 | 1 | | Other | 10 | 6 |
| | 0 (4/1-9/30/23) | | 21 (10/1/23-3/31/24) | | | | 4/1/19-3/31/20 | 4/1/20-3/31/21 |
| 0-500M | 500M-2MM | 2-10MM | 10-50MM | 50-100MM | 100-250MM | | ALL | ALL |
| 1 | 1 | 5 | 10 | 3 | 1 | NUMBER OF STATEMENTS | 14 | 11 |
| % | % | % | % | % | % | ASSETS | % | % |
| | | | 25.1 | | | Cash & Equivalents | 11.9 | 6.1 |
| | | | 9.1 | | | Trade Receivables (net) | 4.8 | .7 |
| | | | 12.2 | | | Inventory | .4 | 8.2 |
| | | | 6.4 | | | All Other Current | 14.3 | 2.5 |
| | | | 52.8 | | | Total Current | 31.5 | 17.5 |
| | | | 31.7 | | | Fixed Assets (net) | 52.8 | 42.0 |
| | | | .6 | | | Intangibles (net) | 1.6 | 1.6 |
| | | | 14.9 | | | All Other Non-Current | 14.1 | 39.0 |
| | | | 100.0 | | | Total | 100.0 | 100.0 |
| | | | | | | LIABILITIES | | |
| | | | 15.2 | | | Notes Payable-Short Term | 1.0 | 10.0 |
| | | | 1.5 | | | Cur. Mat.-L.T.D. | 2.3 | .1 |
| | | | 3.3 | | | Trade Payables | 2.0 | .4 |
| | | | .1 | | | Income Taxes Payable | .0 | .1 |
| | | | 9.7 | | | All Other Current | 11.0 | 1.4 |
| | | | 29.6 | | | Total Current | 16.2 | 12.0 |
| | | | 10.0 | | | Long-Term Debt | 35.4 | 27.5 |
| | | | .0 | | | Deferred Taxes | .0 | .0 |
| | | | 21.4 | | | All Other Non-Current | 4.8 | 7.6 |
| | | | 39.0 | | | Net Worth | 43.5 | 52.8 |
| | | | 100.0 | | | Total Liabilities & Net Worth | 100.0 | 100.0 |
| | | | | | | INCOME DATA | | |
| | | | 100.0 | | | Net Sales | 100.0 | 100.0 |
| | | | | | | Gross Profit | | |
| | | | 56.7 | | | Operating Expenses | 58.7 | 48.6 |
| | | | 43.3 | | | Operating Profit | 41.3 | 51.4 |
| | | | 4.2 | | | All Other Expenses (net) | 20.4 | 6.8 |
| | | | 39.1 | | | Profit Before Taxes | 20.9 | 44.6 |
| | | | | | | RATIOS | | |
| | | | 4.6 | | | | 5.7 | 4.4 |
| | | | 1.4 | | | Current | 1.9 | 2.0 |
| | | | 1.1 | | | | .5 | .2 |
| | | | 4.5 | | | | 3.5 | 3.4 |
| | | | 1.2 | | | Quick | .8 | .9 |
| | | | .2 | | | | .2 | .1 |
| | | 0 | UND | | | | 0 UND | 0 UND |
| | | 0 | UND | | | Sales/Receivables | 0 UND | 0 UND |
| | | 0 | UND | | | | 7 55.2 | 0 UND |
| | | | | | | Cost of Sales/Inventory | | |
| | | | | | | Cost of Sales/Payables | | |
| | | | 1.1 | | | | 2.3 | 1.9 |
| | | | 1.4 | | | Sales/Working Capital | 15.9 | 6.2 |
| | | | NM | | | | -16.0 | -.6 |
| | | | | | | EBIT/Interest | | |
| | | | | | | Net Profit + Depr., Dep., Amort./Cur. Mat. L/T/D | | |
| | | | .0 | | | | .1 | .0 |
| | | | .4 | | | Fixed/Worth | 1.5 | 1.0 |
| | | | 1.6 | | | | 2.8 | 2.2 |
| | | | .4 | | | | .1 | .1 |
| | | | .7 | | | Debt/Worth | 1.2 | .6 |
| | | | 4.9 | | | | 5.4 | 2.7 |
| | | | | | | % Profit Before Taxes/Tangible Net Worth | 15.8 | 15.4 |
| | | | | | | | (13) 3.5 | (10) 3.9 |
| | | | | | | | -1.2 | 1.4 |
| | | | 10.6 | | | | 6.5 | 7.5 |
| | | | 4.8 | | | % Profit Before Taxes/Total Assets | 1.7 | 2.2 |
| | | | 2.1 | | | | -2.9 | .2 |
| | | | UND | | | | UND | UND |
| | | | .9 | | | Sales/Net Fixed Assets | .4 | 1.1 |
| | | | .3 | | | | .1 | .2 |
| | | | .4 | | | | 5.4 | .2 |
| | | | .2 | | | Sales/Total Assets | .1 | .1 |
| | | | .1 | | | | .1 | .0 |
| | | | | | | % Depr., Dep., Amort./Sales | | |
| | | | | | | % Officers', Directors' Owners' Comp/Sales | | |
| 95M | 2075M | 8610M | 96404M | 92426M | 11776M | Net Sales ($) | 76343M | 63040M |
| 1M | 597M | 25013M | 268581M | 229194M | 105881M | Total Assets ($) | 642283M | 588821M |

M = $ thousand   MM = $ million
See Pages viii through xx for Explanation of Ratios and Data

© RMA 2024

# FINANCE—Trusts, Estates, and Agency Accounts  NAICS 525920

## Comparative Historical Data | Current Data Sorted by Sales

| Comparative Historical Data ||| Type of Statement | Current Data Sorted by Sales ||||||
|---|---|---|---|---|---|---|---|---|---|
| | 2 | | Unqualified | | | | 1 | 1 | |
| | 2 | 2 | Reviewed | | | | | | |
| 1 | | 1 | Compiled | | | | 1 | 1 | |
| 1 | 3 | 3 | Tax Returns | 2 | | | 2 | | |
| 5 | 14 | 15 | Other | 2 | 4 | 4 | 21 (10/1/23-3/31/24) | | 3 |
| 4/1/21-3/31/22 ALL | 4/1/22-3/31/23 ALL | 4/1/23-3/31/24 ALL | | 0 (4/1-9/30/23) |||||| 
| | | | | 0-1MM | 1-3MM | 3-5MM | 5-10MM | 10-25MM | 25MM & OVER |
| 7 | 21 | 21 | NUMBER OF STATEMENTS | 4 | 4 | 4 | 4 | | 3 |
| % | % | % | **ASSETS** | % | % | % | % | % | % |
| | 27.2 | 21.2 | Cash & Equivalents | | | | | | |
| | 2.5 | 7.7 | Trade Receivables (net) | | | | | | |
| | 2.3 | 5.8 | Inventory | | | | | | |
| | 4.7 | 4.3 | All Other Current | | | | | | |
| | 36.7 | 38.9 | Total Current | | | | | | |
| | 38.4 | 32.9 | Fixed Assets (net) | | | | | | |
| | .9 | 4.2 | Intangibles (net) | | | | | | |
| | 24.0 | 23.9 | All Other Non-Current | | | | | | |
| | 100.0 | 100.0 | Total | | | | | | |
| | | | **LIABILITIES** | | | | | | |
| | 6.1 | 7.2 | Notes Payable-Short Term | | | | | | |
| | 4.2 | 2.1 | Cur. Mat.-L.T.D. | | | | | | |
| | 1.8 | 2.1 | Trade Payables | | | | | | |
| | .0 | .2 | Income Taxes Payable | | | | | | |
| | 2.9 | 19.2 | All Other Current | | | | | | |
| | 15.0 | 30.9 | Total Current | | | | | | |
| | 32.5 | 26.3 | Long-Term Debt | | | | | | |
| | .0 | .0 | Deferred Taxes | | | | | | |
| | 2.1 | 11.3 | All Other Non-Current | | | | | | |
| | 50.4 | 31.5 | Net Worth | | | | | | |
| | 100.0 | 100.0 | Total Liabilities & Net Worth | | | | | | |
| | | | **INCOME DATA** | | | | | | |
| | 100.0 | 100.0 | Net Sales | | | | | | |
| | | | Gross Profit | | | | | | |
| | 60.2 | 55.3 | Operating Expenses | | | | | | |
| | 39.8 | 44.7 | Operating Profit | | | | | | |
| | 6.8 | 11.4 | All Other Expenses (net) | | | | | | |
| | 33.0 | 33.3 | Profit Before Taxes | | | | | | |
| | | | **RATIOS** | | | | | | |
| | 9.8 | 3.3 | | | | | | | |
| | 4.0 | 1.3 | Current | | | | | | |
| | 1.8 | .9 | | | | | | | |
| | 9.8 | 2.9 | | | | | | | |
| | 3.0 | 1.2 | Quick | | | | | | |
| | .7 | .4 | | | | | | | |
| 0 | UND | 0 | UND | | | | | | |
| 0 | UND | 0 | UND Sales/Receivables | | | | | | |
| 16 | 23.4 | 24 | 15.2 | | | | | | |
| | | | Cost of Sales/Inventory | | | | | | |
| | | | Cost of Sales/Payables | | | | | | |
| | .8 | 1.2 | | | | | | | |
| | 4.5 | 4.6 | Sales/Working Capital | | | | | | |
| | 14.9 | -54.8 | | | | | | | |
| | 13.4 | | | | | | | | |
| (11) | 7.9 | | EBIT/Interest | | | | | | |
| | 2.2 | | | | | | | | |
| | | | Net Profit + Depr., Dep., Amort./Cur. Mat. L/T/D | | | | | | |
| | .0 | .0 | | | | | | | |
| | .5 | .7 | Fixed/Worth | | | | | | |
| | 2.4 | 4.6 | | | | | | | |
| | .1 | .4 | | | | | | | |
| | .4 | 3.0 | Debt/Worth | | | | | | |
| | 3.5 | 14.3 | | | | | | | |
| | 15.0 | 26.8 | % Profit Before Taxes/Tangible Net Worth | | | | | | |
| (19) | 5.0 | (18) | 7.9 | | | | | | |
| | 2.8 | -2.5 | | | | | | | |
| | 13.5 | 12.6 | % Profit Before Taxes/Total Assets | | | | | | |
| | 2.9 | 4.2 | | | | | | | |
| | .7 | -.3 | | | | | | | |
| | UND | UND | | | | | | | |
| | 7.5 | 1.0 | Sales/Net Fixed Assets | | | | | | |
| | .1 | .2 | | | | | | | |
| | 1.7 | .9 | | | | | | | |
| | .1 | .2 | Sales/Total Assets | | | | | | |
| | .1 | .1 | | | | | | | |
| | | .4 | | | | | | | |
| (11) | 18.2 | | % Depr., Dep., Amort./Sales | | | | | | |
| | 35.8 | | | | | | | | |
| | | | % Officers', Directors' Owners' Comp/Sales | | | | | | |
| 27716M | 164898M | 211386M | Net Sales ($) | 1363M | 7650M | 17813M | 25570M | 11776M | 147214M |
| 210471M | 579668M | 629267M | Total Assets ($) | 12749M | 80543M | 139001M | 149637M | 105881M | 141456M |

© RMA 2024    M = $ thousand    MM = $ million
See Pages viii through xx for Explanation of Ratios and Data

## FINANCE—Other Financial Vehicles  NAICS 525990

### Current Data Sorted by Assets | Comparative Historical Data

| 0-500M | 500M-2MM | 2-10MM | 10-50MM | 50-100MM | 100-250MM | Type of Statement | 4/1/19-3/31/20 ALL | 4/1/20-3/31/21 ALL |
|---|---|---|---|---|---|---|---|---|
| | | 2 | 9 | 5 | 28 | Unqualified | 19 | 15 |
| | 1 | | | | | Reviewed | 1 | 1 |
| | 1 | 1 | | | 1 | Compiled | 4 | 1 |
| 3 | 5 | 2 | 1 | | | Tax Returns | 9 | 9 |
| 2 | 12 | 29 | 23 | 12 | 25 | Other | 42 | 47 |
| | 21 (4/1-9/30/23) | | 141 (10/1/23-3/31/24) | | | | | |
| 5 | 19 | 34 | 33 | 17 | 54 | **NUMBER OF STATEMENTS** | 75 | 73 |
| % | % | % | % | % | % | **ASSETS** | % | % |
| | 9.6 | 23.0 | 25.2 | 25.8 | 14.1 | Cash & Equivalents | 19.9 | 17.5 |
| | 15.3 | 10.5 | 13.8 | 15.0 | 13.1 | Trade Receivables (net) | 11.4 | 13.7 |
| | .0 | 5.9 | 4.1 | .6 | 1.5 | Inventory | 1.5 | 2.6 |
| | 15.4 | 16.6 | 9.2 | .7 | 5.8 | All Other Current | 10.1 | 5.6 |
| | 40.3 | 56.0 | 52.3 | 42.0 | 34.6 | Total Current | 42.9 | 39.5 |
| | 29.5 | 15.0 | 6.6 | 25.0 | 14.2 | Fixed Assets (net) | 17.5 | 23.1 |
| | 3.2 | 3.6 | 5.0 | 3.5 | 7.1 | Intangibles (net) | 6.0 | 4.0 |
| | 26.9 | 25.4 | 36.1 | 29.5 | 44.1 | All Other Non-Current | 33.7 | 33.5 |
| | 100.0 | 100.0 | 100.0 | 100.0 | 100.0 | Total | 100.0 | 100.0 |
| | | | | | | **LIABILITIES** | | |
| | 15.5 | 17.1 | 11.7 | 4.5 | 16.3 | Notes Payable-Short Term | 8.1 | 21.9 |
| | 2.7 | .5 | .8 | 5.5 | .8 | Cur. Mat.-L.T.D. | 2.5 | .8 |
| | 2.5 | 5.7 | 2.1 | .8 | 2.6 | Trade Payables | 2.5 | 1.2 |
| | .0 | .2 | .2 | .1 | .1 | Income Taxes Payable | .0 | .1 |
| | 9.3 | 23.8 | 12.7 | 11.5 | 7.2 | All Other Current | 9.5 | 9.8 |
| | 30.1 | 47.3 | 27.5 | 22.3 | 27.0 | Total Current | 22.6 | 33.8 |
| | 15.6 | 13.2 | 14.5 | 17.7 | 15.3 | Long-Term Debt | 17.1 | 26.6 |
| | .0 | .0 | .0 | .0 | .0 | Deferred Taxes | .1 | .0 |
| | 10.0 | .7 | 7.1 | 1.3 | 5.8 | All Other Non-Current | 6.6 | 3.2 |
| | 44.4 | 38.7 | 50.9 | 58.7 | 51.9 | Net Worth | 53.7 | 36.4 |
| | 100.0 | 100.0 | 100.0 | 100.0 | 100.0 | Total Liabilities & Net Worth | 100.0 | 100.0 |
| | | | | | | **INCOME DATA** | | |
| | 100.0 | 100.0 | 100.0 | 100.0 | 100.0 | Net Sales | 100.0 | 100.0 |
| | | | | | | Gross Profit | | |
| | 64.7 | 70.1 | 58.9 | 54.8 | 47.7 | Operating Expenses | 59.0 | 55.9 |
| | 35.3 | 29.9 | 41.1 | 45.2 | 52.3 | Operating Profit | 41.0 | 44.1 |
| | 7.3 | 7.8 | 13.8 | 21.1 | 23.0 | All Other Expenses (net) | 10.0 | 13.3 |
| | 28.0 | 22.1 | 27.4 | 24.0 | 29.3 | Profit Before Taxes | 31.0 | 30.7 |
| | | | | | | **RATIOS** | | |
| | 6.6 | 20.7 | 10.6 | 19.5 | 6.4 | | 7.9 | 6.9 |
| | 1.5 | 1.4 | 2.3 | 1.8 | 1.4 | Current | 2.7 | 1.6 |
| | .2 | .7 | 1.1 | 1.1 | .4 | | .6 | .6 |
| | 2.8 | 9.2 | 4.5 | 19.4 | 3.3 | | 3.9 | 6.0 |
| | .6 | 1.1 | 1.3 | 1.8 | 1.1 | Quick | 1.8 | 1.2 |
| | .1 | .2 | .4 | 1.0 | .2 | | .4 | .4 |
| | 0 UND | 0 UND | 0 UND | 0 UND | 0 UND | | 0 UND | 0 UND |
| | 0 UND | 1 293.4 | 4 96.6 | 0 UND | 2 159.9 | Sales/Receivables | 8 45.3 | 3 141.7 |
| | 43 8.4 | 34 10.7 | 42 8.6 | 46 7.9 | 59 6.2 | | 51 7.2 | 41 9.0 |
| | | | | | | Cost of Sales/Inventory | | |
| | | | | | | Cost of Sales/Payables | | |
| | 3.1 | 2.6 | .4 | .6 | .9 | | .3 | 1.1 |
| | 6.0 | 9.8 | 1.0 | 1.7 | 8.3 | Sales/Working Capital | 3.2 | 5.5 |
| | -3.1 | -9.0 | 97.5 | 17.8 | -1.5 | | -84.4 | -21.3 |
| | 6.3 | 253.6 | 203.8 | | 22.2 | | 25.0 | 17.2 |
| | (11) 3.4 | (22) 20.3 | (19) 20.6 | (24) 5.7 | | EBIT/Interest | (47) 6.2 | (46) 5.8 |
| | .9 | 2.1 | 2.3 | | 2.3 | | 2.2 | 1.9 |
| | | | | | | Net Profit + Depr., Dep., Amort./Cur. Mat. L/T/D | | |
| | .0 | .0 | .0 | .0 | .0 | | .0 | .0 |
| | .0 | .0 | .0 | .0 | .0 | Fixed/Worth | .0 | .0 |
| | 1.8 | .8 | .2 | 1.4 | .2 | | 1.2 | 1.4 |
| | .4 | .1 | .2 | .0 | .2 | | .2 | .4 |
| | .6 | 1.1 | .7 | 1.0 | 1.4 | Debt/Worth | .6 | 1.5 |
| | 2.3 | 9.8 | 1.8 | 3.7 | 6.7 | | 2.3 | 7.5 |
| | 38.6 | 94.6 | 38.9 | 16.0 | 18.8 | | 34.9 | 42.9 |
| | (17) 7.8 | (29) 46.3 | (28) 9.1 | 6.5 | (51) 7.4 | % Profit Before Taxes/Tangible Net Worth | (69) 8.8 | (63) 11.1 |
| | .9 | 8.6 | 1.4 | 1.5 | 2.8 | | 2.8 | 4.1 |
| | 9.7 | 43.4 | 22.7 | 3.7 | 6.3 | | 14.4 | 11.0 |
| | 6.8 | 9.0 | 4.4 | 2.1 | 3.2 | % Profit Before Taxes/Total Assets | 5.0 | 4.6 |
| | .2 | 1.5 | 1.1 | 1.1 | 1.0 | | 1.3 | 1.2 |
| | UND | UND | UND | UND | UND | | UND | UND |
| | 999.8 | 151.4 | UND | UND | UND | Sales/Net Fixed Assets | 89.0 | 293.6 |
| | 1.0 | 8.1 | 18.9 | .5 | 21.4 | | 6.9 | 4.3 |
| | 2.2 | 2.6 | 1.0 | .3 | .3 | | .9 | .7 |
| | .9 | 1.7 | .3 | .1 | .1 | Sales/Total Assets | .2 | .2 |
| | .1 | .2 | .1 | .1 | .1 | | .1 | .1 |
| | | .4 | .4 | | | | .5 | .6 |
| | (12) 3.2 | (11) .9 | | | | % Depr., Dep., Amort./Sales | (34) .9 | (25) 1.1 |
| | | 11.9 | 1.4 | | | | 5.8 | 12.8 |
| | | | | | | % Officers', Directors' Owners' Comp/Sales | | |
| 20770M | 38656M | 260597M | 366863M | 289400M | 3126502M | Net Sales ($) | 1396753M | 925714M |
| 992M | 26811M | 188190M | 737493M | 1233315M | 9188717M | Total Assets ($) | 4466999M | 3804694M |

M = $ thousand    MM = $ million
See Pages viii through xx for Explanation of Ratios and Data

© RMA 2024

## FINANCE—Other Financial Vehicles  NAICS 525990

| Comparative Historical Data | | | Type of Statement | Current Data Sorted by Sales | | | | | |
|---|---|---|---|---|---|---|---|---|---|
| 22 | 32 | 44 | Unqualified | 2 | 7 | 3 | 4 | 16 | 12 |
|  | 2 | 1 | Reviewed |  |  | 1 |  |  |  |
| 3 | 7 | 3 | Compiled | 1 | 1 |  |  |  | 1 |
| 5 | 9 | 11 | Tax Returns | 5 | 2 |  | 4 |  |  |
| 50 | 59 | 103 | Other | 14 | 13 | 12 | 18 | 32 | 14 |
| 4/1/21-3/31/22 ALL | 4/1/22-3/31/23 ALL | 4/1/23-3/31/24 ALL |  | 21 (4/1-9/30/23) | | | 141 (10/1/23-3/31/24) | | |
|  |  |  |  | 0-1MM | 1-3MM | 3-5MM | 5-10MM | 10-25MM | 25MM & OVER |
| 80 | 109 | 162 | NUMBER OF STATEMENTS | 22 | 23 | 16 | 26 | 48 | 27 |
| % | % | % | ASSETS | % | % | % | % | % | % |
| 19.2 | 17.7 | 20.0 | Cash & Equivalents | 12.7 | 26.3 | 12.0 | 23.9 | 19.0 | 23.1 |
| 8.6 | 11.8 | 13.0 | Trade Receivables (net) | 5.6 | 3.6 | 27.2 | 11.2 | 12.1 | 21.8 |
| 2.9 | 3.0 | 2.6 | Inventory | .0 | 3.5 | .0 | 5.3 | 2.5 | 3.4 |
| 11.2 | 12.0 | 9.2 | All Other Current | 6.9 | 4.8 | 12.2 | 5.0 | 14.2 | 8.0 |
| 41.9 | 44.5 | 44.8 | Total Current | 25.2 | 38.2 | 51.5 | 45.5 | 47.8 | 56.3 |
| 17.2 | 16.0 | 15.6 | Fixed Assets (net) | 27.2 | 15.3 | 17.0 | 17.5 | 12.1 | 10.2 |
| 3.5 | 4.6 | 5.1 | Intangibles (net) | 1.2 | .3 | .0 | 7.5 | 3.0 | 16.9 |
| 37.4 | 34.9 | 34.5 | All Other Non-Current | 46.5 | 46.2 | 31.5 | 29.6 | 37.1 | 16.6 |
| 100.0 | 100.0 | 100.0 | Total | 100.0 | 100.0 | 100.0 | 100.0 | 100.0 | 100.0 |
|  |  |  | LIABILITIES |  |  |  |  |  |  |
| 6.0 | 12.0 | 13.8 | Notes Payable-Short Term | 9.8 | 14.3 | 9.8 | 10.0 | 17.9 | 15.7 |
| 3.1 | 3.0 | 1.4 | Cur. Mat.-L.T.D. | 2.5 | .5 | .6 | 3.7 | .3 | 1.7 |
| 5.0 | 2.7 | 3.4 | Trade Payables | 4.8 | 2.0 | 4.2 | 1.1 | 3.2 | 5.9 |
| .1 | .3 | .1 | Income Taxes Payable | .0 | .0 | .3 | .0 | .1 | .2 |
| 6.5 | 10.4 | 12.9 | All Other Current | 9.0 | 3.5 | 2.4 | 18.8 | 13.2 | 24.3 |
| 20.7 | 28.4 | 31.7 | Total Current | 26.0 | 20.3 | 17.2 | 33.6 | 34.6 | 47.8 |
| 21.1 | 18.8 | 14.5 | Long-Term Debt | 20.8 | 12.7 | 12.8 | 16.7 | 13.3 | 12.0 |
| .0 | .0 | .0 | Deferred Taxes | .0 | .0 | .0 | .0 | .0 | .0 |
| 4.9 | 2.5 | 4.9 | All Other Non-Current | 3.5 | 6.5 | 4.4 | .1 | 5.1 | 8.9 |
| 53.2 | 50.3 | 48.9 | Net Worth | 49.6 | 60.5 | 65.6 | 49.5 | 47.0 | 31.3 |
| 100.0 | 100.0 | 100.0 | Total Liabilities & Net Worth | 100.0 | 100.0 | 100.0 | 100.0 | 100.0 | 100.0 |
|  |  |  | INCOME DATA |  |  |  |  |  |  |
| 100.0 | 100.0 | 100.0 | Net Sales | 100.0 | 100.0 | 100.0 | 100.0 | 100.0 | 100.0 |
|  |  |  | Gross Profit |  |  |  |  |  |  |
| 52.4 | 57.2 | 58.4 | Operating Expenses | 56.8 | 48.5 | 59.5 | 56.8 | 55.4 | 74.4 |
| 47.6 | 42.8 | 41.6 | Operating Profit | 43.2 | 51.5 | 40.5 | 43.2 | 44.6 | 25.6 |
| 10.6 | 10.2 | 15.5 | All Other Expenses (net) | 14.8 | 18.0 | 12.5 | 13.6 | 19.6 | 10.1 |
| 37.1 | 32.6 | 26.1 | Profit Before Taxes | 28.4 | 33.6 | 28.1 | 29.6 | 25.0 | 15.5 |
|  |  |  | RATIOS |  |  |  |  |  |  |
| 19.8 | 8.1 | 7.8 |  | 3.7 | 23.3 | 13.8 | 3.3 | 12.5 | 1.8 |
| 2.1 | 1.7 | 1.6 | Current | 1.5 | 2.8 | 6.9 | 1.3 | 1.7 | 1.3 |
| 1.2 | .9 | .9 |  | .2 | 1.0 | 1.4 | .3 | .7 | 1.0 |
| 12.6 | 5.3 | 4.5 |  | 2.7 | 11.9 | 12.5 | 1.9 | 9.5 | 1.6 |
| 1.3 | 1.1 | 1.2 | Quick | .7 | 1.9 | 3.5 | 1.1 | 1.0 | 1.1 |
| .7 | .3 | .3 |  | .1 | .5 | 1.1 | .2 | .2 | .4 |
| 0 UND | 0 UND | 0 UND |  | 0 UND | 0 UND | 0 UND | 0 UND | 0 UND | 4 88.4 |
| 0 999.8 | 0 919.5 | 0 UND | Sales/Receivables | 0 UND | 0 UND | 43 8.4 | 0 UND | 1 352.1 | 45 8.2 |
| 30 12.0 | 42 8.6 | 43 8.4 |  | 5 74.8 | 0 UND | 91 4.0 | 29 12.5 | 42 8.7 | 83 4.4 |
|  |  |  | Cost of Sales/Inventory |  |  |  |  |  |  |
|  |  |  | Cost of Sales/Payables |  |  |  |  |  |  |
| .8 | 1.0 | 1.0 |  | 1.1 | .2 | .9 | 2.8 | 1.4 | 1.7 |
| 2.6 | 3.8 | 6.0 | Sales/Working Capital | 14.4 | 1.5 | 2.9 | 11.2 | 6.4 | 10.4 |
| 16.3 | -39.6 | -27.2 |  | -.8 | 999.8 | 8.1 | -22.1 | -8.3 | -648.2 |
| 24.7 | 16.8 | 58.3 |  |  | 72.9 | 79.0 | 999.8 | 76.5 | 20.6 |
| (42) 10.3 | (57) 5.4 | (85) 7.2 | EBIT/Interest | (10) 5.8 | (12) 17.5 | (15) 19.9 | (23) 7.6 | (19) 3.5 |
| 2.8 | 1.7 | 2.2 |  |  | 2.2 | 1.8 | 3.4 | 3.0 | 1.4 |
|  |  |  | Net Profit + Depr., Dep., Amort./Cur. Mat. L/T/D |  |  |  |  |  |  |
| .0 | .0 | .0 |  | .0 | .0 | .0 | .0 | .0 | .0 |
| .0 | .0 | .0 | Fixed/Worth | .0 | .0 | .0 | .0 | .0 | .0 |
| .1 | .8 | .7 |  | 1.5 | .3 | .1 | .7 | .5 | 1.6 |
| .1 | .1 | .2 |  | .4 | .0 | .0 | .1 | .2 | .7 |
| .9 | 1.2 | 1.0 | Debt/Worth | 1.0 | .5 | .4 | 1.1 | 1.2 | 3.3 |
| 3.3 | 4.7 | 3.3 |  | 4.8 | 1.0 | 2.3 | 4.5 | 2.3 | 24.7 |
| 36.9 | 43.0 | 42.7 | % Profit Before Taxes/Tangible Net Worth | 39.9 | 20.7 | 23.7 | 91.3 | 44.3 | 63.2 |
| (74) 13.2 | (100) 8.9 | (147) 8.9 |  | (20) 7.4 | (22) 2.6 | 12.9 | (23) 8.9 | (44) 8.5 | (22) 33.7 |
| 2.4 | 2.2 | 2.2 |  | .4 | .9 | .9 | 3.3 | 2.9 | 8.8 |
| 13.9 | 11.5 | 12.6 | % Profit Before Taxes/Total Assets | 7.2 | 8.1 | 18.8 | 53.6 | 18.9 | 14.6 |
| 5.0 | 4.4 | 3.6 |  | 2.6 | 2.4 | 2.4 | 3.3 | 4.5 | 5.6 |
| 1.8 | .9 | 1.1 |  | .0 | .8 | .8 | 1.7 | 1.5 | 3.0 |
| UND | UND | UND | Sales/Net Fixed Assets | UND | UND | UND | UND | UND | UND |
| UND | UND | UND |  | UND | UND | UND | 142.6 | UND | 144.7 |
| 23.2 | 8.3 | 11.8 |  | .2 | 189.3 | 24.4 | 8.1 | 18.1 | 9.5 |
| .5 | .9 | 1.4 |  | .2 | .5 | 2.1 | 2.1 | 1.5 | 1.6 |
| .2 | .2 | .2 | Sales/Total Assets | .1 | .1 | .3 | .4 | .2 | .7 |
| .1 | .1 | .1 |  | .1 | .0 | .1 | .1 | .1 | .3 |
| .3 | .4 | .5 |  |  |  |  |  | .4 | .5 |
| (24) 3.5 | (28) 2.2 | (42) 1.9 | % Depr., Dep., Amort./Sales |  |  |  | (12) 1.0 | (10) 1.6 |
| 24.1 | 12.0 | 12.8 |  |  |  |  |  | 2.6 | 6.3 |
|  |  | 3.2 | % Officers', Directors' Owners' Comp/Sales |  |  |  |  |  |  |
|  | (11) | 5.9 |  |  |  |  |  |  |  |
|  |  | 13.3 |  |  |  |  |  |  |  |
| 1317193M | 3294969M | 4102788M | Net Sales ($) | 10154M | 40936M | 64043M | 193256M | 759847M | 3034552M |
| 6377208M | 8571696M | 11375518M | Total Assets ($) | 114587M | 763040M | 700581M | 1455251M | 4828690M | 3513369M |

© RMA 2024  M = $ thousand  MM = $ million
See Pages viii through xx for Explanation of Ratios and Data

# REAL ESTATE AND RENTAL AND LEASING

# REAL ESTATE—Lessors of Residential Buildings and Dwellings  NAICS 531110

## Current Data Sorted by Assets / Comparative Historical Data

| 0-500M | 500M-2MM | 2-10MM | 10-50MM | 50-100MM | 100-250MM | Type of Statement | ALL 4/1/19-3/31/20 | ALL 4/1/20-3/31/21 |
|---|---|---|---|---|---|---|---|---|
| 2 | 4 | 28 | 28 | 13 | 19 | Unqualified | 134 | 104 |
| 1 | 1 | 4 | 7 | 5 | 1 | Reviewed | 18 | 18 |
| 1 | 2 | 13 | 5 | 2 | 2 | Compiled | 48 | 38 |
| 60 | 164 | 170 | 33 | 2 | 1 | Tax Returns | 656 | 496 |
| 57 | 136 | 273 | 158 | 34 | 36 | Other | 880 | 603 |
|  | 76 (4/1-9/30/23) |  | 1,185 (10/1/23-3/31/24) |  |  |  |  |  |
| 120 | 307 | 488 | 231 | 56 | 59 | NUMBER OF STATEMENTS | 1736 | 1259 |
| % | % | % | % | % | % | ASSETS | % | % |
| 24.6 | 8.5 | 7.8 | 7.7 | 11.3 | 9.6 | Cash & Equivalents | 8.4 | 9.6 |
| 1.8 | 1.2 | 1.6 | 5.1 | 8.3 | 8.2 | Trade Receivables (net) | 1.9 | 1.7 |
| .8 | 1.0 | 1.6 | 1.6 | .6 | 2.0 | Inventory | .9 | 1.0 |
| 4.7 | 1.9 | 2.3 | 3.6 | 7.6 | 5.8 | All Other Current | 2.6 | 2.6 |
| 31.9 | 12.6 | 13.3 | 18.0 | 27.9 | 25.6 | Total Current | 13.8 | 14.9 |
| 61.7 | 79.1 | 75.3 | 60.5 | 46.3 | 43.7 | Fixed Assets (net) | 76.2 | 74.9 |
| 1.9 | 1.9 | 2.1 | 3.5 | 4.5 | 3.0 | Intangibles (net) | 1.8 | 1.9 |
| 4.5 | 6.3 | 9.3 | 18.0 | 21.2 | 27.7 | All Other Non-Current | 8.2 | 8.2 |
| 100.0 | 100.0 | 100.0 | 100.0 | 100.0 | 100.0 | Total | 100.0 | 100.0 |
|  |  |  |  |  |  | LIABILITIES |  |  |
| 9.7 | 3.4 | 4.3 | 3.0 | 4.1 | 1.6 | Notes Payable-Short Term | 2.9 | 4.5 |
| 3.8 | 2.5 | 1.8 | 1.7 | 5.3 | 1.7 | Cur. Mat.-L.T.D. | 2.6 | 2.5 |
| 2.1 | 1.4 | 1.4 | 1.5 | 2.9 | 6.1 | Trade Payables | 1.4 | 1.1 |
| .0 | .0 | .0 | .0 | .0 | .1 | Income Taxes Payable | .0 | .1 |
| 30.3 | 6.8 | 6.0 | 5.6 | 9.8 | 7.3 | All Other Current | 6.5 | 6.6 |
| 45.9 | 14.1 | 13.6 | 11.9 | 22.2 | 16.9 | Total Current | 13.3 | 14.8 |
| 58.4 | 74.4 | 62.0 | 48.7 | 37.5 | 41.2 | Long-Term Debt | 67.1 | 65.5 |
| .0 | .0 | .0 | .0 | .0 | .0 | Deferred Taxes | .1 | .0 |
| 7.3 | 3.7 | 5.1 | 5.0 | 4.1 | 5.8 | All Other Non-Current | 5.3 | 5.0 |
| -11.6 | 7.8 | 19.2 | 34.4 | 36.3 | 35.9 | Net Worth | 14.1 | 14.7 |
| 100.0 | 100.0 | 100.0 | 100.0 | 100.0 | 100.0 | Total Liabilties & Net Worth | 100.0 | 100.0 |
|  |  |  |  |  |  | INCOME DATA |  |  |
| 100.0 | 100.0 | 100.0 | 100.0 | 100.0 | 100.0 | Net Sales | 100.0 | 100.0 |
|  |  |  |  |  |  | Gross Profit |  |  |
| 67.6 | 65.4 | 70.4 | 65.1 | 74.7 | 76.2 | Operating Expenses | 68.2 | 68.3 |
| 32.4 | 34.6 | 29.6 | 34.9 | 25.3 | 23.8 | Operating Profit | 31.8 | 31.7 |
| 16.2 | 18.2 | 18.6 | 15.8 | 15.2 | 6.5 | All Other Expenses (net) | 17.1 | 16.6 |
| 16.1 | 16.4 | 11.0 | 19.1 | 10.1 | 17.3 | Profit Before Taxes | 14.8 | 15.1 |
|  |  |  |  |  |  | RATIOS |  |  |
| 3.1 | 3.2 | 3.5 | 3.4 | 3.1 | 3.5 |  | 2.9 | 3.7 |
| 1.0 | 1.3 | 1.0 | 1.5 | 1.2 | 1.6 | Current | 1.0 | 1.2 |
| .2 | .3 | .3 | .7 | .7 | .8 |  | .3 | .4 |
| 2.0 | 3.0 | 2.5 | 2.9 | 1.7 | 2.2 |  | 2.3 | 3.0 |
| .8 | 1.1 | .8 | 1.2 | .9 | 1.1 | Quick  (1731) .7  (1257) 1.0 |  |  |
| .1 | .2 | .2 | .4 | .3 | .6 |  | .2 | .3 |
| 0 UND | 0 UND | 0 UND | 0 UND | 0 UND | 0 UND |  | 0 UND | 0 UND |
| 0 UND | 0 UND | 0 UND | 1 446.5 | 6 62.1 | 10 38.4 | Sales/Receivables | 0 UND | 0 UND |
| 0 UND | 0 UND | 2 163.3 | 10 35.2 | 49 7.5 | 54 6.8 |  | 1 284.1 | 2 156.2 |
|  |  |  |  |  |  | Cost of Sales/Inventory |  |  |
|  |  |  |  |  |  | Cost of Sales/Payables |  |  |
| 5.9 | 4.3 | 4.3 | 2.1 | 1.9 | 1.9 |  | 4.4 | 3.6 |
| UND | 43.9 | UND | 11.1 | 15.4 | 7.1 | Sales/Working Capital | -209.0 | 31.7 |
| -3.8 | -5.1 | -3.6 | -13.6 | -10.8 | -7.3 |  | -5.2 | -4.8 |
| 7.3 | 4.6 | 4.2 | 6.6 | 17.9 | 24.7 |  | 5.0 | 5.4 |
| (52) 2.8 | (164) 2.7 | (241) 2.3 | (91) 2.7 | (25) 4.0 | (36) 4.0 | EBIT/Interest  (848) 2.6  (617) 2.8 |  |  |
| .8 | 1.5 | 1.0 | 1.3 | 1.2 | 1.1 |  | 1.2 | 1.4 |
|  |  |  |  |  |  | Net Profit + Depr., Dep., Amort./Cur. Mat. L/T/D | 4.6 | 4.2 |
|  |  |  |  |  |  |  (27) 3.1  (17) 1.6 |  |  |
|  |  |  |  |  |  |  | 2.4 | .4 |
| .7 | 2.4 | 1.6 | .4 | .0 | .0 |  | 1.6 | 1.5 |
| 3.8 | 5.5 | 4.1 | 2.5 | 1.2 | 1.2 | Fixed/Worth | 3.8 | 4.0 |
| -4.9 | -23.5 | -358.8 | 10.4 | 6.0 | 3.1 |  | -104.7 | 418.2 |
| 1.0 | 1.9 | 1.2 | .7 | .7 | .6 |  | 1.2 | 1.3 |
| 7.4 | 5.6 | 4.2 | 2.5 | 2.2 | 1.6 | Debt/Worth | 3.7 | 3.9 |
| -4.5 | -27.4 | -312.1 | 14.5 | 6.2 | 5.7 |  | -67.8 | -269.1 |
| 104.9 | 39.7 | 27.6 | 22.8 | 18.4 | 29.4 | % Profit Before Taxes/Tangible Net Worth | 26.7 | 28.6 |
| (74) 20.5 | (214) 11.5 | (361) 8.4 | (191) 6.2 | (49) 2.5 | (49) 4.2 |  (1274) 9.2  (940) 9.6 |  |  |
| -1.8 | .8 | -.6 | 1.2 | -3.7 | .9 |  | .5 | .0 |
| 19.1 | 9.6 | 5.8 | 5.7 | 7.1 | 8.4 | % Profit Before Taxes/Total Assets | 7.1 | 7.3 |
| 5.6 | 3.8 | 2.1 | 2.3 | .8 | 2.2 |  | 2.7 | 2.6 |
| -.8 | .1 | -.5 | .1 | -1.5 | .3 |  | -.1 | -.3 |
| 52.8 | .5 | .4 | 1.9 | 33.0 | 44.6 |  | .5 | .6 |
| .6 | .2 | .2 | .3 | .6 | .6 | Sales/Net Fixed Assets | .2 | .2 |
| .2 | .1 | .1 | .1 | .1 | .2 |  | .1 | .1 |
| 1.7 | .4 | .3 | .3 | .6 | .5 |  | .3 | .3 |
| .4 | .2 | .2 | .2 | .2 | .2 | Sales/Total Assets | .2 | .2 |
| .2 | .1 | .1 | .1 | .1 | .1 |  | .1 | .1 |
| 8.5 | 11.4 | 11.5 | 4.0 | .4 | 1.8 | % Depr., Dep., Amort./Sales | 12.2 | 11.9 |
| (80) 15.9 | (234) 17.4 | (339) 20.9 | (124) 14.2 | (33) 7.4 | (36) 10.9 |  (1269) 19.9  (931) 20.6 |  |  |
| 23.5 | 25.0 | 28.9 | 25.1 | 14.6 | 18.3 |  | 28.2 | 29.5 |
|  | 2.3 | 2.5 | 1.8 |  |  | % Officers', Directors' Owners' Comp/Sales | 2.6 | 2.8 |
|  | (21) 5.3 | (36) 4.3 | (19) 5.0 |  |  |  (118) 6.4  (85) 7.2 |  |  |
|  | 9.6 | 9.5 | 7.2 |  |  |  | 11.9 | 17.3 |
| 58796M | 233285M | 780789M | 1400390M | 1857034M | 5136148M | Net Sales ($) | 6742008M | 4882986M |
| 30001M | 356677M | 2382288M | 5155145M | 3928315M | 9985305M | Total Assets ($) | 17795906M | 13258592M |

© RMA 2024

M = $ thousand    MM = $ million
See Pages viii through xx for Explanation of Ratios and Data

# REAL ESTATE—Lessors of Residential Buildings and Dwellings  NAICS 531110

## Comparative Historical Data / Current Data Sorted by Sales

| | | | Type of Statement | | | | | | |
|---|---|---|---|---|---|---|---|---|---|
| 78 | 113 | 94 | Unqualified | 25 | 18 | 9 | 7 | 12 | 23 |
| 17 | 21 | 18 | Reviewed | 4 | 3 | 1 | 1 | 5 | 4 |
| 21 | 27 | 25 | Compiled | 9 | 8 | 1 | 2 | 2 | 5 |
| 524 | 598 | 430 | Tax Returns | 327 | 70 | 12 | 14 | 5 | 2 |
| 602 | 729 | 694 | Other | 343 | 155 | 57 | 60 | 42 | 37 |
| 4/1/21-3/31/22 ALL | 4/1/22-3/31/23 ALL | 4/1/23-3/31/24 ALL | | 76 (4/1-9/30/23) | | | 1,185 (10/1/23-3/31/24) | | |
| | | | | 0-1MM | 1-3MM | 3-5MM | 5-10MM | 10-25MM | 25MM & OVER |
| 1242 | 1488 | 1261 | NUMBER OF STATEMENTS | 708 | 254 | 80 | 82 | 66 | 71 |
| % | % | % | ASSETS | % | % | % | % | % | % |
| 10.4 | 10.1 | 9.8 | Cash & Equivalents | 7.8 | 9.8 | 15.5 | 14.7 | 13.4 | 14.2 |
| 1.6 | 1.7 | 2.8 | Trade Receivables (net) | .7 | 2.1 | 4.4 | 9.3 | 5.6 | 13.8 |
| 1.3 | 1.4 | 1.4 | Inventory | .5 | 1.0 | 1.5 | 6.4 | 4.2 | 2.3 |
| 2.3 | 2.9 | 3.1 | All Other Current | 1.6 | 3.4 | 4.9 | 4.4 | 5.0 | 11.2 |
| 15.6 | 16.0 | 17.0 | Total Current | 10.6 | 16.3 | 26.4 | 34.9 | 28.1 | 41.5 |
| 75.1 | 73.9 | 69.5 | Fixed Assets (net) | 81.5 | 68.6 | 55.4 | 42.2 | 39.0 | 28.2 |
| 1.6 | 1.6 | 2.4 | Intangibles (net) | 1.3 | 3.3 | 3.5 | 3.3 | 5.1 | 6.1 |
| 7.6 | 8.5 | 11.1 | All Other Non-Current | 6.6 | 11.8 | 14.7 | 19.7 | 27.8 | 24.1 |
| 100.0 | 100.0 | 100.0 | Total | 100.0 | 100.0 | 100.0 | 100.0 | 100.0 | 100.0 |
| | | | LIABILITIES | | | | | | |
| 2.7 | 3.0 | 4.2 | Notes Payable-Short Term | 3.5 | 4.8 | 6.0 | 8.1 | 5.2 | 2.2 |
| 2.2 | 2.2 | 2.3 | Cur. Mat.-L.T.D. | 2.5 | 2.1 | 1.8 | 2.0 | 2.7 | 1.7 |
| 1.2 | 1.5 | 1.8 | Trade Payables | .8 | 2.0 | 1.7 | 2.4 | 4.0 | 8.1 |
| .0 | .0 | .0 | Income Taxes Payable | .0 | .0 | .0 | .0 | .0 | .1 |
| 6.8 | 7.0 | 8.7 | All Other Current | 8.1 | 8.3 | 6.2 | 10.1 | 11.3 | 14.5 |
| 12.9 | 13.8 | 17.0 | Total Current | 14.9 | 17.2 | 15.7 | 22.6 | 23.3 | 26.6 |
| 66.2 | 67.0 | 60.2 | Long-Term Debt | 67.5 | 65.3 | 51.2 | 36.3 | 30.4 | 34.7 |
| .0 | .0 | .0 | Deferred Taxes | .0 | .0 | .1 | .0 | .0 | .1 |
| 4.0 | 4.4 | 4.9 | All Other Non-Current | 4.8 | 5.0 | 4.2 | 2.5 | 11.3 | 3.9 |
| 16.8 | 14.9 | 17.8 | Net Worth | 12.8 | 12.6 | 28.8 | 38.5 | 34.9 | 34.7 |
| 100.0 | 100.0 | 100.0 | Total Liabilities & Net Worth | 100.0 | 100.0 | 100.0 | 100.0 | 100.0 | 100.0 |
| | | | INCOME DATA | | | | | | |
| 100.0 | 100.0 | 100.0 | Net Sales | 100.0 | 100.0 | 100.0 | 100.0 | 100.0 | 100.0 |
| | | | Gross Profit | | | | | | |
| 68.0 | 68.9 | 68.4 | Operating Expenses | 65.5 | 67.9 | 72.4 | 72.2 | 79.4 | 80.8 |
| 32.0 | 31.1 | 31.6 | Operating Profit | 34.5 | 32.1 | 27.6 | 27.8 | 20.6 | 19.2 |
| 14.9 | 15.3 | 17.1 | All Other Expenses (net) | 20.8 | 16.8 | 12.5 | 10.7 | 6.7 | 2.1 |
| 17.2 | 15.8 | 14.5 | Profit Before Taxes | 13.7 | 15.3 | 15.1 | 17.1 | 13.9 | 17.1 |
| | | | RATIOS | | | | | | |
| 4.2 | 4.2 | 3.4 | Current | 3.2 | 3.2 | 3.4 | 5.7 | 3.2 | 3.6 |
| 1.4 | 1.4 | 1.2 | | 1.0 | 1.1 | 1.4 | 1.4 | 1.6 | 1.8 |
| .5 | .4 | .4 | | .3 | .4 | .8 | .9 | .6 | .9 |
| 3.4 | 3.2 | 2.7 | Quick | 2.5 | 2.9 | 2.9 | 3.3 | 2.0 | 2.2 |
| (1241) 1.1 | (1487) 1.1 | .9 | | .8 | .8 | 1.1 | 1.2 | .8 | 1.2 |
| .3 | .3 | .2 | | .2 | .3 | .4 | .4 | .4 | .7 |
| 0 UND | 0 UND | 0 UND | Sales/Receivables | 0 UND | 0 UND | 0 UND | 0 UND | 1 329.2 | |
| 0 UND | 0 UND | 0 UND | | 0 UND | 0 UND | 1 522.6 | 2 186.8 | 6 65.0 | 10 36.6 |
| 2 207.3 | 3 135.9 | 3 124.4 | | 0 UND | 3 142.5 | 5 70.1 | 32 11.4 | 31 11.7 | 70 5.2 |
| | | | Cost of Sales/Inventory | | | | | | |
| | | | Cost of Sales/Payables | | | | | | |
| 3.1 | 3.2 | 3.5 | Sales/Working Capital | 3.9 | 4.5 | 3.2 | 1.6 | 2.9 | 2.6 |
| 16.1 | 16.2 | 38.0 | | UND | 71.5 | 14.8 | 8.2 | 9.3 | 9.6 |
| -7.0 | -7.1 | -5.2 | | -3.2 | -5.0 | -20.5 | -28.9 | -18.8 | -32.5 |
| 5.9 | 5.7 | 5.4 | EBIT/Interest | 3.8 | 5.1 | 10.0 | 68.9 | 12.2 | 19.1 |
| (672) 2.9 | (778) 2.8 | (609) 2.6 | | (320) 2.3 | (124) 2.6 | (37) 2.4 | (47) 8.5 | (38) 2.8 | (43) 6.4 |
| 1.5 | 1.4 | 1.2 | | 1.0 | 1.3 | 1.1 | 2.4 | 1.0 | 1.5 |
| 14.4 | 5.7 | 5.1 | Net Profit + Depr., Dep., Amort./Cur. Mat. L/T/D | | | | | | |
| (16) 3.5 | (22) 3.1 | (18) 2.1 | | | | | | | |
| 1.7 | 1.0 | .3 | | | | | | | |
| 1.4 | 1.5 | 1.3 | Fixed/Worth | 2.0 | 1.2 | .3 | .0 | .1 | .0 |
| 3.8 | 4.2 | 3.6 | | 4.7 | 4.1 | 3.5 | 1.0 | 1.1 | .3 |
| -83.2 | -87.4 | UND | | -84.7 | -43.6 | 38.9 | 4.0 | 4.5 | 2.6 |
| 1.1 | 1.1 | 1.1 | Debt/Worth | 1.4 | 1.3 | 1.0 | .5 | .5 | .7 |
| 3.6 | 4.0 | 3.7 | | 4.5 | 4.6 | 4.0 | 1.6 | 1.5 | 2.0 |
| -57.6 | -65.6 | -298.4 | | -61.2 | -20.1 | 79.2 | 10.2 | 11.9 | 5.7 |
| 31.6 | 30.6 | 29.7 | % Profit Before Taxes/Tangible Net Worth | 22.3 | 45.7 | 61.4 | 31.8 | 25.9 | 48.9 |
| (910) 10.4 | (1080) 10.4 | (938) 8.4 | | (514) 7.6 | (180) 9.3 | (63) 8.2 | (69) 11.9 | (54) 4.3 | (58) 22.9 |
| 1.5 | 1.0 | .0 | | -.8 | .8 | -1.7 | 2.6 | -1.8 | 4.9 |
| 8.4 | 7.6 | 7.7 | % Profit Before Taxes/Total Assets | 5.8 | 7.8 | 10.5 | 12.3 | 15.7 | 18.3 |
| 3.0 | 3.0 | 2.6 | | 2.1 | 2.9 | 2.9 | 4.2 | 2.4 | 7.9 |
| .4 | .0 | -.2 | | -.4 | -.2 | -.5 | 1.0 | -.2 | 2.0 |
| .5 | .6 | .7 | Sales/Net Fixed Assets | .3 | .9 | 28.2 | 107.5 | 64.2 | 153.7 |
| .2 | .2 | .2 | | .2 | .3 | .4 | 1.9 | 3.3 | 13.4 |
| .1 | .1 | .1 | | .1 | .2 | .2 | .2 | .3 | .6 |
| .4 | .4 | .4 | Sales/Total Assets | .2 | .4 | .5 | 1.0 | .9 | 1.7 |
| .2 | .2 | .2 | | .2 | .2 | .3 | .3 | .3 | .6 |
| .1 | .1 | .1 | | .1 | .1 | .1 | .2 | .2 | .3 |
| 11.6 | 10.9 | 9.2 | % Depr., Dep., Amort./Sales | 13.4 | 8.5 | 1.0 | .9 | .6 | .2 |
| (911) 19.1 | (1070) 19.1 | (846) 17.4 | | (514) 20.6 | (158) 15.4 | (40) 9.1 | (53) 5.1 | (37) 9.9 | (44) 1.8 |
| 28.1 | 27.6 | 25.8 | | 28.8 | 24.5 | 23.8 | 16.1 | 16.1 | 9.8 |
| 2.9 | 2.8 | 2.5 | % Officers', Directors' Owners' Comp/Sales | 3.3 | 2.6 | 3.8 | 2.4 | | |
| (114) 7.0 | (95) 6.0 | (91) 5.0 | | (32) 7.3 | (22) 5.3 | (10) 8.1 | (14) 2.8 | | |
| 12.5 | 12.1 | 9.1 | | 11.4 | 9.8 | 9.8 | 6.7 | | |
| 5243307M | 8835094M | 9466442M | Net Sales ($) | 265664M | 436157M | 309183M | 590636M | 1008539M | 6856263M |
| 13871124M | 19452410M | 21837731M | Total Assets ($) | 2200458M | 2532899M | 1673292M | 2983503M | 3928845M | 8518734M |

M = $ thousand   MM = $ million
See Pages viii through xx for Explanation of Ratios and Data
© RMA 2024

# REAL ESTATE—Lessors of Nonresidential Buildings (except Miniwarehouses) NAICS 531120

## Current Data Sorted by Assets | Comparative Historical Data

| | | | | | | Type of Statement | | |
|---|---|---|---|---|---|---|---|---|
| 7 | 6 | 24 | 37 | 16 | 14 | Unqualified | 97 | 59 |
| 2 | 7 | 26 | 31 | 8 | 10 | Reviewed | 115 | 63 |
| 8 | 31 | 77 | 44 | 1 | 2 | Compiled | 394 | 151 |
| 111 | 615 | 749 | 161 | 10 | 5 | Tax Returns | 2824 | 1620 |
| 96 | 505 | 1032 | 474 | 79 | 51 | Other | 3713 | 1764 |
| | 174 (4/1-9/30/23) | | 4,065 (10/1/23-3/31/24) | | | | 4/1/19-3/31/20 | 4/1/20-3/31/21 |
| 0-500M | 500M-2MM | 2-10MM | 10-50MM | 50-100MM | 100-250MM | | ALL | ALL |
| 224 | 1164 | 1908 | 747 | 114 | 82 | NUMBER OF STATEMENTS | 7143 | 3657 |
| % | % | % | % | % | % | ASSETS | % | % |
| 20.7 | 7.3 | 6.1 | 6.3 | 9.5 | 5.6 | Cash & Equivalents | 5.9 | 6.8 |
| 1.5 | .9 | 1.0 | 1.5 | 2.1 | 3.2 | Trade Receivables (net) | 1.0 | 1.0 |
| .5 | .2 | .3 | 1.1 | 2.1 | 2.0 | Inventory | .6 | .5 |
| 1.2 | 1.5 | 1.7 | 2.4 | 2.4 | 2.0 | All Other Current | 1.7 | 1.3 |
| 23.9 | 9.9 | 9.1 | 11.3 | 16.1 | 12.8 | Total Current | 9.2 | 9.6 |
| 70.7 | 83.5 | 82.6 | 77.4 | 64.6 | 66.4 | Fixed Assets (net) | 83.4 | 83.0 |
| 1.6 | 1.6 | 2.2 | 2.9 | 2.5 | 4.0 | Intangibles (net) | 2.3 | 2.6 |
| 3.9 | 5.0 | 6.1 | 8.5 | 16.9 | 16.8 | All Other Non-Current | 5.1 | 4.9 |
| 100.0 | 100.0 | 100.0 | 100.0 | 100.0 | 100.0 | Total | 100.0 | 100.0 |
| | | | | | | LIABILITIES | | |
| 4.3 | 1.8 | 2.4 | 1.7 | 3.7 | 4.3 | Notes Payable-Short Term | 2.2 | 3.2 |
| 4.7 | 3.3 | 2.5 | 2.9 | 4.2 | 2.6 | Cur. Mat.-L.T.D. | 3.7 | 3.5 |
| 1.8 | .7 | .6 | 1.1 | 1.3 | 2.7 | Trade Payables | .8 | .7 |
| .3 | .0 | .0 | .0 | .1 | .0 | Income Taxes Payable | .0 | .0 |
| 18.4 | 6.0 | 4.8 | 4.0 | 4.6 | 8.5 | All Other Current | 4.8 | 4.3 |
| 29.4 | 11.8 | 10.3 | 9.8 | 13.9 | 18.1 | Total Current | 11.6 | 11.7 |
| 65.0 | 69.9 | 64.9 | 58.7 | 46.7 | 46.6 | Long-Term Debt | 64.0 | 63.9 |
| .0 | .0 | .0 | .1 | .0 | .1 | Deferred Taxes | .0 | .0 |
| 6.2 | 2.7 | 3.3 | 3.4 | 3.2 | 2.2 | All Other Non-Current | 3.7 | 3.1 |
| -.7 | 15.6 | 21.6 | 28.0 | 36.1 | 33.0 | Net Worth | 20.8 | 21.2 |
| 100.0 | 100.0 | 100.0 | 100.0 | 100.0 | 100.0 | Total Liabilities & Net Worth | 100.0 | 100.0 |
| | | | | | | INCOME DATA | | |
| 100.0 | 100.0 | 100.0 | 100.0 | 100.0 | 100.0 | Net Sales | 100.0 | 100.0 |
| | | | | | | Gross Profit | | |
| 50.4 | 46.9 | 47.6 | 52.1 | 54.4 | 67.2 | Operating Expenses | 47.5 | 49.9 |
| 49.6 | 53.1 | 52.4 | 47.9 | 45.6 | 32.8 | Operating Profit | 52.5 | 50.1 |
| 14.9 | 20.8 | 22.5 | 19.0 | 20.1 | 19.4 | All Other Expenses (net) | 21.9 | 20.3 |
| 34.7 | 32.3 | 29.9 | 28.9 | 25.5 | 13.4 | Profit Before Taxes | 30.7 | 29.8 |
| | | | | | | RATIOS | | |
| 2.5 | 2.7 | 3.2 | 3.3 | 3.2 | 2.6 | | 2.1 | 2.9 |
| 1.0 | .8 | .9 | 1.2 | 1.3 | .9 | Current | .8 | 1.0 |
| .3 | .3 | .3 | .4 | .3 | .2 | | .2 | .3 |
| 2.3 | 2.3 | 2.6 | 2.4 | 2.5 | 2.1 | | 1.7 | 2.4 |
| .9 (1163) | .7 (1906) | .8 | .9 | .8 | .5 | Quick | .6 (3656) | .9 |
| .3 | .2 | .2 | .2 | .2 | .1 | | .2 | .2 |
| 0 UND | 0 UND | 0 UND | 0 UND | 0 UND | 0 UND | | 0 UND | 0 UND |
| 0 UND | 0 UND | 0 UND | 0 UND | 0 836.4 | 6 61.8 | Sales/Receivables | 0 UND | 0 UND |
| 0 UND | 0 UND | 0 UND | 9 41.9 | 17 21.3 | 41 8.9 | | 0 UND | 0 UND |
| | | | | | | Cost of Sales/Inventory | | |
| | | | | | | Cost of Sales/Payables | | |
| 5.7 | 4.8 | 3.9 | 3.1 | 2.0 | 3.0 | | 5.9 | 4.1 |
| UND | -26.2 | -88.5 | 25.4 | 15.1 | -47.3 | Sales/Working Capital | -17.4 | -353.0 |
| -4.1 | -3.4 | -3.1 | -4.4 | -4.3 | -1.0 | | -3.2 | -3.0 |
| 9.1 | 7.9 | 6.8 | 7.8 | 7.7 | 8.1 | | 6.8 | 7.4 |
| 5.5 (103) | 4.8 (543) | 4.3 (761) | 4.0 (312) | 3.9 (44) | 2.8 (28) | EBIT/Interest | 4.2 (2993) | 4.4 (1584) |
| 3.2 | 2.9 | 2.7 | 2.6 | 2.5 | 1.7 | | 2.7 | 2.7 |
| | 3.4 | 2.9 | 4.2 | | | Net Profit + Depr., Dep., | 3.9 | 3.0 |
| (16) | 2.3 (46) | 1.7 (49) | 2.0 | | | Amort./Cur. Mat. L/T/D | 2.1 (224) | 1.9 (60) |
| | 1.2 | .9 | 1.3 | | | | 1.3 | 1.3 |
| 1.1 | 1.8 | 1.9 | 1.6 | .9 | 1.0 | | 1.9 | 1.9 |
| 3.6 | 3.9 | 4.0 | 3.2 | 1.8 | 2.5 | Fixed/Worth | 3.8 | 4.1 |
| -13.0 | -113.3 | 38.6 | 11.6 | 3.8 | 4.8 | | 24.3 | 34.6 |
| .6 | 1.3 | 1.3 | 1.2 | .7 | 1.1 | | 1.3 | 1.3 |
| 3.9 | 3.5 | 3.7 | 2.7 | 1.8 | 2.0 | Debt/Worth | 3.3 | 3.7 |
| -10.6 | -109.1 | 47.1 | 11.9 | 4.5 | 5.8 | | 27.8 | 41.7 |
| 101.0 | 40.4 | 32.4 | 25.2 | 17.4 | 14.9 | % Profit Before Taxes/Tangible | 32.7 | 32.5 |
| 30.2 (157) | 18.3 (864) | 14.5 (1471) | 12.5 (606) | 7.4 (100) | 7.1 (73) | Net Worth | 14.8 (5667) | 15.3 (2847) |
| 12.0 | 7.9 | 5.2 | 4.0 | 1.3 | -.4 | | 6.1 | 5.7 |
| 35.2 | 11.2 | 8.0 | 6.8 | 5.8 | 4.3 | % Profit Before Taxes/Total | 8.6 | 8.2 |
| 11.1 | 5.5 | 4.3 | 3.7 | 2.4 | 2.0 | Assets | 4.5 | 4.2 |
| 2.8 | 2.0 | 1.5 | 1.1 | .3 | -.1 | | 1.7 | 1.5 |
| 3.5 | .3 | .3 | .3 | .4 | .5 | | .3 | .3 |
| .4 | .2 | .2 | .2 | .2 | .2 | Sales/Net Fixed Assets | .2 | .2 |
| .2 | .1 | .1 | .1 | .1 | .1 | | .1 | .1 |
| 1.4 | .3 | .2 | .2 | .2 | .2 | | .2 | .2 |
| .3 | .2 | .1 | .1 | .1 | .1 | Sales/Total Assets | .1 | .1 |
| .2 | .1 | .1 | .1 | .1 | .1 | | .1 | .1 |
| 6.6 | 11.4 | 12.2 | 11.9 | 8.4 | 8.8 | | 12.3 | 13.5 |
| 12.2 (150) | 17.1 (945) | 18.4 (1486) | 19.4 (541) | 17.2 (78) | 20.9 (56) | % Depr., Dep., Amort./Sales | 18.3 (5617) | 19.7 (2837) |
| 21.7 | 24.8 | 25.6 | 26.9 | 38.2 | 34.3 | | 25.8 | 27.9 |
| 4.9 | 2.1 | 2.3 | 1.7 | | | % Officers', Directors' | 2.5 | 2.1 |
| 7.0 (11) | 4.2 (39) | 4.7 (64) | 5.1 (46) | | | Owners' Comp/Sales | 4.9 (283) | 5.2 (125) |
| 19.5 | 8.2 | 11.8 | 13.7 | | | | 11.9 | 11.0 |
| 73037M | 515576M | 2028288M | 4403694M | 3182843M | 4504586M | Net Sales ($) | 15983708M | 6884066M |
| 66557M | 1431911M | 8794811M | 15746423M | 8087273M | 13343157M | Total Assets ($) | 54099331M | 29309284M |

M = $ thousand    MM = $ million
See Pages viii through xx for Explanation of Ratios and Data

© RMA 2024

# REAL ESTATE—Lessors of Nonresidential Buildings (except Miniwarehouses) NAICS 531120

## Comparative Historical Data | Current Data Sorted by Sales

| Comparative Historical Data | | | Type of Statement | Current Data Sorted by Sales | | | | | |
|---|---|---|---|---|---|---|---|---|---|
| 69 | 90 | 104 | Unqualified | 33 | 21 | 12 | 16 | 10 | 12 |
| 51 | 83 | 84 | Reviewed | 23 | 19 | 9 | 14 | 9 | 10 |
| 161 | 179 | 163 | Compiled | 97 | 44 | 11 | 5 | 5 | 1 |
| 1443 | 1833 | 1651 | Tax Returns | 1296 | 262 | 42 | 31 | 16 | 4 |
| 1830 | 2314 | 2237 | Other | 1390 | 469 | 127 | 134 | 69 | 48 |
| 4/1/21-3/31/22 ALL | 4/1/22-3/31/23 ALL | 4/1/23-3/31/24 ALL | | 174 (4/1-9/30/23) | | | 4,065 (10/1/23-3/31/24) | | |
| | | | | 0-1MM | 1-3MM | 3-5MM | 5-10MM | 10-25MM | 25MM & OVER |
| 3554 | 4499 | 4239 | NUMBER OF STATEMENTS | 2839 | 815 | 201 | 200 | 109 | 75 |
| % | % | % | ASSETS | % | % | % | % | % | % |
| 7.6 | 7.6 | 7.3 | Cash & Equivalents | 6.2 | 8.3 | 9.2 | 9.3 | 13.8 | 18.6 |
| 1.3 | 1.2 | 1.2 | Trade Receivables (net) | .5 | .8 | 1.9 | 3.4 | 5.7 | 14.2 |
| .5 | .5 | .5 | Inventory | .1 | .3 | .7 | 2.5 | .7 | 11.9 |
| 1.7 | 1.5 | 1.8 | All Other Current | 1.3 | 2.2 | 2.7 | 4.4 | 4.4 | 2.9 |
| 11.1 | 10.9 | 10.8 | Total Current | 8.1 | 11.5 | 14.6 | 19.6 | 24.6 | 47.6 |
| 81.1 | 80.9 | 80.5 | Fixed Assets (net) | 84.8 | 79.0 | 72.0 | 65.7 | 56.3 | 32.4 |
| 2.0 | 2.1 | 2.1 | Intangibles (net) | 1.7 | 2.7 | 3.6 | 2.9 | 4.2 | 4.6 |
| 5.8 | 6.1 | 6.6 | All Other Non-Current | 5.4 | 6.8 | 9.9 | 11.8 | 14.9 | 15.4 |
| 100.0 | 100.0 | 100.0 | Total | 100.0 | 100.0 | 100.0 | 100.0 | 100.0 | 100.0 |
| | | | LIABILITIES | | | | | | |
| 3.5 | 2.8 | 2.3 | Notes Payable-Short Term | 1.9 | 2.3 | 3.4 | 3.2 | 5.5 | 6.6 |
| 3.0 | 3.1 | 3.0 | Cur. Mat.-L.T.D. | 3.1 | 2.4 | 2.4 | 4.5 | 3.5 | 1.8 |
| .7 | .7 | .8 | Trade Payables | .4 | .8 | 1.0 | 2.6 | 3.3 | 8.0 |
| .0 | .0 | .0 | Income Taxes Payable | .0 | .0 | .1 | .1 | .0 | .1 |
| 4.4 | 5.1 | 5.8 | All Other Current | 5.4 | 5.6 | 4.6 | 6.2 | 11.8 | 14.4 |
| 11.6 | 11.8 | 11.9 | Total Current | 10.8 | 11.2 | 11.4 | 16.5 | 24.2 | 30.9 |
| 63.3 | 64.2 | 64.3 | Long-Term Debt | 66.3 | 69.0 | 56.2 | 50.9 | 40.5 | 32.5 |
| .0 | .0 | .0 | Deferred Taxes | .0 | .1 | .0 | .1 | .3 | .2 |
| 3.8 | 3.3 | 3.3 | All Other Non-Current | 2.9 | 3.6 | 4.4 | 5.4 | 3.4 | 5.0 |
| 21.3 | 20.7 | 20.5 | Net Worth | 20.1 | 16.0 | 27.9 | 27.2 | 31.5 | 31.3 |
| 100.0 | 100.0 | 100.0 | Total Liabilities & Net Worth | 100.0 | 100.0 | 100.0 | 100.0 | 100.0 | 100.0 |
| | | | INCOME DATA | | | | | | |
| 100.0 | 100.0 | 100.0 | Net Sales | 100.0 | 100.0 | 100.0 | 100.0 | 100.0 | 100.0 |
| | | | Gross Profit | | | | | | |
| 49.6 | 49.5 | 48.9 | Operating Expenses | 44.8 | 50.7 | 58.6 | 63.5 | 71.2 | 86.9 |
| 50.4 | 50.5 | 51.1 | Operating Profit | 55.2 | 49.3 | 41.4 | 36.5 | 28.8 | 13.1 |
| 19.8 | 19.8 | 20.9 | All Other Expenses (net) | 23.2 | 18.3 | 16.4 | 14.8 | 12.2 | 2.6 |
| 30.6 | 30.8 | 30.2 | Profit Before Taxes | 32.0 | 31.0 | 25.0 | 21.6 | 16.6 | 10.4 |
| | | | RATIOS | | | | | | |
| 3.7 | 3.2 | 3.0 | | 2.7 | 3.9 | 3.7 | 3.2 | 4.0 | 2.3 |
| 1.2 | 1.0 | 1.0 | Current | .8 | 1.3 | 1.2 | 1.3 | 1.5 | 1.6 |
| .3 | .3 | .3 | | .2 | .4 | .4 | .4 | .3 | 1.1 |
| 3.0 | 2.6 | 2.5 | | 2.3 | 3.0 | 3.1 | 2.3 | 3.0 | 2.0 |
| 1.0 (4494) | .9 (4236) | .8 | Quick | (2837) .7 | (814) 1.0 | .8 | .9 | 1.2 | 1.1 |
| .3 | .2 | .2 | | .2 | .3 | .3 | .3 | .3 | .5 |
| 0 UND | 0 UND | 0 UND | | 0 UND | 0 UND | 0 UND | 0 UND | 0 UND | 3 141.3 |
| 0 UND | 0 UND | 0 UND | Sales/Receivables | 0 UND | 0 UND | 0 UND | 2 193.5 | 5 72.6 | 20 18.6 |
| 0 UND | 0 UND | 0 999.8 | | 0 UND | 3 122.4 | 10 36.8 | 18 20.2 | 29 12.5 | 49 7.5 |
| | | | Cost of Sales/Inventory | | | | | | |
| | | | Cost of Sales/Payables | | | | | | |
| 3.2 | 3.4 | 4.0 | | 4.4 | 3.2 | 3.8 | 3.3 | 3.3 | 4.2 |
| 36.6 | 125.5 | -123.4 | Sales/Working Capital | -24.3 | 19.5 | 30.0 | 21.2 | 18.7 | 9.6 |
| -3.6 | -3.0 | -3.3 | | -2.8 | -5.7 | -6.1 | -5.7 | -3.0 | 163.9 |
| 7.9 | 7.5 | 7.5 | | 7.0 | 7.1 | 7.9 | 11.0 | 10.9 | 31.4 |
| (1593) 4.4 | (2040) 4.3 | (1791) 4.4 | EBIT/Interest | (1085) 4.6 | (384) 4.1 | (111) 3.8 | (106) 4.7 | (51) 3.2 | (54) 6.2 |
| 2.7 | 2.7 | 2.7 | | 2.9 | 2.5 | 2.1 | 2.9 | 1.8 | 2.5 |
| 3.4 | 3.7 | 3.3 | Net Profit + Depr., Dep., Amort./Cur. Mat. L/T/D | 2.7 | 3.5 | | 3.7 | 7.3 | 4.9 |
| (84) 1.9 | (109) 2.1 | (126) 2.0 | | (43) 1.6 | (31) 2.7 | (14) | (15) 1.7 | (15) 2.5 | (14) 1.9 |
| 1.1 | 1.2 | 1.2 | | .9 | 1.3 | | 1.4 | 1.1 | .2 |
| 1.8 | 1.8 | 1.8 | | 2.0 | 1.9 | 1.1 | 1.0 | .2 | .1 |
| 4.0 | 3.8 | 3.6 | Fixed/Worth | 4.0 | 3.9 | 2.8 | 2.5 | 1.9 | .7 |
| 40.3 | 32.6 | 37.0 | | 38.0 | -40.0 | 11.1 | 32.1 | 4.1 | 3.1 |
| 1.2 | 1.3 | 1.2 | | 1.3 | 1.3 | .9 | .8 | .6 | 1.0 |
| 3.6 | 3.4 | 3.3 | Debt/Worth | 3.5 | 3.7 | 2.5 | 2.1 | 1.9 | 2.0 |
| 52.1 | 46.1 | 46.9 | | 46.2 | -42.3 | 12.1 | 45.7 | 6.5 | 7.1 |
| 33.0 | 33.4 | 33.4 | | 32.7 | 34.9 | 33.3 | 32.3 | 28.8 | 78.9 |
| (2732) 15.1 | (3489) 15.5 | (3271) 15.2 | % Profit Before Taxes/Tangible Net Worth | (2199) 15.0 | (598) 16.4 | (164) 14.3 | (153) 13.3 | (93) 11.7 | (64) 27.2 |
| 5.9 | 6.1 | 5.3 | | 5.4 | 6.5 | 4.7 | 1.3 | 1.3 | 9.6 |
| 8.8 | 8.4 | 8.9 | | 8.5 | 9.1 | 9.2 | 11.2 | 9.3 | 24.1 |
| 4.4 | 4.4 | 4.5 | % Profit Before Taxes/Total Assets | 4.4 | 5.0 | 4.5 | 4.9 | 3.2 | 8.5 |
| 1.4 | 1.6 | 1.4 | | 1.4 | 1.9 | 1.2 | .9 | .1 | 2.7 |
| .3 | .3 | .3 | | .2 | .4 | .6 | 1.0 | 19.1 | 43.8 |
| .2 | .2 | .2 | Sales/Net Fixed Assets | .2 | .2 | .2 | .3 | .4 | 8.4 |
| .1 | .1 | .1 | | .1 | .1 | .1 | .2 | .2 | 1.9 |
| .2 | .2 | .2 | | .2 | .3 | .3 | .5 | 1.3 | 2.7 |
| .1 | .1 | .1 | Sales/Total Assets | .1 | .2 | .2 | .2 | .2 | 1.6 |
| .1 | .1 | .1 | | .1 | .1 | .1 | .1 | .1 | .7 |
| 12.6 | 12.2 | 11.4 | | 12.7 | 11.0 | 9.7 | 5.9 | 3.1 | .4 |
| (2686) 18.9 | (3473) 18.6 | (3256) 17.9 | % Depr., Dep., Amort./Sales | (2214) 18.8 | (625) 17.0 | (145) 16.6 | (144) 14.4 | (76) 12.3 | (52) 1.6 |
| 27.3 | 26.4 | 25.6 | | 26.2 | 24.0 | 23.2 | 26.7 | 26.0 | 5.6 |
| 2.2 | 1.4 | 1.9 | | 2.5 | 2.1 | 3.1 | 3.5 | .8 | .1 |
| (163) 5.2 | (189) 4.3 | (175) 4.9 | % Officers', Directors' Owners' Comp/Sales | (59) 5.3 | (42) 5.7 | (16) 5.0 | (29) 5.2 | (12) 3.1 | (17) 1.0 |
| 11.6 | 10.2 | 10.4 | | 13.9 | 12.7 | 13.4 | 12.4 | 6.7 | 2.6 |
| 10257356M | 14472164M | 14708024M | Net Sales ($) | 1086603M | 1404484M | 775001M | 1381116M | 1699347M | 8361473M |
| 32444016M | 45553438M | 47470132M | Total Assets ($) | 8514767M | 9981982M | 5032808M | 8493316M | 8946696M | 6500563M |

© RMA 2024          M = $ thousand   MM = $ million
See Pages viii through xx for Explanation of Ratios and Data

# REAL ESTATE—Lessors of Miniwarehouses and Self-Storage Units  NAICS 531130

## Current Data Sorted by Assets | Comparative Historical Data

| | | | | | | | |
|---|---|---|---|---|---|---|---|
| | | | | 1 | 1 | 3 | **Type of Statement** |
| | | | 1 | 1 | 1 | | Unqualified |
| | | 1 | 2 | 2 | | | Reviewed |
| | 1 | 41 | 5 | | | | Compiled |
| 9 | 21 | 58 | 11 | 5 | 8 | | Tax Returns |
| 5 | 25 | | | | | | Other |
| | 5 (4/1-9/30/23) | | 196 (10/1/23-3/31/24) | | | | |
| 0-500M | 500M-2MM | 2-10MM | 10-50MM | 50-100MM | 100-250MM | | |

| 0-500M | 500M-2MM | 2-10MM | 10-50MM | 50-100MM | 100-250MM | | 4/1/19-3/31/20 ALL | 4/1/20-3/31/21 ALL |
|---|---|---|---|---|---|---|---|---|
| 14 | 47 | 102 | 20 | 7 | 11 | **NUMBER OF STATEMENTS** | 319 | 253 |
| % | % | % | % | % | % | **ASSETS** | % | % |
| 53.3 | 12.4 | 5.8 | 4.4 | | 10.5 | Cash & Equivalents | 9.7 | 11.4 |
| 2.4 | .1 | .5 | 1.9 | | 8.9 | Trade Receivables (net) | 1.2 | 1.1 |
| .0 | 2.1 | .6 | 1.4 | | .4 | Inventory | .3 | .4 |
| 4.3 | 2.8 | 2.9 | .8 | | .5 | All Other Current | 1.5 | 1.1 |
| 60.0 | 17.4 | 9.8 | 8.4 | | 20.3 | Total Current | 12.6 | 13.9 |
| 39.1 | 75.4 | 80.3 | 79.5 | | 42.7 | Fixed Assets (net) | 78.4 | 75.5 |
| .2 | 1.2 | 3.1 | 6.9 | | 3.4 | Intangibles (net) | 3.3 | 3.4 |
| .7 | 6.0 | 6.8 | 5.2 | | 33.5 | All Other Non-Current | 5.7 | 7.2 |
| 100.0 | 100.0 | 100.0 | 100.0 | | 100.0 | Total | 100.0 | 100.0 |
| | | | | | | **LIABILITIES** | | |
| 37.9 | 2.3 | 4.6 | 4.4 | | 6.7 | Notes Payable-Short Term | 3.8 | 3.3 |
| .3 | 2.5 | 1.8 | .8 | | .1 | Cur. Mat.-L.T.D. | 4.3 | 2.6 |
| 2.9 | .2 | .5 | 1.2 | | 1.5 | Trade Payables | 3.5 | 4.5 |
| .0 | .0 | .0 | .0 | | .1 | Income Taxes Payable | .0 | .0 |
| 50.6 | 6.6 | 4.5 | 1.2 | | 4.1 | All Other Current | 5.9 | 3.2 |
| 91.6 | 11.6 | 11.4 | 7.6 | | 12.5 | Total Current | 17.5 | 13.7 |
| 10.4 | 77.2 | 69.7 | 73.9 | | 43.6 | Long-Term Debt | 63.9 | 66.7 |
| .0 | .0 | .0 | .0 | | .0 | Deferred Taxes | .0 | .0 |
| 8.6 | 2.8 | 4.4 | 2.5 | | 2.0 | All Other Non-Current | 4.0 | 3.3 |
| -10.6 | 8.4 | 14.5 | 16.1 | | 41.9 | Net Worth | 14.6 | 16.4 |
| 100.0 | 100.0 | 100.0 | 100.0 | | 100.0 | Total Liabilities & Net Worth | 100.0 | 100.0 |
| | | | | | | **INCOME DATA** | | |
| 100.0 | 100.0 | 100.0 | 100.0 | | 100.0 | Net Sales | 100.0 | 100.0 |
| | | | | | | Gross Profit | | |
| 66.2 | 61.0 | 55.8 | 64.4 | | 65.3 | Operating Expenses | 58.5 | 60.8 |
| 33.8 | 39.0 | 44.2 | 35.6 | | 34.7 | Operating Profit | 41.5 | 39.2 |
| 4.0 | 16.6 | 20.5 | 21.5 | | 18.8 | All Other Expenses (net) | 15.7 | 15.9 |
| 29.8 | 22.4 | 23.7 | 14.1 | | 15.9 | Profit Before Taxes | 25.8 | 23.3 |
| | | | | | | **RATIOS** | | |
| 10.2 | 6.2 | 4.6 | 4.7 | | 1.8 | | 3.0 | 6.5 |
| 5.0 | 1.5 | 1.0 | 1.8 | | .8 | Current | .9 | 1.8 |
| .5 | .6 | .3 | .3 | | .4 | | .3 | .5 |
| 8.2 | 5.0 | 3.6 | 4.5 | | 1.8 | | 2.5 | 5.6 |
| 3.1 | 1.2 | .9 | 1.2 | | .8 | Quick | .8 | 1.7 |
| .5 | .4 | .3 | .2 | | .3 | | .2 | .4 |
| 0 UND | 0 UND | 0 UND | 0 UND | | 0 UND | | 0 UND | 0 UND |
| 0 UND | 0 UND | 0 UND | 0 UND | | 5 72.4 | Sales/Receivables | 0 UND | 0 UND |
| 3 136.5 | 0 UND | 0 UND | 10 35.7 | | 6 57.5 | | 0 UND | 0 UND |
| | | | | | | Cost of Sales/Inventory | | |
| | | | | | | Cost of Sales/Payables | | |
| 5.0 | 3.6 | 5.2 | 5.0 | | 6.7 | | 7.2 | 4.2 |
| 29.8 | 29.5 | UND | 19.8 | | -43.9 | Sales/Working Capital | -99.5 | 17.3 |
| -20.9 | -8.1 | -5.8 | -5.1 | | -14.1 | | -5.6 | -8.1 |
| | | 7.0 | 6.5 | | 4.4 | | 6.7 | 7.0 |
| | (26) 3.7 | (48) 3.8 | (10) 2.2 | | | EBIT/Interest | (190) 4.0 | (123) 3.9 |
| | | 2.3 | 2.6 | | .9 | | 2.7 | 2.3 |
| | | | | | | Net Profit + Depr., Dep., Amort./Cur. Mat. L/T/D | | |
| .0 | 1.4 | 2.1 | 2.0 | | .0 | | 1.8 | 1.5 |
| 1.2 | 5.5 | 6.9 | 13.4 | | .8 | Fixed/Worth | 5.5 | 3.7 |
| -.3 | -27.5 | -12.4 | -12.3 | | 3.3 | | -17.6 | -66.0 |
| .1 | 1.1 | 1.5 | 1.3 | | .8 | | 1.4 | 1.2 |
| 1.9 | 5.0 | 6.0 | 15.7 | | 1.9 | Debt/Worth | 5.6 | 4.1 |
| -8.7 | -42.6 | -23.5 | -15.5 | | 3.5 | | -19.7 | -51.9 |
| 184.3 | 49.6 | 42.1 | 21.6 | | 28.6 | | 55.5 | 42.4 |
| (10) 28.2 | (34) 26.1 | (71) 12.4 | (13) 10.3 | | (10) 7.0 | % Profit Before Taxes/Tangible Net Worth | (231) 22.5 | (180) 16.4 |
| 7.2 | 6.6 | 3.5 | -.8 | | -4.4 | | 6.7 | 3.2 |
| 165.1 | 18.2 | 9.4 | 6.0 | | 10.6 | | 13.2 | 11.6 |
| 49.6 | 5.4 | 4.5 | 2.2 | | 4.4 | % Profit Before Taxes/Total Assets | 6.0 | 5.1 |
| 3.1 | .6 | 1.2 | .1 | | -1.3 | | 1.9 | .9 |
| UND | .8 | .4 | .3 | | 926.0 | | .6 | .5 |
| 65.5 | .3 | .2 | .2 | | .7 | Sales/Net Fixed Assets | .3 | .2 |
| 1.7 | .2 | .1 | .1 | | .2 | | .2 | .2 |
| 18.2 | .5 | .3 | .2 | | .8 | | .5 | .4 |
| 5.1 | .3 | .2 | .2 | | .2 | Sales/Total Assets | .2 | .2 |
| 1.2 | .2 | .1 | .1 | | .1 | | .1 | .1 |
| | | 6.4 | 10.2 | | 12.5 | | 7.5 | 8.1 |
| | (31) 10.7 | (66) 17.1 | (14) 19.7 | | | % Depr., Dep., Amort./Sales | (230) 12.7 | (179) 15.3 |
| | | 16.6 | 26.5 | | 34.4 | | 19.9 | 23.4 |
| | | | | | | | 2.6 | 3.3 |
| | | | | | | % Officers', Directors' Owners' Comp/Sales | (38) 7.2 | (30) 7.6 |
| | | | | | | | 11.7 | 11.1 |
| 10680M | 23610M | 104788M | 165068M | 1347085M | 1350348M | Net Sales ($) | 1808553M | 404013M |
| 2898M | 55081M | 448669M | 491223M | 504097M | 1749561M | Total Assets ($) | 2745676M | 1810709M |

M = $ thousand    MM = $ million
See Pages viii through xx for Explanation of Ratios and Data

© RMA 2024

# REAL ESTATE—Lessors of Miniwarehouses and Self-Storage Units  NAICS 531130

## Comparative Historical Data | Current Data Sorted by Sales

| | | | | Type of Statement | | | | | | |
|---|---|---|---|---|---|---|---|---|---|---|
| 5 | 10 | 5 | | Unqualified | | | 1 | 1 | 1 | 3 |
| 5 | 9 | 3 | | Reviewed | | | 1 | 1 | 1 | |
| 16 | 12 | 5 | | Compiled | | 2 | 2 | | | |
| 115 | 77 | 76 | | Tax Returns | 53 | 19 | 2 | 1 | | 1 |
| 121 | 110 | 112 | | Other | 60 | 33 | 2 | 3 | 6 | 8 |
| 4/1/21-3/31/22 ALL | 4/1/22-3/31/23 ALL | 4/1/23-3/31/24 ALL | | | 5 (4/1-9/30/23) | | | 196 (10/1/23-3/31/24) | | |
| | | | | | 0-1MM | 1-3MM | 3-5MM | 5-10MM | 10-25MM | 25MM & OVER |
| 262 | 218 | 201 | | NUMBER OF STATEMENTS | 114 | 54 | 7 | 6 | 8 | 12 |
| % | % | % | | ASSETS | % | % | % | % | % | % |
| 11.6 | 14.0 | 11.4 | | Cash & Equivalents | 9.2 | 15.0 | | | | 21.4 |
| .6 | 1.2 | 1.3 | | Trade Receivables (net) | .2 | .7 | | | | 11.8 |
| .5 | .5 | 1.0 | | Inventory | 1.2 | .4 | | | | 3.8 |
| 2.3 | 2.7 | 2.6 | | All Other Current | 2.0 | 3.7 | | | | 1.7 |
| 14.9 | 18.5 | 16.3 | | Total Current | 12.6 | 19.9 | | | | 38.8 |
| 74.7 | 73.8 | 73.2 | | Fixed Assets (net) | 80.9 | 69.1 | | | | 38.8 |
| 3.0 | 1.8 | 2.8 | | Intangibles (net) | 1.9 | 3.0 | | | | 5.5 |
| 7.4 | 5.9 | 7.8 | | All Other Non-Current | 4.7 | 7.9 | | | | 17.0 |
| 100.0 | 100.0 | 100.0 | | Total | 100.0 | 100.0 | | | | 100.0 |
| | | | | LIABILITIES | | | | | | |
| 2.5 | 2.8 | 6.8 | | Notes Payable-Short Term | 8.5 | .8 | | | | 15.3 |
| 3.3 | 1.8 | 1.6 | | Cur. Mat.-L.T.D. | 2.0 | 1.7 | | | | .3 |
| .5 | 1.1 | .8 | | Trade Payables | .6 | .6 | | | | 3.7 |
| .0 | .0 | .0 | | Income Taxes Payable | .0 | .0 | | | | .0 |
| 4.8 | 8.2 | 8.5 | | All Other Current | 5.4 | 13.7 | | | | 16.1 |
| 11.1 | 14.0 | 17.6 | | Total Current | 16.5 | 16.9 | | | | 35.4 |
| 72.5 | 62.8 | 64.9 | | Long-Term Debt | 62.5 | 81.0 | | | | 18.2 |
| .0 | .0 | .0 | | Deferred Taxes | .0 | .0 | | | | .0 |
| 2.6 | 3.6 | 3.9 | | All Other Non-Current | 4.7 | 2.9 | | | | 4.0 |
| 13.8 | 19.6 | 13.6 | | Net Worth | 16.2 | -.8 | | | | 42.5 |
| 100.0 | 100.0 | 100.0 | | Total Liabilties & Net Worth | 100.0 | 100.0 | | | | 100.0 |
| | | | | INCOME DATA | | | | | | |
| 100.0 | 100.0 | 100.0 | | Net Sales | 100.0 | 100.0 | | | | 100.0 |
| | | | | Gross Profit | | | | | | |
| 56.6 | 60.7 | 59.3 | | Operating Expenses | 55.9 | 63.0 | | | | 74.2 |
| 43.4 | 39.3 | 40.7 | | Operating Profit | 44.1 | 37.0 | | | | 25.8 |
| 14.0 | 13.5 | 18.0 | | All Other Expenses (net) | 21.4 | 13.8 | | | | 1.6 |
| 29.3 | 25.8 | 22.6 | | Profit Before Taxes | 22.7 | 23.2 | | | | 24.2 |
| | | | | RATIOS | | | | | | |
| 10.4 | 6.9 | 5.6 | | | 4.2 | 13.7 | | | | 1.9 |
| 2.5 | 1.8 | 1.3 | | Current | 1.1 | 2.7 | | | | 1.3 |
| .6 | .4 | .4 | | | .3 | .4 | | | | .8 |
| 8.3 | 6.7 | 4.2 | | | 3.4 | 10.6 | | | | 1.9 |
| 2.0 | 1.6 | 1.0 | | Quick | .9 | 1.9 | | | | 1.0 |
| .5 | .3 | .3 | | | .3 | .4 | | | | .5 |
| 0 UND | 0 UND | 0 UND | | | 0 UND | 0 UND | | | | 0 UND |
| 0 UND | 0 UND | 0 UND | | Sales/Receivables | 0 UND | 0 UND | | | | 4 91.2 |
| 0 UND | 1 419.4 | 1 421.1 | | | 0 UND | 0 UND | | | | 37 9.9 |
| | | | | Cost of Sales/Inventory | | | | | | |
| | | | | Cost of Sales/Payables | | | | | | |
| 3.8 | 3.8 | 4.4 | | | 4.5 | 3.8 | | | | 4.7 |
| 10.7 | 13.8 | 78.3 | | Sales/Working Capital | 261.7 | 28.5 | | | | 34.3 |
| -15.4 | -11.7 | -7.3 | | | -5.7 | -9.2 | | | | -31.4 |
| 7.9 | 6.4 | 6.3 | | | 5.8 | 6.8 | | | | |
| (156) 4.4 | (117) 4.1 | (100) 3.7 | | EBIT/Interest | (45) 3.8 | (34) 4.0 | | | | |
| 2.8 | 2.6 | 2.3 | | | 2.4 | 2.3 | | | | |
| | | | | Net Profit + Depr., Dep., Amort./Cur. Mat. L/T/D | | | | | | |
| 1.7 | 1.3 | 1.4 | | | 1.8 | 1.5 | | | | .0 |
| 4.4 | 3.8 | 5.4 | | Fixed/Worth | 5.7 | 8.0 | | | | 1.0 |
| -18.3 | -248.1 | -30.1 | | | -146.9 | -6.6 | | | | 1.9 |
| 1.4 | 1.2 | 1.3 | | | 1.4 | 1.3 | | | | .6 |
| 4.4 | 3.8 | 5.2 | | Debt/Worth | 5.3 | 7.8 | | | | 1.3 |
| -15.2 | -125.9 | -45.2 | | | -160.8 | -9.2 | | | | 39.9 |
| 51.9 | 55.2 | 43.5 | | | 41.4 | 48.2 | | | | 69.1 |
| (181) 26.0 | (158) 24.1 | (144) 14.8 | | % Profit Before Taxes/Tangible Net Worth | (85) 12.4 | (36) 22.6 | | | (10) | 23.0 |
| 10.4 | 7.5 | 3.5 | | | 2.9 | 4.1 | | | | 4.8 |
| 15.0 | 12.2 | 10.6 | | | 9.4 | 16.3 | | | | 30.6 |
| 7.2 | 6.3 | 4.6 | | % Profit Before Taxes/Total Assets | 4.0 | 7.1 | | | | 7.8 |
| 2.9 | 1.7 | 1.0 | | | .7 | 1.2 | | | | 2.5 |
| .6 | .6 | .7 | | | .4 | 1.1 | | | | 723.9 |
| .3 | .3 | .3 | | Sales/Net Fixed Assets | .2 | .4 | | | | 2.4 |
| .2 | .2 | .1 | | | .1 | .2 | | | | .8 |
| .4 | .5 | .4 | | | .3 | .7 | | | | 1.2 |
| .2 | .2 | .2 | | Sales/Total Assets | .2 | .3 | | | | .9 |
| .2 | .1 | .1 | | | .1 | .2 | | | | .7 |
| 9.3 | 8.2 | 8.7 | | | 10.2 | 5.1 | | | | |
| (186) 13.9 | (142) 13.4 | (126) 14.3 | | % Depr., Dep., Amort./Sales | (71) 16.6 | (34) 11.0 | | | | |
| 21.5 | 21.8 | 23.1 | | | 27.4 | 18.7 | | | | |
| 2.0 | 5.3 | 3.4 | | | | | | | | |
| (30) 4.8 | (23) 6.7 | (17) 4.8 | | % Officers', Directors' Owners' Comp/Sales | | | | | | |
| 8.0 | 16.4 | 14.9 | | | | | | | | |
| 635961M | 976240M | 3001579M | | Net Sales ($) | 50489M | 82146M | 27808M | 45985M | 127265M | 2667886M |
| 2405985M | 2598038M | 3251529M | | Total Assets ($) | 298952M | 348993M | 88849M | 373343M | 790471M | 1350921M |

© RMA 2024  M = $ thousand  MM = $ million
See Pages viii through xx for Explanation of Ratios and Data

# REAL ESTATE—Lessors of Other Real Estate Property  NAICS 531190

## Current Data Sorted by Assets

| Type of Statement | 0-500M | 500M-2MM | 2-10MM | 10-50MM | 50-100MM | 100-250MM |
|---|---|---|---|---|---|---|
| Unqualified | 1 | 2 | 5 | 6 | 3 | 3 |
| Reviewed |  | 2 | 2 | 2 | 2 | 3 |
| Compiled |  | 6 | 9 | 5 |  |  |
| Tax Returns | 14 | 55 | 52 | 17 | 1 | 1 |
| Other | 24 | 67 | 141 | 80 | 13 | 15 |
|  |  | 22 (4/1-9/30/23) |  | 507 (10/1/23-3/31/24) |  |  |
| NUMBER OF STATEMENTS | 39 | 130 | 209 | 110 | 19 | 22 |

|  | % | % | % | % | % | % | |
|---|---|---|---|---|---|---|---|
| **ASSETS** | | | | | | | |
| Cash & Equivalents | 28.7 | 7.2 | 5.9 | 7.5 | 8.1 | 6.8 | |
| Trade Receivables (net) | 3.0 | 1.3 | .6 | 1.8 | 4.3 | 2.5 | |
| Inventory | .6 | .8 | 1.7 | 2.0 | .5 | 7.4 | |
| All Other Current | 2.9 | 1.5 | 1.5 | 1.8 | .6 | 2.5 | |
| Total Current | 35.1 | 10.8 | 9.6 | 13.1 | 13.5 | 19.1 | |
| Fixed Assets (net) | 44.1 | 79.9 | 82.1 | 78.7 | 69.6 | 57.7 | |
| Intangibles (net) | 2.1 | 2.3 | 3.0 | 1.6 | 3.3 | 13.5 | |
| All Other Non-Current | 18.7 | 7.0 | 5.3 | 6.5 | 13.6 | 9.7 | |
| Total | 100.0 | 100.0 | 100.0 | 100.0 | 100.0 | 100.0 | |
| **LIABILITIES** | | | | | | | |
| Notes Payable-Short Term | 2.2 | 6.5 | 1.8 | 3.0 | .8 | 4.9 | |
| Cur. Mat.-L.T.D. | 6.5 | 2.4 | 2.3 | 2.6 | 5.4 | 1.5 | |
| Trade Payables | .9 | .8 | .6 | 1.8 | 2.8 | 4.4 | |
| Income Taxes Payable | .1 | .0 | .0 | .0 | .0 | .0 | |
| All Other Current | 28.9 | 6.8 | 4.8 | 4.6 | 3.8 | 3.7 | |
| Total Current | 38.5 | 16.5 | 9.5 | 12.0 | 12.9 | 14.6 | |
| Long-Term Debt | 44.1 | 60.8 | 59.6 | 52.3 | 52.8 | 40.3 | |
| Deferred Taxes | .0 | .0 | .0 | .1 | .4 | .8 | |
| All Other Non-Current | 5.7 | 2.4 | 4.9 | 3.4 | 3.2 | 3.0 | |
| Net Worth | 11.7 | 20.3 | 26.0 | 32.2 | 30.8 | 41.4 | |
| Total Liabilities & Net Worth | 100.0 | 100.0 | 100.0 | 100.0 | 100.0 | 100.0 | |
| **INCOME DATA** | | | | | | | |
| Net Sales | 100.0 | 100.0 | 100.0 | 100.0 | 100.0 | 100.0 | |
| Gross Profit | | | | | | | |
| Operating Expenses | 66.1 | 50.1 | 49.0 | 53.6 | 57.5 | 57.7 | |
| Operating Profit | 33.9 | 49.9 | 51.0 | 46.4 | 42.5 | 42.3 | |
| All Other Expenses (net) | 9.3 | 19.0 | 23.2 | 20.0 | 20.6 | 17.9 | |
| Profit Before Taxes | 24.6 | 30.9 | 27.7 | 26.3 | 21.9 | 24.4 | |
| **RATIOS** | | | | | | | |
| Current | 2.3 | 2.4 | 2.8 | 4.4 | 3.5 | 2.4 | |
|  | 1.1 | .9 | .9 | 1.2 | 1.4 | 1.3 | |
|  | .4 | .3 | .3 | .4 | .3 | .3 | |
| Quick | 2.3 | 2.2 | 2.3 | 3.3 | 3.4 | 1.6 | |
|  | .8 | .7 | .7 | .9 | .9 | .6 | |
|  | .4 | .2 | .2 | .2 | .2 | .2 | |
| Sales/Receivables | 0 UND | 0 UND | 0 UND | 0 UND | 0 UND | 0 UND | |
|  | 0 UND | 0 UND | 0 UND | 0 UND | 3 108.1 | 1 661.8 | |
|  | 0 UND | 0 UND | 0 UND | 7 49.7 | 18 19.9 | 19 19.2 | |
| Cost of Sales/Inventory | | | | | | | |
| Cost of Sales/Payables | | | | | | | |
| Sales/Working Capital | 12.5 | 4.8 | 5.8 | 2.6 | 4.1 | 4.3 | |
|  | 763.0 | -118.0 | -52.0 | 27.8 | 78.9 | 24.6 | |
|  | -4.9 | -3.1 | -3.6 | -3.9 | -2.9 | -2.8 | |
| EBIT/Interest | 34.9 | 7.9 | 9.1 | 9.0 | 30.3 |  | |
|  | (20) 10.5 | (60) 4.4 | (79) 4.7 | (44) 4.5 | (12) 4.9 |  | |
|  | 2.9 | 2.5 | 2.4 | 2.5 | 2.7 |  | |
| Net Profit + Depr., Dep., Amort./Cur. Mat. L/T/D |  |  |  | 4.8 |  |  | |
|  |  |  | (10) | 2.9 |  |  | |
|  |  |  |  | 1.2 |  |  | |
| Fixed/Worth | .0 | 1.7 | 1.8 | 1.3 | 1.2 | .9 | |
|  | 3.0 | 3.6 | 3.8 | 2.7 | 2.8 | 2.0 | |
|  | UND | 19.8 | 20.9 | 7.1 | 6.4 | -31.0 | |
| Debt/Worth | .6 | 1.0 | 1.0 | .8 | .8 | .9 | |
|  | 2.9 | 3.1 | 3.0 | 2.2 | 1.8 | 2.1 | |
|  | -16.5 | 28.0 | 23.1 | 6.6 | 5.9 | -36.1 | |
| % Profit Before Taxes/Tangible Net Worth | 206.0 | 38.8 | 33.8 | 22.3 | 20.0 | 22.0 | |
|  | (28) 50.4 | (100) 16.7 | (167) 13.6 | (96) 11.9 | (16) 14.3 | (16) 9.0 | |
|  | 20.7 | 5.6 | 3.7 | 2.8 | 1.7 | 2.6 | |
| % Profit Before Taxes/Total Assets | 60.5 | 11.1 | 8.5 | 7.5 | 8.0 | 6.4 | |
|  | 19.6 | 5.4 | 4.0 | 3.2 | 5.7 | 3.2 | |
|  | 2.8 | 1.5 | .9 | .7 | .5 | 1.7 | |
| Sales/Net Fixed Assets | 769.5 | .4 | .3 | .3 | 1.2 | 4.0 | |
|  | 2.9 | .2 | .2 | .1 | .2 | .4 | |
|  | .2 | .1 | .1 | .1 | .1 | .1 | |
| Sales/Total Assets | 3.8 | .3 | .2 | .3 | .3 | .4 | |
|  | .9 | .2 | .1 | .1 | .1 | .1 | |
|  | .2 | .1 | .1 | .1 | .1 | .1 | |
| % Depr., Dep., Amort./Sales | 4.1 | 10.0 | 11.4 | 6.6 | 2.8 | 7.3 | |
|  | (13) 14.0 | (90) 17.6 | (149) 19.5 | (74) 15.3 | (15) 11.8 | (14) 13.9 | |
|  | 16.0 | 26.6 | 28.3 | 26.8 | 26.3 | 20.5 | |
| % Officers', Directors' Owners' Comp/Sales |  |  | 1.2 |  |  |  | |
|  |  | (10) | 2.7 |  |  |  | |
|  |  |  | 13.8 |  |  |  | |
| Net Sales ($) | 22376M | 68706M | 340921M | 725152M | 622145M | 1951336M | |
| Total Assets ($) | 11210M | 164144M | 958795M | 2246467M | 1277754M | 3831425M | |

## Comparative Historical Data

| Type of Statement | | |
|---|---|---|
| Unqualified | 24 | 13 |
| Reviewed | 22 | 7 |
| Compiled | 48 | 30 |
| Tax Returns | 276 | 191 |
| Other | 501 | 321 |
|  | 4/1/19-3/31/20 ALL | 4/1/20-3/31/21 ALL |
| NUMBER OF STATEMENTS | 871 | 562 |

|  | % | % |
|---|---|---|
| **ASSETS** | | |
| Cash & Equivalents | 7.6 | 11.5 |
| Trade Receivables (net) | 2.0 | 1.3 |
| Inventory | 1.2 | 1.3 |
| All Other Current | 1.6 | 1.3 |
| Total Current | 12.5 | 15.4 |
| Fixed Assets (net) | 77.7 | 74.5 |
| Intangibles (net) | 3.0 | 2.7 |
| All Other Non-Current | 6.9 | 7.4 |
| Total | 100.0 | 100.0 |
| **LIABILITIES** | | |
| Notes Payable-Short Term | 4.0 | 3.4 |
| Cur. Mat.-L.T.D. | 3.0 | 3.2 |
| Trade Payables | 1.4 | 1.1 |
| Income Taxes Payable | .1 | .0 |
| All Other Current | 6.4 | 7.2 |
| Total Current | 14.9 | 14.9 |
| Long-Term Debt | 54.1 | 57.8 |
| Deferred Taxes | .0 | .0 |
| All Other Non-Current | 4.6 | 3.9 |
| Net Worth | 26.4 | 23.4 |
| Total Liabilities & Net Worth | 100.0 | 100.0 |
| **INCOME DATA** | | |
| Net Sales | 100.0 | 100.0 |
| Gross Profit | | |
| Operating Expenses | 54.5 | 53.1 |
| Operating Profit | 45.5 | 46.9 |
| All Other Expenses (net) | 20.7 | 17.6 |
| Profit Before Taxes | 24.8 | 29.3 |
| **RATIOS** | | |
| Current | 2.3 | 3.6 |
|  | .8 | 1.2 |
|  | .2 | .3 |
| Quick | 2.0 | 3.0 |
|  | .6 | 1.0 |
|  | .2 | .2 |
| Sales/Receivables | 0 UND | 0 UND |
|  | 0 UND | 0 UND |
|  | 1 537.5 | 1 541.0 |
| Sales/Working Capital | 5.2 | 3.4 |
|  | -21.6 | 22.4 |
|  | -2.8 | -3.0 |
| EBIT/Interest | 7.5 | 7.9 |
|  | (346) 3.9 | (240) 4.4 |
|  | 2.2 | 2.3 |
| Net Profit + Depr., Dep., Amort./Cur. Mat. L/T/D | 3.0 | 5.3 |
|  | (35) 1.8 | (17) 3.2 |
|  | 1.2 | 1.3 |
| Fixed/Worth | 1.5 | 1.3 |
|  | 3.3 | 3.2 |
|  | 22.4 | 22.1 |
| Debt/Worth | 1.0 | 1.0 |
|  | 2.7 | 3.2 |
|  | 31.1 | 61.4 |
| % Profit Before Taxes/Tangible Net Worth | 30.2 | 35.7 |
|  | (688) 12.5 | (431) 14.8 |
|  | 3.4 | 4.7 |
| % Profit Before Taxes/Total Assets | 8.4 | 8.9 |
|  | 3.7 | 4.4 |
|  | .9 | 1.7 |
| Sales/Net Fixed Assets | .4 | .4 |
|  | .2 | .2 |
|  | .1 | .1 |
| Sales/Total Assets | .3 | .3 |
|  | .1 | .2 |
|  | .1 | .1 |
| % Depr., Dep., Amort./Sales | 9.2 | 10.9 |
|  | (651) 17.0 | (381) 18.3 |
|  | 26.1 | 27.5 |
| % Officers', Directors' Owners' Comp/Sales | 2.6 | 2.5 |
|  | (68) 6.5 | (33) 5.9 |
|  | 14.5 | 12.3 |
| Net Sales ($) | 11100991M | 1391517M |
| Total Assets ($) | 9512196M | 5750671M |

© RMA 2024

M = $ thousand   MM = $ million
See Pages viii through xx for Explanation of Ratios and Data

# REAL ESTATE—Lessors of Other Real Estate Property  NAICS 531190

**Comparative Historical Data** | **Current Data Sorted by Sales**

| | | | | | | Type of Statement | | | | | | | | | | |
|---|---|---|---|---|---|---|---|---|---|---|---|---|---|---|---|---|
| | | 12 | | 20 | 20 | Unqualified | 5 | | 5 | | 2 | 1 | | 7 | | 2 |
| | | 9 | | 19 | 9 | Reviewed | 1 | | 1 | | 1 | 1 | | 4 | | |
| | | 22 | | 31 | 20 | Compiled | 13 | | 4 | | 1 | 2 | | 1 | | 3 |
| | | 176 | | 190 | 140 | Tax Returns | 110 | | 19 | | 3 | 4 | | 1 | | 17 |
| | | 258 | | 354 | 340 | Other | 192 | | 78 | | 20 | 20 | | 13 | | |
| | | 4/1/21-3/31/22 ALL | | 4/1/22-3/31/23 ALL | 4/1/23-3/31/24 ALL | | | | 22 (4/1-9/30/23) | | | 507 (10/1/23-3/31/24) | | | | |
| | | | | | | | 0-1MM | | 1-3MM | | 3-5MM | 5-10MM | | 10-25MM | | 25MM & OVER |
| | | 477 | | 614 | 529 | NUMBER OF STATEMENTS | 321 | | 107 | | 26 | 28 | | 25 | | 22 |
| | | % | | % | % | **ASSETS** | % | | % | | % | % | | % | | % |
| | | 9.2 | | 9.2 | 8.3 | Cash & Equivalents | 6.3 | | 10.9 | | 12.0 | 7.2 | | 16.3 | | 13.2 |
| | | 1.7 | | 2.2 | 1.4 | Trade Receivables (net) | .3 | | 1.5 | | 3.4 | 4.8 | | 2.5 | | 9.0 |
| | | 1.6 | | 2.0 | 1.6 | Inventory | .3 | | .1 | | 4.3 | 3.5 | | 5.5 | | 19.4 |
| | | 1.9 | | 2.4 | 1.7 | All Other Current | 1.3 | | 1.8 | | 2.1 | 3.1 | | 2.4 | | 2.6 |
| | | 14.4 | | 15.8 | 13.1 | Total Current | 8.2 | | 14.4 | | 21.8 | 18.7 | | 26.8 | | 44.2 |
| | | 75.1 | | 74.5 | 76.6 | Fixed Assets (net) | 83.7 | | 73.7 | | 69.1 | 69.6 | | 48.9 | | 36.8 |
| | | 2.4 | | 2.2 | 2.9 | Intangibles (net) | 2.3 | | 3.3 | | 2.4 | 1.8 | | 5.4 | | 8.9 |
| | | 8.1 | | 7.5 | 7.4 | All Other Non-Current | 5.8 | | 8.7 | | 6.8 | 9.9 | | 18.9 | | 10.1 |
| | | 100.0 | | 100.0 | 100.0 | Total | 100.0 | | 100.0 | | 100.0 | 100.0 | | 100.0 | | 100.0 |
| | | | | | | **LIABILITIES** | | | | | | | | | | |
| | | 5.2 | | 4.2 | 3.4 | Notes Payable-Short Term | 3.4 | | 1.9 | | 5.9 | 3.2 | | 2.3 | | 7.9 |
| | | 2.4 | | 2.7 | 2.8 | Cur. Mat.-L.T.D. | 2.8 | | 2.2 | | 1.7 | 5.2 | | 4.1 | | 2.8 |
| | | 1.3 | | 1.6 | 1.1 | Trade Payables | .2 | | .9 | | 2.0 | 2.4 | | 3.2 | | 10.1 |
| | | .0 | | .0 | .0 | Income Taxes Payable | .0 | | .0 | | .0 | .0 | | .0 | | .0 |
| | | 5.3 | | 7.7 | 6.9 | All Other Current | 6.1 | | 5.9 | | 5.9 | 20.7 | | 6.0 | | 9.0 |
| | | 14.2 | | 16.2 | 14.2 | Total Current | 12.5 | | 10.9 | | 15.5 | 31.4 | | 15.7 | | 29.8 |
| | | 55.9 | | 56.9 | 56.2 | Long-Term Debt | 59.7 | | 56.3 | | 44.7 | 61.8 | | 38.0 | | 31.7 |
| | | .0 | | .0 | .1 | Deferred Taxes | .0 | | .0 | | .4 | .0 | | .3 | | .9 |
| | | 4.4 | | 4.1 | 3.9 | All Other Non-Current | 3.9 | | 3.7 | | 3.8 | 1.7 | | 8.4 | | 2.0 |
| | | 25.5 | | 22.8 | 25.6 | Net Worth | 23.8 | | 29.1 | | 35.6 | 5.0 | | 37.7 | | 35.7 |
| | | 100.0 | | 100.0 | 100.0 | Total Liabilities & Net Worth | 100.0 | | 100.0 | | 100.0 | 100.0 | | 100.0 | | 100.0 |
| | | | | | | **INCOME DATA** | | | | | | | | | | |
| | | 100.0 | | 100.0 | 100.0 | Net Sales | 100.0 | | 100.0 | | 100.0 | 100.0 | | 100.0 | | 100.0 |
| | | | | | | Gross Profit | | | | | | | | | | |
| | | 53.9 | | 54.9 | 52.2 | Operating Expenses | 47.9 | | 51.5 | | 61.6 | 57.8 | | 65.5 | | 84.5 |
| | | 46.1 | | 45.1 | 47.8 | Operating Profit | 52.1 | | 48.5 | | 38.4 | 42.2 | | 34.5 | | 15.5 |
| | | 17.7 | | 18.5 | 20.2 | All Other Expenses (net) | 24.0 | | 17.4 | | 11.6 | 12.6 | | 15.1 | | 3.5 |
| | | 28.4 | | 26.6 | 27.6 | Profit Before Taxes | 28.1 | | 31.1 | | 26.8 | 29.6 | | 19.4 | | 12.0 |
| | | | | | | **RATIOS** | | | | | | | | | | |
| | | 3.4 | | 3.7 | 2.9 | | 2.4 | | 5.3 | | 4.6 | 3.3 | | 4.6 | | 3.1 |
| | | 1.2 | | 1.3 | 1.0 | Current | .7 | | 1.2 | | 1.2 | .9 | | 1.7 | | 1.9 |
| | | .4 | | .3 | .3 | | .2 | | .6 | | .3 | .2 | | .8 | | 1.1 |
| | | 2.9 | | 2.9 | 2.3 | | 2.1 | | 4.4 | | 3.5 | 1.8 | | 4.0 | | 2.2 |
| (475) | | .9 | | .9 | .7 | Quick | .6 | | 1.1 | | 1.0 | .5 | | .9 | | .9 |
| | | .2 | | .2 | .2 | | .2 | | .4 | | .2 | .1 | | .6 | | .7 |
| 0 | | UND | 0 | UND | 0 UND | | 0 | UND | 0 | UND | 0 UND | 0 | UND | 0 | UND | 0 UND |
| 0 | | UND | 0 | UND | 0 UND | Sales/Receivables | 0 | UND | 0 | UND | 1 604.6 | 3 | 105.9 | 3 | 118.6 | 5 66.9 |
| 1 | | 617.5 | 2 | 194.1 | 2 192.9 | | 0 | UND | 3 | 128.2 | 16 23.5 | 33 | 10.9 | 21 | 17.8 | 29 12.6 |
| | | | | | | Cost of Sales/Inventory | | | | | | | | | | |
| | | | | | | Cost of Sales/Payables | | | | | | | | | | |
| | | 3.6 | | 3.0 | 4.5 | | 5.3 | | 4.4 | | 2.2 | 2.6 | | 3.1 | | 4.3 |
| | | 24.7 | | 26.6 | 763.0 | Sales/Working Capital | -18.7 | | 31.1 | | 8.4 | -84.5 | | 7.4 | | 10.2 |
| | | -3.1 | | -4.2 | -3.5 | | -2.8 | | -9.4 | | -2.1 | -2.2 | | -19.7 | | 76.1 |
| | | 10.3 | | 11.0 | 9.9 | | 7.6 | | 14.5 | | 9.9 | 19.6 | | 50.9 | | 51.1 |
| (212) | | 4.6 | (281) | 4.6 | (224) 4.6 | EBIT/Interest | (122) 4.1 | (40) | 5.4 | (15) | 4.6 | (16) 7.9 | (13) | 6.8 | (18) | 5.1 |
| | | 2.3 | | 2.3 | 2.7 | | 2.4 | | 3.4 | | 2.4 | 3.1 | | 1.9 | | 2.7 |
| | | | | 3.9 | 8.7 | Net Profit + Depr., Dep., | 2.0 | | | | | | | | | |
| | | | (19) | 1.6 | (25) 3.2 | Amort./Cur. Mat. L/T/D | (10) 1.4 | | | | | | | | | |
| | | | | 1.1 | 1.4 | | 1.1 | | | | | | | | | |
| | | 1.5 | | 1.4 | 1.5 | | 1.9 | | 1.2 | | 1.2 | 1.2 | | .1 | | .2 |
| | | 3.2 | | 3.3 | 3.2 | Fixed/Worth | 3.7 | | 2.7 | | 2.3 | 2.7 | | 1.9 | | .9 |
| | | 17.8 | | 20.9 | 13.5 | | 18.7 | | 9.2 | | 17.0 | 6.3 | | 6.4 | | -27.0 |
| | | 1.1 | | 1.0 | 1.0 | | 1.1 | | .8 | | .7 | 1.0 | | .7 | | .8 |
| | | 3.1 | | 3.1 | 2.8 | Debt/Worth | 3.0 | | 2.4 | | 2.4 | 2.5 | | 2.1 | | 1.8 |
| | | 19.7 | | 34.9 | 14.8 | | 35.0 | | 11.8 | | 18.6 | 7.9 | | 7.9 | | -31.9 |
| | | 44.5 | | 33.3 | 32.2 | % Profit Before Taxes/Tangible | 26.1 | | 54.6 | | 48.6 | 31.7 | | 34.1 | | 38.4 |
| (380) | | 17.0 | (481) | 14.7 | (423) 13.9 | Net Worth | (250) 12.7 | (91) | 20.2 | (23) | 14.8 | (22) 14.7 | (21) | 9.8 | (16) | 24.2 |
| | | 4.9 | | 4.0 | 4.3 | | 2.4 | | 7.7 | | 1.7 | 7.6 | | 4.1 | | 12.5 |
| | | 10.7 | | 10.2 | 10.0 | % Profit Before Taxes/Total | 8.2 | | 12.9 | | 19.2 | 14.5 | | 13.3 | | 21.3 |
| | | 4.6 | | 3.9 | 4.2 | Assets | 3.5 | | 5.5 | | 6.3 | 6.6 | | 3.8 | | 8.7 |
| | | 1.2 | | 1.0 | 1.1 | | .9 | | 2.4 | | 1.0 | 2.0 | | 1.2 | | 3.8 |
| | | .5 | | .5 | .4 | | .2 | | .7 | | .7 | 2.4 | | 32.6 | | 32.1 |
| | | .2 | | .2 | .2 | Sales/Net Fixed Assets | .1 | | .2 | | .3 | .3 | | .6 | | 5.3 |
| | | .1 | | .1 | .1 | | .1 | | .1 | | .2 | .1 | | .3 | | 1.1 |
| | | .3 | | .3 | .3 | | .2 | | .5 | | .4 | .5 | | .9 | | 3.4 |
| | | .1 | | .2 | .1 | Sales/Total Assets | .1 | | .2 | | .2 | .2 | | .3 | | 1.5 |
| | | .1 | | .1 | .1 | | .1 | | .1 | | .1 | .1 | | .1 | | .4 |
| | | 9.8 | | 9.6 | 9.7 | | 13.2 | | 9.6 | | 2.4 | 5.7 | | 2.2 | | .4 |
| (340) | | 17.6 | (439) | 17.3 | (355) 17.6 | % Depr., Dep., Amort./Sales | (219) 20.2 | (63) | 15.4 | (19) | 19.3 | (19) 9.6 | (19) | 9.4 | (16) | 1.0 |
| | | 27.2 | | 26.5 | 26.7 | | 29.3 | | 24.1 | | 26.2 | 17.7 | | 16.1 | | 7.3 |
| | | 2.3 | | 2.8 | 1.6 | % Officers', Directors', | 5.3 | | | | | | | | | |
| (30) | | 5.9 | (37) | 5.6 | (29) 4.6 | Owners' Comp/Sales | (13) 10.8 | | | | | | | | | |
| | | 11.8 | | 11.0 | 11.1 | | 25.6 | | | | | | | | | |
| | | 1343320M | | 4765117M | 3730636M | Net Sales ($) | 125310M | | 184662M | | 103944M | 202925M | | 409269M | | 2704526M |
| | | 4895294M | | 8101287M | 8489795M | Total Assets ($) | 1087754M | | 1238029M | | 610627M | 1369831M | | 2068243M | | 2115311M |

© RMA 2024   M = $ thousand   MM = $ million
See Pages viii through xx for Explanation of Ratios and Data

# REAL ESTATE—Offices of Real Estate Agents and Brokers  NAICS 531210

## Current Data Sorted by Assets | Comparative Historical Data

| | | | | | | | | |
|---|---|---|---|---|---|---|---|---|
| | | | 1 | 5 | 3 | 4 | **Type of Statement** | |
| | | | 2 | 3 | | | Unqualified | 17 / 15 |
| | 1 | | 9 | 1 | | | Reviewed | 8 / 7 |
| 33 | 34 | 25 | 3 | 1 | | | Compiled | 20 / 9 |
| 42 | 58 | 84 | 33 | 12 | 12 | | Tax Returns | 122 / 102 |
| | 29 (4/1-9/30/23) | | 339 (10/1/23-3/31/24) | | | | Other | 229 / 208 |
| 0-500M | 500M-2MM | 2-10MM | 10-50MM | 50-100MM | 100-250MM | | | 4/1/19-3/31/20 ALL / 4/1/20-3/31/21 ALL |
| 76 | 94 | 121 | 45 | 16 | 16 | **NUMBER OF STATEMENTS** | 396 | 341 |
| % | % | % | % | % | % | **ASSETS** | % | % |
| 57.0 | 32.2 | 18.5 | 14.8 | 16.4 | 12.0 | Cash & Equivalents | 31.3 | 36.9 |
| 2.0 | 6.8 | 5.9 | 3.8 | 9.8 | 15.1 | Trade Receivables (net) | 6.0 | 4.7 |
| 1.8 | .8 | 2.6 | .1 | 8.1 | .0 | Inventory | 2.2 | 2.1 |
| 4.7 | 6.3 | 6.7 | 5.8 | 2.0 | 10.8 | All Other Current | 5.9 | 5.2 |
| 65.5 | 46.0 | 33.7 | 24.6 | 36.3 | 38.0 | Total Current | 45.4 | 48.9 |
| 16.5 | 31.4 | 43.0 | 39.6 | 28.0 | 45.0 | Fixed Assets (net) | 32.2 | 30.4 |
| 9.4 | 6.5 | 10.1 | 5.9 | 10.5 | 12.6 | Intangibles (net) | 8.0 | 8.9 |
| 8.6 | 16.1 | 13.2 | 29.9 | 25.2 | 4.4 | All Other Non-Current | 14.4 | 11.9 |
| 100.0 | 100.0 | 100.0 | 100.0 | 100.0 | 100.0 | Total | 100.0 | 100.0 |
| | | | | | | **LIABILITIES** | | |
| 10.5 | 4.0 | 3.7 | 3.0 | 8.3 | 10.8 | Notes Payable-Short Term | 8.2 | 14.1 |
| 1.6 | 2.0 | 2.3 | 4.1 | 1.7 | 1.7 | Cur. Mat.-L.T.D. | 3.3 | 2.9 |
| 4.2 | 3.5 | 2.6 | 5.0 | 3.2 | 4.9 | Trade Payables | 4.6 | 2.8 |
| .1 | .0 | .1 | .1 | .0 | .3 | Income Taxes Payable | .2 | .0 |
| 20.3 | 19.2 | 15.1 | 12.6 | 11.3 | 11.7 | All Other Current | 18.8 | 15.5 |
| 36.8 | 28.8 | 23.8 | 25.0 | 24.5 | 29.3 | Total Current | 35.0 | 35.4 |
| 20.9 | 29.2 | 34.8 | 28.3 | 19.4 | 26.5 | Long-Term Debt | 23.2 | 28.2 |
| .1 | .1 | .0 | .0 | .0 | .0 | Deferred Taxes | .0 | .0 |
| 12.7 | 5.2 | 6.7 | 14.1 | 12.5 | 5.1 | All Other Non-Current | 7.4 | 6.6 |
| 29.5 | 36.7 | 34.7 | 32.7 | 43.6 | 39.0 | Net Worth | 34.3 | 29.8 |
| 100.0 | 100.0 | 100.0 | 100.0 | 100.0 | 100.0 | Total Liabilities & Net Worth | 100.0 | 100.0 |
| | | | | | | **INCOME DATA** | | |
| 100.0 | 100.0 | 100.0 | 100.0 | 100.0 | 100.0 | Net Sales | 100.0 | 100.0 |
| | | | | | | Gross Profit | | |
| 87.9 | 78.7 | 76.8 | 84.3 | 85.1 | 84.2 | Operating Expenses | 81.7 | 79.1 |
| 12.1 | 21.3 | 23.2 | 15.7 | 14.9 | 15.8 | Operating Profit | 18.3 | 20.9 |
| 1.1 | 4.0 | 9.5 | 7.3 | 2.2 | 9.0 | All Other Expenses (net) | 4.6 | 4.9 |
| 11.0 | 17.3 | 13.7 | 8.4 | 12.6 | 6.8 | Profit Before Taxes | 13.8 | 16.0 |
| | | | | | | **RATIOS** | | |
| 10.8 | 10.9 | 4.2 | 3.9 | 2.5 | 2.6 | | 3.7 | 3.6 |
| 2.6 | 1.9 | 1.5 | 1.2 | 1.8 | 1.4 | Current | 1.4 | 1.7 |
| 1.0 | .9 | .6 | .4 | 1.3 | .8 | | .7 | .7 |
| 10.1 | 10.4 | 3.6 | 2.7 | 2.2 | 2.6 | | 3.0 | 3.2 |
| 2.3 | 1.6 | 1.1 | .9 | 1.4 | 1.2 | Quick | 1.2 | 1.3 |
| .8 | .6 | .4 | .3 | .9 | .4 | | .5 | .5 |
| 0 UND | 0 UND | 0 UND | 0 999.8 | 0 UND | 0 UND | | 0 UND | 0 UND |
| 0 UND | 0 UND | 0 UND | 3 110.2 | 3 123.2 | 7 52.6 | Sales/Receivables | 0 UND | 0 UND |
| 0 UND | 2 237.8 | 5 67.0 | 18 20.4 | 30 12.2 | 68 5.4 | | 4 85.2 | 4 83.7 |
| | | | | | | Cost of Sales/Inventory | | |
| | | | | | | Cost of Sales/Payables | | |
| 6.0 | 5.6 | 5.4 | 2.8 | 4.1 | 4.4 | | 7.7 | 5.4 |
| 26.9 | 25.4 | 39.7 | 85.2 | 10.7 | 11.7 | Sales/Working Capital | 35.4 | 23.3 |
| UND | -86.3 | -12.4 | -9.4 | 101.2 | -32.4 | | -24.7 | -26.6 |
| 26.1 | 29.3 | 24.4 | 14.5 | 5.1 | 4.6 | | 35.6 | 53.9 |
| (32) 5.2 | (48) 6.3 | (64) 3.7 | (29) 2.5 | (14) 2.3 | (12) 2.9 | EBIT/Interest | (214) 7.8 | (188) 12.1 |
| -7.6 | -.6 | 1.2 | -4.1 | -1.3 | 1.7 | | 2.2 | 3.2 |
| | | | | | | Net Profit + Depr., Dep., Amort./Cur. Mat. L/T/D | 5.3 / 9.9 |
| | | | | | | | (14) 3.1 | (12) 4.4 |
| | | | | | | | .9 | 1.2 |
| .0 | .0 | .1 | .1 | .2 | .1 | | .1 | .0 |
| .1 | .5 | 1.8 | 1.9 | .8 | 2.1 | Fixed/Worth | .6 | .6 |
| 2.0 | 3.2 | 17.1 | 29.4 | NM | NM | | 3.4 | 6.7 |
| .2 | .6 | .8 | .6 | .8 | 1.2 | | .4 | .7 |
| 1.4 | 1.6 | 2.6 | 2.1 | 1.1 | 2.1 | Debt/Worth | 1.6 | 2.3 |
| -4.6 | 6.2 | 514.3 | 76.0 | NM | -10.0 | | 10.2 | UND |
| 171.2 | 110.8 | 61.5 | 30.2 | 53.6 | 23.9 | | 114.1 | 114.0 |
| (55) 57.7 | (80) 38.6 | (92) 23.3 | (36) 15.1 | (12) 9.1 | (11) 10.0 | % Profit Before Taxes/Tangible Net Worth | (318) 41.3 | (258) 55.6 |
| .0 | 10.8 | 4.8 | -2.4 | 1.4 | 2.3 | | 10.2 | 13.3 |
| 71.9 | 35.7 | 17.6 | 9.8 | 7.5 | 7.0 | | 44.5 | 48.1 |
| 31.8 | 13.8 | 5.5 | 3.7 | 2.6 | 2.3 | % Profit Before Taxes/Total Assets | 11.4 | 16.0 |
| -6.6 | 1.6 | 1.1 | -2.8 | -4.5 | .5 | | 2.4 | 2.8 |
| UND | 236.4 | 136.9 | 46.2 | 39.3 | 68.9 | | 218.9 | 553.9 |
| 240.6 | 48.4 | 9.5 | 11.0 | 13.6 | 3.5 | Sales/Net Fixed Assets | 30.8 | 31.0 |
| 42.9 | 1.3 | .2 | .2 | 1.5 | .2 | | 3.0 | 1.4 |
| 12.7 | 6.1 | 3.4 | 3.3 | 2.8 | 1.6 | | 8.7 | 6.3 |
| 5.4 | 2.4 | 1.0 | .6 | .9 | .9 | Sales/Total Assets | 2.7 | 2.3 |
| 1.8 | .4 | .2 | .1 | .5 | .1 | | .5 | .4 |
| .2 | .3 | .3 | .7 | 1.5 | 2.5 | | .3 | .5 |
| (11) .7 | (38) .7 | (59) 4.1 | (34) 4.8 | (12) 2.2 | (10) 9.8 | % Depr., Dep., Amort./Sales | (216) 1.0 | (145) 2.1 |
| 5.2 | 9.9 | 23.0 | 19.4 | 5.7 | 24.1 | | 9.1 | 16.9 |
| 2.0 | 2.7 | 1.3 | | | | | 2.7 | 2.4 |
| (38) 9.6 | (19) 4.4 | (29) 2.5 | | | | % Officers', Directors' Owners' Comp/Sales | (107) 6.7 | (99) 8.2 |
| 18.8 | 14.9 | 6.1 | | | | | 14.8 | 16.0 |
| 164050M | 532748M | 1439570M | 2419026M | 3387043M | 4863339M | Net Sales ($) | 14924656M | 7089274M |
| 16781M | 104398M | 542687M | 981931M | 1186232M | 2364903M | Total Assets ($) | 5209935M | 4463729M |

© RMA 2024

M = $ thousand   MM = $ million
See Pages viii through xx for Explanation of Ratios and Data

# REAL ESTATE—Offices of Real Estate Agents and Brokers  NAICS 531210

## Comparative Historical Data | Current Data Sorted by Sales

| Comparative Historical Data | | | Type of Statement | Current Data Sorted by Sales | | | | | |
|---|---|---|---|---|---|---|---|---|---|
| 8 | 18 | 13 | Unqualified | | 1 | | 3 | 4 | 5 |
| 7 | 11 | 5 | Reviewed | 1 | 1 | | 1 | | 2 |
| 16 | 19 | 13 | Compiled | 3 | 3 | | 2 | 2 | 3 |
| 111 | 126 | 96 | Tax Returns | 44 | 20 | 9 | 4 | 10 | 9 |
| 211 | 273 | 241 | Other | 67 | 44 | 24 | 32 | 27 | 47 |
| 4/1/21-3/31/22 ALL | 4/1/22-3/31/23 ALL | 4/1/23-3/31/24 ALL | | 29 (4/1-9/30/23) | | | 339 (10/1/23-3/31/24) | | |
| | | | | 0-1MM | 1-3MM | 3-5MM | 5-10MM | 10-25MM | 25MM & OVER |
| 353 | 447 | 368 | NUMBER OF STATEMENTS | 115 | 69 | 33 | 42 | 43 | 66 |
| % | % | % | ASSETS | % | % | % | % | % | % |
| 37.3 | 28.5 | 29.1 | Cash & Equivalents | 28.2 | 31.2 | 25.1 | 28.7 | 39.3 | 24.2 |
| 4.7 | 4.8 | 5.6 | Trade Receivables (net) | 2.1 | 4.6 | 9.4 | 10.1 | 5.6 | 8.3 |
| 1.8 | 2.3 | 1.8 | Inventory | .6 | 1.9 | 3.7 | 4.6 | 1.8 | 1.0 |
| 5.8 | 6.7 | 6.1 | All Other Current | 3.0 | 5.2 | 7.3 | 8.6 | 8.9 | 8.1 |
| 49.6 | 42.3 | 42.6 | Total Current | 34.0 | 42.9 | 45.5 | 51.9 | 55.6 | 41.5 |
| 30.0 | 36.1 | 33.6 | Fixed Assets (net) | 52.4 | 33.4 | 21.3 | 22.2 | 18.6 | 24.1 |
| 7.8 | 7.6 | 8.6 | Intangibles (net) | 4.7 | 7.7 | 12.2 | 7.3 | 13.7 | 12.3 |
| 12.7 | 14.0 | 15.2 | All Other Non-Current | 9.0 | 15.9 | 20.9 | 18.6 | 12.1 | 22.2 |
| 100.0 | 100.0 | 100.0 | Total | 100.0 | 100.0 | 100.0 | 100.0 | 100.0 | 100.0 |
| | | | LIABILITIES | | | | | | |
| 8.4 | 7.4 | 5.6 | Notes Payable-Short Term | 4.2 | 7.0 | 6.5 | 3.6 | 9.0 | 5.2 |
| 1.6 | 2.0 | 2.2 | Cur. Mat.-L.T.D. | 2.7 | 1.4 | 2.2 | 2.8 | 2.4 | 1.8 |
| 3.3 | 3.5 | 3.6 | Trade Payables | 2.5 | 2.5 | 5.4 | 2.2 | 3.7 | 6.5 |
| .1 | .1 | .1 | Income Taxes Payable | .1 | .0 | .0 | .1 | .0 | .3 |
| 15.3 | 14.2 | 16.6 | All Other Current | 9.7 | 17.7 | 16.5 | 20.1 | 23.4 | 21.0 |
| 28.7 | 27.1 | 28.2 | Total Current | 19.2 | 28.7 | 30.7 | 28.9 | 38.5 | 34.8 |
| 25.4 | 30.6 | 28.7 | Long-Term Debt | 45.1 | 30.9 | 16.3 | 19.6 | 16.3 | 17.8 |
| .1 | .0 | .1 | Deferred Taxes | .1 | .1 | .0 | .0 | .0 | .0 |
| 5.6 | 8.3 | 8.7 | All Other Non-Current | 9.4 | 6.1 | 5.3 | 8.8 | 14.9 | 7.6 |
| 40.3 | 33.9 | 34.5 | Net Worth | 26.2 | 34.3 | 47.7 | 42.8 | 30.3 | 39.9 |
| 100.0 | 100.0 | 100.0 | Total Liabilities & Net Worth | 100.0 | 100.0 | 100.0 | 100.0 | 100.0 | 100.0 |
| | | | INCOME DATA | | | | | | |
| 100.0 | 100.0 | 100.0 | Net Sales | 100.0 | 100.0 | 100.0 | 100.0 | 100.0 | 100.0 |
| | | | Gross Profit | | | | | | |
| 76.8 | 76.2 | 81.2 | Operating Expenses | 65.8 | 77.5 | 83.3 | 88.8 | 94.2 | 97.5 |
| 23.2 | 23.8 | 18.8 | Operating Profit | 34.2 | 22.5 | 16.7 | 11.2 | 5.8 | 2.5 |
| 4.2 | 6.4 | 5.7 | All Other Expenses (net) | 12.7 | 5.3 | .2 | 3.6 | 2.6 | .2 |
| 19.0 | 17.4 | 13.1 | Profit Before Taxes | 21.5 | 17.2 | 16.5 | 7.6 | 3.2 | 2.3 |
| | | | RATIOS | | | | | | |
| 8.0 | 6.6 | 5.2 | | 7.0 | 7.0 | 4.1 | 7.9 | 5.0 | 2.6 |
| 2.1 | 1.8 | 1.7 | Current | 1.3 | 1.9 | 1.9 | 2.5 | 2.5 | 1.5 |
| 1.0 | .8 | .7 | | .6 | .8 | 1.2 | 1.3 | .8 | .8 |
| 7.4 | 4.8 | 4.2 | | 5.2 | 5.6 | 3.6 | 5.7 | 4.2 | 2.6 |
| (352) 1.7 | 1.4 | 1.3 | Quick | 1.2 | 1.4 | 1.6 | 2.2 | 1.9 | 1.2 |
| .7 | .5 | .5 | | .5 | .5 | .5 | .8 | .6 | .5 |
| 0 UND | 0 UND | 0 UND | | 0 UND | 0 UND | 0 UND | 0 UND | 0 UND | 0 UND |
| 0 UND | 0 UND | 0 UND | Sales/Receivables | 0 UND | 0 UND | 1 402.1 | 2 204.3 | 0 999.8 | 1 244.5 |
| 2 192.1 | 4 93.3 | 4 99.8 | | 0 UND | 4 81.4 | 29 12.8 | 21 17.2 | 12 31.5 | 5 72.0 |
| | | | Cost of Sales/Inventory | | | | | | |
| | | | Cost of Sales/Payables | | | | | | |
| 5.4 | 4.8 | 5.4 | | 4.2 | 3.8 | 5.3 | 3.7 | 7.8 | 19.1 |
| 17.8 | 23.5 | 28.4 | Sales/Working Capital | 29.8 | 17.0 | 10.3 | 11.8 | 25.1 | 84.4 |
| 417.0 | -31.2 | -40.0 | | -9.6 | -35.6 | 61.2 | 79.5 | -105.1 | -106.1 |
| | 86.6 | 43.4 | 15.8 | | 8.6 | 28.3 | 31.0 | 80.2 | 24.4 | 11.7 |
| (191) 22.1 | (232) 9.9 | (199) 3.8 | EBIT/Interest | (41) 4.6 | (35) 5.5 | (24) 6.6 | (22) 9.1 | (24) 1.8 | (53) 2.5 |
| 5.4 | 3.1 | -.6 | | 1.4 | 1.2 | -4.7 | -2.5 | -57.2 | -3.9 |
| | 52.9 | 4.3 | | Net Profit + Depr., Dep., | | | | | | |
| (10) 9.1 | (10) 1.7 | | Amort./Cur. Mat. L/T/D | | | | | | |
| .4 | -.2 | | | | | | | | |
| .0 | .0 | .0 | | .0 | .0 | .0 | .0 | .0 | .1 |
| .5 | .6 | .8 | Fixed/Worth | 2.1 | .4 | .4 | .2 | .3 | .7 |
| 3.4 | 4.8 | 6.2 | | 12.9 | 4.3 | 1.6 | 1.9 | -3.2 | -7.1 |
| .5 | .6 | .7 | | .8 | .9 | .6 | .2 | .5 | .6 |
| 1.5 | 1.8 | 2.0 | Debt/Worth | 2.5 | 2.6 | 1.2 | 1.4 | 1.9 | 1.7 |
| 8.2 | 18.2 | 84.9 | | UND | 12.9 | 2.5 | 10.0 | -4.9 | -25.5 |
| 155.9 | 94.0 | 79.6 | | 57.7 | 139.3 | 83.0 | 108.8 | 97.2 | 55.0 |
| (294) 61.8 | (354) 34.7 | (286) 24.3 | % Profit Before Taxes/Tangible Net Worth | (87) 20.2 | (59) 45.8 | (29) 24.2 | (35) 31.0 | (29) 43.6 | (47) 17.2 |
| 20.1 | 8.4 | 3.5 | | .0 | 8.3 | 14.9 | 3.1 | 6.9 | 2.3 |
| 69.0 | 38.7 | 28.2 | | 17.6 | 49.5 | 29.6 | 32.5 | 28.3 | 20.0 |
| 22.6 | 10.2 | 7.7 | % Profit Before Taxes/Total Assets | 6.0 | 9.2 | 14.1 | 13.8 | 4.0 | 5.4 |
| 7.0 | 2.4 | .0 | | .0 | 2.0 | .6 | .4 | -7.0 | -1.3 |
| 340.2 | 336.2 | 258.4 | | 98.6 | 654.7 | 169.4 | 369.1 | 450.2 | 222.2 |
| 38.4 | 25.0 | 27.3 | Sales/Net Fixed Assets | .6 | 34.8 | 51.1 | 64.4 | 127.0 | 46.2 |
| 2.2 | .3 | .6 | | .2 | .5 | 8.5 | 6.1 | 17.2 | 13.2 |
| 7.2 | 5.0 | 5.4 | | 1.6 | 4.0 | 3.5 | 5.7 | 13.9 | 15.7 |
| 2.3 | 1.6 | 1.6 | Sales/Total Assets | .3 | 1.1 | 2.2 | 2.1 | 4.6 | 4.4 |
| .5 | .2 | .3 | | .1 | .3 | 1.0 | .7 | 1.7 | 1.5 |
| .3 | .4 | .3 | | 8.8 | 1.1 | .3 | .3 | .3 | .2 |
| (184) 1.3 | (215) 3.1 | (164) 2.8 | % Depr., Dep., Amort./Sales | (42) 19.0 | (29) 13.1 | (12) .5 | (19) .5 | (18) .7 | (44) .6 |
| 10.6 | 16.1 | 16.2 | | 31.3 | 22.1 | .9 | 6.2 | 6.4 | 2.7 |
| 1.9 | 2.0 | 1.7 | | 8.4 | 4.3 | 2.5 | 1.7 | .6 | .2 |
| (101) 6.6 | (94) 4.7 | (96) 4.4 | % Officers', Directors' Owners' Comp/Sales | (29) 14.3 | (18) 8.0 | (10) 3.3 | (11) 2.5 | (14) 1.7 | (14) .7 |
| 14.1 | 12.5 | 14.5 | | 21.5 | 17.1 | 4.5 | 10.3 | 8.6 | 1.7 |
| 11059378M | 11427199M | 12805776M | Net Sales ($) | 46491M | 129089M | 128373M | 295287M | 670008M | 11536528M |
| 4381474M | 5507386M | 5196932M | Total Assets ($) | 203514M | 279509M | 172827M | 448203M | 812661M | 3280218M |

© RMA 2024  M = $ thousand  MM = $ million
See Pages viii through xx for Explanation of Ratios and Data

# REAL ESTATE—Residential Property Managers  NAICS 531311

## Current Data Sorted by Assets | Comparative Historical Data

| | | | | | | | Type of Statement | | | |
|---|---|---|---|---|---|---|---|---|---|---|
| | 1 | 2 | 6 | 5 | 2 | 1 | Unqualified | | 17 | 19 |
| | | 1 | 1 | | | | Reviewed | | 12 | 6 |
| | | 1 | 4 | 2 | | 1 | Compiled | | 12 | 13 |
| | 20 | 20 | 31 | 9 | | | Tax Returns | | 91 | 59 |
| | 20 | 37 | 58 | 32 | 5 | 5 | Other | | 164 | 146 |
| | | 26 (4/1-9/30/23) | | 238 (10/1/23-3/31/24) | | | | | 4/1/19-3/31/20 | 4/1/20-3/31/21 |
| | 0-500M | 500M-2MM | 2-10MM | 10-50MM | 50-100MM | 100-250MM | | | ALL | ALL |
| | 41 | 61 | 100 | 48 | 7 | 7 | NUMBER OF STATEMENTS | | 296 | 243 |
| | % | % | % | % | % | % | ASSETS | | % | % |
| | 33.6 | 24.6 | 23.0 | 21.2 | | | Cash & Equivalents | | 26.6 | 30.9 |
| | 6.6 | 7.2 | 5.1 | 14.2 | | | Trade Receivables (net) | | 5.9 | 5.6 |
| | .7 | 1.8 | 3.1 | 4.1 | | | Inventory | | 1.6 | 2.1 |
| | 4.5 | 9.9 | 4.8 | 7.1 | | | All Other Current | | 5.6 | 5.6 |
| | 45.5 | 43.5 | 35.9 | 46.7 | | | Total Current | | 39.7 | 44.2 |
| | 33.1 | 38.5 | 43.5 | 26.5 | | | Fixed Assets (net) | | 40.1 | 38.5 |
| | 7.4 | 3.8 | 6.1 | 11.8 | | | Intangibles (net) | | 6.5 | 6.3 |
| | 14.1 | 14.2 | 14.5 | 15.1 | | | All Other Non-Current | | 13.8 | 11.0 |
| | 100.0 | 100.0 | 100.0 | 100.0 | | | Total | | 100.0 | 100.0 |
| | | | | | | | LIABILITIES | | | |
| | 9.7 | 1.7 | 5.8 | 7.2 | | | Notes Payable-Short Term | | 7.1 | 7.0 |
| | .9 | 3.9 | 2.7 | .8 | | | Cur. Mat.-L.T.D. | | 2.9 | 2.5 |
| | 4.0 | 5.6 | 4.4 | 6.4 | | | Trade Payables | | 4.2 | 3.3 |
| | .1 | .0 | .0 | .0 | | | Income Taxes Payable | | .2 | .0 |
| | 16.9 | 18.8 | 13.2 | 19.6 | | | All Other Current | | 20.0 | 17.4 |
| | 31.4 | 30.0 | 26.1 | 34.0 | | | Total Current | | 34.5 | 30.3 |
| | 68.5 | 27.3 | 38.3 | 21.2 | | | Long-Term Debt | | 30.4 | 36.9 |
| | .0 | .0 | .0 | .0 | | | Deferred Taxes | | .0 | .0 |
| | 10.8 | 4.7 | 5.0 | 3.2 | | | All Other Non-Current | | 5.8 | 5.0 |
| | -10.7 | 38.0 | 30.5 | 41.6 | | | Net Worth | | 29.3 | 27.8 |
| | 100.0 | 100.0 | 100.0 | 100.0 | | | Total Liabilities & Net Worth | | 100.0 | 100.0 |
| | | | | | | | INCOME DATA | | | |
| | 100.0 | 100.0 | 100.0 | 100.0 | | | Net Sales | | 100.0 | 100.0 |
| | | | | | | | Gross Profit | | | |
| | 77.9 | 76.7 | 73.5 | 74.7 | | | Operating Expenses | | 78.0 | 73.1 |
| | 22.1 | 23.3 | 26.5 | 25.3 | | | Operating Profit | | 22.0 | 26.9 |
| | 3.0 | 6.8 | 9.5 | 5.5 | | | All Other Expenses (net) | | 7.8 | 6.3 |
| | 19.1 | 16.5 | 17.0 | 19.9 | | | Profit Before Taxes | | 14.2 | 20.6 |
| | | | | | | | RATIOS | | | |
| | 3.3 | 9.2 | 4.9 | 2.5 | | | | | 2.9 | 5.1 |
| | 1.4 | 2.0 | 1.4 | 1.3 | | | Current | | 1.2 | 1.6 |
| | .5 | .5 | .4 | .8 | | | | | .5 | .8 |
| | 3.3 | 4.3 | 2.6 | 2.3 | | | | | 2.5 | 3.8 |
| | 1.3 | (60) 1.6 | 1.2 | 1.2 | | | Quick | | 1.0 | 1.2 |
| | .4 | .2 | .3 | .3 | | | | | .3 | .4 |
| | 0 UND | 0 UND | 0 UND | 0 UND | | | | | 0 UND | 0 UND |
| | 0 UND | 0 UND | 0 UND | 15 23.9 | | | Sales/Receivables | | 0 UND | 0 UND |
| | 0 UND | 6 58.1 | 13 28.5 | 61 6.0 | | | | | 10 35.2 | 13 27.9 |
| | | | | | | | Cost of Sales/Inventory | | | |
| | | | | | | | Cost of Sales/Payables | | | |
| | 9.9 | 3.9 | 3.2 | 2.3 | | | | | 5.9 | 2.9 |
| | 34.2 | 14.0 | 17.9 | 7.0 | | | Sales/Working Capital | | 29.3 | 11.1 |
| | -65.6 | -7.3 | -5.6 | -15.2 | | | | | -10.4 | -20.6 |
| | 17.2 | 26.8 | 11.5 | 30.6 | | | | | 30.2 | 42.0 |
| (25) | 5.0 | (39) 5.2 | (42) 4.2 | (28) 14.8 | | | EBIT/Interest | (171) | 5.4 | (132) 6.9 |
| | .8 | .1 | 2.2 | 1.3 | | | | | 1.6 | 2.2 |
| | | | | | | | Net Profit + Depr., Dep., Amort./Cur. Mat. L/T/D | | | |
| | .0 | .0 | .1 | .0 | | | | | .1 | .0 |
| | 1.0 | .5 | 1.7 | .2 | | | Fixed/Worth | | 1.3 | 1.2 |
| | -4.1 | 4.0 | 7.9 | 2.0 | | | | | 8.4 | 9.3 |
| | .9 | .3 | .7 | .7 | | | | | .6 | .6 |
| | 6.2 | 2.1 | 2.7 | 2.1 | | | Debt/Worth | | 2.4 | 2.8 |
| | -5.1 | 8.1 | 27.6 | 13.6 | | | | | 31.3 | 54.7 |
| | 304.0 | 60.9 | 55.4 | 61.0 | | | | | 93.1 | 69.6 |
| (25) | 53.3 | (50) 25.5 | (78) 23.5 | (38) 32.6 | | | % Profit Before Taxes/Tangible Net Worth | (232) | 26.3 | (184) 31.5 |
| | 19.9 | .8 | 6.3 | 7.2 | | | | | 4.1 | 11.5 |
| | 91.7 | 19.0 | 22.1 | 17.7 | | | | | 26.7 | 25.0 |
| | 21.6 | 8.7 | 7.1 | 11.3 | | | % Profit Before Taxes/Total Assets | | 6.8 | 8.8 |
| | 5.3 | -.3 | 1.7 | 1.1 | | | | | .5 | 1.9 |
| | UND | 265.1 | 59.5 | 168.1 | | | | | 73.4 | 197.8 |
| | 61.5 | 9.0 | 5.1 | 46.2 | | | Sales/Net Fixed Assets | | 13.3 | 7.3 |
| | 5.1 | .4 | .2 | .5 | | | | | .3 | .4 |
| | 10.3 | 3.2 | 1.8 | .8 | | | | | 3.2 | 1.9 |
| | 3.6 | .8 | .6 | .5 | | | Sales/Total Assets | | 1.1 | .7 |
| | .9 | .2 | .1 | .2 | | | | | .2 | .2 |
| | .5 | .9 | .6 | .8 | | | | | .9 | .7 |
| (15) | 8.1 | (28) 4.6 | (60) 10.8 | (29) 3.6 | | | % Depr., Dep., Amort./Sales | (173) | 5.0 | (117) 6.4 |
| | 15.1 | 14.3 | 19.5 | 16.2 | | | | | 16.7 | 18.3 |
| | 6.2 | 3.8 | 3.1 | 3.1 | | | | | 3.2 | 2.7 |
| (11) | 13.2 | (15) 5.0 | (18) 4.6 | (15) 6.1 | | | % Officers', Directors' Owners' Comp/Sales | (72) | 6.1 | (53) 4.8 |
| | 17.9 | 9.6 | 7.0 | 7.9 | | | | | 14.5 | 14.2 |
| | 47620M | 133296M | 568634M | 719837M | 385379M | 4846700M | Net Sales ($) | | 3150565M | 1693814M |
| | 9578M | 65730M | 469975M | 1029585M | 483840M | 1217986M | Total Assets ($) | | 1840885M | 2229452M |

M = $ thousand    MM = $ million
See Pages viii through xx for Explanation of Ratios and Data

© RMA 2024

# REAL ESTATE—Residential Property Managers NAICS 531311

## Comparative Historical Data

| | | | | | | | Type of Statement | | | | | | | |
|---|---|---|---|---|---|---|---|---|---|---|---|---|---|---|
| | 18 | | 22 | | 17 | | Unqualified | 2 | | 2 | | 3 | 4 | 2 | 4 |
| | 3 | | 2 | | 2 | | Reviewed | 2 | | | | | | | |
| | 5 | | 6 | | 8 | | Compiled | 2 | | | | | 2 | 2 | 2 |
| | 76 | | 92 | | 80 | | Tax Returns | 44 | | 10 | | 11 | 10 | 4 | 1 |
| | 158 | | 170 | | 157 | | Other | 49 | | 34 | | 13 | 18 | 29 | 14 |
| | 4/1/21-3/31/22 ALL | | 4/1/22-3/31/23 ALL | | 4/1/23-3/31/24 ALL | | | 26 (4/1-9/30/23) | | | | | 238 (10/1/23-3/31/24) | | |
| | | | | | | | | 0-1MM | | 1-3MM | | 3-5MM | 5-10MM | 10-25MM | 25MM & OVER |
| | 260 | | 292 | | 264 | | NUMBER OF STATEMENTS | 99 | | 46 | | 27 | 34 | 37 | 21 |
| | % | | % | | % | | ASSETS | % | | % | | % | % | % | % |
| | 28.1 | | 26.6 | | 24.4 | | Cash & Equivalents | 17.6 | | 24.3 | | 25.9 | 32.4 | 35.2 | 23.5 |
| | 7.0 | | 7.9 | | 7.7 | | Trade Receivables (net) | 1.9 | | 9.0 | | 11.2 | 10.8 | 11.7 | 15.2 |
| | 2.9 | | 1.7 | | 2.8 | | Inventory | 1.1 | | 2.8 | | 5.0 | 4.3 | .9 | 8.7 |
| | 8.0 | | 6.4 | | 6.5 | | All Other Current | 3.1 | | 12.2 | | 6.3 | 6.5 | 7.0 | 9.0 |
| | 46.0 | | 42.6 | | 41.4 | | Total Current | 23.7 | | 48.3 | | 48.4 | 54.0 | 54.8 | 56.3 |
| | 37.0 | | 35.8 | | 36.9 | | Fixed Assets (net) | 59.9 | | 36.1 | | 29.4 | 16.3 | 13.2 | 15.6 |
| | 5.2 | | 6.8 | | 7.1 | | Intangibles (net) | 3.7 | | 6.3 | | 8.6 | 11.8 | 8.8 | 11.9 |
| | 11.9 | | 14.9 | | 14.7 | | All Other Non-Current | 12.7 | | 9.4 | | 13.6 | 17.9 | 23.2 | 16.3 |
| | 100.0 | | 100.0 | | 100.0 | | Total | 100.0 | | 100.0 | | 100.0 | 100.0 | 100.0 | 100.0 |
| | | | | | | | LIABILITIES | | | | | | | | |
| | 8.2 | | 4.8 | | 5.5 | | Notes Payable-Short Term | 2.5 | | 8.6 | | 10.4 | 7.0 | 4.6 | 5.7 |
| | 2.0 | | 1.9 | | 2.3 | | Cur. Mat.-L.T.D. | 4.3 | | 1.1 | | .5 | 1.8 | 1.1 | .7 |
| | 2.8 | | 3.9 | | 5.2 | | Trade Payables | 1.6 | | 2.8 | | 8.6 | 7.4 | 10.4 | 10.6 |
| | .0 | | .1 | | .0 | | Income Taxes Payable | .0 | | .0 | | .0 | .0 | .0 | .0 |
| | 15.1 | | 17.8 | | 16.3 | | All Other Current | 14.2 | | 17.3 | | 10.7 | 25.6 | 15.5 | 18.0 |
| | 28.2 | | 28.6 | | 29.4 | | Total Current | 22.7 | | 29.8 | | 30.2 | 41.8 | 31.6 | 34.9 |
| | 32.4 | | 33.2 | | 36.7 | | Long-Term Debt | 55.5 | | 45.5 | | 26.9 | 18.8 | 10.4 | 16.6 |
| | .0 | | .0 | | .0 | | Deferred Taxes | .0 | | .0 | | .0 | .1 | .0 | .0 |
| | 5.9 | | 4.2 | | 5.4 | | All Other Non-Current | 6.0 | | 3.3 | | 7.8 | 5.8 | 5.7 | 2.6 |
| | 33.5 | | 34.1 | | 28.5 | | Net Worth | 15.7 | | 21.4 | | 35.1 | 33.5 | 52.2 | 45.8 |
| | 100.0 | | 100.0 | | 100.0 | | Total Liabilities & Net Worth | 100.0 | | 100.0 | | 100.0 | 100.0 | 100.0 | 100.0 |
| | | | | | | | INCOME DATA | | | | | | | | |
| | 100.0 | | 100.0 | | 100.0 | | Net Sales | 100.0 | | 100.0 | | 100.0 | 100.0 | 100.0 | 100.0 |
| | | | | | | | Gross Profit | | | | | | | | |
| | 73.6 | | 77.5 | | 75.2 | | Operating Expenses | 62.6 | | 77.6 | | 83.1 | 87.5 | 83.9 | 83.6 |
| | 26.4 | | 22.5 | | 24.8 | | Operating Profit | 37.4 | | 22.4 | | 16.9 | 12.5 | 16.1 | 16.4 |
| | 5.0 | | 5.7 | | 6.8 | | All Other Expenses (net) | 14.5 | | 5.6 | | 3.2 | .3 | .2 | .2 |
| | 21.4 | | 16.8 | | 18.0 | | Profit Before Taxes | 22.9 | | 16.8 | | 13.7 | 12.1 | 15.9 | 16.2 |
| | | | | | | | RATIOS | | | | | | | | |
| | 5.2 | | 4.4 | | 3.9 | | | 2.8 | | 6.7 | | 3.5 | 5.9 | 4.7 | 3.4 |
| | 1.9 | | 1.6 | | 1.4 | | Current | 1.2 | | 1.6 | | 2.0 | 1.5 | 1.7 | 1.7 |
| | .9 | | .8 | | .5 | | | .3 | | .5 | | .9 | .6 | .8 | .6 |
| | 4.6 | | 4.2 | | 3.0 | | | 2.5 | | 4.6 | | 3.0 | 4.4 | 4.1 | 3.3 |
| | 1.5 | | 1.2 | (263) | 1.2 | | Quick | .8 | | 1.5 | | 1.6 | (33) 1.3 | 1.4 | .9 |
| | .5 | | .4 | | .3 | | | .2 | | .2 | | .5 | .3 | .6 | .3 |
| 0 | UND | 0 | UND | 0 | UND | | | 0 | UND | 0 | UND | | | | |
| 0 | UND | 0 | UND | 0 | UND | | Sales/Receivables | 0 | UND | 0 | UND | 2 183.4 | 2 185.8 | 8 43.5 | 4 81.7 |
| 10 | 35.9 | 14 | 26.4 | 19 | 19.4 | | | 0 | UND | 21 | 17.4 | 28 13.2 | 38 9.6 | 49 7.5 | 53 6.9 |
| | | | | | | | Cost of Sales/Inventory | | | | | | | | |
| | | | | | | | Cost of Sales/Payables | | | | | | | | |
| | 3.4 | | 3.8 | | 3.9 | | | 4.0 | | 4.2 | | 2.5 | 4.3 | 3.8 | 3.3 |
| | 8.6 | | 13.5 | | 17.4 | | Sales/Working Capital | 68.8 | | 11.7 | | 17.6 | 13.4 | 12.1 | 10.0 |
| | -97.8 | | -31.3 | | -7.9 | | | -3.3 | | -22.3 | | -194.8 | -6.6 | -29.3 | -14.6 |
| | 59.8 | | 34.3 | | 23.5 | | | 7.9 | | 33.2 | | 18.0 | 36.3 | 30.0 | 96.2 |
| (145) | 9.1 | (171) | 11.8 | (145) | 5.2 | | EBIT/Interest | (43) 4.0 | | (29) 4.9 | | (20) 4.7 | (20) 5.2 | (20) 16.3 | (13) 30.4 |
| | 3.6 | | 2.1 | | 1.7 | | | 2.2 | | 1.9 | | 1.2 | .7 | 1.7 | 8.8 |
| | | | | | 23.3 | | | | | | | | | | |
| | | (10) | | | 6.1 | | Net Profit + Depr., Dep., | | | | | | | | |
| | | | | | 2.5 | | Amort./Cur. Mat. L/T/D | | | | | | | | |
| | .0 | | .0 | | .0 | | | .2 | | .0 | | .0 | .0 | .0 | .0 |
| | .7 | | .8 | | .8 | | Fixed/Worth | 2.7 | | .5 | | .8 | .2 | .1 | .2 |
| | 4.5 | | 4.2 | | 6.6 | | | 8.1 | | UND | | -3.9 | NM | .6 | 1.1 |
| | .5 | | .5 | | .6 | | | 1.1 | | .3 | | .6 | .5 | .3 | .5 |
| | 2.2 | | 1.8 | | 2.2 | | Debt/Worth | 3.0 | | 4.1 | | 2.0 | 2.1 | 1.2 | 1.4 |
| | 10.3 | | 10.9 | | 27.6 | | | 23.7 | | -8.6 | | -10.4 | -7.8 | 4.6 | 3.4 |
| | 92.6 | | 87.4 | | 63.2 | | | 42.7 | | 102.6 | | 46.1 | 50.5 | 103.5 | 102.0 |
| (217) | 37.5 | (240) | 28.3 | (203) | 30.7 | | % Profit Before Taxes/Tangible Net Worth | (79) 16.8 | | (32) 43.6 | | (18) 24.4 | (23) 25.4 | (32) 54.3 | (19) 47.3 |
| | 7.1 | | 4.2 | | 6.8 | | | 4.7 | | 8.5 | | -1.7 | 12.6 | 29.9 | 28.8 |
| | 30.9 | | 29.9 | | 22.9 | | | 11.8 | | 35.9 | | 25.2 | 19.5 | 46.2 | 24.8 |
| | 10.4 | | 8.4 | | 10.3 | | % Profit Before Taxes/Total Assets | 4.8 | | 12.2 | | 13.9 | 11.9 | 23.3 | 16.5 |
| | 2.9 | | .6 | | 1.7 | | | .5 | | 1.9 | | 1.3 | .8 | 12.5 | 12.0 |
| | 258.8 | | 421.2 | | 145.9 | | | 9.6 | | 999.8 | | 205.0 | 288.7 | 391.3 | 377.2 |
| | 12.5 | | 21.0 | | 13.1 | | Sales/Net Fixed Assets | .3 | | 16.7 | | 24.3 | 59.1 | 56.6 | 61.8 |
| | .3 | | .3 | | .3 | | | .1 | | 1.1 | | .8 | 18.5 | 15.3 | 9.7 |
| | 2.6 | | 2.6 | | 2.5 | | | .6 | | 3.2 | | 7.0 | 3.3 | 3.1 | 3.0 |
| | .9 | | 1.0 | | .7 | | Sales/Total Assets | .2 | | 1.3 | | 1.2 | 1.3 | 1.8 | 1.3 |
| | .2 | | .2 | | .2 | | | .1 | | .3 | | .4 | .7 | .6 | .6 |
| | 1.3 | | 1.0 | | .6 | | | 10.3 | | 6.4 | | .4 | .2 | .3 | .1 |
| (134) | 6.2 | (146) | 6.4 | (141) | 6.2 | | % Depr., Dep., Amort./Sales | (60) 15.4 | (13) | 12.1 | (15) | 1.6 | (23) .6 | (17) .7 | (13) .8 |
| | 19.6 | | 18.4 | | 16.5 | | | 23.5 | | 22.0 | | 11.8 | 2.1 | 3.1 | 1.6 |
| | 2.1 | | 2.6 | | 3.3 | | | 8.5 | | 5.2 | | | 2.4 | 3.1 | |
| (56) | 4.9 | (77) | 4.9 | (59) | 6.1 | | % Officers', Directors' Owners' Comp/Sales | (10) 14.3 | (13) | 7.7 | | (11) | 3.8 | (13) 3.4 | |
| | 11.5 | | 8.9 | | 9.2 | | | 18.3 | | 9.8 | | | 6.1 | 7.7 | |
| | 2813456M | | 3673053M | | 6701466M | | Net Sales ($) | 42135M | | 93625M | | 109758M | 240963M | 600654M | 5614331M |
| | 2721212M | | 4139437M | | 3276694M | | Total Assets ($) | 211622M | | 243325M | | 167223M | 287082M | 646387M | 1721055M |

© RMA 2024  
M = $ thousand   MM = $ million  
See Pages viii through xx for Explanation of Ratios and Data

# REAL ESTATE—Nonresidential Property Managers  NAICS 531312

## Current Data Sorted by Assets / Comparative Historical Data

| | | | | | | | Type of Statement | | |
|---|---|---|---|---|---|---|---|---|---|
| | 1 | 2 | 3 | 3 | 1 | 1 | Unqualified | 8 | 9 |
| | | 1 | 2 | 1 | | | Reviewed | 8 | 6 |
| | | 6 | 8 | 2 | | | Compiled | 17 | 10 |
| | 4 | 13 | 25 | 4 | 1 | | Tax Returns | 71 | 49 |
| | 9 | 27 | 79 | 32 | 4 | 10 | Other | 169 | 122 |
| | | 12 (4/1-9/30/23) | | 227 (10/1/23-3/31/24) | | | | 4/1/19-3/31/20 | 4/1/20-3/31/21 |
| | 0-500M | 500M-2MM | 2-10MM | 10-50MM | 50-100MM | 100-250MM | | ALL | ALL |
| | 14 | 49 | 117 | 42 | 6 | 11 | NUMBER OF STATEMENTS | 273 | 196 |
| | % | % | % | % | % | % | ASSETS | % | % |
| | 22.9 | 12.8 | 13.3 | 11.4 | | 4.6 | Cash & Equivalents | 13.9 | 19.4 |
| | 4.8 | 6.2 | 5.6 | 6.3 | | 2.6 | Trade Receivables (net) | 4.1 | 3.9 |
| | .9 | .0 | .5 | 1.4 | | 2.8 | Inventory | 1.0 | .8 |
| | 13.1 | 7.6 | 4.1 | 7.8 | | 1.7 | All Other Current | 4.2 | 3.8 |
| | 41.7 | 26.7 | 23.4 | 27.0 | | 11.8 | Total Current | 23.2 | 27.9 |
| | 48.3 | 61.2 | 65.9 | 59.5 | | 46.4 | Fixed Assets (net) | 62.2 | 59.1 |
| | 4.0 | 3.4 | 2.5 | 2.8 | | 22.0 | Intangibles (net) | 4.5 | 3.1 |
| | 6.0 | 8.7 | 8.3 | 10.8 | | 19.7 | All Other Non-Current | 10.1 | 9.8 |
| | 100.0 | 100.0 | 100.0 | 100.0 | | 100.0 | Total | 100.0 | 100.0 |
| | | | | | | | LIABILITIES | | |
| | 8.9 | 4.8 | 3.9 | 4.1 | | 21.3 | Notes Payable-Short Term | 4.6 | 6.3 |
| | 5.4 | 2.7 | 1.8 | 2.8 | | .9 | Cur. Mat.-L.T.D. | 2.9 | 2.6 |
| | 1.4 | 5.3 | 3.1 | 2.3 | | 3.7 | Trade Payables | 2.3 | 1.4 |
| | .1 | .0 | .0 | .1 | | .1 | Income Taxes Payable | .2 | .0 |
| | 5.4 | 8.5 | 3.9 | 8.2 | | 8.6 | All Other Current | 10.1 | 8.9 |
| | 21.2 | 21.4 | 12.7 | 17.5 | | 34.5 | Total Current | 20.1 | 19.2 |
| | 58.0 | 51.3 | 53.1 | 38.6 | | 29.6 | Long-Term Debt | 42.0 | 48.5 |
| | .0 | .0 | .0 | .0 | | .1 | Deferred Taxes | .1 | .0 |
| | 6.4 | 3.1 | 4.3 | 3.9 | | 13.6 | All Other Non-Current | 5.6 | 9.4 |
| | 14.4 | 24.2 | 29.9 | 40.1 | | 22.2 | Net Worth | 32.2 | 22.9 |
| | 100.0 | 100.0 | 100.0 | 100.0 | | 100.0 | Total Liabilities & Net Worth | 100.0 | 100.0 |
| | | | | | | | INCOME DATA | | |
| | 100.0 | 100.0 | 100.0 | 100.0 | | 100.0 | Net Sales | 100.0 | 100.0 |
| | | | | | | | Gross Profit | | |
| | 71.4 | 67.0 | 53.1 | 58.5 | | 62.5 | Operating Expenses | 58.8 | 65.3 |
| | 28.6 | 33.0 | 46.9 | 41.5 | | 37.5 | Operating Profit | 41.2 | 34.7 |
| | 11.6 | 14.4 | 19.6 | 13.9 | | 14.0 | All Other Expenses (net) | 14.1 | 12.3 |
| | 17.1 | 18.6 | 27.2 | 27.6 | | 23.5 | Profit Before Taxes | 27.2 | 22.5 |
| | | | | | | | RATIOS | | |
| | 10.8 | 5.5 | 8.3 | 3.3 | | 1.7 | | 3.7 | 5.4 |
| | 4.0 | 1.0 | 2.3 | 1.6 | | .5 | Current | 1.1 | 1.7 |
| | .4 | .2 | .5 | .8 | | .1 | | .3 | .4 |
| | 6.0 | 4.7 | 5.4 | 2.2 | | 1.3 | | 3.0 | 4.0 |
| | 2.6 | .8 | 1.7 | 1.3 | | .4 | Quick | .8 | 1.5 |
| | .2 | .1 | .4 | .3 | | .0 | | .2 | .3 |
| | 0 UND | 0 UND | 0 UND | 0 UND | | 0 UND | | 0 UND | 0 UND |
| | 0 UND | 0 UND | 0 UND | 0 UND | | 7 55.7 | Sales/Receivables | 0 UND | 0 UND |
| | 6 61.3 | 16 22.8 | 8 45.4 | 38 9.7 | | 31 11.8 | | 3 109.3 | 6 62.7 |
| | | | | | | | Cost of Sales/Inventory | | |
| | | | | | | | Cost of Sales/Payables | | |
| | 2.9 | 1.7 | 1.9 | 3.1 | | 10.1 | | 3.5 | 2.8 |
| | 18.7 | 351.5 | 9.2 | 7.6 | | -16.7 | Sales/Working Capital | 64.3 | 9.8 |
| | -9.7 | -4.9 | -8.1 | -10.1 | | -.5 | | -3.8 | -6.7 |
| | | | 8.3 | 22.6 | | 13.7 | | 10.2 | 11.3 |
| | | (26) 2.4 | (47) 6.3 | (20) 3.9 | | | EBIT/Interest | (130) 4.6 | (103) 4.5 |
| | | .6 | | 3.5 | | 2.9 | | 2.5 | 2.5 |
| | | | | | | | Net Profit + Depr., Dep., Amort./Cur. Mat. L/T/D | 5.0 (11) 2.1 1.7 | |
| | .1 | .5 | 1.0 | .4 | | .7 | | .8 | .8 |
| | 1.2 | 3.0 | 2.7 | 1.7 | | 2.6 | Fixed/Worth | 2.3 | 2.6 |
| | 2.0 | -13.5 | 12.8 | 7.8 | | .0 | | 10.5 | 92.3 |
| | .2 | .6 | 1.0 | .5 | | 1.3 | | .6 | .9 |
| | .5 | 3.7 | 2.5 | 1.5 | | 19.2 | Debt/Worth | 2.2 | 2.7 |
| | NM | -10.1 | 14.4 | 9.6 | | -1.8 | | 14.6 | -87.5 |
| | 56.1 | 68.7 | 58.2 | 34.5 | | | | 39.8 | 49.1 |
| | (11) 17.8 | (33) 22.5 | (99) 17.0 | (35) 12.0 | | | % Profit Before Taxes/Tangible Net Worth | (224) 16.6 | (145) 20.5 |
| | 7.7 | 2.7 | 4.5 | 5.9 | | | | 5.8 | 5.7 |
| | 42.0 | 17.4 | 11.4 | 9.2 | | 9.7 | | 13.1 | 10.7 |
| | 16.5 | 6.0 | 5.1 | 5.3 | | 5.3 | % Profit Before Taxes/Total Assets | 5.2 | 4.9 |
| | 5.8 | .3 | 1.9 | 2.6 | | 1.7 | | 1.5 | .6 |
| | 308.5 | 14.4 | 1.5 | 12.7 | | 15.7 | | 11.2 | 19.2 |
| | 5.9 | .3 | .2 | .3 | | 3.5 | Sales/Net Fixed Assets | .3 | .3 |
| | .6 | .2 | .1 | .1 | | .2 | | .1 | .1 |
| | 7.1 | 1.3 | .4 | .3 | | .5 | | .9 | .8 |
| | 2.1 | .2 | .1 | .2 | | .2 | Sales/Total Assets | .2 | .2 |
| | .4 | .2 | .1 | .1 | | .2 | | .1 | .1 |
| | | 9.5 | 8.2 | 6.9 | | | | 5.5 | 7.0 |
| | | (30) 12.6 | (71) 17.0 | (29) 13.4 | | | % Depr., Dep., Amort./Sales | (184) 14.3 | (134) 15.4 |
| | | 25.7 | | 24.1 | | 29.4 | | 22.5 | 22.4 |
| | | | | | | | | 4.5 | 3.0 |
| | | | | | | | % Officers', Directors' Owners' Comp/Sales | (24) 10.0 | (16) 7.3 |
| | | | | | | | | 19.4 | 12.7 |
| | 16162M | 56226M | 322871M | 553921M | 104031M | 712121M | Net Sales ($) | 3159785M | 746938M |
| | 4148M | 61369M | 528871M | 917400M | 416196M | 1705655M | Total Assets ($) | 2621170M | 1707645M |

M = $ thousand   MM = $ million
See Pages viii through xx for Explanation of Ratios and Data

© RMA 2024

# REAL ESTATE—Nonresidential Property Managers  NAICS 531312

## Comparative Historical Data | Current Data Sorted by Sales

| | | | | Type of Statement | | | | | | |
|---|---|---|---|---|---|---|---|---|---|---|
| 10 | | 8 | 11 | Unqualified | 4 | 2 | 1 | 1 | | 3 |
| 4 | | 4 | 4 | Reviewed | 2 | | 1 | | | 1 |
| 6 | | 14 | 16 | Compiled | 12 | | 2 | 1 | | 1 |
| 48 | | 66 | 47 | Tax Returns | 31 | 8 | 1 | 4 | 3 | |
| 124 | | 173 | 161 | Other | 70 | 40 | 13 | 9 | 17 | 12 |
| 4/1/21-3/31/22 ALL | | 4/1/22-3/31/23 ALL | 4/1/23-3/31/24 ALL | | 12 (4/1-9/30/23) | | | 227 (10/1/23-3/31/24) | | |
| | | | | | 0-1MM | 1-3MM | 3-5MM | 5-10MM | 10-25MM | 25MM & OVER |
| 192 | | 265 | 239 | NUMBER OF STATEMENTS | 119 | 50 | 18 | 15 | 20 | 17 |
| % | | % | % | ASSETS | % | % | % | % | % | % |
| 18.9 | | 14.6 | 12.7 | Cash & Equivalents | 7.8 | 11.8 | 17.8 | 29.4 | 23.8 | 17.1 |
| 5.1 | | 3.4 | 5.6 | Trade Receivables (net) | .9 | 4.4 | 15.6 | 5.9 | 14.6 | 20.2 |
| .8 | | 1.0 | .7 | Inventory | .5 | .2 | .2 | .2 | 2.2 | 2.3 |
| 5.6 | | 6.4 | 5.8 | All Other Current | 3.8 | 10.2 | 9.6 | 3.9 | 5.1 | 5.1 |
| 30.3 | | 25.4 | 24.8 | Total Current | 13.0 | 26.7 | 43.2 | 39.4 | 45.7 | 44.6 |
| 57.6 | | 61.8 | 62.0 | Fixed Assets (net) | 79.4 | 56.5 | 45.6 | 38.2 | 31.5 | 30.2 |
| 3.0 | | 3.3 | 3.7 | Intangibles (net) | 1.0 | 6.0 | .2 | 12.0 | 1.6 | 14.6 |
| 9.0 | | 9.5 | 9.6 | All Other Non-Current | 6.6 | 10.8 | 11.0 | 10.4 | 21.2 | 10.6 |
| 100.0 | | 100.0 | 100.0 | Total | 100.0 | 100.0 | 100.0 | 100.0 | 100.0 | 100.0 |
| | | | | LIABILITIES | | | | | | |
| 5.7 | | 5.4 | 5.1 | Notes Payable-Short Term | 4.1 | 4.2 | 7.1 | 3.4 | 2.7 | 16.6 |
| 2.0 | | 2.0 | 2.3 | Cur. Mat.-L.T.D. | 2.0 | 4.6 | .6 | 2.1 | .6 | 1.9 |
| 2.5 | | 2.2 | 3.3 | Trade Payables | .6 | 3.0 | 9.0 | 2.8 | 10.5 | 8.7 |
| .1 | | .1 | .0 | Income Taxes Payable | .0 | .0 | .0 | .0 | .0 | .1 |
| 10.5 | | 9.8 | 5.9 | All Other Current | 3.6 | 6.8 | 3.3 | 12.5 | 9.8 | 12.1 |
| 20.8 | | 19.6 | 16.6 | Total Current | 10.3 | 18.7 | 20.1 | 20.9 | 23.5 | 39.5 |
| 47.8 | | 49.0 | 49.0 | Long-Term Debt | 60.1 | 52.8 | 41.2 | 34.6 | 20.9 | 14.8 |
| .0 | | .1 | .0 | Deferred Taxes | .0 | .0 | .0 | .0 | .0 | .0 |
| 4.4 | | 6.3 | 4.4 | All Other Non-Current | 3.9 | 4.6 | 1.9 | 5.1 | 6.4 | 7.3 |
| 26.9 | | 25.1 | 29.9 | Net Worth | 25.7 | 23.9 | 36.8 | 39.4 | 49.0 | 38.4 |
| 100.0 | | 100.0 | 100.0 | Total Liabilities & Net Worth | 100.0 | 100.0 | 100.0 | 100.0 | 100.0 | 100.0 |
| | | | | INCOME DATA | | | | | | |
| 100.0 | | 100.0 | 100.0 | Net Sales | 100.0 | 100.0 | 100.0 | 100.0 | 100.0 | 100.0 |
| | | | | Gross Profit | | | | | | |
| 64.7 | | 59.7 | 58.8 | Operating Expenses | 47.6 | 62.0 | 68.5 | 82.8 | 72.3 | 79.9 |
| 35.3 | | 40.3 | 41.2 | Operating Profit | 52.4 | 38.0 | 31.5 | 17.2 | 27.7 | 20.1 |
| 12.1 | | 13.3 | 16.7 | All Other Expenses (net) | 25.2 | 11.0 | 9.4 | 6.0 | 5.7 | 4.1 |
| 23.2 | | 27.0 | 24.5 | Profit Before Taxes | 27.1 | 27.0 | 22.1 | 11.2 | 22.0 | 15.9 |
| | | | | RATIOS | | | | | | |
| 5.7 | | 5.2 | 5.6 | | 6.1 | 4.8 | 8.7 | 6.7 | 5.0 | 2.5 |
| 1.8 | | 1.8 | 1.7 | Current | 1.8 | 1.4 | 3.0 | 1.7 | 1.6 | 1.7 |
| .6 | | .5 | .4 | | .2 | .7 | 1.2 | 1.2 | .3 | .7 |
| 4.6 | | 4.0 | 4.1 | | 4.4 | 2.6 | 6.1 | 6.1 | 4.1 | 2.1 |
| 1.4 | | 1.1 | 1.3 | Quick | 1.3 | .9 | 1.7 | 1.6 | 1.5 | 1.3 |
| .4 | | .2 | .3 | | .2 | .3 | .9 | .9 | .2 | .4 |
| 0 UND | | 0 UND | 0 UND | | 0 UND | 0 UND | 0 UND | 0 UND | 2 172.0 | 0 UND |
| 0 UND | | 0 UND | 0 UND | Sales/Receivables | 0 UND | 0 UND | 0 UND | 2 230.9 | 10 35.5 | 31 11.8 |
| 7 51.2 | | 3 116.3 | 11 34.1 | | 0 UND | 7 55.0 | 73 5.0 | 22 16.6 | 39 9.4 | 51 7.1 |
| | | | | Cost of Sales/Inventory | | | | | | |
| | | | | Cost of Sales/Payables | | | | | | |
| 2.6 | | 2.6 | 2.3 | | 1.6 | 2.3 | 1.8 | 5.0 | 4.8 | 5.9 |
| 9.8 | | 16.0 | 11.5 | Sales/Working Capital | 17.1 | 10.8 | 5.9 | 7.6 | 17.3 | 10.1 |
| -10.4 | | -5.5 | -6.4 | | -4.2 | -13.1 | 282.5 | 28.0 | -12.6 | -27.4 |
| 18.4 | | 12.8 | 14.9 | | 7.7 | 13.9 | | | 37.9 | 160.6 |
| (90) 4.8 | (139) | 4.8 | (107) 4.7 | EBIT/Interest | (40) 4.2 | (30) 4.4 | | (10) | 15.3 | (10) 11.0 |
| 2.3 | | 2.0 | 2.4 | | 2.0 | 1.8 | | | 4.2 | 4.2 |
| | | | | Net Profit + Depr., Dep., Amort./Cur. Mat. L/T/D | | | | | | |
| .5 | | .9 | .8 | | 1.5 | .4 | .0 | .0 | .0 | .1 |
| 2.4 | | 2.7 | 2.4 | Fixed/Worth | 3.1 | 2.3 | 1.1 | 1.9 | .3 | .7 |
| 9.8 | | 10.6 | 13.5 | | 13.5 | -12.2 | 12.2 | 15.5 | 1.7 | NM |
| .9 | | 1.0 | .7 | | 1.0 | .7 | .4 | .2 | .1 | .6 |
| 2.3 | | 3.2 | 2.3 | Debt/Worth | 2.7 | 3.2 | 1.5 | 1.3 | 1.1 | 1.4 |
| 16.4 | | 17.3 | 16.7 | | 15.1 | -8.2 | 13.8 | 15.4 | 6.5 | NM |
| 61.5 | | 57.6 | 51.7 | | 30.5 | 56.9 | 61.0 | 80.1 | 284.1 | 67.4 |
| (154) 21.6 | (209) | 25.3 | (191) 17.4 | % Profit Before Taxes/Tangible Net Worth | (98) 11.4 | (34) 23.9 | (15) 36.7 | (12) 19.0 | (19) 39.0 | (13) 28.5 |
| 5.4 | | 8.0 | 4.6 | | 2.9 | 7.7 | 4.1 | 6.0 | 10.8 | 17.6 |
| 23.2 | | 15.1 | 13.3 | | 7.5 | 18.2 | 28.1 | 27.2 | 35.3 | 36.1 |
| 6.9 | | 5.9 | 5.5 | % Profit Before Taxes/Total Assets | 3.5 | 5.9 | 8.3 | 10.8 | 12.5 | 7.9 |
| 1.4 | | 1.9 | 1.6 | | .3 | 1.4 | 3.3 | 2.8 | 7.3 | 4.7 |
| 23.8 | | 7.7 | 6.3 | | .2 | 13.0 | 34.6 | 197.4 | 865.4 | 149.5 |
| .3 | | .3 | .2 | Sales/Net Fixed Assets | .2 | .5 | 1.8 | 45.4 | 59.2 | 13.0 |
| .1 | | .1 | .1 | | .1 | .2 | .4 | .2 | .3 | 2.1 |
| 1.4 | | 1.4 | .7 | | .2 | .8 | 1.7 | 2.6 | 3.8 | 3.0 |
| .2 | | .2 | .2 | Sales/Total Assets | .1 | .3 | .5 | 1.5 | 1.7 | 1.3 |
| .1 | | .1 | .1 | | .1 | .1 | .2 | .1 | .2 | .4 |
| 4.1 | | 4.6 | 7.2 | | 11.6 | 8.4 | 2.0 | | | 1.4 |
| (117) 16.3 | (155) | 15.0 | (145) 15.0 | % Depr., Dep., Amort./Sales | (78) 18.2 | (29) 17.9 | (11) 5.8 | | (10) | 2.1 |
| 24.8 | | 24.5 | 25.2 | | 26.3 | 26.9 | 16.7 | | | 5.0 |
| 3.5 | | 4.5 | 1.5 | | | | | | | |
| (18) 9.8 | (31) | 8.0 | (14) 2.6 | % Officers', Directors' Owners' Comp/Sales | | | | | | |
| 16.3 | | 13.0 | 6.2 | | | | | | | |
| 1143748M | | 1668936M | 1765332M | Net Sales ($) | 48391M | 86362M | 72425M | 102313M | 301124M | 1154717M |
| 1984105M | | 2344498M | 3633639M | Total Assets ($) | 397715M | 422823M | 234575M | 333045M | 761304M | 1484177M |

© RMA 2024         M = $ thousand    MM = $ million
See Pages viii through xx for Explanation of Ratios and Data

# REAL ESTATE—Other Activities Related to Real Estate  NAICS 531390

## Current Data Sorted by Assets | Comparative Historical Data

| | | | | | | | Type of Statement | | |
|---|---|---|---|---|---|---|---|---|---|
| | | 5 | 9 | 24 | 11 | 16 | Unqualified | 67 | 31 |
| | 1 | 4 | 6 | 11 | 3 | | Reviewed | 27 | 15 |
| | 1 | 5 | 19 | 8 | 1 | 4 | Compiled | 40 | 36 |
| | 22 | 86 | 95 | 32 | 5 | | Tax Returns | 334 | 282 |
| | 33 | 131 | 206 | 149 | 33 | 25 | Other | 538 | 445 |
| | | 58 (4/1-9/30/23) | | 887 (10/1/23-3/31/24) | | | | 4/1/19- 3/31/20 | 4/1/20- 3/31/21 |
| | 0-500M | 500M-2MM | 2-10MM | 10-50MM | 50-100MM | 100-250MM | | ALL | ALL |
| | 57 | 231 | 335 | 224 | 53 | 45 | NUMBER OF STATEMENTS | 1006 | 809 |
| | % | % | % | % | % | % | ASSETS | % | % |
| | 34.6 | 16.2 | 10.3 | 10.5 | 14.4 | 11.9 | Cash & Equivalents | 12.3 | 15.0 |
| | 7.6 | 4.6 | 6.0 | 7.7 | 3.8 | 11.0 | Trade Receivables (net) | 4.7 | 4.9 |
| | 2.6 | 3.6 | 4.1 | 9.5 | 9.1 | 4.8 | Inventory | 7.1 | 6.8 |
| | 12.8 | 6.3 | 5.9 | 7.4 | 10.9 | 10.8 | All Other Current | 5.2 | 5.8 |
| | 57.6 | 30.7 | 26.3 | 35.1 | 38.3 | 38.5 | Total Current | 29.3 | 32.6 |
| | 28.3 | 56.4 | 56.7 | 44.6 | 29.7 | 26.6 | Fixed Assets (net) | 51.0 | 51.1 |
| | 3.9 | 3.8 | 2.3 | 4.4 | 4.0 | 5.0 | Intangibles (net) | 4.2 | 4.2 |
| | 10.2 | 9.1 | 14.7 | 15.9 | 27.9 | 29.9 | All Other Non-Current | 15.4 | 12.2 |
| | 100.0 | 100.0 | 100.0 | 100.0 | 100.0 | 100.0 | Total | 100.0 | 100.0 |
| | | | | | | | LIABILITIES | | |
| | 19.1 | 10.6 | 8.0 | 9.0 | 7.3 | 3.9 | Notes Payable-Short Term | 9.2 | 8.1 |
| | 1.2 | 3.0 | 2.0 | 2.9 | 1.5 | 1.3 | Cur. Mat.-L.T.D. | 3.0 | 2.3 |
| | 7.2 | 3.1 | 3.1 | 2.9 | 2.7 | 6.6 | Trade Payables | 2.8 | 2.5 |
| | .1 | .0 | .0 | .0 | .0 | .0 | Income Taxes Payable | .1 | .1 |
| | 35.6 | 13.2 | 11.4 | 9.5 | 6.1 | 5.7 | All Other Current | 9.5 | 11.2 |
| | 63.2 | 29.8 | 24.4 | 24.4 | 17.6 | 17.5 | Total Current | 24.6 | 24.2 |
| | 35.9 | 45.1 | 47.2 | 36.2 | 29.2 | 30.7 | Long-Term Debt | 41.1 | 41.4 |
| | .0 | .0 | .0 | .5 | .1 | .4 | Deferred Taxes | .1 | .1 |
| | 11.0 | 5.2 | 3.6 | 5.9 | 5.0 | 8.1 | All Other Non-Current | 7.1 | 6.3 |
| | -10.2 | 20.0 | 24.8 | 33.0 | 48.1 | 43.3 | Net Worth | 27.1 | 28.0 |
| | 100.0 | 100.0 | 100.0 | 100.0 | 100.0 | 100.0 | Total Liabilities & Net Worth | 100.0 | 100.0 |
| | | | | | | | INCOME DATA | | |
| | 100.0 | 100.0 | 100.0 | 100.0 | 100.0 | 100.0 | Net Sales | 100.0 | 100.0 |
| | | | | | | | Gross Profit | | |
| | 75.3 | 64.5 | 61.2 | 69.6 | 70.5 | 68.5 | Operating Expenses | 66.2 | 63.6 |
| | 24.7 | 35.5 | 38.8 | 30.4 | 29.5 | 31.5 | Operating Profit | 33.8 | 36.4 |
| | 6.0 | 13.4 | 16.6 | 14.5 | 8.2 | 14.5 | All Other Expenses (net) | 13.6 | 11.9 |
| | 18.7 | 22.1 | 22.3 | 15.9 | 21.3 | 17.0 | Profit Before Taxes | 20.2 | 24.5 |
| | | | | | | | RATIOS | | |
| | 7.5 | 3.6 | 3.9 | 3.3 | 8.7 | 14.3 | | 3.1 | 4.3 |
| | 1.2 | 1.0 | 1.1 | 1.5 | 2.3 | 1.9 | Current | 1.2 | 1.3 |
| | .5 | .3 | .3 | .7 | 1.4 | 1.0 | | .3 | .4 |
| | 5.1 | 2.4 | 2.7 | 2.4 | 4.2 | 4.7 | | 2.1 | 3.0 |
| | 1.1 | .8 (332) | .7 | .8 | 1.5 | 1.4 | Quick | .6 | .8 |
| | .3 | .2 | .2 | .2 | .4 | .5 | | .1 | .2 |
| | 0 UND | 0 UND | 0 UND | 0 UND | 1 371.6 | 0 UND | | 0 UND | 0 UND |
| | 0 UND | 0 UND | 0 UND | 3 138.4 | 13 27.3 | 8 47.9 | Sales/Receivables | 0 UND | 0 UND |
| | 0 UND | 0 UND | 10 37.6 | 38 9.5 | 33 11.2 | 52 7.0 | | 6 61.1 | 8 47.4 |
| | | | | | | | Cost of Sales/Inventory | | |
| | | | | | | | Cost of Sales/Payables | | |
| | 5.5 | 6.1 | 3.2 | 2.0 | .8 | .7 | | 3.4 | 2.4 |
| | 56.3 | 130.0 | 37.3 | 7.9 | 2.3 | 7.3 | Sales/Working Capital | 29.5 | 16.7 |
| | -5.6 | -4.0 | -3.1 | -10.6 | 9.4 | 85.9 | | -4.5 | -4.8 |
| | 13.0 | 16.5 | 10.9 | 8.1 | 15.6 | 16.6 | | 12.9 | 21.1 |
| (26) | 2.6 | (123) 5.7 | (158) 3.6 | (105) 4.1 | (29) 3.0 | (18) 4.2 | EBIT/Interest | (481) 4.2 | (404) 5.5 |
| | -7.5 | 2.0 | 1.3 | .9 | .4 | 2.0 | | 1.9 | 2.4 |
| | | | | 3.5 | | | Net Profit + Depr., Dep., | 3.6 | 7.3 |
| | | | (13) 1.9 | | | | Amort./Cur. Mat. L/T/D | (26) 2.0 | (23) 2.7 |
| | | | | .5 | | | | 1.0 | .2 |
| | .0 | .4 | .1 | .1 | .0 | .0 | | .1 | .1 |
| | 1.2 | 2.5 | 2.4 | 1.2 | .5 | .1 | Fixed/Worth | 2.0 | 1.8 |
| | -1.7 | 34.6 | 10.3 | 5.2 | 2.4 | 2.9 | | 7.6 | 7.1 |
| | .3 | 1.0 | .9 | .9 | .4 | .4 | | .9 | .8 |
| | 7.5 | 3.4 | 3.1 | 2.2 | 1.3 | 1.9 | Debt/Worth | 3.0 | 2.6 |
| | -3.0 | 706.0 | 38.5 | 10.8 | 3.7 | 5.0 | | 22.0 | 13.7 |
| | 103.4 | 67.3 | 48.0 | 32.3 | 31.5 | 27.6 | % Profit Before Taxes/Tangible | 46.1 | 49.0 |
| (35) | 40.8 | (176) 23.1 | (268) 16.6 | (184) 12.6 | (49) 8.7 | (41) 11.5 | Net Worth | (804) 16.1 | (653) 18.5 |
| | 1.7 | 4.0 | 4.7 | .5 | -.1 | .7 | | 3.5 | 6.5 |
| | 58.6 | 20.1 | 9.6 | 9.2 | 11.5 | 8.5 | % Profit Before Taxes/Total | 11.9 | 13.8 |
| | 10.7 | 6.9 | 3.9 | 3.4 | 3.4 | 2.8 | Assets | 4.2 | 5.5 |
| | -3.1 | .1 | .5 | -.2 | -1.2 | .0 | | .6 | 1.4 |
| | UND | 39.8 | 35.1 | 59.0 | 58.4 | 770.9 | | 68.6 | 66.4 |
| | 73.7 | .5 | .4 | 2.0 | 4.2 | 26.7 | Sales/Net Fixed Assets | .6 | .5 |
| | 1.3 | .1 | .1 | .2 | .2 | .5 | | .2 | .2 |
| | 7.0 | 1.9 | .7 | .8 | .5 | .6 | | 1.1 | 1.0 |
| | 1.9 | .3 | .2 | .3 | .3 | .2 | Sales/Total Assets | .2 | .2 |
| | .6 | .1 | .1 | .1 | .1 | .1 | | .1 | .1 |
| | .1 | 6.8 | 4.7 | 1.4 | .5 | .6 | | 1.9 | 2.5 |
| (17) | 6.1 | (126) 14.5 | (187) 15.6 | (122) 5.6 | (30) 3.5 | (26) 2.3 | % Depr., Dep., Amort./Sales | (569) 14.3 | (448) 14.2 |
| | 17.1 | 22.1 | 25.0 | 21.5 | 11.2 | 21.3 | | 23.5 | 24.9 |
| | 1.8 | 2.6 | 2.4 | .7 | | | % Officers', Directors' | 2.4 | 2.8 |
| (15) | 7.3 | (33) 5.1 | (31) 3.4 | (16) 1.1 | | | Owners' Comp/Sales | (126) 6.5 | (99) 7.4 |
| | 17.6 | 13.0 | 9.2 | 11.3 | | | | 15.5 | 17.1 |
| | 52076M | 430509M | 1138749M | 3622241M | 1954300M | 7137976M | Net Sales ($) | 10163251M | 7085261M |
| | 15651M | 282224M | 1579962M | 5255004M | 3751124M | 6925863M | Total Assets ($) | 15448441M | 10077134M |

© RMA 2024

M = $ thousand    MM = $ million
See Pages viii through xx for Explanation of Ratios and Data

# REAL ESTATE—Other Activities Related to Real Estate  NAICS 531390

## Comparative Historical Data / Current Data Sorted by Sales

| | | | | Type of Statement | | | | | | |
|---|---|---|---|---|---|---|---|---|---|---|
| | 49 | 48 | 65 | Unqualified | 5 | 8 | 9 | 6 | 14 | 23 |
| | 22 | 26 | 25 | Reviewed | 5 | 3 | 3 | 2 | 7 | 5 |
| | 25 | 42 | 38 | Compiled | 21 | 5 | 1 | 5 | 4 | 2 |
| | 271 | 325 | 240 | Tax Returns | 141 | 42 | 18 | 23 | 13 | 3 |
| | 470 | 657 | 577 | Other | 213 | 120 | 55 | 67 | 59 | 63 |
| | 4/1/21-3/31/22 ALL | 4/1/22-3/31/23 ALL | 4/1/23-3/31/24 ALL | | 58 (4/1-9/30/23) | | | 887 (10/1/23-3/31/24) | | |
| | | | | | 0-1MM | 1-3MM | 3-5MM | 5-10MM | 10-25MM | 25MM & OVER |
| | 837 | 1098 | 945 | NUMBER OF STATEMENTS | 385 | 178 | 86 | 103 | 97 | 96 |
| | % | % | % | ASSETS | % | % | % | % | % | % |
| | 16.0 | 14.4 | 13.5 | Cash & Equivalents | 8.1 | 12.8 | 24.3 | 17.5 | 18.1 | 18.4 |
| | 5.2 | 5.1 | 6.3 | Trade Receivables (net) | 2.3 | 5.8 | 4.7 | 10.7 | 9.9 | 16.0 |
| | 7.2 | 6.7 | 5.5 | Inventory | 1.2 | 5.2 | 4.8 | 8.6 | 11.5 | 14.6 |
| | 6.1 | 6.2 | 7.3 | All Other Current | 4.0 | 10.1 | 9.4 | 10.9 | 8.0 | 8.9 |
| | 34.5 | 32.4 | 32.6 | Total Current | 15.5 | 33.9 | 43.2 | 47.7 | 47.5 | 57.9 |
| | 49.3 | 50.6 | 49.1 | Fixed Assets (net) | 70.8 | 47.6 | 34.8 | 31.0 | 26.0 | 20.1 |
| | 3.2 | 3.3 | 3.5 | Intangibles (net) | 1.9 | 4.4 | 5.3 | 3.9 | 4.8 | 5.0 |
| | 13.1 | 13.7 | 14.8 | All Other Non-Current | 11.7 | 14.1 | 16.7 | 17.4 | 21.7 | 17.0 |
| | 100.0 | 100.0 | 100.0 | Total | 100.0 | 100.0 | 100.0 | 100.0 | 100.0 | 100.0 |
| | | | | LIABILITIES | | | | | | |
| | 8.1 | 8.2 | 9.3 | Notes Payable-Short Term | 8.6 | 7.1 | 13.7 | 8.2 | 13.2 | 9.6 |
| | 2.5 | 2.2 | 2.4 | Cur. Mat.-L.T.D. | 2.7 | 2.8 | 1.6 | 1.3 | 1.8 | 2.4 |
| | 2.8 | 2.7 | 3.4 | Trade Payables | 1.0 | 3.1 | 5.4 | 3.8 | 4.4 | 10.6 |
| | .1 | .0 | .0 | Income Taxes Payable | .0 | .1 | .0 | .0 | .0 | .1 |
| | 9.9 | 9.3 | 12.3 | All Other Current | 9.0 | 15.5 | 10.8 | 13.8 | 17.9 | 13.1 |
| | 23.3 | 22.4 | 27.4 | Total Current | 21.3 | 28.5 | 31.6 | 27.0 | 37.5 | 35.7 |
| | 39.6 | 44.9 | 41.6 | Long-Term Debt | 56.5 | 44.1 | 35.7 | 28.4 | 19.8 | 18.9 |
| | .1 | .0 | .1 | Deferred Taxes | .0 | .0 | .0 | .0 | .1 | 1.3 |
| | 7.6 | 5.3 | 5.2 | All Other Non-Current | 3.4 | 6.9 | 8.1 | 6.1 | 6.0 | 5.7 |
| | 29.4 | 27.4 | 25.6 | Net Worth | 18.8 | 20.6 | 24.6 | 38.5 | 36.6 | 38.5 |
| | 100.0 | 100.0 | 100.0 | Total Liabilities & Net Worth | 100.0 | 100.0 | 100.0 | 100.0 | 100.0 | 100.0 |
| | | | | INCOME DATA | | | | | | |
| | 100.0 | 100.0 | 100.0 | Net Sales | 100.0 | 100.0 | 100.0 | 100.0 | 100.0 | 100.0 |
| | | | | Gross Profit | | | | | | |
| | 63.9 | 63.6 | 65.7 | Operating Expenses | 50.8 | 66.0 | 74.0 | 77.2 | 80.9 | 89.4 |
| | 36.1 | 36.4 | 34.3 | Operating Profit | 49.2 | 34.0 | 26.0 | 22.8 | 19.1 | 10.6 |
| | 11.3 | 13.1 | 14.1 | All Other Expenses (net) | 21.9 | 13.8 | 12.0 | 7.5 | 4.5 | 2.2 |
| | 24.8 | 23.3 | 20.2 | Profit Before Taxes | 27.3 | 20.2 | 14.0 | 15.3 | 14.6 | 8.4 |
| | | | | RATIOS | | | | | | |
| | 5.2 | 5.0 | 4.1 | | 2.6 | 8.2 | 5.0 | 6.8 | 3.8 | 2.8 |
| | 1.6 | 1.5 | 1.3 | Current | .8 | 1.6 | 1.4 | 2.1 | 1.9 | 1.6 |
| | .6 | .6 | .5 | | .2 | .5 | .7 | 1.0 | .9 | 1.2 |
| | 3.9 | 3.5 | 2.9 | | 2.0 | 3.6 | 4.2 | 4.1 | 3.1 | 1.9 |
| | 1.0 (1097) | 1.0 (942) | .8 | Quick | (384) .6 | .9 | (85) 1.0 | (102) 1.1 | 1.1 | 1.1 |
| | .2 | .3 | .2 | | .2 | .2 | .4 | .4 | .2 | .5 |
| | 0 UND | 0 UND | 0 UND | | 0 UND | 0 UND | 0 UND | 0 UND | 0 UND | 1 399.2 |
| | 0 UND | 0 UND | 0 UND | Sales/Receivables | 0 UND | 0 UND | 0 UND | 5 79.8 | 4 88.7 | 14 25.7 |
| | 6 61.2 | 10 37.6 | 15 23.7 | | 0 UND | 13 28.8 | 15 23.9 | 51 7.1 | 31 11.6 | 54 6.7 |
| | | | | Cost of Sales/Inventory | | | | | | |
| | | | | Cost of Sales/Payables | | | | | | |
| | 2.3 | 2.2 | 2.7 | | 5.2 | 2.2 | 2.0 | 1.6 | 2.5 | 2.6 |
| | 9.9 | 10.7 | 15.6 | Sales/Working Capital | -17.1 | 10.3 | 8.3 | 7.9 | 8.2 | 8.4 |
| | -6.7 | -8.9 | -5.0 | | -1.9 | -4.4 | -15.2 | 364.0 | -39.6 | 24.2 |
| | 21.7 | 19.3 | 12.8 | | 7.1 | 13.7 | 16.9 | 20.8 | 18.1 | 25.9 |
| | (442) 5.7 | (538) 4.7 | (459) 4.3 | EBIT/Interest | (153) 3.9 | (85) 4.0 | (42) 4.5 | (65) 4.4 | (53) 5.6 | (61) 3.5 |
| | 2.9 | 2.3 | 1.2 | | 1.9 | 1.0 | .8 | 1.6 | 1.4 | .4 |
| | 6.6 | 3.8 | 3.8 | Net Profit + Depr., Dep., | | | | | | |
| | (22) 3.5 | (27) 1.4 | (30) 1.7 | Amort./Cur. Mat. L/T/D | | | | | | |
| | 1.2 | 1.1 | .8 | | | | | | | |
| | .1 | .1 | .1 | | 1.4 | .0 | .0 | .0 | .0 | .0 |
| | 1.5 | 1.9 | 1.7 | Fixed/Worth | 3.3 | 1.7 | .3 | .4 | .2 | .3 |
| | 7.1 | 8.2 | 8.9 | | 73.1 | 20.4 | 14.0 | 3.3 | 1.7 | 1.4 |
| | .8 | .9 | .9 | | 1.3 | .8 | .6 | .6 | .7 | .7 |
| | 2.6 | 2.7 | 2.6 | Debt/Worth | 3.9 | 3.3 | 3.7 | 1.9 | 1.6 | 1.6 |
| | 16.4 | 15.5 | 30.8 | | 280.2 | NM | -20.6 | 5.7 | 4.4 | 3.8 |
| | 58.2 | 48.3 | 42.5 | % Profit Before Taxes/Tangible | 29.1 | 62.9 | 45.9 | 55.0 | 48.0 | 47.6 |
| | (687) 18.8 | (907) 16.4 | (753) 16.3 | Net Worth | (295) 12.0 | (134) 19.1 | (63) 7.9 | (91) 14.7 | (86) 21.3 | (84) 25.0 |
| | 6.2 | 4.7 | 2.8 | | 2.7 | 2.2 | .4 | 3.6 | 2.4 | 6.9 |
| | 13.8 | 11.7 | 12.0 | % Profit Before Taxes/Total | 8.5 | 12.6 | 13.6 | 20.8 | 21.0 | 21.3 |
| | 5.3 | 4.5 | 4.2 | Assets | 3.8 | 4.4 | 2.7 | 4.9 | 6.3 | 9.1 |
| | 1.6 | 1.0 | .1 | | .3 | -.4 | -.5 | 1.0 | -.2 | .5 |
| | 76.3 | 101.0 | 73.6 | | .6 | 174.4 | UND | 261.8 | 231.9 | 237.8 |
| | .7 | .5 | 1.0 | Sales/Net Fixed Assets | .2 | 1.0 | 16.4 | 7.3 | 25.5 | 30.9 |
| | .2 | .1 | .2 | | .1 | .2 | .4 | .5 | 1.9 | 4.8 |
| | 1.0 | .9 | 1.0 | | .2 | 1.0 | 1.8 | 3.0 | 2.0 | 2.8 |
| | .2 | .2 | .3 | Sales/Total Assets | .1 | .3 | .4 | .6 | .8 | 1.5 |
| | .1 | .1 | .1 | | .1 | .1 | .1 | .2 | .3 | .6 |
| | 1.8 | 2.4 | 2.0 | | 12.3 | 2.8 | .8 | .7 | .4 | .1 |
| | (446) 12.3 | (580) 13.8 | (508) 11.8 | % Depr., Dep., Amort./Sales | (235) 18.1 | (87) 11.2 | (29) 6.4 | (44) 2.4 | (53) 1.8 | (60) 1.0 |
| | 24.5 | 23.1 | 22.7 | | 28.4 | 21.5 | 24.4 | 10.9 | 9.7 | 2.2 |
| | 1.8 | 2.3 | 2.1 | % Officers', Directors', | 5.3 | 2.3 | 2.9 | 2.6 | 1.0 | |
| | (113) 5.0 | (122) 5.2 | (100) 3.7 | Owners' Comp/Sales | (17) 9.5 | (25) 3.5 | (18) 6.3 | (20) 3.4 | (13) 2.2 | |
| | 13.5 | 12.4 | 9.9 | | 33.1 | 9.3 | 13.3 | 7.4 | 3.3 | |
| | 8365021M | 9500886M | 14335851M | Net Sales ($) | 149629M | 317690M | 328467M | 735566M | 1571349M | 11233150M |
| | 13944725M | 17241809M | 17809828M | Total Assets ($) | 1089001M | 1834869M | 1542340M | 2890196M | 4228721M | 6224701M |

© RMA 2024    M = $ thousand    MM = $ million
See Pages viii through xx for Explanation of Ratios and Data

# REAL ESTATE—Passenger Car Rental  NAICS 532111

## Current Data Sorted by Assets / Comparative Historical Data

| | | | | | | | Type of Statement | | |
|---|---|---|---|---|---|---|---|---|---|
| | | | | 1 | 1 | | Unqualified | 5 | 2 |
| | 2 | | | 3 | | | Reviewed | 6 | 6 |
| 2 | 3 | 1 | 1 | | | | Compiled | 2 | 4 |
| 1 | 4 | 7 | | | 5 | | Tax Returns | 4 | 4 |
| | 3 (4/1-9/30/23) | | 35 (10/1/23-3/31/24) | | | | Other | 29 | 12 |
| 0-500M | 500M-2MM | 2-10MM | 10-50MM | 50-100MM | 100-250MM | | | 4/1/19-3/31/20 ALL | 4/1/20-3/31/21 ALL |
| 3 | 9 | 9 | 6 | 5 | 6 | | NUMBER OF STATEMENTS | 46 | 28 |
| % | % | % | % | % | % | | ASSETS | % | % |
| | | | | | | | Cash & Equivalents | 19.2 | 14.8 |
| | | | | | | | Trade Receivables (net) | 6.6 | 4.6 |
| | | | | | | | Inventory | 17.8 | 13.1 |
| | | | | | | | All Other Current | 3.3 | 3.4 |
| | | | | | | | Total Current | 47.0 | 35.9 |
| | | | | | | | Fixed Assets (net) | 37.5 | 45.3 |
| | | | | | | | Intangibles (net) | 5.0 | 6.4 |
| | | | | | | | All Other Non-Current | 10.5 | 12.4 |
| | | | | | | | Total | 100.0 | 100.0 |
| | | | | | | | **LIABILITIES** | | |
| | | | | | | | Notes Payable-Short Term | 26.1 | 19.4 |
| | | | | | | | Cur. Mat.-L.T.D. | 4.8 | 5.7 |
| | | | | | | | Trade Payables | 2.8 | 5.6 |
| | | | | | | | Income Taxes Payable | .2 | .0 |
| | | | | | | | All Other Current | 20.9 | 4.9 |
| | | | | | | | Total Current | 54.9 | 35.6 |
| | | | | | | | Long-Term Debt | 24.1 | 48.1 |
| | | | | | | | Deferred Taxes | .4 | .6 |
| | | | | | | | All Other Non-Current | 2.9 | 1.2 |
| | | | | | | | Net Worth | 17.7 | 14.5 |
| | | | | | | | Total Liabilities & Net Worth | 100.0 | 100.0 |
| | | | | | | | **INCOME DATA** | | |
| | | | | | | | Net Sales | 100.0 | 100.0 |
| | | | | | | | Gross Profit | | |
| | | | | | | | Operating Expenses | 90.7 | 96.0 |
| | | | | | | | Operating Profit | 9.3 | 4.0 |
| | | | | | | | All Other Expenses (net) | 1.8 | -.6 |
| | | | | | | | Profit Before Taxes | 7.4 | 4.6 |
| | | | | | | | **RATIOS** | | |
| | | | | | | | Current | 1.6 | 2.5 |
| | | | | | | | | 1.1 | 1.4 |
| | | | | | | | | .5 | .4 |
| | | | | | | | Quick | 1.2 | 1.8 |
| | | | | | | | | .6 | .6 |
| | | | | | | | | .1 | .2 |
| | | | | | | | | 0 UND | 0 UND |
| | | | | | | | Sales/Receivables | 13 27.1 | 8 45.5 |
| | | | | | | | | 34 10.6 | 26 14.3 |
| | | | | | | | Cost of Sales/Inventory | | |
| | | | | | | | Cost of Sales/Payables | | |
| | | | | | | | Sales/Working Capital | 5.6 | 2.8 |
| | | | | | | | | 25.6 | 26.3 |
| | | | | | | | | -8.4 | -3.8 |
| | | | | | | | EBIT/Interest | 4.8 | 5.6 |
| | | | | | | | | (34) 3.0 | (25) 1.5 |
| | | | | | | | | 1.4 | -.5 |
| | | | | | | | Net Profit + Depr., Dep., Amort./Cur. Mat. L/T/D | | |
| | | | | | | | Fixed/Worth | .1 | .2 |
| | | | | | | | | 1.2 | 1.7 |
| | | | | | | | | 8.5 | 10.0 |
| | | | | | | | Debt/Worth | .9 | 1.5 |
| | | | | | | | | 4.1 | 3.9 |
| | | | | | | | | 13.9 | 10.2 |
| | | | | | | | % Profit Before Taxes/Tangible Net Worth | 69.6 | 70.3 |
| | | | | | | | | (39) 25.6 | (25) 21.6 |
| | | | | | | | | 5.1 | -3.7 |
| | | | | | | | % Profit Before Taxes/Total Assets | 14.3 | 11.8 |
| | | | | | | | | 5.6 | 1.6 |
| | | | | | | | | .7 | -2.3 |
| | | | | | | | Sales/Net Fixed Assets | 151.9 | 26.8 |
| | | | | | | | | 5.1 | 3.0 |
| | | | | | | | | 1.2 | .7 |
| | | | | | | | Sales/Total Assets | 1.7 | 1.2 |
| | | | | | | | | .9 | .7 |
| | | | | | | | | .5 | .4 |
| | | | | | | | % Depr., Dep., Amort./Sales | 2.0 | 9.6 |
| | | | | | | | | (20) 12.3 | (16) 21.6 |
| | | | | | | | | 30.4 | 42.8 |
| | | | | | | | % Officers', Directors', Owners' Comp/Sales | .6 | |
| | | | | | | | | (13) 2.6 | |
| | | | | | | | | 7.0 | |
| 1298M | 39863M | 90583M | 107146M | 642395M | 1133690M | | Net Sales ($) | 1402065M | 738968M |
| 907M | 9623M | 43794M | 149829M | 369333M | 923575M | | Total Assets ($) | 1473964M | 753257M |

© RMA 2024

M = $ thousand     MM = $ million
See Pages viii through xx for Explanation of Ratios and Data

# REAL ESTATE—Passenger Car Rental  NAICS 532111

**957**

| Comparative Historical Data | | | Type of Statement | Current Data Sorted by Sales | | | | | |
|---|---|---|---|---|---|---|---|---|---|
| 1 | 3 | 2 | Unqualified | | | | | 2 | 2 |
| 1 | 6 | 5 | Reviewed | | | | | 1 | 3 |
| 4 | 4 | 4 | Compiled | 2 | 1 | | 1 | | |
| 4 | 6 | 6 | Tax Returns | 2 | 3 | | 2 | 4 | |
| 13 | 26 | 21 | Other | 1 | 1 | 5 | | | 8 |
| 4/1/21-3/31/22 ALL | 4/1/22-3/31/23 ALL | 4/1/23-3/31/24 ALL | | 0-1MM | 3 (4/1-9/30/23) 1-3MM | 3-5MM | 35 (10/1/23-3/31/24) 5-10MM | 10-25MM | 25MM & OVER |
| 23 | 41 | 38 | NUMBER OF STATEMENTS | 5 | 5 | 5 | 3 | 7 | 13 |
| % | % | % | | % | % | % | % | % | % |
| 15.0 | 27.5 | 18.2 | **ASSETS** Cash & Equivalents | | | | | | 10.9 |
| 13.5 | 5.8 | 8.9 | Trade Receivables (net) | | | | | | 15.7 |
| 7.5 | 9.9 | 4.6 | Inventory | | | | | | 3.6 |
| 2.5 | 6.5 | 7.6 | All Other Current | | | | | | 6.0 |
| 38.5 | 49.8 | 39.2 | Total Current | | | | | | 36.3 |
| 43.0 | 37.0 | 44.6 | Fixed Assets (net) | | | | | | 40.0 |
| 2.1 | 1.1 | 4.0 | Intangibles (net) | | | | | | 2.9 |
| 16.3 | 12.1 | 12.2 | All Other Non-Current | | | | | | 20.8 |
| 100.0 | 100.0 | 100.0 | Total | | | | | | 100.0 |
| | | | **LIABILITIES** | | | | | | |
| 8.4 | 6.8 | 15.2 | Notes Payable-Short Term | | | | | | 13.1 |
| 2.9 | 4.8 | 5.3 | Cur. Mat.-L.T.D. | | | | | | 4.7 |
| 5.2 | 16.9 | 9.6 | Trade Payables | | | | | | 9.0 |
| .7 | .7 | .8 | Income Taxes Payable | | | | | | 1.0 |
| 11.3 | 19.1 | 11.9 | All Other Current | | | | | | 5.6 |
| 28.5 | 48.3 | 42.8 | Total Current | | | | | | 33.4 |
| 28.3 | 16.1 | 29.5 | Long-Term Debt | | | | | | 22.1 |
| .5 | .4 | .6 | Deferred Taxes | | | | | | 1.2 |
| 5.4 | 4.3 | 5.6 | All Other Non-Current | | | | | | 4.1 |
| 37.3 | 30.9 | 21.5 | Net Worth | | | | | | 39.3 |
| 100.0 | 100.0 | 100.0 | Total Liabilities & Net Worth | | | | | | 100.0 |
| | | | **INCOME DATA** | | | | | | |
| 100.0 | 100.0 | 100.0 | Net Sales | | | | | | 100.0 |
| | | | Gross Profit | | | | | | |
| 85.2 | 76.3 | 89.6 | Operating Expenses | | | | | | 84.4 |
| 14.8 | 23.7 | 10.4 | Operating Profit | | | | | | 15.6 |
| 1.4 | .9 | 1.5 | All Other Expenses (net) | | | | | | 1.6 |
| 13.4 | 22.7 | 9.0 | Profit Before Taxes | | | | | | 14.0 |
| | | | **RATIOS** | | | | | | |
| 4.0 | 3.1 | 2.8 | | | | | | | 3.0 |
| 1.3 | 1.4 | 1.1 | Current | | | | | | .7 |
| .3 | .4 | .3 | | | | | | | .3 |
| 3.4 | 2.2 | 1.6 | | | | | | | 1.6 |
| .9 | 1.0 | .7 | Quick | | | | | | .6 |
| .3 | .3 | .2 | | | | | | | .2 |
| 0 UND | 0 UND | 0 UND | | | | | | 3 | 137.9 |
| 14 25.2 | 3 111.8 | 5 76.0 | Sales/Receivables | | | | | 21 | 17.3 |
| 38 9.7 | 19 19.0 | 22 16.7 | | | | | | 36 | 10.2 |
| | | | Cost of Sales/Inventory | | | | | | |
| | | | Cost of Sales/Payables | | | | | | |
| 4.1 | 4.5 | 7.8 | | | | | | | 5.9 |
| 16.8 | 15.0 | 75.4 | Sales/Working Capital | | | | | | -20.3 |
| -2.2 | -18.3 | -2.2 | | | | | | | -2.1 |
| 15.8 | 13.6 | 5.0 | | | | | | | 9.4 |
| (15) 9.1 | (28) 8.1 | (31) 2.5 | EBIT/Interest | | | | | (11) | 3.5 |
| 3.5 | 3.7 | .2 | | | | | | | 1.3 |
| | | | Net Profit + Depr., Dep., Amort./Cur. Mat. L/T/D | | | | | | |
| .1 | .0 | .4 | | | | | | | .1 |
| 1.1 | .5 | 1.8 | Fixed/Worth | | | | | | .9 |
| 4.9 | 2.1 | 5.8 | | | | | | | 4.8 |
| .6 | .6 | .7 | | | | | | | .5 |
| 2.2 | 1.4 | 2.4 | Debt/Worth | | | | | | 1.6 |
| 9.1 | 3.4 | 11.3 | | | | | | | 5.2 |
| 90.3 | 106.9 | 55.7 | | | | | | | 64.6 |
| (20) 43.5 | (38) 56.5 | (30) 17.1 | % Profit Before Taxes/Tangible Net Worth | | | | | (11) | 15.5 |
| 16.4 | 20.5 | 8.7 | | | | | | | 14.1 |
| 23.2 | 54.4 | 11.5 | | | | | | | 18.1 |
| 15.4 | 18.9 | 4.6 | % Profit Before Taxes/Total Assets | | | | | | 9.5 |
| 2.2 | 9.4 | -4.4 | | | | | | | 2.0 |
| 83.1 | 270.4 | 27.3 | | | | | | | 66.2 |
| 2.7 | 5.2 | 3.5 | Sales/Net Fixed Assets | | | | | | 4.7 |
| .9 | 1.3 | .8 | | | | | | | 1.1 |
| 2.3 | 3.0 | 3.1 | | | | | | | 3.3 |
| .9 | 1.1 | 1.1 | Sales/Total Assets | | | | | | 1.0 |
| .6 | .5 | .6 | | | | | | | .5 |
| .5 | | .5 | | | | | | | .5 |
| (10) 9.6 | (20) 18.0 | (22) 16.8 | % Depr., Dep., Amort./Sales | | | | | | |
| 18.3 | 31.1 | 28.8 | | | | | | | |
| | | .6 | | | | | | | |
| | (10) 1.9 | | % Officers', Directors' Owners' Comp/Sales | | | | | | |
| | | 2.6 | | | | | | | |
| 1717828M | 1234555M | 2014975M | Net Sales ($) | 2202M | 9435M | 20679M | 21695M | 113490M | 1847474M |
| 964454M | 954114M | 1497061M | Total Assets ($) | 2711M | 16846M | 22467M | 5684M | 110703M | 1338650M |

© RMA 2024   M = $ thousand   MM = $ million
See Pages viii through xx for Explanation of Ratios and Data

# REAL ESTATE—Passenger Car Leasing  NAICS 532112

## Current Data Sorted by Assets

| | | | | | | | Comparative Historical Data | |
|---|---|---|---|---|---|---|---|---|
| | | | | 1 | 3 | **Type of Statement** | | |
| | | 3 | 2 | 3 | | Unqualified | 9 | 6 |
| | | 2 | 1 | | | Reviewed | 12 | 16 |
| 1 | 1 | 2 | | | | Compiled | 6 | 2 |
| 1 | 3 | 6 | 4 | 7 | 5 | Tax Returns | 9 | 3 |
| | 6 (4/1-9/30/23) | | 39 (10/1/23-3/31/24) | | | Other | 30 | 24 |
| 0-500M | 500M-2MM | 2-10MM | 10-50MM | 50-100MM | 100-250MM | | 4/1/19-3/31/20 ALL | 4/1/20-3/31/21 ALL |
| 2 | 4 | 13 | 7 | 11 | 8 | **NUMBER OF STATEMENTS** | 66 | 51 |
| % | % | % | % | % | % | **ASSETS** | % | % |
| | | 12.3 | | 6.5 | | Cash & Equivalents | 5.4 | 9.0 |
| | | 5.8 | | 15.9 | | Trade Receivables (net) | 8.0 | 11.0 |
| | | 11.2 | | 6.1 | | Inventory | 8.3 | 4.6 |
| | | 1.2 | | 11.4 | | All Other Current | 3.9 | 7.5 |
| | | 30.4 | | 39.9 | | Total Current | 25.6 | 32.2 |
| | | 48.1 | | 49.6 | | Fixed Assets (net) | 42.5 | 37.5 |
| | | .0 | | .6 | | Intangibles (net) | 1.1 | 1.3 |
| | | 21.5 | | 10.0 | | All Other Non-Current | 30.8 | 29.1 |
| | | 100.0 | | 100.0 | | Total | 100.0 | 100.0 |
| | | | | | | **LIABILITIES** | | |
| | | 5.9 | | 10.6 | | Notes Payable-Short Term | 11.3 | 4.1 |
| | | 4.4 | | 6.2 | | Cur. Mat.-L.T.D. | 10.7 | 7.9 |
| | | 4.3 | | 2.0 | | Trade Payables | 1.6 | 2.3 |
| | | .0 | | .2 | | Income Taxes Payable | .1 | .2 |
| | | 9.5 | | 3.7 | | All Other Current | 3.4 | 3.0 |
| | | 24.1 | | 22.7 | | Total Current | 27.1 | 17.4 |
| | | 40.0 | | 43.6 | | Long-Term Debt | 53.1 | 54.5 |
| | | 1.0 | | 1.7 | | Deferred Taxes | .5 | 1.0 |
| | | 1.3 | | .3 | | All Other Non-Current | 4.2 | 2.3 |
| | | 33.6 | | 31.7 | | Net Worth | 15.1 | 24.8 |
| | | 100.0 | | 100.0 | | Total Liabilities & Net Worth | 100.0 | 100.0 |
| | | | | | | **INCOME DATA** | | |
| | | 100.0 | | 100.0 | | Net Sales | 100.0 | 100.0 |
| | | | | | | Gross Profit | | |
| | | 82.8 | | 76.2 | | Operating Expenses | 82.3 | 77.7 |
| | | 17.2 | | 23.8 | | Operating Profit | 17.7 | 22.3 |
| | | 7.3 | | 5.9 | | All Other Expenses (net) | 8.9 | 9.5 |
| | | 9.9 | | 17.9 | | Profit Before Taxes | 8.8 | 12.8 |
| | | | | | | **RATIOS** | | |
| | | 2.6 | | 5.4 | | | 2.8 | 10.0 |
| | | 1.3 | | 1.3 | | Current | 1.1 | 2.1 |
| | | .4 | | .6 | | | .3 | .4 |
| | | 1.7 | | 2.0 | | | 1.5 | 3.8 |
| | | .5 | | 1.2 | | Quick | .7 | 1.5 |
| | | .1 | | .3 | | | .2 | .4 |
| | 0 | UND | 5 | 77.7 | | | 2  196.6 | 1  295.4 |
| | 6 | 58.9 | 13 | 27.2 | | Sales/Receivables | 12  30.5 | 13  27.2 |
| | 13 | 28.9 | 107 | 3.4 | | | 27  13.3 | 49  7.5 |
| | | | | | | Cost of Sales/Inventory | | |
| | | | | | | Cost of Sales/Payables | | |
| | | 3.0 | | .8 | | | 5.0 | 1.3 |
| | | 25.9 | | 6.0 | | Sales/Working Capital | 70.9 | 5.2 |
| | | -2.7 | | -2.0 | | | -2.7 | -9.1 |
| | | 9.0 | | 39.2 | | | 2.6 | 3.3 |
| | (12) | 1.9 | | 2.3 | | EBIT/Interest | (53)  1.6 | (37)  2.0 |
| | | .4 | | 1.5 | | | 1.3 | 1.4 |
| | | | | | | Net Profit + Depr., Dep., Amort./Cur. Mat. L/T/D | | |
| | | .1 | | .1 | | | .1 | .1 |
| | | 1.6 | | 1.6 | | Fixed/Worth | 1.9 | .9 |
| | | 3.6 | | 9.2 | | | 6.3 | 3.5 |
| | | .7 | | .9 | | | 3.0 | 1.9 |
| | | 2.8 | | 4.8 | | Debt/Worth | 7.3 | 5.9 |
| | | 4.2 | | 8.8 | | | 12.9 | 9.0 |
| | | 22.0 | | 28.4 | | % Profit Before Taxes/Tangible Net Worth | 27.1 | 30.9 |
| | (12) | 5.8 | | 22.2 | | | (62)  15.7 | (50)  14.1 |
| | | -15.6 | | 16.6 | | | 7.2 | 6.9 |
| | | 11.4 | | 9.6 | | % Profit Before Taxes/Total Assets | 4.3 | 4.9 |
| | | 4.3 | | 4.5 | | | 2.0 | 2.4 |
| | | -3.4 | | 2.0 | | | .9 | .9 |
| | | 32.9 | | 26.5 | | Sales/Net Fixed Assets | 19.6 | 31.0 |
| | | 1.7 | | .5 | | | 1.4 | 1.7 |
| | | .5 | | .4 | | | .5 | .5 |
| | | 1.6 | | .5 | | Sales/Total Assets | .7 | .6 |
| | | .7 | | .3 | | | .4 | .4 |
| | | .4 | | .3 | | | .2 | .2 |
| | | | | | | % Depr., Dep., Amort./Sales | 2.7 | 6.6 |
| | | | | | | | (42)  27.2 | (30)  16.6 |
| | | | | | | | 65.9 | 57.6 |
| | | | | | | % Officers', Directors' Owners' Comp/Sales | 1.2 | |
| | | | | | | | (12)  2.3 | |
| | | | | | | | 4.3 | |
| 95M | 4101M | 97939M | 35103M | 296222M | 558730M | Net Sales ($) | 1871983M | 886955M |
| 443M | 4126M | 81199M | 169464M | 791310M | 1180993M | Total Assets ($) | 2641660M | 1925985M |

M = $ thousand   MM = $ million
See Pages viii through xx for Explanation of Ratios and Data

© RMA 2024

# REAL ESTATE—Passenger Car Leasing NAICS 532112

## Comparative Historical Data | Current Data Sorted by Sales

| Comparative Historical Data | | | | | Current Data Sorted by Sales | | | | | |
|---|---|---|---|---|---|---|---|---|---|---|
| | | | Type of Statement | | | | | | | |
| 5 | 7 | 4 | Unqualified | | | | 1 | 1 | 5 | 3 |
| 7 | 11 | 8 | Reviewed | | | 2 | 1 | | | 1 |
| 1 | 1 | 3 | Compiled | | | | | | | |
| 4 | 6 | 4 | Tax Returns | 3 | 4 | | | 4 | | 1 |
| 22 | 27 | 26 | Other | 3 | | 3 | 3 | 4 | 3 | 9 |
| 4/1/21-3/31/22 ALL | 4/1/22-3/31/23 ALL | 4/1/23-3/31/24 ALL | | | 6 (4/1-9/30/23) | | | 39 (10/1/23-3/31/24) | | |
| | | | | 0-1MM | 1-3MM | 3-5MM | 5-10MM | 10-25MM | 25MM & OVER | |
| 39 | 52 | 45 | NUMBER OF STATEMENTS | 6 | 6 | 5 | 5 | 9 | 14 | |
| % | % | % | ASSETS | % | % | % | % | % | % | |
| 9.2 | 10.1 | 8.8 | Cash & Equivalents | | | | | | 7.4 | |
| 5.0 | 7.9 | 9.0 | Trade Receivables (net) | | | | | | 8.6 | |
| 1.2 | 3.9 | 6.7 | Inventory | | | | | | 8.1 | |
| 3.2 | 4.3 | 4.0 | All Other Current | | | | | | 7.9 | |
| 18.6 | 26.2 | 28.6 | Total Current | | | | | | 32.0 | |
| 49.1 | 44.4 | 47.4 | Fixed Assets (net) | | | | | | 32.7 | |
| .3 | .3 | .2 | Intangibles (net) | | | | | | .3 | |
| 32.0 | 29.1 | 23.9 | All Other Non-Current | | | | | | 35.0 | |
| 100.0 | 100.0 | 100.0 | Total | | | | | | 100.0 | |
| | | | LIABILITIES | | | | | | | |
| 3.3 | 7.6 | 9.7 | Notes Payable-Short Term | | | | | | 8.5 | |
| 11.2 | 12.4 | 9.6 | Cur. Mat.-L.T.D. | | | | | | 11.9 | |
| 2.3 | 2.0 | 2.7 | Trade Payables | | | | | | 3.1 | |
| .4 | .2 | .2 | Income Taxes Payable | | | | | | .3 | |
| 8.9 | 6.8 | 12.5 | All Other Current | | | | | | 2.0 | |
| 26.1 | 29.0 | 34.6 | Total Current | | | | | | 25.8 | |
| 52.3 | 40.3 | 40.1 | Long-Term Debt | | | | | | 43.6 | |
| .9 | 1.4 | .9 | Deferred Taxes | | | | | | .7 | |
| 1.2 | 2.5 | 1.0 | All Other Non-Current | | | | | | .3 | |
| 19.4 | 26.7 | 23.4 | Net Worth | | | | | | 29.6 | |
| 100.0 | 100.0 | 100.0 | Total Liabilities & Net Worth | | | | | | 100.0 | |
| | | | INCOME DATA | | | | | | | |
| 100.0 | 100.0 | 100.0 | Net Sales | | | | | | 100.0 | |
| | | | Gross Profit | | | | | | | |
| 80.2 | 76.2 | 79.7 | Operating Expenses | | | | | | 83.9 | |
| 19.8 | 23.8 | 20.3 | Operating Profit | | | | | | 16.1 | |
| 8.3 | 5.5 | 9.0 | All Other Expenses (net) | | | | | | 3.0 | |
| 11.6 | 18.3 | 11.3 | Profit Before Taxes | | | | | | 13.1 | |
| | | | RATIOS | | | | | | | |
| 1.5 | 2.1 | 2.5 | | | | | | | 3.0 | |
| .8 | .9 | .6 | Current | | | | | | .9 | |
| .3 | .2 | .1 | | | | | | | .1 | |
| 1.4 | 1.8 | 1.4 | | | | | | | 1.3 | |
| .4 | .5 | .5 | Quick | | | | | | .8 | |
| .2 | .1 | .1 | | | | | | | .1 | |
| 1  373.9 | 2  243.2 | 1  308.2 | | | | | | | 3  104.7 | |
| 11  31.8 | 9  42.8 | 11  33.2 | Sales/Receivables | | | | | | 7  54.7 | |
| 58  6.3 | 32  11.4 | 37  9.9 | | | | | | | 31  11.7 | |
| | | | Cost of Sales/Inventory | | | | | | | |
| | | | Cost of Sales/Payables | | | | | | | |
| 10.0 | 6.4 | 3.0 | | | | | | | 4.7 | |
| -6.1 | -18.2 | -5.9 | Sales/Working Capital | | | | | | NM | |
| -1.1 | -1.2 | -1.3 | | | | | | | -1.2 | |
| 6.0 | 8.6 | 7.8 | | | | | | | 8.6 | |
| (31)  2.9 | (45)  3.3 | (38)  2.0 | EBIT/Interest | | | | | | (13)  2.0 | |
| 1.7 | 1.9 | 1.4 | | | | | | | 1.6 | |
| | | | Net Profit + Depr., Dep., Amort./Cur. Mat. L/T/D | | | | | | | |
| .1 | .2 | .1 | | | | | | | .0 | |
| 1.6 | 1.4 | 1.6 | Fixed/Worth | | | | | | .2 | |
| 5.7 | 5.8 | 5.3 | | | | | | | 5.3 | |
| 1.6 | 1.1 | 1.3 | | | | | | | .8 | |
| 5.3 | 3.9 | 4.6 | Debt/Worth | | | | | | 6.4 | |
| 8.6 | 7.8 | 8.3 | | | | | | | 8.2 | |
| 32.6 | 30.4 | 25.4 | | | | | | | 38.4 | |
| (38)  18.0 | (49)  17.3 | (42)  16.0 | % Profit Before Taxes/Tangible Net Worth | | | | | | 22.8 | |
| 9.2 | 12.2 | 5.4 | | | | | | | 16.4 | |
| 5.8 | 10.2 | 6.8 | | | | | | | 8.7 | |
| 3.3 | 3.5 | 2.9 | % Profit Before Taxes/Total Assets | | | | | | 4.4 | |
| 1.3 | 2.3 | 1.0 | | | | | | | 2.6 | |
| 20.8 | 20.5 | 19.5 | | | | | | | 684.1 | |
| .6 | 1.2 | .9 | Sales/Net Fixed Assets | | | | | | 9.8 | |
| .3 | .4 | .4 | | | | | | | .4 | |
| .5 | .7 | .5 | | | | | | | .6 | |
| .3 | .4 | .3 | Sales/Total Assets | | | | | | .4 | |
| .2 | .3 | .3 | | | | | | | .3 | |
| 1.1 | 3.8 | 4.5 | | | | | | | | |
| (25)  24.2 | (28)  24.9 | (24)  46.5 | % Depr., Dep., Amort./Sales | | | | | | | |
| 66.0 | 56.7 | 63.8 | | | | | | | | |
| | | 1.2 | % Officers', Directors' Owners' Comp/Sales | | | | | | | |
| | (11)  2.3 | | | | | | | | | |
| | | 6.2 | | | | | | | | |
| 607566M | 903340M | 992190M | Net Sales ($) | 1794M | 11419M | 18476M | 38311M | 145672M | 776518M | |
| 1633563M | 2160760M | 2227535M | Total Assets ($) | 6345M | 65408M | 53305M | 104507M | 481640M | 1516330M | |

M = $ thousand    MM = $ million

© RMA 2024

# REAL ESTATE—Truck, Utility Trailer, and RV (Recreational Vehicle) Rental and Leasing  NAICS 532120

## Current Data Sorted by Assets | Comparative Historical Data

| | | | | | | | Type of Statement | | |
|---|---|---|---|---|---|---|---|---|---|
| | | | 2 | 7 | 7 | 13 | Unqualified | 33 | 22 |
| | | | 2 | 17 | 10 | 4 | Reviewed | 34 | 20 |
| | | 1 | 3 | 4 | 1 | 1 | Compiled | 9 | 12 |
| | 2 | 4 | 8 | 3 | 2 | | Tax Returns | 22 | 16 |
| | 3 | 11 | 27 | 24 | 25 | 25 | Other | 148 | 79 |
| | | 43 (4/1-9/30/23) | | 163 (10/1/23-3/31/24) | | | | 4/1/19-3/31/20 | 4/1/20-3/31/21 |
| 0-500M | 500M-2MM | 2-10MM | 10-50MM | 50-100MM | 100-250MM | | | ALL | ALL |
| 5 | 16 | 42 | 55 | 45 | 43 | | NUMBER OF STATEMENTS | 246 | 149 |
| % | % | % | % | % | % | | ASSETS | % | % |
| | 11.0 | 12.8 | 9.0 | 8.5 | 7.4 | | Cash & Equivalents | 8.3 | 11.8 |
| | 5.9 | 6.9 | 6.4 | 7.7 | 7.7 | | Trade Receivables (net) | 8.5 | 8.0 |
| | 11.8 | 12.0 | 11.8 | 10.0 | 15.9 | | Inventory | 10.8 | 7.3 |
| | 2.1 | 1.9 | 3.8 | 2.5 | 4.1 | | All Other Current | 3.7 | 3.4 |
| | 30.8 | 33.6 | 31.0 | 28.7 | 35.0 | | Total Current | 31.3 | 30.5 |
| | 64.0 | 53.8 | 56.5 | 52.2 | 51.3 | | Fixed Assets (net) | 57.5 | 57.6 |
| | .1 | 3.8 | 1.5 | 1.3 | 2.4 | | Intangibles (net) | 1.5 | 2.5 |
| | 5.2 | 8.7 | 11.0 | 17.8 | 11.4 | | All Other Non-Current | 9.8 | 9.4 |
| | 100.0 | 100.0 | 100.0 | 100.0 | 100.0 | | Total | 100.0 | 100.0 |
| | | | | | | | LIABILITIES | | |
| | 1.0 | 9.0 | 7.9 | 10.7 | 8.6 | | Notes Payable-Short Term | 8.4 | 6.2 |
| | 6.6 | 5.6 | 8.3 | 8.8 | 9.6 | | Cur. Mat.-L.T.D. | 11.2 | 10.5 |
| | 15.7 | 3.6 | 2.6 | 3.4 | 3.0 | | Trade Payables | 4.2 | 3.5 |
| | .0 | .1 | .0 | .1 | .1 | | Income Taxes Payable | .0 | .1 |
| | 4.2 | 14.8 | 5.0 | 5.8 | 5.4 | | All Other Current | 6.9 | 7.2 |
| | 27.5 | 33.1 | 23.8 | 28.9 | 26.6 | | Total Current | 30.8 | 27.5 |
| | 52.9 | 33.1 | 27.8 | 37.8 | 40.9 | | Long-Term Debt | 39.6 | 38.3 |
| | .9 | .1 | 1.1 | .2 | .8 | | Deferred Taxes | 1.0 | .7 |
| | .0 | 7.5 | 3.3 | 3.7 | 5.6 | | All Other Non-Current | 2.5 | 2.7 |
| | 18.7 | 26.2 | 43.9 | 29.3 | 26.0 | | Net Worth | 26.0 | 30.8 |
| | 100.0 | 100.0 | 100.0 | 100.0 | 100.0 | | Total Liabilities & Net Worth | 100.0 | 100.0 |
| | | | | | | | INCOME DATA | | |
| | 100.0 | 100.0 | 100.0 | 100.0 | 100.0 | | Net Sales | 100.0 | 100.0 |
| | | | | | | | Gross Profit | | |
| | 83.6 | 80.3 | 80.7 | 91.4 | 83.2 | | Operating Expenses | 84.3 | 82.7 |
| | 16.4 | 19.7 | 19.3 | 8.6 | 16.8 | | Operating Profit | 15.7 | 17.3 |
| | 5.9 | 3.8 | 3.8 | 4.6 | 4.8 | | All Other Expenses (net) | 5.7 | 4.1 |
| | 10.5 | 15.9 | 15.5 | 4.0 | 12.0 | | Profit Before Taxes | 10.0 | 13.1 |
| | | | | | | | RATIOS | | |
| | 3.4 | 3.0 | 2.0 | 1.8 | 1.4 | | | 1.7 | 2.1 |
| | 1.2 | 1.2 | 1.0 | 1.2 | 1.0 | | Current | .9 | 1.2 |
| | .4 | .5 | .4 | .6 | .7 | | | .4 | .5 |
| | 3.3 | 2.9 | 1.0 | 1.2 | .8 | | | 1.0 | 1.6 |
| | .8 | .7 | .5 | .6 | .5 | | Quick | .5 | .6 |
| | .2 | .2 | .2 | .2 | .2 | | | .2 | .3 |
| 0 UND | 0 UND | 3 132.4 | 7 50.3 | 6 59.8 | | | | 3 108.6 | 0 UND |
| 0 UND | 4 95.2 | 13 28.0 | 23 16.0 | 25 14.4 | | | Sales/Receivables | 19 19.3 | 19 19.5 |
| 7 49.5 | 38 9.6 | 39 9.3 | 40 9.2 | 43 8.4 | | | | 41 8.9 | 42 8.6 |
| | | | | | | | Cost of Sales/Inventory | | |
| | | | | | | | Cost of Sales/Payables | | |
| | 11.9 | 3.9 | 3.7 | 7.8 | 6.1 | | | 9.3 | 5.7 |
| | 40.4 | 18.2 | 128.3 | 40.0 | -300.4 | | Sales/Working Capital | -55.4 | 23.6 |
| | -12.4 | -4.0 | -2.9 | -9.5 | -7.7 | | | -4.1 | -3.7 |
| | 8.3 | 5.9 | 4.9 | 7.2 | | | | 6.9 | 8.9 |
| (14) | .9 | (34) 2.1 | (48) 5.5 | (42) 3.0 | (36) 3.5 | | EBIT/Interest | (216) 2.8 | (130) 3.8 |
| | .0 | .7 | 2.1 | 1.4 | 2.2 | | | 1.4 | 1.5 |
| | | | | | | | | 3.8 | 1.9 |
| | | | | | | | Net Profit + Depr., Dep., Amort./Cur. Mat. L/T/D | (30) 1.6 | (12) 1.6 |
| | | | | | | | | 1.1 | 1.0 |
| | .6 | .7 | .6 | .6 | .7 | | | .9 | .9 |
| | 3.2 | 2.1 | 1.4 | 1.7 | 2.1 | | Fixed/Worth | 2.2 | 2.1 |
| | NM | 17.0 | 2.6 | 3.0 | 4.9 | | | 4.9 | 4.5 |
| | 1.5 | .9 | .7 | 1.4 | 1.9 | | | 1.3 | 1.2 |
| | 3.5 | 4.0 | 1.4 | 2.2 | 3.6 | | Debt/Worth | 3.0 | 2.5 |
| | NM | 17.2 | 3.5 | 4.5 | 7.6 | | | 7.5 | 5.2 |
| | 17.7 | 45.2 | 25.0 | 22.8 | 36.5 | | | 31.6 | 37.7 |
| (12) | -2.4 | (33) 13.9 | 14.8 | (41) 14.9 | (38) 18.8 | | % Profit Before Taxes/Tangible Net Worth | (216) 16.0 | (131) 12.7 |
| | -15.5 | 2.4 | 9.1 | 8.6 | 11.7 | | | 7.6 | 5.4 |
| | 4.6 | 10.2 | 11.4 | 7.3 | 9.2 | | | 8.1 | 11.9 |
| | -1.0 | 3.6 | 6.4 | 4.7 | 5.1 | | % Profit Before Taxes/Total Assets | 4.2 | 4.9 |
| | -5.7 | -.6 | 1.6 | 1.4 | 3.2 | | | 1.1 | 1.3 |
| | 6.9 | 4.5 | 3.8 | 5.3 | 6.6 | | | 5.8 | 5.4 |
| | .8 | 1.0 | .7 | 2.1 | 1.4 | | Sales/Net Fixed Assets | 1.2 | .9 |
| | .4 | .5 | .4 | .7 | .5 | | | .5 | .5 |
| | 1.8 | 1.2 | .8 | 1.8 | 1.1 | | | 1.6 | 1.1 |
| | .6 | .5 | .5 | 1.0 | .6 | | Sales/Total Assets | .6 | .5 |
| | .4 | .4 | .3 | .4 | .3 | | | .3 | .3 |
| | 20.2 | 2.3 | 2.6 | .6 | .5 | | | 3.6 | 4.4 |
| (11) | 50.6 | (27) 11.4 | (47) 19.8 | (31) 5.3 | (15) 2.8 | | % Depr., Dep., Amort./Sales | (161) 15.6 | (84) 21.5 |
| | 88.5 | 32.5 | 53.1 | 19.9 | 5.6 | | | 54.3 | 41.8 |
| | | | | | | | | 1.3 | 1.9 |
| | | | | | | | % Officers', Directors' Owners' Comp/Sales | (25) 2.5 | (23) 3.4 |
| | | | | | | | | 10.0 | 6.5 |
| 2692M | 23234M | 181223M | 1194648M | 3978905M | 5306565M | | Net Sales ($) | 10285425M | 6276342M |
| 1448M | 19353M | 191181M | 1492866M | 3178715M | 6693514M | | Total Assets ($) | 12879256M | 7332346M |

© RMA 2024

M = $ thousand   MM = $ million
See Pages viii through xx for Explanation of Ratios and Data

# REAL ESTATE—Truck, Utility Trailer, and RV (Recreational Vehicle) Rental and Leasing  NAICS 532120

## Comparative Historical Data | Current Data Sorted by Sales

| | | | Type of Statement | | | | | | |
|---|---|---|---|---|---|---|---|---|---|
| 22 | 29 | 29 | Unqualified | | 1 | 2 | 2 | 2 | 22 |
| 21 | 28 | 33 | Reviewed | | 2 | 3 | 6 | 6 | 16 |
| 6 | 15 | 10 | Compiled | 1 | 2 | 1 | 4 | | 2 |
| 11 | 15 | 19 | Tax Returns | 8 | 3 | | 5 | 1 | 2 |
| 117 | 103 | 115 | Other | 9 | 24 | 2 | 15 | 16 | 49 |
| 4/1/21-3/31/22 | 4/1/22-3/31/23 | 4/1/23-3/31/24 | | | 43 (4/1-9/30/23) | | | 163 (10/1/23-3/31/24) | |
| ALL | ALL | ALL | | 0-1MM | 1-3MM | 3-5MM | 5-10MM | 10-25MM | 25MM & OVER |
| 177 | 190 | 206 | NUMBER OF STATEMENTS | 18 | 32 | 8 | 32 | 25 | 91 |
| % | % | % | ASSETS | % | % | % | % | % | % |
| 14.5 | 11.6 | 9.9 | Cash & Equivalents | 11.9 | 11.3 | | 12.1 | 7.5 | 8.9 |
| 9.7 | 9.3 | 7.2 | Trade Receivables (net) | 4.3 | 3.4 | | 9.7 | 7.6 | 8.2 |
| 8.6 | 9.6 | 12.4 | Inventory | 5.0 | 7.3 | | 16.7 | 8.1 | 16.4 |
| 4.9 | 3.8 | 3.0 | All Other Current | 3.1 | 3.4 | | 2.9 | 2.8 | 3.0 |
| 37.7 | 34.3 | 32.5 | Total Current | 24.2 | 25.5 | | 41.4 | 25.9 | 36.5 |
| 49.1 | 50.1 | 54.1 | Fixed Assets (net) | 69.4 | 62.2 | | 44.3 | 66.6 | 48.0 |
| 2.3 | 3.6 | 2.0 | Intangibles (net) | .1 | .8 | | 5.7 | .9 | 1.9 |
| 10.9 | 12.0 | 11.4 | All Other Non-Current | 6.3 | 11.5 | | 8.6 | 6.6 | 13.6 |
| 100.0 | 100.0 | 100.0 | Total | 100.0 | 100.0 | | 100.0 | 100.0 | 100.0 |
| | | | LIABILITIES | | | | | | |
| 10.0 | 9.0 | 8.8 | Notes Payable-Short Term | 7.7 | 7.8 | | 6.4 | 3.6 | 11.4 |
| 9.7 | 9.3 | 7.9 | Cur. Mat.-L.T.D. | 7.3 | 5.2 | | 7.2 | 10.2 | 8.7 |
| 4.6 | 4.0 | 4.4 | Trade Payables | 4.8 | 7.8 | | 4.3 | 4.3 | 3.5 |
| .1 | .2 | .1 | Income Taxes Payable | .0 | .1 | | .0 | .0 | .1 |
| 9.0 | 6.6 | 7.5 | All Other Current | 7.3 | 11.9 | | 9.0 | 3.7 | 7.0 |
| 33.4 | 29.1 | 28.7 | Total Current | 27.0 | 32.7 | | 26.9 | 21.7 | 30.6 |
| 36.9 | 35.0 | 35.5 | Long-Term Debt | 49.0 | 41.8 | | 27.8 | 38.6 | 32.9 |
| .5 | .6 | .6 | Deferred Taxes | .9 | .5 | | .4 | .4 | .7 |
| 5.4 | 4.0 | 4.7 | All Other Non-Current | 7.8 | 1.3 | | 4.0 | 3.2 | 5.1 |
| 23.8 | 31.4 | 30.6 | Net Worth | 15.2 | 23.8 | | 41.0 | 36.1 | 30.6 |
| 100.0 | 100.0 | 100.0 | Total Liabilities & Net Worth | 100.0 | 100.0 | | 100.0 | 100.0 | 100.0 |
| | | | INCOME DATA | | | | | | |
| 100.0 | 100.0 | 100.0 | Net Sales | 100.0 | 100.0 | | 100.0 | 100.0 | 100.0 |
| | | | Gross Profit | | | | | | |
| 79.7 | 79.0 | 83.7 | Operating Expenses | 72.7 | 72.5 | | 86.9 | 83.8 | 89.5 |
| 20.3 | 21.0 | 16.3 | Operating Profit | 27.3 | 27.5 | | 13.1 | 16.2 | 10.5 |
| 2.1 | 3.3 | 4.4 | All Other Expenses (net) | 12.5 | 4.6 | | 2.1 | 7.1 | 2.5 |
| 18.2 | 17.7 | 12.0 | Profit Before Taxes | 14.8 | 22.9 | | 11.0 | 9.1 | 7.9 |
| | | | RATIOS | | | | | | |
| 2.2 | 2.2 | 1.9 | | 7.1 | 1.7 | | 3.0 | 1.6 | 1.8 |
| 1.3 | 1.2 | 1.1 | Current | .9 | .7 | | 1.6 | 1.0 | 1.1 |
| .7 | .6 | .6 | | .3 | .2 | | .6 | .4 | .7 |
| 1.5 | 1.5 | 1.2 | | 4.7 | 1.1 | | 2.7 | 1.3 | .8 |
| .8 | .8 | .6 | Quick | .9 | .2 | | .7 | .6 | .5 |
| .4 | .3 | .2 | | .2 | .1 | | .2 | | |
| 0 UND | 0 999.8 | 1 370.7 | | 0 UND | 0 UND | | 1 349.4 | 1 511.9 | 7 51.7 |
| 21 17.7 | 20 18.7 | 15 23.9 | Sales/Receivables | 0 UND | 0 UND | | 12 30.0 | 17 21.8 | 24 15.2 |
| 41 8.8 | 42 8.7 | 39 9.3 | | 31 11.9 | 31 11.6 | | 55 6.6 | 50 7.3 | 39 9.4 |
| | | | Cost of Sales/Inventory | | | | | | |
| | | | Cost of Sales/Payables | | | | | | |
| 5.0 | 6.4 | 6.0 | | 2.5 | 8.9 | | 1.9 | 6.4 | 7.6 |
| 16.1 | 26.9 | 74.1 | Sales/Working Capital | -33.0 | -6.3 | | 7.2 | -999.8 | 62.6 |
| -7.7 | -6.0 | -5.1 | | -2.3 | -1.1 | | -13.4 | -1.9 | -11.8 |
| 18.1 | 15.4 | 8.3 | | 8.3 | 7.7 | | 4.9 | 12.6 | 8.8 |
| (154) 6.2 | (164) 6.7 | (178) 3.2 | EBIT/Interest | (13) 1.8 | (23) 1.4 | (29) | 3.0 | (21) 2.9 | (85) 3.7 |
| 3.1 | 2.8 | 1.3 | | .0 | .7 | | 1.3 | .8 | 2.0 |
| 3.0 | 2.4 | 3.3 | Net Profit + Depr., Dep., | | | | | | 4.2 |
| (16) 2.1 | (24) 1.7 | (24) 1.6 | Amort./Cur. Mat. L/T/D | | | | | (15) | 1.8 |
| 1.1 | .7 | .9 | | | | | | | 1.2 |
| .5 | .7 | .7 | | 1.1 | .8 | | .3 | .8 | .6 |
| 1.6 | 1.6 | 1.7 | Fixed/Worth | 5.0 | 2.8 | | 1.0 | 2.4 | 1.6 |
| 5.2 | 4.4 | 4.4 | | -29.4 | 19.6 | | 2.5 | 4.6 | 3.0 |
| 1.2 | 1.1 | 1.1 | | 2.7 | 1.3 | | .7 | .8 | 1.4 |
| 2.6 | 2.3 | 2.5 | Debt/Worth | 5.9 | 4.0 | | 1.5 | 2.4 | 2.6 |
| 7.0 | 6.0 | 6.1 | | -12.6 | 19.9 | | 3.7 | 5.5 | 4.7 |
| 65.7 | 50.7 | 28.3 | | 51.7 | 38.2 | | 26.3 | 20.5 | 30.3 |
| (151) 35.9 | (167) 29.0 | (181) 15.0 | % Profit Before Taxes/Tangible Net Worth | (12) 17.3 | (25) 13.0 | (30) | 11.4 | (82) 12.1 | 18.0 |
| 15.7 | 17.2 | 7.7 | | -1.8 | -3.7 | | 4.9 | -.5 | 11.7 |
| 19.1 | 16.4 | 9.3 | | 9.3 | 10.0 | | 8.5 | 9.0 | 9.9 |
| 9.9 | 8.3 | 4.9 | % Profit Before Taxes/Total Assets | 3.2 | 2.8 | | 4.8 | 3.2 | 5.5 |
| 4.9 | 3.9 | 1.1 | | -4.4 | -1.1 | | 1.1 | -.2 | 2.9 |
| 12.3 | 14.7 | 5.3 | | 1.0 | 2.3 | | 9.8 | 1.1 | 9.9 |
| 1.7 | 1.7 | 1.1 | Sales/Net Fixed Assets | .6 | .6 | | 1.7 | .6 | 2.1 |
| .7 | .5 | .5 | | .3 | .5 | | .5 | .3 | .8 |
| 1.6 | 1.7 | 1.3 | | .7 | .5 | | 1.2 | .6 | 1.6 |
| .7 | .6 | .6 | Sales/Total Assets | .4 | .5 | | .5 | .5 | 1.0 |
| .4 | .4 | .3 | | .2 | .2 | | .3 | .3 | .5 |
| 1.3 | .9 | 2.2 | | 13.7 | 12.2 | | 5.9 | 6.9 | .5 |
| (97) 16.1 | (114) 11.1 | (133) 11.4 | % Depr., Dep., Amort./Sales | (15) 31.5 | (16) 40.0 | (24) | 14.9 | (20) 32.6 | (52) 3.2 |
| 34.4 | 37.9 | 38.7 | | 84.0 | 53.1 | | 68.9 | 43.4 | 8.1 |
| 1.3 | .9 | 1.3 | | | | | | | |
| (18) 2.7 | (17) 2.9 | (15) 2.7 | % Officers', Directors', Owners' Comp/Sales | | | | | | |
| 4.2 | 4.1 | 7.0 | | | | | | | |
| 7789865M | 10767761M | 10687267M | Net Sales ($) | 8628M | 55470M | 31118M | 235825M | 425971M | 9930255M |
| 8316251M | 10531172M | 11577077M | Total Assets ($) | 29755M | 171351M | 118477M | 628805M | 1324750M | 9303939M |

© RMA 2024  M = $ thousand  MM = $ million  
See Pages viii through xx for Explanation of Ratios and Data

# REAL ESTATE—Consumer Electronics and Appliances Rental  NAICS 532210

## Current Data Sorted by Assets

| 0-500M | 500M-2MM | 2-10MM | 10-50MM | 50-100MM | 100-250MM | | Comparative Historical Data | | |
|---|---|---|---|---|---|---|---|---|---|
| | | | | 1 | 1 | Type of Statement | | 2 | |
| | | | 1 | 1 | | Unqualified | | 1 | |
| | | 2 | | | | Reviewed | | 2 | 4 |
| 1 | | 1 | | | | Compiled | | 10 | 1 |
| | 3 | 8 | | | | Tax Returns | | 37 | 14 |
| | 3 (4/1-9/30/23) | | 1 | 17 (10/1/23-3/31/24) | | Other | | 4/1/19- | 4/1/20- |
| | | | | | | | | 3/31/20 | 3/31/21 |
| 1 | 3 | 11 | 2 | 2 | 1 | NUMBER OF STATEMENTS | | 52 ALL | 19 ALL |
| % | % | % | % | % | % | | | % | % |
| | | | | | | **ASSETS** | | | |
| | | 9.2 | | | | Cash & Equivalents | | 11.8 | 14.2 |
| | | 10.1 | | | | Trade Receivables (net) | | 5.3 | 2.4 |
| | | 3.2 | | | | Inventory | | 22.3 | 19.9 |
| | | 1.4 | | | | All Other Current | | 2.3 | 1.2 |
| | | 24.0 | | | | Total Current | | 41.7 | 37.7 |
| | | 68.7 | | | | Fixed Assets (net) | | 45.0 | 43.1 |
| | | 3.2 | | | | Intangibles (net) | | 5.9 | 6.6 |
| | | 4.1 | | | | All Other Non-Current | | 7.4 | 12.6 |
| | | 100.0 | | | | Total | | 100.0 | 100.0 |
| | | | | | | **LIABILITIES** | | | |
| | | 15.0 | | | | Notes Payable-Short Term | | 28.9 | 14.7 |
| | | 7.7 | | | | Cur. Mat.-L.T.D. | | 9.0 | 4.7 |
| | | 7.5 | | | | Trade Payables | | 5.7 | 8.6 |
| | | .1 | | | | Income Taxes Payable | | .1 | .3 |
| | | 15.7 | | | | All Other Current | | 8.1 | 7.5 |
| | | 46.1 | | | | Total Current | | 51.8 | 35.8 |
| | | 22.5 | | | | Long-Term Debt | | 21.9 | 27.5 |
| | | .0 | | | | Deferred Taxes | | .2 | .0 |
| | | 3.0 | | | | All Other Non-Current | | 4.4 | 12.6 |
| | | 28.5 | | | | Net Worth | | 21.6 | 24.0 |
| | | 100.0 | | | | Total Liabilties & Net Worth | | 100.0 | 100.0 |
| | | | | | | **INCOME DATA** | | | |
| | | 100.0 | | | | Net Sales | | 100.0 | 100.0 |
| | | | | | | Gross Profit | | | |
| | | 83.3 | | | | Operating Expenses | | 89.4 | 85.2 |
| | | 16.7 | | | | Operating Profit | | 10.6 | 14.8 |
| | | 2.1 | | | | All Other Expenses (net) | | 3.3 | 5.0 |
| | | 14.6 | | | | Profit Before Taxes | | 7.4 | 9.8 |
| | | | | | | **RATIOS** | | | |
| | | 15.8 | | | | | | 2.3 | 2.9 |
| | | .3 | | | | Current | | .9 | .8 |
| | | .1 | | | | | | .3 | .4 |
| | | 15.2 | | | | | | 1.5 | .9 |
| | | .1 | | | | Quick | | .2 | .4 |
| | | .0 | | | | | | .0 | .1 |
| | 0 | UND | | | | | 0 | UND | 0 UND |
| | 0 | UND | | | | Sales/Receivables | 0 | UND | 1 494.2 |
| | 33 | 11.2 | | | | | 8 | 47.5 | 4 100.5 |
| | | | | | | Cost of Sales/Inventory | | | |
| | | | | | | Cost of Sales/Payables | | | |
| | | 5.6 | | | | | | 7.9 | 5.3 |
| | | -6.2 | | | | Sales/Working Capital | | -84.1 | -18.7 |
| | | -3.5 | | | | | | -4.4 | -6.7 |
| | | | | | | | | 9.9 | 45.3 |
| | | | | | | EBIT/Interest | (46) | 4.0 | (16) 5.8 |
| | | | | | | | | 1.4 | 3.0 |
| | | | | | | Net Profit + Depr., Dep., Amort./Cur. Mat. L/T/D | | | |
| | | .6 | | | | | | .4 | .3 |
| | | 6.3 | | | | Fixed/Worth | | 2.1 | 2.2 |
| | | -19.5 | | | | | | -2.9 | 12.7 |
| | | 1.4 | | | | | | .6 | 1.3 |
| | | 7.5 | | | | Debt/Worth | | 4.1 | 3.7 |
| | | -22.3 | | | | | | -4.7 | 12.3 |
| | | | | | | % Profit Before Taxes/Tangible Net Worth | | 67.2 | 94.9 |
| | | | | | | | (35) | 35.6 | (15) 69.0 |
| | | | | | | | | 12.1 | 30.0 |
| | | 32.5 | | | | % Profit Before Taxes/Total Assets | | 28.7 | 30.2 |
| | | 4.9 | | | | | | 8.3 | 12.6 |
| | | .1 | | | | | | 2.0 | 6.6 |
| | | 5.2 | | | | | | 19.7 | 25.1 |
| | | 2.9 | | | | Sales/Net Fixed Assets | | 4.5 | 4.3 |
| | | 2.6 | | | | | | 2.7 | 2.3 |
| | | 2.8 | | | | | | 2.6 | 2.5 |
| | | 2.5 | | | | Sales/Total Assets | | 2.1 | 1.8 |
| | | 1.4 | | | | | | 1.6 | 1.2 |
| | | | | | | % Depr., Dep., Amort./Sales | | 2.2 | |
| | | | | | | | (23) | 7.8 | |
| | | | | | | | | 24.3 | |
| | | | | | | % Officers', Directors' Owners' Comp/Sales | | | |
| 554M | 4748M | 150871M | 45521M | 162427M | 157246M | Net Sales ($) | | 1091540M | 470488M |
| 109M | 3058M | 64090M | 47797M | 130298M | 150501M | Total Assets ($) | | 648225M | 325051M |

M = $ thousand  MMM = $ million
See Pages viii through xx for Explanation of Ratios and Data

© RMA 2024

# REAL ESTATE—Consumer Electronics and Appliances Rental  NAICS 532210

## Comparative Historical Data / Current Data Sorted by Sales

| Comparative Historical Data | | | | | Current Data Sorted by Sales | | | | | |
|---|---|---|---|---|---|---|---|---|---|---|
| 1 | 2 | 2 | Type of Statement | | | | | 1 | 2 | |
| | 2 | 2 | Unqualified | | | | | 2 | 1 | 1 |
| 2 | 4 | 3 | Reviewed | | | | | 1 | 4 | |
| 2 | 3 | 1 | Compiled | 1 | | 1 | 2 | 1 | | |
| 17 | 5 | 12 | Tax Returns | | | | | 4 | | 1 |
| 4/1/21- | 4/1/22- | 4/1/23- | Other | | 3 (4/1-9/30/23) | | | 17 (10/1/23-3/31/24) | | |
| 3/31/22 | 3/31/23 | 3/31/24 | | 0-1MM | 1-3MM | 3-5MM | 5-10MM | 10-25MM | 25MM & OVER | |
| ALL | ALL | ALL | | | | | | | | |
| 22 | 16 | 20 | NUMBER OF STATEMENTS | 1 | 4 | 1 | 2 | 8 | 4 | |
| % | % | % | ASSETS | % | % | % | % | % | % | |
| 15.2 | 17.9 | 11.6 | Cash & Equivalents | | | | | | | |
| 2.3 | 7.9 | 8.2 | Trade Receivables (net) | | | | | | | |
| 32.9 | 15.6 | 6.4 | Inventory | | | | | | | |
| 1.7 | 2.4 | 1.2 | All Other Current | | | | | | | |
| 52.1 | 43.8 | 27.4 | Total Current | | | | | | | |
| 35.2 | 34.9 | 57.8 | Fixed Assets (net) | | | | | | | |
| 8.7 | 12.5 | 4.3 | Intangibles (net) | | | | | | | |
| 4.1 | 8.8 | 10.5 | All Other Non-Current | | | | | | | |
| 100.0 | 100.0 | 100.0 | Total | | | | | | | |
| | | | LIABILITIES | | | | | | | |
| 14.5 | 9.2 | 12.5 | Notes Payable-Short Term | | | | | | | |
| 2.5 | 3.0 | 5.0 | Cur. Mat.-L.T.D. | | | | | | | |
| 4.3 | 8.4 | 5.2 | Trade Payables | | | | | | | |
| .2 | .0 | .0 | Income Taxes Payable | | | | | | | |
| 7.6 | 7.8 | 14.6 | All Other Current | | | | | | | |
| 29.1 | 28.4 | 37.4 | Total Current | | | | | | | |
| 17.2 | 21.6 | 20.2 | Long-Term Debt | | | | | | | |
| .4 | .0 | .0 | Deferred Taxes | | | | | | | |
| 3.7 | 5.1 | 3.6 | All Other Non-Current | | | | | | | |
| 49.6 | 44.8 | 38.8 | Net Worth | | | | | | | |
| 100.0 | 100.0 | 100.0 | Total Liabilities & Net Worth | | | | | | | |
| | | | INCOME DATA | | | | | | | |
| 100.0 | 100.0 | 100.0 | Net Sales | | | | | | | |
| | | | Gross Profit | | | | | | | |
| 85.2 | 92.9 | 84.5 | Operating Expenses | | | | | | | |
| 14.8 | 7.1 | 15.5 | Operating Profit | | | | | | | |
| 1.2 | .3 | 2.0 | All Other Expenses (net) | | | | | | | |
| 13.6 | 6.7 | 13.5 | Profit Before Taxes | | | | | | | |
| | | | RATIOS | | | | | | | |
| 4.4 | 9.0 | 5.9 | | | | | | | | |
| 2.7 | 1.5 | .6 | Current | | | | | | | |
| .5 | .5 | .2 | | | | | | | | |
| 1.6 | 5.4 | 5.9 | | | | | | | | |
| .4 | .6 | .2 | Quick | | | | | | | |
| .1 | .3 | .1 | | | | | | | | |
| 0 UND | 0 UND | 0 UND | | | | | | | | |
| 0 738.2 | 5 70.5 | 0 UND | Sales/Receivables | | | | | | | |
| 2 202.6 | 27 13.4 | 31 11.9 | | | | | | | | |
| | | | Cost of Sales/Inventory | | | | | | | |
| | | | Cost of Sales/Payables | | | | | | | |
| 3.8 | 3.4 | 6.2 | | | | | | | | |
| 5.0 | 31.3 | -16.4 | Sales/Working Capital | | | | | | | |
| -11.7 | -18.7 | -4.0 | | | | | | | | |
| 89.4 | 34.4 | 13.9 | | | | | | | | |
| (20) 21.9 | (14) 8.7 | (17) 2.0 | EBIT/Interest | | | | | | | |
| 7.1 | 1.0 | .9 | | | | | | | | |
| | | | Net Profit + Depr., Dep., Amort./Cur. Mat. L/T/D | | | | | | | |
| .2 | .2 | .4 | | | | | | | | |
| .4 | 1.0 | 2.2 | Fixed/Worth | | | | | | | |
| 2.4 | NM | 78.9 | | | | | | | | |
| .4 | .2 | .5 | | | | | | | | |
| 1.1 | .8 | 2.9 | Debt/Worth | | | | | | | |
| 4.3 | NM | 89.5 | | | | | | | | |
| 90.2 | 56.4 | 77.5 | | | | | | | | |
| (20) 54.0 | (12) 27.9 | (16) 31.3 | % Profit Before Taxes/Tangible Net Worth | | | | | | | |
| 24.8 | 1.8 | 15.7 | | | | | | | | |
| 36.7 | 19.6 | 30.9 | | | | | | | | |
| 24.5 | 7.0 | 8.6 | % Profit Before Taxes/Total Assets | | | | | | | |
| 9.1 | -3.9 | .3 | | | | | | | | |
| 23.4 | 18.8 | 8.8 | | | | | | | | |
| 10.0 | 6.4 | 3.1 | Sales/Net Fixed Assets | | | | | | | |
| 2.5 | 2.7 | 2.3 | | | | | | | | |
| 2.5 | 2.3 | 2.7 | | | | | | | | |
| 1.9 | 1.8 | 1.8 | Sales/Total Assets | | | | | | | |
| 1.4 | 1.1 | 1.1 | | | | | | | | |
| 1.8 | | 3.3 | | | | | | | | |
| (13) 3.6 | | (11) 12.9 | % Depr., Dep., Amort./Sales | | | | | | | |
| 19.6 | | 21.9 | | | | | | | | |
| | | | % Officers', Directors' Owners' Comp/Sales | | | | | | | |
| 358334M | 451183M | 521367M | Net Sales ($) | 554M | 5779M | 3119M | 17023M | 144181M | 350711M | |
| 208892M | 379342M | 395853M | Total Assets ($) | 109M | 6483M | 2870M | 8529M | 76779M | 301083M | |

M = $ thousand    MM = $ million
See Pages viii through xx for Explanation of Ratios and Data

© RMA 2024

# REAL ESTATE—Home Health Equipment Rental  NAICS 532283

## Current Data Sorted by Assets

| | | | | | | Type of Statement | | |
|---|---|---|---|---|---|---|---|---|
| | | | | | 1 | Unqualified | | |
| | | 2 | 2 | | | Reviewed | | |
| | | 2 | | | | Compiled | | |
| 3 | 3 | 2 | 1 | | | Tax Returns | | |
| 5 | 6 | 7 | 4 | 3 | 3 | Other | | |
| | 5 (4/1-9/30/23) | | 39 (10/1/23-3/31/24) | | | | | |
| 0-500M | 500M-2MM | 2-10MM | 10-50MM | 50-100MM | 100-250MM | | | |
| 8 | 9 | 11 | 9 | 3 | 4 | NUMBER OF STATEMENTS | | |
| % | % | % | % | % | % | ASSETS | | |
| | | 11.5 | | | | Cash & Equivalents | | |
| | | 36.2 | | | | Trade Receivables (net) | | |
| | | 13.2 | | | | Inventory | | |
| | | 3.7 | | | | All Other Current | | |
| | | 64.6 | | | | Total Current | | |
| | | 30.0 | | | | Fixed Assets (net) | | |
| | | 1.4 | | | | Intangibles (net) | | |
| | | 4.0 | | | | All Other Non-Current | | |
| | | 100.0 | | | | Total | | |
| | | | | | | LIABILITIES | | |
| | | 8.3 | | | | Notes Payable-Short Term | | |
| | | 3.7 | | | | Cur. Mat.-L.T.D. | | |
| | | 17.6 | | | | Trade Payables | | |
| | | .0 | | | | Income Taxes Payable | | |
| | | 6.1 | | | | All Other Current | | |
| | | 35.8 | | | | Total Current | | |
| | | 20.7 | | | | Long-Term Debt | | |
| | | .0 | | | | Deferred Taxes | | |
| | | 1.6 | | | | All Other Non-Current | | |
| | | 42.0 | | | | Net Worth | | |
| | | 100.0 | | | | Total Liabilities & Net Worth | | |
| | | | | | | INCOME DATA | | |
| | | 100.0 | | | | Net Sales | | |
| | | | | | | Gross Profit | | |
| | | 91.4 | | | | Operating Expenses | | |
| | | 8.6 | | | | Operating Profit | | |
| | | .2 | | | | All Other Expenses (net) | | |
| | | 8.5 | | | | Profit Before Taxes | | |
| | | | | | | RATIOS | | |
| | | 3.5 | | | | | | |
| | | 1.9 | | | | Current | | |
| | | 1.5 | | | | | | |
| | | 2.8 | | | | | | |
| | | 1.3 | | | | Quick | | |
| | | 1.0 | | | | | | |
| | 20 | 18.3 | | | | | | |
| | 60 | 6.1 | | | | Sales/Receivables | | |
| | 70 | 5.2 | | | | | | |
| | | | | | | Cost of Sales/Inventory | | |
| | | | | | | Cost of Sales/Payables | | |
| | | 6.1 | | | | | | |
| | | 7.4 | | | | Sales/Working Capital | | |
| | | 25.5 | | | | | | |
| | | | | | | EBIT/Interest | | |
| | | | | | | Net Profit + Depr., Dep., Amort./Cur. Mat. L/T/D | | |
| | | .3 | | | | | | |
| | | .5 | | | | Fixed/Worth | | |
| | | 1.0 | | | | | | |
| | | .7 | | | | | | |
| | | 1.1 | | | | Debt/Worth | | |
| | | 2.3 | | | | | | |
| | | 79.6 | | | | | | |
| | (10) | 42.3 | | | | % Profit Before Taxes/Tangible Net Worth | | |
| | | 30.2 | | | | | | |
| | | 28.0 | | | | | | |
| | | 20.6 | | | | % Profit Before Taxes/Total Assets | | |
| | | 8.8 | | | | | | |
| | | 20.2 | | | | | | |
| | | 12.4 | | | | Sales/Net Fixed Assets | | |
| | | 5.4 | | | | | | |
| | | 3.2 | | | | | | |
| | | 2.4 | | | | Sales/Total Assets | | |
| | | 2.1 | | | | | | |
| | | | | | | % Depr., Dep., Amort./Sales | | |
| | | | | | | % Officers', Directors' Owners' Comp/Sales | | |
| 13947M | 20849M | 127596M | 335406M | 202364M | 555585M | Net Sales ($) | | |
| 2202M | 8322M | 43596M | 221961M | 176623M | 730864M | Total Assets ($) | | |

## Comparative Historical Data

| | Type of Statement | | |
|---|---|---|---|
| 2 | Unqualified | | |
| 1 | Reviewed | | |
| 2 | Compiled | | |
| 2 | Tax Returns | | |
| 10 | Other | 3 | |
| 4/1/19-3/31/20 ALL | | 5 4/1/20-3/31/21 ALL | |
| 17 | NUMBER OF STATEMENTS | 8 | |
| % | ASSETS | % | |
| 5.2 | Cash & Equivalents | | |
| 28.8 | Trade Receivables (net) | | |
| 6.8 | Inventory | | |
| 2.3 | All Other Current | | |
| 43.1 | Total Current | | |
| 38.7 | Fixed Assets (net) | | |
| 15.0 | Intangibles (net) | | |
| 3.2 | All Other Non-Current | | |
| 100.0 | Total | | |
| | LIABILITIES | | |
| 11.6 | Notes Payable-Short Term | | |
| 6.2 | Cur. Mat.-L.T.D. | | |
| 12.5 | Trade Payables | | |
| .0 | Income Taxes Payable | | |
| 7.5 | All Other Current | | |
| 37.9 | Total Current | | |
| 31.2 | Long-Term Debt | | |
| .4 | Deferred Taxes | | |
| 4.2 | All Other Non-Current | | |
| 26.3 | Net Worth | | |
| 100.0 | Total Liabilities & Net Worth | | |
| | INCOME DATA | | |
| 100.0 | Net Sales | | |
| | Gross Profit | | |
| 89.3 | Operating Expenses | | |
| 10.7 | Operating Profit | | |
| 1.9 | All Other Expenses (net) | | |
| 8.8 | Profit Before Taxes | | |
| | RATIOS | | |
| 2.5 | | | |
| 1.0 | Current | | |
| .6 | | | |
| 1.7 | | | |
| .8 | Quick | | |
| .4 | | | |
| 36 | 10.1 | Sales/Receivables | |
| 54 | 6.8 | | |
| 76 | 4.8 | | |
| | Cost of Sales/Inventory | | |
| | Cost of Sales/Payables | | |
| 5.8 | | | |
| 86.9 | Sales/Working Capital | | |
| -13.0 | | | |
| 28.8 | | | |
| (14) 6.1 | EBIT/Interest | | |
| 1.4 | | | |
| | Net Profit + Depr., Dep., Amort./Cur. Mat. L/T/D | | |
| .9 | | | |
| 2.6 | Fixed/Worth | | |
| -2.0 | | | |
| .7 | | | |
| 4.7 | Debt/Worth | | |
| -5.1 | | | |
| 67.1 | | | |
| (12) 30.1 | % Profit Before Taxes/Tangible Net Worth | | |
| 21.3 | | | |
| 22.7 | | | |
| 10.0 | % Profit Before Taxes/Total Assets | | |
| 3.5 | | | |
| 22.8 | | | |
| 6.3 | Sales/Net Fixed Assets | | |
| 2.6 | | | |
| 2.4 | | | |
| 1.6 | Sales/Total Assets | | |
| 1.0 | | | |
| 4.1 | | | |
| (12) 5.4 | % Depr., Dep., Amort./Sales | | |
| 9.4 | | | |
| | % Officers', Directors' Owners' Comp/Sales | | |
| 604218M | Net Sales ($) | 362241M | |
| 529463M | Total Assets ($) | 306438M | |

© RMA 2024

M = $ thousand    MM = $ million
See Pages viii through xx for Explanation of Ratios and Data

# REAL ESTATE—Home Health Equipment Rental  NAICS 532283

| Comparative Historical Data | | | | Current Data Sorted by Sales | | | | | |
|---|---|---|---|---|---|---|---|---|---|
| 1 | | 3 | Type of Statement | | 1 | | | 1 | 2 |
| | | 2 | Unqualified | | 4 | | 2 | | 2 |
| 1 | 2 | 9 | Reviewed | | 8 | 1 | 1 | 1 | 1 |
| 8 | 11 | 28 | Compiled | 1 | 5 | 1 | 2 | 1 | |
| 4/1/21- | 4/1/22- | 4/1/23- | Tax Returns | 2 | 39 (10/1/23-3/31/24) | 1 | 1 | 4 | 10 |
| 3/31/22 | 3/31/23 | 3/31/24 | Other | | | | | | |
| ALL | ALL | ALL | | 0-1MM | 1-3MM | 3-5MM | 5-10MM | 10-25MM | 25MM & OVER |
| 10 | 13 | 44 | NUMBER OF STATEMENTS | 3 | 12 | 2 | 7 | 5 | 15 |
| % | % | % | ASSETS | % | % | % | % | % | % |
| 19.1 | 14.7 | 12.9 | Cash & Equivalents | | 27.4 | | | | 3.9 |
| 18.7 | 12.5 | 24.7 | Trade Receivables (net) | | 24.2 | | | | 26.8 |
| 7.6 | 9.8 | 15.7 | Inventory | | 17.1 | | | | 13.7 |
| 4.3 | 3.9 | 4.3 | All Other Current | | 8.5 | | | | 2.4 |
| 49.7 | 41.0 | 57.5 | Total Current | | 77.2 | | | | 46.7 |
| 35.7 | 27.4 | 29.9 | Fixed Assets (net) | | 18.7 | | | | 32.0 |
| 3.8 | 12.0 | 6.4 | Intangibles (net) | | .1 | | | | 9.4 |
| 10.6 | 19.6 | 6.2 | All Other Non-Current | | 4.0 | | | | 11.9 |
| 100.0 | 100.0 | 100.0 | Total | | 100.0 | | | | 100.0 |
| | | | LIABILITIES | | | | | | |
| 8.1 | 2.7 | 6.7 | Notes Payable-Short Term | | 8.0 | | | | 5.0 |
| 3.2 | 4.5 | 4.4 | Cur. Mat.-L.T.D. | | 3.6 | | | | 5.6 |
| 14.3 | 17.9 | 13.4 | Trade Payables | | 17.1 | | | | 13.6 |
| .0 | .0 | .0 | Income Taxes Payable | | .0 | | | | .1 |
| 10.0 | 5.0 | 13.3 | All Other Current | | 23.0 | | | | 13.5 |
| 35.5 | 30.0 | 37.8 | Total Current | | 51.7 | | | | 37.8 |
| 31.3 | 42.4 | 36.2 | Long-Term Debt | | 46.3 | | | | 30.9 |
| 1.1 | .8 | .2 | Deferred Taxes | | .0 | | | | .6 |
| 7.3 | 1.1 | 13.5 | All Other Non-Current | | 16.7 | | | | 23.0 |
| 24.8 | 25.7 | 12.3 | Net Worth | | -14.7 | | | | 7.7 |
| 100.0 | 100.0 | 100.0 | Total Liabilties & Net Worth | | 100.0 | | | | 100.0 |
| | | | INCOME DATA | | | | | | |
| 100.0 | 100.0 | 100.0 | Net Sales | | 100.0 | | | | 100.0 |
| | | | Gross Profit | | 95.7 | | | | 88.4 |
| 79.1 | 80.2 | 92.2 | Operating Expenses | | 4.3 | | | | 11.6 |
| 20.9 | 19.8 | 7.8 | Operating Profit | | -.8 | | | | 8.5 |
| .7 | 3.0 | 3.5 | All Other Expenses (net) | | 5.1 | | | | 3.1 |
| 20.2 | 16.7 | 4.3 | Profit Before Taxes | | | | | | |
| | | | RATIOS | | | | | | |
| 3.4 | 8.1 | 2.2 | | | 2.8 | | | | 1.6 |
| 1.3 | 1.9 | 1.5 | Current | | 1.3 | | | | 1.2 |
| .7 | .6 | 1.1 | | | .9 | | | | .6 |
| 2.0 | 4.7 | 1.3 | | | 1.5 | | | | 1.2 |
| .9 | .8 | 1.0 | Quick | | 1.0 | | | | .8 |
| .6 | .5 | .6 | | | .4 | | | | .5 |
| 0 UND | 0 UND | 2 208.8 | | 0 UND | | | | 37 9.9 | |
| 45 8.1 | 45 8.2 | 37 9.9 | Sales/Receivables | 3 143.7 | | | | 47 7.7 | |
| 54 6.7 | 72 5.1 | 63 5.8 | | 33 11.1 | | | | 79 4.6 | |
| | | | Cost of Sales/Inventory | | | | | | |
| | | | Cost of Sales/Payables | | | | | | |
| 8.1 | 4.5 | 6.8 | | | 6.5 | | | | 8.0 |
| 56.1 | 10.7 | 18.9 | Sales/Working Capital | | 23.7 | | | | 33.6 |
| -13.6 | -11.2 | 64.3 | | | NM | | | | -14.4 |
| | 69.2 | 13.8 | | | 10.8 | | | | 13.8 |
| (10) 10.0 | (39) 6.5 | EBIT/Interest | (11) 6.5 | | | | | 4.4 | |
| | .8 | .1 | | | 4.1 | | | | -.5 |
| | | | Net Profit + Depr., Dep., Amort./Cur. Mat. L/T/D | | | | | | |
| .3 | .2 | .4 | | | .3 | | | | .6 |
| .8 | .7 | 1.0 | Fixed/Worth | | 1.6 | | | | 2.1 |
| 3.0 | 2.1 | -1.4 | | | -.1 | | | | -.9 |
| 1.2 | .7 | .9 | | | 1.4 | | | | 1.5 |
| 1.7 | 1.6 | 3.0 | Debt/Worth | | 25.7 | | | | 2.9 |
| 4.6 | NM | -3.8 | | | -2.8 | | | | -3.7 |
| | 57.3 | 80.8 | % Profit Before Taxes/Tangible Net Worth | | | | | | |
| | (10) 24.6 | (29) 39.0 | | | | | | | |
| | 2.9 | 20.8 | | | | | | | |
| 31.9 | 30.3 | 26.5 | % Profit Before Taxes/Total Assets | | 34.4 | | | | 18.4 |
| 17.4 | 10.9 | 15.1 | | | 24.4 | | | | 8.8 |
| 4.7 | -1.1 | -3.0 | | | 2.1 | | | | -13.6 |
| 84.8 | 31.2 | 58.1 | | | 376.1 | | | | 16.6 |
| 6.0 | 13.9 | 11.9 | Sales/Net Fixed Assets | | 106.6 | | | | 4.8 |
| 1.9 | 2.8 | 4.4 | | | 11.9 | | | | 2.4 |
| 5.5 | 3.3 | 3.9 | | | 6.2 | | | | 2.1 |
| 1.4 | 1.1 | 2.1 | Sales/Total Assets | | 4.1 | | | | 1.3 |
| .8 | .7 | 1.3 | | | 2.4 | | | | 1.0 |
| | | 2.8 | % Depr., Dep., Amort./Sales | | | | | | |
| | (19) 7.8 | | | | | | | | |
| | | 14.6 | | | | | | | |
| | | 2.1 | % Officers', Directors' Owners' Comp/Sales | | | | | | |
| | (12) 3.8 | | | | | | | | |
| | | 6.2 | | | | | | | |
| 346686M | 470346M | 1255747M | Net Sales ($) | 1924M | 24603M | 8269M | 54357M | 71662M | 1094932M |
| 262157M | 526290M | 1183568M | Total Assets ($) | 1583M | 6808M | 2133M | 60956M | 29245M | 1082843M |

© RMA 2024

M = $ thousand    MM = $ million
See Pages viii through xx for Explanation of Ratios and Data

# REAL ESTATE—Recreational Goods Rental  NAICS 532284

## Current Data Sorted by Assets / Comparative Historical Data

| | | | | | | Type of Statement | | |
|---|---|---|---|---|---|---|---|---|
| | | | | | | Unqualified | | 1 |
| | | 1 | 1 | | | Reviewed | | |
| 2 | 1 | 7 | 4 | | | Compiled | 4 | |
| 3 | 7 | | 13 | | | Tax Returns | 8 | 3 |
| | | 8 (4/1-9/30/23) | | | | Other | | 6 |
| | | | 25 (10/1/23-3/31/24) | | | | 4/1/19- | 4/1/20- |
| 0-500M | 500M-2MM | 2-10MM | 10-50MM | 50-100MM | 100-250MM | | 3/31/20 | 3/31/21 |
| 5 | 9 | 18 | 1 | | | NUMBER OF STATEMENTS | ALL | ALL |
| % | % | % | % | % | % | | 12 | 10 |
| | | | | | | **ASSETS** | % | % |
| | | 4.3 | | | | Cash & Equivalents | 6.9 | 21.0 |
| | | .8 | | D | D | Trade Receivables (net) | 10.8 | 2.2 |
| | | 5.8 | | A | A | Inventory | 14.4 | 4.3 |
| | | .8 | | T | T | All Other Current | 9.0 | 6.2 |
| | | 11.7 | | A | A | Total Current | 41.1 | 33.7 |
| | | 59.4 | | | | Fixed Assets (net) | 45.1 | 52.7 |
| | | 16.7 | | N | N | Intangibles (net) | .4 | 10.3 |
| | | 12.3 | | O | O | All Other Non-Current | 13.5 | 3.3 |
| | | 100.0 | | T | T | Total | 100.0 | 100.0 |
| | | | | | | **LIABILITIES** | | |
| | | 8.5 | | A | A | Notes Payable-Short Term | 27.5 | 12.8 |
| | | 3.4 | | V | V | Cur. Mat.-L.T.D. | 6.5 | .2 |
| | | 13.5 | | A | A | Trade Payables | 6.8 | 1.6 |
| | | .0 | | I | I | Income Taxes Payable | .0 | .4 |
| | | 4.6 | | L | L | All Other Current | 35.7 | 4.5 |
| | | 30.0 | | A | A | Total Current | 76.5 | 19.5 |
| | | 41.5 | | B | B | Long-Term Debt | 70.8 | 21.9 |
| | | .0 | | L | L | Deferred Taxes | .0 | .0 |
| | | 31.7 | | E | E | All Other Non-Current | 10.4 | 4.8 |
| | | -3.2 | | | | Net Worth | -57.7 | 53.8 |
| | | 100.0 | | | | Total Liabilties & Net Worth | 100.0 | 100.0 |
| | | | | | | **INCOME DATA** | | |
| | | 100.0 | | | | Net Sales | 100.0 | 100.0 |
| | | | | | | Gross Profit | | |
| | | 92.7 | | | | Operating Expenses | 85.7 | 76.7 |
| | | 7.3 | | | | Operating Profit | 14.3 | 23.3 |
| | | 6.2 | | | | All Other Expenses (net) | .6 | -1.6 |
| | | 1.1 | | | | Profit Before Taxes | 13.7 | 24.9 |
| | | | | | | **RATIOS** | | |
| | | 2.6 | | | | | 3.2 | 14.2 |
| | | .2 | | | | Current | 1.7 | 2.3 |
| | | .1 | | | | | .4 | .5 |
| | | 2.3 | | | | | 2.1 | 13.9 |
| | | .1 | | | | Quick | .3 | 1.0 |
| | | .0 | | | | | .1 | .4 |
| | | 0 UND | | | | | 0 UND | 0 UND |
| | | 0 UND | | | | Sales/Receivables | 0 UND | 0 UND |
| | | 0 UND | | | | | 15 24.3 | 2 176.4 |
| | | | | | | Cost of Sales/Inventory | | |
| | | | | | | Cost of Sales/Payables | | |
| | | 28.7 | | | | | 9.2 | 8.4 |
| | | -21.1 | | | | Sales/Working Capital | 29.9 | 16.7 |
| | | -4.8 | | | | | NM | -11.3 |
| | | 5.3 | | | | | 14.4 | |
| | (16) | 1.7 | | | | EBIT/Interest | (10) 7.9 | |
| | | -.1 | | | | | 1.9 | |
| | | | | | | Net Profit + Depr., Dep., Amort./Cur. Mat. L/T/D | | |
| | | 45.3 | | | | | .0 | .3 |
| | | -200.7 | | | | Fixed/Worth | 1.0 | 1.4 |
| | | -1.9 | | | | | NM | NM |
| | | 59.7 | | | | | .7 | .4 |
| | | -203.6 | | | | Debt/Worth | 2.7 | .9 |
| | | -6.5 | | | | | -2.1 | NM |
| | | | | | | % Profit Before Taxes/Tangible Net Worth | | |
| | | 14.3 | | | | | 65.3 | 78.0 |
| | | .9 | | | | % Profit Before Taxes/Total Assets | 16.3 | 41.5 |
| | | -3.1 | | | | | 5.9 | 6.0 |
| | | 5.1 | | | | | 785.5 | 42.8 |
| | | 2.5 | | | | Sales/Net Fixed Assets | 3.8 | 2.2 |
| | | .8 | | | | | 3.0 | 1.6 |
| | | 1.5 | | | | | 3.0 | 2.4 |
| | | 1.0 | | | | Sales/Total Assets | 2.6 | 1.4 |
| | | .5 | | | | | 1.8 | 1.2 |
| | | 2.6 | | | | | | |
| | (16) | 12.8 | | | | % Depr., Dep., Amort./Sales | | |
| | | 40.7 | | | | | | |
| | | | | | | % Officers', Directors' Owners' Comp/Sales | | |
| 3708M | 39136M | 69552M | 9656M | | | Net Sales ($) | 20559M | 20140M |
| 1436M | 13121M | 84782M | 11748M | | | Total Assets ($) | 6093M | 16138M |

M = $ thousand    MM = $ million
See Pages viii through xx for Explanation of Ratios and Data

© RMA 2024

# REAL ESTATE—Recreational Goods Rental  NAICS 532284

## Comparative Historical Data | Current Data Sorted by Sales

| | | | Type of Statement | | | | | | |
|---|---|---|---|---|---|---|---|---|---|
| | | | Unqualified | | | | | 1 | |
| 1 | 1 | 1 | Reviewed | | | | | 1 | |
| | 1 | 1 | Compiled | | 1 | | | 1 | |
| 4 | 5 | 7 | Tax Returns | | 3 | 2 | | 1 | |
| 3 | 19 | 24 | Other | 1 | 8 | 4 | | 8 | |
| 4/1/21-3/31/22 ALL | 4/1/22-3/31/23 ALL | 4/1/23-3/31/24 ALL | | 4 | 8 (4/1-9/30/23) | | | 25 (10/1/23-3/31/24) | |
| | | | | 0-1MM | 1-3MM | 3-5MM | 5-10MM | 10-25MM | 25MM & OVER |
| 8 | 26 | 33 | NUMBER OF STATEMENTS | 5 | 11 | 6 | 11 | | |
| % | % | % | ASSETS | % | % | % | % | % | % |
| | 25.9 | 16.1 | Cash & Equivalents | 8.9 | 15.4 | | | | |
| | 4.8 | 1.7 | Trade Receivables (net) | .0 | 1.5 | | | | |
| | 7.0 | 4.9 | Inventory | .1 | 9.7 | | | DATA | DATA |
| | .6 | 1.2 | All Other Current | .3 | 1.4 | | | | |
| | 38.3 | 23.8 | Total Current | 9.2 | 27.9 | | | NOT | NOT |
| | 45.1 | 48.9 | Fixed Assets (net) | 86.3 | 24.7 | | | | |
| | 10.7 | 14.0 | Intangibles (net) | .6 | 13.9 | | | AVAILABLE | AVAILABLE |
| | 5.9 | 13.3 | All Other Non-Current | 3.9 | 33.4 | | | | |
| | 100.0 | 100.0 | Total | 100.0 | 100.0 | | | | |
| | | | LIABILITIES | | | | | | |
| | 7.9 | 9.1 | Notes Payable-Short Term | 6.0 | 17.4 | | | | |
| | 2.0 | 2.3 | Cur. Mat.-L.T.D. | 1.3 | 5.5 | | | | |
| | 5.1 | 12.2 | Trade Payables | 16.2 | 4.5 | | | | |
| | .1 | .0 | Income Taxes Payable | .0 | .0 | | | | |
| | 18.0 | 4.0 | All Other Current | .6 | 4.9 | | | | |
| | 33.2 | 27.5 | Total Current | 24.1 | 32.4 | | | | |
| | 45.2 | 33.9 | Long-Term Debt | 63.9 | 22.7 | | | | |
| | .1 | .0 | Deferred Taxes | .0 | .0 | | | | |
| | 2.8 | 44.3 | All Other Non-Current | 10.3 | 3.7 | | | | |
| | 18.7 | -5.8 | Net Worth | 1.7 | 41.2 | | | | |
| | 100.0 | 100.0 | Total Liabilities & Net Worth | 100.0 | 100.0 | | | | |
| | | | INCOME DATA | | | | | | |
| | 100.0 | 100.0 | Net Sales | 100.0 | 100.0 | | | | |
| | | | Gross Profit | | | | | | |
| | 71.1 | 93.6 | Operating Expenses | 80.8 | 89.5 | | | | |
| | 28.9 | 6.4 | Operating Profit | 19.2 | 10.5 | | | | |
| | 4.3 | 3.4 | All Other Expenses (net) | 12.3 | -1.3 | | | | |
| | 24.6 | 3.0 | Profit Before Taxes | 6.9 | 11.8 | | | | |
| | | | RATIOS | | | | | | |
| | 6.9 | 3.5 | | 3.1 | 3.1 | | | | |
| | 1.6 | .9 | Current | .2 | 1.8 | | | | |
| | .7 | .2 | | .1 | .4 | | | | |
| | 4.6 | 3.0 | | 2.9 | 2.6 | | | | |
| | 1.0 | .6 | Quick | .0 | .8 | | | | |
| | .4 | .0 | | .0 | .1 | | | | |
| | 0 UND | 0 UND | | 0 UND | 0 UND | | | | |
| | 0 UND | 0 UND | Sales/Receivables | 0 UND | 0 UND | | | | |
| 8 | 45.0 | 0 UND | | 0 UND | 1 248.0 | | | | |
| | | | Cost of Sales/Inventory | | | | | | |
| | | | Cost of Sales/Payables | | | | | | |
| | 3.4 | 9.4 | | 16.8 | 6.7 | | | | |
| | 12.0 | -97.0 | Sales/Working Capital | -27.3 | 48.7 | | | | |
| | -26.3 | -4.3 | | -2.9 | -9.4 | | | | |
| | 8.6 | 6.0 | | | 21.8 | | | | |
| (17) | 2.1 | (27) 1.7 | EBIT/Interest | | (10) 5.8 | | | | |
| | -1.2 | .2 | | | 1.5 | | | | |
| | | | Net Profit + Depr., Dep., Amort./Cur. Mat. L/T/D | | | | | | |
| | .5 | .5 | | 59.9 | .3 | | | | |
| | 2.4 | 165.7 | Fixed/Worth | 411.5 | .5 | | | | |
| | 4.8 | -3.4 | | -52.3 | -6.2 | | | | |
| | 1.2 | 1.9 | | 59.8 | .6 | | | | |
| | 3.7 | 166.7 | Debt/Worth | 417.4 | 2.2 | | | | |
| | UND | -6.8 | | -54.0 | -9.6 | | | | |
| | 176.0 | 103.5 | % Profit Before Taxes/Tangible Net Worth | | | | | | |
| (20) | 24.5 | (19) 66.7 | | | | | | | |
| | 7.1 | 12.3 | | | | | | | |
| | 65.9 | 38.2 | % Profit Before Taxes/Total Assets | 12.4 | 60.5 | | | | |
| | 7.7 | 4.6 | | .9 | 38.0 | | | | |
| | -.6 | -1.1 | | .2 | 1.1 | | | | |
| | 26.5 | 29.4 | Sales/Net Fixed Assets | 1.4 | 33.9 | | | | |
| | 2.7 | 4.0 | | 1.0 | 16.3 | | | | |
| | 1.3 | 1.2 | | .3 | 5.0 | | | | |
| | 2.9 | 3.3 | Sales/Total Assets | 1.1 | 3.5 | | | | |
| | 1.1 | 1.1 | | .9 | 2.9 | | | | |
| | .7 | .9 | | .3 | .9 | | | | |
| | 1.0 | 1.6 | % Depr., Dep., Amort./Sales | 2.9 | | | | | |
| (10) | 17.5 | (25) 11.7 | | (10) 19.6 | | | | | |
| | 21.4 | 21.4 | | 53.1 | | | | | |
| | | 5.1 | % Officers', Directors' Owners' Comp/Sales | | | | | | |
| | | (13) 5.6 | | | | | | | |
| | | 6.3 | | | | | | | |
| 43473M | 151768M | 122052M | Net Sales ($) | 3266M | 23294M | 23856M | 71636M | | |
| 67913M | 146870M | 111087M | Total Assets ($) | 2069M | 47901M | 16228M | 44889M | | |

M = $ thousand  MM = $ million
See Pages viii through xx for Explanation of Ratios and Data

© RMA 2024

# REAL ESTATE—All Other Consumer Goods Rental  NAICS 532289

## Current Data Sorted by Assets | Comparative Historical Data

| 0-500M | 500M-2MM | 2-10MM | 10-50MM | 50-100MM | 100-250MM | | | 4/1/19-3/31/20 ALL | 4/1/20-3/31/21 ALL |
|---|---|---|---|---|---|---|---|---|---|
| | | | | | | **Type of Statement** | | | |
| | | 3 | 3 | | | Unqualified | | 3 | 3 |
| | | | 5 | | | Reviewed | | 4 | 2 |
| | | 3 | 1 | | | Compiled | | 7 | 7 |
| 3 | 4 | 3 | | | | Tax Returns | | 16 | 13 |
| 2 | 8 | 17 | | 2 | 3 | Other | | 37 | 25 |
| 5 | 12 (4/1-9/30/23) | 26 | 48 (10/1/23-3/31/24) | 2 | 3 | **NUMBER OF STATEMENTS** | | 67 | 50 |
| % | % | % | % | % | % | **ASSETS** | | % | % |
| | 22.3 | 20.0 | 5.2 | | | Cash & Equivalents | | 11.0 | 22.3 |
| | 7.2 | 8.0 | 5.1 | | | Trade Receivables (net) | | 10.0 | 9.9 |
| | 2.9 | 2.5 | 17.8 | | | Inventory | | 6.6 | 9.5 |
| | 1.3 | 3.6 | 3.7 | | | All Other Current | | 2.9 | 3.4 |
| | 33.7 | 34.1 | 31.8 | | | Total Current | | 30.5 | 45.1 |
| | 49.0 | 44.7 | 56.0 | | | Fixed Assets (net) | | 52.1 | 38.5 |
| | 13.1 | 9.1 | 1.7 | | | Intangibles (net) | | 10.5 | 10.3 |
| | 4.2 | 12.1 | 10.5 | | | All Other Non-Current | | 6.8 | 6.1 |
| | 100.0 | 100.0 | 100.0 | | | Total | | 100.0 | 100.0 |
| | | | | | | **LIABILITIES** | | | |
| | .2 | 3.6 | 11.5 | | | Notes Payable-Short Term | | 16.7 | 6.6 |
| | 1.9 | 4.2 | 9.4 | | | Cur. Mat.-L.T.D. | | 7.9 | 5.1 |
| | 4.4 | 4.8 | 6.8 | | | Trade Payables | | 8.7 | 4.9 |
| | .0 | .1 | .0 | | | Income Taxes Payable | | .1 | .1 |
| | 19.2 | 15.8 | 20.8 | | | All Other Current | | 17.4 | 15.9 |
| | 25.8 | 28.6 | 48.4 | | | Total Current | | 50.8 | 32.7 |
| | 29.9 | 25.3 | 21.2 | | | Long-Term Debt | | 42.1 | 39.1 |
| | .0 | .4 | 1.3 | | | Deferred Taxes | | .4 | .2 |
| | 13.4 | 4.0 | 2.5 | | | All Other Non-Current | | 5.9 | 13.4 |
| | 30.9 | 41.7 | 26.6 | | | Net Worth | | .7 | 14.6 |
| | 100.0 | 100.0 | 100.0 | | | Total Liabilities & Net Worth | | 100.0 | 100.0 |
| | | | | | | **INCOME DATA** | | | |
| | 100.0 | 100.0 | 100.0 | | | Net Sales | | 100.0 | 100.0 |
| | 77.1 | 91.8 | 91.9 | | | Gross Profit | | | |
| | 22.9 | 8.2 | 8.1 | | | Operating Expenses | | 92.7 | 95.5 |
| | 3.5 | .1 | 1.1 | | | Operating Profit | | 7.3 | 4.5 |
| | 19.4 | 8.1 | 7.0 | | | All Other Expenses (net) | | 5.0 | 3.7 |
| | | | | | | Profit Before Taxes | | 2.4 | .8 |
| | | | | | | **RATIOS** | | | |
| | 6.2 | 6.7 | 1.3 | | | | | 1.7 | 2.8 |
| | 3.4 | 1.5 | .7 | | | Current | | .7 | 1.8 |
| | 1.6 | .4 | .2 | | | | | .3 | .5 |
| | 6.1 | 6.3 | .5 | | | | | 1.3 | 2.2 |
| | 2.3 | 1.1 | .2 | | | Quick | | .4 | 1.1 |
| | .4 | .2 | .1 | | | | | .2 | .3 |
| 0 | UND | 0 | UND | 3 | 107.4 | | 0 | UND | 0 UND |
| 0 | UND | 2 | 185.0 | 18 | 20.4 | Sales/Receivables | 11 | 34.1 | 7 50.0 |
| 166 | 2.2 | 23 | 16.2 | 22 | 16.3 | | 27 | 13.5 | 31 11.9 |
| | | | | | | Cost of Sales/Inventory | | | |
| | | | | | | Cost of Sales/Payables | | | |
| | 2.9 | 4.1 | 9.0 | | | | | 12.9 | 3.7 |
| | 5.4 | 18.0 | -12.1 | | | Sales/Working Capital | | -15.6 | 11.0 |
| | 25.8 | -6.6 | -2.7 | | | | | -6.3 | -11.3 |
| | | 23.5 | 7.7 | | | | | 6.5 | 10.9 |
| | (22) | 3.9 | (11) 2.5 | | | EBIT/Interest | (59) | 2.0 | (40) 2.3 |
| | | -8.4 | 1.9 | | | | | -1.6 | -5.5 |
| | | | | | | Net Profit + Depr., Dep., Amort./Cur. Mat. L/T/D | | | |
| | .4 | .5 | .6 | | | | | 1.4 | .4 |
| | 3.1 | 1.8 | 2.6 | | | Fixed/Worth | | 6.9 | 2.3 |
| | -1.0 | 24.8 | 5.0 | | | | | -5.5 | -4.8 |
| | .3 | .4 | 1.8 | | | | | 1.8 | 1.0 |
| | 2.5 | 1.3 | 3.8 | | | Debt/Worth | | 8.3 | 2.8 |
| | -2.4 | 55.8 | 6.3 | | | | | -7.5 | -12.4 |
| | | 49.5 | 61.9 | | | | | 71.4 | 87.2 |
| | (21) | 15.9 | 26.4 | | | % Profit Before Taxes/Tangible Net Worth | (43) | 22.3 | (35) 29.6 |
| | | -4.9 | 8.1 | | | | | .0 | 1.5 |
| | 28.6 | 20.8 | 13.7 | | | | | 12.9 | 17.8 |
| | 8.5 | 9.8 | 5.8 | | | % Profit Before Taxes/Total Assets | | 3.7 | 4.6 |
| | 1.4 | -4.7 | 2.3 | | | | | -6.7 | -9.4 |
| | 4.3 | 12.1 | 6.1 | | | | | 11.8 | 13.0 |
| | 1.5 | 4.7 | 1.8 | | | Sales/Net Fixed Assets | | 3.4 | 6.0 |
| | .5 | 2.0 | .9 | | | | | 1.6 | 2.0 |
| | 1.9 | 2.2 | 1.3 | | | | | 3.1 | 2.5 |
| | .5 | 1.4 | .9 | | | Sales/Total Assets | | 1.6 | 1.5 |
| | .3 | 1.1 | .7 | | | | | 1.0 | .8 |
| | | 3.4 | 3.2 | | | | | 5.9 | 3.4 |
| | (15) | 8.3 | (10) 6.3 | | | % Depr., Dep., Amort./Sales | (40) | 13.3 | (21) 11.0 |
| | | 23.2 | 22.6 | | | | | 23.1 | 32.0 |
| | | 3.9 | | | | | | 2.2 | 1.7 |
| | (10) | 4.4 | | | | % Officers', Directors', Owners' Comp/Sales | (16) | 3.5 | (15) 4.8 |
| | | 8.0 | | | | | | 6.3 | 6.4 |
| 3586M | 18072M | 206705M | 261810M | 209063M | 424645M | Net Sales ($) | | 1665029M | 1139685M |
| 1470M | 14693M | 129381M | 244510M | 154893M | 388216M | Total Assets ($) | | 1241513M | 897236M |

© RMA 2024

M = $ thousand   MM = $ million
See Pages viii through xx for Explanation of Ratios and Data

# REAL ESTATE—All Other Consumer Goods Rental  NAICS 532289

## Comparative Historical Data | Current Data Sorted by Sales

| | | | | | Type of Statement | | | | | | |
|---|---|---|---|---|---|---|---|---|---|---|---|
| | 5 | | 3 | 6 | Unqualified | | | | 2 | 4 | |
| | 2 | | 3 | 5 | Reviewed | | | | 2 | 2 | 3 |
| | 2 | | 5 | 4 | Compiled | | | | 2 | 2 | |
| | 13 | | 10 | 10 | Tax Returns | 5 | 3 | 1 | 1 | 5 | 6 |
| | 29 | | 32 | 35 | Other | 8 | 12 (4/1-9/30/23) | 4 | 48 (10/1/23-3/31/24) | 5 | 6 |
| | 4/1/21- | | 4/1/22- | 4/1/23- | | | | | | | |
| | 3/31/22 | | 3/31/23 | 3/31/24 | | | | | | | |
| | ALL | | ALL | ALL | | 0-1MM | 1-3MM | 3-5MM | 5-10MM | 10-25MM | 25MM & OVER |
| | 51 | | 53 | 60 | NUMBER OF STATEMENTS | 13 | 6 | 5 | 14 | 13 | 9 |
| | % | | % | % | ASSETS | % | % | % | % | % | % |
| | 24.2 | | 18.8 | 15.5 | Cash & Equivalents | 7.7 | | | 10.7 | 11.9 | |
| | 8.1 | | 10.8 | 8.9 | Trade Receivables (net) | 15.4 | | | 7.2 | 6.7 | |
| | 11.3 | | 7.4 | 6.2 | Inventory | 1.7 | | | 6.4 | 11.8 | |
| | 6.3 | | 3.5 | 2.7 | All Other Current | 1.1 | | | .3 | 3.6 | |
| | 49.9 | | 40.6 | 33.3 | Total Current | 25.9 | | | 24.6 | 34.0 | |
| | 40.0 | | 41.0 | 49.8 | Fixed Assets (net) | 59.2 | | | 55.6 | 52.0 | |
| | 6.2 | | 6.3 | 7.4 | Intangibles (net) | 12.3 | | | 10.0 | 1.4 | |
| | 3.9 | | 12.0 | 9.5 | All Other Non-Current | 2.6 | | | 9.8 | 12.5 | |
| | 100.0 | | 100.0 | 100.0 | Total | 100.0 | | | 100.0 | 100.0 | |
| | | | | | LIABILITIES | | | | | | |
| | 9.8 | | 3.4 | 4.5 | Notes Payable-Short Term | .4 | | | 8.5 | 8.0 | |
| | 4.8 | | 3.6 | 5.2 | Cur. Mat.-L.T.D. | 4.2 | | | 6.1 | 3.7 | |
| | 6.5 | | 4.3 | 5.5 | Trade Payables | 1.3 | | | 7.4 | 6.8 | |
| | .1 | | .0 | .1 | Income Taxes Payable | .0 | | | .2 | .0 | |
| | 11.7 | | 12.8 | 21.7 | All Other Current | 26.4 | | | 33.6 | 20.6 | |
| | 32.9 | | 24.0 | 36.8 | Total Current | 32.3 | | | 55.9 | 39.0 | |
| | 41.9 | | 34.2 | 30.1 | Long-Term Debt | 43.1 | | | 20.5 | 17.7 | |
| | .2 | | .1 | .4 | Deferred Taxes | .0 | | | .7 | .9 | |
| | 4.7 | | 4.9 | 5.9 | All Other Non-Current | 12.4 | | | 6.5 | 1.1 | |
| | 20.3 | | 36.8 | 26.8 | Net Worth | 12.2 | | | 16.4 | 41.3 | |
| | 100.0 | | 100.0 | 100.0 | Total Liabilities & Net Worth | 100.0 | | | 100.0 | 100.0 | |
| | | | | | INCOME DATA | | | | | | |
| | 100.0 | | 100.0 | 100.0 | Net Sales | 100.0 | | | 100.0 | 100.0 | |
| | 90.1 | | 84.0 | 89.0 | Gross Profit | 78.8 | | | 95.6 | 92.0 | |
| | 9.9 | | 16.0 | 11.0 | Operating Expenses | 21.2 | | | 4.4 | 8.0 | |
| | .9 | | 2.2 | 1.5 | Operating Profit | 5.0 | | | -.2 | 1.4 | |
| | 9.0 | | 13.8 | 9.6 | All Other Expenses (net) | 16.1 | | | 4.5 | 6.6 | |
| | | | | | Profit Before Taxes | | | | | | |
| | | | | | RATIOS | | | | | | |
| | 3.0 | | 4.1 | 2.9 | | 4.0 | | | 1.4 | 1.7 | |
| | 1.7 | | 2.3 | 1.3 | Current | 2.1 | | | .4 | .8 | |
| | 1.0 | | .9 | .5 | | 1.0 | | | .1 | .2 | |
| | 2.7 | | 4.0 | 2.1 | | 3.9 | | | 1.0 | .9 | |
| | 1.3 | | 1.2 | .6 | Quick | 1.4 | | | .2 | .3 | |
| | .4 | | .4 | .2 | | .4 | | | .1 | .1 | |
| 0 | UND | 0 | UND | 0 UND | | 0 UND | | | 0 UND | 2 241.2 | |
| 8 | 48.0 | 12 | 30.2 | 8 43.2 | Sales/Receivables | 15 24.0 | | | 3 143.4 | 5 72.7 | |
| 26 | 14.3 | 27 | 13.7 | 23 15.8 | | 203 1.8 | | | 25 14.7 | 18 20.1 | |
| | | | | | Cost of Sales/Inventory | | | | | | |
| | | | | | Cost of Sales/Payables | | | | | | |
| | 5.0 | | 3.9 | 4.9 | | 2.5 | | | 15.0 | 6.6 | |
| | 9.4 | | 6.7 | 25.4 | Sales/Working Capital | 7.4 | | | -6.5 | -58.7 | |
| | 92.8 | | -91.9 | -6.5 | | NM | | | -2.4 | -4.8 | |
| | 71.4 | | 42.8 | 12.8 | | 24.1 | | | 6.7 | 17.0 | |
| (44) | 9.4 | (41) | 7.1 | (49) 3.2 | EBIT/Interest | (10) 3.3 | | | (13) 4.6 | (12) 2.2 | |
| | 2.1 | | 1.7 | .9 | | 1.4 | | | -2.3 | -6.0 | |
| | | | | 35.2 | Net Profit + Depr., Dep., | | | | | | |
| | | (11) | 8.7 | Amort./Cur. Mat. L/T/D | | | | | | |
| | | | | 1.3 | | | | | | | |
| | .4 | | .3 | .8 | | 1.4 | | | 1.1 | .6 | |
| | 1.6 | | 1.9 | 2.2 | Fixed/Worth | 3.3 | | | 2.6 | 1.3 | |
| | -2.1 | | 7.7 | 24.1 | | -.7 | | | -1.1 | 5.5 | |
| | .8 | | .6 | .8 | | 1.2 | | | 1.4 | .5 | |
| | 3.5 | | 1.7 | 2.5 | Debt/Worth | 3.1 | | | 2.0 | 1.0 | |
| | -4.3 | | 10.7 | 38.6 | | -2.2 | | | -2.4 | 6.3 | |
| | 114.4 | | 73.7 | 58.3 | % Profit Before Taxes/Tangible | | | | 51.1 | 52.0 | |
| (35) | 49.6 | (45) | 43.2 | (47) 25.0 | Net Worth | | | | (10) 31.3 | (12) 19.5 | |
| | 26.2 | | 17.3 | 5.5 | | | | | -3.2 | -5.3 | |
| | 35.4 | | 29.8 | 16.2 | % Profit Before Taxes/Total | 12.9 | | | 23.3 | 17.5 | |
| | 14.4 | | 12.7 | 7.6 | Assets | 6.9 | | | 9.8 | 8.0 | |
| | 2.0 | | 1.8 | .3 | | -3.0 | | | -7.9 | -3.3 | |
| | 18.6 | | 14.7 | 6.6 | | 4.0 | | | 5.3 | 6.2 | |
| | 6.4 | | 5.4 | 3.1 | Sales/Net Fixed Assets | .8 | | | 3.4 | 5.3 | |
| | 1.9 | | 1.2 | 1.0 | | .4 | | | 1.9 | 1.0 | |
| | 2.3 | | 2.2 | 1.9 | | 1.0 | | | 2.6 | 2.3 | |
| | 1.5 | | 1.4 | 1.2 | Sales/Total Assets | .4 | | | 1.3 | 1.4 | |
| | .9 | | .7 | .7 | | .3 | | | .9 | .9 | |
| | 1.8 | | 1.5 | 3.1 | | | | | | 1.9 | |
| (25) | 7.3 | (32) | 5.1 | (37) 6.9 | % Depr., Dep., Amort./Sales | | | | (10) 4.3 | | |
| | 14.3 | | 10.4 | 22.0 | | | | | | 10.6 | |
| | 2.4 | | 2.3 | 2.8 | | | | | | | |
| (23) | 4.2 | (18) | 5.7 | (18) 4.2 | % Officers', Directors' | | | | | | |
| | 6.5 | | 9.2 | 6.5 | Owners' Comp/Sales | | | | | | |
| | 863150M | | 651793M | 1123881M | Net Sales ($) | 6239M | 11913M | 21374M | 106613M | 191661M | 786081M |
| | 778071M | | 546690M | 933163M | Total Assets ($) | 14219M | 9907M | 14782M | 80085M | 165543M | 648627M |

© RMA 2024  
M = $ thousand    MM = $ million  
See Pages viii through xx for Explanation of Ratios and Data

# REAL ESTATE—General Rental Centers  NAICS 532310

## Current Data Sorted by Assets | Comparative Historical Data

| 0-500M | 500M-2MM | 2-10MM | 10-50MM | 50-100MM | 100-250MM | Type of Statement | 4/1/19-3/31/20 ALL | 4/1/20-3/31/21 ALL |
|---|---|---|---|---|---|---|---|---|
| 1 | 4 | 2 | 3 | 1 | 1 | Unqualified | 2 | 1 |
| 3 | 6 | 7 | 3 | 2 | 1 | Reviewed | 5 | 6 |
|  | 14 (4/1-9/30/23) | 15 | 1 |  |  | Compiled | 8 | 10 |
|  |  |  | 16 | 1 | 2 | Tax Returns | 29 | 11 |
|  |  |  | 55 (10/1/23-3/31/24) |  |  | Other | 37 | 27 |
| 4 | 10 | 24 | 23 | 4 | 4 | **NUMBER OF STATEMENTS** | 81 | 55 |
| % | % | % | % | % | % | **ASSETS** | % | % |
|  | 9.2 | 4.9 | 5.4 |  |  | Cash & Equivalents | 12.2 | 19.8 |
|  | 1.2 | 10.2 | 8.5 |  |  | Trade Receivables (net) | 7.6 | 7.8 |
|  | 4.3 | 8.8 | 6.0 |  |  | Inventory | 10.9 | 11.3 |
|  | .9 | 1.0 | .8 |  |  | All Other Current | 3.7 | 2.0 |
|  | 15.7 | 25.0 | 20.6 |  |  | Total Current | 34.4 | 40.9 |
|  | 53.1 | 64.4 | 72.0 |  |  | Fixed Assets (net) | 51.4 | 47.9 |
|  | 23.1 | 8.6 | 1.4 |  |  | Intangibles (net) | 6.4 | 5.4 |
|  | 8.1 | 1.9 | 6.0 |  |  | All Other Non-Current | 7.8 | 5.9 |
|  | 100.0 | 100.0 | 100.0 |  |  | Total | 100.0 | 100.0 |
|  |  |  |  |  |  | **LIABILITIES** |  |  |
|  | 6.7 | 4.2 | 13.8 |  |  | Notes Payable-Short Term | 10.3 | 13.0 |
|  | 5.5 | 4.0 | 7.2 |  |  | Cur. Mat.-L.T.D. | 6.0 | 6.4 |
|  | 2.0 | 3.9 | 3.3 |  |  | Trade Payables | 3.5 | 4.8 |
|  | .0 | .0 | .0 |  |  | Income Taxes Payable | .0 | .6 |
|  | 2.3 | 7.3 | 6.0 |  |  | All Other Current | 11.8 | 10.0 |
|  | 16.6 | 19.4 | 30.4 |  |  | Total Current | 31.8 | 34.8 |
|  | 67.3 | 43.6 | 37.9 |  |  | Long-Term Debt | 34.6 | 31.6 |
|  | .0 | .0 | .0 |  |  | Deferred Taxes | .2 | .4 |
|  | 1.5 | 1.6 | .7 |  |  | All Other Non-Current | 9.1 | 7.9 |
|  | 14.7 | 35.4 | 31.0 |  |  | Net Worth | 24.3 | 25.4 |
|  | 100.0 | 100.0 | 100.0 |  |  | Total Liabilities & Net Worth | 100.0 | 100.0 |
|  |  |  |  |  |  | **INCOME DATA** |  |  |
|  | 100.0 | 100.0 | 100.0 |  |  | Net Sales | 100.0 | 100.0 |
|  |  |  |  |  |  | Gross Profit |  |  |
|  | 63.2 | 69.5 | 83.8 |  |  | Operating Expenses | 84.6 | 84.8 |
|  | 36.8 | 30.5 | 16.2 |  |  | Operating Profit | 15.4 | 15.2 |
|  | 14.5 | 8.9 | 4.2 |  |  | All Other Expenses (net) | 4.0 | 3.3 |
|  | 22.3 | 21.5 | 12.0 |  |  | Profit Before Taxes | 11.4 | 12.0 |
|  |  |  |  |  |  | **RATIOS** |  |  |
|  | 1.2 | 10.1 | 1.7 |  |  |  | 2.4 | 3.8 |
|  | .4 | 1.6 | .7 |  |  | Current | 1.2 | 1.5 |
|  | .1 | .7 | .3 |  |  |  | .5 | .6 |
|  | 1.1 | 1.8 | 1.4 |  |  |  | 1.5 | 3.4 |
|  | .4 | 1.0 | .5 |  |  | Quick | .7 | .8 |
|  | .1 | .5 | .2 |  |  |  | .2 | .2 |
| 0 | UND | 0 | UND | 13 | 27.2 |  | 0 | UND | 0 | UND |
| 0 | UND | 0 | UND | 31 | 11.8 |  | Sales/Receivables | 13 | 27.1 | 5 | 79.3 |
| 5 | 73.8 | 38 | 9.6 | 68 | 5.4 |  | 26 | 14.0 | 36 | 10.2 |
|  |  |  |  |  |  | Cost of Sales/Inventory |  |  |
|  |  |  |  |  |  | Cost of Sales/Payables |  |  |
|  | NM | 6.3 | 6.8 |  |  |  | 7.9 | 3.4 |
|  | -10.3 | 14.5 | -14.2 |  |  | Sales/Working Capital | 31.9 | 10.5 |
|  | -2.2 | -15.2 | -3.9 |  |  |  | -9.0 | -9.0 |
|  |  | 22.2 | 8.7 |  |  |  | 10.1 | 14.4 |
|  | (17) | 10.2 | (22) 2.5 |  |  | EBIT/Interest | (69) 4.5 | (44) 4.6 |
|  |  | 1.6 | .8 |  |  |  | 1.4 | 2.4 |
|  |  |  |  |  |  | Net Profit + Depr., Dep., Amort./Cur. Mat. L/T/D |  |  |
|  | .9 | .9 | 1.2 |  |  |  | .9 | .6 |
|  | 4.5 | 3.1 | 2.5 |  |  | Fixed/Worth | 2.0 | 1.9 |
|  | -2.6 | NM | 6.3 |  |  |  | 4.6 | 31.2 |
|  | 2.7 | .4 | 1.0 |  |  |  | 1.0 | .8 |
|  | 4.1 | 2.6 | 2.8 |  |  | Debt/Worth | 2.5 | 2.6 |
|  | -4.0 | NM | 5.5 |  |  |  | 9.8 | 42.1 |
|  |  | 61.0 | 52.3 |  |  |  | 46.7 | 84.8 |
|  | (18) | 34.0 | (22) 20.8 |  |  | % Profit Before Taxes/Tangible Net Worth | (67) 17.1 | (43) 39.2 |
|  |  | 16.5 | -1.7 |  |  |  | 4.9 | 12.7 |
|  | 17.9 | 21.3 | 15.1 |  |  |  | 13.1 | 23.1 |
|  | 6.6 | 10.1 | 7.2 |  |  | % Profit Before Taxes/Total Assets | 6.7 | 9.6 |
|  | .1 | 2.2 | -.2 |  |  |  | 2.1 | 2.7 |
|  | 49.3 | 12.5 | 1.6 |  |  |  | 17.0 | 22.6 |
|  | 2.0 | 1.0 | .8 |  |  | Sales/Net Fixed Assets | 3.4 | 3.1 |
|  | .1 | .2 | .6 |  |  |  | 1.0 | 1.1 |
|  | 1.6 | 1.8 | .9 |  |  |  | 2.2 | 2.1 |
|  | .7 | .9 | .7 |  |  | Sales/Total Assets | 1.4 | 1.1 |
|  | .1 | .2 | .5 |  |  |  | .8 | .6 |
|  |  | 11.6 | 13.8 |  |  |  | 8.5 | 9.6 |
|  | (11) | 28.4 | (19) 19.2 |  |  | % Depr., Dep., Amort./Sales | (48) 14.1 | (30) 16.0 |
|  |  | 30.7 | 26.9 |  |  |  | 19.2 | 28.4 |
|  |  |  |  |  |  | % Officers', Directors' Owners' Comp/Sales | 2.8 | 3.3 |
|  |  |  |  |  |  |  | (33) 4.0 | (15) 5.1 |
|  |  |  |  |  |  |  | 8.1 | 6.0 |
| 2821M | 9473M | 115265M | 385019M | 368566M | 583153M | Net Sales ($) | 1024973M | 633333M |
| 789M | 12444M | 115238M | 575655M | 295979M | 751153M | Total Assets ($) | 1210776M | 832205M |

M = $ thousand    MM = $ million
See Pages viii through xx for Explanation of Ratios and Data

© RMA 2024

# REAL ESTATE—General Rental Centers  NAICS 532310

| Comparative Historical Data ||| | Current Data Sorted by Sales ||||||
|---|---|---|---|---|---|---|---|---|---|
| | | | Type of Statement | | | | | | |
| 3 | 2 | 5 | Unqualified | | | | | 3 | 2 |
| 4 | 7 | 6 | Reviewed | | | | | 1 | 5 |
| 15 | 15 | 2 | Compiled | | | | | 1 | |
| 56 | 44 | 13 | Tax Returns | 4 | 5 | 1 | 2 | 1 | 1 |
| | | 43 | Other | 11 | 6 | 1 | 7 | 13 | 3 |
| 4/1/21-3/31/22 | 4/1/22-3/31/23 | 4/1/23-3/31/24 | | 14 (4/1-9/30/23) ||| 55 (10/1/23-3/31/24) |||
| ALL | ALL | ALL | | 0-1MM | 1-3MM | 3-5MM | 5-10MM | 10-25MM | 25MM & OVER |
| 78 | 68 | 69 | NUMBER OF STATEMENTS | 15 | 11 | 5 | 9 | 19 | 10 |
| % | % | % | ASSETS | % | % | % | % | % | % |
| 15.0 | 15.4 | 8.1 | Cash & Equivalents | 11.3 | 11.3 | | | 4.2 | 8.0 |
| 6.1 | 7.0 | 7.9 | Trade Receivables (net) | 2.2 | 3.6 | | | 18.3 | 6.8 |
| 11.7 | 11.3 | 9.3 | Inventory | .6 | 8.5 | | | 10.6 | 19.2 |
| 1.6 | 1.8 | 1.5 | All Other Current | .3 | .6 | | | 1.5 | 5.1 |
| 34.4 | 35.4 | 26.8 | Total Current | 14.4 | 24.0 | | | 34.6 | 39.2 |
| 51.2 | 57.7 | 60.1 | Fixed Assets (net) | 77.1 | 53.1 | | | 58.2 | 44.6 |
| 6.0 | 3.0 | 7.0 | Intangibles (net) | 6.6 | 14.5 | | | 2.1 | 1.5 |
| 8.4 | 3.9 | 6.1 | All Other Non-Current | 1.9 | 8.4 | | | 5.1 | 14.6 |
| 100.0 | 100.0 | 100.0 | Total | 100.0 | 100.0 | | | 100.0 | 100.0 |
| | | | LIABILITIES | | | | | | |
| 5.9 | 6.6 | 8.7 | Notes Payable-Short Term | 6.5 | 4.9 | | | 19.5 | 5.0 |
| 6.6 | 6.6 | 5.5 | Cur. Mat.-L.T.D. | 5.7 | 3.7 | | | 8.5 | 4.3 |
| 4.9 | 3.2 | 3.7 | Trade Payables | .0 | 3.6 | | | 6.9 | 5.6 |
| .4 | .2 | .0 | Income Taxes Payable | .0 | .0 | | | .0 | .0 |
| 4.2 | 6.9 | 6.4 | All Other Current | 12.0 | 3.1 | | | 6.8 | 6.4 |
| 21.9 | 23.5 | 24.4 | Total Current | 24.1 | 15.4 | | | 41.8 | 21.2 |
| 45.0 | 34.5 | 44.2 | Long-Term Debt | 72.9 | 57.5 | | | 26.4 | 29.8 |
| .2 | .4 | .0 | Deferred Taxes | .0 | .0 | | | .0 | .0 |
| 7.4 | 4.9 | 1.8 | All Other Non-Current | .0 | 4.6 | | | .8 | 5.2 |
| 25.4 | 36.8 | 29.7 | Net Worth | 2.9 | 22.5 | | | 31.1 | 43.8 |
| 100.0 | 100.0 | 100.0 | Total Liabilties & Net Worth | 100.0 | 100.0 | | | 100.0 | 100.0 |
| | | | INCOME DATA | | | | | | |
| 100.0 | 100.0 | 100.0 | Net Sales | 100.0 | 100.0 | | | 100.0 | 100.0 |
| 82.1 | 76.9 | 77.4 | Gross Profit | | | | | 90.7 | 84.3 |
| 17.9 | 23.1 | 22.6 | Operating Expenses | 50.0 | 75.0 | | | 9.3 | 15.7 |
| 2.1 | 5.5 | 6.8 | Operating Profit | 50.0 | 25.0 | | | 2.8 | 2.0 |
| 15.8 | 17.6 | 15.8 | All Other Expenses (net) | 20.8 | 5.9 | | | 6.5 | 13.8 |
| | | | Profit Before Taxes | 29.2 | 19.1 | | | | |
| | | | RATIOS | | | | | | |
| 3.4 | 3.8 | 2.4 | | 1.6 | 11.3 | | | 1.6 | 2.9 |
| 1.5 | 1.3 | 1.2 | Current | .5 | 1.3 | | | .7 | 1.6 |
| .6 | .4 | .5 | | .1 | .5 | | | .3 | 1.1 |
| 2.1 | 3.3 | 1.7 | | 1.6 | 4.0 | | | 1.4 | 1.5 |
| .6 (67) | .7 | .7 | Quick | .5 | 1.0 | | | .5 | .9 |
| .3 | .2 | .3 | | .1 | .5 | | | .2 | .4 |
| 0 UND | 0 UND | 0 UND | | 0 UND | 0 UND | | | 20 17.9 | 0 UND |
| 9 39.0 | 12 31.7 | 12 29.4 | Sales/Receivables | 0 UND | 0 UND | | | 33 11.0 | 31 11.7 |
| 41 8.8 | 34 10.6 | 42 8.7 | | 0 UND | 8 43.8 | | | 78 4.7 | 42 8.6 |
| | | | Cost of Sales/Inventory | | | | | | |
| | | | Cost of Sales/Payables | | | | | | |
| 4.8 | 4.0 | 6.2 | | 12.7 | 6.2 | | | 5.8 | 2.7 |
| 16.8 | 18.6 | 52.4 | Sales/Working Capital | -4.1 | 17.9 | | | -14.2 | 9.6 |
| -7.7 | -4.7 | -5.2 | | -.9 | -21.2 | | | -3.5 | 38.9 |
| 24.9 | 36.5 | 13.9 | | | | | | 10.5 | 43.9 |
| (68) 7.9 | (55) 6.4 | (57) 3.8 | EBIT/Interest | | | | | (18) 2.5 | 13.0 |
| 3.1 | 2.8 | 1.0 | | | | | | .7 | 4.2 |
| | | | Net Profit + Depr., Dep., Amort./Cur. Mat. L/T/D | | | | | | |
| .5 | .6 | .9 | | 2.0 | 1.1 | | | .8 | .2 |
| 1.6 | 1.9 | 2.5 | Fixed/Worth | 4.4 | 7.5 | | | 2.5 | 1.0 |
| 20.0 | 4.3 | 7.5 | | 7.6 | -2.3 | | | 15.9 | 3.6 |
| .7 | .7 | 1.0 | | 2.5 | 1.0 | | | 1.0 | .4 |
| 1.8 | 1.9 | 2.8 | Debt/Worth | 3.6 | 8.1 | | | 2.8 | 1.4 |
| 23.3 | 5.2 | 11.8 | | -6.8 | -4.8 | | | 15.6 | 6.4 |
| 58.7 | 49.6 | 41.2 | | 37.6 | | | | 52.5 | |
| (62) 38.1 | (62) 29.5 | (57) 23.6 | % Profit Before Taxes/Tangible Net Worth | (11) 20.1 | | | | (18) 29.3 | |
| 22.6 | 14.6 | .8 | | -15.4 | | | | -5.9 | |
| 26.2 | 21.0 | 16.5 | | 11.5 | 12.3 | | | 21.4 | 15.3 |
| 13.5 | 8.4 | 7.2 | % Profit Before Taxes/Total Assets | 3.6 | 6.0 | | | 7.2 | 9.2 |
| 4.8 | 3.4 | .4 | | .5 | -5.4 | | | -1.3 | 3.1 |
| 12.7 | 11.7 | 8.4 | | 1.7 | 23.3 | | | 8.9 | 18.0 |
| 2.8 | 1.6 | 1.3 | Sales/Net Fixed Assets | .1 | 1.6 | | | 1.3 | 2.4 |
| 1.1 | .6 | .5 | | .1 | .3 | | | .7 | 1.0 |
| 2.2 | 1.6 | 1.4 | | .6 | 2.2 | | | 1.4 | 1.4 |
| 1.1 | 1.0 | .8 | Sales/Total Assets | .1 | .9 | | | .8 | 1.0 |
| .6 | .5 | .3 | | .1 | .3 | | | .6 | .8 |
| 8.0 | 9.1 | 11.5 | | | | | | 14.1 | |
| (43) 16.7 | (37) 17.9 | (34) 19.9 | % Depr., Dep., Amort./Sales | | | | | (13) 20.6 | |
| 28.8 | 24.9 | 29.0 | | | | | | 39.1 | |
| 2.4 | 2.2 | 1.5 | | | | | | | |
| (32) 3.9 | (26) 3.7 | (16) 4.1 | % Officers', Directors' Owners' Comp/Sales | | | | | | |
| 6.0 | 6.3 | 10.2 | | | | | | | |
| 1237394M | 1175385M | 1464297M | Net Sales ($) | 5959M | 19803M | 22446M | 70417M | 328782M | 1016890M |
| 1490870M | 1238263M | 1751258M | Total Assets ($) | 32045M | 49766M | 25493M | 110090M | 416799M | 1117065M |

© RMA 2024

M = $ thousand    MM = $ million
See Pages viii through xx for Explanation of Ratios and Data

# REAL ESTATE—Commercial Air, Rail, and Water Transportation Equipment Rental and Leasing  NAICS 532411

## Current Data Sorted by Assets | Comparative Historical Data

| | | | | | | Type of Statement | | |
|---|---|---|---|---|---|---|---|---|
| | | 1 | 4 | 3 | 7 | Unqualified | 7 | 3 |
| | 1 | 2 | 7 | 2 | | Reviewed | 5 | 3 |
| | 3 | 5 | 3 | | | Compiled | 5 | 5 |
| 1 | 6 | 12 | 2 | | | Tax Returns | 18 | 7 |
| 2 | 8 (4/1-9/30/23) | | 12 | 2 | 2 | Other | 53 | 49 |
| 0-500M | 500M-2MM | 2-10MM | 10-50MM (10/1/23-3/31/24) | 50-100MM | 100-250MM | | 4/1/19-3/31/20 ALL | 4/1/20-3/31/21 ALL |
| 3 | 10 | 20 | 69 28 | 7 | 9 | NUMBER OF STATEMENTS | 88 | 67 |
| % | % | % | % | % | % | ASSETS | % | % |
| | 7.3 | 11.6 | 8.6 | | | Cash & Equivalents | 8.4 | 11.7 |
| | 1.1 | 5.8 | 7.9 | | | Trade Receivables (net) | 7.0 | 7.7 |
| | .1 | 5.6 | 11.4 | | | Inventory | 2.8 | 3.3 |
| | 1.6 | 2.4 | 1.6 | | | All Other Current | 2.3 | 2.9 |
| | 10.1 | 25.5 | 29.5 | | | Total Current | 20.5 | 25.7 |
| | 63.4 | 61.9 | 64.2 | | | Fixed Assets (net) | 71.7 | 65.2 |
| | 12.9 | .6 | .7 | | | Intangibles (net) | 3.4 | 2.3 |
| | 13.5 | 12.0 | 5.6 | | | All Other Non-Current | 4.4 | 6.7 |
| | 100.0 | 100.0 | 100.0 | | | Total | 100.0 | 100.0 |
| | | | | | | LIABILITIES | | |
| | 3.5 | 6.5 | 4.7 | | | Notes Payable-Short Term | 5.1 | 6.9 |
| | 8.0 | 10.8 | 7.8 | | | Cur. Mat.-L.T.D. | 7.2 | 7.1 |
| | .9 | 2.1 | 3.9 | | | Trade Payables | 1.9 | 7.0 |
| | .1 | .0 | .0 | | | Income Taxes Payable | .2 | .0 |
| | .8 | 7.9 | 6.5 | | | All Other Current | 5.4 | 3.6 |
| | 13.3 | 27.4 | 22.9 | | | Total Current | 19.7 | 24.6 |
| | 83.4 | 62.7 | 41.4 | | | Long-Term Debt | 49.9 | 56.1 |
| | .0 | .0 | .0 | | | Deferred Taxes | 1.2 | .8 |
| | 13.9 | 3.8 | 1.5 | | | All Other Non-Current | 1.7 | 8.0 |
| | -10.6 | 6.1 | 34.2 | | | Net Worth | 27.6 | 10.6 |
| | 100.0 | 100.0 | 100.0 | | | Total Liabilties & Net Worth | 100.0 | 100.0 |
| | | | | | | INCOME DATA | | |
| | 100.0 | 100.0 | 100.0 | | | Net Sales | 100.0 | 100.0 |
| | | | | | | Gross Profit | | |
| | 67.5 | 71.1 | 71.2 | | | Operating Expenses | 76.6 | 76.3 |
| | 32.5 | 28.9 | 28.8 | | | Operating Profit | 23.4 | 23.7 |
| | 10.9 | 9.3 | 10.8 | | | All Other Expenses (net) | 9.4 | 10.1 |
| | 21.6 | 19.7 | 18.0 | | | Profit Before Taxes | 14.0 | 13.6 |
| | | | | | | RATIOS | | |
| | 4.2 | 3.6 | 2.5 | | | | 2.7 | 3.2 |
| | .5 | 1.1 | .8 | | | Current | 1.6 | 1.5 |
| | .2 | .4 | .3 | | | | .6 | .5 |
| | 2.1 | 2.8 | 1.4 | | | | 2.1 | 2.7 |
| | .5 | .8 | .7 | | | Quick | 1.1 | 1.0 |
| | .2 | .2 | .3 | | | | .4 | .4 |
| 0 | 0 UND | 0 UND | 0 UND | | | | 0 UND | 0 UND |
| | 0 UND | 0 UND | 21 17.2 | | | Sales/Receivables | 22 16.9 | 20 17.9 |
| | 24 15.0 | 23 15.7 | 40 9.1 | | | | 49 7.4 | 53 6.9 |
| | | | | | | Cost of Sales/Inventory | | |
| | | | | | | Cost of Sales/Payables | | |
| | 2.3 | 2.7 | 3.7 | | | | 4.2 | 3.5 |
| | -43.9 | 142.4 | -8.0 | | | Sales/Working Capital | 12.8 | 16.8 |
| | -1.8 | -3.8 | -1.9 | | | | -6.8 | -5.9 |
| | | 5.0 | 11.2 | | | | 8.9 | 7.2 |
| | (19) | 2.8 (15) | 5.4 | | | EBIT/Interest | (69) 3.4 | (49) 3.5 |
| | | .6 | 2.5 | | | | 2.2 | .8 |
| | | | | | | Net Profit + Depr., Dep., Amort./Cur. Mat. L/T/D | | |
| | 1.2 | 1.3 | .4 | | | | 1.1 | 1.1 |
| | -44.1 | 3.4 | 2.4 | | | Fixed/Worth | 2.2 | 2.6 |
| | -1.2 | 752.7 | 3.9 | | | | 5.9 | -43.4 |
| | .8 | 1.8 | .7 | | | | .8 | 1.1 |
| | -46.0 | 6.0 | 2.1 | | | Debt/Worth | 1.8 | 3.1 |
| | -2.4 | NM | 3.4 | | | | 6.8 | -35.9 |
| | | 42.3 | 25.8 | | | | 25.9 | 34.7 |
| | (15) | 18.8 (24) | 16.8 | | | % Profit Before Taxes/Tangible Net Worth | (72) 11.8 | (48) 11.7 |
| | | 8.2 | 8.8 | | | | 5.0 | .3 |
| | 17.7 | 13.2 | 12.2 | | | | 11.0 | 12.4 |
| | 3.4 | 6.4 | 5.6 | | | % Profit Before Taxes/Total Assets | 4.8 | 2.3 |
| | -1.2 | -1.3 | 3.0 | | | | 1.0 | -1.2 |
| | 4.7 | 6.0 | 20.9 | | | | 1.4 | 1.8 |
| | .4 | .5 | .2 | | | Sales/Net Fixed Assets | .6 | .7 |
| | .2 | .2 | .2 | | | | .2 | .2 |
| | .9 | 1.1 | 1.7 | | | | .8 | .9 |
| | .3 | .4 | .2 | | | Sales/Total Assets | .3 | .4 |
| | .2 | .2 | .1 | | | | .2 | .2 |
| | | 8.9 | 12.5 | | | | 13.3 | 10.2 |
| | (13) | 22.2 (23) | 27.9 | | | % Depr., Dep., Amort./Sales | (60) 29.4 | (49) 22.2 |
| | | 55.7 | 44.3 | | | | 48.4 | 33.1 |
| | | | | | | % Officers', Directors' Owners' Comp/Sales | .4 | |
| | | | | | | | (13) 1.8 | |
| | | | | | | | 3.3 | |
| 1378M | 6498M | 65149M | 501682M | 248175M | 708724M | Net Sales ($) | 1612501M | 513089M |
| 823M | 12404M | 85381M | 765370M | 474768M | 1513267M | Total Assets ($) | 4129619M | 1988658M |

M = $ thousand   MM = $ million
See Pages viii through xx for Explanation of Ratios and Data

© RMA 2024

## REAL ESTATE—Commercial Air, Rail, and Water Transportation Equipment Rental and Leasing  NAICS 532411

**Comparative Historical Data** | **Current Data Sorted by Sales**

| Comparative Historical Data | | | | | Current Data Sorted by Sales | | | | | |
|---|---|---|---|---|---|---|---|---|---|---|
| 2 | 7 | 15 | Type of Statement | | | 3 | 2 | 10 | | |
| 7 | 10 | 11 | Unqualified | | 1 | 3 | 4 | 4 | | |
| 9 | 7 | 4 | Reviewed | | 1 | 1 | | 2 | | |
| 12 | 7 | 11 | Compiled | 1 | | 1 | 1 | | | |
| 44 | 38 | 36 | Tax Returns | 5 | 4 | 1 | 5 | 4 | 4 | |
| | | | Other | 11 | 10 | 2 | | | | |
| 4/1/21- | 4/1/22- | 4/1/23- | | | 8 (4/1-9/30/23) | | 69 (10/1/23-3/31/24) | | | |
| 3/31/22 | 3/31/23 | 3/31/24 | | 0-1MM | 1-3MM | 3-5MM | 5-10MM | 10-25MM | 25MM & OVER | |
| ALL | ALL | ALL | | | | | | | | |
| 74 | 69 | 77 | NUMBER OF STATEMENTS | 17 | 15 | 6 | 13 | 6 | 20 | |
| % | % | % | ASSETS | % | % | % | % | % | % | |
| 14.6 | 11.9 | 8.7 | Cash & Equivalents | 8.9 | 7.4 | | 5.6 | | 9.2 | |
| 6.7 | 10.6 | 6.0 | Trade Receivables (net) | .8 | .5 | | 2.2 | | 14.8 | |
| 7.2 | 8.0 | 6.9 | Inventory | .0 | 3.9 | | 7.0 | | 17.8 | |
| 7.1 | 3.2 | 2.2 | All Other Current | 2.7 | 1.6 | | .2 | | 2.1 | |
| 35.6 | 33.7 | 23.8 | Total Current | 12.5 | 13.5 | | 15.0 | | 43.9 | |
| 54.6 | 56.2 | 65.5 | Fixed Assets (net) | 78.9 | 71.4 | | 76.0 | | 48.1 | |
| 4.1 | 2.0 | 2.3 | Intangibles (net) | 6.7 | 1.7 | | .3 | | 1.4 | |
| 5.7 | 8.0 | 8.4 | All Other Non-Current | 2.0 | 13.4 | | 8.7 | | 6.6 | |
| 100.0 | 100.0 | 100.0 | Total | 100.0 | 100.0 | | 100.0 | | 100.0 | |
| | | | LIABILITIES | | | | | | | |
| 9.8 | 9.3 | 4.5 | Notes Payable-Short Term | .0 | 2.6 | | 4.8 | | 5.6 | |
| 5.7 | 7.1 | 8.0 | Cur. Mat.-L.T.D. | 6.5 | 8.0 | | 3.3 | | 5.1 | |
| 2.9 | 3.3 | 3.0 | Trade Payables | 1.8 | 1.0 | | .6 | | 6.5 | |
| .1 | .1 | .0 | Income Taxes Payable | .0 | .0 | | .0 | | .0 | |
| 6.2 | 5.3 | 5.6 | All Other Current | 5.3 | 8.0 | | 2.6 | | 7.8 | |
| 24.8 | 25.1 | 21.1 | Total Current | 13.6 | 19.6 | | 11.2 | | 25.0 | |
| 49.9 | 52.2 | 54.3 | Long-Term Debt | 79.7 | 53.7 | | 56.7 | | 26.8 | |
| .4 | .3 | .4 | Deferred Taxes | .0 | .0 | | .0 | | .7 | |
| 6.5 | 3.4 | 4.8 | All Other Non-Current | 13.6 | 4.2 | | 1.4 | | 2.3 | |
| 18.4 | 18.9 | 19.4 | Net Worth | -7.0 | 22.6 | | 30.7 | | 45.3 | |
| 100.0 | 100.0 | 100.0 | Total Liabilities & Net Worth | 100.0 | 100.0 | | 100.0 | | 100.0 | |
| | | | INCOME DATA | | | | | | | |
| 100.0 | 100.0 | 100.0 | Net Sales | 100.0 | 100.0 | | 100.0 | | 100.0 | |
| 77.0 | 75.1 | 72.8 | Gross Profit | | | | | | 90.1 | |
| 23.0 | 24.9 | 27.2 | Operating Expenses | 65.6 | 72.1 | | 63.4 | | 9.9 | |
| 5.2 | 7.4 | 9.8 | Operating Profit | 34.4 | 27.9 | | 36.6 | | 4.0 | |
| 17.8 | 17.5 | 17.4 | All Other Expenses (net) | 14.1 | 10.6 | | 12.4 | | 6.0 | |
| | | | Profit Before Taxes | 20.3 | 17.3 | | 24.2 | | | |
| | | | RATIOS | | | | | | | |
| 5.4 | 4.2 | 2.4 | | 3.4 | 1.2 | | 4.2 | | 2.3 | |
| 1.7 | 1.6 | 1.0 | Current | .8 | .5 | | 1.2 | | 1.5 | |
| 1.0 | .7 | .4 | | .2 | .4 | | .3 | | .9 | |
| 3.2 | 2.5 | 1.7 | | 2.4 | .7 | | 3.6 | | 1.9 | |
| 1.1 | 1.3 | .7 | Quick | .6 | .4 | | 1.2 | | .9 | |
| .5 | .6 | .3 | | .1 | .1 | | .3 | | .7 | |
| 0 UND | 5 73.6 | 0 UND | | 0 UND | 0 UND | | 0 UND | | 26 14.2 | |
| 21 17.2 | 26 14.2 | 16 23.5 | Sales/Receivables | 0 UND | 0 UND | | 20 18.6 | | 42 8.7 | |
| 48 7.6 | 57 6.4 | 41 8.9 | | 10 36.0 | 7 50.5 | | 38 9.6 | | 61 6.0 | |
| | | | Cost of Sales/Inventory | | | | | | | |
| | | | Cost of Sales/Payables | | | | | | | |
| 2.5 | 2.4 | 4.0 | | 1.6 | 21.3 | | 2.3 | | 4.0 | |
| 7.1 | 7.5 | -496.3 | Sales/Working Capital | -13.0 | -4.1 | | 42.6 | | 13.5 | |
| -120.9 | -11.2 | -3.2 | | -1.6 | -1.4 | | -1.7 | | -135.7 | |
| 20.2 | 13.9 | 10.6 | | 17.0 | 9.2 | | | | 17.2 | |
| (63) 4.4 | (55) 4.8 | (54) 3.8 | EBIT/Interest | (11) 2.5 | (13) 3.8 | | | | (15) 3.2 | |
| 1.6 | 2.4 | 1.8 | | .2 | .9 | | | | 1.4 | |
| | 5.9 | | Net Profit + Depr., Dep., | | | | | | | |
| | (10) 1.9 | | Amort./Cur. Mat. L/T/D | | | | | | | |
| | .1 | | | | | | | | | |
| .7 | .7 | 1.1 | | 1.8 | 2.0 | | 1.6 | | .1 | |
| 2.0 | 2.1 | 3.1 | Fixed/Worth | 999.8 | 2.9 | | 3.0 | | 1.5 | |
| 4.1 | 5.7 | 8.9 | | -1.8 | 11.3 | | 4.7 | | 4.1 | |
| .9 | .7 | 1.2 | | 1.5 | 1.3 | | 1.3 | | .4 | |
| 2.4 | 2.0 | 2.8 | Debt/Worth | 999.8 | 2.6 | | 2.6 | | 1.1 | |
| 8.4 | 25.5 | 17.9 | | -3.2 | 12.0 | | 4.3 | | 4.5 | |
| 45.3 | 37.4 | 28.1 | % Profit Before Taxes/Tangible | | 124.0 | | 28.9 | | 27.4 | |
| (61) 12.6 | (54) 23.3 | (61) 16.3 | Net Worth | (13) | 25.4 | | (11) 16.6 | | (19) 12.5 | |
| 2.8 | 8.5 | 6.6 | | | 2.2 | | 11.2 | | 5.9 | |
| 19.4 | 17.7 | 10.6 | % Profit Before Taxes/Total | 11.6 | 14.1 | | 9.7 | | 15.3 | |
| 5.3 | 6.6 | 4.9 | Assets | 4.9 | 4.9 | | 4.7 | | 5.3 | |
| .9 | .8 | .3 | | -1.4 | -2.5 | | 3.5 | | 1.4 | |
| 9.0 | 5.4 | 2.3 | | .4 | 1.0 | | .6 | | 22.0 | |
| .9 | .7 | .4 | Sales/Net Fixed Assets | .3 | .3 | | .2 | | 1.6 | |
| .3 | .2 | .2 | | .2 | .2 | | .2 | | .8 | |
| 1.1 | 1.3 | .9 | | .3 | .8 | | .5 | | 1.9 | |
| .5 | .4 | .3 | Sales/Total Assets | .2 | .3 | | .2 | | .9 | |
| .2 | .2 | .2 | | .2 | .2 | | .1 | | .5 | |
| 6.9 | 7.7 | 11.8 | | 16.6 | 12.4 | | 24.2 | | .9 | |
| (48) 31.6 | (50) 16.9 | (51) 23.6 | % Depr., Dep., Amort./Sales | (11) 34.4 | (11) 45.7 | | (10) 32.4 | | (11) 8.3 | |
| 53.5 | 36.8 | 44.3 | | 65.3 | 70.3 | | 49.0 | | 14.5 | |
| 1.0 | 1.2 | 1.5 | % Officers', Directors' | | | | | | | |
| (13) 1.3 | (14) 2.3 | (12) 5.6 | Owners' Comp/Sales | | | | | | | |
| 4.5 | 7.5 | 10.5 | | | | | | | | |
| 989085M | 1373251M | 1531606M | Net Sales ($) | 6887M | 27037M | 25044M | 82430M | 92550M | 1297658M | |
| 2747315M | 2642219M | 2852013M | Total Assets ($) | 33031M | 216624M | 101588M | 401807M | 359331M | 1739632M | |

M = $ thousand    MM = $ million
See Pages viii through xx for Explanation of Ratios and Data

© RMA 2024

# REAL ESTATE—Construction, Mining, and Forestry Machinery and Equipment Rental and Leasing  NAICS 532412

**Current Data Sorted by Assets** | **Comparative Historical Data**

| | | | | | | Type of Statement | | |
|---|---|---|---|---|---|---|---|---|
| | 1 | 2 | 12 | 7 | 8 | Unqualified | 46 | 25 |
| | 2 | 5 | 22 | 11 | 6 | Reviewed | 47 | 29 |
| 1 | 6 | 13 | 10 | | 1 | Compiled | 25 | 10 |
| 1 | 5 | 11 | 4 | | | Tax Returns | 43 | 21 |
| 2 | 8 | 41 | 61 | 22 | 29 | Other | 191 | 103 |
| | 65 (4/1-9/30/23) | | 226 (10/1/23-3/31/24) | | | | 4/1/19- 3/31/20 | 4/1/20- 3/31/21 |
| 0-500M | 500M-2MM | 2-10MM | 10-50MM | 50-100MM | 100-250MM | | ALL | ALL |
| 4 | 22 | 72 | 109 | 40 | 44 | NUMBER OF STATEMENTS | 352 | 188 |
| % | % | % | % | % | % | ASSETS | % | % |
| | 19.2 | 13.8 | 8.0 | 5.3 | 9.8 | Cash & Equivalents | 7.5 | 13.4 |
| | 12.0 | 11.9 | 9.7 | 9.1 | 9.4 | Trade Receivables (net) | 12.2 | 11.3 |
| | 6.7 | 16.3 | 16.6 | 15.9 | 12.5 | Inventory | 17.7 | 17.8 |
| | 1.9 | 1.3 | 2.4 | 2.8 | 1.1 | All Other Current | 1.6 | 1.3 |
| | 39.9 | 43.3 | 36.8 | 33.1 | 32.8 | Total Current | 39.1 | 43.7 |
| | 47.7 | 49.3 | 53.9 | 57.4 | 55.9 | Fixed Assets (net) | 52.3 | 47.6 |
| | 8.1 | 3.4 | 1.8 | 2.3 | 1.8 | Intangibles (net) | 3.2 | 3.3 |
| | 4.4 | 4.0 | 7.5 | 7.1 | 9.5 | All Other Non-Current | 5.5 | 5.3 |
| | 100.0 | 100.0 | 100.0 | 100.0 | 100.0 | Total | 100.0 | 100.0 |
| | | | | | | LIABILITIES | | |
| | 12.7 | 7.4 | 9.6 | 12.5 | 11.5 | Notes Payable-Short Term | 13.9 | 10.5 |
| | 4.2 | 8.5 | 7.6 | 9.2 | 6.9 | Cur. Mat.-L.T.D. | 8.2 | 8.4 |
| | 8.2 | 5.8 | 5.3 | 6.5 | 4.0 | Trade Payables | 5.0 | 5.2 |
| | .0 | .1 | .1 | .1 | .3 | Income Taxes Payable | .4 | .2 |
| | 11.3 | 5.3 | 5.5 | 4.1 | 6.7 | All Other Current | 6.0 | 5.2 |
| | 36.3 | 27.1 | 27.9 | 32.5 | 29.5 | Total Current | 33.5 | 29.4 |
| | 34.0 | 32.3 | 28.8 | 33.0 | 25.4 | Long-Term Debt | 33.4 | 31.6 |
| | .0 | .2 | 1.4 | 2.2 | .8 | Deferred Taxes | 1.0 | 1.0 |
| | 4.5 | 4.8 | 6.9 | 4.7 | 5.2 | All Other Non-Current | 2.6 | 3.8 |
| | 25.2 | 35.6 | 35.1 | 27.5 | 39.2 | Net Worth | 29.5 | 34.1 |
| | 100.0 | 100.0 | 100.0 | 100.0 | 100.0 | Total Liabilities & Net Worth | 100.0 | 100.0 |
| | | | | | | INCOME DATA | | |
| | 100.0 | 100.0 | 100.0 | 100.0 | 100.0 | Net Sales | 100.0 | 100.0 |
| | | | | | | Gross Profit | | |
| | 83.2 | 81.5 | 88.8 | 91.9 | 89.7 | Operating Expenses | 85.8 | 88.5 |
| | 16.8 | 18.5 | 11.2 | 8.1 | 10.3 | Operating Profit | 14.2 | 11.5 |
| | 3.7 | 4.7 | 1.7 | 3.8 | 4.2 | All Other Expenses (net) | 3.8 | 2.6 |
| | 13.1 | 13.8 | 9.5 | 4.3 | 6.1 | Profit Before Taxes | 10.4 | 8.9 |
| | | | | | | RATIOS | | |
| | 2.3 | 2.9 | 2.2 | 1.8 | 1.7 | | 2.1 | 3.0 |
| | 1.2 | 1.6 | 1.3 | 1.0 | 1.2 | Current | 1.2 | 1.5 |
| | .5 | .8 | .7 | .8 | .8 | | .7 | .9 |
| | 2.3 | 2.4 | 1.4 | 1.0 | 1.3 | | 1.5 | 2.2 |
| | 1.1 | 1.0 | .6 | .6 | .7 | Quick | .6 | 1.0 |
| | .2 | .4 | .3 | .2 | .3 | | .2 | .4 |
| 0 UND | 6 60.3 | 22 16.3 | 21 17.6 | 29 12.5 | | | 21 17.8 | 15 24.4 |
| 2 236.9 | 33 11.2 | 38 9.7 | 41 8.8 | 40 9.1 | | Sales/Receivables | 46 8.0 | 39 9.3 |
| 35 10.4 | 54 6.8 | 60 6.1 | 63 5.8 | 56 6.5 | | | 66 5.5 | 61 6.0 |
| | | | | | | Cost of Sales/Inventory | | |
| | | | | | | Cost of Sales/Payables | | |
| | 4.3 | 3.0 | 4.4 | 8.5 | 5.9 | | 4.8 | 3.6 |
| | 33.0 | 12.0 | 11.0 | 97.5 | 17.7 | Sales/Working Capital | 12.9 | 8.0 |
| | -7.0 | -20.3 | -12.9 | -9.0 | -19.0 | | -9.8 | -24.0 |
| | 7.3 | 20.2 | 7.9 | 4.0 | 9.1 | | 8.1 | 9.9 |
| (13) | 4.1 | (60) 6.2 | (101) 3.5 | 2.4 | (40) 3.7 | EBIT/Interest | (328) 3.5 | (169) 3.6 |
| | -.1 | 2.7 | 1.6 | 1.0 | 1.8 | | 1.5 | 1.2 |
| | | | 2.7 | 4.8 | | | 2.8 | 8.3 |
| | | (31) 1.3 | (10) 1.6 | | Net Profit + Depr., Dep., Amort./Cur. Mat. L/T/D | (57) 1.6 | (24) 1.8 |
| | | | .9 | .9 | | | .9 | .8 |
| | .1 | .3 | .7 | .9 | .9 | | .7 | .3 |
| | 2.5 | 1.2 | 1.6 | 2.4 | 1.5 | Fixed/Worth | 1.6 | 1.2 |
| | -6.2 | 7.0 | 3.4 | 5.8 | 2.7 | | 3.7 | 2.9 |
| | .4 | .7 | 1.1 | 1.2 | .8 | | 1.0 | .8 |
| | 3.5 | 1.3 | 1.8 | 3.6 | 1.3 | Debt/Worth | 2.3 | 1.9 |
| | -6.2 | 9.0 | 3.8 | 6.7 | 4.2 | | 5.8 | 4.4 |
| | 104.4 | 38.9 | 30.6 | 27.9 | 22.7 | | 34.9 | 30.8 |
| (15) | 17.9 | (59) 21.0 | (99) 18.7 | (38) 18.0 | (43) 11.3 | % Profit Before Taxes/Tangible Net Worth | (311) 18.3 | (169) 14.3 |
| | -18.9 | 7.2 | 7.6 | 1.6 | 5.8 | | 6.3 | 4.6 |
| | 30.1 | 18.0 | 11.0 | 7.2 | 8.6 | | 10.8 | 10.3 |
| | 3.7 | 7.0 | 6.6 | 3.6 | 5.1 | % Profit Before Taxes/Total Assets | 5.3 | 5.0 |
| | -2.6 | 3.1 | 2.0 | .1 | 1.0 | | 1.1 | .7 |
| | 115.0 | 14.1 | 4.0 | 3.6 | 2.9 | | 8.5 | 16.4 |
| | 2.5 | 2.0 | 1.5 | 1.2 | 1.3 | Sales/Net Fixed Assets | 1.6 | 1.7 |
| | .5 | .7 | .8 | .7 | .7 | | .7 | .8 |
| | 2.1 | 1.5 | 1.2 | 1.1 | 1.2 | | 1.3 | 1.4 |
| | .7 | 1.0 | .8 | .7 | .7 | Sales/Total Assets | .8 | .8 |
| | .4 | .5 | .6 | .6 | .5 | | .5 | .5 |
| | 6.9 | 6.6 | 4.6 | 3.7 | | | 6.0 | 6.7 |
| (13) | 19.4 | (50) 17.3 | (86) 11.2 | (24) 9.5 | | % Depr., Dep., Amort./Sales | (213) 12.3 | (97) 15.8 |
| | 56.8 | 33.1 | 19.4 | 21.2 | | | 23.4 | 32.1 |
| | | 1.2 | .7 | | | | 1.1 | .8 |
| | (18) | 3.3 | (17) 1.5 | | | % Officers', Directors' Owners' Comp/Sales | (65) 2.0 | (34) 2.4 |
| | | 4.6 | 2.2 | | | | 4.8 | 4.9 |
| 1623M | 28726M | 462027M | 2725693M | 2261253M | 5566711M | Net Sales ($) | 13518010M | 6462863M |
| 981M | 25477M | 411089M | 2955476M | 2734509M | 6945748M | Total Assets ($) | 16941161M | 8298234M |

M = $ thousand     MM = $ million
See Pages viii through xx for Explanation of Ratios and Data

© RMA 2024

# REAL ESTATE—Construction, Mining, and Forestry Machinery and Equipment Rental and Leasing  NAICS 532412

## Comparative Historical Data | Current Data Sorted by Sales

| | | | Type of Statement | | | | | | |
|---|---|---|---|---|---|---|---|---|---|
| 23 | 33 | 30 | Unqualified | 1 | 1 | 1 | 3 | 7 | 20 |
| 36 | 42 | 46 | Reviewed | 2 | 1 | 3 | 12 | 14 | 26 |
| 16 | 34 | 31 | Compiled | 4 | 6 | 3 | 12 | 4 | 2 |
| 16 | 21 | 21 | Tax Returns | 9 | 2 | 2 | 3 | 1 | 4 |
| 136 | 150 | 163 | Other | 11 | 13 | 13 | 46 | 46 | 69 |
| 4/1/21-3/31/22 | 4/1/22-3/31/23 | 4/1/23-3/31/24 | | | 65 (4/1-9/30/23) | | | 226 (10/1/23-3/31/24) | |
| ALL | ALL | ALL | | 0-1MM | 1-3MM | 3-5MM | 5-10MM | 10-25MM | 25MM & OVER |
| 227 | 280 | 291 | NUMBER OF STATEMENTS | 27 | 22 | 20 | 29 | 72 | 121 |
| % | % | % | ASSETS | % | % | % | % | % | % |
| 11.7 | 11.5 | 10.4 | Cash & Equivalents | 15.7 | 20.7 | 10.2 | 7.5 | 9.6 | 8.4 |
| 13.4 | 13.2 | 10.5 | Trade Receivables (net) | 7.3 | 7.9 | 15.6 | 14.1 | 10.6 | 10.0 |
| 16.1 | 13.2 | 14.9 | Inventory | 1.4 | 4.0 | 10.4 | 19.3 | 18.8 | 17.2 |
| 2.6 | 2.6 | 2.0 | All Other Current | .8 | 2.1 | 2.2 | .7 | 2.1 | 2.4 |
| 43.7 | 40.5 | 37.8 | Total Current | 25.2 | 34.7 | 38.4 | 41.5 | 41.1 | 38.1 |
| 44.9 | 48.9 | 52.9 | Fixed Assets (net) | 63.7 | 59.1 | 53.4 | 50.5 | 48.6 | 52.4 |
| 2.9 | 3.0 | 2.7 | Intangibles (net) | 6.6 | 3.7 | 1.3 | 5.2 | 1.4 | 2.0 |
| 8.5 | 7.7 | 6.7 | All Other Non-Current | 4.7 | 2.5 | 6.9 | 2.7 | 8.8 | 7.5 |
| 100.0 | 100.0 | 100.0 | Total | 100.0 | 100.0 | 100.0 | 100.0 | 100.0 | 100.0 |
| | | | LIABILITIES | | | | | | |
| 10.7 | 7.8 | 9.9 | Notes Payable-Short Term | 4.0 | 4.3 | 12.7 | 9.5 | 11.4 | 10.8 |
| 8.0 | 8.6 | 7.8 | Cur. Mat.-L.T.D. | 5.6 | 9.2 | 7.9 | 8.9 | 8.8 | 7.3 |
| 5.4 | 5.4 | 5.5 | Trade Payables | 4.8 | 2.0 | 5.4 | 4.8 | 6.5 | 5.9 |
| .2 | .2 | .1 | Income Taxes Payable | .0 | .0 | .4 | .1 | .0 | .2 |
| 5.5 | 7.1 | 5.8 | All Other Current | 3.4 | 12.2 | 7.2 | 3.9 | 4.9 | 6.0 |
| 29.7 | 29.1 | 29.2 | Total Current | 17.9 | 27.7 | 33.5 | 27.1 | 31.7 | 30.2 |
| 32.0 | 32.7 | 30.5 | Long-Term Debt | 45.9 | 19.1 | 42.2 | 28.9 | 28.7 | 28.6 |
| 1.0 | .7 | 1.0 | Deferred Taxes | .1 | .0 | .1 | .6 | 1.1 | 1.5 |
| 4.1 | 3.8 | 5.6 | All Other Non-Current | 6.6 | 4.4 | 4.6 | 5.4 | 3.0 | 7.2 |
| 33.1 | 33.7 | 33.8 | Net Worth | 29.2 | 48.8 | 19.5 | 37.9 | 35.5 | 32.4 |
| 100.0 | 100.0 | 100.0 | Total Liabilities & Net Worth | 100.0 | 100.0 | 100.0 | 100.0 | 100.0 | 100.0 |
| | | | INCOME DATA | | | | | | |
| 100.0 | 100.0 | 100.0 | Net Sales | 100.0 | 100.0 | 100.0 | 100.0 | 100.0 | 100.0 |
| 88.0 | 84.6 | 87.0 | Gross Profit | | | | | | |
| 12.0 | 15.4 | 13.0 | Operating Expenses | 66.7 | 83.5 | 82.5 | 86.1 | 89.2 | 91.8 |
| 1.4 | 2.1 | 3.3 | Operating Profit | 33.3 | 16.5 | 17.5 | 13.9 | 10.8 | 8.2 |
| 10.7 | 13.3 | 9.7 | All Other Expenses (net) | 14.1 | 2.7 | 1.2 | 1.1 | 2.1 | 2.6 |
| | | | Profit Before Taxes | 19.2 | 13.9 | 16.4 | 12.8 | 8.7 | 5.6 |
| | | | RATIOS | | | | | | |
| 2.8 | 2.8 | 2.2 | | 3.5 | 5.1 | 2.1 | 2.4 | 2.2 | 2.0 |
| 1.5 | 1.5 | 1.3 | Current | 1.2 | 1.5 | 1.0 | 1.6 | 1.3 | 1.3 |
| .9 | .8 | .8 | | .4 | .5 | .7 | .9 | .6 | .9 |
| 1.9 | 1.8 | 1.6 | | 2.5 | 3.7 | 1.7 | 2.0 | 1.4 | 1.3 |
| .9 | .8 | .7 | Quick | 1.0 | 1.4 | .9 | .9 | .5 | .7 |
| .4 | .4 | .3 | | .2 | .5 | .3 | .3 | .3 | .3 |
| 20 18.4 | 16 23.4 | 17 22.1 | | 0 UND | 0 UND | 24 15.0 | 38 9.7 | 20 17.9 | 24 15.5 |
| 43 8.5 | 40 9.2 | 36 10.0 | Sales/Receivables | 0 UND | 21 17.0 | 41 9.0 | 50 7.3 | 35 10.4 | 37 9.9 |
| 69 5.3 | 69 5.3 | 57 6.4 | | 26 13.8 | 46 8.0 | 73 5.0 | 66 5.5 | 59 6.2 | 56 6.5 |
| | | | Cost of Sales/Inventory | | | | | | |
| | | | Cost of Sales/Payables | | | | | | |
| 3.7 | 3.7 | 4.4 | | 2.0 | 2.6 | 2.8 | 3.2 | 4.5 | 5.1 |
| 8.4 | 10.1 | 13.0 | Sales/Working Capital | 21.9 | 18.5 | NM | 7.4 | 12.0 | 13.7 |
| -31.0 | -13.1 | -13.3 | | -3.5 | -2.9 | -12.8 | -54.8 | -9.8 | -31.8 |
| 13.1 | 12.2 | 9.0 | | 8.6 | 31.0 | 9.3 | 19.0 | 11.4 | 6.0 |
| (201) 5.2 | (255) 5.5 | (257) 4.0 | EBIT/Interest | (14) 4.8 | (15) 8.6 | (19) 4.2 | (27) 4.6 | (67) 3.8 | (115) 3.2 |
| 1.7 | 2.2 | 1.6 | | .8 | 2.4 | 2.0 | 1.5 | 2.3 | 1.3 |
| 7.8 | 3.2 | 3.5 | Net Profit + Depr., Dep., | | | | | 1.9 | 4.6 |
| (31) 2.2 | (33) 1.9 | (50) 1.7 | Amort./Cur. Mat. L/T/D | | | | (16) 1.0 | (26) 1.9 | |
| 1.2 | 1.4 | .9 | | | | | | .7 | .9 |
| .3 | .5 | .7 | | .7 | .8 | .8 | .3 | .2 | .8 |
| 1.2 | 1.3 | 1.5 | Fixed/Worth | 2.1 | 1.2 | 1.6 | 1.6 | 1.4 | 1.5 |
| 3.6 | 3.6 | 4.6 | | 8.9 | 9.0 | NM | 3.4 | 2.7 | 4.0 |
| .8 | .8 | .8 | | 1.0 | .2 | .8 | .9 | .9 | .9 |
| 1.8 | 1.7 | 1.8 | Debt/Worth | 2.8 | .8 | 2.0 | 1.7 | 1.5 | 2.2 |
| 6.0 | 4.0 | 6.5 | | 13.0 | 9.2 | NM | 3.3 | 4.6 | 5.8 |
| 36.9 | 37.5 | 31.6 | % Profit Before Taxes/Tangible | 101.6 | 39.3 | 32.0 | 50.7 | 36.7 | 25.1 |
| (200) 20.9 | (246) 20.5 | (257) 17.8 | Net Worth | (21) 15.4 | (18) 20.3 | (15) 14.2 | (26) 25.3 | (64) 19.0 | (113) 16.4 |
| 8.1 | 9.2 | 6.8 | | -1.2 | 4.1 | .8 | 10.4 | 7.6 | 7.2 |
| 14.2 | 13.9 | 11.6 | % Profit Before Taxes/Total | 19.2 | 15.7 | 27.1 | 14.0 | 13.3 | 9.5 |
| 7.2 | 8.0 | 5.7 | Assets | 1.6 | 6.3 | 10.8 | 8.5 | 6.0 | 5.2 |
| 1.9 | 3.4 | 1.3 | | -.7 | .8 | 2.3 | 2.9 | 2.7 | 1.3 |
| 18.2 | 11.1 | 7.2 | | 4.9 | 9.6 | 3.2 | 8.7 | 13.3 | 4.0 |
| 2.4 | 1.7 | 1.5 | Sales/Net Fixed Assets | .4 | .8 | 1.4 | 1.7 | 1.6 | 1.6 |
| .8 | .7 | .7 | | .1 | .3 | .8 | .9 | .8 | .8 |
| 1.5 | 1.4 | 1.3 | | .7 | 1.5 | 1.4 | 1.1 | 1.6 | 1.3 |
| .9 | .8 | .8 | Sales/Total Assets | .3 | .5 | .8 | .9 | .8 | .9 |
| .5 | .5 | .5 | | .1 | .3 | .5 | .7 | .6 | .6 |
| 6.3 | 5.4 | 4.8 | | 19.0 | 20.6 | 11.4 | 6.5 | 3.2 | 2.8 |
| (127) 14.0 | (170) 12.3 | (179) 14.0 | % Depr., Dep., Amort./Sales | (19) 33.7 | (16) 28.0 | (12) 17.3 | (21) 16.2 | (54) 13.1 | (57) 8.3 |
| 25.7 | 24.7 | 25.4 | | 56.0 | 60.5 | 40.8 | 27.1 | 24.2 | 13.6 |
| .9 | .6 | .8 | % Officers', Directors' | | | | | .8 | .5 |
| (43) 3.0 | (50) 1.7 | (53) 1.9 | Owners' Comp/Sales | | | | (10) 1.6 | (19) .6 | |
| 4.3 | 4.1 | 4.0 | | | | | | 4.8 | 2.2 |
| 8062376M | 9480229M | 11046033M | Net Sales ($) | 14344M | 42682M | 80773M | 229182M | 1199597M | 9479455M |
| 9589318M | 12266285M | 13073280M | Total Assets ($) | 84354M | 89823M | 128422M | 318744M | 1721904M | 10730033M |

M = $ thousand     MM = $ million
See Pages viii through xx for Explanation of Ratios and Data
© RMA 2024

# REAL ESTATE—Office Machinery and Equipment Rental and Leasing  NAICS 532420

## Current Data Sorted by Assets | Comparative Historical Data

| 0-500M | 500M-2MM | 2-10MM | 10-50MM | 50-100MM | 100-250MM | Type of Statement | | 4/1/19-3/31/20 ALL | 4/1/20-3/31/21 ALL |
|---|---|---|---|---|---|---|---|---|---|
| 1 | | 1 | 1 | 2 | 3 | Unqualified | | 12 | 7 |
| | 1 | | 1 | 1 | | Reviewed | | 3 | 3 |
| 3 | 2 | | | | | Compiled | | 4 | 1 |
| 2 | 5 | | 13 | | | Tax Returns | | 14 | 7 |
| | 7 (4/1-9/30/23) | 10 | 43 (10/1/23-3/31/24) | 1 | 3 | Other | | 37 | 20 |
| 6 | 8 | 10 | 16 | 4 | 6 | NUMBER OF STATEMENTS | | 70 | 38 |
| % | % | % | % | % | % | ASSETS | | % | % |
| | | 15.5 | 6.1 | | | Cash & Equivalents | | 10.4 | 13.5 |
| | | 14.8 | 12.8 | | | Trade Receivables (net) | | 12.4 | 11.6 |
| | | 12.4 | 10.8 | | | Inventory | | 5.4 | 4.7 |
| | | 4.8 | 7.6 | | | All Other Current | | 6.3 | 9.9 |
| | | 47.4 | 37.4 | | | Total Current | | 34.5 | 39.8 |
| | | 35.4 | 40.5 | | | Fixed Assets (net) | | 37.8 | 40.5 |
| | | 7.9 | 14.9 | | | Intangibles (net) | | 6.4 | 4.6 |
| | | 9.3 | 7.2 | | | All Other Non-Current | | 21.3 | 15.2 |
| | | 100.0 | 100.0 | | | Total | | 100.0 | 100.0 |
| | | | | | | LIABILITIES | | | |
| | | 11.2 | 12.2 | | | Notes Payable-Short Term | | 12.4 | 10.9 |
| | | 5.1 | 7.0 | | | Cur. Mat.-L.T.D. | | 12.4 | 9.6 |
| | | 7.7 | 3.8 | | | Trade Payables | | 7.2 | 5.2 |
| | | .0 | .0 | | | Income Taxes Payable | | .2 | .3 |
| | | 9.1 | 12.3 | | | All Other Current | | 11.0 | 9.7 |
| | | 33.2 | 35.4 | | | Total Current | | 43.2 | 35.8 |
| | | 15.3 | 22.8 | | | Long-Term Debt | | 32.6 | 46.6 |
| | | .0 | .0 | | | Deferred Taxes | | .6 | .4 |
| | | 5.1 | 14.0 | | | All Other Non-Current | | 12.9 | 6.2 |
| | | 46.4 | 27.8 | | | Net Worth | | 10.7 | 11.0 |
| | | 100.0 | 100.0 | | | Total Liabilities & Net Worth | | 100.0 | 100.0 |
| | | | | | | INCOME DATA | | | |
| | | 100.0 | 100.0 | | | Net Sales | | 100.0 | 100.0 |
| | | | | | | Gross Profit | | | |
| | | 70.2 | 84.2 | | | Operating Expenses | | 76.2 | 74.7 |
| | | 29.8 | 15.8 | | | Operating Profit | | 23.8 | 25.3 |
| | | 2.9 | 1.8 | | | All Other Expenses (net) | | 7.5 | 4.6 |
| | | 27.0 | 14.0 | | | Profit Before Taxes | | 16.3 | 20.7 |
| | | | | | | RATIOS | | | |
| | | 5.3 | 1.4 | | | | | 2.0 | 2.1 |
| | | 1.5 | 1.0 | | | Current | | 1.1 | 1.3 |
| | | .8 | .4 | | | | | .4 | .4 |
| | | 3.8 | .9 | | | | | 1.5 | 1.8 |
| | | 1.1 | .4 | | | Quick | | .7 | .8 |
| | | .3 | .2 | | | | | .2 | .2 |
| | 15 | 23.7 | 19 | 19.7 | | | 4 | 87.6 | 0 UND |
| | 35 | 10.3 | 35 | 10.4 | | Sales/Receivables | 24 | 15.3 | 33 11.0 |
| | 41 | 8.9 | 47 | 7.8 | | | 45 | 8.1 | 52 7.0 |
| | | | | | | Cost of Sales/Inventory | | | |
| | | | | | | Cost of Sales/Payables | | | |
| | | 5.0 | 7.0 | | | | | 7.5 | 3.0 |
| | | 27.0 | 174.1 | | | Sales/Working Capital | | 42.1 | 20.5 |
| | | -7.7 | -2.8 | | | | | -3.8 | -3.7 |
| | | | 12.1 | | | | | 8.3 | 13.1 |
| | | (14) | 2.8 | | | EBIT/Interest | (55) | 3.6 | (31) 4.3 |
| | | | 1.7 | | | | | 1.2 | 1.8 |
| | | | | | | Net Profit + Depr., Dep., Amort./Cur. Mat. L/T/D | | | |
| | | .0 | .4 | | | | | .2 | .1 |
| | | .6 | 1.8 | | | Fixed/Worth | | 1.5 | 1.8 |
| | | 1.9 | NM | | | | | 8.2 | 31.2 |
| | | .7 | 1.1 | | | | | 1.4 | 1.5 |
| | | 1.1 | 3.8 | | | Debt/Worth | | 3.5 | 2.7 |
| | | 4.4 | NM | | | | | 61.1 | 65.7 |
| | | | 33.6 | | | | | 35.1 | 53.1 |
| | | (12) | 27.6 | | | % Profit Before Taxes/Tangible Net Worth | (55) | 18.4 | (30) 27.0 |
| | | | 12.9 | | | | | 6.3 | 12.7 |
| | | 40.5 | 14.7 | | | | | 11.3 | 15.9 |
| | | 13.5 | 7.9 | | | % Profit Before Taxes/Total Assets | | 4.8 | 7.3 |
| | | 7.6 | 4.1 | | | | | .6 | 2.0 |
| | | 282.7 | 33.5 | | | | | 26.3 | 58.9 |
| | | 17.1 | 4.8 | | | Sales/Net Fixed Assets | | 3.4 | 5.3 |
| | | .9 | .6 | | | | | .9 | .7 |
| | | 2.4 | 1.8 | | | | | 2.2 | 1.7 |
| | | 2.0 | .8 | | | Sales/Total Assets | | .7 | .7 |
| | | .6 | .5 | | | | | .3 | .4 |
| | | | | | | | | 3.5 | 2.2 |
| | | | | | | % Depr., Dep., Amort./Sales | (38) | 13.4 | (17) 15.3 |
| | | | | | | | | 28.6 | 63.1 |
| | | | | | | | | | 11.1 |
| | | | | | | % Officers', Directors' Owners' Comp/Sales | (17) | 1.9 | |
| | | | | | | | | 3.3 | |
| 787M | 13364M | 85056M | 526625M | 246093M | 587152M | Net Sales ($) | | 2147647M | 1799828M |
| 1555M | 7771M | 54847M | 363110M | 283263M | 1026927M | Total Assets ($) | | 3571048M | 2114331M |

© RMA 2024  M = $ thousand    MM = $ million
See Pages viii through xx for Explanation of Ratios and Data

# REAL ESTATE—Office Machinery and Equipment Rental and Leasing  NAICS 532420

## Comparative Historical Data | Current Data Sorted by Sales

| | | | | Type of Statement | | | | | | |
|---|---|---|---|---|---|---|---|---|---|---|
| 8 | 8 | 7 | | Unqualified | 1 | | | 1 | 5 | |
| 10 | 9 | 3 | | Reviewed | | 1 | | 1 | 1 | |
| | 1 | | | Compiled | | | | | | |
| 5 | 6 | 6 | | Tax Returns | 3 | 1 | | 1 | 1 | |
| 30 | 26 | 34 | | Other | 6 | 4 | 1 | 6 | 12 | 5 |
| 4/1/21- | 4/1/22- | 4/1/23- | | | | 7 (4/1-9/30/23) | | 43 (10/1/23-3/31/24) | | |
| 3/31/22 | 3/31/23 | 3/31/24 | | | 0-1MM | 1-3MM | 3-5MM | 5-10MM | 10-25MM | 25MM & OVER |
| ALL | ALL | ALL | | | | | | | | |
| 53 | 50 | 50 | | NUMBER OF STATEMENTS | 10 | 6 | 1 | 9 | 13 | 11 |
| % | % | % | | ASSETS | % | % | % | % | % | % |
| 10.7 | 9.3 | 10.0 | | Cash & Equivalents | 4.0 | | | | 9.5 | 10.4 |
| 14.3 | 16.4 | 10.8 | | Trade Receivables (net) | 4.0 | | | | 16.2 | 15.7 |
| 10.6 | 11.4 | 7.4 | | Inventory | .0 | | | | 11.2 | 12.4 |
| 5.1 | 4.5 | 6.3 | | All Other Current | 7.1 | | | | 1.3 | 8.7 |
| 40.7 | 41.6 | 34.6 | | Total Current | 15.2 | | | | 38.2 | 47.2 |
| 35.3 | 36.5 | 48.8 | | Fixed Assets (net) | 75.1 | | | | 38.3 | 30.6 |
| 5.4 | 4.5 | 7.4 | | Intangibles (net) | .0 | | | | 19.9 | 5.7 |
| 18.6 | 17.4 | 9.3 | | All Other Non-Current | 9.6 | | | | 3.6 | 16.5 |
| 100.0 | 100.0 | 100.0 | | Total | 100.0 | | | | 100.0 | 100.0 |
| | | | | LIABILITIES | | | | | | |
| 9.8 | 12.8 | 9.4 | | Notes Payable-Short Term | 5.4 | | | | 8.0 | 22.3 |
| 5.7 | 9.3 | 13.2 | | Cur. Mat.-L.T.D. | 19.4 | | | | 7.3 | 3.8 |
| 4.5 | 5.9 | 5.9 | | Trade Payables | 1.1 | | | | 7.4 | 3.7 |
| .6 | .3 | .4 | | Income Taxes Payable | .6 | | | | .0 | 1.3 |
| 12.3 | 11.7 | 11.5 | | All Other Current | 13.5 | | | | 8.1 | 6.6 |
| 32.9 | 40.0 | 40.5 | | Total Current | 40.1 | | | | 30.7 | 37.8 |
| 30.1 | 27.8 | 35.4 | | Long-Term Debt | 54.3 | | | | 25.3 | 10.7 |
| .7 | .2 | .2 | | Deferred Taxes | .0 | | | | .0 | .8 |
| 6.5 | 3.5 | 9.0 | | All Other Non-Current | 1.3 | | | | 22.9 | 5.7 |
| 29.7 | 28.5 | 14.9 | | Net Worth | 4.6 | | | | 21.1 | 45.0 |
| 100.0 | 100.0 | 100.0 | | Total Liabilities & Net Worth | 100.0 | | | | 100.0 | 100.0 |
| | | | | INCOME DATA | | | | | | |
| 100.0 | 100.0 | 100.0 | | Net Sales | 100.0 | | | | 100.0 | 100.0 |
| 75.7 | 78.2 | 78.9 | | Gross Profit | | | | | 89.1 | 84.2 |
| | | | | Operating Expenses | 71.2 | | | | 10.9 | 15.8 |
| 24.3 | 21.8 | 21.1 | | Operating Profit | 28.8 | | | | 3.9 | 2.8 |
| 2.1 | 2.6 | 5.4 | | All Other Expenses (net) | 9.0 | | | | 7.1 | 13.0 |
| 22.3 | 19.2 | 15.7 | | Profit Before Taxes | 19.9 | | | | | |
| | | | | RATIOS | | | | | | |
| 2.5 | 2.4 | 2.2 | | | 1.2 | | | | 2.0 | 3.3 |
| 1.3 | 1.2 | 1.0 | | Current | .4 | | | | 1.0 | 1.3 |
| .5 | .3 | .3 | | | .0 | | | | .4 | .7 |
| 1.7 | 1.6 | 1.5 | | | .9 | | | | 1.1 | 1.3 |
| .8 | .6 | .5 | | Quick | .3 | | | | .6 | .7 |
| .2 | .3 | .2 | | | .0 | | | | .3 | .2 |
| 16  22.4 | 14  25.4 | 1  265.9 | | | 0  UND | | | 25  14.7 | 18  20.1 | |
| 32  11.4 | 35  10.3 | 30  12.0 | | Sales/Receivables | 0  UND | | | 37  9.8 | 31  11.7 | |
| 55  6.6 | 59  6.2 | 45  8.1 | | | 89  4.1 | | | 44  8.3 | 104  3.5 | |
| | | | | Cost of Sales/Inventory | | | | | | |
| | | | | Cost of Sales/Payables | | | | | | |
| 3.8 | 5.9 | 6.6 | | | NM | | | | 8.6 | 6.3 |
| 14.0 | 12.4 | 174.1 | | Sales/Working Capital | -2.7 | | | | 99.4 | 8.6 |
| -6.1 | -4.2 | -2.4 | | | -1.9 | | | | -3.2 | -17.7 |
| 16.2 | 18.4 | 15.6 | | | | | | | 5.8 | 19.4 |
| (44)  7.6 | (42)  6.1 | (45)  4.7 | | EBIT/Interest | | | | (11)  2.5 | 5.1 | |
| 3.0 | 3.1 | 1.8 | | | | | | | 1.4 | 2.1 |
| | | | | Net Profit + Depr., Dep., Amort./Cur. Mat. L/T/D | | | | | | |
| .1 | .2 | .3 | | | .8 | | | | .7 | .2 |
| 1.0 | .8 | 1.5 | | Fixed/Worth | 5.3 | | | | 6.5 | .5 |
| 3.9 | 3.9 | -13.2 | | | -5.4 | | | | -.5 | 2.2 |
| 1.0 | 1.1 | 1.0 | | | .3 | | | | 2.0 | .6 |
| 2.2 | 2.7 | 3.1 | | Debt/Worth | 4.9 | | | | 6.6 | 1.4 |
| 8.2 | 8.2 | -16.0 | | | -8.0 | | | | -2.6 | 5.4 |
| 79.6 | 56.7 | 50.5 | | % Profit Before Taxes/Tangible Net Worth | | | | | | 46.7 |
| (48)  39.5 | (43)  29.3 | (37)  31.9 | | | | | | | | 23.3 |
| 16.1 | 11.2 | 7.8 | | | | | | | | 9.3 |
| 19.9 | 20.3 | 16.8 | | % Profit Before Taxes/Total Assets | 19.5 | | | | 15.9 | 12.9 |
| 9.2 | 8.7 | 8.4 | | | 4.0 | | | | 8.2 | 8.9 |
| 4.9 | 3.5 | 1.8 | | | -1.8 | | | | 2.5 | 4.7 |
| 36.3 | 38.6 | 31.2 | | Sales/Net Fixed Assets | 1.3 | | | | 31.0 | 33.1 |
| 6.1 | 6.1 | 2.4 | | | .7 | | | | 5.3 | 2.9 |
| .9 | 1.1 | .7 | | | .4 | | | | .7 | 1.5 |
| 1.8 | 2.0 | 1.8 | | Sales/Total Assets | .9 | | | | 2.3 | 1.8 |
| .8 | .9 | .8 | | | .4 | | | | 1.3 | 1.0 |
| .4 | .4 | .4 | | | .2 | | | | .6 | .4 |
| 2.2 | 1.1 | 3.6 | | % Depr., Dep., Amort./Sales | | | | | | |
| (27)  8.6 | (26)  2.7 | (21)  13.8 | | | | | | | | |
| 22.5 | 14.7 | 62.4 | | | | | | | | |
| | | | | % Officers', Directors' Owners' Comp/Sales | | | | | | |
| 1743066M | 1961235M | 1459077M | | Net Sales ($) | 3828M | 8815M | 4598M | 63558M | 241742M | 1136536M |
| 2456394M | 2273161M | 1737473M | | Total Assets ($) | 13073M | 10098M | 25560M | 173282M | 277000M | 1238460M |

M = $ thousand    MM = $ million
See Pages viii through xx for Explanation of Ratios and Data

© RMA 2024

# REAL ESTATE—Other Commercial and Industrial Machinery and Equipment Rental and Leasing  NAICS 532490

## Current Data Sorted by Assets | Comparative Historical Data

| | | | | | | Type of Statement | | |
|---|---|---|---|---|---|---|---|---|
| | | 5 | 13 | 8 | 14 | Unqualified | 40 | 31 |
| | 1 | 10 | 25 | 10 | 1 | Reviewed | 31 | 20 |
| | 3 | 11 | 13 | | 3 | Compiled | 36 | 17 |
| 4 | 9 | 14 | 4 | | | Tax Returns | 63 | 46 |
| 9 | 30 | 77 | 75 | 29 | 34 | Other | 259 | 166 |
| | 59 (4/1-9/30/23) | | 343 (10/1/23-3/31/24) | | | | 4/1/19-3/31/20 | 4/1/20-3/31/21 |
| 0-500M | 500M-2MM | 2-10MM | 10-50MM | 50-100MM | 100-250MM | | ALL | ALL |
| 13 | 43 | 117 | 130 | 47 | 52 | NUMBER OF STATEMENTS | 429 | 280 |
| % | % | % | % | % | % | ASSETS | % | % |
| 34.2 | 21.7 | 12.2 | 9.0 | 10.2 | 8.3 | Cash & Equivalents | 11.1 | 15.0 |
| 12.7 | 14.1 | 15.4 | 14.7 | 14.6 | 9.5 | Trade Receivables (net) | 13.2 | 13.6 |
| 2.1 | 3.3 | 10.1 | 12.8 | 10.4 | 10.9 | Inventory | 12.2 | 11.7 |
| 6.7 | 2.7 | 2.1 | 2.9 | 2.5 | 4.9 | All Other Current | 2.8 | 3.4 |
| 55.7 | 41.8 | 39.7 | 39.4 | 37.8 | 33.7 | Total Current | 39.3 | 43.6 |
| 32.9 | 48.0 | 49.6 | 47.5 | 47.8 | 43.3 | Fixed Assets (net) | 47.7 | 42.2 |
| .0 | 5.1 | 3.2 | 2.6 | 5.3 | 9.0 | Intangibles (net) | 4.5 | 5.1 |
| 11.4 | 5.1 | 7.4 | 10.4 | 9.1 | 14.0 | All Other Non-Current | 8.5 | 9.1 |
| 100.0 | 100.0 | 100.0 | 100.0 | 100.0 | 100.0 | Total | 100.0 | 100.0 |
| | | | | | | LIABILITIES | | |
| 3.9 | 6.3 | 6.5 | 8.7 | 14.2 | 8.7 | Notes Payable-Short Term | 10.7 | 12.7 |
| 18.6 | 6.8 | 9.8 | 6.7 | 7.9 | 7.5 | Cur. Mat.-L.T.D. | 7.1 | 8.3 |
| 4.7 | 5.0 | 5.8 | 5.0 | 7.2 | 5.1 | Trade Payables | 5.4 | 4.7 |
| 1.3 | .2 | .0 | .1 | .5 | .1 | Income Taxes Payable | .1 | .2 |
| 12.0 | 10.2 | 8.3 | 7.7 | 5.5 | 14.3 | All Other Current | 9.1 | 8.7 |
| 40.4 | 28.4 | 30.4 | 28.1 | 35.2 | 35.7 | Total Current | 32.4 | 34.6 |
| 15.1 | 42.1 | 40.0 | 29.1 | 27.1 | 39.9 | Long-Term Debt | 31.0 | 38.9 |
| 1.4 | .0 | .1 | 1.4 | 2.0 | .5 | Deferred Taxes | .7 | .4 |
| 7.5 | 3.6 | 5.9 | 4.1 | 4.0 | 6.1 | All Other Non-Current | 4.6 | 5.2 |
| 35.6 | 25.9 | 23.5 | 37.4 | 31.7 | 17.7 | Net Worth | 31.3 | 20.9 |
| 100.0 | 100.0 | 100.0 | 100.0 | 100.0 | 100.0 | Total Liabilities & Net Worth | 100.0 | 100.0 |
| | | | | | | INCOME DATA | | |
| 100.0 | 100.0 | 100.0 | 100.0 | 100.0 | 100.0 | Net Sales | 100.0 | 100.0 |
| 79.3 | 71.5 | 80.7 | 83.8 | 81.0 | 83.7 | Gross Profit | 82.3 | 82.9 |
| 20.7 | 28.5 | 19.3 | 16.2 | 19.0 | 16.3 | Operating Expenses | 17.7 | 17.1 |
| .5 | 2.3 | 3.3 | 2.8 | 5.2 | 6.8 | Operating Profit | 3.8 | 3.7 |
| 20.2 | 26.2 | 15.9 | 13.4 | 13.8 | 9.5 | All Other Expenses (net) | 13.9 | 13.4 |
| | | | | | | Profit Before Taxes | | |
| | | | | | | RATIOS | | |
| 10.5 | 4.4 | 3.7 | 3.2 | 1.6 | 1.6 | | 2.7 | 2.9 |
| 2.6 | 1.6 | 1.3 | 1.4 | 1.1 | 1.0 | Current | 1.4 | 1.5 |
| .9 | .6 | .7 | .8 | .6 | .7 | | .7 | .7 |
| 7.3 | 4.1 | 2.5 | 2.4 | 1.3 | .8 | | 1.9 | 2.0 |
| 1.8 | 1.0 | .9 | .9 | .7 | .6 | Quick | .8 | 1.0 |
| .4 | .5 | .4 | .4 | .3 | .2 | | .3 | .4 |
| 0 UND | 0 UND | 0 UND | 17 21.5 | 26 14.0 | 12 29.6 | | 8 44.9 | 4 93.6 |
| 0 UND | 19 19.5 | 33 11.0 | 48 7.6 | 45 8.1 | 38 9.5 | Sales/Receivables | 36 10.1 | 34 10.6 |
| 36 10.2 | 40 9.2 | 64 5.7 | 74 4.9 | 66 5.5 | 59 6.2 | | 63 5.8 | 63 5.8 |
| | | | | | | Cost of Sales/Inventory | | |
| | | | | | | Cost of Sales/Payables | | |
| 3.1 | 4.9 | 4.5 | 3.9 | 4.7 | 6.5 | | 4.0 | 3.5 |
| 15.7 | 18.8 | 12.1 | 9.9 | 33.0 | NM | Sales/Working Capital | 13.6 | 10.4 |
| NM | -12.5 | -16.9 | -11.9 | -8.2 | -4.6 | | -10.2 | -10.5 |
| | 24.0 | 19.3 | 12.1 | 11.0 | 7.3 | | 10.9 | 13.1 |
| (33) | 7.6 | (102) 5.7 | (119) 4.6 | (43) 3.5 | (43) 2.9 | EBIT/Interest | (367) 4.0 | (245) 3.8 |
| | 2.9 | 1.9 | 1.9 | 1.6 | 1.4 | | 1.6 | 1.1 |
| | | | 9.4 | 13.3 | 4.1 | Net Profit + Depr., Dep., | 5.1 | 14.7 |
| | | (30) 3.7 | (10) 3.4 | (10) .8 | | Amort./Cur. Mat. L/T/D | (57) 2.5 | (22) 3.1 |
| | | | 2.0 | 1.2 | -.1 | | 1.3 | 1.0 |
| .1 | .7 | .6 | .4 | .7 | .5 | | .4 | .2 |
| .6 | 1.8 | 2.1 | 1.2 | 1.4 | 2.2 | Fixed/Worth | 1.5 | 1.4 |
| 17.1 | 19.8 | 59.9 | 2.7 | 4.9 | 5.7 | | 4.4 | 5.7 |
| .2 | .8 | .6 | .7 | .9 | 1.9 | | .8 | 1.0 |
| .9 | 2.4 | 2.6 | 1.9 | 2.6 | 3.4 | Debt/Worth | 2.1 | 2.2 |
| NM | 23.9 | 87.5 | 4.6 | 6.4 | 38.7 | | 7.7 | 12.6 |
| 105.4 | 99.3 | 56.7 | 44.9 | 35.1 | 38.8 | | 41.7 | 43.7 |
| (10) 47.8 | (34) 55.2 | (89) 31.2 | (122) 26.2 | (42) 21.8 | (42) 16.6 | % Profit Before Taxes/Tangible Net Worth | (361) 21.3 | (222) 18.1 |
| 23.6 | 15.0 | 10.1 | 10.8 | 9.4 | 3.8 | | 8.9 | 4.0 |
| 66.0 | 48.6 | 26.5 | 16.4 | 14.7 | 11.5 | | 14.3 | 16.5 |
| 40.3 | 16.4 | 10.5 | 8.0 | 7.1 | 3.9 | % Profit Before Taxes/Total Assets | 6.9 | 6.5 |
| 10.3 | 5.9 | 2.8 | 2.3 | 3.2 | -.6 | | 1.8 | .7 |
| 38.8 | 14.7 | 10.7 | 8.2 | 5.3 | 14.4 | | 10.4 | 20.1 |
| 12.3 | 3.5 | 2.5 | 2.4 | 2.0 | 1.7 | Sales/Net Fixed Assets | 2.3 | 2.5 |
| 6.0 | 1.1 | 1.0 | .7 | .8 | .7 | | .7 | .8 |
| 5.9 | 3.0 | 1.8 | 1.5 | 1.3 | 1.2 | | 1.6 | 1.5 |
| 3.6 | 1.4 | 1.3 | .9 | .8 | .6 | Sales/Total Assets | .9 | .8 |
| 1.9 | .6 | .5 | .4 | .4 | .4 | | .4 | .4 |
| | 4.8 | 4.2 | 5.1 | 5.5 | .6 | | 4.3 | 4.4 |
| (19) | 11.9 | (75) 11.6 | (98) 11.4 | (33) 14.2 | (19) 2.7 | % Depr., Dep., Amort./Sales | (274) 12.9 | (169) 15.5 |
| | 46.3 | 30.1 | 23.5 | 26.4 | 14.8 | | 27.3 | 32.1 |
| | | 1.7 | .4 | | | | 1.3 | 1.7 |
| | (23) 3.5 | (19) 1.7 | | | | % Officers', Directors' Owners' Comp/Sales | (83) 2.8 | (53) 3.8 |
| | | 6.5 | 4.2 | | | | 5.4 | 7.7 |
| 13423M | 113507M | 790964M | 3158740M | 3157987M | 6364700M | Net Sales ($) | 10656951M | 6664234M |
| 3577M | 52905M | 627588M | 3129337M | 3270492M | 8435500M | Total Assets ($) | 13701095M | 8614935M |

© RMA 2024

M = $ thousand  MM = $ million
See Pages viii through xx for Explanation of Ratios and Data

## REAL ESTATE—Other Commercial and Industrial Machinery and Equipment Rental and Leasing  NAICS 532490

### Comparative Historical Data / Current Data Sorted by Sales

| | | | | Type of Statement | | | | | | |
|---|---|---|---|---|---|---|---|---|---|---|
| | 36 | 37 | 40 | Unqualified | 1 | 2 | 5 | 5 | 11 | 21 |
| | 27 | 53 | 47 | Reviewed | | | 5 | 5 | 14 | 23 |
| | 13 | 17 | 30 | Compiled | 2 | 3 | 4 | 10 | 4 | 7 |
| | 46 | 52 | 31 | Tax Returns | 7 | 7 | 2 | 10 | 4 | 1 |
| | 186 | 243 | 254 | Other | 24 | 35 | 25 | 41 | 49 | 80 |
| | 4/1/21-3/31/22 ALL | 4/1/22-3/31/23 ALL | 4/1/23-3/31/24 ALL | | 59 (4/1-9/30/23) | | | 343 (10/1/23-3/31/24) | | |
| | | | | | 0-1MM | 1-3MM | 3-5MM | 5-10MM | 10-25MM | 25MM & OVER |
| | 308 | 402 | 402 | NUMBER OF STATEMENTS | 34 | 47 | 36 | 71 | 82 | 132 |
| | % | % | % | ASSETS | % | % | % | % | % | % |
| | 14.3 | 12.8 | 12.1 | Cash & Equivalents | 17.9 | 15.5 | 14.6 | 14.1 | 8.1 | 10.3 |
| | 13.3 | 14.3 | 14.1 | Trade Receivables (net) | 9.2 | 13.9 | 15.1 | 11.9 | 16.7 | 14.8 |
| | 9.9 | 9.4 | 10.1 | Inventory | .2 | 1.1 | 2.5 | 9.6 | 14.2 | 15.7 |
| | 2.5 | 2.5 | 3.0 | All Other Current | 2.7 | 2.1 | 3.6 | 3.8 | 2.0 | 3.4 |
| | 40.2 | 39.0 | 39.4 | Total Current | 30.0 | 32.5 | 35.8 | 39.5 | 40.9 | 44.2 |
| | 48.2 | 49.0 | 47.2 | Fixed Assets (net) | 63.9 | 55.9 | 52.4 | 48.2 | 44.4 | 39.6 |
| | 2.6 | 2.7 | 4.1 | Intangibles (net) | 3.8 | 3.8 | 2.2 | 2.3 | 4.3 | 5.7 |
| | 9.0 | 9.2 | 9.3 | All Other Non-Current | 2.3 | 7.7 | 9.7 | 10.1 | 10.3 | 10.6 |
| | 100.0 | 100.0 | 100.0 | Total | 100.0 | 100.0 | 100.0 | 100.0 | 100.0 | 100.0 |
| | | | | LIABILITIES | | | | | | |
| | 10.2 | 9.6 | 8.3 | Notes Payable-Short Term | 3.1 | 4.4 | 4.0 | 6.5 | 12.8 | 10.3 |
| | 7.5 | 7.1 | 8.2 | Cur. Mat.-L.T.D. | 12.0 | 4.7 | 6.0 | 9.9 | 9.8 | 7.2 |
| | 4.4 | 5.4 | 5.5 | Trade Payables | .6 | 4.7 | 4.0 | 5.8 | 5.4 | 7.3 |
| | .1 | .1 | .2 | Income Taxes Payable | .0 | .1 | .5 | .2 | .1 | .2 |
| | 5.8 | 6.3 | 8.9 | All Other Current | 7.5 | 5.7 | 13.9 | 7.1 | 7.1 | 11.0 |
| | 28.0 | 28.4 | 31.0 | Total Current | 23.2 | 19.6 | 28.3 | 29.5 | 35.2 | 36.0 |
| | 32.6 | 37.0 | 34.4 | Long-Term Debt | 45.5 | 35.4 | 32.4 | 38.3 | 35.9 | 28.6 |
| | .4 | .7 | .8 | Deferred Taxes | .0 | .6 | .0 | 1.6 | .8 | .9 |
| | 3.0 | 5.0 | 4.9 | All Other Non-Current | .9 | 5.3 | 4.4 | 6.7 | 5.6 | 4.7 |
| | 36.0 | 28.9 | 28.9 | Net Worth | 30.4 | 39.2 | 34.9 | 23.9 | 22.5 | 29.8 |
| | 100.0 | 100.0 | 100.0 | Total Liabilities & Net Worth | 100.0 | 100.0 | 100.0 | 100.0 | 100.0 | 100.0 |
| | | | | INCOME DATA | | | | | | |
| | 100.0 | 100.0 | 100.0 | Net Sales | 100.0 | 100.0 | 100.0 | 100.0 | 100.0 | 100.0 |
| | | | | Gross Profit | | | | | | |
| | 80.8 | 80.4 | 81.1 | Operating Expenses | 57.1 | 70.5 | 84.1 | 82.1 | 85.3 | 87.1 |
| | 19.2 | 19.6 | 18.9 | Operating Profit | 42.9 | 29.5 | 15.9 | 17.9 | 14.7 | 12.9 |
| | 2.0 | 4.0 | 3.6 | All Other Expenses (net) | 6.7 | 4.9 | 3.8 | 1.8 | 4.6 | 2.7 |
| | 17.2 | 15.6 | 15.3 | Profit Before Taxes | 36.2 | 24.6 | 12.2 | 16.1 | 10.1 | 10.2 |
| | | | | RATIOS | | | | | | |
| | 2.8 | 3.0 | 2.8 | | 6.2 | 4.4 | 4.5 | 3.0 | 2.6 | 2.1 |
| | 1.4 | 1.4 | 1.3 | Current | 1.1 | 2.2 | 1.3 | 1.3 | 1.2 | 1.2 |
| | .8 | .8 | .7 | | .5 | .5 | .7 | .6 | .8 | .8 |
| | 2.2 | 2.1 | 2.1 | | 3.5 | 4.3 | 3.6 | 2.1 | 1.7 | 1.3 |
| | 1.0 | 1.0 | .8 | Quick | 1.0 | 1.6 | 1.3 | .8 | .8 | .7 |
| | .5 | .4 | .4 | | .4 | .4 | .4 | .5 | .3 | .4 |
| 1 | 292.5 | 2 152.7 | 8 46.5 | | 0 UND | 0 UND | 1 513.3 | 4 87.6 | 18 20.7 | 25 14.5 |
| 37 | 9.8 | 31 11.6 | 36 10.1 | Sales/Receivables | 0 UND | 24 15.1 | 30 12.2 | 34 10.8 | 47 7.8 | 44 8.3 |
| 65 | 5.6 | 63 5.8 | 65 5.6 | | 52 7.0 | 68 5.4 | 72 5.1 | 62 5.9 | 68 5.4 | 62 5.9 |
| | | | | Cost of Sales/Inventory | | | | | | |
| | | | | Cost of Sales/Payables | | | | | | |
| | 3.9 | 4.6 | 4.4 | | 2.2 | 2.5 | 4.7 | 5.2 | 4.8 | 4.8 |
| | 11.3 | 10.8 | 15.7 | Sales/Working Capital | 36.5 | 7.7 | 12.7 | 15.0 | 14.7 | 18.0 |
| | -15.7 | -16.9 | -12.1 | | -9.2 | -4.9 | -13.3 | -14.0 | -9.6 | -14.8 |
| | 16.0 | 17.0 | 13.3 | | 25.0 | 17.3 | 17.3 | 14.7 | 8.5 | 12.1 |
| (266) | 6.4 | (350) 5.9 | (348) 4.9 | EBIT/Interest | (25) 9.0 | (38) 6.2 | (28) 2.9 | (65) 5.7 | (72) 4.5 | (120) 4.3 |
| | 2.9 | 2.3 | 1.9 | | 3.6 | 1.8 | 1.7 | 2.4 | 1.6 | 2.0 |
| | 3.3 | 5.3 | 8.1 | | | | | | 6.5 | 10.6 |
| (36) | 1.7 | (56) 1.9 | (59) 3.1 | Net Profit + Depr., Dep., Amort./Cur. Mat. L/T/D | | | | (15) 3.1 | (31) 3.1 |
| | .7 | 1.0 | 1.3 | | | | | | 1.5 | 1.0 |
| | .4 | .5 | .6 | | 1.0 | .6 | .6 | .6 | .7 | .4 |
| | 1.3 | 1.6 | 1.5 | Fixed/Worth | 2.2 | 1.9 | 1.3 | 2.1 | 1.4 | 1.2 |
| | 3.4 | 4.2 | 5.2 | | 12.4 | 5.2 | 15.4 | 10.5 | 6.5 | 3.0 |
| | .8 | .9 | .8 | | .6 | .4 | .4 | .8 | .9 | 1.1 |
| | 1.9 | 2.2 | 2.4 | Debt/Worth | 2.7 | 1.5 | 1.9 | 3.2 | 2.2 | 2.3 |
| | 4.7 | 6.0 | 8.7 | | 26.5 | 4.5 | 76.5 | 57.4 | 7.2 | 5.8 |
| | 52.2 | 61.6 | 51.6 | | 81.7 | 63.7 | 46.9 | 57.6 | 35.7 | 43.3 |
| (278) | 25.1 | (346) 28.7 | (339) 26.6 | % Profit Before Taxes/Tangible Net Worth | (28) 47.5 | (40) 39.3 | (29) 21.3 | (56) 24.1 | (70) 23.9 | (116) 27.5 |
| | 12.2 | 12.7 | 10.0 | | 14.8 | 10.9 | 5.9 | 10.2 | 6.8 | 10.4 |
| | 19.0 | 19.9 | 19.2 | | 36.0 | 39.7 | 20.5 | 28.6 | 16.4 | 16.8 |
| | 9.1 | 8.5 | 8.5 | % Profit Before Taxes/Total Assets | 11.3 | 9.5 | 5.6 | 10.0 | 7.9 | 7.9 |
| | 3.9 | 2.7 | 2.4 | | 6.8 | 2.0 | -1.2 | 3.1 | 1.2 | 3.2 |
| | 12.5 | 9.6 | 10.6 | | 5.3 | 6.3 | 12.7 | 9.8 | 13.6 | 14.7 |
| | 1.9 | 2.1 | 2.5 | Sales/Net Fixed Assets | .7 | 1.1 | 2.4 | 2.5 | 3.0 | 3.3 |
| | .6 | .8 | .8 | | .2 | .3 | .6 | 1.1 | .8 | 1.4 |
| | 1.6 | 1.7 | 1.7 | | 1.3 | 1.3 | 2.0 | 1.7 | 1.7 | 1.8 |
| | .9 | 1.0 | 1.0 | Sales/Total Assets | .5 | .5 | .9 | 1.1 | 1.0 | 1.2 |
| | .4 | .4 | .5 | | .2 | .3 | .4 | .6 | .5 | .6 |
| | 5.1 | 3.0 | 4.4 | | 8.7 | 11.5 | 2.9 | 4.9 | 4.9 | 2.6 |
| (211) | 12.7 | (274) 11.8 | (249) 11.3 | % Depr., Dep., Amort./Sales | (22) 24.5 | (26) 27.5 | (21) 18.6 | (45) 13.1 | (61) 11.4 | (74) 5.5 |
| | 28.3 | 24.3 | 26.0 | | 56.0 | 65.2 | 48.0 | 29.0 | 23.5 | 12.7 |
| | 1.6 | 1.3 | 1.2 | % Officers', Directors', Owners' Comp/Sales | | | | 1.7 | .4 | .7 |
| (60) | 3.4 | (71) 2.8 | (58) 2.7 | | | | | (19) 3.5 | (14) 1.8 | (12) 2.7 |
| | 9.0 | 8.6 | 6.7 | | | | | 7.5 | 3.4 | 4.9 |
| | 6926054M | 11502899M | 13599321M | Net Sales ($) | 19716M | 87305M | 149494M | 551949M | 1325509M | 11465348M |
| | 9247467M | 13014672M | 15519399M | Total Assets ($) | 57815M | 208694M | 272189M | 1008345M | 2255688M | 11716668M |

M = $ thousand     MM = $ million

© RMA 2024

# REAL ESTATE—Lessors of Nonfinancial Intangible Assets (except Copyrighted Works) NAICS 533110

## Current Data Sorted by Assets | Comparative Historical Data

| | | | | | | | Type of Statement | | |
|---|---|---|---|---|---|---|---|---|---|
| | | | | 2 | 2 | | Unqualified | 8 | 4 |
| | | 1 | 1 | | | | Reviewed | | |
| 1 | 3 | 7 | 2 | | | | Compiled | | 3 |
| | 5 | | | 1 | | | Tax Returns | 7 | 1 |
| | 4 (4/1-9/30/23) | | 29 (10/1/23-3/31/24) | | 1 | | Other | 21 | 11 |
| 0-500M | 500M-2MM | 2-10MM | 10-50MM | 50-100MM | 100-250MM | | | 4/1/19- 3/31/20 | 4/1/20- 3/31/21 |
| 1 | 8 | 8 | 10 | 3 | 3 | NUMBER OF STATEMENTS | | ALL 36 | ALL 19 |
| % | % | % | % | % | % | ASSETS | | % | % |
| | | | 27.5 | | | Cash & Equivalents | | 18.3 | 28.6 |
| | | | 6.7 | | | Trade Receivables (net) | | 11.0 | 7.1 |
| | | | 2.9 | | | Inventory | | 2.7 | 3.3 |
| | | | 1.0 | | | All Other Current | | 8.9 | 7.1 |
| | | | 38.1 | | | Total Current | | 40.8 | 46.1 |
| | | | 13.2 | | | Fixed Assets (net) | | 22.8 | 19.4 |
| | | | 13.0 | | | Intangibles (net) | | 14.7 | 14.9 |
| | | | 35.7 | | | All Other Non-Current | | 21.7 | 19.7 |
| | | | 100.0 | | | Total | | 100.0 | 100.0 |
| | | | | | | LIABILITIES | | | |
| | | | .0 | | | Notes Payable-Short Term | | 6.5 | 4.7 |
| | | | 3.7 | | | Cur. Mat.-L.T.D. | | 2.1 | 1.9 |
| | | | 3.3 | | | Trade Payables | | 6.1 | 7.0 |
| | | | .6 | | | Income Taxes Payable | | .6 | .7 |
| | | | 18.7 | | | All Other Current | | 15.7 | 20.9 |
| | | | 26.4 | | | Total Current | | 31.0 | 35.3 |
| | | | 65.7 | | | Long-Term Debt | | 15.8 | 12.3 |
| | | | .0 | | | Deferred Taxes | | .0 | .5 |
| | | | 19.8 | | | All Other Non-Current | | 4.8 | 14.4 |
| | | | -11.9 | | | Net Worth | | 48.4 | 37.6 |
| | | | 100.0 | | | Total Liabilities & Net Worth | | 100.0 | 100.0 |
| | | | | | | INCOME DATA | | | |
| | | | 100.0 | | | Net Sales | | 100.0 | 100.0 |
| | | | | | | Gross Profit | | | |
| | | | 59.9 | | | Operating Expenses | | 72.1 | 71.1 |
| | | | 40.1 | | | Operating Profit | | 27.9 | 28.9 |
| | | | 2.4 | | | All Other Expenses (net) | | 5.4 | 2.7 |
| | | | 37.7 | | | Profit Before Taxes | | 22.5 | 26.2 |
| | | | | | | RATIOS | | | |
| | | | 67.2 | | | | | 2.9 | 3.1 |
| | | | 1.8 | | | Current | | 1.7 | 1.0 |
| | | | .8 | | | | | .6 | .7 |
| | | | 67.1 | | | | | 2.7 | 1.8 |
| | | | 1.6 | | | Quick | | .9 | .8 |
| | | | .4 | | | | | .2 | .4 |
| | | | 0 UND | | | | | 0 UND | 0 UND |
| | | | 9 41.0 | | | Sales/Receivables | | 5 66.7 | 0 UND |
| | | | 45 8.2 | | | | | 47 7.7 | 25 14.6 |
| | | | | | | Cost of Sales/Inventory | | | |
| | | | | | | Cost of Sales/Payables | | | |
| | | | 1.9 | | | | | 2.6 | 3.0 |
| | | | 8.2 | | | Sales/Working Capital | | 8.9 | 129.5 |
| | | | -60.5 | | | | | -8.8 | -9.4 |
| | | | | | | | | 55.0 | 309.0 |
| | | | | | | EBIT/Interest | (23) | 17.8 | (11) 30.0 |
| | | | | | | | | 1.5 | 4.6 |
| | | | | | | Net Profit + Depr., Dep., Amort./Cur. Mat. L/T/D | | | |
| | | | .0 | | | | | .0 | .0 |
| | | | .0 | | | Fixed/Worth | | .1 | .4 |
| | | | -6.2 | | | | | 1.6 | 13.8 |
| | | | 1.6 | | | | | .3 | .5 |
| | | | NM | | | Debt/Worth | | 1.0 | 2.8 |
| | | | -1.6 | | | | | 4.5 | -3.9 |
| | | | | | | % Profit Before Taxes/Tangible Net Worth | (30) | 63.0 25.2 3.5 | (13) 74.0 38.8 8.5 |
| | | | 53.7 | | | | | 28.1 | 38.0 |
| | | | 7.6 | | | % Profit Before Taxes/Total Assets | | 8.2 | 17.8 |
| | | | .5 | | | | | .3 | 4.0 |
| | | | UND | | | | | UND | UND |
| | | | 356.9 | | | Sales/Net Fixed Assets | | 103.5 | 30.4 |
| | | | 39.5 | | | | | 5.2 | 4.8 |
| | | | 2.2 | | | | | 1.6 | 2.7 |
| | | | .5 | | | Sales/Total Assets | | .7 | .8 |
| | | | .1 | | | | | .3 | .5 |
| | | | | | | % Depr., Dep., Amort./Sales | (18) | .5 4.1 17.4 | |
| | | | | | | % Officers', Directors' Owners' Comp/Sales | | | |
| 750M | 12487M | 37546M | 316858M | 196161M | 185873M | Net Sales ($) | | 787196M | 353753M |
| 233M | 8490M | 48779M | 251062M | 206547M | 446405M | Total Assets ($) | | 802432M | 302732M |

© RMA 2024

M = $ thousand    MM = $ million
See Pages viii through xx for Explanation of Ratios and Data

# REAL ESTATE—Lessors of Nonfinancial Intangible Assets (except Copyrighted Works) NAICS 533110

| Comparative Historical Data ||| | Current Data Sorted by Sales |||||||
|---|---|---|---|---|---|---|---|---|---|
| | | | Type of Statement | | | | | | |
| 4 | 1 | 4 | Unqualified | | | | 2 | 2 | |
| | 1 | 2 | Reviewed | | 2 | | | | |
| 1 | | 6 | Compiled | | | | | | 1 |
| | 2 | | Tax Returns | 3 | 1 | 1 | 1 | 2 | 5 |
| 19 | 25 | 21 | Other | 7 | 4 | 2 | | | |
| 4/1/21-3/31/22 | 4/1/22-3/31/23 | 4/1/23-3/31/24 | | | 4 (4/1-9/30/23) || 29 (10/1/23-3/31/24) |||
| ALL | ALL | ALL | | 0-1MM | 1-3MM | 3-5MM | 5-10MM | 10-25MM | 25MM & OVER |
| 24 | 29 | 33 | NUMBER OF STATEMENTS | 10 | 7 | 3 | 1 | 4 | 8 |
| % | % | % | ASSETS | % | % | % | % | % | % |
| 13.4 | 16.0 | 24.6 | Cash & Equivalents | 23.2 | | | | | |
| 11.4 | 4.8 | 7.4 | Trade Receivables (net) | 6.0 | | | | | |
| 2.2 | .1 | 2.8 | Inventory | .4 | | | | | |
| 2.0 | 8.7 | 3.6 | All Other Current | 5.0 | | | | | |
| 29.1 | 29.5 | 38.4 | Total Current | 34.7 | | | | | |
| 28.4 | 34.9 | 30.3 | Fixed Assets (net) | 32.4 | | | | | |
| 23.7 | 19.5 | 13.6 | Intangibles (net) | 12.3 | | | | | |
| 18.8 | 16.0 | 17.7 | All Other Non-Current | 20.6 | | | | | |
| 100.0 | 100.0 | 100.0 | Total | 100.0 | | | | | |
| | | | LIABILITIES | | | | | | |
| 5.5 | 5.6 | 3.4 | Notes Payable-Short Term | .9 | | | | | |
| .6 | 1.7 | 1.8 | Cur. Mat.-L.T.D. | .3 | | | | | |
| 6.0 | 1.4 | 5.0 | Trade Payables | 1.5 | | | | | |
| .4 | .4 | .5 | Income Taxes Payable | .0 | | | | | |
| 6.1 | 15.9 | 13.7 | All Other Current | 14.5 | | | | | |
| 18.6 | 24.9 | 24.5 | Total Current | 17.2 | | | | | |
| 37.4 | 36.0 | 46.1 | Long-Term Debt | 51.0 | | | | | |
| .0 | .0 | .0 | Deferred Taxes | .0 | | | | | |
| 8.5 | 1.9 | 12.2 | All Other Non-Current | 21.1 | | | | | |
| 35.5 | 37.2 | 17.2 | Net Worth | 10.7 | | | | | |
| 100.0 | 100.0 | 100.0 | Total Liabilties & Net Worth | 100.0 | | | | | |
| | | | INCOME DATA | | | | | | |
| 100.0 | 100.0 | 100.0 | Net Sales | 100.0 | | | | | |
| | | | Gross Profit | | | | | | |
| 73.0 | 56.8 | 67.3 | Operating Expenses | 41.7 | | | | | |
| 27.0 | 43.2 | 32.7 | Operating Profit | 58.3 | | | | | |
| 6.2 | 5.6 | 3.3 | All Other Expenses (net) | 8.0 | | | | | |
| 20.8 | 37.6 | 29.4 | Profit Before Taxes | 50.3 | | | | | |
| | | | RATIOS | | | | | | |
| 3.6 | 3.9 | 5.7 | | 254.8 | | | | | |
| 1.6 | 1.4 | 2.3 | Current | 4.9 | | | | | |
| .7 | .3 | .8 | | 2.0 | | | | | |
| 3.3 | 2.7 | 5.0 | | 254.8 | | | | | |
| 1.4 | .9 | 1.5 | Quick | 2.8 | | | | | |
| .2 | .1 | .5 | | .6 | | | | | |
| 0 UND | 0 UND | 0 UND | | 0 UND | | | | | |
| 26 13.8 | 0 UND | 4 87.6 | Sales/Receivables | 0 UND | | | | | |
| 83 4.4 | 38 9.6 | 31 11.9 | | 4 93.5 | | | | | |
| | | | Cost of Sales/Inventory | | | | | | |
| | | | Cost of Sales/Payables | | | | | | |
| 2.7 | 2.2 | 2.0 | | 1.5 | | | | | |
| 6.8 | 7.6 | 4.7 | Sales/Working Capital | 2.9 | | | | | |
| -12.1 | -5.5 | -35.5 | | NM | | | | | |
| 5.7 | 57.4 | 17.9 | | | | | | | |
| (13) 2.8 | (12) 5.6 | (20) 6.6 | EBIT/Interest | | | | | | |
| -28.9 | 4.0 | 1.9 | | | | | | | |
| | | | Net Profit + Depr., Dep., Amort./Cur. Mat. L/T/D | | | | | | |
| .0 | .0 | .0 | | .0 | | | | | |
| .1 | .7 | .8 | Fixed/Worth | .0 | | | | | |
| 3.4 | 4.7 | 3.4 | | 2.5 | | | | | |
| .5 | .5 | .7 | | 1.1 | | | | | |
| 1.6 | 2.0 | 2.0 | Debt/Worth | 1.7 | | | | | |
| 16.1 | 16.5 | -11.1 | | NM | | | | | |
| 66.7 | 111.2 | 63.6 | % Profit Before Taxes/Tangible Net Worth | | | | | | |
| (19) 30.0 | (23) 42.5 | (22) 32.9 | | | | | | | |
| 6.2 | 14.2 | 10.8 | | | | | | | |
| 18.2 | 35.8 | 23.7 | % Profit Before Taxes/Total Assets | 23.8 | | | | | |
| 4.5 | 11.3 | 12.7 | | 7.5 | | | | | |
| -.5 | 4.6 | .7 | | 1.9 | | | | | |
| 553.2 | 424.2 | UND | | UND | | | | | |
| 25.8 | 13.2 | 26.2 | Sales/Net Fixed Assets | UND | | | | | |
| .6 | .5 | .7 | | .3 | | | | | |
| 1.1 | 1.2 | 2.0 | | .8 | | | | | |
| .3 | .5 | .6 | Sales/Total Assets | .2 | | | | | |
| .2 | .2 | .2 | | .1 | | | | | |
| .2 | 1.0 | .4 | | | | | | | |
| (15) 1.4 | (16) 8.6 | (12) 1.1 | % Depr., Dep., Amort./Sales | | | | | | |
| 13.3 | 20.5 | 17.0 | | | | | | | |
| | | | % Officers', Directors' Owners' Comp/Sales | | | | | | |
| 337544M | 260466M | 749675M | Net Sales ($) | 6300M | 16357M | 12247M | 5314M | 72149M | 637308M |
| 962762M | 523769M | 961516M | Total Assets ($) | 63411M | 45454M | 20230M | 9349M | 374293M | 448779M |

© RMA 2024
M = $ thousand   MM = $ million
See Pages viii through xx for Explanation of Ratios and Data

# PROFESSIONAL, SCIENTIFIC, AND TECHNICAL SERVICES

# PROFESSIONAL SERVICES—Offices of Lawyers  NAICS 541110

## Current Data Sorted by Assets / Comparative Historical Data

| | | | | | | Type of Statement | | |
|---|---|---|---|---|---|---|---|---|
| 2 | 2 | 8 | 19 | 17 | 11 | Unqualified | 56 | 37 |
| 1 | 12 | 28 | 34 | 7 | 6 | Reviewed | 94 | 46 |
| 8 | 17 | 44 | 22 | 3 | | Compiled | 91 | 59 |
| 81 | 108 | 78 | 19 | 1 | | Tax Returns | 414 | 256 |
| 143 | 210 | 298 | 150 | 40 | 35 | Other | 895 | 705 |
| | 126 (4/1-9/30/23) | | 1,278 (10/1/23-3/31/24) | | | | 4/1/19-3/31/20 | 4/1/20-3/31/21 |
| 0-500M | 500M-2MM | 2-10MM | 10-50MM | 50-100MM | 100-250MM | | ALL | ALL |
| 235 | 349 | 456 | 244 | 68 | 52 | NUMBER OF STATEMENTS | 1550 | 1103 |
| % | % | % | % | % | % | ASSETS | % | % |
| 55.1 | 44.6 | 37.9 | 33.9 | 35.3 | 43.4 | Cash & Equivalents | 38.0 | 47.9 |
| 5.3 | 7.9 | 12.9 | 14.9 | 16.4 | 14.4 | Trade Receivables (net) | 12.4 | 9.9 |
| .2 | .2 | 1.0 | .8 | .1 | .8 | Inventory | .8 | .9 |
| 11.3 | 15.2 | 17.2 | 16.1 | 15.3 | 13.8 | All Other Current | 15.3 | 12.2 |
| 71.9 | 67.9 | 69.1 | 65.7 | 67.1 | 72.5 | Total Current | 66.5 | 70.9 |
| 10.9 | 13.9 | 11.6 | 11.7 | 17.4 | 15.7 | Fixed Assets (net) | 16.0 | 13.0 |
| 4.8 | 3.7 | 3.6 | 1.5 | 1.7 | 2.2 | Intangibles (net) | 2.7 | 3.7 |
| 12.4 | 14.5 | 15.7 | 21.1 | 13.8 | 9.6 | All Other Non-Current | 14.7 | 12.4 |
| 100.0 | 100.0 | 100.0 | 100.0 | 100.0 | 100.0 | Total | 100.0 | 100.0 |
| | | | | | | LIABILITIES | | |
| 38.6 | 15.4 | 10.9 | 8.4 | 7.1 | 4.8 | Notes Payable-Short Term | 18.7 | 18.4 |
| 2.8 | 2.4 | 1.8 | 2.0 | 2.5 | .9 | Cur. Mat.-L.T.D. | 3.0 | 3.4 |
| 1.6 | 2.6 | 2.8 | 2.9 | 2.9 | 1.1 | Trade Payables | 2.6 | 2.6 |
| .4 | .2 | .1 | .2 | .0 | .1 | Income Taxes Payable | .3 | .1 |
| 37.6 | 34.5 | 30.2 | 27.8 | 26.9 | 25.7 | All Other Current | 33.6 | 32.7 |
| 81.0 | 55.1 | 45.8 | 41.3 | 39.4 | 32.5 | Total Current | 58.0 | 57.1 |
| 18.5 | 14.7 | 9.6 | 8.0 | 6.3 | 3.8 | Long-Term Debt | 10.2 | 18.3 |
| .0 | .1 | .1 | .5 | .0 | .3 | Deferred Taxes | .1 | .1 |
| 7.2 | 6.3 | 8.0 | 8.0 | 9.0 | 2.9 | All Other Non-Current | 6.6 | 7.0 |
| -6.6 | 23.8 | 36.5 | 42.3 | 45.3 | 60.6 | Net Worth | 25.0 | 17.4 |
| 100.0 | 100.0 | 100.0 | 100.0 | 100.0 | 100.0 | Total Liabilities & Net Worth | 100.0 | 100.0 |
| | | | | | | INCOME DATA | | |
| 100.0 | 100.0 | 100.0 | 100.0 | 100.0 | 100.0 | Net Sales | 100.0 | 100.0 |
| 80.0 | 78.4 | 77.2 | 75.8 | 68.4 | 68.1 | Gross Profit / Operating Expenses | 78.7 | 78.6 |
| 20.0 | 21.6 | 22.8 | 24.2 | 31.6 | 31.9 | Operating Profit | 21.3 | 21.4 |
| .8 | 1.7 | 1.4 | 1.7 | 1.5 | .7 | All Other Expenses (net) | 1.3 | -.2 |
| 19.3 | 19.9 | 21.5 | 22.6 | 30.1 | 31.2 | Profit Before Taxes | 20.0 | 21.6 |
| | | | | | | RATIOS | | |
| 2.6 | 3.4 | 3.7 | 3.9 | 4.6 | 7.6 | | 3.4 | 3.9 |
| 1.2 | 1.3 | 1.6 | 1.8 | 1.7 | 2.8 | Current | 1.4 | 1.5 |
| .6 | .8 | 1.0 | 1.1 | 1.1 | 1.2 | | .8 | .9 |
| 2.5 | 2.6 | 2.9 | 3.0 | 4.5 | 6.6 | | 2.6 | 3.2 |
| 1.0 | 1.0 | 1.1 | 1.3 | 1.6 | 2.1 | Quick | 1.1 | 1.2 |
| .4 | .4 | .5 | .6 | .9 | .8 | | .4 | .6 |
| 0 UND | 0 UND | 0 UND | 0 UND | 0 UND | 0 UND | | 0 UND | 0 UND |
| 0 UND | 0 UND | 0 UND | 3 143.5 | 5 77.6 | 3 110.5 | Sales/Receivables | 0 UND | 0 UND |
| 0 UND | 0 UND | 13 28.0 | 38 9.7 | 33 11.0 | 52 7.0 | | 9 41.2 | 5 73.7 |
| | | | | | | Cost of Sales/Inventory | | |
| | | | | | | Cost of Sales/Payables | | |
| 16.8 | 9.9 | 6.3 | 4.5 | 7.1 | 3.6 | | 8.2 | 6.1 |
| 109.3 | 36.5 | 15.1 | 12.6 | 14.5 | 5.4 | Sales/Working Capital | 32.6 | 18.4 |
| -32.6 | -44.9 | -333.2 | 65.6 | 69.7 | 17.9 | | -56.0 | -66.0 |
| 82.4 | 118.3 | 193.8 | 194.2 | 604.5 | 999.8 | | 170.3 | 206.3 |
| (141) 19.6 | (219) 20.5 | (343) 38.2 | (194) 38.5 | (57) 85.3 | (40) 142.1 | EBIT/Interest | (1136) 32.4 | (752) 41.2 |
| 2.6 | 2.7 | 4.2 | 4.1 | 18.4 | 10.8 | | 4.6 | 4.0 |
| | | | 24.1 | 27.1 | | | 19.8 | 15.3 |
| | | (27) 3.8 | (28) 7.3 | | | Net Profit + Depr., Dep., Amort./Cur. Mat. L/T/D | (85) 2.7 | (45) 2.3 |
| | | | 1.2 | .6 | | | 1.1 | .2 |
| .0 | .0 | .0 | .0 | .1 | .1 | | .0 | .0 |
| .2 | .1 | .1 | .2 | .3 | .2 | Fixed/Worth | .3 | .2 |
| 4.2 | 2.2 | .9 | .6 | .8 | .5 | | 1.8 | 3.2 |
| .6 | .7 | .5 | .4 | .2 | .1 | | .5 | .7 |
| 3.8 | 2.7 | 1.9 | 1.2 | 1.4 | .7 | Debt/Worth | 2.0 | 2.6 |
| -3.3 | UND | 14.3 | 5.0 | 8.0 | 1.9 | | 26.8 | -94.6 |
| 902.4 | 411.3 | 368.5 | 274.5 | 405.4 | 254.2 | | 376.5 | 368.1 |
| (154) 239.3 | (263) 119.1 | (388) 143.8 | (224) 107.9 | (62) 198.2 | 154.3 | % Profit Before Taxes/Tangible Net Worth | (1228) 136.6 | (820) 145.1 |
| 72.7 | 17.2 | 19.7 | 12.5 | 103.7 | 65.1 | | 30.1 | 35.7 |
| 327.6 | 140.4 | 131.0 | 120.2 | 180.9 | 166.7 | | 153.1 | 137.2 |
| 105.0 | 39.4 | 34.9 | 45.6 | 78.0 | 119.6 | % Profit Before Taxes/Total Assets | 47.1 | 44.7 |
| 12.5 | 3.1 | 4.6 | 3.7 | 16.2 | 10.8 | | 5.4 | 4.3 |
| UND | 999.8 | 505.5 | 204.6 | 85.9 | 48.0 | | 356.8 | 691.0 |
| 393.8 | 171.3 | 89.3 | 60.8 | 33.5 | 28.8 | Sales/Net Fixed Assets | 71.9 | 85.4 |
| 76.4 | 41.5 | 33.0 | 27.9 | 16.0 | 17.5 | | 23.0 | 25.8 |
| 20.0 | 8.8 | 5.9 | 5.3 | 5.1 | 4.6 | | 8.8 | 6.4 |
| 9.1 | 4.8 | 3.1 | 2.7 | 2.9 | 3.3 | Sales/Total Assets | 4.5 | 3.5 |
| 4.5 | 2.7 | 1.7 | 1.6 | 1.4 | 1.8 | | 2.4 | 2.0 |
| .1 | .1 | .2 | .2 | .2 | .5 | | .3 | .3 |
| (43) .4 | (133) .3 | (218) .5 | (159) .5 | (54) .8 | (42) .8 | % Depr., Dep., Amort./Sales | (793) .7 | (490) .7 |
| .9 | 1.0 | .9 | .9 | 1.4 | 1.0 | | 1.3 | 1.3 |
| 8.6 | 5.9 | 2.8 | 4.1 | 10.0 | 8.3 | | 7.2 | 7.7 |
| (116) 14.2 | (174) 15.2 | (193) 11.2 | (90) 14.0 | (24) 14.0 | (13) 34.5 | % Officers', Directors' Owners' Comp/Sales | (713) 17.7 | (504) 17.0 |
| 27.0 | 28.5 | 26.4 | 36.7 | 30.1 | 38.9 | | 32.4 | 31.4 |
| 760996M | 2640857M | 9271873M | 22189970M | 17004341M | 31675138M | Net Sales ($) | 93569652M | 47262272M |
| 58508M | 397154M | 2208057M | 5675979M | 4997907M | 7954047M | Total Assets ($) | 21408203M | 13359633M |

© RMA 2024

M = $ thousand    MM = $ million
See Pages viii through xx for Explanation of Ratios and Data

# PROFESSIONAL SERVICES—Offices of Lawyers  NAICS 541110

| Comparative Historical Data | | | Type of Statement | Current Data Sorted by Sales | | | | | |
|---|---|---|---|---|---|---|---|---|---|
| 32 | 56 | 59 | Unqualified | 1 | 2 | 1 | 2 | 7 | 46 |
| 66 | 89 | 88 | Reviewed |  | 2 | 1 | 4 | 16 | 65 |
| 61 | 78 | 94 | Compiled |  | 5 | 5 | 17 | 31 | 34 |
| 255 | 315 | 287 | Tax Returns | 37 | 61 | 35 | 58 | 67 | 29 |
| 650 | 891 | 876 | Other | 68 | 120 | 92 | 144 | 168 | 284 |
| 4/1/21-3/31/22 ALL | 4/1/22-3/31/23 ALL | 4/1/23-3/31/24 ALL |  | 126 (4/1-9/30/23) | | | 1,278 (10/1/23-3/31/24) | | |
|  |  |  |  | 0-1MM | 1-3MM | 3-5MM | 5-10MM | 10-25MM | 25MM & OVER |
| 1064 | 1429 | 1404 | NUMBER OF STATEMENTS | 108 | 190 | 134 | 225 | 289 | 458 |
| % | % | % | ASSETS | % | % | % | % | % | % |
| 44.3 | 42.2 | 41.8 | Cash & Equivalents | 38.4 | 44.9 | 49.2 | 43.5 | 39.5 | 39.8 |
| 11.2 | 10.5 | 11.0 | Trade Receivables (net) | 4.4 | 8.7 | 10.4 | 10.7 | 11.7 | 13.3 |
| .7 | .5 | .6 | Inventory | .2 | .1 | .7 | .7 | .7 | .6 |
| 16.9 | 16.6 | 15.3 | All Other Current | 7.0 | 15.9 | 13.4 | 18.5 | 17.2 | 14.8 |
| 73.1 | 69.9 | 68.7 | Total Current | 50.0 | 69.6 | 73.7 | 73.5 | 69.1 | 68.6 |
| 12.3 | 12.7 | 12.5 | Fixed Assets (net) | 34.6 | 9.8 | 8.2 | 7.6 | 8.7 | 14.6 |
| 2.7 | 3.1 | 3.3 | Intangibles (net) | 4.3 | 4.9 | 4.1 | 4.4 | 2.4 | 2.2 |
| 11.9 | 14.2 | 15.5 | All Other Non-Current | 11.0 | 15.7 | 13.9 | 14.5 | 19.7 | 14.6 |
| 100.0 | 100.0 | 100.0 | Total | 100.0 | 100.0 | 100.0 | 100.0 | 100.0 | 100.0 |
|  |  |  | LIABILITIES |  |  |  |  |  |  |
| 14.4 | 14.3 | 15.8 | Notes Payable-Short Term | 21.0 | 21.5 | 22.8 | 21.1 | 15.2 | 8.0 |
| 2.5 | 3.2 | 2.1 | Cur. Mat.-L.T.D. | 1.4 | 1.7 | 4.1 | 2.2 | 1.8 | 2.1 |
| 1.8 | 2.4 | 2.5 | Trade Payables | .5 | 3.1 | 2.5 | 3.1 | 2.6 | 2.4 |
| .2 | .2 | .2 | Income Taxes Payable | .0 | .0 | .6 | .3 | .0 | .1 |
| 32.2 | 31.6 | 31.8 | All Other Current | 28.3 | 30.7 | 32.8 | 36.9 | 33.1 | 29.3 |
| 51.0 | 51.8 | 52.4 | Total Current | 51.3 | 57.0 | 62.9 | 63.7 | 52.7 | 42.0 |
| 13.0 | 12.7 | 11.7 | Long-Term Debt | 29.7 | 16.7 | 10.7 | 8.9 | 11.2 | 7.3 |
| .2 | .2 | .2 | Deferred Taxes | .0 | .0 | .0 | .1 | .3 | .2 |
| 6.6 | 7.2 | 7.3 | All Other Non-Current | 4.5 | 6.1 | 9.2 | 7.3 | 11.2 | 5.4 |
| 29.2 | 28.2 | 28.5 | Net Worth | 14.5 | 20.2 | 17.2 | 20.0 | 24.6 | 45.1 |
| 100.0 | 100.0 | 100.0 | Total Liabilities & Net Worth | 100.0 | 100.0 | 100.0 | 100.0 | 100.0 | 100.0 |
|  |  |  | INCOME DATA |  |  |  |  |  |  |
| 100.0 | 100.0 | 100.0 | Net Sales | 100.0 | 100.0 | 100.0 | 100.0 | 100.0 | 100.0 |
|  |  |  | Gross Profit |  |  |  |  |  |  |
| 77.2 | 77.1 | 76.9 | Operating Expenses | 64.8 | 79.2 | 80.1 | 81.8 | 79.5 | 73.9 |
| 22.8 | 22.9 | 23.1 | Operating Profit | 35.2 | 20.8 | 19.9 | 18.2 | 20.5 | 26.1 |
| -.2 | 1.1 | 1.4 | All Other Expenses (net) | 8.2 | .6 | .8 | .2 | .6 | 1.4 |
| 23.0 | 21.8 | 21.7 | Profit Before Taxes | 27.0 | 20.2 | 19.1 | 18.0 | 19.9 | 24.7 |
|  |  |  | RATIOS |  |  |  |  |  |  |
| 4.7 | 4.1 | 3.7 |  | 2.9 | 3.0 | 4.4 | 3.4 | 3.5 | 4.5 |
| 1.7 | 1.6 | 1.5 | Current | 1.1 | 1.2 | 1.4 | 1.3 | 1.5 | 1.9 |
| 1.0 | 1.0 | .9 |  | .5 | .8 | .9 | .9 | .9 | 1.1 |
| 3.6 | 3.2 | 3.0 |  | 2.5 | 2.3 | 2.7 | 2.4 | 2.9 | 3.5 |
| 1.3 (1428) | 1.2 | 1.1 | Quick | 1.0 | 1.0 | 1.2 | 1.1 | 1.1 | 1.4 |
| .6 | .5 | .5 |  | .4 | .4 | .6 | .3 | .5 | .7 |
| 0 UND | 0 UND | 0 UND |  | 0 UND | 0 UND | 0 UND | 0 UND | 0 UND | 0 UND |
| 0 UND | 0 UND | 0 UND | Sales/Receivables | 0 UND | 0 UND | 0 UND | 0 UND | 0 UND | 1 285.9 |
| 7 50.3 | 7 54.0 | 8 44.0 |  | 0 UND | 0 UND | 1 393.0 | 7 48.9 | 14 25.7 | 16 23.3 |
|  |  |  | Cost of Sales/Inventory |  |  |  |  |  |  |
|  |  |  | Cost of Sales/Payables |  |  |  |  |  |  |
| 5.4 | 6.0 | 7.3 |  | 6.6 | 8.0 | 8.4 | 7.3 | 7.9 | 6.4 |
| 16.6 | 18.6 | 21.1 | Sales/Working Capital | 59.9 | 43.6 | 24.7 | 28.8 | 19.3 | 15.1 |
| -938.0 | -207.6 | -138.8 |  | -6.6 | -39.2 | -39.4 | -91.8 | -149.9 | 131.8 |
|  |  |  |  | 50.0 | 56.4 | 116.9 | 125.7 | 224.4 | 404.6 |
| 272.1 | 220.3 | 166.7 |  | (53) 6.2 | (124) 11.9 | (95) 20.0 | (147) 30.0 | (212) 35.7 | (363) 70.4 |
| (709) 52.2 | (994) 47.3 | (994) 34.8 | EBIT/Interest | 1.1 | 2.2 | 5.3 | 4.1 | 3.4 | 9.5 |
| 7.6 | 5.6 | 4.1 |  |  |  |  |  |  |  |
| 37.2 | 29.0 | 27.3 | Net Profit + Depr., Dep., |  |  |  |  | 19.4 | 27.6 |
| (44) 13.7 | (65) 4.9 | (76) 4.9 | Amort./Cur. Mat. L/T/D |  |  |  | (17) 3.1 | (54) 8.4 |
| 1.7 | .8 | 1.1 |  |  |  |  |  | .8 | 1.3 |
| .0 | .0 | .0 |  | .0 | .0 | .0 | .0 | .0 | .1 |
| .1 | .2 | .2 | Fixed/Worth | 1.3 | .2 | .1 | .1 | .1 | .3 |
| 1.1 | 1.0 | 1.0 |  | 11.2 | 1.3 | .6 | 1.3 | .7 | .7 |
| .4 | .5 | .5 |  | 1.1 | .6 | .6 | .7 | .5 | .3 |
| 1.9 | 1.8 | 2.0 | Debt/Worth | 4.7 | 3.1 | 2.4 | 3.4 | 2.2 | 1.0 |
| 18.2 | 15.6 | 17.2 |  | UND | -28.6 | -38.6 | -215.2 | 20.5 | 4.4 |
| 336.0 | 345.0 | 391.5 | % Profit Before Taxes/Tangible | 570.6 | 508.6 | 326.9 | 386.2 | 419.7 | 371.3 |
| (847) 137.2 | (1163) 129.0 | (1143) 142.3 | Net Worth | (84) 96.5 | (139) 132.6 | (100) 142.7 | (167) 105.5 | (240) 130.7 | (413) 168.5 |
| 37.5 | 29.1 | 21.9 |  | 10.9 | 24.2 | 34.3 | 24.4 | 18.3 | 27.1 |
| 133.7 | 140.9 | 150.9 | % Profit Before Taxes/Total | 87.7 | 136.2 | 137.7 | 145.7 | 143.5 | 180.8 |
| 46.7 | 43.8 | 49.0 | Assets | 10.0 | 41.6 | 48.1 | 39.4 | 41.4 | 81.9 |
| 9.4 | 6.1 | 5.0 |  | .8 | 5.9 | 12.1 | 4.6 | 3.9 | 7.1 |
| 794.5 | 826.4 | 829.2 |  | UND | UND | UND | 999.8 | 875.6 | 181.5 |
| 94.7 | 95.6 | 100.3 | Sales/Net Fixed Assets | 30.6 | 153.1 | 189.7 | 236.6 | 114.0 | 52.5 |
| 28.7 | 27.2 | 32.5 |  | .2 | 32.9 | 61.6 | 60.7 | 46.1 | 25.3 |
| 6.7 | 7.6 | 7.7 |  | 4.0 | 7.8 | 7.8 | 9.1 | 8.3 | 7.4 |
| 3.5 | 3.6 | 4.0 | Sales/Total Assets | 1.6 | 3.6 | 3.8 | 4.2 | 4.5 | 4.3 |
| 1.9 | 1.9 | 2.1 |  | .2 | 1.7 | 2.2 | 2.1 | 2.3 | 2.6 |
| .2 | .2 | .2 |  | 2.9 | .1 | .2 | .1 | .1 | .3 |
| (480) .6 | (630) .5 | (649) .5 | % Depr., Dep., Amort./Sales | (34) 14.8 | (44) .4 | (33) .4 | (79) .3 | (142) .4 | (317) .6 |
| 1.1 | 1.0 | 1.0 |  | 26.4 | 1.2 | .9 | .6 | .7 | 1.0 |
| 6.7 | 5.2 | 5.2 |  | .0 | 8.2 | 5.4 | 4.6 | 2.8 | 4.7 |
| (468) 16.1 | (631) 14.1 | (610) 13.8 | % Officers', Directors', Owners' Comp/Sales | (28) 17.2 | (99) 15.6 | (64) 10.8 | (110) 17.1 | (137) 12.9 | (172) 14.0 |
| 31.1 | 30.0 | 29.7 |  | 27.9 | 24.1 | 23.1 | 35.3 | 27.5 | 34.8 |
| 57886216M | 69068438M | 83543175M | Net Sales ($) | 54926M | 375438M | 533673M | 1592960M | 4644084M | 76342094M |
| 14463520M | 19381973M | 21291652M | Total Assets ($) | 115992M | 185269M | 223640M | 577959M | 1543198M | 18645594M |

© RMA 2024    M = $ thousand    MM = $ million
See Pages viii through xx for Explanation of Ratios and Data

# PROFESSIONAL SERVICES—All Other Legal Services  NAICS 541199

## Current Data Sorted by Assets | Comparative Historical Data

| | | | | | | | Type of Statement | | |
|---|---|---|---|---|---|---|---|---|---|
| | 1 | | 1 | | 2 | | Unqualified | 4 | 1 |
| | 1 | | 1 | | | | Reviewed | 4 | 1 |
| | 1 | | | | | | Compiled | 3 | |
| | 1 | | | | | | Tax Returns | 12 | |
| 1 | 5 | 8 | 8 | | | | Other | 42 | 15 |
| | 5 (4/1-9/30/23) | | 26 (10/1/23-3/31/24) | | | | | 4/1/19-3/31/20 ALL | 4/1/20-3/31/21 ALL |
| 0-500M | 500M-2MM | 2-10MM | 10-50MM | 50-100MM | 100-250MM | | NUMBER OF STATEMENTS | 65 | 17 |
| 2 | 9 | 8 | 10 | | 2 | | | | |
| % | % | % | % | % | % | | ASSETS | % | % |
| | | | 26.3 | | | | Cash & Equivalents | 37.9 | 42.4 |
| | | | 29.0 | | | | Trade Receivables (net) | 19.5 | 21.8 |
| | | | .0 | D | | | Inventory | 1.7 | .3 |
| | | | 11.3 | A | | | All Other Current | 5.4 | 6.8 |
| | | | 66.6 | T | | | Total Current | 64.5 | 71.3 |
| | | | 8.2 | A | | | Fixed Assets (net) | 15.8 | 5.8 |
| | | | 9.9 | | | | Intangibles (net) | 8.5 | 12.5 |
| | | | 15.3 | N | | | All Other Non-Current | 11.2 | 10.4 |
| | | | 100.0 | O | | | Total | 100.0 | 100.0 |
| | | | | T | | | LIABILITIES | | |
| | | | 10.7 | | | | Notes Payable-Short Term | 10.6 | 20.2 |
| | | | .9 | A | | | Cur. Mat.-L.T.D. | 1.7 | 4.5 |
| | | | 5.7 | V | | | Trade Payables | 6.1 | 6.9 |
| | | | .0 | A | | | Income Taxes Payable | .1 | .6 |
| | | | 13.7 | I | | | All Other Current | 30.8 | 34.4 |
| | | | 30.9 | L | | | Total Current | 49.3 | 66.6 |
| | | | 4.8 | A | | | Long-Term Debt | 20.5 | 61.0 |
| | | | .0 | B | | | Deferred Taxes | .2 | .9 |
| | | | 4.3 | L | | | All Other Non-Current | .9 | .9 |
| | | | 60.1 | E | | | Net Worth | 29.1 | -29.4 |
| | | | 100.0 | | | | Total Liabilities & Net Worth | 100.0 | 100.0 |
| | | | | | | | INCOME DATA | | |
| | | | 100.0 | | | | Net Sales | 100.0 | 100.0 |
| | | | | | | | Gross Profit | | |
| | | | 83.7 | | | | Operating Expenses | 81.0 | 82.4 |
| | | | 16.3 | | | | Operating Profit | 19.0 | 17.6 |
| | | | 3.1 | | | | All Other Expenses (net) | 2.6 | 1.8 |
| | | | 13.2 | | | | Profit Before Taxes | 16.4 | 15.8 |
| | | | | | | | RATIOS | | |
| | | | 4.5 | | | | | 2.9 | 5.4 |
| | | | 2.4 | | | | Current | 1.5 | 1.1 |
| | | | 1.0 | | | | | .9 | .5 |
| | | | 3.7 | | | | | 2.8 | 4.7 |
| | | | 1.7 | | | | Quick | 1.3 | 1.1 |
| | | | .9 | | | | | .8 | .5 |
| | | | 0 UND | | | | | 0 UND | 0 UND |
| | | | 24 15.3 | | | | Sales/Receivables | 2 201.9 | 40 9.2 |
| | | | 73 5.0 | | | | | 64 5.7 | 94 3.9 |
| | | | | | | | Cost of Sales/Inventory | | |
| | | | | | | | Cost of Sales/Payables | | |
| | | | 3.6 | | | | | 5.7 | 2.7 |
| | | | 9.1 | | | | Sales/Working Capital | 23.6 | 55.9 |
| | | | NM | | | | | -179.2 | -34.7 |
| | | | | | | | | 88.7 | |
| | | | | | | | EBIT/Interest | (41) 13.4 | |
| | | | | | | | | 2.6 | |
| | | | | | | | Net Profit + Depr., Dep., Amort./Cur. Mat. L/T/D | | |
| | | | .0 | | | | | .1 | .0 |
| | | | .1 | | | | Fixed/Worth | .3 | 3.2 |
| | | | .2 | | | | | 2.9 | -.1 |
| | | | .3 | | | | | .7 | .6 |
| | | | .7 | | | | Debt/Worth | 2.1 | -40.9 |
| | | | 4.3 | | | | | 78.0 | -2.2 |
| | | | | | | | | 521.1 | |
| | | | | | | | % Profit Before Taxes/Tangible Net Worth | (52) 88.0 | |
| | | | | | | | | 16.6 | |
| | | | 78.4 | | | | | 94.8 | 122.7 |
| | | | 13.2 | | | | % Profit Before Taxes/Total Assets | 28.5 | 9.5 |
| | | | 3.6 | | | | | 4.9 | 1.3 |
| | | | 617.9 | | | | | 506.8 | 963.8 |
| | | | 56.2 | | | | Sales/Net Fixed Assets | 69.3 | 97.1 |
| | | | 19.0 | | | | | 23.4 | 44.4 |
| | | | 2.9 | | | | | 7.5 | 7.5 |
| | | | 2.4 | | | | Sales/Total Assets | 3.0 | 2.4 |
| | | | 1.0 | | | | | 1.8 | .7 |
| | | | | | | | | .3 | |
| | | | | | | | % Depr., Dep., Amort./Sales | (32) .9 | |
| | | | | | | | | 2.1 | |
| | | | | | | | | 5.5 | |
| | | | | | | | % Officers', Directors' Owners' Comp/Sales | (26) 11.6 | |
| | | | | | | | | 21.3 | |
| 5012M | 86470M | 64004M | 477656M | | 220299M | | Net Sales ($) | 1799833M | 292739M |
| 562M | 11643M | 40825M | 199789M | | 413619M | | Total Assets ($) | 870692M | 273358M |

© RMA 2024    M = $ thousand    MM = $ million
See Pages viii through xx for Explanation of Ratios and Data

# PROFESSIONAL SERVICES—All Other Legal Services  NAICS 541199

## Comparative Historical Data | Current Data Sorted by Sales

| Comparative Historical Data | | | | | Current Data Sorted by Sales | | | | | |
|---|---|---|---|---|---|---|---|---|---|---|
| | | | Type of Statement | | | | | | | |
| 1 | 3 | 4 | Unqualified | | | 1 | | | 3 | |
| 1 | 2 | 2 | Reviewed | | | | | 1 | 1 | |
| 2 | 3 | 1 | Compiled | | | | 1 | | | |
| 1 | 1 | 2 | Tax Returns | | 1 | 1 | | | | |
| 15 | 20 | 22 | Other | 1 | 4 | 2 | 5 | 4 | 6 | |
| 4/1/21-3/31/22 ALL | 4/1/22-3/31/23 ALL | 4/1/23-3/31/24 ALL | | 0-1MM | 5 (4/1-9/30/23) 1-3MM | 3-5MM | 26 (10/1/23-3/31/24) 5-10MM | 10-25MM | 25MM & OVER | |
| 20 | 29 | 31 | NUMBER OF STATEMENTS | 1 | 5 | 4 | 6 | 5 | 10 | |
| % | % | % | ASSETS | % | % | % | % | % | % | |
| 33.5 | 41.6 | 33.4 | Cash & Equivalents | | | | | | 25.8 | |
| 13.4 | 16.9 | 20.7 | Trade Receivables (net) | | | | | | 28.4 | |
| .0 | .0 | .6 | Inventory | | | | | | .0 | |
| 11.1 | 9.9 | 7.7 | All Other Current | | | | | | 6.9 | |
| 58.0 | 68.4 | 62.3 | Total Current | | | | | | 61.1 | |
| 10.9 | 7.8 | 15.2 | Fixed Assets (net) | | | | | | 12.6 | |
| 20.3 | 11.0 | 14.2 | Intangibles (net) | | | | | | 23.1 | |
| 10.8 | 12.9 | 8.3 | All Other Non-Current | | | | | | 3.2 | |
| 100.0 | 100.0 | 100.0 | Total | | | | | | 100.0 | |
| | | | **LIABILITIES** | | | | | | | |
| 23.7 | 18.5 | 14.0 | Notes Payable-Short Term | | | | | | 8.2 | |
| .8 | .7 | 4.4 | Cur. Mat.-L.T.D. | | | | | | 10.9 | |
| 3.2 | 4.9 | 3.5 | Trade Payables | | | | | | 5.1 | |
| .0 | .0 | .0 | Income Taxes Payable | | | | | | .0 | |
| 21.5 | 29.0 | 16.5 | All Other Current | | | | | | 14.5 | |
| 49.2 | 53.1 | 38.5 | Total Current | | | | | | 38.8 | |
| 28.9 | 18.3 | 13.8 | Long-Term Debt | | | | | | 11.8 | |
| .0 | .0 | .0 | Deferred Taxes | | | | | | .0 | |
| 3.2 | 7.8 | 2.4 | All Other Non-Current | | | | | | .5 | |
| 18.7 | 20.9 | 45.3 | Net Worth | | | | | | 48.9 | |
| 100.0 | 100.0 | 100.0 | Total Liabilties & Net Worth | | | | | | 100.0 | |
| | | | **INCOME DATA** | | | | | | | |
| 100.0 | 100.0 | 100.0 | Net Sales | | | | | | 100.0 | |
| | | | Gross Profit | | | | | | | |
| 95.5 | 84.1 | 82.2 | Operating Expenses | | | | | | 86.7 | |
| 4.5 | 15.9 | 17.8 | Operating Profit | | | | | | 13.3 | |
| -1.0 | 3.8 | 2.0 | All Other Expenses (net) | | | | | | 6.0 | |
| 5.5 | 12.1 | 15.8 | Profit Before Taxes | | | | | | 7.3 | |
| | | | **RATIOS** | | | | | | | |
| 3.1 | 7.9 | 3.2 | | | | | | | 3.5 | |
| 1.6 | 2.3 | 2.0 | Current | | | | | | 1.9 | |
| 1.2 | .7 | 1.0 | | | | | | | 1.0 | |
| 2.7 | 7.1 | 3.1 | | | | | | | 2.8 | |
| 1.5 | 1.7 | 1.6 | Quick | | | | | | 1.8 | |
| .8 | .5 | .8 | | | | | | | .9 | |
| 0 UND | 0 UND | 0 UND | | | | | | | 0 UND | |
| 3 132.4 | 7 54.0 | 3 128.4 | Sales/Receivables | | | | | | 24 15.3 | |
| 59 6.2 | 61 6.0 | 66 5.5 | | | | | | | 111 3.3 | |
| | | | Cost of Sales/Inventory | | | | | | | |
| | | | Cost of Sales/Payables | | | | | | | |
| 4.6 | 4.0 | 4.4 | | | | | | | 5.3 | |
| 14.5 | 15.5 | 21.9 | Sales/Working Capital | | | | | | 19.3 | |
| 62.0 | -20.9 | -63.9 | | | | | | | NM | |
| 12.0 | 90.1 | 105.1 | | | | | | | | |
| (14) 2.5 | (15) 20.1 | (23) 12.7 | EBIT/Interest | | | | | | | |
| -1.4 | .7 | 2.3 | | | | | | | | |
| | | | Net Profit + Depr., Dep., Amort./Cur. Mat. L/T/D | | | | | | | |
| .0 | .0 | .0 | | | | | | | .0 | |
| .8 | .0 | .1 | Fixed/Worth | | | | | | .2 | |
| -.4 | UND | 1.2 | | | | | | | NM | |
| .6 | .1 | .4 | | | | | | | .3 | |
| 10.4 | 2.6 | .8 | Debt/Worth | | | | | | 1.9 | |
| -5.8 | -3.4 | -7.7 | | | | | | | -2.4 | |
| 31.5 | 254.7 | 104.3 | % Profit Before Taxes/Tangible Net Worth | | | | | | 107.5 | |
| (11) 5.3 | (18) 33.7 | (22) 39.4 | | | | | | | | |
| -7.8 | -10.3 | 11.7 | | | | | | | | |
| 17.4 | 162.8 | 63.4 | % Profit Before Taxes/Total Assets | | | | | | 107.5 | |
| 4.0 | 14.4 | 18.6 | | | | | | | 13.0 | |
| -1.1 | -5.1 | 3.5 | | | | | | | -5.6 | |
| 340.1 | UND | 999.8 | | | | | | | 617.9 | |
| 46.4 | 77.7 | 71.7 | Sales/Net Fixed Assets | | | | | | 56.2 | |
| 14.3 | 24.7 | 18.9 | | | | | | | 15.2 | |
| 3.8 | 5.6 | 3.2 | | | | | | | 4.8 | |
| 2.1 | 2.3 | 2.2 | Sales/Total Assets | | | | | | 2.5 | |
| 1.0 | 1.0 | .9 | | | | | | | .8 | |
| | .6 | .3 | | | | | | | | |
| | (10) .8 | (11) .6 | % Depr., Dep., Amort./Sales | | | | | | | |
| | 1.4 | 1.1 | | | | | | | | |
| | | 7.0 | | | | | | | | |
| | (11) | 9.2 | % Officers', Directors' Owners' Comp/Sales | | | | | | | |
| | | 29.5 | | | | | | | | |
| 380964M | 1342833M | 853441M | Net Sales ($) | 263M | 11832M | 14631M | 46832M | 94288M | 685595M | |
| 463299M | 629047M | 666438M | Total Assets ($) | 583M | 9487M | 8059M | 30049M | 45318M | 572942M | |

© RMA 2024  
M = $ thousand    MM = $ million  
See Pages viii through xx for Explanation of Ratios and Data

# PROFESSIONAL SERVICES—Offices of Certified Public Accountants  NAICS 541211

## Current Data Sorted by Assets | Comparative Historical Data

| | | | | | | | Type of Statement | | | | |
|---|---|---|---|---|---|---|---|---|---|---|---|
| | | 1 | 8 | 6 | | | Unqualified | | 6 | | 4 |
| 30 | 32 | 11 | 2 | | | | Reviewed | | 4 | | 1 |
| 49 | 69 | 113 | 46 | 4 | 13 | | Compiled | | 22 | | 14 |
| | 67 (4/1-9/30/23) | | 317 (10/1/23-3/31/24) | | | | Tax Returns | | 123 | | 59 |
| | | | | | | | Other | | 365 | | 253 |
| 0-500M | 500M-2MM | 2-10MM | 10-50MM | 50-100MM | 100-250MM | | | | 4/1/19-3/31/20 | | 4/1/20-3/31/21 |
| 79 | 102 | 132 | 54 | 4 | 13 | NUMBER OF STATEMENTS | | ALL 520 | | ALL 331 |
| % | % | % | % | % | % | ASSETS | | % | | % |
| 46.0 | 24.2 | 20.5 | 19.0 | | 11.3 | Cash & Equivalents | | 23.3 | | 31.4 |
| 11.9 | 16.1 | 30.4 | 35.3 | | 38.9 | Trade Receivables (net) | | 25.5 | | 22.1 |
| .9 | .8 | 5.0 | 2.9 | | 5.1 | Inventory | | 3.1 | | 2.1 |
| 2.7 | 5.6 | 6.9 | 8.3 | | 10.5 | All Other Current | | 5.4 | | 5.1 |
| 61.5 | 46.7 | 62.8 | 65.6 | | 65.8 | Total Current | | 57.3 | | 60.6 |
| 13.7 | 11.3 | 10.9 | 7.9 | | 8.7 | Fixed Assets (net) | | 15.0 | | 11.5 |
| 12.0 | 28.2 | 16.1 | 16.8 | | 15.2 | Intangibles (net) | | 19.1 | | 19.1 |
| 12.8 | 13.8 | 10.2 | 9.7 | | 10.2 | All Other Non-Current | | 8.6 | | 8.8 |
| 100.0 | 100.0 | 100.0 | 100.0 | | 100.0 | Total | | 100.0 | | 100.0 |
| | | | | | | LIABILITIES | | | | |
| 23.7 | 9.4 | 6.0 | 5.0 | | 4.5 | Notes Payable-Short Term | | 17.9 | | 13.7 |
| 1.7 | 2.0 | 2.3 | 3.4 | | 3.3 | Cur. Mat.-L.T.D. | | 2.7 | | 3.1 |
| 1.1 | .6 | 2.0 | 3.0 | | 2.9 | Trade Payables | | 2.4 | | 1.6 |
| .2 | .0 | .2 | .0 | | 1.3 | Income Taxes Payable | | .1 | | .1 |
| 23.9 | 11.8 | 13.2 | 24.7 | | 26.3 | All Other Current | | 18.2 | | 14.8 |
| 50.6 | 23.8 | 23.7 | 36.0 | | 38.4 | Total Current | | 41.3 | | 33.2 |
| 23.7 | 36.3 | 15.4 | 13.0 | | 13.8 | Long-Term Debt | | 19.8 | | 22.8 |
| .0 | .0 | .4 | .0 | | .2 | Deferred Taxes | | .1 | | .1 |
| 3.4 | 5.3 | 8.8 | 8.6 | | 8.8 | All Other Non-Current | | 7.4 | | 8.5 |
| 22.4 | 34.6 | 51.7 | 42.3 | | 38.9 | Net Worth | | 31.5 | | 35.4 |
| 100.0 | 100.0 | 100.0 | 100.0 | | 100.0 | Total Liabilities & Net Worth | | 100.0 | | 100.0 |
| | | | | | | INCOME DATA | | | | |
| 100.0 | 100.0 | 100.0 | 100.0 | | 100.0 | Net Sales | | 100.0 | | 100.0 |
| | | | | | | Gross Profit | | | | |
| 79.1 | 81.9 | 79.5 | 85.7 | | 81.9 | Operating Expenses | | 82.1 | | 81.4 |
| 20.9 | 18.1 | 20.5 | 14.3 | | 18.1 | Operating Profit | | 17.9 | | 18.6 |
| .3 | 2.2 | 2.7 | 1.7 | | 2.2 | All Other Expenses (net) | | 2.2 | | -.1 |
| 20.6 | 15.9 | 17.8 | 12.6 | | 15.9 | Profit Before Taxes | | 15.7 | | 18.7 |
| | | | | | | RATIOS | | | | |
| 4.7 | 5.8 | 6.2 | 3.0 | | 3.0 | | | 4.2 | | 5.2 |
| 1.8 | 2.8 | 3.3 | 1.9 | | 1.7 | Current | | 1.9 | | 2.1 |
| .8 | .9 | 1.5 | 1.1 | | 1.2 | | | .8 | | 1.1 |
| 4.5 | 5.3 | 5.1 | 2.8 | | 2.0 | | | 3.5 | | 4.4 |
| 1.6 | 2.4 | 2.5 | 1.3 | | 1.5 | Quick | | 1.5 | | 1.9 |
| .8 | .7 | 1.2 | 1.0 | | .8 | | | .7 | | .9 |
| 0 UND | 0 UND | 25 14.6 | 37 9.8 | | 51 7.2 | | 0 | UND | 0 | UND |
| 0 UND | 0 UND | 45 8.2 | 47 7.7 | | 60 6.1 | Sales/Receivables | 32 | 11.4 | 31 | 11.6 |
| 12 31.5 | 38 9.5 | 66 5.5 | 69 5.3 | | 74 4.9 | | 57 | 6.4 | 62 | 5.9 |
| | | | | | | Cost of Sales/Inventory | | | | |
| | | | | | | Cost of Sales/Payables | | | | |
| 9.1 | 5.7 | 3.8 | 5.9 | | 4.6 | | | 5.5 | | 4.5 |
| 42.1 | 13.4 | 5.7 | 10.2 | | 7.3 | Sales/Working Capital | | 13.9 | | 9.3 |
| -124.8 | -87.2 | 16.7 | 35.3 | | 38.3 | | | -78.8 | | 67.7 |
| 92.5 | 43.2 | 72.5 | 64.1 | | 181.8 | | | 62.7 | | 63.6 |
| (54) 26.1 | (85) 7.7 | (102) 14.3 | (42) 17.2 | | (12) 31.0 | EBIT/Interest | (405) | 15.8 | (255) | 24.3 |
| 4.8 | 2.7 | 6.9 | 2.3 | | 2.4 | | | 3.8 | | 5.4 |
| | | 33.2 | | | | | | 6.0 | | 19.6 |
| | (11) | 3.3 | | | | Net Profit + Depr., Dep., Amort./Cur. Mat. L/T/D | (22) | 2.5 | (11) | 1.4 |
| | | 1.4 | | | | | | 1.2 | | .3 |
| .0 | .0 | .0 | .1 | | .2 | | | .0 | | .0 |
| .1 | .0 | .1 | .2 | | .4 | Fixed/Worth | | .3 | | .2 |
| 1.6 | -55.1 | .7 | -2.8 | | 1.7 | | | -23.0 | | 4.0 |
| .2 | .5 | .4 | .7 | | 1.1 | | | .5 | | .7 |
| 1.5 | 6.0 | .9 | 1.9 | | 4.6 | Debt/Worth | | 2.4 | | 2.4 |
| -5.0 | -2.6 | 7.5 | -33.5 | | 7.1 | | | -6.2 | | -9.1 |
| 930.6 | 215.6 | 120.8 | 182.9 | | 312.1 | | | 224.0 | | 274.4 |
| (55) 201.1 | (59) 65.0 | (106) 74.7 | (39) 83.1 | | (12) 110.7 | % Profit Before Taxes/Tangible Net Worth | (353) | 88.0 | (235) | 108.1 |
| 55.6 | 29.6 | 20.8 | 15.0 | | 33.2 | | | 31.0 | | 40.9 |
| 226.4 | 52.8 | 60.9 | 53.7 | | 61.9 | | | 75.3 | | 73.8 |
| 86.1 | 23.2 | 28.8 | 29.3 | | 45.9 | % Profit Before Taxes/Total Assets | | 31.6 | | 39.5 |
| 28.6 | 6.3 | 8.8 | 3.7 | | 1.7 | | | 7.0 | | 9.6 |
| UND | UND | 553.2 | 75.1 | | 52.3 | | | 275.4 | | 556.6 |
| 250.0 | 254.9 | 64.2 | 44.3 | | 40.4 | Sales/Net Fixed Assets | | 53.6 | | 48.5 |
| 41.3 | 23.6 | 21.3 | 24.4 | | 22.0 | | | 20.5 | | 22.0 |
| 11.6 | 4.3 | 3.1 | 3.3 | | 2.6 | | | 5.4 | | 3.8 |
| 6.8 | 2.4 | 2.3 | 2.5 | | 2.3 | Sales/Total Assets | | 2.9 | | 2.4 |
| 3.2 | 1.3 | 1.7 | 2.1 | | 2.0 | | | 1.9 | | 1.7 |
| .2 | .5 | .5 | .8 | | .8 | | | .7 | | .7 |
| (19) .6 | (29) 1.1 | (68) 1.0 | (35) 1.3 | | (11) 1.2 | % Depr., Dep., Amort./Sales | (256) | 1.4 | (152) | 1.4 |
| 1.6 | 2.5 | 1.7 | 2.0 | | 1.5 | | | 2.2 | | 2.3 |
| 7.4 | 7.5 | 5.7 | 9.6 | | | | | 10.3 | | 9.3 |
| (41) 17.0 | (64) 11.3 | (51) 14.9 | (27) 15.5 | | | % Officers', Directors' Owners' Comp/Sales | (289) | 17.2 | (159) | 18.4 |
| 21.9 | 20.3 | 27.4 | 23.6 | | | | | 25.2 | | 26.1 |
| 170987M | 347300M | 1599626M | 3475891M | 631453M | 4952691M | Net Sales ($) | | 12717205M | | 7756160M |
| 18510M | 115627M | 621868M | 1178034M | 305624M | 2126154M | Total Assets ($) | | 4921466M | | 3492811M |

M = $ thousand    MM = $ million
See Pages viii through xx for Explanation of Ratios and Data

© RMA 2024

## PROFESSIONAL SERVICES—Offices of Certified Public Accountants  NAICS 541211

### Comparative Historical Data / Current Data Sorted by Sales

| Comparative Historical Data | | | Type of Statement | Current Data Sorted by Sales | | | | | |
|---|---|---|---|---|---|---|---|---|---|
| 1 | 4 | | Unqualified | | | | | | |
| 1 | 2 | | Reviewed | | | | | 2 | |
| 10 | 20 | 15 | Compiled | | | 2 | 3 | 4 | 6 |
| 66 | 80 | 75 | Tax Returns | 17 | 21 | 14 | 14 | 7 | 2 |
| 253 | 319 | 294 | Other | 41 | 58 | 26 | 52 | 49 | 68 |
| 4/1/21- | 4/1/22- | 4/1/23- | | | 67 (4/1-9/30/23) | | 317 (10/1/23-3/31/24) | | |
| 3/31/22 | 3/31/23 | 3/31/24 | | 0-1MM | 1-3MM | 3-5MM | 5-10MM | 10-25MM | 25MM & OVER |
| ALL | ALL | ALL | NUMBER OF STATEMENTS | | | | | | |
| 331 | 425 | 384 | | 58 | 79 | 42 | 69 | 60 | 76 |
| % | % | % | ASSETS | % | % | % | % | % | % |
| 29.2 | 25.8 | 26.2 | Cash & Equivalents | 34.6 | 27.8 | 33.5 | 24.1 | 24.1 | 17.7 |
| 24.3 | 24.0 | 23.7 | Trade Receivables (net) | 6.8 | 16.6 | 18.5 | 25.7 | 35.8 | 35.6 |
| 3.2 | 2.2 | 2.7 | Inventory | 1.2 | .6 | 1.7 | 4.2 | 4.0 | 4.2 |
| 5.3 | 6.2 | 6.0 | All Other Current | 3.2 | 4.1 | 2.5 | 7.9 | 8.1 | 8.7 |
| 62.0 | 58.1 | 58.7 | Total Current | 45.8 | 49.2 | 56.1 | 61.9 | 72.1 | 66.2 |
| 11.4 | 11.7 | 11.1 | Fixed Assets (net) | 23.9 | 11.7 | 7.8 | 7.8 | 7.3 | 8.3 |
| 17.5 | 19.4 | 18.5 | Intangibles (net) | 18.8 | 23.8 | 24.4 | 18.9 | 11.7 | 14.6 |
| 9.1 | 10.8 | 11.8 | All Other Non-Current | 11.5 | 15.3 | 11.7 | 11.4 | 8.9 | 10.9 |
| 100.0 | 100.0 | 100.0 | Total | 100.0 | 100.0 | 100.0 | 100.0 | 100.0 | 100.0 |
| | | | LIABILITIES | | | | | | |
| 9.5 | 9.3 | 10.3 | Notes Payable-Short Term | 17.2 | 11.4 | 13.0 | 10.2 | 5.5 | 6.4 |
| 2.4 | 2.7 | 2.3 | Cur. Mat.-L.T.D. | .7 | 2.1 | 2.5 | 2.8 | 2.2 | 3.1 |
| 1.7 | 2.0 | 1.7 | Trade Payables | .4 | .8 | 1.3 | .9 | 3.4 | 3.1 |
| .3 | .1 | .1 | Income Taxes Payable | .2 | .0 | .0 | .1 | .2 | .2 |
| 16.4 | 16.2 | 17.0 | All Other Current | 13.6 | 14.2 | 16.8 | 14.3 | 19.2 | 23.4 |
| 30.2 | 30.3 | 31.4 | Total Current | 32.1 | 28.5 | 33.6 | 28.3 | 30.6 | 36.2 |
| 21.1 | 25.9 | 22.1 | Long-Term Debt | 35.5 | 41.0 | 19.8 | 15.2 | 6.9 | 12.0 |
| .2 | .1 | .1 | Deferred Taxes | .0 | .0 | .0 | .2 | .6 | .0 |
| 5.5 | 7.1 | 6.8 | All Other Non-Current | 1.9 | 3.8 | 8.3 | 11.0 | 8.4 | 7.8 |
| 43.0 | 36.6 | 39.5 | Net Worth | 30.6 | 26.7 | 38.3 | 45.2 | 53.5 | 44.0 |
| 100.0 | 100.0 | 100.0 | Total Liabilties & Net Worth | 100.0 | 100.0 | 100.0 | 100.0 | 100.0 | 100.0 |
| | | | INCOME DATA | | | | | | |
| 100.0 | 100.0 | 100.0 | Net Sales | 100.0 | 100.0 | 100.0 | 100.0 | 100.0 | 100.0 |
| | | | Gross Profit | | | | | | |
| 80.6 | 79.2 | 80.9 | Operating Expenses | 70.2 | 81.4 | 84.0 | 82.4 | 82.6 | 84.1 |
| 19.4 | 20.8 | 19.1 | Operating Profit | 29.8 | 18.6 | 16.0 | 17.6 | 17.4 | 15.9 |
| -.6 | 2.9 | 1.9 | All Other Expenses (net) | 4.7 | 1.2 | .8 | 1.6 | 1.1 | 2.0 |
| 20.0 | 17.9 | 17.2 | Profit Before Taxes | 25.1 | 17.3 | 15.2 | 16.0 | 16.3 | 13.9 |
| | | | RATIOS | | | | | | |
| 7.4 | 7.1 | 5.2 | | 5.4 | 7.6 | 5.1 | 5.8 | 6.0 | 3.1 |
| 2.8 | 2.8 | 2.5 | Current | 1.9 | 2.9 | 2.9 | 2.8 | 3.0 | 1.9 |
| 1.3 | 1.2 | 1.1 | | .8 | 1.0 | 1.0 | 1.1 | 1.9 | 1.2 |
| 6.2 | 5.8 | 4.4 | | 4.8 | 6.3 | 4.4 | 5.0 | 4.4 | 2.7 |
| 2.3 | 2.2 | 1.9 | Quick | 1.7 | 2.5 | 2.5 | 2.1 | 2.5 | 1.5 |
| 1.0 | 1.0 | .9 | | .8 | .9 | .8 | .8 | 1.3 | 1.0 |
| 0 UND | 0 UND | 0 UND | | 0 UND | 0 UND | 0 UND | 0 UND | 26 13.8 | 37 9.8 |
| 35 10.4 | 34 10.6 | 32 11.3 | Sales/Receivables | 0 UND | 1 394.4 | 0 UND | 36 10.0 | 47 7.8 | 48 7.6 |
| 58 6.3 | 62 5.9 | 55 6.6 | | 12 29.5 | 43 8.5 | 39 9.3 | 58 6.3 | 69 5.3 | 65 5.6 |
| | | | Cost of Sales/Inventory | | | | | | |
| | | | Cost of Sales/Payables | | | | | | |
| 4.1 | 4.4 | 5.0 | | 6.4 | 4.8 | 5.7 | 4.3 | 4.1 | 6.3 |
| 6.8 | 7.7 | 10.2 | Sales/Working Capital | 13.9 | 15.5 | 17.4 | 8.0 | 5.7 | 9.4 |
| 43.8 | 80.1 | 72.7 | | -112.0 | 903.7 | NM | 84.6 | 16.5 | 30.0 |
| 119.3 | 88.5 | 70.0 | | 29.0 | 40.7 | 52.9 | 128.0 | 127.6 | 64.1 |
| (259) 35.8 | (305) 23.0 | (299) 14.8 | EBIT/Interest | (39) 7.4 | (65) 10.3 | (33) 14.4 | (58) 22.8 | (42) 21.7 | (62) 17.4 |
| 10.0 | 5.0 | 4.0 | | 2.8 | 4.2 | 1.0 | 6.9 | 7.6 | 3.6 |
| | 5.7 | 9.4 | Net Profit + Depr., Dep., | | | | | | 6.8 |
| (21) 3.2 | (22) 3.5 | | Amort./Cur. Mat. L/T/D | | | | | (10) 3.6 | |
| | 1.4 | 1.7 | | | | | | | 2.1 |
| .0 | .0 | .0 | | .0 | .0 | .0 | .0 | .0 | .1 |
| .2 | .1 | .1 | Fixed/Worth | .1 | .1 | .1 | .0 | .1 | .2 |
| 1.2 | 3.2 | 1.9 | | 16.0 | -.9 | .8 | 1.5 | .3 | 1.1 |
| .4 | .4 | .4 | | .3 | .6 | .3 | .5 | .3 | .7 |
| 1.2 | 1.7 | 1.8 | Debt/Worth | 2.9 | 6.5 | 1.8 | 1.3 | .7 | 1.7 |
| 29.8 | -12.2 | -10.8 | | -4.3 | -3.4 | -2.1 | -10.5 | 3.2 | 5.9 |
| 218.1 | 160.5 | 202.2 | % Profit Before Taxes/Tangible | 341.3 | 459.8 | 183.0 | 157.8 | 122.7 | 182.9 |
| (262) 96.2 | (301) 78.8 | (275) 86.6 | Net Worth | (40) 97.4 | (48) 95.5 | (27) 83.2 | (49) 89.1 | (48) 78.1 | (63) 87.2 |
| 39.7 | 26.8 | 26.0 | | 28.2 | 31.0 | 26.1 | 34.7 | 19.9 | 19.3 |
| 74.3 | 68.5 | 70.7 | % Profit Before Taxes/Total | 89.8 | 70.1 | 80.0 | 73.1 | 80.7 | 57.9 |
| 43.9 | 33.1 | 33.7 | Assets | 32.8 | 27.1 | 39.3 | 33.5 | 42.0 | 33.5 |
| 13.2 | 7.6 | 7.7 | | 8.3 | 10.0 | 3.0 | 10.2 | 8.7 | 4.8 |
| 661.0 | 981.5 | 999.8 | | UND | UND | UND | 999.8 | 328.2 | 65.6 |
| 58.8 | 71.1 | 72.5 | Sales/Net Fixed Assets | 46.6 | 143.7 | 242.5 | 266.4 | 67.7 | 41.4 |
| 24.9 | 23.9 | 24.6 | | 4.6 | 19.2 | 40.4 | 39.7 | 28.4 | 24.6 |
| 3.7 | 3.9 | 4.2 | | 4.9 | 3.9 | 7.2 | 4.2 | 4.3 | 3.4 |
| 2.5 | 2.4 | 2.7 | Sales/Total Assets | 2.1 | 2.0 | 4.4 | 2.7 | 2.8 | 2.7 |
| 1.7 | 1.6 | 1.8 | | .6 | 1.3 | 2.1 | 1.9 | 2.2 | 2.2 |
| .6 | .6 | .5 | | 1.6 | .7 | .3 | .2 | .3 | .8 |
| (162) 1.2 | (186) 1.1 | (165) 1.1 | % Depr., Dep., Amort./Sales | (17) 11.1 | (17) 1.2 | (14) .9 | (29) .8 | (35) .6 | (53) 1.3 |
| 1.8 | 2.0 | 1.8 | | 16.4 | 3.4 | | 1.6 | 1.0 | 1.7 |
| 10.4 | 9.3 | 7.2 | % Officers', Directors' | 9.8 | 5.6 | 7.1 | 7.0 | 4.7 | 9.1 |
| (168) 18.1 | (190) 16.3 | (188) 15.0 | Owners' Comp/Sales | (27) 17.8 | (49) 11.2 | (21) 13.2 | (36) 12.3 | (20) 18.7 | (35) 15.5 |
| 27.9 | 24.4 | 23.1 | | 23.7 | 19.8 | 21.3 | 24.1 | 29.2 | 23.8 |
| 10130667M | 12276907M | 11177948M | Net Sales ($) | 29089M | 150465M | 163711M | 523053M | 1003091M | 9308539M |
| 4131520M | 5347032M | 4365817M | Total Assets ($) | 43204M | 82915M | 52855M | 205143M | 355740M | 3625960M |

© RMA 2024  M = $ thousand   MM = $ million
See Pages viii through xx for Explanation of Ratios and Data

## PROFESSIONAL SERVICES—Tax Preparation Services  NAICS 541213

### Current Data Sorted by Assets | Comparative Historical Data

| 0-500M | 500M-2MM | 2-10MM | 10-50MM | 50-100MM | 100-250MM | | | 4/1/19-3/31/20 ALL | 4/1/20-3/31/21 ALL |
|---|---|---|---|---|---|---|---|---|---|
| | | | | | | **Type of Statement** | | | |
| 7 | 2 | | 1 | | | Unqualified | | 3 | 1 |
| 13 | 8 | | 2 | | | Reviewed | | | 1 |
| | 1 (4/1/9-9/30/23) | | 34 (10/1/23-3/31/24) | | | Compiled | | 6 | 4 |
| | | | | | | Tax Returns | | 17 | 19 |
| | | | | | | Other | | | |
| 20 | 10 | 1 | 3 | | 1 | **NUMBER OF STATEMENTS** | | 26 | 25 |
| % | % | % | % | % | % | **ASSETS** | | % | % |
| 39.9 | 44.8 | | | | | Cash & Equivalents | | 22.8 | 40.6 |
| 9.9 | 16.8 | | | | | Trade Receivables (net) | | 22.7 | 8.3 |
| .0 | .3 | | | | | Inventory | | 1.7 | .0 |
| 1.7 | .5 | | | | | All Other Current | | 11.0 | 4.0 |
| 51.5 | 62.4 | | DATA | | | Total Current | | 58.2 | 53.0 |
| 9.3 | 20.6 | | NOT | | | Fixed Assets (net) | | 13.1 | 11.9 |
| 26.4 | 5.8 | | AVAILABLE | | | Intangibles (net) | | 21.1 | 27.0 |
| 12.9 | 11.3 | | | | | All Other Non-Current | | 7.6 | 8.2 |
| 100.0 | 100.0 | | | | | Total | | 100.0 | 100.0 |
| | | | | | | **LIABILITIES** | | | |
| 12.5 | 5.7 | | | | | Notes Payable-Short Term | | 15.2 | 20.8 |
| .0 | 1.3 | | | | | Cur. Mat.-L.T.D. | | 2.8 | 2.3 |
| 1.2 | 4.6 | | | | | Trade Payables | | 11.1 | 4.4 |
| .8 | .0 | | | | | Income Taxes Payable | | .3 | .0 |
| 31.4 | 9.3 | | | | | All Other Current | | 11.9 | 13.3 |
| 45.8 | 20.9 | | | | | Total Current | | 41.3 | 40.8 |
| 40.9 | 12.9 | | | | | Long-Term Debt | | 17.2 | 31.0 |
| .0 | .0 | | | | | Deferred Taxes | | .0 | .0 |
| 13.0 | 12.0 | | | | | All Other Non-Current | | 4.4 | 5.1 |
| .4 | 54.1 | | | | | Net Worth | | 37.0 | 23.0 |
| 100.0 | 100.0 | | | | | Total Liabilties & Net Worth | | 100.0 | 100.0 |
| | | | | | | **INCOME DATA** | | | |
| 100.0 | 100.0 | | | | | Net Sales | | 100.0 | 100.0 |
| | | | | | | Gross Profit | | | |
| 78.6 | 57.8 | | | | | Operating Expenses | | 86.7 | 79.3 |
| 21.4 | 42.2 | | | | | Operating Profit | | 13.3 | 20.7 |
| 1.3 | 1.4 | | | | | All Other Expenses (net) | | 1.6 | .9 |
| 20.1 | 40.7 | | | | | Profit Before Taxes | | 11.8 | 19.8 |
| | | | | | | **RATIOS** | | | |
| 6.7 | 11.8 | | | | | | | 3.9 | 3.9 |
| 1.8 | 3.8 | | | | | Current | | 1.8 | 1.8 |
| .6 | 1.3 | | | | | | | .9 | .8 |
| 6.7 | 11.8 | | | | | | | 3.1 | 3.6 |
| 1.8 | 3.8 | | | | | Quick | | 1.2 | 1.5 |
| .2 | .7 | | | | | | | .4 | .6 |
| 0 UND | 0 UND | | | | | | | 0 UND | 0 UND |
| 0 UND | 1 534.9 | | | | | Sales/Receivables | | 20 18.7 | 0 UND |
| 5 68.3 | 33 11.2 | | | | | | | 85 4.3 | 21 17.4 |
| | | | | | | Cost of Sales/Inventory | | | |
| | | | | | | Cost of Sales/Payables | | | |
| 5.1 | 1.9 | | | | | | | 3.2 | 3.3 |
| 73.9 | 3.5 | | | | | Sales/Working Capital | | 12.3 | 11.0 |
| -101.4 | NM | | | | | | | -318.4 | -98.0 |
| 36.0 | | | | | | | | 11.3 | 46.3 |
| (11) 11.1 | | | | | | EBIT/Interest | (17) | 3.5 | (17) 22.1 |
| 6.1 | | | | | | | | .4 | 4.4 |
| | | | | | | Net Profit + Depr., Dep., Amort./Cur. Mat. L/T/D | | | |
| .0 | .0 | | | | | | | .0 | .0 |
| .1 | .4 | | | | | Fixed/Worth | | .2 | .6 |
| UND | NM | | | | | | | UND | -.2 |
| .4 | .3 | | | | | | | .3 | .7 |
| 4.5 | .5 | | | | | Debt/Worth | | 1.0 | 3.6 |
| -9.8 | NM | | | | | | | -4.0 | -3.5 |
| 545.3 | | | | | | | | 195.9 | 138.4 |
| (14) 114.7 | | | | | | % Profit Before Taxes/Tangible Net Worth | (19) | 32.6 | (14) 102.6 |
| 50.5 | | | | | | | | 8.8 | 79.7 |
| 85.2 | 101.4 | | | | | | | 74.3 | 72.4 |
| 36.8 | 40.5 | | | | | % Profit Before Taxes/Total Assets | | 11.3 | 35.1 |
| 12.4 | 7.7 | | | | | | | -1.0 | 10.5 |
| UND | 90.5 | | | | | | | 466.1 | 244.3 |
| 320.6 | 28.3 | | | | | Sales/Net Fixed Assets | | 24.5 | 24.6 |
| 22.8 | 4.5 | | | | | | | 4.9 | 9.2 |
| 11.1 | 3.5 | | | | | | | 5.4 | 2.8 |
| 2.7 | 1.6 | | | | | Sales/Total Assets | | 2.0 | 1.7 |
| 1.6 | .5 | | | | | | | .9 | 1.2 |
| | | | | | | % Depr., Dep., Amort./Sales | | | |
| | | | | | | % Officers', Directors' Owners' Comp/Sales | | | |
| 11418M | 21083M | 32029M | 61609M | | 120128M | Net Sales ($) | | 806663M | 534126M |
| 3243M | 11833M | 5914M | 42881M | | 209791M | Total Assets ($) | | 645067M | 443796M |

© RMA 2024

M = $ thousand   MM = $ million
See Pages viii through xx for Explanation of Ratios and Data

# PROFESSIONAL SERVICES—Tax Preparation Services  NAICS 541213

## Comparative Historical Data | Current Data Sorted by Sales

| | | | | Type of Statement | | | | | | |
|---|---|---|---|---|---|---|---|---|---|---|
| | | | | Unqualified | | | | | 1 | 1 |
| | | | | Reviewed | | | | | | |
| | | | 2 | Compiled | | | | | | 1 |
| 6 | 11 | 10 | | Tax Returns | 6 | 2 | 1 | | 1 | 1 |
| 11 | 26 | 23 | | Other | 13 | 6 | 1 | 1 | 1 | 1 |
| 4/1/21-3/31/22 | 4/1/22-3/31/23 | 4/1/23-3/31/24 | | | | 1 (4/1-9/30/23) | | 34 (10/1/23-3/31/24) | | |
| ALL | ALL | ALL | | | 0-1MM | 1-3MM | 3-5MM | 5-10MM | 10-25MM | 25MM & OVER |
| 17 | 37 | 35 | | NUMBER OF STATEMENTS | 19 | 8 | 2 | 1 | 2 | 3 |
| % | % | % | | ASSETS | % | % | % | % | % | % |
| 42.5 | 33.5 | 39.6 | | Cash & Equivalents | 39.7 | | | | | |
| 4.0 | 9.2 | 12.8 | | Trade Receivables (net) | 5.2 | | | | | |
| .0 | 1.4 | 1.1 | | Inventory | .0 | | | | | |
| 5.2 | 8.2 | 2.0 | | All Other Current | .9 | | | | | |
| 51.7 | 52.3 | 55.5 | | Total Current | 45.8 | | | | | |
| 12.0 | 11.7 | 11.4 | | Fixed Assets (net) | 12.4 | | | | | |
| 27.4 | 21.6 | 22.3 | | Intangibles (net) | 27.8 | | | | | |
| 8.8 | 14.4 | 10.9 | | All Other Non-Current | 14.1 | | | | | |
| 100.0 | 100.0 | 100.0 | | Total | 100.0 | | | | | |
| | | | | LIABILITIES | | | | | | |
| 15.5 | 25.3 | 9.2 | | Notes Payable-Short Term | 9.1 | | | | | |
| 1.3 | 4.3 | .5 | | Cur. Mat.-L.T.D. | .1 | | | | | |
| 2.8 | 1.6 | 2.9 | | Trade Payables | .8 | | | | | |
| .0 | .3 | .5 | | Income Taxes Payable | .8 | | | | | |
| 7.1 | 6.8 | 26.6 | | All Other Current | 32.2 | | | | | |
| 26.7 | 38.3 | 39.6 | | Total Current | 43.0 | | | | | |
| 24.3 | 27.9 | 28.9 | | Long-Term Debt | 12.4 | | | | | |
| .0 | .0 | .0 | | Deferred Taxes | .0 | | | | | |
| 1.5 | 3.0 | 11.5 | | All Other Non-Current | 13.9 | | | | | |
| 47.5 | 30.8 | 20.1 | | Net Worth | 30.7 | | | | | |
| 100.0 | 100.0 | 100.0 | | Total Liabilities & Net Worth | 100.0 | | | | | |
| | | | | INCOME DATA | | | | | | |
| 100.0 | 100.0 | 100.0 | | Net Sales | 100.0 | | | | | |
| | | | | Gross Profit | | | | | | |
| 77.3 | 78.6 | 74.8 | | Operating Expenses | 67.3 | | | | | |
| 22.7 | 21.4 | 25.2 | | Operating Profit | 32.7 | | | | | |
| -2.8 | .6 | 1.5 | | All Other Expenses (net) | 1.7 | | | | | |
| 25.5 | 20.8 | 23.6 | | Profit Before Taxes | 31.0 | | | | | |
| | | | | RATIOS | | | | | | |
| 7.1 | 6.7 | 8.0 | | | 3.6 | | | | | |
| 3.5 | 2.4 | 2.0 | | Current | 1.5 | | | | | |
| .5 | .7 | .7 | | | .7 | | | | | |
| 7.1 | 5.7 | 8.0 | | | 3.6 | | | | | |
| 2.0 | 1.9 | 1.8 | | Quick | 1.0 | | | | | |
| .4 | .5 | .6 | | | .2 | | | | | |
| 0 UND | 0 UND | 0 UND | | | 0 UND | | | | | |
| 0 UND | 0 UND | 0 UND | | Sales/Receivables | 0 UND | | | | | |
| 7 52.3 | 8 44.7 | 27 13.6 | | | 8 44.7 | | | | | |
| | | | | Cost of Sales/Inventory | | | | | | |
| | | | | Cost of Sales/Payables | | | | | | |
| 4.8 | 3.6 | 3.5 | | | 3.5 | | | | | |
| 9.5 | 11.7 | 11.0 | | Sales/Working Capital | 118.8 | | | | | |
| -23.2 | -69.4 | -272.0 | | | -44.6 | | | | | |
| 102.1 | 104.9 | 43.0 | | | | | | | | |
| (12) 44.1 | (22) 16.1 | (18) 10.5 | | EBIT/Interest | | | | | | |
| 13.0 | 2.7 | 2.1 | | | | | | | | |
| | | | | Net Profit + Depr., Dep., Amort./Cur. Mat. L/T/D | | | | | | |
| .1 | .0 | .0 | | | .0 | | | | | |
| .3 | .1 | .1 | | Fixed/Worth | .1 | | | | | |
| NM | -1.3 | UND | | | UND | | | | | |
| .2 | .1 | .4 | | | .3 | | | | | |
| 1.5 | 1.1 | 1.0 | | Debt/Worth | 3.4 | | | | | |
| -16.2 | -2.6 | -7.5 | | | -16.7 | | | | | |
| 320.4 | 128.8 | 184.5 | | | 545.3 | | | | | |
| (12) 198.6 | (22) 72.4 | (25) 70.4 | | % Profit Before Taxes/Tangible Net Worth | (14) 114.7 | | | | | |
| 50.6 | 21.2 | 30.0 | | | 53.3 | | | | | |
| 112.9 | 96.4 | 72.0 | | | 66.9 | | | | | |
| 62.2 | 37.7 | 29.1 | | % Profit Before Taxes/Total Assets | 43.1 | | | | | |
| 29.1 | 15.5 | 4.5 | | | 10.7 | | | | | |
| 100.9 | UND | UND | | | UND | | | | | |
| 29.3 | 112.1 | 76.6 | | Sales/Net Fixed Assets | 61.0 | | | | | |
| 13.7 | 23.8 | 15.6 | | | 9.7 | | | | | |
| 3.7 | 4.3 | 5.4 | | | 3.4 | | | | | |
| 2.3 | 2.3 | 2.0 | | Sales/Total Assets | 1.9 | | | | | |
| 1.5 | 1.6 | 1.2 | | | 1.0 | | | | | |
| | | .4 | | | | | | | | |
| | (10) | 1.0 | | % Depr., Dep., Amort./Sales | | | | | | |
| | | 5.6 | | | | | | | | |
| | 7.0 | 7.6 | | | | | | | | |
| | (15) 10.1 | (11) 16.7 | | % Officers', Directors' Owners' Comp/Sales | | | | | | |
| | 17.9 | 19.7 | | | | | | | | |
| 68696M | 235313M | 246267M | | Net Sales ($) | 7702M | 11640M | 6927M | 6232M | 27630M | 186136M |
| 26990M | 83270M | 273662M | | Total Assets ($) | 6164M | 4866M | 2377M | 1669M | 26272M | 232314M |

© RMA 2024     M = $ thousand     MM = $ million
See Pages viii through xx for Explanation of Ratios and Data

# PROFESSIONAL SERVICES—Payroll Services  NAICS 541214

## Current Data Sorted by Assets / Comparative Historical Data

| | | | | | | | Type of Statement | | | | |
|---|---|---|---|---|---|---|---|---|---|---|---|
| | | 1 | 4 | 3 | 3 | 3 | Unqualified | | 6 | | 5 |
| | | | 2 | | 1 | | Reviewed | | 4 | | 1 |
| | | | 1 | 1 | | | Compiled | | 2 | | 1 |
| 4 | 1 | | 4 | | | | Tax Returns | | 12 | | 4 |
| 4 | 5 | 11 (4/1-9/30/23) | 9 | 11 | 1 | 3 | Other | | 23 | | 28 |
| 0-500M | 500M-2MM | 2-10MM | 10-50MM | 50-100MM | 100-250MM | | | | 4/1/19-3/31/20 | | 4/1/20-3/31/21 |
| 8 | 7 | 18 | 17 | 4 | 7 | | NUMBER OF STATEMENTS | | 47 ALL | | 39 ALL |
| % | % | % | % | % | % | | ASSETS | | % | | % |
| | | 32.2 | 27.5 | | | | Cash & Equivalents | | 33.1 | | 44.6 |
| | | 21.7 | 8.9 | | | | Trade Receivables (net) | | 14.6 | | 8.2 |
| | | .0 | .0 | | | | Inventory | | .0 | | .8 |
| | | 10.6 | 12.3 | | | | All Other Current | | 12.6 | | 6.3 |
| | | 64.4 | 48.6 | | | | Total Current | | 60.3 | | 59.9 |
| | | 8.5 | 3.4 | | | | Fixed Assets (net) | | 5.6 | | 5.6 |
| | | 10.3 | 6.0 | | | | Intangibles (net) | | 15.6 | | 13.5 |
| | | 16.8 | 42.0 | | | | All Other Non-Current | | 18.5 | | 21.1 |
| | | 100.0 | 100.0 | | | | Total | | 100.0 | | 100.0 |
| | | | | | | | **LIABILITIES** | | | | |
| | | 10.2 | .7 | | | | Notes Payable-Short Term | | 3.1 | | 5.9 |
| | | .5 | .8 | | | | Cur. Mat.-L.T.D. | | .9 | | .5 |
| | | 4.4 | 5.0 | | | | Trade Payables | | 6.7 | | 6.3 |
| | | .0 | .1 | | | | Income Taxes Payable | | .1 | | .5 |
| | | 32.6 | 42.4 | | | | All Other Current | | 39.4 | | 49.4 |
| | | 47.8 | 48.9 | | | | Total Current | | 50.2 | | 62.6 |
| | | 17.0 | 3.2 | | | | Long-Term Debt | | 5.7 | | 13.9 |
| | | .1 | .0 | | | | Deferred Taxes | | .0 | | .1 |
| | | 7.3 | 24.8 | | | | All Other Non-Current | | 5.5 | | 8.2 |
| | | 27.9 | 23.1 | | | | Net Worth | | 38.6 | | 15.3 |
| | | 100.0 | 100.0 | | | | Total Liabilties & Net Worth | | 100.0 | | 100.0 |
| | | | | | | | **INCOME DATA** | | | | |
| | | 100.0 | 100.0 | | | | Net Sales | | 100.0 | | 100.0 |
| | | | | | | | Gross Profit | | | | |
| | | 89.2 | 81.6 | | | | Operating Expenses | | 84.3 | | 91.1 |
| | | 10.8 | 18.4 | | | | Operating Profit | | 15.7 | | 8.9 |
| | | .2 | -1.9 | | | | All Other Expenses (net) | | .6 | | -1.0 |
| | | 10.5 | 20.3 | | | | Profit Before Taxes | | 15.2 | | 9.9 |
| | | | | | | | **RATIOS** | | | | |
| | | 2.4 | 3.8 | | | | | | 3.2 | | 2.4 |
| | | 1.4 | 1.3 | | | | Current | | 1.1 | | 1.1 |
| | | 1.0 | .5 | | | | | | .7 | | .7 |
| | | 2.4 | 3.8 | | | | | | 3.2 | | 2.4 |
| | | 1.0 | 1.1 | | | | Quick | | 1.0 | | .9 |
| | | .6 | .2 | | | | | | .2 | | .2 |
| | | 0 UND | 1 604.1 | | | | | | 0 UND | | 0 UND |
| | | 5 75.2 | 5 70.1 | | | | Sales/Receivables | | 4 91.2 | | 2 217.0 |
| | | 39 9.4 | 18 20.2 | | | | | | 29 12.7 | | 13 29.1 |
| | | | | | | | Cost of Sales/Inventory | | | | |
| | | | | | | | Cost of Sales/Payables | | | | |
| | | 6.3 | 1.7 | | | | | | 8.4 | | 7.8 |
| | | 22.0 | 7.5 | | | | Sales/Working Capital | | 101.0 | | 131.4 |
| | | NM | -3.8 | | | | | | -26.4 | | -7.9 |
| | | 89.4 | | | | | | | 43.9 | | 50.8 |
| | | (10) 11.9 | | | | | EBIT/Interest | | (25) 15.6 | (22) | 9.4 |
| | | 3.2 | | | | | | | 6.0 | | .7 |
| | | | | | | | Net Profit + Depr., Dep., Amort./Cur. Mat. L/T/D | | | | |
| | | .0 | .0 | | | | | | .0 | | .0 |
| | | .1 | .1 | | | | Fixed/Worth | | .1 | | .1 |
| | | .5 | -2.0 | | | | | | 5.4 | | -4.0 |
| | | .7 | 1.3 | | | | | | .8 | | 1.2 |
| | | 6.7 | 11.6 | | | | Debt/Worth | | 5.3 | | 7.8 |
| | | NM | -77.4 | | | | | | -21.3 | | -8.4 |
| | | 148.8 | 131.2 | | | | | | 192.1 | | 147.6 |
| | (14) | 73.3 | (12) 41.0 | | | | % Profit Before Taxes/Tangible Net Worth | (32) | 59.7 | (25) | 45.6 |
| | | 9.7 | 15.3 | | | | | | 17.2 | | 21.3 |
| | | 28.5 | 12.1 | | | | | | 47.3 | | 25.4 |
| | | 14.0 | 5.8 | | | | % Profit Before Taxes/Total Assets | | 10.7 | | 8.8 |
| | | 2.2 | 2.3 | | | | | | 2.5 | | 2.6 |
| | | UND | 150.1 | | | | | | UND | | UND |
| | | 395.9 | 48.1 | | | | Sales/Net Fixed Assets | | 591.7 | | 710.7 |
| | | 83.1 | 12.8 | | | | | | 40.6 | | 30.3 |
| | | 5.5 | .7 | | | | | | 6.3 | | 13.2 |
| | | 2.7 | .3 | | | | Sales/Total Assets | | 1.7 | | 1.7 |
| | | 1.2 | .2 | | | | | | .3 | | .4 |
| | | | .3 | | | | | | .1 | | .0 |
| | | (12) | .7 | | | | % Depr., Dep., Amort./Sales | (14) | .8 | (10) | .9 |
| | | | 1.7 | | | | | | 1.8 | | 2.9 |
| | | | | | | | | | 2.3 | | |
| | | | | | | | % Officers', Directors' Owners' Comp/Sales | (16) | 8.8 | | |
| | | | | | | | | | 13.8 | | |
| 13174M | 175325M | 512709M | 221611M | 88185M | 330593M | | Net Sales ($) | | 1418234M | | 1059858M |
| 1735M | 8256M | 85411M | 401656M | 290241M | 1100324M | | Total Assets ($) | | 899144M | | 1007701M |

M = $ thousand    MM = $ million
See Pages viii through xx for Explanation of Ratios and Data

© RMA 2024

## PROFESSIONAL SERVICES—Payroll Services  NAICS 541214

### Comparative Historical Data | Current Data Sorted by Sales

| Comparative Historical Data | | | | Type of Statement | Current Data Sorted by Sales | | | | | |
|---|---|---|---|---|---|---|---|---|---|---|
| 7 | 8 | 14 | | Unqualified | | | 3 | 1 | 5 | 5 |
|   | 1 | 3 | | Reviewed | | | 1 | 1 |   | 1 |
|   | 2 | 2 | | Compiled | | | 1 |   |   |   |
| 9 | 2 | 9 | | Tax Returns | 3 | 2 | 1 | 1 |   | 2 |
| 14 | 26 | 33 | | Other | 3 | 3 | 5 | 5 | 5 | 12 |
| 4/1/21-3/31/22 ALL | 4/1/22-3/31/23 ALL | 4/1/23-3/31/24 ALL | | | 11 (4/1-9/30/23) | | | 50 (10/1/23-3/31/24) | | |
|   |   |   | | | 0-1MM | 1-3MM | 3-5MM | 5-10MM | 10-25MM | 25MM & OVER |
| 30 | 39 | 61 | | NUMBER OF STATEMENTS | 6 | 5 | 11 | 9 | 10 | 20 |
| % | % | % | | ASSETS | % | % | % | % | % | % |
| 50.0 | 46.6 | 33.3 | | Cash & Equivalents |   |   | 22.9 |   | 16.0 | 40.2 |
| 7.0 | 6.8 | 11.5 | | Trade Receivables (net) |   |   | 7.3 |   | 23.8 | 12.6 |
| .8 | .0 | .0 | | Inventory |   |   | .0 |   | .0 | .0 |
| 18.6 | 21.8 | 12.8 | | All Other Current |   |   | 4.6 |   | 35.5 | 12.4 |
| 76.5 | 75.3 | 57.7 | | Total Current |   |   | 34.8 |   | 75.4 | 65.2 |
| 4.7 | 2.9 | 5.6 | | Fixed Assets (net) |   |   | 9.5 |   | 1.6 | 5.5 |
| 8.1 | 8.0 | 10.5 | | Intangibles (net) |   |   | 7.9 |   | 5.1 | 14.9 |
| 10.7 | 13.8 | 26.2 | | All Other Non-Current |   |   | 47.7 |   | 18.0 | 14.4 |
| 100.0 | 100.0 | 100.0 | | Total |   |   | 100.0 |   | 100.0 | 100.0 |
|   |   |   | | LIABILITIES |   |   |   |   |   |   |
| 2.8 | 3.3 | 5.5 | | Notes Payable-Short Term |   |   | 1.3 |   | 5.3 | 6.7 |
| 2.2 | .7 | 1.6 | | Cur. Mat.-L.T.D. |   |   | .6 |   | .6 | 1.1 |
| 5.1 | 5.2 | 4.3 | | Trade Payables |   |   | 2.4 |   | 7.1 | 1.3 |
| .1 | .8 | .1 | | Income Taxes Payable |   |   | .0 |   | .1 | .2 |
| 41.5 | 42.4 | 40.2 | | All Other Current |   |   | 35.7 |   | 54.6 | 47.4 |
| 51.7 | 52.5 | 51.7 | | Total Current |   |   | 40.0 |   | 67.6 | 56.8 |
| 11.2 | 10.6 | 9.7 | | Long-Term Debt |   |   | 3.4 |   | 22.7 | 11.0 |
| .0 | .1 | .0 | | Deferred Taxes |   |   | .1 |   | .0 | .1 |
| 6.3 | 7.1 | 11.0 | | All Other Non-Current |   |   | 26.3 |   | 5.8 | 3.4 |
| 30.8 | 29.7 | 27.5 | | Net Worth |   |   | 30.1 |   | 4.0 | 28.7 |
| 100.0 | 100.0 | 100.0 | | Total Liabilities & Net Worth |   |   | 100.0 |   | 100.0 | 100.0 |
|   |   |   | | INCOME DATA |   |   |   |   |   |   |
| 100.0 | 100.0 | 100.0 | | Net Sales |   |   | 100.0 |   | 100.0 | 100.0 |
| 86.2 | 84.2 | 86.9 | | Gross Profit |   |   |   |   |   |   |
| 13.8 | 15.8 | 13.1 | | Operating Expenses |   |   | 82.7 |   | 87.3 | 95.1 |
| -.6 | .3 | .5 | | Operating Profit |   |   | 17.3 |   | 12.7 | 4.9 |
| 14.4 | 15.4 | 12.6 | | All Other Expenses (net) |   |   | -2.6 |   | .3 | 2.1 |
|   |   |   | | Profit Before Taxes |   |   | 19.9 |   | 12.3 | 2.7 |
|   |   |   | | RATIOS |   |   |   |   |   |   |
| 3.2 | 3.8 | 2.7 | | |   |   | 3.5 |   | 1.9 | 1.8 |
| 1.2 | 1.3 | 1.1 | | Current |   |   | 1.5 |   | 1.2 | 1.1 |
| 1.1 | 1.0 | .7 | | |   |   | .3 |   | 1.0 | .5 |
| 3.0 | 3.8 | 2.7 | | |   |   | 3.5 |   | 1.9 | 1.8 |
| 1.1 | 1.1 | 1.0 | | Quick |   |   | .8 |   | .6 | .8 |
| .6 | .5 | .3 | | |   |   | .3 |   | .1 | .2 |
| 0 UND | 0 UND | 0 UND | | | 0 UND | | 2 180.0 | | 0 UND | |
| 0 UND | 0 999.8 | 2 150.0 | | Sales/Receivables | 0 999.8 | | 12 29.5 | | 4 104.2 | |
| 36 10.0 | 15 23.8 | 31 11.8 | | | 7 55.0 | | 45 8.1 | | 41 8.8 | |
|   |   |   | | Cost of Sales/Inventory |   |   |   |   |   |   |
|   |   |   | | Cost of Sales/Payables |   |   |   |   |   |   |
| 2.9 | 4.0 | 4.9 | | |   |   | 4.3 |   | 3.9 | 8.7 |
| 5.1 | 10.0 | 26.3 | | Sales/Working Capital |   |   | 14.1 |   | 12.6 | 152.9 |
| 110.1 | 999.8 | -18.2 | | |   |   | -3.3 |   | NM | -7.3 |
|   |   |   | | | | | | | | 6.3 |
| 42.4 | 152.3 | 62.2 | | | | | | | | .7 |
| (12) 5.3 | (15) 13.1 | (34) 16.4 | | EBIT/Interest | | | | | (10) | -1.1 |
| -2.3 | 3.9 | .9 | | | | | | | | |
|   |   |   | | Net Profit + Depr., Dep., Amort./Cur. Mat. L/T/D |   |   |   |   |   |   |
| .0 | .0 | .0 | | | | | .0 | | .0 | .0 |
| .1 | .1 | .1 | | Fixed/Worth | | | .1 | | .1 | .3 |
| 1.3 | 1.5 | .9 | | | | | -1.9 | | NM | -2.4 |
| 1.9 | 1.6 | 1.1 | | | | | .6 | | 4.7 | 1.3 |
| 6.1 | 3.8 | 7.7 | | Debt/Worth | | | 15.2 | | 15.0 | 14.7 |
| 33.6 | 29.0 | -77.4 | | | | | -83.8 | | -8.1 | -7.6 |
| 112.2 | 168.3 | 131.0 | | | | | | | | 149.7 |
| (25) 61.0 | (31) 58.9 | (45) 50.4 | | % Profit Before Taxes/Tangible Net Worth | | | | | (14) | 77.3 |
| 15.0 | 20.4 | 13.6 | | | | | | | | 24.7 |
| 28.8 | 26.5 | 18.8 | | | | | 34.6 | | 15.0 | 20.2 |
| 7.9 | 8.4 | 6.7 | | % Profit Before Taxes/Total Assets | | | 11.5 | | 4.8 | 6.1 |
| 1.1 | 1.3 | 1.0 | | | | | 4.6 | | .0 | -.5 |
| UND | UND | UND | | | | | 395.6 | | 505.0 | 990.2 |
| 222.7 | 452.0 | 100.7 | | Sales/Net Fixed Assets | | | 74.5 | | 40.9 | 66.6 |
| 15.1 | 60.5 | 16.8 | | | | | 11.3 | | 15.3 | 16.6 |
| 3.0 | 7.9 | 4.3 | | | | | 1.3 | | 3.9 | 16.5 |
| .7 | 1.2 | .8 | | Sales/Total Assets | | | .7 | | .4 | 2.4 |
| .3 | .4 | .3 | | | | | .3 | | .3 | .3 |
| .1 | .1 | .1 | | | | | | | | .1 |
| (10) .8 | (10) .3 | (28) .4 | | % Depr., Dep., Amort./Sales | | | | | (12) | .7 |
| 4.5 | .7 | 1.8 | | | | | | | | 4.4 |
| 3.7 | 1.1 | 1.5 | | | | | | | | |
| (11) 6.3 | (14) 4.4 | (13) 3.5 | | % Officers', Directors', Owners' Comp/Sales | | | | | | |
| 34.7 | 6.8 | 6.3 | | | | | | | | |
| 440230M | 706588M | 1341597M | | Net Sales ($) | 1272M | 10278M | 41670M | 64941M | 165403M | 1058033M |
| 585180M | 701330M | 1887623M | | Total Assets ($) | 2251M | 22324M | 79193M | 155791M | 354820M | 1273244M |

© RMA 2024    M = $ thousand    MM = $ million
See Pages viii through xx for Explanation of Ratios and Data

# PROFESSIONAL SERVICES—Other Accounting Services  NAICS 541219

## Current Data Sorted by Assets | Comparative Historical Data

| | | | | | | | Type of Statement | | |
|---|---|---|---|---|---|---|---|---|---|
| | | 1 | | 1 | 1 | 3 | Unqualified | 4 | 3 |
| | | | 2 | 1 | | | Reviewed | 2 | 3 |
| | | | 5 | | | | Compiled | 2 | |
| 12 | 6 | 13 | 16 | 13 | 2 | 7 | Tax Returns | 19 | 16 |
| 23 | 15 (4/1-9/30/23) | | | 91 (10/1/23-3/31/24) | | | Other | 109 | 61 |
| 0-500M | 500M-2MM | 2-10MM | 10-50MM | 50-100MM | | 100-250MM | | 4/1/19-3/31/20 ALL | 4/1/20-3/31/21 ALL |
| 35 | 20 | 23 | 15 | 3 | | 10 | NUMBER OF STATEMENTS | 136 | 83 |
| % | % | % | % | % | | % | ASSETS | % | % |
| 47.5 | 32.1 | 30.6 | 26.3 | | | 9.0 | Cash & Equivalents | 23.3 | 39.3 |
| 12.2 | 23.8 | 25.0 | 31.0 | | | 22.4 | Trade Receivables (net) | 29.5 | 16.4 |
| .0 | 1.2 | 1.3 | 4.3 | | | 1.6 | Inventory | 1.4 | .7 |
| 6.2 | 15.6 | 4.1 | 8.1 | | | 9.0 | All Other Current | 5.6 | 5.5 |
| 65.9 | 72.7 | 60.9 | 69.7 | | | 42.1 | Total Current | 59.9 | 62.0 |
| 13.1 | 7.1 | 16.9 | 11.9 | | | 22.0 | Fixed Assets (net) | 12.1 | 13.0 |
| 7.0 | 5.2 | 12.4 | 5.1 | | | 25.4 | Intangibles (net) | 12.8 | 16.2 |
| 14.1 | 15.1 | 9.8 | 13.3 | | | 10.6 | All Other Non-Current | 15.2 | 8.9 |
| 100.0 | 100.0 | 100.0 | 100.0 | | | 100.0 | Total | 100.0 | 100.0 |
| | | | | | | | LIABILITIES | | |
| 15.5 | 5.5 | 2.2 | 8.8 | | | 2.7 | Notes Payable-Short Term | 14.2 | 10.2 |
| 1.9 | 2.0 | .8 | 1.4 | | | 3.0 | Cur. Mat.-L.T.D. | 1.8 | 2.1 |
| 2.5 | 7.7 | 7.1 | 3.3 | | | 3.1 | Trade Payables | 8.5 | 3.2 |
| 1.5 | .0 | .0 | .0 | | | .2 | Income Taxes Payable | .1 | .2 |
| 23.1 | 20.3 | 16.6 | 30.1 | | | 16.2 | All Other Current | 26.8 | 21.0 |
| 44.4 | 35.5 | 26.6 | 43.6 | | | 25.1 | Total Current | 51.4 | 36.6 |
| 39.9 | 31.0 | 17.8 | 58.8 | | | 24.9 | Long-Term Debt | 14.7 | 20.7 |
| .0 | .0 | .0 | .0 | | | .2 | Deferred Taxes | .3 | .0 |
| 6.0 | 10.9 | 4.9 | 3.3 | | | 7.7 | All Other Non-Current | 5.7 | 7.0 |
| 9.7 | 22.6 | 50.7 | -5.8 | | | 42.1 | Net Worth | 27.8 | 35.7 |
| 100.0 | 100.0 | 100.0 | 100.0 | | | 100.0 | Total Liabilities & Net Worth | 100.0 | 100.0 |
| | | | | | | | INCOME DATA | | |
| 100.0 | 100.0 | 100.0 | 100.0 | | | 100.0 | Net Sales | 100.0 | 100.0 |
| | | | | | | | Gross Profit | | |
| 72.9 | 85.0 | 78.5 | 85.0 | | | 79.9 | Operating Expenses | 87.6 | 83.7 |
| 27.1 | 15.0 | 21.5 | 15.0 | | | 20.1 | Operating Profit | 12.4 | 16.3 |
| 2.8 | 2.8 | 2.9 | 2.5 | | | 8.7 | All Other Expenses (net) | 1.7 | .3 |
| 24.3 | 12.2 | 18.6 | 12.5 | | | 11.4 | Profit Before Taxes | 10.7 | 16.1 |
| | | | | | | | RATIOS | | |
| 10.3 | 12.9 | 16.1 | 2.8 | | | 2.2 | | 3.2 | 4.9 |
| 2.2 | 3.2 | 4.9 | 1.8 | | | 1.8 | Current | 1.7 | 2.0 |
| 1.1 | 1.4 | 1.4 | 1.2 | | | .6 | | .7 | 1.1 |
| 10.2 | 5.8 | 11.9 | 2.1 | | | 1.6 | | 2.9 | 4.9 |
| 2.2 | 1.9 | 4.9 | 1.6 | | | 1.0 | Quick | 1.5 | 1.9 |
| 1.0 | 1.0 | 1.4 | 1.0 | | | .6 | | .6 | 1.0 |
| 0 UND | 0 762.1 | 0 UND | 26 14.2 | | 31 | 11.6 | | 1 494.3 | 0 UND |
| 0 UND | 20 18.6 | 26 14.0 | 45 8.2 | | 51 | 7.2 | Sales/Receivables | 34 10.6 | 13 27.2 |
| 18 19.9 | 38 9.5 | 53 6.9 | 65 5.6 | | 66 | 5.5 | | 55 6.6 | 45 8.2 |
| | | | | | | | Cost of Sales/Inventory | | |
| | | | | | | | Cost of Sales/Payables | | |
| 5.4 | 3.7 | 3.3 | 6.5 | | | 4.5 | | 6.8 | 5.0 |
| 30.5 | 5.8 | 5.0 | 11.6 | | | 8.9 | Sales/Working Capital | 20.5 | 9.9 |
| 999.8 | 28.1 | 352.2 | 20.9 | | | -5.5 | | -38.3 | 59.8 |
| 44.0 | 23.4 | 217.4 | 34.9 | | | | | 53.0 | 87.5 |
| (22) 16.1 | (13) 4.9 | (18) 17.4 | (11) 5.9 | | | | EBIT/Interest | (95) 15.8 | (45) 23.9 |
| 4.8 | 1.3 | 2.1 | 1.2 | | | | | 4.1 | 4.6 |
| | | | | | | | | 30.3 | |
| | | | | | | | Net Profit + Depr., Dep., Amort./Cur. Mat. L/T/D | (10) 18.4 | |
| | | | | | | | | 5.0 | |
| .0 | .0 | .0 | .0 | | | .5 | | .0 | .0 |
| .0 | .0 | .1 | .2 | | | .8 | Fixed/Worth | .2 | .2 |
| .4 | .4 | 2.3 | -.3 | | | -1.9 | | 2.8 | 2.1 |
| .5 | .5 | .1 | .6 | | | 1.4 | | .6 | .5 |
| 3.0 | 2.2 | .6 | 1.6 | | | 4.0 | Debt/Worth | 2.2 | 2.1 |
| -9.2 | 41.6 | 2.4 | -8.6 | | | -5.0 | | -33.6 | -5.7 |
| 761.3 | 227.8 | 80.1 | | | | | | 162.1 | 166.9 |
| (26) 226.4 | (17) 46.3 | (18) 31.1 | | | | | % Profit Before Taxes/Tangible Net Worth | (100) 72.2 | (59) 68.4 |
| 56.8 | 10.0 | 13.4 | | | | | | 19.4 | 27.0 |
| 190.4 | 58.7 | 42.2 | 65.3 | | | 57.0 | | 59.7 | 55.4 |
| 70.4 | 18.1 | 15.3 | 6.8 | | | 6.3 | % Profit Before Taxes/Total Assets | 21.4 | 26.9 |
| 30.2 | 1.8 | 4.2 | 2.4 | | | -.9 | | 6.5 | 5.2 |
| UND | UND | 142.1 | 90.2 | | | 23.5 | | 423.5 | UND |
| UND | 221.6 | 55.8 | 65.7 | | | 9.4 | Sales/Net Fixed Assets | 72.4 | 76.5 |
| 85.9 | 46.8 | 19.0 | 33.2 | | | 5.8 | | 22.8 | 19.8 |
| 20.9 | 4.5 | 4.0 | 3.2 | | | 2.2 | | 6.2 | 4.5 |
| 4.6 | 2.7 | 2.5 | 2.8 | | | 1.2 | Sales/Total Assets | 3.4 | 2.5 |
| 1.6 | 1.5 | 1.0 | 2.1 | | | .4 | | 1.6 | 1.2 |
| | | .3 | | | | | | .4 | .4 |
| | | (11) 1.0 | | | | | % Depr., Dep., Amort./Sales | (61) 1.0 | (30) 1.3 |
| | | 1.7 | | | | | | 3.0 | 3.1 |
| 11.5 | | | | | | | | 3.7 | 4.2 |
| (13) 19.8 | | | | | | | % Officers', Directors' Owners' Comp/Sales | (50) 11.4 | (32) 10.3 |
| 24.4 | | | | | | | | 17.4 | 18.1 |
| 41614M | 75753M | 264497M | 1274232M | 518465M | | 2125987M | Net Sales ($) | 4937257M | 2656292M |
| 7212M | 23655M | 100744M | 336215M | 281477M | | 1464601M | Total Assets ($) | 1942992M | 1145114M |

© RMA 2024  
M = $ thousand  MM = $ million  
See Pages viii through xx for Explanation of Ratios and Data

## PROFESSIONAL SERVICES—Other Accounting Services  NAICS 541219

### Comparative Historical Data | Current Data Sorted by Sales

| Comparative Historical Data | | | | Type of Statement | Current Data Sorted by Sales | | | | | |
|---|---|---|---|---|---|---|---|---|---|---|
| 4 | 2 | 6 | | Unqualified | | | | | 2 | 4 |
| 4 | 3 | 3 | | Reviewed | | | | | 1 | 1 |
| 12 | 23 | 23 | | Compiled | 1 | | 1 | | 2 | |
| 49 | 61 | 74 | | Tax Returns | 8 | 8 | 1 | 4 | 10 | 22 |
| 4/1/21- | 4/1/22- | 4/1/23- | | Other | 19 | 12 | 6 | 5 | | |
| 3/31/22 | 3/31/23 | 3/31/24 | | | 15 (4/1-9/30/23) | | | 91 (10/1/23-3/31/24) | | |
| ALL | ALL | ALL | | | 0-1MM | 1-3MM | 3-5MM | 5-10MM | 10-25MM | 25MM & OVER |
| 69 | 92 | 106 | | NUMBER OF STATEMENTS | 28 | 20 | 7 | 9 | 15 | 27 |
| % | % | % | | ASSETS | % | % | % | % | % | % |
| 37.9 | 33.0 | 33.3 | | Cash & Equivalents | 38.1 | 36.2 | | | 31.3 | 22.1 |
| 18.1 | 21.1 | 21.2 | | Trade Receivables (net) | 7.8 | 20.8 | | | 32.5 | 28.8 |
| .7 | 1.5 | 1.3 | | Inventory | .0 | 1.1 | | | 2.7 | 2.3 |
| 6.1 | 5.9 | 8.2 | | All Other Current | 6.7 | 9.2 | | | 5.3 | 10.2 |
| 62.7 | 61.5 | 64.0 | | Total Current | 52.6 | 67.3 | | | 71.9 | 63.5 |
| 14.1 | 11.0 | 13.3 | | Fixed Assets (net) | 24.6 | 2.5 | | | 16.3 | 12.2 |
| 16.0 | 13.2 | 9.8 | | Intangibles (net) | 8.2 | 6.2 | | | 6.6 | 15.2 |
| 7.1 | 14.3 | 12.9 | | All Other Non-Current | 14.7 | 24.0 | | | 5.3 | 9.1 |
| 100.0 | 100.0 | 100.0 | | Total | 100.0 | 100.0 | | | 100.0 | 100.0 |
| | | | | LIABILITIES | | | | | | |
| 24.6 | 5.9 | 8.1 | | Notes Payable-Short Term | 16.5 | 5.5 | | | 3.3 | 6.0 |
| .9 | 2.2 | 1.7 | | Cur. Mat.-L.T.D. | .6 | 3.4 | | | .3 | 2.0 |
| 2.2 | 6.4 | 4.8 | | Trade Payables | 2.8 | 5.3 | | | 9.4 | 3.8 |
| .0 | .1 | .5 | | Income Taxes Payable | 1.7 | .0 | | | .0 | .1 |
| 24.9 | 24.8 | 21.2 | | All Other Current | 20.9 | 16.4 | | | 22.2 | 23.3 |
| 52.7 | 39.5 | 36.4 | | Total Current | 42.5 | 30.7 | | | 35.2 | 35.2 |
| 25.3 | 25.8 | 34.2 | | Long-Term Debt | 38.5 | 49.6 | | | 9.5 | 42.1 |
| .0 | .0 | .0 | | Deferred Taxes | .0 | .0 | | | .0 | .1 |
| 6.7 | 4.2 | 6.4 | | All Other Non-Current | 8.4 | 8.8 | | | 4.0 | 5.0 |
| 15.3 | 30.5 | 23.0 | | Net Worth | 10.6 | 10.9 | | | 51.4 | 17.6 |
| 100.0 | 100.0 | 100.0 | | Total Liabilities & Net Worth | 100.0 | 100.0 | | | 100.0 | 100.0 |
| | | | | INCOME DATA | | | | | | |
| 100.0 | 100.0 | 100.0 | | Net Sales | 100.0 | 100.0 | | | 100.0 | 100.0 |
| | | | | Gross Profit | | | | | | |
| 81.4 | 81.5 | 79.4 | | Operating Expenses | 67.1 | 81.5 | | | 87.3 | 85.3 |
| 18.6 | 18.5 | 20.6 | | Operating Profit | 32.9 | 18.5 | | | 12.7 | 14.7 |
| .3 | 1.2 | 3.3 | | All Other Expenses (net) | 6.8 | 1.3 | | | 3.1 | 3.3 |
| 18.3 | 17.3 | 17.2 | | Profit Before Taxes | 26.1 | 17.2 | | | 9.6 | 11.4 |
| | | | | RATIOS | | | | | | |
| 5.0 | 5.3 | 6.0 | | | 10.5 | 11.4 | | | 6.7 | 2.5 |
| 2.5 | 2.7 | 2.3 | | Current | 2.7 | 2.8 | | | 2.4 | 1.8 |
| 1.2 | 1.1 | 1.3 | | | .9 | 1.9 | | | 1.3 | 1.2 |
| 4.0 | 4.9 | 5.4 | | | 9.1 | 5.2 | | | 6.4 | 2.3 |
| 2.0 | 2.1 | 1.9 | | Quick | 2.2 | 2.1 | | | 2.2 | 1.4 |
| 1.0 | .9 | 1.0 | | | .6 | 1.6 | | | 1.1 | .9 |
| 0 UND | 0 UND | 0 UND | | | 0 UND | 0 UND | | 21 17.5 | 26 13.9 | |
| 19 19.6 | 25 14.6 | 21 17.0 | | Sales/Receivables | 0 UND | 10 36.3 | | 32 11.3 | 50 7.3 | |
| 43 8.4 | 50 7.3 | 53 6.9 | | | 20 18.1 | 61 6.0 | | 48 7.6 | 65 5.6 | |
| | | | | Cost of Sales/Inventory | | | | | | |
| | | | | Cost of Sales/Payables | | | | | | |
| 4.2 | 4.2 | 4.6 | | | 4.1 | 4.3 | | | 3.3 | 4.7 |
| 9.2 | 9.3 | 9.7 | | Sales/Working Capital | 20.9 | 7.1 | | | 11.2 | 7.9 |
| 34.4 | 50.2 | 69.9 | | | -20.3 | 31.4 | | | 33.8 | 20.9 |
| 86.1 | 64.9 | 45.2 | | | 26.4 | 28.8 | | 312.3 | 31.8 | |
| (42) 28.0 | (61) 26.5 | (74) 9.9 | | EBIT/Interest | (18) 12.1 | (11) 4.9 | | (12) 17.4 | (21) 3.8 | |
| 3.8 | 7.1 | 2.0 | | | 2.8 | 2.2 | | | -.5 | 1.1 |
| | | 17.2 | | | | | | | | 28.6 |
| | (12) | 9.3 | | Net Profit + Depr., Dep., Amort./Cur. Mat. L/T/D | | | | | (10) 10.8 | |
| | | 2.0 | | | | | | | | 1.6 |
| .0 | .0 | .0 | | | .0 | .0 | | | .0 | .2 |
| .3 | .1 | .1 | | Fixed/Worth | .1 | .0 | | | .1 | .5 |
| NM | 1.1 | 1.0 | | | 3.1 | .1 | | | .6 | -.4 |
| .5 | .5 | .5 | | | 1.1 | .3 | | | .1 | 1.2 |
| 3.1 | 2.2 | 1.7 | | Debt/Worth | 3.6 | 1.0 | | | .8 | 1.8 |
| -3.8 | 100.1 | UND | | | UND | NM | | | 2.8 | -8.6 |
| 253.7 | 222.2 | 220.1 | | | 465.4 | 276.3 | | | 42.5 | 122.4 |
| (46) 108.7 | (70) 79.1 | (80) 65.5 | | % Profit Before Taxes/Tangible Net Worth | (21) 117.1 | (15) 155.4 | | (13) 22.8 | (18) 63.4 | |
| 18.9 | 23.5 | 16.1 | | | 20.6 | 42.2 | | | 5.5 | 2.5 |
| 101.3 | 74.9 | 85.9 | | | 125.1 | 90.9 | | | 25.9 | 65.3 |
| 37.2 | 33.9 | 26.7 | | % Profit Before Taxes/Total Assets | 35.7 | 38.4 | | | 13.6 | 9.3 |
| 5.5 | 6.0 | 3.9 | | | 5.3 | 12.5 | | | .0 | 1.5 |
| UND | UND | UND | | | UND | UND | | | 148.7 | 72.3 |
| 41.0 | 71.8 | 80.6 | | Sales/Net Fixed Assets | 140.7 | 999.8 | | | 55.8 | 35.5 |
| 15.4 | 22.6 | 19.3 | | | 5.7 | 149.1 | | | 21.4 | 10.2 |
| 5.1 | 4.5 | 4.9 | | | 10.1 | 4.7 | | | 6.3 | 3.2 |
| 2.4 | 2.7 | 2.9 | | Sales/Total Assets | 2.0 | 3.0 | | | 4.0 | 2.4 |
| 1.2 | 1.2 | 1.3 | | | .6 | 1.6 | | | 2.5 | 1.5 |
| .4 | .4 | .6 | | | | | | | .3 | .6 |
| (20) 1.3 | (34) 1.0 | (44) 1.0 | | % Depr., Dep., Amort./Sales | | | | (10) .6 | (18) .9 | |
| 1.9 | 3.7 | 2.4 | | | | | | | 2.1 | 2.0 |
| 4.5 | 7.6 | 3.8 | | | 9.7 | | | | | |
| (26) 9.2 | (34) 12.5 | (38) 13.4 | | % Officers', Directors', Owners' Comp/Sales | (10) 18.0 | | | | | |
| 18.4 | 20.9 | 20.6 | | | 24.0 | | | | | |
| 1362947M | 2095601M | 4300548M | | Net Sales ($) | 9736M | 39423M | 25261M | 65885M | 222514M | 3937729M |
| 1107563M | 1015544M | 2213904M | | Total Assets ($) | 13059M | 26018M | 11877M | 27943M | 176907M | 1958100M |

© RMA 2024                M = $ thousand    MM = $ million
See Pages viii through xx for Explanation of Ratios and Data

## PROFESSIONAL SERVICES—Architectural Services  NAICS 541310

### Current Data Sorted by Assets | Comparative Historical Data

| | | | | | | | Type of Statement | | |
|---|---|---|---|---|---|---|---|---|---|
| | | | 1 | 2 | 2 | 4 | Unqualified | 11 | 9 |
| | | 5 | 15 | 28 | 2 | 1 | Reviewed | 47 | 22 |
| 2 | 17 | 16 | 14 | 7 | | | Compiled | 21 | 17 |
| 17 | 26 | 39 | 9 | 1 | | | Tax Returns | 63 | 33 |
| 26 | | | 67 | 35 | 13 | 4 | Other | 177 | 149 |
| | 31 (4/1-9/30/23) | | | 279 (10/1/23-3/31/24) | | | | 4/1/19-3/31/20 | 4/1/20-3/31/21 |
| 0-500M | 500M-2MM | 2-10MM | 10-50MM | 50-100MM | 100-250MM | | | ALL | ALL |
| 45 | 60 | 106 | 73 | 17 | 9 | | NUMBER OF STATEMENTS | 319 | 230 |
| % | % | % | % | % | % | | ASSETS | % | % |
| 43.0 | 32.2 | 21.2 | 15.6 | 16.4 | | | Cash & Equivalents | 22.8 | 31.9 |
| 17.1 | 25.4 | 43.2 | 41.0 | 32.0 | | | Trade Receivables (net) | 40.5 | 34.0 |
| .1 | 2.0 | 1.4 | 2.4 | .6 | | | Inventory | 2.0 | 1.8 |
| 3.9 | 3.3 | 5.6 | 7.7 | 10.3 | | | All Other Current | 5.9 | 5.7 |
| 64.1 | 62.9 | 71.4 | 66.7 | 59.3 | | | Total Current | 71.3 | 73.4 |
| 14.6 | 19.8 | 16.5 | 13.4 | 16.9 | | | Fixed Assets (net) | 14.8 | 14.0 |
| 4.4 | 7.3 | 3.4 | 4.3 | 12.4 | | | Intangibles (net) | 4.6 | 4.8 |
| 17.2 | 9.9 | 8.7 | 15.5 | 11.4 | | | All Other Non-Current | 9.2 | 7.9 |
| 100.0 | 100.0 | 100.0 | 100.0 | 100.0 | | | Total | 100.0 | 100.0 |
| | | | | | | | LIABILITIES | | |
| 26.1 | 5.1 | 4.8 | 3.0 | 2.0 | | | Notes Payable-Short Term | 12.1 | 14.9 |
| 1.5 | 2.9 | 1.6 | 2.7 | 3.4 | | | Cur. Mat.-L.T.D. | 2.0 | 2.9 |
| 5.4 | 10.3 | 14.9 | 13.6 | 12.5 | | | Trade Payables | 14.8 | 12.7 |
| .5 | .2 | .1 | .2 | .2 | | | Income Taxes Payable | .6 | .4 |
| 22.0 | 9.6 | 18.8 | 18.3 | 18.1 | | | All Other Current | 19.9 | 18.0 |
| 55.6 | 28.1 | 40.3 | 37.9 | 36.3 | | | Total Current | 49.5 | 49.0 |
| 12.4 | 21.5 | 13.2 | 11.4 | 17.3 | | | Long-Term Debt | 9.5 | 19.1 |
| .0 | .1 | .3 | 1.1 | 1.2 | | | Deferred Taxes | .8 | .6 |
| 21.4 | 6.2 | 4.7 | 10.1 | 11.8 | | | All Other Non-Current | 4.8 | 4.8 |
| 10.9 | 44.1 | 41.4 | 39.5 | 33.5 | | | Net Worth | 35.4 | 26.5 |
| 100.0 | 100.0 | 100.0 | 100.0 | 100.0 | | | Total Liabilities & Net Worth | 100.0 | 100.0 |
| | | | | | | | INCOME DATA | | |
| 100.0 | 100.0 | 100.0 | 100.0 | 100.0 | | | Net Sales | 100.0 | 100.0 |
| | | | | | | | Gross Profit | | |
| 91.7 | 84.5 | 89.9 | 91.8 | 97.8 | | | Operating Expenses | 89.5 | 92.6 |
| 8.3 | 15.5 | 10.1 | 8.2 | 2.2 | | | Operating Profit | 10.5 | 7.4 |
| -.1 | 4.2 | 1.9 | .8 | .0 | | | All Other Expenses (net) | 1.1 | -1.0 |
| 8.4 | 11.3 | 8.2 | 7.3 | 2.2 | | | Profit Before Taxes | 9.4 | 8.3 |
| | | | | | | | RATIOS | | |
| 6.6 | 10.1 | 3.1 | 2.7 | 2.1 | | | | 3.3 | 4.1 |
| 2.1 | 3.5 | 1.9 | 1.7 | 1.7 | | | Current | 1.8 | 2.1 |
| .8 | 1.1 | 1.3 | 1.3 | 1.3 | | | | 1.2 | 1.3 |
| 5.7 | 9.1 | 2.7 | 2.0 | 1.7 | | | | 3.0 | 3.8 |
| 1.7 | 3.0 | 1.7 | 1.4 | 1.3 | | | Quick | 1.6 | 1.8 |
| .7 | 1.1 | 1.2 | 1.1 | 1.1 | | | | 1.0 | 1.1 |
| 0 UND | 0 UND | 39 9.3 | 55 6.6 | 53 6.9 | | | | 0 UND | 0 UND |
| 0 UND | 1 493.0 | 73 5.0 | 73 5.0 | 78 4.7 | | | Sales/Receivables | 62 5.9 | 60 6.1 |
| 25 14.4 | 54 6.7 | 99 3.7 | 99 3.7 | 94 3.9 | | | | 94 3.9 | 83 4.4 |
| | | | | | | | Cost of Sales/Inventory | | |
| | | | | | | | Cost of Sales/Payables | | |
| 7.4 | 4.4 | 4.1 | 4.2 | 5.3 | | | | 5.1 | 4.1 |
| 37.2 | 8.5 | 7.5 | 7.3 | 7.1 | | | Sales/Working Capital | 9.2 | 7.0 |
| -46.9 | 45.1 | 18.0 | 12.4 | 9.3 | | | | 36.6 | 23.1 |
| 57.8 | 62.4 | 90.6 | 68.6 | 42.4 | | | | 70.1 | 82.5 |
| (24) 8.6 | (34) 27.9 | (76) 20.2 | (61) 17.2 | (16) 7.3 | | | EBIT/Interest | (241) 17.1 | (163) 15.0 |
| -10.2 | .9 | 1.1 | 4.5 | 3.4 | | | | 4.8 | -1.2 |
| | | 20.8 | 4.8 | 2.2 | | | Net Profit + Depr., Dep., | 8.7 | 4.7 |
| | (15) 2.7 | (23) 1.7 | (11) 1.6 | | | | Amort./Cur. Mat. L/T/D | (45) 5.0 | (31) 2.0 |
| | | .4 | .7 | -.1 | | | | 2.2 | .8 |
| .0 | .0 | .1 | .1 | .3 | | | | .1 | .1 |
| .3 | .2 | .2 | .4 | .8 | | | Fixed/Worth | .2 | .3 |
| 7.4 | 1.8 | 1.2 | .8 | 1.2 | | | | .8 | 1.3 |
| .3 | .2 | .5 | 1.1 | 1.4 | | | | .5 | .7 |
| .8 | .8 | 1.2 | 1.8 | 2.2 | | | Debt/Worth | 1.3 | 1.6 |
| -6.7 | 8.0 | 4.6 | 3.3 | 6.7 | | | | 4.2 | 8.4 |
| 268.6 | 113.1 | 76.9 | 61.6 | 25.5 | | | | 92.2 | 97.0 |
| (32) 104.6 | (50) 38.9 | (95) 39.4 | (70) 24.7 | (14) 12.4 | | | % Profit Before Taxes/Tangible Net Worth | (268) 38.7 | (188) 38.4 |
| 19.6 | 9.5 | 7.1 | 9.5 | -.2 | | | | 12.8 | 8.6 |
| 160.7 | 65.9 | 31.4 | 21.5 | 10.0 | | | % Profit Before Taxes/Total Assets | 49.8 | 45.5 |
| 38.8 | 33.0 | 13.3 | 8.7 | 3.9 | | | | 16.2 | 17.1 |
| .6 | 2.1 | 1.6 | 3.2 | -1.6 | | | | 4.7 | .6 |
| 798.2 | 247.8 | 87.3 | 50.3 | 25.4 | | | | 96.1 | 98.7 |
| 83.6 | 96.1 | 36.6 | 17.2 | 11.4 | | | Sales/Net Fixed Assets | 38.7 | 34.0 |
| 30.6 | 20.3 | 13.5 | 10.0 | 7.1 | | | | 18.8 | 15.5 |
| 16.1 | 5.6 | 3.3 | 2.6 | 1.8 | | | | 4.5 | 3.9 |
| 6.5 | 3.7 | 2.3 | 1.7 | 1.6 | | | Sales/Total Assets | 2.8 | 2.5 |
| 3.6 | 2.0 | 1.6 | 1.4 | 1.0 | | | | 2.0 | 1.7 |
| .2 | .2 | .5 | .5 | 1.0 | | | | .5 | .6 |
| (12) .7 | (19) 1.2 | (69) 1.0 | (60) .8 | (14) 2.0 | | | % Depr., Dep., Amort./Sales | (210) .9 | (137) 1.2 |
| 1.2 | 4.2 | 1.4 | 1.6 | 2.6 | | | | 1.5 | 2.1 |
| 5.4 | 4.7 | 2.4 | 2.0 | | | | % Officers', Directors' Owners' Comp/Sales | 3.8 | 4.3 |
| (16) 9.0 | (25) 6.9 | (25) 5.5 | (12) 7.4 | | | | | (110) 6.5 | (98) 7.9 |
| 16.9 | 12.2 | 9.3 | 9.9 | | | | | 11.5 | 12.1 |
| 109543M | 299510M | 1295163M | 3071351M | 1812945M | 2059152M | | Net Sales ($) | 8547140M | 4397985M |
| 11104M | 67924M | 543819M | 1607108M | 1182252M | 1590760M | | Total Assets ($) | 3295644M | 2497985M |

M = $ thousand   MM = $ million
See Pages viii through xx for Explanation of Ratios and Data

© RMA 2024

# PROFESSIONAL SERVICES—Architectural Services  NAICS 541310

## Comparative Historical Data / Current Data Sorted by Sales

| Comparative Historical Data | | | | Type of Statement | Current Data Sorted by Sales | | | | | |
|---|---|---|---|---|---|---|---|---|---|---|
| 11 | 15 | 9 | | Unqualified | | | | 2 | 2 | 7 |
| 23 | 40 | 46 | | Reviewed | | | | 9 | 14 | 30 |
| 20 | 28 | 28 | | Compiled | 1 | | 3 | 9 | 9 | 6 |
| 30 | 47 | 43 | | Tax Returns | 5 | 13 | 6 | 12 | 6 | 1 |
| 140 | 178 | 184 | | Other | 18 | 30 | 16 | 31 | 43 | 46 |
| 4/1/21-3/31/22 ALL | 4/1/22-3/31/23 ALL | 4/1/23-3/31/24 ALL | | | \multicolumn{3}{c}{31 (4/1-9/30/23)} | \multicolumn{3}{c}{279 (10/1/23-3/31/24)} | |
| | | | | | 0-1MM | 1-3MM | 3-5MM | 5-10MM | 10-25MM | 25MM & OVER |
| 224 | 308 | 310 | | NUMBER OF STATEMENTS | 24 | 43 | 25 | 54 | 74 | 90 |
| % | % | % | | ASSETS | % | % | % | % | % | % |
| 28.9 | 27.5 | 24.8 | | Cash & Equivalents | 16.8 | 38.6 | 25.3 | 32.5 | 24.1 | 16.2 |
| 34.8 | 36.4 | 34.4 | | Trade Receivables (net) | 23.1 | 23.3 | 26.4 | 37.6 | 37.7 | 40.3 |
| 2.0 | 2.2 | 1.5 | | Inventory | .0 | 1.3 | 2.9 | .4 | 1.7 | 2.0 |
| 6.3 | 5.6 | 5.9 | | All Other Current | .4 | 4.8 | 6.2 | 3.7 | 5.7 | 9.3 |
| 72.0 | 71.7 | 66.6 | | Total Current | 40.3 | 68.1 | 60.7 | 74.1 | 69.2 | 67.9 |
| 14.9 | 13.2 | 16.0 | | Fixed Assets (net) | 45.1 | 14.3 | 17.2 | 12.1 | 12.6 | 13.7 |
| 5.4 | 4.8 | 5.2 | | Intangibles (net) | 3.3 | 6.1 | 7.4 | 3.9 | 4.9 | 5.8 |
| 7.7 | 10.3 | 12.2 | | All Other Non-Current | 11.7 | 11.5 | 14.6 | 9.8 | 13.3 | 12.6 |
| 100.0 | 100.0 | 100.0 | | Total | 100.0 | 100.0 | 100.0 | 100.0 | 100.0 | 100.0 |
| | | | | LIABILITIES | | | | | | |
| 5.8 | 10.7 | 7.3 | | Notes Payable-Short Term | 14.1 | 15.2 | 13.5 | 3.8 | 6.4 | 2.7 |
| 2.8 | 1.7 | 2.2 | | Cur. Mat.-L.T.D. | 1.7 | 2.8 | 2.2 | 1.2 | 2.3 | 2.7 |
| 11.8 | 12.4 | 12.1 | | Trade Payables | 6.7 | 4.1 | 6.7 | 14.1 | 16.7 | 13.8 |
| .2 | .4 | .2 | | Income Taxes Payable | .3 | .3 | .2 | .0 | .4 | .2 |
| 19.1 | 18.3 | 17.6 | | All Other Current | 3.5 | 17.5 | 19.8 | 18.1 | 17.1 | 21.0 |
| 39.7 | 43.6 | 39.4 | | Total Current | 26.3 | 39.9 | 42.3 | 37.1 | 42.8 | 40.3 |
| 15.3 | 12.0 | 14.5 | | Long-Term Debt | 31.0 | 18.7 | 16.1 | 8.5 | 13.0 | 12.5 |
| .5 | .5 | .5 | | Deferred Taxes | .0 | .0 | .3 | .4 | .5 | .9 |
| 5.2 | 5.7 | 9.4 | | All Other Non-Current | 4.3 | 21.2 | .2 | 9.1 | 7.6 | 9.3 |
| 39.4 | 38.2 | 36.2 | | Net Worth | 38.7 | 20.2 | 41.0 | 44.9 | 36.0 | 36.9 |
| 100.0 | 100.0 | 100.0 | | Total Liabilities & Net Worth | 100.0 | 100.0 | 100.0 | 100.0 | 100.0 | 100.0 |
| | | | | INCOME DATA | | | | | | |
| 100.0 | 100.0 | 100.0 | | Net Sales | 100.0 | 100.0 | 100.0 | 100.0 | 100.0 | 100.0 |
| | | | | Gross Profit | | | | | | |
| 89.0 | 89.4 | 90.1 | | Operating Expenses | 70.5 | 87.2 | 91.2 | 93.1 | 92.3 | 92.8 |
| 11.0 | 10.6 | 9.9 | | Operating Profit | 29.5 | 12.8 | 8.8 | 6.9 | 7.7 | 7.2 |
| -1.3 | .5 | 1.7 | | All Other Expenses (net) | 14.9 | 1.6 | .0 | -.5 | .6 | .8 |
| 12.3 | 10.1 | 8.2 | | Profit Before Taxes | 14.6 | 11.2 | 8.8 | 7.4 | 7.1 | 6.4 |
| | | | | RATIOS | | | | | | |
| 3.7 | 3.8 | 3.7 | | | 4.0 | 13.5 | 5.8 | 5.5 | 3.2 | 2.3 |
| 2.2 | 2.0 | 1.9 | | Current | 1.6 | 3.6 | 2.6 | 2.2 | 1.7 | 1.7 |
| 1.3 | 1.3 | 1.3 | | | .7 | 1.0 | 1.7 | 1.5 | 1.2 | 1.3 |
| 3.4 | 3.5 | 3.3 | | | 4.0 | 9.5 | 4.4 | 5.1 | 2.7 | 1.9 |
| 2.0 | 1.8 | 1.7 | | Quick | 1.4 | 3.0 | 2.0 | 2.1 | 1.6 | 1.3 |
| 1.2 | 1.1 | 1.1 | | | .7 | .7 | 1.5 | 1.3 | 1.1 | 1.0 |
| 10  36.5 | 18  20.0 | 1  291.8 | | | 0  UND | 0  UND | 0  UND | 0  UND | 35  10.3 | 55  6.6 |
| 58  6.3 | 65  5.6 | 61  6.0 | | Sales/Receivables | 0  UND | 0  999.8 | 27  13.7 | 66  5.5 | 70  5.2 | 72  5.1 |
| 85  4.3 | 91  4.0 | 89  4.1 | | | 63  5.8 | 56  6.5 | 87  4.2 | 101  3.6 | 91  4.0 | 89  4.1 |
| | | | | Cost of Sales/Inventory | | | | | | |
| | | | | Cost of Sales/Payables | | | | | | |
| 4.1 | 4.2 | 4.5 | | | 3.1 | 4.4 | 4.5 | 4.0 | 5.5 | 4.9 |
| 6.5 | 7.4 | 8.3 | | Sales/Working Capital | 8.8 | 9.6 | 8.4 | 7.0 | 11.0 | 8.0 |
| 15.8 | 18.6 | 21.5 | | | -11.2 | -73.1 | 46.0 | 18.5 | 24.4 | 12.9 |
| 171.5 | 121.0 | 65.7 | | | | 59.9 | 68.7 | 164.7 | 61.9 | 65.7 |
| (162)  42.2 | (203)  27.0 | (218)  17.2 | | EBIT/Interest | (24)  14.5 | (16)  9.5 | (34)  34.9 | (62)  11.9 | (74)  18.0 |
| 9.3 | 4.6 | 3.2 | | | | -7.5 | -3.4 | 3.5 | 1.2 | 4.8 |
| 13.5 | 7.1 | 8.6 | | | | | | | 15.0 | 6.5 |
| (28)  3.9 | (56)  3.7 | (55)  1.7 | | Net Profit + Depr., Dep., Amort./Cur. Mat. L/T/D | | | | (14)  1.4 | (34)  1.8 |
| 2.5 | 1.4 | .7 | | | | | | | .0 | 1.0 |
| .1 | .1 | .1 | | | .0 | .0 | .0 | .0 | .1 | .1 |
| .2 | .2 | .3 | | Fixed/Worth | 1.4 | .1 | .2 | .2 | .3 | .4 |
| .7 | .7 | 1.1 | | | 5.7 | 5.4 | 1.0 | .6 | 1.2 | 1.1 |
| .4 | .4 | .5 | | | .5 | .1 | .4 | .4 | .5 | 1.1 |
| 1.1 | 1.2 | 1.4 | | Debt/Worth | 3.3 | .6 | .8 | .9 | 2.0 | 2.1 |
| 3.3 | 4.3 | 5.1 | | | 8.0 | -13.0 | 3.2 | 3.0 | 8.7 | 3.9 |
| 104.9 | 89.2 | 93.4 | | | 63.6 | 268.6 | 95.1 | 104.4 | 118.6 | 55.1 |
| (190)  50.2 | (264)  38.0 | (268)  33.6 | | % Profit Before Taxes/Tangible Net Worth | (22)  16.2 | (32)  81.6 | (21)  35.9 | (48)  48.7 | (64)  29.8 | (81)  24.6 |
| 18.4 | 8.3 | 8.9 | | | 1.4 | 20.8 | 1.2 | 15.7 | 2.1 | 9.8 |
| 54.6 | 47.7 | 39.1 | | | 26.0 | 130.5 | 62.7 | 41.7 | 39.4 | 18.9 |
| 25.5 | 18.5 | 13.0 | | % Profit Before Taxes/Total Assets | 3.7 | 34.0 | 22.7 | 18.0 | 13.2 | 8.5 |
| 6.1 | 3.1 | 1.9 | | | 1.6 | 4.7 | -.3 | 4.4 | 1.5 | 2.9 |
| 91.8 | 122.5 | 109.6 | | | 103.8 | 342.2 | 982.3 | 160.3 | 91.3 | 42.4 |
| 32.9 | 36.9 | 36.2 | | Sales/Net Fixed Assets | 10.0 | 89.4 | 114.7 | 40.5 | 45.5 | 18.1 |
| 16.7 | 17.4 | 12.4 | | | .2 | 38.1 | 14.8 | 14.4 | 15.7 | 9.6 |
| 3.7 | 3.8 | 3.9 | | | 2.5 | 6.4 | 5.4 | 4.6 | 3.9 | 2.7 |
| 2.6 | 2.3 | 2.4 | | Sales/Total Assets | .6 | 4.0 | 3.7 | 2.9 | 2.3 | 1.9 |
| 1.8 | 1.6 | 1.5 | | | .1 | 2.1 | 1.8 | 1.8 | 1.6 | 1.4 |
| .5 | .5 | .5 | | | .6 | .2 | .6 | .4 | .5 | |
| (136)  1.0 | (184)  .9 | (182)  1.0 | | % Depr., Dep., Amort./Sales | (12)  .9 | (10)  1.5 | (25)  1.0 | (51)  .8 | (78)  1.1 |
| 1.9 | 1.7 | 1.7 | | | | 3.3 | 2.6 | 1.4 | 1.3 | 1.8 |
| 3.5 | 4.8 | 3.6 | | | 6.6 | 4.7 | 2.3 | 1.7 | 3.0 | |
| (82)  6.5 | (90)  9.0 | (81)  7.0 | | % Officers', Directors' Owners' Comp/Sales | (16)  10.9 | (10)  6.8 | (20)  5.4 | (17)  6.1 | (14)  8.1 |
| 12.7 | 13.0 | 11.6 | | | | 15.3 | 11.6 | 9.3 | 8.3 | 12.9 |
| 5106974M | 10193591M | 8647664M | | Net Sales ($) | 9174M | 84865M | 95567M | 417294M | 1142257M | 6898507M |
| 2711803M | 5811780M | 5002967M | | Total Assets ($) | 29241M | 36064M | 47700M | 168189M | 505785M | 4215988M |

© RMA 2024   M = $ thousand   MM = $ million
See Pages viii through xx for Explanation of Ratios and Data

# PROFESSIONAL SERVICES—Landscape Architectural Services  NAICS 541320

## Current Data Sorted by Assets | Comparative Historical Data

| | | | | | | | Type of Statement | | |
|---|---|---|---|---|---|---|---|---|---|
| | | 1 | 1 | 5 | | | Unqualified | 6 | 2 |
| | 1 | 3 | 8 | 2 | | | Reviewed | 13 | 5 |
| | 3 | 9 | 4 | 1 | | | Compiled | 6 | 5 |
| 4 | 9 | 15 | 7 | 1 | | 1 | Tax Returns | 27 | 18 |
| 6 | 15 | 12 (4/1-9/30/23) | 31 | 8 | 2 | | Other | 77 | 66 |
| 0-500M | 500M-2MM | 2-10MM | 10-50MM | 50-100MM | 100-250MM | | | 4/1/19-3/31/20 ALL | 4/1/20-3/31/21 ALL |
| 10 | 28 | 51 | 17 | 2 | 1 | | NUMBER OF STATEMENTS | 129 | 96 |
| % | % | % | % | % | % | | ASSETS | % | % |
| 26.1 | 21.4 | 10.9 | 11.0 | | | | Cash & Equivalents | 18.4 | 23.5 |
| 2.1 | 21.2 | 27.2 | 28.1 | | | | Trade Receivables (net) | 26.3 | 21.3 |
| 9.7 | 1.7 | 4.8 | 1.8 | | | | Inventory | 2.8 | 3.5 |
| 2.9 | 5.4 | 5.5 | 7.8 | | | | All Other Current | 5.1 | 5.1 |
| 40.9 | 49.8 | 48.3 | 48.7 | | | | Total Current | 52.6 | 53.4 |
| 33.0 | 36.6 | 35.7 | 30.6 | | | | Fixed Assets (net) | 31.5 | 28.3 |
| 11.2 | 6.0 | 5.9 | 11.3 | | | | Intangibles (net) | 6.7 | 5.3 |
| 14.9 | 7.5 | 10.1 | 9.5 | | | | All Other Non-Current | 9.2 | 13.0 |
| 100.0 | 100.0 | 100.0 | 100.0 | | | | Total | 100.0 | 100.0 |
| | | | | | | | LIABILITIES | | |
| 51.3 | 8.8 | 5.4 | .9 | | | | Notes Payable-Short Term | 9.8 | 10.3 |
| 19.0 | 6.8 | 4.5 | 4.8 | | | | Cur. Mat.-L.T.D. | 4.3 | 4.2 |
| 2.4 | 4.4 | 9.9 | 10.4 | | | | Trade Payables | 9.2 | 7.1 |
| .1 | .0 | .0 | .2 | | | | Income Taxes Payable | .0 | .1 |
| 20.5 | 9.8 | 8.5 | 11.2 | | | | All Other Current | 10.6 | 8.7 |
| 93.3 | 29.7 | 28.3 | 27.5 | | | | Total Current | 34.0 | 30.3 |
| 64.5 | 35.9 | 26.3 | 22.1 | | | | Long-Term Debt | 30.4 | 37.2 |
| .0 | .0 | .2 | .3 | | | | Deferred Taxes | .2 | .2 |
| 1.2 | 2.6 | 1.8 | 23.2 | | | | All Other Non-Current | 4.7 | 4.0 |
| -59.1 | 31.7 | 43.3 | 27.0 | | | | Net Worth | 30.8 | 28.2 |
| 100.0 | 100.0 | 100.0 | 100.0 | | | | Total Liabilities & Net Worth | 100.0 | 100.0 |
| | | | | | | | INCOME DATA | | |
| 100.0 | 100.0 | 100.0 | 100.0 | | | | Net Sales | 100.0 | 100.0 |
| | | | | | | | Gross Profit | | |
| 94.5 | 87.9 | 87.4 | 91.3 | | | | Operating Expenses | 91.6 | 92.7 |
| 5.5 | 12.1 | 12.6 | 8.7 | | | | Operating Profit | 8.4 | 7.3 |
| -1.7 | 4.1 | 2.0 | 1.7 | | | | All Other Expenses (net) | .5 | -.5 |
| 7.2 | 8.0 | 10.6 | 6.9 | | | | Profit Before Taxes | 7.9 | 7.8 |
| | | | | | | | RATIOS | | |
| 3.4 | 3.7 | 2.9 | 2.3 | | | | | 3.4 | 4.2 |
| .7 | 1.9 | 1.6 | 1.5 | | | | Current | 1.5 | 1.8 |
| .2 | .9 | 1.0 | 1.3 | | | | | .8 | .9 |
| 3.3 | 3.0 | 2.6 | 1.8 | | | | | 2.6 | 3.4 |
| .7 | 1.7 | 1.3 | 1.3 | | | | Quick | 1.3 | 1.4 |
| .1 | .8 | .5 | .9 | | | | | .7 | .6 |
| 0 UND | 0 UND | 13 27.3 | 24 15.4 | | | | | 0 UND | 4 103.0 |
| 0 UND | 18 20.8 | 31 11.8 | 51 7.2 | | | | Sales/Receivables | 31 11.9 | 25 14.7 |
| 0 UND | 41 8.9 | 57 6.4 | 73 5.0 | | | | | 53 6.9 | 49 7.4 |
| | | | | | | | Cost of Sales/Inventory | | |
| | | | | | | | Cost of Sales/Payables | | |
| 22.1 | 6.9 | 5.7 | 5.5 | | | | | 7.5 | 5.2 |
| UND | 13.8 | 13.5 | 10.3 | | | | Sales/Working Capital | 18.4 | 12.3 |
| -22.8 | NM | 999.8 | 22.2 | | | | | -77.8 | -277.6 |
| | 20.9 | 34.6 | 42.9 | | | | | 40.5 | 26.2 |
| | (19) 9.5 | (41) 12.1 | (15) 26.9 | | | | EBIT/Interest | (108) 10.6 | (81) 10.7 |
| | 1.1 | 4.2 | 5.6 | | | | | 3.1 | 2.4 |
| | | | | | | | Net Profit + Depr., Dep., Amort./Cur. Mat. L/T/D | | |
| .1 | .2 | .4 | .4 | | | | | .3 | .2 |
| 1.9 | 1.2 | 1.0 | .9 | | | | Fixed/Worth | 1.0 | .9 |
| -9.7 | NM | 2.5 | NM | | | | | 5.8 | 8.9 |
| 2.2 | .6 | .6 | .9 | | | | | .6 | .9 |
| 125.6 | 1.4 | 1.7 | 1.1 | | | | Debt/Worth | 1.7 | 2.1 |
| -8.4 | -151.5 | 6.5 | NM | | | | | 10.3 | NM |
| | 110.0 | 65.6 | 58.6 | | | | % Profit Before Taxes/Tangible Net Worth | 95.8 | 102.4 |
| | (20) 60.4 | (45) 31.6 | (13) 22.3 | | | | | (102) 49.5 | (72) 43.6 |
| | 25.5 | 13.5 | 14.1 | | | | | 22.8 | 18.7 |
| 74.6 | 56.5 | 27.8 | 19.8 | | | | % Profit Before Taxes/Total Assets | 39.0 | 32.5 |
| 34.2 | 16.7 | 19.2 | 8.8 | | | | | 17.1 | 14.9 |
| -2.5 | 1.3 | 4.2 | 7.0 | | | | | 8.3 | 4.4 |
| UND | 45.3 | 45.2 | 19.4 | | | | Sales/Net Fixed Assets | 40.1 | 54.9 |
| 45.7 | 15.1 | 8.3 | 8.2 | | | | | 14.5 | 12.1 |
| 16.2 | 5.9 | 4.6 | 3.5 | | | | | 7.0 | 5.4 |
| 15.8 | 4.4 | 3.6 | 2.6 | | | | Sales/Total Assets | 4.7 | 3.9 |
| 7.3 | 3.6 | 2.4 | 1.9 | | | | | 3.1 | 2.4 |
| 4.3 | 2.4 | 1.7 | 1.3 | | | | | 2.3 | 1.8 |
| | .3 | 1.4 | 1.0 | | | | % Depr., Dep., Amort./Sales | 1.2 | 1.2 |
| | (15) 2.4 | (26) 2.8 | (16) 2.3 | | | | | (76) 2.2 | (48) 2.9 |
| | 9.5 | 5.2 | 3.3 | | | | | 3.8 | 4.8 |
| | 2.2 | .9 | | | | | % Officers', Directors' Owners' Comp/Sales | 1.8 | 2.4 |
| | (12) 4.3 | (18) 1.8 | | | | | | (57) 4.1 | (41) 4.4 |
| | 10.4 | 3.3 | | | | | | 8.8 | 10.0 |
| 21958M | 122010M | 624048M | 574701M | 202345M | 169306M | | Net Sales ($) | 3177794M | 1062848M |
| 2772M | 31061M | 245214M | 340364M | 116966M | 148676M | | Total Assets ($) | 769816M | 493625M |

© RMA 2024

M = $ thousand    MM = $ million
See Pages viii through xx for Explanation of Ratios and Data

# PROFESSIONAL SERVICES—Landscape Architectural Services  NAICS 541320

| Comparative Historical Data ||| | Current Data Sorted by Sales ||||||
|---|---|---|---|---|---|---|---|---|---|
| | | | **Type of Statement** | | | | | | |
| 1 | 5 | 6 | Unqualified | | 1 | | | 1 | 4 |
| 5 | 7 | 11 | Reviewed | | | 1 | | 7 | 3 |
| 6 | 11 | 9 | Compiled | 1 | | 2 | 2 | 2 | 2 |
| 15 | 30 | 21 | Tax Returns | 2 | 4 | 3 | 7 | 4 | 1 |
| 48 | 76 | 62 | Other | 8 | 12 | 7 | 11 | 12 | 12 |
| 4/1/21-3/31/22 | 4/1/22-3/31/23 | 4/1/23-3/31/24 | | | 12 (4/1-9/30/23) ||| 97 (10/1/23-3/31/24) |||
| ALL | ALL | ALL | | 0-1MM | 1-3MM | 3-5MM | 5-10MM | 10-25MM | 25MM & OVER |
| 75 | 129 | 109 | **NUMBER OF STATEMENTS** | 11 | 17 | 13 | 20 | 26 | 22 |
| % | % | % | **ASSETS** | % | % | % | % | % | % |
| 23.5 | 22.4 | 14.8 | Cash & Equivalents | 11.1 | 24.6 | 11.4 | 14.6 | 15.5 | 10.6 |
| 24.0 | 23.2 | 23.5 | Trade Receivables (net) | .0 | 15.6 | 29.1 | 24.4 | 27.1 | 33.0 |
| 2.8 | 3.0 | 4.0 | Inventory | .0 | 7.2 | 1.1 | 5.1 | 5.6 | 2.1 |
| 4.9 | 5.0 | 5.6 | All Other Current | .4 | 2.1 | 11.5 | 7.0 | 4.3 | 7.7 |
| 55.2 | 53.6 | 47.9 | Total Current | 11.6 | 49.5 | 53.1 | 51.0 | 52.5 | 53.4 |
| 28.9 | 30.3 | 34.9 | Fixed Assets (net) | 58.5 | 35.7 | 26.0 | 33.3 | 33.3 | 31.0 |
| 6.9 | 6.5 | 7.5 | Intangibles (net) | 7.8 | 11.1 | 4.9 | 5.4 | 7.2 | 8.6 |
| 9.0 | 9.6 | 9.7 | All Other Non-Current | 22.1 | 3.8 | 16.0 | 10.2 | 6.9 | 7.0 |
| 100.0 | 100.0 | 100.0 | Total | 100.0 | 100.0 | 100.0 | 100.0 | 100.0 | 100.0 |
| | | | **LIABILITIES** | | | | | | |
| 7.3 | 4.5 | 9.7 | Notes Payable-Short Term | 8.1 | 29.9 | 8.2 | 7.3 | 6.2 | 2.3 |
| 3.9 | 5.0 | 6.4 | Cur. Mat.-L.T.D. | 14.7 | 2.7 | 6.8 | 5.4 | 7.8 | 4.4 |
| 5.3 | 7.6 | 7.8 | Trade Payables | .0 | 4.7 | 7.5 | 8.6 | 8.1 | 13.3 |
| .1 | .1 | .1 | Income Taxes Payable | .0 | .0 | .0 | .0 | .1 | .1 |
| 7.8 | 9.2 | 10.6 | All Other Current | 8.7 | 12.1 | 9.7 | 11.6 | 9.1 | 11.8 |
| 24.4 | 26.4 | 34.7 | Total Current | 31.6 | 49.4 | 32.2 | 33.0 | 31.2 | 31.9 |
| 27.9 | 30.5 | 31.2 | Long-Term Debt | 67.2 | 38.4 | 43.8 | 20.0 | 24.9 | 17.7 |
| .1 | .2 | .2 | Deferred Taxes | .0 | .0 | .0 | .0 | .4 | .3 |
| 4.4 | 5.1 | 5.3 | All Other Non-Current | .0 | 2.2 | 2.0 | 4.5 | 6.0 | 12.4 |
| 43.2 | 37.7 | 28.7 | Net Worth | 1.2 | 10.0 | 22.0 | 42.5 | 37.5 | 37.7 |
| 100.0 | 100.0 | 100.0 | Total Liabilities & Net Worth | 100.0 | 100.0 | 100.0 | 100.0 | 100.0 | 100.0 |
| | | | **INCOME DATA** | | | | | | |
| 100.0 | 100.0 | 100.0 | Net Sales | 100.0 | 100.0 | 100.0 | 100.0 | 100.0 | 100.0 |
| | | | Gross Profit | | | | | | |
| 87.9 | 87.1 | 89.0 | Operating Expenses | 58.0 | 89.5 | 94.3 | 93.6 | 93.0 | 92.1 |
| 12.1 | 12.9 | 11.0 | Operating Profit | 42.0 | 10.5 | 5.7 | 6.4 | 7.0 | 7.9 |
| -1.6 | 1.8 | 2.1 | All Other Expenses (net) | 18.4 | 1.2 | .1 | .0 | .0 | .3 |
| 13.6 | 11.1 | 8.9 | Profit Before Taxes | 23.6 | 9.3 | 5.6 | 6.4 | 7.0 | 7.5 |
| | | | **RATIOS** | | | | | | |
| 5.6 | 4.0 | 2.9 | | 8.3 | 3.1 | 3.9 | 3.4 | 2.9 | 2.5 |
| 2.3 | 2.1 | 1.6 | Current | .6 | 1.7 | 1.3 | 1.6 | 1.7 | 1.6 |
| 1.4 | 1.3 | 1.0 | | .1 | .8 | .8 | .8 | 1.1 | 1.3 |
| 4.5 | 3.3 | 2.6 | | 2.6 | 2.6 | 3.1 | 2.8 | 2.7 | 2.3 |
| 2.0 | 1.8 | 1.3 | Quick | .5 | 1.7 | .9 | 1.6 | 1.5 | 1.3 |
| 1.0 | .9 | .6 | | .1 | .8 | .4 | .3 | .6 | .7 |
| 0 UND | 0 UND | 2 169.2 | | 0 UND | 0 UND | 0 UND | 2 202.4 | 15 24.6 | 30 12.0 |
| 26 14.3 | 25 14.8 | 28 13.2 | Sales/Receivables | 0 UND | 17 21.7 | 33 11.2 | 28 13.0 | 38 9.6 | 61 6.0 |
| 55 6.6 | 58 6.3 | 53 6.9 | | 0 UND | 32 11.3 | 53 6.9 | 55 6.6 | 47 7.7 | 73 5.0 |
| | | | Cost of Sales/Inventory | | | | | | |
| | | | Cost of Sales/Payables | | | | | | |
| 5.0 | 5.9 | 6.4 | | 4.5 | 7.2 | 8.0 | 5.5 | 5.9 | 5.6 |
| 10.2 | 11.3 | 14.7 | Sales/Working Capital | -19.5 | 23.6 | 13.0 | 12.9 | 18.6 | 10.2 |
| 27.6 | 46.8 | UND | | -7.8 | -30.7 | NM | NM | 71.7 | 21.1 |
| 121.8 | 35.5 | 35.4 | | | 35.4 | 11.4 | 35.8 | 33.3 | 58.2 |
| (54) 32.4 | (101) 9.6 | (87) 10.9 | EBIT/Interest | (11) 5.3 | (10) 3.1 | (19) 16.6 | (23) 13.0 | (19) 26.9 |
| 8.3 | 2.5 | 4.1 | | | .8 | -4.9 | 3.3 | 4.9 | 7.0 |
| | 6.3 | 3.2 | Net Profit + Depr., Dep., | | | | | | |
| (15) 3.3 | (12) 2.2 | Amort./Cur. Mat. L/T/D | | | | | | | |
| | 2.0 | 1.0 | | | | | | | |
| .1 | .2 | .4 | | 1.0 | .2 | .1 | .1 | .4 | .4 |
| .6 | .9 | 1.1 | Fixed/Worth | 1.6 | 1.2 | 1.9 | .7 | 1.1 | .6 |
| 2.0 | 4.8 | 5.0 | | 5.1 | NM | -9.6 | 4.3 | 1.8 | 2.7 |
| .4 | .6 | .7 | | .2 | .8 | 1.2 | .3 | .8 | .7 |
| 1.1 | 2.2 | 1.7 | Debt/Worth | 1.7 | 2.5 | 7.9 | 1.2 | 1.7 | 1.1 |
| 3.9 | 16.0 | 14.0 | | 6.5 | -7.2 | -13.6 | 7.3 | 4.7 | 5.5 |
| 109.2 | 96.9 | 79.6 | % Profit Before Taxes/Tangible | | 178.4 | | 70.9 | 115.1 | 60.0 |
| (65) 67.4 | (104) 53.0 | (86) 38.9 | Net Worth | (11) 48.0 | | (16) 31.8 | (23) 55.3 | (18) 28.3 |
| 35.5 | 20.5 | 16.5 | | | 25.8 | | 6.7 | 21.2 | 16.5 |
| 49.3 | 34.7 | 30.7 | % Profit Before Taxes/Total | 30.4 | 34.3 | 55.8 | 27.6 | 31.7 | 22.8 |
| 29.2 | 15.0 | 17.3 | Assets | 6.3 | 17.3 | 27.8 | 15.4 | 21.3 | 13.7 |
| 16.6 | 4.4 | 4.7 | | .1 | -1.1 | -14.1 | 2.9 | 7.2 | 8.1 |
| 43.4 | 49.3 | 41.2 | | 9.2 | 56.5 | 117.2 | 72.0 | 30.1 | 19.1 |
| 13.7 | 12.2 | 10.6 | Sales/Net Fixed Assets | .2 | 14.0 | 47.0 | 12.4 | 8.2 | 10.4 |
| 6.5 | 5.3 | 4.9 | | .1 | 3.2 | 12.2 | 5.9 | 6.6 | 4.0 |
| 3.8 | 4.2 | 3.7 | | 1.7 | 4.6 | 5.9 | 3.6 | 4.1 | 2.8 |
| 2.5 | 2.6 | 2.7 | Sales/Total Assets | .2 | 3.7 | 3.8 | 2.7 | 3.1 | 2.3 |
| 1.9 | 1.7 | 1.7 | | .1 | 1.3 | 2.2 | 1.7 | 2.2 | 1.6 |
| 1.2 | .9 | 1.2 | | | | | .5 | 1.6 | .7 |
| (38) 3.1 | (71) 2.8 | (64) 2.7 | % Depr., Dep., Amort./Sales | | | (11) 2.8 | (18) 2.7 | (18) 2.2 |
| 6.4 | 4.4 | 5.1 | | | | | 4.5 | 4.9 | 3.2 |
| 2.8 | 1.6 | 1.3 | % Officers', Directors' | | | | 1.6 | .8 | |
| (30) 5.5 | (51) 3.5 | (40) 3.2 | Owners' Comp/Sales | | | (12) 3.0 | (10) 1.9 | |
| 10.5 | 10.7 | 8.0 | | | | | 4.0 | 6.4 | |
| 924131M | 2004610M | 1714368M | Net Sales ($) | 5972M | 32216M | 55417M | 152612M | 420074M | 1048077M |
| 411556M | 1015159M | 885053M | Total Assets ($) | 23796M | 37226M | 18410M | 59769M | 161127M | 584725M |

M = $ thousand   MM = $ million
See Pages viii through xx for Explanation of Ratios and Data
© RMA 2024

## PROFESSIONAL SERVICES—Engineering Services  NAICS 541330

### Current Data Sorted by Assets | Comparative Historical Data

| 0-500M | 500M-2MM | 2-10MM | 10-50MM | 50-100MM | 100-250MM | Type of Statement | | | |
|---|---|---|---|---|---|---|---|---|---|
| 1 | 1 | 10 | 49 | 26 | 17 | Unqualified | | 97 | 71 |
| 1 | 3 | 49 | 78 | 14 | 3 | Reviewed | | 168 | 85 |
| 1 | 12 | 31 | 16 | 4 | | Compiled | | 81 | 48 |
| 16 | 42 | 46 | 6 | | 2 | Tax Returns | | 169 | 96 |
| 21 | 93 | 207 | 193 | 48 | 55 | Other | | 634 | 469 |
| | 132 (4/1-9/30/23) | | 913 (10/1/23-3/31/24) | | | | | 4/1/19-3/31/20 | 4/1/20-3/31/21 |
| 40 | 151 | 343 | 342 | 92 | 77 | NUMBER OF STATEMENTS | | ALL 1149 | ALL 769 |
| % | % | % | % | % | % | ASSETS | | % | % |
| 40.0 | 28.2 | 21.2 | 16.8 | 15.4 | 9.3 | Cash & Equivalents | | 18.4 | 28.7 |
| 14.9 | 32.9 | 41.5 | 39.5 | 30.4 | 31.8 | Trade Receivables (net) | | 40.9 | 33.6 |
| 1.6 | 3.1 | 4.5 | 2.8 | 2.3 | 2.6 | Inventory | | 4.1 | 4.1 |
| 2.6 | 5.4 | 6.0 | 10.2 | 12.8 | 7.7 | All Other Current | | 7.2 | 5.5 |
| 59.1 | 69.6 | 73.2 | 69.3 | 60.9 | 51.4 | Total Current | | 70.6 | 71.8 |
| 18.9 | 16.0 | 13.4 | 13.1 | 10.5 | 12.3 | Fixed Assets (net) | | 15.8 | 14.7 |
| 3.1 | 4.9 | 4.1 | 4.9 | 14.1 | 24.6 | Intangibles (net) | | 5.0 | 5.7 |
| 18.9 | 9.5 | 9.3 | 12.8 | 14.4 | 11.7 | All Other Non-Current | | 8.6 | 7.8 |
| 100.0 | 100.0 | 100.0 | 100.0 | 100.0 | 100.0 | Total | | 100.0 | 100.0 |
| | | | | | | LIABILITIES | | | |
| 20.2 | 8.0 | 4.8 | 4.4 | 2.9 | 1.4 | Notes Payable-Short Term | | 8.7 | 7.1 |
| 4.0 | 2.8 | 2.6 | 2.2 | 3.5 | 2.3 | Cur. Mat.-L.T.D. | | 3.0 | 3.3 |
| 9.7 | 7.7 | 10.3 | 11.5 | 7.6 | 8.2 | Trade Payables | | 9.8 | 8.1 |
| .3 | .3 | .1 | .3 | .4 | .1 | Income Taxes Payable | | .4 | .3 |
| 48.5 | 13.5 | 16.0 | 20.6 | 19.4 | 22.0 | All Other Current | | 17.5 | 15.7 |
| 82.6 | 32.3 | 33.9 | 39.0 | 33.9 | 34.0 | Total Current | | 39.4 | 34.4 |
| 25.9 | 17.8 | 10.3 | 9.7 | 15.4 | 20.4 | Long-Term Debt | | 12.6 | 18.9 |
| .0 | .1 | .3 | .4 | .9 | .8 | Deferred Taxes | | .7 | .9 |
| 10.9 | 7.2 | 6.3 | 9.1 | 16.1 | 10.9 | All Other Non-Current | | 6.6 | 6.7 |
| -19.4 | 42.6 | 49.3 | 41.8 | 33.8 | 33.9 | Net Worth | | 40.7 | 39.0 |
| 100.0 | 100.0 | 100.0 | 100.0 | 100.0 | 100.0 | Total Liabilities & Net Worth | | 100.0 | 100.0 |
| | | | | | | INCOME DATA | | | |
| 100.0 | 100.0 | 100.0 | 100.0 | 100.0 | 100.0 | Net Sales | | 100.0 | 100.0 |
| | | | | | | Gross Profit | | | |
| 85.9 | 89.2 | 90.4 | 93.0 | 93.3 | 94.1 | Operating Expenses | | 90.7 | 91.5 |
| 14.1 | 10.8 | 9.6 | 7.0 | 6.7 | 5.9 | Operating Profit | | 9.3 | 8.5 |
| 2.7 | 1.2 | .3 | .4 | 1.1 | 1.7 | All Other Expenses (net) | | 1.3 | .0 |
| 11.4 | 9.6 | 9.3 | 6.6 | 5.7 | 4.1 | Profit Before Taxes | | 8.0 | 8.5 |
| | | | | | | RATIOS | | | |
| 5.0 | 7.0 | 4.8 | 2.9 | 2.9 | 2.2 | | | 3.8 | 4.3 |
| 1.4 | 3.0 | 2.5 | 1.9 | 2.0 | 1.7 | Current | | 2.0 | 2.5 |
| .3 | 1.3 | 1.4 | 1.3 | 1.4 | 1.3 | | | 1.3 | 1.5 |
| 4.7 | 6.1 | 4.1 | 2.5 | 2.2 | 1.9 | | | 3.3 | 3.7 |
| 1.2 | 2.4 | 2.2 | 1.5 | 1.4 | 1.3 | Quick | | 1.6 (768) | 2.1 |
| .3 | 1.0 | 1.1 | 1.1 | 1.0 | .9 | | | 1.0 | 1.2 |
| 0 UND | 0 UND | 36 10.1 | 51 7.2 | 56 6.5 | 58 6.3 | | | 37 9.8 | 31 11.6 |
| 0 UND | 40 9.1 | 65 5.6 | 72 5.1 | 70 5.2 | 76 4.8 | Sales/Receivables | | 62 5.9 | 61 6.0 |
| 27 13.6 | 72 5.1 | 91 4.0 | 94 3.9 | 91 4.0 | 96 3.8 | | | 87 4.2 | 87 4.2 |
| | | | | | | Cost of Sales/Inventory | | | |
| | | | | | | Cost of Sales/Payables | | | |
| 6.6 | 4.3 | 3.6 | 4.0 | 3.6 | 5.2 | | | 4.3 | 3.4 |
| 156.6 | 8.4 | 5.7 | 6.3 | 5.6 | 7.7 | Sales/Working Capital | | 7.7 | 5.5 |
| -16.4 | 41.3 | 15.2 | 13.9 | 11.6 | 15.8 | | | 22.5 | 13.3 |
| 58.3 | 67.7 | 64.3 | 54.8 | 45.8 | 38.6 | | | 59.8 | 77.4 |
| (24) 17.2 | (109) 17.3 | (250) 18.0 | (267) 13.2 | (79) 9.7 | (68) 12.4 | EBIT/Interest | | (906) 14.0 | (601) 16.0 |
| 3.6 | 2.3 | 3.9 | 3.8 | 2.7 | 1.6 | | | 3.7 | 3.2 |
| | | 20.8 | 5.7 | 18.2 | 21.0 | | | 15.0 | 7.7 |
| | (31) | 5.3 (70) | 3.1 (34) | 2.7 (28) | 3.7 | Net Profit + Depr., Dep., Amort./Cur. Mat. L/T/D | | (199) 4.7 | (126) 3.3 |
| | | 1.4 | 1.3 | 1.7 | 1.8 | | | 1.8 | 1.4 |
| .0 | .0 | .0 | .1 | .2 | .2 | | | .1 | .1 |
| .3 | .2 | .2 | .2 | .3 | .8 | Fixed/Worth | | .2 | .2 |
| -5.2 | .8 | .6 | .7 | 1.6 | -.3 | | | .9 | .9 |
| .4 | .2 | .3 | .8 | .9 | 1.3 | | | .5 | .6 |
| 4.5 | 1.0 | .9 | 1.4 | 1.9 | 4.7 | Debt/Worth | | 1.2 | 1.3 |
| -4.2 | 7.3 | 2.4 | 3.4 | 10.0 | -3.6 | | | 3.3 | 4.5 |
| 361.7 | 102.1 | 70.7 | 60.2 | 50.9 | 73.0 | | | 69.6 | 72.3 |
| (26) 146.8 | (125) 48.2 | (306) 34.2 | (313) 31.7 | (75) 23.6 | (52) 23.2 | % Profit Before Taxes/Tangible Net Worth | | (1010) 34.3 | (657) 35.5 |
| 27.6 | 14.8 | 13.7 | 13.5 | 13.2 | 15.8 | | | 12.6 | 10.5 |
| 105.9 | 49.1 | 33.6 | 19.5 | 12.8 | 13.2 | | | 30.8 | 30.0 |
| 32.6 | 23.0 | 16.1 | 11.3 | 8.2 | 6.1 | % Profit Before Taxes/Total Assets | | 13.4 | 11.7 |
| 5.2 | 3.4 | 6.0 | 5.4 | 3.1 | 1.9 | | | 4.1 | 2.7 |
| UND | 337.5 | 216.3 | 89.9 | 40.2 | 38.4 | | | 98.8 | 92.4 |
| 63.5 | 59.8 | 32.3 | 27.4 | 19.7 | 19.9 | Sales/Net Fixed Assets | | 29.7 | 28.0 |
| 24.4 | 16.9 | 12.8 | 10.0 | 11.9 | 9.8 | | | 13.1 | 11.6 |
| 12.4 | 5.0 | 3.2 | 2.5 | 2.0 | 2.1 | | | 3.6 | 3.0 |
| 5.7 | 3.2 | 2.3 | 1.9 | 1.5 | 1.5 | Sales/Total Assets | | 2.5 | 2.1 |
| 2.8 | 2.0 | 1.7 | 1.4 | 1.1 | .9 | | | 1.8 | 1.5 |
| .3 | .4 | .4 | .5 | .9 | .6 | | | .5 | .6 |
| (14) .8 | (53) .8 | (231) .9 | (265) 1.2 | (70) 1.5 | (50) 1.3 | % Depr., Dep., Amort./Sales | | (808) 1.2 | (524) 1.3 |
| 2.8 | 2.5 | 2.1 | 2.3 | 2.5 | 2.4 | | | 2.3 | 2.5 |
| 6.6 | 3.6 | 1.7 | 1.3 | | | | | 3.2 | 3.2 |
| (18) 13.2 | (60) 6.8 | (91) 3.8 | (37) 2.8 | | | % Officers', Directors' Owners' Comp/Sales | | (281) 5.4 | (205) 6.7 |
| 19.8 | 12.0 | 6.8 | 5.8 | | | | | 11.0 | 12.8 |
| 77267M | 809466M | 4820327M | 16994594M | 13909044M | 26560272M | Net Sales ($) | | 44237189M | 26568353M |
| 9781M | 189257M | 1802746M | 7955271M | 6548312M | 11616166M | Total Assets ($) | | 20969664M | 14716494M |

© RMA 2024

M = $ thousand   MM = $ million
See Pages viii through xx for Explanation of Ratios and Data

## PROFESSIONAL SERVICES—Engineering Services  NAICS 541330

### Comparative Historical Data / Current Data Sorted by Sales

| | | | | | Type of Statement | | | | | | |
|---|---|---|---|---|---|---|---|---|---|---|---|
| | 63 | | 104 | 104 | Unqualified | 1 | 1 | | 4 | 8 | 90 |
| | 89 | | 119 | 148 | Reviewed | 2 | 2 | 4 | 11 | 50 | 79 |
| | 37 | | 56 | 64 | Compiled | 1 | 6 | 3 | 15 | 21 | 18 |
| | 101 | | 159 | 112 | Tax Returns | 8 | 22 | 17 | 30 | 27 | 8 |
| | 453 | | 650 | 617 | Other | 17 | 44 | 51 | 83 | 146 | 276 |
| | 4/1/21-3/31/22 ALL | | 4/1/22-3/31/23 ALL | 4/1/23-3/31/24 ALL | | | 132 (4/1-9/30/23) | | | 913 (10/1/23-3/31/24) | |
| | | | | | | 0-1MM | 1-3MM | 3-5MM | 5-10MM | 10-25MM | 25MM & OVER |
| | 743 | | 1088 | 1045 | NUMBER OF STATEMENTS | 29 | 75 | 75 | 143 | 252 | 471 |
| | % | | % | % | ASSETS | % | % | % | % | % | % |
| | 24.8 | | 22.8 | 20.1 | Cash & Equivalents | 26.5 | 24.0 | 28.3 | 22.5 | 23.0 | 15.5 |
| | 36.1 | | 35.3 | 36.9 | Trade Receivables (net) | 10.8 | 30.0 | 31.6 | 39.4 | 39.5 | 38.3 |
| | 3.8 | | 3.7 | 3.3 | Inventory | .5 | 4.1 | 4.6 | 4.4 | 4.0 | 2.4 |
| | 7.2 | | 7.9 | 7.9 | All Other Current | 1.3 | 4.1 | 8.0 | 4.9 | 6.9 | 10.3 |
| | 71.9 | | 69.8 | 68.2 | Total Current | 39.1 | 62.1 | 72.4 | 71.2 | 73.4 | 66.5 |
| | 14.7 | | 14.8 | 13.5 | Fixed Assets (net) | 36.6 | 20.2 | 15.9 | 13.0 | 12.5 | 11.4 |
| | 5.5 | | 5.5 | 6.8 | Intangibles (net) | 1.3 | 6.7 | 4.2 | 6.2 | 3.8 | 9.4 |
| | 7.9 | | 10.0 | 11.5 | All Other Non-Current | 23.0 | 11.0 | 7.4 | 9.6 | 10.2 | 12.7 |
| | 100.0 | | 100.0 | 100.0 | Total | 100.0 | 100.0 | 100.0 | 100.0 | 100.0 | 100.0 |
| | | | | | LIABILITIES | | | | | | |
| | 5.6 | | 6.2 | 5.3 | Notes Payable-Short Term | 10.2 | 15.8 | 4.4 | 5.4 | 5.2 | 3.5 |
| | 2.9 | | 2.8 | 2.6 | Cur. Mat.-L.T.D. | 1.8 | 3.8 | 1.9 | 2.6 | 3.0 | 2.4 |
| | 8.8 | | 9.7 | 9.9 | Trade Payables | 6.6 | 7.1 | 9.5 | 9.0 | 7.9 | 12.0 |
| | .2 | | .2 | .2 | Income Taxes Payable | .0 | .4 | .0 | .3 | .1 | .3 |
| | 15.8 | | 16.9 | 19.1 | All Other Current | 8.8 | 23.3 | 19.2 | 15.1 | 17.8 | 21.0 |
| | 33.3 | | 35.8 | 37.2 | Total Current | 27.3 | 50.3 | 35.1 | 32.4 | 34.1 | 39.2 |
| | 16.2 | | 15.6 | 13.0 | Long-Term Debt | 40.5 | 17.4 | 17.2 | 13.6 | 8.9 | 11.9 |
| | .6 | | .5 | .4 | Deferred Taxes | .0 | .2 | .1 | .3 | .3 | .6 |
| | 7.4 | | 7.4 | 8.7 | All Other Non-Current | 3.2 | 9.1 | 10.3 | 4.8 | 7.6 | 10.5 |
| | 42.6 | | 40.7 | 40.7 | Net Worth | 29.0 | 23.0 | 37.3 | 48.9 | 49.1 | 37.8 |
| | 100.0 | | 100.0 | 100.0 | Total Liabilities & Net Worth | 100.0 | 100.0 | 100.0 | 100.0 | 100.0 | 100.0 |
| | | | | | INCOME DATA | | | | | | |
| | 100.0 | | 100.0 | 100.0 | Net Sales | 100.0 | 100.0 | 100.0 | 100.0 | 100.0 | 100.0 |
| | | | | | Gross Profit | | | | | | |
| | 91.8 | | 90.5 | 91.4 | Operating Expenses | 71.7 | 87.9 | 92.5 | 90.2 | 91.3 | 93.4 |
| | 8.2 | | 9.5 | 8.6 | Operating Profit | 28.3 | 12.1 | 7.5 | 9.8 | 8.7 | 6.6 |
| | -1.6 | | .7 | .7 | All Other Expenses (net) | 11.4 | 1.6 | .1 | -.2 | -.1 | .7 |
| | 9.7 | | 8.8 | 7.9 | Profit Before Taxes | 16.9 | 10.5 | 7.4 | 10.0 | 8.7 | 5.8 |
| | | | | | RATIOS | | | | | | |
| | 4.7 | | 4.5 | 3.7 | | 7.2 | 4.3 | 10.2 | 6.6 | 4.6 | 2.6 |
| | 2.5 | | 2.2 | 2.1 | Current | 1.7 | 1.9 | 3.4 | 2.6 | 2.5 | 1.8 |
| | 1.5 | | 1.4 | 1.3 | | .5 | .7 | 1.3 | 1.3 | 1.5 | 1.3 |
| | 4.0 | | 3.8 | 3.2 | | 7.2 | 3.9 | 8.6 | 5.5 | 4.0 | 2.2 |
| | 2.0 | | 1.9 | 1.6 | Quick | 1.2 | 1.6 | 3.0 | 2.4 | 2.1 | 1.5 |
| | 1.2 | | 1.1 | 1.0 | | .3 | .5 | .9 | 1.1 | 1.2 | 1.0 |
| 37 | 9.9 | 34 | 10.8 | 40 | 9.2 | | 0 UND | 0 UND | 13 28.4 | 32 11.3 | 42 8.7 | 50 7.3 |
| 62 | 5.9 | 62 | 5.9 | 65 | 5.6 | Sales/Receivables | 0 UND | 50 7.3 | 43 8.4 | 64 5.7 | 68 5.4 | 69 5.3 |
| 85 | 4.3 | 87 | 4.2 | 91 | 4.0 | | 46 8.0 | 91 4.0 | 78 4.7 | 96 3.8 | 94 3.9 | 89 4.1 |
| | | | | | Cost of Sales/Inventory | | | | | | |
| | | | | | Cost of Sales/Payables | | | | | | |
| | 3.4 | | 3.6 | 3.9 | | 2.7 | 3.5 | 2.8 | 3.8 | 3.5 | 4.6 |
| | 5.6 | | 6.2 | 6.5 | Sales/Working Capital | 12.3 | 6.5 | 6.1 | 6.0 | 5.5 | 7.3 |
| | 11.6 | | 15.2 | 16.3 | | -12.9 | -27.7 | 22.9 | 17.2 | 11.4 | 15.3 |
| | 111.3 | | 66.5 | 54.4 | | 19.5 | 49.1 | 58.2 | 72.2 | 56.7 | 51.4 |
| (565) | 30.0 | (797) | 19.2 | (797) | 14.1 | EBIT/Interest | (10) 7.0 | (54) 11.9 | (57) 8.4 | (109) 18.6 | (188) 17.9 | (379) 13.1 |
| | 6.2 | | 3.8 | 3.3 | | 2.8 | .8 | 1.7 | 4.3 | 3.1 | 4.0 |
| | 15.3 | | 8.1 | 12.4 | | | | | 17.0 | 12.8 | 11.0 |
| (109) | 5.7 | (168) | 3.4 | (166) | 3.2 | Net Profit + Depr., Dep., Amort./Cur. Mat. L/T/D | | | (12) 3.2 | (31) 2.8 | (119) 3.2 |
| | 2.3 | | 1.3 | 1.4 | | | | | .5 | 1.4 | 1.6 |
| | .1 | | .1 | .1 | | .1 | .0 | .0 | .0 | .0 | .1 |
| | .2 | | .2 | .2 | Fixed/Worth | .4 | .3 | .1 | .2 | .2 | .3 |
| | .7 | | .8 | .8 | | 24.5 | 10.1 | 1.8 | .7 | .6 | .9 |
| | .4 | | .4 | .5 | | .4 | .3 | .2 | .3 | .4 | .9 |
| | 1.0 | | 1.1 | 1.3 | Debt/Worth | 2.0 | 1.4 | .8 | .8 | 1.0 | 1.7 |
| | 2.9 | | 3.5 | 4.8 | | 43.5 | -8.9 | 7.4 | 3.0 | 2.4 | 5.7 |
| | 73.9 | | 67.0 | 69.7 | | 97.5 | 68.6 | 104.6 | 82.0 | 64.3 | 65.0 |
| (657) | 37.7 | (946) | 28.4 | (897) | 32.8 | % Profit Before Taxes/Tangible Net Worth | (23) 34.1 | (54) 31.7 | (64) 33.7 | (124) 35.7 | (230) 30.1 | (402) 33.7 |
| | 14.1 | | 10.9 | 13.9 | | 14.2 | 7.2 | 4.7 | 18.1 | 13.3 | 14.6 |
| | 35.6 | | 30.1 | 27.1 | | 37.1 | 39.8 | 34.9 | 37.3 | 33.6 | 19.2 |
| | 16.7 | | 12.7 | 12.4 | % Profit Before Taxes/Total Assets | 9.9 | 15.6 | 14.4 | 20.0 | 14.1 | 10.6 |
| | 5.2 | | 3.8 | 4.6 | | 2.3 | -1.1 | .8 | 7.2 | 5.9 | 4.8 |
| | 103.8 | | 122.6 | 133.2 | | 71.1 | 293.5 | 441.9 | 217.1 | 148.8 | 87.7 |
| | 27.9 | | 29.2 | 30.7 | Sales/Net Fixed Assets | 20.2 | 32.8 | 48.2 | 31.3 | 32.3 | 28.0 |
| | 12.1 | | 11.7 | 12.1 | | .2 | 7.9 | 11.0 | 13.5 | 12.3 | 12.2 |
| | 3.2 | | 3.2 | 3.1 | | 3.0 | 4.0 | 3.4 | 3.4 | 3.2 | 2.7 |
| | 2.2 | | 2.1 | 2.1 | Sales/Total Assets | 1.3 | 2.3 | 2.2 | 2.3 | 2.2 | 2.0 |
| | 1.5 | | 1.5 | 1.5 | | .2 | 1.5 | 1.7 | 1.6 | 1.6 | 1.4 |
| | .5 | | .6 | .5 | | 2.4 | .6 | .4 | .4 | .4 | .5 |
| (503) | 1.2 | (687) | 1.3 | (683) | 1.1 | % Depr., Dep., Amort./Sales | (13) 15.6 | (35) 1.9 | (31) .7 | (78) .9 | (180) 1.0 | (346) 1.1 |
| | 2.5 | | 2.5 | 2.3 | | 22.4 | 3.3 | 2.8 | 2.0 | 2.3 | 2.1 |
| | 2.7 | | 2.4 | 2.1 | | | 4.2 | 3.4 | 3.1 | 1.4 | .8 |
| (182) | 6.3 | (257) | 5.0 | (216) | 4.7 | % Officers', Directors' Owners' Comp/Sales | | (32) 6.8 | (23) 7.6 | (50) 5.2 | (65) 3.4 | (39) 1.7 |
| | 13.2 | | 9.4 | 9.9 | | | 11.2 | 12.2 | 11.8 | 6.7 | 4.7 |
| | 31694262M | | 39843089M | 63170970M | Net Sales ($) | 14854M | 160318M | 301147M | 1049070M | 4166339M | 57479242M |
| | 16104057M | | 21595993M | 28121533M | Total Assets ($) | 21516M | 95857M | 173963M | 516422M | 2117561M | 25196214M |

© RMA 2024    M = $ thousand    MM = $ million
See Pages viii through xx for Explanation of Ratios and Data

# PROFESSIONAL SERVICES—Surveying and Mapping (except Geophysical) Services  NAICS 541370

## Current Data Sorted by Assets | Comparative Historical Data

| 0-500M | 500M-2MM | 2-10MM | 10-50MM | 50-100MM | 100-250MM | | Type of Statement | | | | |
|---|---|---|---|---|---|---|---|---|---|---|---|
| 1 | 1 | 1 | 1 | | | | Unqualified | | 3 | | 2 |
| 2 | 2 | 2 | 1 | | | | Reviewed | | 2 | | 1 |
| 2 | 2 | 3 | 2 | | | | Compiled | | 2 | | 3 |
| 1 | 3 | 5 | 2 | | 1 | | Tax Returns | | 12 | | 13 |
| 2 | 4 (4/1-9/30/23) | | 26 (10/1/23-3/31/24) | | | | Other | | 26 | | 24 |
| | | | | | | | | | 4/1/19- | | 4/1/20- |
| | | | | | | | | | 3/31/20 | | 3/31/21 |
| 0-500M | 500M-2MM | 2-10MM | 10-50MM | 50-100MM | 100-250MM | | | | ALL | | ALL |
| 3 | 8 | 11 | 7 | | 1 | NUMBER OF STATEMENTS | | | 45 | | 43 |
| % | % | % | % | % | % | | ASSETS | | % | | % |
| | | 17.6 | | | | | Cash & Equivalents | | 15.0 | | 32.7 |
| | | 21.4 | | D | | | Trade Receivables (net) | | 27.9 | | 23.6 |
| | | 2.4 | | A | | | Inventory | | 1.1 | | .2 |
| | | .6 | | T | | | All Other Current | | 4.2 | | 3.9 |
| | | 42.0 | | A | | | Total Current | | 48.2 | | 60.3 |
| | | 44.9 | | | | | Fixed Assets (net) | | 24.4 | | 21.8 |
| | | 8.5 | | N | | | Intangibles (net) | | 14.1 | | 3.3 |
| | | 4.5 | | O | | | All Other Non-Current | | 13.4 | | 14.6 |
| | | 100.0 | | T | | | Total | | 100.0 | | 100.0 |
| | | | | | | | LIABILITIES | | | | |
| | | 3.1 | | A | | | Notes Payable-Short Term | | 7.4 | | 14.1 |
| | | 3.8 | | V | | | Cur. Mat.-L.T.D. | | 3.0 | | 4.1 |
| | | 4.6 | | A | | | Trade Payables | | 4.6 | | 2.8 |
| | | .1 | | I | | | Income Taxes Payable | | .6 | | .1 |
| | | 12.7 | | L | | | All Other Current | | 7.8 | | 10.5 |
| | | 24.2 | | A | | | Total Current | | 23.4 | | 31.5 |
| | | 28.0 | | B | | | Long-Term Debt | | 27.2 | | 35.9 |
| | | .0 | | L | | | Deferred Taxes | | .7 | | .5 |
| | | 2.2 | | E | | | All Other Non-Current | | 3.3 | | 7.4 |
| | | 45.6 | | | | | Net Worth | | 45.4 | | 24.8 |
| | | 100.0 | | | | | Total Liabilties & Net Worth | | 100.0 | | 100.0 |
| | | | | | | | INCOME DATA | | | | |
| | | 100.0 | | | | | Net Sales | | 100.0 | | 100.0 |
| | | | | | | | Gross Profit | | | | |
| | | 88.8 | | | | | Operating Expenses | | 87.5 | | 90.7 |
| | | 11.2 | | | | | Operating Profit | | 12.5 | | 9.3 |
| | | 5.5 | | | | | All Other Expenses (net) | | 2.5 | | -1.5 |
| | | 5.7 | | | | | Profit Before Taxes | | 10.0 | | 10.8 |
| | | | | | | | RATIOS | | | | |
| | | 4.2 | | | | | | | 4.6 | | 7.3 |
| | | 2.1 | | | | | Current | | 2.0 | | 2.6 |
| | | .9 | | | | | | | 1.2 | | 1.2 |
| | | 4.2 | | | | | | | 3.6 | | 6.6 |
| | | 2.0 | | | | | Quick | | 1.8 | | 2.6 |
| | | .9 | | | | | | | .9 | | 1.1 |
| | 23 | 15.9 | | | | | | 0 | UND | 0 | UND |
| | 58 | 6.3 | | | | | Sales/Receivables | 47 | 7.8 | 43 | 8.5 |
| | 111 | 3.3 | | | | | | 87 | 4.2 | 72 | 5.1 |
| | | | | | | | Cost of Sales/Inventory | | | | |
| | | | | | | | Cost of Sales/Payables | | | | |
| | | 3.5 | | | | | | | 5.0 | | 4.2 |
| | | 8.0 | | | | | Sales/Working Capital | | 10.0 | | 6.7 |
| | | -35.3 | | | | | | | 29.9 | | 66.0 |
| | | | | | | | | | 48.2 | | 70.2 |
| | | | | | | | EBIT/Interest | (39) | 17.4 | (38) | 10.5 |
| | | | | | | | | | 3.8 | | .4 |
| | | | | | | | Net Profit + Depr., Dep., | | | | |
| | | | | | | | Amort./Cur. Mat. L/T/D | | | | |
| | | .4 | | | | | | | .2 | | .2 |
| | | 1.4 | | | | | Fixed/Worth | | 1.0 | | .4 |
| | | 3.2 | | | | | | | NM | | UND |
| | | .4 | | | | | | | .5 | | .5 |
| | | 1.5 | | | | | Debt/Worth | | 1.5 | | 1.1 |
| | | 2.5 | | | | | | | NM | | -69.1 |
| | | 44.7 | | | | | | | 74.5 | | 106.9 |
| | (10) | 21.6 | | | | | % Profit Before Taxes/Tangible | (34) | 47.4 | (32) | 49.3 |
| | | 5.6 | | | | | Net Worth | | 17.8 | | 16.9 |
| | | 18.3 | | | | | | | 42.4 | | 69.5 |
| | | 10.7 | | | | | % Profit Before Taxes/Total | | 17.3 | | 22.5 |
| | | -.3 | | | | | Assets | | 4.2 | | -.8 |
| | | 8.1 | | | | | | | 59.7 | | 43.7 |
| | | 5.1 | | | | | Sales/Net Fixed Assets | | 16.9 | | 11.7 |
| | | 2.6 | | | | | | | 6.8 | | 6.8 |
| | | 2.2 | | | | | | | 4.4 | | 4.3 |
| | | 1.5 | | | | | Sales/Total Assets | | 2.5 | | 2.1 |
| | | 1.4 | | | | | | | 1.4 | | 1.4 |
| | | | | | | | | | 1.9 | | 2.2 |
| | | | | | | | % Depr., Dep., Amort./Sales | (23) | 3.6 | (22) | 4.5 |
| | | | | | | | | | 4.4 | | 7.8 |
| | | | | | | | | | 4.1 | | 5.3 |
| | | | | | | | % Officers', Directors' | (18) | 6.8 | (20) | 14.5 |
| | | | | | | | Owners' Comp/Sales | | 22.6 | | 28.7 |
| 4095M | 23431M | 97021M | 209028M | | 107477M | | Net Sales ($) | | 823031M | | 314980M |
| 445M | 8269M | 61718M | 136700M | | 129714M | | Total Assets ($) | | 658909M | | 169238M |

© RMA 2024

M = $ thousand    MM = $ million
See Pages viii through xx for Explanation of Ratios and Data

# PROFESSIONAL SERVICES—Surveying and Mapping (except Geophysical) Services  NAICS 541370

## Comparative Historical Data | Current Data Sorted by Sales

| | | | | Type of Statement | | | | | | |
|---|---|---|---|---|---|---|---|---|---|---|
| | | | | Unqualified | | | | 1 | 1 | 1 |
| | 1 | 1 | 2 | Reviewed | | | | | 3 | 1 |
| | 4 | 4 | 2 | Compiled | | 2 | | 2 | 1 | 1 |
| | 11 | 17 | 6 | Tax Returns | 2 | 1 | 1 | 2 | 3 | 2 |
| | 16 | 20 | 7 | Other | 3 | 2 | | 3 | 3 | |
| | 4/1/21- | 4/1/22- | 4/1/23- | | 0-1MM | 4 (4/1-9/30/23) 1-3MM | 3-5MM | 5-10MM | 26 (10/1/23-3/31/24) 10-25MM | 25MM & OVER |
| | 3/31/22 | 3/31/23 | 3/31/24 | | | | | | | |
| | ALL | ALL | ALL | | | | | | | |
| | 32 | 42 | 30 | NUMBER OF STATEMENTS | 5 | 5 | 1 | 6 | 8 | 5 |
| | % | % | % | ASSETS | % | % | % | % | % | % |
| | 28.0 | 22.2 | 18.8 | Cash & Equivalents | | | | | | |
| | 27.7 | 20.9 | 23.2 | Trade Receivables (net) | | | | | | |
| | 1.7 | 1.5 | 2.9 | Inventory | | | | | | |
| | 6.0 | 2.8 | 2.0 | All Other Current | | | | | | |
| | 63.3 | 47.3 | 46.9 | Total Current | | | | | | |
| | 22.6 | 29.7 | 32.5 | Fixed Assets (net) | | | | | | |
| | 6.7 | 6.9 | 10.1 | Intangibles (net) | | | | | | |
| | 7.4 | 16.1 | 10.6 | All Other Non-Current | | | | | | |
| | 100.0 | 100.0 | 100.0 | Total | | | | | | |
| | | | | LIABILITIES | | | | | | |
| | 3.9 | 6.6 | 5.1 | Notes Payable-Short Term | | | | | | |
| | 1.7 | 4.0 | 5.1 | Cur. Mat.-L.T.D. | | | | | | |
| | 2.4 | 1.3 | 2.4 | Trade Payables | | | | | | |
| | .0 | .2 | .0 | Income Taxes Payable | | | | | | |
| | 9.6 | 8.1 | 7.4 | All Other Current | | | | | | |
| | 17.7 | 20.2 | 20.1 | Total Current | | | | | | |
| | 17.9 | 23.5 | 26.2 | Long-Term Debt | | | | | | |
| | 1.0 | .5 | .2 | Deferred Taxes | | | | | | |
| | .7 | 5.1 | 4.8 | All Other Non-Current | | | | | | |
| | 62.8 | 50.8 | 48.8 | Net Worth | | | | | | |
| | 100.0 | 100.0 | 100.0 | Total Liabilities & Net Worth | | | | | | |
| | | | | INCOME DATA | | | | | | |
| | 100.0 | 100.0 | 100.0 | Net Sales | | | | | | |
| | | | | Gross Profit | | | | | | |
| | 84.7 | 89.0 | 85.5 | Operating Expenses | | | | | | |
| | 15.3 | 11.0 | 14.5 | Operating Profit | | | | | | |
| | -1.7 | .7 | 4.1 | All Other Expenses (net) | | | | | | |
| | 17.0 | 10.3 | 10.4 | Profit Before Taxes | | | | | | |
| | | | | RATIOS | | | | | | |
| | 9.4 | 10.5 | 5.2 | | | | | | | |
| | 4.7 | 3.6 | 2.7 | Current | | | | | | |
| | 2.6 | 1.5 | 1.4 | | | | | | | |
| | 9.4 | 10.0 | 4.6 | | | | | | | |
| | 4.5 | 3.3 | 2.3 | Quick | | | | | | |
| | 2.2 | 1.3 | 1.4 | | | | | | | |
| | 0 UND | 0 UND | 0 UND | | | | | | | |
| | 42 8.7 | 24 15.2 | 51 7.2 | Sales/Receivables | | | | | | |
| | 85 4.3 | 78 4.7 | 83 4.4 | | | | | | | |
| | | | | Cost of Sales/Inventory | | | | | | |
| | | | | Cost of Sales/Payables | | | | | | |
| | 3.0 | 3.1 | 3.4 | | | | | | | |
| | 4.6 | 8.9 | 7.4 | Sales/Working Capital | | | | | | |
| | 7.3 | 77.0 | 38.6 | | | | | | | |
| | 133.5 | 128.0 | 104.7 | | | | | | | |
| (23) | 44.1 | (34) 18.6 | (22) 24.2 | EBIT/Interest | | | | | | |
| | 7.7 | 2.0 | 2.4 | | | | | | | |
| | | | | Net Profit + Depr., Dep., Amort./Cur. Mat. L/T/D | | | | | | |
| | .2 | .2 | .2 | | | | | | | |
| | .3 | .4 | .8 | Fixed/Worth | | | | | | |
| | .7 | 4.9 | 2.6 | | | | | | | |
| | .2 | .2 | .4 | | | | | | | |
| | .5 | .7 | 1.1 | Debt/Worth | | | | | | |
| | 2.0 | 12.9 | 3.4 | | | | | | | |
| | 101.1 | 80.3 | 104.0 | % Profit Before Taxes/Tangible Net Worth | | | | | | |
| (30) | 65.7 | (36) 42.8 | (26) 32.5 | | | | | | | |
| | 12.3 | 13.4 | 15.6 | | | | | | | |
| | 67.7 | 48.9 | 36.7 | % Profit Before Taxes/Total Assets | | | | | | |
| | 33.9 | 16.8 | 14.0 | | | | | | | |
| | 8.5 | .9 | 3.5 | | | | | | | |
| | 31.2 | 20.1 | 50.5 | | | | | | | |
| | 13.7 | 7.7 | 8.2 | Sales/Net Fixed Assets | | | | | | |
| | 6.4 | 5.1 | 4.3 | | | | | | | |
| | 3.2 | 3.9 | 2.8 | | | | | | | |
| | 2.0 | 2.0 | 1.8 | Sales/Total Assets | | | | | | |
| | 1.6 | 1.1 | 1.4 | | | | | | | |
| | 1.5 | 1.9 | 1.5 | | | | | | | |
| (20) | 2.8 | (26) 4.2 | (19) 3.6 | % Depr., Dep., Amort./Sales | | | | | | |
| | 4.5 | 9.2 | 8.8 | | | | | | | |
| | 3.8 | 5.9 | 6.2 | % Officers', Directors' Owners' Comp/Sales | | | | | | |
| (16) | 6.1 | (20) 9.9 | (11) 8.7 | | | | | | | |
| | 16.9 | 16.9 | 15.5 | | | | | | | |
| | 277829M | 433461M | 441052M | Net Sales ($) | 1464M | 10982M | 3364M | 41875M | 136185M | 247182M |
| | 142952M | 316464M | 336846M | Total Assets ($) | 7607M | 5042M | 232M | 19175M | 109474M | 195316M |

© RMA 2024
M = $ thousand    MM = $ million
See Pages viii through xx for Explanation of Ratios and Data

# PROFESSIONAL SERVICES—Testing Laboratories and Services  NAICS 541380

## Current Data Sorted by Assets | Comparative Historical Data

| | | | | | | | Type of Statement | | | | |
|---|---|---|---|---|---|---|---|---|---|---|---|
| | | | 1 | 4 | | 3 | Unqualified | | 11 | | 4 |
| | | 3 | 5 | 1 | | | Reviewed | | 10 | | 5 |
| | | 5 | 2 | | | 1 | Compiled | | 10 | | 6 |
| 3 | 7 | 5 | 1 | | | 1 | Tax Returns | | 28 | | 8 |
| 6 | 14 | 22 | 20 | 4 | | 1 | Other | | 73 | | 49 |
| | 10 (4/1-9/30/23) | | 103 (10/1/23-3/31/24) | | | | | | 4/1/19-3/31/20 | | 4/1/20-3/31/21 |
| 0-500M | 500M-2MM | 2-10MM | 10-50MM | 50-100MM | 100-250MM | | | | ALL | | ALL |
| 9 | 21 | 36 | 32 | 9 | 6 | | NUMBER OF STATEMENTS | | 132 | | 72 |
| % | % | % | % | % | % | | ASSETS | | % | | % |
| | 24.6 | 18.8 | 17.6 | | | | Cash & Equivalents | | 18.0 | | 25.5 |
| | 18.5 | 25.7 | 24.2 | | | | Trade Receivables (net) | | 24.7 | | 26.1 |
| | 1.0 | 3.7 | 2.5 | | | | Inventory | | 4.6 | | 2.3 |
| | 8.9 | 1.6 | 3.6 | | | | All Other Current | | 3.3 | | 2.3 |
| | 53.1 | 49.8 | 47.9 | | | | Total Current | | 50.5 | | 56.3 |
| | 33.5 | 32.3 | 28.7 | | | | Fixed Assets (net) | | 33.7 | | 29.1 |
| | 7.0 | 7.6 | 13.6 | | | | Intangibles (net) | | 9.9 | | 7.9 |
| | 6.5 | 10.4 | 9.8 | | | | All Other Non-Current | | 5.9 | | 6.7 |
| | 100.0 | 100.0 | 100.0 | | | | Total | | 100.0 | | 100.0 |
| | | | | | | | **LIABILITIES** | | | | |
| | 7.2 | 1.9 | 1.8 | | | | Notes Payable-Short Term | | 9.9 | | 10.6 |
| | 2.6 | 2.8 | 3.0 | | | | Cur. Mat.-L.T.D. | | 4.0 | | 2.4 |
| | 8.3 | 5.5 | 6.0 | | | | Trade Payables | | 6.5 | | 7.8 |
| | .1 | .4 | .0 | | | | Income Taxes Payable | | .1 | | .1 |
| | 22.1 | 9.3 | 12.2 | | | | All Other Current | | 10.3 | | 13.4 |
| | 40.3 | 20.0 | 23.0 | | | | Total Current | | 30.7 | | 34.2 |
| | 27.7 | 17.7 | 13.0 | | | | Long-Term Debt | | 19.8 | | 25.8 |
| | .0 | .6 | 1.1 | | | | Deferred Taxes | | .4 | | .6 |
| | 11.9 | 6.9 | 4.8 | | | | All Other Non-Current | | 4.6 | | 5.0 |
| | 20.0 | 54.9 | 58.2 | | | | Net Worth | | 44.5 | | 34.4 |
| | 100.0 | 100.0 | 100.0 | | | | Total Liabilities & Net Worth | | 100.0 | | 100.0 |
| | | | | | | | **INCOME DATA** | | | | |
| | 100.0 | 100.0 | 100.0 | | | | Net Sales | | 100.0 | | 100.0 |
| | | | | | | | Gross Profit | | | | |
| | 91.0 | 86.6 | 91.1 | | | | Operating Expenses | | 87.1 | | 86.8 |
| | 9.0 | 13.4 | 8.9 | | | | Operating Profit | | 12.9 | | 13.2 |
| | 5.4 | .3 | 1.1 | | | | All Other Expenses (net) | | 2.6 | | .7 |
| | 3.6 | 13.1 | 7.8 | | | | Profit Before Taxes | | 10.3 | | 12.5 |
| | | | | | | | **RATIOS** | | | | |
| | 5.0 | 5.8 | 4.0 | | | | | | 3.4 | | 3.6 |
| | 2.1 | 3.1 | 2.3 | | | | Current | | 1.9 | | 2.1 |
| | .9 | 1.7 | 1.2 | | | | | | 1.0 | | 1.1 |
| | 5.0 | 5.5 | 3.3 | | | | | | 3.3 | | 3.5 |
| | 1.8 | 2.6 | 2.1 | | | | Quick | | 1.6 | | 1.8 |
| | .6 | 1.3 | 1.0 | | | | | | .8 | | .9 |
| 0 | UND | 33 | 11.2 | 43 | 8.4 | | | 29 | 12.7 | 31 | 11.9 |
| 15 | 23.6 | 49 | 7.5 | 59 | 6.2 | | Sales/Receivables | 45 | 8.2 | 54 | 6.7 |
| 56 | 6.5 | 69 | 5.3 | 76 | 4.8 | | | 66 | 5.5 | 74 | 4.9 |
| | | | | | | | Cost of Sales/Inventory | | | | |
| | | | | | | | Cost of Sales/Payables | | | | |
| | 4.6 | 3.5 | 3.0 | | | | | | 4.4 | | 4.0 |
| | 9.8 | 6.3 | 6.1 | | | | Sales/Working Capital | | 8.0 | | 7.4 |
| | -517.9 | 9.6 | 30.4 | | | | | | 192.7 | | 183.3 |
| | 61.2 | 40.6 | 66.3 | | | | | | 24.7 | | 59.8 |
| (12) | 1.8 | (33) 15.1 | (27) 4.3 | | | | EBIT/Interest | (101) | 7.2 | (56) | 14.0 |
| | -1.2 | 3.6 | 1.3 | | | | | | 1.9 | | 4.0 |
| | | | 4.5 | | | | Net Profit + Depr., Dep., | | 4.6 | | 16.5 |
| | | (10) | 3.3 | | | | Amort./Cur. Mat. L/T/D | (25) | 2.4 | (14) | 4.6 |
| | | | 1.9 | | | | | | 1.2 | | .9 |
| | .2 | .2 | .2 | | | | | | .3 | | .2 |
| | 2.0 | .6 | .6 | | | | Fixed/Worth | | .8 | | .7 |
| | -3.2 | 1.5 | 1.5 | | | | | | 3.0 | | 3.7 |
| | 1.1 | .2 | .3 | | | | | | .4 | | .6 |
| | 4.1 | .8 | 1.0 | | | | Debt/Worth | | 1.3 | | 1.3 |
| | -9.0 | 2.9 | 2.6 | | | | | | 7.0 | | 19.2 |
| | 118.6 | 59.4 | 34.0 | | | | % Profit Before Taxes/Tangible | | 58.4 | | 93.8 |
| (13) | 45.7 | (32) 35.8 | (29) 16.7 | | | | Net Worth | (110) | 23.4 | (59) | 37.8 |
| | -21.5 | 8.4 | 7.9 | | | | | | 5.6 | | 11.7 |
| | 35.8 | 31.9 | 16.5 | | | | % Profit Before Taxes/Total | | 25.4 | | 43.4 |
| | 3.3 | 15.1 | 6.4 | | | | Assets | | 8.4 | | 17.0 |
| | -14.0 | 3.7 | .9 | | | | | | 1.9 | | 4.2 |
| | 136.3 | 30.0 | 14.3 | | | | | | 20.6 | | 30.5 |
| | 6.9 | 6.0 | 5.1 | | | | Sales/Net Fixed Assets | | 7.2 | | 10.8 |
| | 2.2 | 2.5 | 2.6 | | | | | | 3.2 | | 3.3 |
| | 4.6 | 2.7 | 1.6 | | | | | | 2.6 | | 2.5 |
| | 2.0 | 1.6 | 1.2 | | | | Sales/Total Assets | | 1.9 | | 1.7 |
| | .9 | 1.3 | 1.0 | | | | | | 1.1 | | 1.2 |
| | 6.9 | 1.6 | 2.1 | | | | | | 2.3 | | 1.1 |
| (10) | 12.1 | (27) 3.6 | (28) 3.9 | | | | % Depr., Dep., Amort./Sales | (100) | 3.4 | (50) | 3.1 |
| | 19.9 | 5.2 | 7.2 | | | | | | 6.3 | | 6.5 |
| | | | | | | | % Officers', Directors' | | 3.6 | | 5.3 |
| | | | | | | | Owners' Comp/Sales | (40) | 5.8 | (21) | 6.8 |
| | | | | | | | | | 14.8 | | 15.3 |
| 7409M | 74808M | 379074M | 902667M | 596212M | 1049767M | | Net Sales ($) | | 2909276M | | 1902231M |
| 1473M | 21091M | 186794M | 697897M | 585054M | 777447M | | Total Assets ($) | | 1978221M | | 1276313M |

© RMA 2024  
M = $ thousand    MM = $ million  
See Pages viii through xx for Explanation of Ratios and Data

## PROFESSIONAL SERVICES—Testing Laboratories and Services  NAICS 541380

### Comparative Historical Data | Current Data Sorted by Sales

| | | | | Type of Statement | | | | | | |
|---|---|---|---|---|---|---|---|---|---|---|
| 5 | | 8 | | 12 | Unqualified | | 1 | | 2 | 1 | 8 |
| 4 | | 10 | | 9 | Reviewed | | 1 | | | 4 | 4 |
| 5 | | 2 | | 8 | Compiled | | | 2 | 1 | 1 | 4 |
| 16 | | 12 | | 17 | Tax Returns | 5 | 3 | 3 | 1 | 4 | 1 |
| 42 | | 64 | | 67 | Other | 11 | 5 | 7 | 12 | 18 | 14 |
| 4/1/21-3/31/22 ALL | | 4/1/22-3/31/23 ALL | | 4/1/23-3/31/24 ALL | | 10 (4/1-9/30/23) | | | 103 (10/1/23-3/31/24) | | |
| | | | | | | 0-1MM | 1-3MM | 3-5MM | 5-10MM | 10-25MM | 25MM & OVER |
| 72 | | 96 | | 113 | NUMBER OF STATEMENTS | 16 | 10 | 12 | 16 | 28 | 31 |
| % | | % | | % | ASSETS | % | % | % | % | % | % |
| 22.1 | | 16.3 | | 21.4 | Cash & Equivalents | 33.2 | 16.7 | 25.8 | 14.1 | 21.9 | 18.5 |
| 21.1 | | 21.6 | | 22.8 | Trade Receivables (net) | 12.4 | 11.5 | 20.5 | 27.8 | 25.8 | 27.3 |
| 2.7 | | 3.0 | | 2.7 | Inventory | .7 | .0 | 6.7 | 1.3 | 3.3 | 3.3 |
| 4.2 | | 2.4 | | 3.8 | All Other Current | 7.3 | 2.9 | 1.2 | 3.2 | 4.0 | 3.3 |
| 50.0 | | 43.3 | | 50.7 | Total Current | 53.7 | 31.1 | 54.3 | 46.4 | 55.1 | 52.5 |
| 27.6 | | 33.6 | | 29.3 | Fixed Assets (net) | 29.5 | 49.9 | 23.4 | 29.8 | 27.0 | 26.6 |
| 11.3 | | 12.6 | | 11.3 | Intangibles (net) | 11.9 | 10.4 | 15.1 | 12.2 | 8.5 | 11.9 |
| 11.0 | | 10.5 | | 8.7 | All Other Non-Current | 5.0 | 8.6 | 7.3 | 11.6 | 9.5 | 8.9 |
| 100.0 | | 100.0 | | 100.0 | Total | 100.0 | 100.0 | 100.0 | 100.0 | 100.0 | 100.0 |
| | | | | | LIABILITIES | | | | | | |
| 3.3 | | 8.7 | | 4.1 | Notes Payable-Short Term | 9.9 | 2.9 | 3.9 | 6.0 | 1.5 | 3.0 |
| 5.0 | | 5.3 | | 2.7 | Cur. Mat.-L.T.D. | 2.8 | 2.9 | 3.1 | 1.9 | 2.1 | 3.5 |
| 5.2 | | 5.1 | | 6.4 | Trade Payables | .9 | 5.7 | 6.3 | 6.1 | 7.9 | 8.3 |
| .2 | | .1 | | .2 | Income Taxes Payable | .3 | .3 | .0 | .0 | .4 | .1 |
| 10.6 | | 13.7 | | 13.5 | All Other Current | 12.0 | 16.3 | 24.2 | 14.7 | 10.1 | 11.7 |
| 24.3 | | 32.8 | | 27.0 | Total Current | 25.8 | 28.1 | 37.6 | 28.7 | 22.0 | 26.6 |
| 18.3 | | 22.3 | | 20.8 | Long-Term Debt | 34.8 | 21.3 | 16.0 | 22.1 | 11.1 | 23.3 |
| .2 | | .4 | | .5 | Deferred Taxes | .0 | .3 | .0 | .3 | 1.0 | .7 |
| 1.8 | | 4.8 | | 6.9 | All Other Non-Current | 4.5 | 17.3 | 9.4 | 2.1 | 7.2 | 5.8 |
| 55.3 | | 39.7 | | 44.9 | Net Worth | 34.9 | 33.0 | 37.0 | 46.7 | 58.7 | 43.6 |
| 100.0 | | 100.0 | | 100.0 | Total Liabilties & Net Worth | 100.0 | 100.0 | 100.0 | 100.0 | 100.0 | 100.0 |
| | | | | | INCOME DATA | | | | | | |
| 100.0 | | 100.0 | | 100.0 | Net Sales | 100.0 | 100.0 | 100.0 | 100.0 | 100.0 | 100.0 |
| | | | | | Gross Profit | | | | | | |
| 86.9 | | 86.7 | | 90.0 | Operating Expenses | 78.8 | 85.3 | 90.6 | 86.2 | 94.9 | 94.7 |
| 13.1 | | 13.3 | | 10.0 | Operating Profit | 21.2 | 14.7 | 9.4 | 13.8 | 5.1 | 5.3 |
| 1.2 | | 2.3 | | 1.7 | All Other Expenses (net) | 7.6 | 5.2 | .4 | 1.1 | -.8 | .5 |
| 11.9 | | 10.9 | | 8.3 | Profit Before Taxes | 13.6 | 9.6 | 9.0 | 12.7 | 5.9 | 4.8 |
| | | | | | RATIOS | | | | | | |
| 6.0 | | 4.5 | | 4.6 | | 6.1 | 3.1 | 4.0 | 6.9 | 5.2 | 4.4 |
| 2.4 | | 2.1 | | 2.3 | Current | 2.9 | 1.8 | 2.9 | 1.6 | 2.6 | 1.9 |
| 1.2 | | .8 | | 1.2 | | 1.2 | 1.1 | 1.1 | .6 | 1.7 | 1.2 |
| 5.4 | | 4.0 | | 4.1 | | 6.1 | 2.8 | 4.0 | 6.3 | 4.6 | 3.7 |
| 2.3 | | 1.8 | | 2.1 | Quick | 2.8 | 1.8 | 2.0 | 1.6 | 2.2 | 1.8 |
| 1.0 | | .7 | | 1.0 | | 1.1 | 1.1 | .7 | .4 | 1.3 | 1.0 |
| 12 | 29.4 | 20 | 18.3 | 31 | 11.8 | | 0 | UND | 0 | UND | 0 | UND | 28 | 13.0 | 35 | 10.5 | 51 | 7.2 |
| 52 | 7.0 | 50 | 7.3 | 53 | 6.9 | Sales/Receivables | 18 | 20.0 | 39 | 9.4 | 59 | 6.2 | 50 | 7.3 | 46 | 8.0 | 60 | 6.1 |
| 74 | 4.9 | 72 | 5.1 | 69 | 5.3 | | 52 | 7.0 | 59 | 6.2 | 74 | 4.9 | 72 | 5.1 | 66 | 5.5 | 85 | 4.3 |
| | | | | | Cost of Sales/Inventory | | | | | | |
| | | | | | Cost of Sales/Payables | | | | | | |
| 3.6 | | 3.5 | | 3.5 | | 2.1 | 7.2 | 4.9 | 3.9 | 3.1 | 3.1 |
| 6.4 | | 8.5 | | 7.4 | Sales/Working Capital | 7.2 | 16.2 | 7.1 | 10.1 | 5.3 | 8.4 |
| 35.4 | | -18.6 | | 30.9 | | 26.3 | NM | UND | -26.7 | 11.1 | 21.1 |
| | 77.1 | | 48.3 | | 46.1 | | | | | | 66.9 | | 68.4 | | 65.8 |
| (55) | 17.5 | (73) | 10.0 | (88) | 4.5 | EBIT/Interest | | | | | (11) | 9.6 | (26) | 18.6 | (26) | 4.2 |
| | 4.3 | | 2.0 | | .8 | | | | | | 2.3 | | 2.2 | | .4 |
| | 52.0 | | 11.9 | | 4.8 | | | | | | | | | 13.8 | | |
| (11) | 8.7 | (15) | 3.7 | (22) | 3.1 | Net Profit + Depr., Dep., Amort./Cur. Mat. L/T/D | | | | | (10) | 4.5 | | | | |
| | 6.4 | | 1.2 | | 1.6 | | | | | | | | 2.5 | | | |
| .2 | | .3 | | .2 | | .4 | 1.3 | .1 | .0 | .2 | .3 |
| .5 | | .7 | | .8 | Fixed/Worth | 1.4 | 2.7 | .5 | .7 | .5 | .6 |
| 1.4 | | 2.1 | | 2.3 | | -3.2 | -2.2 | 8.6 | 4.1 | 1.0 | 1.7 |
| .4 | | .4 | | .4 | | .9 | .8 | .3 | .2 | .3 | .3 |
| .9 | | 1.1 | | 1.4 | Debt/Worth | 2.2 | 2.3 | 1.8 | 1.7 | .8 | 1.0 |
| 3.4 | | 5.4 | | 3.6 | | -9.6 | -17.9 | -21.8 | NM | 2.0 | 3.2 |
| | 93.2 | | 47.6 | | 47.8 | | | 171.7 | | | | | | 86.7 | | 40.0 | | 29.8 |
| (67) | 47.6 | (77) | 17.0 | (92) | 25.4 | % Profit Before Taxes/Tangible Net Worth | (11) | 27.1 | | | (12) | 46.8 | | 13.9 | (26) | 11.4 |
| | 18.4 | | 6.0 | | 4.3 | | | -14.0 | | | | | | 31.1 | | 2.5 | | 6.2 |
| 38.3 | | 19.8 | | 22.9 | % Profit Before Taxes/Total Assets | 27.0 | 14.5 | 50.9 | 34.4 | 20.5 | 14.3 |
| 17.2 | | 8.7 | | 6.9 | | 10.4 | .4 | 25.8 | 14.9 | 6.0 | 5.1 |
| 3.7 | | 1.8 | | .7 | | -5.3 | -24.4 | -6.2 | 4.8 | .9 | .8 |
| 25.5 | | 15.7 | | 35.5 | | 105.5 | 16.8 | 323.4 | 218.7 | 21.6 | 17.7 |
| 7.6 | | 6.0 | | 6.5 | Sales/Net Fixed Assets | 10.7 | 5.0 | 37.0 | 9.6 | 5.5 | 6.5 |
| 4.4 | | 3.2 | | 2.7 | | 1.0 | 1.0 | 2.5 | 2.3 | 4.5 | 2.8 |
| 2.3 | | 2.2 | | 2.6 | | 3.0 | 2.7 | 4.9 | 2.7 | 2.0 | 2.7 |
| 1.7 | | 1.4 | | 1.5 | Sales/Total Assets | 1.3 | 1.6 | 1.7 | 1.6 | 1.5 | 1.1 |
| 1.0 | | .8 | | 1.0 | | .6 | .6 | .8 | .7 | 1.2 | 1.0 |
| | 1.7 | | 2.1 | | 2.1 | | | | | | | | | | 2.3 | | 2.0 |
| (51) | 3.7 | (62) | 4.5 | (78) | 4.2 | % Depr., Dep., Amort./Sales | | | | | | | (24) | 3.9 | (27) | 3.8 |
| | 6.3 | | 7.2 | | 7.3 | | | | | | | | | 4.8 | | 6.9 |
| | 2.4 | | 2.3 | | 2.4 | | | | | | | | | | | |
| (26) | 5.3 | (21) | 5.0 | (22) | 4.7 | % Officers', Directors' Owners' Comp/Sales | | | | | | | | | | |
| | 9.4 | | 11.1 | | 8.5 | | | | | | | | | | | |
| 1689475M | | 2320932M | | 3009937M | Net Sales ($) | 8066M | 19049M | 47286M | 112623M | 476299M | 2346614M |
| 1271025M | | 1862098M | | 2269756M | Total Assets ($) | 11200M | 32312M | 33086M | 158071M | 376247M | 1658840M |

© RMA 2024     M = $ thousand     MM = $ million
See Pages viii through xx for Explanation of Ratios and Data

## PROFESSIONAL SERVICES—Interior Design Services  NAICS 541410

### Current Data Sorted by Assets | Comparative Historical Data

| | | | | | | | Type of Statement | | | | |
|---|---|---|---|---|---|---|---|---|---|---|---|
| | | | 1 | | 1 | 1 | Unqualified | | 2 | | 3 |
| | 1 | 2 | | 1 | 1 | | Reviewed | | 3 | | 4 |
| | 3 | 2 | | | | | Compiled | | 6 | | |
| 2 | 6 | 2 | | | | | Tax Returns | | 22 | | 16 |
| 10 | 14 | 24 | 7 | 3 | 1 | | Other | | 62 | | 33 |
| | 5 (4/1-9/30/23) | | 77 (10/1/23-3/31/24) | | | | | | 4/1/19-3/31/20 | | 4/1/20-3/31/21 |
| 0-500M | 500M-2MM | 2-10MM | 10-50MM | 50-100MM | 100-250MM | | | | ALL | | ALL |
| 12 | 24 | 30 | 9 | 5 | 2 | | NUMBER OF STATEMENTS | | 95 | | 56 |
| % | % | % | % | % | % | | ASSETS | | % | | % |
| 40.0 | 24.5 | 29.1 | | | | | Cash & Equivalents | | 23.0 | | 27.9 |
| 11.3 | 15.7 | 23.5 | | | | | Trade Receivables (net) | | 25.1 | | 20.2 |
| 16.8 | 19.9 | 6.0 | | | | | Inventory | | 13.9 | | 17.8 |
| 6.2 | 5.7 | 5.2 | | | | | All Other Current | | 4.0 | | 4.9 |
| 74.4 | 65.7 | 63.8 | | | | | Total Current | | 66.1 | | 70.8 |
| 24.3 | 15.0 | 17.3 | | | | | Fixed Assets (net) | | 18.8 | | 16.8 |
| .0 | 10.0 | 11.4 | | | | | Intangibles (net) | | 5.0 | | 7.3 |
| 1.3 | 9.3 | 7.4 | | | | | All Other Non-Current | | 10.0 | | 5.1 |
| 100.0 | 100.0 | 100.0 | | | | | Total | | 100.0 | | 100.0 |
| | | | | | | | LIABILITIES | | | | |
| 14.1 | 11.3 | 6.1 | | | | | Notes Payable-Short Term | | 12.2 | | 10.7 |
| 1.8 | 1.4 | .6 | | | | | Cur. Mat.-L.T.D. | | 1.5 | | 2.7 |
| 7.7 | 8.4 | 12.2 | | | | | Trade Payables | | 13.3 | | 10.7 |
| .0 | .0 | .0 | | | | | Income Taxes Payable | | .6 | | .0 |
| 41.9 | 33.8 | 32.7 | | | | | All Other Current | | 28.5 | | 26.8 |
| 65.5 | 55.0 | 51.5 | | | | | Total Current | | 56.1 | | 50.9 |
| 25.3 | 13.0 | 8.8 | | | | | Long-Term Debt | | 9.8 | | 21.1 |
| .0 | .2 | .0 | | | | | Deferred Taxes | | .0 | | .0 |
| 11.4 | 5.3 | 9.0 | | | | | All Other Non-Current | | 5.5 | | 6.0 |
| -2.2 | 26.5 | 30.7 | | | | | Net Worth | | 28.6 | | 22.0 |
| 100.0 | 100.0 | 100.0 | | | | | Total Liabilities & Net Worth | | 100.0 | | 100.0 |
| | | | | | | | INCOME DATA | | | | |
| 100.0 | 100.0 | 100.0 | | | | | Net Sales | | 100.0 | | 100.0 |
| | | | | | | | Gross Profit | | | | |
| 84.2 | 88.1 | 90.4 | | | | | Operating Expenses | | 91.8 | | 92.2 |
| 15.8 | 11.9 | 9.6 | | | | | Operating Profit | | 8.2 | | 7.8 |
| 1.4 | .4 | .3 | | | | | All Other Expenses (net) | | 1.1 | | .4 |
| 14.4 | 11.4 | 9.3 | | | | | Profit Before Taxes | | 7.0 | | 7.4 |
| | | | | | | | RATIOS | | | | |
| 2.5 | 2.8 | 2.8 | | | | | | | 1.8 | | 2.5 |
| 1.9 | 1.2 | 1.3 | | | | | Current | | 1.2 | | 1.7 |
| .6 | .7 | .7 | | | | | | | .9 | | 1.1 |
| 2.4 | 1.5 | 2.7 | | | | | | | 1.4 | | 2.2 |
| 1.0 | .7 | 1.0 | | | | | Quick | | .9 | | 1.0 |
| .3 | .5 | .6 | | | | | | | .5 | | .5 |
| 0 UND | 0 UND | 2 155.4 | | | | | | 1 | 291.4 | 0 | UND |
| 1 295.3 | 9 39.3 | 39 9.4 | | | | | Sales/Receivables | 21 | 17.5 | 21 | 17.6 |
| 20 18.3 | 30 12.1 | 66 5.5 | | | | | | 51 | 7.2 | 37 | 9.8 |
| | | | | | | | Cost of Sales/Inventory | | | | |
| | | | | | | | Cost of Sales/Payables | | | | |
| 8.6 | 5.2 | 5.3 | | | | | | | 9.7 | | 5.9 |
| 26.4 | 41.2 | 17.5 | | | | | Sales/Working Capital | | 28.4 | | 11.5 |
| -17.1 | -18.4 | -11.4 | | | | | | | -62.1 | | 36.9 |
| | 89.3 | 134.5 | | | | | | | 48.3 | | 48.8 |
| (21) | 15.9 (20) | 20.2 | | | | | EBIT/Interest | (66) | 11.7 | (41) | 7.2 |
| | 3.7 | 2.9 | | | | | | | 1.4 | | 1.3 |
| | | | | | | | Net Profit + Depr., Dep., Amort./Cur. Mat. L/T/D | | | | |
| .0 | .0 | .1 | | | | | | | .1 | | .1 |
| .0 | .3 | .6 | | | | | Fixed/Worth | | .5 | | .4 |
| 2.5 | NM | -9.9 | | | | | | | 1.7 | | 2.3 |
| .9 | .6 | .6 | | | | | | | 1.0 | | 1.1 |
| 1.7 | 6.6 | 6.3 | | | | | Debt/Worth | | 2.1 | | 2.6 |
| -9.1 | -3.7 | -16.4 | | | | | | | 13.7 | | 34.4 |
| | 229.3 | 124.8 | | | | | | | 102.6 | | 100.3 |
| (15) | 99.3 (22) | 56.6 | | | | | % Profit Before Taxes/Tangible Net Worth | (76) | 41.7 | (44) | 45.3 |
| | 41.6 | 21.4 | | | | | | | 7.2 | | 13.7 |
| 130.3 | 59.3 | 30.1 | | | | | | | 31.1 | | 28.0 |
| 57.6 | 26.3 | 12.0 | | | | | % Profit Before Taxes/Total Assets | | 13.6 | | 9.5 |
| 21.8 | 8.2 | 3.4 | | | | | | | .5 | | .9 |
| UND | 794.1 | 131.0 | | | | | | | 143.9 | | 95.3 |
| UND | 44.4 | 42.4 | | | | | Sales/Net Fixed Assets | | 35.1 | | 38.5 |
| 6.4 | 13.6 | 12.4 | | | | | | | 11.8 | | 12.9 |
| 8.0 | 5.2 | 2.9 | | | | | | | 4.8 | | 4.0 |
| 4.1 | 3.0 | 2.1 | | | | | Sales/Total Assets | | 3.3 | | 2.8 |
| 3.0 | 2.0 | 1.3 | | | | | | | 2.0 | | 1.8 |
| | .6 | .2 | | | | | | | .3 | | .3 |
| (12) | 1.4 (11) | .4 | | | | | % Depr., Dep., Amort./Sales | (51) | .8 | (28) | .8 |
| | 2.1 | 1.1 | | | | | | | 1.9 | | 2.1 |
| | 2.8 | | | | | | | | 2.4 | | 2.6 |
| (13) | 3.8 | | | | | | % Officers', Directors' Owners' Comp/Sales | (34) | 3.8 | (25) | 4.9 |
| | 7.1 | | | | | | | | 9.2 | | 11.8 |
| 15519M | 96631M | 299759M | 432046M | 812211M | 453826M | | Net Sales ($) | | 2058558M | | 1156794M |
| 3385M | 26672M | 143882M | 183533M | 336760M | 275852M | | Total Assets ($) | | 838080M | | 481893M |

M = $ thousand    MM = $ million
See Pages viii through xx for Explanation of Ratios and Data

© RMA 2024

# PROFESSIONAL SERVICES—Interior Design Services  NAICS 541410

## Comparative Historical Data | Current Data Sorted by Sales

| Comparative Historical Data | | | | | Current Data Sorted by Sales | | | | | |
|---|---|---|---|---|---|---|---|---|---|---|
| 1 | 1 | 2 | **Type of Statement** | | | | | 2 | 2 | |
| 4 | 5 | 5 | Unqualified | | | | 1 | 2 | 2 | |
| 2 | 8 | 6 | Reviewed | | | 2 | 3 | 1 | 1 | |
| 15 | 19 | 10 | Compiled | 4 | 2 | 3 | 17 | 9 | 10 | |
| 46 | 58 | 59 | Tax Returns | 8 | 9 | 6 | | | | |
| 4/1/21-3/31/22 ALL | 4/1/22-3/31/23 ALL | 4/1/23-3/31/24 ALL | Other | 5 (4/1-9/30/23) | | | 77 (10/1/23-3/31/24) | | | |
| | | | | 0-1MM | 1-3MM | 3-5MM | 5-10MM | 10-25MM | 25MM & OVER |
| 68 | 91 | 82 | **NUMBER OF STATEMENTS** | 12 | 11 | 11 | 21 | 12 | 15 |
| % | % | % | **ASSETS** | % | % | % | % | % | % |
| 26.7 | 26.3 | 26.5 | Cash & Equivalents | 27.0 | 38.7 | 21.6 | 35.2 | 25.4 | 9.2 |
| 19.1 | 21.2 | 19.7 | Trade Receivables (net) | 5.9 | 12.6 | 13.9 | 19.3 | 33.8 | 29.5 |
| 15.6 | 13.4 | 14.1 | Inventory | 19.6 | 19.1 | 10.1 | 9.3 | 6.8 | 21.4 |
| 6.2 | 7.5 | 5.4 | All Other Current | .6 | 6.6 | 8.7 | 8.3 | 1.6 | 5.1 |
| 67.5 | 68.3 | 65.7 | Total Current | 53.1 | 77.1 | 54.4 | 72.1 | 67.7 | 65.2 |
| 17.9 | 20.3 | 18.2 | Fixed Assets (net) | 34.9 | 12.1 | 23.8 | 14.4 | 11.7 | 15.5 |
| 5.8 | 5.3 | 8.9 | Intangibles (net) | 3.4 | 2.5 | 11.4 | 7.3 | 18.5 | 10.8 |
| 8.7 | 6.1 | 7.2 | All Other Non-Current | 8.5 | 8.3 | 10.3 | 6.2 | 2.1 | 8.5 |
| 100.0 | 100.0 | 100.0 | Total | 100.0 | 100.0 | 100.0 | 100.0 | 100.0 | 100.0 |
| | | | **LIABILITIES** | | | | | | |
| 8.2 | 10.3 | 8.8 | Notes Payable-Short Term | 3.5 | 12.7 | 19.9 | 4.5 | 6.7 | 9.8 |
| 2.4 | 2.1 | 1.5 | Cur. Mat.-L.T.D. | 2.1 | 1.1 | 1.9 | .9 | .1 | 3.1 |
| 9.3 | 9.3 | 10.7 | Trade Payables | 5.3 | 3.5 | 7.1 | 11.1 | 18.7 | 15.9 |
| .3 | .6 | .1 | Income Taxes Payable | .0 | .1 | .0 | .0 | .0 | .2 |
| 33.1 | 31.6 | 31.4 | All Other Current | 26.3 | 21.0 | 57.0 | 31.0 | 39.2 | 18.9 |
| 53.3 | 54.0 | 52.5 | Total Current | 37.2 | 38.3 | 85.8 | 47.5 | 64.8 | 47.9 |
| 19.5 | 19.5 | 13.7 | Long-Term Debt | 31.5 | 10.3 | 14.8 | 14.5 | .2 | 11.1 |
| .1 | .0 | .1 | Deferred Taxes | .0 | .5 | .0 | .0 | .0 | .1 |
| 3.6 | 6.5 | 8.2 | All Other Non-Current | .9 | 8.6 | 12.0 | 3.3 | 18.9 | 9.4 |
| 23.6 | 20.1 | 25.4 | Net Worth | 30.4 | 42.3 | -12.6 | 34.7 | 16.2 | 31.5 |
| 100.0 | 100.0 | 100.0 | Total Liabilities & Net Worth | 100.0 | 100.0 | 100.0 | 100.0 | 100.0 | 100.0 |
| | | | **INCOME DATA** | | | | | | |
| 100.0 | 100.0 | 100.0 | Net Sales | 100.0 | 100.0 | 100.0 | 100.0 | 100.0 | 100.0 |
| | | | Gross Profit | | | | | | |
| 93.0 | 90.7 | 89.5 | Operating Expenses | 78.6 | 81.1 | 87.0 | 91.7 | 94.7 | 99.2 |
| 7.0 | 9.3 | 10.5 | Operating Profit | 21.4 | 18.9 | 13.0 | 8.3 | 5.3 | .8 |
| -1.5 | 1.5 | 1.0 | All Other Expenses (net) | 5.2 | .2 | .6 | -.2 | .4 | .9 |
| 8.5 | 7.8 | 9.4 | Profit Before Taxes | 16.2 | 18.7 | 12.4 | 8.5 | 4.9 | -.1 |
| | | | **RATIOS** | | | | | | |
| 3.1 | 2.4 | 2.5 | | 3.5 | 5.2 | 1.1 | 3.2 | 2.4 | 1.6 |
| 1.3 | 1.4 | 1.3 | Current | 1.5 | 2.1 | .6 | 2.0 | 1.1 | 1.2 |
| .9 | .9 | .8 | | .3 | 1.1 | .5 | 1.1 | .6 | .9 |
| 1.9 | 1.8 | 2.0 | | 1.5 | 3.0 | .7 | 3.0 | 2.2 | 1.2 |
| .9 | .9 | .8 | Quick | .5 | 1.5 | .5 | 1.3 | .8 | .8 |
| .6 | .5 | .5 | | .2 | .6 | .2 | .7 | .6 | .4 |
| 0 UND | 0 UND | 0 UND | | 0 UND | 0 UND | 0 UND | 12 31.7 | 4 93.4 | 12 29.9 |
| 23 16.0 | 22 16.6 | 20 18.0 | Sales/Receivables | 0 UND | 13 29.0 | 0 816.5 | 27 13.5 | 64 5.7 | 43 8.4 |
| 44 8.3 | 54 6.7 | 57 6.4 | | 2 148.4 | 39 9.4 | 37 9.9 | 39 9.4 | 74 4.9 | 65 5.6 |
| | | | Cost of Sales/Inventory | | | | | | |
| | | | Cost of Sales/Payables | | | | | | |
| 8.2 | 6.9 | 6.4 | | 7.7 | 3.7 | 102.5 | 5.4 | 6.7 | 9.0 |
| 20.7 | 17.5 | 21.3 | Sales/Working Capital | 44.3 | 11.7 | -17.8 | 9.2 | 397.9 | 18.6 |
| -97.3 | -48.6 | -24.0 | | -2.7 | 25.2 | -5.2 | 49.9 | -9.3 | -87.2 |
| 129.8 | 74.1 | 84.7 | | | | 127.0 | 93.1 | | 137.3 |
| (43) 26.7 | (66) 15.7 | (61) 15.9 | EBIT/Interest | (10) 14.5 | | (15) 25.7 | | (13) 20.3 | |
| 5.6 | 1.5 | 4.2 | | | | 3.6 | 2.0 | | 2.6 |
| | | | Net Profit + Depr., Dep., Amort./Cur. Mat. L/T/D | | | | | | |
| .1 | .1 | .0 | | .0 | .0 | .2 | .0 | .1 | .1 |
| .4 | .4 | .4 | Fixed/Worth | .5 | .0 | 3.1 | .2 | NM | .6 |
| 7.0 | 8.6 | 16.7 | | 11.9 | .2 | -.2 | 14.9 | -.1 | 1.0 |
| .7 | 1.1 | .7 | | .5 | .3 | .7 | .5 | .7 | 1.5 |
| 3.3 | 2.8 | 2.8 | Debt/Worth | 3.0 | 1.0 | -17.5 | 1.5 | NM | 2.7 |
| 36.8 | 76.4 | -16.1 | | NM | 9.6 | -2.7 | 57.3 | -3.1 | 4.0 |
| 171.1 | 85.3 | 123.0 | % Profit Before Taxes/Tangible Net Worth | | | | 167.1 | | 51.8 |
| (52) 79.4 | (70) 38.1 | (59) 53.6 | | | | | (17) 61.6 | (13) 32.8 | |
| 30.8 | 17.7 | 18.7 | | | | | 20.1 | | .8 |
| 55.2 | 35.1 | 44.5 | % Profit Before Taxes/Total Assets | 47.0 | 91.7 | 85.6 | 49.2 | 37.6 | 15.2 |
| 21.9 | 11.1 | 18.6 | | 20.1 | 30.5 | 27.7 | 25.4 | 11.5 | 6.2 |
| 7.2 | 2.2 | 4.0 | | 2.1 | 22.6 | 4.1 | .7 | .8 | -.7 |
| 142.1 | 93.3 | 294.8 | | UND | UND | 76.0 | 516.9 | 123.9 | 65.2 |
| 47.4 | 28.7 | 36.9 | Sales/Net Fixed Assets | 13.7 | 999.8 | 35.4 | 52.3 | 70.3 | 16.3 |
| 13.5 | 11.5 | 10.5 | | .8 | 12.6 | 5.6 | 13.3 | 25.6 | 9.8 |
| 5.6 | 3.9 | 3.5 | | 3.5 | 5.3 | 5.4 | 3.5 | 3.4 | 2.7 |
| 3.0 | 2.3 | 2.5 | Sales/Total Assets | 1.6 | 2.1 | 2.9 | 2.8 | 2.5 | 2.6 |
| 1.6 | 1.4 | 1.6 | | .6 | 1.7 | 1.2 | 1.5 | 2.1 | 2.0 |
| .1 | .5 | .3 | | | | | .3 | | |
| (32) .9 | (44) 1.0 | (32) 1.1 | % Depr., Dep., Amort./Sales | | | | (10) .6 | | |
| 1.6 | 2.2 | 2.1 | | | | | 1.2 | | |
| 2.8 | 2.3 | 1.9 | | | | | | | |
| (21) 4.8 | (30) 4.9 | (22) 3.0 | % Officers', Directors' Owners' Comp/Sales | | | | | | |
| 10.7 | 8.4 | 5.6 | | | | | | | |
| 1040485M | 2161159M | 2109992M | Net Sales ($) | 7500M | 22375M | 42703M | 150217M | 166131M | 1721066M |
| 586731M | 1037696M | 970084M | Total Assets ($) | 16707M | 19533M | 24018M | 67109M | 62550M | 780167M |

© RMA 2024  
M = $ thousand    MM = $ million  
See Pages viii through xx for Explanation of Ratios and Data

# PROFESSIONAL SERVICES—Industrial Design Services  NAICS 541420

## Current Data Sorted by Assets | Comparative Historical Data

| 0-500M | 500M-2MM | 2-10MM | 10-50MM | 50-100MM | 100-250MM | | 4/1/19-3/31/20 ALL | 4/1/20-3/31/21 ALL |
|---|---|---|---|---|---|---|---|---|
| | | | 1 | | | Type of Statement | | |
| | | | 4 | | | Unqualified | | 2 |
| | | | 2 | | | Reviewed | 1 | 1 |
| | | 2 | | | | Compiled | 1 | 1 |
| | 1 | 2 | 3 | | | Tax Returns | 3 | 2 |
| | 3 | 3 | 3 | | 1 | Other | 17 | 5 |
| | 2 (4/1-9/30/23) | | 20 (10/1/23-3/31/24) | | | | | |
| | | | | | | **NUMBER OF STATEMENTS** | 22 | 11 |
| | 4 | 7 | 10 | | 1 | | | |
| % | % | % | % | % | % | **ASSETS** | % | % |
| | | | 13.3 | | | Cash & Equivalents | 21.0 | 12.4 |
| | | | 42.4 | | | Trade Receivables (net) | 43.2 | 34.4 |
| DATA | DATA | DATA | 3.1 | DATA | DATA | Inventory | 7.4 | 10.2 |
| NOT | NOT | NOT | 8.6 | NOT | NOT | All Other Current | 3.7 | 6.6 |
| AVAILABLE | AVAILABLE | AVAILABLE | 67.4 | AVAILABLE | AVAILABLE | Total Current | 75.2 | 63.6 |
| | | | 14.1 | | | Fixed Assets (net) | 19.4 | 18.3 |
| | | | 8.3 | | | Intangibles (net) | 2.7 | 6.6 |
| | | | 10.2 | | | All Other Non-Current | 2.7 | 11.5 |
| | | | 100.0 | | | Total | 100.0 | 100.0 |
| | | | | | | **LIABILITIES** | | |
| | | | 5.2 | | | Notes Payable-Short Term | 15.3 | 7.0 |
| | | | 1.8 | | | Cur. Mat.-L.T.D. | 2.1 | 1.9 |
| | | | 8.8 | | | Trade Payables | 13.8 | 10.2 |
| | | | .3 | | | Income Taxes Payable | .1 | .0 |
| | | | 22.2 | | | All Other Current | 12.9 | 23.4 |
| | | | 38.4 | | | Total Current | 44.1 | 42.5 |
| | | | 10.6 | | | Long-Term Debt | 12.1 | 18.6 |
| | | | .1 | | | Deferred Taxes | .0 | .0 |
| | | | 9.3 | | | All Other Non-Current | 3.6 | 10.3 |
| | | | 41.7 | | | Net Worth | 40.2 | 28.6 |
| | | | 100.0 | | | Total Liabilities & Net Worth | 100.0 | 100.0 |
| | | | | | | **INCOME DATA** | | |
| | | | 100.0 | | | Net Sales | 100.0 | 100.0 |
| | | | | | | Gross Profit | | |
| | | | 94.2 | | | Operating Expenses | 88.6 | 92.4 |
| | | | 5.8 | | | Operating Profit | 11.4 | 7.6 |
| | | | -.3 | | | All Other Expenses (net) | 1.7 | 1.6 |
| | | | 6.2 | | | Profit Before Taxes | 9.6 | 6.0 |
| | | | | | | **RATIOS** | | |
| | | | 2.6 | | | | 3.3 | 2.4 |
| | | | 1.7 | | | Current | 1.6 | 1.7 |
| | | | 1.4 | | | | 1.2 | 1.0 |
| | | | 2.0 | | | | 3.1 | 2.0 |
| | | | 1.4 | | | Quick | 1.3 | 1.1 |
| | | | 1.1 | | | | .8 | .8 |
| | | | 69   5.3 | | | | 31   11.7 | 52   7.0 |
| | | | 79   4.6 | | | Sales/Receivables | 48   7.6 | 65   5.6 |
| | | | 96   3.8 | | | | 87   4.2 | 99   3.7 |
| | | | | | | Cost of Sales/Inventory | | |
| | | | | | | Cost of Sales/Payables | | |
| | | | 3.9 | | | | 4.2 | 4.2 |
| | | | 6.1 | | | Sales/Working Capital | 7.7 | 10.0 |
| | | | 9.3 | | | | 26.5 | -999.8 |
| | | | | | | | 52.6 | |
| | | | | | | EBIT/Interest | (15) 14.0 | |
| | | | | | | | 7.4 | |
| | | | | | | Net Profit + Depr., Dep., Amort./Cur. Mat. L/T/D | | |
| | | | .2 | | | | .0 | .1 |
| | | | .3 | | | Fixed/Worth | .3 | .4 |
| | | | .8 | | | | 1.7 | -6.0 |
| | | | 1.4 | | | | .4 | 1.0 |
| | | | 1.8 | | | Debt/Worth | 1.2 | 2.2 |
| | | | 2.7 | | | | 5.2 | -12.7 |
| | | | 79.8 | | | | 63.8 | |
| | | | 30.7 | | | % Profit Before Taxes/Tangible Net Worth | (19) 50.6 | |
| | | | 5.2 | | | | 17.6 | |
| | | | 17.4 | | | | 37.1 | 17.6 |
| | | | 9.7 | | | % Profit Before Taxes/Total Assets | 15.2 | 10.2 |
| | | | 1.3 | | | | 9.9 | 3.5 |
| | | | 43.5 | | | | 112.5 | 57.9 |
| | | | 19.8 | | | Sales/Net Fixed Assets | 44.4 | 21.3 |
| | | | 7.8 | | | | 14.3 | 15.4 |
| | | | 2.5 | | | | 3.7 | 2.5 |
| | | | 1.7 | | | Sales/Total Assets | 2.5 | 2.1 |
| | | | 1.3 | | | | 1.8 | 1.7 |
| | | | .9 | | | | | |
| | | | 1.1 | | | % Depr., Dep., Amort./Sales | | |
| | | | 1.8 | | | | | |
| | | | | | | % Officers', Directors' Owners' Comp/Sales | | |
| | 14811M | 64463M | 353596M | | 1048000M | Net Sales ($) | 258943M | 809742M |
| | 5096M | 32247M | 207975M | | 203000M | Total Assets ($) | 97056M | 437915M |

M = $ thousand    MM = $ million
See Pages viii through xx for Explanation of Ratios and Data

© RMA 2024

# PROFESSIONAL SERVICES—Industrial Design Services  NAICS 541420

## Comparative Historical Data | Current Data Sorted by Sales

| Comparative Historical Data | | | Type of Statement | Current Data Sorted by Sales | | | | | |
|---|---|---|---|---|---|---|---|---|---|
| 3 | 1 3 | 1 4 | Unqualified | | | | | 1 | 1 |
| 1 | 1 | 4 | Reviewed | | | | | 1 | 3 |
| | 3 | 3 | Compiled | | 1 | | 2 | 1 | 2 |
| 4 | 9 | 10 | Tax Returns | | 2 | | 1 | 1 | |
| 4/1/21- | 4/1/22- | 4/1/23- | Other | | | | 3 | 1 | 2 |
| 3/31/22 | 3/31/23 | 3/31/24 | | 2 (4/1-9/30/23) | | | 20 (10/1/23-3/31/24) | | |
| ALL | ALL | ALL | | 0-1MM | 1-3MM | 3-5MM | 5-10MM | 10-25MM | 25MM & OVER |
| 8 | 17 | 22 | NUMBER OF STATEMENTS | | 3 | | 6 | 5 | 8 |
| % | % | % | ASSETS | % | % | % | % | % | % |
| | 19.7 | 12.6 | Cash & Equivalents | D | D | | | | |
| | 30.9 | 31.4 | Trade Receivables (net) | A | A | | | | |
| | 11.5 | 12.7 | Inventory | T | T | | | | |
| | 9.8 | 8.8 | All Other Current | A | A | | | | |
| | 71.9 | 65.5 | Total Current | | | | | | |
| | 11.1 | 20.7 | Fixed Assets (net) | N | N | | | | |
| | 5.7 | 3.9 | Intangibles (net) | O | O | | | | |
| | 11.2 | 9.9 | All Other Non-Current | T | T | | | | |
| | 100.0 | 100.0 | Total | | | | | | |
| | | | LIABILITIES | A | A | | | | |
| | 7.6 | 9.5 | Notes Payable-Short Term | V | V | | | | |
| | 1.2 | 2.6 | Cur. Mat.-L.T.D. | A | A | | | | |
| | 11.2 | 11.4 | Trade Payables | I | I | | | | |
| | .6 | .2 | Income Taxes Payable | L | L | | | | |
| | 14.9 | 16.1 | All Other Current | A | A | | | | |
| | 35.6 | 39.8 | Total Current | B | B | | | | |
| | 15.0 | 21.4 | Long-Term Debt | L | L | | | | |
| | .0 | .1 | Deferred Taxes | E | E | | | | |
| | 2.3 | 8.6 | All Other Non-Current | | | | | | |
| | 47.1 | 30.2 | Net Worth | | | | | | |
| | 100.0 | 100.0 | Total Liabilties & Net Worth | | | | | | |
| | | | INCOME DATA | | | | | | |
| | 100.0 | 100.0 | Net Sales | | | | | | |
| | | | Gross Profit | | | | | | |
| | 92.7 | 91.9 | Operating Expenses | | | | | | |
| | 7.3 | 8.1 | Operating Profit | | | | | | |
| | -1.0 | .6 | All Other Expenses (net) | | | | | | |
| | 8.2 | 7.4 | Profit Before Taxes | | | | | | |
| | | | RATIOS | | | | | | |
| | 5.4 | 2.5 | | | | | | | |
| | 1.9 | 1.8 | Current | | | | | | |
| | 1.2 | 1.1 | | | | | | | |
| | 2.4 | 1.6 | | | | | | | |
| | 1.3 | 1.3 | Quick | | | | | | |
| | .8 | .5 | | | | | | | |
| | 1 508.1 | 2 154.7 | | | | | | | |
| | 68 5.4 | 57 6.4 | Sales/Receivables | | | | | | |
| | 101 3.6 | 94 3.9 | | | | | | | |
| | | | Cost of Sales/Inventory | | | | | | |
| | | | Cost of Sales/Payables | | | | | | |
| | 3.9 | 3.5 | | | | | | | |
| | 5.9 | 6.1 | Sales/Working Capital | | | | | | |
| | 12.3 | NM | | | | | | | |
| | 38.2 | 24.5 | | | | | | | |
| (12) | 2.7 | (19) 7.4 | EBIT/Interest | | | | | | |
| | -2.3 | 2.0 | | | | | | | |
| | | | Net Profit + Depr., Dep., Amort./Cur. Mat. L/T/D | | | | | | |
| | .0 | .2 | | | | | | | |
| | .3 | .3 | Fixed/Worth | | | | | | |
| | .8 | NM | | | | | | | |
| | .5 | .9 | | | | | | | |
| | 1.2 | 1.8 | Debt/Worth | | | | | | |
| | 4.0 | NM | | | | | | | |
| | 73.6 | 81.8 | % Profit Before Taxes/Tangible Net Worth | | | | | | |
| (15) | 30.5 | (17) 31.6 | | | | | | | |
| | 1.8 | 5.6 | | | | | | | |
| | 30.9 | 21.5 | % Profit Before Taxes/Total Assets | | | | | | |
| | 11.6 | 8.4 | | | | | | | |
| | -.6 | 1.9 | | | | | | | |
| | 201.8 | 63.7 | | | | | | | |
| | 28.4 | 19.8 | Sales/Net Fixed Assets | | | | | | |
| | 10.8 | 7.8 | | | | | | | |
| | 3.1 | 2.5 | | | | | | | |
| | 1.9 | 1.7 | Sales/Total Assets | | | | | | |
| | 1.2 | 1.5 | | | | | | | |
| | .4 | .9 | | | | | | | |
| (12) | 1.1 | (16) 1.3 | % Depr., Dep., Amort./Sales | | | | | | |
| | 2.7 | 1.8 | | | | | | | |
| | | | % Officers', Directors' Owners' Comp/Sales | | | | | | |
| 142013M | 345060M | 1480870M | Net Sales ($) | | 6044M | | 43747M | 86787M | 1344292M |
| 86313M | 343018M | 448318M | Total Assets ($) | | 3508M | | 22612M | 49400M | 372798M |

© RMA 2024  M = $ thousand   MM = $ million
See Pages viii through xx for Explanation of Ratios and Data

# PROFESSIONAL SERVICES—Graphic Design Services  NAICS 541430

## Current Data Sorted by Assets

| 0-500M | 500M-2MM | 2-10MM | 10-50MM | 50-100MM | 100-250MM | | Comparative Historical Data | | |
|---|---|---|---|---|---|---|---|---|---|
| | | 3 | | 1 | | **Type of Statement** | | 5 | 3 |
| | 4 | 3 | 2 | 3 | | Unqualified | | 6 | 5 |
| 3 | 10 | 9 | 1 | 3 | 1 | Reviewed | | 5 | 1 |
| | 3 (4/1-9/30/23) | | 38 (10/1/23-3/31/24) | | | Compiled | | 17 | 13 |
| | | | | | | Tax Returns | | 60 | 38 |
| | | | | | | Other | | 4/1/19-3/31/20 ALL | 4/1/20-3/31/21 ALL |
| 3 | 14 | 15 | 6 | 3 | | **NUMBER OF STATEMENTS** | | 93 | 60 |
| % | % | % | % | % | % | **ASSETS** | | % | % |
| | 17.2 | 23.2 | | | | Cash & Equivalents | | 22.4 | 30.9 |
| | 30.3 | 28.4 | | | | Trade Receivables (net) | | 28.6 | 18.4 |
| | 7.1 | 9.0 | | | | Inventory | | 4.0 | 5.4 |
| | 7.9 | 3.0 | | | | All Other Current | | 3.5 | 3.3 |
| | 62.5 | 63.7 | | | | Total Current | | 58.4 | 58.0 |
| | 25.7 | 24.3 | | | | Fixed Assets (net) | | 23.9 | 28.2 |
| | .6 | 2.3 | | | | Intangibles (net) | | 7.8 | 9.3 |
| | 11.2 | 9.7 | | | | All Other Non-Current | | 10.0 | 4.4 |
| | 100.0 | 100.0 | | | | Total | | 100.0 | 100.0 |
| | | | | | | **LIABILITIES** | | | |
| | 10.9 | 3.0 | | | | Notes Payable-Short Term | | 13.8 | 6.0 |
| | 1.9 | 4.0 | | | | Cur. Mat.-L.T.D. | | 4.7 | 4.8 |
| | 3.5 | 8.3 | | | | Trade Payables | | 9.8 | 5.7 |
| | .0 | .0 | | | | Income Taxes Payable | | .1 | .0 |
| | 6.6 | 11.9 | | | | All Other Current | | 14.0 | 13.4 |
| | 22.9 | 27.2 | | | | Total Current | | 42.3 | 29.8 |
| | 16.5 | 16.0 | | | | Long-Term Debt | | 16.6 | 25.6 |
| | .0 | .2 | | | | Deferred Taxes | | .1 | .2 |
| | .5 | 4.0 | | | | All Other Non-Current | | 5.7 | 6.6 |
| | 60.1 | 52.5 | | | | Net Worth | | 35.2 | 37.8 |
| | 100.0 | 100.0 | | | | Total Liabilities & Net Worth | | 100.0 | 100.0 |
| | | | | | | **INCOME DATA** | | | |
| | 100.0 | 100.0 | | | | Net Sales | | 100.0 | 100.0 |
| | | | | | | Gross Profit | | | |
| | 89.0 | 85.0 | | | | Operating Expenses | | 89.1 | 92.3 |
| | 11.0 | 15.0 | | | | Operating Profit | | 10.9 | 7.7 |
| | .4 | 2.6 | | | | All Other Expenses (net) | | 2.1 | .2 |
| | 10.6 | 12.4 | | | | Profit Before Taxes | | 8.8 | 7.4 |
| | | | | | | **RATIOS** | | | |
| | 13.6 | 4.4 | | | | | | 3.2 | 5.6 |
| | 3.8 | 2.4 | | | | Current | | 1.6 | 2.4 |
| | 1.2 | 1.2 | | | | | | 1.0 | 1.2 |
| | 7.3 | 3.5 | | | | | | 2.4 | 4.4 |
| | 2.9 | 2.0 | | | | Quick | | 1.4 | 2.0 |
| | 1.0 | 1.2 | | | | | | .7 | .8 |
| 2 | 174.4 | 17 | 22.0 | | | | 5 | 71.6 | 0 UND |
| 22 | 16.8 | 31 | 11.6 | | | Sales/Receivables | 37 | 9.9 | 29 12.8 |
| 94 | 3.9 | 69 | 5.3 | | | | 60 | 6.1 | 51 7.2 |
| | | | | | | Cost of Sales/Inventory | | | |
| | | | | | | Cost of Sales/Payables | | | |
| | 4.1 | 3.8 | | | | | | 6.6 | 4.3 |
| | 13.6 | 5.3 | | | | Sales/Working Capital | | 14.1 | 7.3 |
| | 32.9 | 17.0 | | | | | | 120.6 | 37.1 |
| | 49.2 | 22.3 | | | | | | 24.0 | 19.4 |
| (11) | 14.6 | (12) 4.0 | | | | EBIT/Interest | (72) | 6.8 | (38) 5.2 |
| | 2.8 | -2.8 | | | | | | 2.3 | .3 |
| | | | | | | Net Profit + Depr., Dep., Amort./Cur. Mat. L/T/D | | | |
| | .0 | .1 | | | | | | .1 | .1 |
| | .3 | .2 | | | | Fixed/Worth | | .6 | .7 |
| | 1.2 | .8 | | | | | | 3.5 | 2.3 |
| | .2 | .3 | | | | | | .4 | .5 |
| | .6 | .7 | | | | Debt/Worth | | 1.1 | 1.3 |
| | 1.9 | 3.5 | | | | | | 7.0 | 6.9 |
| | 100.7 | 49.8 | | | | | | 88.8 | 82.0 |
| | 45.3 | 18.3 | | | | % Profit Before Taxes/Tangible Net Worth | (79) | 44.2 | (50) 37.2 |
| | 27.1 | -4.0 | | | | | | 10.7 | 2.6 |
| | 56.0 | 37.0 | | | | % Profit Before Taxes/Total Assets | | 44.3 | 32.1 |
| | 23.8 | 10.7 | | | | | | 13.9 | 14.6 |
| | 10.8 | -2.8 | | | | | | 3.6 | -.4 |
| | 965.1 | 90.1 | | | | | | 131.6 | 54.3 |
| | 20.7 | 17.2 | | | | Sales/Net Fixed Assets | | 21.5 | 13.7 |
| | 4.8 | 7.7 | | | | | | 6.9 | 4.1 |
| | 3.8 | 3.9 | | | | | | 4.3 | 3.1 |
| | 2.5 | 2.5 | | | | Sales/Total Assets | | 2.8 | 2.2 |
| | 1.9 | 1.4 | | | | | | 1.6 | 1.3 |
| | | | | | | | | .6 | 1.1 |
| | | | | | | % Depr., Dep., Amort./Sales | (54) | 1.9 | (41) 2.7 |
| | | | | | | | | 5.9 | 6.4 |
| | | | | | | | | 5.7 | 4.0 |
| | | | | | | % Officers', Directors', Owners' Comp/Sales | (28) | 9.1 | (23) 9.1 |
| | | | | | | | | 13.5 | 14.9 |
| 4948M | 47728M | 150946M | 203143M | 314821M | | Net Sales ($) | | 1097519M | 634818M |
| 908M | 15759M | 55800M | 123384M | 230008M | | Total Assets ($) | | 767975M | 401674M |

Data Not Available for 100-250MM column.

M = $ thousand    MM = $ million
See Pages viii through xx for Explanation of Ratios and Data

© RMA 2024

# PROFESSIONAL SERVICES—Graphic Design Services  NAICS 541430

## Comparative Historical Data | Current Data Sorted by Sales

| Comparative Historical Data ||| Type of Statement | Current Data Sorted by Sales ||||||
|---|---|---|---|---|---|---|---|---|---|
| 1 | 3 | 1 | Unqualified | | | | | | 1 |
| 3 | 5 | 2 | Reviewed | | | | 1 | 1 | 1 |
| 7 | 3 | 3 | Compiled | | | 2 | 1 | 2 | |
| 8 | 7 | 8 | Tax Returns | | 2 | 1 | 3 | 2 | |
| 22 | 33 | 27 | Other | 2 | 8 | 5 | 6 | 1 | 5 |
| 4/1/21-3/31/22 ALL | 4/1/22-3/31/23 ALL | 4/1/23-3/31/24 ALL | | 0-1MM | 3 (4/1-9/30/23) 1-3MM | 3-5MM | 38 (10/1/23-3/31/24) 5-10MM | 10-25MM | 25MM & OVER |
| 41 | 51 | 41 | NUMBER OF STATEMENTS | 2 | 10 | 8 | 9 | 5 | 7 |
| % | % | % | **ASSETS** | % | % | % | % | % | % |
| 24.4 | 20.8 | 21.6 | Cash & Equivalents | | 8.5 | | | | |
| 23.1 | 31.8 | 27.4 | Trade Receivables (net) | | 26.9 | | | | |
| 7.4 | 7.4 | 8.9 | Inventory | | .1 | | | | |
| 6.9 | 6.6 | 5.2 | All Other Current | | 10.9 | | | | |
| 61.8 | 66.6 | 63.2 | Total Current | | 46.4 | | | | |
| 31.8 | 21.7 | 23.9 | Fixed Assets (net) | | 39.6 | | | | |
| 1.8 | 6.8 | 3.6 | Intangibles (net) | | .8 | | | | |
| 4.6 | 4.8 | 9.3 | All Other Non-Current | | 13.1 | | | | |
| 100.0 | 100.0 | 100.0 | Total | | 100.0 | | | | |
| | | | **LIABILITIES** | | | | | | |
| 7.7 | 9.8 | 5.9 | Notes Payable-Short Term | | 13.1 | | | | |
| 4.1 | 1.9 | 2.7 | Cur. Mat.-L.T.D. | | 2.1 | | | | |
| 5.9 | 12.2 | 5.8 | Trade Payables | | 3.5 | | | | |
| .1 | .1 | .0 | Income Taxes Payable | | .0 | | | | |
| 11.2 | 13.6 | 13.5 | All Other Current | | 6.2 | | | | |
| 29.1 | 37.5 | 27.9 | Total Current | | 25.0 | | | | |
| 26.5 | 16.8 | 14.7 | Long-Term Debt | | 20.8 | | | | |
| .0 | .0 | .2 | Deferred Taxes | | .0 | | | | |
| 7.9 | 6.9 | 4.8 | All Other Non-Current | | .7 | | | | |
| 36.5 | 38.7 | 52.4 | Net Worth | | 53.5 | | | | |
| 100.0 | 100.0 | 100.0 | Total Liabilities & Net Worth | | 100.0 | | | | |
| | | | **INCOME DATA** | | | | | | |
| 100.0 | 100.0 | 100.0 | Net Sales | | 100.0 | | | | |
| | | | Gross Profit | | | | | | |
| 91.0 | 93.0 | 88.3 | Operating Expenses | | 78.2 | | | | |
| 9.0 | 7.0 | 11.7 | Operating Profit | | 21.8 | | | | |
| -1.6 | -.4 | 1.9 | All Other Expenses (net) | | 3.7 | | | | |
| 10.6 | 7.3 | 9.7 | Profit Before Taxes | | 18.1 | | | | |
| | | | **RATIOS** | | | | | | |
| 4.0 | 4.3 | 5.4 | | | 4.5 | | | | |
| 2.5 | 1.9 | 2.5 | Current | | 1.5 | | | | |
| 1.5 | 1.3 | 1.2 | | | 1.2 | | | | |
| 3.2 | 3.5 | 3.8 | | | 2.5 | | | | |
| 2.0 | 1.6 | 1.9 | Quick | | 1.2 | | | | |
| 1.0 | .8 | 1.0 | | | 1.0 | | | | |
| 0 UND | 23 16.1 | 5 69.6 | | 0 UND | | | | | |
| 39 9.4 | 48 7.6 | 31 11.6 | Sales/Receivables | 18 20.0 | | | | | |
| 63 5.8 | 74 4.9 | 72 5.1 | | 107 3.4 | | | | | |
| | | | Cost of Sales/Inventory | | | | | | |
| | | | Cost of Sales/Payables | | | | | | |
| 3.4 | 4.9 | 4.3 | | | 4.7 | | | | |
| 7.6 | 8.7 | 10.2 | Sales/Working Capital | | 14.8 | | | | |
| 12.7 | 30.9 | 31.6 | | | 23.9 | | | | |
| 47.4 | 40.3 | 29.9 | | | | | | | |
| (32) 10.2 | (38) 10.6 | (30) 6.6 | EBIT/Interest | | | | | | |
| 3.0 | 1.8 | 2.3 | | | | | | | |
| | | | Net Profit + Depr., Dep., Amort./Cur. Mat. L/T/D | | | | | | |
| .1 | .1 | .1 | | | .0 | | | | |
| .6 | .4 | .4 | Fixed/Worth | | 1.0 | | | | |
| 1.3 | 1.2 | 1.7 | | | 1.7 | | | | |
| .3 | .6 | .3 | | | .3 | | | | |
| .8 | 1.2 | .8 | Debt/Worth | | 1.2 | | | | |
| 2.4 | 6.8 | 3.8 | | | 2.1 | | | | |
| 71.4 | 72.0 | 87.0 | | | 101.9 | | | | |
| (36) 31.9 | (44) 33.3 | (40) 40.6 | % Profit Before Taxes/Tangible Net Worth | | 40.1 | | | | |
| 7.7 | 13.7 | 8.0 | | | 5.6 | | | | |
| 40.4 | 36.4 | 38.5 | | | 57.5 | | | | |
| 15.3 | 13.4 | 11.3 | % Profit Before Taxes/Total Assets | | 20.3 | | | | |
| 4.2 | 3.0 | 4.0 | | | 4.9 | | | | |
| 31.6 | 118.2 | 94.3 | | | 237.9 | | | | |
| 7.8 | 24.3 | 19.9 | Sales/Net Fixed Assets | | 5.6 | | | | |
| 3.5 | 7.5 | 5.6 | | | 1.2 | | | | |
| 2.9 | 3.3 | 3.8 | | | 2.2 | | | | |
| 1.7 | 2.0 | 2.3 | Sales/Total Assets | | 1.7 | | | | |
| 1.1 | 1.5 | 1.5 | | | .6 | | | | |
| 1.1 | .9 | .8 | | | | | | | |
| (31) 2.7 | (32) 1.9 | (26) 2.1 | % Depr., Dep., Amort./Sales | | | | | | |
| 5.8 | 3.5 | 4.0 | | | | | | | |
| 4.2 | 3.0 | 3.1 | | | | | | | |
| (14) 10.3 | (20) 4.9 | (16) 4.3 | % Officers', Directors' Owners' Comp/Sales | | | | | | |
| 14.1 | 12.1 | 11.5 | | | | | | | |
| 650825M | 1723880M | 721586M | Net Sales ($) | 429M | 17197M | 30468M | 59910M | 87308M | 526274M |
| 471353M | 811039M | 425859M | Total Assets ($) | 2313M | 28334M | 11516M | 21860M | 33179M | 328657M |

© RMA 2024  
M = $ thousand    MM = $ million  
See Pages viii through xx for Explanation of Ratios and Data

# PROFESSIONAL SERVICES—Other Specialized Design Services  NAICS 541490

## Current Data Sorted by Assets | Comparative Historical Data

| Type of Statement | | | | | | | | | |
|---|---|---|---|---|---|---|---|---|---|
| | | | | 1 | 1 | | Unqualified | 3 | 2 |
| | | | 1 | 1 | 1 | | Reviewed | 4 | |
| | | 1 | | | | | Compiled | 2 | 2 |
| 1 | 4 | 2 | | | | | Tax Returns | 6 | 10 |
| 1 | 6 | 10 | 3 | 1 | | | Other | 22 | 16 |
| | 5 (4/1–9/30/23) | | 29 (10/1/23–3/31/24) | | | | | 4/1/19– | 4/1/20– |
| | | | | | | | | 3/31/20 | 3/31/21 |
| 0-500M | 500M-2MM | 2-10MM | 10-50MM | 50-100MM | 100-250MM | | | ALL | ALL |
| 2 | 10 | 13 | 6 | 3 | | NUMBER OF STATEMENTS | | 37 | 30 |
| % | % | % | % | % | % | **ASSETS** | | % | % |
| | 25.0 | 15.9 | | | | Cash & Equivalents | | 23.0 | 29.4 |
| | 27.6 | 41.5 | | | | Trade Receivables (net) | | 22.0 | 17.9 |
| | 11.5 | 12.6 | | | | Inventory | | 12.9 | 10.3 |
| | 3.5 | 1.1 | | | | All Other Current | | 4.8 | 3.9 |
| | 67.6 | 71.2 | | | D | Total Current | | 62.7 | 61.5 |
| | 13.7 | 19.2 | | | A | Fixed Assets (net) | | 22.4 | 18.0 |
| | 7.1 | 5.7 | | | T | Intangibles (net) | | 5.2 | 11.8 |
| | 11.6 | 3.9 | | | A | All Other Non-Current | | 9.7 | 8.6 |
| | 100.0 | 100.0 | | | | Total | | 100.0 | 100.0 |
| | | | | | N | **LIABILITIES** | | | |
| | 13.4 | 3.4 | | | O | Notes Payable-Short Term | | 5.0 | 24.3 |
| | 1.0 | 1.9 | | | T | Cur. Mat.-L.T.D. | | 1.9 | 3.7 |
| | 8.2 | 19.7 | | | | Trade Payables | | 17.6 | 5.9 |
| | .3 | .0 | | | A | Income Taxes Payable | | .0 | .6 |
| | 9.0 | 20.9 | | | V | All Other Current | | 16.9 | 16.3 |
| | 31.8 | 46.0 | | | A | Total Current | | 41.4 | 50.8 |
| | 26.5 | 13.2 | | | I | Long-Term Debt | | 11.6 | 35.1 |
| | .0 | .0 | | | L | Deferred Taxes | | .0 | .0 |
| | 1.6 | .4 | | | A | All Other Non-Current | | 3.1 | .6 |
| | 40.1 | 40.5 | | | B | Net Worth | | 43.9 | 13.5 |
| | 100.0 | 100.0 | | | L | Total Liabilities & Net Worth | | 100.0 | 100.0 |
| | | | | | E | **INCOME DATA** | | | |
| | 100.0 | 100.0 | | | | Net Sales | | 100.0 | 100.0 |
| | | | | | | Gross Profit | | | |
| | 94.0 | 93.5 | | | | Operating Expenses | | 91.6 | 91.2 |
| | 6.0 | 6.5 | | | | Operating Profit | | 8.4 | 8.8 |
| | .0 | .0 | | | | All Other Expenses (net) | | .2 | .6 |
| | 6.0 | 6.5 | | | | Profit Before Taxes | | 8.2 | 8.2 |
| | | | | | | **RATIOS** | | | |
| | 5.1 | 2.5 | | | | | | 4.9 | 4.9 |
| | 2.7 | 1.8 | | | | Current | | 1.6 | 1.6 |
| | 1.8 | 1.3 | | | | | | .9 | .9 |
| | 4.5 | 2.3 | | | | | | 5.3 | 4.1 |
| | 2.1 | 1.6 | | | | Quick | (36) | 1.2 | 1.1 |
| | .8 | 1.0 | | | | | | .6 | .5 |
| 1 | 267.2 | 30 | 12.3 | | | | 2 | 237.8 | 0 UND |
| 26 | 13.9 | 74 | 4.9 | | | Sales/Receivables | 19 | 19.6 | 21 17.8 |
| 51 | 7.1 | 101 | 3.6 | | | | 50 | 7.3 | 51 7.2 |
| | | | | | | Cost of Sales/Inventory | | | |
| | | | | | | Cost of Sales/Payables | | | |
| | 3.7 | 4.7 | | | | | | 4.7 | 3.9 |
| | 9.0 | 6.1 | | | | Sales/Working Capital | | 11.3 | 18.9 |
| | 52.3 | 12.6 | | | | | | -51.7 | -32.5 |
| | | | | | | | | 63.3 | 60.8 |
| | | | | | | EBIT/Interest | (25) | 7.3 | (18) 13.6 |
| | | | | | | | | 1.5 | -.5 |
| | | | | | | Net Profit + Depr., Dep., Amort./Cur. Mat. L/T/D | | | |
| | .0 | .0 | | | | | | .1 | .1 |
| | .1 | .0 | | | | Fixed/Worth | | .3 | .4 |
| | .7 | 1.4 | | | | | | 1.9 | -.7 |
| | .5 | .7 | | | | | | .4 | .8 |
| | 1.2 | 1.3 | | | | Debt/Worth | | 1.0 | 2.0 |
| | NM | 3.5 | | | | | | 4.3 | -7.3 |
| | | 66.6 | | | | | | 66.7 | 198.3 |
| | (12) | 23.5 | | | | % Profit Before Taxes/Tangible Net Worth | (29) | 26.4 | (21) 77.5 |
| | | 14.8 | | | | | | 11.8 | 8.9 |
| | 23.3 | 21.3 | | | | % Profit Before Taxes/Total Assets | | 40.1 | 75.9 |
| | 10.6 | 9.0 | | | | | | 11.8 | 15.9 |
| | -5.2 | 3.5 | | | | | | 2.0 | -4.7 |
| | UND | UND | | | | | | 81.3 | 808.7 |
| | 104.3 | 137.2 | | | | Sales/Net Fixed Assets | | 26.6 | 44.8 |
| | 16.1 | 3.7 | | | | | | 8.3 | 9.7 |
| | 5.7 | 2.7 | | | | | | 4.2 | 7.3 |
| | 3.2 | 1.7 | | | | Sales/Total Assets | | 2.6 | 2.5 |
| | 1.7 | 1.3 | | | | | | 1.6 | 1.1 |
| | | | | | | | | .6 | .5 |
| | | | | | | % Depr., Dep., Amort./Sales | (18) | 1.1 | (12) 1.0 |
| | | | | | | | | 2.7 | 8.3 |
| | | | | | | | | 3.6 | |
| | | | | | | % Officers', Directors' Owners' Comp/Sales | (14) | 6.9 | |
| | | | | | | | | 10.5 | |
| 5191M | 29669M | 158045M | 218595M | 281689M | | Net Sales ($) | | 1131672M | 251307M |
| 539M | 9396M | 74410M | 150701M | 240258M | | Total Assets ($) | | 612513M | 245893M |

M = $ thousand    MM = $ million
See Pages viii through xx for Explanation of Ratios and Data

© RMA 2024

# PROFESSIONAL SERVICES—Other Specialized Design Services   NAICS 541490

## Comparative Historical Data | Current Data Sorted by Sales

| | | | | | | | Type of Statement | | | | | | |
|---|---|---|---|---|---|---|---|---|---|---|---|---|---|
| | | 2 | | 3 | | 2 | Unqualified | | | | | | 2 |
| | | | | 2 | | 3 | Reviewed | | | | 1 | | 2 |
| | | 2 | | 4 | | | Compiled | | 2 | 3 | 1 | 1 | 1 |
| | | 3 | | 4 | | 8 | Tax Returns | 1 | 5 | 5 | 5 | 2 | 5 |
| | | 22 | | 27 | | 21 | Other | | | | | | |
| | | 4/1/21-3/31/22 | | 4/1/22-3/31/23 | | 4/1/23-3/31/24 | | | 5 (4/1-9/30/23) | | 29 (10/1/23-3/31/24) | | |
| | | ALL | | ALL | | ALL | | 0-1MM | 1-3MM | 3-5MM | 5-10MM | 10-25MM | 25MM & OVER |
| | | 29 | | 40 | | 34 | NUMBER OF STATEMENTS | 1 | 5 | 8 | 7 | 3 | 10 |
| | | % | | % | | % | ASSETS | % | % | % | % | % | % |
| | | 25.8 | | 24.3 | | 22.5 | Cash & Equivalents | | | | | | 18.0 |
| | | 19.7 | | 23.4 | | 30.3 | Trade Receivables (net) | | | | | | 30.2 |
| | | 5.4 | | 9.7 | | 12.6 | Inventory | | | | | | 13.3 |
| | | 4.7 | | 3.2 | | 1.8 | All Other Current | | | | | | 1.5 |
| | | 55.5 | | 60.6 | | 67.1 | Total Current | | | | | | 63.0 |
| | | 27.8 | | 25.2 | | 15.4 | Fixed Assets (net) | | | | | | 13.8 |
| | | 5.9 | | 7.4 | | 9.1 | Intangibles (net) | | | | | | 16.2 |
| | | 10.8 | | 6.9 | | 8.4 | All Other Non-Current | | | | | | 6.9 |
| | | 100.0 | | 100.0 | | 100.0 | Total | | | | | | 100.0 |
| | | | | | | | LIABILITIES | | | | | | |
| | | 5.3 | | 9.8 | | 6.5 | Notes Payable-Short Term | | | | | | 2.7 |
| | | 3.7 | | 2.8 | | 1.6 | Cur. Mat.-L.T.D. | | | | | | 1.9 |
| | | 6.0 | | 9.8 | | 15.3 | Trade Payables | | | | | | 18.8 |
| | | 1.1 | | .0 | | .1 | Income Taxes Payable | | | | | | .0 |
| | | 13.6 | | 12.4 | | 15.5 | All Other Current | | | | | | 16.4 |
| | | 29.6 | | 34.8 | | 39.0 | Total Current | | | | | | 39.8 |
| | | 26.1 | | 20.3 | | 16.2 | Long-Term Debt | | | | | | 9.1 |
| | | .0 | | .0 | | .0 | Deferred Taxes | | | | | | .0 |
| | | 1.5 | | 6.6 | | 1.6 | All Other Non-Current | | | | | | 3.9 |
| | | 43.0 | | 38.3 | | 43.2 | Net Worth | | | | | | 47.2 |
| | | 100.0 | | 100.0 | | 100.0 | Total Liabilties & Net Worth | | | | | | 100.0 |
| | | | | | | | INCOME DATA | | | | | | |
| | | 100.0 | | 100.0 | | 100.0 | Net Sales | | | | | | 100.0 |
| | | | | | | | Gross Profit | | | | | | |
| | | 79.3 | | 92.2 | | 91.7 | Operating Expenses | | | | | | 94.2 |
| | | 20.7 | | 7.8 | | 8.3 | Operating Profit | | | | | | 5.8 |
| | | .9 | | .3 | | .1 | All Other Expenses (net) | | | | | | .1 |
| | | 19.8 | | 7.5 | | 8.2 | Profit Before Taxes | | | | | | 5.8 |
| | | | | | | | RATIOS | | | | | | |
| | | 3.2 | | 4.9 | | 3.2 | | | | | | | 3.2 |
| | | 1.8 | | 2.1 | | 1.9 | Current | | | | | | 1.5 |
| | | 1.0 | | 1.1 | | 1.2 | | | | | | | .9 |
| | | 2.8 | | 4.2 | | 2.6 | | | | | | | 2.8 |
| | | 1.2 | | 1.6 | | 1.6 | Quick | | | | | | 1.1 |
| | | .7 | | .8 | | .5 | | | | | | | .3 |
| 0 | UND | | 3 | 105.9 | 19 | 19.2 | | | | | | 23 | 16.1 |
| 27 | 13.3 | | 34 | 10.6 | 41 | 8.9 | Sales/Receivables | | | | | 41 | 8.9 |
| 56 | 6.5 | | 54 | 6.8 | 74 | 4.9 | | | | | | 70 | 5.2 |
| | | | | | | | Cost of Sales/Inventory | | | | | | |
| | | | | | | | Cost of Sales/Payables | | | | | | |
| | | 4.2 | | 3.6 | | 4.5 | | | | | | | 5.0 |
| | | 9.4 | | 9.8 | | 7.2 | Sales/Working Capital | | | | | | 14.0 |
| | | NM | | 71.5 | | 26.8 | | | | | | | NM |
| | | 66.8 | | 106.3 | | 32.5 | | | | | | | |
| (17) | 48.1 | | (31) | 13.7 | (22) | 3.7 | EBIT/Interest | | | | | | |
| | 8.3 | | | 2.8 | | 1.6 | | | | | | | |
| | | | | | | | Net Profit + Depr., Dep., Amort./Cur. Mat. L/T/D | | | | | | |
| | | .0 | | .1 | | .0 | | | | | | | .0 |
| | | .3 | | .4 | | .1 | Fixed/Worth | | | | | | .3 |
| | | 3.3 | | 1.5 | | 1.2 | | | | | | | -1.8 |
| | | .4 | | .5 | | .7 | | | | | | | .6 |
| | | 1.7 | | 1.9 | | 1.4 | Debt/Worth | | | | | | 1.4 |
| | | 6.4 | | 13.1 | | 5.7 | | | | | | | -4.3 |
| | | 105.4 | | 77.2 | | 58.6 | % Profit Before Taxes/Tangible Net Worth | | | | | | |
| (25) | 64.4 | | (32) | 48.1 | (28) | 27.0 | | | | | | | |
| | 39.0 | | | 12.6 | | 15.3 | | | | | | | |
| | | 44.6 | | 24.1 | | 19.2 | % Profit Before Taxes/Total Assets | | | | | | 15.2 |
| | | 29.6 | | 13.8 | | 10.6 | | | | | | | 11.5 |
| | | 12.9 | | 2.2 | | 3.5 | | | | | | | 3.8 |
| | | 200.2 | | 73.3 | | UND | Sales/Net Fixed Assets | | | | | | 418.0 |
| | | 20.3 | | 20.9 | | 104.3 | | | | | | | 72.3 |
| | | 3.1 | | 5.4 | | 5.0 | | | | | | | 4.2 |
| | | 3.3 | | 3.6 | | 3.5 | Sales/Total Assets | | | | | | 2.9 |
| | | 2.0 | | 2.1 | | 1.9 | | | | | | | 1.7 |
| | | 1.0 | | 1.5 | | 1.3 | | | | | | | 1.1 |
| | | .3 | | .2 | | .6 | % Depr., Dep., Amort./Sales | | | | | | |
| (10) | .8 | | (19) | .8 | (14) | 1.3 | | | | | | | |
| | 2.8 | | | 5.0 | | 4.5 | | | | | | | |
| | | | | 2.5 | | 1.5 | % Officers', Directors' Owners' Comp/Sales | | | | | | |
| | | | (14) | 3.5 | (14) | 2.9 | | | | | | | |
| | | | | 9.5 | | 5.7 | | | | | | | |
| | | 307411M | | 1220687M | | 693189M | Net Sales ($) | 759M | 9685M | 32547M | 54010M | 40862M | 555326M |
| | | 267179M | | 686656M | | 475304M | Total Assets ($) | 246M | 4765M | 9589M | 40174M | 32017M | 388513M |

© RMA 2024

M = $ thousand    MM = $ million
See Pages viii through xx for Explanation of Ratios and Data

# PROFESSIONAL SERVICES—Custom Computer Programming Services NAICS 541511

## Current Data Sorted by Assets / Comparative Historical Data

| | | | | | | | Type of Statement | | |
|---|---|---|---|---|---|---|---|---|---|
| | | 2 | 5 | 20 | 5 | 9 | Unqualified | 51 | 19 |
| | | 5 | 14 | 17 | 1 | 1 | Reviewed | 41 | 14 |
| | 13 | 22 | 13 | 5 | 1 | 1 | Compiled | 28 | 8 |
| | 17 | 47 | 30 | 3 | 1 | 1 | Tax Returns | 74 | 35 |
| | | 66 (4/1-9/30/23) | 130 | 123 | 21 | 25 | Other | 341 | 232 |
| | | | | 465 (10/1/23-3/31/24) | | | | 4/1/19-3/31/20 | 4/1/20-3/31/21 |
| | 0-500M | 500M-2MM | 2-10MM | 10-50MM | 50-100MM | 100-250MM | | ALL | ALL |
| | 30 | 76 | 192 | 168 | 29 | 36 | NUMBER OF STATEMENTS | 535 | 308 |
| | % | % | % | % | % | % | ASSETS | % | % |
| | 35.5 | 24.9 | 23.4 | 21.9 | 18.8 | 16.8 | Cash & Equivalents | 26.6 | 36.2 |
| | 18.1 | 42.3 | 43.9 | 29.9 | 28.1 | 24.6 | Trade Receivables (net) | 37.9 | 29.9 |
| | .3 | 1.2 | 1.7 | 1.4 | 3.0 | 5.7 | Inventory | 1.3 | 1.5 |
| | 5.3 | 6.1 | 6.5 | 9.7 | 6.3 | 7.1 | All Other Current | 5.4 | 3.6 |
| | 59.2 | 74.5 | 75.5 | 62.9 | 56.2 | 54.2 | Total Current | 71.2 | 71.2 |
| | 8.9 | 7.3 | 5.0 | 6.8 | 10.6 | 9.9 | Fixed Assets (net) | 8.9 | 7.0 |
| | 12.7 | 6.0 | 8.6 | 16.7 | 22.0 | 21.5 | Intangibles (net) | 9.8 | 12.8 |
| | 19.1 | 12.2 | 10.9 | 13.6 | 11.2 | 14.4 | All Other Non-Current | 10.1 | 9.0 |
| | 100.0 | 100.0 | 100.0 | 100.0 | 100.0 | 100.0 | Total | 100.0 | 100.0 |
| | | | | | | | LIABILITIES | | |
| | 13.2 | 9.0 | 7.8 | 4.5 | 3.3 | 1.6 | Notes Payable-Short Term | 8.1 | 8.4 |
| | 5.3 | 1.2 | 1.6 | 2.3 | 2.9 | 1.8 | Cur. Mat.-L.T.D. | 1.9 | 4.3 |
| | 3.1 | 13.3 | 10.2 | 10.9 | 14.5 | 17.4 | Trade Payables | 11.0 | 8.2 |
| | .1 | .7 | .3 | .2 | .9 | .3 | Income Taxes Payable | .3 | .4 |
| | 33.4 | 26.8 | 24.0 | 24.3 | 16.1 | 25.1 | All Other Current | 25.8 | 23.7 |
| | 55.2 | 51.0 | 43.9 | 42.3 | 37.7 | 46.2 | Total Current | 47.1 | 45.0 |
| | 28.8 | 12.2 | 9.5 | 13.7 | 21.6 | 15.6 | Long-Term Debt | 14.0 | 18.7 |
| | .0 | .0 | .2 | .1 | .0 | .2 | Deferred Taxes | .1 | .1 |
| | 14.7 | 6.9 | 10.1 | 10.3 | 6.7 | 6.8 | All Other Non-Current | 7.3 | 7.6 |
| | 1.3 | 30.0 | 36.4 | 33.6 | 34.0 | 31.1 | Net Worth | 31.5 | 28.6 |
| | 100.0 | 100.0 | 100.0 | 100.0 | 100.0 | 100.0 | Total Liabilties & Net Worth | 100.0 | 100.0 |
| | | | | | | | INCOME DATA | | |
| | 100.0 | 100.0 | 100.0 | 100.0 | 100.0 | 100.0 | Net Sales | 100.0 | 100.0 |
| | | | | | | | Gross Profit | | |
| | 94.5 | 94.0 | 94.1 | 94.6 | 99.2 | 92.9 | Operating Expenses | 93.3 | 93.8 |
| | 5.5 | 6.0 | 5.9 | 5.4 | .8 | 7.1 | Operating Profit | 6.7 | 6.2 |
| | 1.2 | .7 | .8 | 1.8 | 3.2 | 1.8 | All Other Expenses (net) | 1.6 | .2 |
| | 4.3 | 5.3 | 5.1 | 3.6 | -2.4 | 5.3 | Profit Before Taxes | 5.1 | 6.0 |
| | | | | | | | RATIOS | | |
| | 4.2 | 4.5 | 4.3 | 2.9 | 2.0 | 1.6 | | 3.3 | 4.2 |
| | 1.7 | 1.9 | 2.0 | 1.8 | 1.5 | 1.2 | Current | 1.7 | 2.1 |
| | .5 | 1.3 | 1.2 | 1.1 | 1.0 | .8 | | 1.0 | 1.1 |
| | 4.1 | 3.5 | 3.9 | 2.6 | 1.8 | 1.6 | | 3.0 | 4.1 |
| | 1.5 | 1.6 | 1.8 | 1.4 | 1.0 | .9 | Quick | 1.6 | 2.0 |
| | .4 | 1.1 | 1.0 | 1.0 | .8 | .5 | | .9 | .9 |
| 0 | UND | 17 | 21.3 | 36 | 10.1 | 32 | 11.3 | 40 | 9.1 | 46 | 7.9 | | 27 | 13.5 | 26 | 14.2 |
| 0 | UND | 41 | 8.8 | 54 | 6.8 | 51 | 7.1 | 60 | 6.1 | 65 | 5.6 | Sales/Receivables | 50 | 7.3 | 47 | 7.8 |
| 26 | 14.1 | 59 | 6.2 | 78 | 4.7 | 69 | 5.3 | 74 | 4.9 | 89 | 4.1 | | 70 | 5.2 | 65 | 5.6 |
| | | | | | | | Cost of Sales/Inventory | | |
| | | | | | | | Cost of Sales/Payables | | |
| | 10.3 | 5.6 | 4.6 | 4.4 | 6.2 | 6.2 | | 5.4 | 4.0 |
| | 86.2 | 12.1 | 8.0 | 8.9 | 13.2 | 13.8 | Sales/Working Capital | 11.7 | 7.3 |
| | -26.7 | 36.6 | 24.0 | 72.4 | NM | -11.4 | | 221.0 | 43.5 |
| | 40.0 | 26.3 | 41.2 | 71.2 | 19.4 | 18.8 | | 48.9 | 64.4 |
| (19) | 4.7 | (41) 10.6 | (135) 9.9 | (114) 10.3 | (22) 2.7 | (28) 4.3 | EBIT/Interest | (352) 11.4 | (208) 13.9 |
| | -.3 | 1.7 | 2.6 | .5 | .6 | -.2 | | 1.2 | .5 |
| | | | | 20.6 | | | | 13.0 | 11.1 |
| | | | (20) | 4.3 | | | Net Profit + Depr., Dep., Amort./Cur. Mat. L/T/D | (36) 4.7 | (26) 2.8 |
| | | | | 1.7 | | | | 1.4 | 1.0 |
| | .0 | .0 | .0 | .0 | .1 | .1 | | .0 | .0 |
| | .2 | .0 | .0 | .1 | .6 | 1.6 | Fixed/Worth | .1 | .1 |
| | -1.0 | .2 | .3 | 1.1 | -.2 | -.1 | | 1.4 | 1.1 |
| | .2 | .5 | .4 | .6 | .8 | 1.4 | | .5 | .6 |
| | 7.3 | 1.8 | 1.2 | 2.3 | 5.1 | 8.5 | Debt/Worth | 1.5 | 2.2 |
| | -3.8 | 4.4 | 5.3 | 61.1 | -4.5 | -3.4 | | 43.6 | -11.7 |
| | 310.6 | 98.0 | 70.6 | 62.8 | 56.7 | 57.2 | | 79.6 | 94.9 |
| (17) | 94.7 | (65) 50.0 | (158) 36.0 | (128) 31.1 | (19) 19.1 | (20) 32.0 | % Profit Before Taxes/Tangible Net Worth | (408) 42.0 | (222) 44.6 |
| | 20.4 | 12.9 | 13.0 | 14.2 | -22.2 | -.5 | | 15.4 | 17.0 |
| | 66.3 | 38.2 | 32.4 | 22.9 | 11.8 | 13.0 | | 36.1 | 33.6 |
| | 43.0 | 18.2 | 13.7 | 10.1 | 2.0 | 6.3 | % Profit Before Taxes/Total Assets | 14.1 | 13.3 |
| | -2.8 | 4.9 | 3.3 | .3 | -8.5 | -2.8 | | .5 | 1.1 |
| | UND | UND | 999.8 | 500.6 | 128.7 | 159.8 | | 634.7 | 999.8 |
| | 618.6 | 614.3 | 343.4 | 118.4 | 33.0 | 47.1 | Sales/Net Fixed Assets | 98.2 | 113.4 |
| | 47.4 | 67.4 | 71.0 | 29.3 | 10.2 | 15.0 | | 28.0 | 28.5 |
| | 13.9 | 5.7 | 3.8 | 2.8 | 2.4 | 2.1 | | 4.4 | 3.5 |
| | 8.8 | 4.1 | 2.8 | 1.8 | 1.5 | .9 | Sales/Total Assets | 2.7 | 2.4 |
| | 3.9 | 2.6 | 2.1 | 1.1 | .9 | .6 | | 1.6 | 1.4 |
| | | | .1 | .0 | .2 | .5 | .1 | | .2 | .2 |
| | | (21) .4 | (69) .2 | (80) .5 | (12) 1.8 | (16) 1.2 | % Depr., Dep., Amort./Sales | (259) .7 | (131) .7 |
| | | 1.2 | .8 | 1.1 | 4.8 | 2.7 | | 1.9 | 2.2 |
| | 2.7 | 1.8 | 1.4 | | | | | 1.6 | 2.5 |
| (11) | 4.3 | (22) 4.8 | (34) 2.7 | | | | % Officers', Directors' Owners' Comp/Sales | (116) 3.5 | (65) 6.3 |
| | 11.4 | 12.3 | 7.2 | | | | | 7.3 | 13.5 |
| | 100182M | 423786M | 2854754M | 8704942M | 5163465M | 8006004M | Net Sales ($) | 19428017M | 9973621M |
| | 9015M | 95004M | 973780M | 3784891M | 2116554M | 5709580M | Total Assets ($) | 11116348M | 5939026M |

M = $ thousand  MM = $ million
See Pages viii through xx for Explanation of Ratios and Data

© RMA 2024

# PROFESSIONAL SERVICES—Custom Computer Programming Services  NAICS 541511

## Comparative Historical Data | Current Data Sorted by Sales

| | | | | | | Type of Statement | | | | | | |
|---|---|---|---|---|---|---|---|---|---|---|---|---|
| | 28 | | 46 | | 39 | Unqualified | | | | 1 | 8 | 30 |
| | 10 | | 25 | | 35 | Reviewed | | 1 | | 5 | 13 | 16 |
| | 10 | | 18 | | 25 | Compiled | | 1 | 3 | 4 | 8 | 9 |
| | 55 | | 89 | | 69 | Tax Returns | 4 | 9 | 8 | 23 | 18 | 7 |
| | 187 | | 315 | | 363 | Other | 7 | 22 | 32 | 57 | 98 | 147 |
| | 4/1/21- | | 4/1/22- | | 4/1/23- | | | 66 (4/1-9/30/23) | | 465 (10/1/23-3/31/24) | | |
| | 3/31/22 | | 3/31/23 | | 3/31/24 | | | | | | | |
| | ALL | | ALL | | ALL | | 0-1MM | 1-3MM | 3-5MM | 5-10MM | 10-25MM | 25MM & OVER |
| | 290 | | 493 | | 531 | NUMBER OF STATEMENTS | 11 | 33 | 43 | 90 | 145 | 209 |
| | % | | % | | % | ASSETS | % | % | % | % | % | % |
| | 31.6 | | 28.5 | | 23.1 | Cash & Equivalents | 17.3 | 26.2 | 26.2 | 25.1 | 23.6 | 21.1 |
| | 33.8 | | 31.9 | | 35.6 | Trade Receivables (net) | 8.2 | 32.4 | 34.0 | 37.9 | 38.8 | 34.7 |
| | 2.2 | | 2.4 | | 1.8 | Inventory | .0 | 1.0 | .6 | 2.8 | 1.2 | 2.2 |
| | 4.2 | | 7.2 | | 7.4 | All Other Current | 7.0 | 6.6 | 3.6 | 6.7 | 8.5 | 7.9 |
| | 71.8 | | 70.1 | | 68.0 | Total Current | 32.6 | 66.3 | 64.5 | 72.5 | 72.1 | 65.9 |
| | 6.8 | | 7.7 | | 6.8 | Fixed Assets (net) | 15.2 | 10.8 | 8.0 | 6.8 | 4.0 | 7.3 |
| | 11.5 | | 12.0 | | 12.6 | Intangibles (net) | 23.9 | 14.4 | 9.0 | 9.4 | 12.7 | 13.9 |
| | 9.9 | | 10.2 | | 12.6 | All Other Non-Current | 28.3 | 8.5 | 18.5 | 11.2 | 11.2 | 12.9 |
| | 100.0 | | 100.0 | | 100.0 | Total | 100.0 | 100.0 | 100.0 | 100.0 | 100.0 | 100.0 |
| | | | | | | LIABILITIES | | | | | | |
| | 4.8 | | 8.0 | | 6.6 | Notes Payable-Short Term | 29.9 | 7.0 | 7.2 | 9.0 | 6.0 | 4.5 |
| | 1.7 | | 1.4 | | 2.1 | Cur. Mat.-L.T.D. | 1.8 | 4.3 | 1.2 | 1.5 | 1.9 | 2.2 |
| | 10.0 | | 10.1 | | 11.2 | Trade Payables | .6 | 9.2 | 10.0 | 9.0 | 9.8 | 14.2 |
| | .2 | | .3 | | .3 | Income Taxes Payable | .1 | .1 | .0 | .5 | .4 | .3 |
| | 20.2 | | 21.6 | | 24.7 | All Other Current | 21.2 | 28.0 | 35.5 | 21.6 | 23.6 | 24.2 |
| | 36.8 | | 41.3 | | 44.8 | Total Current | 53.6 | 48.6 | 54.0 | 41.6 | 41.8 | 45.4 |
| | 15.8 | | 17.7 | | 13.4 | Long-Term Debt | 21.9 | 29.3 | 12.5 | 9.1 | 11.7 | 13.6 |
| | .1 | | .2 | | .1 | Deferred Taxes | .0 | .0 | .0 | .0 | .1 | .2 |
| | 5.4 | | 7.4 | | 9.6 | All Other Non-Current | 7.7 | 15.2 | 10.6 | 8.1 | 11.3 | 8.0 |
| | 41.9 | | 33.4 | | 32.1 | Net Worth | 16.8 | 6.8 | 22.9 | 41.2 | 35.0 | 32.9 |
| | 100.0 | | 100.0 | | 100.0 | Total Liabilities & Net Worth | 100.0 | 100.0 | 100.0 | 100.0 | 100.0 | 100.0 |
| | | | | | | INCOME DATA | | | | | | |
| | 100.0 | | 100.0 | | 100.0 | Net Sales | 100.0 | 100.0 | 100.0 | 100.0 | 100.0 | 100.0 |
| | | | | | | Gross Profit | | | | | | |
| | 89.7 | | 93.1 | | 94.4 | Operating Expenses | 89.0 | 92.8 | 95.5 | 96.1 | 95.9 | 93.1 |
| | 10.3 | | 6.9 | | 5.6 | Operating Profit | 11.0 | 7.2 | 4.5 | 3.9 | 4.1 | 6.9 |
| | -1.0 | | 1.6 | | 1.3 | All Other Expenses (net) | 8.0 | 3.0 | 1.4 | .9 | .9 | 1.2 |
| | 11.3 | | 5.3 | | 4.2 | Profit Before Taxes | 3.0 | 4.3 | 3.2 | 3.0 | 3.2 | 5.7 |
| | | | | | | RATIOS | | | | | | |
| | 4.7 | | 3.9 | | 3.2 | | 2.3 | 4.8 | 7.0 | 3.7 | 3.7 | 2.4 |
| | 2.2 | | 1.9 | | 1.8 | Current | .6 | 2.0 | 2.1 | 2.0 | 2.1 | 1.5 |
| | 1.3 | | 1.2 | | 1.1 | | .1 | 1.3 | .8 | 1.2 | 1.2 | 1.1 |
| | 4.1 | | 3.4 | | 2.9 | | 2.0 | 4.5 | 6.6 | 3.1 | 3.1 | 2.1 |
| | 2.1 | | 1.6 | | 1.5 | Quick | .4 | 1.6 | 2.1 | 1.5 | 1.8 | 1.3 |
| | 1.2 | | .9 | | .8 | | .1 | 1.0 | .8 | .9 | 1.0 | .8 |
| 22 | 16.3 | 19 | 19.2 | 30 | 12.0 | | 0 UND | 9 39.6 | 20 18.1 | 23 16.1 | 34 10.7 | 35 10.3 |
| 43 | 8.5 | 47 | 7.7 | 51 | 7.2 | Sales/Receivables | 2 173.8 | 35 10.3 | 44 8.3 | 50 7.3 | 55 6.6 | 51 7.1 |
| 66 | 5.5 | 68 | 5.4 | 73 | 5.0 | | 36 10.1 | 63 5.8 | 69 5.3 | 79 4.6 | 74 4.9 | 70 5.2 |
| | | | | | | Cost of Sales/Inventory | | | | | | |
| | | | | | | Cost of Sales/Payables | | | | | | |
| | 4.3 | | 4.7 | | 5.0 | | 6.8 | 5.3 | 4.8 | 5.3 | 4.4 | 5.6 |
| | 7.7 | | 9.0 | | 9.8 | Sales/Working Capital | -93.9 | 10.5 | 11.5 | 8.3 | 7.6 | 11.6 |
| | 21.9 | | 39.0 | | 65.1 | | -.9 | 75.1 | -34.3 | 40.4 | 55.2 | 54.2 |
| | 123.2 | | 67.0 | | 40.2 | | | 19.3 | 12.2 | 25.1 | 41.9 | 73.3 |
| (173) | 24.4 | (303) | 12.3 | (359) | 8.3 | EBIT/Interest | (18) 4.7 | (32) 2.5 | (54) 10.9 | (101) 8.1 | (148) 13.3 |
| | 4.1 | | 1.3 | | 1.0 | | | -.5 | -7.5 | 2.6 | .2 | 1.8 |
| | 52.0 | | 9.9 | | 7.3 | | | | | | | 8.8 |
| (18) | 7.1 | (36) | 3.8 | (43) | 2.4 | Net Profit + Depr., Dep., Amort./Cur. Mat. L/T/D | | | | | (35) 2.6 |
| | 3.5 | | .3 | | .8 | | | | | | | .7 |
| | .0 | | .0 | | .0 | | .0 | .0 | .0 | .0 | .0 | .0 |
| | .1 | | .1 | | .1 | Fixed/Worth | .8 | .0 | .0 | .0 | .0 | .2 |
| | .7 | | 1.1 | | .8 | | -.3 | .8 | .3 | .6 | .2 | 2.9 |
| | .4 | | .5 | | .5 | | 3.0 | .8 | .3 | .5 | .5 | .6 |
| | 1.3 | | 1.6 | | 1.8 | Debt/Worth | 12.5 | 3.4 | .9 | 1.2 | 1.5 | 2.5 |
| | 24.3 | | UND | | 42.8 | | -1.4 | -9.0 | 4.3 | 23.4 | 9.3 | 53.2 |
| | 118.3 | | 83.9 | | 76.7 | | | 100.4 | 81.4 | 73.9 | 62.3 | 80.6 |
| (224) | 56.8 | (370) | 44.2 | (407) | 36.2 | % Profit Before Taxes/Tangible Net Worth | (23) 59.2 | (34) 20.1 | (71) 24.5 | (113) 31.5 | (160) 42.6 |
| | 28.6 | | 14.3 | | 12.3 | | | 6.2 | .9 | 7.3 | 12.6 | 18.4 |
| | 48.7 | | 34.3 | | 29.0 | | 32.1 | 45.6 | 29.0 | 29.4 | 31.2 | 27.4 |
| | 22.7 | | 12.8 | | 11.7 | % Profit Before Taxes/Total Assets | 2.9 | 12.2 | 6.2 | 12.1 | 10.8 | 12.7 |
| | 6.3 | | 1.0 | | .5 | | -1.9 | -1.8 | -4.0 | 1.9 | .3 | 1.9 |
| | 999.8 | | 999.8 | | 999.8 | | UND | UND | UND | UND | 999.8 | 391.0 |
| | 109.6 | | 141.7 | | 171.7 | Sales/Net Fixed Assets | 101.3 | 393.8 | 409.8 | 493.3 | 299.3 | 90.0 |
| | 33.3 | | 34.7 | | 38.4 | | 13.7 | 36.5 | 38.3 | 78.8 | 76.5 | 28.1 |
| | 3.8 | | 4.2 | | 3.9 | | 3.2 | 6.0 | 4.8 | 4.5 | 3.7 | 3.5 |
| | 2.8 | | 2.5 | | 2.5 | Sales/Total Assets | 2.3 | 3.5 | 2.6 | 2.7 | 2.6 | 2.3 |
| | 1.6 | | 1.4 | | 1.5 | | .5 | 1.9 | 1.6 | 1.8 | 1.4 | 1.3 |
| | .1 | | .1 | | .1 | | | .3 | .2 | .1 | .1 | .1 |
| (136) | .4 | (204) | .5 | (207) | .4 | % Depr., Dep., Amort./Sales | (13) .6 | (32) .3 | (49) .3 | (102) .4 |
| | 1.3 | | 1.2 | | 1.3 | | | 2.3 | 1.2 | .6 | 1.5 |
| | 1.8 | | 1.9 | | 1.7 | | | 2.6 | 1.8 | 1.2 | .7 |
| (73) | 4.7 | (95) | 4.6 | (78) | 3.3 | % Officers', Directors' Owners' Comp/Sales | (11) 5.0 | (20) 4.6 | (23) 2.6 | (13) 1.1 |
| | 9.9 | | 9.0 | | 7.3 | | | 12.0 | 6.3 | 5.7 | 2.1 |
| 11098637M | | 19387792M | | 25253133M | | Net Sales ($) | 6242M | 71668M | 176882M | 670917M | 2397228M | 21930196M |
| 5993090M | | 11671200M | | 12688824M | | Total Assets ($) | 6696M | 38676M | 84699M | 432263M | 1338053M | 10788437M |

© RMA 2024    M = $ thousand    MM = $ million
See Pages viii through xx for Explanation of Ratios and Data

# PROFESSIONAL SERVICES—Computer Systems Design Services  NAICS 541512

## Current Data Sorted by Assets | Comparative Historical Data

| | | | | | | | Type of Statement | | |
|---|---|---|---|---|---|---|---|---|---|
| | | | 7 | 21 | 5 | 12 | Unqualified | 64 | 28 |
| | | | 10 | 16 | 2 | | Reviewed | 53 | 21 |
| 2 | 3 | | 15 | 9 | 1 | | Compiled | 34 | 14 |
| 5 | 12 | | 20 | 3 | | | Tax Returns | 68 | 29 |
| 59 | 168 | 456 | 252 | 36 | 32 | | Other | 940 | 196 |
| | | 403 (4/1-9/30/23) | | 743 (10/1/23-3/31/24) | | | | 4/1/19-3/31/20 | 4/1/20-3/31/21 |
| 0-500M | 500M-2MM | 2-10MM | 10-50MM | 50-100MM | 100-250MM | | | ALL | ALL |
| 66 | 183 | 508 | 301 | 44 | 44 | | NUMBER OF STATEMENTS | 1159 | 288 |
| % | % | % | % | % | % | | ASSETS | % | % |
| 30.3 | 38.4 | 29.5 | 29.6 | 19.5 | 10.3 | | Cash & Equivalents | 22.8 | 27.1 |
| 36.2 | 39.9 | 42.8 | 41.5 | 31.0 | 18.7 | | Trade Receivables (net) | 43.4 | 36.6 |
| 5.0 | 2.0 | 4.3 | 5.4 | 3.0 | 4.3 | | Inventory | 5.1 | 3.1 |
| 8.3 | 5.2 | 7.5 | 5.3 | 3.0 | 9.5 | | All Other Current | 7.4 | 4.6 |
| 79.8 | 85.5 | 84.0 | 81.9 | 56.4 | 42.8 | | Total Current | 78.8 | 71.4 |
| 13.5 | 7.3 | 6.0 | 4.3 | 4.2 | 5.7 | | Fixed Assets (net) | 8.6 | 8.1 |
| 1.3 | 2.8 | 4.2 | 6.2 | 24.2 | 43.6 | | Intangibles (net) | 6.7 | 11.5 |
| 5.3 | 4.4 | 5.8 | 7.7 | 15.2 | 7.9 | | All Other Non-Current | 6.0 | 9.0 |
| 100.0 | 100.0 | 100.0 | 100.0 | 100.0 | 100.0 | | Total | 100.0 | 100.0 |
| | | | | | | | LIABILITIES | | |
| 42.9 | 13.1 | 5.0 | 2.3 | 2.6 | 1.6 | | Notes Payable-Short Term | 10.1 | 9.7 |
| 1.2 | .5 | .6 | 1.4 | 1.8 | | | Cur. Mat.-L.T.D. | 1.3 | 2.0 |
| 25.5 | 24.9 | 26.0 | 30.6 | 17.6 | 13.2 | | Trade Payables | 23.6 | 14.2 |
| .0 | .0 | .0 | .1 | .4 | 1.1 | | Income Taxes Payable | .2 | .1 |
| 28.2 | 17.5 | 16.1 | 19.3 | 13.8 | 18.4 | | All Other Current | 18.2 | 17.5 |
| 97.8 | 56.0 | 47.7 | 53.8 | 36.3 | 35.3 | | Total Current | 53.3 | 43.6 |
| 22.6 | 7.7 | 5.5 | 2.8 | 10.4 | 26.4 | | Long-Term Debt | 6.9 | 15.5 |
| .0 | .0 | .1 | .2 | .1 | .9 | | Deferred Taxes | .2 | .3 |
| .1 | 3.3 | 4.1 | 4.8 | 7.7 | 6.1 | | All Other Non-Current | 5.2 | 7.2 |
| -20.4 | 33.0 | 42.7 | 38.4 | 45.6 | 31.2 | | Net Worth | 34.3 | 33.5 |
| 100.0 | 100.0 | 100.0 | 100.0 | 100.0 | 100.0 | | Total Liabilities & Net Worth | 100.0 | 100.0 |
| | | | | | | | INCOME DATA | | |
| 100.0 | 100.0 | 100.0 | 100.0 | 100.0 | 100.0 | | Net Sales | 100.0 | 100.0 |
| | | | | | | | Gross Profit | | |
| 94.9 | 93.5 | 93.6 | 92.9 | 97.9 | 95.6 | | Operating Expenses | 94.3 | 92.6 |
| 5.1 | 6.5 | 6.4 | 7.1 | 2.1 | 4.4 | | Operating Profit | 5.7 | 7.4 |
| .5 | 1.0 | .6 | -.1 | 1.3 | 5.8 | | All Other Expenses (net) | .7 | -.1 |
| 4.6 | 5.5 | 5.9 | 7.2 | .8 | -1.5 | | Profit Before Taxes | 5.0 | 7.5 |
| | | | | | | | RATIOS | | |
| 2.7 | 3.4 | 3.1 | 2.2 | 2.7 | 2.0 | | | 2.5 | 3.2 |
| 1.0 | 2.0 | 1.8 | 1.5 | 1.5 | 1.0 | | Current | 1.6 | 1.8 |
| .6 | 1.3 | 1.3 | 1.2 | 1.1 | .9 | | | 1.1 | 1.2 |
| 2.7 | 3.2 | 2.7 | 1.8 | 2.4 | 1.0 | | | 2.1 | 2.7 |
| .7 | 1.8 | 1.6 | 1.3 | 1.4 | .8 | | Quick | 1.3 | 1.6 |
| .4 | 1.2 | 1.0 | 1.0 | .9 | .5 | | | .9 | 1.0 |
| 6  61.7 | 14  25.4 | 27  13.5 | 35  10.3 | 36  10.0 | 38  9.5 | | | 27  13.7 | 33  11.2 |
| 21  17.1 | 27  13.5 | 41  8.9 | 48  7.6 | 57  6.4 | 51  7.1 | | Sales/Receivables | 45  8.1 | 51  7.1 |
| 51  7.2 | 41  9.0 | 58  6.3 | 66  5.5 | 69  5.3 | 72  5.1 | | | 65  5.6 | 73  5.0 |
| | | | | | | | Cost of Sales/Inventory | | |
| | | | | | | | Cost of Sales/Payables | | |
| 7.1 | 6.8 | 5.4 | 6.0 | 5.7 | 4.6 | | | 7.0 | 4.3 |
| 307.9 | 11.6 | 9.3 | 10.8 | 12.3 | 57.4 | | Sales/Working Capital | 14.5 | 8.6 |
| -13.3 | 40.0 | 29.7 | 25.3 | 73.3 | -17.8 | | | 52.2 | 35.1 |
| | 21.9 | 147.5 | 178.0 | 134.2 | 50.4 | 9.6 | | 59.4 | 70.9 |
| (46) 7.4 | (99) 32.2 | (311) 36.9 | (160) 36.1 | (33) 4.1 | (40) 1.2 | | EBIT/Interest | (815) 14.0 | (212) 16.2 |
| .7 | 2.3 | 9.3 | 8.4 | .8 | .2 | | | 2.8 | 3.7 |
| | | | 31.9 | 79.7 | | | Net Profit + Depr., Dep., | | 15.3 | 20.6 |
| | | (17) 4.7 | (29) 44.8 | | | | Amort./Cur. Mat. L/T/D | (81) 4.3 | (29) 5.9 |
| | | 2.2 | 6.7 | | | | | .9 | 1.8 |
| .1 | .0 | .0 | .0 | .0 | .1 | | | .0 | .0 |
| .7 | .0 | .0 | .0 | .1 | -.2 | | Fixed/Worth | .1 | .2 |
| -.2 | .2 | .3 | .3 | NM | -.1 | | | .7 | 1.0 |
| .7 | .4 | .6 | .9 | .6 | 2.6 | | | .7 | .7 |
| 66.8 | .9 | 1.3 | 1.8 | 2.3 | -3.5 | | Debt/Worth | 1.9 | 1.9 |
| -2.7 | 4.6 | 4.1 | 4.2 | -5.0 | -2.1 | | | 8.7 | 16.0 |
| | 391.2 | 101.1 | 85.0 | 73.0 | 64.0 | 36.4 | | 80.4 | 94.7 |
| (35) 108.9 | (155) 41.4 | (454) 37.4 | (273) 43.9 | (31) 37.8 | (13) 16.8 | | % Profit Before Taxes/Tangible Net Worth | (956) 43.0 | (226) 43.1 |
| 21.1 | 5.8 | 17.8 | 21.1 | 14.1 | -7.8 | | | 15.6 | 18.3 |
| 59.5 | 46.3 | 30.7 | 25.0 | 15.2 | 5.9 | | | 30.1 | 29.3 |
| 27.8 | 15.8 | 16.4 | 15.2 | 6.9 | .6 | | % Profit Before Taxes/Total Assets | 13.7 | 13.6 |
| -2.0 | -.6 | 6.8 | 6.4 | 1.2 | -3.9 | | | 3.2 | 3.9 |
| 251.9 | 999.8 | 999.8 | 855.8 | 447.0 | 126.4 | | | 444.6 | 456.9 |
| 93.3 | 280.2 | 217.1 | 236.3 | 162.7 | 66.1 | | Sales/Net Fixed Assets | 102.0 | 81.4 |
| 21.8 | 69.4 | 63.0 | 63.4 | 42.2 | 21.3 | | | 31.9 | 28.0 |
| 9.5 | 6.7 | 4.9 | 3.9 | 2.9 | 1.9 | | | 5.2 | 3.8 |
| 5.6 | 5.0 | 3.5 | 2.9 | 2.0 | 1.0 | | Sales/Total Assets | 3.6 | 2.4 |
| 3.3 | 3.5 | 2.3 | 1.9 | .9 | .6 | | | 2.3 | 1.4 |
| | .2 | .1 | .1 | .1 | .1 | | | .2 | .2 |
| (28) .3 | (41) .2 | (222) .2 | (156) .3 | (22) .3 | | | % Depr., Dep., Amort./Sales | (569) .5 | (152) .6 |
| 1.1 | .7 | .6 | .6 | 1.3 | | | | 1.2 | 1.7 |
| | | 1.2 | 1.0 | .7 | | | | 1.2 | 1.5 |
| | (28) 2.7 | (47) 1.8 | (15) 1.3 | | | | % Officers', Directors' Owners' Comp/Sales | (171) 3.1 | (68) 3.9 |
| | 4.7 | 3.9 | 3.2 | | | | | 6.5 | 8.6 |
| 135731M | 1250160M | 10031802M | 20392657M | 6021950M | 8613861M | | Net Sales ($) | 49322140M | 13456183M |
| 19260M | 236078M | 2628006M | 6924994M | 2999707M | 7302329M | | Total Assets ($) | 18896456M | 7729717M |

© RMA 2024  
M = $ thousand   MM = $ million  
See Pages viii through xx for Explanation of Ratios and Data

# PROFESSIONAL SERVICES—Computer Systems Design Services  NAICS 541512

## Comparative Historical Data | Current Data Sorted by Sales

| | | | | | | | | | | | | | | | |
|---|---|---|---|---|---|---|---|---|---|---|---|---|---|---|---|
| | | | | | | | | | | | | 1 | 4 | 40 | |
| | 19 | | 51 | | 45 | Type of Statement | | | | | | | 9 | 18 | |
| | 16 | | 28 | | 28 | Unqualified | | | 1 | | | 1 | 10 | 12 | |
| | 19 | | 24 | | 30 | Reviewed | | 1 | 2 | | | 5 | 14 | 4 | |
| | 37 | | 52 | | 40 | Compiled | 1 | 2 | 3 | 7 | | 7 | 291 | 400 | |
| | 475 | | 547 | | 1003 | Tax Returns | 5 | 3 | 51 | 60 | | 181 | | | |
| | 4/1/21- | | 4/1/22- | | 4/1/23- | Other | 20 | 51 | | | | | | | |
| | 3/31/22 | | 3/31/23 | | 3/31/24 | | | 403 (4/1-9/30/23) | | | | 743 (10/1/23-3/31/24) | | | |
| | ALL | | ALL | | ALL | | 0-1MM | 1-3MM | 3-5MM | 5-10MM | | 10-25MM | | 25MM & OVER | |
| | 566 | | 702 | | 1146 | NUMBER OF STATEMENTS | 26 | 57 | 67 | 194 | | 328 | | 474 | |
| | % | | % | | % | ASSETS | % | % | % | % | | % | | % | |
| | 30.9 | | 26.7 | | 29.9 | Cash & Equivalents | 24.4 | 29.2 | 36.1 | 32.5 | | 30.9 | | 27.6 | |
| | 38.7 | | 39.1 | | 40.2 | Trade Receivables (net) | 24.0 | 35.7 | 26.0 | 42.0 | | 41.1 | | 42.3 | |
| | 3.2 | | 3.2 | | 4.2 | Inventory | .1 | 6.1 | 2.6 | 3.4 | | 4.9 | | 4.3 | |
| | 6.1 | | 6.9 | | 6.5 | All Other Current | 4.3 | 10.5 | 6.7 | 6.6 | | 7.2 | | 5.6 | |
| | 78.9 | | 75.9 | | 80.8 | Total Current | 52.8 | 81.6 | 71.4 | 84.4 | | 84.1 | | 79.8 | |
| | 7.6 | | 7.8 | | 6.1 | Fixed Assets (net) | 38.3 | 10.3 | 8.9 | 5.9 | | 5.4 | | 4.0 | |
| | 6.3 | | 7.4 | | 6.6 | Intangibles (net) | 4.1 | 2.6 | 14.9 | 4.2 | | 4.2 | | 8.7 | |
| | 7.3 | | 8.9 | | 6.5 | All Other Non-Current | 4.7 | 5.5 | 4.8 | 5.4 | | 6.3 | | 7.5 | |
| | 100.0 | | 100.0 | | 100.0 | Total | 100.0 | 100.0 | 100.0 | 100.0 | | 100.0 | | 100.0 | |
| | | | | | | LIABILITIES | | | | | | | | | |
| | 11.8 | | 9.8 | | 7.5 | Notes Payable-Short Term | 16.1 | 36.5 | 7.9 | 9.1 | | 7.9 | | 2.6 | |
| | 1.2 | | 1.1 | | .9 | Cur. Mat.-L.T.D. | 2.0 | 1.1 | .9 | .4 | | .5 | | 1.3 | |
| | 20.3 | | 18.9 | | 26.2 | Trade Payables | 12.5 | 28.3 | 11.0 | 24.5 | | 22.4 | | 32.1 | |
| | .1 | | .1 | | .1 | Income Taxes Payable | .0 | .0 | .0 | .1 | | .2 | | .2 | |
| | 18.7 | | 20.5 | | 17.9 | All Other Current | 24.0 | 22.3 | 19.7 | 18.9 | | 16.5 | | 17.3 | |
| | 52.1 | | 50.4 | | 52.6 | Total Current | 54.5 | 88.2 | 39.6 | 52.9 | | 47.3 | | 53.5 | |
| | 9.1 | | 8.8 | | 7.1 | Long-Term Debt | 29.5 | 25.0 | 7.3 | 6.2 | | 5.2 | | 5.4 | |
| | .2 | | .1 | | .1 | Deferred Taxes | .0 | .3 | .0 | .1 | | .1 | | .2 | |
| | 5.0 | | 5.3 | | 4.1 | All Other Non-Current | 1.1 | 5.8 | 2.4 | 3.0 | | 4.8 | | 4.3 | |
| | 33.7 | | 35.5 | | 36.1 | Net Worth | 14.9 | -19.3 | 50.7 | 37.8 | | 42.6 | | 36.6 | |
| | 100.0 | | 100.0 | | 100.0 | Total Liabilities & Net Worth | 100.0 | 100.0 | 100.0 | 100.0 | | 100.0 | | 100.0 | |
| | | | | | | INCOME DATA | | | | | | | | | |
| | 100.0 | | 100.0 | | 100.0 | Net Sales | 100.0 | 100.0 | 100.0 | 100.0 | | 100.0 | | 100.0 | |
| | | | | | | Gross Profit | | | | | | | | | |
| | 92.2 | | 93.9 | | 93.7 | Operating Expenses | 77.2 | 95.9 | 93.5 | 93.8 | | 93.0 | | 94.8 | |
| | 7.8 | | 6.1 | | 6.3 | Operating Profit | 22.8 | 4.1 | 6.5 | 6.2 | | 7.0 | | 5.2 | |
| | -1.0 | | .4 | | .7 | All Other Expenses (net) | 8.6 | 1.5 | .5 | .0 | | .4 | | .7 | |
| | 8.9 | | 5.7 | | 5.6 | Profit Before Taxes | 14.2 | 2.6 | 6.0 | 6.3 | | 6.6 | | 4.5 | |
| | | | | | | RATIOS | | | | | | | | | |
| | 3.0 | | 2.9 | | 2.7 | | 2.5 | 3.4 | 3.6 | 2.8 | | 3.8 | | 2.1 | |
| | 1.8 | | 1.7 | | 1.7 | Current | 1.1 | 1.1 | 2.1 | 1.8 | | 2.1 | | 1.5 | |
| | 1.2 | | 1.1 | | 1.2 | | .5 | .6 | 1.4 | 1.2 | | 1.3 | | 1.2 | |
| | 2.6 | | 2.6 | | 2.5 | | 2.5 | 2.9 | 3.4 | 2.6 | | 3.5 | | 1.8 | |
| | 1.5 | (701) | 1.4 | | 1.5 | Quick | 1.1 | .8 | 1.9 | 1.5 | | 1.9 | | 1.3 | |
| | 1.0 | | .9 | | 1.0 | | .4 | .4 | .9 | 1.0 | | 1.1 | | 1.0 | |
| 24 | 14.9 | 26 | 13.9 | 26 | 13.8 | | 0 UND | 11 33.1 | 14 25.3 | 22 16.5 | | 28 13.1 | | 32 11.5 | |
| 45 | 8.1 | 47 | 7.7 | 41 | 8.8 | Sales/Receivables | 19 19.6 | 26 14.3 | 28 13.2 | 37 9.8 | | 42 8.7 | | 45 8.1 | |
| 68 | 5.4 | 68 | 5.4 | 58 | 6.3 | | 87 4.2 | 45 8.1 | 45 8.1 | 56 6.5 | | 61 6.0 | | 58 6.3 | |
| | | | | | | Cost of Sales/Inventory | | | | | | | | | |
| | | | | | | Cost of Sales/Payables | | | | | | | | | |
| | 5.4 | | 5.7 | | 6.0 | | 3.9 | 6.6 | 5.2 | 5.9 | | 4.6 | | 8.1 | |
| | 10.5 | | 11.5 | | 10.7 | Sales/Working Capital | 183.8 | 37.3 | 7.1 | 9.7 | | 7.9 | | 13.0 | |
| | 31.6 | | 45.4 | | 38.7 | | -2.3 | -15.9 | 75.6 | 41.7 | | 19.6 | | 38.1 | |
| | 135.5 | | 88.8 | | 131.9 | | 27.3 | 18.3 | 75.9 | 201.0 | | 100.8 | | 176.0 | |
| (339) | 38.5 | (420) | 23.8 | (689) | 25.7 | EBIT/Interest | (12) 7.6 | (37) 5.1 | (44) 12.5 | (113) 29.2 | (190) | 27.9 | (293) | 35.3 | |
| | 8.9 | | 2.8 | | 3.7 | | 3.4 | .2 | 2.4 | 2.7 | | 6.3 | | 3.9 | |
| | 83.2 | | 25.2 | | 57.6 | Net Profit + Depr., Dep., | | | | | | 63.5 | | 58.2 | |
| (25) | 8.6 | (41) | 11.7 | (55) | 15.5 | Amort./Cur. Mat. L/T/D | | | | (14) | | 42.4 | (40) | 13.7 | |
| | 3.7 | | 1.2 | | 4.6 | | | | | | | 6.1 | | 4.7 | |
| | .0 | | .0 | | .0 | | .0 | .1 | .0 | .0 | | .0 | | .0 | |
| | .1 | | .1 | | .1 | Fixed/Worth | .4 | 1.3 | .1 | .1 | | .0 | | .0 | |
| | .6 | | .6 | | .4 | | 3.4 | -.2 | 23.8 | .3 | | .2 | | .4 | |
| | .6 | | .6 | | .6 | | .6 | .7 | .4 | .6 | | .4 | | 1.0 | |
| | 1.5 | | 1.7 | | 1.6 | Debt/Worth | 3.0 | 176.0 | .8 | 1.3 | | 1.1 | | 1.9 | |
| | 8.2 | | 7.5 | | 6.5 | | NM | -2.9 | 75.1 | 6.7 | | 4.1 | | 5.4 | |
| | 101.5 | | 90.9 | | 85.9 | | 73.0 | 183.0 | 44.7 | 106.7 | | 76.8 | | 84.8 | |
| (464) | 59.4 | (588) | 44.7 | (961) | 41.4 | % Profit Before Taxes/Tangible Net Worth | (20) 23.9 | (29) 66.8 | (52) 21.6 | (168) 40.0 | (291) | 36.7 | (401) | 45.8 | |
| | 30.4 | | 15.5 | | 16.8 | | 11.7 | 11.7 | -1.4 | 7.2 | | 17.8 | | 23.1 | |
| | 41.2 | | 31.8 | | 30.4 | % Profit Before Taxes/Total Assets | 30.0 | 41.5 | 25.3 | 36.2 | | 31.6 | | 26.2 | |
| | 21.1 | | 13.9 | | 14.9 | | 7.1 | 22.0 | 9.4 | 15.5 | | 17.6 | | 14.0 | |
| | 8.8 | | 2.8 | | 4.7 | | .7 | -6.8 | -1.4 | 2.3 | | 7.3 | | 5.7 | |
| | 919.3 | | 999.8 | | 971.9 | | UND | 264.5 | 211.9 | 999.8 | | 999.8 | | 862.6 | |
| | 123.8 | | 122.5 | | 196.9 | Sales/Net Fixed Assets | 10.1 | 96.6 | 76.1 | 263.8 | | 185.0 | | 263.7 | |
| | 29.9 | | 28.9 | | 53.8 | | .2 | 27.7 | 30.9 | 56.7 | | 67.8 | | 66.3 | |
| | 4.4 | | 4.5 | | 5.0 | | 3.1 | 7.6 | 4.7 | 5.3 | | 5.0 | | 4.8 | |
| | 3.1 | | 3.0 | | 3.5 | Sales/Total Assets | 1.5 | 4.9 | 3.3 | 3.7 | | 3.5 | | 3.5 | |
| | 2.1 | | 2.0 | | 2.2 | | .2 | 2.7 | 2.1 | 2.3 | | 2.1 | | 2.3 | |
| | .1 | | .1 | | .1 | | 1.1 | .1 | .1 | .1 | | .1 | | .1 | |
| (231) | .4 | (279) | .4 | (475) | .3 | % Depr., Dep., Amort./Sales | (11) 1.9 | (22) .3 | (22) .2 | (67) .3 | (144) | .2 | (209) | .3 | |
| | 1.0 | | 1.0 | | .6 | | 33.8 | .7 | 1.1 | .6 | | .5 | | .6 | |
| | 1.7 | | 1.6 | | 1.0 | | | 1.9 | | 1.2 | | 1.0 | | .7 | |
| (74) | 3.9 | (103) | 2.8 | (103) | 2.1 | % Officers', Directors' Owners' Comp/Sales | (12) | 3.9 | (26) 2.1 | (30) | | 1.7 | (26) | 1.2 | |
| | 8.3 | | 5.4 | | 4.3 | | | 4.5 | | 4.0 | | 3.6 | | 4.1 | |
| | 20506125M | | 23364270M | | 46446161M | Net Sales ($) | 11786M | 110070M | 267097M | 1471419M | | 5346118M | | 39239671M | |
| | 9677207M | | 12345290M | | 20110374M | Total Assets ($) | 30923M | 34557M | 123275M | 519064M | | 2021079M | | 17381476M | |

© RMA 2024  
M = $ thousand  MM = $ million  
See Pages viii through xx for Explanation of Ratios and Data

# PROFESSIONAL SERVICES—Computer Facilities Management Services  NAICS 541513

## Current Data Sorted by Assets / Comparative Historical Data

| | | | | | | Type of Statement | | |
|---|---|---|---|---|---|---|---|---|
| | | | 1 | | 1 | Unqualified | 6 | 1 |
| | | 1 | 2 | | | Reviewed | 6 | 2 |
| | 1 | 2 | 3 | | | Compiled | 4 | 2 |
| | 2 | 3 | | | | Tax Returns | 6 | 2 |
| 3 | 5 | 12 | 6 | 2 | 3 | Other | 32 | 17 |
| | 5 (4/1-9/30/23) | | 37 (10/1/23-3/31/24) | | | | 4/1/19-3/31/20 | 4/1/20-3/31/21 |
| 0-500M | 500M-2MM | 2-10MM | 10-50MM | 50-100MM | 100-250MM | | ALL | ALL |
| 3 | 8 | 18 | 7 | 2 | 4 | NUMBER OF STATEMENTS | 54 | 24 |
| % | % | % | % | % | % | ASSETS | % | % |
| | | 28.0 | | | | Cash & Equivalents | 13.6 | 31.1 |
| | | 26.6 | | | | Trade Receivables (net) | 40.7 | 38.5 |
| | | 5.8 | | | | Inventory | 3.3 | 3.5 |
| | | 3.5 | | | | All Other Current | 8.2 | 7.1 |
| | | 63.9 | | | | Total Current | 65.8 | 80.2 |
| | | 8.9 | | | | Fixed Assets (net) | 9.3 | 8.8 |
| | | 17.9 | | | | Intangibles (net) | 13.6 | 4.9 |
| | | 9.3 | | | | All Other Non-Current | 11.3 | 6.0 |
| | | 100.0 | | | | Total | 100.0 | 100.0 |
| | | | | | | LIABILITIES | | |
| | | 6.0 | | | | Notes Payable-Short Term | 12.9 | 7.0 |
| | | 2.6 | | | | Cur. Mat.-L.T.D. | 1.6 | 2.2 |
| | | 12.9 | | | | Trade Payables | 19.3 | 18.5 |
| | | .0 | | | | Income Taxes Payable | .3 | .3 |
| | | 16.7 | | | | All Other Current | 17.2 | 33.5 |
| | | 38.3 | | | | Total Current | 51.3 | 61.6 |
| | | 11.1 | | | | Long-Term Debt | 8.9 | 25.3 |
| | | .0 | | | | Deferred Taxes | .1 | .0 |
| | | 7.1 | | | | All Other Non-Current | 6.3 | 6.6 |
| | | 43.6 | | | | Net Worth | 33.3 | 6.5 |
| | | 100.0 | | | | Total Liabilities & Net Worth | 100.0 | 100.0 |
| | | | | | | INCOME DATA | | |
| | | 100.0 | | | | Net Sales | 100.0 | 100.0 |
| | | 46.4 | | | | Gross Profit | 38.9 | 41.5 |
| | | 37.4 | | | | Operating Expenses | 31.8 | 34.2 |
| | | 8.9 | | | | Operating Profit | 7.1 | 7.3 |
| | | -.4 | | | | All Other Expenses (net) | 1.0 | -1.3 |
| | | 9.3 | | | | Profit Before Taxes | 6.1 | 8.6 |
| | | | | | | RATIOS | | |
| | | 3.5 | | | | | 2.3 | 3.3 |
| | | 2.3 | | | | Current | 1.2 | 1.6 |
| | | 1.1 | | | | | .9 | .9 |
| | | 3.3 | | | | | 1.9 | 3.0 |
| | | 2.0 | | | | Quick | 1.0 | 1.5 |
| | | .9 | | | | | .7 | .8 |
| | 21 | 17.4 | | | | | 31 | 11.8 | 23 | 16.2 |
| | 42 | 8.7 | | | | Sales/Receivables | 42 | 8.7 | 42 | 8.6 |
| | 68 | 5.4 | | | | | 59 | 6.2 | 48 | 7.6 |
| | 0 | UND | | | | | 0 | UND | 0 | UND |
| | 0 | UND | | | | Cost of Sales/Inventory | 0 | UND | 0 | UND |
| | 31 | 11.8 | | | | | 4 | 84.9 | 3 | 107.1 |
| | 12 | 31.0 | | | | | 14 | 26.2 | 6 | 63.3 |
| | 36 | 10.0 | | | | Cost of Sales/Payables | 30 | 12.1 | 34 | 10.8 |
| | 61 | 6.0 | | | | | 47 | 7.7 | 42 | 8.6 |
| | | 4.8 | | | | | | 8.1 | | 5.8 |
| | | 6.7 | | | | Sales/Working Capital | | 22.0 | | 12.6 |
| | | NM | | | | | | -126.6 | | NM |
| | | 172.1 | | | | | | 78.4 | | 131.9 |
| | (11) | 7.2 | | | | EBIT/Interest | (45) | 10.1 | (18) | 20.6 |
| | | 5.1 | | | | | | 1.6 | | 2.7 |
| | | | | | | Net Profit + Depr., Dep., Amort./Cur. Mat. L/T/D | | |
| | | .0 | | | | | .0 | .1 |
| | | .3 | | | | Fixed/Worth | .4 | .3 |
| | | NM | | | | | 1.2 | NM |
| | | .5 | | | | | .6 | .8 |
| | | 1.7 | | | | Debt/Worth | 3.5 | 3.1 |
| | | NM | | | | | NM | -5.7 |
| | | 156.5 | | | | | | 143.5 | | 111.8 |
| | (14) | 71.7 | | | | % Profit Before Taxes/Tangible Net Worth | (41) | 66.3 | (17) | 72.6 |
| | | 16.7 | | | | | | 21.5 | | 23.8 |
| | | 34.6 | | | | | 26.2 | 43.2 |
| | | 11.4 | | | | % Profit Before Taxes/Total Assets | 13.9 | 25.7 |
| | | 6.0 | | | | | 3.1 | 5.5 |
| | | 286.3 | | | | | 473.7 | 271.4 |
| | | 94.9 | | | | Sales/Net Fixed Assets | 75.0 | 63.0 |
| | | 26.7 | | | | | 22.8 | 26.4 |
| | | 3.3 | | | | | 4.9 | 4.9 |
| | | 2.2 | | | | Sales/Total Assets | 3.5 | 3.7 |
| | | 1.6 | | | | | 2.0 | 2.6 |
| | | | | | | | | .4 | | .1 |
| | | | | | | % Depr., Dep., Amort./Sales | (26) | .6 | (18) | .5 |
| | | | | | | | | 1.3 | | 1.2 |
| | | | | | | | | 2.8 | |
| | | | | | | % Officers', Directors' Owners' Comp/Sales | (16) | 6.3 | |
| | | | | | | | | 9.4 | |
| 9341M | 40111M | 237890M | 316282M | 223562M | 488249M | Net Sales ($) | 3230109M | 1355235M |
| 970M | 8662M | 101042M | 193220M | 113869M | 480697M | Total Assets ($) | 1150409M | 328722M |

M = $ thousand   MM = $ million
See Pages viii through xx for Explanation of Ratios and Data

© RMA 2024

# PROFESSIONAL SERVICES—Computer Facilities Management Services   NAICS 541513

## Comparative Historical Data | Current Data Sorted by Sales

| | | | | Type of Statement | | | | | | |
|---|---|---|---|---|---|---|---|---|---|---|
| 2 | 3 | 2 | | Unqualified | | | | | | 2 |
| 3 | 3 | 1 | | Reviewed | | | 1 | | | |
| 2 | 4 | 3 | | Compiled | | | 1 | 2 | 2 | |
| 4 | 5 | 5 | | Tax Returns | | | 3 | 2 | 2 | |
| 16 | 25 | 31 | | Other | | 3 | 4 | 2 | 12 | 10 |
| 4/1/21-3/31/22 ALL | 4/1/22-3/31/23 ALL | 4/1/23-3/31/24 ALL | | | 0-1MM | 5 (4/1-9/30/23) 1-3MM | 3-5MM | 5-10MM | 37 (10/1/23-3/31/24) 10-25MM | 25MM & OVER |
| 27 | 40 | 42 | NUMBER OF STATEMENTS | | | 3 | 9 | 4 | 14 | 12 |
| % | % | % | ASSETS | % | % | % | % | % | % | % |
| 25.2 | 21.2 | 20.6 | Cash & Equivalents | | D | | | | 30.1 | 12.5 |
| 30.8 | 33.5 | 29.0 | Trade Receivables (net) | | A | | | | 33.9 | 31.5 |
| 4.2 | 7.1 | 5.1 | Inventory | | T | | | | 7.8 | 2.0 |
| 7.1 | 6.8 | 5.5 | All Other Current | | A | | | | 4.4 | 7.4 |
| 67.2 | 68.5 | 60.2 | Total Current | | | | | | 76.2 | 53.4 |
| 12.0 | 10.8 | 8.8 | Fixed Assets (net) | | N | | | | 5.0 | 3.4 |
| 12.0 | 10.9 | 17.1 | Intangibles (net) | | O | | | | 6.8 | 30.4 |
| 8.8 | 9.8 | 13.9 | All Other Non-Current | | T | | | | 12.0 | 12.8 |
| 100.0 | 100.0 | 100.0 | Total | | | | | | 100.0 | 100.0 |
| | | | LIABILITIES | | A | | | | | |
| 11.9 | 10.5 | 7.1 | Notes Payable-Short Term | | V | | | | 8.5 | 4.1 |
| 2.7 | 1.3 | 2.7 | Cur. Mat.-L.T.D. | | A | | | | 2.0 | 2.5 |
| 15.2 | 13.5 | 12.4 | Trade Payables | | I | | | | 16.9 | 13.9 |
| .1 | .2 | .1 | Income Taxes Payable | | L | | | | .0 | .2 |
| 21.9 | 14.9 | 18.0 | All Other Current | | A | | | | 12.8 | 22.5 |
| 51.8 | 40.4 | 40.2 | Total Current | | B | | | | 40.3 | 43.6 |
| 21.9 | 29.4 | 26.3 | Long-Term Debt | | L | | | | 7.6 | 15.8 |
| .4 | .0 | .1 | Deferred Taxes | | E | | | | .0 | .3 |
| 4.5 | 3.2 | 10.7 | All Other Non-Current | | | | | | 11.5 | 16.6 |
| 21.5 | 26.9 | 22.7 | Net Worth | | | | | | 40.6 | 23.7 |
| 100.0 | 100.0 | 100.0 | Total Liabilties & Net Worth | | | | | | 100.0 | 100.0 |
| | | | INCOME DATA | | | | | | | |
| 100.0 | 100.0 | 100.0 | Net Sales | | | | | | 100.0 | 100.0 |
| 43.5 | 41.3 | 43.1 | Gross Profit | | | | | | 44.6 | 35.0 |
| 38.7 | 34.2 | 36.5 | Operating Expenses | | | | | | 39.9 | 29.2 |
| 4.8 | 7.1 | 6.6 | Operating Profit | | | | | | 4.7 | 5.8 |
| -3.5 | .6 | 1.1 | All Other Expenses (net) | | | | | | -.6 | 3.9 |
| 8.3 | 6.5 | 5.5 | Profit Before Taxes | | | | | | 5.3 | 1.9 |
| | | | RATIOS | | | | | | | |
| 3.4 | 3.0 | 2.7 | | | | | | | 3.3 | 1.7 |
| 1.4 | 1.9 | 1.7 | Current | | | | | | 2.3 | 1.3 |
| .9 | 1.2 | 1.1 | | | | | | | 1.4 | 1.0 |
| 2.8 | 2.4 | 2.7 | | | | | | | 3.1 | 1.6 |
| 1.4 | 1.3 | 1.3 | Quick | | | | | | 2.0 | 1.2 |
| .5 | 1.0 | .8 | | | | | | | 1.0 | .7 |
| 24  15.4 | 31  11.7 | 21  17.3 | | | | | | 24 | 14.9 | 49  7.5 |
| 41  8.8 | 51  7.2 | 49  7.4 | Sales/Receivables | | | | | 51 | 7.2 | 73  5.0 |
| 59  6.2 | 73  5.0 | 74  4.9 | | | | | | 68 | 5.4 | 94  3.9 |
| 0  UND | 0  UND | 0  UND | | | | | | 0 | UND | 0  UND |
| 0  UND | 0  UND | 0  UND | Cost of Sales/Inventory | | | | | 0 | UND | 0  UND |
| 10  38.1 | 12  31.7 | 14  26.3 | | | | | | 47 | 7.8 | 3  107.3 |
| 9  41.0 | 5  71.4 | 8  44.5 | | | | | | 14 | 26.4 | 20  18.7 |
| 30  12.3 | 21  17.7 | 21  17.0 | Cost of Sales/Payables | | | | | 45 | 8.2 | 25  14.7 |
| 45  8.2 | 54  6.8 | 50  7.3 | | | | | | 87 | 4.2 | 51  7.2 |
| 4.9 | 5.2 | 6.3 | | | | | | | 5.2 | 8.2 |
| 16.1 | 7.9 | 12.7 | Sales/Working Capital | | | | | | 6.7 | 12.7 |
| -38.2 | 26.4 | 61.5 | | | | | | | 13.6 | NM |
| 94.1 | 101.8 | 16.3 | | | | | | | 168.6 | |
| (20)  44.7 | (28)  15.0 | (28)  6.2 | EBIT/Interest | | | | | | (12)  117.3 | |
| 3.0 | 2.2 | -.3 | | | | | | | 17.6 | |
| | | | Net Profit + Depr., Dep., Amort./Cur. Mat. L/T/D | | | | | | | |
| .0 | .0 | .1 | | | | | | | .0 | .2 |
| .3 | .1 | .5 | Fixed/Worth | | | | | | .1 | -.2 |
| -1.3 | 2.3 | -.2 | | | | | | | .9 | .0 |
| .4 | .5 | .9 | | | | | | | .6 | 3.0 |
| 2.3 | 2.2 | 2.9 | Debt/Worth | | | | | | 1.1 | -7.8 |
| -5.0 | -7.9 | -6.3 | | | | | | | 15.7 | -2.7 |
| 103.7 | 67.0 | 146.7 | | | | | | | 168.6 | |
| (19)  50.3 | (28)  33.9 | (26)  53.9 | % Profit Before Taxes/Tangible Net Worth | | | | | | (12)  117.3 | |
| 9.8 | 8.4 | 16.7 | | | | | | | 17.6 | |
| 52.7 | 36.2 | 36.7 | % Profit Before Taxes/Total Assets | | | | | | 54.7 | 32.3 |
| 24.9 | 13.7 | 12.0 | | | | | | | 9.3 | -2.8 |
| 1.7 | 1.6 | -4.9 | | | | | | | -1.8 | -5.8 |
| 197.7 | 340.7 | 267.9 | Sales/Net Fixed Assets | | | | | | 881.5 | 257.6 |
| 80.9 | 48.8 | 74.9 | | | | | | | 104.2 | 101.9 |
| 17.4 | 20.1 | 31.1 | | | | | | | 41.2 | 31.9 |
| 3.9 | 4.0 | 3.7 | | | | | | | 3.7 | 2.7 |
| 2.7 | 2.5 | 2.4 | Sales/Total Assets | | | | | | 2.5 | 1.4 |
| 1.5 | 1.7 | 1.4 | | | | | | | 1.9 | .9 |
| .4 | .2 | .3 | | | | | | | | |
| (15)  .7 | (17)  .5 | (16)  .4 | % Depr., Dep., Amort./Sales | | | | | | | |
| 1.6 | 2.0 | 2.2 | | | | | | | | |
| | 2.1 | 1.7 | | | | | | | | |
| | (12)  3.6 | (10)  4.3 | % Officers', Directors' Owners' Comp/Sales | | | | | | | |
| | | 7.5 | 6.6 | | | | | | | |
| 611148M | 1024480M | 1315435M | Net Sales ($) | | 5219M | 34541M | 30295M | 236437M | 1008943M |
| 608695M | 678499M | 898460M | Total Assets ($) | | 2001M | 15691M | 13619M | 125902M | 741247M |

© RMA 2024      M = $ thousand      MM = $ million
See Pages viii through xx for Explanation of Ratios and Data

## PROFESSIONAL SERVICES—Other Computer Related Services  NAICS 541519

### Current Data Sorted by Assets / Comparative Historical Data

| | | | | | | | | Type of Statement | | |
|---|---|---|---|---|---|---|---|---|---|---|
| | | 2 | 3 | 13 | 10 | 4 | | Unqualified | 24 | 16 |
| | | 1 | 11 | 17 | | | | Reviewed | 30 | 16 |
| | | 1 | 11 | 2 | | | | Compiled | 17 | 13 |
| | 14 | 14 | 10 | 2 | | | | Tax Returns | 75 | 35 |
| | 19 | 43 | 88 | 42 | 15 | 16 | | Other | 286 | 173 |
| | | 34 (4/1-9/30/23) | | 304 (10/1/23-3/31/24) | | | | | 4/1/19-3/31/20 | 4/1/20-3/31/21 |
| | 0-500M | 500M-2MM | 2-10MM | 10-50MM | 50-100MM | 100-250MM | | | ALL | ALL |
| | 33 | 61 | 123 | 76 | 25 | 20 | NUMBER OF STATEMENTS | | 432 | 253 |
| | % | % | % | % | % | % | ASSETS | | % | % |
| | 47.0 | 32.3 | 22.3 | 19.1 | 9.2 | 19.4 | Cash & Equivalents | | 23.6 | 32.4 |
| | 24.3 | 36.8 | 41.3 | 35.2 | 26.8 | 25.9 | Trade Receivables (net) | | 37.0 | 28.8 |
| | 1.9 | 1.8 | 2.6 | 3.2 | 5.2 | 2.0 | Inventory | | 4.0 | 4.8 |
| | 4.7 | 4.9 | 3.7 | 7.8 | 8.1 | 3.0 | All Other Current | | 5.5 | 4.3 |
| | 77.9 | 75.8 | 69.9 | 65.3 | 49.3 | 50.4 | Total Current | | 70.0 | 70.4 |
| | 11.9 | 7.4 | 11.6 | 9.8 | 10.9 | 5.9 | Fixed Assets (net) | | 11.5 | 10.8 |
| | 6.9 | 6.9 | 7.3 | 12.8 | 29.5 | 37.3 | Intangibles (net) | | 9.2 | 9.9 |
| | 3.5 | 10.0 | 11.2 | 12.1 | 10.3 | 6.4 | All Other Non-Current | | 9.3 | 9.0 |
| | 100.0 | 100.0 | 100.0 | 100.0 | 100.0 | 100.0 | Total | | 100.0 | 100.0 |
| | | | | | | | LIABILITIES | | | |
| | 21.8 | 7.9 | 4.9 | 5.2 | 4.6 | 2.1 | Notes Payable-Short Term | | 11.7 | 9.5 |
| | 1.8 | 2.1 | 1.2 | 2.1 | 4.1 | 1.2 | Cur. Mat.-L.T.D. | | 2.2 | 3.0 |
| | 7.9 | 13.0 | 14.4 | 16.9 | 19.4 | 9.2 | Trade Payables | | 14.5 | 12.2 |
| | .6 | .0 | .0 | .2 | .2 | .2 | Income Taxes Payable | | .1 | .1 |
| | 25.7 | 30.1 | 18.2 | 18.4 | 18.8 | 16.9 | All Other Current | | 20.0 | 21.6 |
| | 57.8 | 53.1 | 38.6 | 43.0 | 47.1 | 29.7 | Total Current | | 48.6 | 46.5 |
| | 26.3 | 16.6 | 14.4 | 10.4 | 19.7 | 15.9 | Long-Term Debt | | 14.0 | 20.6 |
| | .1 | .0 | .2 | .1 | .2 | .2 | Deferred Taxes | | .2 | .1 |
| | 8.7 | 2.4 | 7.0 | 8.2 | 7.9 | 5.1 | All Other Non-Current | | 5.3 | 8.6 |
| | 7.1 | 28.0 | 39.8 | 38.3 | 25.1 | 49.1 | Net Worth | | 31.9 | 24.1 |
| | 100.0 | 100.0 | 100.0 | 100.0 | 100.0 | 100.0 | Total Liabilities & Net Worth | | 100.0 | 100.0 |
| | | | | | | | INCOME DATA | | | |
| | 100.0 | 100.0 | 100.0 | 100.0 | 100.0 | 100.0 | Net Sales | | 100.0 | 100.0 |
| | | | | | | | Gross Profit | | | |
| | 93.4 | 92.8 | 92.5 | 92.7 | 96.3 | 92.3 | Operating Expenses | | 92.0 | 92.4 |
| | 6.6 | 7.2 | 7.5 | 7.3 | 3.7 | 7.7 | Operating Profit | | 8.0 | 7.6 |
| | .8 | .5 | 1.4 | 1.5 | 3.3 | 1.4 | All Other Expenses (net) | | .9 | .3 |
| | 5.9 | 6.7 | 6.1 | 5.8 | .4 | 6.4 | Profit Before Taxes | | 7.1 | 7.3 |
| | | | | | | | RATIOS | | | |
| | 4.8 | 5.6 | 3.5 | 2.6 | 1.8 | 3.4 | | | 3.1 | 3.4 |
| | 2.1 | 1.8 | 1.9 | 1.6 | 1.1 | 1.7 | Current | | 1.6 | 1.7 |
| | .8 | 1.0 | 1.2 | 1.1 | .8 | 1.1 | | | 1.0 | 1.1 |
| | 4.7 | 5.4 | 2.8 | 2.5 | 1.7 | 3.2 | | | 2.7 | 3.2 |
| | 2.0 | 1.7 | 1.8 | 1.3 | .8 | 1.5 | Quick | | 1.3 | 1.5 |
| | .8 | .9 | 1.1 | .8 | .5 | 1.0 | | | .8 | .9 |
| 0 | UND | 5 | 71.0 | 28 | 13.2 | 39 | 9.4 | 37 | 9.8 | 59 | 6.2 | | 21 | 17.4 | 16 | 23.4 |
| 7 | 52.0 | 30 | 12.0 | 48 | 7.6 | 53 | 6.9 | 53 | 6.9 | 68 | 5.4 | Sales/Receivables | 45 | 8.2 | 38 | 9.6 |
| 34 | 10.6 | 53 | 6.9 | 66 | 5.5 | 73 | 5.0 | 74 | 4.9 | 104 | 3.5 | | 65 | 5.6 | 69 | 5.3 |
| | | | | | | | | Cost of Sales/Inventory | | |
| | | | | | | | | Cost of Sales/Payables | | |
| | 6.0 | 6.4 | 4.9 | 4.1 | 9.2 | 1.9 | | | 6.6 | 4.7 |
| | 31.0 | 14.9 | 10.5 | 11.4 | 61.5 | 7.4 | Sales/Working Capital | | 14.4 | 10.5 |
| | -36.8 | 298.3 | 39.5 | 48.2 | -24.1 | 183.1 | | | 341.1 | 66.2 |
| | 4.3 | 47.6 | 56.2 | 25.0 | 12.3 | 34.9 | | | 38.2 | 41.1 |
| (14) | 2.5 | (36) | 11.1 | (82) | 8.4 | (56) | 8.5 | (21) | 1.0 | (12) | .9 | EBIT/Interest | (305) | 9.0 | (170) | 10.8 |
| | 1.4 | 1.7 | 1.7 | 2.0 | -.3 | -.4 | | | 2.6 | 1.8 |
| | | | | 21.6 | | | | | 7.1 | 3.3 |
| | | | (12) | 4.5 | | | Net Profit + Depr., Dep., Amort./Cur. Mat. L/T/D | (24) | 2.9 | (15) | 2.3 |
| | | | | .4 | | | | | .7 | 1.7 |
| | .0 | .0 | .0 | .0 | .2 | .1 | | | .0 | .0 |
| | .0 | .0 | .1 | .3 | 1.2 | NM | Fixed/Worth | | .2 | .2 |
| | NM | .5 | .6 | 9.5 | -.3 | -.1 | | | 2.2 | 1.9 |
| | .4 | .5 | .5 | .8 | 1.6 | .7 | | | .5 | .9 |
| | 2.5 | 1.4 | 1.4 | 2.2 | -20.4 | NM | Debt/Worth | | 1.9 | 2.6 |
| | -2.1 | 32.9 | 5.7 | 302.7 | -1.9 | -2.5 | | | 41.2 | -36.0 |
| | 174.7 | 76.0 | 68.2 | 82.0 | 37.7 | 36.8 | | | 95.9 | 108.9 |
| (21) | 101.6 | (49) | 35.6 | (103) | 37.1 | (59) | 39.2 | (11) | 15.8 | (10) | 26.8 | % Profit Before Taxes/Tangible Net Worth | (330) | 49.7 | (183) | 60.9 |
| | 28.2 | 14.0 | 7.0 | 18.7 | -6.5 | .3 | | | 19.8 | 17.4 |
| | 73.7 | 36.4 | 28.6 | 20.7 | 11.5 | 13.1 | | | 38.7 | 34.9 |
| | 25.9 | 16.3 | 12.6 | 11.0 | .1 | 9.6 | % Profit Before Taxes/Total Assets | | 15.2 | 11.5 |
| | 5.4 | 3.9 | 2.4 | 2.7 | -5.2 | -2.9 | | | 5.1 | 3.1 |
| | UND | UND | 558.3 | 336.1 | 161.0 | 138.0 | | | 607.6 | 999.8 |
| | 999.8 | 289.8 | 86.9 | 73.5 | 55.5 | 85.1 | Sales/Net Fixed Assets | | 97.5 | 68.2 |
| | 36.0 | 39.5 | 26.4 | 13.0 | 8.5 | 11.0 | | | 27.1 | 21.7 |
| | 14.4 | 5.9 | 4.3 | 3.5 | 2.7 | 1.8 | | | 5.1 | 3.9 |
| | 5.4 | 3.9 | 3.1 | 2.1 | 1.6 | 1.0 | Sales/Total Assets | | 3.3 | 2.4 |
| | 3.5 | 2.8 | 1.9 | 1.2 | .8 | .5 | | | 2.0 | 1.5 |
| | | .1 | .2 | .2 | .2 | | | .2 | .3 |
| | (20) | .4 | (67) | .6 | (45) | .9 | (13) | 1.3 | % Depr., Dep., Amort./Sales | (202) | .6 | (109) | .9 |
| | | 1.1 | 1.4 | 2.1 | 4.0 | | | 1.7 | 2.7 |
| | 3.4 | 1.6 | .7 | | | | | | 2.1 | 2.3 |
| (16) | 5.1 | (21) | 3.9 | (21) | 2.8 | | | | % Officers', Directors' Owners' Comp/Sales | (106) | 4.6 | (63) | 5.9 |
| | 12.1 | 7.6 | 5.1 | | | | | | 8.2 | 10.9 |
| | 69160M | 324337M | 2077315M | 4153043M | 3738086M | 3860429M | Net Sales ($) | | 13030920M | 7334829M |
| | 7546M | 66202M | 605714M | 1702792M | 1846690M | 3260288M | Total Assets ($) | | 5736416M | 4445555M |

© RMA 2024

M = $ thousand     MM = $ million
See Pages viii through xx for Explanation of Ratios and Data

# PROFESSIONAL SERVICES—Other Computer Related Services  NAICS 541519

| Comparative Historical Data | | | | | | Current Data Sorted by Sales | | | | | |
|---|---|---|---|---|---|---|---|---|---|---|---|
| | | | | **Type of Statement** | | | | | | | |
| 27 | | 29 | | 32 | Unqualified | | | 1 | 3 | 4 | 24 |
| 16 | | 22 | | 29 | Reviewed | | 1 | 1 | 1 | 8 | 18 |
| 11 | | 20 | | 14 | Compiled | | | | 6 | 6 | 2 |
| 35 | | 45 | | 40 | Tax Returns | 4 | 11 | 7 | 5 | 11 | 2 |
| 134 | | 195 | | 223 | Other | 15 | 25 | 18 | 39 | 55 | 71 |
| 4/1/21- | | 4/1/22- | | 4/1/23- | | | 34 (4/1-9/30/23) | | 304 (10/1/23-3/31/24) | | |
| 3/31/22 | | 3/31/23 | | 3/31/24 | | | | | | | |
| ALL | | ALL | | ALL | | 0-1MM | 1-3MM | 3-5MM | 5-10MM | 10-25MM | 25MM & OVER |
| 223 | | 311 | | 338 | **NUMBER OF STATEMENTS** | 19 | 37 | 27 | 54 | 84 | 117 |
| % | | % | | % | **ASSETS** | % | % | % | % | % | % |
| 30.6 | | 26.5 | | 24.6 | Cash & Equivalents | 39.4 | 26.9 | 41.7 | 24.8 | 24.8 | 17.4 |
| 33.3 | | 33.9 | | 35.5 | Trade Receivables (net) | 14.5 | 36.8 | 24.4 | 34.5 | 38.6 | 39.2 |
| 2.9 | | 3.1 | | 2.7 | Inventory | .2 | 2.4 | 2.0 | 3.6 | 2.2 | 3.2 |
| 4.2 | | 6.1 | | 5.2 | All Other Current | 5.0 | 4.7 | 4.1 | 3.8 | 4.4 | 6.9 |
| 71.0 | | 69.7 | | 68.0 | Total Current | 59.1 | 70.9 | 72.2 | 66.6 | 70.0 | 66.8 |
| 9.5 | | 11.0 | | 10.1 | Fixed Assets (net) | 29.1 | 12.4 | 13.0 | 12.3 | 7.0 | 6.8 |
| 9.0 | | 10.0 | | 11.8 | Intangibles (net) | 6.8 | 8.1 | 5.3 | 9.4 | 12.1 | 16.3 |
| 10.4 | | 9.3 | | 10.1 | All Other Non-Current | 5.2 | 8.6 | 9.5 | 11.7 | 10.9 | 10.1 |
| 100.0 | | 100.0 | | 100.0 | Total | 100.0 | 100.0 | 100.0 | 100.0 | 100.0 | 100.0 |
| | | | | | **LIABILITIES** | | | | | | |
| 9.8 | | 8.1 | | 7.0 | Notes Payable-Short Term | 6.3 | 17.4 | 17.5 | 6.1 | 2.8 | 4.7 |
| 1.8 | | 2.1 | | 1.8 | Cur. Mat.-L.T.D. | 1.0 | 2.2 | 2.8 | 1.4 | 1.2 | 2.2 |
| 12.8 | | 12.3 | | 14.1 | Trade Payables | 2.2 | 14.5 | 10.2 | 8.9 | 13.8 | 19.5 |
| .2 | | .3 | | .2 | Income Taxes Payable | .7 | .2 | .1 | .1 | .1 | .1 |
| 17.6 | | 17.7 | | 21.1 | All Other Current | 24.6 | 25.1 | 9.5 | 19.4 | 26.6 | 18.7 |
| 42.2 | | 40.6 | | 44.2 | Total Current | 34.8 | 59.4 | 40.0 | 36.0 | 44.6 | 45.3 |
| 13.9 | | 18.7 | | 15.6 | Long-Term Debt | 33.8 | 18.9 | 28.5 | 18.7 | 9.9 | 11.1 |
| .1 | | .2 | | .1 | Deferred Taxes | .2 | .0 | .0 | .1 | .1 | .3 |
| 11.9 | | 6.0 | | 6.5 | All Other Non-Current | 6.1 | 7.7 | .8 | 7.1 | 4.1 | 9.1 |
| 32.0 | | 34.6 | | 33.6 | Net Worth | 25.0 | 14.0 | 30.7 | 38.1 | 41.3 | 34.2 |
| 100.0 | | 100.0 | | 100.0 | Total Liabilties & Net Worth | 100.0 | 100.0 | 100.0 | 100.0 | 100.0 | 100.0 |
| | | | | | **INCOME DATA** | | | | | | |
| 100.0 | | 100.0 | | 100.0 | Net Sales | 100.0 | 100.0 | 100.0 | 100.0 | 100.0 | 100.0 |
| | | | | | Gross Profit | | | | | | |
| 90.6 | | 91.9 | | 93.0 | Operating Expenses | 75.5 | 93.3 | 94.6 | 91.4 | 95.3 | 94.3 |
| 9.4 | | 8.1 | | 7.0 | Operating Profit | 24.5 | 6.7 | 5.4 | 8.6 | 4.7 | 5.7 |
| -.9 | | .8 | | 1.3 | All Other Expenses (net) | 6.0 | 2.0 | .6 | 1.7 | -.2 | 1.5 |
| 10.3 | | 7.3 | | 5.7 | Profit Before Taxes | 18.5 | 4.7 | 4.8 | 6.9 | 4.9 | 4.2 |
| | | | | | **RATIOS** | | | | | | |
| 3.3 | | 3.7 | | 3.1 | | 3.8 | 3.5 | 6.1 | 3.6 | 3.9 | 2.3 |
| 1.8 | | 1.9 | | 1.7 | Current | 2.3 | 1.1 | 2.5 | 2.0 | 2.0 | 1.5 |
| 1.1 | | 1.2 | | 1.0 | | .4 | .8 | 1.0 | 1.2 | 1.1 | 1.1 |
| 3.2 | | 2.8 | | 2.8 | | 3.8 | 2.7 | 5.7 | 3.5 | 3.8 | 2.0 |
| 1.5 | | 1.6 | | 1.5 | Quick | 2.3 | 1.0 | 2.4 | 2.0 | 1.7 | 1.3 |
| .9 | | .9 | | .9 | | .4 | .6 | .8 | .9 | 1.1 | .9 |
| 21  17.0 | | 21  17.5 | | 25  14.7 | | 0  UND | 7  51.6 | 1  253.4 | 23  16.0 | 29  12.5 | 40  9.1 |
| 39  9.3 | | 45  8.1 | | 46  7.9 | Sales/Receivables | 0  952.0 | 28  13.2 | 22  16.6 | 47  7.7 | 48  7.6 | 54  6.7 |
| 62  5.9 | | 64  5.7 | | 68  5.4 | | 31  11.7 | 68  5.4 | 37  9.8 | 68  5.4 | 69  5.3 | 72  5.1 |
| | | | | | Cost of Sales/Inventory | | | | | | |
| | | | | | Cost of Sales/Payables | | | | | | |
| 4.4 | | 5.2 | | 5.7 | | 4.9 | 7.0 | 5.5 | 4.6 | 4.8 | 6.4 |
| 11.4 | | 11.0 | | 12.8 | Sales/Working Capital | 12.0 | 17.4 | 18.4 | 9.7 | 11.2 | 13.5 |
| 45.3 | | 36.4 | | 208.3 | | -2.8 | -23.8 | 390.6 | 24.9 | 53.7 | 99.9 |
| 115.5 | | 72.3 | | 34.1 | | | 6.7 | 26.5 | 99.4 | 81.6 | 23.1 |
| (145)  33.3 | | (206)  16.0 | | (221)  6.7 | EBIT/Interest | (14)  2.2 | (18)  7.6 | (43)  8.7 | (54)  11.8 | (86)  6.5 |
| 7.4 | | 2.2 | | 1.0 | | | -2.4 | .9 | 2.2 | 2.5 | .3 |
| 20.9 | | 14.2 | | 15.0 | | | | | | | 22.5 |
| (11)  4.4 | | (22)  4.6 | | (27)  4.8 | Net Profit + Depr., Dep., Amort./Cur. Mat. L/T/D | | | | | (17)  6.3 |
| 1.7 | | 1.7 | | -.1 | | | | | | | .5 |
| .0 | | .0 | | .0 | | .0 | .0 | .0 | .0 | .0 | .0 |
| .1 | | .1 | | .1 | Fixed/Worth | .0 | .0 | .1 | .2 | .1 | .2 |
| .6 | | .8 | | 1.8 | | 4.9 | 3.4 | .5 | .5 | .7 | -.7 |
| .6 | | .5 | | .6 | | .4 | .5 | .2 | .4 | .6 | .8 |
| 1.7 | | 1.4 | | 2.0 | Debt/Worth | 2.6 | 3.8 | 1.1 | 1.2 | 1.3 | 3.4 |
| 9.6 | | 12.1 | | -103.6 | | -29.2 | -7.0 | 161.0 | 5.4 | 10.3 | -7.0 |
| 113.1 | | 84.2 | | 76.9 | | 91.8 | 102.3 | 96.8 | 68.2 | 81.9 | 68.1 |
| (178)  66.1 | | (248)  45.2 | | (253)  37.7 | % Profit Before Taxes/Tangible Net Worth | (14)  28.2 | (26)  59.1 | (21)  34.6 | (43)  35.6 | (69)  35.1 | (80)  38.2 |
| 30.2 | | 18.2 | | 12.8 | | 7.1 | 15.4 | 9.4 | 12.9 | 6.9 | 15.2 |
| 45.8 | | 33.9 | | 28.3 | | 33.3 | 36.4 | 66.0 | 31.2 | 28.3 | 22.5 |
| 23.9 | | 16.8 | | 11.3 | % Profit Before Taxes/Total Assets | 9.7 | 8.9 | 24.5 | 12.9 | 13.3 | 10.1 |
| 8.6 | | 4.7 | | 2.0 | | .9 | -.3 | 2.4 | 4.0 | 2.3 | .0 |
| 999.8 | | 999.8 | | 827.4 | | UND | UND | 999.8 | 999.8 | 409.2 | 595.4 |
| 116.7 | | 106.7 | | 95.6 | Sales/Net Fixed Assets | UND | 172.5 | 67.4 | 70.9 | 89.9 | 96.8 |
| 27.8 | | 14.6 | | 25.4 | | .2 | 28.8 | 27.4 | 14.4 | 46.2 | 26.1 |
| 4.2 | | 4.5 | | 4.4 | | 4.5 | 4.4 | 8.3 | 3.9 | 5.0 | 3.9 |
| 3.0 | | 2.7 | | 2.9 | Sales/Total Assets | 3.0 | 2.8 | 4.4 | 2.7 | 3.3 | 2.4 |
| 1.6 | | 1.6 | | 1.7 | | .2 | 2.2 | 2.5 | 1.4 | 1.8 | 1.4 |
| .3 | | .4 | | .2 | | | .1 | .2 | .2 | .1 | .2 |
| (86)  .6 | | (128)  1.2 | | (158)  .6 | % Depr., Dep., Amort./Sales | | (12)  .5 | (10)  .6 | (27)  .7 | (48)  .6 | (58)  .4 |
| 1.6 | | 3.1 | | 1.6 | | | 2.9 | 1.3 | 1.4 | 1.5 | 1.6 |
| 1.9 | | 1.0 | | 1.6 | | | 3.8 | | 1.5 | .8 | .4 |
| (59)  5.1 | | (68)  3.4 | | (64)  3.5 | % Officers', Directors' Owners' Comp/Sales | | (16)  7.1 | | (12)  3.0 | (15)  2.1 | (10)  1.2 |
| 9.8 | | 7.0 | | 6.8 | | | 11.0 | | 4.1 | 4.6 | 2.9 |
| 5920450M | | 10944060M | | 14222370M | Net Sales ($) | 9870M | 73230M | 105883M | 410675M | 1410725M | 12211987M |
| 3381156M | | 6107549M | | 7489232M | Total Assets ($) | 25287M | 42990M | 31291M | 229741M | 683023M | 6476900M |

© RMA 2024  M = $ thousand  MM = $ million
See Pages viii through xx for Explanation of Ratios and Data

# PROFESSIONAL SERVICES—Administrative Management and General Management Consulting Services  NAICS 541611

## Current Data Sorted by Assets | Comparative Historical Data

| | | | | | | | Type of Statement | | |
|---|---|---|---|---|---|---|---|---|---|
| 1 | 1 | 12 | 24 | 11 | 5 | | Unqualified | 50 | 26 |
| | 2 | 11 | 14 | 3 | 1 | | Reviewed | 36 | 16 |
| | 3 | 6 | 7 | | 1 | | Compiled | 26 | 12 |
| 24 | 23 | 14 | 8 | | | | Tax Returns | 69 | 31 |
| 40 | 48 | 101 | 82 | 25 | 21 | | Other | 311 | 202 |
| | 54 (4/1-9/30/23) | | 434 (10/1/23-3/31/24) | | | | | 4/1/19-3/31/20 | 4/1/20-3/31/21 |
| 0-500M | 500M-2MM | 2-10MM | 10-50MM | 50-100MM | 100-250MM | | | ALL | ALL |
| 65 | 77 | 144 | 135 | 39 | 28 | | NUMBER OF STATEMENTS | 492 | 287 |
| % | % | % | % | % | % | | ASSETS | % | % |
| 47.5 | 34.6 | 24.7 | 19.0 | 13.9 | 14.7 | | Cash & Equivalents | 24.9 | 35.6 |
| 8.7 | 23.5 | 35.7 | 33.6 | 21.6 | 13.4 | | Trade Receivables (net) | 32.0 | 25.8 |
| 1.8 | 1.5 | 1.4 | 3.1 | 7.8 | 2.2 | | Inventory | 1.8 | 2.1 |
| 7.4 | 6.4 | 7.3 | 6.5 | 7.1 | 2.2 | | All Other Current | 7.0 | 4.3 |
| 65.5 | 66.0 | 69.0 | 62.2 | 50.4 | 32.5 | | Total Current | 65.6 | 67.8 |
| 12.8 | 10.6 | 11.8 | 8.9 | 14.6 | 13.9 | | Fixed Assets (net) | 11.6 | 10.9 |
| 3.5 | 6.1 | 6.7 | 12.1 | 14.9 | 39.9 | | Intangibles (net) | 10.1 | 10.5 |
| 18.1 | 17.4 | 12.5 | 16.7 | 20.1 | 13.7 | | All Other Non-Current | 12.7 | 10.8 |
| 100.0 | 100.0 | 100.0 | 100.0 | 100.0 | 100.0 | | Total | 100.0 | 100.0 |
| | | | | | | | LIABILITIES | | |
| 33.3 | 10.1 | 6.1 | 5.4 | 6.6 | 1.2 | | Notes Payable-Short Term | 11.1 | 11.6 |
| 3.2 | .9 | 1.7 | 3.1 | 2.0 | 4.6 | | Cur. Mat.-L.T.D. | 2.2 | 3.2 |
| 3.5 | 7.9 | 9.8 | 10.4 | 8.8 | 7.1 | | Trade Payables | 9.0 | 8.4 |
| .0 | .1 | .1 | .2 | .3 | .1 | | Income Taxes Payable | .2 | .1 |
| 20.7 | 21.7 | 22.3 | 19.9 | 14.5 | 19.4 | | All Other Current | 24.0 | 22.7 |
| 60.7 | 40.8 | 39.9 | 39.0 | 32.2 | 32.4 | | Total Current | 46.5 | 46.1 |
| 25.2 | 13.7 | 11.0 | 15.3 | 31.5 | 38.2 | | Long-Term Debt | 15.7 | 22.4 |
| .0 | .0 | .1 | .0 | .3 | .2 | | Deferred Taxes | .2 | .2 |
| 2.8 | 5.3 | 6.6 | 12.8 | 9.8 | 4.6 | | All Other Non-Current | 5.3 | 6.1 |
| 11.3 | 40.2 | 42.4 | 32.9 | 26.1 | 24.6 | | Net Worth | 32.2 | 25.3 |
| 100.0 | 100.0 | 100.0 | 100.0 | 100.0 | 100.0 | | Total Liabilities & Net Worth | 100.0 | 100.0 |
| | | | | | | | INCOME DATA | | |
| 100.0 | 100.0 | 100.0 | 100.0 | 100.0 | 100.0 | | Net Sales | 100.0 | 100.0 |
| | | | | | | | Gross Profit | | |
| 89.0 | 87.5 | 86.5 | 87.8 | 87.9 | 92.3 | | Operating Expenses | 88.6 | 88.0 |
| 11.0 | 12.5 | 13.5 | 12.2 | 12.1 | 7.7 | | Operating Profit | 11.4 | 12.0 |
| .6 | 1.0 | 1.3 | 1.6 | 4.5 | 5.2 | | All Other Expenses (net) | 2.1 | .8 |
| 10.4 | 11.5 | 12.2 | 10.6 | 7.6 | 2.5 | | Profit Before Taxes | 9.4 | 11.2 |
| | | | | | | | RATIOS | | |
| 8.5 | 11.2 | 3.8 | 2.8 | 2.5 | 1.5 | | | 3.2 | 3.8 |
| 1.8 | 2.9 | 2.2 | 1.6 | 1.6 | 1.2 | Current | | 1.6 | 1.8 |
| .6 | 1.0 | 1.2 | 1.1 | 1.3 | .7 | | | .9 | 1.1 |
| 7.7 | 6.2 | 3.5 | 2.5 | 1.8 | 1.4 | | | 2.8 | 3.1 |
| 1.3 | 2.7 | 2.1 | 1.4 | 1.2 | 1.0 | Quick | | 1.4 | 1.6 |
| .4 | .9 | 1.0 | .9 | .6 | .6 | | | .7 | 1.0 |
| 0 UND | 0 UND | 12 30.2 | 39 9.4 | 11 34.4 | 18 20.6 | | | 6 63.4 | 0 751.8 |
| 0 UND | 8 45.1 | 39 9.4 | 51 7.1 | 49 7.4 | 45 8.2 | Sales/Receivables | | 39 9.3 | 33 10.9 |
| 12 30.4 | 47 7.7 | 65 5.6 | 74 4.9 | 73 5.0 | 63 5.8 | | | 63 5.8 | 62 5.9 |
| | | | | | | | Cost of Sales/Inventory | | |
| | | | | | | | Cost of Sales/Payables | | |
| 7.6 | 5.3 | 4.6 | 4.4 | 3.8 | 6.7 | | | 5.2 | 4.1 |
| 26.6 | 9.5 | 8.6 | 9.7 | 8.3 | 38.7 | Sales/Working Capital | | 12.8 | 8.6 |
| -24.8 | NM | 35.9 | 49.3 | 26.1 | -11.2 | | | -134.7 | 52.2 |
| 80.0 | 83.8 | 38.6 | 47.5 | 36.2 | 9.4 | | | 44.6 | 62.4 |
| (37) 17.4 | (50) 9.2 | (92) 12.9 | (102) 8.6 | (28) 6.9 | (22) 1.8 | EBIT/Interest | | (335) 7.8 | (185) 13.9 |
| 1.7 | -1.3 | 2.5 | 2.3 | 2.1 | -.2 | | | 2.1 | 2.1 |
| | | | 29.7 | | | | | 13.5 | 35.0 |
| | | (17) 8.5 | | | | Net Profit + Depr., Dep., | (43) 5.5 | (17) 6.4 |
| | | | 2.7 | | | Amort./Cur. Mat. L/T/D | | 1.7 | 2.3 |
| .0 | .0 | .0 | .0 | .0 | .1 | | | .0 | .0 |
| .0 | .0 | .1 | .1 | .4 | 2.1 | Fixed/Worth | | .2 | .2 |
| 1.7 | .3 | .6 | .7 | 4.5 | -.1 | | | 1.8 | 2.5 |
| .1 | .2 | .4 | 1.0 | .9 | 3.5 | | | .6 | .6 |
| 2.1 | .9 | 1.0 | 2.6 | 2.6 | -39.6 | Debt/Worth | | 1.8 | 2.5 |
| -5.6 | 12.1 | 5.3 | 21.7 | 21.2 | -1.4 | | | 30.0 | -25.0 |
| 187.9 | 95.7 | 96.6 | 97.6 | 62.0 | 65.5 | | | 106.7 | 109.4 |
| (45) 103.6 | (59) 45.2 | (123) 56.3 | (110) 38.7 | (31) 27.1 | (12) 22.7 | % Profit Before Taxes/Tangible Net Worth | (381) 48.1 | (209) 44.2 |
| 2.4 | 6.5 | 18.0 | 14.3 | 8.4 | 1.9 | | | 16.0 | 12.0 |
| 109.2 | 48.3 | 44.7 | 23.9 | 16.9 | 8.2 | | | 35.9 | 37.0 |
| 49.1 | 18.9 | 20.6 | 10.9 | 8.9 | 3.3 | % Profit Before Taxes/Total Assets | | 13.7 | 16.2 |
| -.7 | -.4 | 5.3 | 2.0 | .7 | -5.1 | | | 2.7 | 1.8 |
| UND | UND | 999.8 | 579.1 | 159.0 | 135.4 | | | 513.8 | 613.2 |
| 598.7 | 192.0 | 95.9 | 95.5 | 33.1 | 18.5 | Sales/Net Fixed Assets | | 65.4 | 74.4 |
| 46.0 | 21.9 | 21.0 | 22.6 | 7.2 | 5.7 | | | 18.4 | 19.8 |
| 14.7 | 5.3 | 4.5 | 3.2 | 2.0 | 1.8 | | | 4.9 | 4.1 |
| 5.9 | 3.0 | 2.9 | 1.9 | 1.3 | .9 | Sales/Total Assets | | 2.7 | 2.5 |
| 3.1 | 1.5 | 1.7 | 1.0 | 1.0 | .5 | | | 1.4 | 1.3 |
| .1 | .3 | .1 | .2 | .3 | .5 | | | .2 | .2 |
| (14) .4 | (26) 1.4 | (59) .5 | (77) .6 | (23) .7 | (12) 1.2 | % Depr., Dep., Amort./Sales | (262) .7 | (117) .8 |
| 1.8 | 3.3 | 1.8 | 1.5 | 2.1 | 2.2 | | | 2.1 | 2.2 |
| 4.0 | 2.6 | 1.5 | 1.2 | | | | | 3.4 | 3.2 |
| (27) 4.9 | (27) 5.2 | (29) 3.9 | (10) 3.0 | | | % Officers', Directors' Owners' Comp/Sales | (117) 6.0 | (65) 7.9 |
| 21.5 | 9.0 | 5.6 | 15.3 | | | | | 15.2 | 13.4 |
| 145042M | 315346M | 2222220M | 5609685M | 4345026M | 6432696M | | Net Sales ($) | 16840769M | 10818516M |
| 15934M | 82014M | 732450M | 2802472M | 2653781M | 4618297M | | Total Assets ($) | 9482869M | 7161264M |

© RMA 2024  
M = $ thousand   MM = $ million  
See Pages viii through xx for Explanation of Ratios and Data

# PROFESSIONAL SERVICES—Administrative Management and General Management Consulting Services  NAICS 541611

## Comparative Historical Data / Current Data Sorted by Sales

| | | | | Type of Statement | | | | | | |
|---|---|---|---|---|---|---|---|---|---|---|
| | 20 | 47 | 54 | Unqualified | 1 | 4 | 2 | 3 | 13 | 31 |
| | 14 | 28 | 31 | Reviewed | | 2 | 1 | 3 | 10 | 15 |
| | 11 | 19 | 17 | Compiled | | 1 | 2 | 3 | 2 | 9 |
| | 37 | 68 | 69 | Tax Returns | 13 | 15 | 12 | 13 | 12 | 4 |
| | 186 | 275 | 317 | Other | 29 | 43 | 23 | 38 | 64 | 120 |
| | 4/1/21-3/31/22 ALL | 4/1/22-3/31/23 ALL | 4/1/23-3/31/24 ALL | | 54 (4/1-9/30/23) | | | 434 (10/1/23-3/31/24) | | |
| | | | | | 0-1MM | 1-3MM | 3-5MM | 5-10MM | 10-25MM | 25MM & OVER |
| | 268 | 437 | 488 | NUMBER OF STATEMENTS | 43 | 65 | 40 | 60 | 101 | 179 |
| | % | % | % | ASSETS | % | % | % | % | % | % |
| | 30.8 | 26.7 | 26.3 | Cash & Equivalents | 32.1 | 34.0 | 34.3 | 29.0 | 28.6 | 18.1 |
| | 26.9 | 31.4 | 27.2 | Trade Receivables (net) | 11.0 | 8.8 | 23.6 | 27.8 | 33.7 | 34.6 |
| | 1.7 | 2.3 | 2.5 | Inventory | .0 | 3.3 | .5 | 1.5 | 2.0 | 3.8 |
| | 6.4 | 7.5 | 6.7 | All Other Current | 9.5 | 6.4 | 7.6 | 4.6 | 6.1 | 6.8 |
| | 65.8 | 67.9 | 62.6 | Total Current | 52.6 | 52.7 | 65.9 | 62.9 | 70.5 | 63.3 |
| | 13.3 | 10.5 | 11.3 | Fixed Assets (net) | 17.3 | 14.5 | 16.0 | 15.5 | 6.3 | 9.1 |
| | 10.1 | 9.4 | 10.2 | Intangibles (net) | 5.1 | 5.4 | 6.8 | 9.3 | 8.3 | 15.4 |
| | 10.8 | 12.2 | 15.9 | All Other Non-Current | 24.9 | 27.4 | 11.3 | 12.2 | 14.9 | 12.2 |
| | 100.0 | 100.0 | 100.0 | Total | 100.0 | 100.0 | 100.0 | 100.0 | 100.0 | 100.0 |
| | | | | LIABILITIES | | | | | | |
| | 8.4 | 8.9 | 9.9 | Notes Payable-Short Term | 13.3 | 24.8 | 19.0 | 6.1 | 6.6 | 4.8 |
| | 2.8 | 2.1 | 2.4 | Cur. Mat.-L.T.D. | .1 | 3.2 | 4.8 | 1.6 | .9 | 3.1 |
| | 9.0 | 9.8 | 8.6 | Trade Payables | 2.4 | 3.8 | 8.8 | 6.2 | 8.9 | 12.3 |
| | .1 | .1 | .1 | Income Taxes Payable | .0 | .0 | .4 | .1 | .1 | .2 |
| | 22.9 | 19.8 | 20.5 | All Other Current | 22.6 | 21.3 | 24.0 | 12.1 | 22.4 | 20.7 |
| | 43.2 | 40.7 | 41.5 | Total Current | 38.4 | 53.1 | 57.0 | 25.9 | 39.0 | 41.2 |
| | 18.4 | 18.7 | 17.7 | Long-Term Debt | 24.3 | 17.9 | 14.1 | 22.3 | 9.9 | 19.7 |
| | .1 | .1 | .1 | Deferred Taxes | .0 | .0 | .0 | .2 | .1 | .1 |
| | 7.6 | 7.1 | 7.7 | All Other Non-Current | 8.8 | 1.5 | 4.3 | 8.9 | 6.4 | 10.9 |
| | 30.6 | 33.4 | 33.0 | Net Worth | 28.5 | 27.5 | 24.5 | 42.8 | 44.6 | 28.1 |
| | 100.0 | 100.0 | 100.0 | Total Liabilities & Net Worth | 100.0 | 100.0 | 100.0 | 100.0 | 100.0 | 100.0 |
| | | | | INCOME DATA | | | | | | |
| | 100.0 | 100.0 | 100.0 | Net Sales | 100.0 | 100.0 | 100.0 | 100.0 | 100.0 | 100.0 |
| | | | | Gross Profit | | | | | | |
| | 86.6 | 88.6 | 87.8 | Operating Expenses | 75.5 | 82.7 | 91.5 | 89.9 | 87.3 | 91.4 |
| | 13.4 | 11.4 | 12.2 | Operating Profit | 24.5 | 17.3 | 8.5 | 10.1 | 12.7 | 8.6 |
| | -.3 | .8 | 1.7 | All Other Expenses (net) | 3.9 | 1.5 | 3.0 | .6 | .8 | 1.8 |
| | 13.7 | 10.5 | 10.5 | Profit Before Taxes | 20.7 | 15.8 | 5.6 | 9.6 | 11.9 | 6.8 |
| | | | | RATIOS | | | | | | |
| | 3.8 | 4.4 | 3.8 | | 13.4 | 9.0 | 3.2 | 10.5 | 3.8 | 2.5 |
| | 2.1 | 2.0 | 1.8 | Current | 2.4 | 1.4 | 1.9 | 3.1 | 2.5 | 1.5 |
| | 1.2 | 1.2 | 1.1 | | .6 | .3 | .6 | 1.6 | 1.2 | 1.1 |
| | 3.6 | 3.9 | 3.3 | | 5.5 | 7.7 | 3.1 | 9.0 | 3.7 | 2.0 |
| | 1.8 (436) | 1.7 | 1.5 | Quick | 1.7 | 1.1 | 1.5 | 3.0 | 2.2 | 1.3 |
| | .9 | 1.0 | .8 | | .6 | .2 | .5 | 1.3 | 1.1 | .9 |
| 4 | 89.7 | 5  72.5 | 2  239.6 | | 0  UND | 0  UND | 0  UND | 0  UND | 23  15.7 | 28  13.0 |
| 38 | 9.6 | 38  9.6 | 38  9.6 | Sales/Receivables | 0  UND | 0  UND | 24  14.9 | 37  9.9 | 46  8.0 | 47  7.8 |
| 62 | 5.9 | 68  5.4 | 62  5.9 | | 47  7.7 | 12  29.8 | 55  6.6 | 74  4.9 | 70  5.2 | 64  5.7 |
| | | | | Cost of Sales/Inventory | | | | | | |
| | | | | Cost of Sales/Payables | | | | | | |
| | 4.5 | 4.9 | 4.9 | | 3.7 | 5.7 | 6.6 | 4.7 | 3.5 | 5.8 |
| | 8.8 | 9.5 | 10.5 | Sales/Working Capital | 10.3 | 33.8 | 13.9 | 7.9 | 7.6 | 12.1 |
| | 37.7 | 47.5 | 101.0 | | -13.2 | -16.8 | -7.2 | 31.3 | 34.4 | 49.3 |
| | 123.4 | 64.1 | 40.3 | | 105.3 | 27.9 | 73.0 | 41.3 | 100.6 | 37.0 |
| (176) | 27.5 | (284) 14.3 | (331) 9.7 | EBIT/Interest | (21) 10.6 | (41) 7.1 | (24) 2.7 | (46) 9.9 | (65) 21.6 | (134) 7.6 |
| | 6.4 | 2.0 | 1.6 | | 2.0 | .3 | -10.7 | 1.2 | 2.2 | 2.2 |
| | 10.5 | 24.1 | 16.5 | | | | | | | 16.5 |
| (18) | 5.3 | (40) 3.2 | (39) 5.6 | Net Profit + Depr., Dep., Amort./Cur. Mat. L/T/D | | | | | (27) | 5.6 |
| | 1.6 | .7 | 2.1 | | | | | | | 2.1 |
| | .0 | .0 | .0 | | .0 | .0 | .0 | .0 | .0 | .0 |
| | .1 | .1 | .1 | Fixed/Worth | .0 | .1 | .0 | .1 | .1 | .2 |
| | 1.2 | 1.0 | 1.0 | | 2.4 | 1.5 | 3.2 | 1.6 | .2 | 1.9 |
| | .5 | .4 | .5 | | .1 | .2 | .4 | .2 | .4 | 1.0 |
| | 1.5 | 1.3 | 1.7 | Debt/Worth | 1.2 | 1.5 | 1.6 | 1.1 | 1.0 | 3.2 |
| | 27.9 | 13.1 | 25.2 | | -5.5 | 12.7 | -24.2 | 32.2 | 3.7 | -180.6 |
| | 133.4 | 95.1 | 103.5 | | 112.1 | 119.2 | 94.0 | 103.3 | 78.4 | 105.7 |
| (206) | 61.6 | (340) 47.6 | (380) 45.3 | % Profit Before Taxes/Tangible Net Worth | (30) 41.5 | (52) 47.2 | (29) 19.5 | (46) 49.4 | (89) 42.0 | (134) 45.7 |
| | 18.2 | 14.7 | 13.2 | | 4.5 | 6.7 | -8.9 | 10.6 | 20.1 | 16.9 |
| | 49.9 | 40.4 | 39.8 | | 48.0 | 61.8 | 45.8 | 53.0 | 39.5 | 26.0 |
| | 21.4 | 16.7 | 13.7 | % Profit Before Taxes/Total Assets | 7.7 | 13.1 | 6.5 | 14.9 | 21.9 | 12.1 |
| | 6.6 | 2.7 | 1.3 | | .3 | .9 | -9.9 | .1 | 3.9 | 1.7 |
| | 959.4 | 999.8 | 999.8 | | UND | UND | UND | UND | 999.8 | 430.5 |
| | 95.5 | 141.0 | 95.9 | Sales/Net Fixed Assets | 240.0 | 92.5 | 196.8 | 88.3 | 90.2 | 88.9 |
| | 18.2 | 24.7 | 20.2 | | 8.2 | 10.6 | 16.1 | 16.2 | 32.2 | 20.9 |
| | 4.4 | 4.6 | 4.1 | | 3.4 | 6.3 | 5.0 | 5.4 | 4.5 | 3.7 |
| | 2.3 | 2.8 | 2.5 | Sales/Total Assets | 1.1 | 2.3 | 3.0 | 2.7 | 2.6 | 2.6 |
| | 1.2 | 1.5 | 1.3 | | .6 | 1.1 | 1.5 | 1.4 | 1.4 | 1.4 |
| | .3 | .2 | .2 | | | .3 | .1 | .3 | .1 | .2 |
| (132) | .7 | (187) .6 | (211) .6 | % Depr., Dep., Amort./Sales | (19) .8 | (14) .9 | (24) 1.3 | (48) .5 | (98) .5 | |
| | 2.0 | 1.9 | 1.9 | | | 6.2 | 5.1 | 3.7 | 1.3 | 1.5 |
| | 3.2 | 2.5 | 2.2 | | 7.4 | 2.7 | 2.9 | 2.6 | .9 | .8 |
| (58) | 6.3 | (97) 5.9 | (94) 4.6 | % Officers', Directors', Owners' Comp/Sales | (11) 27.5 | (20) 4.6 | (17) 4.6 | (19) 4.6 | (16) 3.9 | (11) 1.4 |
| | 15.2 | 13.3 | 9.8 | | 38.8 | 11.0 | 8.0 | 5.9 | 5.6 | 5.5 |
| | 9927924M | 19011431M | 19070015M | Net Sales ($) | 21390M | 126659M | 160503M | 435822M | 1709377M | 16616264M |
| | 5685121M | 9968305M | 10904948M | Total Assets ($) | 41439M | 202061M | 158291M | 347290M | 1228683M | 8927184M |

© RMA 2024  M = $ thousand  MM = $ million
See Pages viii through xx for Explanation of Ratios and Data

# PROFESSIONAL SERVICES—Human Resources Consulting Services  NAICS 541612

## Current Data Sorted by Assets | Comparative Historical Data

| | | | | | | | | | |
|---|---|---|---|---|---|---|---|---|---|
| | | | 1 | 1 | 1 | **Type of Statement** | | | |
| | 2 | | 1 | | | Unqualified | | 6 | 7 |
| | 2 | | | | | Reviewed | | 1 | |
| 5 | 2 | 10 | 2 | 3 | 2 | Compiled | | 3 | 1 |
| | 5 | | | | | Tax Returns | | 8 | 5 |
| | 7 (4/1-9/30/23) | | 30 (10/1/23-3/31/24) | | | Other | | 48 | 24 |
| 0-500M | 500M-2MM | 2-10MM | 10-50MM | 50-100MM | 100-250MM | | | 4/1/19-3/31/20 ALL | 4/1/20-3/31/21 ALL |
| 5 | 7 | 14 | 4 | 4 | 3 | **NUMBER OF STATEMENTS** | | 66 | 37 |
| % | % | % | % | % | % | **ASSETS** | | % | % |
| | | 21.6 | | | | Cash & Equivalents | | 22.0 | 38.6 |
| | | 29.3 | | | | Trade Receivables (net) | | 35.9 | 23.7 |
| | | .0 | | | | Inventory | | .8 | .7 |
| | | 10.2 | | | | All Other Current | | 10.0 | 8.3 |
| | | 61.0 | | | | Total Current | | 68.7 | 71.3 |
| | | 4.1 | | | | Fixed Assets (net) | | 9.5 | 11.5 |
| | | 19.3 | | | | Intangibles (net) | | 7.1 | 8.6 |
| | | 15.6 | | | | All Other Non-Current | | 14.7 | 8.7 |
| | | 100.0 | | | | Total | | 100.0 | 100.0 |
| | | | | | | **LIABILITIES** | | | |
| | | 4.1 | | | | Notes Payable-Short Term | | 15.4 | 4.2 |
| | | .7 | | | | Cur. Mat.-L.T.D. | | .9 | 1.6 |
| | | 5.7 | | | | Trade Payables | | 10.9 | 6.1 |
| | | .1 | | | | Income Taxes Payable | | .1 | .2 |
| | | 29.3 | | | | All Other Current | | 21.5 | 24.8 |
| | | 39.9 | | | | Total Current | | 48.7 | 36.9 |
| | | 9.0 | | | | Long-Term Debt | | 5.2 | 13.6 |
| | | .0 | | | | Deferred Taxes | | .3 | .2 |
| | | 1.7 | | | | All Other Non-Current | | 7.5 | 8.0 |
| | | 49.3 | | | | Net Worth | | 38.3 | 41.3 |
| | | 100.0 | | | | Total Liabilties & Net Worth | | 100.0 | 100.0 |
| | | | | | | **INCOME DATA** | | | |
| | | 100.0 | | | | Net Sales | | 100.0 | 100.0 |
| | | | | | | Gross Profit | | | |
| | | 99.3 | | | | Operating Expenses | | 93.6 | 95.4 |
| | | .7 | | | | Operating Profit | | 6.4 | 4.6 |
| | | .7 | | | | All Other Expenses (net) | | 1.1 | -.6 |
| | | .0 | | | | Profit Before Taxes | | 5.3 | 5.2 |
| | | | | | | **RATIOS** | | | |
| | | 4.1 | | | | | | 3.0 | 3.9 |
| | | 1.4 | | | | Current | | 1.8 | 1.7 |
| | | .6 | | | | | | 1.0 | 1.1 |
| | | 2.8 | | | | | | 2.6 | 3.7 |
| | | 1.2 | | | | Quick | | 1.5 | 1.5 |
| | | .5 | | | | | | .7 | .9 |
| | | 19  18.9 | | | | | 1 | 278.9 | 5  71.7 |
| | | 45  8.2 | | | | Sales/Receivables | 33 | 11.0 | 29  12.8 |
| | | 73  5.0 | | | | | 49 | 7.5 | 52  7.0 |
| | | | | | | Cost of Sales/Inventory | | | |
| | | | | | | Cost of Sales/Payables | | | |
| | | 5.0 | | | | | | 10.2 | 4.5 |
| | | 12.3 | | | | Sales/Working Capital | | 17.8 | 10.6 |
| | | -19.1 | | | | | | -913.3 | 281.2 |
| | | | | | | | | 48.3 | 68.2 |
| | | | | | | EBIT/Interest | (43) | 11.4 | (22)  40.4 |
| | | | | | | | | 1.4 | 7.4 |
| | | | | | | Net Profit + Depr., Dep., Amort./Cur. Mat. L/T/D | | | |
| | | .0 | | | | | | .0 | .0 |
| | | .1 | | | | Fixed/Worth | | .1 | .2 |
| | | -.2 | | | | | | .9 | 1.2 |
| | | .2 | | | | | | .6 | .7 |
| | | 1.1 | | | | Debt/Worth | | 1.3 | 2.7 |
| | | -9.5 | | | | | | 10.6 | 7.3 |
| | | 24.7 | | | | | | 74.6 | 110.5 |
| | (10) | 5.3 | | | | % Profit Before Taxes/Tangible Net Worth | (51) | 27.0 | (34)  53.4 |
| | | -9.8 | | | | | | 7.7 | 4.6 |
| | | 12.4 | | | | | | 23.1 | 32.1 |
| | | 5.5 | | | | % Profit Before Taxes/Total Assets | | 9.1 | 14.9 |
| | | -4.3 | | | | | | .6 | .4 |
| | | 888.0 | | | | | | UND | 508.3 |
| | | 179.6 | | | | Sales/Net Fixed Assets | | 216.8 | 160.8 |
| | | 46.9 | | | | | | 67.0 | 25.8 |
| | | 4.1 | | | | | | 10.1 | 5.1 |
| | | 2.7 | | | | Sales/Total Assets | | 4.8 | 2.9 |
| | | 1.1 | | | | | | 2.1 | 1.2 |
| | | | | | | | | .1 | .1 |
| | | | | | | % Depr., Dep., Amort./Sales | (36) | .2 | (25)  .3 |
| | | | | | | | | 1.3 | 2.7 |
| | | | | | | | | .9 | .7 |
| | | | | | | % Officers', Directors' Owners' Comp/Sales | (15) | 4.7 | (10)  2.5 |
| | | | | | | | | 8.0 | 12.8 |
| 17164M | 87736M | 408590M | 175985M | 239719M | 8474148M | Net Sales ($) | | 9345098M | 2727152M |
| 1254M | 10154M | 72660M | 67470M | 259585M | 543401M | Total Assets ($) | | 1502810M | 1168406M |

M = $ thousand    MM = $ million
See Pages viii through xx for Explanation of Ratios and Data

© RMA 2024

# PROFESSIONAL SERVICES—Human Resources Consulting Services  NAICS 541612

## Comparative Historical Data | Current Data Sorted by Sales

| Comparative Historical Data ||||| | Current Data Sorted by Sales |||||||
|---|---|---|---|---|---|---|---|---|---|---|---|
| | | | | | Type of Statement | | | | | | |
| | 8 | 7 | 3 | | Unqualified | | | | 2 | | 3 |
| | | 3 | 3 | | Reviewed | | | | 1 | | 1 |
| | 2 | 1 | 2 | | Compiled | | | | | 1 | 1 |
| | 2 | 3 | 2 | | Tax Returns | | | | | 1 | 1 |
| | 32 | 30 | 27 | | Other | | 4 | 4 | 7 | 3 | 9 |
| | 4/1/21-3/31/22 | 4/1/22-3/31/23 | 4/1/23-3/31/24 | | | | 4 (4/1-9/30/23) | | 30 (10/1/23-3/31/24) | | |
| | ALL | ALL | ALL | | | 0-1MM | 1-3MM | 3-5MM | 5-10MM | 10-25MM | 25MM & OVER |
| | 44 | 44 | 37 | | NUMBER OF STATEMENTS | 4 | 4 | 4 | 10 | 5 | 14 |
| | % | % | % | | ASSETS | % | % | % | % | % | % |
| | 35.1 | 38.5 | 28.7 | | Cash & Equivalents | | | | 17.7 | | 23.8 |
| | 33.3 | 28.6 | 27.2 | | Trade Receivables (net) | | | | 40.7 | | 23.2 |
| | .2 | .0 | .0 | | Inventory | D | | | .0 | | .0 |
| | 5.8 | 11.4 | 9.2 | | All Other Current | A | | | 9.9 | | 14.0 |
| | 74.3 | 78.5 | 65.1 | | Total Current | T | | | 68.2 | | 61.0 |
| | 6.9 | 6.3 | 4.2 | | Fixed Assets (net) | A | | | 3.4 | | 5.9 |
| | 8.9 | 4.9 | 15.0 | | Intangibles (net) | | | | 15.2 | | 20.1 |
| | 9.9 | 10.3 | 15.8 | | All Other Non-Current | N | | | 13.1 | | 12.9 |
| | 100.0 | 100.0 | 100.0 | | Total | O | | | 100.0 | | 100.0 |
| | | | | | LIABILITIES | T | | | | | |
| | 2.3 | 5.5 | 6.6 | | Notes Payable-Short Term | | | | 13.5 | | 2.1 |
| | 1.7 | 1.1 | 1.2 | | Cur. Mat.-L.T.D. | A | | | 1.0 | | 2.5 |
| | 8.9 | 8.6 | 4.3 | | Trade Payables | V | | | 6.7 | | 5.1 |
| | .2 | .1 | .0 | | Income Taxes Payable | A | | | .1 | | .0 |
| | 24.3 | 25.8 | 36.8 | | All Other Current | I | | | 62.0 | | 27.7 |
| | 37.3 | 41.0 | 49.0 | | Total Current | L | | | 83.3 | | 37.3 |
| | 17.3 | 7.9 | 11.7 | | Long-Term Debt | A | | | 14.3 | | 17.8 |
| | .0 | .3 | .0 | | Deferred Taxes | B | | | .0 | | .0 |
| | 13.6 | 6.3 | 2.5 | | All Other Non-Current | L | | | 2.3 | | 4.0 |
| | 31.8 | 44.5 | 36.9 | | Net Worth | E | | | .1 | | 40.9 |
| | 100.0 | 100.0 | 100.0 | | Total Liabilities & Net Worth | | | | 100.0 | | 100.0 |
| | | | | | INCOME DATA | | | | | | |
| | 100.0 | 100.0 | 100.0 | | Net Sales | | | | 100.0 | | 100.0 |
| | 91.6 | 95.2 | 96.2 | | Gross Profit | | | | | | |
| | 8.4 | 4.8 | 3.8 | | Operating Expenses | | | | 101.0 | | 97.6 |
| | .4 | 1.1 | .7 | | Operating Profit | | | | -1.0 | | 2.4 |
| | 8.0 | 3.7 | 3.1 | | All Other Expenses (net) | | | | 1.2 | | 1.3 |
| | | | | | Profit Before Taxes | | | | -2.2 | | 1.0 |
| | | | | | RATIOS | | | | | | |
| | 4.3 | 4.0 | 3.7 | | | | | | 1.5 | | 2.3 |
| | 2.4 | 1.9 | 1.3 | | Current | | | | 1.2 | | 1.4 |
| | 1.2 | 1.2 | .7 | | | | | | .5 | | 1.1 |
| | 4.0 | 3.5 | 2.7 | | | | | | 1.5 | | 2.2 |
| | 2.1 | 1.7 | 1.3 | | Quick | | | | 1.0 | | 1.2 |
| | 1.1 | .9 | .6 | | | | | | .4 | | .6 |
| 3 | 139.2 | 1 | 436.3 | 1 | 351.7 | | | | 27 | 13.7 | 2 | 194.6 |
| 43 | 8.4 | 26 | 14.0 | 35 | 10.3 | Sales/Receivables | | | | 43 | 8.4 | 34 | 10.8 |
| 69 | 5.3 | 45 | 8.2 | 63 | 5.8 | | | | | 76 | 4.8 | 62 | 5.9 |
| | | | | | Cost of Sales/Inventory | | | | | | |
| | | | | | Cost of Sales/Payables | | | | | | |
| | 4.3 | 5.9 | 8.4 | | | | | | 12.1 | | 9.3 |
| | 9.1 | 10.0 | 20.0 | | Sales/Working Capital | | | | 50.7 | | 17.4 |
| | 36.9 | 144.7 | -21.6 | | | | | | -6.7 | | NM |
| | 72.4 | 158.0 | 244.4 | | | | | | | | 326.5 |
| (24) | 28.0 | (23) | 14.9 | (24) | 3.3 | EBIT/Interest | | | | | | (11) | 3.3 |
| | 2.3 | 5.1 | -4.7 | | | | | | | | -5.1 |
| | | | | | Net Profit + Depr., Dep., Amort./Cur. Mat. L/T/D | | | | | | |
| | .0 | .0 | .0 | | | | | | .0 | | .1 |
| | .0 | .1 | .1 | | Fixed/Worth | | | | NM | | .3 |
| | .3 | .4 | -.3 | | | | | | .0 | | -.3 |
| | .5 | .4 | .3 | | | | | | 1.7 | | .7 |
| | 1.1 | 1.1 | 1.9 | | Debt/Worth | | | | NM | | 1.9 |
| | 5.8 | 4.3 | -3.3 | | | | | | -1.9 | | -3.0 |
| | 95.9 | 73.8 | 98.3 | | % Profit Before Taxes/Tangible Net Worth | | | | | | |
| (35) | 43.1 | (39) | 28.3 | (25) | 14.6 | | | | | | | |
| | 8.8 | 8.1 | -4.5 | | | | | | | | |
| | 39.8 | 36.3 | 19.8 | | % Profit Before Taxes/Total Assets | | | | 7.8 | | 29.4 |
| | 15.4 | 14.4 | 6.5 | | | | | | 2.8 | | 12.8 |
| | 3.4 | 3.0 | -3.2 | | | | | | -11.7 | | -4.8 |
| | 943.7 | 927.8 | UND | | | | | | UND | | 417.6 |
| | 200.6 | 165.1 | 210.1 | | Sales/Net Fixed Assets | | | | 236.7 | | 92.9 |
| | 45.3 | 40.0 | 57.0 | | | | | | 79.3 | | 29.2 |
| | 6.2 | 7.0 | 6.1 | | | | | | 6.3 | | 11.2 |
| | 3.2 | 4.2 | 3.2 | | Sales/Total Assets | | | | 3.4 | | 3.4 |
| | 1.2 | 2.1 | 1.3 | | | | | | 1.4 | | .9 |
| | .1 | .1 | .1 | | | | | | | | |
| (18) | .3 | (27) | .2 | (15) | .2 | % Depr., Dep., Amort./Sales | | | | | | |
| | 1.1 | .9 | .8 | | | | | | | | |
| | | | | | % Officers', Directors' Owners' Comp/Sales | | | | | | |
| | 3318523M | 3950512M | 9403342M | | Net Sales ($) | 9516M | 15563M | 78777M | 76782M | 9222704M |
| | 1228853M | 1089636M | 954524M | | Total Assets ($) | 3331M | 19152M | 34302M | 19915M | 877824M |

© RMA 2024       M = $ thousand    MM = $ million
See Pages viii through xx for Explanation of Ratios and Data

# PROFESSIONAL SERVICES—Marketing Consulting Services  NAICS 541613

## Current Data Sorted by Assets | Comparative Historical Data

| | | | | | | | Type of Statement | | |
|---|---|---|---|---|---|---|---|---|---|
| | | | 5 | 5 | 2 | 6 | Unqualified | 26 | 10 |
| | | 2 | 5 | 6 | 1 | 1 | Reviewed | 16 | 7 |
| 13 | 7 | 7 | 7 | 2 | | | Compiled | 9 | 4 |
| 10 | 20 | 41 | 47 | 13 | 1 | Tax Returns | 41 | 21 |
| 10 | 30 (4/1-9/30/23) | | 184 (10/1/23-3/31/24) | | 20 | Other | 148 | 100 |
| 0-500M | 500M-2MM | 2-10MM | 10-50MM | 50-100MM | 100-250MM | | 4/1/19-3/31/20 ALL | 4/1/20-3/31/21 ALL |
| 23 | 29 | 58 | 60 | 16 | 28 | NUMBER OF STATEMENTS | 240 | 142 |
| % | % | % | % | % | % | ASSETS | % | % |
| 54.7 | 36.3 | 23.2 | 19.5 | 14.2 | 20.6 | Cash & Equivalents | 23.9 | 31.2 |
| 12.8 | 20.5 | 35.5 | 33.6 | 38.1 | 21.2 | Trade Receivables (net) | 32.3 | 24.5 |
| 1.2 | 5.5 | 6.4 | 3.7 | 1.2 | .6 | Inventory | 2.6 | 3.8 |
| 7.0 | 10.6 | 5.0 | 6.1 | 9.5 | 11.9 | All Other Current | 5.3 | 6.5 |
| 75.8 | 72.8 | 70.0 | 62.9 | 62.9 | 54.2 | Total Current | 64.1 | 66.0 |
| 5.8 | 11.0 | 10.3 | 9.5 | 6.0 | 6.2 | Fixed Assets (net) | 10.7 | 11.0 |
| 3.2 | 11.6 | 7.8 | 17.3 | 22.1 | 30.2 | Intangibles (net) | 15.4 | 15.9 |
| 15.2 | 4.6 | 11.8 | 10.3 | 9.0 | 9.3 | All Other Non-Current | 9.8 | 7.2 |
| 100.0 | 100.0 | 100.0 | 100.0 | 100.0 | 100.0 | Total | 100.0 | 100.0 |
| | | | | | | LIABILITIES | | |
| 42.9 | 5.3 | 7.7 | 4.1 | 3.1 | 1.1 | Notes Payable-Short Term | 15.7 | 11.9 |
| 13.1 | 1.2 | 1.8 | 2.2 | 8.0 | 3.6 | Cur. Mat.-L.T.D. | 4.4 | 1.7 |
| 4.0 | 8.0 | 11.6 | 14.4 | 7.7 | 9.5 | Trade Payables | 12.9 | 9.6 |
| .1 | .0 | .5 | .7 | .1 | .1 | Income Taxes Payable | .1 | .1 |
| 24.8 | 23.9 | 18.8 | 31.1 | 18.7 | 20.0 | All Other Current | 23.3 | 19.7 |
| 84.9 | 38.4 | 40.4 | 52.6 | 37.5 | 34.3 | Total Current | 56.4 | 43.0 |
| 25.3 | 27.4 | 17.0 | 11.2 | 30.4 | 27.4 | Long-Term Debt | 18.2 | 26.1 |
| .0 | .0 | .0 | .0 | .6 | .0 | Deferred Taxes | .1 | .2 |
| 6.0 | 5.1 | 12.2 | 9.6 | 25.4 | 7.7 | All Other Non-Current | 6.5 | 5.5 |
| -16.2 | 29.1 | 30.4 | 26.5 | 6.1 | 30.6 | Net Worth | 18.8 | 25.2 |
| 100.0 | 100.0 | 100.0 | 100.0 | 100.0 | 100.0 | Total Liabilties & Net Worth | 100.0 | 100.0 |
| | | | | | | INCOME DATA | | |
| 100.0 | 100.0 | 100.0 | 100.0 | 100.0 | 100.0 | Net Sales | 100.0 | 100.0 |
| | | | | | | Gross Profit | | |
| 90.4 | 91.9 | 93.0 | 93.8 | 86.4 | 94.2 | Operating Expenses | 91.7 | 90.5 |
| 9.6 | 8.1 | 7.0 | 6.2 | 13.6 | 5.8 | Operating Profit | 8.3 | 9.5 |
| .6 | 1.3 | 1.1 | 1.6 | 1.6 | 3.4 | All Other Expenses (net) | 2.0 | -.1 |
| 9.0 | 6.8 | 5.9 | 4.6 | 12.1 | 2.5 | Profit Before Taxes | 6.3 | 9.6 |
| | | | | | | RATIOS | | |
| 6.1 | 7.1 | 4.0 | 1.9 | 2.9 | 3.0 | | 2.5 | 3.7 |
| 1.9 | 2.0 | 2.2 | 1.3 | 1.8 | 2.1 | Current | 1.3 | 1.8 |
| .7 | 1.1 | 1.1 | 1.0 | 1.0 | .9 | | .8 | 1.1 |
| 6.1 | 3.8 | 3.1 | 1.8 | 2.7 | 2.5 | | 2.1 | 3.4 |
| 1.9 | 1.6 | 1.5 | 1.0 | 1.1 | 1.3 | Quick | 1.2 | 1.6 |
| .3 | .9 | .9 | .9 | .8 | .6 | | .9 | .8 |
| 0 UND | 0 UND | 21 17.6 | 36 10.0 | 35 10.4 | 26 14.0 | | 9 39.7 | 7 48.8 |
| 0 UND | 5 67.1 | 39 9.3 | 55 6.6 | 69 5.3 | 68 5.4 | Sales/Receivables | 41 8.8 | 40 9.1 |
| 0 UND | 46 8.0 | 61 6.0 | 72 5.1 | 101 3.6 | 94 3.9 | | 69 5.3 | 62 5.9 |
| | | | | | | Cost of Sales/Inventory | | |
| | | | | | | Cost of Sales/Payables | | |
| 7.9 | 4.9 | 4.1 | 6.6 | 3.8 | 3.1 | | 7.5 | 4.1 |
| 30.2 | 12.9 | 9.1 | 16.4 | 10.7 | 5.2 | Sales/Working Capital | 19.5 | 9.6 |
| -58.8 | 53.3 | 301.1 | NM | NM | -20.0 | | -40.7 | 57.2 |
| 97.6 | 56.4 | 125.0 | 30.3 | 23.5 | 14.2 | | 30.5 | 49.1 |
| (13) -.3 | (17) 2.0 | (35) 10.0 | (46) 6.4 | (14) 9.0 | (24) 1.4 | EBIT/Interest | (181) 6.8 | (102) 11.0 |
| -5.2 | -4.4 | 2.2 | 1.0 | 5.7 | -.2 | | .4 | 1.8 |
| | | | | | | Net Profit + Depr., Dep., Amort./Cur. Mat. L/T/D | 11.5 | 12.3 |
| | | | | | | | (21) 4.2 | (10) 4.4 |
| | | | | | | | .9 | .9 |
| .0 | .0 | .0 | .1 | .2 | .2 | | .0 | .0 |
| .0 | .0 | .1 | .6 | -1.7 | .5 | Fixed/Worth | .3 | .2 |
| .2 | .7 | .8 | -2.1 | -.2 | -.1 | | -.9 | 5.2 |
| .2 | .3 | .5 | 1.6 | 5.6 | 1.8 | | .8 | .8 |
| 2.1 | 2.5 | 1.8 | 6.7 | -33.8 | 8.1 | Debt/Worth | 4.0 | 2.5 |
| -2.1 | 22.8 | 9.4 | -18.4 | -3.0 | -2.8 | | -3.7 | -5.4 |
| 214.5 | 138.6 | 120.5 | 109.8 | | 98.5 | % Profit Before Taxes/Tangible Net Worth | 119.4 | 118.8 |
| (14) 33.5 | (23) 52.5 | (47) 47.7 | (42) 32.9 | | (16) 24.2 | | (154) 50.5 | (98) 69.7 |
| -40.6 | -7.7 | 18.3 | 16.5 | | -6.7 | | 20.5 | 18.4 |
| 132.5 | 54.5 | 31.7 | 17.1 | 32.4 | 9.1 | % Profit Before Taxes/Total Assets | 34.2 | 49.9 |
| 14.7 | 24.5 | 18.3 | 7.8 | 17.0 | 4.1 | | 11.6 | 19.4 |
| -16.7 | -1.6 | 5.3 | -.1 | 6.2 | -4.1 | | 1.6 | 2.5 |
| UND | UND | 999.8 | 221.3 | 87.0 | 65.0 | | 346.4 | 958.7 |
| UND | 436.8 | 128.9 | 41.3 | 58.4 | 41.2 | Sales/Net Fixed Assets | 70.7 | 69.4 |
| 253.1 | 62.0 | 27.4 | 12.0 | 31.5 | 17.6 | | 23.8 | 22.0 |
| 24.8 | 6.4 | 3.7 | 2.8 | 2.4 | 1.6 | | 4.8 | 4.0 |
| 13.5 | 3.9 | 2.8 | 1.8 | 1.3 | 1.3 | Sales/Total Assets | 2.9 | 2.4 |
| 5.1 | 1.4 | 1.7 | 1.3 | .9 | .8 | | 1.7 | 1.5 |
| | | | .1 | .3 | 1.1 | | .3 | .3 |
| | | (25) .5 | (31) 1.9 | | (14) 1.7 | % Depr., Dep., Amort./Sales | (120) .7 | (63) 1.0 |
| | | | 1.3 | 2.2 | 2.9 | | 1.8 | 2.3 |
| 5.6 | 4.1 | 1.5 | | | | | 3.0 | 3.3 |
| (12) 10.2 | (10) 7.8 | (16) 2.8 | | | | % Officers', Directors' Owners' Comp/Sales | (65) 5.4 | (41) 8.5 |
| 16.1 | 10.6 | 4.4 | | | | | 11.4 | 21.6 |
| 72136M | 178944M | 808265M | 3074866M | 2033855M | 5053751M | Net Sales ($) | 9528398M | 9413191M |
| 4970M | 35917M | 269538M | 1503004M | 1072815M | 4111136M | Total Assets ($) | 5379358M | 3991120M |

© RMA 2024    M = $ thousand    MM = $ million
See Pages viii through xx for Explanation of Ratios and Data

## PROFESSIONAL SERVICES—Marketing Consulting Services  NAICS 541613

### Comparative Historical Data | Current Data Sorted by Sales

| | | | | | | | | | | | | | |
|---|---|---|---|---|---|---|---|---|---|---|---|---|---|
| | 12 | | 17 | | 13 | **Type of Statement** | | | | | 1 | | 12 |
| | 8 | | 13 | | 13 | Unqualified | | | | 1 | 5 | | 7 |
| | 6 | | 10 | | 9 | Reviewed | | | 1 | 3 | 3 | | 1 |
| | 17 | | 32 | | 28 | Compiled | 1 | | 5 | 2 | 6 | | 2 |
| | 100 | | 148 | | 151 | Tax Returns | 7 | 6 | 10 | 18 | 32 | | 77 |
| | 4/1/21- | | 4/1/22- | | 4/1/23- | Other | 4 | 10 | 10 | | | | |
| | 3/31/22 | | 3/31/23 | | 3/31/24 | | 30 (4/1-9/30/23) | | | 184 (10/1/23-3/31/24) | | | |
| | ALL | | ALL | | ALL | | 0-1MM | 1-3MM | 3-5MM | 5-10MM | 10-25MM | | 25MM & OVER |
| | 143 | | 220 | | 214 | **NUMBER OF STATEMENTS** | 12 | 16 | 16 | 24 | 47 | | 99 |
| | % | | % | | % | **ASSETS** | % | % | % | % | % | | % |
| | 34.7 | | 27.4 | | 26.3 | Cash & Equivalents | 32.5 | 38.5 | 41.5 | 30.7 | 26.4 | | 20.0 |
| | 25.3 | | 28.1 | | 28.8 | Trade Receivables (net) | 9.4 | 15.7 | 18.1 | 32.0 | 34.9 | | 31.3 |
| | 2.6 | | 2.0 | | 3.8 | Inventory | 2.4 | 3.9 | 1.4 | 3.1 | 7.6 | | 2.7 |
| | 4.5 | | 6.4 | | 7.5 | All Other Current | 10.7 | 17.3 | 4.7 | 4.6 | 4.2 | | 8.4 |
| | 67.0 | | 63.9 | | 66.4 | Total Current | 55.0 | 75.3 | 65.6 | 70.3 | 73.1 | | 62.4 |
| | 9.8 | | 12.7 | | 8.8 | Fixed Assets (net) | 21.2 | 6.2 | 7.4 | 15.0 | 5.1 | | 8.2 |
| | 16.9 | | 14.2 | | 14.5 | Intangibles (net) | 5.9 | 12.1 | 10.6 | 6.7 | 12.8 | | 19.3 |
| | 6.3 | | 9.2 | | 10.2 | All Other Non-Current | 17.9 | 6.4 | 16.4 | 8.0 | 9.0 | | 10.1 |
| | 100.0 | | 100.0 | | 100.0 | Total | 100.0 | 100.0 | 100.0 | 100.0 | 100.0 | | 100.0 |
| | | | | | | **LIABILITIES** | | | | | | | |
| | 8.0 | | 9.9 | | 9.0 | Notes Payable-Short Term | 9.7 | 36.9 | 22.0 | 10.9 | 5.7 | | 3.3 |
| | 3.0 | | 2.1 | | 3.7 | Cur. Mat.-L.T.D. | 7.7 | 13.8 | .8 | .7 | 2.8 | | 3.3 |
| | 11.5 | | 10.4 | | 10.6 | Trade Payables | 3.4 | 2.0 | 6.9 | 9.6 | 11.8 | | 13.0 |
| | .0 | | .1 | | .4 | Income Taxes Payable | .1 | .0 | .0 | .4 | .6 | | .4 |
| | 19.6 | | 22.8 | | 23.7 | All Other Current | 15.8 | 25.8 | 14.5 | 20.3 | 25.7 | | 25.8 |
| | 42.1 | | 45.2 | | 47.3 | Total Current | 36.7 | 78.6 | 44.2 | 42.0 | 46.5 | | 45.8 |
| | 22.9 | | 16.2 | | 20.0 | Long-Term Debt | 47.1 | 23.1 | 20.7 | 22.1 | 14.5 | | 18.3 |
| | .4 | | .1 | | .1 | Deferred Taxes | .0 | .0 | .0 | .0 | .0 | | .1 |
| | 7.0 | | 8.0 | | 10.2 | All Other Non-Current | 8.7 | 1.4 | 8.6 | 15.1 | 11.1 | | 10.5 |
| | 27.6 | | 30.4 | | 22.3 | Net Worth | 7.5 | -3.0 | 26.5 | 20.8 | 27.9 | | 25.3 |
| | 100.0 | | 100.0 | | 100.0 | Total Liabilities & Net Worth | 100.0 | 100.0 | 100.0 | 100.0 | 100.0 | | 100.0 |
| | | | | | | **INCOME DATA** | | | | | | | |
| | 100.0 | | 100.0 | | 100.0 | Net Sales | 100.0 | 100.0 | 100.0 | 100.0 | 100.0 | | 100.0 |
| | | | | | | Gross Profit | | | | | | | |
| | 90.3 | | 91.2 | | 92.5 | Operating Expenses | 88.0 | 87.9 | 99.0 | 88.9 | 94.7 | | 92.5 |
| | 9.7 | | 8.8 | | 7.5 | Operating Profit | 12.0 | 12.1 | 1.0 | 11.1 | 5.3 | | 7.5 |
| | -.7 | | 1.6 | | 1.5 | All Other Expenses (net) | 4.3 | .7 | 1.4 | 1.0 | 1.5 | | 1.5 |
| | 10.4 | | 7.2 | | 6.0 | Profit Before Taxes | 7.7 | 11.4 | -.4 | 10.1 | 3.8 | | 6.0 |
| | | | | | | **RATIOS** | | | | | | | |
| | 3.6 | | 2.8 | | 3.4 | | 7.8 | 5.9 | 9.8 | 5.1 | 3.3 | | 2.4 |
| | 1.6 | | 1.5 | | 1.6 | Current | 3.7 | 1.9 | 3.7 | 1.8 | 1.9 | | 1.4 |
| | 1.2 | | 1.0 | | 1.0 | | .9 | .9 | 1.4 | 1.0 | 1.1 | | 1.0 |
| | 3.4 | | 2.5 | | 2.6 | | 7.8 | 4.7 | 7.3 | 3.4 | 2.9 | | 2.0 |
| | 1.5 | | 1.3 | | 1.3 | Quick | 3.7 | 1.3 | 3.3 | 1.5 | 1.4 | | 1.1 |
| | 1.0 | | .8 | | .8 | | .3 | .4 | 1.4 | .9 | .8 | | .8 |
| 7 | 54.2 | 5 | 74.6 | 12 | 30.5 | | 0 UND | 0 UND | 0 UND | 0 UND | 33 11.1 | 30 | 12.1 |
| 39 | 9.4 | 40 | 9.1 | 43 | 8.5 | Sales/Receivables | 0 UND | 0 UND | 1 516.9 | 27 13.7 | 49 7.4 | 49 | 7.4 |
| 68 | 5.4 | 70 | 5.2 | 70 | 5.2 | | 19 19.4 | 9 40.9 | 44 8.3 | 49 7.5 | 70 5.2 | 83 | 4.4 |
| | | | | | | Cost of Sales/Inventory | | | | | | | |
| | | | | | | Cost of Sales/Payables | | | | | | | |
| | 5.3 | | 5.2 | | 4.9 | | 4.5 | 6.5 | 3.0 | 4.9 | 4.9 | | 4.9 |
| | 11.4 | | 13.8 | | 11.6 | Sales/Working Capital | 6.8 | 14.4 | 6.0 | 31.7 | 9.5 | | 13.0 |
| | 33.7 | | -179.1 | | UND | | UND | NM | 19.2 | NM | 272.3 | | -143.1 |
| | 98.9 | | 47.8 | | 46.9 | | | 51.0 | | 83.0 | 36.0 | | 30.3 |
| (101) | 16.1 | (144) | 9.6 | (149) | 6.1 | EBIT/Interest | (11) 3.4 | | (15) 3.4 | (29) 7.8 | (78) 6.6 | | |
| | 4.0 | | 1.2 | | .2 | | | -15.5 | | -4.6 | 1.0 | | 1.0 |
| | 7.9 | | 7.8 | | 14.5 | Net Profit + Depr., Dep., | | | | | | | 16.8 |
| (11) | 3.9 | (22) | 3.4 | (18) | 5.4 | Amort./Cur. Mat. L/T/D | | | | | (14) 6.9 | | |
| | 3.2 | | 1.9 | | 1.9 | | | | | | | | 3.6 |
| | .0 | | .0 | | .0 | | .0 | .0 | .0 | .0 | .0 | | .1 |
| | .2 | | .3 | | .2 | Fixed/Worth | .0 | .0 | .1 | .0 | .1 | | .5 |
| | UND | | 5.0 | | 6.0 | | 5.0 | 2.2 | .2 | .6 | -9.6 | | -.7 |
| | 1.1 | | .8 | | 1.0 | | .7 | .3 | .2 | .3 | .5 | | 1.8 |
| | 3.0 | | 2.7 | | 3.5 | Debt/Worth | 5.1 | 4.3 | .9 | 2.3 | 2.3 | | 6.2 |
| | -4.6 | | -11.8 | | -7.1 | | -2.3 | -3.2 | NM | 14.6 | -19.0 | | -5.1 |
| | 208.3 | | 109.4 | | 122.4 | % Profit Before Taxes/Tangible | | 299.1 | 41.8 | 142.3 | 83.6 | | 129.3 |
| (95) | 75.8 | (161) | 48.2 | (149) | 43.3 | Net Worth | (11) 66.7 | (12) 3.1 | (19) 47.4 | (34) 52.0 | (66) 41.5 | | |
| | 30.2 | | 12.4 | | 12.7 | | | 6.2 | -78.8 | 18.8 | 9.0 | | 17.1 |
| | 54.3 | | 37.6 | | 30.8 | | 43.3 | 109.0 | 20.5 | 44.8 | 30.6 | | 25.3 |
| | 22.4 | | 12.5 | | 9.4 | % Profit Before Taxes/Total Assets | 9.0 | 11.2 | -1.6 | 22.0 | 11.6 | | 8.2 |
| | 5.9 | | 1.8 | | -.1 | | -9.2 | -12.4 | -44.1 | 6.5 | .9 | | .1 |
| | 804.0 | | 408.1 | | 999.8 | | UND | UND | UND | UND | 999.8 | | 176.5 |
| | 84.0 | | 81.9 | | 80.9 | Sales/Net Fixed Assets | UND | UND | 144.6 | 311.9 | 168.8 | | 45.7 |
| | 25.3 | | 19.4 | | 24.3 | | 28.2 | 87.8 | 20.9 | 12.2 | 34.3 | | 20.0 |
| | 4.5 | | 3.9 | | 4.2 | | 7.3 | 14.5 | 6.4 | 5.4 | 4.8 | | 2.9 |
| | 2.8 | | 2.4 | | 2.2 | Sales/Total Assets | 2.7 | 3.6 | 2.2 | 3.4 | 2.8 | | 1.8 |
| | 1.3 | | 1.4 | | 1.3 | | .6 | 1.3 | 1.3 | 1.6 | 1.7 | | 1.2 |
| | .2 | | .3 | | .3 | | | | | | .1 | | .3 |
| (61) | .8 | (112) | .8 | (88) | 1.1 | % Depr., Dep., Amort./Sales | | | | (20) .6 | (50) 1.3 | | |
| | 3.0 | | 2.4 | | 2.2 | | | | | | 1.9 | | 2.2 |
| | 2.4 | | 1.4 | | 1.7 | % Officers', Directors' | | | | | | | |
| (37) | 5.9 | (57) | 4.6 | (46) | 4.9 | Owners' Comp/Sales | | | | | | | |
| | 14.4 | | 8.8 | | 10.2 | | | | | | | | |
| | 7110420M | | 8485739M | | 11221817M | Net Sales ($) | 7199M | 28541M | 65466M | 168414M | 787959M | | 10164238M |
| | 3920715M | | 4622387M | | 6997380M | Total Assets ($) | 8843M | 9993M | 34610M | 68580M | 442667M | | 6432687M |

© RMA 2024  M = $ thousand  MM = $ million
See Pages viii through xx for Explanation of Ratios and Data

# PROFESSIONAL SERVICES—Process, Physical Distribution, and Logistics Consulting Services  NAICS 541614

## Current Data Sorted by Assets | Comparative Historical Data

| | | | | | | | | | |
|---|---|---|---|---|---|---|---|---|---|
| | | | 2 | 5 | 5 | 7 | Type of Statement | | |
| | | 1 | 5 | 4 | | 1 | Unqualified | 13 | 8 |
| | | 4 | 7 | | | | Reviewed | 12 | 13 |
| 2 | | | 5 | | | | Compiled | 13 | 5 |
| 6 | | 16 | 28 | 43 | 9 | 14 | Tax Returns | 12 | 11 |
| | 0-500M | 26 (4/1-9/30/23) 500M-2MM | 2-10MM | 139 (10/1/23-3/31/24) 10-50MM | 50-100MM | 100-250MM | Other | 76 4/1/19- 3/31/20 ALL | 65 4/1/20- 3/31/21 ALL |
| 9 | | 21 | 47 | 52 | 14 | 22 | NUMBER OF STATEMENTS | 126 | 102 |
| % | | % | % | % | % | % | ASSETS | % | % |
| | | 27.6 | 16.4 | 12.5 | 24.0 | 9.9 | Cash & Equivalents | 19.5 | 21.9 |
| | | 35.1 | 38.7 | 37.4 | 24.9 | 30.9 | Trade Receivables (net) | 40.8 | 34.4 |
| | | .8 | 7.4 | 6.6 | 7.1 | 4.0 | Inventory | 3.8 | 4.1 |
| | | 2.9 | 6.7 | 5.2 | 3.1 | 10.1 | All Other Current | 3.7 | 2.8 |
| | | 66.4 | 69.3 | 61.7 | 59.0 | 55.0 | Total Current | 67.8 | 63.1 |
| | | 11.5 | 16.3 | 19.0 | 20.5 | 20.7 | Fixed Assets (net) | 17.5 | 17.2 |
| | | 7.9 | 4.9 | 7.2 | 10.4 | 13.7 | Intangibles (net) | 8.6 | 9.6 |
| | | 14.2 | 9.5 | 12.1 | 10.1 | 10.7 | All Other Non-Current | 6.0 | 10.0 |
| | | 100.0 | 100.0 | 100.0 | 100.0 | 100.0 | Total | 100.0 | 100.0 |
| | | | | | | | LIABILITIES | | |
| | | 12.8 | 11.3 | 6.8 | 3.2 | 11.3 | Notes Payable-Short Term | 10.5 | 8.6 |
| | | 1.4 | 1.1 | 4.3 | 4.1 | 6.4 | Cur. Mat.-L.T.D. | 1.6 | 2.5 |
| | | 11.4 | 18.3 | 21.0 | 16.5 | 17.7 | Trade Payables | 17.4 | 15.1 |
| | | .4 | .2 | .2 | .6 | .5 | Income Taxes Payable | .0 | .1 |
| | | 18.7 | 15.8 | 13.5 | 17.1 | 10.4 | All Other Current | 12.5 | 10.8 |
| | | 44.6 | 46.6 | 45.8 | 41.4 | 46.3 | Total Current | 42.0 | 37.0 |
| | | 12.7 | 7.0 | 14.4 | 21.0 | 23.4 | Long-Term Debt | 13.6 | 18.7 |
| | | .0 | .3 | .4 | .2 | .2 | Deferred Taxes | .5 | .2 |
| | | 2.2 | 7.8 | 6.9 | 8.7 | 8.0 | All Other Non-Current | 4.7 | 7.4 |
| | | 40.4 | 38.3 | 32.4 | 28.7 | 22.1 | Net Worth | 39.2 | 36.7 |
| | | 100.0 | 100.0 | 100.0 | 100.0 | 100.0 | Total Liabilities & Net Worth | 100.0 | 100.0 |
| | | | | | | | INCOME DATA | | |
| | | 100.0 | 100.0 | 100.0 | 100.0 | 100.0 | Net Sales | 100.0 | 100.0 |
| | | | | | | | Gross Profit | | |
| | | 94.1 | 92.1 | 92.4 | 96.0 | 97.5 | Operating Expenses | 93.9 | 89.1 |
| | | 5.9 | 7.9 | 7.6 | 4.0 | 2.5 | Operating Profit | 6.1 | 10.9 |
| | | .3 | 1.7 | .8 | 1.2 | 2.0 | All Other Expenses (net) | .8 | .1 |
| | | 5.6 | 6.2 | 6.8 | 2.8 | .5 | Profit Before Taxes | 5.4 | 10.8 |
| | | | | | | | RATIOS | | |
| | | 2.3 | 3.3 | 2.4 | 1.6 | 2.0 | | 2.8 | 3.1 |
| | | 1.5 | 1.7 | 1.3 | 1.4 | 1.3 | Current | 1.6 | 1.8 |
| | | 1.1 | 1.1 | 1.0 | 1.2 | 1.0 | | 1.1 | 1.1 |
| | | 2.3 | 3.0 | 2.1 | 1.4 | 1.6 | | 2.7 | 2.5 |
| | | 1.5 | 1.4 | 1.1 | 1.2 | .9 | Quick | 1.4 | 1.5 |
| | | .7 | .8 | .8 | .9 | .7 | | .9 | .9 |
| | 0 UND | 27 13.6 | 24 15.3 | 22 16.7 | 28 12.9 | | | 27 13.5 | 26 14.2 |
| | 23 16.0 | 38 9.5 | 41 9.0 | 36 10.2 | 38 9.7 | | Sales/Receivables | 42 8.7 | 43 8.4 |
| | 35 10.4 | 53 6.9 | 74 4.9 | 70 5.2 | 47 7.8 | | | 63 5.8 | 68 5.4 |
| | | | | | | | Cost of Sales/Inventory | | |
| | | | | | | | Cost of Sales/Payables | | |
| | | 8.7 | 6.2 | 6.9 | 9.6 | 8.6 | | 6.4 | 4.8 |
| | | 29.8 | 11.5 | 23.2 | 26.8 | 20.0 | Sales/Working Capital | 15.7 | 12.7 |
| | | 379.4 | 163.3 | NM | 48.5 | NM | | 78.9 | 106.2 |
| | | 107.4 | 26.1 | 21.9 | 34.0 | 11.4 | | 23.6 | 36.0 |
| | (15) | 19.9 | (33) 8.9 | (45) 10.4 | (11) 8.2 | 4.1 | EBIT/Interest | (105) 7.8 | (78) 10.3 |
| | | -10.2 | .2 | 1.9 | 1.1 | .3 | | 2.0 | 3.9 |
| | | | | | | | Net Profit + Depr., Dep., Amort./Cur. Mat. L/T/D | 5.7 (16) 3.6 2.6 | 13.6 (13) 5.3 2.6 |
| | | .0 | .0 | .1 | .3 | .6 | | .1 | .0 |
| | | .1 | .3 | .6 | .6 | 2.6 | Fixed/Worth | .4 | .5 |
| | | 149.4 | 1.1 | 1.4 | NM | -1.1 | | 2.3 | 2.0 |
| | | .7 | .6 | 1.2 | 1.9 | 1.8 | | .8 | .8 |
| | | 1.3 | 1.3 | 2.7 | 2.7 | 15.2 | Debt/Worth | 2.1 | 1.8 |
| | | NM | 5.8 | 10.5 | NM | -9.4 | | 11.2 | 5.8 |
| | | 142.2 | 59.6 | 66.4 | 78.5 | 99.1 | | 75.7 | 85.8 |
| | (16) | 82.9 | (42) 25.4 | (46) 38.2 | (11) 19.8 | (12) 15.8 | % Profit Before Taxes/Tangible Net Worth | (107) 36.6 | (83) 44.8 |
| | | -15.5 | .1 | 9.8 | -7.5 | -4.6 | | 12.7 | 12.5 |
| | | 64.7 | 23.7 | 19.4 | 13.2 | 18.3 | | 23.2 | 30.6 |
| | | 36.7 | 9.5 | 10.0 | 7.0 | 5.2 | % Profit Before Taxes/Total Assets | 10.3 | 15.3 |
| | | -4.3 | -.1 | 2.4 | -2.7 | -3.6 | | 1.4 | 5.3 |
| | | UND | 407.4 | 130.5 | 87.4 | 47.4 | | 229.1 | 274.9 |
| | | 354.2 | 38.3 | 28.5 | 41.5 | 12.6 | Sales/Net Fixed Assets | 43.8 | 38.9 |
| | | 29.9 | 10.5 | 7.3 | 8.6 | 4.5 | | 12.0 | 8.7 |
| | | 8.3 | 5.9 | 4.4 | 5.2 | 5.3 | | 5.1 | 4.0 |
| | | 4.9 | 3.4 | 2.0 | 1.8 | 1.7 | Sales/Total Assets | 3.3 | 2.5 |
| | | 3.1 | 2.2 | 1.3 | .7 | .9 | | 1.9 | 1.3 |
| | | | .4 | .2 | .2 | .1 | | .4 | .5 |
| | | (29) | .9 | (42) 1.0 | (11) .6 | (14) .9 | % Depr., Dep., Amort./Sales | (78) 1.1 | (61) 1.7 |
| | | | 2.2 | 3.6 | 3.8 | 3.3 | | 3.5 | 4.1 |
| | | | | | | | % Officers', Directors' Owners' Comp/Sales | 1.3 (32) 2.8 6.1 | 2.0 (18) 4.6 11.1 |
| 26319M | | 127784M | 970921M | 3995067M | 3318672M | 7945052M | Net Sales ($) | 7411797M | 4919088M |
| 2927M | | 23353M | 254944M | 1314293M | 1030724M | 3263094M | Total Assets ($) | 2950869M | 2346678M |

M = $ thousand   MM = $ million
See Pages viii through xx for Explanation of Ratios and Data

© RMA 2024

## PROFESSIONAL SERVICES—Process, Physical Distribution, and Logistics Consulting Services  NAICS 541614

| Comparative Historical Data | | | | | Current Data Sorted by Sales | | | | | |
|---|---|---|---|---|---|---|---|---|---|---|
| | | | Type of Statement | | | | | | | |
| 14 | 13 | 19 | Unqualified | | | | 1 | 2 | 16 | |
| 13 | 17 | 11 | Reviewed | 1 | | | 1 | 1 | 8 | |
| 6 | 13 | 8 | Compiled | | 1 | | 2 | 2 | 3 | |
| 11 | 18 | 11 | Tax Returns | 2 | | 1 | 3 | 4 | 1 | |
| 81 | 98 | 116 | Other | 5 | 6 | 8 | 13 | 23 | 61 | |
| 4/1/21-3/31/22 | 4/1/22-3/31/23 | 4/1/23-3/31/24 | | | 26 (4/1-9/30/23) | | | 139 (10/1/23-3/31/24) | | |
| ALL | ALL | ALL | | 0-1MM | 1-3MM | 3-5MM | 5-10MM | 10-25MM | 25MM & OVER | |
| 125 | 159 | 165 | NUMBER OF STATEMENTS | 8 | 7 | 9 | 20 | 32 | 89 | |
| % | % | % | ASSETS | % | % | % | % | % | % | |
| 19.0 | 20.3 | 17.1 | Cash & Equivalents | | | | 28.2 | 18.8 | 14.0 | |
| 39.7 | 38.5 | 35.0 | Trade Receivables (net) | | | | 24.7 | 35.3 | 39.0 | |
| 6.7 | 5.6 | 5.4 | Inventory | | | | 6.7 | 12.5 | 3.9 | |
| 4.6 | 5.3 | 5.5 | All Other Current | | | | 6.8 | 6.0 | 6.3 | |
| 69.9 | 69.6 | 63.1 | Total Current | | | | 66.4 | 72.6 | 63.2 | |
| 15.1 | 16.9 | 18.6 | Fixed Assets (net) | | | | 18.9 | 12.3 | 17.4 | |
| 7.0 | 4.9 | 7.5 | Intangibles (net) | | | | 3.8 | 8.0 | 8.0 | |
| 8.0 | 8.5 | 10.7 | All Other Non-Current | | | | 10.9 | 7.1 | 11.4 | |
| 100.0 | 100.0 | 100.0 | Total | | | | 100.0 | 100.0 | 100.0 | |
| | | | LIABILITIES | | | | | | | |
| 9.1 | 7.2 | 10.1 | Notes Payable-Short Term | | | | 12.0 | 7.8 | 9.8 | |
| 2.2 | 2.0 | 3.2 | Cur. Mat.-L.T.D. | | | | 1.5 | 4.6 | 3.3 | |
| 18.9 | 16.2 | 17.5 | Trade Payables | | | | 15.9 | 14.4 | 20.8 | |
| .7 | .2 | .3 | Income Taxes Payable | | | | .0 | .2 | .3 | |
| 14.5 | 15.2 | 14.3 | All Other Current | | | | 7.6 | 16.0 | 14.2 | |
| 45.4 | 40.8 | 45.3 | Total Current | | | | 37.0 | 42.9 | 48.4 | |
| 11.9 | 14.7 | 14.3 | Long-Term Debt | | | | 11.6 | 12.8 | 14.0 | |
| .2 | .2 | .2 | Deferred Taxes | | | | .0 | .1 | .2 | |
| 2.8 | 7.9 | 6.7 | All Other Non-Current | | | | 6.4 | 6.4 | 7.5 | |
| 39.7 | 36.4 | 33.5 | Net Worth | | | | 45.0 | 37.8 | 29.9 | |
| 100.0 | 100.0 | 100.0 | Total Liabilities & Net Worth | | | | 100.0 | 100.0 | 100.0 | |
| | | | INCOME DATA | | | | | | | |
| 100.0 | 100.0 | 100.0 | Net Sales | | | | 100.0 | 100.0 | 100.0 | |
| | | | Gross Profit | | | | | | | |
| 91.9 | 91.6 | 93.0 | Operating Expenses | | | | 93.8 | 95.1 | 95.4 | |
| 8.1 | 8.4 | 7.0 | Operating Profit | | | | 6.2 | 4.9 | 4.6 | |
| -.4 | 1.1 | 1.2 | All Other Expenses (net) | | | | .2 | 1.0 | .9 | |
| 8.5 | 7.3 | 5.8 | Profit Before Taxes | | | | 6.0 | 3.9 | 3.7 | |
| | | | RATIOS | | | | | | | |
| 2.9 | 3.6 | 2.4 | | | | | 4.2 | 3.3 | 2.0 | |
| 1.7 | 1.7 | 1.4 | Current | | | | 1.5 | 2.0 | 1.3 | |
| 1.2 | 1.2 | 1.0 | | | | | 1.1 | 1.2 | 1.0 | |
| 2.6 | 3.3 | 2.2 | | | | | 3.3 | 2.3 | 1.6 | |
| 1.4 | 1.4 | 1.2 | Quick | | | | 1.4 | 1.5 | 1.1 | |
| .9 | .9 | .8 | | | | | .8 | .8 | .8 | |
| 29  12.8 | 26  13.9 | 22  16.6 | | | | | 13  28.1 | 28  13.1 | 27  13.5 | |
| 47  7.7 | 41  8.8 | 36  10.0 | Sales/Receivables | | | | 25  14.5 | 39  9.3 | 38  9.7 | |
| 69  5.3 | 59  6.2 | 55  6.6 | | | | | 43  8.5 | 62  5.9 | 55  6.6 | |
| | | | Cost of Sales/Inventory | | | | | | | |
| | | | Cost of Sales/Payables | | | | | | | |
| 5.5 | 5.6 | 8.1 | | | | | 9.6 | 5.5 | 9.2 | |
| 13.7 | 13.7 | 21.7 | Sales/Working Capital | | | | 20.3 | 9.2 | 25.1 | |
| 40.7 | 38.9 | 169.4 | | | | | 89.9 | 35.1 | 169.4 | |
| | | | | | | | 54.0 | 42.0 | 17.3 | |
| (98) 94.9 | (122) 71.0 | (131) 23.2 | EBIT/Interest | (14) 11.0 | (22) 11.9 | (79) 6.8 | | | | |
| 24.6 | 18.3 | 8.3 | | | | | -7.2 | 1.1 | 1.0 | |
| 7.8 | 4.9 | .8 | | | | | | | | |
| | | | | | | | | | 2.6 | |
| 73.5 | 21.3 | 2.3 | Net Profit + Depr., Dep., | | | | | (18) 1.2 | | |
| (16) 14.3 | (24) 4.8 | (25) 1.3 | Amort./Cur. Mat. L/T/D | | | | | | | |
| 2.4 | 1.8 | -.2 | | | | | | | -.1 | |
| .0 | .0 | .1 | | | | | .0 | .0 | .1 | |
| .2 | .3 | .5 | Fixed/Worth | | | | .4 | .2 | .7 | |
| .9 | 1.7 | 2.1 | | | | | 1.0 | 1.0 | 2.5 | |
| .7 | .6 | .9 | | | | | .6 | .8 | 1.4 | |
| 1.8 | 1.9 | 2.3 | Debt/Worth | | | | 1.2 | 1.4 | 3.2 | |
| 7.0 | 8.3 | 15.0 | | | | | 3.4 | 7.8 | 28.2 | |
| 90.9 | 95.8 | 81.6 | | | | | 124.0 | 55.3 | 74.0 | |
| (110) 60.5 | (134) 51.9 | (135) 35.1 | % Profit Before Taxes/Tangible Net Worth | (18) 42.4 | (28) 36.7 | (70) 31.9 | | | | |
| 29.2 | 18.0 | 6.3 | | | | | -21.5 | 3.7 | 8.2 | |
| 28.3 | 30.4 | 23.7 | | | | | 59.6 | 26.2 | 19.4 | |
| 18.1 | 13.8 | 9.8 | % Profit Before Taxes/Total Assets | | | | 15.9 | 10.5 | 8.0 | |
| 7.0 | 4.7 | .3 | | | | | -5.3 | .3 | .2 | |
| 555.6 | 292.0 | 246.8 | | | | | 889.3 | 536.4 | 150.9 | |
| 72.5 | 46.4 | 33.8 | Sales/Net Fixed Assets | | | | 33.4 | 52.2 | 28.3 | |
| 10.4 | 12.4 | 8.9 | | | | | 7.2 | 21.7 | 10.2 | |
| 4.8 | 5.5 | 5.7 | | | | | 7.5 | 5.6 | 6.0 | |
| 2.8 | 2.8 | 2.9 | Sales/Total Assets | | | | 3.0 | 2.9 | 3.4 | |
| 1.9 | 1.8 | 1.4 | | | | | .9 | 1.7 | 1.4 | |
| .1 | .2 | .2 | | | | | | .5 | .2 | |
| (74) .4 | (101) 1.0 | (105) .9 | % Depr., Dep., Amort./Sales | | | | (20) .8 | (66) .6 | | |
| 2.6 | 3.0 | 2.8 | | | | | | 2.6 | 2.3 | |
| .5 | .7 | .9 | | | | | | | .5 | |
| (28) 1.5 | (24) 2.2 | (20) 1.4 | % Officers', Directors' Owners' Comp/Sales | | | | | (12) 1.1 | | |
| 4.3 | 6.2 | 2.9 | | | | | | | 1.7 | |
| 9309730M | 12146063M | 16383815M | Net Sales ($) | 3869M | 15301M | 38657M | 152437M | 536848M | 15636703M | |
| 3463736M | 4223935M | 5889335M | Total Assets ($) | 6223M | 21997M | 34238M | 116064M | 324374M | 5386439M | |

© RMA 2024   M = $ thousand   MM = $ million
See Pages viii through xx for Explanation of Ratios and Data

## PROFESSIONAL SERVICES—Other Management Consulting Services  NAICS 541618

### Current Data Sorted by Assets | Comparative Historical Data

| | | | | | | | Type of Statement | | |
|---|---|---|---|---|---|---|---|---|---|
| | | 1 | 3 | 10 | 3 | 9 | Unqualified | 35 | 13 |
| | | | 5 | 3 | 3 | | Reviewed | 17 | 10 |
| | 1 | 1 | 5 | 1 | | | Compiled | 9 | 4 |
| | 8 | 8 | 6 | 1 | | | Tax Returns | 26 | 20 |
| 1 | 26 | 26 | 41 | 36 | 4 | 10 | Other | 183 | 112 |
| 19 | 16 (4/1-9/30/23) | | | 180 (10/1/23-3/31/24) | | | | 4/1/19- | 4/1/20- |
| 0-500M | 500M-2MM | 2-10MM | 10-50MM | 50-100MM | 100-250MM | | | 3/31/20 ALL | 3/31/21 ALL |
| 20 | 36 | 60 | 51 | 10 | 19 | | NUMBER OF STATEMENTS | 270 | 159 |
| % | % | % | % | % | % | | ASSETS | % | % |
| 29.3 | 27.2 | 20.8 | 20.1 | 14.0 | 9.2 | | Cash & Equivalents | 22.7 | 28.9 |
| 18.6 | 31.6 | 42.3 | 34.6 | 30.2 | 24.9 | | Trade Receivables (net) | 36.3 | 27.2 |
| .3 | 2.6 | 1.9 | 2.5 | .4 | 3.2 | | Inventory | 3.9 | 3.1 |
| 12.8 | 7.0 | 3.8 | 8.9 | 7.9 | 7.1 | | All Other Current | 6.2 | 5.3 |
| 61.0 | 68.3 | 68.8 | 66.1 | 52.6 | 44.4 | | Total Current | 69.2 | 64.5 |
| 16.5 | 20.2 | 13.0 | 10.6 | 9.2 | 6.5 | | Fixed Assets (net) | 12.2 | 12.2 |
| 2.5 | 4.0 | 6.0 | 10.6 | 13.0 | 41.1 | | Intangibles (net) | 10.1 | 16.3 |
| 20.1 | 7.5 | 12.2 | 12.7 | 25.3 | 8.0 | | All Other Non-Current | 8.5 | 7.0 |
| 100.0 | 100.0 | 100.0 | 100.0 | 100.0 | 100.0 | | Total | 100.0 | 100.0 |
| | | | | | | | LIABILITIES | | |
| 56.9 | 8.2 | 5.9 | 4.9 | 2.9 | 2.7 | | Notes Payable-Short Term | 13.6 | 11.1 |
| 1.6 | 1.2 | 2.6 | 4.0 | 4.2 | 5.9 | | Cur. Mat.-L.T.D. | 2.1 | 2.9 |
| 9.5 | 4.7 | 9.7 | 11.2 | 6.0 | 4.8 | | Trade Payables | 13.9 | 8.2 |
| .0 | .0 | .1 | .2 | .2 | .2 | | Income Taxes Payable | .1 | .3 |
| 28.3 | 16.9 | 11.1 | 23.8 | 22.8 | 18.7 | | All Other Current | 19.8 | 18.5 |
| 96.2 | 31.1 | 29.4 | 44.1 | 36.0 | 32.3 | | Total Current | 49.3 | 41.1 |
| 13.7 | 24.3 | 11.1 | 15.8 | 5.3 | 26.1 | | Long-Term Debt | 12.4 | 23.1 |
| .0 | .0 | .0 | .0 | .1 | .7 | | Deferred Taxes | .1 | .2 |
| .6 | 10.8 | 7.1 | 10.7 | 14.8 | 10.2 | | All Other Non-Current | 6.7 | 11.6 |
| -10.4 | 33.7 | 52.4 | 29.4 | 43.8 | 30.8 | | Net Worth | 31.3 | 24.1 |
| 100.0 | 100.0 | 100.0 | 100.0 | 100.0 | 100.0 | | Total Liabilties & Net Worth | 100.0 | 100.0 |
| | | | | | | | INCOME DATA | | |
| 100.0 | 100.0 | 100.0 | 100.0 | 100.0 | 100.0 | | Net Sales | 100.0 | 100.0 |
| | | | | | | | Gross Profit | | |
| 82.7 | 85.3 | 90.1 | 94.6 | 87.9 | 93.7 | | Operating Expenses | 89.5 | 89.0 |
| 17.3 | 14.7 | 9.9 | 5.4 | 12.1 | 6.3 | | Operating Profit | 10.5 | 11.0 |
| 5.6 | .4 | 1.5 | 1.3 | 2.4 | 3.9 | | All Other Expenses (net) | 1.8 | 1.9 |
| 11.8 | 14.3 | 8.4 | 4.1 | 9.8 | 2.4 | | Profit Before Taxes | 8.8 | 9.1 |
| | | | | | | | RATIOS | | |
| 4.9 | 12.2 | 5.3 | 2.5 | 2.4 | 2.8 | | | 3.1 | 4.5 |
| .7 | 2.6 | 2.6 | 1.5 | 1.5 | 1.7 | Current | 1.6 | 1.8 |
| .3 | .8 | 1.5 | 1.0 | 1.1 | 1.2 | | 1.0 | 1.2 |
| 3.5 | 9.4 | 5.0 | 2.1 | 2.3 | 2.4 | | | 2.8 | 3.9 |
| .7 | 2.2 | 2.5 | 1.3 | 1.4 | 1.4 | Quick | (269) 1.3 | 1.6 |
| .1 | .6 | 1.3 | .5 | .6 | .8 | | .9 | 1.0 |
| 0 UND | 0 UND | 33 11.1 | 25 14.4 | 24 14.9 | 46 7.9 | | | 15 24.6 | 8 47.9 |
| 0 UND | 29 12.8 | 51 7.1 | 54 6.7 | 76 4.8 | 60 6.1 | Sales/Receivables | 46 7.9 | 43 8.4 |
| 17 21.7 | 61 6.0 | 73 5.0 | 74 4.9 | 111 3.3 | 99 3.7 | | 74 4.9 | 65 5.6 |
| | | | | | | | Cost of Sales/Inventory | | |
| | | | | | | | Cost of Sales/Payables | | |
| 8.6 | 3.2 | 4.3 | 6.1 | 3.6 | 4.3 | | | 5.0 | 4.5 |
| -91.0 | 7.1 | 7.8 | 12.9 | 13.8 | 8.2 | Sales/Working Capital | 14.3 | 9.2 |
| -5.1 | -67.2 | 20.7 | -46.8 | 87.5 | 21.4 | | 230.4 | 33.5 |
| 76.9 | 44.5 | 56.2 | 42.8 | | 5.5 | | | 39.2 | 51.7 |
| (13) 22.7 | (23) 9.4 | (40) 13.2 | (39) 6.9 | | (15) .6 | EBIT/Interest | (190) 9.1 | (122) 12.6 |
| -.7 | 2.0 | 2.0 | 2.8 | | -1.3 | | 2.1 | 1.2 |
| | | | | | | Net Profit + Depr., Dep., | | 12.8 | 1.5 |
| | | | | | | Amort./Cur. Mat. L/T/D | (20) 4.0 | (11) -1.0 |
| | | | | | | | 2.1 | -8.0 |
| .0 | .0 | .0 | .0 | .0 | .5 | | .0 | .0 |
| .0 | .1 | .1 | .1 | .1 | -.8 | Fixed/Worth | .2 | .2 |
| NM | 2.5 | .6 | 3.5 | .9 | .0 | | 1.6 | -338.0 |
| .4 | .3 | .3 | .8 | .7 | 2.6 | | .6 | .8 |
| 11.7 | 1.5 | .8 | 1.8 | 2.3 | -5.8 | Debt/Worth | 2.3 | 3.0 |
| -3.2 | -15.1 | 3.3 | 171.8 | 3.8 | -1.8 | | 250.9 | -5.0 |
| 176.8 | 100.0 | 77.8 | 67.1 | | | | | 111.7 | 120.2 |
| (11) 77.2 | (26) 40.4 | (56) 42.9 | (39) 35.9 | | | % Profit Before Taxes/Tangible Net Worth | (205) 45.2 | (109) 55.7 |
| 17.6 | 26.9 | 17.6 | 11.4 | | | | 12.5 | 18.2 |
| 119.6 | 49.0 | 40.7 | 19.4 | 24.8 | 25.4 | | 33.5 | 34.4 |
| 37.4 | 23.4 | 21.5 | 7.0 | 14.6 | 3.0 | % Profit Before Taxes/Total Assets | 12.3 | 13.0 |
| -7.5 | 5.7 | 5.6 | .7 | 5.8 | -3.7 | | 2.4 | 3.0 |
| UND | UND | 388.7 | 419.1 | 104.3 | 304.6 | | 582.5 | 482.6 |
| UND | 102.1 | 80.2 | 162.1 | 36.3 | 47.4 | Sales/Net Fixed Assets | 72.9 | 68.9 |
| 61.2 | 14.1 | 17.4 | 30.4 | 10.2 | 12.6 | | 19.1 | 15.0 |
| 9.4 | 4.7 | 4.4 | 3.9 | 2.4 | 1.8 | | 4.3 | 3.7 |
| 5.4 | 2.6 | 2.7 | 2.3 | 1.5 | 1.2 | Sales/Total Assets | 2.7 | 2.3 |
| 1.8 | 1.4 | 1.9 | 1.1 | 1.0 | .6 | | 1.6 | 1.1 |
| | .2 | .1 | .1 | | | | .2 | .3 |
| | (10) .4 | (37) .3 | (25) .3 | | | % Depr., Dep., Amort./Sales | (119) .5 | (69) .7 |
| | 4.7 | 1.0 | 2.2 | | | | 1.4 | 3.6 |
| | 4.7 | 1.5 | | | | | 1.8 | 4.7 |
| (12) 9.2 | (13) 4.1 | | | | | % Officers', Directors' Owners' Comp/Sales | (54) 4.2 | (32) 7.7 |
| 13.4 | 7.4 | | | | | | 12.3 | 14.4 |
| 43378M | 149194M | 1058852M | 3278106M | 1083720M | 6623875M | Net Sales ($) | 12267662M | 6022218M |
| 5555M | 42402M | 337470M | 1193060M | 660490M | 3036108M | Total Assets ($) | 6674802M | 3448096M |

© RMA 2024

M = $ thousand    MM = $ million
See Pages viii through xx for Explanation of Ratios and Data

# PROFESSIONAL SERVICES—Other Management Consulting Services  NAICS 541618

## Comparative Historical Data | Current Data Sorted by Sales

| | | | | Type of Statement | | | | | | |
|---|---|---|---|---|---|---|---|---|---|---|
| 10 | 16 | 26 | | Unqualified | | | | 1 | 4 | 21 |
| 12 | 8 | 11 | | Reviewed | | | | 1 | 2 | 8 |
| 7 | 7 | 7 | | Compiled | | 1 | 1 | 1 | 2 | 2 |
| 13 | 25 | 16 | | Tax Returns | 3 | 6 | 1 | 1 | 4 | 2 |
| 79 | 146 | 136 | | Other | 15 | 14 | 10 | 16 | 33 | 48 |
| 4/1/21-3/31/22 ALL | 4/1/22-3/31/23 ALL | 4/1/23-3/31/24 ALL | | | 16 (4/1-9/30/23) | | | 180 (10/1/23-3/31/24) | | |
| | | | | | 0-1MM | 1-3MM | 3-5MM | 5-10MM | 10-25MM | 25MM & OVER |
| 121 | 202 | 196 | | NUMBER OF STATEMENTS | 18 | 21 | 11 | 20 | 45 | 81 |
| % | % | % | | ASSETS | % | % | % | % | % | % |
| 29.3 | 27.5 | 21.2 | | Cash & Equivalents | 11.4 | 32.5 | 38.8 | 22.2 | 23.2 | 16.7 |
| 33.8 | 31.0 | 33.6 | | Trade Receivables (net) | 7.3 | 30.7 | 25.1 | 38.7 | 36.5 | 38.5 |
| 3.0 | 2.3 | 2.1 | | Inventory | .3 | 3.8 | 3.5 | 2.8 | 1.6 | 1.9 |
| 8.2 | 6.2 | 7.2 | | All Other Current | 12.7 | 9.0 | 3.3 | 3.1 | 5.2 | 8.0 |
| 74.2 | 66.9 | 64.0 | | Total Current | 31.7 | 76.0 | 70.7 | 66.9 | 66.5 | 65.1 |
| 8.1 | 11.6 | 13.2 | | Fixed Assets (net) | 49.9 | 10.1 | 13.6 | 8.8 | 13.0 | 7.0 |
| 7.3 | 10.7 | 10.2 | | Intangibles (net) | 3.8 | 2.2 | 4.7 | 9.6 | 5.9 | 17.0 |
| 10.4 | 10.8 | 12.5 | | All Other Non-Current | 14.6 | 11.7 | 11.0 | 14.8 | 14.5 | 10.9 |
| 100.0 | 100.0 | 100.0 | | Total | 100.0 | 100.0 | 100.0 | 100.0 | 100.0 | 100.0 |
| | | | | LIABILITIES | | | | | | |
| 8.4 | 9.2 | 10.8 | | Notes Payable-Short Term | 18.9 | 35.1 | 2.7 | 17.5 | 5.8 | 4.9 |
| 1.4 | 2.0 | 3.0 | | Cur. Mat.-L.T.D. | 4.0 | 1.6 | 1.2 | 2.6 | 1.9 | 4.1 |
| 8.4 | 8.5 | 8.5 | | Trade Payables | 4.1 | 6.8 | 3.4 | 11.5 | 9.6 | 9.2 |
| .0 | .1 | .1 | | Income Taxes Payable | .0 | .0 | .0 | .0 | .1 | .2 |
| 20.1 | 17.8 | 18.6 | | All Other Current | 19.9 | 12.7 | 14.2 | 10.8 | 17.4 | 23.0 |
| 38.4 | 37.6 | 41.0 | | Total Current | 46.9 | 56.2 | 21.5 | 42.4 | 34.8 | 41.4 |
| 14.3 | 19.0 | 16.2 | | Long-Term Debt | 31.4 | 12.6 | 31.8 | 16.8 | 9.3 | 15.3 |
| .1 | .1 | .1 | | Deferred Taxes | .0 | .0 | .0 | .1 | .0 | .2 |
| 9.4 | 6.5 | 8.7 | | All Other Non-Current | 1.5 | 14.9 | 7.4 | 11.5 | 5.0 | 10.3 |
| 37.8 | 36.8 | 34.1 | | Net Worth | 20.3 | 16.3 | 39.4 | 29.2 | 50.9 | 32.9 |
| 100.0 | 100.0 | 100.0 | | Total Liabilities & Net Worth | 100.0 | 100.0 | 100.0 | 100.0 | 100.0 | 100.0 |
| | | | | INCOME DATA | | | | | | |
| 100.0 | 100.0 | 100.0 | | Net Sales | 100.0 | 100.0 | 100.0 | 100.0 | 100.0 | 100.0 |
| | | | | Gross Profit | | | | | | |
| 88.7 | 88.2 | 89.9 | | Operating Expenses | 69.7 | 86.5 | 85.6 | 96.1 | 90.0 | 94.2 |
| 11.3 | 11.8 | 10.1 | | Operating Profit | 30.3 | 13.5 | 14.4 | 3.9 | 10.0 | 5.8 |
| -1.4 | 1.4 | 1.9 | | All Other Expenses (net) | 13.0 | -.7 | .7 | -1.3 | .7 | 1.8 |
| 12.8 | 10.4 | 8.2 | | Profit Before Taxes | 17.4 | 14.2 | 13.7 | 5.2 | 9.3 | 4.0 |
| | | | | RATIOS | | | | | | |
| 4.3 | 4.0 | 3.9 | | | 2.4 | 17.0 | 6.4 | 8.7 | 4.9 | 2.6 |
| 2.3 | 2.0 | 1.9 | | Current | .5 | 8.0 | 3.8 | 2.1 | 2.1 | 1.7 |
| 1.4 | 1.2 | 1.0 | | | .2 | 1.0 | 2.2 | 1.1 | 1.1 | 1.2 |
| 4.0 | 3.7 | 3.3 | | | 1.9 | 14.1 | 6.0 | 7.5 | 4.8 | 2.4 |
| 2.1 | 1.8 | 1.6 | | Quick | .3 | 2.7 | 3.2 | 2.1 | 2.0 | 1.4 |
| 1.1 | 1.0 | .8 | | | .0 | .7 | 2.0 | .9 | .9 | .9 |
| 10 38.3 | 1 245.2 | 14 25.4 | | | 0 UND | 0 UND | 6 63.4 | 15 24.1 | 34 10.6 | 35 10.5 |
| 44 8.3 | 39 9.3 | 50 7.3 | | Sales/Receivables | 0 UND | 30 12.0 | 16 22.6 | 45 8.2 | 51 7.1 | 56 6.5 |
| 72 5.1 | 65 5.6 | 73 5.0 | | | 0 UND | 107 3.4 | 55 6.6 | 74 4.9 | 74 4.9 | 81 4.5 |
| | | | | Cost of Sales/Inventory | | | | | | |
| | | | | Cost of Sales/Payables | | | | | | |
| 3.9 | 4.4 | 4.5 | | | 20.2 | 2.5 | 3.4 | 4.3 | 4.2 | 6.2 |
| 7.0 | 9.9 | 9.3 | | Sales/Working Capital | -11.9 | 3.3 | 5.8 | 8.4 | 7.7 | 11.8 |
| 18.1 | 94.0 | NM | | | -2.6 | -76.0 | 21.8 | 56.7 | NM | 32.4 |
| 172.8 | 89.0 | 38.7 | | | 21.0 | 71.8 | | 49.8 | 41.9 | 38.0 |
| (82) 23.4 | (139) 19.9 | (138) 8.2 | | EBIT/Interest | (11) 7.0 | (14) 9.5 | (13) 4.1 | (29) 6.2 | (63) 11.3 | |
| 5.5 | 4.6 | 1.1 | | | .1 | .5 | | .1 | 2.3 | .7 |
| | 18.9 | 4.3 | | Net Profit + Depr., Dep., | | | | | | 6.3 |
| (14) 4.7 | (17) 2.0 | | | Amort./Cur. Mat. L/T/D | | | | | (10) 4.1 | |
| .2 | -26.4 | | | | | | | | -12.5 | |
| .0 | .0 | .0 | | | .0 | .0 | .0 | .0 | .0 | .0 |
| .1 | .1 | .1 | | Fixed/Worth | 2.3 | .1 | .1 | .1 | .2 | .1 |
| .4 | 1.3 | 2.5 | | | NM | NM | .2 | 11.6 | 1.0 | 20.4 |
| .4 | .5 | .6 | | | .5 | .2 | .6 | .3 | .3 | .9 |
| 1.3 | 1.5 | 1.6 | | Debt/Worth | 7.3 | 1.0 | .8 | 2.5 | .8 | 2.6 |
| 4.3 | 15.9 | 173.9 | | | -31.8 | -4.6 | 2.0 | -5.3 | 3.1 | -91.6 |
| 96.9 | 100.4 | 88.6 | | % Profit Before Taxes/Tangible | 100.0 | 99.9 | 190.2 | 80.1 | 88.4 | |
| (97) 57.1 | (161) 44.7 | (149) 42.1 | | Net Worth | (13) 40.3 | (14) 34.6 | (14) 33.3 | (39) 35.0 | (60) 49.2 | |
| 23.6 | 14.4 | 16.2 | | | 6.4 | 11.0 | | 5.5 | 13.2 | 18.9 |
| 48.7 | 39.2 | 34.2 | | % Profit Before Taxes/Total | 36.5 | 52.0 | 59.5 | 45.0 | 47.0 | 26.1 |
| 25.1 | 17.7 | 13.5 | | Assets | 11.4 | 12.7 | 30.5 | 21.1 | 13.7 | 10.9 |
| 8.1 | 3.5 | 1.2 | | | -3.9 | 1.1 | 7.0 | -.3 | 3.3 | 1.7 |
| 703.2 | 999.8 | 657.8 | | | UND | UND | UND | 575.9 | 506.4 | 409.7 |
| 122.6 | 127.5 | 101.0 | | Sales/Net Fixed Assets | 3.0 | 199.3 | 106.5 | 102.2 | 59.1 | 143.5 |
| 24.5 | 22.9 | 19.0 | | | .6 | 24.6 | 30.3 | 28.1 | 18.6 | 23.8 |
| 4.3 | 4.6 | 4.1 | | | 2.0 | 4.1 | 4.8 | 5.3 | 3.2 | 4.1 |
| 2.8 | 2.6 | 2.4 | | Sales/Total Assets | 1.0 | 2.0 | 2.5 | 2.7 | 2.5 | 2.5 |
| 1.6 | 1.4 | 1.4 | | | .4 | 1.4 | 1.6 | 1.5 | 1.8 | 1.4 |
| .2 | .2 | .1 | | | | | | | .1 | .1 |
| (56) .6 | (93) .6 | (84) .4 | | % Depr., Dep., Amort./Sales | | | | (29) .3 | (36) .6 | |
| 1.9 | 2.0 | 1.7 | | | | | | | 1.1 | 2.1 |
| 3.0 | 4.2 | 2.4 | | % Officers', Directors' | | | | | 1.3 | |
| (31) 6.1 | (40) 7.6 | (40) 6.4 | | Owners' Comp/Sales | | | | (10) 3.5 | | |
| 17.8 | 17.1 | 11.2 | | | | | | | 7.1 | |
| 4041985M | 8352151M | 12237125M | | Net Sales ($) | 8452M | 38707M | 44283M | 135822M | 723780M | 11286081M |
| 2025274M | 4417031M | 5275085M | | Total Assets ($) | 12708M | 38880M | 39356M | 80777M | 414448M | 4688916M |

M = $ thousand    MM = $ million
See Pages viii through xx for Explanation of Ratios and Data

© RMA 2024

# PROFESSIONAL SERVICES—Environmental Consulting Services  NAICS 541620

## Current Data Sorted by Assets | Comparative Historical Data

| | | | | | | | Type of Statement | | |
|---|---|---|---|---|---|---|---|---|---|
| | | 1 | | 4 | 1 | 2 | Unqualified | 8 | 7 |
| | 1 | 10 | | 5 | | | Reviewed | 14 | 4 |
| | 1 | 1 | | 1 | | | Compiled | 8 | 4 |
| | 7 | 1 | | | | | Tax Returns | 17 | 9 |
| 3 | 10 | 24 | | 22 | 7 | 4 | Other | 79 | 55 |
| | 12 (4/1-9/30/23) | | | 93 (10/1/23-3/31/24) | | | | 4/1/19-3/31/20 | 4/1/20-3/31/21 |
| 0-500M | 500M-2MM | 2-10MM | | 10-50MM | 50-100MM | 100-250MM | | ALL | ALL |
| 3 | 19 | 37 | | 32 | 8 | 6 | NUMBER OF STATEMENTS | 126 | 79 |
| % | % | % | | % | % | % | ASSETS | % | % |
| | 26.6 | 16.2 | | 10.5 | | | Cash & Equivalents | 16.4 | 21.0 |
| | 34.8 | 50.1 | | 32.0 | | | Trade Receivables (net) | 41.6 | 29.2 |
| | .9 | 1.4 | | 1.9 | | | Inventory | 2.5 | 1.5 |
| | 2.8 | 5.8 | | 7.7 | | | All Other Current | 6.0 | 5.0 |
| | 65.0 | 73.5 | | 52.0 | | | Total Current | 66.5 | 56.8 |
| | 26.4 | 14.6 | | 28.1 | | | Fixed Assets (net) | 20.3 | 25.5 |
| | 3.8 | 2.7 | | 10.2 | | | Intangibles (net) | 4.3 | 7.2 |
| | 4.7 | 9.2 | | 9.7 | | | All Other Non-Current | 8.9 | 10.5 |
| | 100.0 | 100.0 | | 100.0 | | | Total | 100.0 | 100.0 |
| | | | | | | | LIABILITIES | | |
| | 7.0 | 8.2 | | 3.9 | | | Notes Payable-Short Term | 8.6 | 5.4 |
| | 4.7 | 2.9 | | 3.3 | | | Cur. Mat.-L.T.D. | 3.8 | 3.1 |
| | 5.4 | 11.6 | | 8.0 | | | Trade Payables | 11.4 | 6.2 |
| | .0 | .0 | | .8 | | | Income Taxes Payable | .2 | .2 |
| | 5.4 | 11.7 | | 9.8 | | | All Other Current | 13.9 | 9.0 |
| | 22.5 | 34.5 | | 25.8 | | | Total Current | 37.9 | 23.8 |
| | 29.6 | 10.5 | | 15.0 | | | Long-Term Debt | 12.0 | 21.5 |
| | .0 | 1.1 | | .3 | | | Deferred Taxes | .4 | .6 |
| | 1.3 | 2.7 | | 8.4 | | | All Other Non-Current | 6.4 | 5.3 |
| | 46.6 | 51.2 | | 50.5 | | | Net Worth | 43.3 | 48.8 |
| | 100.0 | 100.0 | | 100.0 | | | Total Liabilities & Net Worth | 100.0 | 100.0 |
| | | | | | | | INCOME DATA | | |
| | 100.0 | 100.0 | | 100.0 | | | Net Sales | 100.0 | 100.0 |
| | | | | | | | Gross Profit | | |
| | 82.8 | 93.0 | | 93.5 | | | Operating Expenses | 91.0 | 88.9 |
| | 17.2 | 7.0 | | 6.5 | | | Operating Profit | 9.0 | 11.1 |
| | 4.5 | -.4 | | 2.8 | | | All Other Expenses (net) | 1.4 | .5 |
| | 12.6 | 7.4 | | 3.7 | | | Profit Before Taxes | 7.6 | 10.7 |
| | | | | | | | RATIOS | | |
| | 4.1 | 4.1 | | 2.8 | | | | 3.3 | 4.0 |
| | 3.0 | 2.3 | | 1.9 | | | Current | 2.1 | 2.3 |
| | 1.0 | 1.7 | | 1.2 | | | | 1.1 | 1.6 |
| | 3.8 | 3.8 | | 2.3 | | | | 3.2 | 3.6 |
| | 2.8 | 2.2 | | 1.6 | | | Quick | 1.8 | 2.1 |
| | 1.0 | 1.4 | | 1.0 | | | | .9 | 1.4 |
| | 0 UND | 45 8.1 | | 45 8.2 | | | | 36 10.2 | 26 14.3 |
| | 61 6.0 | 66 5.5 | | 64 5.7 | | | Sales/Receivables | 65 5.6 | 58 6.3 |
| | 78 4.7 | 87 4.2 | | 78 4.7 | | | | 89 4.1 | 87 4.2 |
| | | | | | | | Cost of Sales/Inventory | | |
| | | | | | | | Cost of Sales/Payables | | |
| | 3.8 | 4.8 | | 4.5 | | | | 4.9 | 3.6 |
| | 6.9 | 5.5 | | 8.3 | | | Sales/Working Capital | 8.3 | 5.9 |
| | UND | 13.5 | | 23.7 | | | | 48.5 | 16.2 |
| | 10.7 | 72.6 | | 42.2 | | | | 44.8 | 60.8 |
| (11) | 5.5 | (30) 21.6 | (24) | 5.6 | | | EBIT/Interest | (108) 12.8 | (64) 21.3 |
| | 1.0 | 5.0 | | 2.3 | | | | 3.0 | 4.6 |
| | | | | | | | Net Profit + Depr., Dep., | 25.7 | 45.4 |
| | | | | | | | Amort./Cur. Mat. L/T/D | (17) 3.4 | (13) 8.7 |
| | | | | | | | | 1.8 | 1.6 |
| | .0 | .1 | | .1 | | | | .1 | .1 |
| | .2 | .2 | | .6 | | | Fixed/Worth | .3 | .4 |
| | 4.5 | .5 | | 1.9 | | | | 1.5 | 1.6 |
| | .3 | .4 | | .6 | | | | .5 | .4 |
| | 1.0 | .7 | | 1.1 | | | Debt/Worth | 1.1 | 1.1 |
| | 13.2 | 2.3 | | 2.2 | | | | 3.6 | 2.7 |
| | 66.6 | 66.3 | | 35.0 | | | % Profit Before Taxes/Tangible | 61.1 | 69.0 |
| (16) | 28.8 | (34) 39.7 | (29) | 16.2 | | | Net Worth | (113) 31.6 | (70) 33.5 |
| | 3.2 | 12.8 | | 3.5 | | | | 11.8 | 9.8 |
| | 31.9 | 35.9 | | 12.2 | | | % Profit Before Taxes/Total | 29.5 | 30.6 |
| | 15.1 | 23.4 | | 5.8 | | | Assets | 15.2 | 15.5 |
| | 4.2 | 4.9 | | .5 | | | | 3.6 | 5.4 |
| | 167.1 | 79.2 | | 62.9 | | | | 77.1 | 47.4 |
| | 19.0 | 27.8 | | 9.7 | | | Sales/Net Fixed Assets | 25.1 | 13.3 |
| | 6.3 | 12.1 | | 2.5 | | | | 8.4 | 3.6 |
| | 3.9 | 3.4 | | 2.4 | | | | 3.3 | 2.8 |
| | 2.5 | 2.6 | | 1.5 | | | Sales/Total Assets | 2.6 | 1.9 |
| | 1.4 | 1.9 | | 1.2 | | | | 1.7 | 1.1 |
| | .3 | .6 | | .6 | | | | .6 | .9 |
| (10) | 2.9 | (26) 1.3 | (24) | 2.2 | | | % Depr., Dep., Amort./Sales | (90) 1.4 | (64) 1.7 |
| | 9.3 | 2.3 | | 6.5 | | | | 4.8 | 7.0 |
| | | | | | | | % Officers', Directors' | 3.3 | 4.2 |
| | | | | | | | Owners' Comp/Sales | (36) 4.8 | (16) 8.8 |
| | | | | | | | | 10.6 | 17.4 |
| 5406M | 74240M | 584012M | | 1156581M | 3453186M | 1611078M | Net Sales ($) | 2474672M | 1994290M |
| 461M | 27534M | 209505M | | 690958M | 582500M | 1035442M | Total Assets ($) | 1336467M | 1494279M |

© RMA 2024   M = $ thousand   MM = $ million
See Pages viii through xx for Explanation of Ratios and Data

# PROFESSIONAL SERVICES—Environmental Consulting Services  NAICS 541620

## Comparative Historical Data | Current Data Sorted by Sales

| Comparative Historical Data ||| | Current Data Sorted by Sales |||||||
|---|---|---|---|---|---|---|---|---|---|
| 5 | 4 | 8 | **Type of Statement** | | | | 3 | 3 | 5 |
| 11 | 14 | 16 | Unqualified | | | 1 | 3 | 9 | 3 |
| 6 | 4 | 3 | Reviewed | | | | 1 | 2 | |
| 16 | 11 | 8 | Compiled | 2 | 1 | 1 | 3 | 1 | |
| 51 | 72 | 70 | Tax Returns | 4 | 5 | 3 | 9 | 18 | 31 |
| 4/1/21-3/31/22 ALL | 4/1/22-3/31/23 ALL | 4/1/23-3/31/24 ALL | Other | 12 (4/1-9/30/23) ||| 93 (10/1/23-3/31/24) |||
| | | | | 0-1MM | 1-3MM | 3-5MM | 5-10MM | 10-25MM | 25MM & OVER |
| 89 | 105 | 105 | **NUMBER OF STATEMENTS** | 6 | 6 | 5 | 16 | 33 | 39 |
| % | % | % | **ASSETS** | % | % | % | % | % | % |
| 25.4 | 18.6 | 17.6 | Cash & Equivalents | | | | 23.5 | 12.6 | 16.1 |
| 31.8 | 35.8 | 37.3 | Trade Receivables (net) | | | | 44.8 | 46.7 | 35.9 |
| 2.2 | 2.1 | 1.7 | Inventory | | | | .9 | 1.4 | 2.1 |
| 6.4 | 7.9 | 6.1 | All Other Current | | | | 7.5 | 3.6 | 9.1 |
| 65.8 | 64.3 | 62.7 | Total Current | | | | 76.7 | 64.3 | 63.2 |
| 21.0 | 18.9 | 20.5 | Fixed Assets (net) | | | | 20.1 | 20.7 | 14.7 |
| 7.0 | 9.0 | 8.6 | Intangibles (net) | | | | .9 | 5.2 | 14.6 |
| 6.2 | 7.9 | 8.2 | All Other Non-Current | | | | 2.2 | 9.9 | 7.5 |
| 100.0 | 100.0 | 100.0 | Total | | | | 100.0 | 100.0 | 100.0 |
| | | | **LIABILITIES** | | | | | | |
| 4.0 | 6.0 | 5.8 | Notes Payable-Short Term | | | | 6.9 | 5.9 | 2.5 |
| 4.1 | 2.6 | 3.1 | Cur. Mat.-L.T.D. | | | | .9 | 3.9 | 2.2 |
| 7.7 | 9.0 | 8.6 | Trade Payables | | | | 8.8 | 9.1 | 10.2 |
| .1 | .3 | .3 | Income Taxes Payable | | | | .0 | .0 | .9 |
| 15.9 | 11.9 | 9.9 | All Other Current | | | | 7.6 | 11.4 | 12.0 |
| 31.8 | 29.8 | 27.8 | Total Current | | | | 24.2 | 30.4 | 27.8 |
| 19.6 | 20.1 | 16.1 | Long-Term Debt | | | | 18.1 | 13.1 | 12.9 |
| .3 | .1 | .7 | Deferred Taxes | | | | .0 | 1.2 | .8 |
| 6.7 | 7.2 | 4.5 | All Other Non-Current | | | | .1 | 5.3 | 7.0 |
| 41.5 | 42.9 | 51.0 | Net Worth | | | | 57.6 | 50.1 | 51.6 |
| 100.0 | 100.0 | 100.0 | Total Liabilities & Net Worth | | | | 100.0 | 100.0 | 100.0 |
| | | | **INCOME DATA** | | | | | | |
| 100.0 | 100.0 | 100.0 | Net Sales | | | | 100.0 | 100.0 | 100.0 |
| | | | Gross Profit | | | | | | |
| 89.7 | 90.4 | 91.5 | Operating Expenses | | | | 89.2 | 94.1 | 96.6 |
| 10.3 | 9.6 | 8.5 | Operating Profit | | | | 10.8 | 5.9 | 3.4 |
| -1.0 | 1.1 | 1.9 | All Other Expenses (net) | | | | -.7 | -.7 | 1.6 |
| 11.4 | 8.5 | 6.6 | Profit Before Taxes | | | | 11.5 | 6.7 | 1.8 |
| | | | **RATIOS** | | | | | | |
| 4.0 | 3.7 | 3.4 | | | | | 8.5 | 3.4 | 3.3 |
| 2.4 | 2.3 | 2.3 | Current | | | | 3.4 | 2.3 | 2.2 |
| 1.4 | 1.4 | 1.4 | | | | | 1.9 | 1.5 | 1.5 |
| 3.5 | 3.4 | 3.0 | | | | | 7.6 | 3.1 | 2.9 |
| 2.1 | 1.8 | 1.9 | Quick | | | | 3.0 | 2.1 | 1.9 |
| 1.3 | 1.0 | 1.2 | | | | | 1.7 | 1.4 | 1.2 |
| 16  22.7 | 36  10.0 | 41  9.0 | | | | | 22  16.5 | 54  6.8 | 45  8.1 |
| 58  6.3 | 59  6.2 | 64  5.7 | Sales/Receivables | | | | 68  5.4 | 72  5.1 | 63  5.8 |
| 81  4.5 | 83  4.4 | 85  4.3 | | | | | 85  4.3 | 94  3.9 | 78  4.7 |
| | | | Cost of Sales/Inventory | | | | | | |
| | | | Cost of Sales/Payables | | | | | | |
| 3.5 | 4.1 | 4.4 | | | | | 4.2 | 4.4 | 4.3 |
| 6.0 | 6.3 | 6.7 | Sales/Working Capital | | | | 6.0 | 5.4 | 7.9 |
| 12.9 | 15.0 | 18.8 | | | | | 10.8 | 16.8 | 13.9 |
| 151.5 | 73.1 | 41.4 | | | | | 34.1 | 48.2 | 52.3 |
| (75)  33.6 | (81)  15.5 | (76)  10.1 | EBIT/Interest | | (10)  14.3 | | (27)  14.3 | (29)  6.8 | |
| 8.0 | 3.0 | 2.5 | | | | | 5.2 | 2.5 | 1.9 |
| 16.2 | 4.2 | 10.4 | Net Profit + Depr., Dep., | | | | | | |
| (14)  5.6 | (13)  1.2 | (12)  5.5 | Amort./Cur. Mat. L/T/D | | | | | | |
| 2.9 | .6 | 1.9 | | | | | | | |
| .1 | .1 | .1 | | | | | .0 | .1 | .1 |
| .3 | .5 | .3 | Fixed/Worth | | | | .2 | .3 | .2 |
| 1.2 | 2.1 | 1.2 | | | | | 1.0 | 1.4 | 1.1 |
| .4 | .5 | .5 | | | | | .3 | .5 | .6 |
| 1.0 | 1.2 | .9 | Debt/Worth | | | | .6 | 1.3 | 1.0 |
| 4.8 | 6.1 | 2.7 | | | | | 2.5 | 2.3 | 2.6 |
| 88.8 | 82.0 | 52.2 | % Profit Before Taxes/Tangible | | | | 56.1 | 62.8 | 43.2 |
| (74)  49.1 | (84)  40.8 | (93)  28.5 | Net Worth | | (15)  41.4 | | (30)  31.1 | (34)  13.3 | |
| 23.8 | 19.4 | 8.3 | | | | | 16.5 | 11.2 | 5.9 |
| 41.6 | 35.5 | 24.6 | % Profit Before Taxes/Total | | | | 31.7 | 34.4 | 13.9 |
| 23.8 | 14.3 | 9.4 | Assets | | | | 25.2 | 13.1 | 6.6 |
| 6.8 | 3.1 | 2.3 | | | | | 10.3 | 3.7 | 1.4 |
| 74.4 | 102.8 | 97.2 | | | | | 160.3 | 47.1 | 118.7 |
| 20.2 | 20.0 | 20.4 | Sales/Net Fixed Assets | | | | 22.5 | 17.7 | 22.0 |
| 7.4 | 6.2 | 6.7 | | | | | 14.4 | 5.3 | 10.2 |
| 3.1 | 3.1 | 3.1 | | | | | 4.3 | 2.9 | 3.4 |
| 2.3 | 2.1 | 2.1 | Sales/Total Assets | | | | 3.0 | 2.1 | 2.1 |
| 1.5 | 1.3 | 1.4 | | | | | 2.4 | 1.4 | 1.4 |
| .6 | .6 | .6 | | | | | | 1.0 | .4 |
| (63)  1.9 | (64)  1.3 | (66)  1.7 | % Depr., Dep., Amort./Sales | | | | (26)  1.8 | (23)  1.2 | |
| 3.9 | 2.6 | 4.4 | | | | | | 5.1 | 2.1 |
| 4.5 | 3.4 | 1.2 | % Officers', Directors' | | | | | | |
| (22)  7.9 | (22)  5.1 | (21)  3.7 | Owners' Comp/Sales | | | | | | |
| 16.6 | 10.5 | 6.9 | | | | | | | |
| 6718000M | 3184914M | 6884503M | Net Sales ($) | 2590M | 12035M | 19300M | 112049M | 503345M | 6235184M |
| 1841557M | 2019763M | 2546400M | Total Assets ($) | 33215M | 10097M | 8039M | 63217M | 285076M | 2146756M |

© RMA 2024  M = $ thousand   MM = $ million
See Pages viii through xx for Explanation of Ratios and Data

## PROFESSIONAL SERVICES—Other Scientific and Technical Consulting Services  NAICS 541690

**Current Data Sorted by Assets** | **Comparative Historical Data**

| | | | | | | | Type of Statement | | | |
|---|---|---|---|---|---|---|---|---|---|---|
| | | 2 | 9 | 8 | 4 | 3 | Unqualified | | 33 | 8 |
| | | 6 | 6 | 9 | 2 | | Reviewed | | 19 | 9 |
| | | | 9 | 3 | | 1 | Compiled | | 11 | 6 |
| | 3 | 6 | 8 | 2 | | | Tax Returns | | 28 | 13 |
| | 5 | 26 | 50 | 47 | 10 | 8 | Other | | 134 | 77 |
| | | 32 (4/1-9/30/23) | | 189 (10/1/23-3/31/24) | | | | | 4/1/19-3/31/20 | 4/1/20-3/31/21 |
| 0-500M | 500M-2MM | 2-10MM | 10-50MM | 50-100MM | 100-250MM | | | | ALL | ALL |
| 8 | 34 | 82 | 69 | 16 | 12 | | NUMBER OF STATEMENTS | | 225 | 113 |
| % | % | % | % | % | % | | **ASSETS** | | % | % |
| | 41.5 | 24.8 | 17.5 | 15.8 | 9.1 | | Cash & Equivalents | | 20.6 | 29.6 |
| | 38.1 | 39.9 | 34.7 | 34.3 | 13.7 | | Trade Receivables (net) | | 42.1 | 31.4 |
| | 1.0 | 1.4 | 4.1 | 4.6 | 4.7 | | Inventory | | 2.7 | 2.8 |
| | 2.5 | 7.9 | 7.6 | 5.7 | 3.2 | | All Other Current | | 5.1 | 7.1 |
| | 83.1 | 74.0 | 64.0 | 60.4 | 30.7 | | Total Current | | 70.4 | 70.8 |
| | 5.6 | 8.6 | 12.2 | 6.6 | 23.6 | | Fixed Assets (net) | | 12.7 | 10.6 |
| | 7.4 | 6.1 | 14.1 | 25.0 | 38.7 | | Intangibles (net) | | 7.9 | 12.3 |
| | 3.9 | 11.3 | 9.7 | 8.1 | 7.0 | | All Other Non-Current | | 8.9 | 6.3 |
| | 100.0 | 100.0 | 100.0 | 100.0 | 100.0 | | Total | | 100.0 | 100.0 |
| | | | | | | | **LIABILITIES** | | | |
| | 14.3 | 4.0 | 5.1 | 4.0 | 1.1 | | Notes Payable-Short Term | | 10.7 | 9.9 |
| | .9 | .4 | 3.1 | 1.2 | 3.2 | | Cur. Mat.-L.T.D. | | 3.2 | 2.7 |
| | 6.7 | 11.6 | 12.0 | 8.5 | 4.6 | | Trade Payables | | 9.6 | 8.9 |
| | .4 | .1 | .1 | .0 | .0 | | Income Taxes Payable | | .1 | .2 |
| | 14.3 | 23.1 | 16.2 | 19.4 | 28.6 | | All Other Current | | 20.2 | 17.6 |
| | 36.6 | 39.2 | 36.5 | 33.1 | 37.6 | | Total Current | | 43.9 | 39.2 |
| | 13.3 | 9.4 | 13.1 | 17.6 | 47.7 | | Long-Term Debt | | 11.2 | 16.2 |
| | .0 | .3 | .6 | .4 | .0 | | Deferred Taxes | | .2 | .1 |
| | 2.3 | 4.7 | 5.3 | 3.0 | 1.6 | | All Other Non-Current | | 5.0 | 7.1 |
| | 47.7 | 46.4 | 44.5 | 45.9 | 13.2 | | Net Worth | | 39.8 | 37.4 |
| | 100.0 | 100.0 | 100.0 | 100.0 | 100.0 | | Total Liabilities & Net Worth | | 100.0 | 100.0 |
| | | | | | | | **INCOME DATA** | | | |
| | 100.0 | 100.0 | 100.0 | 100.0 | 100.0 | | Net Sales | | 100.0 | 100.0 |
| | | | | | | | Gross Profit | | | |
| | 90.6 | 91.0 | 92.7 | 89.2 | 98.6 | | Operating Expenses | | 90.8 | 91.5 |
| | 9.4 | 9.0 | 7.3 | 10.8 | 1.4 | | Operating Profit | | 9.2 | 8.5 |
| | 1.3 | .4 | 1.3 | .9 | 13.4 | | All Other Expenses (net) | | 1.2 | -.4 |
| | 8.1 | 8.6 | 6.0 | 9.9 | -12.0 | | Profit Before Taxes | | 8.0 | 8.9 |
| | | | | | | | **RATIOS** | | | |
| | 14.4 | 4.5 | 3.3 | 3.2 | 1.5 | | | | 3.2 | 5.1 |
| | 5.7 | 2.3 | 2.1 | 2.1 | 1.0 | | Current | | 1.8 | 2.0 |
| | 1.4 | 1.2 | 1.2 | 1.3 | .6 | | | | 1.1 | 1.0 |
| | 12.7 | 3.6 | 2.8 | 2.6 | 1.2 | | | | 3.1 | 4.9 |
| | 5.5 | 2.1 | 1.8 | 1.7 | 1.0 | | Quick | | 1.5 | 1.6 |
| | 1.4 | 1.1 | 1.0 | 1.0 | .3 | | | | .9 | .8 |
| | 11 34.3 | 25 14.5 | 38 9.7 | 51 7.2 | 42 8.6 | | | 31 | 11.8 | 16 23.3 |
| | 39 9.4 | 44 8.3 | 54 6.7 | 58 6.3 | 66 5.5 | | Sales/Receivables | 53 | 6.9 | 49 7.5 |
| | 52 7.0 | 70 5.2 | 70 5.2 | 76 4.8 | 87 4.2 | | | 76 | 4.8 | 70 5.2 |
| | | | | | | | Cost of Sales/Inventory | | | |
| | | | | | | | Cost of Sales/Payables | | | |
| | 4.0 | 4.6 | 4.6 | 4.4 | 6.4 | | | | 5.6 | 3.9 |
| | 7.0 | 8.1 | 7.7 | 6.3 | 534.0 | | Sales/Working Capital | | 9.9 | 8.2 |
| | 41.3 | 31.4 | 20.0 | 15.7 | -9.2 | | | | 78.4 | 94.2 |
| | 153.3 | 101.5 | 276.8 | 48.1 | 1.0 | | | | 45.7 | 73.6 |
| | (16) 22.6 | (54) 15.0 | (60) 11.8 | (11) 7.1 | -.1 | | EBIT/Interest | (158) | 11.4 | (85) 15.0 |
| | 2.1 | 5.0 | 3.0 | 2.3 | -.9 | | | | 2.1 | 1.4 |
| | | | | | | | Net Profit + Depr., Dep., | | 33.0 | |
| | | | | | | | Amort./Cur. Mat. L/T/D | (21) | 8.8 | |
| | | | | | | | | | 2.5 | |
| | .0 | .0 | .0 | .0 | -1.3 | | | | .0 | .0 |
| | .0 | .0 | .1 | .3 | -.6 | | Fixed/Worth | | .2 | .1 |
| | 2.4 | .3 | .9 | -.9 | .0 | | | | 1.6 | 1.5 |
| | .1 | .4 | .5 | .9 | -5.8 | | | | .5 | .5 |
| | 1.1 | .8 | 1.3 | 3.1 | -3.0 | | Debt/Worth | | 1.3 | 1.4 |
| | -7.9 | 4.4 | 4.4 | -9.6 | -2.3 | | | | 14.3 | -98.2 |
| | 78.4 | 93.9 | 66.1 | 140.3 | | | | | 97.5 | 91.9 |
| | (24) 39.4 | (71) 49.9 | (60) 43.2 | (11) 68.4 | | | % Profit Before Taxes/Tangible Net Worth | (180) | 43.8 | (83) 56.0 |
| | 21.0 | 18.1 | 14.9 | 24.3 | | | | | 15.5 | 21.8 |
| | 43.6 | 40.2 | 30.2 | 28.1 | .2 | | | | 42.5 | 43.3 |
| | 25.0 | 20.1 | 11.9 | 15.9 | -9.0 | | % Profit Before Taxes/Total Assets | | 15.9 | 12.6 |
| | 3.0 | 7.1 | 3.0 | 3.9 | -13.7 | | | | 4.0 | .9 |
| | UND | 999.8 | 170.7 | 494.5 | 37.1 | | | | 300.1 | 967.7 |
| | 256.1 | 188.5 | 84.6 | 125.9 | 9.1 | | Sales/Net Fixed Assets | | 66.0 | 98.6 |
| | 97.7 | 39.7 | 9.8 | 16.4 | 1.7 | | | | 19.2 | 21.2 |
| | 6.3 | 4.3 | 3.3 | 2.7 | .8 | | | | 4.5 | 3.5 |
| | 4.0 | 2.9 | 2.1 | 1.8 | .7 | | Sales/Total Assets | | 3.0 | 2.6 |
| | 2.8 | 1.8 | 1.4 | 1.2 | .5 | | | | 1.9 | 1.3 |
| | | | .1 | .3 | | | | | .2 | .3 |
| | | (44) .3 | (48) .4 | | | | % Depr., Dep., Amort./Sales | (136) | .6 | (55) .7 |
| | | .7 | 1.2 | | | | | | 1.3 | 2.0 |
| | 2.6 | 1.6 | 1.6 | | | | | | 2.3 | 2.8 |
| | (10) 4.1 | (17) 3.5 | (10) 3.6 | | | | % Officers', Directors' Owners' Comp/Sales | (56) | 3.9 | (30) 6.0 |
| | 7.9 | 7.2 | 10.3 | | | | | | 8.0 | 10.1 |
| 11626M | 215019M | 1405774M | 3732159M | 2048234M | 1623012M | | Net Sales ($) | | 8221732M | 3348674M |
| 1779M | 42829M | 439322M | 1573027M | 1032222M | 1818488M | | Total Assets ($) | | 4207849M | 2307212M |

M = $ thousand    MM = $ million
See Pages viii through xx for Explanation of Ratios and Data

© RMA 2024

## PROFESSIONAL SERVICES—Other Scientific and Technical Consulting Services  NAICS 541690

### Comparative Historical Data / Current Data Sorted by Sales

| | | | | Type of Statement | | | | | | |
|---|---|---|---|---|---|---|---|---|---|---|
| 8 | 23 | | 26 | Unqualified | 1 | 1 | 1 | 2 | 5 | 16 |
| 6 | 19 | | 17 | Reviewed | | 1 | | 1 | 4 | 11 |
| 5 | 8 | | 13 | Compiled | | | | 2 | 7 | 4 |
| 12 | 26 | | 19 | Tax Returns | | 5 | 1 | 5 | 3 | 4 |
| 90 | 129 | | 146 | Other | 1 | 11 | 14 | 19 | 32 | 66 |
| 4/1/21-3/31/22 ALL | 4/1/22-3/31/23 ALL | | 4/1/23-3/31/24 ALL | | 4 | | | | | |
| | | | | | 32 (4/1-9/30/23) | | | 189 (10/1/23-3/31/24) | | |
| | | | | | 0-1MM | 1-3MM | 3-5MM | 5-10MM | 10-25MM | 25MM & OVER |
| 121 | 205 | | 221 | NUMBER OF STATEMENTS | 6 | 18 | 16 | 29 | 51 | 101 |
| % | % | | % | ASSETS | % | % | % | % | % | % |
| 26.1 | 28.6 | | 24.1 | Cash & Equivalents | | 40.9 | 30.8 | 24.8 | 24.7 | 19.1 |
| 35.2 | 34.9 | | 35.7 | Trade Receivables (net) | | 25.8 | 23.9 | 40.3 | 38.5 | 37.8 |
| 2.4 | 2.4 | | 2.5 | Inventory | | 1.5 | .7 | .4 | 2.0 | 4.0 |
| 5.3 | 6.1 | | 6.3 | All Other Current | | 6.9 | 10.5 | 5.9 | 5.5 | 6.4 |
| 69.1 | 72.1 | | 68.7 | Total Current | | 75.0 | 65.9 | 71.4 | 70.8 | 67.3 |
| 13.1 | 12.5 | | 10.3 | Fixed Assets (net) | | 12.7 | 15.0 | 12.9 | 5.5 | 9.0 |
| 10.1 | 7.9 | | 11.8 | Intangibles (net) | | 7.4 | 14.1 | 5.9 | 11.7 | 14.6 |
| 7.8 | 7.5 | | 9.2 | All Other Non-Current | | 4.9 | 5.0 | 9.8 | 12.1 | 9.2 |
| 100.0 | 100.0 | | 100.0 | Total | | 100.0 | 100.0 | 100.0 | 100.0 | 100.0 |
| | | | | LIABILITIES | | | | | | |
| 7.5 | 5.2 | | 5.8 | Notes Payable-Short Term | | 4.0 | 5.9 | 12.0 | 4.5 | 4.6 |
| 2.2 | 1.1 | | 1.5 | Cur. Mat.-L.T.D. | | 1.0 | .7 | .6 | 3.3 | 1.2 |
| 8.8 | 9.4 | | 10.3 | Trade Payables | | 6.8 | 7.4 | 7.4 | 10.7 | 12.6 |
| .3 | .4 | | .1 | Income Taxes Payable | | .6 | .2 | .1 | .1 | .1 |
| 18.9 | 18.0 | | 20.6 | All Other Current | | 11.9 | 9.7 | 28.7 | 22.6 | 18.4 |
| 37.8 | 34.1 | | 38.4 | Total Current | | 24.2 | 23.8 | 48.9 | 41.1 | 36.8 |
| 15.7 | 14.8 | | 16.4 | Long-Term Debt | | 28.2 | 16.7 | 25.7 | 11.2 | 14.0 |
| .2 | .3 | | .3 | Deferred Taxes | | .0 | .2 | .0 | .5 | .4 |
| 4.0 | 5.9 | | 4.3 | All Other Non-Current | | 2.4 | 4.9 | 4.1 | 3.4 | 4.1 |
| 42.3 | 44.8 | | 40.5 | Net Worth | | 45.2 | 54.3 | 21.3 | 43.7 | 44.6 |
| 100.0 | 100.0 | | 100.0 | Total Liabilties & Net Worth | | 100.0 | 100.0 | 100.0 | 100.0 | 100.0 |
| | | | | INCOME DATA | | | | | | |
| 100.0 | 100.0 | | 100.0 | Net Sales | | 100.0 | 100.0 | 100.0 | 100.0 | 100.0 |
| | | | | Gross Profit | | | | | | |
| 90.7 | 90.3 | | 91.9 | Operating Expenses | | 89.4 | 95.6 | 90.0 | 91.4 | 92.4 |
| 9.3 | 9.7 | | 8.1 | Operating Profit | | 10.6 | 4.4 | 10.0 | 8.6 | 7.6 |
| -1.1 | 1.1 | | 1.6 | All Other Expenses (net) | | 2.0 | .3 | 1.5 | .6 | 2.0 |
| 10.4 | 8.5 | | 6.5 | Profit Before Taxes | | 8.5 | 4.1 | 8.5 | 8.1 | 5.6 |
| | | | | RATIOS | | | | | | |
| 3.8 | 4.1 | | 4.0 | | | 28.0 | 10.1 | 6.9 | 3.9 | 3.3 |
| 2.1 | 2.4 | | 2.2 | Current | | 3.2 | 4.6 | 1.7 | 2.2 | 1.9 |
| 1.2 | 1.5 | | 1.2 | | | 1.2 | 1.5 | 1.1 | 1.1 | 1.2 |
| 3.6 | 3.9 | | 3.5 | | | 12.7 | 7.2 | 6.5 | 3.4 | 2.8 |
| 1.7 | 2.0 | | 1.8 | Quick | | 3.0 | 3.2 | 1.6 | 1.9 | 1.6 |
| 1.0 | 1.2 | | 1.0 | | | 1.2 | 1.4 | .8 | .9 | 1.0 |
| 30  12.3 | 29  12.5 | 32 | 11.3 | | 0 UND | 15  23.6 | 43  8.5 | 30  12.3 | 36  10.0 | |
| 51  7.2 | 51  7.1 | 48 | 7.6 | Sales/Receivables | 0 UND | 36  10.0 | 51  7.2 | 46  7.9 | 54  6.8 | |
| 78  4.7 | 72  5.1 | 68 | 5.4 | | 64  5.7 | 59  6.2 | 72  5.1 | 70  5.2 | 70  5.2 | |
| | | | | Cost of Sales/Inventory | | | | | | |
| | | | | Cost of Sales/Payables | | | | | | |
| 4.5 | 4.0 | | 4.6 | | | 2.3 | 3.4 | 4.3 | 4.7 | 5.3 |
| 7.4 | 6.7 | | 7.9 | Sales/Working Capital | | 4.2 | 4.6 | 9.1 | 8.5 | 8.0 |
| 30.0 | 13.0 | | 34.6 | | | 98.0 | 10.9 | 119.7 | 149.4 | 32.7 |
| | 125.6 | | 111.7 | 84.7 | | | | 80.7 | 81.9 | 164.8 |
| (87)  26.3 | (125)  22.2 | (156) | 9.7 | EBIT/Interest | | (21)  6.6 | (36)  14.7 | (82)  12.4 | | |
| 4.7 | 2.7 | | 1.4 | | | | .7 | 6.1 | 2.1 | |
| | 22.4 | | 26.4 | Net Profit + Depr., Dep., | | | | | | |
| (11)  7.2 | (10) | | 6.1 | Amort./Cur. Mat. L/T/D | | | | | | |
| 1.6 | | | 3.7 | | | | | | | |
| .0 | .0 | | .0 | | | .0 | .0 | .0 | .0 | .0 |
| .1 | .1 | | .1 | Fixed/Worth | | .2 | .0 | .1 | .0 | .1 |
| 1.1 | .6 | | 1.0 | | | 1.0 | .8 | 2.0 | .3 | 1.6 |
| .4 | .4 | | .4 | | | .1 | .2 | .3 | .4 | .5 |
| 1.1 | 1.0 | | 1.6 | Debt/Worth | | 3.0 | .8 | 2.0 | 1.0 | 1.7 |
| 5.2 | 3.5 | | 9.4 | | | 11.0 | NM | NM | 4.5 | 8.5 |
| 91.3 | 79.3 | | 83.9 | % Profit Before Taxes/Tangible | 41.9 | 57.3 | 93.4 | 87.1 | 84.7 | |
| (99)  53.0 | (172)  39.6 | (172) | 45.8 | Net Worth | (15)  31.1 | (12)  27.2 | (22)  45.0 | (40)  49.6 | (79)  48.7 | |
| 21.5 | 16.6 | | 15.8 | | -16.7 | 6.6 | 12.5 | 15.3 | 20.4 | |
| 39.1 | 41.4 | | 33.4 | % Profit Before Taxes/Total | | 31.3 | 22.1 | 36.1 | 40.9 | 33.1 |
| 21.5 | 18.3 | | 15.9 | Assets | | 18.4 | 10.1 | 11.4 | 19.2 | 15.9 |
| 4.7 | 5.1 | | 2.7 | | | -1.5 | -15.3 | 3.2 | 8.7 | 3.6 |
| 358.2 | 669.4 | | 999.8 | | | UND | UND | 701.0 | 999.8 | 486.2 |
| 73.4 | 111.2 | | 124.1 | Sales/Net Fixed Assets | | 144.0 | 175.6 | 100.3 | 154.3 | 119.5 |
| 11.9 | 18.2 | | 25.3 | | | 7.1 | 17.7 | 28.6 | 60.9 | 16.4 |
| 3.5 | 3.7 | | 3.9 | | | 4.2 | 3.2 | 4.8 | 4.0 | 3.8 |
| 2.6 | 2.5 | | 2.6 | Sales/Total Assets | | 2.2 | 1.7 | 3.1 | 2.6 | 2.6 |
| 1.5 | 1.6 | | 1.5 | | | .7 | 1.3 | 1.5 | 1.6 | 1.5 |
| .2 | .2 | | .2 | | | | | .3 | .1 | .1 |
| (63)  .8 | (84)  .8 | (113) | .4 | % Depr., Dep., Amort./Sales | | (11)  .6 | (27)  .2 | (59)  .3 | | |
| 2.3 | 3.0 | | 1.1 | | | | 5.4 | .6 | 1.0 | |
| 1.7 | 2.6 | | 2.0 | % Officers', Directors' | | | | | 1.6 | .8 |
| (28)  5.0 | (40)  4.7 | (43) | 4.5 | Owners' Comp/Sales | | | | (13)  4.5 | (11)  2.5 | |
| 17.8 | 9.8 | | 10.1 | | | | | | 9.0 | 6.5 |
| 4183070M | 6760726M | | 9035824M | Net Sales ($) | 2056M | 35588M | 64521M | 212694M | 809238M | 7911727M |
| 2653706M | 4028040M | | 4907667M | Total Assets ($) | 5662M | 35705M | 41135M | 122975M | 398506M | 4303684M |

© RMA 2024   M = $ thousand   MM = $ million
See Pages viii through xx for Explanation of Ratios and Data

# PROFESSIONAL SERVICES—Research and Development in Biotechnology (except Nanobiotechnology) NAICS 541714

## Current Data Sorted by Assets | Comparative Historical Data

| 0-500M | 500M-2MM 7 (4/1-9/30/23) | 2-10MM | 10-50MM 30 (10/1/23-3/31/24) | 50-100MM | 100-250MM | Type of Statement | | 4/1/19-3/31/20 ALL | | 4/1/20-3/31/21 ALL |
|---|---|---|---|---|---|---|---|---|---|---|
| | | | | | | Unqualified | | 9 | | 5 |
| | | | | | | Reviewed | | 3 | | 2 |
| | | | | | | Compiled | | 3 | | 2 |
| | | | | | | Tax Returns | | 1 | | 8 |
| | 4 | 1 | 1 | 1 | | Other | | 29 | | 21 |
| | 7 | 2 | 2 | 2 | | | | | | |
| | | 1 | 2 | | | | | | | |
| | | 3 | | | | | | | | |
| | | 8 | 4 | 4 | 4 | | | | | |
| 4 | | 15 | 9 | 5 | 4 | NUMBER OF STATEMENTS | | 45 | | 38 |
| % | % | % | % | % | % | ASSETS | | % | | % |
| | | 23.1 | | | | Cash & Equivalents | | 29.7 | | 36.7 |
| | | 20.4 | | | | Trade Receivables (net) | | 19.5 | | 23.3 |
| | | 7.4 | | | | Inventory | | 4.7 | | 4.5 |
| D | | 1.4 | | | | All Other Current | | 5.1 | | 5.5 |
| A | | 52.3 | | | | Total Current | | 59.1 | | 69.9 |
| T | | 32.5 | | | | Fixed Assets (net) | | 18.5 | | 21.3 |
| A | | 6.9 | | | | Intangibles (net) | | 6.8 | | 4.4 |
| | | 8.4 | | | | All Other Non-Current | | 15.5 | | 4.2 |
| N | | 100.0 | | | | Total | | 100.0 | | 100.0 |
| O | | | | | | LIABILITIES | | | | |
| T | | 7.0 | | | | Notes Payable-Short Term | | 5.7 | | 5.8 |
| | | 1.0 | | | | Cur. Mat.-L.T.D. | | 2.0 | | 6.4 |
| A | | 8.8 | | | | Trade Payables | | 7.2 | | 5.5 |
| V | | .0 | | | | Income Taxes Payable | | .1 | | .4 |
| A | | 17.1 | | | | All Other Current | | 18.0 | | 14.5 |
| I | | 34.0 | | | | Total Current | | 33.0 | | 32.6 |
| L | | 14.9 | | | | Long-Term Debt | | 18.7 | | 24.3 |
| A | | .7 | | | | Deferred Taxes | | .2 | | .1 |
| B | | 8.1 | | | | All Other Non-Current | | 7.5 | | 5.7 |
| L | | 42.2 | | | | Net Worth | | 40.6 | | 37.2 |
| E | | 100.0 | | | | Total Liabilities & Net Worth | | 100.0 | | 100.0 |
| | | | | | | INCOME DATA | | | | |
| | | 100.0 | | | | Net Sales | | 100.0 | | 100.0 |
| | | | | | | Gross Profit | | | | |
| | | 96.4 | | | | Operating Expenses | | 87.6 | | 84.2 |
| | | 3.6 | | | | Operating Profit | | 12.4 | | 15.8 |
| | | 2.9 | | | | All Other Expenses (net) | | 1.7 | | 1.9 |
| | | .7 | | | | Profit Before Taxes | | 10.7 | | 13.9 |
| | | | | | | RATIOS | | | | |
| | | 4.0 | | | | | | 4.6 | | 4.7 |
| | | 1.7 | | | | Current | | 2.0 | | 2.8 |
| | | .8 | | | | | | 1.3 | | 1.4 |
| | | 3.6 | | | | | | 3.3 | | 4.2 |
| | | 1.4 | | | | Quick | | 1.5 | | 2.6 |
| | | .7 | | | | | | .8 | | 1.0 |
| | 29 | 12.4 | | | | | 7 | 51.7 | 0 | UND |
| | 50 | 7.3 | | | | Sales/Receivables | 36 | 10.2 | 53 | 6.9 |
| | 96 | 3.8 | | | | | 65 | 5.6 | 76 | 4.8 |
| | | | | | | Cost of Sales/Inventory | | | | |
| | | | | | | Cost of Sales/Payables | | | | |
| | | 2.9 | | | | | | 3.1 | | 2.7 |
| | | 4.8 | | | | Sales/Working Capital | | 6.0 | | 4.6 |
| | | -17.6 | | | | | | 31.4 | | 11.1 |
| | | | | | | | | 21.5 | | 56.1 |
| | | | | | | EBIT/Interest | (27) | 8.7 | (24) | 16.7 |
| | | | | | | | | 2.6 | | .4 |
| | | | | | | Net Profit + Depr., Dep., Amort./Cur. Mat. L/T/D | | | | |
| | | .1 | | | | | | .1 | | .1 |
| | | 1.3 | | | | Fixed/Worth | | .3 | | .3 |
| | | -21.3 | | | | | | .9 | | 1.4 |
| | | .4 | | | | | | .3 | | .4 |
| | | 1.4 | | | | Debt/Worth | | .8 | | 1.0 |
| | | -24.8 | | | | | | 26.0 | | 2.1 |
| | | 35.5 | | | | | | 48.6 | | 105.1 |
| | (11) | 12.0 | | | | % Profit Before Taxes/Tangible Net Worth | (35) | 21.0 | (32) | 48.4 |
| | | -20.8 | | | | | | 6.4 | | 11.7 |
| | | 18.7 | | | | | | 27.0 | | 47.3 |
| | | 5.2 | | | | % Profit Before Taxes/Total Assets | | 10.5 | | 16.2 |
| | | -1.8 | | | | | | 2.3 | | 1.8 |
| | | 21.2 | | | | | | 80.8 | | 46.0 |
| | | 6.5 | | | | Sales/Net Fixed Assets | | 11.1 | | 13.0 |
| | | 2.6 | | | | | | 4.8 | | 6.4 |
| | | 1.8 | | | | | | 2.6 | | 2.3 |
| | | 1.3 | | | | Sales/Total Assets | | 1.5 | | 1.9 |
| | | 1.0 | | | | | | .9 | | 1.1 |
| | | .9 | | | | | | 1.0 | | .8 |
| | (12) | 3.1 | | | | % Depr., Dep., Amort./Sales | (32) | 2.7 | (32) | 1.6 |
| | | 11.5 | | | | | | 4.2 | | 4.5 |
| | | | | | | % Officers', Directors' Owners' Comp/Sales | | | | |
| 35004M | 104517M | 278587M | 416861M | 817108M | | Net Sales ($) | | 1111126M | | 986545M |
| 6344M | 72123M | 214444M | 348758M | 746395M | | Total Assets ($) | | 1285953M | | 704933M |

M = $ thousand    MM = $ million
See Pages viii through xx for Explanation of Ratios and Data

© RMA 2024

# PROFESSIONAL SERVICES—Research and Development in Biotechnology (except Nanobiotechnology) NAICS 541714

## Comparative Historical Data | Current Data Sorted by Sales

| Comparative Historical Data | | | Type of Statement | Current Data Sorted by Sales | | | | | |
|---|---|---|---|---|---|---|---|---|---|
| 8 | 6 | 3 | Unqualified | | | | 1 | 1 | 2 |
| 2 | 6 | 4 | Reviewed | | | | 1 | 1 | 2 |
| 2 | 1 | 3 | Compiled | | | 2 | 2 | 1 | |
| 5 | 6 | 3 | Tax Returns | 1 | | 2 | | | |
| 19 | 27 | 24 | Other | 1 | 7 | 2 | 5 | 4 | 11 |
| 4/1/21-3/31/22 ALL | 4/1/22-3/31/23 ALL | 4/1/23-3/31/24 ALL | | 0-1MM | 1-3MM (4/1-9/30/23) | 3-5MM | 5-10MM | 10-25MM (10/1/23-3/31/24) | 25MM & OVER |
| 36 | 46 | 37 | **NUMBER OF STATEMENTS** | 2 | 1 | 4 | 8 | 7 | 15 |
| % | % | % | **ASSETS** | % | % | % | % | % | % |
| 27.4 | 30.1 | 23.0 | Cash & Equivalents | | | | | | 22.9 |
| 25.1 | 23.5 | 23.3 | Trade Receivables (net) | | | | | | 26.3 |
| 5.3 | 7.5 | 8.5 | Inventory | | | | | | 9.9 |
| 3.0 | 6.2 | 4.7 | All Other Current | | | | | | 8.5 |
| 60.8 | 67.2 | 59.5 | Total Current | | | | | | 67.6 |
| 26.6 | 17.2 | 24.5 | Fixed Assets (net) | | | | | | 12.5 |
| 6.8 | 4.0 | 7.3 | Intangibles (net) | | | | | | 7.4 |
| 5.7 | 11.5 | 8.7 | All Other Non-Current | | | | | | 12.5 |
| 100.0 | 100.0 | 100.0 | Total | | | | | | 100.0 |
| | | | **LIABILITIES** | | | | | | |
| 4.7 | 2.2 | 3.5 | Notes Payable-Short Term | | | | | | 1.6 |
| 1.5 | 6.3 | 2.2 | Cur. Mat.-L.T.D. | | | | | | .9 |
| 6.5 | 8.3 | 8.7 | Trade Payables | | | | | | 10.2 |
| .0 | .2 | .2 | Income Taxes Payable | | | | | | .1 |
| 15.8 | 18.4 | 20.7 | All Other Current | | | | | | 26.5 |
| 28.5 | 35.4 | 35.3 | Total Current | | | | | | 39.2 |
| 23.6 | 19.9 | 16.8 | Long-Term Debt | | | | | | 14.4 |
| .2 | .1 | .3 | Deferred Taxes | | | | | | .0 |
| 6.3 | 8.6 | 15.5 | All Other Non-Current | | | | | | 29.4 |
| 41.4 | 36.1 | 32.1 | Net Worth | | | | | | 17.0 |
| 100.0 | 100.0 | 100.0 | Total Liabilities & Net Worth | | | | | | 100.0 |
| | | | **INCOME DATA** | | | | | | |
| 100.0 | 100.0 | 100.0 | Net Sales | | | | | | 100.0 |
| | | | Gross Profit | | | | | | 97.3 |
| 87.5 | 89.2 | 93.9 | Operating Expenses | | | | | | 2.7 |
| 12.5 | 10.8 | 6.1 | Operating Profit | | | | | | .4 |
| -.1 | 1.7 | 2.2 | All Other Expenses (net) | | | | | | 2.3 |
| 12.6 | 9.1 | 3.9 | Profit Before Taxes | | | | | | |
| | | | **RATIOS** | | | | | | |
| 7.0 | 5.0 | 3.1 | | | | | | | 2.8 |
| 2.5 | 2.4 | 1.8 | Current | | | | | | 1.9 |
| 1.4 | 1.4 | 1.3 | | | | | | | 1.2 |
| 6.5 | 3.6 | 2.3 | | | | | | | 2.2 |
| 2.0 | 1.9 | 1.4 | Quick | | | | | | 1.1 |
| 1.2 | .9 | .9 | | | | | | | .9 |
| 44  8.3 | 17  21.9 | 38  9.7 | | | | | | 41 | 8.9 |
| 55  6.6 | 53  6.9 | 52  7.0 | Sales/Receivables | | | | | 53 | 6.9 |
| 83  4.4 | 74  4.9 | 81  4.5 | | | | | | 70 | 5.2 |
| | | | Cost of Sales/Inventory | | | | | | |
| | | | Cost of Sales/Payables | | | | | | |
| 1.9 | 2.3 | 2.9 | | | | | | | 2.2 |
| 3.8 | 3.7 | 5.6 | Sales/Working Capital | | | | | | 4.0 |
| 17.6 | 11.6 | 20.0 | | | | | | | 10.7 |
| 26.7 | 120.8 | 42.9 | | | | | | | 104.1 |
| (27) 10.5 | (32) 12.1 | (24) 7.6 | EBIT/Interest | | | | | (12) | 11.9 |
| 1.9 | -1.5 | .4 | | | | | | | .4 |
| | | | Net Profit + Depr., Dep., Amort./Cur. Mat. L/T/D | | | | | | |
| .1 | .1 | .2 | | | | | | | .1 |
| .5 | .3 | .6 | Fixed/Worth | | | | | | .5 |
| 1.6 | .9 | NM | | | | | | | -.4 |
| .5 | .5 | .5 | | | | | | | 1.2 |
| .9 | 1.1 | 1.9 | Debt/Worth | | | | | | 2.2 |
| 2.3 | 4.8 | NM | | | | | | | -14.6 |
| 70.0 | 53.2 | 93.6 | | | | | | | 148.5 |
| (32) 24.0 | (40) 20.4 | (28) 15.2 | % Profit Before Taxes/Tangible Net Worth | | | | | (11) | 9.9 |
| 4.5 | -4.0 | 7.9 | | | | | | | 7.9 |
| 41.4 | 17.8 | 17.9 | | | | | | | 15.5 |
| 8.2 | 9.8 | 6.2 | % Profit Before Taxes/Total Assets | | | | | | 6.6 |
| .6 | -4.0 | -.7 | | | | | | | -2.0 |
| 26.5 | 56.5 | 30.1 | | | | | | | 109.3 |
| 8.2 | 11.1 | 9.3 | Sales/Net Fixed Assets | | | | | | 12.1 |
| 1.7 | 3.9 | 2.9 | | | | | | | 8.3 |
| 2.3 | 1.6 | 2.1 | | | | | | | 2.2 |
| 1.2 | 1.1 | 1.4 | Sales/Total Assets | | | | | | 1.4 |
| .5 | .9 | .9 | | | | | | | .8 |
| 1.3 | .6 | .7 | | | | | | | .4 |
| (26) 2.5 | (37) 1.7 | (27) 2.1 | % Depr., Dep., Amort./Sales | | | | | (10) | 1.0 |
| 6.2 | 4.1 | 8.4 | | | | | | | 4.7 |
| | | 2.9 | % Officers', Directors' Owners' Comp/Sales | | | | | | |
| | (11) 4.7 | | | | | | | | |
| | | 10.3 | | | | | | | |
| 1007572M | 1289833M | 1652077M | Net Sales ($) | 598M | 1890M | 13519M | 51811M | 118653M | 1465606M |
| 1380437M | 1544944M | 1388064M | Total Assets ($) | 8267M | 1722M | 12143M | 72964M | 68029M | 1224939M |

© RMA 2024  M = $ thousand  MM = $ million
See Pages viii through xx for Explanation of Ratios and Data

# 1038 PROFESSIONAL SERVICES—Research and Development in the Physical, Engineering, and Life Sciences (except Nanotechnology and Biotechnology) NAICS 541715

## Current Data Sorted by Assets | Comparative Historical Data

| Type of Statement | | | | | | | | | |
|---|---|---|---|---|---|---|---|---|---|
| | | | | 7 | 2 | 2 | Unqualified | 19 | 16 |
| | | | | 2 | | | Reviewed | 3 | 4 |
| | | | 1 | 1 | | | Compiled | 7 | 1 |
| 1 | 4 | 3 | | | | | Tax Returns | 8 | 5 |
| | | 4 | 11 | 16 | 11 | 8 | Other | 59 | 21 |
| | 22 | (4/1-9/30/23) | | 51 (10/1/23-3/31/24) | | | | 4/1/19-3/31/20 | 4/1/20-3/31/21 |
| 0-500M | 500M-2MM | 2-10MM | 10-50MM | 50-100MM | 100-250MM | | | ALL | ALL |
| 1 | 8 | 15 | 26 | 13 | 10 | | NUMBER OF STATEMENTS | 96 | 47 |
| % | % | % | % | % | % | | ASSETS | % | % |
| | | 24.9 | 22.5 | 14.7 | 21.0 | | Cash & Equivalents | 19.7 | 34.1 |
| | | 17.6 | 21.2 | 19.3 | 16.4 | | Trade Receivables (net) | 26.0 | 21.8 |
| | | 8.3 | 7.2 | 2.4 | 6.4 | | Inventory | 6.2 | 4.6 |
| | | 1.1 | 10.1 | 9.5 | 1.0 | | All Other Current | 6.7 | 3.1 |
| | | 51.8 | 61.1 | 45.9 | 44.8 | | Total Current | 58.6 | 63.6 |
| | | 23.6 | 16.7 | 27.7 | 8.9 | | Fixed Assets (net) | 20.2 | 18.5 |
| | | 5.0 | 4.0 | 12.5 | 13.7 | | Intangibles (net) | 8.5 | 8.3 |
| | | 19.6 | 18.3 | 14.0 | 32.5 | | All Other Non-Current | 12.7 | 9.6 |
| | | 100.0 | 100.0 | 100.0 | 100.0 | | Total | 100.0 | 100.0 |
| | | | | | | | LIABILITIES | | |
| | | 6.7 | 2.5 | 1.0 | .4 | | Notes Payable-Short Term | 4.7 | 11.5 |
| | | .2 | 2.2 | 1.7 | 1.7 | | Cur. Mat.-L.T.D. | 1.6 | 3.9 |
| | | 5.0 | 9.7 | 8.6 | 6.0 | | Trade Payables | 8.4 | 6.7 |
| | | .2 | .6 | .0 | .1 | | Income Taxes Payable | .2 | .2 |
| | | 14.2 | 22.0 | 15.0 | 15.5 | | All Other Current | 18.7 | 20.7 |
| | | 26.2 | 37.0 | 26.4 | 23.7 | | Total Current | 33.5 | 43.1 |
| | | 5.7 | 7.4 | 22.4 | 10.4 | | Long-Term Debt | 11.3 | 17.9 |
| | | .0 | .1 | .9 | .0 | | Deferred Taxes | .3 | .5 |
| | | 3.9 | 20.8 | 4.8 | 12.6 | | All Other Non-Current | 4.1 | 10.8 |
| | | 64.1 | 34.6 | 45.5 | 53.3 | | Net Worth | 50.9 | 27.7 |
| | | 100.0 | 100.0 | 100.0 | 100.0 | | Total Liabilities & Net Worth | 100.0 | 100.0 |
| | | | | | | | INCOME DATA | | |
| | | 100.0 | 100.0 | 100.0 | 100.0 | | Net Sales | 100.0 | 100.0 |
| | | | | | | | Gross Profit | | |
| | | 90.9 | 94.7 | 98.1 | 98.9 | | Operating Expenses | 91.6 | 93.9 |
| | | 9.1 | 5.3 | 1.9 | 1.1 | | Operating Profit | 8.4 | 6.1 |
| | | 2.8 | -.2 | 1.7 | -1.1 | | All Other Expenses (net) | .9 | .3 |
| | | 6.2 | 5.4 | .3 | 2.2 | | Profit Before Taxes | 7.5 | 5.8 |
| | | | | | | | RATIOS | | |
| | | 5.3 | 4.1 | 2.5 | 2.9 | | | 2.9 | 4.4 |
| | | 1.7 | 2.1 | 1.7 | 2.0 | | Current | 1.9 | 1.9 |
| | | 1.1 | 1.3 | 1.5 | 1.3 | | | 1.2 | 1.0 |
| | | 3.3 | 2.4 | 2.4 | 2.9 | | | 2.5 | 3.5 |
| | | 1.6 | 1.5 | 1.3 | 1.5 | | Quick | 1.4 | 1.7 |
| | | .9 | .9 | .9 | 1.3 | | | .8 | .7 |
| | 0 | UND | 24 | 15.0 | 39 | 9.4 | 24 | 15.0 | | 27 | 13.4 | 21 | 17.2 |
| | 21 | 17.3 | 40 | 9.1 | 55 | 6.6 | 46 | 8.0 | Sales/Receivables | 52 | 7.0 | 52 | 7.0 |
| | 58 | 6.3 | 72 | 5.1 | 81 | 4.5 | 68 | 5.4 | | 74 | 4.9 | 74 | 4.9 |
| | | | | | | | Cost of Sales/Inventory | | |
| | | | | | | | Cost of Sales/Payables | | |
| | | 2.2 | 2.5 | 3.6 | 4.3 | | | 3.3 | 2.7 |
| | | 7.2 | 6.1 | 5.4 | 5.7 | | Sales/Working Capital | 7.2 | 6.8 |
| | | 64.7 | 27.4 | 8.6 | 21.4 | | | 30.5 | 310.6 |
| | | | 33.6 | | | | | 45.2 | 56.7 |
| | | (17) | 12.9 | | | | EBIT/Interest | (72) 12.6 | (37) 6.0 |
| | | | 3.0 | | | | | 3.5 | -.9 |
| | | | | | | | | 21.5 | |
| | | | | | | | Net Profit + Depr., Dep., Amort./Cur. Mat. L/T/D | (12) 7.9 | |
| | | | | | | | | 2.5 | |
| | | .0 | .1 | .3 | .1 | | | .1 | .1 |
| | | .0 | .3 | .6 | .1 | | Fixed/Worth | .3 | .4 |
| | | 1.1 | 1.1 | 1.4 | .6 | | | .9 | 3.2 |
| | | .1 | .3 | .8 | .4 | | | .4 | .7 |
| | | .8 | 1.5 | 1.3 | 1.3 | | Debt/Worth | 1.0 | 2.0 |
| | | 1.6 | 5.6 | 3.3 | 4.4 | | | 3.6 | 9.3 |
| | | 63.7 | 84.1 | 30.5 | 86.2 | | | 66.3 | 51.3 |
| | | 24.7 | (21) 10.2 | (12) 9.3 | 2.4 | | % Profit Before Taxes/Tangible Net Worth | (87) 20.1 | (37) 18.0 |
| | | -3.2 | 2.3 | .4 | -22.8 | | | 1.6 | -.8 |
| | | 43.0 | 18.7 | 11.8 | 25.1 | | | 20.3 | 17.8 |
| | | 20.3 | 8.2 | 4.2 | 1.4 | | % Profit Before Taxes/Total Assets | 8.0 | 6.0 |
| | | -1.7 | -.9 | -4.5 | -3.4 | | | .6 | -2.3 |
| | | 652.0 | 74.3 | 26.9 | 114.8 | | | 60.4 | 155.0 |
| | | 78.5 | 19.0 | 4.2 | 29.2 | | Sales/Net Fixed Assets | 18.2 | 25.8 |
| | | 1.8 | 5.5 | 1.7 | 6.2 | | | 3.6 | 3.8 |
| | | 2.3 | 2.6 | 1.3 | 2.4 | | | 2.6 | 2.7 |
| | | 1.4 | 1.4 | .9 | 1.0 | | Sales/Total Assets | 1.5 | 1.5 |
| | | .6 | 1.1 | .6 | .6 | | | .8 | 1.1 |
| | | | .4 | | | | | 1.1 | .8 |
| | | | (17) .9 | | | | % Depr., Dep., Amort./Sales | (58) 2.1 | (31) 2.4 |
| | | | 2.9 | | | | | 4.8 | 4.6 |
| | | | | | | | | 1.8 | |
| | | | | | | | % Officers', Directors' Owners' Comp/Sales | (10) 4.1 | |
| | | | | | | | | 6.2 | |
| 1149M | 20558M | 129466M | 1794143M | 1314131M | 2444828M | | Net Sales ($) | 5377318M | 2794400M |
| 273M | 10581M | 83568M | 635526M | 945079M | 1717394M | | Total Assets ($) | 3898696M | 1647888M |

M = $ thousand  MM = $ million
See Pages viii through xx for Explanation of Ratios and Data

© RMA 2024

# PROFESSIONAL SERVICES—Research and Development in the Physical, Engineering, and Life Sciences (except Nanotechnology and Biotechnology) NAICS 541715

## Comparative Historical Data | Current Data Sorted by Sales

| Comparative Historical Data ||| Type of Statement | Current Data Sorted by Sales ||||||
|---|---|---|---|---|---|---|---|---|---|
| 7 | 11 | 11 | Unqualified | | | | | 3 | 8 |
| 2 | 5 | 2 | Reviewed | | | | | | 2 |
| 1 | 2 | 2 | Compiled | | | | 1 | 1 | 1 |
| 3 | 8 | 8 | Tax Returns | | 6 | | 1 | 1 | 1 |
| 30 | 42 | 50 | Other | 1 | 5 | 2 | 8 | 6 | 28 |
| 4/1/21-3/31/22 | 4/1/22-3/31/23 | 4/1/23-3/31/24 | | 22 (4/1-9/30/23) ||| 51 (10/1/23-3/31/24) |||
| ALL | ALL | ALL | | 0-1MM | 1-3MM | 3-5MM | 5-10MM | 10-25MM | 25MM & OVER |
| 43 | 68 | 73 | NUMBER OF STATEMENTS | 1 | 11 | 2 | 10 | 9 | 40 |
| % | % | % | | % | % | % | % | % | % |
| | | | ASSETS | | | | | | |
| 28.8 | 23.5 | 23.0 | Cash & Equivalents | | 30.4 | | 34.7 | | 17.6 |
| 21.7 | 27.1 | 18.4 | Trade Receivables (net) | | 10.4 | | 13.8 | | 22.9 |
| 5.4 | 11.5 | 8.3 | Inventory | | 21.0 | | 7.4 | | 7.1 |
| 8.2 | 5.7 | 6.0 | All Other Current | | 2.5 | | 2.2 | | 9.2 |
| 64.1 | 67.8 | 55.8 | Total Current | | 64.3 | | 58.1 | | 56.7 |
| 18.2 | 15.9 | 19.7 | Fixed Assets (net) | | 23.8 | | 22.4 | | 16.2 |
| 10.0 | 5.9 | 6.5 | Intangibles (net) | | 1.1 | | 6.5 | | 6.5 |
| 7.7 | 10.5 | 18.0 | All Other Non-Current | | 10.8 | | 13.0 | | 20.5 |
| 100.0 | 100.0 | 100.0 | Total | | 100.0 | | 100.0 | | 100.0 |
| | | | LIABILITIES | | | | | | |
| 6.8 | 4.2 | 3.8 | Notes Payable-Short Term | | 8.6 | | 3.9 | | 2.3 |
| .6 | 1.0 | 1.7 | Cur. Mat.-L.T.D. | | 2.4 | | .3 | | 1.9 |
| 7.9 | 7.9 | 7.6 | Trade Payables | | 4.1 | | 2.6 | | 10.4 |
| .1 | .3 | .3 | Income Taxes Payable | | .0 | | .1 | | .4 |
| 14.6 | 20.9 | 19.0 | All Other Current | | 25.3 | | 5.5 | | 23.0 |
| 30.0 | 34.3 | 32.4 | Total Current | | 40.3 | | 12.4 | | 38.1 |
| 11.0 | 13.6 | 12.9 | Long-Term Debt | | 23.9 | | 22.6 | | 7.1 |
| .2 | .1 | .2 | Deferred Taxes | | .0 | | .0 | | .2 |
| 1.6 | 6.4 | 10.8 | All Other Non-Current | | .3 | | 3.8 | | 17.4 |
| 57.1 | 45.6 | 43.7 | Net Worth | | 35.4 | | 61.3 | | 37.2 |
| 100.0 | 100.0 | 100.0 | Total Liabilties & Net Worth | | 100.0 | | 100.0 | | 100.0 |
| | | | INCOME DATA | | | | | | |
| 100.0 | 100.0 | 100.0 | Net Sales | | 100.0 | | 100.0 | | 100.0 |
| 91.7 | 89.7 | 95.2 | Gross Profit | | 98.8 | | 80.2 | | 97.4 |
| 8.3 | 10.3 | 4.8 | Operating Expenses | | 1.2 | | 19.8 | | 2.6 |
| -1.7 | 1.2 | .9 | Operating Profit | | 2.0 | | 2.8 | | .0 |
| 10.0 | 9.1 | 3.9 | All Other Expenses (net) | | -.8 | | 17.0 | | 2.6 |
| | | | Profit Before Taxes | | | | | | |
| | | | RATIOS | | | | | | |
| 4.7 | 4.0 | 3.6 | | | 18.0 | | 16.1 | | 2.6 |
| 2.1 | 2.3 | 1.9 | Current | | 1.5 | | 4.8 | | 1.7 |
| 1.5 | 1.4 | 1.3 | | | .9 | | 2.2 | | 1.3 |
| 4.0 | 3.3 | 2.4 | | | 1.7 | | 10.8 | | 1.6 |
| 1.9 | 1.7 | 1.5 | Quick | | 1.1 | | 3.1 | | 1.3 |
| 1.2 | 1.0 | .9 | | | .4 | | 1.9 | | .9 |
| 4  86.5 | 25  14.6 | 18  20.2 | | 0  UND | | 9  42.4 | | 32  11.5 | |
| 48  7.6 | 54  6.7 | 41  8.8 | Sales/Receivables | 0  999.8 | | 26  13.9 | | 42  8.7 | |
| 64  5.7 | 78  4.7 | 69  5.3 | | 41  8.8 | | 111  3.3 | | 68  5.4 | |
| | | | Cost of Sales/Inventory | | | | | | |
| | | | Cost of Sales/Payables | | | | | | |
| 2.8 | 2.7 | 3.5 | | | 3.7 | | 1.3 | | 3.9 |
| 6.0 | 5.7 | 6.4 | Sales/Working Capital | | 7.7 | | 3.0 | | 6.6 |
| 12.9 | 15.8 | 23.6 | | | -40.0 | | 6.3 | | 22.0 |
| 123.4 | 46.2 | 32.6 | | | | | | | 34.0 |
| (27) 57.6 | (44) 6.8 | (45) 6.1 | EBIT/Interest | | | | | (28) | 4.8 |
| 7.6 | 1.5 | -4.3 | | | | | | | -2.5 |
| | | | Net Profit + Depr., Dep., Amort./Cur. Mat. L/T/D | | | | | | |
| .1 | .0 | .0 | | | .1 | | .0 | | .1 |
| .1 | .2 | .3 | Fixed/Worth | | .7 | | .0 | | .3 |
| .8 | 1.4 | 1.4 | | | -1.9 | | 1.5 | | 1.3 |
| .3 | .3 | .4 | | | .1 | | .1 | | .8 |
| .8 | .9 | 1.2 | Debt/Worth | | 2.5 | | 1.8 | | 1.4 |
| 2.4 | 4.3 | 4.2 | | | -10.4 | | 2.7 | | 4.5 |
| 65.1 | 45.5 | 63.7 | | | | | 63.8 | | 77.4 |
| (40) 30.4 | (54) 15.3 | (63) 9.9 | % Profit Before Taxes/Tangible Net Worth | | | | 35.3 | (35) | 9.3 |
| 11.4 | -.5 | -3.2 | | | | | 8.3 | | -3.0 |
| 21.5 | 18.3 | 20.1 | | | 30.8 | | 46.8 | | 17.6 |
| 12.2 | 7.8 | 6.3 | % Profit Before Taxes/Total Assets | | -1.2 | | 14.6 | | 5.7 |
| 4.1 | .7 | -3.7 | | | -45.6 | | 6.1 | | -2.4 |
| 190.5 | 143.7 | 91.9 | | | 650.0 | | 591.7 | | 72.5 |
| 26.9 | 34.1 | 21.0 | Sales/Net Fixed Assets | | 22.8 | | 91.9 | | 19.0 |
| 4.0 | 5.1 | 3.2 | | | 1.9 | | 1.5 | | 5.3 |
| 3.4 | 2.9 | 2.4 | | | 3.2 | | 2.5 | | 3.0 |
| 1.8 | 1.7 | 1.3 | Sales/Total Assets | | 1.3 | | 1.2 | | 1.4 |
| 1.1 | .9 | .8 | | | .7 | | .6 | | 1.1 |
| .4 | .4 | .5 | | | | | | | .4 |
| (28) .9 | (37) 1.2 | (45) 1.8 | % Depr., Dep., Amort./Sales | | | | | (26) | .8 |
| 2.7 | 3.2 | 3.2 | | | | | | | 2.3 |
| | | 3.7 | % Officers', Directors' Owners' Comp/Sales | | | | | | |
| | (10) 6.6 | | | | | | | | |
| | | 8.4 | | | | | | | |
| 2379501M | 2590012M | 5704275M | Net Sales ($) | 224M | 22036M | 8231M | 75738M | 165663M | 5432383M |
| 1462537M | 1670835M | 3392421M | Total Assets ($) | 2950M | 20357M | 16931M | 130637M | 257228M | 2964318M |

© RMA 2024

M = $ thousand    MM = $ million

See Pages viii through xx for Explanation of Ratios and Data

# PROFESSIONAL SERVICES—Research and Development in the Social Sciences and Humanities  NAICS 541720

## Current Data Sorted by Assets / Comparative Historical Data

| Type of Statement | | | | | | | | | |
|---|---|---|---|---|---|---|---|---|---|
| | | | | | | Unqualified | | 16 | 4 |
| | | 1 | 6 | 2 | 1 | Reviewed | | 4 | 1 |
| | | | | | | Compiled | | 4 | 2 |
| 1 | 1 | | | | | Tax Returns | | 5 | 2 |
| 1 | 4 | 2 | 5 | 2 | 3 | Other | | 21 | 11 |
| 12 (4/1-9/30/23) | | | 17 (10/1/23-3/31/24) | | | | | 4/1/19- | 4/1/20- |
| 0-500M | 500M-2MM | 2-10MM | 10-50MM | 50-100MM | 100-250MM | | | 3/31/20 | 3/31/21 |
| | | | | | | NUMBER OF STATEMENTS | | ALL | ALL |
| 2 | 5 | 3 | 11 | 4 | 4 | | | 50 | 20 |
| % | % | % | % | % | % | ASSETS | | % | % |
| | | | 19.3 | | | Cash & Equivalents | | 30.3 | 32.6 |
| | | | 17.9 | | | Trade Receivables (net) | | 27.0 | 17.2 |
| | | | 6.6 | | | Inventory | | 1.6 | 3.7 |
| | | | 2.5 | | | All Other Current | | 2.8 | 3.8 |
| | | | 46.4 | | | Total Current | | 61.7 | 57.3 |
| | | | 22.7 | | | Fixed Assets (net) | | 20.7 | 27.1 |
| | | | 15.7 | | | Intangibles (net) | | 6.4 | 4.6 |
| | | | 15.2 | | | All Other Non-Current | | 11.2 | 11.0 |
| | | | 100.0 | | | Total | | 100.0 | 100.0 |
| | | | | | | LIABILITIES | | | |
| | | | 2.3 | | | Notes Payable-Short Term | | 9.6 | 14.5 |
| | | | .5 | | | Cur. Mat.-L.T.D. | | .8 | 2.4 |
| | | | 6.1 | | | Trade Payables | | 6.2 | 4.4 |
| | | | .0 | | | Income Taxes Payable | | .1 | .0 |
| | | | 16.9 | | | All Other Current | | 18.5 | 10.7 |
| | | | 25.8 | | | Total Current | | 35.2 | 32.0 |
| | | | 21.2 | | | Long-Term Debt | | 9.9 | 11.9 |
| | | | .2 | | | Deferred Taxes | | .3 | .0 |
| | | | 19.1 | | | All Other Non-Current | | 5.8 | 1.5 |
| | | | 33.7 | | | Net Worth | | 48.8 | 54.7 |
| | | | 100.0 | | | Total Liabilities & Net Worth | | 100.0 | 100.0 |
| | | | | | | INCOME DATA | | | |
| | | | 100.0 | | | Net Sales | | 100.0 | 100.0 |
| | | | | | | Gross Profit | | | |
| | | | 98.4 | | | Operating Expenses | | 91.5 | 93.4 |
| | | | 1.6 | | | Operating Profit | | 8.5 | 6.6 |
| | | | 3.7 | | | All Other Expenses (net) | | 1.8 | -1.5 |
| | | | -2.1 | | | Profit Before Taxes | | 6.7 | 8.0 |
| | | | | | | RATIOS | | | |
| | | | 3.7 | | | | | 6.4 | 3.4 |
| | | | 2.3 | | | Current | | 2.3 | 2.0 |
| | | | .7 | | | | | 1.0 | 1.4 |
| | | | 3.1 | | | | | 5.8 | 3.4 |
| | | | 1.5 | | | Quick | | 1.8 | 2.0 |
| | | | .6 | | | | | .9 | .8 |
| | | 30 | 12.1 | | | | 4 | 86.3 | 0 UND |
| | | 49 | 7.5 | | | Sales/Receivables | 42 | 8.6 | 34 10.8 |
| | | 57 | 6.4 | | | | 65 | 5.6 | 60 6.1 |
| | | | | | | Cost of Sales/Inventory | | | |
| | | | | | | Cost of Sales/Payables | | | |
| | | | 4.1 | | | | | 2.4 | 3.2 |
| | | | 8.5 | | | Sales/Working Capital | | 7.7 | 7.9 |
| | | | -7.0 | | | | | NM | 15.1 |
| | | | | | | | | 30.0 | 24.6 |
| | | | | | | EBIT/Interest | (32) | 6.8 | (12) 5.1 |
| | | | | | | | | 2.1 | 1.4 |
| | | | | | | Net Profit + Depr., Dep., Amort./Cur. Mat. L/T/D | | | |
| | | | .1 | | | | | .0 | .0 |
| | | | .7 | | | Fixed/Worth | | .2 | .3 |
| | | | -.2 | | | | | 1.9 | 1.7 |
| | | | .3 | | | | | .3 | .3 |
| | | | 1.6 | | | Debt/Worth | | 1.0 | .6 |
| | | | -2.9 | | | | | 3.5 | 2.2 |
| | | | | | | % Profit Before Taxes/Tangible Net Worth | | 41.0 | 23.5 |
| | | | | | | | (43) | 13.9 | (18) 9.0 |
| | | | | | | | | 4.2 | -7.4 |
| | | | 6.4 | | | | | 19.2 | 12.2 |
| | | | -.1 | | | % Profit Before Taxes/Total Assets | | 6.0 | 5.1 |
| | | | -8.9 | | | | | 1.7 | -5.4 |
| | | | 116.7 | | | | | 137.7 | 86.7 |
| | | | 26.5 | | | Sales/Net Fixed Assets | | 25.6 | 35.8 |
| | | | .8 | | | | | 3.4 | 2.3 |
| | | | 1.4 | | | | | 3.1 | 2.3 |
| | | | .9 | | | Sales/Total Assets | | 2.0 | 1.3 |
| | | | .5 | | | | | 1.0 | .9 |
| | | | | | | | | .4 | .5 |
| | | | | | | % Depr., Dep., Amort./Sales | (35) | 1.8 | (13) 1.1 |
| | | | | | | | | 4.0 | 8.7 |
| | | | | | | % Officers', Directors' Owners' Comp/Sales | | | |
| 907M | 15351M | 18390M | 397055M | 192398M | 677551M | Net Sales ($) | | 2581735M | 354993M |
| 492M | 5147M | 14963M | 260171M | 286569M | 619467M | Total Assets ($) | | 1679434M | 358397M |

M = $ thousand    MM = $ million
See Pages viii through xx for Explanation of Ratios and Data

© RMA 2024

# PROFESSIONAL SERVICES—Research and Development in the Social Sciences and Humanities   NAICS 541720

## Comparative Historical Data | Current Data Sorted by Sales

| | | | | Type of Statement | | | | | | |
|---|---|---|---|---|---|---|---|---|---|---|
| 6 | 5 | 10 | | Unqualified | | | 3 | 1 | 6 | |
| | 1 | 1 | | Reviewed | | | | | | |
| | 1 | 2 | | Compiled | 2 | | | | | |
| 14 | 12 | 17 | | Tax Returns | 1 | 5 | 1 | 5 | 5 | |
| 4/1/21- | 4/1/22- | 4/1/23- | | Other | | 12 (4/1-9/30/23) | | 17 (10/1/23-3/31/24) | | |
| 3/31/22 | 3/31/23 | 3/31/24 | | | 0-1MM | 1-3MM | 3-5MM | 5-10MM | 10-25MM | 25MM & OVER |
| ALL | ALL | ALL | NUMBER OF STATEMENTS | 3 | 5 | 4 | 4 | 6 | 11 | |
| 20 | 20 | 29 | | % | % | % | % | % | % |
| % | % | % | **ASSETS** | | | | | | |
| 29.5 | 30.6 | 22.5 | Cash & Equivalents | | | | | | 33.1 |
| 28.7 | 14.9 | 13.3 | Trade Receivables (net) | | | | | | 18.8 |
| .1 | 2.5 | 2.6 | Inventory | | D | | | | 2.4 |
| 6.2 | 5.7 | 6.7 | All Other Current | | A | | | | 5.7 |
| 64.5 | 53.7 | 45.1 | Total Current | | T | | | | 60.1 |
| 13.1 | 24.4 | 18.8 | Fixed Assets (net) | | A | | | | 12.8 |
| 10.8 | 4.7 | 7.3 | Intangibles (net) | | | | | | 10.7 |
| 11.6 | 17.2 | 28.8 | All Other Non-Current | | N | | | | 16.3 |
| 100.0 | 100.0 | 100.0 | Total | | O | | | | 100.0 |
| | | | **LIABILITIES** | | T | | | | |
| 3.2 | .2 | 5.5 | Notes Payable-Short Term | | | | | | 1.2 |
| .7 | 1.6 | .5 | Cur. Mat.-L.T.D. | | A | | | | .4 |
| 9.4 | 9.2 | 4.5 | Trade Payables | | V | | | | 5.7 |
| .2 | .0 | .0 | Income Taxes Payable | | A | | | | .1 |
| 23.1 | 21.4 | 16.2 | All Other Current | | I | | | | 18.3 |
| 36.6 | 32.5 | 26.7 | Total Current | | L | | | | 25.8 |
| 8.6 | 20.5 | 18.2 | Long-Term Debt | | A | | | | 11.1 |
| .0 | .0 | .1 | Deferred Taxes | | B | | | | .0 |
| 15.6 | 13.9 | 12.0 | All Other Non-Current | | L | | | | 25.5 |
| 39.2 | 33.1 | 43.1 | Net Worth | | E | | | | 37.7 |
| 100.0 | 100.0 | 100.0 | Total Liabilities & Net Worth | | | | | | 100.0 |
| | | | **INCOME DATA** | | | | | | |
| 100.0 | 100.0 | 100.0 | Net Sales | | | | | | 100.0 |
| | | | Gross Profit | | | | | | 96.9 |
| 91.1 | 92.9 | 95.2 | Operating Expenses | | | | | | |
| 8.9 | 7.1 | 4.8 | Operating Profit | | | | | | 3.1 |
| -2.5 | 7.8 | 1.9 | All Other Expenses (net) | | | | | | 1.8 |
| 11.3 | -.7 | 2.9 | Profit Before Taxes | | | | | | 1.3 |
| | | | **RATIOS** | | | | | | |
| 4.4 | 9.4 | 5.5 | | | | | | | 5.6 |
| 1.6 | 3.7 | 1.8 | Current | | | | | | 2.3 |
| 1.3 | 1.2 | .8 | | | | | | | .8 |
| 4.2 | 5.6 | 4.1 | | | | | | | 5.6 |
| 1.5 | 3.6 | 1.5 | Quick | | | | | | 1.7 |
| 1.0 | .9 | .6 | | | | | | | .7 |
| 35  10.3 | 1  443.7 | 3  124.8 | | | | | | 30 | 12.1 |
| 55  6.6 | 24  15.2 | 39  9.4 | Sales/Receivables | | | | | 45 | 8.2 |
| 79  4.6 | 65  5.6 | 51  7.2 | | | | | | 57 | 6.4 |
| | | | Cost of Sales/Inventory | | | | | | |
| | | | Cost of Sales/Payables | | | | | | |
| 2.9 | 1.4 | 1.6 | | | | | | | 1.8 |
| 8.7 | 3.2 | 7.0 | Sales/Working Capital | | | | | | 6.9 |
| 15.6 | 29.9 | -32.1 | | | | | | | -12.5 |
| 83.8 | 22.7 | 21.6 | | | | | | | |
| (13) 20.4 | (13) 2.3 | (21) 1.6 | EBIT/Interest | | | | | | |
| 5.2 | -6.7 | -2.0 | | | | | | | |
| | | | Net Profit + Depr., Dep., Amort./Cur. Mat. L/T/D | | | | | | |
| .1 | .0 | .1 | | | | | | | .1 |
| .3 | .6 | .4 | Fixed/Worth | | | | | | .3 |
| 5.9 | NM | 1.4 | | | | | | | -.2 |
| .3 | .2 | .3 | | | | | | | .3 |
| 1.1 | .5 | 1.0 | Debt/Worth | | | | | | 1.6 |
| 44.4 | NM | NM | | | | | | | -2.9 |
| 81.4 | 20.6 | 14.4 | | | | | | | |
| (16) 36.2 | (15) 3.2 | (22) 1.9 | % Profit Before Taxes/Tangible Net Worth | | | | | | |
| 9.5 | -4.0 | -4.3 | | | | | | | |
| 41.6 | 16.8 | 10.1 | | | | | | | 6.7 |
| 10.2 | 3.2 | .7 | % Profit Before Taxes/Total Assets | | | | | | 3.0 |
| 2.9 | -2.9 | -3.3 | | | | | | | -1.8 |
| 81.4 | 126.5 | 59.5 | | | | | | | 38.3 |
| 30.3 | 11.9 | 21.0 | Sales/Net Fixed Assets | | | | | | 21.0 |
| 9.6 | 1.8 | 3.9 | | | | | | | 8.0 |
| 2.6 | 2.2 | 2.0 | | | | | | | 2.0 |
| 2.0 | 1.2 | .9 | Sales/Total Assets | | | | | | 1.2 |
| 1.3 | .6 | .5 | | | | | | | .8 |
| .2 | .7 | .5 | | | | | | | .8 |
| (11) .6 | (17) 3.1 | (22) 1.6 | % Depr., Dep., Amort./Sales | | | | | (10) | 2.1 |
| 2.0 | 9.5 | 5.1 | | | | | | | 3.8 |
| | | | % Officers', Directors' Owners' Comp/Sales | | | | | | |
| 1302254M | 512890M | 1301652M | Net Sales ($) | 1505M | 11270M | | 26772M | 94508M | 1167597M |
| 761183M | 881310M | 1186809M | Total Assets ($) | 1360M | 11697M | | 56929M | 269150M | 847673M |

© RMA 2024  
M = $ thousand   MM = $ million  
See Pages viii through xx for Explanation of Ratios and Data

## PROFESSIONAL SERVICES—Advertising Agencies  NAICS 541810

### Current Data Sorted by Assets | Comparative Historical Data

| 0-500M | 500M-2MM | 2-10MM | 10-50MM | 50-100MM | 100-250MM | | Type of Statement | 4/1/19-3/31/20 ALL | 4/1/20-3/31/21 ALL |
|---|---|---|---|---|---|---|---|---|---|
| 1 | 2 | 7 | 2 | 2 | 2 | | Unqualified | 9 | 11 |
| 8 | 8 | 4 | 7 | 2 | | | Reviewed | 23 | 12 |
| 17 | 19 | 11 | 6 | | | | Compiled | 12 | 8 |
| | 22 (4/1-9/30/23) | 55 | 3 | 13 | 9 | | Tax Returns | 46 | 25 |
| | | | 40 | | | | Other | 158 | 109 |
| | | | 196 (10/1/23-3/31/24) | | | | | | |
| 26 | 29 | 77 | 58 | 17 | 11 | | NUMBER OF STATEMENTS | 248 | 165 |
| % | % | % | % | % | % | | ASSETS | % | % |
| 40.8 | 28.4 | 29.5 | 18.8 | 23.7 | 15.3 | | Cash & Equivalents | 26.5 | 33.0 |
| 13.7 | 34.5 | 35.1 | 33.1 | 31.8 | 37.4 | | Trade Receivables (net) | 38.6 | 30.1 |
| 3.1 | 2.0 | 1.4 | 3.3 | 2.3 | .0 | | Inventory | 1.9 | 1.9 |
| 2.0 | 2.0 | 3.7 | 7.2 | 5.3 | 2.9 | | All Other Current | 5.3 | 3.3 |
| 59.6 | 66.9 | 69.7 | 62.5 | 63.1 | 55.5 | | Total Current | 72.3 | 68.2 |
| 19.3 | 13.9 | 12.9 | 15.9 | 8.8 | 4.1 | | Fixed Assets (net) | 10.4 | 11.1 |
| 4.6 | 8.0 | 7.3 | 7.3 | 19.1 | 35.0 | | Intangibles (net) | 9.1 | 10.3 |
| 16.5 | 11.3 | 10.1 | 14.4 | 9.0 | 5.4 | | All Other Non-Current | 8.2 | 10.3 |
| 100.0 | 100.0 | 100.0 | 100.0 | 100.0 | 100.0 | | Total | 100.0 | 100.0 |
| | | | | | | | LIABILITIES | | |
| 29.2 | 9.0 | 4.2 | 5.6 | .5 | 3.4 | | Notes Payable-Short Term | 10.9 | 13.7 |
| 2.1 | 3.2 | 2.2 | 3.2 | 2.6 | 1.4 | | Cur. Mat.-L.T.D. | 3.0 | 5.0 |
| 7.5 | 22.9 | 18.1 | 20.7 | 26.8 | 27.8 | | Trade Payables | 21.5 | 19.4 |
| .3 | .0 | .5 | .1 | .1 | .1 | | Income Taxes Payable | .1 | .2 |
| 14.6 | 29.8 | 20.5 | 25.4 | 22.6 | 12.9 | | All Other Current | 27.3 | 24.9 |
| 53.7 | 64.9 | 45.5 | 55.0 | 52.5 | 45.5 | | Total Current | 62.8 | 63.4 |
| 22.9 | 39.7 | 18.1 | 12.6 | 15.2 | 36.9 | | Long-Term Debt | 10.8 | 17.9 |
| .0 | .0 | .0 | .0 | .5 | .0 | | Deferred Taxes | .1 | .1 |
| .2 | 1.3 | 6.8 | 13.3 | 14.7 | 8.3 | | All Other Non-Current | 6.9 | 10.8 |
| 23.3 | -5.9 | 29.6 | 19.1 | 17.2 | 9.4 | | Net Worth | 19.4 | 7.7 |
| 100.0 | 100.0 | 100.0 | 100.0 | 100.0 | 100.0 | | Total Liabilties & Net Worth | 100.0 | 100.0 |
| | | | | | | | INCOME DATA | | |
| 100.0 | 100.0 | 100.0 | 100.0 | 100.0 | 100.0 | | Net Sales | 100.0 | 100.0 |
| 85.8 | 88.7 | 89.7 | 93.8 | 97.6 | 100.3 | | Gross Profit | 92.2 | 92.6 |
| 14.2 | 11.3 | 10.3 | 6.2 | 2.4 | -.3 | | Operating Expenses | 7.8 | 7.4 |
| 2.8 | 2.1 | 2.1 | 3.1 | 3.5 | 3.1 | | Operating Profit | 1.0 | -.1 |
| 11.4 | 9.2 | 8.2 | 3.1 | -1.1 | -3.4 | | All Other Expenses (net) | 6.7 | 7.5 |
| | | | | | | | Profit Before Taxes | | |
| | | | | | | | RATIOS | | |
| 3.7 | 2.9 | 3.8 | 1.7 | 1.5 | 1.5 | | | 2.0 | 2.2 |
| 1.4 | 1.3 | 1.6 | 1.2 | 1.2 | 1.2 | | Current | 1.3 | 1.4 |
| .7 | .6 | 1.1 | .9 | 1.0 | 1.1 | | | .9 | .9 |
| 3.7 | 2.9 | 3.2 | 1.5 | 1.4 | 1.4 | | | 1.9 | 2.1 |
| 1.4 | 1.3 | 1.4 | 1.0 | 1.1 | 1.2 | | Quick | 1.1 (164) | 1.3 |
| .4 | .5 | 1.0 | .7 | .8 | 1.0 | | | .8 | .8 |
| 0 UND | 0 UND | 26 13.9 | 33 11.2 | 35 10.4 | 43 8.5 | | | 22 16.6 | 14 25.5 |
| 0 UND | 22 16.4 | 41 8.9 | 53 6.9 | 68 5.4 | 73 5.0 | | Sales/Receivables | 43 8.4 | 39 9.4 |
| 20 17.9 | 38 9.6 | 62 5.9 | 64 5.7 | 118 3.1 | 111 3.3 | | | 72 5.1 | 74 4.9 |
| | | | | | | | Cost of Sales/Inventory | | |
| | | | | | | | Cost of Sales/Payables | | |
| 20.7 | 6.7 | 5.8 | 6.6 | 5.7 | 6.1 | | | 8.0 | 5.7 |
| 155.1 | 31.3 | 13.5 | 19.8 | 13.6 | 26.0 | | Sales/Working Capital | 25.7 | 14.1 |
| -30.8 | -9.9 | 62.1 | -57.1 | -78.1 | 72.1 | | | -55.4 | -40.0 |
| | 11.6 | 23.7 | 54.1 | 37.4 | 48.5 | | | 34.0 | 52.8 |
| (16) 4.6 | (18) 6.1 | (46) 7.4 | (39) 8.5 | (15) 1.6 | | | EBIT/Interest | (163) 8.1 | (119) 9.3 |
| -4.6 | 1.2 | 1.2 | 1.5 | -1.5 | | | | 1.4 | -.3 |
| | | | | | | | Net Profit + Depr., Dep., Amort./Cur. Mat. L/T/D | 16.1 | 8.5 |
| | | | | | | | | (21) 5.3 | (12) 3.7 |
| | | | | | | | | 2.5 | 1.6 |
| .0 | .0 | .0 | .1 | .3 | .0 | | | .1 | .0 |
| .2 | .5 | .2 | .4 | -77.7 | .6 | | Fixed/Worth | .4 | .3 |
| 3.5 | -.7 | 1.6 | 4.2 | -.2 | -.1 | | | -1.4 | -1.8 |
| .3 | 1.3 | .8 | 1.5 | 3.8 | 2.7 | | | 1.1 | 1.2 |
| 2.5 | 5.9 | 2.2 | 4.2 | -277.6 | -3.7 | | Debt/Worth | 5.4 | 6.3 |
| -75.8 | -2.2 | 12.2 | 12.5 | -5.9 | -1.5 | | | -9.1 | -4.8 |
| 225.0 | 204.9 | 97.3 | 90.0 | | | | | 121.9 | 98.7 |
| (19) 96.4 | (17) 105.3 | (61) 40.3 | (48) 33.3 | | | | % Profit Before Taxes/Tangible Net Worth | (160) 50.3 | (104) 51.8 |
| 33.8 | 35.7 | 12.3 | 4.4 | | | | | 15.5 | 13.0 |
| 172.6 | 45.3 | 31.6 | 13.2 | 7.9 | 12.3 | | | 34.4 | 32.6 |
| 21.2 | 17.6 | 12.2 | 7.1 | .5 | .7 | | % Profit Before Taxes/Total Assets | 11.3 | 9.8 |
| 2.3 | 2.8 | 2.4 | .9 | -6.9 | -5.3 | | | 1.3 | .5 |
| UND | 681.0 | 334.8 | 75.3 | 64.7 | 999.8 | | | 244.8 | 433.6 |
| 937.2 | 91.9 | 78.4 | 36.6 | 19.1 | 55.6 | | Sales/Net Fixed Assets | 72.6 | 58.8 |
| 37.5 | 36.8 | 18.7 | 12.1 | 9.0 | 16.2 | | | 20.2 | 16.5 |
| 15.3 | 7.1 | 3.9 | 2.9 | 2.6 | 3.3 | | | 5.0 | 4.6 |
| 6.7 | 4.3 | 2.8 | 2.1 | 1.4 | 2.2 | | Sales/Total Assets | 3.2 | 2.6 |
| 3.2 | 2.2 | 1.7 | 1.1 | .8 | .6 | | | 2.2 | 1.5 |
| | .3 | .2 | .5 | | | | | .3 | .5 |
| | (10) .4 | (47) .5 | (41) .9 | | | | % Depr., Dep., Amort./Sales | (140) .8 | (75) 1.3 |
| | 3.6 | 1.1 | 2.2 | | | | | 1.8 | 2.6 |
| 7.0 | 2.1 | 1.9 | .8 | | | | | 2.3 | 4.0 |
| (11) 10.9 | (15) 5.8 | (23) 3.1 | (14) 1.0 | | | | % Officers', Directors' Owners' Comp/Sales | (72) 5.3 | (43) 6.0 |
| 13.7 | 10.8 | 6.9 | 3.7 | | | | | 10.6 | 13.6 |
| 83132M | 173377M | 1298205M | 2733118M | 2044766M | 3496980M | | Net Sales ($) | 7672419M | 10903992M |
| 7081M | 33585M | 407589M | 1243985M | 1273726M | 1816367M | | Total Assets ($) | 3552746M | 3368783M |

© RMA 2024

M = $ thousand   MM = $ million
See Pages viii through xx for Explanation of Ratios and Data

# PROFESSIONAL SERVICES—Advertising Agencies  NAICS 541810

## Comparative Historical Data | Current Data Sorted by Sales

| Comparative Historical Data ||| Type of Statement | Current Data Sorted by Sales ||||||
|---|---|---|---|---|---|---|---|---|---|
| 9 | 5 | 6 | Unqualified | | | | 1 | 6 | 6 |
| 13 | 26 | 16 | Reviewed | | | | 2 | 5 | 9 |
| 8 | 7 | 13 | Compiled | | | | 4 | 6 | 3 |
| 23 | 32 | 30 | Tax Returns | 4 | 3 | 6 | 4 | 6 | 4 |
| 87 | 128 | 153 | Other | 12 | 16 | 8 | 16 | 40 | 61 |
| 4/1/21-3/31/22 ALL | 4/1/22-3/31/23 ALL | 4/1/23-3/31/24 ALL | | 22 (4/1-9/30/23) ||| 196 (10/1/23-3/31/24) |||
| | | | | 0-1MM | 1-3MM | 3-5MM | 5-10MM | 10-25MM | 25MM & OVER |
| 140 | 198 | 218 | NUMBER OF STATEMENTS | 16 | 25 | 14 | 23 | 57 | 83 |
| % | % | % | **ASSETS** | % | % | % | % | % | % |
| 32.0 | 33.4 | 26.7 | Cash & Equivalents | 24.7 | 28.2 | 31.0 | 33.9 | 31.2 | 20.8 |
| 33.4 | 30.9 | 31.8 | Trade Receivables (net) | 5.3 | 19.0 | 37.1 | 29.0 | 35.3 | 38.1 |
| 1.7 | 2.9 | 2.2 | Inventory | 1.3 | 4.6 | .2 | .0 | 2.3 | 2.5 |
| 5.2 | 4.9 | 4.3 | All Other Current | .0 | 3.1 | 2.1 | 2.6 | 5.9 | 5.2 |
| 72.3 | 72.1 | 65.0 | Total Current | 31.3 | 54.8 | 70.4 | 65.5 | 74.7 | 66.7 |
| 9.6 | 8.9 | 13.8 | Fixed Assets (net) | 48.1 | 17.6 | 10.9 | 12.5 | 9.2 | 10.1 |
| 10.4 | 9.0 | 9.4 | Intangibles (net) | 4.6 | 12.7 | 10.5 | 6.9 | 5.7 | 12.3 |
| 7.7 | 9.9 | 11.9 | All Other Non-Current | 16.0 | 14.8 | 8.1 | 15.1 | 10.5 | 10.9 |
| 100.0 | 100.0 | 100.0 | Total | 100.0 | 100.0 | 100.0 | 100.0 | 100.0 | 100.0 |
| | | | **LIABILITIES** | | | | | | |
| 7.6 | 6.1 | 7.9 | Notes Payable-Short Term | 9.3 | 10.7 | 33.4 | 3.3 | 5.6 | 5.2 |
| 2.4 | 2.2 | 2.6 | Cur. Mat.-L.T.D. | 3.9 | 2.5 | 2.1 | 1.5 | 1.3 | 3.5 |
| 21.0 | 21.7 | 19.3 | Trade Payables | 4.2 | 10.4 | 20.5 | 10.4 | 21.4 | 25.8 |
| .2 | .2 | .2 | Income Taxes Payable | .5 | .0 | .0 | .0 | .7 | .1 |
| 24.2 | 27.0 | 22.1 | All Other Current | 9.8 | 24.5 | 10.7 | 15.4 | 27.3 | 24.0 |
| 55.4 | 57.1 | 52.1 | Total Current | 27.6 | 48.0 | 67.5 | 30.7 | 56.3 | 58.6 |
| 17.3 | 16.6 | 20.8 | Long-Term Debt | 66.6 | 32.3 | 19.0 | 17.0 | 12.2 | 15.8 |
| .1 | .1 | .1 | Deferred Taxes | .0 | .0 | .0 | .0 | .0 | .1 |
| 11.4 | 10.7 | 7.7 | All Other Non-Current | .4 | 1.1 | 5.8 | 1.9 | 3.2 | 16.1 |
| 15.8 | 15.5 | 19.3 | Net Worth | 5.6 | 18.7 | 7.6 | 50.3 | 28.3 | 9.4 |
| 100.0 | 100.0 | 100.0 | Total Liabilities & Net Worth | 100.0 | 100.0 | 100.0 | 100.0 | 100.0 | 100.0 |
| | | | **INCOME DATA** | | | | | | |
| 100.0 | 100.0 | 100.0 | Net Sales | 100.0 | 100.0 | 100.0 | 100.0 | 100.0 | 100.0 |
| | | | Gross Profit | | | | | | |
| 92.4 | 92.3 | 91.3 | Operating Expenses | 53.8 | 91.5 | 95.3 | 93.3 | 92.2 | 96.7 |
| 7.6 | 7.7 | 8.7 | Operating Profit | 46.2 | 8.5 | 4.7 | 6.7 | 7.8 | 3.3 |
| -1.4 | .6 | 2.6 | All Other Expenses (net) | 15.1 | 7.8 | .5 | .3 | .0 | 1.5 |
| 9.0 | 7.1 | 6.1 | Profit Before Taxes | 31.1 | .8 | 4.2 | 6.3 | 7.8 | 1.8 |
| | | | **RATIOS** | | | | | | |
| 2.3 | 2.4 | 2.4 | | 3.3 | 3.7 | 2.6 | 7.4 | 2.3 | 1.5 |
| 1.5 | 1.5 | 1.3 | Current | .7 | 1.4 | 1.3 | 4.4 | 1.6 | 1.2 |
| 1.0 | 1.0 | 1.0 | | .2 | .7 | 1.0 | 1.3 | 1.1 | 1.0 |
| 2.1 | 2.1 | 2.2 | | 3.3 | 3.7 | 2.3 | 7.4 | 2.3 | 1.5 |
| 1.3 | 1.3 | 1.2 | Quick | .6 | 1.4 | 1.3 | 4.4 | 1.3 | 1.1 |
| .8 | .9 | .8 | | .2 | .4 | 1.0 | 1.2 | 1.0 | .8 |
| 12  29.8 | 19  19.7 | 19  19.5 | | 0  UND | 0  UND | 0  UND | 6  61.7 | 23  15.8 | 34  10.7 |
| 41  8.8 | 43  8.5 | 38  9.5 | Sales/Receivables | 0  UND | 18  20.7 | 35  10.4 | 39  9.4 | 41  9.0 | 51  7.2 |
| 69  5.3 | 70  5.2 | 64  5.7 | | 0  UND | 41  8.8 | 140  2.6 | 66  5.5 | 64  5.7 | 73  5.0 |
| | | | Cost of Sales/Inventory | | | | | | |
| | | | Cost of Sales/Payables | | | | | | |
| 6.0 | 6.3 | 6.8 | | 23.3 | 6.0 | 6.4 | 4.0 | 5.3 | 10.5 |
| 15.5 | 13.8 | 19.3 | Sales/Working Capital | -103.9 | 29.0 | 35.4 | 10.0 | 8.9 | 30.0 |
| -200.1 | 169.1 | -107.0 | | -6.1 | -16.9 | -74.2 | 27.0 | 45.5 | -60.9 |
| 120.0 | 53.6 | 31.0 | | | 8.4 | 30.5 | 71.3 | 104.9 | 37.1 |
| (86) 13.7 | (116) 9.1 | (141) 4.6 | EBIT/Interest | (17) 1.7 | (12) 4.1 | (14) 8.6 | (31) 8.0 | (61) 5.0 |
| 3.0 | .7 | .0 | | | -9.9 | -4.0 | -2.1 | 1.1 | -.4 |
| 16.6 | 30.7 | 6.7 | Net Profit + Depr., Dep., | | | | | | |
| (10) 2.9 | (12) 6.0 | (12) 1.7 | Amort./Cur. Mat. L/T/D | | | | | | |
| 1.1 | -.2 | .3 | | | | | | | |
| .0 | .0 | .0 | | .1 | .0 | .0 | .0 | .0 | .1 |
| .3 | .2 | .4 | Fixed/Worth | 1.5 | .5 | .3 | .2 | .1 | .8 |
| -1.7 | 2.4 | 7.6 | | NM | NM | 2.7 | 1.0 | .6 | -.7 |
| 1.0 | 1.1 | 1.1 | | .3 | .7 | 2.0 | .2 | .8 | 2.5 |
| 4.4 | 4.2 | 4.0 | Debt/Worth | 3.2 | 8.0 | 5.2 | .8 | 2.2 | 8.5 |
| -7.7 | -517.7 | -34.1 | | -9.6 | -3.5 | -4.3 | 5.0 | 9.0 | -7.1 |
| 147.9 | 128.4 | 106.1 | | 152.3 | 164.2 | | 105.3 | 92.3 | 108.2 |
| (92) 70.1 | (148) 43.2 | (157) 40.3 | % Profit Before Taxes/Tangible Net Worth | (11) 41.1 | (16) 39.6 | (19) 50.2 | (48) 40.0 | (54) 37.4 |
| 26.9 | 13.4 | 10.1 | | 8.2 | -.2 | | 22.3 | 6.2 | 7.8 |
| 44.4 | 31.7 | 26.1 | | 120.3 | 26.6 | 33.1 | 40.6 | 32.3 | 17.0 |
| 18.5 | 9.6 | 9.9 | % Profit Before Taxes/Total Assets | 16.9 | 7.6 | 10.2 | 24.2 | 10.4 | 7.1 |
| 3.9 | 1.6 | .7 | | 4.1 | -4.3 | -11.7 | 6.6 | 1.9 | .1 |
| 356.7 | 399.2 | 356.7 | | UND | UND | 859.9 | 351.9 | 257.6 | 263.5 |
| 60.7 | 93.5 | 57.1 | Sales/Net Fixed Assets | 6.6 | 83.2 | 97.7 | 54.5 | 68.7 | 47.1 |
| 29.0 | 24.5 | 17.7 | | .2 | 10.9 | 20.8 | 14.2 | 27.4 | 19.6 |
| 4.9 | 4.4 | 4.7 | | 5.6 | 5.9 | 7.2 | 3.6 | 5.0 | 4.1 |
| 3.0 | 2.7 | 2.7 | Sales/Total Assets | 1.6 | 2.6 | 3.9 | 2.4 | 2.8 | 2.5 |
| 1.9 | 1.7 | 1.4 | | .2 | 1.1 | 1.3 | 1.4 | 1.7 | 1.8 |
| .3 | .2 | .3 | | | | | .3 | .3 | .4 |
| (70) .9 | (97) .7 | (114) .8 | % Depr., Dep., Amort./Sales | | | (11) .5 | (35) .6 | (47) .9 |
| 1.4 | 1.7 | 2.1 | | | | | 1.5 | 1.1 | 3.5 |
| 3.1 | 2.0 | 1.6 | | | 6.9 | 2.2 | | 1.6 | .5 |
| (37) 6.7 | (51) 3.7 | (63) 3.5 | % Officers', Directors', Owners' Comp/Sales | (12) 9.4 | (10) 6.4 | (18) 3.0 | (15) 1.0 |
| 14.4 | 9.2 | 9.4 | | | 13.6 | 11.0 | | 9.1 | 1.9 |
| 5944290M | 8472139M | 9829578M | Net Sales ($) | 8502M | 52830M | 57764M | 167533M | 916359M | 8626590M |
| 2745898M | 4611265M | 4782333M | Total Assets ($) | 21605M | 59896M | 32075M | 90837M | 546960M | 4030960M |

© RMA 2024  
M = $ thousand    MM = $ million  
See Pages viii through xx for Explanation of Ratios and Data

# PROFESSIONAL SERVICES—Public Relations Agencies  NAICS 541820

## Current Data Sorted by Assets / Comparative Historical Data

| | | | | | | | Type of Statement | | |
|---|---|---|---|---|---|---|---|---|---|
| | | 1 | | 1 | | 1 | Unqualified | 1 | 1 |
| | | 1 | | | | | Reviewed | 5 | 3 |
| | 1 | 1 | | | | | Compiled | 5 | 3 |
| 2 | | 3 | | | | | Tax Returns | 6 | 3 |
| 2 | 9 | 6 | | 1 | 1 | 3 | Other | 21 | 21 |
| | 4 (4/1-9/30/23) | | 30 (10/1/23-3/31/24) | | | | | 4/1/19-3/31/20 | 4/1/20-3/31/21 |
| 0-500M | 500M-2MM | 2-10MM | 10-50MM | 50-100MM | 100-250MM | | NUMBER OF STATEMENTS | ALL | ALL |
| 4 | 10 | 12 | 2 | 2 | 4 | | | 38 | 31 |
| % | % | % | % | % | % | | ASSETS | % | % |
| | 37.9 | 22.3 | | | | | Cash & Equivalents | 34.0 | 39.7 |
| | 35.1 | 37.9 | | | | | Trade Receivables (net) | 27.1 | 23.4 |
| | .0 | .0 | | | | | Inventory | .1 | .5 |
| | 1.9 | 7.3 | | | | | All Other Current | 6.2 | 5.5 |
| | 74.8 | 67.5 | | | | | Total Current | 67.3 | 69.1 |
| | 2.4 | 6.9 | | | | | Fixed Assets (net) | 13.2 | 10.9 |
| | 6.9 | 18.4 | | | | | Intangibles (net) | 4.9 | 13.8 |
| | 15.8 | 7.2 | | | | | All Other Non-Current | 14.6 | 6.2 |
| | 100.0 | 100.0 | | | | | Total | 100.0 | 100.0 |
| | | | | | | | LIABILITIES | | |
| | 8.3 | 6.1 | | | | | Notes Payable-Short Term | 15.5 | 14.5 |
| | 1.5 | 1.7 | | | | | Cur. Mat.-L.T.D. | 3.6 | 4.3 |
| | 5.5 | 15.0 | | | | | Trade Payables | 11.0 | 12.2 |
| | .0 | .1 | | | | | Income Taxes Payable | .0 | .0 |
| | 9.3 | 23.6 | | | | | All Other Current | 30.9 | 14.6 |
| | 24.5 | 46.5 | | | | | Total Current | 61.0 | 45.5 |
| | 3.3 | 8.3 | | | | | Long-Term Debt | 27.8 | 25.0 |
| | .0 | .2 | | | | | Deferred Taxes | .0 | .0 |
| | 2.9 | 10.5 | | | | | All Other Non-Current | 9.1 | 6.6 |
| | 69.3 | 34.5 | | | | | Net Worth | 2.1 | 22.8 |
| | 100.0 | 100.0 | | | | | Total Liabilities & Net Worth | 100.0 | 100.0 |
| | | | | | | | INCOME DATA | | |
| | 100.0 | 100.0 | | | | | Net Sales | 100.0 | 100.0 |
| | 81.1 | 89.2 | | | | | Gross Profit | | |
| | 18.9 | 10.8 | | | | | Operating Expenses | 92.8 | 91.6 |
| | -.9 | -.3 | | | | | Operating Profit | 7.2 | 8.4 |
| | 19.8 | 11.1 | | | | | All Other Expenses (net) | 1.0 | -.6 |
| | | | | | | | Profit Before Taxes | 6.2 | 9.0 |
| | | | | | | | RATIOS | | |
| | 11.6 | 4.0 | | | | | | 3.0 | 3.9 |
| | 5.1 | 1.7 | | | | | Current | 1.2 | 1.4 |
| | 1.4 | 1.1 | | | | | | .8 | .9 |
| | 11.6 | 4.0 | | | | | | 2.3 | 3.2 |
| | 4.9 | 1.7 | | | | | Quick | 1.0 | 1.3 |
| | 1.2 | 1.0 | | | | | | .6 | .9 |
| | 0 UND | 38  9.7 | | | | | | 0  UND | 2  242.5 |
| | 38  9.5 | 55  6.6 | | | | | Sales/Receivables | 32  11.4 | 34  10.7 |
| | 47  7.7 | 81  4.5 | | | | | | 54  6.8 | 49  7.5 |
| | | | | | | | Cost of Sales/Inventory | | |
| | | | | | | | Cost of Sales/Payables | | |
| | 4.7 | 5.6 | | | | | | 6.6 | 4.7 |
| | 13.4 | 9.6 | | | | | Sales/Working Capital | 41.3 | 13.9 |
| | NM | 112.8 | | | | | | -21.3 | -76.6 |
| | | | | | | | | 62.9 | 211.9 |
| | | | | | | | EBIT/Interest | (26) 15.8 | (20) 29.8 |
| | | | | | | | | 2.8 | 1.2 |
| | | | | | | | Net Profit + Depr., Dep., Amort./Cur. Mat. L/T/D | | |
| | .0 | .0 | | | | | | .1 | .0 |
| | .0 | .2 | | | | | Fixed/Worth | .3 | .2 |
| | .1 | -.5 | | | | | | -1.0 | -.3 |
| | .1 | 1.2 | | | | | | .6 | .9 |
| | .2 | 3.2 | | | | | Debt/Worth | 3.4 | 2.4 |
| | 1.3 | -77.0 | | | | | | -7.4 | -2.7 |
| | | | | | | | | 92.8 | 187.3 |
| | | | | | | | % Profit Before Taxes/Tangible Net Worth | (24) 40.8 | (19) 89.4 |
| | | | | | | | | 16.8 | 26.6 |
| | 115.1 | 49.0 | | | | | | 49.6 | 69.2 |
| | 76.6 | 16.6 | | | | | % Profit Before Taxes/Total Assets | 20.1 | 15.3 |
| | 12.9 | 5.6 | | | | | | 2.6 | 2.9 |
| | UND | 638.4 | | | | | | 372.9 | 226.5 |
| | 818.3 | 153.9 | | | | | Sales/Net Fixed Assets | 57.2 | 55.1 |
| | 70.8 | 33.9 | | | | | | 29.6 | 21.5 |
| | 7.0 | 2.7 | | | | | | 7.6 | 3.7 |
| | 4.6 | 2.2 | | | | | Sales/Total Assets | 3.8 | 3.0 |
| | 2.3 | 2.0 | | | | | | 2.1 | 1.7 |
| | | | | | | | | .2 | .3 |
| | | | | | | | % Depr., Dep., Amort./Sales | (19) .7 | (12) .4 |
| | | | | | | | | 1.1 | 1.2 |
| | | | | | | | | | 4.5 |
| | | | | | | | % Officers', Directors' Owners' Comp/Sales | (13) 10.4 | |
| | | | | | | | | 25.2 | |
| 5927M | 46026M | 143611M | 138869M | 141762M | 271402M | | Net Sales ($) | 699281M | 346407M |
| 971M | 11494M | 61385M | 62233M | 160633M | 511517M | | Total Assets ($) | 258675M | 215379M |

M = $ thousand   MM = $ million
See Pages viii through xx for Explanation of Ratios and Data

© RMA 2024

# PROFESSIONAL SERVICES—Public Relations Agencies  NAICS 541820

## Comparative Historical Data | Current Data Sorted by Sales

| | | | | | | | Type of Statement | | | | | | |
|---|---|---|---|---|---|---|---|---|---|---|---|---|---|
| | 1 | | | | 4 | | Unqualified | | | | 1 | | 3 |
| | 4 | | 2 | | 1 | | Reviewed | | | | 1 | 1 | |
| | 1 | | 3 | | 2 | | Compiled | | | 1 | 3 | 1 | |
| | 2 | | 8 | | 5 | | Tax Returns | | 2 | | 3 | | |
| | 14 | | 38 | | 22 | | Other | 1 | 5 | 2 | 4 | 5 | 5 |
| | 4/1/21- | | 4/1/22- | | 4/1/23- | | | | 4 (4/1-9/30/23) | | 30 (10/1/23-3/31/24) | | |
| | 3/31/22 | | 3/31/23 | | 3/31/24 | | | 0-1MM | 1-3MM | 3-5MM | 5-10MM | 10-25MM | 25MM & OVER |
| | ALL | | ALL | | ALL | NUMBER OF STATEMENTS | 1 | 7 | 2 | 9 | 7 | 8 |
| | 22 | | 51 | | 34 | | | | | | | | |
| | % | | % | | % | ASSETS | % | % | % | % | % | % |
| | 32.8 | | 38.4 | | 24.0 | Cash & Equivalents | | | | | | |
| | 28.0 | | 25.9 | | 27.1 | Trade Receivables (net) | | | | | | |
| | .4 | | .6 | | .0 | Inventory | | | | | | |
| | 3.7 | | 4.3 | | 3.5 | All Other Current | | | | | | |
| | 64.9 | | 69.1 | | 54.6 | Total Current | | | | | | |
| | 7.6 | | 6.6 | | 10.5 | Fixed Assets (net) | | | | | | |
| | 15.6 | | 14.9 | | 17.5 | Intangibles (net) | | | | | | |
| | 11.9 | | 9.4 | | 17.4 | All Other Non-Current | | | | | | |
| | 100.0 | | 100.0 | | 100.0 | Total | | | | | | |
| | | | | | | LIABILITIES | | | | | | |
| | 9.5 | | 6.0 | | 4.9 | Notes Payable-Short Term | | | | | | |
| | 5.9 | | 1.7 | | 1.6 | Cur. Mat.-L.T.D. | | | | | | |
| | 9.0 | | 7.4 | | 7.9 | Trade Payables | | | | | | |
| | .0 | | .2 | | .0 | Income Taxes Payable | | | | | | |
| | 21.8 | | 21.5 | | 12.9 | All Other Current | | | | | | |
| | 46.2 | | 36.9 | | 27.4 | Total Current | | | | | | |
| | 11.4 | | 8.6 | | 8.8 | Long-Term Debt | | | | | | |
| | .0 | | .2 | | .2 | Deferred Taxes | | | | | | |
| | 6.4 | | 7.1 | | 12.3 | All Other Non-Current | | | | | | |
| | 35.9 | | 47.2 | | 51.3 | Net Worth | | | | | | |
| | 100.0 | | 100.0 | | 100.0 | Total Liabilities & Net Worth | | | | | | |
| | | | | | | INCOME DATA | | | | | | |
| | 100.0 | | 100.0 | | 100.0 | Net Sales | | | | | | |
| | | | | | | Gross Profit | | | | | | |
| | 84.6 | | 86.0 | | 83.8 | Operating Expenses | | | | | | |
| | 15.4 | | 14.0 | | 16.2 | Operating Profit | | | | | | |
| | -.5 | | 1.3 | | 1.4 | All Other Expenses (net) | | | | | | |
| | 15.9 | | 12.7 | | 14.8 | Profit Before Taxes | | | | | | |
| | | | | | | RATIOS | | | | | | |
| | 4.2 | | 5.0 | | 5.3 | | | | | | | |
| | 1.7 | | 2.4 | | 1.9 | Current | | | | | | |
| | 1.0 | | 1.2 | | 1.2 | | | | | | | |
| | 4.0 | | 5.0 | | 5.3 | | | | | | | |
| | 1.6 | | 2.2 | | 1.9 | Quick | | | | | | |
| | .7 | | 1.1 | | 1.0 | | | | | | | |
| 8 | 45.3 | 2 | 169.0 | 15 | 24.6 | | | | | | | |
| 43 | 8.4 | 41 | 8.8 | 45 | 8.2 | Sales/Receivables | | | | | | |
| 64 | 5.7 | 62 | 5.9 | 60 | 6.1 | | | | | | | |
| | | | | | | Cost of Sales/Inventory | | | | | | |
| | | | | | | Cost of Sales/Payables | | | | | | |
| | 4.1 | | 4.8 | | 6.2 | | | | | | | |
| | 14.7 | | 11.3 | | 13.4 | Sales/Working Capital | | | | | | |
| | NM | | 42.8 | | 57.3 | | | | | | | |
| | 104.5 | | 59.4 | | 98.1 | | | | | | | |
| (15) | 46.5 | (21) | 9.6 | (21) | 33.9 | EBIT/Interest | | | | | | |
| | 7.8 | | -.3 | | 1.6 | | | | | | | |
| | | | | | | Net Profit + Depr., Dep., Amort./Cur. Mat. L/T/D | | | | | | |
| | .0 | | .0 | | .0 | | | | | | | |
| | .1 | | .1 | | .1 | Fixed/Worth | | | | | | |
| | 1.5 | | -.9 | | NM | | | | | | | |
| | .4 | | .3 | | .3 | | | | | | | |
| | 1.4 | | 1.5 | | 1.3 | Debt/Worth | | | | | | |
| | -2.7 | | -7.7 | | NM | | | | | | | |
| | 132.1 | | 155.0 | | 168.5 | % Profit Before Taxes/Tangible Net Worth | | | | | | |
| (16) | 60.5 | (36) | 66.9 | (26) | 80.0 | | | | | | | |
| | 22.2 | | 30.4 | | 19.9 | | | | | | | |
| | 59.7 | | 62.8 | | 89.8 | % Profit Before Taxes/Total Assets | | | | | | |
| | 37.1 | | 28.2 | | 20.7 | | | | | | | |
| | 6.3 | | 6.1 | | 3.9 | | | | | | | |
| | UND | | 927.0 | | 704.0 | | | | | | | |
| | 106.7 | | 201.8 | | 132.8 | Sales/Net Fixed Assets | | | | | | |
| | 37.7 | | 28.2 | | 27.3 | | | | | | | |
| | 3.5 | | 5.2 | | 4.5 | | | | | | | |
| | 2.7 | | 2.6 | | 2.4 | Sales/Total Assets | | | | | | |
| | 1.5 | | 1.7 | | 1.4 | | | | | | | |
| | .5 | | .2 | | .2 | | | | | | | |
| (10) | .9 | (24) | .4 | (14) | .7 | % Depr., Dep., Amort./Sales | | | | | | |
| | 1.7 | | 1.0 | | 1.1 | | | | | | | |
| | | | 3.5 | | 2.8 | % Officers', Directors' Owners' Comp/Sales | | | | | | |
| | | (15) | 7.1 | (12) | 5.9 | | | | | | | |
| | | | 31.8 | | 17.5 | | | | | | | |
| | 304858M | | 1092573M | | 747597M | Net Sales ($) | 110M | 15268M | 8704M | 64072M | 107410M | 552033M |
| | 249698M | | 804233M | | 808233M | Total Assets ($) | 271M | 4944M | 3258M | 24994M | 40383M | 734383M |

© RMA 2024  M = $ thousand   MM = $ million
See Pages viii through xx for Explanation of Ratios and Data

# PROFESSIONAL SERVICES—Indoor and Outdoor Display Advertising  NAICS 541850

## Current Data Sorted by Assets | Comparative Historical Data

| | | | | | | Type of Statement | | |
|---|---|---|---|---|---|---|---|---|
| | | | 1 | | 1 | Unqualified | 2 | 2 |
| | | | 1 | | | Reviewed | 2 | 4 |
| | | 3 | 1 | 1 | | Compiled | 4 | 2 |
| | 2 | 3 | 10 | | 1 | Tax Returns | 10 | 5 |
| | 4 (4/1-9/30/23) | | 21 (10/1/23-3/31/24) | | | Other | 23 | 16 |
| 0-500M | 500M-2MM | 2-10MM | 10-50MM | 50-100MM | 100-250MM | | 4/1/19-3/31/20 | 4/1/20-3/31/21 |
| | 5 | 4 | 13 | 1 | 2 | NUMBER OF STATEMENTS | ALL 41 | ALL 29 |
| % | % | % | % | % | % | ASSETS | % | % |
| | | | 10.7 | | | Cash & Equivalents | 15.0 | 13.7 |
| D | | | 13.5 | | | Trade Receivables (net) | 18.6 | 10.1 |
| A | | | 10.3 | | | Inventory | 4.4 | 2.1 |
| T | | | 3.0 | | | All Other Current | 4.1 | 2.4 |
| A | | | 37.5 | | | Total Current | 42.2 | 28.3 |
| | | | 36.3 | | | Fixed Assets (net) | 39.7 | 46.6 |
| N | | | 18.2 | | | Intangibles (net) | 10.2 | 19.4 |
| O | | | 8.1 | | | All Other Non-Current | 7.9 | 5.7 |
| T | | | 100.0 | | | Total | 100.0 | 100.0 |
| A | | | | | | LIABILITIES | | |
| V | | | 4.5 | | | Notes Payable-Short Term | 5.8 | 5.7 |
| A | | | 3.3 | | | Cur. Mat.-L.T.D. | 4.0 | 4.0 |
| I | | | 4.7 | | | Trade Payables | 6.3 | 3.1 |
| L | | | .0 | | | Income Taxes Payable | .2 | .0 |
| A | | | 17.5 | | | All Other Current | 10.9 | 18.6 |
| B | | | 30.0 | | | Total Current | 27.3 | 31.5 |
| L | | | 36.1 | | | Long-Term Debt | 37.8 | 41.8 |
| E | | | .0 | | | Deferred Taxes | .2 | .0 |
| | | | 3.9 | | | All Other Non-Current | 1.5 | 4.3 |
| | | | 30.0 | | | Net Worth | 33.2 | 22.3 |
| | | | 100.0 | | | Total Liabilities & Net Worth | 100.0 | 100.0 |
| | | | | | | INCOME DATA | | |
| | | | 100.0 | | | Net Sales | 100.0 | 100.0 |
| | | | | | | Gross Profit | | |
| | | | 83.8 | | | Operating Expenses | 85.3 | 89.1 |
| | | | 16.2 | | | Operating Profit | 14.7 | 10.9 |
| | | | 7.6 | | | All Other Expenses (net) | 2.0 | 4.1 |
| | | | 8.7 | | | Profit Before Taxes | 12.7 | 6.8 |
| | | | | | | RATIOS | | |
| | | | 3.0 | | | | 2.7 | 1.4 |
| | | | 1.3 | | | Current | 1.5 | .9 |
| | | | .9 | | | | .9 | .5 |
| | | | 2.1 | | | | 1.9 | 1.4 |
| | | | 1.1 | | | Quick | 1.2 | .8 |
| | | | .6 | | | | .7 | .5 |
| | | 22 | 16.5 | | | | 9 40.1 | 5 73.1 |
| | | 34 | 10.7 | | | Sales/Receivables | 35 10.4 | 39 9.4 |
| | | 56 | 6.5 | | | | 73 5.0 | 69 5.3 |
| | | | | | | Cost of Sales/Inventory | | |
| | | | | | | Cost of Sales/Payables | | |
| | | | 3.1 | | | | 5.2 | 11.4 |
| | | | 14.6 | | | Sales/Working Capital | 10.5 | -38.3 |
| | | | -42.6 | | | | -523.0 | -6.7 |
| | | | 15.2 | | | | 12.7 | 6.9 |
| | | (12) | 3.5 | | | EBIT/Interest | (34) 4.2 | (22) 2.0 |
| | | | 1.3 | | | | .9 | -.2 |
| | | | | | | Net Profit + Depr., Dep., Amort./Cur. Mat. L/T/D | | |
| | | | .8 | | | | .4 | 1.3 |
| | | | 2.0 | | | Fixed/Worth | 1.5 | 5.3 |
| | | | 19.1 | | | | 18.4 | -6.8 |
| | | | 1.4 | | | | .5 | 1.7 |
| | | | 3.5 | | | Debt/Worth | 3.8 | 9.8 |
| | | | 21.1 | | | | 67.4 | -14.5 |
| | | | 76.1 | | | | 57.3 | 54.5 |
| | | (12) | 33.5 | | | % Profit Before Taxes/Tangible Net Worth | (33) 26.3 | (19) 17.2 |
| | | | 14.5 | | | | 3.7 | -20.0 |
| | | | 10.7 | | | | 23.1 | 7.8 |
| | | | 6.5 | | | % Profit Before Taxes/Total Assets | 6.9 | 2.4 |
| | | | .6 | | | | .3 | -5.8 |
| | | | 11.4 | | | | 26.2 | 3.7 |
| | | | 2.3 | | | Sales/Net Fixed Assets | 2.6 | 1.7 |
| | | | .6 | | | | 1.1 | .6 |
| | | | 1.8 | | | | 2.5 | 1.3 |
| | | | .8 | | | Sales/Total Assets | 1.0 | .6 |
| | | | .3 | | | | .5 | .3 |
| | | | 1.5 | | | | 2.5 | 8.2 |
| | | (12) | 6.7 | | | % Depr., Dep., Amort./Sales | (32) 8.4 | (24) 12.1 |
| | | | 17.9 | | | | 13.5 | 19.8 |
| | | | | | | % Officers', Directors' Owners' Comp/Sales | (14) 3.0 5.0 8.2 | |
| | 10038M | 39386M | 397928M | 57684M | 125262M | Net Sales ($) | 715574M | 419428M |
| | 5941M | 22159M | 356897M | 56023M | 280482M | Total Assets ($) | 650133M | 618387M |

© RMA 2024

M = $ thousand    MM = $ million
See Pages viii through xx for Explanation of Ratios and Data

## PROFESSIONAL SERVICES—Indoor and Outdoor Display Advertising NAICS 541850

### Comparative Historical Data | Current Data Sorted by Sales

| | | | | | | | | | | | | | | |
|---|---|---|---|---|---|---|---|---|---|---|---|---|---|---|
| | 1 | | 1 | | 3 | Type of Statement | | | | | | 1 | | 2 |
| | | | 1 | | 1 | Unqualified | | | | | | | | 1 |
| | 3 | | 2 | | 2 | Reviewed | | | | | 1 | | | 1 |
| | 3 | | 11 | | 3 | Compiled | 2 | | 2 | 1 | | | | |
| | 12 | | 18 | | 16 | Tax Returns | | 2 | | 2 | 5 | 21 | | 5 |
| | 4/1/21- | | 4/1/22- | | 4/1/23- | Other | | 4 (4/1-9/30/23) | | | | (10/1/23-3/31/24) | | |
| | 3/31/22 | | 3/31/23 | | 3/31/24 | | 0-1MM | 1-3MM | 3-5MM | 5-10MM | 10-25MM | | 25MM & OVER | |
| | ALL | | ALL | | ALL | | | | | | | | | |
| | 19 | | 33 | | 25 | NUMBER OF STATEMENTS | 2 | 2 | 3 | 6 | 3 | | 9 | |
| | % | | % | | % | ASSETS | % | % | % | % | % | | % | |
| | 19.4 | | 17.4 | | 14.1 | Cash & Equivalents | | | | | | | | |
| | 16.3 | | 19.6 | | 18.0 | Trade Receivables (net) | | | | | | | | |
| | .5 | | 2.8 | | 8.9 | Inventory | | | | | | | | |
| | 3.0 | | 7.1 | | 3.3 | All Other Current | | | | | | | | |
| | 39.2 | | 46.9 | | 44.4 | Total Current | | | | | | | | |
| | 35.5 | | 33.6 | | 28.9 | Fixed Assets (net) | | | | | | | | |
| | 14.0 | | 12.0 | | 14.2 | Intangibles (net) | | | | | | | | |
| | 11.4 | | 7.4 | | 12.5 | All Other Non-Current | | | | | | | | |
| | 100.0 | | 100.0 | | 100.0 | Total | | | | | | | | |
| | | | | | | LIABILITIES | | | | | | | | |
| | 9.1 | | 3.1 | | 5.5 | Notes Payable-Short Term | | | | | | | | |
| | 4.4 | | 2.6 | | 2.9 | Cur. Mat.-L.T.D. | | | | | | | | |
| | 5.3 | | 10.4 | | 4.4 | Trade Payables | | | | | | | | |
| | .0 | | .0 | | .0 | Income Taxes Payable | | | | | | | | |
| | 13.6 | | 11.3 | | 18.1 | All Other Current | | | | | | | | |
| | 32.3 | | 27.4 | | 30.9 | Total Current | | | | | | | | |
| | 43.4 | | 43.2 | | 29.0 | Long-Term Debt | | | | | | | | |
| | .0 | | .0 | | .0 | Deferred Taxes | | | | | | | | |
| | 4.9 | | 2.6 | | 10.2 | All Other Non-Current | | | | | | | | |
| | 19.4 | | 26.7 | | 29.9 | Net Worth | | | | | | | | |
| | 100.0 | | 100.0 | | 100.0 | Total Liabilities & Net Worth | | | | | | | | |
| | | | | | | INCOME DATA | | | | | | | | |
| | 100.0 | | 100.0 | | 100.0 | Net Sales | | | | | | | | |
| | | | | | | Gross Profit | | | | | | | | |
| | 79.4 | | 72.8 | | 83.6 | Operating Expenses | | | | | | | | |
| | 20.6 | | 27.2 | | 16.4 | Operating Profit | | | | | | | | |
| | 5.2 | | 2.9 | | 6.9 | All Other Expenses (net) | | | | | | | | |
| | 15.4 | | 24.2 | | 9.5 | Profit Before Taxes | | | | | | | | |
| | | | | | | RATIOS | | | | | | | | |
| | 2.6 | | 3.0 | | 3.0 | | | | | | | | | |
| | 1.2 | | 2.1 | | 2.0 | Current | | | | | | | | |
| | .9 | | 1.2 | | 1.0 | | | | | | | | | |
| | 2.6 | | 2.6 | | 2.1 | | | | | | | | | |
| | 1.0 | | 1.7 | | 1.3 | Quick | | | | | | | | |
| | .7 | | .9 | | .8 | | | | | | | | | |
| 1 | 715.6 | 13 | 28.3 | 28 | 13.1 | | | | | | | | | |
| 46 | 7.9 | 46 | 7.9 | 35 | 10.3 | Sales/Receivables | | | | | | | | |
| 140 | 2.6 | 104 | 3.5 | 73 | 5.0 | | | | | | | | | |
| | | | | | | Cost of Sales/Inventory | | | | | | | | |
| | | | | | | Cost of Sales/Payables | | | | | | | | |
| | 3.0 | | 3.3 | | 3.4 | | | | | | | | | |
| | 16.9 | | 7.4 | | 8.0 | Sales/Working Capital | | | | | | | | |
| | -10.2 | | 25.8 | | NM | | | | | | | | | |
| | 29.8 | | 22.1 | | 31.9 | | | | | | | | | |
| (15) | 8.5 | (25) | 7.0 | (20) | 4.7 | EBIT/Interest | | | | | | | | |
| | 1.4 | | 3.1 | | 1.6 | | | | | | | | | |
| | | | | | | Net Profit + Depr., Dep., Amort./Cur. Mat. L/T/D | | | | | | | | |
| | .7 | | .2 | | .3 | | | | | | | | | |
| | 3.4 | | 1.0 | | 1.2 | Fixed/Worth | | | | | | | | |
| | 32.0 | | 5.1 | | 19.1 | | | | | | | | | |
| | 1.0 | | .7 | | 1.0 | | | | | | | | | |
| | 9.2 | | 2.8 | | 2.9 | Debt/Worth | | | | | | | | |
| | 89.6 | | 41.0 | | 21.1 | | | | | | | | | |
| | 45.6 | | 74.7 | | 90.7 | | | | | | | | | |
| (16) | 25.9 | (26) | 33.9 | (21) | 39.7 | % Profit Before Taxes/Tangible Net Worth | | | | | | | | |
| | -10.9 | | 15.2 | | 13.0 | | | | | | | | | |
| | 15.4 | | 28.5 | | 16.1 | | | | | | | | | |
| | 9.1 | | 13.8 | | 8.1 | % Profit Before Taxes/Total Assets | | | | | | | | |
| | .3 | | 4.8 | | 1.8 | | | | | | | | | |
| | 11.8 | | 76.6 | | 23.1 | | | | | | | | | |
| | 3.2 | | 3.6 | | 8.4 | Sales/Net Fixed Assets | | | | | | | | |
| | .5 | | .8 | | 1.1 | | | | | | | | | |
| | .9 | | 1.9 | | 2.1 | | | | | | | | | |
| | .8 | | .9 | | 1.0 | Sales/Total Assets | | | | | | | | |
| | .3 | | .5 | | .3 | | | | | | | | | |
| | 7.7 | | 1.3 | | 1.0 | | | | | | | | | |
| (13) | 9.9 | (20) | 5.9 | (19) | 5.5 | % Depr., Dep., Amort./Sales | | | | | | | | |
| | 24.4 | | 10.3 | | 8.5 | | | | | | | | | |
| | | | 4.5 | | | | | | | | | | | |
| | | (13) | 5.7 | | | % Officers', Directors' Owners' Comp/Sales | | | | | | | | |
| | | | 10.1 | | | | | | | | | | | |
| | 462066M | | 573686M | | 630298M | Net Sales ($) | 209M | 5418M | 10173M | 44101M | 59549M | | 510848M | |
| | 601930M | | 696651M | | 721502M | Total Assets ($) | 1352M | 21921M | 16544M | 77741M | 84647M | | 519297M | |

M = $ thousand    MM = $ million
See Pages viii through xx for Explanation of Ratios and Data

© RMA 2024

# PROFESSIONAL SERVICES—Direct Mail Advertising  NAICS 541860

## Current Data Sorted by Assets

| | | | | | | | Type of Statement | | | | |
|---|---|---|---|---|---|---|---|---|---|---|---|
| | | | 2 | 1 | 1 | | Unqualified | | 3 | | |
| | | | 2 | 3 | | | Reviewed | | 7 | | 4 |
| | | 1 | 6 | | | | Compiled | | 4 | | |
| | | 1 | | 10 | 1 | 2 | Tax Returns | | 6 | | 5 |
| | 7 (4/1-9/30/23) | | 23 (10/1/23-3/31/24) | | | | Other | | 23 | | 17 |
| 0-500M | 500M-2MM | 2-10MM | 10-50MM | 50-100MM | 100-250MM | | | | 4/1/19-3/31/20 ALL | | 4/1/20-3/31/21 ALL |
| | 2 | 10 | 14 | 2 | 2 | | NUMBER OF STATEMENTS | | 43 | | 26 |
| % | % | % | % | % | % | | ASSETS | | % | | % |
| | | 11.3 | 17.6 | | | | Cash & Equivalents | | 15.9 | | 27.2 |
| DATA | | 14.9 | 20.4 | | | | Trade Receivables (net) | | 24.6 | | 26.3 |
| | | 4.5 | 5.3 | | | | Inventory | | 3.6 | | 3.8 |
| DATA | | .8 | 2.3 | | | | All Other Current | | 3.3 | | 2.3 |
| | | 31.4 | 45.5 | | | | Total Current | | 47.3 | | 59.6 |
| NOT | | 31.5 | 24.1 | | | | Fixed Assets (net) | | 34.4 | | 25.1 |
| | | 24.0 | 17.1 | | | | Intangibles (net) | | 7.2 | | 8.4 |
| | | 13.0 | 13.3 | | | | All Other Non-Current | | 11.1 | | 6.9 |
| | | 100.0 | 100.0 | | | | Total | | 100.0 | | 100.0 |
| AVAILABLE | | | | | | | LIABILITIES | | | | |
| | | .8 | 4.3 | | | | Notes Payable-Short Term | | 4.5 | | 5.7 |
| | | 7.2 | 3.7 | | | | Cur. Mat.-L.T.D. | | 3.4 | | 3.0 |
| | | 15.7 | 9.8 | | | | Trade Payables | | 9.3 | | 8.9 |
| | | .0 | .0 | | | | Income Taxes Payable | | .8 | | 1.0 |
| | | 17.8 | 28.1 | | | | All Other Current | | 17.6 | | 29.5 |
| | | 41.5 | 45.9 | | | | Total Current | | 35.6 | | 48.2 |
| | | 25.4 | 18.0 | | | | Long-Term Debt | | 22.2 | | 18.2 |
| | | .7 | .0 | | | | Deferred Taxes | | 1.7 | | .0 |
| | | 29.9 | 13.1 | | | | All Other Non-Current | | 8.4 | | 14.9 |
| | | 2.5 | 23.0 | | | | Net Worth | | 32.2 | | 18.7 |
| | | 100.0 | 100.0 | | | | Total Liabilities & Net Worth | | 100.0 | | 100.0 |
| | | | | | | | INCOME DATA | | | | |
| | | 100.0 | 100.0 | | | | Net Sales | | 100.0 | | 100.0 |
| | | | | | | | Gross Profit | | | | |
| | | 86.9 | 95.5 | | | | Operating Expenses | | 91.4 | | 89.7 |
| | | 13.1 | 4.5 | | | | Operating Profit | | 8.6 | | 10.3 |
| | | 2.1 | 1.3 | | | | All Other Expenses (net) | | 2.2 | | .5 |
| | | 11.0 | 3.2 | | | | Profit Before Taxes | | 6.4 | | 9.8 |
| | | | | | | | RATIOS | | | | |
| | | 2.0 | 1.6 | | | | | | 2.1 | | 2.3 |
| | | .7 | 1.1 | | | | Current | | 1.4 | | 1.2 |
| | | .3 | .5 | | | | | | .8 | | .8 |
| | | 1.4 | 1.4 | | | | | | 1.8 | | 2.2 |
| | | .5 | .8 | | | | Quick | | 1.2 | | 1.0 |
| | | .2 | .5 | | | | | | .7 | | .7 |
| | | 0  UND | 21  17.7 | | | | | 13 | 28.9 | 17 | 21.9 |
| | | 7  49.3 | 32  11.3 | | | | Sales/Receivables | 39 | 9.3 | 41 | 9.0 |
| | | 70  5.2 | 63  5.8 | | | | | 60 | 6.1 | 76 | 4.8 |
| | | | | | | | Cost of Sales/Inventory | | | | |
| | | | | | | | Cost of Sales/Payables | | | | |
| | | 25.0 | 13.4 | | | | | | 7.6 | | 4.4 |
| | | -8.8 | 51.1 | | | | Sales/Working Capital | | 18.9 | | 13.0 |
| | | -2.1 | -5.6 | | | | | | -21.0 | | -29.8 |
| | | | 32.0 | | | | | | 19.6 | | 21.1 |
| | | (13) | 6.3 | | | | EBIT/Interest | (38) | 7.0 | (24) | 9.2 |
| | | | .6 | | | | | | .1 | | 3.2 |
| | | | | | | | Net Profit + Depr., Dep., Amort./Cur. Mat. L/T/D | | | | |
| | | .2 | .1 | | | | | | .3 | | .2 |
| | | 3.8 | 3.9 | | | | Fixed/Worth | | 1.3 | | .6 |
| | | -.6 | -.4 | | | | | | 16.3 | | -2.3 |
| | | 9.4 | 1.2 | | | | | | .8 | | .8 |
| | | NM | 5.4 | | | | Debt/Worth | | 2.8 | | 4.8 |
| | | -1.8 | -2.7 | | | | | | 22.6 | | -6.3 |
| | | | | | | | | | 78.8 | | 74.2 |
| | | | | | | | % Profit Before Taxes/Tangible Net Worth | (35) | 24.0 | (17) | 18.0 |
| | | | | | | | | | 11.6 | | 10.1 |
| | | 15.3 | 18.7 | | | | | | 17.4 | | 17.3 |
| | | 8.5 | 9.3 | | | | % Profit Before Taxes/Total Assets | | 8.4 | | 8.1 |
| | | -2.7 | -1.3 | | | | | | -.7 | | 2.2 |
| | | 409.9 | 87.1 | | | | | | 40.7 | | 33.3 |
| | | 5.9 | 12.1 | | | | Sales/Net Fixed Assets | | 8.6 | | 9.9 |
| | | 2.9 | 4.1 | | | | | | 4.1 | | 5.2 |
| | | 2.4 | 2.7 | | | | | | 4.1 | | 2.6 |
| | | 1.3 | 2.1 | | | | Sales/Total Assets | | 2.1 | | 2.2 |
| | | .8 | 1.2 | | | | | | 1.4 | | 1.2 |
| | | | | | | | | | 2.4 | | 2.0 |
| | | | | | | | % Depr., Dep., Amort./Sales | (30) | 3.8 | (20) | 3.3 |
| | | | | | | | | | 6.5 | | 6.6 |
| | | | | | | | | | 2.6 | | 1.1 |
| | | | | | | | % Officers', Directors' Owners' Comp/Sales | (12) | 5.2 | (13) | 4.0 |
| | | | | | | | | | 7.3 | | 6.1 |
| | 7217M | 73925M | 556747M | 259043M | 548192M | | Net Sales ($) | | 1840466M | | 1259347M |
| | 2240M | 46796M | 278217M | 111055M | 325461M | | Total Assets ($) | | 877621M | | 593230M |

M = $ thousand   MM = $ million
See Pages viii through xx for Explanation of Ratios and Data

© RMA 2024

# PROFESSIONAL SERVICES—Direct Mail Advertising  NAICS 541860

## Comparative Historical Data | Current Data Sorted by Sales

| | | | | | | | | | | | |
|---|---|---|---|---|---|---|---|---|---|---|---|
| 2 | | 2 | | 1 | Type of Statement | | | | | | 1 |
| 7 | | 7 | | 3 | Unqualified | | | | 1 | 1 | 1 |
| | | 1 | | 3 | Reviewed | | | | | 1 | 2 |
| 4 | | 3 | | 3 | Compiled | | | | | 1 | |
| 18 | | 14 | | 20 | Tax Returns | 1 | 1 | | 3 | 3 | 11 |
| 4/1/21-3/31/22 ALL | | 4/1/22-3/31/23 ALL | | 4/1/23-3/31/24 ALL | Other | 1 7 (4/1-9/30/23) | 1 | 2 | 23 (10/1/23-3/31/24) | | |
| | | | | | | 0-1MM | 1-3MM | 3-5MM | 5-10MM | 10-25MM | 25MM & OVER |
| 31 | | 27 | | 30 | NUMBER OF STATEMENTS | 1 | 2 | | 4 | 6 | 15 |
| % | | % | | % | ASSETS | % | % | % | % | % | % |
| 23.1 | | 17.2 | | 15.1 | Cash & Equivalents | | | | | | 20.2 |
| 23.4 | | 20.5 | | 21.6 | Trade Receivables (net) | | | | | | 23.8 |
| 3.6 | | 6.9 | | 5.9 | Inventory | | | | | | 5.6 |
| 4.5 | | 3.8 | | 2.1 | All Other Current | | | | | | 3.2 |
| 54.7 | | 48.5 | | 44.7 | Total Current | | | | | | 52.8 |
| 24.0 | | 28.8 | | 26.2 | Fixed Assets (net) | | | | | | 22.4 |
| 14.8 | | 13.1 | | 17.7 | Intangibles (net) | | | | | | 13.4 |
| 6.4 | | 9.7 | | 11.4 | All Other Non-Current | | | | | | 11.4 |
| 100.0 | | 100.0 | | 100.0 | Total | | | | | | 100.0 |
| | | | | | LIABILITIES | | | | | | |
| 3.5 | | 4.4 | | 4.1 | Notes Payable-Short Term | | | | | | 3.9 |
| 3.3 | | 3.6 | | 4.4 | Cur. Mat.-L.T.D. | | | | | | 2.5 |
| 10.3 | | 6.4 | | 14.0 | Trade Payables | | | | | | 14.6 |
| .0 | | .2 | | .0 | Income Taxes Payable | | | | | | .0 |
| 17.0 | | 16.7 | | 22.9 | All Other Current | | | | | | 25.1 |
| 34.1 | | 31.3 | | 45.3 | Total Current | | | | | | 46.0 |
| 15.2 | | 20.2 | | 18.5 | Long-Term Debt | | | | | | 15.5 |
| .2 | | .3 | | .2 | Deferred Taxes | | | | | | .0 |
| 8.5 | | 16.1 | | 19.3 | All Other Non-Current | | | | | | 16.2 |
| 42.0 | | 32.1 | | 16.7 | Net Worth | | | | | | 22.3 |
| 100.0 | | 100.0 | | 100.0 | Total Liabilities & Net Worth | | | | | | 100.0 |
| | | | | | INCOME DATA | | | | | | |
| 100.0 | | 100.0 | | 100.0 | Net Sales | | | | | | 100.0 |
| | | | | | Gross Profit | | | | | | |
| 90.8 | | 94.1 | | 93.8 | Operating Expenses | | | | | | 97.4 |
| 9.2 | | 5.9 | | 6.2 | Operating Profit | | | | | | 2.6 |
| -1.3 | | -.2 | | 1.4 | All Other Expenses (net) | | | | | | 1.0 |
| 10.4 | | 6.1 | | 4.9 | Profit Before Taxes | | | | | | 1.6 |
| | | | | | RATIOS | | | | | | |
| 2.7 | | 2.7 | | 1.4 | | | | | | | 1.6 |
| 1.4 | | 1.4 | | 1.1 | Current | | | | | | 1.2 |
| .8 | | 1.1 | | .5 | | | | | | | .8 |
| 2.4 | | 1.8 | | 1.3 | | | | | | | 1.6 |
| 1.3 | | 1.1 | | .8 | Quick | | | | | | 1.1 |
| .7 | | .8 | | .3 | | | | | | | .8 |
| 21 17.5 | | 21 17.5 | | 7 50.4 | | | | | | 21 | 17.7 |
| 38 9.7 | | 38 9.6 | | 35 10.5 | Sales/Receivables | | | | | 37 | 9.9 |
| 54 6.7 | | 57 6.4 | | 66 5.5 | | | | | | 62 | 5.9 |
| | | | | | Cost of Sales/Inventory | | | | | | |
| | | | | | Cost of Sales/Payables | | | | | | |
| 5.7 | | 6.1 | | 13.4 | | | | | | | 11.2 |
| 10.3 | | 16.1 | | 41.8 | Sales/Working Capital | | | | | | 16.8 |
| -56.1 | | 115.2 | | -4.1 | | | | | | | -21.5 |
| 96.9 | | 81.9 | | 37.6 | | | | | | | 35.3 |
| (26) 20.9 | | (26) 12.1 | | (24) 2.9 | EBIT/Interest | | | | | (12) | 4.8 |
| 6.0 | | 5.6 | | -1.0 | | | | | | | -4.8 |
| | | | | | Net Profit + Depr., Dep., Amort./Cur. Mat. L/T/D | | | | | | |
| .3 | | .4 | | .3 | | | | | | | .1 |
| .8 | | .9 | | 1.3 | Fixed/Worth | | | | | | 1.4 |
| -3.4 | | 3.2 | | -.6 | | | | | | | -.9 |
| .5 | | 1.0 | | 1.4 | | | | | | | 1.4 |
| 2.1 | | 2.0 | | 9.5 | Debt/Worth | | | | | | 3.9 |
| -10.3 | | 7.9 | | -2.4 | | | | | | | -4.0 |
| 100.2 | | 87.0 | | 77.4 | | | | | | | 74.1 |
| (23) 46.3 | | (22) 40.5 | | (18) 22.0 | % Profit Before Taxes/Tangible Net Worth | | | | | (10) | 21.1 |
| 24.8 | | 21.0 | | -1.9 | | | | | | | -4.4 |
| 26.5 | | 28.3 | | 15.1 | | | | | | | 17.5 |
| 19.0 | | 12.0 | | 7.0 | % Profit Before Taxes/Total Assets | | | | | | 6.6 |
| 6.5 | | 3.6 | | -2.0 | | | | | | | -3.8 |
| 37.8 | | 33.3 | | 55.1 | | | | | | | 69.4 |
| 9.8 | | 8.2 | | 9.7 | Sales/Net Fixed Assets | | | | | | 12.8 |
| 4.6 | | 3.8 | | 4.1 | | | | | | | 5.6 |
| 2.8 | | 3.1 | | 2.7 | | | | | | | 2.7 |
| 1.8 | | 2.0 | | 2.0 | Sales/Total Assets | | | | | | 2.1 |
| 1.3 | | 1.5 | | 1.2 | | | | | | | 1.6 |
| 1.2 | | 1.3 | | .5 | | | | | | | |
| (20) 2.6 | | (21) 3.0 | | (20) 2.1 | % Depr., Dep., Amort./Sales | | | | | | |
| 4.8 | | 4.8 | | 6.7 | | | | | | | |
| | | | | | % Officers', Directors', Owners' Comp/Sales | | | | | | |
| 1071754M | | 1382271M | | 1445124M | Net Sales ($) | 408M | 3585M | 7226M | 29424M | 93663M | 1310818M |
| 632142M | | 667044M | | 763769M | Total Assets ($) | 2477M | 4512M | 5698M | 19573M | 53550M | 677959M |

© RMA 2024  M = $ thousand  MM = $ million
See Pages viii through xx for Explanation of Ratios and Data

# PROFESSIONAL SERVICES—Other Services Related to Advertising  NAICS 541890

## Current Data Sorted by Assets | Comparative Historical Data

| | | | | | | Type of Statement | | |
|---|---|---|---|---|---|---|---|---|
| | | | 3 | 3 | 1 | Unqualified | 8 | 5 |
| | | 1 | 4 | | | Reviewed | 8 | 3 |
| | | 2 | 1 | | | Compiled | 6 | 2 |
| 2 | 3 | 5 | 1 | | | Tax Returns | 12 | 8 |
| 3 | 3 | 12 | 14 | 8 | 2 | Other | 52 | 30 |
| | 2 (4/1-9/30/23) | | 66 (10/1/23-3/31/24) | | | | 4/1/19- | 4/1/20- |
| 0-500M | 500M-2MM | 2-10MM | 10-50MM | 50-100MM | 100-250MM | | 3/31/20 | 3/31/21 |
| | | | | | | NUMBER OF STATEMENTS | 86 ALL | 48 ALL |
| 5 | 6 | 20 | 23 | 11 | 3 | | | |
| % | % | % | % | % | % | ASSETS | % | % |
| | | 23.6 | 16.0 | 2.7 | | Cash & Equivalents | 19.7 | 29.1 |
| | | 34.4 | 33.3 | 19.1 | | Trade Receivables (net) | 30.9 | 21.3 |
| | | 9.8 | 13.3 | 20.3 | | Inventory | 10.0 | 8.8 |
| | | 1.3 | 9.3 | 1.9 | | All Other Current | 4.2 | 2.9 |
| | | 69.1 | 71.9 | 44.1 | | Total Current | 64.8 | 62.1 |
| | | 11.4 | 12.1 | 7.7 | | Fixed Assets (net) | 16.6 | 17.5 |
| | | 9.1 | 7.9 | 42.0 | | Intangibles (net) | 8.8 | 11.6 |
| | | 10.4 | 8.2 | 6.3 | | All Other Non-Current | 9.8 | 8.8 |
| | | 100.0 | 100.0 | 100.0 | | Total | 100.0 | 100.0 |
| | | | | | | LIABILITIES | | |
| | | 8.0 | 2.3 | 2.4 | | Notes Payable-Short Term | 12.8 | 8.5 |
| | | 1.1 | 3.5 | 1.9 | | Cur. Mat.-L.T.D. | 2.0 | 2.6 |
| | | 14.4 | 14.5 | 8.1 | | Trade Payables | 15.3 | 11.5 |
| | | .1 | .5 | .0 | | Income Taxes Payable | .1 | .1 |
| | | 17.9 | 21.8 | 10.0 | | All Other Current | 19.9 | 17.2 |
| | | 41.5 | 42.7 | 22.4 | | Total Current | 50.1 | 39.9 |
| | | 13.1 | 10.7 | 42.9 | | Long-Term Debt | 17.2 | 26.7 |
| | | .0 | .4 | .0 | | Deferred Taxes | .1 | .5 |
| | | 4.9 | 4.7 | 2.3 | | All Other Non-Current | 5.9 | 11.8 |
| | | 40.4 | 41.4 | 32.4 | | Net Worth | 26.8 | 21.1 |
| | | 100.0 | 100.0 | 100.0 | | Total Liabilities & Net Worth | 100.0 | 100.0 |
| | | | | | | INCOME DATA | | |
| | | 100.0 | 100.0 | 100.0 | | Net Sales | 100.0 | 100.0 |
| | | | | | | Gross Profit | | |
| | | 91.8 | 93.7 | 90.3 | | Operating Expenses | 92.7 | 92.9 |
| | | 8.2 | 6.3 | 9.7 | | Operating Profit | 7.3 | 7.1 |
| | | -.3 | -.6 | 9.7 | | All Other Expenses (net) | 1.5 | 2.2 |
| | | 8.5 | 6.8 | .0 | | Profit Before Taxes | 5.8 | 5.0 |
| | | | | | | RATIOS | | |
| | | 3.6 | 3.1 | 2.3 | | | 2.4 | 3.8 |
| | | 1.6 | 1.7 | 2.0 | | Current | 1.4 | 1.8 |
| | | .9 | 1.2 | 1.7 | | | 1.0 | 1.2 |
| | | 3.2 | 1.7 | 1.6 | | | 2.1 | 2.4 |
| | | 1.3 | 1.2 | 1.1 | | Quick | 1.1 | 1.2 |
| | | .6 | .9 | .8 | | | .6 | .8 |
| | | 31  11.8 | 32  11.5 | 24  15.3 | | | 20  18.4 | 8  48.2 |
| | | 46  7.9 | 49  7.4 | 46  7.9 | | Sales/Receivables | 38  9.5 | 34  10.6 |
| | | 58  6.3 | 68  5.4 | 111  3.3 | | | 57  6.4 | 56  6.5 |
| | | | | | | Cost of Sales/Inventory | | |
| | | | | | | Cost of Sales/Payables | | |
| | | 5.7 | 4.1 | 3.9 | | | 6.1 | 4.8 |
| | | 9.9 | 7.5 | 5.5 | | Sales/Working Capital | 11.0 | 7.6 |
| | | -60.1 | 32.5 | 11.4 | | | 254.9 | 25.8 |
| | | 62.4 | 83.9 | 5.5 | | | 19.9 | 18.6 |
| | | (15) 5.6 | (19) 19.3 | 2.6 | | EBIT/Interest | (65) 7.7 | (36) 5.5 |
| | | 3.1 | 1.6 | .5 | | | 2.2 | .5 |
| | | | 28.2 | | | Net Profit + Depr., Dep., | | |
| | | | (10) 7.3 | | | Amort./Cur. Mat. L/T/D | | |
| | | | 5.4 | | | | | |
| | | .0 | .1 | .2 | | | .1 | .1 |
| | | .0 | .3 | -1.4 | | Fixed/Worth | .4 | .7 |
| | | .4 | .7 | .0 | | | 2.8 | -1.0 |
| | | .4 | .7 | 1.2 | | | .7 | 1.0 |
| | | 2.0 | 1.4 | -3.8 | | Debt/Worth | 2.9 | 5.4 |
| | | 6.1 | 4.5 | -2.2 | | | 44.7 | -5.0 |
| | | 89.9 | 59.3 | | | | 61.3 | 105.5 |
| | | (17) 45.1 | (19) 28.3 | | | % Profit Before Taxes/Tangible Net Worth | (69) 41.3 | (31) 54.9 |
| | | 20.3 | 5.4 | | | | 16.4 | 20.3 |
| | | 32.2 | 31.9 | 14.2 | | | 20.9 | 25.1 |
| | | 13.6 | 10.2 | 5.6 | | % Profit Before Taxes/Total Assets | 10.2 | 10.7 |
| | | 4.4 | 1.1 | -1.7 | | | 1.7 | -1.3 |
| | | 999.8 | 70.9 | 146.2 | | | 113.7 | 137.3 |
| | | 464.2 | 27.5 | 91.9 | | Sales/Net Fixed Assets | 33.0 | 27.9 |
| | | 11.9 | 18.2 | 16.4 | | | 12.9 | 8.3 |
| | | 4.2 | 3.0 | 2.4 | | | 4.3 | 3.2 |
| | | 3.0 | 2.3 | 1.3 | | Sales/Total Assets | 3.0 | 2.1 |
| | | 1.8 | 1.6 | .6 | | | 1.9 | 1.3 |
| | | | .2 | | | | .3 | 1.0 |
| | | (21) | .6 | | | % Depr., Dep., Amort./Sales | (55) .9 | (25) 1.6 |
| | | | 2.2 | | | | 1.6 | 3.9 |
| | | | | | | | 1.9 | 2.4 |
| | | | | | | % Officers', Directors' Owners' Comp/Sales | (25) 5.9 | (13) 5.8 |
| | | | | | | | 9.1 | 10.6 |
| 2474M | 16891M | 321908M | 1365439M | 1260591M | 1016417M | Net Sales ($) | 2910966M | 1748988M |
| 882M | 4271M | 113812M | 564725M | 839346M | 510718M | Total Assets ($) | 1740038M | 1037505M |

© RMA 2024

M = $ thousand   MM = $ million
See Pages viii through xx for Explanation of Ratios and Data

## PROFESSIONAL SERVICES—Other Services Related to Advertising  NAICS 541890

| Comparative Historical Data | | | | | Current Data Sorted by Sales | | | | | |
|---|---|---|---|---|---|---|---|---|---|---|
| | | | | Type of Statement | | | | | | |
| 7 | | 8 | 7 | Unqualified | | | | | 1 | 6 |
| 4 | | 4 | 5 | Reviewed | | | | | 1 | 4 |
| 5 | | 4 | 3 | Compiled | | | | | 2 | 1 |
| 8 | | 17 | 11 | Tax Returns | 2 | 1 | 2 | | 4 | 2 |
| 41 | | 44 | 42 | Other | 4 | 3 | 1 | 3 | 7 | 24 |
| 4/1/21- | | 4/1/22- | 4/1/23- | | | 2 (4/1-9/30/23) | | | 66 (10/1/23-3/31/24) | |
| 3/31/22 | | 3/31/23 | 3/31/24 | | 0-1MM | 1-3MM | 3-5MM | 5-10MM | 10-25MM | 25MM & OVER |
| ALL | | ALL | ALL | NUMBER OF STATEMENTS | | | | | | |
| 65 | | 77 | 68 | | 6 | 4 | 3 | 3 | 15 | 37 |
| % | | % | % | **ASSETS** | % | % | % | % | % | % |
| 20.7 | | 22.2 | 18.4 | Cash & Equivalents | | | | | 23.9 | 13.3 |
| 27.3 | | 29.0 | 30.4 | Trade Receivables (net) | | | | | 34.8 | 29.3 |
| 13.3 | | 10.8 | 12.6 | Inventory | | | | | 7.6 | 18.8 |
| 5.2 | | 3.3 | 3.9 | All Other Current | | | | | 1.0 | 6.2 |
| 66.5 | | 65.3 | 65.3 | Total Current | | | | | 67.2 | 67.7 |
| 15.0 | | 17.3 | 11.7 | Fixed Assets (net) | | | | | 5.8 | 10.8 |
| 9.2 | | 7.1 | 13.9 | Intangibles (net) | | | | | 15.7 | 14.2 |
| 9.4 | | 10.3 | 9.1 | All Other Non-Current | | | | | 11.3 | 7.4 |
| 100.0 | | 100.0 | 100.0 | Total | | | | | 100.0 | 100.0 |
| | | | | **LIABILITIES** | | | | | | |
| 6.4 | | 9.8 | 6.2 | Notes Payable-Short Term | | | | | 5.8 | 4.1 |
| 2.2 | | 2.1 | 4.0 | Cur. Mat.-L.T.D. | | | | | 1.2 | 2.8 |
| 11.3 | | 13.3 | 12.2 | Trade Payables | | | | | 14.8 | 14.3 |
| .2 | | .1 | .2 | Income Taxes Payable | | | | | .0 | .3 |
| 15.1 | | 25.4 | 15.7 | All Other Current | | | | | 17.4 | 19.7 |
| 35.2 | | 50.6 | 38.2 | Total Current | | | | | 39.3 | 41.2 |
| 21.7 | | 24.7 | 18.8 | Long-Term Debt | | | | | 11.3 | 21.0 |
| .0 | | .0 | .1 | Deferred Taxes | | | | | .0 | .3 |
| 6.7 | | 3.7 | 4.1 | All Other Non-Current | | | | | 5.2 | 4.5 |
| 36.4 | | 20.9 | 38.7 | Net Worth | | | | | 44.3 | 33.1 |
| 100.0 | | 100.0 | 100.0 | Total Liabilities & Net Worth | | | | | 100.0 | 100.0 |
| | | | | **INCOME DATA** | | | | | | |
| 100.0 | | 100.0 | 100.0 | Net Sales | | | | | 100.0 | 100.0 |
| | | | | Gross Profit | | | | | | |
| 91.9 | | 89.1 | 91.1 | Operating Expenses | | | | | 91.7 | 93.8 |
| 8.1 | | 10.9 | 8.9 | Operating Profit | | | | | 8.3 | 6.2 |
| -1.3 | | .3 | 1.8 | All Other Expenses (net) | | | | | 1.8 | 1.8 |
| 9.4 | | 10.6 | 7.1 | Profit Before Taxes | | | | | 6.5 | 4.5 |
| | | | | **RATIOS** | | | | | | |
| 3.5 | | 3.4 | 2.9 | | | | | | 3.2 | 2.3 |
| 2.0 | | 2.0 | 1.7 | Current | | | | | 1.7 | 1.7 |
| 1.2 | | 1.1 | 1.2 | | | | | | 1.0 | 1.2 |
| 2.5 | | 3.1 | 2.0 | | | | | | 3.2 | 1.6 |
| 1.3 | | 1.3 | 1.3 | Quick | | | | | 1.4 | 1.1 |
| .8 | | .6 | .8 | | | | | | 1.0 | .6 |
| 19  19.5 | 20 | 18.2 | 30  12.3 | | | | | 33 | 11.0 | 25  14.6 |
| 42  8.7 | 37 | 9.9 | 46  7.9 | Sales/Receivables | | | | 49 | 7.4 | 46  7.9 |
| 63  5.8 | 55 | 6.6 | 62  5.9 | | | | | 54 | 6.7 | 64  5.7 |
| | | | | Cost of Sales/Inventory | | | | | | |
| | | | | Cost of Sales/Payables | | | | | | |
| 4.4 | | 5.3 | 5.0 | | | | | | 3.5 | 5.2 |
| 6.9 | | 9.0 | 8.1 | Sales/Working Capital | | | | | 7.2 | 7.8 |
| 18.7 | | 106.2 | 23.4 | | | | | | -228.6 | 23.0 |
| 138.5 | | 37.1 | 36.7 | | | | | | 30.4 | 36.6 |
| (53)  15.3 | (61) | 11.5 | (56)  5.5 | EBIT/Interest | | | | (10) | 4.9 | (33)  4.8 |
| 2.9 | | 4.4 | 1.1 | | | | | | -.3 | 1.2 |
| | | | 35.0 | Net Profit + Depr., Dep., | | | | | | 35.0 |
| | | (12) | 7.3 | Amort./Cur. Mat. L/T/D | | | | | | (12)  7.3 |
| | | | 3.9 | | | | | | | 3.9 |
| .1 | | .0 | .0 | | | | | | .0 | .1 |
| .3 | | .3 | .2 | Fixed/Worth | | | | | .0 | .3 |
| 3.5 | | UND | 1.4 | | | | | | .7 | -2.2 |
| .7 | | .5 | .7 | | | | | | .6 | .8 |
| 1.8 | | 1.7 | 1.7 | Debt/Worth | | | | | 2.7 | 1.7 |
| 108.5 | | -46.2 | NM | | | | | | 41.1 | -7.0 |
| 86.0 | | 81.6 | 81.2 | % Profit Before Taxes/Tangible | | | | | 112.8 | 57.5 |
| (51)  50.1 | (56) | 34.7 | (51)  43.9 | Net Worth | | | | (12) | 63.4 | (26)  30.1 |
| 28.4 | | 16.8 | 23.2 | | | | | | 28.0 | 7.6 |
| 32.9 | | 27.4 | 32.2 | % Profit Before Taxes/Total | | | | | 35.1 | 16.1 |
| 16.9 | | 14.5 | 12.1 | Assets | | | | | 17.5 | 8.0 |
| 3.3 | | 4.9 | 1.4 | | | | | | 2.4 | .1 |
| 140.2 | | 375.5 | 407.0 | | | | | | 999.8 | 129.1 |
| 32.5 | | 27.5 | 58.2 | Sales/Net Fixed Assets | | | | | 385.9 | 33.2 |
| 11.1 | | 10.9 | 13.8 | | | | | | 34.2 | 17.3 |
| 3.7 | | 4.3 | 3.4 | | | | | | 4.0 | 3.0 |
| 2.2 | | 2.6 | 2.3 | Sales/Total Assets | | | | | 3.0 | 2.1 |
| 1.5 | | 1.8 | 1.6 | | | | | | 1.7 | 1.6 |
| .6 | | .7 | .4 | | | | | | | .2 |
| (36)  1.3 | (46) | 1.4 | (36)  1.2 | % Depr., Dep., Amort./Sales | | | | | (25) | .8 |
| 2.3 | | 3.2 | 2.7 | | | | | | | 2.0 |
| 2.2 | | 1.8 | 1.2 | % Officers', Directors' | | | | | | |
| (23)  5.2 | (21) | 4.8 | (17)  2.5 | Owners' Comp/Sales | | | | | | |
| 12.9 | | 12.0 | 5.7 | | | | | | | |
| 2184726M | | 2624128M | 3983720M | Net Sales ($) | 3268M | 8923M | 11334M | 24805M | 260475M | 3674915M |
| 1121009M | | 1138198M | 2033754M | Total Assets ($) | 1390M | 9529M | 2492M | 16384M | 236872M | 1767087M |

© RMA 2024  M = $ thousand  MM = $ million
See Pages viii through xx for Explanation of Ratios and Data

# PROFESSIONAL SERVICES—Marketing Research and Public Opinion Polling  NAICS 541910

## Current Data Sorted by Assets | Comparative Historical Data

| | | | | | | | Type of Statement | | |
|---|---|---|---|---|---|---|---|---|---|
| | | 1 | 1 | 1 | | | Unqualified | 3 | 2 |
| | | 2 | 2 | | | | Reviewed | 4 | 3 |
| | 1 | 3 | | | | | Compiled | 1 | 1 |
| 5 | 2 | 1 | | | | | Tax Returns | 15 | 1 |
| 4 | 4 | 5 | 7 | 2 | 1 | | Other | 29 | 18 |
| | 5 (4/1-9/30/23) | | 38 (10/1/23-3/31/24) | | | | | 4/1/19- | 4/1/20- |
| 0-500M | 500M-2MM | 2-10MM | 10-50MM | 50-100MM | 100-250MM | | | 3/31/20 | 3/31/21 |
| 9 | 8 | 12 | 10 | 3 | 1 | | NUMBER OF STATEMENTS | ALL 52 | ALL 25 |
| % | % | % | % | % | % | | ASSETS | % | % |
| | | 37.3 | 36.9 | | | | Cash & Equivalents | 22.2 | 31.3 |
| | | 39.3 | 33.7 | | | | Trade Receivables (net) | 36.8 | 32.5 |
| | | .1 | 5.9 | | | | Inventory | 1.7 | 2.8 |
| | | 4.1 | 3.6 | | | | All Other Current | 5.6 | 2.9 |
| | | 80.8 | 80.1 | | | | Total Current | 66.3 | 69.5 |
| | | 5.1 | 3.6 | | | | Fixed Assets (net) | 12.7 | 11.9 |
| | | .9 | 6.4 | | | | Intangibles (net) | 10.0 | 15.2 |
| | | 13.1 | 10.0 | | | | All Other Non-Current | 11.0 | 3.3 |
| | | 100.0 | 100.0 | | | | Total | 100.0 | 100.0 |
| | | | | | | | LIABILITIES | | |
| | | 4.7 | 9.7 | | | | Notes Payable-Short Term | 11.5 | 9.1 |
| | | .2 | .4 | | | | Cur. Mat.-L.T.D. | 2.1 | 2.6 |
| | | 18.8 | 10.6 | | | | Trade Payables | 10.1 | 5.6 |
| | | .1 | .0 | | | | Income Taxes Payable | .3 | .3 |
| | | 15.2 | 14.4 | | | | All Other Current | 26.9 | 32.7 |
| | | 39.0 | 35.2 | | | | Total Current | 51.0 | 50.3 |
| | | 4.7 | 2.5 | | | | Long-Term Debt | 21.6 | 20.4 |
| | | .0 | .0 | | | | Deferred Taxes | .4 | .2 |
| | | 7.7 | 2.8 | | | | All Other Non-Current | 17.6 | 14.1 |
| | | 48.6 | 59.5 | | | | Net Worth | 9.3 | 15.1 |
| | | 100.0 | 100.0 | | | | Total Liabilties & Net Worth | 100.0 | 100.0 |
| | | | | | | | INCOME DATA | | |
| | | 100.0 | 100.0 | | | | Net Sales | 100.0 | 100.0 |
| | | | | | | | Gross Profit | | |
| | | 85.4 | 92.6 | | | | Operating Expenses | 88.4 | 95.5 |
| | | 14.6 | 7.4 | | | | Operating Profit | 11.6 | 4.5 |
| | | .3 | 1.3 | | | | All Other Expenses (net) | 1.3 | .4 |
| | | 14.3 | 6.1 | | | | Profit Before Taxes | 10.3 | 4.1 |
| | | | | | | | RATIOS | | |
| | | 5.1 | 78.6 | | | | | 3.2 | 2.7 |
| | | 2.7 | 1.8 | | | | Current | 1.6 | 1.7 |
| | | 1.1 | 1.3 | | | | | .9 | .8 |
| | | 4.8 | 78.5 | | | | | 3.1 | 2.6 |
| | | 2.7 | 1.7 | | | | Quick | 1.4 | 1.5 |
| | | 1.1 | 1.1 | | | | | .7 | .7 |
| | | 25  14.7 | 0  UND | | | | | 21  17.3 | 32  11.3 |
| | | 56  6.5 | 62  5.9 | | | | Sales/Receivables | 48  7.6 | 49  7.5 |
| | | 78  4.7 | 89  4.1 | | | | | 74  4.9 | 70  5.2 |
| | | | | | | | Cost of Sales/Inventory | | |
| | | | | | | | Cost of Sales/Payables | | |
| | | 4.0 | 3.9 | | | | | 7.5 | 5.9 |
| | | 11.7 | 5.3 | | | | Sales/Working Capital | 14.3 | 12.5 |
| | | 39.2 | 11.5 | | | | | -72.1 | -17.9 |
| | | | | | | | | 25.1 | 23.9 |
| | | | | | | | EBIT/Interest | (36) 8.8 | (19) 9.5 |
| | | | | | | | | 3.2 | .8 |
| | | | | | | | Net Profit + Depr., Dep., Amort./Cur. Mat. L/T/D | | |
| | | .0 | .0 | | | | | .0 | .0 |
| | | .1 | .0 | | | | Fixed/Worth | .3 | .4 |
| | | .5 | .1 | | | | | -2.6 | -.5 |
| | | .2 | .1 | | | | | .5 | 1.0 |
| | | .8 | 1.3 | | | | Debt/Worth | 1.9 | 12.2 |
| | | 7.4 | 2.4 | | | | | -3.0 | -2.7 |
| | | 103.5 | 73.9 | | | | | 104.1 | 100.5 |
| | (10) | 64.8 | 39.4 | | | | % Profit Before Taxes/Tangible Net Worth | (34) 57.2 | (13) 41.4 |
| | | 42.2 | -37.9 | | | | | 19.3 | 28.1 |
| | | 49.3 | 54.2 | | | | | 50.3 | 33.3 |
| | | 30.2 | 16.4 | | | | % Profit Before Taxes/Total Assets | 23.0 | 17.7 |
| | | 5.7 | -5.6 | | | | | 3.3 | -1.1 |
| | | 554.2 | 999.8 | | | | | 407.6 | 650.3 |
| | | 194.4 | 363.7 | | | | Sales/Net Fixed Assets | 51.8 | 61.1 |
| | | 30.5 | 67.1 | | | | | 12.3 | 11.8 |
| | | 4.4 | 3.2 | | | | | 4.6 | 3.8 |
| | | 3.0 | 2.2 | | | | Sales/Total Assets | 3.1 | 2.8 |
| | | 2.0 | 1.7 | | | | | 1.6 | 1.4 |
| | | | | | | | | .3 | .3 |
| | | | | | | | % Depr., Dep., Amort./Sales | (26) .8 | (10) 1.6 |
| | | | | | | | | 2.5 | 6.9 |
| | | | | | | | | 2.2 | |
| | | | | | | | % Officers', Directors' Owners' Comp/Sales | (14) 5.2 | |
| | | | | | | | | 14.2 | |
| 22679M | 31356M | 196930M | 637227M | 535008M | 84685M | | Net Sales ($) | 1751776M | 883305M |
| 2048M | 7706M | 66000M | 233653M | 185583M | 121067M | | Total Assets ($) | 1053745M | 632132M |

© RMA 2024

M = $ thousand   MM = $ million
See Pages viii through xx for Explanation of Ratios and Data

## PROFESSIONAL SERVICES—Marketing Research and Public Opinion Polling  NAICS 541910

### Comparative Historical Data / Current Data Sorted by Sales

| | | | | Type of Statement | | | | | | |
|---|---|---|---|---|---|---|---|---|---|---|
| | 2 | 2 | 4 | Unqualified | | 1 | | 1 | | 2 |
| 2 | 3 | 3 | 4 | Reviewed | | | | 1 | | 3 |
| 2 | 3 | 3 | 4 | Compiled | | 1 | | 1 | 2 | |
| 5 | 7 | 7 | 8 | Tax Returns | | 2 | 2 | 2 | 1 | |
| 17 | 19 | 23 | | Other | 1 | 3 | 3 | 2 | 6 | 8 |
| 4/1/21- | 4/1/22- | 4/1/23- | | | | 5 (4/1-9/30/23) | | | 38 (10/1/23-3/31/24) | |
| 3/31/22 | 3/31/23 | 3/31/24 | | | 0-1MM | 1-3MM | 3-5MM | 5-10MM | 10-25MM | 25MM & OVER |
| ALL | ALL | ALL | | NUMBER OF STATEMENTS | | | | | | |
| 26 | 34 | 43 | | | 2 | 7 | 5 | 7 | 9 | 13 |
| % | % | % | | ASSETS | % | % | % | % | % | % |
| 36.6 | 33.3 | 47.4 | | Cash & Equivalents | | | | | | 56.2 |
| 29.8 | 33.7 | 25.7 | | Trade Receivables (net) | | | | | | 19.1 |
| 5.2 | 2.5 | 2.5 | | Inventory | | | | | | 6.6 |
| 1.8 | 4.9 | 4.6 | | All Other Current | | | | | | 2.1 |
| 73.5 | 74.4 | 80.2 | | Total Current | | | | | | 84.0 |
| 6.8 | 4.7 | 5.2 | | Fixed Assets (net) | | | | | | 3.0 |
| 14.3 | 12.6 | 4.7 | | Intangibles (net) | | | | | | 3.1 |
| 5.4 | 8.2 | 9.8 | | All Other Non-Current | | | | | | 9.9 |
| 100.0 | 100.0 | 100.0 | | Total | | | | | | 100.0 |
| | | | | LIABILITIES | | | | | | |
| 7.8 | 6.3 | 9.2 | | Notes Payable-Short Term | | | | | | 5.9 |
| 3.6 | .7 | .7 | | Cur. Mat.-L.T.D. | | | | | | .6 |
| 14.0 | 12.8 | 10.2 | | Trade Payables | | | | | | 8.6 |
| .1 | .0 | .1 | | Income Taxes Payable | | | | | | .2 |
| 29.2 | 26.4 | 21.2 | | All Other Current | | | | | | 12.4 |
| 54.8 | 46.3 | 41.3 | | Total Current | | | | | | 27.6 |
| 29.7 | 4.1 | 9.5 | | Long-Term Debt | | | | | | 2.0 |
| .1 | .4 | .0 | | Deferred Taxes | | | | | | .0 |
| 4.5 | 3.2 | 3.0 | | All Other Non-Current | | | | | | 1.1 |
| 10.8 | 45.9 | 46.2 | | Net Worth | | | | | | 69.3 |
| 100.0 | 100.0 | 100.0 | | Total Liabilties & Net Worth | | | | | | 100.0 |
| | | | | INCOME DATA | | | | | | |
| 100.0 | 100.0 | 100.0 | | Net Sales | | | | | | 100.0 |
| | | | | Gross Profit | | | | | | |
| 87.8 | 92.4 | 89.8 | | Operating Expenses | | | | | | 89.0 |
| 12.2 | 7.6 | 10.2 | | Operating Profit | | | | | | 11.0 |
| .1 | .6 | .2 | | All Other Expenses (net) | | | | | | 1.0 |
| 12.0 | 7.0 | 10.0 | | Profit Before Taxes | | | | | | 10.0 |
| | | | | RATIOS | | | | | | |
| 4.4 | 3.4 | 6.5 | | | | | | | | 250.5 |
| 1.3 | 1.7 | 2.1 | | Current | | | | | | 6.2 |
| .9 | 1.1 | 1.2 | | | | | | | | 1.3 |
| 4.4 | 2.9 | 6.2 | | | | | | | | 250.2 |
| 1.3 | 1.6 | 2.1 | | Quick | | | | | | 6.2 |
| .6 | 1.1 | 1.2 | | | | | | | | 1.2 |
| 0 UND | 0 UND | 0 UND | | | | | | | | 0 UND |
| 38 9.5 | 41 8.8 | 29 12.6 | | Sales/Receivables | | | | | | 26 14.2 |
| 81 4.5 | 74 4.9 | 72 5.1 | | | | | | | | 61 6.0 |
| | | | | Cost of Sales/Inventory | | | | | | |
| | | | | Cost of Sales/Payables | | | | | | |
| 6.1 | 5.1 | 3.7 | | | | | | | | 3.2 |
| 46.7 | 11.4 | 7.3 | | Sales/Working Capital | | | | | | 5.1 |
| -66.8 | 53.4 | 43.7 | | | | | | | | 20.5 |
| 88.0 | 80.9 | 184.6 | | | | | | | | |
| (17) 6.7 | (20) 28.4 | (22) 31.3 | | EBIT/Interest | | | | | | |
| 2.1 | 3.8 | 1.7 | | | | | | | | |
| | | | | Net Profit + Depr., Dep., Amort./Cur. Mat. L/T/D | | | | | | |
| .0 | .0 | .0 | | | | | | | | .0 |
| .1 | .1 | .0 | | Fixed/Worth | | | | | | .0 |
| -.2 | .4 | .2 | | | | | | | | .0 |
| .6 | .5 | .2 | | | | | | | | .0 |
| 18.4 | 1.9 | 1.3 | | Debt/Worth | | | | | | .2 |
| -3.1 | 17.7 | 3.1 | | | | | | | | 2.1 |
| 132.2 | 209.5 | 87.3 | | | | | | | | 76.4 |
| (14) 99.5 | (29) 78.0 | (38) 54.6 | | % Profit Before Taxes/Tangible Net Worth | | | | | | 46.1 |
| 35.6 | 14.9 | 6.4 | | | | | | | | 8.1 |
| 53.3 | 45.3 | 49.2 | | | | | | | | 59.5 |
| 31.8 | 17.4 | 16.8 | | % Profit Before Taxes/Total Assets | | | | | | 17.8 |
| 6.8 | 2.5 | 2.6 | | | | | | | | 4.3 |
| UND | 999.8 | 999.8 | | | | | | | | 999.8 |
| 252.2 | 292.5 | 527.8 | | Sales/Net Fixed Assets | | | | | | 538.6 |
| 59.4 | 34.1 | 42.3 | | | | | | | | 167.0 |
| 6.2 | 5.9 | 5.3 | | | | | | | | 4.1 |
| 2.7 | 2.8 | 3.1 | | Sales/Total Assets | | | | | | 2.7 |
| 2.0 | 1.4 | 2.2 | | | | | | | | 2.0 |
| | .1 | .1 | | | | | | | | |
| (14) .4 | (19) .3 | | | % Depr., Dep., Amort./Sales | | | | | | |
| 1.9 | 1.0 | | | | | | | | | |
| 2.8 | | 2.8 | | % Officers', Directors' Owners' Comp/Sales | | | | | | |
| (11) 4.1 | (15) 5.8 | | | | | | | | | |
| 6.9 | 10.6 | | | | | | | | | |
| 510378M | 1505330M | 1507885M | | Net Sales ($) | 1350M | 11805M | 19335M | 55297M | 149590M | 1270508M |
| 287055M | 771015M | 616057M | | Total Assets ($) | 257M | 3985M | 2353M | 21901M | 74605M | 512956M |

© RMA 2024    M = $ thousand    MM = $ million
See Pages viii through xx for Explanation of Ratios and Data

# PROFESSIONAL SERVICES—Veterinary Services  NAICS 541940

**Current Data Sorted by Assets** | **Comparative Historical Data**

| | | | | | | | Type of Statement | | |
|---|---|---|---|---|---|---|---|---|---|
| | | | 1 | 1 | 1 | 1 | Unqualified | 8 | 10 |
| | | 3 | 1 | | | | Reviewed | 3 | |
| 30 | 53 | 46 | 15 | | | | Compiled | 17 | 28 |
| 21 | 46 | 33 | 33 | 1 | 2 | 1 | Tax Returns | 151 | 157 |
| | 10 (4/1-9/30/23) | | | 206 (10/1/23-3/31/24) | | | Other | 129 | 152 |
| 0-500M | 500M-2MM | 2-10MM | 10-50MM | 50-100MM | 100-250MM | | | 4/1/19-3/31/20 ALL | 4/1/20-3/31/21 ALL |
| 51 | 102 | 50 | 8 | 3 | 2 | | NUMBER OF STATEMENTS | 308 | 347 |
| % | % | % | % | % | % | | ASSETS | % | % |
| 41.8 | 30.7 | 22.3 | | | | | Cash & Equivalents | 28.3 | 39.8 |
| 2.6 | 1.4 | 2.8 | | | | | Trade Receivables (net) | 3.1 | 1.6 |
| 10.5 | 6.6 | 2.3 | | | | | Inventory | 8.7 | 6.4 |
| 1.5 | 1.9 | 5.3 | | | | | All Other Current | 2.4 | 2.6 |
| 56.5 | 40.5 | 32.7 | | | | | Total Current | 42.5 | 50.4 |
| 26.7 | 29.5 | 49.1 | | | | | Fixed Assets (net) | 30.4 | 22.5 |
| 12.4 | 21.1 | 6.8 | | | | | Intangibles (net) | 17.2 | 20.1 |
| 4.4 | 8.8 | 11.4 | | | | | All Other Non-Current | 9.9 | 7.1 |
| 100.0 | 100.0 | 100.0 | | | | | Total | 100.0 | 100.0 |
| | | | | | | | LIABILITIES | | |
| 9.9 | 3.3 | 1.8 | | | | | Notes Payable-Short Term | 8.7 | 10.3 |
| 2.0 | 2.2 | 1.3 | | | | | Cur. Mat.-L.T.D. | 4.5 | 2.6 |
| 7.5 | 2.8 | 3.2 | | | | | Trade Payables | 5.5 | 4.1 |
| .2 | .0 | .0 | | | | | Income Taxes Payable | .0 | .1 |
| 24.1 | 7.6 | 5.2 | | | | | All Other Current | 9.6 | 7.8 |
| 43.7 | 16.0 | 11.5 | | | | | Total Current | 28.3 | 24.8 |
| 43.8 | 43.0 | 39.9 | | | | | Long-Term Debt | 44.3 | 46.7 |
| .0 | .0 | .0 | | | | | Deferred Taxes | .0 | .0 |
| 5.4 | 1.9 | 9.6 | | | | | All Other Non-Current | 4.3 | 6.0 |
| 7.0 | 39.1 | 39.1 | | | | | Net Worth | 23.0 | 22.6 |
| 100.0 | 100.0 | 100.0 | | | | | Total Liabilities & Net Worth | 100.0 | 100.0 |
| | | | | | | | INCOME DATA | | |
| 100.0 | 100.0 | 100.0 | | | | | Net Sales | 100.0 | 100.0 |
| | | | | | | | Gross Profit | | |
| 88.0 | 84.8 | 77.4 | | | | | Operating Expenses | 88.0 | 86.9 |
| 12.0 | 15.2 | 22.6 | | | | | Operating Profit | 12.0 | 13.1 |
| 1.8 | 1.7 | 6.5 | | | | | All Other Expenses (net) | 1.6 | .0 |
| 10.1 | 13.5 | 16.1 | | | | | Profit Before Taxes | 10.4 | 13.1 |
| | | | | | | | RATIOS | | |
| 5.3 | 8.4 | 6.4 | | | | | | 5.0 | 6.5 |
| 2.0 | 3.5 | 2.9 | | | | | Current | 1.9 | 2.6 |
| .6 | 1.4 | 1.4 | | | | | | .7 | 1.2 |
| 5.2 | 6.4 | 5.7 | | | | | | 3.7 | 5.4 |
| 1.6 | 2.5 | 2.0 | | | | | Quick | 1.2 | 2.3 |
| .3 | 1.0 | .9 | | | | | | .4 | 1.0 |
| 0 UND | 0 UND | 0 UND | | | | | | 0 UND | 0 UND |
| 0 UND | 0 UND | 0 UND | | | | | Sales/Receivables | 0 UND | 0 UND |
| 0 UND | 1 348.4 | 2 227.6 | | | | | | 2 201.5 | 1 371.0 |
| | | | | | | | Cost of Sales/Inventory | | |
| | | | | | | | Cost of Sales/Payables | | |
| 13.3 | 6.8 | 3.5 | | | | | | 11.3 | 6.7 |
| 32.5 | 14.5 | 12.9 | | | | | Sales/Working Capital | 29.3 | 12.3 |
| -30.8 | 59.2 | 43.2 | | | | | | -71.2 | 42.7 |
| 102.5 | 39.6 | 52.1 | | | | | | 44.3 | 65.4 |
| (33) 19.1 | (70) 13.6 | (34) 11.7 | | | | | EBIT/Interest | (237) 11.3 | (249) 13.3 |
| 5.6 | 3.8 | 3.2 | | | | | | 2.6 | 4.1 |
| | | | | | | | Net Profit + Depr., Dep., Amort./Cur. Mat. L/T/D | | |
| .1 | .1 | .8 | | | | | | .2 | .1 |
| .6 | .9 | 2.6 | | | | | Fixed/Worth | 1.4 | 1.2 |
| -1.1 | 47.5 | 12.6 | | | | | | -1.7 | -.8 |
| .5 | .4 | .6 | | | | | | .6 | .8 |
| 2.6 | 2.4 | 2.2 | | | | | Debt/Worth | 3.6 | 4.7 |
| -2.7 | -6.4 | 23.4 | | | | | | -3.9 | -2.7 |
| 469.6 | 156.6 | 138.2 | | | | | | 237.0 | 246.3 |
| (35) 126.8 | (69) 72.0 | (41) 49.9 | | | | | % Profit Before Taxes/Tangible Net Worth | (196) 95.2 | (205) 110.6 |
| 26.9 | 29.9 | 10.4 | | | | | | 36.0 | 53.3 |
| 159.0 | 55.5 | 35.8 | | | | | | 78.3 | 69.6 |
| 57.9 | 29.7 | 14.6 | | | | | % Profit Before Taxes/Total Assets | 29.9 | 32.3 |
| 24.3 | 9.1 | 4.0 | | | | | | 7.3 | 10.0 |
| 161.9 | 99.3 | 14.0 | | | | | | 85.9 | 109.9 |
| 54.9 | 19.2 | 4.8 | | | | | Sales/Net Fixed Assets | 23.2 | 27.6 |
| 20.5 | 6.0 | .8 | | | | | | 7.8 | 9.6 |
| 14.7 | 4.9 | 2.9 | | | | | | 7.0 | 5.4 |
| 7.2 | 2.9 | 1.8 | | | | | Sales/Total Assets | 3.8 | 3.0 |
| 4.1 | 1.6 | .5 | | | | | | 1.8 | 1.6 |
| .5 | 1.0 | 1.8 | | | | | | .7 | .7 |
| (18) 1.3 | (42) 1.8 | (31) 3.1 | | | | | % Depr., Dep., Amort./Sales | (146) 1.9 | (154) 1.8 |
| 3.8 | 4.6 | 15.1 | | | | | | 3.7 | 4.5 |
| 5.5 | 4.1 | 3.7 | | | | | | 5.1 | 3.8 |
| (40) 7.8 | (73) 6.4 | (25) 6.1 | | | | | % Officers', Directors' Owners' Comp/Sales | (189) 8.3 | (210) 6.3 |
| 12.8 | 9.3 | 8.4 | | | | | | 12.4 | 10.9 |
| 121801M | 350938M | 361954M | 206070M | 206978M | 272480M | | Net Sales ($) | 6557987M | 3838517M |
| 14807M | 108329M | 197093M | 165419M | 185793M | 372539M | | Total Assets ($) | 1770426M | 1625392M |

© RMA 2024

M = $ thousand   MM = $ million
See Pages viii through xx for Explanation of Ratios and Data

# PROFESSIONAL SERVICES—Veterinary Services  NAICS 541940

## Comparative Historical Data | Current Data Sorted by Sales

| | | | Type of Statement | | | | | | |
|---|---|---|---|---|---|---|---|---|---|
| 5 | 4 | 3 | Unqualified | | | 1 | | 1 | 2 |
| 1 | | 1 | Reviewed | | | | | 1 | |
| 11 | 7 | 4 | Compiled | | | 1 | 2 | 1 | |
| 95 | 127 | 99 | Tax Returns | 14 | 40 | 21 | 18 | 6 | 4 |
| 157 | 139 | 109 | Other | 20 | 33 | 23 | 16 | 13 | |
| 4/1/21-3/31/22 ALL | 4/1/22-3/31/23 ALL | 4/1/23-3/31/24 ALL | | 10 (4/1-9/30/23) | | | 206 (10/1/23-3/31/24) | | |
| | | | | 0-1MM | 1-3MM | 3-5MM | 5-10MM | 10-25MM | 25MM & OVER |
| 269 | 277 | 216 | NUMBER OF STATEMENTS | 34 | 74 | 45 | 36 | 21 | 6 |
| % | % | % | ASSETS | % | % | % | % | % | % |
| 39.0 | 36.0 | 30.5 | Cash & Equivalents | 15.5 | 29.8 | 40.3 | 38.6 | 25.9 | |
| 2.7 | 2.4 | 2.0 | Trade Receivables (net) | .6 | 1.9 | 1.5 | 2.1 | 5.3 | |
| 7.0 | 5.7 | 6.3 | Inventory | 3.1 | 6.9 | 6.1 | 8.9 | 5.2 | |
| 2.1 | 3.5 | 2.6 | All Other Current | 1.0 | 2.2 | 2.0 | 3.5 | 5.9 | |
| 50.7 | 47.6 | 41.4 | Total Current | 20.3 | 40.8 | 50.0 | 53.1 | 42.4 | |
| 26.0 | 28.0 | 34.1 | Fixed Assets (net) | 66.2 | 26.4 | 23.1 | 29.1 | 38.5 | |
| 18.0 | 16.7 | 16.1 | Intangibles (net) | 9.5 | 25.3 | 16.5 | 8.6 | 5.6 | |
| 5.3 | 7.7 | 8.4 | All Other Non-Current | 4.0 | 7.5 | 10.5 | 9.1 | 13.5 | |
| 100.0 | 100.0 | 100.0 | Total | 100.0 | 100.0 | 100.0 | 100.0 | 100.0 | |
| | | | LIABILITIES | | | | | | |
| 5.9 | 9.6 | 4.4 | Notes Payable-Short Term | 6.2 | 4.3 | 5.5 | 3.5 | 1.6 | |
| 2.9 | 2.7 | 1.9 | Cur. Mat.-L.T.D. | 2.2 | 1.9 | 2.3 | 1.3 | 1.4 | |
| 4.0 | 3.7 | 4.1 | Trade Payables | 1.1 | 3.5 | 2.7 | 8.9 | 5.4 | |
| .1 | .0 | .1 | Income Taxes Payable | .0 | .1 | .0 | .1 | .0 | |
| 12.1 | 10.7 | 10.8 | All Other Current | 4.2 | 14.7 | 3.9 | 10.3 | 24.2 | |
| 25.0 | 26.7 | 21.3 | Total Current | 13.7 | 24.5 | 14.4 | 24.1 | 32.7 | |
| 38.3 | 42.7 | 41.7 | Long-Term Debt | 71.3 | 40.8 | 34.9 | 31.5 | 31.4 | |
| .0 | .0 | .0 | Deferred Taxes | .0 | .0 | .0 | .0 | .0 | |
| 5.2 | 4.1 | 5.0 | All Other Non-Current | 2.4 | 4.9 | 2.8 | 6.7 | 8.4 | |
| 31.4 | 26.5 | 32.0 | Net Worth | 12.5 | 29.8 | 47.9 | 37.7 | 27.5 | |
| 100.0 | 100.0 | 100.0 | Total Liabilities & Net Worth | 100.0 | 100.0 | 100.0 | 100.0 | 100.0 | |
| | | | INCOME DATA | | | | | | |
| 100.0 | 100.0 | 100.0 | Net Sales | 100.0 | 100.0 | 100.0 | 100.0 | 100.0 | |
| | | | Gross Profit | | | | | | |
| 83.1 | 87.1 | 84.1 | Operating Expenses | 65.9 | 87.2 | 86.2 | 89.0 | 88.2 | |
| 16.9 | 12.9 | 15.9 | Operating Profit | 34.1 | 12.8 | 13.8 | 11.0 | 11.8 | |
| 1.2 | 2.1 | 2.8 | All Other Expenses (net) | 14.4 | 1.0 | .6 | .3 | .1 | |
| 15.6 | 10.9 | 13.1 | Profit Before Taxes | 19.7 | 11.8 | 13.2 | 10.6 | 11.8 | |
| | | | RATIOS | | | | | | |
| 8.3 | 6.6 | 6.5 | | 6.6 | 6.7 | 12.4 | 6.3 | 4.0 | |
| 2.9 | 2.7 | 2.8 | Current | 1.9 | 2.6 | 5.1 | 2.5 | 1.7 | |
| 1.2 | .9 | 1.3 | | .3 | 1.2 | 2.7 | 1.5 | .8 | |
| 6.2 | 5.2 | 6.0 | | 5.9 | 5.4 | 11.5 | 5.9 | 3.3 | |
| 2.4 | 2.1 | 2.3 | Quick | 1.2 | 2.3 | 4.8 | 1.8 | 1.3 | |
| 1.0 | .6 | .7 | | .2 | .7 | 1.8 | 1.1 | .5 | |
| 0 UND | 0 UND | 0 UND | | 0 UND | 0 UND | 0 UND | 0 UND | 0 UND | |
| 0 UND | 0 UND | 0 UND | Sales/Receivables | 0 UND | 0 UND | 0 UND | 0 999.8 | 0 UND | |
| 1 399.3 | 0 733.3 | 1 281.5 | | 0 UND | 1 428.9 | 0 809.5 | 3 136.5 | 2 194.9 | |
| | | | Cost of Sales/Inventory | | | | | | |
| | | | | | | | | | |
| | | | | | | | | | |
| | | | Cost of Sales/Payables | | | | | | |
| | | | | | | | | | |
| 6.8 | 6.9 | 6.5 | | 2.5 | 6.8 | 6.3 | 8.0 | 10.6 | |
| 12.6 | 15.4 | 16.1 | Sales/Working Capital | 40.8 | 17.5 | 14.3 | 15.6 | 38.4 | |
| 80.5 | -113.2 | 86.1 | | -8.4 | 74.1 | 30.3 | 41.4 | -86.5 | |
| 61.5 | 46.6 | 48.8 | | 15.8 | 30.7 | 103.8 | 92.9 | 90.1 | |
| (176) 19.0 | (198) 11.6 | (146) 13.4 | EBIT/Interest | (16) 4.3 | (56) 10.4 | (31) 17.3 | (25) 20.6 | (13) 50.8 | |
| 6.3 | 3.3 | 3.8 | | 2.2 | 3.7 | 7.7 | 2.4 | 13.8 | |
| | | | Net Profit + Depr., Dep., Amort./Cur. Mat. L/T/D | | | | | | |
| .1 | .1 | .2 | | 1.0 | .1 | .1 | .2 | .4 | |
| .7 | .7 | 1.0 | Fixed/Worth | 4.0 | .8 | .4 | .7 | 1.3 | |
| -6.9 | 27.2 | 22.6 | | 48.8 | -19.9 | 3.8 | 8.5 | 20.4 | |
| .3 | .4 | .5 | | 1.4 | .7 | .2 | .3 | .4 | |
| 2.7 | 2.4 | 2.4 | Debt/Worth | 3.6 | 3.6 | .9 | .7 | 2.0 | |
| -3.5 | -4.3 | -20.8 | | NM | -3.0 | -41.7 | NM | 67.1 | |
| 243.3 | 161.4 | 176.4 | % Profit Before Taxes/Tangible Net Worth | 25.8 | 220.5 | 233.7 | 179.5 | 328.7 | |
| (169) 109.1 | (187) 80.8 | (156) 71.0 | | (26) 9.6 | (47) 82.1 | (33) 126.6 | (27) 94.8 | (18) 80.3 | |
| 51.0 | 27.6 | 20.4 | | .7 | 24.8 | 39.3 | 49.8 | 45.8 | |
| 91.5 | 62.6 | 57.8 | % Profit Before Taxes/Total Assets | 17.2 | 50.9 | 103.7 | 121.8 | 82.6 | |
| 40.9 | 27.3 | 26.3 | | 4.2 | 29.6 | 40.1 | 45.6 | 40.4 | |
| 15.1 | 7.8 | 6.2 | | .7 | 9.5 | 18.3 | 9.4 | 15.7 | |
| 150.3 | 140.2 | 79.3 | | 12.2 | 156.7 | 156.8 | 84.3 | 32.7 | |
| 28.6 | 22.4 | 17.8 | Sales/Net Fixed Assets | .2 | 25.0 | 35.9 | 23.2 | 15.2 | |
| 6.9 | 5.9 | 3.9 | | .1 | 6.1 | 6.7 | 8.9 | 5.0 | |
| 5.7 | 5.7 | 5.3 | | 1.8 | 4.7 | 7.3 | 7.2 | 6.2 | |
| 3.2 | 3.1 | 2.9 | Sales/Total Assets | .1 | 2.4 | 4.0 | 4.5 | 3.4 | |
| 1.7 | 1.7 | 1.4 | | .1 | 1.5 | 2.0 | 2.6 | 2.2 | |
| .9 | .9 | 1.0 | | 3.8 | 1.0 | 1.0 | .5 | .8 | |
| (116) 2.1 | (131) 2.1 | (100) 2.2 | % Depr., Dep., Amort./Sales | (19) 17.9 | (26) 2.7 | (20) 2.0 | (20) 1.2 | (12) 1.7 | |
| 5.4 | 4.4 | 5.7 | | 36.1 | 5.4 | 4.1 | 1.7 | 3.2 | |
| 4.1 | 4.2 | 4.1 | | 8.5 | 6.3 | 3.7 | 2.9 | .9 | |
| (154) 6.6 | (178) 6.4 | (140) 6.6 | % Officers', Directors' Owners' Comp/Sales | (11) 11.8 | (51) 8.7 | (34) 5.9 | (30) 4.4 | (13) 5.9 | |
| 10.1 | 9.9 | 10.1 | | 14.9 | 10.9 | 7.8 | 6.9 | 8.1 | |
| 2432169M | 1484698M | 1520221M | Net Sales ($) | 15617M | 146149M | 174031M | 232225M | 337610M | 614589M |
| 1037706M | 1220556M | 1043980M | Total Assets ($) | 61412M | 76350M | 84406M | 74833M | 143523M | 603456M |

© RMA 2024   M = $ thousand   MM = $ million
See Pages viii through xx for Explanation of Ratios and Data

# PROFESSIONAL SERVICES—All Other Professional, Scientific, and Technical Services   NAICS 541990

## Current Data Sorted by Assets / Comparative Historical Data

| 0-500M | 500M-2MM | 2-10MM | 10-50MM | 50-100MM | 100-250MM | Type of Statement | 4/1/19-3/31/20 ALL | 4/1/20-3/31/21 ALL |
|---|---|---|---|---|---|---|---|---|
| | 5 | 9 | 19 | 4 | 4 | Unqualified | 35 | 23 |
| | 1 | 14 | 9 | 2 | | Reviewed | 34 | 18 |
| 2 | 5 | 9 | 6 | 1 | | Compiled | 33 | 17 |
| 27 | 48 | 37 | 1 | | 1 | Tax Returns | 165 | 118 |
| 36 | 90 | 132 | 85 | 20 | 17 | Other | 380 | 277 |
| | 51 (4/1-9/30/23) | | 533 (10/1/23-3/31/24) | | | | | |
| 65 | 149 | 201 | 120 | 27 | 22 | **NUMBER OF STATEMENTS** | 647 | 453 |
| % | % | % | % | % | % | **ASSETS** | % | % |
| 51.4 | 34.8 | 23.2 | 19.9 | 11.3 | 8.9 | Cash & Equivalents | 26.0 | 34.7 |
| 8.2 | 20.2 | 30.6 | 24.8 | 29.7 | 22.3 | Trade Receivables (net) | 29.8 | 21.7 |
| 2.8 | 4.7 | 6.7 | 6.9 | 4.5 | 9.4 | Inventory | 4.0 | 4.2 |
| 5.4 | 5.6 | 5.9 | 7.2 | 4.7 | 7.0 | All Other Current | 4.5 | 4.5 |
| 67.8 | 65.4 | 66.4 | 58.7 | 50.2 | 47.6 | Total Current | 64.2 | 65.0 |
| 14.2 | 14.6 | 17.8 | 14.6 | 10.4 | 10.2 | Fixed Assets (net) | 16.6 | 17.6 |
| 1.9 | 8.9 | 5.6 | 13.7 | 30.7 | 23.0 | Intangibles (net) | 7.7 | 8.6 |
| 16.2 | 11.1 | 10.2 | 12.9 | 8.6 | 19.2 | All Other Non-Current | 11.5 | 8.7 |
| 100.0 | 100.0 | 100.0 | 100.0 | 100.0 | 100.0 | Total | 100.0 | 100.0 |
| | | | | | | **LIABILITIES** | | |
| 24.9 | 7.1 | 5.3 | 5.3 | 5.8 | 1.9 | Notes Payable-Short Term | 11.8 | 10.9 |
| .8 | 1.9 | 2.2 | 1.9 | 2.3 | 9.3 | Cur. Mat.-L.T.D. | 3.0 | 3.1 |
| 3.8 | 7.4 | 9.0 | 9.3 | 10.6 | 17.3 | Trade Payables | 9.5 | 7.6 |
| .1 | .1 | .0 | .1 | .1 | .1 | Income Taxes Payable | .2 | .2 |
| 29.9 | 16.9 | 16.5 | 18.3 | 17.4 | 9.9 | All Other Current | 18.2 | 17.7 |
| 59.5 | 33.4 | 33.0 | 34.9 | 36.2 | 38.5 | Total Current | 42.7 | 39.5 |
| 23.7 | 18.4 | 15.4 | 12.2 | 19.7 | 14.3 | Long-Term Debt | 16.2 | 26.6 |
| .0 | .0 | .1 | .1 | .9 | .3 | Deferred Taxes | .1 | .1 |
| 5.3 | 1.6 | 7.0 | 12.3 | 6.0 | 13.5 | All Other Non-Current | 6.7 | 5.8 |
| 11.5 | 46.4 | 44.5 | 40.4 | 37.2 | 33.5 | Net Worth | 34.2 | 28.1 |
| 100.0 | 100.0 | 100.0 | 100.0 | 100.0 | 100.0 | Total Liabilities & Net Worth | 100.0 | 100.0 |
| | | | | | | **INCOME DATA** | | |
| 100.0 | 100.0 | 100.0 | 100.0 | 100.0 | 100.0 | Net Sales | 100.0 | 100.0 |
| 90.3 | 85.5 | 88.9 | 91.3 | 93.7 | 88.1 | Gross Profit / Operating Expenses | 88.2 | 91.3 |
| 9.7 | 14.5 | 11.1 | 8.7 | 6.3 | 11.9 | Operating Profit | 11.8 | 8.7 |
| .8 | .1 | 2.2 | 1.4 | 2.3 | 4.4 | All Other Expenses (net) | 1.4 | -.3 |
| 8.9 | 14.4 | 8.9 | 7.3 | 4.0 | 7.5 | Profit Before Taxes | 10.4 | 8.9 |
| | | | | | | **RATIOS** | | |
| 8.1 | 8.9 | 4.6 | 2.9 | 2.4 | 4.1 | | 4.2 | 5.6 |
| 2.0 | 2.5 | 2.4 | 1.6 | 1.4 | 1.6 | Current | 1.9 | 2.0 |
| .9 | .9 | 1.3 | 1.2 | 1.0 | 1.0 | | 1.0 | 1.1 |
| 7.6 | 6.0 | 4.0 | 2.2 | 1.7 | 2.0 | | 3.5 | 4.9 |
| 1.7 | 1.9 | 1.8 | 1.2 | 1.1 | 1.1 | Quick | 1.5 | 1.7 |
| .5 | .8 | .9 | .7 | .8 | .9 | | .8 | .8 |
| 0 UND | 0 UND | 11 34.4 | 24 15.1 | 51 7.2 | 20 18.3 | | 0 UND | 0 UND |
| 0 UND | 1 280.1 | 44 8.3 | 43 8.4 | 66 5.5 | 70 5.2 | Sales/Receivables | 34 10.6 | 26 14.0 |
| 0 UND | 37 9.8 | 63 5.8 | 68 5.4 | 83 4.4 | 91 4.0 | | 63 5.8 | 53 6.9 |
| | | | | | | Cost of Sales/Inventory | | |
| | | | | | | Cost of Sales/Payables | | |
| 8.1 | 5.6 | 4.1 | 3.4 | 4.7 | 2.5 | | 5.6 | 4.4 |
| 28.4 | 12.2 | 8.0 | 8.2 | 15.1 | 7.2 | Sales/Working Capital | 13.2 | 8.6 |
| -132.2 | -209.7 | 24.9 | 26.0 | 55.2 | -94.5 | | 297.5 | 50.1 |
| 12.2 | 56.9 | 49.6 | 20.1 | 17.3 | 7.0 | | 47.5 | 38.4 |
| (30) 2.2 | (99) 14.0 | (153) 11.2 | (95) 6.1 | (25) 6.0 | (14) .9 | EBIT/Interest | (444) 11.9 | (315) 10.0 |
| -2.6 | 2.1 | 3.6 | .9 | .4 | -1.3 | | 2.8 | 1.5 |
| | | | 14.4 | 51.5 | | Net Profit + Depr., Dep., | | 32.0 | 10.2 |
| | (15) 5.7 | (20) 8.8 | | | Amort./Cur. Mat. L/T/D | (35) 5.2 | (24) 5.8 |
| | | 1.7 | 1.7 | | | | 1.6 | 2.3 |
| .0 | .0 | .0 | .1 | .3 | .1 | | .0 | .0 |
| .1 | .2 | .2 | .5 | .8 | 1.5 | Fixed/Worth | .2 | .3 |
| UND | 1.6 | 1.2 | 1.2 | -.9 | -.5 | | 1.7 | 5.9 |
| .3 | .2 | .4 | .8 | 1.6 | 1.0 | | .5 | .6 |
| 2.3 | .9 | 1.0 | 2.0 | 20.6 | 20.7 | Debt/Worth | 1.4 | 2.2 |
| -8.8 | 18.9 | 6.1 | 9.2 | -3.8 | -4.8 | | 10.8 | -125.5 |
| 283.6 | 121.3 | 72.2 | 72.6 | 73.4 | 59.6 | | 104.4 | 100.9 |
| (46) 112.7 | (116) 58.4 | (172) 33.5 | (100) 28.9 | (16) 26.4 | (12) 2.5 | % Profit Before Taxes/Tangible Net Worth | (528) 50.5 | (339) 49.8 |
| 27.2 | 18.3 | 13.1 | 4.3 | 4.9 | -9.5 | | 19.0 | 11.1 |
| 90.3 | 64.0 | 30.5 | 17.5 | 18.6 | 8.2 | | 46.1 | 41.9 |
| 30.3 | 29.6 | 14.0 | 7.7 | 3.7 | 1.8 | % Profit Before Taxes/Total Assets | 18.8 | 14.2 |
| -7.7 | 5.4 | 4.8 | .2 | -2.2 | -2.1 | | 6.0 | 1.1 |
| UND | 999.8 | 263.5 | 70.2 | 46.3 | 113.1 | | 500.0 | 317.0 |
| 743.0 | 75.5 | 44.8 | 20.8 | 19.1 | 46.6 | Sales/Net Fixed Assets | 63.8 | 42.7 |
| 25.1 | 18.2 | 11.8 | 7.2 | 8.5 | 9.9 | | 12.8 | 8.9 |
| 14.1 | 7.1 | 3.7 | 2.4 | 2.0 | 1.7 | | 5.1 | 4.1 |
| 6.1 | 3.7 | 2.6 | 1.5 | 1.3 | .7 | Sales/Total Assets | 3.1 | 2.5 |
| 3.2 | 2.0 | 1.6 | .9 | .7 | .5 | | 1.8 | 1.5 |
| .4 | .2 | .3 | .5 | .6 | .3 | | .3 | .4 |
| (15) 2.3 | (59) 1.2 | (109) .9 | (82) 1.7 | (14) 1.4 | (12) .9 | % Depr., Dep., Amort./Sales | (325) 1.1 | (221) 1.5 |
| 6.3 | 4.5 | 2.7 | 3.7 | 4.9 | 2.3 | | 3.2 | 4.0 |
| 7.7 | 3.0 | 1.9 | 1.6 | | | | 2.7 | 2.7 |
| (26) 13.1 | (74) 4.8 | (63) 3.8 | (11) 3.0 | | | % Officers', Directors' Owners' Comp/Sales | (221) 6.0 | (176) 5.2 |
| 21.6 | 8.4 | 7.4 | 8.9 | | | | 11.8 | 11.4 |
| 123743M | 921906M | 2693641M | 4376315M | 3175958M | 4277693M | Net Sales ($) | 15006605M | 7345393M |
| 13725M | 176618M | 984534M | 2499185M | 2084962M | 3778392M | Total Assets ($) | 5824403M | 4297902M |

© RMA 2024

M = $ thousand    MM = $ million
See Pages viii through xx for Explanation of Ratios and Data

# PROFESSIONAL SERVICES—All Other Professional, Scientific, and Technical Services NAICS 541990

## Comparative Historical Data | Current Data Sorted by Sales

| Comparative Historical Data | | | | Type of Statement | Current Data Sorted by Sales | | | | | |
|---|---|---|---|---|---|---|---|---|---|---|
| 23 | 34 | 41 | | Unqualified | 1 | 3 | 1 | 6 | 8 | 22 |
| 17 | 22 | 26 | | Reviewed | | | 2 | 6 | 8 | 10 |
| 27 | 26 | 23 | | Compiled | 1 | 1 | 2 | 6 | 8 | 5 |
| 113 | 163 | 114 | | Tax Returns | 28 | 17 | 16 | 28 | 22 | 3 |
| 271 | 348 | 380 | | Other | 36 | 45 | 28 | 68 | 104 | 99 |
| 4/1/21-3/31/22 | 4/1/22-3/31/23 | 4/1/23-3/31/24 | | | 51 (4/1-9/30/23) | | | 533 (10/1/23-3/31/24) | | |
| ALL | ALL | ALL | | | 0-1MM | 1-3MM | 3-5MM | 5-10MM | 10-25MM | 25MM & OVER |
| 451 | 593 | 584 | | NUMBER OF STATEMENTS | 66 | 66 | 49 | 114 | 150 | 139 |
| % | % | % | | ASSETS | % | % | % | % | % | % |
| 30.8 | 28.0 | 27.5 | | Cash & Equivalents | 32.2 | 30.8 | 39.2 | 30.9 | 27.1 | 17.4 |
| 24.2 | 24.2 | 23.9 | | Trade Receivables (net) | 6.5 | 12.4 | 19.7 | 26.3 | 28.3 | 32.5 |
| 4.3 | 5.3 | 5.8 | | Inventory | 2.7 | 4.8 | 4.6 | 6.9 | 6.1 | 6.7 |
| 6.2 | 6.5 | 6.0 | | All Other Current | 4.9 | 9.5 | 4.2 | 6.3 | 5.1 | 6.4 |
| 65.5 | 64.0 | 63.3 | | Total Current | 46.3 | 57.5 | 67.7 | 70.4 | 66.6 | 63.0 |
| 17.0 | 17.4 | 15.3 | | Fixed Assets (net) | 32.3 | 18.4 | 16.4 | 13.6 | 9.9 | 12.6 |
| 8.3 | 8.3 | 9.5 | | Intangibles (net) | 4.3 | 9.8 | 8.1 | 4.9 | 10.7 | 14.9 |
| 9.2 | 10.3 | 11.9 | | All Other Non-Current | 17.2 | 14.3 | 7.7 | 11.1 | 12.8 | 9.6 |
| 100.0 | 100.0 | 100.0 | | Total | 100.0 | 100.0 | 100.0 | 100.0 | 100.0 | 100.0 |
| | | | | LIABILITIES | | | | | | |
| 8.7 | 8.6 | 7.8 | | Notes Payable-Short Term | 16.9 | 8.8 | 8.6 | 7.3 | 6.0 | 5.2 |
| 3.6 | 2.5 | 2.2 | | Cur. Mat.-L.T.D. | .8 | 2.4 | 1.6 | 1.8 | 2.0 | 2.3 |
| 8.3 | 8.3 | 8.4 | | Trade Payables | 3.5 | 2.8 | 5.9 | 8.6 | 10.1 | 12.5 |
| .3 | .2 | .1 | | Income Taxes Payable | .1 | .1 | .1 | .1 | .1 | .1 |
| 15.5 | 17.7 | 18.3 | | All Other Current | 25.2 | 18.0 | 16.5 | 16.0 | 18.3 | 17.6 |
| 36.2 | 37.2 | 36.8 | | Total Current | 46.5 | 32.0 | 32.6 | 33.7 | 36.5 | 38.8 |
| 19.6 | 20.6 | 16.6 | | Long-Term Debt | 33.2 | 27.5 | 17.4 | 10.6 | 11.1 | 14.1 |
| .1 | .1 | .1 | | Deferred Taxes | .0 | .0 | .1 | .0 | .1 | .3 |
| 4.6 | 7.0 | 6.7 | | All Other Non-Current | 4.1 | 2.2 | 8.6 | 6.1 | 5.9 | 10.9 |
| 39.4 | 35.1 | 39.7 | | Net Worth | 16.1 | 38.3 | 41.2 | 49.5 | 46.4 | 35.8 |
| 100.0 | 100.0 | 100.0 | | Total Liabilities & Net Worth | 100.0 | 100.0 | 100.0 | 100.0 | 100.0 | 100.0 |
| | | | | INCOME DATA | | | | | | |
| 100.0 | 100.0 | 100.0 | | Net Sales | 100.0 | 100.0 | 100.0 | 100.0 | 100.0 | 100.0 |
| | | | | Gross Profit | | | | | | |
| 88.3 | 89.1 | 88.9 | | Operating Expenses | 75.0 | 81.8 | 90.6 | 90.3 | 92.6 | 93.0 |
| 11.7 | 10.9 | 11.1 | | Operating Profit | 25.0 | 18.2 | 9.4 | 9.7 | 7.4 | 7.0 |
| -1.0 | 1.2 | 1.4 | | All Other Expenses (net) | 7.0 | .7 | .2 | .7 | .2 | 1.6 |
| 12.7 | 9.6 | 9.7 | | Profit Before Taxes | 18.0 | 17.6 | 9.3 | 9.0 | 7.2 | 5.4 |
| | | | | RATIOS | | | | | | |
| 5.5 | 4.8 | 4.5 | | | 4.8 | 8.3 | 7.5 | 6.7 | 4.5 | 2.4 |
| 2.5 | 2.1 | 2.0 | | Current | 1.7 | 2.2 | 2.8 | 2.7 | 2.1 | 1.5 |
| 1.3 | 1.2 | 1.1 | | | .6 | .8 | 1.3 | 1.3 | 1.2 | 1.2 |
| 5.1 | 3.8 | 3.7 | | | 4.0 | 7.4 | 6.1 | 5.5 | 3.7 | 2.0 |
| 2.0 | (592) 1.6 | 1.5 | | Quick | 1.4 | 1.7 | 2.1 | 1.9 | 1.6 | 1.2 |
| .9 | .8 | .8 | | | .3 | .4 | .9 | 1.0 | .8 | .9 |
| 0 UND | 0 UND | 0 UND | | | 0 UND | 0 UND | 0 UND | 2 160.6 | 8 44.6 | 30 12.3 |
| 33 11.2 | 30 12.2 | 32 11.4 | | Sales/Receivables | 0 UND | 0 UND | 14 25.7 | 31 11.7 | 42 8.6 | 51 7.1 |
| 62 5.9 | 57 6.4 | 61 6.0 | | | 0 UND | 33 11.0 | 58 6.3 | 61 6.0 | 61 6.0 | 74 4.9 |
| | | | | Cost of Sales/Inventory | | | | | | |
| | | | | Cost of Sales/Payables | | | | | | |
| 4.2 | 4.7 | 4.6 | | | 4.0 | 4.0 | 3.2 | 4.8 | 4.5 | 6.9 |
| 8.0 | 9.9 | 9.9 | | Sales/Working Capital | 25.1 | 9.5 | 8.6 | 8.7 | 10.6 | 10.2 |
| 31.5 | 57.0 | 62.5 | | | -13.8 | -29.0 | 30.2 | 23.8 | 48.4 | 31.2 |
| | 96.3 | 50.1 | 43.4 | | 7.2 | 43.6 | 71.6 | 62.1 | 40.0 | 26.4 |
| (311) 22.9 | (421) 14.2 | (416) 8.4 | | EBIT/Interest | (26) 3.8 | (42) 8.9 | (35) 7.5 | (83) 10.0 | (115) 14.3 | (115) 6.0 |
| 4.3 | 2.1 | 1.5 | | | 1.3 | 1.1 | -.3 | 2.0 | 3.2 | .5 |
| 17.7 | 9.6 | 14.8 | | Net Profit + Depr., Dep., | | | | | 28.9 | 11.7 |
| (20) 5.7 | (39) 2.3 | (48) 5.3 | | Amort./Cur. Mat. L/T/D | | | | (15) 6.7 | (26) 4.6 |
| 2.3 | .7 | 1.4 | | | | | | | 1.1 | 1.4 |
| .0 | .0 | .0 | | | .0 | .0 | .0 | .0 | .0 | .1 |
| .2 | .2 | .2 | | Fixed/Worth | .4 | .3 | .2 | .1 | .1 | .6 |
| 1.1 | 1.5 | 1.7 | | | 6.4 | NM | 1.4 | .9 | .8 | 7.3 |
| .3 | .4 | .4 | | | .7 | .2 | .2 | .2 | .4 | 1.0 |
| 1.2 | 1.5 | 1.5 | | Debt/Worth | 2.3 | .9 | 1.4 | .8 | 1.1 | 2.1 |
| 6.7 | 20.8 | 19.8 | | | UND | -9.9 | 62.4 | 3.6 | 6.4 | 105.9 |
| 115.3 | 93.4 | 92.8 | | % Profit Before Taxes/Tangible | 119.2 | 111.9 | 138.2 | 92.5 | 74.0 | 77.3 |
| (376) 58.1 | (465) 39.5 | (462) 38.5 | | Net Worth | (51) 20.0 | (49) 65.5 | (38) 53.4 | (96) 39.0 | (123) 33.7 | (105) 35.1 |
| 17.9 | 11.5 | 11.2 | | | 8.7 | 27.3 | 15.2 | 9.3 | 9.0 | 9.4 |
| 53.3 | 41.3 | 36.8 | | % Profit Before Taxes/Total | 28.5 | 63.6 | 51.9 | 47.6 | 31.4 | 23.5 |
| 23.1 | 14.8 | 13.3 | | Assets | 5.8 | 27.4 | 23.1 | 17.7 | 13.7 | 8.1 |
| 5.0 | 2.3 | 2.0 | | | -.4 | 2.7 | 1.4 | 3.2 | 2.2 | 2.0 |
| 342.9 | 720.5 | 396.7 | | | UND | 704.6 | 157.6 | 875.9 | 458.6 | 149.3 |
| 39.6 | 45.6 | 43.1 | | Sales/Net Fixed Assets | 23.6 | 31.7 | 32.5 | 99.7 | 54.6 | 34.4 |
| 9.4 | 10.1 | 11.8 | | | .2 | 7.3 | 17.7 | 14.5 | 19.5 | 10.1 |
| 4.5 | 4.9 | 4.3 | | | 3.8 | 3.5 | 5.2 | 5.1 | 4.7 | 3.8 |
| 2.4 | 2.7 | 2.5 | | Sales/Total Assets | 1.3 | 2.1 | 2.9 | 3.1 | 2.8 | 2.1 |
| 1.5 | 1.5 | 1.4 | | | .2 | 1.4 | 1.6 | 1.8 | 1.5 | 1.3 |
| .4 | .4 | .4 | | | 4.9 | .6 | .4 | .4 | .2 | .4 |
| (221) 1.2 | (281) 1.2 | (291) 1.1 | | % Depr., Dep., Amort./Sales | (24) 16.9 | (29) 2.1 | (27) 1.2 | (42) 1.1 | (86) .6 | (83) 1.0 |
| 3.3 | 3.5 | 3.4 | | | 28.7 | 6.7 | 3.3 | 4.3 | 1.8 | 2.5 |
| 2.6 | 2.2 | 2.9 | | % Officers', Directors' | 7.0 | 4.8 | 4.1 | 2.4 | 1.6 | .7 |
| (157) 5.6 | (188) 5.2 | (176) 4.8 | | Owners' Comp/Sales | (22) 13.1 | (34) 9.0 | (24) 6.6 | (46) 3.7 | (35) 3.0 | (15) 2.8 |
| 13.1 | 11.2 | 9.9 | | | 21.6 | 16.1 | 8.9 | 5.3 | 4.7 | 9.4 |
| 9369862M | 14021786M | 15569256M | | Net Sales ($) | 31947M | 133964M | 197699M | 825826M | 2395198M | 11984622M |
| 5402656M | 7894304M | 9537416M | | Total Assets ($) | 125692M | 196323M | 120632M | 545107M | 1515815M | 7033847M |

© RMA 2024  M = $ thousand  MM = $ million
See Pages viii through xx for Explanation of Ratios and Data

# MANAGEMENT OF COMPANIES AND ENTERPRISES

## MANAGEMENT—Offices of Other Holding Companies  NAICS 551112

| | | | | | | | | Comparative Historical Data | |
|---|---|---|---|---|---|---|---|---|---|
| | | | | | | | Type of Statement | | |
| | | | 4 | 13 | 19 | 29 | Unqualified | 44 | 26 |
| | 1 | | 4 | 8 | 5 | | Reviewed | 19 | 18 |
| | 3 | | 5 | 5 | 1 | | Compiled | 28 | 21 |
| 6 | 22 | | 31 | 9 | 1 | | Tax Returns | 77 | 54 |
| 19 | 72 | | 90 | 82 | 23 | 45 | Other | 266 | 222 |
| | 44 (4/1-9/30/23) | | | 453 (10/1/23-3/31/24) | | | | 4/1/19-3/31/20 | 4/1/20-3/31/21 |
| 0-500M | 500M-2MM | 2-10MM | 10-50MM | 50-100MM | 100-250MM | | | ALL | ALL |
| 25 | 98 | 134 | 117 | 49 | 74 | | NUMBER OF STATEMENTS | 434 | 341 |
| % | % | % | % | % | % | | ASSETS | % | % |
| 28.6 | 10.4 | 8.4 | 12.9 | 15.8 | 10.5 | | Cash & Equivalents | 11.5 | 15.7 |
| 7.7 | 3.7 | 5.8 | 13.0 | 17.4 | 13.5 | | Trade Receivables (net) | 11.1 | 9.0 |
| 2.2 | 1.6 | 3.5 | 6.8 | 11.8 | 7.4 | | Inventory | 6.9 | 5.8 |
| 11.3 | 4.1 | 2.1 | 7.3 | 7.0 | 5.8 | | All Other Current | 4.4 | 3.4 |
| 49.8 | 19.9 | 19.8 | 40.0 | 52.0 | 37.2 | | Total Current | 33.9 | 34.0 |
| 29.9 | 58.1 | 60.3 | 35.3 | 20.3 | 28.6 | | Fixed Assets (net) | 43.2 | 43.3 |
| 6.5 | 6.5 | 11.8 | 10.5 | 13.1 | 16.3 | | Intangibles (net) | 10.2 | 8.4 |
| 13.8 | 15.6 | 8.1 | 14.1 | 14.6 | 17.9 | | All Other Non-Current | 12.7 | 14.3 |
| 100.0 | 100.0 | 100.0 | 100.0 | 100.0 | 100.0 | | Total | 100.0 | 100.0 |
| | | | | | | | LIABILITIES | | |
| 11.7 | 5.6 | 2.0 | 6.7 | 3.4 | 3.1 | | Notes Payable-Short Term | 5.5 | 8.1 |
| 4.4 | 1.8 | 3.3 | 2.8 | 4.8 | 3.0 | | Cur. Mat.-L.T.D. | 3.3 | 3.2 |
| 5.2 | 4.6 | 2.5 | 6.9 | 8.7 | 7.7 | | Trade Payables | 6.2 | 4.9 |
| .0 | .0 | .0 | .1 | .2 | .1 | | Income Taxes Payable | .2 | .1 |
| 30.7 | 11.5 | 10.5 | 11.4 | 17.2 | 10.5 | | All Other Current | 14.9 | 9.7 |
| 51.9 | 23.4 | 18.4 | 27.9 | 34.3 | 24.3 | | Total Current | 30.1 | 26.0 |
| 42.5 | 42.6 | 46.1 | 27.2 | 16.3 | 32.0 | | Long-Term Debt | 33.8 | 37.7 |
| .0 | .0 | .1 | .1 | .6 | .5 | | Deferred Taxes | .4 | .2 |
| 9.5 | 3.4 | 3.4 | 9.4 | 7.1 | 6.4 | | All Other Non-Current | 5.1 | 6.0 |
| -3.9 | 30.5 | 32.0 | 35.4 | 41.7 | 36.8 | | Net Worth | 30.6 | 30.1 |
| 100.0 | 100.0 | 100.0 | 100.0 | 100.0 | 100.0 | | Total Liabilities & Net Worth | 100.0 | 100.0 |
| | | | | | | | INCOME DATA | | |
| 100.0 | 100.0 | 100.0 | 100.0 | 100.0 | 100.0 | | Net Sales | 100.0 | 100.0 |
| | | | | | | | Gross Profit | | |
| 80.1 | 55.5 | 63.2 | 79.0 | 88.8 | 84.4 | | Operating Expenses | 72.7 | 71.9 |
| 19.9 | 44.5 | 36.8 | 21.0 | 11.2 | 15.6 | | Operating Profit | 27.3 | 28.1 |
| 3.2 | 17.6 | 15.9 | 8.2 | 5.6 | 6.6 | | All Other Expenses (net) | 10.0 | 9.4 |
| 16.7 | 26.9 | 20.9 | 12.8 | 5.6 | 9.0 | | Profit Before Taxes | 17.3 | 18.7 |
| | | | | | | | RATIOS | | |
| 6.3 | 3.5 | 2.9 | 2.9 | 3.6 | 2.3 | | | 2.8 | 3.5 |
| 1.5 | 1.0 | 1.5 | 1.5 | 1.5 | 1.7 | | Current | 1.3 | 1.6 |
| .7 | .3 | .4 | .8 | 1.0 | 1.0 | | | .6 | .7 |
| 3.3 | 3.2 | 2.5 | 2.0 | 1.9 | 1.7 | | | 2.0 | 2.7 |
| (24) 1.4 | .7 | .9 | .9 | 1.0 | 1.0 | | Quick | .8 | 1.1 |
| .5 | .2 | .3 | .3 | .5 | .6 | | | .3 | .4 |
| 0 UND | 0 UND | 0 UND | 0 UND | 21 17.5 | 13 29.1 | | | 0 UND | 0 UND |
| 0 UND | 0 UND | 0 UND | 23 15.9 | 31 11.6 | 39 9.4 | | Sales/Receivables | 9 40.9 | 1 615.2 |
| 0 UND | 2 150.6 | 26 14.0 | 47 7.7 | 61 6.0 | 58 6.3 | | | 42 8.7 | 40 9.1 |
| | | | | | | | Cost of Sales/Inventory | | |
| | | | | | | | Cost of Sales/Payables | | |
| 8.2 | 5.0 | 4.3 | 4.6 | 2.6 | 4.1 | | | 5.0 | 3.6 |
| 21.9 | NM | 16.3 | 10.5 | 7.2 | 8.7 | | Sales/Working Capital | 21.0 | 12.6 |
| -367.8 | -3.7 | -5.9 | -29.1 | -139.4 | NM | | | -10.9 | -11.0 |
| 21.8 | 8.8 | 7.9 | 18.5 | 28.8 | 15.1 | | | 15.1 | 13.4 |
| (10) 3.4 | (44) 5.1 | (66) 4.0 | (79) 6.1 | (34) 3.9 | (65) 3.6 | | EBIT/Interest | (281) 5.0 | (212) 4.4 |
| -.8 | 1.1 | .8 | 1.2 | 1.7 | .5 | | | 1.6 | .9 |
| | | | 21.5 | 155.6 | 4.0 | | Net Profit + Depr., Dep., | 8.6 | 6.9 |
| | | (10) 6.6 | (11) 22.8 | (20) 1.9 | | | Amort./Cur. Mat. L/T/D | (48) 2.9 | (33) 3.6 |
| | | 1.8 | 2.2 | .7 | | | | 1.3 | 1.0 |
| .0 | .2 | .8 | .2 | .1 | .2 | | | .3 | .2 |
| .5 | 2.5 | 2.5 | .8 | .6 | 1.1 | | Fixed/Worth | 1.6 | 1.9 |
| UND | 9.0 | 10.0 | 7.5 | 6.3 | NM | | | 12.7 | 19.2 |
| .3 | .7 | .8 | .7 | .6 | 1.0 | | | .7 | .8 |
| 1.1 | 2.4 | 3.1 | 2.8 | 3.3 | 2.4 | | Debt/Worth | 2.8 | 2.9 |
| -2.4 | 50.4 | -152.8 | 14.0 | 21.7 | -38.2 | | | 32.6 | -548.2 |
| 168.7 | 41.3 | 34.5 | 52.8 | 56.1 | 27.2 | | % Profit Before Taxes/Tangible | 52.1 | 47.8 |
| (18) 76.7 | (75) 24.3 | (100) 12.8 | (94) 24.6 | (39) 20.7 | (55) 14.5 | | Net Worth | (335) 19.0 | (255) 17.0 |
| 17.5 | 3.2 | 4.6 | 3.9 | 8.1 | 3.8 | | | 4.8 | 3.9 |
| 56.7 | 15.1 | 11.1 | 16.4 | 13.3 | 9.3 | | % Profit Before Taxes/Total | 14.9 | 12.6 |
| 23.6 | 5.1 | 3.8 | 5.9 | 5.8 | 3.8 | | Assets | 5.5 | 5.0 |
| -.1 | .4 | .7 | .3 | 1.5 | -2.4 | | | .6 | .0 |
| UND | 25.9 | 8.4 | 45.4 | 66.0 | 33.8 | | | 25.0 | 26.5 |
| 68.9 | .3 | .3 | 7.3 | 12.1 | 7.8 | | Sales/Net Fixed Assets | 4.1 | 3.2 |
| 10.0 | .1 | .1 | .8 | 4.1 | 1.5 | | | .2 | .2 |
| 11.1 | .8 | 1.1 | 2.1 | 1.8 | 1.7 | | | 2.3 | 1.7 |
| 4.8 | .2 | .2 | 1.2 | 1.3 | .8 | | Sales/Total Assets | .9 | .5 |
| 1.8 | .1 | .1 | .2 | .6 | .5 | | | .1 | .1 |
| | 7.9 | 4.3 | 1.2 | .5 | .7 | | | 1.6 | 1.8 |
| (53) 15.1 | (77) 19.4 | (73) 3.0 | (37) 2.1 | (37) 2.8 | | | % Depr., Dep., Amort./Sales | (291) 5.0 | (204) 6.1 |
| | 25.1 | 29.4 | 9.6 | 5.7 | 4.8 | | | 16.7 | 19.0 |
| | 5.0 | | | | | | % Officers', Directors' | 1.5 | 1.2 |
| (13) 8.2 | | | | | | | Owners' Comp/Sales | (49) 4.5 | (37) 4.7 |
| | 16.6 | | | | | | | 7.1 | 11.6 |
| 38015M | 106966M | 430782M | 4386682M | 4877595M | 13835155M | | Net Sales ($) | 23306391M | 12519822M |
| 6615M | 119103M | 618079M | 2853107M | 3404661M | 12280133M | | Total Assets ($) | 15342507M | 9800154M |

M = $ thousand    MM = $ million
See Pages viii through xx for Explanation of Ratios and Data

© RMA 2024

## MANAGEMENT—Offices of Other Holding Companies  NAICS 551112

### Comparative Historical Data | Current Data Sorted by Sales

| | | | Type of Statement | | | | | | |
|---|---|---|---|---|---|---|---|---|---|
| 26 | 58 | 65 | Unqualified | | | 1 | 4 | 7 | 53 |
| 15 | 25 | 18 | Reviewed | 2 | | 2 | 2 | 4 | 8 |
| 19 | 20 | 14 | Compiled | 3 | 4 | 2 | | 1 | 4 |
| 43 | 86 | 69 | Tax Returns | 45 | 9 | 4 | 2 | 6 | 3 |
| 229 | 332 | 331 | Other | 114 | 48 | 20 | 30 | 24 | 95 |
| 4/1/21-3/31/22 ALL | 4/1/22-3/31/23 ALL | 4/1/23-3/31/24 ALL | | 44 (4/1-9/30/23) | | | 453 (10/1/23-3/31/24) | | |
| | | | | 0-1MM | 1-3MM | 3-5MM | 5-10MM | 10-25MM | 25MM & OVER |
| 332 | 521 | 497 | NUMBER OF STATEMENTS | 164 | 61 | 29 | 38 | 42 | 163 |
| % | % | % | ASSETS | % | % | % | % | % | % |
| 14.3 | 12.4 | 11.9 | Cash & Equivalents | 7.0 | 12.9 | 11.3 | 16.3 | 20.3 | 13.4 |
| 8.9 | 9.3 | 9.5 | Trade Receivables (net) | 1.1 | 5.1 | 7.4 | 9.7 | 15.6 | 18.2 |
| 4.9 | 6.4 | 5.2 | Inventory | .3 | .6 | 6.9 | 7.7 | 6.5 | 10.8 |
| 4.4 | 3.8 | 5.2 | All Other Current | 2.5 | 7.3 | 7.1 | 4.6 | 4.7 | 7.2 |
| 32.5 | 31.9 | 31.8 | Total Current | 10.9 | 25.9 | 32.6 | 38.3 | 47.0 | 49.6 |
| 44.6 | 46.3 | 43.8 | Fixed Assets (net) | 71.9 | 51.4 | 33.4 | 26.7 | 24.5 | 23.4 |
| 8.0 | 7.7 | 11.0 | Intangibles (net) | 5.8 | 6.7 | 14.6 | 23.0 | 10.3 | 14.5 |
| 14.9 | 14.1 | 13.4 | All Other Non-Current | 11.3 | 16.0 | 19.3 | 12.0 | 18.3 | 12.5 |
| 100.0 | 100.0 | 100.0 | Total | 100.0 | 100.0 | 100.0 | 100.0 | 100.0 | 100.0 |
| | | | LIABILITIES | | | | | | |
| 5.0 | 4.2 | 4.6 | Notes Payable-Short Term | 4.1 | 7.5 | 3.2 | 3.7 | 1.2 | 5.4 |
| 3.3 | 2.5 | 3.0 | Cur. Mat.-L.T.D. | 2.5 | 3.3 | 1.9 | 3.4 | 2.0 | 3.8 |
| 4.9 | 5.3 | 5.5 | Trade Payables | .6 | 5.5 | 5.9 | 5.1 | 6.2 | 10.2 |
| .1 | .1 | .1 | Income Taxes Payable | .0 | .0 | .0 | .0 | .0 | .2 |
| 10.8 | 11.1 | 12.6 | All Other Current | 10.4 | 11.6 | 12.8 | 15.6 | 15.5 | 13.6 |
| 24.1 | 23.2 | 25.8 | Total Current | 17.6 | 28.0 | 23.8 | 27.8 | 25.0 | 33.2 |
| 36.8 | 40.0 | 35.8 | Long-Term Debt | 49.5 | 49.2 | 38.0 | 27.2 | 23.5 | 21.7 |
| .1 | .2 | .2 | Deferred Taxes | .0 | .0 | .2 | .1 | .4 | .4 |
| 4.6 | 6.0 | 5.9 | All Other Non-Current | 2.9 | 5.2 | 10.3 | 7.1 | 6.0 | 8.1 |
| 34.3 | 30.6 | 32.4 | Net Worth | 30.0 | 17.7 | 27.7 | 37.9 | 45.2 | 36.5 |
| 100.0 | 100.0 | 100.0 | Total Liabilities & Net Worth | 100.0 | 100.0 | 100.0 | 100.0 | 100.0 | 100.0 |
| | | | INCOME DATA | | | | | | |
| 100.0 | 100.0 | 100.0 | Net Sales | 100.0 | 100.0 | 100.0 | 100.0 | 100.0 | 100.0 |
| | | | Gross Profit | | | | | | |
| 68.5 | 69.3 | 71.9 | Operating Expenses | 48.0 | 64.5 | 76.6 | 87.0 | 77.7 | 92.9 |
| 31.5 | 30.7 | 28.1 | Operating Profit | 52.0 | 35.5 | 23.4 | 13.0 | 22.3 | 7.1 |
| 9.3 | 10.8 | 11.4 | All Other Expenses (net) | 23.8 | 13.0 | 10.4 | 6.9 | 3.2 | 1.7 |
| 22.2 | 19.9 | 16.7 | Profit Before Taxes | 28.2 | 22.4 | 13.0 | 6.0 | 19.1 | 5.4 |
| | | | RATIOS | | | | | | |
| 3.3 | 3.5 | 2.9 | | 3.5 | 3.2 | 3.7 | 3.3 | 3.3 | 2.4 |
| 1.5 | 1.6 | 1.5 | Current | .9 | 1.8 | 2.2 | 1.7 | 1.8 | 1.5 |
| .5 | .8 | .6 | | .2 | .4 | .8 | 1.0 | 1.1 | 1.0 |
| 2.6 | 2.6 | 2.1 | | 3.2 | 2.6 | 2.7 | 2.2 | 2.7 | 1.7 |
| 1.0 | (520) 1.1 | (496) 1.0 | Quick | .6 | .9 | (28) 1.3 | 1.1 | 1.3 | 1.0 |
| .4 | .4 | .4 | | .1 | .3 | .4 | .6 | .6 | .5 |
| 0 UND | 0 UND | 0 UND | | 0 UND | 0 UND | 0 UND | 0 UND | 0 UND | 17 21.2 |
| 0 863.5 | 2 150.3 | 5 66.8 | Sales/Receivables | 0 UND | 0 UND | 9 41.1 | 18 20.0 | 29 12.5 | 34 10.6 |
| 38 9.5 | 36 10.2 | 41 8.9 | | 0 UND | 18 20.6 | 32 11.4 | 54 6.7 | 55 6.6 | 54 6.8 |
| | | | Cost of Sales/Inventory | | | | | | |
| | | | Cost of Sales/Payables | | | | | | |
| 3.5 | 4.0 | 4.3 | | 4.0 | 2.7 | 2.9 | 4.9 | 3.4 | 5.0 |
| 11.4 | 10.7 | 15.3 | Sales/Working Capital | -94.8 | 15.3 | 10.7 | 15.5 | 8.7 | 10.5 |
| -8.2 | -19.3 | -11.0 | | -2.7 | -7.5 | -20.2 | -922.1 | 89.5 | -140.8 |
| 35.7 | 18.5 | 13.9 | | 7.3 | 8.5 | 8.7 | 8.0 | 74.6 | 19.0 |
| (192) 7.6 | (326) 5.9 | (298) 4.3 | EBIT/Interest | (47) 4.8 | (38) 4.3 | (22) 2.1 | (24) 2.0 | (26) 5.6 | (141) 4.6 |
| 2.0 | 2.0 | .9 | | 2.2 | -.8 | -.2 | .3 | 1.5 | .9 |
| 26.4 | 8.7 | 18.7 | | | | | | | 17.7 |
| (23) 5.1 | (52) 2.9 | (45) 2.3 | Net Profit + Depr., Dep., Amort./Cur. Mat. L/T/D | | | | | (33) | 2.1 |
| 2.4 | 1.4 | 1.0 | | | | | | | 1.0 |
| .2 | .2 | .2 | | 1.1 | .1 | .2 | .0 | .1 | .2 |
| 1.6 | 1.8 | 1.6 | Fixed/Worth | 3.0 | 1.5 | 2.8 | .9 | .4 | .8 |
| 9.9 | 6.9 | 8.4 | | 8.3 | 8.9 | -2.0 | NM | 3.4 | 7.2 |
| .6 | .8 | .7 | | .8 | .6 | .6 | .9 | .3 | .7 |
| 2.5 | 2.4 | 2.7 | Debt/Worth | 2.6 | 2.6 | 5.4 | 2.9 | 1.3 | 2.5 |
| 21.1 | 16.0 | 42.6 | | 12.2 | NM | -3.6 | -10.3 | 8.6 | 29.9 |
| 69.2 | 54.3 | 45.7 | % Profit Before Taxes/Tangible Net Worth | 31.3 | 61.9 | 42.1 | 52.8 | 96.5 | 51.1 |
| (266) 23.1 | (421) 20.5 | (381) 19.3 | | (131) 13.7 | (46) 21.0 | (17) 5.2 | (26) 23.6 | (36) 23.0 | (125) 24.2 |
| 7.9 | 5.4 | 5.1 | | 4.0 | 4.1 | .9 | -2.1 | 11.4 | 10.6 |
| 18.0 | 14.8 | 12.7 | % Profit Before Taxes/Total Assets | 9.0 | 12.5 | 15.5 | 19.8 | 19.8 | 14.8 |
| 6.7 | 5.1 | 4.7 | | 3.3 | 6.6 | 3.2 | 5.6 | 8.5 | 6.7 |
| 1.5 | 1.1 | .3 | | .8 | -.5 | -2.2 | -1.5 | 1.5 | .1 |
| 31.0 | 32.8 | 36.3 | | .4 | 38.5 | 37.0 | 136.0 | 124.1 | 50.9 |
| 2.7 | 3.0 | 4.1 | Sales/Net Fixed Assets | .2 | .6 | 14.6 | 15.0 | 15.4 | 12.6 |
| .2 | .2 | .2 | | .1 | .2 | .7 | 2.2 | 2.6 | 4.2 |
| 1.7 | 1.8 | 1.8 | | .2 | 2.0 | 2.2 | 2.6 | 2.2 | 2.2 |
| .5 | .5 | .7 | Sales/Total Assets | .1 | .2 | 1.0 | 1.1 | 1.1 | 1.6 |
| .1 | .1 | .1 | | .1 | .1 | .4 | .4 | .5 | 1.0 |
| 1.5 | 1.4 | 1.5 | | 12.2 | 3.9 | .6 | .9 | .3 | .7 |
| (199) 6.2 | (326) 5.7 | (286) 5.5 | % Depr., Dep., Amort./Sales | (95) 21.2 | (31) 18.3 | (16) 4.8 | (18) 2.4 | (23) 1.0 | (103) 1.8 |
| 18.6 | 17.7 | 19.2 | | 31.3 | 29.1 | 16.3 | 10.7 | 5.8 | 4.2 |
| 1.2 | 1.0 | 1.5 | | 12.1 | | | | | .2 |
| (38) 4.8 | (60) 2.9 | (45) 4.4 | % Officers', Directors' Owners' Comp/Sales | (14) 17.4 | | | | (13) | .9 |
| 9.2 | 8.0 | 15.4 | | 28.6 | | | | | 3.7 |
| 9282319M | 21569338M | 23675195M | Net Sales ($) | 61057M | 107120M | 112784M | 262547M | 732861M | 22398826M |
| 9552222M | 16518251M | 19281698M | Total Assets ($) | 485709M | 501743M | 459558M | 644987M | 1988731M | 15200970M |

M = $ thousand    MM = $ million
© RMA 2024
See Pages viii through xx for Explanation of Ratios and Data

# MANAGEMENT—Corporate, Subsidiary, and Regional Managing Offices NAICS 551114

## Current Data Sorted by Assets | Comparative Historical Data

| 0-500M | 500M-2MM | 2-10MM | 10-50MM | 50-100MM | 100-250MM | | Type of Statement | | 4/1/19-3/31/20 ALL | | 4/1/20-3/31/21 ALL |
|---|---|---|---|---|---|---|---|---|---|---|---|
| | 1 | | 2 | 2 | 8 | | Unqualified | | 9 | | 4 |
| | | 1 | 3 | | 2 | | Reviewed | | 2 | | 2 |
| | | 2 | | | 1 | | Compiled | | 3 | | 1 |
| | | 2 | | | | | Tax Returns | | 12 | | 2 |
| | 5 | 10 | 13 | 4 | 10 | | Other | | 52 | | 24 |
| | 10 (4/1-9/30/23) | | 56 (10/1/23-3/31/24) | | | | | | | | |
| | 6 | 15 | 18 | 6 | 21 | NUMBER OF STATEMENTS | | | 78 | | 33 |
| % | % | % | % | % | % | ASSETS | | | % | | % |
| | | 10.8 | 9.5 | | 11.3 | Cash & Equivalents | | | 13.6 | | 18.3 |
| DATA | | 17.0 | 10.9 | | 18.6 | Trade Receivables (net) | | | 17.2 | | 19.9 |
| | | 6.1 | 11.1 | | 12.8 | Inventory | | | 6.2 | | 5.2 |
| | | 2.1 | 1.4 | | 10.1 | All Other Current | | | 5.0 | | 5.3 |
| | | 36.0 | 32.9 | | 52.9 | Total Current | | | 42.0 | | 48.6 |
| NOT | | 42.5 | 39.4 | | 23.0 | Fixed Assets (net) | | | 35.7 | | 27.8 |
| | | 11.0 | 7.0 | | 9.6 | Intangibles (net) | | | 8.6 | | 8.5 |
| | | 10.5 | 20.7 | | 14.5 | All Other Non-Current | | | 13.7 | | 15.1 |
| | | 100.0 | 100.0 | | 100.0 | Total | | | 100.0 | | 100.0 |
| AVAILABLE | | | | | | LIABILITIES | | | | | |
| | | .8 | 5.3 | | 6.4 | Notes Payable-Short Term | | | 3.8 | | 4.6 |
| | | 1.1 | 2.1 | | 2.3 | Cur. Mat.-L.T.D. | | | 4.2 | | 4.5 |
| | | 4.3 | 7.2 | | 9.2 | Trade Payables | | | 8.7 | | 5.5 |
| | | .0 | .0 | | .1 | Income Taxes Payable | | | .1 | | .5 |
| | | 18.7 | 8.7 | | 13.1 | All Other Current | | | 25.5 | | 17.1 |
| | | 24.9 | 23.4 | | 31.2 | Total Current | | | 42.2 | | 32.2 |
| | | 29.6 | 26.3 | | 16.8 | Long-Term Debt | | | 25.0 | | 26.3 |
| | | .0 | .2 | | .0 | Deferred Taxes | | | .3 | | .2 |
| | | 6.8 | 5.4 | | 14.2 | All Other Non-Current | | | 3.5 | | 6.9 |
| | | 38.6 | 44.7 | | 37.8 | Net Worth | | | 28.9 | | 34.4 |
| | | 100.0 | 100.0 | | 100.0 | Total Liabilities & Net Worth | | | 100.0 | | 100.0 |
| | | | | | | INCOME DATA | | | | | |
| | | 100.0 | 100.0 | | 100.0 | Net Sales | | | 100.0 | | 100.0 |
| | | | | | | Gross Profit | | | | | |
| | | 77.1 | 84.0 | | 90.5 | Operating Expenses | | | 86.2 | | 80.6 |
| | | 22.9 | 16.0 | | 9.5 | Operating Profit | | | 13.8 | | 19.4 |
| | | 10.9 | 4.4 | | 1.5 | All Other Expenses (net) | | | 3.2 | | 5.7 |
| | | 12.1 | 11.6 | | 8.1 | Profit Before Taxes | | | 10.6 | | 13.7 |
| | | | | | | RATIOS | | | | | |
| | | 5.1 | 2.3 | | 3.3 | Current | | | 3.2 | | 5.2 |
| | | 1.4 | 1.4 | | 2.1 | | | | 1.4 | | 1.4 |
| | | .5 | .9 | | 1.0 | | | | .5 | | .7 |
| | | 4.8 | 1.6 | | 1.5 | Quick | | | 2.5 | | 4.1 |
| | | 1.3 | .9 | | .9 | | | | .9 | | 1.1 |
| | | .1 | .5 | | .6 | | | | .4 | | .4 |
| | 0 | UND | 7 55.1 | 31 | 11.8 | Sales/Receivables | 0 | 999.8 | 0 | UND |
| | 17 | 21.9 | 37 9.8 | 42 | 8.6 | | 20 | 18.7 | 26 | 14.0 |
| | 48 | 7.6 | 54 6.8 | 53 | 6.9 | | 45 | 8.2 | 59 | 6.2 |
| | | | | | | Cost of Sales/Inventory | | | | | |
| | | | | | | Cost of Sales/Payables | | | | | |
| | | 7.2 | 5.6 | | 3.1 | Sales/Working Capital | | | 5.3 | | 2.9 |
| | | 40.9 | 12.2 | | 4.2 | | | | 18.4 | | 19.1 |
| | | -2.2 | NM | | 100.2 | | | | -11.7 | | -10.1 |
| | | | 16.7 | | 47.7 | EBIT/Interest | | | 11.7 | | 20.5 |
| | | (16) | 4.9 | | 12.0 | | (60) | 3.3 | (21) | 4.1 |
| | | | -.4 | | 2.9 | | | -.6 | | .3 |
| | | | | | | Net Profit + Depr., Dep., Amort./Cur. Mat. L/T/D | | 9.0 | | |
| | | | | | | | (14) | 1.5 | | |
| | | | | | | | | -.3 | | |
| | | .1 | .5 | | .2 | Fixed/Worth | | | .1 | | .0 |
| | | 2.3 | .9 | | 1.1 | | | | 1.0 | | .7 |
| | | 7.0 | 1.8 | | 7.6 | | | | 2.6 | | 32.4 |
| | | .6 | .4 | | .6 | Debt/Worth | | | .5 | | .4 |
| | | 2.0 | 1.1 | | 2.9 | | | | 1.6 | | 1.3 |
| | | 32.2 | 1.6 | | NM | | | | 8.5 | | 70.2 |
| | | 67.6 | 13.4 | | 123.2 | % Profit Before Taxes/Tangible Net Worth | | | 41.7 | | 89.8 |
| | (12) | 9.4 | (16) 11.2 | (16) | 21.5 | | (62) | 13.5 | (26) | 23.3 |
| | | -6.3 | -2.4 | | 10.7 | | | | 6.4 | | .8 |
| | | 63.4 | 8.2 | | 12.5 | % Profit Before Taxes/Total Assets | | | 13.2 | | 20.8 |
| | | 3.4 | 4.6 | | 7.9 | | | | 4.6 | | 6.5 |
| | | -2.4 | -3.1 | | 3.5 | | | | -2.5 | | -.8 |
| | | 33.8 | 8.9 | | 16.3 | Sales/Net Fixed Assets | | | 90.1 | | UND |
| | | 12.0 | 3.3 | | 8.7 | | | | 7.6 | | 16.3 |
| | | .1 | 1.3 | | 4.7 | | | | 1.6 | | 2.4 |
| | | 2.9 | 1.6 | | 1.8 | Sales/Total Assets | | | 2.6 | | 2.2 |
| | | 1.4 | 1.1 | | 1.2 | | | | 1.5 | | 1.3 |
| | | .1 | .6 | | .9 | | | | .4 | | .3 |
| | | .5 | 1.3 | | 1.0 | % Depr., Dep., Amort./Sales | | | 1.0 | | 2.6 |
| | (10) | 1.8 | (17) 3.1 | (15) | 1.7 | | (49) | 3.0 | (15) | 6.1 |
| | | 22.2 | 5.9 | | 3.6 | | | | 7.5 | | 16.7 |
| | | | | | | % Officers', Directors' Owners' Comp/Sales | | | 1.1 | | |
| | | | | | | | (12) | 1.5 | | |
| | | | | | | | | 6.1 | | |
| | 81406M | 105896M | 771657M | 485174M | 4478762M | Net Sales ($) | | | 4699636M | | 1908089M |
| | 7235M | 63542M | 499271M | 502429M | 3383810M | Total Assets ($) | | | 3465486M | | 1654946M |

M = $ thousand   MM = $ million
See Pages viii through xx for Explanation of Ratios and Data

© RMA 2024

# MANAGEMENT—Corporate, Subsidiary, and Regional Managing Offices  NAICS 551114

## Comparative Historical Data | Current Data Sorted by Sales

| Comparative Historical Data | | | | | Current Data Sorted by Sales | | | | | |
|---|---|---|---|---|---|---|---|---|---|---|
| | | | **Type of Statement** | | | | | | | |
| 3 | 13 | 13 | Unqualified | | | | | 1 | 12 | |
| 1 | 7 | 6 | Reviewed | | | | | 3 | 3 | |
| 2 | 2 | 3 | Compiled | | | | 1 | 1 | 1 | |
| 2 | 1 | 2 | Tax Returns | 1 | 1 | | 4 | 5 | 22 | |
| 28 | 33 | 42 | Other | 6 | 4 | 1 | 56 | | | |
| 4/1/21-3/31/22 ALL | 4/1/22-3/31/23 ALL | 4/1/23-3/31/24 ALL | | 0-1MM | 10 (4/1-9/30/23) 1-3MM | 3-5MM | (10/1/23-3/31/24) 5-10MM | 10-25MM | 25MM & OVER | |
| 36 | 56 | 66 | **NUMBER OF STATEMENTS** | 7 | 5 | 1 | 5 | 10 | 38 | |
| % | % | % | **ASSETS** | % | % | % | % | % | % | |
| 19.7 | 17.1 | 11.5 | Cash & Equivalents | | | | | 14.1 | 13.0 | |
| 15.2 | 12.8 | 14.5 | Trade Receivables (net) | | | | | 14.0 | 17.0 | |
| 6.3 | 8.2 | 9.1 | Inventory | | | | | 3.9 | 11.2 | |
| 5.5 | 4.8 | 6.1 | All Other Current | | | | | 2.1 | 8.7 | |
| 46.8 | 42.9 | 41.2 | Total Current | | | | | 34.2 | 49.8 | |
| 32.6 | 37.4 | 32.6 | Fixed Assets (net) | | | | | 35.8 | 25.2 | |
| 4.3 | 7.0 | 9.6 | Intangibles (net) | | | | | 16.7 | 11.9 | |
| 16.3 | 12.8 | 16.7 | All Other Non-Current | | | | | 13.3 | 13.0 | |
| 100.0 | 100.0 | 100.0 | Total | | | | | 100.0 | 100.0 | |
| | | | **LIABILITIES** | | | | | | | |
| 4.7 | 3.2 | 4.1 | Notes Payable-Short Term | | | | | 1.4 | 6.1 | |
| 2.2 | 2.5 | 1.8 | Cur. Mat.-L.T.D. | | | | | 1.6 | 2.1 | |
| 7.6 | 6.9 | 8.7 | Trade Payables | | | | | 6.9 | 12.1 | |
| .0 | .2 | .1 | Income Taxes Payable | | | | | .0 | .1 | |
| 18.7 | 12.6 | 14.5 | All Other Current | | | | | 9.9 | 12.5 | |
| 33.2 | 25.4 | 29.1 | Total Current | | | | | 19.7 | 32.9 | |
| 24.6 | 27.0 | 21.5 | Long-Term Debt | | | | | 22.0 | 18.8 | |
| .1 | .1 | .1 | Deferred Taxes | | | | | .0 | .1 | |
| 8.2 | 7.8 | 10.7 | All Other Non-Current | | | | | 2.2 | 12.9 | |
| 33.9 | 39.8 | 38.6 | Net Worth | | | | | 56.1 | 35.4 | |
| 100.0 | 100.0 | 100.0 | Total Liabilities & Net Worth | | | | | 100.0 | 100.0 | |
| | | | **INCOME DATA** | | | | | | | |
| 100.0 | 100.0 | 100.0 | Net Sales | | | | | 100.0 | 100.0 | |
| | | | Gross Profit | | | | | | | |
| 84.3 | 85.9 | 83.7 | Operating Expenses | | | | | 87.2 | 93.3 | |
| 15.7 | 14.1 | 16.3 | Operating Profit | | | | | 12.8 | 6.7 | |
| 1.3 | 3.2 | 5.0 | All Other Expenses (net) | | | | | 1.0 | 1.5 | |
| 14.4 | 10.8 | 11.3 | Profit Before Taxes | | | | | 11.9 | 5.3 | |
| | | | **RATIOS** | | | | | | | |
| 3.9 | 3.3 | 2.8 | | | | | | 2.8 | 2.9 | |
| 1.7 | 1.6 | 1.4 | Current | | | | | 2.0 | 1.5 | |
| .7 | 1.2 | 1.0 | | | | | | 1.1 | 1.0 | |
| 2.6 | 2.3 | 1.6 | | | | | | 2.5 | 1.3 | |
| 1.3 | 1.2 | 1.0 | Quick | | | | | 1.8 | .9 | |
| .6 | .5 | .5 | | | | | | .7 | .6 | |
| 0  UND | 2  148.2 | 6  57.1 | | | | | 3  120.4 | 26  13.9 | | |
| 16  23.2 | 18  20.5 | 34  10.7 | Sales/Receivables | | | | 23  15.7 | 41  8.8 | | |
| 54  6.7 | 42  8.6 | 51  7.2 | | | | | 51  7.2 | 51  7.1 | | |
| | | | Cost of Sales/Inventory | | | | | | | |
| | | | Cost of Sales/Payables | | | | | | | |
| 4.3 | 3.0 | 4.4 | | | | | | 6.1 | 3.7 | |
| 8.0 | 7.2 | 14.1 | Sales/Working Capital | | | | | 8.7 | 6.7 | |
| -20.0 | 38.1 | NM | | | | | | 45.3 | 96.4 | |
| 38.5 | 23.8 | 23.9 | | | | | | | 28.1 | |
| (34) 9.3 | (45) 3.7 | (54) 7.4 | EBIT/Interest | | | | | (36) 8.8 | | |
| 1.9 | .4 | .3 | | | | | | | .0 | |
| | 11.9 | 28.5 | Net Profit + Depr., Dep., | | | | | | 30.3 | |
| | (11) 4.1 | (15) 5.5 | Amort./Cur. Mat. L/T/D | | | | | (14) 6.2 | | |
| | | .8 | | | | | | | 2.8 | |
| .2 | .3 | .3 | | | | | | .2 | .5 | |
| 1.1 | .9 | 1.1 | Fixed/Worth | | | | | .9 | 1.0 | |
| 2.7 | 2.4 | 5.5 | | | | | | 3.4 | NM | |
| .8 | .6 | .6 | | | | | | .4 | .9 | |
| 1.8 | 1.5 | 1.5 | Debt/Worth | | | | | 1.0 | 2.2 | |
| 19.5 | 3.5 | 29.6 | | | | | | 10.7 | -202.6 | |
| | | | | | | | | | 72.5 | |
| 63.0 | 38.1 | 30.8 | % Profit Before Taxes/Tangible | | | | | | | |
| (30) 27.8 | (47) 11.6 | (52) 13.2 | Net Worth | | | | | (28) 19.2 | | |
| 5.3 | -.4 | 5.3 | | | | | | | 8.4 | |
| 31.4 | 17.8 | 10.5 | % Profit Before Taxes/Total | | | | | 24.2 | 10.2 | |
| 8.8 | 3.4 | 7.0 | Assets | | | | | 6.0 | 7.7 | |
| .5 | -.3 | -.2 | | | | | | -.2 | -3.1 | |
| 63.4 | 35.3 | 15.4 | | | | | | 40.1 | 15.7 | |
| 11.3 | 4.0 | 7.9 | Sales/Net Fixed Assets | | | | | 7.5 | 8.3 | |
| 1.3 | 1.0 | 1.9 | | | | | | 1.1 | 3.8 | |
| 3.3 | 1.9 | 2.1 | | | | | | 3.4 | 2.0 | |
| 1.6 | 1.3 | 1.3 | Sales/Total Assets | | | | | 1.5 | 1.3 | |
| .6 | .4 | .7 | | | | | | .6 | 1.0 | |
| 1.1 | .7 | 1.1 | | | | | | | 1.0 | |
| (18) 2.5 | (41) 2.2 | (52) 2.9 | % Depr., Dep., Amort./Sales | | | | | (32) 2.6 | | |
| 13.1 | 8.3 | 6.6 | | | | | | | 6.0 | |
| | | | % Officers', Directors' Owners' Comp/Sales | | | | | | | |
| 2724835M | 4002383M | 5922895M | Net Sales ($) | 2065M | 10917M | 3576M | 34361M | 153602M | 5718374M | |
| 1792487M | 2976454M | 4456287M | Total Assets ($) | 23453M | 77011M | 1326M | 22427M | 176614M | 4155456M | |

© RMA 2024  
M = $ thousand   MM = $ million  
See Pages viii through xx for Explanation of Ratios and Data

# ADMINISTRATIVE AND SUPPORT AND WASTE MANAGEMENT AND REMEDIATION SERVICES

# ADMIN & WASTE MANAGEMENT SERVICES—Office Administrative Services  NAICS 561110

## Current Data Sorted by Assets | Comparative Historical Data

| | | | | | | | Type of Statement | | |
|---|---|---|---|---|---|---|---|---|---|
| | | | 2 | 3 | 1 | 6 | Unqualified | 12 | 10 |
| | | | 2 | 4 | 2 | 1 | Reviewed | 6 | 5 |
| | | 1 | 4 | 1 | | | Compiled | 8 | 3 |
| 10 | 9 | 9 | 9 | 2 | | | Tax Returns | 36 | 20 |
| 7 | 22 | 33 | 20 | 5 | 2 | | Other | 110 | 76 |
| | 17 (4/1-9/30/23) | | 129 (10/1/23-3/31/24) | | | | | 4/1/19-3/31/20 | 4/1/20-3/31/21 |
| 0-500M | 500M-2MM | 2-10MM | 10-50MM | 50-100MM | 100-250MM | | | ALL | ALL |
| 17 | 32 | 50 | 30 | 8 | 9 | | NUMBER OF STATEMENTS | 172 | 114 |
| % | % | % | % | % | % | | ASSETS | % | % |
| 56.8 | 27.2 | 24.1 | 14.5 | | | | Cash & Equivalents | 23.6 | 31.4 |
| .0 | 17.4 | 15.7 | 21.2 | | | | Trade Receivables (net) | 17.3 | 15.2 |
| .0 | 1.0 | 3.7 | 6.6 | | | | Inventory | 1.7 | 2.0 |
| 10.0 | 10.3 | 4.7 | 7.3 | | | | All Other Current | 7.3 | 6.7 |
| 66.8 | 56.0 | 48.2 | 49.6 | | | | Total Current | 49.9 | 55.2 |
| 8.8 | 18.6 | 33.4 | 28.9 | | | | Fixed Assets (net) | 25.1 | 25.7 |
| 4.9 | 4.4 | 7.2 | 4.8 | | | | Intangibles (net) | 10.1 | 8.8 |
| 19.6 | 21.0 | 11.2 | 16.7 | | | | All Other Non-Current | 14.9 | 10.3 |
| 100.0 | 100.0 | 100.0 | 100.0 | | | | Total | 100.0 | 100.0 |
| | | | | | | | LIABILITIES | | |
| 18.1 | 8.8 | 3.6 | 4.1 | | | | Notes Payable-Short Term | 6.4 | 9.6 |
| 4.2 | 2.7 | 2.2 | 3.5 | | | | Cur. Mat.-L.T.D. | 3.2 | 5.3 |
| .5 | 6.9 | 9.9 | 8.5 | | | | Trade Payables | 10.7 | 6.3 |
| .0 | .1 | 1.8 | .3 | | | | Income Taxes Payable | .1 | .2 |
| 20.2 | 22.4 | 16.0 | 13.2 | | | | All Other Current | 19.8 | 20.2 |
| 43.0 | 40.8 | 33.4 | 29.5 | | | | Total Current | 40.2 | 41.6 |
| 19.2 | 23.0 | 24.6 | 27.0 | | | | Long-Term Debt | 24.3 | 30.8 |
| .0 | .0 | .2 | .0 | | | | Deferred Taxes | .1 | .2 |
| 44.3 | 6.1 | 6.3 | 6.7 | | | | All Other Non-Current | 8.1 | 7.0 |
| -6.5 | 30.1 | 35.4 | 36.7 | | | | Net Worth | 27.3 | 20.5 |
| 100.0 | 100.0 | 100.0 | 100.0 | | | | Total Liabilities & Net Worth | 100.0 | 100.0 |
| | | | | | | | INCOME DATA | | |
| 100.0 | 100.0 | 100.0 | 100.0 | | | | Net Sales | 100.0 | 100.0 |
| | | | | | | | Gross Profit | | |
| 97.3 | 81.0 | 78.6 | 81.8 | | | | Operating Expenses | 85.1 | 86.3 |
| 2.7 | 19.0 | 21.4 | 18.2 | | | | Operating Profit | 14.9 | 13.7 |
| -.6 | 1.4 | 4.2 | 7.6 | | | | All Other Expenses (net) | 3.5 | 2.8 |
| 3.3 | 17.6 | 17.3 | 10.5 | | | | Profit Before Taxes | 11.3 | 10.9 |
| | | | | | | | RATIOS | | |
| 8.6 | 4.2 | 3.7 | 3.1 | | | | | 2.7 | 3.6 |
| 1.9 | 1.5 | 1.5 | 1.4 | | | | Current | 1.4 | 1.8 |
| 1.0 | .5 | .7 | 1.1 | | | | | .7 | 1.0 |
| 6.1 | 2.8 | 3.7 | 2.5 | | | | | 2.2 | 3.2 |
| 1.9 | 1.2 | 1.3 | 1.2 | | | | Quick | 1.1 | 1.5 |
| .7 | .3 | .5 | .5 | | | | | .4 | .8 |
| 0 UND | 0 UND | 0 UND | 1 280.0 | | | | | 0 UND | 0 UND |
| 0 UND | 0 UND | 18 20.4 | 43 8.5 | | | | Sales/Receivables | 7 51.4 | 10 37.5 |
| 0 UND | 26 13.9 | 48 7.6 | 73 5.0 | | | | | 40 9.2 | 50 7.3 |
| | | | | | | | Cost of Sales/Inventory | | |
| | | | | | | | Cost of Sales/Payables | | |
| 8.0 | 5.7 | 3.5 | 4.2 | | | | | 5.7 | 3.9 |
| 34.4 | 36.4 | 12.0 | 11.7 | | | | Sales/Working Capital | 26.3 | 11.2 |
| UND | -15.0 | -25.0 | 31.6 | | | | | -29.9 | UND |
| | | 40.1 | 47.4 | 113.9 | | | | 28.2 | 28.6 |
| (19) | 7.7 | (35) 10.7 | (21) 14.1 | | | | EBIT/Interest | (113) 4.3 | (66) 4.9 |
| | | 2.6 | 4.5 | 2.2 | | | | 1.2 | .7 |
| | | | | | | | Net Profit + Depr., Dep., | | 5.3 |
| | | | | | | | Amort./Cur. Mat. L/T/D | (11) 4.8 | |
| | | | | | | | | | 1.9 |
| .0 | .0 | .1 | .1 | | | | | .0 | .0 |
| .0 | .1 | 1.0 | .2 | | | | Fixed/Worth | .7 | .6 |
| UND | 1.7 | -15.2 | 1.8 | | | | | 105.5 | UND |
| .7 | .3 | .5 | 1.0 | | | | | .8 | .8 |
| 1.5 | 1.1 | 1.3 | 2.6 | | | | Debt/Worth | 3.4 | 3.6 |
| -5.5 | 11.5 | -16.7 | 6.5 | | | | | -33.5 | -15.7 |
| 154.3 | 157.2 | 44.5 | 70.2 | | | | % Profit Before Taxes/Tangible | 124.3 | 90.1 |
| (12) 16.2 | (25) 29.5 | (36) 25.8 | (28) 21.5 | | | | Net Worth | (128) 38.2 | (81) 34.9 |
| -14.5 | 5.2 | 7.8 | 10.3 | | | | | 5.8 | 10.6 |
| 36.6 | 68.6 | 26.3 | 21.7 | | | | % Profit Before Taxes/Total | 33.1 | 35.6 |
| .0 | 17.4 | 11.5 | 7.5 | | | | Assets | 8.1 | 7.2 |
| -25.3 | 1.8 | 2.6 | 1.2 | | | | | .6 | -.1 |
| UND | 999.8 | 139.4 | 189.8 | | | | | 398.2 | 140.9 |
| UND | 95.2 | 12.6 | 33.5 | | | | Sales/Net Fixed Assets | 27.9 | 21.2 |
| 80.0 | 12.9 | .5 | 1.8 | | | | | 5.7 | 3.9 |
| 12.8 | 6.7 | 2.9 | 3.3 | | | | | 4.2 | 3.2 |
| 8.1 | 3.4 | 1.3 | 1.6 | | | | Sales/Total Assets | 1.9 | 1.6 |
| 3.0 | 1.5 | .3 | .5 | | | | | .8 | .7 |
| | .1 | .4 | .2 | | | | | .6 | 1.1 |
| (14) | .8 | (31) 2.0 | (22) .7 | | | | % Depr., Dep., Amort./Sales | (97) 2.1 | (63) 2.9 |
| | 2.7 | 8.2 | 5.7 | | | | | 5.7 | 6.5 |
| | 2.5 | | | | | | | 3.1 | 3.4 |
| (13) | 5.7 | | | | | | % Officers', Directors' | (32) 8.9 | (22) 7.2 |
| | 11.9 | | | | | | Owners' Comp/Sales | 25.3 | 13.1 |
| 30863M | 175304M | 655456M | 1605807M | 552170M | 1859014M | | Net Sales ($) | 5806739M | 4330093M |
| 3583M | 39770M | 236567M | 692215M | 489651M | 1382998M | | Total Assets ($) | 3659963M | 3193620M |

© RMA 2024    M = $ thousand    MM = $ million
See Pages viii through xx for Explanation of Ratios and Data

# ADMIN & WASTE MANAGEMENT SERVICES—Office Administrative Services  NAICS 561110

## Comparative Historical Data | Current Data Sorted by Sales

| Comparative Historical Data | | | | | Current Data Sorted by Sales | | | | | |
|---|---|---|---|---|---|---|---|---|---|---|
| | | | | **Type of Statement** | | | | | | |
| 7 | | 15 | 12 | Unqualified | | 1 | | 1 | 2 | 10 |
| 2 | | 9 | 9 | Reviewed | | 2 | | 1 | 2 | 5 |
| 5 | | 12 | 6 | Compiled | 1 | | | 2 | | 1 |
| 15 | | 32 | 30 | Tax Returns | 8 | 10 | 5 | 3 | 4 | |
| 66 | | 91 | 89 | Other | 15 | 12 | 10 | 11 | 21 | 20 |
| 4/1/21-3/31/22 ALL | | 4/1/22-3/31/23 ALL | 4/1/23-3/31/24 ALL | | | 17 (4/1-9/30/23) | | | 129 (10/1/23-3/31/24) | |
| | | | | | 0-1MM | 1-3MM | 3-5MM | 5-10MM | 10-25MM | 25MM & OVER |
| 95 | | 159 | 146 | **NUMBER OF STATEMENTS** | 24 | 25 | 15 | 17 | 29 | 36 |
| % | | % | % | **ASSETS** | % | % | % | % | % | % |
| 29.5 | | 27.7 | 26.7 | Cash & Equivalents | 27.4 | 26.7 | 32.4 | 32.7 | 28.3 | 19.7 |
| 17.7 | | 15.5 | 14.3 | Trade Receivables (net) | .6 | 6.4 | 13.2 | 19.6 | 22.0 | 20.8 |
| 2.3 | | 2.8 | 3.8 | Inventory | .0 | 1.1 | 5.1 | .9 | 7.5 | 6.0 |
| 8.5 | | 10.2 | 7.7 | All Other Current | 7.7 | 3.8 | 11.2 | 5.7 | 4.0 | 12.9 |
| 58.0 | | 56.3 | 52.5 | Total Current | 35.7 | 38.1 | 62.0 | 59.0 | 61.8 | 59.3 |
| 16.6 | | 23.9 | 25.4 | Fixed Assets (net) | 51.3 | 25.2 | 13.5 | 13.7 | 25.6 | 18.5 |
| 12.2 | | 8.3 | 6.0 | Intangibles (net) | .1 | 5.5 | 16.4 | 6.0 | 4.0 | 7.4 |
| 13.2 | | 11.6 | 16.1 | All Other Non-Current | 12.9 | 31.2 | 8.0 | 21.3 | 8.7 | 14.8 |
| 100.0 | | 100.0 | 100.0 | Total | 100.0 | 100.0 | 100.0 | 100.0 | 100.0 | 100.0 |
| | | | | **LIABILITIES** | | | | | | |
| 10.1 | | 10.9 | 6.2 | Notes Payable-Short Term | .1 | 14.5 | 6.8 | 6.1 | 5.9 | 4.5 |
| 3.4 | | 3.1 | 3.0 | Cur. Mat.-L.T.D. | 2.5 | 4.2 | .2 | 3.4 | 2.5 | 4.0 |
| 7.3 | | 9.2 | 7.3 | Trade Payables | 1.3 | 3.7 | 7.5 | 6.0 | 10.2 | 12.0 |
| .0 | | .2 | .7 | Income Taxes Payable | .0 | .0 | .0 | 5.3 | .0 | .3 |
| 21.1 | | 17.2 | 16.8 | All Other Current | 10.4 | 14.3 | 32.9 | 23.3 | 12.8 | 16.2 |
| 42.0 | | 40.5 | 34.0 | Total Current | 14.3 | 36.7 | 47.5 | 44.1 | 31.5 | 37.0 |
| 23.0 | | 19.7 | 24.1 | Long-Term Debt | 38.8 | 40.1 | 10.7 | 9.4 | 17.2 | 21.0 |
| .2 | | .3 | .2 | Deferred Taxes | .0 | .0 | .0 | .0 | .2 | .7 |
| 6.4 | | 6.1 | 11.4 | All Other Non-Current | 25.6 | 10.4 | 18.4 | 8.5 | 3.6 | 7.3 |
| 28.4 | | 33.4 | 30.3 | Net Worth | 21.3 | 12.7 | 23.4 | 38.0 | 47.5 | 34.1 |
| 100.0 | | 100.0 | 100.0 | Total Liabilities & Net Worth | 100.0 | 100.0 | 100.0 | 100.0 | 100.0 | 100.0 |
| | | | | **INCOME DATA** | | | | | | |
| 100.0 | | 100.0 | 100.0 | Net Sales | 100.0 | 100.0 | 100.0 | 100.0 | 100.0 | 100.0 |
| | | | | Gross Profit | | | | | | |
| 86.7 | | 85.6 | 82.7 | Operating Expenses | 62.4 | 77.2 | 89.0 | 87.9 | 87.1 | 91.6 |
| 13.3 | | 14.4 | 17.3 | Operating Profit | 37.6 | 22.8 | 11.0 | 12.1 | 12.9 | 8.4 |
| -.4 | | 1.3 | 3.4 | All Other Expenses (net) | 9.1 | 9.4 | 1.4 | 1.3 | .4 | -.4 |
| 13.7 | | 13.1 | 13.9 | Profit Before Taxes | 28.5 | 13.4 | 9.6 | 10.8 | 12.4 | 8.8 |
| | | | | **RATIOS** | | | | | | |
| 3.9 | | 4.7 | 3.7 | | 15.6 | 2.8 | 6.7 | 5.9 | 3.6 | 3.3 |
| 1.5 | | 1.4 | 1.8 | Current | 2.4 | 1.1 | 2.4 | 1.3 | 1.8 | 1.7 |
| .9 | | .8 | .9 | | .5 | .5 | .5 | .6 | 1.2 | 1.1 |
| 2.6 | | 3.2 | 3.1 | | 9.3 | 2.6 | 3.7 | 5.9 | 3.2 | 2.0 |
| 1.3 | | 1.1 | 1.3 | Quick | 2.0 | 1.1 | 1.9 | 1.2 | 1.5 | 1.1 |
| .6 | | .5 | .5 | | .3 | .4 | .1 | .5 | 1.0 | .5 |
| 0 UND | | 0 UND | 0 UND | | 0 UND | 0 UND | 0 UND | 0 UND | 0 999.8 | 4 100.9 |
| 8 43.4 | | 4 95.8 | 10 37.5 | Sales/Receivables | 0 UND | 0 UND | 1 430.7 | 38 9.5 | 30 12.3 | 36 10.2 |
| 47 7.8 | | 43 8.4 | 46 7.9 | | 0 UND | 36 10.2 | 89 4.1 | 63 5.8 | 42 8.7 | 49 7.4 |
| | | | | Cost of Sales/Inventory | | | | | | |
| | | | | Cost of Sales/Payables | | | | | | |
| 6.4 | | 6.3 | 4.2 | | 1.6 | 6.4 | 4.9 | 4.5 | 4.2 | 6.0 |
| 15.2 | | 15.3 | 14.1 | Sales/Working Capital | 6.6 | 34.4 | 10.2 | 17.5 | 10.6 | 10.9 |
| -150.8 | | -38.7 | -98.5 | | -4.6 | -38.8 | -12.0 | -9.4 | 79.1 | 103.5 |
| 36.0 | | 22.1 | 37.7 | | 23.6 | 4.5 | 83.6 | 88.0 | 67.7 | 41.2 |
| (56) 5.4 | (89) | 6.9 | (90) 8.5 | EBIT/Interest | (10) 8.5 | (13) 2.6 | (10) 11.0 | (11) 21.4 | (18) 19.6 | (28) 8.7 |
| 2.5 | | 1.0 | 2.5 | | 5.4 | -1.4 | .9 | 3.9 | 1.1 | 2.2 |
| | | 3.9 | 3.4 | Net Profit + Depr., Dep., | | | | | | |
| | (10) | 1.5 | (11) 1.6 | Amort./Cur. Mat. L/T/D | | | | | | |
| | | .8 | .7 | | | | | | | |
| .0 | | .0 | .0 | | .0 | .0 | .0 | .0 | .0 | .1 |
| .4 | | .3 | .4 | Fixed/Worth | 1.6 | .3 | .0 | .4 | .2 | .3 |
| 4.9 | | 4.4 | 2.3 | | 2.6 | -9.5 | -.5 | 1.3 | 1.1 | 2.8 |
| .8 | | .5 | .5 | | .3 | 1.0 | .3 | .1 | .4 | .5 |
| 3.1 | | 2.7 | 1.5 | Debt/Worth | 1.3 | 1.7 | 5.0 | .7 | 1.1 | 2.5 |
| 25.2 | | 26.4 | 16.9 | | UND | -8.3 | -2.3 | NM | 2.6 | 57.7 |
| 133.1 | | 92.3 | 73.3 | % Profit Before Taxes/Tangible | 76.0 | 43.6 | | 40.2 | 80.8 | 66.2 |
| (74) 67.6 | (122) | 30.1 | (113) 22.8 | Net Worth | (19) 15.2 | (17) 12.5 | (13) | 22.6 | (27) 26.1 | (28) 30.3 |
| 33.1 | | 9.1 | 5.9 | | 1.2 | -.7 | | 5.2 | 2.3 | 11.0 |
| 40.4 | | 29.7 | 28.3 | % Profit Before Taxes/Total | 25.0 | 16.6 | 51.2 | 28.0 | 38.6 | 26.0 |
| 12.5 | | 7.9 | 9.1 | Assets | 8.6 | 3.7 | 7.9 | 15.5 | 19.3 | 11.0 |
| 2.1 | | .8 | 1.1 | | .2 | -.8 | 1.3 | 3.7 | .6 | 3.5 |
| 767.5 | | 758.1 | 472.9 | | UND | 898.3 | 999.8 | 736.2 | 619.4 | 184.0 |
| 59.4 | | 38.2 | 36.2 | Sales/Net Fixed Assets | .4 | 27.9 | 80.5 | 36.5 | 30.3 | 45.5 |
| 6.5 | | 7.1 | 3.7 | | .2 | 1.4 | 11.1 | 11.4 | 3.0 | 8.4 |
| 4.9 | | 4.1 | 4.1 | | 1.4 | 6.3 | 5.0 | 3.8 | 6.9 | 4.3 |
| 2.2 | | 2.0 | 1.9 | Sales/Total Assets | .3 | 1.5 | 1.9 | 2.7 | 2.4 | 2.3 |
| .9 | | .9 | .5 | | .1 | .2 | 1.0 | 1.2 | 1.2 | 1.3 |
| .4 | | .5 | .2 | | 8.1 | .4 | | .1 | .2 | |
| (44) 1.3 | (78) | 1.4 | (81) 1.2 | % Depr., Dep., Amort./Sales | (10) 9.6 | | (12) .7 | (19) 1.2 | (26) .9 | |
| 6.4 | | 6.9 | 5.8 | | 22.4 | | | 2.3 | 3.6 | 3.0 |
| 2.9 | | 3.1 | 2.0 | % Officers', Directors' | | | | | | |
| (18) 6.8 | (27) | 7.1 | (31) 5.7 | Owners' Comp/Sales | | | | | | |
| 13.2 | | 11.5 | 13.7 | | | | | | | |
| 3335613M | | 4246474M | 4878614M | Net Sales ($) | 10932M | 46112M | 60616M | 115992M | 424683M | 4220279M |
| 1929353M | | 2401241M | 2844784M | Total Assets ($) | 41786M | 106484M | 47556M | 110598M | 462462M | 2075898M |

© RMA 2024  
M = $ thousand    MM = $ million  
See Pages viii through xx for Explanation of Ratios and Data

## ADMIN & WASTE MANAGEMENT SERVICES—Facilities Support Services  NAICS 561210

### Current Data Sorted by Assets

| | | | | | | Type of Statement | | |
|---|---|---|---|---|---|---|---|---|
| | 1 | | 2 | 4 | 1 | Unqualified | | |
| | | 2 | 3 | | | Reviewed | | |
| | | 2 | 2 | | | Compiled | | |
| 2 | 4 | 1 | | | | Tax Returns | | |
| 4 | 7 | 14 | 15 | 8 | 1 | Other | | |
| | 2 (4/1-9/30/23) | | 71 (10/1/23-3/31/24) | | | | | |
| 0-500M | 500M-2MM | 2-10MM | 10-50MM | 50-100MM | 100-250MM | | | |

### Comparative Historical Data

| | | |
|---|---|---|
| 16 | 3 | |
| 4 | 3 | |
| 1 | | |
| 6 | 3 | |
| 53 | 25 | |
| 4/1/19-3/31/20 ALL | 4/1/20-3/31/21 ALL | |

| 0-500M | 500M-2MM | 2-10MM | 10-50MM | 50-100MM | 100-250MM | | 4/1/19-3/31/20 ALL | 4/1/20-3/31/21 ALL |
|---|---|---|---|---|---|---|---|---|
| 6 | 12 | 19 | 22 | 12 | 2 | NUMBER OF STATEMENTS | 80 | 34 |
| % | % | % | % | % | % | ASSETS | % | % |
| | 22.5 | 12.7 | 22.0 | 5.2 | | Cash & Equivalents | 17.5 | 29.3 |
| | 27.6 | 54.1 | 42.0 | 42.5 | | Trade Receivables (net) | 43.0 | 30.3 |
| | .0 | 1.0 | .8 | .6 | | Inventory | 1.9 | .7 |
| | .3 | 7.2 | 8.0 | 8.8 | | All Other Current | 5.0 | 5.6 |
| | 50.4 | 74.9 | 72.9 | 57.1 | | Total Current | 67.3 | 65.9 |
| | 22.8 | 14.9 | 16.9 | 20.3 | | Fixed Assets (net) | 16.6 | 19.7 |
| | 5.7 | 5.6 | 2.2 | 4.3 | | Intangibles (net) | 4.9 | 6.1 |
| | 21.2 | 4.6 | 8.0 | 18.3 | | All Other Non-Current | 11.2 | 8.3 |
| | 100.0 | 100.0 | 100.0 | 100.0 | | Total | 100.0 | 100.0 |
| | | | | | | LIABILITIES | | |
| | 19.4 | 5.6 | 5.1 | 3.3 | | Notes Payable-Short Term | 13.8 | 10.2 |
| | 3.5 | 1.4 | 2.6 | 4.1 | | Cur. Mat.-L.T.D. | 2.1 | 3.9 |
| | 32.9 | 16.7 | 13.8 | 14.9 | | Trade Payables | 12.7 | 14.1 |
| | .0 | .1 | .2 | .0 | | Income Taxes Payable | .1 | .4 |
| | 17.5 | 17.3 | 15.5 | 67.3 | | All Other Current | 20.2 | 18.2 |
| | 73.2 | 41.1 | 37.1 | 89.6 | | Total Current | 49.0 | 46.8 |
| | 35.5 | 20.3 | 9.8 | 25.2 | | Long-Term Debt | 9.5 | 15.9 |
| | .0 | .0 | .3 | .0 | | Deferred Taxes | .4 | .0 |
| | 6.1 | 7.6 | 5.6 | 9.4 | | All Other Non-Current | 3.4 | 3.8 |
| | -14.8 | 31.0 | 47.2 | -24.2 | | Net Worth | 37.6 | 33.4 |
| | 100.0 | 100.0 | 100.0 | 100.0 | | Total Liabilities & Net Worth | 100.0 | 100.0 |
| | | | | | | INCOME DATA | | |
| | 100.0 | 100.0 | 100.0 | 100.0 | | Net Sales | 100.0 | 100.0 |
| | | | | | | Gross Profit | | |
| | 90.2 | 84.3 | 91.6 | 92.7 | | Operating Expenses | 93.7 | 91.6 |
| | 9.8 | 15.7 | 8.4 | 7.3 | | Operating Profit | 6.3 | 8.4 |
| | 6.9 | 4.7 | .1 | 3.2 | | All Other Expenses (net) | .2 | 1.5 |
| | 2.8 | 10.9 | 8.4 | 4.1 | | Profit Before Taxes | 6.2 | 6.9 |
| | | | | | | RATIOS | | |
| | 2.6 | 5.0 | 3.4 | 2.0 | | | 2.5 | 3.0 |
| | .8 | 2.3 | 2.2 | 1.2 | | Current | 1.5 | 1.7 |
| | .3 | 1.3 | 1.1 | .9 | | | 1.1 | 1.1 |
| | 2.5 | 4.2 | 3.1 | 1.9 | | | 2.1 | 2.7 |
| | .8 | 1.5 | 2.0 | 1.0 | | Quick | 1.4 | 1.6 |
| | .3 | 1.3 | 1.0 | .7 | | | 1.0 | .8 |
| 0 UND | 38 9.6 | 32 11.4 | 29 12.4 | | | | 27 13.4 | 14 26.2 |
| 29 12.5 | 54 6.8 | 63 5.8 | 49 7.4 | | | Sales/Receivables | 42 8.7 | 31 11.8 |
| 51 7.2 | 63 5.8 | 73 5.0 | 81 4.5 | | | | 66 5.5 | 53 6.9 |
| | | | | | | Cost of Sales/Inventory | | |
| | | | | | | Cost of Sales/Payables | | |
| | 12.4 | 4.8 | 5.1 | 9.0 | | | 7.7 | 6.4 |
| | -20.4 | 15.1 | 7.8 | 30.8 | | Sales/Working Capital | 18.0 | 11.0 |
| | -5.5 | 29.1 | 60.3 | NM | | | 65.9 | NM |
| | | 114.5 | 77.9 | 33.0 | | | 61.8 | 93.9 |
| | (13) 3.5 | (19) 14.5 | (10) 3.9 | | | EBIT/Interest | (67) 11.9 | (25) 22.1 |
| | | .9 | 5.2 | 1.2 | | | 3.2 | 5.5 |
| | | | | | | | 68.5 | |
| | | | | | | Net Profit + Depr., Dep., Amort./Cur. Mat. L/T/D | (14) 10.3 | |
| | | | | | | | 2.5 | |
| | .0 | .0 | .1 | .2 | | | .1 | .1 |
| | .6 | .3 | .3 | .5 | | Fixed/Worth | .5 | .4 |
| | NM | .7 | 1.3 | NM | | | 1.4 | 4.5 |
| | 1.6 | .6 | .3 | 1.3 | | | .6 | .6 |
| | 21.3 | 1.6 | 1.1 | 2.8 | | Debt/Worth | 1.6 | 1.8 |
| | -2.0 | 7.2 | 5.8 | NM | | | 5.7 | NM |
| | | 50.9 | 55.4 | | | | 78.9 | 78.1 |
| | (15) 35.1 | (19) 38.3 | | | | % Profit Before Taxes/Tangible Net Worth | (68) 40.5 | (26) 45.1 |
| | | 7.5 | 7.5 | | | | 23.2 | 29.2 |
| | 37.4 | 34.3 | 31.9 | 10.5 | | | 28.5 | 26.8 |
| | 7.9 | 14.5 | 19.6 | 9.2 | | % Profit Before Taxes/Total Assets | 12.4 | 14.6 |
| | -24.8 | 3.2 | 5.8 | 1.8 | | | 4.7 | 9.4 |
| | UND | 999.8 | 80.9 | 42.3 | | | 159.4 | 75.8 |
| | 23.2 | 66.0 | 26.6 | 18.1 | | Sales/Net Fixed Assets | 34.8 | 39.4 |
| | 8.7 | 19.2 | 12.7 | 7.0 | | | 13.0 | 6.7 |
| | 5.3 | 4.9 | 3.8 | 3.7 | | | 4.8 | 4.6 |
| | 2.8 | 4.3 | 2.6 | 2.9 | | Sales/Total Assets | 3.4 | 2.8 |
| | 1.7 | 2.7 | 1.7 | 1.9 | | | 2.4 | 2.2 |
| | | .2 | .3 | | | | .2 | .5 |
| | (11) | 1.5 | (18) .8 | | | % Depr., Dep., Amort./Sales | (55) .9 | (20) 1.5 |
| | | 2.0 | 2.5 | | | | 2.3 | 3.5 |
| | | | | | | | .6 | |
| | | | | | | % Officers', Directors' Owners' Comp/Sales | (12) 1.8 | |
| | | | | | | | 3.8 | |
| 18865M | 53651M | 455320M | 1142794M | 2140650M | 551609M | Net Sales ($) | 5044448M | 2500757M |
| 1567M | 14795M | 109865M | 455784M | 760868M | 253154M | Total Assets ($) | 1737611M | 873728M |

M = $ thousand    MM = $ million
See Pages viii through xx for Explanation of Ratios and Data

© RMA 2024

# ADMIN & WASTE MANAGEMENT SERVICES—Facilities Support Services  NAICS 561210

## Comparative Historical Data | Current Data Sorted by Sales

| Comparative Historical Data | | | | | | Current Data Sorted by Sales | | | | | |
|---|---|---|---|---|---|---|---|---|---|---|---|
| 5 | | 9 | | 8 | Type of Statement | | 1 | | | | 7 |
| 1 | | 2 | | 5 | Unqualified | | | | | 1 | 4 |
| | | 1 | | 4 | Reviewed | | | | | 1 | 3 |
| 4 | | 4 | | 7 | Compiled | 2 | | 2 | 1 | 1 | 1 |
| 29 | | 40 | | 49 | Tax Returns | 3 | 3 | 5 | 5 | 4 | 29 |
| 4/1/21-3/31/22 | | 4/1/22-3/31/23 | | 4/1/23-3/31/24 | Other | | 2 (4/1-9/30/23) | | | 71 (10/1/23-3/31/24) | |
| ALL | | ALL | | ALL | | 0-1MM | 1-3MM | 3-5MM | 5-10MM | 10-25MM | 25MM & OVER |
| 39 | | 56 | | 73 | NUMBER OF STATEMENTS | 5 | 4 | 7 | 6 | 7 | 44 |
| % | | % | | % | ASSETS | % | % | % | % | % | % |
| 25.6 | | 19.3 | | 17.8 | Cash & Equivalents | | | | | | 13.6 |
| 30.9 | | 39.6 | | 39.9 | Trade Receivables (net) | | | | | | 47.9 |
| 2.0 | | .5 | | .6 | Inventory | | | | | | .7 |
| 4.3 | | 7.3 | | 6.4 | All Other Current | | | | | | 8.8 |
| 62.7 | | 66.7 | | 64.8 | Total Current | | | | | | 70.9 |
| 17.6 | | 18.9 | | 17.5 | Fixed Assets (net) | | | | | | 14.8 |
| 6.7 | | 3.2 | | 5.7 | Intangibles (net) | | | | | | 3.5 |
| 13.0 | | 11.2 | | 12.0 | All Other Non-Current | | | | | | 10.8 |
| 100.0 | | 100.0 | | 100.0 | Total | | | | | | 100.0 |
| | | | | | LIABILITIES | | | | | | |
| 4.2 | | 7.0 | | 9.2 | Notes Payable-Short Term | | | | | | 5.1 |
| 3.0 | | 2.1 | | 2.5 | Cur. Mat.-L.T.D. | | | | | | 2.8 |
| 9.0 | | 12.3 | | 17.2 | Trade Payables | | | | | | 16.9 |
| .0 | | .2 | | .1 | Income Taxes Payable | | | | | | .1 |
| 20.0 | | 19.6 | | 28.0 | All Other Current | | | | | | 31.5 |
| 36.2 | | 41.2 | | 56.8 | Total Current | | | | | | 56.4 |
| 12.7 | | 20.2 | | 19.6 | Long-Term Debt | | | | | | 14.1 |
| .0 | | .1 | | .1 | Deferred Taxes | | | | | | .1 |
| 4.2 | | 7.3 | | 6.5 | All Other Non-Current | | | | | | 9.0 |
| 46.9 | | 31.2 | | 17.1 | Net Worth | | | | | | 20.4 |
| 100.0 | | 100.0 | | 100.0 | Total Liabilties & Net Worth | | | | | | 100.0 |
| | | | | | INCOME DATA | | | | | | |
| 100.0 | | 100.0 | | 100.0 | Net Sales | | | | | | 100.0 |
| | | | | | Gross Profit | | | | | | |
| 87.0 | | 92.1 | | 90.0 | Operating Expenses | | | | | | 92.4 |
| 13.0 | | 7.9 | | 10.0 | Operating Profit | | | | | | 7.6 |
| .0 | | 1.5 | | 3.2 | All Other Expenses (net) | | | | | | 2.3 |
| 13.0 | | 6.4 | | 6.8 | Profit Before Taxes | | | | | | 5.4 |
| | | | | | RATIOS | | | | | | |
| | 4.0 | | 3.5 | | 3.3 | Current | | | | | | 2.9 |
| | 2.2 | | 1.9 | | 1.5 | | | | | | | 1.5 |
| | 1.2 | | 1.2 | | 1.0 | | | | | | | 1.1 |
| | 3.9 | | 3.1 | | 2.9 | Quick | | | | | | 2.1 |
| | 1.6 | | 1.8 | | 1.4 | | | | | | | 1.4 |
| | 1.1 | | 1.0 | | .8 | | | | | | | .9 |
| 20 | 18.0 | 29 | 12.7 | 24 | 15.4 | Sales/Receivables | | | | | 35 | 10.5 |
| 34 | 10.6 | 49 | 7.4 | 50 | 7.3 | | | | | | 57 | 6.4 |
| 39 | 9.4 | 72 | 5.1 | 66 | 5.5 | | | | | | 68 | 5.4 |
| | | | | | Cost of Sales/Inventory | | | | | | |
| | | | | | Cost of Sales/Payables | | | | | | |
| | 4.1 | | 5.0 | | 5.8 | Sales/Working Capital | | | | | | 6.3 |
| | 12.3 | | 9.6 | | 15.1 | | | | | | | 13.8 |
| | 29.4 | | 59.2 | | NM | | | | | | | 102.6 |
| | 76.5 | | 70.1 | | 43.4 | EBIT/Interest | | | | | | 44.0 |
| (26) | 24.5 | (43) | 11.0 | (54) | 8.7 | | | | | | (36) | 10.5 |
| | 5.6 | | 2.3 | | 1.7 | | | | | | | 1.7 |
| | | | | | Net Profit + Depr., Dep., Amort./Cur. Mat. L/T/D | | | | | | |
| | .1 | | .0 | | .1 | Fixed/Worth | | | | | | .1 |
| | .3 | | .2 | | .5 | | | | | | | .3 |
| | .9 | | 2.4 | | 7.0 | | | | | | | 1.1 |
| | .3 | | .5 | | .7 | Debt/Worth | | | | | | .7 |
| | 1.1 | | 1.1 | | 2.5 | | | | | | | 2.1 |
| | 4.8 | | 5.2 | | -14.8 | | | | | | | 4.7 |
| | 81.0 | | 54.4 | | 59.1 | % Profit Before Taxes/Tangible Net Worth | | | | | | 54.0 |
| (35) | 54.1 | (46) | 24.8 | (53) | 35.1 | | | | | | (36) | 34.8 |
| | 20.1 | | 7.8 | | 7.5 | | | | | | | 8.3 |
| | 52.4 | | 33.7 | | 30.2 | % Profit Before Taxes/Total Assets | | | | | | 26.3 |
| | 13.8 | | 9.8 | | 11.2 | | | | | | | 10.6 |
| | 5.8 | | 2.0 | | 3.5 | | | | | | | 4.9 |
| | 138.2 | | 100.9 | | 147.1 | Sales/Net Fixed Assets | | | | | | 114.9 |
| | 23.4 | | 36.1 | | 36.4 | | | | | | | 34.9 |
| | 11.1 | | 11.5 | | 13.2 | | | | | | | 14.7 |
| | 3.7 | | 4.6 | | 4.4 | Sales/Total Assets | | | | | | 4.5 |
| | 2.6 | | 3.1 | | 3.1 | | | | | | | 3.3 |
| | 1.6 | | 2.0 | | 2.0 | | | | | | | 2.2 |
| | .3 | | .3 | | .3 | % Depr., Dep., Amort./Sales | | | | | | .2 |
| (14) | 1.2 | (35) | .9 | (46) | .9 | | | | | | (34) | .9 |
| | 4.6 | | 2.4 | | 2.1 | | | | | | | 1.7 |
| | | | 1.6 | | 1.9 | % Officers', Directors' Owners' Comp/Sales | | | | | | |
| | | (10) | 3.9 | (15) | 4.1 | | | | | | | |
| | | | 8.5 | | 7.0 | | | | | | | |
| | 2427056M | | 2801075M | | 4362889M | Net Sales ($) | 2607M | 9056M | 26413M | 45929M | 115971M | 4162913M |
| | 844005M | | 1012316M | | 1596033M | Total Assets ($) | 5712M | 5422M | 13204M | 13437M | 47764M | 1510494M |

© RMA 2024     M = $ thousand     MM = $ million
See Pages viii through xx for Explanation of Ratios and Data

# ADMIN & WASTE MANAGEMENT SERVICES—Employment Placement Agencies  NAICS 561311

## Current Data Sorted by Assets

| | | | | | | Type of Statement | Comparative Historical Data | |
|---|---|---|---|---|---|---|---|---|
| | | 4 | 13 | 7 | 2 | Unqualified | 25 | 20 |
| | 1 | 18 | 13 | 1 | | Reviewed | 24 | 15 |
| | 1 | 8 | 4 | 1 | | Compiled | 26 | 7 |
| 9 | 16 | 11 | 1 | | | Tax Returns | 38 | 11 |
| 16 | 23 | 68 | 43 | 19 | 10 | Other | 224 | 95 |
| | 34 (4/1-9/30/23) | | 255 (10/1/23-3/31/24) | | | | 4/1/19-3/31/20 | 4/1/20-3/31/21 |
| 0-500M | 500M-2MM | 2-10MM | 10-50MM | 50-100MM | 100-250MM | | ALL | ALL |
| 25 | 41 | 109 | 74 | 28 | 12 | NUMBER OF STATEMENTS | 337 | 148 |
| % | % | % | % | % | % | ASSETS | % | % |
| 44.5 | 34.5 | 22.2 | 16.3 | 11.9 | 6.1 | Cash & Equivalents | 17.7 | 28.4 |
| 30.5 | 30.1 | 50.2 | 50.5 | 33.4 | 35.3 | Trade Receivables (net) | 52.5 | 39.0 |
| .0 | .0 | .2 | .1 | 2.3 | .0 | Inventory | .2 | .0 |
| 4.3 | 2.9 | 5.4 | 7.5 | 7.3 | 8.2 | All Other Current | 5.3 | 5.5 |
| 79.2 | 67.5 | 78.1 | 74.3 | 54.9 | 49.5 | Total Current | 75.7 | 72.9 |
| 6.8 | 15.0 | 5.4 | 7.1 | 4.1 | 6.2 | Fixed Assets (net) | 6.8 | 6.0 |
| 2.4 | 6.8 | 4.9 | 6.3 | 30.6 | 34.0 | Intangibles (net) | 8.2 | 12.3 |
| 11.5 | 10.7 | 11.6 | 12.3 | 10.5 | 10.3 | All Other Non-Current | 9.2 | 8.7 |
| 100.0 | 100.0 | 100.0 | 100.0 | 100.0 | 100.0 | Total | 100.0 | 100.0 |
| | | | | | | LIABILITIES | | |
| 28.1 | 14.1 | 7.7 | 10.5 | 5.5 | 3.9 | Notes Payable-Short Term | 18.9 | 20.9 |
| .6 | 2.1 | 1.2 | 1.7 | 3.3 | 1.1 | Cur. Mat.-L.T.D. | 1.5 | 3.1 |
| 2.7 | 6.5 | 7.1 | 6.4 | 6.8 | 12.2 | Trade Payables | 7.6 | 7.1 |
| .0 | .6 | .0 | .3 | .2 | .0 | Income Taxes Payable | .1 | .1 |
| 49.5 | 18.0 | 16.3 | 22.1 | 18.3 | 23.9 | All Other Current | 20.8 | 18.2 |
| 80.9 | 41.3 | 32.4 | 41.0 | 34.1 | 41.1 | Total Current | 49.1 | 49.3 |
| 9.4 | 31.7 | 8.2 | 7.1 | 16.9 | 31.4 | Long-Term Debt | 10.1 | 19.3 |
| .0 | .0 | .1 | .1 | .2 | .0 | Deferred Taxes | .1 | .2 |
| 2.3 | 1.6 | 2.4 | 8.2 | 10.2 | 8.2 | All Other Non-Current | 5.6 | 6.4 |
| 7.4 | 25.4 | 56.9 | 43.6 | 38.6 | 19.3 | Net Worth | 35.1 | 24.9 |
| 100.0 | 100.0 | 100.0 | 100.0 | 100.0 | 100.0 | Total Liabilities & Net Worth | 100.0 | 100.0 |
| | | | | | | INCOME DATA | | |
| 100.0 | 100.0 | 100.0 | 100.0 | 100.0 | 100.0 | Net Sales | 100.0 | 100.0 |
| | | | | | | Gross Profit | | |
| 91.9 | 92.7 | 93.8 | 97.6 | 98.1 | 96.4 | Operating Expenses | 95.2 | 97.5 |
| 8.1 | 7.3 | 6.2 | 2.4 | 1.9 | 3.6 | Operating Profit | 4.8 | 2.5 |
| .3 | 2.1 | .0 | .5 | 1.9 | 3.8 | All Other Expenses (net) | .9 | -.1 |
| 7.8 | 5.2 | 6.2 | 1.9 | .0 | -.2 | Profit Before Taxes | 3.9 | 2.5 |
| | | | | | | RATIOS | | |
| 5.6 | 10.6 | 5.9 | 3.8 | 3.5 | 2.8 | | 3.0 | 3.8 |
| 2.1 | 3.0 | 2.6 | 1.9 | 2.1 | 1.1 | Current | 1.6 | 1.8 |
| .8 | .6 | 1.4 | 1.3 | 1.1 | .8 | | 1.2 | 1.0 |
| 5.1 | 10.6 | 5.4 | 3.7 | 3.2 | 2.7 | | 2.8 | 3.6 |
| 2.1 | 3.0 | 2.4 | 1.6 | 1.3 | 1.0 | Quick | 1.6 | 1.6 |
| .8 | .5 | 1.3 | 1.2 | .8 | .6 | | 1.0 | .9 |
| 0  UND | 0  UND | 28  12.9 | 39  9.3 | 32  11.4 | 40  9.1 | | 26  13.9 | 24  15.5 |
| 9  39.5 | 23  15.9 | 37  9.8 | 51  7.1 | 46  7.9 | 54  6.8 | Sales/Receivables | 41  8.8 | 40  9.1 |
| 23  15.6 | 43  8.4 | 57  6.4 | 66  5.5 | 55  6.6 | 72  5.1 | | 59  6.2 | 58  6.3 |
| | | | | | | Cost of Sales/Inventory | | |
| | | | | | | Cost of Sales/Payables | | |
| 14.5 | 6.8 | 5.9 | 6.3 | 6.3 | 11.4 | | 8.8 | 5.7 |
| 35.3 | 14.6 | 9.9 | 10.0 | 13.7 | 51.2 | Sales/Working Capital | 17.3 | 10.8 |
| -127.9 | -32.9 | 20.3 | 25.2 | 113.2 | -41.6 | | 69.7 | 251.6 |
| | 40.3 | 80.3 | 22.4 | 7.4 | 9.0 | | 27.2 | 49.9 |
| (24)  8.5 | (68)  16.7 | (60)  4.0 | (25)  2.2 | 2.7 | | EBIT/Interest | (275)  7.8 | (109)  6.3 |
| | -12.1 | 3.4 | -.8 | .1 | .6 | | 2.5 | .4 |
| | | 52.5 | 23.2 | | | | 19.6 | |
| | (10) 14.5 | (10) 4.8 | | | | Net Profit + Depr., Dep., Amort./Cur. Mat. L/T/D | (20)  9.6 | |
| | | 2.5 | -.8 | | | | 2.1 | |
| .0 | .0 | .0 | .0 | .1 | .7 | | .0 | .0 |
| .0 | .0 | .0 | .1 | .3 | -.3 | Fixed/Worth | .1 | .1 |
| .2 | 2.6 | .1 | .3 | -.1 | -.1 | | .4 | 4.4 |
| .3 | .2 | .3 | .5 | 1.3 | 8.9 | | .6 | 1.0 |
| 1.4 | .6 | .7 | 1.4 | 9.1 | -10.0 | Debt/Worth | 1.8 | 3.2 |
| 59.6 | -9.3 | 1.9 | 3.4 | -2.8 | -2.0 | | 6.9 | -14.5 |
| 339.7 | 137.1 | 64.4 | 49.4 | 104.1 | | | 80.0 | 73.0 |
| (20) 54.7 | (29) 36.6 | (101) 32.0 | (65) 21.3 | (16) 35.2 | | % Profit Before Taxes/Tangible Net Worth | (279) 37.7 | (101) 29.5 |
| 18.9 | 5.7 | 7.4 | 1.5 | 10.8 | | | 14.5 | 5.7 |
| 97.5 | 52.6 | 33.8 | 18.0 | 11.5 | 15.7 | | 29.9 | 22.3 |
| 17.1 | 13.0 | 14.2 | 7.9 | 4.4 | 1.6 | % Profit Before Taxes/Total Assets | 13.0 | 7.3 |
| -6.0 | -9.3 | 2.7 | -1.2 | -3.2 | -3.6 | | 3.0 | -1.5 |
| UND | 999.8 | 999.8 | 396.5 | 341.0 | 168.5 | | 999.8 | 999.8 |
| UND | 301.8 | 257.5 | 147.7 | 82.1 | 42.6 | Sales/Net Fixed Assets | 223.2 | 200.5 |
| 223.4 | 50.3 | 73.2 | 54.6 | 44.7 | 20.5 | | 77.2 | 67.1 |
| 22.1 | 9.7 | 6.5 | 4.9 | 3.9 | 4.2 | | 7.3 | 5.3 |
| 9.5 | 5.2 | 3.9 | 3.7 | 2.9 | 2.2 | Sales/Total Assets | 5.0 | 3.6 |
| 4.4 | 3.1 | 2.7 | 2.5 | 1.2 | 1.7 | | 3.1 | 2.4 |
| | .0 | .1 | .1 | .1 | | | .1 | .1 |
| (17) .3 | (54) .1 | (46) .2 | (12) .2 | | | % Depr., Dep., Amort./Sales | (176) .2 | (70) .2 |
| | 1.1 | .5 | .7 | 1.0 | | | .4 | .6 |
| 3.1 | 1.4 | .5 | 1.0 | | | | 1.1 | 1.2 |
| (12) 7.7 | (17) 2.9 | (31) 1.3 | (14) 1.7 | | | % Officers', Directors', Owners' Comp/Sales | (73) 2.1 | (27) 2.6 |
| 17.7 | 7.4 | 3.6 | 3.0 | | | | 6.2 | 5.0 |
| 71014M | 458004M | 2584486M | 5554074M | 5220591M | 4767100M | Net Sales ($) | 17276331M | 8629878M |
| 5956M | 48156M | 579594M | 1543917M | 2037706M | 1814508M | Total Assets ($) | 5077526M | 2858148M |

© RMA 2024   M = $ thousand   MM = $ million
See Pages viii through xx for Explanation of Ratios and Data

# ADMIN & WASTE MANAGEMENT SERVICES—Employment Placement Agencies  NAICS 561311

## Comparative Historical Data | Current Data Sorted by Sales

| Comparative Historical Data | | | | Type of Statement | Current Data Sorted by Sales | | | | | |
|---|---|---|---|---|---|---|---|---|---|---|
| 11 | 24 | 26 | | Unqualified | | | | 1 | 1 | 24 |
| 14 | 16 | 33 | | Reviewed | | | | 3 | 11 | 19 |
| 9 | 24 | 14 | | Compiled | | | | 1 | 6 | 7 |
| 12 | 38 | 37 | | Tax Returns | 5 | 6 | 3 | 3 | 13 | 7 |
| 109 | 158 | 179 | | Other | 10 | 11 | 9 | 17 | 36 | 96 |
| 4/1/21-3/31/22 ALL | 4/1/22-3/31/23 ALL | 4/1/23-3/31/24 ALL | | | 34 (4/1-9/30/23) | | | 255 (10/1/23-3/31/24) | | |
| | | | | | 0-1MM | 1-3MM | 3-5MM | 5-10MM | 10-25MM | 25MM & OVER |
| 155 | 260 | 289 | | NUMBER OF STATEMENTS | 15 | 17 | 12 | 25 | 67 | 153 |
| % | % | % | | ASSETS | % | % | % | % | % | % |
| 22.8 | 25.3 | 22.7 | | Cash & Equivalents | 29.8 | 34.8 | 39.0 | 15.1 | 35.5 | 15.0 |
| 47.5 | 45.6 | 43.5 | | Trade Receivables (net) | 16.3 | 30.7 | 29.3 | 45.3 | 39.6 | 50.1 |
| .0 | .1 | .3 | | Inventory | .0 | .0 | .0 | .4 | .1 | .5 |
| 5.4 | 6.4 | 5.8 | | All Other Current | 5.2 | 1.5 | 14.0 | 4.1 | 4.9 | 6.3 |
| 75.7 | 77.4 | 72.3 | | Total Current | 51.3 | 67.0 | 82.3 | 64.9 | 80.1 | 71.9 |
| 5.9 | 6.2 | 7.2 | | Fixed Assets (net) | 31.8 | 3.3 | 7.1 | 9.5 | 5.6 | 5.6 |
| 10.1 | 7.0 | 9.0 | | Intangibles (net) | 2.5 | 18.2 | 3.7 | 4.7 | 2.9 | 12.4 |
| 8.3 | 9.4 | 11.5 | | All Other Non-Current | 14.4 | 11.5 | 6.9 | 20.9 | 11.4 | 10.1 |
| 100.0 | 100.0 | 100.0 | | Total | 100.0 | 100.0 | 100.0 | 100.0 | 100.0 | 100.0 |
| | | | | LIABILITIES | | | | | | |
| 9.0 | 11.2 | 10.7 | | Notes Payable-Short Term | 24.1 | 13.7 | 22.8 | 13.0 | 7.1 | 9.3 |
| 2.3 | 1.4 | 1.6 | | Cur. Mat.-L.T.D. | 1.4 | 1.7 | 5.5 | .2 | 1.2 | 1.7 |
| 5.5 | 7.5 | 6.6 | | Trade Payables | 4.1 | 1.2 | .7 | 10.9 | 8.2 | 6.6 |
| .2 | .2 | .2 | | Income Taxes Payable | .0 | .0 | .0 | .0 | .4 | .2 |
| 19.0 | 16.6 | 21.4 | | All Other Current | 14.9 | 60.4 | 31.1 | 14.7 | 14.3 | 21.1 |
| 36.1 | 36.9 | 40.6 | | Total Current | 44.5 | 76.9 | 60.0 | 38.8 | 31.2 | 39.0 |
| 14.2 | 8.7 | 13.2 | | Long-Term Debt | 26.5 | 14.0 | 30.7 | 35.9 | 6.9 | 9.4 |
| .1 | .1 | .1 | | Deferred Taxes | .0 | .0 | .0 | .0 | .0 | .1 |
| 7.3 | 5.9 | 4.8 | | All Other Non-Current | 1.3 | 4.5 | 3.0 | .3 | .9 | 7.6 |
| 42.3 | 48.4 | 41.4 | | Net Worth | 27.7 | 4.6 | 6.2 | 24.9 | 60.9 | 43.8 |
| 100.0 | 100.0 | 100.0 | | Total Liabilities & Net Worth | 100.0 | 100.0 | 100.0 | 100.0 | 100.0 | 100.0 |
| | | | | INCOME DATA | | | | | | |
| 100.0 | 100.0 | 100.0 | | Net Sales | 100.0 | 100.0 | 100.0 | 100.0 | 100.0 | 100.0 |
| | | | | Gross Profit | | | | | | |
| 92.1 | 92.5 | 95.0 | | Operating Expenses | 68.3 | 100.8 | 91.2 | 97.7 | 93.5 | 97.5 |
| 7.9 | 7.5 | 5.0 | | Operating Profit | 31.7 | -.8 | 8.8 | 2.3 | 6.5 | 2.5 |
| -.7 | .5 | .8 | | All Other Expenses (net) | 8.6 | .7 | -.6 | .0 | -.3 | .8 |
| 8.6 | 7.0 | 4.2 | | Profit Before Taxes | 23.2 | -1.5 | 9.3 | 2.3 | 6.8 | 1.8 |
| | | | | RATIOS | | | | | | |
| 5.0 | 6.8 | 4.9 | | | 18.3 | 6.0 | 20.5 | 6.5 | 9.9 | 3.8 |
| 2.4 | 2.8 | 2.3 | | Current | 1.6 | .9 | 1.9 | 1.7 | 3.5 | 2.2 |
| 1.5 | 1.4 | 1.2 | | | .3 | .4 | .7 | 1.1 | 1.7 | 1.3 |
| 5.0 | 6.2 | 4.7 | | | 9.8 | 6.0 | 20.2 | 6.1 | 9.5 | 3.7 |
| 2.3 | 2.7 | 2.1 | | Quick | 1.6 | .9 | 1.9 | 1.7 | 2.7 | 2.0 |
| 1.5 | 1.3 | 1.1 | | | .3 | .4 | .5 | .8 | 1.4 | 1.1 |
| 33 11.2 | 23 15.6 | 23 15.8 | | | 0 UND | 0 UND | 0 UND | 25 14.6 | 19 19.3 | 31 11.6 |
| 47 7.8 | 41 8.9 | 41 8.9 | | Sales/Receivables | 0 UND | 26 13.9 | 7 49.0 | 50 7.3 | 37 9.8 | 46 8.0 |
| 63 5.8 | 61 6.0 | 57 6.4 | | | 30 12.3 | 50 7.3 | 37 9.9 | 68 5.4 | 57 6.4 | 60 6.1 |
| | | | | Cost of Sales/Inventory | | | | | | |
| | | | | Cost of Sales/Payables | | | | | | |
| 5.4 | 5.9 | 6.4 | | | 2.2 | 5.8 | 10.6 | 6.2 | 5.1 | 7.4 |
| 9.3 | 9.5 | 12.5 | | Sales/Working Capital | 6.5 | -256.3 | 34.4 | 11.4 | 9.3 | 12.8 |
| 17.1 | 23.8 | 40.0 | | | -3.2 | -6.1 | -45.0 | 333.5 | 18.8 | 28.6 |
| 107.3 | 79.6 | 27.8 | | | | | | 24.4 | 116.8 | 22.9 |
| (110) 23.1 | (182) 18.0 | (196) 5.9 | | EBIT/Interest | | | (17) 1.6 | (37) 15.9 | (128) 5.4 |
| 5.1 | 4.5 | .5 | | | | | | -12.0 | 4.8 | .5 |
| | 37.4 | 49.4 | | | | | | | | 52.5 |
| | (16) 11.8 | (26) 10.5 | | Net Profit + Depr., Dep., Amort./Cur. Mat. L/T/D | | | | | (22) 15.2 |
| | 3.1 | 2.3 | | | | | | | | 2.3 |
| .0 | .0 | .0 | | | .0 | .0 | .0 | .0 | .0 | .0 |
| .0 | .0 | .1 | | Fixed/Worth | .0 | .0 | .0 | .0 | .0 | .1 |
| .6 | .2 | .3 | | | 1.8 | 1.4 | .1 | .7 | .1 | .5 |
| .4 | .2 | .3 | | | .2 | .3 | .1 | .2 | .2 | .5 |
| 1.2 | .8 | 1.1 | | Debt/Worth | 1.5 | 7.7 | 1.4 | .8 | .6 | 1.3 |
| 18.4 | 4.9 | 7.2 | | | 8.5 | -1.5 | -2.5 | 5.4 | 1.6 | 11.5 |
| 96.4 | 93.5 | 68.8 | | | 60.1 | 332.6 | | 84.7 | 94.8 | 61.3 |
| (123) 54.0 | (230) 42.3 | (235) 30.4 | | % Profit Before Taxes/Tangible Net Worth | (12) 9.3 | (10) 30.3 | (20) 38.4 | (64) 36.4 | (121) 29.0 |
| 29.6 | 14.4 | 8.3 | | | 1.0 | -31.2 | | -5.4 | 6.5 | 12.1 |
| 45.6 | 39.8 | 28.3 | | | 18.9 | 14.7 | 192.3 | 40.0 | 44.7 | 23.8 |
| 21.7 | 16.4 | 10.4 | | % Profit Before Taxes/Total Assets | 4.4 | -.8 | 28.8 | 7.2 | 18.3 | 9.4 |
| 8.1 | 5.5 | .1 | | | .6 | -63.3 | 15.6 | -9.4 | 3.7 | -.2 |
| 999.8 | 999.8 | 999.8 | | | UND | UND | UND | 999.8 | 600.4 | 630.4 |
| 262.3 | 300.7 | 211.8 | | Sales/Net Fixed Assets | 34.4 | 999.8 | UND | 481.3 | 193.8 | 174.6 |
| 90.5 | 77.1 | 55.5 | | | .2 | 101.2 | 422.5 | 106.3 | 55.3 | 55.1 |
| 5.5 | 6.2 | 5.8 | | | 3.6 | 6.9 | 17.0 | 5.0 | 6.2 | 5.6 |
| 3.8 | 4.3 | 3.9 | | Sales/Total Assets | .4 | 4.3 | 11.1 | 3.7 | 3.5 | 4.0 |
| 2.7 | 2.5 | 2.4 | | | .2 | 2.2 | 3.1 | 1.9 | 2.5 | 3.0 |
| .1 | .0 | .1 | | | | | | .0 | .1 | .1 |
| (69) .2 | (116) .2 | (138) .2 | | % Depr., Dep., Amort./Sales | | | (11) .1 | (31) .2 | (84) .2 |
| .3 | .4 | .6 | | | | | | 1.5 | .5 | .5 |
| .8 | .8 | .9 | | | | | | | 1.0 | .6 |
| (35) 1.9 | (67) 2.9 | (77) 2.0 | | % Officers', Directors' Owners' Comp/Sales | | | | (28) 2.0 | (28) 1.5 |
| 4.8 | 5.7 | 4.7 | | | | | | | 3.8 | 2.5 |
| 11956864M | 16897507M | 18655269M | | Net Sales ($) | 7243M | 34783M | 50789M | 188923M | 1089113M | 17284418M |
| 4169148M | 5066322M | 6029837M | | Total Assets ($) | 15253M | 14695M | 11423M | 104673M | 375655M | 5508138M |

© RMA 2024  M = $ thousand  MM = $ million
See Pages viii through xx for Explanation of Ratios and Data

# ADMIN & WASTE MANAGEMENT SERVICES—Executive Search Services  NAICS 561312

## Current Data Sorted by Assets | Comparative Historical Data

| | | | | | | Type of Statement | | |
|---|---|---|---|---|---|---|---|---|
| | | | 1 | 2 | 1 | Unqualified | 2 | 4 |
| | | | 1 | 1 | 1 | Reviewed | 2 | 1 |
| | | 1 | 3 | | | Compiled | 1 | 1 |
| 1 | 3 | | | | | Tax Returns | 2 | |
| 3 | 2 | 3 | | 5 | 1 | Other | 19 | 15 |
| | 6 (4/1-9/30/23) | | 24 (10/1/23-3/31/24) | | | | 4/1/19-3/31/20 | 4/1/20-3/31/21 |
| 0-500M | 500M-2MM | 2-10MM | 10-50MM | 50-100MM | 100-250MM | | ALL | ALL |
| 4 | 5 | 8 | 8 | 2 | 3 | NUMBER OF STATEMENTS | 26 | 21 |
| % | % | % | % | % | % | ASSETS | % | % |
| | | | | | | Cash & Equivalents | 15.2 | 35.2 |
| | | | | | | Trade Receivables (net) | 52.5 | 31.6 |
| | | | | | | Inventory | .4 | .9 |
| | | | | | | All Other Current | 4.2 | 4.0 |
| | | | | | | Total Current | 72.3 | 71.6 |
| | | | | | | Fixed Assets (net) | 4.2 | 6.9 |
| | | | | | | Intangibles (net) | 11.6 | 13.2 |
| | | | | | | All Other Non-Current | 11.9 | 8.3 |
| | | | | | | Total | 100.0 | 100.0 |
| | | | | | | LIABILITIES | | |
| | | | | | | Notes Payable-Short Term | 21.1 | 9.9 |
| | | | | | | Cur. Mat.-L.T.D. | 2.9 | 2.7 |
| | | | | | | Trade Payables | 8.2 | 4.5 |
| | | | | | | Income Taxes Payable | .0 | .1 |
| | | | | | | All Other Current | 22.2 | 15.7 |
| | | | | | | Total Current | 54.4 | 32.8 |
| | | | | | | Long-Term Debt | 4.8 | 29.9 |
| | | | | | | Deferred Taxes | .0 | .0 |
| | | | | | | All Other Non-Current | 8.0 | 3.1 |
| | | | | | | Net Worth | 32.8 | 34.2 |
| | | | | | | Total Liabilities & Net Worth | 100.0 | 100.0 |
| | | | | | | INCOME DATA | | |
| | | | | | | Net Sales | 100.0 | 100.0 |
| | | | | | | Gross Profit | | |
| | | | | | | Operating Expenses | 92.1 | 94.9 |
| | | | | | | Operating Profit | 7.9 | 5.1 |
| | | | | | | All Other Expenses (net) | .2 | -.5 |
| | | | | | | Profit Before Taxes | 7.7 | 5.6 |
| | | | | | | RATIOS | | |
| | | | | | | | 2.9 | 11.3 |
| | | | | | | Current | 1.7 | 2.1 |
| | | | | | | | .9 | 1.3 |
| | | | | | | | 2.7 | 11.3 |
| | | | | | | Quick | 1.4 | 2.0 |
| | | | | | | | .8 | 1.1 |
| | | | | | | Sales/Receivables | 29  12.5 | 3  144.1 |
| | | | | | | | 42  8.6 | 44  8.3 |
| | | | | | | | 56  6.5 | 51  7.2 |
| | | | | | | Cost of Sales/Inventory | | |
| | | | | | | Cost of Sales/Payables | | |
| | | | | | | | 9.9 | 4.5 |
| | | | | | | Sales/Working Capital | 19.0 | 7.5 |
| | | | | | | | -72.7 | 34.8 |
| | | | | | | | 38.3 | 38.2 |
| | | | | | | EBIT/Interest | (22) 9.5 | (15) 9.5 |
| | | | | | | | 2.7 | -.5 |
| | | | | | | Net Profit + Depr., Dep., Amort./Cur. Mat. L/T/D | | |
| | | | | | | | .0 | .0 |
| | | | | | | Fixed/Worth | .1 | .2 |
| | | | | | | | NM | 1.5 |
| | | | | | | | .5 | 1.9 |
| | | | | | | Debt/Worth | 2.9 | 4.4 |
| | | | | | | | NM | -11.3 |
| | | | | | | % Profit Before Taxes/Tangible Net Worth | 219.0 | 76.2 |
| | | | | | | | (20) 67.7 | (15) 44.0 |
| | | | | | | | 21.4 | -19.9 |
| | | | | | | % Profit Before Taxes/Total Assets | 44.0 | 37.9 |
| | | | | | | | 15.8 | 10.7 |
| | | | | | | | 5.5 | -7.3 |
| | | | | | | Sales/Net Fixed Assets | 496.0 | 211.5 |
| | | | | | | | 168.8 | 109.3 |
| | | | | | | | 81.4 | 43.0 |
| | | | | | | Sales/Total Assets | 7.8 | 4.7 |
| | | | | | | | 4.9 | 3.1 |
| | | | | | | | 3.0 | 1.7 |
| | | | | | | % Depr., Dep., Amort./Sales | .1 | .1 |
| | | | | | | | (16) .3 | (10) .4 |
| | | | | | | | .6 | .8 |
| | | | | | | % Officers', Directors' Owners' Comp/Sales | | |
| 7315M | 26122M | 168074M | 463412M | 394155M | 473462M | Net Sales ($) | 1298272M | 2033973M |
| 1205M | 6310M | 47254M | 179859M | 169527M | 550097M | Total Assets ($) | 430492M | 757950M |

© RMA 2024

M = $ thousand    MM = $ million
See Pages viii through xx for Explanation of Ratios and Data

# ADMIN & WASTE MANAGEMENT SERVICES—Executive Search Services  NAICS 561312

**1073**

## Comparative Historical Data / Current Data Sorted by Sales

| | | | | Type of Statement | | | | | | |
|---|---|---|---|---|---|---|---|---|---|---|
| | | 1 | 4 | Unqualified | | | | | 1 | 3 |
| 2 | 2 | 2 | 3 | Reviewed | | | | | | 3 |
| 3 | 4 | 4 | 3 | Compiled | | | | 3 | | |
| 4 | 6 | 6 | 4 | Tax Returns | | 1 | 1 | | | |
| 10 | 13 | 13 | 16 | Other | 2 | 4 | 1 | 1 | 2 | 9 |
| 4/1/21-3/31/22 ALL | | 4/1/22-3/31/23 ALL | 4/1/23-3/31/24 ALL | | 0-1MM | 6 (4/1-9/30/23) 1-3MM | 3-5MM | 24 (10/1/23-3/31/24) 5-10MM | 10-25MM | 25MM & OVER |
| 19 | | 26 | 30 | **NUMBER OF STATEMENTS** | | 6 | 1 | 2 | 6 | 15 |
| % | | % | % | **ASSETS** | % | % | % | % | % | % |
| 44.8 | | 34.8 | 28.8 | Cash & Equivalents | | | | | | 24.5 |
| 31.5 | | 34.2 | 35.2 | Trade Receivables (net) | | | | | | 34.7 |
| .0 | | .0 | .0 | Inventory | D | | | | | .0 |
| 3.4 | | 6.7 | 4.7 | All Other Current | A | | | | | 3.4 |
| 79.6 | | 75.6 | 68.7 | Total Current | T | | | | | 62.5 |
| 3.0 | | 5.6 | 5.2 | Fixed Assets (net) | A | | | | | 4.1 |
| 11.9 | | 8.2 | 13.3 | Intangibles (net) | | | | | | 16.9 |
| 5.5 | | 10.5 | 12.8 | All Other Non-Current | N | | | | | 16.4 |
| 100.0 | | 100.0 | 100.0 | Total | O | | | | | 100.0 |
| | | | | **LIABILITIES** | T | | | | | |
| 5.9 | | 8.1 | 11.0 | Notes Payable-Short Term | A | | | | | 7.7 |
| 1.5 | | 2.0 | 2.6 | Cur. Mat.-L.T.D. | V | | | | | 1.1 |
| 4.8 | | 6.6 | 4.7 | Trade Payables | A | | | | | 2.9 |
| .4 | | .1 | .0 | Income Taxes Payable | I | | | | | .0 |
| 15.5 | | 15.1 | 25.7 | All Other Current | L | | | | | 16.3 |
| 28.1 | | 32.0 | 43.9 | Total Current | A | | | | | 28.1 |
| 15.8 | | 24.9 | 15.1 | Long-Term Debt | B | | | | | 8.6 |
| .2 | | .0 | .2 | Deferred Taxes | L | | | | | .4 |
| 1.9 | | 2.7 | 4.2 | All Other Non-Current | E | | | | | 7.8 |
| 53.9 | | 40.5 | 36.6 | Net Worth | | | | | | 55.1 |
| 100.0 | | 100.0 | 100.0 | Total Liabilties & Net Worth | | | | | | 100.0 |
| | | | | **INCOME DATA** | | | | | | |
| 100.0 | | 100.0 | 100.0 | Net Sales | | | | | | 100.0 |
| | | | | Gross Profit | | | | | | |
| 81.4 | | 88.7 | 97.0 | Operating Expenses | | | | | | 94.6 |
| 18.6 | | 11.3 | 3.0 | Operating Profit | | | | | | 5.4 |
| -2.8 | | .5 | .4 | All Other Expenses (net) | | | | | | .5 |
| 21.4 | | 10.7 | 2.7 | Profit Before Taxes | | | | | | 4.9 |
| | | | | **RATIOS** | | | | | | |
| 6.4 | | 5.2 | 4.3 | | | | | | | 4.2 |
| 2.7 | | 2.2 | 1.8 | Current | | | | | | 2.1 |
| 1.6 | | 1.4 | 1.3 | | | | | | | 1.7 |
| 6.4 | | 5.1 | 4.3 | | | | | | | 4.0 |
| 2.7 | | 2.0 | 1.8 | Quick | | | | | | 1.8 |
| 1.5 | | 1.2 | 1.3 | | | | | | | 1.3 |
| 0 UND | 0 | UND | 25 14.4 | | | | | | 42 | 8.6 |
| 42 8.6 | 30 | 12.3 | 45 8.1 | Sales/Receivables | | | | | 55 | 6.6 |
| 54 6.8 | 54 | 6.8 | 62 5.9 | | | | | | 65 | 5.6 |
| | | | | Cost of Sales/Inventory | | | | | | |
| | | | | Cost of Sales/Payables | | | | | | |
| 3.4 | | 5.6 | 4.6 | | | | | | | 4.2 |
| 7.5 | | 8.4 | 11.5 | Sales/Working Capital | | | | | | 5.2 |
| 14.2 | | 37.9 | 30.5 | | | | | | | 13.7 |
| 315.9 | | 72.6 | 31.3 | | | | | | | 24.3 |
| (13) 63.0 | (15) | 10.4 | (26) 6.8 | EBIT/Interest | | | | | (14) | 6.8 |
| 22.7 | | 3.9 | 1.1 | | | | | | | 1.1 |
| | | | | Net Profit + Depr., Dep., Amort./Cur. Mat. L/T/D | | | | | | |
| .0 | | .0 | .0 | | | | | | | .0 |
| .0 | | .0 | .1 | Fixed/Worth | | | | | | .1 |
| .1 | | NM | .4 | | | | | | | .5 |
| .3 | | .4 | .5 | | | | | | | .4 |
| .8 | | 1.3 | 1.3 | Debt/Worth | | | | | | 1.1 |
| 2.6 | | NM | NM | | | | | | | 1.6 |
| 146.8 | | 164.2 | 40.7 | | | | | | | 42.5 |
| (17) 100.0 | (20) | 41.9 | (23) 30.6 | % Profit Before Taxes/Tangible Net Worth | | | | | (12) | 28.7 |
| 59.0 | | 24.3 | 3.7 | | | | | | | 6.0 |
| 88.0 | | 62.7 | 22.1 | | | | | | | 26.0 |
| 38.6 | | 20.3 | 8.7 | % Profit Before Taxes/Total Assets | | | | | | 8.4 |
| 23.3 | | 10.3 | .3 | | | | | | | .5 |
| UND | | UND | 375.2 | | | | | | | 246.3 |
| 516.7 | | 183.1 | 123.5 | Sales/Net Fixed Assets | | | | | | 101.5 |
| 101.8 | | 66.6 | 29.1 | | | | | | | 27.3 |
| 5.0 | | 6.0 | 4.6 | | | | | | | 4.0 |
| 3.6 | | 3.7 | 3.6 | Sales/Total Assets | | | | | | 1.8 |
| 1.8 | | 2.6 | 1.6 | | | | | | | 1.2 |
| | | .1 | .0 | | | | | | | .1 |
| | (13) | .2 | (21) .2 | % Depr., Dep., Amort./Sales | | | | | (12) | .3 |
| | | | .5 .8 | | | | | | | 1.0 |
| | | | | % Officers', Directors' Owners' Comp/Sales | | | | | | |
| 606663M | | 1064001M | 1532540M | Net Sales ($) | 12163M | 3951M | 17323M | 107256M | | 1391847M |
| 257943M | | 421145M | 954252M | Total Assets ($) | 3285M | 680M | 3550M | 33523M | | 913214M |

© RMA 2024    M = $ thousand    MM = $ million
See Pages viii through xx for Explanation of Ratios and Data

# ADMIN & WASTE MANAGEMENT SERVICES—Temporary Help Services  NAICS 561320

## Current Data Sorted by Assets | Comparative Historical Data

| | | | | | | | Type of Statement | | | | |
|---|---|---|---|---|---|---|---|---|---|---|---|
| | | 1 | 2 | 13 | 2 | 3 | Unqualified | | 24 | | 11 |
| | | 1 | 12 | 14 | 4 | | Reviewed | | 29 | | 17 |
| | 3 | 3 | 14 | 2 | | | Compiled | | 13 | | 7 |
| | 6 | 9 | 3 | 2 | | | Tax Returns | | 25 | | 6 |
| | | 18 | 48 | 40 | 18 | 11 | Other | | 199 | | 104 |
| | | 35 (4/1-9/30/23) | | 194 (10/1/23-3/31/24) | | | | | 4/1/19-3/31/20 | | 4/1/20-3/31/21 |
| 0-500M | 500M-2MM | 2-10MM | 10-50MM | 50-100MM | 100-250MM | | | | ALL | | ALL |
| 9 | 32 | 79 | 71 | 24 | 14 | | NUMBER OF STATEMENTS | | 290 | | 145 |
| % | % | % | % | % | % | | ASSETS | | % | | % |
| | 29.6 | 21.2 | 20.4 | 12.3 | 5.8 | | Cash & Equivalents | | 14.0 | | 30.7 |
| | 45.6 | 48.7 | 49.2 | 47.0 | 39.2 | | Trade Receivables (net) | | 53.8 | | 39.4 |
| | .0 | .0 | .6 | .0 | .0 | | Inventory | | .5 | | .0 |
| | 6.1 | 2.9 | 5.2 | 2.3 | 3.3 | | All Other Current | | 5.8 | | 4.3 |
| | 81.3 | 72.8 | 75.4 | 61.6 | 48.3 | | Total Current | | 74.1 | | 74.3 |
| | 6.6 | 8.1 | 5.1 | 6.3 | 5.1 | | Fixed Assets (net) | | 6.8 | | 5.4 |
| | 5.4 | 5.2 | 10.0 | 21.9 | 34.7 | | Intangibles (net) | | 10.2 | | 11.3 |
| | 6.8 | 13.9 | 9.4 | 10.1 | 12.0 | | All Other Non-Current | | 8.9 | | 9.1 |
| | 100.0 | 100.0 | 100.0 | 100.0 | 100.0 | | Total | | 100.0 | | 100.0 |
| | | | | | | | LIABILITIES | | | | |
| | 14.9 | 8.9 | 10.6 | 4.3 | 9.3 | | Notes Payable-Short Term | | 16.0 | | 11.8 |
| | 1.1 | 1.7 | 2.0 | 1.3 | 12.0 | | Cur. Mat.-L.T.D. | | 1.7 | | 1.7 |
| | 4.5 | 6.4 | 8.4 | 6.8 | 5.7 | | Trade Payables | | 7.1 | | 5.2 |
| | .1 | .0 | .5 | .0 | .0 | | Income Taxes Payable | | .2 | | .1 |
| | 21.9 | 14.3 | 14.0 | 15.8 | 18.8 | | All Other Current | | 19.0 | | 16.5 |
| | 42.5 | 31.4 | 35.4 | 28.2 | 45.8 | | Total Current | | 44.0 | | 35.3 |
| | 10.7 | 5.4 | 8.7 | 13.0 | 14.2 | | Long-Term Debt | | 7.2 | | 18.6 |
| | .0 | .0 | .3 | .1 | .0 | | Deferred Taxes | | .0 | | .2 |
| | 1.8 | 5.8 | 9.2 | 6.3 | 8.0 | | All Other Non-Current | | 7.3 | | 5.4 |
| | 45.1 | 57.4 | 46.4 | 52.4 | 32.0 | | Net Worth | | 41.4 | | 40.4 |
| | 100.0 | 100.0 | 100.0 | 100.0 | 100.0 | | Total Liabilities & Net Worth | | 100.0 | | 100.0 |
| | | | | | | | INCOME DATA | | | | |
| | 100.0 | 100.0 | 100.0 | 100.0 | 100.0 | | Net Sales | | 100.0 | | 100.0 |
| | | | | | | | Gross Profit | | | | |
| | 95.1 | 94.3 | 95.3 | 94.5 | 91.4 | | Operating Expenses | | 94.6 | | 95.2 |
| | 4.9 | 5.7 | 4.7 | 5.5 | 8.6 | | Operating Profit | | 5.4 | | 4.8 |
| | 1.7 | .4 | .2 | .5 | 2.5 | | All Other Expenses (net) | | .6 | | -.6 |
| | 3.3 | 5.2 | 4.5 | 4.9 | 6.1 | | Profit Before Taxes | | 4.8 | | 5.4 |
| | | | | | | | RATIOS | | | | |
| | 4.7 | 9.3 | 4.2 | 6.2 | 1.9 | | | | 3.2 | | 6.9 |
| | 2.6 | 3.5 | 2.3 | 2.5 | 1.3 | | Current | | 1.7 | | 2.4 |
| | 1.2 | 1.7 | 1.4 | 1.3 | .7 | | | | 1.2 | | 1.3 |
| | 4.7 | 9.3 | 4.1 | 5.8 | 1.8 | | | | 3.0 | | 6.4 |
| | 2.2 | 3.5 | 2.0 | 2.2 | 1.1 | | Quick | | 1.6 | | 2.2 |
| | 1.1 | 1.6 | 1.4 | 1.3 | .7 | | | | 1.1 | | 1.2 |
| 0 | 758.6 | 26 | 13.8 | 32 | 11.5 | 36 | 10.2 | 41 | 9.0 | | | | | | |
| 33 | 11.2 | 39 | 9.3 | 39 | 9.3 | 46 | 7.9 | 44 | 8.3 | | Sales/Receivables | | 29 | 12.6 | 26 | 14.2 |
| 50 | 7.3 | 57 | 6.4 | 60 | 6.1 | 52 | 7.0 | 63 | 5.8 | | | | 43 | 8.4 | 43 | 8.4 |
| | | | | | | | | | | | | | 58 | 6.3 | 54 | 6.7 |
| | | | | | | | Cost of Sales/Inventory | | | | |
| | | | | | | | Cost of Sales/Payables | | | | |
| | 7.2 | 5.4 | 5.5 | 5.6 | 9.0 | | | | 9.0 | | 5.0 |
| | 13.6 | 8.3 | 11.6 | 12.1 | 31.3 | | Sales/Working Capital | | 15.6 | | 8.3 |
| | 60.7 | 17.0 | 19.4 | 25.0 | -14.8 | | | | 36.5 | | 23.8 |
| | 26.5 | 46.7 | 39.9 | 40.2 | 18.3 | | | | 26.5 | | 47.5 |
| (19) | 1.0 | (61) | 13.6 | (51) | 7.9 | (21) | 11.0 | 3.9 | | EBIT/Interest | (230) | 7.4 | (114) | 11.2 |
| | -3.6 | 1.9 | 3.2 | 4.5 | 1.0 | | | | 2.4 | | 2.4 |
| | | | | | | | Net Profit + Depr., Dep., Amort./Cur. Mat. L/T/D | | 33.4 | | 15.3 |
| | | | | | | | | (24) | 6.9 | (12) | 5.9 |
| | | | | | | | | | 3.4 | | .6 |
| | .0 | .0 | .0 | .0 | .2 | | | | .0 | | .0 |
| | .0 | .1 | .1 | .1 | -2.4 | | Fixed/Worth | | .1 | | .1 |
| | .2 | .2 | .2 | .7 | -.1 | | | | .3 | | .6 |
| | .5 | .1 | .4 | .4 | 1.6 | | | | .6 | | .5 |
| | .6 | .5 | .9 | 1.3 | -18.8 | | Debt/Worth | | 1.6 | | 2.2 |
| | 32.3 | 2.6 | 2.3 | 4.8 | -3.7 | | | | 4.5 | | 10.8 |
| | 63.8 | 48.8 | 65.9 | 59.1 | | | | | 76.7 | | 79.7 |
| (25) | 19.8 | (71) | 26.3 | (63) | 33.1 | (20) | 43.8 | | % Profit Before Taxes/Tangible Net Worth | (250) | 36.0 | (117) | 40.6 |
| | -3.9 | 4.2 | 12.7 | 23.4 | | | | | 12.3 | | 15.1 |
| | 27.8 | 26.8 | 31.7 | 28.2 | 34.8 | | | | 26.1 | | 23.9 |
| | 7.0 | 9.0 | 16.9 | 11.7 | 6.7 | | % Profit Before Taxes/Total Assets | | 11.3 | | 12.1 |
| | -3.1 | 2.6 | 5.0 | 5.9 | -.8 | | | | 3.0 | | 2.4 |
| | UND | 999.8 | 512.3 | 494.3 | 156.6 | | | | 911.6 | | 838.6 |
| | 686.6 | 131.4 | 194.0 | 114.0 | 60.9 | | Sales/Net Fixed Assets | | 176.4 | | 198.4 |
| | 99.2 | 54.6 | 69.9 | 50.7 | 39.0 | | | | 71.1 | | 63.0 |
| | 7.0 | 5.8 | 5.2 | 4.4 | 3.8 | | | | 6.5 | | 4.7 |
| | 5.1 | 4.3 | 4.2 | 2.9 | 2.6 | | Sales/Total Assets | | 4.7 | | 3.4 |
| | 3.3 | 2.9 | 2.9 | 2.4 | 1.9 | | | | 3.3 | | 2.3 |
| | | .1 | .1 | .2 | | | | | .1 | | .1 |
| | (47) | .2 | (49) | .1 | (15) | .6 | | % Depr., Dep., Amort./Sales | (164) | .2 | (79) | .3 |
| | | .4 | .4 | .9 | | | | | .5 | | .5 |
| | 2.3 | 1.2 | .4 | | | | | | .6 | | .7 |
| (11) | 3.8 | (15) | 1.8 | (11) | .7 | | | % Officers', Directors' Owners' Comp/Sales | (55) | 1.9 | (30) | 1.9 |
| | | | 1.8 | | | | | | 3.2 | | 3.4 |
| 21786M | 262801M | 2055319M | 6520044M | 5748363M | 6605279M | | Net Sales ($) | | 21926008M | | 11331061M |
| 2466M | 42095M | 438906M | 1646888M | 1664462M | 2267234M | | Total Assets ($) | | 5817841M | | 3629182M |

M = $ thousand    MM = $ million

© RMA 2024

# ADMIN & WASTE MANAGEMENT SERVICES—Temporary Help Services  NAICS 561320

| Comparative Historical Data ||| Type of Statement | Current Data Sorted by Sales ||||||
|---|---|---|---|---|---|---|---|---|---|
| 17 | 20 | 21 | Unqualified | | | | | 3 | 18 |
| 13 | 21 | 31 | Reviewed | | | | | 9 | 22 |
| 6 | 20 | 19 | Compiled | | 1 | | 4 | 5 | 9 |
| 6 | 17 | 17 | Tax Returns | 2 | 3 | 3 | 2 | 5 | 2 |
| 96 | 102 | 141 | Other | 5 | 5 | 4 | 16 | 22 | 89 |
| 4/1/21- | 4/1/22- | 4/1/23- | | 35 (4/1-9/30/23) ||| 194 (10/1/23-3/31/24) |||
| 3/31/22 | 3/31/23 | 3/31/24 | | | | | | | |
| ALL | ALL | ALL | | 0-1MM | 1-3MM | 3-5MM | 5-10MM | 10-25MM | 25MM & OVER |
| 138 | 180 | 229 | NUMBER OF STATEMENTS | 7 | 9 | 7 | 22 | 44 | 140 |
| % | % | % | ASSETS | % | % | % | % | % | % |
| 22.4 | 21.7 | 20.3 | Cash & Equivalents | | | | 22.4 | 23.3 | 17.3 |
| 49.7 | 49.2 | 47.1 | Trade Receivables (net) | | | | 44.5 | 44.0 | 50.6 |
| .5 | .6 | .2 | Inventory | | | | .0 | .1 | .3 |
| 4.3 | 4.0 | 3.9 | All Other Current | | | | 5.9 | 3.8 | 4.1 |
| 76.9 | 75.4 | 71.5 | Total Current | | | | 72.8 | 71.1 | 72.2 |
| 5.0 | 7.3 | 7.6 | Fixed Assets (net) | | | | 7.8 | 6.9 | 5.3 |
| 8.6 | 6.6 | 10.0 | Intangibles (net) | | | | 10.0 | 7.5 | 11.9 |
| 9.5 | 10.6 | 10.8 | All Other Non-Current | | | | 9.4 | 14.5 | 10.5 |
| 100.0 | 100.0 | 100.0 | Total | | | | 100.0 | 100.0 | 100.0 |
| | | | LIABILITIES | | | | | | |
| 11.1 | 9.2 | 11.7 | Notes Payable-Short Term | | | | 8.5 | 15.0 | 8.7 |
| 1.5 | 1.4 | 2.5 | Cur. Mat.-L.T.D. | | | | .2 | 2.7 | 2.6 |
| 5.8 | 10.4 | 6.9 | Trade Payables | | | | 4.8 | 5.2 | 8.0 |
| .2 | .1 | .2 | Income Taxes Payable | | | | .0 | .1 | .3 |
| 15.2 | 17.2 | 15.4 | All Other Current | | | | 15.5 | 11.9 | 17.1 |
| 33.9 | 38.3 | 36.5 | Total Current | | | | 29.0 | 34.8 | 36.7 |
| 15.5 | 9.8 | 9.4 | Long-Term Debt | | | | 4.6 | 6.4 | 8.4 |
| .0 | .0 | .1 | Deferred Taxes | | | | .0 | .0 | .2 |
| 7.1 | 4.9 | 6.8 | All Other Non-Current | | | | 7.5 | 7.0 | 7.6 |
| 43.5 | 46.9 | 47.1 | Net Worth | | | | 59.0 | 51.8 | 47.1 |
| 100.0 | 100.0 | 100.0 | Total Liabilities & Net Worth | | | | 100.0 | 100.0 | 100.0 |
| | | | INCOME DATA | | | | | | |
| 100.0 | 100.0 | 100.0 | Net Sales | | | | 100.0 | 100.0 | 100.0 |
| | | | Gross Profit | | | | | | |
| 93.8 | 93.1 | 94.4 | Operating Expenses | | | | 96.1 | 96.3 | 95.1 |
| 6.2 | 6.9 | 5.6 | Operating Profit | | | | 3.9 | 3.7 | 4.9 |
| -1.7 | .4 | .7 | All Other Expenses (net) | | | | .0 | .3 | .4 |
| 7.8 | 6.5 | 5.0 | Profit Before Taxes | | | | 3.9 | 3.4 | 4.6 |
| | | | RATIOS | | | | | | |
| 5.4 | 5.1 | 5.4 | | | | | 8.9 | 8.5 | 4.3 |
| 2.5 | 2.6 | 2.5 | Current | | | | 3.4 | 2.5 | 2.3 |
| 1.6 | 1.4 | 1.3 | | | | | 1.2 | 1.3 | 1.4 |
| 4.9 | 5.0 | 5.3 | | | | | 7.3 | 8.4 | 4.2 |
| 2.3 | 2.4 | 2.2 | Quick | | | | 3.4 | 2.1 | 2.1 |
| 1.5 | 1.2 | 1.3 | | | | | 1.3 | 1.3 | 1.3 |
| 33  10.9 | 30  12.1 | 29  12.8 | | 18  20.1 | | | 27  13.4 | 32  11.3 | |
| 47  7.8 | 43  8.4 | 40  9.1 | Sales/Receivables | 40  9.1 | | | 40  9.1 | 41  9.0 | |
| 63  5.8 | 61  6.0 | 55  6.6 | | 59  6.2 | | | 54  6.7 | 54  6.7 | |
| | | | Cost of Sales/Inventory | | | | | | |
| | | | Cost of Sales/Payables | | | | | | |
| 5.4 | 5.7 | 5.9 | | | | | 5.9 | 5.5 | 6.6 |
| 8.8 | 9.5 | 11.4 | Sales/Working Capital | | | | 7.7 | 11.1 | 11.8 |
| 16.9 | 19.1 | 30.7 | | | | | 44.6 | 32.5 | 32.1 |
| 121.3 | 73.3 | 38.9 | | | | | 49.2 | 48.1 | 41.8 |
| (106) 31.5 | (127) 22.6 | (174) 7.3 | EBIT/Interest | (17) 2.9 | | | (31) 5.4 | (111) 10.7 | |
| 7.4 | 3.7 | 1.9 | | | | | .3 | 1.3 | 3.6 |
| | 27.7 | 116.1 | | | | | | | 98.8 |
| (18) | 18.3 | (19) 20.8 | Net Profit + Depr., Dep., Amort./Cur. Mat. L/T/D | | | | | (16) 21.1 | |
| | 4.5 | 4.7 | | | | | | | 5.7 |
| .0 | .0 | .0 | | | | | .0 | .0 | .0 |
| .1 | .0 | .1 | Fixed/Worth | | | | .1 | .1 | .1 |
| .3 | .3 | .4 | | | | | .1 | .4 | .4 |
| .3 | .3 | .3 | | | | | .2 | .2 | .4 |
| 1.0 | .9 | .8 | Debt/Worth | | | | .5 | .8 | .9 |
| 4.8 | 3.8 | 4.0 | | | | | 2.1 | 4.2 | 4.4 |
| 96.0 | 70.9 | 60.6 | | | | | 66.8 | 48.4 | 64.4 |
| (113) 54.8 | (159) 43.4 | (191) 30.3 | % Profit Before Taxes/Tangible Net Worth | (18) 27.0 | | | (37) 21.7 | (116) 34.0 | |
| 29.5 | 16.5 | 10.5 | | | | | -1.4 | 1.0 | 12.9 |
| 43.7 | 37.2 | 28.4 | | | | | 35.5 | 26.3 | 31.4 |
| 26.2 | 17.0 | 11.6 | % Profit Before Taxes/Total Assets | | | | 13.1 | 7.0 | 14.2 |
| 9.8 | 4.8 | 2.8 | | | | | -.8 | .1 | 5.1 |
| 758.7 | 999.8 | 883.2 | | | | | UND | 999.8 | 510.1 |
| 226.1 | 266.9 | 170.4 | Sales/Net Fixed Assets | | | | 152.5 | 365.6 | 134.9 |
| 63.1 | 65.9 | 55.8 | | | | | 44.9 | 59.7 | 62.3 |
| 5.4 | 5.7 | 5.8 | | | | | 6.0 | 5.8 | 5.9 |
| 3.7 | 3.9 | 4.0 | Sales/Total Assets | | | | 4.2 | 3.7 | 4.3 |
| 2.6 | 2.7 | 2.7 | | | | | 3.0 | 2.5 | 2.9 |
| .1 | .1 | .1 | | | | | .1 | | .1 |
| (74) .2 | (93) .2 | (132) .3 | % Depr., Dep., Amort./Sales | | | | (22) .1 | (94) .2 | |
| .5 | .8 | .6 | | | | | .5 | | .6 |
| 1.4 | .6 | .8 | | | | | 1.3 | | .6 |
| (27) 2.1 | (46) 1.8 | (45) 1.8 | % Officers', Directors' Owners' Comp/Sales | | | | (13) 2.2 | (21) .8 | |
| 3.7 | 3.6 | 5.4 | | | | | 3.7 | | 2.0 |
| 14287243M | 15307126M | 21213592M | Net Sales ($) | 2945M | 15466M | 30151M | 158137M | 771493M | 20235400M |
| 4315123M | 4153332M | 6062051M | Total Assets ($) | 10522M | 9377M | 8268M | 52169M | 263536M | 5718179M |

© RMA 2024

M = $ thousand  MM = $ million
See Pages viii through xx for Explanation of Ratios and Data

# ADMIN & WASTE MANAGEMENT SERVICES—Professional Employer Organizations  NAICS 561330

## Current Data Sorted by Assets | Comparative Historical Data

| | | | | | | | | | |
|---|---|---|---|---|---|---|---|---|---|
| | 1 | | 5 | 2 | 2 | **Type of Statement** | | | |
| | | 2 | | | | Unqualified | 11 | 5 | |
| | | 2 | 1 | | | Reviewed | 2 | | |
| | 3 | 1 | 1 | | | Compiled | 2 | 1 | |
| 4 | 10 | 19 | 15 | 4 | 7 | Tax Returns | 7 | 4 | |
| | 10 (4/1-9/30/23) | | 69 (10/1/23-3/31/24) | | | Other | 48 | 18 | |
| 0-500M | 500M-2MM | 2-10MM | 10-50MM | 50-100MM | 100-250MM | | 4/1/19-3/31/20 ALL | 4/1/20-3/31/21 ALL | |
| 4 | 14 | 24 | 22 | 6 | 9 | **NUMBER OF STATEMENTS** | 70 | 28 | |
| % | % | % | % | % | % | **ASSETS** | % | % | |
| | 53.1 | 24.4 | 36.5 | | | Cash & Equivalents | 34.2 | 40.3 | |
| | 15.4 | 35.0 | 25.7 | | | Trade Receivables (net) | 36.0 | 31.6 | |
| | .0 | .1 | .0 | | | Inventory | .1 | .0 | |
| | 9.9 | 6.2 | 14.5 | | | All Other Current | 6.7 | 8.7 | |
| | 78.4 | 65.7 | 76.7 | | | Total Current | 77.0 | 80.6 | |
| | 1.2 | 11.7 | 2.3 | | | Fixed Assets (net) | 5.2 | 3.6 | |
| | .2 | 3.3 | 8.0 | | | Intangibles (net) | 5.9 | 8.5 | |
| | 20.3 | 19.4 | 13.0 | | | All Other Non-Current | 11.9 | 7.3 | |
| | 100.0 | 100.0 | 100.0 | | | Total | 100.0 | 100.0 | |
| | | | | | | **LIABILITIES** | | | |
| | .6 | 3.0 | .9 | | | Notes Payable-Short Term | 14.5 | 13.8 | |
| | .8 | 2.7 | .1 | | | Cur. Mat.-L.T.D. | 1.9 | .5 | |
| | 7.4 | 3.1 | 2.9 | | | Trade Payables | 10.8 | 4.3 | |
| | .0 | .0 | 1.1 | | | Income Taxes Payable | .5 | .0 | |
| | 31.9 | 26.1 | 36.2 | | | All Other Current | 28.2 | 25.4 | |
| | 40.7 | 35.0 | 41.2 | | | Total Current | 56.0 | 43.9 | |
| | 6.5 | 8.8 | 2.3 | | | Long-Term Debt | 6.5 | 5.2 | |
| | .0 | .0 | .2 | | | Deferred Taxes | .2 | .2 | |
| | .0 | 5.0 | 15.8 | | | All Other Non-Current | 3.6 | 19.7 | |
| | 52.7 | 51.2 | 40.4 | | | Net Worth | 33.8 | 31.0 | |
| | 100.0 | 100.0 | 100.0 | | | Total Liabilities & Net Worth | 100.0 | 100.0 | |
| | | | | | | **INCOME DATA** | | | |
| | 100.0 | 100.0 | 100.0 | | | Net Sales | 100.0 | 100.0 | |
| | | | | | | Gross Profit | | | |
| | 95.5 | 93.1 | 92.8 | | | Operating Expenses | 95.3 | 94.0 | |
| | 4.5 | 6.9 | 7.2 | | | Operating Profit | 4.7 | 6.0 | |
| | -.3 | .4 | -.8 | | | All Other Expenses (net) | -.3 | -.3 | |
| | 4.9 | 6.5 | 8.0 | | | Profit Before Taxes | 5.0 | 6.3 | |
| | | | | | | **RATIOS** | | | |
| | 27.3 | 4.7 | 10.2 | | | | 3.4 | 5.1 | |
| | 2.0 | 1.8 | 2.0 | | | Current | 1.6 | 1.9 | |
| | 1.0 | 1.0 | 1.0 | | | | 1.1 | 1.1 | |
| | 18.5 | 4.7 | 10.2 | | | | 3.3 | 5.1 | |
| | 1.9 | 1.8 | 1.5 | | | Quick | 1.4 | 1.9 | |
| | .9 | .8 | .7 | | | | .9 | 1.0 | |
| | 0 UND | 2 196.3 | 0 795.6 | | | | 1 447.5 | 10 36.4 | |
| | 1 517.5 | 30 12.0 | 3 106.7 | | | Sales/Receivables | 26 13.9 | 30 12.3 | |
| | 5 77.0 | 44 8.3 | 73 5.0 | | | | 40 9.2 | 51 7.2 | |
| | | | | | | Cost of Sales/Inventory | | | |
| | | | | | | Cost of Sales/Payables | | | |
| | 5.8 | 7.8 | 1.7 | | | | 9.4 | 5.9 | |
| | 29.0 | 22.1 | 28.7 | | | Sales/Working Capital | 26.6 | 9.5 | |
| | NM | UND | 315.7 | | | | 266.1 | 130.5 | |
| | | 29.4 | 129.4 | | | | 102.5 | 74.7 | |
| | (12) | 16.5 (11) | 19.5 | | | EBIT/Interest | (43) 16.2 | (16) 15.9 | |
| | | 4.5 | 5.5 | | | | 4.2 | 5.7 | |
| | | | | | | Net Profit + Depr., Dep., Amort./Cur. Mat. L/T/D | | | |
| | .0 | .0 | .0 | | | | .0 | .0 | |
| | .0 | .1 | .0 | | | Fixed/Worth | .0 | .0 | |
| | .0 | .5 | -.6 | | | | .2 | .3 | |
| | .1 | .2 | .4 | | | | .5 | .9 | |
| | 1.0 | 1.2 | 2.5 | | | Debt/Worth | 2.2 | 1.8 | |
| | 4.2 | 4.2 | -59.3 | | | | 7.8 | 48.1 | |
| | 47.2 | 64.1 | 53.9 | | | % Profit Before Taxes/Tangible Net Worth | 92.8 | 112.9 | |
| | (12) 15.3 | (23) 26.0 | (16) 38.3 | | | | (65) 45.8 | (22) 63.7 | |
| | 4.4 | 7.2 | 22.1 | | | | 21.5 | 9.9 | |
| | 18.4 | 31.3 | 21.3 | | | % Profit Before Taxes/Total Assets | 25.8 | 43.2 | |
| | 12.3 | 15.9 | 12.2 | | | | 12.3 | 12.1 | |
| | 2.6 | 1.3 | 4.3 | | | | 5.4 | 1.6 | |
| | UND | 999.8 | 999.8 | | | Sales/Net Fixed Assets | UND | UND | |
| | 999.8 | 236.9 | 400.3 | | | | 835.6 | 700.3 | |
| | 999.8 | 45.6 | 83.1 | | | | 124.9 | 112.6 | |
| | 40.9 | 7.6 | 3.9 | | | Sales/Total Assets | 14.4 | 5.8 | |
| | 7.9 | 3.6 | 2.2 | | | | 6.2 | 3.8 | |
| | 3.9 | 2.3 | 1.2 | | | | 3.9 | 2.1 | |
| | | .1 | .0 | | | % Depr., Dep., Amort./Sales | .1 | .0 | |
| | (10) | .3 (11) | .2 | | | | (28) .2 | (10) .3 | |
| | | .9 | .4 | | | | .7 | .6 | |
| | | | | | | % Officers', Directors' Owners' Comp/Sales | 1.0 | | |
| | | | | | | | (10) 3.5 | | |
| | | | | | | | 7.9 | | |
| 3168M | 541725M | 955898M | 2141367M | 1464222M | 2248876M | Net Sales ($) | 8364692M | 2021855M | |
| 860M | 17713M | 121040M | 518074M | 459397M | 1471822M | Total Assets ($) | 1241176M | 357632M | |

© RMA 2024

M = $ thousand   MM = $ million

See Pages viii through xx for Explanation of Ratios and Data

## ADMIN & WASTE MANAGEMENT SERVICES—Professional Employer Organizations    NAICS 561330

### Comparative Historical Data | Current Data Sorted by Sales

| | | | | Type of Statement | | | | | | |
|---|---|---|---|---|---|---|---|---|---|---|
| | 6 | 17 | 10 | Unqualified | | | | | 1 | 9 |
| | 1 | 2 | 2 | Reviewed | | | | | 1 | 1 |
| | 4 | | 3 | Compiled | | | | | 1 | 2 |
| | 5 | 12 | 5 | Tax Returns | | 1 | | | 3 | 1 |
| | 47 | 52 | 59 | Other | 4 | 4 | 2 | 8 | 11 | 30 |
| | 4/1/21-3/31/22 | 4/1/22-3/31/23 | 4/1/23-3/31/24 | | | 10 (4/1-9/30/23) | | | 69 (10/1/23-3/31/24) | |
| | ALL | ALL | ALL | | 0-1MM | 1-3MM | 3-5MM | 5-10MM | 10-25MM | 25MM & OVER |
| | 63 | 83 | 79 | NUMBER OF STATEMENTS | 4 | 5 | 2 | 8 | 17 | 43 |
| | % | % | % | ASSETS | % | % | % | % | % | % |
| | 27.8 | 37.3 | 33.0 | Cash & Equivalents | | | | | 16.0 | 38.7 |
| | 35.7 | 26.8 | 26.0 | Trade Receivables (net) | | | | | 40.7 | 20.3 |
| | .1 | .0 | .0 | Inventory | | | | | .0 | .0 |
| | 8.5 | 11.7 | 9.7 | All Other Current | | | | | 8.1 | 12.1 |
| | 72.1 | 75.8 | 68.8 | Total Current | | | | | 64.8 | 71.1 |
| | 4.6 | 5.4 | 6.3 | Fixed Assets (net) | | | | | 7.7 | 3.0 |
| | 7.4 | 6.8 | 8.2 | Intangibles (net) | | | | | 4.8 | 9.7 |
| | 16.0 | 12.0 | 16.7 | All Other Non-Current | | | | | 22.7 | 16.2 |
| | 100.0 | 100.0 | 100.0 | Total | | | | | 100.0 | 100.0 |
| | | | | LIABILITIES | | | | | | |
| | 4.2 | 2.4 | 4.0 | Notes Payable-Short Term | | | | | 5.0 | 2.1 |
| | 1.6 | .8 | 1.9 | Cur. Mat.-L.T.D. | | | | | 1.2 | 2.0 |
| | 8.6 | 6.2 | 4.4 | Trade Payables | | | | | 2.9 | 5.9 |
| | .1 | .2 | .3 | Income Taxes Payable | | | | | .0 | .6 |
| | 29.4 | 32.7 | 30.8 | All Other Current | | | | | 18.9 | 39.5 |
| | 43.9 | 42.2 | 41.4 | Total Current | | | | | 28.0 | 50.1 |
| | 9.6 | 8.5 | 7.7 | Long-Term Debt | | | | | 6.7 | 6.8 |
| | .0 | .1 | .1 | Deferred Taxes | | | | | .1 | .1 |
| | 4.8 | 6.0 | 7.5 | All Other Non-Current | | | | | 8.7 | 10.1 |
| | 41.6 | 43.2 | 43.3 | Net Worth | | | | | 56.5 | 32.9 |
| | 100.0 | 100.0 | 100.0 | Total Liabilities & Net Worth | | | | | 100.0 | 100.0 |
| | | | | INCOME DATA | | | | | | |
| | 100.0 | 100.0 | 100.0 | Net Sales | | | | | 100.0 | 100.0 |
| | | | | Gross Profit | | | | | | |
| | 91.6 | 93.7 | 93.6 | Operating Expenses | | | | | 95.2 | 94.8 |
| | 8.4 | 6.3 | 6.4 | Operating Profit | | | | | 4.8 | 5.2 |
| | -1.1 | .0 | .4 | All Other Expenses (net) | | | | | -1.1 | .5 |
| | 9.5 | 6.3 | 5.9 | Profit Before Taxes | | | | | 5.9 | 4.6 |
| | | | | RATIOS | | | | | | |
| | 3.6 | 4.8 | 4.7 | | | | | | 7.0 | 3.1 |
| | 1.7 | 2.0 | 1.6 | Current | | | | | 2.3 | 1.2 |
| | 1.1 | 1.1 | 1.0 | | | | | | 1.1 | 1.0 |
| | 3.6 | 4.4 | 4.7 | | | | | | 7.0 | 2.9 |
| | 1.4 | 1.6 | 1.2 | Quick | | | | | 2.2 | 1.1 |
| | .7 | .9 | .7 | | | | | | .9 | .6 |
| 1 | 325.2 | 0  999.8 | 0  999.8 | | | | | | 3  138.5 | 0  999.8 |
| 41 | 8.9 | 16  22.8 | 10  35.7 | Sales/Receivables | | | | | 38  9.5 | 2  184.7 |
| 78 | 4.7 | 47  7.7 | 54  6.7 | | | | | | 96  3.8 | 42  8.6 |
| | | | | Cost of Sales/Inventory | | | | | | |
| | | | | Cost of Sales/Payables | | | | | | |
| | 4.5 | 5.5 | 5.1 | | | | | | 3.4 | 7.3 |
| | 11.2 | 18.2 | 34.1 | Sales/Working Capital | | | | | 16.6 | 138.9 |
| | 602.9 | 221.8 | -719.8 | | | | | | UND | -436.0 |
| | 100.1 | 198.0 | 44.2 | | | | | | 26.4 | 199.3 |
| (44) | 49.9 | (51) 37.0 | (41) 12.0 | EBIT/Interest | | | | | (13) 10.2 | (23) 9.8 |
| | 20.7 | 9.3 | 4.5 | | | | | | 4.6 | -.2 |
| | | | | Net Profit + Depr., Dep., Amort./Cur. Mat. L/T/D | | | | | | |
| | .0 | .0 | .0 | | | | | | .0 | .0 |
| | .1 | .1 | .1 | Fixed/Worth | | | | | .1 | .1 |
| | .5 | .5 | .7 | | | | | | .4 | -43.2 |
| | .6 | .5 | .4 | | | | | | .2 | .6 |
| | 1.5 | 1.7 | 1.5 | Debt/Worth | | | | | .7 | 3.1 |
| | 6.7 | 11.3 | 19.7 | | | | | | 2.0 | -19.3 |
| | 96.9 | 90.2 | 58.6 | % Profit Before Taxes/Tangible Net Worth | | | | | 38.9 | 64.4 |
| (54) | 49.5 | (73) 43.9 | (61) 27.2 | | | | | | (15) 24.1 | (30) 39.0 |
| | 20.5 | 14.3 | 7.6 | | | | | | 2.6 | 7.0 |
| | 43.3 | 31.4 | 24.0 | % Profit Before Taxes/Total Assets | | | | | 23.2 | 21.2 |
| | 16.2 | 12.5 | 12.1 | | | | | | 17.6 | 10.8 |
| | 6.2 | 3.4 | 1.6 | | | | | | 1.3 | 1.0 |
| | 999.8 | UND | 999.8 | | | | | | 999.8 | 999.8 |
| | 273.1 | 543.5 | 288.0 | Sales/Net Fixed Assets | | | | | 199.9 | 288.0 |
| | 56.4 | 92.6 | 70.2 | | | | | | 19.0 | 83.9 |
| | 5.9 | 10.9 | 7.0 | | | | | | 6.1 | 16.7 |
| | 3.4 | 4.2 | 2.8 | Sales/Total Assets | | | | | 3.1 | 3.1 |
| | 1.6 | 2.3 | 1.4 | | | | | | 1.3 | 1.6 |
| | .0 | .0 | .1 | | | | | | | .0 |
| (29) | .2 | (37) .2 | (32) .3 | % Depr., Dep., Amort./Sales | | | | | (23) | .1 |
| | 1.1 | .6 | 1.0 | | | | | | | .9 |
| | | | | % Officers', Directors' Owners' Comp/Sales | | | | | | |
| | 5333194M | 12362186M | 7355256M | Net Sales ($) | 1092M | 10664M | 7333M | 64355M | 289178M | 6982634M |
| | 2167386M | 2069446M | 2588906M | Total Assets ($) | 2938M | 7832M | 1572M | 41855M | 151202M | 2383507M |

© RMA 2024      M = $ thousand    MM = $ million
See Pages viii through xx for Explanation of Ratios and Data

# ADMIN & WASTE MANAGEMENT SERVICES—Telemarketing Bureaus and Other Contact Centers  NAICS 561422

## Current Data Sorted by Assets | Comparative Historical Data

| | | | | | | Type of Statement | | |
|---|---|---|---|---|---|---|---|---|
| | | 2 | 2 | | 4 | Unqualified | 5 | 1 |
| | | 1 | 1 | | | Reviewed | 2 | 1 |
| | | | | | | Compiled | 2 | |
| 1 | | 1 | | | | Tax Returns | 1 | |
| | 1 | 5 | 5 | 2 | 4 | Other | 19 | 11 |
| | 8 (4/1-9/30/23) | | 21 (10/1/23-3/31/24) | | | | 4/1/19- | 4/1/20- |
| 0-500M | 500M-2MM | 2-10MM | 10-50MM | 50-100MM | 100-250MM | | 3/31/20 | 3/31/21 |
| 1 | 1 | 9 | 8 | 2 | 8 | NUMBER OF STATEMENTS | 29 ALL | 13 ALL |
| % | % | % | % | % | % | ASSETS | % | % |
| | | | | | | Cash & Equivalents | 11.9 | 15.2 |
| | | | | | | Trade Receivables (net) | 41.5 | 46.9 |
| | | | | | | Inventory | .1 | .3 |
| | | | | | | All Other Current | 5.5 | 7.4 |
| | | | | | | Total Current | 59.0 | 69.8 |
| | | | | | | Fixed Assets (net) | 21.2 | 12.2 |
| | | | | | | Intangibles (net) | 13.5 | 11.4 |
| | | | | | | All Other Non-Current | 6.3 | 6.6 |
| | | | | | | Total | 100.0 | 100.0 |
| | | | | | | **LIABILITIES** | | |
| | | | | | | Notes Payable-Short Term | 11.7 | 5.7 |
| | | | | | | Cur. Mat.-L.T.D. | 2.6 | 3.7 |
| | | | | | | Trade Payables | 24.1 | 14.2 |
| | | | | | | Income Taxes Payable | .2 | .4 |
| | | | | | | All Other Current | 11.2 | 13.4 |
| | | | | | | Total Current | 49.8 | 37.4 |
| | | | | | | Long-Term Debt | 29.2 | 27.2 |
| | | | | | | Deferred Taxes | .2 | .0 |
| | | | | | | All Other Non-Current | 2.7 | 6.5 |
| | | | | | | Net Worth | 18.1 | 28.8 |
| | | | | | | Total Liabilties & Net Worth | 100.0 | 100.0 |
| | | | | | | **INCOME DATA** | | |
| | | | | | | Net Sales | 100.0 | 100.0 |
| | | | | | | Gross Profit | | |
| | | | | | | Operating Expenses | 92.2 | 95.5 |
| | | | | | | Operating Profit | 7.8 | 4.5 |
| | | | | | | All Other Expenses (net) | 1.5 | 1.8 |
| | | | | | | Profit Before Taxes | 6.3 | 2.7 |
| | | | | | | **RATIOS** | | |
| | | | | | | Current | 3.1 | 3.7 |
| | | | | | | | 1.5 | 2.3 |
| | | | | | | | 1.0 | 1.3 |
| | | | | | | Quick | 3.0 | 3.6 |
| | | | | | | | 1.5 | 1.8 |
| | | | | | | | .9 | 1.2 |
| | | | | | | Sales/Receivables | 39  9.3 | 50  7.3 |
| | | | | | | | 54  6.7 | 69  5.3 |
| | | | | | | | 68  5.4 | 94  3.9 |
| | | | | | | Cost of Sales/Inventory | | |
| | | | | | | Cost of Sales/Payables | | |
| | | | | | | Sales/Working Capital | 6.9 | 4.7 |
| | | | | | | | 18.1 | 5.8 |
| | | | | | | | -609.0 | 22.9 |
| | | | | | | EBIT/Interest | 18.3 | 34.4 |
| | | | | | | | (25) 2.7 | (11) 7.7 |
| | | | | | | | .8 | -.4 |
| | | | | | | Net Profit + Depr., Dep., Amort./Cur. Mat. L/T/D | | |
| | | | | | | Fixed/Worth | .3 | .1 |
| | | | | | | | 1.1 | .6 |
| | | | | | | | -33.7 | -2.5 |
| | | | | | | Debt/Worth | .4 | 1.2 |
| | | | | | | | 2.5 | 5.5 |
| | | | | | | | -11.2 | -9.3 |
| | | | | | | % Profit Before Taxes/Tangible Net Worth | 80.7 | |
| | | | | | | | (20) 25.5 | |
| | | | | | | | 3.3 | |
| | | | | | | % Profit Before Taxes/Total Assets | 22.4 | 18.0 |
| | | | | | | | 6.2 | 10.2 |
| | | | | | | | -1.0 | -3.1 |
| | | | | | | Sales/Net Fixed Assets | 65.2 | 87.2 |
| | | | | | | | 16.6 | 19.5 |
| | | | | | | | 6.3 | 12.7 |
| | | | | | | Sales/Total Assets | 3.5 | 2.9 |
| | | | | | | | 2.8 | 2.0 |
| | | | | | | | 1.8 | 1.9 |
| | | | | | | % Depr., Dep., Amort./Sales | 1.3 | |
| | | | | | | | (19) 2.1 | |
| | | | | | | | 2.9 | |
| | | | | | | % Officers', Directors' Owners' Comp/Sales | | |
| 6279M | 1360M | 156285M | 375743M | 255328M | 2527920M | Net Sales ($) | 2562766M | 1704827M |
| 472M | 1238M | 46158M | 170157M | 106752M | 1166195M | Total Assets ($) | 1199229M | 798602M |

© RMA 2024  M = $ thousand  MM = $ million
See Pages viii through xx for Explanation of Ratios and Data

# ADMIN & WASTE MANAGEMENT SERVICES—Telemarketing Bureaus and Other Contact Centers  NAICS 561422

| Comparative Historical Data | | | | | Current Data Sorted by Sales | | | | | | |
|---|---|---|---|---|---|---|---|---|---|---|---|
| | | | | **Type of Statement** | | | | | | | |
| | 2 | 4 | 8 | Unqualified | 1 | | | | | 1 | 6 |
| | 2 | 3 | 2 | Reviewed | | | | | | 1 | 1 |
| | 1 | | | Compiled | | | | | | | |
| | 1 | 1 | 2 | Tax Returns | | | 1 | 1 | | | |
| | 13 | 7 | 17 | Other | | 1 | | 1 | 2 | 13 | |
| | 4/1/21-3/31/22 | 4/1/22-3/31/23 | 4/1/23-3/31/24 | | 8 (4/1-9/30/23) | | | 21 (10/1/23-3/31/24) | | | |
| | ALL | ALL | ALL | | 0-1MM | 1-3MM | 3-5MM | 5-10MM | 10-25MM | 25MM & OVER | |
| | 19 | 15 | 29 | **NUMBER OF STATEMENTS** | 1 | 1 | 1 | 2 | 4 | 20 | |
| | % | % | % | **ASSETS** | % | % | % | % | % | % | |
| | 18.8 | 13.6 | 15.0 | Cash & Equivalents | | | | | | 14.4 | |
| | 42.5 | 45.0 | 35.6 | Trade Receivables (net) | | | | | | 37.1 | |
| | .0 | .0 | .3 | Inventory | | | | | | .2 | |
| | 4.9 | 7.9 | 6.3 | All Other Current | | | | | | 4.5 | |
| | 66.3 | 66.4 | 57.2 | Total Current | | | | | | 56.2 | |
| | 11.7 | 11.4 | 10.3 | Fixed Assets (net) | | | | | | 10.8 | |
| | 6.4 | 8.9 | 12.5 | Intangibles (net) | | | | | | 15.1 | |
| | 15.6 | 13.2 | 20.0 | All Other Non-Current | | | | | | 17.9 | |
| | 100.0 | 100.0 | 100.0 | Total | | | | | | 100.0 | |
| | | | | **LIABILITIES** | | | | | | | |
| | 4.2 | 8.8 | 6.8 | Notes Payable-Short Term | | | | | | 5.6 | |
| | 1.1 | 3.6 | 2.6 | Cur. Mat.-L.T.D. | | | | | | 2.8 | |
| | 8.6 | 7.2 | 11.4 | Trade Payables | | | | | | 14.7 | |
| | .9 | .4 | .3 | Income Taxes Payable | | | | | | .4 | |
| | 41.1 | 24.4 | 23.3 | All Other Current | | | | | | 20.3 | |
| | 56.0 | 44.5 | 44.4 | Total Current | | | | | | 43.8 | |
| | 5.7 | 7.5 | 11.1 | Long-Term Debt | | | | | | 14.0 | |
| | .0 | .0 | .4 | Deferred Taxes | | | | | | .6 | |
| | 6.0 | 12.7 | 15.8 | All Other Non-Current | | | | | | 21.0 | |
| | 32.3 | 35.3 | 28.3 | Net Worth | | | | | | 20.6 | |
| | 100.0 | 100.0 | 100.0 | Total Liabilities & Net Worth | | | | | | 100.0 | |
| | | | | **INCOME DATA** | | | | | | | |
| | 100.0 | 100.0 | 100.0 | Net Sales | | | | | | 100.0 | |
| | | | | Gross Profit | | | | | | | |
| | 89.3 | 86.6 | 85.6 | Operating Expenses | | | | | | 93.0 | |
| | 10.7 | 13.4 | 14.4 | Operating Profit | | | | | | 7.0 | |
| | -.8 | -.2 | .4 | All Other Expenses (net) | | | | | | .8 | |
| | 11.5 | 13.6 | 13.9 | Profit Before Taxes | | | | | | 6.3 | |
| | | | | **RATIOS** | | | | | | | |
| | 6.6 | 2.9 | 2.6 | | | | | | | 2.3 | |
| | 2.2 | 1.3 | 1.4 | Current | | | | | | 1.4 | |
| | .7 | 1.0 | .9 | | | | | | | 1.2 | |
| | 6.6 | 2.7 | 2.2 | | | | | | | 1.9 | |
| | 1.9 | 1.2 | 1.2 | Quick | | | | | | 1.2 | |
| | .6 | .8 | .8 | | | | | | | 1.1 | |
| 41 | 8.9 | 43 | 8.4 | 38 | 9.5 | | | | | 45 | 8.2 |
| 58 | 6.3 | 68 | 5.4 | 60 | 6.1 | Sales/Receivables | | | | 60 | 6.1 |
| 79 | 4.6 | 104 | 3.5 | 74 | 4.9 | | | | | 76 | 4.8 |
| | | | | Cost of Sales/Inventory | | | | | | | |
| | | | | Cost of Sales/Payables | | | | | | | |
| | 4.8 | 4.6 | 6.7 | | | | | | | 9.2 | |
| | 7.4 | 16.2 | 21.3 | Sales/Working Capital | | | | | | 18.0 | |
| | -8.7 | -269.8 | -32.1 | | | | | | | 34.3 | |
| | 159.8 | 22.7 | 26.8 | | | | | | | 25.6 | |
| (15) | 37.5 | (11) | 14.0 | (24) | 6.5 | EBIT/Interest | | | | (19) | 6.2 |
| | 9.2 | .4 | -2.1 | | | | | | | 1.0 | |
| | | | | Net Profit + Depr., Dep., Amort./Cur. Mat. L/T/D | | | | | | | |
| | .0 | .0 | .0 | | | | | | | .2 | |
| | .2 | .2 | .3 | Fixed/Worth | | | | | | .3 | |
| | 40.2 | 2.1 | NM | | | | | | | NM | |
| | .4 | .8 | .5 | | | | | | | .8 | |
| | .7 | 3.0 | 2.3 | Debt/Worth | | | | | | 2.3 | |
| | -11.2 | -22.5 | -8.0 | | | | | | | NM | |
| | 117.6 | 107.6 | 102.4 | | | | | | | 113.9 | |
| (14) | 77.0 | (11) | 23.5 | (21) | 61.4 | % Profit Before Taxes/Tangible Net Worth | | | | (15) | 40.5 |
| | 33.1 | 12.2 | 22.1 | | | | | | | 7.1 | |
| | 50.3 | 34.5 | 40.4 | | | | | | | 25.2 | |
| | 24.9 | 14.8 | 15.0 | % Profit Before Taxes/Total Assets | | | | | | 12.1 | |
| | 4.9 | 2.9 | 1.1 | | | | | | | .6 | |
| | 77.5 | 113.7 | 164.6 | | | | | | | 92.6 | |
| | 36.7 | 41.4 | 39.6 | Sales/Net Fixed Assets | | | | | | 27.5 | |
| | 12.6 | 18.0 | 13.4 | | | | | | | 12.9 | |
| | 3.4 | 2.9 | 3.0 | | | | | | | 3.1 | |
| | 2.3 | 2.5 | 2.3 | Sales/Total Assets | | | | | | 2.2 | |
| | 1.9 | 1.3 | 1.6 | | | | | | | 1.7 | |
| | .6 | .8 | .7 | | | | | | | 1.2 | |
| (11) | 1.7 | (12) | 1.7 | (17) | 1.6 | % Depr., Dep., Amort./Sales | | | | (13) | 2.1 |
| | 2.6 | 2.8 | 3.1 | | | | | | | 3.6 | |
| | | | | % Officers', Directors' Owners' Comp/Sales | | | | | | | |
| | 1713652M | 1211649M | 3322915M | Net Sales ($) | 773M | 1360M | 3490M | 16048M | 73744M | 3227500M | |
| | 775526M | 585110M | 1490972M | Total Assets ($) | 2943M | 1238M | 4464M | 4634M | 32729M | 1444964M | |

© RMA 2024    M = $ thousand    MM = $ million

# ADMIN & WASTE MANAGEMENT SERVICES—Collection Agencies  NAICS 561440

## Current Data Sorted by Assets | Comparative Historical Data

| | | | | | | | Type of Statement | | | | |
|---|---|---|---|---|---|---|---|---|---|---|---|
| | 1 | 8 | 7 | 2 | 4 | | Unqualified | | 19 | | 16 |
| 1 | 1 | 4 | 2 | | | | Reviewed | | 17 | | 5 |
| | 1 | 1 | | | | | Compiled | | 5 | | 1 |
| 1 | 2 | 1 | | | | | Tax Returns | | 12 | | 1 |
| 4 | 7 | 9 | 20 | 2 | 9 | | Other | | 41 | | 24 |
| | 9 (4/1-9/30/23) | | 77 (10/1/23-3/31/24) | | | | | | 4/1/19- | | 4/1/20- |
| 0-500M | 500M-2MM | 2-10MM | 10-50MM | 50-100MM | 100-250MM | | NUMBER OF STATEMENTS | | 3/31/20 ALL | | 3/31/21 ALL |
| 6 | 11 | 23 | 29 | 4 | 13 | | | | 94 | | 47 |
| % | % | % | % | % | % | | ASSETS | | % | | % |
| | 50.8 | 21.3 | 12.6 | | 12.4 | | Cash & Equivalents | | 25.9 | | 29.8 |
| | 10.4 | 27.6 | 23.9 | | 21.0 | | Trade Receivables (net) | | 22.4 | | 20.9 |
| | .1 | .0 | 1.7 | | .0 | | Inventory | | 1.1 | | 2.1 |
| | 4.8 | 12.7 | 10.2 | | 2.1 | | All Other Current | | 11.5 | | 13.6 |
| | 66.1 | 61.6 | 48.4 | | 35.6 | | Total Current | | 60.9 | | 66.4 |
| | 15.6 | 15.6 | 12.2 | | 3.3 | | Fixed Assets (net) | | 11.1 | | 7.8 |
| | .3 | 8.7 | 6.8 | | 48.7 | | Intangibles (net) | | 10.8 | | 15.8 |
| | 18.0 | 14.1 | 32.6 | | 12.5 | | All Other Non-Current | | 17.1 | | 9.9 |
| | 100.0 | 100.0 | 100.0 | | 100.0 | | Total | | 100.0 | | 100.0 |
| | | | | | | | LIABILITIES | | | | |
| | 3.8 | 4.9 | 5.7 | | 9.3 | | Notes Payable-Short Term | | 10.3 | | 5.0 |
| | 6.8 | 1.0 | 3.7 | | 3.8 | | Cur. Mat.-L.T.D. | | 3.5 | | 3.8 |
| | 5.3 | 11.9 | 10.1 | | 2.1 | | Trade Payables | | 9.9 | | 9.5 |
| | .1 | .0 | .1 | | .2 | | Income Taxes Payable | | .1 | | .0 |
| | 20.5 | 18.5 | 17.0 | | 13.2 | | All Other Current | | 23.3 | | 19.8 |
| | 36.5 | 36.4 | 36.5 | | 28.5 | | Total Current | | 47.0 | | 38.1 |
| | 48.0 | 11.0 | 10.1 | | 42.1 | | Long-Term Debt | | 9.9 | | 18.4 |
| | .0 | .0 | .5 | | .2 | | Deferred Taxes | | .2 | | .1 |
| | 2.3 | 5.0 | 6.9 | | 12.5 | | All Other Non-Current | | 3.8 | | 3.2 |
| | 13.1 | 47.6 | 46.0 | | 16.6 | | Net Worth | | 39.0 | | 40.3 |
| | 100.0 | 100.0 | 100.0 | | 100.0 | | Total Liabilties & Net Worth | | 100.0 | | 100.0 |
| | | | | | | | INCOME DATA | | | | |
| | 100.0 | 100.0 | 100.0 | | 100.0 | | Net Sales | | 100.0 | | 100.0 |
| | | | | | | | Gross Profit | | | | |
| | 84.0 | 94.3 | 81.6 | | 97.4 | | Operating Expenses | | 87.0 | | 83.6 |
| | 16.0 | 5.7 | 18.4 | | 2.6 | | Operating Profit | | 13.0 | | 16.4 |
| | 1.0 | 2.1 | 1.6 | | 7.8 | | All Other Expenses (net) | | 2.5 | | .9 |
| | 15.0 | 3.6 | 16.8 | | -5.2 | | Profit Before Taxes | | 10.5 | | 15.5 |
| | | | | | | | RATIOS | | | | |
| | 5.3 | 3.6 | 2.7 | | 1.8 | | | | 2.7 | | 3.0 |
| | 1.8 | 1.4 | 1.6 | | 1.2 | | Current | | 1.5 | | 2.1 |
| | 1.4 | 1.1 | .9 | | .8 | | | | .9 | | 1.3 |
| | 5.3 | 2.5 | 1.9 | | 1.5 | | | | 2.0 | | 2.5 |
| | 1.8 | 1.3 | 1.1 | | 1.1 | | Quick | (93) | 1.2 | | 1.7 |
| | 1.2 | .6 | .3 | | .8 | | | | .6 | | 1.0 |
| 0 | UND | 17 | 21.6 | 20 | 18.1 | 49 | 7.5 | | 1 | 426.2 | 11 | 34.1 |
| 3 | 117.0 | 37 | 9.8 | 37 | 9.8 | 59 | 6.2 | Sales/Receivables | 24 | 15.1 | 27 | 13.5 |
| 19 | 19.3 | 57 | 6.4 | 65 | 5.6 | 101 | 3.6 | | 44 | 8.3 | 47 | 7.8 |
| | | | | | | | Cost of Sales/Inventory | | | | |
| | | | | | | | Cost of Sales/Payables | | | | |
| | 8.4 | 3.7 | 2.2 | | 2.9 | | | | 6.2 | | 4.2 |
| | 12.3 | 7.2 | 9.7 | | 31.9 | | Sales/Working Capital | | 14.4 | | 8.2 |
| | 40.6 | 64.2 | NM | | -18.1 | | | | -58.7 | | 18.6 |
| | | 16.4 | 41.4 | | 2.3 | | | | 124.5 | | 121.1 |
| | (18) | 1.5 | (22) | 11.4 | (11) | -.2 | EBIT/Interest | (73) | 11.6 | (44) | 27.1 |
| | | -3.8 | 2.3 | | -2.4 | | | | 4.3 | | 3.8 |
| | | | | | | | Net Profit + Depr., Dep., Amort./Cur. Mat. L/T/D | | | | |
| | .0 | .1 | .0 | | .1 | | | | .0 | | .1 |
| | .1 | .1 | .3 | | -.1 | | Fixed/Worth | | .3 | | .2 |
| | .7 | .3 | .7 | | .0 | | | | .8 | | 1.4 |
| | .3 | .6 | .7 | | 5.5 | | | | .6 | | .7 |
| | .8 | 1.2 | 1.6 | | -1.8 | | Debt/Worth | | 1.6 | | 1.6 |
| | 3.4 | 3.0 | 4.1 | | -1.4 | | | | 5.8 | | 15.7 |
| | | 31.7 | 58.8 | | | | | | 111.9 | | 170.6 |
| | (22) | 5.1 | (28) | 26.1 | | | % Profit Before Taxes/Tangible Net Worth | (81) | 40.8 | (37) | 92.6 |
| | | -18.6 | 11.7 | | | | | | 14.4 | | 41.1 |
| | 59.1 | 10.8 | 19.5 | | 3.7 | | | | 40.0 | | 50.3 |
| | 34.6 | 2.7 | 11.1 | | -6.4 | | % Profit Before Taxes/Total Assets | | 14.0 | | 23.6 |
| | -.5 | -4.2 | 4.7 | | -11.4 | | | | 2.9 | | 3.3 |
| | 999.8 | 196.6 | 155.2 | | 83.6 | | | | 243.2 | | 104.7 |
| | 113.2 | 33.5 | 23.8 | | 14.9 | | Sales/Net Fixed Assets | | 48.5 | | 34.9 |
| | 15.5 | 15.1 | 8.9 | | 12.2 | | | | 21.5 | | 19.3 |
| | 11.0 | 2.9 | 2.3 | | .8 | | | | 4.8 | | 3.5 |
| | 4.6 | 2.3 | 1.2 | | .5 | | Sales/Total Assets | | 2.7 | | 2.3 |
| | 2.1 | 1.2 | .6 | | .4 | | | | 1.6 | | 1.0 |
| | | .3 | .9 | | | | | | .4 | | .3 |
| | (17) | 2.0 | (18) | 1.4 | | | % Depr., Dep., Amort./Sales | (56) | 1.0 | (31) | .8 |
| | | 4.7 | 2.6 | | | | | | 1.8 | | 1.2 |
| | | | | | | | | | 3.0 | | |
| | | | | | | | % Officers', Directors' Owners' Comp/Sales | (16) | 8.2 | | |
| | | | | | | | | | 14.5 | | |
| 6962M | 68986M | 289482M | 896997M | 515275M | 1744433M | | Net Sales ($) | | 2557239M | | 1815301M |
| 1389M | 12812M | 134287M | 696907M | 306169M | 2269640M | | Total Assets ($) | | 1376215M | | 1487440M |

M = $ thousand    MM = $ million
See Pages viii through xx for Explanation of Ratios and Data

© RMA 2024

# ADMIN & WASTE MANAGEMENT SERVICES—Collection Agencies  NAICS 561440

## Comparative Historical Data | Current Data Sorted by Sales

| | | | | | | Type of Statement | | | | | | |
|---|---|---|---|---|---|---|---|---|---|---|---|---|
| | 14 | | 27 | | 21 | Unqualified | | | | 4 | 5 | 12 |
| | 11 | | 9 | | 8 | Reviewed | | 1 | 1 | 3 | 1 | 2 |
| | | | 2 | | 2 | Compiled | | | | 1 | 1 | |
| | 3 | | 6 | | 4 | Tax Returns | | | 2 | 1 | 1 | |
| | 20 | | 44 | | 51 | Other | 5 | 5 | 3 | 7 | 9 | 22 |
| | 4/1/21-3/31/22 ALL | | 4/1/22-3/31/23 ALL | | 4/1/23-3/31/24 ALL | | 9 (4/1-9/30/23) | | | 77 (10/1/23-3/31/24) | | |
| | | | | | | | 0-1MM | 1-3MM | 3-5MM | 5-10MM | 10-25MM | 25MM & OVER |
| | 48 | | 88 | | 86 | NUMBER OF STATEMENTS | 5 | 9 | 5 | 14 | 17 | 36 |
| | % | | % | | % | ASSETS | % | % | % | % | % | % |
| | 32.1 | | 18.9 | | 21.3 | Cash & Equivalents | | | | 23.4 | 27.4 | 14.7 |
| | 17.4 | | 22.9 | | 23.7 | Trade Receivables (net) | | | | 26.5 | 30.1 | 18.9 |
| | 1.5 | | 3.3 | | .6 | Inventory | | | | .1 | .0 | 1.4 |
| | 14.1 | | 13.7 | | 9.3 | All Other Current | | | | 19.7 | 2.1 | 8.3 |
| | 65.1 | | 58.8 | | 54.8 | Total Current | | | | 69.7 | 59.6 | 43.3 |
| | 7.5 | | 9.9 | | 11.5 | Fixed Assets (net) | | | | 6.2 | 8.8 | 10.9 |
| | 13.1 | | 14.8 | | 13.8 | Intangibles (net) | | | | 2.5 | 11.9 | 24.1 |
| | 14.4 | | 16.4 | | 19.9 | All Other Non-Current | | | | 21.6 | 19.8 | 21.7 |
| | 100.0 | | 100.0 | | 100.0 | Total | | | | 100.0 | 100.0 | 100.0 |
| | | | | | | LIABILITIES | | | | | | |
| | 9.4 | | 9.5 | | 7.6 | Notes Payable-Short Term | | | | 5.3 | 10.7 | 3.8 |
| | 1.5 | | 3.4 | | 3.2 | Cur. Mat.-L.T.D. | | | | 1.4 | 4.6 | 4.1 |
| | 5.7 | | 6.8 | | 8.1 | Trade Payables | | | | 11.2 | 9.0 | 8.6 |
| | .1 | | .2 | | .1 | Income Taxes Payable | | | | .1 | .0 | .1 |
| | 21.3 | | 13.3 | | 18.0 | All Other Current | | | | 20.7 | 16.2 | 19.3 |
| | 38.0 | | 33.2 | | 36.9 | Total Current | | | | 38.7 | 40.6 | 35.9 |
| | 28.2 | | 24.7 | | 20.4 | Long-Term Debt | | | | 6.4 | 27.1 | 24.3 |
| | .4 | | .2 | | .2 | Deferred Taxes | | | | .0 | .8 | .1 |
| | 4.9 | | 6.5 | | 7.1 | All Other Non-Current | | | | 4.6 | 3.6 | 10.6 |
| | 28.6 | | 35.3 | | 35.4 | Net Worth | | | | 50.3 | 27.9 | 29.1 |
| | 100.0 | | 100.0 | | 100.0 | Total Liabilities & Net Worth | | | | 100.0 | 100.0 | 100.0 |
| | | | | | | INCOME DATA | | | | | | |
| | 100.0 | | 100.0 | | 100.0 | Net Sales | | | | 100.0 | 100.0 | 100.0 |
| | | | | | | Gross Profit | | | | | | |
| | 85.4 | | 88.5 | | 88.5 | Operating Expenses | | | | 92.8 | 90.2 | 95.0 |
| | 14.6 | | 11.5 | | 11.5 | Operating Profit | | | | 7.2 | 9.8 | 5.0 |
| | 1.6 | | 4.8 | | 2.6 | All Other Expenses (net) | | | | 1.6 | 1.5 | 2.6 |
| | 13.0 | | 6.6 | | 8.9 | Profit Before Taxes | | | | 5.6 | 8.4 | 2.4 |
| | | | | | | RATIOS | | | | | | |
| | 3.7 | | 3.6 | | 2.6 | | | | | 4.7 | 2.5 | 2.3 |
| | 2.2 | | 1.6 | | 1.5 | Current | | | | 1.8 | 1.3 | 1.3 |
| | 1.2 | | 1.1 | | 1.1 | | | | | 1.2 | 1.1 | .7 |
| | 2.3 | | 2.3 | | 2.0 | | | | | 2.0 | 2.4 | 1.8 |
| | 1.5 | | 1.2 | | 1.2 | Quick | | | | 1.1 | 1.3 | 1.0 |
| | 1.0 | | .5 | | .6 | | | | | .5 | .9 | .4 |
| 14 | 25.7 | 9 | 40.5 | 13 | 27.4 | | | | | 8 47.9 | 25 14.4 | 24 15.0 |
| 29 | 12.7 | 35 | 10.5 | 37 | 9.8 | Sales/Receivables | | | | 27 13.3 | 49 7.5 | 38 9.7 |
| 41 | 9.0 | 49 | 7.5 | 59 | 6.2 | | | | | 61 6.0 | 85 4.3 | 56 6.5 |
| | | | | | | Cost of Sales/Inventory | | | | | | |
| | | | | | | Cost of Sales/Payables | | | | | | |
| | 3.1 | | 2.1 | | 3.7 | | | | | 2.4 | 3.9 | 5.5 |
| | 8.8 | | 11.4 | | 13.7 | Sales/Working Capital | | | | 8.0 | 17.4 | 20.7 |
| | 29.5 | | 60.9 | | 69.7 | | | | | 41.9 | 267.4 | -11.3 |
| | 104.8 | | 17.1 | | 19.9 | | | | | 17.0 | 37.9 | 28.9 |
| (35) | 13.9 | (70) | 2.6 | (66) | 4.8 | EBIT/Interest | | | (10) | 3.9 | (13) 3.3 | (29) 2.4 |
| | 1.5 | | -.6 | | -.2 | | | | | -70.4 | -2.7 | -.7 |
| | | | 56.6 | | 5.8 | Net Profit + Depr., Dep., | | | | | | |
| | | (12) | .9 | (13) | 1.8 | Amort./Cur. Mat. L/T/D | | | | | | |
| | | | | | -2.0 | -.1 | | | | | | |
| | .0 | | .0 | | .0 | | | | | .0 | .0 | .1 |
| | .2 | | .2 | | .2 | Fixed/Worth | | | | .1 | .1 | .7 |
| | 1.8 | | .8 | | 1.1 | | | | | .2 | .4 | -.2 |
| | .6 | | .9 | | .7 | | | | | .5 | .7 | 1.0 |
| | 2.1 | | 2.4 | | 2.0 | Debt/Worth | | | | .9 | 1.6 | 4.1 |
| | 59.0 | | 5.5 | | 6.0 | | | | | 3.0 | 4.1 | -2.4 |
| | 127.8 | | 77.3 | | 59.8 | % Profit Before Taxes/Tangible Net Worth | | | | 17.6 | 52.9 | 94.8 |
| (37) | 48.3 | (73) | 23.4 | (70) | 21.8 | | | | | 5.5 | (15) 13.6 | (24) 29.3 |
| | 33.2 | | .5 | | .2 | | | | | -47.2 | -4.7 | 11.4 |
| | 36.4 | | 14.9 | | 15.4 | % Profit Before Taxes/Total Assets | | | | 9.5 | 39.2 | 16.0 |
| | 19.7 | | 3.5 | | 6.0 | | | | | 4.2 | 4.4 | 6.0 |
| | 3.5 | | -3.2 | | -2.0 | | | | | -19.6 | -.4 | -6.8 |
| | 285.5 | | 328.4 | | 177.1 | | | | | 148.5 | 359.0 | 46.4 |
| | 53.0 | | 32.8 | | 31.6 | Sales/Net Fixed Assets | | | | 89.8 | 34.3 | 19.2 |
| | 20.2 | | 10.9 | | 14.2 | | | | | 26.8 | 22.7 | 10.7 |
| | 3.6 | | 2.7 | | 2.6 | | | | | 4.1 | 3.2 | 2.3 |
| | 1.5 | | 1.4 | | 1.6 | Sales/Total Assets | | | | 2.5 | 2.2 | 1.5 |
| | .8 | | .5 | | .6 | | | | | 1.3 | 1.0 | .7 |
| | .4 | | .7 | | .5 | | | | | | .3 | 1.1 |
| (29) | .9 | (47) | 1.3 | (45) | 1.6 | % Depr., Dep., Amort./Sales | | | | (10) 2.1 | (20) 1.6 | |
| | 1.7 | | 2.2 | | 3.3 | | | | | | 2.9 | 4.7 |
| | | | 2.8 | | 1.4 | % Officers', Directors' Owners' Comp/Sales | | | | | | |
| | | (10) | 8.1 | (11) | 4.1 | | | | | | | |
| | | | 13.1 | | 10.4 | | | | | | | |
| | 1774186M | | 2786679M | | 3522135M | Net Sales ($) | 1177M | 20193M | 19096M | 104383M | 284762M | 3092524M |
| | 1706941M | | 3807375M | | 3421204M | Total Assets ($) | 3884M | 42024M | 39656M | 106893M | 262462M | 2966285M |

© RMA 2024  M = $ thousand   MM = $ million
See Pages viii through xx for Explanation of Ratios and Data

# ADMIN & WASTE MANAGEMENT SERVICES—All Other Business Support Services  NAICS 561499

## Current Data Sorted by Assets | Comparative Historical Data

| | | | | | | | Type of Statement | | |
|---|---|---|---|---|---|---|---|---|---|
| | | 2 | 6 | 4 | 6 | | Unqualified | 13 | 3 |
| | 1 | 2 | 6 | | | | Reviewed | 13 | 8 |
| | 1 | 4 | 2 | | | | Compiled | 9 | 5 |
| 3 | 6 | 12 | 1 | | | | Tax Returns | 19 | 17 |
| 4 | 13 | 24 | 19 | 10 | 7 | | Other | 106 | 59 |
| | 16 (4/1-9/30/23) | | 117 (10/1/23-3/31/24) | | | | | 4/1/19-3/31/20 | 4/1/20-3/31/21 |
| 0-500M | 500M-2MM | 2-10MM | 10-50MM | 50-100MM | 100-250MM | | | ALL | ALL |
| 7 | 21 | 44 | 34 | 14 | 13 | NUMBER OF STATEMENTS | | 160 | 92 |
| % | % | % | % | % | % | ASSETS | | % | % |
| | 32.5 | 22.1 | 11.8 | 33.9 | 14.0 | Cash & Equivalents | | 22.4 | 30.3 |
| | 17.7 | 24.9 | 26.6 | 16.5 | 18.2 | Trade Receivables (net) | | 23.9 | 20.0 |
| | 7.5 | 5.7 | 7.4 | 8.3 | 1.5 | Inventory | | 4.5 | 6.5 |
| | 4.1 | 6.5 | 8.2 | 17.1 | 17.3 | All Other Current | | 6.0 | 5.2 |
| | 61.9 | 59.2 | 54.1 | 75.8 | 51.0 | Total Current | | 56.8 | 62.1 |
| | 17.4 | 14.5 | 21.1 | 13.7 | 20.7 | Fixed Assets (net) | | 20.7 | 20.4 |
| | 7.8 | 9.8 | 14.9 | 1.3 | 14.4 | Intangibles (net) | | 14.3 | 7.5 |
| | 13.0 | 16.5 | 9.9 | 9.2 | 13.9 | All Other Non-Current | | 8.2 | 9.9 |
| | 100.0 | 100.0 | 100.0 | 100.0 | 100.0 | Total | | 100.0 | 100.0 |
| | | | | | | LIABILITIES | | | |
| | 9.5 | 5.4 | 7.6 | 6.7 | 5.5 | Notes Payable-Short Term | | 7.2 | 8.1 |
| | 1.3 | 1.4 | 3.8 | 4.0 | 5.2 | Cur. Mat.-L.T.D. | | 2.7 | 2.2 |
| | 5.7 | 10.1 | 10.7 | 14.6 | 6.5 | Trade Payables | | 10.5 | 7.8 |
| | .0 | .1 | .0 | .0 | .2 | Income Taxes Payable | | .6 | .0 |
| | 15.6 | 19.3 | 17.0 | 18.6 | 20.0 | All Other Current | | 20.4 | 17.7 |
| | 32.1 | 36.4 | 39.2 | 44.0 | 37.5 | Total Current | | 41.3 | 35.9 |
| | 19.7 | 18.8 | 14.4 | 14.5 | 33.9 | Long-Term Debt | | 20.5 | 31.4 |
| | .0 | .2 | .4 | .1 | .0 | Deferred Taxes | | .3 | .4 |
| | 3.5 | 17.1 | 6.3 | 10.4 | 14.2 | All Other Non-Current | | 7.2 | 11.5 |
| | 44.6 | 27.5 | 39.7 | 31.0 | 14.5 | Net Worth | | 30.7 | 20.8 |
| | 100.0 | 100.0 | 100.0 | 100.0 | 100.0 | Total Liabilties & Net Worth | | 100.0 | 100.0 |
| | | | | | | INCOME DATA | | | |
| | 100.0 | 100.0 | 100.0 | 100.0 | 100.0 | Net Sales | | 100.0 | 100.0 |
| | | | | | | Gross Profit | | | |
| | 84.0 | 87.7 | 88.5 | 98.9 | 94.5 | Operating Expenses | | 87.4 | 82.9 |
| | 16.0 | 12.3 | 11.5 | 1.1 | 5.5 | Operating Profit | | 12.6 | 17.1 |
| | 1.7 | 4.0 | 3.7 | -.7 | 6.8 | All Other Expenses (net) | | 3.2 | 2.9 |
| | 14.3 | 8.3 | 7.8 | 1.8 | -1.3 | Profit Before Taxes | | 9.4 | 14.2 |
| | | | | | | RATIOS | | | |
| | 12.9 | 3.2 | 1.7 | 3.8 | 2.0 | | | 3.1 | 3.6 |
| | 2.2 | 1.8 | 1.3 | 2.0 | 1.8 | Current | | 1.5 | 1.6 |
| | 1.0 | 1.0 | 1.0 | 1.1 | 1.1 | | | .9 | 1.1 |
| | 12.9 | 2.7 | 1.5 | 2.2 | 1.6 | | | 2.7 | 3.0 |
| | 1.4 | 1.4 | 1.0 | 1.1 | 1.2 | Quick | | 1.2 | 1.3 |
| | .7 | .6 | .5 | .5 | .8 | | | .6 | .8 |
| 0 | UND | 0 | UND | 17 | 20.9 | 7 | 51.3 | 13 | 28.0 | | | 0 | UND | 0 | UND |
| | 8 | 44.3 | 24 | 15.4 | 45 | 8.2 | 46 | 8.0 | 54 | 6.8 | Sales/Receivables | 33 | 11.0 | 20 | 18.3 |
| | 41 | 8.8 | 53 | 6.9 | 69 | 5.3 | 63 | 5.8 | 96 | 3.8 | | 60 | 6.1 | 49 | 7.5 |
| | | | | | | Cost of Sales/Inventory | | | |
| | | | | | | Cost of Sales/Payables | | | |
| | 4.7 | 4.1 | 7.1 | 2.2 | 3.2 | | | 6.4 | 3.9 |
| | 13.6 | 11.2 | 12.7 | 6.4 | 6.9 | Sales/Working Capital | | 15.0 | 10.4 |
| | NM | NM | NM | 51.9 | 26.9 | | | -77.0 | 50.0 |
| | 44.5 | 16.9 | 25.1 | | 4.7 | | | 33.4 | 83.6 |
| (10) | 10.1 | (28) | 6.9 | (29) | 5.6 | | (10) | 1.1 | EBIT/Interest | (117) | 6.1 | (58) | 8.2 |
| | 3.7 | .8 | 3.4 | | -.8 | | | 1.4 | 1.2 |
| | | | | | | Net Profit + Depr., Dep., Amort./Cur. Mat. L/T/D | | 8.4 | 13.5 |
| | | | | | | | (16) | 3.8 | (13) | 6.5 |
| | | | | | | | 2.5 | 1.8 |
| | .0 | .0 | .1 | .0 | .1 | | | .1 | .1 |
| | .1 | .3 | 1.0 | .4 | 1.8 | Fixed/Worth | | .7 | .8 |
| | 1.3 | NM | 8.1 | 2.9 | -.8 | | | 5.8 | -10.9 |
| | .2 | .7 | 1.0 | 1.0 | 1.9 | | | .6 | .8 |
| | 1.9 | 2.1 | 3.3 | 3.2 | 5.5 | Debt/Worth | | 2.8 | 2.5 |
| | 43.6 | -23.9 | 17.0 | 55.2 | -5.9 | | | UND | -22.9 |
| | 99.3 | 109.5 | 106.4 | 27.6 | | | | 100.2 | 74.3 |
| (19) | 56.5 | (31) | 31.8 | (27) | 39.2 | (12) | 4.7 | | % Profit Before Taxes/Tangible Net Worth | (120) | 34.3 | (65) | 32.9 |
| | 6.9 | 9.2 | 13.8 | -39.2 | | | | 8.6 | 9.4 |
| | 50.3 | 22.2 | 16.7 | 9.7 | 8.9 | % Profit Before Taxes/Total Assets | | 25.1 | 33.5 |
| | 33.8 | 10.9 | 8.5 | 3.9 | 3.2 | | | 9.0 | 8.9 |
| | 3.6 | -.4 | 4.3 | -4.2 | -6.7 | | | .8 | 1.2 |
| | UND | 943.6 | 106.3 | 585.7 | 271.6 | Sales/Net Fixed Assets | | 186.5 | 193.9 |
| | 66.1 | 77.0 | 35.6 | 15.9 | 9.4 | | | 27.8 | 32.3 |
| | 6.3 | 9.7 | 3.6 | 7.0 | 2.9 | | | 6.4 | 6.1 |
| | 6.8 | 3.9 | 2.7 | 2.4 | 1.3 | Sales/Total Assets | | 3.8 | 3.8 |
| | 2.3 | 2.0 | 1.4 | 1.4 | .9 | | | 2.3 | 2.2 |
| | 1.0 | .8 | .6 | .6 | .6 | | | 1.0 | .9 |
| | | .2 | .3 | | | | | .5 | .5 |
| | (22) | .6 | (26) | .9 | | | % Depr., Dep., Amort./Sales | (97) | 1.4 | (44) | 2.2 |
| | | 5.1 | 5.1 | | | | | 4.7 | 4.9 |
| | | 1.5 | | | | | | 1.3 | 3.4 |
| | (11) | 4.1 | | | | % Officers', Directors' Owners' Comp/Sales | (39) | 4.3 | (22) | 10.3 |
| | | 4.7 | | | | | | 8.6 | 19.1 |
| 8852M | 122732M | 872606M | 1340750M | 1482332M | 2377418M | Net Sales ($) | | 9782698M | 4879339M |
| 1709M | 25740M | 232638M | 733611M | 942716M | 2338265M | Total Assets ($) | | 4489644M | 2110632M |

© RMA 2024  M = $ thousand  MM = $ million
See Pages viii through xx for Explanation of Ratios and Data

# ADMIN & WASTE MANAGEMENT SERVICES—All Other Business Support Services  NAICS 561499

## Comparative Historical Data | Current Data Sorted by Sales

| Comparative Historical Data | | | Type of Statement | Current Data Sorted by Sales | | | | | |
|---|---|---|---|---|---|---|---|---|---|
| 10 | 20 | 18 | Unqualified | | | | 1 | 3 | 14 |
| 4 | 6 | 9 | Reviewed | 1 | | | 1 | 2 | 5 |
| 4 | 13 | 7 | Compiled | 1 | | | 2 | 3 | 1 |
| 17 | 25 | 22 | Tax Returns | 6 | 6 | 3 | 3 | 4 | |
| 41 | 96 | 77 | Other | 8 | 5 | 5 | 11 | 17 | 31 |
| 4/1/21-3/31/22 ALL | 4/1/22-3/31/23 ALL | 4/1/23-3/31/24 ALL | | 16 (4/1-9/30/23) | | | 117 (10/1/23-3/31/24) | | |
| | | | | 0-1MM | 1-3MM | 3-5MM | 5-10MM | 10-25MM | 25MM & OVER |
| 76 | 160 | 133 | NUMBER OF STATEMENTS | 16 | 11 | 8 | 18 | 29 | 51 |
| % | % | % | ASSETS | % | % | % | % | % | % |
| 30.5 | 21.1 | 22.9 | Cash & Equivalents | 27.4 | 25.2 | | 20.5 | 27.3 | 18.2 |
| 19.4 | 20.7 | 21.7 | Trade Receivables (net) | 11.0 | 10.7 | | 18.1 | 17.6 | 30.6 |
| 3.3 | 8.9 | 6.4 | Inventory | 4.0 | 1.0 | | 5.8 | 9.7 | 6.5 |
| 7.3 | 6.6 | 8.9 | All Other Current | 5.8 | 6.3 | | 3.7 | 6.3 | 14.7 |
| 60.6 | 57.2 | 60.0 | Total Current | 48.2 | 43.1 | | 48.1 | 60.9 | 70.1 |
| 19.4 | 21.3 | 16.8 | Fixed Assets (net) | 29.7 | 35.0 | | 12.0 | 12.2 | 13.3 |
| 9.7 | 10.8 | 10.8 | Intangibles (net) | 14.1 | .0 | | 18.5 | 13.1 | 9.6 |
| 10.4 | 10.7 | 12.4 | All Other Non-Current | 8.0 | 21.9 | | 21.3 | 13.9 | 7.1 |
| 100.0 | 100.0 | 100.0 | Total | 100.0 | 100.0 | | 100.0 | 100.0 | 100.0 |
| | | | LIABILITIES | | | | | | |
| 7.0 | 8.4 | 6.7 | Notes Payable-Short Term | 2.7 | 1.7 | | 6.7 | 8.4 | 7.1 |
| 2.0 | 3.1 | 2.7 | Cur. Mat.-L.T.D. | .3 | 1.2 | | 2.7 | 1.2 | 4.4 |
| 7.2 | 10.2 | 9.3 | Trade Payables | 2.0 | 3.5 | | 4.3 | 7.5 | 15.5 |
| .1 | .2 | .1 | Income Taxes Payable | .0 | .0 | | .3 | .0 | .1 |
| 14.4 | 15.9 | 18.4 | All Other Current | 22.0 | 15.5 | | 15.3 | 18.9 | 20.4 |
| 30.6 | 37.8 | 37.2 | Total Current | 27.0 | 21.8 | | 29.3 | 36.1 | 47.4 |
| 26.8 | 28.0 | 18.2 | Long-Term Debt | 20.5 | 21.0 | | 22.0 | 12.5 | 15.8 |
| .6 | .2 | .2 | Deferred Taxes | .0 | .6 | | .4 | .2 | .0 |
| 8.4 | 7.8 | 10.3 | All Other Non-Current | 9.6 | 5.5 | | 11.2 | 16.8 | 8.4 |
| 33.6 | 26.2 | 34.1 | Net Worth | 42.9 | 51.0 | | 37.1 | 34.4 | 28.3 |
| 100.0 | 100.0 | 100.0 | Total Liabilities & Net Worth | 100.0 | 100.0 | | 100.0 | 100.0 | 100.0 |
| | | | INCOME DATA | | | | | | |
| 100.0 | 100.0 | 100.0 | Net Sales | 100.0 | 100.0 | | 100.0 | 100.0 | 100.0 |
| | | | Gross Profit | | | | | | |
| 80.6 | 87.4 | 89.4 | Operating Expenses | 72.5 | 72.7 | | 90.9 | 97.1 | 93.8 |
| 19.4 | 12.6 | 10.6 | Operating Profit | 27.5 | 27.3 | | 9.1 | 2.9 | 6.2 |
| 1.9 | 3.4 | 3.1 | All Other Expenses (net) | 13.0 | 4.6 | | 2.0 | .6 | 2.0 |
| 17.5 | 9.1 | 7.4 | Profit Before Taxes | 14.5 | 22.7 | | 7.0 | 2.3 | 4.3 |
| | | | RATIOS | | | | | | |
| 6.2 | 4.4 | 2.9 | | 13.9 | 7.8 | | 4.2 | 4.2 | 2.1 |
| 2.1 | 1.5 | 1.6 | Current | 2.5 | 2.3 | | 1.9 | 1.6 | 1.5 |
| 1.1 | 1.0 | 1.1 | | .5 | .7 | | .9 | 1.1 | 1.1 |
| 5.1 | 3.1 | 2.4 | | 13.9 | 7.8 | | 3.5 | 3.2 | 1.7 |
| 1.4 | 1.2 | 1.2 | Quick | .9 | 1.4 | | 1.6 | 1.2 | 1.1 |
| 1.0 | .5 | .6 | | .3 | .6 | | .3 | .5 | .6 |
| 0 UND | 0 UND | 0 UND | | 0 UND | 0 UND | | 0 UND | 0 UND | 16 22.6 |
| 23 15.6 | 26 13.8 | 30 12.3 | Sales/Receivables | 0 UND | 0 UND | | 29 12.8 | 35 10.3 | 47 7.8 |
| 41 9.0 | 59 6.2 | 61 6.0 | | 12 31.7 | 18 20.2 | | 43 8.4 | 58 6.3 | 74 4.9 |
| | | | Cost of Sales/Inventory | | | | | | |
| | | | Cost of Sales/Payables | | | | | | |
| 3.2 | 4.5 | 4.3 | | 1.7 | 3.5 | | 4.2 | 4.1 | 5.5 |
| 9.4 | 10.7 | 9.8 | Sales/Working Capital | 7.5 | 7.2 | | 6.9 | 14.1 | 9.4 |
| 52.3 | -863.5 | 186.2 | | -8.0 | -8.6 | | -47.6 | 92.4 | 90.9 |
| | 64.2 | 23.4 | 18.9 | | | | 7.4 | 14.5 | 30.6 |
| (50) 9.9 | (106) 4.8 | (86) 6.1 | EBIT/Interest | | | (11) 1.3 | (21) 7.6 | (38) 5.4 |
| 1.4 | 1.0 | 1.3 | | | | | -5.2 | -.2 | 2.9 |
| | 121.3 | 6.6 | Net Profit + Depr., Dep., | | | | | | |
| (22) 5.8 | (17) 3.5 | Amort./Cur. Mat. L/T/D | | | | | | | |
| .9 | 1.1 | | | | | | | | |
| .0 | .0 | .0 | | .0 | .0 | | .1 | .0 | .0 |
| .2 | .7 | .5 | Fixed/Worth | .5 | .8 | | 1.0 | .2 | .5 |
| 3.8 | 5.4 | 4.5 | | 11.8 | 2.2 | | -.3 | 2.2 | 10.6 |
| .3 | .9 | .8 | | .2 | .4 | | .7 | .3 | 1.4 |
| 2.1 | 3.3 | 2.4 | Debt/Worth | 2.2 | 1.4 | | 3.3 | 1.4 | 3.8 |
| -26.5 | -14.3 | 107.1 | | 463.3 | 1.9 | | -4.7 | -6.9 | 131.1 |
| 85.5 | 72.8 | 92.5 | | 304.2 | 71.1 | | 137.1 | 44.5 | 117.9 |
| (55) 42.5 | (114) 37.5 | (104) 31.5 | % Profit Before Taxes/Tangible Net Worth | (14) 26.3 | 18.1 | | (12) 52.4 | (21) 23.3 | (39) 44.6 |
| 16.9 | 6.8 | 7.3 | | 5.9 | .6 | | 8.5 | 6.8 | 14.4 |
| 38.8 | 22.6 | 22.8 | | 31.6 | 31.7 | | 33.9 | 19.3 | 18.3 |
| 15.2 | 8.1 | 8.6 | % Profit Before Taxes/Total Assets | 7.4 | 7.7 | | 6.6 | 8.2 | 9.4 |
| 1.8 | .9 | .4 | | -.2 | .5 | | -5.5 | -1.1 | 3.8 |
| 284.7 | 252.0 | 433.6 | | 63.1 | 999.8 | | 204.7 | 445.2 | 740.1 |
| 55.3 | 27.3 | 30.8 | Sales/Net Fixed Assets | 13.8 | 2.6 | | 30.3 | 40.5 | 52.8 |
| 5.7 | 5.5 | 6.3 | | .9 | 1.3 | | 7.8 | 7.1 | 7.7 |
| 3.7 | 3.3 | 3.0 | | 1.9 | 1.1 | | 2.5 | 5.7 | 4.1 |
| 2.2 | 1.8 | 1.8 | Sales/Total Assets | 1.0 | .6 | | 1.5 | 2.0 | 2.1 |
| .9 | .8 | .8 | | .1 | .2 | | .7 | 1.1 | 1.1 |
| .3 | .5 | .3 | | | | | | .2 | .2 |
| (41) 1.5 | (77) 2.5 | (69) 1.6 | % Depr., Dep., Amort./Sales | | | | (16) .6 | (29) 1.0 |
| 4.9 | 4.4 | 4.8 | | | | | | 3.1 | 3.0 |
| 4.1 | 1.4 | 1.6 | % Officers', Directors', Owners' Comp/Sales | | | | | | |
| (17) 6.7 | (29) 2.8 | (25) 4.0 | | | | | | | |
| 16.0 | 6.1 | 9.8 | | | | | | | |
| 5206491M | 11287305M | 6204690M | Net Sales ($) | 9362M | 19821M | 34372M | 130565M | 485036M | 5525534M |
| 1791265M | 6050174M | 4274679M | Total Assets ($) | 25341M | 52514M | 20701M | 149839M | 599076M | 3427208M |

© RMA 2024   M = $ thousand   MM = $ million
See Pages viii through xx for Explanation of Ratios and Data

# ADMIN & WASTE MANAGEMENT SERVICES—Travel Agencies  NAICS 561510

## Current Data Sorted by Assets | Comparative Historical Data

| | | | | | | | Type of Statement | | |
|---|---|---|---|---|---|---|---|---|---|
| | | 1 | | 5 | 1 | 1 | Unqualified | 8 | 5 |
| | 3 | | 6 | 1 | | | Reviewed | 6 | |
| 1 | 1 | | 2 | 1 | | | Compiled | 4 | 1 |
| 2 | 3 | | 5 | | | | Tax Returns | 21 | 7 |
| 4 | 16 | | 23 | 12 | 4 | 1 | Other | 42 | 24 |
| | 23 (4/1-9/30/23) | | | 70 (10/1/23-3/31/24) | | | | 4/1/19-3/31/20 | 4/1/20-3/31/21 |
| 0-500M | 500M-2MM | | 2-10MM | 10-50MM | 50-100MM | 100-250MM | | ALL | ALL |
| 7 | 24 | | 36 | 19 | 5 | 2 | NUMBER OF STATEMENTS | 81 | 37 |
| % | % | | % | % | % | % | ASSETS | % | % |
| | 54.2 | | 53.9 | 30.9 | | | Cash & Equivalents | 39.2 | 42.5 |
| | 19.4 | | 17.7 | 16.5 | | | Trade Receivables (net) | 16.8 | 10.2 |
| | .3 | | .1 | .2 | | | Inventory | .6 | .1 |
| | 8.5 | | 11.9 | 7.9 | | | All Other Current | 7.4 | 6.0 |
| | 82.5 | | 83.6 | 55.5 | | | Total Current | 64.0 | 58.8 |
| | 4.0 | | 4.7 | 15.2 | | | Fixed Assets (net) | 12.3 | 14.7 |
| | 7.3 | | 4.4 | 15.1 | | | Intangibles (net) | 11.9 | 12.7 |
| | 6.2 | | 7.3 | 14.1 | | | All Other Non-Current | 11.8 | 13.8 |
| | 100.0 | | 100.0 | 100.0 | | | Total | 100.0 | 100.0 |
| | | | | | | | LIABILITIES | | |
| | 4.7 | | 2.1 | 2.0 | | | Notes Payable-Short Term | 7.1 | 4.3 |
| | 1.2 | | .7 | 1.2 | | | Cur. Mat.-L.T.D. | .7 | 3.1 |
| | 13.7 | | 14.1 | 17.1 | | | Trade Payables | 12.5 | 9.2 |
| | .6 | | .1 | .8 | | | Income Taxes Payable | 1.2 | .2 |
| | 42.9 | | 37.0 | 26.7 | | | All Other Current | 40.8 | 40.1 |
| | 63.1 | | 54.2 | 47.9 | | | Total Current | 62.3 | 57.0 |
| | 9.3 | | 4.4 | 8.9 | | | Long-Term Debt | 7.9 | 11.0 |
| | .0 | | .0 | .6 | | | Deferred Taxes | .3 | .7 |
| | 5.1 | | 1.4 | 2.8 | | | All Other Non-Current | 7.0 | 6.0 |
| | 22.5 | | 40.0 | 39.8 | | | Net Worth | 22.5 | 25.2 |
| | 100.0 | | 100.0 | 100.0 | | | Total Liabilties & Net Worth | 100.0 | 100.0 |
| | | | | | | | INCOME DATA | | |
| | 100.0 | | 100.0 | 100.0 | | | Net Sales | 100.0 | 100.0 |
| | | | | | | | Gross Profit | | |
| | 94.1 | | 90.9 | 91.1 | | | Operating Expenses | 94.3 | 107.0 |
| | 5.9 | | 9.1 | 8.9 | | | Operating Profit | 5.7 | -7.0 |
| | .1 | | -.3 | 1.5 | | | All Other Expenses (net) | .5 | .0 |
| | 5.9 | | 9.4 | 7.5 | | | Profit Before Taxes | 5.2 | -7.1 |
| | | | | | | | RATIOS | | |
| | 2.7 | | 2.8 | 1.6 | | | | 2.4 | 2.2 |
| | 1.4 | | 1.4 | 1.1 | | | Current | 1.2 | 1.0 |
| | 1.0 | | 1.2 | .6 | | | | .8 | .6 |
| | 2.6 | | 2.2 | 1.5 | | | | 2.2 | 2.1 |
| | 1.4 | | 1.3 | 1.1 | | | Quick | 1.0 | .9 |
| | .7 | | .9 | .5 | | | | .5 | .5 |
| | 0 UND | 0 | 999.8 | 1 482.8 | | | | 1 385.7 | 0 UND |
| | 2 164.5 | 8 | 46.6 | 22 16.9 | | | Sales/Receivables | 12 31.6 | 1 266.0 |
| | 41 9.0 | 47 | 7.8 | 43 8.4 | | | | 34 10.6 | 18 20.2 |
| | | | | | | | Cost of Sales/Inventory | | |
| | | | | | | | Cost of Sales/Payables | | |
| | 8.2 | | 4.4 | 6.0 | | | | 7.7 | 10.5 |
| | 25.3 | | 14.8 | 15.2 | | | Sales/Working Capital | 39.8 | UND |
| | NM | | 45.0 | -19.2 | | | | -14.2 | -10.0 |
| | 43.6 | | 282.0 | 153.8 | | | | 92.6 | 20.5 |
| (13) | 15.2 | (15) | 33.1 | (11) 2.8 | | | EBIT/Interest | (43) 28.5 | (21) -9.4 |
| | 4.5 | | 13.3 | .7 | | | | 2.4 | -54.5 |
| | | | | | | | Net Profit + Depr., Dep., Amort./Cur. Mat. L/T/D | | |
| | .0 | | .0 | .0 | | | | .1 | .3 |
| | .0 | | .0 | .2 | | | Fixed/Worth | .4 | 1.5 |
| | -2.7 | | .2 | 1.2 | | | | UND | -.9 |
| | 1.8 | | .6 | .7 | | | | 1.0 | 1.6 |
| | 9.5 | | 2.4 | 2.1 | | | Debt/Worth | 3.2 | 6.9 |
| | -11.8 | | 5.9 | 70.8 | | | | UND | -12.0 |
| | 213.1 | | 110.6 | 108.6 | | | | 105.5 | 48.1 |
| (16) | 93.3 | (34) | 65.9 | (15) 49.6 | | | % Profit Before Taxes/Tangible Net Worth | (61) 40.9 | (24) -14.5 |
| | 51.6 | | 24.7 | 1.3 | | | | 12.1 | -83.4 |
| | 38.5 | | 31.8 | 32.2 | | | | 23.5 | 5.5 |
| | 19.1 | | 13.0 | 13.5 | | | % Profit Before Taxes/Total Assets | 8.3 | -10.4 |
| | 1.5 | | 6.7 | .3 | | | | 1.6 | -20.7 |
| | UND | | 999.8 | 680.0 | | | | 407.5 | 200.5 |
| | 973.6 | | 457.7 | 46.8 | | | Sales/Net Fixed Assets | 67.7 | 39.4 |
| | 83.7 | | 176.6 | 5.3 | | | | 15.4 | 11.7 |
| | 8.2 | | 8.1 | 2.1 | | | | 6.0 | 5.6 |
| | 4.3 | | 2.8 | 1.5 | | | Sales/Total Assets | 2.7 | 1.4 |
| | 2.2 | | 1.5 | .9 | | | | 1.5 | .9 |
| | | | .1 | .1 | | | | .2 | .2 |
| | | (15) | .2 | (12) .6 | | | % Depr., Dep., Amort./Sales | (47) .5 | (23) .8 |
| | | | .5 | 4.9 | | | | 1.2 | 3.6 |
| | | | | | | | % Officers', Directors' Owners' Comp/Sales | 1.5 | |
| | | | | | | | | (30) 3.8 | |
| | | | | | | | | 7.3 | |
| 34796M | 280492M | | 886186M | 990626M | 320301M | 127172M | Net Sales ($) | 3538111M | 1003065M |
| 2071M | 27622M | | 175159M | 517919M | 280564M | 262632M | Total Assets ($) | 1883196M | 670299M |

© RMA 2024  M = $ thousand   MM = $ million
See Pages viii through xx for Explanation of Ratios and Data

## ADMIN & WASTE MANAGEMENT SERVICES—Travel Agencies  NAICS 561510

### Comparative Historical Data | Current Data Sorted by Sales

| Comparative Historical Data | | | | | Current Data Sorted by Sales | | | | | |
|---|---|---|---|---|---|---|---|---|---|---|
| 3 | 7 | 8 | **Type of Statement** | | | 1 | | 1 | | 7 |
| 3 | 9 | 10 | Unqualified | | 3 | 2 | 3 | 1 | 1 |
| 1 | 10 | 5 | Reviewed | | 1 | 1 | | 1 | 2 |
| 6 | 22 | 10 | Compiled | | 1 | 1 | 4 | 1 | 2 |
| 32 | 56 | 60 | Tax Returns | 1 | 9 | 1 | 11 | 13 | 23 |
| 4/1/21-3/31/22 ALL | 4/1/22-3/31/23 ALL | 4/1/23-3/31/24 ALL | Other | | 9 | 4 | | | |
| | | | | **23 (4/1-9/30/23)** | | | **70 (10/1/23-3/31/24)** | | |
| | | | | 0-1MM | 1-3MM | 3-5MM | 5-10MM | 10-25MM | 25MM & OVER |
| 45 | 104 | 93 | **NUMBER OF STATEMENTS** | 1 | 14 | 9 | 18 | 16 | 35 |
| % | % | % | **ASSETS** | % | % | % | % | % | % |
| 50.4 | 54.5 | 48.5 | Cash & Equivalents | | 52.6 | | 48.8 | 51.6 | 44.6 |
| 14.5 | 13.8 | 16.8 | Trade Receivables (net) | | 23.2 | | 21.3 | 16.8 | 11.7 |
| .6 | .1 | .2 | Inventory | | .0 | | .0 | .2 | .1 |
| 10.3 | 11.6 | 10.0 | All Other Current | | 15.3 | | 10.9 | 4.9 | 10.0 |
| 75.8 | 80.0 | 75.5 | Total Current | | 91.1 | | 81.0 | 73.6 | 66.4 |
| 9.6 | 5.9 | 6.3 | Fixed Assets (net) | | 1.3 | | 5.8 | 11.5 | 7.1 |
| 11.0 | 8.7 | 10.0 | Intangibles (net) | | 7.3 | | 3.1 | 7.5 | 17.7 |
| 3.7 | 5.4 | 8.2 | All Other Non-Current | | .3 | | 10.1 | 7.4 | 8.8 |
| 100.0 | 100.0 | 100.0 | Total | | 100.0 | | 100.0 | 100.0 | 100.0 |
| | | | **LIABILITIES** | | | | | | |
| 6.5 | 4.1 | 5.4 | Notes Payable-Short Term | | .1 | | 7.2 | 1.9 | 3.1 |
| 2.5 | .8 | 1.7 | Cur. Mat.-L.T.D. | | 1.3 | | 3.6 | .5 | 1.6 |
| 15.5 | 17.4 | 15.3 | Trade Payables | | 19.1 | | 19.6 | 12.5 | 13.1 |
| .2 | .2 | .4 | Income Taxes Payable | | .9 | | .2 | .0 | .4 |
| 35.2 | 37.1 | 36.0 | All Other Current | | 38.8 | | 53.1 | 28.0 | 31.2 |
| 59.9 | 59.6 | 58.8 | Total Current | | 60.2 | | 83.8 | 42.8 | 49.4 |
| 9.1 | 10.4 | 6.9 | Long-Term Debt | | 6.6 | | 3.6 | 10.4 | 8.3 |
| .1 | .0 | .1 | Deferred Taxes | | .1 | | .0 | .0 | .3 |
| 11.6 | 7.0 | 3.4 | All Other Non-Current | | 2.1 | | 6.4 | 4.6 | 2.7 |
| 19.3 | 23.0 | 30.8 | Net Worth | | 31.1 | | 6.2 | 42.2 | 39.3 |
| 100.0 | 100.0 | 100.0 | Total Liabilties & Net Worth | | 100.0 | | 100.0 | 100.0 | 100.0 |
| | | | **INCOME DATA** | | | | | | |
| 100.0 | 100.0 | 100.0 | Net Sales | | 100.0 | | 100.0 | 100.0 | 100.0 |
| 95.6 | 92.0 | 91.9 | Gross Profit | | 87.2 | | 92.7 | 93.1 | 93.0 |
| 4.4 | 8.0 | 8.1 | Operating Expenses | | 12.8 | | 7.3 | 6.9 | 7.0 |
| -.8 | -.2 | .1 | Operating Profit | | -.2 | | -.4 | .2 | .4 |
| 5.2 | 8.2 | 8.0 | All Other Expenses (net) | | 13.0 | | 7.7 | 6.8 | 6.6 |
| | | | Profit Before Taxes | | | | | | |
| | | | **RATIOS** | | | | | | |
| 1.8 | 2.8 | 2.2 | | | 1.7 | | 1.9 | 3.3 | 2.0 |
| 1.2 | 1.3 | 1.4 | Current | | 1.4 | | 1.2 | 1.5 | 1.2 |
| .9 | 1.0 | 1.0 | | | 1.3 | | .8 | 1.3 | 1.0 |
| 1.7 | 2.6 | 1.9 | | | 1.6 | | 1.6 | 3.2 | 1.6 |
| 1.0 | 1.3 | 1.3 | Quick | | 1.3 | | .9 | 1.4 | 1.1 |
| .7 | .7 | .7 | | | 1.0 | | .7 | 1.2 | .7 |
| 0 UND | 0 UND | 0 UND | | 1 554.5 | | 0 UND | 0 UND | 0 UND | |
| 4 99.8 | 3 141.4 | 4 83.2 | Sales/Receivables | 26 14.3 | | 8 46.0 | 8 47.7 | 2 191.1 | |
| 48 7.6 | 38 9.7 | 43 8.5 | | 182 2.0 | | 48 7.6 | 41 8.9 | 28 13.1 | |
| | | | Cost of Sales/Inventory | | | | | | |
| | | | Cost of Sales/Payables | | | | | | |
| 5.3 | 4.9 | 6.8 | | | 1.5 | | 8.8 | 6.7 | 8.9 |
| 62.1 | 23.4 | 24.2 | Sales/Working Capital | | 5.8 | | 23.2 | 19.1 | 88.1 |
| -29.8 | -602.3 | 324.0 | | | 18.1 | | -13.9 | 26.8 | -123.3 |
| 68.3 | 95.7 | 115.5 | | | | | 318.9 | | 176.0 |
| (25) 6.6 | (50) 18.0 | (45) 18.5 | EBIT/Interest | | | | (10) 24.0 | (17) 55.0 | |
| -.1 | 6.4 | 1.7 | | | | | -1.7 | | 1.7 |
| | | | Net Profit + Depr., Dep., Amort./Cur. Mat. L/T/D | | | | | | |
| .0 | .0 | .0 | | | .0 | | .0 | .0 | .0 |
| .8 | .1 | .1 | Fixed/Worth | | .0 | | .0 | .0 | .2 |
| -.2 | 1.3 | 1.0 | | | NM | | NM | 1.0 | 1.3 |
| 1.6 | 1.2 | 1.0 | | | 1.5 | | 1.8 | .9 | .9 |
| 8.2 | 4.2 | 3.5 | Debt/Worth | | 2.4 | | 7.1 | 2.1 | 4.9 |
| -4.7 | -9.6 | 23.4 | | | NM | | -33.3 | 3.8 | -75.0 |
| 73.7 | 98.1 | 109.0 | | | 98.9 | | 163.6 | 90.8 | 171.3 |
| (26) 39.1 | (72) 56.7 | (72) 67.2 | % Profit Before Taxes/Tangible Net Worth | (11) 66.3 | | (12) 78.9 | (14) 64.1 | (26) 68.7 | |
| 11.7 | 17.7 | 20.3 | | | 19.2 | | 31.4 | 35.0 | 39.7 |
| 18.0 | 28.7 | 33.3 | | | 27.0 | | 38.0 | 28.1 | 32.3 |
| 8.1 | 15.7 | 14.6 | % Profit Before Taxes/Total Assets | | 12.2 | | 13.0 | 18.3 | 14.3 |
| -1.3 | 2.2 | 4.1 | | | 5.7 | | 2.6 | 5.3 | 2.3 |
| 434.1 | 999.8 | 999.8 | | | UND | | UND | 999.8 | 999.8 |
| 72.2 | 295.6 | 458.0 | Sales/Net Fixed Assets | | 465.7 | | 457.7 | 571.9 | 338.2 |
| 31.5 | 42.9 | 76.3 | | | 55.2 | | 116.0 | 73.7 | 46.8 |
| 8.4 | 7.7 | 6.9 | | | 2.5 | | 5.0 | 8.0 | 12.9 |
| 1.5 | 2.1 | 2.7 | Sales/Total Assets | | 1.5 | | 3.1 | 3.0 | 2.9 |
| .6 | 1.1 | 1.4 | | | .5 | | 1.8 | 1.5 | 1.3 |
| .2 | .0 | .1 | | | | | .0 | .0 | .1 |
| (28) .5 | (44) .3 | (37) .3 | % Depr., Dep., Amort./Sales | | | | (10) .4 | (15) .5 | 1.9 |
| 1.4 | 1.4 | .9 | | | | | | 5.0 | |
| | 1.0 | 1.3 | | | | | | | |
| | (28) 2.8 | (14) 2.5 | % Officers', Directors', Owners' Comp/Sales | | | | | | |
| | 7.9 | 5.1 | | | | | | | |
| 1412215M | 4617038M | 2639573M | Net Sales ($) | 383M | 29273M | 35093M | 135628M | 269583M | 2169613M |
| 768926M | 1320558M | 1265967M | Total Assets ($) | 112M | 33791M | 22907M | 51635M | 134024M | 1023498M |

© RMA 2024   M = $ thousand   MM = $ million
See Pages viii through xx for Explanation of Ratios and Data

# ADMIN & WASTE MANAGEMENT SERVICES—Tour Operators  NAICS 561520

## Current Data Sorted by Assets

| | | | | 1 | | | Comparative Historical Data | |
|---|---|---|---|---|---|---|---|---|
| | | 1 | 1 | 1 | | **Type of Statement** | | |
| 1 | 2 | 2 | 1 | | | Unqualified | 2 | 1 |
| | | 2 | 1 | | | Reviewed | 1 | |
| 1 | 2 | 12 | | | 3 | Compiled | 3 | |
| | 8 (4/1-9/30/23) | | 28 (10/1/23-3/31/24) | | | Tax Returns | 9 | 2 |
| 0-500M | 500M-2MM | 2-10MM | 10-50MM | 50-100MM | 100-250MM | Other | 25 | 8 |
| | | | | | | | 4/1/19- | 4/1/20- |
| | | | | | | | 3/31/20 | 3/31/21 |
| | | | | | | | ALL | ALL |
| 2 | 4 | 17 | 8 | 2 | 3 | **NUMBER OF STATEMENTS** | 40 | 11 |
| % | % | % | % | % | % | **ASSETS** | % | % |
| | | 44.6 | | | | Cash & Equivalents | 33.2 | 29.5 |
| | | 1.0 | | | | Trade Receivables (net) | 8.3 | 14.7 |
| | | .2 | | | | Inventory | 2.3 | .3 |
| | | 13.6 | | | | All Other Current | 10.9 | 16.7 |
| | | 59.4 | | | | Total Current | 54.6 | 61.2 |
| | | 15.5 | | | | Fixed Assets (net) | 29.3 | 18.5 |
| | | 9.2 | | | | Intangibles (net) | 8.2 | 11.6 |
| | | 15.9 | | | | All Other Non-Current | 7.9 | 8.7 |
| | | 100.0 | | | | Total | 100.0 | 100.0 |
| | | | | | | **LIABILITIES** | | |
| | | .1 | | | | Notes Payable-Short Term | 3.3 | 8.8 |
| | | 2.5 | | | | Cur. Mat.-L.T.D. | 16.5 | 11.3 |
| | | 5.1 | | | | Trade Payables | 7.9 | 6.8 |
| | | .0 | | | | Income Taxes Payable | .2 | .0 |
| | | 49.8 | | | | All Other Current | 34.0 | 33.4 |
| | | 57.5 | | | | Total Current | 62.0 | 60.2 |
| | | 7.7 | | | | Long-Term Debt | 23.4 | 53.9 |
| | | .2 | | | | Deferred Taxes | .1 | .0 |
| | | 12.3 | | | | All Other Non-Current | 2.9 | .8 |
| | | 22.3 | | | | Net Worth | 11.5 | -14.9 |
| | | 100.0 | | | | Total Liabilities & Net Worth | 100.0 | 100.0 |
| | | | | | | **INCOME DATA** | | |
| | | 100.0 | | | | Net Sales | 100.0 | 100.0 |
| | | | | | | Gross Profit | | |
| | | 79.8 | | | | Operating Expenses | 93.4 | 104.0 |
| | | 20.2 | | | | Operating Profit | 6.6 | -4.0 |
| | | -.6 | | | | All Other Expenses (net) | -.2 | 3.7 |
| | | 20.8 | | | | Profit Before Taxes | 6.8 | -7.7 |
| | | | | | | **RATIOS** | | |
| | | 2.9 | | | | | 1.7 | 4.5 |
| | | 1.2 | | | | Current | 1.1 | 1.1 |
| | | .8 | | | | | .6 | .3 |
| | | 2.9 | | | | | 1.6 | 4.5 |
| | | .9 | | | | Quick | .8 | 1.0 |
| | | .6 | | | | | .3 | .1 |
| | 0 | 0 | UND | | | | 0 UND | 0 UND |
| | 0 | 0 | UND | | | Sales/Receivables | 1 555.0 | 20 18.0 |
| | 0 | 732.5 | | | | | 13 27.1 | 45 8.1 |
| | | | | | | Cost of Sales/Inventory | | |
| | | | | | | Cost of Sales/Payables | | |
| | | 5.9 | | | | | 8.3 | 3.6 |
| | | 40.7 | | | | Sales/Working Capital | 98.4 | 23.2 |
| | | -13.8 | | | | | -13.1 | -1.1 |
| | | | | | | | 109.4 | |
| | | | | | | EBIT/Interest | (23) 5.8 | |
| | | | | | | | 1.4 | |
| | | | | | | Net Profit + Depr., Dep., | | |
| | | | | | | Amort./Cur. Mat. L/T/D | | |
| | | .0 | | | | | .2 | .0 |
| | | .2 | | | | Fixed/Worth | 1.0 | .4 |
| | | 1.5 | | | | | NM | -.4 |
| | | 2.7 | | | | | .8 | 2.4 |
| | | 5.1 | | | | Debt/Worth | 3.6 | -12.2 |
| | | 20.0 | | | | | -14.0 | -2.0 |
| | | 214.6 | | | | | 94.1 | |
| | | (14) 65.2 | | | | % Profit Before Taxes/Tangible Net Worth | (28) 42.9 | |
| | | 44.8 | | | | | 9.9 | |
| | | 34.5 | | | | | 28.7 | 3.9 |
| | | 13.1 | | | | % Profit Before Taxes/Total Assets | 8.1 | -2.1 |
| | | 4.5 | | | | | .3 | -17.2 |
| | | UND | | | | | 97.3 | UND |
| | | 212.0 | | | | Sales/Net Fixed Assets | 13.4 | 21.3 |
| | | 5.8 | | | | | 4.2 | 2.8 |
| | | 3.3 | | | | | 4.3 | 2.4 |
| | | 1.5 | | | | Sales/Total Assets | 2.1 | 1.1 |
| | | 1.0 | | | | | 1.0 | .3 |
| | | | | | | | .5 | |
| | | | | | | % Depr., Dep., Amort./Sales | (32) 1.9 | |
| | | | | | | | 5.6 | |
| | | | | | | % Officers', Directors' Owners' Comp/Sales | | |
| 541M | 19050M | 281294M | 267023M | 159625M | 598357M | Net Sales ($) | 1289347M | 47112M |
| 565M | 6062M | 92487M | 194453M | 129424M | 478663M | Total Assets ($) | 708230M | 97112M |

© RMA 2024

M = $ thousand   MM = $ million
See Pages viii through xx for Explanation of Ratios and Data

# ADMIN & WASTE MANAGEMENT SERVICES—Tour Operators  NAICS 561520

## Comparative Historical Data | Current Data Sorted by Sales

| | | | | | | | | | | |
|---|---|---|---|---|---|---|---|---|---|---|
| 1 | 3 | 1 | **Type of Statement** | | | | | | | 1 |
| 1 | 2 | 3 | Unqualified | | | | | | 1 | 2 |
| | 3 | 6 | Reviewed | | 2 | | | 1 | 1 | 1 |
| 2 | 5 | 3 | Compiled | 1 | | 1 | 1 | 2 | | |
| 8 | 23 | 23 | Tax Returns | | 4 | | 5 | | | 7 |
| 4/1/21- | 4/1/22- | 4/1/23- | Other | | | | | | | |
| 3/31/22 | 3/31/23 | 3/31/24 | | 0-1MM | 1-3MM | 3-5MM | 5-10MM | 10-25MM | 25MM & OVER | |
| ALL | ALL | ALL | | 8 (4/1-9/30/23) | | | 28 (10/1/23-3/31/24) | | | |
| 12 | 36 | 36 | **NUMBER OF STATEMENTS** | 2 | 6 | 2 | 6 | 9 | 11 | |
| % | % | % | **ASSETS** | % | % | % | % | % | % | |
| 47.8 | 33.0 | 39.9 | Cash & Equivalents | | | | | | 39.5 | |
| 3.9 | 8.8 | 2.3 | Trade Receivables (net) | | | | | | 4.7 | |
| 2.7 | 3.4 | .4 | Inventory | | | | | | 1.0 | |
| 14.6 | 9.4 | 15.0 | All Other Current | | | | | | 16.5 | |
| 69.0 | 54.5 | 57.6 | Total Current | | | | | | 61.7 | |
| 13.4 | 25.2 | 21.1 | Fixed Assets (net) | | | | | | 22.6 | |
| 15.9 | 7.2 | 8.6 | Intangibles (net) | | | | | | 8.7 | |
| 1.7 | 13.2 | 12.7 | All Other Non-Current | | | | | | 7.0 | |
| 100.0 | 100.0 | 100.0 | Total | | | | | | 100.0 | |
| | | | **LIABILITIES** | | | | | | | |
| 1.5 | 2.3 | .3 | Notes Payable-Short Term | | | | | | .5 | |
| 2.0 | 10.4 | 2.8 | Cur. Mat.-L.T.D. | | | | | | 1.9 | |
| 3.0 | 12.9 | 7.6 | Trade Payables | | | | | | 16.0 | |
| .0 | .2 | .2 | Income Taxes Payable | | | | | | .1 | |
| 45.0 | 35.0 | 37.1 | All Other Current | | | | | | 26.9 | |
| 51.5 | 60.7 | 48.1 | Total Current | | | | | | 45.5 | |
| 15.4 | 27.5 | 16.4 | Long-Term Debt | | | | | | 19.0 | |
| .4 | .5 | .1 | Deferred Taxes | | | | | | .1 | |
| 10.7 | 19.7 | 10.5 | All Other Non-Current | | | | | | 13.7 | |
| 22.1 | -8.4 | 25.0 | Net Worth | | | | | | 21.8 | |
| 100.0 | 100.0 | 100.0 | Total Liabilities & Net Worth | | | | | | 100.0 | |
| | | | **INCOME DATA** | | | | | | | |
| 100.0 | 100.0 | 100.0 | Net Sales | | | | | | 100.0 | |
| | | | Gross Profit | | | | | | 93.7 | |
| 89.0 | 87.2 | 82.8 | Operating Expenses | | | | | | 6.3 | |
| 11.0 | 12.8 | 17.2 | Operating Profit | | | | | | -.3 | |
| .5 | .4 | .6 | All Other Expenses (net) | | | | | | 6.6 | |
| 10.6 | 12.4 | 16.6 | Profit Before Taxes | | | | | | | |
| | | | **RATIOS** | | | | | | | |
| 3.7 | 2.6 | 2.7 | | | | | | | 2.1 | |
| 1.5 | 1.0 | 1.2 | Current | | | | | | 1.2 | |
| .8 | .5 | .9 | | | | | | | 1.1 | |
| 3.5 | 1.9 | 2.2 | | | | | | | 1.8 | |
| 1.4 | .8 | 1.0 | Quick | | | | | | 1.1 | |
| .4 | .4 | .6 | | | | | | | .5 | |
| 0 UND | 0 UND | 0 UND | | | | | | | 0 UND | |
| 0 794.4 | 1 341.2 | 0 999.8 | Sales/Receivables | | | | | | 5 75.4 | |
| 13 29.0 | 24 15.0 | 5 69.2 | | | | | | | 27 13.4 | |
| | | | Cost of Sales/Inventory | | | | | | | |
| | | | Cost of Sales/Payables | | | | | | | |
| 3.5 | 4.5 | 3.6 | | | | | | | 3.1 | |
| 4.7 | -197.8 | 36.1 | Sales/Working Capital | | | | | | 37.8 | |
| -4.7 | -12.3 | -20.5 | | | | | | | 111.4 | |
| | 71.3 | 89.0 | | | | | | | | |
| (26) 19.1 | (20) 18.5 | | EBIT/Interest | | | | | | | |
| | 1.3 | 6.3 | | | | | | | | |
| | | | Net Profit + Depr., Dep., Amort./Cur. Mat. L/T/D | | | | | | | |
| .0 | .1 | .0 | | | | | | | .1 | |
| .3 | .7 | .5 | Fixed/Worth | | | | | | .3 | |
| -45.7 | -1.4 | 1.8 | | | | | | | 5.6 | |
| 1.1 | .5 | 1.0 | | | | | | | .8 | |
| -205.3 | 3.7 | 4.8 | Debt/Worth | | | | | | 6.6 | |
| -4.2 | -3.4 | 25.4 | | | | | | | 26.5 | |
| | 96.9 | 127.9 | % Profit Before Taxes/Tangible Net Worth | | | | | | | |
| (22) 43.5 | (29) 58.9 | | | | | | | | | |
| | 8.5 | 25.3 | | | | | | | | |
| 49.8 | 33.1 | 21.0 | % Profit Before Taxes/Total Assets | | | | | | 19.6 | |
| 11.8 | 13.6 | 10.3 | | | | | | | 6.8 | |
| -9.3 | .7 | 4.9 | | | | | | | 3.9 | |
| UND | 215.2 | 999.8 | | | | | | | 541.6 | |
| 75.8 | 17.4 | 53.5 | Sales/Net Fixed Assets | | | | | | 49.4 | |
| 4.9 | 4.0 | 2.5 | | | | | | | 2.1 | |
| 2.8 | 2.8 | 2.4 | | | | | | | 4.3 | |
| 1.1 | 1.7 | 1.3 | Sales/Total Assets | | | | | | 1.9 | |
| .4 | 1.1 | .9 | | | | | | | 1.1 | |
| | .7 | .2 | | | | | | | | |
| (17) 1.7 | (19) 1.3 | | % Depr., Dep., Amort./Sales | | | | | | | |
| | 4.3 | 2.8 | | | | | | | | |
| | | | % Officers', Directors' Owners' Comp/Sales | | | | | | | |
| 121566M | 891065M | 1325890M | Net Sales ($) | 541M | 11824M | 6655M | 43513M | 138281M | 1125076M | |
| 221685M | 617334M | 901654M | Total Assets ($) | 565M | 35071M | 4913M | 36451M | 112321M | 712333M | |

M = $ thousand   MM = $ million
See Pages viii through xx for Explanation of Ratios and Data

© RMA 2024

# ADMIN & WASTE MANAGEMENT SERVICES—All Other Travel Arrangement and Reservation Services  NAICS 561599

## Current Data Sorted by Assets | Comparative Historical Data

| | | | | | | | | | |
|---|---|---|---|---|---|---|---|---|---|
| | | | | 2 | 1 | 4 | **Type of Statement** | | |
| | | | | | 1 | | Unqualified | 11 | 2 |
| | | 1 | | | | | Reviewed | 1 | |
| | | 1 | | | | | Compiled | 4 | |
| | | 1 | | 1 | | | Tax Returns | 4 | 3 |
| | 1 | 2 | 1 | 8 | 3 | | Other | 23 | 14 |
| | 0-500M | 6 (4/1-9/30/23) 500M-2MM | 3 2-10MM | 26 (10/1/23-3/31/24) 10-50MM | 50-100MM | 4 100-250MM | | 4/1/19- 3/31/20 ALL | 4/1/20- 3/31/21 ALL |
| | 1 | 4 | 6 | 10 | 7 | 4 | NUMBER OF STATEMENTS | 43 | 19 |
| | % | % | % | % | % | % | ASSETS | % | % |
| | | | | 21.9 | | | Cash & Equivalents | 37.7 | 27.3 |
| | | | | 20.1 | | | Trade Receivables (net) | 12.0 | 7.7 |
| | | | | 24.9 | | | Inventory | 12.0 | 20.0 |
| | | | | 3.5 | | | All Other Current | 8.1 | 9.5 |
| | | | | 70.4 | | | Total Current | 69.8 | 64.6 |
| | | | | 3.9 | | | Fixed Assets (net) | 11.3 | 10.3 |
| | | | | 8.1 | | | Intangibles (net) | 5.9 | 14.3 |
| | | | | 17.6 | | | All Other Non-Current | 13.0 | 10.8 |
| | | | | 100.0 | | | Total | 100.0 | 100.0 |
| | | | | | | | LIABILITIES | | |
| | | | | 3.8 | | | Notes Payable-Short Term | 5.2 | 10.8 |
| | | | | .5 | | | Cur. Mat.-L.T.D. | 1.8 | 2.6 |
| | | | | 15.2 | | | Trade Payables | 13.5 | 9.1 |
| | | | | .0 | | | Income Taxes Payable | .2 | .2 |
| | | | | 31.5 | | | All Other Current | 19.8 | 40.1 |
| | | | | 51.0 | | | Total Current | 40.4 | 62.8 |
| | | | | 1.3 | | | Long-Term Debt | 6.2 | 15.8 |
| | | | | .0 | | | Deferred Taxes | .4 | .8 |
| | | | | 1.0 | | | All Other Non-Current | 6.8 | 6.1 |
| | | | | 46.8 | | | Net Worth | 46.2 | 14.5 |
| | | | | 100.0 | | | Total Liabilties & Net Worth | 100.0 | 100.0 |
| | | | | | | | INCOME DATA | | |
| | | | | 100.0 | | | Net Sales | 100.0 | 100.0 |
| | | | | | | | Gross Profit | | |
| | | | | 88.5 | | | Operating Expenses | 92.1 | 100.0 |
| | | | | 11.5 | | | Operating Profit | 7.9 | .0 |
| | | | | -1.1 | | | All Other Expenses (net) | .4 | -.6 |
| | | | | 12.6 | | | Profit Before Taxes | 7.5 | .6 |
| | | | | | | | RATIOS | | |
| | | | | 5.4 | | | | 3.0 | 2.9 |
| | | | | 1.3 | | | Current | 1.8 | 1.3 |
| | | | | 1.0 | | | | 1.0 | .8 |
| | | | | 4.0 | | | | 2.4 | 1.8 |
| | | | | .8 | | | Quick | 1.2 | .7 |
| | | | | .2 | | | | .4 | .2 |
| | | | 1 | 290.7 | | | | 3 134.1 | 0 UND |
| | | | 19 | 18.8 | | | Sales/Receivables | 10 38.4 | 18 19.9 |
| | | | 44 | 8.3 | | | | 26 14.0 | 36 10.2 |
| | | | | | | | Cost of Sales/Inventory | | |
| | | | | | | | Cost of Sales/Payables | | |
| | | | | 4.9 | | | | 2.8 | 3.0 |
| | | | | 16.8 | | | Sales/Working Capital | 8.7 | 5.9 |
| | | | | NM | | | | 293.5 | -11.3 |
| | | | | | | | | 73.8 | 19.5 |
| | | | | | | | EBIT/Interest | (26) 9.0 | (13) -1.7 |
| | | | | | | | | -.9 | -8.9 |
| | | | | | | | Net Profit + Depr., Dep., Amort./Cur. Mat. L/T/D | | |
| | | | | .0 | | | | .0 | .0 |
| | | | | .0 | | | Fixed/Worth | .2 | .3 |
| | | | | .1 | | | | .5 | 3.5 |
| | | | | .1 | | | | .5 | 1.2 |
| | | | | 2.0 | | | Debt/Worth | 1.1 | 3.0 |
| | | | | 10.7 | | | | 3.7 | -5.4 |
| | | | | | | | | 73.9 | 49.1 |
| | | | | | | | % Profit Before Taxes/Tangible Net Worth | (40) 23.9 | (11) 7.2 |
| | | | | | | | | 11.7 | -16.9 |
| | | | | 32.8 | | | | 27.8 | 9.0 |
| | | | | 20.2 | | | % Profit Before Taxes/Total Assets | 9.1 | 3.7 |
| | | | | 8.2 | | | | 2.0 | -12.1 |
| | | | | UND | | | | 409.5 | 999.8 |
| | | | | 999.8 | | | Sales/Net Fixed Assets | 40.4 | 31.4 |
| | | | | 136.6 | | | | 12.4 | 10.9 |
| | | | | 3.1 | | | | 3.7 | 1.8 |
| | | | | 2.3 | | | Sales/Total Assets | 2.1 | 1.4 |
| | | | | 1.0 | | | | 1.0 | .7 |
| | | | | | | | | | .1 |
| | | | | | | | % Depr., Dep., Amort./Sales | (31) .9 | |
| | | | | | | | | 2.9 | |
| | | | | | | | % Officers', Directors' Owners' Comp/Sales | | |
| | 4029M | 10765M | 70797M | 529678M | 1429619M | 516194M | Net Sales ($) | 2316450M | 975148M |
| | 121M | 5274M | 35603M | 231506M | 489187M | 647717M | Total Assets ($) | 1466048M | 1015076M |

© RMA 2024

M = $ thousand  MM = $ million
See Pages viii through xx for Explanation of Ratios and Data

# ADMIN & WASTE MANAGEMENT SERVICES—All Other Travel Arrangement and Reservation Services  NAICS 561599

## Comparative Historical Data | Current Data Sorted by Sales

| | | | Type of Statement | | | | | | |
|---|---|---|---|---|---|---|---|---|---|
| | 8 | 7 | Unqualified | | | 1 | | 1 | 5 |
| 1 | 1 | 1 | Reviewed | | | | | | 1 |
| 1 | 1 | 1 | Compiled | | | 1 | | | |
| 2 | | 2 | Tax Returns | | 2 | | 1 | | |
| 12 | 29 | 21 | Other | 1 | 2 | 1 | | 3 | 14 |
| 4/1/21-3/31/22 | 4/1/22-3/31/23 | 4/1/23-3/31/24 | | | 6 (4/1-9/30/23) | | | 26 (10/1/23-3/31/24) | |
| ALL | ALL | ALL | | 0-1MM | 1-3MM | 3-5MM | 5-10MM | 10-25MM | 25MM & OVER |
| 16 | 39 | 32 | NUMBER OF STATEMENTS | 1 | 5 | 2 | | 4 | 20 |
| % | % | % | ASSETS | % | % | % | | % | % |
| 43.0 | 39.1 | 24.1 | Cash & Equivalents | | | | D | | 21.5 |
| 10.1 | 9.9 | 12.9 | Trade Receivables (net) | | | | A | | 16.4 |
| 6.6 | 11.3 | 19.9 | Inventory | | | | T | | 24.8 |
| 3.3 | 8.7 | 5.0 | All Other Current | | | | A | | 5.4 |
| 63.0 | 68.9 | 61.9 | Total Current | | | | | | 68.1 |
| 8.0 | 8.1 | 7.7 | Fixed Assets (net) | | | | N | | 2.5 |
| 8.0 | 11.9 | 16.6 | Intangibles (net) | | | | O | | 13.9 |
| 20.9 | 11.1 | 13.7 | All Other Non-Current | | | | T | | 15.6 |
| 100.0 | 100.0 | 100.0 | Total | | | | | | 100.0 |
| | | | LIABILITIES | | | | A | | |
| 9.4 | 6.0 | 11.6 | Notes Payable-Short Term | | | | V | | 6.5 |
| 2.0 | 1.8 | 2.4 | Cur. Mat.-L.T.D. | | | | A | | 1.4 |
| 11.6 | 13.6 | 11.3 | Trade Payables | | | | I | | 17.3 |
| .1 | .2 | .0 | Income Taxes Payable | | | | L | | .1 |
| 24.5 | 30.1 | 25.0 | All Other Current | | | | A | | 30.0 |
| 47.6 | 51.7 | 50.5 | Total Current | | | | B | | 55.2 |
| 11.2 | 11.6 | 8.7 | Long-Term Debt | | | | L | | 10.8 |
| .7 | .3 | .0 | Deferred Taxes | | | | E | | .0 |
| 13.3 | 7.8 | 3.8 | All Other Non-Current | | | | | | 5.6 |
| 27.3 | 28.6 | 37.0 | Net Worth | | | | | | 28.4 |
| 100.0 | 100.0 | 100.0 | Total Liabilities & Net Worth | | | | | | 100.0 |
| | | | INCOME DATA | | | | | | |
| 100.0 | 100.0 | 100.0 | Net Sales | | | | | | 100.0 |
| | | | Gross Profit | | | | | | |
| 93.1 | 90.6 | 87.5 | Operating Expenses | | | | | | 89.5 |
| 6.9 | 9.4 | 12.5 | Operating Profit | | | | | | 10.5 |
| -3.4 | 2.0 | .3 | All Other Expenses (net) | | | | | | .6 |
| 10.3 | 7.4 | 12.2 | Profit Before Taxes | | | | | | 9.9 |
| | | | RATIOS | | | | | | |
| 2.1 | 2.1 | 3.1 | | | | | | | 2.3 |
| 1.3 | 1.3 | 1.4 | Current | | | | | | 1.5 |
| .9 | 1.0 | .7 | | | | | | | .9 |
| 2.0 | 1.9 | 2.6 | | | | | | | 1.1 |
| 1.0 | 1.0 | .7 | Quick | | | | | | .7 |
| .5 | .5 | .3 | | | | | | | .5 |
| 0 UND | 1 269.7 | 0 832.7 | | | | | | 7 | 50.7 |
| 10 35.5 | 13 27.2 | 17 21.7 | Sales/Receivables | | | | | 19 | 19.0 |
| 41 9.0 | 26 13.9 | 29 12.4 | | | | | | 32 | 11.4 |
| | | | Cost of Sales/Inventory | | | | | | |
| | | | Cost of Sales/Payables | | | | | | |
| 2.5 | 4.1 | 5.5 | | | | | | | 5.7 |
| 30.7 | 9.0 | 10.9 | Sales/Working Capital | | | | | | 13.3 |
| -12.3 | 732.4 | -62.9 | | | | | | | NM |
| 488.2 | 28.8 | 20.8 | | | | | | | 17.9 |
| (12) 15.8 | (18) 11.2 | (20) 8.0 | EBIT/Interest | | | | | (15) | 8.1 |
| 6.6 | 2.9 | 3.5 | | | | | | | 3.3 |
| | | | Net Profit + Depr., Dep., Amort./Cur. Mat. L/T/D | | | | | | |
| .0 | .0 | .0 | | | | | | | .0 |
| .6 | .2 | .0 | Fixed/Worth | | | | | | .0 |
| UND | 1.7 | 1.0 | | | | | | | .3 |
| .9 | 1.0 | .5 | | | | | | | .8 |
| 3.2 | 3.6 | 3.7 | Debt/Worth | | | | | | 6.4 |
| -57.6 | -29.9 | -5.6 | | | | | | | -12.2 |
| 271.5 | 92.2 | 106.3 | | | | | | | 170.6 |
| (11) 33.6 | (29) 41.0 | (22) 47.3 | % Profit Before Taxes/Tangible Net Worth | | | | | (14) | 93.2 |
| 19.0 | -8.0 | 17.2 | | | | | | | 34.8 |
| 21.2 | 26.6 | 31.4 | | | | | | | 28.3 |
| 15.3 | 13.2 | 14.3 | % Profit Before Taxes/Total Assets | | | | | | 16.2 |
| 7.9 | -3.2 | 5.2 | | | | | | | 6.8 |
| 910.3 | 650.7 | 999.8 | | | | | | | 999.8 |
| 129.8 | 80.7 | 636.4 | Sales/Net Fixed Assets | | | | | | 999.8 |
| 10.9 | 10.4 | 29.5 | | | | | | | 117.8 |
| 2.5 | 2.7 | 3.5 | | | | | | | 3.6 |
| 1.3 | 1.7 | 1.9 | Sales/Total Assets | | | | | | 2.1 |
| .6 | .7 | .9 | | | | | | | 1.0 |
| | .4 | .0 | | | | | | | .0 |
| (20) | 1.3 | (14) .5 | % Depr., Dep., Amort./Sales | | | | | (11) | .3 |
| | 2.4 | 1.7 | | | | | | | .8 |
| | | | % Officers', Directors' Owners' Comp/Sales | | | | | | |
| 754147M | 3435108M | 2561082M | Net Sales ($) | 62M | 11190M | 7063M | | 65172M | 2477595M |
| 713276M | 2467720M | 1409408M | Total Assets ($) | 3769M | 13175M | 1726M | | 40931M | 1349807M |

© RMA 2024  
M = $ thousand   MM = $ million  
See Pages viii through xx for Explanation of Ratios and Data

# ADMIN & WASTE MANAGEMENT SERVICES—Security Guards and Patrol Services  NAICS 561612

## Current Data Sorted by Assets

| | | | Type of Statement | | |
|---|---|---|---|---|---|
| | | 1 | Unqualified | | |
| | | 1 | Reviewed | | |
| 1 | 1 | 4 | 1 2 | 1 | 2 Compiled |
| 1 | 1 | 2 | | | Tax Returns |
| 3 | 4 | 22 | 5 | 3 | 3 Other |
| | 3 (4/1-9/30/23) | | 55 (10/1/23-3/31/24) | | |
| 0-500M | 500M-2MM | 2-10MM | 10-50MM | 50-100MM | 100-250MM |
| 5 | 6 | 30 | 8 | 4 | 5 |
| % | % | % | % | % | % |

| 0-500M | 500M-2MM | 2-10MM | 10-50MM | 50-100MM | 100-250MM | | Comparative Historical Data | |
|---|---|---|---|---|---|---|---|---|
| | | | | | | | 6 Unqualified | |
| | | | | | | | 2 Reviewed | 1 |
| | | | | | | | 5 Compiled | 3 |
| | | | | | | | 9 Tax Returns | 1 |
| | | | | | | | 48 Other | 24 |
| | | | | | | | 4/1/19-3/31/20 | 4/1/20-3/31/21 |
| | | | | | | NUMBER OF STATEMENTS | ALL 70 | ALL 29 |
| | | | | | | | % | % |
| | | | | | | **ASSETS** | | |
| | | 16.2 | | | | Cash & Equivalents | 19.7 | 21.4 |
| | | 54.4 | | | | Trade Receivables (net) | 48.5 | 41.4 |
| | | .6 | | | | Inventory | 1.7 | 3.0 |
| | | 4.4 | | | | All Other Current | 5.8 | 4.0 |
| | | 75.6 | | | | Total Current | 75.7 | 69.9 |
| | | 13.9 | | | | Fixed Assets (net) | 10.8 | 11.3 |
| | | 4.5 | | | | Intangibles (net) | 5.4 | 9.8 |
| | | 6.0 | | | | All Other Non-Current | 8.1 | 9.0 |
| | | 100.0 | | | | Total | 100.0 | 100.0 |
| | | | | | | **LIABILITIES** | | |
| | | 13.9 | | | | Notes Payable-Short Term | 23.7 | 11.1 |
| | | .8 | | | | Cur. Mat.-L.T.D. | 2.0 | 3.0 |
| | | 5.7 | | | | Trade Payables | 4.6 | 5.3 |
| | | .6 | | | | Income Taxes Payable | .2 | .0 |
| | | 16.9 | | | | All Other Current | 23.7 | 21.2 |
| | | 37.8 | | | | Total Current | 54.2 | 40.6 |
| | | 11.0 | | | | Long-Term Debt | 16.5 | 21.4 |
| | | 1.3 | | | | Deferred Taxes | .1 | .0 |
| | | 4.5 | | | | All Other Non-Current | 3.0 | 6.1 |
| | | 45.4 | | | | Net Worth | 26.2 | 31.9 |
| | | 100.0 | | | | Total Liabilities & Net Worth | 100.0 | 100.0 |
| | | | | | | **INCOME DATA** | | |
| | | 100.0 | | | | Net Sales | 100.0 | 100.0 |
| | | | | | | Gross Profit | | |
| | | 94.6 | | | | Operating Expenses | 91.7 | 97.1 |
| | | 5.4 | | | | Operating Profit | 8.3 | 2.9 |
| | | 1.4 | | | | All Other Expenses (net) | .8 | .6 |
| | | 4.0 | | | | Profit Before Taxes | 7.5 | 2.4 |
| | | | | | | **RATIOS** | | |
| | | 3.7 | | | | | 3.6 | 6.0 |
| | | 2.0 | | | | Current | 1.6 | 2.0 |
| | | 1.2 | | | | | 1.0 | 1.2 |
| | | 3.4 | | | | | 2.9 | 4.3 |
| | | 2.0 | | | | Quick | 1.4 | 1.8 |
| | | 1.1 | | | | | 1.0 | .9 |
| | 34 | 10.8 | | | | | 28  13.1 | 39  9.4 |
| | 41 | 8.9 | | | | Sales/Receivables | 43  8.4 | 45  8.1 |
| | 49 | 7.4 | | | | | 56  6.5 | 56  6.5 |
| | | | | | | Cost of Sales/Inventory | | |
| | | | | | | Cost of Sales/Payables | | |
| | | 8.0 | | | | | 9.0 | 4.7 |
| | | 14.4 | | | | Sales/Working Capital | 18.3 | 10.1 |
| | | 44.0 | | | | | 179.5 | 26.5 |
| | | 26.8 | | | | | 36.6 | 51.4 |
| | (25) | 6.2 | | | | EBIT/Interest | (62)  8.0 | (23)  8.3 |
| | | 2.5 | | | | | 3.5 | 2.4 |
| | | | | | | Net Profit + Depr., Dep., Amort./Cur. Mat. L/T/D | | |
| | | .0 | | | | | .1 | .1 |
| | | .1 | | | | Fixed/Worth | .2 | .3 |
| | | .8 | | | | | .9 | 1.4 |
| | | .7 | | | | | .6 | 1.0 |
| | | 1.3 | | | | Debt/Worth | 1.9 | 2.7 |
| | | 2.8 | | | | | 6.0 | 10.9 |
| | | 64.8 | | | | | 103.8 | 88.7 |
| | (27) | 27.3 | | | | % Profit Before Taxes/Tangible Net Worth | (59)  48.4 | (25)  43.5 |
| | | 11.4 | | | | | 19.0 | 6.7 |
| | | 22.9 | | | | | 32.7 | 21.7 |
| | | 8.5 | | | | % Profit Before Taxes/Total Assets | 17.6 | 11.7 |
| | | 4.2 | | | | | 6.0 | 2.1 |
| | | 415.4 | | | | | 308.2 | 175.9 |
| | | 98.8 | | | | Sales/Net Fixed Assets | 93.4 | 83.7 |
| | | 31.8 | | | | | 26.2 | 23.0 |
| | | 5.9 | | | | | 6.0 | 4.5 |
| | | 4.7 | | | | Sales/Total Assets | 4.7 | 3.3 |
| | | 3.7 | | | | | 3.0 | 2.4 |
| | | .2 | | | | | .1 | .2 |
| | (18) | .4 | | | | % Depr., Dep., Amort./Sales | (43)  .3 | (20)  .5 |
| | | 1.2 | | | | | 1.1 | 1.2 |
| | | | | | | | 1.5 | |
| | | | | | | % Officers', Directors' Owners' Comp/Sales | (23)  3.9 | |
| | | | | | | | 5.2 | |
| 12048M | 43026M | 756836M | 653273M | 926995M | 2900854M | Net Sales ($) | 3261865M | 899937M |
| 1056M | 6781M | 162800M | 184808M | 285521M | 830651M | Total Assets ($) | 871609M | 257041M |

© RMA 2024   M = $ thousand   MM = $ million
See Pages viii through xx for Explanation of Ratios and Data

# ADMIN & WASTE MANAGEMENT SERVICES—Security Guards and Patrol Services   NAICS 561612

## Comparative Historical Data | Current Data Sorted by Sales

| | | | | | | | | | | 1 | 5 |
|---|---|---|---|---|---|---|---|---|---|---|---|
| | 3 | | 8 | | 6 | Type of Statement | | | | 1 | 2 |
| | | | 1 | | 3 | Unqualified | | | 1 | 2 | 2 |
| | 3 | | 6 | | 5 | Reviewed | | | | 2 | 2 |
| | 5 | | 6 | | 4 | Compiled | | 1 | 1 | 2 | |
| | 19 | | 36 | | 40 | Tax Returns | 1 | 3 | 3 | 11 | 20 |
| | 4/1/21- | | 4/1/22- | | 4/1/23- | Other | | | | | |
| | 3/31/22 | | 3/31/23 | | 3/31/24 | | | 3 (4/1-9/30/23) | | 55 (10/1/23-3/31/24) | |
| | ALL | | ALL | | ALL | | 0-1MM | 1-3MM | 3-5MM | 5-10MM | 10-25MM | 25MM & OVER |
| | 30 | | 57 | | 58 | NUMBER OF STATEMENTS | 1 | 4 | 3 | 5 | 16 | 29 |
| | % | | % | | % | ASSETS | % | % | % | % | % | % |
| | 18.4 | | 18.8 | | 16.4 | Cash & Equivalents | | | | | 26.9 | 6.8 |
| | 42.7 | | 43.0 | | 50.6 | Trade Receivables (net) | | | | | 51.4 | 60.0 |
| | 1.2 | | 1.0 | | .4 | Inventory | | | | | .5 | .5 |
| | 10.6 | | 6.8 | | 4.7 | All Other Current | | | | | 4.2 | 5.1 |
| | 72.9 | | 69.6 | | 72.1 | Total Current | | | | | 83.0 | 72.3 |
| | 8.0 | | 13.5 | | 13.6 | Fixed Assets (net) | | | | | 8.0 | 10.3 |
| | 8.1 | | 11.5 | | 6.9 | Intangibles (net) | | | | | 5.9 | 7.5 |
| | 11.0 | | 5.4 | | 7.3 | All Other Non-Current | | | | | 3.1 | 9.9 |
| | 100.0 | | 100.0 | | 100.0 | Total | | | | | 100.0 | 100.0 |
| | | | | | | LIABILITIES | | | | | | |
| | 10.4 | | 9.2 | | 11.9 | Notes Payable-Short Term | | | | | 14.6 | 10.9 |
| | 3.0 | | 1.7 | | 3.6 | Cur. Mat.-L.T.D. | | | | | .9 | 4.6 |
| | 7.3 | | 7.1 | | 7.0 | Trade Payables | | | | | 3.4 | 8.8 |
| | .1 | | .1 | | .3 | Income Taxes Payable | | | | | 1.1 | .1 |
| | 19.5 | | 13.8 | | 20.3 | All Other Current | | | | | 13.3 | 25.0 |
| | 40.2 | | 32.0 | | 43.1 | Total Current | | | | | 33.3 | 49.3 |
| | 18.0 | | 16.7 | | 17.7 | Long-Term Debt | | | | | 5.8 | 19.8 |
| | .0 | | .3 | | .7 | Deferred Taxes | | | | | 2.3 | .1 |
| | 3.2 | | 3.5 | | 4.2 | All Other Non-Current | | | | | 2.6 | 5.0 |
| | 38.6 | | 47.6 | | 34.3 | Net Worth | | | | | 55.9 | 25.8 |
| | 100.0 | | 100.0 | | 100.0 | Total Liabilities & Net Worth | | | | | 100.0 | 100.0 |
| | | | | | | INCOME DATA | | | | | | |
| | 100.0 | | 100.0 | | 100.0 | Net Sales | | | | | 100.0 | 100.0 |
| | | | | | | Gross Profit | | | | | | |
| | 96.1 | | 94.5 | | 95.1 | Operating Expenses | | | | | 95.1 | 96.1 |
| | 3.9 | | 5.5 | | 4.9 | Operating Profit | | | | | 4.9 | 3.9 |
| | -.1 | | 2.6 | | 1.3 | All Other Expenses (net) | | | | | .8 | 1.1 |
| | 4.0 | | 3.0 | | 3.6 | Profit Before Taxes | | | | | 4.1 | 2.8 |
| | | | | | | RATIOS | | | | | | |
| | 4.1 | | 5.2 | | 2.6 | | | | | | 8.0 | 2.0 |
| | 2.5 | | 2.1 | | 1.7 | Current | | | | | 2.7 | 1.6 |
| | 1.3 | | 1.2 | | 1.1 | | | | | | 1.7 | 1.1 |
| | 2.7 | | 4.7 | | 2.6 | | | | | | 6.0 | 1.9 |
| | 1.4 | | 1.8 | | 1.5 | Quick | | | | | 2.7 | 1.4 |
| | 1.0 | | 1.0 | | 1.0 | | | | | | 1.7 | 1.0 |
| 30 | 12.3 | 24 | 15.1 | 34 | 10.8 | | | | | 33 | 11.1 | 37 | 9.8 |
| 44 | 8.3 | 44 | 8.3 | 42 | 8.6 | Sales/Receivables | | | | 42 | 8.6 | 47 | 7.7 |
| 65 | 5.6 | 57 | 6.4 | 57 | 6.4 | | | | | 58 | 6.3 | 63 | 5.8 |
| | | | | | | Cost of Sales/Inventory | | | | | | |
| | | | | | | Cost of Sales/Payables | | | | | | |
| | 6.5 | | 6.0 | | 10.0 | | | | | | 4.3 | 11.8 |
| | 11.1 | | 14.7 | | 15.1 | Sales/Working Capital | | | | | 9.9 | 15.4 |
| | 28.4 | | 63.2 | | 65.6 | | | | | | 23.4 | 57.7 |
| | 69.2 | | 41.1 | | 16.7 | | | | | | 46.8 | 9.9 |
| (25) | 13.1 | (47) | 10.7 | (51) | 4.7 | EBIT/Interest | | | | (14) | 8.7 | (28) | 4.3 |
| | 3.1 | | .4 | | 2.0 | | | | | | 1.9 | 1.9 |
| | | | | | | Net Profit + Depr., Dep., Amort./Cur. Mat. L/T/D | | | | | | |
| | .1 | | .0 | | .0 | | | | | | .0 | .1 |
| | .2 | | .2 | | .4 | Fixed/Worth | | | | | .1 | .5 |
| | .5 | | 2.0 | | 1.3 | | | | | | .7 | 1.6 |
| | .5 | | .4 | | .9 | | | | | | .3 | 1.4 |
| | 1.9 | | 1.2 | | 1.9 | Debt/Worth | | | | | .7 | 3.4 |
| | 5.7 | | 8.2 | | 10.5 | | | | | | 1.3 | 11.5 |
| | 50.3 | | 66.7 | | 77.0 | | | | | | 32.9 | 88.4 |
| (24) | 33.6 | (48) | 22.6 | (47) | 27.3 | % Profit Before Taxes/Tangible Net Worth | | | | (14) | 16.4 | (23) | 47.4 |
| | 5.0 | | 8.1 | | 11.4 | | | | | | 10.1 | 19.5 |
| | 24.0 | | 22.4 | | 22.6 | | | | | | 20.8 | 21.0 |
| | 12.4 | | 7.5 | | 7.7 | % Profit Before Taxes/Total Assets | | | | | 7.3 | 7.4 |
| | 2.8 | | -1.5 | | 3.8 | | | | | | 5.5 | 3.3 |
| | 188.9 | | 307.7 | | 358.3 | | | | | | 610.9 | 323.2 |
| | 89.8 | | 72.4 | | 68.7 | Sales/Net Fixed Assets | | | | | 102.0 | 62.1 |
| | 44.1 | | 24.9 | | 23.3 | | | | | | 68.7 | 21.3 |
| | 5.3 | | 5.9 | | 6.1 | | | | | | 5.6 | 5.9 |
| | 4.1 | | 4.2 | | 4.6 | Sales/Total Assets | | | | | 4.6 | 3.8 |
| | 2.7 | | 2.1 | | 3.2 | | | | | | 3.1 | 3.3 |
| | .2 | | .2 | | .3 | | | | | | .2 | .2 |
| (18) | .3 | (29) | .5 | (31) | .4 | % Depr., Dep., Amort./Sales | | | | (10) | .4 | (18) | .4 |
| | .9 | | 1.2 | | 1.2 | | | | | | .8 | .9 |
| | | | 1.0 | | 1.0 | % Officers', Directors' Owners' Comp/Sales | | | | | | |
| | | (14) | 1.8 | (15) | 1.6 | | | | | | | |
| | | | | | 3.8 | | | | | | | 3.3 |
| | 1415789M | | 3345145M | | 5293032M | Net Sales ($) | 511M | 7225M | 13991M | 35405M | 289805M | 4946095M |
| | 381055M | | 918724M | | 1471617M | Total Assets ($) | 4594M | 885M | 2755M | 9102M | 77605M | 1376676M |

© RMA 2024    M = $ thousand   MM = $ million
See Pages viii through xx for Explanation of Ratios and Data

# ADMIN & WASTE MANAGEMENT SERVICES—Security Systems Services (except Locksmiths) NAICS 561621

**Current Data Sorted by Assets** | **Comparative Historical Data**

| | | | | | | Type of Statement | | |
|---|---|---|---|---|---|---|---|---|
| | | 5 | 7 | 5 | 3 | Unqualified | 22 | 12 |
| | 2 | 12 | 11 | 1 | | Reviewed | 25 | 10 |
| | 2 | 4 | 1 | | | Compiled | 7 | 4 |
| 4 | 11 | 7 | 1 | 1 | | Tax Returns | 18 | 7 |
| 3 | 16 | 51 | 27 | 11 | 10 | Other | 106 | 53 |
| 0-500M | 30 (4/1-9/30/23) 500M-2MM | 2-10MM | 165 (10/1/23-3/31/24) 10-50MM | 50-100MM | 100-250MM | | 4/1/19- 3/31/20 ALL | 4/1/20- 3/31/21 ALL |
| 7 | 31 | 79 | 47 | 18 | 13 | NUMBER OF STATEMENTS | 178 | 86 |
| % | % | % | % | % | % | ASSETS | % | % |
| | 22.0 | 11.7 | 15.4 | 11.7 | 3.8 | Cash & Equivalents | 13.2 | 19.9 |
| | 23.1 | 25.6 | 24.4 | 23.5 | 8.0 | Trade Receivables (net) | 31.2 | 22.9 |
| | 7.9 | 17.5 | 11.0 | 11.3 | 4.1 | Inventory | 10.0 | 10.9 |
| | 3.4 | 7.2 | 6.5 | 6.9 | 2.1 | All Other Current | 5.5 | 4.2 |
| | 56.4 | 62.0 | 57.4 | 53.4 | 18.0 | Total Current | 59.9 | 58.0 |
| | 21.9 | 15.5 | 12.5 | 8.8 | 13.3 | Fixed Assets (net) | 14.0 | 14.3 |
| | 5.8 | 15.3 | 17.0 | 23.1 | 60.9 | Intangibles (net) | 18.6 | 17.6 |
| | 15.9 | 7.2 | 13.1 | 14.8 | 7.8 | All Other Non-Current | 7.5 | 10.2 |
| | 100.0 | 100.0 | 100.0 | 100.0 | 100.0 | Total | 100.0 | 100.0 |
| | | | | | | LIABILITIES | | |
| | 5.0 | 15.4 | 17.3 | 8.0 | 6.9 | Notes Payable-Short Term | 8.9 | 7.5 |
| | 5.3 | 2.1 | 1.0 | 1.7 | .8 | Cur. Mat.-L.T.D. | 3.1 | 4.0 |
| | 9.6 | 10.9 | 9.5 | 9.7 | 3.0 | Trade Payables | 14.2 | 11.6 |
| | .1 | .0 | .2 | .1 | .0 | Income Taxes Payable | .2 | .1 |
| | 20.8 | 17.0 | 22.7 | 22.6 | 10.3 | All Other Current | 17.9 | 16.1 |
| | 40.9 | 45.4 | 50.7 | 42.1 | 21.0 | Total Current | 44.3 | 39.3 |
| | 51.8 | 28.4 | 16.4 | 12.6 | 44.2 | Long-Term Debt | 27.8 | 40.3 |
| | .1 | .1 | .1 | .0 | .5 | Deferred Taxes | .1 | .1 |
| | 3.5 | 4.6 | 8.4 | 6.9 | 11.0 | All Other Non-Current | 8.0 | 13.6 |
| | 3.6 | 21.6 | 24.5 | 38.4 | 23.4 | Net Worth | 19.8 | 6.8 |
| | 100.0 | 100.0 | 100.0 | 100.0 | 100.0 | Total Liabilities & Net Worth | 100.0 | 100.0 |
| | | | | | | INCOME DATA | | |
| | 100.0 | 100.0 | 100.0 | 100.0 | 100.0 | Net Sales | 100.0 | 100.0 |
| | | | | | | Gross Profit | | |
| | 91.0 | 90.4 | 90.3 | 94.0 | 102.7 | Operating Expenses | 94.3 | 93.9 |
| | 9.0 | 9.6 | 9.7 | 6.0 | -2.7 | Operating Profit | 5.7 | 6.1 |
| | 1.5 | 2.8 | .9 | .3 | 9.0 | All Other Expenses (net) | 2.0 | .1 |
| | 7.6 | 6.8 | 8.8 | 5.7 | -11.7 | Profit Before Taxes | 3.7 | 5.9 |
| | | | | | | RATIOS | | |
| | 4.0 | 4.3 | 1.9 | 2.4 | 1.6 | | 2.5 | 2.7 |
| | 1.7 | 2.3 | 1.3 | 1.4 | 1.0 | Current | 1.5 | 1.8 |
| | .9 | 1.1 | .7 | .9 | .9 | | .9 | .9 |
| | 2.7 | 2.8 | 1.7 | 1.4 | 1.1 | | 1.9 | 2.0 |
| | 1.7 | 1.1 | .8 | .8 | .6 | Quick | 1.0 | 1.3 |
| | .7 | .6 | .5 | .5 | .5 | | .6 | .7 |
| 10 | 35.1 | 27 | 13.5 | 24 | 15.1 | 37 | 9.8 | 30 | 12.0 | | 30 | 12.2 | 23 | 16.1 |
| 26 | 14.3 | 45 | 8.1 | 51 | 7.2 | 56 | 6.5 | 49 | 7.5 | Sales/Receivables | 47 | 7.8 | 41 | 9.0 |
| 41 | 8.8 | 63 | 5.8 | 74 | 4.9 | 74 | 4.9 | 61 | 6.0 | | 66 | 5.5 | 56 | 6.5 |
| | | | | | | Cost of Sales/Inventory | | |
| | | | | | | Cost of Sales/Payables | | |
| | 6.0 | 4.2 | 5.5 | 4.5 | 6.7 | | 5.6 | 4.5 |
| | 16.4 | 6.7 | 10.1 | 11.5 | -144.7 | Sales/Working Capital | 12.6 | 9.4 |
| | -82.8 | 55.6 | -9.4 | -69.6 | -35.1 | | -81.2 | -100.0 |
| | 24.2 | 11.2 | 51.5 | 145.3 | 1.8 | | 18.4 | 18.6 |
| (23) | 4.7 | (66) | 4.1 | (46) | 10.1 | 8.7 | (12) | -.1 | EBIT/Interest | (150) | 5.4 | (73) | 4.8 |
| | .1 | 1.1 | 3.7 | 1.8 | -2.2 | | 1.6 | 1.1 |
| | | | | | | Net Profit + Depr., Dep., Amort./Cur. Mat. L/T/D | | 5.9 |
| | | | | | | | (17) | 2.9 |
| | | | | | | | | 1.6 |
| | .1 | .2 | .3 | .3 | 4.8 | | .1 | .2 |
| | .9 | .7 | .5 | .5 | -.2 | Fixed/Worth | .7 | 2.5 |
| | -.8 | -.3 | -.8 | -2.9 | -.1 | | -.3 | -.2 |
| | .4 | .5 | 1.3 | 1.1 | NM | | .7 | 1.1 |
| | 2.1 | 3.8 | 6.5 | 7.6 | -1.6 | Debt/Worth | 3.6 | 131.1 |
| | -2.7 | -2.8 | -4.3 | -39.2 | -1.4 | | -3.4 | -2.8 |
| | 77.6 | 72.5 | 65.6 | 57.2 | | | 71.6 | 93.6 |
| (21) | 23.3 | (47) | 29.8 | (29) | 45.9 | (13) | 43.0 | | % Profit Before Taxes/Tangible Net Worth | (117) | 30.3 | (44) | 42.5 |
| | -2.9 | 5.0 | 24.5 | 12.9 | | | 11.7 | 12.0 |
| | 45.6 | 22.4 | 23.8 | 16.3 | 3.7 | | 22.5 | 23.1 |
| | 8.7 | 6.6 | 14.2 | 8.9 | -1.7 | % Profit Before Taxes/Total Assets | 10.3 | 10.8 |
| | -1.2 | 1.0 | 5.6 | 1.5 | -11.8 | | 1.2 | .3 |
| | 95.7 | 36.3 | 35.9 | 30.1 | 20.4 | | 64.7 | 54.0 |
| | 26.5 | 20.5 | 20.7 | 19.6 | 8.4 | Sales/Net Fixed Assets | 22.7 | 20.6 |
| | 10.7 | 9.3 | 10.0 | 8.9 | 2.5 | | 11.7 | 11.1 |
| | 4.9 | 2.6 | 2.2 | 2.0 | .7 | | 3.1 | 2.7 |
| | 3.1 | 1.9 | 1.6 | 1.3 | .5 | Sales/Total Assets | 2.3 | 1.9 |
| | 2.2 | 1.4 | 1.0 | .8 | .4 | | 1.3 | 1.3 |
| | .8 | 1.1 | .6 | .8 | | | .7 | .7 |
| (17) | 2.3 | (49) | 2.0 | (31) | 2.4 | (14) | 1.9 | | % Depr., Dep., Amort./Sales | (109) | 1.7 | (61) | 1.8 |
| | 3.1 | 3.6 | 3.7 | 4.0 | | | 3.9 | 3.5 |
| | 3.1 | 2.0 | | | | | 2.1 | 1.4 |
| (12) | 5.6 | (18) | 2.8 | | | | % Officers', Directors' Owners' Comp/Sales | (39) | 3.9 | (18) | 4.1 |
| | 12.1 | 5.2 | | | | | 7.4 | 8.2 |
| 17674M | 146162M | 870332M | 2033293M | 1688396M | 1357221M | Net Sales ($) | 6194176M | 2735366M |
| 2107M | 40310M | 412546M | 1103161M | 1221117M | 2329401M | Total Assets ($) | 3584874M | 1783040M |

© RMA 2024   M = $ thousand   MM = $ million
See Pages viii through xx for Explanation of Ratios and Data

# ADMIN & WASTE MANAGEMENT SERVICES—Security Systems Services (except Locksmiths) NAICS 561621

## Comparative Historical Data / Current Data Sorted by Sales

| | | | | Type of Statement | | | | | | |
|---|---|---|---|---|---|---|---|---|---|---|
| 12 | | 11 | 20 | Unqualified | | 1 | | 1 | 5 | 13 |
| 15 | | 13 | 26 | Reviewed | | 1 | 2 | 8 | 7 | 8 |
| 5 | | 6 | 7 | Compiled | | 2 | 1 | | 3 | 1 |
| 10 | | 13 | 24 | Tax Returns | 2 | 6 | 4 | 7 | 4 | 1 |
| 48 | | 73 | 118 | Other | 5 | 7 | 6 | 35 | 24 | 41 |
| 4/1/21-3/31/22 ALL | | 4/1/22-3/31/23 ALL | 4/1/23-3/31/24 ALL | | 0-1MM | 30 (4/1-9/30/23) 1-3MM | 3-5MM | 165 (10/1/23-3/31/24) 5-10MM | 10-25MM | 25MM & OVER |
| 90 | | 116 | 195 | **NUMBER OF STATEMENTS** | 7 | 17 | 13 | 51 | 43 | 64 |
| % | | % | % | **ASSETS** | % | % | % | % | % | % |
| 15.2 | | 19.0 | 14.5 | Cash & Equivalents | | 25.9 | 11.3 | 14.9 | 13.5 | 12.8 |
| 25.5 | | 28.2 | 23.2 | Trade Receivables (net) | | 18.5 | 24.2 | 21.2 | 30.1 | 22.5 |
| 14.6 | | 11.8 | 12.9 | Inventory | | 5.7 | 13.7 | 16.5 | 17.1 | 9.5 |
| 5.2 | | 7.4 | 6.0 | All Other Current | | 4.3 | 6.9 | 6.2 | 6.9 | 6.0 |
| 60.5 | | 66.4 | 56.5 | Total Current | | 54.4 | 56.1 | 58.8 | 67.6 | 50.8 |
| 13.5 | | 13.0 | 15.0 | Fixed Assets (net) | | 18.8 | 18.8 | 13.5 | 12.5 | 11.9 |
| 18.2 | | 11.5 | 17.8 | Intangibles (net) | | 13.1 | 3.4 | 20.0 | 13.8 | 23.6 |
| 7.9 | | 9.1 | 10.6 | All Other Non-Current | | 13.7 | 21.7 | 7.6 | 6.0 | 13.7 |
| 100.0 | | 100.0 | 100.0 | Total | | 100.0 | 100.0 | 100.0 | 100.0 | 100.0 |
| | | | | **LIABILITIES** | | | | | | |
| 8.9 | | 8.9 | 14.5 | Notes Payable-Short Term | | 3.1 | 18.0 | 19.3 | 12.2 | 14.3 |
| 4.7 | | 2.0 | 2.5 | Cur. Mat.-L.T.D. | | 5.9 | 1.2 | 2.7 | 2.0 | 1.3 |
| 10.7 | | 12.6 | 9.4 | Trade Payables | | 5.0 | 7.0 | 9.3 | 11.9 | 10.3 |
| .1 | | .1 | .1 | Income Taxes Payable | | .2 | .0 | .0 | .2 | .1 |
| 14.7 | | 19.4 | 19.0 | All Other Current | | 18.6 | 27.0 | 18.3 | 20.6 | 18.3 |
| 39.1 | | 42.9 | 45.5 | Total Current | | 32.8 | 53.2 | 49.6 | 46.9 | 44.3 |
| 26.7 | | 21.0 | 29.0 | Long-Term Debt | | 30.8 | 15.3 | 41.2 | 24.0 | 18.8 |
| .1 | | .0 | .1 | Deferred Taxes | | .0 | .1 | .0 | .2 | .1 |
| 9.0 | | 8.7 | 6.0 | All Other Non-Current | | .0 | 8.3 | 4.7 | 3.0 | 10.3 |
| 25.2 | | 27.4 | 19.5 | Net Worth | | 36.5 | 23.1 | 4.5 | 26.0 | 26.6 |
| 100.0 | | 100.0 | 100.0 | Total Liabilities & Net Worth | | 100.0 | 100.0 | 100.0 | 100.0 | 100.0 |
| | | | | **INCOME DATA** | | | | | | |
| 100.0 | | 100.0 | 100.0 | Net Sales | | 100.0 | 100.0 | 100.0 | 100.0 | 100.0 |
| | | | | Gross Profit | | | | | | |
| 93.9 | | 91.0 | 92.0 | Operating Expenses | | 95.2 | 95.8 | 91.0 | 92.8 | 94.0 |
| 6.1 | | 9.0 | 8.0 | Operating Profit | | 4.8 | 4.2 | 9.0 | 7.2 | 6.0 |
| -1.4 | | .9 | 2.2 | All Other Expenses (net) | | .7 | 1.3 | 2.9 | 1.2 | 2.0 |
| 7.5 | | 8.1 | 5.8 | Profit Before Taxes | | 4.1 | 2.9 | 6.1 | 6.1 | 4.0 |
| | | | | **RATIOS** | | | | | | |
| 2.9 | | 2.9 | 2.9 | | | 6.1 | 4.5 | 4.0 | 3.1 | 2.0 |
| 1.6 | | 1.6 | 1.5 | Current | | 3.5 | 1.3 | 1.7 | 1.7 | 1.2 |
| 1.2 | | 1.1 | .9 | | | 1.3 | .6 | .9 | 1.1 | .8 |
| 2.0 | | 2.1 | 2.1 | | | 5.7 | 3.1 | 2.4 | 2.2 | 1.4 |
| 1.0 | | 1.1 | 1.0 | Quick | | 2.7 | 1.2 | .9 | 1.1 | .8 |
| .7 | | .6 | .5 | | | 1.2 | .3 | .7 | .5 | .5 |
| 28 13.2 | 27 | 13.7 | 23 16.1 | | 0 UND | 14 25.9 | 20 18.6 | 35 10.4 | 27 13.5 | |
| 41 8.8 | 44 | 8.3 | 42 8.6 | Sales/Receivables | 40 9.2 | 39 9.4 | 38 9.6 | 48 7.6 | 49 7.4 | |
| 68 5.4 | 73 | 5.0 | 64 5.7 | | 53 6.9 | 51 7.1 | 51 7.1 | 69 5.3 | 74 4.9 | |
| | | | | Cost of Sales/Inventory | | | | | | |
| | | | | Cost of Sales/Payables | | | | | | |
| 4.1 | | 3.9 | 4.9 | | | 4.0 | 5.9 | 4.4 | 4.0 | 5.6 |
| 9.8 | | 9.1 | 9.3 | Sales/Working Capital | | 6.6 | 16.4 | 9.0 | 7.9 | 14.7 |
| 33.8 | | 54.3 | -45.7 | | | 24.2 | -13.4 | -55.7 | 55.6 | -18.0 |
| 41.2 | | 36.7 | 26.8 | | | 15.7 | 61.3 | 14.3 | 29.9 | 41.3 |
| (77) 17.2 | (91) | 12.1 | (171) 4.9 | EBIT/Interest | (13) 4.7 | (10) 9.7 | (45) 4.2 | (39) 6.3 | (61) 4.9 | |
| 1.6 | | 1.6 | 1.2 | | | -5.7 | -1.2 | .3 | 1.8 | 1.3 |
| | | | 18.9 | Net Profit + Depr., Dep., | | | | | | 24.2 |
| | | (23) | 7.2 | Amort./Cur. Mat. L/T/D | | | | | (11) | 12.0 |
| | | | 2.3 | | | | | | | 6.4 |
| .1 | | .1 | .3 | | | .1 | .1 | .4 | .3 | .2 |
| .6 | | .3 | .8 | Fixed/Worth | | .4 | .6 | 3.2 | .4 | .6 |
| -1.9 | | 2.1 | -.5 | | | -.8 | NM | -.2 | -.6 | -.6 |
| 1.0 | | .9 | .8 | | | .3 | .5 | .5 | .7 | 1.3 |
| 3.0 | | 2.3 | 6.5 | Debt/Worth | | 1.4 | 3.1 | 9.3 | 1.7 | 12.1 |
| -6.0 | | 27.1 | -2.8 | | | -3.4 | -23.3 | -1.8 | -3.6 | -2.9 |
| 84.9 | | 91.8 | 73.0 | | | 81.8 | | 91.1 | 56.1 | 73.0 |
| (63) 48.1 | (92) | 38.8 | (117) 42.7 | % Profit Before Taxes/Tangible Net Worth | (12) 13.9 | (28) 39.5 | (28) 25.3 | (37) 51.1 | | |
| 16.1 | | 11.9 | 9.8 | | | 8.9 | | -1.5 | 6.5 | 27.6 |
| 24.6 | | 24.1 | 22.4 | | | 22.1 | 50.3 | 29.2 | 18.8 | 20.6 |
| 13.2 | | 9.7 | 9.3 | % Profit Before Taxes/Total Assets | | 7.8 | 7.6 | 11.1 | 6.4 | 11.8 |
| 2.3 | | 2.7 | 1.1 | | | -8.9 | 2.1 | -3.1 | 2.1 | 1.1 |
| 54.7 | | 86.8 | 38.2 | | | 98.4 | 144.7 | 39.1 | 35.4 | 35.5 |
| 19.5 | | 28.3 | 20.8 | Sales/Net Fixed Assets | | 12.2 | 26.5 | 21.3 | 22.7 | 20.1 |
| 8.4 | | 10.9 | 9.0 | | | 4.7 | 9.9 | 9.7 | 15.3 | 8.6 |
| 2.5 | | 2.8 | 2.6 | | | 2.4 | 4.6 | 3.3 | 2.6 | 2.1 |
| 1.8 | | 1.9 | 1.9 | Sales/Total Assets | | 2.1 | 2.7 | 1.9 | 2.2 | 1.5 |
| 1.1 | | 1.4 | 1.2 | | | 1.1 | 1.9 | 1.3 | 1.6 | .9 |
| .8 | | .6 | .8 | | | | | 1.6 | .4 | .6 |
| (62) 1.7 | (61) | 1.3 | (113) 2.0 | % Depr., Dep., Amort./Sales | | (26) 2.2 | (31) 1.5 | (36) 1.9 | | |
| 5.0 | | 2.7 | 3.7 | | | | | 3.0 | 3.7 | 2.8 |
| 2.0 | | | 1.8 | | | | 1.0 | | 1.8 | |
| (25) 4.1 | (24) | 3.6 | (41) 3.3 | % Officers', Directors', Owners' Comp/Sales | | (10) 2.4 | (10) 2.7 | | | |
| 7.9 | | 6.0 | 7.2 | | | | 2.9 | | 3.6 | |
| 2384963M | | 3584246M | 6113078M | Net Sales ($) | 2726M | 37280M | 53930M | 382781M | 734052M | 4902309M |
| 1849826M | | 2503924M | 5108642M | Total Assets ($) | 14123M | 27438M | 20223M | 212320M | 418140M | 4416398M |

M = $ thousand   MM = $ million
See Pages viii through xx for Explanation of Ratios and Data

© RMA 2024

# ADMIN & WASTE MANAGEMENT SERVICES—Exterminating and Pest Control Services  NAICS 561710

## Current Data Sorted by Assets | Comparative Historical Data

| | | | | | | Type of Statement | | |
|---|---|---|---|---|---|---|---|---|
| | | | 1 | | | Unqualified | 3 | 2 |
| | | | 2 | | | Reviewed | 6 | 1 |
| 7 | 5 | 1 | 1 | | | Compiled | 6 | 2 |
| 6 | 11 | 14 | 11 | 2 | 4 | Tax Returns | 29 | 18 |
| | 8 (4/1-9/30/23) | | 57 (10/1/23-3/31/24) | | | Other | 37 | 31 |
| 0-500M | 500M-2MM | 2-10MM | 10-50MM | 50-100MM | 100-250MM | | 4/1/19-3/31/20 ALL | 4/1/20-3/31/21 ALL |
| 13 | 16 | 15 | 14 | 3 | 4 | NUMBER OF STATEMENTS | 81 | 54 |
| % | % | % | % | % | % | ASSETS | % | % |
| 55.9 | 28.1 | 17.0 | 14.7 | | | Cash & Equivalents | 23.3 | 44.0 |
| 7.6 | 10.0 | 13.2 | 7.1 | | | Trade Receivables (net) | 12.7 | 7.2 |
| 1.4 | 4.4 | 2.3 | 2.4 | | | Inventory | 3.8 | 1.8 |
| 1.9 | 5.2 | 12.9 | 1.7 | | | All Other Current | 4.5 | 2.7 |
| 66.8 | 47.6 | 45.4 | 25.9 | | | Total Current | 44.3 | 55.8 |
| 13.2 | 34.8 | 30.6 | 27.6 | | | Fixed Assets (net) | 28.7 | 21.9 |
| 15.0 | 6.5 | 11.0 | 17.3 | | | Intangibles (net) | 14.6 | 10.3 |
| 5.1 | 11.1 | 13.0 | 29.2 | | | All Other Non-Current | 12.5 | 12.0 |
| 100.0 | 100.0 | 100.0 | 100.0 | | | Total | 100.0 | 100.0 |
| | | | | | | LIABILITIES | | |
| 15.6 | 5.2 | 2.8 | 2.4 | | | Notes Payable-Short Term | 8.0 | 8.6 |
| 10.2 | 3.4 | 4.0 | 4.9 | | | Cur. Mat.-L.T.D. | 3.6 | 4.4 |
| 17.1 | 4.0 | 4.0 | 4.5 | | | Trade Payables | 5.7 | 3.7 |
| .0 | .0 | .0 | .1 | | | Income Taxes Payable | .1 | .1 |
| 20.3 | 8.0 | 6.1 | 8.9 | | | All Other Current | 16.7 | 14.9 |
| 63.2 | 20.6 | 16.8 | 21.0 | | | Total Current | 34.1 | 31.6 |
| 145.3 | 30.0 | 27.1 | 32.8 | | | Long-Term Debt | 32.0 | 33.3 |
| .0 | .0 | .0 | .4 | | | Deferred Taxes | .1 | .1 |
| .0 | 2.7 | .9 | 7.5 | | | All Other Non-Current | 15.2 | 4.2 |
| -108.5 | 46.7 | 55.1 | 38.3 | | | Net Worth | 18.6 | 30.7 |
| 100.0 | 100.0 | 100.0 | 100.0 | | | Total Liabilties & Net Worth | 100.0 | 100.0 |
| | | | | | | INCOME DATA | | |
| 100.0 | 100.0 | 100.0 | 100.0 | | | Net Sales | 100.0 | 100.0 |
| | | | | | | Gross Profit | | |
| 101.2 | 92.8 | 93.1 | 88.5 | | | Operating Expenses | 90.9 | 89.1 |
| -1.2 | 7.2 | 6.9 | 11.5 | | | Operating Profit | 9.1 | 10.9 |
| -.2 | 1.1 | 3.8 | 4.1 | | | All Other Expenses (net) | 1.0 | .4 |
| -1.0 | 6.0 | 3.1 | 7.4 | | | Profit Before Taxes | 8.1 | 10.5 |
| | | | | | | RATIOS | | |
| 7.7 | 6.4 | 9.1 | 2.4 | | | | 4.4 | 5.8 |
| 1.4 | 2.0 | 2.6 | 1.0 | | | Current | 1.5 | 2.1 |
| 1.0 | .8 | .5 | .8 | | | | .6 | 1.1 |
| 7.5 | 4.8 | 4.4 | 2.1 | | | | 3.6 | 5.8 |
| 1.4 | 1.3 | 2.0 | .9 | | | Quick | 1.2 | 2.0 |
| .8 | .6 | .4 | .6 | | | | .4 | 1.0 |
| 0 UND | 0 UND | 0 999.8 | 5 78.5 | | | | 0 UND | 0 UND |
| 0 UND | 0 UND | 11 33.7 | 9 41.9 | | | Sales/Receivables | 10 37.5 | 6 66.2 |
| 1 364.1 | 15 24.2 | 37 9.8 | 28 13.1 | | | | 19 19.2 | 16 23.1 |
| | | | | | | Cost of Sales/Inventory | | |
| | | | | | | Cost of Sales/Payables | | |
| 15.1 | 8.4 | 4.4 | 7.1 | | | | 10.2 | 5.0 |
| 37.3 | 16.7 | 13.9 | NM | | | Sales/Working Capital | 30.9 | 10.8 |
| UND | -71.3 | -17.1 | -25.3 | | | | -30.8 | 90.0 |
| 9.1 | 51.9 | 52.1 | 38.9 | | | | 20.6 | 52.8 |
| (12) -.6 | (13) 17.8 | (12) 13.7 | (11) 17.9 | | | EBIT/Interest | (58) 4.9 | (38) 12.9 |
| -3.4 | 4.0 | 3.4 | 5.9 | | | | 1.6 | 4.8 |
| | | | | | | Net Profit + Depr., Dep., Amort./Cur. Mat. L/T/D | 8.7 (10) 4.1 2.4 | |
| .0 | .2 | .2 | .5 | | | | .4 | .1 |
| .8 | 1.0 | .5 | 1.1 | | | Fixed/Worth | 1.1 | .8 |
| -.1 | 3.0 | 4.0 | NM | | | | -1.8 | 42.0 |
| .4 | .6 | .1 | 1.1 | | | | .8 | .9 |
| -2.6 | 1.5 | .9 | 2.4 | | | Debt/Worth | 2.8 | 2.7 |
| -1.4 | 3.6 | 3.0 | NM | | | | -3.9 | 79.5 |
| | 99.2 | 73.8 | 94.2 | | | | 109.2 | 189.5 |
| (15) | 70.1 | (13) 39.4 | (11) 50.8 | | | % Profit Before Taxes/Tangible Net Worth | (54) 59.1 | (43) 65.5 |
| | 19.7 | -11.4 | 17.2 | | | | 20.0 | 14.5 |
| 29.5 | 47.8 | 36.7 | 20.3 | | | | 49.5 | 47.7 |
| 8.6 | 28.8 | 24.3 | 12.6 | | | % Profit Before Taxes/Total Assets | 17.1 | 22.1 |
| -23.1 | 6.8 | -7.9 | 4.3 | | | | 4.8 | 4.7 |
| 624.3 | 34.1 | 13.5 | 13.8 | | | | 42.8 | 69.3 |
| 187.3 | 23.0 | 9.2 | 9.7 | | | Sales/Net Fixed Assets | 14.4 | 16.3 |
| 34.7 | 5.3 | 6.5 | 6.2 | | | | 8.1 | 7.5 |
| 9.8 | 5.2 | 3.8 | 2.2 | | | | 5.9 | 3.9 |
| 5.8 | 3.4 | 2.6 | 1.8 | | | Sales/Total Assets | 3.3 | 2.4 |
| 3.9 | 2.1 | 1.5 | 1.2 | | | | 1.9 | 1.6 |
| | | | 2.7 | | | | 1.5 | 2.0 |
| | | (11) | 3.6 | | | % Depr., Dep., Amort./Sales | (46) 3.0 | (19) 3.1 |
| | | | 4.1 | | | | 5.6 | 4.5 |
| | | | | | | % Officers', Directors' Owners' Comp/Sales | 2.9 (32) 5.0 9.8 | 2.4 (18) 8.1 15.7 |
| 16415M | 79512M | 180413M | 450594M | 406771M | 1295991M | Net Sales ($) | 1780690M | 961620M |
| 2480M | 21908M | 68270M | 257272M | 202006M | 717481M | Total Assets ($) | 824615M | 526572M |

M = $ thousand    MM = $ million
See Pages viii through xx for Explanation of Ratios and Data

© RMA 2024

# ADMIN & WASTE MANAGEMENT SERVICES—Exterminating and Pest Control Services  NAICS 561710

## Comparative Historical Data | Current Data Sorted by Sales

| | | | Type of Statement | | | | | | |
|---|---|---|---|---|---|---|---|---|---|
| | | 1 | Unqualified | | | | 1 | | |
| 2 | 2 | 2 | Reviewed | | | | | | 2 |
| 4 | 6 | 1 | Compiled | | 2 | 3 | 2 | 1 | 1 |
| 10 | 17 | 13 | Tax Returns | 5 | 10 | 2 | 9 | 9 | 14 |
| 32 | 38 | 48 | Other | 4 | 8 (4/1-9/30/23) | | 57 (10/1/23-3/31/24) | | |
| 4/1/21-3/31/22 | 4/1/22-3/31/23 | 4/1/23-3/31/24 | | 0-1MM | 1-3MM | 3-5MM | 5-10MM | 10-25MM | 25MM & OVER |
| ALL | ALL | ALL | | | | | | | |
| 48 | 63 | 65 | NUMBER OF STATEMENTS | 9 | 12 | 5 | 12 | 10 | 17 |
| % | % | % | ASSETS | % | % | % | % | % | % |
| 34.6 | 29.3 | 27.5 | Cash & Equivalents | | 36.9 | | 27.0 | 16.7 | 18.2 |
| 12.4 | 11.3 | 9.5 | Trade Receivables (net) | | 6.2 | | 11.9 | 6.8 | 12.4 |
| 2.7 | 3.3 | 2.6 | Inventory | | 4.6 | | 2.9 | 3.1 | 1.9 |
| 3.9 | 5.1 | 5.1 | All Other Current | | 7.9 | | 9.8 | .9 | 2.2 |
| 53.6 | 49.0 | 44.7 | Total Current | | 55.6 | | 51.7 | 27.5 | 34.7 |
| 24.9 | 21.2 | 27.7 | Fixed Assets (net) | | 28.9 | | 21.9 | 29.3 | 30.3 |
| 12.1 | 17.1 | 13.2 | Intangibles (net) | | 11.3 | | 10.8 | 20.5 | 13.5 |
| 9.3 | 12.7 | 14.4 | All Other Non-Current | | 4.3 | | 15.6 | 22.7 | 21.4 |
| 100.0 | 100.0 | 100.0 | Total | | 100.0 | | 100.0 | 100.0 | 100.0 |
| | | | LIABILITIES | | | | | | |
| 9.3 | 11.9 | 5.7 | Notes Payable-Short Term | | 14.5 | | 2.2 | 3.3 | 2.3 |
| 3.7 | 3.4 | 5.3 | Cur. Mat.-L.T.D. | | 7.8 | | 3.3 | 8.4 | 4.1 |
| 5.4 | 3.7 | 6.8 | Trade Payables | | 19.2 | | 5.4 | 4.3 | 5.9 |
| .0 | .2 | .0 | Income Taxes Payable | | .0 | | .0 | .0 | .1 |
| 13.2 | 11.6 | 12.3 | All Other Current | | 8.5 | | 9.0 | 7.3 | 18.7 |
| 31.5 | 30.7 | 30.2 | Total Current | | 50.1 | | 19.9 | 23.2 | 31.0 |
| 33.4 | 36.0 | 51.6 | Long-Term Debt | | 83.7 | | 18.8 | 52.8 | 17.7 |
| .0 | .1 | .2 | Deferred Taxes | | .0 | | .0 | .0 | .6 |
| 5.8 | 5.6 | 2.9 | All Other Non-Current | | .3 | | 2.9 | 1.5 | 7.9 |
| 29.2 | 27.6 | 15.0 | Net Worth | | -34.1 | | 58.5 | 22.5 | 42.9 |
| 100.0 | 100.0 | 100.0 | Total Liabilities & Net Worth | | 100.0 | | 100.0 | 100.0 | 100.0 |
| | | | INCOME DATA | | | | | | |
| 100.0 | 100.0 | 100.0 | Net Sales | | 100.0 | | 100.0 | 100.0 | 100.0 |
| 92.9 | 92.4 | 93.8 | Gross Profit | | 90.9 | | 96.0 | 90.7 | 92.7 |
| 7.1 | 7.6 | 6.2 | Operating Expenses | | 9.1 | | 4.0 | 9.3 | 7.3 |
| -1.1 | .0 | 2.0 | Operating Profit | | 1.3 | | -1.0 | 3.3 | .6 |
| 8.2 | 7.5 | 4.3 | All Other Expenses (net) | | 7.8 | | 5.1 | 6.0 | 6.7 |
| | | | Profit Before Taxes | | | | | | |
| | | | RATIOS | | | | | | |
| 4.3 | 5.0 | 5.8 | | | 9.1 | | 9.8 | 2.7 | 1.9 |
| 2.0 | 2.2 | 1.6 | Current | | 4.6 | | 3.1 | .9 | 1.1 |
| .9 | 1.1 | .8 | | | .5 | | 1.6 | .5 | .5 |
| 4.1 | 4.1 | 4.1 | | | 8.4 | | 4.6 | 2.7 | 1.8 |
| 1.8 | 1.8 | 1.3 | Quick | | 1.1 | | 2.3 | .8 | 1.0 |
| .6 | .6 | .6 | | | .3 | | 1.3 | .4 | .4 |
| 0 UND | 0 UND | 0 UND | | 0 UND | | 0 900.6 | 0 UND | 9 42.0 | |
| 8 45.7 | 7 49.1 | 7 55.9 | Sales/Receivables | 0 UND | | 13 28.6 | 7 55.5 | 16 22.8 | |
| 20 18.2 | 25 14.8 | 17 20.9 | | 1 671.5 | | 29 12.6 | 27 13.3 | 26 14.0 | |
| | | | Cost of Sales/Inventory | | | | | | |
| | | | Cost of Sales/Payables | | | | | | |
| 6.7 | 6.6 | 8.2 | | | 3.5 | | 4.5 | 26.4 | 11.3 |
| 16.6 | 13.3 | 29.6 | Sales/Working Capital | | 25.0 | | 8.4 | -47.5 | 89.3 |
| NM | 99.5 | -26.4 | | | -13.4 | | 26.2 | -15.8 | -12.4 |
| | | | | | 38.9 | | | 23.3 | 28.7 |
| 80.3 | 27.3 | 29.7 | EBIT/Interest | (10) | 4.0 | | 14.2 | (13) 6.0 | |
| (39) 14.8 | (50) 11.2 | (52) 10.6 | | | .2 | | 5.2 | 2.8 | |
| 3.3 | 2.7 | 2.1 | | | | | | | |
| | | | Net Profit + Depr., Dep., Amort./Cur. Mat. L/T/D | | | | | | |
| .2 | .1 | .3 | | | .1 | | .1 | 1.1 | .4 |
| .6 | .6 | .8 | Fixed/Worth | | .5 | | .4 | 26.4 | .8 |
| 9.4 | -1.6 | 6.1 | | | 1.7 | | 1.2 | -.7 | 3.8 |
| .9 | .7 | .5 | | | .2 | | .1 | 1.6 | .9 |
| 1.9 | 3.6 | 1.6 | Debt/Worth | | 1.2 | | .7 | 212.1 | 1.3 |
| 49.9 | -5.6 | NM | | | 2.4 | | 1.7 | -2.9 | 6.0 |
| 195.1 | 111.9 | 89.5 | % Profit Before Taxes/Tangible Net Worth | | 78.2 | | 71.5 | | 71.5 |
| (37) 89.0 | (42) 52.4 | (49) 50.8 | | (10) | 23.9 | | 46.3 | (14) | 48.2 |
| 42.5 | 18.9 | 14.0 | | | 7.7 | | 12.6 | | 16.9 |
| 38.2 | 32.5 | 34.6 | % Profit Before Taxes/Total Assets | | 19.9 | | 42.3 | 36.5 | 21.2 |
| 25.7 | 18.1 | 16.6 | | | 7.8 | | 22.9 | 23.3 | 12.6 |
| 9.7 | 6.1 | 2.7 | | | -2.3 | | 6.5 | 15.3 | 5.0 |
| 60.1 | 68.4 | 40.2 | Sales/Net Fixed Assets | | 233.3 | | 50.4 | 16.0 | 11.9 |
| 14.5 | 19.0 | 12.3 | | | 30.6 | | 18.5 | 11.1 | 8.4 |
| 8.2 | 8.5 | 6.2 | | | 3.8 | | 10.6 | 7.3 | 4.9 |
| 5.0 | 4.3 | 4.5 | Sales/Total Assets | | 7.8 | | 4.7 | 4.9 | 3.1 |
| 3.7 | 3.1 | 2.7 | | | 3.3 | | 2.9 | 2.3 | 2.0 |
| 2.2 | 1.5 | 1.5 | | | .9 | | 1.8 | 1.5 | 1.7 |
| 1.6 | .9 | 1.8 | % Depr., Dep., Amort./Sales | | | | | | 2.7 |
| (22) 3.0 | (30) 2.7 | (31) 3.1 | | | | | | (12) | 3.5 |
| 4.6 | 3.8 | 4.7 | | | | | | | 4.0 |
| 2.3 | 2.2 | 1.4 | % Officers', Directors', Owners' Comp/Sales | | | | | | |
| (24) 4.1 | (27) 5.3 | (24) 5.8 | | | | | | | |
| 12.2 | 10.5 | 11.6 | | | | | | | |
| 923816M | 1767213M | 2429696M | Net Sales ($) | 4201M | 23629M | 19365M | 90920M | 157898M | 2133683M |
| 349346M | 837028M | 1269417M | Total Assets ($) | 5685M | 27466M | 7769M | 48365M | 77574M | 1102558M |

M = $ thousand  MM = $ million
See Pages viii through xx for Explanation of Ratios and Data

© RMA 2024

# ADMIN & WASTE MANAGEMENT SERVICES—Janitorial Services  NAICS 561720

## Current Data Sorted by Assets / Comparative Historical Data

| | | | | | | | Type of Statement | | | | |
|---|---|---|---|---|---|---|---|---|---|---|---|
| | 2 | 6 | 4 | 1 | 2 | | Unqualified | | 11 | | 8 |
| | 1 | 10 | 11 | | | | Reviewed | | 10 | | 5 |
| | 1 | 6 | 1 | | | | Compiled | | 11 | | 6 |
| 18 | 10 | 13 | 1 | | | | Tax Returns | | 58 | | 28 |
| 22 | 28 | 49 | 19 | 5 | 7 | | Other | | 152 | | 101 |
| | 28 (4/1-9/30/23) | | 189 (10/1/23-3/31/24) | | | | | | 4/1/19-3/31/20 | | 4/1/20-3/31/21 |
| 0-500M | 500M-2MM | 2-10MM | 10-50MM | 50-100MM | 100-250MM | | NUMBER OF STATEMENTS | | ALL | | ALL |
| 40 | 42 | 84 | 36 | 6 | 9 | | | | 242 | | 148 |
| % | % | % | % | % | % | | ASSETS | | % | | % |
| 31.2 | 29.7 | 21.3 | 19.8 | | | | Cash & Equivalents | | 18.4 | | 30.5 |
| 16.0 | 30.6 | 37.0 | 42.7 | | | | Trade Receivables (net) | | 36.0 | | 27.2 |
| 3.8 | 1.2 | 2.6 | .7 | | | | Inventory | | 1.4 | | 1.3 |
| 5.0 | 2.7 | 4.3 | 2.9 | | | | All Other Current | | 5.6 | | 4.1 |
| 56.0 | 64.2 | 65.1 | 66.2 | | | | Total Current | | 61.4 | | 63.2 |
| 17.7 | 12.8 | 12.1 | 8.9 | | | | Fixed Assets (net) | | 18.1 | | 15.5 |
| 22.4 | 8.7 | 12.7 | 12.9 | | | | Intangibles (net) | | 11.7 | | 12.3 |
| 3.9 | 14.2 | 10.1 | 12.0 | | | | All Other Non-Current | | 8.8 | | 9.1 |
| 100.0 | 100.0 | 100.0 | 100.0 | | | | Total | | 100.0 | | 100.0 |
| | | | | | | | LIABILITIES | | | | |
| 15.3 | 7.1 | 4.2 | 2.8 | | | | Notes Payable-Short Term | | 12.4 | | 8.0 |
| 5.4 | 4.0 | 1.7 | 2.0 | | | | Cur. Mat.-L.T.D. | | 3.6 | | 3.2 |
| 3.6 | 7.7 | 10.1 | 9.7 | | | | Trade Payables | | 10.5 | | 6.6 |
| .0 | .5 | .1 | .2 | | | | Income Taxes Payable | | .3 | | .2 |
| 28.8 | 15.0 | 14.0 | 13.3 | | | | All Other Current | | 18.6 | | 15.6 |
| 53.1 | 34.4 | 30.2 | 27.9 | | | | Total Current | | 45.3 | | 33.6 |
| 32.0 | 23.9 | 14.3 | 10.2 | | | | Long-Term Debt | | 21.8 | | 27.8 |
| .0 | .0 | .1 | .1 | | | | Deferred Taxes | | .2 | | .1 |
| .3 | 7.8 | 5.6 | 5.6 | | | | All Other Non-Current | | 4.2 | | 4.3 |
| 14.5 | 33.8 | 49.9 | 56.2 | | | | Net Worth | | 28.4 | | 34.2 |
| 100.0 | 100.0 | 100.0 | 100.0 | | | | Total Liabilities & Net Worth | | 100.0 | | 100.0 |
| | | | | | | | INCOME DATA | | | | |
| 100.0 | 100.0 | 100.0 | 100.0 | | | | Net Sales | | 100.0 | | 100.0 |
| | | | | | | | Gross Profit | | | | |
| 87.1 | 92.5 | 93.7 | 92.3 | | | | Operating Expenses | | 93.3 | | 91.6 |
| 12.9 | 7.5 | 6.3 | 7.7 | | | | Operating Profit | | 6.7 | | 8.4 |
| 3.4 | .1 | .6 | -.4 | | | | All Other Expenses (net) | | .8 | | -.6 |
| 9.5 | 7.4 | 5.7 | 8.2 | | | | Profit Before Taxes | | 5.9 | | 9.0 |
| | | | | | | | RATIOS | | | | |
| 8.5 | 5.3 | 5.6 | 3.7 | | | | | | 2.6 | | 5.8 |
| 1.4 | 2.5 | 2.6 | 2.6 | | | | Current | | 1.6 | | 2.2 |
| 1.0 | 1.5 | 1.4 | 1.5 | | | | | | 1.0 | | 1.3 |
| 8.0 | 5.3 | 5.0 | 3.4 | | | | | | 2.4 | | 5.0 |
| 1.2 | 2.3 | 2.3 | 2.5 | | | | Quick | | 1.3 | | 2.1 |
| .6 | 1.2 | 1.2 | 1.5 | | | | | | .8 | | 1.1 |
| 0 UND | 12 30.5 | 27 13.7 | 32 11.3 | | | | | | 14 26.9 | | 11 33.6 |
| 0 UND | 23 15.7 | 35 10.3 | 53 6.9 | | | | Sales/Receivables | | 33 11.2 | | 29 12.4 |
| 26 13.8 | 40 9.2 | 51 7.2 | 69 5.3 | | | | | | 50 7.3 | | 49 7.4 |
| | | | | | | | Cost of Sales/Inventory | | | | |
| | | | | | | | Cost of Sales/Payables | | | | |
| 14.4 | 6.9 | 4.6 | 5.0 | | | | | | 10.2 | | 5.8 |
| 55.6 | 13.9 | 9.4 | 8.1 | | | | Sales/Working Capital | | 25.9 | | 10.1 |
| UND | 28.9 | 30.7 | 12.8 | | | | | | -651.4 | | 35.8 |
| 23.1 | 55.1 | 59.4 | 57.2 | | | | | | 35.8 | | 56.8 |
| (30) 10.0 | (32) 10.0 | (70) 15.4 | (32) 18.9 | | | | EBIT/Interest | | (188) 9.4 | (124) | 18.6 |
| .0 | 3.6 | 3.4 | 6.9 | | | | | | 2.9 | | 3.7 |
| | | | | | | | Net Profit + Depr., Dep., Amort./Cur. Mat. L/T/D | | 13.1 | | 20.6 |
| | | | | | | | | (18) | 5.2 | (21) | 5.9 |
| | | | | | | | | | 1.9 | | 2.4 |
| .0 | .0 | .1 | .0 | | | | | | .1 | | .1 |
| 1.1 | .2 | .2 | .2 | | | | Fixed/Worth | | .5 | | .5 |
| -.8 | 3.1 | .6 | .4 | | | | | | 4.4 | | -4.1 |
| .5 | .6 | .4 | .4 | | | | | | .6 | | .8 |
| 16.2 | 1.3 | 1.0 | .8 | | | | Debt/Worth | | 2.2 | | 2.2 |
| -2.7 | -14.3 | 6.5 | 1.8 | | | | | | -27.6 | | -15.1 |
| 870.3 | 143.3 | 87.2 | 65.5 | | | | % Profit Before Taxes/Tangible Net Worth | | 113.0 | | 115.4 |
| (24) 141.7 | (31) 49.5 | (70) 41.7 | (33) 42.6 | | | | | (180) | 51.3 | (106) | 60.9 |
| 71.2 | 21.8 | 15.4 | 27.1 | | | | | | 23.8 | | 27.1 |
| 105.7 | 39.9 | 32.4 | 26.7 | | | | % Profit Before Taxes/Total Assets | | 34.7 | | 42.8 |
| 46.2 | 15.1 | 17.0 | 18.5 | | | | | | 18.6 | | 20.5 |
| 8.9 | 7.1 | 2.3 | 9.8 | | | | | | 6.0 | | 6.7 |
| UND | 355.5 | 119.9 | 153.2 | | | | | | 127.3 | | 93.0 |
| 93.9 | 94.8 | 49.4 | 45.6 | | | | Sales/Net Fixed Assets | | 44.1 | | 32.7 |
| 12.8 | 34.6 | 20.7 | 19.8 | | | | | | 17.3 | | 16.2 |
| 11.1 | 6.9 | 4.8 | 3.8 | | | | | | 6.7 | | 4.7 |
| 4.9 | 5.0 | 3.1 | 3.1 | | | | Sales/Total Assets | | 4.2 | | 3.0 |
| 2.6 | 2.5 | 2.4 | 2.2 | | | | | | 2.6 | | 2.0 |
| 1.3 | .3 | .3 | .3 | | | | | | .5 | | .6 |
| (12) 2.0 | (14) .7 | (53) .8 | (27) .9 | | | | % Depr., Dep., Amort./Sales | (140) | 1.0 | (76) | 1.2 |
| 3.3 | 2.5 | 1.7 | 1.7 | | | | | | 1.7 | | 2.4 |
| 2.5 | 1.9 | 1.1 | | | | | | | 1.6 | | 1.5 |
| (27) 4.5 | (16) 2.8 | (32) 2.1 | | | | | % Officers', Directors' Owners' Comp/Sales | (96) | 3.1 | (50) | 3.1 |
| 10.1 | 9.3 | 4.4 | | | | | | | 5.2 | | 6.6 |
| 64047M | 205224M | 1504550M | 2146458M | 787215M | 2553529M | | Net Sales ($) | | 8452038M | | 5288912M |
| 9605M | 43743M | 391477M | 728486M | 434861M | 1273235M | | Total Assets ($) | | 2717889M | | 2098829M |

© RMA 2024  M = $ thousand   MM = $ million
See Pages viii through xx for Explanation of Ratios and Data

## ADMIN & WASTE MANAGEMENT SERVICES—Janitorial Services  NAICS 561720

### Comparative Historical Data

| | | | | | | Type of Statement | | | | | | |
|---|---|---|---|---|---|---|---|---|---|---|---|---|
| | 8 | | 17 | | 15 | Unqualified | | 2 | | 3 | 2 | 8 |
| | 13 | | 19 | | 22 | Reviewed | | | 1 | 1 | 5 | 15 |
| | 6 | | 11 | | 8 | Compiled | | | 1 | 2 | 2 | 3 |
| | 34 | | 40 | | 42 | Tax Returns | 8 | 10 | 6 | 9 | 5 | 4 |
| | 85 | | 126 | | 130 | Other | 11 | 20 | 17 | 18 | 26 | 38 |
| | 4/1/21-3/31/22 ALL | | 4/1/22-3/31/23 ALL | | 4/1/23-3/31/24 ALL | | | 28 (4/1-9/30/23) | | 189 (10/1/23-3/31/24) | | |
| | | | | | | | 0-1MM | 1-3MM | 3-5MM | 5-10MM | 10-25MM | 25MM & OVER |
| | 146 | | 213 | | 217 | NUMBER OF STATEMENTS | 19 | 32 | 25 | 33 | 40 | 68 |
| | % | | % | | % | ASSETS | % | % | % | % | % | % |
| | 29.5 | | 23.9 | | 23.9 | Cash & Equivalents | 27.4 | 23.1 | 35.5 | 30.0 | 22.1 | 17.1 |
| | 29.4 | | 34.3 | | 32.5 | Trade Receivables (net) | 11.0 | 26.5 | 23.3 | 26.9 | 37.4 | 44.5 |
| | 1.0 | | 1.1 | | 2.1 | Inventory | 5.2 | 1.9 | 1.8 | 1.9 | 3.6 | .5 |
| | 5.4 | | 4.6 | | 4.0 | All Other Current | 5.5 | 3.8 | 2.8 | 5.7 | 3.0 | 3.8 |
| | 65.3 | | 63.8 | | 62.4 | Total Current | 49.0 | 55.3 | 63.4 | 64.6 | 66.2 | 65.9 |
| | 15.3 | | 16.0 | | 12.4 | Fixed Assets (net) | 24.4 | 14.9 | 12.5 | 10.6 | 11.4 | 9.3 |
| | 12.6 | | 10.7 | | 14.5 | Intangibles (net) | 25.2 | 20.7 | 11.4 | 15.1 | 8.6 | 13.1 |
| | 6.8 | | 9.5 | | 10.6 | All Other Non-Current | 1.4 | 9.1 | 12.7 | 9.7 | 13.8 | 11.7 |
| | 100.0 | | 100.0 | | 100.0 | Total | 100.0 | 100.0 | 100.0 | 100.0 | 100.0 | 100.0 |
| | | | | | | LIABILITIES | | | | | | |
| | 8.2 | | 7.1 | | 6.9 | Notes Payable-Short Term | 8.4 | 5.1 | 12.9 | 5.8 | 7.3 | 5.4 |
| | 1.9 | | 2.9 | | 2.9 | Cur. Mat.-L.T.D. | 2.7 | 4.3 | 3.5 | 2.7 | 3.0 | 2.1 |
| | 7.4 | | 9.5 | | 8.2 | Trade Payables | 2.4 | 6.5 | 4.1 | 9.4 | 10.7 | 10.0 |
| | .3 | | .1 | | .2 | Income Taxes Payable | .0 | .0 | .0 | .0 | .7 | .2 |
| | 16.8 | | 15.4 | | 17.0 | All Other Current | 37.3 | 17.0 | 12.6 | 12.8 | 12.4 | 17.7 |
| | 34.6 | | 35.1 | | 35.2 | Total Current | 50.8 | 33.0 | 33.2 | 30.7 | 34.1 | 35.4 |
| | 17.0 | | 18.4 | | 18.4 | Long-Term Debt | 36.0 | 21.9 | 28.8 | 25.2 | 10.1 | 9.5 |
| | .0 | | .1 | | .0 | Deferred Taxes | .0 | .0 | .0 | .0 | .1 | .1 |
| | 4.2 | | 3.8 | | 5.1 | All Other Non-Current | 1.4 | 6.7 | 3.9 | 6.0 | 5.7 | 5.2 |
| | 44.2 | | 42.7 | | 41.3 | Net Worth | 11.7 | 38.4 | 34.1 | 38.1 | 50.0 | 49.8 |
| | 100.0 | | 100.0 | | 100.0 | Total Liabilities & Net Worth | 100.0 | 100.0 | 100.0 | 100.0 | 100.0 | 100.0 |
| | | | | | | INCOME DATA | | | | | | |
| | 100.0 | | 100.0 | | 100.0 | Net Sales | 100.0 | 100.0 | 100.0 | 100.0 | 100.0 | 100.0 |
| | | | | | | Gross Profit | | | | | | |
| | 91.8 | | 92.2 | | 92.2 | Operating Expenses | 76.3 | 91.7 | 91.6 | 93.2 | 94.4 | 95.3 |
| | 8.2 | | 7.8 | | 7.8 | Operating Profit | 23.7 | 8.3 | 8.4 | 6.8 | 5.6 | 4.7 |
| | -1.4 | | .5 | | 1.0 | All Other Expenses (net) | 10.0 | .3 | -.5 | .0 | -.3 | .4 |
| | 9.6 | | 7.3 | | 6.9 | Profit Before Taxes | 13.7 | 8.0 | 8.8 | 6.8 | 5.9 | 4.3 |
| | | | | | | RATIOS | | | | | | |
| | 4.5 | | 4.1 | | 4.9 | | 11.7 | 6.4 | 11.0 | 6.1 | 5.0 | 3.2 |
| | 2.3 | | 2.1 | | 2.2 | Current | 2.2 | 1.6 | 2.7 | 2.8 | 2.5 | 2.0 |
| | 1.4 | | 1.2 | | 1.3 | | 1.0 | 1.0 | 1.6 | 1.5 | 1.5 | 1.3 |
| | 3.9 | | 3.8 | | 4.5 | | 11.4 | 6.2 | 9.2 | 5.7 | 4.5 | 3.1 |
| | 2.1 | | 1.9 | | 2.1 | Quick | 2.2 | 1.5 | 2.6 | 2.6 | 2.2 | 1.8 |
| | 1.2 | | 1.1 | | 1.1 | | .2 | .7 | 1.3 | 1.3 | 1.3 | 1.1 |
| 9 | 41.0 | 15 | 24.2 | 17 | 21.4 | | 0 UND | 0 UND | 0 UND | 14 26.0 | 26 13.8 | 31 11.6 |
| 29 | 12.4 | 37 | 9.8 | 33 | 10.9 | Sales/Receivables | 0 UND | 29 12.7 | 29 12.4 | 27 13.7 | 36 10.1 | 48 7.6 |
| 52 | 7.0 | 64 | 5.7 | 54 | 6.8 | | 25 14.4 | 60 6.1 | 35 10.3 | 49 7.4 | 50 7.3 | 62 5.9 |
| | | | | | | Cost of Sales/Inventory | | | | | | |
| | | | | | | Cost of Sales/Payables | | | | | | |
| | 6.3 | | 5.0 | | 6.1 | | 4.1 | 5.9 | 4.6 | 5.1 | 4.8 | 6.8 |
| | 10.2 | | 10.1 | | 12.6 | Sales/Working Capital | 19.0 | 32.2 | 13.4 | 11.6 | 12.5 | 9.7 |
| | 34.1 | | 44.0 | | 42.8 | | UND | NM | 41.8 | 26.5 | 18.7 | 33.1 |
| | 109.0 | | 58.1 | | 44.4 | | 19.3 | 17.9 | 31.6 | 55.6 | 79.3 | 52.5 |
| (112) | 29.2 | (149) | 14.4 | (179) | 12.5 | EBIT/Interest | (14) 7.5 | (21) 5.0 | (19) 11.1 | (29) 16.9 | (35) 21.8 | (61) 14.9 |
| | 9.7 | | 4.1 | | 3.3 | | 2.3 | .4 | 2.0 | 3.7 | 6.1 | 3.6 |
| | 18.3 | | 36.6 | | 10.4 | Net Profit + Depr., Dep., | | | | | | 9.3 |
| (11) | 8.0 | (22) | 10.0 | (24) | 4.1 | Amort./Cur. Mat. L/T/D | | | | | (17) | 3.7 |
| | 4.1 | | 3.3 | | 2.1 | | | | | | | 2.2 |
| | .1 | | .0 | | .0 | | .1 | .0 | .0 | .1 | .1 | .1 |
| | .3 | | .3 | | .2 | Fixed/Worth | 5.1 | .2 | .1 | .3 | .2 | .2 |
| | 1.6 | | 1.2 | | 1.2 | | -1.2 | 6.1 | .5 | NM | .7 | .5 |
| | .4 | | .4 | | .5 | | 1.8 | .7 | .3 | .5 | .4 | .5 |
| | 1.2 | | 1.4 | | 1.5 | Debt/Worth | UND | 5.9 | .9 | 1.0 | .8 | 1.6 |
| | 9.6 | | 11.1 | | 16.7 | | -2.7 | -12.3 | -13.2 | -5.2 | 3.6 | 3.7 |
| | 140.4 | | 79.9 | | 89.0 | % Profit Before Taxes/Tangible | 753.8 | 235.4 | 87.3 | 141.0 | 73.9 | 73.7 |
| (119) | 61.2 | (169) | 36.6 | (172) | 43.6 | Net Worth | (11) 97.4 | (22) 65.1 | (18) 41.5 | (24) 44.6 | (35) 44.3 | (62) 39.9 |
| | 27.3 | | 12.8 | | 18.0 | | 71.6 | -19.3 | 10.2 | 21.1 | 20.8 | 16.8 |
| | 47.8 | | 33.0 | | 36.6 | % Profit Before Taxes/Total | 60.6 | 65.5 | 52.6 | 35.8 | 32.4 | 27.0 |
| | 24.4 | | 14.5 | | 17.5 | Assets | 26.2 | 15.5 | 17.7 | 17.8 | 19.3 | 11.5 |
| | 10.3 | | 3.8 | | 6.1 | | 2.2 | -.3 | 4.5 | 8.8 | 10.7 | 3.6 |
| | 144.3 | | 149.0 | | 254.3 | | UND | 999.8 | 688.9 | 242.4 | 133.9 | 117.9 |
| | 45.0 | | 40.0 | | 54.2 | Sales/Net Fixed Assets | 72.3 | 69.5 | 97.1 | 55.6 | 51.4 | 48.6 |
| | 15.1 | | 14.8 | | 20.0 | | 9.3 | 12.7 | 35.6 | 24.7 | 18.1 | 22.5 |
| | 5.4 | | 4.8 | | 5.3 | | 4.0 | 5.2 | 8.4 | 5.7 | 5.8 | 4.5 |
| | 3.3 | | 3.0 | | 3.3 | Sales/Total Assets | 2.4 | 3.3 | 5.3 | 3.5 | 3.5 | 3.2 |
| | 2.2 | | 1.8 | | 2.3 | | 1.5 | 1.9 | 1.9 | 2.5 | 2.6 | 2.3 |
| | .5 | | .5 | | .4 | | | 1.2 | | .6 | .4 | .2 |
| (75) | .9 | (104) | 1.1 | (115) | .9 | % Depr., Dep., Amort./Sales | (10) 2.0 | | (18) 1.3 | (21) .8 | (51) .8 |
| | 2.0 | | 2.5 | | 1.9 | | | 2.9 | | 2.1 | 1.8 | 1.3 |
| | 2.1 | | 1.5 | | 1.9 | % Officers', Directors', | | 2.4 | 2.0 | .9 | 1.3 | 1.0 |
| (61) | 3.4 | (73) | 2.7 | (79) | 2.6 | Owners' Comp/Sales | (18) 4.6 | (14) 2.7 | (16) 2.5 | (10) 2.1 | (12) 2.0 |
| | 9.1 | | 5.3 | | 6.4 | | | 11.1 | 6.4 | 4.1 | 3.4 | 3.5 |
| | 5173721M | | 6184938M | | 7261023M | Net Sales ($) | 9240M | 58578M | 96502M | 245644M | 662038M | 6189021M |
| | 1917911M | | 2273109M | | 2881407M | Total Assets ($) | 8373M | 30062M | 37620M | 78497M | 214467M | 2512388M |

M = $ thousand   MM = $ million
See Pages viii through xx for Explanation of Ratios and Data

© RMA 2024

# ADMIN & WASTE MANAGEMENT SERVICES—Landscaping Services  NAICS 561730

## Current Data Sorted by Assets

| | | | | | | Type of Statement | | |
|---|---|---|---|---|---|---|---|---|
| | 1 | 5 | 6 | 7 | 3 | Unqualified | | |
| | 2 | 13 | 17 | | | Reviewed | | |
| 1 | 7 | 20 | 6 | | | Compiled | | |
| 33 | 52 | 28 | 2 | | | Tax Returns | | |
| 42 | 64 | 97 | 50 | 11 | 9 | Other | | |
| | 30 (4/1-9/30/23) | | 446 (10/1/23-3/31/24) | | | | | |
| 0-500M | 500M-2MM | 2-10MM | 10-50MM | 50-100MM | 100-250MM | | | |
| 76 | 126 | 163 | 81 | 18 | 12 | NUMBER OF STATEMENTS | | |

## Comparative Historical Data

| | | | |
|---|---|---|---|
| | 22 | | 14 |
| | 40 | | 17 |
| | 35 | | 22 |
| | 168 | | 122 |
| | 296 | | 218 |
| | 4/1/19-3/31/20 | | 4/1/20-3/31/21 |
| | ALL | | ALL |
| | 561 | | 393 |

| % | % | % | % | % | % | ASSETS | % | % |
|---|---|---|---|---|---|---|---|---|
| 34.4 | 20.0 | 14.2 | 12.7 | 4.3 | 5.5 | Cash & Equivalents | 17.5 | 25.7 |
| 13.1 | 15.7 | 25.7 | 27.5 | 26.5 | 13.6 | Trade Receivables (net) | 22.0 | 17.5 |
| 2.2 | 3.0 | 3.2 | 3.5 | 4.0 | 4.2 | Inventory | 3.1 | 2.7 |
| 4.1 | 2.7 | 2.9 | 6.8 | 5.6 | 3.6 | All Other Current | 3.0 | 2.8 |
| 53.8 | 41.5 | 46.1 | 50.6 | 40.4 | 26.8 | Total Current | 45.6 | 48.7 |
| 36.2 | 39.3 | 41.1 | 33.3 | 28.0 | 34.8 | Fixed Assets (net) | 38.5 | 37.5 |
| 5.1 | 8.7 | 5.5 | 7.5 | 24.3 | 34.1 | Intangibles (net) | 6.1 | 7.3 |
| 5.0 | 10.6 | 7.3 | 8.6 | 7.3 | 4.3 | All Other Non-Current | 9.9 | 6.5 |
| 100.0 | 100.0 | 100.0 | 100.0 | 100.0 | 100.0 | Total | 100.0 | 100.0 |
| | | | | | | LIABILITIES | | |
| 6.5 | 8.6 | 3.9 | 3.2 | 3.3 | 5.9 | Notes Payable-Short Term | 10.6 | 9.9 |
| 6.0 | 5.1 | 5.1 | 6.8 | 5.2 | 4.7 | Cur. Mat.-L.T.D. | 6.6 | 5.8 |
| 5.6 | 5.5 | 6.6 | 9.8 | 10.4 | 1.8 | Trade Payables | 8.1 | 5.7 |
| .2 | .0 | .1 | .1 | .0 | .6 | Income Taxes Payable | .1 | .2 |
| 22.6 | 9.1 | 6.7 | 11.0 | 11.2 | 6.4 | All Other Current | 9.5 | 9.6 |
| 40.9 | 28.3 | 22.5 | 30.9 | 30.1 | 19.5 | Total Current | 34.8 | 31.1 |
| 52.3 | 46.4 | 31.5 | 21.5 | 40.8 | 37.3 | Long-Term Debt | 34.8 | 42.8 |
| .0 | .1 | .2 | .4 | 1.0 | .9 | Deferred Taxes | .3 | .1 |
| 9.6 | 5.6 | 4.0 | 10.7 | 8.5 | 1.9 | All Other Non-Current | 4.1 | 5.4 |
| -2.8 | 19.6 | 41.9 | 36.5 | 19.6 | 40.4 | Net Worth | 26.0 | 20.6 |
| 100.0 | 100.0 | 100.0 | 100.0 | 100.0 | 100.0 | Total Liabilities & Net Worth | 100.0 | 100.0 |
| | | | | | | INCOME DATA | | |
| 100.0 | 100.0 | 100.0 | 100.0 | 100.0 | 100.0 | Net Sales | 100.0 | 100.0 |
| | | | | | | Gross Profit | | |
| 91.9 | 90.3 | 91.0 | 94.4 | 96.8 | 100.2 | Operating Expenses | 91.6 | 91.8 |
| 8.1 | 9.7 | 9.0 | 5.6 | 3.2 | -.2 | Operating Profit | 8.4 | 8.2 |
| 1.9 | 2.5 | .9 | .8 | 2.7 | 2.9 | All Other Expenses (net) | .8 | -.8 |
| 6.2 | 7.3 | 8.2 | 4.8 | .5 | -3.1 | Profit Before Taxes | 7.6 | 9.0 |
| | | | | | | RATIOS | | |
| 5.4 | 7.7 | 3.9 | 2.6 | 1.9 | 2.8 | | 3.0 | 4.4 |
| 2.1 | 1.7 | 2.2 | 1.6 | 1.4 | 1.7 | Current | 1.5 | 2.1 |
| .8 | .7 | 1.3 | 1.1 | 1.1 | .9 | | .8 | 1.1 |
| 4.5 | 7.0 | 3.5 | 2.1 | 1.4 | 2.0 | | 2.7 | 4.0 |
| 1.9 | 1.3 | 1.9 | 1.3 | 1.1 | 1.4 | Quick | 1.3 | 1.8 |
| .8 | .5 | 1.0 | .7 | .8 | .5 | | .6 | .9 |
| 0  UND | 0  UND | 17  21.6 | 36  10.1 | 53  6.9 | 23  15.6 | | 0  UND | 0  UND |
| 0  UND | 7  54.0 | 39  9.4 | 49  7.4 | 64  5.7 | 41  8.9 | Sales/Receivables | 25  14.7 | 22  16.9 |
| 22  16.5 | 29  12.7 | 60  6.1 | 65  5.6 | 76  4.8 | 74  4.9 | | 46  7.9 | 45  8.2 |
| | | | | | | Cost of Sales/Inventory | | |
| | | | | | | Cost of Sales/Payables | | |
| 9.4 | 7.9 | 5.4 | 6.1 | 6.9 | 3.9 | | 8.5 | 5.8 |
| 21.5 | 26.4 | 9.9 | 10.5 | 15.2 | 13.1 | Sales/Working Capital | 24.1 | 11.5 |
| -45.6 | -28.4 | 30.4 | 73.8 | 45.9 | NM | | -37.9 | 123.8 |
| 22.9 | 19.0 | 19.1 | 19.2 | 5.8 | 9.7 | | 22.1 | 24.5 |
| (52) 7.7 | (106) 5.1 | (148) 7.1 | (72) 5.2 | 3.0 | (10) 2.2 | EBIT/Interest | (493) 7.7 | (322) 11.3 |
| 1.3 | 1.1 | 2.2 | 2.0 | .5 | -1.1 | | 2.5 | 3.0 |
| | | 5.7 | 3.4 | | | Net Profit + Depr., Dep., | 8.3 | 3.2 |
| | (11) 1.8 | (24) 2.3 | | | | Amort./Cur. Mat. L/T/D | (47) 3.5 | (17) 2.6 |
| | | .9 | 1.3 | | | | 1.8 | .9 |
| .3 | .3 | .5 | .5 | 1.0 | .8 | | .5 | .5 |
| 4.5 | 2.6 | 1.0 | 1.0 | NM | NM | Fixed/Worth | 1.3 | 1.4 |
| -1.0 | -4.0 | 3.8 | 3.9 | -.4 | -.4 | | 9.6 | -13.5 |
| 1.1 | .6 | .5 | .7 | 1.5 | .8 | | .7 | .9 |
| 24.1 | 6.0 | 1.4 | 1.7 | NM | NM | Debt/Worth | 2.1 | 2.6 |
| -3.3 | -6.2 | 5.4 | 4.6 | -2.2 | -1.7 | | 28.0 | -11.6 |
| 222.8 | 104.8 | 54.5 | 40.1 | | | % Profit Before Taxes/Tangible | 92.5 | 103.4 |
| (44) 69.1 | (78) 43.8 | (139) 23.4 | (65) 19.3 | | | Net Worth | (437) 44.2 | (283) 49.9 |
| 27.9 | 12.3 | 8.6 | 6.9 | | | | 17.6 | 22.2 |
| 43.6 | 31.4 | 23.4 | 19.5 | 8.0 | 6.4 | % Profit Before Taxes/Total | 30.6 | 34.7 |
| 22.5 | 10.9 | 11.8 | 7.4 | 4.2 | 4.4 | Assets | 15.0 | 18.1 |
| 4.8 | .7 | 3.2 | 2.8 | -2.0 | -15.1 | | 4.6 | 6.4 |
| 82.7 | 69.5 | 11.4 | 13.7 | 8.1 | 6.2 | | 24.8 | 22.2 |
| 15.8 | 11.4 | 5.0 | 6.9 | 5.6 | 3.8 | Sales/Net Fixed Assets | 8.9 | 8.1 |
| 6.3 | 3.2 | 3.1 | 4.0 | 4.2 | 3.4 | | 4.4 | 3.8 |
| 6.1 | 4.5 | 2.9 | 2.3 | 1.8 | 1.7 | | 4.5 | 3.6 |
| 4.4 | 2.8 | 2.1 | 1.8 | 1.4 | 1.1 | Sales/Total Assets | 2.8 | 2.5 |
| 2.9 | 1.8 | 1.4 | 1.4 | 1.2 | .6 | | 1.9 | 1.7 |
| 1.7 | 2.8 | 2.2 | 2.6 | 4.3 | | | 2.3 | 2.3 |
| (32) 5.3 | (53) 4.8 | (114) 4.4 | (66) 3.9 | (12) 5.8 | | % Depr., Dep., Amort./Sales | (329) 4.0 | (208) 4.4 |
| 11.1 | 11.5 | 7.8 | 7.6 | 8.0 | | | 6.2 | 7.7 |
| 4.2 | 1.7 | 1.5 | .6 | | | | 2.1 | 1.8 |
| (39) 7.2 | (63) 3.4 | (73) 2.4 | (17) .9 | | | % Officers', Directors' Owners' Comp/Sales | (254) 4.1 | (169) 3.9 |
| 14.5 | 6.4 | 4.7 | 1.9 | | | | 7.3 | 7.0 |
| 94509M | 487141M | 1719384M | 4590083M | 1908845M | 2418698M | Net Sales ($) | 13046306M | 6056319M |
| 19978M | 141248M | 769316M | 1813424M | 1290435M | 1907210M | Total Assets ($) | 4995173M | 2728726M |

© RMA 2024

M = $ thousand   MM = $ million  
See Pages viii through xx for Explanation of Ratios and Data

# ADMIN & WASTE MANAGEMENT SERVICES—Landscaping Services  NAICS 561730

## Comparative Historical Data / Current Data Sorted by Sales

| | | | | Type of Statement | | | | | | |
|---|---|---|---|---|---|---|---|---|---|---|
| 11 | 21 | 22 | | Unqualified | | 1 | | 3 | 2 | 16 |
| 23 | 23 | 32 | | Reviewed | 1 | | 1 | 5 | 11 | 14 |
| 17 | 27 | 34 | | Compiled | 4 | | 2 | 14 | 11 | 3 |
| 133 | 139 | 115 | | Tax Returns | 19 | 37 | 16 | 25 | 15 | 3 |
| 238 | 313 | 273 | | Other | 38 | 47 | 32 | 42 | 50 | 64 |
| 4/1/21-3/31/22 ALL | 4/1/22-3/31/23 ALL | 4/1/23-3/31/24 ALL | | | 30 (4/1-9/30/23) | | | 446 (10/1/23-3/31/24) | | |
| | | | | | 0-1MM | 1-3MM | 3-5MM | 5-10MM | 10-25MM | 25MM & OVER |
| 422 | 523 | 476 | | NUMBER OF STATEMENTS | 62 | 85 | 51 | 89 | 89 | 100 |
| % | % | % | | ASSETS | % | % | % | % | % | % |
| 22.4 | 18.7 | 18.1 | | Cash & Equivalents | 24.5 | 22.9 | 17.8 | 18.9 | 16.8 | 10.8 |
| 17.4 | 20.6 | 21.1 | | Trade Receivables (net) | 7.7 | 17.3 | 17.3 | 20.6 | 30.9 | 26.3 |
| 2.6 | 3.5 | 3.1 | | Inventory | 1.4 | 2.7 | 3.5 | 3.8 | 2.8 | 4.1 |
| 4.8 | 3.5 | 3.8 | | All Other Current | 2.1 | 4.5 | 4.4 | 1.6 | 3.8 | 6.1 |
| 47.2 | 46.3 | 46.2 | | Total Current | 35.8 | 47.4 | 42.9 | 44.9 | 54.3 | 47.2 |
| 38.7 | 37.9 | 37.8 | | Fixed Assets (net) | 53.0 | 37.6 | 42.7 | 35.7 | 33.0 | 32.4 |
| 7.1 | 7.3 | 8.0 | | Intangibles (net) | 4.3 | 8.6 | 8.9 | 5.6 | 5.7 | 13.6 |
| 7.1 | 8.4 | 7.9 | | All Other Non-Current | 6.9 | 6.4 | 5.5 | 13.7 | 7.0 | 6.8 |
| 100.0 | 100.0 | 100.0 | | Total | 100.0 | 100.0 | 100.0 | 100.0 | 100.0 | 100.0 |
| | | | | LIABILITIES | | | | | | |
| 7.6 | 6.1 | 5.5 | | Notes Payable-Short Term | 4.9 | 7.8 | 6.2 | 6.2 | 4.6 | 3.6 |
| 4.9 | 5.0 | 5.6 | | Cur. Mat.-L.T.D. | 6.8 | 3.9 | 4.4 | 6.5 | 5.4 | 6.0 |
| 5.7 | 7.6 | 6.7 | | Trade Payables | 3.1 | 5.2 | 6.9 | 5.8 | 7.7 | 9.9 |
| .1 | .1 | .1 | | Income Taxes Payable | .2 | .0 | .1 | .0 | .3 | .1 |
| 9.3 | 9.5 | 10.8 | | All Other Current | 18.9 | 12.9 | 6.6 | 7.9 | 8.7 | 10.5 |
| 27.7 | 28.2 | 28.6 | | Total Current | 33.8 | 29.9 | 24.1 | 26.5 | 26.7 | 30.2 |
| 39.2 | 40.7 | 37.6 | | Long-Term Debt | 56.5 | 47.7 | 44.3 | 34.4 | 26.7 | 26.1 |
| .2 | .2 | .2 | | Deferred Taxes | .1 | .0 | .4 | .2 | .0 | .6 |
| 4.2 | 4.2 | 6.6 | | All Other Non-Current | 7.5 | 5.7 | 11.1 | 3.8 | 3.0 | 10.1 |
| 28.7 | 26.6 | 27.0 | | Net Worth | 2.1 | 16.6 | 20.2 | 35.2 | 43.5 | 33.0 |
| 100.0 | 100.0 | 100.0 | | Total Liabilities & Net Worth | 100.0 | 100.0 | 100.0 | 100.0 | 100.0 | 100.0 |
| | | | | INCOME DATA | | | | | | |
| 100.0 | 100.0 | 100.0 | | Net Sales | 100.0 | 100.0 | 100.0 | 100.0 | 100.0 | 100.0 |
| | | | | Gross Profit | | | | | | |
| 91.0 | 92.0 | 92.0 | | Operating Expenses | 78.3 | 94.8 | 93.1 | 92.3 | 92.8 | 96.5 |
| 9.0 | 8.0 | 8.0 | | Operating Profit | 21.7 | 5.2 | 6.9 | 7.7 | 7.2 | 3.5 |
| -1.0 | .9 | 1.6 | | All Other Expenses (net) | 8.4 | .2 | .5 | .2 | .1 | 1.4 |
| 10.0 | 7.1 | 6.5 | | Profit Before Taxes | 13.3 | 5.0 | 6.4 | 7.4 | 7.1 | 2.1 |
| | | | | RATIOS | | | | | | |
| 4.7 | 3.8 | 3.8 | | | 4.9 | 5.8 | 5.7 | 4.2 | 4.1 | 2.6 |
| 2.1 | 1.9 | 1.8 | | Current | 1.7 | 1.9 | 1.8 | 2.2 | 2.1 | 1.6 |
| 1.1 | 1.0 | 1.1 | | | .5 | .8 | 1.0 | 1.1 | 1.3 | 1.2 |
| 3.9 | 3.3 | 3.3 | | | 4.9 | 5.0 | 4.0 | 3.9 | 3.6 | 2.0 |
| 1.8 | 1.6 | 1.5 | | Quick | 1.2 | 1.6 | 1.8 | 1.9 | 1.9 | 1.3 |
| .8 | .7 | .8 | | | .4 | .6 | .8 | .8 | 1.0 | .7 |
| 0 UND | 0 UND | 1 422.2 | | | 0 UND | 0 UND | 0 UND | 7 53.3 | 27 13.7 | 33 11.2 |
| 17 21.5 | 24 15.0 | 30 12.1 | | Sales/Receivables | 0 UND | 11 34.4 | 17 22.0 | 26 14.1 | 43 8.4 | 51 7.1 |
| 44 8.3 | 50 7.3 | 56 6.5 | | | 20 18.0 | 33 10.9 | 45 8.2 | 54 6.8 | 66 5.5 | 68 5.4 |
| | | | | Cost of Sales/Inventory | | | | | | |
| | | | | Cost of Sales/Payables | | | | | | |
| 6.1 | 6.5 | 6.4 | | | 8.8 | 7.9 | 6.7 | 6.0 | 5.7 | 6.8 |
| 12.3 | 14.9 | 14.1 | | Sales/Working Capital | 38.9 | 17.5 | 17.2 | 10.6 | 11.1 | 12.0 |
| 127.2 | -277.4 | 151.3 | | | -16.9 | -47.7 | -126.7 | 82.9 | 31.1 | 46.0 |
| 37.4 | 27.0 | 18.7 | | | 11.4 | 11.8 | 19.7 | 19.5 | 21.9 | 18.5 |
| (353) 14.0 | (452) 9.4 | (406) 5.9 | | EBIT/Interest | (35) 5.7 | (73) 3.7 | (45) 6.0 | (79) 5.9 | (83) 10.5 | (91) 4.7 |
| 4.2 | 2.1 | 1.5 | | | 2.0 | .7 | 1.7 | 1.5 | 2.2 | 1.5 |
| 5.8 | 5.2 | 3.4 | | Net Profit + Depr., Dep., | | | | | 7.7 | 3.1 |
| (22) 2.8 | (35) 3.1 | (44) 2.3 | | Amort./Cur. Mat. L/T/D | | | | (11) 2.4 | (29) 2.2 | |
| 1.2 | 1.6 | 1.3 | | | | | | | .6 | 1.3 |
| .4 | .4 | .5 | | | .9 | .3 | .6 | .4 | .4 | .7 |
| 1.1 | 1.3 | 1.3 | | Fixed/Worth | 4.2 | 2.8 | 2.2 | 1.0 | .8 | 1.2 |
| 5.8 | 13.2 | -16.3 | | | -9.3 | -3.1 | -4.2 | 6.2 | 2.4 | -1.9 |
| .7 | .7 | .7 | | | 1.3 | .6 | .9 | .5 | .5 | .8 |
| 1.8 | 2.1 | 2.2 | | Debt/Worth | 5.8 | 8.5 | 4.4 | 1.5 | 1.1 | 2.0 |
| 13.4 | 230.7 | -23.1 | | | -7.3 | -4.6 | -10.4 | 23.8 | 3.8 | -5.0 |
| 105.7 | 84.9 | 69.6 | | % Profit Before Taxes/Tangible | 108.9 | 72.2 | 137.9 | 77.2 | 64.5 | 43.0 |
| (333) 53.1 | (398) 36.8 | (341) 28.9 | | Net Worth | (43) 54.5 | (49) 35.4 | (33) 51.3 | (68) 26.6 | (78) 29.2 | (70) 18.8 |
| 20.4 | 14.6 | 9.5 | | | 13.1 | 8.0 | 12.1 | 8.2 | 9.8 | 7.5 |
| 40.5 | 30.3 | 25.7 | | % Profit Before Taxes/Total | 33.6 | 30.1 | 33.7 | 31.9 | 28.1 | 14.9 |
| 19.1 | 13.9 | 10.7 | | Assets | 13.2 | 10.6 | 11.7 | 13.3 | 14.4 | 6.4 |
| 6.1 | 2.7 | 2.1 | | | 1.4 | .1 | 1.4 | 2.7 | 3.6 | 2.1 |
| 24.1 | 20.5 | 20.8 | | | 17.1 | 74.0 | 24.1 | 27.3 | 20.3 | 11.8 |
| 7.9 | 7.8 | 7.0 | | Sales/Net Fixed Assets | 4.7 | 11.2 | 5.3 | 8.0 | 7.6 | 6.7 |
| 3.9 | 3.8 | 3.6 | | | .9 | 3.9 | 2.6 | 3.7 | 4.3 | 4.0 |
| 4.2 | 4.0 | 3.7 | | | 4.1 | 4.5 | 4.2 | 3.8 | 3.2 | 2.4 |
| 2.5 | 2.5 | 2.3 | | Sales/Total Assets | 2.2 | 3.0 | 2.2 | 2.4 | 2.3 | 1.8 |
| 1.7 | 1.6 | 1.5 | | | .7 | 1.9 | 1.4 | 1.6 | 1.8 | 1.3 |
| 2.2 | 2.1 | 2.6 | | | 5.4 | 3.5 | 1.3 | 2.0 | 2.2 | 2.7 |
| (227) 4.0 | (274) 4.1 | (281) 4.6 | | % Depr., Dep., Amort./Sales | (29) 11.2 | (40) 5.4 | (27) 5.2 | (52) 4.0 | (63) 3.8 | (70) 4.2 |
| 7.2 | 7.4 | 8.5 | | | 20.1 | 12.6 | 10.5 | 6.8 | 5.5 | 7.1 |
| 1.9 | 1.8 | 1.6 | | % Officers', Directors', | 5.8 | 3.3 | 2.0 | 1.4 | 1.2 | .6 |
| (188) 3.5 | (216) 3.6 | (194) 3.2 | | Owners' Comp/Sales | (18) 10.7 | (47) 4.4 | (31) 3.4 | (46) 2.3 | (33) 2.2 | (19) .9 |
| 5.7 | 6.5 | 5.4 | | | 16.8 | 7.2 | 5.2 | 3.9 | 3.3 | 1.8 |
| 9433686M | 8369290M | 11218660M | | Net Sales ($) | 31508M | 164481M | 198021M | 635515M | 1379228M | 8809907M |
| 3827995M | 4842805M | 5941611M | | Total Assets ($) | 44412M | 71883M | 106476M | 277474M | 643253M | 4798113M |

M = $ thousand   MM = $ million
See Pages viii through xx for Explanation of Ratios and Data

© RMA 2024

# ADMIN & WASTE MANAGEMENT SERVICES—Carpet and Upholstery Cleaning Services    NAICS 561740

## Current Data Sorted by Assets

| | | | | | | Type of Statement | | |
|---|---|---|---|---|---|---|---|---|
| | | | | | | Unqualified | | |
| | 1 | 2 | | | | Reviewed | | |
| 1 | 5 | 2 | | | | Compiled | | |
| 4 | 4 | 7 | | 5 | | Tax Returns | | |
| | 1 (4/1-9/30/23) | | 30 (10/1/23-3/31/24) | | | Other | | |
| 0-500M | 500M-2MM | 2-10MM | 10-50MM | 50-100MM | 100-250MM | | | |
| 5 | 10 | 11 | 5 | | | NUMBER OF STATEMENTS | | |
| % | % | % | % | % | % | ASSETS | | |
| | 29.6 | 16.0 | | | | Cash & Equivalents | | |
| | 11.3 | 10.4 | D | | D | Trade Receivables (net) | | |
| | .3 | 4.7 | A | | A | Inventory | | |
| | 7.7 | .6 | T | | T | All Other Current | | |
| | 48.8 | 31.6 | A | | A | Total Current | | |
| | 42.5 | 40.4 | | | | Fixed Assets (net) | | |
| | 2.8 | 16.3 | N | | N | Intangibles (net) | | |
| | 5.9 | 11.7 | O | | O | All Other Non-Current | | |
| | 100.0 | 100.0 | T | | T | Total | | |
| | | | | | | LIABILITIES | | |
| | 10.8 | 5.4 | A | | A | Notes Payable-Short Term | | |
| | 6.8 | 1.9 | V | | V | Cur. Mat.-L.T.D. | | |
| | 2.7 | 2.9 | A | | A | Trade Payables | | |
| | .0 | .0 | I | | I | Income Taxes Payable | | |
| | 5.4 | 11.1 | L | | L | All Other Current | | |
| | 25.6 | 21.3 | A | | A | Total Current | | |
| | 60.5 | 33.1 | B | | B | Long-Term Debt | | |
| | .0 | .0 | L | | L | Deferred Taxes | | |
| | 6.7 | 1.3 | E | | E | All Other Non-Current | | |
| | 7.2 | 44.3 | | | | Net Worth | | |
| | 100.0 | 100.0 | | | | Total Liabilities & Net Worth | | |
| | | | | | | INCOME DATA | | |
| | 100.0 | 100.0 | | | | Net Sales | | |
| | | | | | | Gross Profit | | |
| | 88.2 | 86.6 | | | | Operating Expenses | | |
| | 11.8 | 13.4 | | | | Operating Profit | | |
| | 1.5 | 6.3 | | | | All Other Expenses (net) | | |
| | 10.3 | 7.1 | | | | Profit Before Taxes | | |
| | | | | | | RATIOS | | |
| | 9.0 | 2.7 | | | | | | |
| | 2.4 | 1.7 | | | | Current | | |
| | .9 | .5 | | | | | | |
| | 7.9 | 2.4 | | | | | | |
| | 1.9 | 1.5 | | | | Quick | | |
| | .1 | .5 | | | | | | |
| 0 | UND | 0 | UND | | | | | |
| 0 | UND | 4 | 91.8 | | | Sales/Receivables | | |
| 27 | 13.7 | 46 | 8.0 | | | | | |
| | | | | | | Cost of Sales/Inventory | | |
| | | | | | | Cost of Sales/Payables | | |
| | 5.8 | 7.6 | | | | | | |
| | 12.4 | 12.1 | | | | Sales/Working Capital | | |
| | -164.0 | -12.7 | | | | | | |
| | | 28.2 | | | | | | |
| | (10) | 2.8 | | | | EBIT/Interest | | |
| | | .1 | | | | | | |
| | | | | | | Net Profit + Depr., Dep., Amort./Cur. Mat. L/T/D | | |
| | .8 | .4 | | | | | | |
| | 12.6 | 1.1 | | | | Fixed/Worth | | |
| | -1.3 | 4.2 | | | | | | |
| | .8 | .8 | | | | | | |
| | 89.0 | .9 | | | | Debt/Worth | | |
| | -2.6 | 5.4 | | | | | | |
| | | | | | | % Profit Before Taxes/Tangible Net Worth | | |
| | 61.2 | 10.0 | | | | | | |
| | 38.5 | 5.7 | | | | % Profit Before Taxes/Total Assets | | |
| | 15.7 | 1.9 | | | | | | |
| | 64.3 | 17.1 | | | | | | |
| | 10.2 | 7.7 | | | | Sales/Net Fixed Assets | | |
| | 4.8 | 3.5 | | | | | | |
| | 6.5 | 2.7 | | | | | | |
| | 4.4 | 2.4 | | | | Sales/Total Assets | | |
| | 2.3 | 1.5 | | | | | | |
| | | | | | | % Depr., Dep., Amort./Sales | | |
| | | | | | | % Officers', Directors' Owners' Comp/Sales | | |
| 3700M | 42291M | 107154M | 101436M | | | Net Sales ($) | | |
| 986M | 10125M | 45494M | 79150M | | | Total Assets ($) | | |

## Comparative Historical Data

| | | | |
|---|---|---|---|
| | 1 | | 1 |
| | 1 | | 1 |
| | | | 1 |
| | 10 | | 4 |
| | 29 | | 18 |
| | 4/1/19-3/31/20 | | 4/1/20-3/31/21 |
| | ALL | | ALL |
| | 41 | | 24 |
| | % | | % |
| Cash & Equivalents | 19.1 | | 26.7 |
| Trade Receivables (net) | 17.5 | | 17.8 |
| Inventory | 1.6 | | 4.0 |
| All Other Current | 6.8 | | 5.2 |
| Total Current | 44.9 | | 53.7 |
| Fixed Assets (net) | 36.4 | | 18.2 |
| Intangibles (net) | 12.8 | | 16.7 |
| All Other Non-Current | 5.9 | | 11.4 |
| Total | 100.0 | | 100.0 |
| Notes Payable-Short Term | 10.7 | | 5.5 |
| Cur. Mat.-L.T.D. | 4.6 | | 1.6 |
| Trade Payables | 5.9 | | 5.0 |
| Income Taxes Payable | .1 | | .1 |
| All Other Current | 11.9 | | 7.3 |
| Total Current | 33.1 | | 19.5 |
| Long-Term Debt | 43.3 | | 33.8 |
| Deferred Taxes | .0 | | .0 |
| All Other Non-Current | 4.0 | | 7.1 |
| Net Worth | 19.6 | | 39.7 |
| Total Liabilities & Net Worth | 100.0 | | 100.0 |
| Net Sales | 100.0 | | 100.0 |
| Operating Expenses | 85.7 | | 91.5 |
| Operating Profit | 14.3 | | 8.5 |
| All Other Expenses (net) | 2.7 | | -1.0 |
| Profit Before Taxes | 11.6 | | 9.5 |
| Current — 4.8 | 1.9 | — | 6.7 / 2.6 / 2.1 |

### Historical Ratios

| Ratio | Hist1 | | Hist2 |
|---|---|---|---|
| Current | 4.8 / 1.9 / .8 | | 6.7 / 2.6 / 2.1 |
| Quick | 4.4 / 1.4 / .7 | | 6.7 / 2.1 / 1.4 |
| Sales/Receivables | 0 UND / 15  24.5 / 50  7.3 | | 0 UND / 13  28.1 / 66  5.5 |
| Sales/Working Capital | 8.1 / 17.2 / -45.3 | | 5.3 / 6.6 / 13.3 |
| EBIT/Interest | (30) 50.6 / 13.1 / 4.6 | | (23) 51.3 / 27.9 / 6.7 |
| Fixed/Worth | .5 / 1.2 / -13.8 | | .1 / .5 / 2.5 |
| Debt/Worth | .6 / 1.6 / -22.7 | | .8 / 2.4 / NM |
| % Profit Before Taxes/Tangible Net Worth | (29) 109.0 / 67.7 / 14.1 | | (18) 165.1 / 75.1 / 27.5 |
| % Profit Before Taxes/Total Assets | 58.8 / 23.5 / 4.1 | | 54.7 / 24.3 / 8.5 |
| Sales/Net Fixed Assets | 25.0 / 9.8 / 5.4 | | 84.3 / 18.9 / 7.4 |
| Sales/Total Assets | 3.9 / 2.9 / 1.9 | | 3.6 / 2.5 / 1.6 |
| % Depr., Dep., Amort./Sales | (20) 2.0 / 4.0 / 6.3 | | (11) 1.4 / 4.2 / 5.6 |
| % Officers', Directors' Owners' Comp/Sales | (15) 4.8 / 5.4 / 9.8 | | (12) 2.2 / 4.3 / 11.1 |
| Net Sales ($) | 664660M | | 508052M |
| Total Assets ($) | 364321M | | 286109M |

M = $ thousand    MM = $ million
See Pages viii through xx for Explanation of Ratios and Data

© RMA 2024

# ADMIN & WASTE MANAGEMENT SERVICES—Carpet and Upholstery Cleaning Services  NAICS 561740

## Comparative Historical Data | Current Data Sorted by Sales

| | | | | Type of Statement | | | | | | |
|---|---|---|---|---|---|---|---|---|---|---|
| | | 1 | | Unqualified | | | | | | |
| | 1 | | | Reviewed | | | | | | |
| | 2 | 3 | | Compiled | | | 1 | | 1 | |
| | 7 | 12 | 3 | Tax Returns | | 4 | 1 | 2 | 1 | |
| | 9 | 17 | 8 | Other | 1 | 4 | 1 | 4 | 3 | 3 |
| | 4/1/21- | 4/1/22- | 20 | | 5 | 1 (4/1-9/30/23) | | 30 (10/1/23-3/31/24) | | |
| | 3/31/22 | 3/31/23 | 4/1/23- | | | | | | | |
| | ALL | ALL | 3/31/24 | | | | | | | |
| | | | ALL | | 0-1MM | 1-3MM | 3-5MM | 5-10MM | 10-25MM | 25MM & OVER |
| | 20 | 34 | 31 | NUMBER OF STATEMENTS | 6 | 8 | 3 | 6 | 5 | 3 |
| | % | % | % | ASSETS | % | % | % | % | % | % |
| | 27.8 | 27.0 | 21.7 | Cash & Equivalents | | | | | | |
| | 11.9 | 13.1 | 14.4 | Trade Receivables (net) | | | | | | |
| | 3.2 | 3.5 | 3.6 | Inventory | | | | | | |
| | 14.6 | 7.4 | 6.4 | All Other Current | | | | | | |
| | 57.4 | 51.1 | 46.1 | Total Current | | | | | | |
| | 25.5 | 24.7 | 36.9 | Fixed Assets (net) | | | | | | |
| | 12.4 | 14.2 | 7.5 | Intangibles (net) | | | | | | |
| | 4.8 | 10.0 | 9.5 | All Other Non-Current | | | | | | |
| | 100.0 | 100.0 | 100.0 | Total | | | | | | |
| | | | | LIABILITIES | | | | | | |
| | 5.4 | 2.5 | 8.1 | Notes Payable-Short Term | | | | | | |
| | 2.2 | 4.2 | 3.5 | Cur. Mat.-L.T.D. | | | | | | |
| | 3.8 | 4.6 | 4.1 | Trade Payables | | | | | | |
| | .1 | .1 | .2 | Income Taxes Payable | | | | | | |
| | 6.7 | 9.9 | 7.4 | All Other Current | | | | | | |
| | 18.2 | 21.2 | 23.4 | Total Current | | | | | | |
| | 40.4 | 36.4 | 44.2 | Long-Term Debt | | | | | | |
| | .0 | .0 | .0 | Deferred Taxes | | | | | | |
| | 1.7 | 4.5 | 4.4 | All Other Non-Current | | | | | | |
| | 39.6 | 37.9 | 28.0 | Net Worth | | | | | | |
| | 100.0 | 100.0 | 100.0 | Total Liabilties & Net Worth | | | | | | |
| | | | | INCOME DATA | | | | | | |
| | 100.0 | 100.0 | 100.0 | Net Sales | | | | | | |
| | | | | Gross Profit | | | | | | |
| | 85.5 | 86.4 | 86.6 | Operating Expenses | | | | | | |
| | 14.5 | 13.6 | 13.4 | Operating Profit | | | | | | |
| | -.5 | 2.1 | 4.9 | All Other Expenses (net) | | | | | | |
| | 15.1 | 11.5 | 8.6 | Profit Before Taxes | | | | | | |
| | | | | RATIOS | | | | | | |
| | 12.0 | 4.4 | 3.3 | | | | | | | |
| | 2.5 | 2.5 | 2.2 | Current | | | | | | |
| | 1.5 | .9 | .9 | | | | | | | |
| | 8.0 | 3.2 | 3.4 | | | | | | | |
| | 2.1 | 1.8 | (30) 1.6 | Quick | | | | | | |
| | 1.0 | .8 | .7 | | | | | | | |
| 0 | UND | 0 UND | 0 UND | | | | | | | |
| 0 | UND | 8 45.5 | 4 91.8 | Sales/Receivables | | | | | | |
| 35 | 10.4 | 35 10.3 | 43 8.5 | | | | | | | |
| | | | | Cost of Sales/Inventory | | | | | | |
| | | | | Cost of Sales/Payables | | | | | | |
| | 4.0 | 4.9 | 5.8 | | | | | | | |
| | 6.5 | 9.0 | 10.2 | Sales/Working Capital | | | | | | |
| | 26.3 | -83.5 | -184.6 | | | | | | | |
| | 108.5 | 45.7 | 29.8 | | | | | | | |
| (16) | 21.2 | (27) 7.5 | (22) 5.0 | EBIT/Interest | | | | | | |
| | 6.1 | 2.3 | 2.4 | | | | | | | |
| | | | | Net Profit + Depr., Dep., Amort./Cur. Mat. L/T/D | | | | | | |
| | .2 | .0 | .3 | | | | | | | |
| | .9 | .3 | 1.1 | Fixed/Worth | | | | | | |
| | NM | 12.4 | -39.3 | | | | | | | |
| | .4 | .4 | .8 | | | | | | | |
| | 1.5 | 1.7 | 1.5 | Debt/Worth | | | | | | |
| | NM | -8.2 | -40.4 | | | | | | | |
| | 135.1 | 53.6 | 99.3 | % Profit Before Taxes/Tangible Net Worth | | | | | | |
| (15) | 64.5 | (24) 25.6 | (23) 36.1 | | | | | | | |
| | 41.0 | 8.7 | 11.9 | | | | | | | |
| | 54.0 | 25.1 | 30.4 | % Profit Before Taxes/Total Assets | | | | | | |
| | 26.7 | 8.0 | 12.8 | | | | | | | |
| | 15.5 | 1.5 | 3.7 | | | | | | | |
| | 45.5 | 263.9 | 29.7 | | | | | | | |
| | 19.2 | 31.2 | 8.9 | Sales/Net Fixed Assets | | | | | | |
| | 5.3 | 6.8 | 4.1 | | | | | | | |
| | 4.4 | 3.5 | 4.8 | | | | | | | |
| | 2.7 | 2.3 | 2.4 | Sales/Total Assets | | | | | | |
| | 2.0 | 1.6 | 1.6 | | | | | | | |
| | | 1.5 | 1.3 | | | | | | | |
| | | (15) 3.6 | (18) 3.5 | % Depr., Dep., Amort./Sales | | | | | | |
| | | 20.1 | 10.5 | | | | | | | |
| | 2.4 | 2.0 | | % Officers', Directors' Owners' Comp/Sales | | | | | | |
| (10) | 3.9 | (14) 3.7 | | | | | | | | |
| | 6.2 | 10.4 | | | | | | | | |
| | 125711M | 208682M | 254581M | Net Sales ($) | 2871M | 14258M | 11346M | 45218M | 81455M | 99433M |
| | 54980M | 129104M | 135755M | Total Assets ($) | 17701M | 16637M | 3947M | 13631M | 25705M | 58134M |

© RMA 2024  M = $ thousand   MM = $ million
See Pages viii through xx for Explanation of Ratios and Data

## ADMIN & WASTE MANAGEMENT SERVICES—Other Services to Buildings and Dwellings  NAICS 561790

### Current Data Sorted by Assets | Comparative Historical Data

| | | | | | | Type of Statement | | |
|---|---|---|---|---|---|---|---|---|
| | | | | | | Unqualified | 3 | 3 |
| | | | 2 | 1 | | Reviewed | 5 | 4 |
| | | | 1 | 1 | | Compiled | 5 | |
| 5 | 8 | | 4 | | | Tax Returns | 36 | 23 |
| 10 | 15 | | 17 | 15 | 1 | Other | 51 | 45 |
| | 8 (4/1-9/30/23) | | | 75 (10/1/23-3/31/24) | | | 4/1/19-3/31/20 | 4/1/20-3/31/21 |
| 0-500M | 500M-2MM | 2-10MM | 10-50MM | 50-100MM | 100-250MM | | ALL | ALL |
| 15 | 23 | 24 | 17 | 2 | 2 | NUMBER OF STATEMENTS | 100 | 75 |
| % | % | % | % | % | % | ASSETS | % | % |
| 36.7 | 17.1 | 11.4 | 19.1 | | | Cash & Equivalents | 18.3 | 22.9 |
| 15.9 | 19.7 | 23.4 | 23.7 | | | Trade Receivables (net) | 24.8 | 20.9 |
| .5 | 3.3 | 6.7 | 4.8 | | | Inventory | 5.2 | 4.6 |
| 1.0 | 3.0 | 2.9 | 3.7 | | | All Other Current | 4.8 | 3.1 |
| 54.1 | 43.0 | 44.4 | 51.3 | | | Total Current | 53.1 | 51.5 |
| 32.6 | 25.7 | 24.6 | 14.0 | | | Fixed Assets (net) | 26.7 | 27.8 |
| 6.2 | 20.3 | 15.6 | 19.9 | | | Intangibles (net) | 9.7 | 12.0 |
| 6.9 | 11.0 | 15.3 | 14.9 | | | All Other Non-Current | 10.5 | 8.8 |
| 100.0 | 100.0 | 100.0 | 100.0 | | | Total | 100.0 | 100.0 |
| | | | | | | LIABILITIES | | |
| 15.5 | 3.4 | 14.4 | 4.5 | | | Notes Payable-Short Term | 13.8 | 12.5 |
| 3.5 | 2.5 | 3.7 | 3.2 | | | Cur. Mat.-L.T.D. | 4.6 | 4.3 |
| .6 | 4.0 | 10.2 | 5.7 | | | Trade Payables | 8.4 | 4.8 |
| .1 | .3 | .2 | .0 | | | Income Taxes Payable | .1 | .2 |
| 8.6 | 13.6 | 19.2 | 13.8 | | | All Other Current | 11.3 | 12.9 |
| 28.3 | 23.8 | 47.7 | 27.2 | | | Total Current | 38.2 | 34.7 |
| 46.4 | 38.4 | 23.5 | 13.0 | | | Long-Term Debt | 36.8 | 37.5 |
| .0 | .0 | .0 | .0 | | | Deferred Taxes | .1 | .2 |
| 1.2 | .9 | 1.8 | 8.6 | | | All Other Non-Current | 4.3 | 6.4 |
| 24.1 | 36.9 | 27.0 | 51.2 | | | Net Worth | 20.6 | 21.2 |
| 100.0 | 100.0 | 100.0 | 100.0 | | | Total Liabilities & Net Worth | 100.0 | 100.0 |
| | | | | | | INCOME DATA | | |
| 100.0 | 100.0 | 100.0 | 100.0 | | | Net Sales | 100.0 | 100.0 |
| | | | | | | Gross Profit | | |
| 91.3 | 91.7 | 92.4 | 88.0 | | | Operating Expenses | 92.9 | 91.9 |
| 8.7 | 8.3 | 7.6 | 12.0 | | | Operating Profit | 7.1 | 8.1 |
| -.4 | 1.7 | 2.7 | .2 | | | All Other Expenses (net) | 1.3 | -.5 |
| 9.1 | 6.6 | 4.9 | 11.8 | | | Profit Before Taxes | 5.8 | 8.7 |
| | | | | | | RATIOS | | |
| 11.6 | 3.8 | 1.6 | 3.3 | | | | 3.9 | 4.5 |
| 1.7 | 1.9 | 1.1 | 1.9 | | | Current | 1.5 | 2.1 |
| .9 | 1.0 | .6 | 1.1 | | | | .8 | .8 |
| 11.5 | 3.4 | 1.3 | 3.0 | | | | 3.5 | 4.2 |
| 1.7 | 1.7 | .9 | 1.4 | | | Quick | 1.3 | 1.8 |
| .6 | .7 | .4 | 1.0 | | | | .5 | .7 |
| 0 UND | 0 UND | 5 79.9 | 29 12.7 | | | | 0 UND | 0 UND |
| 0 UND | 22 16.4 | 27 13.4 | 51 7.2 | | | Sales/Receivables | 23 15.6 | 19 19.1 |
| 21 17.0 | 47 7.7 | 63 5.8 | 72 5.1 | | | | 49 7.5 | 55 6.6 |
| | | | | | | Cost of Sales/Inventory | | |
| | | | | | | Cost of Sales/Payables | | |
| 11.3 | 8.5 | 11.1 | 4.3 | | | | 7.4 | 5.7 |
| 34.0 | 19.1 | 99.8 | 6.4 | | | Sales/Working Capital | 20.5 | 10.2 |
| -57.6 | 322.4 | -10.0 | 26.5 | | | | -38.3 | -31.9 |
| 101.8 | 55.5 | 14.2 | 144.8 | | | | 26.8 | 30.3 |
| (12) 3.7 | (20) 7.2 | (22) 7.0 | (15) 23.2 | | | EBIT/Interest | (84) 5.3 | (63) 11.3 |
| -4.4 | 1.0 | .1 | 7.8 | | | | .6 | 2.9 |
| | | | | | | Net Profit + Depr., Dep., Amort./Cur. Mat. L/T/D | | |
| .2 | .4 | .3 | .1 | | | | .2 | .2 |
| 2.4 | 1.2 | .9 | .4 | | | Fixed/Worth | .8 | 1.0 |
| -5.5 | -.4 | -.6 | 1.8 | | | | -48.8 | -16.2 |
| .6 | .8 | 1.2 | .5 | | | | 1.0 | .9 |
| 12.1 | 2.9 | 2.0 | .9 | | | Debt/Worth | 3.2 | 3.7 |
| -6.8 | -2.3 | -2.7 | 26.4 | | | | -6.8 | -7.1 |
| 790.0 | 108.1 | 83.6 | 103.9 | | | | 114.7 | 193.9 |
| (10) 307.9 | (15) 76.3 | (17) 58.6 | (14) 41.2 | | | % Profit Before Taxes/Tangible Net Worth | (69) 57.4 | (51) 68.6 |
| 92.3 | 19.0 | 12.4 | 25.2 | | | | 12.1 | 14.9 |
| 187.2 | 48.7 | 26.2 | 26.7 | | | | 40.4 | 41.2 |
| 36.9 | 13.4 | 12.0 | 13.9 | | | % Profit Before Taxes/Total Assets | 14.1 | 19.2 |
| .0 | .7 | -2.9 | 8.2 | | | | 1.6 | 3.5 |
| 94.0 | 33.6 | 29.1 | 44.3 | | | | 85.2 | 69.0 |
| 23.3 | 19.9 | 16.8 | 14.0 | | | Sales/Net Fixed Assets | 19.1 | 15.5 |
| 8.5 | 12.9 | 6.0 | 6.6 | | | | 7.4 | 6.6 |
| 8.4 | 6.2 | 3.7 | 2.1 | | | | 5.2 | 4.2 |
| 5.8 | 3.0 | 2.5 | 1.5 | | | Sales/Total Assets | 3.0 | 2.8 |
| 2.9 | 1.6 | 1.8 | 1.1 | | | | 1.9 | 1.7 |
| | | .6 | | | | | .7 | .5 |
| | (13) | 1.4 | | | | % Depr., Dep., Amort./Sales | (42) 2.8 | (40) 2.1 |
| | | 6.7 | | | | | 6.3 | 5.0 |
| | | 1.4 | | | | | 2.8 | 2.5 |
| | (10) | 2.0 | | | | % Officers', Directors' Owners' Comp/Sales | (35) 5.5 | (38) 4.8 |
| | | 3.5 | | | | | 11.2 | 8.0 |
| 25992M | 99767M | 321603M | 538902M | 179560M | 288316M | Net Sales ($) | 1137584M | 1555489M |
| 3809M | 29471M | 121643M | 344828M | 166126M | 220256M | Total Assets ($) | 573930M | 682651M |

© RMA 2024

M = $ thousand    MM = $ million
See Pages viii through xx for Explanation of Ratios and Data

# ADMIN & WASTE MANAGEMENT SERVICES—Other Services to Buildings and Dwellings NAICS 561790

## Comparative Historical Data | Current Data Sorted by Sales

| | | | | Type of Statement | | | | | | |
|---|---|---|---|---|---|---|---|---|---|---|
| 3 | 2 | 4 | | Unqualified | | | | 1 | 1 | 4 |
| 6 | 8 | 3 | | Reviewed | | | | | | 1 |
| 1 | 3 | 1 | | Compiled | | | | 1 | 1 | |
| 17 | 18 | 17 | | Tax Returns | 1 | 7 | 3 | 3 | 2 | 1 |
| 40 | 62 | 58 | | Other | 6 | 11 | 7 | 7 | 16 | 11 |
| 4/1/21-3/31/22 | 4/1/22-3/31/23 | 4/1/23-3/31/24 | | | 8 (4/1-9/30/23) | | | 75 (10/1/23-3/31/24) | | |
| ALL | ALL | ALL | | | 0-1MM | 1-3MM | 3-5MM | 5-10MM | 10-25MM | 25MM & OVER |
| 67 | 93 | 83 | | NUMBER OF STATEMENTS | 7 | 18 | 10 | 11 | 20 | 17 |
| % | % | % | | ASSETS | % | % | % | % | % | % |
| 25.3 | 25.0 | 19.1 | | Cash & Equivalents | 26.1 | 24.0 | 24.0 | 15.1 | 14.4 | |
| 22.2 | 17.6 | 21.3 | | Trade Receivables (net) | 18.5 | 12.6 | 25.9 | 24.9 | 28.1 | |
| 4.9 | 4.3 | 4.0 | | Inventory | 1.4 | 4.0 | 4.7 | 4.9 | 6.5 | |
| 7.5 | 4.2 | 2.9 | | All Other Current | .5 | 1.7 | 6.4 | 3.1 | 4.6 | |
| 59.9 | 51.1 | 47.3 | | Total Current | 46.6 | 42.3 | 61.0 | 47.9 | 53.6 | |
| 24.0 | 28.5 | 23.7 | | Fixed Assets (net) | 26.5 | 18.1 | 19.8 | 20.4 | 16.4 | |
| 9.4 | 11.2 | 16.8 | | Intangibles (net) | 17.4 | 28.9 | 7.1 | 18.5 | 15.8 | |
| 6.7 | 9.2 | 12.2 | | All Other Non-Current | 9.6 | 10.7 | 12.1 | 13.1 | 14.2 | |
| 100.0 | 100.0 | 100.0 | | Total | 100.0 | 100.0 | 100.0 | 100.0 | 100.0 | |
| | | | | LIABILITIES | | | | | | |
| 9.6 | 7.6 | 9.0 | | Notes Payable-Short Term | 13.5 | 4.7 | 11.7 | 5.7 | 11.3 | |
| 2.7 | 3.5 | 3.2 | | Cur. Mat.-L.T.D. | 3.7 | 3.8 | 1.2 | 4.6 | 2.9 | |
| 6.5 | 6.8 | 5.7 | | Trade Payables | 1.2 | 4.6 | 8.7 | 6.6 | 10.5 | |
| .4 | .4 | .1 | | Income Taxes Payable | .1 | .3 | .0 | .2 | .3 | |
| 15.6 | 13.1 | 14.2 | | All Other Current | 16.2 | 14.9 | 29.1 | 8.2 | 11.1 | |
| 34.7 | 31.3 | 32.3 | | Total Current | 34.6 | 28.2 | 50.7 | 25.2 | 36.0 | |
| 23.0 | 27.9 | 29.6 | | Long-Term Debt | 40.0 | 38.4 | 20.3 | 21.4 | 17.1 | |
| .4 | .2 | .0 | | Deferred Taxes | .0 | .0 | .0 | .0 | .0 | |
| 5.3 | 5.0 | 3.5 | | All Other Non-Current | .0 | 2.1 | .2 | 6.1 | 7.3 | |
| 36.6 | 35.6 | 34.7 | | Net Worth | 25.4 | 31.3 | 28.8 | 47.3 | 39.5 | |
| 100.0 | 100.0 | 100.0 | | Total Liabilities & Net Worth | 100.0 | 100.0 | 100.0 | 100.0 | 100.0 | |
| | | | | INCOME DATA | | | | | | |
| 100.0 | 100.0 | 100.0 | | Net Sales | 100.0 | 100.0 | 100.0 | 100.0 | 100.0 | |
| | | | | Gross Profit | | | | | | |
| 90.1 | 88.8 | 91.1 | | Operating Expenses | 86.7 | 91.8 | 95.0 | 89.2 | 93.6 | |
| 9.9 | 11.2 | 8.9 | | Operating Profit | 13.3 | 8.2 | 5.0 | 10.8 | 6.4 | |
| -1.4 | 1.9 | 1.4 | | All Other Expenses (net) | .6 | .2 | .4 | .1 | .6 | |
| 11.2 | 9.2 | 7.6 | | Profit Before Taxes | 12.7 | 8.0 | 4.6 | 10.6 | 5.7 | |
| | | | | RATIOS | | | | | | |
| 4.7 | 4.7 | 3.1 | | | 2.7 | 2.8 | 3.5 | 4.0 | 2.7 | |
| 2.3 | 2.0 | 1.6 | | Current | 1.3 | 1.7 | 1.9 | 1.8 | 2.3 | |
| 1.4 | 1.0 | 1.0 | | | .8 | 1.2 | .6 | 1.0 | 1.1 | |
| | | | | | | | | | | |
| 4.2 | 4.4 | 3.0 | | | 2.5 | 2.7 | 3.4 | 4.0 | 2.3 | |
| (66) 1.8 | 1.5 | 1.4 | | Quick | 1.1 | 1.6 | 1.5 | 1.4 | 1.4 | |
| .9 | .7 | .7 | | | .6 | .9 | .6 | .8 | .9 | |
| 0 UND | 0 UND | 2 157.3 | | | 0 UND | 0 UND | 0 UND | 8 47.7 | 25 14.5 | |
| 20 18.3 | 16 22.3 | 26 13.9 | | Sales/Receivables | 10 38.3 | 23 16.1 | 33 11.2 | 43 8.4 | 50 7.3 | |
| 55 6.6 | 54 6.8 | 64 5.7 | | | 55 6.6 | 68 5.4 | 65 5.6 | 64 5.7 | 74 4.9 | |
| | | | | Cost of Sales/Inventory | | | | | | |
| | | | | Cost of Sales/Payables | | | | | | |
| 5.8 | 6.8 | 7.6 | | | 10.8 | 10.7 | 7.4 | 6.8 | 5.2 | |
| 12.0 | 13.5 | 19.5 | | Sales/Working Capital | 198.5 | 18.7 | 19.5 | 14.7 | 8.7 | |
| 78.9 | NM | -353.1 | | | -23.8 | 29.0 | -7.1 | -354.6 | 49.1 | |
| 87.2 | 126.2 | 57.7 | | | 93.3 | | 47.5 | 110.5 | 84.2 | |
| (51) 19.0 | (71) 14.5 | (73) 9.0 | | EBIT/Interest | (13) 6.9 | (10) 1.5 | 22.7 | (15) 10.3 | | |
| 5.0 | 2.5 | 1.0 | | | 1.8 | | -2.4 | 7.5 | 4.1 | |
| | | | | Net Profit + Depr., Dep., Amort./Cur. Mat. L/T/D | | | | | | |
| .1 | .1 | .3 | | | .3 | .8 | .1 | .3 | .2 | |
| .5 | .8 | .8 | | Fixed/Worth | 2.4 | 2.0 | .4 | .6 | .8 | |
| 2.3 | 7.2 | -1.8 | | | -.6 | -.2 | 3.8 | NM | 2.3 | |
| .5 | .5 | .8 | | | .9 | .9 | .6 | .6 | 1.1 | |
| 1.4 | 1.9 | 2.0 | | Debt/Worth | 13.8 | 28.9 | 1.7 | 1.1 | 2.0 | |
| -31.5 | 17.9 | -3.8 | | | -2.2 | -1.7 | 10.4 | NM | 5.4 | |
| 170.7 | 111.8 | 108.1 | | | 720.0 | | | 93.5 | 72.0 | |
| (50) 71.4 | (74) 61.3 | (59) 71.6 | | % Profit Before Taxes/Tangible Net Worth | (11) 95.2 | | (15) 86.4 | (14) 47.4 | | |
| 31.1 | 17.2 | 27.0 | | | 59.4 | | | 42.3 | 28.9 | |
| 64.2 | 49.7 | 36.8 | | % Profit Before Taxes/Total Assets | 94.4 | 61.7 | 62.4 | 47.5 | 23.0 | |
| 29.9 | 14.8 | 14.4 | | | 29.8 | 11.1 | 1.6 | 22.3 | 12.4 | |
| 7.8 | 4.0 | 1.6 | | | 8.3 | -.9 | -4.0 | 11.5 | 7.1 | |
| 71.1 | 69.2 | 38.3 | | Sales/Net Fixed Assets | 96.4 | 35.0 | 69.8 | 33.2 | 41.8 | |
| 29.0 | 19.3 | 17.9 | | | 20.5 | 19.7 | 20.6 | 18.9 | 21.0 | |
| 7.4 | 5.2 | 6.8 | | | 4.7 | 6.3 | 6.2 | 10.4 | 8.5 | |
| 5.8 | 4.9 | 4.4 | | Sales/Total Assets | 8.2 | 6.8 | 6.2 | 4.6 | 2.9 | |
| 3.1 | 2.5 | 2.5 | | | 3.6 | 2.1 | 3.5 | 2.2 | 2.0 | |
| 2.3 | 1.4 | 1.3 | | | 1.8 | 1.0 | 2.2 | 1.3 | 1.2 | |
| .3 | .5 | 1.1 | | | | | | .8 | .8 | |
| (26) 1.4 | (40) 2.1 | (37) 3.0 | | % Depr., Dep., Amort./Sales | | | | (11) 1.5 | (10) 1.9 | |
| 4.8 | 5.6 | 4.6 | | | | | | 4.5 | 3.2 | |
| 2.6 | 1.2 | 2.0 | | % Officers', Directors', Owners' Comp/Sales | 4.7 | | | | | |
| (23) 6.0 | (34) 4.1 | (32) 3.7 | | | (10) 5.8 | | | | | |
| 8.6 | 7.2 | 6.0 | | | 10.7 | | | | | |
| 1266453M | 1681791M | 1454140M | | Net Sales ($) | 3341M | 33129M | 38752M | 78906M | 298940M | 1001072M |
| 519997M | 869302M | 886133M | | Total Assets ($) | 13425M | 13334M | 27891M | 28429M | 148589M | 654465M |

© RMA 2024  M = $ thousand  MM = $ million
See Pages viii through xx for Explanation of Ratios and Data

# ADMIN & WASTE MANAGEMENT SERVICES—Packaging and Labeling Services  NAICS 561910

## Current Data Sorted by Assets | Comparative Historical Data

| | | | | | | | Type of Statement | | | |
|---|---|---|---|---|---|---|---|---|---|---|
| | 1 | | 1 | 4 | | 2 | Unqualified | | 6 | 7 |
| | | | 2 | 7 | | | Reviewed | | 15 | 9 |
| | | | 5 | | 1 | | Compiled | | 5 | 8 |
| | 3 | 4 | 4 | 1 | | | Tax Returns | | 14 | 5 |
| | 2 | 7 | 28 | 12 | 3 | 9 | Other | | 45 | 43 |
| | | 13 (4/1-9/30/23) | | 83 (10/1/23-3/31/24) | | | | | 4/1/19-3/31/20 | 4/1/20-3/31/21 |
| | 0-500M | 500M-2MM | 2-10MM | 10-50MM | 50-100MM | 100-250MM | | | ALL | ALL |
| | 6 | 11 | 40 | 24 | 4 | 11 | NUMBER OF STATEMENTS | | 85 | 72 |
| | % | % | % | % | % | % | ASSETS | | % | % |
| | | 18.1 | 14.6 | 8.9 | | 1.9 | Cash & Equivalents | | 9.0 | 11.4 |
| | | 34.4 | 28.0 | 21.0 | | 16.3 | Trade Receivables (net) | | 26.7 | 29.8 |
| | | 18.4 | 19.9 | 21.8 | | 8.5 | Inventory | | 18.0 | 16.5 |
| | | .2 | 3.0 | 1.3 | | 2.4 | All Other Current | | 2.7 | 2.4 |
| | | 71.0 | 65.7 | 53.0 | | 29.0 | Total Current | | 56.5 | 60.1 |
| | | 12.7 | 17.6 | 30.4 | | 30.0 | Fixed Assets (net) | | 27.4 | 28.3 |
| | | 8.6 | 9.7 | 7.1 | | 21.9 | Intangibles (net) | | 10.4 | 8.3 |
| | | 7.6 | 7.1 | 9.5 | | 19.0 | All Other Non-Current | | 5.7 | 3.2 |
| | | 100.0 | 100.0 | 100.0 | | 100.0 | Total | | 100.0 | 100.0 |
| | | | | | | | LIABILITIES | | | |
| | | 10.8 | 6.6 | 8.9 | | 3.6 | Notes Payable-Short Term | | 10.1 | 11.7 |
| | | 3.6 | 1.8 | 5.9 | | 3.5 | Cur. Mat.-L.T.D. | | 4.2 | 2.3 |
| | | 13.6 | 17.9 | 12.3 | | 8.2 | Trade Payables | | 17.5 | 13.4 |
| | | .3 | .4 | .2 | | .0 | Income Taxes Payable | | .1 | .0 |
| | | 8.2 | 9.3 | 5.3 | | 5.9 | All Other Current | | 13.1 | 13.9 |
| | | 36.4 | 35.9 | 32.7 | | 21.3 | Total Current | | 45.0 | 41.3 |
| | | 20.5 | 13.2 | 16.7 | | 28.6 | Long-Term Debt | | 16.5 | 19.2 |
| | | .0 | .0 | .6 | | .2 | Deferred Taxes | | .2 | .1 |
| | | 6.8 | 3.7 | 6.3 | | 18.2 | All Other Non-Current | | 7.1 | 4.4 |
| | | 36.3 | 47.2 | 43.8 | | 31.7 | Net Worth | | 31.2 | 34.9 |
| | | 100.0 | 100.0 | 100.0 | | 100.0 | Total Liabilties & Net Worth | | 100.0 | 100.0 |
| | | | | | | | INCOME DATA | | | |
| | | 100.0 | 100.0 | 100.0 | | 100.0 | Net Sales | | 100.0 | 100.0 |
| | | | | | | | Gross Profit | | | |
| | | 91.8 | 94.0 | 95.9 | | 99.2 | Operating Expenses | | 95.9 | 92.7 |
| | | 8.2 | 6.0 | 4.1 | | .8 | Operating Profit | | 4.1 | 7.3 |
| | | .7 | .4 | 1.3 | | 4.5 | All Other Expenses (net) | | 1.0 | -.2 |
| | | 7.5 | 5.6 | 2.8 | | -3.6 | Profit Before Taxes | | 3.1 | 7.4 |
| | | | | | | | RATIOS | | | |
| | | 5.8 | 3.0 | 3.1 | | 1.8 | | | 2.5 | 2.7 |
| | | 2.6 | 1.8 | 1.8 | | 1.4 | Current | | 1.6 | 1.5 |
| | | .8 | 1.2 | 1.0 | | 1.1 | | | .9 | 1.1 |
| | | 3.4 | 2.2 | 1.6 | | 1.1 | | | 1.5 | 2.0 |
| | | 1.8 | 1.1 | 1.0 | | 1.0 | Quick | | .9 | 1.0 |
| | | .7 | .7 | .5 | | .7 | | | .5 | .7 |
| | | 28  13.1 | 23  16.0 | 28  13.0 | | 41  8.8 | | | 30  12.2 | 31  11.7 |
| | | 47  7.8 | 34  10.7 | 42  8.6 | | 52  7.0 | Sales/Receivables | | 42  8.7 | 42  8.6 |
| | | 56  6.5 | 47  7.7 | 56  6.5 | | 69  5.3 | | | 56  6.5 | 60  6.1 |
| | | | | | | | Cost of Sales/Inventory | | | |
| | | | | | | | Cost of Sales/Payables | | | |
| | | 3.2 | 6.4 | 5.3 | | 7.9 | | | 7.0 | 5.9 |
| | | 5.9 | 8.9 | 9.0 | | 11.4 | Sales/Working Capital | | 14.1 | 13.1 |
| | | -21.4 | 24.2 | 101.0 | | 37.0 | | | -37.7 | 94.9 |
| | | | 45.9 | 15.3 | | 4.7 | | | 13.4 | 32.2 |
| | | (35) | 7.4  (23) | 1.8 | | 1.8 | EBIT/Interest | (74) | 4.7  (60) | 7.7 |
| | | | 2.4 | -.1 | | .4 | | | -.4 | 1.5 |
| | | | | | | | Net Profit + Depr., Dep., Amort./Cur. Mat. L/T/D | | 12.1 | |
| | | | | | | | | (14) | 5.2 | |
| | | | | | | | | | 1.3 | |
| | | .0 | .0 | .3 | | .9 | | | .2 | .2 |
| | | .2 | .4 | .9 | | 2.2 | Fixed/Worth | | 1.0 | .7 |
| | | 4.1 | .9 | 1.8 | | -2.5 | | | 6.0 | 3.7 |
| | | .4 | .5 | .6 | | 2.0 | | | .9 | .9 |
| | | 1.8 | 1.4 | 1.4 | | 4.9 | Debt/Worth | | 2.2 | 2.2 |
| | | -4.5 | 3.9 | 6.5 | | -6.1 | | | -204.8 | 10.3 |
| | | | 56.2 | 46.9 | | | % Profit Before Taxes/Tangible Net Worth | | 56.2 | 76.1 |
| | | (34) | 33.7  (20) | 21.9 | | | | (63) | 27.4  (59) | 38.7 |
| | | | 5.5 | 1.4 | | | | | 4.7 | 9.7 |
| | | 37.6 | 33.1 | 16.2 | | 5.3 | % Profit Before Taxes/Total Assets | | 18.5 | 23.1 |
| | | 28.3 | 10.3 | 5.0 | | 2.2 | | | 6.8 | 12.2 |
| | | 6.2 | 1.5 | -2.4 | | -4.1 | | | -3.7 | 2.5 |
| | | 338.4 | 161.7 | 19.3 | | 5.0 | | | 42.5 | 38.5 |
| | | 48.7 | 30.0 | 6.0 | | 3.9 | Sales/Net Fixed Assets | | 10.6 | 10.6 |
| | | 14.1 | 10.8 | 3.0 | | 3.1 | | | 4.0 | 3.6 |
| | | 4.0 | 3.4 | 2.2 | | 1.5 | | | 3.4 | 3.5 |
| | | 3.5 | 2.7 | 1.8 | | 1.1 | Sales/Total Assets | | 2.0 | 2.1 |
| | | 1.8 | 1.8 | 1.2 | | .6 | | | 1.5 | 1.5 |
| | | | .4 | 1.7 | | | | | 1.1 | 1.1 |
| | | (27) | 1.4  (21) | 2.9 | | | % Depr., Dep., Amort./Sales | (67) | 3.5  (54) | 2.4 |
| | | | 3.2 | 5.5 | | | | | 5.5 | 6.0 |
| | | | 1.7 | | | | % Officers', Directors' Owners' Comp/Sales | | 1.4 | .8 |
| | | (15) | 2.9 | | | | | (28) | 2.8  (15) | 2.4 |
| | | | 4.1 | | | | | | 4.7 | 4.8 |
| | 9686M | 39715M | 504534M | 951347M | 850035M | 1894982M | Net Sales ($) | | 4170869M | 2753858M |
| | 1532M | 12400M | 183476M | 544587M | 273740M | 1777969M | Total Assets ($) | | 1998243M | 1531242M |

© RMA 2024

M = $ thousand    MM = $ million
See Pages viii through xx for Explanation of Ratios and Data

# ADMIN & WASTE MANAGEMENT SERVICES—Packaging and Labeling Services  NAICS 561910

| Comparative Historical Data | | | | | Current Data Sorted by Sales | | | | | |
|---|---|---|---|---|---|---|---|---|---|---|
| | | | Type of Statement | | | 1 | | 3 | 4 | |
| 2 | 7 | 8 | Unqualified | | | | | 5 | 5 | |
| 15 | 15 | 10 | Reviewed | | | | 1 | 4 | | |
| 7 | 6 | 5 | Compiled | | | | 1 | 1 | | |
| 12 | 14 | 12 | Tax Returns | 2 | 3 | 2 | 3 | 1 | 1 | |
| 38 | 50 | 61 | Other | 1 | 6 | 4 | 14 | 12 | 24 | |
| 4/1/21-3/31/22 | 4/1/22-3/31/23 | 4/1/23-3/31/24 | | | 13 (4/1-9/30/23) | | 83 (10/1/23-3/31/24) | | | |
| ALL | ALL | ALL | | 0-1MM | 1-3MM | 3-5MM | 5-10MM | 10-25MM | 25MM & OVER | |
| 74 | 92 | 96 | NUMBER OF STATEMENTS | 3 | 10 | 6 | 18 | 25 | 34 | |
| % | % | % | ASSETS | % | % | % | % | % | % | |
| 15.6 | 14.7 | 12.5 | Cash & Equivalents | | 18.8 | | 13.1 | 19.3 | 5.4 | |
| 24.9 | 23.5 | 24.6 | Trade Receivables (net) | | 29.7 | | 24.6 | 28.0 | 21.7 | |
| 21.8 | 19.2 | 18.4 | Inventory | | 21.6 | | 16.0 | 20.5 | 18.9 | |
| 1.8 | 2.5 | 2.9 | All Other Current | | .4 | | 4.3 | .8 | 4.6 | |
| 64.0 | 60.0 | 58.6 | Total Current | | 70.4 | | 58.1 | 68.5 | 50.7 | |
| 20.4 | 22.5 | 22.6 | Fixed Assets (net) | | 17.8 | | 16.7 | 18.8 | 28.4 | |
| 11.0 | 10.5 | 9.8 | Intangibles (net) | | 2.4 | | 17.3 | 6.9 | 9.9 | |
| 4.6 | 7.0 | 9.0 | All Other Non-Current | | 9.4 | | 8.0 | 5.7 | 11.0 | |
| 100.0 | 100.0 | 100.0 | Total | | 100.0 | | 100.0 | 100.0 | 100.0 | |
| | | | LIABILITIES | | | | | | | |
| 9.2 | 7.0 | 7.9 | Notes Payable-Short Term | | 8.2 | | 8.1 | 6.0 | 8.0 | |
| 2.3 | 3.2 | 3.1 | Cur. Mat.-L.T.D. | | 1.3 | | 1.4 | 4.4 | 2.4 | |
| 15.7 | 15.2 | 14.6 | Trade Payables | | 13.2 | | 16.5 | 17.2 | 13.3 | |
| .2 | .2 | .2 | Income Taxes Payable | | .0 | | .4 | .5 | .0 | |
| 8.1 | 7.5 | 8.6 | All Other Current | | 7.8 | | 10.1 | 7.3 | 8.0 | |
| 35.5 | 33.2 | 34.4 | Total Current | | 30.5 | | 36.5 | 35.5 | 31.8 | |
| 17.3 | 19.5 | 17.4 | Long-Term Debt | | 18.3 | | 17.4 | 12.0 | 19.8 | |
| .2 | .4 | .2 | Deferred Taxes | | .0 | | .0 | .3 | .3 | |
| 5.7 | 5.2 | 6.2 | All Other Non-Current | | 9.3 | | 6.4 | 2.5 | 8.8 | |
| 41.4 | 41.8 | 41.8 | Net Worth | | 41.8 | | 39.7 | 49.8 | 39.3 | |
| 100.0 | 100.0 | 100.0 | Total Liabilities & Net Worth | | 100.0 | | 100.0 | 100.0 | 100.0 | |
| | | | INCOME DATA | | | | | | | |
| 100.0 | 100.0 | 100.0 | Net Sales | | 100.0 | | 100.0 | 100.0 | 100.0 | |
| | | | Gross Profit | | | | | | | |
| 92.8 | 91.3 | 94.0 | Operating Expenses | | 90.1 | | 98.0 | 94.4 | 95.9 | |
| 7.2 | 8.7 | 6.0 | Operating Profit | | 9.9 | | 2.0 | 5.6 | 4.1 | |
| -.4 | 1.5 | 1.1 | All Other Expenses (net) | | .5 | | .7 | .1 | 2.3 | |
| 7.6 | 7.2 | 4.9 | Profit Before Taxes | | 9.4 | | 1.3 | 5.5 | 1.8 | |
| | | | RATIOS | | | | | | | |
| 3.3 | 3.1 | 3.0 | | | 6.2 | | 2.9 | 4.1 | 2.3 | |
| 2.0 | 2.0 | 1.8 | Current | | 3.7 | | 1.8 | 2.3 | 1.4 | |
| 1.2 | 1.2 | 1.2 | | | 1.7 | | 1.2 | 1.2 | 1.1 | |
| 2.4 | 2.2 | 2.1 | | | 4.7 | | 1.5 | 3.2 | 1.4 | |
| 1.1 | 1.1 | 1.1 | Quick | | 2.2 | | 1.0 | 1.1 | 1.0 | |
| .6 | .6 | .7 | | | 1.0 | | .7 | .7 | .5 | |
| 23 16.1 | 23 15.7 | 24 15.4 | | 0 UND | | | 23 15.8 | 30 12.3 | 26 13.9 | |
| 39 9.4 | 36 10.2 | 39 9.4 | Sales/Receivables | 44 8.3 | | | 34 10.7 | 38 9.6 | 42 8.6 | |
| 57 6.4 | 50 7.3 | 54 6.7 | | 96 3.8 | | | 48 7.6 | 53 6.9 | 56 6.5 | |
| | | | Cost of Sales/Inventory | | | | | | | |
| | | | Cost of Sales/Payables | | | | | | | |
| 5.9 | 5.9 | 5.8 | | | 3.0 | | 6.8 | 4.7 | 7.0 | |
| 9.1 | 9.2 | 9.2 | Sales/Working Capital | | 6.7 | | 8.8 | 8.5 | 11.3 | |
| 23.1 | 29.1 | 31.6 | | | 30.0 | | 23.8 | 25.8 | 52.7 | |
| 47.8 | 28.6 | 23.0 | | | 23.3 | | 23.3 | 31.4 | 17.4 | |
| (54) 8.2 | (73) 6.4 | (84) 4.5 | EBIT/Interest | | (17) 4.8 | | (22) 3.8 | (32) 3.6 | | |
| 3.1 | -1.4 | .6 | | | -1.5 | | 1.3 | .4 | | |
| 6.4 | 6.2 | 13.4 | Net Profit + Depr., Dep., | | | | | | | |
| (13) 4.8 | (13) 1.9 | (12) 3.0 | Amort./Cur. Mat. L/T/D | | | | | | | |
| 1.9 | .9 | .9 | | | | | | | | |
| .1 | .1 | .1 | | | .1 | | .1 | .0 | .4 | |
| .6 | .4 | .5 | Fixed/Worth | | .4 | | .5 | .3 | 1.0 | |
| 2.3 | 1.7 | 1.8 | | | NM | | 2.6 | .9 | 4.2 | |
| .7 | .5 | .7 | | | .2 | | .8 | .4 | 1.1 | |
| 1.8 | 1.9 | 1.6 | Debt/Worth | | 1.5 | | 1.8 | 1.4 | 1.7 | |
| 8.2 | 7.8 | 7.4 | | | NM | | NM | 3.7 | 8.0 | |
| 117.2 | 88.6 | 56.4 | | | 59.6 | | 54.7 | 50.0 | | |
| (61) 47.0 | (78) 41.6 | (76) 27.3 | % Profit Before Taxes/Tangible Net Worth | | (14) 12.8 | (22) | 31.9 | (27) 24.4 | | |
| 16.5 | 5.4 | 5.9 | | | -17.7 | | 8.3 | 8.8 | | |
| 31.5 | 32.4 | 30.8 | % Profit Before Taxes/Total Assets | | 67.8 | | 19.6 | 36.3 | 16.6 | |
| 16.0 | 13.9 | 7.6 | | | 25.1 | | 4.4 | 9.9 | 5.0 | |
| 4.0 | .0 | -.5 | | | -.7 | | -7.2 | 1.8 | -3.6 | |
| 269.2 | 117.7 | 75.7 | | | UND | | 81.2 | 351.1 | 21.9 | |
| 21.0 | 17.0 | 12.8 | Sales/Net Fixed Assets | | 25.4 | | 20.8 | 37.4 | 6.3 | |
| 6.2 | 5.9 | 4.4 | | | 5.4 | | 9.8 | 5.2 | 3.5 | |
| 3.9 | 3.7 | 3.4 | | | 5.4 | | 2.8 | 3.4 | 2.6 | |
| 2.1 | 2.1 | 2.1 | Sales/Total Assets | | 3.2 | | 2.1 | 2.7 | 1.6 | |
| 1.6 | 1.3 | 1.5 | | | 1.7 | | 1.6 | 1.7 | 1.1 | |
| .4 | .6 | 1.1 | | | | | 1.3 | .5 | 1.1 | |
| (44) 2.7 | (63) 2.5 | (65) 2.8 | % Depr., Dep., Amort./Sales | | | (13) | 2.4 (16) | 2.2 (27) | 3.0 | |
| 4.6 | 4.7 | 4.6 | | | | | 3.4 | 3.1 | 5.5 | |
| 1.4 | .9 | 1.8 | % Officers', Directors' Owners' Comp/Sales | | | | | | | |
| (20) 2.2 | (28) 2.1 | (29) 3.0 | | | | | | | | |
| 4.5 | 3.7 | 4.4 | | | | | | | | |
| 2885032M | 5288453M | 4250299M | Net Sales ($) | 2030M | 18742M | 25865M | 135142M | 419183M | 3649337M | |
| 1602694M | 2726915M | 2793704M | Total Assets ($) | 5514M | 13690M | 47348M | 65389M | 194737M | 2467026M | |

© RMA 2024

M = $ thousand    MM = $ million
See Pages viii through xx for Explanation of Ratios and Data

# ADMIN & WASTE MANAGEMENT SERVICES—Convention and Trade Show Organizers  NAICS 561920

## Current Data Sorted by Assets | Comparative Historical Data

| | | | | | | | Type of Statement | | |
|---|---|---|---|---|---|---|---|---|---|
| | | 1 | | 3 | | | Unqualified | 3 | 1 |
| | | | 3 | 4 | | | Reviewed | 3 | |
| | 2 | 6 | 2 | | | | Compiled | 1 | 1 |
| | | 4 | 3 | | | | Tax Returns | 5 | 2 |
| | | 11 (4/1-9/30/23) | 15 | 11 | | 2 | Other | 51 | 19 |
| | 0-500M | 500M-2MM | 2-10MM | 45 (10/1/23-3/31/24) | | | | 4/1/19- | 4/1/20- |
| | | | | 10-50MM | 50-100MM | 100-250MM | | 3/31/20 | 3/31/21 |
| | | | | | | | NUMBER OF STATEMENTS | ALL 63 | ALL 23 |
| | 3 | 10 | 23 | 18 | | 2 | | | |
| | % | % | % | % | % | % | ASSETS | % | % |
| | | 47.8 | 23.3 | 20.2 | | | Cash & Equivalents | 25.1 | 40.5 |
| | | 14.2 | 24.9 | 27.1 | | | Trade Receivables (net) | 24.5 | 9.6 |
| | | .0 | .8 | 5.0 | D | | Inventory | 3.2 | 4.0 |
| | | 5.6 | 4.0 | 14.3 | A | | All Other Current | 7.5 | 6.0 |
| | | 67.6 | 53.0 | 66.6 | T | | Total Current | 60.3 | 60.1 |
| | | 15.9 | 32.9 | 9.6 | A | | Fixed Assets (net) | 20.2 | 23.1 |
| | | 6.5 | 1.6 | 9.7 | | | Intangibles (net) | 7.8 | 4.8 |
| | | 10.0 | 12.5 | 14.2 | N | | All Other Non-Current | 11.7 | 12.1 |
| | | 100.0 | 100.0 | 100.0 | O | | Total | 100.0 | 100.0 |
| | | | | | T | | LIABILITIES | | |
| | | 3.7 | 4.3 | 2.1 | | | Notes Payable-Short Term | 8.4 | 11.2 |
| | | .8 | 7.3 | .8 | A | | Cur. Mat.-L.T.D. | 2.1 | 6.6 |
| | | 1.9 | 7.0 | 8.6 | V | | Trade Payables | 15.9 | 4.9 |
| | | .0 | .0 | .6 | A | | Income Taxes Payable | .3 | .1 |
| | | 20.1 | 28.7 | 46.1 | I | | All Other Current | 26.2 | 24.1 |
| | | 26.5 | 47.3 | 58.2 | L | | Total Current | 52.9 | 46.9 |
| | | 16.2 | 9.8 | 13.6 | A | | Long-Term Debt | 16.6 | 28.7 |
| | | .0 | .0 | .0 | B | | Deferred Taxes | .2 | .2 |
| | | 6.3 | 11.1 | 17.3 | L | | All Other Non-Current | 19.9 | 31.9 |
| | | 50.9 | 31.8 | 10.9 | E | | Net Worth | 10.4 | -7.7 |
| | | 100.0 | 100.0 | 100.0 | | | Total Liabilities & Net Worth | 100.0 | 100.0 |
| | | | | | | | INCOME DATA | | |
| | | 100.0 | 100.0 | 100.0 | | | Net Sales | 100.0 | 100.0 |
| | | | | | | | Gross Profit | | |
| | | 83.4 | 95.3 | 91.9 | | | Operating Expenses | 92.5 | 100.3 |
| | | 16.6 | 4.7 | 8.1 | | | Operating Profit | 7.5 | -.3 |
| | | 3.4 | 3.2 | 2.2 | | | All Other Expenses (net) | 1.4 | 3.2 |
| | | 13.2 | 1.5 | 5.9 | | | Profit Before Taxes | 6.1 | -3.4 |
| | | | | | | | RATIOS | | |
| | | 9.8 | 2.2 | 1.6 | | | | 2.1 | 4.5 |
| | | 3.3 | 1.5 | 1.1 | | | Current | 1.1 | 1.3 |
| | | 1.1 | .4 | .9 | | | | .8 | .8 |
| | | 9.8 | 2.2 | 1.1 | | | | 1.8 | 2.8 |
| | | 3.3 | 1.3 | .9 | | | Quick | .9 | 1.3 |
| | | .8 | .2 | .7 | | | | .6 | .7 |
| | 0 UND | | 14 26.4 | 30 12.3 | | | | 10 37.3 | 0 999.8 |
| | 1 513.2 | | 29 12.4 | 47 7.7 | | | Sales/Receivables | 28 13.1 | 4 102.5 |
| | 26 14.3 | | 64 5.7 | 63 5.8 | | | | 40 9.1 | 34 10.6 |
| | | | | | | | Cost of Sales/Inventory | | |
| | | | | | | | Cost of Sales/Payables | | |
| | | 6.4 | 9.0 | 7.5 | | | | 10.8 | 3.3 |
| | | 14.2 | 16.4 | 84.5 | | | Sales/Working Capital | 71.4 | 14.3 |
| | | NM | -4.3 | -32.4 | | | | -23.6 | -12.3 |
| | | | 187.0 | 97.2 | | | | 32.1 | 7.5 |
| | | (22) | 9.6 | (15) 11.4 | | | EBIT/Interest | (46) 5.8 | (16) 1.5 |
| | | | -.6 | 6.7 | | | | 1.6 | -26.2 |
| | | | | | | | Net Profit + Depr., Dep., Amort./Cur. Mat. L/T/D | | |
| | | .0 | .1 | .1 | | | | .2 | .2 |
| | | .1 | .7 | .2 | | | Fixed/Worth | .8 | 1.7 |
| | | 1.5 | 2.6 | .6 | | | | -3.5 | -.5 |
| | | .4 | .8 | 2.1 | | | | 1.3 | 1.5 |
| | | 1.7 | 2.2 | 6.8 | | | Debt/Worth | 4.3 | -35.2 |
| | | 2.4 | 5.9 | 39.0 | | | | -9.9 | -2.9 |
| | | | 76.5 | 146.8 | | | | 105.4 | 15.0 |
| | | (18) | 31.4 | (15) 53.1 | | | % Profit Before Taxes/Tangible Net Worth | (42) 37.8 | (11) 2.2 |
| | | | -1.1 | 39.6 | | | | 11.6 | -89.7 |
| | | 82.1 | 31.2 | 18.1 | | | | 25.8 | 11.7 |
| | | 19.1 | 5.7 | 12.9 | | | % Profit Before Taxes/Total Assets | 12.4 | .8 |
| | | 4.0 | -2.2 | 2.9 | | | | 2.0 | -51.4 |
| | | UND | 85.8 | 176.7 | | | | 128.2 | 54.4 |
| | | 159.2 | 12.7 | 77.6 | | | Sales/Net Fixed Assets | 31.8 | 14.2 |
| | | 30.9 | 3.0 | 22.9 | | | | 12.5 | 5.2 |
| | | 9.3 | 3.0 | 3.1 | | | | 4.9 | 2.1 |
| | | 3.0 | 2.1 | 2.1 | | | Sales/Total Assets | 3.1 | 1.7 |
| | | 2.1 | 1.6 | 1.3 | | | | 1.5 | .8 |
| | | | .8 | .5 | | | | .4 | .8 |
| | | (14) | 4.8 | (10) 1.5 | | | % Depr., Dep., Amort./Sales | (35) 1.0 | (14) 4.2 |
| | | | 17.7 | 2.8 | | | | 3.4 | 13.5 |
| | | | | | | | % Officers', Directors' Owners' Comp/Sales | 2.1 | |
| | | | | | | | | (13) 3.8 | |
| | | | | | | | | 5.4 | |
| | 4256M | 60199M | 284367M | 1104333M | 379360M | | Net Sales ($) | 2413569M | 379785M |
| | 421M | 12223M | 120536M | 483277M | 402488M | | Total Assets ($) | 1259110M | 345938M |

© RMA 2024

M = $ thousand  MM = $ million
See Pages viii through xx for Explanation of Ratios and Data

# ADMIN & WASTE MANAGEMENT SERVICES—Convention and Trade Show Organizers  NAICS 561920

## Comparative Historical Data | Current Data Sorted by Sales

| | | | | Type of Statement | | | | | | |
|---|---|---|---|---|---|---|---|---|---|---|
| 3 | 6 | 4 | | Unqualified | | 1 | | | 2 | 3 |
| 4 | 2 | 7 | | Reviewed | | 1 | | | | 4 |
| 1 | | 2 | | Compiled | | 1 | | | | 1 |
| 3 | 3 | 11 | | Tax Returns | 3 | 1 | 2 | 2 | 3 | |
| 17 | 30 | 32 | | Other | 2 | 2 | 2 | 1 | 12 | 13 |
| 4/1/21-3/31/22 ALL | 4/1/22-3/31/23 ALL | 4/1/23-3/31/24 ALL | | | 0-1MM | 11 (4/1-9/30/23) 1-3MM | 3-5MM | 5-10MM | 45 (10/1/23-3/31/24) 10-25MM | 25MM & OVER |
| 28 | 41 | 56 | | NUMBER OF STATEMENTS | 5 | 3 | 7 | 3 | 17 | 21 |
| % | % | % | | ASSETS | % | % | % | % | % | % |
| 27.3 | 28.5 | 29.2 | | Cash & Equivalents | | | | | 29.4 | 21.3 |
| 21.2 | 16.9 | 21.9 | | Trade Receivables (net) | | | | | 21.7 | 28.0 |
| 3.2 | 3.1 | 1.9 | | Inventory | | | | | 1.1 | 4.3 |
| 5.7 | 7.4 | 7.3 | | All Other Current | | | | | 11.6 | 9.3 |
| 57.4 | 55.9 | 60.3 | | Total Current | | | | | 63.8 | 62.9 |
| 24.9 | 23.4 | 19.5 | | Fixed Assets (net) | | | | | 32.3 | 7.2 |
| 9.8 | 12.4 | 7.6 | | Intangibles (net) | | | | | .4 | 14.8 |
| 7.9 | 8.3 | 12.6 | | All Other Non-Current | | | | | 3.5 | 15.1 |
| 100.0 | 100.0 | 100.0 | | Total | | | | | 100.0 | 100.0 |
| | | | | LIABILITIES | | | | | | |
| 9.0 | 4.6 | 3.1 | | Notes Payable-Short Term | | | | | 2.7 | .2 |
| 3.7 | 1.5 | 3.5 | | Cur. Mat.-L.T.D. | | | | | 9.3 | 1.1 |
| 9.1 | 6.5 | 9.1 | | Trade Payables | | | | | 7.2 | 7.0 |
| .0 | .2 | .2 | | Income Taxes Payable | | | | | .1 | .5 |
| 30.8 | 30.9 | 45.7 | | All Other Current | | | | | 30.6 | 44.2 |
| 52.7 | 43.6 | 61.6 | | Total Current | | | | | 49.9 | 53.1 |
| 21.2 | 23.7 | 12.6 | | Long-Term Debt | | | | | 14.3 | 13.8 |
| .0 | .0 | .0 | | Deferred Taxes | | | | | .0 | .1 |
| 29.7 | 9.7 | 11.5 | | All Other Non-Current | | | | | 9.6 | 17.0 |
| -3.5 | 22.9 | 14.2 | | Net Worth | | | | | 26.3 | 16.0 |
| 100.0 | 100.0 | 100.0 | | Total Liabilities & Net Worth | | | | | 100.0 | 100.0 |
| | | | | INCOME DATA | | | | | | |
| 100.0 | 100.0 | 100.0 | | Net Sales | | | | | 100.0 | 100.0 |
| 90.4 | 90.3 | 91.7 | | Gross Profit | | | | | 95.2 | 93.3 |
| | | | | Operating Expenses | | | | | | |
| 9.6 | 9.7 | 8.3 | | Operating Profit | | | | | 4.8 | 6.7 |
| .1 | 3.1 | 2.9 | | All Other Expenses (net) | | | | | .3 | 2.2 |
| 9.5 | 6.6 | 5.4 | | Profit Before Taxes | | | | | 4.6 | 4.5 |
| | | | | RATIOS | | | | | | |
| 2.5 | 1.8 | 2.1 | | | | | | | 3.7 | 1.8 |
| 1.5 | 1.1 | 1.2 | | Current | | | | | 1.6 | 1.2 |
| .7 | .7 | .8 | | | | | | | .5 | .9 |
| 2.4 | 1.5 | 1.8 | | | | | | | 2.8 | 1.2 |
| 1.1 | .9 | 1.0 | | Quick | | | | | 1.3 | .9 |
| .5 | .5 | .6 | | | | | | | .3 | .7 |
| 11   32.5 | 0   UND | 10   38.4 | | | | | | | 10   37.0 | 26   14.0 |
| 43   8.4 | 23   16.0 | 31   11.9 | | Sales/Receivables | | | | | 19   19.1 | 47   7.8 |
| 76   4.8 | 39   9.4 | 54   6.7 | | | | | | | 49   7.4 | 65   5.6 |
| | | | | Cost of Sales/Inventory | | | | | | |
| | | | | Cost of Sales/Payables | | | | | | |
| 6.6 | 9.8 | 8.3 | | | | | | | 9.2 | 8.2 |
| 8.8 | 62.6 | 19.9 | | Sales/Working Capital | | | | | 16.4 | 21.3 |
| -8.3 | -12.5 | -21.9 | | | | | | | -9.2 | -36.0 |
| 42.0 | 26.0 | 100.0 | | | | | | | 183.0 | 97.2 |
| (20)   13.9 | (28)   10.7 | (45)   10.6 | | EBIT/Interest | | | | | (15)   21.1 | (19)   11.4 |
| 1.6 | 1.8 | .7 | | | | | | | -2.0 | 5.0 |
| | | | | Net Profit + Depr., Dep., Amort./Cur. Mat. L/T/D | | | | | | |
| .1 | .1 | .0 | | | | | | | .1 | .1 |
| 1.5 | 1.5 | .3 | | Fixed/Worth | | | | | .6 | .3 |
| -12.3 | -.4 | 2.4 | | | | | | | -39.3 | 1.0 |
| 1.0 | 1.3 | 1.2 | | | | | | | 1.0 | 1.9 |
| 310.2 | 7.6 | 2.7 | | Debt/Worth | | | | | 2.8 | 8.3 |
| -3.7 | -5.6 | UND | | | | | | | -70.2 | NM |
| 128.9 | 88.9 | 107.3 | | | | | | | 121.7 | 130.8 |
| (15)   84.5 | (25)   38.5 | (43)   51.7 | | % Profit Before Taxes/Tangible Net Worth | | | | | (12)   76.6 | (16)   51.6 |
| .5 | 5.9 | 14.2 | | | | | | | 30.0 | 39.0 |
| 33.0 | 18.2 | 27.3 | | | | | | | 47.3 | 18.4 |
| 12.2 | 7.3 | 8.1 | | % Profit Before Taxes/Total Assets | | | | | 8.8 | 12.6 |
| -.3 | 2.9 | -.1 | | | | | | | -5.4 | 2.5 |
| 127.4 | 102.2 | 222.5 | | | | | | | 211.3 | 195.1 |
| 21.3 | 28.0 | 43.7 | | Sales/Net Fixed Assets | | | | | 20.0 | 89.0 |
| 4.5 | 8.7 | 10.9 | | | | | | | 2.9 | 26.8 |
| 2.9 | 2.9 | 3.4 | | | | | | | 4.8 | 3.3 |
| 1.7 | 2.1 | 2.4 | | Sales/Total Assets | | | | | 2.3 | 2.4 |
| .9 | 1.0 | 1.6 | | | | | | | 2.0 | 1.3 |
| .8 | .7 | .5 | | | | | | | .7 | |
| (14)   3.7 | (20)   1.7 | (29)   1.4 | | % Depr., Dep., Amort./Sales | | | | | (10)   2.9 | |
| 12.5 | 5.6 | 9.9 | | | | | | | 17.1 | |
| | | 3.4 | | % Officers', Directors' Owners' Comp/Sales | | | | | | |
| | (16)   7.0 | | | | | | | | | |
| | 9.3 | | | | | | | | | |
| 464378M | 2540277M | 1832515M | | Net Sales ($) | 1565M | 6789M | 27765M | 19985M | 242551M | 1533860M |
| 522208M | 1565393M | 1018945M | | Total Assets ($) | 10074M | 4823M | 14871M | 7187M | 95880M | 886110M |

M = $ thousand     MM = $ million
See Pages viii through xx for Explanation of Ratios and Data

© RMA 2024

# ADMIN & WASTE MANAGEMENT SERVICES—All Other Support Services  NAICS 561990

## Current Data Sorted by Assets | Comparative Historical Data

| | | | | | | | Type of Statement | | |
|---|---|---|---|---|---|---|---|---|---|
| | | | 3 | 4 | 2 | 2 | Unqualified | 14 | 12 |
| | | | 3 | 4 | | | Reviewed | 9 | 4 |
| | | 1 | 3 | 1 | | | Compiled | 14 | 7 |
| 3 | | 6 | 7 | 2 | | | Tax Returns | 26 | 14 |
| 5 | | 16 | 24 | 17 | 7 | 8 | Other | 93 | 93 |
| | | 18 (4/1-9/30/23) | | 100 (10/1/23-3/31/24) | | | | 4/1/19-3/31/20 | 4/1/20-3/31/21 |
| 0-500M | 500M-2MM | 2-10MM | 10-50MM | 50-100MM | 100-250MM | | | ALL | ALL |
| 8 | 23 | 40 | 28 | 9 | 10 | | NUMBER OF STATEMENTS | 156 | 130 |
| % | % | % | % | % | % | | ASSETS | % | % |
| | 30.6 | 24.3 | 18.5 | | 6.8 | | Cash & Equivalents | 20.4 | 25.9 |
| | 10.4 | 23.1 | 25.2 | | 9.2 | | Trade Receivables (net) | 18.2 | 20.5 |
| | 1.6 | 5.5 | 8.0 | | 1.4 | | Inventory | 5.8 | 5.4 |
| | 8.7 | 7.7 | 9.7 | | 4.1 | | All Other Current | 7.7 | 5.0 |
| | 51.3 | 60.6 | 61.5 | | 21.4 | | Total Current | 52.1 | 56.8 |
| | 31.9 | 21.2 | 21.4 | | 29.6 | | Fixed Assets (net) | 27.9 | 20.6 |
| | 4.4 | 8.3 | 4.9 | | 34.2 | | Intangibles (net) | 8.4 | 13.2 |
| | 12.4 | 9.9 | 12.2 | | 14.8 | | All Other Non-Current | 11.6 | 9.3 |
| | 100.0 | 100.0 | 100.0 | | 100.0 | | Total | 100.0 | 100.0 |
| | | | | | | | LIABILITIES | | |
| | 3.0 | 4.0 | 14.6 | | 3.6 | | Notes Payable-Short Term | 7.3 | 5.2 |
| | 1.3 | 1.9 | 1.8 | | 1.7 | | Cur. Mat.-L.T.D. | 2.9 | 2.7 |
| | 2.7 | 7.5 | 11.3 | | 5.6 | | Trade Payables | 10.2 | 8.1 |
| | .0 | .1 | .0 | | .0 | | Income Taxes Payable | .1 | .3 |
| | 4.9 | 16.8 | 17.5 | | 4.1 | | All Other Current | 15.2 | 13.3 |
| | 12.0 | 30.2 | 45.2 | | 14.9 | | Total Current | 35.9 | 29.7 |
| | 43.4 | 30.9 | 11.1 | | 16.2 | | Long-Term Debt | 25.0 | 24.9 |
| | .0 | .1 | .1 | | .0 | | Deferred Taxes | .3 | .2 |
| | 3.4 | 9.7 | 4.2 | | 8.3 | | All Other Non-Current | 9.6 | 11.2 |
| | 41.2 | 29.1 | 39.4 | | 60.5 | | Net Worth | 29.2 | 34.0 |
| | 100.0 | 100.0 | 100.0 | | 100.0 | | Total Liabilties & Net Worth | 100.0 | 100.0 |
| | | | | | | | INCOME DATA | | |
| | 100.0 | 100.0 | 100.0 | | 100.0 | | Net Sales | 100.0 | 100.0 |
| | 79.5 | 91.7 | 85.9 | | 95.2 | | Gross Profit | | |
| | 20.5 | 8.3 | 14.1 | | 4.8 | | Operating Expenses | 88.5 | 91.2 |
| | 3.3 | .6 | 2.7 | | 2.3 | | Operating Profit | 11.5 | 8.8 |
| | 17.2 | 7.7 | 11.4 | | 2.5 | | All Other Expenses (net) | 2.9 | 1.5 |
| | | | | | | | Profit Before Taxes | 8.7 | 7.3 |
| | | | | | | | RATIOS | | |
| | 12.7 | 5.5 | 2.7 | | 2.6 | | | 3.2 | 4.3 |
| | 5.6 | 2.6 | 1.8 | | 1.7 | | Current | 1.6 | 2.2 |
| | 2.9 | 1.3 | 1.1 | | 1.0 | | | .9 | 1.2 |
| | 9.6 | 5.1 | 1.8 | | 1.7 | | | 2.3 | 3.3 |
| | 5.6 | 2.2 | 1.3 | | 1.1 | | Quick | 1.1 | 1.5 |
| | 1.6 | .8 | .5 | | .9 | | | .6 | .9 |
| | 0 UND | 4 92.4 | 16 22.5 | | 42 8.7 | | | 3 118.2 | 3 111.2 |
| | 1 686.0 | 24 15.1 | 41 8.9 | | 54 6.8 | | Sales/Receivables | 30 12.2 | 35 10.3 |
| | 23 16.0 | 48 7.6 | 63 5.8 | | 81 4.5 | | | 53 6.9 | 58 6.3 |
| | | | | | | | Cost of Sales/Inventory | | |
| | | | | | | | Cost of Sales/Payables | | |
| | 3.7 | 3.0 | 4.7 | | 4.0 | | | 4.8 | 4.0 |
| | 7.3 | 7.8 | 8.8 | | 6.5 | | Sales/Working Capital | 15.8 | 7.9 |
| | 16.9 | 118.8 | 94.2 | | NM | | | -120.7 | 25.5 |
| | 54.4 | 65.6 | 40.6 | | | | | 26.9 | 22.7 |
| (17) | 7.6 | (32) 13.9 | (22) 11.5 | | | | EBIT/Interest | (117) 6.6 | (96) 4.9 |
| | 3.0 | 1.3 | 5.9 | | | | | 1.5 | -.4 |
| | | | | | | | Net Profit + Depr., Dep., | 7.9 | 6.6 |
| | | | | | | | Amort./Cur. Mat. L/T/D | (20) 3.3 | (13) 1.3 |
| | | | | | | | | 1.5 | .2 |
| | .0 | .0 | .2 | | .8 | | | .1 | .1 |
| | .5 | .2 | .6 | | 1.0 | | Fixed/Worth | .9 | .7 |
| | 3.4 | 2.4 | .8 | | NM | | | 15.9 | 9.4 |
| | .2 | .3 | .9 | | .2 | | | .7 | .7 |
| | .6 | .9 | 1.5 | | .5 | | Debt/Worth | 2.8 | 2.9 |
| | 2.9 | 138.1 | 4.9 | | NM | | | 68.5 | -200.4 |
| | 116.1 | 51.2 | 54.2 | | | | | 57.2 | 77.3 |
| (19) | 37.6 | (31) 30.7 | (26) 35.3 | | | | % Profit Before Taxes/Tangible Net Worth | (119) 31.9 | (97) 26.6 |
| | 2.2 | 6.3 | 17.9 | | | | | 12.4 | -6.7 |
| | 58.3 | 31.6 | 23.2 | | 6.3 | | | 19.0 | 27.1 |
| | 17.1 | 15.6 | 16.4 | | 1.3 | | % Profit Before Taxes/Total Assets | 8.8 | 9.2 |
| | 7.1 | .2 | 5.5 | | -.6 | | | 1.7 | -1.7 |
| | 139.8 | 149.4 | 54.5 | | 7.9 | | | 150.2 | 111.5 |
| | 11.8 | 39.8 | 9.0 | | 1.9 | | Sales/Net Fixed Assets | 12.5 | 19.4 |
| | 4.1 | 7.3 | 5.6 | | .8 | | | 3.8 | 3.7 |
| | 4.6 | 4.2 | 3.0 | | .8 | | | 3.2 | 3.0 |
| | 2.2 | 2.0 | 2.0 | | .4 | | Sales/Total Assets | 1.9 | 1.6 |
| | 1.3 | 1.0 | 1.1 | | .3 | | | .9 | .8 |
| | | .3 | .4 | | | | | .9 | 1.1 |
| | | (27) 1.4 | (20) 1.6 | | | | % Depr., Dep., Amort./Sales | (98) 3.2 | (77) 2.3 |
| | | 4.0 | 3.5 | | | | | 7.2 | 8.7 |
| | | 1.5 | | | | | | 1.3 | 2.2 |
| | | (11) 2.5 | | | | | % Officers', Directors' Owners' Comp/Sales | (44) 4.2 | (24) 5.5 |
| | | 6.9 | | | | | | 8.3 | 8.9 |
| 10303M | 71670M | 562849M | 1820790M | 1237180M | 1025507M | | Net Sales ($) | 4899765M | 4778898M |
| 1886M | 25215M | 200526M | 618166M | 696173M | 1753896M | | Total Assets ($) | 3158318M | 3098062M |

© RMA 2024

M = $ thousand   MM = $ million
See Pages viii through xx for Explanation of Ratios and Data

# ADMIN & WASTE MANAGEMENT SERVICES—All Other Support Services  NAICS 561990

## Comparative Historical Data | Current Data Sorted by Sales

| | | | | | | Type of Statement | | | | | | |
|---|---|---|---|---|---|---|---|---|---|---|---|---|
| | 3 | | 15 | | 11 | Unqualified | | 2 | | 1 | 1 | 7 |
| | 2 | | 9 | | 7 | Reviewed | | 2 | | 2 | 1 | 4 |
| | 4 | | 13 | | 5 | Compiled | | 2 | | 1 | | 2 |
| | 19 | | 26 | | 18 | Tax Returns | 2 | 4 | 2 | 5 | 4 | 1 |
| | 54 | | 82 | | 77 | Other | 9 | 10 | 8 | 11 | 11 | 29 |
| | 4/1/21-3/31/22 ALL | | 4/1/22-3/31/23 ALL | | 4/1/23-3/31/24 ALL | | | 18 (4/1-9/30/23) | | | 100 (10/1/23-3/31/24) | |
| | | | | | | | 0-1MM | 1-3MM | 3-5MM | 5-10MM | 10-25MM | 25MM & OVER |
| | 82 | | 145 | | 118 | NUMBER OF STATEMENTS | 11 | 18 | 10 | 19 | 17 | 43 |
| | % | | % | | % | ASSETS | % | % | % | % | % | % |
| | 27.3 | | 24.9 | | 22.8 | Cash & Equivalents | 19.3 | 29.8 | 28.8 | 35.2 | 20.7 | 14.6 |
| | 15.3 | | 18.8 | | 19.0 | Trade Receivables (net) | 5.2 | 13.0 | 19.4 | 16.7 | 27.7 | 22.6 |
| | 3.4 | | 4.5 | | 4.9 | Inventory | .0 | 2.7 | .0 | 3.7 | 4.3 | 9.1 |
| | 4.9 | | 7.7 | | 7.8 | All Other Current | 2.7 | 10.4 | 5.9 | 14.4 | 5.3 | 6.7 |
| | 50.9 | | 55.8 | | 54.5 | Total Current | 27.3 | 55.8 | 54.1 | 70.0 | 57.9 | 52.9 |
| | 27.5 | | 23.4 | | 23.8 | Fixed Assets (net) | 62.3 | 23.8 | 12.1 | 17.3 | 22.1 | 20.2 |
| | 12.0 | | 11.1 | | 10.0 | Intangibles (net) | .8 | 6.4 | 13.3 | 4.8 | 6.2 | 17.0 |
| | 9.5 | | 9.7 | | 11.7 | All Other Non-Current | 9.7 | 14.0 | 20.6 | 8.0 | 13.7 | 9.9 |
| | 100.0 | | 100.0 | | 100.0 | Total | 100.0 | 100.0 | 100.0 | 100.0 | 100.0 | 100.0 |
| | | | | | | LIABILITIES | | | | | | |
| | 3.0 | | 6.4 | | 8.0 | Notes Payable-Short Term | 2.8 | 17.7 | 7.4 | 4.1 | 2.2 | 9.4 |
| | 3.9 | | 3.3 | | 1.8 | Cur. Mat.-L.T.D. | .9 | 2.9 | 1.4 | .5 | 1.8 | 2.2 |
| | 7.6 | | 10.0 | | 7.0 | Trade Payables | 1.0 | 1.2 | 2.8 | 7.2 | 11.5 | 10.2 |
| | .1 | | .6 | | .1 | Income Taxes Payable | .2 | .0 | .0 | .0 | .2 | .2 |
| | 10.6 | | 14.2 | | 14.1 | All Other Current | 14.9 | 11.4 | 7.6 | 18.3 | 15.9 | 13.9 |
| | 25.2 | | 34.6 | | 31.0 | Total Current | 19.7 | 33.2 | 19.1 | 30.1 | 31.5 | 35.9 |
| | 32.1 | | 22.2 | | 31.1 | Long-Term Debt | 51.6 | 36.6 | 72.5 | 6.7 | 31.6 | 24.5 |
| | .2 | | .2 | | .1 | Deferred Taxes | .0 | .0 | .0 | .2 | .0 | .2 |
| | 3.7 | | 5.4 | | 7.5 | All Other Non-Current | 12.9 | 9.4 | 1.9 | 3.0 | 8.4 | 8.2 |
| | 38.7 | | 37.6 | | 30.3 | Net Worth | 15.8 | 20.8 | 6.4 | 60.0 | 28.5 | 31.1 |
| | 100.0 | | 100.0 | | 100.0 | Total Liabilities & Net Worth | 100.0 | 100.0 | 100.0 | 100.0 | 100.0 | 100.0 |
| | | | | | | INCOME DATA | | | | | | |
| | 100.0 | | 100.0 | | 100.0 | Net Sales | 100.0 | 100.0 | 100.0 | 100.0 | 100.0 | 100.0 |
| | | | | | | Gross Profit | | | | | | |
| | 87.6 | | 86.0 | | 88.2 | Operating Expenses | 55.2 | 85.4 | 89.3 | 91.6 | 94.8 | 93.4 |
| | 12.4 | | 14.0 | | 11.8 | Operating Profit | 44.8 | 14.6 | 10.7 | 8.4 | 5.2 | 6.6 |
| | -.6 | | 1.6 | | 2.0 | All Other Expenses (net) | 9.3 | 2.8 | .6 | .5 | .3 | 1.5 |
| | 12.9 | | 12.4 | | 9.8 | Profit Before Taxes | 35.5 | 11.9 | 10.1 | 7.9 | 4.9 | 5.1 |
| | | | | | | RATIOS | | | | | | |
| | 5.0 | | 4.3 | | 5.2 | | 5.7 | 10.1 | 14.9 | 11.1 | 6.4 | 2.6 |
| | 2.4 | | 1.8 | | 2.4 | Current | 2.6 | 2.9 | 4.6 | 2.6 | 3.8 | 1.8 |
| | 1.1 | | 1.1 | | 1.1 | | .1 | 1.2 | 1.0 | 1.7 | 1.1 | 1.1 |
| | 4.1 | | 2.8 | | 4.4 | | 5.7 | 4.8 | 14.2 | 8.8 | 5.7 | 1.8 |
| | 1.8 | | 1.4 | | 1.6 | Quick | 2.5 | 1.5 | 4.6 | 2.3 | 3.3 | 1.1 |
| | .8 | | .7 | | .7 | | .1 | .3 | 1.0 | 1.0 | .8 | .7 |
| 2 | 215.1 | 2 | 239.4 | 1 | 312.9 | | 0 UND | 0 UND | 0 UND | 4 102.8 | 24 15.3 | 22 16.7 |
| 26 | 14.2 | 32 | 11.5 | 26 | 14.1 | Sales/Receivables | 0 UND | 3 109.1 | 22 16.3 | 15 24.5 | 31 11.7 | 41 9.0 |
| 56 | 6.5 | 48 | 7.6 | 54 | 6.8 | | 1 686.0 | 47 7.8 | 56 6.5 | 53 6.9 | 60 6.1 | 58 6.3 |
| | | | | | | Cost of Sales/Inventory | | | | | | |
| | | | | | | Cost of Sales/Payables | | | | | | |
| | 4.1 | | 4.2 | | 3.9 | | 2.6 | 2.3 | 2.0 | 3.7 | 4.2 | 4.8 |
| | 8.1 | | 9.1 | | 8.0 | Sales/Working Capital | 5.5 | 5.3 | 4.8 | 8.8 | 7.9 | 11.0 |
| | 99.1 | | 55.5 | | 105.9 | | -4.1 | NM | NM | 16.9 | NM | 77.3 |
| | 56.5 | | 41.3 | | 32.8 | | | 47.4 | | 184.2 | 131.7 | 22.0 |
| (62) | 9.7 | (101) | 10.4 | (91) | 8.0 | EBIT/Interest | (14) | 9.7 | (15) | 28.2 | (15) 11.5 | (33) 7.9 |
| | 2.5 | | 1.6 | | 1.5 | | | 1.9 | | 1.3 | 4.8 | 1.3 |
| | | | 10.1 | | 5.4 | Net Profit + Depr., Dep., | | | | | | |
| | | (17) | 3.5 | (10) | 3.5 | Amort./Cur. Mat. L/T/D | | | | | | |
| | | | .3 | | 1.3 | | | | | | | |
| | .2 | | .1 | | .1 | | 1.0 | .0 | .0 | .0 | .1 | .3 |
| | .9 | | .5 | | .6 | Fixed/Worth | 2.3 | .6 | .0 | .3 | .6 | .7 |
| | 3.9 | | 2.9 | | 2.1 | | -2.6 | 36.7 | NM | .5 | -6.4 | 1.4 |
| | .4 | | .5 | | .3 | | .2 | .4 | .2 | .1 | .2 | .7 |
| | 1.6 | | 1.6 | | 1.2 | Debt/Worth | 2.7 | 2.6 | 1.6 | .6 | .6 | 1.6 |
| | 27.6 | | 14.9 | | 7.6 | | -7.6 | NM | -2.2 | 1.8 | -18.3 | 5.7 |
| | 89.5 | | 72.6 | | 55.5 | | | 116.7 | | 114.3 | 69.0 | 46.4 |
| (63) | 38.4 | (118) | 33.2 | (93) | 25.5 | % Profit Before Taxes/Tangible Net Worth | (14) | 29.6 | | 35.5 | (12) 35.5 | (34) 27.8 |
| | 15.8 | | 12.9 | | 5.7 | | | -5.1 | | 2.8 | 17.8 | 4.6 |
| | 34.3 | | 29.0 | | 28.2 | % Profit Before Taxes/Total Assets | 17.1 | 39.8 | 30.2 | 30.5 | 32.8 | 20.9 |
| | 16.1 | | 11.7 | | 10.8 | | 9.9 | 10.9 | 4.8 | 11.9 | 16.7 | 8.3 |
| | 4.3 | | 2.0 | | .5 | | 7.1 | -.7 | -1.6 | .3 | 6.5 | .4 |
| | 44.1 | | 128.0 | | 127.6 | | 71.0 | 125.5 | UND | 266.0 | 59.1 | 73.3 |
| | 8.3 | | 17.6 | | 14.6 | Sales/Net Fixed Assets | .3 | 10.7 | 147.1 | 31.3 | 18.4 | 11.2 |
| | 3.1 | | 4.3 | | 5.4 | | .2 | 6.2 | 17.4 | 6.7 | 7.7 | 4.8 |
| | 2.8 | | 3.0 | | 3.5 | | 1.3 | 3.3 | 4.0 | 4.6 | 4.5 | 3.4 |
| | 1.6 | | 2.1 | | 1.9 | Sales/Total Assets | .3 | 1.9 | .8 | 2.0 | 2.9 | 2.1 |
| | 1.0 | | .9 | | .7 | | .2 | 1.1 | .5 | 1.0 | 1.7 | 1.1 |
| | 1.1 | | .4 | | .4 | | | | | .3 | .3 | 1.4 |
| (57) | 2.9 | (88) | 2.0 | (68) | 1.8 | % Depr., Dep., Amort./Sales | | | (12) 1.5 | (13) 1.3 | (27) 1.4 |
| | 8.2 | | 5.2 | | 5.9 | | | | | 3.6 | 3.6 | 5.3 |
| | 1.5 | | 1.3 | | 2.1 | % Officers', Directors' Owners' Comp/Sales | | | | | | |
| (23) | 4.8 | (40) | 3.1 | (30) | 3.7 | | | | | | | |
| | 9.2 | | 7.8 | | 6.7 | | | | | | | |
| | 2487891M | | 4698715M | | 4728299M | Net Sales ($) | 3734M | 37705M | 40251M | 139318M | 290569M | 4216722M |
| | 2087435M | | 4164759M | | 3295862M | Total Assets ($) | 13715M | 47169M | 45847M | 101220M | 117084M | 2970827M |

M = $ thousand    MM = $ million
See Pages viii through xx for Explanation of Ratios and Data

© RMA 2024

# ADMIN & WASTE MANAGEMENT SERVICES—Solid Waste Collection  NAICS 562111

## Current Data Sorted by Assets | Comparative Historical Data

| | | | | | | Type of Statement | | |
|---|---|---|---|---|---|---|---|---|
| | | 5 | 11 | 8 | 9 | Unqualified | 12 | 11 |
| 1 | | 3 | 6 | 1 | 1 | Reviewed | 21 | 11 |
| 6 | 12 | 6 | 1 | | | Compiled | 15 | 12 |
| 3 | 19 | 13 | 2 | 16 | 21 | Tax Returns | 41 | 30 |
| | 43 (4/1-9/30/23) | 31 | 29 | (10/1/23-3/31/24) | | Other | 102 | 86 |
| 0-500M | 500M-2MM | 2-10MM | 10-50MM | 50-100MM | 100-250MM | | 4/1/19-3/31/20 ALL | 4/1/20-3/31/21 ALL |
| 10 | 31 | 58 | 49 | 25 | 31 | NUMBER OF STATEMENTS | 191 | 150 |
| % | % | % | % | % | % | ASSETS | % | % |
| 29.0 | 23.6 | 16.4 | 15.3 | 8.4 | 5.0 | Cash & Equivalents | 14.9 | 17.0 |
| 13.8 | 14.7 | 15.1 | 13.6 | 9.1 | 9.5 | Trade Receivables (net) | 15.1 | 14.7 |
| .0 | .2 | .2 | .5 | .4 | 1.6 | Inventory | 1.0 | 1.3 |
| 9.4 | 3.4 | 2.0 | 4.4 | 2.0 | 1.8 | All Other Current | 3.2 | 3.1 |
| 52.2 | 41.9 | 33.7 | 33.8 | 19.8 | 17.9 | Total Current | 34.2 | 36.1 |
| 33.0 | 44.3 | 51.3 | 49.3 | 45.1 | 44.8 | Fixed Assets (net) | 50.3 | 47.7 |
| 7.2 | 4.0 | 6.9 | 6.3 | 27.4 | 33.1 | Intangibles (net) | 8.4 | 7.6 |
| 7.6 | 9.8 | 8.0 | 10.6 | 7.7 | 4.2 | All Other Non-Current | 7.1 | 8.7 |
| 100.0 | 100.0 | 100.0 | 100.0 | 100.0 | 100.0 | Total | 100.0 | 100.0 |
| | | | | | | LIABILITIES | | |
| 1.0 | 4.7 | 2.1 | 4.1 | 3.2 | 2.6 | Notes Payable-Short Term | 4.8 | 3.7 |
| 17.0 | 10.0 | 7.6 | 4.1 | 4.8 | 2.8 | Cur. Mat.-L.T.D. | 7.0 | 7.3 |
| 12.3 | 5.2 | 9.2 | 6.7 | 4.8 | 6.2 | Trade Payables | 8.8 | 7.7 |
| .0 | .0 | .0 | .1 | .0 | .0 | Income Taxes Payable | .0 | .0 |
| 18.8 | 8.1 | 8.5 | 8.8 | 4.9 | 5.1 | All Other Current | 10.8 | 6.4 |
| 49.1 | 28.0 | 27.4 | 23.7 | 17.7 | 16.7 | Total Current | 31.4 | 25.2 |
| 64.4 | 43.8 | 38.6 | 26.2 | 31.6 | 43.6 | Long-Term Debt | 37.7 | 41.3 |
| .0 | .0 | .5 | .7 | 1.2 | 1.1 | Deferred Taxes | .5 | .1 |
| .0 | 5.1 | 4.7 | 4.0 | 5.2 | 6.3 | All Other Non-Current | 6.4 | 11.6 |
| -13.5 | 23.2 | 28.9 | 45.3 | 44.3 | 32.3 | Net Worth | 23.9 | 21.8 |
| 100.0 | 100.0 | 100.0 | 100.0 | 100.0 | 100.0 | Total Liabilties & Net Worth | 100.0 | 100.0 |
| | | | | | | INCOME DATA | | |
| 100.0 | 100.0 | 100.0 | 100.0 | 100.0 | 100.0 | Net Sales | 100.0 | 100.0 |
| | | | | | | Gross Profit | | |
| 93.5 | 92.0 | 91.3 | 88.8 | 89.9 | 93.8 | Operating Expenses | 91.9 | 90.7 |
| 6.5 | 8.0 | 8.7 | 11.2 | 10.1 | 6.2 | Operating Profit | 8.1 | 9.3 |
| 1.0 | 2.0 | 1.0 | 2.3 | 3.3 | 4.9 | All Other Expenses (net) | 2.3 | 1.0 |
| 5.6 | 6.0 | 7.7 | 8.9 | 6.8 | 1.3 | Profit Before Taxes | 5.9 | 8.3 |
| | | | | | | RATIOS | | |
| 19.5 | 2.7 | 2.5 | 3.2 | 2.2 | 1.5 | | 2.7 | 2.6 |
| 1.5 | 1.5 | 1.4 | 1.6 | 1.3 | 1.1 | Current | 1.2 | 1.3 |
| .6 | .5 | .7 | 1.0 | .6 | .7 | | .7 | .8 |
| 8.1 | 2.7 | 2.2 | 3.0 | 1.8 | 1.3 | | 2.3 | 2.4 |
| 1.0 | 1.3 | 1.3 | 1.4 | 1.3 | .8 | Quick | 1.0 | 1.1 |
| .3 | .5 | .7 | .9 | .5 | .6 | | .6 | .7 |
| 0 UND | 0 UND | 7 48.9 | 11 31.9 | 27 13.7 | 33 11.0 | | 12 31.0 | 11 34.5 |
| 0 UND | 8 44.6 | 25 14.4 | 31 11.6 | 33 11.2 | 42 8.7 | Sales/Receivables | 29 12.7 | 29 12.4 |
| 23 16.2 | 35 10.4 | 43 8.5 | 44 8.3 | 39 9.4 | 52 7.0 | | 42 8.7 | 41 8.8 |
| | | | | | | Cost of Sales/Inventory | | |
| | | | | | | Cost of Sales/Payables | | |
| 6.6 | 10.6 | 6.7 | 4.9 | 8.1 | 12.8 | | 8.1 | 7.8 |
| 20.6 | 38.5 | 45.2 | 13.3 | 42.1 | 55.6 | Sales/Working Capital | 50.2 | 27.8 |
| -27.3 | -42.5 | -40.3 | NM | -8.3 | -21.8 | | -22.4 | -22.8 |
| | 17.6 | 13.0 | 31.2 | 10.3 | 5.5 | | 11.8 | 17.1 |
| (27) | 6.6 (55) | 4.5 (43) | 6.1 (30) | 4.1 | 1.3 | EBIT/Interest | (169) 4.8 (132) | 6.7 |
| | 1.7 | 2.2 | 1.8 | .8 | -.1 | | 1.8 | 1.5 |
| | | 5.2 | 16.8 | | | Net Profit + Depr., Dep., | 5.9 | 5.0 |
| | (11) 1.8 | (13) 3.5 | | | | Amort./Cur. Mat. L/T/D | (34) 2.6 (17) 3.2 |
| | 1.4 | 2.2 | | | | | 1.7 | 1.7 |
| .1 | .4 | 1.0 | .5 | 1.3 | 3.8 | | .8 | .8 |
| 3.5 | 2.5 | 1.8 | 1.2 | 3.3 | -5.7 | Fixed/Worth | 2.1 | 2.0 |
| -.4 | 21.9 | -11.3 | 2.9 | -7.2 | -1.7 | | 24.5 | -13.0 |
| .6 | 1.0 | 1.0 | .4 | .8 | 3.9 | | .9 | 1.1 |
| 4.6 | 2.8 | 1.8 | 1.3 | 3.7 | -8.8 | Debt/Worth | 2.6 | 2.6 |
| -2.2 | 814.0 | -14.5 | 3.2 | -9.4 | -4.1 | | 85.1 | -18.4 |
| | 96.0 | 79.1 | 49.5 | 43.6 | 60.8 | % Profit Before Taxes/Tangible | 51.3 | 71.3 |
| (24) | 43.2 (43) | 34.8 (43) | 21.9 (17) | 21.6 (12) | 20.9 | Net Worth | (145) 26.6 (107) 39.5 |
| | 27.6 | 10.6 | 9.0 | 16.2 | 4.4 | | 10.1 | 17.4 |
| 41.6 | 32.0 | 21.9 | 17.8 | 12.9 | 7.3 | % Profit Before Taxes/Total | 19.7 | 25.3 |
| 15.3 | 14.4 | 9.9 | 7.9 | 7.5 | 1.9 | Assets | 7.4 | 11.7 |
| -11.7 | 3.0 | 3.8 | 1.3 | -.4 | -5.6 | | 1.3 | 1.3 |
| 58.8 | 34.8 | 9.4 | 5.2 | 2.8 | 2.3 | | 7.4 | 7.9 |
| 12.7 | 4.9 | 3.4 | 2.5 | 2.0 | 1.7 | Sales/Net Fixed Assets | 3.3 | 3.0 |
| 5.3 | 2.2 | 2.0 | 1.6 | 1.4 | 1.3 | | 1.9 | 1.7 |
| 5.7 | 4.6 | 3.0 | 1.8 | 1.1 | 1.0 | | 2.8 | 2.5 |
| 3.8 | 2.8 | 1.9 | 1.3 | .8 | .8 | Sales/Total Assets | 1.6 | 1.6 |
| 1.4 | 1.4 | 1.3 | .9 | .6 | .6 | | 1.2 | .9 |
| | 4.2 | 4.3 | 4.9 | 5.9 | 5.2 | | 5.4 | 5.0 |
| (13) | 8.5 (40) | 6.9 (44) | 6.6 (17) | 8.5 (11) | 6.6 | % Depr., Dep., Amort./Sales | (130) 7.9 (95) 7.3 |
| | 20.6 | 10.0 | 10.8 | 12.6 | 13.5 | | 11.1 | 11.0 |
| | 1.8 | 1.9 | | | | % Officers', Directors' | 1.4 | 1.5 |
| (13) | 5.2 (21) | 2.3 | | | | Owners' Comp/Sales | (67) 3.0 (48) 3.2 |
| | 9.1 | 3.7 | | | | | 5.3 | 6.2 |
| 8769M | 124187M | 670150M | 1530574M | 1692830M | 3862046M | Net Sales ($) | 5050774M | 3502637M |
| 2612M | 34383M | 316439M | 1193186M | 1850331M | 4806865M | Total Assets ($) | 4028243M | 2680699M |

© RMA 2024

M = $ thousand    MM = $ million
See Pages viii through xx for Explanation of Ratios and Data

# ADMIN & WASTE MANAGEMENT SERVICES—Solid Waste Collection  NAICS 562111

## Comparative Historical Data | Current Data Sorted by Sales

| | | | | Type of Statement | | | | | | |
|---|---|---|---|---|---|---|---|---|---|---|
| | 7 | 19 | 33 | Unqualified | | 2 | 1 | 2 | 2 | 26 |
| | 11 | 14 | 11 | Reviewed | | 2 | | 2 | 5 | 4 |
| | 15 | 17 | 8 | Compiled | 1 | | | 1 | 6 | |
| | 31 | 33 | 33 | Tax Returns | 4 | 5 | 7 | 9 | 7 | 1 |
| | 94 | 119 | 119 | Other | 7 | 17 | 6 | 14 | 21 | 54 |
| | 4/1/21-3/31/22 | 4/1/22-3/31/23 | 4/1/23-3/31/24 | | | 43 (4/1-9/30/23) | | | 161 (10/1/23-3/31/24) | |
| | ALL | ALL | ALL | | 0-1MM | 1-3MM | 3-5MM | 5-10MM | 10-25MM | 25MM & OVER |
| | 158 | 202 | 204 | NUMBER OF STATEMENTS | 12 | 24 | 14 | 28 | 41 | 85 |
| | % | % | % | ASSETS | % | % | % | % | % | % |
| | 16.5 | 18.0 | 15.1 | Cash & Equivalents | 16.9 | 13.3 | 24.7 | 20.2 | 21.1 | 9.3 |
| | 14.7 | 13.4 | 13.0 | Trade Receivables (net) | 16.7 | 9.1 | 12.7 | 9.5 | 15.4 | 13.8 |
| | .9 | .6 | .5 | Inventory | .2 | .0 | .2 | .1 | .5 | .8 |
| | 3.5 | 4.5 | 3.1 | All Other Current | 8.6 | .6 | 2.0 | 1.9 | 3.5 | 3.5 |
| | 35.6 | 36.5 | 31.8 | Total Current | 42.3 | 23.0 | 39.7 | 31.6 | 40.5 | 27.3 |
| | 47.2 | 45.1 | 47.1 | Fixed Assets (net) | 43.0 | 68.2 | 39.6 | 45.7 | 43.9 | 45.0 |
| | 9.5 | 10.0 | 12.8 | Intangibles (net) | 6.3 | 2.8 | 3.7 | 10.0 | 8.8 | 21.0 |
| | 7.7 | 8.5 | 8.3 | All Other Non-Current | 8.3 | 6.0 | 17.1 | 12.8 | 6.8 | 6.7 |
| | 100.0 | 100.0 | 100.0 | Total | 100.0 | 100.0 | 100.0 | 100.0 | 100.0 | 100.0 |
| | | | | LIABILITIES | | | | | | |
| | 4.7 | 4.0 | 3.1 | Notes Payable-Short Term | .8 | 5.9 | .7 | .8 | 5.2 | 2.8 |
| | 7.0 | 6.8 | 6.5 | Cur. Mat.-L.T.D. | 10.9 | 7.0 | 15.5 | 7.9 | 6.3 | 3.9 |
| | 6.6 | 7.0 | 7.2 | Trade Payables | 8.1 | 4.2 | 6.1 | 4.1 | 10.7 | 7.3 |
| | .0 | .2 | .0 | Income Taxes Payable | .0 | .0 | .0 | .0 | .0 | .1 |
| | 5.0 | 7.5 | 8.0 | All Other Current | 11.9 | 11.7 | 6.9 | 7.6 | 8.0 | 6.8 |
| | 23.3 | 25.6 | 24.9 | Total Current | 31.6 | 28.8 | 29.2 | 20.5 | 30.3 | 20.9 |
| | 42.8 | 39.3 | 37.6 | Long-Term Debt | 54.5 | 48.4 | 31.7 | 51.1 | 27.4 | 33.6 |
| | .5 | .3 | .6 | Deferred Taxes | .0 | .0 | .4 | .0 | .8 | 1.0 |
| | 8.8 | 8.1 | 4.7 | All Other Non-Current | .0 | 9.1 | .8 | 2.1 | 1.6 | 7.0 |
| | 24.6 | 26.7 | 32.3 | Net Worth | 13.9 | 13.7 | 37.8 | 26.4 | 40.1 | 37.5 |
| | 100.0 | 100.0 | 100.0 | Total Liabilities & Net Worth | 100.0 | 100.0 | 100.0 | 100.0 | 100.0 | 100.0 |
| | | | | INCOME DATA | | | | | | |
| | 100.0 | 100.0 | 100.0 | Net Sales | 100.0 | 100.0 | 100.0 | 100.0 | 100.0 | 100.0 |
| | | | | Gross Profit | | | | | | |
| | 91.8 | 90.3 | 91.1 | Operating Expenses | 88.6 | 90.3 | 83.8 | 91.4 | 93.0 | 92.0 |
| | 8.2 | 9.7 | 8.9 | Operating Profit | 11.4 | 9.7 | 16.2 | 8.6 | 7.0 | 8.0 |
| | .5 | 1.0 | 2.3 | All Other Expenses (net) | 4.7 | 3.9 | 3.2 | .1 | .4 | 3.1 |
| | 7.7 | 8.7 | 6.5 | Profit Before Taxes | 6.7 | 5.8 | 13.1 | 8.5 | 6.6 | 5.0 |
| | | | | RATIOS | | | | | | |
| | 2.8 | 3.0 | 2.6 | | 3.7 | 2.2 | 3.0 | 3.3 | 3.1 | 2.2 |
| | 1.4 | 1.6 | 1.4 | Current | 1.5 | .8 | 1.5 | 1.6 | 1.5 | 1.3 |
| | .9 | .8 | .8 | | .5 | .2 | .4 | 1.1 | 1.0 | .8 |
| | 2.5 | 2.8 | 2.2 | | 3.1 | 2.0 | 3.0 | 3.3 | 3.0 | 1.8 |
| | 1.3 | 1.4 | 1.2 | Quick | 1.0 | .8 | 1.5 | 1.5 | 1.3 | 1.1 |
| | .8 | .7 | .7 | | .4 | .2 | .4 | 1.1 | .8 | .7 |
| | | | | | 0 UND | 0 UND | 0 UND | 0 UND | 6 59.3 | 28 12.9 |
| 9 | 41.2 | 9 40.5 | 11 34.2 | Sales/Receivables | 0 UND | 11 33.7 | 18 19.9 | 22 16.3 | 25 14.4 | 38 9.7 |
| 27 | 13.3 | 28 12.9 | 30 12.2 | | 49 7.5 | 35 10.5 | 39 9.3 | 31 11.9 | 38 9.7 | 48 7.6 |
| 44 | 8.3 | 43 8.5 | 44 8.3 | | | | | | | |
| | | | | Cost of Sales/Inventory | | | | | | |
| | | | | Cost of Sales/Payables | | | | | | |
| | 9.4 | 6.7 | 6.9 | | 3.0 | 11.9 | 7.1 | 5.1 | 6.2 | 7.4 |
| | 22.0 | 18.7 | 24.4 | Sales/Working Capital | 17.6 | -68.3 | 34.2 | 19.6 | 18.7 | 22.7 |
| | -103.2 | -46.6 | -33.2 | | -16.7 | -7.1 | -18.7 | 132.2 | 490.2 | -33.0 |
| | 20.7 | 21.4 | 12.1 | | | 11.9 | 31.1 | 11.0 | 13.9 | 11.3 |
| (141) | 7.1 | (178) 6.8 | (187) 4.1 | EBIT/Interest | (22) 4.2 | (13) 17.6 | (26) 3.8 | (37) 5.9 | (81) 2.7 | |
| | 2.3 | 1.9 | 1.2 | | | 1.6 | 3.7 | 1.7 | 3.2 | .2 |
| | 7.6 | 12.7 | 9.0 | Net Profit + Depr., Dep., | | | | | 4.9 | 9.0 |
| (19) | 3.3 | (45) 3.3 | (43) 2.7 | Amort./Cur. Mat. L/T/D | | | | (10) 2.5 | (23) 2.3 | |
| | 2.9 | 2.0 | 1.6 | | | | | | 1.7 | 1.4 |
| | .7 | .7 | .9 | | .3 | 1.9 | .4 | 1.2 | .6 | 1.2 |
| | 2.0 | 1.7 | 2.3 | Fixed/Worth | 5.9 | 3.2 | .7 | 2.4 | 1.4 | 3.8 |
| | -44.4 | -6.8 | -10.4 | | -4.7 | NM | NM | NM | 2.9 | -3.7 |
| | .9 | .7 | 1.0 | | .7 | 1.0 | .8 | 1.4 | .7 | 1.0 |
| | 2.2 | 2.4 | 2.4 | Debt/Worth | 6.2 | 2.8 | 1.6 | 2.3 | 1.7 | 4.0 |
| | -17.6 | -8.8 | -13.9 | | -12.9 | NM | NM | NM | 3.0 | -6.9 |
| | 73.3 | 59.7 | 65.6 | % Profit Before Taxes/Tangible | | 71.9 | 147.4 | 103.3 | 46.5 | 52.8 |
| (114) | 43.0 | (137) 30.0 | (145) 27.8 | Net Worth | (18) 23.3 | (11) 79.1 | (21) 37.0 | (33) 29.2 | (54) 22.6 | |
| | 19.2 | 16.1 | 12.2 | | | 2.3 | 34.9 | 3.5 | 10.2 | 14.6 |
| | 28.2 | 21.9 | 18.0 | % Profit Before Taxes/Total | 20.1 | 18.3 | 49.9 | 20.3 | 21.0 | 14.3 |
| | 12.5 | 10.5 | 7.8 | Assets | 9.9 | 6.0 | 23.2 | 9.6 | 9.6 | 5.5 |
| | 4.2 | 3.2 | 1.0 | | -15.4 | .9 | 4.9 | 1.3 | 5.2 | -2.6 |
| | 9.1 | 9.1 | 7.4 | | 28.8 | 3.9 | 28.4 | 9.5 | 11.6 | 3.4 |
| | 3.3 | 3.5 | 2.7 | Sales/Net Fixed Assets | 4.6 | 2.2 | 4.2 | 2.8 | 5.0 | 2.2 |
| | 1.9 | 1.7 | 1.7 | | 1.8 | .7 | 2.8 | 1.7 | 2.2 | 1.5 |
| | 2.7 | 2.7 | 2.2 | | 2.8 | 2.8 | 4.6 | 2.4 | 3.3 | 1.5 |
| | 1.6 | 1.5 | 1.4 | Sales/Total Assets | 1.4 | 1.5 | 1.9 | 1.5 | 2.0 | 1.0 |
| | 1.1 | .9 | .8 | | 1.0 | .6 | 1.4 | .7 | 1.4 | .7 |
| | 4.9 | 4.5 | 4.8 | | | 5.6 | | 4.8 | 4.3 | 5.2 |
| (100) | 7.4 | (125) 7.0 | (131) 7.2 | % Depr., Dep., Amort./Sales | (13) 10.3 | | (19) 7.3 | (29) 6.5 | (54) 6.9 | |
| | 11.0 | 9.4 | 11.8 | | | 19.6 | | 13.0 | 9.6 | 12.0 |
| | 1.6 | 1.4 | 1.8 | % Officers', Directors' | | | | 1.0 | 1.7 | |
| (47) | 2.8 | (49) 2.2 | (49) 2.7 | Owners' Comp/Sales | | (10) 1.8 | (17) 2.1 | | | |
| | 5.6 | 4.8 | 5.5 | | | | | 7.0 | 4.2 | |
| | 4551461M | 6632212M | 7888556M | Net Sales ($) | 7294M | 47414M | 55774M | 216615M | 719505M | 6841954M |
| | 4322834M | 6722009M | 8203816M | Total Assets ($) | 5921M | 90222M | 46927M | 204034M | 447656M | 7409056M |

© RMA 2024  
M = $ thousand  MM = $ million  
See Pages viii through xx for Explanation of Ratios and Data

# ADMIN & WASTE MANAGEMENT SERVICES—Other Waste Collection  NAICS 562119

## Current Data Sorted by Assets | Comparative Historical Data

| | | | | | | Type of Statement | | |
|---|---|---|---|---|---|---|---|---|
| | | | 1 | | 1 | Unqualified | 3 | 1 |
| | | | 3 | | | Reviewed | 1 | |
| | | | 1 | | | Compiled | | |
| 1 | 4 | 2 | 12 | | | Tax Returns | 4 | 2 |
| 2 | 7 | 10 | 39 | 3 | | Other | 11 | 4 |
| | 8 (4/1-9/30/23) | | (10/1/23-3/31/24) | | | | 36 | 21 |
| | | | | | | | 4/1/19- | 4/1/20- |
| | | | | | | | 3/31/20 | 3/31/21 |
| 0-500M | 500M-2MM | 2-10MM | 10-50MM | 50-100MM | 100-250MM | | ALL | ALL |
| 3 | 11 | 12 | 17 | 3 | 1 | NUMBER OF STATEMENTS | 55 | 28 |
| % | % | % | % | % | % | ASSETS | % | % |
| | 19.5 | 12.7 | 9.7 | | | Cash & Equivalents | 15.4 | 14.7 |
| | 24.0 | 18.1 | 13.1 | | | Trade Receivables (net) | 20.8 | 14.1 |
| | .7 | .0 | .4 | | | Inventory | 2.3 | 1.0 |
| | 3.4 | 13.2 | 1.1 | | | All Other Current | 3.8 | 2.6 |
| | 47.6 | 44.0 | 24.3 | | | Total Current | 42.3 | 32.4 |
| | 32.6 | 43.8 | 51.0 | | | Fixed Assets (net) | 43.1 | 41.3 |
| | 11.9 | .1 | 15.3 | | | Intangibles (net) | 6.9 | 21.4 |
| | 7.9 | 12.1 | 9.3 | | | All Other Non-Current | 7.9 | 4.8 |
| | 100.0 | 100.0 | 100.0 | | | Total | 100.0 | 100.0 |
| | | | | | | LIABILITIES | | |
| | 4.3 | 3.7 | 6.6 | | | Notes Payable-Short Term | 5.4 | 14.8 |
| | 11.4 | 4.0 | 3.4 | | | Cur. Mat.-L.T.D. | 8.0 | 7.7 |
| | 14.8 | 12.5 | 9.1 | | | Trade Payables | 10.1 | 8.0 |
| | .0 | .1 | .0 | | | Income Taxes Payable | .0 | .0 |
| | 7.1 | 32.8 | 4.4 | | | All Other Current | 9.4 | 6.5 |
| | 37.7 | 53.0 | 23.5 | | | Total Current | 32.9 | 37.0 |
| | 64.5 | 28.5 | 33.6 | | | Long-Term Debt | 30.9 | 42.9 |
| | .0 | .0 | .4 | | | Deferred Taxes | .0 | .3 |
| | .0 | 7.5 | 6.9 | | | All Other Non-Current | 8.8 | 8.7 |
| | -2.1 | 11.1 | 35.6 | | | Net Worth | 27.2 | 11.1 |
| | 100.0 | 100.0 | 100.0 | | | Total Liabilities & Net Worth | 100.0 | 100.0 |
| | | | | | | INCOME DATA | | |
| | 100.0 | 100.0 | 100.0 | | | Net Sales | 100.0 | 100.0 |
| | | | | | | Gross Profit | | |
| | 90.5 | 76.3 | 88.5 | | | Operating Expenses | 91.5 | 93.9 |
| | 9.5 | 23.7 | 11.5 | | | Operating Profit | 8.5 | 6.1 |
| | .2 | .0 | 1.7 | | | All Other Expenses (net) | 1.3 | 1.2 |
| | 9.3 | 23.7 | 9.8 | | | Profit Before Taxes | 7.3 | 4.9 |
| | | | | | | RATIOS | | |
| | 1.7 | 3.7 | 2.8 | | | | 2.4 | 2.0 |
| | 1.0 | 1.9 | 1.1 | | | Current | 1.4 | 1.3 |
| | .8 | .9 | .6 | | | | .7 | .5 |
| | 1.7 | 2.7 | 2.6 | | | | 2.3 | 1.8 |
| | 1.0 | 1.5 | 1.1 | | | Quick | 1.1 | 1.1 |
| | .7 | .9 | .6 | | | | .5 | .5 |
| 16 | 23.3 | 22 16.9 | 18 20.8 | | | | 19 19.5 | 1 266.5 |
| 30 | 12.3 | 33 11.1 | 28 13.1 | | | Sales/Receivables | 37 9.8 | 35 10.5 |
| 49 | 7.4 | 83 4.4 | 40 9.1 | | | | 56 6.5 | 54 6.8 |
| | | | | | | Cost of Sales/Inventory | | |
| | | | | | | Cost of Sales/Payables | | |
| | 18.2 | 3.4 | 9.1 | | | | 7.9 | 7.9 |
| | -514.0 | 9.2 | 42.1 | | | Sales/Working Capital | 41.6 | 21.3 |
| | -15.3 | NM | -14.3 | | | | -22.3 | -8.4 |
| | | 46.8 | 9.4 | | | | 23.5 | 10.1 |
| | (10) | 11.6 | (15) 3.8 | | | EBIT/Interest | (48) 6.0 | (22) 3.4 |
| | | 4.3 | 1.5 | | | | .9 | .1 |
| | | | | | | Net Profit + Depr., Dep., Amort./Cur. Mat. L/T/D | | |
| | .0 | .7 | 1.1 | | | | .6 | .6 |
| | 1.3 | .9 | 2.4 | | | Fixed/Worth | 1.5 | 1.9 |
| | -.5 | 2.9 | -26.2 | | | | 8.5 | -2.7 |
| | .5 | .6 | 1.2 | | | | 1.1 | 1.0 |
| | 2.6 | 1.9 | 3.4 | | | Debt/Worth | 1.9 | 3.9 |
| | -1.9 | 5.1 | -43.0 | | | | 11.2 | -2.4 |
| | | 97.3 | 93.9 | | | | 90.1 | 112.0 |
| | (11) | 65.7 | (12) 41.9 | | | % Profit Before Taxes/Tangible Net Worth | (42) 36.1 | (15) 35.4 |
| | | 42.2 | 23.2 | | | | 10.1 | 10.5 |
| | 30.2 | 36.9 | 25.3 | | | | 36.9 | 18.5 |
| | 13.3 | 23.4 | 14.4 | | | % Profit Before Taxes/Total Assets | 10.1 | 6.3 |
| | 2.0 | 11.8 | 3.5 | | | | .4 | -3.6 |
| | 88.1 | 14.2 | 5.0 | | | | 25.7 | 15.8 |
| | 9.3 | 3.3 | 3.2 | | | Sales/Net Fixed Assets | 4.8 | 3.4 |
| | 1.6 | 1.3 | 1.9 | | | | 2.2 | 1.9 |
| | 4.1 | 2.3 | 1.9 | | | | 3.0 | 2.6 |
| | 1.8 | 1.4 | 1.4 | | | Sales/Total Assets | 2.1 | 1.1 |
| | 1.0 | 1.0 | 1.1 | | | | 1.3 | .8 |
| | | | 2.8 | | | | 2.3 | |
| | | (14) | 7.6 | | | % Depr., Dep., Amort./Sales | (37) 7.6 | |
| | | | 12.6 | | | | 10.0 | |
| | | | | | | % Officers', Directors', Owners' Comp/Sales | 1.4 | |
| | | | | | | | (22) 3.1 | |
| | | | | | | | 4.3 | |
| 2770M | 45409M | 75652M | 659292M | 210956M | 152743M | Net Sales ($) | 1068099M | 1311914M |
| 851M | 13660M | 48801M | 415520M | 214667M | 146247M | Total Assets ($) | 684295M | 1348614M |

© RMA 2024  M = $ thousand   MM = $ million
See Pages viii through xx for Explanation of Ratios and Data

## ADMIN & WASTE MANAGEMENT SERVICES—Other Waste Collection  NAICS 562119

### Comparative Historical Data | Current Data Sorted by Sales

| Comparative Historical Data | | | | | Current Data Sorted by Sales | | | | | |
|---|---|---|---|---|---|---|---|---|---|---|
| | 4 | 2 | **Type of Statement** | | | | | | 2 | |
| 2 | 2 | 3 | Unqualified | | | | | | 3 | |
| 1 | 1 | 1 | Reviewed | | | | | 1 | | |
| 6 | 11 | 7 | Compiled | 2 | 1 | | 1 | 3 | | |
| 21 | 30 | 34 | Tax Returns | 3 | 5 | 7 | 6 | 6 | 9 | |
| 4/1/21-3/31/22 ALL | 4/1/22-3/31/23 ALL | 4/1/23-3/31/24 ALL | Other | 0-1MM | 1-3MM  8 (4/1-9/30/23) | 3-5MM | 5-10MM  39 (10/1/23-3/31/24) | 10-25MM | 25MM & OVER |
| 30 | 48 | 47 | **NUMBER OF STATEMENTS** | 5 | 6 | 7 | 5 | 10 | 14 |
| % | % | % | **ASSETS** | % | % | % | % | % | % |
| 28.0 | 18.9 | 13.4 | Cash & Equivalents | | | | | 8.5 | 11.9 |
| 14.7 | 14.1 | 17.3 | Trade Receivables (net) | | | | | 19.6 | 11.7 |
| 2.8 | 2.0 | .3 | Inventory | | | | | .5 | .4 |
| 5.4 | 4.2 | 4.8 | All Other Current | | | | | 7.3 | 1.0 |
| 50.9 | 39.2 | 35.7 | Total Current | | | | | 35.8 | 25.1 |
| 34.3 | 43.9 | 44.1 | Fixed Assets (net) | | | | | 52.4 | 43.8 |
| 10.3 | 8.8 | 11.2 | Intangibles (net) | | | | | 6.0 | 20.9 |
| 4.4 | 8.1 | 9.0 | All Other Non-Current | | | | | 5.8 | 10.2 |
| 100.0 | 100.0 | 100.0 | Total | | | | | 100.0 | 100.0 |
| | | | **LIABILITIES** | | | | | | |
| 13.0 | 8.6 | 6.7 | Notes Payable-Short Term | | | | | 11.0 | 5.6 |
| 8.3 | 8.5 | 5.3 | Cur. Mat.-L.T.D. | | | | | 2.3 | 3.8 |
| 10.6 | 9.6 | 11.8 | Trade Payables | | | | | 12.5 | 9.5 |
| .0 | .0 | .1 | Income Taxes Payable | | | | | .0 | .0 |
| 17.6 | 6.8 | 12.6 | All Other Current | | | | | 3.1 | 4.9 |
| 49.4 | 33.6 | 36.4 | Total Current | | | | | 28.9 | 23.8 |
| 39.1 | 51.8 | 43.3 | Long-Term Debt | | | | | 24.7 | 36.6 |
| .1 | .2 | .3 | Deferred Taxes | | | | | .7 | .5 |
| 5.7 | 7.9 | 4.9 | All Other Non-Current | | | | | .7 | 9.1 |
| 5.7 | 6.5 | 15.1 | Net Worth | | | | | 44.9 | 29.9 |
| 100.0 | 100.0 | 100.0 | Total Liabilities & Net Worth | | | | | 100.0 | 100.0 |
| | | | **INCOME DATA** | | | | | | |
| 100.0 | 100.0 | 100.0 | Net Sales | | | | | 100.0 | 100.0 |
| | | | Gross Profit | | | | | | |
| 87.7 | 88.9 | 86.0 | Operating Expenses | | | | | 81.9 | 90.6 |
| 12.3 | 11.1 | 14.0 | Operating Profit | | | | | 18.1 | 9.4 |
| -.5 | 1.3 | .9 | All Other Expenses (net) | | | | | 1.3 | 1.5 |
| 12.8 | 9.8 | 13.1 | Profit Before Taxes | | | | | 16.8 | 7.8 |
| | | | **RATIOS** | | | | | | |
| 2.8 | 2.3 | 2.6 | Current | | | | | 3.9 | 1.8 |
| 1.4 | 1.4 | 1.1 | | | | | | 1.6 | 1.2 |
| .6 | .5 | .6 | | | | | | .6 | .6 |
| 1.7 | 2.0 | 2.0 | Quick | | | | | 2.3 | 1.6 |
| 1.0 | 1.3 | 1.1 | | | | | | 1.5 | 1.2 |
| .5 | .5 | .6 | | | | | | .5 | .6 |
| 0   UND | 7   52.2 | 18   20.8 | Sales/Receivables | | | | | 20   18.0 | 14   25.8 |
| 15   25.1 | 20   18.6 | 30   12.2 | | | | | | 38   9.5 | 23   16.2 |
| 31   11.7 | 45   8.1 | 47   7.7 | | | | | | 78   4.7 | 33   11.1 |
| | | | Cost of Sales/Inventory | | | | | | |
| | | | Cost of Sales/Payables | | | | | | |
| 7.4 | 10.3 | 7.9 | Sales/Working Capital | | | | | 7.5 | 12.9 |
| 27.3 | 25.3 | 45.0 | | | | | | 30.5 | 41.5 |
| -17.8 | -12.4 | -14.2 | | | | | | -10.8 | -14.9 |
| 36.4 | 20.4 | 13.8 | EBIT/Interest | | | | | | 16.4 |
| (24) 11.4 | (38) 7.6 | (39) 4.5 | | | | | | | 5.6 |
| 4.3 | .7 | 2.2 | | | | | | | 2.0 |
| | | | Net Profit + Depr., Dep., Amort./Cur. Mat. L/T/D | | | | | | |
| .3 | .7 | .8 | Fixed/Worth | | | | | .6 | 1.3 |
| 1.4 | 2.0 | 2.0 | | | | | | 1.2 | 5.3 |
| UND | NM | -1.9 | | | | | | 8.4 | -4.9 |
| .7 | .9 | 1.0 | Debt/Worth | | | | | .2 | 1.5 |
| 2.9 | 2.9 | 2.9 | | | | | | 1.6 | 9.5 |
| -9.8 | -10.5 | -3.7 | | | | | | 8.6 | -7.3 |
| 164.1 | 52.4 | 96.9 | % Profit Before Taxes/Tangible Net Worth | | | | | | |
| (21) 47.1 | (33) 38.6 | (32) 44.5 | | | | | | | |
| 22.7 | 16.2 | 23.2 | | | | | | | |
| 59.1 | 35.0 | 27.2 | % Profit Before Taxes/Total Assets | | | | | 30.4 | 22.5 |
| 20.3 | 13.3 | 14.4 | | | | | | 21.0 | 12.3 |
| 5.8 | -.2 | 5.0 | | | | | | 5.3 | 4.3 |
| 50.9 | 9.7 | 14.6 | Sales/Net Fixed Assets | | | | | 20.9 | 8.8 |
| 9.7 | 3.6 | 3.9 | | | | | | 2.1 | 4.0 |
| 3.2 | 1.8 | 1.6 | | | | | | .8 | 2.5 |
| 4.6 | 3.9 | 2.4 | Sales/Total Assets | | | | | 1.9 | 2.0 |
| 3.0 | 1.5 | 1.5 | | | | | | 1.4 | 1.5 |
| 2.0 | .9 | 1.0 | | | | | | .6 | 1.1 |
| 2.2 | .4 | 3.6 | % Depr., Dep., Amort./Sales | | | | | | .5 |
| (17) 5.8 | (23) 7.0 | (22) 7.9 | | | | | | (10) | 5.4 |
| 11.9 | 13.1 | 12.6 | | | | | | | 8.6 |
| 1.9 | .6 | 1.6 | % Officers', Directors' Owners' Comp/Sales | | | | | | |
| (11) 3.7 | (17) 2.9 | (14) 2.5 | | | | | | | |
| 5.9 | 4.4 | 4.8 | | | | | | | |
| 675484M | 1071546M | 1146822M | Net Sales ($) | 2949M | 10835M | 27617M | 36071M | 160050M | 909300M |
| 200003M | 838088M | 839746M | Total Assets ($) | 4761M | 6262M | 18651M | 18789M | 168595M | 622688M |

© RMA 2024   M = $ thousand   MM = $ million
See Pages viii through xx for Explanation of Ratios and Data

# ADMIN & WASTE MANAGEMENT SERVICES—Hazardous Waste Treatment and Disposal  NAICS 562211

## Current Data Sorted by Assets | Comparative Historical Data

| | | | | | | Type of Statement | | |
|---|---|---|---|---|---|---|---|---|
| | | | | 2 | 1 | Unqualified | 4 | 5 |
| | | | 2 | 1 | | Reviewed | 4 | 6 |
| | | 2 | 1 | | | Compiled | 2 | |
| 2 | 3 | 2 | | | | Tax Returns | 7 | 1 |
| 2 | 3 | 10 | 5 | 3 | 1 | Other | 22 | 13 |
| | 5 (4/1-9/30/23) | | 33 (10/1/23-3/31/24) | | | | 4/1/19-3/31/20 | 4/1/20-3/31/21 |
| 0-500M | 500M-2MM | 2-10MM | 10-50MM | 50-100MM | 100-250MM | | ALL | ALL |
| 4 | 6 | 14 | 9 | 4 | 1 | NUMBER OF STATEMENTS | 39 | 25 |
| % | % | % | % | % | % | ASSETS | % | % |
| | | 14.1 | | | | Cash & Equivalents | 9.9 | 21.8 |
| | | 36.0 | | | | Trade Receivables (net) | 27.3 | 16.6 |
| | | 2.8 | | | | Inventory | 1.7 | 1.4 |
| | | 5.4 | | | | All Other Current | 2.1 | 3.7 |
| | | 58.2 | | | | Total Current | 41.0 | 43.4 |
| | | 26.2 | | | | Fixed Assets (net) | 39.1 | 39.2 |
| | | 4.5 | | | | Intangibles (net) | 9.8 | 10.8 |
| | | 11.1 | | | | All Other Non-Current | 10.2 | 6.6 |
| | | 100.0 | | | | Total | 100.0 | 100.0 |
| | | | | | | LIABILITIES | | |
| | | 3.2 | | | | Notes Payable-Short Term | 4.3 | 3.7 |
| | | 2.9 | | | | Cur. Mat.-L.T.D. | 5.9 | 10.6 |
| | | 12.2 | | | | Trade Payables | 8.5 | 7.8 |
| | | .1 | | | | Income Taxes Payable | .2 | .2 |
| | | 16.0 | | | | All Other Current | 12.7 | 15.0 |
| | | 34.5 | | | | Total Current | 31.5 | 37.2 |
| | | 20.1 | | | | Long-Term Debt | 27.9 | 37.9 |
| | | .0 | | | | Deferred Taxes | .8 | 1.0 |
| | | 4.3 | | | | All Other Non-Current | 13.4 | 6.1 |
| | | 41.1 | | | | Net Worth | 26.4 | 17.8 |
| | | 100.0 | | | | Total Liabilities & Net Worth | 100.0 | 100.0 |
| | | | | | | INCOME DATA | | |
| | | 100.0 | | | | Net Sales | 100.0 | 100.0 |
| | | | | | | Gross Profit | | |
| | | 90.2 | | | | Operating Expenses | 89.1 | 91.6 |
| | | 9.8 | | | | Operating Profit | 10.9 | 8.4 |
| | | -.2 | | | | All Other Expenses (net) | 3.1 | .4 |
| | | 10.0 | | | | Profit Before Taxes | 7.8 | 7.9 |
| | | | | | | RATIOS | | |
| | | 4.3 | | | | | 2.7 | 2.9 |
| | | 1.6 | | | | Current | 1.4 | 1.3 |
| | | .9 | | | | | .7 | .9 |
| | | 2.8 | | | | | 2.4 | 2.8 |
| | | 1.5 | | | | Quick | 1.2 | 1.3 |
| | | .9 | | | | | .7 | .8 |
| | 27 | 13.5 | | | | | 29 | 12.4 | 8 | 46.8 |
| | 60 | 6.1 | | | | Sales/Receivables | 48 | 7.6 | 42 | 8.7 |
| | 74 | 4.9 | | | | | 78 | 4.7 | 73 | 5.0 |
| | | | | | | Cost of Sales/Inventory | | |
| | | | | | | Cost of Sales/Payables | | |
| | | 4.7 | | | | | 7.7 | 5.2 |
| | | 7.2 | | | | Sales/Working Capital | 15.9 | 23.2 |
| | | -46.4 | | | | | -14.7 | -123.4 |
| | | 29.7 | | | | | 29.5 | 19.5 |
| | (13) | 11.8 | | | | EBIT/Interest | (32) 9.7 | (23) 6.4 |
| | | 4.9 | | | | | 1.2 | 2.7 |
| | | | | | | Net Profit + Depr., Dep., Amort./Cur. Mat. L/T/D | | |
| | | .1 | | | | | .3 | .7 |
| | | .9 | | | | Fixed/Worth | 2.5 | 2.0 |
| | | 1.3 | | | | | -16.3 | -3.9 |
| | | .8 | | | | | .8 | .8 |
| | | 1.3 | | | | Debt/Worth | 3.1 | 2.5 |
| | | 5.7 | | | | | -17.0 | -10.5 |
| | | 86.7 | | | | | 106.0 | 92.1 |
| | (13) | 52.2 | | | | % Profit Before Taxes/Tangible Net Worth | (28) 51.0 | (18) 44.2 |
| | | 21.7 | | | | | 13.9 | 15.3 |
| | | 30.5 | | | | | 21.9 | 26.4 |
| | | 14.6 | | | | % Profit Before Taxes/Total Assets | 8.2 | 14.5 |
| | | 7.2 | | | | | -.5 | -.5 |
| | | 70.4 | | | | | 26.6 | 14.5 |
| | | 9.0 | | | | Sales/Net Fixed Assets | 3.9 | 4.9 |
| | | 3.9 | | | | | 1.3 | 2.3 |
| | | 2.6 | | | | | 3.0 | 2.8 |
| | | 2.0 | | | | Sales/Total Assets | 1.6 | 1.9 |
| | | 1.5 | | | | | .7 | 1.0 |
| | | | | | | | 1.6 | 3.3 |
| | | | | | | % Depr., Dep., Amort./Sales | (29) 3.8 | (16) 5.6 |
| | | | | | | | 10.9 | 12.5 |
| | | | | | | | 2.1 | |
| | | | | | | % Officers', Directors' Owners' Comp/Sales | (11) 2.8 | |
| | | | | | | | 5.3 | |
| 7043M | 25779M | 190153M | 327742M | 428621M | 72920M | Net Sales ($) | 1167031M | 818490M |
| 1303M | 5898M | 84758M | 223042M | 301718M | 105650M | Total Assets ($) | 1025325M | 925746M |

M = $ thousand    MM = $ million
See Pages viii through xx for Explanation of Ratios and Data

© RMA 2024

## ADMIN & WASTE MANAGEMENT SERVICES—Hazardous Waste Treatment and Disposal  NAICS 562211

| Comparative Historical Data | | | | | Current Data Sorted by Sales | | | | | |
|---|---|---|---|---|---|---|---|---|---|---|
| 6 | 4 | 3 | Type of Statement Unqualified | | | | 1 | | 2 | |
| 2 | 4 | 1 | Reviewed | | | | | | 1 | |
| 2 | 2 | 3 | Compiled | | | | 1 | 1 | 1 | |
| 3 | 2 | 7 | Tax Returns | | 2 | 2 | 3 | 4 | 10 | |
| 20 | 26 | 24 | Other | 2 | 1 | 4 | 3 | | | |
| 4/1/21-3/31/22 ALL | 4/1/22-3/31/23 ALL | 4/1/23-3/31/24 ALL | | 5 (4/1-9/30/23) | | | 33 (10/1/23-3/31/24) | | | |
| | | | | 0-1MM | 1-3MM | 3-5MM | 5-10MM | 10-25MM | 25MM & OVER | |
| 33 | 38 | 38 | NUMBER OF STATEMENTS | 2 | 3 | 6 | 8 | 5 | 14 | |
| % | % | % | ASSETS | % | % | % | % | % | % | |
| 13.0 | 15.1 | 19.0 | Cash & Equivalents | | | | | | 10.8 | |
| 11.5 | 18.8 | 25.8 | Trade Receivables (net) | | | | | | 29.2 | |
| 3.0 | 3.1 | 2.1 | Inventory | | | | | | 5.1 | |
| 2.7 | 1.9 | 4.2 | All Other Current | | | | | | 4.7 | |
| 30.3 | 38.9 | 51.2 | Total Current | | | | | | 49.8 | |
| 51.5 | 41.7 | 26.6 | Fixed Assets (net) | | | | | | 22.3 | |
| 8.7 | 12.1 | 9.6 | Intangibles (net) | | | | | | 11.7 | |
| 9.5 | 7.3 | 12.5 | All Other Non-Current | | | | | | 16.2 | |
| 100.0 | 100.0 | 100.0 | Total | | | | | | 100.0 | |
| | | | LIABILITIES | | | | | | | |
| 4.1 | 2.9 | 4.8 | Notes Payable-Short Term | | | | | | 1.2 | |
| 5.3 | 3.1 | 4.4 | Cur. Mat.-L.T.D. | | | | | | 5.3 | |
| 7.1 | 9.9 | 11.6 | Trade Payables | | | | | | 17.1 | |
| .4 | .0 | .4 | Income Taxes Payable | | | | | | .5 | |
| 13.6 | 15.6 | 11.1 | All Other Current | | | | | | 12.1 | |
| 30.6 | 31.5 | 32.3 | Total Current | | | | | | 36.2 | |
| 41.8 | 28.7 | 20.7 | Long-Term Debt | | | | | | 22.1 | |
| .4 | .5 | .1 | Deferred Taxes | | | | | | .2 | |
| 5.1 | 1.7 | 5.6 | All Other Non-Current | | | | | | 9.2 | |
| 22.0 | 37.6 | 41.3 | Net Worth | | | | | | 32.3 | |
| 100.0 | 100.0 | 100.0 | Total Liabilities & Net Worth | | | | | | 100.0 | |
| | | | INCOME DATA | | | | | | | |
| 100.0 | 100.0 | 100.0 | Net Sales | | | | | | 100.0 | |
| | | | Gross Profit | | | | | | 94.6 | |
| 81.5 | 78.3 | 89.4 | Operating Expenses | | | | | | 5.4 | |
| 18.5 | 21.7 | 10.6 | Operating Profit | | | | | | 2.1 | |
| 8.7 | 9.1 | .9 | All Other Expenses (net) | | | | | | 3.3 | |
| 9.9 | 12.6 | 9.7 | Profit Before Taxes | | | | | | | |
| | | | RATIOS | | | | | | | |
| 3.5 | 2.8 | 3.9 | | | | | | | 2.6 | |
| 1.6 | 1.5 | 1.6 | Current | | | | | | 1.2 | |
| .2 | .4 | 1.0 | | | | | | | .9 | |
| 2.4 | 2.4 | 3.1 | | | | | | | 2.2 | |
| 1.4 | 1.4 | 1.5 | Quick | | | | | | .9 | |
| .2 | .3 | .9 | | | | | | | .7 | |
| 24 15.4 | 29 12.6 | 19 19.3 | | | | | | | 32 11.4 | |
| 48 7.6 | 46 8.0 | 39 9.4 | Sales/Receivables | | | | | | 46 7.9 | |
| 63 5.8 | 70 5.2 | 61 6.0 | | | | | | | 59 6.2 | |
| | | | Cost of Sales/Inventory | | | | | | | |
| | | | Cost of Sales/Payables | | | | | | | |
| 4.8 | 4.9 | 5.2 | | | | | | | 6.3 | |
| 12.2 | 14.4 | 11.8 | Sales/Working Capital | | | | | | 57.8 | |
| -4.0 | -1.7 | -214.4 | | | | | | | -42.0 | |
| 16.3 | 49.4 | 29.2 | | | | | | | 18.1 | |
| (24) 5.3 | (26) 20.9 | (30) 8.4 | EBIT/Interest | | | | | | (12) 3.6 | |
| .9 | 5.9 | 3.3 | | | | | | | .6 | |
| 7.4 | 25.0 | | Net Profit + Depr., Dep., | | | | | | | |
| (11) .8 | (12) 1.5 | | Amort./Cur. Mat. L/T/D | | | | | | | |
| .3 | .8 | | | | | | | | | |
| .8 | .4 | .2 | | | | | | | .2 | |
| 3.3 | 1.5 | .6 | Fixed/Worth | | | | | | .6 | |
| -6.8 | -34.0 | 1.7 | | | | | | | NM | |
| .8 | .7 | .7 | | | | | | | .8 | |
| 3.5 | 3.4 | 1.4 | Debt/Worth | | | | | | 1.9 | |
| -11.1 | -37.9 | 26.4 | | | | | | | NM | |
| 66.3 | 75.5 | 77.9 | % Profit Before Taxes/Tangible | | | | | | 65.0 | |
| (23) 39.3 | (28) 46.6 | (31) 29.5 | Net Worth | | | | | | (11) 28.6 | |
| 15.9 | 27.8 | 14.8 | | | | | | | 11.3 | |
| 20.0 | 21.2 | 28.1 | | | | | | | 19.3 | |
| 4.5 | 11.8 | 15.6 | % Profit Before Taxes/Total Assets | | | | | | 7.3 | |
| .0 | 2.9 | 3.3 | | | | | | | -1.1 | |
| 7.5 | 11.3 | 37.9 | | | | | | | 53.9 | |
| 2.3 | 4.2 | 8.3 | Sales/Net Fixed Assets | | | | | | 7.6 | |
| .5 | 1.2 | 4.0 | | | | | | | 4.7 | |
| 1.8 | 1.8 | 3.3 | | | | | | | 3.0 | |
| .8 | 1.2 | 2.1 | Sales/Total Assets | | | | | | 2.0 | |
| .3 | .4 | 1.5 | | | | | | | 1.3 | |
| 4.8 | 1.8 | 2.0 | | | | | | | | |
| (21) 12.3 | (24) 5.9 | (23) 3.9 | % Depr., Dep., Amort./Sales | | | | | | | |
| 21.7 | 18.5 | 6.9 | | | | | | | | |
| | | | % Officers', Directors' Owners' Comp/Sales | | | | | | | |
| 681034M | 1590564M | 1052258M | Net Sales ($) | 1810M | 5706M | 25061M | 60589M | 70417M | 888675M | |
| 800951M | 1567336M | 722369M | Total Assets ($) | 472M | 2426M | 24906M | 70303M | 54403M | 569859M | |

© RMA 2024    M = $ thousand    MM = $ million
See Pages viii through xx for Explanation of Ratios and Data

# ADMIN & WASTE MANAGEMENT SERVICES—Solid Waste Landfill  NAICS 562212

## Current Data Sorted by Assets

| 0-500M | 500M-2MM | 2-10MM | 10-50MM | 50-100MM | 100-250MM | | Comparative Historical Data 4/1/19-3/31/20 ALL | 4/1/20-3/31/21 ALL |
|---|---|---|---|---|---|---|---|---|
| | | | 2 | 1 | | **Type of Statement** | | |
| | | | 1 | | | Unqualified | 5 | 2 |
| | | 3 | 3 | 1 | | Reviewed | 5 | 4 |
| | 1 | 3 | | | | Compiled | 1 | 1 |
| 2 | 1 | 5 | 5 | 3 | 1 | Tax Returns | 7 | 5 |
| | 6 (4/1-9/30/23) | | 23 (10/1/23-3/31/24) | | | Other | 29 | 14 |
| 2 | 2 | 11 | 8 | 5 | 1 | **NUMBER OF STATEMENTS** | 47 | 26 |
| % | % | % | % | % | % | | % | % |
| | | | | | | **ASSETS** | | |
| | | 16.3 | | | | Cash & Equivalents | 11.7 | 14.8 |
| | | 9.7 | | | | Trade Receivables (net) | 13.9 | 12.3 |
| | | .4 | | | | Inventory | 5.1 | 2.8 |
| | | 5.5 | | | | All Other Current | 1.6 | 1.1 |
| | | 31.9 | | | | Total Current | 32.2 | 31.0 |
| | | 44.9 | | | | Fixed Assets (net) | 46.7 | 54.4 |
| | | 9.9 | | | | Intangibles (net) | 10.6 | 7.3 |
| | | 13.3 | | | | All Other Non-Current | 10.4 | 7.4 |
| | | 100.0 | | | | Total | 100.0 | 100.0 |
| | | | | | | **LIABILITIES** | | |
| | | 2.2 | | | | Notes Payable-Short Term | 2.7 | 8.0 |
| | | 5.8 | | | | Cur. Mat.-L.T.D. | 4.5 | 6.6 |
| | | 13.9 | | | | Trade Payables | 8.6 | 5.7 |
| | | .0 | | | | Income Taxes Payable | .1 | .0 |
| | | 7.5 | | | | All Other Current | 5.4 | 5.3 |
| | | 29.4 | | | | Total Current | 21.4 | 25.6 |
| | | 36.7 | | | | Long-Term Debt | 31.1 | 47.5 |
| | | .0 | | | | Deferred Taxes | .4 | .4 |
| | | 16.4 | | | | All Other Non-Current | 7.9 | 6.5 |
| | | 17.5 | | | | Net Worth | 39.2 | 20.1 |
| | | 100.0 | | | | Total Liabilties & Net Worth | 100.0 | 100.0 |
| | | | | | | **INCOME DATA** | | |
| | | 100.0 | | | | Net Sales | 100.0 | 100.0 |
| | | | | | | Gross Profit | | |
| | | 96.6 | | | | Operating Expenses | 90.8 | 93.3 |
| | | 3.4 | | | | Operating Profit | 9.2 | 6.7 |
| | | 1.6 | | | | All Other Expenses (net) | 2.6 | 1.0 |
| | | 1.8 | | | | Profit Before Taxes | 6.7 | 5.8 |
| | | | | | | **RATIOS** | | |
| | | 9.6 | | | | | 2.8 | 3.3 |
| | | .9 | | | | Current | 1.3 | 1.3 |
| | | .6 | | | | | .7 | .5 |
| | | 9.6 | | | | | 2.2 | 3.1 |
| | | .7 | | | | Quick | 1.1 | 1.0 |
| | | .4 | | | | | .5 | .5 |
| | 17 | 21.0 | | | | | 6 57.0 | 16 22.9 |
| | 29 | 12.4 | | | | Sales/Receivables | 30 12.0 | 38 9.6 |
| | 47 | 7.7 | | | | | 51 7.1 | 48 7.6 |
| | | | | | | Cost of Sales/Inventory | | |
| | | | | | | Cost of Sales/Payables | | |
| | | 3.3 | | | | | 7.7 | 5.7 |
| | | -97.3 | | | | Sales/Working Capital | 24.4 | 46.0 |
| | | -5.9 | | | | | -17.3 | -12.6 |
| | | | | | | | 15.9 | 14.9 |
| | | | | | | EBIT/Interest | (41) 3.7 | (23) 3.6 |
| | | | | | | | 1.2 | .7 |
| | | | | | | Net Profit + Depr., Dep., Amort./Cur. Mat. L/T/D | | |
| | | .6 | | | | | .8 | .9 |
| | | 1.6 | | | | Fixed/Worth | 1.3 | 3.0 |
| | | -.8 | | | | | 6.3 | -3.5 |
| | | .8 | | | | | .8 | .9 |
| | | 3.0 | | | | Debt/Worth | 1.8 | 3.5 |
| | | -2.5 | | | | | 7.1 | -5.3 |
| | | | | | | | 44.0 | 63.4 |
| | | | | | | % Profit Before Taxes/Tangible Net Worth | (36) 9.6 | (16) 26.4 |
| | | | | | | | 1.9 | 7.5 |
| | | 8.9 | | | | | 11.8 | 17.5 |
| | | 6.9 | | | | % Profit Before Taxes/Total Assets | 4.0 | 7.2 |
| | | -8.5 | | | | | .4 | -1.1 |
| | | 5.9 | | | | | 4.3 | 3.1 |
| | | 2.0 | | | | Sales/Net Fixed Assets | 2.7 | 2.2 |
| | | 1.1 | | | | | 1.9 | 1.1 |
| | | 1.9 | | | | | 2.1 | 1.6 |
| | | 1.2 | | | | Sales/Total Assets | 1.4 | 1.2 |
| | | .4 | | | | | .9 | .6 |
| | | | | | | | 4.8 | 8.7 |
| | | | | | | % Depr., Dep., Amort./Sales | (35) 8.6 | (20) 13.0 |
| | | | | | | | 13.9 | 17.8 |
| | | | | | | | | 1.2 |
| | | | | | | % Officers', Directors' Owners' Comp/Sales | (13) 2.3 | |
| | | | | | | | 2.9 | |
| 2366M | 3155M | 102322M | 152721M | 367429M | 64306M | Net Sales ($) | 1364333M | 582704M |
| 785M | 3490M | 71610M | 170620M | 312962M | 123998M | Total Assets ($) | 1478784M | 709416M |

M = $ thousand   MM = $ million
See Pages viii through xx for Explanation of Ratios and Data

© RMA 2024

ADMIN & WASTE MANAGEMENT SERVICES—Solid Waste Landfill  NAICS 562212

## Comparative Historical Data / Current Data Sorted by Sales

| | | | | Type of Statement | | | | | | |
|---|---|---|---|---|---|---|---|---|---|---|
| | 1 | 3 | 3 | Unqualified | | 1 | | 1 | | 1 |
| | 3 | 2 | 2 | Reviewed | | | | | 1 | 1 |
| | 2 | 2 | 4 | Compiled | | | | | 3 | 1 |
| | 3 | 4 | 4 | Tax Returns | | 3 | | 2 | 1 | |
| | 14 | 19 | 16 | Other | 1 | 5 | | 23 | 3 | 5 |
| | 4/1/21-3/31/22 ALL | 4/1/22-3/31/23 ALL | 4/1/23-3/31/24 ALL | | 0-1MM | 6 (4/1-9/30/23) 1-3MM | 3-5MM | 23 (10/1/23-3/31/24) 5-10MM | 10-25MM | 25MM & OVER |
| | 23 | 30 | 29 | NUMBER OF STATEMENTS | 1 | 9 | | 3 | 8 | 8 |
| | % | % | % | | % | % | % | % | % | % |
| | | | | **ASSETS** | | | | | | |
| | 21.0 | 14.7 | 14.7 | Cash & Equivalents | | | | | | |
| | 11.1 | 10.2 | 9.7 | Trade Receivables (net) | | | | | | |
| | 1.0 | .4 | .3 | Inventory | | | | | | |
| | 4.7 | 6.7 | 7.3 | All Other Current | | | D | | | |
| | 37.8 | 32.0 | 32.0 | Total Current | | | A | | | |
| | 40.5 | 55.8 | 40.7 | Fixed Assets (net) | | | T | | | |
| | 11.2 | 3.4 | 11.9 | Intangibles (net) | | | A | | | |
| | 10.4 | 8.7 | 15.5 | All Other Non-Current | | | | | | |
| | 100.0 | 100.0 | 100.0 | Total | | | N | | | |
| | | | | **LIABILITIES** | | | O | | | |
| | 2.6 | 7.8 | 3.1 | Notes Payable-Short Term | | | T | | | |
| | 6.3 | 2.8 | 3.8 | Cur. Mat.-L.T.D. | | | | | | |
| | 6.0 | 4.8 | 8.6 | Trade Payables | | | A | | | |
| | .1 | .2 | .2 | Income Taxes Payable | | | V | | | |
| | 6.5 | 13.8 | 5.5 | All Other Current | | | A | | | |
| | 21.5 | 29.5 | 21.3 | Total Current | | | I | | | |
| | 29.1 | 27.2 | 36.5 | Long-Term Debt | | | L | | | |
| | .6 | .0 | .0 | Deferred Taxes | | | A | | | |
| | 12.8 | 16.6 | 19.6 | All Other Non-Current | | | B | | | |
| | 36.1 | 26.7 | 22.6 | Net Worth | | | L | | | |
| | 100.0 | 100.0 | 100.0 | Total Liabilities & Net Worth | | | E | | | |
| | | | | **INCOME DATA** | | | | | | |
| | 100.0 | 100.0 | 100.0 | Net Sales | | | | | | |
| | | | | Gross Profit | | | | | | |
| | 85.1 | 85.1 | 91.6 | Operating Expenses | | | | | | |
| | 14.9 | 14.9 | 8.4 | Operating Profit | | | | | | |
| | -.2 | 3.0 | 2.1 | All Other Expenses (net) | | | | | | |
| | 15.2 | 11.8 | 6.3 | Profit Before Taxes | | | | | | |
| | | | | **RATIOS** | | | | | | |
| | 6.2 | 3.5 | 4.1 | | | | | | | |
| | 1.8 | 1.6 | 1.4 | Current | | | | | | |
| | .6 | .8 | .7 | | | | | | | |
| | 5.9 | 3.3 | 3.3 | | | | | | | |
| | 1.7 | 1.4 | 1.0 | Quick | | | | | | |
| | .5 | .6 | .6 | | | | | | | |
| 18 | 20.3 | 1 | 263.5 | 21 | 17.5 | | | | | |

Sales/Receivables:
| | | | | | | |
|---|---|---|---|---|---|---|
| 18 | 20.3 | 1 | 263.5 | 21 | 17.5 | |
| 35 | 10.3 | 37 | 9.8 | 29 | 12.4 | |
| 54 | 6.8 | 52 | 7.0 | 43 | 8.4 | |

Cost of Sales/Inventory

Cost of Sales/Payables

| | | | | | | |
|---|---|---|---|---|---|---|
| | 1.8 | | 4.9 | | 3.4 | Sales/Working Capital |
| | 7.9 | | 13.1 | | 14.7 | |
| | -13.7 | | -29.3 | | -19.8 | |

| | | | | | | |
|---|---|---|---|---|---|---|
| | 27.4 | | 34.8 | | 9.9 | EBIT/Interest |
| (19) | 5.7 | (27) | 9.4 | (25) | 2.4 | |
| | 2.0 | | 1.1 | | .8 | |

Net Profit + Depr., Dep., Amort./Cur. Mat. L/T/D

| | | | | | | |
|---|---|---|---|---|---|---|
| | .6 | | .8 | | .9 | Fixed/Worth |
| | 1.0 | | 1.3 | | 2.5 | |
| | -6.4 | | 2.0 | | -1.0 | |

| | | | | | | |
|---|---|---|---|---|---|---|
| | .7 | | .6 | | 1.3 | Debt/Worth |
| | 2.3 | | 1.1 | | 3.7 | |
| | -10.5 | | NM | | -4.7 | |

| | | | | | | |
|---|---|---|---|---|---|---|
| | 38.6 | | 50.4 | | 38.6 | % Profit Before Taxes/Tangible Net Worth |
| (15) | 14.8 | (23) | 32.2 | (18) | 12.4 | |
| | 6.9 | | 8.4 | | 4.5 | |

| | | | | | | |
|---|---|---|---|---|---|---|
| | 18.6 | | 25.0 | | 12.0 | % Profit Before Taxes/Total Assets |
| | 8.9 | | 11.1 | | 2.5 | |
| | 1.6 | | -2.1 | | -.3 | |

| | | | | | | |
|---|---|---|---|---|---|---|
| | 4.1 | | 4.0 | | 7.5 | Sales/Net Fixed Assets |
| | 2.5 | | 2.0 | | 2.2 | |
| | 1.2 | | .9 | | 1.1 | |

| | | | | | | |
|---|---|---|---|---|---|---|
| | 1.7 | | 1.8 | | 1.7 | Sales/Total Assets |
| | .8 | | .9 | | 1.1 | |
| | .4 | | .6 | | .5 | |

| | | | | | | |
|---|---|---|---|---|---|---|
| | 6.9 | | 3.8 | | 5.1 | % Depr., Dep., Amort./Sales |
| (17) | 9.1 | (22) | 9.0 | (20) | 7.7 | |
| | 15.1 | | 19.7 | | 12.0 | |

% Officers', Directors' Owners' Comp/Sales

| | | | | | | | | |
|---|---|---|---|---|---|---|---|---|
| 554341M | 678448M | 692299M | Net Sales ($) | 688M | 17973M | | 23978M | 125553M | 524107M |
| 752603M | 711729M | 683465M | Total Assets ($) | 343M | 41133M | | 74287M | 76228M | 491474M |

© RMA 2024

M = $ thousand    MM = $ million
See Pages viii through xx for Explanation of Ratios and Data

# ADMIN & WASTE MANAGEMENT SERVICES—Other Nonhazardous Waste Treatment and Disposal NAICS 562219

## Current Data Sorted by Assets | Comparative Historical Data

| | | | | | | Type of Statement | | |
|---|---|---|---|---|---|---|---|---|
| | | | | 1 | 2 | Unqualified | 1 | 1 |
| | | 3 | 1 | 2 | 1 | Reviewed | 6 | 5 |
| | | 1 | 2 | | | Compiled | 4 | |
| | 1 | 3 | | | | Tax Returns | 5 | 1 |
| | 1 | 6 | 8 | 2 | 3 | Other | 5 | |
| 0-500M | 7 (4/1-9/30/23) 500M-2MM | 2-10MM | 28 (10/1/23-3/31/24) 10-50MM | 50-100MM | 100-250MM | | 29 4/1/19-3/31/20 ALL | 12 4/1/20-3/31/21 ALL |
| | 2 | 13 | 11 | 3 | 6 | NUMBER OF STATEMENTS | 45 | 19 |
| % | % | % | % | % | % | ASSETS | % | % |
| D | | 25.4 | 10.6 | | | Cash & Equivalents | 11.6 | 9.2 |
| A | | 21.1 | 15.6 | | | Trade Receivables (net) | 18.4 | 17.6 |
| T | | 1.3 | 1.8 | | | Inventory | 2.3 | 2.6 |
| A | | 2.0 | 2.9 | | | All Other Current | 1.0 | 2.2 |
| | | 49.8 | 31.0 | | | Total Current | 33.3 | 31.6 |
| N | | 32.0 | 48.2 | | | Fixed Assets (net) | 54.3 | 56.4 |
| O | | 3.6 | 6.3 | | | Intangibles (net) | 5.4 | 6.9 |
| T | | 14.6 | 14.6 | | | All Other Non-Current | 7.1 | 5.1 |
| | | 100.0 | 100.0 | | | Total | 100.0 | 100.0 |
| A | | | | | | LIABILITIES | | |
| V | | 1.7 | 1.1 | | | Notes Payable-Short Term | 9.1 | 5.7 |
| A | | 4.3 | 5.8 | | | Cur. Mat.-L.T.D. | 5.6 | 3.9 |
| I | | 8.9 | 5.9 | | | Trade Payables | 7.3 | 10.4 |
| L | | .1 | .0 | | | Income Taxes Payable | .1 | .0 |
| A | | 10.6 | 5.2 | | | All Other Current | 7.0 | 3.8 |
| B | | 25.5 | 18.1 | | | Total Current | 29.1 | 23.9 |
| L | | 46.2 | 22.2 | | | Long-Term Debt | 32.5 | 39.9 |
| E | | .0 | .7 | | | Deferred Taxes | .2 | .1 |
| | | 4.8 | 12.2 | | | All Other Non-Current | 8.1 | 8.9 |
| | | 23.5 | 46.8 | | | Net Worth | 30.1 | 27.3 |
| | | 100.0 | 100.0 | | | Total Liabilities & Net Worth | 100.0 | 100.0 |
| | | | | | | INCOME DATA | | |
| | | 100.0 | 100.0 | | | Net Sales | 100.0 | 100.0 |
| | | | | | | Gross Profit | | |
| | | 90.0 | 86.8 | | | Operating Expenses | 91.7 | 88.5 |
| | | 10.0 | 13.2 | | | Operating Profit | 8.3 | 11.5 |
| | | 2.5 | 2.5 | | | All Other Expenses (net) | 3.2 | .5 |
| | | 7.5 | 10.7 | | | Profit Before Taxes | 5.1 | 11.0 |
| | | | | | | RATIOS | | |
| | | 3.4 | 1.8 | | | | 2.5 | 2.5 |
| | | 2.4 | 1.2 | | | Current | 1.2 | 1.6 |
| | | 1.6 | .9 | | | | .7 | .8 |
| | | 3.2 | 1.8 | | | | 2.3 | 2.4 |
| | | 2.2 | 1.1 | | | Quick | 1.1 | 1.3 |
| | | 1.6 | .8 | | | | .6 | .6 |
| | | 0 UND | 26 14.1 | | | | 21 17.6 | 29 12.4 |
| | | 52 7.0 | 42 8.7 | | | Sales/Receivables | 37 9.9 | 38 9.6 |
| | | 76 4.8 | 60 6.1 | | | | 55 6.6 | 52 7.0 |
| | | | | | | Cost of Sales/Inventory | | |
| | | | | | | Cost of Sales/Payables | | |
| | | 3.9 | 3.1 | | | | 8.2 | 8.2 |
| | | 5.4 | 28.6 | | | Sales/Working Capital | 21.8 | 14.2 |
| | | 50.7 | -35.4 | | | | -20.5 | -26.4 |
| | | | 7.4 | | | | 8.4 | 22.0 |
| | | (10) | 5.9 | | | EBIT/Interest | (44) 3.6 | 6.1 |
| | | | 3.1 | | | | 1.5 | 3.7 |
| | | | | | | Net Profit + Depr., Dep., Amort./Cur. Mat. L/T/D | | |
| | | .2 | .8 | | | | 1.0 | 1.2 |
| | | .8 | 1.2 | | | Fixed/Worth | 2.0 | 1.8 |
| | | 36.3 | 2.1 | | | | 37.3 | 4.6 |
| | | .7 | .6 | | | | .9 | 1.0 |
| | | 1.9 | 1.5 | | | Debt/Worth | 1.9 | 1.9 |
| | | 45.2 | 2.9 | | | | 62.2 | 7.0 |
| | | 78.6 | 32.5 | | | | 40.6 | 56.0 |
| | | (11) 28.8 | 21.4 | | | % Profit Before Taxes/Tangible Net Worth | (35) 9.0 | (15) 35.7 |
| | | 6.3 | 12.7 | | | | 1.3 | 23.5 |
| | | 23.8 | 10.2 | | | | 14.8 | 22.7 |
| | | 4.0 | 8.3 | | | % Profit Before Taxes/Total Assets | 3.7 | 9.6 |
| | | -.7 | 3.4 | | | | .5 | 4.3 |
| | | 12.4 | 2.9 | | | | 6.5 | 3.9 |
| | | 8.1 | 2.4 | | | Sales/Net Fixed Assets | 2.8 | 2.3 |
| | | 5.3 | .7 | | | | 1.4 | 1.1 |
| | | 2.4 | 1.6 | | | | 2.2 | 2.2 |
| | | 1.9 | 1.1 | | | Sales/Total Assets | 1.3 | 1.1 |
| | | 1.5 | .4 | | | | .9 | .8 |
| | | | | | | | 5.7 | 4.3 |
| | | | | | | % Depr., Dep., Amort./Sales | (35) 7.8 | (13) 6.6 |
| | | | | | | | 11.3 | 14.9 |
| | | | | | | | 1.7 | |
| | | | | | | % Officers', Directors' Owners' Comp/Sales | (15) 2.4 | |
| | | | | | | | 6.8 | |
| | 2233M | 154172M | 242388M | 215457M | 862174M | Net Sales ($) | 853421M | 807722M |
| | 2449M | 73518M | 264065M | 249442M | 783146M | Total Assets ($) | 771393M | 713954M |

© RMA 2024

M = $ thousand    MM = $ million
See Pages viii through xx for Explanation of Ratios and Data

# ADMIN & WASTE MANAGEMENT SERVICES—Other Nonhazardous Waste Treatment and Disposal  NAICS 562219

## Comparative Historical Data | Current Data Sorted by Sales

| Comparative Historical Data ||| Type of Statement | Current Data Sorted by Sales ||||||
|---|---|---|---|---|---|---|---|---|---|
| 3 | 3 | 4 | Unqualified | | | | 1 | 1 | 3 |
| 2 | 4 | 6 | Reviewed | | | | | 2 | 2 |
| | 1 | 1 | Compiled | | | 1 | | | |
| 3 | 3 | 4 | Tax Returns | 1 | | 1 | | 1 | 1 |
| 12 | 14 | 20 | Other | | 3 | 1 | 1 | 7 | 8 |
| 4/1/21- | 4/1/22- | 4/1/23- | | 7 (4/1-9/30/23) ||| 28 (10/1/23-3/31/24) |||
| 3/31/22 | 3/31/23 | 3/31/24 | | 0-1MM | 1-3MM | 3-5MM | 5-10MM | 10-25MM | 25MM & OVER |
| ALL | ALL | ALL | | | | | | | |
| 20 | 25 | 35 | NUMBER OF STATEMENTS | 1 | 3 | 2 | 4 | 11 | 14 |
| % | % | % | ASSETS | % | % | % | % | % | % |
| 18.6 | 17.3 | 16.5 | Cash & Equivalents | | | | | 23.8 | 7.9 |
| 14.6 | 13.5 | 16.2 | Trade Receivables (net) | | | | | 20.1 | 14.4 |
| .9 | 2.5 | 1.7 | Inventory | | | | | 1.4 | 2.6 |
| 1.1 | 3.4 | 2.3 | All Other Current | | | | | 3.2 | 1.6 |
| 35.1 | 36.7 | 36.7 | Total Current | | | | | 48.5 | 26.4 |
| 48.2 | 45.6 | 38.2 | Fixed Assets (net) | | | | | 30.4 | 41.2 |
| 12.8 | 11.9 | 11.5 | Intangibles (net) | | | | | 5.5 | 19.3 |
| 3.9 | 5.8 | 13.5 | All Other Non-Current | | | | | 15.5 | 13.2 |
| 100.0 | 100.0 | 100.0 | Total | | | | | 100.0 | 100.0 |
| | | | LIABILITIES | | | | | | |
| 1.3 | .8 | 1.6 | Notes Payable-Short Term | | | | | .4 | 2.6 |
| 2.9 | 5.5 | 3.9 | Cur. Mat.-L.T.D. | | | | | 2.7 | 4.0 |
| 11.0 | 6.1 | 6.6 | Trade Payables | | | | | 7.1 | 6.4 |
| .0 | .0 | .0 | Income Taxes Payable | | | | | .0 | .0 |
| 5.2 | 7.3 | 8.1 | All Other Current | | | | | 8.3 | 12.8 |
| 20.4 | 19.7 | 20.3 | Total Current | | | | | 18.4 | 25.8 |
| 43.8 | 33.9 | 29.9 | Long-Term Debt | | | | | 41.7 | 20.9 |
| .3 | .2 | .8 | Deferred Taxes | | | | | .7 | 1.4 |
| 7.9 | 1.5 | 7.6 | All Other Non-Current | | | | | 10.4 | 9.4 |
| 27.7 | 44.8 | 41.4 | Net Worth | | | | | 28.8 | 42.5 |
| 100.0 | 100.0 | 100.0 | Total Liabilties & Net Worth | | | | | 100.0 | 100.0 |
| | | | INCOME DATA | | | | | | |
| 100.0 | 100.0 | 100.0 | Net Sales | | | | | 100.0 | 100.0 |
| | | | Gross Profit | | | | | | |
| 90.5 | 92.1 | 89.8 | Operating Expenses | | | | | 86.9 | 94.8 |
| 9.5 | 7.9 | 10.2 | Operating Profit | | | | | 13.1 | 5.2 |
| .6 | 1.1 | 2.6 | All Other Expenses (net) | | | | | 2.3 | 2.5 |
| 8.9 | 6.8 | 7.6 | Profit Before Taxes | | | | | 10.8 | 2.7 |
| | | | RATIOS | | | | | | |
| 3.0 | 6.5 | 2.5 | | | | | | 3.9 | 1.8 |
| 1.7 | 1.7 | 1.8 | Current | | | | | 2.2 | 1.4 |
| 1.1 | 1.0 | 1.1 | | | | | | 1.4 | .8 |
| 2.8 | 5.6 | 2.4 | | | | | | 3.2 | 1.5 |
| 1.5 | 1.5 | 1.5 | Quick | | | | | 2.2 | 1.1 |
| 1.0 | .7 | 1.0 | | | | | | 1.4 | .7 |
| 16  23.3 | 12  30.5 | 25  14.6 | | | | | | 15  23.7 | 32  11.5 |
| 38  9.5 | 38  9.7 | 45  8.2 | Sales/Receivables | | | | | 54  6.8 | 45  8.1 |
| 63  5.8 | 52  7.0 | 65  5.6 | | | | | | 74  4.9 | 62  5.9 |
| | | | Cost of Sales/Inventory | | | | | | |
| | | | Cost of Sales/Payables | | | | | | |
| 5.3 | 5.1 | 3.9 | | | | | | 2.9 | 7.7 |
| 16.4 | 15.7 | 12.2 | Sales/Working Capital | | | | | 5.8 | 23.1 |
| 149.5 | NM | 72.0 | | | | | | 29.5 | -21.2 |
| | | | | | | | | | 6.3 |
| 17.9 | 10.0 | 7.0 | | | | | | | |
| (17)  4.5 | (23)  5.5 | (27)  4.4 | EBIT/Interest | | | | | (12)  2.2 | |
| 1.4 | .1 | .5 | | | | | | | -4.3 |
| | | | Net Profit + Depr., Dep., Amort./Cur. Mat. L/T/D | | | | | | |
| .9 | .5 | .7 | | | | | | .1 | .9 |
| 1.5 | 1.2 | 1.2 | Fixed/Worth | | | | | .8 | 2.1 |
| 40.1 | 3.2 | 2.2 | | | | | | 1.1 | -13.7 |
| .7 | .5 | .6 | | | | | | .7 | .8 |
| 1.3 | 1.0 | 1.4 | Debt/Worth | | | | | 1.5 | 3.1 |
| NM | 5.2 | 3.5 | | | | | | 1.9 | -17.4 |
| 56.8 | 42.5 | 38.0 | | | | | | 76.0 | 25.9 |
| (15)  34.5 | (20)  17.7 | (29)  21.4 | % Profit Before Taxes/Tangible Net Worth | | | | (10)  25.6 | (10)  13.4 | |
| 18.7 | 8.9 | 3.7 | | | | | | 7.7 | -3.9 |
| 15.5 | 13.3 | 12.2 | | | | | | 25.9 | 7.5 |
| 7.1 | 8.3 | 5.6 | % Profit Before Taxes/Total Assets | | | | | 8.3 | 3.5 |
| .8 | -2.0 | -1.0 | | | | | | 2.4 | -3.1 |
| 6.4 | 9.6 | 8.9 | | | | | | 21.4 | 7.9 |
| 1.9 | 2.9 | 2.9 | Sales/Net Fixed Assets | | | | | 6.5 | 2.7 |
| 1.1 | 1.5 | 1.3 | | | | | | 1.9 | 1.1 |
| 1.7 | 1.8 | 1.9 | | | | | | 2.3 | 1.8 |
| 1.1 | 1.1 | 1.1 | Sales/Total Assets | | | | | 1.6 | 1.0 |
| .8 | .8 | .8 | | | | | | .8 | .6 |
| 5.5 | 2.2 | 4.1 | | | | | | | 4.0 |
| (11)  9.7 | (20)  5.9 | (23)  6.5 | % Depr., Dep., Amort./Sales | | | | | (10)  6.4 | |
| 13.5 | 14.5 | 9.5 | | | | | | | 8.6 |
| | | | % Officers', Directors' Owners' Comp/Sales | | | | | | |
| 666979M | 738051M | 1476424M | Net Sales ($) | 556M | 7121M | 7652M | 35231M | 180107M | 1245757M |
| 818583M | 711345M | 1372620M | Total Assets ($) | 580M | 7775M | 19639M | 38767M | 171529M | 1134330M |

M = $ thousand    MM = $ million
See Pages viii through xx for Explanation of Ratios and Data

© RMA 2024

# ADMIN & WASTE MANAGEMENT SERVICES—Remediation Services  NAICS 562910

## Current Data Sorted by Assets | Comparative Historical Data

| 0-500M | 500M-2MM | 2-10MM | 10-50MM | 50-100MM | 100-250MM | Type of Statement | | 4/1/19-3/31/20 ALL | 4/1/20-3/31/21 ALL |
|---|---|---|---|---|---|---|---|---|---|
|  | 1 | 3 | 9 | 1 |  | Unqualified |  | 8 | 5 |
|  | 1 | 5 | 10 | 1 |  | Reviewed |  | 21 | 10 |
|  | 1 | 5 | 4 |  |  | Compiled |  | 6 | 8 |
|  | 6 | 10 |  | 1 |  | Tax Returns |  | 16 | 8 |
| 5 | 12 | 26 | 26 | 4 | 1 | Other |  | 56 | 32 |
|  | 14 (4/1-9/30/23) | | 120 (10/1/23-3/31/24) | | | | | | |
| 8 | 20 | 49 | 49 | 7 | 1 | **NUMBER OF STATEMENTS** |  | 107 | 63 |
| % | % | % | % | % | % | **ASSETS** |  | % | % |
|  | 26.8 | 17.6 | 13.4 |  |  | Cash & Equivalents |  | 14.9 | 18.5 |
|  | 32.7 | 40.9 | 35.8 |  |  | Trade Receivables (net) |  | 37.5 | 30.8 |
|  | 2.5 | .3 | .9 |  |  | Inventory |  | 2.3 | 2.6 |
|  | 5.8 | 4.5 | 9.0 |  |  | All Other Current |  | 6.1 | 5.5 |
|  | 67.9 | 63.4 | 59.1 |  |  | Total Current |  | 60.8 | 57.4 |
|  | 19.5 | 23.1 | 24.8 |  |  | Fixed Assets (net) |  | 23.9 | 27.9 |
|  | 5.8 | 6.9 | 9.1 |  |  | Intangibles (net) |  | 7.1 | 7.0 |
|  | 6.8 | 6.5 | 7.0 |  |  | All Other Non-Current |  | 8.1 | 7.7 |
|  | 100.0 | 100.0 | 100.0 |  |  | Total |  | 100.0 | 100.0 |
|  |  |  |  |  |  | **LIABILITIES** |  |  |  |
|  | 4.7 | 4.5 | 4.1 |  |  | Notes Payable-Short Term |  | 9.0 | 10.6 |
|  | 3.2 | 3.0 | 3.2 |  |  | Cur. Mat.-L.T.D. |  | 2.9 | 3.6 |
|  | 8.1 | 9.1 | 10.3 |  |  | Trade Payables |  | 12.8 | 9.2 |
|  | .3 | .0 | .0 |  |  | Income Taxes Payable |  | .1 | .2 |
|  | 11.3 | 9.7 | 11.2 |  |  | All Other Current |  | 12.1 | 9.2 |
|  | 27.7 | 26.2 | 28.9 |  |  | Total Current |  | 36.8 | 32.7 |
|  | 28.4 | 15.4 | 14.8 |  |  | Long-Term Debt |  | 18.3 | 18.0 |
|  | .6 | .4 | .8 |  |  | Deferred Taxes |  | .2 | .2 |
|  | 5.1 | 4.1 | 3.8 |  |  | All Other Non-Current |  | 2.8 | 5.3 |
|  | 38.3 | 54.0 | 51.7 |  |  | Net Worth |  | 41.9 | 43.8 |
|  | 100.0 | 100.0 | 100.0 |  |  | Total Liabilities & Net Worth |  | 100.0 | 100.0 |
|  |  |  |  |  |  | **INCOME DATA** |  |  |  |
|  | 100.0 | 100.0 | 100.0 |  |  | Net Sales |  | 100.0 | 100.0 |
|  | 91.6 | 94.9 | 87.5 |  |  | Gross Profit |  |  |  |
|  | 8.4 | 5.1 | 12.5 |  |  | Operating Expenses |  | 90.7 | 94.8 |
|  | .1 | -.4 | .6 |  |  | Operating Profit |  | 9.3 | 5.2 |
|  | 8.3 | 5.6 | 11.9 |  |  | All Other Expenses (net) |  | .9 | -.5 |
|  |  |  |  |  |  | Profit Before Taxes |  | 8.4 | 5.7 |
|  |  |  |  |  |  | **RATIOS** |  |  |  |
|  | 14.5 | 6.2 | 3.1 |  |  |  |  | 3.5 | 3.5 |
|  | 3.2 | 2.5 | 2.1 |  |  | Current |  | 1.8 | 2.1 |
|  | 1.9 | 1.8 | 1.6 |  |  |  |  | 1.3 | 1.4 |
|  | 14.1 | 5.8 | 3.0 |  |  |  |  | 3.1 | 3.1 |
|  | 3.0 | 2.4 | 1.7 |  |  | Quick |  | 1.5 | 1.7 |
|  | 1.1 | 1.6 | 1.2 |  |  |  |  | 1.0 | 1.1 |
|  | 0 UND | 45   8.1 | 54   6.8 |  |  |  | 33 | 11.2 | 38   9.7 |
|  | 39   9.3 | 70   5.2 | 72   5.1 |  |  | Sales/Receivables | 58 | 6.3 | 64   5.7 |
|  | 63   5.8 | 96   3.8 | 104  3.5 |  |  |  | 83 | 4.4 | 85   4.3 |
|  |  |  |  |  |  | Cost of Sales/Inventory |  |  |  |
|  |  |  |  |  |  | Cost of Sales/Payables |  |  |  |
|  | 4.4 | 3.9 | 3.9 |  |  |  |  | 4.9 | 3.8 |
|  | 7.4 | 6.0 | 5.8 |  |  | Sales/Working Capital |  | 10.5 | 5.9 |
|  | 24.0 | 12.9 | 11.2 |  |  |  |  | 37.0 | 17.8 |
|  | 90.8 | 37.8 | 63.7 |  |  |  |  | 37.8 | 36.8 |
| (19) | 6.2 | (44) 11.2 | (47) 25.6 |  |  | EBIT/Interest | (96) | 13.0 | (54) 12.7 |
|  | .9 | 4.7 | 5.8 |  |  |  |  | 2.8 | 1.1 |
|  |  |  | 13.1 |  |  | Net Profit + Depr., Dep., |  | 27.4 | 10.7 |
|  |  | (14) 3.7 |  |  |  | Amort./Cur. Mat. L/T/D | (13) | 7.2 | (10) 6.7 |
|  |  |  | 2.1 |  |  |  |  | 3.4 | -1.8 |
|  | .1 | .1 | .2 |  |  |  |  | .1 | .2 |
|  | .4 | .5 | .5 |  |  | Fixed/Worth |  | .4 | .6 |
|  | 5.1 | .8 | .9 |  |  |  |  | 1.5 | 1.6 |
|  | .5 | .4 | .5 |  |  |  |  | .6 | .5 |
|  | 1.4 | .9 | 1.3 |  |  | Debt/Worth |  | 1.3 | 1.0 |
|  | 25.6 | 2.2 | 1.9 |  |  |  |  | 2.8 | 3.7 |
|  | 104.9 | 40.2 | 66.1 |  |  | % Profit Before Taxes/Tangible |  | 74.7 | 42.3 |
| (16) | 61.9 | (46) 26.3 | (44) 38.3 |  |  | Net Worth | (92) | 37.8 | (55) 20.9 |
|  | 25.1 | 6.6 | 24.5 |  |  |  |  | 16.3 | 9.5 |
|  | 47.3 | 20.7 | 28.1 |  |  | % Profit Before Taxes/Total |  | 31.5 | 19.0 |
|  | 22.4 | 12.9 | 15.7 |  |  | Assets |  | 14.3 | 9.5 |
|  | .6 | 2.8 | 8.4 |  |  |  |  | 4.8 | .9 |
|  | 107.4 | 26.2 | 25.0 |  |  |  |  | 48.6 | 23.6 |
|  | 22.6 | 14.3 | 6.6 |  |  | Sales/Net Fixed Assets |  | 15.7 | 9.9 |
|  | 12.4 | 6.3 | 3.7 |  |  |  |  | 7.6 | 3.9 |
|  | 4.4 | 2.8 | 2.2 |  |  |  |  | 3.4 | 2.3 |
|  | 3.3 | 2.4 | 1.5 |  |  | Sales/Total Assets |  | 2.4 | 1.8 |
|  | 2.2 | 1.7 | 1.1 |  |  |  |  | 1.6 | 1.2 |
|  |  | 1.4 | 1.3 |  |  |  |  | .8 | 1.3 |
|  | (38) | 1.8 | (43) 3.0 |  |  | % Depr., Dep., Amort./Sales | (76) | 2.1 | (46) 3.2 |
|  |  | 3.5 | 6.2 |  |  |  |  | 3.7 | 5.3 |
|  |  | 1.9 |  |  |  | % Officers', Directors' |  | 1.3 | 1.6 |
|  | (21) | 3.0 |  |  |  | Owners' Comp/Sales | (38) | 3.4 | (20) 2.8 |
|  |  | 5.2 |  |  |  |  |  | 6.7 | 5.7 |
| 10999M | 75006M | 547310M | 2242711M | 939634M | 123525M | Net Sales ($) |  | 2725258M | 1226922M |
| 2712M | 24074M | 237208M | 1200918M | 475865M | 199454M | Total Assets ($) |  | 1222415M | 866448M |

© RMA 2024

M = $ thousand   MM = $ million
See Pages viii through xx for Explanation of Ratios and Data

# ADMIN & WASTE MANAGEMENT SERVICES—Remediation Services   NAICS 562910

## Comparative Historical Data / Current Data Sorted by Sales

| Comparative Historical Data | | | Type of Statement | Current Data Sorted by Sales | | | | | |
|---|---|---|---|---|---|---|---|---|---|
| 6 | 10 | 13 | Unqualified | | 1 | | 1 | 6 | 5 |
| 19 | 21 | 18 | Reviewed | | 1 | 4 | 4 | 4 | 9 |
| 2 | 5 | 11 | Compiled | 1 | 1 | 2 | 2 | 2 | 3 |
| 6 | 19 | 18 | Tax Returns | 2 | 4 | 4 | 5 | 6 | 1 |
| 46 | 62 | 74 | Other | 3 | 8 | 8 | 11 | 23 | 21 |
| 4/1/21-3/31/22 ALL | 4/1/22-3/31/23 ALL | 4/1/23-3/31/24 ALL | | 0-1MM | 14 (4/1-9/30/23) 1-3MM | 3-5MM | 120 (10/1/23-3/31/24) 5-10MM | 10-25MM | 25MM & OVER |
| 79 | 117 | 134 | NUMBER OF STATEMENTS | 6 | 10 | 15 | 23 | 41 | 39 |
| % | % | % | ASSETS | % | % | % | % | % | % |
| 17.0 | 17.0 | 17.8 | Cash & Equivalents | 23.2 | 24.6 | 18.7 | 17.3 | 10.9 | |
| 32.3 | 35.2 | 36.2 | Trade Receivables (net) | 35.3 | 21.0 | 38.2 | 41.6 | 39.2 | |
| 2.9 | 3.4 | .8 | Inventory | 3.5 | .7 | .6 | .2 | 1.1 | |
| 7.7 | 7.5 | 7.3 | All Other Current | 1.7 | 6.7 | 4.3 | 6.6 | 11.9 | |
| 60.0 | 63.2 | 62.0 | Total Current | 63.8 | 52.9 | 61.8 | 65.7 | 63.1 | |
| 28.2 | 22.7 | 22.6 | Fixed Assets (net) | 23.9 | 26.6 | 20.7 | 22.6 | 19.7 | |
| 6.6 | 6.8 | 8.6 | Intangibles (net) | 9.8 | 9.3 | 10.9 | 4.1 | 11.9 | |
| 5.2 | 7.3 | 6.7 | All Other Non-Current | 2.5 | 11.1 | 6.6 | 7.6 | 5.3 | |
| 100.0 | 100.0 | 100.0 | Total | 100.0 | 100.0 | 100.0 | 100.0 | 100.0 | |
| | | | LIABILITIES | | | | | | |
| 6.7 | 5.8 | 4.5 | Notes Payable-Short Term | 3.5 | 8.4 | 2.0 | 5.9 | 3.1 | |
| 2.7 | 2.7 | 3.5 | Cur. Mat.-L.T.D. | 1.6 | 7.9 | 3.7 | 3.4 | 2.6 | |
| 8.7 | 7.6 | 9.7 | Trade Payables | 8.3 | 5.8 | 8.4 | 7.8 | 15.7 | |
| .0 | .0 | .1 | Income Taxes Payable | .0 | .1 | .2 | .0 | .1 | |
| 9.6 | 9.7 | 12.3 | All Other Current | 37.4 | 6.0 | 9.1 | 11.4 | 11.9 | |
| 27.8 | 25.9 | 30.1 | Total Current | 50.7 | 28.2 | 23.5 | 28.6 | 33.3 | |
| 15.2 | 15.7 | 17.9 | Long-Term Debt | 15.2 | 32.2 | 16.9 | 12.9 | 16.7 | |
| .1 | .2 | .5 | Deferred Taxes | .0 | 1.7 | .6 | .6 | .2 | |
| 4.6 | 3.6 | 3.9 | All Other Non-Current | 6.3 | 4.3 | 4.3 | 3.3 | 2.9 | |
| 52.3 | 54.6 | 47.7 | Net Worth | 27.8 | 33.5 | 54.8 | 54.5 | 46.9 | |
| 100.0 | 100.0 | 100.0 | Total Liabilities & Net Worth | 100.0 | 100.0 | 100.0 | 100.0 | 100.0 | |
| | | | INCOME DATA | | | | | | |
| 100.0 | 100.0 | 100.0 | Net Sales | 100.0 | 100.0 | 100.0 | 100.0 | 100.0 | |
| 90.2 | 90.6 | 91.4 | Gross Profit / Operating Expenses | 92.5 | 94.6 | 92.9 | 92.0 | 89.6 | |
| 9.8 | 9.4 | 8.6 | Operating Profit | 7.5 | 5.4 | 7.1 | 8.0 | 10.4 | |
| .3 | .5 | .3 | All Other Expenses (net) | .8 | -1.4 | -1.0 | -.1 | 1.3 | |
| 9.6 | 9.0 | 8.3 | Profit Before Taxes | 6.7 | 6.8 | 8.1 | 8.1 | 9.2 | |
| | | | RATIOS | | | | | | |
| 4.1 | 5.7 | 4.0 | | 6.5 | 4.2 | 11.4 | 4.1 | 2.8 | |
| 2.4 | 2.5 | 2.3 | Current | 2.4 | 2.4 | 3.2 | 2.4 | 2.0 | |
| 1.5 | 1.6 | 1.6 | | .8 | 1.9 | 1.8 | 1.6 | 1.7 | |
| 3.6 | 4.5 | 3.6 | | 6.5 | 4.1 | 11.4 | 3.6 | 2.4 | |
| 2.1 | 2.2 | 2.1 | Quick | 2.0 | 2.4 | 2.8 | 2.3 | 1.5 | |
| 1.1 | 1.1 | 1.2 | | .8 | .7 | 1.7 | 1.4 | 1.0 | |
| 43  8.5 | 41  8.8 | 43  8.4 | | 40  9.2 | 0  UND | 32  11.5 | 54  6.7 | 50  7.3 | |
| 73  5.0 | 70  5.2 | 62  5.9 | Sales/Receivables | 63  5.8 | 34  10.6 | 62  5.9 | 74  4.9 | 60  6.1 | |
| 94  3.9 | 99  3.7 | 91  4.0 | | 104  3.5 | 70  5.2 | 96  3.8 | 104  3.5 | 83  4.4 | |
| | | | Cost of Sales/Inventory | | | | | | |
| | | | Cost of Sales/Payables | | | | | | |
| 3.4 | 3.4 | 3.9 | | 3.2 | 4.1 | 3.7 | 3.5 | 5.0 | |
| 5.6 | 5.8 | 6.1 | Sales/Working Capital | 6.5 | 6.8 | 5.9 | 5.8 | 6.4 | |
| 10.7 | 10.4 | 12.9 | | -9.3 | 28.3 | 11.3 | 13.4 | 10.1 | |
| 46.5 | 71.2 | 49.3 | | | 40.4 | 97.5 | 33.6 | 152.2 | |
| (65) 19.1 | (90) 19.6 | (123) 13.6 | EBIT/Interest | (13) 6.2 | (21) 15.8 | (38) 9.9 | (38) 29.8 | | |
| 5.8 | 4.4 | 3.0 | | | -2.1 | 6.2 | 4.4 | 5.9 | |
| 24.6 | 13.1 | 15.9 | Net Profit + Depr., Dep., | | | | 27.2 | | |
| (10) 7.9 | (12) 4.7 | (26) 6.7 | Amort./Cur. Mat. L/T/D | | | | (11) 12.3 | | |
| 4.8 | 1.2 | 2.3 | | | | | 1.6 | | |
| .2 | .1 | .1 | | .2 | .2 | .1 | .1 | .1 | |
| .6 | .4 | .5 | Fixed/Worth | 1.4 | .7 | .5 | .4 | .4 | |
| 1.4 | .9 | 1.2 | | -.2 | 8.1 | 1.2 | .7 | .8 | |
| .4 | .3 | .5 | | .8 | .4 | .4 | .4 | .5 | |
| 1.0 | .8 | 1.1 | Debt/Worth | 1.8 | 1.1 | 1.2 | .9 | 1.3 | |
| 2.2 | 2.4 | 2.5 | | -32.5 | 31.6 | 2.5 | 1.8 | 2.7 | |
| 54.9 | 58.5 | 65.0 | % Profit Before Taxes/Tangible | | 53.3 | 59.0 | 43.2 | 69.7 | |
| (72) 34.2 | (108) 31.1 | (118) 31.2 | Net Worth | | (12) 31.2 | (21) 34.6 | (39) 27.7 | (33) 39.1 | |
| 16.7 | 16.0 | 14.6 | | | 3.5 | 15.4 | 11.6 | 19.2 | |
| 26.5 | 29.4 | 27.6 | % Profit Before Taxes/Total | 27.6 | 30.9 | 23.2 | 23.4 | 28.5 | |
| 18.4 | 14.5 | 13.7 | Assets | 6.8 | 20.3 | 16.2 | 14.5 | 13.4 | |
| 5.2 | 5.7 | 3.6 | | -7.9 | -1.2 | 3.2 | 3.3 | 7.1 | |
| 20.3 | 27.5 | 34.3 | | 47.7 | 23.6 | 36.9 | 29.5 | 66.5 | |
| 6.5 | 12.5 | 14.3 | Sales/Net Fixed Assets | 22.6 | 14.3 | 12.0 | 12.4 | 18.3 | |
| 3.9 | 5.4 | 5.3 | | 3.1 | 6.1 | 6.5 | 5.6 | 5.1 | |
| 2.4 | 2.7 | 3.0 | | 3.3 | 4.2 | 3.3 | 2.7 | 2.8 | |
| 1.7 | 1.9 | 2.2 | Sales/Total Assets | 2.3 | 2.8 | 2.4 | 2.2 | 2.0 | |
| 1.1 | 1.3 | 1.4 | | 1.0 | 1.4 | 1.6 | 1.4 | 1.4 | |
| 2.2 | 1.2 | 1.3 | | | | .9 | 1.4 | .8 | |
| (60) 3.4 | (82) 2.4 | (99) 2.1 | % Depr., Dep., Amort./Sales | | (17) 1.9 | (33) 2.1 | (32) 1.9 | | |
| 5.4 | 3.9 | 5.0 | | | | 3.5 | 5.5 | 5.0 | |
| 1.8 | 1.2 | 1.8 | % Officers', Directors' | | | 2.0 | 1.3 | | |
| (24) 3.6 | (35) 2.4 | (36) 3.0 | Owners' Comp/Sales | | (12) 3.0 | (13) 2.3 | | | |
| 4.8 | 6.3 | 6.7 | | | | 8.7 | 3.3 | | |
| 1773071M | 2986291M | 3939185M | Net Sales ($) | 2403M | 21008M | 59761M | 166026M | 667253M | 3022734M |
| 1202959M | 2006837M | 2140231M | Total Assets ($) | 3468M | 16682M | 60073M | 108259M | 370073M | 1581676M |

M = $ thousand    MM = $ million
See Pages viii through xx for Explanation of Ratios and Data

© RMA 2024

# ADMIN & WASTE MANAGEMENT SERVICES—Materials Recovery Facilities  NAICS 562920

**Current Data Sorted by Assets** | **Comparative Historical Data**

| 0-500M | 500M-2MM | 2-10MM | 10-50MM | 50-100MM | 100-250MM | Type of Statement | | 4/1/19-3/31/20 ALL | 4/1/20-3/31/21 ALL |
|---|---|---|---|---|---|---|---|---|---|
| | 1 | 6 | 2 | 3 | 5 | Unqualified | | 8 | 7 |
| | 1 | 3 | 6 | | 1 | Reviewed | | 8 | 3 |
| | | 3 | 1 | | | Compiled | | 6 | |
| | | | 3 | | | Tax Returns | | 11 | 6 |
| | 8 | 12 | 2 | 6 | 4 | Other | | 45 | 42 |
| DATA NOT AVAILABLE | 15 (4/1-9/30/23) 10 | 24 | 17 66 (10/1/23-3/31/24) 28 | 9 | 10 | NUMBER OF STATEMENTS | | 78 | 58 |
| | % | % | % | % | % | ASSETS | | % | % |
| | 5.1 | 14.8 | 13.4 | | 5.1 | Cash & Equivalents | | 9.3 | 10.9 |
| | 21.3 | 17.3 | 14.4 | | 15.2 | Trade Receivables (net) | | 20.3 | 15.7 |
| | 13.7 | 7.5 | 10.9 | | 4.6 | Inventory | | 6.5 | 6.5 |
| | 4.2 | 3.6 | 2.2 | | 3.7 | All Other Current | | 3.4 | 3.0 |
| | 44.3 | 43.2 | 40.8 | | 28.5 | Total Current | | 39.5 | 36.1 |
| | 45.1 | 44.7 | 43.5 | | 43.6 | Fixed Assets (net) | | 45.1 | 51.0 |
| | 2.0 | 1.5 | 6.0 | | 23.3 | Intangibles (net) | | 9.3 | 8.9 |
| | 8.6 | 10.6 | 9.7 | | 4.6 | All Other Non-Current | | 6.1 | 4.1 |
| | 100.0 | 100.0 | 100.0 | | 100.0 | Total | | 100.0 | 100.0 |
| | | | | | | LIABILITIES | | | |
| | 13.3 | 2.0 | 4.7 | | .0 | Notes Payable-Short Term | | 8.2 | 5.8 |
| | 2.2 | 4.2 | 3.3 | | 3.7 | Cur. Mat.-L.T.D. | | 6.0 | 3.2 |
| | 23.3 | 12.6 | 10.5 | | 5.3 | Trade Payables | | 9.9 | 7.1 |
| | .0 | .0 | .1 | | .0 | Income Taxes Payable | | .0 | .0 |
| | 14.6 | 6.3 | 6.9 | | 8.5 | All Other Current | | 10.1 | 5.0 |
| | 53.4 | 25.1 | 25.4 | | 17.5 | Total Current | | 34.2 | 21.1 |
| | 15.8 | 21.1 | 24.1 | | 24.4 | Long-Term Debt | | 28.9 | 33.4 |
| | .0 | .0 | 2.0 | | 1.0 | Deferred Taxes | | .1 | .1 |
| | 14.2 | 2.7 | 3.5 | | 22.8 | All Other Non-Current | | 4.6 | 8.8 |
| | 16.6 | 51.2 | 44.9 | | 34.4 | Net Worth | | 32.3 | 36.6 |
| | 100.0 | 100.0 | 100.0 | | 100.0 | Total Liabilities & Net Worth | | 100.0 | 100.0 |
| | | | | | | INCOME DATA | | | |
| | 100.0 | 100.0 | 100.0 | | 100.0 | Net Sales | | 100.0 | 100.0 |
| | | | | | | Gross Profit | | | |
| | 84.3 | 84.2 | 93.5 | | 93.1 | Operating Expenses | | 91.5 | 89.4 |
| | 15.7 | 15.8 | 6.5 | | 6.9 | Operating Profit | | 8.5 | 10.6 |
| | 4.4 | 2.6 | .3 | | .3 | All Other Expenses (net) | | 1.6 | 3.0 |
| | 11.3 | 13.2 | 6.1 | | 6.6 | Profit Before Taxes | | 6.9 | 7.6 |
| | | | | | | RATIOS | | | |
| | 6.4 | 2.4 | 3.5 | | 4.0 | | | 3.1 | 2.8 |
| | 2.5 | 1.7 | 1.6 | | 2.0 | Current | | 1.2 | 1.8 |
| | .3 | 1.1 | .8 | | 1.2 | | | .7 | .9 |
| | 4.8 | 2.1 | 2.8 | | 4.0 | | | 2.2 | 2.3 |
| | 1.4 | 1.2 | .9 | | 1.4 | Quick | | .9 | 1.2 |
| | .3 | .7 | .5 | | .7 | | | .4 | .6 |
| | 0 UND | 15 23.7 | 15 24.7 | | 29 12.6 | | 22 | 16.4 | 19 19.2 |
| | 22 16.8 | 31 11.9 | 26 13.8 | | 53 6.9 | Sales/Receivables | 35 | 10.5 | 35 10.5 |
| | 91 4.0 | 41 8.9 | 38 9.7 | | 76 4.8 | | 46 | 8.0 | 46 8.0 |
| | | | | | | Cost of Sales/Inventory | | | |
| | | | | | | Cost of Sales/Payables | | | |
| | 4.6 | 8.3 | 3.5 | | 4.4 | | | 7.5 | 5.7 |
| | 21.8 | 22.0 | 16.6 | | 10.3 | Sales/Working Capital | | 51.3 | 14.8 |
| | -5.7 | 183.9 | -34.5 | | NM | | | -20.1 | -48.6 |
| | | 101.7 | 12.9 | | 30.8 | | | 11.7 | 14.2 |
| | (18) | 15.5 (26) | 5.5 | | 5.2 | EBIT/Interest | (71) | 4.6 | (50) 6.1 |
| | | 3.7 | 1.6 | | -.1 | | | .8 | 1.3 |
| | | | | | | Net Profit + Depr., Dep., Amort./Cur. Mat. L/T/D | | 7.2 | 8.5 |
| | | | | | | | (11) | 3.5 | (10) 2.9 |
| | | | | | | | | 2.1 | 1.2 |
| | .5 | .3 | .7 | | 1.1 | | | .6 | .7 |
| | 1.8 | .9 | 1.1 | | 5.2 | Fixed/Worth | | 1.5 | 1.7 |
| | -.9 | 1.4 | 1.8 | | -.8 | | | 7.5 | 8.4 |
| | .6 | .4 | .7 | | .6 | | | .9 | .8 |
| | 1.3 | .9 | 1.1 | | 7.7 | Debt/Worth | | 1.9 | 2.5 |
| | -7.5 | 1.8 | 2.5 | | -2.4 | | | 15.9 | 12.0 |
| | | 83.1 | 34.2 | | | % Profit Before Taxes/Tangible Net Worth | | 52.1 | 65.1 |
| | (23) | 34.7 (25) | 18.9 | | | | (62) | 27.1 | (48) 23.5 |
| | | 16.9 | 8.0 | | | | | 6.5 | 7.0 |
| | 57.1 | 37.3 | 10.5 | | 12.0 | % Profit Before Taxes/Total Assets | | 16.2 | 17.5 |
| | 6.2 | 16.8 | 6.5 | | 5.1 | | | 7.1 | 4.8 |
| | -9.8 | 9.0 | 1.9 | | -3.7 | | | .7 | 1.1 |
| | 56.0 | 13.5 | 10.9 | | 3.3 | | | 9.8 | 5.4 |
| | 13.0 | 6.6 | 3.0 | | 2.0 | Sales/Net Fixed Assets | | 3.9 | 2.5 |
| | .2 | 1.5 | 2.0 | | 1.7 | | | 1.8 | 1.5 |
| | 7.0 | 3.4 | 2.6 | | 1.4 | | | 3.0 | 2.3 |
| | 4.3 | 2.0 | 1.4 | | .9 | Sales/Total Assets | | 1.8 | 1.4 |
| | .1 | .9 | .9 | | .7 | | | 1.2 | .8 |
| | | 4.0 | .7 | | | | | 2.4 | 3.3 |
| | (17) | 4.4 (27) | 3.6 | | | % Depr., Dep., Amort./Sales | (63) | 4.3 | (43) 7.5 |
| | | 10.2 | 7.4 | | | | | 9.3 | 11.0 |
| | | | | | | % Officers', Directors' Owners' Comp/Sales | | 1.7 | |
| | | | | | | | (14) | 3.0 | |
| | | | | | | | | 8.2 | |
| | 52880M | 317457M | 1403195M | 1095649M | 1468767M | Net Sales ($) | | 3356152M | 3506168M |
| | 12833M | 116308M | 719082M | 748479M | 1337139M | Total Assets ($) | | 2016924M | 2526765M |

M = $ thousand   MM = $ million

© RMA 2024

# ADMIN & WASTE MANAGEMENT SERVICES—Materials Recovery Facilities  NAICS 562920

## Comparative Historical Data | Current Data Sorted by Sales

| Comparative Historical Data | | | | Type of Statement | Current Data Sorted by Sales | | | | | |
|---|---|---|---|---|---|---|---|---|---|---|
| 3 | 10 | 10 | | Unqualified | | | | 1 | 1 | 8 |
| 9 | 10 | 14 | | Reviewed | 3 | | | 1 | 4 | 6 |
| 5 | 9 | 5 | | Compiled | | 1 | | 2 | 1 | 1 |
| 7 | 8 | 5 | | Tax Returns | | | | 1 | 1 | 3 |
| 29 | 42 | 47 | | Other | 3 | 2 | 2 | 7 | 9 | 24 |
| 4/1/21-3/31/22 ALL | 4/1/22-3/31/23 ALL | 4/1/23-3/31/24 ALL | | | 0-1MM | 15 (4/1-9/30/23) 1-3MM | 3-5MM | 66 (10/1/23-3/31/24) 5-10MM | 10-25MM | 25MM & OVER |
| 53 | 79 | 81 | | NUMBER OF STATEMENTS | 6 | 3 | 2 | 12 | 16 | 42 |
| % | % | % | | ASSETS | % | % | % | % | % | % |
| 16.4 | 17.7 | 10.8 | | Cash & Equivalents | | | | 11.1 | 10.6 | 11.7 |
| 18.1 | 16.4 | 16.9 | | Trade Receivables (net) | | | | 14.1 | 18.8 | 18.5 |
| 8.1 | 9.6 | 9.7 | | Inventory | | | | 12.5 | 7.1 | 11.1 |
| 3.5 | 2.9 | 2.9 | | All Other Current | | | | 2.4 | 3.7 | 2.1 |
| 46.1 | 46.6 | 40.4 | | Total Current | | | | 40.1 | 40.1 | 43.4 |
| 44.4 | 39.8 | 43.0 | | Fixed Assets (net) | | | | 38.9 | 41.3 | 38.3 |
| 5.8 | 5.5 | 6.7 | | Intangibles (net) | | | | .8 | 7.7 | 9.3 |
| 3.6 | 8.0 | 10.0 | | All Other Non-Current | | | | 20.2 | 10.9 | 8.9 |
| 100.0 | 100.0 | 100.0 | | Total | | | | 100.0 | 100.0 | 100.0 |
| | | | | LIABILITIES | | | | | | |
| 4.7 | 4.5 | 4.1 | | Notes Payable-Short Term | | | | 2.9 | 2.0 | 3.1 |
| 3.6 | 3.4 | 3.3 | | Cur. Mat.-L.T.D. | | | | 4.3 | 2.9 | 3.1 |
| 10.2 | 11.7 | 12.2 | | Trade Payables | | | | 8.9 | 12.7 | 11.5 |
| .0 | .1 | .0 | | Income Taxes Payable | | | | .0 | .0 | .1 |
| 5.7 | 5.9 | 8.4 | | All Other Current | | | | 4.2 | 9.4 | 8.6 |
| 24.2 | 25.6 | 28.1 | | Total Current | | | | 20.2 | 27.1 | 26.3 |
| 36.7 | 30.3 | 21.7 | | Long-Term Debt | | | | 22.0 | 21.8 | 19.8 |
| .3 | .2 | .8 | | Deferred Taxes | | | | .0 | .3 | 1.4 |
| 2.9 | 9.3 | 8.4 | | All Other Non-Current | | | | 2.4 | 7.2 | 9.5 |
| 35.9 | 34.7 | 41.0 | | Net Worth | | | | 55.4 | 43.6 | 43.0 |
| 100.0 | 100.0 | 100.0 | | Total Liabilities & Net Worth | | | | 100.0 | 100.0 | 100.0 |
| | | | | INCOME DATA | | | | | | |
| 100.0 | 100.0 | 100.0 | | Net Sales | | | | 100.0 | 100.0 | 100.0 |
| | | | | Gross Profit | | | | | | |
| 85.7 | 90.5 | 90.2 | | Operating Expenses | | | | 92.0 | 89.7 | 95.0 |
| 14.3 | 9.5 | 9.8 | | Operating Profit | | | | 8.0 | 10.3 | 5.0 |
| .4 | 1.6 | 1.9 | | All Other Expenses (net) | | | | -.2 | -.3 | 1.0 |
| 13.9 | 7.9 | 8.0 | | Profit Before Taxes | | | | 8.3 | 10.5 | 4.0 |
| | | | | RATIOS | | | | | | |
| 4.1 | 3.6 | 3.1 | | | | | | 7.3 | 3.1 | 2.7 |
| 2.2 | 2.1 | 1.8 | | Current | | | | 1.9 | 1.9 | 1.7 |
| 1.2 | 1.2 | 1.0 | | | | | | 1.1 | .7 | 1.0 |
| 2.9 | 3.3 | 2.5 | | | | | | 4.4 | 2.1 | 2.5 |
| 1.6 | 1.4 | 1.2 | | Quick | | | | 1.1 | 1.4 | 1.1 |
| .8 | .7 | .6 | | | | | | .6 | .5 | .7 |
| 12   29.6 | 9   41.0 | 18   20.7 | | | 18   19.8 | | | 5   75.4 | 24   14.9 | |
| 27   13.5 | 22   16.9 | 31   11.9 | | Sales/Receivables | 33   10.9 | | | 20   18.6 | 35   10.5 | |
| 39   9.4 | 38   9.5 | 51   7.2 | | | 46   7.9 | | | 32   11.3 | 53   6.9 | |
| | | | | Cost of Sales/Inventory | | | | | | |
| | | | | Cost of Sales/Payables | | | | | | |
| 5.9 | 6.5 | 5.9 | | | | | | 6.0 | 9.9 | 6.2 |
| 10.8 | 14.1 | 17.0 | | Sales/Working Capital | | | | 25.2 | 15.7 | 13.8 |
| 54.7 | 70.6 | -308.6 | | | | | | 44.0 | -31.7 | 198.9 |
| 52.4 | 32.8 | 18.0 | | | | | | 88.2 | | 17.2 |
| (47) 21.4 | (67) 10.9 | (69) 6.2 | | EBIT/Interest | | | | (11) 5.7 | (40) 6.5 | |
| 8.2 | 3.3 | 1.3 | | | | | | 3.7 | 1.1 | |
| | | 10.6 | 7.5 | | | | | | | 7.6 |
| | (10) 6.1 | (18) 4.6 | | Net Profit + Depr., Dep., Amort./Cur. Mat. L/T/D | | | | | (17) 4.7 | |
| | 4.0 | 1.9 | | | | | | | | 2.0 |
| .5 | .3 | .6 | | | | | | .1 | .6 | .6 |
| 1.1 | .9 | 1.1 | | Fixed/Worth | | | | .5 | 1.0 | 1.0 |
| 8.5 | 3.8 | 3.2 | | | | | | 1.6 | NM | 3.0 |
| .6 | .5 | .6 | | | | | | .6 | .5 | .6 |
| 1.8 | 1.3 | 1.0 | | Debt/Worth | | | | .8 | 1.0 | 1.3 |
| 10.9 | 9.6 | 4.5 | | | | | | .9 | NM | 3.5 |
| 102.2 | 62.4 | 39.1 | | | | | | 42.7 | 78.8 | 37.2 |
| (42) 56.3 | (67) 39.4 | (69) 19.6 | | % Profit Before Taxes/Tangible Net Worth | | | | 19.9 (12) | 36.4 (36) | 19.4 |
| 29.1 | 24.3 | 8.5 | | | | | | 8.7 | 16.6 | 4.0 |
| 43.8 | 28.7 | 18.4 | | | | | | 34.6 | 40.5 | 14.0 |
| 28.2 | 15.6 | 9.2 | | % Profit Before Taxes/Total Assets | | | | 10.6 | 16.1 | 7.1 |
| 13.9 | 4.3 | 1.1 | | | | | | 2.1 | 6.6 | .3 |
| 14.0 | 21.6 | 11.3 | | | | | | 26.2 | 30.4 | 11.2 |
| 5.7 | 7.8 | 4.3 | | Sales/Net Fixed Assets | | | | 9.6 | 8.0 | 3.9 |
| 2.4 | 2.2 | 1.8 | | | | | | 1.2 | 1.7 | 2.1 |
| 3.5 | 3.9 | 3.0 | | | | | | 2.7 | 5.7 | 2.7 |
| 2.1 | 2.3 | 1.4 | | Sales/Total Assets | | | | 1.4 | 2.2 | 1.5 |
| 1.6 | 1.3 | .9 | | | | | | .8 | .9 | .9 |
| 1.6 | 1.2 | 1.9 | | | | | | 2.0 | | .9 |
| (41) 4.0 | (52) 3.3 | (63) 4.3 | | % Depr., Dep., Amort./Sales | | | | (11) 5.9 | (35) 3.6 | |
| 7.2 | 6.1 | 7.4 | | | | | | 7.4 | 5.0 | |
| .7 | .6 | 1.0 | | % Officers', Directors' Owners' Comp/Sales | | | | | | |
| (16) 2.9 | (15) 1.1 | (14) 2.0 | | | | | | | | |
| 8.8 | 3.7 | 6.8 | | | | | | | | |
| 2790356M | 4249010M | 4337948M | | Net Sales ($) | 2066M | 6029M | 8259M | 87720M | 240410M | 3993464M |
| 1162246M | 2081319M | 2933841M | | Total Assets ($) | 15496M | 3568M | 7248M | 79254M | 169633M | 2658642M |

© RMA 2024   M = $ thousand   MM = $ million
See Pages viii through xx for Explanation of Ratios and Data

# ADMIN & WASTE MANAGEMENT SERVICES—Septic Tank and Related Services    NAICS 562991

## Current Data Sorted by Assets | Comparative Historical Data

| Type of Statement | | | |
|---|---|---|---|
| | | | |

Current Data — Type of Statement counts (columns: 0-500M, 500M-2MM, 2-10MM, 10-50MM, 50-100MM, 100-250MM):

|  | 0-500M | 500M-2MM | 2-10MM | 10-50MM | 50-100MM | 100-250MM | Type of Statement | 4/1/19-3/31/20 ALL | 4/1/20-3/31/21 ALL |
|---|---|---|---|---|---|---|---|---|---|
|  |  | 2 | 2 | 2 |  |  | Unqualified | 1 | 1 |
|  |  | 2 | 2 | 2 |  |  | Reviewed | 1 | 1 |
|  | 2 | 11 | 2 | 2 |  |  | Compiled | 4 | 2 |
|  | 2 | 4 | 9 | 3 | 2 |  | Tax Returns | 15 | 3 |
|  |  | 6 (4/1-9/30/23) |  | 39 (10/1/23-3/31/24) | | | Other | 15 | 10 |
|  | 4 | 17 | 15 | 7 | 2 |  | NUMBER OF STATEMENTS | 36 | 17 |
|  | % | % | % | % | % | % | ASSETS | % | % |
|  |  | 21.7 | 24.4 |  |  | D | Cash & Equivalents | 17.9 | 20.0 |
|  |  | 9.3 | 15.2 |  |  | A | Trade Receivables (net) | 12.5 | 13.7 |
|  |  | 1.8 | 1.5 |  |  | T | Inventory | 3.0 | .5 |
|  |  | 6.6 | 3.6 |  |  | A | All Other Current | 2.7 | 3.9 |
|  |  | 39.3 | 44.7 |  |  |  | Total Current | 36.1 | 38.1 |
|  |  | 46.7 | 34.6 |  |  | N | Fixed Assets (net) | 47.1 | 39.1 |
|  |  | 6.5 | 12.8 |  |  | O | Intangibles (net) | 12.5 | 17.6 |
|  |  | 7.5 | 7.9 |  |  | T | All Other Non-Current | 4.3 | 5.2 |
|  |  | 100.0 | 100.0 |  |  |  | Total | 100.0 | 100.0 |
|  |  |  |  |  |  | A | LIABILITIES | | |
|  |  | 6.0 | .6 |  |  | V | Notes Payable-Short Term | 5.9 | 4.6 |
|  |  | 5.5 | 4.9 |  |  | A | Cur. Mat.-L.T.D. | 3.3 | 4.1 |
|  |  | 4.1 | 4.3 |  |  | I | Trade Payables | 4.5 | 2.1 |
|  |  | .2 | .4 |  |  | L | Income Taxes Payable | .0 | .0 |
|  |  | 2.8 | 5.1 |  |  | A | All Other Current | 3.0 | 13.4 |
|  |  | 18.6 | 15.4 |  |  | B | Total Current | 16.8 | 24.2 |
|  |  | 43.6 | 23.6 |  |  | L | Long-Term Debt | 48.2 | 43.7 |
|  |  | .0 | .5 |  |  | E | Deferred Taxes | .0 | .4 |
|  |  | .9 | 15.3 |  |  |  | All Other Non-Current | 5.9 | 2.5 |
|  |  | 37.0 | 45.2 |  |  |  | Net Worth | 29.0 | 29.2 |
|  |  | 100.0 | 100.0 |  |  |  | Total Liabilities & Net Worth | 100.0 | 100.0 |
|  |  |  |  |  |  |  | INCOME DATA | | |
|  |  | 100.0 | 100.0 |  |  |  | Net Sales | 100.0 | 100.0 |
|  |  |  |  |  |  |  | Gross Profit | | |
|  |  | 84.4 | 89.9 |  |  |  | Operating Expenses | 91.1 | 87.2 |
|  |  | 15.6 | 10.1 |  |  |  | Operating Profit | 8.9 | 12.8 |
|  |  | 5.2 | 1.5 |  |  |  | All Other Expenses (net) | 2.7 | -1.6 |
|  |  | 10.4 | 8.6 |  |  |  | Profit Before Taxes | 6.2 | 14.3 |
|  |  |  |  |  |  |  | RATIOS | | |
|  |  | 3.2 | 7.1 |  |  |  |  | 4.8 | 4.4 |
|  |  | 1.3 | 3.3 |  |  |  | Current | 1.8 | 2.1 |
|  |  | .8 | 2.4 |  |  |  |  | 1.1 | 1.3 |
|  |  | 2.5 | 5.1 |  |  |  |  | 3.1 | 4.4 |
|  |  | 1.3 | 3.2 |  |  |  | Quick | 1.8 | 2.0 |
|  |  | .7 | 2.4 |  |  |  |  | .9 | 1.2 |
|  |  | 0  UND | 15  23.8 |  |  |  |  | 0  UND | 0  UND |
|  |  | 0  UND | 33  11.1 |  |  |  | Sales/Receivables | 6  58.3 | 25  14.4 |
|  |  | 27  13.6 | 50  7.3 |  |  |  |  | 37  9.9 | 57  6.4 |
|  |  |  |  |  |  |  | Cost of Sales/Inventory | | |
|  |  |  |  |  |  |  | Cost of Sales/Payables | | |
|  |  | 9.2 | 2.6 |  |  |  |  | 7.2 | 3.7 |
|  |  | 28.4 | 6.5 |  |  |  | Sales/Working Capital | 15.8 | 9.1 |
|  |  | -46.8 | 14.2 |  |  |  |  | 181.6 | 31.2 |
|  |  | 36.3 | 56.9 |  |  |  |  | 18.3 | 14.5 |
|  | (15) | 6.3 | (11) 5.2 |  |  |  | EBIT/Interest | (34) 3.1 | (15) 9.4 |
|  |  | -.4 | 2.4 |  |  |  |  | 1.0 | 4.1 |
|  |  |  |  |  |  |  | Net Profit + Depr., Dep., Amort./Cur. Mat. L/T/D | | |
|  |  | .4 | .4 |  |  |  |  | 1.2 | .8 |
|  |  | 1.6 | .9 |  |  |  | Fixed/Worth | 2.9 | 1.9 |
|  |  | UND | -86.0 |  |  |  |  | -2.3 | -1.8 |
|  |  | .5 | .2 |  |  |  |  | .9 | 1.4 |
|  |  | 2.2 | 1.0 |  |  |  | Debt/Worth | 6.4 | 3.8 |
|  |  | UND | -135.6 |  |  |  |  | -5.6 | -4.4 |
|  |  | 85.7 | 51.5 |  |  |  |  | 79.9 | 143.2 |
|  | (13) | 50.6 | (11) 32.2 |  |  |  | % Profit Before Taxes/Tangible Net Worth | (23) 27.2 | (11) 73.2 |
|  |  | 27.1 | 19.6 |  |  |  |  | 2.5 | 43.6 |
|  |  | 40.9 | 27.2 |  |  |  |  | 27.6 | 38.8 |
|  |  | 18.3 | 9.8 |  |  |  | % Profit Before Taxes/Total Assets | 6.8 | 24.6 |
|  |  | -3.9 | 3.1 |  |  |  |  | .0 | 10.9 |
|  |  | 89.2 | 8.2 |  |  |  |  | 12.0 | 6.9 |
|  |  | 7.3 | 6.1 |  |  |  | Sales/Net Fixed Assets | 4.0 | 5.1 |
|  |  | 1.8 | 3.0 |  |  |  |  | 2.0 | 2.6 |
|  |  | 3.8 | 2.3 |  |  |  |  | 4.1 | 2.4 |
|  |  | 2.4 | 1.6 |  |  |  | Sales/Total Assets | 2.0 | 1.4 |
|  |  | 1.3 | 1.2 |  |  |  |  | 1.2 | 1.1 |
|  |  |  |  |  |  |  |  | 5.3 | 4.5 |
|  |  |  |  |  |  |  | % Depr., Dep., Amort./Sales | (23) 9.4 | (12) 7.0 |
|  |  |  |  |  |  |  |  | 17.7 | 13.4 |
|  |  |  |  |  |  |  |  |  | 3.2 |
|  |  |  |  |  |  |  | % Officers', Directors' Owners' Comp/Sales | (15) 5.7 |  |
|  |  |  |  |  |  |  |  | 7.4 |  |
|  | 1953M | 56770M | 161834M | 118407M | 168773M |  | Net Sales ($) | 202689M | 127339M |
|  | 1077M | 20596M | 79706M | 112980M | 138743M |  | Total Assets ($) | 209895M | 131255M |

© RMA 2024    M = $ thousand    MM = $ million
See Pages viii through xx for Explanation of Ratios and Data

# ADMIN & WASTE MANAGEMENT SERVICES—Septic Tank and Related Services  NAICS 562991

## Comparative Historical Data / Current Data Sorted by Sales

| Comparative Historical Data | | | Type of Statement | Current Data Sorted by Sales | | | | | |
|---|---|---|---|---|---|---|---|---|---|
| 1 | 1 | | Unqualified | | 1 | | 1 | 2 | |
| 6 | 2 | 4 | Reviewed | 3 | 1 | 1 | 1 | 2 | |
| 6 | 3 | 8 | Compiled | 3 | 3 | 4 | 2 | 3 | |
| 21 | 15 | 15 | Tax Returns | 1 | 2 | 2 | 4 | 6 | 3 |
| 4/1/21- | 4/1/22- | 4/1/23- | Other | | | | | | |
| 3/31/22 | 3/31/23 | 3/31/24 | | 0-1MM | 6 (4/1-9/30/23) 1-3MM | 3-5MM | 5-10MM | 39 (10/1/23-3/31/24) 10-25MM | 25MM & OVER |
| ALL 34 | ALL 42 | ALL 45 | NUMBER OF STATEMENTS | 7 | 7 | 7 | 8 | 13 | 3 |
| % | % | % | ASSETS | % | % | % | % | % | % |
| 20.1 | 22.8 | 20.9 | Cash & Equivalents | | | | | 10.8 | |
| 14.0 | 12.0 | 12.6 | Trade Receivables (net) | | | | | 15.3 | |
| .1 | .8 | 1.5 | Inventory | | | | | 3.2 | |
| 6.4 | 4.1 | 3.8 | All Other Current | | | | | 1.8 | |
| 40.6 | 39.6 | 38.8 | Total Current | | | | | 31.1 | |
| 44.3 | 41.6 | 45.5 | Fixed Assets (net) | | | | | 52.7 | |
| 9.1 | 11.6 | 7.8 | Intangibles (net) | | | | | 2.4 | |
| 6.0 | 7.2 | 7.8 | All Other Non-Current | | | | | 13.8 | |
| 100.0 | 100.0 | 100.0 | Total | | | | | 100.0 | |
| | | | LIABILITIES | | | | | | |
| 3.2 | 3.0 | 3.5 | Notes Payable-Short Term | | | | | 2.0 | |
| 5.0 | 5.0 | 5.1 | Cur. Mat.-L.T.D. | | | | | 6.0 | |
| 2.8 | 4.5 | 4.1 | Trade Payables | | | | | 6.0 | |
| .0 | .1 | .2 | Income Taxes Payable | | | | | .0 | |
| 6.3 | 3.5 | 6.0 | All Other Current | | | | | 4.3 | |
| 17.3 | 16.0 | 18.9 | Total Current | | | | | 18.4 | |
| 38.6 | 34.1 | 30.8 | Long-Term Debt | | | | | 28.1 | |
| .1 | .0 | .3 | Deferred Taxes | | | | | .4 | |
| 4.0 | 5.6 | 6.4 | All Other Non-Current | | | | | 6.8 | |
| 40.1 | 44.4 | 43.6 | Net Worth | | | | | 46.4 | |
| 100.0 | 100.0 | 100.0 | Total Liabilities & Net Worth | | | | | 100.0 | |
| | | | INCOME DATA | | | | | | |
| 100.0 | 100.0 | 100.0 | Net Sales | | | | | 100.0 | |
| | | | Gross Profit | | | | | | |
| 84.8 | 88.0 | 86.0 | Operating Expenses | | | | | 90.5 | |
| 15.2 | 12.0 | 14.0 | Operating Profit | | | | | 9.5 | |
| 1.1 | 1.3 | 5.0 | All Other Expenses (net) | | | | | -.9 | |
| 14.0 | 10.6 | 9.1 | Profit Before Taxes | | | | | 10.4 | |
| | | | RATIOS | | | | | | |
| 6.9 | 6.5 | 4.4 | | | | | | 3.8 | |
| 2.1 | 2.5 | 1.7 | Current | | | | | 1.1 | |
| 1.4 | .9 | .8 | | | | | | .7 | |
| 5.9 | 6.4 | 3.3 | | | | | | 3.3 | |
| 2.1 | 2.1 | 1.6 | Quick | | | | | 1.1 | |
| 1.4 | .9 | .8 | | | | | | .6 | |
| 0 UND | 0 UND | 0 UND | | | | | | 23 16.0 | |
| 30 12.2 | 13 28.3 | 28 13.1 | Sales/Receivables | | | | | 34 10.6 | |
| 54 6.7 | 47 7.7 | 40 9.1 | | | | | | 41 9.0 | |
| | | | Cost of Sales/Inventory | | | | | | |
| | | | Cost of Sales/Payables | | | | | | |
| 4.1 | 4.4 | 5.9 | | | | | | 7.2 | |
| 6.9 | 9.5 | 14.2 | Sales/Working Capital | | | | | 30.9 | |
| 21.1 | -303.0 | -54.8 | | | | | | -29.0 | |
| 39.8 | 36.7 | 22.3 | | | | | | 41.1 | |
| (29) 14.6 | (35) 8.4 | (35) 5.5 | EBIT/Interest | | | | | (10) 8.8 | |
| 4.3 | 2.5 | 2.3 | | | | | | 4.4 | |
| | | | Net Profit + Depr., Dep., Amort./Cur. Mat. L/T/D | | | | | | |
| .8 | .5 | .5 | | | | | | .4 | |
| 1.2 | 1.5 | 1.6 | Fixed/Worth | | | | | 1.7 | |
| NM | NM | 9.0 | | | | | | 4.1 | |
| .6 | .3 | .4 | | | | | | .4 | |
| 1.7 | 1.2 | 1.4 | Debt/Worth | | | | | 1.2 | |
| NM | NM | 12.4 | | | | | | 4.1 | |
| 86.6 | 100.1 | 67.7 | | | | | | 41.4 | |
| (26) 36.5 | (32) 50.6 | (37) 32.2 | % Profit Before Taxes/Tangible Net Worth | | | | | (11) 25.8 | |
| 15.5 | 19.5 | 15.3 | | | | | | 13.3 | |
| 33.2 | 30.5 | 29.2 | | | | | | 30.8 | |
| 12.4 | 17.3 | 9.8 | % Profit Before Taxes/Total Assets | | | | | 16.1 | |
| 6.6 | 1.0 | 1.6 | | | | | | 4.7 | |
| 7.9 | 9.5 | 9.3 | | | | | | 7.1 | |
| 3.6 | 4.2 | 4.3 | Sales/Net Fixed Assets | | | | | 3.7 | |
| 2.3 | 2.1 | 1.5 | | | | | | 1.3 | |
| 2.8 | 2.7 | 2.7 | | | | | | 2.4 | |
| 1.7 | 1.6 | 1.7 | Sales/Total Assets | | | | | 1.4 | |
| .9 | 1.0 | 1.0 | | | | | | 1.0 | |
| 4.2 | 5.4 | 6.3 | | | | | | | |
| (16) 6.6 | (24) 9.5 | (26) 9.0 | % Depr., Dep., Amort./Sales | | | | | | |
| 20.4 | 14.8 | 15.2 | | | | | | | |
| 3.0 | 2.9 | 2.3 | | | | | | | |
| (15) 7.4 | (16) 4.9 | (18) 4.2 | % Officers', Directors' Owners' Comp/Sales | | | | | | |
| 10.5 | 8.4 | 7.3 | | | | | | | |
| 237407M | 425845M | 507737M | Net Sales ($) | 2019M | 12614M | 27160M | 58341M | 206547M | 201056M |
| 214657M | 422291M | 353102M | Total Assets ($) | 7940M | 7216M | 14427M | 31301M | 148954M | 143264M |

© RMA 2024  
M = $ thousand   MM = $ million  
See Pages viii through xx for Explanation of Ratios and Data

# ADMIN & WASTE MANAGEMENT SERVICES—All Other Miscellaneous Waste Management Services  NAICS 562998

## Current Data Sorted by Assets | Comparative Historical Data

| | | | | | | | Type of Statement | | |
|---|---|---|---|---|---|---|---|---|---|
| | | 1 | 2 | 4 | 2 | | Unqualified | 9 | 4 |
| | | 1 | 3 | 3 | | | Reviewed | 3 | 2 |
| 3 | | 2 | 2 | 1 | | 1 | Compiled | 3 | 5 |
| 1 | | 8 | 17 | 1 | | 2 | Tax Returns | 14 | 13 |
| | | 6 (4/1-9/30/23) | | 8 | 56 (10/1/23-3/31/24) | | Other | 35 | 32 |
| 0-500M | 500M-2MM | 2-10MM | 10-50MM | 50-100MM | 100-250MM | | | 4/1/19-3/31/20 ALL | 4/1/20-3/31/21 ALL |
| 4 | 12 | 24 | 17 | 2 | 3 | | NUMBER OF STATEMENTS | 64 | 56 |
| % | % | % | % | % | % | | ASSETS | % | % |
| | | 28.5 | 22.7 | 7.9 | | | Cash & Equivalents | 11.0 | 14.9 |
| | | 24.4 | 16.2 | 19.0 | | | Trade Receivables (net) | 25.0 | 16.8 |
| | | 3.7 | 2.1 | 1.5 | | | Inventory | 2.0 | 1.7 |
| | | .1 | 4.9 | 2.9 | | | All Other Current | 2.7 | 5.4 |
| | | 56.6 | 45.9 | 31.3 | | | Total Current | 40.7 | 38.8 |
| | | 36.0 | 36.3 | 40.1 | | | Fixed Assets (net) | 43.0 | 45.6 |
| | | 2.8 | 10.3 | 14.8 | | | Intangibles (net) | 9.6 | 6.8 |
| | | 4.5 | 7.5 | 13.7 | | | All Other Non-Current | 6.8 | 8.7 |
| | | 100.0 | 100.0 | 100.0 | | | Total | 100.0 | 100.0 |
| | | | | | | | LIABILITIES | | |
| | | 3.8 | 3.4 | 2.9 | | | Notes Payable-Short Term | 3.9 | 7.5 |
| | | 3.4 | 6.1 | 4.6 | | | Cur. Mat.-L.T.D. | 4.4 | 5.6 |
| | | 4.8 | 8.8 | 7.3 | | | Trade Payables | 10.7 | 7.2 |
| | | .0 | .0 | .2 | | | Income Taxes Payable | .1 | .0 |
| | | 7.8 | 8.5 | 7.2 | | | All Other Current | 11.2 | 10.2 |
| | | 19.8 | 26.9 | 22.3 | | | Total Current | 30.3 | 30.5 |
| | | 26.5 | 37.4 | 24.4 | | | Long-Term Debt | 29.7 | 37.7 |
| | | .0 | .0 | .0 | | | Deferred Taxes | .5 | .0 |
| | | .1 | 8.2 | 4.4 | | | All Other Non-Current | 5.2 | 4.4 |
| | | 53.7 | 27.6 | 49.0 | | | Net Worth | 34.2 | 27.4 |
| | | 100.0 | 100.0 | 100.0 | | | Total Liabilities & Net Worth | 100.0 | 100.0 |
| | | | | | | | INCOME DATA | | |
| | | 100.0 | 100.0 | 100.0 | | | Net Sales | 100.0 | 100.0 |
| | | | | | | | Gross Profit | | |
| | | 89.0 | 84.3 | 89.9 | | | Operating Expenses | 91.3 | 92.1 |
| | | 11.0 | 15.7 | 10.1 | | | Operating Profit | 8.7 | 7.9 |
| | | .5 | 1.6 | 2.1 | | | All Other Expenses (net) | .9 | -.2 |
| | | 10.4 | 14.1 | 8.0 | | | Profit Before Taxes | 7.8 | 8.1 |
| | | | | | | | RATIOS | | |
| | | 20.8 | 6.2 | 2.6 | | | | 2.8 | 2.6 |
| | | 3.9 | 1.5 | 1.3 | | | Current | 1.6 | 1.5 |
| | | 1.2 | .9 | 1.0 | | | | .9 | 1.0 |
| | | 20.8 | 6.2 | 2.1 | | | | 2.3 | 2.3 |
| | | 3.8 | 1.3 | 1.0 | | | Quick | 1.3 | 1.3 |
| | | 1.2 | .8 | .6 | | | | .7 | .7 |
| | 0 UND | 0 UND | 29 12.8 | | | | | 15 25.0 | 0 UND |
| | 27 13.4 | 24 15.2 | 55 6.6 | | | | Sales/Receivables | 41 8.8 | 28 13.0 |
| | 38 9.5 | 49 7.5 | 91 4.0 | | | | | 65 5.6 | 51 7.2 |
| | | | | | | | Cost of Sales/Inventory | | |
| | | | | | | | Cost of Sales/Payables | | |
| | | 5.6 | 4.7 | 5.4 | | | | 6.4 | 8.6 |
| | | 18.8 | 10.6 | 13.9 | | | Sales/Working Capital | 14.5 | 15.0 |
| | | 110.6 | NM | -228.9 | | | | -70.8 | -482.1 |
| | | 159.3 | | 15.5 | | | | 19.7 | 17.9 |
| | | (21) 17.2 | (15) 6.8 | | | | EBIT/Interest | (55) 6.4 | (50) 7.8 |
| | | | -.5 | -.1 | | | | 1.7 | 1.2 |
| | | | | | | | Net Profit + Depr., Dep., Amort./Cur. Mat. L/T/D | | |
| | | .2 | .4 | .6 | | | | .7 | .8 |
| | | .5 | 1.1 | 1.3 | | | Fixed/Worth | 1.2 | 1.6 |
| | | 2.0 | NM | 3.4 | | | | 4.4 | NM |
| | | .2 | .7 | .6 | | | | .7 | 1.0 |
| | | 1.2 | 2.8 | 1.8 | | | Debt/Worth | 1.6 | 1.9 |
| | | 1.8 | NM | 4.1 | | | | 9.6 | NM |
| | | 90.2 | 352.3 | 46.6 | | | | 76.2 | 95.6 |
| | (10) 78.3 | (18) 61.7 | (14) 18.8 | | | | % Profit Before Taxes/Tangible Net Worth | (51) 20.8 | (42) 38.4 |
| | | 37.4 | 31.3 | -8.6 | | | | 8.9 | 18.0 |
| | | 41.9 | 42.9 | 17.3 | | | | 24.8 | 27.1 |
| | | 32.7 | 22.2 | 13.2 | | | % Profit Before Taxes/Total Assets | 9.8 | 12.1 |
| | | 15.2 | -3.8 | -3.2 | | | | 1.5 | 1.7 |
| | | 27.9 | 29.6 | 6.9 | | | | 14.3 | 23.2 |
| | | 12.8 | 8.3 | 3.5 | | | Sales/Net Fixed Assets | 4.6 | 4.3 |
| | | 4.7 | 1.8 | 1.9 | | | | 1.7 | 2.3 |
| | | 3.8 | 3.2 | 1.8 | | | | 3.3 | 3.3 |
| | | 3.3 | 1.5 | 1.3 | | | Sales/Total Assets | 1.7 | 1.9 |
| | | 1.5 | 1.1 | .5 | | | | 1.0 | 1.3 |
| | | | .9 | 3.7 | | | | 2.9 | 5.3 |
| | | (15) 5.8 | (12) 6.2 | | | | % Depr., Dep., Amort./Sales | (46) 6.2 | (36) 7.5 |
| | | | 12.5 | 18.7 | | | | 10.3 | 10.9 |
| | | | | | | | % Officers', Directors' Owners' Comp/Sales | 1.7 | 2.4 |
| | | | | | | | | (18) 4.8 | (13) 4.3 |
| | | | | | | | | 8.3 | 9.3 |
| 2624M | 39964M | 260796M | 441216M | 92311M | 436032M | | Net Sales ($) | 1693958M | 1053364M |
| 1089M | 12773M | 128791M | 407889M | 156717M | 486619M | | Total Assets ($) | 1369750M | 995380M |

M = $ thousand    MM = $ million
See Pages viii through xx for Explanation of Ratios and Data

© RMA 2024

# ADMIN & WASTE MANAGEMENT SERVICES—All Other Miscellaneous Waste Management Services  NAICS 562998

## Comparative Historical Data | Current Data Sorted by Sales

| Comparative Historical Data | | | | | Current Data Sorted by Sales | | | | | |
|---|---|---|---|---|---|---|---|---|---|---|
| 4 | 4 | 6 | Type of Statement | | | 2 | 1 | 3 | | |
| 2 | 5 | 6 | Unqualified | | 1 | 1 | 1 | 3 | | |
| 4 | 5 | 6 | Reviewed | | | 1 | 3 | 1 | | |
| 12 | 8 | 8 | Compiled | | 1 | 2 | 2 | | | |
| 27 | 53 | 36 | Tax Returns | 2 | 1 | 1 | 2 | 2 | | |
| | | | Other | 4 | 5 | 5 | 8 | 10 | 4 | |
| 4/1/21-3/31/22 ALL | 4/1/22-3/31/23 ALL | 4/1/23-3/31/24 ALL | | 0-1MM | 6 (4/1-9/30/23) 1-3MM | 3-5MM | 56 (10/1/23-3/31/24) 5-10MM | 10-25MM | 25MM & OVER | |
| 49 | 75 | 62 | **NUMBER OF STATEMENTS** | 6 | 6 | 8 | 14 | 17 | 11 | |
| % | % | % | **ASSETS** | % | % | % | % | % | % | |
| 18.4 | 16.1 | 19.9 | Cash & Equivalents | | | | 16.2 | 12.3 | 8.3 | |
| 21.1 | 20.8 | 19.0 | Trade Receivables (net) | | | | 17.1 | 14.9 | 27.5 | |
| .7 | 2.7 | 2.0 | Inventory | | | | .7 | 2.2 | 1.5 | |
| 3.6 | 5.5 | 3.0 | All Other Current | | | | 3.2 | 5.7 | 3.4 | |
| 43.8 | 45.0 | 43.8 | Total Current | | | | 37.1 | 35.1 | 40.7 | |
| 35.5 | 36.9 | 35.8 | Fixed Assets (net) | | | | 43.9 | 38.3 | 27.2 | |
| 11.6 | 9.0 | 11.9 | Intangibles (net) | | | | 5.4 | 20.6 | 16.6 | |
| 9.1 | 9.1 | 8.4 | All Other Non-Current | | | | 13.5 | 6.0 | 15.5 | |
| 100.0 | 100.0 | 100.0 | Total | | | | 100.0 | 100.0 | 100.0 | |
| | | | **LIABILITIES** | | | | | | | |
| 5.3 | 6.8 | 4.2 | Notes Payable-Short Term | | | | 1.0 | 3.3 | 4.7 | |
| 3.7 | 5.6 | 4.9 | Cur. Mat.-L.T.D. | | | | 3.1 | 6.6 | 6.5 | |
| 8.1 | 8.6 | 7.8 | Trade Payables | | | | 6.2 | 6.1 | 12.5 | |
| .1 | .4 | .1 | Income Taxes Payable | | | | .0 | .0 | .3 | |
| 9.5 | 9.6 | 7.5 | All Other Current | | | | 7.5 | 2.0 | 8.7 | |
| 26.7 | 31.0 | 24.6 | Total Current | | | | 17.9 | 18.0 | 32.6 | |
| 32.9 | 30.7 | 28.2 | Long-Term Debt | | | | 40.0 | 31.3 | 19.9 | |
| .0 | .0 | .1 | Deferred Taxes | | | | .0 | .0 | .5 | |
| 3.8 | 2.3 | 6.3 | All Other Non-Current | | | | 14.2 | 3.2 | 11.4 | |
| 36.6 | 36.1 | 40.9 | Net Worth | | | | 27.9 | 47.5 | 35.5 | |
| 100.0 | 100.0 | 100.0 | Total Liabilties & Net Worth | | | | 100.0 | 100.0 | 100.0 | |
| | | | **INCOME DATA** | | | | | | | |
| 100.0 | 100.0 | 100.0 | Net Sales | | | | 100.0 | 100.0 | 100.0 | |
| | | | Gross Profit | | | | | | | |
| 89.8 | 89.9 | 87.1 | Operating Expenses | | | | 89.1 | 88.2 | 92.7 | |
| 10.2 | 10.1 | 12.9 | Operating Profit | | | | 10.9 | 11.8 | 7.3 | |
| -1.0 | 1.3 | 1.6 | All Other Expenses (net) | | | | 1.9 | 1.5 | 2.2 | |
| 11.3 | 8.9 | 11.3 | Profit Before Taxes | | | | 9.0 | 10.3 | 5.1 | |
| | | | **RATIOS** | | | | | | | |
| 3.3 | 3.1 | 5.4 | | | | | 3.7 | 7.4 | 1.8 | |
| 1.6 | 1.6 | 1.4 | Current | | | | 2.3 | 1.8 | 1.3 | |
| 1.3 | 1.0 | 1.0 | | | | | 1.2 | .9 | 1.0 | |
| 2.7 | 2.8 | 5.4 | | | | | 3.7 | 7.0 | 1.4 | |
| 1.5 | 1.4 | 1.3 | Quick | | | | 2.1 | 1.5 | 1.1 | |
| 1.0 | .6 | .8 | | | | | .8 | .7 | .8 | |
| 0 UND | 9 41.9 | 8 46.6 | | | | | 12 31.1 | 1 519.4 | 33 11.2 | |
| 38 9.7 | 36 10.2 | 33 11.1 | Sales/Receivables | | | | 41 8.9 | 33 10.9 | 55 6.6 | |
| 60 6.1 | 59 6.2 | 60 6.1 | | | | | 69 5.3 | 54 6.7 | 74 4.9 | |
| | | | Cost of Sales/Inventory | | | | | | | |
| | | | Cost of Sales/Payables | | | | | | | |
| 6.7 | 6.6 | 5.4 | | | | | 5.7 | 4.9 | 12.0 | |
| 15.0 | 16.3 | 13.1 | Sales/Working Capital | | | | 11.5 | 9.7 | 22.4 | |
| 33.6 | -147.5 | NM | | | | | NM | -227.5 | 139.6 | |
| 37.8 | 26.3 | 56.9 | | | | | 81.9 | 53.0 | 25.5 | |
| (42) 14.3 | (62) 10.1 | (51) 10.1 | EBIT/Interest | | | (10) 3.3 | (16) 9.5 | 9.1 | | |
| 2.9 | 3.7 | .3 | | | | | -.9 | 3.3 | .3 | |
| | | | Net Profit + Depr., Dep., Amort./Cur. Mat. L/T/D | | | | | | | |
| .4 | .4 | .4 | | | | | .3 | .6 | .4 | |
| .8 | .9 | 1.2 | Fixed/Worth | | | | 1.0 | 1.5 | 1.3 | |
| 6.9 | 2.8 | NM | | | | | NM | -276.8 | -1.1 | |
| .5 | .7 | .5 | | | | | .4 | .7 | 1.8 | |
| 1.7 | 1.8 | 1.8 | Debt/Worth | | | | 1.8 | 1.7 | 2.6 | |
| 367.6 | 6.1 | NM | | | | | NM | -378.0 | -3.8 | |
| 95.2 | 81.2 | 86.2 | | | | | 83.7 | 90.4 | | |
| (38) 42.3 | (60) 43.3 | (47) 43.7 | % Profit Before Taxes/Tangible Net Worth | | | (11) 66.7 | (12) 42.0 | | | |
| 17.4 | 17.7 | 15.8 | | | | | 2.2 | 17.4 | | |
| 39.5 | 27.5 | 36.6 | | | | | 35.3 | 33.7 | 17.3 | |
| 16.6 | 14.3 | 16.9 | % Profit Before Taxes/Total Assets | | | | 19.0 | 16.2 | 4.8 | |
| 7.3 | 6.1 | -1.2 | | | | | -6.3 | -.6 | -2.9 | |
| 31.6 | 34.6 | 18.6 | | | | | 20.5 | 17.1 | 15.9 | |
| 6.4 | 5.5 | 4.7 | Sales/Net Fixed Assets | | | | 3.5 | 4.3 | 8.4 | |
| 2.8 | 2.5 | 2.0 | | | | | 1.2 | 2.6 | 3.5 | |
| 2.9 | 3.5 | 3.1 | | | | | 3.4 | 3.0 | 1.9 | |
| 1.9 | 1.6 | 1.5 | Sales/Total Assets | | | | 1.3 | 1.8 | 1.6 | |
| 1.3 | 1.2 | 1.0 | | | | | .4 | 1.1 | 1.1 | |
| 2.7 | 2.3 | 1.9 | | | | | | 3.3 | | |
| (24) 6.4 | (38) 4.9 | (36) 5.7 | % Depr., Dep., Amort./Sales | | | | | (11) 5.8 | | |
| 11.9 | 9.9 | 12.0 | | | | | | 12.4 | | |
| 2.1 | 1.6 | 2.0 | | | | | | | | |
| (14) 4.4 | (19) 2.0 | (19) 3.6 | % Officers', Directors' Owners' Comp/Sales | | | | | | | |
| 10.1 | 3.5 | 11.8 | | | | | | | | |
| 1145992M | 2133768M | 1272943M | Net Sales ($) | 3409M | 12703M | 32670M | 104220M | 279322M | 840619M | |
| 931549M | 1701116M | 1193878M | Total Assets ($) | 4109M | 7696M | 25171M | 151015M | 271457M | 734430M | |

© RMA 2024  M = $ thousand  MM = $ million
See Pages viii through xx for Explanation of Ratios and Data

# EDUCATIONAL SERVICES

# EDUCATION—Elementary and Secondary Schools  NAICS 611110

## Current Data Sorted by Assets

| 2 | 10 | 78 | 335 | 160 | 158 | Type of Statement |
|---|---|---|---|---|---|---|
|  | 1 | 14 | 13 |  |  | Unqualified |
|  |  | 10 | 2 | 1 | 1 | Reviewed |
| 8 | 13 | 15 | 7 |  |  | Compiled |
| 15 | 29 | 83 | 121 | 35 | 27 | Tax Returns |
|  |  |  |  |  |  | Other |

1,010 (4/1-9/30/23)   128 (10/1/23-3/31/24)

| 0-500M | 500M-2MM | 2-10MM | 10-50MM | 50-100MM | 100-250MM | | 
|---|---|---|---|---|---|---|
| 25 | 53 | 200 | 478 | 196 | 186 | NUMBER OF STATEMENTS |
| % | % | % | % | % | % | ASSETS |
| 53.4 | 48.3 | 31.1 | 30.4 | 29.0 | 23.4 | Cash & Equivalents |
| 3.6 | 5.8 | 6.0 | 5.3 | 4.8 | 4.2 | Trade Receivables (net) |
| .0 | 1.5 | .2 | .2 | .1 | .1 | Inventory |
| 7.0 | 7.4 | 5.0 | 4.4 | 2.9 | 4.2 | All Other Current |
| 64.0 | 62.9 | 42.2 | 40.3 | 36.9 | 31.8 | Total Current |
| 18.5 | 19.6 | 47.0 | 46.0 | 47.3 | 46.8 | Fixed Assets (net) |
| 5.2 | 5.2 | 1.6 | 1.0 | 1.3 | 2.7 | Intangibles (net) |
| 12.3 | 12.3 | 9.2 | 12.8 | 14.5 | 18.7 | All Other Non-Current |
| 100.0 | 100.0 | 100.0 | 100.0 | 100.0 | 100.0 | Total |
|  |  |  |  |  |  | LIABILITIES |
| 3.5 | 2.3 | .9 | .5 | .7 | .6 | Notes Payable-Short Term |
| 11.0 | 2.5 | 1.8 | 1.6 | 1.4 | 1.7 | Cur. Mat.-L.T.D. |
| 1.6 | 2.1 | 2.8 | 2.2 | 2.1 | 2.0 | Trade Payables |
| .0 | .0 | 1.0 | .0 | .1 | .0 | Income Taxes Payable |
| 39.2 | 13.7 | 9.1 | 8.2 | 7.4 | 5.4 | All Other Current |
| 55.2 | 20.5 | 15.7 | 12.5 | 11.7 | 9.7 | Total Current |
| 21.0 | 35.2 | 26.0 | 23.2 | 27.4 | 27.9 | Long-Term Debt |
| .0 | .0 | .1 | .2 | .3 | .3 | Deferred Taxes |
| .6 | 7.2 | 10.4 | 19.9 | 22.1 | 33.0 | All Other Non-Current |
| 23.2 | 37.1 | 47.8 | 44.3 | 38.5 | 29.0 | Net Worth |
| 100.0 | 100.0 | 100.0 | 100.0 | 100.0 | 100.0 | Total Liabilities & Net Worth |
|  |  |  |  |  |  | INCOME DATA |
| 100.0 | 100.0 | 100.0 | 100.0 | 100.0 | 100.0 | Net Sales |
|  |  |  |  |  |  | Gross Profit |
| 92.8 | 91.0 | 92.7 | 93.9 | 92.1 | 92.2 | Operating Expenses |
| 7.2 | 9.0 | 7.3 | 6.1 | 7.9 | 7.8 | Operating Profit |
| -1.3 | -.2 | 1.1 | 1.1 | 1.0 | 1.5 | All Other Expenses (net) |
| 8.5 | 9.2 | 6.2 | 5.0 | 6.9 | 6.3 | Profit Before Taxes |
|  |  |  |  |  |  | RATIOS |
| 22.4 | 22.0 | 7.3 | 7.9 | 6.4 | 6.7 |  |
| 5.1 | 3.7 | 3.7 | 3.8 | 3.4 | 3.3 | Current |
| .6 | 1.3 | 1.6 | 1.9 | 1.7 | 1.6 |  |
| 16.6 | 16.1 | 7.2 | 7.3 | 5.6 | 6.2 |  |
| 4.1 | 2.8 | 3.0 | 3.3 | 3.2 | 2.8 | Quick |
| .6 | 1.0 | 1.3 | 1.6 | 1.5 | 1.4 |  |
| 0 UND | 0 UND | 0 UND | 1 333.7 | 1 634.4 | 1 319.6 |  |
| 0 UND | 0 999.8 | 3 115.7 | 7 51.1 | 10 37.5 | 9 38.7 | Sales/Receivables |
| 0 UND | 13 28.6 | 15 23.7 | 26 14.0 | 32 11.3 | 30 12.0 |  |
|  |  |  |  |  |  | Cost of Sales/Inventory |
|  |  |  |  |  |  | Cost of Sales/Payables |
| 7.7 | 2.7 | 2.7 | 2.0 | 1.8 | 1.6 |  |
| 18.5 | 5.3 | 5.0 | 3.8 | 3.2 | 3.1 | Sales/Working Capital |
| -33.8 | 24.7 | 15.9 | 9.0 | 7.3 | 8.8 |  |
|  | 19.7 | 13.3 | 10.9 | 9.7 | 11.4 |  |
| (28) | 7.1 (156) | 4.0 (374) | 3.8 (149) | 3.6 (161) | 3.7 | EBIT/Interest |
|  | 1.9 | .0 | .9 | 1.4 | 1.2 |  |
|  |  |  |  |  |  | Net Profit + Depr., Dep., Amort./Cur. Mat. L/T/D |
| .0 | .0 | .2 | .5 | .5 | .6 |  |
| .2 | .1 | .9 | 1.0 | 1.1 | 1.6 | Fixed/Worth |
| 1.1 | .9 | 2.1 | 2.3 | 3.5 | 25.1 |  |
| .1 | .3 | .4 | .3 | .4 | .5 |  |
| .2 | .7 | .8 | .9 | 1.2 | 2.0 | Debt/Worth |
| -4.0 | 2.8 | 2.7 | 3.1 | 5.1 | 66.9 |  |
| 119.8 | 59.7 | 26.3 | 16.6 | 15.1 | 19.9 | % Profit Before Taxes/Tangible Net Worth |
| (17) 46.6 | (44) 21.7 | (181) 10.8 | (423) 6.7 | (162) 6.1 | (141) 8.6 |  |
| 14.6 | 9.7 | -.6 | -.7 | -.1 | 1.5 |  |
| 72.9 | 31.8 | 12.2 | 7.3 | 6.3 | 5.5 | % Profit Before Taxes/Total Assets |
| 28.5 | 10.6 | 4.5 | 3.0 | 2.7 | 2.7 |  |
| -6.6 | 3.8 | -.7 | -.5 | -.1 | .3 |  |
| UND | 386.2 | 26.3 | 3.1 | 1.5 | 1.3 | Sales/Net Fixed Assets |
| 67.2 | 31.6 | 1.5 | 1.1 | .9 | .8 |  |
| 16.0 | 7.1 | .9 | .7 | .6 | .6 |  |
| 10.3 | 3.2 | 1.7 | 1.0 | .7 | .7 | Sales/Total Assets |
| 5.4 | 2.1 | .9 | .6 | .5 | .4 |  |
| 2.4 | 1.2 | .6 | .4 | .3 | .3 |  |
|  | .6 | 2.6 | 3.6 | 4.1 | 3.8 | % Depr., Dep., Amort./Sales |
| (25) | .9 (134) | 4.0 (361) | 5.4 (147) | 5.8 (146) | 5.7 |  |
|  | 2.0 | 5.7 | 7.7 | 8.0 | 7.5 |  |
|  | 2.4 | 1.0 | .9 | 4.3 |  | % Officers', Directors', Owners' Comp/Sales |
| (17) | 3.5 (18) | 2.7 (23) | 4.6 (10) | 6.7 |  |  |
|  | 5.2 | 5.0 | 16.3 | 10.3 |  |  |
| 35420M | 202078M | 1783095M | 14230452M | 11827511M | 19656377M | Net Sales ($) |
| 6273M | 63491M | 1142245M | 12254677M | 13816080M | 28476478M | Total Assets ($) |

## Comparative Historical Data

| | 936 | 643 |
|---|---|---|
| Unqualified | 41 | 33 |
| Reviewed | 34 | 18 |
| Compiled | 79 | 34 |
| Tax Returns | 311 | 287 |
| Other | | |

| 4/1/19-3/31/20 ALL | 4/1/20-3/31/21 ALL | |
|---|---|---|
| 1401 | 1015 | NUMBER OF STATEMENTS |
| % | % | ASSETS |
| 25.9 | 27.0 | Cash & Equivalents |
| 4.9 | 4.7 | Trade Receivables (net) |
| .1 | .1 | Inventory |
| 3.2 | 3.0 | All Other Current |
| 34.1 | 34.8 | Total Current |
| 50.2 | 49.4 | Fixed Assets (net) |
| 1.7 | 1.5 | Intangibles (net) |
| 14.0 | 14.2 | All Other Non-Current |
| 100.0 | 100.0 | Total |
|  |  | LIABILITIES |
| 1.2 | 2.0 | Notes Payable-Short Term |
| 1.8 | 2.3 | Cur. Mat.-L.T.D. |
| 2.6 | 2.5 | Trade Payables |
| .0 | .0 | Income Taxes Payable |
| 9.1 | 7.8 | All Other Current |
| 14.8 | 14.5 | Total Current |
| 25.5 | 27.7 | Long-Term Debt |
| .1 | .1 | Deferred Taxes |
| 18.8 | 20.9 | All Other Non-Current |
| 40.8 | 36.8 | Net Worth |
| 100.0 | 100.0 | Total Liabilities & Net Worth |
|  |  | INCOME DATA |
| 100.0 | 100.0 | Net Sales |
|  |  | Gross Profit |
| 93.5 | 94.8 | Operating Expenses |
| 6.5 | 5.2 | Operating Profit |
| 2.1 | 2.3 | All Other Expenses (net) |
| 4.4 | 2.9 | Profit Before Taxes |
|  |  | RATIOS |
| 6.0 | 5.7 |  |
| 2.7 | 2.9 | Current |
| 1.3 | 1.4 |  |
| 5.6 | 5.3 |  |
| 2.4 | 2.4 | Quick |
| 1.1 | 1.2 |  |
| 0 999.8 | 0 999.8 |  |
| 5 66.7 | 5 71.8 | Sales/Receivables |
| 22 16.8 | 25 14.7 |  |
|  |  | Cost of Sales/Inventory |
|  |  | Cost of Sales/Payables |
| 2.3 | 2.3 |  |
| 5.2 | 4.2 | Sales/Working Capital |
| 21.3 | 12.9 |  |
| 7.1 | 5.6 |  |
| (1119) 2.6 | (787) 1.9 | EBIT/Interest |
| .4 | -.1 |  |
|  |  | Net Profit + Depr., Dep., Amort./Cur. Mat. L/T/D |
| .5 | .6 |  |
| 1.1 | 1.2 | Fixed/Worth |
| 2.8 | 4.1 |  |
| .4 | .4 |  |
| .9 | 1.1 | Debt/Worth |
| 3.7 | 6.5 |  |
| 12.8 | 12.1 | % Profit Before Taxes/Tangible Net Worth |
| (1178) 4.3 | (833) 3.8 |  |
| -1.0 | -1.7 |  |
| 6.1 | 5.1 | % Profit Before Taxes/Total Assets |
| 2.2 | 1.4 |  |
| -.8 | -1.6 |  |
| 2.8 | 2.4 | Sales/Net Fixed Assets |
| 1.0 | 1.0 |  |
| .7 | .6 |  |
| 1.1 | 1.0 | Sales/Total Assets |
| .6 | .5 |  |
| .4 | .4 |  |
| 3.1 | 3.2 | % Depr., Dep., Amort./Sales |
| (1119) 5.2 | (811) 5.5 |  |
| 7.6 | 7.7 |  |
| 2.5 | 2.9 | % Officers', Directors', Owners' Comp/Sales |
| (104) 4.7 | (66) 4.7 |  |
| 9.1 | 10.2 |  |
| 41418181M | 31299297M | Net Sales ($) |
| 63304872M | 48905260M | Total Assets ($) |

© RMA 2024  
M = $ thousand   MM = $ million  
See Pages viii through xx for Explanation of Ratios and Data

## EDUCATION—Elementary and Secondary Schools NAICS 611110

### Comparative Historical Data

| | | | | | | Current Data Sorted by Sales | | | | | |
|---|---|---|---|---|---|---|---|---|---|---|---|
| | | | **Type of Statement** | | | | | | | | |
| 539 | 719 | 743 | Unqualified | 1 | 11 | 28 | 103 | 220 | 380 | | |
| 31 | 38 | 28 | Reviewed | | 7 | 5 | 8 | 8 | | | |
| 18 | 18 | 14 | Compiled | | 4 | 2 | 5 | 2 | 1 | | |
| 36 | 47 | 43 | Tax Returns | 5 | 15 | 8 | 9 | 6 | | | |
| 280 | 306 | 310 | Other | 19 | 40 | 37 | 64 | 83 | 67 | | |
| 4/1/21-3/31/22 ALL | 4/1/22-3/31/23 ALL | 4/1/23-3/31/24 ALL | | 1,010 (4/1-9/30/23) | | | 128 (10/1/23-3/31/24) | | | | |
| | | | | 0-1MM | 1-3MM | 3-5MM | 5-10MM | 10-25MM | 25MM & OVER | | |
| 904 | 1128 | 1138 | NUMBER OF STATEMENTS | 25 | 77 | 80 | 189 | 319 | 448 | | |
| % | % | % | **ASSETS** | % | % | % | % | % | % | | |
| 28.8 | 30.8 | 30.5 | Cash & Equivalents | 31.8 | 37.1 | 29.4 | 23.9 | 26.1 | 35.4 | | |
| 5.4 | 5.3 | 5.1 | Trade Receivables (net) | .3 | 4.0 | 4.4 | 4.6 | 4.6 | 6.3 | | |
| .1 | .2 | .2 | Inventory | 3.2 | .0 | .0 | .1 | .3 | .2 | | |
| 3.6 | 4.5 | 4.4 | All Other Current | 5.6 | 2.8 | 3.7 | 3.4 | 3.2 | 6.0 | | |
| 38.0 | 40.9 | 40.2 | Total Current | 40.9 | 43.8 | 37.5 | 32.0 | 34.2 | 47.9 | | |
| 48.7 | 43.7 | 44.7 | Fixed Assets (net) | 50.7 | 41.9 | 51.1 | 53.2 | 49.7 | 36.5 | | |
| 1.7 | 1.6 | 1.7 | Intangibles (net) | 3.0 | 3.3 | 1.9 | 1.4 | 1.2 | 1.8 | | |
| 11.5 | 13.7 | 13.4 | All Other Non-Current | 5.4 | 11.0 | 9.5 | 13.4 | 14.9 | 13.8 | | |
| 100.0 | 100.0 | 100.0 | Total | 100.0 | 100.0 | 100.0 | 100.0 | 100.0 | 100.0 | | |
| | | | **LIABILITIES** | | | | | | | | |
| 1.3 | 1.0 | .8 | Notes Payable-Short Term | 3.8 | 1.4 | .6 | .7 | .8 | .5 | | |
| 2.0 | 1.7 | 1.9 | Cur. Mat.-L.T.D. | 1.4 | 5.6 | 1.8 | 1.9 | 1.3 | 1.6 | | |
| 2.1 | 2.5 | 2.2 | Trade Payables | .2 | 1.9 | 1.1 | 1.5 | 1.4 | 3.5 | | |
| .1 | .1 | .2 | Income Taxes Payable | .0 | .0 | .5 | .8 | .0 | .1 | | |
| 8.1 | 8.8 | 8.7 | All Other Current | 9.6 | 14.0 | 10.3 | 7.3 | 7.8 | 8.8 | | |
| 13.5 | 14.1 | 13.8 | Total Current | 15.1 | 22.9 | 14.4 | 12.3 | 11.3 | 14.4 | | |
| 29.7 | 24.7 | 25.7 | Long-Term Debt | 34.9 | 31.8 | 27.6 | 29.1 | 23.6 | 23.9 | | |
| .1 | .2 | .2 | Deferred Taxes | .0 | .0 | .1 | .0 | .2 | .3 | | |
| 21.7 | 18.2 | 19.7 | All Other Non-Current | 1.7 | 7.3 | 11.3 | 12.7 | 20.3 | 27.0 | | |
| 35.1 | 42.8 | 40.6 | Net Worth | 48.3 | 38.0 | 46.7 | 46.0 | 44.6 | 34.4 | | |
| 100.0 | 100.0 | 100.0 | Total Liabilities & Net Worth | 100.0 | 100.0 | 100.0 | 100.0 | 100.0 | 100.0 | | |
| | | | **INCOME DATA** | | | | | | | | |
| 100.0 | 100.0 | 100.0 | Net Sales | 100.0 | 100.0 | 100.0 | 100.0 | 100.0 | 100.0 | | |
| | | | Gross Profit | | | | | | | | |
| 90.4 | 92.3 | 92.9 | Operating Expenses | 83.8 | 91.1 | 94.0 | 93.3 | 93.5 | 93.0 | | |
| 9.6 | 7.7 | 7.1 | Operating Profit | 16.2 | 8.9 | 6.0 | 6.7 | 6.5 | 7.0 | | |
| .7 | 2.3 | 1.0 | All Other Expenses (net) | 4.0 | .4 | .4 | 1.0 | .5 | 1.5 | | |
| 9.0 | 5.3 | 6.0 | Profit Before Taxes | 12.2 | 8.5 | 5.6 | 5.7 | 6.1 | 5.4 | | |
| | | | **RATIOS** | | | | | | | | |
| 7.0 | 7.1 | 7.5 | | 12.0 | 11.9 | 11.2 | 7.7 | 7.8 | 6.8 | | |
| 3.5 | 3.5 | 3.6 | Current | 3.2 | 4.3 | 4.0 | 3.1 | 3.6 | 3.6 | | |
| 1.8 | 1.8 | 1.7 | | .6 | 1.3 | 1.9 | 1.3 | 1.6 | 2.0 | | |
| 6.6 | 6.4 | 7.0 | | 8.2 | 11.9 | 10.3 | 7.1 | 7.3 | 6.2 | | |
| 3.1 | 3.1 | 3.1 | Quick | 2.5 | 4.2 | 3.8 | 2.7 | 3.1 | 3.1 | | |
| 1.5 | 1.6 | 1.5 | | .5 | 1.1 | 1.5 | 1.2 | 1.4 | 1.7 | | |
| 0 999.8 | 0 999.8 | 0 999.8 | | 0 UND | 0 UND | 0 UND | 0 999.8 | 1 318.1 | 1 465.3 | | |
| 7 51.9 | 6 58.6 | 6 57.2 | Sales/Receivables | 0 UND | 0 UND | 3 115.0 | 6 66.2 | 8 43.7 | 8 44.4 | | |
| 33 10.9 | 27 13.4 | 24 15.1 | | 0 835.0 | 9 41.9 | 22 16.7 | 18 19.9 | 30 12.2 | 24 15.3 | | |
| | | | Cost of Sales/Inventory | | | | | | | | |
| | | | Cost of Sales/Payables | | | | | | | | |
| 2.0 | 2.0 | 2.0 | | 1.8 | 2.7 | 1.6 | 2.2 | 1.8 | 2.1 | | |
| 3.6 | 3.9 | 3.9 | Sales/Working Capital | 5.2 | 6.6 | 3.3 | 4.0 | 3.7 | 3.9 | | |
| 7.4 | 9.4 | 10.3 | | -44.7 | 29.9 | 11.8 | 20.7 | 8.5 | 8.9 | | |
| 13.3 | 11.8 | 11.2 | | 8.1 | 13.2 | 9.3 | 10.1 | 10.8 | 13.2 | | |
| (712) 4.4 | (860) 4.1 | (877) 3.8 | EBIT/Interest | (13) 3.0 | (50) 5.7 | (57) 4.0 | (149) 3.3 | (270) 4.2 | (338) 3.8 | | |
| 1.5 | .8 | .9 | | -.6 | .4 | .9 | .4 | .7 | 1.2 | | |
| | | | Net Profit + Depr., Dep., Amort./Cur. Mat. L/T/D | | | | | | | | |
| .6 | .3 | .4 | | .1 | .1 | .6 | .7 | .6 | .0 | | |
| 1.2 | 1.0 | 1.0 | Fixed/Worth | 1.0 | .9 | 1.1 | 1.1 | 1.0 | 1.0 | | |
| 3.6 | 2.7 | 2.8 | | 2.7 | 2.0 | 2.4 | 2.4 | 2.2 | 4.2 | | |
| .4 | .3 | .4 | | .1 | .5 | .4 | .3 | .3 | .4 | | |
| 1.2 | .9 | 1.0 | Debt/Worth | .6 | .9 | .9 | .9 | .9 | 1.2 | | |
| 6.5 | 3.9 | 4.1 | | NM | 3.8 | 3.4 | 3.1 | 3.1 | 8.6 | | |
| 28.3 | 22.0 | 19.9 | % Profit Before Taxes/Tangible Net Worth | 24.9 | 50.5 | 19.4 | 19.5 | 14.9 | 20.3 | | |
| (739) 12.2 | (965) 7.8 | (968) 7.9 | | (19) 15.0 | (65) 18.5 | (72) 10.1 | (169) 7.9 | (281) 6.1 | (362) 8.3 | | |
| 4.6 | -.7 | -.1 | | -.7 | 4.6 | .0 | -.8 | -.3 | .7 | | |
| 10.4 | 8.6 | 8.1 | % Profit Before Taxes/Total Assets | 14.8 | 23.2 | 8.3 | 7.6 | 6.9 | 7.8 | | |
| 4.6 | 3.8 | 3.3 | | 5.6 | 7.8 | 4.2 | 3.0 | 2.8 | 3.2 | | |
| 1.1 | -.5 | -.2 | | -.6 | -.4 | .0 | -.7 | -.3 | .0 | | |
| 2.9 | 6.1 | 4.9 | Sales/Net Fixed Assets | 36.5 | 54.2 | 3.9 | 1.8 | 1.5 | UND | | |
| 1.0 | 1.1 | 1.1 | | 2.3 | 3.9 | 1.2 | 1.0 | .9 | 1.4 | | |
| .7 | .7 | .7 | | .2 | .8 | .7 | .7 | .6 | .8 | | |
| 1.0 | 1.4 | 1.2 | Sales/Total Assets | 1.7 | 2.3 | 1.2 | 1.0 | .8 | 2.0 | | |
| .6 | .6 | .6 | | .8 | 1.0 | .6 | .6 | .5 | .7 | | |
| .4 | .4 | .4 | | .2 | .5 | .4 | .4 | .4 | .5 | | |
| 3.1 | 3.2 | 3.3 | % Depr., Dep., Amort./Sales | .7 | 1.1 | 2.6 | 3.5 | 4.1 | 3.2 | | |
| (700) 5.0 | (798) 5.2 | (820) 5.1 | | (11) 3.5 | (44) 3.1 | (62) 4.3 | (161) 5.3 | (271) 5.7 | (271) 4.9 | | |
| 7.2 | 7.4 | 7.3 | | 11.2 | 5.4 | 6.0 | 7.8 | 8.1 | 6.8 | | |
| 2.5 | 2.7 | 1.8 | % Officers', Directors' Owners' Comp/Sales | | 2.6 | | .8 | | 1.4 | | |
| (61) 4.2 | (95) 5.1 | (83) 4.6 | | (14) 4.8 | | (13) 2.5 | | (35) 6.4 | | | |
| 8.6 | 8.3 | 8.3 | | | 6.0 | | 4.6 | | 16.3 | | |
| 26707454M | 46021627M | 47734933M | Net Sales ($) | 15680M | 146145M | 319216M | 1394260M | 5194332M | 40665300M | | |
| 42065244M | 58657169M | 55759244M | Total Assets ($) | 55145M | 181026M | 542330M | 2901967M | 11595914M | 40482862M | | |

© RMA 2024    M = $ thousand    MM = $ million
See Pages viii through xx for Explanation of Ratios and Data

# EDUCATION—Colleges, Universities, and Professional Schools   NAICS 611310

## Current Data Sorted by Assets | Comparative Historical Data

| Type of Statement | | | | | | | | |
|---|---|---|---|---|---|---|---|---|
| | 1 | 2 | 9 | 25 | 46 | 86 | Unqualified | 293 | 198 |
| | | | | | 1 | 1 | Reviewed | 1 | 1 |
| | | | | | 1 | | Compiled | | |
| | | | | | | 2 | Tax Returns | 2 | 1 |
| | 1 | | 5 | 27 | 20 | 26 | Other | 26 | |
| | 1 | 5 | | 44 (10/1/23-3/31/24) | | | | 77 | 108 |
| | 0-500M | 500M-2MM | 2-10MM | 10-50MM | 50-100MM | 100-250MM | | 4/1/19-3/31/20 ALL | 4/1/20-3/31/21 ALL |
| | 3 | 7 | 14 | 52 | 66 | 116 | NUMBER OF STATEMENTS | 398 | 308 |
| | % | % | % | % | % | % | ASSETS | % | % |
| | | | 24.7 | 16.1 | 16.9 | 12.3 | Cash & Equivalents | 16.8 | 17.8 |
| | | | 5.1 | 5.5 | 6.5 | 3.5 | Trade Receivables (net) | 4.4 | 4.8 |
| | | | .0 | .2 | .2 | .2 | Inventory | .2 | .2 |
| | | | 3.0 | 6.0 | 3.1 | 2.0 | All Other Current | 2.8 | 2.7 |
| | | | 32.7 | 27.7 | 26.7 | 18.0 | Total Current | 24.2 | 25.5 |
| | | | 50.2 | 49.7 | 45.5 | 46.6 | Fixed Assets (net) | 47.1 | 47.1 |
| | | | 3.6 | 1.1 | 1.7 | .9 | Intangibles (net) | 1.7 | 2.1 |
| | | | 13.4 | 21.5 | 26.1 | 34.5 | All Other Non-Current | 27.0 | 25.3 |
| | | | 100.0 | 100.0 | 100.0 | 100.0 | Total | 100.0 | 100.0 |
| | | | | | | | LIABILITIES | | |
| | | | 2.9 | 1.1 | .8 | .9 | Notes Payable-Short Term | 1.3 | 1.3 |
| | | | 2.1 | 2.0 | 1.4 | 1.1 | Cur. Mat.-L.T.D. | 1.4 | 2.1 |
| | | | 2.2 | 2.4 | 2.6 | 2.4 | Trade Payables | 2.7 | 2.3 |
| | | | .0 | .0 | .2 | .0 | Income Taxes Payable | .0 | .1 |
| | | | 7.3 | 9.4 | 5.6 | 4.1 | All Other Current | 6.4 | 6.1 |
| | | | 14.6 | 14.9 | 10.5 | 8.6 | Total Current | 11.8 | 12.0 |
| | | | 25.9 | 31.2 | 19.1 | 18.8 | Long-Term Debt | 24.1 | 23.8 |
| | | | .3 | .0 | .2 | .0 | Deferred Taxes | .0 | .1 |
| | | | 8.5 | 8.1 | 5.9 | 5.1 | All Other Non-Current | 5.8 | 6.6 |
| | | | 50.8 | 45.8 | 64.3 | 67.5 | Net Worth | 58.3 | 57.5 |
| | | | 100.0 | 100.0 | 100.0 | 100.0 | Total Liabilities & Net Worth | 100.0 | 100.0 |
| | | | | | | | INCOME DATA | | |
| | | | 100.0 | 100.0 | 100.0 | 100.0 | Net Sales | 100.0 | 100.0 |
| | | | | | | | Gross Profit | | |
| | | | 95.4 | 91.5 | 99.4 | 101.0 | Operating Expenses | 94.7 | 96.4 |
| | | | 4.6 | 8.5 | .6 | -1.0 | Operating Profit | 5.3 | 3.6 |
| | | | -.5 | 4.5 | .6 | -.8 | All Other Expenses (net) | 2.5 | 2.4 |
| | | | 5.1 | 4.1 | .0 | -.1 | Profit Before Taxes | 2.8 | 1.2 |
| | | | | | | | RATIOS | | |
| | | | 9.3 | 5.3 | 6.3 | 3.6 | | 4.6 | 4.1 |
| | | | 2.6 | 2.1 | 2.4 | 1.8 | Current | 2.0 | 2.2 |
| | | | 1.6 | 1.3 | 1.5 | 1.0 | | 1.1 | 1.2 |
| | | | 9.3 | 3.6 | 4.8 | 3.0 | | 4.2 | 3.9 |
| | | | 2.4 | 1.9 | 1.8 | 1.5 | Quick | 1.7 | 1.9 |
| | | | 1.5 | .8 | 1.0 | .9 | | .8 | 1.0 |
| | | 0 | UND | 5 | 78.9 | 11 | 34.4 | 10 | 35.7 | | 7 | 49.5 | 7 | 51.3 |
| | | 7 | 50.2 | 17 | 21.0 | 21 | 17.8 | 20 | 18.2 | Sales/Receivables | 18 | 20.3 | 18 | 20.7 |
| | | 33 | 11.0 | 33 | 11.1 | 38 | 9.5 | 35 | 10.3 | | 37 | 9.8 | 33 | 11.0 |
| | | | | | | | | Cost of Sales/Inventory | | |
| | | | | | | | | Cost of Sales/Payables | | |
| | | | 1.6 | 1.8 | 1.8 | 2.6 | | 2.1 | 1.9 |
| | | | 3.2 | 4.6 | 5.0 | 6.5 | Sales/Working Capital | 5.2 | 4.4 |
| | | | 7.8 | 18.3 | 10.5 | 413.9 | | 39.0 | 22.9 |
| | | | 17.3 | 6.6 | 6.5 | 4.0 | | 5.6 | 5.8 |
| | | (12) | 3.5 | (30) | 2.3 | (55) | 1.4 | (100) | .7 | EBIT/Interest | (344) | 1.6 | (265) | 1.5 |
| | | | -2.5 | -1.8 | -4.0 | -1.8 | | -.5 | -1.0 |
| | | | | | | | | | 8.1 | 12.6 |
| | | | | | | | | Net Profit + Depr., Dep., Amort./Cur. Mat. L/T/D | (13) | 1.6 | (11) | 1.3 |
| | | | | | | | | | .2 | .3 |
| | | | .5 | .5 | .4 | .5 | | .5 | .5 |
| | | | .9 | .9 | .8 | .7 | Fixed/Worth | .7 | .8 |
| | | | 2.8 | 1.5 | 1.2 | .9 | | 1.2 | 1.2 |
| | | | .5 | .4 | .2 | .2 | | .3 | .3 |
| | | | 1.0 | 1.1 | .5 | .4 | Debt/Worth | .5 | .5 |
| | | | 3.1 | 2.3 | 1.2 | .7 | | 1.0 | 1.1 |
| | | | 23.5 | 10.8 | 5.2 | 3.2 | | 6.2 | 5.2 |
| | | (13) | 6.7 | (46) | 2.7 | | .6 | | -.2 | % Profit Before Taxes/Tangible Net Worth | (378) | 1.3 | (292) | .6 |
| | | | -2.1 | -4.2 | -4.8 | -3.5 | | -1.9 | -2.2 |
| | | | 9.5 | 5.0 | 3.9 | 2.3 | | 3.8 | 3.1 |
| | | | 2.5 | 1.7 | .5 | -.1 | % Profit Before Taxes/Total Assets | .9 | .5 |
| | | | -1.9 | -2.1 | -3.5 | -2.3 | | -1.1 | -1.5 |
| | | | 7.4 | 2.3 | 1.3 | 1.0 | | 1.2 | 1.2 |
| | | | 1.0 | 1.1 | .9 | .8 | Sales/Net Fixed Assets | .8 | .8 |
| | | | .5 | .5 | .6 | .5 | | .6 | .6 |
| | | | .9 | .8 | .5 | .4 | | .6 | .6 |
| | | | .5 | .5 | .4 | .3 | Sales/Total Assets | .4 | .4 |
| | | | .4 | .3 | .3 | .3 | | .3 | .3 |
| | | | 2.4 | 2.4 | 3.6 | 5.4 | | 4.5 | 4.8 |
| | | (12) | 5.1 | (45) | 6.8 | (64) | 6.2 | (107) | 7.4 | % Depr., Dep., Amort./Sales | (361) | 6.5 | (273) | 7.0 |
| | | | 10.7 | 10.8 | 8.3 | 9.8 | | 8.7 | 9.1 |
| | | | | | | | | | 4.5 | 1.2 |
| | | | | | | | | % Officers', Directors', Owners' Comp/Sales | (17) | 9.5 | (16) | 6.1 |
| | | | | | | | | | 14.1 | 14.4 |
| | 1107M | 21529M | 50688M | 1230935M | 2294922M | 8064935M | Net Sales ($) | 20767333M | 15233696M |
| | 554M | 9305M | 81697M | 1630526M | 4808266M | 20205501M | Total Assets ($) | 42506911M | 33080139M |

© RMA 2024

M = $ thousand    MM = $ million
See Pages viii through xx for Explanation of Ratios and Data

# EDUCATION—Colleges, Universities, and Professional Schools   NAICS 611310

## Comparative Historical Data | Current Data Sorted by Sales

| | | | | Type of Statement | | | | | | |
|---|---|---|---|---|---|---|---|---|---|---|
| 159 | | 204 | 169 | Unqualified | 2 | 5 | 9 | 8 | 29 | 116 |
| | | 2 | 1 | Reviewed | | | | | | 1 |
| 2 | | 1 | 1 | Compiled | | | | | | 1 |
| 1 | | 1 | 3 | Tax Returns | 1 | | | | | 2 |
| 75 | | 87 | 84 | Other | 2 | 6 | 5 | 7 | 14 | 50 |
| 4/1/21- | | 4/1/22- | 4/1/23- | | | 214 (4/1-9/30/23) | | 44 (10/1/23-3/31/24) | | |
| 3/31/22 | | 3/31/23 | 3/31/24 | | 0-1MM | 1-3MM | 3-5MM | 5-10MM | 10-25MM | 25MM & OVER |
| ALL | | ALL | ALL | | | | | | | |
| 237 | | 295 | 258 | NUMBER OF STATEMENTS | 5 | 11 | 14 | 15 | 43 | 170 |
| % | | % | % | ASSETS | % | % | % | % | % | % |
| 20.8 | | 19.1 | 15.5 | Cash & Equivalents | | 28.3 | 22.4 | 11.8 | 16.0 | 14.4 |
| 5.9 | | 5.4 | 4.8 | Trade Receivables (net) | | 1.8 | 6.6 | 11.5 | 3.2 | 4.7 |
| .3 | | .1 | .2 | Inventory | | .1 | .0 | .1 | .1 | .2 |
| 3.0 | | 3.6 | 3.3 | All Other Current | | 2.4 | 4.7 | 3.7 | 4.0 | 3.1 |
| 30.0 | | 28.2 | 23.8 | Total Current | | 32.6 | 33.7 | 27.2 | 23.4 | 22.5 |
| 43.7 | | 44.5 | 46.4 | Fixed Assets (net) | | 55.2 | 42.9 | 45.0 | 48.6 | 45.8 |
| 2.3 | | 1.6 | 1.8 | Intangibles (net) | | 1.3 | 4.0 | 1.0 | .6 | 1.3 |
| 24.1 | | 25.7 | 28.0 | All Other Non-Current | | 10.8 | 19.4 | 26.8 | 27.5 | 30.4 |
| 100.0 | | 100.0 | 100.0 | Total | | 100.0 | 100.0 | 100.0 | 100.0 | 100.0 |
| | | | | LIABILITIES | | | | | | |
| 1.2 | | 1.2 | 1.5 | Notes Payable-Short Term | | 1.9 | 4.9 | 2.3 | .9 | .9 |
| 1.2 | | 1.5 | 1.5 | Cur. Mat.-L.T.D. | | 2.2 | 1.8 | 2.6 | .9 | 1.4 |
| 2.5 | | 2.5 | 2.4 | Trade Payables | | 1.2 | 1.6 | 1.5 | 2.0 | 2.8 |
| .1 | | .1 | .1 | Income Taxes Payable | | .0 | .0 | .0 | .0 | .1 |
| 6.8 | | 6.4 | 5.9 | All Other Current | | 5.4 | 9.0 | 5.1 | 2.6 | 6.7 |
| 11.7 | | 11.8 | 11.4 | Total Current | | 10.7 | 17.4 | 11.6 | 6.3 | 11.9 |
| 21.7 | | 20.7 | 22.6 | Long-Term Debt | | 24.1 | 37.1 | 47.1 | 18.6 | 18.7 |
| .1 | | .1 | .1 | Deferred Taxes | | .0 | .3 | .0 | .0 | .1 |
| 5.8 | | 6.0 | 6.1 | All Other Non-Current | | 7.5 | 10.7 | 6.0 | 5.4 | 6.0 |
| 60.8 | | 61.4 | 59.9 | Net Worth | | 57.7 | 34.6 | 35.3 | 69.7 | 63.4 |
| 100.0 | | 100.0 | 100.0 | Total Liabilties & Net Worth | | 100.0 | 100.0 | 100.0 | 100.0 | 100.0 |
| | | | | INCOME DATA | | | | | | |
| 100.0 | | 100.0 | 100.0 | Net Sales | | 100.0 | 100.0 | 100.0 | 100.0 | 100.0 |
| | | | | Gross Profit | | | | | | |
| 88.2 | | 94.9 | 97.7 | Operating Expenses | | 89.4 | 88.9 | 80.0 | 102.0 | 100.2 |
| 11.8 | | 5.1 | 2.3 | Operating Profit | | 10.6 | 11.1 | 20.0 | -2.0 | -.2 |
| .2 | | 4.2 | .7 | All Other Expenses (net) | | .0 | 5.9 | 7.6 | .8 | -.6 |
| 11.7 | | .9 | 1.6 | Profit Before Taxes | | 10.6 | 5.2 | 12.3 | -2.8 | .4 |
| | | | | RATIOS | | | | | | |
| 4.6 | | 5.9 | 4.2 | | | 26.1 | 5.2 | 6.3 | 7.0 | 3.4 |
| 2.7 | | 2.6 | 2.1 | Current | | 5.4 | 2.3 | 2.1 | 3.3 | 1.7 |
| 1.7 | | 1.4 | 1.2 | | | 2.1 | 1.6 | 1.3 | 2.3 | 1.1 |
| 4.3 | | 5.2 | 3.7 | | | 25.5 | 5.1 | 6.1 | 5.8 | 3.0 |
| 2.4 | | 2.1 | 1.7 | Quick | | 5.4 | 2.0 | 2.1 | 2.7 | 1.4 |
| 1.4 | | 1.1 | .9 | | | 2.1 | 1.4 | 1.0 | 1.5 | .9 |
| 7   50.9 | 8 | 46.4 | 9   41.7 | | 0   UND | 4   90.2 | 4   85.2 | 6   60.0 | 11   34.0 | |
| 19   19.2 | 20 | 18.7 | 19   19.2 | Sales/Receivables | 0   UND | 18   20.4 | 11   32.8 | 17   21.4 | 20   18.5 | |
| 37   9.8 | 41 | 9.0 | 34   10.6 | | 10   34.9 | 52   7.0 | 261   1.4 | 35   10.5 | 33   10.9 | |
| | | | | Cost of Sales/Inventory | | | | | | |
| | | | | Cost of Sales/Payables | | | | | | |
| 2.1 | | 1.9 | 2.1 | | | 1.1 | 1.7 | 1.1 | 1.5 | 2.9 |
| 4.5 | | 4.1 | 5.2 | Sales/Working Capital | | 3.0 | 3.8 | 2.0 | 2.7 | 7.5 |
| 9.0 | | 12.9 | 23.1 | | | 7.4 | 11.4 | 17.5 | 5.6 | 58.2 |
| 16.5 | | 7.5 | 5.9 | | | 30.1 | 21.2 | | 4.3 | 5.0 |
| (197)   7.4 | (248) | 1.6 | (207)   1.4 | EBIT/Interest | (10)   3.5 | (11)   3.0 | | (30)   1.0 | (144)   .8 | |
| 2.1 | | -4.5 | -1.9 | | | 1.7 | -1.3 | | -2.3 | -2.4 | |
| | | | | Net Profit + Depr., Dep., Amort./Cur. Mat. L/T/D | | | | | | |
| .4 | | .4 | .5 | | | .5 | .1 | .4 | .4 | .5 |
| .7 | | .7 | .7 | Fixed/Worth | | .8 | .8 | 1.2 | .7 | .7 |
| 1.0 | | 1.1 | 1.2 | | | 1.7 | 2.9 | 3.9 | 1.1 | 1.0 |
| .3 | | .2 | .2 | | | .2 | .5 | .6 | .1 | .2 |
| .5 | | .5 | .6 | Debt/Worth | | .8 | 1.2 | 1.8 | .3 | .5 |
| 1.1 | | 1.1 | 1.2 | | | 1.9 | NM | 8.4 | 1.0 | 1.1 |
| 18.3 | | 8.6 | 6.3 | | | 70.5 | 24.4 | 27.1 | 4.5 | 5.0 |
| (230)   8.7 | (285) | .8 | (249)   .7 | % Profit Before Taxes/Tangible Net Worth | | 20.5 | (11)   5.2 | (12)   4.4 | -.3 | (169)   .1 |
| 1.8 | | -4.7 | -3.9 | | | -.1 | -2.2 | -2.4 | -4.7 | -3.9 |
| 11.2 | | 5.4 | 3.9 | | | 23.4 | 10.2 | 5.3 | 2.6 | 3.0 |
| 5.1 | | .6 | .6 | % Profit Before Taxes/Total Assets | | 6.0 | 1.4 | 2.1 | -.2 | .1 |
| 1.1 | | -2.9 | -2.5 | | | -.1 | -4.0 | -2.0 | -3.9 | -2.5 |
| 1.9 | | 1.4 | 1.4 | | | 4.4 | 26.8 | 2.5 | 1.2 | 1.3 |
| 1.0 | | .9 | .8 | Sales/Net Fixed Assets | | .6 | 1.3 | .8 | .8 | .8 |
| .7 | | .7 | .6 | | | .3 | .5 | .3 | .5 | .6 |
| .7 | | .6 | .6 | | | 1.3 | 1.0 | .6 | .5 | .6 |
| .5 | | .4 | .4 | Sales/Total Assets | | .4 | .5 | .3 | .4 | .4 |
| .3 | | .3 | .3 | | | .2 | .3 | .1 | .2 | .3 |
| 3.9 | | 3.9 | 4.3 | | | | 2.1 | 2.3 | 4.3 | 4.6 |
| (214)   5.7 | (277) | 6.2 | (232)   7.0 | % Depr., Dep., Amort./Sales | | (10)   4.3 | (11)   6.3 | 7.1 | (158)   7.0 | |
| 8.2 | | 8.4 | 9.6 | | | | 7.3 | 12.8 | 11.6 | 8.9 |
| 2.3 | | 2.3 | | % Officers', Directors' Owners' Comp/Sales | | | | | | |
| (11)   9.7 | (10) | 10.6 | | | | | | | | |
| 33.4 | | 28.5 | | | | | | | | |
| 11357004M | | 12185946M | 11664116M | Net Sales ($) | 2187M | 22641M | 53823M | 110861M | 784496M | 10690108M |
| 22905951M | | 28792503M | 26735849M | Total Assets ($) | 19228M | 57297M | 142437M | 482135M | 2698576M | 23336176M |

© RMA 2024  
M = $ thousand   MM = $ million  
See Pages viii through xx for Explanation of Ratios and Data

## EDUCATION—Professional and Management Development Training  NAICS 611430

**Current Data Sorted by Assets** | **Comparative Historical Data**

| 0-500M | 500M-2MM | 2-10MM | 10-50MM | 50-100MM | 100-250MM | | Type of Statement | 4/1/19-3/31/20 ALL | 4/1/20-3/31/21 ALL |
|---|---|---|---|---|---|---|---|---|---|
| 1 | 2 | 1 | 2 | | | | Unqualified | 11 | 4 |
| | | 1 | 1 | | | | Reviewed | 5 | 2 |
| | 4 | 6 | 7 | 2 | 2 | | Compiled | | 1 |
| | | | | | | | Tax Returns | 7 | 3 |
| 1 | 11 (4/1-9/30/23) | | 21 (10/1/23-3/31/24) | | | | Other | 12 | 9 |
| 1 | 6 | 9 | 9 | 2 | 5 | | NUMBER OF STATEMENTS | 35 | 19 |
| % | % | % | % | % | % | | **ASSETS** | % | % |
| | | | | | | | Cash & Equivalents | 30.0 | 39.3 |
| | | | | | | | Trade Receivables (net) | 23.3 | 21.1 |
| | | | | | | | Inventory | 1.1 | 1.6 |
| | | | | | | | All Other Current | 1.8 | 4.7 |
| | | | | | | | Total Current | 56.1 | 66.7 |
| | | | | | | | Fixed Assets (net) | 22.0 | 13.0 |
| | | | | | | | Intangibles (net) | 14.6 | 15.7 |
| | | | | | | | All Other Non-Current | 7.4 | 4.5 |
| | | | | | | | Total | 100.0 | 100.0 |
| | | | | | | | **LIABILITIES** | | |
| | | | | | | | Notes Payable-Short Term | 3.6 | 1.1 |
| | | | | | | | Cur. Mat.-L.T.D. | 1.9 | 2.2 |
| | | | | | | | Trade Payables | 9.8 | 13.4 |
| | | | | | | | Income Taxes Payable | .2 | .3 |
| | | | | | | | All Other Current | 17.0 | 13.0 |
| | | | | | | | Total Current | 32.5 | 29.9 |
| | | | | | | | Long-Term Debt | 17.9 | 24.0 |
| | | | | | | | Deferred Taxes | .1 | .3 |
| | | | | | | | All Other Non-Current | 2.4 | 2.1 |
| | | | | | | | Net Worth | 47.1 | 43.6 |
| | | | | | | | Total Liabilities & Net Worth | 100.0 | 100.0 |
| | | | | | | | **INCOME DATA** | | |
| | | | | | | | Net Sales | 100.0 | 100.0 |
| | | | | | | | Gross Profit | | |
| | | | | | | | Operating Expenses | 92.3 | 94.9 |
| | | | | | | | Operating Profit | 7.7 | 5.1 |
| | | | | | | | All Other Expenses (net) | .8 | -1.3 |
| | | | | | | | Profit Before Taxes | 6.9 | 6.4 |
| | | | | | | | **RATIOS** | | |
| | | | | | | | Current | 5.0 | 7.3 |
| | | | | | | | | 2.0 | 3.4 |
| | | | | | | | | .9 | 1.3 |
| | | | | | | | Quick | 4.9 | 7.0 |
| | | | | | | | | 1.8 | 2.7 |
| | | | | | | | | .8 | 1.2 |
| | | | | | | | Sales/Receivables | 5  77.6 | 0  UND |
| | | | | | | | | 21  17.2 | 27  13.4 |
| | | | | | | | | 46  7.9 | 46  7.9 |
| | | | | | | | Cost of Sales/Inventory | | |
| | | | | | | | Cost of Sales/Payables | | |
| | | | | | | | Sales/Working Capital | 2.3 | 2.7 |
| | | | | | | | | 9.4 | 12.1 |
| | | | | | | | | -65.8 | 29.4 |
| | | | | | | | EBIT/Interest | 36.1 | |
| | | | | | | | | (23) 10.0 | |
| | | | | | | | | .1 | |
| | | | | | | | Net Profit + Depr., Dep., Amort./Cur. Mat. L/T/D | | |
| | | | | | | | Fixed/Worth | .1 | .0 |
| | | | | | | | | .6 | .1 |
| | | | | | | | | 16.2 | 1.7 |
| | | | | | | | Debt/Worth | .4 | .2 |
| | | | | | | | | .8 | 1.0 |
| | | | | | | | | 30.1 | 5.4 |
| | | | | | | | % Profit Before Taxes/Tangible Net Worth | 69.2 | 129.5 |
| | | | | | | | | (27) 36.1 | (15) 21.5 |
| | | | | | | | | -2.2 | 1.3 |
| | | | | | | | % Profit Before Taxes/Total Assets | 33.4 | 36.6 |
| | | | | | | | | 13.6 | 9.7 |
| | | | | | | | | -2.1 | .3 |
| | | | | | | | Sales/Net Fixed Assets | 156.7 | 117.4 |
| | | | | | | | | 22.6 | 46.4 |
| | | | | | | | | 3.2 | 16.1 |
| | | | | | | | Sales/Total Assets | 4.0 | 4.0 |
| | | | | | | | | 2.0 | 2.6 |
| | | | | | | | | .6 | 1.0 |
| | | | | | | | % Depr., Dep., Amort./Sales | .9 | .2 |
| | | | | | | | | (21) 2.0 | (10) .5 |
| | | | | | | | | 4.5 | 1.8 |
| | | | | | | | % Officers', Directors' Owners' Comp/Sales | | |
| 801M | 11973M | 92585M | 442129M | 142750M | 741125M | | Net Sales ($) | 830672M | 429142M |
| 128M | 5501M | 40624M | 228166M | 182508M | 904939M | | Total Assets ($) | 927409M | 636494M |

© RMA 2024

M = $ thousand    MM = $ million
See Pages viii through xx for Explanation of Ratios and Data

# EDUCATION—Professional and Management Development Training  NAICS 611430

**Comparative Historical Data** | **Current Data Sorted by Sales**

| | | | | | | | | | | |
|---|---|---|---|---|---|---|---|---|---|---|
| | | | **Type of Statement** | | | | | | | |
| 3 | 10 | 6 | Unqualified | | | | 1 | | 1 | 5 |
| 1 | 2 | 1 | Reviewed | | | | | | | |
| 2 | 1 | | Compiled | | | | | | | |
| 3 | 3 | 3 | Tax Returns | 1 | 1 | | 1 | | | |
| 12 | 21 | 22 | Other | 2 | 3 | 2 | 3 | 2 | 10 | |
| 4/1/21- | 4/1/22- | 4/1/23- | | | 11 (4/1-9/30/23) | | | 21 (10/1/23-3/31/24) | | |
| 3/31/22 | 3/31/23 | 3/31/24 | | 0-1MM | 1-3MM | 3-5MM | 5-10MM | 10-25MM | 25MM & OVER | |
| ALL | ALL | ALL | | | | | | | | |
| 21 | 37 | 32 | **NUMBER OF STATEMENTS** | 3 | 4 | 2 | 5 | 3 | 15 | |
| % | % | % | **ASSETS** | % | % | % | % | % | % | |
| 41.9 | 45.0 | 25.1 | Cash & Equivalents | | | | | | 16.3 | |
| 12.4 | 14.3 | 18.7 | Trade Receivables (net) | | | | | | 16.8 | |
| .3 | .4 | 1.3 | Inventory | | | | | | 2.8 | |
| 3.5 | 3.3 | 10.3 | All Other Current | | | | | | 7.7 | |
| 58.1 | 63.0 | 55.4 | Total Current | | | | | | 43.6 | |
| 9.0 | 10.3 | 10.3 | Fixed Assets (net) | | | | | | 11.8 | |
| 23.6 | 17.5 | 16.7 | Intangibles (net) | | | | | | 26.6 | |
| 9.4 | 9.3 | 17.6 | All Other Non-Current | | | | | | 18.0 | |
| 100.0 | 100.0 | 100.0 | Total | | | | | | 100.0 | |
| | | | **LIABILITIES** | | | | | | | |
| 1.5 | 9.1 | 2.3 | Notes Payable-Short Term | | | | | | 2.7 | |
| 1.9 | 2.0 | 1.5 | Cur. Mat.-L.T.D. | | | | | | 2.3 | |
| 2.6 | 4.7 | 5.7 | Trade Payables | | | | | | 5.3 | |
| 1.0 | .3 | .0 | Income Taxes Payable | | | | | | .0 | |
| 17.1 | 16.8 | 18.5 | All Other Current | | | | | | 23.0 | |
| 24.0 | 33.0 | 28.0 | Total Current | | | | | | 33.3 | |
| 13.7 | 22.0 | 14.4 | Long-Term Debt | | | | | | 21.8 | |
| .5 | .5 | .2 | Deferred Taxes | | | | | | .4 | |
| 3.3 | 2.7 | 8.7 | All Other Non-Current | | | | | | 13.4 | |
| 58.6 | 41.9 | 48.7 | Net Worth | | | | | | 31.0 | |
| 100.0 | 100.0 | 100.0 | Total Liabilities & Net Worth | | | | | | 100.0 | |
| | | | **INCOME DATA** | | | | | | | |
| 100.0 | 100.0 | 100.0 | Net Sales | | | | | | 100.0 | |
| 90.9 | 87.6 | 92.4 | Gross Profit | | | | | | 95.9 | |
| 9.1 | 12.4 | 7.6 | Operating Expenses | | | | | | 4.1 | |
| .1 | .9 | 2.3 | Operating Profit | | | | | | 4.1 | |
| 9.0 | 11.5 | 5.4 | All Other Expenses (net) | | | | | | -.1 | |
| | | | Profit Before Taxes | | | | | | | |
| | | | **RATIOS** | | | | | | | |
| 8.3 | 11.0 | 7.2 | | | | | | | 2.2 | |
| 2.4 | 2.9 | 2.0 | Current | | | | | | .9 | |
| .9 | 1.2 | .9 | | | | | | | .7 | |
| 8.3 | 10.9 | 4.8 | | | | | | | 1.3 | |
| 2.1 | 2.7 | 1.1 | Quick | | | | | | .8 | |
| .8 | 1.1 | .7 | | | | | | | .5 | |
| 0 UND | 0 UND | 11 32.6 | | | | | | 25 | 14.6 | |
| 26 14.0 | 27 13.7 | 34 10.6 | Sales/Receivables | | | | | 36 | 10.2 | |
| 49 7.4 | 44 8.3 | 53 6.9 | | | | | | 53 | 6.9 | |
| | | | Cost of Sales/Inventory | | | | | | | |
| | | | Cost of Sales/Payables | | | | | | | |
| 2.9 | 2.1 | 3.4 | | | | | | | 4.6 | |
| 4.9 | 6.2 | 8.7 | Sales/Working Capital | | | | | | -48.3 | |
| -34.5 | 129.6 | -36.3 | | | | | | | -10.6 | |
| 64.1 | 30.4 | 71.8 | | | | | | | 47.3 | |
| (14) 9.6 | (23) 6.6 | (21) 5.9 | EBIT/Interest | | | | | (11) | 2.6 | |
| -.8 | -3.0 | -1.1 | | | | | | | -1.3 | |
| | | | Net Profit + Depr., Dep., Amort./Cur. Mat. L/T/D | | | | | | | |
| .0 | .0 | .0 | | | | | | | .0 | |
| .3 | .1 | .0 | Fixed/Worth | | | | | | .6 | |
| 3.0 | 1.1 | 1.4 | | | | | | | -.3 | |
| .3 | .1 | .2 | | | | | | | 1.3 | |
| .5 | 1.0 | 1.4 | Debt/Worth | | | | | | 6.7 | |
| NM | -5.5 | 7.7 | | | | | | | -1.5 | |
| 65.2 | 63.2 | 48.8 | % Profit Before Taxes/Tangible Net Worth | | | | | | | |
| (16) 16.5 | (27) 28.1 | (25) 28.4 | | | | | | | | |
| -16.7 | -.6 | 9.0 | | | | | | | | |
| 26.5 | 43.3 | 24.8 | % Profit Before Taxes/Total Assets | | | | | | 16.8 | |
| 8.7 | 14.4 | 12.1 | | | | | | | 6.5 | |
| -6.8 | -6.1 | .7 | | | | | | | -10.5 | |
| 239.5 | 579.9 | 825.5 | | | | | | | 83.7 | |
| 37.6 | 64.1 | 54.0 | Sales/Net Fixed Assets | | | | | | 31.6 | |
| 10.8 | 21.0 | 9.2 | | | | | | | 4.8 | |
| 2.5 | 2.4 | 2.5 | | | | | | | 2.1 | |
| 1.1 | 1.6 | 1.5 | Sales/Total Assets | | | | | | 1.1 | |
| .4 | .8 | .9 | | | | | | | .6 | |
| | .4 | .2 | | | | | | | | |
| (16) 1.0 | (16) .6 | % Depr., Dep., Amort./Sales | | | | | | | | |
| | 3.8 | 2.5 | | | | | | | | |
| | | | % Officers', Directors' Owners' Comp/Sales | | | | | | | |
| 486522M | 1184461M | 1431363M | Net Sales ($) | 2201M | 9195M | 8544M | 40977M | 53197M | 1317249M | |
| 820840M | 1247482M | 1361866M | Total Assets ($) | 1887M | 5449M | 6915M | 29766M | 14146M | 1303703M | |

© RMA 2024    M = $ thousand    MM = $ million
See Pages viii through xx for Explanation of Ratios and Data

# EDUCATION—Flight Training  NAICS 611512

## Current Data Sorted by Assets

| | | | | | | | Comparative Historical Data | |
|---|---|---|---|---|---|---|---|---|
| | | | | | | **Type of Statement** | | |
| | | | | | | Unqualified | 5 | 1 |
| | | 2 | 3 | | 1 | Reviewed | 3 | 3 |
| | | | | | | Compiled | | |
| | 1 | 1 | | | | Tax Returns | 3 | 1 |
| 1 | 1 | 3 | 7 | 2 | 4 | Other | 7 | 5 |
| | 8 (4/1-9/30/23) | | 18 (10/1/23-3/31/24) | | | | 4/1/19- | 4/1/20- |
| 0-500M | 500M-2MM | 2-10MM | 10-50MM | 50-100MM | 100-250MM | | 3/31/20 | 3/31/21 |
| 1 | 2 | 6 | 10 | 2 | 5 | **NUMBER OF STATEMENTS** | 18 ALL | 10 ALL |
| % | % | % | % | % | % | **ASSETS** | % | % |
| | | | 16.5 | | | Cash & Equivalents | 13.2 | 22.4 |
| | | | 5.7 | | | Trade Receivables (net) | 9.6 | 6.1 |
| | | | 3.8 | | | Inventory | 1.7 | 4.5 |
| | | | 4.2 | | | All Other Current | 5.4 | 2.1 |
| | | | 30.2 | | | Total Current | 29.9 | 35.0 |
| | | | 60.3 | | | Fixed Assets (net) | 56.8 | 54.3 |
| | | | 3.5 | | | Intangibles (net) | 10.4 | 9.4 |
| | | | 6.0 | | | All Other Non-Current | 3.0 | 1.3 |
| | | | 100.0 | | | Total | 100.0 | 100.0 |
| | | | | | | **LIABILITIES** | | |
| | | | 1.4 | | | Notes Payable-Short Term | 4.4 | 9.0 |
| | | | 4.1 | | | Cur. Mat.-L.T.D. | 3.4 | 4.7 |
| | | | 7.7 | | | Trade Payables | 9.7 | 3.6 |
| | | | .2 | | | Income Taxes Payable | .0 | .0 |
| | | | 23.4 | | | All Other Current | 18.1 | 12.2 |
| | | | 36.8 | | | Total Current | 35.6 | 29.5 |
| | | | 34.7 | | | Long-Term Debt | 48.5 | 41.3 |
| | | | .7 | | | Deferred Taxes | .5 | .0 |
| | | | 1.1 | | | All Other Non-Current | 2.3 | .0 |
| | | | 26.7 | | | Net Worth | 13.2 | 29.2 |
| | | | 100.0 | | | Total Liabilities & Net Worth | 100.0 | 100.0 |
| | | | | | | **INCOME DATA** | | |
| | | | 100.0 | | | Net Sales | 100.0 | 100.0 |
| | | | | | | Gross Profit | | |
| | | | 93.0 | | | Operating Expenses | 86.6 | 96.7 |
| | | | 7.0 | | | Operating Profit | 13.4 | 3.3 |
| | | | 1.3 | | | All Other Expenses (net) | 1.8 | -2.6 |
| | | | 5.7 | | | Profit Before Taxes | 11.6 | 5.9 |
| | | | | | | **RATIOS** | | |
| | | | 1.8 | | | | 1.7 | 1.5 |
| | | | 1.1 | | | Current | .6 | 1.0 |
| | | | .3 | | | | .4 | .9 |
| | | | 1.3 | | | | .8 | 1.1 |
| | | | .8 | | | Quick | .4 | .7 |
| | | | .3 | | | | .2 | .6 |
| | | | 0 UND | | | | 0 UND | 7 54.6 |
| | | | 19 18.9 | | | Sales/Receivables | 9 42.0 | 12 30.7 |
| | | | 41 8.8 | | | | 24 15.2 | 35 10.5 |
| | | | | | | Cost of Sales/Inventory | | |
| | | | | | | Cost of Sales/Payables | | |
| | | | 6.5 | | | | 19.5 | 11.2 |
| | | | 48.6 | | | Sales/Working Capital | -11.4 | NM |
| | | | -1.9 | | | | -6.2 | -22.4 |
| | | | 6.7 | | | | 12.6 | 9.0 |
| | | | 4.7 | | | EBIT/Interest | (16) 5.1 | 3.9 |
| | | | -1.2 | | | | -.1 | -1.3 |
| | | | | | | Net Profit + Depr., Dep., Amort./Cur. Mat. L/T/D | | |
| | | | 1.3 | | | | 1.2 | .8 |
| | | | 2.1 | | | Fixed/Worth | 5.7 | 4.8 |
| | | | 10.4 | | | | -9.4 | 5.3 |
| | | | 1.1 | | | | 1.1 | .9 |
| | | | 3.1 | | | Debt/Worth | 5.8 | 5.6 |
| | | | 12.6 | | | | -15.8 | NM |
| | | | | | | | 328.0 | |
| | | | | | | % Profit Before Taxes/Tangible Net Worth | (13) 47.7 | |
| | | | | | | | 25.7 | |
| | | | 11.5 | | | | 20.0 | 12.0 |
| | | | 4.6 | | | % Profit Before Taxes/Total Assets | 9.4 | 6.1 |
| | | | -4.4 | | | | -2.9 | -2.1 |
| | | | 2.8 | | | | 7.3 | 4.8 |
| | | | 1.1 | | | Sales/Net Fixed Assets | 2.0 | 1.1 |
| | | | .8 | | | | .7 | .8 |
| | | | .9 | | | | 3.1 | 1.6 |
| | | | .8 | | | Sales/Total Assets | 1.0 | .6 |
| | | | .6 | | | | .5 | .5 |
| | | | 6.1 | | | | 8.3 | |
| | | | 8.5 | | | % Depr., Dep., Amort./Sales | (12) 11.6 | |
| | | | 9.3 | | | | 14.4 | |
| | | | | | | % Officers', Directors' Owners' Comp/Sales | | |
| 646M | 6746M | 52884M | 191120M | 126023M | 527410M | Net Sales ($) | 368907M | 229791M |
| 424M | 2031M | 26636M | 280358M | 155995M | 1011052M | Total Assets ($) | 538526M | 251881M |

© RMA 2024  
M = $ thousand  MM = $ million  
See Pages viii through xx for Explanation of Ratios and Data

# EDUCATION—Flight Training  NAICS 611512

## Comparative Historical Data

| | | | | | | | | | Current Data Sorted by Sales | | |
|---|---|---|---|---|---|---|---|---|---|---|---|
| | | | | Type of Statement | | | | | | | |
| | 1 | 2 | 6 | Unqualified | | | | 1 | | 3 | 2 |
| | 1 | 1 | | Reviewed | | | | | | | |
| | | 2 | 2 | Compiled | | | | 1 | 1 | | |
| | 14 | 11 | 18 | Tax Returns | | | 1 | 1 | 2 | 8 | 6 |
| | 4/1/21-3/31/22 | 4/1/22-3/31/23 | 4/1/23-3/31/24 | Other | | 8 (4/1-9/30/23) | | | 18 (10/1/23-3/31/24) | | |
| | ALL | ALL | ALL | | 0-1MM | 1-3MM | 3-5MM | 5-10MM | 10-25MM | 25MM & OVER | |
| | 16 | 16 | 26 | NUMBER OF STATEMENTS | 1 | | 3 | 3 | 11 | 8 | |
| | % | % | % | ASSETS | % | % | % | % | % | % | |
| | 21.9 | 23.3 | 18.8 | Cash & Equivalents | | D | | | 21.8 | | |
| | 1.9 | 3.6 | 5.9 | Trade Receivables (net) | | A | | | 9.3 | | |
| | 4.4 | 4.2 | 3.8 | Inventory | | T | | | 2.1 | | |
| | 1.8 | 3.3 | 4.2 | All Other Current | | A | | | 3.3 | | |
| | 30.0 | 34.4 | 32.7 | Total Current | | | | | 36.5 | | |
| | 61.3 | 58.2 | 51.7 | Fixed Assets (net) | | N | | | 48.7 | | |
| | 2.8 | 4.1 | 7.1 | Intangibles (net) | | O | | | 3.1 | | |
| | 6.0 | 3.3 | 8.5 | All Other Non-Current | | T | | | 11.7 | | |
| | 100.0 | 100.0 | 100.0 | Total | | | | | 100.0 | | |
| | | | | LIABILITIES | | A | | | | | |
| | 1.2 | .9 | 1.8 | Notes Payable-Short Term | | V | | | .7 | | |
| | 3.2 | 2.5 | 3.1 | Cur. Mat.-L.T.D. | | A | | | 3.5 | | |
| | 6.3 | 12.7 | 7.4 | Trade Payables | | I | | | 11.3 | | |
| | .0 | .0 | .1 | Income Taxes Payable | | L | | | .2 | | |
| | 18.3 | 18.7 | 20.7 | All Other Current | | A | | | 11.0 | | |
| | 29.0 | 34.7 | 33.1 | Total Current | | B | | | 26.6 | | |
| | 29.5 | 32.2 | 33.0 | Long-Term Debt | | L | | | 29.7 | | |
| | .5 | .6 | .5 | Deferred Taxes | | E | | | .6 | | |
| | 9.7 | 6.4 | 3.1 | All Other Non-Current | | | | | 2.6 | | |
| | 31.4 | 26.0 | 30.3 | Net Worth | | | | | 40.4 | | |
| | 100.0 | 100.0 | 100.0 | Total Liabilities & Net Worth | | | | | 100.0 | | |
| | | | | INCOME DATA | | | | | | | |
| | 100.0 | 100.0 | 100.0 | Net Sales | | | | | 100.0 | | |
| | | | | Gross Profit | | | | | | | |
| | 88.4 | 92.8 | 89.8 | Operating Expenses | | | | | 93.3 | | |
| | 11.6 | 7.2 | 10.2 | Operating Profit | | | | | 6.7 | | |
| | -.8 | 3.5 | 2.6 | All Other Expenses (net) | | | | | .6 | | |
| | 12.4 | 3.6 | 7.6 | Profit Before Taxes | | | | | 6.1 | | |
| | | | | RATIOS | | | | | | | |
| | 2.1 | 1.6 | 1.6 | | | | | | 3.1 | | |
| | 1.1 | 1.1 | 1.0 | Current | | | | | 1.2 | | |
| | .8 | .8 | .6 | | | | | | .8 | | |
| | 1.3 | 1.6 | 1.3 | | | | | | 2.4 | | |
| (15) | .9 | 1.0 | .7 | Quick | | | | | 1.1 | | |
| | .6 | .6 | .4 | | | | | | .6 | | |
| 0 | UND | 0 UND | 0 UND | | | | | 6 | 59.8 | | |
| 5 | 80.3 | 16 23.2 | 12 31.1 | Sales/Receivables | | | | 15 | 25.0 | | |
| 13 | 27.1 | 33 11.0 | 36 10.0 | | | | | 40 | 9.2 | | |
| | | | | Cost of Sales/Inventory | | | | | | | |
| | | | | Cost of Sales/Payables | | | | | | | |
| | 9.1 | 7.6 | 8.2 | | | | | | 2.5 | | |
| | 311.8 | 23.5 | NM | Sales/Working Capital | | | | | 9.2 | | |
| | -18.4 | -11.3 | -10.3 | | | | | | -41.5 | | |
| | 23.0 | 6.1 | 7.9 | | | | | | 10.2 | | |
| (14) | 7.1 | (14) 3.7 | (23) 4.1 | EBIT/Interest | | | | (10) | 5.8 | | |
| | -.3 | -1.6 | 1.5 | | | | | | -1.2 | | |
| | | | | Net Profit + Depr., Dep., Amort./Cur. Mat. L/T/D | | | | | | | |
| | .9 | 1.3 | 1.1 | | | | | | .7 | | |
| | 4.0 | 3.4 | 1.9 | Fixed/Worth | | | | | 1.4 | | |
| | 5.1 | 11.9 | 10.4 | | | | | | 2.7 | | |
| | 1.9 | 1.2 | 1.1 | | | | | | .8 | | |
| | 4.5 | 6.0 | 2.0 | Debt/Worth | | | | | 1.2 | | |
| | 9.9 | 15.2 | 12.6 | | | | | | 3.1 | | |
| | 86.4 | 60.2 | 61.9 | | | | | | 70.9 | | |
| (15) | 60.8 | (14) 25.3 | (21) 28.6 | % Profit Before Taxes/Tangible Net Worth | | | | (10) | 25.5 | | |
| | -4.8 | -1.9 | 6.8 | | | | | | .9 | | |
| | 19.0 | 8.8 | 18.7 | | | | | | 18.4 | | |
| | 9.0 | 6.0 | 6.5 | % Profit Before Taxes/Total Assets | | | | | 8.2 | | |
| | .0 | -3.4 | 1.8 | | | | | | -1.9 | | |
| | 6.6 | 3.8 | 6.7 | | | | | | 3.0 | | |
| | 1.1 | 1.2 | 1.5 | Sales/Net Fixed Assets | | | | | 1.3 | | |
| | .9 | .5 | .6 | | | | | | .6 | | |
| | 1.1 | 1.2 | 1.6 | | | | | | 1.5 | | |
| | .8 | .6 | .9 | Sales/Total Assets | | | | | .8 | | |
| | .7 | .4 | .4 | | | | | | .5 | | |
| | 9.6 | 5.8 | 4.3 | | | | | | 4.0 | | |
| (11) | 10.8 | (15) 9.0 | (19) 8.8 | % Depr., Dep., Amort./Sales | | | | (10) | 8.1 | | |
| | 12.7 | 14.7 | 13.3 | | | | | | 10.5 | | |
| | | | | % Officers', Directors' Owners' Comp/Sales | | | | | | | |
| | 300148M | 398249M | 904829M | Net Sales ($) | 646M | | 10025M | 21587M | 188207M | 684364M | |
| | 421184M | 660915M | 1476496M | Total Assets ($) | 424M | | 9591M | 13674M | 314684M | 1138123M | |

© RMA 2024    M = $ thousand    MM = $ million
See Pages viii through xx for Explanation of Ratios and Data

# EDUCATION—Other Technical and Trade Schools  NAICS 611519

## Current Data Sorted by Assets | Comparative Historical Data

| 0-500M | 500M-2MM | 2-10MM | 10-50MM | 50-100MM | 100-250MM | | | | | |
|---|---|---|---|---|---|---|---|---|---|---|
| | | 3 | | 5 | 1 | Type of Statement | | | | |
| | | 1 | | | 1 | Unqualified | | 24 | | 11 |
| | 1 | 1 | | | | Reviewed | | 2 | | 1 |
| | 2 | 6 | 4 | 3 | 1 | Compiled | | | | |
| 4 | | | | | 2 | Tax Returns | | 5 | | 2 |
| | 11 (4/1-9/30/23) | | 24 (10/1/23-3/31/24) | | | Other | | 28 | | 17 |
| | | | | | | | | 4/1/19- | | 4/1/20- |
| | | | | | | | | 3/31/20 | | 3/31/21 |
| | | | | | | | | ALL | | ALL |
| | | | | | | NUMBER OF STATEMENTS | | 59 | | 31 |
| 4 | 3 | 11 | 9 | 5 | 3 | | | | | |
| % | % | % | % | % | % | ASSETS | | % | | % |
| | | 26.9 | | | | Cash & Equivalents | | 24.2 | | 30.5 |
| | | 14.1 | | | | Trade Receivables (net) | | 25.0 | | 16.4 |
| | | 2.7 | | | | Inventory | | 2.2 | | .5 |
| | | .4 | | | | All Other Current | | 2.4 | | 4.8 |
| | | 44.2 | | | | Total Current | | 53.8 | | 52.2 |
| | | 22.9 | | | | Fixed Assets (net) | | 27.8 | | 26.8 |
| | | 6.3 | | | | Intangibles (net) | | 7.5 | | 7.5 |
| | | 26.6 | | | | All Other Non-Current | | 10.9 | | 13.4 |
| | | 100.0 | | | | Total | | 100.0 | | 100.0 |
| | | | | | | LIABILITIES | | | | |
| | | 1.9 | | | | Notes Payable-Short Term | | 1.8 | | 3.9 |
| | | 1.9 | | | | Cur. Mat.-L.T.D. | | 1.7 | | 1.9 |
| | | 8.3 | | | | Trade Payables | | 7.3 | | 3.0 |
| | | .1 | | | | Income Taxes Payable | | .6 | | .0 |
| | | 8.6 | | | | All Other Current | | 21.0 | | 16.3 |
| | | 20.8 | | | | Total Current | | 32.4 | | 25.1 |
| | | 12.3 | | | | Long-Term Debt | | 15.7 | | 17.6 |
| | | .0 | | | | Deferred Taxes | | .1 | | .2 |
| | | 14.0 | | | | All Other Non-Current | | 10.3 | | 16.9 |
| | | 52.9 | | | | Net Worth | | 41.6 | | 40.1 |
| | | 100.0 | | | | Total Liabilities & Net Worth | | 100.0 | | 100.0 |
| | | | | | | INCOME DATA | | | | |
| | | 100.0 | | | | Net Sales | | 100.0 | | 100.0 |
| | | | | | | Gross Profit | | | | |
| | | 90.7 | | | | Operating Expenses | | 92.7 | | 92.8 |
| | | 9.3 | | | | Operating Profit | | 7.3 | | 7.2 |
| | | .2 | | | | All Other Expenses (net) | | 1.8 | | .2 |
| | | 9.2 | | | | Profit Before Taxes | | 5.5 | | 7.0 |
| | | | | | | RATIOS | | | | |
| | | 5.4 | | | | | | 3.7 | | 8.1 |
| | | 2.4 | | | | Current | | 1.7 | | 1.8 |
| | | 1.2 | | | | | | 1.1 | | 1.2 |
| | | 5.3 | | | | | | 3.2 | | 5.4 |
| | | 2.3 | | | | Quick | | 1.4 | | 1.6 |
| | | 1.2 | | | | | | .9 | | .9 |
| | 8 | 44.2 | | | | | 10 | 37.6 | 2 | 208.7 |
| | 32 | 11.3 | | | | Sales/Receivables | 31 | 11.8 | 21 | 17.8 |
| | 69 | 5.3 | | | | | 83 | 4.4 | 66 | 5.5 |
| | | | | | | Cost of Sales/Inventory | | | | |
| | | | | | | Cost of Sales/Payables | | | | |
| | | 4.1 | | | | | | 3.9 | | 1.9 |
| | | 5.8 | | | | Sales/Working Capital | | 11.5 | | 7.2 |
| | | 20.6 | | | | | | 71.4 | | 20.0 |
| | | | | | | | | 27.3 | | 61.9 |
| | | | | | | EBIT/Interest | (45) | 4.7 | (22) | 6.7 |
| | | | | | | | | 1.4 | | 1.5 |
| | | | | | | Net Profit + Depr., Dep., Amort./Cur. Mat. L/T/D | | | | |
| | | .1 | | | | | | .2 | | .1 |
| | | .3 | | | | Fixed/Worth | | .7 | | .7 |
| | | 1.2 | | | | | | 1.9 | | 3.7 |
| | | .3 | | | | | | .6 | | .6 |
| | | 1.0 | | | | Debt/Worth | | 1.3 | | 1.4 |
| | | 2.3 | | | | | | 8.2 | | 6.0 |
| | | 41.2 | | | | | | 40.9 | | 51.8 |
| | (10) | 7.5 | | | | % Profit Before Taxes/Tangible Net Worth | (51) | 15.8 | (26) | 20.5 |
| | | 3.1 | | | | | | 5.1 | | 3.3 |
| | | 12.3 | | | | | | 15.9 | | 24.9 |
| | | 5.7 | | | | % Profit Before Taxes/Total Assets | | 5.4 | | 3.8 |
| | | 1.5 | | | | | | .8 | | .7 |
| | | 34.7 | | | | | | 37.7 | | 37.9 |
| | | 15.4 | | | | Sales/Net Fixed Assets | | 11.6 | | 9.1 |
| | | 3.3 | | | | | | 2.3 | | 1.6 |
| | | 1.8 | | | | | | 3.0 | | 1.9 |
| | | 1.3 | | | | Sales/Total Assets | | 1.4 | | 1.3 |
| | | .9 | | | | | | .7 | | .5 |
| | | | | | | | | 1.1 | | 1.5 |
| | | | | | | % Depr., Dep., Amort./Sales | (50) | 2.0 | (24) | 3.5 |
| | | | | | | | | 4.9 | | 6.2 |
| | | | | | | % Officers', Directors' Owners' Comp/Sales | | | | |
| 3321M | 3628M | 61946M | 303440M | 341234M | 461349M | Net Sales ($) | | 2691469M | | 1061855M |
| 1129M | 4506M | 45587M | 197618M | 313362M | 596472M | Total Assets ($) | | 1747078M | | 1154483M |

© RMA 2024

M = $ thousand    MM = $ million
See Pages viii through xx for Explanation of Ratios and Data

# EDUCATION—Other Technical and Trade Schools  NAICS 611519

## Comparative Historical Data

| | | | | | | | Type of Statement | | | | | | |
|---|---|---|---|---|---|---|---|---|---|---|---|---|---|
| | 13 | | 12 | | 9 | | Unqualified | | | 3 | 2 | 2 | 2 |
| | 1 | | | | 1 | | Reviewed | | | | | 1 | 1 |
| | 4 | | 3 | | 2 | | Compiled | | 1 | 1 | 1 | | 1 |
| | 22 | | 19 | | 21 | | Tax Returns | | 3 | 1 | 3 | 2 | 7 |
| | 4/1/21- | | 4/1/22- | | 4/1/23- | | Other | 6 | | | | | |
| | 3/31/22 | | 3/31/23 | | 3/31/24 | | | | 11 (4/1-9/30/23) | | 24 (10/1/23-3/31/24) | | |
| | ALL | | ALL | | ALL | | | 0-1MM | 1-3MM | 3-5MM | 5-10MM | 10-25MM | 25MM & OVER |
| | 40 | | 34 | | 35 | NUMBER OF STATEMENTS | 6 | 4 | 4 | 6 | 4 | 11 |
| | % | | % | | % | ASSETS | % | % | % | % | % | % |
| | 26.4 | | 23.4 | | 17.5 | Cash & Equivalents | | | | | | 15.3 |
| | 20.6 | | 18.3 | | 14.5 | Trade Receivables (net) | | | | | | 13.6 |
| | .7 | | 1.0 | | 1.6 | Inventory | | | | | | 1.3 |
| | 6.4 | | 5.6 | | 3.1 | All Other Current | | | | | | 4.4 |
| | 54.2 | | 48.4 | | 36.7 | Total Current | | | | | | 34.6 |
| | 26.7 | | 31.8 | | 30.2 | Fixed Assets (net) | | | | | | 29.5 |
| | 6.5 | | 1.9 | | 9.8 | Intangibles (net) | | | | | | 12.3 |
| | 12.6 | | 17.9 | | 23.3 | All Other Non-Current | | | | | | 23.6 |
| | 100.0 | | 100.0 | | 100.0 | Total | | | | | | 100.0 |
| | | | | | | LIABILITIES | | | | | | |
| | 4.7 | | 1.3 | | 3.7 | Notes Payable-Short Term | | | | | | 1.8 |
| | 3.1 | | 2.2 | | 4.9 | Cur. Mat.-L.T.D. | | | | | | 11.2 |
| | 4.3 | | 3.4 | | 4.4 | Trade Payables | | | | | | 3.8 |
| | 1.4 | | 1.0 | | .0 | Income Taxes Payable | | | | | | .0 |
| | 14.8 | | 13.5 | | 13.6 | All Other Current | | | | | | 15.6 |
| | 28.3 | | 21.4 | | 26.7 | Total Current | | | | | | 32.4 |
| | 19.5 | | 19.9 | | 15.4 | Long-Term Debt | | | | | | 11.0 |
| | .6 | | .2 | | .0 | Deferred Taxes | | | | | | .0 |
| | 15.4 | | 15.3 | | 18.3 | All Other Non-Current | | | | | | 26.7 |
| | 36.3 | | 43.2 | | 39.6 | Net Worth | | | | | | 29.8 |
| | 100.0 | | 100.0 | | 100.0 | Total Liabilities & Net Worth | | | | | | 100.0 |
| | | | | | | INCOME DATA | | | | | | |
| | 100.0 | | 100.0 | | 100.0 | Net Sales | | | | | | 100.0 |
| | | | | | | Gross Profit | | | | | | |
| | 91.7 | | 94.4 | | 92.0 | Operating Expenses | | | | | | 85.2 |
| | 8.3 | | 5.6 | | 8.0 | Operating Profit | | | | | | 14.8 |
| | -1.8 | | .4 | | .7 | All Other Expenses (net) | | | | | | 1.8 |
| | 10.1 | | 5.2 | | 7.3 | Profit Before Taxes | | | | | | 13.0 |
| | | | | | | RATIOS | | | | | | |
| | 3.7 | | 5.3 | | 2.5 | | | | | | | 2.3 |
| | 2.1 | | 2.2 | | 1.5 | Current | | | | | | 1.3 |
| | 1.3 | | 1.3 | | .9 | | | | | | | .7 |
| | 3.0 | | 4.1 | | 2.5 | | | | | | | 2.3 |
| | 1.7 | | 2.0 | | 1.3 | Quick | | | | | | 1.2 |
| | 1.0 | | 1.0 | | .8 | | | | | | | .6 |
| 9 | 42.2 | 2 | 217.3 | 11 | 33.5 | | | | | | 7 | 53.9 |
| 23 | 15.8 | 29 | 12.4 | 32 | 11.3 | Sales/Receivables | | | | | 29 | 12.6 |
| 66 | 5.5 | 57 | 6.4 | 56 | 6.5 | | | | | | 59 | 6.2 |
| | | | | | | Cost of Sales/Inventory | | | | | | |
| | | | | | | Cost of Sales/Payables | | | | | | |
| | 2.7 | | 3.7 | | 5.5 | | | | | | | 6.7 |
| | 6.0 | | 6.0 | | 16.8 | Sales/Working Capital | | | | | | 16.8 |
| | 14.0 | | 31.0 | | -33.0 | | | | | | | -14.7 |
| | 23.0 | | 34.1 | | 40.4 | | | | | | | |
| (27) | 10.6 | (22) | 8.8 | (24) | 9.5 | EBIT/Interest | | | | | | |
| | .7 | | 2.0 | | .0 | | | | | | | |
| | | | | | | Net Profit + Depr., Dep., Amort./Cur. Mat. L/T/D | | | | | | |
| | .3 | | .1 | | .3 | | | | | | | .5 |
| | .7 | | .5 | | .9 | Fixed/Worth | | | | | | 1.2 |
| | 3.1 | | 1.7 | | 2.1 | | | | | | | -1.2 |
| | .6 | | .6 | | .9 | | | | | | | 1.1 |
| | 1.4 | | 1.1 | | 2.1 | Debt/Worth | | | | | | 2.8 |
| | 8.9 | | 2.4 | | 4.5 | | | | | | | -7.7 |
| | 70.7 | | 56.7 | | 62.4 | | | | | | | |
| (33) | 24.8 | (31) | 15.9 | (30) | 31.4 | % Profit Before Taxes/Tangible Net Worth | | | | | | |
| | 10.3 | | 3.8 | | 4.7 | | | | | | | |
| | 25.7 | | 29.7 | | 22.9 | | | | | | | 30.6 |
| | 9.0 | | 6.6 | | 6.2 | % Profit Before Taxes/Total Assets | | | | | | 14.2 |
| | .7 | | 2.1 | | 2.3 | | | | | | | 5.9 |
| | 30.8 | | 41.8 | | 17.1 | | | | | | | 16.4 |
| | 5.2 | | 7.2 | | 10.5 | Sales/Net Fixed Assets | | | | | | 11.6 |
| | 2.6 | | 2.1 | | 1.6 | | | | | | | 2.0 |
| | 2.1 | | 2.9 | | 2.0 | | | | | | | 2.0 |
| | 1.3 | | 1.6 | | 1.2 | Sales/Total Assets | | | | | | 1.1 |
| | .7 | | .8 | | .6 | | | | | | | .6 |
| | 1.2 | | .6 | | 1.4 | | | | | | | |
| (31) | 2.4 | (26) | 2.5 | (26) | 2.6 | % Depr., Dep., Amort./Sales | | | | | | |
| | 4.1 | | 3.8 | | 5.7 | | | | | | | |
| | | | | | | % Officers', Directors' Owners' Comp/Sales | | | | | | |
| | 1360785M | | 855405M | | 1174918M | Net Sales ($) | 4587M | 8815M | 15145M | 40496M | 71808M | 1034067M |
| | 1453896M | | 563861M | | 1158674M | Total Assets ($) | 3732M | 10227M | 50177M | 29505M | 102145M | 962888M |

© RMA 2024  M = $ thousand   MM = $ million
See Pages viii through xx for Explanation of Ratios and Data

# EDUCATION—Fine Arts Schools  NAICS 611610

## Current Data Sorted by Assets / Comparative Historical Data

| | | | | | | Type of Statement | | |
|---|---|---|---|---|---|---|---|---|
| | | 1 | 2 | 4 | | 2 | Unqualified | 18 | 7 |
| | | 1 | | | | | Reviewed | | |
| 1 | | | 1 | | | | Compiled | 1 | 1 |
| 2 | 3 | 3 | | | | | Tax Returns | 5 | 4 |
| 6 | 4 | 4 | 7 | 3 | 3 | 1 | Other | 21 | 12 |
| | 20 (4/1-9/30/23) | | | 21 (10/1/23-3/31/24) | | | | 4/1/19-3/31/20 | 4/1/20-3/31/21 |
| 0-500M | 500M-2MM | 2-10MM | 10-50MM | 50-100MM | 100-250MM | NUMBER OF STATEMENTS | ALL 45 | ALL 24 |
| 9 | 9 | 10 | 7 | 3 | 3 | | | |

| 0-500M | 500M-2MM | 2-10MM | 10-50MM | 50-100MM | 100-250MM | | ALL | ALL |
|---|---|---|---|---|---|---|---|---|
| % | % | % | % | % | % | **ASSETS** | % | % |
| | | 13.8 | | | | Cash & Equivalents | 26.1 | 40.2 |
| | | 2.2 | | | | Trade Receivables (net) | 6.1 | 4.7 |
| | | 2.1 | | | | Inventory | .7 | 1.4 |
| | | 1.9 | | | | All Other Current | 2.7 | 3.4 |
| | | 20.0 | | | | Total Current | 35.7 | 49.8 |
| | | 57.6 | | | | Fixed Assets (net) | 41.4 | 28.8 |
| | | 7.3 | | | | Intangibles (net) | 3.7 | 7.7 |
| | | 15.1 | | | | All Other Non-Current | 19.3 | 13.7 |
| | | 100.0 | | | | Total | 100.0 | 100.0 |
| | | | | | | **LIABILITIES** | | |
| | | 1.6 | | | | Notes Payable-Short Term | 4.9 | 3.1 |
| | | 2.4 | | | | Cur. Mat.-L.T.D. | 1.0 | 1.3 |
| | | 1.1 | | | | Trade Payables | 3.2 | 1.9 |
| | | .0 | | | | Income Taxes Payable | .0 | .0 |
| | | 4.3 | | | | All Other Current | 11.3 | 24.7 |
| | | 9.3 | | | | Total Current | 20.5 | 31.0 |
| | | 31.7 | | | | Long-Term Debt | 19.6 | 37.8 |
| | | .0 | | | | Deferred Taxes | .0 | .0 |
| | | 7.2 | | | | All Other Non-Current | 3.9 | 10.8 |
| | | 51.8 | | | | Net Worth | 56.0 | 20.4 |
| | | 100.0 | | | | Total Liabilities & Net Worth | 100.0 | 100.0 |
| | | | | | | **INCOME DATA** | | |
| | | 100.0 | | | | Net Sales | 100.0 | 100.0 |
| | | | | | | Gross Profit | | |
| | | 89.9 | | | | Operating Expenses | 91.7 | 95.7 |
| | | 10.1 | | | | Operating Profit | 8.3 | 4.3 |
| | | 9.2 | | | | All Other Expenses (net) | 2.0 | -.3 |
| | | .9 | | | | Profit Before Taxes | 6.3 | 4.6 |
| | | | | | | **RATIOS** | | |
| | | 17.7 | | | | | 5.5 | 4.0 |
| | | 3.5 | | | | Current | 1.9 | 2.1 |
| | | .6 | | | | | .7 | 1.1 |
| | | 8.5 | | | | | 5.3 | 4.0 |
| | | 2.8 | | | | Quick | 1.7 | 2.0 |
| | | .4 | | | | | .6 | .9 |
| | | 0 UND | | | | | 0 UND | 0 UND |
| | | 1 380.5 | | | | Sales/Receivables | 10 37.7 | 2 153.2 |
| | | 21 17.4 | | | | | 31 11.7 | 28 13.2 |
| | | | | | | Cost of Sales/Inventory | | |
| | | | | | | Cost of Sales/Payables | | |
| | | 1.4 | | | | | 4.8 | 3.2 |
| | | 12.1 | | | | Sales/Working Capital | 10.5 | 7.0 |
| | | -4.9 | | | | | -45.2 | 91.6 |
| | | | | | | | 12.0 | 4.5 |
| | | | | | | EBIT/Interest | (27) 1.2 | (15) .6 |
| | | | | | | | -3.1 | -24.6 |
| | | | | | | Net Profit + Depr., Dep., Amort./Cur. Mat. L/T/D | | |
| | | .5 | | | | | .1 | .1 |
| | | 1.0 | | | | Fixed/Worth | .6 | .8 |
| | | 2.3 | | | | | 2.3 | NM |
| | | .4 | | | | | .2 | .5 |
| | | .8 | | | | Debt/Worth | .5 | 1.4 |
| | | 2.7 | | | | | 2.5 | NM |
| | | | | | | | 32.6 | 52.2 |
| | | | | | | % Profit Before Taxes/Tangible Net Worth | (41) 3.7 | (18) 15.9 |
| | | | | | | | -.8 | -4.9 |
| | | 2.8 | | | | | 16.2 | 16.4 |
| | | -1.4 | | | | % Profit Before Taxes/Total Assets | 2.2 | 2.0 |
| | | -4.8 | | | | | -1.2 | -15.0 |
| | | 1.6 | | | | | 16.8 | 45.2 |
| | | 1.0 | | | | Sales/Net Fixed Assets | 3.9 | 16.6 |
| | | .3 | | | | | .7 | .5 |
| | | .7 | | | | | 2.4 | 2.6 |
| | | .5 | | | | Sales/Total Assets | 1.1 | 1.7 |
| | | .2 | | | | | .4 | .4 |
| | | | | | | | 1.9 | .3 |
| | | | | | | % Depr., Dep., Amort./Sales | (35) 4.9 | (14) 1.8 |
| | | | | | | | 6.9 | 4.3 |
| | | | | | | % Officers', Directors' Owners' Comp/Sales | | |
| 7450M | 12530M | 31562M | 120620M | 70741M | 54205M | Net Sales ($) | 367900M | 215325M |
| 1732M | 8483M | 41877M | 168525M | 240745M | 417023M | Total Assets ($) | 668153M | 478207M |

© RMA 2024

M = $ thousand   MM = $ million
See Pages viii through xx for Explanation of Ratios and Data

# EDUCATION—Fine Arts Schools NAICS 611610

| Comparative Historical Data | | | | | Current Data Sorted by Sales | | | | | |
|---|---|---|---|---|---|---|---|---|---|---|
| | | | | Type of Statement | | | | | | |
| 7 | | 7 | 9 | Unqualified | | 2 | 3 | 4 | | |
| 1 | | 1 | 1 | Reviewed | 1 | | | | | |
| 1 | | 11 | 1 | Compiled | | 1 | | | 1 | |
| 4 | | 11 | 6 | Tax Returns | 4 | | | 1 | 1 | |
| 23 | | 20 | 24 | Other | 10 | 5 | 3 | 4 | 4 | 2 |
| 4/1/21-3/31/22 | | 4/1/22-3/31/23 | 4/1/23-3/31/24 | | 20 (4/1-9/30/23) | | | 21 (10/1/23-3/31/24) | | |
| ALL | | ALL | ALL | | 0-1MM | 1-3MM | 3-5MM | 5-10MM | 10-25MM | 25MM & OVER |
| 36 | | 38 | 41 | NUMBER OF STATEMENTS | 15 | 9 | 6 | | 9 | 2 |
| % | | % | % | ASSETS | % | % | % | % | % | % |
| 36.8 | | 28.7 | 32.0 | Cash & Equivalents | 38.6 | | | | | |
| 5.6 | | 3.7 | 3.6 | Trade Receivables (net) | 2.6 | | | | | |
| 2.5 | | 2.3 | 3.2 | Inventory | 7.2 | | | | | |
| 2.0 | | 2.4 | 1.4 | All Other Current | 2.7 | | | D | | |
| 46.9 | | 37.1 | 40.2 | Total Current | 51.1 | | | A | | |
| 35.1 | | 42.4 | 35.8 | Fixed Assets (net) | 41.4 | | | T | | |
| 4.5 | | 5.2 | 4.6 | Intangibles (net) | 4.5 | | | A | | |
| 13.5 | | 15.3 | 19.3 | All Other Non-Current | 3.0 | | | | | |
| 100.0 | | 100.0 | 100.0 | Total | 100.0 | | | N | | |
| | | | | LIABILITIES | | | | O | | |
| 3.9 | | 7.0 | 6.9 | Notes Payable-Short Term | 17.3 | | | T | | |
| 3.0 | | 1.2 | 1.5 | Cur. Mat.-L.T.D. | 1.7 | | | | | |
| 1.8 | | .9 | 1.7 | Trade Payables | .7 | | | A | | |
| .1 | | .0 | .0 | Income Taxes Payable | .0 | | | V | | |
| 5.6 | | 7.8 | 4.5 | All Other Current | 4.9 | | | A | | |
| 14.4 | | 17.0 | 14.7 | Total Current | 24.6 | | | I | | |
| 33.5 | | 36.0 | 24.2 | Long-Term Debt | 30.9 | | | L | | |
| .0 | | .0 | .0 | Deferred Taxes | .0 | | | A | | |
| 19.0 | | 2.0 | 6.5 | All Other Non-Current | .9 | | | B | | |
| 33.0 | | 45.0 | 54.7 | Net Worth | 43.6 | | | L | | |
| 100.0 | | 100.0 | 100.0 | Total Liabilities & Net Worth | 100.0 | | | E | | |
| | | | | INCOME DATA | | | | | | |
| 100.0 | | 100.0 | 100.0 | Net Sales | 100.0 | | | | | |
| | | | | Gross Profit | | | | | | |
| 87.4 | | 87.7 | 93.8 | Operating Expenses | 84.2 | | | | | |
| 12.6 | | 12.3 | 6.2 | Operating Profit | 15.8 | | | | | |
| -.2 | | 1.4 | 3.1 | All Other Expenses (net) | 8.2 | | | | | |
| 12.8 | | 10.9 | 3.1 | Profit Before Taxes | 7.6 | | | | | |
| | | | | RATIOS | | | | | | |
| 9.8 | | 11.7 | 12.9 | | 14.4 | | | | | |
| 3.7 | | 4.7 | 4.0 | Current | 4.0 | | | | | |
| 1.8 | | 1.5 | 1.1 | | .7 | | | | | |
| 9.8 | | 9.0 | 10.1 | | 12.7 | | | | | |
| 3.4 | | 3.8 | 4.0 | Quick | 1.4 | | | | | |
| 1.4 | | 1.5 | 1.1 | | .3 | | | | | |
| 0 UND | | 0 UND | 0 UND | | 0 UND | | | | | |
| 1 313.8 | | 0 UND | 4 93.1 | Sales/Receivables | 0 UND | | | | | |
| 38 9.5 | | 23 16.0 | 34 10.7 | | 2 150.0 | | | | | |
| | | | | Cost of Sales/Inventory | | | | | | |
| | | | | Cost of Sales/Payables | | | | | | |
| 2.1 | | 2.3 | 1.7 | | 1.6 | | | | | |
| 4.3 | | 6.6 | 3.4 | Sales/Working Capital | 10.0 | | | | | |
| 9.5 | | NM | 119.1 | | -32.2 | | | | | |
| 36.2 | | 24.6 | 9.3 | | | | | | | |
| (23) 6.0 | (22) | 8.2 | (24) 1.8 | EBIT/Interest | | | | | | |
| .9 | | .6 | -5.3 | | | | | | | |
| | | | | Net Profit + Depr., Dep., Amort./Cur. Mat. L/T/D | | | | | | |
| .2 | | .2 | .2 | | .2 | | | | | |
| .9 | | .9 | .6 | Fixed/Worth | 1.2 | | | | | |
| 3.3 | | 3.0 | 1.9 | | 17.5 | | | | | |
| .5 | | .2 | .2 | | .1 | | | | | |
| 1.4 | | .6 | .7 | Debt/Worth | 1.8 | | | | | |
| 5.2 | | 3.2 | 2.8 | | 18.7 | | | | | |
| 42.9 | | 63.7 | 30.5 | | 40.9 | | | | | |
| (29) 18.5 | (32) | 18.7 | (36) .8 | % Profit Before Taxes/Tangible Net Worth | (12) 8.4 | | | | | |
| 1.3 | | 4.9 | -6.8 | | -29.1 | | | | | |
| 18.5 | | 27.7 | 22.6 | | 36.3 | | | | | |
| 8.8 | | 11.5 | .7 | % Profit Before Taxes/Total Assets | 3.5 | | | | | |
| -.2 | | 1.2 | -4.6 | | -8.2 | | | | | |
| 28.7 | | 30.5 | 33.3 | | 112.7 | | | | | |
| 5.7 | | 2.5 | 1.6 | Sales/Net Fixed Assets | 6.0 | | | | | |
| .5 | | .9 | .8 | | .3 | | | | | |
| 2.4 | | 2.4 | 2.3 | | 3.1 | | | | | |
| .9 | | 1.3 | 1.0 | Sales/Total Assets | 1.4 | | | | | |
| .3 | | .4 | .3 | | .2 | | | | | |
| 1.6 | | .9 | 1.7 | | | | | | | |
| (23) 3.2 | (25) | 3.9 | (27) 4.8 | % Depr., Dep., Amort./Sales | | | | | | |
| 6.7 | | 5.4 | 7.2 | | | | | | | |
| | | 4.2 | | | | | | | | |
| | (12) | 8.2 | | % Officers', Directors' Owners' Comp/Sales | | | | | | |
| | | 15.7 | | | | | | | | |
| 170083M | | 234526M | 297108M | Net Sales ($) | 8217M | 17588M | 24254M | | 164860M | 82189M |
| 387025M | | 489179M | 878385M | Total Assets ($) | 15019M | 20408M | 56294M | | 683931M | 102733M |

© RMA 2024  M = $ thousand  MM = $ million
See Pages viii through xx for Explanation of Ratios and Data

# EDUCATION—Sports and Recreation Instruction  NAICS 611620

## Current Data Sorted by Assets

| | | | | | | Type of Statement | | |
|---|---|---|---|---|---|---|---|---|
| | | | | | 1 | Unqualified | | |
| | | 1 | | 1 | | Reviewed | | |
| | 1 | | | | | Compiled | | |
| 8 | 4 | | | | | Tax Returns | | |
| 12 | 14 | 1 | 5 | | 1 | Other | | |
| | 7 (4/1-9/30/23) | 9 | 50 (10/1/23-3/31/24) | | | | | |
| 0-500M | 500M-2MM | 2-10MM | 10-50MM | 50-100MM | 100-250MM | NUMBER OF STATEMENTS | | |
| 20 | 19 | 10 | 6 | | 2 | | | |

## Comparative Historical Data

| Type of Statement | | |
|---|---|---|
| Unqualified | 6 | 2 |
| Reviewed | | |
| Compiled | 2 | 2 |
| Tax Returns | 25 | 6 |
| Other | 36 | 21 |
| | 4/1/19-3/31/20 ALL | 4/1/20-3/31/21 ALL |
| NUMBER OF STATEMENTS | 69 | 31 |

| % | % | % | % | % | % | ASSETS | % | % |
|---|---|---|---|---|---|---|---|---|
| 37.0 | 30.8 | 19.6 | | | | Cash & Equivalents | 21.3 | 31.6 |
| 4.2 | 1.3 | 6.3 | D | | | Trade Receivables (net) | 2.3 | 2.3 |
| 4.5 | 2.0 | 4.3 | A | | | Inventory | 2.7 | 6.5 |
| 5.0 | 2.5 | 10.2 | T | | | All Other Current | 1.7 | 2.8 |
| 50.8 | 36.5 | 40.4 | A | | | Total Current | 28.0 | 43.3 |
| 31.6 | 39.0 | 45.1 | | | | Fixed Assets (net) | 52.8 | 41.7 |
| 4.9 | 8.3 | 2.2 | N | | | Intangibles (net) | 3.9 | 8.2 |
| 12.7 | 16.3 | 12.4 | O | | | All Other Non-Current | 15.3 | 6.9 |
| 100.0 | 100.0 | 100.0 | T | | | Total | 100.0 | 100.0 |
| | | | | | | LIABILITIES | | |
| 12.5 | 1.5 | .1 | A | | | Notes Payable-Short Term | 13.0 | 6.7 |
| 3.2 | 5.6 | 8.8 | V | | | Cur. Mat.-L.T.D. | 2.5 | 6.8 |
| 6.8 | 6.2 | 9.4 | A | | | Trade Payables | 5.8 | 4.5 |
| .0 | 4.0 | .0 | I | | | Income Taxes Payable | .0 | .1 |
| 35.9 | 7.5 | 25.4 | L | | | All Other Current | 21.2 | 14.2 |
| 58.4 | 24.8 | 43.7 | A | | | Total Current | 42.6 | 32.2 |
| 47.3 | 34.0 | 22.0 | B | | | Long-Term Debt | 35.3 | 34.8 |
| .0 | .0 | .3 | L | | | Deferred Taxes | .0 | .2 |
| 2.7 | 6.7 | 18.8 | E | | | All Other Non-Current | 8.2 | 10.5 |
| -8.3 | 34.6 | 15.2 | | | | Net Worth | 14.0 | 22.3 |
| 100.0 | 100.0 | 100.0 | | | | Total Liabilities & Net Worth | 100.0 | 100.0 |
| | | | | | | INCOME DATA | | |
| 100.0 | 100.0 | 100.0 | | | | Net Sales | 100.0 | 100.0 |
| | | | | | | Gross Profit | | |
| 89.6 | 85.8 | 96.5 | | | | Operating Expenses | 88.0 | 100.4 |
| 10.4 | 14.2 | 3.5 | | | | Operating Profit | 12.0 | -.4 |
| 1.1 | 4.0 | 7.1 | | | | All Other Expenses (net) | 2.3 | -.9 |
| 9.4 | 10.2 | -3.5 | | | | Profit Before Taxes | 9.7 | .5 |
| | | | | | | RATIOS | | |
| 32.1 | 11.4 | 5.4 | | | | | 3.1 | 8.5 |
| 1.4 | 3.4 | .9 | | | | Current | .9 | 1.7 |
| .6 | .5 | .2 | | | | | .4 | .9 |
| 20.0 | 11.3 | 1.7 | | | | | 3.0 | 7.6 |
| 1.3 | 2.7 | .7 | | | | Quick | .7 | 1.4 |
| .4 | .5 | .2 | | | | | .3 | .4 |
| 0 UND | 0 UND | 0 UND | | | | | 0 UND | 0 UND |
| 0 UND | 0 UND | 6 65.0 | | | | Sales/Receivables | 0 UND | 0 UND |
| 0 UND | 0 UND | 29 12.4 | | | | | 2 207.9 | 6 59.4 |
| | | | | | | Cost of Sales/Inventory | | |
| | | | | | | Cost of Sales/Payables | | |
| 2.8 | 4.9 | 1.8 | | | | | 9.7 | 4.3 |
| 44.9 | 20.9 | -42.4 | | | | Sales/Working Capital | -776.8 | 9.5 |
| -46.1 | -15.2 | -2.0 | | | | | -10.4 | -48.7 |
| 59.9 | 61.0 | | | | | | 14.1 | 3.5 |
| (14) 6.3 | (11) 9.7 | | | | | EBIT/Interest | (49) 6.0 | (19) .9 |
| -.3 | .0 | | | | | | 1.0 | -12.3 |
| | | | | | | Net Profit + Depr., Dep., Amort./Cur. Mat. L/T/D | | |
| .0 | .1 | .4 | | | | | .5 | .4 |
| 1.2 | .8 | NM | | | | Fixed/Worth | 1.5 | 1.2 |
| -.9 | 36.4 | -1.7 | | | | | 55.8 | -1.8 |
| .4 | .2 | .3 | | | | | .3 | .5 |
| 1.5 | 2.4 | NM | | | | Debt/Worth | 1.5 | 2.0 |
| -3.4 | -6.0 | -8.4 | | | | | 147.9 | -5.9 |
| 232.4 | 112.3 | | | | | | 84.3 | 25.1 |
| (14) 65.4 | (14) 37.8 | | | | | % Profit Before Taxes/Tangible Net Worth | (53) 19.7 | (21) 7.4 |
| 28.6 | 9.3 | | | | | | .2 | -17.0 |
| 43.6 | 34.6 | 5.3 | | | | % Profit Before Taxes/Total Assets | 30.3 | 9.5 |
| 22.9 | 21.8 | .3 | | | | | 9.0 | -.3 |
| 10.0 | 1.5 | -5.0 | | | | | .2 | -20.6 |
| UND | 32.7 | 6.3 | | | | | 20.2 | 34.9 |
| 27.8 | 4.7 | .9 | | | | Sales/Net Fixed Assets | 3.3 | 3.0 |
| 6.4 | 1.5 | .4 | | | | | 1.2 | 1.1 |
| 5.0 | 3.6 | 1.2 | | | | | 3.4 | 2.8 |
| 3.4 | 1.7 | .5 | | | | Sales/Total Assets | 1.8 | 1.2 |
| 2.3 | .5 | .1 | | | | | .8 | .7 |
| .4 | | | | | | | 1.3 | .8 |
| (10) 1.4 | | | | | | % Depr., Dep., Amort./Sales | (46) 3.2 | (22) 3.8 |
| 2.2 | | | | | | | 7.2 | 6.8 |
| 4.3 | | | | | | | 4.2 | 3.1 |
| (10) 5.8 | | | | | | % Officers', Directors' Owners' Comp/Sales | (25) 7.0 | (12) 7.5 |
| 11.6 | | | | | | | 10.0 | 16.6 |
| 19817M | 35966M | 36497M | 98775M | | 174859M | Net Sales ($) | 469603M | 305269M |
| 4967M | 20150M | 52361M | 153132M | | 329014M | Total Assets ($) | 388518M | 392394M |

M = $ thousand    MM = $ million
See Pages viii through xx for Explanation of Ratios and Data

© RMA 2024

# EDUCATION—Sports and Recreation Instruction  NAICS 611620

## Comparative Historical Data | Current Data Sorted by Sales

| Comparative Historical Data | | | | | Current Data Sorted by Sales | | | | | |
|---|---|---|---|---|---|---|---|---|---|---|
| 1 | 2 | 1 | **Type of Statement** | | | | | | 1 | 1 |
| | 4 | 1 | Unqualified | | | 1 | | | | |
| 1 | 2 | 1 | Reviewed | | 1 | 4 | | 1 | | |
| 19 | 20 | 13 | Compiled | | 7 | 15 | 4 | 3 | 2 | 2 |
| 25 | 43 | 41 | Tax Returns | | 15 | | | | | |
| 4/1/21-3/31/22 ALL | 4/1/22-3/31/23 ALL | 4/1/23-3/31/24 ALL | Other | | 7 (4/1-9/30/23) | | | 50 (10/1/23-3/31/24) | | |
| | | | | | 0-1MM | 1-3MM | 3-5MM | 5-10MM | 10-25MM | 25MM & OVER |
| 46 | 71 | 57 | **NUMBER OF STATEMENTS** | | 22 | 20 | 5 | 4 | 3 | 3 |
| % | % | % | **ASSETS** | | % | % | % | % | % | % |
| 42.1 | 38.0 | 29.0 | Cash & Equivalents | | 28.2 | 31.9 | | | | |
| 2.7 | 3.1 | 3.3 | Trade Receivables (net) | | 5.1 | 2.5 | | | | |
| 1.6 | 1.9 | 3.1 | Inventory | | 2.1 | 2.7 | | | | |
| 5.5 | 6.9 | 4.6 | All Other Current | | 9.8 | 1.3 | | | | |
| 51.9 | 49.9 | 40.0 | Total Current | | 45.2 | 38.3 | | | | |
| 34.4 | 32.3 | 36.6 | Fixed Assets (net) | | 34.8 | 46.2 | | | | |
| 4.6 | 3.8 | 9.0 | Intangibles (net) | | 6.3 | 6.8 | | | | |
| 9.1 | 14.0 | 14.4 | All Other Non-Current | | 13.7 | 8.6 | | | | |
| 100.0 | 100.0 | 100.0 | Total | | 100.0 | 100.0 | | | | |
| | | | **LIABILITIES** | | | | | | | |
| 8.5 | 3.9 | 5.0 | Notes Payable-Short Term | | 9.5 | 2.8 | | | | |
| 1.4 | 1.7 | 5.0 | Cur. Mat.-L.T.D. | | 11.0 | .5 | | | | |
| 1.8 | 3.2 | 6.4 | Trade Payables | | 5.4 | 10.3 | | | | |
| .1 | .2 | 1.3 | Income Taxes Payable | | .0 | .0 | | | | |
| 9.1 | 12.9 | 21.1 | All Other Current | | 10.2 | 32.3 | | | | |
| 21.0 | 21.9 | 38.8 | Total Current | | 36.1 | 45.9 | | | | |
| 39.8 | 39.0 | 39.5 | Long-Term Debt | | 40.9 | 43.2 | | | | |
| .0 | .0 | .1 | Deferred Taxes | | .0 | .0 | | | | |
| 10.6 | 16.2 | 7.5 | All Other Non-Current | | 2.4 | 7.3 | | | | |
| 28.6 | 22.9 | 14.2 | Net Worth | | 20.6 | 3.6 | | | | |
| 100.0 | 100.0 | 100.0 | Total Liabilities & Net Worth | | 100.0 | 100.0 | | | | |
| | | | **INCOME DATA** | | | | | | | |
| 100.0 | 100.0 | 100.0 | Net Sales | | 100.0 | 100.0 | | | | |
| | | | Gross Profit | | | | | | | |
| 84.9 | 84.5 | 88.7 | Operating Expenses | | 88.2 | 87.2 | | | | |
| 15.1 | 15.5 | 11.3 | Operating Profit | | 11.8 | 12.8 | | | | |
| -1.5 | 1.0 | 4.6 | All Other Expenses (net) | | 8.0 | 1.1 | | | | |
| 16.6 | 14.5 | 6.7 | Profit Before Taxes | | 3.8 | 11.7 | | | | |
| | | | **RATIOS** | | | | | | | |
| 12.1 | 10.5 | 11.4 | | | 23.8 | 10.7 | | | | |
| 3.7 | 3.0 | 1.3 | Current | | .9 | 3.0 | | | | |
| 1.1 | 1.2 | .5 | | | .2 | .7 | | | | |
| 9.7 | 10.0 | 7.8 | | | 18.5 | 10.6 | | | | |
| 3.7 | 2.6 | .9 | Quick | | .7 | 2.6 | | | | |
| .6 | .9 | .3 | | | .2 | .7 | | | | |
| 0 UND | 0 UND | 0 UND | | | 0 UND | 0 UND | | | | |
| 0 UND | 0 UND | 0 UND | Sales/Receivables | | 0 UND | 0 UND | | | | |
| 3 137.9 | 6 61.1 | 4 90.7 | | | 8 48.0 | 0 UND | | | | |
| | | | Cost of Sales/Inventory | | | | | | | |
| | | | Cost of Sales/Payables | | | | | | | |
| 3.1 | 3.3 | 3.9 | | | 2.2 | 4.8 | | | | |
| 4.5 | 5.9 | 74.5 | Sales/Working Capital | | -77.1 | 29.3 | | | | |
| 59.2 | 71.9 | -9.7 | | | -3.0 | -46.2 | | | | |
| 50.4 | 62.3 | 34.8 | | | 39.4 | 69.4 | | | | |
| (29) 11.6 | (44) 20.9 | (33) 6.7 | EBIT/Interest | | (12) 1.3 | (12) 14.1 | | | | |
| 3.7 | 5.4 | .0 | | | -2.2 | 4.5 | | | | |
| | | | Net Profit + Depr., Dep., Amort./Cur. Mat. L/T/D | | | | | | | |
| .2 | .1 | .2 | | | .0 | .4 | | | | |
| 1.2 | .8 | 1.6 | Fixed/Worth | | .8 | 2.3 | | | | |
| -3.2 | 3.1 | -1.9 | | | -58.0 | -252.1 | | | | |
| .4 | .4 | .4 | | | .2 | .4 | | | | |
| 1.7 | 1.1 | 3.2 | Debt/Worth | | 3.9 | 3.1 | | | | |
| -13.4 | 9.6 | -4.7 | | | -5.8 | -253.2 | | | | |
| 111.7 | 101.2 | 105.3 | | | 140.0 | 219.7 | | | | |
| (32) 47.1 | (58) 54.0 | (38) 37.8 | % Profit Before Taxes/Tangible Net Worth | | (15) 26.8 | (14) 46.0 | | | | |
| 9.4 | 17.7 | 7.6 | | | -10.1 | 27.0 | | | | |
| 43.8 | 46.8 | 28.0 | | | 22.8 | 42.3 | | | | |
| 17.3 | 18.6 | 11.1 | % Profit Before Taxes/Total Assets | | 3.0 | 23.9 | | | | |
| 5.1 | 3.2 | .3 | | | -3.4 | 15.1 | | | | |
| 60.8 | 64.3 | 40.6 | | | UND | 23.2 | | | | |
| 4.9 | 8.9 | 6.8 | Sales/Net Fixed Assets | | 4.7 | 8.2 | | | | |
| 1.7 | 2.2 | 1.5 | | | .6 | 2.8 | | | | |
| 2.7 | 3.0 | 3.5 | | | 2.8 | 4.6 | | | | |
| 1.7 | 2.0 | 1.7 | Sales/Total Assets | | 1.1 | 2.7 | | | | |
| .9 | .8 | .6 | | | .2 | 1.2 | | | | |
| .8 | 1.6 | .9 | | | .5 | .8 | | | | |
| (25) 3.0 | (37) 3.2 | (32) 2.3 | % Depr., Dep., Amort./Sales | | (13) 1.8 | (10) 2.2 | | | | |
| 6.9 | 5.9 | 5.4 | | | 23.2 | 3.5 | | | | |
| 3.6 | 4.9 | 3.0 | | | | | | | | |
| (15) 7.3 | (23) 7.4 | (18) 5.0 | % Officers', Directors' Owners' Comp/Sales | | | | | | | |
| 9.6 | 12.6 | 11.6 | | | | | | | | |
| 162946M | 379160M | 365914M | Net Sales ($) | | 10453M | 36801M | 18989M | 30765M | 56198M | 212708M |
| 288490M | 558479M | 559624M | Total Assets ($) | | 24358M | 39312M | 32074M | 27060M | 58807M | 378013M |

© RMA 2024    M = $ thousand    MM = $ million
See Pages viii through xx for Explanation of Ratios and Data

# EDUCATION—All Other Miscellaneous Schools and Instruction  NAICS 611699

| Current Data Sorted by Assets | | | | | | | Comparative Historical Data | |
|---|---|---|---|---|---|---|---|---|
| | | | | | | **Type of Statement** | | |
| 2 | 3 | 4 | 8 | 6 | 2 | Unqualified | 34 | 23 |
| | 1 | | | | | Reviewed | 1 | 2 |
| | 1 | 1 | 1 | | | Compiled | 6 | 3 |
| 4 | 6 | 2 | | | 1 | Tax Returns | 27 | 16 |
| 7 | 13 | 10 | 8 | 7 | | Other | 48 | 49 |
| | 44 (4/1-9/30/23) | | 42 (10/1/23-3/31/24) | | | | 4/1/19-3/31/20 | 4/1/20-3/31/21 |
| 0-500M | 500M-2MM | 2-10MM | 10-50MM | 50-100MM | 100-250MM | | ALL | ALL |
| 13 | 24 | 17 | 16 | 14 | 2 | NUMBER OF STATEMENTS | 116 | 93 |
| % | % | % | % | % | % | **ASSETS** | % | % |
| 60.8 | 40.4 | 21.5 | 31.9 | 18.0 | | Cash & Equivalents | 28.3 | 39.1 |
| 3.6 | 10.4 | 6.2 | 5.7 | 6.3 | | Trade Receivables (net) | 8.9 | 4.6 |
| 7.1 | 6.0 | 2.1 | 1.8 | .7 | | Inventory | 2.0 | 1.9 |
| .1 | 3.7 | 1.0 | 7.9 | 3.0 | | All Other Current | 3.9 | 2.9 |
| 71.6 | 60.6 | 30.9 | 47.3 | 28.0 | | Total Current | 43.0 | 48.5 |
| 8.6 | 14.4 | 43.4 | 42.9 | 32.0 | | Fixed Assets (net) | 39.0 | 33.1 |
| .5 | 8.7 | .8 | 2.6 | 6.8 | | Intangibles (net) | 8.0 | 9.4 |
| 19.4 | 16.3 | 24.9 | 7.1 | 33.3 | | All Other Non-Current | 9.9 | 9.0 |
| 100.0 | 100.0 | 100.0 | 100.0 | 100.0 | | Total | 100.0 | 100.0 |
| | | | | | | **LIABILITIES** | | |
| 1.1 | 3.1 | 3.3 | .8 | .2 | | Notes Payable-Short Term | 3.4 | 4.1 |
| 1.8 | 1.4 | 1.6 | .9 | .7 | | Cur. Mat.-L.T.D. | 2.4 | 3.7 |
| 1.4 | 2.7 | 2.3 | 5.1 | 1.4 | | Trade Payables | 4.4 | 2.4 |
| .1 | .2 | .0 | .0 | .1 | | Income Taxes Payable | .1 | .0 |
| 23.3 | 12.3 | 7.7 | 11.5 | 5.0 | | All Other Current | 19.4 | 12.0 |
| 27.6 | 19.7 | 15.0 | 18.3 | 7.4 | | Total Current | 29.7 | 22.2 |
| 24.8 | 14.3 | 30.1 | 16.3 | 16.6 | | Long-Term Debt | 25.1 | 31.6 |
| .0 | .0 | .0 | .0 | .0 | | Deferred Taxes | .1 | .1 |
| 16.3 | 10.3 | 11.5 | 7.9 | 21.6 | | All Other Non-Current | 13.2 | 11.7 |
| 31.3 | 55.6 | 43.4 | 57.4 | 54.3 | | Net Worth | 31.9 | 34.4 |
| 100.0 | 100.0 | 100.0 | 100.0 | 100.0 | | Total Liabilities & Net Worth | 100.0 | 100.0 |
| | | | | | | **INCOME DATA** | | |
| 100.0 | 100.0 | 100.0 | 100.0 | 100.0 | | Net Sales | 100.0 | 100.0 |
| | | | | | | Gross Profit | | |
| 97.1 | 90.6 | 86.2 | 92.6 | 101.8 | | Operating Expenses | 90.7 | 91.9 |
| 2.9 | 9.4 | 13.8 | 7.4 | -1.8 | | Operating Profit | 9.3 | 8.1 |
| -.6 | 1.0 | 3.5 | -1.1 | -1.3 | | All Other Expenses (net) | 1.4 | .9 |
| 3.5 | 8.4 | 10.3 | 8.5 | -.5 | | Profit Before Taxes | 7.8 | 7.2 |
| | | | | | | **RATIOS** | | |
| 48.8 | 29.9 | 12.8 | 4.7 | 8.1 | | | 5.0 | 7.6 |
| 7.2 | 4.5 | 4.9 | 2.8 | 3.0 | | Current | 1.9 | 2.7 |
| 1.5 | .7 | 1.6 | 1.7 | 2.3 | | | .8 | 1.4 |
| 48.8 | 23.4 | 12.8 | 3.4 | 7.8 | | | 4.3 | 7.3 |
| 6.7 | 4.0 | 4.9 | 2.4 | 2.8 | | Quick | 1.7 | 2.5 |
| 1.0 | .3 | 1.5 | 1.3 | 2.1 | | | .6 | 1.1 |
| 0 UND | 0 UND | 0 UND | 6 66.1 | 9 39.2 | | | 0 UND | 0 UND |
| 0 UND | 0 UND | 2 227.6 | 11 33.9 | 24 15.5 | | Sales/Receivables | 7 49.8 | 1 361.4 |
| 4 84.6 | 21 17.7 | 16 22.6 | 31 11.6 | 76 4.8 | | | 33 10.9 | 20 18.7 |
| | | | | | | Cost of Sales/Inventory | | |
| | | | | | | Cost of Sales/Payables | | |
| 2.7 | 2.6 | 2.3 | 2.1 | 1.6 | | | 4.2 | 2.2 |
| 7.8 | 7.2 | 3.2 | 3.0 | 4.4 | | Sales/Working Capital | 13.1 | 6.6 |
| 37.9 | -29.9 | 14.7 | 7.1 | 7.5 | | | -38.1 | 17.9 |
| | 8.3 | 11.5 | 7.2 | 13.6 | | | 30.3 | 10.8 |
| (11) 4.7 | (12) 4.1 | (13) 1.7 | (11) 2.8 | | | EBIT/Interest | (75) 5.4 | (57) 2.4 |
| | -18.8 | -2.6 | .0 | .4 | | | 1.3 | -.2 |
| | | | | | | Net Profit + Depr., Dep., Amort./Cur. Mat. L/T/D | | |
| .0 | .0 | .2 | .0 | .1 | | | .2 | .1 |
| .0 | .0 | .9 | .9 | .5 | | Fixed/Worth | 1.0 | .9 |
| .7 | .9 | 5.4 | 1.3 | 1.5 | | | 5.6 | 4.6 |
| .1 | .1 | .3 | .3 | .1 | | | .3 | .5 |
| .6 | .9 | 1.1 | .5 | .3 | | Debt/Worth | 1.4 | 1.6 |
| 20.9 | 3.4 | 16.6 | 1.1 | 3.3 | | | 17.5 | -26.3 |
| 187.9 | 38.0 | 25.9 | 16.7 | 3.5 | | | 71.1 | 35.5 |
| (11) 10.1 | (21) 22.0 | (14) 9.5 | (15) 5.4 | (13) .6 | | % Profit Before Taxes/Tangible Net Worth | (88) 15.8 | (68) 8.9 |
| -.8 | .1 | -10.2 | -4.8 | -3.6 | | | 2.0 | -.7 |
| 34.7 | 31.7 | 12.9 | 10.9 | 1.8 | | | 26.5 | 15.3 |
| 7.3 | 16.7 | 3.4 | 3.5 | .5 | | % Profit Before Taxes/Total Assets | 8.5 | 3.5 |
| -3.2 | .5 | -5.0 | -2.6 | -4.4 | | | .7 | -1.5 |
| UND | UND | 19.0 | 62.8 | 19.5 | | | 39.3 | 38.1 |
| 364.8 | 90.1 | 1.7 | 1.5 | 1.8 | | Sales/Net Fixed Assets | 6.3 | 6.4 |
| 52.4 | 12.5 | .6 | .6 | .7 | | | 1.2 | .9 |
| 4.5 | 3.6 | 1.0 | 1.3 | .8 | | | 3.4 | 2.6 |
| 2.6 | 2.1 | .6 | .6 | .6 | | Sales/Total Assets | 1.6 | 1.0 |
| 1.7 | 1.3 | .3 | .5 | .3 | | | .7 | .5 |
| | | 2.5 | .7 | 2.9 | | | .8 | 1.6 |
| | (14) 3.5 | (10) 3.8 | (13) 5.9 | | | % Depr., Dep., Amort./Sales | (82) 2.8 | (56) 3.6 |
| | | 11.6 | 5.4 | 7.1 | | | 5.6 | 7.3 |
| | | | | | | | 4.5 | 3.0 |
| | | | | | | % Officers', Directors', Owners' Comp/Sales | (25) 7.0 | (17) 9.0 |
| | | | | | | | 10.6 | 17.9 |
| 14373M | 77469M | 57940M | 316983M | 644345M | 253080M | Net Sales ($) | 2639352M | 965011M |
| 4166M | 29405M | 83319M | 362840M | 926429M | 272986M | Total Assets ($) | 2484772M | 1793024M |

© RMA 2024  
M = $ thousand    MM = $ million  
See Pages viii through xx for Explanation of Ratios and Data

# EDUCATION—All Other Miscellaneous Schools and Instruction NAICS 611699

## Comparative Historical Data | Current Data Sorted by Sales

| | | | | | | Type of Statement | | | | | | |
|---|---|---|---|---|---|---|---|---|---|---|---|---|
| | 13 | | 23 | | 25 | Unqualified | 1 | 3 | 2 | 7 | 6 | 6 |
| | 2 | | | | 1 | Reviewed | | 1 | | | | |
| | 1 | | 2 | | 2 | Compiled | | 2 | | | | |
| | 21 | | 9 | | 13 | Tax Returns | 2 | 8 | | 2 | | 1 |
| | 32 | | 36 | | 45 | Other | 9 | 12 | 6 | 5 | 6 | 7 |
| | 4/1/21-3/31/22 ALL | | 4/1/22-3/31/23 ALL | | 4/1/23-3/31/24 ALL | | 44 (4/1-9/30/23) | | | 42 (10/1/23-3/31/24) | | |
| | | | | | | | 0-1MM | 1-3MM | 3-5MM | 5-10MM | 10-25MM | 25MM & OVER |
| | 69 | | 70 | | 86 | NUMBER OF STATEMENTS | 12 | 26 | 8 | 14 | 12 | 14 |
| | % | | % | | % | ASSETS | % | % | % | % | % | % |
| | 41.4 | | 30.9 | | 34.1 | Cash & Equivalents | 55.8 | 30.2 | | 33.8 | 30.5 | 19.6 |
| | 5.9 | | 8.8 | | 6.9 | Trade Receivables (net) | 3.2 | 8.0 | | 3.0 | 4.7 | 9.1 |
| | 2.0 | | 1.1 | | 3.7 | Inventory | .2 | 6.3 | | 7.1 | .7 | 2.5 |
| | 2.2 | | 4.2 | | 3.2 | All Other Current | .2 | 2.3 | | 4.6 | 3.7 | 6.8 |
| | 51.5 | | 45.0 | | 47.8 | Total Current | 59.5 | 46.9 | | 48.5 | 39.6 | 38.0 |
| | 34.1 | | 33.2 | | 27.6 | Fixed Assets (net) | 28.7 | 23.2 | | 27.5 | 44.3 | 21.3 |
| | 6.4 | | 3.5 | | 4.3 | Intangibles (net) | .0 | 7.7 | | 2.1 | 1.4 | 8.6 |
| | 8.0 | | 18.3 | | 20.3 | All Other Non-Current | 11.8 | 22.2 | | 21.9 | 14.8 | 32.1 |
| | 100.0 | | 100.0 | | 100.0 | Total | 100.0 | 100.0 | | 100.0 | 100.0 | 100.0 |
| | | | | | | LIABILITIES | | | | | | |
| | 4.1 | | .9 | | 1.9 | Notes Payable-Short Term | .3 | 5.0 | | 1.1 | .0 | .9 |
| | 1.0 | | 1.5 | | 1.3 | Cur. Mat.-L.T.D. | 3.3 | 1.2 | | .8 | .7 | .8 |
| | 2.3 | | 4.0 | | 2.7 | Trade Payables | .7 | 1.4 | | 3.3 | 3.7 | 4.3 |
| | .0 | | .2 | | .1 | Income Taxes Payable | .1 | .2 | | .0 | .0 | .1 |
| | 8.2 | | 12.0 | | 11.6 | All Other Current | 11.5 | 12.4 | | 12.9 | 10.4 | 8.6 |
| | 15.7 | | 18.6 | | 17.5 | Total Current | 15.8 | 20.2 | | 18.1 | 14.9 | 14.7 |
| | 28.6 | | 24.8 | | 19.5 | Long-Term Debt | 30.4 | 26.0 | | 16.9 | 17.1 | 13.3 |
| | .0 | | .1 | | .0 | Deferred Taxes | .0 | .0 | | .0 | .0 | .0 |
| | 12.4 | | 12.1 | | 14.4 | All Other Non-Current | 3.4 | 11.9 | | 18.7 | 4.0 | 36.6 |
| | 43.4 | | 44.4 | | 48.6 | Net Worth | 50.4 | 41.9 | | 46.3 | 64.0 | 35.3 |
| | 100.0 | | 100.0 | | 100.0 | Total Liabilities & Net Worth | 100.0 | 100.0 | | 100.0 | 100.0 | 100.0 |
| | | | | | | INCOME DATA | | | | | | |
| | 100.0 | | 100.0 | | 100.0 | Net Sales | 100.0 | 100.0 | | 100.0 | 100.0 | 100.0 |
| | | | | | | Gross Profit | | | | | | |
| | 90.8 | | 92.6 | | 92.9 | Operating Expenses | 79.6 | 93.2 | | 93.9 | 99.2 | 98.0 |
| | 9.2 | | 7.4 | | 7.1 | Operating Profit | 20.4 | 6.8 | | 6.1 | .8 | 2.0 |
| | -.1 | | 2.2 | | .5 | All Other Expenses (net) | 7.6 | -1.2 | | -.9 | -.8 | .0 |
| | 9.3 | | 5.2 | | 6.7 | Profit Before Taxes | 12.8 | 8.0 | | 7.0 | 1.7 | 1.9 |
| | | | | | | RATIOS | | | | | | |
| | 19.2 | | 8.1 | | 9.5 | | 59.8 | 34.0 | | 6.3 | 3.8 | 5.4 |
| | 4.9 | | 3.2 | | 3.7 | Current | 6.4 | 7.0 | | 3.9 | 2.8 | 2.5 |
| | 1.9 | | 1.4 | | 1.7 | | 1.2 | 1.0 | | 1.3 | 2.5 | 1.8 |
| | 14.6 | | 7.0 | | 8.7 | | 59.8 | 27.7 | | 6.3 | 3.7 | 4.2 |
| | 4.9 | | 3.2 | | 3.2 | Quick | 6.3 | 4.4 | | 1.8 | 2.7 | 2.4 |
| | 1.6 | | 1.0 | | 1.1 | | 1.2 | .6 | | 1.1 | 2.1 | 1.4 |
| 0 | UND | 0 | UND | 0 | UND | | 0 | UND | 0 | UND | 9 | 40.7 | 12 | 29.9 |
| 0 | 999.8 | 12 | 31.0 | 6 | 58.2 | Sales/Receivables | 0 | UND | 0 | UND | 3 | 109.7 | 16 | 23.1 | 25 | 14.6 |
| 29 | 12.7 | 36 | 10.1 | 25 | 14.8 | | 0 | UND | 14 | 26.5 | 14 | 25.2 | 35 | 10.4 | 51 | 7.2 |
| | | | | | | Cost of Sales/Inventory | | | | | | |
| | | | | | | Cost of Sales/Payables | | | | | | |
| | 2.8 | | 2.5 | | 2.4 | | 1.6 | 2.3 | | 2.5 | 1.9 | 2.9 |
| | 5.3 | | 6.2 | | 4.9 | Sales/Working Capital | 6.0 | 8.0 | | 7.2 | 3.0 | 5.1 |
| | 12.3 | | 21.5 | | 15.4 | | 44.4 | NM | | 40.5 | 5.5 | 8.8 |
| | 31.8 | | 22.7 | | 11.3 | | | 10.5 | | 11.4 | 8.5 | 61.9 |
| (42) | 3.3 | (48) | 4.7 | (53) | 4.4 | EBIT/Interest | (16) | 6.1 | (10) | 2.1 | (10) | 2.2 | (11) | 4.4 |
| | -.1 | | -2.8 | | .0 | | | .6 | | -.7 | -3.7 | .5 |
| | | | | | | Net Profit + Depr., Dep., Amort./Cur. Mat. L/T/D | | | | | | |
| | .1 | | .1 | | .0 | | .0 | .0 | | .0 | .2 | .0 |
| | .7 | | .6 | | .4 | Fixed/Worth | .0 | .2 | | .4 | .6 | .4 |
| | 2.9 | | 1.7 | | 1.2 | | 15.3 | 1.3 | | 1.5 | .9 | 2.6 |
| | .1 | | .2 | | .2 | | .1 | .0 | | .4 | .2 | .2 |
| | .8 | | .7 | | .7 | Debt/Worth | .8 | .9 | | 1.1 | .5 | 1.5 |
| | 7.7 | | 2.3 | | 3.9 | | 17.9 | 27.9 | | 4.4 | 1.0 | NM |
| | 55.4 | | 51.1 | | 29.0 | % Profit Before Taxes/Tangible Net Worth | 101.7 | 26.9 | | 44.9 | 5.8 | 26.2 |
| (56) | 14.2 | (58) | 3.2 | (75) | 5.9 | | (10) | 10.1 | (21) | 9.8 | (13) | 22.3 | 2.6 | (11) | 1.8 |
| | 2.0 | | -3.2 | | -1.7 | | -5.6 | .1 | | -3.0 | -7.7 | -.5 |
| | 37.6 | | 22.7 | | 16.4 | % Profit Before Taxes/Total Assets | 28.9 | 22.2 | | 33.5 | 4.5 | 7.4 |
| | 10.6 | | 4.0 | | 4.3 | | 6.8 | 9.0 | | 10.0 | 1.8 | .8 |
| | .9 | | -2.4 | | -1.1 | | -.5 | .0 | | -.8 | -3.0 | -5.0 |
| | 151.8 | | 115.7 | | 205.3 | Sales/Net Fixed Assets | UND | 219.0 | | 999.8 | 8.6 | 38.4 |
| | 6.4 | | 3.7 | | 11.6 | | 32.9 | 56.3 | | 19.0 | .9 | 7.7 |
| | 1.2 | | .8 | | 1.3 | | 1.4 | 2.4 | | .8 | .6 | 2.0 |
| | 3.9 | | 2.4 | | 2.1 | | 2.2 | 3.4 | | 3.9 | 1.2 | 1.6 |
| | 1.5 | | 1.3 | | 1.2 | Sales/Total Assets | 1.5 | 1.6 | | 1.1 | .5 | .8 |
| | .7 | | .4 | | .5 | | .4 | .8 | | .6 | .3 | .6 |
| | .9 | | 1.3 | | .9 | | | .6 | | | | 1.1 |
| (41) | 1.9 | (46) | 4.3 | (52) | 2.7 | % Depr., Dep., Amort./Sales | | (14) | 1.3 | | | (12) | 3.4 |
| | 5.9 | | 7.3 | | 5.9 | | | 3.3 | | | | 5.6 |
| | 5.6 | | | | 1.2 | % Officers', Directors' Owners' Comp/Sales | | 1.6 | | | | |
| (13) | 9.8 | | | (17) | 2.9 | | | (10) | 2.7 | | | |
| | 15.8 | | | | 9.7 | | | 9.0 | | | | |
| | 872718M | | 1172581M | | 1364190M | Net Sales ($) | 6994M | 53168M | 28015M | 104108M | 203511M | 968394M |
| | 1097218M | | 1777421M | | 1679145M | Total Assets ($) | 9638M | 53323M | 35863M | 142754M | 398142M | 1039425M |

© RMA 2024

M = $ thousand   MM = $ million
See Pages viii through xx for Explanation of Ratios and Data

# EDUCATION—Educational Support Services  NAICS 611710

## Current Data Sorted by Assets | Comparative Historical Data

| | | | | | | | Type of Statement | | |
|---|---|---|---|---|---|---|---|---|---|
| | | | 5 | 26 | 7 | 8 | Unqualified | 122 | 81 |
| | | | 1 | 1 | | | Reviewed | 6 | 5 |
| | | 2 | 2 | 2 | | | Compiled | 6 | 1 |
| | 4 | 2 | 1 | 1 | | | Tax Returns | 19 | 3 |
| | 6 | 12 | 28 | 15 | 9 | 5 | Other | 93 | 63 |
| | | 69 (4/1-9/30/23) | | 68 (10/1/23-3/31/24) | | | | 4/1/19-3/31/20 | 4/1/20-3/31/21 |
| | 0-500M | 500M-2MM | 2-10MM | 10-50MM | 50-100MM | 100-250MM | | ALL | ALL |
| | 10 | 16 | 37 | 45 | 16 | 13 | NUMBER OF STATEMENTS | 246 | 153 |
| | % | % | % | % | % | % | ASSETS | % | % |
| | 48.1 | 32.8 | 30.8 | 41.5 | 37.0 | 14.9 | Cash & Equivalents | 29.3 | 34.8 |
| | 5.9 | 24.2 | 15.5 | 9.4 | 7.3 | 7.2 | Trade Receivables (net) | 11.2 | 6.7 |
| | 3.2 | 1.7 | .9 | .7 | 2.5 | 2.2 | Inventory | 2.0 | 1.6 |
| | 3.4 | 4.9 | 5.3 | 3.3 | 4.1 | 1.6 | All Other Current | 5.4 | 4.0 |
| | 60.5 | 63.6 | 52.5 | 54.8 | 50.9 | 25.8 | Total Current | 47.8 | 47.1 |
| | 17.9 | 18.1 | 31.1 | 27.4 | 20.8 | 34.4 | Fixed Assets (net) | 34.9 | 36.1 |
| | 1.1 | 4.6 | 4.4 | 2.4 | 7.6 | 25.8 | Intangibles (net) | 3.4 | 1.9 |
| | 20.0 | 13.7 | 12.0 | 15.4 | 20.7 | 14.0 | All Other Non-Current | 13.9 | 14.9 |
| | 100.0 | 100.0 | 100.0 | 100.0 | 100.0 | 100.0 | Total | 100.0 | 100.0 |
| | | | | | | | LIABILITIES | | |
| | 11.3 | 17.7 | 2.3 | .3 | .7 | .2 | Notes Payable-Short Term | 4.0 | 2.2 |
| | .0 | .7 | 1.6 | 2.3 | 1.6 | 1.4 | Cur. Mat.-L.T.D. | 1.8 | 2.0 |
| | 1.6 | 11.7 | 2.6 | 3.4 | 3.3 | 2.2 | Trade Payables | 4.3 | 3.1 |
| | .0 | .0 | .0 | .5 | .2 | .1 | Income Taxes Payable | .0 | .0 |
| | 7.6 | 24.5 | 10.0 | 14.0 | 7.4 | 4.0 | All Other Current | 14.9 | 7.8 |
| | 20.5 | 54.5 | 16.5 | 20.4 | 13.3 | 7.9 | Total Current | 25.0 | 15.2 |
| | 75.5 | 3.6 | 28.6 | 14.9 | 11.1 | 37.0 | Long-Term Debt | 25.3 | 23.6 |
| | .0 | .0 | .2 | .0 | .0 | .2 | Deferred Taxes | .1 | .0 |
| | 4.6 | .5 | 10.2 | 10.9 | 24.4 | 13.2 | All Other Non-Current | 19.7 | 19.7 |
| | -.6 | 41.4 | 44.5 | 53.8 | 51.3 | 41.7 | Net Worth | 29.9 | 41.5 |
| | 100.0 | 100.0 | 100.0 | 100.0 | 100.0 | 100.0 | Total Liabilties & Net Worth | 100.0 | 100.0 |
| | | | | | | | INCOME DATA | | |
| | 100.0 | 100.0 | 100.0 | 100.0 | 100.0 | 100.0 | Net Sales | 100.0 | 100.0 |
| | | | | | | | Gross Profit | | |
| | 91.9 | 93.5 | 83.4 | 90.7 | 99.6 | 86.5 | Operating Expenses | 92.0 | 92.2 |
| | 8.1 | 6.5 | 16.6 | 9.3 | .4 | 13.5 | Operating Profit | 8.0 | 7.8 |
| | .6 | -.9 | 4.4 | -.3 | -2.4 | 7.6 | All Other Expenses (net) | 2.9 | 2.0 |
| | 7.5 | 7.5 | 12.3 | 9.7 | 2.9 | 5.9 | Profit Before Taxes | 5.0 | 5.8 |
| | | | | | | | RATIOS | | |
| | 19.5 | 7.5 | 14.6 | 7.2 | 7.5 | 7.1 | | 8.3 | 14.1 |
| | 2.6 | 1.6 | 4.8 | 3.4 | 2.7 | 4.0 | Current | 2.8 | 4.3 |
| | 1.1 | .7 | 1.7 | 1.6 | 1.9 | 2.1 | | 1.2 | 1.9 |
| | 13.8 | 7.5 | 13.2 | 7.2 | 7.4 | 7.0 | | 7.0 | 12.5 |
| | 2.6 | 1.4 | 4.2 | 2.9 | 2.1 | 4.0 | Quick | 2.2 | 3.4 |
| | 1.1 | .7 | 1.3 | 1.2 | 1.5 | 1.6 | | 1.0 | 1.5 |
| 0 | UND | 1 | 348.7 | 0 | UND | 5 | 69.9 | 3 | 108.4 | 14 | 26.2 | | 0 | UND | 0 | UND |
| 0 | UND | 23 | 15.6 | 23 | 16.2 | 19 | 19.2 | 38 | 9.6 | 51 | 7.1 | Sales/Receivables | 9 | 42.4 | 5 | 73.8 |
| 15 | 23.6 | 58 | 6.3 | 55 | 6.6 | 54 | 6.7 | 55 | 6.6 | 72 | 5.1 | | 36 | 10.1 | 31 | 11.7 |
| | | | | | | | Cost of Sales/Inventory | | |
| | | | | | | | Cost of Sales/Payables | | |
| | 5.7 | 2.5 | 1.7 | 1.5 | .8 | 1.2 | | 2.1 | 1.6 |
| | 31.6 | 14.0 | 3.8 | 3.7 | 2.8 | 2.2 | Sales/Working Capital | 6.0 | 3.0 |
| | 682.7 | -17.0 | 9.7 | 10.6 | 5.7 | 8.5 | | 24.4 | 8.8 |
| | | | 69.4 | 32.6 | | 8.9 | | 16.4 | 13.9 |
| | | (20) | 8.1 | (28) | 9.0 | (10) | 2.9 | EBIT/Interest | (163) | 3.5 | (102) | 2.4 |
| | | | 1.0 | | -.6 | | .2 | | -.1 | .0 |
| | | | | | | | Net Profit + Depr., Dep., | | 5.8 | |
| | | | | | | | Amort./Cur. Mat. L/T/D | (11) | 2.2 | |
| | | | | | | | | -1.2 | |
| | .0 | .0 | .0 | .1 | .0 | .6 | | .1 | .1 |
| | .0 | .2 | .3 | .5 | .5 | 2.0 | Fixed/Worth | .8 | .8 |
| | -2.4 | .8 | 2.1 | 1.1 | 1.6 | .0 | | 6.6 | 2.8 |
| | .3 | .1 | .3 | .2 | .1 | .5 | | .4 | .2 |
| | .8 | .6 | .9 | .5 | .7 | 1.6 | Debt/Worth | 1.4 | 1.1 |
| | -7.2 | 1.8 | 3.5 | 1.5 | 5.1 | -1.8 | | 87.9 | 5.0 |
| | | 60.4 | 37.1 | 27.3 | 7.3 | | | 38.0 | 23.7 |
| | (14) | 27.5 | (33) | 16.9 | (40) | 10.2 | (14) | -2.4 | % Profit Before Taxes/Tangible | (186) | 8.5 | (125) | 4.8 |
| | | -5.5 | | 2.2 | | -4.9 | | -8.5 | Net Worth | | .5 | | -1.3 |
| | 77.5 | 30.2 | 17.0 | 22.1 | 9.3 | 10.1 | % Profit Before Taxes/Total | 11.6 | 9.0 |
| | 32.6 | 16.1 | 5.2 | 5.5 | -.5 | 1.6 | Assets | 2.8 | 2.4 |
| | -7.8 | -10.7 | .2 | -2.9 | -3.9 | -.4 | | -1.1 | -1.6 |
| | UND | 792.6 | 999.8 | 18.9 | 12.5 | 56.5 | | 42.8 | 35.7 |
| | 444.5 | 40.3 | 23.8 | 5.0 | 5.5 | 1.2 | Sales/Net Fixed Assets | 4.5 | 2.1 |
| | 16.2 | 6.8 | 1.2 | 1.7 | 2.1 | .7 | | 1.0 | .8 |
| | 8.8 | 4.4 | 2.8 | 1.6 | .9 | .8 | | 2.7 | 1.6 |
| | 4.9 | 1.8 | 1.0 | .9 | .7 | .4 | Sales/Total Assets | 1.0 | .7 |
| | 2.7 | 1.0 | .3 | .5 | .4 | .2 | | .5 | .4 |
| | | .6 | .6 | .8 | 1.1 | | | .8 | 1.2 |
| | (10) | .9 | (16) | 1.8 | (32) | 2.1 | (14) | 3.3 | % Depr., Dep., Amort./Sales | (162) | 2.4 | (103) | 3.4 |
| | | 2.6 | | 15.0 | | 6.0 | | 6.0 | | | 5.4 | | 6.0 |
| | | | | | | | % Officers', Directors' | | 3.1 | 1.2 |
| | | | | | | | Owners' Comp/Sales | (29) | 4.6 | (11) | 3.2 |
| | | | | | | | | 11.7 | 6.9 |
| | 15973M | 56223M | 293385M | 1573716M | 861140M | 1226865M | Net Sales ($) | 9565366M | 4774358M |
| | 2384M | 22311M | 179449M | 1066595M | 1151814M | 2286036M | Total Assets ($) | 11386212M | 7902545M |

© RMA 2024

M = $ thousand    MM = $ million
See Pages viii through xx for Explanation of Ratios and Data

# EDUCATION—Educational Support Services  NAICS 611710

## Comparative Historical Data / Current Data Sorted by Sales

| | | | | Type of Statement | | | | | | |
|---|---|---|---|---|---|---|---|---|---|---|
| 32 | 54 | 46 | | Unqualified | | 1 | 2 | 4 | 15 | 24 |
| 4 | 1 | 2 | | Reviewed | | | | 1 | | 1 |
| 1 | 3 | 6 | | Compiled | 1 | 1 | 1 | 2 | 1 | |
| 7 | 11 | 8 | | Tax Returns | 3 | 1 | 2 | | 1 | 1 |
| 42 | 68 | 75 | | Other | 11 | 15 | 5 | 10 | 17 | 17 |
| 4/1/21-3/31/22 ALL | 4/1/22-3/31/23 ALL | 4/1/23-3/31/24 ALL | | | 69 (4/1-9/30/23) | | | 68 (10/1/23-3/31/24) | | |
| | | | | | 0-1MM | 1-3MM | 3-5MM | 5-10MM | 10-25MM | 25MM & OVER |
| 86 | 137 | 137 | | NUMBER OF STATEMENTS | 15 | 18 | 10 | 17 | 34 | 43 |
| % | % | % | | ASSETS | % | % | % | % | % | % |
| 38.4 | 36.6 | 35.0 | | Cash & Equivalents | 28.7 | 34.3 | 38.1 | 30.3 | 44.8 | 30.8 |
| 13.8 | 9.2 | 12.1 | | Trade Receivables (net) | 6.2 | 11.6 | 12.5 | 19.3 | 12.3 | 11.3 |
| 1.7 | 3.4 | 1.4 | | Inventory | 2.1 | 1.0 | .0 | 1.9 | .5 | 2.1 |
| 5.4 | 5.3 | 4.0 | | All Other Current | 3.2 | 2.0 | 7.9 | 2.0 | 4.6 | 4.4 |
| 59.4 | 54.5 | 52.4 | | Total Current | 40.2 | 48.9 | 58.4 | 53.5 | 62.2 | 48.6 |
| 28.3 | 26.5 | 26.5 | | Fixed Assets (net) | 39.5 | 32.3 | 21.4 | 26.9 | 24.2 | 22.4 |
| 1.9 | 7.1 | 5.9 | | Intangibles (net) | .5 | .1 | 8.7 | 8.6 | 1.4 | 12.1 |
| 10.4 | 12.0 | 15.1 | | All Other Non-Current | 19.4 | 18.7 | 11.5 | 10.9 | 12.2 | 16.9 |
| 100.0 | 100.0 | 100.0 | | Total | 100.0 | 100.0 | 100.0 | 100.0 | 100.0 | 100.0 |
| | | | | LIABILITIES | | | | | | |
| 3.7 | 2.4 | 3.7 | | Notes Payable-Short Term | 2.8 | 10.6 | 19.4 | 3.2 | .3 | .3 |
| 1.1 | 2.5 | 1.6 | | Cur. Mat.-L.T.D. | 1.1 | .8 | .6 | .9 | 2.1 | 2.2 |
| 4.6 | 5.4 | 3.9 | | Trade Payables | 1.6 | 1.1 | 10.5 | 6.1 | 2.4 | 4.7 |
| .0 | .0 | .2 | | Income Taxes Payable | .0 | .0 | .0 | .0 | .0 | .6 |
| 23.5 | 14.5 | 12.0 | | All Other Current | 3.5 | 5.2 | 24.1 | 10.2 | 13.3 | 14.6 |
| 32.9 | 24.7 | 21.3 | | Total Current | 9.0 | 17.7 | 54.6 | 20.3 | 18.1 | 22.4 |
| 16.3 | 18.2 | 23.3 | | Long-Term Debt | 62.8 | 12.7 | 21.8 | 26.6 | 14.6 | 20.0 |
| .1 | .0 | .1 | | Deferred Taxes | .0 | .0 | .0 | .0 | .2 | .1 |
| 8.8 | 9.5 | 10.9 | | All Other Non-Current | 6.7 | 6.6 | 8.8 | 8.4 | 3.6 | 21.3 |
| 42.0 | 47.5 | 44.4 | | Net Worth | 21.5 | 63.0 | 14.8 | 44.7 | 63.5 | 36.3 |
| 100.0 | 100.0 | 100.0 | | Total Liabilities & Net Worth | 100.0 | 100.0 | 100.0 | 100.0 | 100.0 | 100.0 |
| | | | | INCOME DATA | | | | | | |
| 100.0 | 100.0 | 100.0 | | Net Sales | 100.0 | 100.0 | 100.0 | 100.0 | 100.0 | 100.0 |
| | | | | Gross Profit | | | | | | |
| 85.2 | 89.3 | 89.8 | | Operating Expenses | 79.5 | 83.7 | 95.8 | 86.1 | 92.5 | 93.7 |
| 14.8 | 10.7 | 10.2 | | Operating Profit | 20.5 | 16.3 | 4.2 | 13.9 | 7.5 | 6.3 |
| -1.1 | 2.3 | 1.4 | | All Other Expenses (net) | 11.9 | 1.0 | -.4 | -1.6 | -.6 | 1.2 |
| 15.9 | 8.4 | 8.8 | | Profit Before Taxes | 8.6 | 15.3 | 4.6 | 15.6 | 8.1 | 5.0 |
| | | | | RATIOS | | | | | | |
| 8.5 | 6.6 | 9.0 | | | 14.9 | 19.7 | 5.9 | 14.6 | 10.2 | 5.2 |
| 3.0 | 3.3 | 3.4 | | Current | 3.2 | 2.6 | 2.7 | 6.2 | 5.3 | 2.5 |
| 1.4 | 1.6 | 1.5 | | | 1.1 | .8 | 1.4 | 1.5 | 2.2 | 1.5 |
| 7.7 | 6.2 | 8.4 | | | 14.9 | 19.6 | 5.9 | 13.2 | 9.6 | 5.0 |
| 2.7 | 2.6 | 2.9 | | Quick | 2.7 | 2.6 | 2.4 | 5.5 | 4.9 | 2.1 |
| 1.1 | 1.1 | 1.2 | | | 1.1 | .8 | 1.4 | 1.2 | 1.9 | 1.3 |
| 0 UND | 0 UND | 1 351.8 | | | 0 UND | 0 UND | 0 UND | 5 68.7 | 6 58.7 | 6 62.3 |
| 12 30.5 | 14 26.6 | 23 16.2 | | Sales/Receivables | 0 UND | 32 11.4 | 2 195.2 | 33 11.0 | 38 9.5 | 27 13.3 |
| 42 8.6 | 42 8.6 | 54 6.7 | | | 18 20.3 | 57 6.4 | 63 5.8 | 53 6.9 | 62 5.9 | 55 6.6 |
| | | | | Cost of Sales/Inventory | | | | | | |
| | | | | Cost of Sales/Payables | | | | | | |
| 1.9 | 1.9 | 1.7 | | | 1.4 | 1.0 | 1.6 | 2.9 | 1.1 | 2.7 |
| 4.6 | 4.0 | 4.2 | | Sales/Working Capital | 5.5 | 4.7 | 9.5 | 5.0 | 2.3 | 4.8 |
| 13.6 | 23.6 | 11.9 | | | 74.0 | -52.8 | 289.5 | 14.8 | 4.6 | 11.4 |
| 125.7 | 41.6 | 36.7 | | | | | | 200.8 | 76.0 | 17.0 |
| (44) 16.6 | (80) 6.0 | (80) 5.4 | | EBIT/Interest | | | | (13) 14.0 | (16) 19.2 | (28) 2.6 |
| 4.6 | -.8 | .2 | | | | | | 2.5 | 1.3 | -2.3 |
| | | | | Net Profit + Depr., Dep., Amort./Cur. Mat. L/T/D | | | | | | |
| .0 | .0 | .0 | | | .0 | .0 | .0 | .1 | .0 | .1 |
| .3 | .4 | .4 | | Fixed/Worth | 1.1 | .3 | .1 | .4 | .3 | .8 |
| 1.9 | 1.7 | 1.6 | | | 14.1 | 1.2 | NM | 1.7 | .7 | 6.2 |
| .3 | .3 | .2 | | | .2 | .1 | .2 | .2 | .1 | .4 |
| .8 | .9 | .7 | | Debt/Worth | .9 | .6 | 1.2 | .8 | .3 | 1.1 |
| 3.1 | 4.1 | 3.2 | | | 15.1 | 1.2 | -2.2 | 2.8 | 1.0 | -7.2 |
| 53.7 | 43.5 | 34.7 | | % Profit Before Taxes/Tangible Net Worth | 51.3 | 37.3 | | 83.4 | 32.0 | 22.2 |
| (75) 27.3 | (118) 14.3 | (117) 12.4 | | | (13) 21.2 | 14.3 | | (14) 24.4 | (33) 10.6 | (32) 7.7 |
| 8.2 | .7 | -2.1 | | | .1 | -8.8 | | 6.6 | -2.5 | -6.5 |
| 30.9 | 18.8 | 17.9 | | % Profit Before Taxes/Total Assets | 33.8 | 21.1 | 19.3 | 22.8 | 24.7 | 14.4 |
| 9.9 | 7.5 | 5.2 | | | 1.9 | 6.9 | 3.9 | 6.6 | 5.4 | 4.9 |
| 3.6 | -.1 | -1.6 | | | -5.3 | -4.0 | -5.8 | 2.8 | -1.6 | -2.4 |
| 175.1 | 101.0 | 125.8 | | Sales/Net Fixed Assets | UND | UND | UND | 80.6 | 121.2 | 123.3 |
| 13.3 | 10.8 | 7.9 | | | 6.4 | 12.6 | 66.4 | 19.6 | 6.1 | 6.7 |
| 1.3 | 1.7 | 1.7 | | | .1 | 1.0 | 3.5 | 1.5 | 2.0 | 2.0 |
| 2.4 | 2.4 | 2.0 | | | 3.0 | 1.2 | 7.8 | 3.8 | 1.6 | 1.8 |
| 1.2 | 1.2 | .9 | | Sales/Total Assets | .6 | .9 | 2.6 | 1.7 | .9 | 1.0 |
| .6 | .5 | .4 | | | .1 | .4 | .3 | .6 | .6 | .6 |
| .4 | .5 | .8 | | | 1.4 | | | | .6 | .9 |
| (59) 1.1 | (89) 2.2 | (86) 2.2 | | % Depr., Dep., Amort./Sales | (10) 7.8 | | | | (25) 2.4 | (30) 2.4 |
| 4.8 | 4.2 | 4.8 | | | 24.2 | | | | 7.3 | 4.2 |
| 2.8 | 3.1 | 2.6 | | % Officers', Directors' Owners' Comp/Sales | | | | | | |
| (12) 4.7 | (23) 4.3 | (21) 6.1 | | | | | | | | |
| 6.3 | 11.1 | 13.5 | | | | | | | | |
| 2472944M | 4839918M | 4027302M | | Net Sales ($) | 7924M | 35012M | 35469M | 119913M | 573247M | 3255737M |
| 2050937M | 5183469M | 4708589M | | Total Assets ($) | 31808M | 84902M | 51273M | 165421M | 919720M | 3455465M |

© RMA 2024  M = $ thousand  MM = $ million
See Pages viii through xx for Explanation of Ratios and Data

# HEALTH CARE AND SOCIAL ASSISTANCE

# HEALTH CARE—Offices of Physicians (except Mental Health Specialists) NAICS 621111

## Current Data Sorted by Assets | Comparative Historical Data

| | | | | | | Type of Statement | | |
|---|---|---|---|---|---|---|---|---|
| 1 | 1 | 6 | 38 | 27 | 24 | Unqualified | 119 | 71 |
| 1 | 7 | 15 | 33 | 2 | 2 | Reviewed | 56 | 32 |
| 25 | 52 | 57 | 17 | 2 | | Compiled | 274 | 130 |
| 136 | 191 | 94 | 11 | 2 | 1 | Tax Returns | 652 | 334 |
| 231 | 382 | 323 | 168 | 38 | 40 | Other | 1477 | 1099 |
| | 203 (4/1-9/30/23) | | 1,724 (10/1/23-3/31/24) | | | | 4/1/19- 3/31/20 ALL | 4/1/20- 3/31/21 ALL |
| 0-500M | 500M-2MM | 2-10MM | 10-50MM | 50-100MM | 100-250MM | NUMBER OF STATEMENTS | 2578 | 1666 |
| 394 | 633 | 495 | 267 | 71 | 67 | | | |
| % | % | % | % | % | % | ASSETS | % | % |
| 52.3 | 40.9 | 28.8 | 19.0 | 17.3 | 9.5 | Cash & Equivalents | 34.1 | 44.0 |
| 2.6 | 3.1 | 8.8 | 16.7 | 20.0 | 15.6 | Trade Receivables (net) | 8.2 | 5.5 |
| .6 | 1.4 | 2.0 | 2.0 | 1.3 | 1.4 | Inventory | 1.5 | 1.2 |
| 4.8 | 4.8 | 3.0 | 5.1 | 5.8 | 8.1 | All Other Current | 3.9 | 3.5 |
| 60.3 | 50.3 | 42.7 | 42.8 | 44.5 | 34.6 | Total Current | 47.7 | 54.1 |
| 20.7 | 28.2 | 36.2 | 34.9 | 29.0 | 23.7 | Fixed Assets (net) | 32.7 | 27.6 |
| 5.0 | 6.2 | 7.2 | 6.8 | 9.5 | 28.2 | Intangibles (net) | 6.1 | 7.7 |
| 14.1 | 15.3 | 14.0 | 15.5 | 17.0 | 13.5 | All Other Non-Current | 13.5 | 10.6 |
| 100.0 | 100.0 | 100.0 | 100.0 | 100.0 | 100.0 | Total | 100.0 | 100.0 |
| | | | | | | LIABILITIES | | |
| 23.6 | 11.4 | 5.8 | 2.4 | 1.6 | 2.5 | Notes Payable-Short Term | 15.8 | 18.8 |
| 3.5 | 4.0 | 3.8 | 4.3 | 6.7 | 1.8 | Cur. Mat.-L.T.D. | 4.8 | 4.5 |
| 3.0 | 2.2 | 4.7 | 7.7 | 5.6 | 10.2 | Trade Payables | 3.8 | 2.6 |
| .0 | .1 | .1 | .0 | .1 | .2 | Income Taxes Payable | .1 | .0 |
| 38.2 | 24.3 | 20.5 | 17.5 | 20.3 | 11.3 | All Other Current | 28.0 | 23.0 |
| 68.3 | 42.0 | 34.8 | 31.9 | 34.3 | 26.0 | Total Current | 52.5 | 48.9 |
| 31.7 | 27.9 | 30.6 | 24.0 | 19.5 | 24.0 | Long-Term Debt | 26.5 | 36.6 |
| .0 | .0 | .1 | .2 | .2 | .5 | Deferred Taxes | .2 | .1 |
| 4.2 | 3.9 | 3.6 | 6.2 | 9.1 | 11.6 | All Other Non-Current | 5.1 | 6.2 |
| -4.1 | 26.2 | 30.8 | 37.6 | 36.9 | 37.9 | Net Worth | 15.7 | 8.2 |
| 100.0 | 100.0 | 100.0 | 100.0 | 100.0 | 100.0 | Total Liabilities & Net Worth | 100.0 | 100.0 |
| | | | | | | INCOME DATA | | |
| 100.0 | 100.0 | 100.0 | 100.0 | 100.0 | 100.0 | Net Sales | 100.0 | 100.0 |
| | | | | | | Gross Profit | | |
| 85.8 | 85.1 | 82.2 | 88.9 | 89.8 | 93.9 | Operating Expenses | 86.0 | 86.6 |
| 14.2 | 14.9 | 17.8 | 11.1 | 10.2 | 6.1 | Operating Profit | 14.0 | 13.4 |
| .8 | 1.5 | 3.9 | 2.2 | 2.0 | 3.4 | All Other Expenses (net) | 1.7 | .0 |
| 13.4 | 13.4 | 13.9 | 8.9 | 8.2 | 2.8 | Profit Before Taxes | 12.3 | 13.4 |
| | | | | | | RATIOS | | |
| 4.0 | 4.2 | 3.2 | 2.9 | 2.6 | 2.4 | | 2.9 | 3.7 |
| 1.4 | 1.5 | 1.2 | 1.3 | 1.4 | 1.4 | Current | 1.1 | 1.4 |
| .6 | .6 | .5 | .7 | 1.0 | 1.0 | | .5 | .7 |
| 3.6 | 3.7 | 2.8 | 2.4 | 2.5 | 1.5 | | 2.5 | 3.2 |
| 1.2 | 1.4 | (494) 1.1 | 1.1 | 1.2 | 1.0 | Quick | (2574) 1.0 | (1663) 1.3 |
| .5 | .6 | .4 | .5 | .7 | .6 | | .4 | .6 |
| 0 UND | 0 UND | 0 UND | 0 UND | 16 23.0 | 21 17.2 | | 0 UND | 0 UND |
| 0 UND | 0 UND | 0 UND | 18 19.8 | 33 11.1 | 33 10.9 | Sales/Receivables | 0 UND | 0 UND |
| 0 UND | 0 UND | 1 259.2 | 40 9.2 | 48 7.6 | 47 7.8 | | 2 147.0 | 0 999.8 |
| | | | | | | Cost of Sales/Inventory | | |
| | | | | | | Cost of Sales/Payables | | |
| 20.8 | 12.5 | 10.6 | 8.5 | 3.7 | 5.8 | | 15.9 | 9.0 |
| 86.3 | 50.3 | 64.5 | 33.9 | 17.7 | 20.0 | Sales/Working Capital | 185.8 | 36.0 |
| -46.8 | -54.5 | -26.4 | -33.1 | -71.9 | -132.0 | | -29.6 | -29.6 |
| 47.3 | 65.7 | 56.1 | 46.6 | 31.2 | 9.4 | | 53.5 | 67.9 |
| (226) 11.3 | (426) 14.4 | (351) 11.1 | (194) 7.6 | (60) 9.6 | (56) 2.7 | EBIT/Interest | (1794) 11.0 | (1107) 12.8 |
| .9 | 2.8 | 2.2 | 1.3 | .3 | -1.3 | | 1.7 | 1.3 |
| | | 14.2 | 7.5 | 6.5 | | | 7.9 | 8.5 |
| | | (28) 4.1 | (42) 3.0 | (18) 3.2 | | Net Profit + Depr., Dep., Amort./Cur. Mat. L/T/D | (139) 2.4 | (72) 2.5 |
| | | 1.2 | 1.1 | .5 | | | 1.3 | .3 |
| .0 | .1 | .2 | .3 | .3 | .6 | | .2 | .1 |
| .4 | .7 | 1.1 | 1.0 | .7 | 1.8 | Fixed/Worth | 1.1 | 1.3 |
| -22.0 | 7.7 | 17.4 | 5.2 | 5.2 | -.7 | | -33.5 | -3.8 |
| .4 | .4 | .6 | .7 | .6 | 1.6 | | .6 | 1.0 |
| 2.8 | 2.1 | 2.3 | 2.1 | 1.8 | 4.6 | Debt/Worth | 3.1 | 5.6 |
| -3.5 | -24.3 | 999.8 | 13.0 | -291.1 | -3.4 | | -12.2 | -5.3 |
| 517.5 | 297.0 | 158.9 | 80.2 | 33.2 | 29.6 | | 250.6 | 222.4 |
| (257) 150.0 | (466) 95.2 | (373) 50.8 | (221) 23.2 | (53) 10.6 | (44) 11.4 | % Profit Before Taxes/Tangible Net Worth | (1798) 76.2 | (1039) 78.3 |
| 25.7 | 28.5 | 9.3 | 3.5 | .7 | -5.5 | | 14.3 | 15.9 |
| 179.8 | 104.2 | 49.7 | 21.7 | 14.5 | 6.7 | | 80.8 | 71.7 |
| 57.3 | 32.1 | 14.3 | 6.6 | 4.3 | 1.4 | % Profit Before Taxes/Total Assets | 22.2 | 19.4 |
| 3.6 | 4.8 | 1.9 | .0 | .0 | -2.9 | | 2.0 | .4 |
| UND | 419.5 | 92.0 | 34.3 | 30.0 | 17.0 | | 154.4 | 194.4 |
| 133.8 | 45.7 | 21.1 | 13.2 | 6.8 | 7.5 | Sales/Net Fixed Assets | 32.5 | 32.8 |
| 32.7 | 11.6 | 4.8 | 3.6 | 2.3 | 2.6 | | 9.8 | 8.1 |
| 23.0 | 12.2 | 8.3 | 5.2 | 2.2 | 2.2 | | 13.7 | 8.6 |
| 11.5 | 6.4 | 4.1 | 2.3 | 1.2 | 1.2 | Sales/Total Assets | 6.2 | 4.4 |
| 5.7 | 2.8 | 1.5 | 1.0 | .7 | .7 | | 2.6 | 1.9 |
| .2 | .3 | .4 | .8 | .9 | 1.4 | | .5 | .4 |
| (115) .5 | (281) 1.0 | (309) 1.1 | (214) 1.5 | (60) 2.5 | (37) 2.0 | % Depr., Dep., Amort./Sales | (1516) 1.2 | (896) 1.2 |
| 1.2 | 2.7 | 3.9 | 3.7 | 4.1 | 2.9 | | 2.7 | 3.2 |
| 8.1 | 5.2 | 4.7 | 5.9 | 6.7 | 9.8 | | 8.4 | 8.1 |
| (211) 15.8 | (329) 12.6 | (201) 10.1 | (66) 19.6 | (10) 24.6 | (11) 24.9 | % Officers', Directors' Owners' Comp/Sales | (1156) 17.5 | (754) 16.9 |
| 25.4 | 25.3 | 25.0 | 25.0 | 28.4 | 33.6 | | 29.3 | 31.0 |
| 1687131M | 6406413M | 12607413M | 20359346M | 7891889M | 17215230M | Net Sales ($) | 73995800M | 39294302M |
| 94228M | 697240M | 2232051M | 6138712M | 5060750M | 10731840M | Total Assets ($) | 24069367M | 15392256M |

© RMA 2024

M = $ thousand    MM = $ million
See Pages viii through xx for Explanation of Ratios and Data

# HEALTH CARE—Offices of Physicians (except Mental Health Specialists) NAICS 621111

## Comparative Historical Data | Current Data Sorted by Sales

| | | | Type of Statement | | | | | | |
|---|---|---|---|---|---|---|---|---|---|
| 80 | 97 | 97 | Unqualified | 1 | 3 | 1 | 5 | 11 | 76 |
| 24 | 50 | 60 | Reviewed | | 3 | 1 | 2 | 13 | 41 |
| 149 | 174 | 153 | Compiled | 15 | 10 | 10 | 24 | 51 | 43 |
| 355 | 482 | 435 | Tax Returns | 79 | 86 | 58 | 89 | 77 | 46 |
| 1076 | 1303 | 1182 | Other | 129 | 196 | 113 | 178 | 218 | 348 |
| 4/1/21-3/31/22 ALL | 4/1/22-3/31/23 ALL | 4/1/23-3/31/24 ALL | | 203 (4/1-9/30/23) | | | 1,724 (10/1/23-3/31/24) | | |
| | | | | 0-1MM | 1-3MM | 3-5MM | 5-10MM | 10-25MM | 25MM & OVER |
| 1684 | 2106 | 1927 | NUMBER OF STATEMENTS | 224 | 298 | 183 | 298 | 370 | 554 |
| % | % | % | ASSETS | % | % | % | % | % | % |
| 41.1 | 36.7 | 35.1 | Cash & Equivalents | 24.4 | 38.3 | 38.9 | 41.9 | 41.0 | 29.0 |
| 6.8 | 7.8 | 7.4 | Trade Receivables (net) | 2.2 | 3.9 | 3.9 | 3.3 | 8.4 | 14.0 |
| 1.2 | 1.4 | 1.5 | Inventory | .4 | .6 | 1.5 | 1.4 | 2.1 | 2.0 |
| 4.4 | 4.8 | 4.5 | All Other Current | 5.7 | 5.0 | 3.4 | 3.9 | 3.9 | 5.0 |
| 53.5 | 50.8 | 48.6 | Total Current | 32.8 | 47.7 | 47.7 | 50.5 | 55.4 | 50.0 |
| 28.6 | 30.2 | 29.5 | Fixed Assets (net) | 50.0 | 29.5 | 26.0 | 27.7 | 24.0 | 27.2 |
| 7.4 | 6.7 | 7.2 | Intangibles (net) | 4.1 | 6.3 | 7.3 | 8.2 | 6.9 | 8.4 |
| 10.5 | 12.3 | 14.7 | All Other Non-Current | 13.0 | 16.5 | 19.0 | 13.6 | 13.8 | 14.4 |
| 100.0 | 100.0 | 100.0 | Total | 100.0 | 100.0 | 100.0 | 100.0 | 100.0 | 100.0 |
| | | | LIABILITIES | | | | | | |
| 11.9 | 12.3 | 10.5 | Notes Payable-Short Term | 12.4 | 12.4 | 14.6 | 11.8 | 11.9 | 5.9 |
| 4.4 | 3.9 | 3.9 | Cur. Mat.-L.T.D. | 3.5 | 4.1 | 3.4 | 3.8 | 3.4 | 4.5 |
| 3.3 | 3.7 | 4.2 | Trade Payables | 1.0 | 2.1 | 5.0 | 1.8 | 3.0 | 8.4 |
| .1 | .1 | .1 | Income Taxes Payable | .0 | .0 | .0 | .1 | .1 | .1 |
| 22.9 | 24.4 | 24.6 | All Other Current | 14.9 | 22.2 | 23.4 | 19.7 | 28.6 | 30.2 |
| 42.6 | 44.3 | 43.3 | Total Current | 31.9 | 40.8 | 46.4 | 37.2 | 46.9 | 49.0 |
| 28.3 | 28.8 | 28.4 | Long-Term Debt | 47.6 | 41.0 | 29.3 | 30.1 | 19.0 | 18.9 |
| .1 | .1 | .1 | Deferred Taxes | .0 | .0 | .0 | .0 | .0 | .2 |
| 4.8 | 3.8 | 4.7 | All Other Non-Current | 2.1 | 5.6 | 3.8 | 4.3 | 4.3 | 5.9 |
| 24.2 | 23.0 | 23.6 | Net Worth | 18.4 | 12.5 | 20.4 | 28.3 | 29.8 | 26.0 |
| 100.0 | 100.0 | 100.0 | Total Liabilities & Net Worth | 100.0 | 100.0 | 100.0 | 100.0 | 100.0 | 100.0 |
| | | | INCOME DATA | | | | | | |
| 100.0 | 100.0 | 100.0 | Net Sales | 100.0 | 100.0 | 100.0 | 100.0 | 100.0 | 100.0 |
| | | | Gross Profit | | | | | | |
| 84.3 | 85.3 | 85.5 | Operating Expenses | 63.8 | 80.2 | 85.3 | 85.9 | 90.5 | 93.6 |
| 15.7 | 14.7 | 14.5 | Operating Profit | 36.2 | 19.8 | 14.7 | 14.1 | 9.5 | 6.4 |
| .1 | 1.8 | 2.1 | All Other Expenses (net) | 11.0 | 2.7 | 1.5 | .8 | .1 | .5 |
| 15.7 | 12.9 | 12.4 | Profit Before Taxes | 25.2 | 17.1 | 13.2 | 13.3 | 9.4 | 5.9 |
| | | | RATIOS | | | | | | |
| 4.2 | 3.9 | 3.5 | | 3.4 | 5.4 | 3.2 | 4.6 | 4.0 | 2.2 |
| 1.7 | 1.5 | 1.4 | Current | 1.2 | 2.0 | 1.5 | 1.6 | 1.5 | 1.2 |
| .7 | .7 | .6 | | .3 | .7 | .5 | .7 | .7 | .7 |
| 3.7 | 3.5 | 3.0 | | 2.8 | 4.3 | 2.8 | 4.0 | 3.6 | 1.8 |
| (1683) 1.4 | (2104) 1.2 | (1926) 1.2 | Quick | .9 | 1.6 | 1.3 | (297) 1.4 | 1.3 | 1.0 |
| .6 | .5 | .5 | | .2 | .5 | .5 | .6 | .6 | .6 |
| 0 UND | 0 UND | 0 UND | | 0 UND | 0 UND | 0 UND | 0 UND | 0 UND | 0 UND |
| 0 UND | 0 UND | 0 UND | Sales/Receivables | 0 UND | 0 UND | 0 UND | 0 UND | 0 UND | 1 372.5 |
| 0 999.8 | 1 254.5 | 2 172.2 | | 0 UND | 0 UND | 0 UND | 0 UND | 3 124.0 | 33 10.9 |
| | | | Cost of Sales/Inventory | | | | | | |
| | | | Cost of Sales/Payables | | | | | | |
| 9.9 | 10.7 | 12.2 | | 6.2 | 6.8 | 12.8 | 12.9 | 13.5 | 16.6 |
| 34.2 | 48.1 | 52.6 | Sales/Working Capital | 70.6 | 26.9 | 59.0 | 46.4 | 52.0 | 77.1 |
| -58.1 | -42.8 | -41.5 | | -4.2 | -30.7 | -28.2 | -51.6 | -68.8 | -54.8 |
| 104.3 | 58.4 | 52.3 | | 12.9 | 31.9 | 57.3 | 91.2 | 59.4 | 58.4 |
| (1094) 23.2 | (1433) 11.8 | (1313) 10.4 | EBIT/Interest | (104) 5.3 | (192) 8.7 | (122) 14.8 | (211) 18.5 | (255) 14.7 | (429) 8.9 |
| 4.7 | 1.4 | 1.5 | | 2.9 | .7 | 3.1 | 2.3 | 1.5 | 1.0 |
| 12.7 | 9.5 | 8.9 | Net Profit + Depr., Dep., | | | | | 16.3 | 8.0 |
| (47) 3.9 | (100) 2.1 | (109) 3.2 | Amort./Cur. Mat. L/T/D | | | | (16) 7.2 | (83) 3.2 |
| 1.2 | .3 | 1.1 | | | | | | .7 | 1.3 |
| .1 | .1 | .1 | | .1 | .1 | .0 | .1 | .1 | .3 |
| .7 | .9 | .8 | Fixed/Worth | 2.1 | .9 | .5 | .7 | .5 | .9 |
| 16.4 | 10.6 | 12.6 | | 10.2 | -75.7 | -29.0 | 5.0 | 4.3 | 33.1 |
| .5 | .5 | .6 | | .9 | .5 | .4 | .4 | .4 | .8 |
| 2.3 | 2.2 | 2.3 | Debt/Worth | 2.8 | 2.9 | 1.8 | 1.6 | 2.0 | 2.8 |
| -24.7 | -31.3 | -42.3 | | UND | -7.9 | -8.9 | 347.9 | 69.6 | -44.2 |
| 252.4 | 172.5 | 214.1 | % Profit Before Taxes/Tangible | 102.2 | 292.4 | 255.6 | 411.6 | 231.1 | 109.4 |
| (1224) 88.6 | (1546) 49.3 | (1414) 61.7 | Net Worth | (170) 30.4 | (209) 85.0 | (124) 98.8 | (225) 118.7 | (286) 80.7 | (400) 27.0 |
| 19.9 | 7.4 | 10.6 | | 7.9 | 24.0 | 36.5 | 37.2 | 11.0 | 4.4 |
| 99.2 | 74.0 | 76.5 | % Profit Before Taxes/Total | 57.4 | 90.0 | 93.4 | 126.3 | 71.8 | 37.0 |
| 29.6 | 17.5 | 18.3 | Assets | 8.6 | 25.9 | 35.5 | 45.9 | 23.6 | 7.4 |
| 5.1 | .6 | 1.3 | | 2.3 | 2.4 | 5.1 | 5.9 | .4 | .0 |
| 240.5 | 218.0 | 207.5 | | 179.5 | 134.7 | 953.0 | 207.2 | 341.3 | 143.6 |
| 36.5 | 33.4 | 32.8 | Sales/Net Fixed Assets | 5.6 | 26.2 | 51.6 | 41.1 | 58.4 | 27.7 |
| 9.5 | 8.1 | 8.5 | | .2 | 4.1 | 10.4 | 13.1 | 17.0 | 10.4 |
| 10.3 | 11.0 | 11.1 | | 4.4 | 6.8 | 9.6 | 12.1 | 14.6 | 12.7 |
| 5.2 | 5.0 | 5.1 | Sales/Total Assets | .7 | 3.2 | 4.9 | 6.8 | 8.2 | 5.7 |
| 2.1 | 2.0 | 1.8 | | .1 | 1.3 | 2.6 | 3.7 | 3.5 | 2.1 |
| .4 | .4 | .4 | | 3.6 | .6 | .5 | .2 | .3 | .5 |
| (863) 1.2 | (1110) 1.2 | (1016) 1.2 | % Depr., Dep., Amort./Sales | (100) 13.0 | (115) 2.5 | (75) 1.3 | (141) .8 | (205) .8 | (380) 1.1 |
| 2.8 | 3.2 | 3.0 | | 23.2 | 9.3 | 3.7 | 2.4 | 1.9 | 1.9 |
| 7.6 | 6.6 | 5.8 | % Officers', Directors' | 11.7 | 6.9 | 5.4 | 3.6 | 4.4 | 7.0 |
| (741) 17.6 | (979) 14.6 | (828) 13.7 | Owners' Comp/Sales | (61) 19.7 | (139) 12.1 | (94) 10.3 | (152) 9.8 | (177) 14.8 | (205) 20.4 |
| 29.3 | 26.7 | 25.4 | | 30.6 | 17.6 | 19.1 | 24.7 | 29.0 | 29.5 |
| 43509216M | 62389398M | 66167422M | Net Sales ($) | 118769M | 564530M | 711018M | 2145125M | 6118594M | 56509386M |
| 15064107M | 20866372M | 24954821M | Total Assets ($) | 336022M | 771200M | 410714M | 980359M | 2152511M | 20304015M |

© RMA 2024  M = $ thousand  MM = $ million
See Pages viii through xx for Explanation of Ratios and Data

# HEALTH CARE—Offices of Physicians, Mental Health Specialists  NAICS 621112

## Current Data Sorted by Assets | Comparative Historical Data

| | | | | | | Type of Statement | | | | |
|---|---|---|---|---|---|---|---|---|---|---|
| | | 1 | | | | Unqualified | | 15 | | 8 |
| 1 | | 1 | 2 | 2 | 2 | Reviewed | | | | |
| | | | 1 | | | Compiled | | 7 | | 1 |
| 15 | 3 | 2 | | | | Tax Returns | | 23 | | 15 |
| 16 | 6 | 9 | 5 | 5 | 1 | Other | | 36 | | 55 |
| | 6 (4/1-9/30/23) | | 65 (10/1/23-3/31/24) | | | | | 4/1/19-3/31/20 | | 4/1/20-3/31/21 |
| 0-500M | 500M-2MM | 2-10MM | 10-50MM | 50-100MM | 100-250MM | | | ALL | | ALL |
| 32 | 9 | 12 | 8 | 7 | 3 | NUMBER OF STATEMENTS | | 81 | | 79 |
| % | % | % | % | % | % | ASSETS | | % | | % |
| 60.4 | | 26.3 | | | | Cash & Equivalents | | 39.9 | | 51.6 |
| .0 | | 24.7 | | | | Trade Receivables (net) | | 11.8 | | 5.2 |
| .3 | | .0 | | | | Inventory | | .6 | | .3 |
| 7.3 | | 3.7 | | | | All Other Current | | 4.0 | | 3.5 |
| 68.0 | | 54.7 | | | | Total Current | | 56.3 | | 60.6 |
| 18.8 | | 28.3 | | | | Fixed Assets (net) | | 25.7 | | 21.2 |
| 2.2 | | 10.3 | | | | Intangibles (net) | | 6.9 | | 10.8 |
| 11.1 | | 6.7 | | | | All Other Non-Current | | 11.1 | | 7.4 |
| 100.0 | | 100.0 | | | | Total | | 100.0 | | 100.0 |
| | | | | | | LIABILITIES | | | | |
| 20.8 | | 6.9 | | | | Notes Payable-Short Term | | 14.3 | | 18.6 |
| 2.8 | | 1.8 | | | | Cur. Mat.-L.T.D. | | 4.5 | | 4.4 |
| 22.2 | | 1.0 | | | | Trade Payables | | 5.0 | | 2.0 |
| .9 | | .1 | | | | Income Taxes Payable | | .5 | | .3 |
| 31.7 | | 8.4 | | | | All Other Current | | 13.2 | | 28.1 |
| 78.3 | | 18.1 | | | | Total Current | | 37.5 | | 53.4 |
| 38.4 | | 18.9 | | | | Long-Term Debt | | 19.1 | | 35.3 |
| .0 | | 1.3 | | | | Deferred Taxes | | .2 | | .1 |
| 1.6 | | 6.0 | | | | All Other Non-Current | | 4.0 | | 9.5 |
| -18.4 | | 55.7 | | | | Net Worth | | 39.3 | | 1.8 |
| 100.0 | | 100.0 | | | | Total Liabilities & Net Worth | | 100.0 | | 100.0 |
| | | | | | | INCOME DATA | | | | |
| 100.0 | | 100.0 | | | | Net Sales | | 100.0 | | 100.0 |
| | | | | | | Gross Profit | | | | |
| 82.5 | | 84.4 | | | | Operating Expenses | | 91.5 | | 84.8 |
| 17.5 | | 15.6 | | | | Operating Profit | | 8.5 | | 15.2 |
| 1.8 | | 1.4 | | | | All Other Expenses (net) | | .7 | | -1.2 |
| 15.7 | | 14.2 | | | | Profit Before Taxes | | 7.8 | | 16.4 |
| | | | | | | RATIOS | | | | |
| 3.0 | | 14.3 | | | | | | 6.2 | | 5.0 |
| 1.4 | | 7.6 | | | | Current | | 2.1 | | 1.8 |
| .7 | | 1.3 | | | | | | .9 | | .7 |
| 2.8 | | 14.2 | | | | | | 5.7 | | 4.7 |
| 1.4 | | 6.9 | | | | Quick | | 1.8 | | 1.7 |
| .5 | | 1.3 | | | | | | .9 | | .5 |
| 0 UND | | 0 UND | | | | | | 0 UND | 0 | UND |
| 0 UND | | 41 8.9 | | | | Sales/Receivables | | 0 UND | 0 | UND |
| 0 UND | | 63 5.8 | | | | | | 26 13.9 | 9 | 38.7 |
| | | | | | | Cost of Sales/Inventory | | | | |
| | | | | | | Cost of Sales/Payables | | | | |
| 18.9 | | 3.0 | | | | | | 6.5 | | 6.7 |
| 137.9 | | 4.8 | | | | Sales/Working Capital | | 20.9 | | 16.6 |
| -151.4 | | 180.7 | | | | | | -164.8 | | -273.5 |
| 59.0 | | | | | | | | 23.8 | | 114.4 |
| (17) 27.5 | | | | | | EBIT/Interest | (53) | 5.3 | (53) | 26.0 |
| 17.0 | | | | | | | | 1.6 | | 8.2 |
| | | | | | | Net Profit + Depr., Dep., Amort./Cur. Mat. L/T/D | | | | |
| .0 | | .1 | | | | | | .1 | | .1 |
| .1 | | .4 | | | | Fixed/Worth | | .8 | | .5 |
| 3.9 | | 3.1 | | | | | | 5.9 | | 12.6 |
| .5 | | .3 | | | | | | .2 | | .6 |
| 2.0 | | .8 | | | | Debt/Worth | | 1.3 | | 1.6 |
| -6.7 | | 4.0 | | | | | | 152.0 | | -2.2 |
| 761.4 | | 50.0 | | | | % Profit Before Taxes/Tangible Net Worth | | 179.3 | | 245.0 |
| (21) 99.5 | (10) | 16.6 | | | | | (63) | 40.2 | (55) | 122.5 |
| .6 | | 10.6 | | | | | | 2.4 | | 26.0 |
| 384.7 | | 29.8 | | | | % Profit Before Taxes/Total Assets | | 116.2 | | 142.7 |
| 166.0 | | 8.7 | | | | | | 11.2 | | 36.3 |
| 16.3 | | 2.7 | | | | | | .9 | | 9.2 |
| UND | | 62.0 | | | | | | 228.0 | | 218.4 |
| 529.3 | | 27.6 | | | | Sales/Net Fixed Assets | | 30.7 | | 46.9 |
| 55.2 | | 2.9 | | | | | | 6.0 | | 8.5 |
| 33.0 | | 6.1 | | | | | | 9.6 | | 6.9 |
| 14.4 | | 3.1 | | | | Sales/Total Assets | | 4.9 | | 4.3 |
| 8.8 | | .4 | | | | | | 1.8 | | 2.2 |
| | | | | | | % Depr., Dep., Amort./Sales | | .4 | | .6 |
| | | | | | | | (48) | 1.9 | (31) | 1.4 |
| | | | | | | | | 2.6 | | 2.1 |
| 8.5 | | | | | | % Officers', Directors' Owners' Comp/Sales | | 5.5 | | 3.3 |
| (17) 14.0 | | | | | | | (28) | 12.2 | (33) | 9.7 |
| 25.7 | | | | | | | | 24.0 | | 23.1 |
| 66167M | 39735M | 194835M | 324211M | 909916M | 1124828M | Net Sales ($) | | 2299565M | | 3010799M |
| 4793M | 9429M | 59311M | 159157M | 547890M | 547515M | Total Assets ($) | | 1207178M | | 1155950M |

© RMA 2024

M = $ thousand    MM = $ million
See Pages viii through xx for Explanation of Ratios and Data

## HEALTH CARE—Offices of Physicians, Mental Health Specialists  NAICS 621112

**Comparative Historical Data** | **Current Data Sorted by Sales**

| Comparative Historical Data | | | | | Current Data Sorted by Sales | | | | | |
|---|---|---|---|---|---|---|---|---|---|---|
| 3 | 9 | 8 | Type of Statement | | | | | | | |
| 1 | | 1 | Unqualified | 1 | 1 | | | 1 | 5 | |
| 2 | 7 | | Reviewed | | | | | | 1 | |
| 20 | 25 | 20 | Compiled | | | | | | | |
| 38 | 56 | 42 | Tax Returns | 8 | 5 | 5 | 1 | 1 | | |
| 4/1/21-3/31/22 ALL | 4/1/22-3/31/23 ALL | 4/1/23-3/31/24 ALL | Other | 8 | 9 | 4 | 4 | 4 | 13 | |
| | | | | 6 (4/1-9/30/23) | | | 65 (10/1/23-3/31/24) | | | |
| | | | | 0-1MM | 1-3MM | 3-5MM | 5-10MM | 10-25MM | 25MM & OVER | |
| 64 | 97 | 71 | NUMBER OF STATEMENTS | 17 | 15 | 9 | 5 | 6 | 19 | |
| % | % | % | ASSETS | % | % | % | % | % | % | |
| 46.0 | 38.4 | 42.0 | Cash & Equivalents | 44.5 | 45.7 | | | | 22.4 | |
| 5.7 | 8.7 | 9.5 | Trade Receivables (net) | .1 | 1.5 | | | | 23.8 | |
| .1 | 1.4 | .7 | Inventory | .0 | 1.3 | | | | .7 | |
| 7.9 | 5.9 | 4.6 | All Other Current | 9.5 | 1.2 | | | | 3.6 | |
| 59.7 | 54.4 | 56.8 | Total Current | 54.1 | 49.6 | | | | 50.5 | |
| 23.0 | 23.6 | 24.8 | Fixed Assets (net) | 35.6 | 25.1 | | | | 22.7 | |
| 6.9 | 10.2 | 5.4 | Intangibles (net) | 4.4 | 4.7 | | | | 9.8 | |
| 10.5 | 11.8 | 13.0 | All Other Non-Current | 5.9 | 20.7 | | | | 16.9 | |
| 100.0 | 100.0 | 100.0 | Total | 100.0 | 100.0 | | | | 100.0 | |
| | | | LIABILITIES | | | | | | | |
| 11.7 | 19.6 | 12.2 | Notes Payable-Short Term | 30.9 | 1.3 | | | | 5.7 | |
| 2.6 | 2.5 | 2.2 | Cur. Mat.-L.T.D. | 5.0 | 1.6 | | | | 2.2 | |
| 1.0 | 4.2 | 11.9 | Trade Payables | 36.3 | 1.5 | | | | 6.2 | |
| .6 | .2 | .5 | Income Taxes Payable | 1.7 | .0 | | | | .1 | |
| 20.6 | 20.7 | 20.8 | All Other Current | 14.4 | 20.6 | | | | 14.8 | |
| 36.5 | 47.1 | 47.5 | Total Current | 88.3 | 24.9 | | | | 29.1 | |
| 17.9 | 29.8 | 30.1 | Long-Term Debt | 74.6 | 20.4 | | | | 21.6 | |
| .2 | .2 | .3 | Deferred Taxes | .0 | .0 | | | | 1.3 | |
| 2.4 | 4.8 | 4.6 | All Other Non-Current | .4 | 2.1 | | | | 10.3 | |
| 43.0 | 18.1 | 17.4 | Net Worth | -63.3 | 52.6 | | | | 37.6 | |
| 100.0 | 100.0 | 100.0 | Total Liabilities & Net Worth | 100.0 | 100.0 | | | | 100.0 | |
| | | | INCOME DATA | | | | | | | |
| 100.0 | 100.0 | 100.0 | Net Sales | 100.0 | 100.0 | | | | 100.0 | |
| | | | Gross Profit | | | | | | | |
| 85.8 | 87.5 | 84.1 | Operating Expenses | 69.6 | 85.4 | | | | 97.0 | |
| 14.2 | 12.5 | 15.9 | Operating Profit | 30.4 | 14.6 | | | | 3.0 | |
| -1.5 | .9 | 2.6 | All Other Expenses (net) | 6.7 | 3.5 | | | | -.1 | |
| 15.7 | 11.6 | 13.3 | Profit Before Taxes | 23.7 | 11.1 | | | | 3.1 | |
| | | | RATIOS | | | | | | | |
| 5.3 | 5.7 | 3.9 | | 2.5 | 12.2 | | | | 4.3 | |
| 2.7 | 1.7 | 1.9 | Current | 1.1 | 2.5 | | | | 1.6 | |
| 1.0 | .6 | .7 | | .4 | .8 | | | | .8 | |
| 4.6 | 5.4 | 3.4 | | 1.8 | 12.2 | | | | 3.8 | |
| 2.5 | 1.3 | 1.5 | Quick | 1.0 | 2.5 | | | | 1.6 | |
| .8 | .4 | .6 | | .1 | .7 | | | | .6 | |
| 0 UND | 0 UND | 0 UND | | 0 UND | 0 UND | | | | 23 15.8 | |
| 0 UND | 0 UND | 0 UND | Sales/Receivables | 0 UND | 0 UND | | | | 36 10.1 | |
| 2 196.6 | 20 18.2 | 30 12.3 | | 0 UND | 0 UND | | | | 55 6.6 | |
| | | | Cost of Sales/Inventory | | | | | | | |
| | | | Cost of Sales/Payables | | | | | | | |
| 7.2 | 6.5 | 6.8 | | 16.8 | 4.2 | | | | 4.0 | |
| 25.1 | 24.1 | 20.8 | Sales/Working Capital | 237.5 | 16.0 | | | | 13.2 | |
| 858.3 | -32.2 | -154.6 | | -9.4 | -180.3 | | | | -45.8 | |
| 92.5 | 69.0 | 53.7 | | | | | | | 12.5 | |
| (43) 27.2 | (63) 15.4 | (44) 22.1 | EBIT/Interest | | | | | | (15) 5.2 | |
| 8.6 | 2.3 | 4.9 | | | | | | | .7 | |
| | | | Net Profit + Depr., Dep., Amort./Cur. Mat. L/T/D | | | | | | | |
| .0 | .0 | .1 | | .0 | .0 | | | | .2 | |
| .4 | .3 | .3 | Fixed/Worth | .6 | .3 | | | | .7 | |
| 1.0 | 2.8 | 4.5 | | NM | 4.5 | | | | -1.1 | |
| .3 | .3 | .5 | | 1.1 | .1 | | | | .5 | |
| 1.1 | 1.5 | 1.3 | Debt/Worth | 4.9 | .8 | | | | 1.3 | |
| 3.0 | -9.1 | -31.2 | | -2.6 | 19.4 | | | | -16.1 | |
| 307.0 | 111.3 | 180.5 | | 336.6 | 163.5 | | | | 14.1 | |
| (54) 101.7 | (69) 38.5 | (53) 26.4 | % Profit Before Taxes/Tangible Net Worth | (10) 10.3 | (12) 39.7 | | | | (13) 12.9 | |
| 19.1 | 5.0 | 8.6 | | -5.0 | 4.8 | | | | 7.0 | |
| 183.1 | 54.6 | 144.1 | | 359.1 | 96.0 | | | | 8.8 | |
| 53.4 | 14.4 | 16.3 | % Profit Before Taxes/Total Assets | 103.3 | 21.7 | | | | 4.5 | |
| 15.8 | -.3 | 3.2 | | 1.5 | 1.1 | | | | -.6 | |
| 389.3 | 365.4 | 268.5 | | UND | UND | | | | 43.0 | |
| 34.0 | 37.8 | 47.6 | Sales/Net Fixed Assets | 801.0 | 39.2 | | | | 12.2 | |
| 9.9 | 6.8 | 6.7 | | 2.1 | 4.9 | | | | 5.1 | |
| 10.2 | 9.7 | 13.8 | | 20.0 | 21.5 | | | | 4.7 | |
| 4.6 | 3.1 | 5.0 | Sales/Total Assets | 8.3 | 8.8 | | | | 1.8 | |
| 2.4 | 1.5 | 1.5 | | .8 | 1.2 | | | | 1.4 | |
| .2 | .6 | .4 | | | | | | | .5 | |
| (28) 1.0 | (50) 1.3 | (28) 1.2 | % Depr., Dep., Amort./Sales | | | | | | (14) 1.1 | |
| 2.1 | 2.5 | 3.7 | | | | | | | 1.6 | |
| 6.9 | 6.4 | 7.9 | | | | | | | | |
| (25) 9.6 | (29) 12.4 | (23) 11.8 | % Officers', Directors' Owners' Comp/Sales | | | | | | | |
| 25.3 | 23.5 | 20.6 | | | | | | | | |
| 1052393M | 2767021M | 2659692M | Net Sales ($) | 10074M | 25913M | 34368M | 35548M | 92550M | 2461239M | |
| 475531M | 1299936M | 1328095M | Total Assets ($) | 14669M | 15635M | 2669M | 17074M | 37119M | 1240929M | |

© RMA 2024  
M = $ thousand  MM = $ million  
See Pages viii through xx for Explanation of Ratios and Data

# HEALTH CARE—Offices of Dentists  NAICS 621210

## Current Data Sorted by Assets | Comparative Historical Data

| | | | | | | Type of Statement | | |
|---|---|---|---|---|---|---|---|---|
| 4 | 18 | 19 | 3 | 5 | 7 | Unqualified | 10 | 9 |
| 1 | 1 | 2 | 3 | | | Reviewed | 14 | 4 |
| 12 | 38 | 16 | 3 | | 1 | Compiled | 108 | 140 |
| 167 | 219 | 24 | | 2 | | Tax Returns | 458 | 424 |
| 183 | 306 | 75 | 17 | 6 | 6 | Other | 708 | 930 |
| | 32 (4/1-9/30/23) | | 1,106 (10/1/23-3/31/24) | | | | 4/1/19-3/31/20 ALL | 4/1/20-3/31/21 ALL |
| 0-500M | 500M-2MM | 2-10MM | 10-50MM | 50-100MM | 100-250MM | NUMBER OF STATEMENTS | 1298 | 1507 |
| 367 | 582 | 136 | 26 | 13 | 14 | | | |
| % | % | % | % | % | % | ASSETS | % | % |
| 38.5 | 19.6 | 14.3 | 14.4 | 13.9 | 13.5 | Cash & Equivalents | 25.3 | 35.7 |
| 2.9 | 2.3 | 5.1 | 8.7 | 10.2 | 3.7 | Trade Receivables (net) | 3.0 | 1.7 |
| .4 | .2 | .2 | .2 | .4 | .7 | Inventory | .2 | .3 |
| 5.8 | 6.6 | 3.9 | 6.7 | 3.5 | 5.6 | All Other Current | 3.7 | 2.4 |
| 47.5 | 28.7 | 23.5 | 30.0 | 28.0 | 23.5 | Total Current | 32.3 | 39.9 |
| 25.5 | 26.9 | 35.9 | 29.1 | 37.2 | 31.5 | Fixed Assets (net) | 31.9 | 24.8 |
| 16.9 | 32.3 | 27.2 | 25.8 | 22.4 | 28.3 | Intangibles (net) | 22.7 | 27.9 |
| 10.0 | 12.1 | 13.4 | 15.0 | 12.3 | 16.7 | All Other Non-Current | 13.1 | 7.4 |
| 100.0 | 100.0 | 100.0 | 100.0 | 100.0 | 100.0 | Total | 100.0 | 100.0 |
| | | | | | | LIABILITIES | | |
| 17.5 | 5.5 | 1.6 | 1.5 | 6.8 | 4.2 | Notes Payable-Short Term | 11.6 | 17.3 |
| 5.6 | 4.7 | 4.6 | 5.8 | 2.5 | 6.8 | Cur. Mat.-L.T.D. | 5.9 | 5.4 |
| 2.5 | .5 | 1.1 | 2.7 | 4.0 | 1.6 | Trade Payables | 1.4 | 1.1 |
| .0 | .0 | .0 | .1 | .0 | .0 | Income Taxes Payable | .0 | .0 |
| 23.7 | 10.2 | 9.9 | 15.4 | 15.3 | 11.9 | All Other Current | 16.0 | 11.5 |
| 49.4 | 20.9 | 17.2 | 25.5 | 28.6 | 24.5 | Total Current | 34.9 | 35.4 |
| 57.1 | 60.4 | 58.8 | 62.5 | 81.4 | 60.1 | Long-Term Debt | 50.4 | 59.2 |
| .0 | .0 | .0 | .0 | .0 | .0 | Deferred Taxes | .0 | .0 |
| 7.6 | 3.3 | 4.5 | 19.1 | 5.9 | 16.0 | All Other Non-Current | 5.1 | 4.9 |
| -14.0 | 15.3 | 19.5 | -7.2 | -15.9 | -.6 | Net Worth | 9.5 | .5 |
| 100.0 | 100.0 | 100.0 | 100.0 | 100.0 | 100.0 | Total Liabilities & Net Worth | 100.0 | 100.0 |
| | | | | | | INCOME DATA | | |
| 100.0 | 100.0 | 100.0 | 100.0 | 100.0 | 100.0 | Net Sales | 100.0 | 100.0 |
| | | | | | | Gross Profit | | |
| 86.0 | 82.7 | 77.3 | 88.2 | 88.6 | 90.6 | Operating Expenses | 83.3 | 85.6 |
| 14.0 | 17.3 | 22.7 | 11.8 | 11.4 | 9.4 | Operating Profit | 16.7 | 14.4 |
| 1.4 | 4.0 | 6.6 | 6.7 | 2.5 | 8.0 | All Other Expenses (net) | 2.6 | -.8 |
| 12.6 | 13.3 | 16.1 | 5.0 | 8.9 | 1.4 | Profit Before Taxes | 14.1 | 15.1 |
| | | | | | | RATIOS | | |
| 4.5 | 3.9 | 3.1 | 2.8 | 1.8 | 1.7 | | 3.4 | 4.7 |
| 1.5 | 1.5 | 1.2 | 1.2 | .9 | 1.0 | Current | 1.1 | 1.6 |
| .6 | .5 | .4 | .4 | .8 | .4 | | .4 | .6 |
| 4.1 | 3.1 | 2.5 | 2.2 | 1.7 | 1.1 | | 3.0 | 4.5 |
| 1.3 | (581) 1.1 | 1.0 | .8 | .8 | .6 | Quick (1296) | 1.0 (1506) | 1.5 |
| .4 | .3 | .3 | .4 | .5 | .3 | | .3 | .6 |
| 0 UND | 0 UND | 0 UND | 0 UND | 0 UND | 0 UND | | 0 UND | 0 UND |
| 0 UND | 0 UND | 0 UND | 15 24.1 | 20 18.1 | 18 20.5 | Sales/Receivables | 0 UND | 0 UND |
| 0 UND | 0 UND | 11 34.2 | 32 11.3 | 40 9.1 | 28 12.9 | | 0 UND | 0 UND |
| | | | | | | Cost of Sales/Inventory | | |
| | | | | | | Cost of Sales/Payables | | |
| 17.4 | 9.9 | 8.4 | 8.7 | 70.3 | 20.1 | | 14.0 | 7.3 |
| 78.3 | 41.8 | 55.9 | 37.1 | -165.0 | NM | Sales/Working Capital | 174.3 | 23.1 |
| -33.2 | -20.6 | -8.2 | -7.2 | -17.3 | -7.9 | | -20.0 | -21.3 |
| 38.3 | 21.0 | 17.5 | 7.3 | 49.4 | 8.3 | | 26.9 | 29.6 |
| (253) 8.9 | (488) 7.5 | (110) 6.1 | (24) 3.1 | (12) 3.5 | (12) 2.6 | EBIT/Interest (974) | 9.5 (1170) | 10.1 |
| 2.7 | 2.7 | 2.8 | -.2 | .4 | -.5 | | 2.9 | 2.5 |
| | | | | | | Net Profit + Depr., Dep., Amort./Cur. Mat. L/T/D | 7.4 | 35.9 |
| | | | | | | | (12) 4.1 (12) | 4.8 |
| | | | | | | | 1.6 | 1.3 |
| .1 | .5 | .7 | 3.4 | 1.0 | 1.8 | | .5 | .4 |
| 1.4 | -132.3 | NM | -1.8 | -4.3 | -1.4 | Fixed/Worth | 8.7 | -15.5 |
| -.5 | -.3 | -.7 | -.4 | -.8 | -.2 | | -.5 | -.3 |
| .9 | 2.5 | 1.8 | -25.5 | 1.9 | 3.2 | | 1.1 | 2.4 |
| -49.5 | -6.3 | -17.1 | -5.9 | -5.9 | -3.7 | Debt/Worth | -745.4 | -5.1 |
| -1.9 | -1.6 | -2.3 | -1.9 | -2.2 | -1.8 | | -2.2 | -1.7 |
| 593.1 | 243.5 | 88.9 | | | | % Profit Before Taxes/Tangible Net Worth | 385.9 | 347.6 |
| (181) 184.4 | (246) 103.4 | (64) 44.9 | | | | (648) | 124.3 (598) | 127.6 |
| 60.9 | 39.4 | 9.9 | | | | | 44.1 | 51.6 |
| 143.9 | 49.2 | 27.9 | 22.8 | 16.6 | 43.9 | | 74.0 | 61.1 |
| 50.0 | 21.0 | 13.3 | 5.4 | 9.1 | 2.6 | % Profit Before Taxes/Total Assets | 31.5 | 25.1 |
| 11.6 | 5.9 | 3.3 | -2.8 | -9.0 | -2.9 | | 8.1 | 4.9 |
| 806.7 | 66.6 | 28.7 | 26.2 | 33.2 | 16.5 | | 63.5 | 75.3 |
| 45.3 | 15.3 | 5.9 | 6.2 | 6.4 | 6.9 | Sales/Net Fixed Assets | 16.2 | 16.8 |
| 13.4 | 5.4 | 1.3 | 2.6 | 2.1 | 2.6 | | 6.6 | 6.1 |
| 11.6 | 3.4 | 2.0 | 3.3 | 4.5 | 3.1 | | 5.9 | 4.0 |
| 5.9 | 2.0 | 1.1 | 1.2 | 1.4 | 1.1 | Sales/Total Assets | 3.0 | 2.2 |
| 3.4 | 1.3 | .6 | .7 | 1.1 | .6 | | 1.7 | 1.3 |
| .5 | 1.2 | 1.9 | 1.6 | | | | 1.0 | 1.3 |
| (148) 1.4 | (269) 4.0 | (77) 4.1 | (16) 4.0 | | | % Depr., Dep., Amort./Sales (599) | 2.7 (618) | 3.1 |
| 3.2 | 9.9 | 10.2 | 5.9 | | | | 5.8 | 6.2 |
| 8.3 | 6.6 | 2.4 | 1.2 | | | | 7.8 | 8.1 |
| (204) 14.1 | (355) 10.9 | (43) 4.0 | (10) 6.1 | | | % Officers', Directors' Owners' Comp/Sales (760) | 12.9 (896) | 13.1 |
| 20.5 | 16.3 | 8.5 | 20.1 | | | | 21.0 | 20.4 |
| 631199M | 1418115M | 854049M | 1038141M | 4726780M | 5945481M | Net Sales ($) | 23676592M | 7300360M |
| 93849M | 572377M | 513567M | 623861M | 911308M | 2323777M | Total Assets ($) | 3819613M | 2507508M |

© RMA 2024     M = $ thousand    MM = $ million
See Pages viii through xx for Explanation of Ratios and Data

# HEALTH CARE—Offices of Dentists  NAICS 621210

| Comparative Historical Data ||| Type of Statement | Current Data Sorted by Sales ||||||
|---|---|---|---|---|---|---|---|---|---|
| 19 | 16 | 56 | Unqualified | 10 | 16 | 10 | 5 | 1 | 14 |
| 35 | 6 | 7 | Reviewed | | 2 | | | 3 | 2 |
| 102 | 90 | 70 | Compiled | 13 | 29 | 9 | 10 | 4 | 5 |
| 426 | 533 | 412 | Tax Returns | 89 | 229 | 58 | 31 | 3 | 2 |
| 963 | 796 | 593 | Other | 146 | 279 | 80 | 41 | 22 | 25 |
| 4/1/21-3/31/22 ALL | 4/1/22-3/31/23 ALL | 4/1/23-3/31/24 ALL | | 32 (4/1-9/30/23) |||| 1,106 (10/1/23-3/31/24) ||
| | | | | 0-1MM | 1-3MM | 3-5MM | 5-10MM | 10-25MM | 25MM & OVER |
| 1545 | 1441 | 1138 | NUMBER OF STATEMENTS | 258 | 555 | 157 | 87 | 33 | 48 |
| % | % | % | ASSETS | % | % | % | % | % | % |
| 32.5 | 28.2 | 24.8 | Cash & Equivalents | 20.5 | 24.5 | 30.6 | 33.8 | 21.6 | 18.9 |
| 2.4 | 2.6 | 3.1 | Trade Receivables (net) | 2.4 | 2.5 | 2.9 | 4.3 | 6.8 | 9.6 |
| .3 | .4 | .3 | Inventory | .1 | .3 | .4 | .4 | .4 | .4 |
| 3.6 | 5.5 | 6.0 | All Other Current | 4.4 | 7.0 | 4.7 | 6.9 | 2.8 | 6.3 |
| 38.7 | 36.7 | 34.1 | Total Current | 27.3 | 34.3 | 38.5 | 45.4 | 31.6 | 35.3 |
| 25.2 | 26.8 | 27.8 | Fixed Assets (net) | 38.8 | 23.9 | 24.0 | 21.7 | 40.8 | 27.4 |
| 28.0 | 25.8 | 26.4 | Intangibles (net) | 23.3 | 30.4 | 24.2 | 19.7 | 15.5 | 23.8 |
| 8.0 | 10.6 | 11.7 | All Other Non-Current | 10.5 | 11.4 | 13.3 | 13.3 | 12.1 | 13.6 |
| 100.0 | 100.0 | 100.0 | Total | 100.0 | 100.0 | 100.0 | 100.0 | 100.0 | 100.0 |
| | | | LIABILITIES | | | | | | |
| 9.4 | 10.3 | 8.8 | Notes Payable-Short Term | 10.4 | 9.5 | 5.7 | 10.1 | 3.5 | 4.1 |
| 5.3 | 4.2 | 5.0 | Cur. Mat.-L.T.D. | 5.4 | 4.9 | 5.0 | 3.9 | 8.0 | 5.0 |
| .9 | 1.4 | 1.3 | Trade Payables | .5 | 1.4 | 1.3 | 1.7 | 1.5 | 3.5 |
| .0 | .0 | .0 | Income Taxes Payable | .0 | .0 | .0 | .0 | .0 | .0 |
| 10.6 | 16.2 | 14.7 | All Other Current | 17.7 | 13.1 | 13.0 | 18.1 | 16.0 | 16.0 |
| 26.2 | 32.2 | 29.9 | Total Current | 33.9 | 28.9 | 25.0 | 33.9 | 29.0 | 28.6 |
| 56.9 | 60.1 | 59.4 | Long-Term Debt | 64.7 | 62.4 | 52.6 | 37.7 | 56.3 | 61.6 |
| .0 | .0 | .0 | Deferred Taxes | .0 | .0 | .0 | .0 | .0 | .0 |
| 3.8 | 5.0 | 5.4 | All Other Non-Current | 7.7 | 4.1 | 2.4 | 5.3 | 15.7 | 10.2 |
| 13.1 | 2.7 | 5.3 | Net Worth | -6.3 | 4.6 | 20.1 | 23.1 | -1.0 | -.3 |
| 100.0 | 100.0 | 100.0 | Total Liabilities & Net Worth | 100.0 | 100.0 | 100.0 | 100.0 | 100.0 | 100.0 |
| | | | INCOME DATA | | | | | | |
| 100.0 | 100.0 | 100.0 | Net Sales | 100.0 | 100.0 | 100.0 | 100.0 | 100.0 | 100.0 |
| | | | Gross Profit | | | | | | |
| 82.6 | 85.6 | 83.4 | Operating Expenses | 75.5 | 85.7 | 84.4 | 85.0 | 87.2 | 90.1 |
| 17.4 | 14.4 | 16.6 | Operating Profit | 24.5 | 14.3 | 15.6 | 15.0 | 12.8 | 9.9 |
| .5 | 2.2 | 3.6 | All Other Expenses (net) | 8.6 | 2.1 | 1.2 | 1.9 | 4.3 | 3.2 |
| 16.9 | 12.2 | 13.1 | Profit Before Taxes | 15.9 | 12.2 | 14.4 | 13.1 | 8.5 | 6.7 |
| | | | RATIOS | | | | | | |
| 5.1 | 5.3 | 3.8 | | 3.3 | 4.5 | 4.6 | 3.8 | 2.1 | 2.4 |
| 1.9 | 1.6 | 1.4 | Current | 1.0 | 1.5 | 2.0 | 1.7 | .8 | 1.1 |
| .8 | .6 | .5 | | .3 | .6 | .6 | .7 | .5 | .7 |
| 4.5 | 4.5 | 3.3 | | 3.0 | 3.8 | 4.3 | 3.3 | 1.9 | 2.0 |
| 1.7 (1440) | 1.4 (1137) | 1.1 | Quick | .8 | (554) 1.2 | 1.8 | 1.4 | .8 | .9 |
| .7 | .4 | .4 | | .2 | .3 | .5 | .6 | .4 | .5 |
| 0 UND | 0 UND | 0 UND | | 0 UND | 0 UND | 0 UND | 0 UND | 0 UND | 0 UND |
| 0 UND | 0 UND | 0 UND | Sales/Receivables | 0 UND | 0 UND | 0 UND | 0 UND | 0 UND | 20 18.7 |
| 0 UND | 0 UND | 0 UND | | 0 UND | 0 UND | 0 UND | 0 UND | 19 19.5 | 32 11.5 |
| | | | Cost of Sales/Inventory | | | | | | |
| | | | Cost of Sales/Payables | | | | | | |
| 7.0 | 9.2 | 11.8 | | 11.5 | 10.9 | 11.2 | 13.8 | 20.4 | 15.7 |
| 19.5 | 34.4 | 57.5 | Sales/Working Capital | UND | 47.4 | 36.1 | 39.2 | -151.6 | 185.7 |
| -70.9 | -27.8 | -21.2 | | -5.3 | -30.8 | -44.0 | -74.0 | -10.9 | -17.9 |
| 34.4 | 23.8 | 23.0 | | 9.3 | 22.1 | 34.2 | 97.2 | 41.0 | 16.1 |
| (1151) 11.2 | (1089) 8.1 | (899) 7.3 | EBIT/Interest | (167) 3.9 | (467) 7.6 | (125) 11.8 | (69) 22.9 | (27) 4.9 | (44) 3.6 |
| 3.7 | 1.8 | 2.5 | | .3 | 3.0 | 3.4 | 6.5 | .8 | 1.7 |
| 6.1 | 19.4 | 2.4 | | | | | | | |
| (17) 2.7 | (17) 2.7 | (14) 1.8 | Net Profit + Depr., Dep., Amort./Cur. Mat. L/T/D | | | | | | |
| .7 | 1.1 | .8 | | | | | | | |
| .3 | .2 | .3 | | .7 | .4 | .2 | .1 | 1.8 | .6 |
| 14.4 | 6.2 | 14.5 | Fixed/Worth | 197.1 | -21.1 | 1.5 | .9 | 29.7 | -2.0 |
| -.4 | -.5 | -.4 | | -.4 | -.3 | -.8 | -1.2 | -.8 | -.4 |
| 1.8 | 2.0 | 1.7 | | 2.4 | 2.2 | .8 | .7 | 1.6 | 2.2 |
| -9.5 | -11.2 | -8.7 | Debt/Worth | -13.5 | -4.6 | 17.7 | 4.5 | 162.7 | -5.1 |
| -1.9 | -1.8 | -1.7 | | -1.7 | -1.6 | -2.3 | -2.7 | -4.2 | -2.3 |
| 345.3 | 265.2 | 309.7 | | 225.4 | 375.2 | 288.1 | 305.5 | 349.5 | 297.9 |
| (690) 136.9 | (657) 102.4 | (507) 107.1 | % Profit Before Taxes/Tangible Net Worth | (118) 58.1 | (221) 124.8 | (83) 146.1 | (51) 92.7 | (17) 105.5 | (17) 57.2 |
| 53.9 | 27.5 | 34.9 | | 9.1 | 47.3 | 85.0 | 40.0 | 23.7 | 18.9 |
| 71.2 | 54.2 | 63.4 | % Profit Before Taxes/Total Assets | 35.3 | 62.0 | 102.9 | 94.5 | 84.8 | 30.5 |
| 30.0 | 20.4 | 23.1 | | 7.9 | 25.2 | 45.7 | 46.6 | 23.6 | 8.7 |
| 8.2 | 2.1 | 5.0 | | .0 | 8.7 | 13.3 | 15.8 | -1.6 | 1.0 |
| 78.2 | 113.2 | 102.3 | | 59.1 | 112.3 | 137.7 | 179.8 | 23.5 | 31.3 |
| 15.4 | 18.3 | 18.6 | Sales/Net Fixed Assets | 9.1 | 20.8 | 35.5 | 35.5 | 7.9 | 11.2 |
| 5.7 | 6.3 | 6.0 | | 1.1 | 7.8 | 8.5 | 12.4 | 3.3 | 3.8 |
| 4.2 | 4.8 | 4.9 | | 2.8 | 4.7 | 7.4 | 9.5 | 5.6 | 5.0 |
| 2.2 | 2.5 | 2.6 | Sales/Total Assets | 1.3 | 2.6 | 3.8 | 5.0 | 2.4 | 1.7 |
| 1.2 | 1.4 | 1.4 | | .4 | 1.5 | 2.2 | 2.5 | 1.4 | 1.0 |
| 1.2 | 1.2 | 1.0 | | 3.5 | 1.0 | .6 | .5 | 1.7 | 1.7 |
| (614) 3.4 | (636) 3.2 | (524) 2.9 | % Depr., Dep., Amort./Sales | (116) 11.6 | (242) 2.6 | (77) 1.4 | (42) 1.2 | (22) 2.1 | (25) 3.7 |
| 7.0 | 6.6 | 7.3 | | 20.5 | 5.7 | 4.0 | 2.4 | 3.7 | 5.7 |
| 7.1 | 7.1 | 6.4 | | 7.6 | 7.6 | 5.6 | 2.8 | 2.6 | 1.9 |
| (840) 12.3 | (785) 12.1 | (616) 11.3 | % Officers', Directors' Owners' Comp/Sales | (99) 12.8 | (331) 11.5 | (108) 9.9 | (49) 10.2 | (16) 7.1 | (13) 7.5 |
| 18.9 | 18.8 | 17.5 | | 18.9 | 16.8 | 15.4 | 23.4 | 27.8 | 20.3 |
| 13578300M | 6107660M | 14613765M | Net Sales ($) | 150564M | 997552M | 591898M | 602050M | 513310M | 11758391M |
| 4170839M | 4043774M | 5038739M | Total Assets ($) | 208470M | 478127M | 207062M | 181274M | 518942M | 3444864M |

© RMA 2024  M = $ thousand  MM = $ million
See Pages viii through xx for Explanation of Ratios and Data

# HEALTH CARE—Offices of Chiropractors  NAICS 621310

## Current Data Sorted by Assets | Comparative Historical Data

| 0-500M | 500M-2MM | 2-10MM | 10-50MM | 50-100MM | 100-250MM | Type of Statement | 4/1/19-3/31/20 ALL | 4/1/20-3/31/21 ALL |
|---|---|---|---|---|---|---|---|---|
|  | 1 | 2 |  |  |  | Unqualified |  |  |
|  | 1 | 2 |  |  |  | Reviewed | 1 | 1 |
| 26 | 3 | 2 |  |  |  | Compiled | 10 | 4 |
| 28 | 5 | 10 |  | 1 | 1 | Tax Returns | 65 | 49 |
|  | 4 (4/1-9/30/23) |  | 76 (10/1/23-3/31/24) |  |  | Other | 60 | 64 |
| 54 | 10 | 14 | 1 | 1 | 1 | NUMBER OF STATEMENTS | 136 | 118 |
| % | % | % | % | % | % | ASSETS | % | % |
| 44.3 | 25.2 | 18.6 |  |  |  | Cash & Equivalents | 36.4 | 48.7 |
| 1.6 | 6.2 | 11.6 |  |  |  | Trade Receivables (net) | 5.1 | 4.1 |
| 2.1 | .0 | 1.0 |  |  |  | Inventory | 1.0 | .6 |
| 3.4 | 2.8 | 2.4 |  |  |  | All Other Current | 4.3 | 1.8 |
| 51.4 | 34.3 | 33.6 |  |  |  | Total Current | 46.8 | 55.2 |
| 24.6 | 11.1 | 49.4 | D |  |  | Fixed Assets (net) | 28.6 | 21.2 |
| 14.6 | 34.0 | 11.2 | A |  |  | Intangibles (net) | 12.2 | 16.2 |
| 9.5 | 20.6 | 5.7 | T |  |  | All Other Non-Current | 12.4 | 7.4 |
| 100.0 | 100.0 | 100.0 | A |  |  | Total | 100.0 | 100.0 |
|  |  |  |  |  |  | LIABILITIES |  |  |
| 9.2 | 17.9 | 4.0 | N |  |  | Notes Payable-Short Term | 11.4 | 18.6 |
| 9.2 | 5.8 | 2.0 | O |  |  | Cur. Mat.-L.T.D. | 4.1 | 4.2 |
| .2 | .5 | 3.3 | T |  |  | Trade Payables | 2.8 | 1.6 |
| .0 | .0 | .0 |  |  |  | Income Taxes Payable | .0 | .0 |
| 13.6 | 10.7 | 2.5 | A |  |  | All Other Current | 12.2 | 12.2 |
| 32.2 | 34.8 | 11.9 | V |  |  | Total Current | 30.5 | 36.6 |
| 47.6 | 48.9 | 40.1 | A |  |  | Long-Term Debt | 29.6 | 46.8 |
| .0 | .0 | .0 | I |  |  | Deferred Taxes | .0 | .0 |
| 4.9 | .0 | 1.7 | L |  |  | All Other Non-Current | 4.2 | 4.6 |
| 15.3 | 16.3 | 46.3 | A |  |  | Net Worth | 35.7 | 12.1 |
| 100.0 | 100.0 | 100.0 | B |  |  | Total Liabilities & Net Worth | 100.0 | 100.0 |
|  |  |  | L |  |  | INCOME DATA |  |  |
| 100.0 | 100.0 | 100.0 | E |  |  | Net Sales | 100.0 | 100.0 |
|  |  |  |  |  |  | Gross Profit |  |  |
| 88.8 | 84.1 | 74.8 |  |  |  | Operating Expenses | 82.2 | 82.2 |
| 11.2 | 15.9 | 25.2 |  |  |  | Operating Profit | 17.8 | 17.8 |
| .4 | 3.9 | 11.8 |  |  |  | All Other Expenses (net) | 1.1 | .0 |
| 10.7 | 12.0 | 13.3 |  |  |  | Profit Before Taxes | 16.7 | 17.8 |
|  |  |  |  |  |  | RATIOS |  |  |
| 18.1 | 2.9 | 10.9 |  |  |  |  | 6.0 | 7.5 |
| 3.2 | 1.2 | 2.8 |  |  |  | Current | 2.3 | 2.6 |
| .6 | .2 | .7 |  |  |  |  | .9 | 1.0 |
| 11.4 | 2.0 | 5.4 |  |  |  |  | 5.0 | 7.1 |
| 2.7 | 1.2 | 1.8 |  |  |  | Quick | 1.9 | 2.5 |
| .5 | .2 | .7 |  |  |  |  | .7 | 1.0 |
| 0 UND | 0 UND | 0 UND |  |  |  |  | 0 UND | 0 UND |
| 0 UND | 0 UND | 1 538.6 |  |  |  | Sales/Receivables | 0 UND | 0 UND |
| 0 UND | 0 UND | 89 4.1 |  |  |  |  | 0 UND | 0 UND |
|  |  |  |  |  |  | Cost of Sales/Inventory |  |  |
|  |  |  |  |  |  | Cost of Sales/Payables |  |  |
| 7.4 | 25.7 | 2.2 |  |  |  |  | 10.2 | 4.8 |
| 24.8 | 437.0 | 5.1 |  |  |  | Sales/Working Capital | 31.0 | 11.8 |
| -61.8 | -4.1 | -18.5 |  |  |  |  | -190.4 | UND |
|  |  | 43.8 |  |  |  |  | 46.1 | 58.0 |
| (30) 6.9 | (10) | 87.5 7.0 |  |  |  | EBIT/Interest | (87) 19.1 | (69) 20.0 |
| .6 |  | 3.1 |  |  |  |  | 4.7 | 4.2 |
|  |  |  |  |  |  | Net Profit + Depr., Dep., Amort./Cur. Mat. L/T/D |  |  |
| .1 | .1 | .5 |  |  |  |  | .1 | .1 |
| .5 | NM | 2.1 |  |  |  | Fixed/Worth | .7 | .9 |
| -2.2 | .0 | 4.2 |  |  |  |  | 13.2 | -5.3 |
| .1 | 4.7 | .9 |  |  |  |  | .3 | .8 |
| 1.3 | -24.9 | 2.7 |  |  |  | Debt/Worth | 1.1 | 5.8 |
| -3.2 | -1.2 | 4.8 |  |  |  |  | -13.7 | -4.4 |
| 194.2 |  | 151.7 |  |  |  |  | 353.5 | 342.8 |
| (36) 66.6 | (13) | 21.7 |  |  |  | % Profit Before Taxes/Tangible Net Worth | (100) 173.3 | (76) 158.7 |
| 25.9 |  | 3.4 |  |  |  |  | 63.9 | 51.4 |
| 90.5 | 59.4 | 30.1 |  |  |  |  | 136.8 | 98.7 |
| 37.9 | 19.6 | 8.0 |  |  |  | % Profit Before Taxes/Total Assets | 59.9 | 38.9 |
| 5.2 | 5.1 | 1.3 |  |  |  |  | 21.1 | 12.6 |
| 162.5 | UND | 28.0 |  |  |  |  | 107.1 | 107.8 |
| 39.6 | 112.5 | 2.2 |  |  |  | Sales/Net Fixed Assets | 20.0 | 21.1 |
| 14.5 | 22.6 | .1 |  |  |  |  | 9.6 | 8.3 |
| 7.6 | 5.9 | 1.8 |  |  |  |  | 9.2 | 5.4 |
| 5.0 | 2.8 | .9 |  |  |  | Sales/Total Assets | 4.4 | 2.9 |
| 3.3 | .8 | .1 |  |  |  |  | 2.3 | 1.4 |
| .4 |  |  |  |  |  |  | .7 | .7 |
| (23) 1.1 |  |  |  |  |  | % Depr., Dep., Amort./Sales | (62) 1.7 | (40) 1.6 |
| 2.8 |  |  |  |  |  |  | 2.9 | 4.9 |
| 6.6 |  |  |  |  |  |  | 8.9 | 7.2 |
| (34) 13.4 |  |  |  |  |  | % Officers', Directors' Owners' Comp/Sales | (81) 12.5 | (66) 13.3 |
| 19.4 |  |  |  |  |  |  | 19.5 | 20.5 |
| 52246M | 37037M | 150586M | 28522M | 1360731M |  | Net Sales ($) | 643923M | 332053M |
| 10193M | 9317M | 66326M | 56391M | 216591M |  | Total Assets ($) | 301686M | 309999M |

© RMA 2024

M = $ thousand   MM = $ million
See Pages viii through xx for Explanation of Ratios and Data

# HEALTH CARE—Offices of Chiropractors  NAICS 621310

## Comparative Historical Data / Current Data Sorted by Sales

| Comparative Historical Data | | | | | Current Data Sorted by Sales | | | | | |
|---|---|---|---|---|---|---|---|---|---|---|
| | | 1 | 1 | Type of Statement | | 1 | | | | |
| | | | | Unqualified | | | | | | |
| 3 | 1 | 3 | | Reviewed | | | | 1 | 1 | |
| 40 | 51 | 32 | | Compiled | 1 | | | 1 | 1 | 1 |
| 57 | 67 | 44 | | Tax Returns | 23 | 4 | 2 | 1 | 1 | 1 |
| 4/1/21- | 4/1/22- | 4/1/23- | | Other | 20 | 16 | 5 | | | 2 |
| 3/31/22 | 3/31/23 | 3/31/24 | | | | 4 (4/1-9/30/23) | | 76 (10/1/23-3/31/24) | | |
| ALL | ALL | ALL | | | 0-1MM | 1-3MM | 3-5MM | 5-10MM | 10-25MM | 25MM & OVER |
| 100 | 120 | 80 | NUMBER OF STATEMENTS | 44 | 20 | 7 | 4 | 2 | 3 |
| % | % | % | **ASSETS** | % | % | % | % | % | % |
| 47.4 | 45.0 | 37.2 | Cash & Equivalents | 35.6 | 40.0 | | | | |
| 3.7 | 3.2 | 5.1 | Trade Receivables (net) | 2.1 | 8.1 | | | | |
| .4 | 1.0 | 1.6 | Inventory | 2.3 | .9 | | | | |
| 2.6 | 3.5 | 3.2 | All Other Current | 4.8 | 1.7 | | | | |
| 54.1 | 52.6 | 47.2 | Total Current | 44.8 | 50.8 | | | | |
| 26.0 | 24.0 | 26.8 | Fixed Assets (net) | 29.2 | 24.1 | | | | |
| 11.2 | 14.8 | 16.1 | Intangibles (net) | 17.6 | 13.9 | | | | |
| 8.8 | 8.6 | 10.0 | All Other Non-Current | 8.4 | 11.2 | | | | |
| 100.0 | 100.0 | 100.0 | Total | 100.0 | 100.0 | | | | |
| | | | **LIABILITIES** | | | | | | |
| 16.5 | 16.9 | 9.2 | Notes Payable-Short Term | 8.9 | 10.5 | | | | |
| 2.0 | 2.1 | 7.4 | Cur. Mat.-L.T.D. | 10.3 | 4.6 | | | | |
| 2.7 | .9 | .7 | Trade Payables | .2 | .3 | | | | |
| .0 | .0 | .0 | Income Taxes Payable | .0 | .0 | | | | |
| 14.4 | 14.1 | 11.3 | All Other Current | 7.7 | 21.0 | | | | |
| 35.5 | 34.0 | 28.6 | Total Current | 27.1 | 36.3 | | | | |
| 37.2 | 34.5 | 45.4 | Long-Term Debt | 53.5 | 28.7 | | | | |
| .0 | .1 | .0 | Deferred Taxes | .0 | .0 | | | | |
| 6.6 | 6.1 | 3.6 | All Other Non-Current | 6.1 | .0 | | | | |
| 20.7 | 25.2 | 22.4 | Net Worth | 13.3 | 35.0 | | | | |
| 100.0 | 100.0 | 100.0 | Total Liabilties & Net Worth | 100.0 | 100.0 | | | | |
| | | | **INCOME DATA** | | | | | | |
| 100.0 | 100.0 | 100.0 | Net Sales | 100.0 | 100.0 | | | | |
| | | | Gross Profit | | | | | | |
| 81.3 | 84.4 | 85.4 | Operating Expenses | 83.8 | 88.1 | | | | |
| 18.7 | 15.6 | 14.6 | Operating Profit | 16.2 | 11.9 | | | | |
| -1.1 | .0 | 2.9 | All Other Expenses (net) | 5.2 | -.1 | | | | |
| 19.8 | 15.5 | 11.8 | Profit Before Taxes | 10.9 | 11.9 | | | | |
| | | | **RATIOS** | | | | | | |
| 16.6 | 12.9 | 11.3 | | 16.4 | 6.4 | | | | |
| 2.5 | 2.7 | 2.6 | Current | 2.7 | 2.7 | | | | |
| .8 | .9 | .6 | | .5 | .7 | | | | |
| 14.1 | 11.5 | 7.6 | | 7.6 | 6.3 | | | | |
| 2.5 | 2.4 | 2.0 | Quick | 2.2 | 1.9 | | | | |
| .8 | .6 | .5 | | .3 | .7 | | | | |
| 0 UND | 0 UND | 0 UND | | 0 UND | 0 UND | | | | |
| 0 UND | 0 UND | 0 UND | Sales/Receivables | 0 UND | 0 UND | | | | |
| 0 UND | 0 UND | 0 UND | | 0 UND | 0 UND | | | | |
| | | | Cost of Sales/Inventory | | | | | | |
| | | | Cost of Sales/Payables | | | | | | |
| 4.3 | 6.2 | 6.0 | | 5.0 | 6.5 | | | | |
| 14.0 | 17.4 | 26.2 | Sales/Working Capital | 24.5 | 33.5 | | | | |
| -59.7 | -119.3 | -44.6 | | -14.6 | -64.3 | | | | |
| 49.7 | 38.3 | 44.6 | | 8.0 | 97.8 | | | | |
| (58) 18.7 | (63) 12.8 | (49) 6.7 | EBIT/Interest | (22) 3.6 | (16) 25.0 | | | | |
| 6.3 | 2.0 | .8 | | -.2 | 3.6 | | | | |
| | | | Net Profit + Depr., Dep., Amort./Cur. Mat. L/T/D | | | | | | |
| .2 | .0 | .1 | | .0 | .2 | | | | |
| .9 | .5 | .6 | Fixed/Worth | .7 | .7 | | | | |
| -2.1 | 8.3 | -19.6 | | -2.3 | NM | | | | |
| .6 | .4 | .2 | | .3 | .2 | | | | |
| 4.4 | 1.7 | 1.9 | Debt/Worth | 2.0 | 1.9 | | | | |
| -4.6 | -4.5 | -3.9 | | -2.0 | NM | | | | |
| 341.4 | 217.3 | 174.0 | % Profit Before Taxes/Tangible Net Worth | 194.2 | 137.5 | | | | |
| (70) 135.3 | (84) 102.9 | (55) 60.8 | | (28) 43.1 | (15) 66.1 | | | | |
| 75.3 | 36.2 | 17.7 | | 5.4 | 27.4 | | | | |
| 83.8 | 97.3 | 65.0 | % Profit Before Taxes/Total Assets | 63.9 | 79.4 | | | | |
| 52.5 | 41.6 | 24.7 | | 16.6 | 40.0 | | | | |
| 17.5 | 10.1 | 4.0 | | -.8 | 18.6 | | | | |
| 83.7 | 184.4 | 163.7 | Sales/Net Fixed Assets | 206.8 | 149.2 | | | | |
| 21.2 | 28.0 | 31.6 | | 36.6 | 34.9 | | | | |
| 7.0 | 8.9 | 10.1 | | 8.0 | 13.2 | | | | |
| 4.7 | 6.0 | 6.5 | Sales/Total Assets | 5.7 | 7.5 | | | | |
| 2.7 | 3.6 | 3.9 | | 3.4 | 4.9 | | | | |
| 1.5 | 1.9 | 1.9 | | 1.6 | 2.8 | | | | |
| 1.0 | .5 | .5 | % Depr., Dep., Amort./Sales | 1.1 | .2 | | | | |
| (31) 1.9 | (45) 1.2 | (32) 1.5 | | (14) 2.7 | (13) .5 | | | | |
| 4.7 | 3.3 | 3.2 | | 7.4 | 2.9 | | | | |
| 7.4 | 6.9 | 6.2 | % Officers', Directors' Owners' Comp/Sales | 7.6 | 4.2 | | | | |
| (56) 12.6 | (70) 11.8 | (45) 13.3 | | (24) 16.2 | (12) 7.3 | | | | |
| 18.5 | 18.8 | 20.1 | | 21.9 | 13.5 | | | | |
| 130655M | 422548M | 1629122M | Net Sales ($) | 22026M | 34826M | 25557M | 30184M | 23077M | 1493452M |
| 67370M | 325684M | 358818M | Total Assets ($) | 26960M | 19751M | 13783M | 8043M | 7528M | 282753M |

© RMA 2024    M = $ thousand    MM = $ million
See Pages viii through xx for Explanation of Ratios and Data

# HEALTH CARE—Offices of Optometrists NAICS 621320

## Current Data Sorted by Assets | Comparative Historical Data

| | 0-500M | 500M-2MM | 2-10MM | 10-50MM | 50-100MM | 100-250MM | | 4/1/19-3/31/20 ALL | 4/1/20-3/31/21 ALL |
|---|---|---|---|---|---|---|---|---|---|
| **Type of Statement** | | | | | | | | | |
| Unqualified | | | 2 | 1 | | 1 | | 3 | 2 |
| Reviewed | 1 | 1 | 1 | 2 | | | | 1 | 1 |
| Compiled | 24 | 3 | 1 | 1 | | | | 15 | 3 |
| Tax Returns | 24 | 24 | 6 | | | 1 | | 68 | 50 |
| Other | 32 | 40 | 20 | 4 | 2 | 2 | | 131 | 115 |
| | | 11 (4/1-9/30/23) | | 157 (10/1/23-3/31/24) | | | NUMBER OF STATEMENTS | | |
| | 57 | 68 | 29 | 8 | 2 | 4 | | 218 | 171 |
| | % | % | % | % | % | % | **ASSETS** | % | % |
| | 37.2 | 30.2 | 18.2 | | | | Cash & Equivalents | 26.0 | 39.7 |
| | 2.7 | 4.2 | 3.2 | | | | Trade Receivables (net) | 6.0 | 5.5 |
| | 12.6 | 6.8 | 5.7 | | | | Inventory | 10.8 | 7.8 |
| | 3.9 | 4.0 | 1.6 | | | | All Other Current | 2.0 | 2.0 |
| | 56.4 | 45.3 | 28.7 | | | | Total Current | 44.8 | 55.0 |
| | 23.9 | 32.2 | 41.2 | | | | Fixed Assets (net) | 35.6 | 25.6 |
| | 11.8 | 10.6 | 12.2 | | | | Intangibles (net) | 10.0 | 12.7 |
| | 8.0 | 11.9 | 17.9 | | | | All Other Non-Current | 9.6 | 6.7 |
| | 100.0 | 100.0 | 100.0 | | | | Total | 100.0 | 100.0 |
| | | | | | | | **LIABILITIES** | | |
| | 17.5 | 6.9 | 4.8 | | | | Notes Payable-Short Term | 10.3 | 12.7 |
| | 9.2 | 3.9 | 6.2 | | | | Cur. Mat.-L.T.D. | 6.1 | 5.8 |
| | 4.1 | 2.1 | .8 | | | | Trade Payables | 3.1 | 3.9 |
| | .1 | .1 | .0 | | | | Income Taxes Payable | .1 | .0 |
| | 18.6 | 11.5 | 10.0 | | | | All Other Current | 17.0 | 15.5 |
| | 49.4 | 24.5 | 21.8 | | | | Total Current | 36.6 | 37.9 |
| | 69.2 | 35.4 | 43.7 | | | | Long-Term Debt | 35.6 | 38.8 |
| | .0 | .0 | .0 | | | | Deferred Taxes | .1 | .0 |
| | 3.1 | 1.6 | 7.9 | | | | All Other Non-Current | 5.5 | 5.8 |
| | -21.5 | 38.5 | 26.5 | | | | Net Worth | 22.3 | 17.5 |
| | 100.0 | 100.0 | 100.0 | | | | Total Liabilities & Net Worth | 100.0 | 100.0 |
| | | | | | | | **INCOME DATA** | | |
| | 100.0 | 100.0 | 100.0 | | | | Net Sales | 100.0 | 100.0 |
| | | | | | | | Gross Profit | | |
| | 91.8 | 84.8 | 83.4 | | | | Operating Expenses | 86.2 | 90.2 |
| | 8.2 | 15.2 | 16.6 | | | | Operating Profit | 13.8 | 9.8 |
| | .6 | 2.5 | 3.8 | | | | All Other Expenses (net) | 1.7 | -1.8 |
| | 7.7 | 12.6 | 12.7 | | | | Profit Before Taxes | 12.2 | 11.6 |
| | | | | | | | **RATIOS** | | |
| | 6.9 | 6.5 | 3.4 | | | | | 3.7 | 3.7 |
| | 2.3 | 2.4 | 1.4 | | | | Current | 1.6 | 1.9 |
| | .8 | .9 | .6 | | | | | .6 | 1.0 |
| | 4.3 | 5.1 | 1.9 | | | | | 2.9 | 3.4 |
| | 1.8 | 1.5 | 1.0 | | | | Quick | (217) 1.0 | 1.5 |
| | .3 | .5 | .4 | | | | | .4 | .7 |
| | 0 UND | 0 UND | 0 UND | | | | | 0 UND | 0 UND |
| | 0 UND | 0 UND | 0 UND | | | | Sales/Receivables | 0 UND | 0 UND |
| | 0 UND | 0 UND | 1 330.3 | | | | | 4 83.1 | 9 41.8 |
| | | | | | | | Cost of Sales/Inventory | | |
| | | | | | | | Cost of Sales/Payables | | |
| | 8.2 | 6.5 | 10.4 | | | | | 11.1 | 5.6 |
| | 18.3 | 13.2 | 31.2 | | | | Sales/Working Capital | 51.2 | 13.2 |
| | -57.4 | -54.4 | -28.4 | | | | | -40.7 | 999.8 |
| | 35.0 | 32.2 | 24.2 | | | | | 35.6 | 39.7 |
| (43) | 11.6 | (46) 8.7 | (20) 9.2 | | | | EBIT/Interest | (174) 12.7 | (123) 12.6 |
| | 3.9 | 2.6 | 1.4 | | | | | 3.6 | 3.2 |
| | | | | | | | Net Profit + Depr., Dep., Amort./Cur. Mat. L/T/D | | |
| | .1 | .2 | .4 | | | | | .2 | .2 |
| | 1.2 | 1.0 | 1.1 | | | | Fixed/Worth | 1.6 | 1.5 |
| | -.4 | 5.1 | -6.5 | | | | | -3.4 | -1.5 |
| | .8 | .6 | .8 | | | | | .6 | 1.1 |
| | -11.7 | 1.7 | 3.6 | | | | Debt/Worth | 3.3 | 4.8 |
| | -2.0 | 23.1 | -7.2 | | | | | -5.6 | -5.0 |
| | 179.1 | 151.8 | 88.0 | | | | % Profit Before Taxes/Tangible Net Worth | 255.1 | 171.0 |
| (27) | 84.4 | (53) 77.3 | (19) 50.2 | | | | | (143) 113.5 | (106) 76.6 |
| | 52.5 | 39.6 | 24.6 | | | | | 45.5 | 26.2 |
| | 79.7 | 55.5 | 25.9 | | | | % Profit Before Taxes/Total Assets | 78.4 | 59.0 |
| | 36.1 | 26.2 | 11.5 | | | | | 35.4 | 19.7 |
| | 4.2 | 5.4 | 3.6 | | | | | 11.5 | 3.5 |
| | 421.1 | 72.5 | 85.2 | | | | | 92.8 | 70.4 |
| | 30.3 | 17.3 | 13.9 | | | | Sales/Net Fixed Assets | 20.0 | 20.3 |
| | 12.2 | 6.0 | .7 | | | | | 8.5 | 7.7 |
| | 7.7 | 4.7 | 6.6 | | | | | 9.1 | 5.4 |
| | 4.3 | 3.2 | 1.3 | | | | Sales/Total Assets | 4.7 | 3.0 |
| | 2.7 | 1.8 | .6 | | | | | 2.7 | 1.8 |
| | .7 | .5 | 1.0 | | | | | 1.1 | 1.0 |
| (19) | 1.8 | (30) 2.3 | (13) 1.7 | | | | % Depr., Dep., Amort./Sales | (106) 2.0 | (83) 2.5 |
| | 3.5 | 6.4 | 14.9 | | | | | 3.6 | 5.1 |
| | 5.9 | 4.1 | 7.2 | | | | | 6.0 | 6.8 |
| (40) | 10.6 | (38) 8.9 | (13) 11.1 | | | | % Officers', Directors' Owners' Comp/Sales | (126) 10.6 | (88) 11.0 |
| | 14.0 | 13.8 | 18.6 | | | | | 15.9 | 20.3 |
| | 89750M | 332902M | 410865M | 312794M | 109585M | 1776568M | Net Sales ($) | 1917603M | 1764229M |
| | 15391M | 72866M | 113975M | 251991M | 135457M | 750576M | Total Assets ($) | 778817M | 1131658M |

© RMA 2024

M = $ thousand    MM = $ million
See Pages viii through xx for Explanation of Ratios and Data

# HEALTH CARE—Offices of Optometrists  NAICS 621320

## Comparative Historical Data | Current Data Sorted by Sales

| Comparative Historical Data | | | Type of Statement | Current Data Sorted by Sales | | | | | |
|---|---|---|---|---|---|---|---|---|---|
| 1 | 4 | 4 | Unqualified | | 1 | | 2 | | 1 |
|  | 5 | 3 | Reviewed | | | | | | 3 |
| 6 | 7 | 6 | Compiled | | 1 | 1 | 1 | 1 | 2 |
| 66 | 58 | 55 | Tax Returns | 10 | 27 | 4 | 5 | 6 | 3 |
| 96 | 120 | 100 | Other | 23 | 39 | 10 | 9 | 9 | 10 |
| 4/1/21- | 4/1/22- | 4/1/23- | | 11 (4/1-9/30/23) | | | 157 (10/1/23-3/31/24) | | |
| 3/31/22 | 3/31/23 | 3/31/24 | | 0-1MM | 1-3MM | 3-5MM | 5-10MM | 10-25MM | 25MM & OVER |
| ALL | ALL | ALL | | | | | | | |
| 169 | 194 | 168 | NUMBER OF STATEMENTS | 33 | 68 | 15 | 17 | 16 | 19 |
| % | % | % | ASSETS | % | % | % | % | % | % |
| 38.0 | 33.9 | 28.7 | Cash & Equivalents | 23.8 | 30.4 | 33.1 | 34.7 | 29.6 | 21.9 |
| 4.1 | 3.9 | 3.7 | Trade Receivables (net) | 2.3 | 2.7 | 5.9 | 8.9 | 1.1 | 5.3 |
| 9.6 | 9.0 | 8.3 | Inventory | 9.1 | 8.2 | 4.5 | 16.0 | 7.5 | 3.9 |
| 2.7 | 2.2 | 3.7 | All Other Current | 1.8 | 6.2 | .0 | 2.0 | 2.6 | 3.2 |
| 54.4 | 49.0 | 44.4 | Total Current | 37.0 | 47.4 | 43.6 | 61.6 | 40.9 | 34.4 |
| 23.0 | 30.0 | 31.5 | Fixed Assets (net) | 46.0 | 28.8 | 32.9 | 17.0 | 33.0 | 26.6 |
| 14.8 | 13.5 | 12.3 | Intangibles (net) | 5.4 | 13.7 | 15.2 | 10.1 | 6.5 | 23.8 |
| 7.8 | 7.5 | 11.8 | All Other Non-Current | 11.8 | 10.1 | 8.2 | 11.2 | 19.5 | 15.2 |
| 100.0 | 100.0 | 100.0 | Total | 100.0 | 100.0 | 100.0 | 100.0 | 100.0 | 100.0 |
| | | | LIABILITIES | | | | | | |
| 8.5 | 11.4 | 9.8 | Notes Payable-Short Term | 19.5 | 6.0 | 11.6 | 8.0 | 12.9 | 4.0 |
| 2.4 | 3.1 | 6.1 | Cur. Mat.-L.T.D. | 6.5 | 5.5 | 3.5 | 9.7 | 7.2 | 6.1 |
| 3.4 | 2.4 | 3.0 | Trade Payables | 4.8 | 2.7 | 1.4 | 1.2 | .5 | 6.3 |
| .0 | .0 | .1 | Income Taxes Payable | .1 | .1 | .1 | .0 | .0 | .0 |
| 11.4 | 13.0 | 13.3 | All Other Current | 6.6 | 9.7 | 15.8 | 18.4 | 25.7 | 21.2 |
| 25.7 | 29.8 | 32.4 | Total Current | 37.5 | 24.0 | 32.4 | 37.2 | 46.2 | 37.7 |
| 38.4 | 43.2 | 47.8 | Long-Term Debt | 82.7 | 45.1 | 53.5 | 38.9 | 26.8 | 17.8 |
| .0 | .0 | .0 | Deferred Taxes | .0 | .0 | .0 | .0 | .0 | .0 |
| 3.9 | 3.6 | 4.3 | All Other Non-Current | .2 | 5.5 | .1 | .1 | .5 | 17.8 |
| 32.0 | 23.4 | 15.6 | Net Worth | -20.3 | 25.5 | 14.0 | 23.8 | 26.5 | 26.8 |
| 100.0 | 100.0 | 100.0 | Total Liabilities & Net Worth | 100.0 | 100.0 | 100.0 | 100.0 | 100.0 | 100.0 |
| | | | INCOME DATA | | | | | | |
| 100.0 | 100.0 | 100.0 | Net Sales | 100.0 | 100.0 | 100.0 | 100.0 | 100.0 | 100.0 |
| 88.4 | 87.9 | 88.0 | Gross Profit | | | | | | |
| 11.6 | 12.1 | 12.0 | Operating Expenses | 83.5 | 87.2 | 88.5 | 85.9 | 89.5 | 98.9 |
| -2.1 | 1.2 | 2.2 | Operating Profit | 16.5 | 12.8 | 11.5 | 14.1 | 10.5 | 1.1 |
| 13.7 | 11.0 | 9.8 | All Other Expenses (net) | 5.5 | 1.9 | 1.1 | 2.3 | -1.0 | .8 |
| | | | Profit Before Taxes | 10.9 | 11.0 | 10.4 | 11.7 | 11.6 | .3 |
| | | | RATIOS | | | | | | |
| 8.0 | 6.0 | 5.6 | | 4.5 | 6.2 | 11.4 | 9.1 | 2.6 | 1.2 |
| 3.3 | 2.3 | 2.0 | Current | 2.1 | 2.5 | 2.0 | 2.5 | 1.1 | .7 |
| 1.2 | .9 | .7 | | .7 | .9 | .4 | .8 | .7 | .6 |
| 5.7 | 4.9 | 3.6 | | 3.1 | 4.5 | 8.6 | 8.5 | 1.7 | 1.0 |
| 1.9 | 1.4 | 1.1 | Quick | 1.6 | 1.9 | 2.0 | 1.7 | .9 | .6 |
| .9 | .6 | .4 | | .3 | .5 | .4 | .4 | .2 | .3 |
| 0 UND | 0 UND | 0 UND | | 0 UND | 0 UND | 0 UND | 0 UND | 0 UND | 0 UND |
| 0 UND | 0 UND | 0 UND | Sales/Receivables | 0 UND | 0 UND | 0 UND | 1 274.1 | 0 UND | 1 386.5 |
| 1 277.0 | 0 973.3 | 2 190.2 | | 0 UND | 0 UND | 26 14.1 | 20 18.0 | 0 UND | 25 14.5 |
| | | | Cost of Sales/Inventory | | | | | | |
| | | | Cost of Sales/Payables | | | | | | |
| 5.1 | 7.4 | 7.4 | | 5.4 | 6.5 | 6.5 | 7.3 | 24.6 | 89.4 |
| 10.8 | 18.5 | 20.3 | Sales/Working Capital | 11.3 | 11.7 | 39.5 | 11.5 | 431.5 | -26.3 |
| 104.6 | -818.6 | -30.5 | | -16.5 | NM | -25.9 | -523.7 | -35.4 | -16.8 |
| 61.5 | 36.0 | 28.1 | | 17.8 | 32.2 | 21.5 | 30.3 | | 26.7 |
| (116) 16.3 | (126) 8.6 | (119) 9.2 | EBIT/Interest | (21) 6.3 | (50) 8.7 | (13) 10.8 | (11) 15.7 | (16) 1.9 |
| 4.7 | -.3 | 2.0 | | .4 | 3.2 | 2.8 | 2.6 | | -.5 |
| | | | Net Profit + Depr., Dep., Amort./Cur. Mat. L/T/D | | | | | | |
| .1 | .2 | .2 | | .2 | .2 | .8 | .1 | .1 | .5 |
| .8 | 1.1 | 1.2 | Fixed/Worth | 1.9 | 1.0 | 2.2 | .4 | .9 | 9.8 |
| -2.8 | -1.7 | -2.0 | | -6.5 | -4.0 | -.3 | -1.5 | 2.5 | -.5 |
| .4 | .6 | .7 | | .9 | .6 | 1.1 | .2 | .5 | 2.6 |
| 2.2 | 3.0 | 4.0 | Debt/Worth | 7.0 | 2.7 | 3.6 | 1.3 | 2.6 | 37.8 |
| -6.2 | -4.2 | -4.2 | | -5.5 | -5.6 | -2.8 | -3.9 | -6.8 | -3.0 |
| 137.7 | 151.4 | 151.0 | | 175.5 | 126.0 | | 108.2 | 889.7 | 167.6 |
| (115) 72.3 | (131) 62.4 | (107) 71.9 | % Profit Before Taxes/Tangible Net Worth | (21) 80.4 | (45) 69.0 | (11) 66.0 | (11) 151.0 | (11) 64.6 |
| 25.7 | 15.0 | 33.4 | | 26.1 | 25.1 | | 28.2 | 83.5 | 33.4 |
| 64.9 | 58.0 | 56.1 | | 43.0 | 45.0 | 60.6 | 94.1 | 137.0 | 29.9 |
| 31.2 | 17.1 | 19.8 | % Profit Before Taxes/Total Assets | 8.7 | 19.4 | 24.8 | 38.2 | 63.8 | 3.5 |
| 6.8 | -.1 | 3.2 | | -5.1 | 5.7 | 11.5 | 16.8 | 6.7 | -4.7 |
| 99.4 | 128.7 | 79.5 | | 36.1 | 72.9 | 110.0 | 187.5 | UND | 101.8 |
| 25.0 | 25.2 | 18.1 | Sales/Net Fixed Assets | 7.4 | 22.7 | 10.7 | 30.7 | 25.6 | 12.3 |
| 8.9 | 5.9 | 5.7 | | .6 | 6.7 | 5.9 | 15.9 | 10.4 | 5.9 |
| 5.1 | 6.3 | 6.1 | | 4.1 | 4.9 | 4.3 | 6.6 | 13.7 | 8.2 |
| 2.9 | 3.1 | 3.2 | Sales/Total Assets | 1.9 | 3.1 | 3.5 | 4.1 | 7.9 | 3.3 |
| 1.7 | 1.9 | 1.5 | | .4 | 1.8 | 1.5 | 2.6 | 4.9 | 1.0 |
| .9 | .6 | .8 | | .8 | .7 | | | | 1.1 |
| (67) 1.6 | (79) 2.0 | (72) 2.2 | % Depr., Dep., Amort./Sales | (14) 5.3 | (25) 3.0 | | | (11) 1.7 |
| 3.3 | 4.6 | 6.0 | | 17.5 | 6.3 | | | | 4.0 |
| 6.5 | 6.0 | 5.4 | | 10.1 | 5.1 | 4.7 | | 3.3 | |
| (102) 11.6 | (108) 10.0 | (94) 10.1 | % Officers', Directors' Owners' Comp/Sales | (15) 11.5 | (46) 8.4 | (10) 8.8 | (10) 8.6 | |
| 17.7 | 16.0 | 14.2 | | 16.4 | 11.3 | 17.7 | | 24.8 | |
| 1726765M | 2055772M | 3032464M | Net Sales ($) | 16207M | 127286M | 57181M | 107848M | 237461M | 2486481M |
| 1031768M | 1469442M | 1340256M | Total Assets ($) | 20867M | 70383M | 24315M | 66192M | 87622M | 1070877M |

© RMA 2024

M = $ thousand    MM = $ million
See Pages viii through xx for Explanation of Ratios and Data

# HEALTH CARE—Offices of Mental Health Practitioners (except Physicians) NAICS 621330

## Current Data Sorted by Assets | Comparative Historical Data

| | | | | | | | Type of Statement | | |
|---|---|---|---|---|---|---|---|---|---|
| | | 3 | 3 | 1 | | | Unqualified | 12 | 7 |
| | | 1 | 1 | | | | Reviewed | | |
| 14 | 6 | | | 1 | | | Compiled | 1 | 1 |
| 11 | 12 | 11 | 8 | 2 | 2 | | Tax Returns | 17 | 12 |
| | | 13 (4/1-9/30/23) | | 63 (10/1/23-3/31/24) | | | Other | 41 | 36 |
| 0-500M | 500M-2MM | 2-10MM | 10-50MM | 50-100MM | 100-250MM | | | 4/1/19-3/31/20 ALL | 4/1/20-3/31/21 ALL |
| 25 | 18 | 15 | 12 | 4 | 2 | NUMBER OF STATEMENTS | | 71 | 56 |
| % | % | % | % | % | % | ASSETS | | % | % |
| 62.4 | 22.9 | 32.6 | 24.6 | | | Cash & Equivalents | | 37.1 | 58.6 |
| 4.7 | .9 | 18.7 | 7.2 | | | Trade Receivables (net) | | 13.1 | 9.6 |
| .0 | .0 | .0 | 2.2 | | | Inventory | | .1 | .8 |
| 1.0 | 13.2 | 3.4 | 6.1 | | | All Other Current | | 3.3 | 1.3 |
| 68.2 | 37.0 | 54.7 | 40.1 | | | Total Current | | 53.6 | 70.3 |
| 15.4 | 41.3 | 23.6 | 46.5 | | | Fixed Assets (net) | | 29.6 | 19.5 |
| 9.5 | 8.1 | 2.2 | .4 | | | Intangibles (net) | | 4.4 | 7.4 |
| 7.0 | 13.6 | 19.4 | 13.0 | | | All Other Non-Current | | 12.4 | 2.8 |
| 100.0 | 100.0 | 100.0 | 100.0 | | | Total | | 100.0 | 100.0 |
| | | | | | | LIABILITIES | | | |
| 18.9 | 10.7 | 4.9 | .8 | | | Notes Payable-Short Term | | 8.5 | 10.0 |
| 2.0 | 3.2 | 1.4 | 5.0 | | | Cur. Mat.-L.T.D. | | 4.0 | 19.7 |
| 9.3 | .2 | .7 | 3.3 | | | Trade Payables | | 2.9 | 3.9 |
| .0 | .0 | .1 | .8 | | | Income Taxes Payable | | .1 | .2 |
| 31.8 | 11.5 | 7.8 | 14.3 | | | All Other Current | | 11.1 | 14.2 |
| 62.0 | 25.6 | 15.0 | 24.3 | | | Total Current | | 26.7 | 48.0 |
| 24.2 | 35.1 | 23.3 | 26.8 | | | Long-Term Debt | | 18.1 | 25.6 |
| .0 | .0 | .0 | .0 | | | Deferred Taxes | | .1 | .0 |
| 11.3 | .3 | 12.2 | 1.2 | | | All Other Non-Current | | 12.8 | 14.1 |
| 2.5 | 39.0 | 49.6 | 47.6 | | | Net Worth | | 42.3 | 12.3 |
| 100.0 | 100.0 | 100.0 | 100.0 | | | Total Liabilities & Net Worth | | 100.0 | 100.0 |
| | | | | | | INCOME DATA | | | |
| 100.0 | 100.0 | 100.0 | 100.0 | | | Net Sales | | 100.0 | 100.0 |
| | | | | | | Gross Profit | | | |
| 91.8 | 83.6 | 90.6 | 90.7 | | | Operating Expenses | | 88.8 | 88.6 |
| 8.2 | 16.4 | 9.4 | 9.3 | | | Operating Profit | | 11.2 | 11.4 |
| 1.1 | 2.6 | 3.6 | .6 | | | All Other Expenses (net) | | 1.4 | -.4 |
| 7.1 | 13.8 | 5.8 | 8.7 | | | Profit Before Taxes | | 9.7 | 11.8 |
| | | | | | | RATIOS | | | |
| 12.4 | 10.5 | 11.1 | 3.4 | | | | | 6.8 | 8.3 |
| 2.6 | 2.0 | 4.2 | 1.6 | | | Current | | 2.4 | 3.1 |
| .4 | .3 | 1.7 | 1.0 | | | | | 1.3 | 1.3 |
| 12.4 | 4.8 | 11.1 | 3.3 | | | | | 5.7 | 8.3 |
| 2.6 | 1.1 | 3.5 | 1.3 | | | Quick | | 2.3 | 3.0 |
| .4 | .2 | 1.5 | .7 | | | | | 1.3 | 1.2 |
| 0 UND | 0 UND | 0 UND | 4 102.9 | | | | | 0 UND | 0 UND |
| 0 UND | 0 UND | 36 10.0 | 11 32.6 | | | Sales/Receivables | | 2 241.7 | 0 UND |
| 0 UND | 0 UND | 52 7.0 | 32 11.3 | | | | | 39 9.3 | 31 11.7 |
| | | | | | | Cost of Sales/Inventory | | | |
| | | | | | | Cost of Sales/Payables | | | |
| 10.5 | 9.1 | 2.4 | 7.9 | | | | | 6.9 | 3.4 |
| 32.2 | 34.8 | 5.6 | 16.4 | | | Sales/Working Capital | | 15.4 | 8.5 |
| -81.9 | -17.1 | 146.7 | NM | | | | | 85.4 | 40.0 |
| 34.0 | | | 20.2 | | | | | 44.0 | 46.7 |
| (13) 8.2 | | | 7.4 | | | EBIT/Interest | (52) | 7.1 | (32) 5.6 |
| -16.1 | | | .7 | | | | | 2.1 | 1.0 |
| | | | | | | Net Profit + Depr., Dep., Amort./Cur. Mat. L/T/D | | | |
| .0 | .1 | .0 | .5 | | | | | .1 | .0 |
| .0 | 2.0 | .6 | 1.0 | | | Fixed/Worth | | .4 | .4 |
| -1.4 | -4.0 | -64.8 | 2.2 | | | | | 1.0 | 1.6 |
| .3 | .0 | .2 | .2 | | | | | .3 | .4 |
| .8 | 2.5 | 1.0 | .8 | | | Debt/Worth | | .8 | .9 |
| -2.7 | -6.2 | -69.6 | 2.5 | | | | | 3.0 | -8.3 |
| 242.5 | 93.0 | 33.2 | 56.3 | | | | | 134.4 | 137.6 |
| (16) 167.2 | (11) 44.9 | (11) 17.7 | (10) 8.2 | | | % Profit Before Taxes/Tangible Net Worth | (63) | 33.8 | (40) 39.9 |
| 35.1 | 17.8 | 7.1 | -12.6 | | | | | 7.3 | 6.9 |
| 154.7 | 47.5 | 17.1 | 36.9 | | | | | 79.2 | 79.1 |
| 53.7 | 22.8 | 8.1 | 7.9 | | | % Profit Before Taxes/Total Assets | | 21.5 | 28.2 |
| -31.0 | 7.2 | 3.8 | -.3 | | | | | 3.4 | 1.2 |
| UND | 59.6 | 134.8 | 6.4 | | | | | 299.5 | UND |
| 647.5 | 18.4 | 17.8 | 4.7 | | | Sales/Net Fixed Assets | | 27.3 | 73.1 |
| 73.1 | 3.7 | 4.8 | 1.8 | | | | | 4.0 | 6.8 |
| 21.4 | 4.9 | 3.1 | 2.6 | | | | | 5.9 | 7.5 |
| 11.3 | 3.3 | 2.4 | 1.7 | | | Sales/Total Assets | | 3.1 | 3.1 |
| 4.2 | 1.0 | 1.4 | 1.1 | | | | | 1.6 | 1.6 |
| | | .2 | 1.4 | | | | | .9 | .9 |
| | (10) 1.2 | (11) 2.4 | | | | % Depr., Dep., Amort./Sales | (39) | 1.6 | (24) 1.4 |
| | | 9.5 | 3.0 | | | | | 2.6 | 2.8 |
| 5.5 | | | | | | | | 5.9 | 4.8 |
| (13) 8.6 | | | | | | % Officers', Directors' Owners' Comp/Sales | (27) | 8.4 | (21) 8.1 |
| 15.3 | | | | | | | | 13.2 | 16.0 |
| 67901M | 55308M | 197336M | 527068M | 359134M | 385585M | Net Sales ($) | | 1679206M | 642980M |
| 4463M | 17025M | 76561M | 276260M | 223512M | 318472M | Total Assets ($) | | 869323M | 650049M |

© RMA 2024

M = $ thousand    MM = $ million
See Pages viii through xx for Explanation of Ratios and Data

# HEALTH CARE—Offices of Mental Health Practitioners (except Physicians) NAICS 621330

## Comparative Historical Data | Current Data Sorted by Sales

| Comparative Historical Data ||| Type of Statement | Current Data Sorted by Sales ||||||
|---|---|---|---|---|---|---|---|---|---|
| 5 | 7 | 7 | Unqualified | | | 1 | 1 | 3 | 2 |
| | | | Reviewed | | | | | 1 | 1 |
| 1 | 2 | 2 | Compiled | | | | | 1 | 1 |
| 19 | 22 | 21 | Tax Returns | 6 | 6 | 5 | 2 | 1 | 1 |
| 43 | 53 | 46 | Other | 12 | 6 | 3 | 6 | 7 | 12 |
| 4/1/21- | 4/1/22- | 4/1/23- | | 13 (4/1-9/30/23) ||| 63 (10/1/23-3/31/24) |||
| 3/31/22 | 3/31/23 | 3/31/24 | | | | | | | |
| ALL | ALL | ALL | | 0-1MM | 1-3MM | 3-5MM | 5-10MM | 10-25MM | 25MM & OVER |
| 68 | 84 | 76 | NUMBER OF STATEMENTS | 18 | 12 | 9 | 9 | 12 | 16 |
| % | % | % | **ASSETS** | % | % | % | % | % | % |
| 49.9 | 45.9 | 37.8 | Cash & Equivalents | 43.8 | 53.2 | | | 32.3 | 25.1 |
| 8.6 | 8.9 | 7.3 | Trade Receivables (net) | 1.3 | 9.7 | | | 15.2 | 10.7 |
| .2 | .2 | .4 | Inventory | .0 | .0 | | | .3 | 1.6 |
| 4.4 | 5.4 | 5.3 | All Other Current | 1.7 | 4.2 | | | 3.2 | 5.7 |
| 63.1 | 60.4 | 50.8 | Total Current | 46.8 | 67.1 | | | 51.0 | 43.1 |
| 21.9 | 20.9 | 29.8 | Fixed Assets (net) | 36.0 | 23.3 | | | 25.0 | 34.1 |
| 5.7 | 4.9 | 6.8 | Intangibles (net) | 7.7 | 4.7 | | | 11.9 | 7.3 |
| 9.3 | 13.7 | 12.6 | All Other Non-Current | 9.5 | 4.9 | | | 12.1 | 15.5 |
| 100.0 | 100.0 | 100.0 | Total | 100.0 | 100.0 | | | 100.0 | 100.0 |
| | | | **LIABILITIES** | | | | | | |
| 5.5 | 9.3 | 9.9 | Notes Payable-Short Term | 16.9 | 7.2 | | | 7.2 | 4.4 |
| 6.0 | 1.6 | 2.5 | Cur. Mat.-L.T.D. | 3.3 | .7 | | | .7 | 3.8 |
| 1.7 | 1.4 | 4.0 | Trade Payables | .2 | 19.3 | | | 1.0 | 3.4 |
| .1 | .1 | .2 | Income Taxes Payable | .0 | .0 | | | .0 | .7 |
| 14.5 | 11.3 | 17.7 | All Other Current | 13.9 | 45.8 | | | 10.7 | 15.1 |
| 27.8 | 23.7 | 34.3 | Total Current | 34.2 | 73.0 | | | 19.6 | 27.5 |
| 20.1 | 26.1 | 26.7 | Long-Term Debt | 36.5 | 17.1 | | | 20.5 | 24.3 |
| .1 | .0 | .0 | Deferred Taxes | .0 | .0 | | | .0 | .0 |
| 2.0 | 2.7 | 7.1 | All Other Non-Current | 16.3 | .1 | | | 6.0 | 4.5 |
| 49.8 | 47.5 | 31.9 | Net Worth | 13.0 | 9.8 | | | 53.9 | 43.7 |
| 100.0 | 100.0 | 100.0 | Total Liabilities & Net Worth | 100.0 | 100.0 | | | 100.0 | 100.0 |
| | | | **INCOME DATA** | | | | | | |
| 100.0 | 100.0 | 100.0 | Net Sales | 100.0 | 100.0 | | | 100.0 | 100.0 |
| | | | Gross Profit | | | | | | |
| 83.2 | 87.8 | 90.7 | Operating Expenses | 84.2 | 89.1 | | | 96.7 | 95.1 |
| 16.8 | 12.2 | 9.3 | Operating Profit | 15.8 | 10.9 | | | 3.3 | 4.9 |
| -.4 | 1.6 | 1.8 | All Other Expenses (net) | 6.0 | -.7 | | | .7 | 1.5 |
| 17.2 | 10.6 | 7.5 | Profit Before Taxes | 9.8 | 11.6 | | | 2.6 | 3.4 |
| | | | **RATIOS** | | | | | | |
| 7.4 | 9.8 | 8.1 | | 14.0 | 25.0 | | | 9.3 | 2.9 |
| 4.2 | 4.1 | 2.5 | Current | 2.1 | 2.6 | | | 3.5 | 1.6 |
| 1.5 | 1.3 | 1.0 | | .3 | .7 | | | 1.1 | 1.0 |
| 7.1 | 9.8 | 8.0 | | 13.9 | 11.2 | | | 9.3 | 2.9 |
| 3.4 | 3.6 | 2.0 | Quick | 1.3 | 2.6 | | | 3.0 | 1.3 |
| 1.4 | 1.2 | .6 | | .3 | .7 | | | .9 | .7 |
| 0 UND | 0 UND | 0 UND | | 0 UND | 0 UND | | | 0 UND | 1 369.1 |
| 0 UND | 0 UND | 0 UND | Sales/Receivables | 0 UND | 0 UND | | | 25 14.4 | 10 37.6 |
| 27 13.4 | 23 16.2 | 23 16.1 | | 0 UND | 1 306.7 | | | 43 8.4 | 36 10.0 |
| | | | Cost of Sales/Inventory | | | | | | |
| | | | Cost of Sales/Payables | | | | | | |
| 5.2 | 4.2 | 5.5 | | 3.6 | 13.0 | | | 3.2 | 7.9 |
| 9.8 | 12.9 | 20.2 | Sales/Working Capital | 21.2 | 23.6 | | | 7.2 | 14.9 |
| 58.0 | 52.1 | UND | | -11.5 | NM | | | 759.3 | NM |
| 59.5 | 37.5 | 24.4 | | | | | | | 12.2 |
| (38) 30.2 | (48) 11.9 | (44) 6.9 | EBIT/Interest | | | | | (12) 5.1 | |
| 8.3 | -.1 | -.7 | | | | | | | -.7 |
| | | | Net Profit + Depr., Dep., | | | | | | |
| | | | Amort./Cur. Mat. L/T/D | | | | | | |
| .0 | .0 | .0 | | .0 | .0 | | | .1 | .5 |
| .2 | .2 | .6 | Fixed/Worth | 3.2 | .1 | | | .8 | .7 |
| 1.3 | 1.4 | -8.2 | | -2.9 | 1.4 | | | NM | NM |
| .2 | .2 | .2 | | .2 | .2 | | | .2 | .3 |
| .9 | .8 | .8 | Debt/Worth | NM | .6 | | | .7 | 1.5 |
| 2.6 | 2.2 | -11.6 | | -3.0 | 2.1 | | | NM | NM |
| 181.7 | 152.0 | 116.1 | | | 286.1 | | | | 31.1 |
| (56) 75.3 | (69) 38.7 | (53) 22.8 | % Profit Before Taxes/Tangible Net Worth | (10) 194.4 | | | | (12) 1.8 | |
| 22.2 | 4.9 | 6.9 | | | 35.5 | | | | -28.6 |
| 96.7 | 72.9 | 47.8 | | 44.6 | 162.7 | | | 17.3 | 27.1 |
| 48.1 | 27.1 | 12.3 | % Profit Before Taxes/Total Assets | 5.6 | 56.8 | | | 12.7 | 3.7 |
| 16.6 | 1.5 | 1.1 | | -8.0 | 14.1 | | | 3.0 | -11.9 |
| 794.1 | 731.6 | 585.0 | | UND | UND | | | 331.9 | 48.0 |
| 57.2 | 47.7 | 26.8 | Sales/Net Fixed Assets | 59.9 | 187.1 | | | 15.9 | 6.0 |
| 7.8 | 10.1 | 4.4 | | .9 | 18.3 | | | 5.1 | 3.6 |
| 9.4 | 9.3 | 7.5 | | 7.4 | 14.7 | | | 4.4 | 3.2 |
| 3.8 | 3.9 | 2.9 | Sales/Total Assets | 2.0 | 9.8 | | | 2.2 | 2.0 |
| 1.5 | 1.9 | 1.6 | | .4 | 3.8 | | | 1.4 | 1.5 |
| .5 | .3 | .7 | | | | | | | .4 |
| (30) 1.4 | (33) 1.3 | (36) 2.4 | % Depr., Dep., Amort./Sales | | | | | (11) 1.9 | |
| 2.7 | 2.4 | 4.4 | | | | | | | 2.5 |
| 4.9 | 2.6 | 1.9 | | | | | | | |
| (27) 8.4 | (36) 6.1 | (27) 5.5 | % Officers', Directors' Owners' Comp/Sales | | | | | | |
| 21.2 | 15.2 | 9.6 | | | | | | | |
| 1690188M | 933476M | 1592332M | Net Sales ($) | 8246M | 22000M | 32971M | 59679M | 185217M | 1284219M |
| 655587M | 739301M | 916293M | Total Assets ($) | 10786M | 4408M | 11777M | 35970M | 87111M | 766241M |

© RMA 2024  M = $ thousand   MM = $ million
See Pages viii through xx for Explanation of Ratios and Data

# HEALTH CARE—Offices of Physical, Occupational and Speech Therapists, and Audiologists  NAICS 621340

## Current Data Sorted by Assets

| | | | | | | Type of Statement | | |
|---|---|---|---|---|---|---|---|---|
| | | 2 | 4 | 2 | | Unqualified | 7 | 3 |
| | | 1 | 1 | | | Reviewed | 5 | 1 |
| 2 | 3 | 2 | 4 | | | Compiled | 12 | 2 |
| 21 | 10 | 2 | 1 | 1 | | Tax Returns | 54 | 39 |
| 29 | 21 | 27 | 6 | 2 | 3 | Other | 100 | 80 |
| | 11 (4/1-9/30/23) | | 133 (10/1/23-3/31/24) | | | | 4/1/19-3/31/20 | 4/1/20-3/31/21 |
| 0-500M | 500M-2MM | 2-10MM | 10-50MM | 50-100MM | 100-250MM | | ALL | ALL |
| 52 | 34 | 33 | 16 | 6 | 3 | NUMBER OF STATEMENTS | 178 | 125 |
| % | % | % | % | % | % | **ASSETS** | % | % |
| 50.8 | 36.5 | 19.0 | 22.7 | | | Cash & Equivalents | 36.3 | 50.7 |
| 6.1 | 9.9 | 26.0 | 31.8 | | | Trade Receivables (net) | 17.2 | 15.9 |
| .1 | .0 | .0 | .1 | | | Inventory | .3 | .3 |
| 3.1 | 4.6 | 7.2 | 2.5 | | | All Other Current | 3.4 | 1.9 |
| 60.1 | 51.0 | 52.3 | 57.0 | | | Total Current | 57.2 | 68.8 |
| 18.4 | 29.7 | 26.1 | 23.6 | | | Fixed Assets (net) | 24.8 | 19.5 |
| 8.2 | 10.1 | 11.5 | 7.6 | | | Intangibles (net) | 7.9 | 5.7 |
| 13.2 | 9.2 | 10.1 | 11.7 | | | All Other Non-Current | 10.2 | 6.0 |
| 100.0 | 100.0 | 100.0 | 100.0 | | | Total | 100.0 | 100.0 |
| | | | | | | **LIABILITIES** | | |
| 31.1 | 8.7 | 4.0 | 4.8 | | | Notes Payable-Short Term | 17.9 | 15.1 |
| 3.8 | 2.3 | 1.5 | 2.9 | | | Cur. Mat.-L.T.D. | 3.4 | 3.5 |
| 2.2 | 1.0 | 1.2 | 2.9 | | | Trade Payables | 2.0 | 6.4 |
| 1.0 | .3 | .0 | .0 | | | Income Taxes Payable | .0 | .1 |
| 21.4 | 7.2 | 22.1 | 11.5 | | | All Other Current | 16.4 | 18.0 |
| 59.4 | 19.5 | 28.7 | 22.1 | | | Total Current | 39.8 | 43.2 |
| 37.4 | 27.2 | 29.8 | 13.6 | | | Long-Term Debt | 20.0 | 33.3 |
| .0 | .0 | .0 | .0 | | | Deferred Taxes | .1 | .0 |
| 1.5 | 3.2 | 4.6 | 6.2 | | | All Other Non-Current | 10.3 | 4.9 |
| 1.7 | 50.1 | 36.9 | 58.1 | | | Net Worth | 29.8 | 18.7 |
| 100.0 | 100.0 | 100.0 | 100.0 | | | Total Liabilities & Net Worth | 100.0 | 100.0 |
| | | | | | | **INCOME DATA** | | |
| 100.0 | 100.0 | 100.0 | 100.0 | | | Net Sales | 100.0 | 100.0 |
| | | | | | | Gross Profit | | |
| 91.2 | 82.9 | 88.0 | 93.3 | | | Operating Expenses | 88.2 | 91.6 |
| 8.8 | 17.1 | 12.0 | 6.7 | | | Operating Profit | 11.8 | 8.4 |
| 1.0 | 2.7 | 1.4 | 1.3 | | | All Other Expenses (net) | 1.4 | -.7 |
| 7.8 | 14.3 | 10.7 | 5.4 | | | Profit Before Taxes | 10.4 | 9.0 |
| | | | | | | **RATIOS** | | |
| 5.6 | 8.0 | 3.8 | 4.1 | | | | 8.2 | 6.2 |
| 1.3 | 3.9 | 1.6 | 3.0 | | | Current | 3.0 | 2.2 |
| .4 | .6 | 1.1 | 1.9 | | | | .8 | 1.1 |
| 5.6 | 8.0 | 3.7 | 4.1 | | | | 7.3 | 6.0 |
| 1.2 | 3.2 | 1.4 | 2.6 | | | Quick | 2.4 | 2.2 |
| .4 | .4 | 1.0 | 1.9 | | | | .6 | 1.1 |
| 0 UND | 0 UND | 0 UND | 24 14.9 | | | | 0 UND | 0 UND |
| 0 UND | 0 UND | 15 23.6 | 50 7.3 | | | Sales/Receivables | 0 UND | 0 UND |
| 0 UND | 11 32.2 | 64 5.7 | 74 4.9 | | | | 33 11.1 | 30 12.1 |
| | | | | | | Cost of Sales/Inventory | | |
| | | | | | | Cost of Sales/Payables | | |
| 11.1 | 3.4 | 7.5 | 2.9 | | | | 6.7 | 4.7 |
| 56.8 | 12.7 | 16.1 | 7.7 | | | Sales/Working Capital | 16.0 | 11.2 |
| -42.2 | -103.0 | 174.4 | 42.5 | | | | -56.1 | 92.4 |
| 49.4 | 51.9 | 131.4 | 41.2 | | | | 49.9 | 75.0 |
| (33) 9.6 | (19) 11.3 | (26) 14.2 | (11) 23.0 | | | EBIT/Interest | (114) 9.3 | (77) 15.7 |
| 2.0 | 2.8 | 5.8 | 3.2 | | | | 1.9 | 1.5 |
| | | | | | | Net Profit + Depr., Dep., Amort./Cur. Mat. L/T/D | | |
| .0 | .0 | .0 | .0 | | | | .0 | .1 |
| .4 | .3 | .4 | .1 | | | Fixed/Worth | .3 | .6 |
| UND | 2.8 | 20.8 | 1.6 | | | | 4.0 | -33.3 |
| .2 | .2 | 1.1 | .3 | | | | .2 | .7 |
| 1.3 | 1.2 | 2.8 | .7 | | | Debt/Worth | .9 | 2.8 |
| -4.5 | 14.9 | NM | 2.0 | | | | -59.4 | -7.9 |
| 345.7 | 127.1 | 206.3 | 30.8 | | | % Profit Before Taxes/Tangible Net Worth | 145.4 | 171.3 |
| (36) 87.7 | (28) 67.7 | (25) 64.4 | (15) 21.9 | | | | (132) 60.7 | (86) 85.3 |
| 7.4 | 18.5 | 20.6 | 12.3 | | | | 23.3 | 24.1 |
| 154.9 | 57.9 | 28.7 | 20.0 | | | % Profit Before Taxes/Total Assets | 89.1 | 63.0 |
| 44.8 | 26.8 | 17.4 | 7.1 | | | | 28.1 | 29.0 |
| 5.5 | 5.5 | 5.3 | 4.6 | | | | 6.2 | 2.1 |
| UND | 187.2 | 306.4 | 119.4 | | | Sales/Net Fixed Assets | 389.2 | 197.3 |
| 85.2 | 34.7 | 35.3 | 30.1 | | | | 35.7 | 33.7 |
| 26.0 | 5.9 | 7.8 | 1.7 | | | | 14.1 | 12.0 |
| 14.5 | 5.0 | 4.0 | 3.2 | | | | 9.0 | 4.9 |
| 7.6 | 3.0 | 2.3 | 1.6 | | | Sales/Total Assets | 4.8 | 3.4 |
| 4.2 | 1.4 | 1.3 | 1.0 | | | | 2.6 | 2.4 |
| .4 | .2 | .3 | .5 | | | | .3 | .5 |
| (14) .9 | (17) .7 | (13) .8 | (14) 1.0 | | | % Depr., Dep., Amort./Sales | (93) 1.0 | (67) 1.0 |
| 6.8 | 2.9 | 1.8 | 2.0 | | | | 1.8 | 1.9 |
| 5.4 | 3.0 | | | | | | 3.3 | 4.7 |
| (30) 8.5 | (16) 4.4 | | | | | % Officers', Directors' Owners' Comp/Sales | (78) 7.0 | (50) 10.1 |
| 15.7 | 7.1 | | | | | | 15.6 | 16.2 |
| 104456M | 194350M | 434619M | 1051459M | 2643523M | 1014069M | Net Sales ($) | 2592120M | 1958366M |
| 11709M | 43884M | 139519M | 335745M | 427332M | 565750M | Total Assets ($) | 1041621M | 789490M |

© RMA 2024    M = $ thousand    MM = $ million
See Pages viii through xx for Explanation of Ratios and Data

## HEALTH CARE—Offices of Physical, Occupational and Speech Therapists, and Audiologists  NAICS 621340

### Comparative Historical Data / Current Data Sorted by Sales

| | | | Type of Statement | | | | | | |
|---|---|---|---|---|---|---|---|---|---|
| 5 | 7 | 8 | Unqualified | | | | 1 | 1 | 7 |
| 3 | 4 | 2 | Reviewed | | | | 1 | 1 | 1 |
| 4 | 13 | 11 | Compiled | 1 | 2 | | 1 | 2 | 5 |
| 36 | 67 | 35 | Tax Returns | 8 | 12 | 3 | 6 | 4 | 2 |
| 84 | 84 | 88 | Other | 21 | 21 | 10 | 15 | 9 | 12 |
| 4/1/21-3/31/22 ALL | 4/1/22-3/31/23 ALL | 4/1/23-3/31/24 ALL | | \multicolumn{3}{c}{11 (4/1-9/30/23)} | \multicolumn{3}{c}{133 (10/1/23-3/31/24)} |
| | | | | 0-1MM | 1-3MM | 3-5MM | 5-10MM | 10-25MM | 25MM & OVER |
| 132 | 175 | 144 | NUMBER OF STATEMENTS | 30 | 35 | 13 | 22 | 17 | 27 |
| % | % | % | ASSETS | % | % | % | % | % | % |
| 51.3 | 39.4 | 34.9 | Cash & Equivalents | 38.1 | 51.6 | 42.5 | 23.2 | 28.5 | 19.4 |
| 13.1 | 15.8 | 15.7 | Trade Receivables (net) | 2.1 | 7.9 | 7.5 | 26.0 | 26.1 | 29.9 |
| .1 | .3 | .2 | Inventory | .1 | .1 | .0 | .0 | .1 | 1.0 |
| 1.9 | 4.7 | 4.4 | All Other Current | 2.4 | 4.7 | 11.9 | 4.5 | 3.2 | 3.4 |
| 66.4 | 60.3 | 55.2 | Total Current | 42.7 | 64.3 | 61.9 | 53.7 | 57.9 | 53.7 |
| 20.2 | 18.9 | 23.1 | Fixed Assets (net) | 41.0 | 16.8 | 14.5 | 21.2 | 16.4 | 21.3 |
| 7.0 | 10.5 | 10.0 | Intangibles (net) | 9.5 | 6.9 | 9.0 | 15.8 | 10.8 | 9.6 |
| 6.4 | 10.2 | 11.7 | All Other Non-Current | 6.7 | 12.1 | 14.5 | 9.3 | 14.9 | 15.4 |
| 100.0 | 100.0 | 100.0 | Total | 100.0 | 100.0 | 100.0 | 100.0 | 100.0 | 100.0 |
| | | | LIABILITIES | | | | | | |
| 13.8 | 13.0 | 15.7 | Notes Payable-Short Term | 11.9 | 17.5 | 1.5 | 38.6 | 9.0 | 10.0 |
| 2.4 | 1.9 | 2.6 | Cur. Mat.-L.T.D. | 5.3 | 2.4 | 2.2 | .9 | 1.0 | 2.7 |
| 2.9 | 2.2 | 2.0 | Trade Payables | 2.0 | 1.6 | 1.3 | .4 | 3.0 | 3.6 |
| .1 | 1.6 | .5 | Income Taxes Payable | .0 | 1.5 | .0 | .0 | .6 | .1 |
| 10.2 | 13.3 | 16.4 | All Other Current | 16.4 | 18.7 | 13.5 | 15.1 | 20.6 | 13.4 |
| 29.4 | 32.1 | 37.2 | Total Current | 35.5 | 41.6 | 18.5 | 55.0 | 34.2 | 29.8 |
| 28.4 | 28.3 | 29.8 | Long-Term Debt | 51.8 | 33.5 | 21.9 | 23.5 | 10.9 | 21.1 |
| .0 | .3 | .1 | Deferred Taxes | .0 | .0 | .0 | .0 | .0 | .3 |
| 7.5 | 5.9 | 5.5 | All Other Non-Current | 2.7 | 5.0 | .8 | 1.6 | 2.5 | 16.6 |
| 34.7 | 33.4 | 27.5 | Net Worth | 9.9 | 19.9 | 58.7 | 19.9 | 52.3 | 32.2 |
| 100.0 | 100.0 | 100.0 | Total Liabilities & Net Worth | 100.0 | 100.0 | 100.0 | 100.0 | 100.0 | 100.0 |
| | | | INCOME DATA | | | | | | |
| 100.0 | 100.0 | 100.0 | Net Sales | 100.0 | 100.0 | 100.0 | 100.0 | 100.0 | 100.0 |
| | | | Gross Profit | | | | | | |
| 85.9 | 92.1 | 89.1 | Operating Expenses | 80.8 | 86.7 | 91.2 | 91.5 | 95.3 | 94.5 |
| 14.1 | 7.9 | 10.9 | Operating Profit | 19.2 | 13.3 | 8.8 | 8.5 | 4.7 | 5.5 |
| -.1 | .6 | 1.6 | All Other Expenses (net) | 5.3 | 1.5 | .1 | -.6 | 1.0 | .3 |
| 14.2 | 7.3 | 9.3 | Profit Before Taxes | 13.9 | 11.9 | 8.7 | 9.1 | 3.7 | 5.2 |
| | | | RATIOS | | | | | | |
| 15.2 | 8.1 | 5.2 | | 4.9 | 8.1 | 13.1 | 9.3 | 4.6 | 3.7 |
| 4.1 | 3.3 | 1.9 | Current | 1.0 | 2.8 | 4.6 | 1.4 | 2.0 | 1.8 |
| 1.6 | 1.2 | .8 | | .3 | .6 | 1.5 | .7 | 1.2 | 1.2 |
| 14.3 | 7.1 | 5.0 | | 4.8 | 8.1 | 11.6 | 6.9 | 4.5 | 3.4 |
| 3.9 | 3.0 | 1.6 | Quick | .8 | 1.8 | 2.5 | 1.4 | 1.8 | 1.7 |
| 1.4 | 1.0 | .7 | | .3 | .6 | 1.2 | .6 | 1.2 | .9 |
| 0 UND | 0 UND | 0 UND | | 0 UND | 0 UND | 0 UND | 0 UND | 0 UND | 8 46.4 |
| 0 UND | 0 UND | 0 UND | Sales/Receivables | 0 UND | 0 UND | 0 UND | 20 18.0 | 25 14.5 | 49 7.4 |
| 24 15.4 | 38 9.7 | 41 9.0 | | 0 UND | 0 UND | 0 UND | 64 5.7 | 56 6.5 | 87 4.2 |
| | | | Cost of Sales/Inventory | | | | | | |
| | | | Cost of Sales/Payables | | | | | | |
| 4.5 | 5.3 | 6.9 | | 8.4 | 5.0 | 6.6 | 4.9 | 7.3 | 6.9 |
| 8.5 | 11.7 | 16.8 | Sales/Working Capital | UND | 14.0 | 14.9 | 10.7 | 17.8 | 11.7 |
| 33.3 | 138.3 | -92.6 | | -12.2 | -27.7 | 42.0 | -94.3 | 27.0 | 118.5 |
| | 93.8 | 48.3 | 47.2 | | 45.6 | 51.9 | | 43.5 | 125.1 | 47.0 |
| (76) 22.9 | (110) 9.2 | (96) 10.3 | EBIT/Interest | (16) 11.2 | (23) 8.3 | | (14) 10.6 | (12) 9.8 | (22) 14.0 |
| 3.7 | 1.4 | 3.1 | | 2.7 | 2.5 | | | 3.3 | -.7 | 3.0 |
| | | 17.1 | Net Profit + Depr., Dep., | | | | | | |
| | (10) 3.7 | Amort./Cur. Mat. L/T/D | | | | | | |
| | | 2.4 | | | | | | | |
| .0 | .0 | .0 | | .1 | .0 | .0 | .0 | .1 | .0 |
| .3 | .2 | .4 | Fixed/Worth | 1.7 | .2 | .2 | .2 | .2 | .9 |
| 8.1 | 2.6 | 19.1 | | UND | UND | 1.0 | 65.3 | 1.8 | -6.3 |
| .3 | .2 | .3 | | .3 | .4 | .1 | .2 | .3 | .6 |
| 1.0 | 1.3 | 1.8 | Debt/Worth | 2.1 | 2.4 | .5 | 3.3 | .9 | 2.4 |
| 20.8 | -13.6 | UND | | UND | -14.8 | 13.4 | NM | 4.5 | -18.8 |
| 151.3 | 131.0 | 161.9 | | 217.8 | 200.4 | 193.9 | 237.5 | 122.9 | 83.0 |
| (102) 89.2 | (129) 45.9 | (108) 53.5 | % Profit Before Taxes/Tangible Net Worth | (23) 23.8 | (24) 86.7 | (11) 55.2 | (17) 43.9 | (14) 52.6 | (19) 26.6 |
| 40.3 | 12.8 | 16.2 | | 3.2 | 53.7 | 17.7 | 6.4 | 10.0 | 15.6 |
| 85.6 | 47.8 | 54.8 | | 147.7 | 71.9 | 63.6 | 45.6 | 48.8 | 26.6 |
| 41.9 | 15.8 | 20.7 | % Profit Before Taxes/Total Assets | 7.6 | 41.3 | 28.2 | 14.7 | 21.8 | 9.5 |
| 6.2 | .9 | 4.6 | | 1.3 | 14.1 | 8.8 | 4.6 | -1.3 | 5.7 |
| 330.0 | 466.7 | 308.1 | | UND | UND | UND | UND | 208.4 | 197.3 |
| 50.9 | 47.7 | 54.0 | Sales/Net Fixed Assets | 28.4 | 90.6 | 35.3 | 55.3 | 85.4 | 37.5 |
| 12.9 | 12.0 | 11.7 | | .5 | 14.1 | 18.0 | 12.8 | 17.2 | 8.6 |
| 6.1 | 7.0 | 7.2 | | 11.3 | 7.9 | 8.4 | 4.4 | 9.1 | 5.8 |
| 3.7 | 3.8 | 3.2 | Sales/Total Assets | 2.3 | 4.9 | 3.2 | 3.0 | 3.7 | 1.9 |
| 2.3 | 1.7 | 1.7 | | .5 | 2.9 | 2.1 | 1.9 | 1.5 | 1.5 |
| .3 | .3 | .4 | | .7 | .2 | | | .3 | .2 |
| (50) .7 | (92) .9 | (65) .9 | % Depr., Dep., Amort./Sales | (11) 2.1 | (10) .8 | | (11) .7 | (23) 1.0 |
| 2.2 | 2.6 | 2.5 | | 19.0 | 4.4 | | | 1.9 | 2.3 |
| 3.4 | 3.6 | 2.9 | | 7.0 | 6.2 | | 1.9 | | |
| (50) 7.2 | (85) 7.6 | (61) 6.2 | % Officers', Directors' Owners' Comp/Sales | (12) 11.2 | (18) 7.6 | | (10) 2.7 | | |
| 12.3 | 11.7 | 11.2 | | 18.9 | 14.1 | | 5.9 | | |
| 1906475M | 3310055M | 5442476M | Net Sales ($) | 15469M | 68711M | 50591M | 160946M | 258184M | 4888575M |
| 1143637M | 1528150M | 1523939M | Total Assets ($) | 16786M | 21753M | 17344M | 67285M | 113905M | 1286866M |

© RMA 2024  M = $ thousand   MM = $ million
See Pages viii through xx for Explanation of Ratios and Data

# HEALTH CARE—Offices of Podiatrists  NAICS 621391

## Current Data Sorted by Assets

| | | | | | | Type of Statement | | | |
|---|---|---|---|---|---|---|---|---|---|
| | | | | | | | Unqualified | | |
| | 1 | | | | | | Reviewed | | |
| | 5 | 1 | | | | | Compiled | | |
| | 10 | 7 | 4 | | | | Tax Returns | 4 | 10 |
| | | 2 (4/1-9/30/23) | | 28 (10/1/23-3/31/24) | 1 | 1 | Other | 17 | 16 |
| | | | | | | | | 4/1/19- | 4/1/20- |
| | 0-500M | 500M-2MM | 2-10MM | 10-50MM | 50-100MM | 100-250MM | | 3/31/20 | 3/31/21 |
| | 16 | 8 | 4 | | 1 | 1 | NUMBER OF STATEMENTS | ALL 21 | ALL 26 |

| | % | % | % | | % | % | | % | % |
|---|---|---|---|---|---|---|---|---|---|
| | 40.0 | | | | | | **ASSETS** | | |
| | .1 | | | | | | Cash & Equivalents | 33.7 | 55.2 |
| | .0 | | | | | | Trade Receivables (net) | 2.1 | 1.7 |
| | 8.9 | | | DATA | | | Inventory | 1.3 | .6 |
| | 49.0 | | | NOT | | | All Other Current | 9.8 | 2.5 |
| | 32.3 | | | AVAILABLE | | | Total Current | 46.9 | 60.0 |
| | 13.5 | | | | | | Fixed Assets (net) | 28.6 | 16.7 |
| | 5.2 | | | | | | Intangibles (net) | 8.6 | 15.2 |
| | 100.0 | | | | | | All Other Non-Current | 16.0 | 8.1 |
| | | | | | | | Total | 100.0 | 100.0 |
| | 18.9 | | | | | | **LIABILITIES** | | |
| | 2.9 | | | | | | Notes Payable-Short Term | 29.2 | 16.5 |
| | .8 | | | | | | Cur. Mat.-L.T.D. | 2.9 | 8.1 |
| | .0 | | | | | | Trade Payables | .9 | .3 |
| | 34.5 | | | | | | Income Taxes Payable | .2 | .0 |
| | 57.1 | | | | | | All Other Current | 29.6 | 17.5 |
| | 24.7 | | | | | | Total Current | 62.8 | 42.3 |
| | .0 | | | | | | Long-Term Debt | 21.3 | 38.6 |
| | .0 | | | | | | Deferred Taxes | .0 | .0 |
| | 18.2 | | | | | | All Other Non-Current | 4.9 | 9.8 |
| | 100.0 | | | | | | Net Worth | 11.0 | 9.3 |
| | | | | | | | Total Liabilities & Net Worth | 100.0 | 100.0 |
| | 100.0 | | | | | | **INCOME DATA** | | |
| | | | | | | | Net Sales | 100.0 | 100.0 |
| | 80.1 | | | | | | Gross Profit | | |
| | 19.9 | | | | | | Operating Expenses | 85.8 | 86.2 |
| | -1.1 | | | | | | Operating Profit | 14.2 | 13.8 |
| | 21.0 | | | | | | All Other Expenses (net) | .9 | -3.1 |
| | | | | | | | Profit Before Taxes | 13.3 | 16.8 |
| | | | | | | | **RATIOS** | | |
| | 7.8 | | | | | | | 6.5 | 5.1 |
| | 2.3 | | | | | | Current | 1.8 | 1.4 |
| | .3 | | | | | | | .3 | .9 |
| | 4.1 | | | | | | | 6.4 | 5.1 |
| | 1.4 | | | | | | Quick | 1.0 | 1.3 |
| | .3 | | | | | | | .2 | .8 |
| 0 | UND | | | | | | | 0 UND | 0 UND |
| 0 | UND | | | | | | Sales/Receivables | 0 UND | 0 UND |
| 0 | UND | | | | | | | 0 UND | 0 UND |
| | | | | | | | Cost of Sales/Inventory | | |
| | | | | | | | Cost of Sales/Payables | | |
| | 20.6 | | | | | | | 9.2 | 8.0 |
| | 128.8 | | | | | | Sales/Working Capital | 81.2 | 17.5 |
| | -18.8 | | | | | | | -19.3 | -308.9 |
| | | | | | | | | 43.4 | 80.2 |
| | | | | | | | EBIT/Interest | (15) 4.3 | (17) 24.7 |
| | | | | | | | | -4.3 | 6.6 |
| | | | | | | | Net Profit + Depr., Dep., Amort./Cur. Mat. L/T/D | | |
| | .0 | | | | | | | .1 | .3 |
| | 1.1 | | | | | | Fixed/Worth | .7 | .8 |
| | -4.7 | | | | | | | -5.1 | -.6 |
| | .2 | | | | | | | .2 | 1.4 |
| | 1.7 | | | | | | Debt/Worth | 2.0 | 6.2 |
| | -9.8 | | | | | | | -4.9 | -3.6 |
| | 738.5 | | | | | | | 263.1 | 333.3 |
| (10) | 289.1 | | | | | | % Profit Before Taxes/Tangible Net Worth | (13) 80.4 | (16) 146.5 |
| | 18.6 | | | | | | | 31.7 | 80.8 |
| | 279.3 | | | | | | | 89.2 | 122.7 |
| | 73.5 | | | | | | % Profit Before Taxes/Total Assets | 37.6 | 67.0 |
| | 12.6 | | | | | | | -4.4 | 10.5 |
| | 797.8 | | | | | | | 139.5 | 214.7 |
| | 43.3 | | | | | | Sales/Net Fixed Assets | 21.4 | 47.2 |
| | 17.7 | | | | | | | 9.9 | 14.9 |
| | 13.9 | | | | | | | 8.9 | 7.8 |
| | 10.9 | | | | | | Sales/Total Assets | 4.2 | 5.9 |
| | 4.2 | | | | | | | 2.7 | 3.0 |
| | | | | | | | | .4 | .2 |
| | | | | | | | % Depr., Dep., Amort./Sales | (11) .8 | (12) .8 |
| | | | | | | | | 1.5 | 1.2 |
| | | | | | | | | 4.9 | 8.0 |
| | | | | | | | % Officers', Directors' Owners' Comp/Sales | (10) 13.2 | (16) 11.1 |
| | | | | | | | | 18.5 | 28.5 |
| | 33811M | 36017M | 23134M | | 26859M | 483000M | Net Sales ($) | 47068M | 71383M |
| | 3161M | 8930M | 21740M | | 51035M | 247000M | Total Assets ($) | 9756M | 12809M |

© RMA 2024

M = $ thousand    MM = $ million
See Pages viii through xx for Explanation of Ratios and Data

# HEALTH CARE—Offices of Podiatrists  NAICS 621391

## Comparative Historical Data / Current Data Sorted by Sales

| Comparative Historical Data | | | | Type of Statement | Current Data Sorted by Sales | | | | | |
|---|---|---|---|---|---|---|---|---|---|---|
| | 1 | | | Unqualified | | 1 | | | | |
| 6 | 4 | 1 | | Reviewed | | 3 | | 1 | | |
| 25 | 17 | 6 | | Compiled | 2 | 8 | | 4 | 2 | 2 |
| | | 23 | | Tax Returns | 6 | | 1 | 28 | | |
| 4/1/21-3/31/22 | 4/1/22-3/31/23 | 4/1/23-3/31/24 | | Other | | 2 (4/1-9/30/23) | | (10/1/23-3/31/24) | | |
| ALL | ALL | ALL | | | 0-1MM | 1-3MM | 3-5MM | 5-10MM | 10-25MM | 25MM & OVER |
| 32 | 22 | 30 | | NUMBER OF STATEMENTS | 8 | 12 | 1 | 5 | 2 | 2 |
| % | % | % | | ASSETS | % | % | % | % | % | % |
| 53.8 | 45.4 | 33.8 | | Cash & Equivalents | | 47.8 | | | | |
| 5.4 | .1 | 8.0 | | Trade Receivables (net) | | 6.4 | | | | |
| .4 | .6 | 1.6 | | Inventory | | .0 | | | | |
| 3.2 | 6.7 | 5.6 | | All Other Current | | 2.2 | | | | |
| 62.8 | 52.9 | 49.0 | | Total Current | | 56.3 | | | | |
| 20.1 | 16.7 | 24.5 | | Fixed Assets (net) | | 16.5 | | | | |
| 11.8 | 14.6 | 22.3 | | Intangibles (net) | | 24.8 | | | | |
| 5.2 | 15.8 | 4.2 | | All Other Non-Current | | 2.3 | | | | |
| 100.0 | 100.0 | 100.0 | | Total | | 100.0 | | | | |
| | | | | LIABILITIES | | | | | | |
| 25.1 | 19.5 | 26.4 | | Notes Payable-Short Term | | 21.7 | | | | |
| 6.3 | 1.6 | 1.9 | | Cur. Mat.-L.T.D. | | 3.9 | | | | |
| 1.2 | .8 | 1.2 | | Trade Payables | | .0 | | | | |
| .0 | .1 | .0 | | Income Taxes Payable | | .0 | | | | |
| 8.1 | 36.8 | 21.3 | | All Other Current | | 5.6 | | | | |
| 40.6 | 58.8 | 50.8 | | Total Current | | 31.1 | | | | |
| 24.3 | 29.0 | 32.3 | | Long-Term Debt | | 39.7 | | | | |
| .0 | .0 | .0 | | Deferred Taxes | | .0 | | | | |
| 8.8 | .7 | 2.7 | | All Other Non-Current | | 6.5 | | | | |
| 26.2 | 11.5 | 14.3 | | Net Worth | | 22.7 | | | | |
| 100.0 | 100.0 | 100.0 | | Total Liabilities & Net Worth | | 100.0 | | | | |
| | | | | INCOME DATA | | | | | | |
| 100.0 | 100.0 | 100.0 | | Net Sales | | 100.0 | | | | |
| | | | | Gross Profit | | | | | | |
| 80.5 | 83.5 | 79.8 | | Operating Expenses | | 79.7 | | | | |
| 19.5 | 16.5 | 20.2 | | Operating Profit | | 20.3 | | | | |
| -1.2 | .1 | 2.3 | | All Other Expenses (net) | | .2 | | | | |
| 20.6 | 16.3 | 17.9 | | Profit Before Taxes | | 20.1 | | | | |
| | | | | RATIOS | | | | | | |
| 8.1 | 8.0 | 10.2 | | | | 4.7 | | | | |
| 2.4 | 3.1 | 3.2 | | Current | | 2.7 | | | | |
| .8 | 1.3 | .6 | | | | .7 | | | | |
| 7.3 | 6.6 | 7.8 | | | | 4.6 | | | | |
| 2.1 | 2.6 | 2.8 | | Quick | | 2.7 | | | | |
| .8 | .3 | .5 | | | | .7 | | | | |
| 0 UND | 0 UND | 0 UND | | | | 0 UND | | | | |
| 0 UND | 0 UND | 0 UND | | Sales/Receivables | | 0 UND | | | | |
| 0 UND | 0 UND | 0 UND | | | | 0 UND | | | | |
| | | | | Cost of Sales/Inventory | | | | | | |
| | | | | Cost of Sales/Payables | | | | | | |
| 8.2 | 7.5 | 4.5 | | | | 7.6 | | | | |
| 25.6 | 40.6 | 24.2 | | Sales/Working Capital | | 20.4 | | | | |
| -155.8 | NM | -38.4 | | | | -69.5 | | | | |
| 73.7 | 174.5 | 37.9 | | | | | | | | |
| (17) 23.0 | (14) 48.8 | (16) 6.5 | | EBIT/Interest | | | | | | |
| .8 | -9.9 | .4 | | | | | | | | |
| | | | | Net Profit + Depr., Dep., Amort./Cur. Mat. L/T/D | | | | | | |
| .0 | .0 | .1 | | | | .0 | | | | |
| .6 | .3 | 1.9 | | Fixed/Worth | | 1.2 | | | | |
| NM | .7 | -.3 | | | | -1.2 | | | | |
| .6 | .2 | .3 | | | | .7 | | | | |
| 1.9 | .6 | 5.5 | | Debt/Worth | | NM | | | | |
| -8.3 | -18.7 | -2.0 | | | | -1.9 | | | | |
| 368.2 | 415.1 | 475.0 | | | | | | | | |
| (22) 137.8 | (16) 114.2 | (17) 151.3 | | % Profit Before Taxes/Tangible Net Worth | | | | | | |
| 47.7 | 64.6 | 5.5 | | | | | | | | |
| 138.9 | 104.8 | 94.8 | | | | 233.1 | | | | |
| 55.9 | 60.2 | 40.6 | | % Profit Before Taxes/Total Assets | | 41.1 | | | | |
| 2.5 | .7 | 7.9 | | | | 2.6 | | | | |
| 641.0 | UND | 225.9 | | | | UND | | | | |
| 69.9 | 41.8 | 31.9 | | Sales/Net Fixed Assets | | 102.9 | | | | |
| 15.8 | 19.2 | 14.2 | | | | 24.8 | | | | |
| 9.7 | 8.1 | 12.0 | | | | 11.7 | | | | |
| 4.8 | 5.3 | 3.7 | | Sales/Total Assets | | 6.5 | | | | |
| 2.2 | 2.9 | 1.6 | | | | 1.9 | | | | |
| .3 | | | | | | | | | | |
| (11) .9 | | | | % Depr., Dep., Amort./Sales | | | | | | |
| 2.6 | | | | | | | | | | |
| 6.1 | 7.2 | 4.6 | | | | | | | | |
| (10) 8.6 | (11) 25.0 | (12) 8.6 | | % Officers', Directors' Owners' Comp/Sales | | | | | | |
| 22.7 | 30.2 | 23.0 | | | | | | | | |
| 1309817M | 82535M | 602821M | | Net Sales ($) | 4357M | 25035M | 3188M | 34762M | 25620M | 509859M |
| 109533M | 10758M | 331866M | | Total Assets ($) | 5512M | 8812M | 245M | 11158M | 8104M | 298035M |

M = $ thousand    MM = $ million
See Pages viii through xx for Explanation of Ratios and Data

© RMA 2024

# HEALTH CARE—Offices of All Other Miscellaneous Health Practitioners  NAICS 621399

## Current Data Sorted by Assets | Comparative Historical Data

| | | | | | | | | | |
|---|---|---|---|---|---|---|---|---|---|
| 1 | 1 | 4 | 2 | | 2 | Type of Statement | | | |
| | | | 2 | | | Unqualified | 11 | 5 | |
| 2 | 4 | 5 | 1 | | | Reviewed | 4 | 3 | |
| 28 | 11 | 7 | | | | Compiled | 8 | 9 | |
| 23 | 24 | 18 | 6 | 4 | 5 | Tax Returns | 59 | 37 | |
| | 9 (4/1-9/30/23) | | 141 (10/1/23-3/31/24) | | | Other | 120 | 69 | |
| 0-500M | 500K-2MM | 2-10MM | 10-50MM | 50-100MM | 100-250MM | | 4/1/19-3/31/20 ALL | 4/1/20-3/31/21 ALL | |
| 54 | 40 | 34 | 11 | 4 | 7 | NUMBER OF STATEMENTS | 202 | 123 | |
| % | % | % | % | % | % | ASSETS | % | % | |
| 44.4 | 39.1 | 11.6 | 24.5 | | | Cash & Equivalents | 30.1 | 42.0 | |
| 8.1 | 4.8 | 28.9 | 19.4 | | | Trade Receivables (net) | 14.5 | 9.1 | |
| 4.7 | 3.2 | 2.4 | .0 | | | Inventory | 2.5 | 2.3 | |
| 4.8 | 2.9 | 3.5 | 1.0 | | | All Other Current | 2.6 | 3.6 | |
| 62.1 | 50.0 | 46.5 | 44.9 | | | Total Current | 49.8 | 57.0 | |
| 21.1 | 32.6 | 28.6 | 21.4 | | | Fixed Assets (net) | 29.7 | 21.7 | |
| 5.6 | 8.1 | 8.7 | 8.8 | | | Intangibles (net) | 6.9 | 12.8 | |
| 11.2 | 9.4 | 16.2 | 24.9 | | | All Other Non-Current | 13.6 | 8.5 | |
| 100.0 | 100.0 | 100.0 | 100.0 | | | Total | 100.0 | 100.0 | |
| | | | | | | LIABILITIES | | | |
| 25.9 | 20.4 | 2.6 | .2 | | | Notes Payable-Short Term | 14.2 | 18.7 | |
| 13.9 | 5.9 | 4.5 | 3.5 | | | Cur. Mat.-L.T.D. | 3.5 | 3.1 | |
| 8.5 | 1.4 | 7.1 | 7.0 | | | Trade Payables | 5.5 | 3.4 | |
| .2 | .0 | .0 | .0 | | | Income Taxes Payable | .1 | .1 | |
| 45.8 | 13.4 | 16.3 | 27.2 | | | All Other Current | 24.3 | 24.0 | |
| 94.2 | 41.1 | 30.4 | 37.9 | | | Total Current | 47.5 | 49.1 | |
| 39.3 | 39.2 | 27.2 | 18.4 | | | Long-Term Debt | 29.0 | 37.6 | |
| .0 | .0 | .0 | .0 | | | Deferred Taxes | .0 | .0 | |
| 4.2 | 3.7 | 9.2 | 25.9 | | | All Other Non-Current | 4.9 | 5.8 | |
| -37.7 | 16.0 | 33.2 | 17.7 | | | Net Worth | 18.6 | 7.5 | |
| 100.0 | 100.0 | 100.0 | 100.0 | | | Total Liabilties & Net Worth | 100.0 | 100.0 | |
| | | | | | | INCOME DATA | | | |
| 100.0 | 100.0 | 100.0 | 100.0 | | | Net Sales | 100.0 | 100.0 | |
| | | | | | | Gross Profit | | | |
| 92.4 | 87.6 | 89.1 | 95.2 | | | Operating Expenses | 87.2 | 90.1 | |
| 7.6 | 12.4 | 10.9 | 4.8 | | | Operating Profit | 12.8 | 9.9 | |
| .4 | 3.8 | 2.0 | -.2 | | | All Other Expenses (net) | 1.5 | -.2 | |
| 7.2 | 8.6 | 8.9 | 5.0 | | | Profit Before Taxes | 11.3 | 10.1 | |
| | | | | | | RATIOS | | | |
| 5.5 | 5.7 | 4.1 | 4.0 | | | | 4.0 | 3.8 | |
| 1.2 | 1.7 | 1.8 | 2.0 | | | Current | 1.3 | 1.7 | |
| .4 | .5 | .6 | 1.0 | | | | .5 | .6 | |
| 3.5 | 4.2 | 3.9 | 3.9 | | | | 3.7 | 3.6 | |
| 1.0 | 1.7 | 1.4 | 1.6 | | | Quick | 1.2 (122) | 1.6 | |
| .2 | .4 | .4 | 1.0 | | | | .4 | .6 | |
| 0 UND | 0 UND | 0 UND | 9 40.8 | | | | 0 UND | 0 UND | |
| 0 UND | 0 UND | 29 12.4 | 39 9.4 | | | Sales/Receivables | 0 UND | 0 UND | |
| 0 UND | 0 UND | 61 6.0 | 118 3.1 | | | | 32 11.4 | 14 25.6 | |
| | | | | | | Cost of Sales/Inventory | | | |
| | | | | | | Cost of Sales/Payables | | | |
| 11.6 | 5.2 | 6.5 | 4.3 | | | | 9.5 | 5.9 | |
| 95.0 | 27.0 | 10.5 | 6.0 | | | Sales/Working Capital | 48.1 | 21.6 | |
| -14.0 | -26.2 | -45.8 | 440.1 | | | | -23.5 | -26.8 | |
| 35.0 | 23.3 | 77.1 | | | | | 44.5 | 61.8 | |
| (29) 8.4 | (23) 11.6 | (24) 5.7 | | | | EBIT/Interest | (139) 13.5 | (79) 12.9 | |
| 2.7 | 2.9 | -.9 | | | | | 1.6 | 2.5 | |
| | | | | | | Net Profit + Depr., Dep., Amort./Cur. Mat. L/T/D | 546.0 (12) 4.6 1.2 | | |
| .0 | .1 | .1 | .1 | | | | .1 | .1 | |
| .6 | 1.1 | .4 | .4 | | | Fixed/Worth | .8 | .7 | |
| -1.2 | -7.9 | -6.1 | 1.5 | | | | -17.1 | -1.6 | |
| .8 | .6 | .3 | .8 | | | | .4 | .7 | |
| UND | 2.9 | 1.3 | 2.9 | | | Debt/Worth | 2.2 | 4.5 | |
| -2.0 | -5.3 | -10.3 | 13.3 | | | | -23.6 | -3.6 | |
| 128.6 | 165.3 | 79.5 | | | | | 172.2 | 209.2 | |
| (27) 63.3 | (26) 34.3 | (24) 22.4 | | | | % Profit Before Taxes/Tangible Net Worth | (142) 64.8 | (79) 61.5 | |
| 20.6 | 4.1 | -1.5 | | | | | 7.2 | 10.3 | |
| 81.0 | 69.5 | 29.4 | 16.8 | | | | 80.8 | 75.1 | |
| 30.4 | 21.7 | 5.0 | 5.5 | | | % Profit Before Taxes/Total Assets | 29.3 | 15.2 | |
| -2.4 | -.5 | -4.6 | .0 | | | | 1.7 | -2.5 | |
| UND | 468.0 | 168.0 | 42.1 | | | | 178.9 | 382.7 | |
| 109.9 | 28.5 | 15.6 | 22.4 | | | Sales/Net Fixed Assets | 31.3 | 35.6 | |
| 19.0 | 3.3 | 2.6 | 11.1 | | | | 7.0 | 9.0 | |
| 14.4 | 10.0 | 5.3 | 2.0 | | | | 8.9 | 6.6 | |
| 6.1 | 3.4 | 2.2 | 1.4 | | | Sales/Total Assets | 4.4 | 3.6 | |
| 3.3 | 1.6 | .7 | .9 | | | | 1.8 | 1.9 | |
| .2 | .2 | | .5 | | | | .3 | .3 | |
| (15) .7 | (18) 1.0 | (22) | 1.6 | | | % Depr., Dep., Amort./Sales | (120) 1.5 | (60) 1.5 | |
| 1.6 | 9.0 | | 12.5 | | | | 3.5 | 4.4 | |
| 6.9 | 3.4 | | | | | | 4.2 | 6.4 | |
| (26) 14.3 | (15) 7.2 | | | | | % Officers', Directors' Owners' Comp/Sales | (81) 10.6 | (42) 13.2 | |
| 18.5 | 10.3 | | | | | | 25.0 | 27.3 | |
| 90840M | 408849M | 754761M | 405997M | 259874M | 1298424M | Net Sales ($) | 5709132M | 2099945M | |
| 12053M | 44621M | 182485M | 234580M | 288515M | 1192602M | Total Assets ($) | 1847693M | 935010M | |

M = $ thousand   MM = $ million
See Pages viii through xx for Explanation of Ratios and Data

© RMA 2024

# HEALTH CARE—Offices of All Other Miscellaneous Health Practitioners  NAICS 621399

## Comparative Historical Data / Current Data Sorted by Sales

| Comparative Historical Data | | | | | Current Data Sorted by Sales | | | | | |
|---|---|---|---|---|---|---|---|---|---|---|
| 5 | 8 | 10 | Type of Statement | | | | | | | |
| 4 | 2 | 2 | Unqualified | 1 | 1 | | | | 3 | 5 |
| 7 | 6 | 12 | Reviewed | | | | | | | 2 |
| 40 | 53 | 46 | Compiled | 1 | | 4 | | | 6 | 1 |
| 80 | 84 | 80 | Tax Returns | 12 | 18 | 4 | 10 | | 2 | |
| 4/1/21-3/31/22 ALL | 4/1/22-3/31/23 ALL | 4/1/23-3/31/24 ALL | Other | 17 | 19 | 7 | 8 | | 12 | 17 |
| | | | | | 9 (4/1-9/30/23) | | 141 (10/1/23-3/31/24) | | | |
| | | | | 0-1MM | 1-3MM | 3-5MM | 5-10MM | | 10-25MM | 25MM & OVER |
| 136 | 153 | 150 | NUMBER OF STATEMENTS | 31 | 38 | 15 | 18 | | 23 | 25 |
| % | % | % | ASSETS | % | % | % | % | | % | % |
| 41.6 | 33.9 | 31.6 | Cash & Equivalents | 30.6 | 36.7 | 40.4 | 43.1 | | 21.7 | 20.6 |
| 9.0 | 12.4 | 13.2 | Trade Receivables (net) | 6.3 | 5.7 | 9.7 | 8.0 | | 38.1 | 15.8 |
| 3.0 | 2.7 | 3.3 | Inventory | 4.2 | 4.9 | 4.9 | 1.9 | | 1.9 | 1.0 |
| 5.5 | 5.1 | 3.7 | All Other Current | 6.6 | 1.4 | 9.0 | .4 | | 4.0 | 2.4 |
| 59.0 | 54.1 | 51.7 | Total Current | 47.7 | 48.7 | 64.0 | 53.3 | | 65.7 | 39.8 |
| 21.6 | 21.9 | 25.8 | Fixed Assets (net) | 34.4 | 26.3 | 28.7 | 27.8 | | 13.9 | 22.4 |
| 10.7 | 10.7 | 9.1 | Intangibles (net) | 5.4 | 9.9 | 1.0 | 5.2 | | 11.0 | 18.7 |
| 8.7 | 13.3 | 13.3 | All Other Non-Current | 12.4 | 15.2 | 6.3 | 13.7 | | 9.4 | 19.1 |
| 100.0 | 100.0 | 100.0 | Total | 100.0 | 100.0 | 100.0 | 100.0 | | 100.0 | 100.0 |
| | | | LIABILITIES | | | | | | | |
| 22.2 | 14.9 | 15.5 | Notes Payable-Short Term | 12.3 | 26.6 | 15.7 | 12.6 | | 1.2 | 17.6 |
| 2.5 | 4.0 | 8.0 | Cur. Mat.-L.T.D. | 3.8 | 19.7 | 2.0 | 4.5 | | 6.4 | 3.2 |
| 4.7 | 4.9 | 6.1 | Trade Payables | 4.0 | 4.4 | 14.0 | 3.3 | | 4.5 | 9.9 |
| .0 | .1 | .1 | Income Taxes Payable | .3 | .0 | .0 | .0 | | .0 | .1 |
| 18.5 | 18.8 | 26.6 | All Other Current | 34.5 | 23.6 | 35.3 | 25.8 | | 22.6 | 20.3 |
| 47.9 | 42.7 | 56.2 | Total Current | 54.9 | 74.3 | 67.0 | 46.2 | | 34.7 | 51.1 |
| 27.7 | 34.7 | 33.9 | Long-Term Debt | 33.7 | 47.4 | 30.2 | 42.9 | | 23.1 | 19.4 |
| .0 | .0 | .0 | Deferred Taxes | .1 | .0 | .0 | .0 | | .0 | .2 |
| 4.6 | 5.9 | 7.3 | All Other Non-Current | 5.7 | 5.6 | .0 | 7.6 | | 6.9 | 16.2 |
| 19.8 | 16.7 | 2.5 | Net Worth | 5.6 | -27.3 | 2.9 | 3.3 | | 35.2 | 13.2 |
| 100.0 | 100.0 | 100.0 | Total Liabilities & Net Worth | 100.0 | 100.0 | 100.0 | 100.0 | | 100.0 | 100.0 |
| | | | INCOME DATA | | | | | | | |
| 100.0 | 100.0 | 100.0 | Net Sales | 100.0 | 100.0 | 100.0 | 100.0 | | 100.0 | 100.0 |
| | | | Gross Profit | | | | | | | |
| 84.0 | 90.6 | 90.5 | Operating Expenses | 91.7 | 88.9 | 93.3 | 91.3 | | 87.0 | 92.7 |
| 16.0 | 9.4 | 9.5 | Operating Profit | 8.3 | 11.1 | 6.7 | 8.7 | | 13.0 | 7.3 |
| .6 | .9 | 1.8 | All Other Expenses (net) | 4.9 | 1.7 | -.4 | .4 | | .6 | 1.7 |
| 15.4 | 8.5 | 7.7 | Profit Before Taxes | 3.5 | 9.4 | 7.1 | 8.3 | | 12.4 | 5.5 |
| | | | RATIOS | | | | | | | |
| 5.6 | 3.9 | 4.9 | | 3.3 | 6.2 | 6.6 | 4.8 | | 7.6 | 2.1 |
| 2.0 | 1.6 | 1.5 | Current | 1.4 | 1.1 | 4.1 | 1.9 | | 2.4 | 1.1 |
| .9 | .7 | .6 | | .6 | .3 | 1.5 | .4 | | 1.0 | .5 |
| 4.9 | 3.4 | 3.3 | | 2.3 | 5.8 | 5.5 | 4.8 | | 7.6 | 1.8 |
| 1.8 | 1.4 | 1.4 | Quick | 1.1 | .8 | 2.8 | 1.7 | | 2.2 | 1.1 |
| .7 | .4 | .4 | | .3 | .2 | 1.2 | .3 | | .9 | .5 |
| 0 UND | 0 UND | 0 UND | | 0 UND | 0 UND | 0 UND | 0 UND | 4 | 101.2 | 0 UND |
| 0 UND | 0 UND | 0 UND | Sales/Receivables | 0 UND | 0 UND | 0 UND | 0 UND | 42 | 8.7 | 28 13.0 |
| 22 16.9 | 25 14.4 | 34 10.8 | | 2 174.7 | 3 114.8 | 40 9.2 | 0 UND | 101 | 3.6 | 52 7.0 |
| | | | Cost of Sales/Inventory | | | | | | | |
| | | | Cost of Sales/Payables | | | | | | | |
| 5.6 | 7.4 | 6.6 | | 3.2 | 8.8 | 5.2 | 10.4 | | 5.3 | 8.7 |
| 15.4 | 22.9 | 27.5 | Sales/Working Capital | 27.8 | 534.7 | 13.5 | 32.6 | | 8.8 | 95.7 |
| -69.7 | -46.0 | -21.6 | | -12.7 | -13.2 | 56.6 | -13.7 | | 999.8 | -52.8 |
| | 87.5 | 22.0 | 24.8 | | 16.4 | 32.6 | | 21.9 | | 87.6 | 9.7 |
| (88) 21.3 | (97) 5.9 | (92) 7.5 | EBIT/Interest | (11) 6.2 | (27) 8.1 | | (12) 2.1 | (13) | 73.1 | (20) 3.8 |
| 4.1 | -.2 | .5 | | -6.0 | 3.3 | | -6.7 | | .1 | .0 |
| | | | Net Profit + Depr., Dep., Amort./Cur. Mat. L/T/D | | | | | | | |
| .0 | .1 | .1 | | .0 | .1 | .1 | .0 | | .0 | .3 |
| .6 | 1.2 | .7 | Fixed/Worth | .7 | 2.3 | .5 | 1.7 | | .1 | 1.3 |
| -1.9 | -1.4 | -3.6 | | -8.3 | -.6 | 1.7 | -1.7 | | .5 | -1.9 |
| .3 | .7 | .7 | | .7 | .6 | .5 | 1.1 | | .2 | 3.2 |
| 2.4 | 3.9 | 5.0 | Debt/Worth | 10.2 | UND | 1.1 | 6.1 | | .8 | 6.6 |
| -4.3 | -3.8 | -4.1 | | -4.0 | -2.1 | -10.2 | -3.9 | | -14.6 | -5.5 |
| 296.6 | 178.2 | 124.9 | | 94.2 | 125.9 | 105.9 | 517.8 | | 98.2 | 169.3 |
| (89) 100.0 | (101) 55.9 | (93) 36.7 | % Profit Before Taxes/Tangible Net Worth | (18) 25.6 | (20) 28.5 | (11) 50.1 | (11) 31.9 | (17) | 45.3 | (16) 50.6 |
| 47.3 | 8.9 | 4.1 | | -1.8 | 16.0 | 4.2 | -80.3 | | .4 | 14.8 |
| 80.7 | 45.8 | 53.3 | | 44.6 | 60.1 | 72.1 | 191.2 | | 77.7 | 15.3 |
| 42.7 | 14.2 | 13.3 | % Profit Before Taxes/Total Assets | 4.4 | 23.0 | 24.7 | 33.8 | | 10.8 | 6.1 |
| 12.1 | -1.1 | -1.7 | | -9.8 | 9.2 | 5.0 | -12.6 | | -4.4 | -2.4 |
| 242.0 | 190.2 | 198.0 | | UND | 123.2 | 178.9 | 678.1 | | UND | 132.9 |
| 35.4 | 31.8 | 33.1 | Sales/Net Fixed Assets | 11.0 | 32.9 | 68.1 | 34.4 | | 50.0 | 18.0 |
| 7.8 | 9.7 | 5.8 | | 1.8 | 8.6 | 6.3 | 5.6 | | 17.8 | 5.1 |
| 7.3 | 6.0 | 8.0 | | 4.9 | 10.5 | 14.8 | 10.5 | | 6.0 | 7.5 |
| 3.5 | 3.5 | 3.4 | Sales/Total Assets | 2.0 | 4.1 | 4.1 | 6.3 | | 4.7 | 1.8 |
| 1.5 | 1.7 | 1.5 | | .9 | 1.9 | 2.8 | 2.7 | | 1.6 | .9 |
| .4 | .3 | .3 | | 1.0 | .5 | | | | .4 | .2 |
| (59) 1.1 | (73) 1.3 | (69) 1.2 | % Depr., Dep., Amort./Sales | (10) 8.1 | (18) .9 | | | (12) | 1.5 | (17) 1.2 |
| 2.9 | 3.4 | 5.2 | | 23.2 | 5.6 | | | | 2.7 | 3.4 |
| 4.2 | 3.8 | 4.6 | | | 4.1 | | | | | |
| (45) 12.6 | (59) 9.0 | (48) 9.4 | % Officers', Directors' Owners' Comp/Sales | (11) 16.8 | (18) 8.9 | | | | | |
| 22.8 | 17.9 | 17.4 | | 29.5 | 14.1 | | | | | |
| 3236010M | 2801149M | 3218745M | Net Sales ($) | 13745M | 69547M | 59335M | 131244M | | 325069M | 2619805M |
| 1260967M | 1537495M | 1954856M | Total Assets ($) | 22649M | 35040M | 27814M | 42715M | | 142321M | 1684317M |

© RMA 2024  M = $ thousand  MM = $ million  See Pages viii through xx for Explanation of Ratios and Data

# HEALTH CARE—Outpatient Mental Health and Substance Abuse Centers  NAICS 621420

## Current Data Sorted by Assets | Comparative Historical Data

| | | | | | | Type of Statement | | |
|---|---|---|---|---|---|---|---|---|
| | | | 4 | 23 | 14 | Unqualified | 65 | 30 |
| | | 1 | 1 | 1 | | Reviewed | 1 | |
| | | 3 | | | | Compiled | 3 | 2 |
| | 4 | 2 | 1 | 5 | | Tax Returns | 25 | 6 |
| 1 | 10 | 17 | 22 | 11 | 4 | Other | 71 | 51 |
| 5 | 60 (4/1-9/30/23) | | 68 (10/1/23-3/31/24) | | | | 4/1/19-3/31/20 | 4/1/20-3/31/21 |
| 0-500M | 500M-2MM | 2-10MM | 10-50MM | 50-100MM | 100-250MM | | ALL | ALL |
| 6 | 14 | 27 | 47 | 25 | 9 | NUMBER OF STATEMENTS | 165 | 89 |
| % | % | % | % | % | % | ASSETS | % | % |
| | 36.3 | 24.7 | 24.7 | 31.1 | | Cash & Equivalents | 24.9 | 38.6 |
| | 7.1 | 22.2 | 12.8 | 10.7 | | Trade Receivables (net) | 17.5 | 11.3 |
| | .0 | .0 | .2 | .1 | | Inventory | .1 | .1 |
| | 5.4 | 3.0 | 4.8 | 4.6 | | All Other Current | 3.5 | 3.1 |
| | 48.7 | 49.9 | 42.5 | 46.5 | | Total Current | 45.9 | 53.2 |
| | 24.6 | 39.4 | 38.9 | 35.4 | | Fixed Assets (net) | 38.0 | 28.8 |
| | 10.8 | 1.6 | 3.2 | .4 | | Intangibles (net) | 6.6 | 8.2 |
| | 15.8 | 9.1 | 15.5 | 17.7 | | All Other Non-Current | 9.4 | 9.8 |
| | 100.0 | 100.0 | 100.0 | 100.0 | | Total | 100.0 | 100.0 |
| | | | | | | LIABILITIES | | |
| | 26.3 | 3.6 | 1.0 | 1.7 | | Notes Payable-Short Term | 4.0 | 5.1 |
| | 1.8 | 2.1 | 3.2 | 1.1 | | Cur. Mat.-L.T.D. | 2.6 | 3.7 |
| | 2.3 | 3.5 | 3.9 | 2.3 | | Trade Payables | 4.0 | 2.9 |
| | .1 | .0 | .0 | .0 | | Income Taxes Payable | .0 | .1 |
| | 4.6 | 6.6 | 8.8 | 13.7 | | All Other Current | 13.3 | 10.8 |
| | 35.2 | 15.8 | 16.8 | 18.9 | | Total Current | 24.0 | 22.6 |
| | 24.4 | 22.3 | 18.7 | 13.5 | | Long-Term Debt | 23.9 | 28.3 |
| | .0 | .0 | .0 | .0 | | Deferred Taxes | .0 | .4 |
| | 2.8 | 6.7 | 6.2 | 8.0 | | All Other Non-Current | 4.7 | 3.4 |
| | 37.7 | 55.2 | 58.2 | 59.6 | | Net Worth | 47.3 | 45.4 |
| | 100.0 | 100.0 | 100.0 | 100.0 | | Total Liabilities & Net Worth | 100.0 | 100.0 |
| | | | | | | INCOME DATA | | |
| | 100.0 | 100.0 | 100.0 | 100.0 | | Net Sales | 100.0 | 100.0 |
| | | | | | | Gross Profit | | |
| | 88.6 | 80.7 | 95.7 | 97.1 | | Operating Expenses | 95.5 | 91.7 |
| | 11.4 | 19.3 | 4.3 | 2.9 | | Operating Profit | 4.5 | 8.3 |
| | 1.9 | 3.8 | .7 | -.7 | | All Other Expenses (net) | 1.1 | 1.2 |
| | 9.5 | 15.6 | 3.6 | 3.6 | | Profit Before Taxes | 3.4 | 7.1 |
| | | | | | | RATIOS | | |
| | 18.7 | 12.5 | 5.4 | 4.4 | | | 4.3 | 6.0 |
| | 2.2 | 3.4 | 3.2 | 2.6 | | Current | 2.2 | 2.9 |
| | .1 | 1.7 | 1.6 | 1.5 | | | 1.3 | 1.5 |
| | 15.0 | 12.4 | 5.1 | 4.0 | | | 4.0 | 5.7 |
| | 1.7 | 2.4 | 3.0 | 2.3 | | Quick | 1.9 | 2.7 |
| | .1 | 1.7 | 1.2 | 1.3 | | | 1.1 | 1.4 |
| 0 | UND | 0 | UND | 21 | 17.0 | 23 | 15.7 | 10 | 35.8 | 0 | UND |
| 0 | UND | 40 | 9.2 | 33 | 11.0 | 29 | 12.7 | Sales/Receivables | 33 | 11.2 | 22 | 16.8 |
| 23 | 16.2 | 74 | 4.9 | 53 | 6.9 | 47 | 7.8 | | 50 | 7.3 | 44 | 8.3 |
| | | | | | | Cost of Sales/Inventory | | |
| | | | | | | Cost of Sales/Payables | | |
| | 5.3 | 2.3 | 2.2 | 2.6 | | | 4.5 | 3.3 |
| | 10.9 | 5.5 | 4.3 | 4.3 | | Sales/Working Capital | 8.6 | 6.6 |
| | -18.2 | 18.8 | 14.2 | 10.4 | | | 48.4 | 14.2 |
| | 52.6 | 137.1 | 20.8 | 25.4 | | | 12.5 | 50.9 |
| (11) | 16.6 | (20) 20.4 | (40) 4.0 | (22) 16.1 | | EBIT/Interest | (131) 4.5 | (61) 8.9 |
| | 1.7 | 1.5 | -3.6 | 4.8 | | | .8 | .3 |
| | | | | | | Net Profit + Depr., Dep., Amort./Cur. Mat. L/T/D | | |
| | .0 | .2 | .2 | .5 | | | .4 | .2 |
| | .2 | .5 | .7 | .5 | | Fixed/Worth | .8 | .6 |
| | 1.6 | 2.0 | 1.3 | .8 | | | 1.9 | 2.3 |
| | .3 | .2 | .3 | .3 | | | .4 | .2 |
| | 1.1 | .6 | .6 | .6 | | Debt/Worth | .9 | .8 |
| | -32.4 | 2.3 | 1.8 | 1.1 | | | 2.9 | 41.2 |
| | 178.8 | 69.9 | 15.1 | 13.5 | | | 26.2 | 44.7 |
| (10) | 67.7 | (26) 28.2 | (45) -6.0 | 10.4 | | % Profit Before Taxes/Tangible Net Worth | (143) 9.6 | (68) 10.4 |
| | 9.2 | 10.8 | -4.5 | -.5 | | | 2.5 | 1.0 |
| | 118.5 | 33.9 | 8.9 | 8.5 | | | 11.8 | 22.2 |
| | 7.5 | 15.5 | 2.6 | 6.1 | | % Profit Before Taxes/Total Assets | 4.4 | 6.3 |
| | -.7 | 3.6 | -2.9 | -.3 | | | .1 | -.3 |
| | 727.9 | 19.3 | 11.8 | 5.2 | | | 21.8 | 37.4 |
| | 52.4 | 4.4 | 3.0 | 3.3 | | Sales/Net Fixed Assets | 5.2 | 7.3 |
| | 6.3 | 1.9 | 1.4 | 2.4 | | | 2.2 | 2.4 |
| | 5.3 | 2.9 | 1.8 | 1.3 | | | 3.0 | 3.0 |
| | 3.8 | 1.2 | 1.0 | 1.2 | | Sales/Total Assets | 1.7 | 1.6 |
| | 2.3 | .9 | .7 | 1.0 | | | 1.1 | .8 |
| | | .8 | 1.1 | 1.5 | | | 1.1 | .7 |
| | (18) 1.7 | (45) 2.1 | (24) 2.0 | | % Depr., Dep., Amort./Sales | (130) 2.1 | (61) 1.8 |
| | 3.5 | 3.7 | 2.3 | | | 3.3 | 2.7 |
| | | | | | | % Officers', Directors' Owners' Comp/Sales | 4.5 | |
| | | | | | | | (19) 7.3 | |
| | | | | | | | 16.4 | |
| 15574M | 61351M | 257460M | 1522514M | 2118043M | 1463117M | Net Sales ($) | 4954136M | 2612491M |
| 1436M | 18372M | 142354M | 1243030M | 1743654M | 1342855M | Total Assets ($) | 3785463M | 2069252M |

M = $ thousand    MM = $ million
See Pages viii through xx for Explanation of Ratios and Data

© RMA 2024

# HEALTH CARE—Outpatient Mental Health and Substance Abuse Centers NAICS 621420

| Comparative Historical Data | | | | | Current Data Sorted by Sales | | | | | |
|---|---|---|---|---|---|---|---|---|---|---|
| 35 | 52 | 46 | Type of Statement | | | | | 4 | 10 | 32 |
| 1 | 2 | 2 | Unqualified | | | | | 1 | 1 | |
| 3 | 2 | 3 | Reviewed | | | | | 3 | | |
| 11 | 8 | 8 | Compiled | | | | | 3 | 2 | |
| 66 | 70 | 69 | Tax Returns | 1 | 1 | 1 | 3 | 15 | 12 | 26 |
| 4/1/21-3/31/22 | 4/1/22-3/31/23 | 4/1/23-3/31/24 | Other | 5 | 6 | 5 | 15 | 68 | | |
| ALL | ALL | ALL | | | 60 (4/1-9/30/23) | | | (10/1/23-3/31/24) | | |
| | | | | 0-1MM | 1-3MM | 3-5MM | 5-10MM | 10-25MM | 25MM & OVER | |
| 116 | 134 | 128 | NUMBER OF STATEMENTS | 6 | 7 | 6 | 26 | 25 | 58 | |
| % | % | % | ASSETS | % | % | % | % | % | % | |
| 36.6 | 31.6 | 27.1 | Cash & Equivalents | | | | 28.9 | 33.1 | 26.8 | |
| 17.2 | 15.5 | 14.7 | Trade Receivables (net) | | | | 16.2 | 15.6 | 13.9 | |
| .2 | .1 | .1 | Inventory | | | | .0 | .0 | .2 | |
| 2.5 | 4.7 | 4.1 | All Other Current | | | | 3.4 | 4.9 | 4.8 | |
| 56.5 | 51.9 | 46.0 | Total Current | | | | 48.4 | 53.6 | 45.8 | |
| 28.2 | 33.1 | 35.0 | Fixed Assets (net) | | | | 33.2 | 31.2 | 35.9 | |
| 3.4 | 2.7 | 3.1 | Intangibles (net) | | | | 2.1 | 4.0 | .5 | |
| 11.9 | 12.3 | 15.9 | All Other Non-Current | | | | 16.4 | 11.2 | 17.8 | |
| 100.0 | 100.0 | 100.0 | Total | | | | 100.0 | 100.0 | 100.0 | |
| | | | LIABILITIES | | | | | | | |
| 3.0 | 3.6 | 5.8 | Notes Payable-Short Term | | | | 6.7 | 2.4 | 1.6 | |
| 2.6 | 2.6 | 4.6 | Cur. Mat.-L.T.D. | | | | 2.1 | 1.9 | 2.4 | |
| 5.0 | 3.2 | 3.6 | Trade Payables | | | | 2.5 | 2.0 | 3.9 | |
| .0 | .0 | .0 | Income Taxes Payable | | | | .1 | .0 | .0 | |
| 12.4 | 12.2 | 9.2 | All Other Current | | | | 4.7 | 8.6 | 12.1 | |
| 23.1 | 21.7 | 23.3 | Total Current | | | | 16.0 | 14.9 | 20.1 | |
| 22.9 | 21.5 | 23.2 | Long-Term Debt | | | | 20.7 | 14.6 | 15.8 | |
| .0 | .0 | .0 | Deferred Taxes | | | | .0 | .0 | .0 | |
| 3.2 | 3.4 | 5.8 | All Other Non-Current | | | | 4.5 | 7.1 | 7.0 | |
| 50.8 | 53.3 | 47.7 | Net Worth | | | | 58.8 | 63.4 | 57.1 | |
| 100.0 | 100.0 | 100.0 | Total Liabilities & Net Worth | | | | 100.0 | 100.0 | 100.0 | |
| | | | INCOME DATA | | | | | | | |
| 100.0 | 100.0 | 100.0 | Net Sales | | | | 100.0 | 100.0 | 100.0 | |
| 89.8 | 93.5 | 91.9 | Gross Profit | | | | | | | |
| 10.2 | 6.5 | 8.1 | Operating Expenses | | | | 91.6 | 90.1 | 96.2 | |
| -.8 | .7 | .9 | Operating Profit | | | | 8.4 | 9.9 | 3.8 | |
| 11.0 | 5.8 | 7.2 | All Other Expenses (net) | | | | 1.1 | -.1 | -.7 | |
| | | | Profit Before Taxes | | | | 7.3 | 10.0 | 4.5 | |
| | | | RATIOS | | | | | | | |
| 6.3 | 5.8 | 5.8 | | | | | 12.7 | 8.3 | 4.5 | |
| 3.0 | 3.1 | 2.8 | Current | | | | 3.1 | 4.3 | 2.7 | |
| 1.6 | 1.6 | 1.4 | | | | | 1.5 | 2.6 | 1.6 | |
| 5.9 | 5.6 | 5.6 | | | | | 12.6 | 7.9 | 4.1 | |
| 3.0 | 2.8 | 2.5 | Quick | | | | 2.4 | 4.1 | 2.4 | |
| 1.5 | 1.5 | 1.2 | | | | | 1.2 | 2.5 | 1.3 | |
| 0 UND | 3 121.1 | 8 45.0 | | 0 UND | | 26 14.3 | 18 20.2 | | | |
| 27 13.7 | 29 12.4 | 29 12.7 | Sales/Receivables | 41 8.8 | | 37 9.9 | 31 11.6 | | | |
| 54 6.8 | 54 6.8 | 49 7.4 | | 76 4.8 | | 55 6.6 | 50 7.3 | | | |
| | | | Cost of Sales/Inventory | | | | | | | |
| | | | Cost of Sales/Payables | | | | | | | |
| 3.1 | 2.9 | 2.6 | | | | | 2.4 | 2.0 | 2.8 | |
| 6.0 | 5.3 | 4.7 | Sales/Working Capital | | | | 5.1 | 3.8 | 4.6 | |
| 18.9 | 14.8 | 22.6 | | | | | 40.9 | 6.8 | 13.1 | |
| 56.9 | 22.9 | 34.4 | | | | | 39.9 | 50.5 | 30.8 | |
| (77) 18.5 | (89) 5.5 | (105) 8.4 | EBIT/Interest | (22) 7.5 | (19) 10.2 | (52) 9.0 | | | | |
| 2.4 | -1.4 | 1.0 | | 1.0 | 2.0 | 1.0 | | | | |
| | | | Net Profit + Depr., Dep., Amort./Cur. Mat. L/T/D | | | | | | | |
| .1 | .2 | .2 | | | | | .1 | .2 | .4 | |
| .5 | .6 | .5 | Fixed/Worth | | | | .4 | .6 | .6 | |
| 1.2 | 1.0 | 1.2 | | | | | 1.5 | 1.1 | .8 | |
| .3 | .2 | .3 | | | | | .1 | .2 | .3 | |
| .6 | .6 | .6 | Debt/Worth | | | | .5 | .5 | .6 | |
| 1.8 | 1.5 | 2.1 | | | | | 2.4 | 1.3 | 1.4 | |
| 54.2 | 25.7 | 27.4 | % Profit Before Taxes/Tangible Net Worth | | | | 37.3 | 65.4 | 15.1 | |
| (105) 18.1 | (124) 9.1 | (116) 10.6 | | (24) 23.7 | (24) 12.5 | (57) 9.7 | | | | |
| 3.9 | -.1 | 1.9 | | -4.6 | 3.3 | .7 | | | | |
| 24.9 | 16.7 | 14.7 | % Profit Before Taxes/Total Assets | | | | 22.7 | 19.6 | 10.2 | |
| 12.4 | 5.1 | 6.6 | | | | | 12.9 | 6.8 | 5.9 | |
| 2.3 | -1.0 | .1 | | | | | -1.2 | 1.3 | -.6 | |
| 45.1 | 14.9 | 13.8 | Sales/Net Fixed Assets | | | | 80.9 | 15.2 | 5.9 | |
| 7.3 | 4.8 | 4.1 | | | | | 5.6 | 6.7 | 3.4 | |
| 2.9 | 2.2 | 2.2 | | | | | 1.8 | 1.6 | 2.3 | |
| 2.9 | 2.4 | 2.0 | Sales/Total Assets | | | | 4.1 | 2.0 | 1.7 | |
| 1.6 | 1.4 | 1.2 | | | | | 1.3 | 1.1 | 1.2 | |
| 1.0 | 1.0 | .9 | | | | | .9 | .8 | 1.0 | |
| 1.0 | 1.1 | 1.2 | % Depr., Dep., Amort./Sales | | | | 1.1 | .7 | 1.4 | |
| (81) 1.8 | (107) 1.9 | (104) 2.0 | | (18) 1.6 | (22) 1.8 | (56) 2.0 | | | | |
| 2.9 | 2.9 | 3.1 | | | | | 3.2 | 3.6 | 2.7 | |
| 4.1 | 3.9 | 1.3 | % Officers', Directors' Owners' Comp/Sales | | | | | | | |
| (15) 5.8 | (16) 6.6 | (13) 4.8 | | | | | | | | |
| 11.3 | 13.7 | 10.6 | | | | | | | | |
| 3398300M | 5389920M | 5438059M | Net Sales ($) | 2531M | 14581M | 24494M | 184814M | 431819M | 4779820M | |
| 2941822M | 4410985M | 4491701M | Total Assets ($) | 12584M | 9223M | 26135M | 177826M | 417741M | 3848192M | |

M = $ thousand    MM = $ million
See Pages viii through xx for Explanation of Ratios and Data

© RMA 2024

# HEALTH CARE—HMO Medical Centers  NAICS 621491

## Current Data Sorted by Assets

|  |  |  |  | 2 | 3 |
|---|---|---|---|---|---|
|  |  |  | 1 | 1 |  |
|  |  | 3 | 3 | 3 | 3 |
| 1 | 9 (4/1-9/30/23) | 2-10MM | 12 (10/1/23-3/31/24) | 50-100MM | 100-250MM |
| 0-500M | 500M-2MM | 2-10MM | 10-50MM | 50-100MM | 100-250MM |
| 1 |  | 4 | 4 | 6 | 6 |
| % | % | % | % | % | % |

## Comparative Historical Data

| | 2 | 2 |
|---|---|---|
| | 10 | 2 |
| | 4/1/19-3/31/20 | 4/1/20-3/31/21 |
| | ALL | ALL |
| NUMBER OF STATEMENTS | 12 | 8 |

| | Historical 4/1/19-3/31/20 % | Historical 4/1/20-3/31/21 % |
|---|---|---|
| **ASSETS** | | |
| Cash & Equivalents | 28.3 | |
| Trade Receivables (net) | 10.6 | |
| Inventory | 1.2 | |
| All Other Current | 8.1 | |
| Total Current | 48.3 | |
| Fixed Assets (net) | 25.6 | |
| Intangibles (net) | 6.3 | |
| All Other Non-Current | 19.8 | |
| Total | 100.0 | |
| **LIABILITIES** | | |
| Notes Payable-Short Term | 7.2 | |
| Cur. Mat.-L.T.D. | .8 | |
| Trade Payables | 6.0 | |
| Income Taxes Payable | .0 | |
| All Other Current | 23.6 | |
| Total Current | 37.7 | |
| Long-Term Debt | 10.7 | |
| Deferred Taxes | .1 | |
| All Other Non-Current | 6.5 | |
| Net Worth | 45.1 | |
| Total Liabilities & Net Worth | 100.0 | |
| **INCOME DATA** | | |
| Net Sales | 100.0 | |
| Gross Profit | | |
| Operating Expenses | 93.5 | |
| Operating Profit | 6.5 | |
| All Other Expenses (net) | .0 | |
| Profit Before Taxes | 6.5 | |

**RATIOS**

| | | |
|---|---|---|
| Current | 1.9 | |
| | 1.4 | |
| | .8 | |
| Quick | 1.8 | |
| | .9 | |
| | .6 | |
| Sales/Receivables | 4   89.2 | |
| | 10   37.0 | |
| | 34   10.7 | |
| Cost of Sales/Inventory | | |
| Cost of Sales/Payables | | |
| Sales/Working Capital | 8.4 | |
| | 19.5 | |
| | -135.0 | |
| EBIT/Interest | | |
| Net Profit + Depr., Dep., Amort./Cur. Mat. L/T/D | | |
| Fixed/Worth | .1 | |
| | .6 | |
| | 1.5 | |
| Debt/Worth | .6 | |
| | 1.5 | |
| | 3.3 | |
| % Profit Before Taxes/Tangible Net Worth | 25.4 | |
| | (10)  2.3 | |
| | -17.0 | |
| % Profit Before Taxes/Total Assets | 26.7 | |
| | 6.8 | |
| | -3.8 | |
| Sales/Net Fixed Assets | 78.0 | |
| | 25.3 | |
| | 4.6 | |
| Sales/Total Assets | 4.9 | |
| | 3.0 | |
| | 1.3 | |
| % Depr., Dep., Amort./Sales | | |
| % Officers', Directors' Owners' Comp/Sales | | |

| 0-500M | 500M-2MM | 2-10MM | 10-50MM | 50-100MM | 100-250MM | | Historical | Historical |
|---|---|---|---|---|---|---|---|---|
| 767M | | 20748M | 155164M | 398870M | 1582185M | Net Sales ($) | 1749072M | 865724M |
| 106M | | 23713M | 68350M | 431860M | 977667M | Total Assets ($) | 573111M | 380040M |

M = $ thousand     MM = $ million
See Pages viii through xx for Explanation of Ratios and Data

© RMA 2024

# HEALTH CARE—HMO Medical Centers  NAICS 621491

## Comparative Historical Data / Current Data Sorted by Sales

| Comparative Historical Data | | | | Current Data Sorted by Sales | | | | | |
|---|---|---|---|---|---|---|---|---|---|
| 2 | 7 | 7 | Type of Statement | | 1 | | | | 6 |
| | | 1 | Unqualified | | | | | | 1 |
| | 1 | 1 | Reviewed | | | | | | |
| 1 | 1 | 1 | Compiled | | | | | | |
| 6 | 5 | 13 | Tax Returns | | | | | | 8 |
| 4/1/21-3/31/22 ALL | 4/1/22-3/31/23 ALL | 4/1/23-3/31/24 ALL | Other | 0-1MM | 1 (4/1-9/30/23) 1-3MM | 3-5MM | 12 (10/1/23-3/31/24) 5-10MM | 10-25MM | 25MM & OVER |
| 9 | 14 | 21 | NUMBER OF STATEMENTS | 1 | 1 | 2 | 1 | 1 | 15 |
| % | % | % | ASSETS | % | % | % | % | % | % |
| | 37.3 | 33.2 | Cash & Equivalents | | | | | | 34.4 |
| | 8.7 | 18.0 | Trade Receivables (net) | | | | | | 15.6 |
| | .6 | .7 | Inventory | | | | | | .9 |
| | 7.4 | 9.4 | All Other Current | | | | | | 6.5 |
| | 54.1 | 61.3 | Total Current | | | | | | 57.4 |
| | 16.6 | 23.7 | Fixed Assets (net) | | | | | | 27.1 |
| | 12.5 | 1.6 | Intangibles (net) | | | | | | 1.1 |
| | 16.8 | 13.4 | All Other Non-Current | | | | | | 14.4 |
| | 100.0 | 100.0 | Total | | | | | | 100.0 |
| | | | LIABILITIES | | | | | | |
| | .2 | 2.3 | Notes Payable-Short Term | | | | | | .3 |
| | 1.6 | .8 | Cur. Mat.-L.T.D. | | | | | | .9 |
| | 8.2 | 8.2 | Trade Payables | | | | | | 11.3 |
| | .0 | .0 | Income Taxes Payable | | | | | | .0 |
| | 23.9 | 14.4 | All Other Current | | | | | | 15.4 |
| | 33.9 | 25.7 | Total Current | | | | | | 27.9 |
| | 7.4 | 8.0 | Long-Term Debt | | | | | | 8.2 |
| | .6 | 1.1 | Deferred Taxes | | | | | | 1.5 |
| | 7.6 | 7.9 | All Other Non-Current | | | | | | 10.9 |
| | 50.6 | 57.5 | Net Worth | | | | | | 51.5 |
| | 100.0 | 100.0 | Total Liabilities & Net Worth | | | | | | 100.0 |
| | | | INCOME DATA | | | | | | |
| | 100.0 | 100.0 | Net Sales | | | | | | 100.0 |
| | | | Gross Profit | | | | | | 97.4 |
| | 96.6 | 95.8 | Operating Expenses | | | | | | |
| | 3.4 | 4.2 | Operating Profit | | | | | | 2.6 |
| | -.7 | -.1 | All Other Expenses (net) | | | | | | -.5 |
| | 4.1 | 4.2 | Profit Before Taxes | | | | | | 3.1 |
| | | | RATIOS | | | | | | |
| | 2.5 | 4.6 | | | | | | | 3.8 |
| | 1.5 | 2.9 | Current | | | | | | 2.2 |
| | 1.3 | 1.7 | | | | | | | 1.6 |
| | 2.0 | 4.4 | | | | | | | 3.6 |
| | 1.4 | 1.9 | Quick | | | | | | 1.6 |
| | .9 | 1.4 | | | | | | | 1.3 |
| | 1   387.3 | 4   93.8 | | | | | | 7 | 53.7 |
| | 14   25.5 | 31  11.9 | Sales/Receivables | | | | | | 24  14.9 |
| | 32   11.5 | 69   5.3 | | | | | | 35 | 10.3 |
| | | | Cost of Sales/Inventory | | | | | | |
| | | | Cost of Sales/Payables | | | | | | |
| | 6.5 | 2.0 | | | | | | | 2.5 |
| | 11.0 | 4.0 | Sales/Working Capital | | | | | | 5.5 |
| | 36.0 | 10.7 | | | | | | | 10.9 |
| | 103.3 | 44.0 | | | | | | | 46.1 |
| (11) | 14.7 | (17)  5.0 | EBIT/Interest | | | | | | (13)  5.6 |
| | -7.2 | -7.3 | | | | | | | 1.2 |
| | | | Net Profit + Depr., Dep., Amort./Cur. Mat. L/T/D | | | | | | |
| | .0 | .0 | | | | | | | .4 |
| | .4 | .5 | Fixed/Worth | | | | | | .6 |
| | .7 | .6 | | | | | | | .6 |
| | .4 | .4 | | | | | | | .6 |
| | 1.2 | .7 | Debt/Worth | | | | | | 1.0 |
| | 3.2 | 1.4 | | | | | | | 1.7 |
| | 31.2 | 28.9 | % Profit Before Taxes/Tangible Net Worth | | | | | | 26.4 |
| (12) | 13.5 | 7.7 | | | | | | | 7.7 |
| | -35.3 | -.3 | | | | | | | .7 |
| | 16.6 | 13.7 | % Profit Before Taxes/Total Assets | | | | | | 11.5 |
| | 8.8 | 4.2 | | | | | | | 4.2 |
| | -8.8 | -.2 | | | | | | | .5 |
| | 331.9 | 91.4 | | | | | | | 25.1 |
| | 32.5 | 16.4 | Sales/Net Fixed Assets | | | | | | 4.7 |
| | 4.7 | 2.3 | | | | | | | 2.1 |
| | 3.6 | 2.8 | | | | | | | 2.9 |
| | 1.9 | 1.2 | Sales/Total Assets | | | | | | 1.2 |
| | 1.2 | .8 | | | | | | | .8 |
| | .2 | 1.2 | | | | | | | 1.2 |
| (11) | .7 | (16)  2.5 | % Depr., Dep., Amort./Sales | | | | | | (12)  2.6 |
| | 4.4 | 4.8 | | | | | | | 5.2 |
| | | | % Officers', Directors' Owners' Comp/Sales | | | | | | |
| 880039M | 2329188M | 2157734M | Net Sales ($) | 767M | 2616M | 8249M | 9883M | 20561M | 2115658M |
| 375679M | 953493M | 1501696M | Total Assets ($) | 106M | 2687M | 14069M | 6957M | 25591M | 1452286M |

M = $ thousand   MM = $ million
See Pages viii through xx for Explanation of Ratios and Data

© RMA 2024

# HEALTH CARE—Kidney Dialysis Centers NAICS 621492

## Current Data Sorted by Assets | Comparative Historical Data

| | | | | | | | Type of Statement | | | | |
|---|---|---|---|---|---|---|---|---|---|---|---|
| | | 3 | | | | | Unqualified | | 1 | | 2 |
| | | 2 | 2 | | 1 | | Reviewed | | 1 | | 1 |
| | | 1 | | | | | Compiled | | 3 | | 2 |
| 1 | 1 | 6 | | | | | Tax Returns | | 10 | | 8 |
| 2 | 16 | 29 | 8 | 5 | 2 | | Other | | 20 | | 29 |
| 0-500M | 8 (4/1-9/30/23) 500M-2MM | 2-10MM | 71 (10/1/23-3/31/24) 10-50MM | 50-100MM | 100-250MM | | | | 4/1/19-3/31/20 | | 4/1/20-3/31/21 |
| 3 | 17 | 41 | 10 | 5 | 3 | | NUMBER OF STATEMENTS | | 35 ALL | | 42 ALL |
| % | % | % | % | % | % | | ASSETS | | % | | % |
| | 13.9 | 12.4 | 14.2 | | | | Cash & Equivalents | | 23.7 | | 22.7 |
| | 23.7 | 14.4 | 13.0 | | | | Trade Receivables (net) | | 16.5 | | 10.7 |
| | .6 | .9 | .8 | | | | Inventory | | 3.1 | | 3.2 |
| | .8 | 2.3 | 1.9 | | | | All Other Current | | 1.2 | | 3.1 |
| | 38.9 | 30.0 | 29.9 | | | | Total Current | | 44.5 | | 39.7 |
| | 29.7 | 29.7 | 18.2 | | | | Fixed Assets (net) | | 35.8 | | 29.2 |
| | 9.2 | 7.7 | 15.9 | | | | Intangibles (net) | | 6.2 | | 18.6 |
| | 22.1 | 32.6 | 36.0 | | | | All Other Non-Current | | 13.5 | | 12.5 |
| | 100.0 | 100.0 | 100.0 | | | | Total | | 100.0 | | 100.0 |
| | | | | | | | LIABILITIES | | | | |
| | 9.6 | 5.9 | 4.1 | | | | Notes Payable-Short Term | | 2.9 | | 5.1 |
| | 2.9 | 8.5 | 1.9 | | | | Cur. Mat.-L.T.D. | | 3.3 | | 3.0 |
| | 3.1 | 2.7 | 3.0 | | | | Trade Payables | | 10.0 | | 4.1 |
| | .0 | .0 | .0 | | | | Income Taxes Payable | | .0 | | .0 |
| | 34.0 | 23.5 | 19.1 | | | | All Other Current | | 21.7 | | 17.7 |
| | 49.5 | 40.6 | 28.2 | | | | Total Current | | 37.9 | | 29.9 |
| | 21.0 | 28.1 | 24.0 | | | | Long-Term Debt | | 19.5 | | 24.6 |
| | .0 | .1 | .0 | | | | Deferred Taxes | | .0 | | .0 |
| | 9.1 | 9.0 | 13.8 | | | | All Other Non-Current | | 6.8 | | 2.7 |
| | 20.4 | 22.1 | 34.0 | | | | Net Worth | | 35.9 | | 42.8 |
| | 100.0 | 100.0 | 100.0 | | | | Total Liabilities & Net Worth | | 100.0 | | 100.0 |
| | | | | | | | INCOME DATA | | | | |
| | 100.0 | 100.0 | 100.0 | | | | Net Sales | | 100.0 | | 100.0 |
| | | | | | | | Gross Profit | | | | |
| | 89.4 | 80.3 | 67.4 | | | | Operating Expenses | | 87.3 | | 84.4 |
| | 10.6 | 19.7 | 32.6 | | | | Operating Profit | | 12.7 | | 15.6 |
| | 1.3 | 4.9 | 5.7 | | | | All Other Expenses (net) | | .7 | | 1.4 |
| | 9.4 | 14.8 | 26.9 | | | | Profit Before Taxes | | 12.0 | | 14.1 |
| | | | | | | | RATIOS | | | | |
| | 1.6 | 1.4 | 2.9 | | | | | | 2.1 | | 2.9 |
| | .8 | .8 | 1.2 | | | | Current | | 1.3 | | 1.5 |
| | .4 | .3 | .8 | | | | | | .7 | | .7 |
| | 1.6 | 1.2 | 2.7 | | | | | | 1.8 | | 2.9 |
| | .8 | .7 | 1.2 | | | | Quick | | 1.2 | | 1.1 |
| | .4 | .3 | .7 | | | | | | .7 | | .4 |
| | 0 UND | 0 UND | 0 UND | | | | | | 0 UND | | 0 UND |
| | 35 10.3 | 41 8.8 | 23 15.9 | | | | Sales/Receivables | | 40 9.2 | | 36 10.0 |
| | 46 7.9 | 51 7.1 | 59 6.2 | | | | | | 51 7.1 | | 52 7.0 |
| | | | | | | | Cost of Sales/Inventory | | | | |
| | | | | | | | Cost of Sales/Payables | | | | |
| | 33.9 | 22.0 | 4.4 | | | | | | 6.5 | | 5.8 |
| | -25.6 | -18.7 | 13.0 | | | | Sales/Working Capital | | 13.9 | | 12.3 |
| | -10.8 | -5.5 | NM | | | | | | -34.3 | | -17.5 |
| | 31.4 | 20.5 | | | | | | | 93.8 | | 41.4 |
| (13) | 8.8 | (37) 5.1 | | | | | EBIT/Interest | (26) | 10.1 | (29) | 10.0 |
| | .1 | -1.7 | | | | | | | 1.0 | | .8 |
| | | | | | | | Net Profit + Depr., Dep., Amort./Cur. Mat. L/T/D | | | | |
| | .4 | .2 | .0 | | | | | | .3 | | .3 |
| | 1.5 | 1.0 | .7 | | | | Fixed/Worth | | 1.1 | | 1.0 |
| | -3.2 | 14.8 | 4.0 | | | | | | 2.3 | | -1.5 |
| | 1.0 | 1.4 | 1.6 | | | | | | .7 | | .6 |
| | 13.9 | 2.3 | 4.1 | | | | Debt/Worth | | 1.7 | | 1.8 |
| | -9.9 | 23.7 | NM | | | | | | 7.3 | | -3.9 |
| | 439.6 | 98.8 | | | | | | | 133.8 | | 113.3 |
| (11) | 143.8 | (33) 38.2 | | | | | % Profit Before Taxes/Tangible Net Worth | (30) | 55.8 | (27) | 51.7 |
| | -16.7 | 9.6 | | | | | | | 6.2 | | 6.6 |
| | 36.5 | 23.1 | 17.7 | | | | % Profit Before Taxes/Total Assets | | 63.8 | | 48.0 |
| | 23.1 | 8.8 | 7.8 | | | | | | 16.4 | | 12.3 |
| | -7.7 | -7.4 | 1.4 | | | | | | 1.1 | | 1.3 |
| | 92.9 | 56.2 | UND | | | | | | 23.7 | | 55.4 |
| | 21.9 | 10.0 | 10.2 | | | | Sales/Net Fixed Assets | | 4.4 | | 15.9 |
| | 2.6 | 1.9 | 5.4 | | | | | | 2.6 | | 1.6 |
| | 5.2 | 2.3 | 2.4 | | | | | | 2.9 | | 3.3 |
| | 2.3 | 1.2 | 1.2 | | | | Sales/Total Assets | | 1.6 | | 1.5 |
| | 1.4 | .5 | .3 | | | | | | 1.1 | | .6 |
| | | | 1.7 | | | | | | 1.5 | | .9 |
| | | (28) 5.5 | | | | | % Depr., Dep., Amort./Sales | (28) | 2.5 | (35) | 2.8 |
| | | | 11.1 | | | | | | 5.8 | | 6.3 |
| | | | | | | | % Officers', Directors' Owners' Comp/Sales | | | | |
| 9550M | 58005M | 411907M | 261296M | 301304M | 213269M | | Net Sales ($) | | 871070M | | 1000964M |
| 590M | 21601M | 196471M | 193159M | 424845M | 312349M | | Total Assets ($) | | 735912M | | 1272831M |

M = $ thousand    MM = $ million
See Pages viii through xx for Explanation of Ratios and Data

© RMA 2024

# HEALTH CARE—Kidney Dialysis Centers  NAICS 621492

## Comparative Historical Data | Current Data Sorted by Sales

| Comparative Historical Data | | | | Current Data Sorted by Sales | | | | | | |
|---|---|---|---|---|---|---|---|---|---|---|
| 2 | 3 | 3 | Type of Statement | | | | | | | |
| | 1 | 5 | Unqualified | | | 2 | 1 | | | |
| 2 | 4 | 1 | Reviewed | | | | | | 2 | 3 |
| 5 | 3 | 8 | Compiled | | | | | | 1 | |
| 8 | 24 | 62 | Tax Returns | 1 | 4 | 1 | 1 | 1 | 1 | 11 |
| 4/1/21-3/31/22 ALL | 4/1/22-3/31/23 ALL | 4/1/23-3/31/24 ALL | Other | 4 | 14 | 17 | 9 | 7 | | |
| | | | | | 8 (4/1-9/30/23) | | | 71 (10/1/23-3/31/24) | | |
| | | | | 0-1MM | 1-3MM | 3-5MM | 5-10MM | 10-25MM | | 25MM & OVER |
| 17 | 35 | 79 | NUMBER OF STATEMENTS | 5 | 20 | 18 | 11 | 11 | | 14 |
| % | % | % | ASSETS | % | % | % | % | % | | % |
| 21.6 | 23.6 | 14.6 | Cash & Equivalents | 6.9 | 14.8 | 16.6 | 19.2 | 17.7 | | |
| 13.3 | 15.7 | 15.9 | Trade Receivables (net) | 8.8 | 26.4 | 20.4 | 17.3 | 13.9 | | |
| 2.4 | .8 | .9 | Inventory | .5 | .9 | 1.3 | .8 | 1.6 | | |
| 1.7 | 3.5 | 1.8 | All Other Current | .3 | 1.5 | 2.1 | 4.2 | 2.8 | | |
| 38.9 | 43.6 | 33.2 | Total Current | 16.5 | 43.5 | 40.3 | 41.4 | 36.0 | | |
| 29.1 | 17.8 | 28.6 | Fixed Assets (net) | 35.0 | 30.3 | 24.2 | 22.0 | 29.5 | | |
| 9.8 | 20.6 | 8.5 | Intangibles (net) | 7.6 | 8.7 | 8.9 | 13.2 | 8.5 | | |
| 22.1 | 17.9 | 29.7 | All Other Non-Current | 40.9 | 17.4 | 26.6 | 23.4 | 26.1 | | |
| 100.0 | 100.0 | 100.0 | Total | 100.0 | 100.0 | 100.0 | 100.0 | 100.0 | | |
| | | | LIABILITIES | | | | | | | |
| 1.5 | 12.9 | 7.5 | Notes Payable-Short Term | 8.7 | 9.0 | 15.4 | 4.0 | 2.9 | | |
| 5.1 | 4.9 | 6.1 | Cur. Mat.-L.T.D. | 12.7 | 4.9 | 1.7 | 1.7 | 2.0 | | |
| 2.7 | 2.5 | 2.8 | Trade Payables | 1.8 | 3.3 | 3.9 | 2.0 | 4.2 | | |
| .0 | .0 | .0 | Income Taxes Payable | .0 | .0 | .0 | .0 | .0 | | |
| 24.2 | 32.7 | 24.9 | All Other Current | 19.3 | 32.3 | 46.3 | 16.4 | 15.3 | | |
| 33.5 | 53.0 | 41.2 | Total Current | 42.4 | 49.6 | 67.4 | 24.0 | 24.3 | | |
| 21.7 | 29.4 | 24.7 | Long-Term Debt | 35.7 | 31.7 | 14.0 | 9.9 | 16.8 | | |
| .0 | .2 | .1 | Deferred Taxes | .0 | .0 | .0 | .3 | .4 | | |
| 3.9 | 6.3 | 11.8 | All Other Non-Current | 9.1 | 16.8 | 15.5 | 9.7 | 11.6 | | |
| 41.0 | 11.1 | 22.3 | Net Worth | 12.8 | 1.9 | 3.1 | 56.1 | 46.9 | | |
| 100.0 | 100.0 | 100.0 | Total Liabilities & Net Worth | 100.0 | 100.0 | 100.0 | 100.0 | 100.0 | | |
| | | | INCOME DATA | | | | | | | |
| 100.0 | 100.0 | 100.0 | Net Sales | 100.0 | 100.0 | 100.0 | 100.0 | 100.0 | | |
| | | | Gross Profit | | | | | | | |
| 90.1 | 77.5 | 83.4 | Operating Expenses | 72.6 | 94.2 | 88.4 | 85.6 | 99.9 | | |
| 9.9 | 22.5 | 16.6 | Operating Profit | 27.4 | 5.8 | 11.6 | 14.4 | .1 | | |
| -.1 | 1.6 | 3.6 | All Other Expenses (net) | 8.5 | 1.6 | .9 | .2 | .2 | | |
| 10.0 | 20.9 | 13.0 | Profit Before Taxes | 18.9 | 4.3 | 10.6 | 14.2 | -.1 | | |
| | | | RATIOS | | | | | | | |
| 5.5 | 2.4 | 1.5 | | 1.0 | 1.4 | 1.5 | 3.3 | 2.2 | | |
| 1.6 | .8 | .9 | Current | .5 | .8 | .8 | 1.7 | 1.3 | | |
| .7 | .4 | .4 | | .2 | .6 | .3 | 1.1 | 1.0 | | |
| 4.5 | 2.4 | 1.4 | | 1.0 | 1.3 | 1.3 | 3.3 | 2.0 | | |
| 1.4 | .7 | .9 | Quick | .4 | .8 | .8 | 1.6 | 1.2 | | |
| .5 | .4 | .4 | | .2 | .5 | .3 | 1.1 | .9 | | |
| 0  UND | 0  UND | 0  UND | | 0  UND | 33  11.0 | 0  UND | 0  UND | 18  20.6 | | |
| 45  8.2 | 17  21.8 | 36  10.0 | Sales/Receivables | 37  9.8 | 47  7.7 | 37  9.8 | 17  21.9 | 35  10.4 | | |
| 70  5.2 | 63  5.8 | 51  7.1 | | 47  7.7 | 59  6.2 | 51  7.1 | 64  5.7 | 51  7.2 | | |
| | | | Cost of Sales/Inventory | | | | | | | |
| | | | Cost of Sales/Payables | | | | | | | |
| 5.7 | 5.5 | 16.5 | | NM | 17.8 | 19.1 | 5.4 | 8.7 | | |
| 16.8 | -42.2 | -45.3 | Sales/Working Capital | -8.9 | -21.3 | -32.9 | 11.8 | 28.4 | | |
| -13.9 | -9.4 | -8.2 | | -1.1 | -10.0 | -18.7 | 116.7 | NM | | |
| 37.9 | 18.9 | 27.0 | | 12.7 | 12.8 | 30.5 | | 8.9 | | |
| (12)  8.9 | (27)  4.8 | (69)  5.4 | EBIT/Interest | (17)  2.8 | (15)  4.1 | 13.9 | | 3.9 | | |
| 2.0 | 1.0 | -1.7 | | -1.7 | -2.6 | -6.7 | | -6.0 | | |
| | | | Net Profit + Depr., Dep., Amort./Cur. Mat. L/T/D | | | | | | | |
| .2 | .0 | .2 | | .0 | 1.2 | .4 | .1 | .4 | | |
| .7 | 1.4 | 1.0 | Fixed/Worth | 1.6 | 4.6 | .9 | .3 | .7 | | |
| NM | -.4 | 24.7 | | -2.4 | -2.7 | -1.0 | 1.5 | 2.0 | | |
| .3 | 1.6 | 1.1 | | 1.3 | 1.7 | 1.2 | .7 | .4 | | |
| 2.0 | -8.8 | 2.5 | Debt/Worth | 6.1 | 13.8 | 2.8 | 1.3 | 1.6 | | |
| -22.3 | -2.5 | 999.8 | | -11.9 | -13.2 | -2.7 | 1.7 | 8.6 | | |
| 69.8 | 58.5 | 102.8 | | 200.6 | 217.7 | | 56.9 | 23.4 | | |
| (12)  28.0 | (14)  22.5 | (60)  24.8 | % Profit Before Taxes/Tangible Net Worth | (14)  18.8 | (12)  70.9 | | (10)  43.9 | (12)  7.6 | | |
| 8.2 | -10.1 | .3 | | -36.0 | -78.7 | | 3.8 | -4.0 | | |
| 18.6 | 25.8 | 25.4 | | 16.8 | 29.9 | 41.0 | 31.8 | 9.1 | | |
| 9.1 | 7.7 | 7.8 | % Profit Before Taxes/Total Assets | 6.6 | 8.0 | 27.5 | 16.8 | 2.9 | | |
| 1.9 | .0 | -4.5 | | -11.1 | -5.4 | -8.5 | 1.9 | -3.3 | | |
| 170.8 | 999.8 | 67.4 | | UND | 28.8 | 93.9 | 67.4 | 17.5 | | |
| 7.5 | 28.8 | 10.3 | Sales/Net Fixed Assets | 2.0 | 10.0 | 13.2 | 17.3 | 6.2 | | |
| 1.4 | 3.0 | 2.5 | | 1.2 | 2.7 | 4.1 | 5.8 | .7 | | |
| 2.6 | 6.0 | 2.5 | | 1.0 | 3.5 | 2.7 | 5.8 | 2.5 | | |
| .9 | 1.2 | 1.3 | Sales/Total Assets | .8 | 1.7 | 2.2 | 2.7 | 1.2 | | |
| .6 | .5 | .5 | | .3 | 1.2 | 1.1 | 1.5 | .5 | | |
| 2.4 | 1.9 | 1.7 | | 8.5 | 2.1 | | | 1.1 | | |
| (13)  6.7 | (17)  5.8 | (52)  5.0 | % Depr., Dep., Amort./Sales | (12)  11.9 | (12)  4.0 | | | (13)  3.6 | | |
| 11.4 | 9.7 | 8.8 | | 15.2 | 8.7 | | | 8.3 | | |
| | | 6.2 | % Officers', Directors' Owners' Comp/Sales | | | | | | | |
| | (10)  23.8 | | | | | | | | | |
| | | 29.0 | | | | | | | | |
| 481208M | 473192M | 1255331M | Net Sales ($) | 2352M | 35529M | 70871M | 83752M | 186090M | | 876737M |
| 534511M | 456310M | 1149015M | Total Assets ($) | 17230M | 90396M | 52032M | 47182M | 93428M | | 848747M |

M = $ thousand   MM = $ million  
See Pages viii through xx for Explanation of Ratios and Data

© RMA 2024

# HEALTH CARE—Freestanding Ambulatory Surgical and Emergency Centers  NAICS 621493

## Current Data Sorted by Assets | Comparative Historical Data

| | | | | | | Type of Statement | | |
|---|---|---|---|---|---|---|---|---|
| 1 | 1 | 4 | 6 | 2 | 1 | Unqualified | 14 | 8 |
| 1 | 1 | 1 | 5 |  |  | Reviewed | 15 | 1 |
| 1 | 5 | 5 | 8 |  |  | Compiled | 11 | 15 |
| 4 | 7 | 23 | 7 |  |  | Tax Returns | 51 | 26 |
| 2 | 23 | 68 | 50 | 8 | 6 | Other | 164 | 126 |
|  |  | 34 (4/1-9/30/23) |  | 204 (10/1/23-3/31/24) |  |  | 4/1/19- 3/31/20 | 4/1/20- 3/31/21 |
| 0-500M | 500M-2MM | 2-10MM | 10-50MM | 50-100MM | 100-250MM |  | ALL | ALL |
| 9 | 35 | 101 | 76 | 10 | 7 | NUMBER OF STATEMENTS | 255 | 176 |
| % | % | % | % | % | % | ASSETS | % | % |
|  | 33.7 | 20.9 | 13.5 | 10.7 |  | Cash & Equivalents | 19.1 | 23.0 |
|  | 5.2 | 20.7 | 19.9 | 13.5 |  | Trade Receivables (net) | 16.6 | 17.0 |
|  | 1.8 | 2.6 | 2.4 | 2.8 |  | Inventory | 3.5 | 2.7 |
|  | 1.8 | 2.3 | 4.0 | 5.2 |  | All Other Current | 2.7 | 2.1 |
|  | 42.5 | 46.4 | 39.9 | 32.2 |  | Total Current | 42.0 | 44.8 |
|  | 43.3 | 35.1 | 34.2 | 31.6 |  | Fixed Assets (net) | 39.0 | 38.5 |
|  | 8.1 | 8.6 | 14.7 | 27.6 |  | Intangibles (net) | 11.3 | 10.9 |
|  | 6.2 | 9.9 | 11.2 | 8.6 |  | All Other Non-Current | 7.7 | 5.8 |
|  | 100.0 | 100.0 | 100.0 | 100.0 |  | Total | 100.0 | 100.0 |
|  |  |  |  |  |  | LIABILITIES | | |
|  | 5.5 | 1.9 | 1.6 | .3 |  | Notes Payable-Short Term | 3.4 | 6.5 |
|  | 7.4 | 6.1 | 3.7 | 3.2 |  | Cur. Mat.-L.T.D. | 6.1 | 6.0 |
|  | 5.2 | 5.2 | 5.3 | 7.1 |  | Trade Payables | 5.7 | 4.0 |
|  | .1 | .0 | .0 | .1 |  | Income Taxes Payable | .0 | .0 |
|  | 16.8 | 8.4 | 9.4 | 8.9 |  | All Other Current | 12.2 | 13.4 |
|  | 35.0 | 21.7 | 19.9 | 19.6 |  | Total Current | 27.5 | 30.0 |
|  | 18.4 | 26.2 | 27.2 | 31.2 |  | Long-Term Debt | 26.5 | 31.9 |
|  | .0 | .0 | .0 | .0 |  | Deferred Taxes | .0 | .0 |
|  | .7 | 6.7 | 13.7 | 6.9 |  | All Other Non-Current | 2.6 | 5.7 |
|  | 45.8 | 45.4 | 39.1 | 42.3 |  | Net Worth | 43.4 | 32.5 |
|  | 100.0 | 100.0 | 100.0 | 100.0 |  | Total Liabilties & Net Worth | 100.0 | 100.0 |
|  |  |  |  |  |  | INCOME DATA | | |
|  | 100.0 | 100.0 | 100.0 | 100.0 |  | Net Sales | 100.0 | 100.0 |
|  |  |  |  |  |  | Gross Profit | | |
|  | 87.1 | 75.9 | 72.0 | 90.0 |  | Operating Expenses | 76.5 | 79.1 |
|  | 12.9 | 24.1 | 28.0 | 10.0 |  | Operating Profit | 23.5 | 20.9 |
|  | .6 | 3.1 | 2.4 | 3.8 |  | All Other Expenses (net) | 2.4 | .3 |
|  | 12.3 | 21.0 | 25.5 | 6.1 |  | Profit Before Taxes | 21.1 | 20.7 |
|  |  |  |  |  |  | RATIOS | | |
|  | 3.0 | 4.9 | 4.1 | 3.0 |  |  | 3.0 | 4.1 |
|  | 1.5 | 2.5 | 2.2 | 1.6 |  | Current | 1.7 | 1.8 |
|  | .4 | 1.2 | 1.3 | 1.0 |  |  | 1.0 | 1.0 |
|  | 2.9 | 4.2 | 2.9 | 2.7 |  |  | 2.5 | 3.4 |
|  | 1.3 | 2.0 | 1.8 | 1.1 |  | Quick | 1.5 | 1.5 |
|  | .3 | 1.0 | 1.1 | .6 |  |  | .8 | .8 |
| 0 | UND | 0 | UND | 31 | 11.9 | 0 UND |  | 0 UND |
| 0 | UND | 30 | 12.1 | 42 | 8.7 | 38 9.6 | Sales/Receivables | 31 11.6 | 34 10.6 |
| 5 | 68.9 | 46 | 8.0 | 57 | 6.4 | 57 6.4 |  | 46 8.0 | 53 6.9 |
|  |  |  |  |  |  | Cost of Sales/Inventory | | |
|  |  |  |  |  |  | Cost of Sales/Payables | | |
|  | 13.8 | 6.4 | 4.6 | 6.3 |  |  | 6.5 | 5.1 |
|  | 212.6 | 8.8 | 7.8 | 11.0 |  | Sales/Working Capital | 15.5 | 11.4 |
|  | -31.7 | 28.1 | 21.1 | NM |  |  | -491.5 | 999.8 |
|  | 298.8 | 186.5 | 100.0 |  |  |  | 137.8 | 136.2 |
| (27) | 54.5 | (84) 25.2 | (67) 39.0 |  |  | EBIT/Interest | (213) 36.4 | (149) 30.3 |
|  | -10.7 | 7.9 | 8.6 |  |  |  | 6.8 | 6.5 |
|  |  | 24.3 | 13.5 |  |  |  | 10.8 | 8.5 |
|  | (10) | 6.9 (10) | 12.2 |  |  | Net Profit + Depr., Dep., Amort./Cur. Mat. L/T/D | (30) 7.7 | (16) 4.2 |
|  |  | 2.2 | 5.2 |  |  |  | 1.5 | 2.2 |
|  | .1 | .3 | .5 | .5 |  |  | .4 | .4 |
|  | 1.0 | .9 | 1.3 | 1.7 |  | Fixed/Worth | 1.0 | 1.3 |
|  | 2.2 | 4.9 | 4.7 | -2.6 |  |  | 3.1 | 5.1 |
|  | .2 | .4 | 1.1 | .5 |  |  | .5 | .6 |
|  | .7 | 1.4 | 2.4 | 11.8 |  | Debt/Worth | 1.5 | 1.9 |
|  | 4.6 | 5.6 | 7.3 | -6.7 |  |  | 5.1 | 8.5 |
|  | 346.7 | 199.0 | 193.5 |  |  |  | 175.5 | 191.9 |
| (29) | 123.1 | (84) 91.7 | (64) 144.8 |  |  | % Profit Before Taxes/Tangible Net Worth | (215) 94.7 | (146) 97.7 |
|  | 22.5 | 34.8 | 76.3 |  |  |  | 36.3 | 42.4 |
|  | 166.1 | 91.9 | 51.0 | 36.4 |  |  | 85.1 | 63.9 |
|  | 86.5 | 40.8 | 27.7 | .1 |  | % Profit Before Taxes/Total Assets | 33.7 | 32.8 |
|  | -8.7 | 9.9 | 12.2 | -5.1 |  |  | 6.7 | 10.2 |
|  | 46.0 | 26.6 | 13.5 | 7.8 |  |  | 19.1 | 17.5 |
|  | 9.8 | 8.7 | 4.7 | 3.7 |  | Sales/Net Fixed Assets | 7.9 | 5.9 |
|  | 5.5 | 3.3 | 2.3 | 2.8 |  |  | 2.6 | 2.8 |
|  | 6.6 | 3.6 | 1.8 | 1.8 |  |  | 3.7 | 3.1 |
|  | 4.9 | 2.2 | 1.2 | 1.4 |  | Sales/Total Assets | 2.1 | 1.8 |
|  | 2.5 | 1.2 | .8 | .8 |  |  | 1.0 | 1.0 |
|  | 1.2 | 1.2 | 1.6 |  |  |  | 1.8 | 2.1 |
| (24) | 1.7 | (75) 2.3 | (73) 3.2 |  |  | % Depr., Dep., Amort./Sales | (215) 3.3 | (140) 3.6 |
|  | 4.4 | 5.8 | 5.4 |  |  |  | 5.6 | 6.8 |
|  |  |  |  |  |  | % Officers', Directors' Owners' Comp/Sales | 2.6 | 3.1 |
|  |  |  |  |  |  |  | (26) 6.7 | (15) 5.0 |
|  |  |  |  |  |  |  | 24.2 | 25.3 |
| 38494M | 224336M | 1270918M | 2128161M | 881389M | 895526M | Net Sales ($) | 5415835M | 3505083M |
| 2465M | 46359M | 537891M | 1494347M | 718542M | 1035618M | Total Assets ($) | 3517781M | 2391109M |

© RMA 2024

M = $ thousand    MM = $ million
See Pages viii through xx for Explanation of Ratios and Data

# HEALTH CARE—Freestanding Ambulatory Surgical and Emergency Centers  NAICS 621493

## Comparative Historical Data | Current Data Sorted by Sales

| | | | | Type of Statement | | | | | | |
|---|---|---|---|---|---|---|---|---|---|---|
| 9 | 13 | 14 | | Unqualified | | 1 | | 1 | 4 | 8 |
| 5 | 1 | 7 | | Reviewed | | 1 | | 4 | 4 | 2 |
| 12 | 14 | 19 | | Compiled | | | | 6 | 9 | 3 |
| 23 | 35 | 41 | | Tax Returns | 1 | 5 | 3 | 12 | 13 | 7 |
| 128 | 158 | 157 | | Other | 6 | 10 | 16 | 42 | 40 | 43 |
| 4/1/21-3/31/22 ALL | 4/1/22-3/31/23 ALL | 4/1/23-3/31/24 ALL | | | 0-1MM | 34 (4/1-9/30/23) 1-3MM | 3-5MM | 204 (10/1/23-3/31/24) 5-10MM | 10-25MM | 25MM & OVER |
| 177 | 221 | 238 | NUMBER OF STATEMENTS | 9 | 16 | 19 | 61 | 70 | 63 |
| % | % | % | **ASSETS** | % | % | % | % | % | % |
| 23.2 | 21.5 | 21.7 | Cash & Equivalents | 15.0 | 31.3 | 21.9 | 22.8 | 19.8 |
| 17.3 | 17.0 | 16.8 | Trade Receivables (net) | 5.5 | 10.5 | 14.4 | 21.2 | 21.2 |
| 3.0 | 2.3 | 2.3 | Inventory | .3 | .3 | 2.4 | 2.5 | 3.5 |
| 2.1 | 2.5 | 3.6 | All Other Current | 8.2 | 1.2 | 1.5 | 2.7 | 5.2 |
| 45.5 | 43.3 | 44.3 | Total Current | 28.9 | 43.2 | 40.2 | 49.2 | 49.6 |
| 31.8 | 38.6 | 35.1 | Fixed Assets (net) | 49.8 | 40.8 | 36.9 | 29.3 | 30.3 |
| 13.8 | 10.7 | 10.8 | Intangibles (net) | 10.3 | 1.5 | 13.7 | 12.8 | 9.9 |
| 8.9 | 7.4 | 9.8 | All Other Non-Current | 11.0 | 14.5 | 9.2 | 8.7 | 10.2 |
| 100.0 | 100.0 | 100.0 | Total | 100.0 | 100.0 | 100.0 | 100.0 | 100.0 |
| | | | **LIABILITIES** | | | | | | |
| 4.7 | 5.5 | 2.2 | Notes Payable-Short Term | 5.1 | 3.0 | 2.9 | 1.4 | 1.5 |
| 6.0 | 6.2 | 5.9 | Cur. Mat.-L.T.D. | 17.0 | 1.8 | 6.8 | 6.3 | 3.6 |
| 5.7 | 5.4 | 5.1 | Trade Payables | 1.8 | 1.9 | 6.0 | 5.3 | 6.4 |
| .0 | .0 | .0 | Income Taxes Payable | .0 | .0 | .0 | .0 | .0 |
| 13.1 | 9.8 | 11.5 | All Other Current | 23.2 | 18.0 | 8.6 | 11.1 | 11.2 |
| 29.4 | 27.1 | 24.8 | Total Current | 47.1 | 24.7 | 24.3 | 24.3 | 22.7 |
| 28.1 | 33.5 | 27.4 | Long-Term Debt | 67.6 | 14.7 | 22.2 | 22.6 | 27.8 |
| .0 | .0 | .0 | Deferred Taxes | .0 | .0 | .0 | .0 | .0 |
| 5.1 | 5.0 | 8.3 | All Other Non-Current | 2.6 | 16.6 | 6.3 | 7.9 | 10.4 |
| 37.4 | 34.4 | 39.6 | Net Worth | -17.3 | 44.0 | 47.1 | 45.3 | 39.1 |
| 100.0 | 100.0 | 100.0 | Total Liabilities & Net Worth | 100.0 | 100.0 | 100.0 | 100.0 | 100.0 |
| | | | **INCOME DATA** | | | | | | |
| 100.0 | 100.0 | 100.0 | Net Sales | 100.0 | 100.0 | 100.0 | 100.0 | 100.0 |
| | | | Gross Profit | | | | | | |
| 77.6 | 77.5 | 77.1 | Operating Expenses | 94.1 | 77.7 | 83.4 | 72.0 | 74.4 |
| 22.4 | 22.5 | 22.9 | Operating Profit | 5.9 | 22.3 | 16.6 | 28.0 | 25.6 |
| .5 | 2.3 | 2.6 | All Other Expenses (net) | 4.8 | .7 | 1.7 | 1.3 | 2.4 |
| 21.9 | 20.2 | 20.3 | Profit Before Taxes | 1.1 | 21.7 | 14.8 | 26.6 | 23.2 |
| | | | **RATIOS** | | | | | | |
| 3.6 | 4.5 | 4.3 | Current | 2.7 | 5.5 | 4.0 | 4.8 | 3.8 |
| 1.9 | 2.0 | 2.2 | | .9 | 2.5 | 1.7 | 2.4 | 2.4 |
| .9 | 1.0 | 1.2 | | .1 | .4 | 1.0 | 1.4 | 1.6 |
| 3.2 | 4.1 | 3.6 | Quick | 1.4 | 5.3 | 3.7 | 4.2 | 2.9 |
| 1.6 | 1.7 | 1.8 | | .6 | 2.4 | 1.6 | 2.0 | 1.9 |
| .7 | .9 | .9 | | .1 | .4 | .8 | 1.1 | 1.2 |
| 0 UND | 0 UND | 0 UND | Sales/Receivables | 0 UND | 0 UND | 0 UND | 22 16.6 | 22 16.8 |
| 30 12.1 | 26 13.9 | 31 11.7 | | 0 UND | 0 UND | 30 12.2 | 33 11.2 | 40 9.2 |
| 44 8.3 | 44 8.3 | 46 8.0 | | 1 276.9 | 78 4.7 | 45 8.1 | 45 8.1 | 54 6.7 |
| | | | Cost of Sales/Inventory | | | | | | |
| | | | Cost of Sales/Payables | | | | | | |
| 6.8 | 6.3 | 5.5 | Sales/Working Capital | 8.6 | 3.3 | 6.7 | 6.2 | 5.3 |
| 13.4 | 14.3 | 10.6 | | NM | 14.7 | 14.5 | 9.9 | 8.1 |
| -91.3 | 282.6 | 54.6 | | -4.3 | -49.0 | 591.3 | 27.0 | 20.6 |
| 138.5 | 113.9 | 146.3 | EBIT/Interest | 5.2 | 315.1 | 79.0 | 327.3 | 133.1 |
| (151) 34.7 | (177) 34.2 | (197) 34.4 | | (13) -.7 | (14) 30.7 | (51) 15.2 | (62) 62.9 | (53) 39.0 |
| 7.9 | 7.0 | 6.3 | | -28.7 | 6.9 | 5.6 | 21.0 | 7.4 |
| 24.7 | 13.4 | 13.4 | Net Profit + Depr., Dep., Amort./Cur. Mat. L/T/D | | | | | 13.4 |
| (17) 10.0 | (14) 9.8 | (27) 8.3 | | | | | | (15) 8.3 |
| 5.9 | 1.4 | 2.2 | | | | | | 2.1 |
| .3 | .4 | .4 | Fixed/Worth | 1.0 | .1 | .4 | .4 | .3 |
| 1.2 | 1.1 | 1.1 | | 4.0 | .7 | 1.3 | .9 | 1.1 |
| 6.6 | 6.9 | 5.0 | | -2.6 | 4.4 | 2.8 | 3.3 | 4.7 |
| .6 | .5 | .5 | Debt/Worth | 1.3 | .1 | .5 | .5 | .6 |
| 1.9 | 1.8 | 1.9 | | NM | .4 | 1.8 | 1.8 | 1.9 |
| 23.2 | 11.6 | 7.9 | | -3.6 | 7.0 | 6.9 | 5.8 | 7.8 |
| 225.5 | 186.9 | 202.3 | % Profit Before Taxes/Tangible Net Worth | | 176.3 | 183.6 | 252.2 | 214.0 |
| (137) 120.9 | (177) 109.4 | (194) 116.3 | | (15) | 115.2 | (50) 69.7 | (60) 142.5 | (52) 156.3 |
| 61.7 | 41.2 | 37.4 | | | 39.3 | 19.7 | 78.5 | 82.3 |
| 88.2 | 78.9 | 87.4 | % Profit Before Taxes/Total Assets | 17.4 | 115.5 | 56.4 | 107.5 | 86.1 |
| 40.6 | 32.5 | 33.8 | | -3.3 | 43.5 | 23.2 | 46.1 | 39.7 |
| 15.0 | 8.5 | 8.4 | | -13.3 | 8.3 | 2.7 | 21.6 | 13.2 |
| 28.3 | 27.4 | 24.0 | Sales/Net Fixed Assets | 22.8 | 35.3 | 18.0 | 36.0 | 24.9 |
| 9.9 | 7.6 | 7.5 | | 3.3 | 5.6 | 7.3 | 9.0 | 8.2 |
| 3.3 | 3.1 | 2.9 | | .8 | 1.8 | 3.4 | 3.7 | 3.5 |
| 3.4 | 3.9 | 3.3 | Sales/Total Assets | 2.4 | 3.8 | 3.4 | 3.9 | 3.0 |
| 2.0 | 2.0 | 1.8 | | .9 | 2.1 | 1.8 | 2.2 | 1.8 |
| 1.2 | 1.1 | 1.0 | | .4 | .8 | 1.0 | 1.2 | 1.1 |
| 1.5 | 1.3 | 1.4 | % Depr., Dep., Amort./Sales | | | 1.6 | 1.1 | 1.5 |
| (137) 3.2 | (167) 2.6 | (193) 2.6 | | | (51) 2.5 | (60) 2.2 | (59) 2.8 |
| 5.5 | 5.3 | 4.9 | | | | 5.6 | 4.4 | 4.3 |
| 1.0 | 2.8 | 1.0 | % Officers', Directors' Owners' Comp/Sales | | | | | |
| (21) 2.3 | (22) 9.7 | (15) 7.8 | | | | | | |
| 7.7 | 15.7 | 19.8 | | | | | | |
| 4968919M | 3522130M | 5438824M | Net Sales ($) | 4337M | 26653M | 78527M | 481564M | 1148241M | 3699502M |
| 2380704M | 2256945M | 3835222M | Total Assets ($) | 24195M | 39027M | 67325M | 420892M | 673366M | 2610417M |

M = $ thousand    MM = $ million
See Pages viii through xx for Explanation of Ratios and Data
© RMA 2024

# HEALTH CARE—All Other Outpatient Care Centers  NAICS 621498

## Current Data Sorted by Assets / Comparative Historical Data

| 0-500M | 500M-2MM | 2-10MM | 10-50MM | 50-100MM | 100-250MM | | 4/1/19-3/31/20 ALL | 4/1/20-3/31/21 ALL |
|---|---|---|---|---|---|---|---|---|
| 2 | 1 | 3 | 7 | 10 | 9 | Type of Statement | | |
| | 8 | 3 | 1 | | 1 | Unqualified | 41 | 17 |
| | | 1 | 1 | | | Reviewed | 1 | 4 |
| 11 | | 7 | | | | Compiled | 12 | 5 |
| | 15 | 29 | 35 | 15 | 15 | Tax Returns | 30 | 9 |
| | 46 (4/1-9/30/23) | | 128 (10/1/23-3/31/24) | | | Other | 106 | 87 |
| 13 | 24 | 43 | 44 | 25 | 25 | NUMBER OF STATEMENTS | 190 | 122 |
| % | % | % | % | % | % | ASSETS | % | % |
| 43.3 | 45.9 | 21.0 | 19.4 | 22.2 | 22.0 | Cash & Equivalents | 26.3 | 33.8 |
| 14.4 | 2.8 | 14.1 | 15.2 | 11.7 | 15.0 | Trade Receivables (net) | 14.6 | 13.7 |
| 1.0 | .4 | 2.7 | .8 | 1.4 | 2.0 | Inventory | 1.1 | 1.8 |
| 3.8 | 3.1 | 5.0 | 3.1 | 4.2 | 4.5 | All Other Current | 3.4 | 4.1 |
| 62.4 | 52.1 | 42.8 | 38.6 | 39.4 | 43.5 | Total Current | 45.5 | 53.4 |
| 25.2 | 22.4 | 38.3 | 37.4 | 40.9 | 33.9 | Fixed Assets (net) | 34.2 | 32.2 |
| 6.6 | 7.2 | 7.1 | 12.5 | 6.8 | 9.0 | Intangibles (net) | 11.0 | 6.1 |
| 5.9 | 18.3 | 11.7 | 11.6 | 12.9 | 13.6 | All Other Non-Current | 9.2 | 8.4 |
| 100.0 | 100.0 | 100.0 | 100.0 | 100.0 | 100.0 | Total | 100.0 | 100.0 |
| | | | | | | LIABILITIES | | |
| .1 | 9.3 | 6.6 | 3.6 | .2 | .5 | Notes Payable-Short Term | 6.3 | 7.3 |
| 13.6 | 1.6 | 3.2 | 2.6 | 2.0 | 2.3 | Cur. Mat.-L.T.D. | 3.6 | 3.8 |
| 13.3 | 2.7 | 3.4 | 4.5 | 4.7 | 7.9 | Trade Payables | 5.2 | 8.5 |
| .0 | .0 | .0 | .0 | .0 | .0 | Income Taxes Payable | .0 | .0 |
| 46.8 | 17.4 | 10.7 | 10.8 | 7.6 | 9.9 | All Other Current | 10.5 | 15.0 |
| 73.7 | 31.0 | 24.0 | 21.5 | 14.4 | 20.6 | Total Current | 25.7 | 34.6 |
| 18.8 | 12.8 | 21.9 | 18.8 | 18.9 | 25.1 | Long-Term Debt | 23.3 | 23.1 |
| .0 | .0 | .0 | .0 | .0 | .0 | Deferred Taxes | .1 | .0 |
| 9.5 | .0 | 5.4 | 24.7 | 5.4 | 6.2 | All Other Non-Current | 3.3 | 4.4 |
| -1.9 | 56.2 | 48.8 | 35.0 | 61.2 | 48.1 | Net Worth | 47.6 | 37.9 |
| 100.0 | 100.0 | 100.0 | 100.0 | 100.0 | 100.0 | Total Liabilties & Net Worth | 100.0 | 100.0 |
| | | | | | | INCOME DATA | | |
| 100.0 | 100.0 | 100.0 | 100.0 | 100.0 | 100.0 | Net Sales | 100.0 | 100.0 |
| | | | | | | Gross Profit | | |
| 83.3 | 79.7 | 83.6 | 92.0 | 94.5 | 96.6 | Operating Expenses | 89.0 | 86.3 |
| 16.7 | 20.3 | 16.4 | 8.0 | 5.5 | 3.4 | Operating Profit | 11.0 | 13.7 |
| 1.0 | .0 | 3.2 | 2.6 | -.8 | -.9 | All Other Expenses (net) | .8 | .4 |
| 15.7 | 20.3 | 13.2 | 5.5 | 6.3 | 4.3 | Profit Before Taxes | 10.2 | 13.3 |
| | | | | | | RATIOS | | |
| 4.2 | 5.2 | 4.6 | 3.6 | 5.1 | 4.4 | | 3.7 | 4.1 |
| 1.0 | 2.5 | 2.0 | 2.6 | 2.6 | 2.7 | Current | 2.1 | 2.0 |
| .4 | .6 | .7 | .9 | 2.0 | 1.4 | | 1.2 | 1.1 |
| 4.1 | 4.3 | 4.6 | 3.4 | 4.1 | 4.1 | | 3.4 | 3.7 |
| 1.0 | 1.9 | 1.9 | 2.1 | 2.6 | 2.2 | Quick | 1.8 | 1.7 |
| .4 | .6 | .5 | .8 | 1.4 | 1.1 | | 1.1 | .8 |
| 0 UND | 0 UND | 0 UND | 22 16.3 | 23 15.6 | 30 12.0 | | 0 UND | 0 UND |
| 0 UND | 0 UND | 16 22.9 | 38 9.7 | 33 11.1 | 42 8.6 | Sales/Receivables | 26 14.2 | 24 15.0 |
| 3 113.0 | 0 UND | 38 9.7 | 51 7.2 | 47 7.7 | 54 6.7 | | 45 8.2 | 45 8.2 |
| | | | | | | Cost of Sales/Inventory | | |
| | | | | | | Cost of Sales/Payables | | |
| 11.8 | 7.3 | 4.4 | 3.4 | 2.6 | 2.7 | | 5.0 | 4.0 |
| 999.8 | 28.8 | 8.2 | 7.4 | 5.4 | 4.3 | Sales/Working Capital | 12.3 | 7.7 |
| -19.8 | -39.5 | -29.5 | NM | 9.7 | 21.7 | | 44.2 | 119.8 |
| | 344.7 | 60.8 | 36.1 | 45.5 | 15.3 | | 38.3 | 57.6 |
| (12) 100.0 | (29) 14.4 | (39) 10.2 | (22) 16.7 | (23) 5.1 | EBIT/Interest | (147) 9.9 | (95) 14.6 |
| | 9.9 | 1.2 | -.6 | -2.3 | 1.0 | | 1.6 | 1.4 |
| | | | | | | Net Profit + Depr., Dep., Amort./Cur. Mat. L/T/D | 20.9 (10) 3.5 1.5 | |
| 1.1 | .1 | .4 | .5 | .4 | .6 | | .3 | .3 |
| 3.3 | .3 | .9 | .8 | .7 | .8 | Fixed/Worth | .9 | .8 |
| -.1 | 1.1 | 3.1 | 1.9 | 1.2 | 2.7 | | 1.9 | 2.7 |
| 1.8 | .1 | .4 | .4 | .3 | .3 | | .3 | .5 |
| 6.3 | .5 | 1.0 | .8 | .5 | .6 | Debt/Worth | .8 | 1.2 |
| -2.2 | 12.6 | 3.7 | 2.8 | 1.3 | 4.4 | | 3.6 | 6.4 |
| | 356.6 | 133.8 | 49.0 | 18.5 | 16.4 | % Profit Before Taxes/Tangible Net Worth | 111.9 | 101.0 |
| (21) 112.1 | (38) 44.3 | (38) 10.9 | (24) 4.6 | (20) 7.1 | (160) 18.5 | (98) 21.8 |
| | 37.3 | 2.3 | 2.2 | -7.2 | 2.9 | | 3.8 | 5.6 |
| 274.8 | 108.0 | 51.8 | 18.6 | 13.6 | 8.0 | | 48.4 | 49.6 |
| 53.2 | 47.4 | 11.7 | 4.4 | 2.9 | 2.9 | % Profit Before Taxes/Total Assets | 9.4 | 10.8 |
| -33.4 | 17.9 | 1.2 | -2.3 | -3.8 | .6 | | 1.0 | 2.2 |
| 580.3 | 297.4 | 21.9 | 9.5 | 5.7 | 16.5 | | 42.4 | 21.4 |
| 49.7 | 32.7 | 5.4 | 3.9 | 2.3 | 2.2 | Sales/Net Fixed Assets | 6.4 | 6.9 |
| 22.5 | 10.9 | 2.1 | 2.3 | 1.6 | 1.7 | | 2.7 | 2.4 |
| 18.9 | 8.8 | 2.8 | 1.9 | 1.4 | 1.1 | | 3.6 | 2.8 |
| 7.5 | 4.5 | 1.7 | 1.3 | 1.0 | .9 | Sales/Total Assets | 1.9 | 1.5 |
| 4.5 | 2.6 | 1.0 | .8 | .8 | .8 | | 1.1 | 1.0 |
| | .2 | 1.5 | 2.0 | 2.1 | 2.5 | | 1.5 | 1.3 |
| (11) 1.0 | (32) 2.6 | (40) 2.7 | (24) 3.1 | (19) 3.3 | % Depr., Dep., Amort./Sales | (141) 2.8 | (90) 2.6 |
| | 2.6 | 4.7 | 5.0 | 5.4 | 5.4 | | 4.2 | 3.9 |
| | | | | | | % Officers', Directors' Owners' Comp/Sales | 1.9 (29) 7.2 18.6 | 3.2 (16) 9.8 24.4 |
| 30305M | 133391M | 649235M | 1543503M | 1987261M | 5645920M | Net Sales ($) | 7147016M | 5597569M |
| 3193M | 24248M | 246995M | 1150462M | 1754114M | 3502303M | Total Assets ($) | 4689451M | 3353029M |

M = $ thousand    MM = $ million
See Pages viii through xx for Explanation of Ratios and Data

© RMA 2024

# HEALTH CARE—All Other Outpatient Care Centers  NAICS 621498

## Comparative Historical Data | Current Data Sorted by Sales

| Comparative Historical Data | | | Type of Statement | Current Data Sorted by Sales | | | | | |
|---|---|---|---|---|---|---|---|---|---|
| 21 | 37 | 29 | Unqualified | | | 2 | 2 | 3 | 24 |
| 3 | 8 | 5 | Reviewed | | | 1 | 1 | 1 | 4 |
| 5 | 4 | 3 | Compiled | 1 | | 1 | 6 | 3 | 1 |
| 17 | 20 | 17 | Tax Returns | 2 | 2 | 3 | 6 | 3 | 1 |
| 88 | 118 | 120 | Other | 6 | 15 | 8 | 10 | 28 | 53 |
| 4/1/21-3/31/22 ALL | 4/1/22-3/31/23 ALL | 4/1/23-3/31/24 ALL | | 0-1MM | 46 (4/1-9/30/23) 1-3MM | 3-5MM | 5-10MM | 128 (10/1/23-3/31/24) 10-25MM | 25MM & OVER |
| 134 | 187 | 174 | NUMBER OF STATEMENTS | 9 | 17 | 11 | 20 | 35 | 82 |
| % | % | % | **ASSETS** | % | % | % | % | % | % |
| 30.8 | 26.2 | 26.0 | Cash & Equivalents | | 29.6 | 48.9 | 29.8 | 26.7 | 21.3 |
| 14.8 | 15.8 | 12.6 | Trade Receivables (net) | | 2.5 | 15.5 | 12.0 | 11.9 | 15.2 |
| 1.0 | 1.2 | 1.5 | Inventory | | .0 | .4 | 3.3 | 1.6 | 1.6 |
| 7.1 | 5.6 | 4.0 | All Other Current | | 10.3 | .7 | 3.0 | 2.8 | 4.3 |
| 53.7 | 48.7 | 44.1 | Total Current | | 42.4 | 65.5 | 48.1 | 43.1 | 42.3 |
| 28.4 | 32.7 | 34.6 | Fixed Assets (net) | | 30.6 | 19.9 | 31.1 | 34.4 | 36.5 |
| 10.4 | 7.4 | 8.7 | Intangibles (net) | | 7.6 | 9.4 | 9.9 | 10.1 | 8.8 |
| 7.5 | 11.2 | 12.6 | All Other Non-Current | | 19.4 | 5.2 | 10.9 | 12.4 | 12.4 |
| 100.0 | 100.0 | 100.0 | Total | | 100.0 | 100.0 | 100.0 | 100.0 | 100.0 |
| | | | **LIABILITIES** | | | | | | |
| 3.0 | 2.1 | 3.9 | Notes Payable-Short Term | | 2.0 | 1.5 | 8.9 | 6.8 | 2.6 |
| 4.5 | 3.6 | 3.3 | Cur. Mat.-L.T.D. | | .6 | 1.0 | 4.1 | 2.9 | 2.8 |
| 5.9 | 5.2 | 5.2 | Trade Payables | | 3.5 | 6.5 | 7.4 | 4.5 | 5.6 |
| .0 | .0 | .0 | Income Taxes Payable | | .0 | .0 | .0 | .0 | .0 |
| 15.6 | 16.0 | 13.8 | All Other Current | | 25.2 | 31.2 | 11.3 | 10.6 | 9.3 |
| 29.1 | 26.9 | 26.2 | Total Current | | 31.4 | 40.2 | 31.8 | 24.8 | 20.4 |
| 20.2 | 18.9 | 19.6 | Long-Term Debt | | 33.9 | 5.1 | 10.8 | 17.3 | 21.5 |
| .2 | .0 | .0 | Deferred Taxes | | .0 | .0 | .0 | .0 | .0 |
| 3.4 | 6.5 | 10.0 | All Other Non-Current | | 2.8 | 3.9 | 6.9 | 2.5 | 16.3 |
| 47.1 | 47.7 | 44.2 | Net Worth | | 32.0 | 50.8 | 50.6 | 55.4 | 41.8 |
| 100.0 | 100.0 | 100.0 | Total Liabilities & Net Worth | | 100.0 | 100.0 | 100.0 | 100.0 | 100.0 |
| | | | **INCOME DATA** | | | | | | |
| 100.0 | 100.0 | 100.0 | Net Sales | | 100.0 | 100.0 | 100.0 | 100.0 | 100.0 |
| 84.2 | 83.6 | 88.6 | Gross Profit | | | | | | |
| 15.8 | 16.4 | 11.4 | Operating Expenses | | 84.8 | 75.2 | 96.4 | 85.3 | 94.4 |
| -.5 | .9 | 1.3 | Operating Profit | | 15.2 | 24.8 | 3.6 | 14.7 | 5.6 |
| 16.3 | 15.4 | 10.1 | All Other Expenses (net) | | 2.5 | -.4 | -1.0 | -.2 | 1.0 |
| | | | Profit Before Taxes | | 12.7 | 25.2 | 4.6 | 15.0 | 4.6 |
| | | | **RATIOS** | | | | | | |
| 5.0 | 5.5 | 3.9 | | | 5.9 | 12.1 | 3.7 | 3.5 | 3.9 |
| 2.6 | 2.7 | 2.4 | Current | | 1.0 | 2.4 | 1.9 | 2.6 | 2.7 |
| 1.2 | 1.5 | .9 | | | .4 | .6 | .7 | .8 | 1.5 |
| 4.3 | 4.4 | 3.6 | | | 4.3 | 12.1 | 3.4 | 3.4 | 3.6 |
| 2.3 | 2.3 | 2.0 | Quick | | .8 | 2.2 | 1.7 | 2.0 | 2.3 |
| 1.0 | 1.3 | .8 | | | .2 | .6 | .5 | .8 | 1.2 |
| 0  UND | 0  UND | 0  UND | | 0  UND | 0  UND | 0  UND | 0  UND | 24  15.2 | |
| 24  15.4 | 26  14.0 | 25  14.4 | Sales/Receivables | 0  UND | 0  UND | 17  21.4 | 23  15.8 | 36  10.0 | |
| 41  8.8 | 51  7.2 | 45  8.2 | | 0  UND | 27  13.6 | 45  8.1 | 41  8.8 | 51  7.1 | |
| | | | Cost of Sales/Inventory | | | | | | |
| | | | Cost of Sales/Payables | | | | | | |
| 3.6 | 3.5 | 3.7 | | | 6.6 | 3.6 | 4.2 | 4.7 | 3.4 |
| 7.1 | 7.7 | 8.3 | Sales/Working Capital | | 999.8 | 14.3 | 19.4 | 8.8 | 5.9 |
| 55.1 | 22.3 | -344.0 | | | -24.4 | -24.7 | -31.3 | -20.7 | 24.2 |
| 74.6 | 108.8 | 44.9 | | | 37.9 | | 141.1 | 73.0 | 36.2 |
| (105) 25.7 | (121) 22.8 | (133) 10.2 | EBIT/Interest | (10) 4.8 | | (13) 9.3 | (28) 16.7 | (73) 5.9 | |
| 6.9 | 4.0 | .4 | | | -2.4 | | -.4 | 2.1 | .0 |
| | 21.7 | 17.8 | | | | | | | 19.0 |
| (17) | 11.2 (13) | 11.7 | Net Profit + Depr., Dep., Amort./Cur. Mat. L/T/D | | | | | (11) | 15.5 |
| | 2.5 | 2.7 | | | | | | | 2.0 |
| .2 | .3 | .4 | | | .1 | .0 | .4 | .4 | .4 |
| .5 | .6 | .8 | Fixed/Worth | | .9 | .4 | 1.0 | .6 | .7 |
| 1.6 | 1.2 | 2.5 | | | -10.0 | 2.0 | 2.4 | 1.9 | 1.4 |
| .3 | .3 | .3 | | | .3 | .2 | .4 | .4 | .3 |
| .8 | .8 | .8 | Debt/Worth | | 2.4 | .8 | .9 | .8 | .7 |
| 3.6 | 2.8 | 4.8 | | | -13.3 | 16.0 | 8.6 | 4.7 | 2.1 |
| 99.0 | 133.5 | 103.3 | | | 188.5 | | 317.4 | 193.9 | 22.0 |
| (114) 34.4 | (162) 32.6 | (149) 14.9 | % Profit Before Taxes/Tangible Net Worth | (12) | 38.6 | (17) 43.5 | (34) 41.6 | (70) 8.4 | |
| 13.8 | 7.4 | 2.2 | | | 2.9 | | -2.8 | 4.6 | .8 |
| 45.5 | 45.2 | 35.6 | | | 52.5 | 93.1 | 43.9 | 55.5 | 14.1 |
| 17.1 | 13.3 | 8.2 | % Profit Before Taxes/Total Assets | | 20.7 | 43.0 | 9.6 | 13.3 | 3.1 |
| 5.4 | 2.9 | .3 | | | 2.1 | 9.9 | -3.2 | 2.3 | -1.5 |
| 41.2 | 33.6 | 21.0 | | | 73.6 | UND | 46.0 | 25.7 | 14.9 |
| 10.4 | 6.1 | 4.4 | Sales/Net Fixed Assets | | 24.3 | 35.3 | 10.5 | 4.4 | 3.2 |
| 2.7 | 2.3 | 2.1 | | | 3.6 | 7.3 | 2.9 | 2.5 | 1.8 |
| 3.0 | 3.1 | 2.9 | | | 5.7 | 6.7 | 7.6 | 2.8 | 2.0 |
| 1.8 | 1.6 | 1.3 | Sales/Total Assets | | 3.6 | 3.6 | 1.8 | 1.4 | 1.1 |
| 1.0 | .9 | .9 | | | 1.0 | 1.8 | 1.0 | .9 | .9 |
| 1.0 | 1.3 | 1.7 | | | | | 2.1 | 2.0 | 1.9 |
| (92) 2.3 | (142) 2.5 | (132) 2.7 | % Depr., Dep., Amort./Sales | | | (13) 2.7 | (28) 2.6 | (71) 3.0 | |
| 3.7 | 3.7 | 4.8 | | | | | 3.5 | 4.6 | 5.4 |
| 7.8 | 4.2 | 3.8 | | | | | | | |
| (18) 10.3 | (18) 7.2 | (17) 8.1 | % Officers', Directors' Owners' Comp/Sales | | | | | | |
| 18.5 | 11.3 | 13.6 | | | | | | | |
| 5827778M | 8379568M | 9989615M | Net Sales ($) | 5218M | 34314M | 45370M | 140569M | 591380M | 9172764M |
| 3244412M | 5885189M | 6681315M | Total Assets ($) | 15435M | 18540M | 21182M | 81109M | 465716M | 6079333M |

M = $ thousand     MM = $ million
See Pages viii through xx for Explanation of Ratios and Data

© RMA 2024

# HEALTH CARE—Medical Laboratories  NAICS 621511

## Current Data Sorted by Assets

| | | | | | | | Type of Statement | | |
|---|---|---|---|---|---|---|---|---|---|
| | | | 1 | 6 | | 1 | Unqualified | | |
| | 2 | | 7 | 3 | | | Reviewed | | |
| 1 | 5 | | | | | | Compiled | | |
| 4 | 15 | | 17 | 15 | 7 | 6 | Tax Returns | | |
| 2 | 8 (4/1-9/30/23) | | | 84 (10/1/23-3/31/24) | | | Other | | |
| 0-500M | 500M-2MM | 2-10MM | 10-50MM | 50-100MM | 100-250MM | | NUMBER OF STATEMENTS | | |
| 7 | 22 | 25 | 24 | 7 | 6 | | | | |

## Comparative Historical Data

| | | |
|---|---|---|
| | 8 | 14 |
| | 3 | 1 |
| | 3 | 4 |
| | 22 | 8 |
| | 64 | 41 |
| | 4/1/19-3/31/20 | 4/1/20-3/31/21 |
| | ALL | ALL |
| | 100 | 68 |

| % | % | % | % | % | % | | ASSETS | % | % |
|---|---|---|---|---|---|---|---|---|---|
| | 45.2 | 17.5 | 11.7 | | | | Cash & Equivalents | 24.4 | 27.1 |
| | 14.6 | 34.8 | 36.4 | | | | Trade Receivables (net) | 21.4 | 22.7 |
| | 1.3 | 5.0 | 2.7 | | | | Inventory | 2.8 | 3.4 |
| | 2.4 | 6.7 | 8.7 | | | | All Other Current | 7.4 | 6.5 |
| | 63.4 | 64.0 | 59.4 | | | | Total Current | 55.9 | 59.7 |
| | 20.4 | 13.9 | 18.8 | | | | Fixed Assets (net) | 21.2 | 21.2 |
| | 3.4 | 13.6 | 8.2 | | | | Intangibles (net) | 12.9 | 11.4 |
| | 12.9 | 8.5 | 13.6 | | | | All Other Non-Current | 10.0 | 7.7 |
| | 100.0 | 100.0 | 100.0 | | | | Total | 100.0 | 100.0 |
| | | | | | | | **LIABILITIES** | | |
| | 3.6 | 5.3 | 7.9 | | | | Notes Payable-Short Term | 8.1 | 14.2 |
| | 5.1 | 2.8 | 2.9 | | | | Cur. Mat.-L.T.D. | 3.7 | 1.9 |
| | 2.5 | 7.7 | 8.9 | | | | Trade Payables | 7.6 | 7.8 |
| | .0 | .1 | .3 | | | | Income Taxes Payable | .1 | .1 |
| | 35.4 | 28.1 | 14.7 | | | | All Other Current | 20.6 | 15.6 |
| | 46.5 | 44.1 | 34.7 | | | | Total Current | 40.1 | 39.7 |
| | 25.4 | 13.2 | 15.4 | | | | Long-Term Debt | 23.1 | 25.2 |
| | .0 | .6 | .3 | | | | Deferred Taxes | .2 | .4 |
| | 4.9 | 10.4 | 11.1 | | | | All Other Non-Current | 13.2 | 12.9 |
| | 23.2 | 31.7 | 38.5 | | | | Net Worth | 23.4 | 21.9 |
| | 100.0 | 100.0 | 100.0 | | | | Total Liabilities & Net Worth | 100.0 | 100.0 |
| | | | | | | | **INCOME DATA** | | |
| | 100.0 | 100.0 | 100.0 | | | | Net Sales | 100.0 | 100.0 |
| | | | | | | | Gross Profit | | |
| | 90.6 | 87.1 | 87.4 | | | | Operating Expenses | 86.7 | 82.0 |
| | 9.4 | 12.9 | 12.6 | | | | Operating Profit | 13.3 | 18.0 |
| | .8 | -.9 | .7 | | | | All Other Expenses (net) | 2.6 | .1 |
| | 8.6 | 13.8 | 11.9 | | | | Profit Before Taxes | 10.8 | 17.9 |
| | | | | | | | **RATIOS** | | |
| | 10.3 | 9.4 | 5.0 | | | | | 4.2 | 4.8 |
| | 3.9 | 2.0 | 1.5 | | | | Current | 1.8 | 2.1 |
| | 1.3 | 1.1 | 1.0 | | | | | 1.0 | 1.0 |
| | 7.6 | 8.4 | 4.1 | | | | | 3.6 | 4.4 |
| | 3.5 | 2.0 | 1.3 | | | | Quick | 1.5 | 1.7 |
| | 1.3 | .9 | .7 | | | | | .7 | .8 |
| 0 UND | 5 69.5 | 41 8.8 | | | | | | 0 UND | 0 UND |
| 0 UND | 57 6.4 | 70 5.2 | | | | | Sales/Receivables | 31 11.8 | 42 8.7 |
| 40 9.1 | 79 4.6 | 140 2.6 | | | | | | 56 6.5 | 72 5.1 |
| | | | | | | | Cost of Sales/Inventory | | |
| | | | | | | | Cost of Sales/Payables | | |
| | 5.7 | 3.5 | 2.1 | | | | | 4.9 | 4.3 |
| | 12.0 | 9.0 | 8.2 | | | | Sales/Working Capital | 16.6 | 9.1 |
| | 36.9 | 367.4 | NM | | | | | NM | NM |
| | 31.4 | 100.6 | 57.4 | | | | | 49.4 | 89.2 |
| (15) | 4.1 | (20) 44.2 | (21) 20.8 | | | | EBIT/Interest | (71) 9.0 | (50) 19.8 |
| | .2 | 3.0 | 2.5 | | | | | -.6 | 2.9 |
| | | | | | | | Net Profit + Depr., Dep., | 10.1 | |
| | | | | | | | Amort./Cur. Mat. L/T/D | (10) 4.6 | |
| | | | | | | | | 1.3 | |
| | .0 | .1 | .2 | | | | | .1 | .1 |
| | .2 | .3 | .6 | | | | Fixed/Worth | .6 | .5 |
| | 1.0 | NM | NM | | | | | 163.1 | 2.7 |
| | .2 | .5 | .5 | | | | | .3 | .5 |
| | .9 | 1.2 | 2.0 | | | | Debt/Worth | 1.7 | 1.6 |
| | NM | -7.4 | NM | | | | | -10.9 | UND |
| | 210.3 | 113.2 | 92.2 | | | | | 154.5 | 137.3 |
| (17) | 22.6 | (18) 83.7 | (18) 59.0 | | | | % Profit Before Taxes/Tangible Net Worth | (73) 59.3 | (52) 65.2 |
| | -8.2 | 61.1 | 16.8 | | | | | 16.8 | 23.0 |
| | 70.2 | 65.0 | 40.0 | | | | | 52.8 | 76.8 |
| | 16.4 | 24.6 | 16.8 | | | | % Profit Before Taxes/Total Assets | 17.6 | 19.2 |
| | -2.6 | -10.7 | .6 | | | | | -.8 | 5.5 |
| | UND | 119.5 | 31.2 | | | | | 101.4 | 59.1 |
| | 108.9 | 46.8 | 10.7 | | | | Sales/Net Fixed Assets | 20.5 | 18.5 |
| | 6.7 | 8.4 | 5.4 | | | | | 7.9 | 6.1 |
| | 7.0 | 4.0 | 2.2 | | | | | 4.9 | 4.4 |
| | 3.7 | 2.2 | 1.4 | | | | Sales/Total Assets | 2.4 | 2.0 |
| | 2.4 | 1.5 | .8 | | | | | 1.4 | 1.2 |
| | | | 1.6 | | | | | 1.0 | .7 |
| | | (22) 3.0 | | | | | % Depr., Dep., Amort./Sales | (63) 2.3 | (42) 2.6 |
| | | | 5.5 | | | | | 4.1 | 5.9 |
| | | 1.0 | | | | | | 2.4 | 1.4 |
| | (11) | 2.8 | | | | | % Officers', Directors' Owners' Comp/Sales | (22) 5.6 | (16) 4.7 |
| | | 4.4 | | | | | | 18.1 | 12.6 |
| 13773M | 139669M | 284816M | 958184M | 603503M | 734801M | | Net Sales ($) | 3579784M | 3104359M |
| 1411M | 22544M | 109001M | 562505M | 502088M | 988873M | | Total Assets ($) | 2243737M | 2112189M |

© RMA 2024

M = $ thousand    MM = $ million
See Pages viii through xx for Explanation of Ratios and Data

## HEALTH CARE—Medical Laboratories  NAICS 621511

### Comparative Historical Data | Current Data Sorted by Sales

| Comparative Historical Data | | | | | | Current Data Sorted by Sales | | | | | |
|---|---|---|---|---|---|---|---|---|---|---|---|
| | | | | **Type of Statement** | | | | | | | |
| 6 | 8 | 7 | | Unqualified | | | | 1 | 3 | | 7 |
| 1 | 4 | 4 | | Reviewed | | | 1 | 1 | 1 | | |
| 1 | 4 | 3 | | Compiled | | 1 | 5 | 2 | 5 | | |
| 9 | 16 | 16 | | Tax Returns | 2 | 2 | 8 | 13 | 11 | | 22 |
| 49 | 59 | 62 | | Other | 2 | 6 | | | | | |
| 4/1/21-3/31/22 ALL | 4/1/22-3/31/23 ALL | 4/1/23-3/31/24 ALL | | | 8 (4/1-9/30/23) | | | 84 (10/1/23-3/31/24) | | | |
| | | | | | 0-1MM | 1-3MM | 3-5MM | 5-10MM | 10-25MM | | 25MM & OVER |
| 66 | 91 | 92 | | NUMBER OF STATEMENTS | 4 | 9 | 14 | 16 | 20 | | 29 |
| % | % | % | | **ASSETS** | % | % | % | % | % | | % |
| 30.0 | 24.2 | 22.3 | | Cash & Equivalents | | | 31.9 | 24.1 | 24.0 | | 15.4 |
| 22.5 | 23.3 | 26.2 | | Trade Receivables (net) | | | 22.2 | 34.2 | 27.6 | | 26.7 |
| 3.6 | 2.6 | 2.8 | | Inventory | | | 1.0 | 5.8 | 3.2 | | 2.3 |
| 5.5 | 5.7 | 6.2 | | All Other Current | | | 9.2 | 1.4 | 11.4 | | 6.1 |
| 61.5 | 55.8 | 57.5 | | Total Current | | | 64.4 | 65.4 | 66.2 | | 50.5 |
| 18.2 | 25.4 | 18.4 | | Fixed Assets (net) | | | 14.9 | 20.0 | 12.0 | | 17.4 |
| 10.7 | 9.0 | 11.6 | | Intangibles (net) | | | 9.8 | 3.4 | 9.3 | | 19.5 |
| 9.5 | 9.8 | 12.5 | | All Other Non-Current | | | 10.8 | 11.2 | 12.5 | | 12.6 |
| 100.0 | 100.0 | 100.0 | | Total | | | 100.0 | 100.0 | 100.0 | | 100.0 |
| | | | | **LIABILITIES** | | | | | | | |
| 2.2 | 6.0 | 8.2 | | Notes Payable-Short Term | | | 16.7 | 8.3 | 5.3 | | 3.5 |
| 3.4 | 3.1 | 5.7 | | Cur. Mat.-L.T.D. | | | 1.1 | 2.1 | 2.7 | | 6.4 |
| 9.2 | 7.9 | 7.3 | | Trade Payables | | | 10.6 | 7.3 | 7.9 | | 7.1 |
| .1 | .2 | .1 | | Income Taxes Payable | | | .0 | .1 | .0 | | .3 |
| 18.4 | 14.8 | 23.5 | | All Other Current | | | 18.4 | 10.6 | 27.0 | | 18.1 |
| 33.2 | 32.0 | 44.9 | | Total Current | | | 46.9 | 28.4 | 43.0 | | 35.3 |
| 24.0 | 24.7 | 25.9 | | Long-Term Debt | | | 36.4 | 22.7 | 8.4 | | 22.5 |
| .3 | .4 | .6 | | Deferred Taxes | | | .6 | .0 | .3 | | 1.3 |
| 7.7 | 5.4 | 7.6 | | All Other Non-Current | | | 6.6 | 11.9 | 9.7 | | 5.2 |
| 34.9 | 37.4 | 21.0 | | Net Worth | | | 9.4 | 37.0 | 38.7 | | 35.6 |
| 100.0 | 100.0 | 100.0 | | Total Liabilities & Net Worth | | | 100.0 | 100.0 | 100.0 | | 100.0 |
| | | | | **INCOME DATA** | | | | | | | |
| 100.0 | 100.0 | 100.0 | | Net Sales | | | 100.0 | 100.0 | 100.0 | | 100.0 |
| | | | | Gross Profit | | | | | | | |
| 84.7 | 88.5 | 89.6 | | Operating Expenses | | | 87.2 | 88.2 | 88.7 | | 88.7 |
| 15.3 | 11.5 | 10.4 | | Operating Profit | | | 12.8 | 11.8 | 11.3 | | 11.3 |
| -.2 | 2.7 | 1.7 | | All Other Expenses (net) | | | .9 | 1.0 | -1.6 | | 4.5 |
| 15.5 | 8.8 | 8.7 | | Profit Before Taxes | | | 11.9 | 10.8 | 12.9 | | 6.8 |
| | | | | **RATIOS** | | | | | | | |
| 5.7 | 7.3 | 4.9 | | | | | 17.2 | 16.4 | 6.1 | | 2.3 |
| 2.2 | 2.3 | 1.8 | | Current | | | 2.0 | 4.4 | 2.5 | | 1.4 |
| 1.3 | 1.1 | 1.0 | | | | | .8 | 1.2 | 1.0 | | .8 |
| 5.5 | 6.9 | 4.5 | | | | | 14.8 | 14.3 | 4.7 | | 1.7 |
| 1.9 | 2.1 | 1.5 | | Quick | | | 1.9 | 4.1 | 2.0 | | 1.3 |
| 1.0 | .9 | .7 | | | | | .3 | 1.0 | .9 | | .6 |
| 0 UND | 0 UND | 0 UND | | | 0 UND | 0 UND | 0 UND | 35 10.4 | | | |
| 39 9.3 | 34 10.7 | 42 8.6 | | Sales/Receivables | 0 UND | 60 6.1 | 33 10.9 | 52 7.0 | | | |
| 69 5.3 | 64 5.7 | 70 5.2 | | | 46 8.0 | 114 3.2 | 83 4.4 | 74 4.9 | | | |
| | | | | Cost of Sales/Inventory | | | | | | | |
| | | | | Cost of Sales/Payables | | | | | | | |
| 4.4 | 3.7 | 4.2 | | | | | 5.4 | 2.2 | 4.2 | | 4.6 |
| 7.6 | 9.0 | 12.0 | | Sales/Working Capital | | | 20.2 | 7.3 | 14.5 | | 13.2 |
| 153.5 | 140.0 | -122.0 | | | | | -90.8 | 15.2 | 536.8 | | -22.4 |
| 69.8 | 49.2 | 54.6 | | | | | 54.2 | 480.3 | | | 58.1 |
| (46) 21.7 | (60) 8.3 | (74) 9.5 | | EBIT/Interest | | (15) 5.1 | (13) 66.9 | (26) 20.6 | | | |
| .9 | -.5 | -.7 | | | | | -.3 | 6.9 | | | -1.8 |
| | 40.9 | | | Net Profit + Depr., Dep., | | | | | | | |
| | (10) 3.7 | | | Amort./Cur. Mat. L/T/D | | | | | | | |
| | | .1 | | | | | | | | | |
| .0 | .1 | .1 | | | | | .0 | .2 | .0 | | .2 |
| .4 | .5 | .5 | | Fixed/Worth | | | .0 | .6 | .2 | | .8 |
| 1.8 | 2.6 | -2.1 | | | | | .7 | 1.0 | .7 | | -.4 |
| .2 | .3 | .5 | | | | | .3 | .3 | .2 | | .8 |
| 1.1 | .9 | 2.0 | | Debt/Worth | | | .9 | 1.8 | .8 | | 2.2 |
| 20.8 | 6.3 | -4.4 | | | | | -2.2 | 12.0 | 10.8 | | -3.3 |
| 147.0 | 101.6 | 103.0 | | | | | 154.2 | 100.6 | 174.1 | | 111.4 |
| (52) 71.6 | (76) 36.3 | (63) 54.9 | | % Profit Before Taxes/Tangible Net Worth | (10) 51.8 | (13) 67.5 | (16) 71.3 | (19) 33.3 | | | |
| 22.5 | 4.0 | .0 | | | | | -2.1 | 9.7 | 22.0 | | .7 |
| 69.2 | 45.3 | 43.6 | | | | | 71.8 | 56.9 | 69.6 | | 35.4 |
| 29.6 | 14.0 | 12.1 | | % Profit Before Taxes/Total Assets | | | 9.5 | 14.3 | 21.1 | | 10.9 |
| 1.7 | -2.5 | -8.6 | | | | | -25.1 | -5.1 | 3.5 | | -8.1 |
| 170.3 | 93.3 | 108.2 | | | | | UND | 48.0 | 357.8 | | 25.6 |
| 25.7 | 11.4 | 23.2 | | Sales/Net Fixed Assets | | | 371.9 | 17.8 | 61.7 | | 12.0 |
| 5.2 | 5.1 | 6.0 | | | | | 6.9 | 5.4 | 23.1 | | 6.1 |
| 3.7 | 4.2 | 3.9 | | | | | 7.7 | 3.9 | 6.9 | | 2.4 |
| 2.1 | 1.9 | 2.0 | | Sales/Total Assets | | | 3.3 | 2.4 | 2.1 | | 1.7 |
| 1.3 | 1.2 | 1.2 | | | | | 1.8 | .8 | 1.3 | | .8 |
| .7 | .9 | 1.4 | | | | | | 1.4 | | | 1.7 |
| (36) 2.3 | (55) 2.7 | (48) 2.4 | | % Depr., Dep., Amort./Sales | | (11) 3.2 | (20) 3.7 | | | | |
| 4.8 | 5.7 | 5.3 | | | | | | 6.4 | | | 5.6 |
| 1.4 | 1.4 | 1.7 | | % Officers', Directors' Owners' Comp/Sales | | | | | | | |
| (13) 3.0 | (24) 3.8 | (22) 3.6 | | | | | | | | | |
| 11.4 | 8.1 | 7.0 | | | | | | | | | |
| 2425396M | 3246705M | 2734746M | | Net Sales ($) | 2760M | 17315M | 52981M | 126516M | 344610M | | 2190564M |
| 1735989M | 2477164M | 2186422M | | Total Assets ($) | 1312M | 9051M | 17763M | 94252M | 229076M | | 1834968M |

© RMA 2024     M = $ thousand     MM = $ million
See Pages viii through xx for Explanation of Ratios and Data

# HEALTH CARE—Diagnostic Imaging Centers  NAICS 621512

## Current Data Sorted by Assets

| | | | | | | | Comparative Historical Data | |
|---|---|---|---|---|---|---|---|---|
| | | | | | | **Type of Statement** | | |
| | | 1 | | 6 | 2 | 2 | Unqualified | 12 | 15 |
| | | 2 | | 3 | | 1 | Reviewed | 9 | 4 |
| | 1 | 2 | | 1 | | 1 | Compiled | 12 | 7 |
| 1 | 5 | 4 | | | 8 | | Tax Returns | 35 | 12 |
| 21 | 18 | 27 | | 23 | 8 | 9 | Other | 116 | 95 |
| | 25 (4/1-9/30/23) | | | 113 (10/1/23-3/31/24) | | | | 4/1/19-3/31/20 | 4/1/20-3/31/21 |
| 0-500M | 500M-2MM | 2-10MM | 10-50MM | 50-100MM | 100-250MM | | ALL | ALL |
| 22 | 25 | 35 | 33 | 10 | 13 | NUMBER OF STATEMENTS | 184 | 133 |
| % | % | % | % | % | % | **ASSETS** | % | % |
| 38.4 | 30.8 | 19.9 | 11.3 | 10.8 | 7.5 | Cash & Equivalents | 21.8 | 28.6 |
| 1.9 | 14.8 | 18.1 | 22.2 | 14.8 | 14.5 | Trade Receivables (net) | 17.9 | 13.3 |
| .0 | .0 | .0 | .2 | .1 | .3 | Inventory | .5 | .1 |
| 5.8 | 3.3 | 5.9 | 2.3 | 10.2 | 8.7 | All Other Current | 3.0 | 2.1 |
| 46.1 | 48.9 | 43.9 | 36.1 | 35.9 | 31.0 | Total Current | 43.2 | 44.1 |
| 40.4 | 35.9 | 38.1 | 32.6 | 38.1 | 20.4 | Fixed Assets (net) | 36.5 | 35.8 |
| 6.5 | 5.8 | 6.7 | 19.1 | 6.9 | 34.7 | Intangibles (net) | 11.2 | 11.5 |
| 7.0 | 9.4 | 11.2 | 12.2 | 19.2 | 13.9 | All Other Non-Current | 9.1 | 8.6 |
| 100.0 | 100.0 | 100.0 | 100.0 | 100.0 | 100.0 | Total | 100.0 | 100.0 |
| | | | | | | **LIABILITIES** | | |
| 16.9 | 6.3 | 5.0 | .6 | 1.8 | .3 | Notes Payable-Short Term | 3.8 | 5.9 |
| 17.6 | 7.5 | 6.2 | 6.4 | 5.1 | 4.7 | Cur. Mat.-L.T.D. | 6.5 | 7.9 |
| 43.8 | 5.0 | 2.7 | 4.7 | 4.9 | 2.9 | Trade Payables | 5.0 | 6.4 |
| .0 | .3 | .2 | .2 | .2 | .0 | Income Taxes Payable | .2 | .1 |
| 24.0 | 11.5 | 17.8 | 12.3 | 12.9 | 9.6 | All Other Current | 16.3 | 14.9 |
| 102.2 | 30.6 | 31.8 | 24.2 | 24.8 | 17.5 | Total Current | 31.7 | 35.2 |
| 62.7 | 43.4 | 30.1 | 23.0 | 15.2 | 38.3 | Long-Term Debt | 27.2 | 32.7 |
| .0 | .0 | .0 | .1 | .0 | .0 | Deferred Taxes | .2 | .1 |
| .2 | 2.5 | 11.8 | 9.0 | 10.4 | 12.3 | All Other Non-Current | 4.0 | 2.0 |
| -65.2 | 23.5 | 26.3 | 43.6 | 49.6 | 32.0 | Net Worth | 36.8 | 30.1 |
| 100.0 | 100.0 | 100.0 | 100.0 | 100.0 | 100.0 | Total Liabilities & Net Worth | 100.0 | 100.0 |
| | | | | | | **INCOME DATA** | | |
| 100.0 | 100.0 | 100.0 | 100.0 | 100.0 | 100.0 | Net Sales | 100.0 | 100.0 |
| | | | | | | Gross Profit | | |
| 89.2 | 83.9 | 82.8 | 84.8 | 79.4 | 88.3 | Operating Expenses | 86.5 | 84.8 |
| 10.8 | 16.1 | 17.2 | 15.2 | 20.6 | 11.7 | Operating Profit | 13.5 | 15.2 |
| .2 | 2.4 | 1.4 | 1.2 | .1 | 3.2 | All Other Expenses (net) | 1.1 | .4 |
| 10.6 | 13.6 | 15.8 | 14.0 | 20.5 | 8.4 | Profit Before Taxes | 12.5 | 14.7 |
| | | | | | | **RATIOS** | | |
| 1.9 | 5.6 | 3.5 | 2.8 | 6.1 | 1.8 | | 2.8 | 4.0 |
| .6 | 2.8 | 1.2 | 1.6 | 1.2 | 1.4 | Current | 1.4 | 1.7 |
| .2 | .6 | .7 | .8 | .9 | 1.2 | | .8 | .9 |
| 1.1 | 5.6 | 3.5 | 2.6 | 1.5 | 1.5 | | 2.5 | 3.9 |
| .5 | 2.4 | 1.0 | 1.5 | 1.1 | 1.3 | Quick | 1.3 | 1.5 |
| .2 | .5 | .4 | .7 | .6 | 1.1 | | .7 | .7 |
| 0 UND | 0 UND | 0 UND | 28 12.9 | 13 28.5 | 28 13.2 | | 0 UND | 0 UND |
| 0 UND | 0 UND | 7 52.0 | 41 9.0 | 34 10.6 | 54 6.8 | Sales/Receivables | 29 12.8 | 0 UND |
| 0 UND | 46 7.9 | 39 9.4 | 56 6.5 | 53 6.9 | 79 4.6 | | 49 7.5 | 44 8.3 |
| | | | | | | Cost of Sales/Inventory | | |
| | | | | | | Cost of Sales/Payables | | |
| 57.1 | 4.0 | 7.0 | 4.8 | 5.3 | 6.5 | | 7.1 | 5.0 |
| -51.8 | 17.1 | 39.4 | 17.2 | 19.5 | 12.3 | Sales/Working Capital | 25.9 | 18.5 |
| -8.2 | -89.4 | -34.4 | -46.0 | -234.2 | 28.6 | | -61.7 | -67.7 |
| 125.0 | 27.1 | 98.7 | 29.9 | | 19.1 | | 38.1 | 33.8 |
| (14) 12.1 | (21) 10.5 | (29) 8.6 | (28) 13.5 | | 7.2 | EBIT/Interest | (153) 12.1 | (102) 8.8 |
| 1.0 | 3.1 | 2.6 | 3.4 | | .1 | | 2.1 | .0 |
| | | | | | | Net Profit + Depr., Dep., | | 10.7 |
| | | | | | | Amort./Cur. Mat. L/T/D | (19) 5.1 | |
| | | | | | | | 2.3 | |
| .0 | .1 | .5 | .5 | .5 | 1.0 | | .4 | .4 |
| 1.0 | 1.4 | 1.1 | 1.1 | 1.0 | 2.7 | Fixed/Worth | 1.4 | 1.0 |
| -.3 | NM | 75.8 | 12.0 | 10.8 | -.3 | | 3.6 | 5.3 |
| .4 | .4 | .4 | .7 | .2 | 1.1 | | .7 | .5 |
| -4.1 | 2.2 | 1.7 | 1.8 | 1.7 | 5.1 | Debt/Worth | 2.0 | 2.1 |
| -1.5 | -9.9 | 151.3 | 16.5 | 13.2 | -2.4 | | 7.9 | 12.2 |
| 506.2 | 132.0 | 145.6 | 111.0 | | | % Profit Before Taxes/Tangible | 135.8 | 127.1 |
| (10) 90.2 | (16) 63.7 | (27) 63.5 | (27) 51.8 | | | Net Worth | (149) 57.1 | (105) 54.0 |
| .2 | 17.4 | 11.4 | 20.7 | | | | 12.1 | 9.7 |
| 210.2 | 71.5 | 52.9 | 36.3 | 23.8 | 18.5 | % Profit Before Taxes/Total | 45.9 | 42.9 |
| 63.8 | 34.6 | 24.1 | 18.4 | 12.3 | 6.6 | Assets | 17.9 | 17.1 |
| -19.5 | 6.6 | 5.1 | 4.3 | 7.7 | -7.4 | | 1.6 | -.3 |
| 992.5 | 721.7 | 39.6 | 7.8 | 253.9 | 8.9 | | 24.3 | 21.3 |
| 22.2 | 15.5 | 11.1 | 4.6 | 4.3 | 6.0 | Sales/Net Fixed Assets | 6.8 | 6.5 |
| 6.1 | 5.6 | 3.2 | 2.9 | 2.9 | 3.0 | | 3.5 | 3.6 |
| 16.5 | 4.7 | 5.4 | 2.1 | 1.9 | 1.0 | | 4.1 | 4.0 |
| 6.5 | 3.0 | 2.6 | 1.4 | 1.3 | .8 | Sales/Total Assets | 2.2 | 2.1 |
| 4.2 | 1.7 | 1.3 | .9 | .7 | .6 | | 1.2 | 1.0 |
| .7 | .7 | 1.0 | 4.1 | | | | 3.3 | 2.7 |
| (10) 1.3 | (16) 2.2 | (25) 5.8 | (28) 5.3 | | | % Depr., Dep., Amort./Sales | (132) 5.8 | (98) 5.6 |
| 1.9 | 5.6 | 12.8 | 6.2 | | | | 8.4 | 10.0 |
| | | | | | | % Officers', Directors' | | 3.8 | 1.7 |
| | | | | | | Owners' Comp/Sales | (40) 17.6 | (21) 10.3 |
| | | | | | | | 30.6 | 32.0 |
| 72253M | 130024M | 724949M | 1358509M | 1019625M | 1927883M | Net Sales ($) | 5594176M | 3081210M |
| 6070M | 27701M | 155506M | 782687M | 771007M | 2172641M | Total Assets ($) | 3621660M | 2369983M |

© RMA 2024

M = $ thousand   MM = $ million
See Pages viii through xx for Explanation of Ratios and Data

## HEALTH CARE—Diagnostic Imaging Centers  NAICS 621512

| Comparative Historical Data | | | | Current Data Sorted by Sales | | | | | |
|---|---|---|---|---|---|---|---|---|---|
| 10 | 15 | 11 | Type of Statement | | | | 1 | 2 | 8 |
| 4 | 7 | 6 | Unqualified | | | | 1 | 1 | 5 |
| 7 | 10 | 5 | Reviewed | | | | 1 | 1 | 2 |
| 10 | 20 | 10 | Compiled | 1 | 2 | 3 | 1 | 1 | |
| 74 | 89 | 106 | Tax Returns | 3 | 2 | 3 | 1 | 1 | |
| | | | Other | 7 | 21 | 8 | 16 | 21 | 33 |
| 4/1/21-3/31/22 ALL | 4/1/22-3/31/23 ALL | 4/1/23-3/31/24 ALL | | 25 (4/1-9/30/23) | | | 113 (10/1/23-3/31/24) | | |
| | | | | 0-1MM | 1-3MM | 3-5MM | 5-10MM | 10-25MM | 25MM & OVER |
| 105 | 141 | 138 | NUMBER OF STATEMENTS | 11 | 23 | 11 | 20 | 25 | 48 |
| % | % | % | ASSETS | % | % | % | % | % | % |
| 27.4 | 21.2 | 20.9 | Cash & Equivalents | 11.9 | 32.6 | 22.2 | 32.5 | 24.1 | 10.6 |
| 13.4 | 18.0 | 15.3 | Trade Receivables (net) | 1.1 | 11.3 | 16.2 | 19.3 | 14.5 | 19.1 |
| .2 | .2 | .1 | Inventory | .0 | .0 | .0 | .0 | .1 | .2 |
| 2.2 | 4.7 | 5.1 | All Other Current | 8.1 | 2.5 | 9.3 | 4.3 | 1.9 | 6.8 |
| 43.2 | 44.1 | 41.5 | Total Current | 21.1 | 46.4 | 47.7 | 56.2 | 40.7 | 36.7 |
| 39.0 | 38.4 | 35.1 | Fixed Assets (net) | 60.4 | 42.6 | 44.2 | 20.9 | 32.9 | 30.7 |
| 10.1 | 10.7 | 12.1 | Intangibles (net) | 10.6 | 2.9 | 3.3 | 10.0 | 10.8 | 20.5 |
| 7.6 | 6.9 | 11.3 | All Other Non-Current | 7.9 | 8.2 | 4.8 | 12.9 | 15.7 | 12.1 |
| 100.0 | 100.0 | 100.0 | Total | 100.0 | 100.0 | 100.0 | 100.0 | 100.0 | 100.0 |
| | | | LIABILITIES | | | | | | |
| 4.6 | 8.8 | 5.4 | Notes Payable-Short Term | 34.8 | 1.6 | 1.1 | 1.5 | 2.6 | 4.6 |
| 8.8 | 7.6 | 8.1 | Cur. Mat.-L.T.D. | 4.3 | 14.7 | 16.6 | 7.3 | 5.5 | 5.5 |
| 2.4 | 5.6 | 10.3 | Trade Payables | 57.0 | 17.6 | 1.6 | 4.7 | 3.4 | 4.1 |
| .2 | .1 | .1 | Income Taxes Payable | .0 | .0 | .6 | .0 | .2 | .2 |
| 14.7 | 20.4 | 15.2 | All Other Current | 5.8 | 10.8 | 8.9 | 18.6 | 14.6 | 19.8 |
| 30.6 | 42.5 | 39.2 | Total Current | 101.9 | 44.6 | 28.8 | 32.1 | 26.3 | 34.2 |
| 27.4 | 27.3 | 35.7 | Long-Term Debt | 14.0 | 86.1 | 41.9 | 36.9 | 16.1 | 24.8 |
| .2 | .0 | .0 | Deferred Taxes | .0 | .0 | .0 | .0 | .2 | .0 |
| 6.4 | 4.0 | 7.5 | All Other Non-Current | .0 | 2.5 | .4 | 1.6 | 15.1 | 11.9 |
| 35.5 | 26.2 | 17.6 | Net Worth | -15.9 | -33.2 | 28.9 | 29.5 | 42.3 | 29.1 |
| 100.0 | 100.0 | 100.0 | Total Liabilties & Net Worth | 100.0 | 100.0 | 100.0 | 100.0 | 100.0 | 100.0 |
| | | | INCOME DATA | | | | | | |
| 100.0 | 100.0 | 100.0 | Net Sales | 100.0 | 100.0 | 100.0 | 100.0 | 100.0 | 100.0 |
| | | | Gross Profit | | | | | | |
| 83.7 | 85.0 | 84.8 | Operating Expenses | 72.9 | 87.1 | 76.8 | 78.4 | 86.1 | 90.2 |
| 16.3 | 15.0 | 15.2 | Operating Profit | 27.1 | 12.9 | 23.2 | 21.6 | 13.9 | 9.8 |
| .4 | .6 | 1.4 | All Other Expenses (net) | 5.8 | 1.2 | 2.2 | .6 | .1 | 1.4 |
| 16.0 | 14.4 | 13.8 | Profit Before Taxes | 21.4 | 11.6 | 21.0 | 20.9 | 13.9 | 8.4 |
| | | | RATIOS | | | | | | |
| 4.6 | 2.7 | 3.5 | | 3.4 | 6.4 | 3.3 | 4.8 | 4.4 | 1.6 |
| 1.6 | 1.5 | 1.3 | Current | .3 | 1.9 | 1.7 | 2.2 | 2.3 | 1.1 |
| .9 | .8 | .7 | | .0 | .4 | .8 | .9 | 1.1 | .7 |
| 4.5 | 2.3 | 2.9 | | 3.4 | 6.4 | 3.3 | 4.7 | 4.3 | 1.3 |
| 1.4 | 1.3 | 1.2 | Quick | .3 | 1.1 | 1.2 | 1.3 | 2.3 | 1.0 |
| .9 | .7 | .6 | | .0 | .4 | .5 | .8 | 1.0 | .7 |
| 0 UND | 0 UND | 0 UND | | 0 UND | 0 UND | 0 UND | 0 UND | 0 UND | 13 27.9 |
| 19 19.2 | 26 14.0 | 26 14.2 | Sales/Receivables | 0 UND | 0 UND | 37 9.8 | 0 UND | 28 12.9 | 36 10.2 |
| 46 7.9 | 48 7.6 | 47 7.7 | | 0 UND | 11 31.8 | 51 7.1 | 48 7.6 | 51 7.1 | 53 6.9 |
| | | | Cost of Sales/Inventory | | | | | | |
| | | | Cost of Sales/Payables | | | | | | |
| 5.8 | 5.3 | 5.6 | | 4.9 | 4.3 | 5.5 | 2.9 | 5.0 | 11.1 |
| 23.5 | 24.4 | 29.7 | Sales/Working Capital | -4.3 | 65.2 | 8.3 | 20.1 | 13.2 | 99.4 |
| -145.5 | -45.9 | -43.0 | | -1.3 | -17.7 | -27.3 | -174.8 | NM | -62.4 |
| 41.7 | 52.1 | 44.3 | | | 68.1 | 41.4 | 192.7 | 63.0 | 27.5 |
| (86) 10.2 | (118) 15.2 | (113) 11.3 | EBIT/Interest | (17) 10.5 | (10) 13.6 | (16) 20.4 | (21) 28.8 | (40) 9.9 |
| 3.6 | 4.5 | 3.2 | | | 4.5 | 5.2 | 4.7 | 4.2 | 2.3 |
| | 6.3 | 7.4 | Net Profit + Depr., Dep., | | | | | | |
| (26) 3.4 | (16) 3.5 | Amort./Cur. Mat. L/T/D | | | | | | |
| | 1.7 | 1.6 | | | | | | | |
| .3 | .5 | .4 | | .5 | .1 | .4 | .0 | .4 | .8 |
| 1.2 | 1.2 | 1.2 | Fixed/Worth | 1.8 | 1.5 | 1.2 | .2 | .8 | 2.2 |
| 5.4 | 7.6 | -25.9 | | -1.0 | -.6 | 104.6 | 1.6 | 6.6 | -2.1 |
| .7 | .7 | .6 | | .9 | .1 | .7 | .3 | .3 | 1.3 |
| 1.8 | 1.9 | 2.4 | Debt/Worth | 1.5 | 82.0 | 2.2 | 1.2 | .7 | 3.8 |
| 12.7 | 16.4 | -10.9 | | -1.4 | -2.7 | -24.9 | NM | 10.8 | -6.9 |
| 164.7 | 114.7 | 111.4 | | | 105.4 | | 148.9 | 73.3 | 141.9 |
| (88) 56.6 | (111) 62.7 | (96) 57.1 | % Profit Before Taxes/Tangible Net Worth | (12) 63.5 | | (15) 81.2 | (22) 49.0 | (32) 60.5 |
| 9.7 | 19.4 | 17.2 | | | 12.3 | | 33.6 | 11.1 | 23.5 |
| 58.9 | 41.8 | 50.3 | % Profit Before Taxes/Total Assets | 7.2 | 85.0 | 85.5 | 66.9 | 43.7 | 32.6 |
| 19.9 | 15.1 | 19.8 | | 6.0 | 51.4 | 58.7 | 35.0 | 19.4 | 14.3 |
| 4.5 | 4.5 | 4.3 | | -19.3 | 3.2 | 22.4 | 16.7 | -2.5 | 2.1 |
| 28.6 | 35.1 | 33.9 | | 7.1 | 181.0 | 12.2 | 802.6 | 31.0 | 29.3 |
| 5.7 | 6.1 | 6.3 | Sales/Net Fixed Assets | 2.0 | 12.9 | 5.7 | 29.2 | 7.1 | 6.1 |
| 2.5 | 2.7 | 3.6 | | .2 | 5.8 | 2.8 | 4.2 | 3.3 | 4.0 |
| 4.1 | 3.8 | 4.6 | | 4.0 | 6.7 | 4.6 | 4.6 | 4.1 | 4.0 |
| 2.0 | 1.9 | 2.3 | Sales/Total Assets | .9 | 4.4 | 2.3 | 2.6 | 1.6 | 1.8 |
| .8 | .9 | 1.1 | | .2 | 2.3 | 1.1 | .7 | 1.2 | .9 |
| 1.3 | 2.1 | 1.6 | | | .8 | 1.0 | | 3.5 | 1.6 |
| (70) 5.1 | (105) 5.4 | (89) 4.4 | % Depr., Dep., Amort./Sales | (15) 1.6 | (10) 4.1 | (20) 5.6 | (28) 4.4 |
| 9.9 | 9.7 | 6.2 | | | 5.8 | 12.9 | | 6.2 | 6.4 |
| 5.5 | 4.9 | 3.1 | % Officers', Directors' Owners' Comp/Sales | | | | | | |
| (20) 15.0 | (30) 17.9 | (17) 11.2 | | | | | | | |
| 35.3 | 29.7 | 34.4 | | | | | | | |
| 2433525M | 4628662M | 5233243M | Net Sales ($) | 6320M | 46173M | 40752M | 149712M | 406314M | 4583972M |
| 1392087M | 2674132M | 3915612M | Total Assets ($) | 10990M | 17321M | 25035M | 111670M | 320180M | 3430416M |

© RMA 2024  
M = $ thousand  MM = $ million  
See Pages viii through xx for Explanation of Ratios and Data

# HEALTH CARE—Home Health Care Services  NAICS 621610

## Current Data Sorted by Assets

| | | | | | | | Type of Statement |
|---|---|---|---|---|---|---|---|
| | 3 | 3 | 8 | 10 | 8 | | Unqualified |
| | 2 | 4 | 5 | | | | Reviewed |
| | 2 | 8 | 2 | | | | Compiled |
| 7 | 19 | 13 | 2 | | | | Tax Returns |
| 29 | 49 | 68 | 32 | 10 | 14 | | Other |
| | 46 (4/1-9/30/23) | | | 252 (10/1/23-3/31/24) | | | |
| 0-500M | 500M-2MM | 2-10MM | 10-50MM | 50-100MM | 100-250MM | | |
| 36 | 75 | 96 | 49 | 20 | 22 | NUMBER OF STATEMENTS | |

## Comparative Historical Data

| | | |
|---|---|---|
| 44 | 20 | Unqualified |
| 6 | 3 | Reviewed |
| 13 | 8 | Compiled |
| 55 | 33 | Tax Returns |
| 221 | 115 | Other |
| 4/1/19-3/31/20 ALL | 4/1/20-3/31/21 ALL | |
| 339 | 179 | NUMBER OF STATEMENTS |

### Combined Data

| 0-500M | 500M-2MM | 2-10MM | 10-50MM | 50-100MM | 100-250MM | | 4/1/19-3/31/20 ALL | 4/1/20-3/31/21 ALL |
|---|---|---|---|---|---|---|---|---|
| % | % | % | % | % | % | **ASSETS** | % | % |
| 40.3 | 31.9 | 30.7 | 19.3 | 24.8 | 13.8 | Cash & Equivalents | 23.8 | 39.3 |
| 13.7 | 18.4 | 24.3 | 29.5 | 22.5 | 23.9 | Trade Receivables (net) | 28.4 | 19.9 |
| .5 | 2.3 | 1.3 | 1.3 | 1.2 | 1.6 | Inventory | 1.7 | 1.3 |
| 6.6 | 7.0 | 7.2 | 1.7 | 4.1 | 4.3 | All Other Current | 3.3 | 2.8 |
| 61.1 | 59.6 | 63.5 | 51.8 | 52.6 | 43.6 | Total Current | 57.2 | 63.3 |
| 19.4 | 16.1 | 12.5 | 10.5 | 16.3 | 13.5 | Fixed Assets (net) | 17.2 | 10.8 |
| 7.8 | 9.0 | 8.8 | 23.3 | 18.0 | 26.4 | Intangibles (net) | 13.4 | 15.9 |
| 11.7 | 15.4 | 15.2 | 14.4 | 13.1 | 16.5 | All Other Non-Current | 12.2 | 9.9 |
| 100.0 | 100.0 | 100.0 | 100.0 | 100.0 | 100.0 | Total | 100.0 | 100.0 |
| | | | | | | **LIABILITIES** | | |
| 8.8 | 6.0 | 5.5 | 3.9 | 2.0 | 1.0 | Notes Payable-Short Term | 9.8 | 9.7 |
| 2.9 | 3.6 | 1.5 | 2.7 | 3.1 | 4.4 | Cur. Mat.-L.T.D. | 3.0 | 3.7 |
| 5.7 | 3.3 | 5.0 | 4.6 | 6.3 | 6.1 | Trade Payables | 6.6 | 4.2 |
| .0 | .0 | .1 | .2 | .0 | .1 | Income Taxes Payable | .0 | .2 |
| 33.8 | 11.4 | 14.9 | 18.9 | 17.2 | 15.4 | All Other Current | 17.8 | 15.0 |
| 51.3 | 24.2 | 27.0 | 30.3 | 28.6 | 27.0 | Total Current | 37.3 | 32.8 |
| 51.1 | 19.3 | 19.3 | 16.6 | 26.9 | 31.7 | Long-Term Debt | 17.9 | 24.3 |
| .0 | .0 | .0 | .1 | .0 | .0 | Deferred Taxes | .1 | .0 |
| 8.9 | 2.9 | 5.7 | 8.8 | 6.3 | 5.8 | All Other Non-Current | 3.6 | 4.6 |
| -11.3 | 53.6 | 48.0 | 44.2 | 38.1 | 35.5 | Net Worth | 41.1 | 38.4 |
| 100.0 | 100.0 | 100.0 | 100.0 | 100.0 | 100.0 | Total Liabilities & Net Worth | 100.0 | 100.0 |
| | | | | | | **INCOME DATA** | | |
| 100.0 | 100.0 | 100.0 | 100.0 | 100.0 | 100.0 | Net Sales | 100.0 | 100.0 |
| | | | | | | Gross Profit | | |
| 96.8 | 87.2 | 91.3 | 93.7 | 96.9 | 89.2 | Operating Expenses | 93.4 | 92.5 |
| 3.2 | 12.8 | 8.7 | 6.3 | 3.1 | 10.8 | Operating Profit | 6.6 | 7.5 |
| 1.8 | .7 | .5 | 1.0 | .9 | 2.0 | All Other Expenses (net) | 1.3 | -.5 |
| 1.3 | 12.2 | 8.2 | 5.3 | 2.2 | 8.7 | Profit Before Taxes | 5.3 | 7.9 |
| | | | | | | **RATIOS** | | |
| 9.4 | 10.3 | 8.4 | 3.8 | 3.0 | 3.0 | | 3.5 | 4.8 |
| 2.0 | 2.8 | 2.9 | 2.0 | 1.6 | 2.0 | Current | 1.7 | 2.2 |
| .8 | 1.1 | 1.3 | 1.1 | 1.1 | 1.0 | | 1.0 | 1.3 |
| 6.7 | 9.6 | 8.2 | 3.8 | 2.7 | 2.5 | | 3.4 | 4.8 |
| 2.0 | 2.4 | 2.4 | 1.9 | 1.6 | 1.9 | Quick | 1.6 | 2.1 |
| .7 | .8 | 1.2 | 1.0 | 1.0 | .7 | | .9 | 1.2 |
| 0 UND | 0 UND | 0 UND | 32 11.3 | 17 21.7 | 42 8.7 | | 5 71.9 | 0 UND |
| 0 UND | 0 UND | 27 13.3 | 49 7.4 | 48 7.6 | 51 7.1 | Sales/Receivables | 33 11.2 | 29 12.5 |
| 15 23.7 | 29 12.4 | 51 7.2 | 62 5.9 | 59 6.2 | 74 4.9 | | 52 7.0 | 51 7.2 |
| | | | | | | Cost of Sales/Inventory | | |
| | | | | | | Cost of Sales/Payables | | |
| 6.7 | 6.8 | 4.6 | 5.6 | 5.4 | 4.3 | | 6.9 | 4.3 |
| 28.6 | 14.2 | 7.2 | 9.8 | 9.6 | 8.2 | Sales/Working Capital | 16.2 | 7.3 |
| -217.8 | 735.2 | 23.3 | 49.7 | 109.9 | 137.2 | | 403.5 | 25.0 |
| 17.1 | 84.1 | 40.6 | 30.1 | 6.2 | 7.5 | | 32.1 | 54.0 |
| (23) 2.7 | (43) 18.0 | (61) 12.8 | (38) 2.5 | (15) 1.4 | (19) 3.4 | EBIT/Interest | (242) 9.4 | (121) 12.2 |
| -28.3 | 6.1 | 2.3 | -.4 | -4.2 | 1.1 | | 2.0 | 2.4 |
| | | | | | | Net Profit + Depr., Dep., Amort./Cur. Mat. L/T/D | 5.7 (16) 2.4 -.1 | |
| .0 | .0 | .0 | .1 | .1 | .3 | | .0 | .0 |
| 4.7 | .1 | .1 | .6 | .4 | -1.9 | Fixed/Worth | .3 | .1 |
| -.5 | .7 | .7 | -.2 | -1.0 | -.1 | | 1.2 | 1.6 |
| .5 | .2 | .2 | .5 | .5 | 1.4 | | .4 | .5 |
| 12.7 | .9 | .8 | 1.6 | 1.5 | -18.5 | Debt/Worth | 1.4 | 2.1 |
| -3.0 | 4.0 | 5.4 | -2.9 | -3.7 | -3.6 | | 43.0 | -10.9 |
| 465.6 | 137.1 | 93.1 | 51.7 | 45.9 | 51.1 | | 84.4 | 105.2 |
| (21) 42.7 | (63) 67.2 | (79) 35.2 | (32) 16.0 | (14) 2.8 | (10) 28.4 | % Profit Before Taxes/Tangible Net Worth | (257) 29.5 | (127) 50.3 |
| -44.6 | 19.8 | 7.6 | -.1 | -9.5 | 10.0 | | 7.4 | 13.5 |
| 69.8 | 67.0 | 35.3 | 17.1 | 12.7 | 20.4 | | 38.7 | 36.6 |
| 3.5 | 35.2 | 15.3 | 8.6 | 1.9 | 4.9 | % Profit Before Taxes/Total Assets | 12.9 | 14.5 |
| -43.9 | 6.3 | 3.3 | -2.8 | -5.4 | -.1 | | 2.4 | 3.1 |
| UND | 999.8 | 727.7 | 133.9 | 210.5 | 109.7 | | 548.0 | 762.1 |
| 165.9 | 70.9 | 152.7 | 60.0 | 9.7 | 29.1 | Sales/Net Fixed Assets | 62.0 | 101.0 |
| 27.2 | 21.1 | 23.2 | 20.4 | 6.3 | 8.0 | | 11.8 | 22.3 |
| 11.4 | 6.6 | 4.5 | 3.1 | 2.5 | 2.2 | | 5.8 | 4.4 |
| 5.9 | 3.6 | 2.7 | 2.0 | 1.6 | 1.6 | Sales/Total Assets | 3.5 | 2.4 |
| 2.9 | 1.5 | 1.4 | 1.2 | 1.3 | 1.0 | | 1.5 | 1.5 |
| .2 | .1 | .1 | .1 | .3 | .9 | | .3 | .4 |
| (12) 1.0 | (29) .5 | (48) .3 | (28) .4 | (13) .9 | (10) 1.5 | % Depr., Dep., Amort./Sales | (170) 1.0 | (82) .7 |
| 3.6 | 1.9 | 1.1 | 2.6 | 1.6 | 2.6 | | 2.2 | 1.5 |
| | 3.1 | .6 | | | | | 1.8 | 2.4 |
| | (26) 6.1 | (30) 2.1 | | | | % Officers', Directors' Owners' Comp/Sales | (86) 3.4 | (48) 5.7 |
| | 8.2 | 5.7 | | | | | 6.4 | 11.9 |
| 66209M | 394673M | 1666994M | 2839060M | 2780998M | 4729285M | Net Sales ($) | 9761950M | 7199942M |
| 7731M | 84371M | 494386M | 1304207M | 1335016M | 3097654M | Total Assets ($) | 4876273M | 4177276M |

© RMA 2024    M = $ thousand    MM = $ million
See Pages viii through xx for Explanation of Ratios and Data

# HEALTH CARE—Home Health Care Services  NAICS 621610

| Comparative Historical Data | | | | Current Data Sorted by Sales | | | | | |
|---|---|---|---|---|---|---|---|---|---|
| 21 | 28 | 32 | Type of Statement / Unqualified | 1 | 1 | 1 | 2 | 27 | |
| 3 | 10 | 11 | Reviewed | | 1 | 2 | 3 | 5 | |
| 8 | 9 | 12 | Compiled | | 1 | 3 | 3 | 5 | |
| 33 | 37 | 41 | Tax Returns | 7 | 5 | 8 | 12 | 6 | 3 |
| 121 | 158 | 202 | Other | 24 | 28 | 20 | 29 | 38 | 63 |
| 4/1/21-3/31/22 ALL | 4/1/22-3/31/23 ALL | 4/1/23-3/31/24 ALL | | 46 (4/1-9/30/23) | | 252 (10/1/23-3/31/24) | | | |
| | | | | 0-1MM | 1-3MM | 3-5MM | 5-10MM | 10-25MM | 25MM & OVER |
| 186 | 242 | 298 | NUMBER OF STATEMENTS | 31 | 35 | 30 | 47 | 52 | 103 |
| % | % | % | ASSETS | % | % | % | % | % | % |
| 34.4 | 30.9 | 28.7 | Cash & Equivalents | 30.7 | 23.5 | 42.8 | 34.4 | 27.2 | 23.8 |
| 21.6 | 22.5 | 22.2 | Trade Receivables (net) | 9.6 | 15.4 | 17.9 | 16.9 | 30.1 | 28.1 |
| 1.3 | 1.2 | 1.5 | Inventory | 2.1 | 1.0 | .5 | 2.7 | 1.0 | 1.3 |
| 4.3 | 4.6 | 5.7 | All Other Current | 9.2 | 5.4 | 5.0 | 9.4 | 6.3 | 3.1 |
| 61.6 | 59.2 | 58.1 | Total Current | 51.5 | 45.3 | 66.2 | 63.5 | 64.7 | 56.3 |
| 13.5 | 15.5 | 14.2 | Fixed Assets (net) | 26.9 | 16.8 | 13.6 | 10.8 | 11.8 | 12.6 |
| 15.5 | 12.1 | 13.0 | Intangibles (net) | 5.8 | 16.6 | 6.6 | 11.0 | 7.8 | 19.4 |
| 9.4 | 13.2 | 14.6 | All Other Non-Current | 15.7 | 21.4 | 13.6 | 14.8 | 15.7 | 11.7 |
| 100.0 | 100.0 | 100.0 | Total | 100.0 | 100.0 | 100.0 | 100.0 | 100.0 | 100.0 |
| | | | LIABILITIES | | | | | | |
| 6.9 | 6.4 | 5.2 | Notes Payable-Short Term | 3.8 | 7.3 | 7.2 | 9.3 | 3.2 | 3.5 |
| 2.8 | 2.2 | 2.7 | Cur. Mat.-L.T.D. | 1.0 | 3.7 | 1.3 | 3.0 | 3.1 | 2.9 |
| 5.3 | 4.7 | 4.8 | Trade Payables | 1.6 | 1.3 | 4.5 | 4.2 | 6.4 | 6.3 |
| .2 | .1 | .1 | Income Taxes Payable | .0 | .0 | .0 | .2 | .1 | .1 |
| 19.9 | 17.4 | 17.1 | All Other Current | 35.6 | 10.7 | 16.2 | 11.0 | 17.4 | 16.7 |
| 35.0 | 30.9 | 29.9 | Total Current | 42.1 | 23.0 | 29.3 | 27.7 | 30.3 | 29.6 |
| 29.7 | 19.7 | 24.1 | Long-Term Debt | 35.0 | 51.3 | 16.9 | 12.1 | 20.9 | 20.8 |
| .0 | .0 | .0 | Deferred Taxes | .0 | .0 | .0 | .0 | .0 | .0 |
| 7.6 | 13.1 | 5.9 | All Other Non-Current | 3.8 | 6.6 | .0 | 6.4 | 8.8 | 6.4 |
| 27.7 | 36.4 | 40.0 | Net Worth | 19.1 | 19.2 | 53.7 | 53.7 | 40.0 | 43.2 |
| 100.0 | 100.0 | 100.0 | Total Liabilities & Net Worth | 100.0 | 100.0 | 100.0 | 100.0 | 100.0 | 100.0 |
| | | | INCOME DATA | | | | | | |
| 100.0 | 100.0 | 100.0 | Net Sales | 100.0 | 100.0 | 100.0 | 100.0 | 100.0 | 100.0 |
| | | | Gross Profit | | | | | | |
| 92.1 | 91.5 | 91.6 | Operating Expenses | 88.1 | 87.9 | 94.1 | 91.8 | 89.0 | 94.3 |
| 7.9 | 8.5 | 8.4 | Operating Profit | 11.9 | 12.1 | 5.9 | 8.2 | 11.0 | 5.7 |
| -.8 | .8 | .9 | All Other Expenses (net) | 3.8 | 1.2 | -.6 | .0 | 1.2 | .7 |
| 8.7 | 7.7 | 7.5 | Profit Before Taxes | 8.0 | 10.8 | 6.5 | 8.2 | 9.9 | 5.1 |
| | | | RATIOS | | | | | | |
| 5.6 | 6.6 | 6.3 | Current | 14.2 | 9.1 | 11.1 | 21.4 | 6.2 | 3.2 |
| 2.3 | 2.5 | 2.3 | | 2.0 | 1.6 | 4.1 | 3.2 | 2.7 | 1.9 |
| 1.3 | 1.4 | 1.1 | | .7 | .8 | 1.4 | 1.5 | 1.3 | 1.1 |
| 5.0 | 6.1 | 6.0 | Quick | 8.9 | 9.1 | 10.9 | 14.7 | 5.3 | 3.0 |
| 2.1 | 2.3 | 2.1 | | 1.8 | 1.5 | 4.1 | 2.9 | 2.4 | 1.8 |
| 1.1 | 1.1 | 1.0 | | .2 | .8 | 1.4 | .7 | 1.1 | 1.0 |
| 0 UND | 0 UND | 0 UND | Sales/Receivables | 0 UND | 0 UND | 0 UND | 0 UND | 0 784.3 | 27 13.4 |
| 28 12.9 | 26 14.3 | 27 13.4 | | 0 UND | 0 UND | 0 UND | 15 24.7 | 35 10.5 | 47 7.8 |
| 53 6.9 | 50 7.3 | 51 7.2 | | 15 24.6 | 24 15.5 | 34 10.7 | 37 9.9 | 68 5.4 | 61 6.0 |
| | | | Cost of Sales/Inventory | | | | | | |
| | | | Cost of Sales/Payables | | | | | | |
| 5.0 | 4.2 | 5.3 | Sales/Working Capital | 5.6 | 5.6 | 2.6 | 4.6 | 6.0 | 5.6 |
| 9.3 | 9.0 | 10.4 | | 13.1 | 29.9 | 10.0 | 10.5 | 7.8 | 10.2 |
| 30.1 | 27.7 | 87.9 | | -13.2 | -71.5 | 33.4 | 25.8 | 34.8 | 60.2 |
| 68.2 | 61.3 | 37.2 | EBIT/Interest | 16.5 | 82.0 | 17.5 | 41.4 | 48.8 | 27.0 |
| (120) 13.7 | (157) 13.9 | (199) 6.6 | | (15) 1.8 | (27) 7.2 | (14) 8.1 | (27) 19.5 | (37) 16.1 | (79) 3.7 |
| 2.3 | 2.2 | .9 | | -41.0 | 2.5 | -5.0 | 3.6 | 2.3 | .6 |
| | | 12.1 8.5 | Net Profit + Depr., Dep., Amort./Cur. Mat. L/T/D | | | | | | 11.7 |
| | (10) 7.5 | (16) 2.4 | | | | | | (12) 2.1 | |
| | 1.9 | 1.0 | | | | | | | 1.0 |
| .0 | .0 | .0 | Fixed/Worth | .0 | .0 | .0 | .0 | .0 | .1 |
| .1 | .1 | .2 | | .7 | .1 | .1 | .1 | .1 | .4 |
| 2.2 | 1.0 | 10.9 | | UND | -1.2 | 1.1 | .6 | 1.0 | -.6 |
| .4 | .3 | .3 | Debt/Worth | .5 | .3 | .1 | .1 | .4 | .5 |
| 1.9 | 1.1 | 1.4 | | 2.7 | 5.3 | .7 | .6 | 1.1 | 1.9 |
| -12.9 | 16.7 | -21.3 | | UND | -4.7 | 2.5 | -45.4 | 13.5 | -5.3 |
| 99.3 | 99.3 | 94.4 | % Profit Before Taxes/Tangible Net Worth | 61.3 | 147.4 | 87.7 | 107.1 | 119.2 | 64.2 |
| (132) 39.1 | (186) 34.5 | (219) 35.2 | | (24) 21.6 | (23) 69.1 | (26) 26.3 | (35) 60.3 | (41) 53.3 | (70) 28.4 |
| 10.2 | 5.5 | 5.8 | | -24.8 | 10.6 | 2.5 | 5.8 | 11.9 | 2.1 |
| 44.9 | 43.0 | 37.6 | % Profit Before Taxes/Total Assets | 27.0 | 62.4 | 33.6 | 60.1 | 64.7 | 21.7 |
| 15.8 | 14.9 | 12.6 | | 2.4 | 32.1 | 14.1 | 20.6 | 19.4 | 9.0 |
| 3.6 | 1.4 | -.1 | | -30.5 | -.4 | -3.3 | 3.0 | 6.2 | -.8 |
| 999.8 | 838.4 | 476.7 | Sales/Net Fixed Assets | UND | UND | UND | 598.4 | 298.2 | 170.4 |
| 118.2 | 81.1 | 81.2 | | 27.3 | 102.0 | 76.3 | 82.6 | 117.3 | 60.0 |
| 16.1 | 14.6 | 17.1 | | 4.4 | 21.1 | 22.5 | 33.5 | 23.3 | 9.6 |
| 5.3 | 5.1 | 4.7 | Sales/Total Assets | 3.5 | 6.0 | 7.3 | 6.3 | 6.2 | 3.5 |
| 2.7 | 2.7 | 2.7 | | 1.6 | 2.9 | 3.1 | 2.8 | 3.6 | 2.4 |
| 1.5 | 1.3 | 1.4 | | .4 | 1.3 | 1.4 | 1.5 | 2.0 | 1.4 |
| .2 | .2 | .1 | % Depr., Dep., Amort./Sales | .9 | .2 | .1 | .1 | .1 | .2 |
| (78) .8 | (109) .8 | (140) .5 | | (13) 3.7 | (10) .6 | (11) 1.0 | (21) .3 | (25) .2 | (60) .6 |
| 2.3 | 2.3 | 1.7 | | 6.7 | 4.5 | 3.1 | .7 | .4 | 1.7 |
| 2.4 | 2.0 | 1.2 | % Officers', Directors' Owners' Comp/Sales | | 3.6 | 4.1 | .4 | .9 | .6 |
| (59) 5.3 | (55) 3.8 | (68) 3.7 | | (10) 5.6 | (13) 6.1 | (13) 1.8 | (12) 3.2 | (13) 1.0 | |
| 8.0 | 7.4 | 7.4 | | 7.3 | 8.4 | 5.6 | 7.1 | 2.9 | |
| 7670762M | 5939318M | 12477219M | Net Sales ($) | 16153M | 69236M | 122141M | 327957M | 835009M | 11106723M |
| 3220967M | 3151011M | 6323365M | Total Assets ($) | 18101M | 39021M | 82389M | 140150M | 394163M | 5649541M |

© RMA 2024   M = $ thousand   MM = $ million
See Pages viii through xx for Explanation of Ratios and Data

# HEALTH CARE—Ambulance Services  NAICS 621910

**Current Data Sorted by Assets** | **Comparative Historical Data**

| | | | | | | Type of Statement | | |
|---|---|---|---|---|---|---|---|---|
| | | 1 | 4 | 5 | 3 | 1 | Unqualified | 18 | 3 |
| | | | 1 | 4 | 2 | | Reviewed | 5 | 3 |
| | | | 1 | 2 | | | Compiled | 9 | 2 |
| 2 | 3 | | 2 | | | | Tax Returns | 9 | 6 |
| 3 | 9 | 17 | 7 | 3 | 3 | Other | 53 | 37 |
| 0-500M | 20 (4/1-9/30/23) 500M-2MM | 2-10MM | 53 (10/1/23-3/31/24) 10-50MM | 50-100MM | 100-250MM | | 4/1/19-3/31/20 ALL | 4/1/20-3/31/21 ALL |
| 5 | 13 | 25 | 18 | 8 | 4 | NUMBER OF STATEMENTS | 94 | 51 |
| % | % | % | % | % | % | ASSETS | % | % |
| | 25.2 | 26.0 | 15.9 | | | Cash & Equivalents | 15.2 | 23.7 |
| | 13.0 | 21.8 | 32.8 | | | Trade Receivables (net) | 24.8 | 23.3 |
| | 1.3 | 1.6 | .5 | | | Inventory | 2.2 | 3.8 |
| | 1.8 | 2.5 | 2.6 | | | All Other Current | 5.3 | 3.8 |
| | 41.3 | 51.8 | 51.8 | | | Total Current | 47.5 | 54.5 |
| | 45.6 | 30.7 | 29.1 | | | Fixed Assets (net) | 37.2 | 35.3 |
| | .8 | 7.9 | 4.9 | | | Intangibles (net) | 6.0 | 4.3 |
| | 12.3 | 9.6 | 14.2 | | | All Other Non-Current | 9.3 | 5.9 |
| | 100.0 | 100.0 | 100.0 | | | Total | 100.0 | 100.0 |
| | | | | | | LIABILITIES | | |
| | .5 | 1.6 | .3 | | | Notes Payable-Short Term | 6.6 | 4.7 |
| | 3.0 | 4.5 | 5.1 | | | Cur. Mat.-L.T.D. | 6.5 | 7.4 |
| | .4 | 3.0 | 5.2 | | | Trade Payables | 3.6 | 2.9 |
| | .0 | .1 | .0 | | | Income Taxes Payable | .0 | .1 |
| | 3.1 | 11.5 | 8.3 | | | All Other Current | 9.3 | 10.1 |
| | 7.0 | 20.6 | 18.9 | | | Total Current | 25.9 | 25.2 |
| | 33.5 | 22.4 | 15.8 | | | Long-Term Debt | 28.8 | 33.2 |
| | .0 | .4 | .6 | | | Deferred Taxes | .3 | .3 |
| | 15.1 | 1.2 | 10.3 | | | All Other Non-Current | 5.6 | 3.1 |
| | 44.4 | 55.5 | 54.4 | | | Net Worth | 39.4 | 38.2 |
| | 100.0 | 100.0 | 100.0 | | | Total Liabilities & Net Worth | 100.0 | 100.0 |
| | | | | | | INCOME DATA | | |
| | 100.0 | 100.0 | 100.0 | | | Net Sales | 100.0 | 100.0 |
| | 79.8 | 87.7 | 91.0 | | | Gross Profit | | |
| | | | | | | Operating Expenses | 92.3 | 93.8 |
| | 20.2 | 12.3 | 9.0 | | | Operating Profit | 7.7 | 6.2 |
| | 1.5 | 1.6 | .5 | | | All Other Expenses (net) | 1.7 | -.9 |
| | 18.7 | 10.7 | 8.5 | | | Profit Before Taxes | 5.9 | 7.1 |
| | | | | | | RATIOS | | |
| | 25.1 | 9.8 | 5.8 | | | | 4.6 | 5.2 |
| | 7.8 | 3.4 | 3.3 | | | Current | 2.3 | 3.0 |
| | 2.9 | 1.3 | 1.3 | | | | 1.1 | 1.7 |
| | 24.7 | 9.8 | 4.7 | | | | 3.4 | 4.5 |
| | 7.8 | 3.2 | 2.9 | | | Quick | 1.7 | 2.7 |
| | 1.5 | 1.3 | 1.3 | | | | .9 | 1.0 |
| 0 UND | 0 UND | 40 9.2 | | | | | 0 992.0 | 6 64.0 |
| 0 UND | 55 6.6 | 62 5.9 | | | | Sales/Receivables | 55 6.6 | 63 5.8 |
| 50 7.3 | 91 4.0 | 85 4.3 | | | | | 70 5.2 | 87 4.2 |
| | | | | | | Cost of Sales/Inventory | | |
| | | | | | | Cost of Sales/Payables | | |
| | 3.4 | 2.3 | 2.6 | | | | 4.8 | 2.6 |
| | 5.5 | 5.7 | 4.6 | | | Sales/Working Capital | 8.7 | 4.8 |
| | 21.2 | 20.2 | 22.7 | | | | 107.1 | 15.0 |
| | | 43.1 | 21.8 | | | | 16.0 | 18.3 |
| | (22) | 11.4 | (14) 9.2 | | | EBIT/Interest | (81) 3.6 | (45) 5.6 |
| | | 2.9 | 2.1 | | | | .5 | -1.1 |
| | | | | | | Net Profit + Depr., Dep., | 4.7 | 4.7 |
| | | | | | | Amort./Cur. Mat. L/T/D | (17) 2.1 | (10) 3.9 |
| | | | | | | | 1.8 | 1.2 |
| | .0 | .2 | .3 | | | | .5 | .5 |
| | .7 | .7 | .7 | | | Fixed/Worth | .9 | .7 |
| | 1.8 | 1.4 | 1.5 | | | | 2.5 | 1.4 |
| | .1 | .2 | .3 | | | | .4 | .4 |
| | .2 | .8 | .7 | | | Debt/Worth | 1.3 | 1.1 |
| | 1.6 | 1.6 | 3.5 | | | | 6.0 | 2.4 |
| | 70.7 | 54.1 | 52.9 | | | | 39.0 | 46.0 |
| (11) | 30.6 | (21) 21.2 | (17) 29.3 | | | % Profit Before Taxes/Tangible Net Worth | (78) 16.6 | (43) 14.6 |
| | 3.0 | .9 | 4.9 | | | | 4.5 | -3.6 |
| | 44.7 | 26.0 | 20.9 | | | | 16.1 | 12.4 |
| | 10.3 | 13.3 | 9.6 | | | % Profit Before Taxes/Total Assets | 5.8 | 5.9 |
| | .9 | .5 | 2.1 | | | | -.8 | -3.9 |
| | 119.3 | 127.2 | 9.0 | | | | 11.6 | 11.4 |
| | 3.6 | 9.1 | 6.4 | | | Sales/Net Fixed Assets | 6.8 | 5.6 |
| | 1.9 | 2.6 | 3.6 | | | | 2.8 | 2.1 |
| | 4.3 | 3.0 | 2.0 | | | | 2.8 | 2.2 |
| | 2.0 | 2.0 | 1.6 | | | Sales/Total Assets | 2.0 | 1.5 |
| | .7 | .9 | 1.4 | | | | 1.1 | .9 |
| | | 1.3 | 3.2 | | | | 3.0 | 3.7 |
| | (18) | 3.5 | (16) 4.3 | | | % Depr., Dep., Amort./Sales | (72) 4.2 | (37) 5.6 |
| | | 7.8 | 5.8 | | | | 5.5 | 8.8 |
| | | .6 | | | | | 2.6 | 1.5 |
| | (10) | 1.0 | | | | % Officers', Directors' Owners' Comp/Sales | (18) 3.9 | (10) 3.0 |
| | | 1.9 | | | | | 6.3 | 7.4 |
| 8426M | 36511M | 267292M | 785545M | 760787M | 1074972M | Net Sales ($) | 3633473M | 1433738M |
| 1305M | 15703M | 122364M | 465880M | 574635M | 726561M | Total Assets ($) | 2941796M | 1247646M |

© RMA 2024

M = $ thousand    MM = $ million
See Pages viii through xx for Explanation of Ratios and Data

# HEALTH CARE—Ambulance Services  NAICS 621910

## Comparative Historical Data / Current Data Sorted by Sales

| | | | | | | | | | | |
|---|---|---|---|---|---|---|---|---|---|---|
| | | | | **Type of Statement** | | | | | | |
| 9 | 13 | 14 | | Unqualified | | | 1 | 1 | 2 | 3 | 7 |
| 6 | 6 | 7 | | Reviewed | | | | | | | 7 |
| 2 | 2 | 3 | | Compiled | | | | | 1 | 2 | |
| 4 | 11 | 7 | | Tax Returns | | | 2 | 3 | 1 | 1 | 1 |
| 41 | 41 | 42 | | Other | 6 | 5 | 4 | 7 | 8 | 12 |
| 4/1/21-3/31/22 ALL | 4/1/22-3/31/23 ALL | 4/1/23-3/31/24 ALL | | | | 20 (4/1-9/30/23) | | | 53 (10/1/23-3/31/24) | | |
| | | | | | 0-1MM | 1-3MM | 3-5MM | 5-10MM | 10-25MM | 25MM & OVER |
| 62 | 73 | 73 | | **NUMBER OF STATEMENTS** | 6 | 8 | 8 | 11 | 13 | 27 |
| % | % | % | | **ASSETS** | % | % | % | % | % | % |
| 22.7 | 20.3 | 22.7 | | Cash & Equivalents | | | | 37.3 | 20.6 | 15.2 |
| 28.8 | 24.0 | 24.8 | | Trade Receivables (net) | | | | 25.5 | 27.0 | 32.0 |
| .2 | .5 | 1.0 | | Inventory | | | | 2.9 | .0 | .9 |
| 2.3 | 3.7 | 3.2 | | All Other Current | | | | 2.2 | .2 | 5.3 |
| 53.9 | 48.5 | 51.8 | | Total Current | | | | 67.9 | 47.8 | 53.4 |
| 32.8 | 36.2 | 33.0 | | Fixed Assets (net) | | | | 11.6 | 27.8 | 32.6 |
| 7.6 | 3.8 | 4.6 | | Intangibles (net) | | | | 11.0 | 8.6 | 3.1 |
| 5.7 | 11.5 | 10.6 | | All Other Non-Current | | | | 9.4 | 15.8 | 10.8 |
| 100.0 | 100.0 | 100.0 | | Total | | | | 100.0 | 100.0 | 100.0 |
| | | | | **LIABILITIES** | | | | | | |
| 4.3 | 4.3 | 1.2 | | Notes Payable-Short Term | | | | 1.0 | 1.9 | 1.4 |
| 3.7 | 3.3 | 4.9 | | Cur. Mat.-L.T.D. | | | | 2.2 | 6.6 | 4.9 |
| 3.9 | 3.2 | 4.4 | | Trade Payables | | | | 5.2 | 1.3 | 6.2 |
| .0 | .9 | .0 | | Income Taxes Payable | | | | .1 | .0 | .0 |
| 6.2 | 7.7 | 8.8 | | All Other Current | | | | 7.1 | 5.2 | 15.7 |
| 18.1 | 19.3 | 19.4 | | Total Current | | | | 15.6 | 15.0 | 28.2 |
| 26.7 | 29.5 | 25.2 | | Long-Term Debt | | | | 14.9 | 19.5 | 23.0 |
| .2 | .3 | .4 | | Deferred Taxes | | | | .0 | .2 | .7 |
| 5.0 | 6.4 | 6.6 | | All Other Non-Current | | | | 2.2 | 3.4 | 7.9 |
| 50.1 | 44.5 | 48.4 | | Net Worth | | | | 67.3 | 61.9 | 40.3 |
| 100.0 | 100.0 | 100.0 | | Total Liabilities & Net Worth | | | | 100.0 | 100.0 | 100.0 |
| | | | | **INCOME DATA** | | | | | | |
| 100.0 | 100.0 | 100.0 | | Net Sales | | | | 100.0 | 100.0 | 100.0 |
| | | | | Gross Profit | | | | | | |
| 91.6 | 92.8 | 88.2 | | Operating Expenses | | | | 87.3 | 88.2 | 92.4 |
| 8.4 | 7.2 | 11.8 | | Operating Profit | | | | 12.7 | 11.8 | 7.6 |
| -.4 | .7 | 1.3 | | All Other Expenses (net) | | | | .9 | .0 | 1.4 |
| 8.8 | 6.5 | 10.5 | | Profit Before Taxes | | | | 11.8 | 11.7 | 6.3 |
| | | | | **RATIOS** | | | | | | |
| 8.2 | 6.1 | 8.4 | | | | | | 16.2 | 12.1 | 4.4 |
| 4.6 | 3.2 | 3.7 | | Current | | | | 7.9 | 3.7 | 2.5 |
| 2.3 | 1.4 | 1.3 | | | | | | 2.8 | 1.5 | 1.2 |
| 8.1 | 5.9 | 7.8 | | | | | | 16.2 | 12.1 | 4.1 |
| 4.5 | 3.1 | 2.9 | | Quick | | | | 6.7 | 3.6 | 2.4 |
| 2.1 | 1.3 | 1.3 | | | | | | 2.6 | 1.5 | 1.0 |
| 31  11.6 | 14  25.3 | 0  UND | | Sales/Receivables | | | | 0  UND | 58  6.3 | |
| 60  6.1 | 57  6.4 | 55  6.6 | | | | | | 54  6.7 | 54  6.7 | 68  5.4 |
| 83  4.4 | 83  4.4 | 85  4.3 | | | | | | 101  3.6 | 59  6.2 | 85  4.3 |
| | | | | Cost of Sales/Inventory | | | | | | |
| | | | | Cost of Sales/Payables | | | | | | |
| 2.7 | 2.9 | 2.7 | | | | | | 2.5 | 3.4 | 2.7 |
| 5.1 | 5.7 | 5.7 | | Sales/Working Capital | | | | 5.4 | 7.0 | 5.9 |
| 8.2 | 22.5 | 20.6 | | | | | | 9.2 | 16.0 | 25.1 |
| 27.1 | 19.9 | 24.2 | | | | | | | 43.2 | 30.4 |
| (46)  8.7 | (58)  4.6 | (57)  9.2 | | EBIT/Interest | | | | (12)  22.4 | (24)  4.1 | |
| 2.2 | .0 | 1.7 | | | | | | | 12.2 | 1.3 |
| 13.3 | 14.1 | 5.8 | | Net Profit + Depr., Dep., | | | | | | |
| (12)  4.4 | (13)  2.4 | (11)  2.9 | | Amort./Cur. Mat. L/T/D | | | | | | |
| 1.9 | .2 | 1.8 | | | | | | | | |
| .3 | .3 | .3 | | | | | | .0 | .3 | .5 |
| .8 | .7 | .7 | | Fixed/Worth | | | | .1 | .6 | .9 |
| 1.8 | 1.7 | 1.6 | | | | | | 1.2 | 1.0 | 1.6 |
| .2 | .3 | .2 | | | | | | .1 | .2 | .5 |
| .7 | .7 | .8 | | Debt/Worth | | | | .2 | 1.0 | 1.6 |
| 2.4 | 3.3 | 3.1 | | | | | | 1.9 | 1.3 | 5.1 |
| 46.4 | 36.7 | 59.4 | | % Profit Before Taxes/Tangible | | | | 73.9 | 43.0 | |
| (52)  21.2 | (65)  15.9 | (64)  16.0 | | Net Worth | | | | (12)  42.8 | (24)  13.9 | |
| 9.1 | 1.5 | 2.3 | | | | | | | 11.3 | 2.0 |
| 21.6 | 17.8 | 26.0 | | % Profit Before Taxes/Total | | | | 49.2 | 36.3 | 17.2 |
| 9.4 | 8.1 | 10.2 | | Assets | | | | 20.7 | 23.8 | 7.2 |
| 3.6 | .0 | 1.5 | | | | | | -2.4 | 7.0 | 1.7 |
| 13.0 | 10.5 | 17.0 | | | | | | 280.1 | 13.2 | 11.9 |
| 5.8 | 5.7 | 6.9 | | Sales/Net Fixed Assets | | | | 201.7 | 8.2 | 6.9 |
| 3.2 | 2.7 | 3.1 | | | | | | 12.4 | 4.5 | 3.5 |
| 2.2 | 2.3 | 2.6 | | | | | | 3.8 | 2.7 | 2.3 |
| 1.6 | 1.7 | 1.7 | | Sales/Total Assets | | | | 2.0 | 2.3 | 1.6 |
| .9 | 1.1 | 1.1 | | | | | | 1.3 | 1.4 | 1.2 |
| 3.5 | 3.5 | 2.5 | | | | | | | 1.9 | 2.3 |
| (42)  4.7 | (53)  5.1 | (50)  4.4 | | % Depr., Dep., Amort./Sales | | | | (10)  2.9 | (22)  4.0 | |
| 8.7 | 7.6 | 6.9 | | | | | | | 7.3 | 5.5 |
| | 1.5 | .9 | | % Officers', Directors' | | | | | | |
| (20)  2.7 | (21)  2.7 | | | Owners' Comp/Sales | | | | | | |
| | 6.6 | 6.9 | | | | | | | | |
| 1749528M | 2633137M | 2933533M | | Net Sales ($) | 3020M | 13544M | 30870M | 77133M | 226572M | 2582394M |
| 1290538M | 1872388M | 1906448M | | Total Assets ($) | 8071M | 8397M | 25194M | 39321M | 124361M | 1701104M |

© RMA 2024         M = $ thousand   MM = $ million
See Pages viii through xx for Explanation of Ratios and Data

# HEALTH CARE—Blood and Organ Banks  NAICS 621991

## Current Data Sorted by Assets | Comparative Historical Data

| | | | | | | Type of Statement | | |
|---|---|---|---|---|---|---|---|---|
| | | | 6 | 1 | 3 | Unqualified | 14 | 4 |
| | | | | | | Reviewed | | |
| | | | | | | Compiled | | |
| 1 | 2 (4/1-9/30/23) | 2 | 6 | 1 | 1 | Tax Returns | 2 | 2 |
| 0-500M | 500M-2MM | 2-10MM | 19 (10/1/23-3/31/24) 10-50MM | 50-100MM | 100-250MM | Other | 12 4/1/19-3/31/20 | 9 4/1/20-3/31/21 |
| 1 | | 2 | 12 | 2 | 4 | NUMBER OF STATEMENTS | 28 ALL | 15 ALL |
| % | % | % | % | % | % | ASSETS | % | % |
| | | | 24.9 | | | Cash & Equivalents | 28.2 | 38.1 |
| | | | 21.6 | | | Trade Receivables (net) | 18.1 | 13.8 |
| | D | | 4.4 | | | Inventory | 8.2 | 5.2 |
| | A | | 6.6 | | | All Other Current | 1.5 | 1.7 |
| | T | | 57.4 | | | Total Current | 56.0 | 58.8 |
| | A | | 21.6 | | | Fixed Assets (net) | 29.5 | 16.4 |
| | N | | 1.6 | | | Intangibles (net) | 2.4 | 16.2 |
| | O | | 19.4 | | | All Other Non-Current | 12.1 | 8.7 |
| | T | | 100.0 | | | Total | 100.0 | 100.0 |
| | A | | | | | LIABILITIES | | |
| | V | | .7 | | | Notes Payable-Short Term | 2.0 | 1.7 |
| | A | | 1.0 | | | Cur. Mat.-L.T.D. | 1.0 | .8 |
| | I | | 7.2 | | | Trade Payables | 11.4 | 6.4 |
| | L | | .0 | | | Income Taxes Payable | .2 | .5 |
| | A | | 10.5 | | | All Other Current | 7.3 | 6.2 |
| | B | | 19.4 | | | Total Current | 21.9 | 15.5 |
| | L | | 8.0 | | | Long-Term Debt | 9.7 | 12.9 |
| | E | | .0 | | | Deferred Taxes | .1 | .2 |
| | | | 7.7 | | | All Other Non-Current | 5.7 | 3.4 |
| | | | 64.9 | | | Net Worth | 62.5 | 68.0 |
| | | | 100.0 | | | Total Liabilities & Net Worth | 100.0 | 100.0 |
| | | | | | | INCOME DATA | | |
| | | | 100.0 | | | Net Sales | 100.0 | 100.0 |
| | | | | | | Gross Profit | | |
| | | | 96.9 | | | Operating Expenses | 95.9 | 96.0 |
| | | | 3.1 | | | Operating Profit | 4.1 | 4.0 |
| | | | -3.0 | | | All Other Expenses (net) | -.9 | -1.7 |
| | | | 6.1 | | | Profit Before Taxes | 5.0 | 5.8 |
| | | | | | | RATIOS | | |
| | | | 4.0 | | | | 6.0 | 7.6 |
| | | | 2.9 | | | Current | 3.2 | 5.6 |
| | | | 2.1 | | | | 1.4 | 1.8 |
| | | | 3.6 | | | | 5.8 | 7.6 |
| | | | 2.5 | | | Quick | 2.7 | 5.4 |
| | | | 1.6 | | | | 1.0 | 1.3 |
| | | 48 | 7.6 | | | | 42  8.6 | 38  9.7 |
| | | 62 | 5.9 | | | Sales/Receivables | 51  7.2 | 44  8.3 |
| | | 70 | 5.2 | | | | 63  5.8 | 69  5.3 |
| | | | | | | Cost of Sales/Inventory | | |
| | | | | | | Cost of Sales/Payables | | |
| | | | 2.9 | | | | 1.8 | 1.0 |
| | | | 4.4 | | | Sales/Working Capital | 4.2 | 1.8 |
| | | | 5.6 | | | | 14.1 | 8.5 |
| | | | 48.1 | | | | 29.9 | |
| | | (11) | 10.2 | | | EBIT/Interest | (22) 2.3 | |
| | | | -8.5 | | | | -2.7 | |
| | | | | | | Net Profit + Depr., Dep., Amort./Cur. Mat. L/T/D | | |
| | | | .1 | | | | .3 | .2 |
| | | | .3 | | | Fixed/Worth | .4 | .2 |
| | | | .6 | | | | 1.1 | .5 |
| | | | .2 | | | | .1 | .1 |
| | | | .3 | | | Debt/Worth | .5 | .7 |
| | | | 1.0 | | | | .9 | 1.3 |
| | | | 33.7 | | | | 13.2 | 27.8 |
| | | | 10.0 | | | % Profit Before Taxes/Tangible Net Worth | (25) 3.5 | (14) 11.1 |
| | | | -1.9 | | | | -3.2 | 2.1 |
| | | | 14.9 | | | | 10.9 | 11.1 |
| | | | 5.7 | | | % Profit Before Taxes/Total Assets | 3.5 | 7.1 |
| | | | -1.2 | | | | -2.6 | .0 |
| | | | 16.8 | | | | 8.9 | 25.1 |
| | | | 6.0 | | | Sales/Net Fixed Assets | 4.5 | 7.1 |
| | | | 3.4 | | | | 2.3 | 2.6 |
| | | | 1.6 | | | | 1.8 | 1.3 |
| | | | 1.2 | | | Sales/Total Assets | 1.2 | .8 |
| | | | .9 | | | | .8 | .6 |
| | | | 1.0 | | | | 1.7 | 2.0 |
| | | (11) | 1.6 | | | % Depr., Dep., Amort./Sales | (25) 2.7 | (10) 2.7 |
| | | | 2.6 | | | | 4.3 | 4.0 |
| | | | | | | % Officers', Directors' Owners' Comp/Sales | | |
| 518M | | 13669M | 424381M | 234044M | 502188M | Net Sales ($) | 1599258M | 954940M |
| 101M | | 10663M | 321722M | 182065M | 631646M | Total Assets ($) | 1338976M | 959702M |

© RMA 2024

M = $ thousand    MM = $ million
See Pages viii through xx for Explanation of Ratios and Data

# HEALTH CARE—Blood and Organ Banks  NAICS 621991

## Comparative Historical Data | Current Data Sorted by Sales

| | | | | Type of Statement | | | | | | |
|---|---|---|---|---|---|---|---|---|---|---|
| | | 7 | | Unqualified | | | | | 2 | 8 |
| | 9 | | | Reviewed | | | | | | |
| | | 10 | | Compiled | | | | | | |
| | | | | Tax Returns | | | | | | |
| | | | | Other | 1 | 1 | | | 3 | 6 |
| 7 | 10 | 11 | | | | 2 (4/1-9/30/23) | | 19 (10/1/23-3/31/24) | | |
| 4/1/21- | 4/1/22- | 4/1/23- | | | 0-1MM | 1-3MM | 3-5MM | 5-10MM | 10-25MM | 25MM & OVER |
| 3/31/22 | 3/31/23 | 3/31/24 | | | | | | | | |
| ALL | ALL | ALL | | | | | | | | |
| 14 | 19 | 21 | | NUMBER OF STATEMENTS | 1 | 1 | | | 5 | 14 |
| % | % | % | | ASSETS | % | % | % | % | % | % |
| 31.5 | 22.5 | 25.2 | | Cash & Equivalents | | | D | D | | 30.3 |
| 20.0 | 21.8 | 20.2 | | Trade Receivables (net) | | | A | A | | 20.7 |
| 9.6 | 7.9 | 5.0 | | Inventory | | | T | T | | 7.2 |
| 2.4 | 4.9 | 4.8 | | All Other Current | | | A | A | | 5.6 |
| 63.6 | 57.0 | 55.3 | | Total Current | | | | | | 63.9 |
| 21.4 | 23.5 | 26.8 | | Fixed Assets (net) | | | N | N | | 23.2 |
| 4.0 | .8 | 1.0 | | Intangibles (net) | | | O | O | | 1.2 |
| 11.1 | 18.7 | 17.0 | | All Other Non-Current | | | T | T | | 11.8 |
| 100.0 | 100.0 | 100.0 | | Total | | | | | | 100.0 |
| | | | | LIABILITIES | | | A | A | | |
| 2.3 | 1.8 | 1.7 | | Notes Payable-Short Term | | | V | V | | .1 |
| .7 | .8 | 1.3 | | Cur. Mat.-L.T.D. | | | A | A | | 1.0 |
| 9.6 | 7.4 | 7.6 | | Trade Payables | | | I | I | | 8.6 |
| .0 | .0 | .0 | | Income Taxes Payable | | | L | L | | .0 |
| 16.0 | 12.0 | 16.6 | | All Other Current | | | A | A | | 10.3 |
| 28.5 | 22.1 | 27.2 | | Total Current | | | B | B | | 20.1 |
| 5.6 | 9.9 | 9.3 | | Long-Term Debt | | | L | L | | 7.0 |
| .0 | .0 | .0 | | Deferred Taxes | | | E | E | | .0 |
| 1.6 | 24.7 | 5.9 | | All Other Non-Current | | | | | | 2.9 |
| 64.3 | 43.3 | 57.7 | | Net Worth | | | | | | 70.0 |
| 100.0 | 100.0 | 100.0 | | Total Liabilities & Net Worth | | | | | | 100.0 |
| | | | | INCOME DATA | | | | | | |
| 100.0 | 100.0 | 100.0 | | Net Sales | | | | | | 100.0 |
| | | | | Gross Profit | | | | | | |
| 94.1 | 101.1 | 98.6 | | Operating Expenses | | | | | | 97.1 |
| 5.9 | -1.1 | 1.4 | | Operating Profit | | | | | | 2.9 |
| -3.2 | .1 | -2.6 | | All Other Expenses (net) | | | | | | -2.3 |
| 9.1 | -1.2 | 4.0 | | Profit Before Taxes | | | | | | 5.2 |
| | | | | RATIOS | | | | | | |
| 6.6 | 7.0 | 4.1 | | | | | | | | 4.9 |
| 3.1 | 3.4 | 2.7 | | Current | | | | | | 3.5 |
| 1.8 | 1.8 | 2.0 | | | | | | | | 2.2 |
| 6.4 | 6.9 | 4.0 | | | | | | | | 4.8 |
| 2.6 | 2.6 | 2.5 | | Quick | | | | | | 2.8 |
| 1.1 | 1.2 | 1.4 | | | | | | | | 1.5 |
| 39  9.3 | 42  8.6 | 47  7.8 | | | | | | | 47 | 7.8 |
| 46  7.9 | 53  6.9 | 58  6.3 | | Sales/Receivables | | | | | 57 | 6.4 |
| 69  5.3 | 70  5.2 | 70  5.2 | | | | | | | 69 | 5.3 |
| | | | | Cost of Sales/Inventory | | | | | | |
| | | | | Cost of Sales/Payables | | | | | | |
| 1.6 | 2.3 | 1.4 | | | | | | | | 1.4 |
| 3.1 | 3.9 | 3.7 | | Sales/Working Capital | | | | | | 3.2 |
| 7.8 | 9.0 | 7.1 | | | | | | | | 5.2 |
| 235.2 | 17.1 | 48.1 | | | | | | | | 64.7 |
| (11) 60.4 | (15) 1.8 | (19) 8.6 | | EBIT/Interest | | | | | (13) | 8.2 |
| 14.0 | -1.1 | -8.5 | | | | | | | | -3.5 |
| | | | | Net Profit + Depr., Dep., Amort./Cur. Mat. L/T/D | | | | | | |
| .2 | .1 | .2 | | | | | | | | .2 |
| .3 | .4 | .3 | | Fixed/Worth | | | | | | .3 |
| .4 | .6 | 1.0 | | | | | | | | .4 |
| .1 | .2 | .2 | | | | | | | | .2 |
| .5 | .6 | .4 | | Debt/Worth | | | | | | .4 |
| 1.4 | 1.7 | 1.2 | | | | | | | | .7 |
| 48.9 | 22.3 | 13.9 | | | | | | | | 14.5 |
| (13) 9.8 | (18) .8 | (20) 6.1 | | % Profit Before Taxes/Tangible Net Worth | | | | | | 3.8 |
| 6.7 | -6.1 | -1.9 | | | | | | | | -.4 |
| 24.7 | 6.0 | 10.7 | | % Profit Before Taxes/Total Assets | | | | | | 11.3 |
| 8.8 | .5 | 2.3 | | | | | | | | 2.5 |
| 4.8 | -4.6 | -3.1 | | | | | | | | -.2 |
| 27.8 | 31.0 | 13.9 | | | | | | | | 10.9 |
| 4.2 | 5.4 | 5.2 | | Sales/Net Fixed Assets | | | | | | 5.1 |
| 2.5 | 2.2 | 2.5 | | | | | | | | 2.5 |
| 2.4 | 2.4 | 1.5 | | | | | | | | 1.5 |
| 1.2 | 1.5 | 1.2 | | Sales/Total Assets | | | | | | 1.2 |
| .7 | .8 | .8 | | | | | | | | .9 |
| 1.5 | .9 | 1.1 | | | | | | | | 1.1 |
| (13) 2.9 | (14) 2.7 | (18) 2.3 | | % Depr., Dep., Amort./Sales | | | | | | 2.0 |
| 4.3 | 4.2 | 4.2 | | | | | | | | 3.5 |
| | | | | % Officers', Directors' Owners' Comp/Sales | | | | | | |
| 979387M | 1096253M | 1174800M | | Net Sales ($) | 518M | 1568M | | | 81289M | 1091425M |
| 979879M | 1107999M | 1146197M | | Total Assets ($) | 101M | 5260M | | | 80815M | 1060021M |

© RMA 2024  M = $ thousand   MM = $ million
See Pages viii through xx for Explanation of Ratios and Data

# HEALTH CARE—All Other Miscellaneous Ambulatory Health Care Services  NAICS 621999

## Current Data Sorted by Assets | Comparative Historical Data

| | | | | | | Type of Statement | | |
|---|---|---|---|---|---|---|---|---|
| | | 2 | 7 | 2 | 8 | Unqualified | 18 | 21 |
| | 1 | 1 | 3 | | | Reviewed | 3 | 4 |
| | 2 | 1 | | 1 | | Compiled | 5 | 2 |
| 1 | 9 | 1 | 1 | 8 | | Tax Returns | 15 | 8 |
| 2 | | 26 | 18 | | 10 | Other | 87 | 34 |
| | 22 (4/1-9/30/23) | | 81 (10/1/23-3/31/24) | | | | 4/1/19-3/31/20 | 4/1/20-3/31/21 |
| 0-500M | 500M-2MM | 2-10MM | 10-50MM | 50-100MM | 100-250MM | | ALL | ALL |
| 3 | 12 | 31 | 28 | 11 | 18 | NUMBER OF STATEMENTS | 128 | 69 |
| % | % | % | % | % | % | ASSETS | % | % |
| | 38.9 | 28.5 | 21.1 | 27.1 | 23.0 | Cash & Equivalents | 24.6 | 28.6 |
| | 7.9 | 21.0 | 18.6 | 24.9 | 18.5 | Trade Receivables (net) | 22.0 | 18.9 |
| | .3 | 1.7 | 10.2 | 1.0 | 2.7 | Inventory | 2.5 | 4.6 |
| | 9.0 | 5.0 | 4.6 | 4.5 | 2.2 | All Other Current | 4.5 | 4.6 |
| | 56.2 | 56.2 | 54.5 | 57.6 | 46.3 | Total Current | 53.6 | 56.7 |
| | 20.1 | 27.5 | 19.1 | 15.9 | 14.2 | Fixed Assets (net) | 25.2 | 21.3 |
| | .9 | 6.0 | 15.7 | 17.4 | 25.0 | Intangibles (net) | 12.6 | 12.4 |
| | 22.8 | 10.3 | 10.7 | 9.1 | 14.5 | All Other Non-Current | 8.6 | 9.6 |
| | 100.0 | 100.0 | 100.0 | 100.0 | 100.0 | Total | 100.0 | 100.0 |
| | | | | | | LIABILITIES | | |
| | 5.1 | 1.2 | 2.6 | .7 | .0 | Notes Payable-Short Term | 6.7 | 4.8 |
| | 4.9 | 2.6 | 2.0 | .7 | 2.3 | Cur. Mat.-L.T.D. | 3.1 | 3.2 |
| | 3.5 | 4.4 | 9.9 | 18.9 | 10.6 | Trade Payables | 9.0 | 9.2 |
| | .0 | .4 | .7 | .0 | .6 | Income Taxes Payable | .8 | .2 |
| | 22.4 | 18.5 | 15.3 | 12.6 | 10.1 | All Other Current | 17.3 | 14.5 |
| | 36.0 | 27.1 | 30.5 | 32.9 | 23.5 | Total Current | 37.0 | 31.9 |
| | 20.6 | 22.3 | 17.2 | 15.2 | 33.8 | Long-Term Debt | 27.3 | 26.3 |
| | .0 | .4 | .0 | .0 | 1.3 | Deferred Taxes | .2 | .2 |
| | 4.6 | 6.8 | 3.5 | 8.3 | 5.7 | All Other Non-Current | 3.4 | 6.5 |
| | 38.8 | 43.4 | 48.8 | 43.5 | 35.6 | Net Worth | 32.2 | 35.1 |
| | 100.0 | 100.0 | 100.0 | 100.0 | 100.0 | Total Liabilities & Net Worth | 100.0 | 100.0 |
| | | | | | | INCOME DATA | | |
| | 100.0 | 100.0 | 100.0 | 100.0 | 100.0 | Net Sales | 100.0 | 100.0 |
| | | | | | | Gross Profit | | |
| | 79.1 | 79.1 | 86.7 | 81.5 | 85.9 | Operating Expenses | 91.1 | 87.9 |
| | 20.9 | 20.9 | 13.3 | 18.5 | 14.1 | Operating Profit | 8.9 | 12.1 |
| | .6 | 3.3 | .5 | 9.9 | 5.8 | All Other Expenses (net) | 2.9 | 1.2 |
| | 20.3 | 17.6 | 12.8 | 8.5 | 8.2 | Profit Before Taxes | 6.0 | 10.8 |
| | | | | | | RATIOS | | |
| | 21.0 | 4.8 | 5.1 | 3.0 | 4.7 | | 3.5 | 3.9 |
| | 2.2 | 2.2 | 2.0 | 2.4 | 1.8 | Current | 1.8 | 2.0 |
| | .3 | 1.1 | 1.1 | 1.5 | 1.0 | | 1.1 | 1.2 |
| | 7.8 | 4.7 | 4.1 | 2.9 | 4.2 | | 3.0 | 3.3 |
| | 1.6 | 2.0 | 1.3 | 2.3 | 1.6 | Quick | 1.4 | 1.9 |
| | .3 | 1.0 | .7 | 1.4 | .9 | | .8 | 1.0 |
| 0 UND | 0 999.8 | 12 29.9 | 0 UND | 13 28.3 | | | 5 77.0 | 5 68.7 |
| 0 UND | 33 11.1 | 39 9.3 | 58 6.3 | 51 7.1 | | Sales/Receivables | 31 11.6 | 28 13.0 |
| 0 UND | 62 5.9 | 63 5.8 | 122 3.0 | 99 3.7 | | | 58 6.3 | 57 6.4 |
| | | | | | | Cost of Sales/Inventory | | |
| | | | | | | Cost of Sales/Payables | | |
| | 4.0 | 3.5 | 2.5 | 2.7 | 2.0 | | 5.0 | 4.2 |
| | 103.0 | 7.8 | 7.2 | 6.0 | 7.3 | Sales/Working Capital | 12.3 | 7.9 |
| | -38.8 | 61.4 | 171.4 | 12.1 | NM | | 210.1 | 35.9 |
| | | 133.2 | 141.1 | | 5.4 | | 34.9 | 50.7 |
| | (17) | 47.2 | (20) 14.2 | (15) | 1.6 | EBIT/Interest | (93) 5.5 | (52) 16.6 |
| | | 3.0 | 5.7 | | .2 | | .3 | 2.7 |
| | | | | | | Net Profit + Depr., Dep., | 14.2 | |
| | | | | | | Amort./Cur. Mat. L/T/D | (12) 2.1 | |
| | | | | | | | -.1 | |
| | .0 | .0 | .1 | .1 | .0 | | .2 | .1 |
| | .1 | .3 | .5 | .5 | 3.0 | Fixed/Worth | .6 | .6 |
| | NM | 3.1 | 1.7 | 2.2 | -.3 | | -5.3 | -4.1 |
| | .2 | .5 | .8 | .8 | .9 | | .4 | .4 |
| | 1.2 | 1.1 | 2.1 | 1.8 | NM | Debt/Worth | 2.0 | 1.3 |
| | NM | 10.2 | 16.0 | 35.7 | -4.2 | | -12.2 | -16.6 |
| | | 111.3 | 100.0 | | | | 53.6 | 126.8 |
| | (25) | 57.8 | (23) 35.7 | | | % Profit Before Taxes/Tangible Net Worth | (87) 15.8 | (51) 56.4 |
| | | 15.4 | 10.7 | | | | 2.1 | 10.9 |
| | 262.2 | 56.1 | 23.9 | 13.8 | 11.8 | | 18.9 | 48.0 |
| | 53.9 | 14.1 | 12.9 | 4.7 | 2.1 | % Profit Before Taxes/Total Assets | 5.1 | 13.1 |
| | 16.1 | 1.4 | 2.8 | -5.6 | -5.2 | | -1.1 | 2.1 |
| | UND | 373.3 | 77.9 | 32.0 | 291.6 | | 73.2 | 61.0 |
| | 141.7 | 34.4 | 14.6 | 7.7 | 15.6 | Sales/Net Fixed Assets | 20.3 | 21.7 |
| | 17.2 | 2.3 | 3.3 | 5.3 | 5.0 | | 4.3 | 4.1 |
| | 11.9 | 2.8 | 2.1 | 2.6 | 1.5 | | 4.0 | 3.2 |
| | 3.7 | 1.8 | 1.3 | .8 | 1.0 | Sales/Total Assets | 1.8 | 1.8 |
| | 2.4 | .8 | .9 | .3 | .6 | | 1.1 | 1.0 |
| | | .6 | .5 | | | | .8 | .7 |
| | (15) | .8 | (15) 2.5 | | | % Depr., Dep., Amort./Sales | (89) 1.5 | (40) 1.7 |
| | | 2.8 | 3.8 | | | | 4.8 | 3.3 |
| | | | | | | % Officers', Directors' Owners' Comp/Sales | 2.5 | |
| | | | | | | | (15) 5.0 | |
| | | | | | | | 14.4 | |
| 18829M | 97308M | 428407M | 1109851M | 1175699M | 3548104M | Net Sales ($) | 5173114M | 4622091M |
| 679M | 13284M | 137088M | 650088M | 731741M | 2615323M | Total Assets ($) | 2965612M | 2366645M |

M = $ thousand    MM = $ million
See Pages viii through xx for Explanation of Ratios and Data

© RMA 2024

# HEALTH CARE—All Other Miscellaneous Ambulatory Health Care Services  NAICS 621999

| Comparative Historical Data ||| | | Current Data Sorted by Sales |||||||
|---|---|---|---|---|---|---|---|---|---|---|---|
| | | | | **Type of Statement** | | | | | | | |
| 10 | | 16 | | 19 | Unqualified | | 1 | | 1 | 2 | 15 |
| 4 | | 4 | | 4 | Reviewed | | 1 | | 1 | 2 | 1 |
| 1 | | 2 | | 2 | Compiled | | | | | | 1 |
| 6 | | 10 | | 5 | Tax Returns | | | 2 | 2 | | 1 |
| 36 | | 61 | | 73 | Other | 4 | 6 | 6 | 10 | 18 | 29 |
| 4/1/21-3/31/22 ALL | | 4/1/22-3/31/23 ALL | | 4/1/23-3/31/24 ALL | | | 22 (4/1-9/30/23) | | 81 (10/1/23-3/31/24) | | |
| | | | | | | 0-1MM | 1-3MM | 3-5MM | 5-10MM | 10-25MM | 25MM & OVER |
| 57 | | 93 | | 103 | NUMBER OF STATEMENTS | 4 | 8 | 8 | 14 | 22 | 47 |
| % | | % | | % | **ASSETS** | % | % | % | % | % | % |
| 27.8 | | 20.9 | | 26.6 | Cash & Equivalents | | | | 24.6 | 24.9 | 27.4 |
| 22.6 | | 21.1 | | 18.2 | Trade Receivables (net) | | | | 18.3 | 22.5 | 21.0 |
| 6.7 | | 3.6 | | 3.9 | Inventory | | | | .8 | 8.2 | 3.7 |
| 6.8 | | 4.1 | | 4.9 | All Other Current | | | | 2.1 | 4.8 | 4.9 |
| 63.8 | | 49.7 | | 53.6 | Total Current | | | | 45.9 | 60.4 | 57.1 |
| 15.1 | | 22.3 | | 21.2 | Fixed Assets (net) | | | | 33.4 | 17.4 | 14.4 |
| 9.1 | | 16.2 | | 13.0 | Intangibles (net) | | | | 8.9 | 14.6 | 15.5 |
| 12.0 | | 11.7 | | 12.3 | All Other Non-Current | | | | 11.8 | 7.6 | 13.0 |
| 100.0 | | 100.0 | | 100.0 | Total | | | | 100.0 | 100.0 | 100.0 |
| | | | | **LIABILITIES** | | | | | | | |
| 6.8 | | 7.1 | | 3.2 | Notes Payable-Short Term | | | | 4.8 | 3.4 | .4 |
| 1.7 | | 2.1 | | 2.7 | Cur. Mat.-L.T.D. | | | | 5.5 | 1.0 | 2.0 |
| 10.6 | | 9.4 | | 8.3 | Trade Payables | | | | 7.4 | 6.5 | 12.7 |
| .5 | | .2 | | .4 | Income Taxes Payable | | | | .4 | .6 | .5 |
| 16.7 | | 13.2 | | 16.1 | All Other Current | | | | 16.6 | 17.3 | 18.0 |
| 36.4 | | 32.0 | | 30.7 | Total Current | | | | 34.7 | 28.8 | 33.6 |
| 15.1 | | 20.6 | | 25.1 | Long-Term Debt | | | | 23.5 | 13.1 | 21.8 |
| .5 | | .0 | | .4 | Deferred Taxes | | | | .5 | .0 | .6 |
| 13.6 | | 7.5 | | 7.4 | All Other Non-Current | | | | 8.1 | 5.2 | 5.2 |
| 34.3 | | 39.8 | | 36.5 | Net Worth | | | | 33.1 | 52.9 | 38.8 |
| 100.0 | | 100.0 | | 100.0 | Total Liabilties & Net Worth | | | | 100.0 | 100.0 | 100.0 |
| | | | | **INCOME DATA** | | | | | | | |
| 100.0 | | 100.0 | | 100.0 | Net Sales | | | | 100.0 | 100.0 | 100.0 |
| | | | | Gross Profit | | | | | | | |
| 88.8 | | 87.6 | | 82.6 | Operating Expenses | | | | 77.9 | 80.9 | 89.2 |
| 11.2 | | 12.4 | | 17.4 | Operating Profit | | | | 22.1 | 19.1 | 10.8 |
| .4 | | 1.3 | | 3.3 | All Other Expenses (net) | | | | .3 | 4.5 | 2.4 |
| 10.8 | | 11.1 | | 14.0 | Profit Before Taxes | | | | 21.8 | 14.7 | 8.4 |
| | | | | **RATIOS** | | | | | | | |
| 4.1 | | 3.7 | | 4.4 | | | | | 2.7 | 4.8 | 3.9 |
| 1.8 | | 2.1 | | 2.1 | Current | | | | 1.3 | 2.4 | 1.8 |
| 1.1 | | 1.0 | | 1.0 | | | | | .9 | 1.1 | 1.1 |
| 3.2 | | 3.2 | | 4.1 | | | | | 2.5 | 4.6 | 3.6 |
| 1.3 | | 1.6 | | 1.6 | Quick | | | | 1.2 | 2.3 | 1.6 |
| .8 | | .8 | | .9 | | | | | .9 | 1.0 | .9 |
| 3 | 121.3 | 4 | 97.1 | 0 UND | | 0 | UND | 0 | UND | 9 | 40.5 |
| 37 | 9.9 | 37 | 9.9 | 34 10.8 | Sales/Receivables | 29 | 12.7 | 38 | 9.5 | 45 | 8.1 |
| 69 | 5.3 | 69 | 5.3 | 64 5.7 | | 61 | 6.0 | 70 | 5.2 | 83 | 4.4 |
| | | | | Cost of Sales/Inventory | | | | | | | |
| | | | | Cost of Sales/Payables | | | | | | | |
| 3.9 | | 4.0 | | 2.8 | | | | | 8.4 | 2.8 | 2.8 |
| 9.6 | | 11.0 | | 7.8 | Sales/Working Capital | | | | 63.1 | 7.5 | 7.8 |
| 105.8 | | NM | | 193.6 | | | | | -363.1 | 161.0 | 89.9 |
| | 68.7 | | 44.9 | | 98.1 | | | | | 107.8 | 108.0 | 114.1 |
| (38) | 37.3 | (65) | 6.6 | (68) | 8.2 | EBIT/Interest | | (12) | 45.5 | (12) | 9.4 | (36) | 5.5 |
| | 6.6 | | .6 | | 2.5 | | | | | 5.4 | 5.2 | .7 |
| | | | 37.6 | | 34.1 | Net Profit + Depr., Dep., Amort./Cur. Mat. L/T/D | | | | | | |
| | | (10) | 10.0 | (12) | 10.5 | | | | | | | |
| | | | 2.3 | | 4.2 | | | | | | | |
| .0 | | .1 | | .0 | | | | | .1 | .0 | .1 |
| .4 | | .5 | | .5 | Fixed/Worth | | | | 1.6 | .4 | .4 |
| 2.0 | | 2.8 | | 5.1 | | | | | NM | 1.6 | -2.2 |
| .5 | | .6 | | .5 | | | | | .7 | .3 | .8 |
| 1.2 | | 1.3 | | 1.9 | Debt/Worth | | | | 3.1 | 1.3 | 2.6 |
| 8.9 | | 5.7 | | -17.5 | | | | | NM | 6.7 | -6.2 |
| | 132.9 | | 100.3 | | 105.4 | % Profit Before Taxes/Tangible Net Worth | | | | 420.8 | 218.1 | 100.0 |
| (47) | 56.6 | (75) | 28.5 | (76) | 39.1 | | | (11) | 97.6 | (20) | 48.4 | (31) | 26.1 |
| | 20.7 | | 5.5 | | 13.3 | | | | | 57.8 | 18.6 | 4.0 |
| 43.1 | | 30.4 | | 29.9 | % Profit Before Taxes/Total Assets | | | | 139.9 | 29.5 | 17.0 |
| 18.5 | | 10.5 | | 11.6 | | | | | 34.4 | 11.9 | 10.4 |
| 2.5 | | 2.0 | | 1.2 | | | | | 13.4 | 2.8 | -.7 |
| 658.8 | | 145.6 | | 152.2 | Sales/Net Fixed Assets | | | | 62.0 | 179.3 | 152.2 |
| 43.3 | | 14.2 | | 21.3 | | | | | 14.1 | 12.2 | 21.3 |
| 9.3 | | 2.9 | | 3.8 | | | | | 3.3 | 3.6 | 7.3 |
| 4.3 | | 3.3 | | 3.2 | Sales/Total Assets | | | | 4.7 | 2.1 | 3.4 |
| 2.5 | | 1.5 | | 1.5 | | | | | 2.2 | 1.4 | 1.5 |
| .9 | | .8 | | .8 | | | | | 1.6 | .6 | 1.0 |
| | .3 | | .7 | | .6 | % Depr., Dep., Amort./Sales | | | | | .5 | | .5 |
| (36) | 1.1 | (54) | 2.3 | (51) | 1.7 | | | | | (14) | .9 | (22) | 1.3 |
| | 2.3 | | 4.5 | | 3.5 | | | | | | 3.0 | 4.1 |
| | | | 2.3 | | 1.0 | % Officers', Directors' Owners' Comp/Sales | | | | | | |
| | | (14) | 3.4 | (12) | 3.7 | | | | | | | |
| | | | | | 12.8 | 8.2 | | | | | | |
| 4151244M | | 2832269M | | 6378198M | Net Sales ($) | 2167M | 14398M | 32174M | 100396M | 385617M | 5843446M |
| 2229994M | | 2344065M | | 4148203M | Total Assets ($) | 7805M | 30859M | 18400M | 54102M | 472777M | 3564260M |

© RMA 2024  M = $ thousand  MM = $ million
See Pages viii through xx for Explanation of Ratios and Data

# HEALTH CARE—General Medical and Surgical Hospitals  NAICS 622110

**Current Data Sorted by Assets** | **Comparative Historical Data**

| 0-500M | 500M-2MM | 2-10MM | 10-50MM | 50-100MM | 100-250MM | | Type of Statement | | 4/1/19-3/31/20 ALL | | 4/1/20-3/31/21 ALL |
|---|---|---|---|---|---|---|---|---|---|---|---|
| 1 | 1 | 5 | 29 | 39 | 61 | | Unqualified | | 87 | | 82 |
| | | 1 | 1 | 1 | 1 | | Reviewed | | 7 | | 6 |
| | 1 | 2 | 2 | 1 | 1 | | Compiled | | 6 | | 4 |
| 2 | 3 | 4 | 5 | 1 | | | Tax Returns | | 37 | | 8 |
| 7 | 7 | 26 | 31 | 36 | 51 | | Other | | 136 | | 141 |
| | 140 (4/1-9/30/23) | | 180 (10/1/23-3/31/24) | | | | | | | | |
| 10 | 12 | 38 | 68 | 78 | 114 | NUMBER OF STATEMENTS | | | 273 | | 241 |
| % | % | % | % | % | % | **ASSETS** | | | % | | % |
| 30.7 | 24.8 | 13.2 | 14.9 | 19.7 | 19.5 | Cash & Equivalents | | | 17.8 | | 26.2 |
| 5.7 | 14.7 | 14.1 | 17.1 | 14.7 | 13.0 | Trade Receivables (net) | | | 16.2 | | 13.4 |
| .7 | 1.7 | 5.4 | 2.5 | 2.4 | 1.9 | Inventory | | | 1.9 | | 1.8 |
| 7.8 | 2.6 | 3.0 | 4.2 | 5.8 | 5.2 | All Other Current | | | 4.1 | | 3.0 |
| 44.9 | 43.8 | 35.7 | 38.6 | 42.6 | 39.5 | Total Current | | | 40.0 | | 44.4 |
| 33.0 | 29.4 | 44.1 | 45.0 | 37.3 | 35.8 | Fixed Assets (net) | | | 39.1 | | 35.0 |
| 2.3 | 8.6 | 5.2 | 3.2 | 3.5 | 2.9 | Intangibles (net) | | | 5.7 | | 4.6 |
| 19.8 | 18.1 | 15.0 | 13.1 | 16.6 | 21.8 | All Other Non-Current | | | 15.1 | | 16.1 |
| 100.0 | 100.0 | 100.0 | 100.0 | 100.0 | 100.0 | Total | | | 100.0 | | 100.0 |
| | | | | | | **LIABILITIES** | | | | | |
| 14.8 | 4.7 | 4.3 | 1.1 | .5 | .1 | Notes Payable-Short Term | | | 3.0 | | 1.8 |
| .8 | 4.4 | 4.0 | 3.4 | 2.4 | 2.2 | Cur. Mat.-L.T.D. | | | 2.8 | | 3.3 |
| 1.6 | 5.6 | 7.1 | 6.9 | 8.9 | 6.0 | Trade Payables | | | 7.9 | | 7.0 |
| .0 | .0 | .0 | .0 | .2 | .0 | Income Taxes Payable | | | 1.6 | | .3 |
| 25.7 | 15.1 | 14.7 | 10.8 | 12.3 | 10.3 | All Other Current | | | 9.3 | | 14.4 |
| 42.9 | 29.8 | 30.0 | 22.2 | 24.3 | 18.7 | Total Current | | | 24.6 | | 26.9 |
| 29.7 | 35.4 | 37.1 | 29.8 | 22.4 | 20.6 | Long-Term Debt | | | 29.4 | | 28.7 |
| .0 | .0 | .0 | .1 | .0 | .0 | Deferred Taxes | | | .1 | | .1 |
| 17.1 | 4.5 | 8.1 | 7.1 | 8.1 | 5.7 | All Other Non-Current | | | 6.1 | | 7.6 |
| 10.4 | 30.3 | 24.8 | 40.9 | 45.2 | 55.0 | Net Worth | | | 39.8 | | 36.8 |
| 100.0 | 100.0 | 100.0 | 100.0 | 100.0 | 100.0 | Total Liabilities & Net Worth | | | 100.0 | | 100.0 |
| | | | | | | **INCOME DATA** | | | | | |
| 100.0 | 100.0 | 100.0 | 100.0 | 100.0 | 100.0 | Net Sales | | | 100.0 | | 100.0 |
| | | | | | | Gross Profit | | | | | |
| 88.0 | 85.4 | 74.7 | 91.8 | 94.4 | 98.3 | Operating Expenses | | | 90.6 | | 92.9 |
| 12.0 | 14.6 | 25.3 | 8.2 | 5.6 | 1.7 | Operating Profit | | | 9.4 | | 7.1 |
| 3.0 | 2.2 | 5.9 | 1.5 | -.5 | .1 | All Other Expenses (net) | | | 1.9 | | .0 |
| 9.1 | 12.4 | 19.4 | 6.7 | 6.1 | 1.7 | Profit Before Taxes | | | 7.5 | | 7.0 |
| | | | | | | **RATIOS** | | | | | |
| 3.1 | 2.8 | 2.7 | 3.1 | 4.6 | 4.0 | | | | 3.5 | | 3.2 |
| 1.9 | 2.0 | 1.3 | 1.9 | 2.1 | 2.3 | Current | | | 2.2 | | 1.8 |
| .5 | .9 | .6 | 1.0 | 1.2 | 1.3 | | | | 1.3 | | 1.1 |
| 2.3 | 2.8 | 2.2 | 2.8 | 4.1 | 3.4 | | | | 3.0 | | 2.8 |
| 1.7 | 1.7 | 1.1 | 1.4 | 1.9 | 1.8 | Quick | | | 1.8 | | 1.6 |
| .5 | .8 | .3 | .8 | 1.0 | 1.0 | | | | 1.0 | | 1.0 |
| 0 UND | 0 UND | 0 UND | 33 11.2 | 31 11.8 | 36 10.2 | | | 30 | 12.3 | 31 | 11.9 |
| 0 UND | 6 57.3 | 24 14.9 | 46 7.9 | 43 8.4 | 45 8.2 | Sales/Receivables | | 43 | 8.4 | 41 | 8.8 |
| 31 11.8 | 60 6.1 | 39 9.4 | 60 6.1 | 55 6.6 | 57 6.4 | | | 59 | 6.2 | 54 | 6.8 |
| | | | | | | Cost of Sales/Inventory | | | | | |
| | | | | | | Cost of Sales/Payables | | | | | |
| 7.8 | 4.8 | 6.9 | 3.9 | 2.5 | 2.5 | | | | 3.8 | | 2.7 |
| 78.9 | 10.6 | 19.4 | 9.5 | 6.4 | 5.4 | Sales/Working Capital | | | 7.0 | | 5.9 |
| -55.2 | NM | -10.0 | 82.4 | 27.5 | 15.0 | | | | 23.5 | | 41.8 |
| | | 179.7 | 32.2 | 18.7 | 7.8 | | | | 13.7 | | 22.0 |
| | (26) | 27.2 | (58) 4.2 | (70) 5.3 | (110) 2.8 | EBIT/Interest | | (228) | 3.8 | (208) | 5.2 |
| | | 1.8 | -1.0 | -2.2 | -3.1 | | | | -.9 | | 1.3 |
| | | | | | | Net Profit + Depr., Dep., Amort./Cur. Mat. L/T/D | | | 18.4 | | 13.8 |
| | | | | | | | | (23) | 5.3 | (13) | 4.2 |
| | | | | | | | | | 2.2 | | .9 |
| .5 | .2 | .3 | .5 | .4 | .5 | | | | .5 | | .5 |
| 2.3 | 1.1 | 1.0 | 1.1 | .9 | .7 | Fixed/Worth | | | .8 | | .8 |
| -1.1 | -1.7 | -2.5 | 3.5 | 1.5 | 1.0 | | | | 1.8 | | 2.1 |
| .5 | .5 | .5 | .5 | .5 | .5 | | | | .5 | | .6 |
| 18.2 | 22.9 | 1.8 | 1.5 | 1.0 | .8 | Debt/Worth | | | 1.1 | | 1.3 |
| -5.6 | -5.8 | -4.3 | 4.6 | 3.1 | 1.6 | | | | 3.1 | | 3.8 |
| | | 137.0 | 37.7 | 31.9 | 9.6 | | | | 26.2 | | 30.2 |
| | (26) | 53.5 | (59) 8.6 | (73) 5.3 | (111) 2.6 | % Profit Before Taxes/Tangible Net Worth | | (241) | 6.8 | (206) | 9.1 |
| | | -9.7 | -5.6 | -1.4 | -7.4 | | | | -1.1 | | 2.0 |
| 134.4 | 45.4 | 63.9 | 11.0 | 11.7 | 5.0 | | | | 11.8 | | 10.6 |
| 4.1 | 19.2 | 12.8 | 3.9 | 3.3 | 1.2 | % Profit Before Taxes/Total Assets | | | 3.1 | | 3.8 |
| -18.5 | 1.3 | -2.5 | -2.6 | -2.0 | -3.4 | | | | -1.1 | | .3 |
| UND | 69.5 | 17.2 | 5.5 | 4.6 | 3.8 | | | | 7.0 | | 6.1 |
| 17.1 | 30.6 | 8.4 | 2.7 | 3.0 | 2.7 | Sales/Net Fixed Assets | | | 2.8 | | 2.7 |
| 3.6 | 1.6 | 1.0 | 1.6 | 2.1 | 2.0 | | | | 1.8 | | 1.8 |
| 15.8 | 4.8 | 2.9 | 1.7 | 1.5 | 1.3 | | | | 1.8 | | 1.6 |
| 2.6 | 2.7 | 1.8 | 1.2 | 1.0 | .9 | Sales/Total Assets | | | 1.1 | | .9 |
| 1.4 | .9 | .5 | .8 | .8 | .7 | | | | .7 | | .6 |
| | | 1.1 | 2.5 | 2.6 | 3.1 | | | | 2.9 | | 3.0 |
| | (34) | 3.3 | (66) 4.0 | (76) 4.0 | (91) 4.2 | % Depr., Dep., Amort./Sales | | (229) | 4.2 | (208) | 4.6 |
| | | 10.1 | 6.2 | 5.2 | 5.4 | | | | 6.0 | | 6.0 |
| | | | | | | % Officers', Directors' Owners' Comp/Sales | | | 11.7 | | 5.5 |
| | | | | | | | | (29) | 19.6 | (18) | 14.4 |
| | | | | | | | | | 32.0 | | 30.3 |
| 14915M | 34388M | 552689M | 2413115M | 7638732M | 19186552M | Net Sales ($) | | | 20158273M | | 19167387M |
| 2424M | 11657M | 214814M | 1951731M | 5892435M | 18556920M | Total Assets ($) | | | 19223315M | | 20013144M |

© RMA 2024    M = $ thousand    MM = $ million
See Pages viii through xx for Explanation of Ratios and Data

# HEALTH CARE—General Medical and Surgical Hospitals  NAICS 622110

| Comparative Historical Data | | | Type of Statement | Current Data Sorted by Sales | | | | | |
|---|---|---|---|---|---|---|---|---|---|
| 93 | 160 | 136 | Unqualified | 2 | 2 | 1 | 3 | 7 | 121 |
| 7 | 5 | 4 | Reviewed | | | | | | 4 |
| 4 | 7 | 7 | Compiled | | | | 1 | | 3 |
| 7 | 14 | 15 | Tax Returns | 5 | 2 | 2 | 1 | 4 | 1 |
| 138 | 165 | 158 | Other | 6 | 6 | 8 | 10 | 21 | 107 |
| 4/1/21-3/31/22 ALL | 4/1/22-3/31/23 ALL | 4/1/23-3/31/24 ALL | | 0-1MM | 140 (4/1-9/30/23) 1-3MM | 3-5MM | 180 (10/1/23-3/31/24) 5-10MM | 10-25MM | 25MM & OVER |
| 249 | 351 | 320 | NUMBER OF STATEMENTS | 15 | 11 | 11 | 15 | 32 | 236 |
| % | % | % | ASSETS | % | % | % | % | % | % |
| 23.7 | 20.5 | 18.4 | Cash & Equivalents | 8.7 | 22.8 | 21.3 | 14.8 | 16.0 | 19.2 |
| 15.0 | 14.8 | 14.3 | Trade Receivables (net) | 7.8 | 5.4 | 10.2 | 5.1 | 18.5 | 15.3 |
| 2.0 | 2.0 | 2.5 | Inventory | .6 | .0 | 2.8 | 2.2 | 5.4 | 2.4 |
| 4.0 | 4.2 | 4.8 | All Other Current | 4.5 | 2.1 | 2.3 | 5.3 | 4.1 | 5.2 |
| 44.7 | 41.6 | 40.0 | Total Current | 21.6 | 30.3 | 36.7 | 27.4 | 44.0 | 42.0 |
| 35.8 | 36.8 | 38.8 | Fixed Assets (net) | 58.2 | 56.4 | 37.1 | 42.4 | 34.8 | 37.1 |
| 4.2 | 3.3 | 3.6 | Intangibles (net) | .1 | .1 | 7.9 | 12.9 | 7.0 | 2.7 |
| 15.3 | 18.3 | 17.7 | All Other Non-Current | 20.0 | 13.2 | 18.3 | 17.3 | 14.2 | 18.3 |
| 100.0 | 100.0 | 100.0 | Total | 100.0 | 100.0 | 100.0 | 100.0 | 100.0 | 100.0 |
| | | | LIABILITIES | | | | | | |
| 2.0 | 2.1 | 1.6 | Notes Payable-Short Term | 6.7 | 9.1 | 6.6 | 2.5 | 2.7 | .4 |
| 2.8 | 3.3 | 2.8 | Cur. Mat.-L.T.D. | 2.7 | 3.4 | 6.2 | 2.9 | 3.5 | 2.5 |
| 7.4 | 6.9 | 6.9 | Trade Payables | 1.6 | 1.1 | 6.0 | 3.4 | 7.8 | 7.6 |
| .1 | .1 | .1 | Income Taxes Payable | .0 | .0 | .0 | .0 | .0 | .1 |
| 12.6 | 10.3 | 12.1 | All Other Current | 13.7 | 2.3 | 16.8 | 20.9 | 11.7 | 11.7 |
| 25.0 | 22.7 | 23.3 | Total Current | 24.7 | 16.0 | 35.6 | 29.7 | 25.8 | 22.3 |
| 27.6 | 27.2 | 25.8 | Long-Term Debt | 63.1 | 66.6 | 27.9 | 47.0 | 15.5 | 21.5 |
| .1 | .1 | .0 | Deferred Taxes | .0 | .0 | .0 | .0 | .0 | .0 |
| 5.9 | 5.9 | 7.2 | All Other Non-Current | 3.5 | 14.1 | 7.9 | 4.2 | 8.3 | 7.1 |
| 41.5 | 44.2 | 43.7 | Net Worth | 8.7 | 3.2 | 28.6 | 19.1 | 50.4 | 49.2 |
| 100.0 | 100.0 | 100.0 | Total Liabilties & Net Worth | 100.0 | 100.0 | 100.0 | 100.0 | 100.0 | 100.0 |
| | | | INCOME DATA | | | | | | |
| 100.0 | 100.0 | 100.0 | Net Sales | 100.0 | 100.0 | 100.0 | 100.0 | 100.0 | 100.0 |
| | | | Gross Profit | | | | | | |
| 91.5 | 95.4 | 92.3 | Operating Expenses | 65.5 | 74.7 | 85.1 | 75.8 | 84.1 | 97.4 |
| 8.5 | 4.6 | 7.7 | Operating Profit | 34.5 | 25.3 | 14.9 | 24.2 | 15.9 | 2.6 |
| -.4 | 1.7 | 1.1 | All Other Expenses (net) | 11.1 | 13.4 | 3.7 | 6.0 | -.4 | -.4 |
| 8.9 | 3.0 | 6.6 | Profit Before Taxes | 23.3 | 11.9 | 11.2 | 18.2 | 16.2 | 3.0 |
| | | | RATIOS | | | | | | |
| 3.2 | 3.6 | 3.7 | | 2.2 | 3.8 | 2.3 | 2.3 | 3.4 | 3.9 |
| 2.0 | 1.9 | 2.0 | Current | 1.3 | 1.6 | 1.4 | 1.1 | 2.1 | 2.1 |
| 1.3 | 1.3 | 1.1 | | .1 | .7 | .3 | .5 | 1.3 | 1.2 |
| 2.9 | 3.1 | 2.9 | | 2.1 | 2.0 | 2.3 | 1.5 | 2.8 | 3.2 |
| 1.6 | 1.5 | 1.6 | Quick | 1.3 | 1.6 | 1.3 | .8 | 1.6 | 1.8 |
| 1.0 | 1.0 | .9 | | .1 | .2 | .2 | .3 | .9 | 1.0 |
| 33  11.2 | 31  11.6 | 31  11.9 | | 0  UND | 0  UND | 0  UND | 0  UND | 34  10.8 | 35  10.5 |
| 42  8.7 | 43  8.4 | 42  8.7 | Sales/Receivables | 0  UND | 0  UND | 24  15.5 | 23  15.8 | 42  8.6 | 45  8.2 |
| 54  6.7 | 56  6.5 | 55  6.6 | | 31  11.8 | 0  UND | 63  5.8 | 40  9.1 | 52  7.0 | 56  6.5 |
| | | | Cost of Sales/Inventory | | | | | | |
| | | | Cost of Sales/Payables | | | | | | |
| 2.8 | 3.0 | 3.0 | | 2.5 | 19.2 | 9.9 | 4.0 | 4.4 | 2.7 |
| 6.0 | 7.1 | 7.5 | Sales/Working Capital | 16.5 | 110.7 | 61.5 | 85.0 | 8.0 | 6.5 |
| 17.6 | 22.9 | 62.6 | | -2.0 | -10.9 | -1.5 | -15.2 | 26.4 | 27.1 |
| 31.4 | 13.5 | 21.4 | | | | | 50.9 | 142.8 | 16.8 |
| (220)  7.7 | (310)  2.6 | (280)  4.0 | EBIT/Interest | | | (12)  4.4 | (27)  31.8 | (220)  3.4 |
| 2.1 | -4.1 | -2.1 | | | | | 2.7 | 2.0 | -3.0 |
| 13.0 | 6.1 | 12.1 | | | | | | | 21.5 |
| (11)  4.1 | (23)  3.3 | (22)  3.8 | Net Profit + Depr., Dep., Amort./Cur. Mat. L/T/D | | | | | (17)  3.2 |
| 1.0 | 1.5 | 1.2 | | | | | | | 1.0 |
| .4 | .4 | .5 | | 1.0 | .1 | .4 | .4 | .4 | .5 |
| .7 | .7 | .8 | Fixed/Worth | 10.4 | 2.0 | 3.6 | 7.3 | .6 | .7 |
| 1.7 | 1.4 | 1.8 | | -2.7 | -1.2 | -1.8 | -1.3 | 1.3 | 1.3 |
| .6 | .5 | .5 | | 1.0 | .3 | .5 | .8 | .4 | .5 |
| 1.0 | 1.0 | 1.0 | Debt/Worth | 33.3 | 3.2 | 2.8 | 9.9 | .9 | .9 |
| 3.5 | 2.5 | 3.1 | | -3.7 | -2.3 | -5.0 | -3.0 | 2.5 | 2.3 |
| 39.7 | 20.2 | 21.0 | | | | | | 121.7 | 14.6 |
| (222)  12.8 | (316)  3.3 | (282)  4.9 | % Profit Before Taxes/Tangible Net Worth | | | | (29)  49.8 | (223)  4.1 |
| 4.1 | -6.9 | -6.9 | | | | | | 3.1 | -7.1 |
| 13.8 | 7.8 | 10.2 | % Profit Before Taxes/Total Assets | 16.4 | 42.9 | 27.0 | 11.0 | 58.8 | 8.3 |
| 5.9 | 1.6 | 3.0 | | 4.9 | 3.3 | 6.0 | 8.6 | 22.6 | 2.1 |
| 1.1 | -4.3 | -2.7 | | .4 | -15.3 | -3.9 | 1.7 | 3.2 | -3.1 |
| 5.8 | 5.1 | 5.9 | Sales/Net Fixed Assets | 5.6 | 48.6 | 46.4 | 52.1 | 11.4 | 4.9 |
| 2.9 | 2.9 | 3.0 | | 1.3 | 3.8 | 7.7 | 3.0 | 5.4 | 2.9 |
| 1.9 | 1.8 | 1.9 | | .2 | .2 | .8 | .4 | 2.3 | 2.1 |
| 1.5 | 1.5 | 1.6 | Sales/Total Assets | 1.5 | 7.8 | 3.5 | 2.0 | 2.7 | 1.5 |
| 1.0 | 1.0 | 1.1 | | .3 | 2.4 | 1.2 | .9 | 1.6 | 1.0 |
| .7 | .7 | .7 | | .1 | .2 | .4 | .2 | 1.0 | .8 |
| 2.8 | 2.9 | 2.6 | | | | | 4.0 | 1.9 | 2.7 |
| (224)  4.2 | (305)  4.2 | (278)  4.0 | % Depr., Dep., Amort./Sales | | | (11)  14.6 | (31)  2.9 | (210)  4.0 |
| 5.6 | 5.7 | 5.5 | | | | | 19.8 | 4.5 | 5.2 |
| 4.1 | 8.6 | 4.9 | | | | | | | 10.5 |
| (17)  13.3 | (24)  16.1 | (18)  12.4 | % Officers', Directors' Owners' Comp/Sales | | | | | (10)  14.7 |
| 31.5 | 35.3 | 19.8 | | | | | | | 25.5 |
| 21985514M | 31031546M | 29840391M | Net Sales ($) | 6492M | 21204M | 44070M | 101508M | 584103M | 29083014M |
| 22188695M | 29262930M | 26629981M | Total Assets ($) | 23991M | 71876M | 79858M | 409331M | 496272M | 25548653M |

© RMA 2024   M = $ thousand   MM = $ million  
See Pages viii through xx for Explanation of Ratios and Data

# HEALTH CARE—Psychiatric and Substance Abuse Hospitals  NAICS 622210

## Current Data Sorted by Assets | Comparative Historical Data

| 0-500M | 500M-2MM | 2-10MM | 10-50MM | 50-100MM | 100-250MM | | Type of Statement | | 22 4/1/19-3/31/20 ALL | | 27 4/1/20-3/31/21 ALL |
|---|---|---|---|---|---|---|---|---|---|---|---|
| | | | | 5 | 6 | | Unqualified | | 10 | | 8 |
| | | | 1 | | | | Reviewed | | 2 | | |
| 1 | 1 | | 8 | 5 | 2 | | Compiled | | 2 | | |
| 1 | 3 | 2 | 24 (10/1/23-3/31/24) | | | | Tax Returns | | 3 | | |
| | 11 (4/1-9/30/23) | | | | | | Other | | | | |
| 2 | 4 | 2 | 14 | 5 | 8 | | NUMBER OF STATEMENTS | | 39 | | 35 |
| % | % | % | % | % | % | | ASSETS | | % | | % |
| | | | 13.9 | | | | Cash & Equivalents | | 17.6 | | 22.1 |
| | | | 12.8 | | | | Trade Receivables (net) | | 23.0 | | 20.3 |
| | | | .2 | | | | Inventory | | .2 | | .4 |
| | | | 1.8 | | | | All Other Current | | 3.6 | | 3.0 |
| | | | 28.7 | | | | Total Current | | 44.3 | | 45.8 |
| | | | 45.3 | | | | Fixed Assets (net) | | 38.4 | | 42.2 |
| | | | 6.4 | | | | Intangibles (net) | | 7.3 | | 4.9 |
| | | | 19.6 | | | | All Other Non-Current | | 10.0 | | 7.1 |
| | | | 100.0 | | | | Total | | 100.0 | | 100.0 |
| | | | | | | | LIABILITIES | | | | |
| | | | .5 | | | | Notes Payable-Short Term | | 2.2 | | 5.5 |
| | | | 1.7 | | | | Cur. Mat.-L.T.D. | | 1.3 | | 1.8 |
| | | | 3.3 | | | | Trade Payables | | 5.3 | | 5.7 |
| | | | .0 | | | | Income Taxes Payable | | .0 | | .1 |
| | | | 13.8 | | | | All Other Current | | 10.0 | | 14.4 |
| | | | 19.2 | | | | Total Current | | 18.9 | | 27.5 |
| | | | 24.1 | | | | Long-Term Debt | | 24.0 | | 29.3 |
| | | | .0 | | | | Deferred Taxes | | .1 | | .0 |
| | | | 24.2 | | | | All Other Non-Current | | 5.9 | | 6.6 |
| | | | 32.4 | | | | Net Worth | | 51.2 | | 36.7 |
| | | | 100.0 | | | | Total Liabilties & Net Worth | | 100.0 | | 100.0 |
| | | | | | | | INCOME DATA | | | | |
| | | | 100.0 | | | | Net Sales | | 100.0 | | 100.0 |
| | | | | | | | Gross Profit | | | | |
| | | | 96.9 | | | | Operating Expenses | | 94.1 | | 95.1 |
| | | | 3.1 | | | | Operating Profit | | 5.9 | | 4.9 |
| | | | -.6 | | | | All Other Expenses (net) | | 4.0 | | .0 |
| | | | 3.7 | | | | Profit Before Taxes | | 1.9 | | 4.9 |
| | | | | | | | RATIOS | | | | |
| | | | 3.1 | | | | | | 5.4 | | 3.8 |
| | | | 1.3 | | | | Current | | 2.7 | | 2.4 |
| | | | .5 | | | | | | 1.5 | | 1.5 |
| | | | 3.1 | | | | | | 5.3 | | 2.5 |
| | | | 1.2 | | | | Quick | | 2.0 | | 1.7 |
| | | | .5 | | | | | | 1.4 | | 1.2 |
| | | | 27  13.4 | | | | | 24 | 15.2 | 24 | 14.9 |
| | | | 40  9.1 | | | | Sales/Receivables | 47 | 7.7 | 46 | 8.0 |
| | | | 52  7.0 | | | | | 73 | 5.0 | 64 | 5.7 |
| | | | | | | | Cost of Sales/Inventory | | | | |
| | | | | | | | Cost of Sales/Payables | | | | |
| | | | 4.3 | | | | | | 3.5 | | 3.3 |
| | | | 76.6 | | | | Sales/Working Capital | | 6.7 | | 6.2 |
| | | | -10.1 | | | | | | 21.9 | | 19.2 |
| | | | 6.9 | | | | | | 16.2 | | 15.4 |
| | | | (13)  3.1 | | | | EBIT/Interest | (35) | 6.0 | (29) | 4.0 |
| | | | -2.5 | | | | | | .3 | | .8 |
| | | | | | | | Net Profit + Depr., Dep., Amort./Cur. Mat. L/T/D | | | | |
| | | | .6 | | | | | | .4 | | .6 |
| | | | .9 | | | | Fixed/Worth | | .8 | | 1.2 |
| | | | NM | | | | | | 5.6 | | 5.0 |
| | | | .3 | | | | | | .3 | | .6 |
| | | | 1.0 | | | | Debt/Worth | | .6 | | 2.3 |
| | | | NM | | | | | | 6.5 | | 11.8 |
| | | | 16.2 | | | | | | 31.3 | | 42.3 |
| | | | (11)  5.2 | | | | % Profit Before Taxes/Tangible Net Worth | (33) | 5.9 | (29) | 5.2 |
| | | | -.2 | | | | | | -10.0 | | 1.0 |
| | | | 7.7 | | | | | | 11.7 | | 12.9 |
| | | | 3.1 | | | | % Profit Before Taxes/Total Assets | | 5.0 | | 3.0 |
| | | | -1.0 | | | | | | -6.8 | | -.1 |
| | | | 7.0 | | | | | | 13.3 | | 12.9 |
| | | | 1.8 | | | | Sales/Net Fixed Assets | | 4.5 | | 2.3 |
| | | | 1.1 | | | | | | 1.7 | | 1.3 |
| | | | 1.2 | | | | | | 2.4 | | 3.0 |
| | | | .8 | | | | Sales/Total Assets | | 1.5 | | 1.3 |
| | | | .7 | | | | | | .8 | | .7 |
| | | | 1.6 | | | | | | 1.4 | | 1.4 |
| | | | (13)  2.7 | | | | % Depr., Dep., Amort./Sales | (32) | 2.1 | (28) | 3.2 |
| | | | 5.6 | | | | | | 4.0 | | 5.0 |
| | | | | | | | % Officers', Directors' Owners' Comp/Sales | | | | |
| 4283M | 28872M | 44274M | 475925M | 331848M | 1702111M | | Net Sales ($) | | 2008896M | | 2397545M |
| 163M | 5356M | 10500M | 490672M | 380924M | 1134897M | | Total Assets ($) | | 1315320M | | 1538246M |

M = $ thousand   MM = $ million
See Pages viii through xx for Explanation of Ratios and Data

© RMA 2024

# HEALTH CARE—Psychiatric and Substance Abuse Hospitals  NAICS 622210

## Comparative Historical Data | Current Data Sorted by Sales

| Comparative Historical Data | | | Type of Statement | Current Data Sorted by Sales | | | | | |
|---|---|---|---|---|---|---|---|---|---|
| 12 | 12 | 11 | Unqualified | | | | | 1 | 10 |
|  |  | 1 | Reviewed | | | | | | 1 |
|  | 1 | 1 | Compiled | | | | | | |
| 1 | 1 | 2 | Tax Returns | 1 | 1 | | 2 | 9 | 9 |
| 11 | 17 | 21 | Other | | | 1 | | | |
| 4/1/21- | 4/1/22- | 4/1/23- | | 11 (4/1-9/30/23) | | | 24 (10/1/23-3/31/24) | | |
| 3/31/22 | 3/31/23 | 3/31/24 | | 0-1MM | 1-3MM | 3-5MM | 5-10MM | 10-25MM | 25MM & OVER |
| ALL | ALL | ALL | | | | | | | |
| 24 | 31 | 35 | NUMBER OF STATEMENTS | 1 | 1 | 1 | 2 | 10 | 20 |
| % | % | % | ASSETS | % | % | % | % | % | % |
| 23.3 | 20.7 | 19.1 | Cash & Equivalents | | | | | 6.9 | 18.8 |
| 21.4 | 11.0 | 14.1 | Trade Receivables (net) | | | | | 10.7 | 15.8 |
| .1 | .1 | .1 | Inventory | | | | | .0 | .2 |
| 4.8 | 5.8 | 4.1 | All Other Current | | | | | 1.2 | 4.1 |
| 49.6 | 37.6 | 37.4 | Total Current | | | | | 18.9 | 38.9 |
| 36.3 | 42.4 | 35.4 | Fixed Assets (net) | | | | | 41.0 | 35.5 |
| 6.6 | 6.7 | 9.0 | Intangibles (net) | | | | | 16.5 | 7.4 |
| 7.5 | 13.3 | 18.1 | All Other Non-Current | | | | | 23.6 | 18.2 |
| 100.0 | 100.0 | 100.0 | Total | | | | | 100.0 | 100.0 |
| | | | LIABILITIES | | | | | | |
| 4.0 | 7.8 | 7.4 | Notes Payable-Short Term | | | | | 10.4 | 4.8 |
| 1.3 | .4 | 2.5 | Cur. Mat.-L.T.D. | | | | | 2.4 | 3.1 |
| 3.2 | 3.1 | 3.2 | Trade Payables | | | | | 2.9 | 3.6 |
| .1 | .0 | .0 | Income Taxes Payable | | | | | .0 | .0 |
| 13.7 | 14.1 | 12.1 | All Other Current | | | | | 8.7 | 14.8 |
| 22.3 | 25.4 | 25.1 | Total Current | | | | | 24.4 | 26.3 |
| 18.5 | 16.1 | 26.7 | Long-Term Debt | | | | | 25.7 | 26.3 |
| .0 | .0 | .0 | Deferred Taxes | | | | | .0 | .0 |
| 3.6 | 11.0 | 13.8 | All Other Non-Current | | | | | 6.4 | 18.7 |
| 55.6 | 47.5 | 34.4 | Net Worth | | | | | 43.4 | 28.6 |
| 100.0 | 100.0 | 100.0 | Total Liabilities & Net Worth | | | | | 100.0 | 100.0 |
| | | | INCOME DATA | | | | | | |
| 100.0 | 100.0 | 100.0 | Net Sales | | | | | 100.0 | 100.0 |
| | | | Gross Profit | | | | | | |
| 91.9 | 90.3 | 93.2 | Operating Expenses | | | | | 93.8 | 94.2 |
| 8.1 | 9.7 | 6.8 | Operating Profit | | | | | 6.2 | 5.8 |
| -2.1 | .9 | .3 | All Other Expenses (net) | | | | | -.5 | .8 |
| 10.2 | 8.8 | 6.5 | Profit Before Taxes | | | | | 6.6 | 5.0 |
| | | | RATIOS | | | | | | |
| 4.5 | 8.2 | 3.4 | | | | | | 2.3 | 2.9 |
| 3.3 | 2.4 | 1.5 | Current | | | | | .9 | 1.5 |
| 1.6 | 1.1 | .8 | | | | | | .5 | 1.0 |
| 4.3 | 5.4 | 2.9 | | | | | | 2.3 | 2.2 |
| 2.5 | 2.1 | 1.3 | Quick | | | | | .9 | 1.3 |
| 1.3 | .8 | .8 | | | | | | .4 | .8 |
| 22  16.5 | 20  18.0 | 15  24.9 | | | | | | 14  26.2 | 31  11.6 |
| 45  8.1 | 33  11.0 | 35  10.4 | Sales/Receivables | | | | | 33  10.9 | 39  9.4 |
| 63  5.8 | 57  6.4 | 49  7.4 | | | | | | 46  8.0 | 51  7.2 |
| | | | Cost of Sales/Inventory | | | | | | |
| | | | Cost of Sales/Payables | | | | | | |
| 3.8 | 2.4 | 5.5 | | | | | | 13.2 | 4.8 |
| 5.7 | 7.2 | 18.4 | Sales/Working Capital | | | | | NM | 12.7 |
| 11.6 | 21.5 | -30.1 | | | | | | -9.9 | NM |
| 40.1 | 8.8 | 10.4 | | | | | | | 9.8 |
| (18) 10.1 | (23) 1.6 | (32) 4.7 | EBIT/Interest | | | | | | 4.1 |
| 1.4 | -11.7 | 1.9 | | | | | | | 2.2 |
| | | | Net Profit + Depr., Dep., Amort./Cur. Mat. L/T/D | | | | | | |
| .4 | .4 | .6 | | | | | | .4 | .7 |
| .8 | .7 | 1.0 | Fixed/Worth | | | | | 10.1 | .9 |
| 1.3 | 1.4 | -999.8 | | | | | | -1.1 | 22.4 |
| .3 | .2 | .6 | | | | | | .3 | .7 |
| .8 | .5 | 1.4 | Debt/Worth | | | | | 10.9 | 1.3 |
| 2.3 | 3.0 | -999.8 | | | | | | -8.0 | 65.3 |
| 45.3 | 48.2 | 98.3 | % Profit Before Taxes/Tangible Net Worth | | | | | | 38.6 |
| (22) 22.6 | (26) 4.3 | (26) 11.1 | | | | | | (16) | 6.7 |
| 1.6 | -6.2 | 2.0 | | | | | | | 2.4 |
| 21.6 | 9.5 | 16.1 | % Profit Before Taxes/Total Assets | | | | | 22.9 | 14.2 |
| 13.9 | 1.5 | 5.0 | | | | | | 4.5 | 3.9 |
| .8 | -4.9 | 1.3 | | | | | | -1.0 | 1.4 |
| 14.4 | 10.5 | 17.2 | | | | | | 43.8 | 8.0 |
| 4.6 | 2.7 | 4.6 | Sales/Net Fixed Assets | | | | | 3.6 | 3.4 |
| 2.2 | 1.4 | 2.1 | | | | | | 1.0 | 2.1 |
| 2.4 | 2.0 | 2.7 | | | | | | 4.0 | 1.6 |
| 1.7 | 1.1 | 1.2 | Sales/Total Assets | | | | | .8 | 1.2 |
| 1.0 | .6 | .8 | | | | | | .4 | .9 |
| 1.0 | 1.7 | .8 | | | | | | | .8 |
| (21) 2.2 | (20) 3.2 | (27) 2.2 | % Depr., Dep., Amort./Sales | | | | | (19) | 2.2 |
| 3.9 | 4.7 | 5.2 | | | | | | | 5.1 |
| | | | % Officers', Directors' Owners' Comp/Sales | | | | | | |
| 1526107M | 1378893M | 2587313M | Net Sales ($) | 510M | 1852M | 3773M | 14464M | 185955M | 2380759M |
| 864977M | 1304025M | 2022512M | Total Assets ($) | 48M | 637M | 115M | 3086M | 265436M | 1753190M |

M = $ thousand   MM = $ million
See Pages viii through xx for Explanation of Ratios and Data
© RMA 2024

# HEALTH CARE—Specialty (except Psychiatric and Substance Abuse) Hospitals  NAICS 622310

## Current Data Sorted by Assets | Comparative Historical Data

| | | | | | | Type of Statement | | | | |
|---|---|---|---|---|---|---|---|---|---|---|
| | | | 1 | 3 | 4 | Unqualified | | 20 | | 16 |
| | | | 1 | | 1 | Reviewed | | 1 | | 2 |
| | | | 2 | | | Compiled | | 3 | | 4 |
| | 1 | | 1 | | | Tax Returns | | 8 | | 4 |
| 1 | 5 | 6 | 11 | 8 | 4 | Other | | 30 | | 41 |
| 0-500M | 12 (4/1-9/30/23) 500M-2MM | 2-10MM | 37 (10/1/23-3/31/24) 10-50MM | 50-100MM | 100-250MM | | | 4/1/19-3/31/20 ALL | | 4/1/20-3/31/21 ALL |
| 1 | 6 | 6 | 16 | 11 | 9 | NUMBER OF STATEMENTS | | 62 | | 67 |
| % | % | % | % | % | % | ASSETS | | % | | % |
| | | | 18.3 | 12.4 | | Cash & Equivalents | | 20.2 | | 23.3 |
| | | | 20.0 | 15.5 | | Trade Receivables (net) | | 17.0 | | 24.0 |
| | | | 1.7 | 2.0 | | Inventory | | 1.2 | | 1.2 |
| | | | 6.4 | 3.3 | | All Other Current | | 2.6 | | 2.9 |
| | | | 46.4 | 33.2 | | Total Current | | 41.0 | | 51.4 |
| | | | 33.9 | 37.4 | | Fixed Assets (net) | | 39.6 | | 35.2 |
| | | | 1.3 | 9.8 | | Intangibles (net) | | 7.5 | | 7.2 |
| | | | 18.3 | 19.6 | | All Other Non-Current | | 11.9 | | 6.2 |
| | | | 100.0 | 100.0 | | Total | | 100.0 | | 100.0 |
| | | | | | | LIABILITIES | | | | |
| | | | .8 | 4.3 | | Notes Payable-Short Term | | 6.4 | | 5.9 |
| | | | 7.2 | 2.5 | | Cur. Mat.-L.T.D. | | 5.4 | | 4.5 |
| | | | 4.8 | 4.9 | | Trade Payables | | 5.6 | | 5.3 |
| | | | .0 | .0 | | Income Taxes Payable | | .3 | | .1 |
| | | | 17.5 | 15.7 | | All Other Current | | 11.7 | | 20.0 |
| | | | 30.3 | 27.4 | | Total Current | | 29.4 | | 35.8 |
| | | | 20.5 | 35.6 | | Long-Term Debt | | 24.8 | | 26.3 |
| | | | 2.0 | .0 | | Deferred Taxes | | .3 | | .4 |
| | | | 10.9 | 4.7 | | All Other Non-Current | | 2.2 | | 4.0 |
| | | | 36.2 | 32.3 | | Net Worth | | 43.4 | | 33.5 |
| | | | 100.0 | 100.0 | | Total Liabilities & Net Worth | | 100.0 | | 100.0 |
| | | | | | | INCOME DATA | | | | |
| | | | 100.0 | 100.0 | | Net Sales | | 100.0 | | 100.0 |
| | | | | | | Gross Profit | | | | |
| | | | 87.8 | 72.3 | | Operating Expenses | | 85.6 | | 83.9 |
| | | | 12.2 | 27.7 | | Operating Profit | | 14.4 | | 16.1 |
| | | | 6.5 | 7.2 | | All Other Expenses (net) | | 2.0 | | 1.7 |
| | | | 5.7 | 20.5 | | Profit Before Taxes | | 12.4 | | 14.4 |
| | | | | | | RATIOS | | | | |
| | | | 2.2 | 2.0 | | | | 3.5 | | 3.6 |
| | | | 1.6 | 1.4 | | Current | | 1.8 | | 1.7 |
| | | | 1.4 | 1.1 | | | | 1.1 | | .9 |
| | | | 2.0 | 2.0 | | | | 3.1 | | 3.1 |
| | | | 1.3 | 1.2 | | Quick | | 1.4 | | 1.6 |
| | | | 1.0 | .6 | | | | .9 | | .8 |
| | | 15 | 24.7 | 0 | UND | | 1 | 372.0 | 16 | 23.0 |
| | | 38 | 9.5 | 49 | 7.5 | Sales/Receivables | 41 | 9.0 | 44 | 8.3 |
| | | 54 | 6.8 | 79 | 4.6 | | 58 | 6.3 | 72 | 5.1 |
| | | | | | | Cost of Sales/Inventory | | | | |
| | | | | | | Cost of Sales/Payables | | | | |
| | | | 6.9 | 7.6 | | | | 5.6 | | 3.8 |
| | | | 13.4 | 14.9 | | Sales/Working Capital | | 12.2 | | 9.2 |
| | | | 28.1 | 124.8 | | | | 287.9 | | -86.6 |
| | | | 21.5 | | | | | 33.3 | | 29.1 |
| | | | (12) 6.3 | | | EBIT/Interest | (52) | 10.7 | (56) | 9.8 |
| | | | 1.1 | | | | | 2.1 | | 1.2 |
| | | | | | | Net Profit + Depr., Dep., Amort./Cur. Mat. L/T/D | | | | |
| | | | .4 | .8 | | | | .4 | | .5 |
| | | | 1.1 | 1.5 | | Fixed/Worth | | 1.0 | | 1.2 |
| | | | 1.6 | 1.7 | | | | 3.3 | | 3.4 |
| | | | .8 | .8 | | | | .4 | | .7 |
| | | | 1.9 | 2.4 | | Debt/Worth | | 1.2 | | 2.1 |
| | | | 4.2 | 7.9 | | | | 4.6 | | 9.2 |
| | | | 42.3 | | | | | 181.1 | | 125.8 |
| | | | (15) 15.4 | | | % Profit Before Taxes/Tangible Net Worth | (51) | 39.6 | (57) | 31.3 |
| | | | 4.8 | | | | | 1.7 | | 9.7 |
| | | | 10.6 | 33.6 | | | | 48.0 | | 24.3 |
| | | | 5.4 | 8.7 | | % Profit Before Taxes/Total Assets | | 12.6 | | 12.0 |
| | | | -1.9 | -.1 | | | | 1.7 | | .9 |
| | | | 14.3 | 11.8 | | | | 15.6 | | 18.8 |
| | | | 5.5 | 4.3 | | Sales/Net Fixed Assets | | 4.4 | | 5.0 |
| | | | 4.2 | .4 | | | | 1.6 | | 1.6 |
| | | | 2.6 | 2.0 | | | | 3.4 | | 2.7 |
| | | | 1.9 | 1.5 | | Sales/Total Assets | | 1.6 | | 1.3 |
| | | | 1.2 | .2 | | | | .7 | | .6 |
| | | | 1.8 | | | | | 1.3 | | 1.5 |
| | | | (11) 2.3 | | | % Depr., Dep., Amort./Sales | (59) | 3.1 | (60) | 2.9 |
| | | | 3.4 | | | | | 5.6 | | 6.1 |
| | | | | | | | | | | 1.0 |
| | | | | | | % Officers', Directors' Owners' Comp/Sales | | | (11) | 5.7 |
| | | | | | | | | | | 17.1 |
| 1344M | 16474M | 43060M | 812943M | 1050116M | 1293574M | Net Sales ($) | | 3368985M | | 3343077M |
| 447M | 6782M | 38341M | 464609M | 788903M | 1417170M | Total Assets ($) | | 3039058M | | 2581105M |

M = $ thousand    MM = $ million
See Pages viii through xx for Explanation of Ratios and Data

© RMA 2024

# HEALTH CARE—Specialty (except Psychiatric and Substance Abuse) Hospitals  NAICS 622310

**Comparative Historical Data** | **Current Data Sorted by Sales**

| | | | Type of Statement | | | | | | |
|---|---|---|---|---|---|---|---|---|---|
| 9 | 19 | 8 | Unqualified | | | | | | 8 |
| 2 | 1 | 2 | Reviewed | | | | | | 2 |
| 1 | 1 | 2 | Compiled | | | | | | 2 |
| | 4 | 2 | Tax Returns | | | | | | 1 |
| 43 | 27 | 35 | Other | 2 | 1 | 2 | 4 | 3 | 17 |
| | | | | | 7 | | | | |
| | | | | | 12 (4/1-9/30/23) | | 37 (10/1/23-3/31/24) | | |
| 4/1/21- | 4/1/22- | 4/1/23- | | 0-1MM | 1-3MM | 3-5MM | 5-10MM | 10-25MM | 25MM & OVER |
| 3/31/22 | 3/31/23 | 3/31/24 | | | | | | | |
| ALL | ALL | ALL | | | | | | | |
| 55 | 52 | 49 | NUMBER OF STATEMENTS | 2 | 8 | 2 | 4 | 3 | 30 |
| % | % | % | **ASSETS** | % | % | % | % | % | % |
| 22.0 | 15.5 | 14.8 | Cash & Equivalents | | | | | | 15.5 |
| 18.6 | 19.7 | 17.5 | Trade Receivables (net) | | | | | | 19.5 |
| 1.6 | 1.3 | 1.6 | Inventory | | | | | | 2.0 |
| 6.1 | 5.5 | 5.6 | All Other Current | | | | | | 4.2 |
| 48.3 | 41.9 | 39.4 | Total Current | | | | | | 41.2 |
| 25.4 | 33.9 | 33.3 | Fixed Assets (net) | | | | | | 30.1 |
| 7.9 | 6.0 | 6.0 | Intangibles (net) | | | | | | 6.6 |
| 18.4 | 18.2 | 21.3 | All Other Non-Current | | | | | | 22.1 |
| 100.0 | 100.0 | 100.0 | Total | | | | | | 100.0 |
| | | | **LIABILITIES** | | | | | | |
| .4 | 5.2 | 7.4 | Notes Payable-Short Term | | | | | | 2.0 |
| 2.5 | 2.3 | 3.5 | Cur. Mat.-L.T.D. | | | | | | 3.5 |
| 8.2 | 8.0 | 5.5 | Trade Payables | | | | | | 6.3 |
| .1 | .0 | .0 | Income Taxes Payable | | | | | | .0 |
| 16.4 | 13.8 | 12.1 | All Other Current | | | | | | 16.2 |
| 27.5 | 29.4 | 28.4 | Total Current | | | | | | 28.0 |
| 25.1 | 29.4 | 25.4 | Long-Term Debt | | | | | | 24.3 |
| .0 | .5 | .7 | Deferred Taxes | | | | | | .1 |
| 5.8 | 10.8 | 10.5 | All Other Non-Current | | | | | | 14.9 |
| 41.6 | 30.0 | 34.9 | Net Worth | | | | | | 32.7 |
| 100.0 | 100.0 | 100.0 | Total Liabilities & Net Worth | | | | | | 100.0 |
| | | | **INCOME DATA** | | | | | | |
| 100.0 | 100.0 | 100.0 | Net Sales | | | | | | 100.0 |
| 79.1 | 93.5 | 82.5 | Gross Profit | | | | | | 91.8 |
| 20.9 | 6.5 | 17.5 | Operating Expenses | | | | | | 8.2 |
| 3.1 | 1.8 | 4.8 | Operating Profit | | | | | | .3 |
| 17.8 | 4.8 | 12.7 | All Other Expenses (net) | | | | | | 7.9 |
| | | | Profit Before Taxes | | | | | | |
| | | | **RATIOS** | | | | | | |
| 3.0 | 2.7 | 2.3 | | | | | | | 2.0 |
| 1.8 | 1.8 | 1.5 | Current | | | | | | 1.6 |
| 1.2 | 1.0 | 1.3 | | | | | | | 1.3 |
| 2.5 | 2.5 | 2.0 | | | | | | | 1.8 |
| 1.6 | 1.6 | 1.3 | Quick | | | | | | 1.3 |
| .9 | .8 | .9 | | | | | | | 1.0 |
| 13  28.5 | 21  17.6 | 0  UND | | | | | | 35 | 10.4 |
| 39  9.4 | 45  8.2 | 40  9.2 | Sales/Receivables | | | | | 49 | 7.5 |
| 57  6.4 | 64  5.7 | 55  6.6 | | | | | | 54 | 6.7 |
| | | | Cost of Sales/Inventory | | | | | | |
| | | | Cost of Sales/Payables | | | | | | |
| 4.3 | 5.5 | 6.3 | | | | | | | 7.1 |
| 8.7 | 7.7 | 13.8 | Sales/Working Capital | | | | | | 11.7 |
| 32.6 | NM | 28.4 | | | | | | | 28.0 |
| 102.9 | 25.9 | 26.2 | | | | | | | 25.5 |
| (38) 19.5 | (44) 2.8 | (36) 5.8 | EBIT/Interest | | | | | (26) | 8.6 |
| 5.0 | -8.4 | 1.0 | | | | | | | 2.6 |
| | | | Net Profit + Depr., Dep., Amort./Cur. Mat. L/T/D | | | | | | |
| .3 | .3 | .3 | | | | | | | .5 |
| .5 | 1.2 | 1.1 | Fixed/Worth | | | | | | 1.2 |
| 1.5 | 5.9 | 2.1 | | | | | | | 2.1 |
| .7 | .5 | .7 | | | | | | | 1.2 |
| 1.4 | 2.4 | 2.1 | Debt/Worth | | | | | | 2.4 |
| 5.0 | 11.7 | 6.1 | | | | | | | 7.4 |
| 143.1 | 55.5 | 52.3 | | | | | | | 59.5 |
| (48) 47.8 | (42) 5.4 | (41) 16.9 | % Profit Before Taxes/Tangible Net Worth | | | | | (25) | 16.9 |
| 11.4 | -7.0 | 4.2 | | | | | | | 5.7 |
| 41.9 | 16.2 | 16.2 | | | | | | | 16.1 |
| 19.1 | 1.3 | 5.7 | % Profit Before Taxes/Total Assets | | | | | | 7.0 |
| 5.0 | -5.2 | .7 | | | | | | | .8 |
| 33.2 | 17.4 | 20.2 | | | | | | | 11.8 |
| 10.1 | 5.3 | 5.6 | Sales/Net Fixed Assets | | | | | | 5.2 |
| 3.6 | 2.1 | 2.5 | | | | | | | 3.8 |
| 2.4 | 2.9 | 2.2 | | | | | | | 2.2 |
| 1.4 | 1.4 | 1.4 | Sales/Total Assets | | | | | | 1.6 |
| .6 | .8 | .8 | | | | | | | 1.0 |
| 1.6 | 1.6 | 1.6 | | | | | | | 1.8 |
| (37) 2.5 | (41) 3.0 | (31) 2.7 | % Depr., Dep., Amort./Sales | | | | | (24) | 2.8 |
| 4.5 | 5.0 | 3.5 | | | | | | | 3.5 |
| | .4 | | % Officers', Directors' Owners' Comp/Sales | | | | | | |
| (10) | 1.3 | | | | | | | | |
| | 6.9 | | | | | | | | |
| 5140886M | 3088068M | 3217511M | Net Sales ($) | 1377M | 16273M | 9667M | 33056M | 52853M | 3104285M |
| 4068026M | 2862496M | 2716252M | Total Assets ($) | 10008M | 130415M | 2156M | 77731M | 98865M | 2397077M |

M = $ thousand    MM = $ million
See Pages viii through xx for Explanation of Ratios and Data

© RMA 2024

# HEALTH CARE—Nursing Care Facilities (Skilled Nursing Facilities) NAICS 623110

## Current Data Sorted by Assets | Comparative Historical Data

| | | | | | | Type of Statement | | |
|---|---|---|---|---|---|---|---|---|
| 1 | 1 | 8 | 35 | 12 | 15 | Unqualified | 118 | 79 |
| | 1 | 26 | 12 | 1 | 6 | Reviewed | 65 | 17 |
| | 5 | 10 | 6 | 1 | 3 | Compiled | 36 | 22 |
| 4 | 5 | 5 | 2 | | | Tax Returns | 54 | 18 |
| 15 | 41 | 177 | 141 | 31 | 34 | Other | 359 | 318 |
| | 150 (4/1-9/30/23) | | 448 (10/1/23-3/31/24) | | | | 4/1/19-3/31/20 | 4/1/20-3/31/21 |
| 0-500M | 500M-2MM | 2-10MM | 10-50MM | 50-100MM | 100-250MM | | ALL | ALL |
| 20 | 53 | 226 | 196 | 45 | 58 | **NUMBER OF STATEMENTS** | 632 | 454 |
| % | % | % | % | % | % | **ASSETS** | % | % |
| 23.3 | 19.5 | 16.2 | 9.7 | 11.4 | 7.9 | Cash & Equivalents | 15.1 | 22.6 |
| 18.7 | 33.7 | 25.7 | 16.2 | 19.4 | 14.4 | Trade Receivables (net) | 22.9 | 17.2 |
| 1.0 | .1 | .1 | .1 | .1 | .4 | Inventory | .2 | .2 |
| 1.1 | 4.9 | 6.9 | 10.4 | 3.9 | 1.4 | All Other Current | 2.8 | 2.9 |
| 44.1 | 58.2 | 49.0 | 36.4 | 34.8 | 24.1 | Total Current | 41.0 | 42.9 |
| 32.3 | 26.5 | 29.3 | 43.2 | 42.9 | 46.3 | Fixed Assets (net) | 40.2 | 37.9 |
| 6.5 | 2.2 | 7.4 | 8.4 | 10.1 | 9.4 | Intangibles (net) | 5.6 | 8.5 |
| 16.8 | 13.2 | 14.3 | 12.0 | 12.2 | 20.2 | All Other Non-Current | 13.2 | 10.7 |
| 100.0 | 100.0 | 100.0 | 100.0 | 100.0 | 100.0 | Total | 100.0 | 100.0 |
| | | | | | | **LIABILITIES** | | |
| 6.7 | 13.2 | 3.0 | 3.5 | 2.7 | 2.1 | Notes Payable-Short Term | 5.0 | 5.5 |
| 11.6 | 1.4 | 3.1 | 4.1 | 5.1 | 2.4 | Cur. Mat.-L.T.D. | 2.7 | 3.8 |
| 20.1 | 12.9 | 13.3 | 5.7 | 6.6 | 5.0 | Trade Payables | 10.1 | 6.7 |
| .0 | .0 | .1 | .0 | .0 | .0 | Income Taxes Payable | .0 | .1 |
| 30.4 | 47.7 | 21.3 | 13.5 | 16.8 | 13.4 | All Other Current | 20.2 | 22.4 |
| 68.8 | 75.2 | 40.8 | 26.8 | 31.3 | 22.9 | Total Current | 38.0 | 38.4 |
| 16.5 | 35.8 | 51.3 | 48.9 | 40.1 | 45.4 | Long-Term Debt | 32.5 | 36.6 |
| .0 | .0 | .0 | .0 | .0 | .1 | Deferred Taxes | .0 | .1 |
| 30.7 | 13.1 | 12.4 | 14.4 | 7.9 | 17.8 | All Other Non-Current | 7.2 | 8.5 |
| -16.1 | -24.1 | -4.5 | 9.9 | 20.7 | 13.7 | Net Worth | 22.3 | 16.4 |
| 100.0 | 100.0 | 100.0 | 100.0 | 100.0 | 100.0 | Total Liabilties & Net Worth | 100.0 | 100.0 |
| | | | | | | **INCOME DATA** | | |
| 100.0 | 100.0 | 100.0 | 100.0 | 100.0 | 100.0 | Net Sales | 100.0 | 100.0 |
| | | | | | | Gross Profit | | |
| 90.3 | 88.0 | 89.7 | 90.3 | 91.5 | 92.6 | Operating Expenses | 92.4 | 91.2 |
| 9.7 | 12.0 | 10.3 | 9.7 | 8.5 | 7.4 | Operating Profit | 7.6 | 8.8 |
| 3.7 | 2.3 | 2.8 | 5.4 | 5.2 | 5.9 | All Other Expenses (net) | 3.6 | 2.2 |
| 6.0 | 9.7 | 7.5 | 4.3 | 3.3 | 1.5 | Profit Before Taxes | 4.0 | 6.6 |
| | | | | | | **RATIOS** | | |
| 2.9 | 2.8 | 2.5 | 3.2 | 2.2 | 1.8 | | 2.4 | 2.5 |
| .8 | 1.4 | 1.3 | 1.3 | 1.3 | 1.1 | Current | 1.4 | 1.4 |
| .4 | .4 | .9 | .6 | .8 | .8 | | .8 | .7 |
| 2.8 | 2.4 | 2.2 | 1.9 | 1.8 | 1.8 | | 2.3 | 2.3 |
| .8 | 1.3 | 1.2 | 1.0 | 1.2 | 1.0 | Quick | 1.3 | 1.3 |
| .4 | .4 | .8 | .5 | .8 | .6 | | .7 | .6 |
| 0 UND | 1 482.7 | 24 15.0 | 22 16.9 | 25 14.5 | 33 10.9 | | 19 19.7 | 16 23.1 |
| 8 48.2 | 32 11.5 | 38 9.5 | 36 10.0 | 36 10.1 | 41 8.8 | Sales/Receivables | 35 10.4 | 31 11.7 |
| 33 10.9 | 46 7.9 | 52 7.0 | 54 6.7 | 58 6.3 | 53 6.9 | | 49 7.4 | 48 7.6 |
| | | | | | | Cost of Sales/Inventory | | |
| | | | | | | Cost of Sales/Payables | | |
| 22.0 | 7.9 | 7.3 | 4.0 | 6.4 | 9.2 | | 7.8 | 5.1 |
| UND | 32.9 | 19.7 | 23.5 | 19.7 | NM | Sales/Working Capital | 20.2 | 13.2 |
| -12.7 | -14.4 | -46.2 | -10.0 | -45.8 | -10.6 | | -26.3 | -14.6 |
| | 67.9 | 48.0 | 19.6 | 11.5 | 4.6 | | 10.5 | 17.7 |
| (32) | 19.5 | (145) 4.3 | (152) 2.7 | (39) 3.1 | (49) 1.3 | EBIT/Interest | (487) 2.5 | (362) 3.3 |
| | -4.6 | -2.0 | .5 | .7 | .5 | | .4 | .1 |
| | | 4.6 | 38.3 | | | Net Profit + Depr., Dep., | 9.0 | 12.5 |
| | (15) | .4 | (16) 2.5 | | | Amort./Cur. Mat. L/T/D | (17) 1.7 | (28) 2.8 |
| | | -3.9 | -.4 | | | | 1.2 | .4 |
| .2 | .1 | .3 | .6 | 1.0 | 1.2 | | .4 | .4 |
| NM | .5 | 1.5 | 3.9 | 2.9 | 8.1 | Fixed/Worth | 1.6 | 1.7 |
| -.6 | -.7 | -.9 | -6.7 | -14.8 | -7.0 | | -18.1 | -5.4 |
| 1.4 | .7 | 1.0 | 2.2 | 1.6 | 2.5 | | .7 | 1.0 |
| -16.8 | 4.4 | 2.9 | 7.5 | 3.7 | 20.7 | Debt/Worth | 2.9 | 3.9 |
| -2.5 | -2.2 | -3.2 | -9.7 | -80.0 | -21.5 | | -26.0 | -9.4 |
| | 83.3 | 57.5 | 43.7 | 40.8 | 28.3 | % Profit Before Taxes/Tangible | 46.7 | 63.7 |
| (30) | 31.8 | (146) 21.3 | (127) 14.3 | (33) 9.2 | (36) 8.8 | Net Worth | (452) 15.7 | (313) 18.4 |
| | 3.9 | .4 | .2 | -.3 | -2.2 | | 2.4 | 1.4 |
| 45.5 | 30.6 | 19.5 | 8.9 | 9.9 | 4.6 | % Profit Before Taxes/Total | 13.8 | 14.7 |
| 14.7 | 10.1 | 7.9 | 3.2 | 4.1 | 1.1 | Assets | 4.1 | 4.1 |
| .3 | -9.6 | -2.0 | -1.1 | -.9 | -.9 | | -1.1 | -1.2 |
| 126.1 | 149.9 | 43.2 | 24.2 | 23.9 | 4.7 | | 28.1 | 26.8 |
| 41.1 | 30.7 | 16.3 | 2.1 | 1.9 | 1.8 | Sales/Net Fixed Assets | 4.9 | 4.1 |
| 12.0 | 10.8 | 3.7 | .8 | .8 | .8 | | 1.3 | 1.1 |
| 13.7 | 6.2 | 3.1 | 1.6 | 2.3 | 1.1 | | 3.7 | 2.4 |
| 6.5 | 3.7 | 2.2 | .9 | .8 | .7 | Sales/Total Assets | 1.7 | 1.2 |
| 1.4 | 1.5 | 1.4 | .6 | .5 | .5 | | .7 | .6 |
| .4 | .5 | .5 | .6 | .5 | 1.5 | | .8 | .9 |
| (10) .6 | (37) .7 | (192) 1.0 | (181) 2.0 | (40) 3.1 | (44) 3.5 | % Depr., Dep., Amort./Sales | (564) 2.3 | (385) 2.9 |
| 3.9 | 1.9 | 2.8 | 5.7 | 7.2 | 8.7 | | 5.3 | 7.0 |
| | | 4.4 | .6 | | | % Officers', Directors' | 1.6 | 2.3 |
| | (15) | 5.0 | (11) 2.6 | | | Owners' Comp/Sales | (70) 4.2 | (58) 4.5 |
| | | 10.1 | 16.0 | | | | 9.2 | 9.7 |
| 42278M | 295187M | 2745470M | 5342497M | 5126101M | 8660036M | Net Sales ($) | 21012825M | 14603793M |
| 4882M | 70217M | 1269675M | 4581564M | 3299009M | 9279872M | Total Assets ($) | 17326169M | 15587362M |

© RMA 2024    M = $ thousand    MM = $ million
See Pages viii through xx for Explanation of Ratios and Data

# HEALTH CARE—Nursing Care Facilities (Skilled Nursing Facilities) NAICS 623110

| Comparative Historical Data ||| | Type of Statement | Current Data Sorted by Sales ||||||
|---|---|---|---|---|---|---|---|---|---|---|
| 56 | 85 | 72 | | Unqualified | 1 | 1 | 4 | 7 | 28 | 31 |
| 54 | 36 | 46 | | Reviewed | 1 | 3 | | 6 | 24 | 12 |
| 10 | 14 | 25 | | Compiled | | | | 8 | 12 | 4 |
| 22 | 31 | 16 | | Tax Returns | 1 | 6 | 2 | 4 | 3 | |
| 331 | 378 | 439 | | Other | 20 | 30 | 26 | 90 | 157 | 116 |
| 4/1/21-3/31/22 | 4/1/22-3/31/23 | 4/1/23-3/31/24 | | | | 150 (4/1-9/30/23) ||| 448 (10/1/23-3/31/24) |||
| ALL | ALL | ALL | | | 0-1MM | 1-3MM | 3-5MM | 5-10MM | 10-25MM | 25MM & OVER |
| 473 | 544 | 598 | | NUMBER OF STATEMENTS | 24 | 40 | 32 | 115 | 224 | 163 |
| % | % | % | | ASSETS | % | % | % | % | % | % |
| 18.9 | 16.8 | 13.4 | | Cash & Equivalents | 8.7 | 11.9 | 18.2 | 15.9 | 13.2 | 12.2 |
| 18.3 | 16.9 | 21.5 | | Trade Receivables (net) | 9.1 | 10.8 | 14.9 | 21.4 | 22.2 | 26.3 |
| .1 | .2 | .2 | | Inventory | .0 | .0 | .6 | .2 | .1 | .2 |
| 5.3 | 3.5 | 6.9 | | All Other Current | 4.2 | 2.0 | 4.4 | 5.4 | 11.0 | 4.6 |
| 42.6 | 37.4 | 42.0 | | Total Current | 21.9 | 24.8 | 38.2 | 42.9 | 46.4 | 43.3 |
| 39.0 | 40.7 | 36.4 | | Fixed Assets (net) | 53.8 | 53.6 | 40.7 | 35.4 | 33.4 | 33.7 |
| 6.4 | 6.5 | 7.6 | | Intangibles (net) | 3.1 | 4.0 | 8.6 | 11.4 | 5.4 | 9.4 |
| 12.1 | 15.5 | 13.9 | | All Other Non-Current | 21.0 | 17.6 | 12.5 | 10.3 | 14.8 | 13.7 |
| 100.0 | 100.0 | 100.0 | | Total | 100.0 | 100.0 | 100.0 | 100.0 | 100.0 | 100.0 |
| | | | | LIABILITIES | | | | | | |
| 3.0 | 3.2 | 4.1 | | Notes Payable-Short Term | .0 | 2.0 | 4.5 | 6.4 | 3.2 | 4.6 |
| 2.9 | 4.4 | 3.6 | | Cur. Mat.-L.T.D. | 13.4 | 3.3 | 9.7 | 3.3 | 2.3 | 3.2 |
| 8.3 | 8.0 | 9.7 | | Trade Payables | .7 | 5.0 | 15.2 | 10.0 | 11.0 | 9.1 |
| .1 | .0 | .0 | | Income Taxes Payable | .0 | .0 | .0 | .1 | .1 | .0 |
| 18.3 | 21.9 | 20.3 | | All Other Current | 16.3 | 20.0 | 14.1 | 26.8 | 19.8 | 18.2 |
| 32.5 | 37.5 | 37.7 | | Total Current | 30.4 | 30.3 | 43.5 | 46.6 | 36.4 | 35.0 |
| 35.9 | 35.0 | 46.5 | | Long-Term Debt | 53.3 | 52.9 | 33.3 | 40.2 | 47.2 | 50.2 |
| .0 | .0 | .0 | | Deferred Taxes | .0 | .0 | .0 | .0 | .0 | .0 |
| 9.2 | 9.1 | 13.9 | | All Other Non-Current | 11.9 | 23.7 | 3.2 | 9.5 | 18.1 | 11.4 |
| 22.4 | 18.4 | 1.8 | | Net Worth | 4.4 | -6.9 | 20.0 | 3.8 | -1.7 | 3.3 |
| 100.0 | 100.0 | 100.0 | | Total Liabilities & Net Worth | 100.0 | 100.0 | 100.0 | 100.0 | 100.0 | 100.0 |
| | | | | INCOME DATA | | | | | | |
| 100.0 | 100.0 | 100.0 | | Net Sales | 100.0 | 100.0 | 100.0 | 100.0 | 100.0 | 100.0 |
| | | | | Gross Profit | | | | | | |
| 90.5 | 90.5 | 90.2 | | Operating Expenses | 50.4 | 63.4 | 89.6 | 95.5 | 94.4 | 93.1 |
| 9.5 | 9.5 | 9.8 | | Operating Profit | 49.6 | 36.6 | 10.4 | 4.5 | 5.6 | 6.9 |
| 2.1 | 4.2 | 4.1 | | All Other Expenses (net) | 16.4 | 13.0 | 8.7 | 2.1 | 2.5 | 2.8 |
| 7.4 | 5.3 | 5.7 | | Profit Before Taxes | 33.2 | 23.6 | 1.6 | 2.3 | 3.0 | 4.1 |
| | | | | RATIOS | | | | | | |
| 2.8 | 2.7 | 2.6 | | | 3.3 | 2.6 | 4.1 | 2.5 | 3.0 | 2.1 |
| 1.6 | 1.3 | 1.3 | | Current | 1.5 | 1.1 | 1.3 | 1.3 | 1.3 | 1.3 |
| .9 | .5 | .8 | | | .1 | .3 | .6 | .5 | .9 | .8 |
| 2.3 | 2.4 | 2.0 | | | 2.9 | 2.4 | 2.2 | 2.1 | 1.9 | 1.8 |
| 1.4 | 1.2 | 1.2 | | Quick | 1.2 | 1.0 | 1.2 | 1.2 | 1.2 | 1.2 |
| .8 | .5 | .6 | | | .1 | .3 | .6 | .4 | .7 | .8 |
| 17  21.6 | 11  32.4 | 21  17.1 | | | 0  UND | 0  UND | 0  UND | 18  20.0 | 26  14.0 | 34  10.6 |
| 33  10.9 | 33  11.2 | 37  9.9 | | Sales/Receivables | 0  UND | 0  UND | 4  90.4 | 34  10.6 | 38  9.6 | 44  8.3 |
| 47  7.7 | 49  7.5 | 53  6.9 | | | 56  6.5 | 13  27.6 | 37  9.8 | 47  7.8 | 53  6.9 | 60  6.1 |
| | | | | Cost of Sales/Inventory | | | | | | |
| | | | | Cost of Sales/Payables | | | | | | |
| 4.9 | 6.1 | 6.5 | | | 2.3 | 6.3 | 6.6 | 8.1 | 5.3 | 8.0 |
| 12.7 | 23.9 | 23.1 | | Sales/Working Capital | 14.1 | 101.7 | 33.8 | 22.8 | 21.1 | 23.1 |
| -45.4 | -10.1 | -19.5 | | | -1.3 | -4.5 | -30.3 | -9.1 | -31.9 | -26.8 |
| 27.8 | 8.3 | 21.1 | | | | | 25.8 | 40.8 | 29.0 | 25.0 | 11.6 |
| (337)  3.6 | (365)  1.3 | (426)  3.1 | | EBIT/Interest | (20)  4.4 | (21)  3.8 | (69)  1.7 | (177)  3.2 | (134)  3.0 |
| .7 | -1.4 | .0 | | | | 1.5 | .3 | -4.0 | -1.1 | .9 |
| 22.7 | 8.2 | 4.9 | | | | | | 2.4 | 49.8 | 29.4 |
| (20)  3.2 | (31)  2.5 | (46)  1.5 | | Net Profit + Depr., Dep., Amort./Cur. Mat. L/T/D | | (11)  -.7 | (14)  1.7 | (18)  1.9 |
| 1.8 | .6 | -.5 | | | | | -2.2 | -1.8 | .6 |
| .3 | .4 | .4 | | | .7 | .3 | .2 | .3 | .4 | .7 |
| 1.4 | 1.9 | 2.8 | | Fixed/Worth | 3.2 | 5.0 | 1.6 | 3.4 | 2.0 | 3.8 |
| -18.8 | -8.6 | -1.9 | | | -1.4 | -2.3 | -2.9 | -.7 | -7.3 | -1.3 |
| .7 | .8 | 1.4 | | | .8 | 1.3 | .6 | .9 | 1.5 | 1.8 |
| 2.9 | 3.3 | 5.9 | | Debt/Worth | 5.2 | 9.7 | 2.2 | 4.8 | 5.5 | 7.3 |
| -32.4 | -13.5 | -5.2 | | | -3.8 | -3.0 | -5.2 | -2.7 | -11.2 | -4.6 |
| 60.5 | 46.2 | 50.3 | | % Profit Before Taxes/Tangible Net Worth | 78.9 | 66.2 | 43.5 | 63.2 | 42.1 | 53.2 |
| (343)  22.3 | (379)  12.8 | (381)  16.8 | | | (16)  12.6 | (23)  23.7 | (22)  16.6 | (68)  25.4 | (154)  13.0 | (98)  18.8 |
| 1.8 | -5.4 | .2 | | | 1.1 | 13.0 | -6.7 | -.4 | -6.0 | 2.3 |
| 18.3 | 14.9 | 14.5 | | % Profit Before Taxes/Total Assets | 15.9 | 16.8 | 18.3 | 17.2 | 11.8 | 11.7 |
| 5.7 | 2.4 | 4.1 | | | 4.9 | 5.8 | 4.8 | 2.8 | 3.7 | 4.6 |
| -.5 | -3.2 | -1.1 | | | 1.2 | 2.5 | -.1 | -6.7 | -2.7 | .0 |
| 28.9 | 28.5 | 32.7 | | | 9.0 | 29.9 | 73.6 | 46.6 | 36.3 | 26.7 |
| 4.1 | 3.4 | 8.2 | | Sales/Net Fixed Assets | .7 | 1.0 | 9.4 | 10.7 | 13.1 | 7.1 |
| 1.0 | .9 | 1.2 | | | .2 | .3 | .9 | 1.7 | 1.6 | 1.6 |
| 2.8 | 2.7 | 2.7 | | | .6 | 2.0 | 3.7 | 2.8 | 2.9 | 2.7 |
| 1.2 | 1.1 | 1.4 | | Sales/Total Assets | .3 | .5 | 1.6 | 1.7 | 1.5 | 1.4 |
| .6 | .5 | .7 | | | .1 | .2 | .5 | .8 | .8 | .8 |
| .8 | .8 | .5 | | | 6.8 | 3.2 | .5 | .6 | .5 | .5 |
| (421)  2.4 | (461)  3.1 | (504)  1.4 | | % Depr., Dep., Amort./Sales | (16)  18.7 | (27)  15.6 | (25)  1.6 | (97)  1.1 | (203)  1.1 | (136)  1.5 |
| 6.0 | 7.1 | 5.1 | | | 32.2 | 22.9 | 7.5 | 4.9 | 3.7 | 3.8 |
| 1.7 | 1.2 | 1.8 | | | | | | | 1.9 | .4 |
| (38)  5.0 | (62)  3.7 | (44)  5.0 | | % Officers', Directors' Owners' Comp/Sales | | | | (13)  5.0 | (11)  1.8 |
| 10.2 | 6.2 | 10.1 | | | | | | | 10.1 | 7.2 |
| 17056634M | 26185798M | 22211569M | | Net Sales ($) | 10744M | 68265M | 127425M | 909225M | 3588039M | 17507871M |
| 16248026M | 17896270M | 18505219M | | Total Assets ($) | 94451M | 281072M | 224372M | 940782M | 3871154M | 13093388M |

© RMA 2024  M = $ thousand  MM = $ million
See Pages viii through xx for Explanation of Ratios and Data

# HEALTH CARE—Residential Intellectual and Developmental Disability Facilities  NAICS 623210

## Current Data Sorted by Assets | Comparative Historical Data

| | | | | | | Type of Statement | | |
|---|---|---|---|---|---|---|---|---|
| | | 7 | 29 | 6 | 4 | Unqualified | 66 | 22 |
| | 1 | 1 | | | | Reviewed | 1 | 1 |
| | | 1 | | | | Compiled | 2 | 3 |
| 1 | 2 | | | | | Tax Returns | 7 | 2 |
| 2 | 5 | 17 | 26 | 5 | 2 | Other | 52 | 55 |
| | 57 (4/1-9/30/23) | | 52 (10/1/23-3/31/24) | | | | 4/1/19-3/31/20 | 4/1/20-3/31/21 |
| 0-500M | 500M-2MM | 2-10MM | 10-50MM | 50-100MM | 100-250MM | | ALL | ALL |
| 3 | 8 | 26 | 55 | 11 | 6 | NUMBER OF STATEMENTS | 128 | 83 |
| % | % | % | % | % | % | ASSETS | % | % |
| | | 26.8 | 30.6 | 21.5 | | Cash & Equivalents | 22.2 | 30.9 |
| | | 14.7 | 15.2 | 10.6 | | Trade Receivables (net) | 14.2 | 12.7 |
| | | .0 | .1 | .3 | | Inventory | .2 | .1 |
| | | 2.1 | 1.5 | .9 | | All Other Current | 2.1 | 2.9 |
| | | 43.6 | 47.4 | 33.4 | | Total Current | 38.7 | 46.6 |
| | | 43.0 | 38.4 | 26.9 | | Fixed Assets (net) | 48.0 | 39.5 |
| | | 2.8 | .6 | 5.2 | | Intangibles (net) | 2.6 | 4.1 |
| | | 10.6 | 13.6 | 34.6 | | All Other Non-Current | 10.7 | 9.9 |
| | | 100.0 | 100.0 | 100.0 | | Total | 100.0 | 100.0 |
| | | | | | | LIABILITIES | | |
| | | .7 | .4 | .0 | | Notes Payable-Short Term | 2.7 | 2.7 |
| | | 2.2 | 1.6 | .7 | | Cur. Mat.-L.T.D. | 3.0 | 4.2 |
| | | 3.1 | 2.1 | 2.1 | | Trade Payables | 4.5 | 2.4 |
| | | .1 | .1 | .0 | | Income Taxes Payable | .1 | .0 |
| | | 11.1 | 11.5 | 9.5 | | All Other Current | 11.4 | 13.5 |
| | | 17.2 | 15.6 | 12.4 | | Total Current | 21.6 | 22.8 |
| | | 20.9 | 17.2 | 17.9 | | Long-Term Debt | 22.2 | 25.6 |
| | | .0 | .0 | .0 | | Deferred Taxes | .0 | .1 |
| | | 2.2 | 2.9 | 21.2 | | All Other Non-Current | 3.7 | 4.5 |
| | | 59.7 | 64.2 | 48.5 | | Net Worth | 52.4 | 47.1 |
| | | 100.0 | 100.0 | 100.0 | | Total Liabilties & Net Worth | 100.0 | 100.0 |
| | | | | | | INCOME DATA | | |
| | | 100.0 | 100.0 | 100.0 | | Net Sales | | |
| | | | | | | Gross Profit | | |
| | | 94.4 | 95.1 | 87.4 | | Operating Expenses | 93.8 | 93.7 |
| | | 5.6 | 4.9 | 12.6 | | Operating Profit | 6.2 | 6.3 |
| | | -.5 | -.3 | 5.2 | | All Other Expenses (net) | 1.3 | -.3 |
| | | 6.1 | 5.2 | 7.5 | | Profit Before Taxes | 4.8 | 6.6 |
| | | | | | | RATIOS | | |
| | | 3.6 | 5.6 | 3.7 | | | 3.5 | 3.5 |
| | | 2.9 | 2.7 | 2.3 | | Current | 2.1 | 2.2 |
| | | 1.7 | 2.0 | 1.0 | | | 1.0 | 1.4 |
| | | 3.3 | 5.6 | 3.7 | | | 3.3 | 3.3 |
| | | 2.9 | 2.7 | 2.3 | | Quick | 1.8 | 2.1 |
| | | 1.7 | 1.6 | 1.0 | | | .9 | 1.2 |
| | | 13  29.1 | 30  12.3 | 24  14.9 | | | 16  22.5 | 19  19.2 |
| | | 27  13.3 | 36  10.2 | 33  10.9 | | Sales/Receivables | 30  12.1 | 30  12.3 |
| | | 36  10.1 | 48  7.6 | 38  9.6 | | | 41  8.9 | 36  10.1 |
| | | | | | | Cost of Sales/Inventory | | |
| | | | | | | Cost of Sales/Payables | | |
| | | 3.8 | 2.4 | 2.8 | | | 4.7 | 3.4 |
| | | 7.4 | 4.3 | 7.5 | | Sales/Working Capital | 10.8 | 6.6 |
| | | 15.1 | 9.3 | 687.4 | | | UND | 32.1 |
| | | 22.5 | 20.8 | | | | 15.0 | 20.3 |
| | (22) | 4.3 | (49) 8.7 | | | EBIT/Interest | (112) 4.7 | (72) 6.7 |
| | | -.8 | .8 | | | | 1.4 | 1.9 |
| | | | | | | Net Profit + Depr., Dep., Amort./Cur. Mat. L/T/D | | |
| | | .3 | .3 | .4 | | | .5 | .5 |
| | | .7 | .6 | .7 | | Fixed/Worth | .9 | .9 |
| | | 1.3 | .8 | .9 | | | 1.7 | 1.5 |
| | | .3 | .3 | .6 | | | .3 | .5 |
| | | .7 | .4 | .9 | | Debt/Worth | .7 | 1.0 |
| | | 1.3 | .9 | 3.1 | | | 2.1 | 2.6 |
| | | 28.2 | 13.9 | 13.1 | | | 18.8 | 27.0 |
| | | 10.5 | (53) 4.2 | (10) 8.6 | | % Profit Before Taxes/Tangible Net Worth | (117) 7.9 | (76) 12.2 |
| | | .1 | -.1 | 3.6 | | | 1.2 | 4.2 |
| | | 18.3 | 10.6 | 7.5 | | | 9.0 | 10.7 |
| | | 7.3 | 3.5 | 3.7 | | % Profit Before Taxes/Total Assets | 4.6 | 5.7 |
| | | .1 | .0 | 1.4 | | | .6 | 2.1 |
| | | 11.0 | 6.0 | 9.9 | | | 7.0 | 7.9 |
| | | 4.0 | 3.5 | 5.2 | | Sales/Net Fixed Assets | 3.3 | 3.5 |
| | | 2.4 | 2.1 | 2.9 | | | 1.8 | 2.0 |
| | | 2.2 | 1.6 | 1.5 | | | 2.3 | 2.0 |
| | | 1.6 | 1.3 | 1.0 | | Sales/Total Assets | 1.5 | 1.2 |
| | | 1.3 | .8 | .8 | | | .9 | .9 |
| | | 1.1 | 1.5 | 1.5 | | | 1.5 | 1.7 |
| | (22) | 2.3 | (10) 2.0 | 1.7 | | % Depr., Dep., Amort./Sales | (119) 2.7 | (75) 2.3 |
| | | 3.6 | 3.1 | 3.2 | | | 4.1 | 3.5 |
| | | | | | | % Officers', Directors' Owners' Comp/Sales | 1.7 | |
| | | | | | | | (10) 5.1 | |
| | | | | | | | 9.2 | |
| 8195M | 30412M | 255638M | 1561117M | 943898M | 1109582M | Net Sales ($) | 3236616M | 2903750M |
| 1231M | 9846M | 153198M | 1192684M | 820150M | 892943M | Total Assets ($) | 2283602M | 2218012M |

© RMA 2024  M = $ thousand  MM = $ million
See Pages viii through xx for Explanation of Ratios and Data

# HEALTH CARE—Residential Intellectual and Developmental Disability Facilities  NAICS 623210

## Comparative Historical Data / Current Data Sorted by Sales

| | | | | | | Type of Statement | | | | | | | |
|---|---|---|---|---|---|---|---|---|---|---|---|---|---|
| | | 41 | | 51 | 46 | Unqualified | | | | 8 | 17 | 21 | |
| | | 2 | | | 2 | Reviewed | 1 | | | | 1 | | |
| | | 2 | | 2 | 1 | Compiled | | | | 1 | | | |
| | | 1 | | 5 | 3 | Tax Returns | 2 | | | 1 | | | |
| | | 51 | | 42 | 57 | Other | 2 | 2 | 5 | 13 | 17 | 18 | |
| | | 4/1/21-3/31/22 ALL | | 4/1/22-3/31/23 ALL | 4/1/23-3/31/24 ALL | | | 57 (4/1-9/30/23) | | | 52 (10/1/23-3/31/24) | | |
| | | | | | | | 0-1MM | 1-3MM | 3-5MM | 5-10MM | 10-25MM | 25MM & OVER |
| | | | | | | NUMBER OF STATEMENTS | 5 | 2 | 5 | 23 | 35 | 39 |
| | | 97 | | 100 | 109 | | | | | | | |
| | | % | | % | % | ASSETS | % | % | % | % | % | % |
| | | 31.2 | | 32.6 | 27.8 | Cash & Equivalents | | | | 35.5 | 25.3 | 29.2 |
| | | 12.3 | | 12.1 | 13.6 | Trade Receivables (net) | | | | 13.7 | 16.5 | 14.5 |
| | | .2 | | .2 | .1 | Inventory | | | | .1 | .0 | .3 |
| | | 1.9 | | 2.5 | 2.2 | All Other Current | | | | .9 | 2.2 | 3.2 |
| | | 45.6 | | 47.3 | 43.7 | Total Current | | | | 50.1 | 44.1 | 47.2 |
| | | 36.8 | | 36.5 | 38.2 | Fixed Assets (net) | | | | 34.0 | 43.3 | 31.5 |
| | | 3.1 | | 2.4 | 2.7 | Intangibles (net) | | | | 2.7 | .9 | 1.9 |
| | | 14.6 | | 13.8 | 15.4 | All Other Non-Current | | | | 13.2 | 11.7 | 19.3 |
| | | 100.0 | | 100.0 | 100.0 | Total | | | | 100.0 | 100.0 | 100.0 |
| | | | | | | LIABILITIES | | | | | | |
| | | 5.4 | | 2.6 | 1.4 | Notes Payable-Short Term | | | | 4.6 | .3 | .4 |
| | | 1.9 | | 1.6 | 1.6 | Cur. Mat.-L.T.D. | | | | 1.6 | 2.2 | 1.2 |
| | | 3.1 | | 3.5 | 2.5 | Trade Payables | | | | 2.1 | 2.1 | 3.5 |
| | | .1 | | .0 | .1 | Income Taxes Payable | | | | .1 | .1 | .0 |
| | | 14.6 | | 14.6 | 10.8 | All Other Current | | | | 9.5 | 12.2 | 12.7 |
| | | 25.0 | | 22.3 | 16.4 | Total Current | | | | 18.0 | 17.0 | 17.9 |
| | | 21.6 | | 15.3 | 20.5 | Long-Term Debt | | | | 20.2 | 18.9 | 13.3 |
| | | .0 | | .0 | .0 | Deferred Taxes | | | | .0 | .0 | .0 |
| | | 2.9 | | 4.7 | 5.1 | All Other Non-Current | | | | 1.7 | 2.3 | 11.0 |
| | | 50.4 | | 57.6 | 58.0 | Net Worth | | | | 60.2 | 61.7 | 57.7 |
| | | 100.0 | | 100.0 | 100.0 | Total Liabilties & Net Worth | | | | 100.0 | 100.0 | 100.0 |
| | | | | | | INCOME DATA | | | | | | |
| | | 100.0 | | 100.0 | 100.0 | Net Sales | | | | 100.0 | 100.0 | 100.0 |
| | | | | | | Gross Profit | | | | | | |
| | | 89.9 | | 93.0 | 93.1 | Operating Expenses | | | | 96.7 | 96.3 | 96.5 |
| | | 10.1 | | 7.0 | 6.9 | Operating Profit | | | | 3.3 | 3.7 | 3.5 |
| | | -.9 | | .9 | .8 | All Other Expenses (net) | | | | -2.4 | -.3 | -.5 |
| | | 11.0 | | 6.2 | 6.1 | Profit Before Taxes | | | | 5.7 | 4.0 | 4.0 |
| | | | | | | RATIOS | | | | | | |
| | | 4.5 | | 4.7 | 4.4 | Current | | | | 7.9 | 5.6 | 4.2 |
| | | 2.6 | | 2.9 | 2.7 | | | | | 3.2 | 2.7 | 2.5 |
| | | 1.4 | | 1.6 | 1.7 | | | | | 2.2 | 1.6 | 1.7 |
| | | 4.3 | | 4.7 | 4.4 | Quick | | | | 7.9 | 4.7 | 4.1 |
| | | 2.5 | | 2.8 | 2.6 | | | | | 3.1 | 2.6 | 2.4 |
| | | 1.3 | | 1.4 | 1.5 | | | | | 2.2 | 1.4 | 1.5 |
| 13 | 28.1 | 17 | 22.0 | 21 | 17.6 | Sales/Receivables | | | 9 | 40.6 | 28 | 13.2 | 27 | 13.4 |
| 30 | 12.3 | 31 | 11.7 | 31 | 11.6 | | | | 30 | 12.3 | 33 | 11.2 | 33 | 10.9 |
| 42 | 8.6 | 42 | 8.7 | 43 | 8.4 | | | | 49 | 7.5 | 45 | 8.1 | 43 | 8.5 |
| | | | | | | Cost of Sales/Inventory | | | | | | |
| | | | | | | Cost of Sales/Payables | | | | | | |
| | | 3.2 | | 3.1 | 3.3 | Sales/Working Capital | | | | 3.1 | 3.4 | 3.1 |
| | | 5.3 | | 5.4 | 6.3 | | | | | 6.6 | 6.5 | 6.0 |
| | | 16.9 | | 22.2 | 15.1 | | | | | 12.7 | 17.7 | 12.2 |
| | | 27.2 | | 21.5 | 19.8 | EBIT/Interest | | | | 27.8 | 17.6 | 20.2 |
| (71) | 9.7 | (78) | 5.7 | (91) | 7.3 | | | | (18) | 11.9 | (32) | 7.1 | (34) | 8.2 |
| | | 3.0 | | -1.4 | 1.0 | | | | | -4.5 | .9 | 1.5 |
| | | | | | | Net Profit + Depr., Dep., Amort./Cur. Mat. L/T/D | | | | | | |
| | | .3 | | .3 | .3 | Fixed/Worth | | | | .2 | .4 | .3 |
| | | .6 | | .5 | .7 | | | | | .6 | .8 | .5 |
| | | 1.2 | | 1.0 | 1.1 | | | | | 1.0 | 1.4 | .7 |
| | | .3 | | .3 | .3 | Debt/Worth | | | | .2 | .3 | .3 |
| | | .7 | | .5 | .5 | | | | | .5 | .6 | .6 |
| | | 1.7 | | 1.2 | 1.2 | | | | | 1.1 | 1.2 | 1.0 |
| | | 31.4 | | 19.8 | 18.2 | % Profit Before Taxes/Tangible Net Worth | | | | 26.2 | 20.1 | 14.3 |
| (92) | 17.6 | (96) | 6.2 | (102) | 6.5 | | | | (22) | 11.8 | (34) | 3.3 | (38) | 8.7 |
| | | 7.6 | | -.9 | .6 | | | | | 2.6 | .3 | 2.8 |
| | | 18.7 | | 10.7 | 11.4 | % Profit Before Taxes/Total Assets | | | | 19.2 | 11.1 | 9.6 |
| | | 9.1 | | 3.5 | 4.4 | | | | | 7.8 | 2.2 | 4.6 |
| | | 3.3 | | -.1 | .2 | | | | | .7 | .1 | 1.4 |
| | | 9.0 | | 9.4 | 6.6 | Sales/Net Fixed Assets | | | | 17.1 | 4.3 | 7.6 |
| | | 4.1 | | 4.1 | 3.9 | | | | | 4.8 | 2.9 | 4.9 |
| | | 2.1 | | 2.5 | 2.3 | | | | | 1.8 | 2.1 | 3.2 |
| | | 1.9 | | 2.1 | 1.8 | Sales/Total Assets | | | | 2.0 | 1.6 | 2.0 |
| | | 1.4 | | 1.4 | 1.4 | | | | | 1.3 | 1.4 | 1.5 |
| | | .9 | | .9 | .8 | | | | | .7 | 1.0 | 1.1 |
| | | 1.3 | | 1.4 | 1.5 | % Depr., Dep., Amort./Sales | | | | .8 | 1.8 | 1.3 |
| (80) | 2.2 | (89) | 2.1 | (98) | 2.1 | | | | (18) | 1.7 | (33) | 2.2 | (38) | 1.9 |
| | | 3.8 | | 3.1 | 3.3 | | | | | 3.7 | 3.2 | 2.6 |
| | | | | | | % Officers', Directors' Owners' Comp/Sales | | | | | | |
| | | 5271264M | | 6280701M | 3908842M | Net Sales ($) | 1947M | 3111M | 17441M | 177972M | 605067M | 3103304M |
| | | 2974593M | | 3162044M | 3070052M | Total Assets ($) | 4979M | 26293M | 63889M | 164616M | 502867M | 2307408M |

M = $ thousand    MM = $ million
See Pages viii through xx for Explanation of Ratios and Data
© RMA 2024

# HEALTH CARE—Residential Mental Health and Substance Abuse Facilities  NAICS 623220

## Current Data Sorted by Assets | Comparative Historical Data

| | | | 9 | 22 | 10 | 6 | Type of Statement | | 62 | 16 |
|---|---|---|---|---|---|---|---|---|---|---|
| | | | 2 | 2 | | | Unqualified | | | |
| | 1 | 2 | 3 | | | | Reviewed | | 5 | 2 |
| | | 3 | | | | | Compiled | | 2 | 3 |
| | | | | | | | Tax Returns | | 14 | 4 |
| 3 | 9 | | 18 | 28 | 9 | 4 | Other | | 66 | 51 |
| | | 59 (4/1-9/30/23) | | 72 (10/1/23-3/31/24) | | | | | 4/1/19-3/31/20 | 4/1/20-3/31/21 |
| 0-500M | 500M-2MM | 2-10MM | 10-50MM | 50-100MM | 100-250MM | | | | ALL | ALL |
| 4 | 14 | 32 | 52 | 19 | 10 | | NUMBER OF STATEMENTS | | 149 | 76 |
| % | % | % | % | % | % | | ASSETS | | % | % |
| | 22.6 | 17.1 | 20.0 | 23.9 | 11.2 | | Cash & Equivalents | | 20.4 | 25.2 |
| | 27.5 | 12.9 | 15.8 | 13.2 | 14.9 | | Trade Receivables (net) | | 17.6 | 17.1 |
| | .0 | .1 | .1 | .1 | .1 | | Inventory | | .1 | .1 |
| | 3.0 | 2.5 | 1.2 | 2.0 | 2.1 | | All Other Current | | 4.4 | 4.0 |
| | 53.2 | 32.6 | 37.2 | 39.1 | 28.3 | | Total Current | | 42.6 | 46.3 |
| | 41.8 | 53.1 | 44.7 | 37.4 | 43.7 | | Fixed Assets (net) | | 45.3 | 40.3 |
| | 1.5 | 3.3 | 2.9 | 7.6 | 1.2 | | Intangibles (net) | | 3.4 | 4.4 |
| | 3.5 | 10.9 | 15.2 | 15.9 | 26.8 | | All Other Non-Current | | 8.7 | 9.0 |
| | 100.0 | 100.0 | 100.0 | 100.0 | 100.0 | | Total | | 100.0 | 100.0 |
| | | | | | | | **LIABILITIES** | | | |
| | 6.7 | 6.3 | .6 | 1.0 | 1.8 | | Notes Payable-Short Term | | 2.9 | 5.2 |
| | 3.7 | 5.1 | 1.5 | 1.2 | 1.1 | | Cur. Mat.-L.T.D. | | 1.7 | 2.2 |
| | 6.6 | 1.4 | 3.7 | 3.3 | 3.0 | | Trade Payables | | 4.6 | 4.5 |
| | .0 | .0 | .1 | .0 | .0 | | Income Taxes Payable | | .0 | .1 |
| | 6.8 | 8.2 | 12.3 | 10.1 | 10.1 | | All Other Current | | 13.1 | 15.4 |
| | 23.8 | 21.0 | 18.2 | 15.6 | 16.0 | | Total Current | | 22.4 | 27.5 |
| | 23.4 | 34.5 | 18.1 | 18.3 | 23.4 | | Long-Term Debt | | 24.5 | 25.3 |
| | .0 | .0 | .1 | .0 | .0 | | Deferred Taxes | | .1 | .0 |
| | 4.5 | 1.9 | 5.6 | 5.3 | 9.3 | | All Other Non-Current | | 4.3 | 6.6 |
| | 48.2 | 42.6 | 58.0 | 60.8 | 51.3 | | Net Worth | | 48.8 | 40.7 |
| | 100.0 | 100.0 | 100.0 | 100.0 | 100.0 | | Total Liabilties & Net Worth | | 100.0 | 100.0 |
| | | | | | | | **INCOME DATA** | | | |
| | 100.0 | 100.0 | 100.0 | 100.0 | 100.0 | | Net Sales | | 100.0 | 100.0 |
| | | | | | | | Gross Profit | | | |
| | 86.4 | 87.5 | 94.7 | 95.3 | 99.0 | | Operating Expenses | | 95.4 | 92.7 |
| | 13.6 | 12.5 | 5.3 | 4.7 | 1.0 | | Operating Profit | | 4.6 | 7.3 |
| | 1.0 | 4.4 | -1.4 | -.5 | 1.0 | | All Other Expenses (net) | | .6 | .0 |
| | 12.6 | 8.1 | 6.8 | 5.2 | .0 | | Profit Before Taxes | | 4.1 | 7.3 |
| | | | | | | | **RATIOS** | | | |
| | 8.6 | 3.6 | 4.1 | 4.1 | 3.1 | | | | 4.4 | 4.5 |
| | 3.6 | 2.2 | 2.2 | 2.9 | 1.7 | | Current | | 2.1 | 2.7 |
| | .9 | .4 | 1.4 | 1.8 | 1.2 | | | | 1.3 | 1.5 |
| | 8.5 | 3.3 | 4.1 | 3.7 | 3.0 | | | | 4.3 | 4.4 |
| | 2.8 | 1.9 | 2.2 | 2.6 | 1.5 | | Quick | | 1.8 | 2.4 |
| | .9 | .4 | 1.2 | 1.8 | 1.1 | | | | 1.1 | 1.4 |
| 0 | UND | 0 | UND | 32 | 11.5 | 27 | 13.6 | 25 | 14.4 | | | 21 | 17.1 | 9 | 39.1 |
| 18 | 19.9 | 23 | 16.2 | 45 | 8.2 | 55 | 6.6 | 42 | 8.6 | | Sales/Receivables | 37 | 9.9 | 36 | 10.1 |
| 118 | 3.1 | 49 | 7.4 | 65 | 5.6 | 68 | 5.4 | 64 | 5.7 | | | 53 | 6.9 | 53 | 6.9 |
| | | | | | | | Cost of Sales/Inventory | | | |
| | | | | | | | Cost of Sales/Payables | | | |
| | 4.1 | 4.7 | 3.4 | 2.8 | 4.4 | | | | 4.4 | 3.1 |
| | 7.3 | 8.1 | 7.9 | 4.8 | 12.0 | | Sales/Working Capital | | 8.0 | 6.1 |
| | NM | -11.9 | 20.2 | 7.5 | 50.1 | | | | 35.8 | 15.1 |
| | 18.4 | 16.6 | 41.3 | 17.8 | | | | | 8.7 | 31.5 |
| (10) | 5.6 | (25) 5.7 | (40) 8.9 | (18) 8.2 | | | EBIT/Interest | (117) | 2.3 | (55) 6.7 |
| | 2.0 | 1.9 | 1.0 | 4.4 | | | | | .5 | 1.3 |
| | | | | | | | Net Profit + Depr., Dep., Amort./Cur. Mat. L/T/D | | 50.1 | |
| | | | | | | | | (10) | 3.4 | |
| | | | | | | | | | 1.8 | |
| | .1 | .5 | .5 | .5 | .4 | | | | .5 | .5 |
| | .9 | 1.2 | .8 | .6 | 1.0 | | Fixed/Worth | | 1.0 | .9 |
| | 3.1 | 2.7 | 1.4 | 1.3 | 1.9 | | | | 2.0 | 2.6 |
| | .3 | .6 | .3 | .3 | .6 | | | | .4 | .4 |
| | .7 | 1.4 | .6 | .6 | 1.3 | | Debt/Worth | | .9 | 1.1 |
| | 5.9 | 2.7 | 1.6 | 1.5 | 2.1 | | | | 2.6 | 4.3 |
| | 74.8 | 74.4 | 19.2 | 15.0 | 6.6 | | | | 21.3 | 29.6 |
| (13) | 20.5 | (28) 21.9 | (48) 9.8 | (17) 7.7 | 4.3 | | % Profit Before Taxes/Tangible Net Worth | (135) | 6.9 | (64) 11.0 |
| | 4.1 | 1.0 | 1.2 | 3.7 | -9.7 | | | | -.6 | 1.5 |
| | 30.3 | 24.0 | 13.2 | 8.2 | 3.4 | | | | 12.0 | 15.6 |
| | 12.8 | 9.1 | 5.7 | 4.2 | 1.8 | | % Profit Before Taxes/Total Assets | | 3.4 | 4.7 |
| | 3.8 | 1.6 | .7 | 2.4 | -3.0 | | | | -.5 | .0 |
| | 91.8 | 7.2 | 5.1 | 4.1 | 4.2 | | | | 9.3 | 8.7 |
| | 4.4 | 3.3 | 2.6 | 2.6 | 3.1 | | Sales/Net Fixed Assets | | 3.1 | 3.4 |
| | 1.1 | 1.5 | 1.3 | 2.1 | 1.2 | | | | 1.6 | 1.4 |
| | 3.7 | 2.0 | 1.7 | 1.2 | 1.4 | | | | 2.4 | 1.9 |
| | 1.7 | 1.5 | 1.1 | 1.0 | 1.2 | | Sales/Total Assets | | 1.5 | 1.3 |
| | .7 | 1.0 | .7 | .8 | .9 | | | | .9 | .8 |
| | .7 | 1.1 | 2.0 | 1.2 | | | | | 1.4 | 1.1 |
| (11) | 2.8 | (24) 2.1 | (51) 2.5 | 2.3 | | | % Depr., Dep., Amort./Sales | (128) | 2.5 | (60) 2.2 |
| | 4.0 | 3.8 | 3.7 | 3.2 | | | | | 4.2 | 4.4 |
| | | | | | | | % Officers', Directors' Owners' Comp/Sales | | 3.0 | |
| | | | | | | | | (18) | 5.5 | |
| | | | | | | | | | 12.4 | |
| 4228M | 59113M | 249218M | 1624982M | 1340609M | 1444363M | | Net Sales ($) | | 4244539M | 1533998M |
| 1397M | 17470M | 168230M | 1247561M | 1303006M | 1343964M | | Total Assets ($) | | 3595253M | 1818032M |

© RMA 2024  
M = $ thousand  MM = $ million  
See Pages viii through xx for Explanation of Ratios and Data

# HEALTH CARE—Residential Mental Health and Substance Abuse Facilities  NAICS 623220

## Comparative Historical Data | Current Data Sorted by Sales

| | | | | | Type of Statement | | | | | | |
|---|---|---|---|---|---|---|---|---|---|---|---|
| | 27 | | 42 | 47 | Unqualified | 1 | 1 | 2 | 8 | 11 | 24 |
| | 6 | | 6 | 4 | Reviewed | | | | 2 | 2 | |
| | 1 | | 2 | 6 | Compiled | | 2 | 1 | 2 | 1 | |
| | 7 | | 6 | 3 | Tax Returns | 2 | 1 | | | | |
| | 47 | | 59 | 71 | Other | 6 | 4 | 4 | 13 | 20 | 24 |
| | 4/1/21-3/31/22 ALL | | 4/1/22-3/31/23 ALL | 4/1/23-3/31/24 ALL | | | 59 (4/1-9/30/23) | | | 72 (10/1/23-3/31/24) | |
| | | | | | | 0-1MM | 1-3MM | 3-5MM | 5-10MM | 10-25MM | 25MM & OVER |
| | 88 | | 115 | 131 | NUMBER OF STATEMENTS | 9 | 8 | 7 | 25 | 34 | 48 |
| | % | | % | % | ASSETS | % | % | % | % | % | % |
| | 25.6 | | 24.6 | 20.0 | Cash & Equivalents | | | | 17.4 | 22.3 | 20.3 |
| | 17.7 | | 14.2 | 15.9 | Trade Receivables (net) | | | | 15.2 | 13.8 | 16.7 |
| | .0 | | .0 | .1 | Inventory | | | | .1 | .1 | .1 |
| | 2.1 | | 2.0 | 1.9 | All Other Current | | | | 2.7 | 2.7 | 1.6 |
| | 45.4 | | 40.8 | 37.9 | Total Current | | | | 35.5 | 39.0 | 38.7 |
| | 45.2 | | 46.4 | 45.1 | Fixed Assets (net) | | | | 54.6 | 39.3 | 39.8 |
| | 1.1 | | 2.3 | 3.3 | Intangibles (net) | | | | 1.7 | 6.7 | 2.5 |
| | 8.3 | | 10.4 | 13.6 | All Other Non-Current | | | | 8.2 | 15.1 | 19.0 |
| | 100.0 | | 100.0 | 100.0 | Total | | | | 100.0 | 100.0 | 100.0 |
| | | | | | LIABILITIES | | | | | | |
| | 4.1 | | 1.7 | 3.1 | Notes Payable-Short Term | | | | 2.8 | 7.0 | .8 |
| | 1.9 | | 1.8 | 2.5 | Cur. Mat.-L.T.D. | | | | 6.0 | .9 | 1.5 |
| | 2.9 | | 4.0 | 3.3 | Trade Payables | | | | 1.2 | 2.3 | 4.5 |
| | .0 | | .0 | .1 | Income Taxes Payable | | | | .0 | .0 | .1 |
| | 11.9 | | 9.5 | 9.9 | All Other Current | | | | 8.3 | 6.8 | 15.1 |
| | 20.7 | | 17.0 | 18.8 | Total Current | | | | 18.3 | 17.0 | 22.0 |
| | 23.4 | | 27.0 | 23.5 | Long-Term Debt | | | | 30.1 | 13.4 | 19.7 |
| | .1 | | .0 | .0 | Deferred Taxes | | | | .0 | .0 | .1 |
| | 9.2 | | 5.9 | 4.6 | All Other Non-Current | | | | .7 | 5.4 | 7.3 |
| | 46.5 | | 50.1 | 53.0 | Net Worth | | | | 50.9 | 64.2 | 50.9 |
| | 100.0 | | 100.0 | 100.0 | Total Liabilities & Net Worth | | | | 100.0 | 100.0 | 100.0 |
| | | | | | INCOME DATA | | | | | | |
| | 100.0 | | 100.0 | 100.0 | Net Sales | | | | 100.0 | 100.0 | 100.0 |
| | | | | | Gross Profit | | | | | | |
| | 90.5 | | 90.5 | 92.3 | Operating Expenses | | | | 92.7 | 91.2 | 96.9 |
| | 9.5 | | 9.5 | 7.7 | Operating Profit | | | | 7.3 | 8.8 | 3.1 |
| | -.8 | | 2.1 | 1.1 | All Other Expenses (net) | | | | .4 | -.9 | -.7 |
| | 10.3 | | 7.4 | 6.6 | Profit Before Taxes | | | | 6.8 | 9.8 | 3.8 |
| | | | | | RATIOS | | | | | | |
| | 7.2 | | 4.8 | 4.1 | | | | | 4.8 | 5.5 | 3.1 |
| | 2.8 | | 2.5 | 2.4 | Current | | | | 2.6 | 2.9 | 1.9 |
| | 1.3 | | 1.4 | 1.2 | | | | | .9 | 1.9 | 1.3 |
| | 7.1 | | 4.5 | 3.8 | | | | | 4.4 | 5.0 | 3.0 |
| | 2.3 | | 2.4 | 2.3 | Quick | | | | 2.2 | 2.8 | 1.9 |
| | 1.2 | | 1.3 | 1.2 | | | | | .9 | 1.7 | 1.2 |
| 9 | 38.8 | 12 | 29.4 | 21 | 17.1 | | | | 14 | 25.7 | 17 | 20.9 | 27 | 13.4 |
| 35 | 10.5 | 36 | 10.2 | 38 | 9.6 | Sales/Receivables | | | | 30 | 12.3 | 46 | 7.9 | 43 | 8.5 |
| 53 | 6.9 | 58 | 6.3 | 62 | 5.9 | | | | | 69 | 5.3 | 60 | 6.1 | 62 | 5.9 |
| | | | | | Cost of Sales/Inventory | | | | | | |
| | | | | | Cost of Sales/Payables | | | | | | |
| | 3.9 | | 3.2 | 3.9 | | | | | 3.5 | 3.0 | 4.0 |
| | 6.7 | | 6.7 | 7.1 | Sales/Working Capital | | | | 7.1 | 5.6 | 8.8 |
| | 17.7 | | 29.9 | 23.0 | | | | | NM | 9.3 | 20.1 |
| | 37.4 | | 14.0 | 20.6 | | | | | 10.9 | 50.9 | 19.4 |
| (65) | 10.2 | (90) | 4.6 | (102) | 6.4 | EBIT/Interest | | | (22) | 2.6 | (27) | 18.6 | (39) | 6.2 |
| | 1.9 | | -.9 | 1.9 | | | | | 1.3 | 3.1 | 2.8 |
| | | | | | Net Profit + Depr., Dep., Amort./Cur. Mat. L/T/D | | | | | | |
| | .5 | | .4 | .5 | | | | | .5 | .3 | .5 |
| | .9 | | .8 | .8 | Fixed/Worth | | | | 1.1 | .6 | .7 |
| | 1.6 | | 1.5 | 1.7 | | | | | 2.2 | 1.4 | 1.4 |
| | .3 | | .3 | .4 | | | | | .5 | .2 | .5 |
| | .8 | | .7 | .8 | Debt/Worth | | | | .7 | .4 | .9 |
| | 2.0 | | 1.7 | 1.9 | | | | | 2.1 | 1.2 | 1.9 |
| | 47.6 | | 22.7 | 23.5 | | | | | 26.9 | 28.1 | 15.3 |
| (79) | 15.8 | (110) | 8.0 | (120) | 9.4 | % Profit Before Taxes/Tangible Net Worth | | | (23) | 5.4 | (30) | 15.3 | (45) | 5.6 |
| | 3.4 | | -3.4 | 1.2 | | | | | .7 | 7.9 | .6 |
| | 21.1 | | 14.1 | 14.4 | | | | | 20.0 | 15.4 | 7.8 |
| | 9.1 | | 5.3 | 5.4 | % Profit Before Taxes/Total Assets | | | | 3.7 | 10.0 | 3.1 |
| | 2.0 | | -2.2 | .7 | | | | | .6 | 4.7 | -.2 |
| | 11.2 | | 6.2 | 5.4 | | | | | 4.5 | 9.1 | 5.0 |
| | 2.6 | | 2.8 | 3.2 | Sales/Net Fixed Assets | | | | 2.6 | 3.6 | 3.5 |
| | 1.4 | | 1.2 | 1.4 | | | | | 1.1 | 1.6 | 2.4 |
| | 2.5 | | 1.8 | 1.7 | | | | | 1.9 | 1.6 | 1.7 |
| | 1.3 | | 1.1 | 1.2 | Sales/Total Assets | | | | 1.1 | 1.1 | 1.3 |
| | .8 | | .7 | .8 | | | | | .7 | .7 | .9 |
| | 1.7 | | 1.7 | 1.3 | | | | | 1.7 | 1.3 | 1.2 |
| (71) | 2.9 | (98) | 2.5 | (113) | 2.4 | % Depr., Dep., Amort./Sales | | | (22) | 2.9 | (30) | 2.4 | (46) | 2.2 |
| | 4.6 | | 4.0 | 3.7 | | | | | 5.1 | 3.0 | 2.8 |
| | | | 3.1 | | | | | | | | |
| | | (12) | 7.0 | | % Officers', Directors', Owners' Comp/Sales | | | | | | |
| | | | 28.6 | | | | | | | | |
| | 1902624M | | 3350016M | 4722513M | Net Sales ($) | 5006M | 12133M | 31599M | 184492M | 561056M | 3928227M |
| | 1591598M | | 2880172M | 4081628M | Total Assets ($) | 22076M | 11991M | 39210M | 238740M | 642754M | 3126857M |

© RMA 2024  M = $ thousand  MM = $ million
See Pages viii through xx for Explanation of Ratios and Data

# HEALTH CARE—Continuing Care Retirement Communities  NAICS 623311

## Current Data Sorted by Assets | Comparative Historical Data

| | | | | | | Type of Statement | | |
|---|---|---|---|---|---|---|---|---|
| | 2 | 2 | 16 | 15 | 21 | Unqualified | 147 | 80 |
| | | 6 | 2 | | | Reviewed | 7 | 1 |
| | | 2 | | 1 | 3 | Compiled | 9 | 2 |
| 1 | 1 | 3 | 2 | | | Tax Returns | 30 | 5 |
| 2 | 13 | 22 | 52 | 21 | 37 | Other | 166 | 158 |
| | 65 (4/1-9/30/23) | | 159 (10/1/23-3/31/24) | | | | 4/1/19-3/31/20 | 4/1/20-3/31/21 |
| 0-500M | 500M-2MM | 2-10MM | 10-50MM | 50-100MM | 100-250MM | | ALL | ALL |
| 3 | 16 | 35 | 72 | 37 | 61 | NUMBER OF STATEMENTS | 359 | 246 |
| % | % | % | % | % | % | ASSETS | % | % |
| | 25.6 | 11.3 | 11.2 | 13.0 | 12.4 | Cash & Equivalents | 15.1 | 17.8 |
| | 16.4 | 4.1 | 5.4 | 3.1 | 1.7 | Trade Receivables (net) | 4.6 | 4.2 |
| | .0 | .3 | .1 | .0 | .1 | Inventory | .2 | .1 |
| | 9.8 | 3.8 | 3.7 | .9 | 2.4 | All Other Current | 1.6 | 2.5 |
| | 51.8 | 19.6 | 20.3 | 17.0 | 16.6 | Total Current | 21.5 | 24.5 |
| | 37.4 | 64.7 | 65.2 | 65.2 | 63.6 | Fixed Assets (net) | 60.7 | 59.7 |
| | 6.8 | 1.3 | 2.3 | 1.6 | 2.6 | Intangibles (net) | 1.6 | 2.5 |
| | 4.0 | 14.4 | 12.2 | 16.1 | 17.3 | All Other Non-Current | 16.3 | 13.3 |
| | 100.0 | 100.0 | 100.0 | 100.0 | 100.0 | Total | 100.0 | 100.0 |
| | | | | | | LIABILITIES | | |
| | .6 | .8 | .8 | .1 | .1 | Notes Payable-Short Term | 2.0 | .5 |
| | 1.0 | 2.9 | 4.2 | 2.4 | 5.2 | Cur. Mat.-L.T.D. | 2.4 | 2.4 |
| | 9.5 | 6.0 | 3.0 | 1.6 | 1.4 | Trade Payables | 3.7 | 3.0 |
| | .0 | .0 | .0 | .0 | .0 | Income Taxes Payable | .0 | .0 |
| | 20.4 | 7.1 | 7.3 | 6.1 | 6.0 | All Other Current | 12.2 | 8.9 |
| | 31.5 | 16.8 | 15.3 | 10.3 | 12.7 | Total Current | 20.3 | 14.8 |
| | 19.9 | 60.2 | 54.8 | 47.0 | 39.6 | Long-Term Debt | 46.2 | 46.8 |
| | .0 | .0 | .0 | .0 | .0 | Deferred Taxes | .0 | .0 |
| | 34.4 | 24.0 | 14.7 | 23.4 | 30.0 | All Other Non-Current | 23.1 | 21.8 |
| | 14.3 | -1.0 | 15.2 | 19.3 | 17.8 | Net Worth | 10.4 | 16.5 |
| | 100.0 | 100.0 | 100.0 | 100.0 | 100.0 | Total Liabilities & Net Worth | 100.0 | 100.0 |
| | | | | | | INCOME DATA | | |
| | 100.0 | 100.0 | 100.0 | 100.0 | 100.0 | Net Sales | 100.0 | 100.0 |
| | | | | | | Gross Profit | | |
| | 77.7 | 84.7 | 89.1 | 97.5 | 94.1 | Operating Expenses | 92.5 | 93.5 |
| | 22.3 | 15.3 | 10.9 | 2.5 | 5.9 | Operating Profit | 7.5 | 6.5 |
| | 7.2 | 4.2 | 9.1 | 1.6 | 7.0 | All Other Expenses (net) | 4.6 | 3.4 |
| | 15.1 | 11.1 | 1.8 | .8 | -1.0 | Profit Before Taxes | 2.9 | 3.1 |
| | | | | | | RATIOS | | |
| | 7.7 | 2.6 | 3.5 | 4.2 | 3.8 | | 2.8 | 3.8 |
| | 2.2 | 1.3 | 1.6 | 2.1 | 1.5 | Current | 1.3 | 2.0 |
| | .5 | .5 | .7 | 1.1 | 1.0 | | .6 | 1.0 |
| | 4.4 | 2.0 | 2.9 | 3.9 | 3.6 | | 2.6 | 3.7 |
| | 1.5 | 1.0 | 1.2 | 2.0 | 1.4 | Quick | 1.2 | 1.9 |
| | .4 | .4 | .5 | 1.0 | .6 | | .5 | .8 |
| 0 | UND | 0 | UND | 1 | 348.9 | 8 | 43.6 | 7 | 51.3 | | 4 | 99.1 | 5 | 69.9 |
| 5 | 72.7 | 7 | 49.9 | 15 | 23.6 | 21 | 17.0 | 13 | 28.4 | Sales/Receivables | 14 | 26.0 | 15 | 23.9 |
| 56 | 6.5 | 23 | 15.7 | 28 | 12.9 | 35 | 10.4 | 24 | 14.9 | | 24 | 14.9 | 27 | 13.7 |
| | | | | | | Cost of Sales/Inventory | | |
| | | | | | | Cost of Sales/Payables | | |
| | 2.5 | 7.2 | 3.4 | 2.3 | 1.6 | | 3.5 | 2.3 |
| | 9.3 | 38.0 | 9.4 | 5.2 | 7.1 | Sales/Working Capital | 23.0 | 6.0 |
| | -7.9 | -11.5 | -20.9 | 122.5 | NM | | -15.8 | UND |
| | | 7.0 | 2.9 | 3.1 | 2.4 | | 3.6 | 4.2 |
| | (27) | 2.5 | (58) 1.7 | (34) 1.1 | (51) 1.0 | EBIT/Interest | (299) 1.6 | (217) 1.6 |
| | | .8 | .8 | .2 | .3 | | .4 | .3 |
| | | | | | | Net Profit + Depr., Dep., Amort./Cur. Mat. L/T/D | | |
| | .1 | 1.0 | 2.0 | 1.5 | 1.7 | | 1.3 | 1.2 |
| | .6 | 4.3 | 5.5 | 5.1 | 3.0 | Fixed/Worth | 4.0 | 4.1 |
| | 10.3 | -2.6 | -14.0 | 77.5 | 312.0 | | -6.9 | -6.5 |
| | .3 | .6 | 2.5 | 1.5 | 1.6 | | 1.3 | 1.5 |
| | 3.8 | 4.0 | 6.2 | 6.2 | 4.1 | Debt/Worth | 5.5 | 5.5 |
| | NM | -5.3 | -25.9 | 100.6 | NM | | -11.7 | -10.4 |
| | 69.3 | 27.2 | 29.1 | 9.5 | 8.8 | | 19.0 | 17.1 |
| (12) | 48.2 | (21) 9.3 | (51) 2.9 | (29) -.9 | (46) 2.5 | % Profit Before Taxes/Tangible Net Worth | (241) 5.7 | (169) 5.4 |
| | 14.2 | -1.3 | -4.5 | -8.6 | -3.1 | | -3.1 | -3.0 |
| | 26.2 | 19.4 | 4.2 | 2.7 | 1.7 | | 4.6 | 4.5 |
| | 14.4 | 5.1 | .8 | .2 | .0 | % Profit Before Taxes/Total Assets | 1.0 | 1.1 |
| | 2.4 | -.2 | -1.1 | -1.9 | -2.5 | | -1.3 | -1.6 |
| | 41.1 | 2.4 | 1.6 | .8 | .7 | | 1.4 | 1.4 |
| | 15.7 | 1.1 | .7 | .5 | .4 | Sales/Net Fixed Assets | .6 | .7 |
| | .6 | .5 | .4 | .4 | .3 | | .4 | .4 |
| | 4.2 | 1.9 | .7 | .4 | .3 | | .8 | .7 |
| | .9 | .9 | .5 | .3 | .3 | Sales/Total Assets | .4 | .4 |
| | .3 | .5 | .3 | .3 | .2 | | .3 | .3 |
| | | 5.9 | 4.7 | 7.6 | 8.8 | | 6.2 | 6.5 |
| | (21) | 9.0 | (70) 7.9 | (34) 10.5 | (55) 12.4 | % Depr., Dep., Amort./Sales | (328) 9.7 | (216) 9.5 |
| | | 10.8 | 11.8 | 13.5 | 18.6 | | 14.7 | 14.3 |
| | | | | | | | 1.2 | 2.6 |
| | | | | | | % Officers', Directors' Owners' Comp/Sales | (13) 5.0 | (12) 5.8 |
| | | | | | | | 15.5 | 11.3 |
| 6369M | 41740M | 226935M | 1133219M | 1048863M | 3436160M | Net Sales ($) | 13286338M | 6512948M |
| 880M | 20263M | 179657M | 1937291M | 2859033M | 9527268M | Total Assets ($) | 23068465M | 16166274M |

© RMA 2024

M = $ thousand    MM = $ million
See Pages viii through xx for Explanation of Ratios and Data

# HEALTH CARE—Continuing Care Retirement Communities  NAICS 623311

## Comparative Historical Data | Current Data Sorted by Sales

| | | | | Type of Statement | | | | | | |
|---|---|---|---|---|---|---|---|---|---|---|
| 65 | | 66 | 56 | Unqualified | 2 | | 1 | 3 | 18 | 32 |
| 4 | | 4 | 8 | Reviewed | | 1 | 3 | 2 | 2 | |
| 4 | | 7 | 6 | Compiled | | | 1 | | 2 | 3 |
| 14 | | 19 | 7 | Tax Returns | | 2 | 2 | 1 | | |
| 170 | | 183 | 147 | Other | 9 | 13 | 14 | 18 | 44 | 49 |
| 4/1/21-3/31/22 ALL | | 4/1/22-3/31/23 ALL | 4/1/23-3/31/24 ALL | | | 65 (4/1-9/30/23) | | | 159 (10/1/23-3/31/24) | |
| | | | | | 0-1MM | 1-3MM | 3-5MM | 5-10MM | 10-25MM | 25MM & OVER |
| 257 | | 279 | 224 | NUMBER OF STATEMENTS | 13 | 17 | 20 | 24 | 66 | 84 |
| % | | % | % | ASSETS | % | % | % | % | % | % |
| 20.1 | | 18.3 | 13.3 | Cash & Equivalents | 9.0 | 14.4 | 12.4 | 14.6 | 12.5 | 14.2 |
| 4.6 | | 5.4 | 5.1 | Trade Receivables (net) | 16.7 | 8.8 | 2.7 | 4.4 | 2.6 | 5.2 |
| .1 | | .1 | .2 | Inventory | .0 | 1.4 | .0 | .0 | .2 | .1 |
| 1.8 | | 3.6 | 3.3 | All Other Current | 3.0 | 1.5 | 6.7 | 5.0 | 3.2 | 2.6 |
| 26.6 | | 27.4 | 21.9 | Total Current | 28.6 | 26.2 | 21.7 | 24.1 | 18.5 | 22.2 |
| 59.8 | | 57.7 | 61.8 | Fixed Assets (net) | 56.5 | 68.1 | 57.5 | 63.4 | 65.9 | 58.8 |
| 1.7 | | 1.5 | 2.4 | Intangibles (net) | 12.0 | 2.3 | 1.8 | .7 | 2.4 | 1.5 |
| 11.9 | | 13.4 | 13.8 | All Other Non-Current | 2.8 | 3.2 | 18.9 | 11.9 | 13.2 | 17.5 |
| 100.0 | | 100.0 | 100.0 | Total | 100.0 | 100.0 | 100.0 | 100.0 | 100.0 | 100.0 |
| | | | | LIABILITIES | | | | | | |
| .5 | | .8 | .4 | Notes Payable-Short Term | .5 | 1.3 | .1 | .3 | .8 | .1 |
| 2.3 | | 3.1 | 3.7 | Cur. Mat.-L.T.D. | 2.4 | 2.8 | 1.4 | 2.0 | 4.4 | 4.6 |
| 3.1 | | 5.8 | 3.2 | Trade Payables | 5.1 | 2.1 | 2.9 | 5.1 | 2.8 | 3.0 |
| .0 | | .0 | .0 | Income Taxes Payable | .0 | .0 | .1 | .0 | .0 | .0 |
| 8.7 | | 10.7 | 8.3 | All Other Current | 5.4 | 11.1 | 12.0 | 9.3 | 7.3 | 7.7 |
| 14.7 | | 20.3 | 15.6 | Total Current | 13.5 | 17.3 | 16.5 | 16.7 | 15.3 | 15.4 |
| 48.0 | | 44.9 | 47.0 | Long-Term Debt | 43.5 | 57.1 | 64.5 | 52.6 | 48.6 | 38.4 |
| .0 | | .0 | .0 | Deferred Taxes | .0 | .0 | .0 | .0 | .0 | .0 |
| 21.0 | | 17.7 | 22.9 | All Other Non-Current | 6.0 | 7.7 | 29.0 | 6.4 | 28.6 | 27.5 |
| 16.4 | | 17.0 | 14.4 | Net Worth | 37.0 | 17.9 | -10.0 | 24.3 | 7.4 | 18.7 |
| 100.0 | | 100.0 | 100.0 | Total Liabilities & Net Worth | 100.0 | 100.0 | 100.0 | 100.0 | 100.0 | 100.0 |
| | | | | INCOME DATA | | | | | | |
| 100.0 | | 100.0 | 100.0 | Net Sales | 100.0 | 100.0 | 100.0 | 100.0 | 100.0 | 100.0 |
| | | | | Gross Profit | | | | | | |
| 93.0 | | 95.7 | 90.3 | Operating Expenses | 59.1 | 77.2 | 87.6 | 89.9 | 93.2 | 96.3 |
| 7.0 | | 4.3 | 9.7 | Operating Profit | 40.9 | 22.8 | 12.4 | 10.1 | 6.8 | 3.7 |
| 2.5 | | 4.9 | 6.3 | All Other Expenses (net) | 17.4 | 12.0 | 6.9 | 7.9 | 7.2 | 2.0 |
| 4.5 | | -.6 | 3.4 | Profit Before Taxes | 23.5 | 10.7 | 5.5 | 2.2 | -.4 | 1.6 |
| | | | | RATIOS | | | | | | |
| 4.0 | | 3.7 | 3.6 | | 19.9 | 4.0 | 2.6 | 2.8 | 3.8 | 3.5 |
| 2.0 | | 1.7 | 1.6 | Current | 1.3 | 1.0 | .9 | 1.6 | 1.7 | 1.7 |
| .9 | | .7 | .8 | | .2 | .4 | .6 | .8 | .7 | 1.0 |
| 3.8 | | 3.4 | 3.3 | | 10.2 | 3.7 | 2.2 | 2.5 | 3.5 | 3.5 |
| 1.8 | (278) | 1.5 | 1.3 | Quick | 1.3 | .9 | .9 | 1.2 | 1.6 | 1.5 |
| .7 | | .5 | .5 | | .2 | .3 | .5 | .6 | .5 | .7 |
| 3  130.5 | | 3  105.3 | 3  127.0 | | 0  UND | 0  UND | 1  686.2 | 0  941.7 | 5  67.5 | 9  38.5 |
| 13  28.3 | | 12  29.6 | 12  30.3 | Sales/Receivables | 1  456.5 | 1  303.7 | 4  90.4 | 3  107.7 | 16  22.3 | 18  19.9 |
| 24  15.0 | | 28  13.0 | 27  13.4 | | 107  3.4 | 21  17.1 | 10  38.1 | 29  12.7 | 26  14.2 | 29  12.4 |
| | | | | Cost of Sales/Inventory | | | | | | |
| | | | | Cost of Sales/Payables | | | | | | |
| 2.1 | | 2.9 | 2.8 | | 1.4 | 3.7 | 7.7 | 4.9 | 2.5 | 2.5 |
| 6.9 | | 11.5 | 8.8 | Sales/Working Capital | 6.1 | 985.0 | -95.5 | 17.5 | 6.3 | 7.4 |
| -59.3 | | -18.8 | -21.1 | | -3.2 | -5.5 | -25.1 | -28.6 | -14.9 | 158.0 |
| 4.8 | | 2.5 | 3.3 | | | 5.4 | 5.4 | 5.2 | 2.2 | 3.0 |
| (214) 1.6 | (214) | .7 | (174) 1.4 | EBIT/Interest | (12) 3.6 | (13) 1.4 | (16) 2.6 | (55) 1.2 | (75) 1.2 |
| .1 | | -1.3 | .5 | | | 1.3 | .3 | 1.0 | .4 | .3 |
| | | | | Net Profit + Depr., Dep., Amort./Cur. Mat. L/T/D | | | | | | |
| 1.1 | | 1.0 | 1.3 | | .1 | 1.1 | .6 | .9 | 2.0 | 1.4 |
| 3.2 | | 3.5 | 3.9 | Fixed/Worth | 1.3 | 4.6 | 521.1 | 3.1 | 5.3 | 2.9 |
| -13.3 | | -18.0 | -78.6 | | 11.7 | -28.8 | -2.3 | NM | -60.9 | 36.3 |
| 1.1 | | 1.0 | 1.5 | | .1 | .6 | .6 | .6 | 2.4 | 1.5 |
| 4.7 | | 4.2 | 5.3 | Debt/Worth | 4.6 | 6.9 | 551.0 | 3.4 | 6.6 | 4.1 |
| -20.6 | | -19.0 | -63.4 | | NM | -22.1 | -4.0 | NM | -69.9 | 145.1 |
| 31.4 | | 20.7 | 21.2 | | 60.7 | | 132.8 | 33.4 | 14.6 | 9.5 |
| (184) 7.8 | (191) | 1.4 | (161) 3.6 | % Profit Before Taxes/Tangible Net Worth | (10) 23.7 | (11) 21.6 | (18) 14.7 | (48) 2.0 | (65) 2.3 |
| -3.3 | | -11.8 | -2.8 | | 4.8 | | -6.5 | -.5 | -2.7 | -4.6 |
| 7.2 | | 4.6 | 4.2 | | 14.9 | 7.2 | 19.3 | 14.9 | 1.6 | 3.1 |
| 1.8 | | -.1 | .8 | % Profit Before Taxes/Total Assets | 3.2 | 4.4 | 2.6 | 4.6 | .4 | .5 |
| -1.5 | | -4.6 | -1.2 | | 1.0 | -2.0 | -1.6 | -.4 | -2.6 | -1.7 |
| 1.5 | | 1.8 | 1.3 | | 24.4 | 1.2 | 23.1 | 3.7 | .9 | 1.2 |
| .7 | | .6 | .6 | Sales/Net Fixed Assets | .3 | .6 | .8 | 1.0 | .5 | .6 |
| .4 | | .4 | .4 | | .2 | .3 | .5 | .4 | .3 | .4 |
| .8 | | 1.0 | .7 | | .6 | .9 | 2.0 | 2.0 | .6 | .6 |
| .4 | | .4 | .4 | Sales/Total Assets | .2 | .5 | .6 | .4 | .4 | .3 |
| .3 | | .3 | .3 | | .1 | .3 | .4 | .3 | .2 | .3 |
| 6.4 | | 6.1 | 6.4 | | | 8.3 | 4.9 | 4.4 | 7.0 | 6.4 |
| (230) 10.2 | (232) | 10.1 | (187) 9.5 | % Depr., Dep., Amort./Sales | (11) 9.5 | (11) 9.0 | (19) 8.1 | (62) 9.7 | (76) 9.2 |
| 14.3 | | 15.3 | 14.4 | | | 18.9 | 10.8 | 13.0 | 15.5 | 13.6 |
| 3.0 | | 2.5 | 3.0 | | | | | | | |
| (10) 5.6 | (12) | 5.0 | (16) 4.4 | % Officers', Directors' Owners' Comp/Sales | | | | | | |
| 18.4 | | 8.3 | 7.9 | | | | | | | |
| 6330283M | | 5576915M | 5893286M | Net Sales ($) | 7330M | 34255M | 83094M | 172396M | 1134316M | 4461895M |
| 15962411M | | 15579990M | 14524392M | Total Assets ($) | 51636M | 111009M | 146524M | 421678M | 4016427M | 9777118M |

© RMA 2024  
M = $ thousand    MM = $ million  
See Pages viii through xx for Explanation of Ratios and Data

# HEALTH CARE—Assisted Living Facilities for the Elderly  NAICS 623312

**Current Data Sorted by Assets** | **Comparative Historical Data**

| 0-500M | 500M-2MM | 2-10MM | 10-50MM | 50-100MM | 100-250MM | | 4/1/19-3/31/20 ALL | 4/1/20-3/31/21 ALL |
|---|---|---|---|---|---|---|---|---|
| 1 | 2 | 2 | 6 | 11 | 2 | Type of Statement | | |
| 1 | 2 | 3 | 11 | 3 | 1 | Unqualified | 46 | 31 |
| 1 | 5 | 4 | 1 | | | Reviewed | 16 | 6 |
| 8 | 4 | 7 | 5 | | | Compiled | 24 | 3 |
| 17 | 40 | 58 | 70 | 23 | 13 | Tax Returns | 49 | 12 |
| | 47 (4/1-9/30/23) | | 257 (10/1/23-3/31/24) | | | Other | 200 | 122 |
| 27 | 53 | 78 | 93 | 37 | 16 | **NUMBER OF STATEMENTS** | 335 | 174 |
| % | % | % | % | % | % | **ASSETS** | % | % |
| 28.7 | 24.9 | 13.9 | 6.8 | 5.7 | 11.6 | Cash & Equivalents | 13.6 | 20.7 |
| 18.0 | 9.5 | 5.2 | 1.8 | 1.1 | 1.8 | Trade Receivables (net) | 7.1 | 3.9 |
| .2 | .2 | .1 | .0 | .0 | .0 | Inventory | .2 | .2 |
| 5.3 | 3.5 | 3.7 | 1.7 | 3.1 | 1.8 | All Other Current | 5.1 | 2.6 |
| 52.1 | 38.1 | 22.8 | 10.4 | 9.9 | 15.2 | Total Current | 25.9 | 27.4 |
| 19.0 | 35.9 | 57.4 | 80.8 | 79.2 | 65.1 | Fixed Assets (net) | 56.9 | 57.4 |
| 9.1 | 5.9 | 5.8 | 3.1 | 2.6 | .2 | Intangibles (net) | 4.8 | 4.7 |
| 19.7 | 20.1 | 13.9 | 5.8 | 8.2 | 19.5 | All Other Non-Current | 12.3 | 10.5 |
| 100.0 | 100.0 | 100.0 | 100.0 | 100.0 | 100.0 | Total | 100.0 | 100.0 |
| | | | | | | **LIABILITIES** | | |
| 3.6 | 1.9 | 2.3 | .4 | .9 | .1 | Notes Payable-Short Term | 3.4 | 3.4 |
| 3.1 | 1.4 | 5.0 | 3.0 | 2.2 | .7 | Cur. Mat.-L.T.D. | 2.9 | 2.4 |
| 24.9 | 10.4 | 3.1 | 1.7 | 1.5 | 8.3 | Trade Payables | 7.0 | 3.2 |
| .0 | .0 | .2 | .0 | .0 | .1 | Income Taxes Payable | .0 | .0 |
| 63.2 | 45.6 | 14.5 | 7.8 | 7.3 | 23.9 | All Other Current | 23.0 | 20.0 |
| 94.8 | 59.4 | 25.1 | 12.9 | 11.9 | 33.1 | Total Current | 36.3 | 29.1 |
| 37.1 | 46.9 | 64.8 | 70.9 | 63.3 | 44.7 | Long-Term Debt | 55.2 | 60.9 |
| .0 | .0 | .0 | .0 | .1 | .0 | Deferred Taxes | .0 | .0 |
| 24.8 | 10.9 | 13.8 | 4.6 | 12.5 | 17.5 | All Other Non-Current | 7.9 | 12.3 |
| -56.7 | -17.1 | -3.8 | 11.6 | 12.3 | 4.7 | Net Worth | .7 | -2.2 |
| 100.0 | 100.0 | 100.0 | 100.0 | 100.0 | 100.0 | Total Liabilities & Net Worth | 100.0 | 100.0 |
| | | | | | | **INCOME DATA** | | |
| 100.0 | 100.0 | 100.0 | 100.0 | 100.0 | 100.0 | Net Sales | 100.0 | 100.0 |
| | | | | | | Gross Profit | | |
| 101.6 | 93.7 | 87.0 | 82.4 | 88.5 | 81.1 | Operating Expenses | 86.8 | 90.3 |
| -1.6 | 6.3 | 13.0 | 17.6 | 11.5 | 18.9 | Operating Profit | 13.2 | 9.7 |
| 2.4 | 4.0 | 7.3 | 17.7 | 14.1 | 11.0 | All Other Expenses (net) | 8.4 | 6.6 |
| -4.0 | 2.3 | 5.7 | -.1 | -2.6 | 7.9 | Profit Before Taxes | 4.8 | 3.1 |
| | | | | | | **RATIOS** | | |
| 1.8 | 2.8 | 3.0 | 2.1 | 2.9 | 1.2 | | 2.5 | 2.8 |
| .6 | 1.1 | 1.1 | .8 | 1.2 | .9 | Current | 1.0 | 1.3 |
| .3 | .4 | .3 | .4 | .4 | .3 | | .4 | .5 |
| 1.4 | 2.7 | 2.2 | 1.6 | 2.0 | 1.0 | | 1.9 | 2.4 |
| .6 | .9 | .8 | .7 | .9 | .7 | Quick | .8 (173) | 1.1 |
| .3 | .4 | .2 | .2 | .3 | .3 | | .2 | .4 |
| 0 UND | 0 UND | 0 UND | 0 839.6 | 1 272.1 | 0 UND | | 0 UND | 0 999.8 |
| 0 UND | 2 236.0 | 2 175.8 | 4 96.2 | 4 82.8 | 7 53.6 | Sales/Receivables | 3 120.9 | 5 73.2 |
| 8 46.8 | 12 31.2 | 18 19.9 | 11 32.3 | 13 28.1 | 20 18.3 | | 19 19.7 | 18 19.8 |
| | | | | | | Cost of Sales/Inventory | | |
| | | | | | | Cost of Sales/Payables | | |
| 44.5 | 8.4 | 6.4 | 10.4 | 6.2 | 18.2 | | 9.4 | 5.6 |
| -43.1 | 367.1 | 96.5 | -60.0 | 15.3 | -83.6 | Sales/Working Capital | -338.0 | 25.7 |
| -8.3 | -9.1 | -6.6 | -5.7 | -5.8 | -3.8 | | -10.7 | -10.1 |
| 15.7 | 6.1 | 4.2 | 3.1 | 1.5 | | | 5.3 | 3.8 |
| (17) 1.1 | (27) 3.5 | (59) 2.4 | (54) 1.6 | (24) .9 | | EBIT/Interest | (217) 2.0 | (119) 1.5 |
| -4.4 | -2.9 | .2 | .6 | .3 | | | .5 | .3 |
| | | | | | | Net Profit + Depr., Dep., Amort./Cur. Mat. L/T/D | | |
| .0 | .1 | .8 | 3.1 | 2.7 | 2.6 | | 1.1 | 1.2 |
| .7 | 5.3 | 7.4 | 7.6 | 7.0 | 4.0 | Fixed/Worth | 6.8 | 5.5 |
| -.5 | -.8 | -2.8 | -12.5 | -7.0 | -5.3 | | -3.2 | -4.2 |
| 2.1 | 2.1 | 2.4 | 2.5 | 2.2 | 3.1 | | 1.4 | 2.2 |
| -4.9 | -70.7 | 35.2 | 8.5 | 7.0 | 4.4 | Debt/Worth | 9.8 | 10.0 |
| -1.5 | -3.0 | -3.7 | -15.2 | -9.1 | -7.1 | | -5.1 | -5.8 |
| | 177.0 | 64.3 | 26.3 | 11.2 | | % Profit Before Taxes/Tangible Net Worth | 83.2 | 66.4 |
| (26) | 39.2 (42) | 24.0 (63) | 5.8 (22) | .8 | | | (201) 20.3 | (102) 15.9 |
| | 10.6 | 5.3 | -17.2 | -11.4 | | | -2.2 | -3.7 |
| 44.9 | 22.3 | 9.4 | 4.3 | 1.5 | 9.8 | | 14.6 | 8.2 |
| 7.1 | 5.0 | 4.6 | .6 | -.2 | 2.1 | % Profit Before Taxes/Total Assets | 3.1 | 1.8 |
| -116.7 | -8.9 | -3.0 | -3.7 | -2.6 | -1.1 | | -2.2 | -3.0 |
| UND | 414.2 | 10.7 | .5 | .6 | 9.5 | | 25.6 | 9.3 |
| 101.6 | 8.3 | 1.1 | .3 | .3 | .5 | Sales/Net Fixed Assets | 1.0 | .8 |
| 19.9 | 2.2 | .7 | .2 | .2 | .2 | | .4 | .4 |
| 13.3 | 5.5 | 1.4 | .4 | .5 | .5 | | 3.7 | 1.9 |
| 8.2 | 2.5 | .8 | .3 | .2 | .3 | Sales/Total Assets | .7 | .5 |
| 3.1 | 1.1 | .5 | .2 | .2 | .2 | | .3 | .3 |
| .2 | .3 | 4.8 | 9.6 | 6.6 | | | 2.4 | 4.1 |
| (12) .5 | (32) 3.9 | (53) 7.9 | (66) 12.8 | (29) 13.6 | | % Depr., Dep., Amort./Sales | (240) 8.2 | (125) 9.2 |
| 2.4 | 7.2 | 13.6 | 17.6 | 20.8 | | | 13.2 | 14.5 |
| | | | 2.5 | | | | 3.2 | 3.0 |
| | | | (16) 4.8 | | | % Officers', Directors' Owners' Comp/Sales | (41) 5.0 | (19) 5.0 |
| | | | 5.8 | | | | 18.2 | 10.0 |
| 42933M | 200426M | 408247M | 776711M | 834772M | 2780355M | Net Sales ($) | 3888541M | 1839696M |
| 6171M | 61395M | 416120M | 2283015M | 2554806M | 2456684M | Total Assets ($) | 6353906M | 3919274M |

M = $ thousand   MM = $ million
See Pages viii through xx for Explanation of Ratios and Data

© RMA 2024

# HEALTH CARE—Assisted Living Facilities for the Elderly  NAICS 623312

## Comparative Historical Data / Current Data Sorted by Sales

| Comparative Historical Data | | | | | Current Data Sorted by Sales | | | | | |
|---|---|---|---|---|---|---|---|---|---|---|
| | | | **Type of Statement** | | | | | | | |
| 17 | 37 | 27 | Unqualified | 1 | 2 | 4 | 4 | 8 | 8 | |
| 8 | 11 | 21 | Reviewed | | 3 | 3 | 9 | 3 | 3 | |
| 6 | 18 | 11 | Compiled | | | 9 | 1 | 1 | | |
| 37 | 42 | 24 | Tax Returns | 9 | 7 | 4 | 3 | 1 | | |
| 196 | 254 | 221 | Other | 14 | 47 | 38 | 65 | 37 | 20 | |
| 4/1/21-3/31/22 ALL | 4/1/22-3/31/23 ALL | 4/1/23-3/31/24 ALL | | 47 (4/1-9/30/23) | | | 257 (10/1/23-3/31/24) | | | |
| | | | | 0-1MM | 1-3MM | 3-5MM | 5-10MM | 10-25MM | 25MM & OVER | |
| 264 | 362 | 304 | **NUMBER OF STATEMENTS** | 24 | 68 | 50 | 81 | 50 | 31 | |
| % | % | % | **ASSETS** | % | % | % | % | % | % | |
| 16.1 | 17.4 | 13.8 | Cash & Equivalents | 6.7 | 23.4 | 10.2 | 12.6 | 10.1 | 13.5 | |
| 4.4 | 4.3 | 5.4 | Trade Receivables (net) | 3.1 | 8.5 | 5.5 | 3.9 | 5.6 | 3.6 | |
| .2 | .1 | .1 | Inventory | .0 | .1 | .0 | .1 | .0 | .0 | |
| 2.7 | 3.2 | 3.0 | All Other Current | 3.5 | 1.6 | 3.2 | 3.1 | 4.9 | 2.3 | |
| 23.4 | 25.1 | 22.3 | Total Current | 13.2 | 33.7 | 18.9 | 19.7 | 20.7 | 19.5 | |
| 63.6 | 59.7 | 60.5 | Fixed Assets (net) | 59.2 | 47.9 | 74.2 | 61.1 | 63.6 | 60.2 | |
| 3.2 | 3.4 | 4.6 | Intangibles (net) | 14.1 | 4.6 | 1.8 | 4.4 | 3.8 | 3.5 | |
| 9.9 | 11.8 | 12.6 | All Other Non-Current | 13.5 | 13.8 | 5.1 | 14.9 | 11.9 | 16.8 | |
| 100.0 | 100.0 | 100.0 | Total | 100.0 | 100.0 | 100.0 | 100.0 | 100.0 | 100.0 | |
| | | | **LIABILITIES** | | | | | | | |
| 1.8 | 1.0 | 1.5 | Notes Payable-Short Term | 3.2 | 2.4 | .8 | 1.4 | .5 | 1.1 | |
| 5.0 | 3.7 | 3.0 | Cur. Mat.-L.T.D. | 3.7 | 3.8 | 4.4 | 1.3 | 3.8 | 1.8 | |
| 4.7 | 3.8 | 6.0 | Trade Payables | 2.1 | 7.9 | 5.5 | 5.0 | 7.8 | 5.2 | |
| .3 | .0 | .1 | Income Taxes Payable | .0 | .0 | .0 | .0 | .3 | .1 | |
| 18.4 | 16.2 | 21.8 | All Other Current | 24.5 | 28.2 | 14.7 | 28.0 | 10.7 | 18.9 | |
| 30.2 | 24.7 | 32.3 | Total Current | 33.5 | 42.3 | 25.3 | 35.7 | 23.2 | 27.1 | |
| 63.6 | 58.8 | 59.9 | Long-Term Debt | 77.0 | 51.0 | 82.3 | 57.4 | 53.3 | 46.6 | |
| .0 | .0 | .0 | Deferred Taxes | .0 | .0 | .0 | .0 | .0 | .1 | |
| 14.0 | 10.3 | 11.5 | All Other Non-Current | 5.6 | 13.9 | 10.9 | 6.8 | 17.6 | 14.0 | |
| -7.9 | 6.3 | -3.7 | Net Worth | -16.0 | -7.2 | -18.5 | .0 | 5.9 | 12.2 | |
| 100.0 | 100.0 | 100.0 | Total Liabilities & Net Worth | 100.0 | 100.0 | 100.0 | 100.0 | 100.0 | 100.0 | |
| | | | **INCOME DATA** | | | | | | | |
| 100.0 | 100.0 | 100.0 | Net Sales | 100.0 | 100.0 | 100.0 | 100.0 | 100.0 | 100.0 | |
| | | | Gross Profit | | | | | | | |
| 89.8 | 87.9 | 87.9 | Operating Expenses | 80.5 | 86.9 | 92.5 | 88.0 | 89.4 | 86.1 | |
| 10.2 | 12.1 | 12.1 | Operating Profit | 19.5 | 13.1 | 7.5 | 12.0 | 10.6 | 13.9 | |
| 6.8 | 9.2 | 10.5 | All Other Expenses (net) | 20.8 | 9.7 | 9.9 | 9.7 | 10.6 | 6.9 | |
| 3.5 | 2.8 | 1.6 | Profit Before Taxes | -1.3 | 3.4 | -2.4 | 2.3 | .0 | 7.0 | |
| | | | **RATIOS** | | | | | | | |
| 2.8 | 3.0 | 2.4 | | 3.5 | 2.7 | 2.9 | 1.6 | 3.0 | 2.1 | |
| 1.1 | 1.1 | 1.0 | Current | .5 | 1.3 | .9 | .7 | 1.2 | 1.2 | |
| .4 | .4 | .4 | | .2 | .4 | .4 | .3 | .3 | .8 | |
| 2.7 | 2.5 | 2.0 | | 2.4 | 2.7 | 1.8 | 1.2 | 2.3 | 1.5 | |
| .9 | 1.0 | .8 | Quick | .4 | 1.2 | .7 | .7 | .9 | .9 | |
| .3 | .4 | .3 | | .2 | .3 | .3 | .2 | .3 | .5 | |
| 0 UND | 0 UND | 0 UND | | 0 UND | 0 UND | 1 488.6 | 0 999.8 | 1 318.1 | 2 159.5 | |
| 4 87.0 | 3 132.5 | 3 135.1 | Sales/Receivables | 0 UND | 0 UND | 4 86.5 | 3 139.5 | 6 59.6 | 8 45.2 | |
| 16 23.3 | 16 22.3 | 13 29.1 | | 2 148.8 | 9 38.9 | 20 18.4 | 7 52.8 | 24 15.5 | 30 12.2 | |
| | | | Cost of Sales/Inventory | | | | | | | |
| | | | Cost of Sales/Payables | | | | | | | |
| 7.4 | 6.4 | 8.8 | | 12.9 | 5.6 | 9.7 | 18.8 | 6.0 | 8.4 | |
| 189.7 | 123.7 | -164.0 | Sales/Working Capital | -10.5 | 51.8 | -85.8 | -31.3 | 32.4 | 30.7 | |
| -6.6 | -8.1 | -6.8 | | -2.8 | -9.0 | -7.6 | -7.3 | -3.9 | -8.2 | |
| 2.7 | 3.1 | 4.2 | | 2.8 | 5.1 | 2.7 | 4.4 | 6.7 | 3.1 | |
| (178) 1.4 | (214) 1.1 | (189) 1.6 | EBIT/Interest | (11) .1 | (41) 3.3 | (34) .9 | (47) 2.2 | (32) 1.6 | (24) 1.4 | |
| .1 | -.1 | .3 | | -6.9 | .4 | .0 | .4 | .5 | .6 | |
| | | | Net Profit + Depr., Dep., Amort./Cur. Mat. L/T/D | | | | | | | |
| 2.1 | 1.1 | 1.7 | | 4.9 | .6 | 4.4 | .5 | 2.5 | 1.3 | |
| 5.8 | 4.9 | 6.2 | Fixed/Worth | 15.5 | 3.6 | 10.7 | 5.1 | 7.0 | 3.5 | |
| -3.1 | -4.1 | -3.9 | | -2.4 | -2.2 | -2.9 | -4.0 | -8.0 | -13.8 | |
| 2.3 | 1.7 | 2.4 | | 4.7 | 1.9 | 4.8 | 2.0 | 2.6 | 2.4 | |
| 11.1 | 9.1 | 15.1 | Debt/Worth | 28.2 | -16.3 | 117.7 | 14.8 | 8.7 | 4.8 | |
| -4.5 | -5.4 | -4.9 | | -4.5 | -3.0 | -5.4 | -4.7 | -8.1 | -20.8 | |
| 48.0 | 38.5 | 48.3 | % Profit Before Taxes/Tangible Net Worth | 40.2 | 50.2 | 42.7 | 73.3 | 39.8 | 57.5 | |
| (154) 10.9 | (224) 6.9 | (171) 12.0 | | (13) 17.6 | (32) 23.8 | (28) -1.8 | (46) 22.7 | (32) 12.5 | (20) 10.4 | |
| -2.0 | -10.7 | -5.5 | | -12.3 | 3.9 | -30.1 | -6.2 | -9.0 | .7 | |
| 7.5 | 8.1 | 8.5 | % Profit Before Taxes/Total Assets | 3.8 | 11.7 | 7.3 | 9.7 | 8.2 | 5.8 | |
| 1.7 | 1.1 | 1.7 | | .5 | 5.0 | -.6 | 2.6 | 1.2 | 2.8 | |
| -2.0 | -3.4 | -3.6 | | -11.2 | -4.0 | -5.7 | -3.7 | -3.4 | .3 | |
| 5.9 | 10.6 | 10.0 | | 8.8 | 135.4 | 1.2 | 53.9 | 6.7 | 2.7 | |
| .6 | .8 | .9 | Sales/Net Fixed Assets | .6 | 2.7 | .7 | .6 | .4 | 1.0 | |
| .3 | .3 | .3 | | .1 | .6 | .3 | .3 | .3 | .5 | |
| 1.5 | 1.8 | 1.7 | | 1.7 | 3.8 | .9 | 2.5 | 1.0 | .8 | |
| .5 | .5 | .5 | Sales/Total Assets | .3 | 1.2 | .5 | .5 | .3 | .5 | |
| .3 | .2 | .3 | | .1 | .4 | .3 | .3 | .2 | .3 | |
| 4.5 | 4.7 | 3.9 | | 3.3 | 2.9 | 4.6 | 4.5 | 3.8 | 3.0 | |
| (189) 9.3 | (251) 9.9 | (200) 9.5 | % Depr., Dep., Amort./Sales | (21) 15.7 | (39) 7.7 | (37) 9.1 | (46) 10.5 | (35) 12.9 | (22) 6.0 | |
| 16.4 | 17.8 | 15.8 | | 31.1 | 13.6 | 14.8 | 15.4 | 20.7 | 9.4 | |
| 2.7 | 3.0 | 2.1 | | | | | 2.4 | | | |
| (37) 5.0 | (38) 5.0 | (33) 4.4 | % Officers', Directors' Owners' Comp/Sales | | | | (11) 4.7 | | | |
| 9.1 | 7.0 | 8.1 | | | | | 9.4 | | | |
| 2019300M | 3609546M | 5043444M | Net Sales ($) | 13889M | 129487M | 198890M | 569863M | 706418M | 3424897M | |
| 5646152M | 8422479M | 7778191M | Total Assets ($) | 59997M | 314327M | 556445M | 1435835M | 2130391M | 3281196M | |

© RMA 2024

M = $ thousand    MM = $ million

See Pages viii through xx for Explanation of Ratios and Data

# HEALTH CARE—Other Residential Care Facilities   NAICS 623990

| | | | Current Data Sorted by Assets | | | | | Comparative Historical Data | |
|---|---|---|---|---|---|---|---|---|---|
| | | 1 | 4 | 14 | 2 | 1 | Type of Statement | | |
| | | | 2 | | | | Unqualified | 38 | 10 |
| | 1 | | | 1 | | | Reviewed | | 1 |
| 2 | 1 | 5 | 9 | 11 | 3 | 2 | Compiled | 3 | 1 |
| 2 | | | | | | | Tax Returns | 12 | 3 |
| | | 31 (4/1-9/30/23) | | 30 (10/1/23-3/31/24) | | | Other | 40 | 36 |
| 0-500M | 500M-2MM | 2-10MM | 10-50MM | 50-100MM | 100-250MM | | | 4/1/19-3/31/20 ALL | 4/1/20-3/31/21 ALL |
| 4 | 8 | 15 | 26 | 5 | 3 | | NUMBER OF STATEMENTS | 93 | 51 |
| % | % | % | % | % | % | | ASSETS | % | % |
| | | 33.2 | 19.9 | | | | Cash & Equivalents | 18.8 | 24.9 |
| | | 21.8 | 10.5 | | | | Trade Receivables (net) | 11.3 | 7.4 |
| | | .1 | .0 | | | | Inventory | .3 | .1 |
| | | 2.2 | 4.4 | | | | All Other Current | 2.8 | 2.0 |
| | | 57.4 | 34.8 | | | | Total Current | 33.3 | 34.3 |
| | | 34.2 | 43.0 | | | | Fixed Assets (net) | 48.6 | 49.0 |
| | | 1.4 | 2.2 | | | | Intangibles (net) | 4.6 | 5.3 |
| | | 7.0 | 20.1 | | | | All Other Non-Current | 13.5 | 11.3 |
| | | 100.0 | 100.0 | | | | Total | 100.0 | 100.0 |
| | | | | | | | LIABILITIES | | |
| | | 6.0 | .7 | | | | Notes Payable-Short Term | 4.6 | 1.2 |
| | | 1.4 | 1.2 | | | | Cur. Mat.-L.T.D. | 2.4 | 1.7 |
| | | 3.5 | 3.2 | | | | Trade Payables | 3.7 | 4.2 |
| | | .5 | .0 | | | | Income Taxes Payable | .0 | .1 |
| | | 6.5 | 5.7 | | | | All Other Current | 10.8 | 9.4 |
| | | 17.9 | 10.8 | | | | Total Current | 21.6 | 16.6 |
| | | 21.6 | 14.7 | | | | Long-Term Debt | 29.0 | 27.4 |
| | | .2 | .0 | | | | Deferred Taxes | .1 | .0 |
| | | 8.0 | 6.2 | | | | All Other Non-Current | 6.9 | 7.7 |
| | | 52.4 | 68.2 | | | | Net Worth | 42.5 | 48.3 |
| | | 100.0 | 100.0 | | | | Total Liabilities & Net Worth | 100.0 | 100.0 |
| | | | | | | | INCOME DATA | | |
| | | 100.0 | 100.0 | | | | Net Sales | 100.0 | 100.0 |
| | | | | | | | Gross Profit | | |
| | | 91.0 | 93.5 | | | | Operating Expenses | 94.3 | 91.5 |
| | | 9.0 | 6.5 | | | | Operating Profit | 5.7 | 8.5 |
| | | 3.1 | .2 | | | | All Other Expenses (net) | 1.4 | 4.4 |
| | | 5.9 | 6.3 | | | | Profit Before Taxes | 4.3 | 4.1 |
| | | | | | | | RATIOS | | |
| | | 4.2 | 4.5 | | | | Current | 4.1 | 4.2 |
| | | 2.8 | 3.6 | | | | | 1.8 | 2.8 |
| | | 2.1 | 2.1 | | | | | .8 | 1.1 |
| | | 3.9 | 4.1 | | | | Quick | 3.8 | 4.0 |
| | | 2.8 | 2.7 | | | | | 1.6 | 2.6 |
| | | 2.1 | 2.0 | | | | | .7 | 1.1 |
| | | 14  26.2 | 19  19.6 | | | | Sales/Receivables | 4   89.7 | 0   UND |
| | | 28  13.0 | 34  10.8 | | | | | 24  15.5 | 11  32.9 |
| | | 51  7.1 | 50  7.3 | | | | | 41  8.9 | 32  11.4 |
| | | | | | | | Cost of Sales/Inventory | | |
| | | | | | | | Cost of Sales/Payables | | |
| | | 2.8 | 2.4 | | | | Sales/Working Capital | 5.8 | 3.2 |
| | | 5.2 | 5.1 | | | | | 14.5 | 10.3 |
| | | 8.4 | 8.5 | | | | | -60.9 | 425.0 |
| | | 17.9 | 38.3 | | | | EBIT/Interest | 11.1 | 19.7 |
| | | (13) 13.1 | (19) 18.2 | | | | | (74) 3.5 | (37) 6.3 |
| | | 3.8 | 1.8 | | | | | 1.3 | 1.8 |
| | | | | | | | Net Profit + Depr., Dep., Amort./Cur. Mat. L/T/D | | |
| | | .2 | .4 | | | | Fixed/Worth | .5 | .6 |
| | | .5 | .6 | | | | | 1.3 | 1.1 |
| | | 1.1 | .8 | | | | | 3.3 | 4.3 |
| | | .3 | .1 | | | | Debt/Worth | .3 | .4 |
| | | .7 | .3 | | | | | 1.1 | .9 |
| | | 3.3 | .6 | | | | | 10.9 | 6.4 |
| | | 46.1 | 14.6 | | | | % Profit Before Taxes/Tangible Net Worth | 24.8 | 34.9 |
| | | 10.7 | (23) 6.2 | | | | | (76) 8.5 | (47) 10.8 |
| | | 4.3 | 2.4 | | | | | .3 | 2.8 |
| | | 23.4 | 11.0 | | | | % Profit Before Taxes/Total Assets | 11.1 | 15.3 |
| | | 7.1 | 4.4 | | | | | 3.8 | 4.2 |
| | | 2.5 | .6 | | | | | .2 | 1.6 |
| | | 28.9 | 4.3 | | | | Sales/Net Fixed Assets | 15.0 | 9.2 |
| | | 6.0 | 2.5 | | | | | 2.3 | 2.0 |
| | | 3.2 | 1.2 | | | | | 1.3 | 1.0 |
| | | 3.3 | 1.5 | | | | Sales/Total Assets | 2.2 | 2.1 |
| | | 2.1 | .7 | | | | | 1.1 | .9 |
| | | .9 | .5 | | | | | .6 | .6 |
| | | .7 | 2.2 | | | | % Depr., Dep., Amort./Sales | 1.6 | 1.5 |
| | | (12) 1.6 | (25) 2.9 | | | | | (77) 3.0 | (42) 3.7 |
| | | 3.2 | 5.6 | | | | | 5.9 | 6.2 |
| | | | | | | | % Officers', Directors' Owners' Comp/Sales | 2.2 | |
| | | | | | | | | (16) 4.3 | |
| | | | | | | | | 10.1 | |
| 6251M | 28898M | 161907M | 760056M | 200224M | 374510M | | Net Sales ($) | 2251053M | 1651736M |
| 815M | 9496M | 76281M | 812362M | 320998M | 354179M | | Total Assets ($) | 2243588M | 1375191M |

© RMA 2024

M = $ thousand    MM = $ million
See Pages viii through xx for Explanation of Ratios and Data

# HEALTH CARE—Other Residential Care Facilities  NAICS 623990

| Comparative Historical Data ||| Type of Statement | Current Data Sorted by Sales ||||||
|---|---|---|---|---|---|---|---|---|---|
| 13 | 22 | 22 | Unqualified | 1 | 1 | 1 | 3 | 5 | 11 |
| 1 | | | Reviewed | | | | | | |
| 2 | 3 | 3 | Compiled | | | | 2 | | 1 |
| 8 | 7 | 4 | Tax Returns | 1 | 2 | | | | 1 |
| 40 | 34 | 32 | Other | 4 | 4 | 1 | 7 | 3 | 13 |
| 4/1/21- | 4/1/22- | 4/1/23- | | | 31 (4/1-9/30/23) ||| 30 (10/1/23-3/31/24) |||
| 3/31/22 | 3/31/23 | 3/31/24 | | 0-1MM | 1-3MM | 3-5MM | 5-10MM | 10-25MM | 25MM & OVER |
| ALL | ALL | ALL | | | | | | | |
| 64 | 66 | 61 | NUMBER OF STATEMENTS | 6 | 7 | 4 | 12 | 8 | 26 |
| % | % | % | ASSETS | % | % | % | % | % | % |
| 21.1 | 25.7 | 27.2 | Cash & Equivalents | | | | 36.9 | | 22.7 |
| 10.5 | 13.7 | 11.8 | Trade Receivables (net) | | | | 12.1 | | 16.7 |
| .1 | .0 | .1 | Inventory | | | | .0 | | .0 |
| 5.5 | 2.8 | 3.3 | All Other Current | | | | 1.2 | | 3.9 |
| 37.2 | 42.3 | 42.3 | Total Current | | | | 50.2 | | 43.3 |
| 44.6 | 43.0 | 40.0 | Fixed Assets (net) | | | | 44.8 | | 35.0 |
| 5.1 | 3.1 | 3.6 | Intangibles (net) | | | | 2.1 | | 3.7 |
| 13.1 | 11.7 | 14.1 | All Other Non-Current | | | | 2.9 | | 18.0 |
| 100.0 | 100.0 | 100.0 | Total | | | | 100.0 | | 100.0 |
| | | | LIABILITIES | | | | | | |
| 2.5 | 1.9 | 7.5 | Notes Payable-Short Term | | | | 3.0 | | 2.1 |
| 1.6 | 2.0 | 1.6 | Cur. Mat.-L.T.D. | | | | 1.4 | | 1.4 |
| 7.5 | 3.3 | 3.0 | Trade Payables | | | | 2.3 | | 3.9 |
| .0 | .0 | .1 | Income Taxes Payable | | | | .6 | | .0 |
| 15.7 | 15.1 | 10.9 | All Other Current | | | | 5.1 | | 9.0 |
| 27.4 | 22.3 | 23.1 | Total Current | | | | 12.3 | | 16.3 |
| 45.4 | 26.8 | 16.6 | Long-Term Debt | | | | 21.4 | | 12.9 |
| .1 | .0 | .1 | Deferred Taxes | | | | .2 | | .2 |
| 5.8 | 11.9 | 8.0 | All Other Non-Current | | | | 8.9 | | 5.0 |
| 21.6 | 38.9 | 52.1 | Net Worth | | | | 57.2 | | 65.6 |
| 100.0 | 100.0 | 100.0 | Total Liabilities & Net Worth | | | | 100.0 | | 100.0 |
| | | | INCOME DATA | | | | | | |
| 100.0 | 100.0 | 100.0 | Net Sales | | | | 100.0 | | 100.0 |
| | | | Gross Profit | | | | | | |
| 87.6 | 96.1 | 92.7 | Operating Expenses | | | | 96.0 | | 96.6 |
| 12.4 | 3.9 | 7.3 | Operating Profit | | | | 4.0 | | 3.4 |
| 2.0 | 1.1 | 1.0 | All Other Expenses (net) | | | | -1.2 | | .2 |
| 10.4 | 2.8 | 6.3 | Profit Before Taxes | | | | 5.2 | | 3.2 |
| | | | RATIOS | | | | | | |
| 6.2 | 6.7 | 5.7 | | | | | 13.3 | | 4.1 |
| 2.3 | 2.5 | 2.8 | Current | | | | 4.9 | | 2.4 |
| .9 | 1.4 | 1.8 | | | | | 2.4 | | 1.7 |
| 4.8 | 5.5 | 4.6 | | | | | 12.3 | | 3.8 |
| 1.9 | 2.3 | 2.7 | Quick | | | | 4.5 | | 2.3 |
| .8 | 1.1 | 1.5 | | | | | 2.4 | | 1.6 |
| 0 UND | 1 552.6 | 8 48.4 | | | | | 0 UND | 35 10.4 |
| 17 21.6 | 35 10.5 | 29 12.5 | Sales/Receivables | | | | 14 25.6 | 46 8.0 |
| 36 10.0 | 54 6.8 | 46 7.9 | | | | | 19 18.8 | 52 7.0 |
| | | | Cost of Sales/Inventory | | | | | | |
| | | | Cost of Sales/Payables | | | | | | |
| 2.9 | 3.1 | 2.9 | | | | | 3.4 | | 2.9 |
| 8.6 | 6.3 | 5.4 | Sales/Working Capital | | | | 5.3 | | 5.2 |
| NM | 38.7 | 16.1 | | | | | 16.7 | | 8.8 |
| 31.1 | 14.8 | 19.1 | | | | | 17.0 | | 37.4 |
| (45) 6.4 | (51) 2.2 | (48) 8.2 | EBIT/Interest | | | | (10) 10.2 | (21) 12.3 |
| 1.6 | -3.2 | 1.4 | | | | | 4.0 | | 1.5 |
| | | | Net Profit + Depr., Dep., Amort./Cur. Mat. L/T/D | | | | | | |
| .4 | .4 | .3 | | | | | .2 | | .3 |
| 1.1 | .8 | .6 | Fixed/Worth | | | | .7 | | .5 |
| -862.3 | 2.1 | 1.2 | | | | | 1.1 | | .8 |
| .4 | .3 | .2 | | | | | .1 | | .2 |
| 1.7 | 1.0 | .5 | Debt/Worth | | | | .5 | | .4 |
| -755.3 | 3.5 | 1.8 | | | | | 3.6 | | 1.0 |
| 75.5 | 23.9 | 21.8 | | | | | 56.6 | | 14.2 |
| (46) 18.6 | (58) 9.1 | (55) 8.0 | % Profit Before Taxes/Tangible Net Worth | | | | (10) 13.2 | (25) 6.6 |
| 6.4 | -4.6 | .6 | | | | | 1.3 | | 3.0 |
| 21.3 | 12.3 | 15.1 | | | | | 28.3 | | 11.4 |
| 7.0 | 2.0 | 4.7 | % Profit Before Taxes/Total Assets | | | | 7.3 | | 4.7 |
| 1.2 | -3.6 | .3 | | | | | -.2 | | .8 |
| 16.9 | 17.3 | 9.3 | | | | | 24.3 | | 5.6 |
| 2.9 | 2.5 | 3.2 | Sales/Net Fixed Assets | | | | 7.0 | | 3.2 |
| 1.0 | 1.2 | 1.4 | | | | | 3.2 | | 1.9 |
| 2.6 | 2.7 | 2.2 | | | | | 5.0 | | 1.5 |
| 1.1 | 1.1 | 1.2 | Sales/Total Assets | | | | 2.1 | | 1.1 |
| .6 | .6 | .6 | | | | | 1.5 | | .7 |
| 1.2 | 1.5 | 1.2 | | | | | | | 2.1 |
| (46) 3.1 | (57) 3.1 | (50) 2.8 | % Depr., Dep., Amort./Sales | | | | | (25) 2.7 |
| 6.3 | 5.6 | 4.8 | | | | | | | 3.5 |
| | | 2.7 | % Officers', Directors' Owners' Comp/Sales | | | | | | |
| | (10) 4.0 | | | | | | | | |
| | | 10.7 | | | | | | | |
| 1493492M | 1778257M | 1531846M | Net Sales ($) | 3588M | 12378M | 7722M | 88441M | 121034M | 1298683M |
| 1235036M | 1515977M | 1574131M | Total Assets ($) | 26733M | 34849M | 26097M | 70302M | 154170M | 1261980M |

© RMA 2024  M = $ thousand  MM = $ million
See Pages viii through xx for Explanation of Ratios and Data

# HEALTH CARE—Child and Youth Services  NAICS 624110

**Current Data Sorted by Assets** | **Comparative Historical Data**

| | | | | | | | Type of Statement | | | | |
|---|---|---|---|---|---|---|---|---|---|---|---|
| | | | 18 | 32 | 9 | 7 | Unqualified | | 119 | | 53 |
| | | | 4 | | | | Reviewed | | 1 | | |
| 1 | 2 | | 1 | | | | Compiled | | 4 | | 4 |
| 2 | 4 | | 6 | | | | Tax Returns | | 19 | | 8 |
| 8 | 11 | | 25 | 17 | 10 | 3 | Other | | 76 | | 70 |
| | 102 (4/1-9/30/23) | | | 58 (10/1/23-3/31/24) | | | | | 4/1/19-3/31/20 | | 4/1/20-3/31/21 |
| 0-500M | 500M-2MM | 2-10MM | 10-50MM | 50-100MM | 100-250MM | | | | ALL | | ALL |
| 11 | 17 | 54 | 49 | 19 | 10 | | NUMBER OF STATEMENTS | | 219 | | 135 |
| % | % | % | % | % | % | | ASSETS | | % | | % |
| 59.4 | 15.8 | 22.7 | 20.2 | 19.1 | 8.7 | | Cash & Equivalents | | 26.2 | | 32.0 |
| 5.4 | 17.2 | 23.1 | 15.1 | 20.0 | 19.4 | | Trade Receivables (net) | | 16.3 | | 16.3 |
| .0 | .0 | .1 | .0 | .0 | 7.7 | | Inventory | | .1 | | .3 |
| 1.7 | 1.8 | 3.9 | 4.0 | 2.8 | 3.6 | | All Other Current | | 3.3 | | 3.3 |
| 66.4 | 34.8 | 49.8 | 39.4 | 41.9 | 39.3 | | Total Current | | 45.8 | | 52.0 |
| 21.9 | 40.1 | 32.2 | 36.3 | 35.1 | 24.1 | | Fixed Assets (net) | | 38.1 | | 32.1 |
| 7.7 | 11.0 | 1.6 | 2.1 | 1.9 | .1 | | Intangibles (net) | | 1.1 | | 3.7 |
| 4.1 | 14.2 | 16.4 | 22.3 | 21.1 | 36.5 | | All Other Non-Current | | 14.9 | | 12.3 |
| 100.0 | 100.0 | 100.0 | 100.0 | 100.0 | 100.0 | | Total | | 100.0 | | 100.0 |
| | | | | | | | LIABILITIES | | | | |
| 4.6 | 5.5 | 3.7 | 2.1 | 1.6 | 2.3 | | Notes Payable-Short Term | | 4.2 | | 5.6 |
| .5 | 1.3 | 2.0 | 1.8 | 1.6 | 1.4 | | Cur. Mat.-L.T.D. | | 1.4 | | 1.7 |
| 2.3 | 5.7 | 7.5 | 4.6 | 5.7 | 5.6 | | Trade Payables | | 6.2 | | 6.6 |
| .0 | .1 | .1 | .0 | .0 | .0 | | Income Taxes Payable | | .0 | | .0 |
| 16.6 | 6.4 | 10.1 | 8.7 | 14.1 | 13.9 | | All Other Current | | 11.0 | | 10.0 |
| 23.9 | 18.9 | 23.4 | 17.2 | 23.0 | 23.2 | | Total Current | | 22.9 | | 23.9 |
| 18.8 | 37.5 | 14.6 | 10.5 | 13.3 | 7.7 | | Long-Term Debt | | 16.5 | | 19.0 |
| .0 | .0 | .0 | .0 | .0 | .0 | | Deferred Taxes | | .0 | | .0 |
| 2.2 | .5 | 7.1 | 10.2 | 3.7 | 16.1 | | All Other Non-Current | | 4.8 | | 6.8 |
| 55.1 | 43.1 | 55.0 | 62.0 | 59.9 | 52.9 | | Net Worth | | 55.9 | | 50.2 |
| 100.0 | 100.0 | 100.0 | 100.0 | 100.0 | 100.0 | | Total Liabilities & Net Worth | | 100.0 | | 100.0 |
| | | | | | | | INCOME DATA | | | | |
| 100.0 | 100.0 | 100.0 | 100.0 | 100.0 | 100.0 | | Net Sales | | 100.0 | | 100.0 |
| | | | | | | | Gross Profit | | | | |
| 91.2 | 92.8 | 98.1 | 98.6 | 95.5 | 97.0 | | Operating Expenses | | 96.9 | | 95.0 |
| 8.8 | 7.2 | 1.9 | 1.4 | 4.5 | 3.0 | | Operating Profit | | 3.1 | | 5.0 |
| .2 | 4.3 | -.1 | -1.1 | -.9 | -1.8 | | All Other Expenses (net) | | .6 | | -.1 |
| 8.6 | 2.9 | 2.0 | 2.4 | 5.3 | 4.9 | | Profit Before Taxes | | 2.4 | | 5.1 |
| | | | | | | | RATIOS | | | | |
| 9.0 | 5.2 | 5.5 | 4.0 | 2.4 | 4.9 | | | | 4.9 | | 5.3 |
| 5.2 | 2.0 | 2.8 | 2.5 | 1.8 | 1.2 | | Current | | 2.4 | | 2.6 |
| 1.6 | 1.2 | 1.7 | 1.6 | 1.3 | 1.0 | | | | 1.4 | | 1.6 |
| 9.0 | 5.1 | 5.0 | 3.8 | 2.4 | 2.4 | | | | 4.4 | | 4.7 |
| 3.9 | 1.5 | 2.8 | 2.5 | 1.7 | 1.0 | | Quick | | 2.2 | | 2.5 |
| 1.6 | .7 | 1.2 | 1.3 | 1.3 | .9 | | | | 1.2 | | 1.5 |
| 0 UND | 0 UND | 21 17.2 | 17 21.5 | 37 9.8 | 32 11.5 | | | 11 | 32.7 | 11 | 33.7 |
| 0 UND | 25 14.4 | 46 7.9 | 37 9.9 | 46 8.0 | 64 5.7 | | Sales/Receivables | 32 | 11.5 | 34 | 10.7 |
| 19 19.4 | 53 6.9 | 74 4.9 | 63 5.8 | 64 5.7 | 101 3.6 | | | 55 | 6.6 | 45 | 8.1 |
| | | | | | | | Cost of Sales/Inventory | | | | |
| | | | | | | | Cost of Sales/Payables | | | | |
| 5.6 | 3.4 | 2.7 | 3.5 | 4.7 | 3.3 | | | | 3.4 | | 2.8 |
| 6.2 | 8.4 | 4.5 | 5.8 | 8.1 | 24.9 | | Sales/Working Capital | | 7.2 | | 5.8 |
| 18.8 | 78.7 | 11.4 | 16.6 | 40.8 | NM | | | | 20.2 | | 12.0 |
| | 11.7 | 19.0 | 22.8 | 19.0 | 50.4 | | | | 13.4 | | 20.3 |
| (11) | 4.3 | (33) 2.8 | (37) 6.9 | (15) 4.6 | 5.3 | | EBIT/Interest | (158) | 3.2 | (91) | 5.0 |
| | 2.0 | -2.3 | -3.8 | .1 | 1.1 | | | | -.4 | | -.9 |
| | | | | | | | Net Profit + Depr., Dep., Amort./Cur. Mat. L/T/D | | | | |
| .0 | .1 | .1 | .4 | .4 | .2 | | | | .2 | | .2 |
| .4 | 1.5 | .5 | .6 | .5 | .3 | | Fixed/Worth | | .6 | | .6 |
| 1.2 | UND | 1.2 | 1.0 | 1.0 | 1.2 | | | | 1.2 | | 1.0 |
| .1 | .2 | .2 | .2 | .4 | .2 | | | | .2 | | .3 |
| .5 | .9 | .5 | .4 | .8 | .9 | | Debt/Worth | | .6 | | .8 |
| UND | UND | 2.7 | 1.6 | 1.1 | 3.5 | | | | 1.7 | | 2.1 |
| | 113.3 | 18.0 | 14.8 | 25.7 | 18.0 | | % Profit Before Taxes/Tangible Net Worth | | 14.2 | | 20.8 |
| (14) | 22.1 | (51) 5.4 | (48) 6.4 | 11.1 | 7.2 | | | (208) | 3.5 | (123) | 5.7 |
| | -2.6 | -1.5 | -2.1 | -1.0 | 2.1 | | | | -2.2 | | -1.6 |
| 59.4 | 16.7 | 8.1 | 7.4 | 11.4 | 6.1 | | % Profit Before Taxes/Total Assets | | 7.9 | | 11.0 |
| 25.9 | 3.5 | 2.7 | 3.0 | 4.3 | 3.2 | | | | 2.0 | | 3.1 |
| 3.8 | -2.4 | -1.3 | -2.0 | -.6 | .3 | | | | -1.8 | | -1.3 |
| UND | 109.8 | 33.3 | 10.1 | 8.5 | 11.7 | | Sales/Net Fixed Assets | | 17.1 | | 37.6 |
| 562.0 | 4.3 | 5.2 | 3.1 | 3.9 | 4.8 | | | | 3.2 | | 4.5 |
| 3.9 | .9 | 1.5 | 1.6 | 1.4 | 2.5 | | | | 1.5 | | 2.0 |
| 7.3 | 2.5 | 2.2 | 1.8 | 1.7 | 1.4 | | | | 2.4 | | 2.6 |
| 4.2 | 1.4 | 1.1 | 1.0 | 1.2 | 1.1 | | Sales/Total Assets | | 1.3 | | 1.4 |
| 1.8 | .5 | .7 | .6 | .6 | .9 | | | | .7 | | .7 |
| | | .5 | 1.0 | 1.1 | 1.3 | | | | 1.2 | | .9 |
| | (42) 1.5 | (44) 2.2 | (16) 2.3 | 1.5 | | | % Depr., Dep., Amort./Sales | (178) | 2.4 | (104) | 2.3 |
| | 4.3 | 3.6 | 3.4 | 1.6 | | | | | 4.3 | | 3.8 |
| | | | | | | | % Officers', Directors' Owners' Comp/Sales | | 3.2 | | 3.7 |
| | | | | | | | | (24) | 5.4 | (13) | 7.9 |
| | | | | | | | | | 9.3 | | 9.9 |
| 9796M | 37374M | 519160M | 1470175M | 1807643M | 1913843M | | Net Sales ($) | | 5616060M | | 3985614M |
| 2602M | 22020M | 322215M | 1163472M | 1332439M | 1654292M | | Total Assets ($) | | 4714960M | | 2926218M |

© RMA 2024      M = $ thousand   MM = $ million
See Pages viii through xx for Explanation of Ratios and Data

# HEALTH CARE—Child and Youth Services  NAICS 624110

| Comparative Historical Data | | | Type of Statement | Current Data Sorted by Sales | | | | | |
|---|---|---|---|---|---|---|---|---|---|
| 52 | 66 | 66 | Unqualified | | 2 | 6 | 11 | 17 | 30 |
| 1 | 2 | 4 | Reviewed | 1 | 1 | 1 | | | 1 |
| 1 | 1 | 4 | Compiled | 1 | 3 | | | | |
| 7 | 10 | 12 | Tax Returns | 4 | 2 | 1 | 3 | 2 | |
| 71 | 76 | 74 | Other | 11 | 9 | 8 | 11 | 14 | 21 |
| 4/1/21-3/31/22 ALL | 4/1/22-3/31/23 ALL | 4/1/23-3/31/24 ALL | | 102 (4/1-9/30/23) | | | 58 (10/1/23-3/31/24) | | |
| | | | | 0-1MM | 1-3MM | 3-5MM | 5-10MM | 10-25MM | 25MM & OVER |
| 132 | 155 | 160 | NUMBER OF STATEMENTS | 17 | 17 | 16 | 25 | 33 | 52 |
| % | % | % | ASSETS | % | % | % | % | % | % |
| 32.1 | 32.0 | 22.4 | Cash & Equivalents | 36.0 | 22.8 | 23.1 | 25.1 | 16.7 | 20.0 |
| 13.9 | 15.7 | 18.2 | Trade Receivables (net) | 3.5 | 12.2 | 21.0 | 14.6 | 23.1 | 22.8 |
| .4 | .7 | .5 | Inventory | .0 | .0 | .0 | .1 | .0 | 1.6 |
| 2.6 | 3.1 | 3.4 | All Other Current | 2.9 | 1.5 | 6.2 | 3.8 | 2.0 | 4.0 |
| 49.1 | 51.6 | 44.6 | Total Current | 42.4 | 36.5 | 50.3 | 43.6 | 41.9 | 48.3 |
| 33.2 | 33.8 | 33.4 | Fixed Assets (net) | 48.3 | 33.9 | 29.9 | 37.8 | 31.9 | 28.4 |
| 2.1 | 1.8 | 3.1 | Intangibles (net) | .1 | 14.1 | 5.7 | 2.6 | .3 | 1.7 |
| 15.6 | 12.8 | 18.9 | All Other Non-Current | 9.2 | 15.5 | 14.1 | 16.0 | 26.0 | 21.6 |
| 100.0 | 100.0 | 100.0 | Total | 100.0 | 100.0 | 100.0 | 100.0 | 100.0 | 100.0 |
| | | | LIABILITIES | | | | | | |
| 4.4 | 1.6 | 3.1 | Notes Payable-Short Term | 2.6 | 4.7 | 1.6 | 1.1 | 3.3 | 4.1 |
| 1.6 | 1.0 | 1.7 | Cur. Mat.-L.T.D. | 2.3 | 1.1 | .6 | 2.5 | 1.0 | 2.0 |
| 5.5 | 5.3 | 5.7 | Trade Payables | 3.5 | 8.0 | 2.6 | 4.2 | 6.2 | 7.1 |
| .0 | .0 | .0 | Income Taxes Payable | .1 | .2 | .0 | .0 | .0 | .0 |
| 10.6 | 9.7 | 10.4 | All Other Current | 9.4 | 6.6 | 4.5 | 9.3 | 8.6 | 15.6 |
| 22.0 | 17.7 | 21.0 | Total Current | 17.8 | 20.6 | 9.3 | 17.1 | 19.1 | 28.8 |
| 13.7 | 15.3 | 15.5 | Long-Term Debt | 34.2 | 30.5 | 9.5 | 11.7 | 12.9 | 9.7 |
| .0 | .0 | .0 | Deferred Taxes | .0 | .0 | .0 | .0 | .0 | .0 |
| 8.4 | 5.3 | 7.2 | All Other Non-Current | 1.3 | 2.7 | 3.2 | 5.2 | 9.4 | 11.3 |
| 55.9 | 61.7 | 56.3 | Net Worth | 46.6 | 46.2 | 78.0 | 66.0 | 58.5 | 50.1 |
| 100.0 | 100.0 | 100.0 | Total Liabilities & Net Worth | 100.0 | 100.0 | 100.0 | 100.0 | 100.0 | 100.0 |
| | | | INCOME DATA | | | | | | |
| 100.0 | 100.0 | 100.0 | Net Sales | 100.0 | 100.0 | 100.0 | 100.0 | 100.0 | 100.0 |
| | | | Gross Profit | | | | | | |
| 88.1 | 93.2 | 96.8 | Operating Expenses | 88.9 | 95.2 | 101.0 | 100.7 | 95.4 | 97.8 |
| 11.9 | 6.8 | 3.2 | Operating Profit | 11.1 | 4.8 | -1.0 | -.7 | 4.6 | 2.2 |
| -.7 | 2.1 | -.1 | All Other Expenses (net) | 5.4 | .6 | -.6 | -1.4 | -.6 | -1.0 |
| 12.5 | 4.6 | 3.3 | Profit Before Taxes | 5.7 | 4.2 | -.3 | .7 | 5.3 | 3.2 |
| | | | RATIOS | | | | | | |
| 7.4 | 8.0 | 5.2 | | 6.1 | 5.6 | 9.5 | 6.1 | 4.6 | 2.6 |
| 3.2 | 3.8 | 2.5 | Current | 3.2 | 1.9 | 5.0 | 3.9 | 2.8 | 1.8 |
| 1.7 | 1.8 | 1.4 | | .9 | 1.5 | 3.0 | 1.6 | 1.7 | 1.1 |
| 7.2 | 6.9 | 4.3 | | 6.1 | 5.6 | 9.3 | 5.5 | 4.2 | 2.4 |
| 3.1 | 3.5 | 2.4 | Quick | 3.2 | 1.9 | 4.3 | 3.7 | 2.8 | 1.4 |
| 1.4 | 1.6 | 1.2 | | .2 | 1.2 | 3.0 | 1.5 | 1.6 | 1.0 |
| 9  39.7 | 17  22.1 | 15  23.8 | | 0  UND | 0  UND | 34  10.7 | 14  26.1 | 24  15.3 | 31  11.7 |
| 28  13.0 | 35  10.4 | 38  9.5 | Sales/Receivables | 0  UND | 0  999.8 | 53  6.9 | 49  7.5 | 46  8.0 | 42  8.7 |
| 45  8.1 | 56  6.5 | 66  5.5 | | 23  15.9 | 41  8.8 | 85  4.3 | 72  5.1 | 72  5.1 | 65  5.6 |
| | | | Cost of Sales/Inventory | | | | | | |
| | | | Cost of Sales/Payables | | | | | | |
| 2.8 | 2.0 | 3.3 | | 3.4 | 2.8 | 2.2 | 2.1 | 3.5 | 4.9 |
| 5.2 | 4.2 | 6.1 | Sales/Working Capital | 6.2 | 7.8 | 2.8 | 4.1 | 6.1 | 11.2 |
| 14.5 | 10.8 | 23.8 | | UND | 49.7 | 4.1 | 13.1 | 16.2 | 36.3 |
| 36.0 | 25.0 | 19.8 | | 15.0 | 12.5 | | 23.0 | 18.9 | 29.2 |
| (83) 14.4 | (90) 4.0 | (113) 4.1 | EBIT/Interest | (10) 2.6 | (14) 4.8 | (15) .6 | (25) 8.4 | (43) 6.5 | |
| -.1 | -4.5 | -1.7 | | 1.7 | -3.7 | | -13.8 | -2.9 | .6 |
| | | | Net Profit + Depr., Dep., Amort./Cur. Mat. L/T/D | | | | | | |
| .1 | .2 | .2 | | .0 | .2 | .0 | .2 | .3 | .2 |
| .5 | .5 | .5 | Fixed/Worth | 1.4 | .9 | .3 | .6 | .4 | .5 |
| .9 | 1.0 | 1.1 | | 131.6 | 6.7 | .8 | 1.2 | 1.1 | 1.0 |
| .1 | .2 | .2 | | .3 | .2 | .1 | .1 | .2 | .4 |
| .4 | .4 | .6 | Debt/Worth | .7 | 1.4 | .3 | .4 | .5 | 1.0 |
| 1.3 | 1.1 | 2.1 | | 146.1 | NM | .5 | .9 | 1.5 | 2.5 |
| 36.6 | 20.3 | 20.5 | | 60.9 | 19.5 | 9.1 | 12.3 | 20.4 | 22.8 |
| (122) 14.2 | (146) 2.4 | (151) 8.0 | % Profit Before Taxes/Tangible Net Worth | (16) 28.1 | (13) -.9 | (15) 3.7 | .1 | (32) 8.9 | (50) 9.2 |
| 2.9 | -6.2 | -1.4 | | 7.4 | -9.5 | -5.6 | -6.7 | -1.0 | 3.2 |
| 22.1 | 11.0 | 8.7 | | 28.8 | 12.1 | 7.7 | 7.9 | 9.0 | 7.5 |
| 9.1 | 1.3 | 3.5 | % Profit Before Taxes/Total Assets | 4.7 | 1.0 | 3.0 | .1 | 6.3 | 3.8 |
| 1.3 | -3.6 | -.8 | | .1 | -6.4 | -5.0 | -2.5 | -.3 | .3 |
| 28.6 | 19.9 | 19.3 | | UND | 72.1 | 342.5 | 15.9 | 17.3 | 15.6 |
| 3.9 | 3.8 | 4.3 | Sales/Net Fixed Assets | 1.4 | 5.9 | 3.2 | 3.8 | 3.1 | 5.5 |
| 1.5 | 1.6 | 1.7 | | .5 | 1.6 | 1.2 | 1.5 | 1.7 | 2.7 |
| 2.6 | 2.0 | 2.1 | | 3.3 | 3.1 | 1.5 | 1.4 | 2.2 | 2.5 |
| 1.1 | 1.1 | 1.1 | Sales/Total Assets | .9 | 1.0 | .9 | .8 | 1.1 | 1.6 |
| .6 | .7 | .6 | | .5 | .6 | .5 | .6 | .6 | 1.0 |
| 1.3 | .5 | .7 | | | | .7 | .7 | .7 | .7 |
| (90) 2.2 | (124) 1.7 | (122) 1.7 | % Depr., Dep., Amort./Sales | | (12) 2.8 | (23) 1.6 | (29) 2.0 | (44) 1.5 | |
| 4.8 | 3.7 | 3.3 | | | | 4.9 | 3.5 | 2.8 | 2.3 |
| 4.1 | 4.0 | 3.2 | % Officers', Directors' Owners' Comp/Sales | | | | | | |
| (15) 7.3 | (14) 5.0 | (16) 5.5 | | | | | | | |
| 12.9 | 9.5 | 14.5 | | | | | | | |
| 2958645M | 5023102M | 5757991M | Net Sales ($) | 8417M | 36727M | 66591M | 187480M | 567042M | 4891734M |
| 2519956M | 3682684M | 4497040M | Total Assets ($) | 18325M | 40361M | 95251M | 230734M | 672712M | 3439657M |

© RMA 2024  M = $ thousand  MM = $ million
See Pages viii through xx for Explanation of Ratios and Data

# HEALTH CARE—Services for the Elderly and Persons with Disabilities  NAICS 624120

## Current Data Sorted by Assets | Comparative Historical Data

| 0-500M | 500M-2MM | 2-10MM | 10-50MM | 50-100MM | 100-250MM | | | 4/1/19-3/31/20 ALL | 4/1/20-3/31/21 ALL |
|---|---|---|---|---|---|---|---|---|---|
| 1 | 1 | 17 | 25 | 7 | 5 | Type of Statement | Unqualified | 115 | 40 |
|  |  |  | 2 |  | 2 |  | Reviewed | 8 | 1 |
|  |  |  |  |  |  |  | Compiled | 8 |  |
| 3 | 1 | 5 | 1 |  | 3 |  | Tax Returns | 15 | 12 |
| 3 | 11 | 29 | 28 | 9 | 2 |  | Other | 92 | 67 |
|  | 88 (4/1-9/30/23) |  | 67 (10/1/23-3/31/24) |  |  |  |  |  |  |
| 7 | 13 | 51 | 56 | 16 | 12 | NUMBER OF STATEMENTS |  | 238 | 120 |
| % | % | % | % | % | % | ASSETS |  | % | % |
|  | 49.0 | 25.4 | 32.9 | 25.8 | 12.9 | Cash & Equivalents |  | 24.1 | 31.2 |
|  | 21.1 | 14.7 | 15.8 | 15.4 | 20.2 | Trade Receivables (net) |  | 17.4 | 12.6 |
|  | 1.5 | .5 | .5 | .0 | .0 | Inventory |  | .6 | .4 |
|  | .4 | 4.4 | 3.0 | 3.0 | 3.1 | All Other Current |  | 3.5 | 3.0 |
|  | 72.0 | 45.0 | 52.2 | 44.2 | 36.1 | Total Current |  | 45.6 | 47.3 |
|  | 17.3 | 43.1 | 32.6 | 36.3 | 19.4 | Fixed Assets (net) |  | 39.1 | 36.2 |
|  | .8 | 1.2 | 1.4 | 3.1 | 29.0 | Intangibles (net) |  | 3.4 | 2.7 |
|  | 9.9 | 10.8 | 13.9 | 16.4 | 15.6 | All Other Non-Current |  | 11.9 | 13.8 |
|  | 100.0 | 100.0 | 100.0 | 100.0 | 100.0 | Total |  | 100.0 | 100.0 |
|  |  |  |  |  |  | LIABILITIES |  |  |  |
|  | 3.2 | .6 | .7 | 1.8 | .0 | Notes Payable-Short Term |  | 2.0 | 3.8 |
|  | 1.4 | 1.8 | 1.2 | 2.4 | 1.3 | Cur. Mat.-L.T.D. |  | 2.3 | 2.4 |
|  | 6.1 | 5.3 | 5.2 | 4.9 | 14.3 | Trade Payables |  | 5.4 | 4.5 |
|  | .0 | .1 | .0 | .0 | .0 | Income Taxes Payable |  | .1 | .0 |
|  | 11.3 | 9.4 | 10.0 | 10.8 | 20.1 | All Other Current |  | 14.9 | 12.2 |
|  | 22.0 | 17.2 | 17.2 | 19.8 | 35.8 | Total Current |  | 24.7 | 22.9 |
|  | 12.4 | 22.7 | 15.2 | 18.7 | 18.9 | Long-Term Debt |  | 21.0 | 25.7 |
|  | .1 | .0 | .1 | .0 | 1.1 | Deferred Taxes |  | .0 | .0 |
|  | 3.6 | 4.4 | 7.7 | 6.6 | 17.2 | All Other Non-Current |  | 6.0 | 12.1 |
|  | 62.0 | 55.7 | 59.8 | 54.9 | 26.9 | Net Worth |  | 48.2 | 39.2 |
|  | 100.0 | 100.0 | 100.0 | 100.0 | 100.0 | Total Liabilities & Net Worth |  | 100.0 | 100.0 |
|  |  |  |  |  |  | INCOME DATA |  |  |  |
|  | 100.0 | 100.0 | 100.0 | 100.0 | 100.0 | Net Sales |  | 100.0 | 100.0 |
|  |  |  |  |  |  | Gross Profit |  |  |  |
|  | 95.5 | 97.9 | 98.5 | 96.1 | 96.5 | Operating Expenses |  | 95.7 | 97.9 |
|  | 4.5 | 2.1 | 1.5 | 3.9 | 3.5 | Operating Profit |  | 4.3 | 2.1 |
|  | 1.5 | -.3 | -1.0 | -.5 | 2.0 | All Other Expenses (net) |  | .9 | .3 |
|  | 3.1 | 2.4 | 2.5 | 4.4 | 1.5 | Profit Before Taxes |  | 3.4 | 1.8 |
|  |  |  |  |  |  | RATIOS |  |  |  |
|  | 32.1 | 5.2 | 6.3 | 3.5 | 1.7 | Current |  | 4.2 | 4.8 |
|  | 5.1 | 2.5 | 3.4 | 2.4 | 1.2 |  |  | 2.2 | 2.4 |
|  | 1.3 | 1.5 | 2.1 | 1.3 | .6 |  |  | 1.2 | 1.5 |
|  | 28.2 | 4.7 | 5.5 | 3.3 | 1.7 | Quick |  | 3.8 | 4.4 |
|  | 5.0 | 2.3 | 3.1 | 2.3 | 1.1 |  |  | 1.9 | 2.3 |
|  | 1.3 | 1.1 | 2.0 | 1.3 | .6 |  |  | 1.0 | 1.1 |
| 0 UND | 17 21.0 | 22 16.3 | 17 21.1 | 12 30.6 |  | Sales/Receivables | 8 46.2 | 2 152.7 |  |
| 9 41.5 | 29 12.4 | 33 11.1 | 33 10.9 | 29 12.5 |  |  | 29 12.7 | 25 14.5 |  |
| 42 8.6 | 43 8.5 | 49 7.5 | 44 8.3 | 44 8.3 |  |  | 41 9.0 | 41 9.0 |  |
|  |  |  |  |  |  | Cost of Sales/Inventory |  |  |  |
|  |  |  |  |  |  | Cost of Sales/Payables |  |  |  |
|  | 4.0 | 3.0 | 2.7 | 3.8 | 13.4 | Sales/Working Capital |  | 4.9 | 3.6 |
|  | 6.0 | 6.0 | 4.1 | 7.5 | 511.5 |  |  | 9.9 | 6.9 |
|  | NM | 16.8 | 8.2 | 19.1 | -40.0 |  |  | 49.9 | 27.7 |
|  |  | 11.9 | 28.5 | 12.8 |  | EBIT/Interest |  | 14.6 | 18.8 |
|  | (36) | 3.2 | (46) 8.5 | (13) 3.0 |  |  | (178) 2.3 | (80) 3.1 |  |
|  |  | -1.7 | -1.1 | -11.5 |  |  |  | -.6 | -1.2 |
|  |  |  |  |  |  | Net Profit + Depr., Dep., Amort./Cur. Mat. L/T/D |  |  |  |
|  | .0 | .4 | .3 | .2 | .0 | Fixed/Worth |  | .3 | .3 |
|  | .0 | .7 | .5 | .9 | 1.7 |  |  | .7 | .7 |
|  | 1.9 | 1.4 | .9 | 1.3 | -.1 |  |  | 1.8 | 1.9 |
|  | .1 | .3 | .3 | .6 | 2.8 | Debt/Worth |  | .3 | .4 |
|  | .2 | .6 | .6 | .9 | NM |  |  | .7 | .9 |
|  | 4.3 | 1.4 | 1.3 | 1.1 | -1.6 |  |  | 2.3 | 3.8 |
|  | 85.5 | 17.4 | 14.7 | 8.0 |  | % Profit Before Taxes/Tangible Net Worth |  | 21.6 | 26.9 |
| (12) | 2.8 | (47) 5.9 | (54) 6.9 | (15) 2.9 |  |  | (217) 4.6 | (105) 8.1 |  |
|  | -27.9 | -2.3 | -2.1 | -9.7 |  |  |  | -1.9 | -1.7 |
|  | 32.2 | 9.1 | 9.2 | 5.0 | 4.7 | % Profit Before Taxes/Total Assets |  | 10.4 | 11.3 |
|  | -1.8 | 3.4 | 4.0 | 1.8 | 1.7 |  |  | 1.9 | 2.5 |
|  | -20.7 | -1.5 | -1.5 | -7.3 | .0 |  |  | -2.0 | -1.5 |
|  | UND | 7.8 | 11.7 | 14.7 | UND | Sales/Net Fixed Assets |  | 19.6 | 27.5 |
|  | 128.9 | 4.0 | 4.0 | 3.7 | 108.9 |  |  | 5.4 | 4.6 |
|  | 9.1 | 1.4 | 2.6 | 2.2 | 3.3 |  |  | 2.3 | 1.5 |
|  | 5.2 | 2.1 | 1.8 | 1.8 | 2.2 | Sales/Total Assets |  | 3.2 | 2.9 |
|  | 3.5 | 1.4 | 1.3 | 1.5 | 1.5 |  |  | 1.8 | 1.4 |
|  | 2.4 | .8 | 1.0 | 1.1 | 1.0 |  |  | 1.1 | .7 |
|  |  | 1.0 | .9 | 1.7 |  | % Depr., Dep., Amort./Sales |  | 1.1 | 1.1 |
|  | (45) | 2.1 | (54) 1.6 | (14) 2.8 |  |  | (207) 2.3 | (92) 2.4 |  |
|  |  | 3.6 | 2.6 | 3.2 |  |  |  | 3.7 | 4.5 |
|  |  |  |  |  |  | % Officers', Directors' Owners' Comp/Sales |  | 2.0 | 3.5 |
|  |  |  |  |  |  |  | (31) 6.8 | (14) 5.2 |  |
|  |  |  |  |  |  |  |  | 11.5 | 7.7 |
| 12334M | 46502M | 489641M | 2117214M | 2215840M | 3388172M | Net Sales ($) |  | 9529112M | 3666763M |
| 1406M | 13339M | 303562M | 1386662M | 1098474M | 1894920M | Total Assets ($) |  | 4335475M | 2069926M |

M = $ thousand  MM = $ million
See Pages viii through xx for Explanation of Ratios and Data

© RMA 2024

# HEALTH CARE—Services for the Elderly and Persons with Disabilities   NAICS 624120

**Comparative Historical Data** | **Current Data Sorted by Sales**

| Comparative Historical Data | | | | Type of Statement | Current Data Sorted by Sales | | | | | |
|---|---|---|---|---|---|---|---|---|---|---|
| 40 | | 67 | 56 | Unqualified | 1 | 1 | 2 | 7 | 19 | 26 |
| 2 | | 2 | 2 | Reviewed | | | | | 1 | 1 |
| 3 | | 3 | 2 | Compiled | | | | | | 2 |
| 5 | | 10 | 13 | Tax Returns | 3 | 4 | | 1 | 2 | 3 |
| 64 | | 87 | 82 | Other | 3 | 10 | 8 | 12 | 19 | 30 |
| 4/1/21-3/31/22 | | 4/1/22-3/31/23 | 4/1/23-3/31/24 | | 88 (4/1-9/30/23) | | | 67 (10/1/23-3/31/24) | | |
| ALL | | ALL | ALL | | 0-1MM | 1-3MM | 3-5MM | 5-10MM | 10-25MM | 25MM & OVER |
| 114 | | 169 | 155 | NUMBER OF STATEMENTS | 7 | 15 | 10 | 20 | 41 | 62 |
| % | | % | % | | % | % | % | % | % | % |
| | | | | **ASSETS** | | | | | | |
| 33.7 | | 32.8 | 30.1 | Cash & Equivalents | 37.7 | 41.9 | 33.8 | 28.2 | 26.8 | |
| 13.3 | | 14.0 | 16.0 | Trade Receivables (net) | 7.6 | 16.2 | 15.8 | 13.7 | 20.0 | |
| .5 | | .7 | .5 | Inventory | .1 | 2.0 | 1.1 | .7 | .0 | |
| 3.1 | | 3.4 | 3.1 | All Other Current | .4 | 4.1 | 2.8 | 5.0 | 2.8 | |
| 50.5 | | 50.9 | 49.6 | Total Current | 45.8 | 64.2 | 53.5 | 47.6 | 49.7 | |
| 36.4 | | 34.6 | 34.1 | Fixed Assets (net) | 41.5 | 22.2 | 38.0 | 35.8 | 30.0 | |
| 3.1 | | 1.7 | 3.5 | Intangibles (net) | 2.3 | .2 | 1.5 | 1.3 | 6.8 | |
| 10.0 | | 12.8 | 12.8 | All Other Non-Current | 10.3 | 13.4 | 7.0 | 15.3 | 13.5 | |
| 100.0 | | 100.0 | 100.0 | Total | 100.0 | 100.0 | 100.0 | 100.0 | 100.0 | |
| | | | | **LIABILITIES** | | | | | | |
| 3.0 | | 4.4 | 1.4 | Notes Payable-Short Term | 1.3 | 2.6 | 1.7 | .8 | .6 | |
| 1.1 | | 1.9 | 1.7 | Cur. Mat.-L.T.D. | 1.9 | .3 | .8 | 1.6 | 1.6 | |
| 5.3 | | 4.9 | 6.0 | Trade Payables | 4.1 | 5.8 | 3.6 | 4.4 | 8.7 | |
| .0 | | .0 | .0 | Income Taxes Payable | .0 | .0 | .2 | .0 | .0 | |
| 10.1 | | 12.2 | 10.8 | All Other Current | 8.6 | 7.5 | 8.6 | 9.0 | 13.8 | |
| 19.5 | | 23.3 | 19.9 | Total Current | 15.8 | 16.2 | 15.0 | 15.9 | 24.7 | |
| 17.2 | | 19.4 | 18.3 | Long-Term Debt | 18.8 | 11.2 | 16.7 | 18.6 | 17.5 | |
| .0 | | .0 | .1 | Deferred Taxes | .1 | .0 | .0 | .0 | .3 | |
| 7.3 | | 4.2 | 8.4 | All Other Non-Current | 25.8 | 3.4 | 3.2 | 3.9 | 10.4 | |
| 56.0 | | 53.1 | 53.2 | Net Worth | 39.5 | 69.2 | 65.1 | 61.6 | 47.2 | |
| 100.0 | | 100.0 | 100.0 | Total Liabilities & Net Worth | 100.0 | 100.0 | 100.0 | 100.0 | 100.0 | |
| | | | | **INCOME DATA** | | | | | | |
| 100.0 | | 100.0 | 100.0 | Net Sales | 100.0 | 100.0 | 100.0 | 100.0 | 100.0 | |
| | | | | Gross Profit | | | | | | |
| 90.7 | | 95.2 | 97.9 | Operating Expenses | 94.4 | 92.2 | 101.1 | 98.8 | 97.9 | |
| 9.3 | | 4.8 | 2.1 | Operating Profit | 5.6 | 7.8 | -1.1 | 1.2 | 2.1 | |
| -1.3 | | .5 | -.3 | All Other Expenses (net) | -.6 | .1 | -1.2 | -1.2 | -.1 | |
| 10.6 | | 4.2 | 2.3 | Profit Before Taxes | 6.2 | 7.7 | .1 | 2.4 | 2.2 | |
| | | | | **RATIOS** | | | | | | |
| 7.6 | | 6.1 | 5.4 | | 31.6 | 16.9 | 6.6 | 5.4 | 3.1 | |
| 2.7 | | 3.1 | 2.6 | Current | 5.1 | 5.8 | 4.1 | 3.3 | 2.3 | |
| 1.6 | | 1.7 | 1.5 | | .9 | 1.4 | 2.1 | 2.0 | 1.5 | |
| 6.9 | | 5.8 | 4.7 | | 30.5 | 15.2 | 6.3 | 4.8 | 3.0 | |
| 2.6 | | 2.9 | 2.5 | Quick | 5.0 | 5.5 | 3.9 | 2.9 | 2.1 | |
| 1.4 | | 1.5 | 1.3 | | .8 | 1.4 | 1.7 | 1.4 | 1.3 | |
| 2  172.7 | 9 | 41.6 | 17  22.1 | | 0  UND | 0  UND | 18  20.7 | 19  19.5 | 22  16.5 | |
| 21  17.2 | 30 | 12.0 | 29  12.4 | Sales/Receivables | 13  28.4 | 13  28.4 | 36  10.0 | 29  12.4 | 35  10.5 | |
| 42  8.6 | 47 | 7.8 | 43  8.4 | | 30  12.0 | 54  6.8 | 58  6.3 | 37  9.8 | 47  7.7 | |
| | | | | Cost of Sales/Inventory | | | | | | |
| | | | | Cost of Sales/Payables | | | | | | |
| 2.4 | | 2.9 | 3.5 | | 1.4 | 2.0 | 2.3 | 3.2 | 4.4 | |
| 5.3 | | 5.2 | 6.0 | Sales/Working Capital | 4.0 | 4.9 | 5.9 | 4.9 | 8.2 | |
| 17.3 | | 13.3 | 17.5 | | -21.0 | 33.0 | 10.3 | 10.0 | 17.7 | |
| 46.7 | | 17.7 | 18.4 | | | | 9.3 | 20.5 | 16.9 | |
| (73)  14.8 | (122) | 2.8 | (116)  3.4 | EBIT/Interest | (15)  1.8 | (35)  9.0 | (47)  2.8 | | | |
| 4.6 | | -5.3 | -1.3 | | | -2.8 | -1.0 | -.4 | | |
| | | | | Net Profit + Depr., Dep., Amort./Cur. Mat. L/T/D | | | | | | |
| .2 | | .2 | .2 | | .1 | .0 | .2 | .3 | .2 | |
| .6 | | .5 | .6 | Fixed/Worth | .6 | .1 | .7 | .5 | .7 | |
| 1.3 | | 1.0 | 1.2 | | 6.2 | .8 | 1.1 | 1.0 | 1.3 | |
| .2 | | .2 | .3 | | .0 | .1 | .2 | .3 | .6 | |
| .6 | | .6 | .7 | Debt/Worth | .2 | .2 | .7 | .4 | 1.0 | |
| 1.3 | | 1.4 | 1.8 | | 6.9 | 1.1 | 1.1 | 1.0 | 2.7 | |
| 32.9 | | 21.9 | 16.6 | | 19.8 | | 18.1 | 11.0 | 18.7 | |
| (106)  15.8 | (158) | 5.9 | (140)  6.9 | % Profit Before Taxes/Tangible Net Worth | (13)  2.7 | | 4.2 | (37)  4.8 | (54)  7.1 | |
| 3.6 | | -3.2 | -2.2 | | -14.7 | | -13.3 | -.5 | -.3 | |
| 17.7 | | 13.5 | 9.1 | | 12.3 | 28.0 | 8.8 | 7.6 | 9.4 | |
| 8.8 | | 2.8 | 3.3 | % Profit Before Taxes/Total Assets | -1.1 | 5.8 | 2.5 | 3.4 | 2.6 | |
| 1.7 | | -2.4 | -2.3 | | -6.1 | -3.1 | -9.6 | .6 | -.5 | |
| 19.2 | | 14.8 | 19.3 | | 13.9 | UND | 15.0 | 7.4 | 25.6 | |
| 4.1 | | 4.5 | 4.9 | Sales/Net Fixed Assets | 2.8 | 68.1 | 2.8 | 4.5 | 6.3 | |
| 1.7 | | 2.0 | 2.5 | | 1.2 | 1.3 | 1.8 | 2.8 | 2.9 | |
| 2.5 | | 2.1 | 2.3 | | 2.0 | 3.9 | 1.6 | 2.1 | 2.2 | |
| 1.3 | | 1.4 | 1.5 | Sales/Total Assets | .8 | 2.9 | 1.2 | 1.4 | 1.6 | |
| .7 | | .9 | 1.0 | | .5 | .5 | 1.0 | 1.1 | 1.2 | |
| 1.1 | | 1.2 | .9 | | .9 | | 1.3 | 1.1 | .8 | |
| (85)  2.3 | (138) | 2.0 | (124)  1.8 | % Depr., Dep., Amort./Sales | (11)  2.6 | (15)  2.4 | (38)  1.8 | (51)  1.7 | | |
| 3.9 | | 3.2 | 3.2 | | 7.3 | | 3.6 | 2.6 | 2.9 | |
| 3.3 | | 2.2 | .2 | | | | | | | |
| (12)  4.3 | (19) | 4.3 | (11)  2.8 | % Officers', Directors' Owners' Comp/Sales | | | | | | |
| 10.8 | | 9.8 | 12.9 | | | | | | | |
| 4726965M | | 5887944M | 8269703M | Net Sales ($) | 3426M | 29459M | 41916M | 137328M | 678962M | 7378612M |
| 2439967M | | 4110965M | 4698363M | Total Assets ($) | 7025M | 106125M | 37224M | 113435M | 563080M | 3871474M |

© RMA 2024    M = $ thousand    MM = $ million
See Pages viii through xx for Explanation of Ratios and Data

# HEALTH CARE—Other Individual and Family Services NAICS 624190

## Current Data Sorted by Assets | Comparative Historical Data

| | | | | | | | Type of Statement | | |
|---|---|---|---|---|---|---|---|---|---|
| | | 4 | 27 | 67 | 21 | 4 | Unqualified | 207 | 86 |
| | | | | 3 | | | Reviewed | 4 | |
| | | | | | | | Compiled | 4 | |
| | 2 | 1 | 2 | 1 | | | Tax Returns | 13 | 12 |
| | 15 | 17 | 47 | 65 | 17 | 6 | Other | 145 | 115 |
| | | 176 (4/1-9/30/23) | | 123 (10/1/23-3/31/24) | | | | 4/1/19- | 4/1/20- |
| | | | | | | | | 3/31/20 | 3/31/21 |
| | 0-500M | 500M-2MM | 2-10MM | 10-50MM | 50-100MM | 100-250MM | NUMBER OF STATEMENTS | ALL | ALL |
| | 17 | 22 | 76 | 136 | 38 | 10 | | 373 | 213 |
| | % | % | % | % | % | % | ASSETS | % | % |
| | 60.1 | 27.4 | 27.5 | 23.7 | 19.3 | 24.5 | Cash & Equivalents | 23.1 | 32.1 |
| | 16.7 | 20.8 | 15.5 | 16.1 | 14.5 | 19.8 | Trade Receivables (net) | 17.1 | 13.0 |
| | .0 | .0 | .5 | .5 | 1.0 | .0 | Inventory | .8 | .8 |
| | 3.8 | 8.7 | 3.0 | 3.0 | 1.7 | .9 | All Other Current | 3.6 | 2.8 |
| | 80.5 | 57.0 | 46.6 | 43.3 | 36.5 | 45.2 | Total Current | 44.6 | 48.8 |
| | 8.9 | 23.0 | 38.3 | 36.5 | 33.5 | 23.5 | Fixed Assets (net) | 40.3 | 36.0 |
| | 5.3 | .0 | 1.6 | 3.3 | 1.4 | 3.2 | Intangibles (net) | 1.2 | 1.6 |
| | 4.9 | 20.0 | 13.5 | 16.9 | 28.6 | 28.2 | All Other Non-Current | 13.9 | 13.6 |
| | 100.0 | 100.0 | 100.0 | 100.0 | 100.0 | 100.0 | Total | 100.0 | 100.0 |
| | | | | | | | LIABILITIES | | |
| | 11.8 | 7.7 | 1.6 | 1.1 | .8 | 1.3 | Notes Payable-Short Term | 2.9 | 3.0 |
| | .9 | .5 | 2.1 | 1.6 | 1.3 | 1.3 | Cur. Mat.-L.T.D. | 1.5 | 2.9 |
| | 12.5 | 4.3 | 2.9 | 3.8 | 6.2 | 8.3 | Trade Payables | 5.1 | 4.3 |
| | .0 | .0 | .0 | .0 | .0 | .0 | Income Taxes Payable | .0 | .0 |
| | 14.1 | 12.2 | 10.1 | 9.9 | 11.7 | 11.4 | All Other Current | 10.8 | 13.3 |
| | 39.3 | 24.6 | 16.7 | 16.5 | 20.0 | 22.3 | Total Current | 20.3 | 23.5 |
| | 2.2 | 3.0 | 17.4 | 13.0 | 15.3 | 18.1 | Long-Term Debt | 14.4 | 21.0 |
| | .0 | .0 | .1 | .0 | .0 | .0 | Deferred Taxes | .0 | .0 |
| | 2.1 | 8.8 | 5.7 | 5.2 | 5.4 | 21.1 | All Other Non-Current | 3.8 | 3.7 |
| | 56.1 | 63.6 | 60.1 | 65.4 | 59.3 | 38.6 | Net Worth | 61.4 | 51.8 |
| | 100.0 | 100.0 | 100.0 | 100.0 | 100.0 | 100.0 | Total Liabilities & Net Worth | 100.0 | 100.0 |
| | | | | | | | INCOME DATA | | |
| | 100.0 | 100.0 | 100.0 | 100.0 | 100.0 | 100.0 | Net Sales | 100.0 | 100.0 |
| | | | | | | | Gross Profit | | |
| | 87.1 | 100.5 | 96.9 | 99.1 | 97.5 | 95.9 | Operating Expenses | 97.3 | 95.8 |
| | 12.9 | -.5 | 3.1 | .9 | 2.5 | 4.1 | Operating Profit | 2.7 | 4.2 |
| | .0 | -.3 | 1.4 | -.4 | -1.3 | -2.2 | All Other Expenses (net) | .4 | -.3 |
| | 12.9 | -.3 | 1.7 | 1.4 | 3.8 | 6.3 | Profit Before Taxes | 2.4 | 4.5 |
| | | | | | | | RATIOS | | |
| | 8.6 | 9.6 | 8.3 | 5.8 | 4.1 | 5.3 | | 5.4 | 4.6 |
| | 2.8 | 3.9 | 4.2 | 2.8 | 2.0 | 2.4 | Current | 2.5 | 2.9 |
| | 1.1 | 1.2 | 2.0 | 1.7 | 1.1 | 1.2 | | 1.3 | 1.6 |
| | 8.2 | 7.4 | 7.8 | 5.4 | 3.8 | 5.3 | | 4.8 | 4.5 |
| | 2.8 | 2.5 | 3.6 | 2.6 | 1.9 | 2.4 | Quick | 2.2 | 2.7 |
| | 1.0 | .9 | 1.5 | 1.5 | 1.0 | 1.2 | | 1.1 | 1.5 |
| 0 | UND | 0 UND | 5 71.1 | 25 14.8 | 19 18.9 | 26 14.2 | | 13 28.8 | 4 82.5 |
| 1 | 263.0 | 34 10.7 | 31 11.8 | 41 8.9 | 43 8.5 | 55 6.6 | Sales/Receivables | 35 10.5 | 29 12.4 |
| 10 | 35.7 | 61 6.0 | 56 6.5 | 63 5.8 | 58 6.3 | 81 4.5 | | 55 6.6 | 49 7.5 |
| | | | | | | | Cost of Sales/Inventory | | |
| | | | | | | | Cost of Sales/Payables | | |
| | 4.6 | 2.6 | 2.5 | 2.6 | 4.2 | 2.9 | | 3.5 | 2.5 |
| | 22.0 | 6.1 | 5.2 | 5.4 | 6.8 | 5.3 | Sales/Working Capital | 6.7 | 4.8 |
| | UND | 66.2 | 9.4 | 11.9 | 57.6 | 34.1 | | 23.2 | 11.2 |
| | | | 14.8 | 15.9 | 24.1 | | | 10.0 | 20.1 |
| | | (47) | 2.4 (98) | 4.7 (26) | 3.8 | | EBIT/Interest | (233) 2.7 (144) | 4.4 |
| | | | -7.1 | -1.4 | -7.8 | | | -.5 | -.2 |
| | | | | | | | Net Profit + Depr., Dep., | | |
| | | | | | | | Amort./Cur. Mat. L/T/D | | |
| | .0 | .0 | .3 | .3 | .3 | .1 | | .3 | .3 |
| | .1 | .3 | .6 | .6 | .6 | .7 | Fixed/Worth | .6 | .5 |
| | .5 | .6 | .9 | .9 | .8 | 1.3 | | 1.1 | 1.0 |
| | .1 | .2 | .1 | .2 | .3 | .7 | | .2 | .3 |
| | .5 | .4 | .4 | .4 | .5 | 1.3 | Debt/Worth | .5 | .6 |
| | 4.7 | 1.2 | 1.0 | 1.0 | 1.2 | 251.6 | | 1.2 | 1.4 |
| | 999.8 | 12.5 | 18.7 | 12.3 | 9.0 | | | 11.8 | 14.8 |
| (15) | 35.8 | -1.5 (73) | 1.0 (131) | 3.2 | 1.6 | | % Profit Before Taxes/Tangible | (360) 2.6 (201) | 4.2 |
| | 19.5 | -8.3 | -8.5 | -4.0 | -2.7 | | Net Worth | -1.9 | -1.8 |
| | 128.3 | 6.7 | 11.1 | 7.7 | 3.6 | 6.7 | | 6.8 | 9.4 |
| | 27.0 | -1.3 | .6 | 1.7 | .9 | 4.7 | % Profit Before Taxes/Total | 1.4 | 2.4 |
| | 15.3 | -7.2 | -5.3 | -2.7 | -1.6 | .5 | Assets | -1.3 | -1.5 |
| | UND | 82.6 | 10.3 | 7.1 | 6.5 | 278.8 | | 11.0 | 12.0 |
| | 121.5 | 20.2 | 3.6 | 3.5 | 3.4 | 3.8 | Sales/Net Fixed Assets | 3.4 | 3.6 |
| | 39.3 | 3.3 | 1.9 | 2.0 | 1.8 | 1.9 | | 1.4 | 1.5 |
| | 16.4 | 3.1 | 2.0 | 1.7 | 1.7 | 2.2 | | 2.4 | 1.9 |
| | 7.6 | 1.6 | 1.2 | 1.1 | 1.0 | 1.1 | Sales/Total Assets | 1.2 | 1.2 |
| | 1.7 | .9 | .7 | .8 | .7 | .6 | | .7 | .7 |
| | | .4 | .9 | 1.2 | 1.0 | | | 1.1 | 1.1 |
| | (12) | .8 (61) | 1.9 (124) | 2.2 (34) | 1.6 | | % Depr., Dep., Amort./Sales | (325) 2.1 (177) | 2.0 |
| | | 1.7 | 3.0 | 3.2 | 3.5 | | | 3.9 | 3.7 |
| | | | | | | | % Officers', Directors' | 2.9 | 3.6 |
| | | | | | | | Owners' Comp/Sales | (21) 6.1 (18) | 9.5 |
| | | | | | | | | 9.3 | 27.6 |
| | 28910M | 58283M | 600376M | 4421062M | 3746464M | 2138505M | Net Sales ($) | 10090606M | 5827544M |
| | 2538M | 27268M | 393474M | 3183650M | 2739377M | 1603903M | Total Assets ($) | 8297710M | 4337675M |

© RMA 2024

M = $ thousand    MM = $ million
See Pages viii through xx for Explanation of Ratios and Data

# HEALTH CARE—Other Individual and Family Services   NAICS 624190

## Comparative Historical Data | Current Data Sorted by Sales

| Type of Statement | | | | | | | | | |
|---|---|---|---|---|---|---|---|---|---|
| 84 | 157 | 123 | Unqualified | 1 | 8 | 11 | 20 | 30 | 53 |
| 2 | 5 | 3 | Reviewed | | | | | 1 | 2 |
| 4 | 2 | | Compiled | | | | | | |
| 6 | 7 | 6 | Tax Returns | 1 | 4 | 1 | | | |
| 118 | 151 | 167 | Other | 16 | 20 | 16 | 22 | 31 | 62 |
| 4/1/21-3/31/22 ALL | 4/1/22-3/31/23 ALL | 4/1/23-3/31/24 ALL | | 176 (4/1-9/30/23) | | | 123 (10/1/23-3/31/24) | | |
| | | | | 0-1MM | 1-3MM | 3-5MM | 5-10MM | 10-25MM | 25MM & OVER |
| 214 | 322 | 299 | NUMBER OF STATEMENTS | 18 | 32 | 28 | 42 | 62 | 117 |
| % | % | % | ASSETS | % | % | % | % | % | % |
| 31.0 | 28.6 | 26.5 | Cash & Equivalents | 39.1 | 29.3 | 32.7 | 28.2 | 28.2 | 20.7 |
| 16.0 | 16.6 | 16.2 | Trade Receivables (net) | 5.4 | 12.9 | 14.1 | 12.1 | 17.4 | 20.2 |
| .8 | .8 | .5 | Inventory | .0 | .3 | .5 | .6 | .1 | .8 |
| 4.0 | 3.4 | 3.3 | All Other Current | 3.1 | 7.3 | 3.1 | 1.5 | 3.1 | 2.9 |
| 51.8 | 49.5 | 46.5 | Total Current | 47.7 | 49.8 | 50.4 | 42.3 | 49.0 | 44.5 |
| 32.1 | 32.8 | 33.6 | Fixed Assets (net) | 27.6 | 33.7 | 31.3 | 40.9 | 33.6 | 32.4 |
| 2.3 | 1.1 | 2.5 | Intangibles (net) | 4.3 | .2 | 1.6 | 1.3 | 2.2 | 3.7 |
| 13.8 | 16.6 | 17.4 | All Other Non-Current | 19.9 | 16.2 | 16.7 | 15.5 | 15.3 | 19.4 |
| 100.0 | 100.0 | 100.0 | Total | 100.0 | 100.0 | 100.0 | 100.0 | 100.0 | 100.0 |
| | | | LIABILITIES | | | | | | |
| 1.2 | 1.9 | 2.3 | Notes Payable-Short Term | 4.5 | 3.8 | 5.4 | .9 | 1.5 | 1.8 |
| 1.2 | 1.4 | 1.6 | Cur. Mat.-L.T.D. | 1.0 | .2 | 1.0 | 1.6 | 2.1 | 1.8 |
| 4.9 | 4.6 | 4.6 | Trade Payables | .5 | 6.7 | 4.4 | 2.3 | 4.0 | 5.8 |
| .0 | .0 | .0 | Income Taxes Payable | .0 | .0 | .0 | .0 | .0 | .0 |
| 12.8 | 10.8 | 10.7 | All Other Current | 12.2 | 8.4 | 6.1 | 6.0 | 11.6 | 13.3 |
| 20.2 | 18.6 | 19.1 | Total Current | 18.2 | 19.1 | 16.8 | 10.7 | 19.2 | 22.7 |
| 12.8 | 13.2 | 13.2 | Long-Term Debt | 12.0 | 9.4 | 11.8 | 14.9 | 11.6 | 15.1 |
| .0 | .0 | .0 | Deferred Taxes | .0 | .0 | .0 | .0 | .1 | .0 |
| 3.6 | 4.0 | 6.0 | All Other Non-Current | 10.2 | 4.3 | 6.4 | 2.0 | 5.1 | 7.6 |
| 63.3 | 64.1 | 61.7 | Net Worth | 59.4 | 67.2 | 65.0 | 72.5 | 64.0 | 54.6 |
| 100.0 | 100.0 | 100.0 | Total Liabilities & Net Worth | 100.0 | 100.0 | 100.0 | 100.0 | 100.0 | 100.0 |
| | | | INCOME DATA | | | | | | |
| 100.0 | 100.0 | 100.0 | Net Sales | 100.0 | 100.0 | 100.0 | 100.0 | 100.0 | 100.0 |
| | | | Gross Profit | | | | | | |
| 92.3 | 98.2 | 97.6 | Operating Expenses | 91.8 | 99.1 | 100.0 | 96.2 | 96.8 | 98.5 |
| 7.7 | 1.8 | 2.4 | Operating Profit | 8.2 | .9 | .0 | 3.8 | 3.2 | 1.5 |
| -.9 | -.1 | -.1 | All Other Expenses (net) | 4.3 | -.2 | .7 | .0 | -.3 | -.8 |
| 8.6 | 1.9 | 2.5 | Profit Before Taxes | 3.8 | 1.1 | -.7 | 3.9 | 3.5 | 2.3 |
| | | | RATIOS | | | | | | |
| 6.5 | 6.2 | 6.3 | | 12.3 | 11.8 | 8.9 | 9.4 | 6.3 | 3.8 |
| 3.2 | 3.2 | 2.9 | Current | 3.3 | 5.1 | 5.3 | 4.0 | 3.3 | 2.1 |
| 1.7 | 1.9 | 1.6 | | .4 | 1.6 | 2.5 | 2.7 | 1.7 | 1.4 |
| 5.6 | 5.6 | 5.9 | | 9.4 | 9.3 | 8.1 | 9.3 | 6.0 | 3.3 |
| 3.1 | 3.0 | 2.7 | Quick | 3.3 | 4.1 | 4.7 | 3.8 | 2.7 | 2.0 |
| 1.6 | 1.7 | 1.3 | | .4 | .9 | 2.2 | 2.5 | 1.5 | 1.2 |
| 7   50.3 | 15   23.7 | 12   29.3 | | 0   UND | 0   UND | 18   20.5 | 14   26.1 | 19   19.0 | 27   13.5 |
| 34   10.8 | 37   9.8 | 38   9.6 | Sales/Receivables | 0   UND | 9   41.8 | 35   10.3 | 33   10.9 | 41   8.8 | 44   8.3 |
| 55   6.6 | 61   6.0 | 59   6.2 | | 10   37.5 | 49   7.4 | 65   5.6 | 66   5.5 | 68   5.4 | 59   6.2 |
| | | | Cost of Sales/Inventory | | | | | | |
| | | | Cost of Sales/Payables | | | | | | |
| 2.5 | 2.5 | 2.7 | | 2.4 | 2.0 | 1.8 | 1.7 | 2.2 | 4.5 |
| 5.0 | 4.9 | 5.7 | Sales/Working Capital | 34.5 | 4.5 | 3.1 | 4.1 | 5.4 | 6.9 |
| 11.9 | 9.8 | 14.3 | | -6.1 | 21.3 | 6.4 | 7.5 | 13.2 | 19.3 |
| 51.7 | 12.5 | 15.0 | | | 12.8 | 5.6 | 35.0 | 50.6 | 12.6 |
| (119)   13.7 | (215)   3.0 | (190)   3.7 | EBIT/Interest | (15)   -1.3 | (15)   2.5 | (25)   3.0 | (42)   2.5 | (87)   4.8 |
| 3.2 | -2.0 | -2.7 | | | -13.6 | -7.1 | -9.4 | -8.5 | .6 |
| | | | Net Profit + Depr., Dep., Amort./Cur. Mat. L/T/D | | | | | | |
| .1 | .2 | .2 | | .0 | .1 | .2 | .3 | .2 | .4 |
| .4 | .5 | .6 | Fixed/Worth | .2 | .5 | .5 | .6 | .4 | .6 |
| .8 | .8 | .9 | | 1.6 | .8 | .8 | .9 | .9 | .9 |
| .2 | .2 | .2 | | .1 | .1 | .2 | .1 | .2 | .3 |
| .4 | .5 | .5 | Debt/Worth | .3 | .3 | .4 | .3 | .4 | .7 |
| 1.0 | .9 | 1.1 | | 1.7 | .9 | 1.0 | .7 | 1.0 | 1.5 |
| 27.8 | 14.4 | 15.0 | | 28.0 | 19.7 | 19.5 | 16.0 | 14.3 | 12.9 |
| (203)   12.6 | (316)   2.1 | (288)   3.1 | % Profit Before Taxes/Tangible Net Worth | (16)   10.0 | (30)   3.5 | 1.4 | -.3 | (61)   5.2 | (111)   3.1 |
| 4.3 | -3.4 | -5.0 | | -1.7 | -6.9 | -7.6 | -7.2 | -5.2 | -.9 |
| 19.0 | 8.6 | 8.8 | | 31.7 | 9.4 | 10.4 | 11.5 | 9.2 | 6.5 |
| 8.7 | 1.3 | 1.4 | % Profit Before Taxes/Total Assets | 6.2 | 2.3 | .2 | -.2 | 3.6 | 1.6 |
| 2.4 | -2.3 | -2.8 | | -1.5 | -5.2 | -6.3 | -5.7 | -3.0 | -.6 |
| 30.6 | 16.4 | 11.4 | | 296.8 | 93.4 | 29.0 | 5.2 | 8.8 | 9.9 |
| 5.1 | 4.7 | 4.1 | Sales/Net Fixed Assets | 16.0 | 2.7 | 3.5 | 2.8 | 4.5 | 4.9 |
| 1.9 | 2.0 | 2.0 | | 1.0 | 1.3 | 1.7 | 1.5 | 2.1 | 2.7 |
| 2.4 | 2.1 | 1.9 | | 2.7 | 1.9 | 1.5 | 1.7 | 1.9 | 2.1 |
| 1.4 | 1.2 | 1.2 | Sales/Total Assets | 1.2 | 1.0 | .8 | .9 | 1.1 | 1.5 |
| .7 | .7 | .8 | | .4 | .5 | .5 | .6 | .8 | 1.0 |
| .7 | 1.0 | 1.0 | | | .8 | .7 | 1.2 | .9 | 1.0 |
| (168)   1.7 | (262)   1.9 | (241)   1.9 | % Depr., Dep., Amort./Sales | (19)   3.0 | (22)   1.8 | (35)   2.2 | (54)   2.0 | (106)   1.7 |
| 3.2 | 3.3 | 3.1 | | | 6.2 | 4.1 | 3.3 | 3.3 | 2.9 |
| 2.4 | 2.9 | 3.5 | | | | | | | |
| (13)   5.7 | (20)   6.6 | (10)   4.5 | % Officers', Directors' Owners' Comp/Sales | | | | | | |
| 9.7 | 15.5 | 11.2 | | | | | | | |
| 7189705M | 10893375M | 10993600M | Net Sales ($) | 8052M | 66811M | 109191M | 315640M | 1011635M | 9482271M |
| 4558903M | 8862406M | 7950210M | Total Assets ($) | 18510M | 99829M | 178212M | 472269M | 1056940M | 6124450M |

© RMA 2024   M = $ thousand   MM = $ million
See Pages viii through xx for Explanation of Ratios and Data

# HEALTH CARE—Community Food Services  NAICS 624210

## Current Data Sorted by Assets

| | | | | | | Type of Statement | | |
|---|---|---|---|---|---|---|---|---|
| | | | 1 | 9 | 7 | Unqualified | 30 | 18 |
| | | | | 1 | | Reviewed | 1 | 1 |
| | | | | 1 | | Compiled | | |
| | | | | | | Tax Returns | 1 | 1 |
| 1 | 1 | 6 | 10 | | 2 | Other | 16 | 16 |
| | 30 (4/1-9/30/23) | | 9 (10/1/23-3/31/24) | | | | 4/1/19- | 4/1/20- |
| | | | | | | | 3/31/20 | 3/31/21 |
| 0-500M | 500M-2MM | 2-10MM | 10-50MM | 50-100MM | 100-250MM | | ALL | ALL |
| 1 | 1 | 7 | 21 | 9 | | NUMBER OF STATEMENTS | 48 | 36 |

## Comparative Historical Data

| 0-500M | 500M-2MM | 2-10MM | 10-50MM | 50-100MM | 100-250MM | | ALL | ALL |
|---|---|---|---|---|---|---|---|---|
| % | % | % | % | % | % | **ASSETS** | % | % |
| | | | 29.3 | | | Cash & Equivalents | 19.4 | 34.4 |
| | | | 7.9 | | | Trade Receivables (net) | 5.4 | 4.0 |
| | | | 6.5 | | | Inventory | 13.8 | 8.8 |
| | | | 1.4 | | DATA | All Other Current | 2.2 | 2.4 |
| | | | 45.1 | | NOT | Total Current | 40.8 | 49.5 |
| | | | 35.0 | | AVAILABLE | Fixed Assets (net) | 46.3 | 36.7 |
| | | | .0 | | | Intangibles (net) | .1 | .0 |
| | | | 19.9 | | | All Other Non-Current | 12.8 | 13.7 |
| | | | 100.0 | | | Total | 100.0 | 100.0 |
| | | | | | | **LIABILITIES** | | |
| | | | 2.6 | | | Notes Payable-Short Term | .6 | 3.1 |
| | | | .6 | | | Cur. Mat.-L.T.D. | .6 | 1.1 |
| | | | 2.7 | | | Trade Payables | 4.3 | 2.5 |
| | | | .0 | | | Income Taxes Payable | .0 | .0 |
| | | | 4.3 | | | All Other Current | 3.4 | 3.5 |
| | | | 10.2 | | | Total Current | 8.9 | 10.2 |
| | | | 8.6 | | | Long-Term Debt | 13.1 | 11.5 |
| | | | .0 | | | Deferred Taxes | .0 | .0 |
| | | | 3.4 | | | All Other Non-Current | 2.0 | 1.3 |
| | | | 77.7 | | | Net Worth | 76.1 | 77.0 |
| | | | 100.0 | | | Total Liabilities & Net Worth | 100.0 | 100.0 |
| | | | | | | **INCOME DATA** | | |
| | | | 100.0 | | | Net Sales | 100.0 | 100.0 |
| | | | | | | Gross Profit | | |
| | | | 99.3 | | | Operating Expenses | 93.9 | 81.1 |
| | | | .7 | | | Operating Profit | 6.1 | 18.9 |
| | | | -.6 | | | All Other Expenses (net) | .8 | 3.5 |
| | | | 1.3 | | | Profit Before Taxes | 5.3 | 15.3 |
| | | | | | | **RATIOS** | | |
| | | | 17.8 | | | | 11.9 | 25.5 |
| | | | 9.4 | | | Current | 6.4 | 7.1 |
| | | | 3.7 | | | | 3.3 | 3.8 |
| | | | 14.3 | | | | 6.5 | 22.5 |
| | | | 8.3 | | | Quick | 3.4 | 5.2 |
| | | | 2.9 | | | | 2.0 | 2.5 |
| | | 2 | 228.2 | | | | 2  204.7 | 0  UND |
| | | 11 | 31.9 | | | Sales/Receivables | 10  38.0 | 3  109.0 |
| | | 41 | 8.8 | | | | 32  11.5 | 14  25.6 |
| | | | | | | Cost of Sales/Inventory | | |
| | | | | | | Cost of Sales/Payables | | |
| | | | 2.7 | | | | 2.1 | 2.0 |
| | | | 4.2 | | | Sales/Working Capital | 4.0 | 3.8 |
| | | | 7.0 | | | | 11.4 | 6.0 |
| | | | 242.9 | | | | 35.5 | 83.9 |
| | | | (14)  5.8 | | | EBIT/Interest | (30)  8.1 | (23)  50.0 |
| | | | -15.0 | | | | 1.9 | 17.4 |
| | | | | | | Net Profit + Depr., Dep., Amort./Cur. Mat. L/T/D | | |
| | | | .2 | | | | .4 | .3 |
| | | | .3 | | | Fixed/Worth | .6 | .4 |
| | | | .8 | | | | .8 | .6 |
| | | | .0 | | | | .1 | .1 |
| | | | .1 | | | Debt/Worth | .3 | .2 |
| | | | .7 | | | | .6 | .4 |
| | | | 13.4 | | | % Profit Before Taxes/Tangible Net Worth | 14.4 | 38.7 |
| | | | 3.4 | | | | 7.8 | (35) 27.6 |
| | | | -3.6 | | | | .0 | 13.4 |
| | | | 11.5 | | | % Profit Before Taxes/Total Assets | 11.3 | 31.9 |
| | | | 3.3 | | | | 5.9 | 22.7 |
| | | | -2.6 | | | | .0 | 9.3 |
| | | | 7.7 | | | | 7.4 | 9.4 |
| | | | 5.7 | | | Sales/Net Fixed Assets | 2.4 | 4.8 |
| | | | 1.5 | | | | .9 | 1.8 |
| | | | 2.1 | | | | 2.8 | 2.7 |
| | | | 1.4 | | | Sales/Total Assets | 1.2 | 1.3 |
| | | | .6 | | | | .5 | .6 |
| | | | .9 | | | | .7 | .7 |
| | | | 1.5 | | | % Depr., Dep., Amort./Sales | (40) 2.1 | (32) 1.6 |
| | | | 3.0 | | | | 4.4 | 2.6 |
| | | | | | | % Officers', Directors' Owners' Comp/Sales | | |
| 634M | 2374M | 54171M | 778187M | 736387M | | Net Sales ($) | 1750539M | 1536398M |
| 398M | 1105M | 38068M | 541784M | 573051M | | Total Assets ($) | 1056852M | 1001255M |

© RMA 2024

M = $ thousand    MM = $ million
See Pages viii through xx for Explanation of Ratios and Data

# HEALTH CARE—Community Food Services  NAICS 624210

## Comparative Historical Data | Current Data Sorted by Sales

| | | | Type of Statement | | | | | | |
|---|---|---|---|---|---|---|---|---|---|
| 17 | 23 | 17 | Unqualified | | 1 | 2 | 1 | 3 | 10 |
| | 1 | 1 | Reviewed | | | 1 | | | |
| | 1 | 1 | Compiled | | | | | 1 | |
| 1 | 1 | | Tax Returns | | | | | | |
| 13 | 14 | 20 | Other | 1 | 1 | 1 | 3 | 4 | 10 |
| 4/1/21-3/31/22 ALL | 4/1/22-3/31/23 ALL | 4/1/23-3/31/24 ALL | | 0-1MM | 30 (4/1-9/30/23) 1-3MM | 3-5MM | 5-10MM | 9 (10/1/23-3/31/24) 10-25MM | 25MM & OVER |
| 31 | 40 | 39 | NUMBER OF STATEMENTS | 1 | 2 | 3 | 5 | 8 | 20 |
| % | % | % | ASSETS | % | % | % | % | % | % |
| 37.3 | 36.4 | 29.1 | Cash & Equivalents | | | | | | 34.0 |
| 2.9 | 5.1 | 7.2 | Trade Receivables (net) | | | | | | 7.3 |
| 10.1 | 10.4 | 6.9 | Inventory | | | | | | 9.7 |
| 3.5 | 2.0 | 1.6 | All Other Current | | | | | | 2.1 |
| 53.8 | 53.9 | 44.8 | Total Current | | | | | | 53.2 |
| 31.4 | 30.1 | 34.3 | Fixed Assets (net) | | | | | | 29.4 |
| .0 | .2 | .0 | Intangibles (net) | | | | | | .0 |
| 14.8 | 15.8 | 20.8 | All Other Non-Current | | | | | | 17.3 |
| 100.0 | 100.0 | 100.0 | Total | | | | | | 100.0 |
| | | | LIABILITIES | | | | | | |
| .1 | 2.3 | 1.8 | Notes Payable-Short Term | | | | | | 2.7 |
| .2 | .7 | .5 | Cur. Mat.-L.T.D. | | | | | | .8 |
| 2.2 | 2.9 | 2.7 | Trade Payables | | | | | | 3.8 |
| .0 | .0 | .0 | Income Taxes Payable | | | | | | .0 |
| 3.5 | 4.3 | 5.2 | All Other Current | | | | | | 4.7 |
| 6.1 | 10.2 | 10.3 | Total Current | | | | | | 12.0 |
| 6.0 | 5.6 | 8.0 | Long-Term Debt | | | | | | 8.9 |
| .0 | .1 | .0 | Deferred Taxes | | | | | | .0 |
| 6.4 | 2.0 | 2.0 | All Other Non-Current | | | | | | 3.7 |
| 81.6 | 82.2 | 79.8 | Net Worth | | | | | | 75.4 |
| 100.0 | 100.0 | 100.0 | Total Liabilities & Net Worth | | | | | | 100.0 |
| | | | INCOME DATA | | | | | | |
| 100.0 | 100.0 | 100.0 | Net Sales | | | | | | 100.0 |
| | | | Gross Profit | | | | | | |
| 88.2 | 92.3 | 100.1 | Operating Expenses | | | | | | 95.7 |
| 11.8 | 7.7 | -.1 | Operating Profit | | | | | | 4.3 |
| -.5 | 1.0 | -1.4 | All Other Expenses (net) | | | | | | -.6 |
| 12.3 | 6.7 | 1.3 | Profit Before Taxes | | | | | | 4.9 |
| | | | RATIOS | | | | | | |
| 24.9 | 26.7 | 18.4 | | | | | | | 17.3 |
| 14.6 | 10.7 | 9.4 | Current | | | | | | 8.0 |
| 5.3 | 4.9 | 3.8 | | | | | | | 4.0 |
| 17.4 | 20.8 | 15.2 | | | | | | | 14.2 |
| 9.4 | 7.6 | 8.3 | Quick | | | | | | 6.6 |
| 4.6 | 3.5 | 2.8 | | | | | | | 3.0 |
| 0 UND | 0 749.8 | 2 169.9 | | | | | | 4 | 95.6 |
| 4 102.8 | 8 44.6 | 11 33.1 | Sales/Receivables | | | | | 10 | 36.1 |
| 8 48.2 | 17 22.0 | 38 9.5 | | | | | | 23 | 16.2 |
| | | | Cost of Sales/Inventory | | | | | | |
| | | | Cost of Sales/Payables | | | | | | |
| 2.5 | 2.1 | 2.5 | | | | | | | 2.6 |
| 4.6 | 3.8 | 4.5 | Sales/Working Capital | | | | | | 4.3 |
| 6.4 | 5.8 | 7.0 | | | | | | | 7.0 |
| 316.1 | 70.1 | 86.7 | | | | | | | 92.8 |
| (19) 87.2 | (24) 33.1 | (24) 11.8 | EBIT/Interest | | | | | (17) | 11.8 |
| 16.6 | 3.4 | -.8 | | | | | | | 2.6 |
| | | | Net Profit + Depr., Dep., Amort./Cur. Mat. L/T/D | | | | | | |
| .2 | .2 | .2 | | | | | | | .2 |
| .3 | .3 | .3 | Fixed/Worth | | | | | | .3 |
| .5 | .5 | .7 | | | | | | | .6 |
| .0 | .0 | .1 | | | | | | | .1 |
| .1 | .1 | .1 | Debt/Worth | | | | | | .2 |
| .2 | .3 | .3 | | | | | | | .7 |
| 37.6 | 19.3 | 12.6 | | | | | | | 18.9 |
| (30) 24.7 | (39) 4.4 | 4.1 | % Profit Before Taxes/Tangible Net Worth | | | | | | 10.6 |
| 10.1 | -2.1 | -1.4 | | | | | | | 2.3 |
| 36.3 | 15.0 | 11.2 | | | | | | | 12.3 |
| 20.0 | 4.0 | 3.3 | % Profit Before Taxes/Total Assets | | | | | | 8.2 |
| 6.6 | -4.3 | -1.3 | | | | | | | 1.6 |
| 13.8 | 16.2 | 7.0 | | | | | | | 8.0 |
| 8.3 | 6.4 | 4.6 | Sales/Net Fixed Assets | | | | | | 5.9 |
| 4.2 | 1.9 | 2.1 | | | | | | | 4.4 |
| 2.9 | 2.3 | 1.9 | | | | | | | 2.4 |
| 2.1 | 1.3 | 1.3 | Sales/Total Assets | | | | | | 1.8 |
| 1.0 | .7 | .7 | | | | | | | 1.3 |
| .6 | .8 | 1.0 | | | | | | | .9 |
| (28) 1.2 | (33) 1.7 | (37) 1.6 | % Depr., Dep., Amort./Sales | | | | | | 1.2 |
| 2.2 | 3.1 | 3.5 | | | | | | | 1.7 |
| | | | % Officers', Directors' Owners' Comp/Sales | | | | | | |
| 2325627M | 1538121M | 1571753M | Net Sales ($) | 634M | 4137M | 12161M | 34352M | 132831M | 1387638M |
| 1053675M | 1042692M | 1154406M | Total Assets ($) | 398M | 3309M | 43480M | 52315M | 194881M | 860023M |

© RMA 2024  M = $ thousand   MM = $ million
See Pages viii through xx for Explanation of Ratios and Data

# HEALTH CARE—Temporary Shelters  NAICS 624221

## Current Data Sorted by Assets

| | | | | | | | Comparative Historical Data | |
|---|---|---|---|---|---|---|---|---|
| | | | | | | Type of Statement | | |
| | | | | | | Unqualified | 29 | 14 |
| | 2 | 8 | 12 | 6 | 1 | Reviewed | 1 | 2 |
| 1 | | | | | | Compiled | 3 | |
| | | 3 | | | | Tax Returns | 1 | 3 |
| | 6 | 11 | 7 | 2 | | Other | 17 | 13 |
| | 36 (4/1-9/30/23) | | 23 (10/1/23-3/31/24) | | | | 4/1/19-3/31/20 | 4/1/20-3/31/21 |
| 0-500M | 500M-2MM | 2-10MM | 10-50MM | 50-100MM | 100-250MM | | ALL | ALL |
| 1 | 8 | 22 | 19 | 8 | 1 | NUMBER OF STATEMENTS | 51 | 32 |
| % | % | % | % | % | % | ASSETS | % | % |
| | | 17.9 | 20.8 | | | Cash & Equivalents | 18.8 | 25.7 |
| | | 13.4 | 7.1 | | | Trade Receivables (net) | 9.3 | 5.5 |
| | | .5 | .1 | | | Inventory | .3 | .8 |
| | | 3.6 | 3.5 | | | All Other Current | 1.6 | 4.5 |
| | | 35.4 | 31.5 | | | Total Current | 30.0 | 36.6 |
| | | 46.2 | 48.4 | | | Fixed Assets (net) | 56.2 | 53.5 |
| | | 1.7 | 1.8 | | | Intangibles (net) | .4 | .0 |
| | | 16.8 | 18.2 | | | All Other Non-Current | 13.5 | 10.0 |
| | | 100.0 | 100.0 | | | Total | 100.0 | 100.0 |
| | | | | | | LIABILITIES | | |
| | | .4 | 1.2 | | | Notes Payable-Short Term | 1.2 | 1.4 |
| | | 1.4 | .5 | | | Cur. Mat.-L.T.D. | 1.1 | .7 |
| | | 3.8 | 1.8 | | | Trade Payables | 3.6 | 1.8 |
| | | .0 | .0 | | | Income Taxes Payable | .0 | .2 |
| | | 4.1 | 7.1 | | | All Other Current | 4.3 | 4.5 |
| | | 9.8 | 10.6 | | | Total Current | 10.3 | 8.6 |
| | | 11.5 | 15.1 | | | Long-Term Debt | 15.8 | 20.2 |
| | | .0 | .0 | | | Deferred Taxes | .0 | .0 |
| | | 1.4 | 1.6 | | | All Other Non-Current | 1.4 | 3.6 |
| | | 77.3 | 72.7 | | | Net Worth | 72.5 | 67.7 |
| | | 100.0 | 100.0 | | | Total Liabilities & Net Worth | 100.0 | 100.0 |
| | | | | | | INCOME DATA | | |
| | | 100.0 | 100.0 | | | Net Sales | 100.0 | 100.0 |
| | | | | | | Gross Profit | | |
| | | 92.5 | 97.3 | | | Operating Expenses | 94.1 | 92.8 |
| | | 7.5 | 2.7 | | | Operating Profit | 5.9 | 7.2 |
| | | -.1 | .4 | | | All Other Expenses (net) | -.4 | -1.8 |
| | | 7.6 | 2.2 | | | Profit Before Taxes | 6.3 | 9.0 |
| | | | | | | RATIOS | | |
| | | 12.5 | 9.9 | | | | 5.2 | 8.4 |
| | | 4.1 | 3.7 | | | Current | 2.8 | 4.4 |
| | | 2.0 | 2.1 | | | | 1.7 | 2.8 |
| | | 10.6 | 9.6 | | | | 4.9 | 8.1 |
| | | 3.4 | 3.7 | | | Quick | 2.7 | 4.0 |
| | | 1.5 | 1.3 | | | | 1.4 | 2.1 |
| | | 11  33.0 | 9  42.5 | | | | 5  75.5 | 0  734.7 |
| | | 35  10.5 | 41  9.0 | | | Sales/Receivables | 28  12.9 | 18  20.2 |
| | | 70  5.2 | 49  7.4 | | | | 41  8.8 | 54  6.7 |
| | | | | | | Cost of Sales/Inventory | | |
| | | | | | | Cost of Sales/Payables | | |
| | | 1.7 | 1.5 | | | | 2.8 | 1.7 |
| | | 4.2 | 3.1 | | | Sales/Working Capital | 6.5 | 3.3 |
| | | 9.6 | 6.8 | | | | 13.9 | 6.2 |
| | | 36.8 | 30.6 | | | | 15.0 | 12.9 |
| | | (16)  3.3 | (12)  8.2 | | | EBIT/Interest | (32)  2.7 | (18)  3.9 |
| | | -6.7 | -1.4 | | | | -3.0 | 1.9 |
| | | | | | | Net Profit + Depr., Dep., Amort./Cur. Mat. L/T/D | | |
| | | .3 | .4 | | | | .5 | .5 |
| | | .7 | .7 | | | Fixed/Worth | .8 | .8 |
| | | .9 | 1.1 | | | | 1.2 | 1.3 |
| | | .1 | .1 | | | | .1 | .1 |
| | | .3 | .3 | | | Debt/Worth | .4 | .4 |
| | | .5 | .9 | | | | .6 | 1.0 |
| | | 18.8 | 8.0 | | | | 18.3 | 21.8 |
| | | 4.9 | (18) .7 | | | % Profit Before Taxes/Tangible Net Worth | 3.0 | 8.3 |
| | | -2.7 | -4.0 | | | | -3.9 | .8 |
| | | 12.2 | 7.6 | | | | 10.3 | 16.2 |
| | | 3.8 | .8 | | | % Profit Before Taxes/Total Assets | 2.0 | 6.2 |
| | | -2.0 | -2.9 | | | | -3.2 | .6 |
| | | 3.7 | 2.9 | | | | 2.9 | 3.0 |
| | | 1.5 | 1.2 | | | Sales/Net Fixed Assets | 1.3 | 1.1 |
| | | .9 | .6 | | | | .8 | .6 |
| | | 1.4 | .7 | | | | 1.3 | .9 |
| | | .8 | .5 | | | Sales/Total Assets | .8 | .7 |
| | | .5 | .4 | | | | .5 | .4 |
| | | 1.5 | 1.9 | | | | 2.0 | 1.9 |
| | | 3.5 | (16) 3.6 | | | % Depr., Dep., Amort./Sales | (43) 3.8 | (30) 3.9 |
| | | 5.0 | 5.3 | | | | 6.2 | 5.9 |
| | | | | | | % Officers', Directors' Owners' Comp/Sales | | |
| 1143M | 13612M | 105949M | 301258M | 280425M | 22248M | Net Sales ($) | 603227M | 243167M |
| 333M | 8794M | 123932M | 492314M | 624297M | 101852M | Total Assets ($) | 774309M | 419462M |

M = $ thousand   MM = $ million

# HEALTH CARE—Temporary Shelters  NAICS 624221

## Comparative Historical Data | Current Data Sorted by Sales

| Comparative Historical Data ||| Type of Statement | Current Data Sorted by Sales ||||||
|---|---|---|---|---|---|---|---|---|---|
| 17 | 17 | 29 | Unqualified | 1 | 2 | 5 | 4 | 9 | 8 |
| 1 | 1 | 1 | Reviewed | | 1 | | | | |
| | | | Compiled | | | | | | |
| 3 | 1 | 3 | Tax Returns | | 1 | 2 | | | |
| 16 | 25 | 26 | Other | 4 | 6 | 7 | 3 | 4 | 2 |
| 4/1/21-3/31/22 | 4/1/22-3/31/23 | 4/1/23-3/31/24 | | 36 (4/1-9/30/23) ||| 23 (10/1/23-3/31/24) |||
| ALL | ALL | ALL | | 0-1MM | 1-3MM | 3-5MM | 5-10MM | 10-25MM | 25MM & OVER |
| 37 | 44 | 59 | **NUMBER OF STATEMENTS** | 5 | 10 | 14 | 7 | 13 | 10 |
| % | % | % | **ASSETS** | % | % | % | % | % | % |
| 30.2 | 19.7 | 18.6 | Cash & Equivalents | | 30.1 | 9.8 | | 21.3 | 7.5 |
| 7.8 | 10.1 | 11.9 | Trade Receivables (net) | | 14.1 | 17.1 | | 12.4 | 5.4 |
| 2.5 | .3 | .2 | Inventory | | .1 | .7 | | .1 | .2 |
| 2.9 | 5.2 | 3.0 | All Other Current | | 1.7 | 4.5 | | 4.3 | 3.1 |
| 43.3 | 35.2 | 33.8 | Total Current | | 46.0 | 32.1 | | 38.0 | 16.3 |
| 45.8 | 46.5 | 48.9 | Fixed Assets (net) | | 45.4 | 43.9 | | 41.4 | 61.4 |
| .0 | .1 | 1.2 | Intangibles (net) | | .0 | 2.1 | | 3.0 | .0 |
| 11.0 | 18.2 | 16.2 | All Other Non-Current | | 8.6 | 21.8 | | 17.7 | 22.4 |
| 100.0 | 100.0 | 100.0 | Total | | 100.0 | 100.0 | | 100.0 | 100.0 |
| | | | **LIABILITIES** | | | | | | |
| 2.7 | 2.0 | 1.0 | Notes Payable-Short Term | | .8 | 1.3 | | 1.2 | .2 |
| .8 | 1.7 | 1.6 | Cur. Mat.-L.T.D. | | 1.7 | .8 | | .6 | 1.2 |
| 1.7 | 2.6 | 2.9 | Trade Payables | | 1.8 | 3.7 | | 4.0 | 2.6 |
| .0 | .0 | .0 | Income Taxes Payable | | .0 | .0 | | .0 | .0 |
| 7.9 | 10.2 | 6.0 | All Other Current | | 4.3 | 8.4 | | 6.6 | 2.8 |
| 13.0 | 16.5 | 11.5 | Total Current | | 8.7 | 14.1 | | 12.5 | 6.8 |
| 10.3 | 11.9 | 14.7 | Long-Term Debt | | 4.2 | 11.7 | | 16.7 | 16.8 |
| .0 | .0 | .0 | Deferred Taxes | | .0 | .0 | | .0 | .0 |
| 1.2 | 1.4 | 2.4 | All Other Non-Current | | 2.4 | 2.0 | | 1.6 | 6.1 |
| 75.4 | 70.2 | 71.5 | Net Worth | | 84.8 | 72.1 | | 69.2 | 70.3 |
| 100.0 | 100.0 | 100.0 | Total Liabilities & Net Worth | | 100.0 | 100.0 | | 100.0 | 100.0 |
| | | | **INCOME DATA** | | | | | | |
| 100.0 | 100.0 | 100.0 | Net Sales | | 100.0 | 100.0 | | 100.0 | 100.0 |
| | | | Gross Profit | | | | | | |
| 81.6 | 91.0 | 93.6 | Operating Expenses | | 100.2 | 93.9 | | 97.0 | 90.2 |
| 18.4 | 9.0 | 6.4 | Operating Profit | | -.2 | 6.1 | | 3.0 | 9.8 |
| -1.6 | -.2 | .8 | All Other Expenses (net) | | -.4 | -.2 | | -.2 | -.8 |
| 20.0 | 9.2 | 5.6 | Profit Before Taxes | | .3 | 6.3 | | 3.1 | 10.5 |
| | | | **RATIOS** | | | | | | |
| 22.4 | 10.4 | 9.7 | | | 16.6 | 7.3 | | 5.8 | 5.0 |
| 6.0 | 4.7 | 4.0 | Current | | 11.7 | 3.6 | | 3.7 | 2.6 |
| 2.6 | 2.1 | 1.5 | | | 5.2 | 1.8 | | 1.7 | 1.0 |
| 17.5 | 8.7 | 9.4 | | | 15.9 | 4.6 | | 5.3 | 3.4 |
| 5.9 | 3.8 | 3.0 | Quick | | 10.9 | 1.9 | | 3.6 | 1.7 |
| 2.5 | 1.9 | 1.3 | | | 5.2 | 1.3 | | 1.6 | .5 |
| 0 UND | 2 240.3 | 10 35.0 | | 0 UND | 16 23.3 | | 6 61.6 | 0 UND | |
| 5 73.4 | 24 14.9 | 35 10.4 | Sales/Receivables | 38 9.6 | 28 12.9 | | 41 9.0 | 26 14.3 | |
| 45 8.1 | 54 6.7 | 54 6.8 | | 57 6.4 | 68 5.4 | | 51 7.1 | 46 7.9 | |
| | | | Cost of Sales/Inventory | | | | | | |
| | | | Cost of Sales/Payables | | | | | | |
| 1.8 | 1.8 | 1.9 | | | 1.7 | 2.6 | | 2.1 | 3.1 |
| 3.3 | 3.7 | 3.9 | Sales/Working Capital | | 1.9 | 5.6 | | 3.1 | 12.0 |
| 5.8 | 5.8 | 10.8 | | | 7.8 | 10.3 | | 10.2 | NM |
| 88.7 | 25.6 | 30.8 | | | | 42.5 | | | |
| (18) 23.4 | (27) 6.0 | (39) 3.0 | EBIT/Interest | | (11) | 3.5 | | | |
| 4.9 | -6.1 | -2.1 | | | | -17.8 | | | |
| | | | Net Profit + Depr., Dep., Amort./Cur. Mat. L/T/D | | | | | | |
| .3 | .3 | .4 | | | .4 | .2 | | .3 | .6 |
| .6 | .7 | .8 | Fixed/Worth | | .6 | .8 | | .6 | .9 |
| .8 | 1.0 | 1.0 | | | .8 | 1.1 | | 1.1 | 1.0 |
| .0 | .1 | .1 | | | .0 | .1 | | .2 | .1 |
| .3 | .3 | .3 | Debt/Worth | | .1 | .3 | | .5 | .2 |
| .5 | .7 | .7 | | | .4 | .6 | | .7 | .9 |
| 37.9 | 16.1 | 14.0 | | | 6.7 | 16.8 | | 17.1 | 15.1 |
| (36) 16.4 | (43) 8.6 | (58) 3.7 | % Profit Before Taxes/Tangible Net Worth | | 3.6 | 2.0 | (12) | 3.8 | 6.2 |
| 6.4 | -3.2 | -5.2 | | | -6.0 | -17.8 | | -3.0 | -5.3 |
| 25.1 | 10.3 | 9.6 | | | 6.4 | 11.8 | | 11.7 | 10.4 |
| 12.9 | 3.8 | 2.3 | % Profit Before Taxes/Total Assets | | 2.7 | 1.6 | | 4.1 | 4.8 |
| 4.7 | -3.8 | -3.2 | | | -4.5 | -12.7 | | -1.7 | -3.5 |
| 5.8 | 3.2 | 3.3 | | | 27.9 | 15.9 | | 5.0 | 1.6 |
| 2.5 | 1.3 | 1.3 | Sales/Net Fixed Assets | | 1.6 | 1.4 | | 1.6 | 1.0 |
| .9 | .7 | .6 | | | .9 | .8 | | .8 | .5 |
| 1.4 | 1.1 | 1.2 | | | 1.8 | 1.5 | | 1.3 | .9 |
| .8 | .7 | .6 | Sales/Total Assets | | .8 | .7 | | .6 | .5 |
| .6 | .4 | .4 | | | .5 | .4 | | .4 | .4 |
| 1.4 | 1.5 | 1.7 | | | | 1.2 | | 1.0 | 2.4 |
| (29) 2.5 | (39) 3.7 | (51) 3.4 | % Depr., Dep., Amort./Sales | | (13) | 3.7 | (11) | 3.3 | 3.9 |
| 6.2 | 6.3 | 5.4 | | | | 5.1 | | 5.5 | 7.3 |
| | | | % Officers', Directors' Owners' Comp/Sales | | | | | | |
| 355400M | 942853M | 724635M | Net Sales ($) | 3076M | 22356M | 58084M | 50907M | 213165M | 377047M |
| 457114M | 1163670M | 1351522M | Total Assets ($) | 8392M | 39122M | 87423M | 119068M | 402649M | 694868M |

© RMA 2024   M = $ thousand   MM = $ million
See Pages viii through xx for Explanation of Ratios and Data

# HEALTH CARE—Other Community Housing Services  NAICS 624229

## Current Data Sorted by Assets

| | | | | | | | Type of Statement | | |
|---|---|---|---|---|---|---|---|---|---|
| | | 3 | 7 | 23 | 9 | 7 | Unqualified | 53 | 36 |
| | | | | 1 | 1 | 1 | Reviewed | | 1 |
| | 1 | | | 1 | | | Compiled | 2 | 1 |
| | 2 | 9 | 14 | 24 | 11 | 2 | Tax Returns | 3 | 1 |
| | | 74 (4/1-9/30/23) | | 42 (10/1/23-3/31/24) | | | Other | 36 | 35 |
| | 0-500M | 500M-2MM | 2-10MM | 10-50MM | 50-100MM | 100-250MM | | 4/1/19-3/31/20 ALL | 4/1/20-3/31/21 ALL |
| | 3 | 12 | 21 | 49 | 21 | 10 | NUMBER OF STATEMENTS | 94 | 74 |
| | % | % | % | % | % | % | ASSETS | % | % |
| | | 24.2 | 16.5 | 19.0 | 15.4 | 8.0 | Cash & Equivalents | 16.7 | 21.7 |
| | | 9.3 | 8.0 | 10.6 | 4.8 | 3.2 | Trade Receivables (net) | 10.2 | 5.3 |
| | | .0 | 3.3 | 3.3 | 7.1 | 6.0 | Inventory | 1.6 | 1.9 |
| | | 6.2 | 3.5 | 4.1 | 4.4 | 2.2 | All Other Current | 4.8 | 2.8 |
| | | 39.7 | 31.4 | 37.0 | 31.8 | 19.2 | Total Current | 33.2 | 31.7 |
| | | 50.9 | 44.0 | 41.1 | 36.5 | 38.3 | Fixed Assets (net) | 44.8 | 42.4 |
| | | 6.2 | 1.6 | 1.7 | 3.2 | .1 | Intangibles (net) | 2.1 | 1.6 |
| | | 3.1 | 23.0 | 20.3 | 28.5 | 42.3 | All Other Non-Current | 20.0 | 24.2 |
| | | 100.0 | 100.0 | 100.0 | 100.0 | 100.0 | Total | 100.0 | 100.0 |
| | | | | | | | LIABILITIES | | |
| | | 3.9 | 1.1 | 2.1 | 2.2 | 3.5 | Notes Payable-Short Term | 2.1 | 2.7 |
| | | 1.4 | .9 | 1.2 | 1.2 | 1.7 | Cur. Mat.-L.T.D. | 1.9 | 1.7 |
| | | 1.1 | 3.3 | 3.7 | 3.4 | 1.5 | Trade Payables | 3.2 | 1.8 |
| | | .0 | .0 | .0 | .0 | .0 | Income Taxes Payable | .0 | .0 |
| | | 5.8 | 7.9 | 6.2 | 4.3 | 1.1 | All Other Current | 7.3 | 4.3 |
| | | 12.2 | 13.1 | 13.2 | 11.1 | 7.8 | Total Current | 14.6 | 10.5 |
| | | 28.1 | 31.9 | 20.8 | 30.3 | 42.8 | Long-Term Debt | 29.1 | 27.3 |
| | | .0 | .0 | .0 | .0 | .0 | Deferred Taxes | .0 | .0 |
| | | 3.6 | 2.0 | 4.1 | 6.9 | 10.7 | All Other Non-Current | 2.3 | 2.3 |
| | | 56.1 | 53.0 | 61.9 | 51.6 | 38.7 | Net Worth | 54.1 | 59.9 |
| | | 100.0 | 100.0 | 100.0 | 100.0 | 100.0 | Total Liabilities & Net Worth | 100.0 | 100.0 |
| | | | | | | | INCOME DATA | | |
| | | 100.0 | 100.0 | 100.0 | 100.0 | 100.0 | Net Sales | 100.0 | 100.0 |
| | | | | | | | Gross Profit | | |
| | | 69.9 | 87.5 | 91.3 | 89.5 | 86.6 | Operating Expenses | 93.0 | 86.5 |
| | | 30.1 | 12.5 | 8.7 | 10.5 | 13.4 | Operating Profit | 7.0 | 13.5 |
| | | 7.8 | 2.4 | .6 | .0 | 8.3 | All Other Expenses (net) | .9 | 1.8 |
| | | 22.3 | 10.1 | 8.1 | 10.6 | 5.1 | Profit Before Taxes | 6.1 | 11.7 |
| | | | | | | | RATIOS | | |
| | | 12.8 | 11.7 | 6.9 | 5.6 | 6.2 | | 6.1 | 6.2 |
| | | 2.9 | 2.1 | 3.1 | 2.3 | 2.3 | Current | 2.4 | 3.3 |
| | | .9 | .9 | 1.7 | 1.5 | 1.5 | | 1.2 | 1.7 |
| | | 11.4 | 8.5 | 4.6 | 2.5 | 4.9 | | 4.0 | 5.2 |
| | | 2.2 | 1.7 | 2.6 | 1.5 | 1.4 | Quick | 1.9 | 3.1 |
| | | .6 | .7 | 1.4 | .8 | .6 | | .9 | 1.4 |
| | 0 | UND | 7 | 52.8 | 8 | 48.6 | 3 | 113.1 | 0 | UND | | 1 | 372.4 | 1 | 469.2 |
| | 5 | 71.0 | 25 | 14.4 | 26 | 13.8 | 20 | 18.6 | 14 | 25.5 | Sales/Receivables | 15 | 24.7 | 11 | 33.0 |
| | 17 | 21.9 | 58 | 6.3 | 56 | 6.5 | 39 | 9.3 | 43 | 8.4 | | 52 | 7.0 | 41 | 9.0 |
| | | | | | | | Cost of Sales/Inventory | | |
| | | | | | | | Cost of Sales/Payables | | |
| | | 3.2 | 1.3 | 1.8 | 1.0 | 1.0 | | 1.7 | 1.6 |
| | | 10.7 | 6.7 | 2.9 | 2.8 | 1.5 | Sales/Working Capital | 5.2 | 3.3 |
| | | NM | NM | 7.7 | 4.5 | NM | | 16.4 | 8.8 |
| | | | 15.8 | 33.7 | 4.3 | | | 7.6 | 9.8 |
| | | (15) | 4.0 | (34) | 9.2 | (16) | 2.2 | EBIT/Interest | (68) | 2.2 | (53) | 2.4 |
| | | | -8.3 | -1.4 | 1.6 | | | .3 | .5 |
| | | | | | | | Net Profit + Depr., Dep., Amort./Cur. Mat. L/T/D | | |
| | | .2 | .3 | .3 | .1 | .1 | | .2 | .2 |
| | | .9 | .5 | .6 | .7 | 1.5 | Fixed/Worth | .6 | .7 |
| | | 1.9 | 2.6 | 1.0 | 1.8 | 2.4 | | 2.0 | 1.4 |
| | | .2 | .2 | .2 | .7 | .8 | | .3 | .3 |
| | | .6 | .3 | .5 | .8 | 2.8 | Debt/Worth | .7 | .6 |
| | | 1.3 | 7.7 | 1.2 | 1.3 | 4.0 | | 2.0 | 1.5 |
| | | 66.5 | 21.1 | 11.2 | 9.6 | 8.1 | % Profit Before Taxes/Tangible Net Worth | 11.0 | 9.3 |
| | (10) | 28.3 | (17) | 6.5 | (47) | 4.5 | 4.3 | 3.9 | | (91) | 3.0 | 5.2 |
| | | 5.4 | -7.4 | -1.1 | 2.2 | -1.1 | | -1.4 | .1 |
| | | 43.8 | 12.9 | 7.4 | 5.0 | 1.9 | % Profit Before Taxes/Total Assets | 5.7 | 5.8 |
| | | 10.9 | 4.4 | 1.8 | 1.9 | .9 | | 1.3 | 3.1 |
| | | 4.5 | -3.1 | -1.3 | .8 | -.7 | | -1.0 | .0 |
| | | 14.8 | 3.4 | 6.7 | 11.9 | 15.4 | | 4.3 | 7.7 |
| | | 3.6 | 1.3 | 1.4 | 1.1 | .7 | Sales/Net Fixed Assets | 1.1 | 1.1 |
| | | .5 | .6 | .6 | .4 | .3 | | .5 | .5 |
| | | 1.5 | .8 | .9 | .5 | .4 | | .8 | .6 |
| | | .8 | .5 | .5 | .3 | .2 | Sales/Total Assets | .4 | .4 |
| | | .4 | .4 | .3 | .2 | .1 | | .2 | .2 |
| | | | 1.2 | .7 | 1.1 | 1.5 | | 1.5 | 1.1 |
| | | (16) | 2.4 | (37) | 2.6 | (18) | 4.1 | 6.3 | % Depr., Dep., Amort./Sales | (73) | 3.4 | (60) | 4.1 |
| | | | 3.3 | 5.8 | 8.9 | 20.9 | | 11.6 | 10.1 |
| | | | | | | | % Officers', Directors' Owners' Comp/Sales | | |
| | 22556M | 20259M | 79905M | 778051M | 648774M | 382434M | Net Sales ($) | 1288631M | 988623M |
| | 789M | 15946M | 111798M | 1158282M | 1372793M | 1546084M | Total Assets ($) | 2236160M | 2501904M |

M = $ thousand   MM = $ million
See Pages viii through xx for Explanation of Ratios and Data

© RMA 2024

# HEALTH CARE—Other Community Housing Services  NAICS 624229

## Comparative Historical Data | Current Data Sorted by Sales

| Comparative Historical Data ||| Type of Statement | Current Data Sorted by Sales ||||||
|---|---|---|---|---|---|---|---|---|---|
| 46 | 54 | 49 | Unqualified | 2 | 4 | 8 | 2 | 20 | 13 |
| 2 | 1 | 3 | Reviewed |  |  | 1 |  | 1 | 1 |
| 2 | 1 | 1 | Compiled |  |  |  |  | 1 |  |
| 3 | 2 | 1 | Tax Returns |  |  |  |  | 1 |  |
| 41 | 55 | 62 | Other | 10 | 10 | 9 | 9 | 15 | 9 |
| 4/1/21-3/31/22 ALL | 4/1/22-3/31/23 ALL | 4/1/23-3/31/24 ALL |  | 74 (4/1-9/30/23) |||  42 (10/1/23-3/31/24) |||
|  |  |  |  | 0-1MM | 1-3MM | 3-5MM | 5-10MM | 10-25MM | 25MM & OVER |
| 94 | 113 | 116 | NUMBER OF STATEMENTS | 12 | 14 | 18 | 11 | 38 | 23 |
| % | % | % | ASSETS | % | % | % | % | % | % |
| 19.2 | 20.8 | 18.9 | Cash & Equivalents | 16.4 | 27.3 | 15.3 | 18.0 | 18.1 | 19.7 |
| 5.8 | 6.6 | 8.0 | Trade Receivables (net) | 3.2 | 6.7 | 3.4 | 4.9 | 8.0 | 16.6 |
| 2.0 | 3.0 | 3.8 | Inventory | .0 | 1.8 | 2.6 | 3.9 | 5.4 | 5.3 |
| 5.6 | 4.1 | 4.0 | All Other Current | .6 | 3.3 | 6.6 | 3.2 | 5.8 | 1.5 |
| 32.6 | 34.4 | 34.8 | Total Current | 20.2 | 39.1 | 28.0 | 29.9 | 37.3 | 43.1 |
| 38.5 | 37.4 | 41.1 | Fixed Assets (net) | 65.8 | 42.0 | 49.4 | 39.3 | 35.9 | 30.7 |
| 2.3 | 1.4 | 2.2 | Intangibles (net) | 6.3 | 1.3 | 2.7 | 1.4 | 1.8 | 1.4 |
| 26.7 | 26.8 | 21.9 | All Other Non-Current | 7.6 | 17.6 | 19.9 | 29.5 | 25.0 | 24.7 |
| 100.0 | 100.0 | 100.0 | Total | 100.0 | 100.0 | 100.0 | 100.0 | 100.0 | 100.0 |
|  |  |  | LIABILITIES |  |  |  |  |  |  |
| 2.3 | 2.6 | 2.2 | Notes Payable-Short Term | 3.1 | 1.4 | 1.4 | .5 | 3.7 | 1.0 |
| 2.0 | 1.2 | 1.2 | Cur. Mat.-L.T.D. | .3 | 1.8 | 1.7 | .3 | .7 | 2.1 |
| 2.7 | 2.2 | 3.0 | Trade Payables | .9 | 1.7 | 2.2 | .8 | 3.5 | 5.8 |
| .0 | .1 | .0 | Income Taxes Payable | .1 | .0 | .0 | .0 | .0 | .0 |
| 6.5 | 7.4 | 7.1 | All Other Current | 11.5 | 7.2 | 4.3 | 4.0 | 9.0 | 5.5 |
| 13.6 | 13.5 | 13.5 | Total Current | 15.8 | 12.0 | 9.5 | 5.6 | 16.9 | 14.4 |
| 32.7 | 30.9 | 26.7 | Long-Term Debt | 36.6 | 35.2 | 31.3 | 19.8 | 25.4 | 18.4 |
| .0 | .0 | .0 | Deferred Taxes | .0 | .0 | .0 | .0 | .0 | .0 |
| 3.4 | 3.9 | 4.6 | All Other Non-Current | 1.6 | 1.0 | 2.8 | 6.8 | 6.3 | 6.1 |
| 50.4 | 51.6 | 55.1 | Net Worth | 46.0 | 51.8 | 56.4 | 67.8 | 51.4 | 61.1 |
| 100.0 | 100.0 | 100.0 | Total Liabilities & Net Worth | 100.0 | 100.0 | 100.0 | 100.0 | 100.0 | 100.0 |
|  |  |  | INCOME DATA |  |  |  |  |  |  |
| 100.0 | 100.0 | 100.0 | Net Sales | 100.0 | 100.0 | 100.0 | 100.0 | 100.0 | 100.0 |
|  |  |  | Gross Profit |  |  |  |  |  |  |
| 84.4 | 87.4 | 88.0 | Operating Expenses | 84.2 | 75.4 | 93.9 | 65.1 | 92.5 | 96.4 |
| 15.6 | 12.6 | 12.0 | Operating Profit | 15.8 | 24.6 | 6.1 | 34.9 | 7.5 | 3.6 |
| 2.2 | 3.4 | 2.2 | All Other Expenses (net) | 4.6 | 7.9 | 1.6 | 6.4 | .3 | -.8 |
| 13.3 | 9.1 | 9.8 | Profit Before Taxes | 11.2 | 16.7 | 4.5 | 28.5 | 7.3 | 4.3 |
|  |  |  | RATIOS |  |  |  |  |  |  |
| 7.9 | 9.3 | 6.9 |  | 4.1 | 16.5 | 13.5 | 15.5 | 4.9 | 6.8 |
| 3.2 | 3.3 | 2.7 | Current | 1.3 | 1.9 | 2.6 | 7.4 | 2.9 | 2.3 |
| 1.3 | 1.8 | 1.4 |  | .5 | .7 | 1.0 | 2.1 | 1.5 | 1.8 |
| 4.8 | 6.8 | 5.3 |  | 3.5 | 13.3 | 7.4 | 9.0 | 3.8 | 5.1 |
| 2.2 | 2.5 | 1.9 | Quick | 1.3 | 1.5 | 1.3 | 4.2 | 1.8 | 2.0 |
| 1.0 | 1.3 | .9 |  | .5 | .6 | .6 | 2.1 | .8 | 1.1 |
| 0 UND | 2 175.1 | 4 98.9 |  | 0 UND | 0 UND | 3 121.1 | 3 135.5 | 11 32.2 | 5 78.9 |
| 11 31.9 | 18 20.5 | 21 17.7 | Sales/Receivables | 16 22.7 | 6 59.2 | 17 21.0 | 11 33.8 | 21 17.3 | 48 7.6 |
| 41 8.8 | 41 8.9 | 52 7.0 |  | 34 10.8 | 47 7.8 | 52 7.0 | 29 12.7 | 38 9.5 | 69 5.3 |
|  |  |  | Cost of Sales/Inventory |  |  |  |  |  |  |
|  |  |  | Cost of Sales/Payables |  |  |  |  |  |  |
| 1.5 | 1.1 | 1.5 |  | 3.7 | 1.4 | 1.3 | 1.5 | 1.1 | 1.8 |
| 3.5 | 2.8 | 3.7 | Sales/Working Capital | UND | 3.3 | 4.9 | 2.9 | 2.9 | 3.9 |
| 16.8 | 8.6 | 10.1 |  | -6.5 | -38.1 | NM | 8.0 | 6.0 | 7.4 |
| 19.1 | 23.6 | 20.5 |  |  | 18.0 |  | 8.8 | 33.6 |  |
| (64) 6.4 | (78) 4.8 | (82) 3.3 | EBIT/Interest | (15) 4.0 |  | (26) 2.5 | (18) 2.9 |  |  |
| 1.5 | .5 | -.3 |  |  | -1.0 |  | .9 | -2.6 |  |
|  |  |  | Net Profit + Depr., Dep., Amort./Cur. Mat. L/T/D |  |  |  |  |  |  |
| .1 | .2 | .2 |  | .9 | .2 | .4 | .2 | .1 | .1 |
| .5 | .6 | .6 | Fixed/Worth | 1.2 | .5 | .7 | .4 | .6 | .4 |
| 1.2 | 1.4 | 1.4 |  | UND | NM | 2.3 | .9 | 1.8 | 1.0 |
| .3 | .2 | .3 |  | .2 | .2 | .2 | .2 | .4 | .3 |
| .6 | .6 | .7 | Debt/Worth | .9 | .5 | .5 | .4 | 1.0 | .7 |
| 1.7 | 2.2 | 2.0 |  | UND | NM | 2.2 | .8 | 3.4 | 1.1 |
| 20.6 | 15.6 | 15.0 |  |  | 62.4 | 7.2 | 43.0 | 10.7 | 9.0 |
| (86) 7.3 | (107) 6.4 | (108) 4.7 | % Profit Before Taxes/Tangible Net Worth | (11) 13.5 | (16) 4.4 | 18.6 | 4.3 | 2.7 |  |
| 1.1 | -1.1 | -1.0 |  |  | -5.0 | -1.4 | 4.9 | -.9 | -5.4 |
| 10.2 | 9.5 | 9.3 |  | 8.2 | 31.0 | 7.7 | 29.4 | 5.1 | 5.5 |
| 5.3 | 2.7 | 2.6 | % Profit Before Taxes/Total Assets | 4.3 | 9.8 | 2.6 | 13.5 | 1.8 | 1.0 |
| .5 | -.9 | -.8 |  | -1.7 | -3.4 | -1.0 | 4.2 | -.6 | -2.4 |
| 6.9 | 5.7 | 8.3 |  | 1.0 | 10.2 | 2.3 | 5.6 | 14.0 | 10.2 |
| 1.8 | 1.6 | 1.3 | Sales/Net Fixed Assets | .4 | 1.4 | .9 | 2.5 | 1.1 | 5.8 |
| .7 | .6 | .5 |  | .3 | .7 | .4 | 1.1 | .5 | 1.1 |
| .9 | .8 | .8 |  | .7 | 1.1 | .6 | 1.0 | .7 | 2.1 |
| .4 | .4 | .4 | Sales/Total Assets | .4 | .5 | .4 | .5 | .4 | .6 |
| .3 | .2 | .2 |  | .2 | .2 | .2 | .3 | .2 | .4 |
| 1.0 | 1.1 | 1.0 |  |  | 1.2 | 1.9 |  | .7 | .7 |
| (72) 2.2 | (88) 2.9 | (86) 2.6 | % Depr., Dep., Amort./Sales | (11) 3.4 | (11) 2.6 | (32) 4.4 | (21) 1.6 |  |  |
| 6.4 | 6.7 | 7.0 |  |  | 6.9 | 16.8 |  | 8.8 | 5.0 |
|  |  |  | % Officers', Directors' Owners' Comp/Sales |  |  |  |  |  |  |
| 964552M | 1561774M | 1931979M | Net Sales ($) | 7440M | 25149M | 72536M | 85475M | 579091M | 1162288M |
| 2528295M | 4384486M | 4205692M | Total Assets ($) | 31068M | 61782M | 281722M | 262652M | 1752592M | 1815876M |

© RMA 2024    M = $ thousand    MM = $ million
See Pages viii through xx for Explanation of Ratios and Data

# HEALTH CARE—Vocational Rehabilitation Services  NAICS 624310

## Current Data Sorted by Assets

| | | | | | | |
|---|---|---|---|---|---|---|
| | | 1 | 5 | 15 | 2 | 2 |
| | | | 1 | | | |
| | 2 | 2 | | 1 | | |
| 3 | 5 | 18 | 21 | 4 | 9 | |
| | | 39 (4/1-9/30/23) | | 52 (10/1/23-3/31/24) | | |
| 0-500M | 500M-2MM | 2-10MM | 10-50MM | 50-100MM | 100-250MM | |
| 4 | 7 | 26 | 37 | 6 | 11 | |

## Comparative Historical Data

| Type of Statement | | |
|---|---|---|
| Unqualified | 63 | 40 |
| Reviewed | 1 | |
| Compiled | 1 | 1 |
| Tax Returns | 18 | 7 |
| Other | 54 | 40 |
| | 4/1/19-3/31/20 ALL | 4/1/20-3/31/21 ALL |
| NUMBER OF STATEMENTS | 137 | 88 |

| Current % | % | % | % | % | % | | Historical % | % |
|---|---|---|---|---|---|---|---|---|
| | | 28.6 | 25.6 | | 21.0 | **ASSETS** Cash & Equivalents | 28.5 | 36.8 |
| | | 11.7 | 21.3 | | 18.7 | Trade Receivables (net) | 15.8 | 12.1 |
| | | .2 | 2.2 | | 3.3 | Inventory | 2.3 | 1.2 |
| | | 6.2 | 3.9 | | 1.7 | All Other Current | 4.1 | 5.3 |
| | | 46.7 | 52.9 | | 44.7 | Total Current | 50.7 | 55.5 |
| | | 40.8 | 32.5 | | 32.4 | Fixed Assets (net) | 36.9 | 29.8 |
| | | 2.7 | 3.5 | | 2.1 | Intangibles (net) | 2.0 | 1.3 |
| | | 9.8 | 11.0 | | 20.8 | All Other Non-Current | 10.4 | 13.4 |
| | | 100.0 | 100.0 | | 100.0 | Total | 100.0 | 100.0 |
| | | | | | | **LIABILITIES** | | |
| | | 3.3 | 2.5 | | .8 | Notes Payable-Short Term | 1.5 | 2.6 |
| | | 1.2 | 2.3 | | .8 | Cur. Mat.-L.T.D. | 1.5 | 2.2 |
| | | 4.6 | 4.6 | | 12.8 | Trade Payables | 5.3 | 5.3 |
| | | .1 | .0 | | .0 | Income Taxes Payable | .0 | .1 |
| | | 12.0 | 15.6 | | 9.4 | All Other Current | 9.8 | 9.6 |
| | | 21.2 | 25.0 | | 23.9 | Total Current | 18.1 | 19.7 |
| | | 20.2 | 12.5 | | 6.7 | Long-Term Debt | 14.6 | 14.8 |
| | | .0 | .0 | | .0 | Deferred Taxes | .0 | .0 |
| | | 4.1 | 7.4 | | 10.1 | All Other Non-Current | 4.8 | 3.4 |
| | | 54.6 | 55.1 | | 59.3 | Net Worth | 62.4 | 62.1 |
| | | 100.0 | 100.0 | | 100.0 | Total Liabilties & Net Worth | 100.0 | 100.0 |
| | | | | | | **INCOME DATA** | | |
| | | 100.0 | 100.0 | | 100.0 | Net Sales | 100.0 | 100.0 |
| | | | | | | Gross Profit | | |
| | | 89.6 | 96.2 | | 95.4 | Operating Expenses | 98.1 | 96.8 |
| | | 10.4 | 3.8 | | 4.6 | Operating Profit | 1.9 | 3.2 |
| | | 5.1 | .1 | | -.9 | All Other Expenses (net) | -.5 | -1.2 |
| | | 5.3 | 3.7 | | 5.5 | Profit Before Taxes | 2.4 | 4.3 |
| | | | | | | **RATIOS** | | |
| | | 12.0 | 5.3 | | 3.2 | | 5.6 | 6.8 |
| | | 3.8 | 3.1 | | 2.6 | Current | 3.3 | 3.5 |
| | | 1.6 | 1.7 | | 1.2 | | 2.2 | 1.9 |
| | | 8.9 | 4.8 | | 2.9 | | 4.9 | 6.3 |
| | | 2.4 | 2.7 | | 1.9 | Quick | 2.9 | 3.2 |
| | | 1.5 | 1.4 | | 1.2 | | 1.8 | 1.7 |
| | | 0 UND | 31 11.7 | 12 | 29.8 | | 11 34.6 | 11 32.3 |
| | | 28 13.1 | 49 7.5 | 30 | 12.3 | Sales/Receivables | 28 13.2 | 27 13.7 |
| | | 53 6.9 | 72 5.1 | 40 | 9.1 | | 48 7.6 | 47 7.8 |
| | | | | | | Cost of Sales/Inventory | | |
| | | | | | | Cost of Sales/Payables | | |
| | | 1.8 | 2.5 | | 3.0 | | 2.7 | 2.3 |
| | | 4.9 | 4.7 | | 5.6 | Sales/Working Capital | 6.3 | 4.5 |
| | | 11.1 | 12.4 | | 11.7 | | 11.6 | 9.6 |
| | | 70.1 | 48.5 | | | | 12.3 | 25.3 |
| | | (21) 5.4 | (29) 13.2 | | | EBIT/Interest | (101) 3.7 | (65) 3.3 |
| | | -.4 | 1.9 | | | | .3 | -3.9 |
| | | | | | | Net Profit + Depr., Dep., Amort./Cur. Mat. L/T/D | | |
| | | .3 | .3 | | .1 | | .2 | .2 |
| | | .8 | .5 | | .8 | Fixed/Worth | .6 | .4 |
| | | 1.2 | 1.2 | | .9 | | 1.0 | .7 |
| | | .2 | .3 | | .3 | | .2 | .2 |
| | | .7 | .5 | | .4 | Debt/Worth | .5 | .4 |
| | | 1.4 | 1.6 | | 1.9 | | .9 | 1.0 |
| | | 18.7 | 12.3 | | 9.5 | | 9.5 | 14.5 |
| | | (23) 9.8 | (35) 7.5 | | 7.5 | % Profit Before Taxes/Tangible Net Worth | (132) 4.7 | (86) 4.2 |
| | | -7.6 | 2.4 | | 4.3 | | -1.4 | -2.9 |
| | | 14.5 | 8.9 | | 6.2 | | 6.4 | 9.5 |
| | | 3.6 | 5.4 | | 4.2 | % Profit Before Taxes/Total Assets | 2.5 | 2.3 |
| | | -2.5 | 1.5 | | 1.3 | | -1.2 | -1.7 |
| | | 7.9 | 7.5 | | 13.4 | | 11.5 | 34.1 |
| | | 2.7 | 3.6 | | 4.7 | Sales/Net Fixed Assets | 4.1 | 4.5 |
| | | 1.7 | 2.2 | | 1.2 | | 1.8 | 1.8 |
| | | 1.8 | 1.8 | | 1.5 | | 2.5 | 2.3 |
| | | 1.0 | 1.2 | | 1.0 | Sales/Total Assets | 1.4 | 1.2 |
| | | .7 | .8 | | .6 | | .8 | .7 |
| | | .9 | 1.5 | | | | 1.4 | .9 |
| | | (22) 2.8 | (33) 2.3 | | | % Depr., Dep., Amort./Sales | (125) 2.6 | (76) 2.4 |
| | | 4.4 | 2.9 | | | | 3.8 | 3.7 |
| | | | | | | % Officers', Directors' Owners' Comp/Sales | | 2.5 |
| | | | | | | | | (14) 4.2 |
| | | | | | | | | 10.9 |
| 2735M | 25027M | 176531M | 1312003M | 305588M | 2023283M | Net Sales ($) | 4013915M | 2078310M |
| 1087M | 7155M | 157693M | 868736M | 431935M | 1573118M | Total Assets ($) | 2754988M | 1830962M |

M = $ thousand   MM = $ million
See Pages viii through xx for Explanation of Ratios and Data

© RMA 2024

# HEALTH CARE—Vocational Rehabilitation Services  NAICS 624310

## Comparative Historical Data | Current Data Sorted by Sales

| | | | | Type of Statement | | | | | | |
|---|---|---|---|---|---|---|---|---|---|---|
| 33 | 29 | 25 | | Unqualified | 1 | | 1 | 5 | 6 | 12 |
| | | | | Reviewed | | | | | | |
| | 1 | 1 | | Compiled | | 1 | | | | 1 |
| 6 | 2 | 5 | | Tax Returns | 1 | 2 | | 1 | 1 | 23 |
| 37 | 65 | 60 | | Other | 4 | 5 | 3 | 11 | 14 | |
| 4/1/21-3/31/22 ALL | 4/1/22-3/31/23 ALL | 4/1/23-3/31/24 ALL | | | 0-1MM | 39 (4/1-9/30/23) 1-3MM | 3-5MM | 52 (10/1/23-3/31/24) 5-10MM | 10-25MM | 25MM & OVER |
| 76 | 97 | 91 | | NUMBER OF STATEMENTS | 6 | 8 | 4 | 17 | 20 | 36 |
| % | % | % | | ASSETS | % | % | % | % | % | % |
| 36.5 | 30.4 | 28.7 | | Cash & Equivalents | | | | 46.1 | 23.2 | 23.7 |
| 11.5 | 17.3 | 15.6 | | Trade Receivables (net) | | | | 8.5 | 22.9 | 19.2 |
| 2.5 | 2.1 | 1.4 | | Inventory | | | | .3 | 2.3 | 2.2 |
| 3.0 | 3.6 | 4.8 | | All Other Current | | | | 6.8 | 2.5 | 3.4 |
| 53.5 | 53.5 | 50.5 | | Total Current | | | | 61.8 | 51.0 | 48.4 |
| 32.2 | 32.8 | 33.2 | | Fixed Assets (net) | | | | 20.8 | 36.1 | 32.0 |
| 2.5 | 2.0 | 3.7 | | Intangibles (net) | | | | 6.0 | 2.7 | 2.5 |
| 11.8 | 11.7 | 12.6 | | All Other Non-Current | | | | 11.4 | 10.2 | 17.1 |
| 100.0 | 100.0 | 100.0 | | Total | | | | 100.0 | 100.0 | 100.0 |
| | | | | LIABILITIES | | | | | | |
| 1.5 | 3.8 | 4.4 | | Notes Payable-Short Term | | | | 1.4 | 5.2 | 1.9 |
| .9 | 1.2 | 1.6 | | Cur. Mat.-L.T.D. | | | | 1.1 | 2.0 | 2.0 |
| 2.8 | 4.3 | 5.0 | | Trade Payables | | | | 2.9 | 8.2 | 6.2 |
| .1 | .1 | .0 | | Income Taxes Payable | | | | .0 | .1 | .0 |
| 7.8 | 10.6 | 14.5 | | All Other Current | | | | 9.0 | 15.9 | 14.0 |
| 13.1 | 20.0 | 25.5 | | Total Current | | | | 14.4 | 31.4 | 24.1 |
| 12.0 | 14.6 | 14.3 | | Long-Term Debt | | | | 5.7 | 16.1 | 11.9 |
| .0 | .0 | .0 | | Deferred Taxes | | | | .0 | .0 | .0 |
| 1.9 | 2.4 | 10.8 | | All Other Non-Current | | | | 5.1 | 9.9 | 7.6 |
| 73.0 | 63.1 | 49.4 | | Net Worth | | | | 74.8 | 42.6 | 56.4 |
| 100.0 | 100.0 | 100.0 | | Total Liabilities & Net Worth | | | | 100.0 | 100.0 | 100.0 |
| | | | | INCOME DATA | | | | | | |
| 100.0 | 100.0 | 100.0 | | Net Sales | | | | 100.0 | 100.0 | 100.0 |
| | | | | Gross Profit | | | | | | |
| 89.6 | 92.1 | 94.3 | | Operating Expenses | | | | 98.1 | 95.0 | 96.2 |
| 10.4 | 7.9 | 5.7 | | Operating Profit | | | | 1.9 | 5.0 | 3.8 |
| -2.3 | .9 | 1.4 | | All Other Expenses (net) | | | | -1.1 | 1.7 | -1.0 |
| 12.7 | 7.0 | 4.3 | | Profit Before Taxes | | | | 3.0 | 3.3 | 4.8 |
| | | | | RATIOS | | | | | | |
| 8.9 | 7.4 | 7.4 | | Current | | | | 11.0 | 5.3 | 3.7 |
| 4.5 | 3.4 | 3.1 | | | | | | 7.4 | 2.9 | 2.6 |
| 2.6 | 2.0 | 1.6 | | | | | | 2.7 | 1.3 | 1.4 |
| 8.3 | 6.0 | 5.3 | | Quick | | | | 10.7 | 5.1 | 3.7 |
| 4.2 | 3.2 | 2.5 | | | | | | 5.7 | 2.2 | 1.9 |
| 2.4 | 1.6 | 1.3 | | | | | | 2.4 | 1.3 | 1.1 |
| 6  62.5 | 7  52.5 | 4  100.9 | | Sales/Receivables | 0  UND | 31  11.8 | 13  28.9 | | | |
| 27  13.6 | 34  10.8 | 34  10.7 | | | 19  19.0 | 55  6.6 | 39  9.4 | | | |
| 45  8.1 | 57  6.4 | 63  5.8 | | | 38  9.5 | 74  4.9 | 72  5.1 | | | |
| | | | | Cost of Sales/Inventory | | | | | | |
| | | | | Cost of Sales/Payables | | | | | | |
| 2.0 | 1.9 | 2.4 | | Sales/Working Capital | | | | 1.3 | 2.5 | 3.1 |
| 3.3 | 4.2 | 5.4 | | | | | | 2.0 | 5.2 | 6.2 |
| 7.0 | 8.6 | 11.8 | | | | | | 11.1 | 11.6 | 15.1 |
| 146.7 | 30.7 | 48.1 | | EBIT/Interest | | | | 97.9 | 89.1 | 49.4 |
| (53) 40.0 | (69) 6.6 | (66) 6.2 | | | (11) 7.1 | (16) 10.4 | (27) 13.5 | | | |
| 9.5 | -1.0 | 1.3 | | | | | | -9.0 | -.7 | 2.2 |
| | | | | Net Profit + Depr., Dep., Amort./Cur. Mat. L/T/D | | | | | | |
| .2 | .1 | .3 | | Fixed/Worth | | | | .1 | .5 | .3 |
| .4 | .5 | .6 | | | | | | .3 | .7 | .7 |
| .8 | .9 | 1.0 | | | | | | .4 | 1.1 | 1.1 |
| .1 | .1 | .2 | | Debt/Worth | | | | .1 | .3 | .4 |
| .3 | .4 | .6 | | | | | | .4 | .6 | .6 |
| .7 | 1.1 | 1.6 | | | | | | .7 | 1.6 | 1.9 |
| 36.1 | 18.3 | 15.7 | | % Profit Before Taxes/Tangible Net Worth | | | | 15.0 | 20.4 | 12.3 |
| (74) 17.8 | (92) 8.1 | (84) 8.2 | | | | | | 2.0 (18) 9.6 | (35) 8.2 | |
| 9.3 | -1.8 | .7 | | | | | | -7.8 | -5.2 | 3.2 |
| 24.5 | 16.3 | 10.0 | | % Profit Before Taxes/Total Assets | | | | 13.4 | 14.8 | 7.4 |
| 13.4 | 5.5 | 5.6 | | | | | | 1.8 | 6.9 | 5.2 |
| 6.8 | -1.2 | -.2 | | | | | | -3.9 | -9.4 | 1.7 |
| 12.5 | 12.9 | 13.1 | | Sales/Net Fixed Assets | | | | 57.3 | 7.8 | 17.3 |
| 3.9 | 3.9 | 3.7 | | | | | | 6.6 | 3.7 | 4.1 |
| 1.9 | 1.7 | 2.0 | | | | | | 2.2 | 2.3 | 2.0 |
| 1.8 | 1.7 | 1.8 | | Sales/Total Assets | | | | 2.4 | 1.9 | 1.8 |
| 1.2 | 1.1 | 1.1 | | | | | | 1.0 | 1.3 | 1.3 |
| .8 | .7 | .8 | | | | | | .8 | .9 | .9 |
| 1.2 | 1.0 | 1.3 | | % Depr., Dep., Amort./Sales | | | | .7 | 1.1 | 1.5 |
| (65) 2.6 | (83) 2.4 | (71) 2.4 | | | (12) 2.3 | (16) 2.0 | (32) 2.4 | | | |
| 3.8 | 3.4 | 3.5 | | | | | | 3.6 | 3.3 | 3.0 |
| 1.5 | 1.0 | | | % Officers', Directors' Owners' Comp/Sales | | | | | | |
| (10) 3.0 | (11) 3.0 | | | | | | | | | |
| 14.3 | 4.2 | | | | | | | | | |
| 2885458M | 3132357M | 3845167M | | Net Sales ($) | 3936M | 13292M | 16022M | 123532M | 339388M | 3348997M |
| 2497680M | 3019473M | 3039724M | | Total Assets ($) | 7182M | 24099M | 36272M | 116636M | 419323M | 2436212M |

© RMA 2024  
M = $ thousand    MM = $ million  
See Pages viii through xx for Explanation of Ratios and Data

# HEALTH CARE—Child Care Services  NAICS 624410

## Current Data Sorted by Assets / Comparative Historical Data

| | | | | | | | Type of Statement | | | | |
|---|---|---|---|---|---|---|---|---|---|---|---|
| 1 | 3 | 11 | 6 | 1 | 3 | | Unqualified | | 44 | | 30 |
| 1 | | | 1 | | | | Reviewed | | 5 | | 3 |
| 5 | 8 | 10 | 1 | | | | Compiled | | 34 | | 12 |
| 38 | 47 | 27 | 2 | | 2 | | Tax Returns | | 158 | | 62 |
| 62 | 68 | 76 | 14 | 6 | 4 | | Other | | 207 | | 155 |
| | 51 (4/1-9/30/23) | | 346 (10/1/23-3/31/24) | | | | | | 4/1/19-3/31/20 ALL | | 4/1/20-3/31/21 ALL |
| 0-500M | 500M-2MM | 2-10MM | 10-50MM | 50-100MM | 100-250MM | | | | | | |
| 107 | 126 | 124 | 24 | 7 | 9 | | NUMBER OF STATEMENTS | | 448 | | 262 |
| % | % | % | % | % | % | | ASSETS | | % | | % |
| 47.6 | 35.1 | 19.0 | 16.6 | | | | Cash & Equivalents | | 28.6 | | 42.9 |
| 1.6 | 1.6 | 1.8 | 10.0 | | | | Trade Receivables (net) | | 3.8 | | 3.0 |
| .2 | .0 | .0 | .0 | | | | Inventory | | .2 | | .1 |
| 3.1 | 1.5 | 2.2 | 6.3 | | | | All Other Current | | 3.6 | | 2.6 |
| 52.6 | 38.3 | 23.0 | 32.9 | | | | Total Current | | 36.2 | | 48.6 |
| 30.6 | 30.5 | 61.8 | 53.9 | | | | Fixed Assets (net) | | 44.2 | | 33.8 |
| 9.5 | 9.4 | 5.0 | 2.1 | | | | Intangibles (net) | | 8.1 | | 9.3 |
| 7.3 | 21.8 | 10.2 | 11.1 | | | | All Other Non-Current | | 11.5 | | 8.3 |
| 100.0 | 100.0 | 100.0 | 100.0 | | | | Total | | 100.0 | | 100.0 |
| | | | | | | | LIABILITIES | | | | |
| 5.5 | 2.0 | 1.3 | 2.9 | | | | Notes Payable-Short Term | | 4.7 | | 11.2 |
| 1.9 | 2.5 | 2.3 | 2.7 | | | | Cur. Mat.-L.T.D. | | 2.5 | | 3.1 |
| 1.8 | .6 | 1.5 | 6.1 | | | | Trade Payables | | 3.1 | | 1.5 |
| .0 | .0 | .0 | .0 | | | | Income Taxes Payable | | .1 | | .0 |
| 38.4 | 12.5 | 6.8 | 8.6 | | | | All Other Current | | 16.3 | | 19.2 |
| 47.7 | 17.6 | 11.8 | 20.3 | | | | Total Current | | 26.6 | | 35.1 |
| 35.9 | 31.1 | 55.7 | 28.8 | | | | Long-Term Debt | | 35.0 | | 37.2 |
| .0 | .0 | .0 | .0 | | | | Deferred Taxes | | .0 | | .0 |
| 9.7 | 8.6 | 2.6 | 13.4 | | | | All Other Non-Current | | 7.3 | | 6.4 |
| 6.6 | 42.7 | 29.9 | 37.4 | | | | Net Worth | | 30.9 | | 21.2 |
| 100.0 | 100.0 | 100.0 | 100.0 | | | | Total Liabilities & Net Worth | | 100.0 | | 100.0 |
| | | | | | | | INCOME DATA | | | | |
| 100.0 | 100.0 | 100.0 | 100.0 | | | | Net Sales | | 100.0 | | 100.0 |
| | | | | | | | Gross Profit | | | | |
| 93.1 | 86.2 | 73.9 | 77.6 | | | | Operating Expenses | | 85.2 | | 89.6 |
| 6.9 | 13.8 | 26.1 | 22.4 | | | | Operating Profit | | 14.8 | | 10.4 |
| -.9 | 2.6 | 9.4 | 6.9 | | | | All Other Expenses (net) | | 4.1 | | 1.1 |
| 7.8 | 11.2 | 16.6 | 15.5 | | | | Profit Before Taxes | | 10.7 | | 9.3 |
| | | | | | | | RATIOS | | | | |
| 8.0 | 13.9 | 6.4 | 4.8 | | | | | | 5.8 | | 8.2 |
| 2.7 | 4.5 | 2.1 | 1.6 | | | Current | | | 1.6 | | 2.3 |
| .8 | 1.1 | .4 | .9 | | | | | | .6 | | .9 |
| 7.2 | 13.6 | 5.6 | 4.0 | | | | | | 5.3 | | 7.4 |
| 2.4 | 4.0 | 1.9 | 1.0 | | | Quick | | | 1.5 | | 2.1 |
| .8 | 1.0 | .4 | .2 | | | | | | .5 | | .8 |
| 0  UND | 0  UND | 0  UND | 0  UND | | | | | 0 | UND | 0 | UND |
| 0  UND | 0  UND | 0  UND | 7  50.8 | | | Sales/Receivables | | 0 | UND | 0 | UND |
| 0  UND | 0  UND | 0  UND | 24  15.4 | | | | | 3 | 141.4 | 3 | 121.8 |
| | | | | | | | Cost of Sales/Inventory | | | | |
| | | | | | | | Cost of Sales/Payables | | | | |
| 11.7 | 4.2 | 3.5 | 3.2 | | | | | | 8.8 | | 4.2 |
| 34.6 | 11.2 | 8.6 | 8.6 | | | Sales/Working Capital | | | 32.1 | | 11.0 |
| -102.3 | 175.3 | -9.0 | NM | | | | | | -34.9 | | -116.7 |
| 44.1 | 30.9 | 9.4 | 178.6 | | | | | | 29.6 | | 23.4 |
| (47) 14.6 | (68) 7.5 | (75) 3.9 | (16) 8.2 | | | EBIT/Interest | | (285) | 6.5 | (140) | 3.6 |
| 2.2 | .6 | 1.8 | 2.9 | | | | | | 2.0 | | .0 |
| | | | | | | | | | 32.4 | | |
| | | | | | | | Net Profit + Depr., Dep., Amort./Cur. Mat. L/T/D | (11) | 4.2 | | |
| | | | | | | | | | .9 | | |
| .1 | .0 | .8 | .6 | | | | | | .3 | | .1 |
| .7 | .5 | 4.2 | 1.8 | | | Fixed/Worth | | | 1.3 | | .9 |
| -13.8 | 12.9 | 40.4 | 2.7 | | | | | | 20.2 | | UND |
| .2 | .2 | 1.1 | 1.0 | | | | | | .4 | | .5 |
| 1.7 | .9 | 3.8 | 2.3 | | | Debt/Worth | | | 2.0 | | 2.1 |
| -2.9 | 24.3 | 111.8 | 5.3 | | | | | | 153.1 | | -17.1 |
| 167.4 | 80.9 | 72.3 | 31.3 | | | | | | 125.3 | | 107.8 |
| (73) 77.1 | (98) 37.7 | (96) 24.7 | (23) 13.1 | | | % Profit Before Taxes/Tangible Net Worth | (341) | 42.8 | (189) | 44.3 |
| 2.5 | 8.6 | 9.7 | 2.1 | | | | | | 10.7 | | 7.5 |
| 89.9 | 41.9 | 16.7 | 10.6 | | | | | | 45.0 | | 39.9 |
| 37.7 | 16.5 | 6.4 | 3.7 | | | % Profit Before Taxes/Total Assets | | | 13.8 | | 8.7 |
| 2.0 | .3 | 1.7 | 1.5 | | | | | | 2.9 | | -.4 |
| 253.0 | 160.8 | 4.1 | 3.8 | | | | | | 43.7 | | 71.9 |
| 36.1 | 14.7 | 1.0 | 1.2 | | | Sales/Net Fixed Assets | | | 11.2 | | 14.3 |
| 12.7 | 3.8 | .3 | .3 | | | | | | 1.3 | | 1.9 |
| 10.3 | 3.0 | 1.0 | 1.8 | | | | | | 5.4 | | 3.7 |
| 6.5 | 1.9 | .7 | .8 | | | Sales/Total Assets | | | 2.6 | | 2.1 |
| 3.5 | 1.2 | .3 | .2 | | | | | | .9 | | .9 |
| .5 | .8 | 1.8 | .7 | | | | | | .8 | | .9 |
| (51) 1.4 | (65) 2.3 | (82) 4.6 | (19) 2.5 | | | % Depr., Dep., Amort./Sales | (273) | 2.3 | (143) | 2.4 |
| 3.2 | 6.1 | 11.4 | 3.9 | | | | | | 5.4 | | 7.4 |
| 2.8 | 2.3 | 2.7 | | | | | | | 2.8 | | 4.0 |
| (39) 5.0 | (44) 4.0 | (28) 3.7 | | | | % Officers', Directors' Owners' Comp/Sales | (150) | 5.4 | (78) | 6.5 |
| 8.9 | 5.9 | 6.8 | | | | | | | 8.4 | | 10.5 |
| 183325M | 280717M | 467548M | 869640M | 712396M | 4965713M | | Net Sales ($) | | 3079361M | | 1450291M |
| 27629M | 142953M | 497774M | 535679M | 514707M | 1440689M | | Total Assets ($) | | 1853058M | | 1297055M |

M = $ thousand    MM = $ million
See Pages viii through xx for Explanation of Ratios and Data

© RMA 2024

# HEALTH CARE—Child Care Services  NAICS 624410

## Comparative Historical Data | Current Data Sorted by Sales

| Comparative Historical Data | | | Type of Statement | Current Data Sorted by Sales | | | | | |
|---|---|---|---|---|---|---|---|---|---|
| 25 | 24 | 25 | Unqualified | 1 | 3 | 6 | 4 | 3 | 8 |
| 3 | 4 | 2 | Reviewed | | 1 | | | | 1 |
| 12 | 16 | 24 | Compiled | 4 | 12 | 6 | 1 | 1 | |
| 68 | 123 | 116 | Tax Returns | 22 | 76 | 12 | 3 | 1 | 2 |
| 187 | 194 | 230 | Other | 54 | 105 | 28 | 19 | 8 | 16 |
| 4/1/21-3/31/22 ALL | 4/1/22-3/31/23 ALL | 4/1/23-3/31/24 ALL | | 51 (4/1-9/30/23) | | | 346 (10/1/23-3/31/24) | | |
| | | | | 0-1MM | 1-3MM | 3-5MM | 5-10MM | 10-25MM | 25MM & OVER |
| 295 | 361 | 397 | NUMBER OF STATEMENTS | 81 | 197 | 52 | 27 | 13 | 27 |
| % | % | % | ASSETS | % | % | % | % | % | % |
| 42.5 | 36.1 | 32.1 | Cash & Equivalents | 24.8 | 34.1 | 34.6 | 39.4 | 29.4 | 28.7 |
| 2.6 | 3.2 | 2.4 | Trade Receivables (net) | 1.5 | .8 | 1.9 | 4.6 | 6.9 | 13.1 |
| .0 | .5 | .1 | Inventory | .2 | .0 | .0 | .0 | .0 | .0 |
| 3.1 | 3.2 | 2.7 | All Other Current | 2.1 | 2.1 | 4.6 | .7 | 1.0 | 8.3 |
| 48.2 | 43.0 | 37.2 | Total Current | 28.6 | 37.0 | 41.1 | 44.6 | 37.3 | 50.1 |
| 35.0 | 39.8 | 41.8 | Fixed Assets (net) | 60.0 | 37.5 | 36.0 | 37.0 | 50.2 | 30.3 |
| 6.5 | 6.9 | 7.4 | Intangibles (net) | 4.3 | 10.8 | 4.6 | 3.6 | 3.0 | 3.0 |
| 10.3 | 10.3 | 13.6 | All Other Non-Current | 7.1 | 14.7 | 18.3 | 14.7 | 9.5 | 16.6 |
| 100.0 | 100.0 | 100.0 | Total | 100.0 | 100.0 | 100.0 | 100.0 | 100.0 | 100.0 |
| | | | LIABILITIES | | | | | | |
| 5.2 | 5.3 | 2.7 | Notes Payable-Short Term | 4.2 | 2.8 | 1.8 | .7 | .2 | 2.7 |
| 2.0 | 2.4 | 2.4 | Cur. Mat.-L.T.D. | 2.2 | 2.6 | 1.5 | 1.3 | 4.7 | 3.8 |
| 1.4 | 2.4 | 1.7 | Trade Payables | .4 | 1.1 | .8 | 1.7 | 4.6 | 10.8 |
| .1 | .0 | .0 | Income Taxes Payable | .0 | .0 | .0 | .0 | .0 | .0 |
| 14.4 | 11.9 | 17.3 | All Other Current | 13.6 | 15.1 | 37.2 | 16.8 | 7.7 | 11.3 |
| 23.0 | 22.1 | 24.2 | Total Current | 20.4 | 21.6 | 41.3 | 20.5 | 17.3 | 28.6 |
| 37.2 | 37.1 | 40.0 | Long-Term Debt | 56.8 | 40.6 | 32.1 | 21.9 | 29.9 | 22.9 |
| .1 | .0 | .0 | Deferred Taxes | .0 | .0 | .0 | .0 | .0 | .1 |
| 6.0 | 6.7 | 7.8 | All Other Non-Current | 2.9 | 10.4 | 2.6 | 4.7 | 3.2 | 18.9 |
| 33.6 | 34.0 | 28.0 | Net Worth | 19.8 | 27.4 | 24.0 | 52.9 | 49.6 | 29.5 |
| 100.0 | 100.0 | 100.0 | Total Liabilities & Net Worth | 100.0 | 100.0 | 100.0 | 100.0 | 100.0 | 100.0 |
| | | | INCOME DATA | | | | | | |
| 100.0 | 100.0 | 100.0 | Net Sales | 100.0 | 100.0 | 100.0 | 100.0 | 100.0 | 100.0 |
| | | | Gross Profit | | | | | | |
| 83.7 | 83.2 | 83.9 | Operating Expenses | 68.4 | 87.0 | 88.0 | 89.5 | 88.5 | 92.9 |
| 16.3 | 16.8 | 16.1 | Operating Profit | 31.6 | 13.0 | 12.0 | 10.5 | 11.5 | 7.1 |
| 1.8 | 2.6 | 4.0 | All Other Expenses (net) | 18.0 | 1.0 | -1.7 | -.4 | .5 | .4 |
| 14.5 | 14.2 | 12.1 | Profit Before Taxes | 13.6 | 12.0 | 13.7 | 11.0 | 11.0 | 6.7 |
| | | | RATIOS | | | | | | |
| 11.5 | 12.5 | 8.8 | | 6.3 | 12.9 | 10.9 | 4.4 | 7.8 | 3.6 |
| 3.1 | 2.9 | 2.6 | Current | 1.6 | 4.0 | 1.8 | 3.7 | 4.3 | 1.6 |
| 1.1 | 1.1 | .8 | | .5 | .9 | .6 | 1.5 | .7 | 1.1 |
| 11.1 | 11.5 | 8.2 | | 5.4 | 11.1 | 5.6 | 4.4 | 7.3 | 2.1 |
| 2.7 | 2.6 | 2.3 | Quick | 1.3 | 3.6 | 1.7 | 3.7 | 4.2 | 1.2 |
| 1.0 | .9 | .7 | | .4 | .7 | .5 | 1.5 | .7 | .9 |
| 0 UND | 0 UND | 0 UND | | 0 UND | 0 UND | 0 UND | 0 UND | 0 UND | 0 999.8 |
| 0 UND | 0 UND | 0 UND | Sales/Receivables | 0 UND | 0 UND | 0 UND | 0 UND | 4 93.0 | 14 25.4 |
| 0 UND | 0 999.8 | 0 UND | | 0 UND | 0 UND | 0 UND | 16 22.2 | 17 22.1 | 24 14.9 |
| | | | Cost of Sales/Inventory | | | | | | |
| | | | Cost of Sales/Payables | | | | | | |
| 3.9 | 3.7 | 5.0 | | 5.0 | 5.0 | 8.2 | 4.4 | 2.4 | 6.0 |
| 8.4 | 9.8 | 18.5 | Sales/Working Capital | 27.0 | 19.7 | 39.4 | 6.3 | 4.4 | 19.9 |
| 73.1 | 129.4 | -81.1 | | -8.9 | -265.7 | -32.6 | 28.9 | -84.4 | 165.5 |
| 47.3 | 59.1 | 28.8 | | 15.5 | 32.0 | 57.2 | 28.8 | 287.0 | 36.7 |
| (157) 13.4 | (220) 9.5 | (216) 6.6 | EBIT/Interest | (21) 4.0 | (123) 4.2 | (28) 8.8 | (17) 9.4 | (10) 12.0 | (17) 10.9 |
| 3.6 | 2.5 | 1.9 | | .2 | 1.8 | 1.1 | 5.3 | 4.1 | 3.6 |
| | | 27.4 | Net Profit + Depr., Dep., | | | | | | |
| | (10) 2.8 | | Amort./Cur. Mat. L/T/D | | | | | | |
| | | 1.2 | | | | | | | |
| .1 | .1 | .1 | | .4 | .1 | .1 | .2 | .5 | .2 |
| .9 | 1.1 | 1.1 | Fixed/Worth | 3.8 | 1.2 | .8 | .7 | 1.5 | .7 |
| 12.4 | 6.7 | 17.3 | | NM | -22.5 | 9.0 | 1.6 | 4.2 | 1.7 |
| .4 | .4 | .3 | | .9 | .3 | .2 | .3 | .2 | .5 |
| 2.3 | 2.0 | 2.1 | Debt/Worth | 4.8 | 2.1 | 1.2 | 1.1 | 1.3 | 1.7 |
| 195.8 | 9.8 | 124.0 | | -38.6 | -13.0 | 11.3 | 1.9 | 3.8 | 5.4 |
| 99.4 | 99.1 | 89.9 | | 49.0 | 99.8 | 123.4 | 87.0 | 53.4 | 30.6 |
| (224) 39.2 | (293) 40.0 | (303) 28.8 | % Profit Before Taxes/Tangible Net Worth | (58) 11.7 | (141) 41.8 | (43) 44.4 | (26) 25.0 | (11) 27.3 | (24) 11.4 |
| 10.6 | 8.8 | 6.8 | | -2.3 | 14.9 | 6.8 | .5 | 10.8 | .8 |
| 44.6 | 39.6 | 37.5 | | 14.1 | 42.0 | 76.3 | 58.8 | 19.2 | 11.0 |
| 15.6 | 12.0 | 10.2 | % Profit Before Taxes/Total Assets | 3.1 | 15.5 | 24.6 | 13.7 | 12.4 | 3.6 |
| 3.3 | 2.4 | 1.3 | | -.5 | 3.9 | 1.0 | .3 | 5.6 | .8 |
| 60.9 | 47.7 | 55.1 | | 23.7 | 68.0 | 117.8 | 35.5 | 32.5 | 70.4 |
| 11.2 | 7.5 | 9.0 | Sales/Net Fixed Assets | .4 | 14.1 | 10.7 | 6.6 | 2.4 | 6.4 |
| 1.4 | 1.2 | 1.0 | | .1 | 1.4 | 2.6 | 1.7 | 1.2 | 2.9 |
| 3.4 | 3.2 | 4.0 | | 2.3 | 4.3 | 6.8 | 3.7 | 3.2 | 3.5 |
| 1.9 | 1.5 | 1.6 | Sales/Total Assets | .4 | 1.7 | 2.6 | 2.0 | 1.1 | 1.6 |
| .7 | .7 | .7 | | .1 | .9 | 1.0 | 1.1 | .6 | .7 |
| .8 | 1.2 | 1.1 | | 3.4 | 1.2 | .6 | 1.2 | .6 | .3 |
| (159) 2.7 | (205) 2.8 | (229) 2.5 | % Depr., Dep., Amort./Sales | (47) 13.1 | (104) 2.7 | (29) 1.7 | (15) 1.8 | (12) 1.9 | (22) .8 |
| 6.2 | 7.7 | 5.8 | | 25.3 | 4.8 | 2.8 | 2.7 | 3.6 | 2.9 |
| 2.6 | 3.0 | 2.4 | | | 3.0 | 2.1 | | | |
| (82) 4.4 | (107) 5.8 | (117) 4.0 | % Officers', Directors' Owners' Comp/Sales | (77) | (17) 3.6 | | | | |
| 9.5 | 9.5 | 6.9 | | | 6.8 | 4.9 | | | |
| 2688604M | 3444002M | 7479339M | Net Sales ($) | 36704M | 385389M | 187266M | 175671M | 184332M | 6509977M |
| 1723635M | 2141780M | 3159431M | Total Assets ($) | 147946M | 389649M | 126035M | 120446M | 177737M | 2197618M |

© RMA 2024   M = $ thousand   MM = $ million
See Pages viii through xx for Explanation of Ratios and Data

# ARTS, ENTERTAINMENT, AND RECREATION

ENTERTAINMENT—Theater Companies and Dinner Theaters  NAICS 711110

**Current Data Sorted by Assets** | **Comparative Historical Data**

| | | | | | | | | | |
|---|---|---|---|---|---|---|---|---|---|
| | | | | | | Type of Statement | | | |
| | | 2 | 8 | 6 | 4 | 2 | Unqualified | 44 | 24 |
| | | | 1 | | 1 | | Reviewed | 4 | 2 |
| | | | 1 | | | | Compiled | 1 | |
| 2 | | 13 | 8 | 1 | | | Tax Returns | 4 | 1 |
| | 1 | | | 7 | 5 | 1 | Other | 25 | 15 |
| 0-500M | 500M-2MM | 32 (4/1-9/30/23) 2-10MM | 10-50MM | 20 (10/1/23-3/31/24) 50-100MM | 100-250MM | | 4/1/19-3/31/20 ALL | 4/1/20-3/31/21 ALL |
| 2 | 6 | 17 | 14 | 10 | 3 | NUMBER OF STATEMENTS | 78 | 42 |
| % | % | % | % | % | % | ASSETS | % | % |
| | | 33.8 | 10.4 | 14.9 | | Cash & Equivalents | 20.4 | 32.8 |
| | | 2.2 | 6.4 | 3.8 | | Trade Receivables (net) | 6.9 | 7.1 |
| | | .1 | 1.7 | .3 | | Inventory | .8 | .6 |
| | | 4.4 | 3.8 | .6 | | All Other Current | 5.7 | 2.8 |
| | | 40.5 | 22.3 | 19.5 | | Total Current | 33.8 | 43.3 |
| | | 35.5 | 43.0 | 45.0 | | Fixed Assets (net) | 44.2 | 38.1 |
| | | 3.9 | .5 | 3.8 | | Intangibles (net) | 2.4 | .4 |
| | | 20.1 | 34.2 | 31.7 | | All Other Non-Current | 19.6 | 18.2 |
| | | 100.0 | 100.0 | 100.0 | | Total | 100.0 | 100.0 |
| | | | | | | LIABILITIES | | |
| | | 2.0 | 2.1 | 3.4 | | Notes Payable-Short Term | 2.2 | 6.5 |
| | | 1.8 | 3.5 | .2 | | Cur. Mat.-L.T.D. | 2.0 | .7 |
| | | 3.0 | .7 | 1.4 | | Trade Payables | 4.1 | 3.1 |
| | | .0 | .0 | .0 | | Income Taxes Payable | .2 | .3 |
| | | 9.5 | 13.9 | 3.2 | | All Other Current | 13.7 | 12.8 |
| | | 16.2 | 20.2 | 8.2 | | Total Current | 22.2 | 23.4 |
| | | 15.8 | 10.4 | 16.2 | | Long-Term Debt | 16.9 | 19.6 |
| | | .0 | .0 | .0 | | Deferred Taxes | .0 | .0 |
| | | 7.0 | 5.4 | 6.6 | | All Other Non-Current | 4.4 | 5.4 |
| | | 61.0 | 63.9 | 69.0 | | Net Worth | 56.5 | 51.6 |
| | | 100.0 | 100.0 | 100.0 | | Total Liabilities & Net Worth | 100.0 | 100.0 |
| | | | | | | INCOME DATA | | |
| | | 100.0 | 100.0 | 100.0 | | Net Sales | 100.0 | 100.0 |
| | | 101.1 | 106.0 | 87.7 | | Gross Profit Operating Expenses | 91.4 | 94.2 |
| | | -1.1 | -6.0 | 12.3 | | Operating Profit | 8.6 | 5.8 |
| | | -1.7 | 4.1 | -2.0 | | All Other Expenses (net) | 1.5 | .6 |
| | | .7 | -10.2 | 14.3 | | Profit Before Taxes | 7.1 | 5.2 |
| | | | | | | RATIOS | | |
| | | 22.4 | 1.7 | 5.7 | | | 5.8 | 10.7 |
| | | 4.3 | 1.0 | 2.9 | | Current | 1.6 | 2.9 |
| | | 1.1 | .5 | 1.5 | | | .6 | 1.2 |
| | | 22.4 | 1.4 | 5.7 | | | 4.2 | 10.6 |
| | | 3.6 | .8 | 2.8 | | Quick | 1.1 | 2.5 |
| | | .8 | .3 | 1.5 | | | .4 | 1.0 |
| | | 1 707.1 | 1 285.6 | 4 102.1 | | | 0 UND | 5 75.4 |
| | | 10 38.1 | 15 24.2 | 35 10.4 | | Sales/Receivables | 11 33.2 | 19 19.2 |
| | | 28 13.1 | 51 7.1 | 94 3.9 | | | 38 9.7 | 66 5.5 |
| | | | | | | Cost of Sales/Inventory | | |
| | | | | | | Cost of Sales/Payables | | |
| | | 1.5 | 4.4 | 2.9 | | | 2.5 | 1.6 |
| | | 2.4 | NM | 4.1 | | Sales/Working Capital | 14.2 | 3.9 |
| | | NM | -5.4 | 21.6 | | | -12.5 | 29.9 |
| | | | | | | | 14.9 | 1.2 |
| | | | | | | EBIT/Interest | (50) 1.9 | (21) -3.5 |
| | | | | | | | -2.5 | -17.0 |
| | | | | | | Net Profit + Depr., Dep., Amort./Cur. Mat. L/T/D | | |
| | | .1 | .2 | .5 | | | .2 | .2 |
| | | .4 | .7 | .8 | | Fixed/Worth | .8 | .7 |
| | | .8 | 1.0 | 1.1 | | | 1.4 | 1.2 |
| | | .1 | .2 | .2 | | | .1 | .2 |
| | | .6 | .5 | .3 | | Debt/Worth | .5 | .5 |
| | | 1.0 | 1.3 | .9 | | | 2.1 | 1.5 |
| | | 8.7 | 12.7 | | | | 27.3 | 9.9 |
| | | (16) -2.0 | -10.5 | | | % Profit Before Taxes/Tangible Net Worth | (72) 4.4 | (39) -2.0 |
| | | -17.0 | -32.0 | | | | -2.6 | -20.8 |
| | | 4.7 | 9.3 | 15.9 | | | 11.7 | 6.5 |
| | | .4 | -3.9 | 3.2 | | % Profit Before Taxes/Total Assets | 2.5 | -1.8 |
| | | -12.7 | -16.3 | .4 | | | -2.3 | -5.8 |
| | | 125.7 | 3.4 | 6.1 | | | 8.3 | 10.7 |
| | | 2.4 | 1.8 | .5 | | Sales/Net Fixed Assets | 2.3 | 2.0 |
| | | 1.1 | .4 | .4 | | | .6 | .7 |
| | | 1.3 | 1.1 | .6 | | | 1.7 | 1.2 |
| | | .7 | .5 | .3 | | Sales/Total Assets | .7 | .6 |
| | | .5 | .3 | .2 | | | .3 | .3 |
| | | 1.7 | 2.0 | | | | 1.6 | 2.2 |
| | | (11) 3.5 | (12) 4.9 | | | % Depr., Dep., Amort./Sales | (63) 3.8 | (36) 3.7 |
| | | 8.5 | 13.5 | | | | 8.6 | 8.9 |
| | | | | | | % Officers', Directors' Owners' Comp/Sales | | |
| 1387M | 8538M | 69555M | 155114M | 323645M | 290616M | Net Sales ($) | 1650779M | 481310M |
| 457M | 5520M | 87418M | 288003M | 739617M | 495472M | Total Assets ($) | 2238712M | 1186871M |

© RMA 2024

M = $ thousand    MM = $ million
See Pages viii through xx for Explanation of Ratios and Data

## ENTERTAINMENT—Theater Companies and Dinner Theaters  NAICS 711110

### Comparative Historical Data / Current Data Sorted by Sales

| | | | | | | | | | |
|---|---|---|---|---|---|---|---|---|---|
| 12 | 24 | 22 | Type of Statement Unqualified | 1 | 2 | 3 | 7 | 8 | 1 |
| 1 | 2 | 1 | Reviewed | | | | | | 1 |
| | 1 | 1 | Compiled | | | | 1 | | |
| 5 | 6 | 4 | Tax Returns | 3 | | | 4 | 1 | |
| 12 | 21 | 24 | Other | 3 | 4 | 4 | 4 | 6 | 3 |
| 4/1/21-3/31/22 ALL | 4/1/22-3/31/23 ALL | 4/1/23-3/31/24 ALL | | | 32 (4/1-9/30/23) | | | 20 (10/1/23-3/31/24) | |
| | | | | 0-1MM | 1-3MM | 3-5MM | 5-10MM | 10-25MM | 25MM & OVER |
| 30 | 54 | 52 | NUMBER OF STATEMENTS | 7 | 6 | 7 | 12 | 15 | 5 |
| % | % | % | **ASSETS** | % | % | % | % | % | % |
| 37.2 | 28.3 | 23.3 | Cash & Equivalents | | | | 29.6 | 12.2 | |
| 2.6 | 5.6 | 4.2 | Trade Receivables (net) | | | | 2.3 | 7.2 | |
| 1.7 | .3 | .7 | Inventory | | | | .1 | .1 | |
| 4.5 | 2.5 | 4.2 | All Other Current | | | | 5.0 | 3.3 | |
| 46.0 | 36.7 | 32.3 | Total Current | | | | 37.1 | 22.8 | |
| 40.5 | 43.7 | 38.7 | Fixed Assets (net) | | | | 40.8 | 41.0 | |
| 1.2 | 5.1 | 3.2 | Intangibles (net) | | | | 5.0 | .4 | |
| 12.3 | 14.6 | 25.8 | All Other Non-Current | | | | 17.2 | 35.8 | |
| 100.0 | 100.0 | 100.0 | Total | | | | 100.0 | 100.0 | |
| | | | **LIABILITIES** | | | | | | |
| 5.5 | .8 | 2.3 | Notes Payable-Short Term | | | | .5 | 4.5 | |
| .3 | 1.2 | 1.6 | Cur. Mat.-L.T.D. | | | | 2.6 | 1.5 | |
| 2.7 | 3.4 | 2.4 | Trade Payables | | | | 3.2 | .8 | |
| .0 | .0 | .0 | Income Taxes Payable | | | | .0 | .0 | |
| 5.8 | 10.3 | 9.7 | All Other Current | | | | 9.5 | 12.9 | |
| 14.3 | 15.6 | 16.1 | Total Current | | | | 15.8 | 19.8 | |
| 16.8 | 13.7 | 14.9 | Long-Term Debt | | | | 17.9 | 6.2 | |
| .2 | .0 | .0 | Deferred Taxes | | | | .0 | .0 | |
| 5.2 | 7.2 | 6.3 | All Other Non-Current | | | | 9.7 | 3.6 | |
| 63.1 | 63.4 | 62.7 | Net Worth | | | | 56.6 | 70.3 | |
| 100.0 | 100.0 | 100.0 | Total Liabilities & Net Worth | | | | 100.0 | 100.0 | |
| | | | **INCOME DATA** | | | | | | |
| 100.0 | 100.0 | 100.0 | Net Sales | | | | 100.0 | 100.0 | |
| | | | Gross Profit | | | | | | |
| 84.2 | 97.8 | 99.5 | Operating Expenses | | | | 109.3 | 103.9 | |
| 15.8 | 2.2 | .5 | Operating Profit | | | | -9.3 | -3.9 | |
| .5 | 1.3 | .0 | All Other Expenses (net) | | | | 3.1 | -3.2 | |
| 15.2 | .9 | .5 | Profit Before Taxes | | | | -12.4 | -.7 | |
| | | | **RATIOS** | | | | | | |
| 15.5 | 6.4 | 5.5 | | | | | 5.8 | 2.2 | |
| 4.0 | 3.5 | 2.1 | Current | | | | 2.1 | 1.3 | |
| 1.7 | 1.5 | .9 | | | | | .7 | .8 | |
| 9.7 | 5.8 | 4.1 | | | | | 5.1 | 1.9 | |
| 3.0 | 3.0 | 1.6 | Quick | | | | 2.0 | 1.2 | |
| 1.3 | 1.4 | .6 | | | | | .6 | .8 | |
| 0 UND | 0 956.5 | 0 844.6 | | | | | 0 UND | 4 98.4 | |
| 4 94.1 | 12 30.3 | 10 37.2 | Sales/Receivables | | | | 9 40.9 | 38 9.5 | |
| 56 6.5 | 35 10.4 | 42 8.6 | | | | | 11 32.0 | 85 4.3 | |
| | | | Cost of Sales/Inventory | | | | | | |
| | | | Cost of Sales/Payables | | | | | | |
| 1.3 | 1.9 | 2.5 | | | | | 2.2 | 3.5 | |
| 2.3 | 3.9 | 5.2 | Sales/Working Capital | | | | 5.1 | 31.2 | |
| 4.1 | 14.4 | -60.3 | | | | | NM | -8.0 | |
| 113.1 | 86.3 | 13.9 | | | | | | 15.8 | |
| (18) 10.2 | (33) .8 | (32) 1.3 | EBIT/Interest | | | | | (11) 3.5 | |
| -2.5 | -24.5 | -19.4 | | | | | | -.2 | |
| | | | Net Profit + Depr., Dep., Amort./Cur. Mat. L/T/D | | | | | | |
| .3 | .3 | .2 | | | | | .2 | .3 | |
| .6 | .7 | .6 | Fixed/Worth | | | | .6 | .8 | |
| 1.1 | 1.4 | 1.0 | | | | | 1.0 | 1.0 | |
| .1 | .1 | .2 | | | | | .1 | .2 | |
| .5 | .2 | .6 | Debt/Worth | | | | .4 | .3 | |
| 1.2 | 1.2 | 1.0 | | | | | 1.4 | .7 | |
| 33.8 | 19.6 | 12.9 | | | | | .7 | 8.7 | |
| (29) 14.4 | (48) 1.5 | (49) .1 | % Profit Before Taxes/Tangible Net Worth | | | | (11) -18.7 | 1.3 | |
| -.9 | -6.8 | -20.2 | | | | | -30.9 | -16.0 | |
| 19.7 | 11.1 | 7.1 | | | | | 1.3 | 7.1 | |
| 7.8 | .1 | .2 | % Profit Before Taxes/Total Assets | | | | -6.4 | .7 | |
| -.7 | -6.8 | -10.3 | | | | | -19.1 | -9.8 | |
| 8.7 | 8.9 | 7.0 | | | | | 22.0 | 3.1 | |
| 1.3 | 1.5 | 2.0 | Sales/Net Fixed Assets | | | | 1.3 | 1.7 | |
| .4 | .5 | .5 | | | | | .7 | .4 | |
| 1.2 | 1.4 | 1.1 | | | | | 1.5 | 1.0 | |
| .4 | .6 | .7 | Sales/Total Assets | | | | .7 | .4 | |
| .2 | .3 | .3 | | | | | .4 | .2 | |
| 3.2 | 1.6 | 1.9 | | | | | | 1.0 | |
| (22) 8.4 | (43) 3.8 | (39) 4.2 | % Depr., Dep., Amort./Sales | | | | (13) 4.3 | | |
| 11.8 | 8.7 | 9.4 | | | | | | 9.6 | |
| | | | % Officers', Directors' Owners' Comp/Sales | | | | | | |
| 326069M | 729581M | 848855M | Net Sales ($) | 3909M | 11016M | 27210M | 78343M | 250256M | 478121M |
| 968099M | 1479106M | 1616487M | Total Assets ($) | 14309M | 8902M | 64382M | 160772M | 744928M | 623194M |

M = $ thousand   MM = $ million
See Pages viii through xx for Explanation of Ratios and Data

© RMA 2024

# ENTERTAINMENT—Sports Teams and Clubs  NAICS 711211

## Current Data Sorted by Assets | Comparative Historical Data

| | | | | | | Type of Statement | | |
|---|---|---|---|---|---|---|---|---|
| | 1 | 1 | 3 | | 11 | Unqualified | 27 | 12 |
| | | 2 | 1 | | | Reviewed | 2 | |
| | 2 | | | | | Compiled | 4 | |
| 2 | 2 | 4 | | | | Tax Returns | 20 | 5 |
| 6 | 9 | 8 | 5 | 2 | 11 | Other | 36 | 25 |
| | 31 (4/1-9/30/23) | | 39 (10/1/23-3/31/24) | | | | 4/1/19-3/31/20 | 4/1/20-3/31/21 |
| 0-500M | 500M-2MM | 2-10MM | 10-50MM | 50-100MM | 100-250MM | | ALL | ALL |
| 8 | 14 | 15 | 9 | 2 | 22 | NUMBER OF STATEMENTS | 89 | 42 |
| % | % | % | % | % | % | **ASSETS** | % | % |
| | 40.2 | 29.7 | | | 12.5 | Cash & Equivalents | 19.9 | 22.3 |
| | 12.2 | 7.9 | | | 11.1 | Trade Receivables (net) | 8.5 | 8.7 |
| | 6.4 | 1.3 | | | .4 | Inventory | 1.2 | 1.2 |
| | 1.2 | 1.7 | | | 5.4 | All Other Current | 4.5 | 3.9 |
| | 60.0 | 40.7 | | | 29.4 | Total Current | 34.0 | 36.1 |
| | 21.3 | 36.4 | | | 16.1 | Fixed Assets (net) | 24.6 | 27.7 |
| | 8.7 | 15.6 | | | 19.0 | Intangibles (net) | 24.5 | 16.0 |
| | 10.0 | 7.4 | | | 35.5 | All Other Non-Current | 16.9 | 20.3 |
| | 100.0 | 100.0 | | | 100.0 | Total | 100.0 | 100.0 |
| | | | | | | **LIABILITIES** | | |
| | 7.2 | 3.1 | | | 11.1 | Notes Payable-Short Term | 9.7 | 20.1 |
| | 3.2 | .9 | | | 2.0 | Cur. Mat.-L.T.D. | 3.1 | 18.2 |
| | 7.4 | 4.7 | | | 11.8 | Trade Payables | 6.1 | 6.2 |
| | .3 | .1 | | | .0 | Income Taxes Payable | .1 | .0 |
| | 60.6 | 33.1 | | | 24.1 | All Other Current | 26.1 | 26.0 |
| | 78.6 | 42.0 | | | 49.0 | Total Current | 45.0 | 70.5 |
| | 11.6 | 23.6 | | | 79.2 | Long-Term Debt | 42.4 | 56.2 |
| | .0 | .0 | | | .0 | Deferred Taxes | .0 | .0 |
| | 3.0 | 4.0 | | | 24.6 | All Other Non-Current | 18.5 | 19.7 |
| | 6.7 | 30.4 | | | -52.7 | Net Worth | -6.0 | -46.3 |
| | 100.0 | 100.0 | | | 100.0 | Total Liabilities & Net Worth | 100.0 | 100.0 |
| | | | | | | **INCOME DATA** | | |
| | 100.0 | 100.0 | | | 100.0 | Net Sales | 100.0 | 100.0 |
| | | | | | | Gross Profit | | |
| | 98.2 | 93.5 | | | 87.8 | Operating Expenses | 92.5 | 98.8 |
| | 1.8 | 6.5 | | | 12.2 | Operating Profit | 7.5 | 1.2 |
| | .4 | .8 | | | 4.8 | All Other Expenses (net) | 4.2 | 6.0 |
| | 1.4 | 5.7 | | | 7.4 | Profit Before Taxes | 3.4 | -4.7 |
| | | | | | | **RATIOS** | | |
| | 4.8 | 7.1 | | | 1.4 | | 2.1 | 2.0 |
| | 1.6 | 2.2 | | | .6 | Current | .7 | .7 |
| | .2 | .5 | | | .4 | | .4 | .3 |
| | 3.5 | 7.1 | | | 1.1 | | 1.8 | 1.5 |
| | 1.3 | 1.9 | | | .6 | Quick | .6 | .5 |
| | .2 | .4 | | | .3 | | .2 | .2 |
| | 0 UND | 2  172.5 | | 10  38.3 | | | 2  166.3 | 0  UND |
| | 5  73.3 | 13  27.9 | | 27  13.6 | | Sales/Receivables | 12  31.1 | 11  33.5 |
| | 17  21.6 | 47  7.8 | | 61  6.0 | | | 42  8.7 | 45  8.2 |
| | | | | | | Cost of Sales/Inventory | | |
| | | | | | | Cost of Sales/Payables | | |
| | 6.3 | 2.5 | | | 15.1 | | 8.5 | 5.1 |
| | NM | 8.7 | | | -5.7 | Sales/Working Capital | -11.6 | -28.9 |
| | -4.5 | -6.4 | | | -3.1 | | -3.0 | -1.6 |
| | | 15.7 | | | 3.6 | | 9.3 | 1.5 |
| | (11) | 6.2 | | (19) | 1.2 | EBIT/Interest | (64) 2.3 | (30) -1.6 |
| | | 1.1 | | | -.2 | | -1.9 | -4.8 |
| | | | | | | Net Profit + Depr., Dep., Amort./Cur. Mat. L/T/D | | |
| | .1 | .4 | | | -5.9 | | .3 | .6 |
| | .9 | 1.5 | | | -.2 | Fixed/Worth | 10.0 | -81.2 |
| | -.3 | -.3 | | | .0 | | -.2 | -.3 |
| | .5 | 1.0 | | | -21.0 | | 1.0 | 2.6 |
| | 1.5 | 1.9 | | | -2.6 | Debt/Worth | 112.3 | -14.6 |
| | -1.8 | -3.4 | | | -1.6 | | -1.7 | -1.7 |
| | | | | | | % Profit Before Taxes/Tangible Net Worth | 35.7 | 83.7 |
| | | | | | | | (45) 10.0 | (17) 7.8 |
| | | | | | | | 2.5 | -16.0 |
| | 33.9 | 22.0 | | | 11.8 | % Profit Before Taxes/Total Assets | 10.0 | 3.7 |
| | 7.0 | 7.9 | | | 2.3 | | 2.8 | -4.0 |
| | -22.0 | .2 | | | -5.0 | | -5.7 | -19.1 |
| | 336.7 | 31.4 | | | 56.2 | | 73.0 | 43.2 |
| | 65.6 | 4.5 | | | 18.9 | Sales/Net Fixed Assets | 8.5 | 15.1 |
| | 13.2 | 1.0 | | | 5.9 | | 3.2 | 1.2 |
| | 5.6 | 2.2 | | | 1.5 | | 1.8 | 1.8 |
| | 4.4 | 1.2 | | | 1.1 | Sales/Total Assets | 1.2 | .8 |
| | 3.1 | .9 | | | .6 | | .5 | .5 |
| | .2 | 1.1 | | | .5 | | 1.0 | 1.1 |
| | (12) .4 | (11) 2.5 | | (17) | 1.0 | % Depr., Dep., Amort./Sales | (60) 2.6 | (32) 3.3 |
| | 3.7 | 7.2 | | | 2.2 | | 6.8 | 9.4 |
| | | | | | | | 3.7 | |
| | | | | | | % Officers', Directors' Owners' Comp/Sales | (12) 7.2 | |
| | | | | | | | 13.5 | |
| 7887M | 60163M | 81861M | 144247M | 115314M | 4519735M | Net Sales ($) | 7765618M | 2240394M |
| 1183M | 13401M | 60344M | 189614M | 190128M | 3966030M | Total Assets ($) | 6330224M | 2765783M |

© RMA 2024   M = $ thousand   MM = $ million
See Pages viii through xx for Explanation of Ratios and Data

# ENTERTAINMENT—Sports Teams and Clubs  NAICS 711211

| Comparative Historical Data | | | Type of Statement | Current Data Sorted by Sales | | | | | |
|---|---|---|---|---|---|---|---|---|---|
| 10 | 19 | 16 | Unqualified | | | | 2 | 2 | 10 |
| 2 | 1 | 3 | Reviewed | | 1 | | 1 | 1 | |
| | 2 | 2 | Compiled | | 1 | 1 | | | |
| 8 | 7 | 8 | Tax Returns | 1 | 1 | 4 | 2 | | |
| 24 | 35 | 41 | Other | 7 | 5 | 1 | 9 | 6 | 13 |
| 4/1/21-3/31/22 ALL | 4/1/22-3/31/23 ALL | 4/1/23-3/31/24 ALL | | 0-1MM | 1-3MM | 3-5MM | 5-10MM | 10-25MM | 25MM & OVER |
| | | | | | 31 (4/1-9/30/23) | | 39 (10/1/23-3/31/24) | | |
| 44 | 64 | 70 | NUMBER OF STATEMENTS | 8 | 8 | 8 | 14 | 9 | 23 |
| % | % | % | ASSETS | % | % | % | % | % | % |
| 25.6 | 21.0 | 27.6 | Cash & Equivalents | | | | 19.1 | | 15.3 |
| 9.4 | 9.1 | 9.5 | Trade Receivables (net) | | | | 13.9 | | 12.2 |
| 1.7 | 1.6 | 1.9 | Inventory | | | | 2.3 | | .3 |
| 4.0 | 4.5 | 2.6 | All Other Current | | | | 1.8 | | 5.6 |
| 40.7 | 36.2 | 41.6 | Total Current | | | | 37.1 | | 33.5 |
| 26.4 | 30.4 | 26.1 | Fixed Assets (net) | | | | 31.4 | | 18.4 |
| 19.3 | 13.4 | 14.8 | Intangibles (net) | | | | 23.9 | | 15.6 |
| 13.5 | 19.9 | 17.4 | All Other Non-Current | | | | 7.6 | | 32.5 |
| 100.0 | 100.0 | 100.0 | Total | | | | 100.0 | | 100.0 |
| | | | LIABILITIES | | | | | | |
| 9.9 | 6.8 | 5.9 | Notes Payable-Short Term | | | | 2.7 | | 10.6 |
| 1.1 | 7.5 | 3.7 | Cur. Mat.-L.T.D. | | | | 2.9 | | 3.7 |
| 7.0 | 8.6 | 7.5 | Trade Payables | | | | 6.0 | | 12.2 |
| .2 | .0 | .1 | Income Taxes Payable | | | | .2 | | .0 |
| 22.5 | 31.1 | 33.6 | All Other Current | | | | 51.6 | | 25.4 |
| 40.7 | 54.1 | 50.7 | Total Current | | | | 63.4 | | 52.0 |
| 51.7 | 44.8 | 38.7 | Long-Term Debt | | | | 15.9 | | 78.2 |
| .0 | .0 | .0 | Deferred Taxes | | | | .0 | | .0 |
| 19.2 | 26.7 | 10.4 | All Other Non-Current | | | | 4.5 | | 26.0 |
| -11.6 | -25.5 | .1 | Net Worth | | | | 16.2 | | -56.1 |
| 100.0 | 100.0 | 100.0 | Total Liabilities & Net Worth | | | | 100.0 | | 100.0 |
| | | | INCOME DATA | | | | | | |
| 100.0 | 100.0 | 100.0 | Net Sales | | | | 100.0 | | 100.0 |
| | | | Gross Profit | | | | | | |
| 91.0 | 92.5 | 90.9 | Operating Expenses | | | | 96.1 | | 90.0 |
| 9.0 | 7.5 | 9.1 | Operating Profit | | | | 3.9 | | 10.0 |
| 1.9 | 4.4 | 2.2 | All Other Expenses (net) | | | | .5 | | 2.7 |
| 7.1 | 3.1 | 7.0 | Profit Before Taxes | | | | 3.4 | | 7.2 |
| | | | RATIOS | | | | | | |
| 2.3 | 1.8 | 3.3 | | | | | 3.4 | | 1.4 |
| .9 | .8 | 1.0 | Current | | | | 1.9 | | .6 |
| .5 | .4 | .4 | | | | | .4 | | .4 |
| 2.2 | 1.5 | 2.7 | | | | | 3.3 | | 1.0 |
| .9 | .7 | .8 | Quick | | | | 1.5 | | .5 |
| .4 | .3 | .3 | | | | | .4 | | .3 |
| 1  323.3 | 6  58.5 | 0  UND | | | | | 5  68.6 | | 10  35.4 |
| 24  14.9 | 23  15.7 | 12  30.2 | Sales/Receivables | | | | 17  21.6 | | 36  10.0 |
| 59  6.2 | 54  6.8 | 40  9.2 | | | | | 26  14.1 | | 61  6.0 |
| | | | Cost of Sales/Inventory | | | | | | |
| | | | Cost of Sales/Payables | | | | | | |
| 5.5 | 9.1 | 7.0 | | | | | 7.5 | | 15.3 |
| -119.9 | -23.9 | UND | Sales/Working Capital | | | | 20.2 | | -5.5 |
| -3.7 | -3.3 | -3.7 | | | | | -5.9 | | -3.0 |
| 12.9 | 10.8 | 16.0 | | | | | 151.8 | | 3.6 |
| (36) 2.8 | (48) 3.1 | (51) 3.0 | EBIT/Interest | | | | (10) 4.2 | (20) | 1.8 |
| -.1 | .1 | -.2 | | | | | -3.9 | | -.2 |
| | | | Net Profit + Depr., Dep., Amort./Cur. Mat. L/T/D | | | | | | |
| .2 | .8 | .5 | | | | | .6 | | -4.0 |
| 6.0 | 11.0 | 9.3 | Fixed/Worth | | | | 1.2 | | -.2 |
| -.2 | -.2 | -.2 | | | | | -.3 | | .0 |
| 1.1 | 1.7 | 1.0 | | | | | .5 | | -7.6 |
| -12.7 | UND | UND | Debt/Worth | | | | 7.7 | | -2.8 |
| -1.9 | -1.9 | -2.3 | | | | | -2.6 | | -1.6 |
| 103.1 | 41.9 | 90.4 | % Profit Before Taxes/Tangible Net Worth | | | | | | |
| (20) 24.5 | (32) 5.9 | (35) 20.2 | | | | | | | |
| -.5 | -11.0 | 2.1 | | | | | | | |
| 16.2 | 14.1 | 20.4 | % Profit Before Taxes/Total Assets | | | | 26.3 | | 12.5 |
| 3.7 | 2.0 | 6.3 | | | | | 6.6 | | 1.8 |
| -2.8 | -8.4 | -2.8 | | | | | -6.6 | | -10.0 |
| 165.9 | 64.5 | 77.6 | | | | | 46.5 | | 42.7 |
| 7.1 | 8.5 | 13.4 | Sales/Net Fixed Assets | | | | 13.0 | | 18.5 |
| 2.7 | 2.2 | 2.4 | | | | | 4.5 | | 4.4 |
| 2.0 | 2.2 | 3.0 | | | | | 5.2 | | 1.5 |
| 1.1 | 1.2 | 1.4 | Sales/Total Assets | | | | 2.2 | | 1.2 |
| .5 | .5 | .8 | | | | | 1.0 | | .8 |
| 1.4 | .5 | .5 | | | | | .8 | | .5 |
| (29) 4.1 | (47) 1.1 | (51) 1.3 | % Depr., Dep., Amort./Sales | | | | (11) 2.9 | (17) | 1.0 |
| 16.6 | 4.6 | 5.0 | | | | | 5.0 | | 2.2 |
| | | | % Officers', Directors' Owners' Comp/Sales | | | | | | |
| 3022876M | 5598530M | 4929207M | Net Sales ($) | 3552M | 16797M | 29474M | 99734M | 144115M | 4635535M |
| 3182720M | 5385397M | 4420700M | Total Assets ($) | 6660M | 10704M | 16539M | 89868M | 439935M | 3856994M |

© RMA 2024

M = $ thousand    MM = $ million
See Pages viii through xx for Explanation of Ratios and Data

# ENTERTAINMENT—Promoters of Performing Arts, Sports, and Similar Events with Facilities NAICS 711310

| Current Data Sorted by Assets | | | | | | | Comparative Historical Data | |
|---|---|---|---|---|---|---|---|---|
| 1 | | 3 | 5 | 5 | 5 | Type of Statement | | |
| | | | 2 | | | Unqualified | 32 | 11 |
| | | | 1 | | | Reviewed | 6 | 1 |
| 2 | 1 | 2 | 1 | | | Compiled | 6 | 2 |
| 2 | 12 | 18 | 13 | 4 | 3 | Tax Returns | 12 | 3 |
| | 20 (4/1-9/30/23) | | 60 (10/1/23-3/31/24) | | | Other | 46 | 28 |
| 0-500M | 500M-2MM | 2-10MM | 10-50MM | 50-100MM | 100-250MM | | 4/1/19-3/31/20 ALL | 4/1/20-3/31/21 ALL |
| 5 | 13 | 23 | 22 | 9 | 8 | NUMBER OF STATEMENTS | 102 | 45 |
| % | % | % | % | % | % | ASSETS | % | % |
| | 50.7 | 26.7 | 28.1 | | | Cash & Equivalents | 22.6 | 24.1 |
| | 8.0 | 5.5 | 7.0 | | | Trade Receivables (net) | 6.6 | 5.2 |
| | .1 | 2.9 | 3.4 | | | Inventory | 1.1 | .8 |
| | 5.3 | 6.9 | 1.8 | | | All Other Current | 3.9 | 5.0 |
| | 64.2 | 42.0 | 40.3 | | | Total Current | 34.3 | 35.1 |
| | 26.9 | 37.7 | 38.9 | | | Fixed Assets (net) | 47.9 | 47.1 |
| | 1.5 | 10.5 | 3.6 | | | Intangibles (net) | 3.4 | 3.6 |
| | 7.4 | 9.8 | 17.2 | | | All Other Non-Current | 14.4 | 14.3 |
| | 100.0 | 100.0 | 100.0 | | | Total | 100.0 | 100.0 |
| | | | | | | LIABILITIES | | |
| | 3.1 | 5.7 | 1.8 | | | Notes Payable-Short Term | 2.0 | 2.4 |
| | .0 | 1.2 | 2.6 | | | Cur. Mat.-L.T.D. | 1.4 | 1.2 |
| | 14.5 | 1.9 | 7.6 | | | Trade Payables | 5.2 | 4.2 |
| | .0 | .0 | .0 | | | Income Taxes Payable | .1 | .4 |
| | 17.3 | 15.2 | 13.8 | | | All Other Current | 14.9 | 10.7 |
| | 35.0 | 24.0 | 25.8 | | | Total Current | 23.6 | 18.9 |
| | 20.4 | 29.9 | 20.8 | | | Long-Term Debt | 21.9 | 29.9 |
| | .0 | .0 | .0 | | | Deferred Taxes | .3 | .4 |
| | 10.0 | 4.9 | 7.5 | | | All Other Non-Current | 8.4 | 8.0 |
| | 34.6 | 41.1 | 45.9 | | | Net Worth | 45.8 | 42.8 |
| | 100.0 | 100.0 | 100.0 | | | Total Liabilities & Net Worth | 100.0 | 100.0 |
| | | | | | | INCOME DATA | | |
| | 100.0 | 100.0 | 100.0 | | | Net Sales | 100.0 | 100.0 |
| | | | | | | Gross Profit | | |
| | 89.3 | 85.1 | 94.2 | | | Operating Expenses | 88.5 | 94.2 |
| | 10.7 | 14.9 | 5.8 | | | Operating Profit | 11.5 | 5.8 |
| | .4 | 5.2 | 1.1 | | | All Other Expenses (net) | 3.2 | 6.7 |
| | 10.3 | 9.7 | 4.7 | | | Profit Before Taxes | 8.3 | -.8 |
| | | | | | | RATIOS | | |
| | 11.9 | 12.8 | 2.4 | | | | 3.6 | 5.4 |
| | 4.2 | 2.5 | 2.1 | | | Current | 1.6 | 1.2 |
| | .9 | .7 | 1.2 | | | | .6 | .6 |
| | 10.7 | 12.8 | 2.3 | | | | 3.4 | 4.8 |
| | 3.9 | 1.9 | 1.8 | | | Quick | 1.2 | 1.1 |
| | .8 | .5 | 1.1 | | | | .5 | .5 |
| | 0 UND | 0 UND | 3 117.5 | | | | 0 UND | 0 UND |
| | 4 97.6 | 6 59.5 | 13 27.4 | | | Sales/Receivables | 6 64.5 | 5 67.7 |
| | 10 35.0 | 28 13.2 | 32 11.5 | | | | 33 10.9 | 28 13.0 |
| | | | | | | Cost of Sales/Inventory | | |
| | | | | | | Cost of Sales/Payables | | |
| | 3.7 | 2.2 | 3.5 | | | | 3.2 | 2.6 |
| | 11.8 | 4.7 | 7.2 | | | Sales/Working Capital | 11.8 | 20.6 |
| | -51.1 | -22.0 | 17.5 | | | | -15.3 | -10.1 |
| | | 28.1 | 34.8 | | | | 21.2 | 9.2 |
| | (11) | 4.3 | (16) 4.9 | | | EBIT/Interest | (67) 3.7 | (28) 1.2 |
| | | 2.0 | .0 | | | | -.7 | -11.9 |
| | | | | | | Net Profit + Depr., Dep., Amort./Cur. Mat. L/T/D | | |
| | .2 | .2 | .1 | | | | .3 | .1 |
| | .7 | 1.2 | .5 | | | Fixed/Worth | .9 | 1.0 |
| | NM | 6.1 | 2.3 | | | | 3.1 | 3.9 |
| | .1 | .6 | .4 | | | | .1 | .2 |
| | 1.0 | 1.7 | 1.2 | | | Debt/Worth | .6 | 1.0 |
| | NM | 9.8 | 8.9 | | | | 7.0 | 9.1 |
| | 193.6 | 71.8 | 46.3 | | | | 48.7 | 12.4 |
| | (10) 49.4 | (18) 23.1 | (19) 10.0 | | | % Profit Before Taxes/Tangible Net Worth | (85) 5.4 | (37) -.4 |
| | 9.8 | 5.3 | -2.7 | | | | -1.2 | -9.4 |
| | 60.9 | 27.8 | 12.9 | | | | 17.1 | 4.4 |
| | 26.4 | 9.3 | 5.4 | | | % Profit Before Taxes/Total Assets | 3.7 | -.3 |
| | 7.9 | 1.9 | -.1 | | | | -1.3 | -5.8 |
| | 141.4 | 35.9 | 51.2 | | | | 15.8 | 102.1 |
| | 15.5 | 7.2 | 2.3 | | | Sales/Net Fixed Assets | 1.6 | 1.0 |
| | 8.0 | 1.5 | 1.1 | | | | .6 | .2 |
| | 5.7 | 2.4 | 1.8 | | | | 2.1 | 1.6 |
| | 3.6 | 1.2 | .8 | | | Sales/Total Assets | .7 | .5 |
| | 2.0 | .4 | .4 | | | | .3 | .2 |
| | | 1.2 | 1.3 | | | | 1.9 | 1.5 |
| | (13) | 2.8 | (18) 3.5 | | | % Depr., Dep., Amort./Sales | (76) 5.1 | (28) 6.7 |
| | | 15.7 | 9.9 | | | | 11.3 | 24.3 |
| | | | | | | % Officers', Directors' Owners' Comp/Sales | 2.0 | |
| | | | | | | | (14) 6.9 | |
| | | | | | | | 13.4 | |
| 8819M | 62415M | 187473M | 868052M | 930230M | 1844203M | Net Sales ($) | 2276410M | 911153M |
| 1475M | 16018M | 118804M | 606056M | 724237M | 1470032M | Total Assets ($) | 3477637M | 1142828M |

M = $ thousand    MM = $ million
See Pages viii through xx for Explanation of Ratios and Data

© RMA 2024

# ENTERTAINMENT—Promoters of Performing Arts, Sports, and Similar Events with Facilities  NAICS 711310

## Comparative Historical Data / Current Data Sorted by Sales

| | | | Type of Statement | | | | | | |
|---|---|---|---|---|---|---|---|---|---|
| 11 | 25 | 19 | Unqualified | 1 | 3 | 1 | 1 | 3 | 10 |
| 3 | 3 | 2 | Reviewed | | | | 1 | | 1 |
| 5 | 2 | 1 | Compiled | | | | | | 1 |
| 11 | 12 | 6 | Tax Returns | | 3 | | 2 | 2 | |
| 22 | 38 | 52 | Other | 6 | 6 | 4 | 11 | 10 | 15 |
| 4/1/21-3/31/22 ALL | 4/1/22-3/31/23 ALL | 4/1/23-3/31/24 ALL | | 0-1MM | 20 (4/1-9/30/23) 1-3MM | 3-5MM | 60 (10/1/23-3/31/24) 5-10MM | 10-25MM | 25MM & OVER |
| 52 | 80 | 80 | NUMBER OF STATEMENTS | 8 | 12 | 5 | 13 | 15 | 27 |
| % | % | % | ASSETS | % | % | % | % | % | % |
| 41.6 | 28.6 | 29.5 | Cash & Equivalents | | 26.2 | 40.0 | 32.1 | 26.0 | |
| 5.4 | 7.1 | 6.0 | Trade Receivables (net) | | 4.6 | 6.4 | 4.8 | 8.0 | |
| 2.7 | 1.0 | 3.3 | Inventory | | 1.8 | .1 | 2.8 | 7.3 | |
| 3.5 | 2.8 | 4.6 | All Other Current | | 10.0 | 1.7 | 6.4 | 3.7 | |
| 53.2 | 39.6 | 43.5 | Total Current | | 42.7 | 48.2 | 46.2 | 45.0 | |
| 33.8 | 38.3 | 37.4 | Fixed Assets (net) | | 31.5 | 36.5 | 31.7 | 33.7 | |
| 1.8 | 5.2 | 7.1 | Intangibles (net) | | 10.4 | 2.0 | 12.9 | 8.1 | |
| 11.2 | 16.9 | 12.0 | All Other Non-Current | | 15.4 | 13.3 | 9.3 | 13.3 | |
| 100.0 | 100.0 | 100.0 | Total | | 100.0 | 100.0 | 100.0 | 100.0 | |
| | | | LIABILITIES | | | | | | |
| 9.3 | 4.6 | 3.9 | Notes Payable-Short Term | | 9.5 | 7.8 | .9 | 3.1 | |
| .4 | 1.1 | 2.3 | Cur. Mat.-L.T.D. | | .1 | 1.2 | .4 | 4.0 | |
| 10.0 | 5.9 | 6.1 | Trade Payables | | 14.8 | 2.8 | 3.7 | 8.0 | |
| .0 | .8 | .0 | Income Taxes Payable | | .0 | .0 | .1 | .0 | |
| 17.0 | 21.5 | 15.5 | All Other Current | | 7.5 | 11.4 | 24.6 | 16.5 | |
| 36.8 | 33.9 | 27.8 | Total Current | | 32.0 | 23.1 | 29.6 | 31.6 | |
| 19.4 | 22.3 | 21.3 | Long-Term Debt | | 21.9 | 25.1 | 9.3 | 18.9 | |
| .4 | .0 | .0 | Deferred Taxes | | .0 | .0 | .0 | .0 | |
| 15.0 | 11.6 | 8.4 | All Other Non-Current | | 6.2 | 7.4 | 6.8 | 12.5 | |
| 28.4 | 32.2 | 42.5 | Net Worth | | 39.8 | 44.4 | 54.3 | 37.0 | |
| 100.0 | 100.0 | 100.0 | Total Liabilities & Net Worth | | 100.0 | 100.0 | 100.0 | 100.0 | |
| | | | INCOME DATA | | | | | | |
| 100.0 | 100.0 | 100.0 | Net Sales | | 100.0 | 100.0 | 100.0 | 100.0 | |
| | | | Gross Profit | | | | | | |
| 86.3 | 86.2 | 89.2 | Operating Expenses | | 100.4 | 90.2 | 94.8 | 86.8 | |
| 13.7 | 13.8 | 10.8 | Operating Profit | | -.4 | 9.8 | 5.2 | 13.2 | |
| 2.2 | 5.0 | 3.5 | All Other Expenses (net) | | 1.1 | .3 | 1.4 | 4.7 | |
| 11.5 | 8.8 | 7.3 | Profit Before Taxes | | -1.5 | 9.4 | 3.8 | 8.6 | |
| | | | RATIOS | | | | | | |
| 5.0 | 5.7 | 4.5 | | | 12.5 | 6.6 | 2.2 | 2.5 | |
| 2.3 | 1.8 | 1.8 | Current | | 2.4 | 2.4 | 1.4 | 1.6 | |
| 1.1 | .9 | .8 | | | .5 | .8 | 1.2 | .7 | |
| 5.0 | 5.3 | 3.9 | | | 10.8 | 6.6 | 2.2 | 2.1 | |
| 2.0 | 1.6 | 1.4 | Quick | | 1.4 | 2.2 | 1.1 | 1.4 | |
| 1.0 | .6 | .6 | | | .4 | .8 | .6 | .3 | |
| 0 UND | 0 999.8 | 1 317.9 | | 0 UND | 1 318.8 | 1 308.7 | 7 54.7 | | |
| 2 235.8 | 9 40.2 | 9 42.5 | Sales/Receivables | 6 64.2 | 7 51.5 | 4 81.6 | 15 24.4 | | |
| 27 13.5 | 30 12.3 | 24 15.0 | | 24 15.4 | 11 32.5 | 33 11.2 | 33 10.9 | | |
| | | | Cost of Sales/Inventory | | | | | | |
| | | | Cost of Sales/Payables | | | | | | |
| 2.0 | 2.5 | 3.5 | | | 1.5 | 2.5 | 3.7 | 4.4 | |
| 8.0 | 6.1 | 8.6 | Sales/Working Capital | | 3.1 | 8.4 | 11.0 | 10.1 | |
| 115.3 | -32.8 | -46.8 | | | -6.8 | -52.8 | 18.4 | -12.3 | |
| 135.2 | 44.0 | 22.0 | | | | | | 25.2 | |
| (32) 18.7 | (55) 9.3 | (47) 7.7 | EBIT/Interest | | | | | (20) 9.9 | |
| .6 | -2.8 | 1.6 | | | | | | 1.9 | |
| | | | Net Profit + Depr., Dep., Amort./Cur. Mat. L/T/D | | | | | | |
| .1 | .2 | .2 | | | .0 | .3 | .4 | .1 | |
| .6 | .8 | .8 | Fixed/Worth | | 1.4 | 1.0 | .6 | .7 | |
| 1.5 | 5.1 | 3.9 | | | NM | 3.1 | 1.2 | 37.7 | |
| .2 | .2 | .5 | | | .1 | .4 | .2 | .7 | |
| 1.6 | 1.1 | 1.6 | Debt/Worth | | .9 | 1.0 | 1.0 | 2.5 | |
| 7.0 | 39.6 | 9.9 | | | NM | 8.0 | 6.7 | 97.4 | |
| 99.1 | 52.8 | 83.7 | | | 154.0 | 72.4 | 121.2 | | |
| (42) 24.1 | (61) 11.4 | (66) 26.0 | % Profit Before Taxes/Tangible Net Worth | | (12) 32.6 | (12) 31.1 | (22) 34.9 | | |
| -.8 | .7 | 3.4 | | | .5 | 2.2 | 8.5 | | |
| 23.2 | 23.3 | 26.9 | % Profit Before Taxes/Total Assets | | 19.6 | 65.9 | 27.1 | 22.9 | |
| 8.6 | 4.7 | 8.7 | | | 2.4 | 10.6 | 8.4 | 11.9 | |
| -1.4 | -2.4 | 1.2 | | | -5.1 | 1.7 | .7 | 3.4 | |
| 87.0 | 33.5 | 41.1 | | | 53.6 | 64.3 | 44.0 | 122.4 | |
| 9.1 | 4.8 | 4.8 | Sales/Net Fixed Assets | | 13.5 | 7.2 | 17.5 | 2.4 | |
| .6 | .8 | 1.2 | | | 1.8 | 1.6 | 1.2 | 1.2 | |
| 3.2 | 2.2 | 3.2 | | | 2.5 | 5.7 | 3.2 | 3.3 | |
| .9 | .9 | 1.3 | Sales/Total Assets | | .6 | 1.7 | 1.3 | 1.4 | |
| .3 | .3 | .4 | | | .3 | 1.1 | .4 | .6 | |
| 1.5 | 1.2 | .6 | | | | | | .3 | |
| (37) 4.7 | (60) 3.4 | (52) 2.7 | % Depr., Dep., Amort./Sales | | | | (21) 2.6 | | |
| 14.9 | 9.3 | 9.6 | | | | | | 7.6 | |
| | 6.5 | .8 | % Officers', Directors' Owners' Comp/Sales | | | | | | |
| (11) 14.3 | (16) 4.2 | | | | | | | | |
| | 19.5 | 6.4 | | | | | | | |
| 1020440M | 2682889M | 3901192M | Net Sales ($) | 4563M | 26615M | 19703M | 95644M | 227927M | 3526740M |
| 1301921M | 2861685M | 2936622M | Total Assets ($) | 14605M | 49718M | 50169M | 86841M | 377880M | 2357409M |

© RMA 2024

M = $ thousand    MM = $ million
See Pages viii through xx for Explanation of Ratios and Data

# ENTERTAINMENT—Independent Artists, Writers, and Performers  NAICS 711510

## Current Data Sorted by Assets

|  |  | 1 | 1 |  |  |
|---|---|---|---|---|---|
|  |  | 1 | 1 |  |  |
| 4 | 1 |  |  |  |  |
| 4 | 6 | 9 | 4 |  |  |
|  | 0 (4/1-9/30/23) |  | 31 (10/1/23-3/31/24) |  |  |
| 0-500M | 500M-2MM | 2-10MM | 10-50MM | 50-100MM | 100-250MM |
| 8 | 7 | 10 | 6 |  |  |
| % | % | % | % | % | % |

## Comparative Historical Data

| Type of Statement | | |
|---|---|---|
| Unqualified | 1 | |
| Reviewed | 1 | |
| Compiled | 1 | 1 |
| Tax Returns | 5 | 11 |
| Other | 27 | 17 |
| | 4/1/19-3/31/20 | 4/1/20-3/31/21 |
| NUMBER OF STATEMENTS | ALL 35 | ALL 29 |

| Assets Columns | | | | | | | Assets | Hist 1 | Hist 2 |
|---|---|---|---|---|---|---|---|---|---|
|  |  | 19.4 |  | DATA | DATA | Cash & Equivalents | 37.8 | 28.2 |
|  |  | 11.2 |  | | | Trade Receivables (net) | 8.0 | 4.2 |
|  |  | .8 |  | | | Inventory | 3.8 | 5.2 |
|  |  | 13.7 |  | | | All Other Current | 5.3 | 3.1 |
|  |  | 45.0 |  | | | Total Current | 54.8 | 40.6 |
|  |  | 28.2 |  | NOT | NOT | Fixed Assets (net) | 28.0 | 33.1 |
|  |  | 5.3 |  | | | Intangibles (net) | 3.2 | 10.7 |
|  |  | 21.4 |  | AVAILABLE | AVAILABLE | All Other Non-Current | 14.0 | 15.4 |
|  |  | 100.0 |  | | | Total | 100.0 | 100.0 |
|  |  |  |  | | | **LIABILITIES** | | |
|  |  | 7.4 |  | | | Notes Payable-Short Term | 12.8 | 5.0 |
|  |  | 12.3 |  | | | Cur. Mat.-L.T.D. | 1.6 | 5.5 |
|  |  | 7.4 |  | | | Trade Payables | 7.3 | 7.2 |
|  |  | .0 |  | | | Income Taxes Payable | .3 | 4.1 |
|  |  | 7.1 |  | | | All Other Current | 16.9 | 25.7 |
|  |  | 34.2 |  | | | Total Current | 38.9 | 47.5 |
|  |  | 42.8 |  | | | Long-Term Debt | 16.6 | 24.5 |
|  |  | .0 |  | | | Deferred Taxes | .2 | .0 |
|  |  | 25.2 |  | | | All Other Non-Current | 3.2 | 2.7 |
|  |  | -2.2 |  | | | Net Worth | 41.1 | 25.3 |
|  |  | 100.0 |  | | | Total Liabilities & Net Worth | 100.0 | 100.0 |
|  |  |  |  | | | **INCOME DATA** | | |
|  |  | 100.0 |  | | | Net Sales | 100.0 | 100.0 |
|  |  |  |  | | | Gross Profit | | |
|  |  | 77.3 |  | | | Operating Expenses | 80.5 | 88.5 |
|  |  | 22.7 |  | | | Operating Profit | 19.5 | 11.5 |
|  |  | 7.8 |  | | | All Other Expenses (net) | 3.4 | .7 |
|  |  | 14.9 |  | | | Profit Before Taxes | 16.1 | 10.8 |
|  |  |  |  | | | **RATIOS** | | |
|  |  | 2.1 |  | | | | 8.1 | 5.6 |
|  |  | 1.0 |  | | | Current | 1.7 | .9 |
|  |  | .7 |  | | | | .8 | .3 |
|  |  | 1.9 |  | | | | 7.6 | 4.2 |
|  |  | .9 |  | | | Quick | 1.4 | .7 |
|  |  | .2 |  | | | | .5 | .1 |
| | 0 | UND | | | | | 0 UND | 0 UND |
| | 0 | 853.7 | | | | Sales/Receivables | 0 999.8 | 0 UND |
| | 15 | 24.3 | | | | | 9 40.2 | 0 UND |
| | | | | | | Cost of Sales/Inventory | | |
| | | | | | | Cost of Sales/Payables | | |
|  |  | 16.7 |  | | | | 5.2 | 4.8 |
|  |  | 567.0 |  | | | Sales/Working Capital | 12.8 | -57.7 |
|  |  | -12.2 |  | | | | -38.0 | -5.3 |
|  |  |  |  | | | | 49.3 | 55.8 |
|  |  |  |  | | | EBIT/Interest | (20) 15.9 | (17) 7.5 |
|  |  |  |  | | | | 4.9 | -2.5 |
|  |  |  |  | | | Net Profit + Depr., Dep., Amort./Cur. Mat. L/T/D | | |
|  |  | .0 |  | | | | .0 | .1 |
|  |  | .3 |  | | | Fixed/Worth | .3 | 1.1 |
|  |  | NM |  | | | | 1.2 | 4.7 |
|  |  | 2.0 |  | | | | .1 | .6 |
|  |  | 206.4 |  | | | Debt/Worth | .7 | 2.4 |
|  |  | -4.1 |  | | | | 5.9 | 25.7 |
|  |  |  |  | | | | 95.1 | 85.0 |
|  |  |  |  | | | % Profit Before Taxes/Tangible Net Worth | (30) 53.3 | (23) 58.4 |
|  |  |  |  | | | | 11.0 | -30.1 |
|  |  | 46.3 |  | | | | 48.8 | 37.5 |
|  |  | 24.5 |  | | | % Profit Before Taxes/Total Assets | 25.0 | 9.8 |
|  |  | -1.0 |  | | | | 6.3 | -12.5 |
|  |  | UND |  | | | | UND | 121.1 |
|  |  | 26.8 |  | | | Sales/Net Fixed Assets | 28.2 | 12.6 |
|  |  | 2.5 |  | | | | 3.2 | 1.5 |
|  |  | 4.2 |  | | | | 8.5 | 4.1 |
|  |  | 1.7 |  | | | Sales/Total Assets | 3.3 | 1.3 |
|  |  | .6 |  | | | | 1.2 | .5 |
|  |  |  |  | | | | .8 | .3 |
|  |  |  |  | | | % Depr., Dep., Amort./Sales | (11) 3.3 | (11) 1.9 |
|  |  |  |  | | | | 9.5 | 7.2 |
|  |  |  |  | | | | 11.5 | 3.3 |
|  |  |  |  | | | % Officers', Directors', Owners' Comp/Sales | (11) 20.3 | (13) 13.7 |
|  |  |  |  | | | | 26.0 | 17.7 |
| 3899M | 29103M | 106615M | 187230M |  |  | Net Sales ($) | 1525424M | 129979M |
| 1206M | 8520M | 38140M | 127841M |  |  | Total Assets ($) | 329372M | 283662M |

© RMA 2024     M = $ thousand     MM = $ million

See Pages viii through xx for Explanation of Ratios and Data

# ENTERTAINMENT—Independent Artists, Writers, and Performers  NAICS 711510

| Comparative Historical Data | | | | Current Data Sorted by Sales | | | | | |
|---|---|---|---|---|---|---|---|---|---|
| | | | Type of Statement | | | | | | |
| | | 2 | Unqualified | | | | | 1 | 1 |
| | 2 | 1 | Reviewed | | | | | | 1 |
| 6 | 1 | | Compiled | | | | 1 | | |
| 10 | 8 | 5 | Tax Returns | 3 | 1 | | 5 | 4 | 2 |
| 4/1/21-3/31/22 | 20 4/1/22-3/31/23 | 23 4/1/23-3/31/24 | Other | 6 | 0 (4/1-9/30/23) 3 | 3 | 31 (10/1/23-3/31/24) | | |
| ALL | ALL | ALL | | 0-1MM | 1-3MM | 3-5MM | 5-10MM | 10-25MM | 25MM & OVER |
| 16 | 31 | 31 | NUMBER OF STATEMENTS | 9 | 4 | 3 | 6 | 5 | 4 |
| % | % | % | ASSETS | % | % | % | % | % | % |
| 28.2 | 31.1 | 33.7 | Cash & Equivalents | | | | | | |
| 1.7 | 5.8 | 8.9 | Trade Receivables (net) | | | | | | |
| 5.7 | 7.9 | 3.4 | Inventory | | | | | | |
| 15.3 | 7.0 | 6.7 | All Other Current | | | | | | |
| 50.9 | 51.8 | 52.7 | Total Current | | | | | | |
| 36.7 | 19.7 | 20.9 | Fixed Assets (net) | | | | | | |
| 5.8 | 10.8 | 3.5 | Intangibles (net) | | | | | | |
| 6.4 | 17.6 | 22.8 | All Other Non-Current | | | | | | |
| 100.0 | 100.0 | 100.0 | Total | | | | | | |
| | | | LIABILITIES | | | | | | |
| 9.0 | 8.3 | 18.7 | Notes Payable-Short Term | | | | | | |
| 1.2 | 1.9 | 5.8 | Cur. Mat.-L.T.D. | | | | | | |
| 1.7 | 5.3 | 4.7 | Trade Payables | | | | | | |
| .0 | 2.1 | .0 | Income Taxes Payable | | | | | | |
| 8.0 | 11.2 | 15.3 | All Other Current | | | | | | |
| 19.9 | 28.8 | 44.5 | Total Current | | | | | | |
| 22.1 | 14.3 | 45.6 | Long-Term Debt | | | | | | |
| .0 | .0 | .0 | Deferred Taxes | | | | | | |
| 4.9 | 6.1 | 10.6 | All Other Non-Current | | | | | | |
| 53.1 | 50.8 | -.7 | Net Worth | | | | | | |
| 100.0 | 100.0 | 100.0 | Total Liabilties & Net Worth | | | | | | |
| | | | INCOME DATA | | | | | | |
| 100.0 | 100.0 | 100.0 | Net Sales | | | | | | |
| | | | Gross Profit | | | | | | |
| 74.7 | 76.6 | 86.5 | Operating Expenses | | | | | | |
| 25.3 | 23.4 | 13.5 | Operating Profit | | | | | | |
| 5.1 | 1.3 | 4.3 | All Other Expenses (net) | | | | | | |
| 20.1 | 22.2 | 9.3 | Profit Before Taxes | | | | | | |
| | | | RATIOS | | | | | | |
| 10.0 | 13.2 | 5.0 | | | | | | | |
| 4.1 | 2.4 | 1.1 | Current | | | | | | |
| 1.3 | .9 | .6 | | | | | | | |
| 7.2 | 7.2 | 4.1 | | | | | | | |
| (15) 5.0 | 1.4 | .9 | Quick | | | | | | |
| 1.8 | .6 | .4 | | | | | | | |
| 0 UND | 0 UND | 0 UND | | | | | | | |
| 0 UND | 0 UND | 1 707.6 | Sales/Receivables | | | | | | |
| 0 UND | 22 16.9 | 32 11.3 | | | | | | | |
| | | | Cost of Sales/Inventory | | | | | | |
| | | | Cost of Sales/Payables | | | | | | |
| 3.5 | 3.5 | 7.4 | | | | | | | |
| 7.7 | 11.5 | 297.9 | Sales/Working Capital | | | | | | |
| UND | -47.7 | -11.4 | | | | | | | |
| | 54.8 | 12.2 | | | | | | | |
| | (13) 15.5 | (17) 5.1 | EBIT/Interest | | | | | | |
| | 2.7 | -.9 | | | | | | | |
| | | | Net Profit + Depr., Dep., Amort./Cur. Mat. L/T/D | | | | | | |
| .1 | .0 | .0 | | | | | | | |
| 1.0 | .1 | .1 | Fixed/Worth | | | | | | |
| UND | 1.0 | 2.2 | | | | | | | |
| .1 | .3 | .5 | | | | | | | |
| .5 | 1.1 | 3.2 | Debt/Worth | | | | | | |
| UND | 6.5 | -17.3 | | | | | | | |
| 190.1 | 99.6 | 568.8 | % Profit Before Taxes/Tangible Net Worth | | | | | | |
| (13) 66.0 | (26) 62.0 | (23) 67.1 | | | | | | | |
| 22.0 | 12.5 | 29.8 | | | | | | | |
| 128.5 | 52.5 | 51.2 | % Profit Before Taxes/Total Assets | | | | | | |
| 30.7 | 27.7 | 22.8 | | | | | | | |
| 3.6 | 4.9 | .0 | | | | | | | |
| 85.7 | 999.8 | UND | | | | | | | |
| 9.1 | 81.5 | 70.0 | Sales/Net Fixed Assets | | | | | | |
| 2.1 | 5.0 | 5.8 | | | | | | | |
| 4.3 | 3.0 | 4.3 | | | | | | | |
| 2.0 | 2.3 | 2.1 | Sales/Total Assets | | | | | | |
| .7 | .9 | 1.0 | | | | | | | |
| | | .1 | | | | | | | |
| | (10) | 1.1 | % Depr., Dep., Amort./Sales | | | | | | |
| | | 4.6 | | | | | | | |
| | 3.2 | | | | | | | | |
| | (18) 13.0 | | % Officers', Directors' Owners' Comp/Sales | | | | | | |
| | 21.4 | | | | | | | | |
| 157546M | 254120M | 326847M | Net Sales ($) | 3873M | 5916M | 10900M | 42682M | 82608M | 180868M |
| 64302M | 194446M | 175707M | Total Assets ($) | 6400M | 3994M | 7244M | 15328M | 60373M | 82368M |

© RMA 2024   M = $ thousand   MM = $ million
See Pages viii through xx for Explanation of Ratios and Data

# ENTERTAINMENT—Museums  NAICS 712110

| Current Data Sorted by Assets | | | | | | | Comparative Historical Data | | |
|---|---|---|---|---|---|---|---|---|---|
| 1 | | 3 | 13 | 10 | 6 | **Type of Statement** Unqualified | 43 | 19 | |
| | 1 | 2 | 1 | | | Reviewed | | | |
| | | 3 | 1 | | | Compiled | 4 | 2 | |
| | | 3 | 1 | | 1 | Tax Returns | 6 | 2 | |
| 3 | 5 | 3 | 16 | 4 | 5 | Other | 41 | 22 | |
| | 39 (4/1-9/30/23) | | 40 (10/1/23-3/31/24) | | | | 4/1/19-3/31/20 ALL | 4/1/20-3/31/21 ALL | |
| 0-500M | 500M-2MM | 2-10MM | 10-50MM | 50-100MM | 100-250MM | | | | |
| 4 | 6 | 11 | 32 | 14 | 12 | **NUMBER OF STATEMENTS** | 94 | 45 | |
| % | % | % | % | % | % | **ASSETS** | % | % | |
| | | 21.3 | 11.7 | 11.7 | 17.6 | Cash & Equivalents | 14.0 | 17.4 | |
| | | 4.9 | 7.2 | 1.9 | 1.2 | Trade Receivables (net) | 4.9 | 3.6 | |
| | | 1.5 | 2.8 | .4 | .7 | Inventory | 1.0 | 2.5 | |
| | | 7.1 | 1.4 | 2.2 | 4.0 | All Other Current | 2.3 | 1.9 | |
| | | 34.8 | 23.1 | 16.2 | 23.5 | Total Current | 22.2 | 25.3 | |
| | | 42.9 | 42.0 | 47.2 | 48.0 | Fixed Assets (net) | 49.3 | 51.9 | |
| | | .0 | 7.4 | .2 | .0 | Intangibles (net) | .3 | .3 | |
| | | 22.2 | 27.4 | 36.5 | 28.5 | All Other Non-Current | 28.2 | 22.5 | |
| | | 100.0 | 100.0 | 100.0 | 100.0 | Total | 100.0 | 100.0 | |
| | | | | | | **LIABILITIES** | | | |
| | | 1.3 | .9 | 1.1 | .5 | Notes Payable-Short Term | 1.2 | 1.7 | |
| | | .4 | .8 | 1.4 | .5 | Cur. Mat.-L.T.D. | 1.2 | .9 | |
| | | 4.0 | 4.3 | 1.1 | .9 | Trade Payables | 2.8 | 1.1 | |
| | | .0 | .0 | .0 | .2 | Income Taxes Payable | .0 | .1 | |
| | | 3.8 | 6.0 | .8 | 1.9 | All Other Current | 3.8 | 3.9 | |
| | | 9.5 | 11.9 | 4.4 | 4.0 | Total Current | 9.0 | 7.6 | |
| | | 22.2 | 9.2 | 11.0 | 5.1 | Long-Term Debt | 9.1 | 17.6 | |
| | | .0 | .0 | .1 | .4 | Deferred Taxes | .0 | .0 | |
| | | 6.0 | 3.8 | 2.0 | 5.4 | All Other Non-Current | 3.7 | 9.7 | |
| | | 62.3 | 75.1 | 82.5 | 85.2 | Net Worth | 78.1 | 65.1 | |
| | | 100.0 | 100.0 | 100.0 | 100.0 | Total Liabilities & Net Worth | 100.0 | 100.0 | |
| | | | | | | **INCOME DATA** | | | |
| | | 100.0 | 100.0 | 100.0 | 100.0 | Net Sales | 100.0 | 100.0 | |
| | | | | | | Gross Profit | | | |
| | | 104.3 | 96.2 | 86.9 | 100.5 | Operating Expenses | 94.0 | 101.6 | |
| | | -4.3 | 3.8 | 13.1 | -.5 | Operating Profit | 6.0 | -1.6 | |
| | | -.3 | -1.1 | 3.8 | 1.2 | All Other Expenses (net) | 2.7 | -1.3 | |
| | | -4.0 | 4.9 | 9.4 | -1.7 | Profit Before Taxes | 3.3 | -.3 | |
| | | | | | | **RATIOS** | | | |
| | | 18.4 | 6.8 | 8.6 | 9.6 | | 7.2 | 9.0 | |
| | | 5.5 | 2.9 | 2.6 | 5.3 | Current | 3.1 | 3.0 | |
| | | 1.4 | 1.1 | 1.2 | 1.9 | | 1.4 | 1.2 | |
| | | 8.5 | 4.5 | 6.7 | 8.6 | | 6.1 | 7.7 | |
| | | 3.8 | 2.3 | 2.1 | 4.9 | Quick | 2.5 | 2.6 | |
| | | 1.2 | .9 | .6 | 1.7 | | .8 | 1.1 | |
| | | 0  UND | 10  36.2 | 3  106.2 | 0  UND | | 0  967.6 | 0  UND | |
| | | 2  172.7 | 32  11.4 | 13  28.4 | 6  57.9 | Sales/Receivables | 7  54.9 | 7  49.8 | |
| | | 19  19.5 | 65  5.6 | 35  10.5 | 30  12.0 | | 40  9.2 | 32  11.4 | |
| | | | | | | Cost of Sales/Inventory | | | |
| | | | | | | Cost of Sales/Payables | | | |
| | | 1.9 | 1.9 | 1.2 | .9 | | 1.9 | 1.4 | |
| | | 2.8 | 4.6 | 4.3 | 1.3 | Sales/Working Capital | 3.7 | 3.9 | |
| | | 18.6 | 40.0 | NM | 21.9 | | 37.3 | 16.5 | |
| | | | 9.3 | 16.1 | | | 20.4 | 5.5 | |
| | | (20) | 1.7 | (10)  6.4 | | EBIT/Interest | (61)  1.6 | (32)  -1.9 | |
| | | | -6.6 | 2.8 | | | -11.2 | -16.3 | |
| | | | | | | Net Profit + Depr., Dep., Amort./Cur. Mat. L/T/D | | | |
| | | .4 | .3 | .4 | .4 | | .3 | .4 | |
| | | .5 | .7 | .6 | .7 | Fixed/Worth | .7 | .8 | |
| | | 1.0 | .9 | .7 | .8 | | .9 | 1.1 | |
| | | .1 | .0 | .1 | .0 | | .0 | .1 | |
| | | .2 | .2 | .1 | .1 | Debt/Worth | .1 | .2 | |
| | | 1.5 | .5 | .3 | .2 | | .4 | .5 | |
| | | 27.9 | 5.1 | 7.0 | 1.9 | | 6.5 | 3.1 | |
| | (10) | 7.3 | (28)  .9 | 2.4 | -.6 | % Profit Before Taxes/Tangible Net Worth | (91)  -.2 | (42)  -.2 | |
| | | -10.3 | -2.9 | -.7 | -3.7 | | -3.5 | -4.9 | |
| | | 18.7 | 4.7 | 4.4 | 1.7 | | 5.8 | 2.8 | |
| | | -1.0 | 1.7 | 1.7 | -.6 | % Profit Before Taxes/Total Assets | .0 | -.2 | |
| | | -9.1 | -.6 | -.6 | -3.1 | | -3.1 | -4.3 | |
| | | 5.4 | 3.4 | .8 | .7 | | 1.5 | 1.5 | |
| | | 1.5 | 1.0 | .5 | .5 | Sales/Net Fixed Assets | .6 | .5 | |
| | | .4 | .3 | .3 | .3 | | .4 | .3 | |
| | | 1.5 | .7 | .3 | .3 | | .6 | .4 | |
| | | .6 | .3 | .2 | .2 | Sales/Total Assets | .3 | .2 | |
| | | .4 | .2 | .2 | .1 | | .2 | .1 | |
| | | | 5.3 | 3.5 | 8.6 | | 5.9 | 4.8 | |
| | | (25) | 9.6 | (11)  11.6 | (11)  15.9 | % Depr., Dep., Amort./Sales | (78)  10.5 | (36)  12.9 | |
| | | | 17.8 | 14.8 | 21.3 | | 15.4 | 23.4 | |
| | | | | | | % Officers', Directors' Owners' Comp/Sales | | | |
| 4457M | 6678M | 39571M | 371116M | 224990M | 441710M | Net Sales ($) | 1099705M | 412167M | |
| 808M | 6186M | 47695M | 891667M | 1049736M | 1804126M | Total Assets ($) | 3764698M | 1578811M | |

M = $ thousand    MM = $ million
See Pages viii through xx for Explanation of Ratios and Data

© RMA 2024

# ENTERTAINMENT—Museums  NAICS 712110

| Comparative Historical Data | | | Type of Statement | Current Data Sorted by Sales | | | | | |
|---|---|---|---|---|---|---|---|---|---|
| 24 | 32 | 33 | Unqualified | | 4 | 2 | 9 | 14 | 4 |
| | 2 | 1 | Reviewed | | | | | | 1 |
| 2 | 1 | 4 | Compiled | 1 | 1 | 1 | | 1 | |
| 1 | 3 | 5 | Tax Returns | 1 | | 1 | 3 | | |
| 26 | 24 | 36 | Other | 7 | 2 | 4 | 10 | 5 | 8 |
| 4/1/21-3/31/22 ALL | 4/1/22-3/31/23 ALL | 4/1/23-3/31/24 ALL | | | 39 (4/1-9/30/23) | | | 40 (10/1/23-3/31/24) | |
| | | | | 0-1MM | 1-3MM | 3-5MM | 5-10MM | 10-25MM | 25MM & OVER |
| 53 | 62 | 79 | NUMBER OF STATEMENTS | 9 | 7 | 8 | 19 | 23 | 13 |
| % | % | % | ASSETS | % | % | % | % | % | % |
| 17.8 | 21.2 | 16.7 | Cash & Equivalents | | | | 11.0 | 11.8 | 20.1 |
| 4.8 | 4.8 | 4.5 | Trade Receivables (net) | | | | 3.6 | 4.2 | 8.5 |
| 1.1 | 1.9 | 3.8 | Inventory | | | | .3 | 4.1 | .8 |
| 2.8 | 3.0 | 3.0 | All Other Current | | | | 1.6 | 3.8 | 2.1 |
| 26.6 | 30.9 | 28.1 | Total Current | | | | 16.4 | 23.9 | 31.5 |
| 48.6 | 43.6 | 42.4 | Fixed Assets (net) | | | | 37.1 | 43.4 | 45.8 |
| .5 | 1.1 | 3.0 | Intangibles (net) | | | | 9.0 | .1 | 5.2 |
| 24.3 | 24.4 | 26.4 | All Other Non-Current | | | | 37.5 | 32.6 | 17.5 |
| 100.0 | 100.0 | 100.0 | Total | | | | 100.0 | 100.0 | 100.0 |
| | | | LIABILITIES | | | | | | |
| 4.8 | .9 | 1.2 | Notes Payable-Short Term | | | | 2.0 | .9 | .4 |
| 1.0 | .6 | .7 | Cur. Mat.-L.T.D. | | | | .8 | 1.1 | .6 |
| 1.7 | 4.7 | 3.1 | Trade Payables | | | | 2.0 | 3.4 | 5.9 |
| .0 | .0 | .0 | Income Taxes Payable | | | | .0 | .0 | .2 |
| 4.8 | 4.6 | 5.0 | All Other Current | | | | 2.3 | 5.1 | 5.1 |
| 12.4 | 10.7 | 10.0 | Total Current | | | | 7.1 | 10.5 | 12.2 |
| 18.6 | 8.5 | 11.8 | Long-Term Debt | | | | 8.8 | 11.8 | 5.9 |
| .0 | .0 | .1 | Deferred Taxes | | | | .0 | .0 | .4 |
| 3.1 | 1.7 | 3.5 | All Other Non-Current | | | | 3.7 | 2.5 | 5.5 |
| 65.9 | 79.1 | 74.6 | Net Worth | | | | 80.4 | 75.3 | 75.9 |
| 100.0 | 100.0 | 100.0 | Total Liabilities & Net Worth | | | | 100.0 | 100.0 | 100.0 |
| | | | INCOME DATA | | | | | | |
| 100.0 | 100.0 | 100.0 | Net Sales | | | | 100.0 | 100.0 | 100.0 |
| | | | Gross Profit | | | | | | |
| 86.3 | 91.2 | 96.1 | Operating Expenses | | | | 99.5 | 90.1 | 93.6 |
| 13.7 | 8.8 | 3.9 | Operating Profit | | | | .5 | 9.9 | 6.4 |
| -1.7 | 5.2 | .4 | All Other Expenses (net) | | | | -2.3 | 3.1 | .6 |
| 15.4 | 3.6 | 3.6 | Profit Before Taxes | | | | 2.8 | 6.8 | 5.8 |
| | | | RATIOS | | | | | | |
| 7.8 | 7.2 | 8.4 | | | | | 7.5 | 8.3 | 6.0 |
| 3.1 | 3.8 | 3.3 | Current | | | | 1.4 | 3.2 | 3.4 |
| 1.4 | 1.9 | 1.3 | | | | | .8 | 1.3 | 1.3 |
| 6.9 | 6.6 | 6.5 | | | | | 4.9 | 6.2 | 5.7 |
| 2.9 | 3.5 | 2.8 | Quick | | | | .9 | 3.1 | 3.4 |
| 1.1 | 1.3 | .8 | | | | | .5 | 1.0 | 1.2 |
| 6   59.4 | 4   93.5 | 2   172.7 | | | | | 3   120.0 | 4   101.6 | 8   46.1 |
| 20   18.2 | 15   24.7 | 14   26.7 | Sales/Receivables | | | | 23   16.2 | 17   21.6 | 26   13.8 |
| 48   7.6 | 35   10.3 | 41   9.0 | | | | | 57   6.4 | 29   12.4 | 38   9.6 |
| | | | Cost of Sales/Inventory | | | | | | |
| | | | Cost of Sales/Payables | | | | | | |
| 1.2 | 1.0 | 1.5 | | | | | 1.6 | 1.6 | 1.1 |
| 3.0 | 2.5 | 3.5 | Sales/Working Capital | | | | 29.4 | 3.4 | 3.4 |
| 11.3 | 8.1 | 29.4 | | | | | -10.6 | 9.3 | 27.2 |
| 55.2 | 16.1 | 12.2 | | | | | 3.2 | 13.6 | 781.3 |
| (42) 11.9 | (45) .6 | (47) 1.8 | EBIT/Interest | | | (13) 1.1 | (14) 7.9 | (10) 14.4 |
| 1.8 | -14.4 | -6.3 | | | | | -7.0 | 1.3 | -2.1 |
| | | | Net Profit + Depr., Dep., Amort./Cur. Mat. L/T/D | | | | | | |
| .3 | .2 | .3 | | | | | .2 | .3 | .7 |
| .7 | .6 | .7 | Fixed/Worth | | | | .7 | .5 | .7 |
| 1.1 | .8 | .9 | | | | | .9 | .9 | .8 |
| .1 | .0 | .1 | | | | | .0 | .1 | .1 |
| .3 | .2 | .2 | Debt/Worth | | | | .1 | .2 | .3 |
| .8 | .4 | .5 | | | | | .7 | .4 | .4 |
| 16.6 | 10.7 | 7.3 | | | | | 4.4 | 5.7 | 12.9 |
| (49) 4.5 | (61) .4 | (74) 1.2 | % Profit Before Taxes/Tangible Net Worth | | (17) .5 | (22) 2.1 | (12) 5.4 |
| .8 | -3.4 | -2.6 | | | | | -3.7 | -1.1 | -2.7 |
| 13.1 | 7.1 | 6.1 | | | | | 2.4 | 5.0 | 12.7 |
| 4.1 | .1 | 1.4 | % Profit Before Taxes/Total Assets | | | | .9 | 1.8 | 4.7 |
| .8 | -3.1 | -1.8 | | | | | -3.3 | -.8 | -1.9 |
| 1.8 | 2.7 | 3.4 | | | | | 30.8 | 1.3 | 3.0 |
| .7 | .7 | .8 | Sales/Net Fixed Assets | | | | .7 | .8 | .6 |
| .3 | .3 | .4 | | | | | .3 | .4 | .5 |
| .5 | .7 | .7 | | | | | .3 | .4 | .8 |
| .3 | .3 | .3 | Sales/Total Assets | | | | .2 | .3 | .4 |
| .2 | .2 | .2 | | | | | .2 | .2 | .3 |
| 5.2 | 5.0 | 5.1 | | | | | 11.8 | 3.4 | 6.4 |
| (40) 11.5 | (51) 8.3 | (58) 9.7 | % Depr., Dep., Amort./Sales | | (12) 19.5 | (20) 7.4 | (12) 10.0 |
| 18.7 | 17.5 | 17.3 | | | | | 24.4 | 14.1 | 15.9 |
| | | | % Officers', Directors' Owners' Comp/Sales | | | | | | |
| 1001262M | 708453M | 1088522M | Net Sales ($) | 4244M | 15598M | 32179M | 149341M | 349747M | 537413M |
| 3189530M | 2718907M | 3800218M | Total Assets ($) | 11486M | 39647M | 95788M | 869731M | 1453803M | 1329763M |

© RMA 2024

M = $ thousand    MM = $ million
See Pages viii through xx for Explanation of Ratios and Data

# ENTERTAINMENT—Zoos and Botanical Gardens  NAICS 712130

## Current Data Sorted by Assets | Comparative Historical Data

| 0-500M | 5 (4/1-9/30/23) 500M-2MM | 2-10MM | 21 (10/1/23-3/31/24) 10-50MM | 50-100MM | 100-250MM | Type of Statement | 5 4/1/19-3/31/20 ALL | 3 4/1/20-3/31/21 ALL |
|---|---|---|---|---|---|---|---|---|
| | | | 5 | | | Unqualified | 11 | 6 |
| | 1 | 1 | 1 | 1 | | Reviewed | | |
| | | | | | | Compiled | | |
| | | | 5 | 1 | 2 | Tax Returns | 5 | 1 |
| | | | | 2 | | Other | | 3 |
| 1 | 1 | 1 | 11 | 8 | 5 | NUMBER OF STATEMENTS | 16 | 10 |
| % | % | % | % | % | % | ASSETS | % | % |
| | | | 34.2 | | | Cash & Equivalents | 27.0 | 30.5 |
| D | | | 3.5 | | | Trade Receivables (net) | 4.6 | 2.6 |
| A | | | .4 | | | Inventory | .6 | .4 |
| T | | | 3.0 | | | All Other Current | 4.1 | 2.0 |
| A | | | 41.1 | | | Total Current | 36.2 | 35.4 |
| | | | 47.6 | | | Fixed Assets (net) | 51.6 | 47.9 |
| N | | | .0 | | | Intangibles (net) | .1 | .1 |
| O | | | 11.3 | | | All Other Non-Current | 12.1 | 16.5 |
| T | | | 100.0 | | | Total | 100.0 | 100.0 |
| A | | | | | | LIABILITIES | | |
| V | | | .0 | | | Notes Payable-Short Term | 2.5 | 4.5 |
| A | | | .6 | | | Cur. Mat.-L.T.D. | .8 | .5 |
| I | | | 3.8 | | | Trade Payables | 1.6 | .6 |
| L | | | .0 | | | Income Taxes Payable | .0 | .0 |
| A | | | 6.0 | | | All Other Current | 3.3 | 8.5 |
| B | | | 10.4 | | | Total Current | 8.2 | 14.1 |
| L | | | 6.2 | | | Long-Term Debt | 9.6 | 12.8 |
| E | | | .1 | | | Deferred Taxes | .0 | .0 |
| | | | 2.3 | | | All Other Non-Current | 3.6 | 6.5 |
| | | | 81.0 | | | Net Worth | 78.5 | 66.6 |
| | | | 100.0 | | | Total Liabilities & Net Worth | 100.0 | 100.0 |
| | | | | | | INCOME DATA | | |
| | | | 100.0 | | | Net Sales | 100.0 | 100.0 |
| | | | | | | Gross Profit | | |
| | | | 94.8 | | | Operating Expenses | 79.9 | 79.1 |
| | | | 5.2 | | | Operating Profit | 20.1 | 20.9 |
| | | | 8.3 | | | All Other Expenses (net) | 5.0 | 6.5 |
| | | | -3.1 | | | Profit Before Taxes | 15.1 | 14.4 |
| | | | | | | RATIOS | | |
| | | | 5.5 | | | | 17.2 | 9.7 |
| | | | 3.0 | | | Current | 6.4 | 3.6 |
| | | | 2.4 | | | | 1.8 | 2.1 |
| | | | 5.0 | | | | 16.3 | 9.3 |
| | | | 2.6 | | | Quick | 4.8 | 3.4 |
| | | | 2.3 | | | | 1.3 | 1.8 |
| | | 1 | 453.1 | | | | 0 UND | 0 UND |
| | | 3 | 112.7 | | | Sales/Receivables | 0 UND | 1 401.3 |
| | | 32 | 11.5 | | | | 9 39.1 | 17 21.4 |
| | | | | | | Cost of Sales/Inventory | | |
| | | | | | | Cost of Sales/Payables | | |
| | | | 1.6 | | | | .6 | 1.3 |
| | | | 2.8 | | | Sales/Working Capital | 1.2 | 1.9 |
| | | | 5.7 | | | | 9.2 | 4.1 |
| | | | | | | | 50.2 | |
| | | | | | | EBIT/Interest | (10) 3.7 | |
| | | | | | | | -.7 | |
| | | | | | | Net Profit + Depr., Dep., Amort./Cur. Mat. L/T/D | | |
| | | | .2 | | | | .2 | .5 |
| | | | .5 | | | Fixed/Worth | .7 | .7 |
| | | | 1.0 | | | | 1.0 | .9 |
| | | | .1 | | | | .1 | .0 |
| | | | .2 | | | Debt/Worth | .3 | .3 |
| | | | .3 | | | | .4 | 1.5 |
| | | | 3.3 | | | | 13.8 | |
| | | | -.8 | | | % Profit Before Taxes/Tangible Net Worth | 6.4 | |
| | | | -10.5 | | | | -1.1 | |
| | | | 2.9 | | | | 11.6 | 10.9 |
| | | | -.8 | | | % Profit Before Taxes/Total Assets | 5.8 | 3.5 |
| | | | -8.0 | | | | -.9 | -3.6 |
| | | | 8.4 | | | | 2.3 | 4.1 |
| | | | 1.0 | | | Sales/Net Fixed Assets | .6 | .6 |
| | | | .6 | | | | .5 | .4 |
| | | | 1.1 | | | | .5 | 1.0 |
| | | | .5 | | | Sales/Total Assets | .3 | .3 |
| | | | .4 | | | | .2 | .2 |
| | | | 2.0 | | | | 5.1 | |
| | | | 5.5 | | | % Depr., Dep., Amort./Sales | (13) 9.2 | |
| | | | 9.4 | | | | 14.0 | |
| | | | | | | % Officers', Directors' Owners' Comp/Sales | | |
| | 2382M | 15645M | 249260M | 265395M | 172864M | Net Sales ($) | 209365M | 149983M |
| | 580M | 5176M | 381143M | 637670M | 825863M | Total Assets ($) | 756875M | 564973M |

© RMA 2024

M = $ thousand    MM = $ million
See Pages viii through xx for Explanation of Ratios and Data

# ENTERTAINMENT—Zoos and Botanical Gardens  NAICS 712130

| Comparative Historical Data ||| | Current Data Sorted by Sales |||||||
|---|---|---|---|---|---|---|---|---|---|
| 5 | 17 | 12 | Type of Statement | | | | 1 | 7 | 4 |
|  |  | 3 | Unqualified | | | | 2 |  | 1 |
|  |  |  | Reviewed | | | | | | |
| 2 | 1 | 2 | Compiled | | | | 1 | 1 | |
| 9 | 6 | 9 | Tax Returns | 1 | | 1 | 2 | | 5 |
| 4/1/21-3/31/22 | 4/1/22-3/31/23 | 4/1/23-3/31/24 | Other | 5 (4/1-9/30/23) | 1 | | 21 (10/1/23-3/31/24) | | |
| ALL | ALL | ALL |  | 0-1MM | 1-3MM | 3-5MM | 5-10MM | 10-25MM | 25MM & OVER |
| 16 | 24 | 26 | NUMBER OF STATEMENTS | 1 | 1 | 1 | 12 | 10 |
| % | % | % | **ASSETS** | % | % | % | % | % | % |
| 26.6 | 30.8 | 29.4 | Cash & Equivalents | | | | | 25.4 | 43.2 |
| 2.5 | 2.6 | 6.2 | Trade Receivables (net) | D | | | | 2.8 | 4.4 |
| .6 | .6 | 1.1 | Inventory | A | | | | .6 | .1 |
| 1.2 | 4.1 | 3.7 | All Other Current | T | | | | 2.7 | 6.4 |
| 30.9 | 38.1 | 40.4 | Total Current | A | | | | 31.5 | 54.1 |
| 37.4 | 35.4 | 45.4 | Fixed Assets (net) |   | | | | 54.1 | 30.9 |
| 4.9 | .2 | .0 | Intangibles (net) | N | | | | .0 | .1 |
| 26.8 | 26.3 | 14.1 | All Other Non-Current | O | | | | 14.4 | 15.0 |
| 100.0 | 100.0 | 100.0 | Total | T | | | | 100.0 | 100.0 |
| | | | **LIABILITIES** | | | | | | |
| .4 | .1 | 1.0 | Notes Payable-Short Term | A | | | | .5 | .3 |
| 1.2 | .2 | .5 | Cur. Mat.-L.T.D. | V | | | | .6 | .1 |
| 1.6 | 1.7 | 4.3 | Trade Payables | A | | | | 4.0 | 4.0 |
| .0 | .1 | .0 | Income Taxes Payable | I | | | | .0 | .0 |
| 2.9 | 4.0 | 5.3 | All Other Current | L | | | | 5.8 | 6.2 |
| 6.2 | 6.1 | 11.1 | Total Current | A | | | | 10.9 | 10.6 |
| 15.6 | 2.7 | 2.9 | Long-Term Debt | B | | | | 4.4 | .4 |
| .0 | .0 | .0 | Deferred Taxes | L | | | | .0 | .0 |
| 1.8 | 1.7 | 3.9 | All Other Non-Current | E | | | | 5.4 | 3.8 |
| 76.4 | 89.5 | 82.1 | Net Worth | | | | | 79.3 | 85.2 |
| 100.0 | 100.0 | 100.0 | Total Liabilities & Net Worth | | | | | 100.0 | 100.0 |
| | | | **INCOME DATA** | | | | | | |
| 100.0 | 100.0 | 100.0 | Net Sales | | | | | 100.0 | 100.0 |
| | | | Gross Profit | | | | | | |
| 69.0 | 88.2 | 91.6 | Operating Expenses | | | | | 84.6 | 93.6 |
| 31.0 | 11.8 | 8.4 | Operating Profit | | | | | 15.4 | 6.4 |
| 6.0 | 6.7 | 4.7 | All Other Expenses (net) | | | | | 6.8 | 3.4 |
| 25.0 | 5.1 | 3.7 | Profit Before Taxes | | | | | 8.6 | 3.1 |
| | | | **RATIOS** | | | | | | |
| 13.2 | 12.0 | 7.9 | | | | | | 12.2 | 8.3 |
| 6.6 | 4.8 | 3.6 | Current | | | | | 3.6 | 5.1 |
| 1.2 | 3.9 | 2.5 | | | | | | 1.7 | 3.3 |
| 13.1 | 11.9 | 7.2 | | | | | | 12.0 | 8.1 |
| 5.9 | 4.3 | 3.1 | Quick | | | | | 3.3 | 4.7 |
| 1.0 | 2.5 | 2.2 | | | | | | 1.4 | 2.5 |
| 3  107.0 | 3  112.5 | 1  301.1 | | | | | 3  143.1 | 0  UND |
| 8  44.1 | 13  28.1 | 11  33.6 | Sales/Receivables | | | | 11  33.6 | 13  28.6 |
| 36  10.1 | 34  10.7 | 36  10.0 | | | | | 31  11.6 | 36  10.0 |
| | | | Cost of Sales/Inventory | | | | | | |
| | | | Cost of Sales/Payables | | | | | | |
| 1.7 | 1.4 | 1.4 | | | | | | 1.5 | .9 |
| 2.3 | 1.7 | 2.1 | Sales/Working Capital | | | | | 2.2 | 1.6 |
| 39.2 | 2.9 | 5.3 | | | | | | 8.4 | 2.1 |
| | | 28.4 | | | | | | 48.1 | |
| | (15) 5.3 | EBIT/Interest | | | | | (10) 9.0 | |
| | | -5.7 | | | | | | -8.0 | |
| | | | Net Profit + Depr., Dep., Amort./Cur. Mat. L/T/D | | | | | | |
| .0 | .1 | .1 | | | | | | .4 | .0 |
| .5 | .3 | .6 | Fixed/Worth | | | | | .7 | .2 |
| .9 | .8 | .9 | | | | | | 1.0 | .8 |
| .1 | .0 | .1 | | | | | | .1 | .1 |
| .2 | .1 | .1 | Debt/Worth | | | | | .1 | .2 |
| .3 | .2 | .3 | | | | | | .3 | .3 |
| 34.7 | 7.2 | 5.1 | % Profit Before Taxes/Tangible Net Worth | | | | | 5.1 | 5.4 |
| (15) 13.7 | 1.2 | 2.2 | | | | | | 2.5 | 2.3 |
| 2.0 | -.9 | -2.7 | | | | | | -.8 | -13.6 |
| 26.7 | 6.9 | 4.6 | % Profit Before Taxes/Total Assets | | | | | 4.8 | 3.9 |
| 11.0 | 1.0 | 2.0 | | | | | | 2.4 | 2.0 |
| 1.5 | -.8 | -2.2 | | | | | | -.7 | -11.6 |
| 24.0 | 12.0 | 9.8 | Sales/Net Fixed Assets | | | | | 1.2 | 25.8 |
| 1.4 | .8 | .7 | | | | | | .8 | 7.4 |
| .5 | .4 | .4 | | | | | | .4 | .4 |
| .7 | .7 | .8 | Sales/Total Assets | | | | | .8 | .8 |
| .5 | .3 | .4 | | | | | | .4 | .4 |
| .2 | .2 | .2 | | | | | | .3 | .2 |
| 1.5 | 1.1 | 2.1 | % Depr., Dep., Amort./Sales | | | | | 2.9 | .9 |
| (13) 8.5 | (20) 6.6 | (25) 6.0 | | | | | | 5.6 | 5.2 |
| 16.0 | 13.0 | 12.0 | | | | | | 9.7 | 12.3 |
| | | | % Officers', Directors' Owners' Comp/Sales | | | | | | |
| 452288M | 645639M | 705546M | Net Sales ($) | | 2382M | 3770M | 15903M | 232753M | 450738M |
| 1077914M | 2064963M | 1850432M | Total Assets ($) | | 580M | 31466M | 53494M | 695211M | 1069681M |

© RMA 2024            M = $ thousand    MM = $ million
See Pages viii through xx for Explanation of Ratios and Data

# ENTERTAINMENT—Amusement and Theme Parks  NAICS 713110

## Current Data Sorted by Assets | Comparative Historical Data

| | | | | | | Type of Statement | | | | |
|---|---|---|---|---|---|---|---|---|---|---|
| | | | 3 | 3 | 1 | Unqualified | | 8 | | 2 |
| | | | 4 | | | Reviewed | | 6 | | 9 |
| | | 1 | | | | Compiled | | 3 | | 2 |
| 1 | 2 | 2 | | | | Tax Returns | | 18 | | 5 |
| 1 | 3 | 7 | 10 | 3 | 2 | Other | | 36 | | 15 |
| | 10 (4/1-9/30/23) | | 33 (10/1/23-3/31/24) | | | | | 4/1/19-3/31/20 | | 4/1/20-3/31/21 |
| 0-500M | 500M-2MM | 2-10MM | 10-50MM | 50-100MM | 100-250MM | | | ALL | | ALL |
| 2 | 5 | 10 | 17 | 6 | 3 | NUMBER OF STATEMENTS | | 71 | | 33 |
| % | % | % | % | % | % | ASSETS | | % | | % |
| | | 12.5 | 13.3 | | | Cash & Equivalents | | 15.5 | | 26.1 |
| | | 7.4 | 1.4 | | | Trade Receivables (net) | | 2.1 | | 2.5 |
| | | .8 | 3.6 | | | Inventory | | 1.9 | | 4.4 |
| | | 11.4 | 2.4 | | | All Other Current | | 2.3 | | .5 |
| | | 32.0 | 20.8 | | | Total Current | | 21.9 | | 33.6 |
| | | 47.5 | 56.6 | | | Fixed Assets (net) | | 65.4 | | 57.2 |
| | | 8.6 | 8.2 | | | Intangibles (net) | | 4.6 | | 6.8 |
| | | 11.8 | 14.4 | | | All Other Non-Current | | 8.1 | | 2.4 |
| | | 100.0 | 100.0 | | | Total | | 100.0 | | 100.0 |
| | | | | | | LIABILITIES | | | | |
| | | .2 | .0 | | | Notes Payable-Short Term | | 2.6 | | 4.9 |
| | | 1.3 | 3.8 | | | Cur. Mat.-L.T.D. | | 5.1 | | 3.6 |
| | | 11.0 | 4.4 | | | Trade Payables | | 3.7 | | 1.3 |
| | | .1 | .4 | | | Income Taxes Payable | | .0 | | .3 |
| | | 37.9 | 8.8 | | | All Other Current | | 17.6 | | 25.0 |
| | | 50.4 | 17.4 | | | Total Current | | 29.0 | | 35.2 |
| | | 30.6 | 36.0 | | | Long-Term Debt | | 41.2 | | 25.2 |
| | | .2 | .5 | | | Deferred Taxes | | .3 | | .3 |
| | | 8.5 | 10.0 | | | All Other Non-Current | | 6.3 | | 8.0 |
| | | 10.4 | 36.1 | | | Net Worth | | 23.2 | | 31.4 |
| | | 100.0 | 100.0 | | | Total Liabilties & Net Worth | | 100.0 | | 100.0 |
| | | | | | | INCOME DATA | | | | |
| | | 100.0 | 100.0 | | | Net Sales | | 100.0 | | 100.0 |
| | | | | | | Gross Profit | | | | |
| | | 92.7 | 87.8 | | | Operating Expenses | | 87.0 | | 109.3 |
| | | 7.3 | 12.2 | | | Operating Profit | | 13.0 | | -9.3 |
| | | 2.7 | 2.2 | | | All Other Expenses (net) | | 4.0 | | -.1 |
| | | 4.6 | 10.0 | | | Profit Before Taxes | | 9.0 | | -9.2 |
| | | | | | | RATIOS | | | | |
| | | 2.2 | 1.6 | | | | | 2.2 | | 3.3 |
| | | 1.0 | .9 | | | Current | | .6 | | 1.5 |
| | | .5 | .7 | | | | | .3 | | .4 |
| | | 1.6 | 1.2 | | | | | 2.1 | | 2.9 |
| | | .7 | (16) .6 | | | Quick | | .5 | | 1.4 |
| | | .4 | .4 | | | | | .2 | | .3 |
| | | 0 UND | 0 996.0 | | | | | 0 UND | | 0 UND |
| | | 1 516.6 | 1 404.5 | | | Sales/Receivables | | 1 548.1 | | 1 446.8 |
| | | 22 16.7 | 7 54.5 | | | | | 5 78.3 | | 13 27.8 |
| | | | | | | Cost of Sales/Inventory | | | | |
| | | | | | | Cost of Sales/Payables | | | | |
| | | 11.2 | 16.7 | | | | | 14.6 | | 3.5 |
| | | NM | -67.3 | | | Sales/Working Capital | | -24.2 | | 19.0 |
| | | -5.7 | -24.3 | | | | | -5.8 | | -5.3 |
| | | | 13.1 | | | | | 7.8 | | 9.6 |
| | | (15) | 6.0 | | | EBIT/Interest | (56) | 3.9 | (25) | -1.8 |
| | | | 2.5 | | | | | 1.3 | | -24.7 |
| | | | | | | Net Profit + Depr., Dep., | | 6.6 | | |
| | | | | | | Amort./Cur. Mat. L/T/D | (10) | 3.2 | | |
| | | | | | | | | 2.5 | | |
| | | 1.0 | 1.1 | | | | | 1.1 | | .7 |
| | | 3.5 | 2.8 | | | Fixed/Worth | | 2.0 | | 1.6 |
| | | -2.0 | NM | | | | | -476.4 | | 16.8 |
| | | 1.7 | .9 | | | | | .7 | | .4 |
| | | 6.6 | 2.9 | | | Debt/Worth | | 1.7 | | .9 |
| | | -10.0 | NM | | | | | -575.4 | | 19.1 |
| | | | 61.0 | | | | | 48.1 | | 22.9 |
| | | (13) | 43.3 | | | % Profit Before Taxes/Tangible Net Worth | (53) | 18.1 | (26) | -7.9 |
| | | | 10.8 | | | | | 6.8 | | -67.8 |
| | | 26.4 | 20.3 | | | | | 18.9 | | 13.9 |
| | | 7.1 | 9.1 | | | % Profit Before Taxes/Total Assets | | 8.8 | | -7.3 |
| | | -6.5 | 1.6 | | | | | 1.0 | | -23.9 |
| | | 109.5 | 2.4 | | | | | 3.9 | | 4.7 |
| | | 3.5 | 2.0 | | | Sales/Net Fixed Assets | | 1.6 | | 1.9 |
| | | 1.2 | .9 | | | | | .7 | | .7 |
| | | 2.2 | 1.4 | | | | | 1.9 | | 1.5 |
| | | 1.1 | .9 | | | Sales/Total Assets | | 1.2 | | 1.0 |
| | | .9 | .6 | | | | | .5 | | .5 |
| | | | 2.9 | | | | | 5.1 | | 5.4 |
| | | (15) | 10.0 | | | % Depr., Dep., Amort./Sales | (59) | 11.1 | (28) | 14.7 |
| | | | 13.6 | | | | | 19.1 | | 24.0 |
| | | | | | | | | 2.4 | | |
| | | | | | | % Officers', Directors' Owners' Comp/Sales | (19) | 4.9 | | |
| | | | | | | | | 9.9 | | |
| 2798M | 16079M | 72639M | 485423M | 300735M | 193083M | Net Sales ($) | | 1357696M | | 317500M |
| 417M | 6691M | 46579M | 412021M | 344334M | 443904M | Total Assets ($) | | 1570120M | | 554468M |

© RMA 2024    M = $ thousand   MM = $ million
See Pages viii through xx for Explanation of Ratios and Data

# ENTERTAINMENT—Amusement and Theme Parks  NAICS 713110

## Comparative Historical Data | Current Data Sorted by Sales

| | | | | | | Type of Statement | | | | | | | |
|---|---|---|---|---|---|---|---|---|---|---|---|---|---|
| | | 3 | | 9 | | 7 | Unqualified | | | | 1 | 1 | 6 |
| | | 4 | | 7 | | 4 | Reviewed | | | 1 | | 2 | |
| | | 3 | | 3 | | 1 | Compiled | | | 1 | | | |
| | | 6 | | 6 | | 5 | Tax Returns | | 1 | 2 | 1 | 1 | |
| | | 14 | | 22 | | 26 | Other | | 4 | 4 | 4 | 4 | 10 |
| | | 4/1/21- | | 4/1/22- | | 4/1/23- | | | 10 (4/1-9/30/23) | | | 33 (10/1/23-3/31/24) | |
| | | 3/31/22 | | 3/31/23 | | 3/31/24 | | 0-1MM | 1-3MM | 3-5MM | 5-10MM | 10-25MM | 25MM & OVER |
| | | ALL | | ALL | | ALL | | | | | | | |
| | | 30 | | 47 | | 43 | NUMBER OF STATEMENTS | | 5 | 8 | 6 | 8 | 16 |
| | | % | | % | | % | | % | % | % | % | % | % |
| | | | | | | | ASSETS | | | | | | |
| | | 34.3 | | 25.5 | | 17.0 | Cash & Equivalents | | | | | | 14.8 |
| | | 1.0 | | 1.0 | | 2.9 | Trade Receivables (net) | | | | | | 1.9 |
| | | 3.9 | | 1.9 | | 2.2 | Inventory | | | | | | 4.6 |
| | | 3.5 | | 4.3 | | 5.5 | All Other Current | | | | | | 2.5 |
| | | 42.7 | | 32.7 | | 27.6 | Total Current | | | | | | 23.9 |
| | | 48.1 | | 51.3 | | 53.9 | Fixed Assets (net) | | | | | | 66.7 |
| | | 3.0 | | 6.0 | | 6.0 | Intangibles (net) | | | | | | 1.9 |
| | | 6.2 | | 10.1 | | 12.5 | All Other Non-Current | | | | | | 7.4 |
| | | 100.0 | | 100.0 | | 100.0 | Total | | | | | | 100.0 |
| | | | | | | | LIABILITIES | | | | | | |
| | | 5.9 | | 1.9 | | .5 | Notes Payable-Short Term | | | | | | .0 |
| | | 1.4 | | 2.4 | | 2.7 | Cur. Mat.-L.T.D. | | | | | | 4.1 |
| | | 1.4 | | 4.4 | | 5.1 | Trade Payables | | | | | | 5.2 |
| | | .0 | | .1 | | .2 | Income Taxes Payable | | | | | | .1 |
| | | 12.6 | | 22.8 | | 20.0 | All Other Current | | | | | | 13.4 |
| | | 21.4 | | 31.6 | | 28.5 | Total Current | | | | | | 22.8 |
| | | 34.9 | | 44.8 | | 39.1 | Long-Term Debt | | | | | | 33.8 |
| | | .0 | | .2 | | .2 | Deferred Taxes | | | | | | .0 |
| | | .9 | | 7.6 | | 7.6 | All Other Non-Current | | | | | | 2.4 |
| | | 42.7 | | 15.7 | | 24.6 | Net Worth | | | | | | 40.9 |
| | | 100.0 | | 100.0 | | 100.0 | Total Liabilities & Net Worth | | | | | | 100.0 |
| | | | | | | | INCOME DATA | | | | | | |
| | | 100.0 | | 100.0 | | 100.0 | Net Sales | | | | | | 100.0 |
| | | | | | | | Gross Profit | | | | | | |
| | | 84.7 | | 80.6 | | 89.1 | Operating Expenses | | | | | | 86.5 |
| | | 15.3 | | 19.4 | | 10.9 | Operating Profit | | | | | | 13.5 |
| | | .0 | | 3.5 | | 1.9 | All Other Expenses (net) | | | | | | .9 |
| | | 15.3 | | 15.9 | | 9.0 | Profit Before Taxes | | | | | | 12.6 |
| | | | | | | | RATIOS | | | | | | |
| | | 7.3 | | 4.2 | | 1.8 | | | | | | | 1.7 |
| | | 2.0 | | 1.2 | | 1.1 | Current | | | | | | 1.0 |
| | | .6 | | .6 | | .6 | | | | | | | .6 |
| | | 6.6 | | 3.6 | | 1.5 | | | | | | | 1.2 |
| | | 1.7 | | .8 | (42) | .7 | Quick | | | | | | .6 |
| | | .5 | | .4 | | .4 | | | | | | | .3 |
| 0 | UND | | 0 | UND | | 0 | 999.8 | Sales/Receivables | | | | 0 | 851.0 |
| 0 | UND | | 1 | 419.3 | 1 | 280.0 | | | | | | 4 | 84.0 |
| 5 | 68.5 | | 3 | 116.6 | 8 | 43.7 | | | | | | 12 | 30.2 |
| | | | | | | | Cost of Sales/Inventory | | | | | | |
| | | | | | | | Cost of Sales/Payables | | | | | | |
| | | 2.9 | | 3.4 | | 8.5 | | | | | | | 8.7 |
| | | 8.4 | | 27.8 | | 282.3 | Sales/Working Capital | | | | | | NM |
| | | -9.1 | | -15.8 | | -20.8 | | | | | | | -31.0 |
| | | 36.3 | | 17.8 | | 13.0 | | | | | | | 8.7 |
| (22) | 10.2 | (39) | 9.0 | (37) | 4.1 | EBIT/Interest | | | | | (14) | 3.7 |
| | | 1.7 | | 3.2 | | 2.1 | | | | | | | 3.4 |
| | | | | 9.3 | | 11.9 | Net Profit + Depr., Dep., | | | | | | |
| | | | (13) | 5.1 | (12) | 3.9 | Amort./Cur. Mat. L/T/D | | | | | | |
| | | | | 4.4 | | 2.7 | | | | | | | |
| | | .2 | | .7 | | 1.1 | | | | | | | 1.0 |
| | | 1.3 | | 1.9 | | 2.4 | Fixed/Worth | | | | | | 1.9 |
| | | 3.6 | | 999.8 | | 14.6 | | | | | | | 2.9 |
| | | .2 | | .7 | | 1.0 | | | | | | | 1.1 |
| | | 1.2 | | 2.6 | | 2.3 | Debt/Worth | | | | | | 1.6 |
| | | 4.4 | | -18.0 | | -53.5 | | | | | | | 3.4 |
| | | 71.0 | | 66.1 | | 47.2 | | | | | | | 47.2 |
| (26) | 51.9 | (35) | 31.9 | (32) | 29.8 | % Profit Before Taxes/Tangible Net Worth | | | | | (15) | 30.5 |
| | | 8.8 | | 10.4 | | 11.1 | | | | | | | 22.7 |
| | | 43.8 | | 25.9 | | 23.0 | | | | | | | 22.3 |
| | | 16.3 | | 11.3 | | 8.9 | % Profit Before Taxes/Total Assets | | | | | | 9.0 |
| | | 6.0 | | 4.7 | | -.6 | | | | | | | 7.4 |
| | | 8.9 | | 8.1 | | 4.9 | | | | | | | 2.1 |
| | | 2.8 | | 1.8 | | 2.1 | Sales/Net Fixed Assets | | | | | | 1.7 |
| | | .7 | | .8 | | .9 | | | | | | | .9 |
| | | 2.1 | | 1.5 | | 1.8 | | | | | | | 1.4 |
| | | 1.2 | | .8 | | 1.0 | Sales/Total Assets | | | | | | 1.0 |
| | | .5 | | .5 | | .7 | | | | | | | .8 |
| | | 3.8 | | 4.6 | | 4.1 | | | | | | | 5.5 |
| (22) | 10.1 | (33) | 7.5 | (33) | 8.1 | % Depr., Dep., Amort./Sales | | | | | (15) | 9.4 |
| | | 17.7 | | 14.5 | | 11.4 | | | | | | | 10.5 |
| | | 2.6 | | | | | % Officers', Directors' | | | | | | |
| (11) | 3.7 | | | | | Owners' Comp/Sales | | | | | | |
| | | 12.0 | | | | | | | | | | | |
| | | 454590M | | 1013210M | | 1070757M | Net Sales ($) | | 9542M | 31793M | 44172M | 127505M | 857745M |
| | | 512332M | | 1353626M | | 1253946M | Total Assets ($) | | 6786M | 29946M | 59242M | 135731M | 1022241M |

© RMA 2024   M = $ thousand   MM = $ million
See Pages viii through xx for Explanation of Ratios and Data

# ENTERTAINMENT—Casinos (except Casino Hotels) NAICS 713210

## Current Data Sorted by Assets | Comparative Historical Data

| | | | | | | | | Type of Statement | | | | |
|---|---|---|---|---|---|---|---|---|---|---|---|---|
| | | | | | 5 | 1 | 10 | Unqualified | | 15 | | 16 |
| | | | | | 1 | | | Reviewed | | 1 | | 3 |
| | | | | | 1 | | | Compiled | | 2 | | 1 |
| | 2 | 5 | 2 | 1 | 2 | | 7 | Tax Returns | | 8 | | 3 |
| | | 5 | 4 | | 8 | | | Other | | 42 | | 27 |
| | | 15 (4/1-9/30/23) | | | 39 (10/1/23-3/31/24) | | | | | 4/1/19-3/31/20 | | 4/1/20-3/31/21 |
| | 0-500M | 500M-2MM | 2-10MM | 10-50MM | 50-100MM | | 100-250MM | | | ALL | | ALL |
| | 2 | 10 | 6 | 8 | 11 | | 17 | NUMBER OF STATEMENTS | | 68 | | 50 |
| | % | % | % | % | % | | % | ASSETS | | % | | % |
| | | 29.7 | | | 34.1 | | 24.9 | Cash & Equivalents | | 25.7 | | 25.7 |
| | | 3.3 | | | 1.3 | | 1.2 | Trade Receivables (net) | | 1.4 | | 1.1 |
| | | 4.5 | | | .5 | | .9 | Inventory | | 1.2 | | 1.6 |
| | | 15.9 | | | 2.7 | | 2.2 | All Other Current | | 2.2 | | 1.9 |
| | | 53.5 | | | 38.5 | | 29.2 | Total Current | | 30.5 | | 30.3 |
| | | 29.7 | | | 51.4 | | 65.5 | Fixed Assets (net) | | 59.1 | | 62.4 |
| | | 10.9 | | | 3.3 | | 4.2 | Intangibles (net) | | 6.0 | | 2.1 |
| | | 6.0 | | | 6.8 | | 1.1 | All Other Non-Current | | 4.4 | | 5.2 |
| | | 100.0 | | | 100.0 | | 100.0 | Total | | 100.0 | | 100.0 |
| | | | | | | | | LIABILITIES | | | | |
| | | 22.1 | | | 17.0 | | .0 | Notes Payable-Short-Term | | .6 | | 1.0 |
| | | 5.9 | | | 1.6 | | 3.1 | Cur. Mat.-L.T.D. | | 3.5 | | 4.7 |
| | | 6.0 | | | 3.1 | | 2.0 | Trade Payables | | 2.9 | | 2.0 |
| | | .1 | | | .0 | | .0 | Income Taxes Payable | | .1 | | .0 |
| | | 40.6 | | | 9.9 | | 12.2 | All Other Current | | 11.5 | | 14.5 |
| | | 74.7 | | | 31.5 | | 17.3 | Total Current | | 18.5 | | 22.2 |
| | | 23.7 | | | 16.7 | | 29.5 | Long-Term Debt | | 28.1 | | 24.2 |
| | | .0 | | | .0 | | .0 | Deferred Taxes | | .0 | | .0 |
| | | 12.1 | | | 3.3 | | 1.7 | All Other Non-Current | | 2.7 | | 1.2 |
| | | -10.5 | | | 48.5 | | 51.4 | Net Worth | | 50.7 | | 52.3 |
| | | 100.0 | | | 100.0 | | 100.0 | Total Liabilities & Net Worth | | 100.0 | | 100.0 |
| | | | | | | | | INCOME DATA | | | | |
| | | 100.0 | | | 100.0 | | 100.0 | Net Sales | | 100.0 | | 100.0 |
| | | | | | | | | Gross Profit | | | | |
| | | 94.8 | | | 75.3 | | 65.4 | Operating Expenses | | 81.8 | | 84.6 |
| | | 5.2 | | | 24.7 | | 34.6 | Operating Profit | | 18.2 | | 15.4 |
| | | -1.5 | | | 1.2 | | 2.1 | All Other Expenses (net) | | 2.6 | | 2.1 |
| | | 6.6 | | | 23.4 | | 32.5 | Profit Before Taxes | | 15.6 | | 13.3 |
| | | | | | | | | RATIOS | | | | |
| | | 2.3 | | | 5.0 | | 2.6 | | | 3.0 | | 3.9 |
| | | .8 | | | 1.6 | | 1.5 | Current | | 1.6 | | 1.7 |
| | | .4 | | | 1.5 | | 1.3 | | | .9 | | .9 |
| | | 1.4 | | | 4.8 | | 2.6 | | | 2.8 | | 3.3 |
| | | .6 | | | 1.5 | | 1.3 | Quick | | 1.4 | | 1.5 |
| | | .1 | | | 1.2 | | 1.2 | | | .8 | | .7 |
| | 0 | UND | | 1 | 377.3 | 1 | 513.0 | | 0 | 999.8 | 0 | 999.8 |
| | 0 | UND | | 3 | 106.2 | 5 | 69.3 | Sales/Receivables | 2 | 159.7 | 3 | 113.6 |
| | 0 | UND | | 8 | 43.2 | 7 | 53.6 | | 4 | 89.6 | 6 | 65.4 |
| | | | | | | | | Cost of Sales/Inventory | | | | |
| | | | | | | | | Cost of Sales/Payables | | | | |
| | | 41.9 | | | 1.7 | | 4.8 | | | 8.0 | | 4.3 |
| | | -543.0 | | | 7.5 | | 9.6 | Sales/Working Capital | | 19.7 | | 10.7 |
| | | -7.6 | | | 15.8 | | 28.5 | | | NM | | -42.0 |
| | | | | | | | 68.1 | | | 40.9 | | 39.4 |
| | | | | | (16) | | 14.5 | EBIT/Interest | (57) | 9.6 | (40) | 7.4 |
| | | | | | | | 7.3 | | | 2.2 | | 1.6 |
| | | | | | | | | Net Profit + Depr., Dep., Amort./Cur. Mat. L/T/D | | | | |
| | | .4 | | | .6 | | .8 | | | .8 | | .8 |
| | | 2.2 | | | .8 | | 1.3 | Fixed/Worth | | 1.3 | | 1.2 |
| | | -.4 | | | 3.2 | | 3.5 | | | 2.1 | | 1.9 |
| | | .6 | | | .2 | | .2 | | | .3 | | .3 |
| | | NM | | | .4 | | 1.0 | Debt/Worth | | .7 | | .7 |
| | | -1.8 | | | 3.1 | | 3.3 | | | 2.0 | | 2.0 |
| | | | | | | | 98.1 | | | 67.4 | | 56.4 |
| | | | | | (16) | | 49.5 | % Profit Before Taxes/Tangible Net Worth | (62) | 35.1 | (47) | 19.4 |
| | | | | | | | 27.1 | | | 9.8 | | 4.4 |
| | | 22.3 | | | 38.1 | | 33.8 | | | 32.8 | | 20.4 |
| | | 8.5 | | | 18.2 | | 24.0 | % Profit Before Taxes/Total Assets | | 17.8 | | 10.1 |
| | | -6.3 | | | 9.9 | | 17.6 | | | 4.2 | | 2.0 |
| | | 118.5 | | | 3.9 | | 1.7 | | | 6.4 | | 2.9 |
| | | 36.0 | | | 1.8 | | 1.2 | Sales/Net Fixed Assets | | 1.5 | | 1.1 |
| | | 12.6 | | | 1.1 | | .9 | | | 1.1 | | .8 |
| | | 13.9 | | | 1.2 | | 1.0 | | | 3.0 | | 1.2 |
| | | 10.2 | | | 1.0 | | .8 | Sales/Total Assets | | 1.1 | | .7 |
| | | 3.5 | | | .6 | | .7 | | | .8 | | .6 |
| | | | | | | | 4.6 | | | 2.5 | | 3.2 |
| | | | | | (12) | | 5.9 | % Depr., Dep., Amort./Sales | (57) | 5.4 | (38) | 8.4 |
| | | | | | | | 7.7 | | | 7.6 | | 11.1 |
| | | | | | | | | % Officers', Directors' Owners' Comp/Sales | | | | |
| | 17938M | 92408M | 67623M | 326599M | 806356M | | 2641198M | Net Sales ($) | | 4454237M | | 2890009M |
| | 624M | 10670M | 30001M | 262935M | 771483M | | 2947370M | Total Assets ($) | | 4486122M | | 3700136M |

© RMA 2024

M = $ thousand   MM = $ million
See Pages viii through xx for Explanation of Ratios and Data

# ENTERTAINMENT—Casinos (except Casino Hotels) NAICS 713210

## Comparative Historical Data | Current Data Sorted by Sales

| Comparative Historical Data | | | Type of Statement | Current Data Sorted by Sales | | | | | |
|---|---|---|---|---|---|---|---|---|---|
| 20 | 17 | 16 | Unqualified | | | | | 2 | 14 |
| 1 | 3 | 1 | Reviewed | | | | | 1 | 1 |
| 2 | | 1 | Compiled | | | | | 2 | 1 |
| 8 | 7 | 10 | Tax Returns | | | | 1 | 8 | |
| 21 | 24 | 26 | Other | 2 | | 1 | 2 | 5 | 16 |
| 4/1/21-3/31/22 ALL | 4/1/22-3/31/23 ALL | 4/1/23-3/31/24 ALL | | | 15 (4/1-9/30/23) | | | 39 (10/1/23-3/31/24) | |
| | | | | 0-1MM | 1-3MM | 3-5MM | 5-10MM | 10-25MM | 25MM & OVER |
| 52 | 51 | 54 | NUMBER OF STATEMENTS | 2 | | 1 | 4 | 15 | 32 |
| % | % | % | ASSETS | % | | % | % | % | % |
| 35.5 | 33.4 | 33.9 | Cash & Equivalents | | | | | 47.3 | 28.8 |
| .9 | 1.8 | 1.4 | Trade Receivables (net) | | DATA | | | 1.4 | 1.3 |
| 1.1 | .9 | 1.4 | Inventory | | | | | 1.4 | .7 |
| 2.9 | 2.1 | 4.9 | All Other Current | | NOT | | | 6.1 | 2.6 |
| 40.4 | 38.3 | 41.7 | Total Current | | | | | 56.1 | 33.4 |
| 50.2 | 50.5 | 47.4 | Fixed Assets (net) | | AVAILABLE | | | 22.7 | 60.0 |
| 4.8 | 6.7 | 5.6 | Intangibles (net) | | | | | 11.9 | 3.5 |
| 4.6 | 4.6 | 5.3 | All Other Non-Current | | | | | 9.2 | 3.0 |
| 100.0 | 100.0 | 100.0 | Total | | | | | 100.0 | 100.0 |
| | | | LIABILITIES | | | | | | |
| .1 | 3.5 | 7.5 | Notes Payable-Short Term | | | | | 2.0 | 5.8 |
| 7.3 | 5.4 | 2.7 | Cur. Mat.-L.T.D. | | | | | 4.8 | 2.2 |
| 2.6 | 4.5 | 3.1 | Trade Payables | | | | | 3.1 | 2.6 |
| .0 | .0 | .0 | Income Taxes Payable | | | | | .0 | .0 |
| 8.6 | 9.2 | 16.4 | All Other Current | | | | | 26.4 | 11.3 |
| 18.6 | 22.5 | 29.7 | Total Current | | | | | 36.3 | 22.0 |
| 33.9 | 21.8 | 21.8 | Long-Term Debt | | | | | 23.3 | 21.7 |
| .0 | .0 | .0 | Deferred Taxes | | | | | .0 | .0 |
| 2.5 | 1.0 | 4.2 | All Other Non-Current | | | | | 7.8 | 2.5 |
| 44.9 | 54.7 | 44.3 | Net Worth | | | | | 32.6 | 53.9 |
| 100.0 | 100.0 | 100.0 | Total Liabilities & Net Worth | | | | | 100.0 | 100.0 |
| | | | INCOME DATA | | | | | | |
| 100.0 | 100.0 | 100.0 | Net Sales | | | | | 100.0 | 100.0 |
| | | | Gross Profit | | | | | | |
| 71.6 | 75.2 | 77.4 | Operating Expenses | | | | | 90.9 | 69.0 |
| 28.4 | 24.8 | 22.6 | Operating Profit | | | | | 9.1 | 31.0 |
| .6 | 2.4 | .5 | All Other Expenses (net) | | | | | -1.3 | 1.4 |
| 27.8 | 22.4 | 22.1 | Profit Before Taxes | | | | | 10.4 | 29.7 |
| | | | RATIOS | | | | | | |
| 3.9 | 4.1 | 4.4 | | | | | | 4.6 | 3.4 |
| 2.9 | 2.3 | 1.8 | Current | | | | | 3.9 | 1.6 |
| 1.7 | 1.3 | 1.3 | | | | | | .9 | 1.3 |
| 3.7 | 3.4 | 4.0 | | | | | | 4.5 | 3.3 |
| 2.4 | 2.1 | 1.5 | Quick | | | | | 3.9 | 1.5 |
| 1.4 | 1.1 | .9 | | | | | | .9 | 1.0 |
| 0 UND | 0 UND | 0 UND | | | | | | 0 UND | 1 409.3 |
| 1 290.1 | 2 155.1 | 1 273.0 | Sales/Receivables | | | | | 0 UND | 5 75.1 |
| 3 121.7 | 6 62.7 | 5 67.2 | | | | | | 0 UND | 7 54.4 |
| | | | Cost of Sales/Inventory | | | | | | |
| | | | Cost of Sales/Payables | | | | | | |
| 4.1 | 4.9 | 4.2 | | | | | | 4.3 | 4.3 |
| 5.9 | 10.9 | 10.6 | Sales/Working Capital | | | | | 10.4 | 8.6 |
| 21.5 | 35.5 | 53.6 | | | | | | -999.8 | 19.2 |
| 98.4 | 51.3 | 89.0 | | | | | | 172.0 | 108.9 |
| (36) 28.3 | (36) 23.2 | (44) 18.3 | EBIT/Interest | | | | | (12) 22.4 | (28) 32.8 |
| 10.2 | 7.9 | 5.6 | | | | | | 6.2 | 7.3 |
| | | | Net Profit + Depr., Dep., Amort./Cur. Mat. L/T/D | | | | | | |
| .6 | .5 | .4 | | | | | | .0 | .7 |
| 1.0 | 1.0 | .9 | Fixed/Worth | | | | | .4 | 1.0 |
| 1.8 | 2.1 | 3.0 | | | | | | 2.9 | 2.9 |
| .3 | .3 | .2 | | | | | | .3 | .2 |
| .9 | .7 | .8 | Debt/Worth | | | | | 1.1 | .6 |
| 2.3 | 2.3 | 4.2 | | | | | | -5.9 | 2.4 |
| 149.4 | 106.7 | 85.2 | | | | | | 176.2 | 87.1 |
| (44) 74.6 | (46) 52.1 | (46) 48.3 | % Profit Before Taxes/Tangible Net Worth | | | | | (11) 82.5 | (29) 49.1 |
| 35.7 | 27.5 | 19.2 | | | | | | 19.3 | 26.5 |
| 73.3 | 39.3 | 38.6 | | | | | | 64.8 | 37.8 |
| 35.4 | 21.4 | 22.9 | % Profit Before Taxes/Total Assets | | | | | 27.0 | 24.4 |
| 18.2 | 14.9 | 12.5 | | | | | | 14.4 | 16.6 |
| 5.8 | 8.9 | 20.1 | | | | | | 999.8 | 2.8 |
| 2.5 | 2.3 | 2.0 | Sales/Net Fixed Assets | | | | | 59.0 | 1.5 |
| 1.3 | 1.1 | 1.1 | | | | | | 8.5 | 1.0 |
| 2.1 | 2.1 | 2.2 | | | | | | 12.0 | 1.3 |
| 1.2 | 1.2 | 1.1 | Sales/Total Assets | | | | | 7.1 | .9 |
| .8 | .7 | .7 | | | | | | 1.4 | .7 |
| 2.5 | 2.4 | 1.6 | | | | | | | 2.9 |
| (40) 4.5 | (38) 4.7 | (39) 4.9 | % Depr., Dep., Amort./Sales | | | | | (24) 5.6 | |
| 6.5 | 7.0 | 7.3 | | | | | | | 7.5 |
| | | | % Officers', Directors' Owners' Comp/Sales | | | | | | |
| 2724577M | 3253207M | 3952122M | Net Sales ($) | 662M | | 3283M | 28397M | 219667M | 3700113M |
| 2793249M | 3606506M | 4023083M | Total Assets ($) | 1841M | | 5574M | 8262M | 127361M | 3880045M |

© RMA 2024  M = $ thousand  MM = $ million
See Pages viii through xx for Explanation of Ratios and Data

# ENTERTAINMENT—Other Gambling Industries  NAICS 713290

## Current Data Sorted by Assets | Comparative Historical Data

| 0-500M | 500M-2MM | 2-10MM | 10-50MM | 50-100MM | 100-250MM | | | | |
|---|---|---|---|---|---|---|---|---|---|
| | 2 | | 1 | | | Type of Statement | | | |
| | 3 | 4 | 5 | | | Unqualified | 7 | | 14 |
| | | | 6 | | 1 | Reviewed | | | |
| | | | | 4 | | Compiled | | | |
| | | | | 3 | 2 | Tax Returns | 5 | | 3 |
| | 5 (4/1-9/30/23) | | 31 (10/1/23-3/31/24) | | | Other | 40 | | 23 |
| | | | | | | | 4/1/19-3/31/20 | | 4/1/20-3/31/21 |
| | 5 | 6 | 11 | 7 | 7 | NUMBER OF STATEMENTS | 52 ALL | | 40 ALL |

| % | % | % | % | % | % | ASSETS | % | | % |
|---|---|---|---|---|---|---|---|---|---|
| | | | 36.9 | | | Cash & Equivalents | 19.6 | | 24.2 |
| | | | 7.2 | | | Trade Receivables (net) | 6.3 | | 9.3 |
| | | | 4.2 | | | Inventory | 3.1 | | 4.7 |
| | | | 8.0 | | | All Other Current | 1.2 | | 9.6 |
| | | | 56.2 | | | Total Current | 30.3 | | 47.8 |
| | | | 32.2 | | | Fixed Assets (net) | 51.4 | | 29.9 |
| | | | 5.8 | | | Intangibles (net) | 12.0 | | 13.1 |
| | | | 5.7 | | | All Other Non-Current | 6.3 | | 9.1 |
| | | | 100.0 | | | Total | 100.0 | | 100.0 |

DATA NOT AVAILABLE (for 0-500M column)

### LIABILITIES

| | | | | | | | | | |
|---|---|---|---|---|---|---|---|---|---|
| | | | 3.7 | | | Notes Payable-Short Term | 1.1 | | 2.8 |
| | | | 2.3 | | | Cur. Mat.-L.T.D. | 7.6 | | 3.3 |
| | | | 7.6 | | | Trade Payables | 7.7 | | 6.2 |
| | | | .2 | | | Income Taxes Payable | .3 | | .1 |
| | | | 30.3 | | | All Other Current | 8.5 | | 14.6 |
| | | | 44.1 | | | Total Current | 25.3 | | 27.0 |
| | | | 20.0 | | | Long-Term Debt | 25.9 | | 26.7 |
| | | | .0 | | | Deferred Taxes | .0 | | .0 |
| | | | 43.8 | | | All Other Non-Current | 3.6 | | 10.3 |
| | | | -7.9 | | | Net Worth | 45.2 | | 36.0 |
| | | | 100.0 | | | Total Liabilities & Net Worth | 100.0 | | 100.0 |

### INCOME DATA

| | | | | | | | | | |
|---|---|---|---|---|---|---|---|---|---|
| | | | 100.0 | | | Net Sales | 100.0 | | 100.0 |
| | | | 86.4 | | | Gross Profit | | | |
| | | | 86.4 | | | Operating Expenses | 77.1 | | 86.2 |
| | | | 13.6 | | | Operating Profit | 22.9 | | 13.8 |
| | | | 3.6 | | | All Other Expenses (net) | 3.6 | | 1.7 |
| | | | 10.0 | | | Profit Before Taxes | 19.4 | | 12.2 |

### RATIOS

| | | | | | | | | | |
|---|---|---|---|---|---|---|---|---|---|
| | | | 3.9 | | | | 2.9 | | 2.8 |
| | | | 2.5 | | | Current | 1.3 | | 1.9 |
| | | | 1.0 | | | | .7 | | 1.0 |
| | | | 3.8 | | | | 2.9 | | 2.5 |
| | | | 2.4 | | | Quick | 1.1 | | 1.3 |
| | | | .6 | | | | .5 | | .6 |
| | | | 0 UND | | | | 0 903.4 | 0 | 999.8 |
| | | | 3 114.7 | | | Sales/Receivables | 3 108.6 | 5 | 70.2 |
| | | | 57 6.4 | | | | 15 23.7 | 38 | 9.7 |
| | | | | | | Cost of Sales/Inventory | | | |
| | | | | | | Cost of Sales/Payables | | | |
| | | | 4.4 | | | | 6.9 | | 3.5 |
| | | | 10.2 | | | Sales/Working Capital | 33.6 | | 7.9 |
| | | | 54.0 | | | | -18.6 | | 252.4 |
| | | | | | | | 63.7 | | 36.5 |
| | | | | | | EBIT/Interest | (46) 13.5 | (33) | 7.4 |
| | | | | | | | 5.9 | | 1.8 |
| | | | | | | Net Profit + Depr., Dep., Amort./Cur. Mat. L/T/D | | | |
| | | | .5 | | | | .6 | | .1 |
| | | | .8 | | | Fixed/Worth | 1.1 | | .8 |
| | | | -1.7 | | | | 2.6 | | 2.0 |
| | | | .5 | | | | .2 | | .7 |
| | | | 1.1 | | | Debt/Worth | 1.0 | | 1.1 |
| | | | -2.8 | | | | 5.4 | | 8.7 |
| | | | | | | | 89.9 | | 64.0 |
| | | | | | | % Profit Before Taxes/Tangible Net Worth | (43) 49.7 | (31) | 25.7 |
| | | | | | | | 25.6 | | 7.5 |
| | | | 54.5 | | | | 36.6 | | 23.7 |
| | | | 35.0 | | | % Profit Before Taxes/Total Assets | 24.0 | | 11.1 |
| | | | -4.3 | | | | 7.4 | | 1.2 |
| | | | 8.3 | | | | 5.5 | | 33.2 |
| | | | 6.8 | | | Sales/Net Fixed Assets | 2.1 | | 5.4 |
| | | | 3.5 | | | | 1.2 | | 1.4 |
| | | | 2.7 | | | | 2.2 | | 2.3 |
| | | | 1.4 | | | Sales/Total Assets | 1.1 | | 1.0 |
| | | | 1.0 | | | | .8 | | .5 |
| | | | | | | | 3.4 | | .7 |
| | | | | | | % Depr., Dep., Amort./Sales | (27) 5.5 | (27) | 3.5 |
| | | | | | | | 8.4 | | 9.3 |
| | | | | | | % Officers', Directors' Owners' Comp/Sales | | | |
| | 60118M | 184752M | 531698M | 1244728M | 1580874M | Net Sales ($) | 4755175M | | 1204884M |
| | 4882M | 35825M | 316443M | 477863M | 1238305M | Total Assets ($) | 4297641M | | 1569247M |

© RMA 2024

M = $ thousand    MM = $ million
See Pages viii through xx for Explanation of Ratios and Data

# ENTERTAINMENT—Other Gambling Industries  NAICS 713290

**Comparative Historical Data** | **Current Data Sorted by Sales**

| | | | | Type of Statement | | | | | | |
|---|---|---|---|---|---|---|---|---|---|---|
| | 13 | 6 | 14 | Unqualified | | | | 1 | 1 | 12 |
| | 1 | 1 | | Reviewed | | | | | | 2 |
| | | | 2 | Compiled | | | | | | |
| | 1 | 7 | 2 | Tax Returns | | | | 1 | 1 | |
| | 19 | 22 | 18 | Other | | 5 (4/1-9/30/23) | | 2 | 5 | 10 |
| | 4/1/21- | 4/1/22- | 4/1/23- | | 1 | | | | | |
| | 3/31/22 | 3/31/23 | 3/31/24 | | | | | 31 (10/1/23-3/31/24) | | |
| | ALL | ALL | ALL | | 0-1MM | 1-3MM | 3-5MM | 5-10MM | 10-25MM | 25MM & OVER |
| | 34 | 36 | 36 | NUMBER OF STATEMENTS | 1 | | | 4 | 7 | 24 |
| | % | % | % | **ASSETS** | % | % | % | % | % | % |
| | 33.9 | 34.9 | 36.1 | Cash & Equivalents | | | | | | 38.0 |
| | 4.5 | 5.9 | 8.7 | Trade Receivables (net) | D | D | | | | 6.7 |
| | 2.0 | 3.4 | 6.6 | Inventory | A | A | | | | 6.7 |
| | 4.5 | 4.2 | 4.8 | All Other Current | T | T | | | | 5.7 |
| | 44.8 | 48.4 | 56.1 | Total Current | A | A | | | | 57.2 |
| | 32.2 | 29.7 | 30.3 | Fixed Assets (net) | | | | | | 28.5 |
| | 16.5 | 14.5 | 7.0 | Intangibles (net) | N | N | | | | 6.3 |
| | 6.5 | 7.4 | 6.5 | All Other Non-Current | O | O | | | | 8.1 |
| | 100.0 | 100.0 | 100.0 | Total | T | T | | | | 100.0 |
| | | | | **LIABILITIES** | | | | | | |
| | 2.3 | 7.3 | 5.6 | Notes Payable-Short Term | A | A | | | | .9 |
| | 4.3 | 8.6 | 1.7 | Cur. Mat.-L.T.D. | V | V | | | | 1.7 |
| | 3.8 | 7.3 | 6.4 | Trade Payables | A | A | | | | 5.9 |
| | .1 | .0 | .1 | Income Taxes Payable | I | I | | | | .1 |
| | 11.6 | 12.7 | 22.3 | All Other Current | L | L | | | | 21.1 |
| | 22.1 | 35.8 | 36.0 | Total Current | A | A | | | | 29.8 |
| | 28.3 | 35.5 | 23.2 | Long-Term Debt | B | B | | | | 19.4 |
| | .1 | .1 | .0 | Deferred Taxes | L | L | | | | .0 |
| | 11.3 | 11.3 | 16.1 | All Other Non-Current | E | E | | | | 4.7 |
| | 38.3 | 17.3 | 24.7 | Net Worth | | | | | | 46.1 |
| | 100.0 | 100.0 | 100.0 | Total Liabilities & Net Worth | | | | | | 100.0 |
| | | | | **INCOME DATA** | | | | | | |
| | 100.0 | 100.0 | 100.0 | Net Sales | | | | | | 100.0 |
| | | | | Gross Profit | | | | | | |
| | 73.7 | 80.3 | 81.9 | Operating Expenses | | | | | | 73.0 |
| | 26.3 | 19.7 | 18.1 | Operating Profit | | | | | | 27.0 |
| | 2.5 | 4.6 | 2.8 | All Other Expenses (net) | | | | | | 4.5 |
| | 23.9 | 15.1 | 15.2 | Profit Before Taxes | | | | | | 22.5 |
| | | | | **RATIOS** | | | | | | |
| | 4.7 | 3.5 | 3.8 | | | | | | | 4.1 |
| | 2.1 | 1.7 | 2.2 | Current | | | | | | 2.6 |
| | 1.0 | .9 | 1.0 | | | | | | | 1.3 |
| | 4.4 | 3.4 | 2.8 | | | | | | | 3.3 |
| | 1.8 | 1.3 | 1.4 | Quick | | | | | | 1.9 |
| | 1.0 | .7 | .9 | | | | | | | 1.2 |
| 0 | UND | 0 UND | 0 UND | | | | | | 0 | UND |
| 2 | 148.5 | 4 95.0 | 5 67.3 | Sales/Receivables | | | | | 4 | 90.0 |
| 22 | 16.3 | 17 21.6 | 50 7.3 | | | | | | 38 | 9.7 |
| | | | | Cost of Sales/Inventory | | | | | | |
| | | | | Cost of Sales/Payables | | | | | | |
| | 3.2 | 4.4 | 5.8 | | | | | | | 5.7 |
| | 16.7 | 16.7 | 11.7 | Sales/Working Capital | | | | | | 6.7 |
| | NM | -33.6 | 188.0 | | | | | | | 29.3 |
| | 93.9 | 41.7 | 128.8 | | | | | | | 456.7 |
| (24) | 15.6 | (26) 8.5 | (21) 17.6 | EBIT/Interest | | | | | (15) | 39.1 |
| | 4.0 | 2.1 | 4.8 | | | | | | | 14.0 |
| | | | | Net Profit + Depr., Dep., Amort./Cur. Mat. L/T/D | | | | | | |
| | .3 | .4 | .2 | | | | | | | .2 |
| | 1.0 | 1.0 | .8 | Fixed/Worth | | | | | | .7 |
| | -5.6 | -1.7 | -3.2 | | | | | | | NM |
| | .3 | .5 | .3 | | | | | | | .2 |
| | 1.7 | 3.5 | .9 | Debt/Worth | | | | | | .6 |
| | -4.1 | -3.0 | -13.6 | | | | | | | NM |
| | 137.4 | 153.4 | 155.9 | | | | | | | 165.2 |
| (24) | 68.9 | (22) 57.0 | (26) 52.7 | % Profit Before Taxes/Tangible Net Worth | | | | | (18) | 52.7 |
| | 39.2 | 26.3 | 34.4 | | | | | | | 38.9 |
| | 55.6 | 44.9 | 63.6 | | | | | | | 62.9 |
| | 26.3 | 18.7 | 28.9 | % Profit Before Taxes/Total Assets | | | | | | 30.6 |
| | 13.8 | 1.6 | 9.0 | | | | | | | 16.3 |
| | 46.5 | 65.3 | 134.3 | | | | | | | 134.3 |
| | 7.9 | 6.4 | 7.6 | Sales/Net Fixed Assets | | | | | | 7.6 |
| | 2.1 | 1.7 | 3.4 | | | | | | | 3.7 |
| | 2.8 | 5.0 | 5.4 | | | | | | | 3.0 |
| | 1.2 | 1.0 | 1.8 | Sales/Total Assets | | | | | | 1.6 |
| | .7 | .7 | 1.0 | | | | | | | .9 |
| | 1.1 | 2.1 | .2 | | | | | | | .1 |
| (20) | 3.9 | (18) 4.1 | (22) 2.1 | % Depr., Dep., Amort./Sales | | | | | (17) | 1.7 |
| | 8.8 | 10.8 | 7.8 | | | | | | | 5.3 |
| | | | | % Officers', Directors' Owners' Comp/Sales | | | | | | |
| | 1183643M | 1641289M | 3602170M | Net Sales ($) | | | 3859M | 25571M | 123111M | 3449629M |
| | 1145617M | 1763989M | 2073318M | Total Assets ($) | | | 2015M | 12707M | 136221M | 1922375M |

M = $ thousand    MM = $ million
See Pages viii through xx for Explanation of Ratios and Data
© RMA 2024

# ENTERTAINMENT—Golf Courses and Country Clubs  NAICS 713910

## Current Data Sorted by Assets | Comparative Historical Data

| | | | | | | Type of Statement | | |
|---|---|---|---|---|---|---|---|---|
| 2 | 1 | 10 | 68 | 16 | 7 | Unqualified | 118 | 67 |
| | 1 | 11 | 17 | 1 | | Reviewed | 33 | 26 |
| 1 | 4 | 9 | 8 | | 1 | Compiled | 28 | 13 |
| 6 | 13 | 13 | 4 | | | Tax Returns | 49 | 44 |
| 20 | 26 | 84 | 146 | 17 | 11 | Other | 193 | 147 |
| | 115 (4/1-9/30/23) | | 382 (10/1/23-3/31/24) | | | | 4/1/19-3/31/20 ALL | 4/1/20-3/31/21 ALL |
| 0-500M | 500M-2MM | 2-10MM | 10-50MM | 50-100MM | 100-250MM | | | |
| 29 | 45 | 127 | 243 | 34 | 19 | NUMBER OF STATEMENTS | 421 | 297 |
| % | % | % | % | % | % | ASSETS | % | % |
| 27.0 | 24.7 | 16.4 | 12.8 | 16.0 | 8.1 | Cash & Equivalents | 10.5 | 14.8 |
| 3.2 | 4.5 | 7.1 | 6.0 | 5.3 | 3.5 | Trade Receivables (net) | 4.5 | 5.4 |
| 7.2 | 2.8 | 2.8 | 2.2 | 1.5 | 9.2 | Inventory | 2.1 | 2.2 |
| 4.4 | 2.5 | 2.4 | 2.4 | 2.7 | .8 | All Other Current | 1.3 | 1.3 |
| 41.9 | 34.5 | 28.7 | 23.4 | 25.5 | 21.7 | Total Current | 18.5 | 23.6 |
| 48.0 | 52.3 | 62.3 | 69.0 | 69.1 | 61.7 | Fixed Assets (net) | 72.6 | 68.6 |
| 2.2 | 9.1 | 2.6 | 1.0 | 1.3 | 2.9 | Intangibles (net) | 1.7 | 2.3 |
| 7.8 | 4.1 | 6.4 | 6.6 | 4.1 | 13.7 | All Other Non-Current | 7.2 | 5.5 |
| 100.0 | 100.0 | 100.0 | 100.0 | 100.0 | 100.0 | Total | 100.0 | 100.0 |
| | | | | | | LIABILITIES | | |
| 17.4 | .6 | .9 | .8 | 1.2 | .9 | Notes Payable-Short Term | 1.9 | 1.8 |
| 2.9 | 5.6 | 2.3 | 2.0 | 1.3 | 1.4 | Cur. Mat.-L.T.D. | 3.4 | 3.4 |
| 6.8 | 5.9 | 3.2 | 2.4 | 2.0 | 3.5 | Trade Payables | 3.2 | 3.6 |
| .0 | .1 | .0 | .0 | 1.0 | .0 | Income Taxes Payable | .1 | .0 |
| 28.0 | 20.7 | 11.5 | 9.2 | 12.7 | 8.9 | All Other Current | 12.9 | 12.4 |
| 55.1 | 32.9 | 17.9 | 14.5 | 18.2 | 14.7 | Total Current | 21.5 | 21.3 |
| 38.4 | 38.3 | 33.6 | 21.9 | 12.9 | 29.6 | Long-Term Debt | 34.2 | 35.5 |
| .0 | .0 | .2 | .1 | .1 | .2 | Deferred Taxes | .0 | .0 |
| 9.8 | 9.8 | 14.9 | 14.7 | 15.1 | 18.5 | All Other Non-Current | 13.0 | 12.5 |
| -3.4 | 19.0 | 33.5 | 48.7 | 53.7 | 36.9 | Net Worth | 31.2 | 30.8 |
| 100.0 | 100.0 | 100.0 | 100.0 | 100.0 | 100.0 | Total Liabilities & Net Worth | 100.0 | 100.0 |
| | | | | | | INCOME DATA | | |
| 100.0 | 100.0 | 100.0 | 100.0 | 100.0 | 100.0 | Net Sales | 100.0 | 100.0 |
| | | | | | | Gross Profit | | |
| 97.0 | 89.9 | 93.4 | 95.7 | 95.9 | 96.4 | Operating Expenses | 98.9 | 97.4 |
| 3.0 | 10.1 | 6.6 | 4.3 | 4.1 | 3.6 | Operating Profit | 1.1 | 2.6 |
| .5 | 1.1 | .4 | -.5 | -.1 | 3.4 | All Other Expenses (net) | .8 | -.9 |
| 2.5 | 9.0 | 6.3 | 4.8 | 4.2 | .3 | Profit Before Taxes | .3 | 3.5 |
| | | | | | | RATIOS | | |
| 4.7 | 3.1 | 2.8 | 2.7 | 3.1 | 2.3 | | 2.0 | 2.9 |
| .8 | 1.4 | 1.8 | 1.6 | 1.6 | 1.7 | Current | 1.2 | 1.5 |
| .3 | .4 | 1.1 | 1.0 | .9 | .8 | | .6 | .8 |
| 4.0 | 2.3 | 2.5 | 2.0 | 2.7 | 2.1 | | 1.6 | 2.4 |
| .6 | 1.0 | 1.4 | 1.3 | 1.2 | 1.0 | Quick | .9 | 1.3 |
| .2 | .3 | .8 | .8 | .7 | .4 | | .4 | .7 |
| 0 UND | 0 UND | 1 277.4 | 14 26.1 | 11 33.8 | 8 46.9 | | 2 170.6 | 3 125.6 |
| 0 UND | 0 UND | 24 15.1 | 31 11.8 | 22 16.6 | 17 21.3 | Sales/Receivables | 19 19.7 | 21 17.0 |
| 7 54.1 | 8 45.1 | 37 9.8 | 46 7.9 | 52 7.0 | 28 13.0 | | 35 10.4 | 41 9.0 |
| | | | | | | Cost of Sales/Inventory | | |
| | | | | | | Cost of Sales/Payables | | |
| 5.5 | 7.8 | 4.8 | 3.2 | 2.9 | 3.6 | | 7.3 | 4.4 |
| -305.6 | 20.3 | 10.1 | 7.4 | 8.1 | 12.7 | Sales/Working Capital | 40.0 | 11.1 |
| -11.9 | -9.1 | 53.3 | 121.1 | -21.7 | -40.5 | | -11.0 | -24.3 |
| 5.4 | 13.7 | 10.8 | 12.8 | 15.4 | 8.3 | | 3.9 | 7.8 |
| (13) 2.0 | (32) 4.1 | (93) 3.8 | (190) 4.2 | (26) 4.1 | (16) 2.3 | EBIT/Interest | (350) 1.2 | (239) 2.2 |
| -1.3 | 1.3 | .4 | .2 | -7.0 | .2 | | -.6 | -.6 |
| | | | 8.9 | | | | 4.7 | 4.2 |
| | | (17) 2.3 | | | | Net Profit + Depr., Dep., Amort./Cur. Mat. L/T/D | (28) 3.1 | (19) 2.5 |
| | | | 1.6 | | | | 1.0 | .3 |
| .8 | .9 | 1.0 | .9 | .9 | 1.1 | | 1.1 | 1.0 |
| 9.1 | 2.6 | 1.6 | 1.3 | 1.1 | 1.7 | Fixed/Worth | 1.6 | 1.6 |
| -1.7 | -1.9 | 5.2 | 1.9 | 1.8 | 4.1 | | 4.2 | 5.5 |
| .4 | .7 | .6 | .4 | .3 | .7 | | .4 | .5 |
| 14.8 | 3.0 | 1.2 | .8 | .6 | 2.1 | Debt/Worth | 1.2 | 1.3 |
| -3.5 | -4.4 | 8.0 | 1.6 | 1.3 | 4.1 | | 5.1 | 6.6 |
| 288.5 | 64.7 | 30.0 | 13.3 | 13.4 | 20.3 | | 7.4 | 14.3 |
| (18) 8.5 | (27) 19.9 | (102) 9.7 | (220) 5.4 | (30) 3.1 | (17) 9.4 | % Profit Before Taxes/Tangible Net Worth | (338) .9 | (236) 4.9 |
| -.7 | 5.9 | -2.4 | -1.7 | -3.8 | -4.0 | | -4.5 | -2.6 |
| 23.5 | 31.2 | 12.4 | 7.0 | 7.3 | 6.4 | | 3.6 | 7.5 |
| 5.0 | 8.1 | 3.9 | 3.2 | 1.8 | 2.9 | % Profit Before Taxes/Total Assets | .2 | 2.1 |
| -3.0 | .9 | -1.6 | -1.0 | -2.6 | -2.0 | | -2.7 | -2.0 |
| 25.6 | 10.5 | 2.4 | 1.1 | 1.1 | 1.5 | | 1.4 | 1.5 |
| 6.6 | 2.7 | 1.3 | .8 | .7 | .8 | Sales/Net Fixed Assets | .8 | .8 |
| 1.4 | 1.6 | .9 | .6 | .5 | .5 | | .5 | .5 |
| 6.0 | 2.7 | 1.3 | .7 | .6 | .7 | | .9 | 1.0 |
| 3.1 | 1.4 | .9 | .5 | .4 | .4 | Sales/Total Assets | .6 | .6 |
| .6 | 1.1 | .6 | .4 | .4 | .3 | | .4 | .4 |
| 3.5 | 3.5 | 3.7 | 6.4 | 7.0 | 5.0 | | 6.2 | 6.5 |
| (19) 8.3 | (28) 6.8 | (88) 6.6 | (211) 9.2 | (29) 10.0 | (10) 8.5 | % Depr., Dep., Amort./Sales | (373) 9.2 | (252) 9.2 |
| 12.5 | 9.7 | 10.0 | 12.0 | 14.1 | 12.8 | | 12.6 | 13.0 |
| | 1.6 | 2.0 | | | | | 3.3 | 3.0 |
| | (10) 3.8 | (10) 4.6 | | | | % Officers', Directors' Owners' Comp/Sales | (47) 6.2 | (38) 6.4 |
| | 6.7 | 17.0 | | | | | 12.2 | 14.1 |
| 28215M | 94023M | 664718M | 3487385M | 1415226M | 1636501M | Net Sales ($) | 4180584M | 2154083M |
| 5922M | 49559M | 680180M | 5995431M | 2395343M | 3056058M | Total Assets ($) | 7907203M | 4167029M |

© RMA 2024

M = $ thousand    MM = $ million
See Pages viii through xx for Explanation of Ratios and Data

## ENTERTAINMENT—Golf Courses and Country Clubs  NAICS 713910

| Comparative Historical Data ||| Type of Statement | Current Data Sorted by Sales ||||||
|---|---|---|---|---|---|---|---|---|---|
| 62 | 92 | 104 | Unqualified | 2 | 1 | 6 | 28 | 40 | 27 |
| 25 | 36 | 30 | Reviewed |   | 2 | 6 | 12 | 9 | 1 |
| 17 | 21 | 23 | Compiled | 2 | 6 | 1 | 9 | 3 | 2 |
| 34 | 46 | 36 | Tax Returns | 9 | 13 | 5 | 8 | 1 |   |
| 231 | 267 | 304 | Other | 15 | 46 | 41 | 73 | 97 | 32 |
| 4/1/21-3/31/22 ALL | 4/1/22-3/31/23 ALL | 4/1/23-3/31/24 ALL |   | 115 (4/1-9/30/23) ||| 382 (10/1/23-3/31/24) |||
|   |   |   |   | 0-1MM | 1-3MM | 3-5MM | 5-10MM | 10-25MM | 25MM & OVER |
| 369 | 462 | 497 | NUMBER OF STATEMENTS | 28 | 68 | 59 | 130 | 150 | 62 |
| % | % | % | ASSETS | % | % | % | % | % | % |
| 16.6 | 16.8 | 15.7 | Cash & Equivalents | 20.3 | 19.8 | 16.9 | 13.7 | 14.8 | 14.3 |
| 5.7 | 6.0 | 5.8 | Trade Receivables (net) | 1.4 | 3.8 | 5.4 | 7.6 | 6.2 | 5.7 |
| 2.3 | 3.0 | 2.9 | Inventory | 1.8 | 4.5 | 2.3 | 2.3 | 3.2 | 3.0 |
| 2.0 | 2.9 | 2.5 | All Other Current | 1.8 | 2.5 | 2.5 | 2.9 | 2.2 | 2.9 |
| 26.7 | 28.7 | 26.9 | Total Current | 25.2 | 30.5 | 27.1 | 26.4 | 26.4 | 25.9 |
| 65.3 | 62.9 | 64.3 | Fixed Assets (net) | 63.3 | 56.4 | 63.7 | 68.0 | 65.6 | 62.8 |
| 1.6 | 2.2 | 2.3 | Intangibles (net) | 4.3 | 6.6 | 2.7 | 1.3 | 1.0 | 1.7 |
| 6.4 | 6.3 | 6.5 | All Other Non-Current | 7.2 | 6.5 | 6.5 | 4.3 | 7.0 | 9.7 |
| 100.0 | 100.0 | 100.0 | Total | 100.0 | 100.0 | 100.0 | 100.0 | 100.0 | 100.0 |
|   |   |   | LIABILITIES |   |   |   |   |   |   |
| 1.0 | .9 | 1.8 | Notes Payable-Short Term | 13.6 | 2.9 | .6 | .6 | 1.0 | 1.0 |
| 2.5 | 2.4 | 2.4 | Cur. Mat.-L.T.D. | 2.6 | 3.5 | 2.6 | 2.6 | 2.0 | 1.5 |
| 3.1 | 3.3 | 3.2 | Trade Payables | 2.9 | 5.0 | 3.7 | 2.7 | 2.7 | 3.1 |
| .1 | .2 | .1 | Income Taxes Payable | .0 | .0 | .0 | .0 | .0 | .6 |
| 11.9 | 12.0 | 12.2 | All Other Current | 19.1 | 19.8 | 7.5 | 11.2 | 9.8 | 13.0 |
| 18.5 | 18.7 | 19.7 | Total Current | 38.3 | 31.2 | 14.4 | 17.0 | 15.5 | 19.1 |
| 33.0 | 28.4 | 27.0 | Long-Term Debt | 33.4 | 40.3 | 29.9 | 27.1 | 21.5 | 20.1 |
| .1 | .1 | .1 | Deferred Taxes | .0 | .0 | .3 | .0 | .2 | .2 |
| 13.0 | 12.6 | 14.2 | All Other Non-Current | 10.1 | 8.2 | 12.7 | 12.2 | 19.0 | 16.6 |
| 35.3 | 40.3 | 39.0 | Net Worth | 18.0 | 20.3 | 42.7 | 43.7 | 43.8 | 43.9 |
| 100.0 | 100.0 | 100.0 | Total Liabilities & Net Worth | 100.0 | 100.0 | 100.0 | 100.0 | 100.0 | 100.0 |
|   |   |   | INCOME DATA |   |   |   |   |   |   |
| 100.0 | 100.0 | 100.0 | Net Sales | 100.0 | 100.0 | 100.0 | 100.0 | 100.0 | 100.0 |
|   |   |   | Gross Profit |   |   |   |   |   |   |
| 92.4 | 92.5 | 94.7 | Operating Expenses | 93.8 | 95.0 | 92.5 | 95.7 | 94.9 | 94.2 |
| 7.6 | 7.5 | 5.3 | Operating Profit | 6.2 | 5.0 | 7.5 | 4.3 | 5.1 | 5.8 |
| -1.2 | .1 | .1 | All Other Expenses (net) | 2.4 | 1.0 | .2 | .0 | -1.1 | 1.0 |
| 8.8 | 7.4 | 5.2 | Profit Before Taxes | 3.8 | 4.0 | 7.3 | 4.4 | 6.2 | 4.8 |
|   |   |   | RATIOS |   |   |   |   |   |   |
| 3.7 | 3.6 | 2.8 |   | 4.6 | 3.0 | 3.5 | 2.6 | 2.8 | 2.5 |
| 1.9 | 2.0 | 1.6 | Current | 1.0 | 1.4 | 1.9 | 1.6 | 1.7 | 1.7 |
| 1.0 | 1.0 | .9 |   | .3 | .4 | 1.2 | 1.0 | 1.1 | .9 |
| 3.2 | 2.9 | 2.3 |   | 4.3 | 2.0 | 3.3 | 2.3 | 2.1 | 2.1 |
| (368) 1.6 | (461) 1.4 | 1.3 | Quick | .8 | 1.1 | 1.4 | 1.3 | 1.4 | 1.1 |
| .8 | .8 | .7 |   | .2 | .3 | .7 | .8 | .8 | .7 |
| 3 141.2 | 3 105.7 | 4 96.2 |   | 0 UND | 0 UND | 0 999.8 | 12 30.4 | 16 23.2 | 8 46.6 |
| 21 17.1 | 19 18.8 | 23 15.7 | Sales/Receivables | 0 UND | 1 558.8 | 14 26.8 | 29 12.6 | 31 11.8 | 20 18.3 |
| 39 9.3 | 37 9.9 | 38 9.5 |   | 2 165.9 | 17 21.1 | 36 10.2 | 45 8.1 | 47 7.8 | 36 10.0 |
|   |   |   | Cost of Sales/Inventory |   |   |   |   |   |   |
|   |   |   |   |   |   |   |   |   |   |
|   |   |   |   |   |   |   |   |   |   |
|   |   |   | Cost of Sales/Payables |   |   |   |   |   |   |
|   |   |   |   |   |   |   |   |   |   |
| 3.6 | 3.6 | 3.9 |   | 3.9 | 7.8 | 3.8 | 4.0 | 3.3 | 3.6 |
| 7.4 | 8.3 | 9.8 | Sales/Working Capital | -207.9 | 17.6 | 8.6 | 9.2 | 7.9 | 10.0 |
| 194.0 | 473.8 | -104.7 |   | -10.5 | -11.7 | 36.9 | 123.0 | 38.5 | -36.1 |
| 11.7 | 17.5 | 12.8 |   | 9.2 | 10.5 | 14.9 | 8.0 | 13.3 | 21.3 |
| (302) 4.7 | (358) 5.8 | (370) 3.9 | EBIT/Interest | (16) 1.6 | (46) 2.8 | (48) 4.1 | (91) 3.2 | (118) 5.6 | (51) 3.7 |
| 1.9 | 1.2 | .4 |   | .7 | .2 | .1 | .3 | 1.1 | .3 |
| 11.1 | 10.2 | 8.4 |   |   |   |   |   | 11.1 | 14.9 |
| (22) 4.2 | (27) 6.3 | (33) 3.2 | Net Profit + Depr., Dep., Amort./Cur. Mat. L/T/D |   |   |   |   | (11) 2.2 | (10) 8.3 |
| 3.8 | 2.7 | 1.3 |   |   |   |   |   | 1.8 | 3.4 |
| 1.0 | .9 | .9 |   | .9 | 1.0 | .9 | 1.0 | .9 | .9 |
| 1.5 | 1.3 | 1.4 | Fixed/Worth | 4.5 | 1.8 | 1.4 | 1.4 | 1.3 | 1.2 |
| 4.6 | 2.3 | 3.3 |   | -4.0 | -3.4 | 2.8 | 2.2 | 1.9 | 2.7 |
| .4 | .4 | .5 |   | .4 | .6 | .5 | .5 | .4 | .4 |
| 1.2 | .9 | 1.0 | Debt/Worth | 5.1 | 1.7 | 1.1 | .9 | .8 | .9 |
| 7.2 | 3.8 | 4.0 |   | -6.2 | -8.7 | 2.6 | 2.4 | 2.0 | 4.0 |
| 27.1 | 23.3 | 18.9 |   | 45.0 | 29.6 | 32.0 | 15.9 | 14.8 | 22.7 |
| (302) 10.6 | (388) 7.1 | (414) 6.5 | % Profit Before Taxes/Tangible Net Worth | (19) 6.7 | (45) 9.8 | (50) 8.5 | (115) 5.0 | (132) 6.3 | (53) 9.4 |
| 1.8 | .4 | -2.0 |   | -3.6 | -.3 | -4.4 | -2.3 | -1.2 | -1.2 |
| 13.1 | 12.1 | 9.5 |   | 7.4 | 14.6 | 13.2 | 8.3 | 8.8 | 8.4 |
| 5.9 | 4.7 | 3.4 | % Profit Before Taxes/Total Assets | 3.3 | 4.1 | 4.5 | 3.0 | 3.4 | 4.3 |
| 1.2 | .0 | -1.2 |   | -2.2 | -2.9 | -2.1 | -1.0 | -.3 | -1.6 |
| 1.6 | 1.8 | 1.8 |   | 3.3 | 6.8 | 2.3 | 1.3 | 1.2 | 1.5 |
| .9 | 1.0 | 1.0 | Sales/Net Fixed Assets | 1.7 | 2.0 | 1.1 | .9 | .8 | .9 |
| .6 | .7 | .6 |   | .8 | 1.0 | .7 | .6 | .6 | .6 |
| 1.0 | 1.0 | 1.0 |   | 1.8 | 2.5 | 1.3 | .9 | .8 | .9 |
| .7 | .7 | .7 | Sales/Total Assets | 1.0 | 1.1 | .8 | .6 | .6 | .6 |
| .5 | .5 | .5 |   | .5 | .7 | .5 | .4 | .4 | .4 |
| 4.9 | 5.3 | 5.4 |   | 6.7 | 3.6 | 3.9 | 5.7 | 6.4 | 4.9 |
| (319) 7.9 | (383) 7.9 | (385) 8.6 | % Depr., Dep., Amort./Sales | (24) 9.4 | (43) 7.5 | (39) 7.4 | (99) 8.8 | (131) 9.3 | (49) 7.4 |
| 10.8 | 10.6 | 11.6 |   | 14.5 | 10.4 | 10.3 | 11.1 | 12.5 | 11.9 |
| 2.4 | 1.3 | 2.1 |   |   |   |   |   |   |   |
| (32) 5.1 | (34) 6.6 | (32) 4.5 | % Officers', Directors', Owners' Comp/Sales |   |   |   |   |   |   |
| 22.4 | 18.2 | 7.6 |   |   |   |   |   |   |   |
| 4471810M | 5689938M | 7326068M | Net Sales ($) | 12384M | 142734M | 232617M | 944908M | 2320600M | 3672825M |
| 6896299M | 9327678M | 12182493M | Total Assets ($) | 14887M | 200359M | 349038M | 1821778M | 4287698M | 5508733M |

© RMA 2024  M = $ thousand  MM = $ million
See Pages viii through xx for Explanation of Ratios and Data

# ENTERTAINMENT—Skiing Facilities  NAICS 713920

## Current Data Sorted by Assets | Comparative Historical Data

| 0-500M | 500M-2MM | 2-10MM | 10-50MM | 50-100MM | 100-250MM | Type of Statement | | 4/1/19-3/31/20 | | 4/1/20-3/31/21 |
|---|---|---|---|---|---|---|---|---|---|---|
| | 12 (4/1-9/30/23) | 2 | 3 10 (10/1/23-3/31/24) | 2 | 3 | | | 14 ALL | | 15 ALL |
| | | | 1 | | | Unqualified | | 5 | | 5 |
| | | 1 | 5 | 2 | | Reviewed | | 5 | | 2 |
| | | 1 | 1 | 1 | | Compiled | | 3 | | |
| | | | | | | Tax Returns | | 7 | | |
| | | | 3 | | 3 | Other | | | | |
| | | 4 | 10 | 5 | 3 | NUMBER OF STATEMENTS | | 34 | | 22 |
| % | % | % | % | % | % | ASSETS | | % | | % |
| D | D | | 18.2 | | | Cash & Equivalents | | 17.9 | | 18.4 |
| A | A | | 1.4 | | | Trade Receivables (net) | | 1.3 | | 1.5 |
| T | T | | 2.3 | | | Inventory | | 4.4 | | 2.2 |
| A | A | | 2.8 | | | All Other Current | | 3.1 | | 1.5 |
| | | | 24.7 | | | Total Current | | 26.7 | | 23.6 |
| N | N | | 69.1 | | | Fixed Assets (net) | | 61.9 | | 68.4 |
| O | O | | 3.0 | | | Intangibles (net) | | 6.0 | | 2.9 |
| T | T | | 3.2 | | | All Other Non-Current | | 5.5 | | 5.1 |
| | | | 100.0 | | | Total | | 100.0 | | 100.0 |
| A | A | | | | | LIABILITIES | | | | |
| V | V | | 1.3 | | | Notes Payable-Short Term | | 4.7 | | 1.3 |
| A | A | | 2.2 | | | Cur. Mat.-L.T.D. | | 5.3 | | 1.6 |
| I | I | | 2.9 | | | Trade Payables | | 5.5 | | 3.3 |
| L | L | | .3 | | | Income Taxes Payable | | .1 | | .1 |
| A | A | | 13.1 | | | All Other Current | | 16.0 | | 11.3 |
| B | B | | 19.8 | | | Total Current | | 31.6 | | 17.6 |
| L | L | | 29.7 | | | Long-Term Debt | | 19.4 | | 31.3 |
| E | E | | .3 | | | Deferred Taxes | | .7 | | .9 |
| | | | 12.4 | | | All Other Non-Current | | 2.5 | | .7 |
| | | | 37.8 | | | Net Worth | | 45.7 | | 49.5 |
| | | | 100.0 | | | Total Liabilities & Net Worth | | 100.0 | | 100.0 |
| | | | | | | INCOME DATA | | | | |
| | | | 100.0 | | | Net Sales | | 100.0 | | 100.0 |
| | | | | | | Gross Profit | | | | |
| | | | 90.7 | | | Operating Expenses | | 89.6 | | 86.0 |
| | | | 9.3 | | | Operating Profit | | 10.4 | | 14.0 |
| | | | 2.3 | | | All Other Expenses (net) | | .8 | | 1.9 |
| | | | 7.1 | | | Profit Before Taxes | | 9.6 | | 12.1 |
| | | | | | | RATIOS | | | | |
| | | | 2.7 | | | | | 1.7 | | 2.6 |
| | | | 1.1 | | | Current | | 1.0 | | 1.2 |
| | | | .6 | | | | | .6 | | .7 |
| | | | 2.3 | | | | | 1.4 | | 2.1 |
| | | | .9 | | | Quick | | .7 | | 1.1 |
| | | | .2 | | | | | .4 | | .5 |
| | | 1 | 368.3 | | | | 0 | UND | 0 | UND |
| | | 7 | 56.0 | | | Sales/Receivables | 1 | 482.3 | 3 | 136.3 |
| | | 11 | 33.3 | | | | 9 | 39.4 | 11 | 33.5 |
| | | | | | | Cost of Sales/Inventory | | | | |
| | | | | | | Cost of Sales/Payables | | | | |
| | | | 3.0 | | | | | 9.1 | | 3.8 |
| | | | NM | | | Sales/Working Capital | | -112.0 | | 29.4 |
| | | | -5.9 | | | | | -9.8 | | -8.2 |
| | | | | | | | | 17.2 | | 10.5 |
| | | | | | | EBIT/Interest | (25) | 5.0 | (18) | 6.8 |
| | | | | | | | | 2.2 | | 1.7 |
| | | | | | | Net Profit + Depr., Dep., Amort./Cur. Mat. L/T/D | | | | |
| | | | .8 | | | | | .9 | | .9 |
| | | | 1.9 | | | Fixed/Worth | | 1.3 | | 1.3 |
| | | | 6.0 | | | | | 3.3 | | 2.8 |
| | | | .5 | | | | | .4 | | .3 |
| | | | 1.7 | | | Debt/Worth | | .9 | | .9 |
| | | | 7.1 | | | | | 4.2 | | 3.2 |
| | | | | | | | | 34.0 | | 25.4 |
| | | | | | | % Profit Before Taxes/Tangible Net Worth | (29) | 18.9 | (20) | 15.9 |
| | | | | | | | | 5.4 | | 2.6 |
| | | | 16.3 | | | | | 13.9 | | 12.9 |
| | | | 9.1 | | | % Profit Before Taxes/Total Assets | | 9.4 | | 8.6 |
| | | | -2.1 | | | | | .8 | | .5 |
| | | | 1.7 | | | | | 2.3 | | 1.4 |
| | | | 1.2 | | | Sales/Net Fixed Assets | | 1.6 | | .9 |
| | | | .8 | | | | | 1.0 | | .7 |
| | | | .9 | | | | | 1.4 | | .9 |
| | | | .8 | | | Sales/Total Assets | | .9 | | .7 |
| | | | .6 | | | | | .7 | | .5 |
| | | | 6.4 | | | | | 6.5 | | 7.3 |
| | | | 7.7 | | | % Depr., Dep., Amort./Sales | (31) | 8.1 | (19) | 9.2 |
| | | | 12.0 | | | | | 10.8 | | 12.0 |
| | | | | | | % Officers', Directors' Owners' Comp/Sales | | | | |
| | 15028M | 200045M | 167204M | | 394214M | Net Sales ($) | | 596354M | | 508616M |
| | 21266M | 272339M | 304522M | | 464160M | Total Assets ($) | | 683566M | | 831083M |

M = $ thousand MM = $ million
See Pages viii through xx for Explanation of Ratios and Data

© RMA 2024

## ENTERTAINMENT—Skiing Facilities  NAICS 713920

### Comparative Historical Data / Current Data Sorted by Sales

| | | | | Type of Statement | | | | | | |
|---|---|---|---|---|---|---|---|---|---|---|
| 4 | 4 | 3 | | Unqualified | | | | | 1 | 2 |
| 5 | 2 | 7 | | Reviewed | | | | 2 | 3 | 2 |
| 1 | 2 | 2 | | Compiled | | | | 1 | 1 | |
| | 1 | | | Tax Returns | | | | | | |
| 7 | 19 | 10 | | Other | 2 | 12 (4/1-9/30/23) | | 1 | 1 | 6 |
| 4/1/21-3/31/22 ALL | 4/1/22-3/31/23 ALL | 4/1/23-3/31/24 ALL | | | 0-1MM | 1-3MM | 3-5MM | 10 (10/1/23-3/31/24) 5-10MM | 10-25MM | 25MM & OVER |
| 17 | 28 | 22 | | NUMBER OF STATEMENTS | 2 | | | 4 | 6 | 10 |
| % | % | % | | ASSETS | % | % | % | % | % | % |
| 22.9 | 21.1 | 15.2 | | Cash & Equivalents | | | | | | 12.9 |
| 1.3 | 1.8 | 1.5 | | Trade Receivables (net) | | D | D | | | 2.1 |
| 1.9 | 1.9 | 2.4 | | Inventory | | A | A | | | 2.8 |
| 3.3 | 2.8 | 2.8 | | All Other Current | | T | T | | | 3.5 |
| 29.5 | 27.6 | 21.9 | | Total Current | | A | A | | | 21.3 |
| 62.4 | 61.5 | 67.4 | | Fixed Assets (net) | | | | | | 68.9 |
| 2.6 | 3.5 | 3.7 | | Intangibles (net) | | N | N | | | 5.8 |
| 5.5 | 7.5 | 7.0 | | All Other Non-Current | | O | O | | | 4.0 |
| 100.0 | 100.0 | 100.0 | | Total | | T | T | | | 100.0 |
| | | | | LIABILITIES | | | | | | |
| .5 | .0 | .6 | | Notes Payable-Short Term | | A | A | | | .0 |
| 1.6 | 1.5 | 1.8 | | Cur. Mat.-L.T.D. | | V | V | | | 1.1 |
| 3.0 | 5.1 | 2.6 | | Trade Payables | | A | A | | | 2.5 |
| .3 | .2 | .1 | | Income Taxes Payable | | I | I | | | .0 |
| 16.4 | 13.6 | 14.0 | | All Other Current | | L | L | | | 18.0 |
| 21.8 | 20.6 | 19.0 | | Total Current | | A | A | | | 21.7 |
| 23.8 | 24.2 | 24.9 | | Long-Term Debt | | B | B | | | 19.4 |
| .8 | .3 | .4 | | Deferred Taxes | | L | L | | | .6 |
| 8.9 | 8.8 | 7.8 | | All Other Non-Current | | E | E | | | 3.4 |
| 44.8 | 46.1 | 47.8 | | Net Worth | | | | | | 54.9 |
| 100.0 | 100.0 | 100.0 | | Total Liabilities & Net Worth | | | | | | 100.0 |
| | | | | INCOME DATA | | | | | | |
| 100.0 | 100.0 | 100.0 | | Net Sales | | | | | | 100.0 |
| | | | | Gross Profit | | | | | | |
| 80.7 | 79.8 | 83.8 | | Operating Expenses | | | | | | 87.6 |
| 19.3 | 20.2 | 16.2 | | Operating Profit | | | | | | 12.4 |
| -1.7 | 3.6 | 4.2 | | All Other Expenses (net) | | | | | | .8 |
| 21.0 | 16.6 | 12.0 | | Profit Before Taxes | | | | | | 11.6 |
| | | | | RATIOS | | | | | | |
| 2.5 | 4.3 | 1.9 | | | | | | | | 1.2 |
| 1.3 | 1.2 | 1.1 | | Current | | | | | | .9 |
| .8 | .7 | .6 | | | | | | | | .6 |
| 2.3 | 3.6 | 1.4 | | | | | | | | .9 |
| 1.0 | 1.0 | .8 | | Quick | | | | | | .7 |
| .7 | .5 | .2 | | | | | | | | .3 |
| 1  290.2 | 0  UND | 1  471.3 | | | | | | | 4 | 97.5 |
| 4  91.2 | 2  154.8 | 6  62.9 | | Sales/Receivables | | | | | 9 | 42.5 |
| 9  41.1 | 10  37.0 | 12  30.0 | | | | | | | 16 | 22.9 |
| | | | | Cost of Sales/Inventory | | | | | | |
| | | | | Cost of Sales/Payables | | | | | | |
| 5.5 | 4.0 | 8.3 | | | | | | | | 15.9 |
| 16.4 | 31.4 | NM | | Sales/Working Capital | | | | | | -47.0 |
| -18.0 | -10.5 | -6.6 | | | | | | | | -8.2 |
| 49.1 | 22.5 | 22.4 | | | | | | | | 175.0 |
| (16) 17.2 | (24) 10.4 | (19) 9.4 | | EBIT/Interest | | | | | | 13.8 |
| 3.9 | 2.6 | 1.5 | | | | | | | | 1.6 |
| | | | | Net Profit + Depr., Dep., Amort./Cur. Mat. L/T/D | | | | | | |
| .9 | .9 | .9 | | | | | | | | .9 |
| 1.3 | 1.7 | 1.6 | | Fixed/Worth | | | | | | 1.4 |
| 3.8 | 2.5 | 2.4 | | | | | | | | 1.9 |
| .4 | .6 | .5 | | | | | | | | .5 |
| .9 | 1.2 | 1.0 | | Debt/Worth | | | | | | .8 |
| 4.4 | 2.1 | 1.9 | | | | | | | | 1.3 |
| 114.2 | 55.9 | 38.7 | | | | | | | | 36.2 |
| (16) 31.6 | (27) 28.7 | (21) 19.0 | | % Profit Before Taxes/Tangible Net Worth | | | | | | 18.2 |
| 20.9 | 12.9 | 5.7 | | | | | | | | 5.6 |
| 24.7 | 18.9 | 16.3 | | | | | | | | 14.4 |
| 15.5 | 12.5 | 8.9 | | % Profit Before Taxes/Total Assets | | | | | | 8.9 |
| 7.5 | 4.9 | 1.7 | | | | | | | | 2.7 |
| 2.1 | 3.4 | 1.7 | | | | | | | | 1.4 |
| 1.1 | 1.1 | 1.1 | | Sales/Net Fixed Assets | | | | | | 1.0 |
| .8 | .7 | .6 | | | | | | | | .8 |
| .9 | 1.4 | .9 | | | | | | | | .9 |
| .7 | .7 | .8 | | Sales/Total Assets | | | | | | .7 |
| .6 | .5 | .5 | | | | | | | | .5 |
| 6.7 | 6.8 | 6.3 | | | | | | | | |
| (16) 8.0 | (21) 8.3 | (20) 9.9 | | % Depr., Dep., Amort./Sales | | | | | | |
| 11.5 | 12.1 | 16.4 | | | | | | | | |
| | | | | % Officers', Directors' Owners' Comp/Sales | | | | | | |
| 483991M | 846794M | 776491M | | Net Sales ($) | 1147M | | | 31074M | 111001M | 633269M |
| 701074M | 1158096M | 1062287M | | Total Assets ($) | 9331M | | | 49275M | 150483M | 853198M |

M = $ thousand    MM = $ million
See Pages viii through xx for Explanation of Ratios and Data

© RMA 2024

# ENTERTAINMENT—Marinas  NAICS 713930

## Current Data Sorted by Assets / Comparative Historical Data

| | | | | | | Type of Statement | | |
|---|---|---|---|---|---|---|---|---|
| | | | | | | Unqualified | 6 | 8 |
| 2 | | 1 | 6 | 1 | | Reviewed | 8 | 1 |
| | 2 | 3 | 3 | 2 | | Compiled | 7 | 4 |
| 6 | 6 | 7 | 2 | | | Tax Returns | 24 | 14 |
| 6 | 12 | 4 | 25 | | 4 | Other | 64 | 39 |
| | 4 (4/1-9/30/23) | 26 | 114 (10/1/23-3/31/24) | | | | 4/1/19-3/31/20 | 4/1/20-3/31/21 |
| 0-500M | 500M-2MM | 2-10MM | 10-50MM | 50-100MM | 100-250MM | | ALL | ALL |
| 14 | 20 | 41 | 36 | 3 | 4 | NUMBER OF STATEMENTS | 109 | 66 |
| % | % | % | % | % | % | ASSETS | % | % |
| 32.7 | 20.7 | 9.8 | 9.0 | | | Cash & Equivalents | 11.2 | 18.9 |
| 7.7 | 9.2 | 4.1 | 1.3 | | | Trade Receivables (net) | 4.4 | 3.8 |
| 1.6 | 9.5 | 11.7 | 14.3 | | | Inventory | 8.6 | 5.9 |
| .7 | 5.8 | 1.6 | 2.7 | | | All Other Current | 1.2 | 1.0 |
| 42.8 | 45.2 | 27.2 | 27.3 | | | Total Current | 25.4 | 29.6 |
| 42.3 | 42.9 | 60.5 | 49.3 | | | Fixed Assets (net) | 60.0 | 56.6 |
| 2.5 | 6.0 | 3.7 | 7.0 | | | Intangibles (net) | 5.0 | 7.1 |
| 12.4 | 5.9 | 8.6 | 16.4 | | | All Other Non-Current | 9.6 | 6.7 |
| 100.0 | 100.0 | 100.0 | 100.0 | | | Total | 100.0 | 100.0 |
| | | | | | | **LIABILITIES** | | |
| 9.1 | 3.9 | 7.7 | 7.3 | | | Notes Payable-Short Term | 5.4 | 6.2 |
| 14.6 | 8.5 | 3.7 | 2.9 | | | Cur. Mat.-L.T.D. | 4.4 | 4.5 |
| 2.2 | 4.2 | 7.7 | 1.6 | | | Trade Payables | 3.8 | 3.2 |
| .0 | .0 | .0 | .0 | | | Income Taxes Payable | .0 | .0 |
| 33.2 | 6.3 | 9.5 | 10.3 | | | All Other Current | 15.0 | 12.0 |
| 59.1 | 22.9 | 28.7 | 22.1 | | | Total Current | 28.6 | 25.8 |
| 51.9 | 53.2 | 54.0 | 44.8 | | | Long-Term Debt | 52.1 | 45.4 |
| .0 | .0 | .0 | .0 | | | Deferred Taxes | .0 | .0 |
| 6.9 | 1.4 | 5.2 | .7 | | | All Other Non-Current | 6.2 | 9.0 |
| -18.2 | 22.5 | 12.2 | 32.4 | | | Net Worth | 13.1 | 19.7 |
| 100.0 | 100.0 | 100.0 | 100.0 | | | Total Liabilities & Net Worth | 100.0 | 100.0 |
| | | | | | | **INCOME DATA** | | |
| 100.0 | 100.0 | 100.0 | 100.0 | | | Net Sales | 100.0 | 100.0 |
| | | | | | | Gross Profit | | |
| 89.8 | 80.5 | 84.3 | 82.8 | | | Operating Expenses | 81.2 | 79.6 |
| 10.2 | 19.5 | 15.7 | 17.2 | | | Operating Profit | 18.8 | 20.4 |
| -1.3 | 1.6 | 9.2 | 9.3 | | | All Other Expenses (net) | 6.9 | 5.0 |
| 11.6 | 18.0 | 6.5 | 8.0 | | | Profit Before Taxes | 11.9 | 15.4 |
| | | | | | | **RATIOS** | | |
| 12.9 | 3.7 | 3.7 | 2.0 | | | | 2.3 | 3.5 |
| 1.8 | 2.2 | 1.7 | 1.5 | | | Current | 1.2 | 1.3 |
| .1 | 1.0 | .2 | .9 | | | | .6 | .5 |
| 11.9 | 3.0 | 3.1 | 1.8 | | | | 1.8 | 2.6 |
| 1.8 | 1.1 | .5 | .9 | | | Quick | .8 | 1.2 |
| .1 | .7 | .1 | .1 | | | | .2 | .3 |
| 0 UND | 0 UND | 1 288.3 | 1 270.2 | | | | 2 152.2 | 0 UND |
| 0 UND | 7 51.9 | 8 46.0 | 5 79.8 | | | Sales/Receivables | 12 31.0 | 6 57.2 |
| 6 61.9 | 26 14.1 | 23 15.7 | 11 32.6 | | | | 30 12.2 | 25 14.6 |
| | | | | | | Cost of Sales/Inventory | | |
| | | | | | | Cost of Sales/Payables | | |
| 2.9 | 4.7 | 3.6 | 5.0 | | | | 5.1 | 4.0 |
| 290.5 | 14.1 | 7.4 | 8.1 | | | Sales/Working Capital | 27.2 | 17.7 |
| -6.9 | NM | -3.2 | -288.5 | | | | -6.4 | -5.2 |
| | | 31.6 | 23.5 | 5.4 | 7.7 | | 6.4 | 14.0 |
| (10) 4.2 | (17) 6.2 | (33) 2.0 | (27) 4.8 | | | EBIT/Interest | (84) 2.9 | (55) 3.7 |
| -4.1 | 1.5 | -.1 | 1.8 | | | | 1.4 | 2.0 |
| | | | | | | Net Profit + Depr., Dep., Amort./Cur. Mat. L/T/D | | |
| .2 | .1 | 1.0 | .7 | | | | 1.1 | 1.2 |
| NM | 1.5 | 3.3 | 2.1 | | | Fixed/Worth | 4.2 | 2.3 |
| -.6 | 5.7 | -5.7 | 7.8 | | | | -2.9 | -2.5 |
| .2 | 1.2 | 1.2 | 1.5 | | | | .9 | .9 |
| NM | 1.8 | 4.0 | 3.5 | | | Debt/Worth | 5.2 | 2.7 |
| -2.8 | NM | -7.3 | 7.3 | | | | -6.5 | -4.3 |
| | 119.5 | 46.2 | 44.4 | | | | 48.1 | 58.4 |
| (15) | 63.7 (26) | 8.5 (32) | 12.8 | | | % Profit Before Taxes/Tangible Net Worth | (72) 15.1 (40) | 16.3 |
| | 20.6 | -2.9 | 5.1 | | | | 5.9 | 5.9 |
| 56.2 | 50.1 | 9.7 | 11.2 | | | | 10.2 | 16.7 |
| 17.4 | 11.4 | 4.1 | 3.2 | | | % Profit Before Taxes/Total Assets | 5.5 | 7.4 |
| -8.6 | 2.5 | -2.1 | .4 | | | | .7 | 2.7 |
| UND | 77.7 | 5.6 | 4.2 | | | | 3.8 | 4.1 |
| 6.0 | 2.8 | .6 | .8 | | | Sales/Net Fixed Assets | 1.0 | 1.1 |
| 2.4 | .8 | .3 | .3 | | | | .4 | .5 |
| 6.1 | 2.5 | 1.1 | .7 | | | | 1.1 | 1.2 |
| 2.3 | 1.3 | .4 | .5 | | | Sales/Total Assets | .6 | .6 |
| 1.1 | .6 | .2 | .2 | | | | .3 | .3 |
| | | 2.6 | 1.7 | | | | 4.0 | 1.6 |
| | (31) | 8.8 (27) | 12.0 | | | % Depr., Dep., Amort./Sales | (82) 10.2 (43) | 7.7 |
| | | 17.9 | 20.6 | | | | 14.6 | 13.9 |
| | | | | | | | 1.9 | 2.1 |
| | | | | | | % Officers', Directors' Owners' Comp/Sales | (19) 4.0 (16) | 5.3 |
| | | | | | | | 6.4 | 7.5 |
| 9577M | 33831M | 162255M | 458721M | 111646M | 99906M | Net Sales ($) | 412273M | 488228M |
| 2919M | 20520M | 233236M | 768722M | 259580M | 560925M | Total Assets ($) | 697831M | 788100M |

© RMA 2024

M = $ thousand    MM = $ million
See Pages viii through xx for Explanation of Ratios and Data

# ENTERTAINMENT—Marinas  NAICS 713930

## Comparative Historical Data | Current Data Sorted by Sales

| | | | | Type of Statement | | | | | | |
|---|---|---|---|---|---|---|---|---|---|---|
| 2 | 2 | 2 | | Unqualified | | 1 | | | | 1 |
| 2 | 7 | 13 | | Reviewed | 1 | 1 | 2 | 5 | 3 | 1 |
| 8 | 6 | 12 | | Compiled | 1 | 5 | | 1 | 4 | 1 |
| 13 | 26 | 18 | | Tax Returns | 11 | 2 | 1 | 2 | 2 | |
| 59 | 58 | 73 | | Other | 17 | 25 | 5 | 14 | 8 | 4 |
| 4/1/21-3/31/22 ALL | 4/1/22-3/31/23 ALL | 4/1/23-3/31/24 ALL | | | | 4 (4/1-9/30/23) | | | 114 (10/1/23-3/31/24) | |
| | | | | | 0-1MM | 1-3MM | 3-5MM | 5-10MM | 10-25MM | 25MM & OVER |
| 84 | 99 | 118 | | NUMBER OF STATEMENTS | 30 | 34 | 8 | 22 | 17 | 7 |
| % | % | % | | ASSETS | % | % | % | % | % | % |
| 16.9 | 13.6 | 13.9 | | Cash & Equivalents | 22.4 | 9.9 | | 16.5 | 9.2 | |
| 2.9 | 3.1 | 4.4 | | Trade Receivables (net) | 6.0 | 3.0 | | 3.9 | 3.8 | |
| 6.7 | 9.4 | 10.4 | | Inventory | 1.9 | 7.1 | | 1.5 | 25.7 | |
| .5 | 3.1 | 2.5 | | All Other Current | 1.1 | 4.4 | | 2.3 | .8 | |
| 27.0 | 29.1 | 31.1 | | Total Current | 31.4 | 24.4 | | 24.2 | 39.5 | |
| 56.8 | 53.9 | 52.0 | | Fixed Assets (net) | 53.3 | 60.6 | | 52.8 | 46.0 | |
| 6.2 | 3.3 | 5.5 | | Intangibles (net) | 2.5 | 7.6 | | 6.7 | 5.2 | |
| 10.0 | 13.6 | 11.4 | | All Other Non-Current | 12.8 | 7.4 | | 16.2 | 9.3 | |
| 100.0 | 100.0 | 100.0 | | Total | 100.0 | 100.0 | | 100.0 | 100.0 | |
| | | | | LIABILITIES | | | | | | |
| 4.8 | 5.4 | 6.7 | | Notes Payable-Short Term | 4.8 | 6.4 | | 1.3 | 13.8 | |
| 2.8 | 3.1 | 5.9 | | Cur. Mat.-L.T.D. | 2.1 | 6.2 | | 2.6 | 5.4 | |
| 3.6 | 4.5 | 4.2 | | Trade Payables | 6.3 | 4.0 | | 1.7 | 1.5 | |
| .1 | .0 | .0 | | Income Taxes Payable | .0 | .0 | | .0 | .0 | |
| 13.5 | 9.5 | 11.6 | | All Other Current | 20.3 | 8.6 | | 9.3 | 6.7 | |
| 24.8 | 22.6 | 28.4 | | Total Current | 33.6 | 25.3 | | 14.9 | 27.5 | |
| 54.6 | 49.5 | 49.5 | | Long-Term Debt | 54.5 | 52.0 | | 51.2 | 23.6 | |
| .2 | .0 | .0 | | Deferred Taxes | .0 | .0 | | .0 | .0 | |
| 3.1 | 5.1 | 4.2 | | All Other Non-Current | 3.2 | 3.7 | | 1.1 | 6.3 | |
| 17.4 | 22.8 | 17.9 | | Net Worth | 8.6 | 19.1 | | 32.8 | 42.6 | |
| 100.0 | 100.0 | 100.0 | | Total Liabilities & Net Worth | 100.0 | 100.0 | | 100.0 | 100.0 | |
| | | | | INCOME DATA | | | | | | |
| 100.0 | 100.0 | 100.0 | | Net Sales | 100.0 | 100.0 | | 100.0 | 100.0 | |
| | | | | Gross Profit | | | | | | |
| 78.1 | 82.4 | 84.2 | | Operating Expenses | 80.2 | 83.0 | | 84.8 | 90.0 | |
| 21.9 | 17.6 | 15.8 | | Operating Profit | 19.8 | 17.0 | | 15.2 | 10.0 | |
| 4.5 | 4.8 | 6.9 | | All Other Expenses (net) | 7.2 | 9.2 | | 7.5 | 4.5 | |
| 17.4 | 12.9 | 8.9 | | Profit Before Taxes | 12.6 | 7.8 | | 7.7 | 5.6 | |
| | | | | RATIOS | | | | | | |
| 4.7 | 3.0 | 3.1 | | | 9.0 | 2.7 | | 3.4 | 2.0 | |
| 1.8 | 1.6 | 1.6 | | Current | 1.6 | 1.5 | | 2.2 | 1.6 | |
| .6 | .7 | .6 | | | .2 | .3 | | .7 | 1.3 | |
| 3.4 | 2.6 | 2.5 | | | 7.5 | 2.0 | | 3.0 | 1.5 | |
| 1.5 | 1.1 | 1.0 | | Quick | 1.3 | .7 | | 2.0 | .5 | |
| .3 | .2 | .2 | | | .3 | .1 | | .7 | .2 | |
| 0 UND | 0 UND | 0 UND | | | 0 UND | 0 UND | | 1 313.3 | 5 79.9 | |
| 3 108.2 | 5 70.3 | 5 74.0 | | Sales/Receivables | 0 UND | 7 54.1 | | 3 135.8 | 12 29.4 | |
| 19 19.4 | 12 29.4 | 16 23.3 | | | 14 26.3 | 19 18.9 | | 9 42.0 | 17 21.9 | |
| | | | | Cost of Sales/Inventory | | | | | | |
| | | | | Cost of Sales/Payables | | | | | | |
| 4.4 | 4.8 | 4.2 | | | 2.0 | 5.6 | | 4.3 | 4.1 | |
| 11.4 | 9.1 | 9.3 | | Sales/Working Capital | 22.5 | 13.2 | | 7.7 | 7.4 | |
| -7.5 | -14.4 | -9.3 | | | -6.8 | -3.2 | | -39.5 | 19.6 | |
| 13.6 | 13.6 | 7.8 | | | 17.9 | 7.6 | | 16.0 | 7.9 | |
| (66) 4.2 | (82) 3.6 | (93) 2.9 | | EBIT/Interest | (17) 2.4 | (29) 2.2 | | (17) 5.4 | (15) 4.3 | |
| 2.3 | 1.9 | .9 | | | -1.4 | .7 | | 2.0 | 1.8 | |
| | | | | Net Profit + Depr., Dep., Amort./Cur. Mat. L/T/D | | | | | | |
| .9 | .6 | .7 | | | .9 | 1.1 | | .9 | .4 | |
| 3.8 | 2.3 | 2.1 | | Fixed/Worth | 2.3 | 2.9 | | 4.1 | 1.0 | |
| -3.3 | -27.3 | -16.6 | | | -1.6 | -12.3 | | 14.1 | 2.8 | |
| .8 | .8 | 1.1 | | | .9 | 1.2 | | .8 | .8 | |
| 5.4 | 3.3 | 3.5 | | Debt/Worth | 3.8 | 5.5 | | 4.4 | 1.7 | |
| -5.4 | -66.1 | -11.7 | | | -3.7 | -9.0 | | 20.5 | 3.3 | |
| 92.1 | 69.1 | 54.3 | | | 63.6 | 70.3 | | 91.4 | 39.0 | |
| (56) 27.3 | (72) 22.9 | (85) 12.7 | | % Profit Before Taxes/Tangible Net Worth | (19) 8.1 | (22) 11.4 | | (19) 15.8 | (16) 15.6 | |
| 11.4 | 6.1 | -1.5 | | | -11.9 | -1.5 | | 5.3 | 6.0 | |
| 19.1 | 16.7 | 14.8 | | | 23.8 | 9.1 | | 15.3 | 17.4 | |
| 9.9 | 5.8 | 4.9 | | % Profit Before Taxes/Total Assets | 5.4 | 2.9 | | 7.6 | 3.7 | |
| 2.7 | 1.3 | -.9 | | | -5.2 | -.6 | | .0 | 2.0 | |
| 5.0 | 6.8 | 8.5 | | | 10.1 | 2.7 | | 4.4 | 9.8 | |
| .9 | 1.1 | 1.1 | | Sales/Net Fixed Assets | 2.2 | .5 | | 1.1 | 1.1 | |
| .5 | .4 | .4 | | | .2 | .3 | | .4 | .4 | |
| 1.6 | 1.6 | 1.4 | | | 1.9 | .8 | | .7 | 1.4 | |
| .6 | .5 | .6 | | Sales/Total Assets | .9 | .4 | | .5 | .8 | |
| .3 | .3 | .2 | | | .1 | .2 | | .4 | .2 | |
| 4.4 | 2.2 | 2.6 | | | 6.3 | 6.8 | | 3.1 | .8 | |
| (52) 10.1 | (67) 7.0 | (74) 9.7 | | % Depr., Dep., Amort./Sales | (10) 24.7 | (23) 12.0 | | (17) 13.9 | (16) 6.0 | |
| 15.4 | 14.2 | 19.6 | | | 35.6 | 18.7 | | 20.1 | 12.6 | |
| 1.5 | 1.7 | 1.1 | | % Officers', Directors' Owners' Comp/Sales | | | | | | |
| (16) 4.0 | (19) 3.4 | (21) 2.0 | | | | | | | | |
| 5.3 | 5.7 | 4.3 | | | | | | | | |
| 949023M | 696186M | 875936M | | Net Sales ($) | 15528M | 68154M | 29313M | 159881M | 288907M | 314153M |
| 1050061M | 1140330M | 1845902M | | Total Assets ($) | 42242M | 217644M | 39349M | 380037M | 734767M | 431863M |

© RMA 2024        M = $ thousand    MM = $ million
See Pages viii through xx for Explanation of Ratios and Data

# ENTERTAINMENT—Fitness and Recreational Sports Centers  NAICS 713940

## Current Data Sorted by Assets | Comparative Historical Data

| | | | | | | | Type of Statement | | |
|---|---|---|---|---|---|---|---|---|---|
| 1 | 1 | | 3 | 9 | 10 | 9 | Unqualified | 36 | 21 |
| 1 | | 1 | 8 | 10 | 1 | | Reviewed | 14 | 7 |
| 1 | | 3 | 8 | 2 | | | Compiled | 22 | 16 |
| 26 | 20 | | 22 | 5 | | | Tax Returns | 102 | 45 |
| 46 | 41 | | 60 | 40 | 11 | 14 | Other | 240 | 149 |
| | 43 (4/1-9/30/23) | | | 309 (10/1/23-3/31/24) | | | | 4/1/19-3/31/20 | 4/1/20-3/31/21 |
| 0-500M | 500M-2MM | 2-10MM | 10-50MM | 50-100MM | 100-250MM | | | ALL | ALL |
| 75 | 65 | 101 | 66 | 22 | 23 | | NUMBER OF STATEMENTS | 414 | 238 |
| % | % | % | % | % | % | | ASSETS | % | % |
| 33.6 | 21.8 | 11.7 | 14.8 | 12.8 | 7.2 | | Cash & Equivalents | 13.9 | 21.3 |
| 2.5 | 3.9 | 4.4 | 2.8 | 2.2 | 1.6 | | Trade Receivables (net) | 2.8 | 2.6 |
| 1.2 | 1.7 | 1.0 | 1.0 | .4 | .2 | | Inventory | 1.3 | 1.0 |
| 3.7 | 5.4 | 3.1 | 1.9 | 1.1 | 1.7 | | All Other Current | 4.0 | 2.7 |
| 41.1 | 32.8 | 20.2 | 20.6 | 16.5 | 10.8 | | Total Current | 21.9 | 27.6 |
| 38.6 | 45.0 | 63.3 | 61.3 | 53.7 | 58.0 | | Fixed Assets (net) | 61.9 | 56.7 |
| 12.1 | 7.4 | 5.5 | 7.5 | 11.0 | 4.2 | | Intangibles (net) | 8.8 | 8.5 |
| 8.1 | 14.8 | 10.9 | 10.6 | 18.8 | 27.1 | | All Other Non-Current | 7.4 | 7.2 |
| 100.0 | 100.0 | 100.0 | 100.0 | 100.0 | 100.0 | | Total | 100.0 | 100.0 |
| | | | | | | | LIABILITIES | | |
| 13.2 | 7.6 | 2.4 | 1.1 | .8 | 1.1 | | Notes Payable-Short Term | 4.7 | 5.7 |
| 4.9 | 3.8 | 5.0 | 3.0 | 3.9 | 2.3 | | Cur. Mat.-L.T.D. | 4.9 | 5.5 |
| 7.1 | 2.3 | 2.3 | 2.7 | 2.2 | 2.9 | | Trade Payables | 3.2 | 4.2 |
| .1 | .1 | .1 | .3 | .1 | .0 | | Income Taxes Payable | .1 | .1 |
| 21.6 | 15.3 | 13.8 | 9.4 | 7.2 | 8.1 | | All Other Current | 14.5 | 13.0 |
| 46.9 | 29.2 | 23.6 | 16.4 | 14.2 | 14.3 | | Total Current | 27.3 | 28.7 |
| 55.4 | 48.2 | 44.7 | 43.6 | 32.1 | 55.0 | | Long-Term Debt | 45.4 | 52.8 |
| .0 | .0 | .0 | .0 | .4 | .0 | | Deferred Taxes | .1 | .0 |
| 19.4 | 20.7 | 12.4 | 13.3 | 18.5 | 24.9 | | All Other Non-Current | 10.8 | 9.7 |
| -21.7 | 1.9 | 19.3 | 26.7 | 34.9 | 5.8 | | Net Worth | 16.3 | 8.8 |
| 100.0 | 100.0 | 100.0 | 100.0 | 100.0 | 100.0 | | Total Liabilities & Net Worth | 100.0 | 100.0 |
| | | | | | | | INCOME DATA | | |
| 100.0 | 100.0 | 100.0 | 100.0 | 100.0 | 100.0 | | Net Sales | 100.0 | 100.0 |
| | | | | | | | Gross Profit | | |
| 89.4 | 83.0 | 83.0 | 89.8 | 92.4 | 89.3 | | Operating Expenses | 87.9 | 96.2 |
| 10.6 | 17.0 | 17.0 | 10.2 | 7.6 | 10.7 | | Operating Profit | 12.1 | 3.8 |
| 1.7 | 5.8 | 5.2 | 2.2 | 1.2 | 7.3 | | All Other Expenses (net) | 4.3 | 2.1 |
| 8.9 | 11.2 | 11.8 | 7.9 | 6.5 | 3.3 | | Profit Before Taxes | 7.8 | 1.7 |
| | | | | | | | RATIOS | | |
| 6.4 | 4.6 | 4.5 | 2.2 | 2.9 | 1.9 | | | 2.5 | 3.2 |
| 1.9 | 1.5 | 1.0 | 1.4 | 1.3 | .8 | Current | | .9 | 1.1 |
| .5 | .6 | .4 | .6 | .8 | .3 | | | .4 | .4 |
| 6.0 | 3.9 | 3.2 | 2.0 | 2.8 | 1.2 | | | 2.0 | 3.0 |
| 1.4 | 1.2 | .9 | 1.1 | 1.1 | .7 | Quick | | .7 | .9 |
| .4 | .4 | .3 | .5 | .7 | .3 | | | .2 | .4 |
| 0 UND | 0 UND | 0 UND | 0 999.8 | 2 194.4 | 0 999.8 | | | 0 UND | 0 UND |
| 0 UND | 0 UND | 2 174.1 | 3 115.2 | 8 48.0 | 5 75.1 | Sales/Receivables | | 0 741.6 | 0 UND |
| 0 UND | 10 36.6 | 16 22.6 | 11 34.2 | 21 17.7 | 19 19.2 | | | 8 47.2 | 10 35.2 |
| | | | | | | | Cost of Sales/Inventory | | |
| | | | | | | | Cost of Sales/Payables | | |
| 8.3 | 6.0 | 5.4 | 8.6 | 4.5 | 11.2 | | | 9.9 | 4.9 |
| 23.8 | 25.8 | 410.9 | 24.3 | 14.1 | -35.1 | Sales/Working Capital | | -140.0 | 96.3 |
| -11.7 | -16.8 | -6.8 | -25.0 | -29.6 | -4.6 | | | -9.8 | -6.5 |
| 9.8 | 11.0 | 6.8 | 14.0 | 6.4 | 3.6 | | | 9.2 | 5.4 |
| (44) 2.5 | (44) 1.6 | (76) 2.7 | (61) 4.0 | (21) 3.4 | 2.4 | EBIT/Interest | (332) 3.0 | (194) 1.0 |
| .1 | -.5 | 1.0 | 1.7 | .8 | .5 | | | .6 | -3.6 |
| | | | | | | | Net Profit + Depr., Dep., | 6.4 | 21.3 |
| | | | | | | | Amort./Cur. Mat. L/T/D | (24) 3.2 | (12) 1.8 |
| | | | | | | | | 1.3 | -.4 |
| .3 | .4 | 1.2 | 1.1 | .9 | 1.6 | | | 1.1 | 1.2 |
| 19.4 | 1.5 | 3.1 | 2.5 | 1.3 | 18.3 | Fixed/Worth | | 2.8 | 4.1 |
| -.7 | -8.6 | -15.6 | 8.4 | -2.0 | -1.6 | | | -7.0 | -2.7 |
| .8 | .7 | 1.2 | 1.0 | .6 | 1.8 | | | .9 | 1.0 |
| -30.9 | 4.9 | 4.7 | 2.9 | 1.4 | 28.8 | Debt/Worth | | 3.2 | 6.2 |
| -2.1 | -3.9 | -19.0 | 8.2 | -3.3 | -9.6 | | | -7.8 | -4.9 |
| 211.0 | 172.0 | 43.5 | 55.9 | 18.9 | 26.2 | | % Profit Before Taxes/Tangible | 77.6 | 39.7 |
| (35) 86.3 | (43) 43.7 | (71) 19.9 | (53) 24.2 | (15) 8.1 | (15) 11.2 | | Net Worth | (286) 24.7 | (142) 8.0 |
| 19.1 | 8.2 | 3.8 | 9.3 | 1.7 | 1.2 | | | 1.8 | -4.3 |
| 54.9 | 36.8 | 13.6 | 16.4 | 8.7 | 6.0 | | % Profit Before Taxes/Total | 23.1 | 12.5 |
| 19.4 | 9.2 | 5.9 | 5.6 | 4.7 | 2.7 | | Assets | 6.1 | 1.0 |
| -4.3 | -2.3 | .1 | 1.3 | -.5 | -1.1 | | | -.6 | -8.3 |
| 56.2 | 34.1 | 2.4 | 2.6 | 2.4 | 1.6 | | | 6.8 | 4.1 |
| 10.8 | 4.9 | 1.1 | 1.2 | .9 | .7 | Sales/Net Fixed Assets | | 1.8 | 1.4 |
| 3.7 | 1.3 | .4 | .7 | .6 | .6 | | | .7 | .7 |
| 4.7 | 2.7 | 1.1 | 1.2 | .7 | .6 | | | 2.5 | 1.6 |
| 2.8 | 1.5 | .6 | .7 | .6 | .4 | Sales/Total Assets | | 1.1 | .8 |
| 2.0 | .8 | .3 | .5 | .4 | .4 | | | .6 | .4 |
| 1.6 | 2.8 | 4.0 | 4.2 | 4.8 | 7.3 | | | 3.9 | 3.9 |
| (36) 4.0 | (34) 6.6 | (78) 8.4 | (57) 6.8 | (20) 6.4 | (17) 8.7 | % Depr., Dep., Amort./Sales | (302) 6.8 | (161) 8.6 |
| 8.6 | 11.0 | 15.0 | 10.0 | 10.6 | 11.7 | | | 11.3 | 14.6 |
| 4.7 | 2.1 | 2.2 | 2.2 | | | | % Officers', Directors' | 3.3 | 2.7 |
| (28) 9.6 | (15) 4.6 | (24) 5.7 | (10) 4.0 | | | | Owners' Comp/Sales | (90) 5.3 | (50) 6.3 |
| 13.9 | 9.8 | 10.2 | 16.5 | | | | | 11.4 | 11.5 |
| 66596M | 141012M | 439107M | 1352419M | 944991M | 1773848M | | Net Sales ($) | 5078939M | 2346238M |
| 17943M | 75297M | 503671M | 1395828M | 1618470M | 3314805M | | Total Assets ($) | 6421286M | 3888158M |

© RMA 2024

M = $ thousand  MM = $ million
See Pages viii through xx for Explanation of Ratios and Data

# ENTERTAINMENT—Fitness and Recreational Sports Centers NAICS 713940

| Comparative Historical Data | | | | Current Data Sorted by Sales | | | | | |
|---|---|---|---|---|---|---|---|---|---|
| 24 | 33 | 32 | Type of Statement | | | | | | |
| | | | Unqualified | 1 | | 1 | 6 | 8 | 16 |
| 9 | 25 | 21 | Reviewed | 1 | 2 | 5 | 3 | 7 | 3 |
| 11 | 20 | 14 | Compiled | 2 | 3 | 1 | 5 | 1 | 2 |
| 47 | 71 | 73 | Tax Returns | 30 | 26 | 8 | 4 | 4 | 1 |
| 158 | 213 | 212 | Other | 51 | 64 | 21 | 19 | 21 | 36 |
| 4/1/21-3/31/22 ALL | 4/1/22-3/31/23 ALL | 4/1/23-3/31/24 ALL | | 43 (4/1-9/30/23) | | | 309 (10/1/23-3/31/24) | | |
| | | | | 0-1MM | 1-3MM | 3-5MM | 5-10MM | 10-25MM | 25MM & OVER |
| 249 | 362 | 352 | NUMBER OF STATEMENTS | 85 | 95 | 36 | 37 | 41 | 58 |
| % | % | % | ASSETS | % | % | % | % | % | % |
| 22.9 | 21.6 | 18.6 | Cash & Equivalents | 21.5 | 20.6 | 15.4 | 19.4 | 15.9 | 14.4 |
| 2.1 | 2.4 | 3.3 | Trade Receivables (net) | 1.5 | 4.0 | 5.0 | 5.8 | 2.6 | 2.6 |
| 1.1 | 1.3 | 1.1 | Inventory | .6 | 1.0 | 2.3 | 1.8 | .7 | 1.0 |
| 3.7 | 4.2 | 3.2 | All Other Current | 4.0 | 4.8 | 1.0 | 2.1 | 1.2 | 3.1 |
| 29.9 | 29.5 | 26.2 | Total Current | 27.6 | 30.4 | 23.7 | 29.1 | 20.4 | 21.0 |
| 55.2 | 53.4 | 53.3 | Fixed Assets (net) | 52.5 | 53.0 | 52.8 | 52.1 | 61.6 | 50.5 |
| 6.9 | 8.9 | 7.9 | Intangibles (net) | 11.3 | 7.0 | 3.9 | 6.2 | 8.3 | 7.6 |
| 8.0 | 8.3 | 12.5 | All Other Non-Current | 8.5 | 9.6 | 19.6 | 12.6 | 9.7 | 20.8 |
| 100.0 | 100.0 | 100.0 | Total | 100.0 | 100.0 | 100.0 | 100.0 | 100.0 | 100.0 |
| | | | LIABILITIES | | | | | | |
| 3.6 | 2.9 | 5.2 | Notes Payable-Short Term | 6.0 | 10.1 | 5.4 | 1.1 | 2.0 | .9 |
| 3.5 | 3.5 | 4.1 | Cur. Mat.-L.T.D. | 4.4 | 4.0 | 6.6 | 2.9 | 3.5 | 3.5 |
| 1.5 | 4.1 | 3.5 | Trade Payables | 5.1 | 2.4 | 3.9 | 2.7 | 2.8 | 3.3 |
| .1 | .1 | .1 | Income Taxes Payable | .0 | .0 | .4 | .0 | .1 | .3 |
| 14.2 | 17.1 | 14.1 | All Other Current | 13.9 | 15.2 | 7.9 | 24.4 | 11.8 | 11.7 |
| 22.9 | 27.6 | 27.1 | Total Current | 29.5 | 31.8 | 24.2 | 31.2 | 20.2 | 19.7 |
| 52.3 | 51.4 | 47.3 | Long-Term Debt | 66.0 | 43.8 | 40.1 | 37.5 | 35.9 | 44.4 |
| .0 | .0 | .0 | Deferred Taxes | .0 | .0 | .0 | .0 | .1 | .0 |
| 8.2 | 13.9 | 16.8 | All Other Non-Current | 3.1 | 19.2 | 37.1 | 11.1 | 16.1 | 24.3 |
| 16.5 | 7.1 | 8.8 | Net Worth | 1.4 | 5.1 | -1.4 | 20.2 | 27.6 | 11.5 |
| 100.0 | 100.0 | 100.0 | Total Liabilities & Net Worth | 100.0 | 100.0 | 100.0 | 100.0 | 100.0 | 100.0 |
| | | | INCOME DATA | | | | | | |
| 100.0 | 100.0 | 100.0 | Net Sales | 100.0 | 100.0 | 100.0 | 100.0 | 100.0 | 100.0 |
| | | | Gross Profit | | | | | | |
| 86.2 | 87.6 | 86.6 | Operating Expenses | 79.6 | 87.9 | 86.7 | 92.2 | 88.3 | 90.0 |
| 13.8 | 12.4 | 13.4 | Operating Profit | 20.4 | 12.1 | 13.3 | 7.8 | 11.7 | 10.0 |
| 1.7 | 3.6 | 3.9 | All Other Expenses (net) | 7.6 | 3.3 | 1.2 | 1.5 | 1.7 | 4.3 |
| 12.0 | 8.8 | 9.5 | Profit Before Taxes | 12.8 | 8.8 | 12.1 | 6.2 | 10.0 | 5.7 |
| | | | RATIOS | | | | | | |
| 4.6 | 3.2 | 3.5 | | 4.9 | 6.7 | 4.1 | 6.2 | 1.9 | 2.2 |
| 1.6 | 1.4 | 1.3 | Current | 1.2 | 1.9 | 1.2 | 1.3 | 1.0 | 1.0 |
| .7 | .6 | .5 | | .4 | .5 | .7 | .6 | .5 | .7 |
| 4.0 | 2.8 | 3.0 | | 3.6 | 6.2 | 2.5 | 5.9 | 1.8 | 2.0 |
| 1.4 | 1.3 | 1.0 | Quick | 1.0 | 1.3 | 1.1 | 1.0 | .9 | .9 |
| .6 | .5 | .4 | | .2 | .3 | .6 | .4 | .3 | .4 |
| 0 UND | 0 UND | 0 UND | | 0 UND | 0 UND | 0 748.0 | 0 999.8 | 0 UND | 1 402.7 |
| 0 UND | 0 UND | 1 434.0 | Sales/Receivables | 0 UND | 0 UND | 9 41.3 | 4 92.9 | 3 117.1 | 5 76.3 |
| 13 28.3 | 9 39.5 | 11 32.6 | | 0 UND | 12 31.5 | 16 22.3 | 18 20.6 | 10 35.4 | 19 19.3 |
| | | | Cost of Sales/Inventory | | | | | | |
| | | | Cost of Sales/Payables | | | | | | |
| 3.9 | 6.0 | 6.5 | | 6.7 | 5.1 | 10.8 | 4.5 | 10.2 | 9.6 |
| 16.5 | 24.4 | 35.1 | Sales/Working Capital | 73.5 | 14.5 | 43.6 | 51.3 | -139.0 | 164.8 |
| -16.3 | -12.2 | -11.5 | | -5.8 | -11.5 | -23.5 | -9.7 | -14.1 | -15.8 |
| 15.2 | 9.8 | 8.0 | | 5.7 | 7.7 | 7.2 | 13.6 | 20.9 | 6.3 |
| (193) 3.8 | (273) 3.1 | (269) 2.8 | EBIT/Interest | (51) 1.6 | (67) 2.1 | (30) 2.7 | (28) 3.2 | (36) 6.4 | (57) 3.0 |
| 1.6 | .3 | .9 | | .1 | .9 | .6 | .6 | 2.7 | 1.4 |
| | | 12.2 13.8 | Net Profit + Depr., Dep., | | | | | | 13.9 |
| | (28) 3.7 | (23) 8.6 | Amort./Cur. Mat. L/T/D | | | | | (12) | 10.4 |
| | | 1.4 3.0 | | | | | | | 3.7 |
| .9 | .9 | .9 | | .9 | .7 | .7 | .8 | .9 | 1.0 |
| 2.3 | 3.3 | 2.8 | Fixed/Worth | 8.3 | 3.1 | 2.4 | 1.9 | 2.5 | 2.9 |
| -6.7 | -2.8 | -5.2 | | -1.8 | -6.4 | NM | -4.7 | 25.2 | -1.4 |
| .8 | 1.0 | 1.0 | | 1.0 | .7 | 1.1 | .8 | 1.0 | 1.0 |
| 2.8 | 6.0 | 4.6 | Debt/Worth | 20.0 | 4.9 | 3.9 | 2.0 | 3.0 | 4.3 |
| -8.9 | -4.1 | -6.6 | | -3.5 | -7.5 | -16.7 | -7.2 | 26.1 | -6.6 |
| 56.8 | 55.0 | 68.5 | % Profit Before Taxes/Tangible Net Worth | 105.5 | 61.6 | 108.2 | 46.2 | 88.5 | 36.2 |
| (169) 22.1 | (223) 19.2 | (232) 25.1 | | (45) 23.3 | (64) 18.5 | (25) 30.2 | (26) 28.4 | (33) 41.3 | (39) 14.9 |
| 4.2 | 1.9 | 5.7 | | 3.8 | 3.6 | 13.8 | 9.2 | 14.4 | 3.8 |
| 20.1 | 26.9 | 19.4 | % Profit Before Taxes/Total Assets | 23.9 | 27.5 | 20.3 | 24.4 | 18.8 | 11.1 |
| 7.4 | 6.3 | 6.2 | | 5.5 | 6.0 | 10.3 | 11.2 | 7.5 | 5.7 |
| .7 | -.4 | .1 | | -3.7 | .0 | 1.6 | -.3 | 2.5 | .9 |
| 6.4 | 7.4 | 7.6 | | 15.2 | 16.4 | 7.2 | 5.1 | 3.0 | 3.2 |
| 1.4 | 1.8 | 1.8 | Sales/Net Fixed Assets | 2.6 | 1.6 | 1.9 | 1.9 | 1.3 | 1.4 |
| .6 | .7 | .7 | | .7 | .5 | .6 | 1.1 | .8 | .7 |
| 1.8 | 2.0 | 2.2 | | 2.8 | 2.8 | 2.5 | 1.7 | 1.3 | 1.2 |
| .8 | 1.0 | .9 | Sales/Total Assets | 1.4 | 1.0 | .8 | 1.0 | .8 | .7 |
| .4 | .5 | .5 | | .3 | .4 | .5 | .5 | .6 | .4 |
| 4.0 | 4.0 | 3.8 | | 3.1 | 2.7 | 3.5 | 3.4 | 4.4 | 4.8 |
| (168) 8.9 | (247) 7.7 | (242) 7.3 | % Depr., Dep., Amort./Sales | (51) 8.7 | (58) 6.5 | (24) 8.3 | (24) 5.6 | (37) 7.4 | (48) 7.3 |
| 13.5 | 11.5 | 11.3 | | 20.3 | 12.6 | 9.7 | 9.8 | 11.2 | 11.0 |
| 4.7 | 3.2 | 2.6 | | 7.0 | 2.0 | 2.0 | 3.9 | | |
| (42) 7.0 | (74) 6.7 | (80) 6.9 | % Officers', Directors' Owners' Comp/Sales | (23) 10.3 | (25) 7.4 | (10) 4.8 | (10) 6.8 | | |
| 11.0 | 10.7 | 11.1 | | 16.9 | 10.3 | 7.6 | 10.6 | | |
| 3087781M | 4709535M | 4717973M | Net Sales ($) | 39512M | 171105M | 141141M | 251604M | 665317M | 3449294M |
| 4360700M | 6935595M | 6926014M | Total Assets ($) | 77926M | 286968M | 194847M | 330676M | 865576M | 5170021M |

© RMA 2024  
M = $ thousand  MM = $ million  
See Pages viii through xx for Explanation of Ratios and Data

# ENTERTAINMENT—Bowling Centers NAICS 713950

**Current Data Sorted by Assets** | **Comparative Historical Data**

| | | | | | | Type of Statement | | |
|---|---|---|---|---|---|---|---|---|
| | | | | 1 | 1 | Unqualified | | 1 |
| | | 1 | | 1 | | Reviewed | 3 | 1 |
| | 1 | 4 | | | | Compiled | 11 | 2 |
| 7 | 1 | 10 | | | | Tax Returns | 24 | 5 |
| 1 | 3 | | 2 | | | Other | 28 | 22 |
| | 11 (4/1-9/30/23) | | 22 (10/1/23-3/31/24) | | | | 4/1/19-3/31/20 | 4/1/20-3/31/21 |
| 0-500M | 500M-2MM | 2-10MM | 10-50MM | 50-100MM | 100-250MM | | ALL | ALL |
| 8 | 5 | 15 | 2 | 2 | 1 | NUMBER OF STATEMENTS | 66 | 31 |
| % | % | % | % | % | % | ASSETS | % | % |
| | | 19.9 | | | | Cash & Equivalents | 12.6 | 27.9 |
| | | .9 | | | | Trade Receivables (net) | 1.4 | 1.3 |
| | | 1.9 | | | | Inventory | 2.1 | 2.8 |
| | | 1.7 | | | | All Other Current | 2.0 | 2.4 |
| | | 24.4 | | | | Total Current | 18.0 | 34.5 |
| | | 61.7 | | | | Fixed Assets (net) | 68.2 | 51.5 |
| | | 1.1 | | | | Intangibles (net) | 3.1 | 7.1 |
| | | 12.8 | | | | All Other Non-Current | 10.8 | 7.0 |
| | | 100.0 | | | | Total | 100.0 | 100.0 |
| | | | | | | LIABILITIES | | |
| | | .8 | | | | Notes Payable-Short Term | 8.7 | 3.1 |
| | | 1.7 | | | | Cur. Mat.-L.T.D. | 5.0 | 8.6 |
| | | 2.5 | | | | Trade Payables | 5.0 | 3.4 |
| | | .2 | | | | Income Taxes Payable | .0 | .0 |
| | | 12.4 | | | | All Other Current | 7.5 | 19.7 |
| | | 17.6 | | | | Total Current | 26.3 | 34.8 |
| | | 62.1 | | | | Long-Term Debt | 64.0 | 73.8 |
| | | .5 | | | | Deferred Taxes | .5 | .3 |
| | | 3.3 | | | | All Other Non-Current | 14.6 | 16.2 |
| | | 16.5 | | | | Net Worth | -5.3 | -25.1 |
| | | 100.0 | | | | Total Liabilities & Net Worth | 100.0 | 100.0 |
| | | | | | | INCOME DATA | | |
| | | 100.0 | | | | Net Sales | 100.0 | 100.0 |
| | | | | | | Gross Profit | | |
| | | 85.1 | | | | Operating Expenses | 87.4 | 103.9 |
| | | 14.9 | | | | Operating Profit | 12.6 | -3.9 |
| | | 2.7 | | | | All Other Expenses (net) | 5.7 | .3 |
| | | 12.2 | | | | Profit Before Taxes | 6.9 | -4.2 |
| | | | | | | RATIOS | | |
| | | 2.5 | | | | | 2.1 | 3.5 |
| | | 1.9 | | | | Current | .7 | 1.4 |
| | | .8 | | | | | .2 | .6 |
| | | 2.1 | | | | | 1.8 | 2.6 |
| | | 1.5 | | | | Quick | (65) .6 | 1.0 |
| | | .5 | | | | | .2 | .4 |
| | 0 | UND | | | | | 0 UND | 0 UND |
| | 0 | 999.8 | | | | Sales/Receivables | 0 UND | 0 UND |
| | 8 | 45.7 | | | | | 1 345.2 | 1 595.2 |
| | | | | | | Cost of Sales/Inventory | | |
| | | | | | | Cost of Sales/Payables | | |
| | | 6.4 | | | | | 13.6 | 5.3 |
| | | 13.1 | | | | Sales/Working Capital | -38.3 | 13.8 |
| | | -135.6 | | | | | -9.4 | -6.6 |
| | | 6.8 | | | | | 4.4 | 2.2 |
| | (12) | 4.2 | | | | EBIT/Interest | (56) 2.3 | (23) .7 |
| | | 1.8 | | | | | 1.1 | -1.5 |
| | | | | | | Net Profit + Depr., Dep., Amort./Cur. Mat. L/T/D | | |
| | | .9 | | | | | 2.0 | 1.8 |
| | | 3.4 | | | | Fixed/Worth | 18.2 | 41.7 |
| | | -18.3 | | | | | -2.8 | -1.3 |
| | | 1.3 | | | | | 1.7 | 2.2 |
| | | 3.8 | | | | Debt/Worth | 18.3 | 47.2 |
| | | -22.8 | | | | | -4.0 | -4.2 |
| | | | | | | | 86.1 | 24.6 |
| | | | | | | % Profit Before Taxes/Tangible Net Worth | (36) 23.9 | (16) 8.4 |
| | | | | | | | 8.6 | -23.0 |
| | | 16.9 | | | | | 12.8 | 4.4 |
| | | 9.0 | | | | % Profit Before Taxes/Total Assets | 5.5 | -1.1 |
| | | 5.2 | | | | | 1.1 | -12.0 |
| | | 3.1 | | | | | 5.6 | 10.2 |
| | | 1.3 | | | | Sales/Net Fixed Assets | 1.5 | 2.3 |
| | | .7 | | | | | .9 | .7 |
| | | 1.3 | | | | | 2.4 | 2.4 |
| | | .9 | | | | Sales/Total Assets | 1.1 | 1.1 |
| | | .5 | | | | | .7 | .5 |
| | | 2.7 | | | | | 4.1 | 2.9 |
| | (12) | 4.5 | | | | % Depr., Dep., Amort./Sales | (57) 7.0 | (20) 7.9 |
| | | 9.8 | | | | | 9.9 | 13.4 |
| | | | | | | | 1.1 | 1.5 |
| | | | | | | % Officers', Directors' Owners' Comp/Sales | (20) 3.1 | (11) 3.6 |
| | | | | | | | 6.4 | 10.6 |
| 10561M | 16233M | 64138M | 423465M | 57386M | 75749M | Net Sales ($) | 1844279M | 111542M |
| 2061M | 6411M | 70314M | 47540M | 113907M | 114882M | Total Assets ($) | 598161M | 193062M |

© RMA 2024

M = $ thousand   MM = $ million
See Pages viii through xx for Explanation of Ratios and Data

# ENTERTAINMENT—Bowling Centers  NAICS 713950

## Comparative Historical Data / Current Data Sorted by Sales

| | | | | | | | | | | |
|---|---|---|---|---|---|---|---|---|---|---|
| **Type of Statement** | | | | | | | | | | |
| Unqualified | 1 | 1 | 2 | | | | 1 | | | 2 |
| Reviewed | 1 | 2 | 1 | | | | | | | 1 |
| Compiled | 5 | 2 | 2 | | 1 | 4 | | 1 | 1 | |
| Tax Returns | 13 | 17 | 12 | | 6 | 4 | 6 | 5 | | 1 |
| Other | 17 | 24 | 16 | | | | | | | |
| | 4/1/21-3/31/22 ALL | 4/1/22-3/31/23 ALL | 4/1/23-3/31/24 ALL | | 0-1MM | 11 (4/1-9/30/23) 1-3MM | 3-5MM | 22 (10/1/23-3/31/24) 5-10MM | 10-25MM | 25MM & OVER |
| **NUMBER OF STATEMENTS** | 37 | 45 | 33 | | 7 | 9 | 7 | 6 | | 4 |

| | % | % | % | | % | % | % | % | % | % |
|---|---|---|---|---|---|---|---|---|---|---|
| **ASSETS** | | | | | | | | | | |
| Cash & Equivalents | 29.6 | 34.9 | 28.9 | | | | | | | |
| Trade Receivables (net) | .8 | 1.0 | .5 | | | | | | | |
| Inventory | 2.6 | 1.6 | 2.4 | | | | | | | |
| All Other Current | 3.1 | 2.9 | 4.3 | | | | | | | |
| Total Current | 36.2 | 40.5 | 36.1 | | | | | | | |
| Fixed Assets (net) | 48.8 | 40.0 | 46.9 | | | | | | DATA NOT AVAILABLE | |
| Intangibles (net) | 6.6 | 5.8 | 3.7 | | | | | | | |
| All Other Non-Current | 8.4 | 13.6 | 13.4 | | | | | | | |
| Total | 100.0 | 100.0 | 100.0 | | | | | | | |
| **LIABILITIES** | | | | | | | | | | |
| Notes Payable-Short Term | 4.1 | 1.0 | 7.1 | | | | | | | |
| Cur. Mat.-L.T.D. | 2.8 | 2.4 | 2.0 | | | | | | | |
| Trade Payables | 2.0 | 1.7 | 3.3 | | | | | | | |
| Income Taxes Payable | .0 | .0 | 1.0 | | | | | | | |
| All Other Current | 13.5 | 9.2 | 12.0 | | | | | | | |
| Total Current | 22.4 | 14.3 | 25.4 | | | | | | | |
| Long-Term Debt | 65.2 | 53.2 | 53.2 | | | | | | | |
| Deferred Taxes | .0 | .1 | .2 | | | | | | | |
| All Other Non-Current | 4.2 | 13.5 | 3.6 | | | | | | | |
| Net Worth | 8.2 | 18.9 | 17.7 | | | | | | | |
| Total Liabilities & Net Worth | 100.0 | 100.0 | 100.0 | | | | | | | |
| **INCOME DATA** | | | | | | | | | | |
| Net Sales | 100.0 | 100.0 | 100.0 | | | | | | | |
| Gross Profit | | | | | | | | | | |
| Operating Expenses | 85.7 | 81.4 | 87.9 | | | | | | | |
| Operating Profit | 14.3 | 18.6 | 12.1 | | | | | | | |
| All Other Expenses (net) | -1.3 | 1.7 | 2.5 | | | | | | | |
| Profit Before Taxes | 15.7 | 16.9 | 9.7 | | | | | | | |

| | | | | **RATIOS** | | | | | | |
|---|---|---|---|---|---|---|---|---|---|---|
| Current | 5.6 | 8.1 | 2.5 | | | | | | | |
| | 2.7 | 3.2 | 1.8 | | | | | | | |
| | 1.2 | 1.3 | .7 | | | | | | | |
| Quick | 4.7 | 7.6 | 2.1 | | | | | | | |
| | 2.5 | 2.5 | 1.2 | | | | | | | |
| | 1.0 | .7 | .4 | | | | | | | |
| Sales/Receivables | 0 UND | 0 UND | 0 UND | | | | | | | |
| | 0 UND | 0 UND | 0 UND | | | | | | | |
| | 1 726.1 | 3 139.9 | 1 277.1 | | | | | | | |
| Cost of Sales/Inventory | | | | | | | | | | |
| Cost of Sales/Payables | | | | | | | | | | |
| Sales/Working Capital | 3.4 | 3.5 | 5.2 | | | | | | | |
| | 6.3 | 5.7 | 17.2 | | | | | | | |
| | 39.5 | 48.4 | -76.3 | | | | | | | |
| EBIT/Interest | 13.9 | 30.1 | 9.0 | | | | | | | |
| | (30) 5.6 | (30) 6.4 | (25) 4.0 | | | | | | | |
| | 3.2 | 2.7 | 1.3 | | | | | | | |
| Net Profit + Depr., Dep., Amort./Cur. Mat. L/T/D | | | | | | | | | | |
| Fixed/Worth | .9 | .3 | .3 | | | | | | | |
| | 2.6 | 2.0 | 2.7 | | | | | | | |
| | -2.5 | 88.5 | -13.7 | | | | | | | |
| Debt/Worth | 1.3 | 1.1 | 1.2 | | | | | | | |
| | 4.9 | 3.1 | 2.8 | | | | | | | |
| | -5.2 | 186.7 | -19.3 | | | | | | | |
| % Profit Before Taxes/Tangible Net Worth | 96.9 | 115.3 | 79.7 | | | | | | | |
| | (23) 57.1 | (35) 56.6 | (22) 40.8 | | | | | | | |
| | 25.0 | 37.8 | 28.7 | | | | | | | |
| % Profit Before Taxes/Total Assets | 19.9 | 34.9 | 25.4 | | | | | | | |
| | 16.3 | 19.2 | 9.0 | | | | | | | |
| | 5.7 | 7.6 | 2.6 | | | | | | | |
| Sales/Net Fixed Assets | 7.2 | 9.4 | 73.6 | | | | | | | |
| | 2.0 | 3.3 | 2.8 | | | | | | | |
| | 1.4 | 1.5 | .9 | | | | | | | |
| Sales/Total Assets | 1.7 | 2.0 | 2.3 | | | | | | | |
| | 1.1 | 1.3 | 1.2 | | | | | | | |
| | .7 | .7 | .7 | | | | | | | |
| % Depr., Dep., Amort./Sales | 2.4 | 1.2 | 1.8 | | | | | | | |
| | (31) 6.1 | (33) 5.1 | (25) 5.0 | | | | | | | |
| | 8.8 | 7.9 | 10.7 | | | | | | | |
| % Officers', Directors' Owners' Comp/Sales | 1.8 | 1.7 | .7 | | | | | | | |
| | (13) 4.7 | (17) 4.7 | (11) 3.4 | | | | | | | |
| | 7.7 | 6.5 | 6.4 | | | | | | | |
| Net Sales ($) | 376990M | 175200M | 647532M | | 4224M | 19685M | 30147M | 44174M | | 549302M |
| Total Assets ($) | 392602M | 258723M | 355115M | | 3641M | 18963M | 31466M | 34998M | | 266047M |

M = $ thousand    MM = $ million
See Pages viii through xx for Explanation of Ratios and Data

© RMA 2024

# ENTERTAINMENT—All Other Amusement and Recreation Industries  NAICS 713990

## Current Data Sorted by Assets | Comparative Historical Data

| | | | | | | | Type of Statement | | |
|---|---|---|---|---|---|---|---|---|---|
| | 1 | 1 | 2 | 5 | 1 | 8 | Unqualified | 12 | 9 |
| | | 1 | 3 | 1 | 2 | | Reviewed | 12 | 2 |
| | 1 | 2 | 1 | | | | Compiled | 12 | 3 |
| | 15 | 19 | 17 | 2 | | 10 | Tax Returns | 69 | 33 |
| | 16 | 37 | 45 | 10 | 6 | 10 | Other | 125 | 64 |
| | | 28 (4/1-9/30/23) | | 178 (10/1/23-3/31/24) | | | | 4/1/19-3/31/20 | 4/1/20-3/31/21 |
| | 0-500M | 500M-2MM | 2-10MM | 10-50MM | 50-100MM | 100-250MM | NUMBER OF STATEMENTS | ALL 230 | ALL 111 |
| | 33 | 60 | 68 | 18 | 9 | 18 | | | |
| | % | % | % | % | % | % | | % | % |
| | | | | | | | **ASSETS** | | |
| | 49.1 | 27.3 | 18.6 | 22.1 | | 8.4 | Cash & Equivalents | 16.0 | 22.9 |
| | 2.9 | 3.2 | 3.2 | 2.7 | | 2.6 | Trade Receivables (net) | 2.8 | 1.8 |
| | 9.4 | 5.9 | 8.0 | 5.5 | | 3.0 | Inventory | 7.1 | 6.7 |
| | 6.8 | 2.3 | 4.0 | 4.9 | | 1.1 | All Other Current | 2.8 | 4.2 |
| | 68.3 | 38.7 | 33.8 | 35.1 | | 15.0 | Total Current | 28.7 | 35.7 |
| | 22.7 | 38.0 | 49.8 | 52.7 | | 57.9 | Fixed Assets (net) | 55.6 | 47.8 |
| | 5.6 | 5.0 | 6.6 | 6.1 | | 11.1 | Intangibles (net) | 7.2 | 8.2 |
| | 3.5 | 18.3 | 9.8 | 6.1 | | 16.1 | All Other Non-Current | 8.5 | 8.4 |
| | 100.0 | 100.0 | 100.0 | 100.0 | | 100.0 | Total | 100.0 | 100.0 |
| | | | | | | | **LIABILITIES** | | |
| | 10.1 | 2.8 | 6.6 | .3 | | 1.6 | Notes Payable-Short Term | 6.6 | 9.3 |
| | 2.9 | 3.3 | 3.9 | 3.4 | | 10.0 | Cur. Mat.-L.T.D. | 3.9 | 2.2 |
| | 1.7 | 4.9 | 3.7 | 6.2 | | 4.2 | Trade Payables | 4.9 | 3.4 |
| | .2 | .1 | .1 | .4 | | .3 | Income Taxes Payable | .1 | .1 |
| | 16.1 | 32.1 | 9.7 | 16.5 | | 5.4 | All Other Current | 16.9 | 15.7 |
| | 31.0 | 43.2 | 24.1 | 26.9 | | 21.5 | Total Current | 32.3 | 30.7 |
| | 28.4 | 32.0 | 36.7 | 28.2 | | 51.3 | Long-Term Debt | 36.1 | 42.5 |
| | .0 | .0 | .1 | .1 | | .8 | Deferred Taxes | .0 | .1 |
| | 6.2 | 6.3 | 7.1 | 7.5 | | 16.8 | All Other Non-Current | 13.1 | 10.7 |
| | 34.3 | 18.4 | 32.0 | 37.3 | | 9.7 | Net Worth | 18.5 | 16.0 |
| | 100.0 | 100.0 | 100.0 | 100.0 | | 100.0 | Total Liabilties & Net Worth | 100.0 | 100.0 |
| | | | | | | | **INCOME DATA** | | |
| | 100.0 | 100.0 | 100.0 | 100.0 | | 100.0 | Net Sales | 100.0 | 100.0 |
| | | | | | | | Gross Profit | | |
| | 85.8 | 88.0 | 87.3 | 90.9 | | 90.2 | Operating Expenses | 86.7 | 95.0 |
| | 14.2 | 12.0 | 12.7 | 9.1 | | 9.8 | Operating Profit | 13.3 | 5.0 |
| | .4 | 2.3 | 2.0 | 3.8 | | 5.2 | All Other Expenses (net) | 3.1 | 2.1 |
| | 13.9 | 9.7 | 10.7 | 5.3 | | 4.6 | Profit Before Taxes | 10.2 | 2.9 |
| | | | | | | | **RATIOS** | | |
| | 11.2 | 3.6 | 3.4 | 2.7 | | 1.2 | | 2.5 | 5.3 |
| | 2.7 | 1.4 | 1.7 | 1.2 | | .9 | Current | 1.1 | 1.8 |
| | 1.8 | .5 | .5 | .8 | | .4 | | .5 | .8 |
| | 10.2 | 2.9 | 2.5 | 2.3 | | 1.1 | | 1.9 | 3.2 |
| | 1.9 | 1.0 | 1.2 | .9 | | .6 | Quick | .8 | 1.2 |
| | .8 | .4 | .3 | .3 | | .2 | | .3 | .4 |
| 0 | UND | 0 UND | 0 UND | 0 UND | 1 | 564.6 | | 0 UND | 0 UND |
| 0 | UND | 0 UND | 0 952.4 | 1 585.3 | 5 | 67.6 | Sales/Receivables | 0 UND | 0 UND |
| 0 | UND | 0 809.2 | 11 32.9 | 7 53.5 | 18 | 20.2 | | 5 67.5 | 5 72.1 |
| | | | | | | | Cost of Sales/Inventory | | |
| | | | | | | | Cost of Sales/Payables | | |
| | 3.5 | 6.5 | 4.1 | 3.5 | | 10.3 | | 9.5 | 4.1 |
| | 16.8 | 56.3 | 12.6 | 42.1 | | -42.9 | Sales/Working Capital | 65.8 | 10.6 |
| | 53.2 | -10.3 | -10.2 | -18.5 | | -5.0 | | -9.1 | -24.9 |
| | 45.7 | 51.4 | 10.8 | 9.6 | | 9.5 | | 15.1 | 11.8 |
| (20) | 13.0 | (38) 8.9 | (56) 4.0 | (12) 2.4 | (17) | 2.2 | EBIT/Interest | (173) 3.8 | (77) 3.3 |
| | 1.5 | 1.6 | .8 | -1.4 | | -.6 | | .9 | -.5 |
| | | | | | | | Net Profit + Depr., Dep., Amort./Cur. Mat. L/T/D | | |
| | .0 | .1 | .6 | .7 | | 1.4 | | .9 | .5 |
| | .2 | 1.2 | 1.8 | 1.5 | | 6.4 | Fixed/Worth | 2.0 | 1.5 |
| | 1.0 | -31.8 | -20.1 | NM | | NM | | -4.5 | -8.7 |
| | .3 | .5 | .7 | .5 | | .7 | | .7 | .5 |
| | .9 | 2.6 | 2.1 | 1.8 | | 14.4 | Debt/Worth | 2.8 | 2.9 |
| | NM | -5.9 | -19.1 | -45.4 | | NM | | -7.8 | -5.6 |
| | 138.0 | 108.1 | 60.2 | 20.4 | | 87.0 | | 71.9 | 54.8 |
| (25) | 58.2 | (40) 30.2 | (48) 21.2 | (13) 5.2 | (14) | 29.7 | % Profit Before Taxes/Tangible Net Worth | (157) 25.1 | (74) 11.6 |
| | .0 | -2.1 | 5.2 | -16.3 | | -2.8 | | 6.8 | .2 |
| | 84.0 | 34.4 | 19.3 | 9.1 | | 8.4 | | 21.2 | 15.6 |
| | 34.3 | 12.7 | 6.7 | 2.5 | | 2.3 | % Profit Before Taxes/Total Assets | 8.2 | 4.3 |
| | .0 | -.1 | -.4 | -4.1 | | -2.4 | | .1 | -5.3 |
| | UND | 81.4 | 6.9 | 8.2 | | 2.2 | | 8.6 | 11.8 |
| | 29.6 | 10.7 | 1.8 | 1.6 | | 1.1 | Sales/Net Fixed Assets | 2.5 | 2.1 |
| | 7.4 | 1.5 | 1.0 | .8 | | .6 | | 1.1 | .7 |
| | 7.7 | 4.1 | 1.8 | 1.4 | | .6 | | 2.3 | 1.9 |
| | 3.0 | 2.1 | .9 | .8 | | .6 | Sales/Total Assets | 1.3 | 1.0 |
| | 1.9 | 1.0 | .6 | .4 | | .4 | | .7 | .4 |
| | .8 | | 2.8 | 3.9 | | 4.6 | | 2.2 | 2.8 |
| (12) | 2.4 | (26) 3.6 | (41) 4.1 | (15) 7.1 | (11) | 5.8 | % Depr., Dep., Amort./Sales | (154) 6.4 | (71) 8.4 |
| | 3.7 | 9.7 | 8.6 | 10.5 | | 7.6 | | 10.4 | 12.2 |
| | 3.8 | 1.5 | 2.0 | | | | | 2.5 | 2.8 |
| (11) | 9.5 | (13) 2.9 | (16) 5.1 | | | | % Officers', Directors' Owners' Comp/Sales | (60) 5.4 | (24) 5.5 |
| | 18.1 | 10.1 | 11.6 | | | | | 10.4 | 7.3 |
| | 36860M | 188735M | 368114M | 520593M | 546629M | 1893677M | Net Sales ($) | 2166803M | 1010810M |
| | 9117M | 68874M | 325844M | 470857M | 604081M | 3137828M | Total Assets ($) | 1923466M | 1370969M |

© RMA 2024

M = $ thousand    MM = $ million
See Pages viii through xx for Explanation of Ratios and Data

# ENTERTAINMENT—All Other Amusement and Recreation Industries  NAICS 713990

## Comparative Historical Data | Current Data Sorted by Sales

| Comparative Historical Data | | | Type of Statement | Current Data Sorted by Sales | | | | | |
|---|---|---|---|---|---|---|---|---|---|
| 14 | 20 | 18 | Unqualified | 2 | 1 | 1 | 2 | 1 | 11 |
| 7 | 4 | 7 | Reviewed |  | 2 | 1 | 2 | 1 | 1 |
| 12 | 10 | 4 | Compiled |  | 3 | 1 |  |  |  |
| 40 | 48 | 53 | Tax Returns | 13 | 19 | 6 | 9 | 5 | 1 |
| 80 | 91 | 124 | Other | 23 | 30 | 21 | 19 | 12 | 19 |
| 4/1/21-3/31/22 | 4/1/22-3/31/23 | 4/1/23-3/31/24 |  | 28 (4/1-9/30/23) | | | 178 (10/1/23-3/31/24) | | |
| ALL | ALL | ALL |  | 0-1MM | 1-3MM | 3-5MM | 5-10MM | 10-25MM | 25MM & OVER |
| 153 | 173 | 206 | NUMBER OF STATEMENTS | 38 | 55 | 30 | 32 | 19 | 32 |
| % | % | % | ASSETS | % | % | % | % | % | % |
| 32.2 | 29.8 | 25.1 | Cash & Equivalents | 40.7 | 24.0 | 19.4 | 26.6 | 24.4 | 12.6 |
| 3.4 | 3.1 | 3.2 | Trade Receivables (net) | 5.1 | 2.5 | 3.4 | 1.9 | .9 | 4.7 |
| 7.0 | 5.8 | 6.9 | Inventory | 5.7 | 5.3 | 4.9 | 13.2 | 7.7 | 6.3 |
| 3.1 | 2.6 | 3.8 | All Other Current | 4.4 | 3.2 | 6.2 | 1.6 | 6.3 | 2.5 |
| 45.6 | 41.2 | 39.0 | Total Current | 55.9 | 35.0 | 33.8 | 43.4 | 39.3 | 26.1 |
| 41.2 | 40.4 | 42.3 | Fixed Assets (net) | 33.5 | 45.0 | 55.2 | 34.4 | 35.6 | 47.6 |
| 4.6 | 6.5 | 6.6 | Intangibles (net) | 3.3 | 8.7 | 3.1 | 3.8 | 7.8 | 12.5 |
| 8.6 | 11.9 | 12.1 | All Other Non-Current | 7.3 | 11.3 | 7.8 | 18.4 | 17.2 | 13.8 |
| 100.0 | 100.0 | 100.0 | Total | 100.0 | 100.0 | 100.0 | 100.0 | 100.0 | 100.0 |
|  |  |  | LIABILITIES |  |  |  |  |  |  |
| 4.1 | 6.3 | 4.9 | Notes Payable-Short Term | 12.5 | 2.2 | 4.2 | 4.7 | 4.7 | 1.3 |
| 3.1 | 2.2 | 3.9 | Cur. Mat.-L.T.D. | 1.7 | 4.7 | 6.0 | 1.8 | 2.9 | 6.2 |
| 4.5 | 3.1 | 4.2 | Trade Payables | 3.8 | 2.9 | 1.8 | 5.5 | 5.8 | 6.7 |
| .0 | .1 | .1 | Income Taxes Payable | .2 | .1 | .0 | .1 | .3 | .2 |
| 18.8 | 14.7 | 17.7 | All Other Current | 17.5 | 25.5 | 6.1 | 23.0 | 14.8 | 12.0 |
| 30.5 | 26.4 | 30.9 | Total Current | 35.7 | 35.4 | 18.1 | 35.2 | 28.3 | 26.4 |
| 33.1 | 41.3 | 33.8 | Long-Term Debt | 31.7 | 36.5 | 38.8 | 23.7 | 31.4 | 38.5 |
| .1 | .1 | .1 | Deferred Taxes | .0 | .0 | .3 | .0 | .0 | .5 |
| 12.3 | 8.8 | 8.4 | All Other Non-Current | 10.9 | 3.0 | 6.2 | 6.4 | 13.0 | 15.8 |
| 24.1 | 23.4 | 26.9 | Net Worth | 21.7 | 25.2 | 36.6 | 34.7 | 27.2 | 18.8 |
| 100.0 | 100.0 | 100.0 | Total Liabilities & Net Worth | 100.0 | 100.0 | 100.0 | 100.0 | 100.0 | 100.0 |
|  |  |  | INCOME DATA |  |  |  |  |  |  |
| 100.0 | 100.0 | 100.0 | Net Sales | 100.0 | 100.0 | 100.0 | 100.0 | 100.0 | 100.0 |
|  |  |  | Gross Profit |  |  |  |  |  |  |
| 84.1 | 86.1 | 87.8 | Operating Expenses | 85.0 | 89.3 | 81.1 | 92.9 | 89.3 | 88.8 |
| 15.9 | 13.9 | 12.2 | Operating Profit | 15.0 | 10.7 | 18.9 | 7.1 | 10.7 | 11.2 |
| .6 | 1.7 | 2.1 | All Other Expenses (net) | 3.3 | 1.8 | 2.2 | 1.2 | 1.0 | 3.0 |
| 15.2 | 12.1 | 10.1 | Profit Before Taxes | 11.7 | 8.9 | 16.7 | 5.9 | 9.7 | 8.2 |
|  |  |  | RATIOS |  |  |  |  |  |  |
| 6.0 | 5.4 | 3.5 |  | 8.2 | 4.4 | 4.2 | 3.1 | 2.3 | 1.6 |
| 2.2 | 2.4 | 1.6 | Current | 2.2 | 1.6 | 2.4 | 1.9 | 1.2 | 1.0 |
| 1.0 | .9 | .7 |  | 1.0 | .5 | .6 | .5 | .9 | .5 |
| 4.1 | 5.0 | 2.7 |  | 8.0 | 3.2 | 2.8 | 2.5 | 2.1 | 1.4 |
| 1.5 | 1.6 | 1.1 | Quick | 1.8 | 1.0 | 1.7 | .9 | .9 | .7 |
| .7 | .6 | .4 |  | .5 | .4 | .5 | .2 | .3 | .3 |
| 0 UND | 0 UND | 0 UND |  | 0 UND | 0 UND | 0 UND | 0 UND | 0 UND | 1 518.7 |
| 0 999.8 | 0 UND | 0 UND | Sales/Receivables | 0 UND | 0 UND | 0 UND | 0 825.3 | 0 923.6 | 11 33.7 |
| 7 49.6 | 3 111.7 | 7 51.0 |  | 1 386.5 | 0 UND | 14 26.2 | 2 181.8 | 4 83.7 | 20 18.4 |
|  |  |  | Cost of Sales/Inventory |  |  |  |  |  |  |
|  |  |  | Cost of Sales/Payables |  |  |  |  |  |  |
| 3.4 | 3.8 | 5.2 |  | 2.1 | 5.4 | 4.1 | 5.5 | 6.3 | 9.8 |
| 7.3 | 9.6 | 28.1 | Sales/Working Capital | 6.5 | 37.9 | 16.0 | 13.5 | 69.9 | 111.1 |
| 595.2 | -72.6 | -20.5 |  | 148.2 | -9.0 | -40.3 | -8.5 | -36.7 | -7.5 |
|  | 58.4 | 19.6 | 16.9 |  | 15.5 | 21.1 | 20.0 | 38.6 | 10.6 | 11.9 |
| (103) 9.9 | (119) 7.0 | (152) 5.5 | EBIT/Interest | (20) 4.6 | (42) 4.4 | (25) 9.0 | (23) 4.3 | (13) 7.0 | (29) 4.0 |
| 2.6 | 1.8 | 1.0 |  | -1.8 | 1.0 | 3.4 | .7 | -1.7 | 1.1 |
|  |  |  | Net Profit + Depr., Dep., Amort./Cur. Mat. L/T/D |  |  |  |  |  |  |
| .3 | .4 | .3 |  | .0 | .6 | .7 | .0 | .2 | 1.3 |
| 1.1 | 1.1 | 1.4 | Fixed/Worth | .6 | 1.5 | 1.9 | .4 | 2.9 | 2.3 |
| 6.1 | 11.6 | 47.3 |  | -7.9 | -24.9 | 7.7 | 2.3 | -.6 | NM |
| .4 | .4 | .5 |  | .3 | .6 | .4 | .5 | .4 | .9 |
| 2.0 | 2.2 | 2.0 | Debt/Worth | 1.4 | 1.9 | 1.3 | 2.3 | 112.2 | 2.7 |
| 37.1 | UND | -17.6 |  | -5.3 | -5.4 | 8.2 | NM | -4.0 | NM |
|  | 96.8 | 69.1 | 72.4 | % Profit Before Taxes/Tangible Net Worth | 63.6 | 68.0 | 97.3 | 72.0 | 70.3 | 84.9 |
| (117) 41.9 | (131) 28.7 | (147) 24.7 |  | (26) 13.4 | (38) 26.2 | (25) 40.5 | (24) 20.3 | (10) 12.4 | (24) 30.1 |
| 16.3 | 7.3 | .0 |  | -7.4 | -.1 | 12.8 | 3.6 | -8.8 | 2.9 |
| 40.4 | 31.4 | 28.6 | % Profit Before Taxes/Total Assets | 31.6 | 31.6 | 35.6 | 29.1 | 41.7 | 12.3 |
| 16.7 | 12.4 | 8.3 |  | 7.3 | 10.6 | 15.1 | 5.3 | 11.8 | 4.5 |
| 5.9 | 2.4 | .0 |  | -4.9 | .0 | 7.3 | .0 | -3.2 | .3 |
| 18.7 | 20.4 | 33.0 | Sales/Net Fixed Assets | UND | 20.1 | 21.8 | 830.9 | 49.3 | 6.5 |
| 3.5 | 4.7 | 3.3 |  | 6.8 | 3.5 | 1.7 | 8.4 | 4.7 | 1.5 |
| 1.2 | 1.4 | 1.2 |  | .8 | 1.2 | 1.1 | 1.4 | 2.3 | .7 |
| 2.3 | 2.5 | 2.6 | Sales/Total Assets | 2.9 | 2.6 | 3.9 | 5.2 | 2.5 | 1.3 |
| 1.2 | 1.5 | 1.3 |  | 1.2 | 1.4 | 1.0 | 1.9 | 1.8 | .6 |
| .6 | .7 | .6 |  | .3 | .9 | .8 | .8 | .6 | .5 |
| 2.6 | 2.0 | 1.9 |  | 2.4 | 1.6 | .9 | 2.1 | .3 | 3.8 |
| (93) 4.9 | (107) 4.6 | (114) 4.5 | % Depr., Dep., Amort./Sales | (13) 4.9 | (29) 3.4 | (19) 4.0 | (16) 3.8 | (12) 3.7 | (25) 5.8 |
| 9.8 | 9.7 | 7.9 |  | 14.9 | 8.7 | 8.3 | 8.3 | 10.2 | 7.6 |
| 2.3 | 2.9 | 2.5 | % Officers', Directors' Owners' Comp/Sales |  | 3.5 |  |  |  |  |
| (37) 4.6 | (52) 5.6 | (42) 6.0 |  | (11) 8.5 |  |  |  |  |  |
| 11.2 | 11.7 | 11.0 |  | 11.9 |  |  |  |  |  |
| 1930019M | 2481935M | 3554608M | Net Sales ($) | 22538M | 105501M | 116231M | 224198M | 291219M | 2794921M |
| 2005928M | 2589053M | 4616601M | Total Assets ($) | 38582M | 104760M | 110877M | 165854M | 314025M | 3882503M |

© RMA 2024   M = $ thousand   MM = $ million
See Pages viii through xx for Explanation of Ratios and Data

# ACCOMMODATION AND FOOD SERVICES

# RESTAURANT/LODGING—Hotels (except Casino Hotels) and Motels  NAICS 721110

## Current Data Sorted by Assets | Comparative Historical Data

| | | | | | | | Type of Statement | | | | |
|---|---|---|---|---|---|---|---|---|---|---|---|
| | | | 10 | 16 | 5 | 5 | Unqualified | | 26 | | 14 |
| | | 2 | 12 | 20 | 3 | 4 | Reviewed | | 42 | | 14 |
| | 2 | 5 | 22 | 14 | | | Compiled | | 69 | | 34 |
| | 11 | 45 | 135 | 39 | 4 | 1 | Tax Returns | | 341 | | 217 |
| | 9 | 41 | 168 | 178 | 21 | 20 | Other | | 587 | | 353 |
| | | 54 (4/1-9/30/23) | | | 738 (10/1/23-3/31/24) | | | | 4/1/19-3/31/20 | | 4/1/20-3/31/21 |
| | 0-500M | 500M-2MM | 2-10MM | 10-50MM | 50-100MM | 100-250MM | NUMBER OF STATEMENTS | | ALL | | ALL |
| | 22 | 93 | 347 | 267 | 33 | 30 | | | 1065 | | 632 |
| | % | % | % | % | % | % | ASSETS | | % | | % |
| | 42.0 | 22.0 | 11.8 | 9.2 | 6.2 | 9.8 | Cash & Equivalents | | 11.1 | | 15.5 |
| | 8.1 | 3.9 | 1.9 | 2.3 | 3.6 | 2.1 | Trade Receivables (net) | | 1.9 | | 2.1 |
| | 3.6 | 1.1 | .4 | .4 | 1.0 | 1.2 | Inventory | | .5 | | .5 |
| | 5.0 | 4.0 | 2.2 | 4.8 | 1.4 | 1.8 | All Other Current | | 2.4 | | 2.1 |
| | 58.8 | 31.0 | 16.5 | 16.7 | 12.1 | 14.9 | Total Current | | 16.0 | | 20.2 |
| | 28.7 | 52.9 | 72.6 | 71.5 | 75.0 | 64.3 | Fixed Assets (net) | | 73.6 | | 69.8 |
| | 4.8 | 5.0 | 4.3 | 4.1 | 7.6 | 9.0 | Intangibles (net) | | 4.7 | | 4.0 |
| | 7.8 | 11.1 | 6.5 | 7.6 | 5.2 | 11.8 | All Other Non-Current | | 5.7 | | 6.0 |
| | 100.0 | 100.0 | 100.0 | 100.0 | 100.0 | 100.0 | Total | | 100.0 | | 100.0 |
| | | | | | | | LIABILITIES | | | | |
| | 2.2 | 2.1 | 2.0 | 1.0 | 1.2 | 6.9 | Notes Payable-Short Term | | 2.2 | | 4.7 |
| | .5 | 1.3 | 1.9 | 4.6 | 2.0 | 3.5 | Cur. Mat.-L.T.D. | | 2.8 | | 2.6 |
| | 2.9 | 3.8 | 1.9 | 2.0 | 1.7 | 1.6 | Trade Payables | | 2.5 | | 2.1 |
| | .0 | .0 | .1 | .1 | .0 | .3 | Income Taxes Payable | | .1 | | .1 |
| | 25.7 | 16.4 | 7.6 | 5.2 | 8.4 | 10.1 | All Other Current | | 8.1 | | 8.5 |
| | 31.3 | 23.6 | 13.4 | 12.9 | 13.3 | 22.4 | Total Current | | 15.6 | | 18.1 |
| | 46.1 | 44.5 | 72.8 | 63.3 | 59.9 | 39.9 | Long-Term Debt | | 64.8 | | 66.0 |
| | .0 | .0 | .2 | .1 | .0 | .6 | Deferred Taxes | | .1 | | .0 |
| | 7.3 | 16.1 | 5.1 | 5.3 | 5.9 | 9.1 | All Other Non-Current | | 5.9 | | 5.5 |
| | 15.3 | 15.7 | 8.4 | 18.5 | 20.9 | 28.0 | Net Worth | | 13.6 | | 10.4 |
| | 100.0 | 100.0 | 100.0 | 100.0 | 100.0 | 100.0 | Total Liabilties & Net Worth | | 100.0 | | 100.0 |
| | | | | | | | INCOME DATA | | | | |
| | 100.0 | 100.0 | 100.0 | 100.0 | 100.0 | 100.0 | Net Sales | | 100.0 | | 100.0 |
| | | | | | | | Gross Profit | | | | |
| | 92.8 | 86.3 | 81.4 | 80.7 | 79.5 | 84.3 | Operating Expenses | | 82.6 | | 94.4 |
| | 7.2 | 13.7 | 18.6 | 19.3 | 20.5 | 15.7 | Operating Profit | | 17.4 | | 5.6 |
| | 1.7 | 5.0 | 8.3 | 9.6 | 11.2 | 7.0 | All Other Expenses (net) | | 8.6 | | 7.7 |
| | 5.5 | 8.7 | 10.2 | 9.7 | 9.4 | 8.7 | Profit Before Taxes | | 8.8 | | -2.1 |
| | | | | | | | RATIOS | | | | |
| | 11.4 | 7.5 | 4.6 | 3.7 | 1.6 | 2.0 | | | 2.6 | | 3.8 |
| | 2.2 | 2.0 | 1.9 | 1.5 | .9 | .9 | Current | | 1.1 | | 1.4 |
| | 1.0 | .7 | .6 | .5 | .4 | .4 | | | .4 | | .6 |
| | 8.4 | 6.7 | 3.9 | 2.8 | 1.1 | 1.6 | | | 2.1 | | 3.3 |
| | 1.5 | 1.4 | 1.5 | 1.1 | .7 | .8 | Quick | | .8 | | 1.2 |
| | .7 | .6 | .5 | .4 | .3 | .2 | | | .3 | | .5 |
| | 0 UND | 0 UND | 0 UND | 1 320.1 | 2 174.7 | 4 96.2 | | | 0 UND | | 0 UND |
| | 0 UND | 0 UND | 1 276.0 | 4 94.1 | 6 58.9 | 8 47.8 | Sales/Receivables | | 2 186.4 | | 3 144.7 |
| | 4 98.1 | 4 84.9 | 6 62.8 | 10 36.5 | 12 29.8 | 13 27.6 | | | 7 49.1 | | 9 41.5 |
| | | | | | | | Cost of Sales/Inventory | | | | |
| | | | | | | | Cost of Sales/Payables | | | | |
| | 7.4 | 6.9 | 4.5 | 4.0 | 9.4 | 4.7 | | | 8.4 | | 3.7 |
| | 19.6 | 21.6 | 17.1 | 17.9 | -100.7 | -100.7 | Sales/Working Capital | | 188.4 | | 15.6 |
| | UND | -54.2 | -18.4 | -10.8 | -9.5 | -8.7 | | | -9.6 | | -8.6 |
| | 23.1 | 11.0 | 4.0 | 4.1 | 8.2 | 11.2 | | | 4.0 | | 2.8 |
| (10) | 2.6 | (60) 2.8 | (288) 2.4 | (218) 2.3 | (24) 3.6 | (26) 2.4 | EBIT/Interest | (852) | 2.1 | (462) | 1.0 |
| | -.2 | .6 | 1.2 | 1.1 | 1.7 | .5 | | | .9 | | -.7 |
| | | | | 4.4 | | | | | 5.5 | | 4.0 |
| | | | (20) 2.6 | | | | Net Profit + Depr., Dep., Amort./Cur. Mat. L/T/D | (44) | 2.8 | (13) | -.2 |
| | | | | 1.0 | | | | | 1.3 | | -1.8 |
| | .1 | .6 | 2.7 | 2.0 | 1.6 | 1.8 | | | 2.1 | | 1.8 |
| | .5 | 2.7 | 9.5 | 5.3 | 10.8 | 3.2 | Fixed/Worth | | 5.3 | | 6.1 |
| | UND | -7.2 | -7.1 | -44.8 | -7.5 | -9.4 | | | -12.0 | | -10.3 |
| | .3 | .6 | 2.7 | 1.9 | 1.8 | 1.2 | | | 1.8 | | 1.8 |
| | 1.2 | 7.3 | 12.3 | 6.2 | 12.0 | 3.2 | Debt/Worth | | 5.9 | | 7.4 |
| | -9.5 | -9.3 | -9.2 | -48.4 | -10.6 | -11.8 | | | -12.3 | | -12.6 |
| | 297.0 | 72.8 | 68.3 | 41.6 | 47.2 | 26.1 | | | 48.1 | | 26.7 |
| (16) | 84.1 | (61) 26.0 | (207) 22.5 | (194) 15.2 | (19) 9.2 | (20) 8.2 | % Profit Before Taxes/Tangible Net Worth | (712) | 16.1 | (422) | 3.9 |
| | 28.2 | 3.2 | 5.7 | -.7 | 2.9 | .1 | | | 2.0 | | -16.2 |
| | 56.8 | 26.4 | 11.3 | 8.5 | 8.2 | 6.0 | | | 10.3 | | 5.2 |
| | 14.6 | 9.3 | 5.3 | 4.0 | 5.2 | 1.6 | % Profit Before Taxes/Total Assets | | 4.1 | | -.2 |
| | -11.8 | -1.4 | .3 | -.6 | 1.2 | -1.6 | | | -.4 | | -5.0 |
| | UND | 29.0 | 1.1 | .9 | 1.1 | 1.0 | | | 1.2 | | .9 |
| | 37.2 | 2.9 | .6 | .5 | .3 | .6 | Sales/Net Fixed Assets | | .6 | | .4 |
| | 9.1 | .7 | .5 | .3 | .3 | .4 | | | .4 | | .3 |
| | 6.7 | 3.2 | .7 | .6 | .7 | .5 | | | .8 | | .5 |
| | 4.7 | 1.2 | .5 | .4 | .5 | .3 | Sales/Total Assets | | .5 | | .3 |
| | 3.2 | .6 | .4 | .3 | .3 | .3 | | | .3 | | .2 |
| | .4 | 2.2 | 5.3 | 5.5 | 5.5 | 3.2 | | | 5.5 | | 6.8 |
| (12) | 1.1 | (60) 5.0 | (269) 7.9 | (209) 8.5 | (25) 8.6 | (27) 8.8 | % Depr., Dep., Amort./Sales | (829) | 8.8 | (481) | 11.7 |
| | 2.0 | 9.4 | 11.8 | 13.7 | 11.4 | 11.5 | | | 14.2 | | 17.5 |
| | | 2.5 | 2.0 | 2.5 | | | | | 2.5 | | 3.0 |
| | | (31) 5.2 | (63) 3.6 | (19) 6.7 | | | % Officers', Directors' Owners' Comp/Sales | (217) | 4.4 | (141) | 4.9 |
| | | 7.9 | 6.0 | 15.5 | | | | | 8.1 | | 7.8 |
| | 25085M | 230822M | 1342477M | 2942466M | 1227085M | 2401146M | Net Sales ($) | | 11026322M | | 3302973M |
| | 5539M | 120136M | 1912966M | 5458954M | 2340924M | 4738086M | Total Assets ($) | | 14778267M | | 8325615M |

© RMA 2024  M = $ thousand    MM = $ million
See Pages viii through xx for Explanation of Ratios and Data

## RESTAURANT/LODGING—Hotels (except Casino Hotels) and Motels NAICS 721110

### Comparative Historical Data | Current Data Sorted by Sales

| Comparative Historical Data | | | | Type of Statement | Current Data Sorted by Sales | | | | | |
|---|---|---|---|---|---|---|---|---|---|---|
| 34 | | 42 | 36 | Unqualified | | 8 | 3 | 7 | 5 | 13 |
| 16 | | 27 | 41 | Reviewed | 1 | 4 | 5 | 14 | 6 | 11 |
| 50 | | 48 | 43 | Compiled | 5 | 12 | 12 | 10 | 4 | |
| 281 | | 269 | 235 | Tax Returns | 40 | 105 | 49 | 27 | 10 | 4 |
| 467 | | 478 | 437 | Other | 33 | 111 | 95 | 80 | 73 | 45 |
| 4/1/21-3/31/22 ALL | | 4/1/22-3/31/23 ALL | 4/1/23-3/31/24 ALL | | 54 (4/1-9/30/23) | | | 738 (10/1/23-3/31/24) | | |
| 848 | | 864 | 792 | NUMBER OF STATEMENTS | 79 | 240 | 164 | 138 | 98 | 73 |
| | | | | | 0-1MM | 1-3MM | 3-5MM | 5-10MM | 10-25MM | 25MM & OVER |
| % | | % | % | ASSETS | % | % | % | % | % | % |
| 17.8 | | 15.1 | 12.7 | Cash & Equivalents | 12.4 | 11.2 | 12.1 | 13.3 | 15.2 | 14.8 |
| 2.1 | | 2.8 | 2.5 | Trade Receivables (net) | 2.6 | 1.3 | 2.0 | 2.2 | 5.2 | 5.1 |
| .5 | | .7 | .6 | Inventory | 1.0 | .1 | .1 | 1.0 | 1.3 | 1.5 |
| 3.1 | | 2.5 | 3.3 | All Other Current | 2.7 | 2.8 | 3.6 | 3.0 | 4.7 | 4.0 |
| 23.5 | | 21.1 | 19.2 | Total Current | 18.7 | 15.4 | 17.8 | 19.5 | 26.4 | 25.3 |
| 66.9 | | 68.0 | 68.5 | Fixed Assets (net) | 64.9 | 73.7 | 71.8 | 68.2 | 63.0 | 56.0 |
| 3.5 | | 3.9 | 4.7 | Intangibles (net) | 4.4 | 4.3 | 4.0 | 4.6 | 3.7 | 9.0 |
| 6.2 | | 7.1 | 7.6 | All Other Non-Current | 12.0 | 6.6 | 6.4 | 7.8 | 7.0 | 9.7 |
| 100.0 | | 100.0 | 100.0 | Total | 100.0 | 100.0 | 100.0 | 100.0 | 100.0 | 100.0 |
| | | | | LIABILITIES | | | | | | |
| 2.4 | | 1.9 | 1.8 | Notes Payable-Short Term | 3.1 | 1.0 | .7 | 1.4 | 3.9 | 3.6 |
| 2.5 | | 3.1 | 2.8 | Cur. Mat.-L.T.D. | 1.4 | 1.9 | 1.6 | 3.7 | 6.9 | 2.2 |
| 2.3 | | 2.2 | 2.2 | Trade Payables | .6 | 1.6 | 1.4 | 2.7 | 3.9 | 4.4 |
| .1 | | .1 | .1 | Income Taxes Payable | .0 | .0 | .1 | .1 | .1 | .2 |
| 7.8 | | 8.3 | 8.4 | All Other Current | 9.1 | 7.4 | 5.4 | 6.8 | 13.4 | 14.2 |
| 15.1 | | 15.6 | 15.3 | Total Current | 14.1 | 11.9 | 9.3 | 14.9 | 28.2 | 24.7 |
| 65.0 | | 63.5 | 63.8 | Long-Term Debt | 63.2 | 70.6 | 71.7 | 62.4 | 56.6 | 36.3 |
| .0 | | .0 | .1 | Deferred Taxes | 1.1 | .0 | .0 | .0 | .0 | .4 |
| 5.4 | | 6.8 | 6.7 | All Other Non-Current | 8.2 | 7.1 | 5.2 | 5.9 | 7.7 | 7.7 |
| 14.4 | | 14.1 | 14.1 | Net Worth | 13.4 | 10.5 | 13.8 | 16.9 | 7.5 | 31.0 |
| 100.0 | | 100.0 | 100.0 | Total Liabilities & Net Worth | 100.0 | 100.0 | 100.0 | 100.0 | 100.0 | 100.0 |
| | | | | INCOME DATA | | | | | | |
| 100.0 | | 100.0 | 100.0 | Net Sales | 100.0 | 100.0 | 100.0 | 100.0 | 100.0 | 100.0 |
| | | | | Gross Profit | | | | | | |
| 78.9 | | 80.1 | 82.1 | Operating Expenses | 79.3 | 83.1 | 78.6 | 81.7 | 85.6 | 85.8 |
| 21.1 | | 19.9 | 17.9 | Operating Profit | 20.7 | 16.9 | 21.4 | 18.3 | 14.4 | 14.2 |
| 4.3 | | 7.1 | 8.2 | All Other Expenses (net) | 14.4 | 8.1 | 8.0 | 7.0 | 8.2 | 5.2 |
| 16.8 | | 12.8 | 9.6 | Profit Before Taxes | 6.3 | 8.8 | 13.4 | 11.3 | 6.1 | 9.0 |
| | | | | RATIOS | | | | | | |
| 5.5 | | 4.6 | 4.1 | | 4.6 | 5.2 | 5.4 | 3.7 | 3.0 | 2.0 |
| 2.1 | | 1.8 | 1.6 | Current | 1.9 | 1.8 | 2.0 | 1.4 | 1.2 | 1.0 |
| .8 | | .7 | .6 | | .6 | .5 | .7 | .6 | .4 | .5 |
| 4.8 | | 4.0 | 3.2 | | 3.9 | 4.6 | 4.2 | 2.9 | 2.3 | 1.6 |
| (846) 1.6 | (862) | 1.4 | 1.2 | Quick | 1.3 | 1.5 | 1.6 | 1.1 | .9 | .8 |
| .6 | | .5 | .5 | | .5 | .4 | .6 | .5 | .3 | .4 |
| 0 UND | 0 | UND | 0 UND | | 0 UND | 0 UND | 0 UND | 1 455.0 | 2 190.2 | 3 114.1 |
| 3 137.9 | 3 | 134.5 | 3 143.0 | Sales/Receivables | 0 UND | 1 467.4 | 2 163.6 | 4 96.3 | 5 76.2 | 7 50.6 |
| 9 42.1 | 8 | 43.7 | 8 46.0 | | 0 UND | 5 70.7 | 7 52.2 | 9 42.4 | 9 38.8 | 13 27.4 |
| | | | | Cost of Sales/Inventory | | | | | | |
| | | | | Cost of Sales/Payables | | | | | | |
| 3.4 | | 4.4 | 5.0 | | 5.0 | 4.9 | 4.3 | 5.3 | 4.3 | 9.0 |
| 9.2 | | 13.5 | 20.5 | Sales/Working Capital | 14.0 | 17.9 | 17.2 | 25.8 | 36.3 | 130.0 |
| -22.8 | | -20.1 | -15.6 | | -15.9 | -13.0 | -31.9 | -14.3 | -10.5 | -11.2 |
| 7.0 | | 5.3 | 4.4 | | 3.1 | 3.8 | 4.5 | 4.4 | 4.3 | 9.0 |
| (683) 3.9 | (698) | 2.9 | (626) 2.4 | EBIT/Interest | (44) 1.4 | (194) 2.0 | (143) 2.8 | (107) 2.5 | (78) 2.2 | (60) 3.6 |
| 2.1 | | 1.6 | 1.1 | | .1 | 1.0 | 1.6 | 1.3 | .9 | 1.2 |
| 4.6 | | 6.1 | 4.3 | | | | | | | 4.0 |
| (20) 2.0 | (34) | 3.4 | (35) 2.6 | Net Profit + Depr., Dep., Amort./Cur. Mat. L/T/D | | | | | (12) | 2.9 |
| 1.0 | | 1.2 | 1.4 | | | | | | | 2.0 |
| 1.7 | | 1.7 | 1.8 | | 1.2 | 2.1 | 2.7 | 1.9 | 1.3 | .9 |
| 5.4 | | 5.6 | 6.2 | Fixed/Worth | 6.5 | 8.9 | 8.3 | 6.2 | 3.8 | 2.2 |
| -10.9 | | -19.8 | -9.3 | | -24.0 | -7.4 | -7.7 | -18.6 | -7.4 | -11.7 |
| 1.9 | | 1.7 | 1.8 | | 2.0 | 1.9 | 2.5 | 1.6 | 2.1 | .9 |
| 7.0 | | 6.4 | 7.6 | Debt/Worth | 8.2 | 10.3 | 9.1 | 7.7 | 5.2 | 3.3 |
| -15.4 | | -21.7 | -11.8 | | -14.7 | -10.3 | -10.2 | -20.3 | -8.1 | -13.0 |
| 82.1 | | 70.8 | 57.2 | % Profit Before Taxes/Tangible Net Worth | 70.1 | 60.0 | 52.7 | 61.8 | 42.0 | 57.7 |
| (563) 34.6 | (607) | 26.3 | (517) 18.6 | | (53) 25.9 | (150) 19.0 | (98) 22.9 | (99) 24.6 | (66) 11.6 | (51) 15.0 |
| 10.4 | | 6.8 | 3.9 | | -1.0 | 3.9 | 5.9 | 5.6 | -1.6 | 5.6 |
| 17.1 | | 14.3 | 11.2 | % Profit Before Taxes/Total Assets | 9.3 | 9.7 | 12.2 | 11.3 | 11.4 | 13.6 |
| 8.2 | | 6.0 | 4.5 | | .9 | 3.5 | 6.5 | 5.5 | 4.4 | 5.0 |
| 2.3 | | 1.3 | -.2 | | -1.9 | -.5 | 2.1 | -.5 | -.6 | .2 |
| 1.2 | | 1.4 | 1.4 | | 1.8 | 1.1 | .9 | 2.0 | 2.7 | 5.1 |
| .6 | | .7 | .6 | Sales/Net Fixed Assets | .5 | .6 | .6 | .7 | .9 | 1.1 |
| .3 | | .4 | .4 | | .2 | .4 | .4 | .4 | .4 | .6 |
| .7 | | .8 | .8 | | .7 | .7 | .6 | .8 | 1.2 | 1.3 |
| .4 | | .5 | .5 | Sales/Total Assets | .4 | .5 | .4 | .5 | .7 | .7 |
| .3 | | .3 | .3 | | .2 | .3 | .3 | .3 | .4 | .4 |
| 5.1 | | 4.8 | 4.9 | | 3.8 | 5.4 | 6.1 | 4.3 | 3.2 | 3.2 |
| (616) 8.8 | (639) | 8.0 | (602) 7.9 | % Depr., Dep., Amort./Sales | (54) 10.2 | (181) 8.0 | (123) 8.9 | (108) 7.1 | (77) 7.9 | (59) 5.7 |
| 14.2 | | 12.6 | 12.0 | | 16.7 | 12.2 | 13.3 | 11.0 | 11.7 | 10.0 |
| 2.3 | | 2.3 | 2.0 | % Officers', Directors', Owners' Comp/Sales | 3.6 | 2.0 | 1.2 | 2.0 | | |
| (154) 4.6 | (140) | 4.5 | (129) 4.0 | | (22) 5.1 | (51) 3.3 | (18) 4.1 | (22) 5.8 | | |
| 8.2 | | 8.6 | 6.8 | | 9.7 | 6.6 | 6.2 | 12.8 | | |
| 14031561M | | 8145744M | 8169081M | Net Sales ($) | 51551M | 484266M | 632904M | 955376M | 1497536M | 4547448M |
| 14128934M | | 14999297M | 14576605M | Total Assets ($) | 195064M | 1199584M | 1639507M | 2116420M | 2794871M | 6631159M |

© RMA 2024  M = $ thousand  MM = $ million
See Pages viii through xx for Explanation of Ratios and Data

# RESTAURANT/LODGING—Casino Hotels  NAICS 721120

**Current Data Sorted by Assets** | **Comparative Historical Data**

| | | | | | | | | | |
|---|---|---|---|---|---|---|---|---|---|
| | | | | 4 | 2 | 7 | Type of Statement | | |
| | | | | | | | Unqualified | 23 | 22 |
| | | | | | | | Reviewed | 2 | |
| | | | | | | | Compiled | | |
| | | | | | 1 | | Tax Returns | 9 | 1 |
| | | 1 | | 4 | 9 | 11 | Other | 29 | 26 |
| | 19 (4/1-9/30/23) | | | 20 (10/1/23-3/31/24) | | | | 4/1/19- | 4/1/20- |
| 0-500M | 500M-2MM | 2-10MM | 10-50MM | 50-100MM | 100-250MM | | | 3/31/20 | 3/31/21 |
| | | 1 | 9 | 11 | 18 | | NUMBER OF STATEMENTS | ALL 63 | ALL 49 |
| % | % | % | % | % | % | | ASSETS | % | % |
| | | | | 26.0 | 28.0 | | Cash & Equivalents | 17.9 | 20.6 |
| D | D | | | 2.2 | 1.7 | | Trade Receivables (net) | 1.5 | 1.1 |
| A | A | | | .5 | .6 | | Inventory | .6 | .6 |
| T | T | | | 1.2 | 1.0 | | All Other Current | 2.1 | 1.2 |
| A | A | | | 29.8 | 31.3 | | Total Current | 22.2 | 23.4 |
| | | | | 62.1 | 58.2 | | Fixed Assets (net) | 69.6 | 68.9 |
| N | N | | | 2.8 | 1.1 | | Intangibles (net) | 4.7 | 4.0 |
| O | O | | | 5.3 | 9.4 | | All Other Non-Current | 3.5 | 3.7 |
| T | T | | | 100.0 | 100.0 | | Total | 100.0 | 100.0 |
| | | | | | | | LIABILITIES | | |
| A | A | | | .0 | .8 | | Notes Payable-Short Term | 1.3 | .7 |
| V | V | | | 9.2 | 7.6 | | Cur. Mat.-L.T.D. | 4.0 | 8.0 |
| A | A | | | 1.5 | 2.1 | | Trade Payables | 3.2 | 2.5 |
| I | I | | | .0 | .0 | | Income Taxes Payable | .2 | .0 |
| L | L | | | 7.6 | 17.3 | | All Other Current | 8.6 | 7.8 |
| A | A | | | 18.3 | 27.8 | | Total Current | 17.2 | 19.0 |
| B | B | | | 11.8 | 23.8 | | Long-Term Debt | 26.1 | 29.1 |
| L | L | | | .8 | .1 | | Deferred Taxes | .1 | .1 |
| E | E | | | 1.8 | .8 | | All Other Non-Current | 7.8 | 7.8 |
| | | | | 67.4 | 47.6 | | Net Worth | 48.8 | 44.1 |
| | | | | 100.0 | 100.0 | | Total Liabilities & Net Worth | 100.0 | 100.0 |
| | | | | | | | INCOME DATA | | |
| | | | | 100.0 | 100.0 | | Net Sales | 100.0 | 100.0 |
| | | | | | | | Gross Profit | | |
| | | | | 81.4 | 67.5 | | Operating Expenses | 81.6 | 82.8 |
| | | | | 18.6 | 32.5 | | Operating Profit | 18.4 | 17.2 |
| | | | | 1.1 | 3.9 | | All Other Expenses (net) | 3.0 | 2.5 |
| | | | | 17.5 | 28.6 | | Profit Before Taxes | 15.4 | 14.6 |
| | | | | | | | RATIOS | | |
| | | | | 6.3 | 2.5 | | | 2.3 | 2.3 |
| | | | | 3.2 | 1.5 | | Current | 1.2 | 1.3 |
| | | | | 1.0 | 1.0 | | | .8 | .8 |
| | | | | 6.3 | 2.4 | | | 1.9 | 2.2 |
| | | | | 2.6 | 1.4 | | Quick | 1.1 | 1.3 |
| | | | | .9 | .9 | | | .7 | .7 |
| | | | | 2  222.4 | 3  142.7 | | | 1  399.8 | 1  280.2 |
| | | | | 4  82.1 | 5  70.2 | | Sales/Receivables | 2  146.1 | 4  84.9 |
| | | | | 10  38.3 | 7  50.7 | | | 5  76.1 | 6  59.3 |
| | | | | | | | Cost of Sales/Inventory | | |
| | | | | | | | Cost of Sales/Payables | | |
| | | | | 2.7 | 5.2 | | | 9.5 | 5.6 |
| | | | | 4.9 | 7.6 | | Sales/Working Capital | 26.2 | 11.9 |
| | | | | -277.6 | NM | | | -27.2 | -14.7 |
| | | | | | 45.7 | | | 24.6 | 11.9 |
| | | | | (15) | 22.7 | | EBIT/Interest | (52)  6.4 | (41)  6.4 |
| | | | | | 7.3 | | | 2.1 | 2.2 |
| | | | | | | | Net Profit + Depr., Dep., Amort./Cur. Mat. L/T/D | | |
| | | | | .6 | .7 | | | 1.0 | 1.1 |
| | | | | .8 | 1.1 | | Fixed/Worth | 1.6 | 1.9 |
| | | | | 1.7 | 2.1 | | | 3.0 | 3.4 |
| | | | | .2 | .6 | | | .3 | .5 |
| | | | | .3 | .9 | | Debt/Worth | 1.0 | 1.4 |
| | | | | 1.2 | 3.1 | | | 2.7 | 3.4 |
| | | | | 42.5 | 84.5 | | | 59.9 | 62.0 |
| | | | | (10)  22.2 | (17)  56.2 | | % Profit Before Taxes/Tangible Net Worth | (57)  32.3 | (45)  21.6 |
| | | | | 16.0 | 32.0 | | | 10.8 | 7.4 |
| | | | | 22.8 | 40.4 | | | 22.6 | 24.0 |
| | | | | 15.9 | 29.6 | | % Profit Before Taxes/Total Assets | 12.8 | 6.9 |
| | | | | 10.9 | 18.0 | | | 3.9 | 1.9 |
| | | | | 2.1 | 3.3 | | | 1.7 | 1.5 |
| | | | | 1.4 | 1.4 | | Sales/Net Fixed Assets | 1.3 | 1.0 |
| | | | | 1.1 | 1.1 | | | 1.0 | .8 |
| | | | | 1.0 | 1.2 | | | 1.2 | .9 |
| | | | | .9 | 1.1 | | Sales/Total Assets | .9 | .7 |
| | | | | .7 | .8 | | | .8 | .6 |
| | | | | 4.7 | 2.6 | | | 4.8 | 7.3 |
| | | | | (10)  6.6 | (11)  5.1 | | % Depr., Dep., Amort./Sales | (45)  6.2 | (35)  9.6 |
| | | | | 8.4 | 6.9 | | | 8.6 | 13.1 |
| | | | | | | | % Officers', Directors' Owners' Comp/Sales | | |
| | | 6562M | 269007M | 945379M | 3225450M | | Net Sales ($) | 5735742M | 3727097M |
| | | 7770M | 226510M | 929560M | 3005608M | | Total Assets ($) | 5883427M | 5200157M |

M = $ thousand    MM = $ million
See Pages viii through xx for Explanation of Ratios and Data

© RMA 2024

# RESTAURANT/LODGING—Casino Hotels  NAICS 721120

## Comparative Historical Data | Current Data Sorted by Sales

| Comparative Historical Data | | | | | Current Data Sorted by Sales | | | | | |
|---|---|---|---|---|---|---|---|---|---|---|
| 17 | 24 | 13 | Type of Statement | | | | | | 3 | 10 |
| 1 | 1 | | Unqualified | | | | | | | |
| 1 | | | Reviewed | | | | | | | |
| 2 | | 1 | Compiled | | | | | | | 1 |
| 30 | 26 | 25 | Tax Returns | | | | | | 2 | 22 |
| 4/1/21-3/31/22 | 4/1/22-3/31/23 | 4/1/23-3/31/24 | Other | 0-1MM | 19 (4/1-9/30/23) 1-3MM | 3-5MM | 20 (10/1/23-3/31/24) 5-10MM | 10-25MM | 25MM & OVER | |
| ALL | ALL | ALL | | | | | | | | |
| 51 | 51 | 39 | NUMBER OF STATEMENTS | | | | 1 | 5 | 33 | |
| % | % | % | ASSETS | % | % | % | % | % | % | |
| 24.7 | 20.5 | 27.6 | Cash & Equivalents | | | | | | 28.3 | |
| 2.4 | 1.8 | 1.9 | Trade Receivables (net) | D | D | D | | | 2.2 | |
| .8 | .8 | 1.2 | Inventory | A | A | A | | | .9 | |
| 1.6 | 1.7 | 1.4 | All Other Current | T | T | T | | | 1.1 | |
| 29.5 | 24.8 | 32.1 | Total Current | A | A | A | | | 32.5 | |
| 61.4 | 62.3 | 59.7 | Fixed Assets (net) | | | | | | 58.8 | |
| 6.8 | 4.0 | 1.4 | Intangibles (net) | N | N | N | | | .8 | |
| 2.3 | 8.9 | 6.8 | All Other Non-Current | O | O | O | | | 7.9 | |
| 100.0 | 100.0 | 100.0 | Total | T | T | T | | | 100.0 | |
| | | | LIABILITIES | A | A | A | | | | |
| 1.0 | .6 | 1.2 | Notes Payable-Short Term | V | V | V | | | .5 | |
| 3.2 | 11.0 | 6.6 | Cur. Mat.-L.T.D. | A | A | A | | | 7.6 | |
| 2.1 | 2.6 | 2.2 | Trade Payables | I | I | I | | | 2.0 | |
| .0 | .0 | .0 | Income Taxes Payable | L | L | L | | | .0 | |
| 8.5 | 10.0 | 13.0 | All Other Current | A | A | A | | | 13.6 | |
| 14.7 | 24.2 | 23.0 | Total Current | B | B | B | | | 23.7 | |
| 27.2 | 24.3 | 16.9 | Long-Term Debt | L | L | L | | | 17.1 | |
| .1 | .0 | .3 | Deferred Taxes | E | E | E | | | .3 | |
| 5.4 | 5.6 | 2.2 | All Other Non-Current | | | | | | 2.3 | |
| 52.7 | 45.9 | 57.8 | Net Worth | | | | | | 56.5 | |
| 100.0 | 100.0 | 100.0 | Total Liabilties & Net Worth | | | | | | 100.0 | |
| | | | INCOME DATA | | | | | | | |
| 100.0 | 100.0 | 100.0 | Net Sales | | | | | | 100.0 | |
| | | | Gross Profit | | | | | | | |
| 71.3 | 73.7 | 74.2 | Operating Expenses | | | | | | 71.2 | |
| 28.7 | 26.3 | 25.8 | Operating Profit | | | | | | 28.8 | |
| -.5 | 1.3 | 2.1 | All Other Expenses (net) | | | | | | 2.3 | |
| 29.2 | 25.0 | 23.7 | Profit Before Taxes | | | | | | 26.5 | |
| | | | RATIOS | | | | | | | |
| 2.9 | 2.1 | 3.4 | | | | | | | 3.3 | |
| 1.9 | 1.2 | 1.6 | Current | | | | | | 2.1 | |
| 1.1 | .7 | 1.0 | | | | | | | 1.0 | |
| 2.8 | 1.9 | 3.1 | | | | | | | 2.9 | |
| 1.6 | 1.1 | 1.5 | Quick | | | | | | 2.0 | |
| .9 | .6 | .7 | | | | | | | 1.0 | |
| 2  199.7 | 2  156.1 | 2  222.4 | | | | | | | 2  165.4 | |
| 4  104.1 | 5  80.3 | 4  84.1 | Sales/Receivables | | | | | | 5  80.9 | |
| 6  60.4 | 7  50.7 | 7  51.6 | | | | | | | 7  49.8 | |
| | | | Cost of Sales/Inventory | | | | | | | |
| | | | Cost of Sales/Payables | | | | | | | |
| 4.5 | 7.0 | 4.4 | | | | | | | 4.6 | |
| 11.2 | 35.0 | 8.1 | Sales/Working Capital | | | | | | 7.1 | |
| 115.2 | -12.1 | -277.6 | | | | | | | NM | |
| 48.8 | 25.1 | 40.1 | | | | | | | 45.7 | |
| (41)  17.6 | (42)  13.6 | (31)  19.2 | EBIT/Interest | | | | | (27) | 21.2 | |
| 8.6 | 5.6 | 7.3 | | | | | | | 7.6 | |
| | | | Net Profit + Depr., Dep., Amort./Cur. Mat. L/T/D | | | | | | | |
| 1.0 | 1.0 | .7 | | | | | | | .6 | |
| 1.4 | 1.5 | 1.1 | Fixed/Worth | | | | | | 1.0 | |
| 2.3 | 2.9 | 1.5 | | | | | | | 1.5 | |
| .4 | .6 | .3 | | | | | | | .3 | |
| 1.2 | 1.1 | .7 | Debt/Worth | | | | | | .7 | |
| 2.7 | 3.3 | 1.3 | | | | | | | 1.4 | |
| 119.9 | 102.1 | 76.3 | % Profit Before Taxes/Tangible Net Worth | | | | | | 78.2 | |
| (49)  65.9 | (46)  46.2 | (37)  41.6 | | | | | | (32) | 46.5 | |
| 29.2 | 23.6 | 19.0 | | | | | | | 22.7 | |
| 46.1 | 31.0 | 31.4 | % Profit Before Taxes/Total Assets | | | | | | 38.8 | |
| 25.2 | 23.9 | 22.8 | | | | | | | 24.3 | |
| 15.5 | 12.1 | 14.2 | | | | | | | 15.7 | |
| 2.3 | 1.9 | 2.6 | | | | | | | 2.9 | |
| 1.5 | 1.3 | 1.5 | Sales/Net Fixed Assets | | | | | | 1.7 | |
| 1.1 | 1.0 | 1.1 | | | | | | | 1.2 | |
| 1.2 | 1.1 | 1.2 | | | | | | | 1.2 | |
| 1.0 | .9 | 1.0 | Sales/Total Assets | | | | | | 1.0 | |
| .7 | .8 | .8 | | | | | | | .9 | |
| 3.7 | 3.1 | 3.9 | | | | | | | 3.8 | |
| (38)  5.9 | (39)  5.9 | (31)  5.2 | % Depr., Dep., Amort./Sales | | | | | (25) | 5.2 | |
| 7.6 | 7.5 | 6.7 | | | | | | | 6.8 | |
| | | | % Officers', Directors' Owners' Comp/Sales | | | | | | | |
| 4727743M | 5033475M | 4446398M | Net Sales ($) | | | | 6562M | 80752M | 4359084M | |
| 4779754M | 5339191M | 4169448M | Total Assets ($) | | | | 7770M | 159813M | 4001865M | |

© RMA 2024                    M = $ thousand    MM = $ million
See Pages viii through xx for Explanation of Ratios and Data

# RESTAURANT/LODGING—Bed-and-Breakfast Inns  NAICS 721191

## Current Data Sorted by Assets

| | | | | | | | Type of Statement | | Comparative Historical Data | |
|---|---|---|---|---|---|---|---|---|---|---|
| | | | | 1 | | | Unqualified | | | |
| 1 | | | | | | | Reviewed | | | |
| 2 | 7 | | 4 | | | | Compiled | | 17 | 7 |
| 3 | 2 | | 3 | 2 | | | Tax Returns | | 7 | 2 |
| | 0 (4/1-9/30/23) | | | 25 (10/1/23-3/31/24) | | | Other | | 4/1/19- | 4/1/20- |
| 0-500M | 500M-2MM | 2-10MM | 10-50MM | 50-100MM | 100-250MM | | | | 3/31/20 | 3/31/21 |
| 6 | 9 | 7 | 3 | | | | NUMBER OF STATEMENTS | | 24 ALL | 9 ALL |
| % | % | % | % | % | % | | ASSETS | | % | % |
| | | | | D | D | | Cash & Equivalents | | 15.0 | |
| | | | | A | A | | Trade Receivables (net) | | .3 | |
| | | | | T | T | | Inventory | | .9 | |
| | | | | A | A | | All Other Current | | 1.0 | |
| | | | | | | | Total Current | | 17.2 | |
| | | | | N | N | | Fixed Assets (net) | | 76.0 | |
| | | | | O | O | | Intangibles (net) | | 4.0 | |
| | | | | T | T | | All Other Non-Current | | 2.9 | |
| | | | | | | | Total | | 100.0 | |
| | | | | A | A | | LIABILITIES | | | |
| | | | | V | V | | Notes Payable-Short Term | | 5.5 | |
| | | | | A | A | | Cur. Mat.-L.T.D. | | 1.5 | |
| | | | | I | I | | Trade Payables | | 2.3 | |
| | | | | L | L | | Income Taxes Payable | | .3 | |
| | | | | A | A | | All Other Current | | 39.1 | |
| | | | | B | B | | Total Current | | 48.7 | |
| | | | | L | L | | Long-Term Debt | | 53.8 | |
| | | | | E | E | | Deferred Taxes | | .0 | |
| | | | | | | | All Other Non-Current | | 31.5 | |
| | | | | | | | Net Worth | | -33.9 | |
| | | | | | | | Total Liabilities & Net Worth | | 100.0 | |
| | | | | | | | INCOME DATA | | | |
| | | | | | | | Net Sales | | 100.0 | |
| | | | | | | | Gross Profit | | | |
| | | | | | | | Operating Expenses | | 93.9 | |
| | | | | | | | Operating Profit | | 6.1 | |
| | | | | | | | All Other Expenses (net) | | 6.2 | |
| | | | | | | | Profit Before Taxes | | -.1 | |
| | | | | | | | RATIOS | | | |
| | | | | | | | | | 1.7 | |
| | | | | | | | Current | | .5 | |
| | | | | | | | | | .1 | |
| | | | | | | | | | 1.2 | |
| | | | | | | | Quick | | .4 | |
| | | | | | | | | | .1 | |
| | | | | | | | | | 0  UND | |
| | | | | | | | Sales/Receivables | | 0  UND | |
| | | | | | | | | | 0  UND | |
| | | | | | | | Cost of Sales/Inventory | | | |
| | | | | | | | Cost of Sales/Payables | | | |
| | | | | | | | | | 22.1 | |
| | | | | | | | Sales/Working Capital | | -13.0 | |
| | | | | | | | | | -5.2 | |
| | | | | | | | | | 5.7 | |
| | | | | | | | EBIT/Interest | | (17) 1.6 | |
| | | | | | | | | | -.7 | |
| | | | | | | | Net Profit + Depr., Dep., Amort./Cur. Mat. L/T/D | | | |
| | | | | | | | | | 2.2 | |
| | | | | | | | Fixed/Worth | | NM | |
| | | | | | | | | | -.7 | |
| | | | | | | | | | 1.6 | |
| | | | | | | | Debt/Worth | | -145.1 | |
| | | | | | | | | | -1.8 | |
| | | | | | | | | | 31.2 | |
| | | | | | | | % Profit Before Taxes/Tangible Net Worth | | (11) 8.5 | |
| | | | | | | | | | -1.6 | |
| | | | | | | | | | 10.2 | |
| | | | | | | | % Profit Before Taxes/Total Assets | | .9 | |
| | | | | | | | | | -5.1 | |
| | | | | | | | | | 6.6 | |
| | | | | | | | Sales/Net Fixed Assets | | 1.0 | |
| | | | | | | | | | .4 | |
| | | | | | | | | | 3.8 | |
| | | | | | | | Sales/Total Assets | | .8 | |
| | | | | | | | | | .4 | |
| | | | | | | | | | 5.0 | |
| | | | | | | | % Depr., Dep., Amort./Sales | | (18) 11.7 | |
| | | | | | | | | | 18.1 | |
| | | | | | | | % Officers', Directors' Owners' Comp/Sales | | | |
| 2397M | 7467M | 10081M | 14707M | | | | Net Sales ($) | | 17137M | 6799M |
| 1209M | 9082M | 23982M | 51835M | | | | Total Assets ($) | | 18424M | 16891M |

© RMA 2024

M = $ thousand     MM = $ million
See Pages viii through xx for Explanation of Ratios and Data

# RESTAURANT/LODGING—Bed-and-Breakfast Inns  NAICS 721191

## Comparative Historical Data | Current Data Sorted by Sales

| | | | Type of Statement | | | | | | |
|---|---|---|---|---|---|---|---|---|---|
| | | 1 | Unqualified | | 1 | | | | |
| | | 1 | Reviewed | | | | | | |
| 8 | 14 | 13 | Compiled | 1 | 7 | | | | |
| 13 | 10 | 10 | Tax Returns | 6 | 2 | 1 | | 1 | |
| 4/1/21-3/31/22 | 4/1/22-3/31/23 | 4/1/23-3/31/24 | Other | 6 | | | | | |
| ALL | ALL | ALL | | 0 (4/1-9/30/23) | | | | 25 (10/1/23-3/31/24) | |
| | | | | 0-1MM | 1-3MM | 3-5MM | 5-10MM | 10-25MM | 25MM & OVER |
| 21 | 24 | 25 | NUMBER OF STATEMENTS | 13 | 9 | 2 | 1 | | |
| % | % | % | ASSETS | % | % | % | % | % | % |
| 24.4 | 16.8 | 22.4 | Cash & Equivalents | 25.8 | | | | D | D |
| 1.7 | 1.2 | .4 | Trade Receivables (net) | .0 | | | | A | A |
| .7 | 1.0 | .8 | Inventory | .4 | | | | T | T |
| 7.5 | 6.8 | 3.3 | All Other Current | .0 | | | | A | A |
| 34.3 | 25.8 | 26.9 | Total Current | 26.2 | | | | | |
| 58.4 | 60.2 | 65.7 | Fixed Assets (net) | 63.0 | | | | N | N |
| 4.2 | 1.9 | 3.4 | Intangibles (net) | 4.3 | | | | O | O |
| 3.1 | 12.0 | 4.0 | All Other Non-Current | 6.5 | | | | T | T |
| 100.0 | 100.0 | 100.0 | Total | 100.0 | | | | | |
| | | | LIABILITIES | | | | | A | A |
| .6 | 3.7 | 3.1 | Notes Payable-Short Term | 5.8 | | | | V | V |
| 1.2 | 1.2 | 1.6 | Cur. Mat.-L.T.D. | .9 | | | | A | A |
| 1.1 | .8 | 2.9 | Trade Payables | 4.0 | | | | I | I |
| .0 | .0 | .0 | Income Taxes Payable | .0 | | | | L | L |
| 14.4 | 11.2 | 22.6 | All Other Current | 38.3 | | | | A | A |
| 17.2 | 16.9 | 30.1 | Total Current | 49.1 | | | | B | B |
| 54.6 | 87.3 | 65.7 | Long-Term Debt | 38.5 | | | | L | L |
| .0 | .0 | .0 | Deferred Taxes | .0 | | | | E | E |
| 11.0 | 5.8 | 4.1 | All Other Non-Current | 4.7 | | | | | |
| 17.2 | -10.1 | .1 | Net Worth | 7.7 | | | | | |
| 100.0 | 100.0 | 100.0 | Total Liabilties & Net Worth | 100.0 | | | | | |
| | | | INCOME DATA | | | | | | |
| 100.0 | 100.0 | 100.0 | Net Sales | 100.0 | | | | | |
| | | | Gross Profit | | | | | | |
| 81.3 | 80.9 | 80.1 | Operating Expenses | 82.9 | | | | | |
| 18.7 | 19.1 | 19.9 | Operating Profit | 17.1 | | | | | |
| 2.9 | 7.6 | 10.5 | All Other Expenses (net) | 12.4 | | | | | |
| 15.8 | 11.4 | 9.4 | Profit Before Taxes | 4.8 | | | | | |
| | | | RATIOS | | | | | | |
| 8.4 | 6.0 | 3.2 | | .5 | | | | | |
| 4.2 | 1.6 | 1.0 | Current | .4 | | | | | |
| .7 | .7 | .3 | | .1 | | | | | |
| 6.7 | 2.4 | 2.4 | | .5 | | | | | |
| 1.3 | .9 | .5 | Quick | .3 | | | | | |
| .5 | .3 | .2 | | .1 | | | | | |
| 0 UND | 0 UND | 0 UND | | 0 UND | | | | | |
| 0 UND | 0 UND | 0 UND | Sales/Receivables | 0 UND | | | | | |
| 0 UND | 5 72.4 | 4 96.3 | | 0 UND | | | | | |
| | | | Cost of Sales/Inventory | | | | | | |
| | | | Cost of Sales/Payables | | | | | | |
| 3.8 | 3.4 | 5.8 | | -25.3 | | | | | |
| 8.8 | 21.5 | -68.1 | Sales/Working Capital | -9.7 | | | | | |
| -19.2 | -39.6 | -9.1 | | -3.3 | | | | | |
| 8.3 | 6.0 | 6.5 | | | | | | | |
| (12) 4.2 | (19) 1.8 | (19) 3.2 | EBIT/Interest | | | | | | |
| .0 | 1.0 | 1.0 | | | | | | | |
| | | | Net Profit + Depr., Dep., Amort./Cur. Mat. L/T/D | | | | | | |
| .7 | 1.9 | 1.8 | | .8 | | | | | |
| 1.9 | 3.8 | 4.4 | Fixed/Worth | 2.5 | | | | | |
| NM | -2.2 | -8.0 | | -43.6 | | | | | |
| .6 | 1.7 | 1.2 | | .8 | | | | | |
| 2.1 | 6.3 | 10.2 | Debt/Worth | 10.2 | | | | | |
| NM | -3.3 | -3.9 | | -3.9 | | | | | |
| 105.4 | 50.0 | 36.2 | | | | | | | |
| (16) 41.6 | (15) 5.0 | (15) 25.4 | % Profit Before Taxes/Tangible Net Worth | | | | | | |
| 13.0 | -7.2 | .1 | | | | | | | |
| 24.2 | 13.5 | 20.2 | | 21.5 | | | | | |
| 8.7 | 4.5 | 5.8 | % Profit Before Taxes/Total Assets | .6 | | | | | |
| 2.1 | -.2 | -.9 | | -6.0 | | | | | |
| 5.7 | 4.8 | 3.2 | | 22.5 | | | | | |
| 1.9 | .8 | .7 | Sales/Net Fixed Assets | 1.0 | | | | | |
| .4 | .4 | .3 | | .3 | | | | | |
| 1.7 | 1.1 | 1.6 | | 2.3 | | | | | |
| .8 | .6 | .5 | Sales/Total Assets | .6 | | | | | |
| .4 | .4 | .3 | | .3 | | | | | |
| 2.8 | 1.4 | 1.3 | | | | | | | |
| (13) 5.4 | (17) 4.1 | (11) 7.8 | % Depr., Dep., Amort./Sales | | | | | | |
| 10.3 | 13.8 | 13.5 | | | | | | | |
| | | | % Officers', Directors' Owners' Comp/Sales | | | | | | |
| 48088M | 30400M | 34652M | Net Sales ($) | 4792M | 15153M | 9272M | 5435M | | |
| 71122M | 81643M | 86108M | Total Assets ($) | 9151M | 25122M | 34961M | 16874M | | |

M = $ thousand   MM = $ million
See Pages viii through xx for Explanation of Ratios and Data
© RMA 2024

# RESTAURANT/LODGING—All Other Traveler Accommodation  NAICS 721199

## Current Data Sorted by Assets | Comparative Historical Data

| 0-500M | 500M-2MM | 2-10MM | 10-50MM | 50-100MM | 100-250MM | | Type of Statement | | 4/1/19-3/31/20 ALL | | 4/1/20-3/31/21 ALL |
|---|---|---|---|---|---|---|---|---|---|---|---|
| 6 | 1 | 1 | 1 | | | | Unqualified | | 2 | | 2 |
| 2 | 5 | 2 | 5 | | | | Reviewed | | 4 | | 3 |
| | 2 (4/1-9/30/23) | 10 | 31 (10/1/23-3/31/24) | | | | Compiled | | 5 | | 4 |
| | | | | | | | Tax Returns | | 14 | | 12 |
| | | | | | | | Other | | | | |
| 8 | 6 | 13 | 6 | | | **NUMBER OF STATEMENTS** | | | 25 | | 21 |
| % | % | % | % | % | % | | **ASSETS** | | % | | % |
| | | 26.0 | DATA | DATA | | Cash & Equivalents | | | 24.1 | | 24.7 |
| | | .8 | | | | Trade Receivables (net) | | | 18.2 | | .9 |
| | | .6 | | | | Inventory | | | 2.9 | | 8.3 |
| | | 2.3 | | | | All Other Current | | | 2.5 | | 4.5 |
| | | 29.7 | | | | Total Current | | | 47.7 | | 38.4 |
| | | 49.8 | NOT | NOT | | Fixed Assets (net) | | | 38.2 | | 49.3 |
| | | 9.8 | | | | Intangibles (net) | | | 4.6 | | 5.1 |
| | | 10.8 | | | | All Other Non-Current | | | 9.5 | | 7.2 |
| | | 100.0 | | | | Total | | | 100.0 | | 100.0 |
| | | | AVAILABLE | AVAILABLE | | **LIABILITIES** | | | | | |
| | | 1.1 | | | | Notes Payable-Short Term | | | 4.4 | | 3.3 |
| | | 1.1 | | | | Cur. Mat.-L.T.D. | | | 1.8 | | 1.8 |
| | | 1.1 | | | | Trade Payables | | | 12.5 | | 2.0 |
| | | .0 | | | | Income Taxes Payable | | | .1 | | 1.2 |
| | | 14.1 | | | | All Other Current | | | 16.0 | | 11.5 |
| | | 17.4 | | | | Total Current | | | 34.8 | | 19.9 |
| | | 30.4 | | | | Long-Term Debt | | | 19.6 | | 51.5 |
| | | .0 | | | | Deferred Taxes | | | .6 | | .0 |
| | | 11.0 | | | | All Other Non-Current | | | 7.7 | | 9.9 |
| | | 41.2 | | | | Net Worth | | | 37.3 | | 18.7 |
| | | 100.0 | | | | Total Liabilties & Net Worth | | | 100.0 | | 100.0 |
| | | | | | | **INCOME DATA** | | | | | |
| | | 100.0 | | | | Net Sales | | | 100.0 | | 100.0 |
| | | | | | | Gross Profit | | | | | |
| | | 84.0 | | | | Operating Expenses | | | 92.9 | | 84.9 |
| | | 16.0 | | | | Operating Profit | | | 7.1 | | 15.1 |
| | | 5.7 | | | | All Other Expenses (net) | | | 3.9 | | 7.3 |
| | | 10.2 | | | | Profit Before Taxes | | | 3.1 | | 7.8 |
| | | | | | | **RATIOS** | | | | | |
| | | 2.8 | | | | | | | 4.6 | | 10.4 |
| | | 1.5 | | | | Current | | | 1.7 | | 1.9 |
| | | .7 | | | | | | | .8 | | 1.0 |
| | | 2.4 | | | | | | | 3.3 | | 6.1 |
| | (12) | 1.5 | | | | Quick | | | 1.2 | | 1.2 |
| | | 1.0 | | | | | | | .6 | | .4 |
| | 0 | UND | | | | | 0 | UND | 0 | UND | |
| | 0 | 999.8 | | | | Sales/Receivables | 5 | 74.5 | 0 | UND | |
| | 7 | 54.0 | | | | | 36 | 10.0 | 2 | 183.6 | |
| | | | | | | Cost of Sales/Inventory | | | | | |
| | | | | | | Cost of Sales/Payables | | | | | |
| | | 6.2 | | | | | | | 9.2 | | 3.4 |
| | | 13.9 | | | | Sales/Working Capital | | | 21.6 | | 8.2 |
| | | -213.2 | | | | | | | -65.7 | | 553.3 |
| | | | | | | | | | 20.9 | | 36.9 |
| | | | | | | EBIT/Interest | (14) | | 2.0 | (10) | 2.9 |
| | | | | | | | | | -.8 | | -1.4 |
| | | | | | | Net Profit + Depr., Dep., Amort./Cur. Mat. L/T/D | | | | | |
| | | .5 | | | | | | | .1 | | .1 |
| | | 2.1 | | | | Fixed/Worth | | | 1.3 | | 3.5 |
| | | 11.5 | | | | | | | 2.6 | | NM |
| | | .9 | | | | | | | .6 | | .9 |
| | | 1.6 | | | | Debt/Worth | | | 1.6 | | 3.1 |
| | | 10.9 | | | | | | | 9.9 | | NM |
| | | 72.8 | | | | | | | 51.7 | | 88.7 |
| | (11) | 28.3 | | | | % Profit Before Taxes/Tangible Net Worth | (21) | | 9.8 | (16) | 37.2 |
| | | 7.0 | | | | | | | -5.8 | | 16.2 |
| | | 25.7 | | | | | | | 23.6 | | 22.4 |
| | | 7.1 | | | | % Profit Before Taxes/Total Assets | | | 4.1 | | 5.5 |
| | | 1.4 | | | | | | | -3.2 | | -.1 |
| | | 316.1 | | | | | | | 161.6 | | 37.4 |
| | | 2.9 | | | | Sales/Net Fixed Assets | | | 19.5 | | 1.7 |
| | | .5 | | | | | | | .8 | | .4 |
| | | 2.0 | | | | | | | 3.9 | | 1.9 |
| | | 1.3 | | | | Sales/Total Assets | | | 2.0 | | .7 |
| | | .4 | | | | | | | .5 | | .3 |
| | | | | | | | | | 1.0 | | 4.3 |
| | | | | | | % Depr., Dep., Amort./Sales | (15) | | 2.7 | (13) | 13.1 |
| | | | | | | | | | 9.7 | | 21.0 |
| | | | | | | % Officers', Directors' Owners' Comp/Sales | | | | | |
| 17308M | 21041M | 115590M | 135782M | | | Net Sales ($) | | | 1075298M | | 275962M |
| 1873M | 6881M | 52304M | 174027M | | | Total Assets ($) | | | 833005M | | 481834M |

© RMA 2024

M = $ thousand    MM = $ million
See Pages viii through xx for Explanation of Ratios and Data

# RESTAURANT/LODGING—All Other Traveler Accommodation  NAICS 721199

## Comparative Historical Data | Current Data Sorted by Sales

| | | | | Type of Statement | | | | | | |
|---|---|---|---|---|---|---|---|---|---|---|
| | 1 | | | Unqualified | | | | | | |
| | | | | Reviewed | | | | | 1 | |
| | 1 | 3 | 1 | Compiled | | | 1 | | | |
| | 3 | 12 | 10 | Tax Returns | 5 | 3 | 1 | 1 | 1 | |
| | 20 | 24 | 22 | Other | 4 | 2 | 1 | 8 | 4 | 3 |
| | 4/1/21-3/31/22 ALL | 4/1/22-3/31/23 ALL | 4/1/23-3/31/24 ALL | | 2 (4/1-9/30/23) | | | 31 (10/1/23-3/31/24) | | |
| | | | | | 0-1MM | 1-3MM | 3-5MM | 5-10MM | 10-25MM | 25MM & OVER |
| | 25 | 39 | 33 | NUMBER OF STATEMENTS | 9 | 5 | 3 | 8 | 5 | 3 |
| | % | % | % | ASSETS | % | % | % | % | % | % |
| | 27.3 | 36.2 | 30.0 | Cash & Equivalents | | | | | | |
| | 2.1 | 6.2 | 3.7 | Trade Receivables (net) | | | | | | |
| | .6 | 2.0 | 4.0 | Inventory | | | | | | |
| | 3.3 | 4.0 | 5.5 | All Other Current | | | | | | |
| | 33.3 | 48.4 | 43.1 | Total Current | | | | | | |
| | 54.9 | 37.6 | 40.3 | Fixed Assets (net) | | | | | | |
| | 1.9 | 2.0 | 8.9 | Intangibles (net) | | | | | | |
| | 9.9 | 12.0 | 7.6 | All Other Non-Current | | | | | | |
| | 100.0 | 100.0 | 100.0 | Total | | | | | | |
| | | | | LIABILITIES | | | | | | |
| | 7.2 | 6.5 | 10.3 | Notes Payable-Short Term | | | | | | |
| | 1.2 | .8 | 3.7 | Cur. Mat.-L.T.D. | | | | | | |
| | .6 | 3.4 | 1.6 | Trade Payables | | | | | | |
| | .1 | .2 | .4 | Income Taxes Payable | | | | | | |
| | 21.0 | 37.4 | 29.4 | All Other Current | | | | | | |
| | 30.2 | 48.4 | 45.3 | Total Current | | | | | | |
| | 35.0 | 21.6 | 40.5 | Long-Term Debt | | | | | | |
| | .0 | .0 | .0 | Deferred Taxes | | | | | | |
| | 2.9 | 4.3 | 9.1 | All Other Non-Current | | | | | | |
| | 31.9 | 25.8 | 5.1 | Net Worth | | | | | | |
| | 100.0 | 100.0 | 100.0 | Total Liabilities & Net Worth | | | | | | |
| | | | | INCOME DATA | | | | | | |
| | 100.0 | 100.0 | 100.0 | Net Sales | | | | | | |
| | | | | Gross Profit | | | | | | |
| | 77.2 | 82.0 | 85.3 | Operating Expenses | | | | | | |
| | 22.8 | 18.0 | 14.7 | Operating Profit | | | | | | |
| | 6.6 | 8.1 | 4.9 | All Other Expenses (net) | | | | | | |
| | 16.1 | 10.0 | 9.8 | Profit Before Taxes | | | | | | |
| | | | | RATIOS | | | | | | |
| | 3.1 | 2.2 | 2.9 | | | | | | | |
| | 1.1 | 1.2 | 1.3 | Current | | | | | | |
| | .5 | .6 | .4 | | | | | | | |
| | 2.1 | 1.7 | 2.4 | | | | | | | |
| | 1.0 | 1.1 | (32) 1.1 | Quick | | | | | | |
| | .5 | .3 | .4 | | | | | | | |
| 0 | UND | 0 UND | 0 UND | | | | | | | |
| 0 | UND | 0 UND | 0 UND | Sales/Receivables | | | | | | |
| 2 | 180.6 | 28 13.0 | 7 54.0 | | | | | | | |
| | | | | Cost of Sales/Inventory | | | | | | |
| | | | | Cost of Sales/Payables | | | | | | |
| | 5.5 | 4.1 | 6.0 | | | | | | | |
| | 192.0 | 26.6 | 39.9 | Sales/Working Capital | | | | | | |
| | -7.0 | -14.1 | -8.3 | | | | | | | |
| | 47.0 | 74.1 | 42.9 | | | | | | | |
| (16) | 12.6 | (19) 26.3 | (20) 5.5 | EBIT/Interest | | | | | | |
| | 2.3 | 3.2 | 1.2 | | | | | | | |
| | | | | Net Profit + Depr., Dep., Amort./Cur. Mat. L/T/D | | | | | | |
| | .7 | .2 | .1 | | | | | | | |
| | 2.5 | 1.2 | 2.1 | Fixed/Worth | | | | | | |
| | 18.7 | -23.3 | 111.4 | | | | | | | |
| | .8 | .8 | 1.0 | | | | | | | |
| | 2.8 | 2.8 | 3.0 | Debt/Worth | | | | | | |
| | 19.3 | -25.1 | -13.2 | | | | | | | |
| | 68.7 | 95.4 | 104.9 | | | | | | | |
| (21) | 26.6 | (28) 25.9 | (24) 33.2 | % Profit Before Taxes/Tangible Net Worth | | | | | | |
| | 10.7 | 7.8 | 7.0 | | | | | | | |
| | 18.1 | 27.1 | 32.4 | | | | | | | |
| | 9.1 | 4.4 | 11.8 | % Profit Before Taxes/Total Assets | | | | | | |
| | 2.4 | .6 | .4 | | | | | | | |
| | 15.1 | 47.3 | 191.4 | | | | | | | |
| | 1.2 | 11.8 | 8.2 | Sales/Net Fixed Assets | | | | | | |
| | .3 | .7 | .8 | | | | | | | |
| | 1.7 | 3.1 | 4.1 | | | | | | | |
| | .7 | 1.5 | 1.8 | Sales/Total Assets | | | | | | |
| | .3 | .4 | .5 | | | | | | | |
| | 5.9 | 1.4 | 1.2 | | | | | | | |
| (12) | 9.8 | (17) 5.9 | (16) 3.6 | % Depr., Dep., Amort./Sales | | | | | | |
| | 20.3 | 17.5 | 6.2 | | | | | | | |
| | | | | % Officers', Directors' Owners' Comp/Sales | | | | | | |
| | 408239M | 435928M | 289721M | Net Sales ($) | 4570M | 10152M | 12440M | 55197M | 77825M | 129537M |
| | 491122M | 504665M | 235085M | Total Assets ($) | 16535M | 6804M | 6751M | 42375M | 106821M | 55799M |

© RMA 2024   M = $ thousand   MM = $ million
See Pages viii through xx for Explanation of Ratios and Data

# RESTAURANT/LODGING—RV (Recreational Vehicle) Parks and Campgrounds  NAICS 721211

## Current Data Sorted by Assets | Comparative Historical Data

| | | | | | | | Type of Statement | | | | |
|---|---|---|---|---|---|---|---|---|---|---|---|
| | | | 1 | | 1 | | Unqualified | | 3 | | 3 |
| | | | 1 | | | | Reviewed | | 4 | | 1 |
| | | | 7 | 3 | | | Compiled | | 12 | | 3 |
| 3 | 8 | | 6 | 1 | | | Tax Returns | | 32 | | 16 |
| 4 | 5 | | 13 | 4 | | | Other | | 29 | | 24 |
| | 1 (4/1-9/30/23) | | | 56 (10/1/23-3/31/24) | | | | | 4/1/19-3/31/20 | | 4/1/20-3/31/21 |
| 0-500M | 500M-2MM | 2-10MM | 10-50MM | 50-100MM | 100-250MM | | | | ALL | | ALL |
| 7 | 13 | 28 | 8 | | 1 | | NUMBER OF STATEMENTS | | 80 | | 47 |
| % | % | % | % | % | % | | ASSETS | | % | | % |
| | 17.7 | 11.0 | | | | | Cash & Equivalents | | 11.5 | | 14.8 |
| | .0 | 1.3 | | DATA NOT AVAILABLE | | | Trade Receivables (net) | | 3.5 | | 2.7 |
| | .7 | .7 | | | | | Inventory | | 2.7 | | 2.6 |
| | 4.1 | 5.6 | | | | | All Other Current | | 1.9 | | .8 |
| | 22.6 | 18.7 | | | | | Total Current | | 19.7 | | 20.8 |
| | 59.9 | 52.6 | | | | | Fixed Assets (net) | | 63.5 | | 68.3 |
| | 6.9 | 7.7 | | | | | Intangibles (net) | | 11.1 | | 5.7 |
| | 10.7 | 21.0 | | | | | All Other Non-Current | | 5.7 | | 5.2 |
| | 100.0 | 100.0 | | | | | Total | | 100.0 | | 100.0 |
| | | | | | | | LIABILITIES | | | | |
| | 10.5 | 1.4 | | | | | Notes Payable-Short Term | | 6.5 | | 3.0 |
| | 1.7 | 1.2 | | | | | Cur. Mat.-L.T.D. | | 3.4 | | 8.9 |
| | .4 | .7 | | | | | Trade Payables | | 1.0 | | 1.1 |
| | .2 | .1 | | | | | Income Taxes Payable | | .0 | | .0 |
| | 19.8 | 11.2 | | | | | All Other Current | | 12.3 | | 15.5 |
| | 32.6 | 14.6 | | | | | Total Current | | 23.1 | | 28.5 |
| | 32.6 | 42.4 | | | | | Long-Term Debt | | 45.8 | | 51.4 |
| | .0 | .0 | | | | | Deferred Taxes | | .0 | | .1 |
| | .2 | 4.4 | | | | | All Other Non-Current | | 17.1 | | 13.6 |
| | 34.5 | 38.7 | | | | | Net Worth | | 13.9 | | 6.3 |
| | 100.0 | 100.0 | | | | | Total Liabilities & Net Worth | | 100.0 | | 100.0 |
| | | | | | | | INCOME DATA | | | | |
| | 100.0 | 100.0 | | | | | Net Sales | | 100.0 | | 100.0 |
| | | | | | | | Gross Profit | | | | |
| | 93.5 | 75.3 | | | | | Operating Expenses | | 80.8 | | 79.5 |
| | 6.5 | 24.7 | | | | | Operating Profit | | 19.2 | | 20.5 |
| | 6.2 | 5.2 | | | | | All Other Expenses (net) | | 8.3 | | 4.0 |
| | .3 | 19.5 | | | | | Profit Before Taxes | | 10.9 | | 16.5 |
| | | | | | | | RATIOS | | | | |
| | 1.2 | 7.6 | | | | | | | 1.9 | | 3.3 |
| | .8 | 1.0 | | | | | Current | | .8 | | 1.4 |
| | .5 | .5 | | | | | | | .3 | | .5 |
| | 1.2 | 5.0 | | | | | | | 1.5 | | 2.9 |
| | .5 | .8 | | | | | Quick | | .6 | | 1.2 |
| | .2 | .2 | | | | | | | .2 | | .2 |
| | 0 UND | 0 UND | | | | | | 0 | UND | 0 | UND |
| | 0 UND | 0 UND | | | | | Sales/Receivables | 0 | UND | 0 | UND |
| | 0 UND | 0 UND | | | | | | 3 | 109.2 | 2 | 146.6 |
| | | | | | | | Cost of Sales/Inventory | | | | |
| | | | | | | | Cost of Sales/Payables | | | | |
| | 65.5 | 6.0 | | | | | | | 7.4 | | 5.3 |
| | -22.3 | NM | | | | | Sales/Working Capital | | -35.8 | | 14.9 |
| | -4.9 | -7.8 | | | | | | | -6.0 | | -14.0 |
| | 2.3 | 8.3 | | | | | | | 4.2 | | 6.5 |
| | (11) 1.6 | (19) 4.4 | | | | | EBIT/Interest | (62) | 2.6 | (37) | 3.9 |
| | .5 | 1.4 | | | | | | | .9 | | 2.2 |
| | | | | | | | Net Profit + Depr., Dep., Amort./Cur. Mat. L/T/D | | | | |
| | .8 | .5 | | | | | | | 1.4 | | 1.2 |
| | 2.2 | 2.1 | | | | | Fixed/Worth | | 6.4 | | 4.8 |
| | 11.4 | 11.8 | | | | | | | -9.0 | | -12.1 |
| | .8 | .6 | | | | | | | 1.2 | | 1.9 |
| | 4.4 | 2.5 | | | | | Debt/Worth | | 5.9 | | 3.9 |
| | 24.9 | 14.3 | | | | | | | -14.6 | | -13.4 |
| | 25.2 | 55.5 | | | | | | | 32.2 | | 67.8 |
| | (11) 3.6 | (23) 42.7 | | | | | % Profit Before Taxes/Tangible Net Worth | (51) | 14.8 | (32) | 21.0 |
| | -42.9 | 13.7 | | | | | | | 3.2 | | 5.9 |
| | 4.2 | 22.4 | | | | | | | 11.4 | | 21.6 |
| | .5 | 10.3 | | | | | % Profit Before Taxes/Total Assets | | 3.9 | | 7.8 |
| | -4.2 | 1.2 | | | | | | | -.4 | | 1.5 |
| | 4.6 | 4.8 | | | | | | | 2.5 | | 2.7 |
| | 1.3 | .8 | | | | | Sales/Net Fixed Assets | | .6 | | .8 |
| | .7 | .5 | | | | | | | .4 | | .3 |
| | 1.3 | 1.1 | | | | | | | 1.0 | | 1.1 |
| | .8 | .5 | | | | | Sales/Total Assets | | .4 | | .5 |
| | .5 | .2 | | | | | | | .3 | | .3 |
| | 4.3 | 3.0 | | | | | | | 4.5 | | 4.3 |
| | (10) 9.7 | (22) 6.6 | | | | | % Depr., Dep., Amort./Sales | (60) | 9.4 | (35) | 11.7 |
| | 13.4 | 10.3 | | | | | | | 21.0 | | 17.8 |
| | | | | | | | | | 5.1 | | 2.6 |
| | | | | | | | % Officers', Directors', Owners' Comp/Sales | (30) | 7.7 | (15) | 7.5 |
| | | | | | | | | | 12.7 | | 11.9 |
| 11786M | 11908M | 110162M | 77916M | | 52991M | | Net Sales ($) | | 354178M | | 305889M |
| 1682M | 12028M | 149437M | 194167M | | 122237M | | Total Assets ($) | | 532528M | | 493536M |

© RMA 2024  M = $ thousand   MM = $ million
See Pages viii through xx for Explanation of Ratios and Data

# RESTAURANT/LODGING—RV (Recreational Vehicle) Parks and Campgrounds  NAICS 721211

## Comparative Historical Data / Current Data Sorted by Sales

| Comparative Historical Data | | | Type of Statement | Current Data Sorted by Sales | | | | | |
|---|---|---|---|---|---|---|---|---|---|
| 1 | 1 | 2 | Unqualified | | | | 1 | 1 | |
| | | 1 | Reviewed | | | 1 | | | |
| 8 | 12 | 10 | Compiled | | 7 | 1 | 1 | 1 | 1 |
| 22 | 20 | 18 | Tax Returns | 10 | 3 | 2 | 2 | 1 | |
| 27 | 25 | 26 | Other | 8 | 10 | 2 | 4 | 2 | |
| 4/1/21-3/31/22 ALL | 4/1/22-3/31/23 ALL | 4/1/23-3/31/24 ALL | | 0-1MM | 1 (4/1-9/30/23) 1-3MM | 3-5MM | 56 (10/1/23-3/31/24) 5-10MM | 10-25MM | 25MM & OVER |
| 58 | 58 | 57 | NUMBER OF STATEMENTS | 18 | 20 | 5 | 7 | 5 | 2 |
| % | % | % | ASSETS | % | % | % | % | % | % |
| 17.2 | 22.2 | 16.5 | Cash & Equivalents | 15.8 | 9.9 | | | | |
| 1.5 | 1.1 | 1.9 | Trade Receivables (net) | .0 | 1.7 | | | | |
| 2.4 | 1.7 | 1.4 | Inventory | .7 | 2.3 | | | | |
| 3.7 | 2.4 | 3.8 | All Other Current | 3.9 | .1 | | | | |
| 24.8 | 27.5 | 23.5 | Total Current | 20.4 | 14.1 | | | | |
| 57.7 | 50.1 | 52.6 | Fixed Assets (net) | 56.4 | 58.1 | | | | |
| 5.7 | 9.9 | 8.8 | Intangibles (net) | 12.4 | 9.4 | | | | |
| 11.8 | 12.6 | 15.1 | All Other Non-Current | 10.9 | 18.5 | | | | |
| 100.0 | 100.0 | 100.0 | Total | 100.0 | 100.0 | | | | |
| | | | LIABILITIES | | | | | | |
| 1.0 | 3.7 | 3.9 | Notes Payable-Short Term | 3.4 | 6.9 | | | | |
| 2.1 | 3.6 | 1.1 | Cur. Mat.-L.T.D. | 1.8 | .9 | | | | |
| .8 | 1.2 | 1.4 | Trade Payables | 1.2 | .5 | | | | |
| .0 | .0 | .1 | Income Taxes Payable | .1 | .1 | | | | |
| 15.9 | 12.1 | 21.5 | All Other Current | 25.8 | 22.1 | | | | |
| 19.8 | 20.6 | 28.1 | Total Current | 32.3 | 30.7 | | | | |
| 49.5 | 46.7 | 36.0 | Long-Term Debt | 46.2 | 33.5 | | | | |
| .0 | .0 | .0 | Deferred Taxes | .0 | .0 | | | | |
| 11.4 | 5.5 | 3.5 | All Other Non-Current | .8 | 3.5 | | | | |
| 19.3 | 27.2 | 32.4 | Net Worth | 20.7 | 32.3 | | | | |
| 100.0 | 100.0 | 100.0 | Total Liabilties & Net Worth | 100.0 | 100.0 | | | | |
| | | | INCOME DATA | | | | | | |
| 100.0 | 100.0 | 100.0 | Net Sales | 100.0 | 100.0 | | | | |
| | | | Gross Profit | | | | | | |
| 74.1 | 80.2 | 82.1 | Operating Expenses | 84.4 | 82.0 | | | | |
| 25.9 | 19.8 | 17.9 | Operating Profit | 15.6 | 18.0 | | | | |
| 6.5 | 5.5 | 4.8 | All Other Expenses (net) | 8.9 | 4.6 | | | | |
| 19.4 | 14.3 | 13.1 | Profit Before Taxes | 6.7 | 13.5 | | | | |
| | | | RATIOS | | | | | | |
| 6.5 | 5.5 | 3.7 | | 3.2 | 2.6 | | | | |
| 1.2 | 1.1 | .9 | Current | 1.0 | .6 | | | | |
| .5 | .5 | .5 | | .6 | .1 | | | | |
| 4.2 | 5.0 | 3.1 | | 2.8 | 2.3 | | | | |
| .9 | 1.0 | .8 | Quick | .8 | .4 | | | | |
| .3 | .3 | .2 | | .3 | .1 | | | | |
| 0 UND | 0 UND | 0 UND | | 0 UND | 0 UND | | | | |
| 0 UND | 0 UND | 0 UND | Sales/Receivables | 0 UND | 0 UND | | | | |
| 0 UND | 0 UND | 0 UND | | 0 UND | 0 UND | | | | |
| | | | Cost of Sales/Inventory | | | | | | |
| | | | Cost of Sales/Payables | | | | | | |
| 3.7 | 7.8 | 9.3 | | 18.8 | NM | | | | |
| 37.6 | 72.3 | -89.8 | Sales/Working Capital | NM | -16.6 | | | | |
| -19.0 | -8.4 | -6.9 | | -4.1 | -1.6 | | | | |
| 8.1 | 9.3 | 8.2 | | 4.0 | 5.7 | | | | |
| (43) 4.7 | (43) 4.2 | (42) 2.5 | EBIT/Interest | (13) 1.6 | (16) 3.5 | | | | |
| 2.5 | 1.9 | 1.0 | | .8 | 1.3 | | | | |
| | | | Net Profit + Depr., Dep., Amort./Cur. Mat. L/T/D | | | | | | |
| 1.0 | .7 | .8 | | .8 | 1.0 | | | | |
| 3.1 | 2.3 | 2.2 | Fixed/Worth | 9.5 | 2.9 | | | | |
| -13.8 | -6.9 | 13.8 | | -16.8 | 4.9 | | | | |
| .9 | .7 | .6 | | 1.0 | 1.0 | | | | |
| 3.6 | 3.6 | 2.4 | Debt/Worth | 15.5 | 2.5 | | | | |
| -17.1 | -8.0 | 16.8 | | -7.4 | 4.5 | | | | |
| 74.5 | 79.2 | 54.4 | | 30.0 | 56.9 | | | | |
| (42) 23.6 | (42) 43.4 | (46) 25.5 | % Profit Before Taxes/Tangible Net Worth | (12) 7.3 | (17) 35.5 | | | | |
| 9.4 | 12.4 | 2.8 | | -8.4 | -3.8 | | | | |
| 16.2 | 19.7 | 19.3 | | 8.6 | 18.5 | | | | |
| 7.8 | 9.8 | 7.5 | % Profit Before Taxes/Total Assets | 1.6 | 8.8 | | | | |
| 2.7 | 2.1 | .0 | | -1.0 | .7 | | | | |
| 3.8 | 5.6 | 6.2 | | 4.7 | 4.6 | | | | |
| .8 | 1.3 | 1.3 | Sales/Net Fixed Assets | .6 | .9 | | | | |
| .4 | .5 | .5 | | .3 | .5 | | | | |
| 1.1 | 1.5 | 1.2 | | .9 | 1.7 | | | | |
| .5 | .8 | .7 | Sales/Total Assets | .4 | .6 | | | | |
| .3 | .4 | .3 | | .2 | .4 | | | | |
| 4.6 | 3.3 | 3.7 | | 5.2 | 5.1 | | | | |
| (43) 8.7 | (43) 6.5 | (41) 6.6 | % Depr., Dep., Amort./Sales | (12) 10.7 | (14) 7.4 | | | | |
| 16.0 | 13.0 | 12.4 | | 21.0 | 12.3 | | | | |
| 1.9 | 1.7 | 1.5 | | | | | | | |
| (17) 3.7 | (19) 2.8 | (18) 5.2 | % Officers', Directors' Owners' Comp/Sales | | | | | | |
| 13.0 | 5.6 | 11.7 | | | | | | | |
| 148135M | 225656M | 264763M | Net Sales ($) | 9766M | 39323M | 21310M | 52736M | 59048M | 82580M |
| 244740M | 344667M | 479551M | Total Assets ($) | 33066M | 95080M | 33400M | 94495M | 68862M | 154648M |

© RMA 2024    M = $ thousand   MM = $ million
See Pages viii through xx for Explanation of Ratios and Data

# RESTAURANT/LODGING—Recreational and Vacation Camps (except Campgrounds) NAICS 721214

## Current Data Sorted by Assets | Comparative Historical Data

| | | | | | | | Type of Statement | | |
|---|---|---|---|---|---|---|---|---|---|
| | | | 1 | 1 | 1 | | Unqualified | 8 | 2 |
| | | 1 | 1 | 1 | | | Reviewed | 5 | 1 |
| | | 2 | | 1 | | | Compiled | 1 | 1 |
| 1 | 1 | 1 | 3 | | | | Tax Returns | 9 | 3 |
| 3 | 4 | 10 (4/1-9/30/23) | 11 | 5 | 2 | 1 | Other | 28 | 10 |
| 0-500M | 500M-2MM | 2-10MM | 10-50MM | 50-100MM | 100-250MM | | | 4/1/19-3/31/20 | 4/1/20-3/31/21 |
| 4 | 7 | 16 | | 8 | 3 | 1 | NUMBER OF STATEMENTS | 51 ALL | 17 ALL |
| % | % | % | | % | % | % | ASSETS | % | % |
| | | 21.1 | | | | | Cash & Equivalents | 21.4 | 31.4 |
| | | 1.3 | | | | | Trade Receivables (net) | 1.7 | 1.4 |
| | | 6.0 | | | | | Inventory | .9 | .5 |
| | | .4 | | | | | All Other Current | 3.2 | .6 |
| | | 28.8 | | | | | Total Current | 27.2 | 33.9 |
| | | 59.8 | | | | | Fixed Assets (net) | 60.8 | 58.2 |
| | | 8.7 | | | | | Intangibles (net) | 4.0 | 1.1 |
| | | 2.7 | | | | | All Other Non-Current | 8.0 | 6.8 |
| | | 100.0 | | | | | Total | 100.0 | 100.0 |
| | | | | | | | LIABILITIES | | |
| | | 2.5 | | | | | Notes Payable-Short Term | 3.2 | 1.7 |
| | | 1.0 | | | | | Cur. Mat.-L.T.D. | 1.0 | 1.9 |
| | | 1.5 | | | | | Trade Payables | 2.0 | 4.3 |
| | | .3 | | | | | Income Taxes Payable | .0 | .0 |
| | | 22.1 | | | | | All Other Current | 13.4 | 17.2 |
| | | 27.4 | | | | | Total Current | 19.6 | 25.1 |
| | | 37.9 | | | | | Long-Term Debt | 18.3 | 34.6 |
| | | .0 | | | | | Deferred Taxes | .1 | .0 |
| | | .7 | | | | | All Other Non-Current | 6.7 | 6.1 |
| | | 34.0 | | | | | Net Worth | 55.3 | 34.2 |
| | | 100.0 | | | | | Total Liabilities & Net Worth | 100.0 | 100.0 |
| | | | | | | | INCOME DATA | | |
| | | 100.0 | | | | | Net Sales | 100.0 | 100.0 |
| | | | | | | | Gross Profit | | |
| | | 93.3 | | | | | Operating Expenses | 88.0 | 86.3 |
| | | 6.7 | | | | | Operating Profit | 12.0 | 13.7 |
| | | 6.3 | | | | | All Other Expenses (net) | 2.7 | 4.8 |
| | | .4 | | | | | Profit Before Taxes | 9.4 | 8.9 |
| | | | | | | | RATIOS | | |
| | | 2.6 | | | | | | 4.4 | 13.5 |
| | | 1.1 | | | | | Current | 1.7 | 2.2 |
| | | .2 | | | | | | .6 | .8 |
| | | 1.5 | | | | | | 3.4 | 13.5 |
| | | .7 | | | | | Quick | 1.5 | 2.0 |
| | | .2 | | | | | | .5 | .8 |
| | | 0 UND | | | | | | 0 UND | 0 UND |
| | | 0 UND | | | | | Sales/Receivables | 0 999.8 | 0 UND |
| | | 4 97.9 | | | | | | 3 124.6 | 1 488.9 |
| | | | | | | | Cost of Sales/Inventory | | |
| | | | | | | | Cost of Sales/Payables | | |
| | | 1.8 | | | | | | 3.6 | 2.3 |
| | | 141.0 | | | | | Sales/Working Capital | 14.8 | 20.2 |
| | | -3.6 | | | | | | -11.5 | -68.5 |
| | | 4.9 | | | | | | 12.2 | 5.2 |
| | (11) | 3.6 | | | | | EBIT/Interest | (35) 4.8 | (13) 1.1 |
| | | 1.2 | | | | | | -.2 | -12.7 |
| | | | | | | | Net Profit + Depr., Dep., Amort./Cur. Mat. L/T/D | | |
| | | .8 | | | | | | .7 | .7 |
| | | 1.2 | | | | | Fixed/Worth | .9 | 1.4 |
| | | -9.4 | | | | | | 2.4 | 14.3 |
| | | .4 | | | | | | .2 | .4 |
| | | 4.8 | | | | | Debt/Worth | .5 | 3.9 |
| | | -12.7 | | | | | | 4.4 | 20.5 |
| | | 14.5 | | | | | | 38.9 | 53.4 |
| | (11) | 1.8 | | | | | % Profit Before Taxes/Tangible Net Worth | (46) 8.6 | (15) .2 |
| | | -1.8 | | | | | | .0 | -19.1 |
| | | 6.7 | | | | | | 15.7 | 11.3 |
| | | 1.3 | | | | | % Profit Before Taxes/Total Assets | 4.8 | 3.8 |
| | | -1.3 | | | | | | .0 | -1.4 |
| | | 3.4 | | | | | | 4.7 | 8.5 |
| | | 1.1 | | | | | Sales/Net Fixed Assets | 1.5 | 1.1 |
| | | .6 | | | | | | .6 | .4 |
| | | 1.1 | | | | | | 1.7 | 1.6 |
| | | .7 | | | | | Sales/Total Assets | .8 | .6 |
| | | .4 | | | | | | .5 | .3 |
| | | 4.8 | | | | | | 3.1 | 6.9 |
| | (14) | 6.7 | | | | | % Depr., Dep., Amort./Sales | (37) 7.3 | (13) 8.5 |
| | | 10.3 | | | | | | 9.3 | 13.5 |
| | | | | | | | | 2.7 | |
| | | | | | | | % Officers', Directors' Owners' Comp/Sales | (18) 3.8 | |
| | | | | | | | | 7.0 | |
| 2245M | 13105M | 67127M | 91462M | 75763M | 82092M | | Net Sales ($) | 286531M | 51562M |
| 927M | 8233M | 85261M | 186526M | 172111M | 104127M | | Total Assets ($) | 337752M | 96327M |

M = $ thousand    MM = $ million
See Pages viii through xx for Explanation of Ratios and Data

© RMA 2024

# RESTAURANT/LODGING—Recreational and Vacation Camps (except Campgrounds) NAICS 721214

## Comparative Historical Data | Current Data Sorted by Sales

| | | | | Type of Statement | | | | | | |
|---|---|---|---|---|---|---|---|---|---|---|
| 2 | 2 | 3 | | Unqualified | | | | 1 | 2 | |
| 1 | 3 | 2 | | Reviewed | | | | 1 | 1 | |
| 1 | 1 | 3 | | Compiled | | | 2 | | 1 | |
| 3 | 4 | 5 | | Tax Returns | | 1 | 2 | | | |
| 24 | 16 | 26 | | Other | 2 | 5 | 4 | 6 | 1 | 3 |
| 4/1/21-3/31/22 ALL | 4/1/22-3/31/23 ALL | 4/1/23-3/31/24 ALL | | | 7 | 10 (4/1-9/30/23) | | 29 (10/1/23-3/31/24) | | |
| | | | | | 0-1MM | 1-3MM | 3-5MM | 5-10MM | 10-25MM | 25MM & OVER |
| 31 | 26 | 39 | NUMBER OF STATEMENTS | | 9 | 6 | 8 | 8 | 5 | 3 |
| % | % | % | ASSETS | | % | % | % | % | % | % |
| 22.9 | 25.7 | 19.5 | Cash & Equivalents | | | | | | | |
| 3.8 | 1.6 | 1.3 | Trade Receivables (net) | | | | | | | |
| 2.4 | 2.5 | 3.4 | Inventory | | | | | | | |
| 3.2 | 1.5 | .8 | All Other Current | | | | | | | |
| 32.3 | 31.3 | 25.0 | Total Current | | | | | | | |
| 41.8 | 46.6 | 52.8 | Fixed Assets (net) | | | | | | | |
| 13.3 | 12.1 | 12.0 | Intangibles (net) | | | | | | | |
| 12.6 | 10.0 | 10.2 | All Other Non-Current | | | | | | | |
| 100.0 | 100.0 | 100.0 | Total | | | | | | | |
| | | | LIABILITIES | | | | | | | |
| 8.0 | 4.7 | 1.8 | Notes Payable-Short Term | | | | | | | |
| 4.8 | 1.3 | 1.9 | Cur. Mat.-L.T.D. | | | | | | | |
| 2.7 | 1.3 | 2.3 | Trade Payables | | | | | | | |
| .0 | .1 | .3 | Income Taxes Payable | | | | | | | |
| 29.4 | 14.5 | 16.1 | All Other Current | | | | | | | |
| 45.0 | 21.9 | 22.4 | Total Current | | | | | | | |
| 41.9 | 33.0 | 35.0 | Long-Term Debt | | | | | | | |
| .3 | .0 | .0 | Deferred Taxes | | | | | | | |
| 2.7 | 5.4 | 19.7 | All Other Non-Current | | | | | | | |
| 10.0 | 39.8 | 22.9 | Net Worth | | | | | | | |
| 100.0 | 100.0 | 100.0 | Total Liabilities & Net Worth | | | | | | | |
| | | | INCOME DATA | | | | | | | |
| 100.0 | 100.0 | 100.0 | Net Sales | | | | | | | |
| | | | Gross Profit | | | | | | | |
| 82.6 | 89.4 | 88.6 | Operating Expenses | | | | | | | |
| 17.4 | 10.6 | 11.4 | Operating Profit | | | | | | | |
| .9 | -.2 | 3.9 | All Other Expenses (net) | | | | | | | |
| 16.5 | 10.8 | 7.5 | Profit Before Taxes | | | | | | | |
| | | | RATIOS | | | | | | | |
| 3.6 | 4.2 | 2.7 | | | | | | | | |
| 1.3 | 1.9 | 1.2 | Current | | | | | | | |
| .6 | .7 | .3 | | | | | | | | |
| 2.9 | 3.4 | 2.1 | | | | | | | | |
| (30) 1.1 | 1.5 | .8 | Quick | | | | | | | |
| .5 | .6 | .2 | | | | | | | | |
| 0 UND | 0 UND | 0 UND | | | | | | | | |
| 0 UND | 0 UND | 0 UND | Sales/Receivables | | | | | | | |
| 7 52.4 | 2 158.8 | 6 62.5 | | | | | | | | |
| | | | Cost of Sales/Inventory | | | | | | | |
| | | | Cost of Sales/Payables | | | | | | | |
| 3.7 | 3.1 | 2.8 | | | | | | | | |
| 32.5 | 10.8 | 49.9 | Sales/Working Capital | | | | | | | |
| -7.0 | -16.8 | -5.4 | | | | | | | | |
| 12.4 | 12.1 | 7.6 | | | | | | | | |
| (18) 7.0 | (17) 4.1 | (28) 3.5 | EBIT/Interest | | | | | | | |
| 2.9 | -2.5 | 1.3 | | | | | | | | |
| | | | Net Profit + Depr., Dep., Amort./Cur. Mat. L/T/D | | | | | | | |
| .5 | .8 | .8 | | | | | | | | |
| 1.2 | 1.2 | 1.5 | Fixed/Worth | | | | | | | |
| -.5 | -3.4 | -2.0 | | | | | | | | |
| .4 | .2 | .3 | | | | | | | | |
| 5.2 | 1.0 | 2.1 | Debt/Worth | | | | | | | |
| -2.0 | -5.1 | -4.5 | | | | | | | | |
| 36.0 | 55.3 | 23.5 | | | | | | | | |
| (19) 13.3 | (18) 19.4 | (26) 10.0 | % Profit Before Taxes/Tangible Net Worth | | | | | | | |
| 1.7 | 4.8 | .6 | | | | | | | | |
| 21.9 | 21.9 | 11.0 | | | | | | | | |
| 12.3 | 9.4 | 4.1 | % Profit Before Taxes/Total Assets | | | | | | | |
| 1.6 | .6 | .6 | | | | | | | | |
| 8.2 | 8.5 | 4.9 | | | | | | | | |
| 4.1 | 3.2 | 1.9 | Sales/Net Fixed Assets | | | | | | | |
| .7 | .7 | .7 | | | | | | | | |
| 1.4 | 2.1 | 1.2 | | | | | | | | |
| .7 | .8 | .7 | Sales/Total Assets | | | | | | | |
| .4 | .5 | .4 | | | | | | | | |
| 1.2 | 2.2 | 2.8 | | | | | | | | |
| (18) 4.1 | (16) 4.9 | (30) 5.5 | % Depr., Dep., Amort./Sales | | | | | | | |
| 9.4 | 10.9 | 10.2 | | | | | | | | |
| 1.1 | | 3.4 | | | | | | | | |
| (11) 4.4 | | (10) 6.0 | % Officers', Directors', Owners' Comp/Sales | | | | | | | |
| 8.2 | | 7.4 | | | | | | | | |
| 302623M | 324666M | 331794M | Net Sales ($) | | 4430M | 9874M | 33504M | 59513M | 75955M | 148518M |
| 605908M | 511238M | 557185M | Total Assets ($) | | 14592M | 12166M | 62571M | 91117M | 176368M | 200371M |

© RMA 2024  M = $ thousand   MM = $ million
See Pages viii through xx for Explanation of Ratios and Data

# RESTAURANT/LODGING—Rooming and Boarding Houses, Dormitories, and Workers' Camps  NAICS 721310

**Current Data Sorted by Assets** | **Comparative Historical Data**

| 0-500M | 500M-2MM | 2-10MM | 10-50MM | 50-100MM | 100-250MM | Type of Statement | | 4/1/19-3/31/20 ALL | 4/1/20-3/31/21 ALL |
|---|---|---|---|---|---|---|---|---|---|
| | 1 | 1 | 3 | | 2 | Unqualified | | 7 | 2 |
| | 2 | 2 | | | | Reviewed | | 1 | 1 |
| | 1 | 8 | 1 | | | Compiled | | | 1 |
| | | | 4 | 2 | | Tax Returns | | 8 | 3 |
| | 16 (4/1-9/30/23) | | 12 (10/1/23-3/31/24) | | | Other | | 7 | 7 |
| | | | | | | NUMBER OF STATEMENTS | | 23 | 14 |
| | 4 | 12 | 8 | 2 | 2 | | | | |
| % | % | % | % | % | % | ASSETS | | % | % |
| | | 15.3 | | | | Cash & Equivalents | | 15.7 | 11.8 |
| D | | 7.1 | | | | Trade Receivables (net) | | 5.4 | 2.3 |
| A | | .0 | | | | Inventory | | .1 | 2.5 |
| T | | 1.6 | | | | All Other Current | | .7 | .1 |
| A | | 24.0 | | | | Total Current | | 21.9 | 16.7 |
| | | 70.0 | | | | Fixed Assets (net) | | 71.1 | 80.7 |
| N | | .5 | | | | Intangibles (net) | | 3.0 | .5 |
| O | | 5.5 | | | | All Other Non-Current | | 4.0 | 2.2 |
| T | | 100.0 | | | | Total | | 100.0 | 100.0 |
| | | | | | | LIABILITIES | | | |
| A | | 1.3 | | | | Notes Payable-Short Term | | 1.1 | 3.2 |
| V | | 1.1 | | | | Cur. Mat.-L.T.D. | | 4.4 | .7 |
| A | | 2.6 | | | | Trade Payables | | 1.8 | 1.9 |
| I | | .5 | | | | Income Taxes Payable | | .0 | .0 |
| L | | 5.2 | | | | All Other Current | | 5.2 | 1.2 |
| A | | 10.7 | | | | Total Current | | 12.5 | 7.0 |
| B | | 30.2 | | | | Long-Term Debt | | 45.1 | 51.2 |
| L | | .0 | | | | Deferred Taxes | | .1 | .0 |
| E | | 6.8 | | | | All Other Non-Current | | 3.7 | 1.0 |
| | | 52.3 | | | | Net Worth | | 38.5 | 40.8 |
| | | 100.0 | | | | Total Liabilities & Net Worth | | 100.0 | 100.0 |
| | | | | | | INCOME DATA | | | |
| | | 100.0 | | | | Net Sales | | 100.0 | 100.0 |
| | | | | | | Gross Profit | | | |
| | | 84.7 | | | | Operating Expenses | | 84.2 | 79.9 |
| | | 15.3 | | | | Operating Profit | | 15.8 | 20.1 |
| | | 12.2 | | | | All Other Expenses (net) | | 10.3 | 15.6 |
| | | 3.1 | | | | Profit Before Taxes | | 5.5 | 4.5 |
| | | | | | | RATIOS | | | |
| | | 9.8 | | | | | | 2.9 | 18.2 |
| | | 2.3 | | | | Current | | 1.6 | 3.5 |
| | | 1.2 | | | | | | 1.0 | 1.6 |
| | | 9.8 | | | | | | 2.9 | 18.1 |
| | | 2.3 | | | | Quick | | 1.5 | 3.5 |
| | | 1.1 | | | | | | 1.0 | 1.5 |
| | 0 | UND | | | | | 0 | UND | 0 UND |
| | 0 | UND | | | | Sales/Receivables | 4 | 91.3 | 2 178.8 |
| | 72 | 5.1 | | | | | 36 | 10.2 | 21 17.5 |
| | | | | | | Cost of Sales/Inventory | | | |
| | | | | | | Cost of Sales/Payables | | | |
| | | 1.7 | | | | | | 2.9 | 1.5 |
| | | 5.8 | | | | Sales/Working Capital | | 13.4 | 3.8 |
| | | 31.1 | | | | | | 51.7 | 18.6 |
| | | | | | | | | 5.6 | |
| | | | | | | EBIT/Interest | (16) | 1.8 | |
| | | | | | | | | 1.4 | |
| | | | | | | Net Profit + Depr., Dep., Amort./Cur. Mat. L/T/D | | | |
| | | .8 | | | | | | 1.4 | 1.2 |
| | | 1.3 | | | | Fixed/Worth | | 1.8 | 2.0 |
| | | 3.5 | | | | | | 3.5 | 5.8 |
| | | .2 | | | | | | .7 | .7 |
| | | .8 | | | | Debt/Worth | | 1.5 | 1.5 |
| | | 4.7 | | | | | | 3.3 | 5.0 |
| | | 31.2 | | | | | | 23.1 | 31.5 |
| | | 2.7 | | | | % Profit Before Taxes/Tangible Net Worth | (20) | 4.6 | (13) 1.8 |
| | | -5.7 | | | | | | .8 | -4.6 |
| | | 6.6 | | | | | | 5.9 | 5.3 |
| | | 1.3 | | | | % Profit Before Taxes/Total Assets | | 1.4 | 1.3 |
| | | -2.5 | | | | | | .2 | -2.4 |
| | | .7 | | | | | | .5 | .4 |
| | | .3 | | | | Sales/Net Fixed Assets | | .3 | .2 |
| | | .1 | | | | | | .2 | .2 |
| | | .4 | | | | | | .4 | .3 |
| | | .2 | | | | Sales/Total Assets | | .3 | .2 |
| | | .1 | | | | | | .2 | .1 |
| | | | | | | | | 10.2 | 15.8 |
| | | | | | | % Depr., Dep., Amort./Sales | (21) | 16.2 | (11) 21.3 |
| | | | | | | | | 26.4 | 44.6 |
| | | | | | | % Officers', Directors', Owners' Comp/Sales | | | |
| | 11697M | 64723M | 68296M | 47606M | 64142M | Net Sales ($) | | 948330M | 24946M |
| | 5158M | 56645M | 181844M | 173065M | 228151M | Total Assets ($) | | 400350M | 105833M |

M = $ thousand    MM = $ million
See Pages viii through xx for Explanation of Ratios and Data

© RMA 2024

# RESTAURANT/LODGING—Rooming and Boarding Houses, Dormitories, and Workers' Camps  NAICS 721310

## Comparative Historical Data | Current Data Sorted by Sales

| Comparative Historical Data | | | Type of Statement | Current Data Sorted by Sales | | | | | |
|---|---|---|---|---|---|---|---|---|---|
| 1 | 7 | 6 | Unqualified | 1 | 1 | 2 | | | 2 |
| 1 | | | Reviewed | | | | | | |
| 3 | 2 | 2 | Compiled | | | | | | 1 |
| 6 | 5 | 5 | Tax Returns | 1 | | | 1 | | |
| 6 | 9 | 15 | Other | 3 | 1 | 2 | 1 | 2 | 2 |
| 4/1/21-3/31/22 ALL | 4/1/22-3/31/23 ALL | 4/1/23-3/31/24 ALL | | 7 | 16 (4/1-9/30/23) | | 12 (10/1/23-3/31/24) | | |
| | | | | 0-1MM | 1-3MM | 3-5MM | 5-10MM | 10-25MM | 25MM & OVER |
| 17 | 23 | 28 | NUMBER OF STATEMENTS | 11 | 3 | 3 | 3 | 3 | 5 |
| % | % | % | ASSETS | % | % | % | % | % | % |
| 18.7 | 16.4 | 17.0 | Cash & Equivalents | 8.2 | | | | | |
| .7 | 3.1 | 4.7 | Trade Receivables (net) | .6 | | | | | |
| 3.6 | .0 | .0 | Inventory | .0 | | | | | |
| 1.7 | 2.5 | 1.3 | All Other Current | .3 | | | | | |
| 24.7 | 22.0 | 23.0 | Total Current | 9.2 | | | | | |
| 73.8 | 68.7 | 72.0 | Fixed Assets (net) | 88.3 | | | | | |
| .4 | 4.0 | 1.0 | Intangibles (net) | .2 | | | | | |
| 1.0 | 5.3 | 3.9 | All Other Non-Current | 2.3 | | | | | |
| 100.0 | 100.0 | 100.0 | Total | 100.0 | | | | | |
| | | | LIABILITIES | | | | | | |
| .8 | .1 | 2.4 | Notes Payable-Short Term | .0 | | | | | |
| 1.8 | 2.2 | 2.2 | Cur. Mat.-L.T.D. | 1.3 | | | | | |
| 1.1 | 3.5 | 2.0 | Trade Payables | .8 | | | | | |
| .0 | .1 | .2 | Income Taxes Payable | .0 | | | | | |
| 5.6 | 6.2 | 3.5 | All Other Current | 1.4 | | | | | |
| 9.3 | 12.1 | 10.3 | Total Current | 3.4 | | | | | |
| 44.6 | 55.1 | 37.2 | Long-Term Debt | 21.6 | | | | | |
| .0 | .0 | .0 | Deferred Taxes | .0 | | | | | |
| 6.2 | 2.2 | 5.8 | All Other Non-Current | 7.5 | | | | | |
| 39.9 | 30.6 | 46.8 | Net Worth | 67.5 | | | | | |
| 100.0 | 100.0 | 100.0 | Total Liabilities & Net Worth | 100.0 | | | | | |
| | | | INCOME DATA | | | | | | |
| 100.0 | 100.0 | 100.0 | Net Sales | 100.0 | | | | | |
| | | | Gross Profit | | | | | | |
| 81.0 | 76.0 | 88.2 | Operating Expenses | 91.0 | | | | | |
| 19.0 | 24.0 | 11.8 | Operating Profit | 9.0 | | | | | |
| 7.0 | 13.5 | 10.6 | All Other Expenses (net) | 11.9 | | | | | |
| 12.0 | 10.5 | 1.2 | Profit Before Taxes | -2.8 | | | | | |
| | | | RATIOS | | | | | | |
| 7.9 | 10.3 | 6.6 | | 10.8 | | | | | |
| 2.5 | 2.8 | 2.4 | Current | 2.5 | | | | | |
| 1.4 | 1.2 | 1.2 | | 1.2 | | | | | |
| 4.3 | 10.3 | 6.6 | | 10.8 | | | | | |
| 2.4 | 2.1 | 2.4 | Quick | 2.5 | | | | | |
| 1.4 | 1.0 | .9 | | .7 | | | | | |
| 0 UND | 0 UND | 0 UND | | 0 UND | | | | | |
| 0 UND | 2 200.1 | 2 204.3 | Sales/Receivables | 0 UND | | | | | |
| 5 71.0 | 20 18.7 | 47 7.7 | | 0 UND | | | | | |
| | | | Cost of Sales/Inventory | | | | | | |
| | | | Cost of Sales/Payables | | | | | | |
| 2.0 | 1.5 | 1.7 | | 1.5 | | | | | |
| 4.4 | 2.6 | 5.2 | Sales/Working Capital | 4.6 | | | | | |
| 14.7 | 33.8 | 23.2 | | 37.4 | | | | | |
| 23.7 | 7.3 | 5.1 | | | | | | | |
| (11) 4.3 | (18) 2.9 | (20) 1.9 | EBIT/Interest | | | | | | |
| -.4 | 1.4 | .2 | | | | | | | |
| | | | Net Profit + Depr., Dep., Amort./Cur. Mat. L/T/D | | | | | | |
| 1.2 | 1.4 | .9 | | .9 | | | | | |
| 1.8 | 2.3 | 1.5 | Fixed/Worth | 1.1 | | | | | |
| 4.0 | 26.5 | 4.1 | | 2.0 | | | | | |
| .6 | 1.0 | .2 | | .2 | | | | | |
| 1.2 | 1.8 | 1.0 | Debt/Worth | .4 | | | | | |
| 3.4 | 369.7 | 5.0 | | 1.0 | | | | | |
| 29.9 | 50.1 | 13.8 | | 3.0 | | | | | |
| (15) 11.2 | (18) 9.2 | (25) .9 | % Profit Before Taxes/Tangible Net Worth | .8 | | | | | |
| -2.2 | 2.3 | -5.2 | | -5.2 | | | | | |
| 14.2 | 8.8 | 5.3 | | 2.0 | | | | | |
| 2.0 | 2.4 | .7 | % Profit Before Taxes/Total Assets | .5 | | | | | |
| -2.8 | .8 | -2.6 | | -4.5 | | | | | |
| .7 | .6 | .6 | | .3 | | | | | |
| .3 | .3 | .3 | Sales/Net Fixed Assets | .2 | | | | | |
| .1 | .2 | .2 | | .1 | | | | | |
| .6 | .3 | .3 | | .2 | | | | | |
| .2 | .2 | .2 | Sales/Total Assets | .2 | | | | | |
| .1 | .1 | .1 | | .1 | | | | | |
| 5.2 | 14.4 | 10.5 | | | | | | | |
| (11) 17.6 | (17) 19.8 | (22) 26.6 | % Depr., Dep., Amort./Sales | | | | | | |
| 21.7 | 29.3 | 36.6 | | | | | | | |
| | | | % Officers', Directors', Owners' Comp/Sales | | | | | | |
| 89088M | 383249M | 256464M | Net Sales ($) | 5633M | 5402M | 11769M | 19949M | 36396M | 177315M |
| 245065M | 446119M | 644863M | Total Assets ($) | 36805M | 33057M | 52269M | 88312M | 98930M | 335490M |

© RMA 2024   M = $ thousand   MM = $ million
See Pages viii through xx for Explanation of Ratios and Data

# RESTAURANT/LODGING—Food Service Contractors  NAICS 722310

## Current Data Sorted by Assets

| | | | | | | Type of Statement |
|---|---|---|---|---|---|---|
| | | 2 | 4 | 1 | 2 | Unqualified |
| | | 4 | 1 | | | Reviewed |
| | | 4 | | 1 | | Compiled |
| 6 | 8 | 5 | 12 | | 8 | Tax Returns |
| 5 | 5 | 12 | 12 | 5 | | Other |
| | 17 (4/1-9/30/23) | | 68 (10/1/23-3/31/24) | | | |
| 0-500M | 500M-2MM | 2-10MM | 10-50MM | 50-100MM | 100-250MM | |
| 11 | 13 | 27 | 17 | 7 | 10 | NUMBER OF STATEMENTS |

## Comparative Historical Data

| | | |
|---|---|---|
| 6 | 5 | Unqualified |
| 6 | 7 | Reviewed |
| 5 | 1 | Compiled |
| 28 | 15 | Tax Returns |
| 54 | 39 | Other |
| 4/1/19-3/31/20 ALL | 4/1/20-3/31/21 ALL | |
| 99 | 67 | |

| % | % | % | % | % | % | | % | % |
|---|---|---|---|---|---|---|---|---|
| | | | | | | **ASSETS** | | |
| 25.3 | 32.6 | 16.1 | 16.3 | | 6.1 | Cash & Equivalents | 20.5 | 31.1 |
| 12.9 | 8.6 | 18.9 | 27.4 | | 15.1 | Trade Receivables (net) | 17.1 | 12.2 |
| 9.6 | 7.5 | 7.7 | 18.8 | | 8.2 | Inventory | 9.4 | 9.5 |
| 3.2 | 7.6 | 1.1 | 5.6 | | 4.6 | All Other Current | 5.6 | 3.9 |
| 51.0 | 56.3 | 43.8 | 68.1 | | 33.9 | Total Current | 52.6 | 56.7 |
| 7.6 | 21.5 | 35.4 | 20.6 | | 28.2 | Fixed Assets (net) | 26.5 | 26.7 |
| 20.1 | 10.5 | 11.6 | 4.2 | | 25.4 | Intangibles (net) | 10.0 | 9.2 |
| 21.4 | 11.7 | 9.2 | 7.1 | | 12.5 | All Other Non-Current | 10.9 | 7.4 |
| 100.0 | 100.0 | 100.0 | 100.0 | | 100.0 | Total | 100.0 | 100.0 |
| | | | | | | **LIABILITIES** | | |
| 6.3 | .0 | 4.2 | 8.5 | | 2.9 | Notes Payable-Short Term | 6.6 | 9.0 |
| 10.9 | 6.5 | 6.0 | 4.7 | | 1.3 | Cur. Mat.-L.T.D. | 2.8 | 3.7 |
| 14.8 | 9.9 | 12.7 | 22.7 | | 14.8 | Trade Payables | 12.8 | 9.9 |
| .0 | .0 | .0 | .1 | | .0 | Income Taxes Payable | .3 | .0 |
| 22.4 | 23.1 | 12.7 | 16.2 | | 20.3 | All Other Current | 22.8 | 14.6 |
| 54.3 | 39.5 | 35.6 | 52.3 | | 39.3 | Total Current | 45.2 | 37.3 |
| 33.2 | 38.9 | 34.3 | 25.0 | | 28.9 | Long-Term Debt | 22.2 | 25.2 |
| .0 | .0 | .0 | .3 | | .0 | Deferred Taxes | .1 | .1 |
| 1.4 | 12.9 | .7 | 3.4 | | 17.6 | All Other Non-Current | 6.5 | 5.9 |
| 11.1 | 8.7 | 29.4 | 19.0 | | 14.1 | Net Worth | 26.0 | 31.6 |
| 100.0 | 100.0 | 100.0 | 100.0 | | 100.0 | Total Liabilities & Net Worth | 100.0 | 100.0 |
| | | | | | | **INCOME DATA** | | |
| 100.0 | 100.0 | 100.0 | 100.0 | | 100.0 | Net Sales | 100.0 | 100.0 |
| | | | | | | Gross Profit | | |
| 94.8 | 89.1 | 91.7 | 89.5 | | 96.7 | Operating Expenses | 93.3 | 94.1 |
| 5.2 | 10.9 | 8.3 | 10.5 | | 3.3 | Operating Profit | 6.7 | 5.9 |
| 1.4 | 1.8 | 2.1 | .8 | | 2.0 | All Other Expenses (net) | .4 | .5 |
| 3.8 | 9.2 | 6.2 | 9.7 | | 1.4 | Profit Before Taxes | 6.3 | 5.4 |
| | | | | | | **RATIOS** | | |
| 3.1 | 31.6 | 2.7 | 1.8 | | 1.7 | | 2.8 | 2.8 |
| 1.2 | 3.8 | 1.7 | 1.4 | | .8 | Current | 1.3 | 1.7 |
| .2 | .5 | .8 | 1.1 | | .6 | | .8 | .8 |
| 3.0 | 22.2 | 2.2 | 1.5 | | 1.1 | | 2.2 | 2.1 |
| 1.1 | 2.0 | 1.5 | 1.0 | | .5 | Quick | .9 | 1.5 |
| .1 | .3 | .5 | .6 | | .2 | | .4 | .5 |
| 0  UND | 0  UND | 4  91.3 | 13  28.5 | | 8  44.8 | | 0  UND | 0  UND |
| 0  UND | 0  UND | 26  13.9 | 27  13.3 | | 18  20.1 | Sales/Receivables | 5  69.8 | 8  45.0 |
| 37  9.9 | 16  23.2 | 36  10.1 | 43  8.4 | | 51  7.1 | | 25  14.8 | 26  13.8 |
| | | | | | | Cost of Sales/Inventory | | |
| | | | | | | Cost of Sales/Payables | | |
| 6.5 | 5.1 | 8.5 | 7.1 | | 8.6 | | 13.7 | 6.3 |
| 71.3 | 13.2 | 14.3 | 14.3 | | -33.2 | Sales/Working Capital | 27.9 | 13.6 |
| -17.4 | -9.1 | -19.3 | 88.6 | | -17.3 | | -38.1 | -26.6 |
| | | 24.2 | 16.8 | | 4.8 | | 23.2 | 28.3 |
| | (25) | 4.7 | (15) 5.0 | | 3.2 | EBIT/Interest | (76) 5.3 | (49) 7.7 |
| | | 1.3 | 2.5 | | .3 | | 2.1 | .1 |
| | | | | | | | 4.8 | |
| | | | | | | Net Profit + Depr., Dep., | (10) 3.5 | |
| | | | | | | Amort./Cur. Mat. L/T/D | .6 | |
| .0 | .1 | .4 | .1 | | NM | | .2 | .2 |
| .2 | 1.7 | 1.1 | .8 | | -2.0 | Fixed/Worth | 1.1 | .5 |
| 1.0 | -.5 | -13.0 | 2.4 | | -.8 | | 16.8 | 5.9 |
| .9 | .3 | .7 | 1.0 | | NM | | .9 | 1.0 |
| 3.0 | UND | 2.5 | 2.8 | | -4.4 | Debt/Worth | 3.9 | 2.3 |
| -2.5 | -3.0 | -20.5 | 7.8 | | -3.5 | | -28.2 | 20.8 |
| | | 54.4 | 84.1 | | | | 147.6 | 84.2 |
| | (20) | 29.0 | (15) 37.6 | | | % Profit Before Taxes/Tangible Net Worth | (72) 63.3 | (54) 43.4 |
| | | 9.4 | 6.4 | | | | 24.4 | 5.9 |
| 52.4 | 61.1 | 18.5 | 24.2 | | 6.3 | | 34.4 | 24.9 |
| 17.3 | 15.1 | 5.3 | 8.1 | | 4.9 | % Profit Before Taxes/Total Assets | 13.0 | 7.7 |
| -3.4 | -6.6 | 1.1 | 3.0 | | -1.6 | | 3.5 | -1.3 |
| UND | 300.3 | 27.4 | 74.9 | | 18.0 | | 77.5 | 82.4 |
| 130.6 | 34.8 | 6.0 | 15.5 | | 8.5 | Sales/Net Fixed Assets | 18.6 | 23.2 |
| 23.1 | 4.1 | 2.2 | 11.6 | | 5.9 | | 8.0 | 4.6 |
| 9.7 | 6.6 | 3.2 | 4.6 | | 2.9 | | 5.7 | 4.8 |
| 6.5 | 2.6 | 1.8 | 3.1 | | 2.3 | Sales/Total Assets | 3.7 | 2.9 |
| 3.3 | 1.7 | 1.0 | 1.2 | | 1.4 | | 2.2 | 1.3 |
| | | .7 | .3 | | | | .4 | .3 |
| | (23) | 1.4 | (14) .8 | | | % Depr., Dep., Amort./Sales | (61) 1.4 | (47) 1.5 |
| | | 3.9 | 1.8 | | | | 3.3 | 5.6 |
| | | | | | | | 1.2 | 2.5 |
| | | | | | | % Officers', Directors' Owners' Comp/Sales | (32) 2.3 | (17) 4.0 |
| | | | | | | | 5.6 | 7.6 |
| 13913M | 54299M | 377344M | 1389022M | 1420709M | 3521523M | Net Sales ($) | 7001331M | 3649463M |
| 2418M | 12954M | 161643M | 431297M | 476252M | 1542515M | Total Assets ($) | 2590816M | 1466663M |

M = $ thousand    MM = $ million
See Pages viii through xx for Explanation of Ratios and Data

© RMA 2024

## RESTAURANT/LODGING—Food Service Contractors  NAICS 722310

### Comparative Historical Data / Current Data Sorted by Sales

| Comparative Historical Data | | | | Type of Statement | Current Data Sorted by Sales | | | | | |
|---|---|---|---|---|---|---|---|---|---|---|
| 6 | 6 | 9 | | Unqualified | | | | | 4 | 5 |
| 6 | 5 | 5 | | Reviewed | | | | 2 | | 3 |
| 6 | 1 | 5 | | Compiled | | | | | 3 | 1 |
| 17 | 16 | 19 | | Tax Returns | 1 | | | 3 | 2 | |
| 30 | 49 | 47 | | Other | 3 | 9 | 2 | 3 | 11 | 22 |
| 4/1/21-3/31/22 ALL | 4/1/22-3/31/23 ALL | 4/1/23-3/31/24 ALL | | | 5 | 3 | 3 | 3 | | |
| | | | | | 17 (4/1-9/30/23) | | | 68 (10/1/23-3/31/24) | | |
| | | | | | 0-1MM | 1-3MM | 3-5MM | 5-10MM | 10-25MM | 25MM & OVER |
| 65 | 77 | 85 | | NUMBER OF STATEMENTS | 9 | 12 | 5 | 8 | 20 | 31 |
| % | % | % | | ASSETS | % | % | % | % | % | % |
| 31.9 | 23.2 | 19.4 | | Cash & Equivalents | 31.0 | | | | 23.0 | 15.7 |
| 15.8 | 20.1 | 17.8 | | Trade Receivables (net) | 10.0 | | | | 21.9 | 24.3 |
| 9.0 | 10.0 | 10.3 | | Inventory | 3.9 | | | | 14.7 | 11.3 |
| 4.0 | 6.0 | 3.6 | | All Other Current | 1.5 | | | | 2.9 | 3.7 |
| 60.7 | 59.3 | 51.2 | | Total Current | 46.4 | | | | 62.5 | 55.0 |
| 21.7 | 20.3 | 24.8 | | Fixed Assets (net) | 8.8 | | | | 18.5 | 21.6 |
| 9.5 | 7.9 | 12.2 | | Intangibles (net) | 24.1 | | | | 9.0 | 11.1 |
| 8.1 | 12.5 | 11.8 | | All Other Non-Current | 20.7 | | | | 9.9 | 12.3 |
| 100.0 | 100.0 | 100.0 | | Total | 100.0 | | | | 100.0 | 100.0 |
| | | | | LIABILITIES | | | | | | |
| 5.2 | 4.0 | 4.5 | | Notes Payable-Short Term | 5.8 | | | | 4.1 | 6.8 |
| 3.8 | 4.1 | 5.8 | | Cur. Mat.-L.T.D. | 13.1 | | | | 6.0 | 3.5 |
| 11.5 | 11.1 | 14.9 | | Trade Payables | 12.2 | | | | 18.7 | 17.3 |
| .1 | .1 | .0 | | Income Taxes Payable | .0 | | | | .0 | .1 |
| 11.4 | 19.8 | 17.5 | | All Other Current | 23.2 | | | | 11.9 | 19.6 |
| 31.9 | 39.1 | 42.7 | | Total Current | 54.3 | | | | 40.7 | 47.2 |
| 31.6 | 22.5 | 30.9 | | Long-Term Debt | 43.3 | | | | 28.5 | 23.5 |
| .0 | .0 | .1 | | Deferred Taxes | .0 | | | | .1 | .1 |
| 5.1 | 4.9 | 5.5 | | All Other Non-Current | 13.9 | | | | 1.9 | 7.7 |
| 31.4 | 33.5 | 20.8 | | Net Worth | -11.6 | | | | 28.8 | 21.5 |
| 100.0 | 100.0 | 100.0 | | Total Liabilities & Net Worth | 100.0 | | | | 100.0 | 100.0 |
| | | | | INCOME DATA | | | | | | |
| 100.0 | 100.0 | 100.0 | | Net Sales | 100.0 | | | | 100.0 | 100.0 |
| | | | | Gross Profit | | | | | | |
| 93.6 | 93.2 | 91.8 | | Operating Expenses | 95.1 | | | | 90.3 | 94.6 |
| 6.4 | 6.8 | 8.2 | | Operating Profit | 4.9 | | | | 9.7 | 5.4 |
| -1.4 | 1.5 | 1.5 | | All Other Expenses (net) | .8 | | | | .4 | .9 |
| 7.8 | 5.3 | 6.7 | | Profit Before Taxes | 4.1 | | | | 9.4 | 4.5 |
| | | | | RATIOS | | | | | | |
| 4.5 | 4.4 | 2.6 | | | 2.8 | | | | 3.8 | 1.8 |
| 1.9 | 1.7 | 1.5 | | Current | 1.0 | | | | 1.9 | 1.3 |
| 1.2 | .9 | .7 | | | .3 | | | | 1.4 | .7 |
| 3.7 | 2.7 | 2.1 | | | 2.8 | | | | 2.8 | 1.4 |
| 1.5 | 1.3 | 1.1 | | Quick | .9 | | | | 1.8 | 1.1 |
| .7 | .5 | .4 | | | .3 | | | | 1.0 | .4 |
| 0 UND | 0 UND | 1 290.1 | | | 0 UND | | | | 11 32.4 | 12 29.7 |
| 6 57.6 | 17 21.0 | 15 24.1 | | Sales/Receivables | 0 UND | | | | 20 18.2 | 30 12.3 |
| 30 12.2 | 37 9.9 | 38 9.6 | | | 19 19.4 | | | | 43 8.5 | 39 9.3 |
| | | | | Cost of Sales/Inventory | | | | | | |
| | | | | Cost of Sales/Payables | | | | | | |
| 6.2 | 7.0 | 6.8 | | | 9.3 | | | | 5.9 | 11.0 |
| 13.2 | 13.0 | 17.5 | | Sales/Working Capital | NM | | | | 8.7 | 27.9 |
| 57.8 | -180.6 | -20.3 | | | -13.7 | | | | 14.3 | -19.6 |
| 49.1 | 49.0 | 22.4 | | | | | | | 39.8 | 17.3 |
| (54) 16.8 | (52) 7.6 | (71) 4.9 | | EBIT/Interest | | | | | (18) 5.6 | (29) 4.8 |
| 3.4 | -.5 | 1.6 | | | | | | | 2.6 | 3.2 |
| | 22.4 | 8.6 | | Net Profit + Depr., Dep., | | | | | | |
| | (10) 8.9 | (15) 4.2 | | Amort./Cur. Mat. L/T/D | | | | | | |
| | 4.1 | 1.2 | | | | | | | | |
| .1 | .0 | .2 | | | .0 | | | | .2 | .2 |
| .3 | .4 | 1.0 | | Fixed/Worth | .2 | | | | .6 | 1.1 |
| 1.9 | 4.7 | -2.3 | | | NM | | | | 2.7 | -2.0 |
| .6 | .6 | .8 | | | .9 | | | | .5 | 1.2 |
| 1.8 | 1.9 | 3.0 | | Debt/Worth | NM | | | | 3.2 | 3.0 |
| NM | 21.4 | -4.5 | | | -1.4 | | | | 18.0 | -4.3 |
| 114.8 | 63.1 | 75.4 | | | | | | | 99.2 | 72.9 |
| (49) 66.4 | (61) 29.2 | (59) 32.1 | | % Profit Before Taxes/Tangible Net Worth | | | | | (17) 52.3 | (20) 34.7 |
| 11.4 | 5.6 | 9.2 | | | | | | | 19.8 | 11.9 |
| 41.7 | 26.3 | 23.3 | | | 50.3 | | | | 29.8 | 15.5 |
| 19.6 | 9.7 | 8.1 | | % Profit Before Taxes/Total Assets | 14.3 | | | | 12.7 | 6.8 |
| 1.2 | -2.5 | 2.4 | | | -6.7 | | | | 4.5 | 3.6 |
| 139.4 | 223.8 | 73.9 | | | UND | | | | 74.0 | 43.5 |
| 30.7 | 20.4 | 14.2 | | Sales/Net Fixed Assets | 167.9 | | | | 15.0 | 17.5 |
| 10.7 | 7.4 | 4.7 | | | 16.7 | | | | 7.4 | 7.3 |
| 5.2 | 4.7 | 4.6 | | | 7.5 | | | | 4.4 | 4.7 |
| 3.3 | 2.5 | 2.6 | | Sales/Total Assets | 3.8 | | | | 2.3 | 2.9 |
| 1.7 | 1.3 | 1.4 | | | 2.1 | | | | 1.5 | 1.9 |
| .3 | .5 | .5 | | | | | | | .6 | .3 |
| (40) 1.4 | (49) 1.3 | (57) 1.3 | | % Depr., Dep., Amort./Sales | | | | | (13) 1.1 | (23) 1.9 |
| 4.8 | 3.2 | 3.1 | | | | | | | 1.4 | 2.9 |
| 1.1 | 1.5 | 1.3 | | | | | | | | |
| (20) 2.9 | (23) 3.4 | (20) 2.4 | | % Officers', Directors', Owners' Comp/Sales | | | | | | |
| 6.2 | 5.7 | 6.1 | | | | | | | | |
| 2653117M | 3606304M | 6776810M | | Net Sales ($) | 3222M | 21942M | 20059M | 60031M | 329787M | 6341769M |
| 943011M | 1224930M | 2627079M | | Total Assets ($) | 8778M | 7952M | 13158M | 50076M | 201329M | 2345786M |

© RMA 2024      M = $ thousand    MM = $ million
See Pages viii through xx for Explanation of Ratios and Data

# RESTAURANT/LODGING—Caterers NAICS 722320

## Current Data Sorted by Assets | Comparative Historical Data

| 0-500M | 500M-2MM | 2-10MM | 10-50MM | 50-100MM | 100-250MM | | | ALL 4/1/19-3/31/20 | | ALL 4/1/20-3/31/21 |
|---|---|---|---|---|---|---|---|---|---|---|
| | 2 | | 1 | | | Type of Statement | | | | |
| | 1 | 1 | 1 | 1 | | Unqualified | | 2 | | |
| 1 | | 3 | 1 | | | Reviewed | | 2 | | 1 |
| 5 | 13 | 3 | 3 | | | Compiled | | 9 | | 5 |
| 8 | 8 | 4 | 3 | 1 | 2 | Tax Returns | | 30 | | 12 |
| | | 28 | 7 | | | Other | | 71 | | 24 |
| | 11 (4/1-9/30/23) | | 84 (10/1/23-3/31/24) | | | | | | | |
| 14 | 24 | 39 | 13 | 3 | 2 | NUMBER OF STATEMENTS | | 114 | | 42 |
| % | % | % | % | % | % | ASSETS | | % | | % |
| 27.2 | 26.6 | 22.3 | 18.4 | | | Cash & Equivalents | | 25.9 | | 26.6 |
| 9.5 | 8.5 | 5.6 | 8.3 | | | Trade Receivables (net) | | 10.3 | | 4.8 |
| .9 | 2.1 | 2.7 | 2.4 | | | Inventory | | 4.1 | | 2.8 |
| 3.5 | 3.8 | 7.2 | 4.3 | | | All Other Current | | 4.1 | | 2.6 |
| 41.1 | 41.0 | 37.8 | 33.4 | | | Total Current | | 44.4 | | 36.8 |
| 35.6 | 38.7 | 40.8 | 52.4 | | | Fixed Assets (net) | | 42.0 | | 46.1 |
| 19.2 | 6.1 | 6.9 | 5.1 | | | Intangibles (net) | | 3.6 | | 9.5 |
| 4.1 | 14.2 | 14.5 | 9.1 | | | All Other Non-Current | | 10.1 | | 7.6 |
| 100.0 | 100.0 | 100.0 | 100.0 | | | Total | | 100.0 | | 100.0 |
| | | | | | | LIABILITIES | | | | |
| 15.6 | 12.1 | .6 | 8.4 | | | Notes Payable-Short Term | | 9.7 | | 14.5 |
| .0 | 2.7 | 2.7 | 1.1 | | | Cur. Mat.-L.T.D. | | 4.5 | | 3.2 |
| 6.0 | 3.2 | 4.4 | 7.9 | | | Trade Payables | | 10.2 | | 6.2 |
| 1.1 | .1 | .1 | .1 | | | Income Taxes Payable | | .1 | | .1 |
| 40.4 | 22.8 | 21.1 | 19.2 | | | All Other Current | | 23.0 | | 22.3 |
| 63.2 | 41.0 | 28.9 | 36.6 | | | Total Current | | 47.5 | | 46.3 |
| 65.7 | 36.8 | 39.0 | 26.0 | | | Long-Term Debt | | 30.8 | | 48.0 |
| .0 | .0 | .1 | .0 | | | Deferred Taxes | | .1 | | .0 |
| 31.8 | 4.1 | 7.4 | .6 | | | All Other Non-Current | | 7.3 | | 4.2 |
| -60.5 | 18.0 | 24.6 | 36.7 | | | Net Worth | | 14.3 | | 1.5 |
| 100.0 | 100.0 | 100.0 | 100.0 | | | Total Liabilities & Net Worth | | 100.0 | | 100.0 |
| | | | | | | INCOME DATA | | | | |
| 100.0 | 100.0 | 100.0 | 100.0 | | | Net Sales | | 100.0 | | 100.0 |
| | | | | | | Gross Profit | | | | |
| 91.5 | 95.7 | 87.2 | 90.3 | | | Operating Expenses | | 90.8 | | 105.6 |
| 8.5 | 4.3 | 12.8 | 9.7 | | | Operating Profit | | 9.2 | | -5.6 |
| .5 | 2.5 | 3.5 | 5.1 | | | All Other Expenses (net) | | 3.0 | | .0 |
| 8.0 | 1.8 | 9.3 | 4.5 | | | Profit Before Taxes | | 6.2 | | -5.6 |
| | | | | | | RATIOS | | | | |
| 4.5 | 4.2 | 5.7 | 2.8 | | | | | 1.9 | | 5.8 |
| .8 | 1.4 | 1.8 | 1.2 | | | Current | | 1.0 | | 1.1 |
| .4 | .4 | 1.1 | .5 | | | | | .5 | | .3 |
| 3.7 | 3.4 | 3.3 | 2.7 | | | | | 1.8 | | 5.8 |
| .7 | 1.1 | 1.2 | 1.0 | | | Quick | | .8 | | .9 |
| .3 | .4 | .4 | .4 | | | | | .4 | | .3 |
| 0 UND | 0 UND | 0 UND | 2 156.9 | | | | | 0 UND | 0 UND | |
| 0 UND | 2 152.3 | 6 63.1 | 9 39.5 | | | Sales/Receivables | | 2 230.7 | 0 UND | |
| 10 36.5 | 11 33.0 | 20 18.2 | 66 5.5 | | | | | 18 20.3 | 9 39.3 | |
| | | | | | | Cost of Sales/Inventory | | | | |
| | | | | | | Cost of Sales/Payables | | | | |
| 8.2 | 8.1 | 4.0 | 4.2 | | | | | 18.4 | | 4.1 |
| -58.5 | 67.6 | 7.4 | 15.0 | | | Sales/Working Capital | | NM | | NM |
| -11.2 | -7.9 | 194.9 | -7.2 | | | | | -15.1 | | -5.4 |
| | 4.1 | 19.5 | | | | | | 32.7 | | 1.1 |
| (14) | .2 | (30) 11.1 | | | | EBIT/Interest | (87) | 10.0 | (29) | -2.4 |
| | -6.7 | 2.9 | | | | | | 2.3 | | -8.7 |
| | | | | | | Net Profit + Depr., Dep., Amort./Cur. Mat. L/T/D | | | | |
| .3 | .3 | .4 | .6 | | | | | .4 | | .7 |
| NM | .9 | 2.9 | 1.6 | | | Fixed/Worth | | 1.9 | | 15.4 |
| -.3 | -1.2 | -11.8 | NM | | | | | -8.6 | | -1.2 |
| 4.2 | .3 | .6 | .7 | | | | | .9 | | 1.5 |
| -2.2 | 1.3 | 2.2 | 2.1 | | | Debt/Worth | | 3.4 | | 17.1 |
| -1.3 | -5.0 | -18.8 | NM | | | | | -12.3 | | -2.5 |
| | 54.1 | 52.2 | 43.3 | | | | | 111.4 | | 72.6 |
| (15) | 3.2 | (27) 16.5 | (10) 6.0 | | | % Profit Before Taxes/Tangible Net Worth | (78) | 43.1 | (24) | 13.6 |
| | -19.0 | 5.8 | -10.6 | | | | | 14.1 | | -51.2 |
| 81.5 | 12.5 | 14.0 | 13.5 | | | | | 35.6 | | 4.6 |
| 26.2 | .1 | 7.6 | 2.8 | | | % Profit Before Taxes/Total Assets | | 12.4 | | -10.8 |
| -44.4 | -6.8 | 3.4 | -3.0 | | | | | 2.8 | | -28.1 |
| 88.7 | 62.1 | 15.7 | 8.3 | | | | | 46.2 | | 12.5 |
| 17.9 | 8.1 | 4.9 | 3.3 | | | Sales/Net Fixed Assets | | 11.1 | | 3.3 |
| 7.7 | 3.8 | 1.8 | .8 | | | | | 4.0 | | 1.7 |
| 7.1 | 3.7 | 2.5 | 1.9 | | | | | 6.3 | | 2.3 |
| 3.9 | 2.8 | 1.6 | 1.1 | | | Sales/Total Assets | | 3.6 | | 1.5 |
| 2.6 | 1.6 | .7 | .7 | | | | | 1.5 | | .8 |
| | .8 | .7 | 1.7 | | | | | 1.0 | | 1.1 |
| (15) | 1.4 | (27) 2.4 | (11) 2.8 | | | % Depr., Dep., Amort./Sales | (75) | 2.0 | (28) | 3.6 |
| | 4.8 | 6.7 | 4.6 | | | | | 5.2 | | 6.6 |
| | 1.0 | 2.2 | | | | | | 1.9 | | 3.6 |
| (12) | 5.4 | (16) 3.7 | | | | % Officers', Directors' Owners' Comp/Sales | (46) | 3.9 | (18) | 5.1 |
| | 9.9 | 7.5 | | | | | | 6.6 | | 7.9 |
| 14169M | 85117M | 322814M | 263035M | 203974M | 1211300M | Net Sales ($) | | 3020704M | | 338612M |
| 3387M | 28494M | 194884M | 234703M | 204967M | 477562M | Total Assets ($) | | 1061564M | | 261861M |

M = $ thousand   MM = $ million
See Pages viii through xx for Explanation of Ratios and Data
© RMA 2024

# RESTAURANT/LODGING—Caterers NAICS 722320

## Comparative Historical Data | Current Data Sorted by Sales

| Comparative Historical Data | | | Type of Statement | Current Data Sorted by Sales | | | | | |
|---|---|---|---|---|---|---|---|---|---|
| 1 | 4 | 5 | Unqualified | | 1 | 1 | 1 | 1 | 2 |
| 2 | 8 | 6 | Reviewed | | 1 | 1 | 1 | 1 | 3 |
| | 1 | 5 | Compiled | | 2 | 1 | 1 | 1 | 1 |
| 15 | 27 | 25 | Tax Returns | 7 | 4 | 4 | 6 | 4 | |
| 17 | 51 | 54 | Other | 9 | 10 | 9 | 13 | 9 | 4 |
| 4/1/21-3/31/22 ALL | 4/1/22-3/31/23 ALL | 4/1/23-3/31/24 ALL | | 11 (4/1-9/30/23) | | | 84 (10/1/23-3/31/24) | | |
| | | | | 0-1MM | 1-3MM | 3-5MM | 5-10MM | 10-25MM | 25MM & OVER |
| 35 | 91 | 95 | NUMBER OF STATEMENTS | 16 | 17 | 14 | 22 | 16 | 10 |
| % | % | % | ASSETS | % | % | % | % | % | % |
| 50.0 | 29.3 | 23.2 | Cash & Equivalents | 11.9 | 21.7 | 28.3 | 31.7 | 23.7 | 17.0 |
| 8.3 | 9.7 | 7.8 | Trade Receivables (net) | 5.3 | 8.5 | 4.0 | 8.6 | 8.7 | 12.9 |
| 1.3 | 2.3 | 2.2 | Inventory | .2 | 2.0 | 2.1 | 2.0 | 4.6 | 1.9 |
| 2.5 | 4.5 | 5.5 | All Other Current | 5.9 | 3.6 | .6 | 7.5 | 8.7 | 6.0 |
| 62.1 | 45.8 | 38.7 | Total Current | 23.3 | 35.8 | 35.0 | 49.7 | 45.7 | 37.8 |
| 20.6 | 32.0 | 41.2 | Fixed Assets (net) | 54.0 | 43.5 | 39.2 | 32.0 | 39.6 | 42.0 |
| 7.6 | 5.2 | 8.3 | Intangibles (net) | 7.6 | 13.8 | 12.3 | 5.7 | 5.9 | 4.4 |
| 9.7 | 16.9 | 11.8 | All Other Non-Current | 15.1 | 6.9 | 13.5 | 12.5 | 8.8 | 15.8 |
| 100.0 | 100.0 | 100.0 | Total | 100.0 | 100.0 | 100.0 | 100.0 | 100.0 | 100.0 |
| | | | LIABILITIES | | | | | | |
| 14.2 | 4.2 | 6.8 | Notes Payable-Short Term | 9.0 | 8.5 | 7.8 | 10.5 | .9 | .0 |
| 4.1 | 2.7 | 2.1 | Cur. Mat.-L.T.D. | .7 | 1.6 | 1.7 | 2.1 | 2.5 | 4.7 |
| 4.3 | 5.4 | 5.0 | Trade Payables | 4.9 | 2.6 | 1.9 | 4.3 | 7.5 | 11.1 |
| .1 | .2 | .2 | Income Taxes Payable | .1 | .9 | .0 | .1 | .1 | .0 |
| 18.6 | 19.0 | 23.8 | All Other Current | 36.6 | 25.1 | 14.5 | 27.3 | 17.6 | 16.9 |
| 41.3 | 31.6 | 37.9 | Total Current | 51.2 | 38.7 | 25.9 | 44.3 | 28.6 | 32.7 |
| 36.3 | 38.3 | 40.0 | Long-Term Debt | 72.9 | 48.2 | 32.2 | 27.9 | 29.0 | 28.6 |
| .1 | .0 | .2 | Deferred Taxes | .0 | .0 | .0 | .0 | .0 | 1.8 |
| 4.7 | 8.0 | 9.7 | All Other Non-Current | 29.0 | 1.3 | 14.7 | 5.2 | 1.8 | 8.7 |
| 17.7 | 22.1 | 12.2 | Net Worth | -53.0 | 11.8 | 27.2 | 22.6 | 40.7 | 28.1 |
| 100.0 | 100.0 | 100.0 | Total Liabilities & Net Worth | 100.0 | 100.0 | 100.0 | 100.0 | 100.0 | 100.0 |
| | | | INCOME DATA | | | | | | |
| 100.0 | 100.0 | 100.0 | Net Sales | 100.0 | 100.0 | 100.0 | 100.0 | 100.0 | 100.0 |
| | | | Gross Profit | | | | | | |
| 91.2 | 91.7 | 90.9 | Operating Expenses | 77.0 | 94.7 | 86.2 | 96.0 | 96.4 | 93.5 |
| 8.8 | 8.3 | 9.1 | Operating Profit | 23.0 | 5.3 | 13.8 | 4.0 | 3.6 | 6.5 |
| -1.2 | .3 | 2.9 | All Other Expenses (net) | 11.4 | 1.7 | 5.6 | .0 | -1.2 | .5 |
| 10.0 | 8.0 | 6.2 | Profit Before Taxes | 11.6 | 3.6 | 8.3 | 3.9 | 4.8 | 6.0 |
| | | | RATIOS | | | | | | |
| 5.5 | 3.5 | 3.7 | | 4.8 | 2.6 | 6.9 | 6.4 | 3.4 | 3.4 |
| 1.6 | 1.8 | 1.4 | Current | .8 | 1.1 | 3.4 | 1.8 | 1.7 | 1.0 |
| 1.0 | .9 | .6 | | .3 | .5 | 1.1 | .7 | .9 | .5 |
| 5.5 | 3.1 | 2.8 | | .8 | 2.4 | 6.4 | 4.3 | 2.5 | 2.5 |
| 1.4 | 1.4 | 1.0 | Quick | .5 | .8 | 2.6 | 1.5 | .9 | .8 |
| 1.0 | .7 | .4 | | .2 | .3 | 1.1 | .2 | .5 | .4 |
| 0 UND | 0 UND | 0 UND | | 0 UND | 0 UND | 0 UND | 0 UND | 2 196.9 | 4 91.0 |
| 4 92.4 | 4 95.8 | 5 69.5 | Sales/Receivables | 0 UND | 3 118.8 | 5 80.3 | 6 59.2 | 7 50.4 | 20 18.6 |
| 29 12.5 | 25 14.8 | 20 18.6 | | 0 UND | 25 14.7 | 14 26.4 | 20 18.6 | 27 13.4 | 39 9.3 |
| | | | Cost of Sales/Inventory | | | | | | |
| | | | Cost of Sales/Payables | | | | | | |
| 3.9 | 4.4 | 4.7 | | 6.7 | 5.2 | 4.7 | 4.6 | 4.4 | 3.7 |
| 9.2 | 15.3 | 19.3 | Sales/Working Capital | -58.5 | 110.8 | 9.2 | 10.4 | 17.2 | NM |
| -240.0 | -28.8 | -20.2 | | -5.1 | -19.2 | 39.0 | -43.3 | NM | -17.1 |
| 78.4 | 30.4 | 27.3 | | | | | 93.9 | 79.8 | 38.7 |
| (30) 15.9 | (63) 10.5 | (62) 5.1 | EBIT/Interest | | (15) 11.9 | (13) 14.8 | 10.0 | | |
| 4.8 | 1.5 | -.5 | | | | | .7 | .9 | -.7 |
| | | | Net Profit + Depr., Dep., Amort./Cur. Mat. L/T/D | | | | | | |
| .1 | .2 | .4 | | 1.2 | .5 | .7 | .0 | .4 | .4 |
| .5 | 1.0 | 1.7 | Fixed/Worth | -9.7 | 1.4 | 2.8 | .5 | 1.4 | 2.2 |
| 43.5 | -4.6 | -4.1 | | -.4 | -1.7 | -1.6 | -9.5 | 7.8 | -5.9 |
| 1.1 | .6 | .6 | | 2.4 | .6 | .9 | .3 | .6 | .6 |
| 4.2 | 2.2 | 2.8 | Debt/Worth | -5.8 | 5.1 | 3.0 | .9 | 1.4 | 2.7 |
| -18.3 | -8.4 | -6.4 | | -1.7 | -4.3 | -3.1 | -15.9 | 12.9 | -15.9 |
| 189.0 | 72.6 | 57.2 | | | 161.8 | | 42.2 | 90.2 | |
| (25) 65.1 | (64) 31.7 | (60) 13.7 | % Profit Before Taxes/Tangible Net Worth | (11) 10.2 | | (16) 14.0 | (14) 20.7 | | |
| 19.0 | 9.5 | -1.9 | | | .0 | | -1.4 | -7.8 | |
| 40.6 | 26.9 | 16.1 | | 13.4 | 39.4 | 13.7 | 18.7 | 14.8 | 30.9 |
| 12.8 | 9.4 | 4.9 | % Profit Before Taxes/Total Assets | .9 | 3.4 | 4.6 | 9.6 | 6.7 | 6.8 |
| 4.0 | 1.5 | -1.3 | | -4.3 | -2.0 | 1.2 | -.6 | -1.5 | -2.2 |
| 48.3 | 33.2 | 20.2 | | 19.3 | 15.5 | 27.0 | 89.9 | 12.8 | 14.0 |
| 12.5 | 9.3 | 6.4 | Sales/Net Fixed Assets | 4.3 | 6.4 | 3.8 | 12.0 | 6.4 | 5.5 |
| 5.5 | 2.3 | 2.6 | | .2 | 3.5 | 1.7 | 2.7 | 3.3 | 2.9 |
| 3.3 | 3.6 | 3.2 | | 3.8 | 3.6 | 2.9 | 3.6 | 3.0 | 3.2 |
| 1.5 | 2.0 | 2.0 | Sales/Total Assets | .5 | 2.3 | 1.7 | 2.0 | 2.0 | 2.1 |
| .9 | 1.0 | .9 | | .1 | 1.2 | .7 | 1.5 | 1.2 | .9 |
| .6 | 1.0 | 1.2 | | | 1.5 | | .4 | 1.2 | |
| (17) 1.6 | (50) 1.7 | (62) 2.5 | % Depr., Dep., Amort./Sales | (10) 3.6 | | (15) 2.2 | (12) 2.2 | | |
| 6.1 | 4.9 | 5.6 | | | 6.7 | | 6.7 | 4.0 | |
| 2.0 | 2.1 | 2.2 | | | | | 4.2 | 2.2 | |
| (12) 3.7 | (39) 4.0 | (36) 4.8 | % Officers', Directors', Owners' Comp/Sales | | (10) 7.0 | (12) 4.1 | | | |
| 6.3 | 7.6 | 10.0 | | | | | 11.6 | 9.6 | |
| 406098M | 884058M | 2100409M | Net Sales ($) | 8026M | 29261M | 54452M | 153597M | 267419M | 1587654M |
| 213092M | 589322M | 1143997M | Total Assets ($) | 25953M | 37269M | 72021M | 83155M | 149997M | 775602M |

© RMA 2024
M = $ thousand  MM = $ million
See Pages viii through xx for Explanation of Ratios and Data

# RESTAURANT/LODGING—Drinking Places (Alcoholic Beverages) NAICS 722410

## Current Data Sorted by Assets | Comparative Historical Data

| 0-500M | 500M-2MM | 2-10MM | 10-50MM | 50-100MM | 100-250MM | | | 4/1/19-3/31/20 ALL | 4/1/20-3/31/21 ALL |
|---|---|---|---|---|---|---|---|---|---|
| 1 | | | | 1 | 1 | Type of Statement | | | |
| | | 1 | 1 | | | Unqualified | | 3 | 2 |
| | 5 | 3 | 1 | | | Reviewed | | 3 | 1 |
| 19 | 12 | 4 | | | | Compiled | | 8 | 4 |
| 30 | 26 | 22 | 6 | 3 | 2 | Tax Returns | | 47 | 26 |
| | 7 (4/1-9/30/23) | | 131 (10/1/23-3/31/24) | | | Other | | 98 | 68 |
| 50 | 43 | 30 | 8 | 4 | 3 | NUMBER OF STATEMENTS | | 159 | 101 |
| % | % | % | % | % | % | **ASSETS** | | % | % |
| 34.1 | 28.5 | 11.2 | | | | Cash & Equivalents | | 16.9 | 23.6 |
| 1.6 | .7 | 1.6 | | | | Trade Receivables (net) | | 1.6 | 1.1 |
| 9.4 | 5.7 | 5.1 | | | | Inventory | | 9.3 | 8.5 |
| 1.4 | 3.7 | 17.8 | | | | All Other Current | | 3.0 | 3.5 |
| 46.4 | 38.6 | 35.7 | | | | Total Current | | 30.7 | 36.7 |
| 33.5 | 34.4 | 52.8 | | | | Fixed Assets (net) | | 44.6 | 40.9 |
| 13.6 | 11.2 | 6.7 | | | | Intangibles (net) | | 12.6 | 12.6 |
| 6.5 | 15.8 | 4.8 | | | | All Other Non-Current | | 12.2 | 9.8 |
| 100.0 | 100.0 | 100.0 | | | | Total | | 100.0 | 100.0 |
| | | | | | | **LIABILITIES** | | | |
| 2.6 | 3.6 | 1.0 | | | | Notes Payable-Short Term | | 7.1 | 10.2 |
| 2.3 | 1.7 | 5.2 | | | | Cur. Mat.-L.T.D. | | 1.9 | 4.1 |
| 2.1 | 2.0 | 2.9 | | | | Trade Payables | | 6.0 | 4.7 |
| .0 | .1 | .0 | | | | Income Taxes Payable | | .2 | .1 |
| 21.7 | 15.6 | 16.1 | | | | All Other Current | | 20.4 | 11.8 |
| 28.7 | 23.2 | 25.2 | | | | Total Current | | 35.6 | 31.0 |
| 40.6 | 32.7 | 37.4 | | | | Long-Term Debt | | 37.6 | 48.1 |
| .0 | .0 | .0 | | | | Deferred Taxes | | .1 | .0 |
| 8.0 | 1.7 | 4.4 | | | | All Other Non-Current | | 9.5 | 19.2 |
| 22.5 | 42.4 | 33.0 | | | | Net Worth | | 17.3 | 1.7 |
| 100.0 | 100.0 | 100.0 | | | | Total Liabilities & Net Worth | | 100.0 | 100.0 |
| | | | | | | **INCOME DATA** | | | |
| 100.0 | 100.0 | 100.0 | | | | Net Sales | | 100.0 | 100.0 |
| 63.4 | 62.0 | 63.8 | | | | Gross Profit | | 63.9 | 59.0 |
| 55.6 | 53.1 | 55.5 | | | | Operating Expenses | | 57.4 | 63.2 |
| 7.7 | 8.9 | 8.3 | | | | Operating Profit | | 6.5 | -4.3 |
| -.1 | .1 | 1.7 | | | | All Other Expenses (net) | | 1.0 | -.2 |
| 7.9 | 8.8 | 6.6 | | | | Profit Before Taxes | | 5.5 | -4.1 |
| | | | | | | **RATIOS** | | | |
| 4.4 | 7.8 | 2.8 | | | | | | 2.9 | 4.9 |
| 2.4 | 2.2 | 1.8 | | | | Current | | 1.4 | 1.9 |
| 1.7 | .7 | .6 | | | | | | .5 | .8 |
| 3.2 | 6.7 | 1.5 | | | | | | 2.0 | 3.4 |
| (49) 1.7 | 1.4 | .4 | | | | Quick | (158) | .7 | 1.2 |
| 1.2 | .3 | .1 | | | | | | .2 | .4 |
| 0 UND | 0 UND | 0 UND | | | | | | 0 UND | 0 UND |
| 0 UND | 0 UND | 0 UND | | | | Sales/Receivables | | 0 UND | 0 UND |
| 0 UND | 0 UND | 3 145.6 | | | | | | 0 999.8 | 0 UND |
| 6 63.9 | 9 40.4 | 4 99.1 | | | | | | 8 43.1 | 7 49.0 |
| 14 25.9 | 17 21.7 | 16 22.8 | | | | Cost of Sales/Inventory | | 17 21.2 | 28 13.2 |
| 38 9.6 | 29 12.6 | 56 6.5 | | | | | | 36 10.2 | 44 8.3 |
| 0 UND | 0 UND | 5 73.9 | | | | | | 0 UND | 0 UND |
| 0 UND | 2 197.5 | 18 20.8 | | | | Cost of Sales/Payables | | 9 42.3 | 0 837.0 |
| 4 100.2 | 9 40.3 | 47 7.7 | | | | | | 30 12.3 | 26 13.9 |
| 9.8 | 10.1 | 4.3 | | | | | | 17.2 | 6.5 |
| 18.4 | 20.1 | 11.5 | | | | Sales/Working Capital | | 59.0 | 21.3 |
| 60.9 | -28.0 | -25.0 | | | | | | -18.9 | -28.9 |
| 27.6 | 30.6 | 7.5 | | | | | | 15.4 | 10.7 |
| (21) 8.0 | (26) 9.9 | (17) 1.8 | | | | EBIT/Interest | (94) | 3.9 | (61) 1.0 |
| 2.1 | 1.0 | -.6 | | | | | | .9 | -7.9 |
| | | | | | | Net Profit + Depr., Dep., Amort./Cur. Mat. L/T/D | | | |
| .3 | .2 | .2 | | | | | | .4 | .5 |
| .8 | .8 | 1.2 | | | | Fixed/Worth | | 2.2 | 2.9 |
| UND | 9.1 | NM | | | | | | -2.7 | -1.3 |
| .2 | .4 | .3 | | | | | | .5 | .5 |
| 1.9 | 2.1 | 1.2 | | | | Debt/Worth | | 2.9 | 7.9 |
| -3.0 | 8.9 | -75.4 | | | | | | -5.0 | -3.4 |
| 221.3 | 92.5 | 52.5 | | | | | | 106.4 | 44.8 |
| (35) 88.1 | (34) 41.7 | (22) 14.5 | | | | % Profit Before Taxes/Tangible Net Worth | (103) | 62.6 | (59) 11.3 |
| 22.9 | 16.7 | 1.4 | | | | | | 12.5 | -26.6 |
| 72.3 | 48.3 | 18.5 | | | | | | 35.9 | 16.1 |
| 30.0 | 22.5 | 8.3 | | | | % Profit Before Taxes/Total Assets | | 11.5 | .0 |
| -6.0 | 2.8 | -3.1 | | | | | | -1.3 | -21.5 |
| 51.3 | 63.6 | 8.3 | | | | | | 46.4 | 27.2 |
| 21.7 | 12.9 | 2.3 | | | | Sales/Net Fixed Assets | | 7.6 | 7.5 |
| 7.4 | 4.1 | 1.0 | | | | | | 2.6 | 2.0 |
| 7.1 | 4.6 | 1.6 | | | | | | 5.0 | 3.8 |
| 4.2 | 2.5 | 1.0 | | | | Sales/Total Assets | | 2.9 | 1.9 |
| 2.4 | 1.7 | .6 | | | | | | 1.6 | 1.1 |
| 1.0 | .5 | .5 | | | | | | 1.2 | 1.2 |
| (22) 2.3 | (18) 1.2 | (15) 3.4 | | | | % Depr., Dep., Amort./Sales | (98) | 2.0 | (60) 2.9 |
| 2.8 | 3.5 | 8.5 | | | | | | 4.8 | 5.7 |
| 3.1 | 4.5 | | | | | | | 2.1 | 2.2 |
| (16) 5.1 | (14) 4.9 | | | | | % Officers', Directors' Owners' Comp/Sales | (47) | 3.6 | (25) 4.8 |
| 11.5 | 8.4 | | | | | | | 6.7 | 8.1 |
| 58799M | 132674M | 139985M | 140548M | 601771M | 791901M | Net Sales ($) | | 2742182M | 1033741M |
| 13434M | 44592M | 114991M | 132492M | 293008M | 542661M | Total Assets ($) | | 832431M | 529289M |

© RMA 2024

M = $ thousand    MM = $ million
See Pages viii through xx for Explanation of Ratios and Data

# RESTAURANT/LODGING—Drinking Places (Alcoholic Beverages) NAICS 722410

## Comparative Historical Data | Current Data Sorted by Sales

| | | | Type of Statement | | | | | | |
|---|---|---|---|---|---|---|---|---|---|
| 1 | 1 | 3 | Unqualified | | 1 | | | | 2 |
| | | 2 | Reviewed | | 1 | | | | 1 |
| 7 | 5 | 9 | Compiled | 1 | 1 | 3 | 3 | 1 | |
| 37 | 56 | 35 | Tax Returns | 15 | 12 | 6 | 2 | | |
| 54 | 63 | 89 | Other | 18 | 33 | 19 | 8 | 5 | 6 |
| 4/1/21-3/31/22 ALL | 4/1/22-3/31/23 ALL | 4/1/23-3/31/24 ALL | | 7 (4/1-9/30/23) | | | 131 (10/1/23-3/31/24) | | |
| | | | | 0-1MM | 1-3MM | 3-5MM | 5-10MM | 10-25MM | 25MM & OVER |
| 99 | 125 | 138 | **NUMBER OF STATEMENTS** | 34 | 48 | 28 | 13 | 6 | 9 |
| % | % | % | **ASSETS** | % | % | % | % | % | % |
| 31.6 | 29.9 | 24.7 | Cash & Equivalents | 33.8 | 25.0 | 19.1 | 31.7 | | |
| 1.6 | 2.3 | 1.9 | Trade Receivables (net) | 1.1 | 1.7 | .3 | 1.3 | | |
| 6.9 | 7.5 | 6.7 | Inventory | 8.2 | 9.0 | 4.2 | 3.6 | | |
| 7.2 | 5.0 | 6.2 | All Other Current | 1.3 | 6.2 | 8.6 | 5.6 | | |
| 47.3 | 44.8 | 39.6 | Total Current | 44.4 | 41.8 | 32.1 | 42.2 | | |
| 37.9 | 37.2 | 38.4 | Fixed Assets (net) | 35.2 | 38.7 | 40.5 | 38.9 | | |
| 10.8 | 9.0 | 9.9 | Intangibles (net) | 13.5 | 10.9 | 10.9 | 3.4 | | |
| 3.9 | 9.0 | 12.1 | All Other Non-Current | 7.0 | 8.7 | 16.4 | 15.6 | | |
| 100.0 | 100.0 | 100.0 | Total | 100.0 | 100.0 | 100.0 | 100.0 | | |
| | | | **LIABILITIES** | | | | | | |
| 4.1 | 3.0 | 2.3 | Notes Payable-Short Term | 5.4 | 2.1 | .8 | .9 | | |
| 2.0 | 1.8 | 2.9 | Cur. Mat.-L.T.D. | 2.5 | 2.2 | 2.3 | 5.5 | | |
| 4.1 | 3.8 | 2.8 | Trade Payables | 1.9 | 2.4 | 2.0 | 3.8 | | |
| .1 | .0 | .1 | Income Taxes Payable | .0 | .0 | .1 | .2 | | |
| 20.8 | 18.3 | 18.4 | All Other Current | 23.5 | 20.0 | 16.9 | 10.9 | | |
| 31.1 | 26.9 | 26.5 | Total Current | 33.3 | 26.8 | 22.0 | 21.3 | | |
| 41.6 | 36.4 | 34.7 | Long-Term Debt | 37.0 | 42.7 | 23.9 | 42.3 | | |
| .0 | .0 | .0 | Deferred Taxes | .0 | .0 | .0 | .0 | | |
| 5.1 | 8.1 | 6.0 | All Other Non-Current | 12.3 | 1.9 | 3.0 | .0 | | |
| 22.2 | 28.6 | 32.7 | Net Worth | 17.1 | 28.7 | 51.0 | 36.4 | | |
| 100.0 | 100.0 | 100.0 | Total Liabilities & Net Worth | 100.0 | 100.0 | 100.0 | 100.0 | | |
| | | | **INCOME DATA** | | | | | | |
| 100.0 | 100.0 | 100.0 | Net Sales | 100.0 | 100.0 | 100.0 | 100.0 | | |
| 63.2 | 61.8 | 63.0 | Gross Profit | 62.4 | 66.9 | 62.6 | 60.6 | | |
| 51.2 | 53.9 | 54.8 | Operating Expenses | 51.6 | 61.6 | 53.9 | 49.4 | | |
| 12.0 | 7.9 | 8.2 | Operating Profit | 10.8 | 5.4 | 8.7 | 11.2 | | |
| -2.3 | -.2 | .5 | All Other Expenses (net) | 1.3 | -.1 | .0 | .7 | | |
| 14.3 | 8.1 | 7.7 | Profit Before Taxes | 9.5 | 5.5 | 8.6 | 10.5 | | |
| | | | **RATIOS** | | | | | | |
| 10.8 | 8.6 | 4.6 | | 5.8 | 3.6 | 4.1 | 5.4 | | |
| 2.4 | 2.6 | 2.2 | Current | 3.1 | 2.0 | 2.0 | 3.0 | | |
| 1.1 | 1.0 | .8 | | .7 | .7 | .8 | 1.3 | | |
| 5.7 | 6.6 | 3.2 | | 4.7 | 2.4 | 2.9 | 4.5 | | |
| 1.8 | 1.9 (137) | 1.4 | Quick | (33) 2.3 | 1.3 | 1.3 | 1.7 | | |
| .7 | .5 | .3 | | .6 | .3 | .3 | .3 | | |
| 0 UND | 0 UND | 0 UND | | 0 UND | 0 UND | 0 UND | 0 UND | | |
| 0 UND | 0 UND | 0 UND | Sales/Receivables | 0 UND | 0 UND | 0 UND | 0 UND | | |
| 1 703.5 | 1 541.3 | 1 370.1 | | 0 UND | 0 UND | 0 999.8 | 1 333.6 | | |
| 4 87.9 | 1 250.4 | 6 59.5 | | 0 UND | 12 31.5 | 0 UND | 0 UND | | |
| 14 26.3 | 13 27.8 | 16 23.1 | Cost of Sales/Inventory | 21 17.8 | 20 18.6 | 14 26.7 | 10 37.8 | | |
| 30 12.1 | 32 11.5 | 44 8.3 | | 64 5.7 | 44 8.3 | 23 16.1 | 20 18.2 | | |
| 0 UND | 0 UND | 0 UND | | 0 UND | 0 UND | 0 790.3 | 5 UND | | |
| 0 UND | 0 UND | 3 127.1 | Cost of Sales/Payables | 0 UND | 0 UND | 4 83.3 | 5 67.1 | | |
| 18 20.6 | 23 16.1 | 22 16.8 | | 10 37.7 | 27 13.4 | 17 21.4 | 50 7.3 | | |
| 4.1 | 6.2 | 8.3 | | 5.4 | 12.0 | 13.7 | 8.9 | | |
| 12.8 | 18.2 | 18.4 | Sales/Working Capital | 10.7 | 29.6 | 22.0 | 13.7 | | |
| 66.4 | 490.8 | -90.3 | | -179.0 | -29.7 | -74.4 | 47.6 | | |
| 77.6 | 53.1 | 22.5 | | 9.0 | 25.5 | 72.8 | | | |
| (64) 18.0 | (72) 5.2 | (77) 5.9 | EBIT/Interest | (20) 6.1 | (21) 3.4 | (17) 4.1 | | | |
| 2.5 | .5 | 1.1 | | 1.3 | -1.3 | 1.9 | | | |
| | | | Net Profit + Depr., Dep., Amort./Cur. Mat. L/T/D | | | | | | |
| .3 | .2 | .2 | | .1 | .3 | .2 | .2 | | |
| 1.5 | 1.0 | .9 | Fixed/Worth | 1.0 | .8 | .9 | .8 | | |
| -3.7 | 5.8 | 6.7 | | 7.7 | -4.6 | 4.2 | 3.1 | | |
| .4 | .4 | .3 | | .7 | .3 | .1 | .4 | | |
| 2.1 | 2.2 | 1.8 | Debt/Worth | 2.7 | .8 | 1.5 | .9 | | |
| -6.2 | UND | 110.2 | | -2.9 | -5.1 | 6.2 | 5.6 | | |
| 134.9 | 143.5 | 94.8 | | 114.9 | 151.0 | 83.5 | 210.1 | | |
| (67) 63.0 | (94) 51.4 | (106) 41.7 | % Profit Before Taxes/Tangible Net Worth | (25) 50.0 | (32) 38.4 | (23) 36.0 | (11) 62.3 | | |
| 29.0 | 11.2 | 9.9 | | 13.5 | 4.7 | 4.2 | 12.8 | | |
| 44.5 | 42.2 | 36.0 | | 31.2 | 44.9 | 45.5 | 66.8 | | |
| 25.9 | 12.2 | 16.8 | % Profit Before Taxes/Total Assets | 18.5 | 16.9 | 17.0 | 28.6 | | |
| 8.8 | 1.1 | .9 | | -1.8 | -5.8 | 1.9 | 7.7 | | |
| 32.2 | 76.4 | 38.0 | | 57.9 | 43.9 | 57.9 | 55.7 | | |
| 6.1 | 9.0 | 11.2 | Sales/Net Fixed Assets | 18.7 | 12.8 | 7.5 | 13.2 | | |
| 2.5 | 2.8 | 2.3 | | 1.9 | 4.4 | 3.4 | 3.2 | | |
| 3.9 | 4.8 | 4.3 | | 3.7 | 4.8 | 5.3 | 6.5 | | |
| 2.0 | 2.3 | 2.4 | Sales/Total Assets | 1.5 | 3.4 | 2.3 | 2.9 | | |
| 1.1 | 1.3 | 1.2 | | 1.1 | 1.5 | 1.2 | 1.5 | | |
| 1.5 | .8 | 1.0 | | 1.0 | 1.0 | .6 | | | |
| (52) 3.1 | (58) 1.9 | (66) 2.5 | % Depr., Dep., Amort./Sales | (17) 2.6 | (20) 2.3 | (12) 1.9 | | | |
| 6.5 | 4.4 | 4.1 | | 3.9 | 5.7 | 3.0 | | | |
| 2.7 | 2.7 | 2.7 | | | 2.6 | | | | |
| (29) 4.1 | (42) 6.6 | (38) 4.8 | % Officers', Directors' Owners' Comp/Sales | | (16) 5.4 | | | | |
| 7.8 | 11.9 | 7.1 | | | 11.9 | | | | |
| 2001830M | 1594041M | 1865678M | Net Sales ($) | 21574M | 92788M | 104612M | 82955M | 85213M | 1478536M |
| 716279M | 957041M | 1141178M | Total Assets ($) | 16063M | 58699M | 73166M | 42025M | 97853M | 853372M |

© RMA 2024     M = $ thousand     MM = $ million
See Pages viii through xx for Explanation of Ratios and Data

# RESTAURANT/LODGING—Full-Service Restaurants  NAICS 722511

## Current Data Sorted by Assets | Comparative Historical Data

| | | | | | | | Type of Statement | | |
|---|---|---|---|---|---|---|---|---|---|
| 2 | 9 | 5 | 9 | 14 | 15 | | Unqualified | 44 | 28 |
| 8 | 1 | 10 | 21 | 10 | 1 | | Reviewed | 43 | 40 |
| 6 | 18 | 23 | 14 | 1 | 1 | | Compiled | 142 | 63 |
| 221 | 178 | 88 | 4 | | 1 | | Tax Returns | 595 | 325 |
| 180 | 294 | 197 | 92 | 35 | 30 | | Other | 960 | 717 |
| | 91 (4/1-9/30/23) | | 1,397 (10/1/23-3/31/24) | | | | | 4/1/19-3/31/20 ALL | 4/1/20-3/31/21 ALL |
| 0-500M | 500M-2MM | 2-10MM | 10-50MM | 50-100MM | 100-250MM | | NUMBER OF STATEMENTS | 1784 | 1173 |
| 417 | 500 | 323 | 140 | 60 | 48 | | ASSETS | | |
| % | % | % | % | % | % | | | % | % |
| 39.2 | 29.0 | 21.1 | 17.2 | 11.7 | 8.8 | | Cash & Equivalents | 21.3 | 30.1 |
| 1.3 | 2.3 | 2.1 | 2.2 | 1.5 | 1.8 | | Trade Receivables (net) | 1.8 | 1.8 |
| 7.2 | 4.6 | 3.1 | 2.8 | 2.1 | 1.8 | | Inventory | 6.0 | 4.3 |
| 3.6 | 4.0 | 5.2 | 3.8 | 3.3 | 2.3 | | All Other Current | 3.3 | 3.2 |
| 51.3 | 39.9 | 31.4 | 25.9 | 18.5 | 14.8 | | Total Current | 32.4 | 39.4 |
| 31.9 | 33.0 | 39.3 | 44.1 | 45.4 | 40.2 | | Fixed Assets (net) | 45.7 | 37.4 |
| 8.5 | 10.5 | 10.0 | 13.0 | 9.2 | 17.7 | | Intangibles (net) | 10.2 | 11.2 |
| 8.4 | 16.5 | 19.2 | 17.0 | 27.0 | 27.3 | | All Other Non-Current | 11.7 | 12.0 |
| 100.0 | 100.0 | 100.0 | 100.0 | 100.0 | 100.0 | | Total | 100.0 | 100.0 |
| | | | | | | | LIABILITIES | | |
| 6.6 | 3.8 | 2.2 | 2.0 | .3 | .5 | | Notes Payable-Short Term | 6.1 | 9.7 |
| 2.2 | 2.0 | 2.1 | 3.4 | 5.7 | 3.6 | | Cur. Mat.-L.T.D. | 3.1 | 3.8 |
| 5.9 | 5.2 | 5.3 | 5.3 | 4.9 | 4.8 | | Trade Payables | 9.1 | 6.6 |
| .6 | .1 | .1 | .1 | .1 | .0 | | Income Taxes Payable | .3 | .3 |
| 28.0 | 16.7 | 17.6 | 13.6 | 11.9 | 25.4 | | All Other Current | 21.7 | 18.3 |
| 43.2 | 27.8 | 27.2 | 24.4 | 22.9 | 34.3 | | Total Current | 40.2 | 38.6 |
| 37.1 | 32.0 | 30.8 | 28.4 | 36.7 | 33.8 | | Long-Term Debt | 31.3 | 47.2 |
| .0 | .0 | .0 | .0 | .0 | .2 | | Deferred Taxes | .0 | .1 |
| 15.3 | 7.1 | 6.9 | 10.2 | 25.3 | 26.8 | | All Other Non-Current | 10.4 | 14.8 |
| 4.4 | 33.0 | 35.1 | 37.0 | 15.0 | 4.9 | | Net Worth | 18.0 | -.7 |
| 100.0 | 100.0 | 100.0 | 100.0 | 100.0 | 100.0 | | Total Liabilities & Net Worth | 100.0 | 100.0 |
| | | | | | | | INCOME DATA | | |
| 100.0 | 100.0 | 100.0 | 100.0 | 100.0 | 100.0 | | Net Sales | 100.0 | 100.0 |
| 62.8 | 62.2 | 61.9 | 61.0 | 66.9 | 62.4 | | Gross Profit | 61.8 | 61.4 |
| 58.8 | 56.6 | 54.6 | 55.1 | 62.9 | 59.1 | | Operating Expenses | 56.3 | 63.2 |
| 4.1 | 5.5 | 7.3 | 5.9 | 4.1 | 3.3 | | Operating Profit | 5.5 | -1.8 |
| -.1 | .3 | .1 | -.1 | .9 | 1.2 | | All Other Expenses (net) | 1.0 | -.9 |
| 4.2 | 5.2 | 7.2 | 6.0 | 3.1 | 2.1 | | Profit Before Taxes | 4.5 | -.8 |
| | | | | | | | RATIOS | | |
| 4.0 | 5.3 | 2.9 | 2.4 | 1.3 | 1.0 | | | 2.0 | 3.5 |
| 1.6 | 1.7 | 1.2 | 1.1 | .7 | .6 | | Current | .9 | 1.4 |
| .7 | .7 | .6 | .5 | .4 | .3 | | | .4 | .6 |
| 3.1 | 4.5 | 2.1 | 1.6 | .9 | .8 | | | 1.5 | 3.0 |
| (416) 1.1 | (499) 1.2 | (322) .9 | .8 | (59) .5 | .4 | | Quick | (1777) .6 | 1.1 |
| .4 | .4 | .3 | .4 | .3 | .2 | | | .2 | .4 |
| 0 UND | 0 UND | 0 UND | 0 999.8 | 0 UND | 0 UND | | | 0 UND | 0 UND |
| 0 UND | 0 UND | 0 UND | 1 271.2 | 2 147.2 | 2 202.3 | | Sales/Receivables | 0 UND | 0 UND |
| 0 UND | 1 418.1 | 2 149.2 | 6 59.2 | 5 70.7 | 8 48.0 | | | 1 323.1 | 2 204.9 |
| 1 252.8 | 3 134.7 | 4 89.3 | 8 48.3 | 10 36.4 | 7 55.3 | | | 4 84.1 | 4 83.1 |
| 6 57.8 | 8 45.0 | 9 40.5 | 11 33.6 | 14 26.2 | 11 32.3 | | Cost of Sales/Inventory | 9 39.0 | 10 36.3 |
| 12 31.1 | 15 24.5 | 18 20.7 | 20 18.5 | 19 18.8 | 23 16.0 | | | 17 21.8 | 19 19.3 |
| 0 UND | 0 UND | 2 151.4 | 10 35.7 | 20 18.6 | 15 24.8 | | | 0 UND | 0 UND |
| 0 UND | 6 62.7 | 16 22.4 | 21 17.1 | 36 10.1 | 40 9.1 | | Cost of Sales/Payables | 13 28.4 | 14 26.7 |
| 12 30.9 | 20 17.9 | 37 9.8 | 41 9.0 | 52 7.0 | 51 7.1 | | | 31 11.8 | 33 10.7 |
| 17.2 | 8.4 | 8.1 | 12.0 | 33.0 | NM | | | 26.1 | 8.5 |
| 67.0 | 34.2 | 48.5 | 68.7 | -31.9 | -19.7 | | Sales/Working Capital | -243.3 | 34.8 |
| -52.8 | -39.0 | -23.2 | -17.0 | -11.0 | -6.9 | | | -16.0 | -17.1 |
| 28.0 | 24.7 | 21.5 | 14.0 | 7.6 | 7.2 | | | 16.1 | 11.3 |
| (187) 4.6 | (286) 4.9 | (246) 5.4 | (120) 5.6 | (58) 2.9 | (45) 3.4 | | EBIT/Interest | (1179) 4.7 | (764) 1.1 |
| -1.1 | .1 | 1.2 | 1.9 | .6 | .6 | | | .5 | -6.6 |
| | | 24.4 | 22.9 | 4.4 | 13.5 | | | 4.4 | 1.5 |
| | (16) 4.4 | (19) 6.2 | (22) 3.4 | (11) 5.5 | | | Net Profit + Depr., Dep., Amort./Cur. Mat. L/T/D | (63) 2.4 | (37) -.1 |
| | | .5 | 2.5 | .6 | 1.8 | | | 1.1 | -1.4 |
| .2 | .2 | .4 | .7 | 1.8 | 1.8 | | | .6 | .6 |
| 1.0 | .9 | 1.2 | 1.5 | 8.0 | -9.8 | | Fixed/Worth | 2.1 | 3.7 |
| -1.5 | UND | 26.8 | 8.8 | -4.2 | -.9 | | | -2.9 | -1.0 |
| .4 | .4 | .5 | .8 | 2.8 | 2.6 | | | .6 | 1.4 |
| 2.2 | 1.7 | 2.1 | 2.1 | 12.4 | -17.3 | | Debt/Worth | 3.2 | 11.6 |
| -3.3 | -18.4 | -146.5 | 17.1 | -8.6 | -3.3 | | | -5.1 | -3.1 |
| 217.5 | 93.4 | 77.4 | 55.7 | 64.9 | 45.1 | | | 130.9 | 85.2 |
| (261) 80.8 | (362) 41.1 | (241) 32.7 | (113) 24.4 | (36) 32.8 | (22) 16.5 | | % Profit Before Taxes/Tangible Net Worth | (1159) 49.8 | (646) 28.5 |
| 16.7 | 9.3 | 13.5 | 7.4 | 11.6 | 5.1 | | | 14.0 | -11.3 |
| 88.9 | 40.6 | 25.8 | 17.3 | 10.2 | 9.0 | | | 40.5 | 20.9 |
| 28.5 | 14.6 | 11.4 | 7.9 | 3.2 | 3.5 | | % Profit Before Taxes/Total Assets | 12.7 | 1.7 |
| -4.0 | .1 | 2.2 | 1.1 | -.9 | -1.0 | | | -.2 | -15.7 |
| 128.4 | 50.4 | 18.7 | 10.3 | 5.2 | 8.2 | | | 34.2 | 29.6 |
| 37.1 | 15.0 | 7.2 | 4.1 | 2.9 | 2.9 | | Sales/Net Fixed Assets | 9.4 | 8.7 |
| 12.2 | 5.8 | 3.0 | 2.4 | 2.2 | 1.7 | | | 3.7 | 3.2 |
| 11.6 | 4.6 | 3.0 | 2.4 | 1.6 | 1.4 | | | 6.8 | 4.1 |
| 7.1 | 3.1 | 1.8 | 1.7 | 1.3 | 1.0 | | Sales/Total Assets | 3.6 | 2.3 |
| 4.7 | 2.0 | 1.2 | 1.2 | 1.0 | .8 | | | 1.9 | 1.3 |
| .4 | .7 | 1.1 | 1.8 | 2.6 | 2.4 | | | 1.0 | 1.1 |
| (211) .9 | (265) 1.4 | (200) 2.1 | (110) 2.9 | (56) 3.3 | (30) 3.9 | | % Depr., Dep., Amort./Sales | (1205) 2.1 | (722) 2.6 |
| 2.2 | 2.8 | 4.0 | 4.1 | 4.8 | 6.1 | | | 3.8 | 4.6 |
| 2.2 | 2.2 | 1.3 | .5 | | | | | 1.9 | 2.1 |
| (183) 4.2 | (165) 3.6 | (88) 2.5 | (16) 1.1 | | | | % Officers', Directors' Owners' Comp/Sales | (636) 3.3 | (397) 4.1 |
| 7.4 | 6.3 | 5.5 | 3.6 | | | | | 5.7 | 7.0 |
| 813648M | 1834291M | 3211461M | 6249556M | 5942021M | 10704602M | | Net Sales ($) | 32997989M | 14049266M |
| 108112M | 528825M | 1404911M | 3566744M | 4348725M | 7423445M | | Total Assets ($) | 14492670M | 10154954M |

M = $ thousand    MM = $ million
See Pages viii through xx for Explanation of Ratios and Data

© RMA 2024

# RESTAURANT/LODGING—Full-Service Restaurants  NAICS 722511

## Comparative Historical Data | Current Data Sorted by Sales

| Comparative Historical Data | | | Type of Statement | Current Data Sorted by Sales | | | | | |
|---|---|---|---|---|---|---|---|---|---|
| 26 | 36 | 54 | Unqualified | 3 | 4 | 3 | 5 | 4 | 35 |
| 38 | 45 | 51 | Reviewed | | 7 | 2 | 3 | 10 | 29 |
| 63 | 81 | 63 | Compiled | | 8 | 14 | 13 | 12 | 16 |
| 324 | 523 | 492 | Tax Returns | 48 | 228 | 108 | 78 | 22 | 8 |
| 648 | 796 | 828 | Other | 65 | 280 | 138 | 119 | 81 | 145 |
| 4/1/21-3/31/22 ALL | 4/1/22-3/31/23 ALL | 4/1/23-3/31/24 ALL | | 91 (4/1-9/30/23) | | | 1,397 (10/1/23-3/31/24) | | |
| | | | | 0-1MM | 1-3MM | 3-5MM | 5-10MM | 10-25MM | 25MM & OVER |
| 1099 | 1481 | 1488 | NUMBER OF STATEMENTS | 116 | 527 | 265 | 218 | 129 | 233 |
| % | % | % | ASSETS | % | % | % | % | % | % |
| 37.0 | 32.2 | 27.7 | Cash & Equivalents | 31.4 | 32.6 | 29.6 | 27.6 | 23.7 | 14.6 |
| 1.5 | 2.0 | 1.9 | Trade Receivables (net) | 2.3 | 1.4 | 1.5 | 2.4 | 3.3 | 2.0 |
| 3.8 | 4.5 | 4.6 | Inventory | 4.7 | 5.4 | 5.2 | 4.2 | 4.5 | 2.8 |
| 4.4 | 4.6 | 4.0 | All Other Current | 4.1 | 3.8 | 4.5 | 4.6 | 4.2 | 3.4 |
| 46.6 | 43.2 | 38.3 | Total Current | 42.4 | 43.3 | 40.8 | 38.8 | 35.8 | 22.8 |
| 33.1 | 32.9 | 35.8 | Fixed Assets (net) | 37.3 | 34.1 | 31.4 | 34.6 | 39.1 | 43.3 |
| 10.4 | 8.8 | 10.3 | Intangibles (net) | 9.9 | 10.9 | 9.2 | 7.7 | 9.8 | 12.9 |
| 9.8 | 15.0 | 15.6 | All Other Non-Current | 10.3 | 11.7 | 18.6 | 18.8 | 15.3 | 21.0 |
| 100.0 | 100.0 | 100.0 | Total | 100.0 | 100.0 | 100.0 | 100.0 | 100.0 | 100.0 |
| | | | LIABILITIES | | | | | | |
| 4.6 | 3.7 | 3.8 | Notes Payable-Short Term | 7.4 | 4.5 | 6.0 | 1.4 | 1.7 | 1.5 |
| 2.8 | 2.3 | 2.4 | Cur. Mat.-L.T.D. | 1.1 | 2.5 | 1.5 | 2.0 | 2.5 | 4.2 |
| 5.8 | 5.4 | 5.4 | Trade Payables | 5.0 | 4.1 | 6.0 | 6.4 | 7.0 | 5.8 |
| .2 | .2 | .2 | Income Taxes Payable | .8 | .3 | .2 | .0 | .1 | .1 |
| 16.9 | 17.9 | 19.9 | All Other Current | 18.2 | 20.4 | 23.7 | 19.5 | 18.1 | 16.5 |
| 30.3 | 29.5 | 31.7 | Total Current | 32.4 | 31.8 | 37.4 | 29.2 | 29.4 | 28.1 |
| 37.9 | 34.9 | 33.1 | Long-Term Debt | 47.0 | 36.9 | 30.1 | 26.6 | 24.8 | 31.5 |
| .0 | .0 | .0 | Deferred Taxes | .0 | .0 | .0 | .0 | .0 | .1 |
| 10.9 | 9.5 | 11.0 | All Other Non-Current | 28.6 | 8.2 | 8.8 | 5.2 | 8.6 | 17.9 |
| 20.8 | 26.1 | 24.2 | Net Worth | -8.1 | 23.0 | 23.7 | 38.9 | 37.3 | 22.4 |
| 100.0 | 100.0 | 100.0 | Total Liabilities & Net Worth | 100.0 | 100.0 | 100.0 | 100.0 | 100.0 | 100.0 |
| | | | INCOME DATA | | | | | | |
| 100.0 | 100.0 | 100.0 | Net Sales | 100.0 | 100.0 | 100.0 | 100.0 | 100.0 | 100.0 |
| 62.0 | 60.1 | 62.4 | Gross Profit | 64.2 | 62.5 | 61.6 | 61.3 | 64.5 | 62.0 |
| 53.8 | 55.2 | 57.0 | Operating Expenses | 61.9 | 58.0 | 55.4 | 53.2 | 57.1 | 57.6 |
| 8.2 | 4.9 | 5.4 | Operating Profit | 2.4 | 4.5 | 6.2 | 8.1 | 7.4 | 4.4 |
| -2.3 | -.9 | .2 | All Other Expenses (net) | .4 | .2 | .2 | .1 | -.7 | .4 |
| 10.5 | 5.8 | 5.3 | Profit Before Taxes | 1.9 | 4.3 | 6.0 | 8.0 | 8.1 | 4.0 |
| | | | RATIOS | | | | | | |
| 6.2 | 4.6 | 3.7 | | 5.4 | 5.7 | 3.4 | 4.0 | 2.3 | 1.5 |
| 2.1 | 1.9 | 1.4 | Current | 1.7 | 1.8 | 1.2 | 1.6 | 1.2 | .9 |
| .9 | .8 | .6 | | .5 | .7 | .6 | .7 | .7 | .5 |
| | | | | | | | | | |
| 5.2 | 3.8 | 2.7 | | 2.9 | 4.7 | 2.2 | 2.7 | 1.8 | 1.1 |
| (1098) 1.7 | (1479) 1.4 | (1484) 1.0 | Quick | (525) .9 | (264) 1.3 | .9 | 1.3 | (232) 1.0 | .6 |
| .6 | .5 | .4 | | .4 | .3 | .3 | .5 | .4 | .3 |
| | | | | | | | | | |
| 0 UND | 0 UND | 0 UND | | 0 UND | 0 UND | 0 UND | 0 UND | 0 UND | 0 UND |
| 0 UND | 0 UND | 0 UND | Sales/Receivables | 0 UND | 0 UND | 0 UND | 0 UND | 824.8 | 1 259.5 |
| 1 354.8 | 1 318.6 | 1 271.6 | | 0 UND | 0 UND | 999.8 | 2 174.8 | 5 71.0 | 5 66.7 |
| | | | | | | | | | |
| 4 98.0 | 3 111.4 | 4 99.4 | | 0 UND | 3 120.0 | 3 129.7 | 2 161.0 | 7 51.9 | 7 52.7 |
| 9 41.9 | 8 45.3 | 9 42.8 | Cost of Sales/Inventory | 6 60.7 | 8 47.7 | 8 46.6 | 7 48.7 | 10 34.9 | 11 32.0 |
| 16 23.4 | 15 24.4 | 15 23.9 | | 22 16.5 | 14 26.8 | 14 26.5 | 14 25.6 | 20 18.6 | 18 19.8 |
| | | | | | | | | | |
| 0 UND | 0 UND | 0 UND | | 0 UND | 0 UND | 0 UND | 0 UND | 10 36.9 | 13 29.0 |
| 12 29.5 | 9 42.4 | 9 39.8 | Cost of Sales/Payables | 0 UND | 2 241.2 | 6 56.4 | 12 31.5 | 18 20.5 | 27 13.7 |
| 30 12.1 | 25 14.6 | 27 13.6 | | 13 28.5 | 15 23.6 | 24 15.0 | 30 12.3 | 37 9.9 | 46 8.0 |
| | | | | | | | | | |
| 5.6 | 7.9 | 11.6 | | 6.8 | 8.8 | 13.7 | 10.4 | 12.9 | 21.6 |
| 16.0 | 25.1 | 57.8 | Sales/Working Capital | 50.9 | 38.8 | 74.5 | 37.2 | 63.9 | -65.7 |
| -123.1 | -70.4 | -27.9 | | -30.5 | -39.7 | -25.8 | -50.8 | -30.5 | -12.7 |
| | | | | | | | | | |
| 45.2 | 28.1 | 19.9 | | 7.4 | 17.1 | 20.4 | 52.4 | 38.9 | 11.2 |
| (701) 13.4 | (883) 7.5 | (942) 4.9 | EBIT/Interest | (56) 1.8 | (297) 3.7 | (150) 5.6 | (127) 8.3 | (104) 11.2 | (208) 4.5 |
| 3.6 | .2 | .5 | | -3.3 | -.8 | 1.2 | 2.3 | 3.4 | .7 |
| | | | | | | | | | |
| 31.8 | 11.3 | 12.9 | Net Profit + Depr., Dep., | | | | | | 13.0 |
| (32) 5.0 | (59) 5.1 | (79) 3.7 | Amort./Cur. Mat. L/T/D | | | | | (50) | 3.5 |
| 1.5 | 1.3 | 1.0 | | | | | | | 1.0 |
| | | | | | | | | | |
| .3 | .2 | .3 | | .2 | .2 | .2 | .2 | .6 | 1.2 |
| 1.3 | 1.1 | 1.3 | Fixed/Worth | 2.7 | 1.1 | 1.0 | .7 | 1.2 | 3.7 |
| -5.2 | UND | -7.5 | | -1.4 | -7.1 | -7.7 | 6.7 | 4.2 | -3.9 |
| | | | | | | | | | |
| .6 | .4 | .5 | | .5 | .4 | .6 | .3 | .6 | 1.4 |
| 2.6 | 1.9 | 2.3 | Debt/Worth | 5.8 | 2.2 | 2.2 | .9 | 1.5 | 6.2 |
| -7.5 | -21.8 | -9.4 | | -2.8 | -7.7 | -10.1 | 11.6 | 8.1 | -8.0 |
| | | | | | | | | | |
| 157.3 | 102.9 | 105.3 | | 89.2 | 106.5 | 162.1 | 102.0 | 119.0 | 64.7 |
| (758) 70.8 | (1078) 40.5 | (1035) 39.8 | % Profit Before Taxes/Tangible Net Worth | (65) 45.5 | (359) 39.3 | (184) 51.8 | (168) 46.0 | (105) 45.6 | (154) 26.5 |
| 27.7 | 10.7 | 9.2 | | 9.0 | 4.5 | 14.6 | 16.3 | 14.1 | 7.8 |
| | | | | | | | | | |
| 51.3 | 40.1 | 36.4 | % Profit Before Taxes/Total Assets | 36.3 | 39.8 | 49.0 | 53.8 | 40.3 | 12.8 |
| 24.0 | 13.9 | 12.3 | | 7.8 | 11.9 | 17.3 | 23.1 | 16.2 | 5.9 |
| 7.3 | .6 | .1 | | -16.9 | -2.5 | 2.2 | 6.3 | 5.2 | -.7 |
| | | | | | | | | | |
| 42.1 | 54.3 | 43.6 | | 54.8 | 69.9 | 63.0 | 44.7 | 21.4 | 9.3 |
| 10.6 | 13.4 | 11.7 | Sales/Net Fixed Assets | 13.7 | 17.5 | 20.5 | 14.4 | 8.8 | 4.1 |
| 3.9 | 4.6 | 4.2 | | 4.3 | 6.1 | 7.1 | 5.1 | 3.7 | 2.5 |
| | | | | | | | | | |
| 4.3 | 5.4 | 5.5 | | 5.8 | 6.5 | 6.9 | 5.2 | 4.6 | 2.6 |
| 2.5 | 2.9 | 3.0 | Sales/Total Assets | 3.0 | 3.6 | 3.9 | 3.0 | 2.7 | 1.6 |
| 1.5 | 1.6 | 1.6 | | 1.3 | 2.0 | 1.9 | 1.8 | 1.4 | 1.1 |
| | | | | | | | | | |
| .9 | .8 | .9 | | .6 | .5 | .7 | 1.0 | 2.0 | |
| (623) 2.0 | (840) 1.7 | (872) 1.9 | % Depr., Dep., Amort./Sales | (59) 2.3 | (270) 1.3 | (153) 1.2 | (115) 1.6 | (91) 2.3 | (184) 3.1 |
| 3.6 | 3.4 | 3.4 | | 4.0 | 2.8 | 2.5 | 3.2 | 3.5 | 4.4 |
| | | | | | | | | | |
| 1.9 | 2.0 | 1.8 | % Officers', Directors' Owners' Comp/Sales | 5.6 | 2.7 | 1.6 | 1.3 | .8 | .5 |
| (344) 3.6 | (535) 3.8 | (456) 3.6 | | (33) 7.8 | (209) 4.3 | (94) 2.6 | (73) 2.3 | (26) 2.3 | (21) 1.2 |
| 6.4 | 6.7 | 6.5 | | 13.7 | 7.4 | 4.6 | 4.4 | 4.2 | 4.5 |
| | | | | | | | | | |
| 18637167M | 24963496M | 28755579M | Net Sales ($) | 74562M | 1046510M | 1017712M | 1547181M | 2077051M | 22992563M |
| 10174269M | 13716522M | 17380762M | Total Assets ($) | 41438M | 406758M | 396056M | 627443M | 1185543M | 14723524M |

© RMA 2024  M = $ thousand  MM = $ million
See Pages viii through xx for Explanation of Ratios and Data

# RESTAURANT/LODGING—Limited-Service Restaurants  NAICS 722513

## Current Data Sorted by Assets | Comparative Historical Data

| 0-500M | 500M-2MM | 2-10MM | 10-50MM | 50-100MM | 100-250MM | | | | |
|---|---|---|---|---|---|---|---|---|---|
| | | | | | | **Type of Statement** | | | |
| 1 | 1 | 4 | 24 | 17 | 46 | Unqualified | | 61 | 64 |
| 8 | 18 | 13 | 47 | 9 | 3 | Reviewed | | 54 | 27 |
| 26 | 92 | 160 | 121 | 9 | 1 | Compiled | | 534 | 360 |
| 106 | 107 | 44 | 9 | 1 | 1 | Tax Returns | | 375 | 215 |
| 132 | 221 | 229 | 168 | 71 | 62 | Other | | 944 | 693 |
| | 185 (4/1-9/30/23) | | 1,566 (10/1/23-3/31/24) | | | | | 4/1/19-3/31/20 ALL | 4/1/20-3/31/21 ALL |
| 273 | 439 | 450 | 369 | 107 | 113 | **NUMBER OF STATEMENTS** | | 1968 | 1359 |
| % | % | % | % | % | % | **ASSETS** | | % | % |
| 32.6 | 24.3 | 23.5 | 17.8 | 9.5 | 6.1 | Cash & Equivalents | | 19.9 | 31.0 |
| 2.0 | 1.9 | 1.9 | 2.3 | 1.9 | 1.5 | Trade Receivables (net) | | 1.4 | 1.4 |
| 4.6 | 2.9 | 2.4 | 2.0 | 1.3 | 1.3 | Inventory | | 3.2 | 2.4 |
| 4.4 | 4.5 | 2.4 | 3.4 | 2.4 | 1.6 | All Other Current | | 2.0 | 2.1 |
| 43.6 | 33.5 | 30.1 | 25.4 | 15.1 | 10.5 | Total Current | | 26.5 | 36.9 |
| 28.7 | 33.5 | 33.4 | 31.6 | 37.9 | 47.2 | Fixed Assets (net) | | 42.1 | 35.1 |
| 17.3 | 19.1 | 28.1 | 30.5 | 25.7 | 21.4 | Intangibles (net) | | 23.0 | 20.9 |
| 10.5 | 13.9 | 8.4 | 12.4 | 21.3 | 20.9 | All Other Non-Current | | 8.4 | 7.1 |
| 100.0 | 100.0 | 100.0 | 100.0 | 100.0 | 100.0 | Total | | 100.0 | 100.0 |
| | | | | | | **LIABILITIES** | | | |
| 6.7 | 1.8 | 1.5 | 1.5 | .9 | .5 | Notes Payable-Short Term | | 3.1 | 3.8 |
| 4.9 | 4.0 | 6.4 | 7.5 | 9.1 | 4.6 | Cur. Mat.-L.T.D. | | 7.0 | 6.2 |
| 7.1 | 4.7 | 4.3 | 4.5 | 3.9 | 3.3 | Trade Payables | | 6.1 | 4.4 |
| .1 | .2 | .1 | .0 | .0 | .0 | Income Taxes Payable | | .1 | .2 |
| 30.0 | 14.1 | 11.6 | 10.4 | 9.9 | 7.8 | All Other Current | | 17.2 | 13.6 |
| 48.8 | 24.9 | 23.9 | 23.9 | 23.8 | 16.3 | Total Current | | 33.4 | 28.2 |
| 42.9 | 36.7 | 39.1 | 46.3 | 47.5 | 54.9 | Long-Term Debt | | 43.1 | 46.6 |
| .0 | .0 | .0 | .0 | .1 | .0 | Deferred Taxes | | .1 | .1 |
| 12.7 | 10.7 | 5.6 | 6.5 | 13.8 | 20.1 | All Other Non-Current | | 8.2 | 9.3 |
| -4.5 | 27.8 | 31.4 | 23.3 | 14.9 | 8.8 | Net Worth | | 15.2 | 15.9 |
| 100.0 | 100.0 | 100.0 | 100.0 | 100.0 | 100.0 | Total Liabilities & Net Worth | | 100.0 | 100.0 |
| | | | | | | **INCOME DATA** | | | |
| 100.0 | 100.0 | 100.0 | 100.0 | 100.0 | 100.0 | Net Sales | | 100.0 | 100.0 |
| 57.6 | 58.5 | 63.7 | 64.5 | 62.8 | 59.1 | Gross Profit | | 64.7 | 64.6 |
| 52.8 | 53.2 | 58.3 | 58.3 | 58.4 | 54.4 | Operating Expenses | | 58.9 | 58.8 |
| 4.8 | 5.3 | 5.4 | 6.1 | 4.4 | 4.7 | Operating Profit | | 5.8 | 5.9 |
| .0 | .4 | .8 | 1.2 | 1.4 | 1.6 | All Other Expenses (net) | | 1.0 | -.4 |
| 4.7 | 4.9 | 4.6 | 4.9 | 3.1 | 3.1 | Profit Before Taxes | | 4.8 | 6.3 |
| | | | | | | **RATIOS** | | | |
| 3.6 | 3.2 | 2.5 | 1.7 | 1.1 | .8 | | | 1.8 | 2.8 |
| 1.5 | 1.4 | 1.2 | 1.0 | .6 | .5 | Current | | .9 | 1.4 |
| .5 | .6 | .6 | .6 | .3 | .3 | | | .4 | .8 |
| 3.1 | 2.4 | 2.1 | 1.4 | .9 | .6 | | | 1.4 | 2.4 |
| 1.1 | 1.1 | 1.0 | .8 | .4 | .3 | Quick | | .7 | 1.3 |
| .3 | .4 | .5 | .4 | .2 | .2 | | | .3 | .7 |
| 0 UND | 0 UND | 0 UND | 0 UND | 1 572.3 | 0 999.8 | | | 0 UND | 0 UND |
| 0 UND | 0 UND | 0 851.0 | 1 436.6 | 2 180.1 | 2 168.8 | Sales/Receivables | | 0 999.8 | 0 UND |
| 1 565.8 | 2 169.9 | 3 118.0 | 4 92.3 | 5 67.4 | 4 86.1 | | | 1 381.4 | 1 282.5 |
| 1 248.1 | 3 109.3 | 6 65.3 | 6 61.5 | 5 70.1 | 5 75.3 | | | 6 65.8 | 5 72.1 |
| 5 78.5 | 6 57.5 | 8 44.1 | 8 43.9 | 7 49.5 | 7 54.4 | Cost of Sales/Inventory | | 8 43.7 | 8 44.2 |
| 9 39.3 | 10 38.0 | 11 34.5 | 10 35.3 | 10 34.8 | 9 39.1 | | | 11 34.4 | 11 33.4 |
| 0 UND | 1 713.0 | 3 108.0 | 8 47.1 | 8 46.5 | 10 35.5 | | | 2 147.1 | 1 268.8 |
| 2 210.2 | 5 68.9 | 12 31.7 | 17 21.6 | 21 17.0 | 24 15.1 | Cost of Sales/Payables | | 14 26.9 | 12 30.3 |
| 10 34.9 | 17 21.4 | 23 16.0 | 34 10.6 | 41 8.8 | 44 8.3 | | | 27 13.5 | 28 13.1 |
| 15.4 | 12.1 | 13.4 | 17.7 | 156.2 | -58.4 | | | 29.8 | 10.5 |
| 69.9 | 50.7 | 72.8 | 237.5 | -21.2 | -15.7 | Sales/Working Capital | | -145.5 | 28.7 |
| -31.2 | -33.0 | -27.4 | -19.2 | -8.6 | -9.6 | | | -17.7 | -54.4 |
| 25.2 | 19.4 | 13.5 | 10.2 | 7.3 | 4.2 | | | 11.8 | 18.9 |
| (150) 5.4 | (310) 5.0 | (391) 4.6 | (344) 4.3 | (103) 2.8 | (108) 1.8 | EBIT/Interest | (1659) | 4.7 (1118) | 7.0 |
| -.2 | .7 | 1.6 | 1.6 | 1.0 | .8 | | | 1.6 | 2.5 |
| | 11.4 | 3.9 | 4.6 | 5.3 | 2.1 | | | 5.0 | 5.2 |
| (12) | 2.8 (28) | 2.4 (39) | 3.0 (23) | 1.8 (18) | 1.2 | Net Profit + Depr., Dep., Amort./Cur. Mat. L/T/D | (103) | 2.4 (61) | 2.6 |
| | 1.0 | 1.4 | 1.3 | 1.0 | .8 | | | 1.6 | 1.2 |
| .2 | .3 | .7 | 1.1 | 2.5 | 7.0 | | | 1.1 | .9 |
| 1.4 | 1.6 | 4.0 | -14.3 | -6.1 | -7.3 | Fixed/Worth | | 37.5 | 8.9 |
| -.6 | -2.0 | -.6 | -.5 | -.8 | -1.1 | | | -.9 | -1.0 |
| .7 | .5 | 1.1 | 1.9 | 3.7 | 14.8 | | | 1.5 | 1.7 |
| 14.8 | 3.2 | 8.0 | -13.1 | -8.3 | -11.5 | Debt/Worth | | UND | 28.7 |
| -2.1 | -4.6 | -2.6 | -2.1 | -2.8 | -3.7 | | | -2.5 | -3.1 |
| 295.4 | 127.0 | 85.6 | 70.7 | 68.7 | 75.5 | | | 146.9 | 159.5 |
| (148) 95.9 | (280) 51.0 | (257) 35.9 | (171) 30.5 | (42) 34.7 | (43) 15.4 | % Profit Before Taxes/Tangible Net Worth | (985) | 53.7 (718) | 68.9 |
| 29.4 | 16.7 | 9.1 | 16.7 | 12.3 | 2.0 | | | 21.2 | 24.4 |
| 70.8 | 34.4 | 20.7 | 16.8 | 11.9 | 7.7 | | | 26.2 | 31.0 |
| 25.7 | 13.3 | 9.9 | 8.4 | 4.0 | 2.2 | % Profit Before Taxes/Total Assets | | 11.5 | 14.4 |
| -1.4 | .7 | 1.7 | 2.8 | .1 | -.3 | | | 2.2 | 3.9 |
| 192.9 | 41.1 | 28.3 | 22.7 | 8.6 | 4.6 | | | 18.4 | 23.8 |
| 27.1 | 13.6 | 12.0 | 9.3 | 4.5 | 2.7 | Sales/Net Fixed Assets | | 8.7 | 8.7 |
| 11.1 | 5.1 | 4.7 | 3.5 | 2.6 | 1.3 | | | 4.2 | 3.8 |
| 8.7 | 4.8 | 3.9 | 2.8 | 1.9 | 1.3 | | | 4.9 | 3.8 |
| 5.7 | 2.9 | 2.6 | 2.0 | 1.3 | .9 | Sales/Total Assets | | 2.9 | 2.4 |
| 3.5 | 1.7 | 1.5 | 1.4 | .9 | .7 | | | 1.9 | 1.5 |
| .5 | .9 | 1.6 | 2.1 | 2.7 | 3.6 | | | 2.0 | 1.9 |
| (152) 1.2 | (286) 2.0 | (291) 2.8 | (262) 3.4 | (95) 3.6 | (70) 4.9 | % Depr., Dep., Amort./Sales | (1466) | 3.3 (969) | 3.3 |
| 2.3 | 3.6 | 4.4 | 4.7 | 5.3 | 6.3 | | | 5.0 | 5.1 |
| 2.2 | 1.5 | .6 | .4 | .2 | | | | .9 | .9 |
| (107) 4.0 | (150) 2.9 | (152) 1.2 | (116) .6 | (15) 1.3 | | % Officers', Directors' Owners' Comp/Sales | (656) | 2.1 (453) | 2.0 |
| 8.9 | 4.7 | 2.2 | 1.6 | 5.2 | | | | 4.2 | 4.5 |
| 443775M | 1677352M | 6747001M | 18893480M | 12851950M | 24777895M | Net Sales ($) | | 52820651M | 37353055M |
| 73656M | 468602M | 2304373M | 8872760M | 7689488M | 17683326M | Total Assets ($) | | 25150135M | 21145161M |

M = $ thousand    MM = $ million
See Pages viii through xx for Explanation of Ratios and Data

© RMA 2024

# RESTAURANT/LODGING—Limited-Service Restaurants  NAICS 722513

## Comparative Historical Data | Current Data Sorted by Sales

| Comparative Historical Data | | | Type of Statement | Current Data Sorted by Sales | | | | | |
|---|---|---|---|---|---|---|---|---|---|
| 66 | 67 | 93 | Unqualified | 1 | 3 | | 2 | 6 | 81 |
| 45 | 49 | 98 | Reviewed | 7 | 21 | 1 | 5 | 16 | 48 |
| 267 | 353 | 409 | Compiled | 5 | 40 | 64 | 63 | 102 | 135 |
| 199 | 246 | 268 | Tax Returns | 41 | 111 | 52 | 25 | 24 | 15 |
| 773 | 759 | 883 | Other | 77 | 214 | 77 | 69 | 127 | 319 |
| 4/1/21-3/31/22 ALL | 4/1/22-3/31/23 ALL | 4/1/23-3/31/24 ALL | | 185 (4/1-9/30/23) | | | 1,566 (10/1/23-3/31/24) | | |
| | | | | 0-1MM | 1-3MM | 3-5MM | 5-10MM | 10-25MM | 25MM & OVER |
| 1350 | 1474 | 1751 | NUMBER OF STATEMENTS | 131 | 389 | 194 | 164 | 275 | 598 |
| % | % | % | ASSETS | % | % | % | % | % | % |
| 28.3 | 24.3 | 21.9 | Cash & Equivalents | 24.4 | 23.1 | 27.2 | 25.0 | 25.3 | 16.5 |
| 2.1 | 2.3 | 2.0 | Trade Receivables (net) | 1.6 | 1.6 | 2.0 | 1.9 | 1.9 | 2.3 |
| 2.6 | 2.8 | 2.6 | Inventory | 3.0 | 2.9 | 2.9 | 3.1 | 2.9 | 2.1 |
| 4.0 | 4.2 | 3.4 | All Other Current | 4.5 | 4.2 | 3.6 | 3.7 | 3.2 | 2.5 |
| 36.9 | 33.7 | 29.9 | Total Current | 33.5 | 31.8 | 35.6 | 33.7 | 33.3 | 23.4 |
| 32.5 | 31.0 | 33.4 | Fixed Assets (net) | 32.5 | 35.2 | 33.0 | 30.2 | 28.4 | 35.9 |
| 22.2 | 23.3 | 24.1 | Intangibles (net) | 22.1 | 17.7 | 22.6 | 26.2 | 27.7 | 26.9 |
| 8.3 | 12.1 | 12.6 | All Other Non-Current | 11.8 | 15.3 | 8.8 | 9.9 | 10.6 | 13.8 |
| 100.0 | 100.0 | 100.0 | Total | 100.0 | 100.0 | 100.0 | 100.0 | 100.0 | 100.0 |
| | | | LIABILITIES | | | | | | |
| 2.2 | 2.6 | 2.3 | Notes Payable-Short Term | 10.6 | 1.6 | 1.9 | 1.8 | 2.1 | 1.2 |
| 5.7 | 5.5 | 5.8 | Cur. Mat.-L.T.D. | 4.4 | 3.6 | 5.1 | 6.3 | 6.4 | 7.5 |
| 4.5 | 4.4 | 4.8 | Trade Payables | 2.0 | 4.4 | 5.7 | 5.4 | 5.8 | 4.7 |
| .1 | .1 | .1 | Income Taxes Payable | .1 | .1 | .3 | .1 | .2 | .0 |
| 13.0 | 13.0 | 14.5 | All Other Current | 20.0 | 20.2 | 15.2 | 11.1 | 14.1 | 10.5 |
| 25.5 | 25.6 | 27.5 | Total Current | 37.1 | 30.0 | 28.2 | 24.7 | 28.4 | 24.0 |
| 42.8 | 41.8 | 42.1 | Long-Term Debt | 51.7 | 41.3 | 33.2 | 33.3 | 39.3 | 47.3 |
| .1 | .0 | .0 | Deferred Taxes | .0 | .0 | .0 | .0 | .0 | .0 |
| 6.3 | 8.4 | 9.6 | All Other Non-Current | 16.4 | 12.4 | 4.8 | 9.4 | 6.0 | 9.6 |
| 25.3 | 24.1 | 20.7 | Net Worth | -5.2 | 16.4 | 33.8 | 32.6 | 26.3 | 19.2 |
| 100.0 | 100.0 | 100.0 | Total Liabilities & Net Worth | 100.0 | 100.0 | 100.0 | 100.0 | 100.0 | 100.0 |
| | | | INCOME DATA | | | | | | |
| 100.0 | 100.0 | 100.0 | Net Sales | 100.0 | 100.0 | 100.0 | 100.0 | 100.0 | 100.0 |
| 63.5 | 60.5 | 61.2 | Gross Profit | 57.6 | 56.8 | 62.4 | 63.4 | 63.6 | 62.9 |
| 56.0 | 56.0 | 55.9 | Operating Expenses | 56.3 | 51.0 | 55.3 | 55.7 | 58.7 | 58.0 |
| 7.5 | 4.4 | 5.3 | Operating Profit | 1.3 | 5.8 | 7.1 | 7.7 | 4.8 | 4.9 |
| -2.2 | .0 | .8 | All Other Expenses (net) | .9 | 1.1 | .4 | .6 | .2 | .9 |
| 9.7 | 4.4 | 4.6 | Profit Before Taxes | .4 | 4.7 | 6.7 | 7.0 | 4.6 | 4.1 |
| | | | RATIOS | | | | | | |
| 3.2 | 2.9 | 2.4 | | 6.0 | 3.1 | 2.9 | 2.5 | 2.4 | 1.5 |
| 1.6 | 1.4 | 1.1 | Current | 1.4 | 1.4 | 1.2 | 1.3 | 1.3 | .8 |
| .8 | .6 | .5 | | .4 | .4 | .6 | .6 | .7 | .5 |
| 2.7 | 2.3 | 1.8 | | 5.7 | 2.4 | 2.5 | 2.0 | 2.0 | 1.3 |
| 1.3 | 1.0 | .8 | Quick | .9 | 1.1 | 1.0 | 1.0 | 1.0 | .6 |
| .6 | .4 | .3 | | .2 | .3 | .4 | .4 | .5 | .3 |
| 0 UND | 0 UND | 0 UND | | 0 UND | 0 UND | 0 UND | 0 UND | 0 UND | 0 999.8 |
| 0 999.8 | 0 999.8 | 0 999.8 | Sales/Receivables | 0 UND | 0 UND | 0 UND | 0 999.8 | 1 635.8 | 1 291.5 |
| 2 183.1 | 3 131.7 | 3 118.5 | | 0 UND | 1 287.2 | 2 199.4 | 3 118.5 | 3 106.0 | 4 87.7 |
| 5 71.0 | 4 87.6 | 4 84.4 | | 0 UND | 2 147.3 | 4 89.4 | 5 72.2 | 6 59.9 | 6 64.2 |
| 8 43.7 | 8 47.1 | 7 49.5 | Cost of Sales/Inventory | 5 68.6 | 5 77.5 | 7 52.8 | 8 47.3 | 8 44.3 | 8 46.0 |
| 11 33.0 | 11 34.6 | 10 35.8 | | 15 25.1 | 10 38.1 | 9 38.5 | 10 35.5 | 11 34.5 | 10 35.8 |
| 2 214.1 | 1 308.6 | 2 164.3 | | 0 UND | 0 UND | 1 322.3 | 3 110.6 | 4 95.7 | 9 41.3 |
| 12 29.4 | 10 38.2 | 11 34.7 | Cost of Sales/Payables | 0 UND | 4 82.9 | 6 60.7 | 12 30.6 | 11 32.7 | 18 20.5 |
| 27 13.7 | 24 15.0 | 25 14.5 | | 7 56.1 | 15 25.1 | 22 16.6 | 25 14.5 | 27 13.7 | 36 10.1 |
| 9.1 | 11.9 | 15.6 | | 10.3 | 13.6 | 13.6 | 13.3 | 13.4 | 26.2 |
| 24.6 | 51.7 | 179.1 | Sales/Working Capital | 57.9 | 69.9 | 89.7 | 61.1 | 46.2 | -70.9 |
| -58.1 | -27.9 | -19.3 | | -16.5 | -18.3 | -38.9 | -31.5 | -34.4 | -15.6 |
| 33.6 | 13.6 | 11.5 | | 5.8 | 16.8 | 19.1 | 19.1 | 13.0 | 9.1 |
| (1128) 12.1 | (1180) 4.7 | (1406) 4.2 | EBIT/Interest | (86) 1.3 | (253) 4.3 | (125) 4.1 | (136) 5.5 | (245) 5.1 | (561) 3.9 |
| 4.7 | 1.1 | 1.2 | | -4.7 | .2 | 1.5 | 2.2 | 1.5 | 1.4 |
| | 11.8 | 4.2 | Net Profit + Depr., Dep., | | | 1.8 | 5.7 | | 4.6 |
| (75) 5.2 | (100) 2.5 | (122) 2.0 | Amort./Cur. Mat. L/T/D | | (10) 1.1 | | (20) 3.3 | (75) 1.9 |
| 3.1 | 1.3 | 1.1 | | | .6 | | 1.7 | 1.1 |
| .6 | .5 | .6 | | .3 | .4 | .3 | .3 | .7 | 1.6 |
| 2.7 | 3.2 | 5.2 | Fixed/Worth | 26.9 | 2.0 | 1.5 | 1.5 | 3.4 | -7.6 |
| -1.1 | -.8 | -.7 | | -.5 | -1.1 | -2.1 | -.8 | -.6 | -.7 |
| 1.0 | .9 | 1.1 | | 2.0 | .6 | .5 | .7 | 1.2 | 2.5 |
| 5.2 | 8.8 | 18.1 | Debt/Worth | -15.2 | 5.5 | 2.8 | 2.7 | 9.7 | -13.2 |
| -3.3 | -2.8 | -2.7 | | -2.0 | -2.8 | -3.7 | -2.6 | -2.6 | -2.7 |
| 152.6 | 88.0 | 112.1 | | 106.5 | 127.3 | 188.5 | 125.7 | 94.9 | 75.3 |
| (794) 79.7 | (832) 35.6 | (941) 43.1 | % Profit Before Taxes/Tangible Net Worth | (61) 25.4 | (226) 46.5 | (126) 62.1 | (106) 45.7 | (156) 47.8 | (266) 36.7 |
| 38.8 | 10.2 | 13.8 | | -6.1 | 12.9 | 20.3 | 16.0 | 17.4 | 12.5 |
| 44.4 | 24.1 | 26.1 | | 19.3 | 34.3 | 40.2 | 38.9 | 24.9 | 16.6 |
| 22.0 | 9.3 | 9.6 | % Profit Before Taxes/Total Assets | 1.8 | 12.1 | 14.9 | 14.3 | 10.0 | 7.6 |
| 9.2 | .7 | 1.0 | | -11.9 | -.8 | 4.8 | 4.4 | 2.5 | 1.2 |
| 25.4 | 31.4 | 30.4 | | 65.8 | 36.4 | 53.6 | 53.6 | 37.9 | 17.6 |
| 10.0 | 11.2 | 11.0 | Sales/Net Fixed Assets | 11.1 | 11.7 | 14.8 | 16.4 | 15.8 | 7.5 |
| 4.7 | 4.8 | 4.1 | | 3.3 | 4.5 | 5.5 | 5.7 | 6.2 | 3.1 |
| 3.8 | 4.1 | 4.2 | | 4.2 | 5.1 | 6.0 | 4.7 | 4.7 | 3.1 |
| 2.5 | 2.5 | 2.5 | Sales/Total Assets | 2.1 | 2.8 | 3.4 | 2.8 | 2.8 | 2.0 |
| 1.6 | 1.5 | 1.4 | | 1.3 | 1.5 | 1.6 | 1.7 | 1.7 | 1.2 |
| 1.6 | 1.3 | 1.4 | | 1.6 | .9 | .8 | 1.0 | 1.5 | 2.1 |
| (922) 2.9 | (975) 2.6 | (1156) 2.7 | % Depr., Dep., Amort./Sales | (68) 2.8 | (256) 1.9 | (128) 2.0 | (101) 2.2 | (169) 2.7 | (434) 3.4 |
| 4.7 | 4.3 | 4.4 | | 6.3 | 4.0 | 3.6 | 3.7 | 4.4 | 4.9 |
| 1.0 | .9 | .7 | | 2.7 | 2.2 | 1.3 | .9 | .6 | .3 |
| (461) 2.0 | (503) 2.0 | (548) 1.8 | % Officers', Directors' Owners' Comp/Sales | (50) 4.4 | (122) 3.5 | (68) 2.9 | (62) 1.7 | (90) 1.2 | (156) .6 |
| 4.3 | 4.3 | 4.0 | | 10.3 | 6.0 | 4.6 | 2.7 | 1.9 | 1.6 |
| 44542072M | 48149051M | 65391453M | Net Sales ($) | 89033M | 723309M | 749350M | 1205591M | 4566477M | 58057693M |
| 23994861M | 28438107M | 37092205M | Total Assets ($) | 58722M | 417320M | 315094M | 604086M | 2112409M | 33584574M |

© RMA 2024  M = $ thousand   MM = $ million
See Pages viii through xx for Explanation of Ratios and Data

# RESTAURANT/LODGING—Snack and Nonalcoholic Beverage Bars  NAICS 722515

## Current Data Sorted by Assets

| | | | | | | Type of Statement | | |
|---|---|---|---|---|---|---|---|---|
| | | | | 1 | 2 | Unqualified | | |
| | | | 1 | | | Reviewed | | |
| 2 | 1 | 2 | 1 | | | Compiled | | |
| 35 | 13 | 5 | | | | Tax Returns | | |
| 34 | 26 | 24 | | | 4 | Other | | |
| | 7 (4/1-9/30/23) | | 3 | | | | | |
| | | | 147 (10/1/23-3/31/24) | | | | | |
| 0-500M | 500M-2MM | 2-10MM | 10-50MM | 50-100MM | 100-250MM | | | |
| 71 | 40 | 31 | 5 | 1 | 6 | NUMBER OF STATEMENTS | | |

## Comparative Historical Data

| | | | |
|---|---|---|---|
| | 2 | 1 | |
| | 4 | 2 | |
| | 6 | 3 | |
| | 40 | 21 | |
| | 79 | 40 | |
| | 4/1/19-3/31/20 ALL | 4/1/20-3/31/21 ALL | |
| | 131 | 67 | |

| Current | | | | | | | Historical | |
|---|---|---|---|---|---|---|---|---|
| % | % | % | % | % | % | **ASSETS** | % | % |
| 32.5 | 20.9 | 9.8 | | | | Cash & Equivalents | 18.0 | 29.6 |
| 2.3 | .6 | 1.4 | | | | Trade Receivables (net) | 1.6 | 1.0 |
| 4.7 | 2.5 | 3.1 | | | | Inventory | 4.9 | 3.5 |
| 5.4 | 3.0 | 5.5 | | | | All Other Current | 2.3 | 2.0 |
| 44.9 | 27.1 | 19.9 | | | | Total Current | 26.8 | 36.1 |
| 35.8 | 51.7 | 30.0 | | | | Fixed Assets (net) | 41.6 | 43.2 |
| 12.0 | 12.5 | 11.2 | | | | Intangibles (net) | 17.7 | 15.7 |
| 7.4 | 8.7 | 38.8 | | | | All Other Non-Current | 13.9 | 4.9 |
| 100.0 | 100.0 | 100.0 | | | | Total | 100.0 | 100.0 |
| | | | | | | **LIABILITIES** | | |
| 9.7 | 3.6 | 3.2 | | | | Notes Payable-Short Term | 9.9 | 11.7 |
| 3.3 | 2.7 | 2.0 | | | | Cur. Mat.-L.T.D. | 3.7 | 4.3 |
| 5.6 | .8 | 2.8 | | | | Trade Payables | 5.6 | 3.9 |
| .2 | .0 | .1 | | | | Income Taxes Payable | .1 | .2 |
| 29.6 | 6.3 | 23.1 | | | | All Other Current | 19.5 | 25.7 |
| 48.4 | 13.5 | 31.2 | | | | Total Current | 38.9 | 45.8 |
| 44.3 | 48.3 | 27.7 | | | | Long-Term Debt | 28.3 | 37.1 |
| .0 | .0 | .0 | | | | Deferred Taxes | .1 | .0 |
| 12.5 | 8.5 | 21.8 | | | | All Other Non-Current | 8.8 | 3.6 |
| -5.1 | 29.6 | 19.3 | | | | Net Worth | 23.9 | 13.4 |
| 100.0 | 100.0 | 100.0 | | | | Total Liabilities & Net Worth | 100.0 | 100.0 |
| | | | | | | **INCOME DATA** | | |
| 100.0 | 100.0 | 100.0 | | | | Net Sales | 100.0 | 100.0 |
| | | | | | | Gross Profit | | |
| 93.7 | 92.0 | 91.7 | | | | Operating Expenses | 92.3 | 94.1 |
| 6.3 | 8.0 | 8.3 | | | | Operating Profit | 7.7 | 5.9 |
| 1.3 | 2.8 | 2.6 | | | | All Other Expenses (net) | 1.5 | -1.3 |
| 5.0 | 5.2 | 5.6 | | | | Profit Before Taxes | 6.2 | 7.1 |
| | | | | | | **RATIOS** | | |
| 6.8 | 5.6 | 2.0 | | | | | 2.0 | 3.4 |
| 3.0 | 2.1 | .7 | | | | Current | .9 | 1.3 |
| .9 | .7 | .0 | | | | | .5 | .6 |
| 4.8 | 5.3 | 1.5 | | | | | 1.6 | 2.8 |
| 1.5 | 1.3 | .2 | | | | Quick | (130) .6 | 1.1 |
| .3 | .6 | .0 | | | | | .2 | .4 |
| 0 UND | 0 UND | 0 UND | | | | | 0 UND | 0 UND |
| 0 UND | 0 UND | 0 UND | | | | Sales/Receivables | 0 UND | 0 UND |
| 0 UND | 0 UND | 2 162.4 | | | | | 1 249.4 | 2 212.1 |
| | | | | | | Cost of Sales/Inventory | | |
| | | | | | | Cost of Sales/Payables | | |
| 12.6 | 6.6 | 20.7 | | | | | 20.1 | 10.8 |
| 49.5 | 26.6 | -64.4 | | | | Sales/Working Capital | -217.6 | 33.0 |
| -78.2 | -46.4 | -.9 | | | | | -19.0 | -19.3 |
| 21.0 | 10.4 | 19.9 | | | | | 15.6 | 20.3 |
| (34) 8.2 | (30) 3.8 | (16) 4.3 | | | | EBIT/Interest | (93) 4.1 | (50) 11.5 |
| -.6 | .3 | .7 | | | | | .4 | 2.2 |
| | | | | | | Net Profit + Depr., Dep., Amort./Cur. Mat. L/T/D | | |
| .3 | .5 | .0 | | | | | .8 | 1.0 |
| 1.0 | 2.3 | 1.1 | | | | Fixed/Worth | 2.0 | 2.4 |
| -4.2 | 145.5 | 28.0 | | | | | -2.3 | -5.3 |
| .2 | .9 | 1.7 | | | | | 1.1 | 1.2 |
| 4.3 | 6.2 | 4.9 | | | | Debt/Worth | 4.6 | 3.1 |
| -3.3 | -17.3 | 242.2 | | | | | -4.3 | -8.8 |
| 257.6 | 73.4 | 59.3 | | | | | 103.9 | 148.0 |
| (44) 95.9 | (27) 36.9 | (24) 20.0 | | | | % Profit Before Taxes/Tangible Net Worth | (82) 43.4 | (46) 50.2 |
| 12.7 | 4.7 | 8.7 | | | | | 14.3 | 31.4 |
| 86.3 | 18.5 | 13.4 | | | | | 35.2 | 37.9 |
| 40.4 | 8.3 | 4.4 | | | | % Profit Before Taxes/Total Assets | 10.9 | 16.7 |
| -4.8 | -3.4 | -.5 | | | | | -.4 | 2.5 |
| 106.8 | 12.1 | 100.9 | | | | | 28.3 | 14.0 |
| 23.1 | 4.4 | 13.5 | | | | Sales/Net Fixed Assets | 7.6 | 6.2 |
| 11.0 | 2.0 | 3.7 | | | | | 3.3 | 2.4 |
| 9.5 | 2.5 | 2.5 | | | | | 5.5 | 3.7 |
| 5.7 | 1.7 | 1.1 | | | | Sales/Total Assets | 2.5 | 2.0 |
| 3.2 | 1.3 | .4 | | | | | 1.3 | 1.3 |
| .7 | 2.2 | 1.5 | | | | | 1.8 | 2.3 |
| (42) 1.7 | (26) 4.1 | (20) 1.9 | | | | % Depr., Dep., Amort./Sales | (76) 4.1 | (39) 4.0 |
| 3.4 | 6.5 | 4.4 | | | | | 6.1 | 5.2 |
| 3.1 | 3.0 | | | | | | 2.5 | 1.9 |
| (21) 5.2 | (16) 4.5 | | | | | % Officers', Directors' Owners' Comp/Sales | (40) 4.7 | (22) 6.2 |
| 11.0 | 8.3 | | | | | | 10.2 | 10.2 |
| 79722M | 72952M | 233827M | 132420M | 88075M | 1191318M | Net Sales ($) | 2378530M | 1252534M |
| 15150M | 37499M | 144774M | 124837M | 64817M | 913676M | Total Assets ($) | 832545M | 802817M |

M = $ thousand  MM = $ million
See Pages viii through xx for Explanation of Ratios and Data

© RMA 2024

## RESTAURANT/LODGING—Snack and Nonalcoholic Beverage Bars  NAICS 722515

| Comparative Historical Data | | | Type of Statement | Current Data Sorted by Sales | | | | | |
|---|---|---|---|---|---|---|---|---|---|
| 2 | 4 | 3 | Unqualified | | | | | 1 | 2 |
| 1 | 6 | 1 | Reviewed | | | | | 2 | 1 |
| 12 | 10 | 6 | Compiled | | 3 | | | 2 | 1 |
| 25 | 38 | 53 | Tax Returns | 24 | 24 | 1 | 2 | 2 | |
| 40 | 83 | 91 | Other | 23 | 45 | 6 | 4 | 8 | 5 |
| 4/1/21-3/31/22 ALL | 4/1/22-3/31/23 ALL | 4/1/23-3/31/24 ALL | | 7 (4/1-9/30/23) | | | 147 (10/1/23-3/31/24) | | |
| | | | | 0-1MM | 1-3MM | 3-5MM | 5-10MM | 10-25MM | 25MM & OVER |
| 80 | 141 | 154 | NUMBER OF STATEMENTS | 47 | 72 | 7 | 6 | 13 | 9 |
| % | % | % | ASSETS | % | % | % | % | % | % |
| 27.0 | 20.8 | 23.7 | Cash & Equivalents | 28.9 | 22.7 | | | 19.4 | |
| 1.8 | 1.6 | 1.7 | Trade Receivables (net) | .8 | 1.9 | | | 1.5 | |
| 4.9 | 4.3 | 4.0 | Inventory | 4.1 | 2.9 | | | 3.1 | |
| 3.3 | 5.1 | 4.6 | All Other Current | 6.0 | 2.3 | | | 12.1 | |
| 37.1 | 31.8 | 33.9 | Total Current | 39.8 | 29.8 | | | 36.2 | |
| 39.4 | 37.3 | 38.7 | Fixed Assets (net) | 42.5 | 36.8 | | | 30.8 | |
| 15.2 | 13.2 | 11.8 | Intangibles (net) | 11.9 | 12.0 | | | 14.2 | |
| 8.3 | 17.7 | 15.7 | All Other Non-Current | 5.9 | 21.4 | | | 18.8 | |
| 100.0 | 100.0 | 100.0 | Total | 100.0 | 100.0 | | | 100.0 | |
| | | | LIABILITIES | | | | | | |
| 13.3 | 7.5 | 6.1 | Notes Payable-Short Term | 13.1 | 2.9 | | | 1.1 | |
| 3.6 | 3.2 | 3.1 | Cur. Mat.-L.T.D. | 1.9 | 3.0 | | | 1.7 | |
| 4.8 | 3.9 | 3.7 | Trade Payables | 5.3 | 2.5 | | | 4.4 | |
| .0 | .2 | .1 | Income Taxes Payable | .0 | .2 | | | .2 | |
| 9.1 | 18.7 | 21.9 | All Other Current | 24.5 | 24.9 | | | 10.8 | |
| 30.8 | 33.5 | 34.9 | Total Current | 44.8 | 33.5 | | | 18.2 | |
| 38.6 | 35.2 | 40.8 | Long-Term Debt | 57.6 | 30.4 | | | 29.6 | |
| .0 | .1 | .0 | Deferred Taxes | .0 | .0 | | | .1 | |
| 5.2 | 11.6 | 13.4 | All Other Non-Current | 2.5 | 17.0 | | | 27.1 | |
| 25.2 | 19.5 | 11.0 | Net Worth | -4.8 | 19.2 | | | 25.0 | |
| 100.0 | 100.0 | 100.0 | Total Liabilties & Net Worth | 100.0 | 100.0 | | | 100.0 | |
| | | | INCOME DATA | | | | | | |
| 100.0 | 100.0 | 100.0 | Net Sales | 100.0 | 100.0 | | | 100.0 | |
| | | | Gross Profit | | | | | | |
| 92.1 | 92.2 | 92.8 | Operating Expenses | 95.3 | 90.1 | | | 92.6 | |
| 7.9 | 7.8 | 7.2 | Operating Profit | 4.7 | 9.9 | | | 7.4 | |
| -1.3 | 1.5 | 1.9 | All Other Expenses (net) | 3.8 | 1.1 | | | .7 | |
| 9.2 | 6.3 | 5.2 | Profit Before Taxes | .9 | 8.8 | | | 6.7 | |
| | | | RATIOS | | | | | | |
| 3.8 | 3.4 | 5.4 | | 6.4 | 5.3 | | | 6.5 | |
| 1.4 | 1.1 | 1.8 | Current | 3.4 | 1.4 | | | 1.9 | |
| .6 | .4 | .5 | | .9 | .3 | | | .8 | |
| 3.3 | 2.2 | 4.1 | | 4.4 | 4.8 | | | 2.8 | |
| 1.1 | .9 | 1.1 | Quick | 1.8 | .8 | | | 1.5 | |
| .3 | .3 | .2 | | .3 | .1 | | | .3 | |
| 0 UND | 0 UND | 0 UND | | 0 UND | 0 UND | | | 0 UND | |
| 0 UND | 0 UND | 0 UND | Sales/Receivables | 0 UND | 0 UND | | | 0 UND | |
| 0 999.8 | 2 206.0 | 0 UND | | 0 UND | 0 UND | | | 4 103.8 | |
| | | | Cost of Sales/Inventory | | | | | | |
| | | | Cost of Sales/Payables | | | | | | |
| 10.0 | 9.5 | 11.3 | | 8.0 | 13.4 | | | 4.8 | |
| 30.7 | 56.0 | 57.0 | Sales/Working Capital | 36.7 | 88.3 | | | 34.5 | |
| -22.8 | -10.4 | -19.4 | | -78.2 | -7.8 | | | -85.2 | |
| 42.9 | 23.0 | 16.2 | | 5.7 | 39.5 | | | 126.1 | |
| (62) 11.3 | (106) 6.0 | (91) 4.5 | EBIT/Interest | (27) .2 | (33) 11.3 | | | (11) 21.7 | |
| 2.2 | -.5 | .1 | | -3.1 | 1.7 | | | 3.2 | |
| | | | Net Profit + Depr., Dep., Amort./Cur. Mat. L/T/D | | | | | | |
| .6 | .6 | .3 | | .0 | .3 | | | .1 | |
| 1.7 | 1.9 | 1.7 | Fixed/Worth | 2.3 | 1.1 | | | .6 | |
| UND | -21.0 | -24.2 | | -2.4 | 11.6 | | | NM | |
| .8 | 1.1 | .8 | | .2 | .8 | | | .6 | |
| 2.2 | 3.2 | 5.3 | Debt/Worth | 3.9 | 5.3 | | | 1.3 | |
| -11.2 | -17.3 | -7.8 | | -3.3 | -29.8 | | | NM | |
| 118.2 | 90.3 | 134.3 | | 92.2 | 227.0 | | | 65.3 | |
| (58) 65.1 | (102) 26.7 | (104) 37.4 | % Profit Before Taxes/Tangible Net Worth | (27) 29.6 | (53) 67.5 | | | (10) 38.1 | |
| 23.9 | .3 | 7.8 | | .8 | 17.8 | | | 17.1 | |
| 42.6 | 28.8 | 43.4 | | 46.4 | 50.8 | | | 23.5 | |
| 22.6 | 6.8 | 10.6 | % Profit Before Taxes/Total Assets | 7.6 | 14.0 | | | 16.7 | |
| 3.7 | -.8 | -1.3 | | -10.8 | 1.5 | | | 7.0 | |
| 23.8 | 20.8 | 71.9 | | 141.2 | 94.4 | | | 19.5 | |
| 8.4 | 8.2 | 12.5 | Sales/Net Fixed Assets | 13.2 | 15.1 | | | 10.2 | |
| 3.5 | 3.2 | 3.3 | | 1.6 | 5.3 | | | 6.4 | |
| 3.8 | 3.4 | 5.7 | | 6.7 | 7.0 | | | 3.0 | |
| 2.6 | 1.8 | 2.5 | Sales/Total Assets | 2.3 | 2.8 | | | 2.5 | |
| 1.5 | .9 | 1.3 | | 1.0 | 1.3 | | | 1.3 | |
| 1.1 | 1.5 | 1.3 | | 1.4 | .8 | | | 1.2 | |
| (50) 2.3 | (79) 3.5 | (97) 2.4 | % Depr., Dep., Amort./Sales | (27) 3.8 | (45) 2.4 | | | (11) 1.7 | |
| 4.6 | 5.7 | 4.7 | | 11.6 | 4.1 | | | 2.1 | |
| 3.4 | 2.2 | 2.1 | | 4.3 | 2.8 | | | | |
| (18) 6.3 | (36) 6.1 | (46) 4.4 | % Officers', Directors' Owners' Comp/Sales | (11) 6.4 | (21) 4.8 | | | | |
| 8.3 | 10.2 | 9.2 | | 13.9 | 9.5 | | | | |
| 2034251M | 1211555M | 1798314M | Net Sales ($) | 27528M | 118283M | 25895M | 36772M | 207720M | 1382116M |
| 531435M | 835996M | 1300753M | Total Assets ($) | 20903M | 114260M | 13842M | 12243M | 117101M | 1022404M |

© RMA 2024   M = $ thousand   MM = $ million
See Pages viii through xx for Explanation of Ratios and Data

# OTHER SERVICES (EXCEPT PUBLIC ADMINISTRATION)

# OTHER SERVICES—General Automotive Repair  NAICS 811111

## Current Data Sorted by Assets / Comparative Historical Data

| | | | | | | | Type of Statement | | |
|---|---|---|---|---|---|---|---|---|---|
| | | 1 | | 1 | | | Unqualified | 7 | 7 |
| | | | 1 | 1 | | | Reviewed | 7 | 5 |
| 4 | 3 | 4 | | | | 1 | Compiled | 32 | 10 |
| 59 | 43 | 23 | 1 | | | | Tax Returns | 159 | 111 |
| 46 | 72 | 43 | 15 | 1 | 3 | | Other | 180 | 160 |
| | 21 (4/1-9/30/23) | | 301 (10/1/23-3/31/24) | | | | | 4/1/19- 3/31/20 | 4/1/20- 3/31/21 |
| 0-500M | 500M-2MM | 2-10MM | 10-50MM | 50-100MM | 100-250MM | | NUMBER OF STATEMENTS | ALL | ALL |
| 109 | 119 | 71 | 18 | 1 | 4 | | | 385 | 293 |
| % | % | % | % | % | % | | ASSETS | % | % |
| 45.0 | 22.0 | 15.7 | 16.9 | | | | Cash & Equivalents | 24.7 | 34.6 |
| 5.8 | 7.0 | 9.6 | 8.5 | | | | Trade Receivables (net) | 10.2 | 8.3 |
| 10.7 | 8.6 | 19.3 | 17.3 | | | | Inventory | 15.4 | 11.5 |
| 2.4 | 3.3 | 2.0 | .5 | | | | All Other Current | 2.7 | 3.1 |
| 63.9 | 40.9 | 46.6 | 43.1 | | | | Total Current | 52.9 | 57.4 |
| 22.9 | 34.8 | 34.1 | 43.9 | | | | Fixed Assets (net) | 33.1 | 29.0 |
| 8.2 | 15.6 | 9.6 | 10.2 | | | | Intangibles (net) | 6.2 | 6.9 |
| 4.9 | 8.7 | 9.7 | 2.7 | | | | All Other Non-Current | 7.8 | 6.7 |
| 100.0 | 100.0 | 100.0 | 100.0 | | | | Total | 100.0 | 100.0 |
| | | | | | | | LIABILITIES | | |
| 12.8 | 7.3 | 6.0 | 5.7 | | | | Notes Payable-Short Term | 10.6 | 13.9 |
| 5.9 | 2.1 | 2.6 | 3.3 | | | | Cur. Mat.-L.T.D. | 4.6 | 2.0 |
| 8.7 | 7.6 | 9.0 | 8.4 | | | | Trade Payables | 10.9 | 7.7 |
| .2 | .0 | .2 | .1 | | | | Income Taxes Payable | .1 | .1 |
| 22.3 | 9.4 | 6.2 | 6.4 | | | | All Other Current | 12.7 | 14.6 |
| 49.8 | 26.5 | 24.1 | 23.8 | | | | Total Current | 38.9 | 38.3 |
| 42.6 | 40.1 | 32.5 | 24.7 | | | | Long-Term Debt | 31.4 | 34.0 |
| .0 | .0 | .0 | .1 | | | | Deferred Taxes | .1 | .1 |
| 11.4 | 4.0 | 2.0 | 5.9 | | | | All Other Non-Current | 5.8 | 7.9 |
| -3.7 | 29.4 | 41.5 | 45.4 | | | | Net Worth | 23.8 | 19.7 |
| 100.0 | 100.0 | 100.0 | 100.0 | | | | Total Liabilities & Net Worth | 100.0 | 100.0 |
| | | | | | | | INCOME DATA | | |
| 100.0 | 100.0 | 100.0 | 100.0 | | | | Net Sales | 100.0 | 100.0 |
| | | | | | | | Gross Profit | | |
| 91.8 | 85.1 | 85.8 | 85.9 | | | | Operating Expenses | 91.9 | 92.7 |
| 8.2 | 14.9 | 14.2 | 14.1 | | | | Operating Profit | 8.1 | 7.3 |
| 1.9 | 4.5 | 2.1 | 3.5 | | | | All Other Expenses (net) | 1.6 | .2 |
| 6.3 | 10.4 | 12.0 | 10.5 | | | | Profit Before Taxes | 6.5 | 7.1 |
| | | | | | | | RATIOS | | |
| 5.8 | 4.8 | 4.4 | 3.3 | | | | | 3.2 | 4.2 |
| 2.4 | 1.6 | 2.1 | 1.9 | | | | Current | 1.4 | 2.1 |
| .8 | .8 | 1.2 | 1.2 | | | | | .8 | 1.0 |
| 4.8 | 3.8 | 2.6 | 2.4 | | | | | 2.0 | 3.2 |
| 1.6 | 1.2 | 1.0 | 1.0 | | | | Quick | .9 (292) | 1.4 |
| .5 | .5 | .4 | .5 | | | | | .4 | .6 |
| 0 UND | 0 UND | 0 UND | 1 272.9 | | | | | 0 UND | 0 UND |
| 0 UND | 1 727.0 | 9 39.8 | 10 37.1 | | | | Sales/Receivables | 3 115.4 | 2 157.2 |
| 3 127.8 | 8 44.9 | 26 13.8 | 31 11.7 | | | | | 16 23.1 | 13 28.9 |
| | | | | | | | Cost of Sales/Inventory | | |
| | | | | | | | Cost of Sales/Payables | | |
| 9.4 | 7.9 | 4.5 | 5.2 | | | | | 9.9 | 6.1 |
| 24.8 | 23.3 | 11.8 | 9.7 | | | | Sales/Working Capital | 38.2 | 13.7 |
| -86.7 | -46.1 | 69.2 | 35.0 | | | | | -38.3 | UND |
| 18.5 | 22.1 | 19.9 | 55.6 | | | | | 19.1 | 20.1 |
| (72) 2.8 | (90) 9.3 | (54) 7.5 | (12) 14.7 | | | | EBIT/Interest | (269) 5.1 | (185) 6.0 |
| -.2 | 3.1 | 2.7 | 7.6 | | | | | 1.2 | 1.4 |
| | | | | | | | Net Profit + Depr., Dep., Amort./Cur. Mat. L/T/D | 4.3 (19) 1.8 1.1 | |
| .0 | .3 | .3 | .5 | | | | | .2 | .2 |
| .7 | 1.9 | .9 | 1.0 | | | | Fixed/Worth | 1.0 | 1.2 |
| -2.0 | -2.5 | 9.3 | 3.2 | | | | | UND | -28.7 |
| .3 | 1.0 | .6 | .5 | | | | | .7 | .8 |
| 3.6 | 3.2 | 1.5 | 1.5 | | | | Debt/Worth | 2.3 | 2.9 |
| -3.0 | -6.1 | 9.0 | 4.0 | | | | | -38.5 | -14.4 |
| 161.3 | 106.6 | 69.6 | 51.4 | | | | | 99.4 | 114.6 |
| (65) 89.6 | (81) 56.6 | (57) 35.3 | (16) 37.9 | | | | % Profit Before Taxes/Tangible Net Worth | (284) 36.9 | (210) 48.7 |
| 14.2 | 23.4 | 15.2 | 19.2 | | | | | 9.1 | 12.0 |
| 70.7 | 30.7 | 27.6 | 25.7 | | | | | 34.1 | 34.7 |
| 21.2 | 19.3 | 14.8 | 13.8 | | | | % Profit Before Taxes/Total Assets | 11.5 | 14.6 |
| -7.1 | 5.4 | 3.1 | 8.1 | | | | | 1.6 | .7 |
| 772.2 | 39.9 | 35.8 | 16.6 | | | | | 72.6 | 98.5 |
| 43.8 | 13.7 | 8.3 | 5.6 | | | | Sales/Net Fixed Assets | 18.1 | 20.3 |
| 17.1 | 2.5 | 2.4 | 2.6 | | | | | 5.4 | 6.6 |
| 9.4 | 3.7 | 2.8 | 2.7 | | | | | 7.0 | 5.6 |
| 6.1 | 2.2 | 1.9 | 2.1 | | | | Sales/Total Assets | 3.8 | 3.2 |
| 3.3 | 1.3 | 1.1 | 1.2 | | | | | 2.1 | 1.9 |
| .5 | 1.1 | 1.4 | 1.1 | | | | | .7 | .7 |
| (41) 1.5 | (56) 2.6 | (33) 2.3 | (15) 1.5 | | | | % Depr., Dep., Amort./Sales | (214) 1.9 | (154) 1.7 |
| 2.7 | 5.2 | 5.1 | 3.1 | | | | | 4.0 | 3.6 |
| 3.3 | 2.2 | .9 | | | | | | 2.7 | 3.0 |
| (63) 6.4 | (56) 3.3 | (27) 1.9 | | | | | % Officers', Directors' Owners' Comp/Sales | (202) 5.5 | (143) 5.8 |
| 10.2 | 4.8 | 3.2 | | | | | | 8.9 | 10.2 |
| 141273M | 314061M | 591048M | 605208M | 120000M | 2241660M | | Net Sales ($) | 10172366M | 1137376M |
| 25350M | 127127M | 286142M | 341900M | 98200M | 701079M | | Total Assets ($) | 2053315M | 742255M |

© RMA 2024

M = $ thousand    MM = $ million
See Pages viii through xx for Explanation of Ratios and Data

## OTHER SERVICES—General Automotive Repair NAICS 811111

### Comparative Historical Data / Current Data Sorted by Sales

| Comparative Historical Data | | | Type of Statement | Current Data Sorted by Sales | | | | | |
|---|---|---|---|---|---|---|---|---|---|
| 3 | 6 | 3 | Unqualified | | 1 | | | 1 | 2 |
| 5 | 5 | 2 | Reviewed | | | | | 1 | 1 |
| 16 | 17 | 11 | Compiled | 1 | 4 | 2 | 1 | 2 | 1 |
| 134 | 152 | 126 | Tax Returns | 44 | 50 | 11 | 12 | 8 | 1 |
| 159 | 194 | 180 | Other | 30 | 71 | 28 | 22 | 14 | 15 |
| 4/1/21-3/31/22 ALL | 4/1/22-3/31/23 ALL | 4/1/23-3/31/24 ALL | | 21 (4/1-9/30/23) | | | 301 (10/1/23-3/31/24) | | |
| | | | | 0-1MM | 1-3MM | 3-5MM | 5-10MM | 10-25MM | 25MM & OVER |
| 317 | 374 | 322 | NUMBER OF STATEMENTS | 75 | 126 | 41 | 35 | 25 | 20 |
| % | % | % | ASSETS | % | % | % | % | % | % |
| 33.4 | 31.3 | 27.9 | Cash & Equivalents | 29.8 | 30.3 | 30.3 | 23.5 | 22.8 | 14.8 |
| 7.6 | 7.6 | 7.4 | Trade Receivables (net) | 3.5 | 8.7 | 3.5 | 10.9 | 11.5 | 10.0 |
| 12.2 | 11.9 | 12.1 | Inventory | 6.0 | 10.9 | 11.7 | 19.3 | 22.7 | 18.6 |
| 2.7 | 3.2 | 2.5 | All Other Current | 2.3 | 2.9 | 1.7 | 3.3 | 3.0 | .9 |
| 56.0 | 54.1 | 49.9 | Total Current | 41.6 | 52.8 | 47.0 | 57.0 | 60.0 | 44.3 |
| 29.8 | 28.8 | 31.1 | Fixed Assets (net) | 43.2 | 27.8 | 26.4 | 26.0 | 21.4 | 37.6 |
| 6.8 | 8.3 | 11.7 | Intangibles (net) | 8.1 | 12.6 | 19.9 | 8.3 | 7.3 | 14.5 |
| 7.5 | 8.7 | 7.2 | All Other Non-Current | 7.1 | 6.8 | 6.6 | 8.7 | 11.3 | 3.7 |
| 100.0 | 100.0 | 100.0 | Total | 100.0 | 100.0 | 100.0 | 100.0 | 100.0 | 100.0 |
| | | | LIABILITIES | | | | | | |
| 9.9 | 7.0 | 8.7 | Notes Payable-Short Term | 8.2 | 10.9 | 9.2 | 5.0 | 5.7 | 5.7 |
| 2.3 | 3.4 | 3.6 | Cur. Mat.-L.T.D. | 6.7 | 2.9 | 1.7 | 3.2 | 2.5 | 2.3 |
| 8.0 | 9.1 | 8.3 | Trade Payables | 7.0 | 7.6 | 5.0 | 12.2 | 15.1 | 8.9 |
| .9 | .3 | .1 | Income Taxes Payable | .0 | .3 | .0 | .0 | .1 | .0 |
| 8.1 | 12.5 | 12.9 | All Other Current | 17.1 | 13.7 | 12.0 | 8.9 | 7.8 | 7.3 |
| 29.2 | 32.3 | 33.6 | Total Current | 39.0 | 35.3 | 28.0 | 29.4 | 31.1 | 24.3 |
| 31.2 | 36.0 | 38.5 | Long-Term Debt | 49.4 | 42.6 | 37.9 | 23.9 | 17.2 | 25.9 |
| .0 | .1 | .0 | Deferred Taxes | .0 | .0 | .0 | .0 | .0 | .3 |
| 4.4 | 5.6 | 6.1 | All Other Non-Current | 16.2 | 1.8 | 4.4 | 4.5 | 4.1 | 4.7 |
| 35.2 | 26.0 | 21.8 | Net Worth | -4.5 | 20.3 | 29.7 | 42.3 | 47.6 | 44.8 |
| 100.0 | 100.0 | 100.0 | Total Liabilities & Net Worth | 100.0 | 100.0 | 100.0 | 100.0 | 100.0 | 100.0 |
| | | | INCOME DATA | | | | | | |
| 100.0 | 100.0 | 100.0 | Net Sales | 100.0 | 100.0 | 100.0 | 100.0 | 100.0 | 100.0 |
| | | | Gross Profit | | | | | | |
| 90.0 | 90.0 | 87.7 | Operating Expenses | 80.0 | 89.4 | 88.5 | 89.9 | 94.4 | 92.8 |
| 10.0 | 10.0 | 12.3 | Operating Profit | 20.0 | 10.6 | 11.5 | 10.1 | 5.6 | 7.2 |
| .0 | 1.1 | 3.0 | All Other Expenses (net) | 7.7 | 2.1 | 2.4 | 1.1 | -1.5 | .8 |
| 10.0 | 8.9 | 9.3 | Profit Before Taxes | 12.3 | 8.5 | 9.1 | 9.1 | 7.1 | 6.4 |
| | | | RATIOS | | | | | | |
| 5.3 | 5.2 | 4.8 | | 5.0 | 6.0 | 4.8 | 5.2 | 3.9 | 3.1 |
| 2.5 | 2.3 | 1.8 | Current | 1.8 | 1.8 | 1.5 | 2.1 | 1.9 | 1.8 |
| 1.2 | 1.1 | .9 | | .5 | .9 | .9 | 1.3 | 1.2 | 1.3 |
| 4.0 | 4.0 | 3.8 | | 4.0 | 4.4 | 3.9 | 2.8 | 2.7 | 1.8 |
| 1.7 | 1.6 | 1.2 | Quick | 1.3 | 1.5 | 1.0 | 1.4 | 1.0 | 1.0 |
| (316) | (373) | | | | | | | | |
| .7 | .6 | .5 | | .4 | .5 | .6 | .8 | .5 | .6 |
| 0 UND | 0 UND | 0 UND | | 0 UND | 0 UND | 0 UND | 0 999.8 | 0 999.8 | 2 221.0 |
| 2 198.5 | 1 373.6 | 1 549.5 | Sales/Receivables | 0 UND | 1 701.7 | 1 727.0 | 8 44.5 | 13 28.3 | 11 33.3 |
| 13 27.1 | 10 34.8 | 12 29.2 | | 1 244.3 | 12 29.8 | 7 53.2 | 20 18.2 | 27 13.6 | 35 10.4 |
| | | | Cost of Sales/Inventory | | | | | | |
| | | | Cost of Sales/Payables | | | | | | |
| 5.8 | 6.0 | 7.0 | | 9.7 | 6.8 | 10.2 | 4.9 | 6.0 | 6.3 |
| 11.4 | 14.5 | 20.2 | Sales/Working Capital | 43.0 | 24.1 | 22.6 | 12.9 | 11.8 | 14.4 |
| 62.8 | 107.4 | -100.0 | | -8.0 | -100.0 | NM | 36.9 | 46.5 | 41.3 |
| 57.0 | 37.5 | 21.1 | | 5.2 | 18.2 | 29.3 | 59.4 | 36.3 | 30.6 |
| (228) 17.6 | (257) 10.6 | (231) 6.5 | EBIT/Interest | (46) 2.3 | (90) 6.8 | (34) 14.3 | (28) 12.3 | (20) 8.1 | (13) 7.6 |
| 3.6 | 2.8 | 1.8 | | -.2 | .9 | 4.1 | 3.7 | 2.0 | 3.0 |
| | | 25.4 | Net Profit + Depr., Dep., | | | | | | |
| | (11) 4.5 | | Amort./Cur. Mat. L/T/D | | | | | | |
| | | 3.9 | | | | | | | |
| .1 | .1 | .1 | | .3 | .1 | .5 | .2 | .1 | .4 |
| .7 | .7 | 1.1 | Fixed/Worth | 4.0 | .9 | 1.6 | .8 | .4 | 1.0 |
| 6.0 | 7.3 | -3.6 | | -2.8 | -3.2 | -.6 | 3.1 | 2.2 | NM |
| .5 | .5 | .6 | | 1.3 | .4 | 1.1 | .5 | .4 | .4 |
| 2.0 | 2.3 | 2.9 | Debt/Worth | 7.2 | 2.6 | 4.1 | 1.5 | 1.1 | 1.3 |
| 25.4 | -17.5 | -6.1 | | -3.8 | -3.4 | -2.8 | 5.2 | 3.4 | NM |
| 121.1 | 110.0 | 110.1 | | 110.7 | 122.1 | 110.3 | 118.2 | 80.2 | 54.2 |
| (246) 56.8 | (274) 46.5 | (220) 51.6 | % Profit Before Taxes/Tangible Net Worth | (45) 38.2 | (84) 60.1 | (27) 62.5 | (28) 57.5 | (21) 30.7 | (15) 46.3 |
| 26.8 | 13.3 | 20.2 | | 7.0 | 20.9 | 23.8 | 33.2 | 3.5 | 30.2 |
| 49.5 | 39.9 | 36.0 | | 27.9 | 42.7 | 41.7 | 31.8 | 27.9 | 25.8 |
| 21.2 | 18.9 | 17.8 | % Profit Before Taxes/Total Assets | 5.4 | 21.1 | 25.1 | 22.3 | 18.5 | 14.8 |
| 7.8 | 4.8 | 2.9 | | -4.5 | 2.0 | 7.9 | 7.7 | 1.2 | 8.9 |
| 61.1 | 137.1 | 74.5 | | 104.9 | 118.1 | 70.5 | 49.0 | 158.6 | 17.3 |
| 17.4 | 22.6 | 18.2 | Sales/Net Fixed Assets | 9.3 | 23.2 | 20.4 | 11.4 | 27.7 | 9.4 |
| 5.5 | 6.0 | 5.3 | | .7 | 7.1 | 6.4 | 6.7 | 9.8 | 3.2 |
| 5.3 | 5.5 | 5.2 | | 5.4 | 6.0 | 5.4 | 4.3 | 4.2 | 3.4 |
| 3.2 | 3.0 | 2.7 | Sales/Total Assets | 1.7 | 3.3 | 2.7 | 2.7 | 2.9 | 2.4 |
| 1.8 | 1.7 | 1.6 | | .6 | 1.9 | 1.7 | 1.9 | 2.2 | 1.3 |
| .9 | .7 | .8 | | .8 | .6 | .8 | .8 | .4 | 1.0 |
| (165) 1.7 | (184) 1.8 | (145) 2.2 | % Depr., Dep., Amort./Sales | (34) 3.0 | (55) 2.3 | (15) 1.5 | (15) 3.1 | (12) 1.5 | (14) 1.5 |
| 3.5 | 3.7 | 3.8 | | 12.3 | 3.2 | 2.6 | 6.6 | 2.4 | 2.3 |
| 3.3 | 2.8 | 2.1 | | 4.7 | 2.6 | 1.4 | 1.8 | .6 | |
| (175) 5.6 | (186) 4.5 | (149) 3.6 | % Officers', Directors' Owners' Comp/Sales | (31) 8.2 | (69) 4.1 | (20) 2.4 | (16) 2.5 | (10) 1.0 | |
| 9.3 | 7.2 | 7.0 | | 11.1 | 6.8 | 3.8 | 3.4 | 4.5 | |
| 3836173M | 1614999M | 4013250M | Net Sales ($) | 40871M | 232972M | 151820M | 238608M | 391614M | 2957365M |
| 1496853M | 785321M | 1579798M | Total Assets ($) | 48512M | 126813M | 67572M | 125180M | 147370M | 1064351M |

© RMA 2024  M = $ thousand  MM = $ million
See Pages viii through xx for Explanation of Ratios and Data

# OTHER SERVICES—Specialized Automotive Repair  NAICS 811114

## Current Data Sorted by Assets

| | 0-500M | 500M-2MM | 2-10MM | 10-50MM | 50-100MM | 100-250MM | | Comparative Historical Data | |
|---|---|---|---|---|---|---|---|---|---|
| Type of Statement | | | | | | | | | |
| Unqualified | | 1 | 1 | | 1 | | | 1 | 2 |
| Reviewed | | | 1 | | | | | | |
| Compiled | | 6 | 2 | 3 | | | | 7 | 9 |
| Tax Returns | 3 | 11 | 6 | 3 | | 1 | | 16 | 20 |
| Other | | 2 (4/1-9/30/23) | | 38 (10/1/23-3/31/24) | | | | 20 4/1/19-3/31/20 | 20 4/1/20-3/31/21 |
| | | | | | | | | ALL | ALL |
| NUMBER OF STATEMENTS | 3 | 18 | 10 | 6 | 2 | 1 | | 44 | 31 |
| | % | % | % | % | % | % | ASSETS | % | % |
| | | 18.5 | 22.5 | | | | Cash & Equivalents | 20.0 | 30.8 |
| | | 17.5 | 16.9 | | | | Trade Receivables (net) | 18.8 | 8.2 |
| | | 13.8 | 9.8 | | | | Inventory | 18.3 | 10.9 |
| | | 2.5 | 1.6 | | | | All Other Current | 2.3 | 2.2 |
| | | 52.3 | 50.8 | | | | Total Current | 59.3 | 52.1 |
| | | 25.1 | 33.2 | | | | Fixed Assets (net) | 28.4 | 26.6 |
| | | 12.8 | 12.8 | | | | Intangibles (net) | 4.1 | 9.5 |
| | | 9.8 | 3.1 | | | | All Other Non-Current | 8.2 | 11.8 |
| | | 100.0 | 100.0 | | | | Total | 100.0 | 100.0 |
| | | | | | | | LIABILITIES | | |
| | | 3.7 | 4.5 | | | | Notes Payable-Short Term | 10.8 | 8.8 |
| | | 1.2 | 3.6 | | | | Cur. Mat.-L.T.D. | 4.2 | 1.6 |
| | | 6.3 | 13.2 | | | | Trade Payables | 12.8 | 9.8 |
| | | .0 | .3 | | | | Income Taxes Payable | .2 | .2 |
| | | 5.9 | 6.2 | | | | All Other Current | 17.2 | 10.0 |
| | | 17.2 | 27.9 | | | | Total Current | 45.0 | 30.4 |
| | | 26.6 | 34.6 | | | | Long-Term Debt | 20.0 | 31.0 |
| | | .0 | .0 | | | | Deferred Taxes | .0 | .0 |
| | | 1.5 | 2.7 | | | | All Other Non-Current | 4.4 | 5.6 |
| | | 54.7 | 34.8 | | | | Net Worth | 30.5 | 33.0 |
| | | 100.0 | 100.0 | | | | Total Liabilities & Net Worth | 100.0 | 100.0 |
| | | | | | | | INCOME DATA | | |
| | | 100.0 | 100.0 | | | | Net Sales | 100.0 | 100.0 |
| | | | | | | | Gross Profit | | |
| | | 90.2 | 91.9 | | | | Operating Expenses | 95.8 | 96.6 |
| | | 9.8 | 8.1 | | | | Operating Profit | 4.2 | 3.4 |
| | | .7 | .9 | | | | All Other Expenses (net) | .2 | -1.3 |
| | | 9.1 | 7.2 | | | | Profit Before Taxes | 4.0 | 4.7 |
| | | | | | | | RATIOS | | |
| | | 5.3 | 3.4 | | | | | 3.5 | 4.7 |
| | | 3.1 | 1.7 | | | | Current | 1.8 | 2.8 |
| | | 1.8 | .8 | | | | | .9 | 1.2 |
| | | 4.0 | 2.5 | | | | | 2.7 | 3.8 |
| | | 2.0 | .8 | | | | Quick | 1.0 | 1.4 |
| | | 1.2 | .6 | | | | | .3 | .6 |
| | 0 | UND | 2 | 180.3 | | | | 1 | 302.3 | 0 | UND |
| | 9 | 38.9 | 30 | 12.3 | | | Sales/Receivables | 15 | 24.6 | 9 | 39.3 |
| | 34 | 10.7 | 59 | 6.2 | | | | 34 | 10.6 | 23 | 16.1 |
| | | | | | | | Cost of Sales/Inventory | | |
| | | | | | | | Cost of Sales/Payables | | |
| | | 6.3 | 3.2 | | | | | 6.8 | 4.4 |
| | | 12.4 | 14.8 | | | | Sales/Working Capital | 15.0 | 9.5 |
| | | 32.6 | -26.7 | | | | | -36.9 | 65.5 |
| | | 32.0 | | | | | | 22.2 | 19.4 |
| | (14) | 13.7 | | | | | EBIT/Interest | (36) | 4.2 | (18) | 6.4 |
| | | 5.2 | | | | | | .4 | 2.1 |
| | | | | | | | Net Profit + Depr., Dep., Amort./Cur. Mat. L/T/D | | |
| | | .1 | .1 | | | | | .1 | .1 |
| | | .4 | 1.8 | | | | Fixed/Worth | .7 | .4 |
| | | 1.5 | NM | | | | | 3.4 | -30.0 |
| | | .5 | .6 | | | | | .7 | .6 |
| | | .9 | 1.4 | | | | Debt/Worth | 1.8 | 1.7 |
| | | 2.6 | NM | | | | | 6.2 | -30.5 |
| | | 126.1 | | | | | | 79.5 | 68.2 |
| | (16) | 57.0 | | | | | % Profit Before Taxes/Tangible Net Worth | (37) | 42.2 | (22) | 36.6 |
| | | 17.1 | | | | | | 17.6 | 7.0 |
| | | 35.2 | 27.4 | | | | | 32.9 | 31.3 |
| | | 22.9 | 6.4 | | | | % Profit Before Taxes/Total Assets | 8.4 | 14.2 |
| | | 9.0 | .8 | | | | | -1.0 | 2.3 |
| | | 73.6 | 50.3 | | | | | 93.2 | 39.9 |
| | | 24.8 | 9.7 | | | | Sales/Net Fixed Assets | 22.3 | 24.0 |
| | | 5.9 | 2.6 | | | | | 5.7 | 6.1 |
| | | 5.0 | 3.4 | | | | | 5.0 | 4.7 |
| | | 2.4 | 1.6 | | | | Sales/Total Assets | 3.1 | 2.6 |
| | | 1.8 | 1.0 | | | | | 1.6 | 1.3 |
| | | | | | | | | 1.0 | 1.0 |
| | | | | | | | % Depr., Dep., Amort./Sales | (31) | 1.9 | (17) | 2.5 |
| | | | | | | | | 4.4 | 5.3 |
| | | | | | | | | 1.9 | 1.5 |
| | | | | | | | % Officers', Directors' Owners' Comp/Sales | (23) | 4.2 | (11) | 4.1 |
| | | | | | | | | 9.3 | 10.3 |
| | 4993M | 69156M | 86597M | 192035M | 266560M | 1528000M | Net Sales ($) | 374317M | 274534M |
| | 792M | 20681M | 31010M | 118051M | 137930M | 235000M | Total Assets ($) | 247145M | 160738M |

M = $ thousand    MM = $ million
See Pages viii through xx for Explanation of Ratios and Data

© RMA 2024

## OTHER SERVICES—Specialized Automotive Repair  NAICS 811114

### Comparative Historical Data | Current Data Sorted by Sales

| Comparative Historical Data ||| Type of Statement | Current Data Sorted by Sales |||||| |
|---|---|---|---|---|---|---|---|---|---|
| 1 | 1 | 2 | Unqualified | 1 | 1 | | | | 1 |
| 1 | 1 | 1 | Reviewed | | | | 1 | | |
| 2 | 4 | 1 | Compiled | | | | 1 | 3 | 1 |
| 13 | 14 | 11 | Tax Returns | 4 | 2 | 1 | 6 | 2 | 5 |
| 24 4/1/21- 3/31/22 | 20 4/1/22- 3/31/23 | 25 4/1/23- 3/31/24 | Other | 8 | 3 | | | | |
| ALL | ALL | ALL | | 1 | 2 (4/1-9/30/23) ||| 38 (10/1/23-3/31/24) |||
| | | | | 0-1MM | 1-3MM | 3-5MM | 5-10MM | 10-25MM | 25MM & OVER |
| 40 | 40 | 40 | NUMBER OF STATEMENTS | 1 | 13 | 6 | 8 | 5 | 7 |
| % | % | % | ASSETS | % | % | % | % | % | % |
| 36.5 | 23.5 | 19.7 | Cash & Equivalents | | 16.0 | | | | |
| 11.6 | 15.1 | 15.0 | Trade Receivables (net) | | 8.5 | | | | |
| 12.2 | 19.2 | 14.9 | Inventory | | 7.6 | | | | |
| 3.7 | 1.9 | 2.9 | All Other Current | | 1.2 | | | | |
| 64.0 | 59.6 | 52.6 | Total Current | | 33.3 | | | | |
| 20.3 | 23.4 | 26.3 | Fixed Assets (net) | | 31.2 | | | | |
| 5.5 | 6.1 | 12.2 | Intangibles (net) | | 28.0 | | | | |
| 10.2 | 10.8 | 9.0 | All Other Non-Current | | 7.5 | | | | |
| 100.0 | 100.0 | 100.0 | Total | | 100.0 | | | | |
| | | | LIABILITIES | | | | | | |
| 7.2 | 8.8 | 8.9 | Notes Payable-Short Term | | 3.1 | | | | |
| .8 | 1.7 | 2.1 | Cur. Mat.-L.T.D. | | 1.4 | | | | |
| 9.4 | 12.3 | 8.2 | Trade Payables | | 4.4 | | | | |
| .1 | .2 | .1 | Income Taxes Payable | | .0 | | | | |
| 13.9 | 9.4 | 8.3 | All Other Current | | 7.6 | | | | |
| 31.4 | 32.4 | 27.7 | Total Current | | 16.5 | | | | |
| 27.3 | 19.4 | 24.7 | Long-Term Debt | | 41.7 | | | | |
| .0 | .0 | .0 | Deferred Taxes | | .0 | | | | |
| 5.7 | 6.5 | 5.2 | All Other Non-Current | | 3.0 | | | | |
| 35.6 | 41.6 | 42.4 | Net Worth | | 38.8 | | | | |
| 100.0 | 100.0 | 100.0 | Total Liabilities & Net Worth | | 100.0 | | | | |
| | | | INCOME DATA | | | | | | |
| 100.0 | 100.0 | 100.0 | Net Sales | | 100.0 | | | | |
| | | | Gross Profit | | | | | | |
| 91.2 | 95.3 | 92.0 | Operating Expenses | | 85.6 | | | | |
| 8.8 | 4.7 | 8.0 | Operating Profit | | 14.4 | | | | |
| -2.0 | -.5 | .9 | All Other Expenses (net) | | 1.9 | | | | |
| 10.9 | 5.2 | 7.2 | Profit Before Taxes | | 12.5 | | | | |
| | | | RATIOS | | | | | | |
| 6.0 | 4.0 | 3.7 | | | 3.7 | | | | |
| 2.4 | 1.9 | 2.3 | Current | | 2.3 | | | | |
| 1.5 | 1.4 | 1.1 | | | .9 | | | | |
| 4.6 | 3.2 | 2.8 | | | 3.0 | | | | |
| 1.5 | 1.5 | 1.5 | Quick | | 1.6 | | | | |
| .9 | .5 | .6 | | | .6 | | | | |
| 0 UND | 1 473.8 | 0 UND | | | 0 UND | | | | |
| 3 108.9 | 19 19.7 | 14 25.7 | Sales/Receivables | | 0 869.7 | | | | |
| 25 14.6 | 53 6.9 | 43 8.5 | | | 58 6.3 | | | | |
| | | | Cost of Sales/Inventory | | | | | | |
| | | | Cost of Sales/Payables | | | | | | |
| 4.5 | 4.2 | 6.1 | | | 5.2 | | | | |
| 9.7 | 10.4 | 10.8 | Sales/Working Capital | | 20.8 | | | | |
| 25.8 | 20.7 | 357.7 | | | NM | | | | |
| 42.7 | 17.1 | 24.4 | | | | | | | |
| (24) 10.7 | (28) 3.0 | (30) 10.1 | EBIT/Interest | | | | | | |
| 4.4 | 1.1 | 3.0 | | | | | | | |
| | | | Net Profit + Depr., Dep., Amort./Cur. Mat. L/T/D | | | | | | |
| .1 | .1 | .2 | | | .5 | | | | |
| .4 | .5 | .5 | Fixed/Worth | | 1.0 | | | | |
| 3.0 | 1.6 | 2.8 | | | NM | | | | |
| .5 | .5 | .5 | | | .8 | | | | |
| 1.3 | 1.5 | 1.2 | Debt/Worth | | 2.6 | | | | |
| 10.6 | 5.3 | 3.7 | | | NM | | | | |
| 238.4 | 68.3 | 86.4 | % Profit Before Taxes/Tangible Net Worth | | 162.1 | | | | |
| (34) 70.8 | (33) 26.8 | (34) 30.7 | | (10) | 86.6 | | | | |
| 24.1 | 3.9 | 10.3 | | | 54.8 | | | | |
| 46.9 | 30.3 | 28.7 | % Profit Before Taxes/Total Assets | | 34.0 | | | | |
| 29.1 | 9.3 | 13.3 | | | 22.9 | | | | |
| 12.7 | .5 | 2.1 | | | 2.1 | | | | |
| 128.5 | 57.5 | 55.5 | Sales/Net Fixed Assets | | 27.5 | | | | |
| 39.5 | 17.2 | 21.3 | | | 12.8 | | | | |
| 11.5 | 5.1 | 4.1 | | | 2.7 | | | | |
| 6.3 | 3.7 | 4.0 | Sales/Total Assets | | 2.2 | | | | |
| 2.8 | 1.7 | 2.2 | | | 1.8 | | | | |
| 2.1 | 1.4 | 1.5 | | | 1.0 | | | | |
| .2 | .5 | .7 | % Depr., Dep., Amort./Sales | | | | | | |
| (23) 1.8 | (23) 1.9 | (18) 2.0 | | | | | | | |
| 4.5 | 5.9 | 4.6 | | | | | | | |
| 2.7 | 2.0 | 1.2 | % Officers', Directors' Owners' Comp/Sales | | | | | | |
| (19) 5.6 | (18) 4.6 | (11) 1.8 | | | | | | | |
| 6.9 | 9.2 | 7.1 | | | | | | | |
| 201763M | 659741M | 2147341M | Net Sales ($) | 222M | 21661M | 23683M | 55006M | 93494M | 1953275M |
| 98115M | 360478M | 543464M | Total Assets ($) | 236M | 16215M | 8848M | 14906M | 64539M | 438720M |

© RMA 2024  M = $ thousand  MM = $ million
See Pages viii through xx for Explanation of Ratios and Data

# OTHER SERVICES—Automotive Body, Paint, and Interior Repair and Maintenance  NAICS 811121

## Current Data Sorted by Assets | Comparative Historical Data

| | | | | | | | | | |
|---|---|---|---|---|---|---|---|---|---|
| | | | | 2 | | | Type of Statement | | |
| | | | 4 | 3 | | | Unqualified | 5 | 1 |
| 2 | 2 | | 3 | 2 | | | Reviewed | 7 | 3 |
| 14 | 21 | | 8 | 2 | | | Compiled | 11 | 4 |
| 18 | 28 | | 35 | 2 | | 1 | Tax Returns | 76 | 43 |
| | 15 (4/1-9/30/23) | | | 8 | 1 | | Other | 102 | 90 |
| | | | | 139 (10/1/23-3/31/24) | | | | 4/1/19- | 4/1/20- |
| | | | | | | | | 3/31/20 | 3/31/21 |
| 0-500M | 500M-2MM | 2-10MM | 10-50MM | 50-100MM | 100-250MM | | | ALL | ALL |
| 34 | 51 | 50 | 17 | 1 | 1 | | NUMBER OF STATEMENTS | 201 | 141 |
| % | % | % | % | % | % | | ASSETS | % | % |
| 34.8 | 32.0 | 21.3 | 18.1 | | | | Cash & Equivalents | 24.1 | 30.2 |
| 13.8 | 9.4 | 10.5 | 12.0 | | | | Trade Receivables (net) | 13.1 | 10.0 |
| 10.7 | 5.0 | 8.8 | 17.5 | | | | Inventory | 8.4 | 7.0 |
| 4.2 | 7.4 | 5.5 | 3.4 | | | | All Other Current | 5.1 | 3.4 |
| 63.5 | 53.8 | 46.1 | 51.0 | | | | Total Current | 50.6 | 50.6 |
| 29.0 | 26.2 | 42.1 | 30.1 | | | | Fixed Assets (net) | 32.2 | 29.7 |
| 4.4 | 10.1 | 3.3 | 8.2 | | | | Intangibles (net) | 7.8 | 9.8 |
| 3.1 | 9.8 | 8.4 | 10.7 | | | | All Other Non-Current | 9.4 | 9.8 |
| 100.0 | 100.0 | 100.0 | 100.0 | | | | Total | 100.0 | 100.0 |
| | | | | | | | LIABILITIES | | |
| 19.7 | 4.7 | 4.0 | 3.1 | | | | Notes Payable-Short Term | 14.6 | 16.8 |
| 4.1 | 1.5 | 1.5 | 1.2 | | | | Cur. Mat.-L.T.D. | 3.2 | 3.6 |
| 7.3 | 8.5 | 9.1 | 9.0 | | | | Trade Payables | 12.7 | 9.0 |
| .1 | .1 | .1 | .0 | | | | Income Taxes Payable | .2 | .1 |
| 20.1 | 20.0 | 9.9 | 14.5 | | | | All Other Current | 15.2 | 14.1 |
| 51.3 | 34.8 | 24.6 | 27.8 | | | | Total Current | 45.8 | 43.5 |
| 37.5 | 20.8 | 29.1 | 16.6 | | | | Long-Term Debt | 21.4 | 30.8 |
| .0 | .0 | .0 | .0 | | | | Deferred Taxes | .0 | .0 |
| 6.4 | 4.1 | 4.5 | 15.2 | | | | All Other Non-Current | 9.5 | 6.2 |
| 4.8 | 40.3 | 41.9 | 40.4 | | | | Net Worth | 23.3 | 19.4 |
| 100.0 | 100.0 | 100.0 | 100.0 | | | | Total Liabilities & Net Worth | 100.0 | 100.0 |
| | | | | | | | INCOME DATA | | |
| 100.0 | 100.0 | 100.0 | 100.0 | | | | Net Sales | 100.0 | 100.0 |
| | | | | | | | Gross Profit | | |
| 92.9 | 90.6 | 77.7 | 92.2 | | | | Operating Expenses | 92.6 | 93.9 |
| 7.1 | 9.4 | 22.3 | 7.8 | | | | Operating Profit | 7.4 | 6.1 |
| 1.9 | 2.9 | 6.5 | -1.2 | | | | All Other Expenses (net) | 1.2 | -.2 |
| 5.2 | 6.5 | 15.8 | 9.0 | | | | Profit Before Taxes | 6.2 | 6.3 |
| | | | | | | | RATIOS | | |
| 3.3 | 4.6 | 4.1 | 2.6 | | | | | 2.3 | 3.6 |
| 1.4 | 2.4 | 2.0 | 1.6 | | | | Current | 1.3 | 1.4 |
| .8 | 1.0 | .8 | 1.2 | | | | | .7 | .6 |
| 2.8 | 4.6 | 3.0 | 1.7 | | | | | 1.9 | 2.8 |
| 1.3 | 1.6 | 1.4 | 1.1 | | | | Quick | .8 | 1.0 |
| .3 | .5 | .5 | .7 | | | | | .4 | .4 |
| 0 UND | 0 UND | 0 UND | 9 42.9 | | | | | 0 UND | 0 UND |
| 3 117.2 | 5 71.9 | 8 43.2 | 21 17.2 | | | | Sales/Receivables | 8 47.7 | 7 51.4 |
| 12 29.3 | 14 26.3 | 31 11.7 | 31 11.9 | | | | | 16 22.8 | 17 22.0 |
| | | | | | | | Cost of Sales/Inventory | | |
| | | | | | | | Cost of Sales/Payables | | |
| 14.9 | 5.5 | 4.0 | 4.3 | | | | | 12.2 | 8.9 |
| 28.6 | 13.5 | 9.6 | 8.4 | | | | Sales/Working Capital | 45.6 | 29.4 |
| -71.7 | 999.8 | -23.1 | 63.6 | | | | | -31.5 | -17.8 |
| 21.8 | 81.2 | 48.0 | 72.6 | | | | | 24.1 | 44.8 |
| (21) 5.9 | (36) 16.7 | (34) 10.3 | (15) 30.1 | | | | EBIT/Interest | (144) 6.9 | (107) 7.1 |
| .7 | 1.8 | 2.8 | 2.4 | | | | | 1.8 | 1.5 |
| | | | | | | | Net Profit + Depr., Dep., Amort./Cur. Mat. L/T/D | | |
| .1 | .2 | .2 | .3 | | | | | .4 | .3 |
| 1.0 | .6 | 1.1 | .9 | | | | Fixed/Worth | 1.2 | 1.4 |
| -4.6 | 5.2 | 4.0 | 3.6 | | | | | -16.0 | -1.4 |
| .8 | .4 | .5 | .7 | | | | | .8 | 1.0 |
| 3.2 | 1.2 | 1.5 | 1.9 | | | | Debt/Worth | 3.2 | 3.1 |
| -5.5 | 12.0 | 5.3 | 7.7 | | | | | -20.2 | -5.5 |
| 194.1 | 94.7 | 73.3 | 110.1 | | | | | 106.5 | 96.8 |
| (23) 105.1 | (39) 48.0 | (45) 38.5 | (15) 60.7 | | | | % Profit Before Taxes/Tangible Net Worth | (144) 44.5 | (96) 41.4 |
| 36.8 | 27.6 | 12.2 | 18.2 | | | | | 15.6 | 21.0 |
| 92.3 | 36.4 | 32.2 | 31.9 | | | | | 36.4 | 35.1 |
| 46.4 | 20.6 | 13.7 | 16.9 | | | | % Profit Before Taxes/Total Assets | 12.3 | 12.2 |
| .3 | 1.5 | 3.9 | 7.1 | | | | | 3.4 | 2.1 |
| 145.2 | 57.4 | 24.4 | 22.1 | | | | | 62.7 | 42.7 |
| 28.7 | 16.4 | 6.1 | 9.1 | | | | Sales/Net Fixed Assets | 16.8 | 18.0 |
| 16.9 | 5.2 | 1.4 | 3.8 | | | | | 6.8 | 7.7 |
| 11.6 | 4.9 | 2.6 | 2.8 | | | | | 6.7 | 5.9 |
| 7.7 | 3.1 | 2.0 | 1.8 | | | | Sales/Total Assets | 3.9 | 3.5 |
| 3.3 | 1.7 | .9 | 1.3 | | | | | 2.2 | 2.1 |
| .3 | .3 | .3 | .4 | | | | | .7 | .4 |
| (17) 1.4 | (25) 1.4 | (28) 1.7 | (14) 2.1 | | | | % Depr., Dep., Amort./Sales | (124) 1.5 | (79) 1.1 |
| 3.4 | 4.2 | 3.9 | 3.4 | | | | | 2.7 | 2.8 |
| 2.6 | 2.1 | 1.0 | | | | | | 1.7 | 2.6 |
| (17) 4.0 | (25) 3.8 | (18) 2.5 | | | | | % Officers', Directors' Owners' Comp/Sales | (107) 3.7 | (70) 4.1 |
| 5.4 | 7.9 | 3.3 | | | | | | 6.1 | 7.5 |
| 56972M | 204168M | 437100M | 602105M | 65181M | 2958505M | | Net Sales ($) | 7499704M | 2013379M |
| 7924M | 55174M | 224690M | 297441M | 59636M | 223544M | | Total Assets ($) | 772640M | 677141M |

M = $ thousand    MM = $ million
See Pages viii through xx for Explanation of Ratios and Data

© RMA 2024

# OTHER SERVICES—Automotive Body, Paint, and Interior Repair and Maintenance  NAICS 811121

## Comparative Historical Data | Current Data Sorted by Sales

| | | | Type of Statement | | | | | | |
|---|---|---|---|---|---|---|---|---|---|
| 1 | 3 | 2 | Unqualified | | | | 1 | 1 | 1 |
| 2 | 2 | 7 | Reviewed | | | | | 5 | 2 |
| 3 | 7 | 9 | Compiled | 1 | 4 | 1 | 8 | 2 | 1 |
| 37 | 55 | 46 | Tax Returns | 3 | 17 | 11 | 21 | 3 | 4 |
| 82 | 96 | 90 | Other | 22 | 17 | 13 | 21 | 9 | 8 |
| 4/1/21-3/31/22 ALL | 4/1/22-3/31/23 ALL | 4/1/23-3/31/24 ALL | | | 15 (4/1-9/30/23) | | | 139 (10/1/23-3/31/24) | |
| | | | | 0-1MM | 1-3MM | 3-5MM | 5-10MM | 10-25MM | 25MM & OVER |
| 125 | 163 | 154 | NUMBER OF STATEMENTS | 26 | 38 | 25 | 30 | 19 | 16 |
| % | % | % | ASSETS | % | % | % | % | % | % |
| 27.9 | 30.3 | 27.3 | Cash & Equivalents | 20.8 | 30.4 | 32.9 | 31.1 | 26.3 | 15.7 |
| 9.8 | 11.0 | 11.0 | Trade Receivables (net) | 9.2 | 8.7 | 10.0 | 7.5 | 21.4 | 15.5 |
| 9.0 | 10.0 | 8.8 | Inventory | 7.4 | 7.5 | 5.5 | 9.9 | 11.3 | 14.6 |
| 5.3 | 4.2 | 5.5 | All Other Current | 4.0 | 3.1 | 7.7 | 7.2 | 8.9 | 3.5 |
| 52.0 | 55.5 | 52.7 | Total Current | 41.3 | 49.8 | 56.1 | 55.8 | 67.8 | 49.3 |
| 29.4 | 28.6 | 33.1 | Fixed Assets (net) | 45.2 | 38.0 | 23.4 | 31.6 | 20.6 | 34.5 |
| 9.4 | 7.5 | 6.3 | Intangibles (net) | 7.1 | 5.4 | 7.4 | 6.2 | 6.0 | 6.0 |
| 9.2 | 8.4 | 7.9 | All Other Non-Current | 6.4 | 6.8 | 13.1 | 6.4 | 5.5 | 10.3 |
| 100.0 | 100.0 | 100.0 | Total | 100.0 | 100.0 | 100.0 | 100.0 | 100.0 | 100.0 |
| | | | LIABILITIES | | | | | | |
| 8.3 | 11.3 | 7.6 | Notes Payable-Short Term | 11.1 | 11.6 | 6.7 | 5.0 | 2.9 | 3.9 |
| 2.3 | 3.3 | 2.1 | Cur. Mat.-L.T.D. | 1.1 | 4.4 | .8 | 1.2 | 1.5 | 2.7 |
| 8.8 | 9.9 | 8.4 | Trade Payables | 5.1 | 4.6 | 11.0 | 10.4 | 14.4 | 8.3 |
| .6 | .2 | .1 | Income Taxes Payable | .0 | .1 | .0 | .1 | .2 | .0 |
| 12.9 | 13.0 | 15.9 | All Other Current | 17.8 | 14.7 | 19.7 | 13.2 | 9.8 | 21.9 |
| 32.9 | 37.7 | 34.0 | Total Current | 35.1 | 35.4 | 38.2 | 29.9 | 28.8 | 36.7 |
| 38.9 | 27.1 | 27.9 | Long-Term Debt | 44.7 | 40.2 | 16.3 | 15.9 | 14.3 | 28.3 |
| .2 | .0 | .0 | Deferred Taxes | .0 | .0 | .0 | .0 | .0 | .0 |
| 4.5 | 5.5 | 5.9 | All Other Non-Current | 3.9 | 6.0 | 1.1 | 4.6 | 9.4 | 14.5 |
| 23.6 | 29.7 | 32.2 | Net Worth | 16.3 | 18.4 | 44.5 | 49.6 | 47.4 | 20.5 |
| 100.0 | 100.0 | 100.0 | Total Liabilities & Net Worth | 100.0 | 100.0 | 100.0 | 100.0 | 100.0 | 100.0 |
| | | | INCOME DATA | | | | | | |
| 100.0 | 100.0 | 100.0 | Net Sales | 100.0 | 100.0 | 100.0 | 100.0 | 100.0 | 100.0 |
| | | | Gross Profit | | | | | | |
| 92.2 | 90.9 | 87.2 | Operating Expenses | 67.4 | 93.5 | 88.2 | 90.9 | 88.9 | 93.6 |
| 7.8 | 9.1 | 12.8 | Operating Profit | 32.6 | 6.5 | 11.8 | 9.1 | 11.1 | 6.4 |
| -.9 | .5 | 3.4 | All Other Expenses (net) | 19.8 | .3 | .6 | .8 | -1.9 | -.7 |
| 8.7 | 8.6 | 9.5 | Profit Before Taxes | 12.8 | 6.2 | 11.2 | 8.3 | 12.9 | 7.2 |
| | | | RATIOS | | | | | | |
| 4.4 | 4.4 | 3.7 | | 2.9 | 5.1 | 3.6 | 5.5 | 3.6 | 2.6 |
| 2.2 | 1.8 | 1.8 | Current | 1.1 | 1.8 | 1.5 | 2.3 | 2.0 | 1.5 |
| 1.0 | 1.0 | .9 | | .6 | .6 | .9 | 1.3 | 1.6 | 1.1 |
| 3.4 | 3.2 | 3.0 | | 2.8 | 5.1 | 2.5 | 3.2 | 3.3 | 1.9 |
| 1.5 | 1.2 | 1.3 | Quick | .9 | 1.4 | 1.1 | 1.7 | 1.6 | 1.0 |
| .6 | .6 | .5 | | .3 | .3 | .6 | .7 | .8 | .7 |
| 0 UND | 0 UND | 0 UND | | 0 UND | 0 UND | 0 UND | 0 UND | 17 21.8 | 8 44.9 |
| 7 52.3 | 6 63.1 | 7 53.3 | Sales/Receivables | 5 67.5 | 0 UND | 3 109.1 | 5 68.5 | 29 12.7 | 13 27.7 |
| 20 18.5 | 16 23.1 | 22 16.5 | | 52 7.0 | 11 32.1 | 10 38.0 | 13 29.1 | 37 9.8 | 27 13.3 |
| | | | Cost of Sales/Inventory | | | | | | |
| | | | | | | | | | |
| | | | | | | | | | |
| | | | Cost of Sales/Payables | | | | | | |
| | | | | | | | | | |
| | | | | | | | | | |
| 6.6 | 7.7 | 5.8 | | 4.7 | 7.9 | 7.1 | 4.2 | 4.3 | 7.4 |
| 14.2 | 18.9 | 15.1 | Sales/Working Capital | NM | 21.0 | 24.2 | 11.8 | 6.3 | 16.4 |
| NM | -999.8 | -95.8 | | -5.4 | -22.0 | -69.0 | 64.1 | 14.1 | 106.8 |
| 50.0 | 30.9 | 58.6 | | 20.6 | 19.8 | 54.2 | 66.1 | 131.5 | 131.9 |
| (86) 17.5 | (101) 11.4 | (107) 10.5 | EBIT/Interest | (10) 3.9 | (28) 4.3 | (16) 25.8 | (24) 10.3 | (14) 43.6 | (15) 30.1 |
| 3.5 | 2.8 | 1.7 | | .0 | .1 | 2.8 | 2.8 | 13.5 | .8 |
| | | | Net Profit + Depr., Dep., Amort./Cur. Mat. L/T/D | | | | | | |
| | | | | | | | | | |
| | | | | | | | | | |
| .3 | .2 | .2 | | .1 | .3 | .1 | .3 | .1 | .4 |
| 1.3 | .8 | .9 | Fixed/Worth | 3.7 | 1.2 | .4 | .6 | .3 | 1.1 |
| -9.9 | 26.4 | 6.7 | | NM | -7.1 | 3.9 | 2.3 | 1.7 | NM |
| 1.1 | .6 | .6 | | 1.0 | .7 | .4 | .5 | .5 | 1.0 |
| 2.9 | 2.1 | 1.9 | Debt/Worth | 4.0 | 2.2 | 1.4 | 1.0 | 1.1 | 2.0 |
| -17.8 | 363.7 | 22.6 | | -5.7 | -24.8 | 11.0 | 3.2 | 6.6 | NM |
| 108.8 | 113.8 | 98.5 | | 92.6 | 120.2 | 144.1 | 77.5 | 128.6 | 104.5 |
| (87) 67.5 | (125) 43.9 | (122) 50.6 | % Profit Before Taxes/Tangible Net Worth | (19) 33.8 | (26) 45.0 | (21) 68.8 | (27) 43.8 | (17) 55.0 | (12) 71.5 |
| 35.4 | 15.5 | 17.5 | | 17.8 | 1.1 | 24.5 | 7.0 | 29.5 | 37.7 |
| 41.2 | 38.8 | 41.4 | | 20.8 | 57.2 | 52.6 | 40.8 | 62.4 | 38.1 |
| 18.5 | 16.2 | 20.0 | % Profit Before Taxes/Total Assets | 5.7 | 19.1 | 27.7 | 20.8 | 24.7 | 18.7 |
| 5.7 | 3.1 | 2.2 | | -.3 | -1.0 | 11.4 | 5.3 | 15.1 | .4 |
| 47.6 | 85.2 | 48.2 | | 40.7 | 25.1 | 91.1 | 41.7 | 87.3 | 25.3 |
| 16.7 | 16.9 | 13.9 | Sales/Net Fixed Assets | 1.8 | 12.5 | 43.6 | 12.0 | 24.6 | 12.1 |
| 6.3 | 7.1 | 4.5 | | .3 | 4.8 | 11.7 | 5.6 | 5.2 | 4.4 |
| 4.6 | 5.9 | 4.7 | | 1.7 | 6.2 | 8.3 | 4.4 | 2.9 | 4.1 |
| 2.7 | 3.3 | 2.6 | Sales/Total Assets | .7 | 3.1 | 4.1 | 2.5 | 2.6 | 2.4 |
| 1.5 | 2.0 | 1.4 | | .1 | 1.5 | 1.9 | 2.0 | 1.6 | 1.8 |
| .7 | .6 | .6 | | 1.7 | .6 | .0 | .1 | | 1.0 |
| (58) 1.7 | (83) 1.4 | (84) 1.6 | % Depr., Dep., Amort./Sales | (12) 10.6 | (23) 1.5 | (10) 1.1 | (18) 1.3 | (12) 1.8 | |
| 3.1 | 3.0 | 3.6 | | 17.6 | 3.3 | 2.4 | 3.6 | | 3.1 |
| 1.7 | 2.0 | 2.0 | | | 3.2 | 1.9 | 2.2 | | |
| (56) 3.8 | (81) 3.7 | (66) 3.3 | % Officers', Directors' Owners' Comp/Sales | (20) 4.4 | (16) 3.3 | (14) 3.0 | | | |
| 7.5 | 7.6 | 5.6 | | | 8.6 | 4.8 | 4.5 | | |
| 7449484M | 1053715M | 4324031M | Net Sales ($) | 10553M | 74464M | 95159M | 219445M | 294214M | 3630196M |
| 566832M | 468758M | 868409M | Total Assets ($) | 30708M | 35312M | 42596M | 103946M | 129024M | 526823M |

© RMA 2024          M = $ thousand     MM = $ million
See Pages viii through xx for Explanation of Ratios and Data

## OTHER SERVICES—Automotive Oil Change and Lubrication Shops  NAICS 811191

### Current Data Sorted by Assets | Comparative Historical Data

| | | | | | | Type of Statement | | |
|---|---|---|---|---|---|---|---|---|
| | | 1 | | 1 | | Unqualified | 2 | |
| 1 | 1 | | 2 | | 1 | Reviewed | 4 | 1 |
| 6 | 2 | 6 | | | | Compiled | 8 | 6 |
| 5 | 7 | 9 | 5 | 2 | | Tax Returns | 28 | 21 |
| | 3 (4/1-9/30/23) | | 47 (10/1/23-3/31/24) | | | Other | 48 | 24 |
| 0-500M | 500M-2MM | 2-10MM | 10-50MM | 50-100MM | 100-250MM | | 4/1/19-3/31/20 ALL | 4/1/20-3/31/21 ALL |
| 12 | 10 | 16 | 7 | 3 | 2 | NUMBER OF STATEMENTS | 90 | 52 |
| % | % | % | % | % | % | ASSETS | % | % |
| 51.5 | 19.6 | 18.3 | | | | Cash & Equivalents | 19.9 | 22.0 |
| 11.7 | 3.1 | 2.7 | | | | Trade Receivables (net) | 4.2 | 1.5 |
| 7.2 | 2.4 | 7.0 | | | | Inventory | 11.6 | 10.4 |
| .7 | 3.1 | 1.7 | | | | All Other Current | 1.3 | 3.2 |
| 71.2 | 28.2 | 29.7 | | | | Total Current | 37.1 | 37.1 |
| 2.5 | 64.2 | 48.0 | | | | Fixed Assets (net) | 45.6 | 38.2 |
| 7.7 | 4.0 | 16.7 | | | | Intangibles (net) | 10.6 | 14.5 |
| 18.6 | 3.5 | 5.6 | | | | All Other Non-Current | 6.6 | 10.2 |
| 100.0 | 100.0 | 100.0 | | | | Total | 100.0 | 100.0 |
| | | | | | | LIABILITIES | | |
| 2.4 | 4.5 | 2.4 | | | | Notes Payable-Short Term | 7.6 | 8.5 |
| 1.3 | 14.7 | 5.9 | | | | Cur. Mat.-L.T.D. | 3.6 | 3.8 |
| 4.9 | 4.0 | 6.5 | | | | Trade Payables | 8.1 | 3.7 |
| .4 | .0 | .1 | | | | Income Taxes Payable | .2 | .0 |
| 40.4 | 28.4 | 6.5 | | | | All Other Current | 15.4 | 16.4 |
| 49.4 | 51.6 | 21.3 | | | | Total Current | 34.9 | 32.4 |
| 36.2 | 118.4 | 59.8 | | | | Long-Term Debt | 44.7 | 41.7 |
| .0 | .0 | .0 | | | | Deferred Taxes | .0 | .0 |
| 7.1 | 2.8 | 3.9 | | | | All Other Non-Current | 10.0 | 5.3 |
| 7.4 | -72.9 | 14.9 | | | | Net Worth | 10.5 | 20.6 |
| 100.0 | 100.0 | 100.0 | | | | Total Liabilities & Net Worth | 100.0 | 100.0 |
| | | | | | | INCOME DATA | | |
| 100.0 | 100.0 | 100.0 | | | | Net Sales | 100.0 | 100.0 |
| | | | | | | Gross Profit | | |
| 89.9 | 71.7 | 76.5 | | | | Operating Expenses | 85.6 | 94.9 |
| 10.1 | 28.3 | 23.5 | | | | Operating Profit | 14.4 | 5.1 |
| .1 | 9.1 | 7.6 | | | | All Other Expenses (net) | 5.3 | .7 |
| 9.9 | 19.3 | 15.9 | | | | Profit Before Taxes | 9.1 | 4.4 |
| | | | | | | RATIOS | | |
| 7.5 | 2.1 | 3.1 | | | | | 3.4 | 3.9 |
| 3.0 | .8 | 1.5 | | | | Current | 1.4 | 1.7 |
| .6 | .1 | .4 | | | | | .6 | .4 |
| 7.5 | 1.4 | 2.6 | | | | | 1.9 | 2.4 |
| 2.8 | .8 | 1.0 | | | | Quick | .9 | .9 |
| .5 | .1 | .3 | | | | | .4 | .2 |
| 0  UND | 0  UND | 0  UND | | | | | 0  UND | 0  UND |
| 2  223.8 | 1  356.3 | 1  382.8 | | | | Sales/Receivables | 1  630.0 | 1  454.5 |
| 3  113.5 | 5  70.5 | 3  120.9 | | | | | 3  120.0 | 4  96.1 |
| | | | | | | Cost of Sales/Inventory | | |
| | | | | | | Cost of Sales/Payables | | |
| 10.5 | 24.8 | 5.3 | | | | | 13.0 | 6.4 |
| 44.3 | -126.7 | 22.8 | | | | Sales/Working Capital | 40.6 | 17.1 |
| -40.5 | -.7 | -7.5 | | | | | -26.5 | -9.7 |
| | | 23.4 | | | | | 14.0 | 14.9 |
| | (13) | 6.2 | | | | EBIT/Interest | (66) 4.4 | (34) 6.1 |
| | | 4.2 | | | | | 1.7 | .8 |
| | | | | | | Net Profit + Depr., Dep., Amort./Cur. Mat. L/T/D | | |
| .0 | 1.3 | .9 | | | | | .6 | .5 |
| UND | NM | 37.1 | | | | Fixed/Worth | 4.4 | 2.5 |
| -.2 | -.5 | -.6 | | | | | -2.9 | -1.5 |
| .3 | 2.1 | 1.0 | | | | | 1.0 | 1.3 |
| -10.0 | NM | 48.2 | | | | Debt/Worth | 11.0 | 3.4 |
| -3.1 | -1.6 | -2.3 | | | | | -4.1 | -4.3 |
| | | | | | | % Profit Before Taxes/Tangible Net Worth | 116.4 | 93.2 |
| | | | | | | | (53) 43.5 | (36) 35.8 |
| | | | | | | | 14.1 | -1.5 |
| 66.6 | 33.0 | 38.4 | | | | | 34.8 | 20.3 |
| 30.5 | 12.1 | 15.5 | | | | % Profit Before Taxes/Total Assets | 9.8 | 8.0 |
| 6.6 | -1.2 | 3.6 | | | | | .7 | -2.1 |
| UND | 51.7 | 17.5 | | | | | 74.7 | 53.4 |
| UND | 1.5 | 4.6 | | | | Sales/Net Fixed Assets | 8.2 | 8.2 |
| 243.1 | .5 | .4 | | | | | 1.1 | 1.3 |
| 15.6 | 2.5 | 3.1 | | | | | 6.3 | 3.5 |
| 6.7 | 1.2 | 1.8 | | | | Sales/Total Assets | 2.3 | 1.9 |
| 5.2 | .5 | .3 | | | | | .9 | .8 |
| | | 2.3 | | | | | 1.0 | .8 |
| | (10) | 4.2 | | | | % Depr., Dep., Amort./Sales | (55) 2.5 | (36) 2.4 |
| | | 13.8 | | | | | 5.4 | 6.1 |
| | | | | | | % Officers', Directors' Owners' Comp/Sales | 3.0 | 1.7 |
| | | | | | | | (28) 4.0 | (21) 8.0 |
| | | | | | | | 8.4 | 10.5 |
| 17537M | 18357M | 142627M | 226170M | 159281M | 132128M | Net Sales ($) | 931785M | 347425M |
| 2654M | 10711M | 82915M | 177128M | 191606M | 275877M | Total Assets ($) | 547094M | 298579M |

© RMA 2024   M = $ thousand   MM = $ million
See Pages viii through xx for Explanation of Ratios and Data

## OTHER SERVICES—Automotive Oil Change and Lubrication Shops  NAICS 811191

### Comparative Historical Data | Current Data Sorted by Sales

| | | | Type of Statement | | | | | | |
|---|---|---|---|---|---|---|---|---|---|
| 1 | 3 | 2 | Unqualified | | | | | 1 | 1 |
| 2 | 2 | 3 | Reviewed | | 2 | | | 2 | 1 |
| 3 | 2 | 2 | Compiled | | 6 | 2 | 2 | 1 | |
| 18 | 19 | 14 | Tax Returns | 3 | 6 | 2 | 2 | 7 | 6 |
| 27 | 20 | 29 | Other | 7 | 7 | | 2 | | |
| 4/1/21- 3/31/22 | 4/1/22- 3/31/23 | 4/1/23- 3/31/24 | | | 3 (4/1-9/30/23) | | | 47 (10/1/23-3/31/24) | |
| ALL | ALL | ALL | | 0-1MM | 1-3MM | 3-5MM | 5-10MM | 10-25MM | 25MM & OVER |
| 51 | 46 | 50 | NUMBER OF STATEMENTS | 10 | 15 | 2 | 4 | 11 | 8 |
| % | % | % | ASSETS | % | % | % | % | % | % |
| 23.9 | 25.6 | 24.7 | Cash & Equivalents | 25.9 | 31.7 | | | 13.2 | |
| 3.9 | 3.2 | 4.5 | Trade Receivables (net) | .2 | 10.0 | | | 3.6 | |
| 12.1 | 8.7 | 5.4 | Inventory | .0 | 7.2 | | | 9.9 | |
| 4.5 | 2.1 | 1.7 | All Other Current | .0 | 2.3 | | | 2.9 | |
| 44.5 | 39.5 | 36.2 | Total Current | 26.2 | 51.2 | | | 29.5 | |
| 40.7 | 41.7 | 41.4 | Fixed Assets (net) | 60.3 | 30.0 | | | 42.7 | |
| 11.0 | 8.8 | 11.0 | Intangibles (net) | 5.7 | 5.0 | | | 15.7 | |
| 3.9 | 10.0 | 11.5 | All Other Non-Current | 7.8 | 13.8 | | | 12.2 | |
| 100.0 | 100.0 | 100.0 | Total | 100.0 | 100.0 | | | 100.0 | |
| | | | LIABILITIES | | | | | | |
| 4.5 | 4.6 | 2.3 | Notes Payable-Short Term | .1 | 2.8 | | | 1.2 | |
| 3.7 | 4.7 | 6.6 | Cur. Mat.-L.T.D. | 13.3 | 3.5 | | | 6.6 | |
| 5.7 | 4.6 | 4.7 | Trade Payables | .7 | 5.1 | | | 8.1 | |
| .1 | .0 | .1 | Income Taxes Payable | .0 | .4 | | | .2 | |
| 7.1 | 9.5 | 18.5 | All Other Current | 40.0 | 26.0 | | | 8.0 | |
| 21.0 | 23.5 | 32.2 | Total Current | 54.2 | 37.8 | | | 24.0 | |
| 48.3 | 55.9 | 60.9 | Long-Term Debt | 100.8 | 57.2 | | | 49.7 | |
| .0 | .0 | .0 | Deferred Taxes | .0 | .0 | | | .0 | |
| 13.0 | 7.3 | 7.1 | All Other Non-Current | 3.9 | 6.0 | | | 3.3 | |
| 17.7 | 13.4 | -.2 | Net Worth | -58.9 | -1.0 | | | 23.0 | |
| 100.0 | 100.0 | 100.0 | Total Liabilties & Net Worth | 100.0 | 100.0 | | | 100.0 | |
| | | | INCOME DATA | | | | | | |
| 100.0 | 100.0 | 100.0 | Net Sales | 100.0 | 100.0 | | | 100.0 | |
| | | | Gross Profit | | | | | | |
| 84.5 | 87.1 | 82.2 | Operating Expenses | 66.8 | 78.5 | | | 92.7 | |
| 15.5 | 12.9 | 17.8 | Operating Profit | 33.2 | 21.5 | | | 7.3 | |
| 1.8 | 1.4 | 4.8 | All Other Expenses (net) | 14.4 | 5.1 | | | -1.2 | |
| 13.7 | 11.5 | 13.1 | Profit Before Taxes | 18.8 | 16.4 | | | 8.5 | |
| | | | RATIOS | | | | | | |
| 4.9 | 9.4 | 3.4 | | 2.2 | 3.9 | | | 2.1 | |
| 2.6 | 2.0 | 1.3 | Current | .8 | 1.0 | | | 1.4 | |
| 1.3 | .9 | .5 | | .1 | .4 | | | .6 | |
| 3.3 | 6.3 | 2.7 | | 2.2 | 3.5 | | | 1.4 | |
| 1.7 | 1.8 | 1.0 | Quick | .8 | 1.0 | | | .5 | |
| .6 | .6 | .2 | | .1 | .4 | | | .1 | |
| 0 UND | 0 UND | 0 UND | | 0 UND | 0 UND | | | 0 999.8 | |
| 1 532.3 | 1 628.5 | 1 322.0 | Sales/Receivables | 0 UND | 2 218.7 | | | 3 131.0 | |
| 3 114.3 | 2 153.4 | 4 103.3 | | 0 UND | 9 39.4 | | | 7 54.3 | |
| | | | Cost of Sales/Inventory | | | | | | |
| | | | Cost of Sales/Payables | | | | | | |
| 4.8 | 5.1 | 8.3 | | 45.5 | 7.0 | | | 19.2 | |
| 14.0 | 11.3 | 50.7 | Sales/Working Capital | UND | -237.8 | | | 36.1 | |
| 51.1 | -119.0 | -13.1 | | -.7 | -13.5 | | | -28.9 | |
| 45.0 | 33.2 | 19.5 | | | | | | 27.6 | |
| (40) 11.0 | (38) 8.4 | (36) 5.2 | EBIT/Interest | | | | | (10) 10.8 | |
| 4.5 | 2.8 | 2.4 | | | | | | 3.7 | |
| | | | Net Profit + Depr., Dep., Amort./Cur. Mat. L/T/D | | | | | | |
| .3 | .1 | .3 | | 2.7 | .0 | | | .2 | |
| 2.5 | 1.8 | 14.3 | Fixed/Worth | UND | -8.5 | | | 1.4 | |
| -2.2 | -6.1 | -.8 | | -4.9 | -.3 | | | -1.0 | |
| .8 | .6 | 1.4 | | 2.1 | .3 | | | .6 | |
| 5.4 | 5.1 | 53.1 | Debt/Worth | UND | -11.2 | | | 2.0 | |
| -4.0 | -8.6 | -3.4 | | -6.4 | -3.1 | | | -2.2 | |
| 132.3 | 147.4 | 165.7 | % Profit Before Taxes/Tangible Net Worth | | | | | | |
| (32) 52.8 | (29) 48.2 | (27) 49.0 | | | | | | | |
| 24.1 | 27.3 | 20.9 | | | | | | | |
| 43.8 | 37.9 | 37.0 | % Profit Before Taxes/Total Assets | 134.0 | 42.0 | | | 39.1 | |
| 20.7 | 16.5 | 12.1 | | 6.6 | 18.2 | | | 20.9 | |
| 8.0 | 7.9 | 3.4 | | -2.7 | 7.2 | | | 3.6 | |
| 69.7 | 88.8 | 159.8 | Sales/Net Fixed Assets | UND | 472.3 | | | 38.3 | |
| 3.4 | 5.3 | 5.5 | | 1.0 | 52.5 | | | 4.7 | |
| 1.6 | 1.3 | 1.3 | | .1 | .9 | | | 2.4 | |
| 3.8 | 3.6 | 4.2 | Sales/Total Assets | 11.0 | 6.4 | | | 3.5 | |
| 1.6 | 1.6 | 1.7 | | .9 | 3.3 | | | 3.0 | |
| 1.1 | .9 | .9 | | .1 | .7 | | | 1.5 | |
| .9 | 1.1 | 1.5 | % Depr., Dep., Amort./Sales | | | | | | |
| (32) 2.4 | (25) 2.5 | (28) 4.9 | | | | | | | |
| 6.0 | 8.5 | 12.4 | | | | | | | |
| 1.9 | 2.2 | | % Officers', Directors' Owners' Comp/Sales | | | | | | |
| (19) 5.3 | (18) 3.5 | | | | | | | | |
| 10.0 | | 7.5 | | | | | | | |
| 405763M | 501966M | 696100M | Net Sales ($) | 4786M | 24289M | 7601M | 29641M | 201315M | 428468M |
| 266171M | 427808M | 740891M | Total Assets ($) | 16484M | 27266M | 2260M | 17522M | 238126M | 439233M |

© RMA 2024  M = $ thousand   MM = $ million
See Pages viii through xx for Explanation of Ratios and Data

## OTHER SERVICES—Car Washes  NAICS 811192

### Current Data Sorted by Assets

| | | | | | | Type of Statement |
|---|---|---|---|---|---|---|
| | | 3 | 6 | 1 | 7 | Unqualified |
| 3 | 10 | 9 | 1 | 1 | 1 | Reviewed |
| 23 | 33 | 22 | 2 | | | Compiled |
| 20 | 34 | 72 | 16 | 13 | 9 | Tax Returns |
| | 15 (4/1-9/30/23) | | 271 (10/1/23-3/31/24) | | | Other |
| 0-500M | 500M-2MM | 2-10MM | 10-50MM | 50-100MM | 100-250MM | |
| 46 | 77 | 106 | 25 | 15 | 17 | NUMBER OF STATEMENTS |

| % | % | % | % | % | % | ASSETS |
|---|---|---|---|---|---|---|
| 42.5 | 14.3 | 7.8 | 7.5 | 4.8 | 4.7 | Cash & Equivalents |
| 2.8 | 1.1 | 1.0 | 2.1 | .5 | 1.0 | Trade Receivables (net) |
| 2.2 | 1.9 | .8 | 1.1 | .6 | 2.4 | Inventory |
| 5.2 | .9 | 1.1 | .7 | 1.1 | 3.3 | All Other Current |
| 52.7 | 18.1 | 10.7 | 11.4 | 7.0 | 11.3 | Total Current |
| 32.1 | 64.0 | 70.4 | 66.9 | 73.2 | 76.9 | Fixed Assets (net) |
| 8.6 | 9.8 | 11.7 | 9.0 | 16.1 | 6.3 | Intangibles (net) |
| 6.6 | 8.0 | 7.2 | 12.8 | 3.7 | 5.5 | All Other Non-Current |
| 100.0 | 100.0 | 100.0 | 100.0 | 100.0 | 100.0 | Total |

| | | | | | | LIABILITIES |
|---|---|---|---|---|---|---|
| 12.0 | 2.2 | 2.8 | .8 | .2 | 5.0 | Notes Payable-Short Term |
| 5.8 | 6.1 | 2.6 | 3.9 | 2.0 | 2.8 | Cur. Mat.-L.T.D. |
| 2.7 | 1.6 | 4.0 | 1.9 | 3.3 | 2.9 | Trade Payables |
| .1 | .0 | .0 | .0 | .0 | .0 | Income Taxes Payable |
| 21.6 | 8.4 | 6.5 | 5.3 | 4.7 | 9.4 | All Other Current |
| 42.1 | 18.4 | 16.0 | 11.9 | 10.3 | 20.2 | Total Current |
| 47.5 | 95.4 | 74.3 | 48.2 | 51.7 | 41.8 | Long-Term Debt |
| .0 | .0 | .0 | .3 | .0 | .0 | Deferred Taxes |
| 13.5 | 4.7 | 5.1 | 6.9 | 10.7 | 4.8 | All Other Non-Current |
| -3.0 | -18.5 | 4.7 | 32.7 | 27.2 | 33.2 | Net Worth |
| 100.0 | 100.0 | 100.0 | 100.0 | 100.0 | 100.0 | Total Liabilities & Net Worth |

| | | | | | | INCOME DATA |
|---|---|---|---|---|---|---|
| 100.0 | 100.0 | 100.0 | 100.0 | 100.0 | 100.0 | Net Sales |
| | | | | | | Gross Profit |
| 88.7 | 76.7 | 77.8 | 73.0 | 86.0 | 93.3 | Operating Expenses |
| 11.3 | 23.3 | 22.2 | 27.0 | 14.0 | 6.7 | Operating Profit |
| 3.7 | 6.7 | 10.4 | 8.9 | 11.6 | 5.6 | All Other Expenses (net) |
| 7.6 | 16.6 | 11.9 | 18.1 | 2.4 | 1.2 | Profit Before Taxes |

| | | | | | | RATIOS |
|---|---|---|---|---|---|---|
| 9.6 | 4.2 | 2.4 | 1.9 | 1.2 | 1.0 | |
| 1.6 | 1.0 | .8 | 1.0 | .6 | .4 | Current |
| .7 | .3 | .2 | .5 | .2 | .1 | |
| 8.5 | 4.0 | 2.0 | 1.7 | 1.0 | .6 | |
| 1.3 | .8 | .6 | .9 | .5 | .3 | Quick |
| .3 | .2 | .2 | .3 | .2 | .1 | |
| 0 UND | 0 UND | 0 UND | 0 UND | 0 UND | 1 669.0 | |
| 0 UND | 0 UND | 0 UND | 0 999.8 | 1 538.4 | 1 408.3 | Sales/Receivables |
| 0 UND | 0 UND | 0 999.8 | 3 128.8 | 4 85.5 | 8 47.7 | |
| | | | | | | Cost of Sales/Inventory |
| | | | | | | Cost of Sales/Payables |
| 11.2 | 10.0 | 13.7 | 12.1 | 44.5 | NM | |
| 39.0 | -795.7 | -40.6 | -999.8 | -22.8 | -7.6 | Sales/Working Capital |
| -23.4 | -13.9 | -5.1 | -9.9 | -6.2 | -2.3 | |
| 29.7 | 10.6 | 6.0 | 7.4 | 3.0 | 5.2 | |
| (16) 4.8 | (60) 4.7 | (83) 3.3 | (21) 5.2 | (11) 1.9 | (15) 2.7 | EBIT/Interest |
| .3 | 1.2 | 1.1 | 1.6 | -.2 | -.3 | |
| | | | | | | Net Profit + Depr., Dep., Amort./Cur. Mat. L/T/D |
| .1 | 2.6 | 3.3 | 1.3 | 2.8 | 1.8 | |
| .9 | -6.3 | 14.1 | 3.6 | 5.7 | 2.9 | Fixed/Worth |
| -1.4 | -.7 | -3.3 | NM | -3.7 | 20.2 | |
| .3 | 2.3 | 3.2 | .9 | 2.1 | 1.0 | |
| 2.9 | -9.9 | 16.9 | 2.9 | 6.7 | 2.7 | Debt/Worth |
| -2.6 | -2.0 | -4.6 | NM | -5.0 | 20.2 | |
| 231.3 | 95.1 | 56.8 | 30.3 | | 27.0 | % Profit Before Taxes/Tangible Net Worth |
| (30) 89.0 | (30) 61.5 | (59) 18.6 | (19) 19.5 | (14) | 9.0 | |
| -1.0 | 14.2 | 2.6 | 4.8 | | -10.4 | |
| 70.0 | 45.2 | 13.8 | 12.2 | 5.0 | 6.7 | % Profit Before Taxes/Total Assets |
| 15.6 | 16.7 | 4.2 | 4.9 | 1.6 | 1.8 | |
| -5.3 | .8 | -.3 | 1.5 | -4.4 | -2.5 | |
| UND | 3.9 | 1.4 | 2.0 | 1.5 | 1.0 | |
| 37.4 | 1.7 | .6 | .6 | .9 | .5 | Sales/Net Fixed Assets |
| 7.4 | 1.0 | .3 | .4 | .3 | .3 | |
| 9.3 | 1.9 | .8 | .9 | .8 | .7 | |
| 5.0 | 1.1 | .4 | .4 | .6 | .4 | Sales/Total Assets |
| 2.7 | .7 | .3 | .2 | .3 | .2 | |
| .8 | 1.7 | 7.3 | 1.2 | 6.7 | 2.3 | |
| (23) 1.5 | (55) 4.9 | (74) 13.1 | (20) 7.1 | (13) 8.6 | (10) 9.0 | % Depr., Dep., Amort./Sales |
| 6.7 | 12.6 | 18.9 | 9.7 | 17.2 | 14.6 | |
| 3.0 | 2.9 | 2.5 | | | | % Officers', Directors' Owners' Comp/Sales |
| (13) 5.1 | (17) 3.6 | (13) 4.1 | | | | |
| 12.1 | 5.9 | 6.4 | | | | |
| 49057M | 146420M | 317487M | 385762M | 660210M | 1464325M | Net Sales ($) |
| 9705M | 97131M | 435599M | 635913M | 1121699M | 2689910M | Total Assets ($) |

### Comparative Historical Data

| | | | | Type of Statement |
|---|---|---|---|---|
| | 6 | | 4 | Unqualified |
| | 15 | | 7 | Reviewed |
| | 32 | | 26 | Compiled |
| | 87 | | 48 | Tax Returns |
| | 132 | | 126 | Other |
| | 4/1/19-3/31/20 ALL | | 4/1/20-3/31/21 ALL | |
| | 272 | | 211 | NUMBER OF STATEMENTS |

| | % | | % | ASSETS |
|---|---|---|---|---|
| | 15.0 | | 19.2 | Cash & Equivalents |
| | 1.8 | | 2.3 | Trade Receivables (net) |
| | 1.6 | | 1.7 | Inventory |
| | 2.7 | | 2.2 | All Other Current |
| | 21.2 | | 25.4 | Total Current |
| | 65.4 | | 61.2 | Fixed Assets (net) |
| | 6.3 | | 6.7 | Intangibles (net) |
| | 7.1 | | 6.7 | All Other Non-Current |
| | 100.0 | | 100.0 | Total |

| | | | | LIABILITIES |
|---|---|---|---|---|
| | 3.7 | | 5.6 | Notes Payable-Short Term |
| | 3.6 | | 3.5 | Cur. Mat.-L.T.D. |
| | 1.8 | | 2.1 | Trade Payables |
| | .1 | | .1 | Income Taxes Payable |
| | 8.6 | | 8.9 | All Other Current |
| | 17.8 | | 20.3 | Total Current |
| | 55.3 | | 68.4 | Long-Term Debt |
| | .0 | | .0 | Deferred Taxes |
| | 5.4 | | 15.3 | All Other Non-Current |
| | 21.5 | | -4.0 | Net Worth |
| | 100.0 | | 100.0 | Total Liabilities & Net Worth |

| | | | | INCOME DATA |
|---|---|---|---|---|
| | 100.0 | | 100.0 | Net Sales |
| | | | | Gross Profit |
| | 80.3 | | 78.3 | Operating Expenses |
| | 19.7 | | 21.7 | Operating Profit |
| | 6.5 | | 6.0 | All Other Expenses (net) |
| | 13.2 | | 15.6 | Profit Before Taxes |

| | | | | RATIOS |
|---|---|---|---|---|
| | 3.2 | | 3.7 | |
| | 1.2 | | 1.2 | Current |
| | .4 | | .5 | |
| | 2.9 | | 3.3 | |
| (271) | .9 | | 1.1 | Quick |
| | .3 | | .4 | |
| 0 | UND | 0 | UND | |
| 0 | UND | 0 | UND | Sales/Receivables |
| 1 | 411.3 | 1 | 548.0 | |
| | | | | Cost of Sales/Inventory |
| | | | | Cost of Sales/Payables |
| | 9.6 | | 6.8 | |
| | 69.9 | | 41.7 | Sales/Working Capital |
| | -10.1 | | -10.3 | |
| | 6.6 | | 9.5 | |
| (204) | 3.5 | (153) | 4.3 | EBIT/Interest |
| | 1.4 | | 1.7 | |
| | 19.0 | | | |
| (11) | 3.5 | | | Net Profit + Depr., Dep., Amort./Cur. Mat. L/T/D |
| | 1.2 | | | |
| | 1.0 | | 1.5 | |
| | 4.2 | | 5.6 | Fixed/Worth |
| | -27.6 | | -5.8 | |
| | 1.0 | | 2.0 | |
| | 4.6 | | 8.1 | Debt/Worth |
| | -21.3 | | -6.3 | |
| | 72.7 | | 116.2 | % Profit Before Taxes/Tangible Net Worth |
| (183) | 30.0 | (133) | 43.1 | |
| | 6.6 | | 11.5 | |
| | 21.3 | | 23.8 | % Profit Before Taxes/Total Assets |
| | 7.4 | | 10.1 | |
| | 1.8 | | 1.5 | |
| | 3.9 | | 5.9 | |
| | 1.0 | | .9 | Sales/Net Fixed Assets |
| | .5 | | .4 | |
| | 1.6 | | 1.8 | |
| | .7 | | .7 | Sales/Total Assets |
| | .4 | | .3 | |
| | 4.1 | | 2.9 | |
| (198) | 9.3 | (124) | 7.5 | % Depr., Dep., Amort./Sales |
| | 15.4 | | 14.9 | |
| | 2.8 | | 2.7 | % Officers', Directors' Owners' Comp/Sales |
| (68) | 4.9 | (42) | 5.2 | |
| | 7.8 | | 7.6 | |
| | 1978530M | | 1127573M | Net Sales ($) |
| | 2288743M | | 1944054M | Total Assets ($) |

M = $ thousand   MM = $ million
See Pages viii through xx for Explanation of Ratios and Data

© RMA 2024

# OTHER SERVICES—Car Washes  NAICS 811192

| Comparative Historical Data ||| Type of Statement | Current Data Sorted by Sales ||||||
|---|---|---|---|---|---|---|---|---|---|
| 5 | 6 | 8 | Unqualified | | | | | 2 | 6 |
| 8 | 7 | 11 | Reviewed | | 3 | | 1 | 2 | 5 |
| 17 | 17 | 23 | Compiled | 3 | 14 | 1 | 3 | 2 | |
| 71 | 74 | 80 | Tax Returns | 31 | 40 | 4 | 2 | 3 | 2 |
| 119 | 137 | 164 | Other | 43 | 60 | 20 | 8 | 16 | 17 |
| 4/1/21-3/31/22 ALL | 4/1/22-3/31/23 ALL | 4/1/23-3/31/24 ALL | | 15 (4/1-9/30/23) ||| 271 (10/1/23-3/31/24) |||
| | | | | 0-1MM | 1-3MM | 3-5MM | 5-10MM | 10-25MM | 25MM & OVER |
| 220 | 241 | 286 | NUMBER OF STATEMENTS | 77 | 117 | 25 | 14 | 25 | 28 |
| % | % | % | ASSETS | % | % | % | % | % | % |
| 17.9 | 17.8 | 14.8 | Cash & Equivalents | 16.2 | 17.2 | 12.8 | 6.4 | 10.2 | 10.6 |
| 1.6 | 1.7 | 1.4 | Trade Receivables (net) | 1.1 | 1.0 | .1 | .6 | 6.2 | .9 |
| 1.3 | 1.5 | 1.4 | Inventory | .3 | 1.1 | 3.4 | .8 | 3.5 | 2.9 |
| 3.2 | 1.9 | 1.8 | All Other Current | 1.9 | 2.1 | .6 | 1.1 | .6 | 3.1 |
| 24.0 | 22.9 | 19.4 | Total Current | 19.4 | 21.3 | 16.8 | 8.9 | 20.6 | 17.5 |
| 63.4 | 63.3 | 62.7 | Fixed Assets (net) | 67.2 | 58.9 | 56.7 | 75.3 | 61.6 | 66.7 |
| 6.0 | 6.5 | 10.4 | Intangibles (net) | 8.1 | 10.9 | 17.4 | 8.7 | 7.3 | 11.6 |
| 6.5 | 7.4 | 7.5 | All Other Non-Current | 5.3 | 8.9 | 9.2 | 7.1 | 10.5 | 4.1 |
| 100.0 | 100.0 | 100.0 | Total | 100.0 | 100.0 | 100.0 | 100.0 | 100.0 | 100.0 |
| | | | LIABILITIES | | | | | | |
| 2.7 | 4.4 | 3.9 | Notes Payable-Short Term | 8.5 | 2.2 | .3 | 5.8 | 1.2 | 3.2 |
| 3.3 | 3.4 | 4.2 | Cur. Mat.-L.T.D. | 3.8 | 5.5 | 3.4 | 3.6 | 1.8 | 2.6 |
| 2.6 | 2.7 | 2.9 | Trade Payables | 1.1 | 1.9 | 1.0 | 1.4 | 13.7 | 4.3 |
| .0 | .0 | .0 | Income Taxes Payable | .0 | .0 | .0 | .0 | .1 | .0 |
| 10.9 | 10.5 | 9.4 | All Other Current | 16.3 | 6.1 | 7.1 | 4.2 | 9.5 | 8.9 |
| 19.5 | 21.0 | 20.4 | Total Current | 29.9 | 15.7 | 11.8 | 15.0 | 26.3 | 19.1 |
| 62.1 | 69.6 | 70.3 | Long-Term Debt | 61.0 | 82.5 | 63.7 | 94.2 | 69.2 | 39.3 |
| .0 | .1 | .0 | Deferred Taxes | .0 | .0 | .0 | .0 | .0 | .3 |
| 12.9 | 9.0 | 6.8 | All Other Non-Current | 6.9 | 6.9 | 9.5 | 2.8 | 6.5 | 6.2 |
| 5.5 | .4 | 2.5 | Net Worth | 2.3 | -5.1 | 15.0 | -12.0 | -2.1 | 35.2 |
| 100.0 | 100.0 | 100.0 | Total Liabilities & Net Worth | 100.0 | 100.0 | 100.0 | 100.0 | 100.0 | 100.0 |
| | | | INCOME DATA | | | | | | |
| 100.0 | 100.0 | 100.0 | Net Sales | 100.0 | 100.0 | 100.0 | 100.0 | 100.0 | 100.0 |
| | | | Gross Profit | | | | | | |
| 77.5 | 80.5 | 80.2 | Operating Expenses | 77.7 | 78.5 | 77.8 | 69.8 | 91.3 | 91.3 |
| 22.5 | 19.5 | 19.8 | Operating Profit | 22.3 | 21.5 | 22.2 | 30.2 | 8.7 | 8.7 |
| 4.5 | 6.6 | 8.0 | All Other Expenses (net) | 12.5 | 6.2 | 4.5 | 14.7 | 6.5 | 3.6 |
| 18.1 | 12.9 | 11.9 | Profit Before Taxes | 9.8 | 15.2 | 17.7 | 15.5 | 2.2 | 5.1 |
| | | | RATIOS | | | | | | |
| 4.1 | 3.3 | 2.7 | | 4.1 | 5.8 | 2.9 | 1.7 | 1.9 | 1.4 |
| 1.2 | 1.2 | .9 | Current | .6 | 1.0 | 1.0 | .7 | 1.0 | .7 |
| .5 | .4 | .3 | | .2 | .4 | .5 | .1 | .3 | .3 |
| 3.6 | 2.6 | 2.3 | | 3.8 | 4.0 | 1.9 | 1.6 | 1.6 | 1.0 |
| 1.0 | 1.0 | .7 | Quick | .6 | .8 | 1.0 | .6 | .8 | .5 |
| .3 | .4 | .2 | | .1 | .2 | .3 | .1 | .2 | .3 |
| 0 UND | 0 UND | 0 UND | | 0 UND | 0 UND | 0 UND | 0 UND | 0 999.8 | 0 942.0 |
| 0 UND | 0 UND | 0 UND | Sales/Receivables | 0 UND | 0 UND | 0 UND | 0 999.8 | 1 290.1 | 1 476.6 |
| 0 999.8 | 0 778.9 | 1 626.9 | | 0 UND | 0 UND | 0 UND | 6 58.5 | 6 65.5 | 4 93.1 |
| | | | Cost of Sales/Inventory | | | | | | |
| | | | Cost of Sales/Payables | | | | | | |
| 7.4 | 10.0 | 12.6 | | 8.9 | 11.5 | 12.1 | 19.5 | 20.5 | 28.9 |
| 54.5 | 71.5 | -110.0 | Sales/Working Capital | -15.7 | -795.7 | 43.8 | -40.5 | -174.3 | -24.2 |
| -11.8 | -11.6 | -6.8 | | -3.2 | -14.7 | -21.3 | -2.1 | -5.8 | -5.6 |
| 10.7 | 7.9 | 7.2 | | 5.3 | 8.4 | 9.6 | | 7.2 | 5.3 |
| (158) 5.5 | (176) 4.4 | (206) 3.4 | EBIT/Interest | (34) 2.4 | (93) 3.5 | (23) 5.4 | (20) 4.5 | (27) 2.9 |
| 2.4 | 1.4 | 1.1 | | .2 | 1.4 | 1.1 | | .8 | .0 |
| | 5.4 | 13.6 | Net Profit + Depr., Dep., | | | | | | |
| (18) 3.1 | (18) 3.8 | Amort./Cur. Mat. L/T/D | | | | | | | |
| | 1.2 | 1.6 | | | | | | | |
| 1.1 | 1.3 | 1.7 | | 1.6 | 1.5 | 1.9 | 2.4 | 1.1 | 1.7 |
| 5.5 | 4.9 | 7.3 | Fixed/Worth | 6.3 | 17.3 | -39.2 | -20.6 | 5.2 | 3.2 |
| -4.3 | -3.1 | -2.2 | | -3.3 | -1.2 | -1.6 | -2.3 | -13.7 | 22.5 |
| 1.3 | 1.5 | 1.8 | | 2.2 | 2.2 | 1.4 | 1.6 | 1.6 | 1.0 |
| 7.0 | 6.1 | 13.9 | Debt/Worth | 11.6 | 18.7 | -43.5 | -21.9 | 4.4 | 2.7 |
| -5.6 | -3.6 | -4.0 | | -3.8 | -2.6 | -4.4 | -3.6 | -17.7 | 23.1 |
| 112.1 | 100.1 | 72.7 | | 64.2 | 108.6 | 76.1 | | 67.0 | 36.7 |
| (141) 47.3 | (146) 36.3 | (161) 23.8 | % Profit Before Taxes/Tangible Net Worth | (43) 14.9 | (62) 55.2 | (12) 51.9 | (16) 13.4 | (22) 16.2 |
| 18.4 | 4.2 | .8 | | -3.3 | 8.4 | 31.1 | | -9.9 | -8.7 |
| 33.2 | 26.9 | 21.8 | | 12.2 | 42.4 | 32.4 | 13.5 | 18.3 | 8.6 |
| 12.7 | 6.9 | 5.5 | % Profit Before Taxes/Total Assets | 2.9 | 11.4 | 16.4 | 3.3 | 4.3 | 5.2 |
| 3.9 | -.1 | -.6 | | -2.8 | .8 | .8 | 1.5 | -1.7 | -2.0 |
| 4.0 | 4.8 | 4.9 | | 4.4 | 12.4 | 23.8 | 2.3 | 14.4 | 1.9 |
| .9 | 1.0 | 1.1 | Sales/Net Fixed Assets | .5 | 1.8 | 1.1 | .8 | .8 | 1.1 |
| .4 | .5 | .5 | | .2 | .7 | .8 | .3 | .3 | .5 |
| 1.7 | 1.7 | 1.8 | | 1.6 | 2.1 | 1.4 | 1.3 | 3.0 | 1.3 |
| .7 | .7 | .7 | Sales/Total Assets | .4 | .9 | .8 | .5 | .7 | .7 |
| .4 | .4 | .4 | | .2 | .5 | .5 | .2 | .3 | .5 |
| 5.0 | 4.1 | 1.9 | | 4.2 | 1.5 | 4.9 | 1.0 | 2.0 | 3.5 |
| (141) 9.4 | (165) 10.7 | (195) 7.7 | % Depr., Dep., Amort./Sales | (45) 10.8 | (83) 6.8 | (17) 12.8 | (13) 1.8 | (18) 9.3 | (19) 6.6 |
| 18.8 | 20.2 | 15.5 | | 20.1 | 15.5 | 20.1 | 15.0 | 14.7 | 8.6 |
| 2.8 | 3.6 | 2.9 | | 3.3 | 3.0 | | | | |
| (51) 5.2 | (57) 6.1 | (49) 4.1 | % Officers', Directors' Owners' Comp/Sales | (17) 5.1 | (17) 4.0 | | | | |
| 10.4 | 11.9 | 6.9 | | 11.0 | 5.9 | | | | |
| 1510958M | 1798352M | 3023261M | Net Sales ($) | 43858M | 208071M | 91517M | 91137M | 398973M | 2189705M |
| 2152367M | 2832733M | 4989957M | Total Assets ($) | 132167M | 302555M | 144333M | 346220M | 1052096M | 3012586M |

© RMA 2024   M = $ thousand   MM = $ million
See Pages viii through xx for Explanation of Ratios and Data

## OTHER SERVICES—All Other Automotive Repair and Maintenance  NAICS 811198

### Current Data Sorted by Assets

| | | | | | | Type of Statement |
|---|---|---|---|---|---|---|
| | | 1 | 1 | | | Unqualified |
| 2 | 2 | 2 | 1 | 1 | | Reviewed |
| 5 | 2 | 4 | | | | Compiled |
| 6 | 12 | 15 | 3 | | 1 | Tax Returns |
| | 4 (4/1-9/30/23) | | 54 (10/1/23-3/31/24) | | | Other |
| 0-500M | 500M-2MM | 2-10MM | 10-50MM | 50-100MM | 100-250MM | |
| 13 | 16 | 22 | 5 | 1 | 1 | NUMBER OF STATEMENTS |

### Comparative Historical Data

| | | | |
|---|---|---|---|
| | 1 | 2 | |
| | 3 | | |
| | 5 | 1 | |
| | 29 | 12 | |
| | 43 | 34 | |
| | 4/1/19-3/31/20 | 4/1/20-3/31/21 | |
| | ALL | ALL | |
| | 81 | 49 | |

| 0-500M | 500M-2MM | 2-10MM | 10-50MM | 50-100MM | 100-250MM | | 4/1/19-3/31/20 ALL | 4/1/20-3/31/21 ALL |
|---|---|---|---|---|---|---|---|---|
| % | % | % | % | % | % | **ASSETS** | % | % |
| 17.6 | 16.7 | 18.9 | | | | Cash & Equivalents | 20.4 | 29.9 |
| 12.1 | 19.4 | 18.2 | | | | Trade Receivables (net) | 15.1 | 10.7 |
| 18.9 | 24.7 | 24.1 | | | | Inventory | 14.6 | 9.8 |
| 2.6 | 1.9 | 1.6 | | | | All Other Current | 2.7 | 2.0 |
| 51.2 | 62.6 | 62.7 | | | | Total Current | 52.7 | 52.5 |
| 31.2 | 19.6 | 26.8 | | | | Fixed Assets (net) | 30.2 | 29.4 |
| 7.2 | 6.5 | 5.0 | | | | Intangibles (net) | 12.2 | 11.5 |
| 10.4 | 11.3 | 5.4 | | | | All Other Non-Current | 4.8 | 6.5 |
| 100.0 | 100.0 | 100.0 | | | | Total | 100.0 | 100.0 |
| | | | | | | **LIABILITIES** | | |
| 8.5 | 10.3 | 8.6 | | | | Notes Payable-Short Term | 19.5 | 14.6 |
| 3.4 | 1.4 | 1.1 | | | | Cur. Mat.-L.T.D. | 3.2 | 3.3 |
| 5.2 | 8.7 | 9.9 | | | | Trade Payables | 8.6 | 6.6 |
| .3 | .1 | .0 | | | | Income Taxes Payable | .2 | .1 |
| 2.7 | 6.7 | 3.9 | | | | All Other Current | 14.5 | 15.7 |
| 20.0 | 27.2 | 23.5 | | | | Total Current | 46.1 | 40.3 |
| 35.5 | 28.6 | 19.6 | | | | Long-Term Debt | 31.2 | 38.5 |
| .0 | .0 | .0 | | | | Deferred Taxes | .0 | .0 |
| 22.5 | 1.2 | 1.8 | | | | All Other Non-Current | 7.5 | 15.7 |
| 21.9 | 43.0 | 55.1 | | | | Net Worth | 15.2 | 5.4 |
| 100.0 | 100.0 | 100.0 | | | | Total Liabilities & Net Worth | 100.0 | 100.0 |
| | | | | | | **INCOME DATA** | | |
| 100.0 | 100.0 | 100.0 | | | | Net Sales | 100.0 | 100.0 |
| | | | | | | Gross Profit | | |
| 97.3 | 89.6 | 90.6 | | | | Operating Expenses | 89.2 | 90.6 |
| 2.7 | 10.4 | 9.4 | | | | Operating Profit | 10.8 | 9.4 |
| 1.1 | 2.3 | 1.3 | | | | All Other Expenses (net) | 3.1 | .8 |
| 1.5 | 8.2 | 8.2 | | | | Profit Before Taxes | 7.7 | 8.5 |
| | | | | | | **RATIOS** | | |
| 9.0 | 4.9 | 9.4 | | | | | 3.9 | 6.5 |
| 2.1 | 2.2 | 2.8 | | | | Current | 1.6 | 2.1 |
| .9 | 1.2 | 1.9 | | | | | .8 | .8 |
| 3.1 | 3.5 | 6.5 | | | | | 2.9 | 5.9 |
| 1.2 | 1.3 | 2.1 | | | | Quick | .8 | 1.6 |
| .4 | .4 | .9 | | | | | .4 | .5 |
| 0 UND | 0 UND | 0 UND | | | | | 0 UND | 0 UND |
| 0 UND | 6 57.6 | 10 37.7 | | | | Sales/Receivables | 11 33.5 | 7 50.6 |
| 13 28.4 | 31 11.7 | 41 9.0 | | | | | 28 13.2 | 20 18.0 |
| | | | | | | Cost of Sales/Inventory | | |
| | | | | | | Cost of Sales/Payables | | |
| 7.2 | 6.7 | 3.4 | | | | | 6.9 | 7.0 |
| 32.4 | 9.5 | 6.4 | | | | Sales/Working Capital | 17.0 | 13.2 |
| NM | 49.6 | 13.0 | | | | | -39.5 | -35.7 |
| | | 26.5 | | | | | 14.5 | 35.7 |
| | (18) | 9.9 | | | | EBIT/Interest | (56) 6.2 | (32) 9.2 |
| | | 5.9 | | | | | 2.3 | 2.1 |
| | | | | | | Net Profit + Depr., Dep., Amort./Cur. Mat. L/T/D | | |
| .0 | .1 | .1 | | | | | .2 | .2 |
| .6 | .6 | .2 | | | | Fixed/Worth | 1.0 | 1.8 |
| 1.9 | 2.1 | .8 | | | | | -10.4 | -.6 |
| .1 | .6 | .5 | | | | | .7 | .9 |
| 1.0 | 1.2 | .8 | | | | Debt/Worth | 2.8 | 4.6 |
| 6.1 | 4.3 | 2.3 | | | | | -6.8 | -2.9 |
| 89.2 | 113.9 | 56.8 | | | | | 92.8 | 87.8 |
| (11) 74.5 | (15) 15.8 | 23.6 | | | | % Profit Before Taxes/Tangible Net Worth | (57) 48.8 | (31) 50.2 |
| -4.8 | 3.9 | 12.0 | | | | | 16.6 | 22.0 |
| 50.6 | 31.1 | 31.0 | | | | | 39.8 | 40.2 |
| 10.8 | 5.3 | 10.3 | | | | % Profit Before Taxes/Total Assets | 15.3 | 14.5 |
| -10.8 | 2.5 | 2.9 | | | | | 3.4 | 3.1 |
| UND | 195.8 | 64.7 | | | | | 72.5 | 60.5 |
| 27.4 | 21.7 | 14.8 | | | | Sales/Net Fixed Assets | 29.3 | 18.4 |
| 6.1 | 8.4 | 9.4 | | | | | 7.4 | 6.1 |
| 8.3 | 6.9 | 3.2 | | | | | 5.5 | 5.0 |
| 3.6 | 2.6 | 2.1 | | | | Sales/Total Assets | 3.5 | 3.2 |
| 2.3 | 1.5 | 1.6 | | | | | 1.7 | 1.4 |
| | | .6 | | | | | .5 | .8 |
| | (10) | 1.8 | | | | % Depr., Dep., Amort./Sales | (45) 1.2 | (18) 3.0 |
| | | 2.7 | | | | | 6.6 | 6.3 |
| | | | | | | | 2.6 | 3.7 |
| | | | | | | % Officers', Directors' Owners' Comp/Sales | (42) 4.8 | (21) 5.6 |
| | | | | | | | 7.9 | 7.7 |
| 17924M | 58960M | 239832M | 219029M | 285131M | 170928M | Net Sales ($) | 681793M | 444481M |
| 3731M | 18373M | 102793M | 140069M | 73767M | 135090M | Total Assets ($) | 387484M | 382779M |

M = $ thousand   MM = $ million
See Pages viii through xx for Explanation of Ratios and Data

© RMA 2024

## OTHER SERVICES—All Other Automotive Repair and Maintenance  NAICS 811198

**Comparative Historical Data** | | | | **Current Data Sorted by Sales** | | | | |

| | | | Type of Statement | | | | | | |
|---|---|---|---|---|---|---|---|---|---|
| 4 | 5 | 2 | Unqualified | | | | 1 | | 1 |
| 1 | | | Reviewed | | 3 | | 2 | 1 | |
| 2 | 5 | 8 | Compiled | 1 | 3 | | 1 | 2 | 1 |
| 19 | 21 | 11 | Tax Returns | 4 | 7 | 3 | 10 | 8 | 5 |
| 27 | 27 | 37 | Other | 4 | | | 54 | | |
| 4/1/21- | 4/1/22- | 4/1/23- | | 0-1MM | 4 (4/1-9/30/23) | 3-5MM | (10/1/23-3/31/24) | | |
| 3/31/22 | 3/31/23 | 3/31/24 | | | 1-3MM | | 5-10MM | 10-25MM | 25MM & OVER |
| ALL | ALL | ALL | | | | | | | |
| 53 | 58 | 58 | NUMBER OF STATEMENTS | 9 | 13 | 4 | 14 | 11 | 7 |
| % | % | % | **ASSETS** | % | % | % | % | % | % |
| 26.0 | 30.9 | 16.6 | Cash & Equivalents | | 18.0 | | 18.9 | 25.6 | |
| 10.2 | 12.0 | 17.4 | Trade Receivables (net) | | 11.9 | | 14.4 | 26.3 | |
| 15.4 | 14.3 | 20.6 | Inventory | | 25.8 | | 29.2 | 8.7 | |
| 3.1 | 3.8 | 2.2 | All Other Current | | .5 | | 6.2 | 1.1 | |
| 54.7 | 60.9 | 56.7 | Total Current | | 56.3 | | 68.7 | 61.6 | |
| 31.6 | 22.4 | 27.7 | Fixed Assets (net) | | 18.5 | | 24.4 | 30.6 | |
| 9.1 | 8.4 | 6.0 | Intangibles (net) | | 8.1 | | 2.0 | 2.9 | |
| 4.6 | 8.2 | 9.5 | All Other Non-Current | | 17.1 | | 4.9 | 4.9 | |
| 100.0 | 100.0 | 100.0 | Total | | 100.0 | | 100.0 | 100.0 | |
| | | | **LIABILITIES** | | | | | | |
| 6.3 | 5.9 | 8.3 | Notes Payable-Short Term | | 7.5 | | 8.1 | 10.7 | |
| 4.7 | 2.2 | 2.4 | Cur. Mat.-L.T.D. | | .8 | | .8 | 1.1 | |
| 6.8 | 4.8 | 8.3 | Trade Payables | | 4.6 | | 10.4 | 9.4 | |
| .2 | .1 | .1 | Income Taxes Payable | | .4 | | .0 | .1 | |
| 6.8 | 7.8 | 5.3 | All Other Current | | 3.9 | | 6.6 | 3.9 | |
| 24.8 | 20.8 | 24.3 | Total Current | | 17.2 | | 25.9 | 25.1 | |
| 31.0 | 28.3 | 26.2 | Long-Term Debt | | 25.5 | | 13.5 | 17.7 | |
| .0 | .1 | .0 | Deferred Taxes | | .0 | | .0 | .0 | |
| 3.7 | 6.7 | 6.3 | All Other Non-Current | | 3.9 | | .9 | .5 | |
| 40.6 | 44.1 | 43.1 | Net Worth | | 53.4 | | 59.6 | 56.7 | |
| 100.0 | 100.0 | 100.0 | Total Liabilities & Net Worth | | 100.0 | | 100.0 | 100.0 | |
| | | | **INCOME DATA** | | | | | | |
| 100.0 | 100.0 | 100.0 | Net Sales | | 100.0 | | 100.0 | 100.0 | |
| 92.0 | 88.5 | 91.8 | Gross Profit | | 89.6 | | 94.1 | 94.0 | |
| 8.0 | 11.5 | 8.2 | Operating Expenses | | 10.4 | | 5.9 | 6.0 | |
| -.1 | .8 | 1.4 | Operating Profit | | .8 | | -.8 | .2 | |
| 8.1 | 10.7 | 6.8 | All Other Expenses (net) | | 9.6 | | 6.7 | 5.9 | |
| | | | Profit Before Taxes | | | | | | |
| | | | **RATIOS** | | | | | | |
| 4.7 | 9.8 | 4.8 | | | 16.5 | | 9.0 | 13.6 | |
| 2.5 | 3.3 | 2.3 | Current | | 2.5 | | 3.1 | 2.8 | |
| 1.4 | 1.9 | 1.3 | | | 1.5 | | 1.7 | 1.6 | |
| 3.2 | 7.4 | 3.1 | | | 12.5 | | 3.7 | 13.1 | |
| 1.6 | 2.2 | 1.3 | Quick | | 1.3 | | 2.1 | 2.8 | |
| .8 | 1.1 | .6 | | | .6 | | .8 | 1.6 | |
| 0 UND | 0 UND | 0 UND | | 0 UND | | | 0 UND | 0 UND | |
| 3 108.0 | 5 67.4 | 9 38.6 | Sales/Receivables | 3 104.4 | | 16 22.4 | 14 26.3 | | |
| 17 21.5 | 23 15.6 | 39 9.4 | | 13 28.4 | | 29 12.7 | 59 6.2 | | |
| | | | Cost of Sales/Inventory | | | | | | |
| | | | Cost of Sales/Payables | | | | | | |
| 6.6 | 5.0 | 5.3 | | | 6.6 | | 3.6 | 7.0 | |
| 11.6 | 9.6 | 10.8 | Sales/Working Capital | | 9.2 | | 6.1 | 12.5 | |
| 38.4 | 29.4 | 36.8 | | | 34.5 | | 17.0 | 14.9 | |
| 47.4 | 28.4 | 17.4 | | | | | | 22.4 | |
| (43) 11.4 | (37) 7.2 | (39) 8.1 | EBIT/Interest | | | | (10) 8.4 | | |
| 3.0 | 2.7 | 2.8 | | | | | | 6.0 | |
| | | | Net Profit + Depr., Dep., Amort./Cur. Mat. L/T/D | | | | | | |
| .2 | .1 | .1 | | | .0 | | .1 | .1 | |
| .8 | .4 | .4 | Fixed/Worth | | .8 | | .2 | .4 | |
| 11.0 | 2.8 | 1.5 | | | 2.2 | | .6 | .9 | |
| .6 | .3 | .5 | | | .2 | | .3 | .4 | |
| 1.7 | 1.1 | 1.2 | Debt/Worth | | 1.2 | | .7 | .5 | |
| 11.7 | 6.6 | 2.7 | | | 6.9 | | 1.6 | 2.2 | |
| 76.4 | 126.7 | 79.3 | | | 182.3 | | 67.5 | 55.5 | |
| (43) 50.0 | (50) 66.4 | (55) 27.1 | % Profit Before Taxes/Tangible Net Worth | | 89.2 | | 18.4 | 26.5 | |
| 18.5 | 18.7 | 8.5 | | | 10.8 | | 5.6 | 8.5 | |
| 43.5 | 49.0 | 31.0 | | | 54.6 | | 35.6 | 30.3 | |
| 14.1 | 15.4 | 9.0 | % Profit Before Taxes/Total Assets | | 19.2 | | 14.6 | 10.4 | |
| 6.5 | 4.5 | 2.1 | | | 2.4 | | 2.1 | 5.6 | |
| 61.8 | 175.0 | 124.5 | | | UND | | 85.7 | 72.2 | |
| 11.3 | 31.2 | 15.7 | Sales/Net Fixed Assets | | 27.4 | | 21.7 | 11.5 | |
| 4.9 | 7.6 | 7.5 | | | 9.1 | | 12.9 | 7.9 | |
| 5.2 | 6.0 | 3.8 | | | 6.4 | | 7.5 | 4.5 | |
| 2.7 | 3.3 | 2.4 | Sales/Total Assets | | 3.6 | | 2.3 | 3.3 | |
| 1.5 | 1.6 | 1.5 | | | 2.1 | | 1.9 | 2.0 | |
| 1.0 | 1.2 | .5 | | | | | | | |
| (30) 3.4 | (29) 2.5 | (27) 1.5 | % Depr., Dep., Amort./Sales | | | | | | |
| 7.9 | 5.4 | 4.7 | | | | | | | |
| 2.5 | 3.3 | 2.5 | | | | | | | |
| (22) 5.1 | (23) 5.5 | (11) 3.8 | % Officers', Directors' Owners' Comp/Sales | | | | | | |
| 7.9 | 10.6 | 5.7 | | | | | | | |
| 1014416M | 788713M | 991804M | Net Sales ($) | 4036M | 22185M | 14518M | 90071M | 163491M | 697503M |
| 747963M | 424573M | 473823M | Total Assets ($) | 7753M | 8282M | 9408M | 48757M | 55161M | 344462M |

M = $ thousand   MM = $ million
See Pages viii through xx for Explanation of Ratios and Data

© RMA 2024

# OTHER SERVICES—Electronic and Precision Equipment Repair and Maintenance  NAICS 811210

**Current Data Sorted by Assets** | **Comparative Historical Data**

| | | | | | | | Type of Statement | | | | |
|---|---|---|---|---|---|---|---|---|---|---|---|
| | | | 1 | 1 | 3 | | Unqualified | | 6 | | 4 |
| | | 3 | 5 | | | | Reviewed | | 11 | | 4 |
| | 8 | 6 | 3 | | | | Compiled | | 7 | | 2 |
| 3 | 13 | 5 | | 6 | | | Tax Returns | | 17 | | 14 |
| 3 | 14 (4/1-9/30/23) | 23 | 8 (10/1/23-3/31/24) | | 3 | | Other | | 65 | | 34 |
| 0-500M | 500M-2MM | 2-10MM | 10-50MM | 50-100MM | 100-250MM | | | | 4/1/19-3/31/20 ALL | | 4/1/20-3/31/21 ALL |
| 6 | 21 | 37 | 17 | 7 | 6 | | NUMBER OF STATEMENTS | | 106 | | 58 |
| % | % | % | % | % | % | | **ASSETS** | | % | | % |
| | 24.5 | 19.3 | 14.2 | | | | Cash & Equivalents | | 18.7 | | 25.9 |
| | 14.7 | 26.8 | 23.6 | | | | Trade Receivables (net) | | 30.3 | | 23.2 |
| | 23.5 | 14.3 | 20.1 | | | | Inventory | | 16.5 | | 16.9 |
| | 3.0 | 3.3 | 4.0 | | | | All Other Current | | 3.4 | | 1.9 |
| | 65.7 | 63.7 | 62.0 | | | | Total Current | | 68.8 | | 67.9 |
| | 18.3 | 19.1 | 14.2 | | | | Fixed Assets (net) | | 15.4 | | 16.8 |
| | 5.9 | 7.5 | 13.7 | | | | Intangibles (net) | | 7.3 | | 8.8 |
| | 10.1 | 9.8 | 10.1 | | | | All Other Non-Current | | 8.4 | | 6.4 |
| | 100.0 | 100.0 | 100.0 | | | | Total | | 100.0 | | 100.0 |
| | | | | | | | **LIABILITIES** | | | | |
| | 13.1 | 4.6 | 6.1 | | | | Notes Payable-Short Term | | 8.3 | | 7.0 |
| | 2.5 | 2.8 | 4.3 | | | | Cur. Mat.-L.T.D. | | 3.2 | | 3.2 |
| | 13.1 | 9.9 | 10.9 | | | | Trade Payables | | 14.2 | | 9.6 |
| | .0 | .0 | .1 | | | | Income Taxes Payable | | .1 | | .1 |
| | 10.2 | 9.0 | 12.4 | | | | All Other Current | | 15.5 | | 10.5 |
| | 38.9 | 26.3 | 33.8 | | | | Total Current | | 41.3 | | 30.3 |
| | 19.9 | 12.4 | 13.0 | | | | Long-Term Debt | | 16.5 | | 17.1 |
| | .0 | .0 | .0 | | | | Deferred Taxes | | .2 | | .0 |
| | 3.6 | 5.3 | 8.4 | | | | All Other Non-Current | | 10.7 | | 7.7 |
| | 37.7 | 56.0 | 44.8 | | | | Net Worth | | 31.3 | | 44.8 |
| | 100.0 | 100.0 | 100.0 | | | | Total Liabilities & Net Worth | | 100.0 | | 100.0 |
| | | | | | | | **INCOME DATA** | | | | |
| | 100.0 | 100.0 | 100.0 | | | | Net Sales | | 100.0 | | 100.0 |
| | 90.5 | 89.5 | 97.6 | | | | Gross Profit | | | | |
| | 9.5 | 10.5 | 2.4 | | | | Operating Expenses | | 93.0 | | 93.3 |
| | .5 | 1.2 | .8 | | | | Operating Profit | | 7.0 | | 6.7 |
| | 9.0 | 9.4 | 1.6 | | | | All Other Expenses (net) | | 1.3 | | 1.0 |
| | | | | | | | Profit Before Taxes | | 5.7 | | 5.6 |
| | | | | | | | **RATIOS** | | | | |
| | 4.3 | 5.1 | 2.9 | | | | | | 3.2 | | 5.3 |
| | 2.1 | 3.0 | 1.9 | | | | Current | | 1.8 | | 2.4 |
| | 1.2 | 1.2 | 1.3 | | | | | | 1.3 | | 1.3 |
| | 2.7 | 4.3 | 1.5 | | | | | | 2.3 | | 2.7 |
| | 1.2 | 2.0 | 1.2 | | | | Quick | | 1.4 | | 1.7 |
| | .7 | .9 | .8 | | | | | | .8 | | .9 |
| | 0  UND | 25  14.4 | 40  9.2 | | | | | 22 | 16.4 | 6 | 60.2 |
| | 7  49.5 | 42  8.6 | 42  8.6 | | | | Sales/Receivables | 42 | 8.7 | 37 | 9.9 |
| | 33  11.2 | 57  6.4 | 49  7.5 | | | | | 59 | 6.2 | 54 | 6.7 |
| | | | | | | | Cost of Sales/Inventory | | | | |
| | | | | | | | Cost of Sales/Payables | | | | |
| | 6.7 | 4.1 | 5.1 | | | | | | 4.5 | | 4.1 |
| | 14.0 | 5.7 | 7.0 | | | | Sales/Working Capital | | 8.7 | | 8.5 |
| | 78.7 | 23.8 | 20.8 | | | | | | 29.3 | | 20.0 |
| | 41.0 | 31.3 | 14.4 | | | | | | 37.9 | | 91.7 |
| (16) | 16.8 | (27) 15.8 | (16) 4.5 | | | | EBIT/Interest | (81) | 12.0 | (45) | 20.7 |
| | 3.8 | 6.6 | .4 | | | | | | 1.5 | | 3.5 |
| | | | | | | | Net Profit + Depr., Dep., Amort./Cur. Mat. L/T/D | | 7.3 | | |
| | | | | | | | | (15) | 1.6 | | |
| | | | | | | | | | -2.0 | | |
| | .1 | .1 | .2 | | | | | | .1 | | .1 |
| | .3 | .4 | .4 | | | | Fixed/Worth | | .4 | | .3 |
| | 3.5 | .7 | 1.2 | | | | | | NM | | 1.0 |
| | .5 | .3 | .8 | | | | | | .6 | | .6 |
| | 1.3 | .7 | 2.7 | | | | Debt/Worth | | 1.4 | | 1.3 |
| | 10.4 | 1.8 | 12.2 | | | | | | -72.5 | | 3.0 |
| | 96.3 | 56.7 | 26.1 | | | | | | 57.2 | | 68.2 |
| (17) | 56.7 | (35) 36.6 | (16) 18.2 | | | | % Profit Before Taxes/Tangible Net Worth | (79) | 33.4 | (50) | 34.5 |
| | 29.3 | 21.1 | -22.0 | | | | | | 12.5 | | 10.1 |
| | 37.4 | 28.0 | 10.2 | | | | | | 24.1 | | 26.9 |
| | 23.1 | 20.0 | 6.6 | | | | % Profit Before Taxes/Total Assets | | 12.4 | | 14.0 |
| | 7.5 | 7.9 | -1.7 | | | | | | 2.2 | | 3.3 |
| | 160.7 | 47.5 | 59.9 | | | | | | 121.3 | | 111.9 |
| | 55.4 | 23.5 | 20.5 | | | | Sales/Net Fixed Assets | | 24.0 | | 25.8 |
| | 9.8 | 7.2 | 7.3 | | | | | | 12.3 | | 10.9 |
| | 5.7 | 3.2 | 2.2 | | | | | | 4.1 | | 2.9 |
| | 3.6 | 2.5 | 2.0 | | | | Sales/Total Assets | | 2.5 | | 2.4 |
| | 2.6 | 1.5 | 1.4 | | | | | | 1.7 | | 1.7 |
| | | .3 | .5 | | | | | | .5 | | .4 |
| | (20) | 1.2 | (13) 1.8 | | | | % Depr., Dep., Amort./Sales | (59) | 1.6 | (35) | 1.2 |
| | | 5.3 | 5.4 | | | | | | 3.0 | | 3.2 |
| | | 1.7 | | | | | | | 1.6 | | 1.4 |
| | (13) | 2.2 | | | | | % Officers', Directors', Owners' Comp/Sales | (34) | 4.2 | (15) | 5.0 |
| | | 3.2 | | | | | | | 6.8 | | 14.4 |
| 8953M | 97932M | 470199M | 625221M | 747829M | 1455826M | | Net Sales ($) | | 2067640M | | 1390791M |
| 1169M | 23057M | 187047M | 335439M | 504176M | 959209M | | Total Assets ($) | | 1239413M | | 727503M |

© RMA 2024     M = $ thousand    MM = $ million
See Pages viii through xx for Explanation of Ratios and Data

## OTHER SERVICES—Electronic and Precision Equipment Repair and Maintenance NAICS 811210

### Comparative Historical Data | Current Data Sorted by Sales

| | | | | Type of Statement | | | | | | |
|---|---|---|---|---|---|---|---|---|---|---|
| 2 | 6 | 5 | | Unqualified | | | | 3 | 1 | 5 |
| 5 | 8 | 8 | | Reviewed | | | | 2 | 5 | 4 |
| 1 | 8 | 9 | | Compiled | | | | 6 | 4 | 2 |
| 18 | 17 | 16 | | Tax Returns | 3 | 3 | | 12 | 10 | |
| 45 | 45 | 56 | | Other | 1 | 7 | 8 | 80 | | 18 |
| 4/1/21-3/31/22 ALL | 4/1/22-3/31/23 ALL | 4/1/23-3/31/24 ALL | | | 0-1MM | 14 (4/1-9/30/23) 1-3MM | 3-5MM | (10/1/23-3/31/24) 5-10MM | 10-25MM | 25MM & OVER |
| 71 | 84 | 94 | | NUMBER OF STATEMENTS | 4 | 10 | 8 | 23 | 20 | 29 |
| % | % | % | | ASSETS | % | % | % | % | % | % |
| 21.5 | 26.6 | 19.2 | | Cash & Equivalents | 18.3 | | | 21.3 | 28.5 | 9.0 |
| 27.2 | 25.3 | 21.3 | | Trade Receivables (net) | 14.9 | | | 21.9 | 25.2 | 24.7 |
| 14.2 | 15.6 | 16.5 | | Inventory | 12.2 | | | 13.8 | 14.9 | 17.6 |
| 2.8 | 1.9 | 3.2 | | All Other Current | 1.9 | | | 2.9 | 5.6 | 2.8 |
| 65.7 | 69.4 | 60.2 | | Total Current | 47.3 | | | 59.8 | 74.2 | 54.2 |
| 15.9 | 16.1 | 16.6 | | Fixed Assets (net) | 31.5 | | | 20.9 | 12.3 | 8.4 |
| 12.9 | 7.9 | 13.2 | | Intangibles (net) | 5.8 | | | 10.6 | 3.9 | 28.2 |
| 5.4 | 6.6 | 10.0 | | All Other Non-Current | 15.3 | | | 8.6 | 9.7 | 9.2 |
| 100.0 | 100.0 | 100.0 | | Total | 100.0 | | | 100.0 | 100.0 | 100.0 |
| | | | | LIABILITIES | | | | | | |
| 6.8 | 9.8 | 9.1 | | Notes Payable-Short Term | 31.4 | | | 7.1 | 7.8 | 3.6 |
| 2.2 | 4.2 | 4.6 | | Cur. Mat.-L.T.D. | 18.8 | | | 4.0 | 1.8 | 3.5 |
| 9.3 | 9.4 | 10.8 | | Trade Payables | 13.1 | | | 11.0 | 10.0 | 12.2 |
| .0 | .0 | .0 | | Income Taxes Payable | .0 | | | .1 | .1 | .0 |
| 11.1 | 12.5 | 12.1 | | All Other Current | 14.7 | | | 8.0 | 9.6 | 13.2 |
| 29.4 | 36.0 | 36.6 | | Total Current | 77.9 | | | 30.2 | 29.4 | 32.5 |
| 23.2 | 18.7 | 17.3 | | Long-Term Debt | 36.0 | | | 15.7 | 4.8 | 19.6 |
| .1 | .0 | .0 | | Deferred Taxes | .0 | | | .0 | .0 | .0 |
| 10.7 | 5.6 | 6.3 | | All Other Non-Current | .3 | | | 6.5 | 3.9 | 10.5 |
| 36.5 | 39.7 | 39.9 | | Net Worth | -14.2 | | | 47.7 | 61.8 | 37.4 |
| 100.0 | 100.0 | 100.0 | | Total Liabilities & Net Worth | 100.0 | | | 100.0 | 100.0 | 100.0 |
| | | | | INCOME DATA | | | | | | |
| 100.0 | 100.0 | 100.0 | | Net Sales | 100.0 | | | 100.0 | 100.0 | 100.0 |
| | | | | Gross Profit | | | | | | |
| 92.5 | 89.7 | 93.6 | | Operating Expenses | 96.1 | | | 92.4 | 92.3 | 98.7 |
| 7.5 | 10.3 | 6.4 | | Operating Profit | 3.9 | | | 7.6 | 7.7 | 1.3 |
| 1.2 | .9 | 1.5 | | All Other Expenses (net) | .0 | | | .0 | .0 | 3.1 |
| 6.3 | 9.3 | 4.9 | | Profit Before Taxes | 3.9 | | | 7.6 | 7.7 | -1.7 |
| | | | | RATIOS | | | | | | |
| 4.8 | 3.9 | 4.1 | | | 4.0 | | | 4.9 | 6.7 | 3.1 |
| 2.8 | 2.6 | 2.1 | | Current | 1.3 | | | 2.4 | 3.6 | 1.7 |
| 1.4 | 1.3 | 1.2 | | | .2 | | | .9 | 1.5 | 1.1 |
| 3.9 | 3.0 | 2.7 | | | 2.1 | | | 4.2 | 4.9 | 1.4 |
| 2.1 | 1.9 | 1.2 | | Quick | .8 | | | 1.4 | 2.7 | 1.1 |
| .9 | .9 | .8 | | | .2 | | | .8 | .9 | .8 |
| 33  11.1 | 14  26.7 | 17  21.6 | | | 0  UND | | | 23  15.7 | 0  754.3 | 41  9.0 |
| 49  7.4 | 41  8.9 | 41  9.0 | | Sales/Receivables | 23  16.2 | | | 39  9.3 | 38  9.5 | 44  8.3 |
| 68  5.4 | 63  5.8 | 54  6.7 | | | 40  9.1 | | | 56  6.5 | 54  6.8 | 59  6.2 |
| | | | | Cost of Sales/Inventory | | | | | | |
| | | | | Cost of Sales/Payables | | | | | | |
| 3.3 | 4.3 | 4.8 | | | 11.7 | | | 4.2 | 4.7 | 5.1 |
| 5.5 | 7.2 | 9.3 | | Sales/Working Capital | 35.4 | | | 8.5 | 6.7 | 8.0 |
| 16.1 | 34.8 | 50.4 | | | -6.8 | | | -117.8 | 23.5 | 44.8 |
| 58.0 | 117.6 | 26.0 | | | | | | 25.3 | 46.6 | 15.3 |
| (53) 10.9 | (57) 15.1 | (74) 7.1 | | EBIT/Interest | (16) 11.9 | | (15) | 17.8 | (27) | 3.1 |
| .8 | 3.1 | 1.0 | | | | | | .9 | 6.6 | -1.1 |
| | | | 12.7 | Net Profit + Depr., Dep., | | | | | | |
| | | (14) | 3.8 | Amort./Cur. Mat. L/T/D | | | | | | |
| | | | 2.6 | | | | | | | |
| .1 | .0 | .1 | | | .1 | | | .2 | .1 | .2 |
| .4 | .3 | .4 | | Fixed/Worth | NM | | | .5 | .2 | .4 |
| 14.1 | 1.1 | 2.0 | | | -.4 | | | 1.9 | .4 | -.8 |
| .6 | .4 | .5 | | | .8 | | | .4 | .3 | 1.1 |
| 1.5 | 1.1 | 1.5 | | Debt/Worth | NM | | | 1.2 | .5 | 5.9 |
| 310.5 | 5.4 | 13.5 | | | -2.2 | | | 7.0 | 1.3 | -5.1 |
| 80.5 | 87.0 | 56.5 | | % Profit Before Taxes/Tangible | | | | 71.5 | 62.2 | 26.1 |
| (54) 35.6 | (69) 38.5 | (76) 31.6 | | Net Worth | (20) | | | 43.0 | 35.2 | (20) 20.3 |
| 8.9 | 18.7 | 17.0 | | | | | | 11.5 | 24.7 | -43.2 |
| 31.9 | 40.8 | 25.4 | | % Profit Before Taxes/Total | 38.9 | | | 22.9 | 32.6 | 10.5 |
| 9.9 | 15.4 | 10.2 | | Assets | 15.3 | | | 11.7 | 24.2 | 4.8 |
| .7 | 6.1 | 2.8 | | | -52.5 | | | 6.5 | 8.4 | -4.9 |
| 93.8 | 183.5 | 76.2 | | | 118.9 | | | 51.9 | 81.2 | 75.4 |
| 21.4 | 28.0 | 28.3 | | Sales/Net Fixed Assets | 17.6 | | | 25.3 | 27.8 | 35.0 |
| 10.7 | 10.0 | 9.5 | | | 6.4 | | | 6.2 | 16.7 | 15.8 |
| 3.0 | 4.0 | 3.6 | | | 7.8 | | | 3.9 | 3.3 | 2.9 |
| 1.7 | 2.4 | 2.5 | | Sales/Total Assets | 3.0 | | | 2.3 | 2.8 | 1.9 |
| 1.2 | 1.6 | 1.5 | | | 1.7 | | | 1.4 | 2.4 | 1.1 |
| 1.0 | .4 | .3 | | | | | | .4 | .2 | .2 |
| (45) 2.1 | (44) 1.9 | (48) 1.3 | | % Depr., Dep., Amort./Sales | | | (14) | 1.2 | (11) .5 | (16) 1.4 |
| 3.9 | 3.5 | 5.0 | | | | | | 5.5 | 2.9 | 3.0 |
| 2.7 | 1.3 | 2.1 | | | | | | | 1.6 | |
| (23) 3.9 | (28) 3.5 | (27) 2.7 | | % Officers', Directors', Owners' Comp/Sales | | | | (10) | 2.2 | |
| 7.5 | 6.6 | 4.7 | | | | | | | | |
| 1543403M | 2095934M | 3405960M | | Net Sales ($) | 1734M | 21938M | 32090M | 170412M | 318686M | 2861100M |
| 1096825M | 1205834M | 2010097M | | Total Assets ($) | 3713M | 7532M | 13317M | 96769M | 114455M | 1774311M |

© RMA 2024  M = $ thousand  MM = $ million
See Pages viii through xx for Explanation of Ratios and Data

# 1300 OTHER SERVICES—Commercial & Industrial Machinery & Equip. (except Auto. & Electronic) Repair & Maintenance  NAICS 811310

**Current Data Sorted by Assets** | **Comparative Historical Data**

| | | | | | | | Type of Statement | | |
|---|---|---|---|---|---|---|---|---|---|
| | | | 2 | 6 | 3 | 5 | Unqualified | 12 | 7 |
| | 1 | | 11 | 13 | 2 | | Reviewed | 34 | 18 |
| 1 | 1 | 28 | 13 | 3 | 1 | | Compiled | 25 | 18 |
| 10 | 28 | 19 | 19 | 2 | | | Tax Returns | 70 | 35 |
| 7 | 27 | 53 | 36 | | 5 | 10 | Other | 159 | 112 |
| | | 39 (4/1-9/30/23) | | 220 (10/1/23-3/31/24) | | | | 4/1/19- | 4/1/20- |
| 0-500M | 500M-2MM | 2-10MM | 10-50MM | 50-100MM | 100-250MM | | | 3/31/20 | 3/31/21 |
| 18 | 57 | 98 | 60 | 11 | 15 | | NUMBER OF STATEMENTS | ALL 300 | ALL 190 |
| % | % | % | % | % | % | | ASSETS | % | % |
| 27.8 | 21.5 | 14.6 | 12.0 | 6.1 | 3.4 | | Cash & Equivalents | 14.3 | 19.5 |
| 18.5 | 21.3 | 28.6 | 31.8 | 28.1 | 21.0 | | Trade Receivables (net) | 28.7 | 23.6 |
| 16.1 | 11.8 | 16.8 | 13.1 | 15.8 | 14.8 | | Inventory | 17.3 | 17.2 |
| 1.1 | 1.9 | 4.1 | 5.6 | 8.5 | 3.6 | | All Other Current | 3.8 | 3.8 |
| 63.5 | 56.5 | 64.1 | 62.4 | 58.5 | 42.7 | | Total Current | 64.1 | 64.2 |
| 20.5 | 31.3 | 20.8 | 21.1 | 13.9 | 21.1 | | Fixed Assets (net) | 23.5 | 23.3 |
| 1.1 | 6.1 | 6.0 | 9.0 | 15.3 | 26.5 | | Intangibles (net) | 4.9 | 5.0 |
| 14.8 | 6.1 | 9.1 | 7.5 | 12.2 | 9.7 | | All Other Non-Current | 7.5 | 7.5 |
| 100.0 | 100.0 | 100.0 | 100.0 | 100.0 | 100.0 | | Total | 100.0 | 100.0 |
| | | | | | | | LIABILITIES | | |
| 24.7 | 6.0 | 6.2 | 6.6 | 2.5 | 6.0 | | Notes Payable-Short Term | 12.6 | 12.3 |
| .5 | 1.5 | 3.2 | 2.9 | 3.4 | 3.4 | | Cur. Mat.-L.T.D. | 4.4 | 2.9 |
| 10.6 | 7.2 | 11.3 | 10.4 | 8.7 | 6.7 | | Trade Payables | 11.4 | 10.0 |
| .0 | .0 | .1 | .3 | .8 | .1 | | Income Taxes Payable | .1 | .2 |
| 24.7 | 15.5 | 12.4 | 13.1 | 15.2 | 14.1 | | All Other Current | 13.1 | 11.9 |
| 60.4 | 30.2 | 33.2 | 33.2 | 30.6 | 30.3 | | Total Current | 41.7 | 37.3 |
| 19.8 | 30.8 | 15.8 | 18.1 | 10.6 | 41.3 | | Long-Term Debt | 18.7 | 25.2 |
| .0 | .0 | .0 | .4 | .4 | .9 | | Deferred Taxes | .1 | .1 |
| 3.9 | 2.1 | 4.1 | 4.9 | 12.2 | 2.6 | | All Other Non-Current | 4.2 | 4.3 |
| 15.9 | 36.8 | 46.9 | 43.5 | 46.1 | 24.9 | | Net Worth | 35.3 | 33.0 |
| 100.0 | 100.0 | 100.0 | 100.0 | 100.0 | 100.0 | | Total Liabilties & Net Worth | 100.0 | 100.0 |
| | | | | | | | INCOME DATA | | |
| 100.0 | 100.0 | 100.0 | 100.0 | 100.0 | 100.0 | | Net Sales | 100.0 | 100.0 |
| | | | | | | | Gross Profit | | |
| 92.5 | 87.7 | 90.8 | 92.3 | 90.0 | 93.8 | | Operating Expenses | 92.6 | 91.8 |
| 7.5 | 12.3 | 9.2 | 7.7 | 10.0 | 6.2 | | Operating Profit | 7.4 | 8.2 |
| .9 | 3.5 | 1.0 | .6 | 1.4 | 3.0 | | All Other Expenses (net) | 1.1 | -.1 |
| 6.6 | 8.8 | 8.2 | 7.0 | 8.6 | 3.2 | | Profit Before Taxes | 6.3 | 8.3 |
| | | | | | | | RATIOS | | |
| 2.6 | 6.2 | 3.7 | 3.1 | 3.2 | 2.2 | | | 3.4 | 3.5 |
| 1.2 | 2.2 | 2.1 | 2.0 | 1.6 | 1.6 | | Current | 1.7 | 2.0 |
| .6 | 1.1 | 1.2 | 1.4 | 1.4 | 1.2 | | | 1.1 | 1.2 |
| 2.3 | 5.8 | 2.7 | 2.4 | 2.3 | 1.4 | | | 2.4 | 2.6 |
| .8 | 1.3 | 1.3 | 1.3 | 1.0 | 1.0 | | Quick | 1.1 | 1.3 |
| .3 | .7 | .6 | .9 | .9 | .9 | | | .6 | .7 |
| 0 UND | 0 UND | 27 13.6 | 41 8.9 | 50 7.3 | 47 7.8 | | | 23 15.9 | 18 19.8 |
| 0 UND | 23 15.6 | 46 7.9 | 54 6.8 | 62 5.9 | 57 6.4 | | Sales/Receivables | 41 8.8 | 37 9.8 |
| 22 16.5 | 51 7.1 | 66 5.5 | 76 4.8 | 85 4.3 | 74 4.9 | | | 62 5.9 | 58 6.3 |
| | | | | | | | Cost of Sales/Inventory | | |
| | | | | | | | | | |
| | | | | | | | Cost of Sales/Payables | | |
| 12.6 | 5.3 | 3.8 | 4.3 | 2.9 | 4.5 | | | 5.0 | 4.1 |
| 40.4 | 15.7 | 6.4 | 7.5 | 7.9 | 9.7 | | Sales/Working Capital | 10.5 | 7.9 |
| -23.6 | 80.0 | 18.2 | 16.0 | 9.4 | 28.0 | | | 54.7 | 24.6 |
| 21.8 | 35.2 | 37.1 | 54.1 | 38.0 | 5.0 | | | 22.2 | 26.7 |
| (15) 8.0 | (46) 9.2 | (86) 12.4 | (52) 10.7 | (10) 7.5 | 3.0 | | EBIT/Interest | (257) 7.5 | (153) 8.1 |
| 1.4 | 3.0 | 2.5 | 2.8 | 1.0 | 1.4 | | | 1.9 | 1.4 |
| | | | 27.9 | | | | | 10.6 | 9.4 |
| | | (13) 6.1 | | | | | Net Profit + Depr., Dep., Amort./Cur. Mat. L/T/D | (24) 2.4 | (15) 2.7 |
| | | | 1.9 | | | | | 1.6 | 1.5 |
| .1 | .2 | .2 | .2 | .2 | .7 | | | .1 | .1 |
| .4 | .7 | .4 | .6 | .5 | -1.2 | | Fixed/Worth | .5 | .5 |
| UND | 3.5 | 1.0 | 1.4 | 1.3 | -.5 | | | 1.5 | 1.7 |
| .8 | .5 | .4 | .7 | .9 | 4.8 | | | .6 | .6 |
| 4.9 | 1.5 | .9 | 1.5 | 1.6 | -11.4 | | Debt/Worth | 1.5 | 1.7 |
| UND | 15.6 | 4.2 | 4.0 | 11.9 | -3.2 | | | 6.3 | 20.7 |
| 400.0 | 85.8 | 68.8 | 59.0 | 82.2 | | | | 63.0 | 65.7 |
| (15) 101.6 | (44) 38.7 | (84) 22.0 | (49) 27.7 | (10) 31.3 | | | % Profit Before Taxes/Tangible Net Worth | (253) 24.7 | (150) 30.1 |
| 50.0 | 10.1 | 8.4 | 16.9 | 14.9 | | | | 8.9 | 9.0 |
| 68.4 | 28.8 | 22.6 | 19.4 | 18.9 | 11.0 | | | 27.1 | 28.1 |
| 34.6 | 15.5 | 11.2 | 12.1 | 8.2 | 3.5 | | % Profit Before Taxes/Total Assets | 10.4 | 12.0 |
| 5.9 | 2.9 | 2.7 | 6.0 | .7 | 1.1 | | | 2.0 | 2.5 |
| 885.2 | 60.8 | 54.7 | 24.5 | 26.2 | 20.0 | | | 56.3 | 54.0 |
| 63.2 | 13.5 | 17.4 | 11.5 | 17.1 | 10.7 | | Sales/Net Fixed Assets | 17.8 | 16.8 |
| 17.6 | 4.6 | 7.1 | 4.8 | 5.8 | 5.9 | | | 6.3 | 6.5 |
| 8.8 | 3.5 | 3.0 | 2.8 | 2.0 | 1.9 | | | 3.4 | 3.3 |
| 5.3 | 2.8 | 2.2 | 2.0 | 1.2 | 1.5 | | Sales/Total Assets | 2.5 | 2.3 |
| 3.0 | 1.8 | 1.5 | 1.3 | .9 | 1.0 | | | 1.6 | 1.4 |
| | 1.3 | .9 | .8 | | | | | .9 | .9 |
| | (30) 2.7 | (58) 1.6 | (54) 1.8 | | | | % Depr., Dep., Amort./Sales | (179) 1.9 | (112) 1.9 |
| | 8.2 | 3.4 | 3.5 | | | | | 3.5 | 3.2 |
| 4.3 | 2.6 | 1.5 | .5 | | | | | 1.9 | 2.2 |
| (11) 8.4 | (27) 4.6 | (35) 2.7 | (13) .8 | | | | % Officers', Directors', Owners' Comp/Sales | (120) 3.6 | (68) 3.9 |
| 11.0 | 7.3 | 4.1 | 1.4 | | | | | 6.9 | 7.9 |
| 25833M | 202196M | 1063239M | 2670078M | 1123685M | 3969275M | | Net Sales ($) | 7227379M | 6807387M |
| 4550M | 71152M | 459839M | 1343231M | 792544M | 2680351M | | Total Assets ($) | 3889262M | 2482689M |

M = $ thousand    MM = $ million
See Pages viii through xx for Explanation of Ratios and Data

© RMA 2024

# OTHER SERVICES—Commercial & Industrial Machinery & Equip. (except Auto. & Electronic) Repair & Maintenance NAICS 811310

## 1301

| Comparative Historical Data | | | Type of Statement | Current Data Sorted by Sales | | | | | |
|---|---|---|---|---|---|---|---|---|---|
| 4 | 14 | 16 | Unqualified | | | 1 | 1 | 1 | 14 |
| 17 | 35 | 27 | Reviewed | | | 4 | 4 | 9 | 13 |
| 16 | 27 | 19 | Compiled | | 1 | 2 | 7 | 6 | 3 |
| 44 | 67 | 59 | Tax Returns | 10 | 14 | 13 | 12 | 10 | |
| 115 | 143 | 138 | Other | 10 | 17 | 14 | 21 | 30 | 46 |
| 4/1/21- | 4/1/22- | 4/1/23- | | | 39 (4/1-9/30/23) | | | 220 (10/1/23-3/31/24) | |
| 3/31/22 | 3/31/23 | 3/31/24 | | 0-1MM | 1-3MM | 3-5MM | 5-10MM | 10-25MM | 25MM & OVER |
| ALL | ALL | ALL | | | | | | | |
| 196 | 286 | 259 | NUMBER OF STATEMENTS | 20 | 32 | 30 | 45 | 56 | 76 |
| % | % | % | ASSETS | % | % | % | % | % | % |
| 17.5 | 16.9 | 15.4 | Cash & Equivalents | 12.6 | 18.5 | 22.6 | 18.7 | 14.4 | 10.9 |
| 24.8 | 26.3 | 26.6 | Trade Receivables (net) | 11.4 | 20.2 | 24.0 | 24.1 | 31.1 | 32.4 |
| 17.0 | 16.3 | 14.7 | Inventory | 9.4 | 16.5 | 8.9 | 15.5 | 21.7 | 11.8 |
| 4.5 | 3.4 | 3.9 | All Other Current | .4 | 4.5 | 1.1 | 3.4 | 3.0 | 6.5 |
| 63.8 | 62.8 | 60.5 | Total Current | 33.8 | 59.7 | 56.6 | 61.7 | 70.2 | 61.7 |
| 22.3 | 23.0 | 22.9 | Fixed Assets (net) | 51.2 | 28.5 | 22.0 | 19.4 | 18.1 | 19.0 |
| 7.1 | 5.0 | 8.0 | Intangibles (net) | 2.1 | 6.0 | 13.5 | 5.3 | 7.2 | 10.3 |
| 6.8 | 9.2 | 8.6 | All Other Non-Current | 13.0 | 5.8 | 7.9 | 13.6 | 4.5 | 9.1 |
| 100.0 | 100.0 | 100.0 | Total | 100.0 | 100.0 | 100.0 | 100.0 | 100.0 | 100.0 |
| | | | LIABILITIES | | | | | | |
| 9.4 | 7.4 | 7.4 | Notes Payable-Short Term | 7.5 | 13.7 | 6.1 | 7.4 | 7.0 | 5.4 |
| 3.1 | 3.7 | 2.6 | Cur. Mat.-L.T.D. | 1.6 | 2.2 | 3.7 | 2.0 | 2.8 | 2.7 |
| 10.0 | 10.6 | 9.7 | Trade Payables | 3.3 | 9.2 | 7.1 | 8.0 | 14.0 | 10.6 |
| .2 | .2 | .1 | Income Taxes Payable | .0 | .0 | .0 | .1 | .2 | .3 |
| 10.9 | 11.2 | 14.3 | All Other Current | 18.6 | 17.9 | 19.1 | 10.4 | 11.2 | 14.4 |
| 33.6 | 33.2 | 34.2 | Total Current | 31.0 | 43.0 | 36.1 | 27.8 | 35.2 | 33.5 |
| 21.2 | 20.0 | 21.2 | Long-Term Debt | 38.3 | 24.3 | 32.6 | 12.7 | 17.9 | 18.2 |
| .2 | .3 | .2 | Deferred Taxes | .1 | .0 | .0 | .0 | .4 | .3 |
| 3.8 | 4.4 | 4.1 | All Other Non-Current | 4.4 | 4.0 | 1.2 | 3.5 | 5.8 | 4.3 |
| 41.1 | 42.2 | 40.4 | Net Worth | 26.3 | 28.7 | 30.1 | 55.9 | 40.8 | 43.8 |
| 100.0 | 100.0 | 100.0 | Total Liabilities & Net Worth | 100.0 | 100.0 | 100.0 | 100.0 | 100.0 | 100.0 |
| | | | INCOME DATA | | | | | | |
| 100.0 | 100.0 | 100.0 | Net Sales | 100.0 | 100.0 | 100.0 | 100.0 | 100.0 | 100.0 |
| | | | Gross Profit | | | | | | |
| 93.1 | 91.7 | 90.7 | Operating Expenses | 66.4 | 91.4 | 93.2 | 94.7 | 92.5 | 92.2 |
| 6.9 | 8.3 | 9.3 | Operating Profit | 33.6 | 8.6 | 6.8 | 5.3 | 7.5 | 7.8 |
| -1.4 | .1 | 1.6 | All Other Expenses (net) | 16.4 | .1 | .2 | -.2 | .2 | 1.0 |
| 8.3 | 8.1 | 7.7 | Profit Before Taxes | 17.2 | 8.4 | 6.6 | 5.6 | 7.3 | 6.8 |
| | | | RATIOS | | | | | | |
| 3.5 | 3.7 | 3.6 | | 2.3 | 5.6 | 4.3 | 4.9 | 3.5 | 3.0 |
| 2.1 | 2.1 | 2.0 | Current | 1.0 | 1.7 | 2.0 | 2.3 | 2.2 | 1.8 |
| 1.3 | 1.4 | 1.2 | | .5 | 1.0 | .9 | 1.4 | 1.5 | 1.3 |
| 2.6 | 2.7 | 2.5 | | 2.0 | 3.6 | 4.3 | 4.7 | 2.5 | 2.1 |
| 1.3 | 1.5 | 1.3 | Quick | .7 | 1.2 | 1.8 | 1.6 | 1.3 | 1.2 |
| .7 | .8 | .8 | | .3 | .5 | .6 | .9 | .8 | .9 |
| 24  15.0 | 19  19.5 | 22  16.7 | | 0  UND | 0  UND | 12  29.2 | 18  20.7 | 31  11.8 | 43  8.4 |
| 45  8.1 | 45  8.2 | 45  8.1 | Sales/Receivables | 0  UND | 31  11.9 | 37  9.8 | 39  9.4 | 43  8.4 | 55  6.6 |
| 66  5.5 | 64  5.7 | 65  5.6 | | 21  17.6 | 59  6.2 | 63  5.8 | 62  5.9 | 69  5.3 | 72  5.1 |
| | | | Cost of Sales/Inventory | | | | | | |
| | | | Cost of Sales/Payables | | | | | | |
| 3.7 | 4.1 | 4.4 | | 5.4 | 3.7 | 6.2 | 4.3 | 4.2 | 4.4 |
| 6.7 | 7.3 | 8.5 | Sales/Working Capital | 115.2 | 13.4 | 14.2 | 7.1 | 6.6 | 8.5 |
| 17.3 | 20.2 | 28.0 | | -39.8 | NM | -144.9 | 17.9 | 14.6 | 19.6 |
| 38.4 | 44.7 | 32.7 | | 11.8 | 37.3 | 25.0 | 29.7 | 32.1 | 52.0 |
| (164) 11.6 | (238) 12.9 | (224) 8.3 | EBIT/Interest | (12) 5.0 | (28) 9.9 | (24) 9.1 | (41) 10.9 | (53) 8.3 | (66) 9.7 |
| 3.5 | 3.3 | 2.5 | | 1.2 | 3.1 | 2.7 | 2.2 | 2.4 | 2.7 |
| 11.1 | 6.1 | 14.5 | Net Profit + Depr., Dep., | | | | | | 20.8 |
| (19) 4.9 | (30) 3.0 | (34) 5.5 | Amort./Cur. Mat. L/T/D | | | | | (23) 5.3 | |
| 2.1 | 1.4 | 1.8 | | | | | | | 1.4 |
| .1 | .1 | .2 | | .1 | .3 | .2 | .1 | .2 | .2 |
| .5 | .4 | .5 | Fixed/Worth | 1.9 | 1.2 | .5 | .3 | .4 | .5 |
| 2.2 | 1.4 | 2.4 | | UND | UND | -1.9 | .7 | 1.2 | 3.5 |
| .5 | .5 | .6 | | .9 | .6 | .8 | .3 | .7 | .7 |
| 1.2 | 1.3 | 1.5 | Debt/Worth | 3.9 | 2.6 | 1.8 | .7 | 1.5 | 1.5 |
| 8.8 | 3.8 | 7.9 | | UND | UND | -4.2 | 1.7 | 4.1 | 7.1 |
| 70.4 | 70.3 | 70.1 | | 88.4 | 97.4 | 104.5 | 40.5 | 84.1 | 59.6 |
| (161) 33.3 | (247) 32.9 | (209) 29.8 | % Profit Before Taxes/Tangible Net Worth | (15) 26.0 | (24) 57.8 | (21) 27.5 | (41) 15.5 | (46) 25.1 | (62) 32.2 |
| 15.4 | 10.2 | 11.2 | | 1.8 | 29.1 | 8.5 | 8.5 | 8.4 | 17.3 |
| 30.3 | 29.5 | 23.8 | | 17.1 | 40.8 | 30.4 | 20.1 | 22.2 | 20.0 |
| 11.5 | 13.8 | 11.9 | % Profit Before Taxes/Total Assets | 4.8 | 21.1 | 13.7 | 10.5 | 11.3 | 12.1 |
| 4.4 | 2.9 | 3.2 | | .6 | 5.0 | 2.7 | 3.1 | 3.0 | 4.9 |
| 48.3 | 64.9 | 36.7 | | 72.5 | 58.3 | 66.0 | 54.8 | 44.3 | 25.9 |
| 15.5 | 15.4 | 15.7 | Sales/Net Fixed Assets | 1.0 | 12.9 | 18.7 | 15.2 | 17.4 | 13.9 |
| 6.6 | 6.3 | 5.9 | | .2 | 4.4 | 6.8 | 6.7 | 7.3 | 8.2 |
| 3.0 | 3.3 | 3.1 | | 2.0 | 3.7 | 3.5 | 3.0 | 3.1 | 3.0 |
| 2.0 | 2.3 | 2.2 | Sales/Total Assets | .3 | 2.4 | 2.7 | 2.4 | 2.3 | 2.1 |
| 1.3 | 1.4 | 1.4 | | .2 | 1.5 | 1.7 | 1.6 | 1.6 | 1.4 |
| 1.0 | .8 | 1.0 | | 6.5 | .3 | .8 | 1.4 | 1.0 | .8 |
| (137) 2.0 | (171) 2.1 | (166) 1.9 | % Depr., Dep., Amort./Sales | (10) 10.8 | (15) 2.9 | (13) 1.6 | (25) 2.2 | (41) 1.9 | (62) 1.7 |
| 3.9 | 4.2 | 4.0 | | 20.5 | 5.6 | 2.4 | 4.1 | 4.4 | 2.5 |
| 2.5 | 1.6 | 1.5 | | | 4.0 | 3.4 | 2.2 | .8 | |
| (71) 4.0 | (119) 3.0 | (87) 3.0 | % Officers', Directors', Owners' Comp/Sales | | (14) 5.4 | (14) 4.6 | (22) 3.7 | (24) 1.4 | |
| 7.2 | 5.3 | 6.1 | | | 8.1 | 8.7 | 4.9 | 2.7 | |
| 5336008M | 7270948M | 9054306M | Net Sales ($) | 9223M | 67110M | 118696M | 315426M | 878997M | 7664854M |
| 3085385M | 4049653M | 5351667M | Total Assets ($) | 23384M | 40244M | 53419M | 171863M | 487351M | 4575406M |

© RMA 2024  M = $ thousand  MM = $ million
See Pages viii through xx for Explanation of Ratios and Data

# OTHER SERVICES—Other Personal and Household Goods Repair and Maintenance  NAICS 811490

**Current Data Sorted by Assets** | **Comparative Historical Data**

| | | | | | | Type of Statement | | |
|---|---|---|---|---|---|---|---|---|
| | | | | | | Unqualified | | |
| | | 2 | | | | Reviewed | 2 | 1 |
| 9 | 7 | 2 | | | | Compiled | | 1 |
| 10 | 7 | 8 | 3 | 1 | | Tax Returns | 29 | 26 |
| | 3 (4/1-9/30/23) | | 46 (10/1/23-3/31/24) | | | Other | 35 | 17 |
| 0-500M | 500M-2MM | 2-10MM | 10-50MM | 50-100MM | 100-250MM | | 4/1/19-3/31/20 ALL | 4/1/20-3/31/21 ALL |
| 19 | 14 | 12 | 3 | 1 | | NUMBER OF STATEMENTS | 66 | 45 |
| % | % | % | % | % | % | ASSETS | % | % |
| 28.8 | 16.7 | 13.8 | | | | Cash & Equivalents | 22.9 | 27.8 |
| 15.8 | 22.1 | 28.0 | | | D | Trade Receivables (net) | 20.0 | 20.5 |
| 4.7 | 24.8 | 8.3 | | | A | Inventory | 9.6 | 6.5 |
| 3.8 | 3.7 | 1.2 | | | T | All Other Current | 1.3 | 4.5 |
| 53.1 | 67.2 | 51.4 | | | A | Total Current | 53.8 | 59.3 |
| 30.3 | 14.2 | 28.8 | | | | Fixed Assets (net) | 28.0 | 24.0 |
| 10.1 | 7.3 | 7.9 | | | N | Intangibles (net) | 5.5 | 9.8 |
| 6.6 | 11.3 | 11.9 | | | O | All Other Non-Current | 12.7 | 6.8 |
| 100.0 | 100.0 | 100.0 | | | T | Total | 100.0 | 100.0 |
| | | | | | A | LIABILITIES | | |
| 13.7 | 9.6 | 9.9 | | | V | Notes Payable-Short Term | 10.6 | 12.6 |
| 5.2 | 1.4 | 2.1 | | | A | Cur. Mat.-L.T.D. | 4.4 | 3.0 |
| 8.9 | 10.5 | 10.6 | | | I | Trade Payables | 11.8 | 8.9 |
| .0 | .0 | .0 | | | L | Income Taxes Payable | .2 | .0 |
| 15.6 | 12.6 | 14.1 | | | A | All Other Current | 17.1 | 15.2 |
| 43.5 | 34.1 | 36.7 | | | B | Total Current | 44.0 | 39.8 |
| 41.9 | 24.7 | 24.2 | | | L | Long-Term Debt | 26.4 | 46.6 |
| .0 | .0 | .0 | | | E | Deferred Taxes | .0 | .0 |
| 21.5 | 4.4 | 13.3 | | | | All Other Non-Current | 4.1 | 8.8 |
| -6.9 | 36.8 | 25.7 | | | | Net Worth | 25.5 | 4.6 |
| 100.0 | 100.0 | 100.0 | | | | Total Liabilties & Net Worth | 100.0 | 100.0 |
| | | | | | | INCOME DATA | | |
| 100.0 | 100.0 | 100.0 | | | | Net Sales | 100.0 | 100.0 |
| | | | | | | Gross Profit | | |
| 99.4 | 85.3 | 91.8 | | | | Operating Expenses | 91.7 | 93.4 |
| .6 | 14.7 | 8.2 | | | | Operating Profit | 8.3 | 6.6 |
| -.1 | 2.1 | 4.1 | | | | All Other Expenses (net) | .9 | -1.6 |
| .7 | 12.6 | 4.1 | | | | Profit Before Taxes | 7.4 | 8.2 |
| | | | | | | RATIOS | | |
| 3.6 | 5.0 | 2.6 | | | | | 4.3 | 4.7 |
| 1.2 | 1.6 | 1.6 | | | | Current | 1.7 | 2.2 |
| .3 | 1.2 | .8 | | | | | .8 | 1.1 |
| 3.0 | 4.6 | 2.5 | | | | | 3.9 | 4.1 |
| .8 | .9 | 1.2 | | | | Quick | 1.2 | 1.8 |
| .3 | .3 | .4 | | | | | .5 | .7 |
| 0  UND | 0  UND | 15  23.6 | | | | | 0  UND | 0  UND |
| 0  UND | 0  UND | 31  11.7 | | | | Sales/Receivables | 9  39.6 | 16  22.3 |
| 19  18.8 | 51  7.2 | 54  6.7 | | | | | 38  9.5 | 37  9.9 |
| | | | | | | Cost of Sales/Inventory | | |
| | | | | | | Cost of Sales/Payables | | |
| 14.1 | 4.7 | 7.1 | | | | | 6.7 | 8.4 |
| 48.4 | 9.4 | 30.5 | | | | Sales/Working Capital | 27.0 | 13.9 |
| -26.3 | NM | -25.7 | | | | | -51.2 | 164.9 |
| 22.6 | 31.8 | | | | | | 32.4 | 30.3 |
| (14)  2.7 | (13)  6.1 | | | | | EBIT/Interest | (50)  7.3 | (35)  11.4 |
| -.1 | 2.5 | | | | | | 1.7 | 2.1 |
| | | | | | | Net Profit + Depr., Dep., Amort./Cur. Mat. L/T/D | | |
| .0 | .0 | .1 | | | | | .2 | .1 |
| 4.1 | .3 | .8 | | | | Fixed/Worth | .6 | 1.8 |
| -3.8 | 4.1 | -4.0 | | | | | -4.6 | -.9 |
| .9 | .5 | .4 | | | | | .5 | 1.4 |
| 113.0 | 2.6 | 1.6 | | | | Debt/Worth | 1.5 | 11.2 |
| -2.7 | 50.7 | -9.2 | | | | | -8.3 | -3.5 |
| 530.6 | 233.4 | | | | | | 152.9 | 173.7 |
| (10)  68.5 | (12)  106.8 | | | | | % Profit Before Taxes/Tangible Net Worth | (47)  51.4 | (24)  75.4 |
| 7.4 | 30.6 | | | | | | 15.5 | 50.9 |
| 35.5 | 64.1 | 34.1 | | | | | 41.1 | 55.9 |
| 9.0 | 17.2 | 9.4 | | | | % Profit Before Taxes/Total Assets | 21.1 | 29.3 |
| -2.9 | 6.9 | 1.9 | | | | | 3.9 | 2.8 |
| 612.0 | 272.5 | 140.3 | | | | | 79.0 | 206.3 |
| 66.9 | 91.6 | 12.6 | | | | Sales/Net Fixed Assets | 20.5 | 23.4 |
| 6.6 | 26.7 | 7.4 | | | | | 7.3 | 10.7 |
| 12.1 | 4.3 | 4.1 | | | | | 6.0 | 5.7 |
| 5.7 | 3.7 | 3.1 | | | | Sales/Total Assets | 3.8 | 3.4 |
| 2.6 | 2.4 | 1.6 | | | | | 2.3 | 1.8 |
| | | | | | | | .8 | .3 |
| | | | | | | % Depr., Dep., Amort./Sales | (28)  2.4 | (17)  1.9 |
| | | | | | | | 4.3 | 7.2 |
| | | | | | | | 2.8 | 2.0 |
| | | | | | | % Officers', Directors' Owners' Comp/Sales | (34)  5.5 | (25)  3.6 |
| | | | | | | | 8.6 | 9.2 |
| 30188M | 53581M | 155218M | 100655M | 23623M | | Net Sales ($) | 1628365M | 207110M |
| 5311M | 17086M | 49893M | 58522M | 64607M | | Total Assets ($) | 339867M | 90105M |

© RMA 2024

M = $ thousand    MM = $ million
See Pages viii through xx for Explanation of Ratios and Data

# OTHER SERVICES—Other Personal and Household Goods Repair and Maintenance  NAICS 811490

## Comparative Historical Data | Current Data Sorted by Sales

| | | | Type of Statement | | | | | |
|---|---|---|---|---|---|---|---|---|
| 2 | 1 | | Unqualified | | | | | 1 |
| 3 | 1 | 2 | Reviewed | | | | 1 | 1 |
| 18 | 29 | 18 | Compiled | 6 | 3 | 3 | 5 | 2 |
| 18 | 35 | 29 | Tax Returns | 3 | 11 | 4 | 5 | 4 |
| 4/1/21- | 4/1/22- | 4/1/23- | Other | | 3 (4/1-9/30/23) | | 46 (10/1/23-3/31/24) | |
| 3/31/22 | 3/31/23 | 3/31/24 | | 0-1MM | 1-3MM | 3-5MM | 5-10MM | 10-25MM | 25MM & OVER |
| ALL | ALL | ALL | | | | | | | |
| 41 | 68 | 49 | NUMBER OF STATEMENTS | 9 | 14 | 7 | 11 | 4 | 4 |
| % | % | % | ASSETS | % | % | % | % | % | % |
| 28.4 | 26.3 | 20.2 | Cash & Equivalents | | 30.8 | | 9.6 | | |
| 23.0 | 23.8 | 20.5 | Trade Receivables (net) | | 15.4 | | 26.6 | | |
| 9.1 | 13.1 | 12.5 | Inventory | | 15.2 | | 12.0 | | |
| 1.4 | 1.9 | 2.8 | All Other Current | | 3.0 | | 1.9 | | |
| 62.0 | 65.1 | 55.9 | Total Current | | 64.5 | | 50.1 | | |
| 29.6 | 20.8 | 24.7 | Fixed Assets (net) | | 19.3 | | 18.6 | | |
| 4.8 | 8.2 | 10.4 | Intangibles (net) | | 9.5 | | 11.4 | | |
| 3.6 | 5.8 | 9.0 | All Other Non-Current | | 6.7 | | 19.9 | | |
| 100.0 | 100.0 | 100.0 | Total | | 100.0 | | 100.0 | | |
| | | | **LIABILITIES** | | | | | | |
| 13.1 | 11.7 | 10.5 | Notes Payable-Short Term | | 8.1 | | 9.4 | | |
| 3.7 | 2.7 | 2.9 | Cur. Mat.-L.T.D. | | 5.4 | | 1.2 | | |
| 5.6 | 7.8 | 10.3 | Trade Payables | | 7.1 | | 7.2 | | |
| .3 | .0 | .0 | Income Taxes Payable | | .0 | | .0 | | |
| 9.4 | 18.6 | 13.2 | All Other Current | | 14.6 | | 7.0 | | |
| 32.1 | 40.8 | 37.0 | Total Current | | 35.2 | | 24.9 | | |
| 31.8 | 35.9 | 30.5 | Long-Term Debt | | 34.8 | | 25.7 | | |
| .0 | .2 | .0 | Deferred Taxes | | .0 | | .0 | | |
| 5.2 | 5.1 | 12.8 | All Other Non-Current | | 30.9 | | 16.7 | | |
| 30.8 | 17.9 | 19.7 | Net Worth | | -1.0 | | 32.7 | | |
| 100.0 | 100.0 | 100.0 | Total Liabilties & Net Worth | | 100.0 | | 100.0 | | |
| | | | **INCOME DATA** | | | | | | |
| 100.0 | 100.0 | 100.0 | Net Sales | | 100.0 | | 100.0 | | |
| | | | Gross Profit | | | | | | |
| 96.3 | 90.4 | 92.5 | Operating Expenses | | 90.9 | | 90.1 | | |
| 3.7 | 9.6 | 7.5 | Operating Profit | | 9.1 | | 9.9 | | |
| -2.3 | 1.1 | 1.8 | All Other Expenses (net) | | .4 | | .6 | | |
| 6.0 | 8.5 | 5.7 | Profit Before Taxes | | 8.7 | | 9.4 | | |
| | | | **RATIOS** | | | | | | |
| 5.6 | 6.4 | 3.3 | | | 4.8 | | 4.9 | | |
| 2.2 | 2.7 | 1.5 | Current | | 2.5 | | 1.6 | | |
| 1.3 | 1.2 | .8 | | | .7 | | .9 | | |
| | | | | | | | | | |
| 4.6 | 4.2 | 2.8 | | | 4.8 | | 4.4 | | |
| 1.9 | 1.5 | 1.1 | Quick | | 1.8 | | 1.5 | | |
| 1.0 | .8 | .3 | | | .3 | | .5 | | |
| 0 UND | 0 UND | 0 UND | | 0 UND | | 4 100.6 | | | |
| 11 34.1 | 20 18.4 | 14 26.0 | Sales/Receivables | 0 UND | | 18 20.8 | | | |
| 31 11.8 | 55 6.6 | 36 10.0 | | 14 26.1 | | 64 5.7 | | | |
| | | | Cost of Sales/Inventory | | | | | | |
| | | | | | | | | | |
| | | | Cost of Sales/Payables | | | | | | |
| | | | | | | | | | |
| 5.6 | 4.1 | 6.1 | | | 5.2 | | 6.7 | | |
| 13.9 | 8.2 | 19.8 | Sales/Working Capital | | 13.4 | | 20.7 | | |
| 45.1 | 50.6 | -46.5 | | | -48.3 | | -139.5 | | |
| 47.5 | 16.5 | 27.5 | | | 34.0 | | 63.3 | | |
| (31) 7.0 | (44) 7.3 | (39) 6.1 | EBIT/Interest | (10) 4.8 | | (10) 4.3 | | | |
| 1.6 | .7 | 1.1 | | | .5 | | .4 | | |
| | | | Net Profit + Depr., Dep., Amort./Cur. Mat. L/T/D | | | | | | |
| | | | | | | | | | |
| .1 | .0 | .0 | | | .0 | | .0 | | |
| .6 | .3 | .9 | Fixed/Worth | | 1.5 | | .3 | | |
| NM | 4.4 | -9.4 | | | -9.2 | | -.8 | | |
| .6 | .5 | .6 | | | .6 | | .4 | | |
| 1.6 | 2.1 | 3.3 | Debt/Worth | | 8.4 | | 1.9 | | |
| -15.7 | -26.8 | -8.7 | | | -8.6 | | -5.4 | | |
| 132.5 | 89.3 | 155.1 | % Profit Before Taxes/Tangible Net Worth | | | | | | |
| (30) 50.3 | (48) 54.5 | (33) 49.7 | | | | | | | |
| 3.7 | 22.3 | 10.2 | | | | | | | |
| 41.5 | 41.6 | 35.2 | % Profit Before Taxes/Total Assets | | 64.1 | | 89.1 | | |
| 18.2 | 22.3 | 13.9 | | | 11.6 | | 11.8 | | |
| -.5 | 3.8 | .5 | | | -.4 | | 1.3 | | |
| 114.9 | 262.3 | 274.8 | Sales/Net Fixed Assets | | 363.1 | | 281.4 | | |
| 23.0 | 26.7 | 41.5 | | | 73.1 | | 153.3 | | |
| 6.7 | 11.7 | 8.1 | | | 11.3 | | 9.4 | | |
| 6.4 | 5.4 | 5.4 | Sales/Total Assets | | 7.1 | | 3.9 | | |
| 3.4 | 2.7 | 3.6 | | | 4.7 | | 3.5 | | |
| 2.2 | 2.0 | 1.9 | | | 2.8 | | 2.6 | | |
| .6 | 1.0 | .3 | % Depr., Dep., Amort./Sales | | | | | | |
| (17) 1.5 | (25) 2.3 | (17) 2.5 | | | | | | | |
| 4.1 | 5.6 | 8.6 | | | | | | | |
| 1.9 | 2.8 | 2.8 | % Officers', Directors' Owners' Comp/Sales | | | | | | |
| (24) 5.7 | (34) 4.1 | (16) 3.6 | | | | | | | |
| 15.2 | 7.3 | 9.6 | | | | | | | |
| 264117M | 337481M | 363265M | Net Sales ($) | 4658M | 26859M | 25098M | 80601M | 77175M | 148874M |
| 94366M | 184897M | 195419M | Total Assets ($) | 7983M | 7723M | 6421M | 28463M | 84111M | 60718M |

© RMA 2024     M = $ thousand     MM = $ million
See Pages viii through xx for Explanation of Ratios and Data

# OTHER SERVICES—Beauty Salons  NAICS 812112

**Current Data Sorted by Assets** | **Comparative Historical Data**

| | | | | | | Type of Statement | | |
|---|---|---|---|---|---|---|---|---|
| 1 | 1 | | 1 | | 1 | Unqualified | 4 | 2 |
| | | | | 1 | | Reviewed | 1 | 1 |
| | 1 | | | | | Compiled | 9 | 1 |
| 23 | 4 | 2 | | | | Tax Returns | 44 | 33 |
| 25 | 25 | 6 | 1 | 1 | 1 | Other | 76 | 67 |
| | 3 (4/1–9/30/23) | | 91 (10/1/23–3/31/24) | | | | 4/1/19–3/31/20 | 4/1/20–3/31/21 |
| 0-500M | 500M-2MM | 2-10MM | 10-50MM | 50-100MM | 100-250MM | | ALL | ALL |
| 49 | 31 | 8 | 2 | 2 | 2 | NUMBER OF STATEMENTS | 134 | 104 |
| % | % | % | % | % | % | ASSETS | % | % |
| 39.7 | 21.1 | | | | | Cash & Equivalents | 20.5 | 30.7 |
| 1.7 | .3 | | | | | Trade Receivables (net) | .8 | 2.1 |
| 10.7 | 3.9 | | | | | Inventory | 11.1 | 6.6 |
| 1.4 | 3.2 | | | | | All Other Current | 1.4 | 1.6 |
| 53.6 | 28.5 | | | | | Total Current | 33.8 | 41.1 |
| 28.2 | 47.6 | | | | | Fixed Assets (net) | 42.5 | 34.6 |
| 8.0 | 16.1 | | | | | Intangibles (net) | 12.1 | 15.5 |
| 10.2 | 7.8 | | | | | All Other Non-Current | 11.5 | 8.8 |
| 100.0 | 100.0 | | | | | Total | 100.0 | 100.0 |
| | | | | | | LIABILITIES | | |
| 27.4 | 3.9 | | | | | Notes Payable-Short Term | 7.8 | 16.4 |
| 3.0 | 4.5 | | | | | Cur. Mat.-L.T.D. | 2.5 | 5.4 |
| 2.6 | 2.7 | | | | | Trade Payables | 2.9 | 2.0 |
| .4 | .0 | | | | | Income Taxes Payable | .0 | .3 |
| 31.9 | 34.3 | | | | | All Other Current | 29.1 | 17.8 |
| 65.2 | 45.4 | | | | | Total Current | 42.3 | 41.9 |
| 44.1 | 37.7 | | | | | Long-Term Debt | 34.8 | 50.7 |
| .0 | .0 | | | | | Deferred Taxes | .0 | .0 |
| 2.0 | 7.8 | | | | | All Other Non-Current | 10.6 | 9.5 |
| -11.2 | 9.2 | | | | | Net Worth | 12.4 | -2.1 |
| 100.0 | 100.0 | | | | | Total Liabilities & Net Worth | 100.0 | 100.0 |
| | | | | | | INCOME DATA | | |
| 100.0 | 100.0 | | | | | Net Sales | 100.0 | 100.0 |
| | | | | | | Gross Profit | | |
| 88.3 | 91.1 | | | | | Operating Expenses | 91.7 | 92.9 |
| 11.7 | 8.9 | | | | | Operating Profit | 8.3 | 7.1 |
| 1.9 | 4.9 | | | | | All Other Expenses (net) | 3.1 | 1.2 |
| 9.9 | 4.0 | | | | | Profit Before Taxes | 5.2 | 5.9 |
| | | | | | | RATIOS | | |
| 5.5 | 1.4 | | | | | | 2.0 | 4.1 |
| 1.9 | .5 | | | | | Current | 1.0 | 1.4 |
| .4 | .2 | | | | | | .4 | .4 |
| 5.1 | 1.0 | | | | | | 1.4 | 3.0 |
| 1.6 | .4 | | | | | Quick | .6 | 1.1 |
| .3 | .1 | | | | | | .2 | .4 |
| 0 UND | 0 UND | | | | | | 0 UND | 0 UND |
| 0 UND | 0 UND | | | | | Sales/Receivables | 0 UND | 0 UND |
| 0 UND | 0 UND | | | | | | 0 UND | 0 UND |
| | | | | | | Cost of Sales/Inventory | | |
| | | | | | | Cost of Sales/Payables | | |
| 7.6 | 48.1 | | | | | | 15.8 | 7.2 |
| 29.0 | -20.4 | | | | | Sales/Working Capital | 295.2 | 25.0 |
| -12.0 | -3.3 | | | | | | -13.5 | -6.6 |
| 13.3 | 13.0 | | | | | | 14.4 | 7.5 |
| (26) 2.5 | (24) 4.7 | | | | | EBIT/Interest | (100) 4.8 | (72) 1.0 |
| -.7 | -.4 | | | | | | 1.0 | -3.5 |
| | | | | | | Net Profit + Depr., Dep., Amort./Cur. Mat. L/T/D | | |
| .0 | 1.6 | | | | | | .7 | .3 |
| .5 | 15.4 | | | | | Fixed/Worth | 3.7 | 2.4 |
| 3.3 | -1.2 | | | | | | -1.7 | -1.0 |
| .4 | 1.8 | | | | | | .8 | 1.3 |
| 3.1 | 14.5 | | | | | Debt/Worth | 4.8 | 15.0 |
| -6.9 | -3.7 | | | | | | -4.0 | -2.6 |
| 145.6 | 175.3 | | | | | | 68.4 | 72.4 |
| (33) 49.1 | (16) 50.4 | | | | | % Profit Before Taxes/Tangible Net Worth | (80) 22.9 | (55) 26.8 |
| -22.1 | 11.4 | | | | | | 4.0 | -7.3 |
| 53.8 | 23.1 | | | | | | 22.2 | 25.6 |
| 20.4 | 11.0 | | | | | % Profit Before Taxes/Total Assets | 10.8 | 1.8 |
| -12.3 | -.7 | | | | | | .3 | -12.5 |
| UND | 12.2 | | | | | | 23.6 | 45.4 |
| 24.8 | 4.2 | | | | | Sales/Net Fixed Assets | 9.9 | 8.3 |
| 6.6 | 1.6 | | | | | | 3.0 | 2.1 |
| 8.3 | 3.8 | | | | | | 5.7 | 4.0 |
| 3.2 | 1.5 | | | | | Sales/Total Assets | 3.1 | 1.9 |
| 2.2 | 1.0 | | | | | | 1.3 | .7 |
| .5 | .3 | | | | | | .8 | 1.3 |
| (27) 1.7 | (16) 2.2 | | | | | % Depr., Dep., Amort./Sales | (89) 1.8 | (49) 2.6 |
| 3.2 | 8.7 | | | | | | 4.5 | 5.5 |
| 4.6 | 1.7 | | | | | | 2.0 | 3.4 |
| (24) 6.3 | (10) 4.8 | | | | | % Officers', Directors' Owners' Comp/Sales | (52) 3.8 | (36) 6.9 |
| 11.9 | 7.9 | | | | | | 8.9 | 11.3 |
| 35007M | 78396M | 72144M | 146054M | 177299M | 343715M | Net Sales ($) | 1277503M | 490122M |
| 10154M | 31451M | 34618M | 84213M | 113418M | 332955M | Total Assets ($) | 924225M | 305647M |

M = $ thousand   MM = $ million
See Pages viii through xx for Explanation of Ratios and Data

© RMA 2024

## OTHER SERVICES—Beauty Salons  NAICS 812112

### Comparative Historical Data | Current Data Sorted by Sales

| | | | | | | Type of Statement | | | | | | |
|---|---|---|---|---|---|---|---|---|---|---|---|---|
| | | 3 | | 1 | | 4 | Unqualified | 1 | | | 1 | | 2 |
| | | 1 | | 1 | | 1 | Reviewed | | | | | | 1 |
| | | | | | | 3 | Compiled | | | 1 | | | |
| | | 23 | | 36 | | 29 | Tax Returns | 18 | 8 | | 1 | 2 | |
| | | 63 | | 62 | | 59 | Other | 26 | 19 | 4 | 4 | 3 | 3 |
| | | 4/1/21- | | 4/1/22- | | 4/1/23- | | 3 (4/1-9/30/23) | | | 91 (10/1/23-3/31/24) | | |
| | | 3/31/22 | | 3/31/23 | | 3/31/24 | | 0-1MM | 1-3MM | 3-5MM | 5-10MM | 10-25MM | 25MM & OVER |
| | | ALL | | ALL | | ALL | NUMBER OF STATEMENTS | | | | | | |
| | | 90 | | 103 | | 94 | | 45 | 27 | 5 | 6 | 5 | 6 |
| | | % | | % | | % | ASSETS | % | % | % | % | % | % |
| | | 35.0 | | 32.2 | | 30.3 | Cash & Equivalents | 28.9 | 36.6 | | | | |
| | | .9 | | 1.3 | | 1.5 | Trade Receivables (net) | .0 | 3.3 | | | | |
| | | 5.8 | | 7.2 | | 8.3 | Inventory | 9.6 | 4.6 | | | | |
| | | 2.8 | | 4.1 | | 2.3 | All Other Current | .6 | 2.8 | | | | |
| | | 44.6 | | 44.9 | | 42.3 | Total Current | 39.2 | 47.2 | | | | |
| | | 38.2 | | 34.5 | | 33.3 | Fixed Assets (net) | 42.3 | 29.7 | | | | |
| | | 9.5 | | 10.8 | | 12.2 | Intangibles (net) | 10.7 | 12.5 | | | | |
| | | 7.8 | | 9.8 | | 12.2 | All Other Non-Current | 7.8 | 10.6 | | | | |
| | | 100.0 | | 100.0 | | 100.0 | Total | 100.0 | 100.0 | | | | |
| | | | | | | | LIABILITIES | | | | | | |
| | | 4.4 | | 14.6 | | 15.9 | Notes Payable-Short Term | 19.7 | 19.7 | | | | |
| | | 4.6 | | 2.6 | | 3.4 | Cur. Mat.-L.T.D. | 4.6 | 1.6 | | | | |
| | | 6.3 | | 2.5 | | 2.7 | Trade Payables | 2.4 | 1.1 | | | | |
| | | .0 | | .0 | | .2 | Income Taxes Payable | .4 | .0 | | | | |
| | | 21.8 | | 16.6 | | 30.8 | All Other Current | 29.8 | 38.7 | | | | |
| | | 37.2 | | 36.3 | | 53.0 | Total Current | 56.9 | 61.1 | | | | |
| | | 51.9 | | 44.4 | | 39.2 | Long-Term Debt | 56.0 | 21.0 | | | | |
| | | .0 | | .0 | | .1 | Deferred Taxes | .0 | .0 | | | | |
| | | 7.8 | | 10.8 | | 5.5 | All Other Non-Current | 6.9 | 1.4 | | | | |
| | | 3.2 | | 8.5 | | 2.3 | Net Worth | -19.6 | 16.5 | | | | |
| | | 100.0 | | 100.0 | | 100.0 | Total Liabilties & Net Worth | 100.0 | 100.0 | | | | |
| | | | | | | | INCOME DATA | | | | | | |
| | | 100.0 | | 100.0 | | 100.0 | Net Sales | 100.0 | 100.0 | | | | |
| | | | | | | | Gross Profit | | | | | | |
| | | 84.5 | | 89.7 | | 90.0 | Operating Expenses | 85.9 | 93.9 | | | | |
| | | 15.5 | | 10.3 | | 10.0 | Operating Profit | 14.1 | 6.1 | | | | |
| | | -.2 | | 2.0 | | 2.8 | All Other Expenses (net) | 4.7 | 1.3 | | | | |
| | | 15.7 | | 8.2 | | 7.2 | Profit Before Taxes | 9.4 | 4.9 | | | | |
| | | | | | | | RATIOS | | | | | | |
| | | 6.0 | | 5.8 | | 3.6 | | 4.2 | 3.9 | | | | |
| | | 2.3 | | 1.9 | | 1.0 | Current | 1.0 | 1.4 | | | | |
| | | .5 | | .8 | | .3 | | .3 | .3 | | | | |
| | | 4.1 | | 3.5 | | 2.4 | | 3.1 | 3.9 | | | | |
| | | 1.8 | | 1.3 | | .8 | Quick | .6 | .5 | | | | |
| | | .4 | | .4 | | .2 | | .2 | .2 | | | | |
| 0 | UND | | 0 | UND | 0 | UND | | 0 | UND | 0 | UND | | |
| 0 | UND | | 0 | UND | 0 | UND | Sales/Receivables | 0 | UND | 0 | UND | | |
| 0 | UND | | 0 | UND | 0 | UND | | 0 | UND | 0 | UND | | |
| | | | | | | | Cost of Sales/Inventory | | | | | | |
| | | | | | | | Cost of Sales/Payables | | | | | | |
| | | 6.0 | | 5.2 | | 9.9 | | 10.4 | 9.6 | | | | |
| | | 14.1 | | 20.5 | | 182.1 | Sales/Working Capital | UND | 33.3 | | | | |
| | | -11.6 | | -57.7 | | -7.1 | | -6.3 | -4.3 | | | | |
| | | 53.3 | | 8.9 | | 12.1 | | 11.3 | 8.6 | | | | |
| (64) | | 11.3 | (58) | 2.5 | (60) | 2.6 | EBIT/Interest | (24) 2.5 | (18) 3.6 | | | | |
| | | 2.5 | | -.2 | | -.6 | | -.7 | -2.5 | | | | |
| | | | | | | | Net Profit + Depr., Dep., Amort./Cur. Mat. L/T/D | | | | | | |
| | | .4 | | .1 | | .3 | | .2 | .1 | | | | |
| | | 2.5 | | 1.1 | | 1.8 | Fixed/Worth | 1.7 | 1.8 | | | | |
| | | -3.6 | | 21.2 | | -3.6 | | -18.7 | -2.4 | | | | |
| | | .9 | | .6 | | .8 | | .4 | .9 | | | | |
| | | 4.8 | | 4.1 | | 5.7 | Debt/Worth | 5.5 | 3.8 | | | | |
| | | -5.6 | | -12.5 | | -5.1 | | -4.7 | -3.9 | | | | |
| | | 193.4 | | 98.4 | | 115.8 | % Profit Before Taxes/Tangible Net Worth | 145.6 | 82.5 | | | | |
| (56) | | 70.1 | (72) | 21.4 | (59) | 39.9 | | (29) 50.0 | (15) 39.9 | | | | |
| | | 20.7 | | -2.5 | | 1.1 | | -3.6 | -18.6 | | | | |
| | | 53.3 | | 33.4 | | 35.8 | % Profit Before Taxes/Total Assets | 44.2 | 33.3 | | | | |
| | | 24.4 | | 8.5 | | 11.0 | | 11.0 | 9.1 | | | | |
| | | 1.1 | | -1.2 | | -3.1 | | -7.6 | -9.1 | | | | |
| | | 39.3 | | 125.7 | | 73.0 | | 104.0 | 49.1 | | | | |
| | | 8.6 | | 9.0 | | 11.1 | Sales/Net Fixed Assets | 6.8 | 8.6 | | | | |
| | | 1.8 | | 2.9 | | 3.4 | | 1.9 | 3.7 | | | | |
| | | 4.4 | | 3.4 | | 4.8 | | 5.8 | 4.4 | | | | |
| | | 2.0 | | 2.0 | | 2.5 | Sales/Total Assets | 2.2 | 2.9 | | | | |
| | | 1.0 | | 1.1 | | 1.5 | | 1.0 | 1.5 | | | | |
| | | 1.2 | | 1.6 | | .6 | | .9 | .5 | | | | |
| (45) | | 2.9 | (49) | 3.3 | (52) | 1.8 | % Depr., Dep., Amort./Sales | (24) 2.5 | (12) 1.7 | | | | |
| | | 7.2 | | 5.6 | | 5.6 | | 10.0 | 2.5 | | | | |
| | | 4.6 | | 3.2 | | 4.2 | % Officers', Directors' Owners' Comp/Sales | 5.7 | 4.2 | | | | |
| (30) | | 6.8 | (37) | 7.4 | (36) | 6.1 | | (13) 7.5 | (15) 5.4 | | | | |
| | | 9.0 | | 11.9 | | 8.6 | | 18.3 | 8.4 | | | | |
| | | 1685650M | | 1103708M | | 852615M | Net Sales ($) | 22035M | 40881M | 18600M | 39928M | 64103M | 667068M |
| | | 867760M | | 547620M | | 606809M | Total Assets ($) | 15137M | 19860M | 5030M | 15356M | 20840M | 530586M |

© RMA 2024          M = $ thousand    MM = $ million
See Pages viii through xx for Explanation of Ratios and Data

# OTHER SERVICES—Other Personal Care Services  NAICS 812199

**Current Data Sorted by Assets** | **Comparative Historical Data**

| | | | | | | Type of Statement | | |
|---|---|---|---|---|---|---|---|---|
| 2 | | 1 | 1 | 1 | | Unqualified | 2 | 2 |
| | | 1 | | | | Reviewed | | |
| | | 2 | | | | Compiled | 4 | 3 |
| 10 | 7 | 1 | | | | Tax Returns | 17 | 16 |
| 18 | 11 | 14 | 5 | 1 | 2 | Other | 48 | 36 |
| | 2 (4/1-9/30/23) | | 76 (10/1/23-3/31/24) | | | | 4/1/19-3/31/20 | 4/1/20-3/31/21 |
| 0-500M | 500M-2MM | 2-10MM | 10-50MM | 50-100MM | 100-250MM | | ALL | ALL |
| 30 | 18 | 19 | 7 | 2 | 2 | NUMBER OF STATEMENTS | 71 | 57 |
| % | % | % | % | % | % | **ASSETS** | % | % |
| 35.3 | 37.9 | 26.2 | | | | Cash & Equivalents | 25.7 | 40.4 |
| .3 | .0 | 6.5 | | | | Trade Receivables (net) | 4.4 | 2.3 |
| 6.5 | 4.6 | 4.5 | | | | Inventory | 3.7 | 5.0 |
| 1.4 | .4 | 1.1 | | | | All Other Current | 1.3 | 2.4 |
| 43.4 | 42.9 | 38.3 | | | | Total Current | 35.1 | 50.1 |
| 33.8 | 27.6 | 31.0 | | | | Fixed Assets (net) | 41.8 | 25.5 |
| 13.3 | 11.4 | 8.3 | | | | Intangibles (net) | 15.1 | 16.6 |
| 9.4 | 18.1 | 22.4 | | | | All Other Non-Current | 8.0 | 7.8 |
| 100.0 | 100.0 | 100.0 | | | | Total | 100.0 | 100.0 |
| | | | | | | **LIABILITIES** | | |
| 14.4 | 6.3 | 4.1 | | | | Notes Payable-Short Term | 7.8 | 5.9 |
| 3.7 | 3.2 | 2.2 | | | | Cur. Mat.-L.T.D. | 3.8 | 3.8 |
| 2.0 | 2.7 | 2.7 | | | | Trade Payables | 3.8 | 6.3 |
| .0 | .0 | .0 | | | | Income Taxes Payable | .0 | .0 |
| 18.9 | 47.6 | 24.0 | | | | All Other Current | 15.5 | 20.8 |
| 39.0 | 59.9 | 33.0 | | | | Total Current | 30.9 | 36.8 |
| 63.6 | 35.8 | 24.4 | | | | Long-Term Debt | 35.8 | 38.8 |
| .0 | .0 | .0 | | | | Deferred Taxes | .1 | .3 |
| 2.6 | 11.7 | 5.4 | | | | All Other Non-Current | 4.8 | 6.8 |
| -5.2 | -7.4 | 37.3 | | | | Net Worth | 28.4 | 17.2 |
| 100.0 | 100.0 | 100.0 | | | | Total Liabilities & Net Worth | 100.0 | 100.0 |
| | | | | | | **INCOME DATA** | | |
| 100.0 | 100.0 | 100.0 | | | | Net Sales | 100.0 | 100.0 |
| | | | | | | Gross Profit | | |
| 86.8 | 94.2 | 88.8 | | | | Operating Expenses | 89.0 | 91.9 |
| 13.2 | 5.8 | 11.2 | | | | Operating Profit | 11.0 | 8.1 |
| 1.0 | 1.1 | 5.2 | | | | All Other Expenses (net) | 2.5 | .7 |
| 12.2 | 4.7 | 6.0 | | | | Profit Before Taxes | 8.5 | 7.4 |
| | | | | | | **RATIOS** | | |
| 6.0 | 3.4 | 5.5 | | | | | 2.5 | 3.9 |
| 2.2 | 1.4 | 1.7 | | | | Current | 1.1 | 1.4 |
| .5 | .8 | .4 | | | | | .4 | .7 |
| 3.9 | 2.8 | 3.9 | | | | | 2.2 | 2.7 |
| 1.7 | 1.3 | 1.3 | | | | Quick | .9 | 1.1 |
| .3 | .7 | .4 | | | | | .3 | .5 |
| 0 UND | 0 UND | 0 UND | | | | | 0 UND | 0 UND |
| 0 UND | 0 UND | 2 169.9 | | | | Sales/Receivables | 0 UND | 0 UND |
| 0 UND | 0 UND | 14 26.5 | | | | | 1 330.8 | 0 UND |
| | | | | | | Cost of Sales/Inventory | | |
| | | | | | | Cost of Sales/Payables | | |
| 7.1 | 5.6 | 4.2 | | | | | 10.1 | 5.6 |
| 18.6 | 36.3 | 11.1 | | | | Sales/Working Capital | 95.9 | 18.0 |
| -19.8 | -35.0 | -8.2 | | | | | -14.5 | -27.7 |
| 22.1 | 24.9 | 18.3 | | | | | 22.5 | 21.9 |
| (20) 3.5 | (15) 1.4 | (11) 5.6 | | | | EBIT/Interest | (52) 8.0 | (39) 4.4 |
| 2.0 | .6 | -1.2 | | | | | 1.3 | -1.3 |
| | | | | | | Net Profit + Depr., Dep., Amort./Cur. Mat. L/T/D | | |
| .0 | .2 | .1 | | | | | .6 | .2 |
| 1.5 | 1.3 | .4 | | | | Fixed/Worth | 1.8 | 5.8 |
| -.7 | -.7 | 10.4 | | | | | -3.5 | -.6 |
| .4 | .8 | .7 | | | | | .6 | .8 |
| 2.2 | 5.7 | 1.7 | | | | Debt/Worth | 4.1 | 23.1 |
| -2.4 | -3.8 | 17.0 | | | | | -5.7 | -2.9 |
| 251.5 | 76.1 | 52.0 | | | | | 164.0 | 126.0 |
| (19) 106.9 | (10) 17.2 | (15) 14.6 | | | | % Profit Before Taxes/Tangible Net Worth | (46) 61.2 | (30) 62.2 |
| 21.2 | .7 | .2 | | | | | 19.3 | 20.0 |
| 78.0 | 26.9 | 16.9 | | | | | 44.8 | 61.2 |
| 23.3 | 2.0 | 6.9 | | | | % Profit Before Taxes/Total Assets | 18.2 | 18.1 |
| 5.9 | -1.0 | -5.9 | | | | | 2.4 | -4.5 |
| 180.9 | 53.1 | 19.3 | | | | | 24.7 | 36.4 |
| 15.6 | 11.3 | 5.6 | | | | Sales/Net Fixed Assets | 5.8 | 14.0 |
| 6.2 | 4.3 | 3.4 | | | | | 2.9 | 4.7 |
| 6.9 | 2.9 | 1.8 | | | | | 4.1 | 3.2 |
| 4.1 | 2.2 | 1.2 | | | | Sales/Total Assets | 1.9 | 2.1 |
| 1.6 | .9 | .6 | | | | | 1.1 | 1.2 |
| 1.6 | | 3.1 | | | | | 1.6 | 1.1 |
| (10) 2.6 | (11) | 5.3 | | | | % Depr., Dep., Amort./Sales | (38) 4.0 | (21) 2.7 |
| 5.7 | | 6.0 | | | | | 7.7 | 5.4 |
| | | | | | | % Officers', Directors' Owners' Comp/Sales | 2.7 | 2.2 |
| | | | | | | | (22) 4.1 | (18) 5.4 |
| | | | | | | | 8.3 | 9.9 |
| 31786M | 42737M | 102687M | 157542M | 50454M | 218037M | Net Sales ($) | 470539M | 527375M |
| 8518M | 19610M | 87901M | 153403M | 154539M | 281897M | Total Assets ($) | 314851M | 369999M |

© RMA 2024

M = $ thousand    MM = $ million
See Pages viii through xx for Explanation of Ratios and Data

# OTHER SERVICES—Other Personal Care Services  NAICS 812199

## Comparative Historical Data | Current Data Sorted by Sales

| Comparative Historical Data | | | Type of Statement | Current Data Sorted by Sales | | | | | |
|---|---|---|---|---|---|---|---|---|---|
| 4 | 2 | 5 | Unqualified | 2 | | | | 2 | 1 |
|  | 1 | 1 | Reviewed |  |  |  | 1 |  |  |
| 3 | 1 | 2 | Compiled |  | 1 | 1 |  |  |  |
| 18 | 22 | 19 | Tax Returns |  | 7 | 1 | 2 | 1 |  |
| 38 | 42 | 51 | Other | 8 | 15 | 6 | 7 | 7 | 3 |
| 4/1/21-3/31/22 | 4/1/22-3/31/23 | 4/1/23-3/31/24 |  | 13 | 2 (4/1-9/30/23) | | 76 (10/1/23-3/31/24) | | |
| ALL | ALL | ALL |  | 0-1MM | 1-3MM | 3-5MM | 5-10MM | 10-25MM | 25MM & OVER |
| 63 | 68 | 78 | **NUMBER OF STATEMENTS** | 23 | 23 | 8 | 10 | 10 | 4 |
| % | % | % | **ASSETS** | % | % | % | % | % | % |
| 31.6 | 33.1 | 30.7 | Cash & Equivalents | 27.1 | 35.9 |  | 34.2 | 14.9 |  |
| 3.2 | 1.9 | 2.4 | Trade Receivables (net) | .2 | 1.8 |  | 8.1 | 5.1 |  |
| 4.0 | 4.5 | 5.6 | Inventory | 4.7 | 6.5 |  | 5.0 | 4.4 |  |
| 1.7 | 2.2 | 1.0 | All Other Current | .7 | 1.3 |  | 1.6 | .5 |  |
| 40.4 | 41.7 | 39.7 | Total Current | 32.7 | 45.5 |  | 48.8 | 24.9 |  |
| 34.7 | 28.4 | 29.3 | Fixed Assets (net) | 41.8 | 26.5 |  | 19.9 | 23.0 |  |
| 17.2 | 17.3 | 14.5 | Intangibles (net) | 7.5 | 18.1 |  | 8.5 | 27.1 |  |
| 7.7 | 12.6 | 16.6 | All Other Non-Current | 18.0 | 9.9 |  | 22.7 | 25.0 |  |
| 100.0 | 100.0 | 100.0 | Total | 100.0 | 100.0 |  | 100.0 | 100.0 |  |
|  |  |  | **LIABILITIES** |  |  |  |  |  |  |
| 12.5 | 8.4 | 8.3 | Notes Payable-Short Term | 14.4 | 4.6 |  | 12.0 | 2.3 |  |
| 4.5 | 2.1 | 3.1 | Cur. Mat.-L.T.D. | 4.3 | 2.5 |  | 1.5 | 4.2 |  |
| 2.7 | 4.3 | 2.9 | Trade Payables | 1.1 | 1.9 |  | 3.7 | 3.2 |  |
| .0 | .1 | .0 | Income Taxes Payable | .0 | .0 |  | .0 | .0 |  |
| 21.7 | 26.5 | 26.1 | All Other Current | 8.3 | 39.5 |  | 34.3 | 16.4 |  |
| 41.3 | 41.4 | 40.4 | Total Current | 28.1 | 48.6 |  | 51.5 | 26.1 |  |
| 42.1 | 38.0 | 41.4 | Long-Term Debt | 56.9 | 62.2 |  | 8.8 | 23.1 |  |
| .2 | .1 | .0 | Deferred Taxes | .0 | .0 |  | .0 | .0 |  |
| 5.1 | 8.6 | 10.1 | All Other Non-Current | 10.6 | 2.8 |  | .2 | 35.8 |  |
| 11.3 | 12.0 | 8.1 | Net Worth | 4.5 | -13.7 |  | 39.6 | 15.0 |  |
| 100.0 | 100.0 | 100.0 | Total Liabilties & Net Worth | 100.0 | 100.0 |  | 100.0 | 100.0 |  |
|  |  |  | **INCOME DATA** |  |  |  |  |  |  |
| 100.0 | 100.0 | 100.0 | Net Sales | 100.0 | 100.0 |  | 100.0 | 100.0 |  |
|  |  |  | Gross Profit |  |  |  |  |  |  |
| 87.0 | 91.0 | 90.4 | Operating Expenses | 84.1 | 92.0 |  | 89.5 | 95.3 |  |
| 13.0 | 9.0 | 9.6 | Operating Profit | 15.9 | 8.0 |  | 10.5 | 4.7 |  |
| 1.3 | 1.3 | 2.4 | All Other Expenses (net) | 4.2 | 1.4 |  | 1.9 | 4.1 |  |
| 11.8 | 7.7 | 7.2 | Profit Before Taxes | 11.7 | 6.6 |  | 8.6 | .5 |  |
|  |  |  | **RATIOS** |  |  |  |  |  |  |
| 7.4 | 6.5 | 4.7 |  | 5.6 | 6.1 |  | 2.9 | 1.2 |  |
| 1.6 | 1.6 | 1.4 | Current | 1.8 | 3.3 |  | 1.4 | .9 |  |
| .6 | .6 | .6 |  | .5 | .6 |  | .3 | .6 |  |
| 7.4 | 5.4 | 3.1 |  | 3.1 | 4.6 |  | 2.8 | 1.1 |  |
| 1.5 | 1.1 | 1.2 | Quick | 1.5 | 2.3 |  | .9 | .8 |  |
| .4 | .3 | .4 |  | .5 | .3 |  | .2 | .3 |  |
| 0 UND | 0 UND | 0 UND |  | 0 UND | 0 UND |  | 0 UND | 0 UND |  |
| 0 UND | 0 UND | 0 UND | Sales/Receivables | 0 UND | 0 UND |  | 0 UND | 6 56.2 |  |
| 3 129.9 | 0 748.3 | 2 161.5 |  | 0 UND | 0 UND |  | 50 7.3 | 31 11.8 |  |
|  |  |  | Cost of Sales/Inventory |  |  |  |  |  |  |
|  |  |  | Cost of Sales/Payables |  |  |  |  |  |  |
| 5.0 | 7.2 | 6.7 |  | 5.6 | 5.9 |  | 4.6 | 39.7 |  |
| 16.1 | 35.4 | 34.0 | Sales/Working Capital | 17.4 | 16.1 |  | 16.8 | -33.8 |  |
| -9.7 | -10.6 | -16.9 |  | -32.6 | -20.1 |  | -5.6 | -9.8 |  |
|  |  |  |  | 23.7 | 9.1 |  |  |  |  |
| 49.1 | 16.5 | 16.3 |  | (15) 3.9 | (17) 2.0 |  |  |  |  |
| (41) 9.1 | (43) 6.6 | (52) 3.5 | EBIT/Interest | 1.0 | -.2 |  |  |  |  |
| 2.2 | .5 | .6 |  |  |  |  |  |  |  |
|  |  |  | Net Profit + Depr., Dep., Amort./Cur. Mat. L/T/D |  |  |  |  |  |  |
| .3 | .2 | .2 |  | .1 | .0 |  | .0 | .9 |  |
| 6.3 | 1.8 | 1.5 | Fixed/Worth | 1.9 | .8 |  | .4 | -1.8 |  |
| -1.3 | -1.4 | -1.5 |  | -.9 | -.5 |  | 3.6 | -.8 |  |
| .6 | .7 | .8 |  | .5 | .4 |  | .6 | 1.7 |  |
| 21.6 | 5.7 | 2.7 | Debt/Worth | 8.6 | 2.1 |  | 1.7 | -7.1 |  |
| -3.4 | -3.6 | -4.3 |  | -3.9 | -2.0 |  | 12.7 | -3.1 |  |
| 161.4 | 97.7 | 169.3 |  | 159.2 | 251.5 |  |  |  |  |
| (36) 86.3 | (41) 43.2 | (49) 22.9 | % Profit Before Taxes/Tangible Net Worth | (14) 33.8 | (15) 18.3 |  |  |  |  |
| 50.4 | 2.0 | 4.7 |  | 12.4 | -3.2 |  |  |  |  |
| 64.7 | 38.3 | 31.6 |  | 70.1 | 42.5 |  | 44.8 | 6.1 |  |
| 25.9 | 10.6 | 7.2 | % Profit Before Taxes/Total Assets | 18.6 | 8.5 |  | 14.6 | 3.3 |  |
| 2.8 | -3.8 | .1 |  | .1 | -1.4 |  | -3.7 | -8.2 |  |
| 25.7 | 57.0 | 33.9 |  | 30.2 | 166.3 |  | 428.6 | 6.8 |  |
| 8.3 | 10.0 | 9.6 | Sales/Net Fixed Assets | 7.7 | 15.5 |  | 14.7 | 4.3 |  |
| 3.2 | 3.5 | 4.2 |  | 1.7 | 5.3 |  | 6.3 | 3.4 |  |
| 3.3 | 3.4 | 3.2 |  | 3.2 | 5.8 |  | 2.8 | 1.4 |  |
| 1.8 | 2.2 | 1.7 | Sales/Total Assets | 1.5 | 2.7 |  | 1.7 | 1.1 |  |
| 1.1 | 1.2 | .9 |  | .9 | 1.4 |  | 1.1 | .6 |  |
| 1.8 | 1.4 | 1.6 |  |  | 1.7 |  |  |  |  |
| (29) 2.9 | (32) 2.5 | (38) 3.3 | % Depr., Dep., Amort./Sales | (10) 2.9 |  |  |  |  |  |
| 6.7 | 5.4 | 5.9 |  |  | 3.6 |  |  |  |  |
| 2.5 | 3.9 | 3.3 | % Officers', Directors' Owners' Comp/Sales |  | 4.1 |  |  |  |  |
| (18) 6.4 | (29) 6.2 | (20) 5.9 |  | (11) | 6.6 |  |  |  |  |
| 8.8 | 8.9 | 9.9 |  |  | 9.8 |  |  |  |  |
| 427757M | 547722M | 603243M | Net Sales ($) | 12026M | 40913M | 28594M | 60823M | 158524M | 302363M |
| 323108M | 551728M | 705868M | Total Assets ($) | 14524M | 23334M | 14282M | 40276M | 256164M | 357288M |

© RMA 2024   M = $ thousand   MM = $ million
See Pages viii through xx for Explanation of Ratios and Data

## OTHER SERVICES—Funeral Homes and Funeral Services  NAICS 812210

### Current Data Sorted by Assets | Comparative Historical Data

| | | | | | | Type of Statement | | |
|---|---|---|---|---|---|---|---|---|
| | | 2 | 1 | | 1 | Unqualified | 4 | 4 |
| | | 4 | 1 | | | Reviewed | 4 | 3 |
| 1 | 3 | 7 | | 1 | | Compiled | 15 | 12 |
| 17 | 24 | 11 | 1 | | | Tax Returns | 63 | 49 |
| 5 | 19 | 17 | 5 | 4 | 2 | Other | 83 | 68 |
| | 19 (4/1-9/30/23) | | 107 (10/1/23-3/31/24) | | | | 4/1/19- 3/31/20 | 4/1/20- 3/31/21 |
| 0-500M | 500M-2MM | 2-10MM | 10-50MM | 50-100MM | 100-250MM | | ALL | ALL |
| 23 | 46 | 41 | 8 | 5 | 3 | NUMBER OF STATEMENTS | 169 | 136 |
| % | % | % | % | % | % | ASSETS | % | % |
| 19.6 | 18.0 | 13.3 | | | | Cash & Equivalents | 15.3 | 20.1 |
| 7.7 | 9.4 | 6.4 | | | | Trade Receivables (net) | 12.1 | 9.3 |
| 4.1 | 2.8 | 1.2 | | | | Inventory | 3.1 | 2.6 |
| 3.9 | 1.4 | 2.6 | | | | All Other Current | 2.2 | 3.6 |
| 35.4 | 31.6 | 23.5 | | | | Total Current | 32.7 | 35.6 |
| 40.1 | 37.5 | 55.6 | | | | Fixed Assets (net) | 40.2 | 41.3 |
| 9.7 | 13.3 | 9.8 | | | | Intangibles (net) | 9.9 | 12.5 |
| 14.9 | 17.6 | 11.0 | | | | All Other Non-Current | 17.2 | 10.6 |
| 100.0 | 100.0 | 100.0 | | | | Total | 100.0 | 100.0 |
| | | | | | | LIABILITIES | | |
| 11.8 | 2.2 | 1.3 | | | | Notes Payable-Short Term | 4.1 | 8.1 |
| 4.3 | 3.9 | 3.1 | | | | Cur. Mat.-L.T.D. | 3.3 | 3.6 |
| 8.1 | 3.6 | 2.7 | | | | Trade Payables | 5.1 | 3.8 |
| .1 | .1 | .0 | | | | Income Taxes Payable | .1 | .1 |
| 31.6 | 7.5 | 10.1 | | | | All Other Current | 7.6 | 8.0 |
| 56.1 | 17.3 | 17.2 | | | | Total Current | 20.2 | 23.7 |
| 21.5 | 35.0 | 45.1 | | | | Long-Term Debt | 31.6 | 37.3 |
| .0 | .3 | .1 | | | | Deferred Taxes | .3 | .1 |
| 2.2 | 4.0 | 8.3 | | | | All Other Non-Current | 20.4 | 10.2 |
| 20.2 | 43.4 | 29.3 | | | | Net Worth | 27.5 | 28.7 |
| 100.0 | 100.0 | 100.0 | | | | Total Liabilities & Net Worth | 100.0 | 100.0 |
| | | | | | | INCOME DATA | | |
| 100.0 | 100.0 | 100.0 | | | | Net Sales | 100.0 | 100.0 |
| | | | | | | Gross Profit | | |
| 99.4 | 92.5 | 89.7 | | | | Operating Expenses | 89.2 | 84.6 |
| .6 | 7.5 | 10.3 | | | | Operating Profit | 10.8 | 15.4 |
| 1.6 | 3.4 | 4.3 | | | | All Other Expenses (net) | 3.9 | 2.5 |
| -1.0 | 4.0 | 6.0 | | | | Profit Before Taxes | 6.8 | 12.9 |
| | | | | | | RATIOS | | |
| 2.6 | 7.2 | 3.4 | | | | | 3.9 | 4.5 |
| 1.0 | 2.8 | 1.5 | | | | Current | 1.8 | 2.1 |
| .1 | .8 | .7 | | | | | .7 | .8 |
| 2.4 | 6.4 | 3.3 | | | | | 3.4 | 3.9 |
| .7 | 2.0 | 1.3 | | | | Quick | 1.4 | 1.7 |
| .1 | .8 | .4 | | | | | .5 | .5 |
| 0  UND | 0  UND | 0  UND | | | | | 5  72.4 | 0  UND |
| 0  UND | 11  32.9 | 21  17.6 | | | | Sales/Receivables | 20  18.4 | 18  20.5 |
| 22  16.6 | 33  11.0 | 28  13.1 | | | | | 38  9.5 | 36  10.2 |
| | | | | | | Cost of Sales/Inventory | | |
| | | | | | | Cost of Sales/Payables | | |
| 10.4 | 5.0 | 4.8 | | | | | 5.0 | 4.6 |
| UND | 13.2 | 28.9 | | | | Sales/Working Capital | 14.7 | 11.5 |
| -6.2 | -21.9 | -30.0 | | | | | -29.4 | -24.7 |
| 12.3 | 13.2 | 6.2 | | | | | 13.8 | 22.9 |
| (17) 2.9 | (32) 2.2 | (38) 3.0 | | | | EBIT/Interest | (124) 6.3 | (108) 7.4 |
| -2.2 | .8 | 1.1 | | | | | 1.9 | 2.4 |
| | | | | | | Net Profit + Depr., Dep., Amort./Cur. Mat. L/T/D | 6.6 | 9.5 |
| | | | | | | | (17) 2.0 | (12) 2.9 |
| | | | | | | | 1.7 | 2.4 |
| .2 | .4 | 1.0 | | | | | .5 | .7 |
| 1.0 | .8 | 2.1 | | | | Fixed/Worth | 1.5 | 1.7 |
| -.8 | NM | 20.7 | | | | | NM | -5.9 |
| .2 | .2 | 1.2 | | | | | .6 | .8 |
| .8 | 1.6 | 2.1 | | | | Debt/Worth | 1.8 | 3.5 |
| -2.9 | -7.9 | 21.8 | | | | | NM | -12.9 |
| 38.9 | 21.0 | 22.9 | | | | | 47.1 | 81.9 |
| (16) 20.6 | (34) 7.1 | (33) 11.1 | | | | % Profit Before Taxes/Tangible Net Worth | (127) 16.1 | (91) 35.7 |
| .3 | -4.1 | -.7 | | | | | 5.1 | 16.4 |
| 20.1 | 11.5 | 10.0 | | | | | 17.1 | 23.2 |
| 6.9 | 4.8 | 4.2 | | | | % Profit Before Taxes/Total Assets | 5.9 | 12.3 |
| -22.8 | -.7 | -.1 | | | | | .9 | 2.7 |
| 39.7 | 13.1 | 4.9 | | | | | 14.0 | 15.4 |
| 10.6 | 7.1 | 1.7 | | | | Sales/Net Fixed Assets | 3.8 | 4.1 |
| 5.6 | 3.0 | .8 | | | | | 1.5 | 1.4 |
| 5.4 | 2.6 | 1.5 | | | | | 2.5 | 2.4 |
| 3.8 | 1.6 | 1.0 | | | | Sales/Total Assets | 1.2 | 1.2 |
| 1.4 | 1.0 | .6 | | | | | .6 | .7 |
| .7 | 1.2 | 2.0 | | | | | 1.5 | 1.7 |
| (17) 2.2 | (34) 2.2 | (38) 3.1 | | | | % Depr., Dep., Amort./Sales | (139) 3.6 | (95) 3.6 |
| 4.6 | 5.7 | 5.7 | | | | | 5.9 | 6.9 |
| 4.0 | 5.5 | 2.6 | | | | | 5.3 | 4.9 |
| (14) 8.1 | (29) 8.5 | (18) 4.4 | | | | % Officers', Directors' Owners' Comp/Sales | (100) 8.2 | (78) 8.1 |
| 16.5 | 17.4 | 9.7 | | | | | 13.9 | 12.9 |
| 27366M | 111129M | 188875M | 120449M | 174290M | 149772M | Net Sales ($) | 2238231M | 474865M |
| 7193M | 56335M | 176473M | 188386M | 368886M | 469611M | Total Assets ($) | 1255520M | 641706M |

M = $ thousand    MM = $ million
See Pages viii through xx for Explanation of Ratios and Data

© RMA 2024

## OTHER SERVICES—Funeral Homes and Funeral Services   NAICS 812210

**Comparative Historical Data** | **Current Data Sorted by Sales**

| | | | Type of Statement | | | | | | |
|---|---|---|---|---|---|---|---|---|---|
| 6 | 6 | 4 | Unqualified | | 1 | 1 | | 1 | 1 |
| 3 | 5 | 5 | Reviewed | | 1 | 1 | 1 | 2 | |
| 15 | 13 | 12 | Compiled | | 3 | 6 | 2 | | 1 |
| 55 | 70 | 53 | Tax Returns | 17 | 25 | 4 | 6 | 1 | |
| 57 | 62 | 52 | Other | 13 | 16 | 3 | 11 | 3 | 6 |
| 4/1/21-3/31/22 ALL | 4/1/22-3/31/23 ALL | 4/1/23-3/31/24 ALL | | 19 (4/1-9/30/23) | | | 107 (10/1/23-3/31/24) | | |
| | | | | 0-1MM | 1-3MM | 3-5MM | 5-10MM | 10-25MM | 25MM & OVER |
| 136 | 156 | 126 | NUMBER OF STATEMENTS | 30 | 46 | 15 | 20 | 7 | 8 |
| % | % | % | ASSETS | % | % | % | % | % | % |
| 22.2 | 21.1 | 15.4 | Cash & Equivalents | 12.6 | 17.2 | 16.0 | 19.7 | | |
| 12.1 | 10.3 | 8.0 | Trade Receivables (net) | 4.1 | 9.1 | 7.6 | 10.5 | | |
| 2.9 | 3.1 | 2.6 | Inventory | 1.0 | 3.1 | 2.8 | 3.1 | | |
| 3.7 | 3.6 | 2.6 | All Other Current | 2.9 | 3.2 | 1.2 | .4 | | |
| 40.8 | 38.1 | 28.6 | Total Current | 20.5 | 32.7 | 27.6 | 33.7 | | |
| 34.9 | 35.2 | 44.2 | Fixed Assets (net) | 41.8 | 48.5 | 45.1 | 38.7 | | |
| 13.0 | 11.1 | 11.5 | Intangibles (net) | 16.1 | 8.3 | 7.5 | 15.0 | | |
| 11.3 | 15.6 | 15.7 | All Other Non-Current | 21.6 | 10.6 | 19.8 | 12.7 | | |
| 100.0 | 100.0 | 100.0 | Total | 100.0 | 100.0 | 100.0 | 100.0 | | |
| | | | LIABILITIES | | | | | | |
| 4.2 | 3.8 | 3.6 | Notes Payable-Short Term | 8.4 | 2.6 | 1.1 | 2.2 | | |
| 3.5 | 2.5 | 3.7 | Cur. Mat.-L.T.D. | 4.9 | 2.9 | 3.0 | 4.2 | | |
| 3.3 | 3.9 | 3.9 | Trade Payables | 1.9 | 4.2 | 2.8 | 7.2 | | |
| .2 | .3 | .1 | Income Taxes Payable | .1 | .1 | .0 | .0 | | |
| 9.4 | 8.0 | 12.6 | All Other Current | 25.6 | 6.0 | 8.8 | 14.9 | | |
| 20.5 | 18.5 | 23.9 | Total Current | 40.9 | 15.8 | 15.7 | 28.5 | | |
| 32.1 | 37.4 | 35.1 | Long-Term Debt | 41.5 | 36.2 | 38.4 | 25.5 | | |
| .0 | .1 | .1 | Deferred Taxes | .0 | .0 | .8 | .2 | | |
| 9.8 | 6.7 | 7.1 | All Other Non-Current | 6.2 | 3.0 | 6.1 | 14.5 | | |
| 37.5 | 37.3 | 33.7 | Net Worth | 11.4 | 45.0 | 39.0 | 31.3 | | |
| 100.0 | 100.0 | 100.0 | Total Liabilities & Net Worth | 100.0 | 100.0 | 100.0 | 100.0 | | |
| | | | INCOME DATA | | | | | | |
| 100.0 | 100.0 | 100.0 | Net Sales | 100.0 | 100.0 | 100.0 | 100.0 | | |
| | | | Gross Profit | | | | | | |
| 84.8 | 88.9 | 92.7 | Operating Expenses | 88.5 | 94.5 | 95.9 | 93.6 | | |
| 15.2 | 11.1 | 7.3 | Operating Profit | 11.5 | 5.5 | 4.1 | 6.4 | | |
| .1 | 1.3 | 3.8 | All Other Expenses (net) | 9.3 | 2.2 | .4 | .0 | | |
| 15.1 | 9.8 | 3.6 | Profit Before Taxes | 2.2 | 3.3 | 3.6 | 6.5 | | |
| | | | RATIOS | | | | | | |
| 6.4 | 8.2 | 3.9 | | 5.8 | 5.1 | 3.9 | 3.4 | | |
| 2.7 | 2.9 | 1.7 | Current | 1.3 | 2.0 | 1.9 | 1.5 | | |
| 1.1 | 1.2 | .6 | | .1 | .6 | .8 | .8 | | |
| 5.3 | 6.5 | 3.6 | | 4.3 | 4.3 | 3.6 | 3.1 | | |
| 2.2 | 2.2 | 1.4 | Quick | .9 | 1.6 | 1.4 | 1.3 | | |
| .9 | .9 | .4 | | .1 | .4 | .8 | .8 | | |
| 0 UND | 0 UND | 0 UND | | 0 UND | 0 UND | 0 UND | 0 UND | | |
| 18 20.4 | 17 20.9 | 14 25.4 | Sales/Receivables | 0 UND | 13 28.1 | 18 20.3 | 21 17.0 | | |
| 39 9.4 | 34 10.8 | 31 11.8 | | 34 10.7 | 29 12.6 | 25 14.8 | 28 12.9 | | |
| | | | Cost of Sales/Inventory | | | | | | |
| | | | Cost of Sales/Payables | | | | | | |
| 3.8 | 3.7 | 5.1 | | 5.1 | 4.3 | 6.6 | 8.1 | | |
| 7.9 | 7.6 | 16.4 | Sales/Working Capital | NM | 16.4 | 14.8 | 28.3 | | |
| 36.1 | 47.1 | -26.2 | | -2.3 | -48.1 | -22.7 | -37.3 | | |
| 33.4 | 35.0 | 9.9 | | 9.1 | 9.4 | 9.0 | 12.9 | | |
| (111) 10.7 | (124) 5.7 | (101) 2.2 | EBIT/Interest | (20) .6 | (35) 2.8 | (14) 2.5 | (18) 3.8 | | |
| 3.9 | 1.4 | .7 | | -4.7 | 1.1 | 1.1 | 1.6 | | |
| | 8.8 | 4.2 | Net Profit + Depr., Dep., | | | | | | |
| (13) 5.1 | | (19) 1.7 | Amort./Cur. Mat. L/T/D | | | | | | |
| | 3.8 | .6 | | | | | | | |
| .4 | .4 | .5 | | .2 | .4 | .5 | .8 | | |
| 1.4 | 1.1 | 1.3 | Fixed/Worth | 5.8 | 1.1 | 1.2 | 1.5 | | |
| -9.2 | -163.9 | 28.3 | | -.6 | 8.8 | -11.1 | NM | | |
| .4 | .3 | .5 | | .3 | .3 | .4 | 1.5 | | |
| 2.6 | 1.9 | 1.9 | Debt/Worth | 9.1 | 1.2 | 1.6 | 2.0 | | |
| -68.5 | -263.8 | 80.6 | | -2.0 | 11.0 | -14.3 | NM | | |
| 111.1 | 47.0 | 23.3 | | 33.3 | 28.0 | 13.0 | 207.7 | | |
| (97) 45.0 | (116) 20.9 | (96) 9.7 | % Profit Before Taxes/Tangible Net Worth | (16) 14.2 | (40) 12.9 | (11) .5 | (15) 19.7 | | |
| 25.7 | 5.3 | -3.0 | | -.7 | -10.1 | -.9 | 4.4 | | |
| 32.7 | 19.8 | 12.0 | | 15.2 | 11.3 | 10.8 | 22.1 | | |
| 16.6 | 8.0 | 3.2 | % Profit Before Taxes/Total Assets | 1.9 | 5.5 | .6 | 6.0 | | |
| 4.9 | 1.4 | -2.3 | | -5.8 | -2.4 | .0 | 1.6 | | |
| 14.0 | 20.2 | 10.0 | | 15.5 | 11.1 | 7.2 | 13.8 | | |
| 6.0 | 6.5 | 4.5 | Sales/Net Fixed Assets | 4.5 | 4.9 | 4.8 | 6.0 | | |
| 1.9 | 1.9 | 1.2 | | .7 | 1.2 | 3.1 | 2.0 | | |
| 2.4 | 2.6 | 2.4 | | 1.5 | 2.9 | 2.6 | 2.9 | | |
| 1.4 | 1.4 | 1.3 | Sales/Total Assets | .9 | 1.5 | 1.5 | 2.0 | | |
| .8 | .7 | .6 | | .4 | .7 | 1.1 | 1.0 | | |
| 1.5 | 1.3 | 1.4 | | 1.6 | .8 | 1.7 | 2.0 | | |
| (106) 3.6 | (106) 3.0 | (103) 2.8 | % Depr., Dep., Amort./Sales | (19) 4.0 | (38) 2.1 | (13) 2.9 | (19) 2.6 | | |
| 6.7 | 6.3 | 5.6 | | 13.5 | 5.5 | 3.7 | 3.7 | | |
| 4.5 | 4.5 | 3.3 | | 4.8 | 3.2 | 5.3 | 2.9 | | |
| (85) 7.4 | (77) 8.1 | (63) 6.9 | % Officers', Directors' Owners' Comp/Sales | (12) 4.8 | (28) 6.4 | (10) 8.7 | (11) 4.5 | | |
| 13.7 | 13.9 | 13.3 | | 18.8 | 9.9 | 13.0 | 11.2 | | |
| 703391M | 733843M | 771881M | Net Sales ($) | 16943M | 94388M | 60863M | 147799M | 127826M | 324062M |
| 1232614M | 1329417M | 1266884M | Total Assets ($) | 29313M | 94582M | 41533M | 111638M | 151321M | 838497M |

© RMA 2024   M = $ thousand   MM = $ million
See Pages viii through xx for Explanation of Ratios and Data

# OTHER SERVICES—Coin-Operated Laundries and Drycleaners  NAICS 812310

## Current Data Sorted by Assets | Comparative Historical Data

| | | | | | | Type of Statement | | |
|---|---|---|---|---|---|---|---|---|
| | | 1 | | | | Unqualified | 1 | |
| | 1 | 3 | | | | Reviewed | 5 | 5 |
| 3 | 3 | 10 | | 2 | | Compiled | 12 | 20 |
| 4 | 6 | | | | | Tax Returns | 23 | 11 |
| | 2 (4/1-9/30/23) | | 33 (10/1/23-3/31/24) | | | Other | 4/1/19-3/31/20 | 4/1/20-3/31/21 |
| 0-500M | 500M-2MM | 2-10MM | 10-50MM | 50-100MM | 100-250MM | | ALL | ALL |
| 7 | 11 | 15 | 2 | | | NUMBER OF STATEMENTS | 41 | 36 |
| % | % | % | % | % | % | ASSETS | % | % |
| | 9.5 | 20.7 | D | D | | Cash & Equivalents | 12.2 | 20.1 |
| | .0 | 4.7 | A | A | | Trade Receivables (net) | .9 | 1.9 |
| | .3 | 2.2 | T | T | | Inventory | 1.5 | 1.0 |
| | 6.3 | 3.8 | A | A | | All Other Current | 1.9 | 1.2 |
| | 16.1 | 31.4 | | | | Total Current | 16.5 | 24.2 |
| | 52.9 | 49.3 | N | N | | Fixed Assets (net) | 62.0 | 51.4 |
| | 24.6 | 7.6 | O | O | | Intangibles (net) | 12.9 | 12.5 |
| | 6.4 | 11.7 | T | T | | All Other Non-Current | 8.5 | 11.8 |
| | 100.0 | 100.0 | | | | Total | 100.0 | 100.0 |
| | | | A | A | | LIABILITIES | | |
| | 6.5 | 2.9 | V | V | | Notes Payable-Short Term | 9.6 | 7.0 |
| | 11.7 | 5.7 | A | A | | Cur. Mat.-L.T.D. | 4.9 | 1.0 |
| | .9 | 3.1 | I | I | | Trade Payables | 1.6 | 1.3 |
| | .1 | .0 | L | L | | Income Taxes Payable | .1 | .5 |
| | 1.7 | 3.4 | A | A | | All Other Current | 3.9 | 13.0 |
| | 20.9 | 15.1 | B | B | | Total Current | 20.1 | 22.8 |
| | 81.8 | 35.6 | L | L | | Long-Term Debt | 54.6 | 66.1 |
| | .0 | .0 | E | E | | Deferred Taxes | .1 | .0 |
| | .0 | 2.8 | | | | All Other Non-Current | 6.1 | 14.1 |
| | -2.7 | 46.5 | | | | Net Worth | 19.0 | -3.1 |
| | 100.0 | 100.0 | | | | Total Liabilities & Net Worth | 100.0 | 100.0 |
| | | | | | | INCOME DATA | | |
| | 100.0 | 100.0 | | | | Net Sales | 100.0 | 100.0 |
| | | | | | | Gross Profit | | |
| | 91.5 | 79.6 | | | | Operating Expenses | 76.0 | 91.2 |
| | 8.5 | 20.4 | | | | Operating Profit | 24.0 | 8.8 |
| | 3.1 | 2.9 | | | | All Other Expenses (net) | 6.7 | 2.0 |
| | 5.4 | 17.5 | | | | Profit Before Taxes | 17.3 | 6.8 |
| | | | | | | RATIOS | | |
| | 1.5 | 9.4 | | | | | 2.6 | 7.4 |
| | .7 | 2.6 | | | | Current | .8 | 1.9 |
| | .3 | .9 | | | | | .2 | .8 |
| | 1.5 | 2.8 | | | | | 2.2 | 5.6 |
| | .3 | 1.8 | | | | Quick | .6 | 1.4 |
| | .3 | .9 | | | | | .2 | .4 |
| 0 UND | 0 UND | | | | | | 0 UND | 0 UND |
| 0 UND | 0 UND | | | | | Sales/Receivables | 0 UND | 0 UND |
| 0 UND | 1 342.4 | | | | | | 0 UND | 0 UND |
| | | | | | | Cost of Sales/Inventory | | |
| | | | | | | Cost of Sales/Payables | | |
| | 22.1 | 3.1 | | | | | 6.8 | 6.4 |
| | -44.0 | 13.7 | | | | Sales/Working Capital | -68.8 | 19.8 |
| | -7.0 | -64.4 | | | | | -5.6 | -73.1 |
| | 6.1 | 68.0 | | | | | 19.9 | 6.6 |
| (10) | 2.1 | (13) 21.6 | | | | EBIT/Interest | (32) 5.2 | (28) 3.0 |
| | -2.4 | 2.4 | | | | | 1.6 | -.6 |
| | | | | | | Net Profit + Depr., Dep., Amort./Cur. Mat. L/T/D | | |
| | 1.4 | .8 | | | | | 1.5 | .6 |
| | 9.6 | 1.2 | | | | Fixed/Worth | 3.9 | 2.2 |
| | -.4 | 11.6 | | | | | -1.5 | -2.3 |
| | .6 | .4 | | | | | .9 | 1.4 |
| | 16.5 | .9 | | | | Debt/Worth | 4.0 | 19.6 |
| | -1.5 | 12.6 | | | | | -4.4 | -2.5 |
| | | 137.1 | | | | | 62.6 | 117.1 |
| | (12) | 64.8 | | | | % Profit Before Taxes/Tangible Net Worth | (25) 15.6 | (20) 37.8 |
| | | 19.4 | | | | | 6.7 | 2.1 |
| | 18.4 | 66.4 | | | | | 30.9 | 21.6 |
| | 7.0 | 27.6 | | | | % Profit Before Taxes/Total Assets | 6.7 | 4.6 |
| | -4.7 | 3.3 | | | | | 1.5 | -2.6 |
| | 4.4 | 8.8 | | | | | 4.8 | 10.5 |
| | 2.2 | 3.0 | | | | Sales/Net Fixed Assets | 1.9 | 2.7 |
| | 1.1 | 1.2 | | | | | .2 | .9 |
| | 1.9 | 2.6 | | | | | 2.1 | 2.1 |
| | .8 | 1.8 | | | | Sales/Total Assets | 1.0 | 1.1 |
| | .5 | .6 | | | | | .2 | .6 |
| | | 3.3 | | | | | 5.2 | 2.0 |
| | (11) | 8.4 | | | | % Depr., Dep., Amort./Sales | (27) 9.5 | (18) 6.7 |
| | | 21.6 | | | | | 17.1 | 21.7 |
| | | | | | | | 2.9 | 2.6 |
| | | | | | | % Officers', Directors' Owners' Comp/Sales | (11) 5.1 | (10) 5.6 |
| | | | | | | | 9.1 | 17.0 |
| 5787M | 14307M | 94748M | 36581M | | | Net Sales ($) | 156194M | 41636M |
| 2310M | 10588M | 53248M | 32897M | | | Total Assets ($) | 159948M | 45962M |

© RMA 2024

M = $ thousand    MM = $ million

See Pages viii through xx for Explanation of Ratios and Data

## OTHER SERVICES—Coin-Operated Laundries and Drycleaners  NAICS 812310

**Comparative Historical Data** / **Current Data Sorted by Sales**

| | | | | Type of Statement | | | | | | |
|---|---|---|---|---|---|---|---|---|---|---|
| 1 | 2 | 1 | | Unqualified | 1 | | | | | |
| 7 | 1 | 3 | | Reviewed | | | | | 1 | |
| 32 | 22 | 9 | | Compiled | 1 | 1 | 4 | 1 | | |
| 17 | 27 | 22 | | Tax Returns | 3 | 1 | 1 | 4 | 4 | |
| 4/1/21-3/31/22 ALL | 4/1/22-3/31/23 ALL | 4/1/23-3/31/24 ALL | | Other | 7 | 6 | | | | |
| | | | | | 2 (4/1-9/30/23) | | | 33 (10/1/23-3/31/24) | | |
| | | | | | 0-1MM | 1-3MM | 3-5MM | 5-10MM | 10-25MM | 25MM & OVER |
| 57 | 54 | 35 | NUMBER OF STATEMENTS | | 12 | 8 | 5 | 5 | 5 | |
| % | % | % | **ASSETS** | | % | % | % | % | % | % |
| 19.4 | 15.0 | 19.8 | Cash & Equivalents | | 6.9 | | | | | D |
| .4 | 1.7 | 2.1 | Trade Receivables (net) | | .0 | | | | | A |
| 1.7 | 1.6 | 1.2 | Inventory | | .3 | | | | | T |
| 3.2 | 2.0 | 4.5 | All Other Current | | 3.5 | | | | | A |
| 24.7 | 20.3 | 27.6 | Total Current | | 10.7 | | | | | |
| 42.2 | 53.8 | 50.5 | Fixed Assets (net) | | 57.0 | | | | | N |
| 18.1 | 18.2 | 14.6 | Intangibles (net) | | 28.6 | | | | | O |
| 15.0 | 7.7 | 7.3 | All Other Non-Current | | 3.7 | | | | | T |
| 100.0 | 100.0 | 100.0 | Total | | 100.0 | | | | | |
| | | | **LIABILITIES** | | | | | | | A |
| 4.1 | 5.9 | 3.5 | Notes Payable-Short Term | | .5 | | | | | V |
| 2.4 | 1.7 | 7.8 | Cur. Mat.-L.T.D. | | 2.0 | | | | | A |
| .8 | 2.1 | 1.8 | Trade Payables | | .3 | | | | | I |
| .2 | .1 | .0 | Income Taxes Payable | | .0 | | | | | L |
| 8.1 | 4.2 | 4.8 | All Other Current | | 3.4 | | | | | A |
| 15.6 | 13.9 | 17.9 | Total Current | | 6.4 | | | | | B |
| 51.9 | 61.7 | 67.9 | Long-Term Debt | | 54.1 | | | | | L |
| .0 | .0 | .0 | Deferred Taxes | | .0 | | | | | E |
| 7.1 | 12.7 | 1.2 | All Other Non-Current | | 2.5 | | | | | |
| 25.5 | 11.6 | 13.0 | Net Worth | | 37.1 | | | | | |
| 100.0 | 100.0 | 100.0 | Total Liabilities & Net Worth | | 100.0 | | | | | |
| | | | **INCOME DATA** | | | | | | | |
| 100.0 | 100.0 | 100.0 | Net Sales | | 100.0 | | | | | |
| | | | Gross Profit | | | | | | | |
| 76.7 | 86.3 | 84.5 | Operating Expenses | | 91.1 | | | | | |
| 23.3 | 13.7 | 15.5 | Operating Profit | | 8.9 | | | | | |
| 4.9 | 4.7 | 3.7 | All Other Expenses (net) | | 6.9 | | | | | |
| 18.3 | 9.0 | 11.8 | Profit Before Taxes | | 2.0 | | | | | |
| | | | **RATIOS** | | | | | | | |
| 13.3 | 7.9 | 11.6 | | | 20.4 | | | | | |
| 2.4 | 2.2 | 1.5 | Current | | 1.2 | | | | | |
| .8 | .6 | .7 | | | .4 | | | | | |
| 7.1 | 5.1 | 3.6 | | | 10.3 | | | | | |
| 2.4 | 1.6 | 1.2 | Quick | | 1.1 | | | | | |
| .4 | .4 | .6 | | | .3 | | | | | |
| 0 UND | 0 UND | 0 UND | | | 0 UND | | | | | |
| 0 UND | 0 UND | 0 UND | Sales/Receivables | | 0 UND | | | | | |
| 0 UND | 2 183.8 | 0 UND | | | 0 UND | | | | | |
| | | | Cost of Sales/Inventory | | | | | | | |
| | | | Cost of Sales/Payables | | | | | | | |
| 3.6 | 9.2 | 5.1 | | | 4.4 | | | | | |
| 18.7 | 27.2 | 22.1 | Sales/Working Capital | | NM | | | | | |
| -77.3 | -20.9 | -26.6 | | | -11.5 | | | | | |
| 40.1 | 16.3 | 36.4 | | | | | | | | |
| (36) 6.2 | (45) 4.9 | (28) 4.4 | EBIT/Interest | | | | | | | |
| 2.0 | .6 | 1.8 | | | | | | | | |
| | | | Net Profit + Depr., Dep., Amort./Cur. Mat. L/T/D | | | | | | | |
| .4 | 1.2 | .8 | | | 1.1 | | | | | |
| 2.2 | 4.0 | 1.9 | Fixed/Worth | | -18.5 | | | | | |
| -1.0 | -1.0 | -2.4 | | | -1.0 | | | | | |
| .5 | .9 | .4 | | | .5 | | | | | |
| 3.6 | 31.4 | 2.1 | Debt/Worth | | -23.4 | | | | | |
| -2.6 | -2.4 | -4.1 | | | -2.4 | | | | | |
| 92.5 | 88.7 | 107.3 | | | | | | | | |
| (32) 49.1 | (28) 17.2 | (22) 52.6 | % Profit Before Taxes/Tangible Net Worth | | | | | | | |
| 18.2 | 3.1 | 13.5 | | | | | | | | |
| 34.3 | 31.3 | 44.9 | | | 14.8 | | | | | |
| 17.1 | 7.2 | 16.0 | % Profit Before Taxes/Total Assets | | 1.7 | | | | | |
| 5.1 | -.9 | 2.3 | | | -6.1 | | | | | |
| 10.2 | 5.4 | 7.6 | | | 3.6 | | | | | |
| 3.3 | 2.3 | 2.7 | Sales/Net Fixed Assets | | 1.1 | | | | | |
| 1.3 | .9 | 1.1 | | | .4 | | | | | |
| 1.8 | 2.0 | 2.6 | | | .8 | | | | | |
| 1.0 | 1.1 | 1.5 | Sales/Total Assets | | .6 | | | | | |
| .5 | .5 | .6 | | | .3 | | | | | |
| 2.5 | 6.0 | 7.2 | | | 7.3 | | | | | |
| (31) 10.8 | (31) 9.4 | (22) 11.2 | % Depr., Dep., Amort./Sales | | (10) 19.9 | | | | | |
| 18.0 | 22.2 | 21.8 | | | 30.1 | | | | | |
| 3.1 | 2.4 | 2.8 | % Officers', Directors' Owners' Comp/Sales | | | | | | | |
| (14) 4.2 | (12) 4.4 | (15) 3.9 | | | | | | | | |
| 10.2 | 8.4 | 6.9 | | | | | | | | |
| 151244M | 495328M | 151423M | Net Sales ($) | | 4972M | 14537M | 18083M | 36552M | 77279M | |
| 260507M | 537006M | 99043M | Total Assets ($) | | 9551M | 14495M | 13060M | 17139M | 44798M | |

© RMA 2024  M = $ thousand  MM = $ million
See Pages viii through xx for Explanation of Ratios and Data

## OTHER SERVICES—Drycleaning and Laundry Services (except Coin-Operated) NAICS 812320

### Current Data Sorted by Assets | Comparative Historical Data

| 0-500M | 500M-2MM | 2-10MM | 10-50MM | 50-100MM | 100-250MM | | | | | | |
|---|---|---|---|---|---|---|---|---|---|---|---|
| 1 | | 1 | 2 | | | Type of Statement | | | | | |
| | | 2 | 4 | | | Unqualified | 4 | | 2 | | |
| | | 1 | 1 | | | Reviewed | 2 | | 3 | | |
| 6 | 4 | 1 | 12 | | | Compiled | 10 | | 8 | | |
| 4 | 4 | 12 | 7 | 2 | 2 | Tax Returns | 18 | | 11 | | |
| | 5 (4/1-9/30/23) | | 48 (10/1/23-3/31/24) | | | Other | 49 | | 26 | | |
| | | | | | | | 4/1/19-3/31/20 ALL | | 4/1/20-3/31/21 ALL | | |
| 11 | 8 | 17 | 13 | 2 | 2 | NUMBER OF STATEMENTS | 83 | | 50 | | |
| % | % | % | % | % | % | ASSETS | % | | % | | |
| 48.2 | | 10.3 | 11.2 | | | Cash & Equivalents | 12.6 | | 25.5 | | |
| .4 | | 9.3 | 12.5 | | | Trade Receivables (net) | 10.3 | | 8.7 | | |
| .6 | | 1.7 | 2.2 | | | Inventory | 5.4 | | 3.3 | | |
| 4.3 | | .5 | 12.9 | | | All Other Current | .7 | | 2.4 | | |
| 53.5 | | 21.8 | 38.8 | | | Total Current | 29.0 | | 39.9 | | |
| 29.1 | | 48.4 | 42.5 | | | Fixed Assets (net) | 45.3 | | 39.2 | | |
| 9.8 | | 12.9 | 4.8 | | | Intangibles (net) | 12.6 | | 14.6 | | |
| 7.6 | | 17.0 | 13.9 | | | All Other Non-Current | 13.1 | | 6.3 | | |
| 100.0 | | 100.0 | 100.0 | | | Total | 100.0 | | 100.0 | | |
| | | | | | | LIABILITIES | | | | | |
| 11.3 | | 5.8 | 4.3 | | | Notes Payable-Short Term | 6.2 | | 10.2 | | |
| 12.0 | | 3.0 | 3.9 | | | Cur. Mat.-L.T.D. | 5.2 | | 6.3 | | |
| .0 | | 3.6 | 3.6 | | | Trade Payables | 5.7 | | 4.3 | | |
| .0 | | .0 | .0 | | | Income Taxes Payable | .0 | | .3 | | |
| 23.3 | | 14.0 | 8.6 | | | All Other Current | 10.2 | | 9.1 | | |
| 46.7 | | 26.4 | 20.3 | | | Total Current | 27.3 | | 30.2 | | |
| 116.6 | | 36.3 | 26.8 | | | Long-Term Debt | 41.9 | | 48.5 | | |
| .0 | | .0 | .0 | | | Deferred Taxes | .1 | | .1 | | |
| 8.4 | | 1.9 | 8.9 | | | All Other Non-Current | 9.2 | | 18.9 | | |
| -71.7 | | 35.4 | 44.0 | | | Net Worth | 21.4 | | 2.2 | | |
| 100.0 | | 100.0 | 100.0 | | | Total Liabilties & Net Worth | 100.0 | | 100.0 | | |
| | | | | | | INCOME DATA | | | | | |
| 100.0 | | 100.0 | 100.0 | | | Net Sales | 100.0 | | 100.0 | | |
| | | | | | | Gross Profit | | | | | |
| 95.8 | | 89.0 | 89.8 | | | Operating Expenses | 93.8 | | 100.6 | | |
| 4.2 | | 11.0 | 10.2 | | | Operating Profit | 6.2 | | -.6 | | |
| 2.2 | | 1.8 | 2.1 | | | All Other Expenses (net) | 1.9 | | .4 | | |
| 2.0 | | 9.2 | 8.1 | | | Profit Before Taxes | 4.3 | | -1.1 | | |
| | | | | | | RATIOS | | | | | |
| 14.9 | | 3.0 | 4.5 | | | | 2.5 | | 4.3 | | |
| 1.0 | | 1.4 | 1.7 | | | Current | 1.0 | | 1.9 | | |
| .3 | | .3 | .9 | | | | .5 | | .8 | | |
| 14.9 | | 2.7 | 2.2 | | | | 2.2 | | 3.6 | | |
| 1.0 | | 1.4 | 1.3 | | | Quick | .8 | | 1.9 | | |
| .1 | | .2 | .7 | | | | .3 | | .6 | | |
| 0 UND | 0 UND | 8 | 47.9 | | | | 0 UND | 0 | UND | | |
| 0 UND | 9 | 41.2 | 32 | 11.5 | | Sales/Receivables | 7 54.4 | 4 | 83.9 | | |
| 0 UND | 39 | 9.4 | 54 | 6.7 | | | 30 12.2 | 35 | 10.5 | | |
| | | | | | | Cost of Sales/Inventory | | | | | |
| | | | | | | Cost of Sales/Payables | | | | | |
| 5.8 | | 9.2 | 4.5 | | | | 9.5 | | 5.4 | | |
| UND | | 44.6 | 7.9 | | | Sales/Working Capital | 423.1 | | 13.5 | | |
| -13.1 | | -5.4 | NM | | | | -10.4 | | -15.9 | | |
| | | 17.2 | 30.1 | | | | 10.8 | | 7.2 | | |
| | | 5.0 | 5.5 | | | EBIT/Interest | (72) 3.3 | (46) | .8 | | |
| | | .0 | 1.9 | | | | .4 | | -6.0 | | |
| | | | | | | Net Profit + Depr., Dep., Amort./Cur. Mat. L/T/D | 6.3 | | | | |
| | | | | | | | (10) 2.4 | | | | |
| | | | | | | | .8 | | | | |
| .0 | | .9 | .5 | | | | .8 | | .6 | | |
| 5.4 | | 1.6 | .9 | | | Fixed/Worth | 2.1 | | 3.5 | | |
| -1.7 | | 5.2 | 3.3 | | | | -3.4 | | -1.1 | | |
| 2.3 | | 1.3 | .5 | | | | .8 | | 1.0 | | |
| -20.2 | | 2.3 | 1.7 | | | Debt/Worth | 3.3 | | 13.7 | | |
| -1.3 | | 13.3 | 5.0 | | | | -4.8 | | -3.5 | | |
| | | 171.0 | 57.6 | | | | 67.6 | | 72.5 | | |
| | (14) | 57.3 | (12) 20.0 | | | % Profit Before Taxes/Tangible Net Worth | (58) 22.4 | (30) | 13.9 | | |
| | | 18.6 | 8.4 | | | | 4.2 | | -15.4 | | |
| 36.9 | | 22.5 | 15.9 | | | | 18.4 | | 17.2 | | |
| 10.5 | | 12.2 | 8.6 | | | % Profit Before Taxes/Total Assets | 6.1 | | -.3 | | |
| -9.4 | | -5.4 | 1.8 | | | | -1.3 | | -29.4 | | |
| UND | | 8.3 | 10.5 | | | | 12.8 | | 22.7 | | |
| 24.2 | | 3.0 | 3.6 | | | Sales/Net Fixed Assets | 5.4 | | 5.5 | | |
| 6.5 | | 2.6 | 2.0 | | | | 2.4 | | 1.8 | | |
| 8.3 | | 2.2 | 1.8 | | | | 2.9 | | 3.0 | | |
| 5.7 | | 1.6 | 1.3 | | | Sales/Total Assets | 1.8 | | 1.6 | | |
| 3.2 | | 1.4 | .9 | | | | 1.1 | | .9 | | |
| | | 2.2 | 3.4 | | | | 1.9 | | 1.8 | | |
| | (12) | 5.4 | 5.2 | | | % Depr., Dep., Amort./Sales | (68) 4.9 | (32) | 4.1 | | |
| | | 8.7 | 6.3 | | | | 8.0 | | 6.5 | | |
| | | | | | | % Officers', Directors' Owners' Comp/Sales | 2.5 | | 3.2 | | |
| | | | | | | | (36) 6.8 | (20) | 4.7 | | |
| | | | | | | | 11.5 | | 8.9 | | |
| 10847M | 17678M | 130794M | 353047M | 152064M | 165962M | Net Sales ($) | 2071297M | | 294252M | | |
| 2273M | 8482M | 82476M | 263848M | 134593M | 292738M | Total Assets ($) | 898108M | | 222269M | | |

© RMA 2024  M = $ thousand  MM = $ million
See Pages viii through xx for Explanation of Ratios and Data

## OTHER SERVICES—Drycleaning and Laundry Services (except Coin-Operated) NAICS 812320

### Comparative Historical Data | Current Data Sorted by Sales

| | | | | Type of Statement | | | | | | |
|---|---|---|---|---|---|---|---|---|---|---|
| 1 | | 3 | 3 | Unqualified | | | 1 | | 1 | 1 |
| 2 | | 4 | 6 | Reviewed | | | | | 5 | 1 |
| 2 | | 2 | 2 | Compiled | 1 | | | 1 | | |
| 8 | | 23 | 11 | Tax Returns | 6 | 3 | 2 | | | |
| 24 | | 27 | 31 | Other | 4 | 3 | 4 | 6 | 8 | 6 |
| 4/1/21-3/31/22 ALL | | 4/1/22-3/31/23 ALL | 4/1/23-3/31/24 ALL | | 0-1MM | 5 (4/1-9/30/23) 1-3MM | 3-5MM | 48 (10/1/23-3/31/24) 5-10MM | 10-25MM | 25MM & OVER |
| 37 | | 59 | 53 | NUMBER OF STATEMENTS | 11 | 7 | 6 | 7 | 14 | 8 |
| % | | % | % | ASSETS | % | % | % | % | % | % |
| 22.3 | | 17.6 | 18.4 | Cash & Equivalents | 43.3 | | | | 11.0 | |
| 9.5 | | 9.9 | 9.0 | Trade Receivables (net) | 4.4 | | | | 11.3 | |
| 5.4 | | 4.2 | 1.9 | Inventory | 1.9 | | | | 2.9 | |
| 6.2 | | 2.4 | 6.4 | All Other Current | 8.5 | | | | 9.9 | |
| 43.6 | | 34.1 | 35.8 | Total Current | 58.1 | | | | 35.1 | |
| 34.5 | | 36.5 | 37.9 | Fixed Assets (net) | 21.3 | | | | 45.7 | |
| 11.5 | | 13.8 | 12.9 | Intangibles (net) | 18.0 | | | | 5.6 | |
| 10.5 | | 15.6 | 13.3 | All Other Non-Current | 2.6 | | | | 13.5 | |
| 100.0 | | 100.0 | 100.0 | Total | 100.0 | | | | 100.0 | |
| | | | | LIABILITIES | | | | | | |
| 6.8 | | 17.3 | 5.6 | Notes Payable-Short Term | 7.6 | | | | 1.5 | |
| 6.9 | | 5.3 | 5.7 | Cur. Mat.-L.T.D. | 9.7 | | | | 4.9 | |
| 3.5 | | 3.8 | 3.2 | Trade Payables | 3.0 | | | | 4.9 | |
| .0 | | .0 | .0 | Income Taxes Payable | .0 | | | | .0 | |
| 10.9 | | 8.0 | 16.0 | All Other Current | 36.5 | | | | 7.3 | |
| 28.2 | | 34.4 | 30.5 | Total Current | 56.7 | | | | 18.5 | |
| 55.7 | | 45.4 | 48.4 | Long-Term Debt | 78.4 | | | | 30.7 | |
| .3 | | .2 | .0 | Deferred Taxes | .0 | | | | .0 | |
| 3.8 | | 3.6 | 6.6 | All Other Non-Current | 10.2 | | | | 7.5 | |
| 12.0 | | 16.3 | 14.5 | Net Worth | -45.3 | | | | 43.2 | |
| 100.0 | | 100.0 | 100.0 | Total Liabilities & Net Worth | 100.0 | | | | 100.0 | |
| | | | | INCOME DATA | | | | | | |
| 100.0 | | 100.0 | 100.0 | Net Sales | 100.0 | | | | 100.0 | |
| | | | | Gross Profit | | | | | | |
| 93.2 | | 90.4 | 90.8 | Operating Expenses | 97.1 | | | | 92.8 | |
| 6.8 | | 9.6 | 9.2 | Operating Profit | 2.9 | | | | 7.2 | |
| -3.6 | | 1.7 | 1.8 | All Other Expenses (net) | 2.9 | | | | 1.9 | |
| 10.4 | | 8.0 | 7.4 | Profit Before Taxes | .0 | | | | 5.3 | |
| | | | | RATIOS | | | | | | |
| 4.9 | | 4.1 | 4.1 | | 14.9 | | | | 3.0 | |
| 1.6 | | 1.2 | 1.4 | Current | 1.0 | | | | 1.7 | |
| .5 | | .5 | .4 | | .4 | | | | .9 | |
| 3.2 | | 3.5 | 2.4 | | 14.9 | | | | 2.1 | |
| 1.4 | | 1.1 | 1.2 | Quick | 1.0 | | | | 1.5 | |
| .4 | | .4 | .2 | | .1 | | | | .7 | |
| 0 UND | | 0 UND | 0 UND | | 0 UND | | | 5 | 68.4 | |
| 9 41.2 | | 8 44.1 | 9 41.3 | Sales/Receivables | 0 UND | | | 36 | 10.1 | |
| 43 8.5 | | 38 9.5 | 43 8.5 | | 0 UND | | | 50 | 7.3 | |
| | | | | Cost of Sales/Inventory | | | | | | |
| | | | | Cost of Sales/Payables | | | | | | |
| 4.5 | | 6.5 | 6.8 | | 4.0 | | | | 5.6 | |
| 11.2 | | 39.9 | 34.8 | Sales/Working Capital | 112.8 | | | | 8.8 | |
| -14.2 | | -9.2 | -12.8 | | -5.9 | | | | NM | |
| 22.4 | | 23.7 | 15.5 | | | | | | 8.9 | |
| (25) 6.2 | (51) | 4.6 | (48) 5.5 | EBIT/Interest | | | | | 4.4 | |
| 1.6 | | 1.1 | 1.4 | | | | | | -.7 | |
| | | | | Net Profit + Depr., Dep., Amort./Cur. Mat. L/T/D | | | | | | |
| .3 | | .6 | .6 | | .0 | | | | .6 | |
| 1.0 | | 2.0 | 1.1 | Fixed/Worth | .6 | | | | .9 | |
| 17.0 | | -4.4 | UND | | -.3 | | | | 6.0 | |
| .9 | | .9 | .9 | | .7 | | | | .4 | |
| 2.6 | | 3.6 | 2.4 | Debt/Worth | -2.0 | | | | 2.0 | |
| 52.1 | | -4.4 | -10.8 | | -1.5 | | | | 7.0 | |
| 96.4 | | 45.4 | 73.6 | | | | | | 46.3 | |
| (29) 38.7 | (39) | 29.9 | (38) 24.9 | % Profit Before Taxes/Tangible Net Worth | | | | (12) | 17.1 | |
| 14.3 | | 1.5 | 13.9 | | | | | | 8.4 | |
| 35.9 | | 19.2 | 21.4 | | 12.1 | | | | 12.2 | |
| 13.9 | | 5.7 | 9.8 | % Profit Before Taxes/Total Assets | 7.3 | | | | 7.3 | |
| 3.2 | | -.2 | 3.7 | | -9.9 | | | | .1 | |
| 23.8 | | 27.2 | 13.3 | | UND | | | | 8.2 | |
| 8.8 | | 5.1 | 6.4 | Sales/Net Fixed Assets | 24.2 | | | | 3.4 | |
| 1.8 | | 2.1 | 2.8 | | 6.4 | | | | 1.8 | |
| 2.6 | | 2.2 | 2.5 | | 7.8 | | | | 1.7 | |
| 1.7 | | 1.4 | 1.6 | Sales/Total Assets | 2.1 | | | | 1.5 | |
| 1.0 | | 1.0 | 1.2 | | 1.3 | | | | .9 | |
| 1.3 | | 1.6 | 3.2 | | | | | | 4.3 | |
| (18) 5.1 | (40) | 4.0 | (35) 4.1 | % Depr., Dep., Amort./Sales | | | | (12) | 6.0 | |
| 8.6 | | 6.9 | 6.3 | | | | | | 13.4 | |
| 2.2 | | 2.1 | 2.8 | | | | | | | |
| (15) 4.8 | (19) | 5.9 | (19) 6.1 | % Officers', Directors' Owners' Comp/Sales | | | | | | |
| 8.0 | | 10.1 | 8.7 | | | | | | | |
| 3405337M | | 576745M | 830392M | Net Sales ($) | 6937M | 12533M | 24939M | 45772M | 236938M | 503273M |
| 629699M | | 461467M | 784410M | Total Assets ($) | 3251M | 8776M | 18592M | 22560M | 199266M | 531965M |

© RMA 2024  
M = $ thousand   MM = $ million  
See Pages viii through xx for Explanation of Ratios and Data

# OTHER SERVICES—Linen Supply   NAICS 812331

**Current Data Sorted by Assets** | **Comparative Historical Data**

| | | | | | | Type of Statement | | |
|---|---|---|---|---|---|---|---|---|
| | | | 4 | | | Unqualified | 4 | 1 |
| | 1 | | 3 | 2 | | Reviewed | 8 | 4 |
| 1 | 1 | | 1 | | | Compiled | 6 | 2 |
| | 4 | 1 | 1 | | | Tax Returns | 8 | 1 |
| | 7 (4/1-9/30/23) | 4 | 9 | 1 | 2 | Other | 25 | 17 |
| 0-500M | 500M-2MM | 2-10MM | 10-50MM | 50-100MM | 100-250MM | | 4/1/19-3/31/20 ALL | 4/1/20-3/31/21 ALL |
| 1 | 5 | 7 | 16 | 3 | 2 | NUMBER OF STATEMENTS | 51 | 25 |
| % | % | % | % | % | % | ASSETS | % | % |
| | | | 13.3 | | | Cash & Equivalents | 11.1 | 22.1 |
| | | | 11.1 | | | Trade Receivables (net) | 19.0 | 14.6 |
| | | | 10.0 | | | Inventory | 10.6 | 8.4 |
| | | | 2.0 | | | All Other Current | 2.8 | 1.9 |
| | | | 36.5 | | | Total Current | 43.5 | 46.9 |
| | | | 40.3 | | | Fixed Assets (net) | 42.1 | 42.7 |
| | | | 10.9 | | | Intangibles (net) | 5.0 | 4.6 |
| | | | 12.4 | | | All Other Non-Current | 9.5 | 5.8 |
| | | | 100.0 | | | Total | 100.0 | 100.0 |
| | | | | | | LIABILITIES | | |
| | | | 4.2 | | | Notes Payable-Short Term | 4.8 | 3.6 |
| | | | 2.6 | | | Cur. Mat.-L.T.D. | 3.1 | 3.3 |
| | | | 7.1 | | | Trade Payables | 9.9 | 5.6 |
| | | | .1 | | | Income Taxes Payable | .1 | .0 |
| | | | 9.4 | | | All Other Current | 8.9 | 5.8 |
| | | | 23.3 | | | Total Current | 26.7 | 18.4 |
| | | | 29.4 | | | Long-Term Debt | 19.5 | 29.4 |
| | | | 1.4 | | | Deferred Taxes | .2 | .5 |
| | | | 5.5 | | | All Other Non-Current | 4.3 | 2.0 |
| | | | 40.3 | | | Net Worth | 49.2 | 49.7 |
| | | | 100.0 | | | Total Liabilities & Net Worth | 100.0 | 100.0 |
| | | | | | | INCOME DATA | | |
| | | | 100.0 | | | Net Sales | 100.0 | 100.0 |
| | | | | | | Gross Profit | | |
| | | | 94.6 | | | Operating Expenses | 94.5 | 94.9 |
| | | | 5.4 | | | Operating Profit | 5.5 | 5.1 |
| | | | .0 | | | All Other Expenses (net) | .3 | -.2 |
| | | | 5.5 | | | Profit Before Taxes | 5.2 | 5.3 |
| | | | | | | RATIOS | | |
| | | | 3.2 | | | | 2.4 | 4.9 |
| | | | 1.8 | | | Current | 1.6 | 2.2 |
| | | | 1.4 | | | | 1.1 | 1.5 |
| | | | 2.8 | | | | 1.7 | 2.6 |
| | | | 1.7 | | | Quick | 1.3 | 1.8 |
| | | | .7 | | | | .6 | 1.2 |
| | | | 19  18.8 | | | | 23  16.0 | 13  27.6 |
| | | | 30  12.3 | | | Sales/Receivables | 31  11.6 | 30  12.1 |
| | | | 36  10.2 | | | | 41  9.0 | 43  8.4 |
| | | | | | | Cost of Sales/Inventory | | |
| | | | | | | Cost of Sales/Payables | | |
| | | | 4.7 | | | | 7.1 | 3.9 |
| | | | 10.3 | | | Sales/Working Capital | 12.6 | 6.4 |
| | | | 18.5 | | | | 69.0 | 10.1 |
| | | | 11.1 | | | | 16.8 | 8.5 |
| | | | (14) 5.3 | | | EBIT/Interest | (45) 6.3 | (22) 1.8 |
| | | | .8 | | | | 2.0 | -6.2 |
| | | | | | | Net Profit + Depr., Dep., Amort./Cur. Mat. L/T/D | | |
| | | | .7 | | | | .4 | .4 |
| | | | .9 | | | Fixed/Worth | .9 | 1.1 |
| | | | 4.2 | | | | 1.6 | 1.5 |
| | | | .6 | | | | .6 | .6 |
| | | | 1.0 | | | Debt/Worth | 1.0 | .9 |
| | | | 20.1 | | | | 2.7 | 1.9 |
| | | | 21.8 | | | | 48.2 | 54.7 |
| | | | (14) 16.0 | | | % Profit Before Taxes/Tangible Net Worth | (48) 19.8 | (24) 8.6 |
| | | | -.6 | | | | 1.7 | -7.8 |
| | | | 11.2 | | | | 23.1 | 18.8 |
| | | | 6.4 | | | % Profit Before Taxes/Total Assets | 8.9 | 4.0 |
| | | | -.3 | | | | 1.4 | -7.0 |
| | | | 7.0 | | | | 12.7 | 14.2 |
| | | | 3.5 | | | Sales/Net Fixed Assets | 4.7 | 3.2 |
| | | | 1.9 | | | | 2.7 | 1.7 |
| | | | 2.0 | | | | 2.6 | 2.2 |
| | | | 1.4 | | | Sales/Total Assets | 1.9 | 1.4 |
| | | | 1.0 | | | | 1.6 | .9 |
| | | | 4.6 | | | | 2.0 | 3.6 |
| | | | (12) 6.0 | | | % Depr., Dep., Amort./Sales | (38) 3.8 | (20) 8.7 |
| | | | 7.3 | | | | 7.2 | 12.2 |
| | | | | | | % Officers', Directors' Owners' Comp/Sales | (16) 1.6 / 2.6 / 4.2 | |
| 652M | 17635M | 59265M | 543168M | 144103M | 276010M | Net Sales ($) | 1749771M | 487208M |
| 78M | 6868M | 38259M | 383139M | 179669M | 375617M | Total Assets ($) | 881299M | 360170M |

© RMA 2024    M = $ thousand    MM = $ million
See Pages viii through xx for Explanation of Ratios and Data

# OTHER SERVICES—Linen Supply  NAICS 812331

## Comparative Historical Data | Current Data Sorted by Sales

| | | | | | | | | | | | |
|---|---|---|---|---|---|---|---|---|---|---|---|
| | | | | Type of Statement | | | | | | | |
| | 3 | 2 | 4 | Unqualified | | | | 1 | | 1 | 2 |
| | 3 | 8 | 6 | Reviewed | | | | | | 3 | 3 |
| | | 3 | 2 | Compiled | | 2 | | | | | |
| | 4 | 8 | 2 | Tax Returns | | | 1 | | | | |
| | 7 | 16 | 20 | Other | | 1 | 2 | 2 | 1 | 4 | 11 |
| | 4/1/21-3/31/22 ALL | 4/1/22-3/31/23 ALL | 4/1/23-3/31/24 ALL | | | 7 (4/1-9/30/23) | | | 27 (10/1/23-3/31/24) | | |
| | | | | | 0-1MM | 1-3MM | 3-5MM | 5-10MM | 10-25MM | 25MM & OVER | |
| | 17 | 37 | 34 | NUMBER OF STATEMENTS | 3 | 2 | 4 | 1 | 8 | 16 | |
| | % | % | % | ASSETS | % | % | % | % | % | % | |
| | 18.3 | 15.3 | 13.9 | Cash & Equivalents | | | | | | 12.7 | |
| | 19.3 | 16.0 | 14.9 | Trade Receivables (net) | | | | | | 10.9 | |
| | 11.3 | 17.2 | 9.8 | Inventory | | | | | | 11.4 | |
| | 1.7 | 3.3 | 1.6 | All Other Current | | | | | | 2.2 | |
| | 50.6 | 51.8 | 40.2 | Total Current | | | | | | 37.3 | |
| | 32.6 | 32.3 | 40.1 | Fixed Assets (net) | | | | | | 33.6 | |
| | 3.9 | 4.3 | 10.4 | Intangibles (net) | | | | | | 13.2 | |
| | 12.9 | 11.7 | 9.4 | All Other Non-Current | | | | | | 15.9 | |
| | 100.0 | 100.0 | 100.0 | Total | | | | | | 100.0 | |
| | | | | LIABILITIES | | | | | | | |
| | 6.7 | 10.2 | 7.6 | Notes Payable-Short Term | | | | | | 4.1 | |
| | 3.2 | 3.9 | 3.1 | Cur. Mat.-L.T.D. | | | | | | 2.2 | |
| | 7.8 | 8.9 | 7.1 | Trade Payables | | | | | | 7.5 | |
| | .0 | .3 | .1 | Income Taxes Payable | | | | | | .0 | |
| | 11.4 | 5.5 | 12.5 | All Other Current | | | | | | 10.6 | |
| | 29.1 | 28.8 | 30.3 | Total Current | | | | | | 24.4 | |
| | 26.2 | 24.9 | 33.4 | Long-Term Debt | | | | | | 32.9 | |
| | .0 | .0 | .9 | Deferred Taxes | | | | | | .4 | |
| | .7 | 4.7 | 3.6 | All Other Non-Current | | | | | | 5.0 | |
| | 44.0 | 41.6 | 31.7 | Net Worth | | | | | | 37.3 | |
| | 100.0 | 100.0 | 100.0 | Total Liabilities & Net Worth | | | | | | 100.0 | |
| | | | | INCOME DATA | | | | | | | |
| | 100.0 | 100.0 | 100.0 | Net Sales | | | | | | 100.0 | |
| | | | | Gross Profit | | | | | | | |
| | 93.7 | 89.2 | 89.5 | Operating Expenses | | | | | | 94.6 | |
| | 6.3 | 10.8 | 10.5 | Operating Profit | | | | | | 5.4 | |
| | .4 | 1.1 | 2.3 | All Other Expenses (net) | | | | | | -.6 | |
| | 5.9 | 9.6 | 8.2 | Profit Before Taxes | | | | | | 5.9 | |
| | | | | RATIOS | | | | | | | |
| | 3.3 | 4.4 | 3.4 | | | | | | | 3.2 | |
| | 1.7 | 2.3 | 1.9 | Current | | | | | | 1.8 | |
| | 1.0 | 1.4 | 1.4 | | | | | | | 1.4 | |
| | 2.4 | 3.0 | 3.0 | | | | | | | 2.8 | |
| | 1.2 | 1.5 | 1.5 | Quick | | | | | | 1.2 | |
| | .9 | .6 | .7 | | | | | | | .6 | |
| 24 | 14.9 | 17 | 21.8 | 20 | 18.0 | Sales/Receivables | | | | | 27 | 13.7 |
| 34 | 10.8 | 32 | 11.5 | 30 | 12.3 | | | | | | 31 | 11.8 |
| 42 | 8.7 | 44 | 8.3 | 40 | 9.4 | | | | | | 41 | 8.9 |
| | | | | Cost of Sales/Inventory | | | | | | | |
| | | | | Cost of Sales/Payables | | | | | | | |
| | 4.3 | 4.2 | 3.8 | | | | | | | 3.7 | |
| | 15.5 | 7.9 | 8.9 | Sales/Working Capital | | | | | | 12.3 | |
| | NM | 16.3 | 18.5 | | | | | | | 21.9 | |
| | 30.6 | 18.6 | 15.6 | | | | | | | 11.8 | |
| (13) | 3.7 | (31) 10.4 | (31) 7.9 | EBIT/Interest | | | | | (14) | 3.0 | |
| | -3.2 | 3.5 | 1.1 | | | | | | | .3 | |
| | | | | Net Profit + Depr., Dep., Amort./Cur. Mat. L/T/D | | | | | | | |
| | .2 | .1 | .6 | | | | | | | .7 | |
| | .6 | .7 | .9 | Fixed/Worth | | | | | | .9 | |
| | 1.7 | 1.8 | 5.0 | | | | | | | 22.0 | |
| | .4 | .6 | .7 | | | | | | | .7 | |
| | 1.2 | 1.2 | 1.4 | Debt/Worth | | | | | | 1.1 | |
| | 4.1 | 3.9 | 10.6 | | | | | | | 33.1 | |
| | 74.0 | 52.4 | 35.1 | % Profit Before Taxes/Tangible Net Worth | | | | | | 24.4 | |
| (15) | 36.9 | (34) 26.4 | (28) 18.7 | | | | | | (13) | 17.0 | |
| | .6 | 11.5 | 2.5 | | | | | | | -1.7 | |
| | 29.5 | 20.1 | 20.2 | % Profit Before Taxes/Total Assets | | | | | | 11.5 | |
| | 6.6 | 10.0 | 8.5 | | | | | | | 5.7 | |
| | -7.9 | 3.5 | .2 | | | | | | | -.5 | |
| | 19.6 | 57.1 | 8.3 | | | | | | | 7.0 | |
| | 6.3 | 6.4 | 4.3 | Sales/Net Fixed Assets | | | | | | 4.4 | |
| | 3.3 | 2.4 | 1.8 | | | | | | | 2.0 | |
| | 2.6 | 2.8 | 2.1 | | | | | | | 2.0 | |
| | 2.2 | 1.6 | 1.4 | Sales/Total Assets | | | | | | 1.2 | |
| | 1.4 | 1.2 | .9 | | | | | | | .8 | |
| | .4 | .3 | 3.5 | | | | | | | 4.6 | |
| (11) | 5.6 | (22) 3.1 | (25) 5.9 | % Depr., Dep., Amort./Sales | | | | | (12) | 5.8 | |
| | 14.4 | 6.3 | 11.0 | | | | | | | 12.8 | |
| | | 1.2 | | | | | | | | | |
| | | (12) 1.8 | | % Officers', Directors' Owners' Comp/Sales | | | | | | | |
| | | | 4.0 | | | | | | | | |
| | 694966M | 1364974M | 1040833M | Net Sales ($) | 1231M | 3520M | 15912M | 6483M | 126773M | 886914M | |
| | 582085M | 966795M | 983630M | Total Assets ($) | 6869M | 1849M | 16938M | 1893M | 90894M | 865187M | |

© RMA 2024  
M = $ thousand  MM = $ million  
See Pages viii through xx for Explanation of Ratios and Data

# OTHER SERVICES—Pet Care (except Veterinary) Services NAICS 812910

**Current Data Sorted by Assets** / **Comparative Historical Data**

| | | | | | | | Type of Statement | | |
|---|---|---|---|---|---|---|---|---|---|
| | | | 1 | 2 | | | Unqualified | 3 | 3 |
| | | 1 | | 1 | | | Reviewed | 1 | 1 |
| 16 | 10 | 4 | 1 | | | | Compiled | 1 | 1 |
| 22 | 8 | 11 | 6 | 2 | 1 | | Tax Returns | 26 | 18 |
| | 7 (4/1-9/30/23) | | 79 (10/1/23-3/31/24) | | | | Other | 62 | 36 |
| 0-500M | 500M-2MM | 2-10MM | 10-50MM | 50-100MM | 100-250MM | | | 4/1/19-3/31/20 ALL | 4/1/20-3/31/21 ALL |
| 38 | 19 | 16 | 10 | 2 | 1 | NUMBER OF STATEMENTS | | 93 | 59 |
| % | % | % | % | % | % | **ASSETS** | | % | % |
| 40.1 | 18.5 | 11.3 | 22.4 | | | Cash & Equivalents | | 24.1 | 31.2 |
| 1.4 | 1.2 | .5 | 3.4 | | | Trade Receivables (net) | | 2.7 | 2.8 |
| 2.5 | 2.9 | .1 | 9.0 | | | Inventory | | 2.5 | 4.8 |
| 7.4 | 5.0 | 2.1 | .2 | | | All Other Current | | .7 | 1.9 |
| 51.4 | 27.6 | 14.1 | 35.0 | | | Total Current | | 30.0 | 40.8 |
| 32.7 | 54.2 | 71.7 | 37.3 | | | Fixed Assets (net) | | 50.3 | 45.0 |
| 4.3 | 8.2 | 5.4 | 6.3 | | | Intangibles (net) | | 8.4 | 5.6 |
| 11.6 | 10.0 | 8.9 | 21.4 | | | All Other Non-Current | | 11.3 | 8.6 |
| 100.0 | 100.0 | 100.0 | 100.0 | | | Total | | 100.0 | 100.0 |
| | | | | | | **LIABILITIES** | | | |
| 7.4 | 2.0 | 1.8 | 5.1 | | | Notes Payable-Short Term | | 8.3 | 10.3 |
| 5.3 | 4.8 | .8 | 1.6 | | | Cur. Mat.-L.T.D. | | 1.7 | 4.9 |
| 18.1 | 7.0 | .9 | 4.4 | | | Trade Payables | | 3.8 | 4.5 |
| .0 | .0 | .0 | .0 | | | Income Taxes Payable | | .0 | .1 |
| 14.8 | 5.6 | 7.2 | 3.1 | | | All Other Current | | 12.3 | 5.8 |
| 45.6 | 19.4 | 10.7 | 14.1 | | | Total Current | | 26.2 | 25.6 |
| 38.8 | 54.1 | 51.5 | 9.3 | | | Long-Term Debt | | 29.8 | 43.4 |
| .0 | .0 | .0 | .0 | | | Deferred Taxes | | .0 | .0 |
| 9.6 | 2.0 | .2 | 9.6 | | | All Other Non-Current | | 9.0 | 8.4 |
| 6.2 | 24.5 | 37.5 | 66.9 | | | Net Worth | | 35.0 | 22.6 |
| 100.0 | 100.0 | 100.0 | 100.0 | | | Total Liabilities & Net Worth | | 100.0 | 100.0 |
| | | | | | | **INCOME DATA** | | | |
| 100.0 | 100.0 | 100.0 | 100.0 | | | Net Sales | | 100.0 | 100.0 |
| | | | | | | Gross Profit | | | |
| 91.0 | 89.5 | 78.1 | 100.6 | | | Operating Expenses | | 87.7 | 96.2 |
| 9.0 | 10.5 | 21.9 | -.6 | | | Operating Profit | | 12.3 | 3.8 |
| .9 | 3.5 | 9.4 | .3 | | | All Other Expenses (net) | | 3.6 | .2 |
| 8.0 | 7.0 | 12.4 | -.9 | | | Profit Before Taxes | | 8.6 | 3.7 |
| | | | | | | **RATIOS** | | | |
| 8.2 | 6.0 | 4.5 | 6.9 | | | | | 5.4 | 6.6 |
| 3.2 | 1.0 | 1.4 | 3.0 | | | Current | | 1.2 | 3.1 |
| .9 | .5 | .2 | .5 | | | | | .3 | .7 |
| 7.5 | 5.8 | 4.1 | 6.4 | | | | | 5.1 | 6.6 |
| 2.9 | .9 | 1.2 | 2.5 | | | Quick | | 1.1 | 1.7 |
| .4 | .3 | .2 | .3 | | | | | .2 | .5 |
| 0 UND | 0 UND | 0 UND | 0 UND | | | | | 0 UND | 0 UND |
| 0 UND | 0 UND | 0 UND | 4 95.1 | | | Sales/Receivables | | 0 UND | 0 UND |
| 0 UND | 0 UND | 1 257.5 | 22 16.3 | | | | | 1 554.5 | 1 652.0 |
| | | | | | | Cost of Sales/Inventory | | | |
| | | | | | | Cost of Sales/Payables | | | |
| 7.2 | 10.9 | 4.8 | 1.3 | | | | | 5.6 | 4.3 |
| 15.5 | -999.8 | 33.3 | 4.2 | | | Sales/Working Capital | | 87.5 | 12.2 |
| -27.6 | -24.8 | -16.4 | -7.9 | | | | | -10.0 | -50.4 |
| 21.7 | 7.5 | 7.4 | | | | | | 16.3 | 17.6 |
| (21) 5.4 | (15) 2.8 | (10) 4.0 | | | | EBIT/Interest | (66) | 4.7 | (38) 3.0 |
| -.2 | -1.9 | 1.5 | | | | | | 1.3 | -.1 |
| | | | | | | Net Profit + Depr., Dep., Amort./Cur. Mat. L/T/D | | | |
| .2 | 1.3 | 1.0 | .2 | | | | | .5 | .5 |
| .6 | 7.5 | 2.9 | .7 | | | Fixed/Worth | | 1.4 | 1.4 |
| -3.4 | -17.3 | -34.4 | 1.2 | | | | | 12.2 | 13.2 |
| .2 | 1.9 | .6 | .1 | | | | | .4 | .4 |
| 1.4 | 8.8 | 2.3 | .4 | | | Debt/Worth | | 1.7 | 3.1 |
| -5.5 | -20.2 | -39.8 | 1.3 | | | | | NM | -38.8 |
| 110.5 | 100.4 | 29.8 | | | | | | 88.4 | 59.6 |
| (25) 40.6 | (13) 26.8 | (11) 7.6 | | | | % Profit Before Taxes/Tangible Net Worth | (70) | 30.1 | (44) 8.2 |
| 9.3 | -47.8 | .9 | | | | | | 6.3 | -7.1 |
| 80.3 | 26.6 | 9.7 | 5.1 | | | | | 28.6 | 26.6 |
| 25.6 | 12.8 | 6.4 | -1.3 | | | % Profit Before Taxes/Total Assets | | 7.8 | 2.8 |
| -3.1 | -4.3 | .9 | -6.7 | | | | | 1.0 | -2.1 |
| 97.4 | 20.1 | 2.5 | 8.4 | | | | | 19.5 | 22.9 |
| 26.0 | 3.2 | .7 | 2.7 | | | Sales/Net Fixed Assets | | 4.4 | 5.3 |
| 6.3 | 1.5 | .5 | .5 | | | | | .9 | 1.1 |
| 7.9 | 3.0 | 1.0 | 1.1 | | | | | 3.6 | 3.9 |
| 4.0 | 1.7 | .6 | .7 | | | Sales/Total Assets | | 1.5 | 2.2 |
| 2.4 | 1.3 | .3 | .3 | | | | | .5 | .5 |
| .7 | 1.2 | | | | | | | 1.4 | 1.3 |
| (19) 4.1 | (11) 3.0 | | | | | % Depr., Dep., Amort./Sales | (65) | 4.6 | (33) 3.2 |
| 7.9 | 10.8 | | | | | | | 9.5 | 6.4 |
| 8.2 | | | | | | | | 5.1 | 3.1 |
| (16) 11.6 | | | | | | % Officers', Directors' Owners' Comp/Sales | (41) | 7.5 | (20) 6.3 |
| 17.4 | | | | | | | | 11.4 | 12.3 |
| 39661M | 73209M | 42091M | 175565M | 369107M | 110963M | Net Sales ($) | | 1175618M | 273969M |
| 9225M | 16680M | 55986M | 291279M | 125956M | 126639M | Total Assets ($) | | 696921M | 406057M |

© RMA 2024

M = $ thousand    MM = $ million
See Pages viii through xx for Explanation of Ratios and Data

# OTHER SERVICES—Pet Care (except Veterinary) Services  NAICS 812910

## Comparative Historical Data | Current Data Sorted by Sales

| | | | | Type of Statement | | | | | | |
|---|---|---|---|---|---|---|---|---|---|---|
| 4 | 3 | 3 | | Unqualified | 1 | | 1 | | 1 | |
| | 2 | 1 | | Reviewed | | | | 1 | | |
| 2 | 3 | 1 | | Compiled | | 1 | | | | |
| 13 | 32 | 31 | | Tax Returns | 17 | 9 | 3 | 1 | 1 | 1 |
| 43 | 46 | 50 | | Other | 17 | 16 | 4 | 4 | 4 | 5 |
| 4/1/21-3/31/22 ALL | 4/1/22-3/31/23 ALL | 4/1/23-3/31/24 ALL | | | 0-1MM | 1-3MM | 7 (4/1-9/30/23) 3-5MM | 5-10MM | 79 (10/1/23-3/31/24) 10-25MM | 25MM & OVER |
| 62 | 86 | 86 | NUMBER OF STATEMENTS | | 35 | 26 | 8 | 5 | 6 | 6 |
| % | % | % | ASSETS | | % | % | % | % | % | % |
| 34.2 | 31.1 | 26.7 | Cash & Equivalents | | 28.7 | 32.3 | | | | |
| .7 | 2.3 | 2.0 | Trade Receivables (net) | | .6 | .0 | | | | |
| .6 | 1.6 | 3.6 | Inventory | | 2.2 | 1.1 | | | | |
| 3.8 | 3.1 | 4.9 | All Other Current | | 5.7 | 3.6 | | | | |
| 39.4 | 38.1 | 37.1 | Total Current | | 37.2 | 37.1 | | | | |
| 48.1 | 44.0 | 45.0 | Fixed Assets (net) | | 53.8 | 36.8 | | | | |
| 5.3 | 9.8 | 6.3 | Intangibles (net) | | 5.9 | 5.6 | | | | |
| 7.2 | 8.1 | 11.6 | All Other Non-Current | | 3.1 | 20.5 | | | | |
| 100.0 | 100.0 | 100.0 | Total | | 100.0 | 100.0 | | | | |
| | | | LIABILITIES | | | | | | | |
| 6.4 | 3.7 | 5.4 | Notes Payable-Short Term | | 7.6 | 2.1 | | | | |
| 2.0 | 1.9 | 3.8 | Cur. Mat.-L.T.D. | | 4.0 | 4.0 | | | | |
| .7 | 2.7 | 10.5 | Trade Payables | | 18.1 | 2.0 | | | | |
| .2 | .0 | .0 | Income Taxes Payable | | .0 | .1 | | | | |
| 9.1 | 12.0 | 10.0 | All Other Current | | 15.5 | 5.3 | | | | |
| 18.4 | 20.3 | 29.7 | Total Current | | 45.2 | 13.5 | | | | |
| 34.3 | 35.2 | 40.2 | Long-Term Debt | | 46.2 | 49.4 | | | | |
| .0 | .0 | .0 | Deferred Taxes | | .0 | .0 | | | | |
| 3.9 | 9.1 | 6.8 | All Other Non-Current | | 6.5 | 5.4 | | | | |
| 43.5 | 35.5 | 23.4 | Net Worth | | 2.2 | 31.7 | | | | |
| 100.0 | 100.0 | 100.0 | Total Liabilities & Net Worth | | 100.0 | 100.0 | | | | |
| | | | INCOME DATA | | | | | | | |
| 100.0 | 100.0 | 100.0 | Net Sales | | 100.0 | 100.0 | | | | |
| | | | Gross Profit | | | | | | | |
| 85.5 | 87.4 | 89.6 | Operating Expenses | | 84.8 | 88.5 | | | | |
| 14.5 | 12.6 | 10.4 | Operating Profit | | 15.2 | 11.5 | | | | |
| -1.1 | 1.6 | 3.2 | All Other Expenses (net) | | 5.3 | 1.6 | | | | |
| 15.6 | 11.0 | 7.2 | Profit Before Taxes | | 9.9 | 9.9 | | | | |
| | | | RATIOS | | | | | | | |
| 11.0 | 11.1 | 6.5 | | | 5.2 | 14.6 | | | | |
| 3.1 | 4.0 | 2.1 | Current | | 1.1 | 5.2 | | | | |
| 1.1 | .7 | .5 | | | .3 | 2.0 | | | | |
| 9.1 | 10.4 | 6.3 | | | 3.5 | 14.6 | | | | |
| 2.9 | 3.5 | 1.6 | Quick | | .9 | 5.2 | | | | |
| 1.0 | .5 | .3 | | | .2 | 1.7 | | | | |
| 0 UND | 0 UND | 0 UND | | | 0 UND | 0 UND | | | | |
| 0 UND | 0 UND | 0 UND | Sales/Receivables | | 0 UND | 0 UND | | | | |
| 0 756.2 | 2 185.0 | 0 897.6 | | | 0 UND | 0 UND | | | | |
| | | | Cost of Sales/Inventory | | | | | | | |
| | | | Cost of Sales/Payables | | | | | | | |
| 4.5 | 4.4 | 6.2 | | | 6.0 | 7.2 | | | | |
| 7.8 | 13.6 | 20.9 | Sales/Working Capital | | 189.0 | 11.1 | | | | |
| 66.9 | -30.9 | -25.5 | | | -13.4 | 70.9 | | | | |
| 53.0 | 16.0 | 7.6 | | | 10.1 | 7.8 | | | | |
| (40) 8.4 | (48) 6.7 | (58) 2.4 | EBIT/Interest | | (18) 3.4 | (16) 3.4 | | | | |
| 2.3 | 1.4 | -1.0 | | | 1.2 | -3.3 | | | | |
| | | | Net Profit + Depr., Dep., Amort./Cur. Mat. L/T/D | | | | | | | |
| .6 | .4 | .4 | | | .4 | .4 | | | | |
| 1.2 | 1.7 | 1.3 | Fixed/Worth | | 1.5 | 1.5 | | | | |
| 10.0 | 36.2 | -50.8 | | | -8.6 | -2.5 | | | | |
| .2 | .4 | .4 | | | .2 | .5 | | | | |
| .9 | 2.6 | 2.3 | Debt/Worth | | 8.1 | 2.3 | | | | |
| 20.5 | -11.8 | -17.4 | | | -7.1 | -5.8 | | | | |
| 73.6 | 130.1 | 64.6 | | | 102.2 | 84.2 | | | | |
| (50) 33.4 | (64) 45.7 | (60) 23.4 | % Profit Before Taxes/Tangible Net Worth | | (21) 40.6 | (19) 28.5 | | | | |
| 8.2 | 8.0 | -7.2 | | | -3.0 | 7.8 | | | | |
| 31.4 | 37.6 | 32.6 | | | 44.6 | 47.9 | | | | |
| 20.2 | 17.2 | 8.5 | % Profit Before Taxes/Total Assets | | 11.1 | 19.5 | | | | |
| 4.9 | 3.1 | -2.3 | | | -1.4 | -2.9 | | | | |
| 9.9 | 22.0 | 35.1 | | | 47.1 | 51.5 | | | | |
| 3.4 | 5.5 | 6.3 | Sales/Net Fixed Assets | | 4.4 | 19.5 | | | | |
| 1.2 | 1.2 | 1.3 | | | .6 | 3.1 | | | | |
| 2.5 | 3.3 | 4.1 | | | 4.2 | 7.1 | | | | |
| 1.3 | 1.6 | 2.0 | Sales/Total Assets | | 1.8 | 3.0 | | | | |
| .7 | .8 | .9 | | | .5 | 1.6 | | | | |
| 1.9 | 2.6 | 1.4 | | | 2.9 | .8 | | | | |
| (36) 4.2 | (46) 4.4 | (50) 4.2 | % Depr., Dep., Amort./Sales | | (19) 6.6 | (12) 2.2 | | | | |
| 7.7 | 10.5 | 8.4 | | | 12.7 | 4.7 | | | | |
| 4.0 | 3.9 | 4.5 | | | 10.7 | 3.4 | | | | |
| (22) 7.4 | (29) 8.7 | (31) 10.8 | % Officers', Directors' Owners' Comp/Sales | | (13) 12.8 | (11) 10.8 | | | | |
| 12.9 | 13.3 | 16.3 | | | 21.6 | 14.5 | | | | |
| 244986M | 386216M | 810596M | Net Sales ($) | | 20867M | 44701M | 30070M | 33465M | 87957M | 593536M |
| 383785M | 440674M | 625765M | Total Assets ($) | | 27346M | 21749M | 39388M | 26677M | 177094M | 333511M |

© RMA 2024

M = $ thousand    MM = $ million
See Pages viii through xx for Explanation of Ratios and Data

# OTHER SERVICES—Parking Lots and Garages  NAICS 812930

## Current Data Sorted by Assets | Comparative Historical Data

| | | | | | | Type of Statement | | |
|---|---|---|---|---|---|---|---|---|
| | | | 1 | 1 | 4 | Unqualified | 8 | 2 |
| | | 1 | 1 | | 1 | Reviewed | 2 | |
| | 1 | 1 | | | | Compiled | 2 | |
| 4 | | 1 | | | | Tax Returns | 4 | 1 |
| 2 | 4 | 8 | 16 | 3 | 2 | Other | 32 | 25 |
| | 7 (4/1-9/30/23) | | 42 (10/1/23-3/31/24) | | | | 4/1/19-3/31/20 | 4/1/20-3/31/21 |
| 0-500M | 500M-2MM | 2-10MM | 10-50MM | 50-100MM | 100-250MM | | ALL | ALL |
| 6 | 5 | 10 | 17 | 4 | 7 | NUMBER OF STATEMENTS | 48 | 28 |
| % | % | % | % | % | % | ASSETS | % | % |
| | | 29.5 | 10.0 | | | Cash & Equivalents | 12.5 | 16.5 |
| | | 20.4 | 16.4 | | | Trade Receivables (net) | 12.1 | 5.4 |
| | | .0 | 1.2 | | | Inventory | .1 | 1.3 |
| | | 8.0 | 5.3 | | | All Other Current | 6.0 | 4.8 |
| | | 57.8 | 32.9 | | | Total Current | 30.7 | 27.9 |
| | | 19.7 | 33.6 | | | Fixed Assets (net) | 49.7 | 52.3 |
| | | 6.6 | 11.0 | | | Intangibles (net) | 5.8 | 11.6 |
| | | 15.8 | 22.5 | | | All Other Non-Current | 13.8 | 8.2 |
| | | 100.0 | 100.0 | | | Total | 100.0 | 100.0 |
| | | | | | | LIABILITIES | | |
| | | .9 | 1.1 | | | Notes Payable-Short Term | 4.2 | 7.6 |
| | | 2.5 | 1.6 | | | Cur. Mat.-L.T.D. | 5.2 | 3.0 |
| | | 19.9 | 6.2 | | | Trade Payables | 5.2 | 6.4 |
| | | .0 | .0 | | | Income Taxes Payable | .1 | .0 |
| | | 12.5 | 18.4 | | | All Other Current | 12.7 | 12.3 |
| | | 35.8 | 27.3 | | | Total Current | 27.3 | 29.2 |
| | | 28.2 | 48.5 | | | Long-Term Debt | 46.9 | 66.2 |
| | | .0 | .1 | | | Deferred Taxes | .0 | .0 |
| | | 2.2 | 4.6 | | | All Other Non-Current | 8.6 | 2.6 |
| | | 33.8 | 19.5 | | | Net Worth | 17.2 | 2.0 |
| | | 100.0 | 100.0 | | | Total Liabilities & Net Worth | 100.0 | 100.0 |
| | | | | | | INCOME DATA | | |
| | | 100.0 | 100.0 | | | Net Sales | 100.0 | 100.0 |
| | | | | | | Gross Profit | | |
| | | 87.3 | 74.5 | | | Operating Expenses | 71.0 | 87.9 |
| | | 12.7 | 25.5 | | | Operating Profit | 29.0 | 12.1 |
| | | -.2 | 13.6 | | | All Other Expenses (net) | 12.7 | 7.1 |
| | | 12.9 | 11.9 | | | Profit Before Taxes | 16.3 | 5.0 |
| | | | | | | RATIOS | | |
| | | 2.2 | 2.0 | | | | 2.6 | 3.7 |
| | | 1.5 | 1.1 | | | Current | 1.1 | 1.3 |
| | | .5 | .7 | | | | .5 | .5 |
| | | 1.7 | 1.7 | | | | 1.7 | 2.1 |
| | | 1.1 | 1.0 | | | Quick | .9 | .8 |
| | | .4 | .5 | | | | .2 | .4 |
| | 3 | 134.4 | 1  264.5 | | | | 0  UND | 0  UND |
| | 6 | 66.3 | 20  17.9 | | | Sales/Receivables | 11  34.2 | 1  384.8 |
| | 64 | 5.7 | 57  6.4 | | | | 30  12.2 | 17  21.3 |
| | | | | | | Cost of Sales/Inventory | | |
| | | | | | | Cost of Sales/Payables | | |
| | | 5.3 | 6.8 | | | | 6.0 | 5.0 |
| | | 20.5 | 67.3 | | | Sales/Working Capital | 74.3 | 18.2 |
| | | -22.5 | -17.5 | | | | -14.3 | -8.4 |
| | | | 47.4 | | | | 31.8 | 3.2 |
| | | | (10) 9.1 | | | EBIT/Interest | (34) 6.7 | (14) 1.1 |
| | | | 4.0 | | | | 2.9 | -19.2 |
| | | | | | | Net Profit + Depr., Dep., Amort./Cur. Mat. L/T/D | | |
| | | .1 | .3 | | | | .8 | 1.3 |
| | | .2 | 1.8 | | | Fixed/Worth | 2.6 | -510.9 |
| | | NM | -1.3 | | | | NM | -.7 |
| | | .6 | 1.0 | | | | 1.0 | 1.0 |
| | | 2.1 | 4.3 | | | Debt/Worth | 2.2 | -530.9 |
| | | NM | -11.6 | | | | NM | -2.3 |
| | | | 81.9 | | | | 66.7 | 9.8 |
| | | | (12) 48.7 | | | % Profit Before Taxes/Tangible Net Worth | (36) 24.8 | (13) .9 |
| | | | 4.0 | | | | 12.1 | -12.4 |
| | | 35.2 | 19.9 | | | | 18.5 | 4.6 |
| | | 13.3 | 7.8 | | | % Profit Before Taxes/Total Assets | 8.5 | .9 |
| | | 8.5 | .3 | | | | 4.2 | -9.1 |
| | | 230.9 | 46.6 | | | | 26.3 | 19.6 |
| | | 38.8 | 6.9 | | | Sales/Net Fixed Assets | 1.4 | .6 |
| | | 7.6 | .3 | | | | .2 | .2 |
| | | 3.8 | 2.5 | | | | 3.7 | 2.8 |
| | | 2.6 | .7 | | | Sales/Total Assets | .8 | .4 |
| | | 1.5 | .1 | | | | .2 | .1 |
| | | | 1.0 | | | | 1.0 | 1.3 |
| | | | (13) 2.7 | | | % Depr., Dep., Amort./Sales | (32) 3.7 | (15) 5.4 |
| | | | 20.2 | | | | 16.9 | 9.0 |
| | | | | | | % Officers', Directors' Owners' Comp/Sales | | |
| 12037M | 10314M | 196280M | 719272M | 509452M | 2474207M | Net Sales ($) | 2806917M | 458519M |
| 1573M | 5457M | 55724M | 459788M | 331510M | 1344619M | Total Assets ($) | 1525302M | 842045M |

© RMA 2024  M = $ thousand  MM = $ million
See Pages viii through xx for Explanation of Ratios and Data

## OTHER SERVICES—Parking Lots and Garages  NAICS 812930

### Comparative Historical Data / Current Data Sorted by Sales

| | | | | Type of Statement | | | | | | |
|---|---|---|---|---|---|---|---|---|---|---|
| | | 7 | 6 | Unqualified | | | | | 1 | 5 |
| | 5 | 9 | 2 | Reviewed | | | | | 2 | |
| | 1 | 3 | 1 | Compiled | | | | | | |
| | 4 | 3 | 5 | Tax Returns | 1 | | 1 | | 1 | |
| | 25 | 7 | 35 | Other | 1 | 2 | | 5 | | |
| | 4/1/21-3/31/22 ALL | 4/1/22-3/31/23 ALL | 4/1/23-3/31/24 ALL | | 3 | 7 | 3 | | | 10 |
| | | | | | | 7 (4/1-9/30/23) | | | 42 (10/1/23-3/31/24) | |
| | | | | | 0-1MM | 1-3MM | 3-5MM | 5-10MM | 10-25MM | 25MM & OVER |
| | 42 | 65 | 49 | NUMBER OF STATEMENTS | 5 | 9 | 4 | 5 | 11 | 15 |
| | % | % | % | ASSETS | % | % | % | % | % | % |
| | 24.2 | 25.3 | 20.0 | Cash & Equivalents | | | | | 20.4 | 18.4 |
| | 19.2 | 11.2 | 15.3 | Trade Receivables (net) | | | | | 10.5 | 27.3 |
| | .3 | .7 | .4 | Inventory | | | | | .0 | 1.4 |
| | 4.9 | 6.1 | 7.1 | All Other Current | | | | | 9.5 | 5.0 |
| | 48.6 | 43.3 | 42.8 | Total Current | | | | | 40.4 | 52.1 |
| | 33.3 | 32.1 | 33.3 | Fixed Assets (net) | | | | | 40.1 | 20.1 |
| | 11.4 | 11.1 | 8.4 | Intangibles (net) | | | | | 5.8 | 12.6 |
| | 6.7 | 13.5 | 15.5 | All Other Non-Current | | | | | 13.7 | 15.2 |
| | 100.0 | 100.0 | 100.0 | Total | | | | | 100.0 | 100.0 |
| | | | | LIABILITIES | | | | | | |
| | 5.9 | 11.2 | 2.2 | Notes Payable-Short Term | | | | | 1.4 | 2.4 |
| | 2.5 | 4.8 | 4.1 | Cur. Mat.-L.T.D. | | | | | 2.1 | 4.0 |
| | 9.8 | 6.0 | 7.9 | Trade Payables | | | | | 11.9 | 14.1 |
| | .1 | .0 | .0 | Income Taxes Payable | | | | | .0 | .0 |
| | 15.1 | 14.8 | 15.4 | All Other Current | | | | | 14.1 | 23.6 |
| | 33.3 | 36.9 | 29.6 | Total Current | | | | | 29.6 | 44.1 |
| | 37.5 | 45.1 | 45.2 | Long-Term Debt | | | | | 53.0 | 23.7 |
| | .0 | .0 | .0 | Deferred Taxes | | | | | .0 | .1 |
| | 2.4 | 5.0 | 7.8 | All Other Non-Current | | | | | 4.5 | 8.6 |
| | 26.7 | 13.1 | 17.3 | Net Worth | | | | | 12.9 | 23.5 |
| | 100.0 | 100.0 | 100.0 | Total Liabilities & Net Worth | | | | | 100.0 | 100.0 |
| | | | | INCOME DATA | | | | | | |
| | 100.0 | 100.0 | 100.0 | Net Sales | | | | | 100.0 | 100.0 |
| | | | | Gross Profit | | | | | | |
| | 80.3 | 81.3 | 81.9 | Operating Expenses | | | | | 76.3 | 93.5 |
| | 19.7 | 18.7 | 18.1 | Operating Profit | | | | | 23.7 | 6.5 |
| | 6.4 | 5.5 | 8.0 | All Other Expenses (net) | | | | | 7.1 | 1.8 |
| | 13.3 | 13.1 | 10.1 | Profit Before Taxes | | | | | 16.7 | 4.8 |
| | | | | RATIOS | | | | | | |
| | 4.4 | 4.6 | 2.2 | | | | | | 2.4 | 2.0 |
| | 1.4 | 1.7 | 1.3 | Current | | | | | 1.6 | 1.1 |
| | .8 | .9 | .8 | | | | | | .6 | 1.0 |
| | 3.8 | 3.6 | 2.0 | | | | | | 2.4 | 1.3 |
| | 1.2 | 1.5 | 1.1 | Quick | | | | | 1.4 | 1.0 |
| | .7 | .6 | .6 | | | | | | .3 | .8 |
| 2 | 213.4 | 0 UND | 1 579.4 | | | | | 0 | UND | 26 14.3 |
| 24 | 15.4 | 9 41.7 | 16 23.4 | Sales/Receivables | | | | 5 | 73.5 | 38 9.6 |
| 57 | 6.4 | 36 10.2 | 47 7.8 | | | | | 29 | 12.4 | 54 6.7 |
| | | | | Cost of Sales/Inventory | | | | | | |
| | | | | Cost of Sales/Payables | | | | | | |
| | 4.4 | 4.8 | 6.8 | | | | | | 6.2 | 7.0 |
| | 19.9 | 16.6 | 39.7 | Sales/Working Capital | | | | | 13.6 | 67.3 |
| | -18.3 | -42.1 | -60.1 | | | | | | -7.6 | -203.4 |
| | 37.2 | 21.6 | 30.8 | | | | | | | 53.7 |
| (28) | 16.4 | (42) 7.1 | (32) 6.6 | EBIT/Interest | | | | | (13) | 9.9 |
| | 6.5 | 1.5 | 2.3 | | | | | | | 6.1 |
| | | 24.7 | | Net Profit + Depr., Dep., | | | | | | |
| | | (11) 3.9 | | Amort./Cur. Mat. L/T/D | | | | | | |
| | | 1.2 | | | | | | | | |
| | .3 | .2 | .2 | | | | | | .1 | .2 |
| | 1.6 | 1.9 | 2.2 | Fixed/Worth | | | | | 2.3 | 1.1 |
| | NM | -1.4 | -.8 | | | | | | -2.1 | -1.6 |
| | 1.1 | .9 | 1.3 | | | | | | 1.6 | 1.6 |
| | 2.8 | 3.4 | 4.3 | Debt/Worth | | | | | 2.9 | 7.5 |
| | -94.2 | -4.7 | -4.8 | | | | | | -3.2 | -5.1 |
| | 147.0 | 41.2 | 71.1 | % Profit Before Taxes/Tangible | | | | | | 92.8 |
| (31) | 29.2 | (36) 25.5 | (30) 35.8 | Net Worth | | | | | (10) | 64.6 |
| | 7.4 | 4.4 | 9.4 | | | | | | | 36.0 |
| | 28.2 | 22.3 | 20.8 | % Profit Before Taxes/Total | | | | | 18.5 | 18.8 |
| | 11.3 | 10.9 | 11.5 | Assets | | | | | 7.8 | 16.9 |
| | 3.8 | .3 | 1.9 | | | | | | 4.3 | 5.8 |
| | 43.9 | 86.0 | 95.6 | | | | | | 123.6 | 67.7 |
| | 11.2 | 18.1 | 16.2 | Sales/Net Fixed Assets | | | | | 3.1 | 22.8 |
| | .6 | .7 | .6 | | | | | | .1 | 9.7 |
| | 3.2 | 3.8 | 3.5 | | | | | | 3.0 | 3.7 |
| | 1.3 | 1.6 | 1.8 | Sales/Total Assets | | | | | .7 | 2.7 |
| | .5 | .4 | .3 | | | | | | .1 | 1.6 |
| | .8 | .6 | .7 | | | | | | | .3 |
| (30) | 1.5 | (42) 1.6 | (29) 1.6 | % Depr., Dep., Amort./Sales | | | | | (10) | 1.0 |
| | 4.3 | 5.4 | 19.2 | | | | | | | 2.6 |
| | | 1.2 | | % Officers', Directors' | | | | | | |
| | | (11) 4.2 | | Owners' Comp/Sales | | | | | | |
| | | 5.1 | | | | | | | | |
| | 1246231M | 3414691M | 3921562M | Net Sales ($) | 2679M | 18963M | 15739M | 41196M | 178728M | 3664257M |
| | 1188573M | 2146573M | 2198671M | Total Assets ($) | 17523M | 109925M | 7534M | 135650M | 487211M | 1440828M |

© RMA 2024  
M = $ thousand    MM = $ million  
See Pages viii through xx for Explanation of Ratios and Data

## OTHER SERVICES—All Other Personal Services NAICS 812990

### Current Data Sorted by Assets | Comparative Historical Data

| | | | | | | | Type of Statement | | |
|---|---|---|---|---|---|---|---|---|---|
| | 1 | 1 | 1 | | 2 | 4 | Unqualified | 10 | 7 |
| | | 2 | 2 | | | | Reviewed | 5 | 1 |
| | | 2 | 2 | | | | Compiled | | |
| | 14 | 19 | 8 | 1 | | | Tax Returns | 14 | 8 |
| | 27 | 44 | 28 | 16 | 4 | | Other | 106 | 64 |
| | | 16 (4/1-9/30/23) | | 160 (10/1/23-3/31/24) | | | | 140 | 99 |
| | | | | | | | | 4/1/19- | 4/1/20- |
| | | | | | | | | 3/31/20 | 3/31/21 |
| | 0-500M | 500M-2MM | 2-10MM | 10-50MM | 50-100MM | 100-250MM | | ALL | ALL |
| | 41 | 66 | 41 | 18 | 6 | 4 | NUMBER OF STATEMENTS | 275 | 179 |
| | % | % | % | % | % | % | ASSETS | % | % |
| | 42.4 | 30.9 | 24.2 | 25.5 | | | Cash & Equivalents | 25.5 | 33.9 |
| | 7.2 | 12.4 | 17.1 | 13.2 | | | Trade Receivables (net) | 12.5 | 9.7 |
| | 2.7 | 3.9 | 5.3 | 9.2 | | | Inventory | 5.0 | 3.1 |
| | 3.4 | 2.6 | 5.8 | 10.0 | | | All Other Current | 3.7 | 3.2 |
| | 55.8 | 49.9 | 52.3 | 57.8 | | | Total Current | 46.6 | 49.9 |
| | 24.4 | 28.6 | 32.3 | 27.0 | | | Fixed Assets (net) | 34.3 | 31.0 |
| | 9.5 | 11.5 | 5.4 | 2.5 | | | Intangibles (net) | 8.4 | 10.4 |
| | 10.3 | 10.1 | 10.0 | 12.6 | | | All Other Non-Current | 10.7 | 8.7 |
| | 100.0 | 100.0 | 100.0 | 100.0 | | | Total | 100.0 | 100.0 |
| | | | | | | | LIABILITIES | | |
| | 13.9 | 7.6 | 2.4 | 7.3 | | | Notes Payable-Short Term | 8.2 | 10.8 |
| | 4.8 | 4.0 | 2.5 | 3.3 | | | Cur. Mat.-L.T.D. | 3.3 | 4.2 |
| | 7.8 | 6.1 | 9.2 | 12.5 | | | Trade Payables | 6.6 | 5.0 |
| | .3 | .1 | .0 | .0 | | | Income Taxes Payable | .3 | .2 |
| | 28.8 | 15.0 | 13.8 | 13.2 | | | All Other Current | 21.2 | 16.8 |
| | 55.5 | 32.8 | 28.0 | 36.3 | | | Total Current | 39.7 | 36.8 |
| | 46.9 | 29.5 | 33.2 | 19.8 | | | Long-Term Debt | 35.5 | 41.5 |
| | .0 | .0 | .0 | .0 | | | Deferred Taxes | .0 | .0 |
| | 5.3 | 6.4 | 7.6 | 6.0 | | | All Other Non-Current | 9.5 | 9.5 |
| | -7.8 | 31.3 | 31.3 | 37.9 | | | Net Worth | 15.3 | 12.1 |
| | 100.0 | 100.0 | 100.0 | 100.0 | | | Total Liabilities & Net Worth | 100.0 | 100.0 |
| | | | | | | | INCOME DATA | | |
| | 100.0 | 100.0 | 100.0 | 100.0 | | | Net Sales | 100.0 | 100.0 |
| | | | | | | | Gross Profit | | |
| | 89.6 | 86.4 | 88.8 | 85.4 | | | Operating Expenses | 86.0 | 87.3 |
| | 10.4 | 13.6 | 11.2 | 14.6 | | | Operating Profit | 14.0 | 12.7 |
| | .7 | 1.7 | 5.1 | 5.0 | | | All Other Expenses (net) | 2.4 | .2 |
| | 9.7 | 11.9 | 6.1 | 9.6 | | | Profit Before Taxes | 11.6 | 12.5 |
| | | | | | | | RATIOS | | |
| | 4.2 | 3.8 | 4.8 | 2.7 | | | | 3.6 | 4.2 |
| | 1.1 | 1.3 | 1.9 | 1.7 | | | Current | 1.3 | 1.6 |
| | .5 | .8 | .7 | 1.1 | | | | .6 | .8 |
| | 4.1 | 3.4 | 4.7 | 2.5 | | | | 3.1 | 3.6 |
| | 1.0 | 1.1 | 1.6 | 1.3 | | | Quick | .9 | 1.4 |
| | .3 | .5 | .5 | .3 | | | | .4 | .7 |
| 0 | UND | 0 UND | 0 UND | 1 359.7 | | | | 0 UND | 0 UND |
| 0 | UND | 0 UND | 16 23.0 | 10 37.0 | | | Sales/Receivables | 0 UND | 0 UND |
| 3 | 115.9 | 17 21.7 | 49 7.5 | 36 10.2 | | | | 23 15.6 | 22 16.9 |
| | | | | | | | Cost of Sales/Inventory | | |
| | | | | | | | Cost of Sales/Payables | | |
| | 12.3 | 6.1 | 3.7 | 4.8 | | | | 9.5 | 6.2 |
| | 224.0 | 29.4 | 11.6 | 10.0 | | | Sales/Working Capital | 42.4 | 17.6 |
| | -15.5 | -34.8 | -12.5 | 42.6 | | | | -21.0 | -31.8 |
| | 11.0 | 23.4 | 29.8 | 127.2 | | | | 33.8 | 49.2 |
| (22) | 4.5 | (48) 12.0 | (20) 8.6 | (13) 4.9 | | | EBIT/Interest | (186) 8.9 | (120) 9.4 |
| | .8 | 2.8 | .1 | .8 | | | | 3.3 | 2.1 |
| | | | | | | | Net Profit + Depr., Dep., | 38.5 | |
| | | | | | | | Amort./Cur. Mat. L/T/D | (15) 10.5 | |
| | | | | | | | | 3.9 | |
| | .0 | .1 | .1 | .0 | | | | .1 | .1 |
| | 3.2 | 1.2 | .4 | .3 | | | Fixed/Worth | 1.3 | 1.1 |
| | -.7 | -1.7 | -60.0 | 2.9 | | | | -6.1 | -12.5 |
| | .6 | .6 | .4 | .6 | | | | .7 | 1.1 |
| | 44.0 | 3.9 | 4.0 | 1.2 | | | Debt/Worth | 3.5 | 3.9 |
| | -2.5 | -7.0 | -11.7 | 5.5 | | | | -7.1 | -5.3 |
| | 246.4 | 109.7 | 59.2 | 57.2 | | | % Profit Before Taxes/Tangible | 184.7 | 167.9 |
| (22) | 78.0 | (42) 61.3 | (29) 31.0 | (16) 21.3 | | | Net Worth | (189) 68.2 | (121) 65.2 |
| | 28.0 | 22.0 | 6.5 | 7.1 | | | | 24.2 | 24.0 |
| | 96.4 | 45.9 | 20.3 | 16.6 | | | % Profit Before Taxes/Total | 59.6 | 47.9 |
| | 36.9 | 19.2 | 4.1 | 6.1 | | | Assets | 20.7 | 20.4 |
| | 2.8 | 3.8 | -.6 | 1.0 | | | | 5.1 | 2.9 |
| | UND | 79.7 | 177.6 | 230.3 | | | | 104.8 | 101.0 |
| | 39.5 | 18.0 | 22.6 | 63.8 | | | Sales/Net Fixed Assets | 19.0 | 15.8 |
| | 15.9 | 4.2 | 1.5 | .6 | | | | 4.6 | 3.7 |
| | 7.6 | 3.8 | 2.8 | 2.3 | | | | 5.4 | 4.1 |
| | 5.1 | 2.4 | 1.3 | 1.2 | | | Sales/Total Assets | 3.0 | 2.4 |
| | 3.4 | 1.6 | .6 | .4 | | | | 1.2 | 1.2 |
| | .3 | .5 | .5 | .1 | | | | .9 | .4 |
| (12) | 1.5 | (39) 1.3 | (21) 2.4 | (12) .8 | | | % Depr., Dep., Amort./Sales | (142) 2.4 | (94) 2.7 |
| | 2.6 | 5.9 | 14.2 | 1.1 | | | | 5.5 | 7.3 |
| | 6.2 | 1.5 | | | | | % Officers', Directors' | 2.7 | 2.2 |
| (13) | 7.1 | (29) 3.5 | | | | | Owners' Comp/Sales | (106) 6.3 | (75) 6.6 |
| | 12.9 | 6.5 | | | | | | 12.0 | 12.0 |
| | 34292M | 233264M | 396997M | 652700M | 471722M | 256992M | Net Sales ($) | 4648363M | 1753215M |
| | 7127M | 78050M | 168693M | 410579M | 438095M | 608316M | Total Assets ($) | 1576044M | 1018838M |

© RMA 2024    M = $ thousand    MM = $ million
See Pages viii through xx for Explanation of Ratios and Data

## OTHER SERVICES—All Other Personal Services  NAICS 812990

| Comparative Historical Data | | | | | Current Data Sorted by Sales | | | | | |
|---|---|---|---|---|---|---|---|---|---|---|
| 6 | 9 | 9 | Type of Statement Unqualified | | | | 3 | 3 | | 6 |
| 2 | 3 | 2 | Reviewed | | | 1 | 1 | 1 | | |
| 9 | 12 | 4 | Compiled | 1 | 1 | 1 | 1 | 1 | | |
| 51 | 58 | 42 | Tax Returns | 21 | 8 | 7 | 5 | 1 | | |
| 89 | 110 | 119 | Other | 24 | 37 | 12 | 19 | 11 | 16 |
| 4/1/21-3/31/22 ALL | 4/1/22-3/31/23 ALL | 4/1/23-3/31/24 ALL | | 16 (4/1-9/30/23) | | | 160 (10/1/23-3/31/24) | | | |
| | | | | 0-1MM | 1-3MM | 3-5MM | 5-10MM | 10-25MM | 25MM & OVER |
| 157 | 192 | 176 | NUMBER OF STATEMENTS | 46 | 46 | 21 | 29 | 12 | 22 |
| % | % | % | ASSETS | % | % | % | % | % | % |
| 34.4 | 29.5 | 30.1 | Cash & Equivalents | 35.4 | 26.8 | 33.9 | 29.9 | 24.4 | 25.4 |
| 8.9 | 14.0 | 11.9 | Trade Receivables (net) | 2.3 | 8.5 | 12.3 | 22.7 | 25.9 | 16.7 |
| 3.9 | 6.1 | 4.9 | Inventory | 1.3 | 4.0 | 2.3 | 7.3 | 14.3 | 8.3 |
| 3.7 | 4.4 | 4.2 | All Other Current | 2.8 | 4.7 | 2.8 | 3.1 | 8.6 | 6.6 |
| 50.8 | 53.9 | 51.0 | Total Current | 41.8 | 44.0 | 51.2 | 63.0 | 73.2 | 56.9 |
| 34.7 | 25.6 | 28.6 | Fixed Assets (net) | 39.0 | 28.0 | 30.1 | 26.3 | 18.6 | 15.3 |
| 6.0 | 8.1 | 9.7 | Intangibles (net) | 10.3 | 12.1 | 8.1 | 3.9 | 4.5 | 15.7 |
| 8.4 | 12.4 | 10.6 | All Other Non-Current | 8.8 | 15.9 | 10.6 | 6.9 | 3.7 | 12.1 |
| 100.0 | 100.0 | 100.0 | Total | 100.0 | 100.0 | 100.0 | 100.0 | 100.0 | 100.0 |
| | | | LIABILITIES | | | | | | |
| 5.7 | 9.6 | 7.6 | Notes Payable-Short Term | 5.7 | 9.7 | 11.5 | 6.5 | 11.8 | 2.4 |
| 3.0 | 3.0 | 3.8 | Cur. Mat.-L.T.D. | 3.9 | 5.3 | 5.7 | 2.0 | .2 | 3.0 |
| 4.3 | 5.7 | 7.9 | Trade Payables | 5.9 | 4.1 | 4.4 | 15.2 | 7.8 | 14.1 |
| .3 | .2 | .1 | Income Taxes Payable | .2 | .1 | .0 | .0 | .0 | .1 |
| 21.5 | 16.4 | 17.5 | All Other Current | 23.4 | 15.1 | 21.2 | 14.9 | 13.6 | 12.6 |
| 34.8 | 34.8 | 36.9 | Total Current | 39.1 | 34.3 | 42.8 | 38.7 | 33.3 | 32.2 |
| 35.4 | 30.0 | 33.8 | Long-Term Debt | 53.1 | 31.5 | 29.1 | 26.6 | 12.9 | 23.9 |
| .0 | .1 | .0 | Deferred Taxes | .0 | .0 | .0 | .1 | .0 | .0 |
| 6.6 | 5.5 | 6.6 | All Other Non-Current | 5.9 | 10.7 | 2.5 | 4.1 | 2.1 | 8.8 |
| 23.2 | 29.6 | 22.6 | Net Worth | 1.8 | 23.6 | 25.7 | 30.6 | 51.6 | 35.0 |
| 100.0 | 100.0 | 100.0 | Total Liabilties & Net Worth | 100.0 | 100.0 | 100.0 | 100.0 | 100.0 | 100.0 |
| | | | INCOME DATA | | | | | | |
| 100.0 | 100.0 | 100.0 | Net Sales | 100.0 | 100.0 | 100.0 | 100.0 | 100.0 | 100.0 |
| | | | Gross Profit | | | | | | |
| 84.4 | 87.8 | 88.1 | Operating Expenses | 81.6 | 86.6 | 88.6 | 94.2 | 90.7 | 94.9 |
| 15.6 | 12.2 | 11.9 | Operating Profit | 18.4 | 13.4 | 11.4 | 5.8 | 9.3 | 5.1 |
| .2 | 1.6 | 2.9 | All Other Expenses (net) | 5.7 | 2.0 | .9 | 1.4 | .7 | 3.6 |
| 15.4 | 10.6 | 9.0 | Profit Before Taxes | 12.7 | 11.4 | 10.5 | 4.4 | 8.6 | 1.5 |
| | | | RATIOS | | | | | | |
| 5.7 | 5.6 | 3.7 | | 6.4 | 3.2 | 4.2 | 3.5 | 5.7 | 3.3 |
| 1.8 | 2.0 | 1.5 | Current | 1.1 | 1.1 | 1.1 | 1.9 | 2.3 | 1.8 |
| 1.0 | .9 | .7 | | .3 | .5 | .7 | .9 | 1.5 | .3 |
| 4.8 | 5.2 | 3.6 | | 6.4 | 3.1 | 4.1 | 2.6 | 5.3 | 3.1 |
| 1.6 | 1.7 | 1.2 | Quick | 1.1 | 1.0 | .9 | 1.6 | 1.9 | 1.6 |
| .6 | .6 | .4 | | .2 | .4 | .6 | .6 | 1.3 | .2 |
| 0 UND | 0 UND | 0 UND | | 0 UND | 0 UND | 0 UND | 0 UND | 0 UND | 4 87.9 |
| 0 UND | 4 93.1 | 0 UND | Sales/Receivables | 0 UND | 0 UND | 1 350.6 | 9 42.6 | 19 19.6 | 26 13.8 |
| 19 19.4 | 33 11.0 | 28 13.1 | | 0 UND | 15 24.7 | 26 13.8 | 48 7.6 | 57 6.4 | 39 9.4 |
| | | | Cost of Sales/Inventory | | | | | | |
| | | | Cost of Sales/Payables | | | | | | |
| 4.6 | 4.5 | 6.2 | | 8.3 | 6.7 | 7.5 | 5.8 | 4.2 | 6.8 |
| 11.5 | 11.8 | 22.3 | Sales/Working Capital | UND | 163.3 | 48.4 | 8.2 | 9.9 | 12.1 |
| -436.0 | -112.1 | -16.4 | | -7.1 | -15.0 | -16.2 | -55.9 | 17.1 | -6.6 |
| 31.0 | 43.2 | 22.4 | | 9.8 | 13.5 | 25.5 | 22.7 | | 44.4 |
| (99) 10.4 | (113) 9.5 | (112) 7.5 | EBIT/Interest | (22) 3.5 | (28) 6.1 | (19) 11.6 | (17) 16.4 | (17) | 5.4 |
| 3.0 | 2.0 | 1.3 | | 1.2 | 1.0 | 1.9 | 1.2 | | -.3 |
| | 14.6 | 301.4 | Net Profit + Depr., Dep., | | | | | | |
| (11) | 2.4 | (11) 18.2 | Amort./Cur. Mat. L/T/D | | | | | | |
| | 1.2 | 3.5 | | | | | | | |
| .1 | .0 | .1 | | .1 | .2 | .2 | .1 | .0 | .0 |
| 1.1 | .4 | 1.2 | Fixed/Worth | 8.1 | 4.5 | 3.2 | .2 | .2 | .1 |
| 63.3 | 6.8 | -2.6 | | -2.5 | -.8 | -1.1 | 3.3 | .5 | -2.7 |
| .5 | .4 | .6 | | .8 | .3 | .7 | .7 | .5 | .5 |
| 2.1 | 1.7 | 4.4 | Debt/Worth | 17.0 | 14.1 | 6.9 | 2.8 | .9 | 2.1 |
| -560.0 | NM | -7.1 | | -4.1 | -4.1 | -6.2 | 9.6 | 3.9 | -2.9 |
| 140.9 | 140.0 | 91.7 | % Profit Before Taxes/Tangible | 94.7 | 114.5 | 154.8 | 72.4 | 101.3 | 72.0 |
| (117) 63.2 | (144) 55.7 | (112) 42.4 | Net Worth | (26) 53.9 | (24) 39.4 | (13) 47.6 | (24) 36.0 | 62.4 | (13) 31.0 |
| 22.2 | 15.0 | 10.7 | | 12.4 | 10.4 | -18.0 | 5.2 | 21.7 | 10.8 |
| 53.7 | 49.0 | 39.9 | | 54.2 | 47.2 | 37.6 | 28.7 | 46.5 | 20.8 |
| 23.4 | 16.0 | 13.4 | % Profit Before Taxes/Total Assets | 16.1 | 13.7 | 19.3 | 5.1 | 21.1 | 6.3 |
| 4.6 | 2.2 | 1.2 | | .2 | .7 | 3.1 | .7 | 10.0 | -6.2 |
| 61.4 | 407.0 | 129.1 | | 460.8 | 91.6 | 58.3 | 142.5 | 308.7 | 340.0 |
| 10.1 | 27.7 | 26.1 | Sales/Net Fixed Assets | 10.0 | 18.1 | 19.5 | 53.8 | 36.3 | 63.8 |
| 2.3 | 5.9 | 4.2 | | 1.4 | 4.4 | 4.8 | 9.4 | 9.3 | 4.2 |
| 4.5 | 4.7 | 4.2 | | 5.2 | 3.8 | 3.5 | 4.2 | 4.2 | 5.0 |
| 2.1 | 2.3 | 2.3 | Sales/Total Assets | 2.4 | 1.8 | 2.7 | 2.8 | 2.9 | 1.6 |
| .9 | 1.1 | 1.1 | | .4 | 1.3 | 1.1 | 1.5 | 1.4 | .7 |
| 1.0 | .6 | .5 | | 1.6 | .7 | .3 | .3 | | .2 |
| (71) 2.9 | (90) 1.7 | (91) 1.3 | % Depr., Dep., Amort./Sales | (20) 5.4 | (21) 2.3 | (12) 1.1 | (17) .7 | (15) | .7 |
| 6.1 | 6.5 | 6.0 | | 20.0 | 6.7 | 2.3 | 2.1 | | 5.9 |
| 2.9 | 3.0 | 1.7 | | | 3.7 | 1.8 | | | |
| (58) 6.4 | (68) 4.9 | (52) 4.4 | % Officers', Directors' Owners' Comp/Sales | | (18) 6.4 | (13) 6.3 | | | |
| 10.6 | 8.5 | 7.4 | | | 10.3 | 7.3 | | | |
| 1551935M | 3519204M | 2045967M | Net Sales ($) | 22944M | 81261M | 82581M | 208903M | 202962M | 1447316M |
| 1012394M | 2029313M | 1710860M | Total Assets ($) | 40102M | 62328M | 51932M | 265195M | 95119M | 1196184M |

© RMA 2024    M = $ thousand    MM = $ million
See Pages viii through xx for Explanation of Ratios and Data

## OTHER SERVICES—Religious Organizations  NAICS 813110

### Current Data Sorted by Assets / Comparative Historical Data

| | | | | | | Type of Statement | | |
|---|---|---|---|---|---|---|---|---|
| 3 | 3 | 14 | 57 | 27 | 21 | Unqualified | 255 | 127 |
| 1 | 2 | 25 | 17 | 1 | | Reviewed | 128 | 43 |
| 5 | 4 | 35 | 12 | | | Compiled | 116 | 69 |
| | 1 | 2 | 2 | | | Tax Returns | 31 | 6 |
| 37 | 67 | 240 | 123 | 32 | 9 | Other | 794 | 556 |
| | 246 (4/1-9/30/23) | | 494 (10/1/23-3/31/24) | | | | 4/1/19-3/31/20 | 4/1/20-3/31/21 |
| 0-500M | 500M-2MM | 2-10MM | 10-50MM | 50-100MM | 100-250MM | | ALL | ALL |
| 46 | 77 | 316 | 211 | 60 | 30 | NUMBER OF STATEMENTS | 1324 | 801 |
| % | % | % | % | % | % | ASSETS | % | % |
| 68.2 | 28.7 | 17.4 | 16.3 | 21.8 | 29.3 | Cash & Equivalents | 16.4 | 20.2 |
| 1.8 | 1.8 | .7 | 1.2 | 4.4 | 4.0 | Trade Receivables (net) | 1.1 | 1.1 |
| .9 | .3 | .2 | .2 | .7 | .7 | Inventory | .2 | .2 |
| 1.5 | 2.1 | .8 | 1.2 | 4.1 | 4.6 | All Other Current | 1.3 | 1.4 |
| 72.4 | 32.9 | 19.0 | 18.9 | 31.0 | 38.6 | Total Current | 19.0 | 22.8 |
| 21.0 | 60.5 | 76.9 | 72.9 | 46.8 | 28.4 | Fixed Assets (net) | 74.5 | 69.6 |
| .6 | .8 | .3 | .3 | .1 | .3 | Intangibles (net) | .2 | .5 |
| 6.0 | 5.8 | 3.7 | 7.9 | 22.1 | 32.7 | All Other Non-Current | 6.3 | 7.1 |
| 100.0 | 100.0 | 100.0 | 100.0 | 100.0 | 100.0 | Total | 100.0 | 100.0 |
| | | | | | | LIABILITIES | | |
| 1.8 | .7 | .7 | .5 | .4 | 1.3 | Notes Payable-Short Term | 1.1 | 1.7 |
| 3.6 | 1.3 | 1.9 | .9 | .7 | .1 | Cur. Mat.-L.T.D. | 2.1 | 1.7 |
| 2.1 | .9 | .6 | .9 | 2.7 | 1.5 | Trade Payables | .9 | .9 |
| .0 | .0 | .0 | .0 | .0 | .0 | Income Taxes Payable | .0 | .1 |
| 23.3 | 3.9 | 1.7 | 3.1 | 6.4 | 15.1 | All Other Current | 3.4 | 3.9 |
| 30.7 | 6.8 | 4.8 | 5.4 | 10.1 | 18.0 | Total Current | 7.6 | 8.3 |
| 16.1 | 29.1 | 29.7 | 18.0 | 12.4 | 8.0 | Long-Term Debt | 26.6 | 25.6 |
| .0 | .0 | .0 | .0 | .0 | .0 | Deferred Taxes | .0 | .0 |
| .0 | 4.6 | 1.0 | 1.8 | 7.3 | 11.7 | All Other Non-Current | 1.9 | 1.7 |
| 53.1 | 59.5 | 64.5 | 74.8 | 70.1 | 62.3 | Net Worth | 63.9 | 64.5 |
| 100.0 | 100.0 | 100.0 | 100.0 | 100.0 | 100.0 | Total Liabilities & Net Worth | 100.0 | 100.0 |
| | | | | | | INCOME DATA | | |
| 100.0 | 100.0 | 100.0 | 100.0 | 100.0 | 100.0 | Net Sales | 100.0 | 100.0 |
| | | | | | | Gross Profit | | |
| 90.3 | 81.5 | 87.6 | 87.1 | 91.5 | 89.3 | Operating Expenses | 87.3 | 84.3 |
| 9.7 | 18.5 | 12.4 | 12.9 | 8.5 | 10.7 | Operating Profit | 12.7 | 15.7 |
| 1.9 | 5.4 | 4.4 | 1.5 | 3.2 | 3.8 | All Other Expenses (net) | 4.9 | 3.7 |
| 7.8 | 13.1 | 8.0 | 11.4 | 5.3 | 6.9 | Profit Before Taxes | 7.8 | 12.0 |
| | | | | | | RATIOS | | |
| 25.6 | 23.3 | 17.4 | 15.2 | 10.5 | 25.8 | | 10.1 | 12.8 |
| 4.4 | 6.9 | 5.3 | 5.5 | 4.1 | 5.5 | Current | 3.7 | 4.4 |
| 1.1 | 1.5 | 1.9 | 2.3 | 2.5 | 1.2 | | 1.5 | 1.7 |
| 25.4 | 21.1 | 17.0 | 14.0 | 10.4 | 25.0 | | 9.6 | 12.4 |
| 4.4 | 6.0 | 5.0 | 5.2 | 4.0 | 5.5 | Quick | 3.4 | 4.0 |
| 1.0 | 1.4 | 1.7 | 2.0 | 1.7 | 1.1 | | 1.3 | 1.7 |
| 0 UND | 0 UND | 0 UND | 0 UND | 0 UND | 0 UND | | 0 UND | 0 UND |
| 0 UND | 0 UND | 0 UND | 0 UND | 10 38.3 | 10 36.2 | Sales/Receivables | 0 UND | 0 UND |
| 0 UND | 0 UND | 0 UND | 2 228.0 | 38 9.6 | 42 8.7 | | 1 434.5 | 1 508.0 |
| | | | | | | Cost of Sales/Inventory | | |
| | | | | | | Cost of Sales/Payables | | |
| 1.5 | 1.4 | 1.7 | 1.4 | 1.3 | .5 | | 2.4 | 1.9 |
| 4.1 | 3.7 | 3.6 | 2.9 | 2.7 | 1.1 | Sales/Working Capital | 4.9 | 3.5 |
| 283.8 | 19.8 | 11.2 | 7.7 | 6.6 | 7.0 | | 17.4 | 9.6 |
| 7.1 | 5.7 | 4.8 | 10.6 | 47.7 | 10.4 | | 5.1 | 7.8 |
| (15) 1.8 | (39) 1.8 | (226) 2.0 | (144) 2.7 | (38) 5.9 | (15) 5.4 | EBIT/Interest | (945) 2.2 | (518) 3.1 |
| .0 | -.5 | .3 | .4 | -.3 | -8.6 | | .8 | 1.3 |
| | | | | | | Net Profit + Depr., Dep., Amort./Cur. Mat. L/T/D | | |
| .0 | .5 | .9 | .7 | .2 | .1 | | .9 | .8 |
| .1 | 1.1 | 1.2 | 1.0 | .6 | .2 | Fixed/Worth | 1.2 | 1.1 |
| 1.1 | 2.0 | 1.7 | 1.3 | 1.0 | .7 | | 1.7 | 1.6 |
| .0 | .1 | .2 | .1 | .1 | .1 | | .2 | .2 |
| .3 | .5 | .5 | .2 | .4 | .2 | Debt/Worth | .5 | .4 |
| 3.6 | 1.6 | 1.0 | .5 | .8 | 1.4 | | 1.0 | 1.0 |
| 65.5 | 18.1 | 8.7 | 8.0 | 7.3 | 5.5 | | 7.8 | 11.2 |
| (42) 15.3 | (70) 6.1 | (308) 2.1 | (207) 3.4 | 2.4 | (29) 3.8 | % Profit Before Taxes/Tangible Net Worth | (1301) 2.6 | (790) 4.3 |
| 3.4 | -1.0 | -1.6 | -.2 | -1.4 | -.1 | | -.5 | .6 |
| 27.0 | 13.0 | 5.1 | 6.0 | 6.2 | 3.7 | % Profit Before Taxes/Total Assets | 4.7 | 6.3 |
| 8.9 | 3.6 | 1.4 | 2.1 | 1.5 | 1.5 | | 1.6 | 2.6 |
| -3.7 | -1.1 | -1.0 | -.1 | -.8 | -.3 | | -.4 | .4 |
| UND | 7.1 | .6 | .6 | 2.7 | 12.2 | | .7 | .8 |
| UND | .5 | .4 | .4 | .7 | 1.6 | Sales/Net Fixed Assets | .4 | .4 |
| 3.9 | .3 | .3 | .2 | .2 | .4 | | .2 | .2 |
| 5.3 | .8 | .5 | .4 | .5 | .4 | | .5 | .5 |
| 1.6 | .4 | .3 | .3 | .3 | .3 | Sales/Total Assets | .3 | .3 |
| .9 | .3 | .2 | .2 | .2 | .1 | | .2 | .2 |
| | 2.4 | 4.1 | 4.8 | 1.4 | 1.0 | | 4.6 | 3.8 |
| | (23) 8.2 | (138) 8.7 | (136) 8.8 | (47) 5.7 | (19) 2.4 | % Depr., Dep., Amort./Sales | (738) 8.6 | (368) 8.1 |
| | 12.8 | 13.1 | 13.5 | 10.4 | 4.8 | | 12.4 | 13.1 |
| | | 7.7 | 3.5 | | | | 4.2 | 6.1 |
| | (18) 14.2 | (14) 28.4 | | | | % Officers', Directors' Owners' Comp/Sales | (114) 9.6 | (62) 16.2 |
| | | 23.2 | 41.1 | | | | 20.9 | 32.3 |
| 19068M | 64593M | 597074M | 1627641M | 2418300M | 1310356M | Net Sales ($) | 8595413M | 5200324M |
| 10546M | 94665M | 1642496M | 4483482M | 4325413M | 4518873M | Total Assets ($) | 23766061M | 14477670M |

© RMA 2024

M = $ thousand   MM = $ million
See Pages viii through xx for Explanation of Ratios and Data

## OTHER SERVICES—Religious Organizations  NAICS 813110

| Comparative Historical Data | | | | | Current Data Sorted by Sales | | | | | |
|---|---|---|---|---|---|---|---|---|---|---|
| 125 | 129 | 125 | **Type of Statement** | | 5 | 13 | 8 | 29 | 40 | 30 |
| 47 | 42 | 46 | Unqualified | | | | | | | |
| 52 | 61 | 56 | Reviewed | | 6 | 18 | 11 | 8 | 2 | 1 |
| 3 | 11 | 5 | Compiled | | 19 | 20 | 7 | 7 | 3 | 1 |
| 498 | 564 | 508 | Tax Returns | | 2 | 1 | 2 | | | |
| 4/1/21- | 4/1/22- | 4/1/23- | Other | | 179 | 165 | 64 | 56 | 19 | 25 |
| 3/31/22 | 3/31/23 | 3/31/24 | | | | 246 (4/1-9/30/23) | | 494 (10/1/23-3/31/24) | | |
| ALL | ALL | ALL | | | 0-1MM | 1-3MM | 3-5MM | 5-10MM | 10-25MM | 25MM & OVER |
| 725 | 807 | 740 | **NUMBER OF STATEMENTS** | | 211 | 217 | 92 | 100 | 64 | 56 |
| % | % | % | **ASSETS** | | % | % | % | % | % | % |
| 21.9 | 23.8 | 22.3 | Cash & Equivalents | | 25.6 | 18.7 | 22.1 | 20.8 | 20.0 | 28.7 |
| 1.2 | 1.4 | 1.5 | Trade Receivables (net) | | .6 | .8 | 1.7 | 1.8 | 2.3 | 5.3 |
| .1 | .3 | .3 | Inventory | | .1 | .0 | .7 | .4 | .1 | 1.4 |
| 1.1 | 1.0 | 1.5 | All Other Current | | 1.1 | .7 | 1.4 | 1.9 | 3.0 | 4.3 |
| 24.3 | 26.6 | 25.5 | Total Current | | 27.4 | 20.2 | 26.0 | 24.9 | 25.4 | 39.7 |
| 70.4 | 65.8 | 66.2 | Fixed Assets (net) | | 67.8 | 75.8 | 67.7 | 63.5 | 52.8 | 40.7 |
| .3 | .3 | .4 | Intangibles (net) | | .4 | .1 | .7 | .6 | .0 | .9 |
| 5.0 | 7.3 | 7.9 | All Other Non-Current | | 4.5 | 4.0 | 5.6 | 11.0 | 21.9 | 18.7 |
| 100.0 | 100.0 | 100.0 | Total | | 100.0 | 100.0 | 100.0 | 100.0 | 100.0 | 100.0 |
| | | | **LIABILITIES** | | | | | | | |
| 1.8 | 1.6 | .7 | Notes Payable-Short Term | | .9 | .7 | .6 | .4 | .3 | 1.2 |
| 1.4 | 1.2 | 1.5 | Cur. Mat.-L.T.D. | | 2.3 | 1.4 | 1.3 | 1.0 | .8 | .6 |
| .8 | .9 | 1.0 | Trade Payables | | .6 | .4 | .9 | 1.2 | 1.7 | 3.8 |
| .0 | .0 | .0 | Income Taxes Payable | | .0 | .0 | .0 | .0 | .0 | .0 |
| 3.6 | 4.6 | 4.6 | All Other Current | | 6.8 | 1.8 | 2.2 | 7.7 | 3.6 | 6.4 |
| 7.6 | 8.2 | 7.8 | Total Current | | 10.6 | 4.3 | 5.0 | 10.3 | 6.4 | 12.0 |
| 26.4 | 23.4 | 23.2 | Long-Term Debt | | 26.3 | 27.8 | 22.5 | 19.8 | 14.4 | 10.3 |
| .0 | .0 | .0 | Deferred Taxes | | .0 | .0 | .0 | .0 | .0 | .0 |
| 1.2 | 2.4 | 2.5 | All Other Non-Current | | 1.6 | 1.2 | 3.4 | 2.1 | 6.2 | 5.9 |
| 64.7 | 65.9 | 66.6 | Net Worth | | 61.4 | 66.7 | 69.2 | 67.8 | 73.0 | 71.8 |
| 100.0 | 100.0 | 100.0 | Total Liabilties & Net Worth | | 100.0 | 100.0 | 100.0 | 100.0 | 100.0 | 100.0 |
| | | | **INCOME DATA** | | | | | | | |
| 100.0 | 100.0 | 100.0 | Net Sales | | 100.0 | 100.0 | 100.0 | 100.0 | 100.0 | 100.0 |
| | | | Gross Profit | | | | | | | |
| 81.5 | 86.8 | 87.4 | Operating Expenses | | 83.4 | 89.2 | 81.1 | 90.0 | 93.7 | 94.0 |
| 18.5 | 13.2 | 12.6 | Operating Profit | | 16.6 | 10.8 | 18.9 | 10.0 | 6.3 | 6.0 |
| 3.1 | 4.2 | 3.4 | All Other Expenses (net) | | 6.2 | 3.8 | 2.4 | 1.0 | 1.1 | .0 |
| 15.4 | 9.0 | 9.2 | Profit Before Taxes | | 10.5 | 7.0 | 16.5 | 9.1 | 5.2 | 6.0 |
| | | | **RATIOS** | | | | | | | |
| 15.6 | 18.1 | 16.6 | | | 18.1 | 24.6 | 22.0 | 13.9 | 8.2 | 11.0 |
| 5.2 | 5.1 | 5.3 | Current | | 4.1 | 5.8 | 9.0 | 5.9 | 3.8 | 4.0 |
| 2.2 | 1.8 | 1.9 | | | 1.0 | 2.3 | 3.9 | 2.6 | 1.9 | 2.2 |
| 15.4 | 16.4 | 15.5 | | | 18.0 | 18.6 | 21.1 | 13.7 | 7.9 | 8.0 |
| 5.0 | 4.7 | 4.9 | Quick | | 3.7 | 5.5 | 7.6 | 5.7 | 3.4 | 3.7 |
| 2.1 | 1.6 | 1.7 | | | 1.0 | 2.2 | 3.5 | 2.6 | 1.3 | 1.5 |
| 0 UND | 0 UND | 0 UND | | | 0 UND | 0 UND | 0 UND | 0 UND | 0 UND | 0 999.8 |
| 0 UND | 0 UND | 0 UND | Sales/Receivables | | 0 UND | 0 UND | 0 UND | 0 UND | 1 273.9 | 10 37.7 |
| 1 719.4 | 1 382.7 | 1 351.8 | | | 0 UND | 0 UND | 3 128.7 | 2 187.5 | 23 15.6 | 38 9.6 |
| | | | Cost of Sales/Inventory | | | | | | | |
| | | | Cost of Sales/Payables | | | | | | | |
| 1.8 | 1.6 | 1.5 | | | 1.5 | 1.5 | 1.4 | 1.4 | 1.6 | 1.5 |
| 3.2 | 3.2 | 3.0 | Sales/Working Capital | | 4.2 | 3.1 | 2.5 | 2.9 | 3.4 | 2.8 |
| 7.3 | 8.6 | 10.4 | | | UND | 7.7 | 5.6 | 7.8 | 8.6 | 8.7 |
| 10.2 | 6.4 | 6.8 | | | 4.5 | 3.8 | 12.8 | 18.4 | 11.4 | 28.2 |
| (484) 4.1 | (503) 2.3 | (477) 2.2 | EBIT/Interest | | (126) 1.9 | (146) 1.8 | (62) 4.5 | (61) 2.4 | (48) 1.7 | (34) 7.8 |
| 1.8 | .5 | .1 | | | .1 | -.1 | 1.1 | .1 | -4.2 | .4 |
| | | | Net Profit + Depr., Dep., Amort./Cur. Mat. L/T/D | | | | | | | |
| .8 | .6 | .7 | | | .7 | .9 | .7 | .6 | .3 | .2 |
| 1.1 | 1.0 | 1.0 | Fixed/Worth | | 1.2 | 1.1 | 1.0 | .9 | .7 | .6 |
| 1.6 | 1.5 | 1.5 | | | 1.8 | 1.7 | 1.3 | 1.3 | 1.1 | .9 |
| .1 | .1 | .1 | | | .1 | .1 | .1 | .1 | .1 | .1 |
| .4 | .4 | .4 | Debt/Worth | | .4 | .4 | .4 | .3 | .3 | .3 |
| 1.0 | .9 | .9 | | | 1.1 | .9 | .8 | .7 | .6 | .7 |
| 14.1 | 10.3 | 9.8 | % Profit Before Taxes/Tangible Net Worth | | 11.2 | 7.7 | 15.7 | 8.0 | 7.6 | 10.8 |
| (710) 6.3 | (786) 2.8 | (716) 3.3 | | | (202) 3.2 | (211) 1.8 | (89) 7.1 | (96) 2.8 | (63) 2.5 | (55) 4.1 |
| 1.6 | -.9 | -.8 | | | -.6 | -1.6 | .3 | -1.1 | -2.2 | .7 |
| 8.9 | 6.6 | 6.5 | % Profit Before Taxes/Total Assets | | 7.4 | 4.8 | 9.7 | 4.8 | 6.1 | 6.6 |
| 3.9 | 1.9 | 1.8 | | | 1.7 | 1.3 | 4.9 | 1.5 | 1.1 | 3.2 |
| 1.0 | -.7 | -.8 | | | -.9 | -.9 | .2 | -.7 | -1.8 | .4 |
| .8 | 1.1 | 1.0 | | | 1.0 | .6 | .9 | 1.1 | 1.7 | 7.5 |
| .4 | .4 | .5 | Sales/Net Fixed Assets | | .3 | .4 | .5 | .5 | .7 | 1.9 |
| .2 | .2 | .2 | | | .2 | .2 | .3 | .4 | .5 | .7 |
| .5 | .5 | .5 | | | .5 | .5 | .6 | .5 | .5 | 1.1 |
| .3 | .3 | .3 | Sales/Total Assets | | .3 | .3 | .4 | .3 | .4 | .5 |
| .2 | .2 | .2 | | | .2 | .2 | .2 | .2 | .2 | .4 |
| 3.5 | 3.2 | 3.6 | | | 4.4 | 5.2 | 2.4 | 4.0 | 3.4 | .9 |
| (333) 8.1 | (384) 7.3 | (372) 7.6 | % Depr., Dep., Amort./Sales | | (64) 8.7 | (87) 10.3 | (49) 6.3 | (72) 7.7 | (54) 7.5 | (46) 2.5 |
| 12.4 | 11.4 | 12.4 | | | 15.0 | 15.3 | 9.7 | 13.1 | 11.7 | 6.3 |
| 8.4 | 5.6 | 6.9 | % Officers', Directors' Owners' Comp/Sales | | 10.0 | 4.2 | | | | |
| (43) 17.8 | (70) 11.8 | (49) 17.8 | | | (21) 17.8 | (12) 15.4 | | | | |
| 29.9 | 20.3 | 32.1 | | | 26.1 | 23.8 | | | | |
| 4669532M | 6026495M | 6037032M | Net Sales ($) | | 114232M | 386434M | 354818M | 714067M | 1036467M | 3431014M |
| 12002683M | 15972649M | 15075475M | Total Assets ($) | | 541114M | 1648508M | 1404573M | 2964624M | 3483486M | 5033170M |

M = $ thousand   MM = $ million
See Pages viii through xx for Explanation of Ratios and Data
© RMA 2024

# OTHER SERVICES—Grantmaking Foundations  NAICS 813211

| | | | Current Data Sorted by Assets | | | | Comparative Historical Data | |
|---|---|---|---|---|---|---|---|---|
| | | | | | | Type of Statement | | |
| 1 | | 1 | 18 | 5 | 10 | Unqualified | 40 | 26 |
| | | | | | | Reviewed | 1 | 1 |
| | | | | | | Compiled | 1 | 1 |
| | | | 1 | | | Tax Returns | 6 | 2 |
| 1 | 2 | 6 | 11 | 6 | 3 | Other | 30 | 17 |
| | 41 (4/1-9/30/23) | | 24 (10/1/23-3/31/24) | | | | 4/1/19-3/31/20 | 4/1/20-3/31/21 |
| 0-500M | 500M-2MM | 2-10MM | 10-50MM | 50-100MM | 100-250MM | | ALL | ALL |
| 2 | 2 | 8 | 29 | 11 | 13 | NUMBER OF STATEMENTS | 78 | 47 |
| % | % | % | % | % | % | ASSETS | % | % |
| | | | 25.1 | 41.1 | 24.6 | Cash & Equivalents | 34.7 | 32.0 |
| | | | 7.5 | 9.0 | 4.3 | Trade Receivables (net) | 8.2 | 9.0 |
| | | | .5 | 3.3 | .0 | Inventory | .7 | 1.4 |
| | | | 1.4 | 4.0 | 3.9 | All Other Current | 3.5 | 3.1 |
| | | | 34.4 | 57.4 | 32.8 | Total Current | 47.1 | 45.5 |
| | | | 34.8 | 16.0 | 22.8 | Fixed Assets (net) | 29.0 | 26.8 |
| | | | .5 | .2 | .1 | Intangibles (net) | .3 | .4 |
| | | | 30.4 | 26.4 | 44.3 | All Other Non-Current | 23.5 | 27.4 |
| | | | 100.0 | 100.0 | 100.0 | Total | 100.0 | 100.0 |
| | | | | | | LIABILITIES | | |
| | | | .7 | 1.1 | 2.0 | Notes Payable-Short Term | 1.7 | .7 |
| | | | 7.0 | 1.8 | 2.1 | Cur. Mat.-L.T.D. | 2.0 | 2.2 |
| | | | 1.4 | 3.0 | 1.3 | Trade Payables | 3.3 | 4.5 |
| | | | .0 | .0 | .0 | Income Taxes Payable | .0 | .0 |
| | | | 3.7 | 8.2 | 6.5 | All Other Current | 5.6 | 7.1 |
| | | | 12.8 | 14.1 | 12.0 | Total Current | 12.6 | 14.6 |
| | | | 17.1 | 10.8 | 21.4 | Long-Term Debt | 13.8 | 16.5 |
| | | | .0 | .1 | .0 | Deferred Taxes | .0 | .0 |
| | | | .6 | 2.1 | 4.4 | All Other Non-Current | 2.6 | 5.6 |
| | | | 69.5 | 72.9 | 62.2 | Net Worth | 71.0 | 63.3 |
| | | | 100.0 | 100.0 | 100.0 | Total Liabilities & Net Worth | 100.0 | 100.0 |
| | | | | | | INCOME DATA | | |
| | | | 100.0 | 100.0 | 100.0 | Net Sales | 100.0 | 100.0 |
| | | | | | | Gross Profit | | |
| | | | 78.3 | 86.7 | 66.2 | Operating Expenses | 85.5 | 87.7 |
| | | | 21.7 | 13.3 | 33.8 | Operating Profit | 14.5 | 12.3 |
| | | | 4.5 | 5.7 | 7.7 | All Other Expenses (net) | 4.4 | 3.7 |
| | | | 17.2 | 7.6 | 26.0 | Profit Before Taxes | 10.1 | 8.6 |
| | | | | | | RATIOS | | |
| | | | 17.2 | 7.7 | 7.6 | | 16.4 | 9.1 |
| | | | 5.4 | 2.9 | 2.4 | Current | 5.1 | 3.9 |
| | | | 1.7 | 1.9 | 1.0 | | 1.8 | 2.0 |
| | | | 13.7 | 7.4 | 7.4 | | 13.2 | 7.5 |
| | | | 4.6 | 2.2 | 1.8 | Quick | 4.7 | 3.6 |
| | | | 1.2 | 1.2 | .5 | | 1.1 | 1.6 |
| | | 2 | 197.4 | 1   708.4 | 0   UND | | 0   UND | 2   187.6 |
| | | 23 | 15.7 | 51   7.1 | 11   32.9 | Sales/Receivables | 5   75.9 | 23   16.1 |
| | | 48 | 7.6 | 74   4.9 | 76   4.8 | | 45   8.1 | 41   8.9 |
| | | | | | | Cost of Sales/Inventory | | |
| | | | | | | Cost of Sales/Payables | | |
| | | | 1.0 | .7 | .6 | | .8 | .7 |
| | | | 2.5 | 1.8 | 4.6 | Sales/Working Capital | 1.9 | 1.8 |
| | | | 35.6 | 3.8 | NM | | 17.1 | 4.9 |
| | | | 9.7 | | | | 5.5 | 17.4 |
| | | | (17)  2.2 | | | EBIT/Interest | (33)  2.6 | (24)  4.0 |
| | | | 1.0 | | | | -.2 | 1.6 |
| | | | | | | Net Profit + Depr., Dep., Amort./Cur. Mat. L/T/D | | |
| | | | .1 | .1 | .0 | | .0 | .0 |
| | | | .4 | .1 | .1 | Fixed/Worth | .2 | .2 |
| | | | 1.0 | .4 | .9 | | .7 | .8 |
| | | | .0 | .1 | .2 | | .1 | .1 |
| | | | .2 | .2 | .5 | Debt/Worth | .2 | .3 |
| | | | .8 | .9 | 1.5 | | 1.0 | 1.3 |
| | | | 10.6 | 7.9 | 11.2 | | 9.8 | 11.7 |
| | | | (28)  4.6 | 1.8 | 4.0 | % Profit Before Taxes/Tangible Net Worth | (77)  2.1 | (46)  3.8 |
| | | | .6 | -3.2 | 2.0 | | -1.7 | .6 |
| | | | 6.4 | 4.6 | 10.8 | | 4.6 | 6.6 |
| | | | 1.6 | 1.6 | 1.8 | % Profit Before Taxes/Total Assets | 1.2 | 1.8 |
| | | | .4 | -3.0 | .7 | | -.9 | -.8 |
| | | | 13.6 | 20.8 | 18.3 | | 105.8 | 26.2 |
| | | | 1.3 | 6.0 | 3.6 | Sales/Net Fixed Assets | 5.9 | 4.0 |
| | | | .7 | 1.2 | .6 | | .7 | .6 |
| | | | .6 | .9 | .6 | | .7 | .8 |
| | | | .2 | .6 | .2 | Sales/Total Assets | .4 | .3 |
| | | | .1 | .2 | .1 | | .1 | .1 |
| | | | 1.1 | | .6 | | .9 | .4 |
| | | | (18)  3.1 | | (12)  2.4 | % Depr., Dep., Amort./Sales | (54)  3.4 | (34)  2.8 |
| | | | 9.0 | | 13.8 | | 10.2 | 10.3 |
| | | | | | | % Officers', Directors' Owners' Comp/Sales | | |
| 1122M | 2481M | 34958M | 339632M | 733910M | 782744M | Net Sales ($) | 1069504M | 994471M |
| 544M | 2599M | 25274M | 818330M | 858137M | 2139425M | Total Assets ($) | 2701529M | 2862370M |

M = $ thousand   MM = $ million
See Pages viii through xx for Explanation of Ratios and Data

© RMA 2024

# OTHER SERVICES—Grantmaking Foundations  NAICS 813211

| Comparative Historical Data | | | | | Current Data Sorted by Sales | | | | | |
|---|---|---|---|---|---|---|---|---|---|---|
| | | | | Type of Statement | | | | | | |
| 23 | 34 | 35 | | Unqualified | 1 | | 5 | 10 | 9 | 10 |
| 1 | | | | Reviewed | | | | | | |
| | 1 | | | Compiled | | | | | | |
| | | 1 | | Tax Returns | | 1 | | | | |
| 1 | | 1 | | Other | 3 | 6 | 4 | 3 | 5 | 8 |
| 26 4/1/21-3/31/22 ALL | 23 4/1/22-3/31/23 ALL | 29 4/1/23-3/31/24 ALL | | | 0-1MM | 41 (4/1-9/30/23) 1-3MM | 3-5MM | 24 (10/1/23-3/31/24) 5-10MM | 10-25MM | 25MM & OVER |
| 51 | 58 | 65 | | NUMBER OF STATEMENTS | 4 | 7 | 9 | 13 | 14 | 18 |
| % | % | % | | **ASSETS** | % | % | % | % | % | % |
| 29.5 | 35.5 | 31.3 | | Cash & Equivalents | | | | 23.7 | 28.1 | 41.5 |
| 6.4 | 8.9 | 8.7 | | Trade Receivables (net) | | | | 6.5 | 3.2 | 12.3 |
| 1.2 | 1.6 | 1.0 | | Inventory | | | | .9 | .0 | 2.1 |
| 4.9 | 4.9 | 2.8 | | All Other Current | | | | 1.3 | 5.2 | 3.4 |
| 42.0 | 50.9 | 43.8 | | Total Current | | | | 32.4 | 36.6 | 59.3 |
| 29.2 | 26.7 | 25.6 | | Fixed Assets (net) | | | | 27.4 | 34.2 | 16.9 |
| .5 | 1.2 | .4 | | Intangibles (net) | | | | .6 | .2 | .1 |
| 28.4 | 21.3 | 30.2 | | All Other Non-Current | | | | 39.6 | 28.9 | 23.7 |
| 100.0 | 100.0 | 100.0 | | Total | | | | 100.0 | 100.0 | 100.0 |
| | | | | **LIABILITIES** | | | | | | |
| 1.9 | .9 | 1.8 | | Notes Payable-Short Term | | | | 6.3 | .7 | .9 |
| .7 | 1.5 | 4.2 | | Cur. Mat.-L.T.D. | | | | 1.1 | 2.5 | 1.2 |
| 5.1 | 2.8 | 2.1 | | Trade Payables | | | | 2.4 | 1.5 | 3.1 |
| .1 | .0 | .0 | | Income Taxes Payable | | | | .1 | .0 | .0 |
| 5.0 | 8.4 | 7.3 | | All Other Current | | | | 1.3 | 8.4 | 8.2 |
| 12.8 | 13.6 | 15.5 | | Total Current | | | | 11.2 | 13.1 | 13.4 |
| 17.8 | 16.9 | 16.0 | | Long-Term Debt | | | | 16.8 | 25.2 | 8.6 |
| .0 | .0 | .0 | | Deferred Taxes | | | | .0 | .0 | .0 |
| 5.7 | 5.5 | 2.8 | | All Other Non-Current | | | | 1.1 | 1.1 | 3.6 |
| 63.6 | 63.9 | 65.8 | | Net Worth | | | | 70.9 | 60.5 | 74.3 |
| 100.0 | 100.0 | 100.0 | | Total Liabilities & Net Worth | | | | 100.0 | 100.0 | 100.0 |
| | | | | **INCOME DATA** | | | | | | |
| 100.0 | 100.0 | 100.0 | | Net Sales | | | | 100.0 | 100.0 | 100.0 |
| | | | | Gross Profit | | | | | | |
| 72.3 | 93.6 | 79.6 | | Operating Expenses | | | | 76.0 | 78.7 | 86.3 |
| 27.7 | 6.4 | 20.4 | | Operating Profit | | | | 24.0 | 21.3 | 13.7 |
| .8 | 3.1 | 4.7 | | All Other Expenses (net) | | | | 9.9 | 3.1 | -1.9 |
| 27.0 | 3.3 | 15.6 | | Profit Before Taxes | | | | 14.1 | 18.2 | 15.6 |
| | | | | **RATIOS** | | | | | | |
| 8.8 | 12.0 | 11.2 | | | | | | 30.0 | 6.1 | 9.1 |
| 4.4 | 4.4 | 4.0 | | Current | | | | 6.9 | 3.0 | 4.7 |
| 2.1 | 2.0 | 1.5 | | | | | | 1.2 | 1.0 | 2.4 |
| 8.5 | 10.5 | 9.8 | | | | | | 23.8 | 6.0 | 8.9 |
| 3.6 | 3.4 | 3.1 | | Quick | | | | 4.6 | 1.7 | 4.6 |
| 1.6 | 1.3 | 1.2 | | | | | | 1.0 | .6 | 2.0 |
| 0 UND | 2 191.9 | 1 650.9 | | | 4 101.2 | 0 UND | | | 6 58.5 | |
| 14 25.8 | 22 16.3 | 15 24.6 | | Sales/Receivables | 15 24.6 | 6 64.9 | | | 37 9.9 | |
| 35 10.5 | 56 6.5 | 52 7.0 | | | 64 5.7 | 43 8.5 | | | 74 4.9 | |
| | | | | Cost of Sales/Inventory | | | | | | |
| | | | | Cost of Sales/Payables | | | | | | |
| 1.6 | .6 | 1.0 | | | | | | .6 | .9 | 1.1 |
| 3.3 | 1.7 | 2.5 | | Sales/Working Capital | | | | 2.5 | 4.7 | 2.2 |
| 6.2 | 7.9 | 10.6 | | | | | | NM | NM | 4.6 |
| 94.8 | 8.3 | 11.5 | | | | | | | | 23.1 |
| (26) 7.1 | (26) -.7 | (34) 2.4 | | EBIT/Interest | | | | | (12) 5.9 | |
| 2.6 | -5.3 | -.5 | | | | | | | | -11.2 |
| | | | | Net Profit + Depr., Dep., Amort./Cur. Mat. L/T/D | | | | | | |
| .0 | .0 | .0 | | | | | | .1 | .0 | .1 |
| .3 | .3 | .2 | | Fixed/Worth | | | | .4 | .5 | .1 |
| 1.0 | .9 | .8 | | | | | | .7 | 1.0 | .4 |
| .1 | .1 | .1 | | | | | | .0 | .3 | .1 |
| .2 | .5 | .3 | | Debt/Worth | | | | .1 | .5 | .2 |
| 1.3 | 1.0 | 1.2 | | | | | | 2.4 | 1.2 | .6 |
| 22.1 | 13.0 | 14.4 | | % Profit Before Taxes/Tangible Net Worth | | | | 14.4 | 9.0 | 12.2 |
| (49) 11.5 | (55) .3 | (63) 4.0 | | | | | | 5.2 | 5.6 | 2.8 |
| 5.9 | -5.6 | .5 | | | | | | -2.3 | 1.3 | -1.9 |
| 11.4 | 5.9 | 7.8 | | % Profit Before Taxes/Total Assets | | | | 7.8 | 6.3 | 11.3 |
| 7.2 | .0 | 1.6 | | | | | | 1.2 | 3.0 | 1.4 |
| 1.5 | -3.9 | .3 | | | | | | -2.0 | .3 | -1.6 |
| 32.7 | 75.6 | 28.9 | | Sales/Net Fixed Assets | | | | 4.9 | 31.6 | 19.6 |
| 2.5 | 4.2 | 5.2 | | | | | | .9 | 1.3 | 7.0 |
| .8 | 1.1 | .9 | | | | | | .5 | .7 | 2.5 |
| 1.1 | 1.0 | .8 | | Sales/Total Assets | | | | .3 | .7 | 1.2 |
| .4 | .5 | .3 | | | | | | .2 | .4 | .9 |
| .2 | .2 | .2 | | | | | | .1 | .1 | .4 |
| .7 | .4 | .8 | | | | | | | .8 | .6 |
| (37) 2.3 | (45) 2.3 | (44) 3.0 | | % Depr., Dep., Amort./Sales | | | | (13) 5.6 | (15) 1.5 | |
| 7.3 | 9.2 | 6.7 | | | | | | | 7.7 | 3.2 |
| | | | | % Officers', Directors' Owners' Comp/Sales | | | | | | |
| 1324022M | 1277896M | 1894847M | | Net Sales ($) | 2364M | 12966M | 34422M | 86550M | 257289M | 1501256M |
| 3244175M | 2896489M | 3844309M | | Total Assets ($) | 8572M | 44071M | 250005M | 584691M | 1111218M | 1845752M |

© RMA 2024  M = $ thousand   MM = $ million
See Pages viii through xx for Explanation of Ratios and Data

# OTHER SERVICES—Voluntary Health Organizations  NAICS 813212

## Current Data Sorted by Assets | Comparative Historical Data

| | | | | | | | | | |
|---|---|---|---|---|---|---|---|---|---|
| | | | | | | | **Type of Statement** | | |
| | | | 4 | 2 | 1 | 1 | Unqualified | 19 | 12 |
| | | | | | | | Reviewed | 1 | 1 |
| | | 1 | | | | | Compiled | | |
| | | | | | | | Tax Returns | 2 | 1 |
| 4 | 4 | 7 | 8 | | | | Other | 16 | 12 |
| | 14 (4/1-9/30/23) | | 18 (10/1/23-3/31/24) | | | | | 4/1/19- | 4/1/20- |
| 0-500M | 500M-2MM | 2-10MM | 10-50MM | 50-100MM | 100-250MM | | | 3/31/20 | 3/31/21 |
| 4 | 4 | 12 | 10 | 1 | 1 | | **NUMBER OF STATEMENTS** | 38 ALL | 26 ALL |
| % | % | % | % | % | % | | **ASSETS** | % | % |
| | | 25.0 | 34.8 | | | | Cash & Equivalents | 26.6 | 30.5 |
| | | 20.0 | 14.2 | | | | Trade Receivables (net) | 19.3 | 16.3 |
| | | .1 | .2 | | | | Inventory | 2.1 | .3 |
| | | 4.5 | 9.1 | | | | All Other Current | 3.4 | 4.8 |
| | | 49.6 | 58.4 | | | | Total Current | 51.3 | 51.9 |
| | | 26.3 | 28.2 | | | | Fixed Assets (net) | 33.5 | 31.6 |
| | | 1.6 | .3 | | | | Intangibles (net) | 2.4 | .7 |
| | | 22.5 | 13.1 | | | | All Other Non-Current | 12.9 | 15.8 |
| | | 100.0 | 100.0 | | | | Total | 100.0 | 100.0 |
| | | | | | | | **LIABILITIES** | | |
| | | 3.3 | .0 | | | | Notes Payable-Short Term | 2.0 | 2.5 |
| | | .4 | .8 | | | | Cur. Mat.-L.T.D. | 2.1 | 2.0 |
| | | 6.5 | 4.8 | | | | Trade Payables | 5.8 | 6.5 |
| | | .0 | .0 | | | | Income Taxes Payable | .0 | .0 |
| | | 9.7 | 7.0 | | | | All Other Current | 9.4 | 11.2 |
| | | 19.8 | 12.5 | | | | Total Current | 19.3 | 22.2 |
| | | 6.0 | 17.4 | | | | Long-Term Debt | 8.1 | 13.3 |
| | | .0 | .0 | | | | Deferred Taxes | .0 | .0 |
| | | 10.4 | 4.7 | | | | All Other Non-Current | 3.8 | 5.3 |
| | | 63.8 | 65.3 | | | | Net Worth | 68.7 | 59.2 |
| | | 100.0 | 100.0 | | | | Total Liabilities & Net Worth | 100.0 | 100.0 |
| | | | | | | | **INCOME DATA** | | |
| | | 100.0 | 100.0 | | | | Net Sales | 100.0 | 100.0 |
| | | | | | | | Gross Profit | | |
| | | 94.2 | 84.6 | | | | Operating Expenses | 98.3 | 94.0 |
| | | 5.8 | 15.4 | | | | Operating Profit | 1.7 | 6.0 |
| | | -2.8 | .0 | | | | All Other Expenses (net) | -.8 | -.4 |
| | | 8.6 | 15.4 | | | | Profit Before Taxes | 2.5 | 6.4 |
| | | | | | | | **RATIOS** | | |
| | | 4.0 | 16.8 | | | | | 5.5 | 5.7 |
| | | 2.6 | 4.7 | | | | Current | 2.8 | 2.9 |
| | | 1.8 | 2.2 | | | | | 1.6 | 1.6 |
| | | 4.0 | 9.1 | | | | | 5.4 | 4.6 |
| | | 2.3 | 4.3 | | | | Quick | 2.6 | 2.3 |
| | | 1.6 | 2.2 | | | | | 1.5 | 1.4 |
| | 4 | 83.4 | 0 UND | | | | | 4  98.1 | 3  126.1 |
| | 40 | 9.2 | 18  20.8 | | | | Sales/Receivables | 29  12.8 | 28  13.2 |
| | 61 | 6.0 | 64  5.7 | | | | | 42  8.6 | 43  8.5 |
| | | | | | | | Cost of Sales/Inventory | | |
| | | | | | | | Cost of Sales/Payables | | |
| | | 2.8 | 1.2 | | | | | 3.2 | 3.1 |
| | | 4.7 | 3.0 | | | | Sales/Working Capital | 6.9 | 6.2 |
| | | 10.3 | 5.6 | | | | | 14.8 | 12.3 |
| | | | | | | | | 20.3 | 18.8 |
| | | | | | | | EBIT/Interest | (22) 8.6 | (13) 8.3 |
| | | | | | | | | .7 | 1.4 |
| | | | | | | | Net Profit + Depr., Dep., | | |
| | | | | | | | Amort./Cur. Mat. L/T/D | | |
| | | .1 | .1 | | | | | .1 | .1 |
| | | .2 | .6 | | | | Fixed/Worth | .5 | .4 |
| | | .6 | .7 | | | | | 1.0 | .8 |
| | | .3 | .3 | | | | | .1 | .2 |
| | | .6 | .6 | | | | Debt/Worth | .4 | .7 |
| | | 1.0 | 1.1 | | | | | .9 | 1.7 |
| | | 35.8 | 34.1 | | | | % Profit Before Taxes/Tangible | 17.2 | 27.2 |
| | | 14.5 | 20.8 | | | | Net Worth | (37) 2.4 | (25) 8.7 |
| | | -1.3 | 5.3 | | | | | -5.0 | -3.2 |
| | | 21.9 | 22.1 | | | | % Profit Before Taxes/Total | 11.7 | 21.6 |
| | | 8.2 | 12.4 | | | | Assets | 2.1 | 3.3 |
| | | -1.2 | 4.0 | | | | | -3.9 | -2.4 |
| | | 76.2 | 257.9 | | | | | 45.8 | 23.1 |
| | | 16.3 | 3.9 | | | | Sales/Net Fixed Assets | 8.7 | 10.0 |
| | | 2.2 | 2.4 | | | | | 1.2 | 1.8 |
| | | 2.0 | 1.5 | | | | | 2.5 | 2.3 |
| | | 1.6 | 1.2 | | | | Sales/Total Assets | 1.3 | 1.6 |
| | | .6 | .6 | | | | | .6 | .9 |
| | | | | | | | | .5 | .5 |
| | | | | | | | % Depr., Dep., Amort./Sales | (32) 1.4 | (20) .9 |
| | | | | | | | | 3.0 | 2.4 |
| | | | | | | | % Officers', Directors' | | |
| | | | | | | | Owners' Comp/Sales | | |
| 2553M | 10597M | 99002M | 231675M | 66739M | 54832M | | Net Sales ($) | 3852725M | 971116M |
| 572M | 5320M | 70165M | 226428M | 87964M | 137850M | | Total Assets ($) | 1190299M | 737736M |

M = $ thousand    MM = $ million
See Pages viii through xx for Explanation of Ratios and Data

© RMA 2024

## OTHER SERVICES—Voluntary Health Organizations  NAICS 813212

| Comparative Historical Data | | | | Current Data Sorted by Sales | | | | | |
|---|---|---|---|---|---|---|---|---|---|
| | | | Type of Statement | | | | | | |
| 11 | 11 | 8 | Unqualified | | | | 2 | 4 | 2 |
| | 1 | 1 | Reviewed | | | | | | |
| | | 1 | Compiled | | | 1 | | | |
| | 1 | | Tax Returns | | | | | | |
| 21 | 21 | 23 | Other | 3 | 7 | | 4 | 7 | 2 |
| 4/1/21- | 4/1/22- | 4/1/23- | | | 14 (4/1-9/30/23) | | 18 (10/1/23-3/31/24) | | |
| 3/31/22 | 3/31/23 | 3/31/24 | | 0-1MM | 1-3MM | 3-5MM | 5-10MM | 10-25MM | 25MM & OVER |
| ALL | ALL | ALL | | | | | | | |
| 32 | 34 | 32 | NUMBER OF STATEMENTS | 3 | 7 | 1 | 6 | 11 | 4 |
| % | % | % | ASSETS | % | % | % | % | % | % |
| 26.9 | 30.2 | 31.0 | Cash & Equivalents | | | | | 28.5 | |
| 16.2 | 19.4 | 15.0 | Trade Receivables (net) | | | | | 17.9 | |
| 1.3 | .8 | .5 | Inventory | | | | | .2 | |
| 4.8 | 7.9 | 6.0 | All Other Current | | | | | 10.1 | |
| 49.2 | 58.3 | 52.5 | Total Current | | | | | 56.7 | |
| 32.9 | 25.5 | 29.0 | Fixed Assets (net) | | | | | 25.4 | |
| 1.8 | .4 | .7 | Intangibles (net) | | | | | .2 | |
| 16.2 | 15.8 | 17.8 | All Other Non-Current | | | | | 17.7 | |
| 100.0 | 100.0 | 100.0 | Total | | | | | 100.0 | |
| | | | LIABILITIES | | | | | | |
| 1.5 | 2.7 | 3.0 | Notes Payable-Short Term | | | | | 1.9 | |
| 1.1 | .3 | 4.2 | Cur. Mat.-L.T.D. | | | | | .7 | |
| 5.8 | 8.6 | 7.5 | Trade Payables | | | | | 5.8 | |
| .0 | .0 | .0 | Income Taxes Payable | | | | | .0 | |
| 8.7 | 7.3 | 14.3 | All Other Current | | | | | 8.3 | |
| 17.1 | 18.9 | 29.1 | Total Current | | | | | 16.7 | |
| 12.3 | 10.6 | 13.0 | Long-Term Debt | | | | | 15.9 | |
| .1 | .0 | .0 | Deferred Taxes | | | | | .0 | |
| 4.5 | 2.2 | 8.0 | All Other Non-Current | | | | | 8.8 | |
| 66.0 | 68.3 | 50.0 | Net Worth | | | | | 58.7 | |
| 100.0 | 100.0 | 100.0 | Total Liabilities & Net Worth | | | | | 100.0 | |
| | | | INCOME DATA | | | | | | |
| 100.0 | 100.0 | 100.0 | Net Sales | | | | | 100.0 | |
| | | | Gross Profit | | | | | | |
| 93.7 | 94.2 | 92.7 | Operating Expenses | | | | | 90.3 | |
| 6.3 | 5.8 | 7.3 | Operating Profit | | | | | 9.7 | |
| -1.5 | 2.9 | -1.3 | All Other Expenses (net) | | | | | .1 | |
| 7.8 | 2.9 | 8.6 | Profit Before Taxes | | | | | 9.6 | |
| | | | RATIOS | | | | | | |
| 5.5 | 16.5 | 6.4 | | | | | | 5.4 | |
| 3.3 | 5.1 | 3.5 | Current | | | | | 3.8 | |
| 1.7 | 1.7 | 1.9 | | | | | | 2.0 | |
| 5.4 | 14.0 | 5.5 | | | | | | 4.8 | |
| 2.3 | 4.9 | 3.5 | Quick | | | | | 3.6 | |
| 1.6 | 1.3 | 1.6 | | | | | | 1.9 | |
| 21  17.0 | 0  UND | 4  87.8 | | | | | 8  45.1 | | |
| 36  10.2 | 35  10.4 | 32  11.5 | Sales/Receivables | | | | 50  7.3 | | |
| 47  7.8 | 72  5.1 | 57  6.4 | | | | | 62  5.9 | | |
| | | | Cost of Sales/Inventory | | | | | | |
| | | | Cost of Sales/Payables | | | | | | |
| 3.3 | 1.3 | 2.5 | | | | | | 1.3 | |
| 4.6 | 3.6 | 4.6 | Sales/Working Capital | | | | | 3.4 | |
| 10.2 | 10.3 | 9.8 | | | | | | 6.2 | |
| 17.2 | 144.5 | 38.4 | | | | | | | |
| (16)  10.7 | (15)  3.3 | (18)  14.8 | EBIT/Interest | | | | | | |
| 2.4 | -13.7 | 3.7 | | | | | | | |
| | | | Net Profit + Depr., Dep., Amort./Cur. Mat. L/T/D | | | | | | |
| .1 | .1 | .0 | | | | | | .1 | |
| .5 | .3 | .5 | Fixed/Worth | | | | | .5 | |
| .9 | .6 | 1.1 | | | | | | .6 | |
| .2 | .1 | .3 | | | | | | .3 | |
| .5 | .3 | .7 | Debt/Worth | | | | | .7 | |
| 1.1 | 1.3 | 1.7 | | | | | | 1.2 | |
| 25.9 | 14.1 | 30.8 | % Profit Before Taxes/Tangible Net Worth | | | | | 21.4 | |
| 7.1 | 6.3 | (29)  18.4 | | | | | | 18.4 | |
| 2.8 | -6.1 | 3.6 | | | | | | 2.0 | |
| 13.8 | 11.8 | 17.7 | % Profit Before Taxes/Total Assets | | | | | 12.4 | |
| 5.0 | 3.9 | 10.5 | | | | | | 9.8 | |
| 1.5 | -5.5 | 2.4 | | | | | | 1.5 | |
| 31.2 | 46.1 | 73.8 | | | | | | 36.9 | |
| 4.2 | 7.7 | 7.8 | Sales/Net Fixed Assets | | | | | 4.7 | |
| 2.0 | 2.1 | 2.1 | | | | | | 2.6 | |
| 1.7 | 2.2 | 2.0 | | | | | | 2.0 | |
| 1.1 | 1.1 | 1.2 | Sales/Total Assets | | | | | 1.4 | |
| .6 | .6 | .6 | | | | | | .6 | |
| .7 | .6 | .2 | | | | | | | |
| (23)  2.4 | (21)  .9 | (20)  .7 | % Depr., Dep., Amort./Sales | | | | | | |
| 4.0 | 2.7 | 3.0 | | | | | | | |
| | | | % Officers', Directors' Owners' Comp/Sales | | | | | | |
| 1005948M | 510960M | 465398M | Net Sales ($) | 1452M | 12478M | 4183M | 42913M | 187864M | 216508M |
| 1022724M | 433217M | 528299M | Total Assets ($) | 425M | 21133M | 5464M | 29084M | 193220M | 278973M |

M = $ thousand    MM = $ million
See Pages viii through xx for Explanation of Ratios and Data

© RMA 2024

# OTHER SERVICES—Other Grantmaking and Giving Services  NAICS 813219

## Current Data Sorted by Assets | Comparative Historical Data

| Type of Statement | | | | | | | |
|---|---|---|---|---|---|---|---|
| | | | | | | Unqualified | 35  17 |
| 1 | 1 | 6 | 11 | 3 | 2 | Reviewed | 1 |
| | | 1 | | | | Compiled | 1  1 |
| | | | | | | Tax Returns | 4  1 |
| 1 | 3 | 10 | 5 | 4 | 2 | Other | 23  27 |
| | 34 (4/1-9/30/23) | | 16 (10/1/23-3/31/24) | | | | 4/1/19- 4/1/20- |
| 0-500M | 500M-2MM | 2-10MM | 10-50MM | 50-100MM | 100-250MM | | 3/31/20  3/31/21 |
| 2 | 5 | 16 | 16 | 7 | 4 | NUMBER OF STATEMENTS | 63 ALL  47 ALL |

| | | | | | | | | |
|---|---|---|---|---|---|---|---|---|
| % | % | % | % | % | % | ASSETS | % | % |
| | | 27.3 | 24.7 | | | Cash & Equivalents | 36.5 | 35.3 |
| | | 21.7 | 7.3 | | | Trade Receivables (net) | 11.1 | 10.2 |
| | | 2.6 | .5 | | | Inventory | 1.3 | 2.2 |
| | | .6 | 1.4 | | | All Other Current | 1.7 | 4.5 |
| | | 52.2 | 33.9 | | | Total Current | 50.6 | 52.2 |
| | | 30.3 | 30.0 | | | Fixed Assets (net) | 31.0 | 33.3 |
| | | 1.7 | .0 | | | Intangibles (net) | .8 | 1.9 |
| | | 15.8 | 36.0 | | | All Other Non-Current | 17.5 | 12.5 |
| | | 100.0 | 100.0 | | | Total | 100.0 | 100.0 |
| | | | | | | **LIABILITIES** | | |
| | | 1.1 | .2 | | | Notes Payable-Short Term | 2.0 | 2.4 |
| | | .6 | 1.4 | | | Cur. Mat.-L.T.D. | 1.0 | 2.6 |
| | | 8.1 | 4.0 | | | Trade Payables | 4.0 | 4.6 |
| | | .0 | .7 | | | Income Taxes Payable | .0 | .0 |
| | | 5.6 | 2.6 | | | All Other Current | 7.7 | 6.9 |
| | | 15.4 | 9.0 | | | Total Current | 14.8 | 16.6 |
| | | 10.5 | 20.7 | | | Long-Term Debt | 13.7 | 15.0 |
| | | .0 | .0 | | | Deferred Taxes | .0 | .0 |
| | | 7.4 | 5.0 | | | All Other Non-Current | 5.0 | 5.7 |
| | | 66.6 | 65.3 | | | Net Worth | 66.5 | 62.7 |
| | | 100.0 | 100.0 | | | Total Liabilities & Net Worth | 100.0 | 100.0 |
| | | | | | | **INCOME DATA** | | |
| | | 100.0 | 100.0 | | | Net Sales | 100.0 | 100.0 |
| | | | | | | Gross Profit | | |
| | | 84.2 | 100.3 | | | Operating Expenses | 93.8 | 89.2 |
| | | 15.8 | -.3 | | | Operating Profit | 6.2 | 10.8 |
| | | -.3 | 1.1 | | | All Other Expenses (net) | .5 | .3 |
| | | 16.1 | -1.4 | | | Profit Before Taxes | 5.7 | 10.5 |
| | | | | | | **RATIOS** | | |
| | | 31.3 | 12.0 | | | | 14.1 | 8.6 |
| | | 7.3 | 4.7 | | | Current | 4.0 | 3.2 |
| | | 2.5 | 1.5 | | | | 1.9 | 1.8 |
| | | 31.3 | 11.8 | | | | 13.7 | 5.7 |
| | | 7.2 | 4.4 | | | Quick | 3.7 | 3.1 |
| | | 2.3 | 1.5 | | | | 1.6 | 1.6 |
| | | 1    450.4 | 2    186.4 | | | | 3    110.1 | 0    999.8 |
| | | 36    10.0 | 26    14.2 | | | Sales/Receivables | 21    17.7 | 20    18.5 |
| | | 96    3.8 | 111    3.3 | | | | 48    7.6 | 41    9.0 |
| | | | | | | Cost of Sales/Inventory | | |
| | | | | | | Cost of Sales/Payables | | |
| | | 1.2 | 1.4 | | | | 1.4 | 2.0 |
| | | 3.5 | 3.4 | | | Sales/Working Capital | 3.5 | 4.9 |
| | | 5.4 | 9.2 | | | | 12.6 | 9.2 |
| | | | 4.4 | | | | 9.6 | 22.0 |
| | | (10) | -1.1 | | | EBIT/Interest | (29)  1.7 | (26)  8.2 |
| | | | -64.8 | | | | -3.0 | 3.5 |
| | | | | | | Net Profit + Depr., Dep., Amort./Cur. Mat. L/T/D | | |
| | | .1 | .1 | | | | .0 | .0 |
| | | .3 | .4 | | | Fixed/Worth | .4 | .5 |
| | | .9 | 1.1 | | | | 1.0 | 1.0 |
| | | .2 | .1 | | | | .1 | .2 |
| | | .4 | .4 | | | Debt/Worth | .3 | .5 |
| | | .7 | 1.1 | | | | 1.1 | 1.2 |
| | | 27.9 | 2.9 | | | % Profit Before Taxes/Tangible Net Worth | 14.8 | 23.2 |
| | (15) | 15.0 | -1.5 | | | | (61)  3.5 | (45)  8.7 |
| | | -2.3 | -5.5 | | | | -3.3 | .2 |
| | | 15.2 | 2.0 | | | % Profit Before Taxes/Total Assets | 7.8 | 15.0 |
| | | 5.7 | -1.0 | | | | 1.5 | 4.4 |
| | | -3.2 | -2.8 | | | | -2.2 | .1 |
| | | 80.4 | 7.2 | | | | 66.5 | 32.6 |
| | | 8.1 | 2.6 | | | Sales/Net Fixed Assets | 5.8 | 5.2 |
| | | 1.2 | 1.1 | | | | 1.6 | 1.6 |
| | | 2.2 | 1.2 | | | | 1.7 | 2.2 |
| | | .9 | .6 | | | Sales/Total Assets | .8 | 1.2 |
| | | .5 | .2 | | | | .3 | .5 |
| | | | 1.2 | | | | .7 | .5 |
| | | (14) | 2.3 | | | % Depr., Dep., Amort./Sales | (48)  2.1 | (33)  2.0 |
| | | | 6.6 | | | | 4.2 | 3.7 |
| | | | | | | % Officers', Directors' Owners' Comp/Sales | | |
| 897M | 10764M | 77129M | 237865M | 281815M | 185605M | Net Sales ($) | 1208155M | 831807M |
| 379M | 6812M | 65340M | 378975M | 440775M | 678279M | Total Assets ($) | 1727181M | 936466M |

© RMA 2024   M = $ thousand   MM = $ million
See Pages viii through xx for Explanation of Ratios and Data

## OTHER SERVICES—Other Grantmaking and Giving Services  NAICS 813219

### Comparative Historical Data | Current Data Sorted by Sales

| | | | | Type of Statement | | | | | | |
|---|---|---|---|---|---|---|---|---|---|---|
| 13 | 26 | 24 | | Unqualified | 1 | 3 | 3 | 4 | 6 | 7 |
| 1 | 1 | 1 | | Reviewed | | | | | | |
| 1 | 1 | | | Compiled | | 1 | | | | |
| 22 | 23 | 25 | | Tax Returns | | | | | | |
| 4/1/21-3/31/22 | 4/1/22-3/31/23 | 4/1/23-3/31/24 | | Other | 4 | 4 | 7 | 4 | 2 | 4 |
| ALL | ALL | ALL | | | 34 (4/1-9/30/23) | | | 16 (10/1/23-3/31/24) | | |
| | | | | | 0-1MM | 1-3MM | 3-5MM | 5-10MM | 10-25MM | 25MM & OVER |
| 37 | 51 | 50 | NUMBER OF STATEMENTS | 5 | 8 | 10 | 8 | 8 | 11 |
| % | % | % | ASSETS | % | % | % | % | % | % |
| 44.8 | 35.4 | 32.0 | Cash & Equivalents | | | 24.4 | | | 33.6 |
| 14.5 | 14.9 | 12.5 | Trade Receivables (net) | | | 18.2 | | | 6.6 |
| 1.6 | .6 | 1.3 | Inventory | | | .7 | | | 1.2 |
| 2.0 | 3.5 | 2.2 | All Other Current | | | 1.5 | | | 2.5 |
| 62.9 | 54.4 | 48.0 | Total Current | | | 44.8 | | | 43.8 |
| 24.7 | 21.9 | 23.7 | Fixed Assets (net) | | | 20.5 | | | 24.2 |
| 3.9 | .1 | 3.2 | Intangibles (net) | | | .0 | | | 7.6 |
| 8.4 | 23.7 | 25.1 | All Other Non-Current | | | 34.7 | | | 24.4 |
| 100.0 | 100.0 | 100.0 | Total | | | 100.0 | | | 100.0 |
| | | | LIABILITIES | | | | | | |
| 2.3 | 1.4 | 3.0 | Notes Payable-Short Term | | | 1.4 | | | 1.4 |
| 1.1 | .5 | 1.0 | Cur. Mat.-L.T.D. | | | 1.2 | | | 1.1 |
| 4.9 | 4.9 | 5.2 | Trade Payables | | | 1.5 | | | 3.8 |
| .0 | .1 | .3 | Income Taxes Payable | | | 1.2 | | | .0 |
| 4.7 | 4.6 | 3.9 | All Other Current | | | 6.5 | | | 2.5 |
| 13.0 | 11.5 | 13.3 | Total Current | | | 11.7 | | | 8.9 |
| 8.5 | 10.4 | 13.2 | Long-Term Debt | | | 14.6 | | | 14.6 |
| .0 | .0 | .0 | Deferred Taxes | | | .0 | | | .0 |
| 4.6 | 8.0 | 7.9 | All Other Non-Current | | | 12.5 | | | 12.6 |
| 73.8 | 70.1 | 65.6 | Net Worth | | | 61.2 | | | 64.0 |
| 100.0 | 100.0 | 100.0 | Total Liabilities & Net Worth | | | 100.0 | | | 100.0 |
| | | | INCOME DATA | | | | | | |
| 100.0 | 100.0 | 100.0 | Net Sales | | | 100.0 | | | 100.0 |
| | | | Gross Profit | | | | | | |
| 77.5 | 90.1 | 93.3 | Operating Expenses | | | 101.4 | | | 87.5 |
| 22.5 | 9.9 | 6.7 | Operating Profit | | | -1.4 | | | 12.5 |
| -2.3 | 4.0 | .1 | All Other Expenses (net) | | | -.7 | | | -.6 |
| 24.8 | 6.0 | 6.5 | Profit Before Taxes | | | -.7 | | | 13.1 |
| | | | RATIOS | | | | | | |
| 22.1 | 14.8 | 16.1 | | | | 9.0 | | | 16.0 |
| 8.7 | 5.6 | 5.3 | Current | | | 5.0 | | | 5.6 |
| 2.9 | 4.0 | 2.0 | | | | 2.8 | | | 1.3 |
| 19.0 | 13.4 | 15.0 | | | | 8.9 | | | 14.2 |
| 7.4 | 5.0 | 4.8 | Quick | | | 4.6 | | | 4.7 |
| 2.4 | 2.7 | 1.9 | | | | 2.7 | | | 1.1 |
| 0  UND | 2  222.1 | 7  50.9 | | | | 33  11.0 | | 7  49.7 |
| 20  18.5 | 32  11.5 | 35  10.3 | Sales/Receivables | | | 69  5.3 | | 14  25.7 |
| 63  5.8 | 72  5.1 | 91  4.0 | | | | 140  2.6 | | 47  7.7 |
| | | | Cost of Sales/Inventory | | | | | | |
| | | | Cost of Sales/Payables | | | | | | |
| 1.3 | 1.2 | 1.1 | | | | .6 | | | 1.6 |
| 2.3 | 2.0 | 3.8 | Sales/Working Capital | | | 3.5 | | | 4.0 |
| 7.8 | 4.0 | 7.4 | | | | 4.2 | | | 24.3 |
| 452.9 | 23.5 | 13.8 | | | | | | | |
| (21) 43.5 | (25) 7.0 | (20) 1.4 | EBIT/Interest | | | | | | |
| 8.0 | -1.1 | -4.5 | | | | | | | |
| | | | Net Profit + Depr., Dep., Amort./Cur. Mat. L/T/D | | | | | | |
| .0 | .0 | .0 | | | | .0 | | | .0 |
| .2 | .2 | .3 | Fixed/Worth | | | .2 | | | .3 |
| .8 | .7 | .7 | | | | .8 | | | .7 |
| .1 | .1 | .2 | | | | .2 | | | .0 |
| .3 | .3 | .4 | Debt/Worth | | | .6 | | | .7 |
| .7 | .9 | 1.0 | | | | 1.2 | | | .9 |
| 39.3 | 18.1 | 15.3 | | | | 7.3 | | | 16.5 |
| (36) 21.4 | 6.6 | (48) .2 | % Profit Before Taxes/Tangible Net Worth | | | -.4 | | (10) 9.6 |
| 7.5 | -2.9 | -5.3 | | | | -12.5 | | | -1.3 |
| 29.6 | 8.1 | 12.1 | | | | 4.1 | | | 13.5 |
| 15.0 | 3.3 | .0 | % Profit Before Taxes/Total Assets | | | -.5 | | | 6.6 |
| 5.0 | -1.9 | -3.4 | | | | -10.3 | | | -.7 |
| 151.6 | 112.4 | 77.4 | | | | 42.2 | | | 33.2 |
| 8.9 | 6.3 | 6.6 | Sales/Net Fixed Assets | | | 8.6 | | | 3.5 |
| 2.2 | 1.5 | 1.5 | | | | 1.4 | | | 1.7 |
| 2.3 | 1.2 | 1.3 | | | | 1.3 | | | 1.3 |
| 1.1 | .7 | .8 | Sales/Total Assets | | | .9 | | | .7 |
| .5 | .3 | .4 | | | | .1 | | | .5 |
| .5 | .4 | 1.2 | | | | | | | |
| (25) 1.3 | (37) 1.9 | (32) 2.1 | % Depr., Dep., Amort./Sales | | | | | | |
| 2.3 | 4.6 | 4.4 | | | | | | | |
| | | | % Officers', Directors' Owners' Comp/Sales | | | | | | |
| 714423M | 957331M | 794075M | Net Sales ($) | 2623M | 15670M | 36296M | 55560M | 129764M | 554162M |
| 1071267M | 1686337M | 1570560M | Total Assets ($) | 9190M | 68880M | 272470M | 209781M | 115848M | 894391M |

© RMA 2024  
M = $ thousand    MM = $ million  
See Pages viii through xx for Explanation of Ratios and Data

# OTHER SERVICES—Environment, Conservation and Wildlife Organizations  NAICS 813312

## Current Data Sorted by Assets | Comparative Historical Data

| | | | | | | Type of Statement | | |
|---|---|---|---|---|---|---|---|---|
| | | | 2 | 4 | 3 | Unqualified | 23 | 10 |
| | | | | | | Reviewed | | |
| 1 | 1 | 2 | 3 | | | Compiled | 3 | 2 |
| 1 | 13 (4/1-9/30/23) | 3 | 8 | 15 (10/1/23-3/31/24) | 3 | Tax Returns | 24 | 12 |
| 0-500M | 500M-2MM | 2-10MM | 10-50MM | 50-100MM | 100-250MM | Other | 4/1/19-3/31/20 ALL | 4/1/20-3/31/21 ALL |
| 2 | 1 | 7 | 12 | 3 | 3 | NUMBER OF STATEMENTS | 50 | 24 |
| % | % | % | % | % | % | ASSETS | % | % |
| | | | 23.0 | | | Cash & Equivalents | 26.0 | 33.1 |
| | | | 11.6 | | | Trade Receivables (net) | 11.0 | 10.1 |
| | | | .4 | | | Inventory | 1.3 | .8 |
| | | | 2.3 | | | All Other Current | 5.5 | 3.4 |
| | | | 37.3 | | | Total Current | 43.8 | 47.4 |
| | | | 39.0 | | | Fixed Assets (net) | 32.3 | 30.9 |
| | | | .0 | | | Intangibles (net) | .4 | .7 |
| | | | 23.7 | | | All Other Non-Current | 23.5 | 21.0 |
| | | | 100.0 | | | Total | 100.0 | 100.0 |
| | | | | | | LIABILITIES | | |
| | | | 1.0 | | | Notes Payable-Short Term | .8 | .5 |
| | | | 1.3 | | | Cur. Mat.-L.T.D. | 1.0 | 1.9 |
| | | | 2.9 | | | Trade Payables | 4.5 | 3.7 |
| | | | .0 | | | Income Taxes Payable | .0 | .0 |
| | | | 4.4 | | | All Other Current | 7.4 | 8.0 |
| | | | 9.6 | | | Total Current | 13.8 | 14.1 |
| | | | 4.5 | | | Long-Term Debt | 4.7 | 12.3 |
| | | | .1 | | | Deferred Taxes | .0 | .0 |
| | | | 2.4 | | | All Other Non-Current | 2.4 | 2.4 |
| | | | 83.4 | | | Net Worth | 79.1 | 71.2 |
| | | | 100.0 | | | Total Liabilities & Net Worth | 100.0 | 100.0 |
| | | | | | | INCOME DATA | | |
| | | | 100.0 | | | Net Sales | 100.0 | 100.0 |
| | | | | | | Gross Profit | | |
| | | | 85.5 | | | Operating Expenses | 90.8 | 84.5 |
| | | | 14.5 | | | Operating Profit | 9.2 | 15.5 |
| | | | -.5 | | | All Other Expenses (net) | -.9 | .9 |
| | | | 15.0 | | | Profit Before Taxes | 10.1 | 14.6 |
| | | | | | | RATIOS | | |
| | | | 9.0 | | | | 8.4 | 7.9 |
| | | | 4.5 | | | Current | 4.6 | 2.9 |
| | | | 2.8 | | | | 1.8 | 1.9 |
| | | | 9.0 | | | | 6.8 | 7.3 |
| | | | 3.6 | | | Quick | 4.0 | 2.9 |
| | | | 2.6 | | | | 1.4 | 1.8 |
| | | | 5 74.5 | | | | 1 428.5 | 1 665.6 |
| | | | 19 19.0 | | | Sales/Receivables | 19 19.1 | 28 13.1 |
| | | | 69 5.3 | | | | 56 6.5 | 68 5.4 |
| | | | | | | Cost of Sales/Inventory | | |
| | | | | | | Cost of Sales/Payables | | |
| | | | 1.1 | | | | 1.8 | 1.3 |
| | | | 3.2 | | | Sales/Working Capital | 3.4 | 4.1 |
| | | | 7.8 | | | | 11.0 | 7.3 |
| | | | | | | | 40.1 | 66.1 |
| | | | | | | EBIT/Interest | (16) 10.9 | (12) 12.0 |
| | | | | | | | 2.4 | 4.2 |
| | | | | | | Net Profit + Depr., Dep., Amort./Cur. Mat. L/T/D | | |
| | | | .2 | | | | .1 | .1 |
| | | | .5 | | | Fixed/Worth | .4 | .2 |
| | | | .6 | | | | .6 | .6 |
| | | | .1 | | | | .0 | .1 |
| | | | .1 | | | Debt/Worth | .1 | .4 |
| | | | .4 | | | | .4 | 1.0 |
| | | | 21.6 | | | | 10.5 | 20.6 |
| | | | 6.9 | | | % Profit Before Taxes/Tangible Net Worth | 3.9 | 9.7 |
| | | | .5 | | | | -.1 | 1.1 |
| | | | 16.8 | | | | 7.3 | 13.2 |
| | | | 5.1 | | | % Profit Before Taxes/Total Assets | 3.1 | 6.1 |
| | | | .5 | | | | -.1 | .4 |
| | | | 5.1 | | | | 45.6 | 36.7 |
| | | | 2.9 | | | Sales/Net Fixed Assets | 2.2 | 2.0 |
| | | | .7 | | | | 1.0 | .6 |
| | | | .9 | | | | 1.9 | 1.7 |
| | | | .5 | | | Sales/Total Assets | .6 | .5 |
| | | | .4 | | | | .4 | .3 |
| | | | 1.0 | | | | .7 | .2 |
| | | (10) | 3.2 | | | % Depr., Dep., Amort./Sales | (34) 2.4 | (20) 2.1 |
| | | | 7.5 | | | | 4.5 | 6.6 |
| | | | | | | % Officers', Directors' Owners' Comp/Sales | | |
| 1178M | 1368M | 39206M | 225457M | 55809M | 209765M | Net Sales ($) | 998182M | 357057M |
| 661M | 620M | 43309M | 292181M | 182917M | 409198M | Total Assets ($) | 1484411M | 524497M |

M = $ thousand    MM = $ million
See Pages viii through xx for Explanation of Ratios and Data

© RMA 2024

## OTHER SERVICES—Environment, Conservation and Wildlife Organizations  NAICS 813312

| Comparative Historical Data | | | | | Current Data Sorted by Sales | | | | | |
|---|---|---|---|---|---|---|---|---|---|---|
| | | | | Type of Statement | | | | | | |
| 8 | 10 | 9 | | Unqualified | | 3 | 1 | 3 | 2 | |
| 1 | | | | Reviewed | | | | | | |
| 1 | | | | Compiled | | | | | | |
| 1 | 1 | 4 | | Tax Returns | 2 | | 2 | 1 | | |
| 17 | 18 | 15 | | Other | | 1 | | | | 5 |
| 4/1/21- | 4/1/22- | 4/1/23- | | | 2 | 2 | 2 | 3 | 3 | |
| 3/31/22 | 3/31/23 | 3/31/24 | | | | 13 (4/1-9/30/23) | | 15 (10/1/23-3/31/24) | | |
| ALL | ALL | ALL | | | 0-1MM | 1-3MM | 3-5MM | 5-10MM | 10-25MM | 25MM & OVER |
| 28 | 29 | 28 | NUMBER OF STATEMENTS | 2 | 3 | 5 | 5 | 6 | 7 | |
| % | % | % | ASSETS | % | % | % | % | % | % | |
| 40.6 | 30.6 | 26.6 | Cash & Equivalents | | | | | | | |
| 7.9 | 7.5 | 10.8 | Trade Receivables (net) | | | | | | | |
| .8 | 1.1 | .3 | Inventory | | | | | | | |
| 2.3 | 5.6 | 6.1 | All Other Current | | | | | | | |
| 51.6 | 44.9 | 43.7 | Total Current | | | | | | | |
| 33.9 | 28.4 | 35.9 | Fixed Assets (net) | | | | | | | |
| .0 | 1.9 | .1 | Intangibles (net) | | | | | | | |
| 14.6 | 24.9 | 20.3 | All Other Non-Current | | | | | | | |
| 100.0 | 100.0 | 100.0 | Total | | | | | | | |
| | | | LIABILITIES | | | | | | | |
| 1.5 | 1.0 | .9 | Notes Payable-Short Term | | | | | | | |
| .2 | .1 | .8 | Cur. Mat.-L.T.D. | | | | | | | |
| 3.6 | 3.5 | 2.8 | Trade Payables | | | | | | | |
| .0 | .0 | .0 | Income Taxes Payable | | | | | | | |
| 9.4 | 8.6 | 4.4 | All Other Current | | | | | | | |
| 14.7 | 13.1 | 8.9 | Total Current | | | | | | | |
| 10.2 | 1.1 | 6.6 | Long-Term Debt | | | | | | | |
| .0 | .0 | .0 | Deferred Taxes | | | | | | | |
| 1.0 | .3 | 2.0 | All Other Non-Current | | | | | | | |
| 74.2 | 85.5 | 82.5 | Net Worth | | | | | | | |
| 100.0 | 100.0 | 100.0 | Total Liabilties & Net Worth | | | | | | | |
| | | | INCOME DATA | | | | | | | |
| 100.0 | 100.0 | 100.0 | Net Sales | | | | | | | |
| | | | Gross Profit | | | | | | | |
| 87.0 | 89.3 | 87.8 | Operating Expenses | | | | | | | |
| 13.0 | 10.7 | 12.2 | Operating Profit | | | | | | | |
| -3.4 | -.3 | -1.3 | All Other Expenses (net) | | | | | | | |
| 16.4 | 11.0 | 13.6 | Profit Before Taxes | | | | | | | |
| | | | RATIOS | | | | | | | |
| 21.4 | 15.7 | 11.1 | | | | | | | | |
| 8.1 | 4.0 | 5.9 | Current | | | | | | | |
| 3.3 | 2.7 | 2.9 | | | | | | | | |
| 15.6 | 15.5 | 9.8 | | | | | | | | |
| 8.1 | 3.0 | 4.7 | Quick | | | | | | | |
| 3.3 | 2.1 | 2.6 | | | | | | | | |
| 1  434.6 | 1  554.7 | 5  75.6 | | | | | | | | |
| 20  18.1 | 19  18.9 | 16  22.6 | Sales/Receivables | | | | | | | |
| 41  8.9 | 37  9.9 | 62  5.9 | | | | | | | | |
| | | | Cost of Sales/Inventory | | | | | | | |
| | | | Cost of Sales/Payables | | | | | | | |
| 1.2 | 1.2 | .9 | | | | | | | | |
| 1.9 | 2.0 | 2.0 | Sales/Working Capital | | | | | | | |
| 5.0 | 5.0 | 6.5 | | | | | | | | |
| 234.0 | 144.6 | 197.2 | | | | | | | | |
| (11) 41.8 | (10) 56.3 | (12) 12.0 | EBIT/Interest | | | | | | | |
| 11.9 | -5.5 | 7.7 | | | | | | | | |
| | | | Net Profit + Depr., Dep., Amort./Cur. Mat. L/T/D | | | | | | | |
| .1 | .0 | .1 | | | | | | | | |
| .4 | .2 | .4 | Fixed/Worth | | | | | | | |
| .7 | .6 | .7 | | | | | | | | |
| .0 | .0 | .0 | | | | | | | | |
| .1 | .1 | .1 | Debt/Worth | | | | | | | |
| .5 | .2 | .3 | | | | | | | | |
| 31.1 | 19.0 | 20.5 | | | | | | | | |
| (27) 10.8 | 3.4 | 5.6 | % Profit Before Taxes/Tangible Net Worth | | | | | | | |
| 5.3 | .0 | .0 | | | | | | | | |
| 20.7 | 16.2 | 16.1 | | | | | | | | |
| 9.8 | 3.3 | 5.1 | % Profit Before Taxes/Total Assets | | | | | | | |
| 3.8 | .0 | -.1 | | | | | | | | |
| 44.0 | 19.6 | 9.5 | | | | | | | | |
| 3.7 | 4.3 | 2.4 | Sales/Net Fixed Assets | | | | | | | |
| 1.0 | .8 | .6 | | | | | | | | |
| 1.2 | 1.2 | 1.1 | | | | | | | | |
| .8 | .6 | .5 | Sales/Total Assets | | | | | | | |
| .4 | .3 | .3 | | | | | | | | |
| 1.1 | .6 | .7 | | | | | | | | |
| (18) 2.5 | (19) 1.5 | (21) 2.6 | % Depr., Dep., Amort./Sales | | | | | | | |
| 5.3 | 3.5 | 3.9 | | | | | | | | |
| | | | % Officers', Directors' Owners' Comp/Sales | | | | | | | |
| 548910M | 393344M | 532783M | Net Sales ($) | 982M | 4374M | 19674M | 36553M | 101293M | 369907M | |
| 793853M | 1044845M | 928886M | Total Assets ($) | 8910M | 4180M | 49128M | 150478M | 261467M | 454723M | |

© RMA 2024           M = $ thousand    MM = $ million
See Pages viii through xx for Explanation of Ratios and Data

# OTHER SERVICES—Other Social Advocacy Organizations  NAICS 813319

## Current Data Sorted by Assets | Comparative Historical Data

| | | | | | | Type of Statement | | |
|---|---|---|---|---|---|---|---|---|
| | | | 24 | 29 | 8 | 8 | Unqualified | 105 | 45 |
| | | 1 | | | | | Reviewed | 4 | |
| | | | 1 | 1 | | | Compiled | 1 | 4 |
| 1 | | 4 | 30 | 17 | 1 | | Tax Returns | 13 | 4 |
| 3 | 12 | 30 | 17 | 2 | 6 | Other | 89 | 56 |
| 0-500M | 83 (4/1-9/30/23) | | 64 (10/1/23-3/31/24) | | | | 4/1/19- | 4/1/20- |
| | 500M-2MM | 2-10MM | 10-50MM | 50-100MM | 100-250MM | | 3/31/20 | 3/31/21 |
| 4 | 12 | 59 | 47 | 11 | 14 | NUMBER OF STATEMENTS | 212 ALL | 109 ALL |
| % | % | % | % | % | % | ASSETS | % | % |
| | 39.0 | 33.5 | 21.3 | 20.1 | 15.5 | Cash & Equivalents | 29.6 | 35.8 |
| | 5.3 | 13.8 | 9.0 | 12.4 | 5.3 | Trade Receivables (net) | 14.6 | 13.0 |
| | .5 | 2.2 | 1.5 | 1.4 | 3.4 | Inventory | 1.6 | 3.1 |
| | .4 | 4.4 | 5.9 | .7 | 1.7 | All Other Current | 4.0 | 3.3 |
| | 45.2 | 53.9 | 37.7 | 34.5 | 26.0 | Total Current | 49.8 | 55.2 |
| | 30.4 | 32.5 | 34.8 | 38.7 | 31.8 | Fixed Assets (net) | 32.6 | 32.3 |
| | .9 | 1.0 | 5.0 | .0 | .1 | Intangibles (net) | .7 | 1.1 |
| | 23.6 | 12.6 | 22.5 | 26.8 | 42.0 | All Other Non-Current | 17.0 | 11.4 |
| | 100.0 | 100.0 | 100.0 | 100.0 | 100.0 | Total | 100.0 | 100.0 |
| | | | | | | LIABILITIES | | |
| | 7.1 | .7 | .7 | .1 | 1.7 | Notes Payable-Short Term | 2.9 | 2.8 |
| | .0 | .7 | 2.4 | 2.1 | 1.9 | Cur. Mat.-L.T.D. | 1.9 | 2.0 |
| | 3.4 | 5.0 | 4.5 | 7.9 | 3.4 | Trade Payables | 5.8 | 4.3 |
| | .0 | .0 | .0 | .0 | .0 | Income Taxes Payable | .0 | .0 |
| | 1.7 | 11.4 | 8.8 | 4.3 | 3.3 | All Other Current | 9.3 | 12.8 |
| | 12.1 | 17.8 | 16.5 | 14.4 | 10.3 | Total Current | 20.0 | 22.0 |
| | .5 | 14.9 | 17.5 | 15.4 | 17.7 | Long-Term Debt | 14.9 | 19.8 |
| | .0 | .0 | .0 | .0 | .0 | Deferred Taxes | .0 | .0 |
| | 2.1 | 5.8 | 5.9 | 7.6 | 11.3 | All Other Non-Current | 3.3 | 2.4 |
| | 85.3 | 61.5 | 60.1 | 62.6 | 60.6 | Net Worth | 61.9 | 55.8 |
| | 100.0 | 100.0 | 100.0 | 100.0 | 100.0 | Total Liabilties & Net Worth | 100.0 | 100.0 |
| | | | | | | INCOME DATA | | |
| | 100.0 | 100.0 | 100.0 | 100.0 | 100.0 | Net Sales | 100.0 | 100.0 |
| | | | | | | Gross Profit | | |
| | 97.3 | 96.2 | 94.2 | 90.1 | 101.4 | Operating Expenses | 96.6 | 92.2 |
| | 2.7 | 3.8 | 5.8 | 9.9 | -1.4 | Operating Profit | 3.4 | 7.8 |
| | 3.4 | 1.0 | .6 | .3 | -1.5 | All Other Expenses (net) | .7 | 1.2 |
| | -.7 | 2.8 | 5.2 | 9.6 | .1 | Profit Before Taxes | 2.8 | 6.7 |
| | | | | | | RATIOS | | |
| | 64.6 | 12.5 | 5.2 | 6.1 | 6.5 | | 6.8 | 6.7 |
| | 8.3 | 3.7 | 2.9 | 4.1 | 2.8 | Current | 3.1 | 3.7 |
| | 2.7 | 1.6 | 1.7 | 1.3 | 1.5 | | 1.6 | 1.6 |
| | 64.1 | 12.1 | 4.4 | 5.6 | 6.3 | | 6.1 | 5.5 |
| | 8.3 | 3.4 | 2.3 | 4.0 | 2.4 | Quick | 2.7 | 3.2 |
| | 2.7 | 1.0 | 1.5 | 1.3 | 1.3 | | 1.1 | 1.3 |
| 0 | UND | 5 | 77.8 | 5 | 76.2 | 5 | 72.4 | 13 | 28.1 | | 4 | 87.9 | 0 | UND |
| 1 | 524.0 | 24 | 15.4 | 23 | 16.1 | 27 | 13.6 | 24 | 15.0 | Sales/Receivables | 26 | 14.3 | 26 | 14.1 |
| 25 | 14.7 | 53 | 6.9 | 49 | 7.5 | 61 | 6.0 | 56 | 6.5 | | 52 | 7.0 | 52 | 7.0 |
| | | | | | | Cost of Sales/Inventory | | |
| | | | | | | Cost of Sales/Payables | | |
| | 1.5 | 1.4 | 1.8 | 2.0 | 2.9 | | 2.1 | 1.7 |
| | 4.6 | 3.0 | 3.7 | 5.5 | 7.7 | Sales/Working Capital | 4.5 | 3.6 |
| | 7.1 | 10.7 | 6.3 | 16.4 | 9.8 | | 11.8 | 8.5 |
| | | 21.1 | 22.9 | | | | 12.3 | 15.9 |
| | (29) | .5 | (26) | 2.1 | | EBIT/Interest | (127) | 3.0 | (55) | 3.9 |
| | | -6.8 | -1.8 | | | | -1.3 | 1.1 |
| | | | | | | Net Profit + Depr., Dep., Amort./Cur. Mat. L/T/D | | |
| | .0 | .1 | .1 | .3 | .2 | | .1 | .0 |
| | .3 | .5 | .6 | .5 | .5 | Fixed/Worth | .4 | .5 |
| | .7 | .9 | 1.0 | .8 | 1.6 | | .9 | 1.2 |
| | .0 | .1 | .3 | .2 | .1 | | .2 | .3 |
| | .1 | .5 | .6 | .6 | .4 | Debt/Worth | .4 | .5 |
| | .3 | 1.4 | 1.4 | 1.2 | 1.8 | | 1.2 | 1.9 |
| | 6.4 | 10.4 | 11.8 | 12.2 | 3.9 | | 13.4 | 17.0 |
| | .4 | (54) | 3.1 | (45) | 4.4 | 1.0 | (13) | .5 | % Profit Before Taxes/Tangible Net Worth | (205) | 3.7 | (104) | 5.7 |
| | -11.7 | -7.4 | -2.8 | -2.4 | -4.2 | | -4.1 | -.2 |
| | 5.4 | 7.4 | 7.5 | 10.8 | 2.6 | | 6.6 | 8.4 |
| | .4 | .1 | 1.4 | .5 | .4 | % Profit Before Taxes/Total Assets | 2.0 | 3.1 |
| | -10.9 | -4.0 | -.5 | -1.7 | -2.2 | | -3.0 | -.2 |
| | 74.7 | 35.1 | 17.7 | 6.0 | 4.2 | | 44.5 | 66.4 |
| | 11.4 | 4.2 | 2.2 | 4.9 | 1.7 | Sales/Net Fixed Assets | 4.4 | 5.2 |
| | .9 | 1.3 | 1.0 | .7 | 1.4 | | 1.4 | 1.1 |
| | 3.5 | 1.6 | 1.2 | 2.2 | 1.1 | | 2.0 | 1.7 |
| | .6 | .9 | .7 | .5 | .6 | Sales/Total Assets | .9 | .9 |
| | .4 | .5 | .4 | .3 | .3 | | .5 | .4 |
| | | .8 | .6 | 1.1 | 1.8 | | .7 | .9 |
| | (42) | 1.8 | (37) | 1.8 | (10) | 1.4 | 2.7 | % Depr., Dep., Amort./Sales | (163) | 1.8 | (77) | 2.0 |
| | | 3.1 | 3.9 | 8.7 | 4.5 | | 4.2 | 4.4 |
| | | | | | | % Officers', Directors' Owners' Comp/Sales | .3 | |
| | | | | | | | (11) | 7.5 | |
| | | | | | | | 20.9 | |
| 2650M | 30231M | 379863M | 1131205M | 906102M | 1884303M | Net Sales ($) | 5030386M | 1377453M |
| 1300M | 14252M | 307821M | 1307088M | 783719M | 1898467M | Total Assets ($) | 4762164M | 2321857M |

© RMA 2024

M = $ thousand   MM = $ million
See Pages viii through xx for Explanation of Ratios and Data

## OTHER SERVICES—Other Social Advocacy Organizations  NAICS 813319

### Comparative Historical Data / Current Data Sorted by Sales

| Comparative Historical Data | | | | | | Current Data Sorted by Sales | | | | | |
|---|---|---|---|---|---|---|---|---|---|---|---|
| | | | Type of Statement | | | | | | | | |
| 55 | 70 | 69 | Unqualified | | | 7 | 9 | 13 | 15 | 25 | |
| | | 1 | Reviewed | | | 1 | | | 1 | | |
| 3 | 1 | 1 | Compiled | | | | | | | | |
| 5 | 6 | 6 | Tax Returns | | 1 | 2 | 2 | 1 | | | |
| 55 | 67 | 70 | Other | | 11 | 12 | 9 | 12 | 12 | 14 | |
| 4/1/21-3/31/22 ALL | 4/1/22-3/31/23 ALL | 4/1/23-3/31/24 ALL | | | 83 (4/1-9/30/23) | | | 64 (10/1/23-3/31/24) | | | |
| | | | | | 0-1MM | 1-3MM | 3-5MM | 5-10MM | 10-25MM | 25MM & OVER |
| 118 | 144 | 147 | NUMBER OF STATEMENTS | | 12 | 22 | 20 | 27 | 27 | 39 |
| % | % | % | ASSETS | | % | % | % | % | % | % |
| 39.8 | 35.7 | 28.1 | Cash & Equivalents | | 40.0 | 26.8 | 29.2 | 33.2 | 27.8 | 21.3 |
| 13.7 | 15.2 | 10.5 | Trade Receivables (net) | | 2.4 | 4.7 | 9.9 | 12.3 | 13.3 | 13.5 |
| 2.6 | 3.0 | 1.8 | Inventory | | 2.7 | .6 | 3.4 | .6 | 1.4 | 2.6 |
| 3.7 | 4.8 | 3.9 | All Other Current | | .4 | 3.1 | 6.2 | 5.4 | 3.5 | 3.5 |
| 59.8 | 58.7 | 44.4 | Total Current | | 45.6 | 35.2 | 48.7 | 51.6 | 46.0 | 40.8 |
| 23.0 | 26.2 | 33.4 | Fixed Assets (net) | | 32.6 | 54.2 | 29.1 | 34.1 | 27.7 | 27.5 |
| .9 | .9 | 2.1 | Intangibles (net) | | .8 | .4 | 4.3 | 3.2 | .8 | 2.4 |
| 16.3 | 14.2 | 20.2 | All Other Non-Current | | 21.0 | 10.2 | 18.0 | 11.1 | 25.5 | 29.3 |
| 100.0 | 100.0 | 100.0 | Total | | 100.0 | 100.0 | 100.0 | 100.0 | 100.0 | 100.0 |
| | | | LIABILITIES | | | | | | | |
| 3.0 | 2.1 | 1.3 | Notes Payable-Short Term | | 2.0 | 3.0 | .7 | 1.0 | 1.1 | .7 |
| 1.8 | 1.1 | 1.4 | Cur. Mat.-L.T.D. | | .0 | .4 | 1.0 | 1.3 | 3.3 | 1.4 |
| 6.9 | 6.5 | 4.9 | Trade Payables | | 2.1 | 3.0 | 3.4 | 4.2 | 7.6 | 6.5 |
| .0 | .0 | .0 | Income Taxes Payable | | .0 | .0 | .0 | .0 | .0 | .0 |
| 9.5 | 9.5 | 8.2 | All Other Current | | 3.5 | 3.4 | 6.8 | 7.6 | 10.7 | 11.6 |
| 21.3 | 19.2 | 15.8 | Total Current | | 7.6 | 9.8 | 11.9 | 14.1 | 22.6 | 20.2 |
| 10.6 | 12.4 | 14.9 | Long-Term Debt | | .8 | 32.6 | 9.8 | 17.1 | 10.7 | 13.0 |
| .0 | .0 | .0 | Deferred Taxes | | .0 | .0 | .0 | .0 | .0 | .0 |
| 3.6 | 3.2 | 6.1 | All Other Non-Current | | 2.1 | 1.9 | 9.4 | 6.6 | 4.2 | 9.0 |
| 64.5 | 65.1 | 63.2 | Net Worth | | 89.4 | 55.7 | 68.9 | 62.2 | 62.4 | 57.8 |
| 100.0 | 100.0 | 100.0 | Total Liabilities & Net Worth | | 100.0 | 100.0 | 100.0 | 100.0 | 100.0 | 100.0 |
| | | | INCOME DATA | | | | | | | |
| 100.0 | 100.0 | 100.0 | Net Sales | | 100.0 | 100.0 | 100.0 | 100.0 | 100.0 | 100.0 |
| | | | Gross Profit | | | | | | | |
| 89.6 | 92.9 | 95.6 | Operating Expenses | | 96.9 | 91.4 | 96.5 | 90.6 | 100.3 | 97.4 |
| 10.4 | 7.1 | 4.4 | Operating Profit | | 3.1 | 8.6 | 3.5 | 9.4 | -.3 | 2.6 |
| -1.2 | 1.5 | .7 | All Other Expenses (net) | | 3.7 | 3.4 | 1.8 | 1.7 | -1.7 | -1.2 |
| 11.7 | 5.7 | 3.6 | Profit Before Taxes | | -.6 | 5.2 | 1.7 | 7.7 | 1.5 | 3.8 |
| | | | RATIOS | | | | | | | |
| 9.6 | 10.3 | 8.3 | | | 96.0 | 12.6 | 12.3 | 12.5 | 4.1 | 5.6 |
| 4.0 | 3.6 | 3.4 | Current | | 19.7 | 4.3 | 3.6 | 4.6 | 2.0 | 2.7 |
| 2.1 | 2.1 | 1.7 | | | 3.3 | .8 | 2.4 | 2.1 | 1.2 | 1.6 |
| 9.0 | 8.2 | 7.0 | | | 89.9 | 10.4 | 10.9 | 11.4 | 3.5 | 4.5 |
| 3.2 | 3.0 | 3.0 | Quick | | 9.3 | 3.2 | 3.2 | 4.5 | 1.9 | 2.5 |
| 1.9 | 1.7 | 1.4 | | | 3.3 | .8 | 2.1 | 1.8 | 1.1 | 1.5 |
| 1  290.8 | 5  72.6 | 5  80.3 | | | 0  UND | 0  UND | 0  UND | 8  44.3 | 6  59.3 | 16  22.8 |
| 20  18.5 | 30  12.1 | 23  16.2 | Sales/Receivables | | 0  UND | 7  55.5 | 25  14.4 | 29  12.5 | 21  17.2 | 28  13.2 |
| 49  7.5 | 60  6.1 | 49  7.4 | | | 20  18.6 | 14  25.8 | 51  7.2 | 63  5.8 | 53  6.9 | 56  6.5 |
| | | | Cost of Sales/Inventory | | | | | | | |
| | | | Cost of Sales/Payables | | | | | | | |
| 1.7 | 1.5 | 1.8 | | | 1.2 | 1.5 | 1.3 | 1.7 | 3.1 | 2.6 |
| 3.2 | 3.5 | 3.8 | Sales/Working Capital | | 2.3 | 2.8 | 3.6 | 2.9 | 5.9 | 5.5 |
| 6.8 | 6.3 | 9.3 | | | 4.6 | -27.8 | 5.1 | 4.7 | 22.0 | 10.7 |
| 43.4 | 16.0 | 16.3 | | | 7.4 | | 21.1 | 14.1 | 26.4 | |
| (59)  14.0 | (77)  3.1 | (74)  1.2 | EBIT/Interest | | (12)  -.8 | | (17)  5.8 | (13)  .6 | (22)  2.4 | |
| 2.7 | -1.4 | -3.0 | | | -5.5 | | -1.2 | -7.4 | -.5 | |
| | | | Net Profit + Depr., Dep., Amort./Cur. Mat. L/T/D | | | | | | | |
| .0 | .0 | .1 | | | .0 | .5 | .1 | .0 | .0 | .2 |
| .2 | .2 | .5 | Fixed/Worth | | .3 | .8 | .3 | .6 | .3 | .6 |
| .7 | .7 | .9 | | | .7 | 1.9 | .8 | 1.5 | .7 | .8 |
| .2 | .2 | .2 | | | .0 | .1 | .1 | .2 | .2 | .3 |
| .4 | .4 | .5 | Debt/Worth | | .0 | .7 | .3 | .6 | .6 | .6 |
| 1.1 | 1.0 | 1.3 | | | .2 | 3.5 | 1.4 | 1.5 | 1.2 | 1.6 |
| 33.5 | 14.4 | 10.0 | | | 5.1 | 8.9 | 10.0 | 12.3 | 9.8 | 14.4 |
| (115)  16.6 | (141)  4.4 | (139)  2.5 | % Profit Before Taxes/Tangible Net Worth | | -.8 | (18)  .2 | (19)  .0 | (26)  5.7 | 3.8 | (37)  2.5 |
| 2.7 | -2.9 | -4.3 | | | -11.7 | -6.9 | -10.4 | -4.4 | -7.2 | -2.5 |
| 23.2 | 7.8 | 7.1 | | | 4.7 | 7.2 | 7.8 | 7.5 | 7.6 | 9.4 |
| 7.5 | 2.6 | .8 | % Profit Before Taxes/Total Assets | | -.7 | -.8 | .3 | 3.5 | 1.5 | 1.0 |
| 1.4 | -2.1 | -2.6 | | | -11.6 | -3.9 | -6.0 | -2.0 | -2.8 | -1.4 |
| 118.0 | 85.1 | 24.9 | | | 69.2 | 5.9 | 18.9 | 34.8 | 97.7 | 8.3 |
| 15.7 | 7.3 | 3.3 | Sales/Net Fixed Assets | | 8.4 | 1.0 | 3.1 | 3.8 | 7.2 | 4.9 |
| 2.1 | 1.6 | 1.2 | | | .7 | .4 | 1.4 | .7 | 1.4 | 1.6 |
| 2.0 | 2.0 | 1.4 | | | .7 | .8 | 1.1 | 1.3 | 2.3 | 2.1 |
| 1.1 | 1.0 | .7 | Sales/Total Assets | | .5 | .5 | .8 | .7 | .9 | 1.0 |
| .6 | .5 | .4 | | | .3 | .4 | .5 | .3 | .6 | .6 |
| .6 | .7 | .9 | | | 1.8 | .9 | .5 | .6 | 1.0 | |
| (89)  1.2 | (106)  2.1 | (107)  1.9 | % Depr., Dep., Amort./Sales | | (15)  1.9 | (16)  1.7 | (21)  1.2 | (18)  2.1 | (36)  1.7 | |
| 3.3 | 3.8 | 3.7 | | | 8.1 | 3.6 | 4.9 | 5.3 | 2.7 | |
| | | | % Officers', Directors' Owners' Comp/Sales | | | | | | | |
| 2110502M | 4033283M | 4334354M | Net Sales ($) | | 6346M | 41850M | 81789M | 199485M | 428995M | 3575889M |
| 2554914M | 3681450M | 4312647M | Total Assets ($) | | 20113M | 134366M | 145528M | 418692M | 521209M | 3072739M |

© RMA 2024  
M = $ thousand  MM = $ million  
See Pages viii through xx for Explanation of Ratios and Data

# OTHER SERVICES—Civic and Social Organizations  NAICS 813410

## Current Data Sorted by Assets | Comparative Historical Data

| | | | | | | Type of Statement | | |
|---|---|---|---|---|---|---|---|---|
| 1 | 6 | 33 | 56 | 17 | 7 | Unqualified | 153 | 80 |
|   | 2 |  2 |  2 |    |   | Reviewed    |   6 |  5 |
| 1 | 2 |  2 |  2 |    |   | Compiled    |  11 |  4 |
| 5 | 5 |    |    |    |   | Tax Returns |  28 | 10 |
| 17| 32| 55 | 48 | 15 | 10| Other       | 129 | 101 |

| 0-500M | 500M-2MM | 2-10MM | 10-50MM | 50-100MM | 100-250MM | | 4/1/19-3/31/20 ALL | 4/1/20-3/31/21 ALL |
|---|---|---|---|---|---|---|---|---|
| 174 (4/1-9/30/23) | | | 142 (10/1/23-3/31/24) | | | | | |
| 24 | 47 | 92 | 104 | 32 | 17 | NUMBER OF STATEMENTS | 327 | 200 |
| % | % | % | % | % | % | ASSETS | % | % |
| 53.5 | 48.8 | 31.7 | 23.6 | 28.6 | 13.8 | Cash & Equivalents | 24.3 | 29.8 |
| 12.3 | 10.1 | 9.8 | 4.9 | 4.9 | 5.9 | Trade Receivables (net) | 6.9 | 6.8 |
| 1.3 | .3 | 2.1 | 1.3 | .8 | .5 | Inventory | 1.3 | 1.0 |
| 3.0 | 4.8 | 5.1 | 2.2 | 2.1 | .6 | All Other Current | 3.4 | 3.2 |
| 70.1 | 64.0 | 48.7 | 32.1 | 36.4 | 20.8 | Total Current | 35.9 | 40.8 |
| 25.0 | 29.6 | 35.8 | 40.6 | 44.0 | 57.3 | Fixed Assets (net) | 46.0 | 42.0 |
| .9 | 2.1 | 1.4 | 1.3 | .5 | 3.5 | Intangibles (net) | 1.2 | .7 |
| 4.1 | 4.2 | 14.2 | 26.1 | 19.1 | 18.4 | All Other Non-Current | 17.0 | 16.4 |
| 100.0 | 100.0 | 100.0 | 100.0 | 100.0 | 100.0 | Total | 100.0 | 100.0 |
| | | | | | | LIABILITIES | | |
| 10.7 | 3.2 | 1.0 | .7 | 1.0 | .5 | Notes Payable-Short Term | 1.3 | 1.9 |
| 1.8 | .5 | 1.5 | .9 | 2.0 | 1.2 | Cur. Mat.-L.T.D. | 1.2 | 1.7 |
| 4.2 | 2.7 | 3.6 | 2.9 | 2.0 | 2.5 | Trade Payables | 4.2 | 3.6 |
| .0 | .4 | .0 | .0 | .0 | .0 | Income Taxes Payable | .1 | .0 |
| 4.6 | 9.6 | 8.1 | 7.1 | 8.5 | 2.3 | All Other Current | 6.3 | 8.2 |
| 21.4 | 16.4 | 14.1 | 11.6 | 13.6 | 6.5 | Total Current | 13.1 | 15.4 |
| 6.8 | 9.6 | 14.2 | 11.9 | 16.5 | 26.0 | Long-Term Debt | 16.3 | 19.0 |
| .0 | .0 | .2 | .0 | .0 | .0 | Deferred Taxes | .1 | .1 |
| .1 | 7.6 | 4.0 | 3.9 | 4.6 | 3.9 | All Other Non-Current | 3.9 | 4.0 |
| 71.6 | 66.4 | 67.6 | 72.6 | 65.3 | 63.6 | Net Worth | 66.6 | 61.5 |
| 100.0 | 100.0 | 100.0 | 100.0 | 100.0 | 100.0 | Total Liabilities & Net Worth | 100.0 | 100.0 |
| | | | | | | INCOME DATA | | |
| 100.0 | 100.0 | 100.0 | 100.0 | 100.0 | 100.0 | Net Sales | 100.0 | 100.0 |
| | | | | | | Gross Profit | | |
| 95.4 | 96.1 | 99.2 | 95.8 | 94.0 | 101.8 | Operating Expenses | 95.3 | 93.5 |
| 4.6 | 3.9 | .8 | 4.2 | 6.0 | -1.8 | Operating Profit | 4.7 | 6.5 |
| .0 | 1.0 | -.1 | .0 | 1.1 | -.9 | All Other Expenses (net) | 1.4 | 1.3 |
| 4.6 | 2.9 | .9 | 4.2 | 4.9 | -.9 | Profit Before Taxes | 3.3 | 5.2 |
| | | | | | | RATIOS | | |
| 43.3 | 30.2 | 12.9 | 6.9 | 7.1 | 5.6 | | 7.7 | 7.9 |
| 4.0 | 8.7 | 4.0 | 3.5 | 4.8 | 3.5 | Current | 3.2 | 3.6 |
| 1.0 | 2.6 | 1.9 | 1.5 | 1.3 | 1.5 | | 1.6 | 1.5 |
| 43.3 | 28.6 | 9.1 | 6.1 | 7.1 | 5.3 | | 7.0 | 7.1 |
| 4.0 | 7.2 | 3.1 | 3.0 | 4.4 | 3.0 | Quick | 2.7 | 3.2 |
| .8 | 2.4 | 1.6 | 1.2 | 1.0 | 1.1 | | 1.6 | 1.3 |
| 0 UND | 0 UND | 1 492.4 | 3 126.6 | 4 93.4 | 11 32.3 | | 1 421.0 | 2 230.3 |
| 0 UND | 4 95.6 | 18 20.0 | 14 25.6 | 13 27.4 | 17 21.4 | Sales/Receivables | 10 37.8 | 18 20.3 |
| 14 26.5 | 31 11.9 | 46 7.9 | 38 9.7 | 35 10.3 | 73 5.0 | | 31 11.9 | 37 9.8 |
| | | | | | | Cost of Sales/Inventory | | |
| | | | | | | Cost of Sales/Payables | | |
| 2.3 | 1.5 | 1.5 | 1.8 | 1.4 | 1.8 | | 1.8 | 1.5 |
| 5.1 | 2.7 | 3.1 | 3.2 | 2.3 | 5.9 | Sales/Working Capital | 4.9 | 3.8 |
| NM | 7.4 | 7.6 | 16.7 | 64.2 | 21.8 | | 16.4 | 9.7 |
| | 27.0 | 9.9 | 14.3 | 7.4 | 2.0 | | 5.6 | 12.1 |
| (21) | 5.2 | (44) 1.3 | (60) 3.8 | (23) 1.3 | (15) .4 | EBIT/Interest | (193) 2.1 | (124) 2.6 |
| | -12.5 | -5.0 | -1.5 | -2.4 | -.6 | | -1.8 | -.9 |
| | | | | | | Net Profit + Depr., Dep., Amort./Cur. Mat. L/T/D | | |
| .0 | .0 | .1 | .2 | .3 | .7 | | .2 | .2 |
| .1 | .3 | .4 | .5 | .7 | 1.0 | Fixed/Worth | .7 | .7 |
| 1.0 | .8 | .9 | .9 | .9 | 1.2 | | 1.2 | 1.2 |
| .0 | .0 | .1 | .1 | .2 | .3 | | .1 | .2 |
| .4 | .2 | .3 | .3 | .5 | .5 | Debt/Worth | .3 | .4 |
| .8 | 1.3 | .9 | .7 | .9 | .9 | | .9 | 1.2 |
| 42.3 | 21.4 | 12.5 | 7.4 | 5.7 | 1.5 | | 8.6 | 10.3 |
| (23) 15.5 | (46) 4.0 | .5 | (100) 2.1 | (31) 1.6 | (15) .2 | % Profit Before Taxes/Tangible Net Worth | (317) 1.7 | (192) 2.8 |
| -12.7 | -14.3 | -13.8 | -3.1 | -1.8 | -2.0 | | -2.7 | -1.6 |
| 31.4 | 15.6 | 7.9 | 4.9 | 3.2 | 1.0 | | 5.7 | 5.4 |
| 9.6 | 1.0 | .3 | 1.7 | 1.0 | -.5 | % Profit Before Taxes/Total Assets | 1.1 | 1.4 |
| -15.7 | -6.5 | -6.6 | -2.2 | -1.2 | -1.4 | | -2.0 | -1.7 |
| UND | 79.9 | 25.7 | 4.8 | 4.2 | 1.0 | | 6.1 | 14.5 |
| 40.0 | 6.0 | 2.7 | 1.4 | 1.1 | .7 | Sales/Net Fixed Assets | 1.4 | 1.6 |
| 3.9 | 1.8 | 1.0 | .7 | .6 | .5 | | .6 | .5 |
| 4.0 | 2.3 | 1.4 | .8 | .8 | .6 | | 1.2 | .9 |
| 2.4 | 1.2 | .9 | .5 | .5 | .4 | Sales/Total Assets | .6 | .5 |
| 1.3 | .7 | .4 | .3 | .3 | .3 | | .3 | .3 |
| | .7 | .8 | 1.8 | 3.3 | 4.7 | | 1.9 | 1.2 |
| (26) | 2.4 | (63) 3.1 | (90) 3.8 | (30) 6.3 | (15) 8.3 | % Depr., Dep., Amort./Sales | (252) 4.4 | (147) 4.3 |
| | 5.4 | 6.0 | 6.7 | 9.4 | 11.7 | | 8.9 | 9.5 |
| | | | | | | | 4.3 | 2.6 |
| | | | | | | % Officers', Directors' Owners' Comp/Sales | (22) 6.9 | (15) 6.4 |
| | | | | | | | 12.5 | 28.6 |
| 16923M | 128553M | 506082M | 1547825M | 1408578M | 1323004M | Net Sales ($) | 4678350M | 2832354M |
| 6863M | 56427M | 478880M | 2374221M | 2229277M | 2485996M | Total Assets ($) | 7693839M | 5066607M |

M = $ thousand   MM = $ million
See Pages viii through xx for Explanation of Ratios and Data

© RMA 2024

## OTHER SERVICES—Civic and Social Organizations  NAICS 813410

### Comparative Historical Data | Current Data Sorted by Sales

| | | | | | Type of Statement | | | | | | |
|---|---|---|---|---|---|---|---|---|---|---|---|
| | 63 | | 115 | | 120 | Unqualified | 6 | 23 | 8 | 28 | 28 | 27 |
| | 4 | | 3 | | 4 | Reviewed | 1 | 1 | 1 | | | 1 |
| | 5 | | 2 | | 5 | Compiled | 2 | 2 | | 1 | | |
| | 5 | | 18 | | 10 | Tax Returns | 7 | 3 | | | | |
| | 100 | | 152 | | 177 | Other | 23 | 46 | 21 | 34 | 26 | 27 |
| | 4/1/21-3/31/22 ALL | | 4/1/22-3/31/23 ALL | | 4/1/23-3/31/24 ALL | | 174 (4/1-9/30/23) | | | 142 (10/1/23-3/31/24) | | |
| | 177 | | 290 | | 316 | NUMBER OF STATEMENTS | 39 | 75 | 30 | 63 | 54 | 55 |
| | | | | | | | 0-1MM | 1-3MM | 3-5MM | 5-10MM | 10-25MM | 25MM & OVER |
| | % | | % | | % | ASSETS | % | % | % | % | % | % |
| | 32.4 | | 29.1 | | 32.0 | Cash & Equivalents | 49.8 | 35.0 | 33.2 | 26.9 | 24.0 | 28.2 |
| | 5.8 | | 7.8 | | 7.7 | Trade Receivables (net) | 3.9 | 10.0 | 7.9 | 4.6 | 11.0 | 7.7 |
| | .9 | | 1.0 | | 1.3 | Inventory | 3.2 | .5 | 1.6 | 1.0 | 1.4 | .9 |
| | 2.9 | | 3.3 | | 3.4 | All Other Current | 4.7 | 3.1 | 2.7 | 4.7 | 2.1 | 2.9 |
| | 42.0 | | 41.3 | | 44.4 | Total Current | 61.6 | 48.6 | 45.5 | 37.3 | 38.6 | 39.7 |
| | 40.8 | | 41.3 | | 37.6 | Fixed Assets (net) | 32.6 | 36.0 | 36.0 | 44.3 | 34.9 | 39.3 |
| | 1.2 | | 1.1 | | 1.4 | Intangibles (net) | .3 | 1.9 | 4.9 | .1 | .6 | 2.0 |
| | 16.0 | | 16.3 | | 16.6 | All Other Non-Current | 5.5 | 13.5 | 13.7 | 18.3 | 25.9 | 19.0 |
| | 100.0 | | 100.0 | | 100.0 | Total | 100.0 | 100.0 | 100.0 | 100.0 | 100.0 | 100.0 |
| | | | | | | LIABILITIES | | | | | | |
| | .7 | | 1.3 | | 1.9 | Notes Payable-Short Term | 7.0 | 1.7 | 1.8 | .7 | 1.0 | .9 |
| | 1.1 | | 1.3 | | 1.2 | Cur. Mat.-L.T.D. | 1.3 | 1.3 | 1.1 | 1.1 | 1.3 | 1.2 |
| | 2.3 | | 4.2 | | 3.1 | Trade Payables | .8 | 3.1 | 3.8 | 2.5 | 4.2 | 3.8 |
| | .1 | | .0 | | .1 | Income Taxes Payable | .0 | .0 | .6 | .0 | .0 | .0 |
| | 8.0 | | 5.6 | | 7.5 | All Other Current | 8.8 | 5.9 | 5.1 | 4.8 | 9.1 | 11.5 |
| | 12.2 | | 12.3 | | 13.7 | Total Current | 17.9 | 11.9 | 12.3 | 9.1 | 15.5 | 17.4 |
| | 17.3 | | 17.2 | | 13.1 | Long-Term Debt | 10.1 | 14.2 | 12.9 | 13.9 | 9.2 | 16.6 |
| | .0 | | .0 | | .1 | Deferred Taxes | .0 | .1 | .3 | .0 | .0 | .0 |
| | 3.9 | | 3.2 | | 4.3 | All Other Non-Current | 3.2 | 2.7 | 10.1 | 3.3 | 3.2 | 6.0 |
| | 66.6 | | 67.3 | | 68.9 | Net Worth | 68.7 | 71.1 | 64.4 | 73.7 | 72.1 | 60.0 |
| | 100.0 | | 100.0 | | 100.0 | Total Liabilities & Net Worth | 100.0 | 100.0 | 100.0 | 100.0 | 100.0 | 100.0 |
| | | | | | | INCOME DATA | | | | | | |
| | 100.0 | | 100.0 | | 100.0 | Net Sales | 100.0 | 100.0 | 100.0 | 100.0 | 100.0 | 100.0 |
| | | | | | | Gross Profit | | | | | | |
| | 88.6 | | 93.0 | | 97.0 | Operating Expenses | 93.3 | 98.3 | 95.8 | 98.0 | 96.3 | 97.8 |
| | 11.4 | | 7.0 | | 3.0 | Operating Profit | 6.7 | 1.7 | 4.2 | 2.0 | 3.7 | 2.2 |
| | -.8 | | 2.3 | | .2 | All Other Expenses (net) | 2.1 | .5 | 2.3 | -.6 | -.7 | -1.2 |
| | 12.2 | | 4.6 | | 2.9 | Profit Before Taxes | 4.6 | 1.2 | 1.9 | 2.6 | 4.4 | 3.4 |
| | | | | | | RATIOS | | | | | | |
| | 12.3 | | 10.6 | | 11.2 | | 42.0 | 15.3 | 15.3 | 9.3 | 6.8 | 5.1 |
| | 4.3 | | 4.5 | | 4.3 | Current | 9.5 | 6.6 | 5.7 | 4.3 | 3.0 | 3.3 |
| | 2.0 | | 2.0 | | 1.6 | | 1.3 | 2.0 | 1.5 | 2.0 | 1.4 | 1.5 |
| | 11.0 | | 9.4 | | 9.1 | | 36.8 | 13.0 | 15.0 | 7.2 | 5.9 | 5.0 |
| | 4.1 | | 3.8 | | 3.4 | Quick | 7.9 | 5.5 | 3.4 | 3.3 | 2.5 | 3.0 |
| | 1.6 | | 1.6 | | 1.4 | | 1.0 | 1.7 | 1.3 | 1.7 | 1.3 | 1.0 |
| 1 | 255.0 | 1 | 432.6 | 1 | 298.6 | | 0 UND | 0 UND | 0 UND | 2 150.4 | 6 59.7 | 10 37.5 |
| 13 | 27.2 | 15 | 24.7 | 13 | 28.6 | Sales/Receivables | 0 UND | 20 18.7 | 9 38.5 | 10 38.4 | 19 18.8 | 23 15.6 |
| 37 | 9.8 | 45 | 8.1 | 40 | 9.2 | | 11 33.3 | 58 6.3 | 38 9.5 | 36 10.1 | 43 8.4 | 44 8.3 |
| | | | | | | Cost of Sales/Inventory | | | | | | |
| | | | | | | Cost of Sales/Payables | | | | | | |
| | 1.2 | | 1.4 | | 1.6 | | 1.0 | 1.3 | 1.5 | 2.1 | 1.7 | 2.1 |
| | 2.4 | | 2.8 | | 3.1 | Sales/Working Capital | 2.2 | 2.6 | 2.9 | 3.4 | 4.4 | 3.9 |
| | 5.3 | | 8.3 | | 12.2 | | 17.0 | 5.5 | 19.0 | 10.0 | 19.7 | 22.3 |
| | 27.7 | | 11.4 | | 12.7 | | 27.3 | 14.0 | 11.3 | 15.2 | 12.1 | 7.4 |
| (107) | 8.4 | (174) | 2.8 | (172) | 1.8 | EBIT/Interest | (17) 6.0 | (39) .7 | (13) 2.2 | (34) 2.2 | (30) 1.9 | (39) 1.3 |
| | .7 | | -3.3 | | -2.1 | | .0 | -7.7 | -1.4 | -2.7 | -2.3 | -.2 |
| | | | | | | Net Profit + Depr., Dep., Amort./Cur. Mat. L/T/D | | | | | | |
| | .2 | | .2 | | .1 | | .0 | .1 | .1 | .3 | .2 | .3 |
| | .6 | | .6 | | .5 | Fixed/Worth | .3 | .4 | .5 | .6 | .4 | .7 |
| | 1.1 | | 1.0 | | .9 | | .9 | .9 | 1.1 | .9 | .7 | 1.1 |
| | .1 | | .1 | | .1 | | .0 | .1 | .1 | .1 | .1 | .3 |
| | .4 | | .4 | | .3 | Debt/Worth | .2 | .2 | .2 | .3 | .3 | .6 |
| | 1.0 | | .8 | | .8 | | 1.1 | .9 | 1.2 | .6 | .7 | 1.0 |
| | 17.4 | | 14.1 | | 12.0 | % Profit Before Taxes/Tangible Net Worth | 32.6 | 11.7 | 11.1 | 7.6 | 12.6 | 8.0 |
| (172) | 8.3 | (283) | 1.7 | (307) | 1.5 | | (38) 8.7 | .5 | (28) .0 | 1.2 | (53) 1.4 | (50) 2.8 |
| | .9 | | -4.2 | | -5.8 | | -9.9 | -11.3 | -14.6 | -4.3 | -4.7 | -.6 |
| | 12.3 | | 7.6 | | 7.8 | % Profit Before Taxes/Total Assets | 18.8 | 10.1 | 6.6 | 6.0 | 10.3 | 5.1 |
| | 5.9 | | 1.0 | | 1.0 | | 1.4 | .4 | .0 | .9 | 1.1 | 1.5 |
| | .4 | | -3.0 | | -3.9 | | -6.5 | -6.6 | -9.2 | -3.5 | -3.7 | -1.1 |
| | 7.5 | | 5.4 | | 12.0 | | UND | 41.9 | 29.5 | 5.0 | 9.7 | 8.0 |
| | 1.2 | | 1.5 | | 2.1 | Sales/Net Fixed Assets | 10.0 | 2.1 | 2.1 | 1.7 | 2.3 | 1.8 |
| | .5 | | .6 | | .8 | | 1.1 | .8 | .8 | .7 | .9 | .8 |
| | 1.0 | | 1.0 | | 1.3 | | 1.9 | 1.4 | 1.7 | 1.2 | 1.2 | 1.2 |
| | .5 | | .6 | | .7 | Sales/Total Assets | .7 | .7 | .8 | .6 | .7 | .7 |
| | .3 | | .3 | | .4 | | .3 | .3 | .4 | .4 | .4 | .5 |
| | 2.3 | | 2.2 | | 1.5 | | 1.6 | 2.3 | .8 | 1.2 | 1.7 | 1.5 |
| (140) | 4.8 | (222) | 5.0 | (228) | 3.8 | % Depr., Dep., Amort./Sales | (15) 3.4 | (44) 4.6 | (21) 2.9 | (51) 4.0 | (46) 3.6 | (51) 3.8 |
| | 9.3 | | 9.0 | | 7.2 | | 12.3 | 9.6 | 5.5 | 7.0 | 6.0 | 8.4 |
| | | | 5.5 | | 7.5 | % Officers', Directors' Owners' Comp/Sales | | | | | | |
| | | (16) | 6.8 | (11) | 18.4 | | | | | | | |
| | | | 10.3 | | 31.4 | | | | | | | |
| | 2302860M | | 4055632M | | 4930965M | Net Sales ($) | 21728M | 145967M | 117208M | 454761M | 870009M | 3321292M |
| | 4973769M | | 7987114M | | 7631664M | Total Assets ($) | 48282M | 422870M | 256347M | 929427M | 1696494M | 4278244M |

© RMA 2024    M = $ thousand    MM = $ million
See Pages viii through xx for Explanation of Ratios and Data

# OTHER SERVICES—Business Associations  NAICS 813910

## Current Data Sorted by Assets | Comparative Historical Data

| | | | | | | Type of Statement | | |
|---|---|---|---|---|---|---|---|---|
| 1 | 1 | 15 | 15 | 5 | 4 | Unqualified | 83 | 29 |
| | 1 | | | 1 | | Reviewed | 2 | 5 |
| 2 | | 1 | | | | Compiled | 3 | 1 |
| 1 | | 1 | | | | Tax Returns | 8 | 1 |
| 1 | | | | | | Other | | |
| 4 | 11 | 14 | 21 | 2 | 3 | | 91 | 54 |
| | 32 (4/1-9/30/23) | | 70 (10/1/23-3/31/24) | | | | 4/1/19-3/31/20 | 4/1/20-3/31/21 |
| 0-500M | 500M-2MM | 2-10MM | 10-50MM | 50-100MM | 100-250MM | | ALL | ALL |
| 5 | 15 | 31 | 36 | 8 | 7 | NUMBER OF STATEMENTS | 187 | 90 |
| % | % | % | % | % | % | ASSETS | % | % |
| | 60.3 | 44.6 | 34.6 | | | Cash & Equivalents | 44.2 | 42.4 |
| | 7.5 | 7.1 | 9.9 | | | Trade Receivables (net) | 8.2 | 11.3 |
| | 1.2 | 1.5 | 1.2 | | | Inventory | 1.3 | 2.9 |
| | 6.5 | 3.8 | 7.0 | | | All Other Current | 4.8 | 5.0 |
| | 75.4 | 57.1 | 52.8 | | | Total Current | 58.4 | 61.5 |
| | 13.8 | 23.6 | 21.2 | | | Fixed Assets (net) | 21.9 | 21.0 |
| | .2 | 1.5 | 2.6 | | | Intangibles (net) | 1.4 | 1.4 |
| | 10.6 | 17.9 | 23.4 | | | All Other Non-Current | 18.3 | 16.0 |
| | 100.0 | 100.0 | 100.0 | | | Total | 100.0 | 100.0 |
| | | | | | | LIABILITIES | | |
| | 6.0 | 2.3 | 2.7 | | | Notes Payable-Short Term | 2.8 | 2.4 |
| | 1.3 | 1.0 | 1.2 | | | Cur. Mat.-L.T.D. | 2.1 | .8 |
| | 4.8 | 5.8 | 7.0 | | | Trade Payables | 5.6 | 4.9 |
| | .0 | .0 | .0 | | | Income Taxes Payable | .0 | .9 |
| | 20.0 | 13.7 | 19.7 | | | All Other Current | 20.1 | 18.6 |
| | 32.0 | 22.9 | 30.6 | | | Total Current | 30.6 | 27.6 |
| | 21.3 | 14.5 | 8.3 | | | Long-Term Debt | 10.8 | 17.0 |
| | .0 | .0 | .0 | | | Deferred Taxes | .2 | .0 |
| | 3.9 | 7.4 | 8.9 | | | All Other Non-Current | 10.6 | 9.6 |
| | 42.7 | 55.3 | 52.2 | | | Net Worth | 47.7 | 45.7 |
| | 100.0 | 100.0 | 100.0 | | | Total Liabilities & Net Worth | 100.0 | 100.0 |
| | | | | | | INCOME DATA | | |
| | 100.0 | 100.0 | 100.0 | | | Net Sales | 100.0 | 100.0 |
| | | | | | | Gross Profit | | |
| | 91.9 | 94.4 | 89.2 | | | Operating Expenses | 95.9 | 89.0 |
| | 8.1 | 5.6 | 10.8 | | | Operating Profit | 4.1 | 11.0 |
| | -.7 | -.9 | -.2 | | | All Other Expenses (net) | .9 | 1.6 |
| | 8.8 | 6.6 | 11.0 | | | Profit Before Taxes | 3.3 | 9.4 |
| | | | | | | RATIOS | | |
| | 6.9 | 13.2 | 5.0 | | | | 7.4 | 7.3 |
| | 4.0 | 3.3 | 2.2 | | | Current | 3.0 | 3.1 |
| | 1.7 | 1.4 | 1.1 | | | | 1.2 | 1.7 |
| | 6.9 | 12.5 | 4.9 | | | | 7.1 | 6.7 |
| | 3.7 | 2.8 | 2.0 | | | Quick | 2.8 | 2.9 |
| | 1.7 | 1.2 | .9 | | | | 1.0 | 1.5 |
| | 0  999.8 | 1  337.8 | 3  107.6 | | | | 2  193.0 | 3  113.8 |
| | 11  34.6 | 7  52.5 | 16  22.4 | | | Sales/Receivables | 11  32.3 | 18  20.2 |
| | 25  14.4 | 21  17.1 | 81  4.5 | | | | 29  12.4 | 56  6.5 |
| | | | | | | Cost of Sales/Inventory | | |
| | | | | | | Cost of Sales/Payables | | |
| | 1.2 | 1.2 | 1.6 | | | | 1.3 | 1.3 |
| | 2.2 | 2.2 | 3.1 | | | Sales/Working Capital | 3.7 | 2.3 |
| | 4.1 | 13.1 | 18.1 | | | | 23.1 | 11.0 |
| | | 15.1 | 18.3 | | | | 14.3 | 25.4 |
| | (15) | 10.7 | (20) 3.9 | | | EBIT/Interest | (83) 3.3 | (43) 7.4 |
| | | 2.7 | 2.1 | | | | .7 | 1.5 |
| | | | | | | Net Profit + Depr., Dep., Amort./Cur. Mat. L/T/D | | |
| | .0 | .1 | .0 | | | | .0 | .0 |
| | .1 | .3 | .2 | | | Fixed/Worth | .2 | .1 |
| | .2 | .7 | .6 | | | | .9 | .6 |
| | .2 | .2 | .3 | | | | .3 | .3 |
| | 1.2 | .4 | 1.1 | | | Debt/Worth | .7 | .6 |
| | 3.2 | 1.4 | 2.0 | | | | 1.6 | 2.8 |
| | 27.5 | 18.6 | 19.9 | | | % Profit Before Taxes/Tangible Net Worth | 12.3 | 26.9 |
| | (13) 8.7 | (29) 5.0 | (35) 6.9 | | | | (170) 3.8 | (81) 8.1 |
| | -14.0 | .2 | 1.9 | | | | -.7 | 1.3 |
| | 11.6 | 13.5 | 11.0 | | | % Profit Before Taxes/Total Assets | 7.2 | 12.6 |
| | 3.2 | 3.7 | 3.7 | | | | 1.9 | 4.2 |
| | -6.0 | -.7 | .9 | | | | -1.0 | .4 |
| | UND | 35.7 | 41.0 | | | | 83.0 | 212.6 |
| | 48.0 | 4.6 | 7.3 | | | Sales/Net Fixed Assets | 11.6 | 9.9 |
| | 7.7 | 2.1 | 2.6 | | | | 2.4 | 1.8 |
| | 1.7 | 1.3 | 1.1 | | | | 1.7 | 1.4 |
| | 1.1 | .8 | .7 | | | Sales/Total Assets | .9 | .9 |
| | .7 | .7 | .4 | | | | .5 | .4 |
| | | 1.1 | .5 | | | | .8 | .9 |
| | (24) | 1.5 | (27) 1.7 | | | % Depr., Dep., Amort./Sales | (135) 1.7 | (63) 2.0 |
| | | 2.7 | 3.3 | | | | 4.0 | 5.1 |
| | | | | | | % Officers', Directors' Owners' Comp/Sales | | |
| 3666M | 20691M | 200349M | 742008M | 942215M | 3446310M | Net Sales ($) | 3588932M | 2058456M |
| 1553M | 18870M | 171486M | 878606M | 556020M | 1370853M | Total Assets ($) | 4928159M | 2054063M |

© RMA 2024  
M = $ thousand  MM = $ million  
See Pages viii through xx for Explanation of Ratios and Data

## OTHER SERVICES—Business Associations  NAICS 813910

| Comparative Historical Data ||| Type of Statement | Current Data Sorted by Sales |||||||
|---|---|---|---|---|---|---|---|---|---|
| 37 | 44 | 41 | Unqualified | 1 | 6 | 6 | 8 | 10 | 10 |
| 5 | 2 | 3 | Reviewed |  | 1 |  | 1 |  | 1 |
| 1 | 3 | 2 | Compiled |  |  | 2 |  |  |  |
| 3 | 7 | 1 | Tax Returns |  | 1 |  |  |  |  |
| 49 | 74 | 55 | Other | 8 | 11 | 4 | 12 | 8 | 12 |
| 4/1/21-3/31/22 ALL | 4/1/22-3/31/23 ALL | 4/1/23-3/31/24 ALL |  |  | 32 (4/1-9/30/23) ||| 70 (10/1/23-3/31/24) |||
|  |  |  |  | 0-1MM | 1-3MM | 3-5MM | 5-10MM | 10-25MM | 25MM & OVER |
| 95 | 130 | 102 | NUMBER OF STATEMENTS | 9 | 21 | 10 | 21 | 18 | 23 |
| % | % | % | ASSETS | % | % | % | % | % | % |
| 44.9 | 45.9 | 40.9 | Cash & Equivalents | 42.6 | 45.0 | 42.4 | 35.4 | 35.9 |  |
| 9.3 | 9.4 | 11.2 | Trade Receivables (net) | 9.5 | 14.0 | 13.3 | 8.8 | 11.7 |  |
| 1.4 | 2.7 | 2.0 | Inventory | .8 | .1 | .2 | 1.9 | 6.3 |  |
| 6.5 | 5.6 | 5.5 | All Other Current | 9.5 | 1.0 | 2.0 | 2.3 | 8.9 |  |
| 62.1 | 63.6 | 59.6 | Total Current | 62.5 | 60.1 | 57.9 | 48.4 | 62.8 |  |
| 21.1 | 18.3 | 19.4 | Fixed Assets (net) | 19.4 | 22.5 | 22.1 | 25.8 | 11.3 |  |
| 1.5 | 1.4 | 2.1 | Intangibles (net) | .1 | 2.3 | 2.4 | 3.7 | 3.0 |  |
| 15.2 | 16.8 | 18.9 | All Other Non-Current | 18.0 | 15.1 | 17.6 | 22.1 | 22.9 |  |
| 100.0 | 100.0 | 100.0 | Total | 100.0 | 100.0 | 100.0 | 100.0 | 100.0 |  |
|  |  |  | **LIABILITIES** |  |  |  |  |  |  |
| 2.5 | 2.8 | 3.4 | Notes Payable-Short Term | 1.3 | .7 | 3.4 | 5.4 | 2.4 |  |
| 2.0 | 1.6 | 1.0 | Cur. Mat.-L.T.D. | .5 | 1.4 | 1.1 | 1.3 | .6 |  |
| 6.3 | 6.3 | 7.7 | Trade Payables | 3.8 | 1.9 | 5.0 | 7.7 | 16.0 |  |
| .1 | .0 | .0 | Income Taxes Payable | .0 | .0 | .0 | .0 | .0 |  |
| 14.9 | 12.8 | 19.2 | All Other Current | 14.9 | 18.0 | 16.4 | 17.3 | 26.4 |  |
| 25.8 | 23.5 | 31.3 | Total Current | 20.5 | 21.9 | 25.9 | 31.7 | 45.4 |  |
| 14.6 | 12.7 | 12.2 | Long-Term Debt | 16.9 | 14.1 | 12.1 | 5.8 | 7.9 |  |
| .0 | .1 | .0 | Deferred Taxes | .0 | .0 | .0 | .0 | .0 |  |
| 7.5 | 12.9 | 9.5 | All Other Non-Current | 5.5 | 7.3 | 4.2 | 10.1 | 16.0 |  |
| 52.1 | 50.9 | 47.0 | Net Worth | 57.1 | 56.6 | 57.8 | 52.4 | 30.7 |  |
| 100.0 | 100.0 | 100.0 | Total Liabilities & Net Worth | 100.0 | 100.0 | 100.0 | 100.0 | 100.0 |  |
|  |  |  | **INCOME DATA** |  |  |  |  |  |  |
| 100.0 | 100.0 | 100.0 | Net Sales | 100.0 | 100.0 | 100.0 | 100.0 | 100.0 |  |
|  |  |  | Gross Profit |  |  |  |  |  |  |
| 89.0 | 95.1 | 92.7 | Operating Expenses | 98.4 | 91.3 | 80.8 | 91.3 | 100.9 |  |
| 11.0 | 4.9 | 7.3 | Operating Profit | 1.6 | 8.7 | 19.2 | 8.7 | -.9 |  |
| .2 | 2.6 | -.2 | All Other Expenses (net) | .1 | -1.2 | 3.1 | -.5 | -2.4 |  |
| 10.7 | 2.3 | 7.6 | Profit Before Taxes | 1.5 | 9.9 | 16.1 | 9.3 | 1.5 |  |
|  |  |  | **RATIOS** |  |  |  |  |  |  |
| 9.0 | 9.5 | 5.3 |  | 10.0 | 22.7 | 5.9 | 5.3 | 2.4 |  |
| 3.5 | 3.6 | 2.3 | Current | 3.7 | 2.9 | 2.8 | 1.6 | 1.5 |  |
| 1.5 | 1.7 | 1.2 |  | 2.1 | 2.0 | 1.3 | .9 | 1.1 |  |
| 8.0 | 9.3 | 5.3 |  | 9.8 | 21.8 | 5.9 | 5.2 | 2.4 |  |
| 3.0 | 3.1 | 2.2 | Quick | 3.7 | 2.9 | 2.5 | 1.2 | 1.3 |  |
| 1.4 | 1.5 | 1.1 |  | 1.9 | 1.9 | 1.2 | .8 | .4 |  |
| 1 359.7 | 1 426.2 | 2 182.5 |  | 1 246.7 | 0 UND | 2 146.2 | 0 UND | 3 137.6 |  |
| 13 28.8 | 12 29.3 | 13 28.1 | Sales/Receivables | 16 22.5 | 7 54.2 | 16 23.1 | 16 22.4 | 6 64.6 |  |
| 43 8.5 | 37 9.9 | 43 8.5 |  | 33 11.1 | 126 2.9 | 78 4.7 | 43 8.5 | 24 14.9 |  |
|  |  |  | Cost of Sales/Inventory |  |  |  |  |  |  |
|  |  |  | Cost of Sales/Payables |  |  |  |  |  |  |
| 1.4 | 1.3 | 1.6 |  | 1.3 | 1.2 | 1.2 | 1.7 | 2.9 |  |
| 2.5 | 2.7 | 3.1 | Sales/Working Capital | 2.2 | 1.8 | 2.2 | 6.3 | 13.4 |  |
| 11.0 | 6.8 | 16.5 |  | 5.4 | 5.9 | 9.0 | -13.6 | 74.1 |  |
|  | 70.0 | 27.9 | 15.1 |  |  |  |  | 15.4 | 78.9 |
| (42) 7.8 | (60) 4.1 | (51) 4.5 | EBIT/Interest |  |  |  | (10) 8.3 | (12) 3.9 |  |
| 3.5 | 1.0 | 1.9 |  |  |  |  |  | 2.0 | 2.0 |
|  |  |  | Net Profit + Depr., Dep., Amort./Cur. Mat. L/T/D |  |  |  |  |  |  |
| .0 | .0 | .0 |  | .0 | .1 | .0 | .1 | .0 |  |
| .2 | .2 | .2 | Fixed/Worth | .1 | .3 | .2 | .3 | .1 |  |
| .7 | .6 | .7 |  | .6 | .6 | .8 | 1.4 | 1.0 |  |
| .2 | .3 | .3 |  | .1 | .3 | .2 | .2 | 1.1 |  |
| .6 | .7 | 1.2 | Debt/Worth | .8 | .5 | .9 | 1.0 | 2.0 |  |
| 1.9 | 2.7 | 4.1 |  | 2.6 | 3.1 | 2.0 | 4.4 | 4.6 |  |
| 19.1 | 15.1 | 19.9 |  | 10.1 | 29.4 | 25.6 | 10.7 | 20.0 |  |
| (86) 10.8 | (120) 3.2 | (96) 6.1 | % Profit Before Taxes/Tangible Net Worth | 3.9 | 8.8 | 16.0 | (16) 2.7 | (21) 6.9 |  |
| 4.7 | -5.6 | .0 |  | -19.0 | 3.8 | 6.1 | -2.6 | -.3 |  |
| 12.5 | 7.0 | 9.7 |  | 4.4 | 15.4 | 13.5 | 10.2 | 7.4 |  |
| 6.3 | 1.8 | 3.0 | % Profit Before Taxes/Total Assets | 1.3 | 3.3 | 4.8 | 2.0 | 1.5 |  |
| 1.9 | -3.9 | -.6 |  | -7.3 | 1.2 | 2.8 | -1.1 | -1.7 |  |
| 84.3 | 194.0 | 78.0 |  | 140.6 | 30.0 | 40.8 | 10.1 | 359.3 |  |
| 12.0 | 12.4 | 10.8 | Sales/Net Fixed Assets | 24.7 | 4.6 | 4.6 | 6.1 | 41.6 |  |
| 1.9 | 2.9 | 2.9 |  | 1.6 | 1.6 | 2.4 | 2.8 | 4.3 |  |
| 1.6 | 1.5 | 1.5 |  | 1.6 | 1.0 | 1.1 | 1.5 | 3.1 |  |
| .8 | .9 | .8 | Sales/Total Assets | .8 | .8 | .7 | .9 | 1.4 |  |
| .6 | .5 | .5 |  | .4 | .4 | .4 | .7 | .7 |  |
| .9 | .9 | .6 |  | .7 |  | .6 | .8 | .2 |  |
| (59) 1.8 | (86) 2.0 | (74) 1.5 | % Depr., Dep., Amort./Sales | (15) 1.3 | (15) 1.7 | (15) 1.3 | (18) .8 |  |  |
| 2.9 | 4.8 | 3.3 |  | 3.5 |  | 2.9 | 3.2 | 2.5 |  |
|  |  |  | % Officers', Directors' Owners' Comp/Sales |  |  |  |  |  |  |
| 2095589M | 2299608M | 5355239M | Net Sales ($) | 5621M | 37128M | 36487M | 142072M | 319884M | 4814047M |
| 2315771M | 2397752M | 2997388M | Total Assets ($) | 7298M | 88729M | 101974M | 333580M | 370678M | 2095129M |

© RMA 2024    M = $ thousand    MM = $ million
See Pages viii through xx for Explanation of Ratios and Data

# OTHER SERVICES—Professional Organizations  NAICS 813920

## Current Data Sorted by Assets | Comparative Historical Data

| | | | | | | Type of Statement | | |
|---|---|---|---|---|---|---|---|---|
| | | 5 | 12 | 2 | 4 | Unqualified | 52 | 21 |
| 1 | 2 | | | | | Reviewed | 3 | 2 |
| 1 | | 1 | | 1 | | Compiled | 1 | 2 |
| | | 7 | 5 | | 2 | Tax Returns | 7 | 4 |
| | 2 | | | | | Other | 35 | 36 |
| | 24 (4/1-9/30/23) | | 21 (10/1/23-3/31/24) | | | | 4/1/19-3/31/20 | 4/1/20-3/31/21 |
| 0-500M | 500M-2MM | 2-10MM | 10-50MM | 50-100MM | 100-250MM | | ALL | ALL |
| 2 | 4 | 13 | 17 | 3 | 6 | NUMBER OF STATEMENTS | 98 | 65 |
| % | % | % | % | % | % | ASSETS | % | % |
| | | 46.6 | 44.7 | | | Cash & Equivalents | 50.1 | 46.1 |
| | | 12.5 | 15.2 | | | Trade Receivables (net) | 7.1 | 6.0 |
| | | .2 | 2.0 | | | Inventory | .4 | .5 |
| | | 2.3 | 1.3 | | | All Other Current | 3.1 | 2.2 |
| | | 61.7 | 63.1 | | | Total Current | 60.7 | 54.8 |
| | | 29.6 | 17.4 | | | Fixed Assets (net) | 18.8 | 22.9 |
| | | .4 | .3 | | | Intangibles (net) | 2.2 | 3.3 |
| | | 8.3 | 19.2 | | | All Other Non-Current | 18.2 | 19.0 |
| | | 100.0 | 100.0 | | | Total | 100.0 | 100.0 |
| | | | | | | LIABILITIES | | |
| | | .7 | .7 | | | Notes Payable-Short Term | .9 | 2.8 |
| | | 2.7 | .6 | | | Cur. Mat.-L.T.D. | .7 | 1.0 |
| | | 6.0 | 6.1 | | | Trade Payables | 7.9 | 5.3 |
| | | .0 | .0 | | | Income Taxes Payable | .0 | .0 |
| | | 17.5 | 12.1 | | | All Other Current | 18.4 | 18.2 |
| | | 26.9 | 19.5 | | | Total Current | 27.9 | 27.3 |
| | | 14.4 | 6.3 | | | Long-Term Debt | 9.8 | 15.6 |
| | | .0 | .0 | | | Deferred Taxes | .1 | .0 |
| | | 9.2 | 14.6 | | | All Other Non-Current | 12.2 | 7.2 |
| | | 49.5 | 59.6 | | | Net Worth | 50.0 | 49.9 |
| | | 100.0 | 100.0 | | | Total Liabilities & Net Worth | 100.0 | 100.0 |
| | | | | | | INCOME DATA | | |
| | | 100.0 | 100.0 | | | Net Sales | 100.0 | 100.0 |
| | | | | | | Gross Profit | | |
| | | 94.7 | 96.0 | | | Operating Expenses | 96.6 | 94.3 |
| | | 5.3 | 4.0 | | | Operating Profit | 3.4 | 5.7 |
| | | -.5 | .6 | | | All Other Expenses (net) | .2 | -1.0 |
| | | 5.8 | 3.4 | | | Profit Before Taxes | 3.2 | 6.6 |
| | | | | | | RATIOS | | |
| | | 5.5 | 7.4 | | | | 8.3 | 5.2 |
| | | 3.4 | 2.8 | | | Current | 2.3 | 2.4 |
| | | 1.5 | 2.2 | | | | 1.4 | 1.4 |
| | | 5.3 | 7.4 | | | | 8.2 | 5.2 |
| | | 2.8 | 2.6 | | | Quick | 2.1 | 2.2 |
| | | 1.5 | 1.9 | | | | 1.3 | 1.3 |
| | | 4   86.6 | 11   34.2 | | | | 4   94.9 | 0   UND |
| | | 26  14.1 | 34  10.7 | | | Sales/Receivables | 14  26.8 | 8   46.7 |
| | | 81   4.5 | 78   4.7 | | | | 31  11.8 | 25  14.5 |
| | | | | | | Cost of Sales/Inventory | | |
| | | | | | | Cost of Sales/Payables | | |
| | | .9 | 1.3 | | | | 1.1 | 1.4 |
| | | 1.8 | 2.0 | | | Sales/Working Capital | 3.4 | 3.3 |
| | | 13.2 | 4.6 | | | | 10.3 | 15.1 |
| | | | | | | | 21.9 | 23.6 |
| | | | | | | EBIT/Interest | (39)  6.9 | (25)  6.1 |
| | | | | | | | .3 | -1.6 |
| | | | | | | Net Profit + Depr., Dep., Amort./Cur. Mat. L/T/D | | |
| | | .1 | .0 | | | | .0 | .0 |
| | | .3 | .2 | | | Fixed/Worth | .2 | .2 |
| | | 1.4 | .4 | | | | .5 | .8 |
| | | .4 | .3 | | | | .4 | .3 |
| | | .7 | .8 | | | Debt/Worth | .7 | .8 |
| | | 2.9 | 1.2 | | | | 1.5 | 1.3 |
| | | 11.7 | 15.5 | | | | 11.0 | 18.6 |
| | | 5.0 | 1.4 | | | % Profit Before Taxes/Tangible Net Worth | (90)  4.9 | (60)  6.2 |
| | | -7.8 | -4.6 | | | | -3.7 | -1.4 |
| | | 6.4 | 9.2 | | | | 6.9 | 13.0 |
| | | 3.1 | 1.2 | | | % Profit Before Taxes/Total Assets | 2.9 | 3.6 |
| | | -2.9 | -2.5 | | | | -1.3 | -1.4 |
| | | 29.6 | 28.4 | | | | 36.8 | 85.4 |
| | | 3.9 | 9.3 | | | Sales/Net Fixed Assets | 9.8 | 7.0 |
| | | 1.7 | 2.7 | | | | 3.9 | 2.1 |
| | | 1.3 | 1.1 | | | | 1.5 | 1.6 |
| | | .7 | .7 | | | Sales/Total Assets | .7 | .7 |
| | | .4 | .6 | | | | .5 | .5 |
| | | .6 | .9 | | | | 1.0 | 1.1 |
| | | (11)  2.2 | (16)  1.8 | | | % Depr., Dep., Amort./Sales | (79)  2.0 | (48)  2.1 |
| | | 6.5 | 3.2 | | | | 2.9 | 4.1 |
| | | | | | | % Officers', Directors' Owners' Comp/Sales | | |
| 1439M | 15110M | 63819M | 379719M | 115363M | 525992M | Net Sales ($) | 3506599M | 1923814M |
| 380M | 2759M | 69141M | 386825M | 218442M | 877927M | Total Assets ($) | 3569332M | 1563927M |

© RMA 2024   M = $ thousand   MM = $ million
See Pages viii through xx for Explanation of Ratios and Data

## OTHER SERVICES—Professional Organizations  NAICS 813920

### Comparative Historical Data | Current Data Sorted by Sales

| | | | | Type of Statement | | | | | | |
|---|---|---|---|---|---|---|---|---|---|---|
| | 17 | 26 | 23 | Unqualified | | 2 | | 4 | 8 | 9 |
| | | 1 | | Reviewed | | | | | | |
| | 1 | | 3 | Compiled | | | 1 | 1 | | |
| | 4 | 2 | 3 | Tax Returns | 1 | | | | | 1 |
| | 29 | 28 | 16 | Other | 1 | 1 | 3 | 2 | 4 | 3 |
| | 4/1/21-3/31/22 | 4/1/22-3/31/23 | 4/1/23-3/31/24 | | 2 | 2 | | | | |
| | ALL | ALL | ALL | | 24 (4/1-9/30/23) | | | 21 (10/1/23-3/31/24) | | |
| | | | | | 0-1MM | 1-3MM | 3-5MM | 5-10MM | 10-25MM | 25MM & OVER |
| | 51 | 59 | 45 | NUMBER OF STATEMENTS | 4 | 5 | 4 | 7 | 12 | 13 |
| | % | % | % | ASSETS | % | % | % | % | % | % |
| | 44.0 | 46.3 | 45.4 | Cash & Equivalents | | | | | 52.7 | 44.4 |
| | 8.8 | 9.0 | 12.3 | Trade Receivables (net) | | | | | 8.9 | 11.7 |
| | 1.2 | .7 | 1.0 | Inventory | | | | | .3 | 2.5 |
| | 3.8 | 4.2 | 1.9 | All Other Current | | | | | 2.9 | 2.2 |
| | 57.7 | 60.2 | 60.6 | Total Current | | | | | 64.8 | 60.8 |
| | 18.8 | 19.3 | 21.6 | Fixed Assets (net) | | | | | 12.2 | 17.8 |
| | 4.8 | 3.2 | 2.1 | Intangibles (net) | | | | | .4 | 1.0 |
| | 18.7 | 17.3 | 15.8 | All Other Non-Current | | | | | 22.6 | 20.5 |
| | 100.0 | 100.0 | 100.0 | Total | | | | | 100.0 | 100.0 |
| | | | | LIABILITIES | | | | | | |
| | 5.0 | 2.2 | 4.5 | Notes Payable-Short Term | | | | | .3 | 1.1 |
| | 1.0 | 1.6 | 1.4 | Cur. Mat.-L.T.D. | | | | | .4 | .6 |
| | 6.6 | 3.8 | 5.3 | Trade Payables | | | | | 8.1 | 4.9 |
| | .1 | .0 | .0 | Income Taxes Payable | | | | | .0 | .0 |
| | 18.1 | 14.3 | 14.3 | All Other Current | | | | | 17.1 | 11.6 |
| | 30.8 | 22.0 | 25.5 | Total Current | | | | | 25.9 | 18.2 |
| | 17.6 | 11.7 | 12.1 | Long-Term Debt | | | | | 3.5 | 6.6 |
| | .0 | .1 | .0 | Deferred Taxes | | | | | .0 | .0 |
| | 6.2 | 6.5 | 9.8 | All Other Non-Current | | | | | 11.4 | 14.7 |
| | 45.4 | 59.7 | 52.6 | Net Worth | | | | | 59.2 | 60.6 |
| | 100.0 | 100.0 | 100.0 | Total Liabilities & Net Worth | | | | | 100.0 | 100.0 |
| | | | | INCOME DATA | | | | | | |
| | 100.0 | 100.0 | 100.0 | Net Sales | | | | | 100.0 | 100.0 |
| | | | | Gross Profit | | | | | | |
| | 90.9 | 93.7 | 93.9 | Operating Expenses | | | | | 96.0 | 101.1 |
| | 9.1 | 6.3 | 6.1 | Operating Profit | | | | | 4.0 | -1.1 |
| | .4 | 6.0 | -.7 | All Other Expenses (net) | | | | | .5 | -2.3 |
| | 8.6 | .3 | 6.7 | Profit Before Taxes | | | | | 3.6 | 1.2 |
| | | | | RATIOS | | | | | | |
| | 4.1 | 8.6 | 6.1 | | | | | | 4.4 | 5.5 |
| | 1.9 | 2.9 | 3.2 | Current | | | | | 2.5 | 3.6 |
| | 1.0 | 1.5 | 1.7 | | | | | | 1.9 | 1.7 |
| | 3.9 | 7.8 | 5.6 | | | | | | 4.3 | 5.0 |
| | 1.8 | 2.8 | 2.8 | Quick | | | | | 2.3 | 3.6 |
| | .9 | 1.4 | 1.3 | | | | | | 1.7 | 1.1 |
| 5 | 67.9 | 1 329.0 | 6 61.9 | | | | | 8 | 43.5 | 9 40.6 |
| 17 | 21.9 | 17 22.0 | 26 14.1 | Sales/Receivables | | | | 18 | 20.8 | 27 13.3 |
| 35 | 10.4 | 47 7.8 | 62 5.9 | | | | | 41 | 9.0 | 47 7.7 |
| | | | | Cost of Sales/Inventory | | | | | | |
| | | | | Cost of Sales/Payables | | | | | | |
| | 1.9 | .9 | 1.2 | | | | | | 1.3 | .9 |
| | 4.2 | 2.1 | 2.3 | Sales/Working Capital | | | | | 2.1 | 1.9 |
| | -341.3 | 9.4 | 12.2 | | | | | | 3.9 | 7.6 |
| | 41.5 | 11.2 | 16.2 | | | | | | | |
| (21) | 4.6 | (28) 1.0 | (22) 7.2 | EBIT/Interest | | | | | | |
| | -.8 | -8.5 | -3.1 | | | | | | | |
| | | 4.3 | | Net Profit + Depr., Dep., | | | | | | |
| | | (11) 2.4 | | Amort./Cur. Mat. L/T/D | | | | | | |
| | | -15.7 | | | | | | | | |
| | .0 | .0 | .1 | | | | | | .0 | .1 |
| | .1 | .1 | .2 | Fixed/Worth | | | | | .2 | .1 |
| | .7 | .4 | .9 | | | | | | .4 | .8 |
| | .5 | .3 | .3 | | | | | | .3 | .3 |
| | .9 | .6 | .7 | Debt/Worth | | | | | .7 | .5 |
| | 1.9 | 1.1 | 1.5 | | | | | | 1.0 | 1.2 |
| | 24.2 | 12.4 | 19.9 | % Profit Before Taxes/Tangible | | | | | 18.1 | 8.2 |
| (46) | 10.7 | (56) .8 | (43) 3.5 | Net Worth | | | | | 2.2 | 1.8 |
| | 1.5 | -8.9 | -5.6 | | | | | | -2.6 | -9.6 |
| | 11.2 | 6.6 | 10.1 | % Profit Before Taxes/Total | | | | | 7.0 | 6.3 |
| | 4.5 | .1 | 2.8 | Assets | | | | | 1.7 | 1.2 |
| | -.1 | -6.4 | -2.7 | | | | | | -1.3 | -4.1 |
| | 427.3 | 49.1 | 24.3 | | | | | | 34.5 | 12.4 |
| | 14.7 | 7.4 | 6.7 | Sales/Net Fixed Assets | | | | | 10.5 | 5.3 |
| | 2.0 | 2.4 | 2.1 | | | | | | 4.2 | 3.0 |
| | 1.8 | 1.0 | 1.3 | | | | | | 1.2 | 1.0 |
| | .7 | .6 | .7 | Sales/Total Assets | | | | | .8 | .7 |
| | .4 | .4 | .6 | | | | | | .6 | .5 |
| | .8 | 1.1 | 1.0 | | | | | | 1.3 | 1.1 |
| (29) | 1.9 | (46) 2.0 | (38) 2.0 | % Depr., Dep., Amort./Sales | | | | (11) | 2.0 | (11) 2.1 |
| | 3.8 | 4.6 | 3.1 | | | | | | 4.3 | 2.7 |
| | | | | % Officers', Directors' Owners' Comp/Sales | | | | | | |
| | 1025243M | 1147009M | 1101442M | Net Sales ($) | 3066M | 11295M | 15610M | 52894M | 177649M | 840928M |
| | 1265654M | 1911318M | 1555474M | Total Assets ($) | 5755M | 25076M | 10850M | 54541M | 237561M | 1221691M |

© RMA 2024  M = $ thousand   MM = $ million
See Pages viii through xx for Explanation of Ratios and Data

# OTHER SERVICES—Labor Unions and Similar Labor Organizations  NAICS 813930

## Current Data Sorted by Assets

| | | | | | | Type of Statement | | |
|---|---|---|---|---|---|---|---|---|
| 1 | 1 | 7 | 8 | 4 | 2 | Unqualified | | |
| | | 1 | | | | Reviewed | | |
| | | 3 | | | | Compiled | | |
| | | | 1 | | | Tax Returns | | |
| 2 | 2 | 3 | 15 (10/1/23-3/31/24) | 1 | 1 | Other | | |
| | 23 (4/1-9/30/23) | | | | | | | |
| 0-500M | 500M-2MM | 2-10MM | 10-50MM | 50-100MM | 100-250MM | | | |
| 3 | 3 | 14 | 10 | 5 | 3 | NUMBER OF STATEMENTS | | |
| % | % | % | % | % | % | ASSETS | | |
| | | 49.3 | 46.2 | | | Cash & Equivalents | | |
| | | 5.8 | 1.7 | | | Trade Receivables (net) | | |
| | | .1 | .0 | | | Inventory | | |
| | | 1.1 | 1.0 | | | All Other Current | | |
| | | 56.3 | 48.9 | | | Total Current | | |
| | | 37.7 | 32.0 | | | Fixed Assets (net) | | |
| | | .0 | .0 | | | Intangibles (net) | | |
| | | 6.0 | 19.1 | | | All Other Non-Current | | |
| | | 100.0 | 100.0 | | | Total | | |
| | | | | | | LIABILITIES | | |
| | | .0 | .0 | | | Notes Payable-Short Term | | |
| | | 1.4 | 1.8 | | | Cur. Mat.-L.T.D. | | |
| | | 3.2 | .7 | | | Trade Payables | | |
| | | .0 | .0 | | | Income Taxes Payable | | |
| | | 9.6 | 3.0 | | | All Other Current | | |
| | | 14.2 | 5.5 | | | Total Current | | |
| | | 16.5 | 4.4 | | | Long-Term Debt | | |
| | | .0 | .0 | | | Deferred Taxes | | |
| | | 4.8 | 4.2 | | | All Other Non-Current | | |
| | | 64.5 | 85.9 | | | Net Worth | | |
| | | 100.0 | 100.0 | | | Total Liabilities & Net Worth | | |
| | | | | | | INCOME DATA | | |
| | | 100.0 | 100.0 | | | Net Sales | | |
| | | | | | | Gross Profit | | |
| | | 85.9 | 91.5 | | | Operating Expenses | | |
| | | 14.1 | 8.5 | | | Operating Profit | | |
| | | 2.6 | -1.7 | | | All Other Expenses (net) | | |
| | | 11.5 | 10.2 | | | Profit Before Taxes | | |
| | | | | | | RATIOS | | |
| | | 93.8 | 13.4 | | | | | |
| | | 6.4 | 8.7 | | | Current | | |
| | | 1.9 | 4.8 | | | | | |
| | | 93.8 | 12.5 | | | | | |
| | | 6.4 | 8.7 | | | Quick | | |
| | | 1.9 | 4.8 | | | | | |
| | | 0 UND | 0 UND | | | | | |
| | | 0 UND | 0 UND | | | Sales/Receivables | | |
| | | 0 UND | 27 13.3 | | | | | |
| | | | | | | Cost of Sales/Inventory | | |
| | | | | | | Cost of Sales/Payables | | |
| | | 1.0 | .8 | | | | | |
| | | 2.5 | 1.0 | | | Sales/Working Capital | | |
| | | 4.1 | 2.9 | | | | | |
| | | | | | | EBIT/Interest | | |
| | | | | | | Net Profit + Depr., Dep., Amort./Cur. Mat. L/T/D | | |
| | | .1 | .0 | | | | | |
| | | .6 | .4 | | | Fixed/Worth | | |
| | | 1.6 | .6 | | | | | |
| | | .0 | .0 | | | | | |
| | | .5 | .1 | | | Debt/Worth | | |
| | | 2.5 | .3 | | | | | |
| | | 12.8 | 15.7 | | | % Profit Before Taxes/Tangible Net Worth | | |
| | | 4.8 | 6.2 | | | | | |
| | | 1.4 | -.5 | | | | | |
| | | 7.2 | 12.6 | | | % Profit Before Taxes/Total Assets | | |
| | | 3.1 | 4.6 | | | | | |
| | | 1.2 | -.5 | | | | | |
| | | 23.9 | 31.7 | | | | | |
| | | 3.2 | 1.3 | | | Sales/Net Fixed Assets | | |
| | | .6 | .7 | | | | | |
| | | 1.5 | .6 | | | | | |
| | | .5 | .5 | | | Sales/Total Assets | | |
| | | .3 | .4 | | | | | |
| | | 2.4 | | | | | | |
| | | (10) 5.1 | | | | % Depr., Dep., Amort./Sales | | |
| | | 13.6 | | | | | | |
| | | | | | | % Officers', Directors' Owners' Comp/Sales | | |
| 1141M | 3006M | 67949M | 95224M | 135131M | 208251M | Net Sales ($) | | |
| 550M | 3065M | 81383M | 216272M | 327195M | 555252M | Total Assets ($) | | |

## Comparative Historical Data

| | | | |
|---|---|---|---|
| 23 | | 14 | |
| 2 | | 1 | |
| | | | |
| 3 | | 3 | |
| 19 | | 11 | |
| 4/1/19-3/31/20 | | 4/1/20-3/31/21 | |
| ALL | | ALL | |
| 47 | | 29 | |
| % | | % | |
| 54.3 | | 61.2 | |
| 4.2 | | 1.7 | |
| .0 | | .0 | |
| 1.0 | | .9 | |
| 59.5 | | 63.9 | |
| 23.8 | | 24.3 | |
| .5 | | .0 | |
| 16.2 | | 11.8 | |
| 100.0 | | 100.0 | |
| | | | |
| .7 | | 2.6 | |
| 3.1 | | .4 | |
| 3.3 | | 6.4 | |
| .0 | | .1 | |
| 7.4 | | 5.3 | |
| 14.5 | | 14.8 | |
| 5.6 | | 6.6 | |
| .0 | | .0 | |
| 6.2 | | 2.0 | |
| 73.6 | | 76.6 | |
| 100.0 | | 100.0 | |
| | | | |
| 100.0 | | 100.0 | |
| | | | |
| 88.3 | | 84.7 | |
| 11.7 | | 15.3 | |
| .0 | | -1.2 | |
| 11.7 | | 16.4 | |
| | | | |
| 61.6 | | 214.3 | |
| 9.0 | | 19.2 | |
| 2.3 | | 3.0 | |
| 61.6 | | 214.3 | |
| 8.9 | | 18.6 | |
| 2.2 | | 2.9 | |
| 0 UND | | 0 UND | |
| 0 999.8 | | 0 774.0 | |
| 18 20.1 | | 24 15.2 | |
| | | | |
| | | | |
| 1.0 | | .7 | |
| 2.0 | | 1.2 | |
| 7.8 | | 2.7 | |
| 103.7 | | 117.7 | |
| (19) 5.7 | | (10) 14.3 | |
| -.7 | | 2.4 | |
| | | | |
| .0 | | .0 | |
| .1 | | .2 | |
| .7 | | .5 | |
| .0 | | .0 | |
| .2 | | .2 | |
| .8 | | .7 | |
| 15.7 | | 19.7 | |
| (45) 7.9 | | 11.3 | |
| 1.2 | | 4.0 | |
| 11.6 | | 15.4 | |
| 6.8 | | 9.0 | |
| .0 | | 2.5 | |
| 996.7 | | 344.3 | |
| 11.4 | | 3.6 | |
| 2.0 | | 1.3 | |
| 1.4 | | .8 | |
| .8 | | .6 | |
| .3 | | .5 | |
| .9 | | 1.3 | |
| (30) 1.8 | | (18) 2.0 | |
| 3.7 | | 3.2 | |
| | | | |
| 1459217M | | 486773M | |
| 1506331M | | 765649M | |

M = $ thousand   MM = $ million
See Pages viii through xx for Explanation of Ratios and Data

© RMA 2024

# OTHER SERVICES—Labor Unions and Similar Labor Organizations  NAICS 813930

## Comparative Historical Data | Current Data Sorted by Sales

| | | | | Type of Statement | | | | | | |
|---|---|---|---|---|---|---|---|---|---|---|
| 15 | | 21 | 23 | Unqualified | 2 | 2 | 3 | 6 | 6 | 4 |
| 2 | | 3 | 1 | Reviewed | | | 1 | | | |
| | | | 3 | Compiled | | | | | | |
| | | 2 | 1 | Tax Returns | 1 | 1 | 1 | 1 | | |
| 12 | | 11 | 10 | Other | 4 | 1 | 2 | 1 | 1 | 1 |
| 4/1/21- | | 4/1/22- | 4/1/23- | | | 23 (4/1-9/30/23) | | | 15 (10/1/23-3/31/24) | |
| 3/31/22 | | 3/31/23 | 3/31/24 | | | | | | | |
| ALL | | ALL | ALL | | 0-1MM | 1-3MM | 3-5MM | 5-10MM | 10-25MM | 25MM & OVER |
| 29 | | 37 | 38 | NUMBER OF STATEMENTS | 7 | 4 | 7 | 8 | 7 | 5 |
| % | | % | % | ASSETS | % | % | % | % | % | % |
| 57.3 | | 51.3 | 54.5 | Cash & Equivalents | | | | | | |
| 3.3 | | 2.3 | 2.8 | Trade Receivables (net) | | | | | | |
| .0 | | .0 | .0 | Inventory | | | | | | |
| 1.3 | | 2.3 | 1.1 | All Other Current | | | | | | |
| 61.9 | | 55.9 | 58.5 | Total Current | | | | | | |
| 26.3 | | 33.3 | 27.8 | Fixed Assets (net) | | | | | | |
| .1 | | .1 | 1.3 | Intangibles (net) | | | | | | |
| 11.7 | | 10.6 | 12.5 | All Other Non-Current | | | | | | |
| 100.0 | | 100.0 | 100.0 | Total | | | | | | |
| | | | | LIABILITIES | | | | | | |
| 1.1 | | .0 | .0 | Notes Payable-Short Term | | | | | | |
| .6 | | 1.6 | 1.0 | Cur. Mat.-L.T.D. | | | | | | |
| 1.8 | | 1.3 | 3.2 | Trade Payables | | | | | | |
| .2 | | .0 | .0 | Income Taxes Payable | | | | | | |
| 12.8 | | 6.8 | 10.6 | All Other Current | | | | | | |
| 16.6 | | 9.8 | 14.8 | Total Current | | | | | | |
| 6.6 | | 8.7 | 7.8 | Long-Term Debt | | | | | | |
| .2 | | .0 | .0 | Deferred Taxes | | | | | | |
| 9.9 | | .0 | 3.0 | All Other Non-Current | | | | | | |
| 66.8 | | 81.4 | 74.3 | Net Worth | | | | | | |
| 100.0 | | 100.0 | 100.0 | Total Liabilities & Net Worth | | | | | | |
| | | | | INCOME DATA | | | | | | |
| 100.0 | | 100.0 | 100.0 | Net Sales | | | | | | |
| | | | | Gross Profit | | | | | | |
| 89.0 | | 86.5 | 87.7 | Operating Expenses | | | | | | |
| 11.0 | | 13.5 | 12.3 | Operating Profit | | | | | | |
| -2.5 | | 1.4 | .5 | All Other Expenses (net) | | | | | | |
| 13.5 | | 12.1 | 11.7 | Profit Before Taxes | | | | | | |
| | | | | RATIOS | | | | | | |
| 40.5 | | 69.9 | 71.7 | | | | | | | |
| 8.0 | | 11.3 | 10.1 | Current | | | | | | |
| 2.7 | | 3.4 | 2.8 | | | | | | | |
| 36.5 | | 56.8 | 71.7 | | | | | | | |
| 7.9 | | 11.2 | 10.1 | Quick | | | | | | |
| 2.7 | | 3.1 | 2.8 | | | | | | | |
| 0 | UND | 0 UND | 0 UND | | | | | | | |
| 0 | UND | 0 UND | 0 UND | Sales/Receivables | | | | | | |
| 8 | 47.9 | 1 507.5 | 4 90.0 | | | | | | | |
| | | | | Cost of Sales/Inventory | | | | | | |
| | | | | Cost of Sales/Payables | | | | | | |
| .7 | | .8 | .8 | | | | | | | |
| 1.2 | | 1.4 | 1.3 | Sales/Working Capital | | | | | | |
| 2.8 | | 3.1 | 4.1 | | | | | | | |
| 122.4 | | 10.6 | 35.3 | | | | | | | |
| (12) 9.2 | (12) | 6.3 | (13) 12.5 | EBIT/Interest | | | | | | |
| 2.7 | | 1.2 | 4.0 | | | | | | | |
| | | | | Net Profit + Depr., Dep., Amort./Cur. Mat. L/T/D | | | | | | |
| .0 | | .0 | .0 | | | | | | | |
| .2 | | .3 | .4 | Fixed/Worth | | | | | | |
| .8 | | .8 | .8 | | | | | | | |
| .0 | | .0 | .0 | | | | | | | |
| .3 | | .1 | .1 | Debt/Worth | | | | | | |
| 1.0 | | .3 | .7 | | | | | | | |
| 18.0 | | 12.5 | 13.4 | | | | | | | |
| (28) 11.3 | | 7.0 | (37) 6.9 | % Profit Before Taxes/Tangible Net Worth | | | | | | |
| 2.2 | | .1 | .4 | | | | | | | |
| 17.7 | | 9.0 | 8.8 | | | | | | | |
| 8.9 | | 3.2 | 3.3 | % Profit Before Taxes/Total Assets | | | | | | |
| 1.1 | | .0 | -.1 | | | | | | | |
| 90.1 | | 36.4 | 296.5 | | | | | | | |
| 5.4 | | 3.3 | 5.2 | Sales/Net Fixed Assets | | | | | | |
| 1.0 | | .6 | .9 | | | | | | | |
| .8 | | .8 | 1.0 | | | | | | | |
| .6 | | .5 | .5 | Sales/Total Assets | | | | | | |
| .4 | | .4 | .3 | | | | | | | |
| .6 | | 1.1 | 1.7 | | | | | | | |
| (23) 3.4 | (26) | 4.2 | (26) 3.8 | % Depr., Dep., Amort./Sales | | | | | | |
| 5.7 | | 7.6 | 9.8 | | | | | | | |
| | | | | % Officers', Directors' Owners' Comp/Sales | | | | | | |
| 642746M | | 513833M | 510702M | Net Sales ($) | 4029M | 6044M | 25778M | 52826M | 103142M | 318883M |
| 1009885M | | 1145497M | 1183717M | Total Assets ($) | 14729M | 15299M | 52593M | 211039M | 199195M | 690862M |

© RMA 2024     M = $ thousand     MM = $ million
See Pages viii through xx for Explanation of Ratios and Data

# OTHER SERVICES—Other Similar Organizations (except Business, Professional, Labor, and Political Organizations) NAICS 813990

## Current Data Sorted by Assets | Comparative Historical Data

| | | | | | | Type of Statement | | |
|---|---|---|---|---|---|---|---|---|
| 2 | 8 | 21 | 18 | 9 | 1 | Unqualified | 44 | 40 |
| 3 | 2 | 2 | 2 | | | Reviewed | 18 | 6 |
| 1 | 1 | 1 | | | | Compiled | 24 | 9 |
| 5 | 1 | 1 | | | | Tax Returns | 12 | 6 |
| 18 | 36 | 29 | 11 | 2 | 1 | Other | 181 | 85 |
| | 42 (4/1-9/30/23) | | 133 (10/1/23-3/31/24) | | | | 4/1/19-3/31/20 | 4/1/20-3/31/21 |
| 0-500M | 500M-2MM | 2-10MM | 10-50MM | 50-100MM | 100-250MM | | ALL | ALL |
| 29 | 48 | 54 | 31 | 11 | 2 | NUMBER OF STATEMENTS | 279 | 146 |
| % | % | % | % | % | % | ASSETS | % | % |
| 71.2 | 62.7 | 53.3 | 30.1 | 22.9 | | Cash & Equivalents | 61.4 | 51.8 |
| 8.0 | 2.8 | 3.6 | 4.3 | 7.0 | | Trade Receivables (net) | 5.6 | 5.5 |
| .0 | .0 | .8 | .7 | .3 | | Inventory | .2 | .7 |
| 4.5 | 8.5 | 8.7 | 3.0 | 1.7 | | All Other Current | 4.2 | 3.4 |
| 83.7 | 74.1 | 66.4 | 38.1 | 31.9 | | Total Current | 71.4 | 61.4 |
| 5.2 | 6.5 | 21.2 | 44.0 | 44.5 | | Fixed Assets (net) | 16.6 | 23.5 |
| .3 | .2 | .5 | .0 | 2.4 | | Intangibles (net) | .6 | 1.8 |
| 10.9 | 19.2 | 11.8 | 17.9 | 21.2 | | All Other Non-Current | 11.4 | 13.3 |
| 100.0 | 100.0 | 100.0 | 100.0 | 100.0 | | Total | 100.0 | 100.0 |
| | | | | | | LIABILITIES | | |
| 12.9 | 2.7 | 1.8 | 2.4 | .0 | | Notes Payable-Short Term | 5.9 | 3.5 |
| 6.8 | 3.9 | 2.5 | 1.9 | 3.1 | | Cur. Mat.-L.T.D. | 4.6 | 2.8 |
| 6.4 | 4.8 | 5.4 | 3.6 | 4.5 | | Trade Payables | 5.3 | 4.0 |
| .0 | .5 | .1 | .0 | .7 | | Income Taxes Payable | .0 | .1 |
| 31.1 | 24.8 | 17.6 | 9.9 | 8.0 | | All Other Current | 11.8 | 11.3 |
| 57.2 | 36.7 | 27.4 | 17.8 | 16.3 | | Total Current | 27.7 | 21.8 |
| 49.1 | 26.5 | 14.0 | 16.0 | 14.4 | | Long-Term Debt | 23.7 | 45.1 |
| .0 | .0 | .1 | .0 | .0 | | Deferred Taxes | .0 | .0 |
| 8.5 | 19.1 | 18.8 | 12.1 | 1.8 | | All Other Non-Current | 12.8 | 6.6 |
| -14.8 | 17.6 | 39.8 | 54.1 | 67.4 | | Net Worth | 35.8 | 26.5 |
| 100.0 | 100.0 | 100.0 | 100.0 | 100.0 | | Total Liabilities & Net Worth | 100.0 | 100.0 |
| | | | | | | INCOME DATA | | |
| 100.0 | 100.0 | 100.0 | 100.0 | 100.0 | | Net Sales | 100.0 | 100.0 |
| | | | | | | Gross Profit | | |
| 90.3 | 88.5 | 89.3 | 89.3 | 85.6 | | Operating Expenses | 91.3 | 90.4 |
| 9.7 | 11.5 | 10.7 | 10.7 | 14.4 | | Operating Profit | 8.7 | 9.6 |
| 7.6 | 10.4 | 1.8 | 5.1 | .3 | | All Other Expenses (net) | 4.1 | 3.1 |
| 2.1 | 1.1 | 8.8 | 5.7 | 14.2 | | Profit Before Taxes | 4.6 | 6.5 |
| | | | | | | RATIOS | | |
| 5.0 | 7.5 | 8.2 | 8.1 | 4.9 | | | 15.9 | 7.6 |
| 2.3 | 2.8 | 3.9 | 2.6 | 2.7 | | Current | 3.9 | 3.7 |
| 1.0 | 1.4 | 1.6 | 1.3 | 1.3 | | | 1.4 | 1.5 |
| 5.0 | 7.0 | 7.8 | 7.9 | 4.9 | | | 14.0 | 6.9 |
| 2.3 | 2.4 | 3.1 | 2.3 | 1.7 | | Quick | 3.8 | 3.2 |
| .9 | 1.2 | 1.4 | 1.0 | 1.1 | | | 1.3 | 1.3 |
| 0 UND | 0 UND | 0 UND | 2 198.8 | 3 123.6 | | | 0 UND | 0 UND |
| 0 UND | 1 500.6 | 2 150.6 | 5 66.7 | 12 30.2 | | Sales/Receivables | 4 96.5 | 5 73.4 |
| 7 50.1 | 5 76.3 | 18 20.0 | 14 25.3 | 68 5.4 | | | 15 24.1 | 20 18.7 |
| | | | | | | Cost of Sales/Inventory | | |
| | | | | | | Cost of Sales/Payables | | |
| 2.6 | 1.8 | 1.2 | 1.5 | 1.0 | | | 1.3 | 1.2 |
| 5.5 | 3.9 | 2.3 | 2.5 | 1.8 | | Sales/Working Capital | 2.9 | 2.8 |
| UND | 23.2 | 6.1 | 21.1 | 20.0 | | | 8.0 | 7.9 |
| 6.6 | 7.7 | 30.0 | 14.4 | | | | 11.2 | 14.7 |
| (10) 1.8 | (15) 1.0 | (26) 7.1 | (19) 1.9 | | | EBIT/Interest | (106) 2.8 | (80) 4.6 |
| -.8 | -11.6 | .9 | .2 | | | | .2 | .8 |
| | | | | | | Net Profit + Depr., Dep., Amort./Cur. Mat. L/T/D | | |
| .0 | .0 | .0 | .3 | .4 | | | .0 | .0 |
| .0 | .0 | .1 | .7 | .7 | | Fixed/Worth | .0 | .1 |
| .1 | .0 | .7 | 1.0 | .9 | | | .7 | 1.0 |
| .3 | .6 | .5 | .3 | .1 | | | .2 | .2 |
| 1.7 | 3.1 | 1.3 | .6 | .2 | | Debt/Worth | 1.0 | 1.1 |
| -3.4 | 344.1 | 4.8 | 3.5 | 1.9 | | | 5.5 | 8.3 |
| 178.2 | 45.7 | 43.5 | 10.1 | 9.8 | | % Profit Before Taxes/Tangible Net Worth | 20.9 | 23.9 |
| (20) 22.2 | (37) 12.0 | (48) 16.0 | (30) 3.0 | (10) 6.7 | | | (240) 6.3 | (115) 7.8 |
| -14.2 | -28.8 | 2.6 | -4.8 | .3 | | | -3.6 | -1.4 |
| 27.6 | 10.6 | 13.0 | 6.1 | 7.7 | | % Profit Before Taxes/Total Assets | 10.0 | 12.9 |
| 5.2 | 2.8 | 5.7 | 1.8 | 5.0 | | | 2.3 | 4.3 |
| -18.7 | -17.2 | .4 | -1.8 | 1.2 | | | -2.2 | -1.2 |
| UND | UND | UND | 11.4 | 2.8 | | | UND | UND |
| UND | UND | 61.4 | 1.5 | .9 | | Sales/Net Fixed Assets | UND | 58.6 |
| UND | 188.9 | 1.8 | .7 | .5 | | | 6.9 | 1.4 |
| 3.0 | 2.3 | 1.3 | 1.0 | .5 | | | 1.8 | 1.5 |
| 1.7 | 1.4 | .9 | .6 | .4 | | Sales/Total Assets | 1.1 | .8 |
| 1.2 | 1.0 | .5 | .4 | .2 | | | .6 | .4 |
| | | .3 | 2.0 | | | | .9 | 1.1 |
| | (25) | 1.9 | (26) 5.7 | | | % Depr., Dep., Amort./Sales | (80) 4.5 | (61) 4.5 |
| | | 5.9 | 8.8 | | | | 8.4 | 9.9 |
| | | | | | | % Officers', Directors' Owners' Comp/Sales | 3.2 | |
| | | | | | | | (22) 5.7 | |
| | | | | | | | 10.1 | |
| 13370M | 97446M | 252078M | 584137M | 360443M | 980374M | Net Sales ($) | 1142687M | 816722M |
| 7005M | 56469M | 263903M | 747869M | 731836M | 247771M | Total Assets ($) | 1880045M | 1591214M |

© RMA 2024   M = $ thousand   MM = $ million
See Pages viii through xx for Explanation of Ratios and Data

## OTHER SERVICES—Other Similar Organizations (except Business, Professional, Labor, and Political Organizations) NAICS 813990

### Comparative Historical Data | Current Data Sorted by Sales

| Comparative Historical Data ||| Type of Statement | Current Data Sorted by Sales ||||||
|---|---|---|---|---|---|---|---|---|---|
| 54 | 64 | 59 | Unqualified | 7 | 6 | 9 | 11 | 18 | 8 |
| 10 | 7 | 9 | Reviewed | 4 | 1 | 1 | 2 | 1 | |
| 5 | 7 | 3 | Compiled | 1 | 1 | 1 | | | |
| 8 | 9 | 7 | Tax Returns | 6 | | | 1 | | |
| 136 | 212 | 97 | Other | 27 | 36 | 12 | 13 | 4 | 5 |
| 4/1/21- 3/31/22 ALL | 4/1/22- 3/31/23 ALL | 4/1/23- 3/31/24 ALL | | 42 (4/1-9/30/23) ||| 133 (10/1/23-3/31/24) |||
| | | | | 0-1MM | 1-3MM | 3-5MM | 5-10MM | 10-25MM | 25MM & OVER |
| 213 | 299 | 175 | NUMBER OF STATEMENTS | 45 | 44 | 23 | 27 | 23 | 13 |
| % | % | % | ASSETS | % | % | % | % | % | % |
| 60.5 | 62.0 | 52.6 | Cash & Equivalents | 60.8 | 62.5 | 52.5 | 51.6 | 37.1 | 19.7 |
| 5.9 | 5.2 | 4.8 | Trade Receivables (net) | 4.6 | 4.4 | 2.7 | 4.5 | 2.3 | 15.8 |
| .1 | .7 | .4 | Inventory | .0 | .0 | .1 | 1.6 | .4 | 1.1 |
| 4.6 | 6.7 | 6.4 | All Other Current | 6.6 | 5.7 | 7.3 | 8.8 | 6.2 | 1.7 |
| 71.2 | 74.7 | 64.2 | Total Current | 72.1 | 72.6 | 62.6 | 66.4 | 46.0 | 38.3 |
| 17.5 | 13.0 | 20.2 | Fixed Assets (net) | 14.6 | 9.2 | 22.7 | 22.7 | 35.0 | 40.8 |
| 1.1 | 1.3 | .4 | Intangibles (net) | .2 | .7 | .2 | .0 | .0 | 2.0 |
| 10.3 | 11.0 | 15.2 | All Other Non-Current | 13.0 | 17.5 | 14.5 | 10.9 | 19.0 | 18.9 |
| 100.0 | 100.0 | 100.0 | Total | 100.0 | 100.0 | 100.0 | 100.0 | 100.0 | 100.0 |
| | | | LIABILITIES | | | | | | |
| 5.4 | 5.2 | 3.9 | Notes Payable-Short Term | 9.9 | 1.1 | .0 | 3.9 | .0 | 5.6 |
| 4.6 | 2.2 | 3.5 | Cur. Mat.-L.T.D. | 5.5 | 2.2 | 4.3 | 3.3 | 2.7 | 1.1 |
| 3.8 | 5.3 | 5.0 | Trade Payables | 4.7 | 3.9 | 5.1 | 7.3 | 4.4 | 5.4 |
| .2 | .3 | .2 | Income Taxes Payable | .0 | .5 | .0 | .2 | .0 | .6 |
| 11.2 | 15.2 | 21.1 | All Other Current | 21.5 | 25.4 | 22.1 | 16.5 | 12.0 | 29.2 |
| 25.1 | 28.3 | 33.6 | Total Current | 41.6 | 33.2 | 31.6 | 31.2 | 19.1 | 41.9 |
| 40.5 | 44.5 | 23.5 | Long-Term Debt | 38.8 | 21.0 | 27.6 | 17.5 | 11.6 | 5.0 |
| .0 | .0 | .0 | Deferred Taxes | .0 | .0 | .0 | .2 | .0 | .0 |
| 10.0 | 11.7 | 14.7 | All Other Non-Current | 12.1 | 22.2 | 15.6 | 14.1 | 8.1 | 9.8 |
| 24.4 | 15.5 | 28.1 | Net Worth | 7.4 | 23.6 | 25.2 | 37.0 | 61.2 | 43.3 |
| 100.0 | 100.0 | 100.0 | Total Liabilties & Net Worth | 100.0 | 100.0 | 100.0 | 100.0 | 100.0 | 100.0 |
| | | | INCOME DATA | | | | | | |
| 100.0 | 100.0 | 100.0 | Net Sales | 100.0 | 100.0 | 100.0 | 100.0 | 100.0 | 100.0 |
| | | | Gross Profit | | | | | | |
| 86.7 | 88.2 | 89.1 | Operating Expenses | 85.2 | 89.2 | 96.5 | 92.1 | 88.8 | 83.9 |
| 13.3 | 11.8 | 10.9 | Operating Profit | 14.8 | 10.8 | 3.5 | 7.9 | 11.2 | 16.1 |
| 6.9 | 7.1 | 5.6 | All Other Expenses (net) | 9.9 | 7.1 | 2.5 | 2.9 | -.1 | 7.3 |
| 6.4 | 4.7 | 5.2 | Profit Before Taxes | 4.9 | 3.7 | 1.0 | 5.1 | 11.4 | 8.8 |
| | | | RATIOS | | | | | | |
| 14.0 | 15.0 | 6.7 | | 6.4 | 10.3 | 7.7 | 3.9 | 8.1 | 3.2 |
| 5.7 | 4.2 | 2.8 | Current | 3.1 | 2.5 | 3.9 | 2.9 | 4.2 | 1.3 |
| 1.9 | 1.5 | 1.3 | | 1.1 | 1.5 | 1.5 | 1.6 | 1.3 | 1.0 |
| 13.2 | 13.5 | 6.3 | | 6.0 | 9.2 | 7.7 | 3.6 | 7.9 | 2.8 |
| 5.5 | 4.0 | 2.5 | Quick | 2.5 | 2.4 | 2.8 | 2.7 | 3.8 | 1.1 |
| 1.7 | 1.3 | 1.1 | | 1.0 | 1.4 | 1.3 | 1.3 | 1.1 | .8 |
| 0 UND | 0 UND | 0 UND | | 0 UND | 0 UND | 0 UND | 0 999.8 | 0 999.8 | 5 78.4 |
| 4 87.0 | 3 106.7 | 3 141.9 | Sales/Receivables | 0 UND | 2 146.6 | 1 244.9 | 3 119.4 | 5 75.5 | 18 20.5 |
| 19 19.2 | 16 22.3 | 12 29.7 | | 6 62.7 | 16 22.4 | 11 33.8 | 20 17.9 | 12 29.7 | 35 10.5 |
| | | | Cost of Sales/Inventory | | | | | | |
| | | | Cost of Sales/Payables | | | | | | |
| 1.2 | 1.0 | 1.5 | | 1.3 | 1.2 | 1.9 | 1.5 | 1.0 | 4.9 |
| 2.0 | 2.0 | 3.2 | Sales/Working Capital | 3.9 | 2.7 | 3.9 | 2.5 | 2.9 | 23.4 |
| 6.2 | 7.4 | 15.4 | | 41.7 | 13.7 | 6.7 | 6.2 | 6.2 | -283.6 |
| 6.7 | 10.4 | 13.5 | | 5.7 | 18.5 | 10.8 | 39.1 | 45.0 | |
| (103) 3.0 | (140) 2.6 | (76) 4.0 | EBIT/Interest | (17) 1.5 | (18) 3.6 | (12) 2.4 | (11) 3.1 | (10) 14.0 | |
| -.7 | -1.2 | .2 | | -1.8 | -1.8 | -2.7 | -4.7 | 7.8 | |
| | | | Net Profit + Depr., Dep., Amort./Cur. Mat. L/T/D | | | | | | |
| .0 | .0 | .0 | | .0 | .0 | .0 | .0 | .0 | .3 |
| .0 | .0 | .0 | Fixed/Worth | .0 | .0 | .3 | .1 | .6 | .8 |
| .7 | .5 | .8 | | .6 | .2 | 1.1 | .8 | .9 | 1.5 |
| .2 | .3 | .3 | | .3 | .9 | .2 | .5 | .1 | .2 |
| 1.3 | 1.6 | 1.3 | Debt/Worth | 1.4 | 3.2 | 1.2 | 1.1 | .6 | .5 |
| 778.0 | -53.8 | 9.6 | | UND | 49.7 | 15.4 | 8.5 | 1.6 | 5.6 |
| 19.2 | 20.7 | 37.2 | | 71.9 | 42.5 | 23.9 | 51.2 | 15.8 | 11.4 |
| (161) 5.3 | (221) 4.7 | (146) 8.7 | % Profit Before Taxes/Tangible Net Worth | (35) 14.4 | (36) 13.2 | (18) 7.6 | (23) 9.7 | (11) 6.6 | 7.4 |
| -4.1 | -3.6 | -.8 | | -9.1 | .0 | -3.4 | -3.4 | .4 | -24.7 |
| 13.2 | 10.5 | 10.5 | | 20.1 | 10.4 | 8.9 | 20.5 | 8.6 | 7.3 |
| 4.6 | 1.6 | 3.7 | % Profit Before Taxes/Total Assets | 5.2 | 3.3 | 2.8 | 5.0 | 4.1 | 5.6 |
| -1.5 | -3.0 | -3.6 | | -11.9 | -2.5 | -17.4 | -1.8 | .2 | -10.6 |
| UND | UND | UND | | UND | UND | UND | UND | 50.1 | 29.6 |
| UND | UND | 537.0 | Sales/Net Fixed Assets | UND | UND | 27.9 | 26.8 | 1.5 | 2.1 |
| 1.8 | 8.0 | 2.1 | | 83.6 | 79.1 | 1.8 | 2.9 | .7 | .9 |
| 1.6 | 1.6 | 1.8 | | 2.0 | 1.7 | 2.7 | 1.8 | 1.0 | 2.2 |
| .9 | .9 | 1.0 | Sales/Total Assets | 1.2 | 1.1 | 1.0 | 1.1 | .5 | .9 |
| .5 | .4 | .6 | | .7 | .7 | .7 | .6 | .4 | .5 |
| 1.4 | 1.4 | .9 | | | | 1.5 | .1 | 1.8 | .5 |
| (59) 5.1 | (69) 4.9 | (67) 3.6 | % Depr., Dep., Amort./Sales | | (10) 3.3 | (14) 1.9 | (19) 5.5 | (10) 5.1 | |
| 10.7 | 10.5 | 8.4 | | | 8.5 | 8.5 | 9.7 | 7.9 | |
| | 3.3 | | | | | | | | |
| (11) | 5.4 | | % Officers', Directors' Owners' Comp/Sales | | | | | | |
| | 21.4 | | | | | | | | |
| 1417979M | 1536849M | 2287848M | Net Sales ($) | 23091M | 84287M | 88629M | 201785M | 332478M | 1557578M |
| 1667101M | 2415573M | 2054853M | Total Assets ($) | 36206M | 106323M | 107464M | 310620M | 736574M | 757666M |

© RMA 2024  M = $ thousand   MM = $ million
See Pages viii through xx for Explanation of Ratios and Data

# PUBLIC ADMINISTRATION

# PUBLIC ADMINISTRATION—Executive Offices  NAICS 921110

## Current Data Sorted by Assets | Comparative Historical Data

| 0-500M | 500M-2MM | 2-10MM | 10-50MM | 50-100MM | 100-250MM | | 4/1/19-3/31/20 ALL | 4/1/20-3/31/21 ALL |
|---|---|---|---|---|---|---|---|---|
| | | | 3 | 37 | 21 | Type of Statement Unqualified | 105 | 68 |
| | | | | | 32 | Reviewed | | |
| | | | | | 1 | Compiled | | |
| | | | | | | Tax Returns | | |
| 2 | 5 | 4 | 7 | 3 | 3 | Other | 15 | 11 |
|  94 (4/1-9/30/23) | | | 24 (10/1/23-3/31/24) | | | | | |
| 2 | 5 | 7 | 44 | 24 | 36 | NUMBER OF STATEMENTS | 120 | 79 |
| % | % | % | % | % | % | ASSETS | % | % |
| | | | 48.9 | 42.5 | 31.2 | Cash & Equivalents | 35.2 | 37.2 |
| | | | 7.1 | 6.2 | 3.1 | Trade Receivables (net) | 5.8 | 5.6 |
| | | | .1 | .2 | .2 | Inventory | .2 | .1 |
| | | | 10.0 | 7.5 | 4.5 | All Other Current | 5.3 | 6.4 |
| | | | 66.1 | 56.5 | 39.0 | Total Current | 46.6 | 49.3 |
| | | | 27.4 | 30.8 | 50.9 | Fixed Assets (net) | 45.4 | 42.8 |
| | | | .5 | .4 | .3 | Intangibles (net) | .7 | .6 |
| | | | 6.0 | 12.3 | 9.8 | All Other Non-Current | 7.3 | 7.2 |
| | | | 100.0 | 100.0 | 100.0 | Total | 100.0 | 100.0 |
| | | | | | | LIABILITIES | | |
| | | | .0 | .4 | .1 | Notes Payable-Short Term | .0 | .1 |
| | | | 1.4 | 1.0 | 1.8 | Cur. Mat.-L.T.D. | 2.4 | 1.6 |
| | | | 3.6 | 3.0 | 2.4 | Trade Payables | 2.8 | 2.2 |
| | | | .2 | .0 | .1 | Income Taxes Payable | .1 | .1 |
| | | | 7.0 | 8.2 | 2.5 | All Other Current | 3.3 | 4.4 |
| | | | 12.3 | 12.6 | 6.9 | Total Current | 8.6 | 8.3 |
| | | | 16.9 | 16.0 | 23.1 | Long-Term Debt | 19.2 | 14.3 |
| | | | .0 | .0 | .7 | Deferred Taxes | .0 | .0 |
| | | | 10.5 | 10.2 | 15.0 | All Other Non-Current | 15.2 | 11.5 |
| | | | 60.3 | 61.3 | 54.3 | Net Worth | 57.0 | 65.9 |
| | | | 100.0 | 100.0 | 100.0 | Total Liabilities & Net Worth | 100.0 | 100.0 |
| | | | | | | INCOME DATA | | |
| | | | 100.0 | 100.0 | 100.0 | Net Sales | 100.0 | 100.0 |
| | | | | | | Gross Profit | | |
| | | | 87.9 | 84.2 | 79.9 | Operating Expenses | 88.7 | 89.4 |
| | | | 12.1 | 15.8 | 20.1 | Operating Profit | 11.3 | 10.6 |
| | | | 3.7 | 3.2 | 1.8 | All Other Expenses (net) | 2.5 | 4.9 |
| | | | 8.4 | 12.7 | 18.3 | Profit Before Taxes | 8.8 | 5.7 |
| | | | | | | RATIOS | | |
| | | | 14.0 | 13.3 | 9.9 | | 9.6 | 12.8 |
| | | | 7.6 | 5.7 | 5.3 | Current | 5.7 | 6.5 |
| | | | 3.8 | 2.8 | 3.9 | | 3.1 | 4.4 |
| | | | 12.9 | 12.5 | 9.2 | | 8.8 | 10.8 |
| | | | 6.6 | 5.2 | 4.4 | Quick | 4.9 | 5.9 |
| | | | 3.7 | 1.6 | 3.1 | | 2.7 | 3.8 |
| | | | 8  45.2 | 13  27.3 | 9  39.0 | | 7  53.2 | 6  63.5 |
| | | | 24  15.1 | 30  12.0 | 29  12.7 | Sales/Receivables | 23  15.6 | 25  14.5 |
| | | | 40  9.1 | 55  6.6 | 62  5.9 | | 45  8.1 | 52  7.0 |
| | | | | | | Cost of Sales/Inventory | | |
| | | | | | | Cost of Sales/Payables | | |
| | | | 1.0 | 1.0 | .8 | | 1.0 | .8 |
| | | | 1.5 | 1.7 | 1.2 | Sales/Working Capital | 1.7 | 1.5 |
| | | | 2.1 | 4.8 | 2.1 | | 2.9 | 2.4 |
| | | | 32.8 | 14.7 | 15.2 | | 14.9 | 11.0 |
| | | | (32)  9.5 | (22)  6.9 | (33)  7.7 | EBIT/Interest | (96)  3.5 | (61)  4.2 |
| | | | 1.8 | 2.1 | 4.3 | | 1.2 | 1.1 |
| | | | | | | Net Profit + Depr., Dep., Amort./Cur. Mat. L/T/D | | |
| | | | .0 | .0 | .7 | | .0 | .0 |
| | | | .3 | .7 | 1.1 | Fixed/Worth | .9 | .9 |
| | | | 1.1 | 1.1 | 1.6 | | 1.6 | 1.2 |
| | | | .2 | .2 | .3 | | .2 | .2 |
| | | | .5 | .6 | .7 | Debt/Worth | .5 | .3 |
| | | | 1.3 | 1.2 | 1.4 | | 1.7 | 1.1 |
| | | | 12.8 | 16.0 | 12.5 | | 12.5 | 10.2 |
| | | | (43)  4.5 | 9.4 | (33)  8.6 | % Profit Before Taxes/Tangible Net Worth | (112)  4.9 | (76)  4.2 |
| | | | -5.4 | 2.8 | 4.7 | | .9 | .0 |
| | | | 7.3 | 12.1 | 6.7 | | 7.6 | 5.6 |
| | | | 3.5 | 6.7 | 4.4 | % Profit Before Taxes/Total Assets | 2.7 | 2.8 |
| | | | -3.8 | 1.5 | 1.8 | | .3 | -.6 |
| | | | UND | UND | 1.7 | | UND | UND |
| | | | 17.6 | .9 | .5 | Sales/Net Fixed Assets | .7 | .8 |
| | | | .6 | .5 | .4 | | .3 | .4 |
| | | | 1.3 | 1.4 | .5 | | 1.1 | 1.1 |
| | | | .6 | .4 | .3 | Sales/Total Assets | .4 | .4 |
| | | | .3 | .3 | .2 | | .2 | .2 |
| | | | 7.3 | 7.3 | 7.6 | | 6.6 | 7.3 |
| | | | (18)  10.3 | (12)  9.3 | (29)  10.1 | % Depr., Dep., Amort./Sales | (69)  11.5 | (48)  12.7 |
| | | | 14.6 | 10.2 | 13.0 | | 18.7 | 21.3 |
| | | | | | | | 3.7 | |
| | | | | | | % Officers', Directors' Owners' Comp/Sales | (10)  6.6 | |
| | | | | | | | 10.2 | |
| 1393M | 18103M | 32033M | 1177480M | 1854117M | 2318596M | Net Sales ($) | 5207204M | 3538926M |
| 863M | 5888M | 36010M | 1315473M | 1779741M | 5663383M | Total Assets ($) | 8513817M | 5291548M |

M = $ thousand   MM = $ million
See Pages viii through xx for Explanation of Ratios and Data
© RMA 2024

# PUBLIC ADMINISTRATION—Executive Offices  NAICS 921110

## Comparative Historical Data | Current Data Sorted by Sales

| Comparative Historical Data ||| Type of Statement | Current Data Sorted by Sales ||||||
|---|---|---|---|---|---|---|---|---|---|
| 59 | 102 | 93 | Unqualified | 1 | 1 | 5 | 6 | 22 | 58 |
|  | 1 |  | Reviewed |  |  |  |  |  |  |
| 1 | 1 | 1 | Compiled |  |  |  |  |  | 1 |
|  |  |  | Tax Returns |  |  |  |  |  |  |
| 23 | 33 | 24 | Other | 3 | 4 | 3 | 2 | 6 | 6 |
| 4/1/21-3/31/22 | 4/1/22-3/31/23 | 4/1/23-3/31/24 |  | 94 (4/1-9/30/23) |||| 24 (10/1/23-3/31/24) ||
| ALL | ALL | ALL |  | 0-1MM | 1-3MM | 3-5MM | 5-10MM | 10-25MM | 25MM & OVER |
| 83 | 137 | 118 | NUMBER OF STATEMENTS | 4 | 5 | 8 | 8 | 28 | 65 |
| % | % | % | ASSETS | % | % | % | % | % | % |
| 41.7 | 45.8 | 43.6 | Cash & Equivalents |  |  |  |  | 35.5 | 45.1 |
| 6.5 | 5.1 | 5.2 | Trade Receivables (net) |  |  |  |  | 7.3 | 5.6 |
| .1 | .2 | .2 | Inventory |  |  |  |  | .1 | .2 |
| 8.7 | 7.5 | 7.7 | All Other Current |  |  |  |  | 6.4 | 8.4 |
| 57.1 | 58.6 | 56.8 | Total Current |  |  |  |  | 49.3 | 59.4 |
| 31.2 | 32.1 | 33.3 | Fixed Assets (net) |  |  |  |  | 42.0 | 31.2 |
| .3 | .5 | .3 | Intangibles (net) |  |  |  |  | .2 | .3 |
| 11.4 | 8.8 | 9.6 | All Other Non-Current |  |  |  |  | 8.6 | 9.2 |
| 100.0 | 100.0 | 100.0 | Total |  |  |  |  | 100.0 | 100.0 |
|  |  |  | LIABILITIES |  |  |  |  |  |  |
| 1.2 | .1 | 1.0 | Notes Payable-Short Term |  |  |  |  | .3 | .1 |
| 2.2 | 1.3 | 1.4 | Cur. Mat.-L.T.D. |  |  |  |  | 1.7 | 1.2 |
| 2.6 | 2.5 | 3.5 | Trade Payables |  |  |  |  | 5.5 | 3.5 |
| .0 | .0 | .1 | Income Taxes Payable |  |  |  |  | .3 | .1 |
| 4.8 | 6.1 | 7.0 | All Other Current |  |  |  |  | 10.9 | 6.4 |
| 10.8 | 10.0 | 13.1 | Total Current |  |  |  |  | 18.7 | 11.1 |
| 14.4 | 17.7 | 18.0 | Long-Term Debt |  |  |  |  | 22.3 | 14.9 |
| .0 | .0 | .3 | Deferred Taxes |  |  |  |  | .0 | .4 |
| 17.6 | 10.5 | 11.8 | All Other Non-Current |  |  |  |  | 15.6 | 11.8 |
| 57.3 | 61.8 | 56.8 | Net Worth |  |  |  |  | 43.3 | 61.9 |
| 100.0 | 100.0 | 100.0 | Total Liabilities & Net Worth |  |  |  |  | 100.0 | 100.0 |
|  |  |  | INCOME DATA |  |  |  |  |  |  |
| 100.0 | 100.0 | 100.0 | Net Sales |  |  |  |  | 100.0 | 100.0 |
|  |  |  | Gross Profit |  |  |  |  |  |  |
| 84.7 | 81.8 | 84.8 | Operating Expenses |  |  |  |  | 82.6 | 85.4 |
| 15.3 | 18.2 | 15.2 | Operating Profit |  |  |  |  | 17.4 | 14.6 |
| 5.3 | 5.3 | 3.8 | All Other Expenses (net) |  |  |  |  | 2.8 | 3.3 |
| 10.0 | 12.9 | 11.4 | Profit Before Taxes |  |  |  |  | 14.6 | 11.4 |
|  |  |  | RATIOS |  |  |  |  |  |  |
| 12.4 | 10.1 | 11.8 |  |  |  |  |  | 13.2 | 10.5 |
| 6.3 | 6.4 | 6.5 | Current |  |  |  |  | 4.9 | 6.9 |
| 3.7 | 3.9 | 3.4 |  |  |  |  |  | 2.5 | 3.9 |
| 9.9 | 9.3 | 10.7 |  |  |  |  |  | 9.2 | 10.1 |
| 5.6 | 6.0 | 5.6 | Quick |  |  |  |  | 4.3 | 5.6 |
| 2.8 | 2.9 | 3.1 |  |  |  |  |  | 2.2 | 3.1 |
| 4  94.9 | 10  38.0 | 7  52.6 |  |  |  |  |  | 14  25.6 | 7  49.7 |
| 32  11.4 | 27  13.7 | 25  14.7 | Sales/Receivables |  |  |  |  | 30  12.1 | 24  15.2 |
| 51  7.1 | 42  8.6 | 43  8.5 |  |  |  |  |  | 81  4.5 | 41  9.0 |
|  |  |  | Cost of Sales/Inventory |  |  |  |  |  |  |
|  |  |  | Cost of Sales/Payables |  |  |  |  |  |  |
| .9 | .9 | .9 |  |  |  |  |  | .9 | 1.0 |
| 1.6 | 1.4 | 1.4 | Sales/Working Capital |  |  |  |  | 1.3 | 1.6 |
| 2.7 | 2.2 | 2.6 |  |  |  |  |  | 2.7 | 2.8 |
| 22.5 | 26.7 | 15.5 |  |  |  |  |  | 20.7 | 13.2 |
| (64)  7.4 | (103)  8.0 | (93)  7.7 | EBIT/Interest |  |  |  |  | (26)  10.0 | (51)  6.5 |
| 1.8 | 1.9 | 2.5 |  |  |  |  |  | 1.2 | 2.7 |
|  |  |  | Net Profit + Depr., Dep., Amort./Cur. Mat. L/T/D |  |  |  |  |  |  |
| .0 | .0 | .0 |  |  |  |  |  | .3 | .0 |
| .6 | .6 | .7 | Fixed/Worth |  |  |  |  | 1.0 | .7 |
| 1.2 | 1.1 | 1.2 |  |  |  |  |  | 1.6 | 1.1 |
| .2 | .2 | .2 |  |  |  |  |  | .5 | .2 |
| .5 | .5 | .6 | Debt/Worth |  |  |  |  | .7 | .5 |
| 1.5 | 1.1 | 1.3 |  |  |  |  |  | 3.1 | 1.2 |
| 19.0 | 17.9 | 13.7 | % Profit Before Taxes/Tangible Net Worth |  |  |  |  | 14.0 | 13.8 |
| (77)  10.7 | (131)  11.6 | (112)  7.4 |  |  |  |  |  | (27)  6.8 | (62)  7.9 |
| 2.8 | 3.3 | 2.1 |  |  |  |  |  | -.6 | 3.0 |
| 12.0 | 13.3 | 8.4 | % Profit Before Taxes/Total Assets |  |  |  |  | 8.2 | 10.1 |
| 5.5 | 6.9 | 3.8 |  |  |  |  |  | 3.7 | 4.2 |
| 1.7 | 1.9 | .8 |  |  |  |  |  | .0 | 1.6 |
| UND | UND | UND |  |  |  |  |  | UND | UND |
| 1.5 | 1.3 | 1.0 | Sales/Net Fixed Assets |  |  |  |  | .7 | 1.9 |
| .4 | .5 | .4 |  |  |  |  |  | .4 | .5 |
| 1.2 | 1.1 | 1.1 |  |  |  |  |  | .6 | 1.4 |
| .5 | .5 | .5 | Sales/Total Assets |  |  |  |  | .4 | .6 |
| .3 | .3 | .3 |  |  |  |  |  | .2 | .3 |
| 6.5 | 6.5 | 7.3 |  |  |  |  |  | 7.4 | 7.2 |
| (42)  10.4 | (72)  10.0 | (62)  9.8 | % Depr., Dep., Amort./Sales |  |  |  |  | (16)  9.6 | (34)  9.1 |
| 13.5 | 14.9 | 12.9 |  |  |  |  |  | 12.5 | 12.1 |
|  | 3.2 | .8 | % Officers', Directors' Owners' Comp/Sales |  |  |  |  |  |  |
|  | (10)  10.2 | (11)  11.1 |  |  |  |  |  |  |  |
|  | 22.4 | 28.9 |  |  |  |  |  |  |  |
| 3608537M | 5604623M | 5401722M | Net Sales ($) | 2544M | 7959M | 31847M | 57699M | 444904M | 4856769M |
| 5444571M | 9110792M | 8801358M | Total Assets ($) | 7373M | 10919M | 120757M | 208407M | 1380304M | 7073598M |

© RMA 2024  M = $ thousand  MM = $ million
See Pages viii through xx for Explanation of Ratios and Data

# PUBLIC ADMINISTRATION—Legislative Bodies  NAICS 921120

## Current Data Sorted by Assets | Comparative Historical Data

| | | | | | | | Type of Statement | | |
|---|---|---|---|---|---|---|---|---|---|
| | 1 | 1 | | 12 | 11 | 17 | Unqualified | 106 | 74 |
| | | | | | | | Reviewed | | |
| | | | | | | | Compiled | 2 | 1 |
| | | | | | | | Tax Returns | 1 | |
| | 1 | 1 | | | 3 | | Other | 12 | 10 |
| | | 40 (4/1-9/30/23) | | 7 (10/1/23-3/31/24) | | | | 4/1/19- | 4/1/20- |
| | | | | | | | | 3/31/20 | 3/31/21 |
| | 0-500M | 500M-2MM | 2-10MM | 10-50MM | 50-100MM | 100-250MM | | ALL | ALL |
| | 2 | 2 | | 12 | 14 | 17 | NUMBER OF STATEMENTS | 121 | 85 |
| | % | % | % | % | % | % | ASSETS | % | % |
| | | | | 31.6 | 28.2 | 27.0 | Cash & Equivalents | 25.1 | 25.4 |
| | | | D | 3.6 | 5.7 | 6.1 | Trade Receivables (net) | 5.5 | 5.6 |
| | | | A | .5 | .1 | .3 | Inventory | .2 | .3 |
| | | | T | 10.3 | 16.1 | 5.8 | All Other Current | 6.6 | 6.1 |
| | | | A | 46.0 | 50.1 | 39.1 | Total Current | 37.5 | 37.3 |
| | | | | 38.2 | 42.2 | 52.4 | Fixed Assets (net) | 54.7 | 54.8 |
| | | | N | 4.3 | .0 | .7 | Intangibles (net) | .7 | .5 |
| | | | O | 11.5 | 7.7 | 7.7 | All Other Non-Current | 7.2 | 7.4 |
| | | | T | 100.0 | 100.0 | 100.0 | Total | 100.0 | 100.0 |
| | | | | | | | LIABILITIES | | |
| | | | A | 2.7 | .7 | .2 | Notes Payable-Short Term | .3 | .2 |
| | | | V | 2.1 | 1.8 | 1.9 | Cur. Mat.-L.T.D. | 2.3 | 1.9 |
| | | | A | 1.7 | 1.4 | 1.3 | Trade Payables | 2.0 | 1.7 |
| | | | I | .0 | .0 | .0 | Income Taxes Payable | .0 | .0 |
| | | | L | 5.1 | 7.2 | 3.1 | All Other Current | 4.9 | 5.6 |
| | | | A | 11.6 | 11.2 | 6.5 | Total Current | 9.5 | 9.4 |
| | | | B | 14.2 | 14.9 | 20.7 | Long-Term Debt | 26.2 | 22.2 |
| | | | L | .0 | .0 | .0 | Deferred Taxes | .0 | .0 |
| | | | E | 11.5 | 15.3 | 20.3 | All Other Non-Current | 16.2 | 17.5 |
| | | | | 62.6 | 58.7 | 52.5 | Net Worth | 48.1 | 50.9 |
| | | | | 100.0 | 100.0 | 100.0 | Total Liabilities & Net Worth | 100.0 | 100.0 |
| | | | | | | | INCOME DATA | | |
| | | | | 100.0 | 100.0 | 100.0 | Net Sales | 100.0 | 100.0 |
| | | | | | | | Gross Profit | | |
| | | | | 88.7 | 88.0 | 81.4 | Operating Expenses | 91.6 | 90.3 |
| | | | | 11.3 | 12.0 | 18.6 | Operating Profit | 8.4 | 9.7 |
| | | | | 3.5 | 3.0 | 1.3 | All Other Expenses (net) | 3.3 | 5.3 |
| | | | | 7.8 | 9.0 | 17.2 | Profit Before Taxes | 5.0 | 4.4 |
| | | | | | | | RATIOS | | |
| | | | | 11.8 | 9.5 | 9.8 | | 6.5 | 7.3 |
| | | | | 6.3 | 4.6 | 6.4 | Current | 4.4 | 4.8 |
| | | | | 2.7 | 2.3 | 4.1 | | 2.8 | 2.7 |
| | | | | 9.4 | 5.8 | 9.0 | | 5.2 | 6.2 |
| | | | | 5.7 | 4.1 | 5.5 | Quick | 3.7 | 4.4 |
| | | | | 2.4 | 1.9 | 3.5 | | 1.9 | 1.8 |
| | | | 3 | 141.8 | 12 | 30.1 | 22 | 16.4 | Sales/Receivables | 11 | 33.5 | 18 | 20.7 |
| | | | 16 | 22.9 | 32 | 11.3 | 37 | 9.8 | | 36 | 10.2 | 37 | 9.9 |
| | | | 49 | 7.4 | 66 | 5.5 | 130 | 2.8 | | 81 | 4.5 | 85 | 4.3 |
| | | | | | | | Cost of Sales/Inventory | | |
| | | | | | | | Cost of Sales/Payables | | |
| | | | | .6 | 1.1 | .7 | | .9 | .9 |
| | | | | 1.4 | 1.5 | .9 | Sales/Working Capital | 1.4 | 1.4 |
| | | | | 2.1 | 3.3 | 1.3 | | 3.3 | 2.7 |
| | | | | 46.8 | 8.2 | 20.2 | | 6.9 | 6.6 |
| | | | (11) | 18.3 | (12) | 4.6 | (16) | 6.3 | EBIT/Interest | (108) | 2.8 | (77) | 2.3 |
| | | | | 6.6 | 2.1 | 3.0 | | .9 | -.1 |
| | | | | | | | Net Profit + Depr., Dep., Amort./Cur. Mat. L/T/D | | |
| | | | | .0 | .0 | .8 | | .8 | .8 |
| | | | | .6 | .9 | 1.0 | Fixed/Worth | 1.1 | 1.0 |
| | | | | .9 | 1.3 | 1.4 | | 2.0 | 1.6 |
| | | | | .3 | .3 | .4 | | .4 | .4 |
| | | | | .5 | .7 | .9 | Debt/Worth | .8 | .7 |
| | | | | 1.6 | 1.0 | 1.8 | | 2.3 | 2.0 |
| | | | | 11.9 | 19.6 | 14.5 | % Profit Before Taxes/Tangible Net Worth | 10.1 | 8.7 |
| | | | (11) | 8.1 | 3.2 | 8.4 | | (114) | 3.8 | (81) | 2.1 |
| | | | | -1.5 | 1.4 | 3.3 | | .1 | -1.3 |
| | | | | 7.3 | 6.7 | 5.9 | % Profit Before Taxes/Total Assets | 4.3 | 3.3 |
| | | | | 5.8 | 1.9 | 3.4 | | 1.8 | 1.3 |
| | | | | -.7 | .8 | 1.6 | | -.1 | -.7 |
| | | | | UND | UND | .7 | | 1.2 | 1.0 |
| | | | | 1.0 | .7 | .5 | Sales/Net Fixed Assets | .5 | .5 |
| | | | | .4 | .3 | .3 | | .3 | .3 |
| | | | | .6 | 1.0 | .3 | | .6 | .5 |
| | | | | .4 | .4 | .3 | Sales/Total Assets | .3 | .3 |
| | | | | .2 | .2 | .2 | | .2 | .2 |
| | | | | | | 6.5 | | 7.0 | 6.8 |
| | | | | | (15) | 11.1 | % Depr., Dep., Amort./Sales | (96) | 12.5 | (67) | 12.3 |
| | | | | | | 15.9 | | 20.2 | 19.2 |
| | | | | | | | % Officers', Directors' Owners' Comp/Sales | | |
| 1328M | 5396M | | 136716M | 591760M | 807756M | Net Sales ($) | 4389408M | 3226141M |
| 509M | 1491M | | 344001M | 1029560M | 2703781M | Total Assets ($) | 10707552M | 7378113M |

M = $ thousand    MM = $ million
See Pages viii through xx for Explanation of Ratios and Data

© RMA 2024

# PUBLIC ADMINISTRATION—Legislative Bodies  NAICS 921120

| Comparative Historical Data ||| | Current Data Sorted by Sales ||||||
|---|---|---|---|---|---|---|---|---|---|
| 68 | 69 | 41 | **Type of Statement**<br>Unqualified | 1 | | | | 1 | |
|  | 2 | 1 | Reviewed | 1 | | | | | |
|  |  |  | Compiled | | | | | | |
|  |  |  | Tax Returns | | | | | | |
| 8<br>4/1/21-<br>3/31/22<br>ALL | 6<br>4/1/22-<br>3/31/23<br>ALL | 5<br>4/1/23-<br>3/31/24<br>ALL | Other | | 1<br>40 (4/1-9/30/23) || | 1<br>7 (10/1/23-3/31/24) || 2 |
|  |  |  |  | 0-1MM | 1-3MM | 3-5MM | 5-10MM | 10-25MM | 25MM & OVER |
| 76 | 77 | 47 | **NUMBER OF STATEMENTS** | 2 | 2 | 1 | 5 | 15 | 22 |
| % | % | % | **ASSETS** | % | % | % | % | % | % |
| 33.2 | 37.1 | 33.6 | Cash & Equivalents | | | | | 28.1 | 31.2 |
| 6.4 | 5.9 | 5.0 | Trade Receivables (net) | | | | | 4.5 | 6.7 |
| .3 | .2 | .3 | Inventory | | | | | .6 | .2 |
| 6.9 | 6.1 | 9.6 | All Other Current | | | | | 8.1 | 14.2 |
| 46.8 | 49.3 | 48.5 | Total Current | | | | | 41.3 | 52.2 |
| 44.1 | 41.1 | 41.3 | Fixed Assets (net) | | | | | 45.9 | 38.9 |
| .7 | 1.2 | 1.4 | Intangibles (net) | | | | | 3.5 | .5 |
| 8.4 | 8.4 | 8.9 | All Other Non-Current | | | | | 9.3 | 8.3 |
| 100.0 | 100.0 | 100.0 | Total | | | | | 100.0 | 100.0 |
|  |  |  | **LIABILITIES** | | | | | | |
| .2 | .2 | 1.0 | Notes Payable-Short Term | | | | | 3.1 | .0 |
| 1.4 | 1.8 | 1.8 | Cur. Mat.-L.T.D. | | | | | 2.1 | 1.5 |
| 2.9 | 2.6 | 1.5 | Trade Payables | | | | | 1.7 | 1.4 |
| .0 | .0 | .0 | Income Taxes Payable | | | | | .0 | .0 |
| 5.7 | 5.2 | 5.4 | All Other Current | | | | | 5.1 | 6.1 |
| 10.2 | 9.7 | 9.6 | Total Current | | | | | 12.0 | 9.0 |
| 20.2 | 17.7 | 15.5 | Long-Term Debt | | | | | 15.7 | 17.7 |
| .1 | .2 | .0 | Deferred Taxes | | | | | .0 | .0 |
| 18.2 | 14.2 | 14.9 | All Other Non-Current | | | | | 10.5 | 22.6 |
| 51.4 | 58.2 | 60.0 | Net Worth | | | | | 61.8 | 50.7 |
| 100.0 | 100.0 | 100.0 | Total Liabilties & Net Worth | | | | | 100.0 | 100.0 |
|  |  |  | **INCOME DATA** | | | | | | |
| 100.0 | 100.0 | 100.0 | Net Sales | | | | | 100.0 | 100.0 |
|  |  |  | Gross Profit | | | | | | |
| 86.7 | 86.7 | 86.2 | Operating Expenses | | | | | 85.5 | 84.8 |
| 13.3 | 13.3 | 13.8 | Operating Profit | | | | | 14.5 | 15.2 |
| 4.5 | 2.9 | 2.2 | All Other Expenses (net) | | | | | 2.8 | 2.8 |
| 8.8 | 10.4 | 11.6 | Profit Before Taxes | | | | | 11.7 | 12.4 |
|  |  |  | **RATIOS** | | | | | | |
| 11.9 | 11.3 | 11.7 |  | | | | | 8.8 | 12.8 |
| 5.7 | 5.7 | 5.9 | Current | | | | | 6.4 | 5.9 |
| 3.1 | 2.9 | 3.1 |  | | | | | 2.2 | 3.4 |
| 9.8 | 9.0 | 7.5 |  | | | | | 7.5 | 8.0 |
| 5.0 | 5.3 | 5.1 | Quick | | | | | 6.0 | 5.0 |
| 2.4 | 2.5 | 3.0 |  | | | | | 1.9 | 3.3 |
| 13  28.3 | 9  38.6 | 10  37.4 |  | | | | | 17  21.6 | 14  25.8 |
| 34  10.7 | 33  11.1 | 28  13.2 | Sales/Receivables | | | | | 39  9.3 | 26  13.9 |
| 76  4.8 | 68  5.4 | 62  5.9 |  | | | | | 78  4.7 | 118  3.1 |
|  |  |  | Cost of Sales/Inventory | | | | | | |
|  |  |  | Cost of Sales/Payables | | | | | | |
| .7 | .8 | .8 |  | | | | | .8 | .8 |
| 1.3 | 1.2 | 1.3 | Sales/Working Capital | | | | | 1.5 | 1.1 |
| 2.8 | 2.7 | 2.3 |  | | | | | 1.7 | 1.7 |
| 13.9 | 17.3 | 19.0 |  | | | | | 47.4 | 13.2 |
| (63)  4.3 | (59)  8.3 | (39)  6.6 | EBIT/Interest | | | | | (14)  8.1 | (19)  5.6 |
| 1.2 | 1.3 | 2.7 |  | | | | | 3.5 | 2.7 |
|  |  |  | Net Profit + Depr., Dep., Amort./Cur. Mat. L/T/D | | | | | | |
| .4 | .0 | .1 |  | | | | | .1 | .3 |
| .9 | .8 | .9 | Fixed/Worth | | | | | .9 | .9 |
| 1.4 | 1.1 | 1.2 |  | | | | | 1.1 | 1.4 |
| .3 | .3 | .3 |  | | | | | .3 | .5 |
| .7 | .6 | .6 | Debt/Worth | | | | | .6 | .9 |
| 2.1 | 1.0 | 1.4 |  | | | | | 1.0 | 2.0 |
| 20.3 | 13.2 | 12.2 | % Profit Before Taxes/Tangible Net Worth | | | | | 11.4 | 19.9 |
| (74)  8.2 | (75)  6.4 | (46)  6.7 |  | | | | | (14)  6.1 | 8.2 |
| -.1 | 2.0 | 1.6 |  | | | | | .8 | 2.3 |
| 7.4 | 7.0 | 6.7 | % Profit Before Taxes/Total Assets | | | | | 7.1 | 6.0 |
| 3.9 | 3.8 | 3.3 |  | | | | | 2.8 | 3.3 |
| -.1 | 1.1 | .8 |  | | | | | .4 | 1.2 |
| 2.2 | UND | 16.1 |  | | | | | 16.1 | 5.5 |
| .6 | .6 | .7 | Sales/Net Fixed Assets | | | | | .4 | .7 |
| .4 | .3 | .3 |  | | | | | .2 | .5 |
| .7 | .8 | .7 |  | | | | | .5 | .8 |
| .3 | .3 | .3 | Sales/Total Assets | | | | | .2 | .3 |
| .2 | .2 | .2 |  | | | | | .2 | .3 |
| 5.6 | 7.0 | 6.6 |  | | | | | 7.0 | 6.1 |
| (52)  11.1 | (47)  12.0 | (32)  11.2 | % Depr., Dep., Amort./Sales | | | | | (10)  13.8 | (16)  7.9 |
| 15.2 | 17.3 | 16.5 |  | | | | | 17.8 | 11.4 |
|  |  |  | % Officers', Directors' Owners' Comp/Sales | | | | | | |
| 3052282M | 2436272M | 1542956M | Net Sales ($) | 696M | 2919M | 3532M | 35042M | 263304M | 1237463M |
| 6341632M | 5809594M | 4079342M | Total Assets ($) | 13097M | 1073M | 892M | 149534M | 1052302M | 2862444M |

© RMA 2024  
M = $ thousand    MM = $ million  
See Pages viii through xx for Explanation of Ratios and Data

# PUBLIC ADMINISTRATION—Public Finance Activities  NAICS 921130

## Current Data Sorted by Assets | Comparative Historical Data

| | | | | | | Type of Statement | | |
|---|---|---|---|---|---|---|---|---|
| 2 | 5 | 6 | 8 | 12 | | Unqualified | 33 | 35 |
| | | | | | | Reviewed | | |
| | 1 | | 4 | | | Compiled | | |
| | 4 | 1 | 7 (10/1/23-3/31/24) | 1 | | Tax Returns | | |
| | 37 (4/1-9/30/23) | | | | | Other | 6 | 10 |
| | | | | | | | 4/1/19- | 4/1/20- |
| 0-500M | 500M-2MM | 2-10MM | 10-50MM | 50-100MM | 100-250MM | | 3/31/20 | 3/31/21 |
| 7 | 6 | 10 | 8 | 13 | | NUMBER OF STATEMENTS | 39 ALL | 45 ALL |
| % | % | % | % | % | % | ASSETS | % | % |
| | | | 20.8 | | 37.5 | Cash & Equivalents | 31.5 | 33.7 |
| | | | 4.4 | | 1.8 | Trade Receivables (net) | 5.2 | 6.1 |
| | | | 1.1 | | .5 | Inventory | .2 | .2 |
| | | | 5.6 | | 6.0 | All Other Current | 10.0 | 3.1 |
| D | | | 32.0 | | 45.6 | Total Current | 46.9 | 43.1 |
| A | | | 41.8 | | 47.7 | Fixed Assets (net) | 45.2 | 46.8 |
| T | | | .0 | | .0 | Intangibles (net) | 2.2 | .0 |
| A | | | 26.2 | | 6.7 | All Other Non-Current | 5.7 | 10.1 |
| | | | 100.0 | | 100.0 | Total | 100.0 | 100.0 |
| N | | | | | | LIABILITIES | | |
| O | | | .0 | | .0 | Notes Payable-Short Term | 2.8 | .8 |
| T | | | 3.1 | | 2.3 | Cur. Mat.-L.T.D. | 4.1 | 1.5 |
| | | | 5.8 | | 2.2 | Trade Payables | 2.9 | 2.2 |
| A | | | .0 | | .0 | Income Taxes Payable | .0 | .0 |
| V | | | 3.1 | | 4.0 | All Other Current | 6.1 | 2.6 |
| A | | | 12.0 | | 8.5 | Total Current | 15.9 | 7.1 |
| I | | | 30.8 | | 18.2 | Long-Term Debt | 25.3 | 25.5 |
| L | | | .0 | | .0 | Deferred Taxes | .0 | .2 |
| A | | | 6.5 | | 16.6 | All Other Non-Current | 5.3 | 8.6 |
| B | | | 50.7 | | 56.7 | Net Worth | 53.5 | 58.6 |
| L | | | 100.0 | | 100.0 | Total Liabilities & Net Worth | 100.0 | 100.0 |
| E | | | | | | INCOME DATA | | |
| | | | 100.0 | | 100.0 | Net Sales | 100.0 | 100.0 |
| | | | | | | Gross Profit | | |
| | | | 67.9 | | 79.0 | Operating Expenses | 78.7 | 83.2 |
| | | | 32.1 | | 21.0 | Operating Profit | 21.3 | 16.8 |
| | | | 4.5 | | .2 | All Other Expenses (net) | 11.4 | 6.2 |
| | | | 27.5 | | 20.8 | Profit Before Taxes | 9.9 | 10.6 |
| | | | | | | RATIOS | | |
| | | | 9.0 | | 12.0 | | 8.3 | 9.6 |
| | | | 4.0 | | 7.4 | Current | 5.2 | 4.7 |
| | | | 1.6 | | 3.6 | | 2.1 | 2.5 |
| | | | 7.0 | | 9.5 | | 8.1 | 9.1 |
| | | | 3.2 | | 7.4 | Quick | 3.9 | 4.7 |
| | | | .9 | | 2.2 | | 1.5 | 2.3 |
| | | | 0  UND | | 1  552.1 | | 3  119.4 | 0  UND |
| | | | 4  83.9 | | 12  31.4 | Sales/Receivables | 22  16.8 | 15  25.0 |
| | | | 69  5.3 | | 27  13.7 | | 42  8.7 | 49  7.5 |
| | | | | | | Cost of Sales/Inventory | | |
| | | | | | | Cost of Sales/Payables | | |
| | | | 1.1 | | .7 | | 1.2 | 1.2 |
| | | | 2.9 | | 1.3 | Sales/Working Capital | 1.7 | 2.2 |
| | | | 15.9 | | 2.2 | | 4.5 | 4.2 |
| | | | | | 45.4 | | 21.8 | 14.4 |
| | | | | | 17.4 | EBIT/Interest | (24) 5.9 | (31) 5.9 |
| | | | | | 4.9 | | 1.9 | 2.3 |
| | | | | | | Net Profit + Depr., Dep., Amort./Cur. Mat. L/T/D | | |
| | | | .4 | | .7 | | .3 | .0 |
| | | | .8 | | .9 | Fixed/Worth | 1.1 | .9 |
| | | | 2.1 | | 1.1 | | 1.5 | 1.3 |
| | | | .2 | | .5 | | .2 | .3 |
| | | | 1.1 | | .7 | Debt/Worth | .6 | .5 |
| | | | 3.4 | | 1.2 | | 2.9 | 1.1 |
| | | | 81.3 | | 28.6 | | 16.7 | 10.2 |
| | | | 7.7 | | 13.2 | % Profit Before Taxes/Tangible Net Worth | (36) 5.7 | (42) 5.6 |
| | | | .8 | | 7.3 | | 1.5 | .9 |
| | | | 33.1 | | 12.2 | | 7.3 | 5.8 |
| | | | 3.1 | | 8.5 | % Profit Before Taxes/Total Assets | 3.9 | 3.1 |
| | | | .5 | | 4.8 | | .4 | .6 |
| | | | 47.8 | | 1.2 | | 44.5 | UND |
| | | | 1.2 | | .9 | Sales/Net Fixed Assets | .8 | .6 |
| | | | .4 | | .6 | | .4 | .4 |
| | | | .7 | | .6 | | .9 | 1.0 |
| | | | .3 | | .4 | Sales/Total Assets | .4 | .4 |
| | | | .2 | | .3 | | .2 | .2 |
| | | | | | 4.0 | | 5.4 | 5.3 |
| | | | (12) | | 6.0 | % Depr., Dep., Amort./Sales | (24) 8.8 | (29) 9.2 |
| | | | | | 8.5 | | 16.4 | 19.8 |
| | | | | | | % Officers', Directors' Owners' Comp/Sales | | |
| | 12281M | 47263M | 228036M | 289584M | 1228095M | Net Sales ($) | 1429734M | 1265700M |
| | 7599M | 34787M | 202818M | 571777M | 2135051M | Total Assets ($) | 2366766M | 2956704M |

M = $ thousand    MM = $ million
See Pages viii through xx for Explanation of Ratios and Data

© RMA 2024

# PUBLIC ADMINISTRATION—Public Finance Activities  NAICS 921130

| Comparative Historical Data ||| Type of Statement | Current Data Sorted by Sales ||||||
|---|---|---|---|---|---|---|---|---|---|
| 28 | 31 | 33 | Unqualified | 1 | 3 | 1 | 6 | 4 | 18 |
|  | 1 |  | Reviewed |  |  |  |  |  |  |
| 2 | 2 | 1 | Compiled |  |  |  |  |  |  |
| 5 | 18 | 10 | Tax Returns | 1 |  |  |  |  |  |
| 4/1/21-3/31/22 | 4/1/22-3/31/23 | 4/1/23-3/31/24 | Other | 3 | 2 | 1 | 2 | 1 | 1 |
| ALL | ALL | ALL |  | 0-1MM | 37 (4/1-9/30/23) 1-3MM | 3-5MM | 7 (10/1/23-3/31/24) 5-10MM | 10-25MM | 25MM & OVER |
| 35 | 52 | 44 | NUMBER OF STATEMENTS | 5 | 5 | 2 | 8 | 5 | 19 |
| % | % | % | ASSETS | % | % | % | % | % | % |
| 30.7 | 39.1 | 33.7 | Cash & Equivalents |  |  |  |  |  | 36.5 |
| 10.3 | 9.2 | 8.4 | Trade Receivables (net) |  |  |  |  |  | 2.1 |
| .1 | .1 | .4 | Inventory |  |  |  |  |  | .3 |
| 7.3 | 8.7 | 6.7 | All Other Current |  |  |  |  |  | 9.3 |
| 48.4 | 57.1 | 49.2 | Total Current |  |  |  |  |  | 48.3 |
| 45.1 | 30.4 | 35.1 | Fixed Assets (net) |  |  |  |  |  | 40.0 |
| .8 | 1.8 | 1.1 | Intangibles (net) |  |  |  |  |  | .0 |
| 5.7 | 10.8 | 14.6 | All Other Non-Current |  |  |  |  |  | 11.7 |
| 100.0 | 100.0 | 100.0 | Total |  |  |  |  |  | 100.0 |
|  |  |  | LIABILITIES |  |  |  |  |  |  |
| 2.0 | 1.4 | 1.9 | Notes Payable-Short Term |  |  |  |  |  | .0 |
| 1.3 | 2.0 | 2.1 | Cur. Mat.-L.T.D. |  |  |  |  |  | 1.8 |
| 2.7 | 4.0 | 3.8 | Trade Payables |  |  |  |  |  | 4.3 |
| .0 | .0 | .0 | Income Taxes Payable |  |  |  |  |  | .0 |
| 4.5 | 7.8 | 3.1 | All Other Current |  |  |  |  |  | 4.3 |
| 10.4 | 15.3 | 10.8 | Total Current |  |  |  |  |  | 10.5 |
| 39.5 | 26.8 | 31.2 | Long-Term Debt |  |  |  |  |  | 16.3 |
| .0 | .0 | .0 | Deferred Taxes |  |  |  |  |  | .0 |
| 14.4 | 12.6 | 15.9 | All Other Non-Current |  |  |  |  |  | 27.3 |
| 35.7 | 45.4 | 42.1 | Net Worth |  |  |  |  |  | 45.9 |
| 100.0 | 100.0 | 100.0 | Total Liabilities & Net Worth |  |  |  |  |  | 100.0 |
|  |  |  | INCOME DATA |  |  |  |  |  |  |
| 100.0 | 100.0 | 100.0 | Net Sales |  |  |  |  |  | 100.0 |
|  |  |  | Gross Profit |  |  |  |  |  |  |
| 80.1 | 82.6 | 74.8 | Operating Expenses |  |  |  |  |  | 80.8 |
| 19.9 | 17.4 | 25.2 | Operating Profit |  |  |  |  |  | 19.2 |
| 10.0 | 6.0 | 5.9 | All Other Expenses (net) |  |  |  |  |  | 1.2 |
| 9.9 | 11.5 | 19.3 | Profit Before Taxes |  |  |  |  |  | 18.0 |
|  |  |  | RATIOS |  |  |  |  |  |  |
| 11.9 | 11.7 | 12.6 |  |  |  |  |  |  | 12.2 |
| 4.2 | 4.0 | 6.6 | Current |  |  |  |  |  | 7.4 |
| 2.5 | 2.1 | 2.5 |  |  |  |  |  |  | 3.0 |
| 10.4 | 9.7 | 11.7 |  |  |  |  |  |  | 11.6 |
| 3.5 | 3.6 | 5.7 | Quick |  |  |  |  |  | 7.4 |
| 2.2 | 2.0 | 1.9 |  |  |  |  |  |  | 1.8 |
| 1  284.8 | 1  295.1 | 2  156.6 |  |  |  |  |  | 2 | 155.9 |
| 12  30.5 | 18  20.7 | 16  23.5 | Sales/Receivables |  |  |  |  | 10 | 37.7 |
| 62  5.9 | 48  7.6 | 46  7.9 |  |  |  |  |  | 23 | 15.9 |
|  |  |  | Cost of Sales/Inventory |  |  |  |  |  |  |
|  |  |  | Cost of Sales/Payables |  |  |  |  |  |  |
| 1.2 | 1.0 | .8 |  |  |  |  |  |  | .8 |
| 2.1 | 2.0 | 1.7 | Sales/Working Capital |  |  |  |  |  | 1.6 |
| 3.4 | 4.8 | 3.7 |  |  |  |  |  |  | 3.5 |
| 9.1 | 26.1 | 41.4 |  |  |  |  |  |  | 45.4 |
| (26)  4.0 | (38)  6.5 | (33)  10.6 | EBIT/Interest |  |  |  |  | (18) | 15.9 |
| 1.8 | 1.2 | 2.9 |  |  |  |  |  |  | 4.0 |
|  |  |  | Net Profit + Depr., Dep., Amort./Cur. Mat. L/T/D |  |  |  |  |  |  |
| .0 | .0 | .0 |  |  |  |  |  |  | .5 |
| 1.2 | .6 | .8 | Fixed/Worth |  |  |  |  |  | .9 |
| 1.8 | 1.0 | 1.2 |  |  |  |  |  |  | 1.2 |
| .4 | .4 | .4 |  |  |  |  |  |  | .5 |
| .8 | .7 | .8 | Debt/Worth |  |  |  |  |  | .8 |
| 2.0 | 1.7 | 2.3 |  |  |  |  |  |  | 2.5 |
| 19.1 | 14.6 | 21.2 |  |  |  |  |  |  | 29.4 |
| (33)  6.8 | (47)  6.9 | (41)  9.3 | % Profit Before Taxes/Tangible Net Worth |  |  |  |  | (18) | 15.4 |
| .9 | .6 | 2.4 |  |  |  |  |  |  | 6.4 |
| 7.9 | 9.5 | 10.5 |  |  |  |  |  |  | 13.0 |
| 3.7 | 3.8 | 5.0 | % Profit Before Taxes/Total Assets |  |  |  |  |  | 7.6 |
| .6 | .3 | 1.0 |  |  |  |  |  |  | 2.6 |
| UND | UND | UND |  |  |  |  |  |  | 2.2 |
| .7 | 6.3 | 1.3 | Sales/Net Fixed Assets |  |  |  |  |  | 1.1 |
| .4 | .6 | .6 |  |  |  |  |  |  | .7 |
| .7 | 1.6 | .9 |  |  |  |  |  |  | .7 |
| .5 | .5 | .4 | Sales/Total Assets |  |  |  |  |  | .4 |
| .2 | .3 | .3 |  |  |  |  |  |  | .3 |
| 5.7 | 4.0 | 3.1 |  |  |  |  |  |  | 3.5 |
| (21)  10.2 | (22)  8.4 | (29)  5.1 | % Depr., Dep., Amort./Sales |  |  |  |  | (17) | 4.6 |
| 15.8 | 9.9 | 8.4 |  |  |  |  |  |  | 7.5 |
|  |  |  | % Officers', Directors' Owners' Comp/Sales |  |  |  |  |  |  |
| 1433098M | 1677678M | 1805259M | Net Sales ($) | 2163M | 9325M | 7396M | 53410M | 71717M | 1661248M |
| 2622112M | 2528619M | 2952032M | Total Assets ($) | 5175M | 78902M | 3336M | 211399M | 107365M | 2545855M |

© RMA 2024  
M = $ thousand   MM = $ million  
See Pages viii through xx for Explanation of Ratios and Data

# PUBLIC ADMINISTRATION—Executive and Legislative Offices, Combined  NAICS 921140

## Current Data Sorted by Assets

| 1 | 2 | 7 | 3 | 13 | | | | |
|---|---|---|---|---|---|---|---|---|
| | | | 2 | | **Type of Statement** | | | |
| | | | 8 (10/1/23-3/31/24) | | Unqualified | | 38 | 23 |
| | 20 (4/1-9/30/23) | | | | Reviewed | | | |
| | | | | | Compiled | | | 1 |
| | | | | | Tax Returns | | | |
| | | | | | Other | | 7 | 7 |
| 0-500M | 500M-2MM | 2-10MM | 10-50MM | 50-100MM | 100-250MM | | 4/1/19-3/31/20 | 4/1/20-3/31/21 |
| 1 | 1 | 2 | 9 | 3 | 13 | **NUMBER OF STATEMENTS** | ALL 45 | ALL 31 |
| % | % | % | % | % | % | **ASSETS** | % | % |

| | | | | | | | | |
|---|---|---|---|---|---|---|---|---|
| | | | | | 30.3 | Cash & Equivalents | 34.2 | 28.5 |
| | | | | | 4.8 | Trade Receivables (net) | 5.8 | 4.0 |
| | | | | | .1 | Inventory | .2 | .2 |
| | | | | | 1.9 | All Other Current | 7.3 | 3.0 |
| | | | | | 37.1 | Total Current | 47.5 | 35.7 |
| | | | | | 46.0 | Fixed Assets (net) | 43.7 | 51.6 |
| | | | | | 1.3 | Intangibles (net) | .3 | 1.2 |
| | | | | | 15.6 | All Other Non-Current | 8.5 | 11.5 |
| | | | | | 100.0 | Total | 100.0 | 100.0 |

DATA NOT AVAILABLE

**LIABILITIES**

| | | | | | | | | |
|---|---|---|---|---|---|---|---|---|
| | | | | | .0 | Notes Payable-Short Term | .1 | .1 |
| | | | | | 2.4 | Cur. Mat.-L.T.D. | 2.3 | 1.8 |
| | | | | | 1.3 | Trade Payables | 3.8 | 1.4 |
| | | | | | .0 | Income Taxes Payable | .0 | .0 |
| | | | | | 2.3 | All Other Current | 4.9 | 1.7 |
| | | | | | 6.0 | Total Current | 11.1 | 5.0 |
| | | | | | 28.5 | Long-Term Debt | 16.3 | 23.9 |
| | | | | | .0 | Deferred Taxes | .0 | .0 |
| | | | | | 12.5 | All Other Non-Current | 17.0 | 15.2 |
| | | | | | 52.9 | Net Worth | 55.7 | 55.9 |
| | | | | | 100.0 | Total Liabilities & Net Worth | 100.0 | 100.0 |

**INCOME DATA**

| | | | | | | | | |
|---|---|---|---|---|---|---|---|---|
| | | | | | 100.0 | Net Sales | 100.0 | 100.0 |
| | | | | | | Gross Profit | | |
| | | | | | 87.6 | Operating Expenses | 87.8 | 89.8 |
| | | | | | 12.4 | Operating Profit | 12.2 | 10.2 |
| | | | | | -1.3 | All Other Expenses (net) | 4.8 | 5.2 |
| | | | | | 13.7 | Profit Before Taxes | 7.5 | 4.9 |

**RATIOS**

| | | | | | | | | | | |
|---|---|---|---|---|---|---|---|---|---|---|
| | | | | | 11.6 | Current | | 11.6 | | 12.8 |
| | | | | | 6.2 | | | 5.8 | | 6.2 |
| | | | | | 3.4 | | | 3.0 | | 3.5 |
| | | | | | 11.2 | Quick | | 9.0 | | 11.8 |
| | | | | | 5.0 | | | 5.1 | | 5.4 |
| | | | | | 3.3 | | | 2.6 | | 3.3 |
| | | | | 1 | 511.6 | Sales/Receivables | 11 | 32.5 | 3 | 142.5 |
| | | | | 42 | 8.6 | | 31 | 11.6 | 35 | 10.4 |
| | | | | 78 | 4.7 | | 60 | 6.1 | 74 | 4.9 |
| | | | | | | Cost of Sales/Inventory | | | | |
| | | | | | | Cost of Sales/Payables | | | | |
| | | | | | .7 | Sales/Working Capital | | 1.1 | | .8 |
| | | | | | 1.1 | | | 1.6 | | 1.2 |
| | | | | | 2.6 | | | 2.4 | | 2.8 |
| | | | | | 21.9 | EBIT/Interest | | 10.7 | | 9.1 |
| | | | | (12) | 4.0 | | (37) | 3.5 | (29) | 3.7 |
| | | | | | 2.2 | | | 1.2 | | .3 |
| | | | | | | Net Profit + Depr., Dep., Amort./Cur. Mat. L/T/D | | | | |
| | | | | | .4 | Fixed/Worth | | .0 | | .7 |
| | | | | | .9 | | | 1.0 | | .9 |
| | | | | | 1.3 | | | 1.5 | | 1.7 |
| | | | | | .5 | Debt/Worth | | .3 | | .2 |
| | | | | | .6 | | | .5 | | .5 |
| | | | | | 1.8 | | | 1.5 | | 2.3 |
| | | | | | 16.3 | % Profit Before Taxes/Tangible Net Worth | | 8.1 | | 8.8 |
| | | | | (12) | 4.8 | | (42) | 4.3 | (29) | 3.5 |
| | | | | | 3.4 | | | .3 | | .8 |
| | | | | | 7.1 | % Profit Before Taxes/Total Assets | | 5.3 | | 4.5 |
| | | | | | 3.2 | | | 2.9 | | 2.2 |
| | | | | | 1.6 | | | .2 | | -.4 |
| | | | | | UND | Sales/Net Fixed Assets | | UND | | 1.6 |
| | | | | | .5 | | | .6 | | .5 |
| | | | | | .4 | | | .4 | | .3 |
| | | | | | .4 | Sales/Total Assets | | .9 | | .5 |
| | | | | | .3 | | | .4 | | .3 |
| | | | | | .2 | | | .3 | | .2 |
| | | | | | 7.3 | % Depr., Dep., Amort./Sales | | 5.6 | | 6.0 |
| | | | | (10) | 10.7 | | (26) | 9.7 | (23) | 10.1 |
| | | | | | 17.0 | | | 14.7 | | 17.7 |
| | | | | | | % Officers', Directors' Owners' Comp/Sales | | | | |
| | 2107M | 6712M | 119943M | 246379M | 657783M | Net Sales ($) | | 2303787M | | 1081372M |
| | 728M | 11019M | 201194M | 225587M | 2168074M | Total Assets ($) | | 4014523M | | 2634178M |

M = $ thousand   MM = $ million
See Pages viii through xx for Explanation of Ratios and Data

© RMA 2024

# PUBLIC ADMINISTRATION—Executive and Legislative Offices, Combined  NAICS 921140

## Comparative Historical Data | Current Data Sorted by Sales

| | | | | | Type of Statement | | | | | | |
|---|---|---|---|---|---|---|---|---|---|---|---|
| | 22 | | 23 | | 26 | Unqualified | | 5 | 1 | 2 | 3 | 15 |
| | 1 | | 1 | | | Reviewed | | | | | | |
| | 5 | | 5 | | 2 | Compiled | | | | | 1 | |
| | | | | | | Tax Returns | | 20 (4/1-9/30/23) | | | 8 (10/1/23-3/31/24) | |
| | 4/1/21-3/31/22 ALL | | 4/1/22-3/31/23 ALL | | 4/1/23-3/31/24 ALL | Other | 0-1MM | 1-3MM | 3-5MM | 5-10MM | 10-25MM | 25MM & OVER |
| | 28 | | 29 | | 28 | NUMBER OF STATEMENTS | 5 | 5 | 2 | 2 | 4 | 15 |
| | % | | % | | % | **ASSETS** | % | % | % | % | % | % |
| | 37.5 | | 41.3 | | 38.3 | Cash & Equivalents | D | | | | | 37.2 |
| | 4.4 | | 3.9 | | 2.9 | Trade Receivables (net) | A | | | | | 4.2 |
| | .1 | | .1 | | .6 | Inventory | T | | | | | .1 |
| | 4.8 | | 2.6 | | 2.3 | All Other Current | A | | | | | 3.8 |
| | 46.8 | | 47.8 | | 44.1 | Total Current | | | | | | 45.3 |
| | 42.8 | | 39.1 | | 43.0 | Fixed Assets (net) | N | | | | | 39.9 |
| | 1.5 | | 1.0 | | .6 | Intangibles (net) | O | | | | | 1.1 |
| | 9.0 | | 12.1 | | 12.3 | All Other Non-Current | T | | | | | 13.7 |
| | 100.0 | | 100.0 | | 100.0 | Total | | | | | | 100.0 |
| | | | | | | **LIABILITIES** | A | | | | | |
| | .0 | | .0 | | .0 | Notes Payable-Short Term | V | | | | | .0 |
| | 2.1 | | 2.8 | | 3.0 | Cur. Mat.-L.T.D. | A | | | | | 2.2 |
| | 1.5 | | 2.4 | | 1.5 | Trade Payables | I | | | | | 2.0 |
| | .0 | | .1 | | .0 | Income Taxes Payable | L | | | | | .0 |
| | 2.4 | | 2.1 | | 2.4 | All Other Current | A | | | | | 3.3 |
| | 6.0 | | 7.3 | | 7.0 | Total Current | B | | | | | 7.5 |
| | 27.8 | | 26.4 | | 34.2 | Long-Term Debt | L | | | | | 24.7 |
| | .0 | | .0 | | .0 | Deferred Taxes | E | | | | | .0 |
| | 17.3 | | 13.4 | | 8.3 | All Other Non-Current | | | | | | 11.3 |
| | 48.8 | | 52.9 | | 50.4 | Net Worth | | | | | | 56.5 |
| | 100.0 | | 100.0 | | 100.0 | Total Liabilities & Net Worth | | | | | | 100.0 |
| | | | | | | **INCOME DATA** | | | | | | |
| | 100.0 | | 100.0 | | 100.0 | Net Sales | | | | | | 100.0 |
| | | | | | | Gross Profit | | | | | | |
| | 83.4 | | 89.6 | | 91.4 | Operating Expenses | | | | | | 87.3 |
| | 16.6 | | 10.4 | | 8.6 | Operating Profit | | | | | | 12.7 |
| | 5.2 | | 2.6 | | 1.7 | All Other Expenses (net) | | | | | | 1.5 |
| | 11.4 | | 7.8 | | 6.9 | Profit Before Taxes | | | | | | 11.3 |
| | | | | | | **RATIOS** | | | | | | |
| | 10.9 | | 12.8 | | 11.0 | | | | | | | 11.2 |
| | 7.6 | | 7.5 | | 5.9 | Current | | | | | | 6.2 |
| | 3.9 | | 3.9 | | 3.7 | | | | | | | 3.7 |
| | 10.7 | | 12.7 | | 10.5 | | | | | | | 10.4 |
| | 6.8 | | 6.5 | | 5.3 | Quick | | | | | | 5.0 |
| | 3.8 | | 3.8 | | 3.6 | | | | | | | 3.4 |
| 0 | 814.8 | 0 | UND | 0 | UND | | | | | | 0 | 782.7 |
| 22 | 16.7 | 19 | 19.2 | 21 | 17.0 | Sales/Receivables | | | | | 30 | 12.0 |
| 91 | 4.0 | 70 | 5.2 | 61 | 6.0 | | | | | | 74 | 4.9 |
| | | | | | | Cost of Sales/Inventory | | | | | | |
| | | | | | | Cost of Sales/Payables | | | | | | |
| | .8 | | .7 | | .7 | | | | | | | .7 |
| | 1.2 | | 1.2 | | 1.4 | Sales/Working Capital | | | | | | 1.3 |
| | 2.8 | | 2.5 | | 2.7 | | | | | | | 2.8 |
| | 11.6 | | 27.9 | | 13.0 | | | | | | | 12.8 |
| (24) | 3.6 | (26) | 3.6 | (26) | 4.0 | EBIT/Interest | | | | | (14) | 4.0 |
| | 2.7 | | 2.0 | | .2 | | | | | | | 2.1 |
| | | | | | | Net Profit + Depr., Dep., Amort./Cur. Mat. L/T/D | | | | | | |
| | .0 | | .0 | | .0 | | | | | | | .0 |
| | .9 | | .8 | | .9 | Fixed/Worth | | | | | | .9 |
| | 3.0 | | 1.1 | | 1.2 | | | | | | | 1.3 |
| | .3 | | .2 | | .4 | | | | | | | .4 |
| | .8 | | .6 | | .6 | Debt/Worth | | | | | | .6 |
| | 5.1 | | 1.6 | | 1.8 | | | | | | | 1.7 |
| | 20.2 | | 11.9 | | 9.7 | | | | | | | 19.2 |
| (26) | 6.0 | (27) | 6.7 | (26) | 4.5 | % Profit Before Taxes/Tangible Net Worth | | | | | (14) | 4.8 |
| | 3.6 | | -.5 | | -3.2 | | | | | | | 3.0 |
| | 6.8 | | 5.8 | | 6.3 | | | | | | | 7.9 |
| | 3.2 | | 3.3 | | 2.4 | % Profit Before Taxes/Total Assets | | | | | | 3.2 |
| | 1.8 | | .1 | | -1.5 | | | | | | | 1.5 |
| | UND | | UND | | UND | | | | | | | UND |
| | .8 | | .8 | | .6 | Sales/Net Fixed Assets | | | | | | .6 |
| | .5 | | .4 | | .3 | | | | | | | .4 |
| | .6 | | .8 | | .6 | | | | | | | .6 |
| | .4 | | .4 | | .3 | Sales/Total Assets | | | | | | .3 |
| | .3 | | .2 | | .2 | | | | | | | .2 |
| | 5.5 | | 5.7 | | 7.2 | | | | | | | 7.3 |
| (17) | 8.0 | (17) | 10.3 | (18) | 11.6 | % Depr., Dep., Amort./Sales | | | | | (10) | 10.7 |
| | 13.1 | | 13.3 | | 18.3 | | | | | | | 17.0 |
| | | | | | | % Officers', Directors' Owners' Comp/Sales | | | | | | |
| | 1108908M | | 1357283M | | 1032924M | Net Sales ($) | | 12649M | 7225M | 14759M | 67456M | 930835M |
| | 2385826M | | 2795670M | | 2606602M | Total Assets ($) | | 50826M | 22223M | 98482M | 145372M | 2289699M |

© RMA 2024

M = $ thousand    MM = $ million

See Pages viii through xx for Explanation of Ratios and Data

# PUBLIC ADMINISTRATION—Other General Government Support  NAICS 921190

## Current Data Sorted by Assets | Comparative Historical Data

| 0-500M | 500M-2MM | 2-10MM | 10-50MM | 50-100MM | 100-250MM | | | 4/1/19-3/31/20 ALL | 4/1/20-3/31/21 ALL |
|---|---|---|---|---|---|---|---|---|---|
| | 4 | 4 | 21 | 16 | 24 | Type of Statement | Unqualified | 138 | 110 |
| | | | 1 | | | | Reviewed | 1 | |
| 1 | | | | | | | Compiled | 3 | 1 |
| | | | | | | | Tax Returns | 3 | |
| | 72 (4/1-9/30/23) | 4 | 18 (10/1/23-3/31/24) | 4 | 1 | | Other | 37 | 21 |
| 1 | 8 | 8 | 28 | 20 | 25 | NUMBER OF STATEMENTS | | 182 | 132 |
| % | % | % | % | % | % | **ASSETS** | | % | % |
| | | | 31.6 | 39.3 | 28.6 | Cash & Equivalents | | 29.7 | 25.8 |
| | | | 12.8 | 7.7 | 4.0 | Trade Receivables (net) | | 9.1 | 7.4 |
| | | | .3 | .5 | .2 | Inventory | | .5 | .5 |
| | | | 10.4 | 2.7 | 2.9 | All Other Current | | 6.5 | 3.8 |
| | | | 55.0 | 50.2 | 35.6 | Total Current | | 45.8 | 37.5 |
| | | | 37.4 | 40.6 | 52.0 | Fixed Assets (net) | | 41.9 | 51.4 |
| | | | .6 | .0 | .1 | Intangibles (net) | | .2 | .7 |
| | | | 7.0 | 9.2 | 12.3 | All Other Non-Current | | 12.1 | 10.3 |
| | | | 100.0 | 100.0 | 100.0 | Total | | 100.0 | 100.0 |
| | | | | | | **LIABILITIES** | | | |
| | | | 1.2 | .2 | .1 | Notes Payable-Short Term | | .4 | .1 |
| | | | 1.9 | 1.7 | 2.2 | Cur. Mat.-L.T.D. | | 2.8 | 1.9 |
| | | | 5.7 | 2.0 | 1.9 | Trade Payables | | 4.0 | 3.3 |
| | | | .0 | .0 | .0 | Income Taxes Payable | | .1 | .1 |
| | | | 11.4 | 6.3 | 5.0 | All Other Current | | 8.1 | 8.0 |
| | | | 20.2 | 10.1 | 9.1 | Total Current | | 15.4 | 13.4 |
| | | | 19.9 | 24.1 | 24.5 | Long-Term Debt | | 18.2 | 22.3 |
| | | | .0 | .0 | .0 | Deferred Taxes | | .3 | |
| | | | 9.1 | 18.6 | 18.9 | All Other Non-Current | | 24.2 | 27.8 |
| | | | 50.8 | 47.1 | 47.5 | Net Worth | | 42.0 | 36.4 |
| | | | 100.0 | 100.0 | 100.0 | Total Liabilties & Net Worth | | 100.0 | 100.0 |
| | | | | | | **INCOME DATA** | | | |
| | | | 100.0 | 100.0 | 100.0 | Net Sales | | 100.0 | 100.0 |
| | | | | | | Gross Profit | | | |
| | | | 89.5 | 89.2 | 79.6 | Operating Expenses | | 90.3 | 90.4 |
| | | | 10.5 | 10.8 | 20.4 | Operating Profit | | 9.7 | 9.6 |
| | | | 1.9 | 4.6 | 1.7 | All Other Expenses (net) | | 3.5 | 2.8 |
| | | | 8.7 | 6.1 | 18.7 | Profit Before Taxes | | 6.3 | 6.8 |
| | | | | | | **RATIOS** | | | |
| | | | 9.2 | 10.1 | 7.1 | | | 7.3 | 7.6 |
| | | | 4.7 | 5.4 | 5.3 | Current | | 4.1 | 4.2 |
| | | | 1.9 | 2.3 | 2.7 | | | 2.2 | 2.5 |
| | | | 9.2 | 9.4 | 6.6 | | | 6.6 | 7.4 |
| | | | 4.4 | 5.0 | 4.5 | Quick | | 3.4 | 3.8 |
| | | | 1.4 | 2.2 | 2.4 | | | 1.7 | 2.1 |
| | | | 7  53.2 | 1  301.5 | 11  34.5 | | | 5  77.3 | 2  149.8 |
| | | | 33  10.9 | 33  11.1 | 38  9.7 | Sales/Receivables | | 28  12.9 | 27  13.4 |
| | | | 89  4.1 | 62  5.9 | 61  6.0 | | | 49  7.4 | 51  7.1 |
| | | | | | | Cost of Sales/Inventory | | | |
| | | | | | | Cost of Sales/Payables | | | |
| | | | 1.0 | 1.1 | .8 | | | 1.4 | 1.2 |
| | | | 1.6 | 1.9 | 1.5 | Sales/Working Capital | | 2.1 | 2.0 |
| | | | 4.6 | 3.6 | 2.7 | | | 5.9 | 4.2 |
| | | | 26.9 | 11.2 | 24.4 | | | 8.9 | 8.3 |
| | | (22) | 5.7 | (16) 6.2 | (23) 6.6 | EBIT/Interest | (129) | 3.3 | (106) 3.0 |
| | | | 2.4 | 1.0 | 3.4 | | | .7 | .4 |
| | | | | | | Net Profit + Depr., Dep., Amort./Cur. Mat. L/T/D | | | |
| | | | .1 | .0 | .7 | | | .0 | .7 |
| | | | .8 | .9 | 1.2 | Fixed/Worth | | .9 | 1.1 |
| | | | 1.6 | 2.5 | 2.1 | | | 1.6 | 1.9 |
| | | | .3 | .3 | .4 | | | .3 | .4 |
| | | | .9 | .8 | .8 | Debt/Worth | | .7 | .9 |
| | | | 2.0 | 4.0 | 2.6 | | | 2.6 | 3.3 |
| | | | 13.4 | 11.8 | 14.0 | % Profit Before Taxes/Tangible Net Worth | | 11.9 | 11.7 |
| | | (24) | 7.8 | (17) 7.2 | (22) 10.6 | | (158) | 3.7 | (109) 3.9 |
| | | | .3 | 1.2 | 4.4 | | | -.2 | .2 |
| | | | 8.9 | 6.1 | 8.3 | % Profit Before Taxes/Total Assets | | 5.3 | 5.5 |
| | | | 3.7 | 3.2 | 5.7 | | | 2.4 | 2.3 |
| | | | .2 | .3 | 2.3 | | | -.2 | -.4 |
| | | | 393.7 | UND | 1.1 | | | UND | 1.4 |
| | | | .9 | 1.1 | .4 | Sales/Net Fixed Assets | | 1.1 | .7 |
| | | | .5 | .6 | .3 | | | .4 | .3 |
| | | | 1.2 | 1.0 | .5 | | | 1.4 | .6 |
| | | | .4 | .6 | .3 | Sales/Total Assets | | .5 | .4 |
| | | | .3 | .4 | .2 | | | .3 | .2 |
| | | | 5.5 | 5.1 | 4.1 | | | 4.1 | 4.2 |
| | | (19) | 8.3 | (13) 7.2 | (22) 8.4 | % Depr., Dep., Amort./Sales | (114) | 7.8 | (102) 8.6 |
| | | | 15.8 | 13.5 | 14.4 | | | 13.6 | 13.8 |
| | | | | | | % Officers', Directors' Owners' Comp/Sales | | | |
| 2772M | 15374M | 97816M | 550772M | 1552517M | 1337351M | Net Sales ($) | | 7410702M | 5001312M |
| 71M | 8372M | 37917M | 643803M | 1454225M | 4051034M | Total Assets ($) | | 10644239M | 9873422M |

© RMA 2024  M = $ thousand  MM = $ million
See Pages viii through xx for Explanation of Ratios and Data

# PUBLIC ADMINISTRATION—Other General Government Support  NAICS 921190

## Comparative Historical Data | Current Data Sorted by Sales

| Comparative Historical Data ||| Type of Statement | Current Data Sorted by Sales ||||||
|---|---|---|---|---|---|---|---|---|---|
| 83 | 99 | 69 | Unqualified | 2 | 6 | 3 | 9 | 10 | 39 |
|  | 2 | 1 | Reviewed |  |  |  |  |  | 1 |
| 1 | 1 |  | Compiled |  |  |  |  |  |  |
| 1 |  | 1 | Tax Returns |  | 1 |  | 3 | 2 | 8 |
| 25 | 38 | 19 | Other | 2 | 72 (4/1-9/30/23) | 2 | 18 (10/1/23-3/31/24) ||  |
| 4/1/21-3/31/22 | 4/1/22-3/31/23 | 4/1/23-3/31/24 |  | 0-1MM | 1-3MM | 3-5MM | 5-10MM | 10-25MM | 25MM & OVER |
| ALL | ALL | ALL | NUMBER OF STATEMENTS |  |  |  |  |  |  |
| 110 | 140 | 90 |  | 4 | 9 | 5 | 12 | 12 | 48 |
| % | % | % | ASSETS | % | % | % | % | % | % |
| 32.7 | 37.8 | 38.4 | Cash & Equivalents |  |  |  | 31.1 | 30.1 | 34.6 |
| 10.9 | 12.3 | 10.3 | Trade Receivables (net) |  |  |  | 9.9 | 9.5 | 11.0 |
| .4 | .2 | .3 | Inventory |  |  |  | .5 | .2 | .3 |
| 4.4 | 5.1 | 4.7 | All Other Current |  |  |  | 1.7 | 10.2 | 5.8 |
| 48.3 | 55.4 | 53.7 | Total Current |  |  |  | 43.2 | 50.1 | 51.7 |
| 39.2 | 32.8 | 36.7 | Fixed Assets (net) |  |  |  | 50.4 | 41.3 | 37.2 |
| 1.5 | 1.2 | .2 | Intangibles (net) |  |  |  | .1 | 0.0 | .4 |
| 11.0 | 10.6 | 9.4 | All Other Non-Current |  |  |  | 6.3 | 8.6 | 10.8 |
| 100.0 | 100.0 | 100.0 | Total |  |  |  | 100.0 | 100.0 | 100.0 |
|  |  |  | LIABILITIES |  |  |  |  |  |  |
| 1.9 | .8 | .5 | Notes Payable-Short Term |  |  |  | .4 | .8 | .7 |
| 1.7 | 1.7 | 2.2 | Cur. Mat.-L.T.D. |  |  |  | 2.0 | 1.9 | 2.0 |
| 3.9 | 5.0 | 3.1 | Trade Payables |  |  |  | 1.9 | 5.6 | 3.3 |
| .0 | .0 | .0 | Income Taxes Payable |  |  |  | .0 | .0 | .0 |
| 8.4 | 8.6 | 8.1 | All Other Current |  |  |  | 12.8 | 7.8 | 8.3 |
| 15.9 | 16.1 | 13.9 | Total Current |  |  |  | 17.0 | 16.0 | 14.3 |
| 17.5 | 20.8 | 19.5 | Long-Term Debt |  |  |  | 15.8 | 22.7 | 20.7 |
| .0 | .2 | .1 | Deferred Taxes |  |  |  | .0 | .0 | .2 |
| 20.1 | 12.2 | 12.9 | All Other Non-Current |  |  |  | 14.1 | 6.6 | 17.6 |
| 46.4 | 50.7 | 53.6 | Net Worth |  |  |  | 53.1 | 54.6 | 47.2 |
| 100.0 | 100.0 | 100.0 | Total Liabilities & Net Worth |  |  |  | 100.0 | 100.0 | 100.0 |
|  |  |  | INCOME DATA |  |  |  |  |  |  |
| 100.0 | 100.0 | 100.0 | Net Sales |  |  |  | 100.0 | 100.0 | 100.0 |
|  |  |  | Gross Profit |  |  |  | 90.3 | 88.0 | 85.4 |
| 84.7 | 85.9 | 86.2 | Operating Expenses |  |  |  |  |  |  |
| 15.3 | 14.1 | 13.8 | Operating Profit |  |  |  | 9.7 | 12.0 | 14.6 |
| 2.9 | 3.9 | 1.9 | All Other Expenses (net) |  |  |  | 1.3 | 1.0 | 2.2 |
| 12.4 | 10.2 | 11.9 | Profit Before Taxes |  |  |  | 8.3 | 11.0 | 12.4 |
|  |  |  | RATIOS |  |  |  |  |  |  |
| 9.9 | 10.7 | 10.3 |  |  |  |  | 9.2 | 6.8 | 8.4 |
| 4.1 | 4.1 | 5.3 | Current |  |  |  | 7.1 | 4.3 | 4.6 |
| 2.0 | 2.4 | 2.5 |  |  |  |  | 2.4 | 1.9 | 2.5 |
| 9.7 | 10.4 | 9.7 |  |  |  |  | 8.9 | 6.1 | 8.1 |
| 4.0 | 3.8 | 5.0 | Quick |  |  |  | 6.5 | 4.3 | 4.3 |
| 1.8 | 2.0 | 2.3 |  |  |  |  | 2.4 | 1.7 | 2.1 |
| 5  68.9 | 3  145.1 | 4  94.2 |  | 7  53.2 | 13  28.2 | 7  55.4 ||||
| 30  12.1 | 26  13.8 | 33  11.2 | Sales/Receivables | 31  11.9 | 33  10.9 | 35  10.4 ||||
| 62  5.9 | 59  6.2 | 65  5.6 |  | 61  6.0 | 43  8.5 | 66  5.5 ||||
|  |  |  | Cost of Sales/Inventory |  |  |  |  |  |  |
|  |  |  | Cost of Sales/Payables |  |  |  |  |  |  |
| 1.0 | 1.0 | 1.0 |  |  |  |  | .7 | 1.3 | 1.1 |
| 1.9 | 2.0 | 1.7 | Sales/Working Capital |  |  |  | 1.3 | 2.1 | 2.0 |
| 4.3 | 5.7 | 3.5 |  |  |  |  | 2.5 | 3.7 | 5.5 |
|  47.7 |  20.3 |  21.0 |  |  |  |  | 24.9 | 29.0 | 21.0 |
| (76)  6.3 | (101)  6.1 | (67)  6.1 | EBIT/Interest | (10)  8.3 | (10)  6.0 | (39)  6.6 ||||
|  3.2 |  1.1 |  2.4 |  | -3.3 | 1.8 | 2.5 ||||
|  |  |  | Net Profit + Depr., Dep., Amort./Cur. Mat. L/T/D |  |  |  |  |  |  |
| .2 | .0 | .0 |  |  |  |  | .6 | .1 | .0 |
| 1.0 | .7 | .8 | Fixed/Worth |  |  |  | 1.0 | 1.0 | .9 |
| 1.7 | 1.3 | 1.3 |  |  |  |  | 1.6 | 2.1 | 1.9 |
| .4 | .3 | .3 |  |  |  |  | .4 | .2 | .3 |
| .8 | .7 | .8 | Debt/Worth |  |  |  | .9 | .9 | .8 |
| 2.8 | 1.8 | 1.5 |  |  |  |  | 1.6 | 2.4 | 2.8 |
|  18.2 |  19.7 |  14.7 |  |  |  |  | 10.6 | 13.9 | 17.3 |
| (90)  8.4 | (124)  6.4 | (80)  9.1 | % Profit Before Taxes/Tangible Net Worth | (11)  7.1 | (11)  8.4 | (41)  9.4 ||||
|  4.1 |  -.5 |  1.2 |  |  | .1 | 1.4 | 2.9 |||
| 9.1 | 10.4 | 8.9 |  |  |  |  | 7.0 | 12.2 | 8.5 |
| 5.0 | 3.8 | 4.9 | % Profit Before Taxes/Total Assets |  |  |  | 4.3 | 4.2 | 5.0 |
| 1.8 | .3 | .9 |  |  |  |  | -3.4 | 1.1 | 2.2 |
| 103.6 | UND | 999.8 |  |  |  |  | .9 | 346.1 | 952.8 |
| 1.0 | 2.2 | 1.1 | Sales/Net Fixed Assets |  |  |  | .6 | 1.0 | 1.1 |
| .4 | .5 | .5 |  |  |  |  | .4 | .4 | .4 |
| 1.3 | 1.7 | 1.0 |  |  |  |  | .4 | 1.2 | 1.0 |
| .5 | .6 | .5 | Sales/Total Assets |  |  |  | .3 | .5 | .6 |
| .2 | .3 | .3 |  |  |  |  | .3 | .3 | .3 |
|  2.4 |  2.1 |  3.4 |  |  |  |  | 5.8 |  | 2.2 |
| (77)  6.7 | (81)  6.7 | (60)  7.5 | % Depr., Dep., Amort./Sales |  |  | (11)  7.8 | (34)  6.5 |||
|  11.9 |  11.1 |  13.5 |  |  |  |  | 13.6 |  | 12.3 |
|  |  |  | % Officers', Directors' Owners' Comp/Sales |  |  |  |  |  |  |
| 3485530M | 5468058M | 3556602M | Net Sales ($) | 2808M | 15733M | 20135M | 86192M | 225887M | 3205847M |
| 6558817M | 6982247M | 6195422M | Total Assets ($) | 3943M | 51020M | 46570M | 290820M | 544913M | 5258156M |

M = $ thousand    MM = $ million
See Pages viii through xx for Explanation of Ratios and Data

© RMA 2024

# PUBLIC ADMINISTRATION—Fire Protection  NAICS 922160

**Current Data Sorted by Assets** | **Comparative Historical Data**

| | | | | | | | Type of Statement | | | | |
|---|---|---|---|---|---|---|---|---|---|---|---|
| | | 1 | 7 | 9 | 4 | | Unqualified | | 21 | | 24 |
| | | | | 3 | | | Reviewed | | 3 | | 3 |
| | | 4 | 2 | | | | Compiled | | | | 3 |
| 1 | 2 | 5 | 7 | | 1 | | Tax Returns | | 6 | | 1 |
| | 30 (4/1-9/30/23) | | 17 (10/1/23-3/31/24) | | | | Other | | 19 | | 9 |
| 0-500M | 500M-2MM | 2-10MM | 10-50MM | 50-100MM | 100-250MM | | | | 4/1/19- | | 4/1/20- |
| | | | | | | | | | 3/31/20 | | 3/31/21 |
| 1 | 7 | 14 | 19 | 4 | 2 | | NUMBER OF STATEMENTS | | 49 ALL | | 40 ALL |
| % | % | % | % | % | % | | **ASSETS** | | % | | % |
| | | 30.7 | 22.4 | | | | Cash & Equivalents | | 29.6 | | 30.0 |
| | | 7.9 | 10.1 | | | | Trade Receivables (net) | | 14.3 | | 10.3 |
| | | 1.2 | 2.0 | | | | Inventory | | 2.3 | | 2.0 |
| | | 1.9 | 5.8 | | | | All Other Current | | 5.3 | | 3.2 |
| | | 41.7 | 40.4 | | | | Total Current | | 51.5 | | 45.5 |
| | | 51.6 | 48.1 | | | | Fixed Assets (net) | | 38.9 | | 46.3 |
| | | 1.2 | .3 | | | | Intangibles (net) | | .1 | | 1.6 |
| | | 5.5 | 11.3 | | | | All Other Non-Current | | 9.5 | | 6.7 |
| | | 100.0 | 100.0 | | | | Total | | 100.0 | | 100.0 |
| | | | | | | | **LIABILITIES** | | | | |
| | | .3 | .6 | | | | Notes Payable-Short Term | | 2.1 | | 1.2 |
| | | 2.5 | 3.0 | | | | Cur. Mat.-L.T.D. | | 2.1 | | 3.0 |
| | | 2.4 | 4.0 | | | | Trade Payables | | 4.6 | | 1.4 |
| | | .0 | .0 | | | | Income Taxes Payable | | .1 | | .1 |
| | | 2.3 | 6.0 | | | | All Other Current | | 8.9 | | 8.6 |
| | | 7.5 | 13.7 | | | | Total Current | | 17.8 | | 14.3 |
| | | 13.6 | 31.6 | | | | Long-Term Debt | | 17.0 | | 21.0 |
| | | .3 | .0 | | | | Deferred Taxes | | .2 | | .2 |
| | | 2.2 | 8.4 | | | | All Other Non-Current | | 24.2 | | 12.2 |
| | | 76.5 | 46.4 | | | | Net Worth | | 40.8 | | 52.3 |
| | | 100.0 | 100.0 | | | | Total Liabilities & Net Worth | | 100.0 | | 100.0 |
| | | | | | | | **INCOME DATA** | | | | |
| | | 100.0 | 100.0 | | | | Net Sales | | 100.0 | | 100.0 |
| | | | | | | | Gross Profit | | | | |
| | | 78.2 | 85.0 | | | | Operating Expenses | | 95.1 | | 86.3 |
| | | 21.8 | 15.0 | | | | Operating Profit | | 4.9 | | 13.7 |
| | | .8 | 1.7 | | | | All Other Expenses (net) | | 1.5 | | .5 |
| | | 20.9 | 13.3 | | | | Profit Before Taxes | | 3.4 | | 13.2 |
| | | | | | | | **RATIOS** | | | | |
| | | 19.3 | 6.5 | | | | | | 15.9 | | 9.9 |
| | | 7.0 | 4.4 | | | Current | | 4.0 | | 5.0 |
| | | 2.9 | 2.1 | | | | | | 2.0 | | 2.7 |
| | | 19.3 | 5.2 | | | | | | 14.4 | | 9.8 |
| | | 5.8 | 3.8 | | | Quick | | 3.8 | | 4.3 |
| | | 2.4 | 1.7 | | | | | | 1.7 | | 2.5 |
| | | 0 UND | 3 129.3 | | | | | | 0 UND | 0 | UND |
| | | 0 UND | 22 16.8 | | | Sales/Receivables | | 11 32.2 | 17 | 21.2 |
| | | 47 7.8 | 39 9.4 | | | | | | 46 7.9 | 52 | 7.0 |
| | | | | | | | Cost of Sales/Inventory | | | | |
| | | | | | | | Cost of Sales/Payables | | | | |
| | | 1.2 | 1.2 | | | | | | 1.2 | | .9 |
| | | 2.2 | 2.7 | | | Sales/Working Capital | | 2.8 | | 1.7 |
| | | 4.3 | 5.4 | | | | | | 6.8 | | 3.7 |
| | | 30.0 | 9.9 | | | | | | 15.3 | | 13.0 |
| | | (10) 14.5 | (17) 5.6 | | | EBIT/Interest | | (36) 4.6 | (33) | 6.2 |
| | | 7.3 | 1.5 | | | | | | -1.8 | | 2.8 |
| | | | | | | | Net Profit + Depr., Dep., Amort./Cur. Mat. L/T/D | | | | |
| | | .5 | .6 | | | | | | .1 | | .6 |
| | | .7 | 1.0 | | | Fixed/Worth | | .8 | | .9 |
| | | 1.0 | 1.9 | | | | | | 2.1 | | 1.5 |
| | | .1 | .6 | | | | | | .2 | | .3 |
| | | .3 | 1.2 | | | Debt/Worth | | .8 | | .5 |
| | | .6 | 1.7 | | | | | | 2.6 | | 1.7 |
| | | 34.9 | 22.9 | | | | | | 13.8 | | 25.3 |
| | | 12.0 | (17) 13.6 | | | % Profit Before Taxes/Tangible Net Worth | | (42) 4.0 | (36) | 8.9 |
| | | 7.5 | 2.0 | | | | | | -3.0 | | 4.2 |
| | | 15.4 | 11.7 | | | | | | 7.1 | | 12.7 |
| | | 10.8 | 7.5 | | | % Profit Before Taxes/Total Assets | | 2.0 | | 5.4 |
| | | 5.6 | 1.1 | | | | | | -3.9 | | .5 |
| | | 5.4 | 1.2 | | | | | | 34.3 | | 2.2 |
| | | .9 | .7 | | | Sales/Net Fixed Assets | | 2.0 | | 1.1 |
| | | .4 | .5 | | | | | | .7 | | .6 |
| | | 1.3 | .6 | | | | | | 2.2 | | 1.0 |
| | | .5 | .4 | | | Sales/Total Assets | | .7 | | .5 |
| | | .3 | .3 | | | | | | .4 | | .3 |
| | | | 3.1 | | | | | | 2.0 | | 4.5 |
| | | (18) | 8.7 | | | % Depr., Dep., Amort./Sales | | (31) 4.9 | (35) | 7.2 |
| | | | 11.8 | | | | | | 10.1 | | 13.4 |
| | | | | | | | % Officers', Directors' Owners' Comp/Sales | | | | |
| 1130M | 11119M | 68653M | 242129M | 114268M | 233929M | | Net Sales ($) | | 543422M | | 311932M |
| 484M | 8127M | 71195M | 370731M | 310573M | 249441M | | Total Assets ($) | | 542446M | | 484520M |

© RMA 2024  M = $ thousand  MM = $ million
See Pages viii through xx for Explanation of Ratios and Data

# PUBLIC ADMINISTRATION—Fire Protection NAICS 922160

| Comparative Historical Data ||| | Current Data Sorted by Sales |||||||
|---|---|---|---|---|---|---|---|---|---|
| | | | **Type of Statement** | | | | | | |
| 13 | 26 | 22 | Unqualified | 1 | 4 | | 8 | 5 | 4 |
| 3 | 3 | 3 | Reviewed | | 1 | 2 | | | |
| 1 | 1 | | Compiled | | | | | | |
| 6 | 6 | 6 | Tax Returns | 1 | 5 | | 2 | 4 | 3 |
| 15 | 20 | 16 | Other | 2 | 5 | | 2 | 4 | 3 |
| 4/1/21-3/31/22 ALL | 4/1/22-3/31/23 ALL | 4/1/23-3/31/24 ALL | | 0-1MM | 30 (4/1-9/30/23) 1-3MM | 3-5MM | 17 (10/1/23-3/31/24) 5-10MM | 10-25MM | 25MM & OVER |
| 38 | 56 | 47 | NUMBER OF STATEMENTS | 4 | 15 | 2 | 10 | 9 | 7 |
| % | % | % | **ASSETS** | % | % | % | % | % | % |
| 30.1 | 36.4 | 29.6 | Cash & Equivalents | | 36.0 | | 29.1 | | |
| 8.3 | 13.2 | 9.2 | Trade Receivables (net) | | 5.1 | | 5.5 | | |
| 3.0 | 1.9 | 1.4 | Inventory | | .1 | | 1.1 | | |
| 1.4 | 3.0 | 4.1 | All Other Current | | 2.3 | | 1.3 | | |
| 42.8 | 54.5 | 44.3 | Total Current | | 43.5 | | 37.0 | | |
| 45.5 | 34.6 | 42.6 | Fixed Assets (net) | | 35.0 | | 55.2 | | |
| .5 | .2 | 4.6 | Intangibles (net) | | 9.8 | | .3 | | |
| 11.2 | 10.7 | 8.5 | All Other Non-Current | | 11.6 | | 7.5 | | |
| 100.0 | 100.0 | 100.0 | Total | | 100.0 | | 100.0 | | |
| | | | **LIABILITIES** | | | | | | |
| .7 | 2.4 | .5 | Notes Payable-Short Term | | .5 | | 1.2 | | |
| 2.0 | 1.2 | 2.7 | Cur. Mat.-L.T.D. | | 2.6 | | 2.8 | | |
| 3.8 | 3.2 | 3.1 | Trade Payables | | 1.7 | | 3.3 | | |
| .0 | .1 | .0 | Income Taxes Payable | | .0 | | .0 | | |
| 2.5 | 5.7 | 5.7 | All Other Current | | 4.8 | | 3.0 | | |
| 9.0 | 12.6 | 12.0 | Total Current | | 9.5 | | 10.3 | | |
| 18.5 | 17.3 | 23.0 | Long-Term Debt | | 17.5 | | 34.5 | | |
| .0 | .1 | .1 | Deferred Taxes | | .0 | | .0 | | |
| 21.5 | 13.2 | 5.5 | All Other Non-Current | | 1.6 | | 4.8 | | |
| 51.1 | 56.8 | 59.5 | Net Worth | | 71.4 | | 50.5 | | |
| 100.0 | 100.0 | 100.0 | Total Liabilties & Net Worth | | 100.0 | | 100.0 | | |
| | | | **INCOME DATA** | | | | | | |
| 100.0 | 100.0 | 100.0 | Net Sales | | 100.0 | | 100.0 | | |
| | | | Gross Profit | | | | | | |
| 86.7 | 85.4 | 84.1 | Operating Expenses | | 86.4 | | 83.9 | | |
| 13.3 | 14.6 | 15.9 | Operating Profit | | 13.6 | | 16.1 | | |
| .6 | -.3 | 1.5 | All Other Expenses (net) | | 1.6 | | 2.2 | | |
| 12.7 | 14.8 | 14.4 | Profit Before Taxes | | 12.0 | | 13.9 | | |
| | | | **RATIOS** | | | | | | |
| 13.7 | 17.1 | 10.5 | | | 41.4 | | 5.8 | | |
| 7.1 | 6.4 | 4.5 | Current | | 6.9 | | 4.4 | | |
| 3.3 | 2.8 | 2.4 | | | 3.0 | | 2.1 | | |
| 13.5 | 16.7 | 10.4 | | | 40.5 | | 5.5 | | |
| 7.0 | 5.4 | 4.3 | Quick | | 4.5 | | 4.0 | | |
| 2.9 | 2.6 | 2.1 | | | 2.5 | | 2.0 | | |
| 0 UND | 0 UND | 0 UND | | 0 UND | | 2 221.3 | | | |
| 4 84.2 | 15 24.2 | 22 16.8 | Sales/Receivables | 0 UND | | 19 19.5 | | | |
| 25 14.5 | 51 7.2 | 51 7.2 | | 33 10.9 | | 39 9.3 | | | |
| | | | Cost of Sales/Inventory | | | | | | |
| | | | Cost of Sales/Payables | | | | | | |
| 1.1 | 1.0 | 1.3 | | | 1.9 | | 1.1 | | |
| 2.1 | 2.7 | 2.4 | Sales/Working Capital | | 2.4 | | 2.6 | | |
| 4.4 | 5.8 | 4.4 | | | 3.8 | | 4.5 | | |
| 21.6 | 38.9 | 13.1 | | | 36.4 | | | | |
| (31) 8.7 | (40) 16.3 | (40) 6.0 | EBIT/Interest | (11) | 5.6 | | | | |
| 2.7 | 3.0 | 2.3 | | | 1.9 | | | | |
| | | | Net Profit + Depr., Dep., Amort./Cur. Mat. L/T/D | | | | | | |
| .5 | .1 | .3 | | | .2 | | .7 | | |
| .9 | .5 | .8 | Fixed/Worth | | .5 | | 1.1 | | |
| 1.4 | 1.1 | 1.1 | | | 1.0 | | 1.9 | | |
| .2 | .2 | .3 | | | .0 | | .5 | | |
| .6 | .6 | .7 | Debt/Worth | | .3 | | .7 | | |
| 1.5 | 1.2 | 1.7 | | | 1.3 | | 1.7 | | |
| 26.8 | 31.4 | 22.0 | % Profit Before Taxes/Tangible | | 14.8 | | | | |
| (33) 9.8 | (51) 21.3 | (43) 10.8 | Net Worth | (13) | 8.3 | | | | |
| 4.3 | 6.6 | 6.2 | | | 3.7 | | | | |
| 15.0 | 18.8 | 11.7 | % Profit Before Taxes/Total | | 12.6 | | 10.8 | | |
| 7.4 | 10.3 | 7.1 | Assets | | 5.8 | | 7.3 | | |
| -.2 | 3.2 | 3.2 | | | 2.4 | | -.1 | | |
| 5.3 | 35.7 | 24.4 | | | 67.0 | | 1.2 | | |
| 1.2 | 1.9 | 1.0 | Sales/Net Fixed Assets | | 2.4 | | .8 | | |
| .5 | .8 | .6 | | | .7 | | .5 | | |
| 1.2 | 2.0 | 1.6 | | | 1.6 | | .6 | | |
| .5 | .6 | .5 | Sales/Total Assets | | 1.1 | | .5 | | |
| .3 | .4 | .3 | | | .3 | | .3 | | |
| 4.4 | 2.0 | 3.1 | | | | | | | |
| (27) 6.8 | (36) 5.3 | (34) 7.6 | % Depr., Dep., Amort./Sales | | | | | | |
| 14.1 | 12.5 | 11.8 | | | | | | | |
| | .5 | | % Officers', Directors' | | | | | | |
| | (10) 2.4 | | Owners' Comp/Sales | | | | | | |
| | 5.7 | | | | | | | | |
| 393094M | 515784M | 671228M | Net Sales ($) | 2897M | 27394M | 7509M | 73879M | 140151M | 419398M |
| 602558M | 731816M | 1010551M | Total Assets ($) | 12711M | 56518M | 24179M | 165033M | 274755M | 477355M |

© RMA 2024  M = $ thousand  MM = $ million
See Pages viii through xx for Explanation of Ratios and Data

# PUBLIC ADMINISTRATION—Administration of Education Programs  NAICS 923110

## Current Data Sorted by Assets | Comparative Historical Data

| | 0-500M | 1<br>23 (4/1-9/30/23)<br>500M-2MM | 3<br>2-10MM | 9<br>1<br>1<br>2 (10/1/23-3/31/24)<br>10-50MM | 3<br>1<br>50-100MM | 5<br>1<br>100-250MM | | Type of Statement | 34<br>1<br>11<br>4/1/19-<br>3/31/20<br>ALL | 24<br>1<br>1<br>5<br>4/1/20-<br>3/31/21<br>ALL |
|---|---|---|---|---|---|---|---|---|---|---|
| | | 1 | 3 | 11 | 4 | 6 | NUMBER OF STATEMENTS | | 46 | 31 |
| | % | % | % | % | % | % | ASSETS | | % | % |
| D | | | | 25.3 | | | Cash & Equivalents | | 29.4 | 27.2 |
| A | | | | 2.0 | | | Trade Receivables (net) | | 9.5 | 4.2 |
| T | | | | .6 | | | Inventory | | .2 | .1 |
| A | | | | 9.0 | | | All Other Current | | 9.4 | 5.6 |
| | | | | 36.9 | | | Total Current | | 48.5 | 37.1 |
| N | | | | 42.3 | | | Fixed Assets (net) | | 36.1 | 45.7 |
| O | | | | .5 | | | Intangibles (net) | | 2.5 | .4 |
| T | | | | 20.4 | | | All Other Non-Current | | 12.9 | 16.7 |
| | | | | 100.0 | | | Total | | 100.0 | 100.0 |
| A | | | | | | | LIABILITIES | | | |
| V | | | | 1.2 | | | Notes Payable-Short Term | | 3.3 | .7 |
| A | | | | 4.1 | | | Cur. Mat.-L.T.D. | | 1.7 | 1.4 |
| I | | | | 2.6 | | | Trade Payables | | 3.5 | 2.3 |
| L | | | | .0 | | | Income Taxes Payable | | .0 | .0 |
| A | | | | 8.9 | | | All Other Current | | 11.2 | 5.1 |
| B | | | | 16.7 | | | Total Current | | 19.7 | 9.5 |
| L | | | | 16.6 | | | Long-Term Debt | | 16.0 | 25.0 |
| E | | | | .2 | | | Deferred Taxes | | .0 | .5 |
| | | | | 46.4 | | | All Other Non-Current | | 29.4 | 43.9 |
| | | | | 20.2 | | | Net Worth | | 35.0 | 21.1 |
| | | | | 100.0 | | | Total Liabilities & Net Worth | | 100.0 | 100.0 |
| | | | | | | | INCOME DATA | | | |
| | | | | 100.0 | | | Net Sales | | 100.0 | 100.0 |
| | | | | | | | Gross Profit | | | |
| | | | | 96.4 | | | Operating Expenses | | 93.2 | 91.9 |
| | | | | 3.6 | | | Operating Profit | | 6.8 | 8.1 |
| | | | | .5 | | | All Other Expenses (net) | | 1.5 | 5.3 |
| | | | | 3.1 | | | Profit Before Taxes | | 5.2 | 2.8 |
| | | | | | | | RATIOS | | | |
| | | | | 4.6 | | | | | 7.0 | 6.1 |
| | | | | 3.1 | | | Current | | 3.5 | 3.5 |
| | | | | 1.8 | | | | | 1.5 | 2.4 |
| | | | | 3.7 | | | | | 6.8 | 5.6 |
| | | | | 2.3 | | | Quick | | 2.7 | 2.8 |
| | | | | 1.5 | | | | | 1.1 | 2.0 |
| | | | 0 | UND | | | | 2 | 234.9 | 0 | 999.8 |
| | | | 2 | 180.6 | | | Sales/Receivables | 10 | 35.2 | 10 | 36.0 |
| | | | 35 | 10.5 | | | | 35 | 10.3 | 41 | 8.8 |
| | | | | | | | Cost of Sales/Inventory | | | |
| | | | | | | | Cost of Sales/Payables | | | |
| | | | | 2.1 | | | | | 2.1 | 1.8 |
| | | | | 4.1 | | | Sales/Working Capital | | 4.3 | 2.4 |
| | | | | 10.0 | | | | | 10.9 | 5.0 |
| | | | | | | | | | 7.7 | 7.0 |
| | | | | | | | EBIT/Interest | (27) | 2.4 | (22) | 1.5 |
| | | | | | | | | | -.6 | -4.0 |
| | | | | | | | Net Profit + Depr., Dep.,<br>Amort./Cur. Mat. L/T/D | | | |
| | | | | .0 | | | | | .1 | .7 |
| | | | | 1.8 | | | Fixed/Worth | | .8 | 2.2 |
| | | | | -2.2 | | | | | 2.6 | -5.1 |
| | | | | .7 | | | | | .4 | 1.3 |
| | | | | 2.4 | | | Debt/Worth | | 1.5 | 3.3 |
| | | | | -4.2 | | | | | 6.0 | -9.5 |
| | | | | | | | | | 19.8 | 18.6 |
| | | | | | | | % Profit Before Taxes/Tangible<br>Net Worth | (37) | 5.9 | (22) | 8.0 |
| | | | | | | | | | -2.9 | -3.5 |
| | | | | 6.8 | | | | | 10.4 | 6.1 |
| | | | | 2.0 | | | % Profit Before Taxes/Total<br>Assets | | 1.7 | 2.1 |
| | | | | -4.9 | | | | | -1.6 | -4.6 |
| | | | | 21.7 | | | | | 152.1 | 14.2 |
| | | | | .8 | | | Sales/Net Fixed Assets | | 2.4 | 1.0 |
| | | | | .6 | | | | | 1.0 | .6 |
| | | | | .7 | | | | | 1.6 | .8 |
| | | | | .5 | | | Sales/Total Assets | | .8 | .5 |
| | | | | .4 | | | | | .5 | .4 |
| | | | | | | | | | 1.4 | 1.8 |
| | | | | | | | % Depr., Dep., Amort./Sales | (31) | 4.0 | (24) | 4.6 |
| | | | | | | | | | 7.6 | 7.0 |
| | | | | | | | % Officers', Directors'<br>Owners' Comp/Sales | | | |
| | | 1431M | 28649M | 268127M | 334125M | 861603M | Net Sales ($) | | 2442969M | 1829963M |
| | | 1536M | 9088M | 371034M | 255690M | 958446M | Total Assets ($) | | 2458467M | 2993271M |

M = $ thousand    MM = $ million
See Pages viii through xx for Explanation of Ratios and Data

© RMA 2024

## PUBLIC ADMINISTRATION—Administration of Education Programs  NAICS 923110

### Comparative Historical Data | Current Data Sorted by Sales

| | | | | | | | Type of Statement | | | | | | |
|---|---|---|---|---|---|---|---|---|---|---|---|---|---|
| | 27 | | 27 | | 17 | | Unqualified | | | | 1 | 6 | 10 |
| | 1 | | 1 | | 1 | | Reviewed | | | | 1 | | |
| | | | | | 1 | | Compiled | | | | | | |
| | 4 | | 8 | | 7 | | Tax Returns | | | | | | |
| | 4/1/21-3/31/22 ALL | | 4/1/22-3/31/23 ALL | | 4/1/23-3/31/24 ALL | | Other | 0-1MM | 23 (4/1-9/30/23) 1-3MM | 3-5MM | 2 (10/1/23-3/31/24) 1 5-10MM | 2 10-25MM | 2 25MM & OVER |
| | 32 | | 37 | | 25 | | NUMBER OF STATEMENTS | | 2 | | 3 | 8 | 12 |
| | % | | % | | % | | ASSETS | % | % | % | % | % | % |
| | 29.5 | | 33.1 | | 38.3 | | Cash & Equivalents | D | | D | | | 48.7 |
| | 5.9 | | 11.0 | | 7.0 | | Trade Receivables (net) | A | | A | | | 11.8 |
| | .1 | | .2 | | 1.2 | | Inventory | T | | T | | | .1 |
| | 3.0 | | 5.6 | | 6.1 | | All Other Current | A | | A | | | 9.7 |
| | 38.4 | | 49.8 | | 52.6 | | Total Current | | | | | | 70.3 |
| | 44.5 | | 30.4 | | 32.1 | | Fixed Assets (net) | N | | N | | | 18.3 |
| | .4 | | .3 | | .2 | | Intangibles (net) | O | | O | | | .0 |
| | 16.6 | | 19.5 | | 15.1 | | All Other Non-Current | T | | T | | | 11.4 |
| | 100.0 | | 100.0 | | 100.0 | | Total | | | | | | 100.0 |
| | | | | | | | LIABILITIES | A | | A | | | |
| | 2.6 | | 2.4 | | 3.5 | | Notes Payable-Short Term | V | | V | | | .0 |
| | 1.6 | | .9 | | 3.3 | | Cur. Mat.-L.T.D. | A | | A | | | 3.2 |
| | 1.7 | | 4.3 | | 2.9 | | Trade Payables | I | | I | | | 3.0 |
| | .3 | | .5 | | .0 | | Income Taxes Payable | L | | L | | | .0 |
| | 6.9 | | 7.8 | | 10.4 | | All Other Current | A | | A | | | 14.0 |
| | 13.1 | | 15.9 | | 20.0 | | Total Current | B | | B | | | 20.1 |
| | 17.8 | | 12.4 | | 20.9 | | Long-Term Debt | L | | L | | | 23.1 |
| | .0 | | 4.2 | | .1 | | Deferred Taxes | E | | E | | | .0 |
| | 42.7 | | 37.2 | | 34.7 | | All Other Non-Current | | | | | | 21.1 |
| | 26.3 | | 30.3 | | 24.3 | | Net Worth | | | | | | 35.6 |
| | 100.0 | | 100.0 | | 100.0 | | Total Liabilities & Net Worth | | | | | | 100.0 |
| | | | | | | | INCOME DATA | | | | | | |
| | 100.0 | | 100.0 | | 100.0 | | Net Sales | | | | | | 100.0 |
| | | | | | | | Gross Profit | | | | | | 90.0 |
| | 94.2 | | 92.6 | | 93.7 | | Operating Expenses | | | | | | 10.0 |
| | 5.8 | | 7.4 | | 6.3 | | Operating Profit | | | | | | -.7 |
| | 1.5 | | 1.9 | | .0 | | All Other Expenses (net) | | | | | | 10.7 |
| | 4.3 | | 5.5 | | 6.3 | | Profit Before Taxes | | | | | | |
| | | | | | | | RATIOS | | | | | | |
| | 5.9 | | 5.8 | | 8.0 | | | | | | | | 12.2 |
| | 3.2 | | 3.5 | | 3.8 | | Current | | | | | | 5.1 |
| | 1.7 | | 1.9 | | 1.8 | | | | | | | | 2.2 |
| | 5.4 | | 5.7 | | 8.0 | | | | | | | | 11.7 |
| | 2.9 | | 2.9 | | 3.2 | | Quick | | | | | | 4.3 |
| | 1.4 | | 1.5 | | 1.3 | | | | | | | | 1.7 |
| 1 | 402.5 | 1 | 656.4 | 0 | UND | | | | | | | 0 | UND |
| 14 | 26.7 | 14 | 26.7 | 8 | 46.6 | | Sales/Receivables | | | | | 16 | 22.8 |
| 34 | 10.7 | 49 | 7.5 | 42 | 8.6 | | | | | | | 74 | 4.9 |
| | | | | | | | Cost of Sales/Inventory | | | | | | |
| | | | | | | | Cost of Sales/Payables | | | | | | |
| | 1.9 | | 2.3 | | 2.0 | | | | | | | | 2.0 |
| | 2.9 | | 3.5 | | 2.5 | | Sales/Working Capital | | | | | | 2.2 |
| | 5.1 | | 6.6 | | 7.1 | | | | | | | | 4.4 |
| | 7.2 | | 19.6 | | 13.2 | | | | | | | | |
| (25) | 3.1 | (22) | 8.3 | (16) | 5.1 | | EBIT/Interest | | | | | | |
| | .5 | | 2.6 | | 2.2 | | | | | | | | |
| | | | | | | | Net Profit + Depr., Dep., Amort./Cur. Mat. L/T/D | | | | | | |
| | .5 | | .0 | | .0 | | | | | | | | .0 |
| | 2.0 | | .8 | | 1.3 | | Fixed/Worth | | | | | | .4 |
| | -5.7 | | NM | | -2.6 | | | | | | | | -3.5 |
| | .5 | | .6 | | .3 | | | | | | | | .3 |
| | 2.1 | | 1.5 | | 1.3 | | Debt/Worth | | | | | | 1.0 |
| | -10.2 | | NM | | -9.0 | | | | | | | | -12.8 |
| | 17.8 | | 26.8 | | 25.9 | | % Profit Before Taxes/Tangible Net Worth | | | | | | |
| (22) | 9.9 | (28) | 10.1 | (17) | 10.9 | | | | | | | | |
| | 1.4 | | 1.3 | | 4.2 | | | | | | | | |
| | 7.7 | | 10.5 | | 9.1 | | | | | | | | 26.1 |
| | 2.4 | | 4.8 | | 5.2 | | % Profit Before Taxes/Total Assets | | | | | | 8.8 |
| | -.5 | | -.7 | | -2.6 | | | | | | | | -.6 |
| | 2.9 | | 53.5 | | UND | | | | | | | | UND |
| | .9 | | 3.5 | | 2.1 | | Sales/Net Fixed Assets | | | | | | 7.3 |
| | .6 | | 1.1 | | .7 | | | | | | | | 1.8 |
| | .7 | | 1.8 | | 1.7 | | | | | | | | 2.0 |
| | .5 | | .8 | | .7 | | Sales/Total Assets | | | | | | 1.0 |
| | .4 | | .5 | | .4 | | | | | | | | .6 |
| | 3.9 | | .8 | | .9 | | | | | | | | |
| (24) | 5.3 | (22) | 2.9 | (17) | 4.4 | | % Depr., Dep., Amort./Sales | | | | | | |
| | 7.5 | | 5.1 | | 6.5 | | | | | | | | |
| | | | | | | | % Officers', Directors' Owners' Comp/Sales | | | | | | |
| | 1999232M | | 2456784M | | 1493935M | | Net Sales ($) | | 2784M | | 25868M | 135091M | 1330192M |
| | 2841905M | | 2704718M | | 1595794M | | Total Assets ($) | | 3614M | | 53911M | 262186M | 1276083M |

© RMA 2024  
M = $ thousand  MM = $ million  
See Pages viii through xx for Explanation of Ratios and Data

# PUBLIC ADMINISTRATION—Administration of Public Health Programs  NAICS 923120

## Current Data Sorted by Assets | Comparative Historical Data

| | | | | | | Type of Statement | | |
|---|---|---|---|---|---|---|---|---|
| | | | | | | Unqualified | 22 | 17 |
| | | | 7 | 1 | 4 | Reviewed | | |
| | | | | | | Compiled | 1 | |
| | | | 1 | | | Tax Returns | 2 | 1 |
| 1 | 2 | 4 | 1 | 1 | 1 | Other | 6 | 5 |
| | 17 (4/1-9/30/23) | | 6 (10/1/23-3/31/24) | | | | 4/1/19- | 4/1/20- |
| 0-500M | 500M-2MM | 2-10MM | 10-50MM | 50-100MM | 100-250MM | | 3/31/20 | 3/31/21 |
| | | | | | | NUMBER OF STATEMENTS | ALL | ALL |
| 1 | 2 | 4 | 9 | 2 | 5 | | 31 | 23 |
| % | % | % | % | % | % | ASSETS | % | % |
| | | | | | | Cash & Equivalents | 28.0 | 28.5 |
| | | | | | | Trade Receivables (net) | 20.1 | 15.3 |
| | | | | | | Inventory | .8 | .4 |
| | | | | | | All Other Current | 7.6 | 4.7 |
| | | | | | | Total Current | 56.5 | 48.9 |
| | | | | | | Fixed Assets (net) | 27.3 | 31.5 |
| | | | | | | Intangibles (net) | 3.3 | 3.5 |
| | | | | | | All Other Non-Current | 12.9 | 16.2 |
| | | | | | | Total | 100.0 | 100.0 |
| | | | | | | LIABILITIES | | |
| | | | | | | Notes Payable-Short Term | 3.2 | 1.4 |
| | | | | | | Cur. Mat.-L.T.D. | .6 | .9 |
| | | | | | | Trade Payables | 8.5 | 7.0 |
| | | | | | | Income Taxes Payable | .0 | .0 |
| | | | | | | All Other Current | 18.5 | 16.6 |
| | | | | | | Total Current | 30.8 | 25.9 |
| | | | | | | Long-Term Debt | 12.4 | 14.1 |
| | | | | | | Deferred Taxes | .0 | .0 |
| | | | | | | All Other Non-Current | 6.1 | 6.6 |
| | | | | | | Net Worth | 50.7 | 53.5 |
| | | | | | | Total Liabilities & Net Worth | 100.0 | 100.0 |
| | | | | | | INCOME DATA | | |
| | | | | | | Net Sales | 100.0 | 100.0 |
| | | | | | | Gross Profit | | |
| | | | | | | Operating Expenses | 98.9 | 100.7 |
| | | | | | | Operating Profit | 1.1 | -.7 |
| | | | | | | All Other Expenses (net) | -.5 | -1.4 |
| | | | | | | Profit Before Taxes | 1.6 | .6 |
| | | | | | | RATIOS | | |
| | | | | | | | 5.2 | 3.6 |
| | | | | | | Current | 2.1 | 2.3 |
| | | | | | | | 1.1 | 1.2 |
| | | | | | | | 4.9 | 3.4 |
| | | | | | | Quick | 1.9 | 2.0 |
| | | | | | | | 1.0 | 1.1 |
| | | | | | | | 23  16.2 | 7  50.4 |
| | | | | | | Sales/Receivables | 45  8.1 | 33  10.9 |
| | | | | | | | 64  5.7 | 51  7.2 |
| | | | | | | Cost of Sales/Inventory | | |
| | | | | | | Cost of Sales/Payables | | |
| | | | | | | | 2.4 | 3.4 |
| | | | | | | Sales/Working Capital | 4.9 | 6.6 |
| | | | | | | | 55.2 | 17.3 |
| | | | | | | | 11.7 | 10.8 |
| | | | | | | EBIT/Interest | (21) 4.8 | (14) 3.3 |
| | | | | | | | 1.5 | -.7 |
| | | | | | | Net Profit + Depr., Dep., Amort./Cur. Mat. L/T/D | | |
| | | | | | | | .1 | .2 |
| | | | | | | Fixed/Worth | .5 | .6 |
| | | | | | | | .8 | 1.1 |
| | | | | | | | .3 | .3 |
| | | | | | | Debt/Worth | .9 | .8 |
| | | | | | | | 2.4 | 2.3 |
| | | | | | | | 14.6 | 21.0 |
| | | | | | | % Profit Before Taxes/Tangible Net Worth | (29) 5.1 | (22) 3.1 |
| | | | | | | | -.2 | .0 |
| | | | | | | | 6.8 | 9.5 |
| | | | | | | % Profit Before Taxes/Total Assets | 2.5 | 2.1 |
| | | | | | | | -.3 | .0 |
| | | | | | | | 103.0 | 20.9 |
| | | | | | | Sales/Net Fixed Assets | 8.7 | 4.6 |
| | | | | | | | 2.2 | 1.5 |
| | | | | | | | 3.1 | 2.1 |
| | | | | | | Sales/Total Assets | 1.4 | 1.1 |
| | | | | | | | .6 | .5 |
| | | | | | | | .4 | .8 |
| | | | | | | % Depr., Dep., Amort./Sales | (26) 2.3 | (18) 1.6 |
| | | | | | | | 6.2 | 3.5 |
| | | | | | | % Officers', Directors' Owners' Comp/Sales | | |
| 3476M | 3105M | 25439M | 363942M | 199352M | 840565M | Net Sales ($) | 3397476M | 1819499M |
| 269M | 2116M | 21982M | 168865M | 159674M | 905024M | Total Assets ($) | 2224139M | 1355111M |

M = $ thousand    MM = $ million
See Pages viii through xx for Explanation of Ratios and Data

© RMA 2024

# PUBLIC ADMINISTRATION—Administration of Public Health Programs  NAICS 923120

## Comparative Historical Data | Current Data Sorted by Sales

| | | | | Type of Statement | | | | | | |
|---|---|---|---|---|---|---|---|---|---|---|
| | 15 | 11 | 12 | Unqualified | | | | | 3 | 9 |
| | | | | Reviewed | | | | | | |
| | | | | Compiled | | | | | | 1 |
| | | 1 | 1 | Tax Returns | | | | | | 3 |
| | 9 | 13 | 10 | Other | | 2 | 2 | 3 | | |
| | 4/1/21-3/31/22 | 4/1/22-3/31/23 | 4/1/23-3/31/24 | | | 17 (4/1-9/30/23) | | 6 (10/1/23-3/31/24) | | |
| | ALL | ALL | ALL | | 0-1MM | 1-3MM | 3-5MM | 5-10MM | 10-25MM | 25MM & OVER |
| | 24 | 25 | 23 | NUMBER OF STATEMENTS | | 2 | 2 | 3 | 3 | 13 |
| | % | % | % | ASSETS | % | % | % | % | % | % |
| | 31.1 | 28.0 | 34.7 | Cash & Equivalents | | | | | | 28.5 |
| | 13.8 | 20.3 | 12.9 | Trade Receivables (net) | D | | | | | 10.6 |
| | 1.1 | .0 | 3.4 | Inventory | A | | | | | 5.6 |
| | 5.6 | 7.1 | 5.8 | All Other Current | T | | | | | 8.7 |
| | 51.6 | 55.4 | 56.8 | Total Current | A | | | | | 53.6 |
| | 28.6 | 25.2 | 23.0 | Fixed Assets (net) | | | | | | 22.1 |
| | 2.9 | 2.7 | 1.3 | Intangibles (net) | N | | | | | 2.3 |
| | 16.9 | 16.8 | 18.9 | All Other Non-Current | O | | | | | 22.1 |
| | 100.0 | 100.0 | 100.0 | Total | T | | | | | 100.0 |
| | | | | LIABILITIES | A | | | | | |
| | .3 | .3 | 4.8 | Notes Payable-Short Term | V | | | | | .8 |
| | 1.3 | .2 | 1.1 | Cur. Mat.-L.T.D. | A | | | | | 1.6 |
| | 5.3 | 4.5 | 8.0 | Trade Payables | I | | | | | 10.4 |
| | .0 | .0 | .0 | Income Taxes Payable | L | | | | | .0 |
| | 14.1 | 17.0 | 8.7 | All Other Current | A | | | | | 8.8 |
| | 21.0 | 22.0 | 22.6 | Total Current | B | | | | | 21.6 |
| | 8.2 | 18.4 | 12.6 | Long-Term Debt | L | | | | | 17.0 |
| | .0 | .1 | .0 | Deferred Taxes | E | | | | | .1 |
| | 21.0 | 11.2 | 10.4 | All Other Non-Current | | | | | | 14.9 |
| | 49.9 | 48.3 | 54.3 | Net Worth | | | | | | 46.4 |
| | 100.0 | 100.0 | 100.0 | Total Liabilties & Net Worth | | | | | | 100.0 |
| | | | | INCOME DATA | | | | | | |
| | 100.0 | 100.0 | 100.0 | Net Sales | | | | | | 100.0 |
| | | | | Gross Profit | | | | | | 98.8 |
| | 96.3 | 92.4 | 96.2 | Operating Expenses | | | | | | 1.2 |
| | 3.7 | 7.6 | 3.8 | Operating Profit | | | | | | -.9 |
| | -.5 | 1.9 | .3 | All Other Expenses (net) | | | | | | 2.1 |
| | 4.2 | 5.7 | 3.5 | Profit Before Taxes | | | | | | |
| | | | | RATIOS | | | | | | |
| | 4.4 | 5.5 | 5.7 | | | | | | | 5.5 |
| | 2.5 | 2.3 | 3.5 | Current | | | | | | 2.8 |
| | 1.5 | 1.2 | 1.6 | | | | | | | 1.2 |
| | 4.2 | 5.5 | 5.4 | | | | | | | 5.4 |
| | 2.2 | 1.8 | 2.3 | Quick | | | | | | 1.8 |
| | 1.2 | 1.1 | 1.1 | | | | | | | .9 |
| 12 | 30.2 | 14  25.4 | 10  38.0 | | | | | | 7 | 52.4 |
| 27 | 13.5 | 43  8.5 | 31  11.6 | Sales/Receivables | | | | | 29 | 12.7 |
| 39 | 9.3 | 64  5.7 | 56  6.5 | | | | | | 43 | 8.4 |
| | | | | Cost of Sales/Inventory | | | | | | |
| | | | | Cost of Sales/Payables | | | | | | |
| | 3.1 | 2.6 | 2.0 | | | | | | | 2.4 |
| | 6.1 | 5.9 | 5.0 | Sales/Working Capital | | | | | | 7.0 |
| | 12.1 | 32.0 | 10.4 | | | | | | | 33.3 |
| | 61.5 | 43.5 | 21.9 | | | | | | | |
| (11) | 15.4 | (14) 1.6 | (12) 3.1 | EBIT/Interest | | | | | | |
| | 4.2 | -1.2 | -1.9 | | | | | | | |
| | | | | Net Profit + Depr., Dep., Amort./Cur. Mat. L/T/D | | | | | | |
| | .1 | .1 | .2 | | | | | | | .2 |
| | .4 | .4 | .5 | Fixed/Worth | | | | | | .6 |
| | 1.1 | 2.1 | 1.0 | | | | | | | 1.5 |
| | .3 | .5 | .4 | | | | | | | .5 |
| | .7 | .9 | .7 | Debt/Worth | | | | | | 1.1 |
| | 1.2 | 3.0 | 1.4 | | | | | | | 3.0 |
| | 19.0 | 16.9 | 10.4 | | | | | | | 12.0 |
| (21) | 10.0 | (22) 4.7 | (20) 4.4 | % Profit Before Taxes/Tangible Net Worth | | | | | (11) | 9.4 |
| | 5.0 | .2 | -6.0 | | | | | | | -13.6 |
| | 10.8 | 10.3 | 7.8 | | | | | | | 8.4 |
| | 5.8 | 1.3 | 2.8 | % Profit Before Taxes/Total Assets | | | | | | 4.7 |
| | 2.6 | .0 | -3.8 | | | | | | | -4.1 |
| | 101.1 | 176.1 | 82.0 | | | | | | | 98.7 |
| | 6.5 | 9.4 | 6.4 | Sales/Net Fixed Assets | | | | | | 10.3 |
| | 1.4 | 2.8 | 3.5 | | | | | | | 2.9 |
| | 2.3 | 2.4 | 2.0 | | | | | | | 2.3 |
| | 1.5 | 1.5 | 1.4 | Sales/Total Assets | | | | | | 1.4 |
| | .7 | .9 | 1.1 | | | | | | | 1.0 |
| | .8 | .2 | .2 | | | | | | | .1 |
| (17) | 2.4 | (17) 1.6 | (17) 2.0 | % Depr., Dep., Amort./Sales | | | | | (11) | 2.0 |
| | 4.7 | 2.4 | 2.7 | | | | | | | 2.5 |
| | | | | % Officers', Directors' Owners' Comp/Sales | | | | | | |
| | 2153281M | 1631328M | 1435879M | Net Sales ($) | | 3105M | 8318M | 20597M | 59548M | 1344311M |
| | 1489890M | 1040868M | 1257930M | Total Assets ($) | | 2116M | 8856M | 13395M | 182600M | 1050963M |

© RMA 2024   M = $ thousand    MM = $ million
See Pages viii through xx for Explanation of Ratios and Data

# PUBLIC ADMINISTRATION—Administration of Housing Programs  NAICS 925110

## Current Data Sorted by Assets | Comparative Historical Data

| 3 | 6 | 16 | 2 | 7 | Type of Statement | | |
|---|---|---|---|---|---|---|---|
| | | | | 1 | Unqualified | 31 | 21 |
| | | | | | Reviewed | | |
| | | 1 | | | Compiled | 1 | |
| 1 | 1 | 10 | 6 | 5 | Tax Returns | 1 | |
| | 42 (4/1-9/30/23) | 20 (10/1/23-3/31/24) | 3 | | Other | 25 | 20 |
| 0-500M | 500M-2MM | 2-10MM | 10-50MM | 50-100MM | 100-250MM | 4/1/19-3/31/20 | 4/1/20-3/31/21 |
| 1 | 4 | 16 | 23 | 5 | 13 | NUMBER OF STATEMENTS  58 ALL | 41 ALL |
| % | % | % | % | % | % | ASSETS  % | % |
| | | 18.4 | 19.1 | | 12.6 | Cash & Equivalents  22.4 | 19.6 |
| | | 1.7 | 1.7 | | 2.6 | Trade Receivables (net)  2.3 | 2.4 |
| | | .4 | 1.1 | | .1 | Inventory  .3 | .3 |
| | | .9 | 6.3 | | 4.9 | All Other Current  2.6 | 4.4 |
| | | 21.4 | 28.1 | | 20.2 | Total Current  27.6 | 26.7 |
| | | 57.5 | 49.4 | | 48.7 | Fixed Assets (net)  48.1 | 48.8 |
| | | .0 | .1 | | 1.7 | Intangibles (net)  3.0 | 2.5 |
| | | 21.0 | 22.3 | | 29.5 | All Other Non-Current  21.3 | 21.9 |
| | | 100.0 | 100.0 | | 100.0 | Total  100.0 | 100.0 |
| | | | | | | LIABILITIES | |
| | | .7 | .1 | | .2 | Notes Payable-Short Term  .8 | 1.6 |
| | | 8.1 | 3.6 | | 3.1 | Cur. Mat.-L.T.D.  6.8 | 2.4 |
| | | 3.2 | 2.2 | | 1.0 | Trade Payables  2.1 | 2.4 |
| | | .0 | .0 | | .0 | Income Taxes Payable  .0 | .0 |
| | | 3.7 | 3.7 | | 2.2 | All Other Current  5.9 | 4.6 |
| | | 15.6 | 9.6 | | 6.5 | Total Current  15.6 | 10.9 |
| | | 36.5 | 39.6 | | 26.9 | Long-Term Debt  36.8 | 33.4 |
| | | .0 | .0 | | .0 | Deferred Taxes  .0 | .0 |
| | | 7.0 | 10.3 | | 13.9 | All Other Non-Current  6.2 | 5.3 |
| | | 40.9 | 40.5 | | 52.7 | Net Worth  41.5 | 50.3 |
| | | 100.0 | 100.0 | | 100.0 | Total Liabilities & Net Worth  100.0 | 100.0 |
| | | | | | | INCOME DATA | |
| | | 100.0 | 100.0 | | 100.0 | Net Sales  | |
| | | | | | | Gross Profit | |
| | | 93.8 | 85.1 | | 76.8 | Operating Expenses  88.9 | 84.8 |
| | | 6.2 | 14.9 | | 23.2 | Operating Profit  11.1 | 15.2 |
| | | 11.5 | 7.6 | | .5 | All Other Expenses (net)  4.0 | 3.8 |
| | | -5.3 | 7.3 | | 22.7 | Profit Before Taxes  7.1 | 11.4 |
| | | | | | | RATIOS | |
| | | 5.4 | 8.6 | | 5.5 |  9.2 | 7.8 |
| | | 2.8 | 3.3 | | 2.9 | Current  3.7 | 2.8 |
| | | .2 | 1.2 | | 1.6 |  1.0 | 1.2 |
| | | 5.3 | 8.3 | | 4.8 |  8.8 | 7.3 |
| | | 1.9 | 2.7 | | 2.8 | Quick  3.6 | 2.6 |
| | | .2 | 1.0 | | 1.2 |  .8 | .9 |
| | | 2  184.5 | 0  UND | | 4  85.2 |  2  154.5 | 3  132.4 |
| | | 9  42.4 | 9  42.9 | | 12  30.8 | Sales/Receivables  10  38.0 | 7  54.0 |
| | | 17  21.1 | 23  16.2 | | 78  4.7 |  24  15.1 | 33  11.2 |
| | | | | | | Cost of Sales/Inventory | |
| | | | | | | Cost of Sales/Payables | |
| | | 1.8 | 1.7 | | 1.2 |  1.1 | 1.7 |
| | | 7.6 | 4.3 | | 2.6 | Sales/Working Capital  3.9 | 4.1 |
| | | -2.2 | 18.1 | | 6.1 |  NM | 27.7 |
| | | 1.7 | 29.5 | | 5.1 |  5.4 | 12.0 |
| | (13) | .6 | (17) 2.2 | | (11) 1.2 | EBIT/Interest  (43) 1.6 | (29) 3.7 |
| | | -4.9 | -.1 | | -1.1 |  .2 | .0 |
| | | | | | | Net Profit + Depr., Dep., Amort./Cur. Mat. L/T/D | |
| | | .6 | .3 | | .5 |  .4 | .4 |
| | | 1.7 | .9 | | 1.1 | Fixed/Worth  1.0 | .8 |
| | | 7.6 | 1.8 | | 2.0 |  2.3 | 2.2 |
| | | .3 | .3 | | .4 |  .3 | .3 |
| | | 2.3 | .6 | | 1.0 | Debt/Worth  1.0 | .9 |
| | | 7.5 | 6.4 | | 2.1 |  3.0 | 2.3 |
| | | 2.6 | 6.9 | | 23.4 |  9.5 | 15.0 |
| | (14) | -2.5 | (21) .5 | | 4.6 | % Profit Before Taxes/Tangible Net Worth  (52) 1.4 | (38) 2.4 |
| | | -14.7 | -3.1 | | -.7 |  -1.6 | -1.6 |
| | | .7 | 4.1 | | 10.6 |  3.8 | 6.4 |
| | | -1.5 | .4 | | 3.3 | % Profit Before Taxes/Total Assets  .5 | 1.1 |
| | | -4.1 | -1.7 | | -.4 |  -1.2 | -1.1 |
| | | 3.0 | 3.5 | | 1.5 |  2.0 | 2.1 |
| | | .6 | 1.5 | | .4 | Sales/Net Fixed Assets  1.0 | .8 |
| | | .3 | .5 | | .3 |  .5 | .3 |
| | | .8 | .8 | | .4 |  .7 | .6 |
| | | .4 | .5 | | .2 | Sales/Total Assets  .4 | .4 |
| | | .2 | .2 | | .1 |  .2 | .2 |
| | | 3.3 | 2.9 | | 1.5 |  3.7 | 2.6 |
| | (13) | 7.2 | (20) 7.1 | | (11) 9.3 | % Depr., Dep., Amort./Sales  (53) 7.2 | (33) 7.6 |
| | | 16.2 | 15.4 | | 11.1 |  13.3 | 14.9 |
| | | | | | | % Officers', Directors' Owners' Comp/Sales | |
| 2378M | 9813M | 54673M | 517452M | 148608M | 616442M | Net Sales ($)  782544M | 589133M |
| 494M | 4843M | 101249M | 556555M | 393197M | 1954286M | Total Assets ($)  1766001M | 1450660M |

M = $ thousand    MM = $ million
See Pages viii through xx for Explanation of Ratios and Data

© RMA 2024

# PUBLIC ADMINISTRATION—Administration of Housing Programs  NAICS 925110

| Comparative Historical Data | | | | Current Data Sorted by Sales | | | | | |
|---|---|---|---|---|---|---|---|---|---|
| 27 | 30 | 34 | **Type of Statement** | 4 | 3 | 2 | 6 | 12 | 7 |
|  | 1 |  | Unqualified |  |  |  |  |  |  |
|  |  | 1 | Reviewed |  |  |  |  |  |  |
| 1 |  | 1 | Compiled |  |  |  | 1 |  |  |
| 21 | 26 | 26 | Tax Returns |  |  |  |  | 1 |  |
| 4/1/21- | 4/1/22- | 4/1/23- | Other | 4 | 9 |  | 1 | 8 | 4 |
| 3/31/22 | 3/31/23 | 3/31/24 |  |  | 42 (4/1-9/30/23) | | | 20 (10/1/23-3/31/24) | |
| ALL | ALL | ALL |  | 0-1MM | 1-3MM | 3-5MM | 5-10MM | 10-25MM | 25MM & OVER |
| 49 | 57 | 62 | NUMBER OF STATEMENTS | 8 | 12 | 2 | 8 | 21 | 11 |
| % | % | % | **ASSETS** | % | % | % | % | % | % |
| 18.1 | 20.5 | 19.1 | Cash & Equivalents | 21.0 |  |  |  | 16.1 | 18.2 |
| 2.0 | 1.9 | 2.8 | Trade Receivables (net) | 3.4 |  |  |  | 2.4 | 2.6 |
| 2.9 | 2.6 | .5 | Inventory | .0 |  |  |  | .6 | .1 |
| 3.4 | 6.2 | 4.0 | All Other Current | 2.4 |  |  |  | 3.2 | 10.8 |
| 26.3 | 31.2 | 26.5 | Total Current | 26.9 |  |  |  | 22.3 | 31.6 |
| 52.3 | 43.9 | 50.8 | Fixed Assets (net) | 57.4 |  |  |  | 48.3 | 46.2 |
| 2.9 | .6 | .4 | Intangibles (net) | .0 |  |  |  | .2 | 1.9 |
| 18.4 | 24.3 | 22.3 | All Other Non-Current | 15.8 |  |  |  | 29.2 | 20.3 |
| 100.0 | 100.0 | 100.0 | Total | 100.0 |  |  |  | 100.0 | 100.0 |
|  |  |  | **LIABILITIES** |  |  |  |  |  |  |
| 2.6 | 7.4 | .4 | Notes Payable-Short Term | .5 |  |  |  | .3 | .1 |
| 1.4 | 1.8 | 4.3 | Cur. Mat.-L.T.D. | 14.4 |  |  |  | 3.0 | .4 |
| 2.4 | 1.7 | 2.0 | Trade Payables | 3.1 |  |  |  | 1.8 | 1.4 |
| .0 | .0 | .0 | Income Taxes Payable | .0 |  |  |  | .0 | .0 |
| 5.3 | 4.8 | 4.1 | All Other Current | 3.9 |  |  |  | 3.9 | 4.4 |
| 11.8 | 15.8 | 10.9 | Total Current | 21.8 |  |  |  | 9.0 | 6.3 |
| 41.8 | 40.0 | 31.6 | Long-Term Debt | 37.4 |  |  |  | 38.0 | 13.8 |
| .0 | .0 | .0 | Deferred Taxes | .0 |  |  |  | .0 | .0 |
| 7.2 | 7.0 | 10.5 | All Other Non-Current | 4.6 |  |  |  | 12.5 | 11.2 |
| 39.3 | 37.2 | 47.0 | Net Worth | 36.1 |  |  |  | 40.5 | 68.7 |
| 100.0 | 100.0 | 100.0 | Total Liabilities & Net Worth | 100.0 |  |  |  | 100.0 | 100.0 |
|  |  |  | **INCOME DATA** |  |  |  |  |  |  |
| 100.0 | 100.0 | 100.0 | Net Sales | 100.0 |  |  |  | 100.0 | 100.0 |
|  |  |  | Gross Profit |  |  |  |  |  |  |
| 89.6 | 87.3 | 87.7 | Operating Expenses | 81.2 |  |  |  | 84.3 | 95.5 |
| 10.4 | 12.7 | 12.3 | Operating Profit | 18.8 |  |  |  | 15.7 | 4.5 |
| 3.6 | 4.0 | 5.8 | All Other Expenses (net) | 17.6 |  |  |  | 1.3 | -1.2 |
| 6.8 | 8.7 | 6.5 | Profit Before Taxes | 1.1 |  |  |  | 14.3 | 5.6 |
|  |  |  | **RATIOS** |  |  |  |  |  |  |
| 6.0 | 7.7 | 6.5 |  | 4.5 |  |  |  | 7.1 | 7.1 |
| 2.0 | 3.6 | 3.0 | Current | 1.4 |  |  |  | 1.6 | 4.8 |
| .9 | 1.5 | 1.1 |  | .3 |  |  |  | 1.0 | 3.2 |
| 5.4 | 6.8 | 5.8 |  | 4.5 |  |  |  | 6.9 | 6.3 |
| 2.0 | 2.8 | 2.8 | Quick | .9 |  |  |  | 1.5 | 3.9 |
| .8 | 1.0 | .9 |  | .2 |  |  |  | .8 | 2.7 |
| 3  135.3 | 1  581.3 | 2  211.8 |  | 0  UND |  |  |  | 1  253.5 | 6  58.1 |
| 10  37.5 | 7  51.8 | 9  40.7 | Sales/Receivables | 6  66.2 |  |  |  | 12  29.5 | 12  30.8 |
| 16  23.2 | 20  18.6 | 21  17.4 |  | 19  19.2 |  |  |  | 31  11.6 | 19  18.9 |
|  |  |  | Cost of Sales/Inventory |  |  |  |  |  |  |
|  |  |  | Cost of Sales/Payables |  |  |  |  |  |  |
| 2.0 | 1.3 | 1.7 |  | 1.1 |  |  |  | 2.0 | 3.3 |
| 4.0 | 2.4 | 4.1 | Sales/Working Capital | 9.3 |  |  |  | 5.5 | 4.0 |
| -98.8 | 10.1 | 36.9 |  | -1.5 |  |  |  | NM | 5.8 |
|  19.1 |  13.8 |  8.9 |  |  |  |  |  |  13.1 |  159.2 |
| (35)  4.7 | (42)  4.7 | (48)  1.1 | EBIT/Interest |  |  |  |  | (19)  2.7 | 5.1 |
|  .5 |  1.2 |  -.4 |  |  |  |  |  |  .7 |  -2.0 |
|  |  |  | Net Profit + Depr., Dep., Amort./Cur. Mat. L/T/D |  |  |  |  |  |  |
| .5 | .2 | .4 |  | .5 |  |  |  | .4 | .4 |
| 1.1 | .8 | .9 | Fixed/Worth | 1.6 |  |  |  | .8 | .8 |
| 1.9 | 1.6 | 2.2 |  | 5.5 |  |  |  | 1.7 | 1.1 |
| .4 | .4 | .3 |  | .4 |  |  |  | .4 | .3 |
| .9 | .9 | .7 | Debt/Worth | 3.7 |  |  |  | .7 | .4 |
| 2.1 | 2.2 | 3.4 |  | 6.4 |  |  |  | 2.1 | .7 |
|  9.9 |  8.9 |  8.5 | % Profit Before Taxes/Tangible |  7.6 |  |  |  |  15.9 |  6.6 |
| (45)  5.8 | (54)  3.7 | (58)  .6 | Net Worth | (11)  .1 |  |  |  | (19)  3.3 |  .7 |
|  -.3 |  .2 |  -3.9 |  |  -5.7 |  |  |  |  -1.3 |  -1.5 |
| 6.0 | 5.5 | 4.1 | % Profit Before Taxes/Total | 1.7 |  |  |  | 5.8 | 3.6 |
| 1.9 | 1.9 | .4 | Assets | .0 |  |  |  | 2.3 | .5 |
| -.8 | .1 | -1.7 |  | -1.7 |  |  |  | -.5 | -1.1 |
| 2.3 | 5.0 | 2.3 |  | 2.9 |  |  |  | 2.2 | 2.2 |
| 1.0 | .8 | .8 | Sales/Net Fixed Assets | .4 |  |  |  | 1.0 | 1.2 |
| .3 | .3 | .4 |  | .2 |  |  |  | .3 | .7 |
| .6 | .6 | .7 |  | .5 |  |  |  | .7 | .9 |
| .4 | .3 | .4 | Sales/Total Assets | .2 |  |  |  | .4 | .6 |
| .2 | .1 | .2 |  | .1 |  |  |  | .2 | .4 |
|  2.8 |  1.9 |  2.6 |  |  |  |  |  |  2.9 |  |
| (42)  6.8 | (42)  5.6 | (52)  7.6 | % Depr., Dep., Amort./Sales |  |  |  |  | (20)  5.5 |  |
|  16.8 |  13.1 |  15.0 |  |  |  |  |  |  11.3 |  |
|  |  |  | % Officers', Directors' Owners' Comp/Sales |  |  |  |  |  |  |
| 750273M | 1487150M | 1349366M | Net Sales ($) | 5265M | 25968M | 6835M | 60377M | 358466M | 892455M |
| 1817127M | 3511732M | 3010624M | Total Assets ($) | 31976M | 128071M | 23960M | 171696M | 1431281M | 1223640M |

© RMA 2024  M = $ thousand  MM = $ million
See Pages viii through xx for Explanation of Ratios and Data

# PUBLIC ADMINISTRATION—Administration of Urban Planning and Community and Rural Development  NAICS 925120

## Current Data Sorted by Assets / Comparative Historical Data

| | | | | | | | Type of Statement | | | | |
|---|---|---|---|---|---|---|---|---|---|---|---|
| | | 2 | 5 | 5 | 2 | 4 | Unqualified | | 22 | | 17 |
| | | | | | | | Reviewed | | 2 | | 1 |
| | | | | 1 | | | Compiled | | 2 | | |
| | 1 | 1 | 4 | 4 | 2 | 2 | Tax Returns | | 2 | | |
| | | 22 (4/1-9/30/23) | | 11 (10/1/23-3/31/24) | | | Other | | 14 | | 12 |
| 0-500M | 500M-2MM | 2-10MM | 10-50MM | 50-100MM | 100-250MM | | | | 4/1/19-3/31/20 | | 4/1/20-3/31/21 |
| 1 | 3 | 10 | 9 | 4 | 6 | | NUMBER OF STATEMENTS | | ALL 42 | | ALL 30 |
| % | % | % | % | % | % | | **ASSETS** | | % | | % |
| | | 18.1 | | | | | Cash & Equivalents | | 24.8 | | 26.7 |
| | | 21.1 | | | | | Trade Receivables (net) | | 9.2 | | 7.5 |
| | | .2 | | | | | Inventory | | .2 | | 1.7 |
| | | 14.2 | | | | | All Other Current | | 8.2 | | 4.5 |
| | | 53.6 | | | | | Total Current | | 42.4 | | 40.4 |
| | | 22.9 | | | | | Fixed Assets (net) | | 36.3 | | 29.9 |
| | | .4 | | | | | Intangibles (net) | | .9 | | 5.7 |
| | | 23.1 | | | | | All Other Non-Current | | 20.4 | | 23.9 |
| | | 100.0 | | | | | Total | | 100.0 | | 100.0 |
| | | | | | | | **LIABILITIES** | | | | |
| | | 4.5 | | | | | Notes Payable-Short Term | | 2.8 | | 2.4 |
| | | 1.5 | | | | | Cur. Mat.-L.T.D. | | 1.3 | | 3.1 |
| | | 6.8 | | | | | Trade Payables | | 4.1 | | 1.9 |
| | | .0 | | | | | Income Taxes Payable | | .0 | | .0 |
| | | 13.0 | | | | | All Other Current | | 5.5 | | 6.2 |
| | | 25.8 | | | | | Total Current | | 13.7 | | 13.5 |
| | | 27.4 | | | | | Long-Term Debt | | 24.8 | | 23.7 |
| | | .1 | | | | | Deferred Taxes | | .2 | | .0 |
| | | 13.7 | | | | | All Other Non-Current | | 8.0 | | 7.0 |
| | | 32.9 | | | | | Net Worth | | 53.4 | | 55.9 |
| | | 100.0 | | | | | Total Liabilities & Net Worth | | 100.0 | | 100.0 |
| | | | | | | | **INCOME DATA** | | | | |
| | | 100.0 | | | | | Net Sales | | 100.0 | | 100.0 |
| | | | | | | | Gross Profit | | | | |
| | | 62.1 | | | | | Operating Expenses | | 87.4 | | 79.8 |
| | | 37.9 | | | | | Operating Profit | | 12.6 | | 20.2 |
| | | 10.3 | | | | | All Other Expenses (net) | | 7.1 | | 3.7 |
| | | 27.6 | | | | | Profit Before Taxes | | 5.5 | | 16.5 |
| | | | | | | | **RATIOS** | | | | |
| | | 9.7 | | | | | | | 10.7 | | 8.6 |
| | | 2.0 | | | | | Current | | 4.1 | | 4.1 |
| | | 1.1 | | | | | | | 1.5 | | 2.0 |
| | | 7.0 | | | | | | | 7.4 | | 8.3 |
| | | 1.3 | | | | | Quick | | 3.8 | | 3.0 |
| | | .4 | | | | | | | 1.4 | | 1.2 |
| | 0 | UND | | | | | | 0 | UND | 0 | 994.7 |
| | 70 | 5.2 | | | | | Sales/Receivables | 21 | 17.0 | 16 | 22.8 |
| | 96 | 3.8 | | | | | | 51 | 7.2 | 89 | 4.1 |
| | | | | | | | Cost of Sales/Inventory | | | | |
| | | | | | | | Cost of Sales/Payables | | | | |
| | | .7 | | | | | | | .8 | | .6 |
| | | 7.1 | | | | | Sales/Working Capital | | 1.7 | | 1.8 |
| | | NM | | | | | | | 11.8 | | 4.1 |
| | | | | | | | | | 14.0 | | 13.0 |
| | | | | | | | EBIT/Interest | (25) | 3.4 | (19) | 3.7 |
| | | | | | | | | | .7 | | .7 |
| | | | | | | | Net Profit + Depr., Dep., Amort./Cur. Mat. L/T/D | | | | |
| | | .0 | | | | | | | .1 | | .0 |
| | | .6 | | | | | Fixed/Worth | | .8 | | .5 |
| | | 2.6 | | | | | | | 1.4 | | 1.6 |
| | | .7 | | | | | | | .3 | | .2 |
| | | 1.9 | | | | | Debt/Worth | | .8 | | .6 |
| | | 5.4 | | | | | | | 1.7 | | 3.1 |
| | | | | | | | | | 8.9 | | 12.5 |
| | | | | | | | % Profit Before Taxes/Tangible Net Worth | (41) | 3.8 | (28) | 3.6 |
| | | | | | | | | | -4.5 | | -.3 |
| | | 31.1 | | | | | | | 5.5 | | 5.6 |
| | | 7.3 | | | | | % Profit Before Taxes/Total Assets | | 1.3 | | 2.0 |
| | | 1.7 | | | | | | | -1.7 | | -.3 |
| | | UND | | | | | | | 14.8 | | 38.1 |
| | | 24.9 | | | | | Sales/Net Fixed Assets | | 2.8 | | 2.8 |
| | | 3.2 | | | | | | | .3 | | .4 |
| | | 1.9 | | | | | | | .9 | | .7 |
| | | .6 | | | | | Sales/Total Assets | | .3 | | .2 |
| | | .3 | | | | | | | .1 | | .1 |
| | | | | | | | | | 1.0 | | .9 |
| | | | | | | | % Depr., Dep., Amort./Sales | (31) | 1.9 | (19) | 2.4 |
| | | | | | | | | | 5.0 | | 13.4 |
| | | | | | | | % Officers', Directors' Owners' Comp/Sales | | | | |
| 44M | 4881M | 40476M | 75976M | 60072M | 152787M | | Net Sales ($) | | 614333M | | 300292M |
| 61M | 3285M | 53123M | 213576M | 326387M | 1078310M | | Total Assets ($) | | 1735652M | | 1053344M |

M = $ thousand   MM = $ million
See Pages viii through xx for Explanation of Ratios and Data

© RMA 2024

## PUBLIC ADMINISTRATION—Administration of Urban Planning and Community and Rural Development  NAICS 925120

### Comparative Historical Data / Current Data Sorted by Sales

| | | | | Type of Statement | | | | | | |
|---|---|---|---|---|---|---|---|---|---|---|
| | 14 | 18 | 18 | Unqualified | 1 | 3 | 1 | 5 | 5 | 3 |
| | 1 | | | Reviewed | | | | | | |
| | 1 | | 1 | Compiled | | | | 1 | | |
| | 16 | 16 | 14 | Tax Returns | 3 | 3 | 1 | 3 | 4 | |
| | 4/1/21- | 4/1/22- | 4/1/23- | Other | | | | | | |
| | 3/31/22 | 3/31/23 | 3/31/24 | | 22 (4/1-9/30/23) | | | 11 (10/1/23-3/31/24) | | |
| | ALL | ALL | ALL | | 0-1MM | 1-3MM | 3-5MM | 5-10MM | 10-25MM | 25MM & OVER |
| | 32 | 34 | 33 | NUMBER OF STATEMENTS | 4 | 6 | 2 | 9 | 9 | 3 |
| | % | % | % | ASSETS | % | % | % | % | % | % |
| | 19.7 | 22.1 | 22.3 | Cash & Equivalents | | | | | | |
| | 5.4 | 8.4 | 10.6 | Trade Receivables (net) | | | | | | |
| | .0 | .3 | .2 | Inventory | | | | | | |
| | 9.5 | 5.9 | 10.8 | All Other Current | | | | | | |
| | 34.6 | 36.7 | 43.9 | Total Current | | | | | | |
| | 31.8 | 32.6 | 27.6 | Fixed Assets (net) | | | | | | |
| | 2.6 | .7 | 3.8 | Intangibles (net) | | | | | | |
| | 31.0 | 30.0 | 24.7 | All Other Non-Current | | | | | | |
| | 100.0 | 100.0 | 100.0 | Total | | | | | | |
| | | | | LIABILITIES | | | | | | |
| | 3.2 | 2.3 | 7.0 | Notes Payable-Short Term | | | | | | |
| | 2.5 | 2.0 | 3.2 | Cur. Mat.-L.T.D. | | | | | | |
| | 2.7 | 3.6 | 3.3 | Trade Payables | | | | | | |
| | .1 | .0 | .0 | Income Taxes Payable | | | | | | |
| | 4.2 | 4.5 | 6.6 | All Other Current | | | | | | |
| | 12.6 | 12.5 | 20.1 | Total Current | | | | | | |
| | 23.1 | 28.3 | 33.1 | Long-Term Debt | | | | | | |
| | .0 | .4 | .2 | Deferred Taxes | | | | | | |
| | 6.6 | 7.0 | 12.5 | All Other Non-Current | | | | | | |
| | 57.7 | 51.8 | 34.0 | Net Worth | | | | | | |
| | 100.0 | 100.0 | 100.0 | Total Liabilities & Net Worth | | | | | | |
| | | | | INCOME DATA | | | | | | |
| | 100.0 | 100.0 | 100.0 | Net Sales | | | | | | |
| | | | | Gross Profit | | | | | | |
| | 70.0 | 77.8 | 75.7 | Operating Expenses | | | | | | |
| | 30.0 | 22.2 | 24.3 | Operating Profit | | | | | | |
| | 6.9 | 7.8 | 6.7 | All Other Expenses (net) | | | | | | |
| | 23.1 | 14.4 | 17.7 | Profit Before Taxes | | | | | | |
| | | | | RATIOS | | | | | | |
| | 12.3 | 17.1 | 7.2 | | | | | | | |
| | 4.0 | 2.9 | 2.6 | Current | | | | | | |
| | 1.5 | 1.5 | 1.0 | | | | | | | |
| | 9.4 | 6.9 | 5.1 | | | | | | | |
| | 1.8 | 2.6 | 1.7 | Quick | | | | | | |
| | .5 | 1.3 | .6 | | | | | | | |
| 1 | 526.2 | 2 190.1 | 0 UND | | | | | | | |
| 13 | 28.8 | 26 13.8 | 9 40.6 | Sales/Receivables | | | | | | |
| 46 | 8.0 | 52 7.0 | 73 5.0 | | | | | | | |
| | | | | Cost of Sales/Inventory | | | | | | |
| | | | | Cost of Sales/Payables | | | | | | |
| | .4 | .7 | .7 | | | | | | | |
| | 1.7 | 1.8 | 2.4 | Sales/Working Capital | | | | | | |
| | 3.6 | 11.4 | NM | | | | | | | |
| | 25.1 | 23.1 | 9.9 | | | | | | | |
| (18) | 7.6 | (21) 4.2 | (19) 3.3 | EBIT/Interest | | | | | | |
| | 2.8 | 1.4 | 1.0 | | | | | | | |
| | | | | Net Profit + Depr., Dep., Amort./Cur. Mat. L/T/D | | | | | | |
| | .0 | .0 | .0 | | | | | | | |
| | .4 | .6 | .2 | Fixed/Worth | | | | | | |
| | 1.3 | 1.1 | 1.8 | | | | | | | |
| | .2 | .4 | .5 | | | | | | | |
| | .8 | .9 | 1.8 | Debt/Worth | | | | | | |
| | 1.7 | 2.3 | 3.8 | | | | | | | |
| | 32.8 | 16.6 | 24.1 | | | | | | | |
| (31) | 6.1 | (33) 5.5 | (28) 6.1 | % Profit Before Taxes/Tangible Net Worth | | | | | | |
| | .9 | 1.6 | .8 | | | | | | | |
| | 10.9 | 7.8 | 8.9 | | | | | | | |
| | 2.5 | 2.6 | 2.0 | % Profit Before Taxes/Total Assets | | | | | | |
| | .2 | .4 | .1 | | | | | | | |
| | 127.3 | 40.5 | 999.8 | | | | | | | |
| | 4.8 | 1.8 | 12.5 | Sales/Net Fixed Assets | | | | | | |
| | .3 | .3 | .5 | | | | | | | |
| | .5 | .7 | .9 | | | | | | | |
| | .1 | .2 | .3 | Sales/Total Assets | | | | | | |
| | .1 | .1 | .1 | | | | | | | |
| | .5 | .5 | .3 | | | | | | | |
| (14) | 4.4 | (16) 3.6 | (17) 1.6 | % Depr., Dep., Amort./Sales | | | | | | |
| | 14.5 | 10.0 | 12.4 | | | | | | | |
| | | | | % Officers', Directors' Owners' Comp/Sales | | | | | | |
| | 227053M | 328222M | 334236M | Net Sales ($) | 1142M | 11989M | 6784M | 58380M | 140590M | 115351M |
| | 993182M | 1707308M | 1674742M | Total Assets ($) | 12882M | 141680M | 42553M | 124719M | 780479M | 572429M |

© RMA 2024

M = $ thousand    MM = $ million
See Pages viii through xx for Explanation of Ratios and Data

# PUBLIC ADMINISTRATION—Administration of General Economic Programs  NAICS 926110

## Current Data Sorted by Assets | Comparative Historical Data

| 0-500M | 500M-2MM | 2-10MM | 10-50MM | 50-100MM | 100-250MM | Type of Statement | | |
|---|---|---|---|---|---|---|---|---|
| | | 3 | 6 | 15 | 3 | 3 | Unqualified | 34 | 26 |
| | | | | 2 | | | Reviewed | 1 | |
| | | | | | | | Compiled | 1 | 3 |
| | | | | | | | Tax Returns | 2 | 2 |
| | | 3 | 6 | 9 | 2 | 1 | Other | 13 | 20 |
| | | | 30 (4/1-9/30/23) | 23 (10/1/23-3/31/24) | | | | 4/1/19-3/31/20 | 4/1/20-3/31/21 |
| 0-500M | 500M-2MM | 2-10MM | 10-50MM | 50-100MM | 100-250MM | | ALL | ALL |
| | 6 | 12 | 26 | 5 | 4 | NUMBER OF STATEMENTS | 51 | 51 |
| % | % | % | % | % | % | ASSETS | % | % |
| | | 30.1 | 38.3 | | | Cash & Equivalents | 23.8 | 31.9 |
| | | 14.0 | 12.2 | | | Trade Receivables (net) | 8.9 | 5.3 |
| | | .0 | 1.0 | | | Inventory | 1.4 | 1.5 |
| | | 5.9 | 8.7 | | | All Other Current | 6.4 | 4.5 |
| | | 50.1 | 60.2 | | | Total Current | 40.5 | 43.2 |
| | | 30.1 | 21.0 | | | Fixed Assets (net) | 40.3 | 38.4 |
| | | .3 | .9 | | | Intangibles (net) | .3 | .1 |
| | | 19.6 | 17.9 | | | All Other Non-Current | 18.9 | 18.3 |
| | | 100.0 | 100.0 | | | Total | 100.0 | 100.0 |
| | | | | | | LIABILITIES | | |
| | | .3 | .9 | | | Notes Payable-Short Term | 1.6 | 3.1 |
| | | 1.3 | 2.8 | | | Cur. Mat.-L.T.D. | 2.9 | 1.5 |
| | | 2.4 | 6.2 | | | Trade Payables | 4.8 | 2.3 |
| | | .0 | .0 | | | Income Taxes Payable | .1 | .1 |
| | | 2.3 | 15.3 | | | All Other Current | 5.5 | 6.1 |
| | | 6.3 | 25.2 | | | Total Current | 14.9 | 13.1 |
| | | 25.5 | 15.3 | | | Long-Term Debt | 24.7 | 26.8 |
| | | .0 | .2 | | | Deferred Taxes | .1 | .1 |
| | | 7.4 | 1.6 | | | All Other Non-Current | 6.9 | 3.1 |
| | | 60.8 | 57.8 | | | Net Worth | 53.4 | 57.0 |
| | | 100.0 | 100.0 | | | Total Liabilities & Net Worth | 100.0 | 100.0 |
| | | | | | | INCOME DATA | | |
| | | 100.0 | 100.0 | | | Net Sales | 100.0 | 100.0 |
| | | | | | | Gross Profit | | |
| | | 61.2 | 80.2 | | | Operating Expenses | 84.7 | 81.8 |
| | | 38.8 | 19.8 | | | Operating Profit | 15.3 | 18.2 |
| | | 3.1 | 4.4 | | | All Other Expenses (net) | 8.2 | 6.4 |
| | | 35.7 | 15.4 | | | Profit Before Taxes | 7.1 | 11.8 |
| | | | | | | RATIOS | | |
| | | 23.9 | 9.4 | | | | 5.3 | 10.7 |
| | | 14.2 | 3.0 | | | Current | 2.4 | 5.6 |
| | | 3.6 | 1.4 | | | | 1.2 | 2.0 |
| | | 22.5 | 9.3 | | | | 3.9 | 10.4 |
| | | 6.9 | 2.3 | | | Quick | 2.0 | 3.9 |
| | | 3.4 | 1.1 | | | | 1.1 | 1.7 |
| | 38 | 9.6 | 0 UND | | | | 0 999.8 | 0 UND |
| | 55 | 6.6 | 34 10.8 | | | Sales/Receivables | 19 19.3 | 8 48.2 |
| | 91 | 4.0 | 74 4.9 | | | | 55 6.6 | 39 9.3 |
| | | | | | | Cost of Sales/Inventory | | |
| | | | | | | Cost of Sales/Payables | | |
| | | .5 | .8 | | | | .9 | .5 |
| | | 1.3 | 2.3 | | | Sales/Working Capital | 4.0 | 1.8 |
| | | 2.7 | 5.7 | | | | 12.3 | 5.9 |
| | | | 966.4 | | | | 13.0 | 15.0 |
| | | (13) | 45.8 | | | EBIT/Interest | (33) 2.3 | (36) 2.8 |
| | | | 6.5 | | | | 1.1 | 1.1 |
| | | | | | | Net Profit + Depr., Dep., Amort./Cur. Mat. L/T/D | | |
| | | .0 | .0 | | | | .1 | .1 |
| | | .5 | .1 | | | Fixed/Worth | .6 | .7 |
| | | .9 | .7 | | | | 1.4 | 1.3 |
| | | .3 | .1 | | | | .3 | .2 |
| | | .5 | .8 | | | Debt/Worth | .9 | .6 |
| | | 2.1 | 1.8 | | | | 1.8 | 1.7 |
| | | 34.1 | 33.2 | | | | 8.0 | 11.0 |
| | (11) | 23.1 | 8.2 | | | % Profit Before Taxes/Tangible Net Worth | (48) 2.1 | (50) 5.7 |
| | | 7.3 | 1.4 | | | | -1.0 | .4 |
| | | 30.0 | 27.0 | | | | 4.5 | 8.3 |
| | | 9.7 | 3.7 | | | % Profit Before Taxes/Total Assets | 1.2 | 2.5 |
| | | 3.8 | .1 | | | | -.3 | .1 |
| | | UND | 438.5 | | | | 29.1 | 28.6 |
| | | 4.9 | 10.1 | | | Sales/Net Fixed Assets | 2.8 | 2.1 |
| | | .6 | 2.9 | | | | .3 | .2 |
| | | .8 | 1.5 | | | | 1.2 | .9 |
| | | .5 | .5 | | | Sales/Total Assets | .5 | .2 |
| | | .2 | .4 | | | | .2 | .1 |
| | | | .8 | | | | .9 | 1.0 |
| | | (18) | 2.8 | | | % Depr., Dep., Amort./Sales | (41) 4.3 | (35) 8.1 |
| | | | 6.4 | | | | 12.5 | 16.3 |
| | | | | | | % Officers', Directors' Owners' Comp/Sales | | |
| | 5919M | 39359M | 537960M | 136183M | 74823M | Net Sales ($) | 1400667M | 516372M |
| | 7569M | 71112M | 677697M | 380376M | 701077M | Total Assets ($) | 2507207M | 1544411M |

Data Not Available for 0-500M column.

M = $ thousand  MM = $ million
See Pages viii through xx for Explanation of Ratios and Data

© RMA 2024

# PUBLIC ADMINISTRATION—Administration of General Economic Programs  NAICS 926110

## Comparative Historical Data / Current Data Sorted by Sales

| | | | | Type of Statement | | | | | | |
|---|---|---|---|---|---|---|---|---|---|---|
| 15 | 20 | 30 | | Unqualified | 3 | 4 | 4 | 4 | 11 | 4 |
| | | | | Reviewed | | | | | | |
| 2 | 2 | 2 | | Compiled | | | | 2 | | |
| | 1 | | | Tax Returns | | | | | | |
| 15 | 20 | 21 | | Other | 3 | 4 | 2 | 1 | 5 | 6 |
| 4/1/21- | 4/1/22- | 4/1/23- | | | | 30 (4/1-9/30/23) | | | 23 (10/1/23-3/31/24) | |
| 3/31/22 | 3/31/23 | 3/31/24 | | | 0-1MM | 1-3MM | 3-5MM | 5-10MM | 10-25MM | 25MM & OVER |
| ALL | ALL | ALL | | | | | | | | |
| 32 | 43 | 53 | | NUMBER OF STATEMENTS | 6 | 8 | 6 | 7 | 16 | 10 |
| % | % | % | | ASSETS | % | % | % | % | % | % |
| 29.6 | 36.1 | 35.8 | | Cash & Equivalents | | | | | 31.1 | 52.5 |
| 4.6 | 8.7 | 10.6 | | Trade Receivables (net) | | | | | 5.7 | 23.6 |
| .9 | 2.0 | 1.9 | | Inventory | | | | | 5.0 | .3 |
| 6.7 | 3.9 | 7.5 | | All Other Current | | | | | 14.0 | 5.4 |
| 41.8 | 50.7 | 55.7 | | Total Current | | | | | 55.7 | 81.8 |
| 40.1 | 31.4 | 25.2 | | Fixed Assets (net) | | | | | 17.8 | 16.2 |
| .7 | 1.6 | .6 | | Intangibles (net) | | | | | .3 | .0 |
| 17.4 | 16.3 | 18.5 | | All Other Non-Current | | | | | 26.2 | 2.0 |
| 100.0 | 100.0 | 100.0 | | Total | | | | | 100.0 | 100.0 |
| | | | | LIABILITIES | | | | | | |
| 1.2 | .6 | .8 | | Notes Payable-Short Term | | | | | 1.6 | .0 |
| 1.7 | 1.2 | 2.0 | | Cur. Mat.-L.T.D. | | | | | 2.0 | 2.4 |
| 2.6 | 4.2 | 5.1 | | Trade Payables | | | | | 7.3 | 11.2 |
| .1 | .0 | .0 | | Income Taxes Payable | | | | | .1 | .0 |
| 7.2 | 5.1 | 10.6 | | All Other Current | | | | | 14.5 | 23.0 |
| 12.8 | 11.0 | 18.5 | | Total Current | | | | | 25.4 | 36.6 |
| 21.8 | 17.7 | 19.7 | | Long-Term Debt | | | | | 18.1 | 3.6 |
| .0 | .0 | .1 | | Deferred Taxes | | | | | .3 | .0 |
| 4.5 | 5.6 | 3.0 | | All Other Non-Current | | | | | 2.5 | 1.5 |
| 60.8 | 65.7 | 58.7 | | Net Worth | | | | | 53.7 | 58.4 |
| 100.0 | 100.0 | 100.0 | | Total Liabilities & Net Worth | | | | | 100.0 | 100.0 |
| | | | | INCOME DATA | | | | | | |
| 100.0 | 100.0 | 100.0 | | Net Sales | | | | | 100.0 | 100.0 |
| | | | | Gross Profit | | | | | | |
| 80.8 | 75.2 | 73.2 | | Operating Expenses | | | | | 60.0 | 97.3 |
| 19.2 | 24.8 | 26.8 | | Operating Profit | | | | | 40.0 | 2.7 |
| 3.0 | 8.3 | 4.5 | | All Other Expenses (net) | | | | | 8.5 | .5 |
| 16.2 | 16.5 | 22.3 | | Profit Before Taxes | | | | | 31.5 | 2.2 |
| | | | | RATIOS | | | | | | |
| 8.3 | 11.3 | 16.8 | | | | | | | 8.2 | 7.8 |
| 3.5 | 4.7 | 3.7 | | Current | | | | | 3.6 | 2.4 |
| 1.5 | 2.9 | 1.8 | | | | | | | 1.1 | 1.4 |
| 6.0 | 11.3 | 13.2 | | | | | | | 3.4 | 7.1 |
| 3.3 | 4.5 | 3.0 | | Quick | | | | | 1.5 | 2.3 |
| 1.1 | 2.1 | 1.2 | | | | | | | .9 | 1.0 |
| 0 UND | 2 204.7 | 0 853.6 | | | | | | | 0 UND | 0 UND |
| 6 65.4 | 22 16.4 | 37 9.8 | | Sales/Receivables | | | | | 15 23.7 | 46 7.9 |
| 41 8.8 | 72 5.1 | 70 5.2 | | | | | | | 62 5.9 | 74 4.9 |
| | | | | Cost of Sales/Inventory | | | | | | |
| | | | | Cost of Sales/Payables | | | | | | |
| 1.2 | .7 | .6 | | | | | | | .7 | 2.4 |
| 2.2 | 1.8 | 1.8 | | Sales/Working Capital | | | | | 1.7 | 3.3 |
| 6.8 | 4.0 | 3.7 | | | | | | | 751.0 | NM |
| 21.0 | 73.5 | 185.3 | | | | | | | | |
| (20) 5.3 | (24) 12.7 | (30) 14.1 | | EBIT/Interest | | | | | | |
| 1.3 | -1.4 | .9 | | | | | | | | |
| | | | | Net Profit + Depr., Dep., | | | | | | |
| | | | | Amort./Cur. Mat. L/T/D | | | | | | |
| .1 | .1 | .0 | | | | | | | .0 | .0 |
| .7 | .4 | .2 | | Fixed/Worth | | | | | .1 | .1 |
| 1.2 | 1.1 | .8 | | | | | | | .6 | .7 |
| .2 | .1 | .2 | | | | | | | .3 | .1 |
| .5 | .5 | .6 | | Debt/Worth | | | | | 1.2 | .8 |
| 1.4 | 1.0 | 1.9 | | | | | | | 2.1 | 1.8 |
| 12.2 | 18.5 | 29.4 | | | | | | | 34.4 | 31.5 |
| (31) 5.5 | (42) 5.0 | (52) 11.4 | | % Profit Before Taxes/Tangible | | | | | 14.8 | 12.7 |
| -.8 | -.9 | 1.6 | | Net Worth | | | | | 3.6 | -8.0 |
| 9.8 | 14.0 | 21.2 | | | | | | | 27.4 | 21.1 |
| 3.9 | 2.9 | 4.4 | | % Profit Before Taxes/Total | | | | | 4.7 | 9.1 |
| -.2 | -.3 | .8 | | Assets | | | | | 1.8 | -2.7 |
| 8.2 | 13.7 | 380.1 | | | | | | | UND | 506.0 |
| 2.9 | 3.9 | 7.0 | | Sales/Net Fixed Assets | | | | | 7.6 | 184.8 |
| .3 | .9 | .6 | | | | | | | 3.5 | 7.1 |
| 1.3 | 1.4 | 1.1 | | | | | | | .6 | 2.6 |
| .4 | .5 | .5 | | Sales/Total Assets | | | | | .5 | 1.5 |
| .1 | .2 | .2 | | | | | | | .3 | .9 |
| .7 | .6 | .6 | | | | | | | .2 | |
| (28) 2.4 | (35) 1.2 | (33) 2.2 | | % Depr., Dep., Amort./Sales | | | | | (11) 1.3 | |
| 7.8 | 4.3 | 9.6 | | | | | | | 3.1 | |
| | | | | % Officers', Directors', | | | | | | |
| | | | | Owners' Comp/Sales | | | | | | |
| 410127M | 667328M | 794244M | | Net Sales ($) | 2668M | 16894M | 24286M | 47138M | 250826M | 452432M |
| 943824M | 1584401M | 1837831M | | Total Assets ($) | 14809M | 90634M | 71921M | 314167M | 811083M | 535217M |

© RMA 2024   M = $ thousand   MM = $ million
See Pages viii through xx for Explanation of Ratios and Data

# CONSTRUCTION—PERCENTAGE OF COMPLETION BASIS OF ACCOUNTING*

# CONSTRUCTION-% OF COMPLETION—New Single-Family Housing Construction (except For-Sale Builders) NAICS 236115

**Current Data Sorted by Revenue** | **Comparative Historical Data**

| | | | | | Type of Statement | | | | | |
|---|---|---|---|---|---|---|---|---|---|---|
| 1 | 2 | 4 | 5 | 12 | Unqualified | 3 | 3 | 2 | 3 | 12 |
| | 1 | 2 | | 3 | Reviewed | 6 | 9 | 4 | 11 | 3 |
| 1 | 23 | 7 | 1 | 32 | Compiled | 6 | 4 | 6 | 3 | 3 |
| 3 | 28 | 12 | 13 | 56 | Tax Returns | 13 | 17 | 17 | 47 | 32 |
| | | | | | Other | 19 | 42 | 42 | 49 | 56 |
| 8 (4/1-9/30/23) | | 95 (10/1/23-3/31/24) | | | | 4/1/19-3/31/20 | 4/1/20-3/31/21 | 4/1/21-3/31/22 | 4/1/22-3/31/23 | 4/1/23-3/31/24 |
| 0-1MM | 1-10MM | 10-50MM | 50 & OVER | ALL | | ALL | ALL | ALL | ALL | ALL |
| 5 | 54 | 25 | 19 | 103 | **NUMBER OF STATEMENTS** | 47 | 75 | 71 | 113 | 103 |
| % | % | % | % | % | **ASSETS** | % | % | % | % | % |
| | 17.4 | 14.6 | 15.0 | 15.8 | Cash & Equivalents | 12.3 | 17.5 | 20.8 | 18.3 | 15.8 |
| | 5.1 | 6.6 | 11.6 | 6.4 | A/R - Progress Billings | 14.2 | 8.2 | 8.9 | 6.1 | 6.4 |
| | .0 | .6 | 3.6 | .8 | A/R - Current Retention | .6 | .1 | .6 | .3 | .8 |
| | 43.8 | 47.7 | 50.2 | 46.9 | Inventory | 37.8 | 44.1 | 33.5 | 44.9 | 46.9 |
| | 1.7 | 5.3 | 1.3 | 2.4 | Cost & Est. Earnings In Excess Billings | 3.6 | 2.8 | 4.4 | 3.2 | 2.4 |
| | 6.0 | 6.5 | 7.3 | 6.1 | All Other Current | 5.1 | 6.3 | 8.2 | 6.3 | 6.1 |
| | 74.0 | 81.3 | 89.1 | 78.4 | Total Current | 73.6 | 79.0 | 76.4 | 79.2 | 78.4 |
| | 15.9 | 6.2 | 6.0 | 11.7 | Fixed Assets (net) | 10.1 | 9.1 | 12.8 | 10.5 | 11.7 |
| | .8 | 1.8 | .7 | 1.1 | Joint Ventures & Investments | 2.3 | 3.5 | 3.0 | 2.8 | 1.1 |
| | .3 | .2 | .8 | .4 | Intangibles (net) | 4.6 | .1 | .2 | .8 | .4 |
| | 9.0 | 10.5 | 3.4 | 8.5 | All Other Non-Current | 9.5 | 8.4 | 7.6 | 6.8 | 8.5 |
| | 100.0 | 100.0 | 100.0 | 100.0 | Total | 100.0 | 100.0 | 100.0 | 100.0 | 100.0 |
| | | | | | **LIABILITIES** | | | | | |
| | 22.2 | 28.6 | 19.8 | 25.0 | Notes Payable-Short Term | 24.8 | 29.0 | 23.8 | 20.5 | 25.0 |
| | 4.6 | 9.0 | 10.1 | 6.5 | A/P - Trade | 11.3 | 9.6 | 10.2 | 6.0 | 6.5 |
| | .0 | .5 | 1.8 | .4 | A/P - Retention | .3 | .5 | .0 | .1 | .4 |
| | .2 | 5.7 | 2.6 | 2.0 | Billings in Excess of Costs & Est. Earnings | 5.1 | 4.4 | 5.2 | 3.0 | 2.0 |
| | .0 | .0 | .3 | .1 | Income Taxes Payable | .0 | .0 | .1 | .1 | .1 |
| | 3.2 | 1.9 | .7 | 2.3 | Cur. Mat.-L/T/D | 3.0 | 3.1 | 2.5 | 2.7 | 2.3 |
| | 10.5 | 11.3 | 11.8 | 10.5 | All Other Current | 8.2 | 11.0 | 13.0 | 12.0 | 10.5 |
| | 40.7 | 57.0 | 47.1 | 46.8 | Total Current | 52.8 | 57.7 | 54.8 | 44.4 | 46.8 |
| | 15.3 | 2.6 | 6.0 | 10.7 | Long-Term Debt | 15.7 | 11.6 | 17.1 | 14.8 | 10.7 |
| | .1 | .0 | .1 | .0 | Deferred Taxes | .0 | .2 | .0 | .0 | .0 |
| | 9.9 | 3.5 | 9.2 | 8.1 | All Other Non-Current | 4.0 | 6.3 | 6.0 | 11.3 | 8.1 |
| | 34.1 | 36.9 | 37.7 | 34.4 | Net Worth | 27.5 | 24.2 | 22.1 | 29.6 | 34.4 |
| | 100.0 | 100.0 | 100.0 | 100.0 | Total Liabilities & Net Worth | 100.0 | 100.0 | 100.0 | 100.0 | 100.0 |
| | | | | | **INCOME DATA** | | | | | |
| | 100.0 | 100.0 | 100.0 | 100.0 | Contract Revenues | 100.0 | 100.0 | 100.0 | 100.0 | 100.0 |
| | 22.0 | 16.7 | 20.0 | 20.4 | Gross Profit | 18.7 | 16.1 | 18.2 | 18.9 | 20.4 |
| | 15.6 | 9.9 | 10.3 | 13.1 | Operating Expenses | 12.2 | 11.0 | 11.6 | 11.6 | 13.1 |
| | 6.4 | 6.9 | 9.7 | 7.3 | Operating Profit | 6.5 | 5.1 | 6.6 | 7.3 | 7.3 |
| | .0 | .4 | .8 | .3 | All Other Expenses (net) | .9 | .0 | -.6 | .2 | .3 |
| | 6.4 | 6.5 | 8.9 | 6.9 | Profit Before Taxes | 5.6 | 5.2 | 7.2 | 7.1 | 6.9 |
| | | | | | **RATIOS** | | | | | |
| | 3.8 | 1.8 | 3.1 | 3.0 | | 2.1 | 2.2 | 2.1 | 5.0 | 3.0 |
| | 1.9 | 1.4 | 2.0 | 1.7 | Current | 1.3 | 1.3 | 1.4 | 1.7 | 1.7 |
| | 1.3 | 1.1 | 1.3 | 1.2 | | 1.0 | 1.1 | 1.1 | 1.2 | 1.2 |
| | 1.6 | .7 | 1.4 | 1.0 | | 1.6 | .7 | 1.4 | 1.3 | 1.0 |
| (26) | .0 | (20) .0 | (18) .3 | (65) .0 | Receivables/Payables | (35) .3 | (50) .0 | (49) .5 | (75) .0 | (65) .0 |
| | .0 | .0 | .0 | .0 | | .0 | .0 | .0 | .0 | .0 |
| | 0 UND | 0 UND | 0 UND | 0 UND | | 0 UND | 0 UND | 0 UND | 0 UND | 0 UND |
| | 0 UND | 0 UND | 3 134.8 | 0 UND | Revenues/Receivables | 0 UND | 0 UND | 0 999.8 | 0 UND | 0 UND |
| | 0 UND | 0 UND | 47 7.7 | 2 169.2 | | 38 9.5 | 2 157.5 | 11 32.5 | 2 199.6 | 2 169.2 |
| | 0 UND | 0 UND | 14 26.3 | 0 UND | | 0 UND | 0 UND | 0 UND | 0 UND | 0 UND |
| | 0 UND | 12 30.8 | 17 21.8 | 11 34.1 | Cost of Revenues/Payables | 14 26.7 | 8 45.9 | 8 48.5 | 3 114.2 | 11 34.1 |
| | 23 16.2 | 30 12.0 | 22 16.8 | 23 16.0 | | 30 12.1 | 27 13.5 | 21 17.1 | 19 18.8 | 23 16.0 |
| | 3.8 | 4.8 | 1.8 | 3.8 | | 5.7 | 4.8 | 4.7 | 2.6 | 3.8 |
| | 5.7 | 8.4 | 6.5 | 6.5 | Revenues/Working Capital | 11.8 | 10.3 | 13.0 | 7.9 | 6.5 |
| | 20.0 | 22.9 | 8.8 | 17.1 | | 104.5 | 43.0 | 33.3 | 20.4 | 17.1 |
| | 29.8 | 84.2 | 17.3 | 32.2 | | 13.3 | 37.7 | 135.6 | 45.0 | 32.2 |
| (37) | 5.8 | (16) 12.1 | (15) 7.4 | (72) 6.4 | EBIT/Interest | (35) 5.0 | (57) 10.3 | (53) 37.1 | (88) 13.2 | (72) 6.4 |
| | 2.2 | 3.6 | 3.8 | 3.0 | | 1.6 | 3.9 | 7.7 | 4.4 | 3.0 |
| | | | | | Net Profit + Depr., Dep., Amort./Cur. Mat. L/T/D | | | | | |
| | .0 | .0 | .0 | .0 | | .0 | .0 | .0 | .0 | .0 |
| | .1 | .1 | .1 | .1 | Fixed/Worth | .2 | .1 | .2 | .0 | .1 |
| | 1.3 | .2 | .3 | .5 | | 1.1 | .7 | .5 | .4 | .5 |
| | .9 | 1.1 | .8 | .9 | | 1.5 | 1.3 | .9 | 1.0 | .9 |
| | 2.0 | 2.3 | 1.8 | 2.1 | Debt/Worth | 3.3 | 4.3 | 3.1 | 2.5 | 2.1 |
| | 9.2 | 3.9 | 9.1 | 7.7 | | 12.6 | 15.5 | 8.1 | 6.2 | 7.7 |
| | 87.2 | 65.7 | 56.8 | 68.5 | | 66.0 | 73.0 | 98.6 | 85.2 | 68.5 |
| (48) | 33.1 | (24) 36.7 | (18) 44.3 | (94) 34.3 | % Profit Before Taxes/ Tangible Net Worth | (40) 32.6 | (65) 38.9 | (66) 49.5 | (106) 35.9 | (94) 34.3 |
| | 7.4 | 15.4 | 15.9 | 11.9 | | 6.5 | 20.6 | 26.4 | 16.9 | 11.9 |
| | 23.0 | 16.7 | 19.5 | 18.3 | | 18.5 | 18.5 | 23.2 | 22.3 | 18.3 |
| | 9.8 | 11.8 | 11.7 | 10.7 | % Profit Before Taxes/ Total Assets | 8.4 | 7.6 | 11.4 | 11.5 | 10.7 |
| | 3.3 | 5.1 | 6.7 | 3.5 | | 2.3 | 2.9 | 4.8 | 3.8 | 3.5 |
| | .5 | .2 | | .2 | | .3 | .1 | .1 | .1 | .2 |
| (23) | 1.4 | (11) .4 | (39) | .6 | % Depr., Dep., Amort./ Revenues | (25) 1.2 | (30) .3 | (35) .4 | (39) .3 | (39) .6 |
| | 2.4 | .9 | | 2.0 | | 1.2 | .6 | .8 | .9 | 2.0 |
| | 2.0 | .5 | | 1.4 | | .6 | .6 | 1.4 | 1.1 | 1.4 |
| (30) | 3.2 | (11) 1.0 | (44) | 2.9 | % Officers', Directors' Owners' Comp/Revenues | (18) 1.7 | (29) 1.9 | (30) 1.9 | (47) 2.4 | (44) 2.9 |
| | 5.7 | 2.0 | | 5.4 | | 5.4 | 4.4 | 5.2 | 5.4 | 5.4 |
| 2628M | 246520M | 616428M | 954350526M | 955216102M | Contract Revenues ($) | 1273927M | 58863963M | 170237998M | 17675287M | 955216102M |
| 5167M | 178868M | 417262M | 548978682M | 549579979M | Total Assets ($) | 736259M | 43071082M | 123998738M | 16818978M | 549579979M |

© RMA 2024

M = $ thousand  MM = $ million
See Pages viii through xx for Explanation of Ratios and Data

# CONSTRUCTION-% OF COMPLETION—New Multifamily Housing Construction (except For-Sale Builders) NAICS 236116

## Current Data Sorted by Revenue | Comparative Historical Data

| | | | | | Type of Statement | | | | | |
|---|---|---|---|---|---|---|---|---|---|---|
| | | | 2 | 2 | Unqualified | 2 | 3 | 1 | 2 | 2 |
| 1 | | 1 | 4 | 6 | Reviewed | 5 | 10 | 4 | 9 | 6 |
| | | 1 | | 1 | Compiled | 1 | | | | 1 |
| | 3 | 2 | | 6 | Tax Returns | | 4 | 2 | 4 | 6 |
| 1 | 1 | | 9 | 10 | Other | 3 | 12 | 8 | 16 | 10 |
| | | | | | | 4/1/19- | 4/1/20- | 4/1/21- | 4/1/22- | 4/1/23- |
| 2 (4/1-9/30/23) | | 23 (10/1/23-3/31/24) | | | | 3/31/20 | 3/31/21 | 3/31/22 | 3/31/23 | 3/31/24 |
| 0-1MM | 1-10MM | 10-50MM | 50 & OVER | ALL | | ALL | ALL | ALL | ALL | ALL |
| 1 | 5 | 4 | 15 | 25 | NUMBER OF STATEMENTS | 20 | 29 | 15 | 31 | 25 |
| % | % | % | % | % | ASSETS | % | % | % | % | % |
| | | | 17.8 | 14.1 | Cash & Equivalents | 21.1 | 18.3 | 22.4 | 20.9 | 14.1 |
| | | | 47.4 | 30.9 | A/R - Progress Billings | 27.4 | 29.4 | 25.7 | 44.4 | 30.9 |
| | | | 6.2 | 3.7 | A/R - Current Retention | 9.7 | 4.6 | 4.4 | 4.6 | 3.7 |
| | | | 5.4 | 27.0 | Inventory | 4.8 | 19.6 | 19.2 | 7.2 | 27.0 |
| | | | 2.5 | 2.3 | Cost & Est. Earnings In Excess Billings | 3.6 | 3.2 | 2.3 | 4.9 | 2.3 |
| | | | 3.1 | 4.2 | All Other Current | 16.3 | 10.5 | 11.0 | 3.3 | 4.2 |
| | | | 82.3 | 82.3 | Total Current | 82.8 | 85.6 | 85.0 | 85.3 | 82.3 |
| | | | 3.9 | 7.7 | Fixed Assets (net) | 6.9 | 7.3 | 3.7 | 7.7 | 7.7 |
| | | | 5.1 | 3.2 | Joint Ventures & Investments | .7 | 2.3 | 2.2 | .1 | 3.2 |
| | | | .0 | .1 | Intangibles (net) | .6 | .0 | .0 | .6 | .1 |
| | | | 8.6 | 6.8 | All Other Non-Current | 9.0 | 4.7 | 9.1 | 6.5 | 6.8 |
| | | | 100.0 | 100.0 | Total | 100.0 | 100.0 | 100.0 | 100.0 | 100.0 |
| | | | | | LIABILITIES | | | | | |
| | | | .0 | 6.1 | Notes Payable-Short Term | 4.4 | 10.2 | 17.9 | 7.7 | 6.1 |
| | | | 40.8 | 25.1 | A/P - Trade | 35.4 | 26.5 | 24.8 | 32.0 | 25.1 |
| | | | 4.4 | 3.0 | A/P - Retention | 3.0 | 2.1 | 4.3 | 4.0 | 3.0 |
| | | | 5.9 | 3.9 | Billings in Excess of Costs & Est. Earnings | 7.1 | 11.6 | 6.7 | 7.9 | 3.9 |
| | | | .2 | .1 | Income Taxes Payable | .0 | .0 | .0 | .1 | .1 |
| | | | 1.8 | 1.5 | Cur. Mat.-L/T/D | .4 | 1.1 | .5 | .7 | 1.5 |
| | | | 5.0 | 11.0 | All Other Current | 7.7 | 6.6 | 3.6 | 16.2 | 11.0 |
| | | | 58.2 | 50.5 | Total Current | 58.1 | 58.1 | 57.8 | 68.6 | 50.5 |
| | | | 9.9 | 11.4 | Long-Term Debt | 5.4 | 6.7 | 11.2 | 6.0 | 11.4 |
| | | | .0 | .0 | Deferred Taxes | .0 | .0 | .0 | .0 | .0 |
| | | | 4.4 | 8.3 | All Other Non-Current | 2.4 | 2.2 | 2.7 | 5.9 | 8.3 |
| | | | 27.6 | 29.7 | Net Worth | 34.2 | 33.0 | 28.3 | 19.5 | 29.7 |
| | | | 100.0 | 100.0 | Total Liabilties & Net Worth | 100.0 | 100.0 | 100.0 | 100.0 | 100.0 |
| | | | | | INCOME DATA | | | | | |
| | | | 100.0 | 100.0 | Contract Revenues | 100.0 | 100.0 | 100.0 | 100.0 | 100.0 |
| | | | 17.9 | 19.2 | Gross Profit | 11.0 | 17.7 | 19.4 | 12.4 | 19.2 |
| | | | 10.2 | 8.9 | Operating Expenses | 6.9 | 11.6 | 10.8 | 6.8 | 8.9 |
| | | | 7.7 | 10.3 | Operating Profit | 4.1 | 6.0 | 8.6 | 5.6 | 10.3 |
| | | | -.4 | -.3 | All Other Expenses (net) | -.3 | -.4 | -1.8 | .0 | -.3 |
| | | | 8.1 | 10.7 | Profit Before Taxes | 4.3 | 6.5 | 10.4 | 5.6 | 10.7 |
| | | | | | RATIOS | | | | | |
| | | | 1.5 | 2.6 | | 1.9 | 2.0 | 1.4 | 1.6 | 2.6 |
| | | | 1.3 | 1.3 | Current | 1.3 | 1.5 | 1.3 | 1.3 | 1.3 |
| | | | 1.2 | 1.2 | | 1.2 | 1.2 | 1.1 | 1.1 | 1.2 |
| | | | 1.9 | 1.3 | | 1.8 | 1.5 | 1.4 | 2.5 | 1.3 |
| | | (14) | 1.1 | (22) 1.0 | Receivables/Payables | (18) 1.2 | (23) 1.1 | (11) 1.1 | (29) 1.2 | (22) 1.0 |
| | | | .9 | .0 | | .4 | .5 | .7 | 1.0 | .0 |
| | | 63 | 5.8 | 0 UND | | 0 UND | 0 UND | 0 UND | 23 15.7 | 0 UND |
| | | 72 | 5.1 | 53 6.9 | Revenues/Receivables | 34 10.6 | 46 8.0 | 47 7.7 | 58 6.3 | 53 6.9 |
| | | 104 | 3.5 | 79 4.6 | | 53 6.9 | 62 5.9 | 68 5.4 | 87 4.2 | 79 4.6 |
| | | 49 | 7.4 | 1 288.2 | | 16 22.6 | 1 319.3 | 0 UND | 10 36.0 | 1 288.2 |
| | | 70 | 5.2 | 31 11.9 | Cost of Revenues/Payables | 46 8.0 | 42 8.7 | 50 7.3 | 48 7.6 | 31 11.9 |
| | | 87 | 4.2 | 73 5.0 | | 63 5.8 | 62 5.9 | 74 4.9 | 78 4.7 | 73 5.0 |
| | | | 9.6 | 2.9 | | 8.0 | 6.3 | 4.4 | 9.2 | 2.9 |
| | | | 14.1 | 12.0 | Revenues/Working Capital | 20.5 | 11.0 | 15.8 | 14.9 | 12.0 |
| | | | 22.3 | 21.1 | | 43.5 | 18.1 | 30.6 | 43.0 | 21.1 |
| | | | 115.7 | 212.9 | | 100.8 | 126.1 | 101.4 | 753.0 | 212.9 |
| | | (10) | 31.2 | (17) 14.8 | EBIT/Interest | (11) 28.8 | (19) 46.3 | (11) 45.8 | (20) 44.7 | (17) 14.8 |
| | | | 1.4 | 2.4 | | 6.8 | 15.4 | 2.9 | 13.5 | 2.4 |
| | | | | | Net Profit + Depr., Dep., Amort./Cur. Mat. L/T/D | | | | | |
| | | | .0 | .0 | | .0 | .0 | .0 | .0 | .0 |
| | | | .0 | .0 | Fixed/Worth | .1 | .1 | .1 | .1 | .0 |
| | | | .1 | .3 | | .2 | .3 | .3 | .3 | .3 |
| | | | 1.9 | 1.6 | | 1.0 | 1.1 | .5 | 1.5 | 1.6 |
| | | | 3.2 | 3.0 | Debt/Worth | 2.9 | 2.6 | 3.3 | 2.8 | 3.0 |
| | | | 5.0 | 4.5 | | 5.5 | 4.3 | 4.2 | 5.6 | 4.5 |
| | | | 56.2 | 69.6 | | 113.8 | 104.6 | 57.1 | 82.7 | 69.6 |
| | | (14) | 42.1 | (23) 50.1 | % Profit Before Taxes/ Tangible Net Worth | (28) 48.2 | (14) 64.0 | (28) 27.9 | (23) 54.9 | (23) 50.1 |
| | | | 23.6 | 37.5 | | 20.1 | 23.4 | 12.7 | 27.9 | 37.5 |
| | | | 16.9 | 24.8 | | 18.6 | 25.0 | 25.5 | 21.9 | 24.8 |
| | | | 11.6 | 12.6 | % Profit Before Taxes/ Total Assets | 14.9 | 18.2 | 8.3 | 13.1 | 12.6 |
| | | | 3.1 | 5.2 | | 8.5 | 5.6 | 3.6 | 7.4 | 5.2 |
| | | | | .1 | | .1 | .2 | .2 | .1 | .1 |
| | | | (12) | .2 | % Depr., Dep., Amort./ Revenues | (14) .2 | (18) .3 | (12) .4 | (22) .2 | (12) .2 |
| | | | | .5 | | .4 | .4 | .6 | .6 | .5 |
| | | | | .4 | | | .2 | | .6 | .4 |
| | | | (10) | .9 | % Officers', Directors' Owners' Comp/Revenues | | (11) 1.5 | | (10) 2.4 | (10) .9 |
| | | | | 4.5 | | | 5.2 | | 3.6 | 4.5 |
| 275M | 20823M | 145015M | 27989910M | 28156023M | Contract Revenues ($) | 2673270M | 2614113M | 1650155M | 3259766M | 28156023M |
| 274M | 9435M | 63087M | 20344359M | 20417155M | Total Assets ($) | 800144M | 1041078M | 1053363M | 1120150M | 20417155M |

© RMA 2024

M = $ thousand    MM = $ million
See Pages viii through xx for Explanation of Ratios and Data

# CONSTRUCTION-% OF COMPLETION—New Housing For-Sale Builders  NAICS 236117

## Current Data Sorted by Revenue | Comparative Historical Data

| | | | | | | Type of Statement | | | | | |
|---|---|---|---|---|---|---|---|---|---|---|---|
| 1 | | | | 1 | 2 | Unqualified | 1 | 3 | 3 | 4 | |
| 1 | | | 1 | 1 | 3 | Reviewed | 5 | 3 | 1 | 12 | 2 |
| | | 1 | | | 1 | Compiled | 4 | 1 | 9 | 6 | 3 |
| 1 | 2 | 3 | | 10 | 16 | Tax Returns | 1 | 3 | 6 | 3 | 1 |
| | | | | | | Other | 13 | 22 | 17 | 25 | 16 |
| | 1 (4/1-9/30/23) | | 21 (10/1/23-3/31/24) | | | | 4/1/19-3/31/20 | 4/1/20-3/31/21 | 4/1/21-3/31/22 | 4/1/22-3/31/23 | 4/1/23-3/31/24 |
| 0-1MM | 1-10MM | 10-50MM | 50 & OVER | | ALL | | ALL | ALL | ALL | ALL | ALL |
| 3 | 3 | 4 | 12 | | 22 | NUMBER OF STATEMENTS | 24 | 32 | 36 | 50 | 22 |
| % | % | % | % | | % | ASSETS | % | % | % | % | % |
| | | | 15.0 | | 13.7 | Cash & Equivalents | 9.5 | 14.4 | 12.0 | 13.8 | 13.7 |
| | | | 15.7 | | 12.5 | A/R - Progress Billings | 3.1 | 3.0 | 3.8 | 7.9 | 12.5 |
| | | | .0 | | .0 | A/R - Current Retention | .0 | .2 | .1 | .1 | .0 |
| | | | 30.3 | | 44.2 | Inventory | 56.2 | 54.6 | 57.9 | 54.6 | 44.2 |
| | | | 10.0 | | 5.5 | Cost & Est. Earnings In Excess Billings | 3.6 | .7 | 4.1 | 2.9 | 5.5 |
| | | | 6.2 | | 6.3 | All Other Current | 2.7 | 6.9 | 6.0 | 2.1 | 6.3 |
| | | | 77.3 | | 82.2 | Total Current | 75.1 | 79.8 | 83.8 | 81.3 | 82.2 |
| | | | 11.4 | | 10.9 | Fixed Assets (net) | 9.9 | 7.2 | 5.9 | 8.5 | 10.9 |
| | | | 1.8 | | 1.1 | Joint Ventures & Investments | 1.2 | 5.4 | 2.0 | 1.7 | 1.1 |
| | | | .6 | | .3 | Intangibles (net) | 2.7 | .2 | .2 | .3 | .3 |
| | | | 9.0 | | 5.6 | All Other Non-Current | 11.0 | 7.4 | 8.1 | 8.2 | 5.6 |
| | | | 100.0 | | 100.0 | Total | 100.0 | 100.0 | 100.0 | 100.0 | 100.0 |
| | | | | | | LIABILITIES | | | | | |
| | | | 14.2 | | 20.5 | Notes Payable-Short Term | 39.0 | 25.6 | 29.3 | 25.6 | 20.5 |
| | | | 11.9 | | 8.7 | A/P - Trade | 9.2 | 14.5 | 6.5 | 10.2 | 8.7 |
| | | | .0 | | .0 | A/P - Retention | .1 | .0 | .0 | .0 | .0 |
| | | | 8.1 | | 5.7 | Billings in Excess of Costs & Est. Earnings | 2.9 | 8.4 | 5.7 | 4.5 | 5.7 |
| | | | .1 | | .1 | Income Taxes Payable | .1 | .0 | .0 | .1 | .1 |
| | | | 6.4 | | 6.9 | Cur. Mat.-L/T/D | 3.6 | 4.2 | .4 | 3.1 | 6.9 |
| | | | 8.8 | | 6.4 | All Other Current | 6.0 | 4.5 | 6.9 | 7.3 | 6.4 |
| | | | 49.5 | | 48.2 | Total Current | 61.0 | 57.3 | 48.8 | 50.9 | 48.2 |
| | | | 10.2 | | 7.3 | Long-Term Debt | 17.1 | 10.9 | 12.6 | 12.6 | 7.3 |
| | | | .0 | | .0 | Deferred Taxes | .0 | .0 | .0 | .0 | .0 |
| | | | 2.9 | | 7.0 | All Other Non-Current | 10.0 | 2.3 | 4.9 | 2.8 | 7.0 |
| | | | 37.4 | | 37.6 | Net Worth | 12.0 | 29.5 | 33.5 | 33.4 | 37.6 |
| | | | 100.0 | | 100.0 | Total Liabilities & Net Worth | 100.0 | 100.0 | 100.0 | 100.0 | 100.0 |
| | | | | | | INCOME DATA | | | | | |
| | | | 100.0 | | 100.0 | Contract Revenues | 100.0 | 100.0 | 100.0 | 100.0 | 100.0 |
| | | | 14.2 | | 17.2 | Gross Profit | 19.1 | 16.2 | 17.7 | 19.5 | 17.2 |
| | | | 8.4 | | 10.6 | Operating Expenses | 13.3 | 8.8 | 9.8 | 9.7 | 10.6 |
| | | | 5.8 | | 6.6 | Operating Profit | 5.8 | 7.4 | 7.9 | 9.7 | 6.6 |
| | | | .4 | | .8 | All Other Expenses (net) | 1.8 | .9 | -.7 | -.3 | .8 |
| | | | 5.4 | | 5.7 | Profit Before Taxes | 4.0 | 6.5 | 8.6 | 10.0 | 5.7 |
| | | | | | | RATIOS | | | | | |
| | | | 2.3 | | 2.3 | | 1.8 | 1.9 | 2.5 | 3.4 | 2.3 |
| | | | 1.4 | | 1.7 | Current | 1.3 | 1.4 | 1.6 | 1.6 | 1.7 |
| | | | 1.3 | | 1.4 | | 1.1 | 1.0 | 1.3 | 1.1 | 1.4 |
| | | | 6.6 | | UND | | .8 | .7 | .9 | .9 | UND |
| | | (11) | .5 | (21) | .9 | Receivables/Payables | (20) .1 | (28) .0 | (26) .1 | (46) .2 | (21) .9 |
| | | | .0 | | .0 | | .0 | .0 | .0 | .0 | .0 |
| | | 0 | UND | 0 | UND | | 0 UND | 0 UND | 0 UND | 0 UND | 0 UND |
| | | 10 | 37.6 | 7 | 50.3 | Revenues/Receivables | 1 622.5 | 0 836.6 | 0 UND | 1 304.8 | 7 50.3 |
| | | 45 | 8.1 | 45 | 8.2 | | 10 37.3 | 3 117.4 | 4 91.3 | 11 33.2 | 45 8.2 |
| | | 0 | UND | 0 | UND | | 8 46.3 | 3 117.1 | 0 UND | 7 53.3 | 0 UND |
| | | 10 | 37.1 | 12 | 29.5 | Cost of Revenues/Payables | 23 16.1 | 18 19.8 | 15 24.2 | 17 21.1 | 12 29.5 |
| | | 29 | 12.8 | 32 | 11.5 | | 40 9.1 | 38 9.6 | 28 13.1 | 30 12.1 | 32 11.5 |
| | | | 3.8 | | 2.4 | | 3.6 | 5.0 | 3.0 | 2.9 | 2.4 |
| | | | 4.7 | | 3.8 | Revenues/Working Capital | 6.4 | 10.8 | 5.1 | 5.8 | 3.8 |
| | | | 12.2 | | 6.7 | | 39.8 | -117.1 | 9.3 | 17.2 | 6.7 |
| | | | 24.0 | | | | 10.7 | 26.9 | 75.2 | 92.6 | 24.0 |
| | | | (15) | | 3.1 | EBIT/Interest | (23) 4.1 | (23) 9.5 | (26) 15.5 | (39) 18.6 | (15) 3.1 |
| | | | 1.0 | | | | 2.0 | 3.4 | 5.8 | 5.4 | 1.0 |
| | | | | | | Net Profit + Depr., Dep., Amort./Cur. Mat. L/T/D | | | | | |
| | | | .0 | | .0 | | .0 | .0 | .0 | .0 | .0 |
| | | | .0 | | .0 | Fixed/Worth | .1 | .1 | .0 | .0 | .0 |
| | | | .5 | | .5 | | 1.1 | .7 | .2 | .3 | .5 |
| | | | 1.0 | | .7 | | 1.8 | 1.3 | 1.5 | 1.0 | .7 |
| | | | 1.9 | | 1.7 | Debt/Worth | 3.2 | 2.3 | 2.4 | 2.2 | 1.7 |
| | | | 2.9 | | 2.8 | | 11.0 | 7.6 | 3.2 | 4.8 | 2.8 |
| | | | 45.1 | | 42.9 | | 39.7 | 84.5 | 65.1 | 72.3 | 42.9 |
| | | | 17.6 | (21) | 21.7 | % Profit Before Taxes/ Tangible Net Worth | (20) 24.7 | (29) 60.5 | (35) 40.5 | (48) 44.1 | (21) 21.7 |
| | | | 5.1 | | 4.2 | | 12.8 | 28.5 | 24.4 | 26.5 | 4.2 |
| | | | 14.8 | | 14.7 | | 14.1 | 22.5 | 18.6 | 22.9 | 14.7 |
| | | | 8.3 | | 6.5 | % Profit Before Taxes/ Total Assets | 6.9 | 13.5 | 13.3 | 13.6 | 6.5 |
| | | | 1.5 | | .8 | | 2.9 | 5.7 | 5.5 | 8.3 | .8 |
| | | | | | | | .2 | .1 | .1 | .0 | |
| | | | | | | % Depr., Dep., Amort./Revenues | (13) .4 | (12) .2 | (12) .4 | (23) .2 | |
| | | | | | | | .6 | .5 | .5 | .6 | |
| | | | | | | % Officers', Directors' Owners' Comp/Revenues | | | | | |
| 227M | 15778M | 112261M | 515520965M | | 515649231M | Contract Revenues ($) | 8924801M | 1464095M | 157000539M | 47558109M | 515649231M |
| 219M | 16644M | 109649M | 325203571M | | 325330083M | Total Assets ($) | 12421997M | 860942M | 72018589M | 40326406M | 325330083M |

© RMA 2024  
M = $ thousand  MM = $ million  
See Pages viii through xx for Explanation of Ratios and Data

## CONSTRUCTION-% OF COMPLETION—Residential Remodelers  NAICS 236118

### Current Data Sorted by Revenue | Comparative Historical Data

| | | | | | Type of Statement | | | | | |
|---|---|---|---|---|---|---|---|---|---|---|
| | | | | | Unqualified | | 1 | 1 | 2 | |
| | | | 2 | 2 | Reviewed | 1 | 3 | 3 | 5 | 2 |
| | | | | | Compiled | 3 | 2 | 2 | 1 | |
| 5 | 6 | 3 | 1 | 15 | Tax Returns | 5 | 2 | 5 | 15 | 15 |
| 1 | 5 | 3 | 3 | 12 | Other | 7 | 5 | 17 | 17 | 12 |
| | | | | | | 4/1/19- | 4/1/20- | 4/1/21- | 4/1/22- | 4/1/23- |
| | 3 (4/1-9/30/23) | | 26 (10/1/23-3/31/24) | | | 3/31/20 | 3/31/21 | 3/31/22 | 3/31/23 | 3/31/24 |
| 0-1MM | 1-10MM | 10-50MM | 50 & OVER | ALL | | ALL | ALL | ALL | ALL | ALL |
| 6 | 11 | 8 | 4 | 29 | **NUMBER OF STATEMENTS** | 16 | 13 | 16 | 40 | 29 |
| % | % | % | % | % | **ASSETS** | % | % | % | % | % |
| | 45.8 | | | 33.3 | Cash & Equivalents | 13.9 | 24.9 | 33.7 | 22.3 | 33.3 |
| | 4.6 | | | 22.0 | A/R - Progress Billings | 38.7 | 27.1 | 15.9 | 22.1 | 22.0 |
| | .0 | | | .7 | A/R - Current Retention | .0 | .0 | .0 | 1.1 | .7 |
| | 5.2 | | | 5.4 | Inventory | .6 | 1.0 | 5.7 | 7.9 | 5.4 |
| | 7.1 | | | 5.2 | Cost & Est. Earnings In Excess Billings | 7.8 | 6.6 | 6.0 | 4.9 | 5.2 |
| | 11.4 | | | 6.2 | All Other Current | 2.6 | 10.7 | 8.5 | 2.6 | 6.2 |
| | 74.1 | | | 72.8 | Total Current | 63.6 | 70.2 | 69.7 | 61.1 | 72.8 |
| | 17.7 | | | 19.6 | Fixed Assets (net) | 21.8 | 14.1 | 22.2 | 21.5 | 19.6 |
| | 2.5 | | | 1.8 | Joint Ventures & Investments | .0 | 1.7 | 1.4 | 3.5 | 1.8 |
| | 1.2 | | | .6 | Intangibles (net) | 1.9 | .4 | 4.9 | 2.9 | .6 |
| | 4.6 | | | 5.2 | All Other Non-Current | 12.7 | 13.5 | 1.8 | 11.0 | 5.2 |
| | 100.0 | | | 100.0 | Total | 100.0 | 100.0 | 100.0 | 100.0 | 100.0 |
| | | | | | **LIABILITIES** | | | | | |
| | 3.1 | | | 4.3 | Notes Payable-Short Term | 15.4 | 5.2 | 15.5 | 11.4 | 4.3 |
| | 3.6 | | | 13.6 | A/P - Trade | 12.5 | 18.0 | 7.1 | 16.3 | 13.6 |
| | .0 | | | .7 | A/P - Retention | .3 | .0 | .0 | .4 | .7 |
| | 6.7 | | | 11.7 | Billings in Excess of Costs & Est. Earnings | 9.6 | 17.1 | 7.1 | 18.0 | 11.7 |
| | .2 | | | .1 | Income Taxes Payable | .5 | .6 | .4 | .1 | .1 |
| | 2.7 | | | 1.9 | Cur. Mat.-L/T/D | 3.7 | 2.2 | 3.4 | .5 | 1.9 |
| | 17.4 | | | 12.2 | All Other Current | 10.0 | 8.7 | 7.6 | 14.1 | 12.2 |
| | 33.7 | | | 44.6 | Total Current | 51.9 | 51.8 | 41.2 | 60.8 | 44.6 |
| | 57.7 | | | 35.5 | Long-Term Debt | 27.8 | 16.2 | 10.1 | 21.4 | 35.5 |
| | .0 | | | .0 | Deferred Taxes | .1 | 1.5 | 1.1 | .4 | .0 |
| | 2.0 | | | 7.2 | All Other Non-Current | 3.6 | 4.7 | 1.9 | 7.0 | 7.2 |
| | 6.7 | | | 12.7 | Net Worth | 16.6 | 25.9 | 45.7 | 10.4 | 12.7 |
| | 100.0 | | | 100.0 | Total Liabilties & Net Worth | 100.0 | 100.0 | 100.0 | 100.0 | 100.0 |
| | | | | | **INCOME DATA** | | | | | |
| | 100.0 | | | 100.0 | Contract Revenues | 100.0 | 100.0 | 100.0 | 100.0 | 100.0 |
| | 34.1 | | | 29.8 | Gross Profit | 36.0 | 33.3 | 30.4 | 28.1 | 29.8 |
| | 26.2 | | | 23.8 | Operating Expenses | 31.3 | 28.6 | 25.6 | 24.4 | 23.8 |
| | 7.9 | | | 6.1 | Operating Profit | 4.7 | 4.7 | 4.9 | 3.8 | 6.1 |
| | -.1 | | | -.3 | All Other Expenses (net) | .6 | -1.7 | -2.7 | -.5 | -.3 |
| | 8.0 | | | 6.3 | Profit Before Taxes | 4.1 | 6.4 | 7.6 | 4.3 | 6.3 |
| | | | | | **RATIOS** | | | | | |
| | 20.5 | | | 7.3 | | 1.8 | 3.5 | 3.1 | 2.0 | 7.3 |
| | 3.0 | | | 1.7 | Current | 1.3 | 1.9 | 2.4 | 1.2 | 1.7 |
| | 1.5 | | | 1.1 | | .8 | 1.0 | 1.5 | .5 | 1.1 |
| | | | | 3.9 | | 8.9 | 3.2 | 37.0 | 3.2 | 3.9 |
| | | | (18) | 1.7 | Receivables/Payables | (13) 4.7 | (12) 2.3 | (11) 2.0 | (28) 1.4 | (18) 1.7 |
| | | | | 1.0 | | 2.1 | .7 | .5 | .6 | 1.0 |
| 0 | UND | | 0 | UND | | 10 36.0 | 0 UND | 0 UND | 0 UND | 0 UND |
| 0 | UND | | 2 | 151.5 | Revenues/Receivables | 35 10.4 | 31 11.7 | 6 65.7 | 11 34.5 | 2 151.5 |
| 2 | 151.5 | | 47 | 7.8 | | 70 5.2 | 68 5.4 | 36 10.0 | 52 7.0 | 47 7.8 |
| 0 | UND | | 0 | UND | | 4 91.4 | 11 32.2 | 0 UND | 0 UND | 0 UND |
| 0 | UND | | 7 | 51.5 | Cost of Revenues/Payables | 12 31.5 | 23 15.8 | 1 387.6 | 15 24.8 | 7 51.5 |
| 13 | 27.4 | | 24 | 15.5 | | 22 16.4 | 42 8.6 | 14 26.2 | 35 10.3 | 24 15.5 |
| | 2.9 | | | 9.1 | | 7.8 | 5.2 | 6.0 | 11.9 | 9.1 |
| | 21.8 | | | 21.8 | Revenues/Working Capital | 35.6 | 8.7 | 10.6 | 48.2 | 21.8 |
| | 41.4 | | | 102.8 | | -51.1 | NM | 20.1 | -26.9 | 102.8 |
| | | | | 66.9 | | 13.8 | 94.0 | 332.9 | 66.2 | 66.9 |
| | | | (21) | 9.7 | EBIT/Interest | (15) 6.0 | (11) 40.7 | (13) 65.4 | (28) 14.7 | (21) 9.7 |
| | | | | 2.5 | | 1.1 | 3.0 | 10.9 | 3.7 | 9.7 |
| | | | | | Net Profit + Depr., Dep., Amort./Cur. Mat. L/T/D | | | | | |
| | .0 | | | .1 | | .2 | .1 | .1 | .2 | .1 |
| | .3 | | | .4 | Fixed/Worth | 1.3 | .3 | .3 | .5 | .4 |
| | 1.3 | | | 7.7 | | 20.4 | 1.2 | 1.4 | 3.7 | 7.7 |
| | .6 | | | .9 | | 1.1 | .4 | .6 | 1.3 | .9 |
| | 1.4 | | | 1.8 | Debt/Worth | 8.5 | 1.2 | 1.3 | 4.0 | 1.8 |
| | 7.5 | | | 82.3 | | NM | 8.2 | 2.7 | 12.0 | 82.3 |
| | 266.0 | | | 118.6 | | 192.4 | 63.0 | 75.7 | 136.6 | 118.6 |
| | (10) 37.5 | | (24) | 62.2 | % Profit Before Taxes/ Tangible Net Worth | (12) 29.5 | (11) 37.2 | (14) 54.2 | (32) 47.3 | (24) 62.2 |
| | 14.0 | | | 27.6 | | -2.3 | 15.8 | 42.9 | 20.3 | 27.6 |
| | 101.4 | | | 36.4 | | 25.5 | 27.5 | 41.6 | 21.9 | 36.4 |
| | 18.6 | | | 18.4 | % Profit Before Taxes/ Total Assets | 10.6 | 15.4 | 20.0 | 14.7 | 18.4 |
| | 6.1 | | | 6.5 | | .9 | 6.2 | 12.9 | 2.8 | 6.5 |
| | | | | .4 | | .9 | .6 | .5 | .2 | .4 |
| | | | (13) | .8 | % Depr., Dep., Amort./ Revenues | (11) 1.6 | (11) .9 | (12) .8 | (29) .5 | (13) .8 |
| | | | | 2.1 | | 2.0 | 1.4 | 1.9 | 1.8 | 2.1 |
| | | | | 1.7 | | 2.8 | | | 1.9 | 1.7 |
| | | | (18) | 3.6 | % Officers', Directors' Owners' Comp/Revenues | (10) 3.7 | | | (22) 3.9 | (18) 3.6 |
| | | | | 6.7 | | 4.4 | | | 4.9 | 6.7 |
| 3907M | 45544M | 138464M | 270010892M | 270198807M | Contract Revenues ($) | 9493754M | 294867M | 297344M | 812977M | 270198807M |
| 2102M | 15773M | 29640M | 93860146M | 93907661M | Total Assets ($) | 2548289M | 116695M | 92203M | 267418M | 93907661M |

© RMA 2024   M = $ thousand   MM = $ million
See Pages viii through xx for Explanation of Ratios and Data

## CONSTRUCTION - % OF COMPLETION — Industrial Building Construction  NAICS 236210

**Current Data Sorted by Revenue** | **Comparative Historical Data**

| | | | | | Type of Statement | | | | | |
|---|---|---|---|---|---|---|---|---|---|---|
| | | | 4 | 4 | Unqualified | 6 | 1 | 5 | 5 | 4 |
| 1 | 1 | 6 | 5 | 13 | Reviewed | 14 | 16 | 12 | 20 | 13 |
| | | | | | Compiled | | | 1 | 1 | |
| | | 1 | 1 | 2 | Tax Returns | 1 | 2 | 2 | 1 | 2 |
| | | 1 | 3 | 11 | 15 | Other | 19 | 15 | 27 | 23 | 15 |
| 4 (4/1-9/30/23) | | 30 (10/1/23-3/31/24) | | | | 4/1/19-3/31/20 | 4/1/20-3/31/21 | 4/1/21-3/31/22 | 4/1/22-3/31/23 | 4/1/23-3/31/24 |
| 0-1MM | 1-10MM | 10-50MM | 50 & OVER | ALL | NUMBER OF STATEMENTS | ALL | ALL | ALL | ALL | ALL |
| 1 | 3 | 10 | 20 | 34 | | 40 | 35 | 46 | 50 | 34 |
| % | % | % | % | % | ASSETS | % | % | % | % | % |
| | | 21.6 | 18.5 | 19.4 | Cash & Equivalents | 18.6 | 20.6 | 18.6 | 18.1 | 19.4 |
| | | 33.7 | 39.0 | 34.9 | A/R - Progress Billings | 43.2 | 39.9 | 41.0 | 42.1 | 34.9 |
| | | 4.6 | 3.8 | 3.7 | A/R - Current Retention | 3.7 | 3.6 | 3.4 | 3.3 | 3.7 |
| | | 4.7 | 2.4 | 2.8 | Inventory | .7 | 4.3 | 1.4 | 2.7 | 2.8 |
| | | 5.5 | 3.7 | 7.6 | Cost & Est. Earnings In Excess Billings | 5.2 | 3.0 | 4.6 | 6.1 | 7.6 |
| | | 6.9 | 3.3 | 4.3 | All Other Current | 4.9 | 5.1 | 6.8 | 4.9 | 4.3 |
| | | 77.0 | 70.6 | 72.6 | Total Current | 76.3 | 76.6 | 75.8 | 77.2 | 72.6 |
| | | 14.5 | 16.2 | 16.8 | Fixed Assets (net) | 17.9 | 15.5 | 12.1 | 15.3 | 16.8 |
| | | 2.8 | .5 | 1.1 | Joint Ventures & Investments | .3 | .3 | .6 | .4 | 1.1 |
| | | .4 | 3.7 | 2.3 | Intangibles (net) | .3 | .3 | 4.4 | .6 | 2.3 |
| | | 5.3 | 9.0 | 7.0 | All Other Non-Current | 5.2 | 7.5 | 7.2 | 6.6 | 7.0 |
| | | 100.0 | 100.0 | 100.0 | Total | 100.0 | 100.0 | 100.0 | 100.0 | 100.0 |
| | | | | | LIABILITIES | | | | | |
| | | 3.0 | 1.3 | 3.0 | Notes Payable-Short Term | 3.2 | 5.4 | 2.5 | 3.9 | 3.0 |
| | | 12.6 | 35.1 | 26.4 | A/P - Trade | 30.6 | 24.8 | 29.4 | 27.1 | 26.4 |
| | | 2.1 | 1.7 | 1.7 | A/P - Retention | 1.6 | .7 | .8 | 1.0 | 1.7 |
| | | 21.5 | 17.0 | 16.7 | Billings in Excess of Costs & Est. Earnings | 9.9 | 10.0 | 9.7 | 14.1 | 16.7 |
| | | .0 | .0 | .0 | Income Taxes Payable | .3 | .0 | .4 | .1 | .0 |
| | | 1.4 | 1.2 | 1.1 | Cur. Mat.-L/T/D | 1.5 | 2.2 | 1.1 | 1.4 | 1.1 |
| | | 9.1 | 5.6 | 8.1 | All Other Current | 5.0 | 7.5 | 5.5 | 7.0 | 8.1 |
| | | 49.7 | 61.9 | 57.0 | Total Current | 51.9 | 50.6 | 49.5 | 54.7 | 57.0 |
| | | 6.7 | 5.6 | 7.5 | Long-Term Debt | 5.3 | 9.0 | 10.1 | 8.6 | 7.5 |
| | | .0 | .2 | .1 | Deferred Taxes | .2 | .0 | .4 | .1 | .1 |
| | | 2.5 | 5.2 | 4.0 | All Other Non-Current | 4.4 | 3.1 | 2.9 | 1.8 | 4.0 |
| | | 41.2 | 27.0 | 31.2 | Net Worth | 38.1 | 37.3 | 37.0 | 34.8 | 31.2 |
| | | 100.0 | 100.0 | 100.0 | Total Liabilities & Net Worth | 100.0 | 100.0 | 100.0 | 100.0 | 100.0 |
| | | | | | INCOME DATA | | | | | |
| | | 100.0 | 100.0 | 100.0 | Contract Revenues | 100.0 | 100.0 | 100.0 | 100.0 | 100.0 |
| | | 19.6 | 12.4 | 15.1 | Gross Profit | 13.8 | 14.5 | 13.0 | 13.1 | 15.1 |
| | | 12.8 | 9.4 | 10.8 | Operating Expenses | 10.0 | 9.9 | 9.6 | 10.2 | 10.8 |
| | | 6.8 | 3.0 | 4.3 | Operating Profit | 3.8 | 4.6 | 3.4 | 2.9 | 4.3 |
| | | -.3 | -.3 | -.3 | All Other Expenses (net) | .3 | -.6 | -2.4 | -.2 | -.3 |
| | | 7.1 | 3.2 | 4.6 | Profit Before Taxes | 3.6 | 5.3 | 5.8 | 3.1 | 4.6 |
| | | | | | RATIOS | | | | | |
| | | 1.9 | 1.5 | 1.7 | | 2.2 | 2.1 | 2.1 | 1.9 | 1.7 |
| | | 1.5 | 1.1 | 1.2 | Current | 1.3 | 1.4 | 1.5 | 1.3 | 1.2 |
| | | 1.2 | 1.0 | 1.0 | | 1.1 | 1.2 | 1.2 | 1.1 | 1.0 |
| | | 19.3 | 2.0 | 2.6 | | 2.9 | 3.3 | 2.8 | 2.8 | 2.6 |
| | | 2.4 | 1.2 (33) | 1.4 | Receivables/Payables | 1.5 (34) | 2.1 | 1.6 (49) | 1.4 (33) | 1.4 |
| | | 1.4 | .8 | 1.0 | | 1.1 | 1.2 | 1.1 | 1.0 | 1.0 |
| | | 46 8.0 | 45 8.1 | 42 8.7 | | 47 7.7 | 36 10.2 | 45 8.2 | 41 8.8 | 42 8.7 |
| | | 64 5.7 | 63 5.8 | 62 5.9 | Revenues/Receivables | 57 6.4 | 57 6.4 | 65 5.6 | 63 5.8 | 62 5.9 |
| | | 81 4.5 | 83 4.4 | 83 4.4 | | 76 4.8 | 78 4.7 | 79 4.6 | 87 4.2 | 83 4.4 |
| | | 3 108.0 | 43 8.4 | 28 13.2 | | 24 15.2 | 20 18.2 | 16 22.6 | 20 17.9 | 28 13.2 |
| | | 29 12.5 | 57 6.4 | 43 8.5 | Cost of Revenues/Payables | 47 7.7 | 33 11.1 | 49 7.4 | 44 8.3 | 43 8.5 |
| | | 38 9.7 | 72 5.1 | 68 5.4 | | 66 5.5 | 45 8.2 | 65 5.6 | 62 5.9 | 68 5.4 |
| | | 3.9 | 7.9 | 6.2 | | 7.1 | 6.5 | 5.3 | 8.2 | 6.2 |
| | | 9.2 | 50.3 | 19.3 | Revenues/Working Capital | 16.2 | 13.5 | 10.3 | 14.4 | 19.3 |
| | | 19.2 | -614.5 | 98.1 | | 42.0 | 27.1 | 24.6 | 33.0 | 98.1 |
| | | | 65.7 | 68.6 | | 112.6 | 48.5 | 134.3 | 123.6 | 68.6 |
| | | | 26.3 (30) | 23.4 | EBIT/Interest | (28) 11.5 (28) | 15.7 (36) | 34.8 (39) | 24.1 (30) | 23.4 |
| | | | 12.8 | 5.5 | | 6.9 | 3.5 | 8.0 | 1.1 | 5.5 |
| | | | | | Net Profit + Depr., Dep., Amort./Cur. Mat. L/T/D | | | | | |
| | | .1 | .2 | .2 | | .1 | .1 | .1 | .2 | .2 |
| | | .3 | .5 | .3 | Fixed/Worth | .4 | .3 | .3 | .4 | .3 |
| | | .8 | 1.5 | 1.1 | | .8 | .7 | .9 | .9 | 1.1 |
| | | .9 | 1.2 | 1.0 | | .6 | .7 | .8 | .9 | 1.0 |
| | | 1.6 | 4.8 | 2.5 | Debt/Worth | 2.1 | 1.8 | 2.1 | 2.2 | 2.5 |
| | | 3.2 | 13.6 | 8.3 | | 4.8 | 3.2 | 6.2 | 5.8 | 8.3 |
| | | 64.3 | 154.7 | 73.3 | | 43.5 | 56.9 | 64.9 | 56.4 | 73.3 |
| | | 24.2 (19) | 28.4 (32) | 27.5 | % Profit Before Taxes/ Tangible Net Worth | (39) 24.5 (34) | 33.7 (42) | 41.3 (48) | 22.3 (32) | 27.5 |
| | | 6.8 | 15.7 | 15.6 | | 9.9 | 9.7 | 20.9 | 3.8 | 15.6 |
| | | 21.5 | 13.7 | 14.2 | | 15.1 | 16.8 | 19.3 | 15.8 | 14.2 |
| | | 7.4 | 10.4 | 10.4 | % Profit Before Taxes/ Total Assets | 8.1 | 10.4 | 13.8 | 5.3 | 10.4 |
| | | 2.6 | 3.7 | 3.9 | | 3.7 | 4.7 | 3.1 | .3 | 3.9 |
| | | .4 | .2 | .2 | | .3 | .2 | .2 | .2 | .2 |
| | | 1.2 (15) | .4 (27) | .6 | % Depr., Dep., Amort./ Revenues | (32) .5 (25) | .6 (32) | .5 (36) | .6 (27) | .6 |
| | | 3.5 | .8 | 1.8 | | 2.2 | 1.4 | 1.4 | 1.9 | 1.8 |
| | | | | | % Officers', Directors' Owners' Comp/Revenues | | 1.6 | .8 | | |
| | | | | | | (12) 2.2 (13) | 1.3 | | | |
| | | | | | | 4.0 | 2.5 | | | |
| 35M | 15442M | 219993M | 8014925M | 8250395M | Contract Revenues ($) | 140127311M | 47802952M | 8121149M | 6225976M | 8250395M |
| 17M | 3521M | 143343M | 3670338M | 3817219M | Total Assets ($) | 36134209M | 10865977M | 3995367M | 2985740M | 3817219M |

© RMA 2024   M = $ thousand   MM = $ million
See Pages viii through xx for Explanation of Ratios and Data

# CONSTRUCTION-% OF COMPLETION—Commercial and Institutional Building Construction  NAICS 236220

## Current Data Sorted by Revenue | Comparative Historical Data

| | | | | | Type of Statement | | | | | |
|---|---|---|---|---|---|---|---|---|---|---|
| | | | | | Unqualified | 27 | 33 | 32 | 51 | 15 |
| 7 | 16 | 2 | 13 | 15 | Reviewed | 100 | 94 | 104 | 155 | 104 |
| | 2 | 52 | 29 | 104 | Compiled | 10 | 7 | 13 | 12 | 11 |
| 1 | 4 | 6 | 3 | 11 | Tax Returns | 7 | 7 | 5 | 15 | 9 |
| 1 | 18 | 4 | 109 | 9 | Other | 109 | 93 | 125 | 128 | 162 |
| | | 34 | | 162 | | 4/1/19- | 4/1/20- | 4/1/21- | 4/1/22- | 4/1/23- |
| 49 (4/1-9/30/23) | | 252 (10/1/23-3/31/24) | | | | 3/31/20 | 3/31/21 | 3/31/22 | 3/31/23 | 3/31/24 |
| 0-1MM | 1-10MM | 10-50MM | 50 & OVER | ALL | | ALL | ALL | ALL | ALL | ALL |
| 9 | 40 | 98 | 154 | 301 | NUMBER OF STATEMENTS | 253 | 234 | 279 | 361 | 301 |
| % | % | % | % | % | **ASSETS** | % | % | % | % | % |
| | 31.5 | 25.8 | 23.3 | 25.6 | Cash & Equivalents | 21.7 | 29.5 | 27.0 | 25.1 | 25.6 |
| | 23.4 | 42.4 | 47.8 | 42.3 | A/R - Progress Billings | 46.4 | 41.6 | 42.8 | 42.0 | 42.3 |
| | 2.5 | 4.5 | 4.6 | 4.4 | A/R - Current Retention | 5.1 | 3.8 | 4.3 | 4.8 | 4.4 |
| | 1.9 | .6 | .5 | .7 | Inventory | 1.2 | .8 | .9 | .8 | .7 |
| | 6.8 | 5.9 | 6.3 | 6.1 | Cost & Est. Earnings In Excess Billings | 6.0 | 4.7 | 5.4 | 6.0 | 6.1 |
| | 5.6 | 4.9 | 4.5 | 4.7 | All Other Current | 3.4 | 4.7 | 5.6 | 5.1 | 4.7 |
| | 71.8 | 84.1 | 86.9 | 83.6 | Total Current | 83.8 | 85.2 | 86.1 | 83.9 | 83.6 |
| | 20.9 | 9.3 | 6.0 | 9.2 | Fixed Assets (net) | 9.5 | 9.8 | 8.8 | 9.1 | 9.2 |
| | .0 | .3 | .4 | .3 | Joint Ventures & Investments | .4 | .3 | .4 | .4 | .3 |
| | 1.5 | .4 | 2.1 | 1.4 | Intangibles (net) | .4 | .2 | 1.0 | 1.3 | 1.4 |
| | 5.9 | 5.9 | 4.6 | 5.4 | All Other Non-Current | 5.9 | 4.5 | 3.7 | 5.2 | 5.4 |
| | 100.0 | 100.0 | 100.0 | 100.0 | Total | 100.0 | 100.0 | 100.0 | 100.0 | 100.0 |
| | | | | | **LIABILITIES** | | | | | |
| | 2.7 | 2.8 | .9 | 2.0 | Notes Payable-Short Term | 3.5 | 2.6 | 1.6 | 1.9 | 2.0 |
| | 10.3 | 29.0 | 39.8 | 32.0 | A/P - Trade | 38.1 | 31.6 | 36.5 | 33.9 | 32.0 |
| | 1.8 | 2.5 | 3.8 | 3.0 | A/P - Retention | 3.2 | 2.5 | 2.6 | 2.3 | 3.0 |
| | 8.6 | 11.7 | 15.0 | 12.9 | Billings in Excess of Costs & Est. Earnings | 10.0 | 10.3 | 10.9 | 11.3 | 12.9 |
| | .6 | .4 | .1 | .3 | Income Taxes Payable | .1 | .1 | .1 | .2 | .3 |
| | .8 | 1.1 | .7 | .8 | Cur. Mat.-L/T/D | 1.2 | 1.5 | .9 | 1.0 | .8 |
| | 11.4 | 6.3 | 10.1 | 8.9 | All Other Current | 6.2 | 8.3 | 7.2 | 7.2 | 8.9 |
| | 36.3 | 53.6 | 70.3 | 59.9 | Total Current | 62.3 | 56.9 | 59.9 | 57.8 | 59.9 |
| | 18.9 | 4.2 | 4.2 | 6.2 | Long-Term Debt | 3.8 | 7.1 | 4.8 | 5.4 | 6.2 |
| | .4 | .4 | .1 | .3 | Deferred Taxes | .3 | .3 | .2 | .2 | .3 |
| | 2.5 | 3.7 | 2.4 | 2.9 | All Other Non-Current | 1.7 | 2.0 | 2.1 | 2.9 | 2.9 |
| | 41.9 | 38.1 | 23.0 | 30.8 | Net Worth | 31.8 | 33.7 | 33.1 | 33.7 | 30.8 |
| | 100.0 | 100.0 | 100.0 | 100.0 | Total Liabilities & Net Worth | 100.0 | 100.0 | 100.0 | 100.0 | 100.0 |
| | | | | | **INCOME DATA** | | | | | |
| | 100.0 | 100.0 | 100.0 | 100.0 | Contract Revenues | 100.0 | 100.0 | 100.0 | 100.0 | 100.0 |
| | 25.0 | 14.6 | 9.1 | 13.2 | Gross Profit | 12.7 | 13.3 | 11.4 | 12.6 | 13.2 |
| | 18.7 | 9.2 | 6.3 | 9.0 | Operating Expenses | 9.3 | 10.6 | 8.6 | 9.6 | 9.0 |
| | 6.3 | 5.4 | 2.7 | 4.2 | Operating Profit | 3.3 | 2.7 | 2.8 | 3.0 | 4.2 |
| | -.6 | -.5 | -.2 | -.4 | All Other Expenses (net) | -.2 | -1.6 | -2.6 | -.5 | -.4 |
| | 6.8 | 6.0 | 3.0 | 4.6 | Profit Before Taxes | 3.5 | 4.3 | 5.3 | 3.5 | 4.6 |
| | | | | | **RATIOS** | | | | | |
| | 3.5 | 2.0 | 1.4 | 1.7 | | 1.7 | 2.0 | 1.9 | 1.9 | 1.7 |
| | 2.2 | 1.5 | 1.2 | 1.3 | Current | 1.3 | 1.5 | 1.4 | 1.4 | 1.3 |
| | 1.4 | 1.3 | 1.1 | 1.2 | | 1.1 | 1.2 | 1.2 | 1.2 | 1.2 |
| | 10.6 | 2.3 | 1.6 | 2.2 | | 1.8 | 2.3 | 1.8 | 2.0 | 2.2 |
| (34) | 2.4 | (96) 1.5 | 1.2 (291) | 1.2 | Receivables/Payables | 1.2 (231) | 1.3 (276) | 1.2 (356) | 1.3 (291) | 1.2 |
| | 1.0 | 1.1 | .9 | 1.0 | | 1.0 | 1.0 | .9 | 1.0 | 1.0 |
| 9 | 40.5 | 43 8.5 | 47 7.8 | 42 8.7 | | 45 8.2 | 38 9.5 | 45 8.1 | 46 7.9 | 42 8.7 |
| 33 | 11.1 | 59 6.2 | 62 5.9 | 60 6.1 | Revenues/Receivables | 61 6.0 | 57 6.4 | 62 5.9 | 66 5.5 | 60 6.1 |
| 78 | 4.7 | 81 4.5 | 78 4.7 | 79 4.6 | | 79 4.6 | 78 4.7 | 81 4.5 | 83 4.4 | 79 4.6 |
| 0 | UND | 27 13.4 | 38 9.5 | 25 14.7 | | 31 11.8 | 23 15.7 | 36 10.1 | 32 11.5 | 25 14.7 |
| 14 | 25.5 | 45 8.1 | 62 5.9 | 50 7.3 | Cost of Revenues/Payables | 53 6.9 | 43 8.4 | 54 6.7 | 56 6.5 | 50 7.3 |
| 44 | 8.3 | 70 5.2 | 81 4.5 | 78 4.7 | | 72 5.1 | 66 5.5 | 74 4.9 | 78 4.7 | 78 4.7 |
| | 4.2 | 5.2 | 13.3 | 7.4 | | 8.4 | 6.6 | 5.8 | 6.2 | 7.4 |
| | 6.3 | 10.3 | 18.6 | 14.8 | Revenues/Working Capital | 18.2 | 10.8 | 11.2 | 12.4 | 14.8 |
| | 34.9 | 18.7 | 37.3 | 29.2 | | 38.1 | 22.2 | 27.0 | 27.0 | 29.2 |
| | 113.0 | 271.7 | 169.7 | 187.9 | | 95.2 | 176.8 | 266.0 | 162.6 | 187.9 |
| (29) | 24.8 | (66) 38.4 | (121) 39.7 (217) | 38.3 | EBIT/Interest | (192) 20.8 | (166) 42.0 (191) | 55.0 (246) | 24.4 (217) | 38.3 |
| | 1.5 | 6.3 | 9.6 | 6.8 | | 5.0 | 6.6 | 11.0 | 6.3 | 6.8 |
| | | 62.3 | 103.0 | 65.6 | | 15.4 | 19.3 | 69.0 | 17.2 | 65.6 |
| | (12) | 9.8 (16) | 12.6 (32) | 9.6 | Net Profit + Depr., Dep., Amort./Cur. Mat. L/T/D | (32) 5.0 | (24) 7.0 (19) | 21.0 (40) | 8.0 (32) | 9.6 |
| | | 1.6 | 5.5 | 2.7 | | 1.4 | 1.6 | 7.6 | 2.0 | 2.7 |
| | .1 | .1 | .1 | .1 | | .1 | .1 | .1 | .1 | .1 |
| | .3 | .2 | .2 | .2 | Fixed/Worth | .2 | .2 | .2 | .2 | .2 |
| | 1.0 | .4 | .4 | .5 | | .5 | .4 | .5 | .4 | .5 |
| | .6 | .9 | 2.2 | 1.3 | | 1.2 | 1.0 | 1.0 | 1.0 | 1.3 |
| | 1.1 | 1.7 | 4.2 | 2.7 | Debt/Worth | 2.6 | 1.9 | 2.2 | 2.3 | 2.7 |
| | 3.4 | 3.3 | 6.5 | 5.6 | | 4.7 | 4.4 | 5.5 | 4.8 | 5.6 |
| | 59.4 | 65.1 | 60.0 | 63.5 | % Profit Before Taxes/ Tangible Net Worth | 56.0 | 62.0 | 63.1 | 53.0 | 63.5 |
| (37) | 24.6 | (95) 33.9 | (142) 35.9 (283) | 34.6 | | (244) 31.8 | (224) 35.8 (265) | 38.6 (345) | 28.3 (283) | 34.6 |
| | .5 | 15.5 | 19.8 | 15.2 | | 12.5 | 9.8 | 18.9 | 10.8 | 15.2 |
| | 32.5 | 22.7 | 12.2 | 19.2 | % Profit Before Taxes/ Total Assets | 17.1 | 20.1 | 21.5 | 16.7 | 19.2 |
| | 8.8 | 12.0 | 6.5 | 8.6 | | 8.3 | 10.5 | 11.1 | 7.4 | 8.6 |
| | -.6 | 5.7 | 3.5 | 3.8 | | 3.2 | 3.4 | 4.1 | 3.1 | 3.8 |
| | .3 | .2 | .1 | .1 | % Depr., Dep., Amort./ Revenues | .2 | .2 | .2 | .2 | .1 |
| (30) | .7 | (82) .4 | (122) .2 (237) | .3 | | (204) .4 | (190) .5 (223) | .4 (283) | .4 (237) | .3 |
| | 1.4 | .7 | .5 | .7 | | 1.1 | 1.1 | 1.0 | .8 | .7 |
| | 1.7 | .7 | 1.1 | .8 | % Officers', Directors' Owners' Comp/Revenues | .7 | .9 | .5 | .7 | .8 |
| (18) | 3.2 | (35) 1.2 | (25) 2.0 (80) | 1.8 | | (62) 1.2 | (58) 1.8 (60) | 1.3 (98) | 1.7 (80) | 1.8 |
| | 4.9 | 1.8 | 2.1 | 2.6 | | 2.7 | 3.7 | 3.0 | 3.4 | 2.6 |
| 1603M | 210099M | 2503527M | 199016220M | 201731449M | Contract Revenues ($) | 337026887M | 289481682M | 400537148M | 75063922M | 201731449M |
| 572M | 105252M | 1000203M | 67955276M | 69061303M | Total Assets ($) | 132142734M | 107735809M | 128783924M | 34280086M | 69061303M |

© RMA 2024

M = $ thousand    MM = $ million

See Pages viii through xx for Explanation of Ratios and Data

## CONSTRUCTION-% OF COMPLETION—Water and Sewer Line and Related Structures Construction NAICS 237110

**Current Data Sorted by Revenue** | **Comparative Historical Data**

| | | | | | Type of Statement | | | | | |
|---|---|---|---|---|---|---|---|---|---|---|
| | 5 | 9 | 7 3 | 7 17 | Unqualified Reviewed | 4 9 | 2 11 | 2 17 | 10 18 | 7 17 |
| | 1 | 11 | 25 | 1 36 | Compiled Tax Returns Other | 1 1 32 | 21 | 2 21 | 3 2 26 | 1 36 |
| 10 (4/1-9/30/23) | | 51 (10/1/23-3/31/24) | | | | 4/1/19-3/31/20 | 4/1/20-3/31/21 | 4/1/21-3/31/22 | 4/1/22-3/31/23 | 4/1/23-3/31/24 |
| 0-1MM | 1-10MM | 10-50MM | 50 & OVER | ALL | | ALL | ALL | ALL | ALL | ALL |
| 6 | 20 | 35 | | 61 | NUMBER OF STATEMENTS | 47 | 34 | 42 | 59 | 61 |
| % | % | % | % | % | ASSETS | % | % | % | % | % |
| D | | 19.3 | 12.6 | 17.0 | Cash & Equivalents | 16.5 | 22.4 | 23.1 | 17.7 | 17.0 |
| A | | 24.8 | 39.7 | 32.8 | A/R - Progress Billings | 31.6 | 27.7 | 27.8 | 32.1 | 32.8 |
| T | | 2.8 | 2.5 | 2.7 | A/R - Current Retention | 2.4 | 3.0 | 3.8 | 2.6 | 2.7 |
| A | | 3.5 | .7 | 1.8 | Inventory | 1.2 | 1.6 | 1.7 | 2.6 | 1.8 |
| | | 6.1 | 8.6 | 7.1 | Cost & Est. Earnings In Excess Billings | 5.8 | 5.8 | 3.6 | 4.6 | 7.1 |
| N | | 1.0 | 2.9 | 2.0 | All Other Current | 2.4 | 2.9 | 2.6 | 2.2 | 2.0 |
| O | | 57.5 | 67.0 | 63.5 | Total Current | 59.9 | 63.5 | 62.6 | 61.8 | 63.5 |
| T | | 33.8 | 25.2 | 28.1 | Fixed Assets (net) | 34.0 | 31.0 | 31.8 | 30.1 | 28.1 |
| | | .2 | .1 | .2 | Joint Ventures & Investments | .0 | .0 | .0 | .3 | .2 |
| A | | 3.3 | 1.6 | 2.0 | Intangibles (net) | 1.2 | 1.4 | 1.0 | .8 | 2.0 |
| V | | 5.2 | 6.1 | 6.2 | All Other Non-Current | 5.0 | 4.1 | 4.5 | 7.0 | 6.2 |
| A | | 100.0 | 100.0 | 100.0 | Total | 100.0 | 100.0 | 100.0 | 100.0 | 100.0 |
| I | | | | | LIABILITIES | | | | | |
| L | | 3.6 | 2.3 | 2.8 | Notes Payable-Short Term | 1.9 | 2.2 | 1.6 | 2.6 | 2.8 |
| A | | 10.8 | 20.9 | 16.2 | A/P - Trade | 17.0 | 13.4 | 12.9 | 16.6 | 16.2 |
| B | | .0 | .3 | .2 | A/P - Retention | .4 | .1 | .3 | .1 | .2 |
| L | | 6.6 | 14.5 | 10.7 | Billings in Excess of Costs & Est. Earnings | 8.8 | 6.4 | 8.5 | 7.8 | 10.7 |
| E | | .2 | .3 | .2 | Income Taxes Payable | .1 | .3 | .1 | .3 | .2 |
| | | 6.1 | 3.2 | 4.1 | Cur. Mat.-L/T/D | 5.0 | 4.3 | 3.7 | 4.0 | 4.1 |
| | | 6.8 | 6.1 | 6.0 | All Other Current | 4.7 | 4.7 | 3.6 | 5.2 | 6.0 |
| | | 34.2 | 47.7 | 40.3 | Total Current | 37.8 | 31.6 | 30.7 | 36.6 | 40.3 |
| | | 15.4 | 12.6 | 13.7 | Long-Term Debt | 11.5 | 14.1 | 10.3 | 10.5 | 13.7 |
| | | .9 | .5 | .6 | Deferred Taxes | .4 | .4 | .7 | .5 | .6 |
| | | 1.5 | 14.0 | 8.6 | All Other Non-Current | 2.9 | .3 | 3.4 | 1.5 | 8.6 |
| | | 48.0 | 25.2 | 36.8 | Net Worth | 47.4 | 53.6 | 54.9 | 50.9 | 36.8 |
| | | 100.0 | 100.0 | 100.0 | Total Liabilities & Net Worth | 100.0 | 100.0 | 100.0 | 100.0 | 100.0 |
| | | | | | INCOME DATA | | | | | |
| | | 100.0 | 100.0 | 100.0 | Contract Revenues | 100.0 | 100.0 | 100.0 | 100.0 | 100.0 |
| | | 18.8 | 13.3 | 17.7 | Gross Profit | 22.5 | 24.2 | 23.6 | 21.1 | 17.7 |
| | | 12.8 | 7.1 | 11.3 | Operating Expenses | 15.5 | 14.3 | 16.0 | 14.2 | 11.3 |
| | | 6.0 | 6.2 | 6.4 | Operating Profit | 7.1 | 9.9 | 7.5 | 7.0 | 6.4 |
| | | -1.3 | .4 | -.3 | All Other Expenses (net) | .7 | -1.6 | -2.6 | -.2 | -.3 |
| | | 7.4 | 5.8 | 6.7 | Profit Before Taxes | 6.4 | 11.5 | 10.1 | 7.2 | 6.7 |
| | | | | | RATIOS | | | | | |
| | | 2.5 | 1.5 | 2.1 | | 2.2 | 3.3 | 3.4 | 2.7 | 2.1 |
| | | 1.8 | 1.3 | 1.4 | Current | 1.5 | 1.9 | 1.9 | 1.6 | 1.4 |
| | | 1.1 | 1.2 | 1.2 | | 1.3 | 1.4 | 1.5 | 1.3 | 1.2 |
| | | 5.9 | 3.0 | 3.2 | | 3.1 | 4.2 | 4.5 | 4.0 | 3.2 |
| | | 2.9 | 1.9 | (60) 2.2 | Receivables/Payables | 2.3 | 2.3 | 2.8 | (57) 2.1 | (60) 2.2 |
| | | 1.9 | 1.6 | 1.7 | | 1.5 | 1.6 | 1.7 | 1.6 | 1.7 |
| | 28 | 13.0 54 | 6.7 51 | 7.2 | | 41 9.0 | 45 8.2 | 60 6.1 | 52 7.0 | 51 7.2 |
| | 57 | 6.4 65 | 5.6 65 | 5.6 | Revenues/Receivables | 58 6.3 | 63 5.8 | 76 4.8 | 78 4.7 | 65 5.6 |
| | 74 | 4.9 81 | 4.5 81 | 4.5 | | 81 4.5 | 79 4.6 | 85 4.3 | 91 4.0 | 81 4.5 |
| | 14 | 26.4 24 | 15.1 18 | 20.4 | | 23 15.8 | 19 19.5 | 19 19.7 | 20 18.1 | 18 20.4 |
| | 25 | 14.6 41 | 9.0 37 | 9.8 | Cost of Revenues/Payables | 37 9.9 | 28 12.9 | 33 11.2 | 38 9.7 | 37 9.8 |
| | 41 | 9.0 53 | 6.9 51 | 7.2 | | 57 6.4 | 54 6.8 | 49 7.4 | 57 6.4 | 51 7.2 |
| | | 4.9 | 8.6 | 5.5 | | 6.0 | 3.9 | 3.6 | 4.7 | 5.5 |
| | | 8.6 | 13.8 | 11.3 | Revenues/Working Capital | 9.5 | 6.5 | 5.4 | 7.6 | 11.3 |
| | | 30.2 | 22.0 | 22.5 | | 20.7 | 11.1 | 9.8 | 17.5 | 22.5 |
| | | 81.3 | 30.5 | 33.4 | | 70.9 | 214.3 | 144.3 | 121.1 | 33.4 |
| | | 15.5 | 9.7 (60) | 12.8 | EBIT/Interest | (42) 15.6 | (32) 38.1 | (37) 53.4 | (54) 23.9 | (60) 12.8 |
| | | 3.9 | 4.0 | 3.7 | | 4.2 | 13.0 | 11.0 | 5.6 | 3.7 |
| | | | 4.4 | 4.5 | | | | | 7.8 | 4.5 |
| | | (10) | 3.3 (17) | 2.6 | Net Profit + Depr., Dep., Amort./Cur. Mat. L/T/D | | | | (11) 5.7 (17) | 2.6 |
| | | | 1.9 | 1.1 | | | | | 1.9 | 1.1 |
| | | .3 | .4 | .4 | | .4 | .3 | .3 | .2 | .4 |
| | | .7 | .9 | .7 | Fixed/Worth | .6 | .6 | .6 | .6 | .7 |
| | | 1.4 | 1.4 | 1.3 | | 1.1 | .9 | .9 | 1.0 | 1.3 |
| | | .6 | 1.4 | .8 | | .5 | .5 | .4 | .5 | .8 |
| | | 1.1 | 2.6 | 2.1 | Debt/Worth | 1.2 | .8 | .8 | 1.1 | 2.1 |
| | | 3.2 | 4.3 | 3.3 | | 2.0 | 1.5 | 1.3 | 1.8 | 3.3 |
| | | 67.2 | 42.7 | 52.7 | | 36.9 | 54.7 | 46.0 | 42.5 | 52.7 |
| | | 33.9 (32) | 29.3 (58) | 29.3 | % Profit Before Taxes/ Tangible Net Worth | (45) 23.3 | 40.5 (41) | 32.9 (58) | 28.0 (58) | 29.3 |
| | | 10.0 | 17.4 | 10.3 | | 7.1 | 17.4 | 14.3 | 14.9 | 10.3 |
| | | 36.4 | 17.6 | 18.4 | | 21.0 | 28.5 | 21.5 | 22.0 | 18.4 |
| | | 16.1 | 9.4 | 10.5 | % Profit Before Taxes/ Total Assets | 10.5 | 21.2 | 13.9 | 13.3 | 10.5 |
| | | 3.2 | 4.0 | 4.2 | | 3.1 | 9.7 | 8.0 | 5.6 | 4.2 |
| | | 1.5 | .1 | .2 | | 2.3 | 2.0 | 2.1 | 2.3 | .2 |
| | (18) | 2.9 (28) | .6 (50) | 2.0 | % Depr., Dep., Amort./ Revenues | (38) 3.9 | (29) 4.1 | (36) 3.9 | (50) 3.5 | (50) 2.0 |
| | | 6.3 | 2.7 | 4.2 | | 5.5 | 4.8 | 5.2 | 5.3 | 4.2 |
| | | | | .8 | | | .7 | | .6 | .8 |
| | | | (12) | 1.7 | % Officers', Directors' Owners' Comp/Revenues | | (13) 2.0 | (19) | 1.4 (12) | 1.7 |
| | | | | 3.3 | | | 4.8 | | 3.8 | 3.3 |
| | 29998M | 626895M | 26674073M | 27330966M | Contract Revenues ($) | 41864032M | 57985584M | 1922449M | 6794169M | 27330966M |
| | 20051M | 373091M | 13101033M | 13494175M | Total Assets ($) | 27475211M | 37218302M | 1264498M | 3677600M | 13494175M |

© RMA 2024 M = $ thousand MM = $ million
See Pages viii through xx for Explanation of Ratios and Data

# CONSTRUCTION-% OF COMPLETION—Power and Communication Line and Related Structures Construction  NAICS 237130

**Current Data Sorted by Revenue** | **Comparative Historical Data**

| | | | | | Type of Statement | | | | | |
|---|---|---|---|---|---|---|---|---|---|---|
| | | | 3 | 3 | Unqualified | | 2 | 2 | 3 | 3 |
| | | 3 | | 3 | Reviewed | 5 | 5 | 3 | 4 | 3 |
| | 2 | | | | Compiled | | | 1 | 4 | |
| | 2 | 5 | 20 | 2 | Tax Returns | 3 | 2 | | | 2 |
| 3 (4/1-9/30/23) | | | 32 (10/1/23-3/31/24) | 27 | Other | 20 | 14 | 18 | 9 | 27 |
| 0-1MM | 1-10MM | 10-50MM | 50 & OVER | ALL | | 4/1/19-3/31/20 ALL | 4/1/20-3/31/21 ALL | 4/1/21-3/31/22 ALL | 4/1/22-3/31/23 ALL | 4/1/23-3/31/24 ALL |
| | 4 | 8 | 23 | 35 | NUMBER OF STATEMENTS | 28 | 23 | 24 | 20 | 35 |
| % | % | % | % | % | ASSETS | % | % | % | % | % |
| D A T A   N O T   A V A I L A B L E | | | 6.6 | 15.5 | Cash & Equivalents | 11.9 | 13.1 | 11.6 | 12.9 | 15.5 |
| | | | 21.1 | 21.1 | A/R - Progress Billings | 28.9 | 33.3 | 29.9 | 26.3 | 21.1 |
| | | | .7 | .8 | A/R - Current Retention | 1.7 | .6 | .9 | .5 | .8 |
| | | | 2.4 | 1.7 | Inventory | 2.0 | 1.4 | 3.2 | 3.9 | 1.7 |
| | | | 9.5 | 8.0 | Cost & Est. Earnings In Excess Billings | 6.6 | 5.1 | 6.5 | 7.1 | 8.0 |
| | | | 6.4 | 5.0 | All Other Current | 6.0 | 6.1 | 5.6 | 5.8 | 5.0 |
| | | | 46.7 | 52.1 | Total Current | 57.0 | 59.6 | 57.6 | 56.5 | 52.1 |
| | | | 23.4 | 26.1 | Fixed Assets (net) | 27.7 | 23.9 | 23.6 | 28.2 | 26.1 |
| | | | .0 | .0 | Joint Ventures & Investments | .3 | .0 | .0 | .1 | .0 |
| | | | 21.1 | 14.5 | Intangibles (net) | 11.9 | 11.3 | 15.3 | 7.9 | 14.5 |
| | | | 8.8 | 7.3 | All Other Non-Current | 3.2 | 5.0 | 3.5 | 7.2 | 7.3 |
| | | | 100.0 | 100.0 | Total | 100.0 | 100.0 | 100.0 | 100.0 | 100.0 |
| | | | | | LIABILITIES | | | | | |
| | | | 1.4 | 1.6 | Notes Payable-Short Term | 5.5 | 7.2 | 4.8 | 4.9 | 1.6 |
| | | | 8.9 | 8.7 | A/P - Trade | 11.0 | 8.5 | 9.5 | 8.5 | 8.7 |
| | | | .0 | .1 | A/P - Retention | .6 | .5 | .2 | .2 | .1 |
| | | | 3.6 | 3.8 | Billings in Excess of Costs & Est. Earnings | 2.2 | 3.1 | 4.0 | 4.4 | 3.8 |
| | | | .0 | .1 | Income Taxes Payable | .0 | .1 | .1 | .2 | .1 |
| | | | 2.7 | 2.7 | Cur. Mat.-L/T/D | 4.0 | 4.0 | 3.8 | 4.2 | 2.7 |
| | | | 9.7 | 8.7 | All Other Current | 11.5 | 7.6 | 8.0 | 6.7 | 8.7 |
| | | | 26.4 | 25.8 | Total Current | 34.8 | 31.0 | 30.6 | 29.1 | 25.8 |
| | | | 26.7 | 23.1 | Long-Term Debt | 21.7 | 20.7 | 18.5 | 25.1 | 23.1 |
| | | | 1.7 | 1.1 | Deferred Taxes | .5 | .5 | 1.6 | .5 | 1.1 |
| | | | 11.8 | 8.3 | All Other Non-Current | 7.0 | 6.2 | 2.7 | 3.8 | 8.3 |
| | | | 33.5 | 41.7 | Net Worth | 36.1 | 41.6 | 46.6 | 41.5 | 41.7 |
| | | | 100.0 | 100.0 | Total Liabilties & Net Worth | 100.0 | 100.0 | 100.0 | 100.0 | 100.0 |
| | | | | | INCOME DATA | | | | | |
| | | | 100.0 | 100.0 | Contract Revenues | 100.0 | 100.0 | 100.0 | 100.0 | 100.0 |
| | | | 21.4 | 29.1 | Gross Profit | 25.5 | 29.4 | 22.4 | 25.6 | 29.1 |
| | | | 14.4 | 19.8 | Operating Expenses | 20.6 | 23.0 | 16.8 | 19.2 | 19.8 |
| | | | 7.0 | 9.4 | Operating Profit | 4.9 | 6.4 | 5.6 | 6.4 | 9.4 |
| | | | 4.0 | 2.9 | All Other Expenses (net) | 1.8 | -.3 | .0 | 1.6 | 2.9 |
| | | | 3.0 | 6.5 | Profit Before Taxes | 3.0 | 6.7 | 5.7 | 4.7 | 6.5 |
| | | | | | RATIOS | | | | | |
| | | | 2.1 | 3.0 | | 2.4 | 2.6 | 2.4 | 2.7 | 3.0 |
| | | | 1.5 | 1.6 | Current | 1.7 | 1.9 | 2.0 | 1.9 | 1.6 |
| | | | 1.4 | 1.3 | | 1.3 | 1.5 | 1.5 | 1.4 | 1.3 |
| | | | 4.4 | 5.5 | | 4.8 | 6.1 | 5.2 | 4.7 | 5.5 |
| | | | 3.6 (33) | 3.6 | Receivables/Payables | (26) 3.0 | (22) 3.8 | 3.1 | 3.6 | (33) 3.6 |
| | | | 1.5 | 1.8 | | 2.1 | 2.6 | 2.0 | 2.1 | 1.8 |
| | | 43 8.4 | 38 9.5 | | 40 9.2 | 52 7.0 | 49 7.5 | 32 11.4 | 38 9.5 | | |
| | | 49 7.5 | 48 7.6 | Revenues/Receivables | 54 6.8 | 62 5.9 | 60 6.1 | 54 6.7 | 48 7.6 | | |
| | | 57 6.4 | 60 6.1 | | 72 5.1 | 81 4.5 | 76 4.8 | 73 5.0 | 60 6.1 | | |
| | | 14 26.6 | 12 29.4 | | 13 27.4 | 14 27.0 | 16 22.4 | 16 23.4 | 12 29.4 | | |
| | | 24 15.1 | 24 15.1 | Cost of Revenues/Payables | 21 17.6 | 20 18.3 | 23 16.0 | 22 16.4 | 24 15.1 | | |
| | | 40 9.1 | 40 9.1 | | 38 9.6 | 34 10.7 | 38 9.6 | 36 10.2 | 40 9.1 | | |
| | | | 6.4 | 5.7 | | 5.3 | 4.6 | 5.2 | 5.0 | 5.7 |
| | | | 10.3 | 9.6 | Revenues/Working Capital | 8.8 | 6.1 | 6.6 | 6.1 | 9.6 |
| | | | 13.3 | 12.8 | | 16.8 | 10.3 | 8.3 | 13.9 | 12.8 |
| | | | 13.4 | 39.8 | | 26.8 | 29.2 | 45.3 | 62.1 | 39.8 |
| | | (21) 2.4 | (32) 6.3 | EBIT/Interest | (27) 3.7 | (21) 7.1 | (20) 9.6 | (19) 2.9 | (32) 6.3 |
| | | | -.3 | 1.2 | | .4 | 2.1 | 2.4 | -.4 | 1.2 |
| | | | | | Net Profit + Depr., Dep., Amort./Cur. Mat. L/T/D | | | | | |
| | | | .6 | .3 | | .4 | .4 | .5 | .3 | .3 |
| | | | 1.2 | .8 | Fixed/Worth | 1.0 | .5 | .6 | .9 | .8 |
| | | | -2.8 | 5.5 | | NM | 2.0 | 1.5 | 5.9 | 5.5 |
| | | | 1.6 | .6 | | .7 | .7 | .6 | .5 | .6 |
| | | | 2.3 | 2.1 | Debt/Worth | 2.4 | 1.7 | 1.7 | 1.6 | 2.1 |
| | | | -9.3 | 19.7 | | NM | 15.9 | 2.9 | 8.1 | 19.7 |
| | | | 59.3 | 59.6 | | 35.0 | 56.7 | 51.1 | 47.1 | 59.6 |
| | | (16) 35.2 | (28) 45.4 | % Profit Before Taxes/ Tangible Net Worth | (21) 18.6 | (19) 36.3 | (20) 22.2 | (17) 24.6 | (28) 45.4 |
| | | | 11.9 | 18.1 | | 2.5 | 17.7 | 11.8 | -2.1 | 18.1 |
| | | | 11.7 | 23.1 | | 15.1 | 21.1 | 17.8 | 18.8 | 23.1 |
| | | | 5.4 | 7.9 | % Profit Before Taxes/ Total Assets | 5.3 | 14.4 | 10.3 | 3.9 | 7.9 |
| | | | -6.1 | 1.2 | | -1.2 | 3.2 | 1.3 | -2.8 | 1.2 |
| | | | | 2.1 | | 1.8 | 1.7 | 1.7 | 1.1 | 2.1 |
| | | | (10) 2.9 | % Depr., Dep., Amort./ Revenues | (17) 4.2 | (15) 3.3 | (12) 2.5 | (15) 2.6 | (10) 2.9 |
| | | | | 10.3 | | 6.7 | 6.3 | 4.2 | 5.7 | 10.3 |
| | | | | | % Officers', Directors' Owners' Comp/Revenues | | | | | |
| | 14794M | 172101M | 60067314M | 60254209M | Contract Revenues ($) | 12093208M | 4794030M | 9778750M | 2984912M | 60254209M |
| | 5677M | 120670M | 54887947M | 55014294M | Total Assets ($) | 6980036M | 2878945M | 9872178M | 3147071M | 55014294M |

© RMA 2024  
M = $ thousand    MM = $ million  
See Pages viii through xx for Explanation of Ratios and Data

# CONSTRUCTION-% OF COMPLETION—Highway, Street, and Bridge Construction  NAICS 237310

## Current Data Sorted by Revenue | Comparative Historical Data

| | | | | | | Type of Statement | | | | | |
|---|---|---|---|---|---|---|---|---|---|---|---|
| | 2 | 3 | 11 | | 16 | Unqualified | 17 | 15 | 20 | 30 | 16 |
| | 4 | 11 | 5 | | 20 | Reviewed | 23 | 29 | 37 | 46 | 20 |
| | | 1 | 1 | | 2 | Compiled | 3 | 1 | 2 | 2 | 2 |
| | 1 | 1 | 1 | | 3 | Tax Returns | 4 | 3 | 1 | 4 | 3 |
| | 5 | 23 | 78 | | 106 | Other | 66 | 55 | 75 | 74 | 106 |
| | | | | | | | 4/1/19- | 4/1/20- | 4/1/21- | 4/1/22- | 4/1/23- |
| 30 (4/1-9/30/23) | | | 117 (10/1/23-3/31/24) | | | | 3/31/20 | 3/31/21 | 3/31/22 | 3/31/23 | 3/31/24 |
| 0-1MM | 1-10MM | 10-50MM | 50 & OVER | | ALL | | ALL | ALL | ALL | ALL | ALL |
| | 12 | 39 | 96 | | 147 | NUMBER OF STATEMENTS | 113 | 103 | 135 | 156 | 147 |
| % | % | % | % | | % | ASSETS | % | % | % | % | % |
| | 29.5 | 29.6 | 18.6 | | 22.4 | Cash & Equivalents | 17.5 | 23.7 | 21.8 | 19.9 | 22.4 |
| D | 24.1 | 19.3 | 25.7 | | 23.9 | A/R - Progress Billings | 26.6 | 24.9 | 24.0 | 25.0 | 23.9 |
| A | 1.3 | 1.8 | 1.3 | | 1.4 | A/R - Current Retention | 1.9 | 1.4 | 2.1 | 2.0 | 1.4 |
| T | .5 | 2.7 | 2.8 | | 2.6 | Inventory | 3.0 | 2.9 | 2.8 | 3.9 | 2.6 |
| A | 3.2 | 5.8 | 5.1 | | 5.1 | Cost & Est. Earnings In Excess Billings | 5.4 | 3.0 | 5.2 | 5.1 | 5.1 |
| N | 7.3 | 4.3 | 4.7 | | 4.8 | All Other Current | 2.0 | 3.1 | 4.2 | 3.7 | 4.8 |
| O | 65.9 | 63.5 | 58.1 | | 60.1 | Total Current | 56.4 | 58.9 | 60.1 | 59.7 | 60.1 |
| T | 27.4 | 28.5 | 30.1 | | 29.4 | Fixed Assets (net) | 34.2 | 32.8 | 30.8 | 30.8 | 29.4 |
| | .5 | .0 | .1 | | .1 | Joint Ventures & Investments | .6 | .4 | .3 | .3 | .1 |
| A | 1.1 | .8 | 5.8 | | 4.1 | Intangibles (net) | 2.4 | 2.2 | 3.1 | 1.8 | 4.1 |
| V | 5.1 | 7.2 | 6.0 | | 6.2 | All Other Non-Current | 6.4 | 5.6 | 5.8 | 7.4 | 6.2 |
| A | 100.0 | 100.0 | 100.0 | | 100.0 | Total | 100.0 | 100.0 | 100.0 | 100.0 | 100.0 |
| I | | | | | | LIABILITIES | | | | | |
| L | 3.9 | 1.2 | 1.7 | | 1.7 | Notes Payable-Short Term | 4.0 | 2.4 | 2.2 | 2.9 | 1.7 |
| A | 18.3 | 10.7 | 14.5 | | 13.8 | A/P - Trade | 13.5 | 9.9 | 12.4 | 13.4 | 13.8 |
| B | .1 | .1 | .3 | | .2 | A/P - Retention | .3 | .1 | .3 | .2 | .2 |
| L | 1.0 | 5.9 | 9.8 | | 8.1 | Billings in Excess of Costs & Est. Earnings | 6.2 | 6.1 | 5.7 | 6.3 | 8.1 |
| E | .2 | .2 | .1 | | .1 | Income Taxes Payable | .1 | .2 | .1 | .1 | .1 |
| | 5.0 | 3.4 | 3.1 | | 3.3 | Cur. Mat.-L/T/D | 4.4 | 4.1 | 4.0 | 3.9 | 3.3 |
| | 6.8 | 5.0 | 6.3 | | 6.0 | All Other Current | 5.3 | 4.9 | 4.9 | 4.9 | 6.0 |
| | 35.3 | 26.6 | 35.7 | | 33.3 | Total Current | 33.8 | 27.7 | 29.7 | 31.7 | 33.3 |
| | 17.2 | 12.7 | 11.6 | | 12.3 | Long-Term Debt | 15.2 | 15.4 | 13.4 | 11.1 | 12.3 |
| | 1.1 | .7 | .6 | | .6 | Deferred Taxes | .9 | .9 | .5 | .6 | .6 |
| | 2.7 | 4.9 | 5.3 | | 5.0 | All Other Non-Current | 2.8 | 2.4 | 2.9 | 3.6 | 5.0 |
| | 43.6 | 55.2 | 46.8 | | 48.8 | Net Worth | 47.2 | 53.6 | 53.5 | 52.8 | 48.8 |
| | 100.0 | 100.0 | 100.0 | | 100.0 | Total Liabilities & Net Worth | 100.0 | 100.0 | 100.0 | 100.0 | 100.0 |
| | | | | | | INCOME DATA | | | | | |
| | 100.0 | 100.0 | 100.0 | | 100.0 | Contract Revenues | 100.0 | 100.0 | 100.0 | 100.0 | 100.0 |
| | 29.7 | 19.0 | 14.0 | | 16.6 | Gross Profit | 17.1 | 17.4 | 17.8 | 17.7 | 16.6 |
| | 23.3 | 12.0 | 9.5 | | 11.3 | Operating Expenses | 12.1 | 12.1 | 13.0 | 13.3 | 11.3 |
| | 6.4 | 7.0 | 4.5 | | 5.3 | Operating Profit | 5.0 | 5.3 | 4.9 | 4.4 | 5.3 |
| | -.7 | -.8 | -.1 | | -.3 | All Other Expenses (net) | -.2 | -1.0 | -2.4 | -.4 | -.3 |
| | 7.0 | 7.8 | 4.6 | | 5.6 | Profit Before Taxes | 5.2 | 6.3 | 7.2 | 4.8 | 5.6 |
| | | | | | | RATIOS | | | | | |
| | 6.6 | 4.5 | 2.1 | | 2.7 | | 2.3 | 3.3 | 3.1 | 3.0 | 2.7 |
| | 1.9 | 2.2 | 1.5 | | 1.7 | Current | 1.6 | 2.1 | 2.0 | 1.7 | 1.7 |
| | 1.4 | 1.5 | 1.3 | | 1.4 | | 1.2 | 1.5 | 1.5 | 1.4 | 1.4 |
| | 7.2 | 4.3 | 2.8 | | 3.1 | | 3.2 | 4.2 | 3.6 | 3.5 | 3.1 |
| | 3.0 | 2.1 | 1.9 | | 2.0 | Receivables/Payables | 1.9 (102) | 2.7 | 2.2 (155) | 2.4 | 2.0 |
| | 1.4 | 1.4 | 1.3 | | 1.3 | | 1.4 | 1.5 | 1.5 | 1.5 | 1.3 |
| | 33  11.2 | 21  17.5 | 39  9.3 | 35 | 10.5 | | 34  10.6 | 31  11.6 | 38  9.5 | 38  9.7 | 35  10.5 |
| | 52  7.0 | 37  9.8 | 55  6.6 | 52 | 7.0 | Revenues/Receivables | 54  6.7 | 54  6.7 | 53  6.9 | 59  6.2 | 52  7.0 |
| | 87  4.2 | 66  5.5 | 73  5.0 | 73 | 5.0 | | 72  5.1 | 78  4.7 | 79  4.6 | 83  4.4 | 73  5.0 |
| | 9  39.7 | 11  33.3 | 21  17.4 | 17 | 21.8 | | 17  21.4 | 13  28.2 | 18  20.3 | 16  22.5 | 17  21.8 |
| | 22  16.5 | 21  17.7 | 32  11.4 | 29 | 12.5 | Cost of Revenues/Payables | 26  14.0 | 24  15.1 | 29  12.6 | 29  13.4 | 29  12.5 |
| | 54  6.7 | 37  9.8 | 43  8.4 | 41 | 8.8 | | 39  9.4 | 38  9.7 | 47  7.7 | 45  8.1 | 41  8.8 |
| | 2.3 | 2.7 | 5.7 | | 4.4 | | 5.4 | 3.9 | 3.9 | 3.7 | 4.4 |
| | 5.9 | 5.0 | 8.8 | | 7.9 | Revenues/Working Capital | 10.7 | 6.5 | 5.9 | 7.2 | 7.9 |
| | 24.0 | 10.2 | 14.4 | | 13.9 | | 21.7 | 10.3 | 9.8 | 11.3 | 13.9 |
| | 23.8 | 113.9 | 47.0 | | 61.7 | | 26.1 | 35.0 | 80.2 | 62.6 | 61.7 |
| | (10)  7.4 | (35)  14.7 | (93)  10.3 | (138) | 11.5 | EBIT/Interest | (105)  7.7 | (90)  14.6 | (124)  19.7 | (146)  15.4 | (138)  11.5 |
| | -1.9 | 2.3 | 3.8 | | 3.1 | | 2.8 | 3.3 | 3.4 | 2.7 | 3.1 |
| | | | 34.0 | | 16.5 | | 5.2 | 12.2 | 11.6 | 6.6 | 16.5 |
| | | (18) | 5.0 | (28) | 8.0 | Net Profit + Depr., Dep., Amort./Cur. Mat. L/T/D | (19)  3.1 | (16)  4.5 | (23)  3.3 | (27)  3.5 | (28)  8.0 |
| | | | 2.0 | | 2.5 | | 2.0 | 1.8 | 1.8 | 1.6 | 2.5 |
| | .3 | .3 | .5 | | .4 | | .5 | .4 | .3 | .3 | .4 |
| | .5 | .5 | .7 | | .7 | Fixed/Worth | .8 | .6 | .6 | .6 | .7 |
| | 1.4 | .8 | 1.1 | | 1.1 | | 1.3 | 1.0 | 1.0 | .9 | 1.1 |
| | .3 | .3 | .7 | | .5 | | .6 | .5 | .5 | .5 | .5 |
| | .7 | .7 | 1.3 | | 1.2 | Debt/Worth | 1.1 | .9 | .9 | .9 | 1.2 |
| | 2.2 | 1.5 | 2.4 | | 2.1 | | 2.2 | 1.5 | 1.5 | 1.5 | 2.1 |
| | 31.2 | 33.4 | 32.2 | | 31.9 | | 29.4 | 37.5 | 35.4 | 26.1 | 31.9 |
| | (10)  14.0 | (38)  16.7 | (90)  21.9 | (138) | 20.9 | % Profit Before Taxes/ Tangible Net Worth | (109)  17.1 | (101)  19.0 | (131)  20.7 | (151)  16.1 | (138)  20.9 |
| | 5.0 | 4.9 | 9.3 | | 7.9 | | 7.0 | 10.5 | 8.5 | 4.5 | 7.9 |
| | 15.0 | 17.9 | 15.1 | | 15.2 | | 13.2 | 17.2 | 19.6 | 14.6 | 15.2 |
| | 7.8 | 9.5 | 9.2 | | 9.1 | % Profit Before Taxes/ Total Assets | 7.5 | 9.3 | 10.8 | 7.5 | 9.1 |
| | 2.2 | 1.5 | 3.2 | | 2.8 | | 1.9 | 4.1 | 3.0 | 1.4 | 2.8 |
| | | 2.5 | .5 | | 1.2 | | 2.5 | 2.7 | 2.1 | 2.1 | 1.2 |
| | (35) | 4.0 | (57)  2.1 | (101) | 2.7 | % Depr., Dep., Amort./ Revenues | (94)  3.8 | (83)  3.7 | (107)  3.6 | (126)  3.7 | (101)  2.7 |
| | | 5.2 | 3.2 | | 4.0 | | 5.3 | 5.1 | 5.2 | 5.1 | 4.0 |
| | | .6 | .2 | | .5 | | 1.0 | .9 | .7 | 1.0 | .5 |
| | (16) | 1.3 | (17)  1.3 | (39) | 1.4 | % Officers', Directors' Owners' Comp/Revenues | (30)  2.0 | (32)  2.2 | (38)  1.3 | (53)  1.7 | (39)  1.4 |
| | | 3.0 | 2.1 | | 3.0 | | 3.0 | 3.0 | 2.4 | 3.0 | 3.0 |
| | 72589M | 1066074M | 92445986M | | 93584649M | Contract Revenues ($) | 60742165M | 20338257M | 40912360M | 47575096M | 93584649M |
| | 60076M | 643721M | 49663288M | | 50367085M | Total Assets ($) | 28419740M | 11802659M | 27570483M | 29817872M | 50367085M |

© RMA 2024    M = $ thousand    MM = $ million
See Pages viii through xx for Explanation of Ratios and Data

# CONSTRUCTION-% OF COMPLETION—Other Heavy and Civil Engineering Construction  NAICS 237990

## Current Data Sorted by Revenue | Comparative Historical Data

| | | | | | Type of Statement | | | | | |
|---|---|---|---|---|---|---|---|---|---|---|
| | | 2 | 10 | 12 | Unqualified | 10 | 8 | 12 | 15 | 12 |
| 1 | 2 | 10 | 3 | 16 | Reviewed | 11 | 23 | 23 | 28 | 16 |
| | | 1 | 1 | 2 | Compiled | | 1 | 1 | | 2 |
| 1 | 1 | | | 2 | Tax Returns | | 2 | 1 | 3 | 2 |
| 1 | 2 | 19 | 26 | 48 | Other | 22 | 26 | 33 | 32 | 48 |
| | | | | | | 4/1/19- | 4/1/20- | 4/1/21- | 4/1/22- | 4/1/23- |
| 12 (4/1-9/30/23) | | | 68 (10/1/23-3/31/24) | | | 3/31/20 | 3/31/21 | 3/31/22 | 3/31/23 | 3/31/24 |
| 0-1MM | 1-10MM | 10-50MM | 50 & OVER | ALL | | ALL | ALL | ALL | ALL | ALL |
| 3 | 5 | 32 | 40 | 80 | NUMBER OF STATEMENTS | 43 | 60 | 70 | 78 | 80 |
| % | % | % | % | % | ASSETS | % | % | % | % | % |
| | | 18.5 | 10.8 | 14.4 | Cash & Equivalents | 13.1 | 21.9 | 22.0 | 19.5 | 14.4 |
| | | 33.4 | 26.6 | 28.9 | A/R - Progress Billings | 31.9 | 30.7 | 27.0 | 29.1 | 28.9 |
| | | 1.2 | 1.2 | 1.1 | A/R - Current Retention | 2.2 | 1.7 | 1.7 | 1.5 | 1.1 |
| | | 4.2 | 1.2 | 2.5 | Inventory | 3.1 | 1.4 | 1.4 | 1.9 | 2.5 |
| | | 5.0 | 6.8 | 5.7 | Cost & Est. Earnings In Excess Billings | 5.5 | 5.6 | 5.0 | 4.5 | 5.7 |
| | | 3.1 | 5.2 | 4.0 | All Other Current | 6.8 | 5.3 | 5.1 | 4.2 | 4.0 |
| | | 65.3 | 51.8 | 56.6 | Total Current | 62.7 | 66.8 | 62.2 | 60.6 | 56.6 |
| | | 26.9 | 36.8 | 33.1 | Fixed Assets (net) | 29.3 | 27.7 | 29.9 | 32.8 | 33.1 |
| | | .0 | .6 | .3 | Joint Ventures & Investments | 1.2 | .5 | .4 | .4 | .3 |
| | | 1.6 | 2.5 | 1.9 | Intangibles (net) | 1.6 | 1.5 | 2.4 | .9 | 1.9 |
| | | 6.1 | 8.2 | 8.1 | All Other Non-Current | 5.3 | 3.7 | 5.0 | 5.4 | 8.1 |
| | | 100.0 | 100.0 | 100.0 | Total | 100.0 | 100.0 | 100.0 | 100.0 | 100.0 |
| | | | | | LIABILITIES | | | | | |
| | | 3.9 | 1.0 | 3.0 | Notes Payable-Short Term | 5.7 | 4.8 | 3.1 | 3.5 | 3.0 |
| | | 17.0 | 13.5 | 14.9 | A/P - Trade | 18.8 | 18.0 | 15.1 | 14.8 | 14.9 |
| | | .1 | .7 | .4 | A/P - Retention | .1 | .6 | .2 | .2 | .4 |
| | | 7.4 | 8.8 | 8.1 | Billings in Excess of Costs & Est. Earnings | 5.5 | 6.1 | 9.7 | 9.1 | 8.1 |
| | | .1 | .0 | .1 | Income Taxes Payable | .1 | .2 | .2 | .2 | .1 |
| | | 3.0 | 4.2 | 3.4 | Cur. Mat.-L/T/D | 4.8 | 4.8 | 4.3 | 3.4 | 3.4 |
| | | 11.0 | 7.9 | 8.8 | All Other Current | 7.7 | 6.0 | 5.5 | 5.1 | 8.8 |
| | | 42.4 | 36.2 | 38.7 | Total Current | 42.7 | 40.5 | 38.2 | 36.9 | 38.7 |
| | | 13.1 | 15.8 | 15.8 | Long-Term Debt | 15.2 | 15.8 | 14.6 | 12.6 | 15.8 |
| | | .2 | 2.1 | 1.1 | Deferred Taxes | .4 | .3 | .6 | .1 | 1.1 |
| | | 1.2 | 3.5 | 2.9 | All Other Non-Current | .9 | 2.5 | 2.8 | 2.9 | 2.9 |
| | | 43.1 | 42.4 | 41.5 | Net Worth | 40.8 | 40.9 | 43.6 | 47.5 | 41.5 |
| | | 100.0 | 100.0 | 100.0 | Total Liabilities & Net Worth | 100.0 | 100.0 | 100.0 | 100.0 | 100.0 |
| | | | | | INCOME DATA | | | | | |
| | | 100.0 | 100.0 | 100.0 | Contract Revenues | 100.0 | 100.0 | 100.0 | 100.0 | 100.0 |
| | | 23.8 | 15.7 | 20.5 | Gross Profit | 20.4 | 19.9 | 21.3 | 18.9 | 20.5 |
| | | 14.7 | 9.1 | 13.3 | Operating Expenses | 16.4 | 12.3 | 14.0 | 14.0 | 13.3 |
| | | 9.1 | 6.6 | 7.3 | Operating Profit | 4.0 | 7.6 | 7.3 | 4.8 | 7.3 |
| | | -.3 | .6 | .2 | All Other Expenses (net) | .5 | -.7 | -2.0 | -1.2 | .2 |
| | | 9.4 | 6.0 | 7.1 | Profit Before Taxes | 3.5 | 8.4 | 9.2 | 6.1 | 7.1 |
| | | | | | RATIOS | | | | | |
| | | 2.4 | 1.8 | 2.0 | | 2.2 | 2.5 | 2.3 | 2.2 | 2.0 |
| | | 1.6 | 1.5 | 1.6 | Current | 1.4 | 1.8 | 1.7 | 1.5 | 1.6 |
| | | 1.3 | 1.1 | 1.1 | | 1.1 | 1.4 | 1.3 | 1.3 | 1.1 |
| | | 3.5 | 3.0 | 3.1 | | 4.1 | 3.7 | 3.6 | 3.2 | 3.1 |
| | | (31) 2.1 | 2.2 (78) | 2.1 | Receivables/Payables | 2.6 | 2.5 | 2.1 (77) | 2.0 (78) | 2.1 |
| | | 1.6 | 1.3 | 1.3 | | 1.1 | 1.4 | 1.2 | 1.5 | 1.3 |
| | | 43 8.5 | 41 8.8 | 40 9.2 | | 47 7.7 | 46 8.0 | 40 9.1 | 45 8.2 | 40 9.2 |
| | | 74 4.9 | 68 5.4 | 69 5.3 | Revenues/Receivables | 61 6.0 | 62 5.9 | 63 5.8 | 62 5.9 | 69 5.3 |
| | | 91 4.0 | 87 4.2 | 89 4.1 | | 81 4.5 | 74 4.9 | 85 4.3 | 85 4.3 | 89 4.1 |
| | | 20 18.1 | 26 14.0 | 23 15.8 | | 21 17.2 | 19 18.8 | 24 15.3 | 20 18.6 | 23 15.8 |
| | | 35 10.5 | 41 9.0 | 39 9.3 | Cost of Revenues/Payables | 39 9.4 | 29 12.5 | 34 10.7 | 37 9.9 | 39 9.3 |
| | | 56 6.5 | 55 6.6 | 56 6.5 | | 57 6.4 | 54 6.7 | 55 6.6 | 51 7.1 | 56 6.5 |
| | | 4.2 | 6.2 | 5.6 | | 6.3 | 4.4 | 4.4 | 5.2 | 5.6 |
| | | 8.0 | 9.3 | 8.6 | Revenues/Working Capital | 13.3 | 7.0 | 7.0 | 8.4 | 8.6 |
| | | 18.7 | 37.9 | 27.6 | | 34.6 | 10.4 | 12.8 | 16.5 | 27.6 |
| | | 38.1 | 65.5 | 35.0 | | 27.0 | 44.4 | 51.9 | 28.4 | 35.0 |
| | | (26) 15.8 | (38) 13.1 | (71) 12.2 | EBIT/Interest | (41) 6.7 | (53) 18.0 | (61) 18.2 | (68) 16.1 | (71) 12.2 |
| | | 5.8 | 3.9 | 4.1 | | 2.1 | 5.2 | 5.6 | 4.6 | 4.1 |
| | | | 4.1 | 12.1 | Net Profit + Depr., Dep., | | | 10.0 | | 12.1 |
| | | | (10) 1.1 | (16) 1.4 | Amort./Cur. Mat. L/T/D | | | (10) 4.0 | | (16) 1.4 |
| | | | .4 | .7 | | | | 2.0 | | .7 |
| | | .3 | .5 | .4 | | .3 | .4 | .3 | .3 | .4 |
| | | .7 | 1.0 | .9 | Fixed/Worth | .8 | .7 | .8 | .7 | .9 |
| | | 1.1 | 1.3 | 1.3 | | 1.6 | 1.1 | 1.1 | 1.1 | 1.3 |
| | | .6 | 1.1 | 1.0 | | 1.0 | .7 | .7 | .7 | 1.0 |
| | | 1.3 | 1.6 | 1.5 | Debt/Worth | 1.7 | 1.5 | 1.2 | 1.1 | 1.5 |
| | | 2.5 | 2.3 | 2.5 | | 3.2 | 2.5 | 2.6 | 2.1 | 2.5 |
| | | 61.8 | 34.6 | 42.6 | | 54.2 | 69.5 | 49.8 | 38.5 | 42.6 |
| | | (29) 31.2 | 18.7 (76) | 25.0 | % Profit Before Taxes/ Tangible Net Worth | (41) 25.5 | (56) 33.3 | (65) 26.1 | 18.7 (76) | 25.0 |
| | | 12.7 | 9.6 | 11.0 | | 7.0 | 13.4 | 13.0 | 7.3 | 11.0 |
| | | 23.4 | 16.8 | 19.5 | | 13.7 | 25.8 | 18.7 | 15.3 | 19.5 |
| | | 13.5 | 6.6 | 8.3 | % Profit Before Taxes/ Total Assets | 9.0 | 12.6 | 12.4 | 8.4 | 8.3 |
| | | 6.1 | 3.3 | 3.9 | | 3.0 | 4.9 | 4.2 | 3.9 | 3.9 |
| | | .5 | .0 | .2 | | 1.0 | 1.6 | .8 | .8 | .2 |
| | | (29) 2.8 | (26) .2 | (61) 1.5 | % Depr., Dep., Amort./ Revenues | (33) 2.8 | (46) 2.7 | (52) 2.8 | (67) 2.7 | (61) 1.5 |
| | | 4.1 | 1.2 | 3.6 | | 6.7 | 4.7 | 6.9 | 5.2 | 3.6 |
| | | | | .9 | % Officers', Directors' Owners' Comp/Revenues | | .6 | 1.2 | .8 | .9 |
| | | | (13) 2.1 | | | (15) 1.3 | (14) 1.8 | (21) 1.3 | (13) 2.1 | |
| | | | | 2.8 | | | 2.7 | 2.4 | | 2.8 |
| 913M | 24215M | 814429M | 17211170M | 18050727M | Contract Revenues ($) | 21223864M | 3297645M | 14891019M | 7829350M | 18050727M |
| 332M | 14780M | 564752M | 14921265M | 15501129M | Total Assets ($) | 20404846M | 2335729M | 8652985M | 4855115M | 15501129M |

© RMA 2024  M = $ thousand  MM = $ million
See Pages viii through xx for Explanation of Ratios and Data

# CONSTRUCTION-% OF COMPLETION—Poured Concrete Foundation and Structure Contractors  NAICS 238110

**Current Data Sorted by Revenue** | **Comparative Historical Data**

| | | | | | Type of Statement | | | | | |
|---|---|---|---|---|---|---|---|---|---|---|
| | | 2 | | 2 | Unqualified | 1 | | | 2 | 2 |
| | 2 | 9 | 3 | 14 | Reviewed | 9 | 9 | 7 | 18 | 14 |
| | | 2 | | 2 | Compiled | 4 | 2 | 3 | 5 | 2 |
| | 4 | 1 | | 5 | Tax Returns | 2 | 3 | 8 | 8 | 5 |
| | | 9 | 13 | 22 | Other | 17 | 15 | 14 | 17 | 22 |
| | 6 (4/1-9/30/23) | | 39 (10/1/23-3/31/24) | | | 4/1/19- 3/31/20 | 4/1/20- 3/31/21 | 4/1/21- 3/31/22 | 4/1/22- 3/31/23 | 4/1/23- 3/31/24 |
| 0-1MM | 1-10MM | 10-50MM | 50 & OVER | ALL | NUMBER OF STATEMENTS | ALL 33 | ALL 29 | ALL 32 | ALL 50 | ALL 45 |
| | 6 | 23 | 16 | 45 | | | | | | |
| % | % | % | % | % | ASSETS | % | % | % | % | % |
| | | 16.1 | 18.9 | 19.3 | Cash & Equivalents | 10.9 | 17.1 | 18.2 | 20.4 | 19.3 |
| D | | 34.2 | 46.1 | 35.0 | A/R - Progress Billings | 45.9 | 43.2 | 37.8 | 36.6 | 35.0 |
| A | | 4.9 | 4.1 | 4.0 | A/R - Current Retention | 3.0 | 3.6 | 2.8 | 2.7 | 4.0 |
| T | | .3 | 2.9 | 1.2 | Inventory | .7 | .5 | 1.8 | 1.3 | 1.2 |
| A | | 6.0 | 8.5 | 6.2 | Cost & Est. Earnings In Excess Billings | 5.5 | 2.7 | 5.7 | 7.1 | 6.2 |
| N | | 4.7 | 3.5 | 3.8 | All Other Current | 2.5 | 3.5 | 3.2 | 6.1 | 3.8 |
| O | | 66.2 | 84.0 | 69.4 | Total Current | 68.4 | 70.6 | 69.5 | 74.3 | 69.4 |
| T | | 23.7 | 11.4 | 22.6 | Fixed Assets (net) | 23.8 | 24.4 | 22.8 | 18.8 | 22.6 |
| | | .0 | .2 | .1 | Joint Ventures & Investments | .1 | .1 | .3 | .0 | .1 |
| A | | 3.5 | .3 | 1.9 | Intangibles (net) | 2.5 | .5 | 5.4 | 1.4 | 1.9 |
| V | | 6.6 | 4.1 | 6.0 | All Other Non-Current | 4.9 | 4.3 | 2.1 | 5.4 | 6.0 |
| A | | 100.0 | 100.0 | 100.0 | Total | 100.0 | 100.0 | 100.0 | 100.0 | 100.0 |
| I | | | | | LIABILITIES | | | | | |
| L | | 2.5 | 2.5 | 7.9 | Notes Payable-Short Term | 9.3 | 4.3 | 4.6 | 2.8 | 7.9 |
| A | | 17.2 | 18.8 | 15.9 | A/P - Trade | 21.4 | 13.0 | 14.9 | 15.8 | 15.9 |
| B | | .1 | 1.4 | .6 | A/P - Retention | .4 | .2 | .4 | .2 | .6 |
| L | | 9.4 | 10.2 | 8.7 | Billings in Excess of Costs & Est. Earnings | 4.7 | 9.0 | 5.9 | 5.1 | 8.7 |
| E | | .3 | .2 | .2 | Income Taxes Payable | .0 | .4 | .1 | .1 | .2 |
| | | 4.5 | .9 | 3.2 | Cur. Mat.-L/T/D | 3.3 | 3.8 | 1.9 | 4.7 | 3.2 |
| | | 7.8 | 6.8 | 6.6 | All Other Current | 9.4 | 11.6 | 7.8 | 11.2 | 6.6 |
| | | 41.8 | 40.8 | 43.1 | Total Current | 48.4 | 42.2 | 35.7 | 39.9 | 43.1 |
| | | 10.4 | 6.2 | 10.2 | Long-Term Debt | 10.3 | 11.8 | 20.5 | 10.5 | 10.2 |
| | | .5 | .0 | .3 | Deferred Taxes | .1 | .3 | .4 | .5 | .3 |
| | | 3.0 | 3.1 | 2.6 | All Other Non-Current | 3.1 | .5 | 1.5 | 3.3 | 2.6 |
| | | 44.4 | 49.9 | 43.8 | Net Worth | 37.7 | 45.2 | 42.1 | 45.7 | 43.8 |
| | | 100.0 | 100.0 | 100.0 | Total Liabilities & Net Worth | 100.0 | 100.0 | 100.0 | 100.0 | 100.0 |
| | | | | | INCOME DATA | | | | | |
| | | 100.0 | 100.0 | 100.0 | Contract Revenues | 100.0 | 100.0 | 100.0 | 100.0 | 100.0 |
| | | 20.6 | 17.1 | 21.2 | Gross Profit | 20.0 | 27.1 | 23.1 | 21.0 | 21.2 |
| | | 13.5 | 8.2 | 13.4 | Operating Expenses | 14.3 | 18.2 | 14.8 | 16.6 | 13.4 |
| | | 7.1 | 9.0 | 7.8 | Operating Profit | 5.7 | 8.9 | 8.3 | 4.4 | 7.8 |
| | | -.3 | -.3 | -.1 | All Other Expenses (net) | -.3 | -1.6 | -1.3 | -1.3 | -.1 |
| | | 7.4 | 9.3 | 7.9 | Profit Before Taxes | 6.0 | 10.5 | 9.6 | 5.7 | 7.9 |
| | | | | | RATIOS | | | | | |
| | | 2.4 | 3.4 | 3.0 | | 2.5 | 2.8 | 2.7 | 3.2 | 3.0 |
| | | 1.6 | 2.3 | 1.6 | Current | 1.5 | 1.9 | 2.1 | 2.1 | 1.6 |
| | | 1.3 | 1.4 | 1.3 | | 1.2 | 1.4 | 1.5 | 1.5 | 1.3 |
| | | 6.2 | 3.7 | 4.5 | | 3.7 | 6.4 | 3.5 | 4.7 | 4.5 |
| | (22) | 3.1 | 3.1 | (40) 3.1 | Receivables/Payables | (32) 2.9 | (25) 4.2 | (28) 2.4 | (46) 2.6 | (40) 3.1 |
| | | 1.9 | 2.3 | 2.0 | | 2.1 | 2.5 | 2.0 | 1.7 | 2.0 |
| | 46 | 7.9 | 65 5.6 | 47 7.8 | | 44 8.3 | 49 7.4 | 27 13.7 | 37 9.8 | 47 7.8 |
| | 65 | 5.6 | 79 4.6 | 69 5.3 | Revenues/Receivables | 78 4.7 | 79 4.6 | 57 6.4 | 66 5.5 | 69 5.3 |
| | 78 | 4.7 | 91 4.0 | 81 4.5 | | 107 3.4 | 107 3.4 | 81 4.5 | 101 3.6 | 81 4.5 |
| | 15 | 25.1 | 23 15.7 | 16 23.0 | | 15 24.6 | 10 37.5 | 13 29.1 | 11 32.1 | 16 23.0 |
| | 21 | 17.0 | 31 11.8 | 26 14.2 | Cost of Revenues/Payables | 40 9.1 | 26 14.1 | 24 15.1 | 23 15.6 | 26 14.2 |
| | 39 | 9.3 | 39 9.3 | 39 9.4 | | 52 7.0 | 43 8.5 | 41 8.9 | 53 6.9 | 39 9.4 |
| | | 6.6 | 3.0 | 5.2 | | 6.1 | 4.7 | 5.6 | 3.8 | 5.2 |
| | | 9.7 | 5.5 | 9.3 | Revenues/Working Capital | 9.2 | 6.9 | 8.0 | 7.3 | 9.3 |
| | | 17.9 | 9.2 | 19.4 | | 36.9 | 11.5 | 14.6 | 10.7 | 19.4 |
| | | 90.1 | 845.9 | 103.3 | | 26.0 | 202.3 | 100.9 | 73.3 | 103.3 |
| | (22) | 25.2 | (15) 39.3 | (43) 28.8 | EBIT/Interest | (28) 13.3 | (21) 48.8 | (28) 41.3 | (44) 22.5 | (43) 28.8 |
| | | 5.4 | 4.6 | 4.6 | | 1.4 | 9.8 | 18.3 | 4.1 | 4.6 |
| | | | | | Net Profit + Depr., Dep., Amort./Cur. Mat. L/T/D | | | | (11) 9.5 4.8 .7 | |
| | | .1 | .1 | .2 | | .2 | .1 | .2 | .2 | .2 |
| | | .4 | .3 | .3 | Fixed/Worth | .5 | .4 | .4 | .3 | .3 |
| | | 1.0 | .4 | .8 | | 1.0 | .7 | .9 | .8 | .8 |
| | | .9 | .4 | .7 | | .7 | .6 | .8 | .5 | .7 |
| | | 1.3 | 1.1 | 1.1 | Debt/Worth | 1.7 | 1.1 | 1.1 | 1.1 | 1.1 |
| | | 2.2 | 1.9 | 2.1 | | 4.4 | 3.0 | 3.1 | 2.2 | 2.1 |
| | | 88.9 | 47.9 | 88.3 | | 53.9 | 65.8 | 76.5 | 58.6 | 88.3 |
| | (22) | 34.7 | 29.5 | (43) 30.3 | % Profit Before Taxes/ Tangible Net Worth | (29) 31.8 | (27) 47.8 | (27) 45.8 | (46) 25.1 | (43) 30.3 |
| | | 13.8 | 23.1 | 19.2 | | 7.1 | 33.3 | 28.7 | 12.7 | 19.2 |
| | | 29.0 | 21.2 | 30.4 | | 25.1 | 41.7 | 33.4 | 26.8 | 30.4 |
| | | 16.3 | 15.2 | 16.3 | % Profit Before Taxes/ Total Assets | 13.7 | 23.2 | 22.6 | 13.6 | 16.3 |
| | | 6.4 | 11.4 | 8.5 | | 2.5 | 11.3 | 15.1 | 5.0 | 8.5 |
| | | .4 | .5 | .5 | | .6 | .7 | .8 | .6 | .5 |
| | (20) | 1.4 | (15) .7 | (40) 1.1 | % Depr., Dep., Amort./ Revenues | (30) 1.6 | (24) 1.6 | (22) 1.5 | (43) 1.4 | (40) 1.1 |
| | | 4.5 | 1.3 | 3.2 | | 2.7 | 3.8 | 3.0 | 3.2 | 3.2 |
| | | | | .5 | | 1.0 | .7 | .7 | .9 | .5 |
| | | | (18) | 1.2 | % Officers', Directors' Owners' Comp/Revenues | (11) 1.5 | (11) 1.2 | (12) 2.2 | (21) 2.1 | (18) 1.2 |
| | | | | 2.8 | | 3.9 | 1.4 | 3.0 | 3.2 | 2.8 |
| | 20257M | 584914M | 26121352M | 26726523M | Contract Revenues ($) | 990132M | 9284100M | 47792184M | 2192153M | 26726523M |
| | 10211M | 276900M | 16063296M | 16350407M | Total Assets ($) | 420834M | 4258156M | 18487635M | 891747M | 16350407M |

© RMA 2024  M = $ thousand  MM = $ million
See Pages viii through xx for Explanation of Ratios and Data

# CONSTRUCTION-% OF COMPLETION—Structural Steel and Precast Concrete Contractors  NAICS 238120

## Current Data Sorted by Revenue | Comparative Historical Data

| | | | | | | Type of Statement | | | | | |
|---|---|---|---|---|---|---|---|---|---|---|---|
| | | 1 | | | | Unqualified | | 2 | | 2 | |
| | | | 6 | 3 | 10 | Reviewed | 5 | 11 | 5 | 12 | 10 |
| | | 1 | | | 1 | Compiled | 2 | 4 | 1 | 3 | 1 |
| | | | | 1 | 1 | Tax Returns | 1 | | | 3 | 1 |
| | 2 | | 4 | 2 | 8 | Other | 5 | 5 | 5 | 7 | 8 |
| | 2 (4/1-9/30/23) | | 18 (10/1/23-3/31/24) | | | | 4/1/19-3/31/20 | 4/1/20-3/31/21 | 4/1/21-3/31/22 | 4/1/22-3/31/23 | 4/1/23-3/31/24 |
| 0-1MM | 1-10MM | 10-50MM | | 50 & OVER | ALL | | ALL | ALL | ALL | ALL | ALL |
| | 3 | 11 | | 6 | 20 | NUMBER OF STATEMENTS | 13 | 22 | 11 | 27 | 20 |
| % | % | % | | % | % | ASSETS | % | % | % | % | % |
| | | 20.3 | | | 17.0 | Cash & Equivalents | 18.4 | 21.7 | 20.9 | 12.8 | 17.0 |
| | | 42.6 | | | 49.7 | A/R - Progress Billings | 41.0 | 35.2 | 46.8 | 51.2 | 49.7 |
| | | 6.8 | | | 3.7 | A/R - Current Retention | 4.8 | 3.2 | 4.9 | 4.4 | 3.7 |
| | | 2.2 | | | 1.4 | Inventory | 1.6 | 1.6 | 4.7 | 4.2 | 1.4 |
| | | 9.8 | | | 7.0 | Cost & Est. Earnings In Excess Billings | 5.1 | 1.4 | 4.8 | 3.7 | 7.0 |
| | | 2.4 | | | 3.2 | All Other Current | 2.8 | 2.9 | 1.4 | 4.4 | 3.2 |
| | | 84.0 | | | 82.0 | Total Current | 73.7 | 66.0 | 83.4 | 80.7 | 82.0 |
| | | 10.2 | | | 11.1 | Fixed Assets (net) | 20.0 | 25.2 | 11.0 | 11.4 | 11.1 |
| | | .0 | | | .1 | Joint Ventures & Investments | .0 | .7 | .2 | .2 | .1 |
| | | .0 | | | 1.7 | Intangibles (net) | .2 | 1.6 | .0 | 1.9 | 1.7 |
| | | 5.8 | | | 5.1 | All Other Non-Current | 6.1 | 6.5 | 4.4 | 5.9 | 5.1 |
| | | 100.0 | | | 100.0 | Total | 100.0 | 100.0 | 100.0 | 100.0 | 100.0 |
| | | | | | | LIABILITIES | | | | | |
| | | 3.3 | | | 4.2 | Notes Payable-Short Term | 5.1 | 4.8 | .9 | 2.8 | 4.2 |
| | | 17.5 | | | 18.7 | A/P - Trade | 16.1 | 11.5 | 17.6 | 15.6 | 18.7 |
| | | 1.1 | | | .6 | A/P - Retention | .1 | .3 | .0 | .3 | .6 |
| | | 8.5 | | | 9.7 | Billings in Excess of Costs & Est. Earnings | 9.0 | 7.7 | 5.0 | 13.2 | 9.7 |
| | | .0 | | | .1 | Income Taxes Payable | .1 | .0 | .0 | .2 | .1 |
| | | 1.5 | | | 1.3 | Cur. Mat.-L/T/D | 2.4 | 3.6 | .9 | 1.3 | 1.3 |
| | | 7.7 | | | 7.4 | All Other Current | 5.3 | 9.1 | 11.4 | 9.2 | 7.4 |
| | | 39.5 | | | 42.0 | Total Current | 38.2 | 37.0 | 35.8 | 42.7 | 42.0 |
| | | 5.1 | | | 6.2 | Long-Term Debt | 6.7 | 15.0 | 4.6 | 5.9 | 6.2 |
| | | .0 | | | .1 | Deferred Taxes | .0 | .5 | .0 | .3 | .1 |
| | | 4.6 | | | 4.8 | All Other Non-Current | .8 | 2.7 | 3.6 | 3.4 | 4.8 |
| | | 50.8 | | | 47.0 | Net Worth | 54.4 | 44.8 | 56.1 | 47.6 | 47.0 |
| | | 100.0 | | | 100.0 | Total Liabilities & Net Worth | 100.0 | 100.0 | 100.0 | 100.0 | 100.0 |
| | | | | | | INCOME DATA | | | | | |
| | | 100.0 | | | 100.0 | Contract Revenues | 100.0 | 100.0 | 100.0 | 100.0 | 100.0 |
| | | 18.9 | | | 19.5 | Gross Profit | 19.2 | 25.2 | 16.3 | 18.0 | 19.5 |
| | | 11.0 | | | 14.4 | Operating Expenses | 12.5 | 17.8 | 8.0 | 13.6 | 14.4 |
| | | 7.9 | | | 5.2 | Operating Profit | 6.7 | 7.4 | 8.4 | 4.4 | 5.2 |
| | | .1 | | | -.4 | All Other Expenses (net) | -.3 | -1.3 | -3.2 | .5 | -.4 |
| | | 7.8 | | | 5.5 | Profit Before Taxes | 7.0 | 8.7 | 11.6 | 3.9 | 5.5 |
| | | | | | | RATIOS | | | | | |
| | | 2.5 | | | 2.6 | | 3.4 | 3.2 | 3.3 | 2.5 | 2.6 |
| | | 2.4 | | | 2.0 | Current | 1.8 | 1.7 | 2.3 | 2.0 | 2.0 |
| | | 1.8 | | | 1.7 | | 1.4 | 1.2 | 1.6 | 1.5 | 1.7 |
| | | 4.0 | | | 4.5 | | 5.7 | 20.6 | 4.8 | 5.4 | 4.5 |
| | | 2.8 | | | 3.0 | Receivables/Payables | 3.3 | (21) 4.2 | 3.0 | 3.3 | 3.0 |
| | | 2.2 | | | 2.2 | | 2.2 | 2.5 | 1.9 | 2.4 | 2.2 |
| | | 60  6.1 | | 62 | 5.9 | | 48  7.6 | 70  5.2 | 45  8.2 | 69  5.3 | 62  5.9 |
| | | 68  5.4 | | 81 | 4.5 | Revenues/Receivables | 78  4.7 | 87  4.2 | 83  4.4 | 89  4.1 | 81  4.5 |
| | | 114  3.2 | | 114 | 3.2 | | 122  3.0 | 101  3.6 | 111  3.3 | 107  3.4 | 114  3.2 |
| | | 26  13.8 | | 21 | 17.4 | | 23  15.7 | 4  91.7 | 19  19.0 | 17  22.1 | 21  17.4 |
| | | 35  10.3 | | 30 | 12.2 | Cost of Revenues/Payables | 29  12.5 | 24  15.3 | 36  10.1 | 29  12.8 | 30  12.2 |
| | | 59  6.2 | | 57 | 6.4 | | 52  7.0 | 51  7.1 | 43  8.5 | 41  9.0 | 57  6.4 |
| | | 4.0 | | | 4.2 | | 3.7 | 3.1 | 3.4 | 5.0 | 4.2 |
| | | 5.4 | | | 5.9 | Revenues/Working Capital | 5.1 | 5.7 | 4.9 | 6.0 | 5.9 |
| | | 6.2 | | | 6.7 | | 10.4 | 42.3 | 8.5 | 8.5 | 6.7 |
| | | 42.1 | | | 37.6 | | 58.3 | 68.9 | | 137.6 | 37.6 |
| | (10) | 20.4 | | (19) | 19.3 | EBIT/Interest | (11) 20.8 | (20) 14.0 | | (22) 19.2 | (19) 19.3 |
| | | 9.7 | | | 4.3 | | 2.5 | 6.2 | | 8.2 | 4.3 |
| | | | | | | Net Profit + Depr., Dep., Amort./Cur. Mat. L/T/D | | | | | |
| | | .0 | | | .1 | | .1 | .1 | .0 | .1 | .1 |
| | | .2 | | | .2 | Fixed/Worth | .2 | .5 | .1 | .2 | .2 |
| | | .3 | | | .4 | | .7 | 1.0 | .4 | .4 | .4 |
| | | .6 | | | .6 | | .4 | .7 | .4 | .7 | .6 |
| | | .9 | | | 1.1 | Debt/Worth | .8 | 1.2 | .6 | 1.0 | 1.1 |
| | | 1.5 | | | 1.8 | | 1.7 | 2.7 | 1.3 | 1.8 | 1.8 |
| | | 62.8 | | | 60.5 | | 44.6 | 50.4 | 72.2 | 49.4 | 60.5 |
| | | 29.4 | | (18) | 25.9 | % Profit Before Taxes/ Tangible Net Worth | 32.3 | 23.0 | 39.1 | 17.0 (18) | 25.9 |
| | | 10.2 | | | 1.7 | | 14.3 | 9.4 | 26.7 | 6.7 | 1.7 |
| | | 34.7 | | | 32.4 | | 25.8 | 23.1 | 40.5 | 20.2 | 32.4 |
| | | 13.6 | | | 9.6 | % Profit Before Taxes/ Total Assets | 19.6 | 10.6 | 22.3 | 7.0 | 9.6 |
| | | 6.4 | | | 1.4 | | 3.4 | 2.6 | 15.6 | 2.9 | 1.4 |
| | | | | | .3 | | 1.2 | .9 | | .6 | .3 |
| | | | | (15) | .8 | % Depr., Dep., Amort./ Revenues | (11) 1.3 | (18) 2.2 | | (23) 1.1 | (15) .8 |
| | | | | | 1.9 | | 3.7 | 4.7 | | 1.5 | 1.9 |
| | | | | | | % Officers', Directors' Owners' Comp/Revenues | | | | | |
| | 24510M | 254064M | 424215M | | 702789M | Contract Revenues ($) | 341005M | 378810M | 514017M | 990393M | 702789M |
| | 13962M | 121724M | 168318M | | 304004M | Total Assets ($) | 196245M | 215097M | 214617M | 427371M | 304004M |

© RMA 2024    M = $ thousand    MM = $ million
See Pages viii through xx for Explanation of Ratios and Data

## CONSTRUCTION-% OF COMPLETION—Glass and Glazing Contractors  NAICS 238150

### Current Data Sorted by Revenue / Comparative Historical Data

| | | | | | Type of Statement | | | | | |
|---|---|---|---|---|---|---|---|---|---|---|
| | 1 | 7 | 2 | 10 | Unqualified | 5 | 6 | 4 | 14 | 10 |
| | 1 | 1 | 1 | 3 | Reviewed | | | | | 3 |
| | 1 | | | 1 | Compiled | 1 | | 1 | | 1 |
| | 1 | 5 | 5 | 11 | Tax Returns | | | | 1 | |
| | 2 (4/1-9/30/23) | 23 (10/1/23-3/31/24) | | | Other | 2 | 5 | 6 | 8 | 11 |
| 0-1MM | 1-10MM | 10-50MM | 50 & OVER | ALL | | 4/1/19-3/31/20 ALL | 4/1/20-3/31/21 ALL | 4/1/21-3/31/22 ALL | 4/1/22-3/31/23 ALL | 4/1/23-3/31/24 ALL |
| | 4 | 13 | 8 | 25 | NUMBER OF STATEMENTS | 8 | 11 | 11 | 23 | 25 |
| % | % | % | % | % | ASSETS | % | % | % | % | % |
| | | 17.5 | | 19.2 | Cash & Equivalents | 9.5 | 11.6 | 9.3 | 19.2 | |
| | | 39.1 | | 36.4 | A/R - Progress Billings | 42.2 | 33.6 | 43.3 | 36.4 | |
| D | | 8.4 | | 6.5 | A/R - Current Retention | 10.1 | 13.2 | 6.3 | 6.5 | |
| A | | 3.3 | | 3.1 | Inventory | 2.4 | 7.8 | 4.0 | 3.1 | |
| T | | 4.1 | | 5.0 | Cost & Est. Earnings In Excess Billings | 6.8 | 5.9 | 5.5 | 5.0 | |
| A | | 2.4 | | 1.4 | All Other Current | 6.4 | 1.4 | 5.8 | 1.4 | |
| | | 74.8 | | 71.7 | Total Current | 77.5 | 73.4 | 74.4 | 71.7 | |
| N | | 9.1 | | 9.8 | Fixed Assets (net) | 14.4 | 10.5 | 8.6 | 9.8 | |
| O | | .1 | | .1 | Joint Ventures & Investments | .1 | .1 | .0 | .1 | |
| T | | 4.4 | | 7.0 | Intangibles (net) | 6.7 | 5.6 | 3.1 | 7.0 | |
| | | 11.5 | | 11.5 | All Other Non-Current | 1.3 | 10.4 | 14.2 | 11.5 | |
| A | | 100.0 | | 100.0 | Total | 100.0 | 100.0 | 100.0 | 100.0 | |
| V | | | | | LIABILITIES | | | | | |
| A | | 2.2 | | 1.8 | Notes Payable-Short Term | 12.5 | 4.6 | 7.7 | 1.8 | |
| I | | 10.8 | | 10.5 | A/P - Trade | 12.3 | 15.1 | 14.3 | 10.5 | |
| L | | .2 | | .5 | A/P - Retention | .0 | .0 | .0 | .5 | |
| A | | 8.3 | | 7.5 | Billings in Excess of Costs & Est. Earnings | 8.8 | 14.9 | 10.8 | 7.5 | |
| B | | .3 | | .2 | Income Taxes Payable | .3 | .1 | .2 | .2 | |
| L | | 1.2 | | 1.7 | Cur. Mat.-L/T/D | 2.3 | 2.7 | 4.4 | 1.7 | |
| E | | 6.1 | | 7.4 | All Other Current | 9.6 | 5.8 | 9.3 | 7.4 | |
| | | 29.1 | | 29.6 | Total Current | 45.9 | 43.3 | 46.9 | 29.6 | |
| | | 2.9 | | 7.1 | Long-Term Debt | 17.0 | 11.7 | 7.0 | 7.1 | |
| | | .2 | | .2 | Deferred Taxes | .9 | .3 | .1 | .2 | |
| | | 6.6 | | 16.4 | All Other Non-Current | 3.3 | 7.7 | 7.9 | 16.4 | |
| | | 61.2 | | 46.8 | Net Worth | 32.9 | 37.1 | 38.4 | 46.8 | |
| | | 100.0 | | 100.0 | Total Liabilities & Net Worth | 100.0 | 100.0 | 100.0 | 100.0 | |
| | | | | | INCOME DATA | | | | | |
| | | 100.0 | | 100.0 | Contract Revenues | 100.0 | 100.0 | 100.0 | 100.0 | |
| | | 27.8 | | 29.1 | Gross Profit | 21.2 | 26.0 | 22.7 | 29.1 | |
| | | 21.3 | | 21.7 | Operating Expenses | 21.0 | 23.1 | 21.7 | 21.7 | |
| | | 6.5 | | 7.4 | Operating Profit | .2 | 3.0 | 1.0 | 7.4 | |
| | | -.9 | | .0 | All Other Expenses (net) | -2.1 | -4.1 | -1.7 | .0 | |
| | | 7.4 | | 7.3 | Profit Before Taxes | 2.3 | 7.0 | 2.7 | 7.3 | |
| | | | | | RATIOS | | | | | |
| | | 7.8 | | 4.3 | | 2.5 | 2.6 | 2.7 | 4.3 | |
| | | 1.9 | | 2.0 | Current | 1.8 | 2.1 | 1.9 | 2.0 | |
| | | 1.6 | | 1.7 | | 1.2 | 1.3 | 1.2 | 1.7 | |
| | | 13.8 | | 10.4 | | 24.3 | 7.6 | 6.4 | 10.4 | |
| | | 6.2 | | (24) 5.0 | Receivables/Payables | 7.1 | 4.1 | (22) 4.3 | (24) 5.0 | |
| | | 2.9 | | 2.6 | | 1.6 | 2.3 | 2.7 | 2.6 | |
| | 65 | 5.6 | 64 | 5.7 | | 70 5.2 | 73 5.0 | 76 4.8 | 64 5.7 | |
| | 85 | 4.3 | 81 | 4.5 | Revenues/Receivables | 81 4.5 | 87 4.2 | 96 3.8 | 81 4.5 | |
| | 122 | 2.9 | 107 | 3.4 | | 91 4.0 | 99 3.7 | 114 3.2 | 107 3.4 | |
| | 10 | 38.0 | 13 | 27.6 | | 5 79.5 | 21 17.4 | 17 22.0 | 13 27.6 | |
| | 17 | 21.0 | 20 | 18.3 | Cost of Revenues/Payables | 12 30.5 | 27 13.3 | 25 14.8 | 20 18.3 | |
| | 43 | 8.4 | 38 | 9.6 | | 43 8.5 | 49 7.4 | 41 8.9 | 38 9.6 | |
| | | 2.6 | | 2.8 | | 5.1 | 3.7 | 3.4 | 2.8 | |
| | | 4.0 | | 5.8 | Revenues/Working Capital | 9.2 | 6.7 | 6.3 | 5.8 | |
| | | 9.6 | | 9.0 | | 17.9 | 18.2 | 21.4 | 9.0 | |
| | | 255.4 | | 59.8 | | 30.2 | 44.7 | 24.9 | 59.8 | |
| | | (10) 49.4 | | (19) 24.7 | EBIT/Interest | 9.6 | (10) 12.2 | (19) 5.9 | (19) 24.7 | |
| | | 17.3 | | 3.5 | | 2.1 | -1.2 | -.1 | 3.5 | |
| | | | | | Net Profit + Depr., Dep., Amort./Cur. Mat. L/T/D | | | | | |
| | | .0 | | .1 | | .2 | .1 | .1 | .1 | |
| | | .1 | | .1 | Fixed/Worth | .3 | .2 | .2 | .1 | |
| | | .2 | | 1.4 | | 1.3 | 1.6 | 1.0 | 1.4 | |
| | | .1 | | .3 | | .8 | .6 | .8 | .3 | |
| | | .9 | | 1.0 | Debt/Worth | 2.1 | 1.0 | 1.7 | 1.0 | |
| | | 2.1 | | 6.7 | | 9.2 | 12.9 | 6.1 | 6.7 | |
| | | 52.1 | | 53.1 | | | 39.5 | | 53.1 | |
| | | 28.8 | | (21) 30.4 | % Profit Before Taxes/ Tangible Net Worth | | (21) 16.8 | (21) 30.4 | | |
| | | 11.5 | | 13.6 | | | 7.9 | 13.6 | | |
| | | 18.5 | | 21.3 | | 13.4 | 24.3 | 13.0 | 21.3 | |
| | | 13.2 | | 13.2 | % Profit Before Taxes/ Total Assets | 7.0 | 15.7 | 8.3 | 13.2 | |
| | | 7.8 | | 6.0 | | 2.1 | -2.0 | 1.9 | 6.0 | |
| | | | | .5 | | .4 | .3 | .2 | .5 | |
| | | | (16) | .8 | % Depr., Dep., Amort./ Revenues | (10) 1.2 | (10) .8 | (18) .9 | (16) .8 | |
| | | | | 1.5 | | 2.3 | 1.8 | 1.5 | 1.5 | |
| | | | | | % Officers', Directors' Owners' Comp/Revenues | | | | | |
| | 20673M | 268164M | 2820415M | 28498252M | Contract Revenues ($) | 448434M | 314552M | 587148M | 470139M | 28498252M |
| | 17674M | 157304M | 18982265M | 19157243M | Total Assets ($) | 211689M | 144097M | 269242M | 274050M | 19157243M |

M = $ thousand     MM = $ million
See Pages viii through xx for Explanation of Ratios and Data

© RMA 2024

# CONSTRUCTION-% OF COMPLETION—Roofing Contractors  NAICS 238160

## Current Data Sorted by Revenue | Comparative Historical Data

| | | | | | | Type of Statement | | | | | |
|---|---|---|---|---|---|---|---|---|---|---|---|
| | | | 3 | 3 | | Unqualified | 1 | | 1 | 1 | 3 |
| | 2 | 7 | 3 | 12 | | Reviewed | 14 | 15 | 16 | 17 | 12 |
| | 1 | 3 | | 4 | | Compiled | 2 | 1 | 3 | 2 | 4 |
| | 3 | | | 3 | | Tax Returns | 2 | 2 | 8 | 7 | 3 |
| 1 | 4 | 5 | 5 | 15 | | Other | 9 | 16 | 18 | 17 | 15 |
| | 4 (4/1-9/30/23) | 33 (10/1/23-3/31/24) | | | | | 4/1/19- 3/31/20 | 4/1/20- 3/31/21 | 4/1/21- 3/31/22 | 4/1/22- 3/31/23 | 4/1/23- 3/31/24 |
| 0-1MM | 1-10MM | 10-50MM | 50 & OVER | ALL | | | ALL | ALL | ALL | ALL | ALL |
| 1 | 10 | 15 | 11 | 37 | | NUMBER OF STATEMENTS | 28 | 34 | 45 | 44 | 37 |
| % | % | % | % | % | | ASSETS | % | % | % | % | % |
| | 32.5 | 16.5 | 17.6 | 21.0 | | Cash & Equivalents | 15.1 | 23.1 | 22.0 | 17.7 | 21.0 |
| | 33.2 | 40.6 | 33.6 | 36.8 | | A/R - Progress Billings | 48.3 | 38.9 | 35.2 | 34.8 | 36.8 |
| | .3 | 4.3 | 3.3 | 2.8 | | A/R - Current Retention | 3.5 | 1.1 | 3.6 | 3.4 | 2.8 |
| | .9 | 2.7 | 3.5 | 2.4 | | Inventory | 4.2 | 3.1 | 5.0 | 6.1 | 2.4 |
| | .8 | 5.4 | 9.1 | 5.9 | | Cost & Est. Earnings In Excess Billings | 6.1 | 4.7 | 5.1 | 7.5 | 5.9 |
| | 3.7 | 5.7 | 1.0 | 3.6 | | All Other Current | 4.3 | 5.2 | 6.1 | 4.8 | 3.6 |
| | 71.4 | 75.3 | 68.0 | 72.5 | | Total Current | 81.6 | 76.1 | 77.0 | 74.3 | 72.5 |
| | 21.0 | 17.7 | 5.5 | 14.8 | | Fixed Assets (net) | 14.3 | 19.8 | 15.1 | 17.1 | 14.8 |
| | .0 | .6 | .0 | .2 | | Joint Ventures & Investments | .2 | .2 | .8 | 1.1 | .2 |
| | 2.5 | .4 | 21.1 | 7.1 | | Intangibles (net) | 1.2 | .7 | 2.9 | 1.4 | 7.1 |
| | 5.1 | 6.0 | 5.4 | 5.4 | | All Other Non-Current | 2.8 | 3.1 | 4.2 | 6.0 | 5.4 |
| | 100.0 | 100.0 | 100.0 | 100.0 | | Total | 100.0 | 100.0 | 100.0 | 100.0 | 100.0 |
| | | | | | | LIABILITIES | | | | | |
| | 6.0 | 1.1 | 3.1 | 3.0 | | Notes Payable-Short Term | 6.8 | 7.8 | 4.7 | 7.1 | 3.0 |
| | 8.7 | 10.2 | 9.4 | 9.3 | | A/P - Trade | 16.8 | 13.8 | 14.3 | 13.3 | 9.3 |
| | .0 | .0 | .0 | .0 | | A/P - Retention | | .2 | .1 | .0 | .0 |
| | 13.3 | 13.3 | 9.3 | 12.3 | | Billings in Excess of Costs & Est. Earnings | 8.4 | 6.8 | 6.0 | 8.8 | 12.3 |
| | .0 | .1 | .0 | .1 | | Income Taxes Payable | .6 | .2 | .3 | .1 | .1 |
| | .4 | .7 | .7 | .6 | | Cur. Mat.-L/T/D | 1.9 | 2.1 | .8 | .9 | .6 |
| | 4.7 | 5.9 | 10.8 | 6.9 | | All Other Current | 15.6 | 15.3 | 8.9 | 8.3 | 6.9 |
| | 33.2 | 31.4 | 33.4 | 32.2 | | Total Current | 50.3 | 46.2 | 35.2 | 38.4 | 32.2 |
| | 8.4 | 8.8 | 10.1 | 9.1 | | Long-Term Debt | 5.2 | 13.4 | 8.5 | 14.4 | 9.1 |
| | .1 | .5 | .0 | .2 | | Deferred Taxes | .5 | .3 | .1 | .3 | .2 |
| | 8.4 | 6.0 | 5.1 | 6.2 | | All Other Non-Current | .9 | 1.5 | 2.0 | 4.8 | 6.2 |
| | 49.9 | 53.2 | 51.4 | 52.2 | | Net Worth | 43.1 | 38.8 | 54.1 | 42.1 | 52.2 |
| | 100.0 | 100.0 | 100.0 | 100.0 | | Total Liabilties & Net Worth | 100.0 | 100.0 | 100.0 | 100.0 | 100.0 |
| | | | | | | INCOME DATA | | | | | |
| | 100.0 | 100.0 | 100.0 | 100.0 | | Contract Revenues | 100.0 | 100.0 | 100.0 | 100.0 | 100.0 |
| | 44.2 | 26.5 | 29.0 | 32.5 | | Gross Profit | 28.7 | 28.3 | 29.4 | 26.6 | 32.5 |
| | 33.1 | 14.7 | 19.2 | 21.3 | | Operating Expenses | 22.0 | 23.7 | 22.2 | 22.4 | 21.3 |
| | 11.1 | 11.8 | 9.8 | 11.2 | | Operating Profit | 6.7 | 4.7 | 7.2 | 4.2 | 11.2 |
| | -.1 | -.8 | 2.3 | .3 | | All Other Expenses (net) | .2 | -2.0 | -3.7 | .0 | .3 |
| | 11.2 | 12.6 | 7.5 | 10.8 | | Profit Before Taxes | 6.5 | 6.6 | 10.9 | 4.2 | 10.8 |
| | | | | | | RATIOS | | | | | |
| | 4.2 | 4.1 | 2.0 | 3.9 | | Current | 2.2 | 3.1 | 3.7 | 3.2 | 3.9 |
| | 2.1 | 2.7 | 1.9 | 2.0 | | | 1.6 | 1.9 | 2.3 | 2.0 | 2.0 |
| | 1.3 | 1.6 | 1.6 | 1.6 | | | 1.4 | 1.4 | 1.6 | 1.5 | 1.6 |
| | | 126.6 | 5.9 | 9.6 | | Receivables/Payables | 8.2 | 5.1 | 5.7 | 5.2 | 9.6 |
| | | (14) 6.2 | 4.5 | (35) 4.7 | | | 3.4 (32) | 3.2 (43) | 2.7 (40) | 3.1 (35) | 4.7 |
| | | 1.9 | 2.6 | 2.5 | | | 2.1 | 1.9 | 1.8 | 1.8 | 2.5 |
| 17 | 21.4 | 58 6.3 | 36 10.1 | 33 11.1 | | Revenues/Receivables | 51 7.2 | 44 8.3 | 34 10.7 | 27 13.5 | 33 11.1 |
| 34 | 10.6 | 78 4.7 | 61 6.0 | 64 5.7 | | | 73 5.0 | 58 6.3 | 63 5.8 | 56 6.5 | 64 5.7 |
| 57 | 6.4 | 107 3.4 | 85 4.3 | 83 4.4 | | | 87 4.2 | 73 5.0 | 83 4.4 | 78 4.7 | 83 4.4 |
| 0 | UND | 0 999.8 | 14 26.0 | 4 93.3 | | Cost of Revenues/Payables | 14 25.8 | 10 36.7 | 14 25.5 | 11 32.7 | 4 93.3 |
| 16 | 22.5 | 14 25.3 | 18 20.1 | 16 23.1 | | | 27 13.3 | 23 15.8 | 24 15.5 | 23 15.6 | 16 23.1 |
| 31 | 11.8 | 29 12.6 | 31 11.7 | 29 12.4 | | | 45 8.2 | 37 9.8 | 44 8.3 | 37 9.8 | 29 12.4 |
| | 7.5 | 3.7 | 5.2 | 4.3 | | Revenues/Working Capital | 5.6 | 5.8 | 4.3 | 5.3 | 4.3 |
| | 11.4 | 4.7 | 8.2 | 7.4 | | | 9.6 | 9.0 | 5.8 | 8.5 | 7.4 |
| | 23.7 | 7.7 | 9.4 | 11.4 | | | 21.3 | 19.1 | 16.0 | 17.4 | 11.4 |
| | | 352.0 | 273.2 | 217.5 | | EBIT/Interest | 49.8 | 70.7 | 285.1 | 68.8 | 217.5 |
| | | (11) 84.4 | (10) 9.6 | (27) 79.1 | | | (23) 23.9 | (28) 11.0 | (33) 72.4 | (34) 16.5 | (27) 79.1 |
| | | 32.2 | 1.8 | 6.3 | | | 4.6 | 4.0 | 25.9 | 3.3 | 6.3 |
| | | | | | | Net Profit + Depr., Dep., Amort./Cur. Mat. L/T/D | | | | | |
| | .1 | .1 | .1 | .1 | | Fixed/Worth | .1 | .2 | .1 | .1 | .1 |
| | .5 | .3 | .2 | .3 | | | .2 | .4 | .2 | .3 | .3 |
| | NM | .4 | -.2 | .7 | | | .8 | .7 | .5 | .8 | .7 |
| | .3 | .3 | .9 | .4 | | Debt/Worth | .8 | .8 | .4 | .5 | .4 |
| | .6 | .6 | 1.3 | .9 | | | 1.3 | 1.3 | .9 | 1.2 | .9 |
| | NM | 1.9 | -5.6 | 3.0 | | | 2.4 | 2.3 | 1.7 | 4.3 | 3.0 |
| | | 62.8 | | 70.0 | | % Profit Before Taxes/ Tangible Net Worth | 60.6 | 69.8 | 88.0 | 54.7 | 70.0 |
| | | (14) 52.4 | (30) | 48.9 | | | (26) 29.0 | (33) 36.5 | (43) 31.3 | (40) 26.7 | (30) 48.9 |
| | | 23.5 | | 23.7 | | | 12.7 | 9.6 | 18.0 | 7.4 | 23.7 |
| | 55.0 | 43.2 | 25.8 | 43.9 | | % Profit Before Taxes/ Total Assets | 25.4 | 38.4 | 44.1 | 23.2 | 43.9 |
| | 33.0 | 29.2 | 10.0 | 24.1 | | | 14.3 | 13.7 | 23.2 | 11.4 | 24.1 |
| | 12.3 | 16.7 | 3.8 | 9.7 | | | 4.6 | 2.8 | 9.4 | 2.1 | 9.7 |
| | | .3 | | .5 | | % Depr., Dep., Amort./ Revenues | .5 | .7 | .5 | .5 | .5 |
| | | (13) .7 | | (24) 1.1 | | | (24) .9 | (26) 1.3 | (30) 1.0 | (32) .8 | (24) 1.1 |
| | | 1.3 | | 1.5 | | | 1.9 | 2.2 | 1.7 | 1.9 | 1.5 |
| | | | | | | % Officers', Directors' Owners' Comp/Revenues | | .9 | 1.4 | .9 | |
| | | | | | | | | (10) 1.8 | (18) 2.2 | (15) 2.8 | |
| | | | | | | | | 3.7 | 3.6 | 8.0 | |
| 23M | 55297M | 350398M | 28008039M | 28413757M | | Contract Revenues ($) | 1578167M | 1615839M | 9509254M | 1896090M | 28413757M |
| 10M | 19174M | 152063M | 4905642M | 5076889M | | Total Assets ($) | 807123M | 879571M | 5686897M | 1138717M | 5076889M |

© RMA 2024  M = $ thousand   MM = $ million
See Pages viii through xx for Explanation of Ratios and Data

## CONSTRUCTION-% OF COMPLETION—Electrical Contractors and Other Wiring Installation Contractors  NAICS 238210

### Current Data Sorted by Revenue / Comparative Historical Data

| | | | | | | Type of Statement | | | | | |
|---|---|---|---|---|---|---|---|---|---|---|---|
| | 1 | 1 | 5 | 6 | | Unqualified | 10 | 4 | 3 | 12 | 6 |
| | 10 | 39 | 6 | 56 | | Reviewed | 65 | 58 | 58 | 73 | 56 |
| | 4 | 8 | | 12 | | Compiled | 6 | 5 | 5 | 12 | 12 |
| | 7 | 4 | | 11 | | Tax Returns | 4 | 5 | 3 | 13 | 11 |
| | 12 | 25 | 31 | 68 | | Other | 47 | 45 | 59 | 49 | 68 |
| | 25 (4/1-9/30/23) | | 128 (10/1/23-3/31/24) | | | | 4/1/19-3/31/20 | 4/1/20-3/31/21 | 4/1/21-3/31/22 | 4/1/22-3/31/23 | 4/1/23-3/31/24 |
| 0-1MM | 1-10MM | 10-50MM | 50 & OVER | ALL | | | ALL | ALL | ALL | ALL | ALL |
| 1 | 33 | 77 | 42 | 153 | | NUMBER OF STATEMENTS | 132 | 117 | 128 | 159 | 153 |
| % | % | % | % | % | | ASSETS | % | % | % | % | % |
| | 28.1 | 19.0 | 11.7 | 19.2 | | Cash & Equivalents | 13.5 | 24.9 | 18.1 | 19.0 | 19.2 |
| | 36.7 | 46.4 | 50.8 | 45.5 | | A/R - Progress Billings | 49.2 | 42.4 | 45.0 | 46.2 | 45.5 |
| | 3.3 | 3.8 | 3.2 | 3.5 | | A/R - Current Retention | 3.8 | 2.3 | 3.8 | 2.8 | 3.5 |
| | 1.1 | 2.5 | 1.7 | 2.0 | | Inventory | 2.7 | 2.4 | 3.4 | 2.5 | 2.0 |
| | 4.8 | 7.4 | 9.3 | 7.4 | | Cost & Est. Earnings In Excess Billings | 8.4 | 4.5 | 8.9 | 6.1 | 7.4 |
| | 2.9 | 4.5 | 2.1 | 3.5 | | All Other Current | 1.8 | 3.4 | 4.4 | 4.6 | 3.5 |
| | 76.9 | 83.6 | 78.9 | 81.0 | | Total Current | 79.4 | 80.0 | 83.7 | 81.3 | 81.0 |
| | 13.6 | 10.3 | 8.5 | 10.4 | | Fixed Assets (net) | 12.8 | 12.9 | 11.2 | 11.9 | 10.4 |
| | .0 | .0 | .4 | .1 | | Joint Ventures & Investments | .5 | .4 | .4 | .3 | .1 |
| | 4.3 | .9 | 3.2 | 2.3 | | Intangibles (net) | 2.8 | 1.5 | 1.2 | 1.2 | 2.3 |
| | 5.3 | 5.2 | 9.0 | 6.2 | | All Other Non-Current | 4.5 | 5.2 | 3.6 | 5.4 | 6.2 |
| | 100.0 | 100.0 | 100.0 | 100.0 | | Total | 100.0 | 100.0 | 100.0 | 100.0 | 100.0 |
| | | | | | | LIABILITIES | | | | | |
| | 7.4 | 4.6 | 1.3 | 4.3 | | Notes Payable-Short Term | 8.5 | 9.8 | 5.1 | 6.2 | 4.3 |
| | 11.9 | 15.2 | 15.3 | 14.5 | | A/P - Trade | 16.9 | 13.6 | 16.3 | 14.8 | 14.5 |
| | .1 | .2 | .1 | .1 | | A/P - Retention | .1 | .1 | .1 | .1 | .1 |
| | 7.4 | 13.8 | 20.4 | 14.3 | | Billings in Excess of Costs & Est. Earnings | 9.5 | 9.4 | 11.9 | 11.2 | 14.3 |
| | .0 | .1 | .1 | .1 | | Income Taxes Payable | .1 | .2 | .1 | .1 | .1 |
| | 2.7 | 1.3 | 2.4 | 1.9 | | Cur. Mat.-L/T/D | 1.9 | 2.9 | 1.3 | 1.8 | 1.9 |
| | 7.6 | 8.4 | 10.5 | 8.8 | | All Other Current | 9.4 | 9.1 | 9.3 | 8.5 | 8.8 |
| | 37.1 | 43.6 | 50.2 | 44.0 | | Total Current | 46.5 | 45.0 | 44.1 | 42.7 | 44.0 |
| | 10.7 | 5.8 | 3.5 | 6.2 | | Long-Term Debt | 6.8 | 12.5 | 7.1 | 7.7 | 6.2 |
| | .1 | .2 | .2 | .2 | | Deferred Taxes | .6 | .2 | .2 | .2 | .2 |
| | 2.4 | 4.5 | 4.1 | 3.9 | | All Other Non-Current | 3.5 | 2.7 | 2.3 | 3.0 | 3.9 |
| | 49.6 | 45.9 | 42.0 | 45.7 | | Net Worth | 42.5 | 39.5 | 46.3 | 46.4 | 45.7 |
| | 100.0 | 100.0 | 100.0 | 100.0 | | Total Liabilities & Net Worth | 100.0 | 100.0 | 100.0 | 100.0 | 100.0 |
| | | | | | | INCOME DATA | | | | | |
| | 100.0 | 100.0 | 100.0 | 100.0 | | Contract Revenues | 100.0 | 100.0 | 100.0 | 100.0 | 100.0 |
| | 31.5 | 20.8 | 17.6 | 22.2 | | Gross Profit | 22.8 | 22.3 | 20.6 | 20.7 | 22.2 |
| | 22.6 | 14.8 | 12.4 | 15.8 | | Operating Expenses | 16.6 | 18.0 | 15.9 | 16.9 | 15.8 |
| | 8.9 | 6.0 | 5.2 | 6.5 | | Operating Profit | 6.2 | 4.4 | 4.7 | 3.8 | 6.5 |
| | .1 | -.4 | -.2 | -.2 | | All Other Expenses (net) | .2 | -2.8 | -3.8 | -.7 | -.2 |
| | 8.8 | 6.4 | 5.4 | 6.7 | | Profit Before Taxes | 6.0 | 7.2 | 8.6 | 4.5 | 6.7 |
| | | | | | | RATIOS | | | | | |
| | 5.2 | 2.7 | 2.0 | 2.7 | | | 2.7 | 2.6 | 2.7 | 3.1 | 2.7 |
| | 2.7 | 2.0 | 1.5 | 1.9 | | Current | 1.7 | 1.9 | 1.9 | 2.0 | 1.9 |
| | 1.5 | 1.5 | 1.3 | 1.4 | | | 1.3 | 1.4 | 1.5 | 1.5 | 1.4 |
| | 8.1 | 6.0 | 5.5 | 5.9 | | | 6.0 | 6.4 | 5.1 | 6.1 | 5.9 |
| (27) | 4.7 | (76) 3.3 | 3.4 | (146) 3.5 | | Receivables/Payables | (131) 3.5 | (114) 3.4 | (126) 3.1 | (153) 3.6 | (146) 3.5 |
| | 2.5 | 2.1 | 2.6 | 2.3 | | | 2.1 | 2.5 | 2.3 | 2.4 | 2.3 |
| 29 | 12.8 | 56 6.5 | 79 4.6 | 57 6.4 | | | 59 6.2 | 53 6.9 | 57 6.4 | 62 5.9 | 57 6.4 |
| 73 | 5.0 | 79 4.6 | 94 3.9 | 85 4.3 | | Revenues/Receivables | 76 4.8 | 69 5.3 | 74 4.9 | 78 4.7 | 85 4.3 |
| 104 | 3.5 | 101 3.6 | 107 3.4 | 101 3.6 | | | 91 4.0 | 87 4.2 | 94 3.9 | 96 3.8 | 101 3.6 |
| 0 | UND | 17 21.3 | 23 16.2 | 16 23.2 | | | 14 25.2 | 10 34.8 | 19 19.6 | 14 25.9 | 16 23.2 |
| 18 | 20.6 | 29 12.4 | 33 11.2 | 29 12.5 | | Cost of Revenues/Payables | 26 13.9 | 23 16.0 | 27 13.5 | 25 14.5 | 29 12.5 |
| 41 | 9.0 | 40 9.2 | 41 8.8 | 40 9.1 | | | 44 8.3 | 38 9.6 | 41 8.8 | 38 9.5 | 40 9.1 |
| | 3.5 | 3.9 | 5.7 | 4.3 | | | 4.8 | 4.7 | 4.2 | 4.3 | 4.3 |
| | 6.8 | 5.8 | 8.3 | 6.8 | | Revenues/Working Capital | 8.4 | 6.4 | 6.5 | 6.4 | 6.8 |
| | 10.9 | 9.5 | 12.3 | 10.4 | | | 13.9 | 10.5 | 10.7 | 10.0 | 10.4 |
| | 138.3 | 88.0 | 133.6 | 104.8 | | | 74.3 | 83.3 | 126.7 | 73.7 | 104.8 |
| (26) | 15.8 | (65) 16.1 | (39) 31.7 | (130) 23.9 | | EBIT/Interest | (118) 18.3 | (94) 26.1 | (97) 39.2 | (134) 18.8 | (130) 23.9 |
| | 3.1 | 4.0 | 7.8 | 4.6 | | | 6.7 | 7.3 | 13.3 | 4.0 | 4.6 |
| | | | | 21.9 | | | 7.2 | 15.1 | 50.3 | 25.3 | 21.9 |
| | | | (15) 9.9 | | | Net Profit + Depr., Dep., Amort./Cur. Mat. L/T/D | (19) 4.6 | (15) 8.5 | (10) 20.3 | (15) 7.9 | (15) 9.9 |
| | | | | .2 | | | 2.8 | 2.6 | 7.0 | 4.1 | .2 |
| | .1 | .1 | .1 | .1 | | | .1 | .1 | .1 | .1 | .1 |
| | .2 | .2 | .2 | .2 | | Fixed/Worth | .2 | .3 | .2 | .2 | .2 |
| | .6 | .3 | .3 | .3 | | | .5 | .4 | .4 | .4 | .3 |
| | .4 | .4 | .8 | .6 | | | .7 | .9 | .6 | .5 | .6 |
| | 1.0 | 1.1 | 1.6 | 1.1 | | Debt/Worth | 1.4 | 1.4 | 1.1 | 1.0 | 1.1 |
| | 2.2 | 2.0 | 2.8 | 2.3 | | | 2.7 | 2.5 | 2.3 | 2.3 | 2.3 |
| | 68.5 | 45.6 | 45.0 | 47.0 | | | 62.4 | 70.5 | 70.4 | 42.9 | 47.0 |
| (29) | 39.0 | (72) 20.7 | (41) 30.4 | (143) 28.4 | | % Profit Before Taxes/ Tangible Net Worth | (123) 32.2 | (109) 39.5 | (124) 41.0 | (150) 17.6 | (143) 28.4 |
| | 7.3 | 8.8 | 14.9 | 9.5 | | | 13.7 | 18.1 | 22.0 | 5.7 | 9.5 |
| | 37.6 | 24.3 | 13.7 | 23.7 | | | 25.7 | 29.2 | 33.2 | 20.1 | 23.7 |
| | 22.0 | 11.7 | 10.0 | 11.7 | | % Profit Before Taxes/ Total Assets | 12.0 | 16.3 | 18.1 | 8.8 | 11.7 |
| | 1.8 | 3.3 | 6.3 | 3.9 | | | 5.5 | 7.6 | 9.6 | 2.4 | 3.9 |
| | .4 | .5 | .1 | .4 | | | .5 | .7 | .6 | .5 | .4 |
| (22) | 1.1 | (60) .8 | (36) .6 | (118) .8 | | % Depr., Dep., Amort./ Revenues | (103) .9 | (82) 1.0 | (96) .8 | (120) .8 | (118) .8 |
| | 1.8 | 1.4 | 1.3 | 1.5 | | | 1.5 | 1.8 | 1.6 | 1.4 | 1.5 |
| | 2.3 | .6 | | 1.1 | | | 1.2 | 1.2 | 1.4 | 1.2 | 1.1 |
| (16) | 3.5 | (30) 1.7 | | (48) 2.2 | | % Officers', Directors' Owners' Comp/Revenues | (53) 2.3 | (40) 2.4 | (42) 2.5 | (57) 2.7 | (48) 2.2 |
| | 5.2 | 3.2 | | 3.9 | | | 4.1 | 5.1 | 4.5 | 4.5 | 3.9 |
| 10M | 191407M | 2041626M | 28457663M | 30693715M | | Contract Revenues ($) | 145648609M | 258304980M | 164651956M | 34685934M | 30693715M |
| 11M | 87364M | 914343M | 14771180M | 15772898M | | Total Assets ($) | 54138065M | 133968556M | 82906402M | 14304064M | 15772898M |

M = $ thousand    MM = $ million
See Pages viii through xx for Explanation of Ratios and Data

© RMA 2024

## CONSTRUCTION-% OF COMPLETION—Plumbing, Heating, and Air-Conditioning Contractors  NAICS 238220

### Current Data Sorted by Revenue | Comparative Historical Data

| | | | | | | Type of Statement | | | | | |
|---|---|---|---|---|---|---|---|---|---|---|---|
| | | 1 | 3 | 4 | | Unqualified | 8 | 12 | 7 | 12 | 4 |
| | 10 | 52 | 16 | 78 | | Reviewed | 86 | 66 | 84 | 90 | 78 |
| | 2 | 4 | 6 | 6 | | Compiled | 4 | 4 | 10 | 10 | 6 |
| | 12 | 2 | | 14 | | Tax Returns | 10 | 7 | 7 | 15 | 14 |
| 2 | 12 | 30 | 29 | 73 | | Other | 47 | 46 | 54 | 50 | 73 |
| 21 (4/1-9/30/23) | | 154 (10/1/23-3/31/24) | | | | | 4/1/19-3/31/20 | 4/1/20-3/31/21 | 4/1/21-3/31/22 | 4/1/22-3/31/23 | 4/1/23-3/31/24 |
| 0-1MM | 1-10MM | 10-50MM | 50 & OVER | ALL | | | ALL | ALL | ALL | ALL | ALL |
| 2 | 36 | 89 | 48 | 175 | | NUMBER OF STATEMENTS | 155 | 135 | 162 | 177 | 175 |
| % | % | % | % | % | | ASSETS | % | % | % | % | % |
| | 26.3 | 20.2 | 14.3 | 19.6 | | Cash & Equivalents | 15.2 | 23.6 | 19.4 | 19.9 | 19.6 |
| | 22.7 | 44.8 | 49.9 | 41.7 | | A/R - Progress Billings | 47.3 | 43.8 | 43.1 | 41.3 | 41.7 |
| | 2.7 | 4.2 | 4.0 | 4.0 | | A/R - Current Retention | 4.7 | 4.0 | 4.2 | 4.6 | 4.0 |
| | 4.5 | 3.5 | 2.1 | 3.3 | | Inventory | 3.6 | 2.6 | 4.4 | 4.0 | 3.3 |
| | 3.3 | 5.4 | 6.7 | 5.5 | | Cost & Est. Earnings In Excess Billings | 6.1 | 4.3 | 6.6 | 5.4 | 5.5 |
| | 1.5 | 3.6 | 2.9 | 2.9 | | All Other Current | 2.1 | 3.8 | 3.7 | 4.1 | 2.9 |
| | 61.0 | 81.6 | 79.9 | 77.0 | | Total Current | 79.0 | 82.1 | 81.6 | 79.4 | 77.0 |
| | 23.2 | 10.2 | 11.2 | 13.1 | | Fixed Assets (net) | 12.1 | 11.2 | 11.3 | 10.7 | 13.1 |
| | 3.5 | .0 | .0 | .8 | | Joint Ventures & Investments | .2 | .1 | .1 | .1 | .8 |
| | 5.5 | 1.4 | 2.4 | 2.5 | | Intangibles (net) | 3.9 | 1.8 | 2.5 | 4.0 | 2.5 |
| | 6.8 | 6.8 | 6.5 | 6.7 | | All Other Non-Current | 4.8 | 4.9 | 4.5 | 5.8 | 6.7 |
| | 100.0 | 100.0 | 100.0 | 100.0 | | Total | 100.0 | 100.0 | 100.0 | 100.0 | 100.0 |
| | | | | | | LIABILITIES | | | | | |
| | 6.3 | 2.7 | 2.5 | 3.6 | | Notes Payable-Short Term | 4.9 | 4.3 | 4.4 | 4.3 | 3.6 |
| | 10.8 | 18.1 | 18.8 | 16.9 | | A/P - Trade | 21.0 | 16.8 | 17.7 | 17.4 | 16.9 |
| | .0 | .4 | 1.4 | .6 | | A/P - Retention | .5 | .6 | .5 | .5 | .6 |
| | 2.6 | 13.0 | 18.9 | 12.5 | | Billings in Excess of Costs & Est. Earnings | 10.3 | 12.9 | 12.1 | 11.5 | 12.5 |
| | .0 | .6 | .0 | .3 | | Income Taxes Payable | .1 | .1 | .1 | .2 | .3 |
| | 2.6 | 1.2 | 1.3 | 1.5 | | Cur. Mat.-L/T/D | 1.6 | 1.8 | 1.5 | 1.9 | 1.5 |
| | 6.7 | 9.0 | 10.4 | 8.8 | | All Other Current | 10.3 | 9.8 | 10.1 | 8.9 | 8.8 |
| | 28.9 | 44.9 | 53.3 | 44.2 | | Total Current | 48.7 | 46.3 | 46.4 | 44.7 | 44.2 |
| | 26.3 | 4.0 | 7.0 | 9.4 | | Long-Term Debt | 7.2 | 12.5 | 6.4 | 8.5 | 9.4 |
| | .0 | .2 | .0 | .1 | | Deferred Taxes | .3 | .2 | .1 | .2 | .1 |
| | 5.0 | 4.2 | 6.2 | 4.8 | | All Other Non-Current | 2.8 | 1.2 | 1.7 | 2.4 | 4.8 |
| | 39.8 | 46.7 | 33.5 | 41.5 | | Net Worth | 41.1 | 39.7 | 45.2 | 44.1 | 41.5 |
| | 100.0 | 100.0 | 100.0 | 100.0 | | Total Liabilities & Net Worth | 100.0 | 100.0 | 100.0 | 100.0 | 100.0 |
| | | | | | | INCOME DATA | | | | | |
| | 100.0 | 100.0 | 100.0 | 100.0 | | Contract Revenues | 100.0 | 100.0 | 100.0 | 100.0 | 100.0 |
| | 43.4 | 22.5 | 20.0 | 26.0 | | Gross Profit | 22.4 | 22.5 | 22.5 | 22.3 | 26.0 |
| | 36.4 | 15.2 | 13.4 | 19.0 | | Operating Expenses | 17.4 | 17.6 | 18.0 | 18.1 | 19.0 |
| | 7.0 | 7.3 | 6.6 | 7.0 | | Operating Profit | 5.0 | 4.9 | 4.5 | 4.2 | 7.0 |
| | .1 | -.5 | .4 | -.1 | | All Other Expenses (net) | .2 | -1.8 | -3.5 | -.5 | -.1 |
| | 7.0 | 7.8 | 6.3 | 7.1 | | Profit Before Taxes | 4.8 | 6.7 | 8.0 | 4.7 | 7.1 |
| | | | | | | RATIOS | | | | | |
| | 5.0 | 2.6 | 1.7 | 2.5 | | Current | 2.2 | 2.6 | 2.5 | 2.4 | 2.5 |
| | 2.5 | 1.8 | 1.5 | 1.7 | | | 1.6 | 1.8 | 1.8 | 1.8 | 1.7 |
| | 1.5 | 1.4 | 1.3 | 1.4 | | | 1.3 | 1.4 | 1.4 | 1.4 | 1.4 |
| | 5.1 | 4.8 | 3.5 | 4.4 | | Receivables/Payables | 4.6 | 4.2 | 4.3 | 4.1 | 4.4 |
| (28) | 2.3 | 3.2 | 2.9 | (167) 3.1 | | | (152) 2.7 | (131) 3.0 | (159) 2.9 | (172) 3.0 | (167) 3.1 |
| | .2 | 1.9 | 2.4 | 1.9 | | | 1.8 | 2.3 | 2.0 | 1.9 | 1.9 |
| 0 UND | 55 6.6 | 74 4.9 | 51 7.2 | | | Revenues/Receivables | 51 7.1 | 55 6.6 | 50 7.3 | 53 6.9 | 51 7.2 |
| 33 11.0 | 76 4.8 | 87 4.2 | 76 4.8 | | | | 72 5.1 | 73 5.0 | 74 4.9 | 76 4.8 | 76 4.8 |
| 66 5.5 | 99 3.7 | 101 3.6 | 96 3.8 | | | | 85 4.3 | 91 4.0 | 87 4.2 | 91 4.0 | 96 3.8 |
| 0 UND | 21 17.6 | 28 12.9 | 19 19.0 | | | Cost of Revenues/Payables | 20 18.5 | 21 17.8 | 19 19.6 | 20 18.6 | 19 19.0 |
| 18 20.6 | 31 11.7 | 37 9.9 | 32 11.5 | | | | 31 11.8 | 31 11.8 | 30 12.0 | 31 11.8 | 32 11.5 |
| 32 11.3 | 46 7.9 | 45 8.2 | 45 8.2 | | | | 45 8.2 | 42 8.6 | 46 7.9 | 43 8.4 | 45 8.2 |
| | 4.1 | 4.4 | 6.7 | 4.8 | | Revenues/Working Capital | 6.4 | 4.4 | 4.4 | 4.4 | 4.8 |
| | 11.2 | 6.1 | 8.8 | 7.7 | | | 11.0 | 6.9 | 7.5 | 7.3 | 7.7 |
| | 26.9 | 10.5 | 13.7 | 13.4 | | | 16.9 | 11.0 | 11.4 | 11.8 | 13.4 |
| | 30.0 | 174.7 | 182.1 | 164.7 | | EBIT/Interest | 72.8 | 136.0 | 189.0 | 96.3 | 164.7 |
| (33) | 14.0 | (72) 36.2 | (40) 36.2 | (147) 25.2 | | | (133) 23.8 | (107) 39.5 | (127) 66.9 | (135) 20.5 | (147) 25.2 |
| | 7.1 | 8.1 | 8.9 | 7.2 | | | 5.3 | 9.5 | 14.7 | 5.2 | 7.2 |
| | | 15.4 | | 16.1 | | Net Profit + Depr., Dep., Amort./Cur. Mat. L/T/D | 30.1 | 13.1 | 43.1 | 12.3 | 16.1 |
| | (15) | 4.7 | (24) | 6.2 | | | (20) 11.2 | (17) 3.6 | (12) 9.9 | (26) 5.6 | (24) 6.2 |
| | | 3.3 | | 3.7 | | | 2.6 | 1.6 | 4.7 | 3.0 | 3.7 |
| | .2 | .1 | .2 | .1 | | Fixed/Worth | .1 | .1 | .1 | .1 | .1 |
| | .5 | .2 | .3 | .2 | | | .3 | .2 | .2 | .2 | .2 |
| | 12.0 | .4 | .7 | .5 | | | .5 | .5 | .4 | .4 | .5 |
| | .4 | .6 | 1.3 | .6 | | Debt/Worth | .8 | .8 | .6 | .6 | .6 |
| | 1.4 | 1.1 | 1.7 | 1.4 | | | 1.6 | 1.5 | 1.2 | 1.2 | 1.4 |
| | 29.9 | 2.2 | 3.5 | 2.9 | | | 3.4 | 3.0 | 2.2 | 2.3 | 2.9 |
| | 89.3 | 58.7 | 61.7 | 58.2 | | % Profit Before Taxes/ Tangible Net Worth | 51.5 | 56.5 | 71.1 | 45.4 | 58.2 |
| (28) | 38.1 | (86) 32.0 | (43) 41.6 | (159) 36.4 | | | (140) 27.8 | (129) 31.2 | (152) 41.1 | (161) 22.1 | (159) 36.4 |
| | 8.1 | 15.1 | 23.3 | 16.6 | | | 14.5 | 10.3 | 22.9 | 6.8 | 16.6 |
| | 45.8 | 29.9 | 22.8 | 29.7 | | % Profit Before Taxes/ Total Assets | 19.2 | 25.0 | 28.8 | 18.3 | 29.7 |
| | 19.3 | 12.8 | 12.2 | 13.4 | | | 10.9 | 12.1 | 18.7 | 9.7 | 13.4 |
| | 3.0 | 6.7 | 5.5 | 6.1 | | | 4.6 | 4.5 | 9.1 | 2.7 | 6.1 |
| | 1.2 | .5 | .4 | .5 | | % Depr., Dep., Amort./ Revenues | .5 | .5 | .5 | .5 | .5 |
| (23) | 1.8 | (72) .8 | (38) .7 | (134) .9 | | | (134) .9 | (110) .9 | (131) 1.0 | (147) .9 | (134) .9 |
| | 2.5 | 1.2 | 1.1 | 1.4 | | | 1.3 | 1.5 | 1.4 | 1.4 | 1.4 |
| | 3.7 | .6 | | .8 | | % Officers', Directors' Owners' Comp/Revenues | .8 | 1.2 | .8 | .9 | .8 |
| (21) | 4.9 | (33) 1.2 | | (61) 2.1 | | | (48) 1.8 | (45) 2.0 | (51) 1.2 | (58) 2.2 | (61) 2.1 |
| | 6.9 | 2.2 | | 4.5 | | | 3.7 | 4.3 | 3.4 | 4.5 | 4.5 |
| 189M | 178102M | 2225956M | 17680753M | 20085000M | | Contract Revenues ($) | 179264305M | 114771492M | 14047671M | 9849513M | 20085000M |
| 85M | 75288M | 1041559M | 8314460M | 9431392M | | Total Assets ($) | 70675611M | 50498996M | 6863731M | 5230910M | 9431392M |

© RMA 2024  
M = $ thousand   MM = $ million  
See Pages viii through xx for Explanation of Ratios and Data

# CONSTRUCTION-% OF COMPLETION—Drywall and Insulation Contractors  NAICS 238310

## Current Data Sorted by Revenue | Comparative Historical Data

| | | | | | Type of Statement | | | | | |
|---|---|---|---|---|---|---|---|---|---|---|
| | | | 2 | 2 | Unqualified | 3 | 3 | | 2 | 2 |
| 4 | 10 | 3 | 17 | Reviewed | 16 | 9 | 9 | 25 | 17 |
| 1 | 3 | | 4 | Compiled | | | | 3 | 4 |
| 2 | 1 | | 3 | Tax Returns | | | | 1 | 3 |
| 2 | 2 | 15 | 19 | Other | 2 | 1 | 1 | 21 | 19 |
| | | | | | | 16 | 12 | 13 | 21 | 19 |
| 3 (4/1-9/30/23) | 42 (10/1/23-3/31/24) | | | | 4/1/19- | 4/1/20- | 4/1/21- | 4/1/22- | 4/1/23- |
| | | | | | | 3/31/20 | 3/31/21 | 3/31/22 | 3/31/23 | 3/31/24 |
| 0-1MM | 1-10MM | 10-50MM | 50 & OVER | ALL | | ALL | ALL | ALL | ALL | ALL |
| | 9 | 16 | 20 | 45 | NUMBER OF STATEMENTS | 37 | 25 | 23 | 52 | 45 |
| % | % | % | % | % | ASSETS | % | % | % | % | % |
| D | | 21.6 | 12.1 | 18.7 | Cash & Equivalents | 11.0 | 23.5 | 17.8 | 17.4 | 18.7 |
| A | | 53.4 | 51.8 | 48.0 | A/R - Progress Billings | 55.3 | 46.1 | 49.8 | 46.7 | 48.0 |
| T | | 3.6 | 5.9 | 4.9 | A/R - Current Retention | 6.5 | 2.4 | 5.3 | 4.8 | 4.9 |
| A | | 1.4 | 2.7 | 2.9 | Inventory | 2.7 | 4.6 | 2.9 | 1.5 | 2.9 |
| | | 4.6 | 6.2 | 4.9 | Cost & Est. Earnings In Excess Billings | 5.2 | 3.9 | 2.8 | 4.6 | 4.9 |
| N | | 3.6 | 1.3 | 2.3 | All Other Current | 2.6 | 3.5 | 3.1 | 6.5 | 2.3 |
| O | | 88.2 | 79.9 | 81.7 | Total Current | 83.3 | 84.0 | 81.7 | 81.3 | 81.7 |
| T | | 6.0 | 4.6 | 7.0 | Fixed Assets (net) | 7.6 | 6.0 | 6.0 | 7.2 | 7.0 |
| | | .5 | .0 | .2 | Joint Ventures & Investments | .6 | 1.6 | .6 | 1.6 | .2 |
| A | | .2 | 9.4 | 4.3 | Intangibles (net) | .7 | 3.3 | 5.2 | 3.3 | 4.3 |
| V | | 5.1 | 6.1 | 6.9 | All Other Non-Current | 7.8 | 5.1 | 6.5 | 6.6 | 6.9 |
| A | | 100.0 | 100.0 | 100.0 | Total | 100.0 | 100.0 | 100.0 | 100.0 | 100.0 |
| I | | | | | LIABILITIES | | | | | |
| L | | 3.4 | 4.2 | 3.8 | Notes Payable-Short Term | 9.4 | 6.6 | 2.2 | 4.7 | 3.8 |
| A | | 11.6 | 15.8 | 12.0 | A/P - Trade | 14.2 | 10.9 | 9.5 | 12.1 | 12.0 |
| B | | .0 | .3 | .1 | A/P - Retention | .7 | .2 | .1 | .3 | .1 |
| L | | 13.9 | 12.8 | 11.6 | Billings in Excess of Costs & Est. Earnings | 12.6 | 13.6 | 9.8 | 10.4 | 11.6 |
| E | | .1 | .1 | .1 | Income Taxes Payable | .0 | .4 | .0 | .3 | .1 |
| | | 1.7 | 1.2 | 1.6 | Cur. Mat.-L/T/D | .7 | 2.1 | .6 | .8 | 1.6 |
| | | 5.6 | 10.0 | 7.5 | All Other Current | 9.1 | 10.2 | 8.7 | 10.0 | 7.5 |
| | | 36.2 | 44.4 | 36.7 | Total Current | 46.8 | 44.1 | 30.9 | 38.5 | 36.7 |
| | | 4.3 | 10.7 | 8.1 | Long-Term Debt | 5.1 | 12.0 | 4.6 | 7.7 | 8.1 |
| | | .6 | .3 | .4 | Deferred Taxes | .5 | .4 | .3 | .3 | .4 |
| | | 3.5 | 2.8 | 5.4 | All Other Non-Current | .6 | 2.7 | .7 | 1.7 | 5.4 |
| | | 55.5 | 41.8 | 49.4 | Net Worth | 47.0 | 40.8 | 63.6 | 51.7 | 49.4 |
| | | 100.0 | 100.0 | 100.0 | Total Liabilities & Net Worth | 100.0 | 100.0 | 100.0 | 100.0 | 100.0 |
| | | | | | INCOME DATA | | | | | |
| | | 100.0 | 100.0 | 100.0 | Contract Revenues | 100.0 | 100.0 | 100.0 | 100.0 | 100.0 |
| | | 19.0 | 16.6 | 19.1 | Gross Profit | 22.4 | 21.5 | 24.6 | 21.2 | 19.1 |
| | | 13.7 | 11.1 | 13.6 | Operating Expenses | 16.5 | 14.7 | 17.1 | 16.1 | 13.6 |
| | | 5.3 | 5.5 | 5.5 | Operating Profit | 5.8 | 6.7 | 7.4 | 5.1 | 5.5 |
| | | -2.3 | .3 | -1.0 | All Other Expenses (net) | -.3 | -1.1 | -4.0 | -1.3 | -1.0 |
| | | 7.6 | 5.2 | 6.5 | Profit Before Taxes | 6.2 | 7.8 | 11.4 | 6.4 | 6.5 |
| | | | | | RATIOS | | | | | |
| | | 3.5 | 2.9 | 3.2 | | 2.6 | 2.7 | 4.9 | 3.4 | 3.2 |
| | | 2.5 | 1.7 | 2.4 | Current | 1.9 | 1.8 | 2.4 | 2.5 | 2.4 |
| | | 2.0 | 1.4 | 1.6 | | 1.3 | 1.4 | 1.9 | 1.6 | 1.6 |
| | | 6.7 | 5.2 | 6.9 | | 7.0 | 23.0 | 14.5 | 7.7 | 6.9 |
| | | 5.2 | 3.8 (43) | 4.8 | Receivables/Payables | 5.3 | 5.2 | 5.7 (50) | 4.4 (43) | 4.8 |
| | | 4.3 | 2.7 | 3.1 | | 2.8 | 3.3 | 3.7 | 3.1 | 3.1 |
| | 63 5.8 | 70 5.2 | 61 6.0 | | 59 6.2 | 54 6.8 | 47 7.7 | 64 5.7 | 61 6.0 |
| | 89 4.1 | 85 4.3 | 85 4.3 | Revenues/Receivables | 83 4.4 | 74 4.9 | 79 4.6 | 81 4.5 | 85 4.3 |
| | 104 3.5 | 96 3.8 | 96 3.8 | | 104 3.5 | 99 3.7 | 96 3.8 | 101 3.6 | 96 3.8 |
| | 15 24.4 | 20 18.3 | 14 26.9 | | 14 26.3 | 6 60.9 | 9 39.2 | 12 29.2 | 14 26.9 |
| | 23 15.7 | 25 14.5 | 22 16.9 | Cost of Revenues/Payables | 21 17.4 | 18 20.4 | 20 18.7 | 22 17.3 | 22 16.9 |
| | 26 14.2 | 37 9.8 | 28 13.1 | | 36 10.2 | 28 13.0 | 25 14.4 | 29 12.4 | 28 13.1 |
| | | 2.9 | 4.1 | 3.6 | | 5.4 | 4.3 | 4.2 | 3.6 | 3.6 |
| | | 4.5 | 8.4 | 5.4 | Revenues/Working Capital | 7.3 | 6.7 | 6.1 | 5.9 | 5.4 |
| | | 6.0 | 11.6 | 11.5 | | 14.0 | 10.3 | 9.6 | 10.0 | 11.5 |
| | | | 16.1 | 31.1 | | 65.7 | 95.6 | 584.1 | 127.5 | 31.1 |
| | | (18) 10.2 | (35) 11.6 | EBIT/Interest | (30) 21.5 | (19) 17.9 | (16) 105.1 | (37) 31.4 | (35) 11.6 |
| | | | 1.6 | 1.7 | | 4.5 | 8.1 | 58.7 | 6.0 | 1.7 |
| | | | | | Net Profit + Depr., Dep., Amort./Cur. Mat. L/T/D | | | | | |
| | | .0 | .0 | .0 | | .1 | .1 | .0 | .0 | .0 |
| | | .1 | .2 | .2 | Fixed/Worth | .1 | .1 | .1 | .1 | .2 |
| | | .2 | .5 | .3 | | .2 | .3 | .2 | .3 | .3 |
| | | .4 | 1.1 | .5 | | .6 | .8 | .2 | .4 | .5 |
| | | .8 | 1.8 | 1.0 | Debt/Worth | 1.1 | 1.8 | .6 | .9 | 1.0 |
| | | 1.0 | 10.3 | 2.7 | | 2.4 | 3.5 | 1.1 | 2.3 | 2.7 |
| | | 35.0 | 73.1 | 52.1 | | 60.5 | 90.7 | 77.8 | 64.0 | 52.1 |
| | (15) 24.6 | (18) 15.2 | (42) 22.9 | % Profit Before Taxes/ Tangible Net Worth | (36) 26.5 | 43.2 (22) | 48.6 (49) | 24.1 (42) | 22.9 |
| | | 11.8 | 7.9 | 10.2 | | 15.6 | 20.8 | 19.3 | 10.2 | 10.2 |
| | | 29.1 | 18.3 | 28.5 | | 24.2 | 31.7 | 49.5 | 25.7 | 28.5 |
| | | 14.0 | 6.9 | 13.0 | % Profit Before Taxes/ Total Assets | 11.2 | 17.2 | 31.0 | 16.2 | 13.0 |
| | | 7.3 | 1.0 | 2.6 | | 6.2 | 4.6 | 10.9 | 4.6 | 2.6 |
| | | .3 | .1 | .2 | | .2 | .2 | .2 | .4 | .2 |
| | (15) .6 | (16) .3 | (40) .5 | % Depr., Dep., Amort./ Revenues | (30) .5 | (21) .5 | (15) .4 | (34) .6 | (40) .5 |
| | | .8 | .5 | .8 | | .9 | .8 | .8 | .9 | .8 |
| | | | | .8 | | 1.5 | | | .8 | .8 |
| | | | (13) 1.2 | % Officers', Directors' Owners' Comp/Revenues | (16) 2.3 | | (17) 1.9 | (13) 1.2 |
| | | | | 2.5 | | 3.3 | | | 5.4 | 2.5 |
| | 48745M | 342216M | 10023893M | 10414854M | Contract Revenues ($) | 12261826M | 965060M | 10702192M | 1981606M | 10414854M |
| | 20560M | 154059M | 7978371M | 8152990M | Total Assets ($) | 3187513M | 389246M | 2975715M | 881985M | 8152990M |

© RMA 2024    M = $ thousand    MM = $ million
See Pages viii through xx for Explanation of Ratios and Data

# CONSTRUCTION-% OF COMPLETION—Flooring Contractors  NAICS 238330

## Current Data Sorted by Revenue | Comparative Historical Data

| | | | | | Type of Statement | | | | | |
|---|---|---|---|---|---|---|---|---|---|---|
| | | | | | Unqualified | | | | 1 | |
| | | 5 | | 5 | Reviewed | 7 | | 2 | 7 | 5 |
| | 4 | | | 4 | Compiled | 2 | | 4 | 2 | 4 |
| | 2 | | | 2 | Tax Returns | | 6 | | 4 | 2 |
| | 2 | 5 | 2 | 9 | Other | 1 | | 7 | 7 | 9 |
| 1 (4/1-9/30/23) | | 19 (10/1/23-3/31/24) | | | | 4/1/19-3/31/20 | 4/1/20-3/31/21 | 4/1/21-3/31/22 | 4/1/22-3/31/23 | 4/1/23-3/31/24 |
| 0-1MM | 1-10MM | 10-50MM | 50 & OVER | ALL | NUMBER OF STATEMENTS | ALL | ALL | ALL | ALL | ALL |
| | 8 | 10 | 2 | 20 | | 10 | 6 | 13 | 21 | 20 |
| % | % | % | % | % | ASSETS | % | % | % | % | % |
| | | 15.2 | | 13.5 | Cash & Equivalents | 19.2 | | 14.9 | 12.9 | 13.5 |
| | | 42.0 | | 31.8 | A/R - Progress Billings | 45.4 | | 49.8 | 44.6 | 31.8 |
| | | 3.3 | | 2.1 | A/R - Current Retention | 4.3 | | 2.6 | 2.8 | 2.1 |
| DATA NOT AVAILABLE | | 9.6 | | 13.0 | Inventory | 2.5 | | 10.8 | 10.0 | 13.0 |
| | | 7.3 | | 7.3 | Cost & Est. Earnings In Excess Billings | 8.0 | | 7.2 | 9.4 | 7.3 |
| | | 5.1 | | 5.8 | All Other Current | .1 | | 6.0 | 4.9 | 5.8 |
| | | 82.4 | | 73.5 | Total Current | 79.6 | | 91.3 | 84.6 | 73.5 |
| | | 9.9 | | 9.9 | Fixed Assets (net) | 9.7 | | 4.3 | 7.1 | 9.9 |
| | | .4 | | .2 | Joint Ventures & Investments | .0 | | .2 | .1 | .2 |
| | | 1.2 | | 7.4 | Intangibles (net) | 1.0 | | .2 | 1.3 | 7.4 |
| | | 6.0 | | 8.9 | All Other Non-Current | 9.7 | | 4.1 | 7.0 | 8.9 |
| | | 100.0 | | 100.0 | Total | 100.0 | | 100.0 | 100.0 | 100.0 |
| | | | | | LIABILITIES | | | | | |
| | | 7.0 | | 6.2 | Notes Payable-Short Term | 4.3 | | 10.5 | 12.2 | 6.2 |
| | | 13.9 | | 10.0 | A/P - Trade | 11.1 | | 11.6 | 15.3 | 10.0 |
| | | .0 | | .0 | A/P - Retention | .5 | | .0 | .0 | .0 |
| | | 5.7 | | 3.4 | Billings in Excess of Costs & Est. Earnings | 11.9 | | 10.4 | 6.9 | 3.4 |
| | | .2 | | .2 | Income Taxes Payable | | | .3 | .4 | .2 |
| | | 1.6 | | 1.4 | Cur. Mat.-L/T/D | 1.2 | | .4 | .7 | 1.4 |
| | | 11.0 | | 23.8 | All Other Current | 6.5 | | 6.1 | 10.5 | 23.8 |
| | | 39.3 | | 45.1 | Total Current | 35.5 | | 39.4 | 46.0 | 45.1 |
| | | 10.8 | | 17.5 | Long-Term Debt | 6.3 | | 6.0 | 12.8 | 17.5 |
| | | .3 | | .1 | Deferred Taxes | .0 | | .2 | .1 | .1 |
| | | 1.2 | | 6.1 | All Other Non-Current | 2.0 | | .9 | 3.0 | 6.1 |
| | | 48.4 | | 31.2 | Net Worth | 56.2 | | 53.4 | 38.2 | 31.2 |
| | | 100.0 | | 100.0 | Total Liabilities & Net Worth | 100.0 | | 100.0 | 100.0 | 100.0 |
| | | | | | INCOME DATA | | | | | |
| | | 100.0 | | 100.0 | Contract Revenues | 100.0 | | 100.0 | 100.0 | 100.0 |
| | | 25.3 | | 30.3 | Gross Profit | 27.4 | | 26.8 | 25.0 | 30.3 |
| | | 19.2 | | 24.7 | Operating Expenses | 18.3 | | 22.9 | 21.7 | 24.7 |
| | | 6.1 | | 5.6 | Operating Profit | 9.1 | | 3.9 | 3.2 | 5.6 |
| | | -.2 | | .4 | All Other Expenses (net) | .0 | | -3.3 | -.5 | .4 |
| | | 6.3 | | 5.2 | Profit Before Taxes | 9.1 | | 7.2 | 3.8 | 5.2 |
| | | | | | RATIOS | | | | | |
| | | 3.5 | | 2.9 | | 4.0 | | 6.4 | 3.1 | 2.9 |
| | | 2.2 | | 2.1 | Current | 2.5 | | 2.3 | 2.0 | 2.1 |
| | | 1.4 | | 1.3 | | 1.4 | | 1.5 | 1.3 | 1.3 |
| | | 6.1 | | 5.9 | | | | 7.5 | 6.4 | 5.9 |
| | | 3.8 | (17) | 3.7 | Receivables/Payables | | | 4.7 | (19) 3.3 | (17) 3.7 |
| | | 2.1 | | 2.2 | | | | 3.2 | 2.7 | 2.2 |
| | 50 | 7.3 | 20 | 18.2 | | 36 10.0 | | 59 6.2 | 55 6.6 | 20 18.2 |
| | 60 | 6.1 | 49 | 7.4 | Revenues/Receivables | 68 5.4 | | 73 5.0 | 89 4.1 | 49 7.4 |
| | 83 | 4.4 | 79 | 4.6 | | 94 3.9 | | 101 3.6 | 101 3.6 | 79 4.6 |
| | 13 | 27.5 | 9 | 40.1 | | 9 42.3 | | 10 38.0 | 13 27.3 | 9 40.1 |
| | 23 | 15.7 | 15 | 23.7 | Cost of Revenues/Payables | 19 19.1 | | 23 16.2 | 25 14.8 | 15 23.7 |
| | 35 | 10.3 | 31 | 11.9 | | 37 9.9 | | 33 11.2 | 43 8.5 | 31 11.9 |
| | | 4.2 | | 4.8 | | 3.9 | | 4.0 | 3.9 | 4.8 |
| | | 6.4 | | 6.8 | Revenues/Working Capital | 5.3 | | 5.3 | 6.2 | 6.8 |
| | | 10.6 | | 11.6 | | 16.0 | | 7.2 | 11.8 | 11.6 |
| | | | | 47.9 | | | | | 91.2 | 47.9 |
| | | | (17) | 9.3 | EBIT/Interest | | | (18) 14.2 | (17) | 9.3 |
| | | | | 3.4 | | | | | 2.9 | 3.4 |
| | | | | | Net Profit + Depr., Dep., Amort./Cur. Mat. L/T/D | | | | | |
| | | .1 | | .1 | | .1 | | .0 | .1 | .1 |
| | | .1 | | .2 | Fixed/Worth | .1 | | .1 | .1 | .2 |
| | | .2 | | 2.3 | | .2 | | .1 | .7 | 2.3 |
| | | .5 | | .7 | | .3 | | .4 | .6 | .7 |
| | | 1.3 | | 1.9 | Debt/Worth | .7 | | 1.0 | 2.0 | 1.9 |
| | | 3.0 | | 6.8 | | 1.8 | | 1.8 | 4.1 | 6.8 |
| | | 60.0 | | 105.1 | | 94.9 | | 54.9 | 31.2 | 105.1 |
| | | 26.9 | (17) | 39.8 | % Profit Before Taxes/ Tangible Net Worth | 52.7 | | 40.3 | (18) 17.6 | (17) 39.8 |
| | | 16.2 | | 23.6 | | 28.9 | | 17.9 | 6.8 | 23.6 |
| | | 20.2 | | 20.8 | | 33.6 | | 23.9 | 16.3 | 20.8 |
| | | 16.2 | | 17.7 | % Profit Before Taxes/ Total Assets | 23.2 | | 19.0 | 8.1 | 17.7 |
| | | 4.8 | | 8.6 | | 21.6 | | 8.5 | .6 | 8.6 |
| | | | | .4 | | | | | .1 | .4 |
| | | | (11) | .7 | % Depr., Dep., Amort./ Revenues | | | (20) | .3 (11) | .7 |
| | | | | 1.5 | | | | | .7 | 1.5 |
| | | | | | % Officers', Directors' Owners' Comp/Revenues | | | | 2.1 | |
| | | | | | | | | (11) | 2.4 | |
| | | | | | | | | | 4.2 | |
| | 40114M | 195223M | 439538M | 674875M | Contract Revenues ($) | 172958M | 134317M | 290635M | 632332M | 674875M |
| | 12518M | 90670M | 300625M | 403813M | Total Assets ($) | 68348M | 49441M | 120046M | 299891M | 403813M |

© RMA 2024   M = $ thousand   MM = $ million
See Pages viii through xx for Explanation of Ratios and Data

# CONSTRUCTION-% OF COMPLETION—Site Preparation Contractors NAICS 238910

## Current Data Sorted by Revenue / Comparative Historical Data

| | | | | | Type of Statement | | | | | |
|---|---|---|---|---|---|---|---|---|---|---|
| | | 1 | 1 | 2 | Unqualified | 3 | 6 | 7 | 16 | 2 |
| | 7 | 21 | 7 | 35 | Reviewed | 38 | 37 | 35 | 53 | 35 |
| | 1 | 2 | | 3 | Compiled | 4 | 2 | 2 | 7 | 3 |
| 1 | 12 | | 2 | 15 | Tax Returns | 6 | 3 | 4 | 9 | 15 |
| 3 | 9 | 28 | 25 | 65 | Other | 34 | 44 | 53 | 65 | 65 |
| | 32 (4/1-9/30/23) | | 88 (10/1/23-3/31/24) | | | 4/1/19-3/31/20 | 4/1/20-3/31/21 | 4/1/21-3/31/22 | 4/1/22-3/31/23 | 4/1/23-3/31/24 |
| 0-1MM | 1-10MM | 10-50MM | 50 & OVER | ALL | | ALL | ALL | ALL | ALL | ALL |
| 4 | 29 | 52 | 35 | 120 | NUMBER OF STATEMENTS | 85 | 92 | 101 | 150 | 120 |
| % | % | % | % | % | ASSETS | % | % | % | % | % |
| | 22.5 | 12.2 | 12.2 | 15.5 | Cash & Equivalents | 14.3 | 19.0 | 16.8 | 15.0 | 15.5 |
| | 14.7 | 33.0 | 25.5 | 25.3 | A/R - Progress Billings | 34.4 | 32.4 | 30.5 | 32.5 | 25.3 |
| | 2.3 | 4.0 | 3.1 | 3.2 | A/R - Current Retention | 2.8 | 1.6 | 2.3 | 2.7 | 3.2 |
| | 3.5 | 1.0 | 1.0 | 1.6 | Inventory | .7 | 1.1 | 1.4 | 1.2 | 1.6 |
| | 4.9 | 3.8 | 2.9 | 3.7 | Cost & Est. Earnings In Excess Billings | 3.8 | 2.1 | 3.7 | 4.2 | 3.7 |
| | 1.4 | 2.7 | 2.9 | 2.4 | All Other Current | 2.1 | 3.1 | 3.1 | 3.3 | 2.4 |
| | 49.3 | 56.7 | 47.6 | 51.6 | Total Current | 58.3 | 59.3 | 57.8 | 58.9 | 51.6 |
| | 38.9 | 35.9 | 37.1 | 37.7 | Fixed Assets (net) | 36.2 | 36.2 | 36.1 | 33.5 | 37.7 |
| | .0 | .1 | .7 | .4 | Joint Ventures & Investments | .1 | .2 | .5 | .8 | .4 |
| | .9 | 1.8 | 6.5 | 2.9 | Intangibles (net) | .4 | .3 | .9 | .7 | 2.9 |
| | 11.0 | 5.5 | 8.1 | 7.5 | All Other Non-Current | 4.9 | 3.9 | 4.7 | 6.1 | 7.5 |
| | 100.0 | 100.0 | 100.0 | 100.0 | Total | 100.0 | 100.0 | 100.0 | 100.0 | 100.0 |
| | | | | | LIABILITIES | | | | | |
| | 17.8 | 2.8 | 1.1 | 5.9 | Notes Payable-Short Term | 4.4 | 3.0 | 4.7 | 3.2 | 5.9 |
| | 5.4 | 13.1 | 12.6 | 10.6 | A/P - Trade | 16.8 | 12.8 | 13.9 | 13.7 | 10.6 |
| | .0 | .2 | .1 | .1 | A/P - Retention | .1 | .2 | .1 | .2 | .1 |
| | 2.8 | 5.2 | 8.9 | 5.5 | Billings in Excess of Costs & Est. Earnings | 6.0 | 6.5 | 6.7 | 6.2 | 5.5 |
| | .3 | .1 | .2 | .2 | Income Taxes Payable | .0 | .1 | .2 | .2 | .2 |
| | 6.6 | 5.8 | 5.5 | 5.7 | Cur. Mat.-L/T/D | 5.8 | 5.1 | 5.1 | 5.0 | 5.7 |
| | 7.4 | 4.5 | 4.4 | 5.2 | All Other Current | 7.7 | 6.4 | 4.3 | 3.9 | 5.2 |
| | 40.2 | 31.7 | 32.9 | 33.3 | Total Current | 40.8 | 34.0 | 35.1 | 32.3 | 33.3 |
| | 57.0 | 16.6 | 18.5 | 27.4 | Long-Term Debt | 20.2 | 22.1 | 16.6 | 17.4 | 27.4 |
| | .6 | .3 | .8 | .5 | Deferred Taxes | .7 | .9 | .5 | .7 | .5 |
| | 4.1 | 2.4 | 4.5 | 3.6 | All Other Non-Current | 3.0 | 1.8 | 2.7 | 3.7 | 3.6 |
| | -1.8 | 49.0 | 43.3 | 35.3 | Net Worth | 35.3 | 41.0 | 45.1 | 45.9 | 35.3 |
| | 100.0 | 100.0 | 100.0 | 100.0 | Total Liabilities & Net Worth | 100.0 | 100.0 | 100.0 | 100.0 | 100.0 |
| | | | | | INCOME DATA | | | | | |
| | 100.0 | 100.0 | 100.0 | 100.0 | Contract Revenues | 100.0 | 100.0 | 100.0 | 100.0 | 100.0 |
| | 37.8 | 22.2 | 22.6 | 27.4 | Gross Profit | 22.0 | 20.5 | 22.6 | 21.1 | 27.4 |
| | 33.3 | 15.2 | 15.2 | 20.5 | Operating Expenses | 16.0 | 15.9 | 16.7 | 15.3 | 20.5 |
| | 4.5 | 7.0 | 7.3 | 6.9 | Operating Profit | 6.0 | 4.6 | 5.9 | 5.9 | 6.9 |
| | -.5 | -.3 | .0 | -.2 | All Other Expenses (net) | .1 | -1.6 | -3.5 | -.7 | -.2 |
| | 5.0 | 7.2 | 7.3 | 7.2 | Profit Before Taxes | 6.0 | 6.2 | 9.4 | 6.6 | 7.2 |
| | | | | | RATIOS | | | | | |
| | 6.1 | 2.5 | 1.8 | 2.6 | | 2.0 | 2.4 | 2.4 | 2.7 | 2.6 |
| | 1.3 | 1.8 | 1.3 | 1.6 | Current | 1.5 | 1.8 | 1.7 | 1.9 | 1.6 |
| | .7 | 1.4 | 1.1 | 1.2 | | 1.2 | 1.4 | 1.3 | 1.3 | 1.2 |
| | 9.2 | 4.9 | 3.2 | 4.1 | | 3.2 | 4.4 | 4.0 | 4.7 | 4.1 |
| (17) | 3.0 | 3.0 | (34) 2.4 | (104) 2.8 | Receivables/Payables | (81) 2.3 | (91) 2.9 | (97) 2.5 | (143) 2.6 | (104) 2.8 |
| | 2.0 | 1.9 | 1.8 | 1.9 | | 1.6 | 1.9 | 1.6 | 1.8 | 1.9 |
| 0 | UND | 65 5.6 | 63 5.8 | 42 8.6 | | 47 7.7 | 47 7.8 | 50 7.3 | 57 6.4 | 42 8.6 |
| 20 | 18.2 | 79 4.6 | 76 4.8 | 72 5.1 | Revenues/Receivables | 72 5.1 | 69 5.3 | 73 5.0 | 76 4.8 | 72 5.1 |
| 81 | 4.5 | 96 3.8 | 94 3.9 | 94 3.9 | | 91 4.0 | 87 4.2 | 94 3.9 | 96 3.8 | 94 3.9 |
| 0 | UND | 17 21.0 | 28 13.1 | 13 28.1 | | 22 16.4 | 19 19.7 | 21 17.5 | 18 20.0 | 13 28.1 |
| 1 | 396.2 | 35 10.5 | 35 10.5 | 30 12.1 | Cost of Revenues/Payables | 38 9.7 | 27 13.3 | 34 10.8 | 31 11.6 | 30 12.1 |
| 25 | 14.6 | 49 7.5 | 56 6.5 | 43 8.4 | | 51 7.1 | 40 9.1 | 49 7.4 | 47 7.7 | 43 8.4 |
| | 5.1 | 4.6 | 6.3 | 5.5 | | 6.7 | 5.1 | 4.5 | 3.9 | 5.5 |
| | 41.4 | 6.6 | 13.2 | 9.0 | Revenues/Working Capital | 11.3 | 7.7 | 8.1 | 7.8 | 9.0 |
| | -42.9 | 12.1 | 32.0 | 22.6 | | 28.7 | 13.7 | 19.9 | 16.6 | 22.6 |
| | 10.4 | 26.9 | 41.4 | 30.8 | | 32.8 | 47.8 | 57.2 | 36.3 | 30.8 |
| (26) | 3.9 | (48) 10.6 | (33) 15.2 | (111) 10.3 | EBIT/Interest | (81) 7.7 | (83) 14.4 | (83) 19.7 | (132) 14.5 | (111) 10.3 |
| | -2.8 | 2.3 | 3.7 | 2.1 | | 2.0 | 4.6 | 9.7 | 4.2 | 2.1 |
| | | | | 2.8 | | | | | 5.7 | 2.8 |
| | | | (13) 1.6 | Net Profit + Depr., Dep., Amort./Cur. Mat. L/T/D | | | (17) 3.5 | (13) 1.6 |
| | | | | .1 | | | | | 1.1 | .1 |
| | .4 | .4 | .7 | .5 | | .5 | .5 | .4 | .4 | .5 |
| | 1.4 | .7 | 1.0 | .9 | Fixed/Worth | .9 | .8 | .8 | .7 | .9 |
| | -13.3 | 1.2 | 2.0 | 2.0 | | 1.3 | 1.2 | 1.4 | 1.1 | 2.0 |
| | .6 | .5 | .8 | .5 | | .7 | .7 | .6 | .6 | .5 |
| | 3.2 | 1.1 | 1.7 | 1.6 | Debt/Worth | 1.5 | 1.1 | 1.1 | 1.0 | 1.6 |
| | -11.7 | 2.1 | 3.6 | 3.6 | | 2.9 | 1.9 | 2.0 | 2.0 | 3.6 |
| | 93.5 | 42.2 | 43.9 | 44.2 | | 39.7 | 38.1 | 50.7 | 39.8 | 44.2 |
| (20) | 16.6 | (50) 25.5 | (33) 31.1 | (107) 27.9 | % Profit Before Taxes/ Tangible Net Worth | (74) 23.9 | (88) 25.3 | (96) 29.9 | (144) 22.7 | (107) 27.9 |
| | 9.5 | 6.9 | 13.1 | 11.0 | | 10.8 | 7.7 | 18.9 | 11.1 | 11.0 |
| | 17.4 | 19.9 | 15.3 | 19.5 | | 17.1 | 18.4 | 24.1 | 19.5 | 19.5 |
| | 5.6 | 11.3 | 9.4 | 10.1 | % Profit Before Taxes/ Total Assets | 9.6 | 11.4 | 14.4 | 10.8 | 10.1 |
| | -9.1 | 2.7 | 6.1 | 2.8 | | 2.2 | 3.5 | 8.8 | 3.8 | 2.8 |
| | 4.0 | 2.5 | 1.1 | 2.2 | | 2.4 | 2.5 | 2.3 | 1.4 | 2.2 |
| (15) | 6.6 | (43) 3.7 | (16) 3.3 | (75) 4.1 | % Depr., Dep., Amort./ Revenues | (72) 4.2 | (76) 4.0 | (82) 4.0 | (128) 3.5 | (75) 4.1 |
| | 10.7 | 6.4 | 4.9 | 6.6 | | 6.0 | 6.3 | 6.3 | 5.3 | 6.6 |
| | 1.3 | .6 | | .9 | | 1.1 | 1.1 | .8 | 1.0 | .9 |
| (19) | 3.9 | (12) 1.0 | (37) 2.4 | % Officers', Directors' Owners' Comp/Revenues | (33) 2.3 | (27) 2.0 | (35) 2.2 | (44) 1.8 | (37) 2.4 |
| | 5.4 | 2.1 | | 4.9 | | 4.0 | 5.2 | 4.2 | 3.6 | 4.9 |
| 2008M | 142954M | 1240874M | 154682864M | 156068700M | Contract Revenues ($) | 168718715M | 200849943M | 106527653M | 6704923M | 156068700M |
| 824M | 85065M | 776411M | 108927525M | 109789825M | Total Assets ($) | 145806401M | 170670324M | 44212117M | 3888169M | 109789825M |

© RMA 2024  
M = $ thousand  MM = $ million  
See Pages viii through xx for Explanation of Ratios and Data

## CONSTRUCTION-% OF COMPLETION—All Other Specialty Trade Contractors  NAICS 238990

**1389**

### Current Data Sorted by Revenue | Comparative Historical Data

| | | | | | Type of Statement | | | | | |
|---|---|---|---|---|---|---|---|---|---|---|
| | 8 | 2<br>22<br>3 | 4<br>5 | 6<br>35<br>3 | Unqualified<br>Reviewed<br>Compiled | 7<br>21<br>6 | 5<br>23<br>3 | 4<br>21<br>8 | 11<br>38<br>4 | 6<br>35<br>3 |
| 1 | 11<br>16 | 2<br>17 | 12 | 13<br>46 | Tax Returns<br>Other | 8<br>27 | 7<br>47 | 10<br>55 | 14<br>60 | 13<br>46 |
| | 14 (4/1-9/30/23) | | 89 (10/1/23-3/31/24) | | | 4/1/19-<br>3/31/20 | 4/1/20-<br>3/31/21 | 4/1/21-<br>3/31/22 | 4/1/22-<br>3/31/23 | 4/1/23-<br>3/31/24 |
| 0-1MM | 1-10MM | 10-50MM | 50 & OVER | ALL | | ALL | ALL | ALL | ALL | ALL |
| 1 | 35 | 46 | 21 | 103 | NUMBER OF STATEMENTS | 69 | 85 | 98 | 127 | 103 |
| % | % | % | % | % | ASSETS | % | % | % | % | % |
| | 23.9 | 16.7 | 19.0 | 20.1 | Cash & Equivalents | 13.2 | 17.9 | 16.5 | 16.1 | 20.1 |
| | 24.4 | 38.8 | 33.8 | 32.5 | A/R - Progress Billings | 38.7 | 35.6 | 38.0 | 32.2 | 32.5 |
| | 1.5 | 1.6 | 2.3 | 1.7 | A/R - Current Retention | 2.0 | 1.3 | 1.4 | 1.6 | 1.7 |
| | 4.5 | 3.0 | .9 | 3.3 | Inventory | 2.6 | 3.0 | 4.1 | 4.0 | 3.3 |
| | 2.9 | 5.3 | 6.8 | 4.7 | Cost & Est. Earnings<br>In Excess Billings | 7.0 | 3.0 | 3.9 | 4.6 | 4.7 |
| | 3.6 | 5.7 | 2.9 | 4.4 | All Other Current | 2.1 | 4.8 | 5.7 | 6.4 | 4.4 |
| | 60.8 | 71.0 | 65.7 | 66.7 | Total Current | 65.6 | 65.7 | 69.6 | 65.0 | 66.7 |
| | 26.0 | 16.1 | 19.3 | 19.9 | Fixed Assets (net) | 20.9 | 25.0 | 20.7 | 21.4 | 19.9 |
| | .0 | .0 | .0 | .0 | Joint Ventures & Investments | .9 | .3 | .3 | .8 | .0 |
| | 3.7 | 1.9 | 4.1 | 2.9 | Intangibles (net) | 2.7 | 3.3 | 2.1 | 3.0 | 2.9 |
| | 9.5 | 11.0 | 11.0 | 10.4 | All Other Non-Current | 10.0 | 5.7 | 7.3 | 9.7 | 10.4 |
| | 100.0 | 100.0 | 100.0 | 100.0 | Total | 100.0 | 100.0 | 100.0 | 100.0 | 100.0 |
| | | | | | LIABILITIES | | | | | |
| | 8.7 | 2.8 | 1.4 | 4.5 | Notes Payable-Short Term | 6.0 | 5.2 | 6.9 | 5.6 | 4.5 |
| | 6.2 | 12.0 | 17.9 | 11.1 | A/P - Trade | 18.2 | 12.3 | 14.9 | 14.6 | 11.1 |
| | .1 | .1 | .3 | .1 | A/P - Retention | .0 | .0 | .1 | .0 | .1 |
| | 3.2 | 9.4 | 8.5 | 7.0 | Billings in Excess of Costs<br>& Est. Earnings | 7.4 | 6.8 | 8.1 | 7.4 | 7.0 |
| | .4 | .2 | .3 | .3 | Income Taxes Payable | .1 | .1 | .1 | .3 | .3 |
| | 2.4 | 3.5 | 2.1 | 2.8 | Cur. Mat.-L/T/D | 3.9 | 2.7 | 3.3 | 3.4 | 2.8 |
| | 4.2 | 7.6 | 8.0 | 6.6 | All Other Current | 9.2 | 7.8 | 5.1 | 7.3 | 6.6 |
| | 25.2 | 35.6 | 38.5 | 32.5 | Total Current | 44.8 | 35.0 | 38.4 | 38.6 | 32.5 |
| | 28.4 | 12.9 | 11.4 | 19.6 | Long-Term Debt | 15.6 | 24.6 | 13.9 | 16.1 | 19.6 |
| | .5 | .2 | 1.2 | .5 | Deferred Taxes | .3 | .4 | .5 | .2 | .5 |
| | 3.6 | 7.9 | 6.3 | 6.0 | All Other Non-Current | 4.5 | 4.0 | 3.5 | 10.2 | 6.0 |
| | 42.3 | 43.4 | 42.6 | 41.4 | Net Worth | 34.8 | 36.0 | 43.8 | 34.9 | 41.4 |
| | 100.0 | 100.0 | 100.0 | 100.0 | Total Liabilities & Net Worth | 100.0 | 100.0 | 100.0 | 100.0 | 100.0 |
| | | | | | INCOME DATA | | | | | |
| | 100.0 | 100.0 | 100.0 | 100.0 | Contract Revenues | 100.0 | 100.0 | 100.0 | 100.0 | 100.0 |
| | 36.8 | 27.8 | 19.0 | 29.3 | Gross Profit | 24.6 | 29.1 | 24.9 | 27.2 | 29.3 |
| | 29.5 | 17.0 | 11.3 | 20.1 | Operating Expenses | 20.0 | 23.2 | 19.1 | 22.8 | 20.1 |
| | 7.3 | 10.8 | 7.7 | 9.3 | Operating Profit | 4.5 | 5.8 | 5.8 | 4.4 | 9.3 |
| | .0 | .6 | .3 | .3 | All Other Expenses (net) | .3 | -.9 | -2.4 | -1.2 | .3 |
| | 7.3 | 10.2 | 7.3 | 8.9 | Profit Before Taxes | 4.2 | 6.7 | 8.2 | 5.6 | 8.9 |
| | | | | | RATIOS | | | | | |
| | 5.1 | 2.8 | 2.0 | 3.0 | | 2.6 | 2.9 | 2.9 | 2.5 | 3.0 |
| | 2.1 | 2.1 | 1.7 | 2.0 | Current | 1.5 | 1.9 | 1.8 | 1.8 | 2.0 |
| | 1.5 | 1.4 | 1.4 | 1.5 | | 1.0 | 1.3 | 1.3 | 1.2 | 1.5 |
| | 7.6 | 7.5 | 2.6 | 6.2 | | 4.8 | 8.2 | 6.1 | 5.0 | 6.2 |
| (25) | 3.3 | (44) 4.5 | 2.1 | (90) 3.0 | Receivables/Payables | (66) 2.7 | (79) 3.8 | (95) 2.9 | (115) 2.4 | (90) 3.0 |
| | 2.1 | 2.6 | 1.7 | 2.1 | | 1.7 | 2.2 | 1.8 | 1.4 | 2.1 |
| | 0 UND | 54 6.7 | 41 9.0 | 38 9.5 | | 41 8.8 | 40 9.1 | 47 7.7 | 29 12.6 | 38 9.5 |
| | 51 7.1 | 76 4.8 | 70 5.2 | 69 5.3 | Revenues/Receivables | 65 5.6 | 65 5.6 | 68 5.4 | 64 5.7 | 69 5.3 |
| | 81 4.5 | 87 4.2 | 85 4.3 | 83 4.4 | | 91 4.0 | 91 4.0 | 96 3.8 | 87 4.2 | 83 4.4 |
| | 0 UND | 13 27.6 | 32 11.3 | 9 42.9 | | 11 33.0 | 9 40.5 | 13 27.5 | 10 38.1 | 9 42.9 |
| | 8 46.7 | 22 16.7 | 38 9.7 | 24 15.5 | Cost of Revenues/Payables | 27 13.3 | 21 17.6 | 28 13.2 | 26 13.8 | 24 15.5 |
| | 30 12.1 | 34 10.6 | 43 8.5 | 40 9.2 | | 60 6.1 | 37 9.9 | 50 7.3 | 51 7.1 | 40 9.2 |
| | 3.9 | 3.7 | 5.5 | 4.1 | | 6.2 | 4.3 | 4.4 | 4.8 | 4.1 |
| | 5.6 | 5.3 | 9.0 | 6.7 | Revenues/Working Capital | 11.9 | 6.5 | 7.9 | 9.5 | 6.7 |
| | 34.8 | 13.7 | 11.8 | 14.2 | | -224.3 | 16.2 | 14.7 | 19.9 | 14.2 |
| | 89.2 | 62.2 | 195.2 | 67.9 | | 41.8 | 56.9 | 86.0 | 26.6 | 67.9 |
| (33) | 9.2 | (38) 19.6 | (18) 34.2 | (90) 12.4 | EBIT/Interest | (60) 8.9 | (76) 15.1 | (81) 19.8 | (102) 10.7 | (90) 12.4 |
| | 2.3 | 5.8 | 8.6 | 4.2 | | 1.0 | 2.5 | 5.5 | 1.5 | 4.2 |
| | | | | 13.2 | | 6.9 | 16.9 | 29.3 | 7.2 | 13.2 |
| | | | (14) | 4.7 | Net Profit + Depr., Dep.,<br>Amort./Cur. Mat. L/T/D | (13) 1.8 | (11) 7.8 | (13) 5.3 | (20) 3.3 | (14) 4.7 |
| | | | | 1.9 | | -.3 | .6 | 3.9 | 1.8 | 1.9 |
| | .1 | .1 | .2 | .1 | | .2 | .2 | .2 | .2 | .1 |
| | .4 | .2 | .4 | .3 | Fixed/Worth | .5 | .5 | .4 | .4 | .3 |
| | 1.1 | .6 | .7 | 1.0 | | 1.7 | 1.1 | .7 | 1.0 | 1.0 |
| | .6 | .6 | .7 | .6 | | .7 | .6 | .6 | .7 | .6 |
| | 1.0 | 1.0 | 1.1 | 1.1 | Debt/Worth | 1.5 | 1.1 | 1.1 | 1.4 | 1.1 |
| | 3.3 | 2.7 | 2.3 | 2.7 | | 3.3 | 2.6 | 2.2 | 3.6 | 2.7 |
| | 76.1 | 65.9 | 51.3 | 62.3 | | 68.3 | 47.4 | 47.7 | 44.6 | 62.3 |
| (32) | 33.7 | (42) 34.0 | (18) 38.2 | (92) 35.2 | % Profit Before Taxes/<br>Tangible Net Worth | (61) 22.1 | (74) 29.6 | (90) 31.5 | (111) 20.3 | (92) 35.2 |
| | 6.8 | 14.6 | 23.5 | 10.6 | | 6.6 | 9.6 | 10.2 | 4.9 | 10.6 |
| | 29.1 | 34.5 | 20.1 | 31.9 | | 23.0 | 22.1 | 26.1 | 20.2 | 31.9 |
| | 14.1 | 14.6 | 14.9 | 14.5 | % Profit Before Taxes/<br>Total Assets | 10.7 | 11.9 | 12.7 | 7.4 | 14.5 |
| | 3.5 | 7.0 | 5.0 | 5.0 | | 1.4 | 4.0 | 4.6 | 1.0 | 5.0 |
| | 1.3 | .5 | .3 | .7 | | .7 | .8 | .8 | .5 | .7 |
| (24) | 2.6 | (38) .9 | (14) 1.5 | (76) 1.2 | % Depr., Dep., Amort./<br>Revenues | (50) 1.5 | (64) 1.3 | (65) 1.9 | (98) 1.2 | (76) 1.2 |
| | 4.9 | 1.5 | 2.3 | 2.6 | | 2.7 | 3.0 | 3.6 | 2.6 | 2.6 |
| | 1.5 | .7 | | .9 | % Officers', Directors' | 1.9 | 1.2 | 1.3 | 1.0 | .9 |
| (19) | 2.7 | (14) 1.2 | (36) | 1.7 | Owners' Comp/Revenues | (18) 3.5 | (29) 3.0 | (41) 2.0 | (43) 1.9 | (36) 1.7 |
| | 5.4 | 2.8 | | | | 4.0 | 6.4 | 4.1 | 2.9 | 2.8 |
| 346M | 203505M | 1200668M | 4392283M | 5796802M | Contract Revenues ($) | 71002785M | 51011160M | 22400165M | 5167080M | 5796802M |
| 49M | 109568M | 651705M | 4176451M | 4937773M | Total Assets ($) | 35806393M | 62710375M | 11728661M | 3133830M | 4937773M |

© RMA 2024  M = $ thousand   MM = $ million
See Pages viii through xx for Explanation of Ratios and Data

# TEXT—KEY WORD INDEX OF INDUSTRIES APPEARING IN THE STATEMENT STUDIES

## STATEMENT STUDIES KEY WORD INDEX

*A complete description of each industry category listed below begins on page 31.*

### A

Adhesive Manufacturing, 332-333, mfg
Administration of Education Programs, 1358-1359, pub admin
Administration of General Economic Programs, 1366-1367, pub admin
Administration of Housing Programs, 1362-1363, pub admin
Administration of Public Health Programs, 1360-1361, pub admin
Administration of Urban Planning and Community and Rural Development, 1364-1365, pub admin
Administrative Management and General Management Consulting Services, 1022-1023, prof serv
Advertising Agencies, 1042-1043, prof serv
Air and Gas Compressor Manufacturing, 468-469, mfg
Air-Conditioning and Warm Air Heating Equipment and Commercial and Industrial Refrigeration Equipment Manufacturing, 456-457, mfg
Aircraft Engine and Engine Parts Manufacturing, 544-545, mfg
Aircraft Manufacturing, 542-543, mfg
All Other Amusement and Recreation Industries, 1254-1255, ent
All Other Automotive Repair and Maintenance, 1296-1297, other
All Other Basic Organic Chemical Manufacturing, 318-319, mfg
All Other Business Support Services, 1082-1083, Admin
All Other Consumer Goods Rental, 968-969, R/E
All Other Converted Paper Product Manufacturing, 306-307, mfg
All Other General Merchandise Retailers, 760-761, rtl
All Other Health and Personal Care Retailers, 768-769, rtl
All Other Home Furnishings Retailers, 756-757, rtl
All Other Industrial Machinery Manufacturing, 448-449, mfg
All Other Insurance Related Activities, 930-931, fin
All Other Legal Services, 986-987, prof serv
All Other Miscellaneous Ambulatory Health Care Services, 1188-1189, HC
All Other Miscellaneous Chemical Product and Preparation Manufacturing, 340-341, mfg
All Other Miscellaneous Crop Farming, 100-101, ag
All Other Miscellaneous Electrical Equipment and Component Manufacturing, 522-523, mfg
All Other Miscellaneous Fabricated Metal Product Manufacturing, 434-435, mfg
All Other Miscellaneous Food Manufacturing, 254-255, mfg
All Other Miscellaneous General Purpose Machinery Manufacturing, 484-485, mfg
All Other Miscellaneous Manufacturing, 584-585, mfg
All Other Miscellaneous Retailers, 794-795, rtl
All Other Miscellaneous Schools and Instruction, 1144-1145, edu
All Other Miscellaneous Textile Product Mills, 270-271, mfg
All Other Miscellaneous Waste Management Services, 1126-1127, Admin
All Other Miscellaneous Wood Product Manufacturing, 292-293, mfg
All Other Outpatient Care Centers, 1176-1177, HC
All Other Personal Services, 1320-1321, other
All Other Plastics Product Manufacturing, 354-355, mfg
All Other Professional, Scientific, and Technical Services, 1056-1057, prof serv
All Other Rubber Product Manufacturing, 358-359, mfg
All Other Specialty Food Retailers, 748-749, rtl
All Other Specialty Trade Contractors, 216-217, cons-g
All Other Specialty Trade Contractors, 1389, cons-%
All Other Support Activities for Transportation, 848-849, trans
All Other Support Services, 1108-1109, Admin
All Other Telecommunications, 886-887, info
All Other Transit and Ground Passenger Transportation, 824-825, trans
All Other Transportation Equipment Manufacturing, 554-555, mfg
All Other Travel Arrangement and Reservation Services, 1088-1089, Admin
All Other Traveler Accommodation, 1264-1265, rest/lodg
Ambulance Services, 1184-1185, HC
Amusement and Theme Parks, 1238-1239, ent
Analytical Laboratory Instrument Manufacturing, 508-509, mfg
Animal (except Poultry) Slaughtering, 236-237, mfg
Apparel Accessories and Other Apparel Manufacturing, 276-277, mfg
Apple Orchards, 92-93, ag
Architectural Services, 996-997, prof serv
Asphalt Paving Mixture and Block Manufacturing, 312-313, mfg
Assisted Living Facilities for the Elderly, 1204-1205, HC
Audio and Video Equipment Manufacturing, 494-495, mfg
Automobile and Light Duty Motor Vehicle Manufacturing, 524-525, mfg
Automobile and Other Motor Vehicle Merchant Wholesalers, 588-589, wsle
Automotive Body, Paint, and Interior Repair and Maintenance, 1290-1291, other
Automotive Oil Change and Lubrication Shops, 1292-1293, other
Automotive Parts and Accessories Retailers, 726-727, rtl

### B

Baked Goods Retailers, 746-747, rtl
Ball and Roller Bearing Manufacturing, 428-429, mfg
Bare Printed Circuit Board Manufacturing, 496-497, mfg
Beauty Salons, 1304-1305, other
Bed-and-Breakfast Inns, 1262-1263, rest/lodg
Beef Cattle Ranching and Farming, 102-103, ag
Beer and Ale Merchant Wholesalers, 700-701, wsle
Beer, Wine, and Liquor Retailers, 750-751, rtl
Blood and Organ Banks, 1186-1187, HC
Boat Building, 550-551, mfg
Boat Dealers, 722-723, rtl
Bolt, Nut, Screw, Rivet, and Washer Manufacturing, 414-415, mfg
Book Publishers, 870-871, info
Bowling Centers, 1252-1253, ent
Breweries, 258-259, mfg
Brick, Stone, and Related Construction Material Merchant Wholesalers, 602-603, wsle
Broadwoven Fabric Mills, 264-265, mfg
Business Associations, 1336-1337, other

### C

Car Washes, 1294-1295, other
Carpet and Rug Mills, 268-269, mfg
Carpet and Upholstery Cleaning Services, 1100-1101, Admin
Casino Hotels, 1260-1261, rest/lodg
Casinos (except Casino Hotels), 1240-1241, ent
Caterers, 1274-1275, rest/lodg
Cattle Feedlots, 104-105, ag
Charter Bus Industry, 822-823, trans
Cheese Manufacturing, 232-233, mfg
Child and Youth Services, 1208-1209, HC
Child Care Services, 1222-1223, HC
Civic and Social Organizations, 1334-1335, other
Clothing and Clothing Accessories Merchant Wholesalers, 668-669, wsle
Clothing and Clothing Accessories Retailers, 776-777, rtl
Coffee and Tea Manufacturing, 248-249, mfg
Coin-Operated Laundries and Drycleaners, 1310-1311, other
Collection Agencies, 1080-1081, Admin
Colleges, Universities, and Professional Schools, 1132-1133, edu
Commercial Air, Rail, and Water Transportation Equipment Rental and Leasing, 972-973, R/E
Commercial and Industrial Machinery and Equipment (except Automotive and Electronic) Repair and Maintenance, 1300-1301, other
Commercial and Institutional Building Construction, 168-169, cons-g
Commercial and Institutional Building Construction, 1375, cons-%
Commercial and Service Industry Machinery Manufacturing, 450-451, mfg
Commercial Bakeries, 244-245, mfg
Commercial Printing (except Screen and Books), 308-309, mfg
Commercial Screen Printing, 310-311, mfg
Commercial, Industrial, and Institutional Electric Lighting Fixture Manufacturing, 512-513, mfg
Community Food Services, 1214-1215, HC
Computer and Computer Peripheral Equipment and Software Merchant Wholesalers, 610-611, wsle
Computer Facilities Management Services, 1018-1019, prof serv
Computer Systems Design Services, 1016-1017, prof serv
Computer Terminal and Other Computer Peripheral Equipment Manufacturing, 488-489, mfg
Computing Infrastructure Providers, Data Processing, Web Hosting, and Related Services, 888-889, info
Concrete Block and Brick Manufacturing, 364-365, mfg
Confectionery Merchant Wholesalers, 678-679, wsle
Construction and Mining (except Oil Well) Machinery and Equipment Merchant Wholesalers, 634-635, wsle
Construction Machinery Manufacturing, 440-441, mfg
Construction Sand and Gravel Mining, 134-135, mng
Construction, Mining, and Forestry Machinery and Equipment Rental and Leasing, 974-975, R/E
Consumer Electronics and Appliances Rental, 962-963, R/E
Consumer Lending, 896-897, fin
Continuing Care Retirement Communities, 1202-1203, HC
Convenience Retailers, 742-743, rtl
Convention and Trade Show Organizers, 1106-1107, Admin
Conveyor and Conveying Equipment Manufacturing, 472-473, mfg
Corporate, Subsidiary, and Regional Managing Offices, 1062-1063, mgmt
Corrugated and Solid Fiber Box Manufacturing, 296-297, mfg
Cosmetics, Beauty Supplies, and Perfume Retailers, 764-765, rtl
Cotton Ginning, 112-113, ag

## STATEMENT STUDIES KEY WORD INDEX
*A complete description of each industry category listed below begins on page 31.*

Couriers and Express Delivery Services, 850-851, trans
Crude Petroleum Extraction, 126-127, mng
Crushed and Broken Limestone Mining and Quarrying, 130-131, mng
Custom Architectural Woodwork and Millwork Manufacturing, 564-565, mfg
Custom Computer Programming Services, 1014-1015, prof serv
Cut and Sew Apparel Contractors, 272-273, mfg
Cut and Sew Apparel Manufacturing (except Contractors), 274-275, mfg
Cut Stone and Stone Product Manufacturing, 368-369, mfg
Cutting Tool and Machine Tool Accessory Manufacturing, 462-463, mfg

### D

Dairy Cattle and Milk Production, 106-107, ag
Dairy Product (except Dried or Canned) Merchant Wholesalers, 674-675, wsle
Deep Sea Freight Transportation, 804-805, trans
Dental Equipment and Supplies Manufacturing, 572-573, mfg
Diagnostic Imaging Centers, 1180-1181, HC
Direct Health and Medical Insurance Carriers, 918-919, fin
Direct Mail Advertising, 1048-1049, prof serv
Direct Property and Casualty Insurance Carriers, 920-921, fin
Distilleries, 262-263, mfg
Dog and Cat Food Manufacturing, 220-221, mfg
Drilling Oil and Gas Wells, 136-137, mng
Drinking Places (Alcoholic Beverages), 1276-1277, rest/lodg
Drugs and Druggists' Sundries Merchant Wholesalers, 662-663, wsle
Drycleaning and Laundry Services (except Coin-Operated), 1312-1313, other
Drywall and Insulation Contractors, 202-203, cons-g
Drywall and Insulation Contractors, 1386, cons-%

### E

Educational Support Services, 1146-1147, edu
Electric Power Distribution, 150-151, util
Electrical Apparatus and Equipment, Wiring Supplies, and Related Equipment Merchant Wholesalers, 620-621, wsle
Electrical Contractors and Other Wiring Installation Contractors, 196-197, cons-g
Electrical Contractors and Other Wiring Installation Contractors, 1384, cons-%
Electronic and Precision Equipment Repair and Maintenance, 1298-1299, other
Electronic Computer Manufacturing, 486-487, mfg
Electronics and Appliance Retailers, 758-759, rtl
Electroplating, Plating, Polishing, Anodizing, and Coloring, 420-421, mfg
Elementary and Secondary Schools, 1130-1131, edu
Employment Placement Agencies, 1070-1071, Admin
Engineering Services, 1000-1001, prof serv
Environment, Conservation and Wildlife Organizations, 1330-1331, other
Environmental Consulting Services, 1032-1033, prof serv
Executive and Legislative Offices, Combined, 1352-1353, pub admin
Executive Offices, 1346-1347, pub admin
Executive Search Services, 1072-1073, Admin
Exterminating and Pest Control Services, 1094-1095, Admin

### F

Fabricated Pipe and Pipe Fitting Manufacturing, 432-433, mfg
Fabricated Structural Metal Manufacturing, 390-391, mfg
Facilities Support Services, 1068-1069, Admin
Farm and Garden Machinery and Equipment Merchant Wholesalers, 636-637, wsle
Farm Machinery and Equipment Manufacturing, 436-437, mfg
Farm Management Services, 118-119, ag
Farm Product Warehousing and Storage, 858-859, trans
Farm Supplies Merchant Wholesalers, 704-705, wsle
Fertilizer (Mixing Only) Manufacturing, 322-323, mfg
Financial Transactions Processing, Reserve, and Clearinghouse Activities, 904-905, fin
Fine Arts Schools, 1140-1141, edu
Finish Carpentry Contractors, 210-211, cons-g
Fire Protection, 1356-1357, pub admin
Fish and Seafood Merchant Wholesalers, 680-681, wsle
Fitness and Recreational Sports Centers, 1250-1251, ent
Flight Training, 1136-1137, edu
Floor Covering Retailers, 754-755, rtl
Flooring Contractors, 206-207, cons-g
Flooring Contractors, 1387, cons-%
Flour Milling, 224-225, mfg
Flower, Nursery Stock, and Florists' Supplies Merchant Wholesalers, 706-707, wsle
Fluid Milk Manufacturing, 230-231, mfg
Fluid Power Valve and Hose Fitting Manufacturing, 424-425, mfg
Folding Paperboard Box Manufacturing, 298-299, mfg
Food (Health) Supplement Retailers, 766-767, rtl
Food Product Machinery Manufacturing, 446-447, mfg
Food Service Contractors, 1272-1273, rest/lodg
Footwear Merchant Wholesalers, 666-667, wsle
Fossil Fuel Electric Power Generation, 142-143, util
Framing Contractors, 186-187, cons-g
Freestanding Ambulatory Surgical and Emergency Centers, 1174-1175, HC
Freight Transportation Arrangement, 844-845, trans
Fresh Fruit and Vegetable Merchant Wholesalers, 684-685, wsle
Frozen Specialty Food Manufacturing, 226-227, mfg
Fruit and Vegetable Canning, 228-229, mfg
Fuel Dealers, 774-775, rtl
Full-Service Restaurants, 1278-1279, rest/lodg
Funeral Homes and Funeral Services, 1308-1309, other
Furniture Merchant Wholesalers, 596-597, wsle
Furniture Retailers, 752-753, rtl

### G

Gasket, Packing, and Sealing Device Manufacturing, 580-581, mfg
Gasoline Stations with Convenience Stores, 770-771, rtl
General Automotive Repair, 1286-1287, other
General Freight Trucking, Local, 808-809, trans
General Freight Trucking, Long-Distance, Less Than Truckload, 812-813, trans
General Freight Trucking, Long-Distance, Truckload, 810-811, trans
General Line Grocery Merchant Wholesalers, 670-671, wsle
General Medical and Surgical Hospitals, 1190-1191, HC
General Rental Centers, 970-971, R/E
General Warehousing and Storage, 854-855, trans
Gift, Novelty, and Souvenir Retailers, 788-789, rtl
Glass and Glazing Contractors, 190-191, cons-g
Glass and Glazing Contractors, 1382, cons-%
Glass Product Manufacturing Made of Purchased Glass, 360-361, mfg
Golf Courses and Country Clubs, 1244-1245, ent
Grain and Field Bean Merchant Wholesalers, 688-689, wsle
Grantmaking Foundations, 1324-1325, other
Grape Vineyards, 94-95, ag
Graphic Design Services, 1010-1011, prof serv

### H

Hardware Manufacturing, 404-405, mfg
Hardware Merchant Wholesalers, 626-627, wsle
Hardware Retailers, 732-733, rtl
Hardwood Veneer and Plywood Manufacturing, 282-283, mfg
Hazardous Waste Treatment and Disposal, 1114-1115, Admin
Heating Equipment (except Warm Air Furnaces) Manufacturing, 454-455, mfg
Highway, Street, and Bridge Construction, 178-179, cons-g
Highway, Street, and Bridge Construction, 1378, cons-%
HMO Medical Centers, 1170-1171, HC
Home Centers, 730-731, rtl
Home Furnishing Merchant Wholesalers, 598-599, wsle
Home Health Care Services, 1182-1183, HC
Home Health Equipment Rental, 964-965, R/E
Hotels (except Casino Hotels) and Motels, 1258-1259, rest/lodg
Household Appliances, Electric Housewares, and Consumer Electronics Merchant Wholesalers, 622-623, wsle
Household Furniture (except Wood and Upholstered) Manufacturing, 560-561, mfg
Human Resources Consulting Services, 1024-1025, prof serv

### I

Ice Cream and Frozen Dessert Manufacturing, 234-235, mfg
Independent Artists, Writers, and Performers, 1232-1233, ent
Indoor and Outdoor Display Advertising, 1046-1047, prof serv
Industrial and Commercial Fan and Blower and Air Purification Equipment Manufacturing, 452-453, mfg
Industrial and Personal Service Paper Merchant Wholesalers, 660-661, wsle
Industrial Building Construction, 166-167, cons-g
Industrial Building Construction, 1374, cons-%
Industrial Design Services, 1008-1009, prof serv
Industrial Machinery and Equipment Merchant Wholesalers, 638-639, wsle
Industrial Mold Manufacturing, 458-459, mfg
Industrial Process Furnace and Oven Manufacturing, 482-483, mfg
Industrial Supplies Merchant Wholesalers, 640-641, wsle
Industrial Truck, Tractor, Trailer, and Stacker Machinery Manufacturing, 476-477, mfg
Industrial Valve Manufacturing, 422-423, mfg
Inland Water Freight Transportation, 806-807, trans
Institutional Furniture Manufacturing, 562-563, mfg

# STATEMENT STUDIES KEY WORD INDEX

*A complete description of each industry category listed below begins on page 31.*

Instruments and Related Products Manufacturing for Measuring, Displaying, and Controlling Industrial Process Variables, 506-507, mfg
Insurance Agencies and Brokerages, 926-927, fin
Interior Design Services, 1006-1007, prof serv
International, Secondary Market, and All Other Nondepository Credit Intermediation, 900-901, fin
Investment Banking and Securities Intermediation, 908-909, fin
Iron and Steel Forging, 382-383, mfg
Iron and Steel Mills and Ferroalloy Manufacturing, 370-371, mfg
Iron and Steel Pipe and Tube Manufacturing from Purchased Steel, 372-373, mfg

## J
Janitorial Services, 1096-1097, Admin
Jewelry and Silverware Manufacturing, 574-575, mfg
Jewelry Retailers, 780-781, rtl
Jewelry, Watch, Precious Stone, and Precious Metal Merchant Wholesalers, 652-653, wsle

## K
Kidney Dialysis Centers, 1172-1173, HC

## L
Labor Unions and Similar Labor Organizations, 1340-1341, other
Land Subdivision, 176-177, cons-g
Landscape Architectural Services, 998-999, prof serv
Landscaping Services, 1098-1099, Admin
Lawn and Garden Tractor and Home Lawn and Garden Equipment Manufacturing, 438-439, mfg
Legislative Bodies, 1348-1349, pub admin
Lessors of Miniwarehouses and Self-Storage Units, 944-945, R/E
Lessors of Nonfinancial Intangible Assets (except Copyrighted Works), 980-981, R/E
Lessors of Nonresidential Buildings (except Miniwarehouses), 942-943, R/E
Lessors of Other Real Estate Property, 946-947, R/E
Lessors of Residential Buildings and Dwellings, 940-941, R/E
Limited-Service Restaurants, 1280-1281, rest/lodg
Linen Supply, 1314-1315, other
Local Messengers and Local Delivery, 852-853, trans
Logging, 110-111, ag
Lumber, Plywood, Millwork, and Wood Panel Merchant Wholesalers, 600-601, wsle

## M
Machine Shops, 410-411, mfg
Machine Tool Manufacturing, 464-465, mfg
Marinas, 1248-1249, ent
Marine Cargo Handling, 834-835, trans
Marketing Consulting Services, 1026-1027, prof serv
Marketing Research and Public Opinion Polling, 1052-1053, prof serv
Masonry Contractors, 188-189, cons-g
Materials Recovery Facilities, 1122-1123, Admin
Measuring, Dispensing, and Other Pumping Equipment Manufacturing, 470-471, mfg
Meat and Meat Product Merchant Wholesalers, 682-683, wsle
Meat Processed from Carcasses, 238-239, mfg
Meat Retailers, 744-745, rtl
Media Streaming Distribution Services, Social Networks, and Other Media Networks and Content Providers, 878-879, info
Medical Laboratories, 1178-1179, HC

Medical, Dental, and Hospital Equipment and Supplies Merchant Wholesalers, 614-615, wsle
Medicinal and Botanical Manufacturing, 326-327, mfg
Metal Coating, Engraving (except Jewelry and Silverware), and Allied Services to Manufacturers, 418-419, mfg
Metal Crown, Closure, and Other Metal Stamping (except Automotive), 384-385, mfg
Metal Heat Treating, 416-417, mfg
Metal Service Centers and Other Metal Merchant Wholesalers, 618-619, wsle
Metal Tank (Heavy Gauge) Manufacturing, 400-401, mfg
Metal Window and Door Manufacturing, 394-395, mfg
Mining Machinery and Equipment Manufacturing, 442-443, mfg
Miscellaneous Financial Investment Activities, 916-917, fin
Miscellaneous Intermediation, 910-911, fin
Mortgage and Nonmortgage Loan Brokers, 902-903, fin
Motion Picture and Video Production, 864-865, info
Motion Picture Theaters (except Drive-Ins), 866-867, info
Motor and Generator Manufacturing, 516-517, mfg
Motor Vehicle Body Manufacturing, 526-527, mfg
Motor Vehicle Electrical and Electronic Equipment Manufacturing, 534-535, mfg
Motor Vehicle Gasoline Engine and Engine Parts Manufacturing, 532-533, mfg
Motor Vehicle Metal Stamping, 538-539, mfg
Motor Vehicle Parts (Used) Merchant Wholesalers, 594-595, wsle
Motor Vehicle Seating and Interior Trim Manufacturing, 536-537, mfg
Motor Vehicle Supplies and New Parts Merchant Wholesalers, 590-591, wsle
Motor Vehicle Towing, 840-841, trans
Motorcycle, ATV, and All Other Motor Vehicle Dealers, 724-725, rtl
Motorcycle, Bicycle, and Parts Manufacturing, 552-553, mfg
Museums, 1234-1235, ent
Music Publishers, 868-869, info
Musical Instrument and Supplies Retailers, 784-785, rtl
Musical Instrument Manufacturing, 582-583, mfg

## N
Natural Gas Distribution, 152-153, util
Natural Gas Extraction, 128-129, mng
Navigational Services to Shipping, 836-837, trans
New Car Dealers, 716-717, rtl
New Housing For-Sale Builders, 162-163, cons-g
New Housing For-Sale Builders, 1372, cons-%
New Multifamily Housing Construction (except For-Sale Builders), 160-161, cons-g
New Multifamily Housing Construction (except For-Sale Builders), 1371, cons-%
New Single-Family Housing Construction (except For-Sale Builders), 158-159, cons-g
New Single-Family Housing Construction (except For-Sale Builders), 1370, cons-%
Nonferrous Metal Die-Casting Foundries, 380-381, mfg
Nonresidential Property Managers, 952-953, R/E
Nonscheduled Chartered Passenger Air Transportation, 800-801, trans
Nursery and Tree Production, 98-99, ag
Nursery, Garden Center, and Farm Supply Retailers, 738-739, rtl

Nursing Care Facilities (Skilled Nursing Facilities), 1196-1197, HC

## O
Office Administrative Services, 1066-1067, Admin
Office Equipment Merchant Wholesalers, 608-609, wsle
Office Machinery and Equipment Rental and Leasing, 976-977, R/E
Office Supplies and Stationery Retailers, 786-787, rtl
Offices of All Other Miscellaneous Health Practitioners, 1166-1167, HC
Offices of Certified Public Accountants, 988-989, prof serv
Offices of Chiropractors, 1156-1157, HC
Offices of Dentists, 1154-1155, HC
Offices of Lawyers, 984-985, prof serv
Offices of Mental Health Practitioners (except Physicians), 1160-1161, HC
Offices of Optometrists, 1158-1159, HC
Offices of Other Holding Companies, 1060-1061, mgmt
Offices of Physical, Occupational and Speech Therapists, and Audiologists, 1162-1163, HC
Offices of Physicians (except Mental Health Specialists), 1150-1151, HC
Offices of Physicians, Mental Health Specialists, 1152-1153, HC
Offices of Podiatrists, 1164-1165, HC
Offices of Real Estate Agents and Brokers, 948-949, R/E
Oil and Gas Field Machinery and Equipment Manufacturing, 444-445, mfg
Oil and Gas Pipeline and Related Structures Construction, 172-173, cons-g
Open-End Investment Funds, 932-933, fin
Ornamental and Architectural Metal Work Manufacturing, 398-399, mfg
Other Accounting Services, 994-995, prof serv
Other Activities Related to Credit Intermediation, 906-907, fin
Other Activities Related to Real Estate, 954-955, R/E
Other Aircraft Parts and Auxiliary Equipment Manufacturing, 546-547, mfg
Other Airport Operations, 826-827, trans
Other Aluminum Rolling, Drawing, and Extruding, 378-379, mfg
Other Animal Food Manufacturing, 222-223, mfg
Other Basic Inorganic Chemical Manufacturing, 316-317, mfg
Other Building Equipment Contractors, 200-201, cons-g
Other Building Finishing Contractors, 212-213, cons-g
Other Building Material Dealers, 734-735, rtl
Other Chemical and Allied Products Merchant Wholesalers, 694-695, wsle
Other Commercial and Industrial Machinery and Equipment Rental and Leasing, 978-979, R/E
Other Commercial Equipment Merchant Wholesalers, 612-613, wsle
Other Communications Equipment Manufacturing, 492-493, mfg
Other Community Housing Services, 1218-1219, HC
Other Computer Related Services, 1020-1021, prof serv
Other Concrete Product Manufacturing, 366-367, mfg
Other Construction Material Merchant Wholesalers, 606-607, wsle
Other Crushed and Broken Stone Mining and Quarrying, 132-133, mng
Other Direct Insurance (except Life, Health, and Medical) Carriers, 922-923, fin
Other Electric Power Generation, 148-149, util

## STATEMENT STUDIES KEY WORD INDEX
*A complete description of each industry category listed below begins on page 31.*

Other Electronic Component Manufacturing, 502-503, mfg
Other Electronic Parts and Equipment Merchant Wholesalers, 624-625, wsle
Other Fabricated Wire Product Manufacturing, 408-409, mfg
Other Farm Product Raw Material Merchant Wholesalers, 690-691, wsle
Other Financial Vehicles, 936-937, fin
Other Foundation, Structure, and Building Exterior Contractors, 194-195, cons-g
Other Gambling Industries, 1242-1243, ent
Other Gasoline Stations, 772-773, rtl
Other General Government Support, 1354-1355, pub admin
Other Grantmaking and Giving Services, 1328-1329, other
Other Grocery and Related Products Merchant Wholesalers, 686-687, wsle
Other Heavy and Civil Engineering Construction, 180-181, cons-g
Other Heavy and Civil Engineering Construction, 1379, cons-%
Other Individual and Family Services, 1212-1213, HC
Other Leather and Allied Product Manufacturing, 278-279, mfg
Other Management Consulting Services, 1030-1031, prof serv
Other Measuring and Controlling Device Manufacturing, 510-511, mfg
Other Metal Container Manufacturing, 402-403, mfg
Other Metal Valve and Pipe Fitting Manufacturing, 426-427, mfg
Other Millwork (including Flooring), 286-287, mfg
Other Miscellaneous Durable Goods Merchant Wholesalers, 654-655, wsle
Other Miscellaneous Nondurable Goods Merchant Wholesalers, 710-711, wsle
Other Motor Vehicle Parts Manufacturing, 540-541, mfg
Other Nonhazardous Waste Treatment and Disposal, 1118-1119, Admin
Other Nonscheduled Air Transportation, 802-803, trans
Other Personal and Household Goods Repair and Maintenance, 1302-1303, other
Other Personal Care Services, 1306-1307, other
Other Professional Equipment and Supplies Merchant Wholesalers, 616-617, wsle
Other Residential Care Facilities, 1206-1207, HC
Other Scientific and Technical Consulting Services, 1034-1035, prof serv
Other Services Related to Advertising, 1050-1051, prof serv
Other Services to Buildings and Dwellings, 1102-1103, Admin
Other Similar Organizations (except Business, Professional, Labor, and Political Organizations), 1342-1343, other
Other Snack Food Manufacturing, 246-247, mfg
Other Social Advocacy Organizations, 1332-1333, other
Other Specialized Design Services, 1012-1013, prof serv
Other Support Activities for Air Transportation, 828-829, trans
Other Support Activities for Road Transportation, 842-843, trans
Other Support Activities for Water Transportation, 838-839, trans
Other Technical and Trade Schools, 1138-1139, edu
Other Vegetable (except Potato) and Melon Farming, 90-91, ag
Other Warehousing and Storage, 860-861, trans
Other Waste Collection, 1112-1113, Admin

Outdoor Power Equipment Retailers, 736-737, rtl
Outpatient Mental Health and Substance Abuse Centers, 1168-1169, HC
Overhead Traveling Crane, Hoist, and Monorail System Manufacturing, 474-475, mfg

## P

Packaged Frozen Food Merchant Wholesalers, 672-673, wsle
Packaging and Labeling Services, 1104-1105, Admin
Packaging Machinery Manufacturing, 480-481, mfg
Packing and Crating, 846-847, trans
Paint and Coating Manufacturing, 330-331, mfg
Painting and Wall Covering Contractors, 204-205, cons-g
Paper Bag and Coated and Treated Paper Manufacturing, 300-301, mfg
Paper Mills, 294-295, mfg
Parking Lots and Garages, 1318-1319, other
Passenger Car Leasing, 958-959, R/E
Passenger Car Rental, 956-957, R/E
Payroll Services, 992-993, prof serv
Perishable Prepared Food Manufacturing, 252-253, mfg
Pesticide and Other Agricultural Chemical Manufacturing, 324-325, mfg
Pet and Pet Supplies Retailers, 792-793, rtl
Pet Care (except Veterinary) Services, 1316-1317, other
Petroleum and Petroleum Products Merchant Wholesalers (except Bulk Stations and Terminals), 698-699, wsle
Petroleum Bulk Stations and Terminals, 696-697, wsle
Petroleum Lubricating Oil and Grease Manufacturing, 314-315, mfg
Pharmaceutical Preparation Manufacturing, 328-329, mfg
Pharmacies and Drug Retailers, 762-763, rtl
Pharmacy Benefit Management and Other Third Party Administration of Insurance and Pension Funds, 928-929, fin
Piece Goods, Notions, and Other Dry Goods Merchant Wholesalers, 664-665, wsle
Plastics Bag and Pouch Manufacturing, 342-343, mfg
Plastics Bottle Manufacturing, 352-353, mfg
Plastics Material and Resin Manufacturing, 320-321, mfg
Plastics Materials and Basic Forms and Shapes Merchant Wholesalers, 692-693, wsle
Plastics Packaging Film and Sheet (including Laminated) Manufacturing, 344-345, mfg
Plastics Pipe and Pipe Fitting Manufacturing, 346-347, mfg
Plate Work Manufacturing, 392-393, mfg
Plumbing and Heating Equipment and Supplies (Hydronics) Merchant Wholesalers, 628-629, wsle
Plumbing, Heating, and Air-Conditioning Contractors, 198-199, cons-g
Plumbing, Heating, and Air-Conditioning Contractors, 1385, cons-%
Polish and Other Sanitation Good Manufacturing, 336-337, mfg
Polystyrene Foam Product Manufacturing, 348-349, mfg
Port and Harbor Operations, 832-833, trans
Portfolio Management and Investment Advice, 912-913, fin
Postharvest Crop Activities (except Cotton Ginning), 116-117, ag
Potato Farming, 88-89, ag
Poultry and Poultry Product Merchant Wholesalers, 676-677, wsle
Poured Concrete Foundation and Structure Contractors, 182-183, cons-g

Poured Concrete Foundation and Structure Contractors, 1380, cons-%
Power and Communication Line and Related Structures Construction, 174-175, cons-g
Power and Communication Line and Related Structures Construction, 1377, cons-%
Power, Distribution, and Specialty Transformer Manufacturing, 514-515, mfg
Precision Turned Product Manufacturing, 412-413, mfg
Prefabricated Metal Building and Component Manufacturing, 388-389, mfg
Prefabricated Wood Building Manufacturing, 290-291, mfg
Printed Circuit Assembly (Electronic Assembly) Manufacturing, 500-501, mfg
Printing and Writing Paper Merchant Wholesalers, 656-657, wsle
Process, Physical Distribution, and Logistics Consulting Services, 1028-1029, prof serv
Professional and Management Development Training, 1134-1135, edu
Professional Employer Organizations, 1076-1077, Admin
Professional Organizations, 1338-1339, other
Promoters of Performing Arts, Sports, and Similar Events with Facilities, 1230-1231, ent
Psychiatric and Substance Abuse Hospitals, 1192-1193, HC
Public Finance Activities, 1350-1351, pub admin
Public Relations Agencies, 1044-1045, prof serv

## R

Radio and Television Broadcasting and Wireless Communications Equipment Manufacturing, 490-491, mfg
Radio Broadcasting Stations, 874-875, info
Ready-Mix Concrete Manufacturing, 362-363, mfg
Real Estate Credit, 898-899, fin
Recreational and Vacation Camps (except Campgrounds), 1268-1269, rest/lodg
Recreational Goods Rental, 966-967, R/E
Recreational Vehicle Dealers, 720-721, rtl
Recyclable Material Merchant Wholesalers, 650-651, wsle
Refrigerated Warehousing and Storage, 856-857, trans
Refrigeration Equipment and Supplies Merchant Wholesalers, 632-633, wsle
Reinsurance Carriers, 924-925, fin
Relay and Industrial Control Manufacturing, 520-521, mfg
Religious Organizations, 1322-1323, other
Remediation Services, 1120-1121, Admin
Research and Development in Biotechnology (except Nanobiotechnology), 1036-1037, prof serv
Research and Development in the Physical, Engineering, and Life Sciences (except Nanotechnology and Biotechnology), 1038-1039, prof serv
Research and Development in the Social Sciences and Humanities, 1040-1041, prof serv
Residential Intellectual and Developmental Disability Facilities, 1198-1199, HC
Residential Mental Health and Substance Abuse Facilities, 1200-1201, HC
Residential Property Managers, 950-951, R/E
Residential Remodelers, 164-165, cons-g
Residential Remodelers, 1373, cons-%
Retail Bakeries, 242-243, mfg
Rolled Steel Shape Manufacturing, 374-375, mfg
Rolling Mill and Other Metalworking Machinery Manufacturing, 466-467, mfg
Roofing Contractors, 192-193, cons-g
Roofing Contractors, 1383, cons-%
Roofing, Siding, and Insulation Material Merchant Wholesalers, 604-605, wsle

## STATEMENT STUDIES KEY WORD INDEX
*A complete description of each industry category listed below begins on page 31.*

Rooming and Boarding Houses, Dormitories, and Workers' Camps, 1270-1271, rest/lodg
Rubber and Plastics Hoses and Belting Manufacturing, 356-357, mfg
RV (Recreational Vehicle) Parks and Campgrounds, 1266-1267, rest/lodg

### S
Sales Financing, 894-895, fin
Sanitary Paper Product Manufacturing, 304-305, mfg
Saw Blade and Handtool Manufacturing, 386-387, mfg
Sawmills, 280-281, mfg
Scheduled Passenger Air Transportation, 798-799, trans
School and Employee Bus Transportation, 820-821, trans
Seafood Product Preparation and Packaging, 240-241, mfg
Search, Detection, Navigation, Guidance, Aeronautical, and Nautical System and Instrument Manufacturing, 504-505, mfg
Secondary Smelting and Alloying of Aluminum, 376-377, mfg
Security Guards and Patrol Services, 1090-1091, Admin
Security Systems Services (except Locksmiths), 1092-1093, Admin
Semiconductor and Related Device Manufacturing, 498-499, mfg
Septic Tank and Related Services, 1124-1125, Admin
Service Establishment Equipment and Supplies Merchant Wholesalers, 642-643, wsle
Services for the Elderly and Persons with Disabilities, 1210-1211, HC
Sheet Metal Work Manufacturing, 396-397, mfg
Ship Building and Repairing, 548-549, mfg
Shoe Retailers, 778-779, rtl
Showcase, Partition, Shelving, and Locker Manufacturing, 566-567, mfg
Sign Manufacturing, 578-579, mfg
Site Preparation Contractors, 214-215, cons-g
Site Preparation Contractors, 1388, cons-%
Skiing Facilities, 1246-1247, ent
Small Arms, Ordnance, and Ordnance Accessories Manufacturing, 430-431, mfg
Snack and Nonalcoholic Beverage Bars, 1282-1283, rest/lodg
Soap and Other Detergent Manufacturing, 334-335, mfg
Soft Drink Manufacturing, 256-257, mfg
Software Publishers, 872-873, info
Soil Preparation, Planting, and Cultivating, 114-115, ag
Solar Electric Power Generation, 144-145, util
Solid Waste Collection, 1110-1111, Admin
Solid Waste Landfill, 1116-1117, Admin
Soybean Farming, 86-87, ag
Special Die and Tool, Die Set, Jig, and Fixture Manufacturing, 460-461, mfg
Specialized Automotive Repair, 1288-1289, other
Specialized Freight (except Used Goods) Trucking, Local, 816-817, trans
Specialized Freight (except Used Goods) Trucking, Long-Distance, 818-819, trans
Specialty (except Psychiatric and Substance Abuse) Hospitals, 1194-1195, HC
Spice and Extract Manufacturing, 250-251, mfg
Sporting and Athletic Goods Manufacturing, 576-577, mfg
Sporting and Recreational Goods and Supplies Merchant Wholesalers, 646-647, wsle
Sporting Goods Retailers, 782-783, rtl
Sports and Recreation Instruction, 1142-1143, edu
Sports Teams and Clubs, 1228-1229, ent
Spring Manufacturing, 406-407, mfg
Stationery and Office Supplies Merchant Wholesalers, 658-659, wsle
Stationery Product Manufacturing, 302-303, mfg
Structural Steel and Precast Concrete Contractors, 184-185, cons-g
Structural Steel and Precast Concrete Contractors, 1381, cons-%
Supermarkets and Other Grocery Retailers (except Convenience Retailers), 740-741, rtl
Support Activities for Animal Production, 120-121, ag
Support Activities for Forestry, 122-123, ag
Support Activities for Oil and Gas Operations, 138-139, mng
Support Activities for Rail Transportation, 830-831, trans
Surgical and Medical Instrument Manufacturing, 568-569, mfg
Surgical Appliance and Supplies Manufacturing, 570-571, mfg
Surveying and Mapping (except Geophysical) Services, 1002-1003, prof serv
Switchgear and Switchboard Apparatus Manufacturing, 518-519, mfg

### T
Tax Preparation Services, 990-991, prof serv
Telecommunications Resellers, 884-885, info
Telemarketing Bureaus and Other Contact Centers, 1078-1079, Admin
Television Broadcasting Stations, 876-877, info
Temporary Help Services, 1074-1075, Admin
Temporary Shelters, 1216-1217, HC
Testing Laboratories and Services, 1004-1005, prof serv
Textile and Fabric Finishing Mills, 266-267, mfg
Theater Companies and Dinner Theaters, 1226-1227, ent
Tile and Terrazzo Contractors, 208-209, cons-g
Timber Tract Operations, 108-109, ag
Tire and Tube Merchant Wholesalers, 592-593, wsle
Tire Dealers, 728-729, rtl
Tobacco Product and Electronic Cigarette Merchant Wholesalers, 708-709, wsle
Toilet Preparation Manufacturing, 338-339, mfg
Tour Operators, 1086-1087, Admin
Toy and Hobby Goods and Supplies Merchant Wholesalers, 648-649, wsle
Transportation Equipment and Supplies (except Motor Vehicle) Merchant Wholesalers, 644-645, wsle
Travel Agencies, 1084-1085, Admin
Travel Trailer and Camper Manufacturing, 530-531, mfg
Tree Nut Farming, 96-97, ag
Truck Trailer Manufacturing, 528-529, mfg
Truck, Utility Trailer, and RV (Recreational Vehicle) Rental and Leasing, 960-961, R/E
Trust, Fiduciary, and Custody Activities, 914-915, fin
Trusts, Estates, and Agency Accounts, 934-935, fin

### U
Upholstered Household Furniture Manufacturing, 558-559, mfg
Urethane and Other Foam Product (except Polystyrene) Manufacturing, 350-351, mfg
Used Car Dealers, 718-719, rtl
Used Household and Office Goods Moving, 814-815, trans
Used Merchandise Retailers, 790-791, rtl

### V
Veterinary Services, 1054-1055, prof serv
Vocational Rehabilitation Services, 1220-1221, HC
Voluntary Health Organizations, 1326-1327, other

### W
Warm Air Heating and Air-Conditioning Equipment and Supplies Merchant Wholesalers, 630-631, wsle
Water and Sewer Line and Related Structures Construction, 170-171, cons-g
Water and Sewer Line and Related Structures Construction, 1376, cons-%
Water Supply and Irrigation Systems, 154-155, util
Web Search Portals and All Other Information Services, 890-891, info
Welding and Soldering Equipment Manufacturing, 478-479, mfg
Wholesale Trade Agents and Brokers, 712-713, wsle
Wind Electric Power Generation, 146-147, util
Wine and Distilled Alcoholic Beverage Merchant Wholesalers, 702-703, wsle
Wineries, 260-261, mfg
Wired Telecommunications Carriers, 880-881, info
Wireless Telecommunications Carriers (except Satellite), 882-883, info
Wood Container and Pallet Manufacturing, 288-289, mfg
Wood Kitchen Cabinet and Countertop Manufacturing, 556-557, mfg
Wood Window and Door Manufacturing, 284-285, mfg

### Z
Zoos and Botanical Gardens, 1236-1237, ent

# CONSTRUCTION FINANCIAL MANAGEMENT ASSOCIATION DATA

# About the Construction Financial Management Association (CFMA)
## Web site: www.cfma.org

Once again, we are delighted to include excerpts from *CFMA's 2024 Construction Industry Financial Benchmarker*. CFMA is **The Source and Resource for Construction Financial Professionals** and has more than **9,700** members in 100 chapters throughout the U.S. and Canada. CFMA's 2024 Financial Benchmarker Website includes aggregate financial data broken down by industry classification, region, revenue and can be accessed at www.financialbenchmarker.com.

The 2024 Annual Survey Questionnaire was distributed to approximately 9,000 firms including CFMA member construction firms, non-member construction firms as well as member CPA and CICPAC firms that represent both member and non-member construction companies (mostly companies that are based in or have significant employment in the U.S. and Canada. Responses were received through June 16, 2024. In all, data from 1,290 companies were included in the study. Companies that submitted data for other sections of the Online Questionnaire and general information that enabled us to classify the respondents were included in those appropriate sections' results. The data submitted were compiled and analyzed by a third-party vendor, in cooperation with CFMA, and was not engaged to and did not audit or review this information and, accordingly, does not express an opinion or any other form of assurance on it.

Fiscal year-end closing dates reflected in the CFMA survey range from 3/31/22 through 3/31/23. The CFMA data are most comparable to the RMA contractor data from 4/1/22 through 3/31/23 appearing in this edition.

The survey respondents were classified into four categories of construction based on the type of work performed. Classification was based on the level of contract volume reported for various NAICS codes. A contractor was included in a classification if at least one half of its annual contract revenue was attributable to that classification. CFMA categorized certain NAICS codes together. The classifications and NAICS codes included in each are as follows:

## NAICS Codes
### RESIDENTIAL CONTRACTORS:

236115 New Single-Family Housing Construction (Except Operative Builders)
236116 New Multifamily Housing Construction (Except Operative Builders)
236117 New Housing Operative Builders
236118 Residential Remodelers

### INDUSTRIAL AND NONRESIDENTIAL CONTRACTORS:

236210 Industrial Building Construction
236220 Commercial and Institutional Building Construction

### HEAVY AND HIGHWAY CONTRACTORS:

237110 Water and Sewer Line and Related Structures Construction
237120 Oil and Gas Pipeline and Related Structures Construction
237130 Power and Communication Line and Related Structures Construction
237310 Highway, Street, and Bridge Construction
237990 Other Heavy and Civil Engineering Construction

### SPECIALTY TRADES CONTRACTORS:

238110 Poured Concrete Foundation and Structure Contractors
238120 Structural Steel and Precast Concrete Contractors
238130 Framing Contractors
238140 Masonry Contractors
238150 Glass and Glazing Contractors
238160 Roofing Contractors
238170 Siding Contractors
238190 Other Foundation, Structure, and Building Exterior Contractors
238210 Electrical Contractors
238220 Plumbing, Heating, and Air-Conditioning Contractors
238290 Other Building Equipment Contractors
238310 Drywall and Insulation Contractors
238320 Painting and Wall Covering Contractors

238330 Flooring Contractors
238340 Tile and Terrazzo Contractors
238350 Finish Carpentry Contractors
238390 Other Building Finishing Contractors
238910 Site Preparation Contractors
238990 All Other Specialty Trade Contractors
561621 Security Systems Services (except Locksmiths)
562910 Environmental Remediation Services

The CFMA financial data includes balance sheets, statements of earnings, and financial ratios. The balance sheets and statements of earnings represent a weighted average of all companies included in each classification. Percentages are presented for each dollar amount in the financial statements. Due to rounding, the totals may not agree to the sum of various accounts. Such variations are few and insignificant.

The financial ratios are calculated from the composite balance sheets and statements of earnings data. They are not averages of ratios for all companies included in the classification.

If you wish to purchase 2024 Financial Benchmarking reports (*www.financialbenchmarker.com*) or have questions regarding the data, contact Mike Elek; Construction Financial Management Association, 100 Village Blvd, Suite 200, Princeton, NJ 08540; Phone 609-452-8000; E-mail melek@cfma.org.

## Interpretation of the Construction Financial Management Association (CFMA) Data

CFMA's data should only be regarded as general information. It cannot be used to establish industry norms for a number of reasons, including the following:

(1) The financial statements used in the composite are not selected by any random or statistically reliable method. CFMA members voluntarily submitted their financial data. Note that contractors' statements have no upper asset/sales limit.

(2) Many companies provide varied services; CFMA includes a contractor in a classification if at least one-half (1/2) of its annual contract revenue was completed within that classification.

(3) Some of the NAICS group samples may be rather small in relation to the total number of firms in a given industry category. A relatively small sample can increase the chances that some of our composites do not fully represent an industry group.

(4) There is the chance that an extreme statement can be present in a sample, causing a disproportionate influence on the industry composite. This is particularly true in a relatively small sample.

(5) Companies within the same industry may differ in their method of operations, which in turn can directly influence their financial statements. Since such differences affect financial data included in our sample, our composite calculations could be significantly affected.

(6) Other considerations that can result in variation among different companies engaged in the same general line of business are: different labor markets; geographical location; different accounting methods; quality of service rendered; sources and methods of financing; and terms of sale.

The use of CFMA data may be helpful when considered with other methods of financial analysis. Nevertheless, RMA and CFMA do not recommend the use of CFMA's data to establish norms or parameters for a given industry or grouping, or the industry as a whole. Although CFMA believes that its data is accurate and representative within the confines of the aforementioned reasons, RMA and CFMA specifically make no representations regarding the accuracy of representativeness of the figures printed in this supplement of the RMA Annual Statement Studies.

**Reprinted with permission © 2024 by the Construction Financial Management Association.**

**CAUTION:** ALL RIGHTS RESERVED. NO PART OF THIS BOOK MAY BE QUOTED, REPRODUCED, DISSEMINATED, OR USED IN ANY FORM OR BY ANY MEANS, ELECTRONIC OR MECHANICAL, INCLUDING PHOTOCOPYING, RECORDING, OR ANY INFORMATION STORAGE AND RETRIEVAL SYSTEMS, WITHOUT THE EXPRESS WRITTEN PERMISSION OF RMA.

# CFMA's ANNUAL FINANCIAL SURVEY - 2024

|  |  | Residential | Industrial & Non-Residential | Heavy & Highway | Specialty Trade |
|---|---|---|---|---|---|
|  | All Companies | All Companies | All Companies | All Companies | All Companies |
| **FINANCIAL INFORMATION** | | | | | |
| **KEY RATIOS - ALL SHOWN AS MEDIANS EXCEPT INVENTORY DAYS** | | | | | |
| Number of Participants | 1,290 | 39 | 310 | 212 | 513 |
| **LIQUIDITY RATIOS** | | | | | |
| Current Ratio | 1.6 | 1.5 | 1.3 | 1.7 | 1.9 |
| Quick Ratio | 1.4 | 1.2 | 1.2 | 1.5 | 1.6 |
| Days of Cash | 23.5 | 23.7 | 27.5 | 32.9 | 19.4 |
| Working Capital Turnover | **7.4** | 12.4 | **13.9** | **7.0** | **6.0** |
| **PROFITABILITY RATIOS** | | | | | |
| Return on Assets | 12% | 12.4% | 9.1% | 11.7% | 13.4% |
| Return on Equity | 31% | 44.9% | 31.6% | 25.0% | 31.4% |
| Times Interest Earned | 25.6 | 87.1 | 40.3 | 17.9 | 24.0 |
| EBIT to Total Revenue | 6.5% | 6.5% | 4.0% | 7.8% | 7.2% |
| EBITDA to Total Revenue | 8.3% | 7.1% | 4.7% | 11.5% | 9.0% |
| **LEVERAGE RATIOS** | | | | | |
| Debt to Equity | 1.3 | 1.9 | 2.6 | 0.9 | 1.1 |
| Revenue to Equity | 5.4 | 8.5 | 11.1 | 3.6 | 4.9 |
| Asset Turnover | 2.3 | 3.0 | 2.9 | 1.8 | 2.3 |
| Fixed Asset Ratio | 23.7% | 6.2% | 15.3% | 55.5% | 22.5% |
| Equity to SG&A Expenses | 1.9 | 2.3 | 1.8 | 3.2 | 1.6 |
| Underbillings to Equity | 8.0% | 2.2% | 8.0% | 5.5% | 9.5% |
| Average Backlog to Equity | 4.4 | 13.4 | 9.6 | 3.0 | 3.3 |
| **EFFICIENCY RATIOS** | | | | | |
| Average Backlog to Working Capital | 5.9 | 16.3 | 12.8 | 5.0 | 4.3 |
| Average Months in Backlog | 8.7 | 13.1 | 10.0 | 8.7 | 7.9 |
| Days in Accounts Receivable | 56.6 | 42.0 | 50.3 | 51.8 | 64.3 |
| Days in Inventory | 6.4 | 47.8 | 1.6 | 5.7 | 4.8 |
| Days in Accounts Payable | 33.0 | 33.9 | 46.7 | 27.6 | 26.3 |
| Operating Cycle | 52.7 | 32.7 | 33.7 | 64.4 | 64.1 |
| **PRODUCTIVITY RATIOS (000)** | | | | | |
| Revenue per FTE Employee | $450,086 | $1,294,021 | $1,263,092 | $451,859 | $303,681 |
| Gross Profit per FTE Employee | $70,642 | $135,170 | $88,294 | $67,712 | $61,542 |
| Revenue per Production FTE Employee | $597,363 | $1,997,477 | $1,714,669 | $579,527 | $402,228 |
| Gross Profit per Production FTE Employee | $97,690 | $195,881 | $127,649 | $93,584 | $78,841 |
| **SALES MEASURES** | | | | | |
| Total Revenue ($000s) | 37,567 | 62,559 | 60,676 | 41,078 | 27,881 |
| Sales Growth | 10% | 21% | 10% | 10% | 10% |

## CFMA's ANNUAL FINANCIAL SURVEY - 2024 (continued)

| | | Residential | Industrial & Non-Residential | Heavy & Highway | Specialty Trade |
|---|---|---|---|---|---|
| | All Companies | All Companies | All Companies | All Companies | All Companies |
| **DETAILED FINANCIAL VALUES - ALL SHOWN AS AVERAGES** | | | | | |
| **BALANCE SHEET (% of Total Assets)** | | | | | |
| **Current Assets:** | | | | | |
| Cash and cash equivalents | 19.4% | 21.1% | 24.2% | 20.2% | 16.7% |
| Marketable securities and short-term investments | 2.9% | 3.1% | 3.8% | 3.0% | 2.0% |
| Contract Receivables currently due | 36.2% | 33.3% | 40.2% | 26.7% | 38.7% |
| Retainages on contracts | 3.1% | 4.3% | 3.6% | 2.2% | 3.2% |
| Unbilled work | 0.3% | 0.0% | 0.2% | 0.2% | 0.4% |
| Other receivables | 1.2% | 0.5% | 1.2% | 0.6% | 1.6% |
| (Less) Allowance for doubtful accounts | 0.1% | 0.1% | 0.1% | 0.1% | 0.2% |
| Total Accounts Receivable, Net | 40.6% | 38.1% | 45.2% | 29.6% | 43.8% |
| **Contract Assets:** | | | | | |
| Costs and recognized earnings in excess of billings on uncompleted contracts | 5.4% | 5.2% | 4.4% | 4.9% | 6.0% |
| Retainage | 4.1% | 2.4% | 6.4% | 2.6% | 3.4% |
| Other | 0.4% | 0.0% | 0.3% | 0.5% | 0.4% |
| Total Contract Assets | 9.9% | 7.6% | 11.1% | 8.0% | 9.8% |
| Notes receivable, current | 0.3% | 0.2% | 0.4% | 0.3% | 0.2% |
| Inventories | 2.3% | 15.8% | 0.4% | 2.0% | 2.0% |
| Investments in and advances to construction joint ventures | 0.2% | 0.1% | 0.5% | 0.1% | 0.0% |
| Income taxes | 0.1% | 0.0% | 0.0% | 0.0% | 0.1% |
| Other current assets | 1.8% | 3.0% | 1.5% | 1.7% | 1.8% |
| Total Current Assets | 77.3% | 88.9% | 87.2% | 64.9% | 76.5% |
| **Noncurrent Assets:** | | | | | |
| Total Property Plant & Equipment | 39.4% | 13.9% | 20.2% | 74.2% | 37.8% |
| (Less) accumulated depreciation | 24.0% | 7.8% | 12.7% | 45.0% | 23.3% |
| Property, Plant and Equipment, Net | 15.4% | 6.1% | 7.5% | 29.1% | 14.5% |
| Finance Lease Right-of-Use Asset | 0.5% | 0.1% | 0.3% | 0.6% | 0.7% |
| (Less) Accumulated Amortization - Finance Lease Right-of-Use Asset | 0.1% | 0.0% | 0.1% | 0.1% | 0.1% |
| Finance Lease Right-of-Use Asset, Net | 0.4% | 0.1% | 0.2% | 0.5% | 0.6% |
| Operating Lease Right-of-Use Asset | 3.0% | 1.4% | 2.0% | 1.8% | 3.5% |
| Long-term investments | 0.4% | 0.1% | 0.4% | 0.4% | 0.4% |
| Notes receivable | 0.8% | 0.5% | 0.7% | 1.1% | 0.8% |
| Investments in and advances to construction joint ventures | 0.2% | 0.1% | 0.5% | 0.1% | 0.0% |
| Investments in unconsolidated affiliates | 0.1% | 0.0% | 0.1% | 0.1% | 0.0% |
| Deferred income taxes | 0.1% | 0.0% | 0.1% | 0.1% | 0.2% |
| Goodwill | 1.0% | 0.0% | 0.2% | 0.6% | 1.9% |
| Other Intangible assets | 0.2% | 0.0% | 0.1% | 0.1% | 0.3% |
| Other Noncurrent Assets | 1.3% | 2.6% | 1.2% | 1.2% | 1.2% |
| Total Other Noncurrent Assets | 2.4% | 2.6% | 1.5% | 1.9% | 3.4% |
| Total Noncurrent Assets | 22.7% | 11.1% | 12.8% | 35.1% | 23.5% |
| **Total Assets** | **100.0%** | **100.0%** | **100.0%** | **100.0%** | **100.0%** |

## CFMA's ANNUAL FINANCIAL SURVEY - 2024 (continued)

| | All Companies | Residential All Companies | Industrial & Non-Residential All Companies | Heavy & Highway All Companies | Specialty Trade All Companies |
|---|---|---|---|---|---|
| **Current Liabilities:** | | | | | |
| Trade, including currently due subcontractors | 20.0% | 27.1% | 33.1% | 12.8% | 13.9% |
| Subcontractors retainages | 3.0% | 4.3% | 8.9% | 1.1% | 0.6% |
| Other payables | 1.0% | 0.4% | 0.9% | 0.9% | 1.0% |
| Total Accounts Payable | 24.0% | 31.8% | 42.9% | 14.8% | 15.5% |
| Accrued expenses | 4.7% | 3.3% | 4.3% | 4.2% | 5.5% |
| *Contract Liabilities:* | | | | | |
| Billings in excess of costs and recognized earnings on uncompleted contracts | 10.4% | 9.2% | 11.0% | 9.7% | 11.1% |
| Retainage | 0.2% | 0.1% | 0.7% | 0.1% | -0.3% |
| Other | 0.3% | 0.2% | 0.1% | 0.2% | 0.5% |
| Total contract liabilities | 10.8% | 9.5% | 11.9% | 9.9% | 11.3% |
| Income taxes Payable | 0.1% | 0.0% | 0.1% | 0.2% | 0.2% |
| Total Other Current Liabilities | 1.5% | 3.8% | 1.2% | 0.8% | 1.6% |
| Notes payable (current portion) and lines of credit | 2.8% | 7.9% | 1.3% | 2.4% | 3.3% |
| Finance Lease Liability (current portion) | 0.1% | 0.0% | 0.1% | 0.1% | 0.2% |
| Operating Lease Liability (current portion) | 0.7% | 0.5% | 0.5% | 0.5% | 0.9% |
| Current maturities of long-term debt | 1.4% | 1.4% | 0.6% | 2.9% | 1.4% |
| Total Current Liabilities | 46.1% | 58.1% | 62.7% | 35.8% | 39.7% |
| **Noncurrent Liabilities:** | | | | | |
| Long-term debt, excluding current maturities | 6.8% | 3.0% | 3.7% | 9.5% | 7.5% |
| Deferred income taxes | 0.1% | 0.0% | 0.1% | 0.1% | 0.2% |
| Finance Lease Liability (noncurrent portion) | 0.3% | 0.1% | 0.2% | 0.3% | 0.4% |
| Operating Lease Liability (noncurrent portion) | 2.4% | 1.0% | 1.6% | 1.5% | 2.8% |
| Other | 0.4% | 0.0% | 0.3% | 0.5% | 0.4% |
| Total Noncurrent Liabilities | 11.1% | 4.7% | 6.3% | 13.3% | 12.8% |
| Total Liabilities | 57.2% | 62.8% | 69.0% | 49.1% | 52.5% |
| **Equity:** | | | | | |
| Common stock, par value | 1.3% | 0.5% | 1.1% | 1.9% | 1.4% |
| Preferred stock, stated value | 0.1% | 0.0% | 0.1% | 0.1% | 0.1% |
| (Less) treasury stock | 1.5% | 2.1% | 0.6% | 1.6% | 2.1% |
| Additional paid-in capital | 3.2% | 1.7% | 2.6% | 3.3% | 3.7% |
| Retained earnings (accumulated deficit) | 35.2% | 25.3% | 24.1% | 41.5% | 40.0% |
| Net Corporate Stock | 38.2% | 25.4% | 27.2% | 45.2% | 43.0% |
| Partnership/LLC Capital | 4.1% | 10.8% | 4.2% | 5.2% | 3.3% |
| Noncontrolling Interests | 0.1% | 0.1% | 0.1% | 0.4% | 0.1% |
| Other equity | 0.4% | 0.8% | -0.4% | 0.2% | 1.1% |
| Total Equity | 42.8% | 37.2% | 31.1% | 50.9% | 47.5% |
| **Total Liabilities and Equity** | 100.0% | 100.0% | 100.0% | 100.0% | 100.0% |

## CFMA's ANNUAL FINANCIAL SURVEY - 2024 (continued)

| | | Residential | Industrial & Non-Residential | Heavy & Highway | Specialty Trade |
|---|---|---|---|---|---|
| | All Companies | All Companies | All Companies | All Companies | All Companies |
| **Statement of Operations** | | | | | |
| Total Revenue | 100.0% | 100.0% | 100.0% | 100.0% | 100.0% |
| **Direct Costs** | | | | | |
| Direct Labor | 17.5% | 9.4% | 9.1% | 17.2% | 23.8% |
| Materials | 21.2% | 15.3% | 10.9% | 22.7% | 27.2% |
| Subcontracts | 30.0% | 53.8% | 62.0% | 21.1% | 12.9% |
| Equipment | 3.6% | 0.7% | 0.9% | 8.2% | 3.7% |
| Other Direct Costs | 7.0% | 5.4% | 5.1% | 10.2% | 6.7% |
| Total Direct Costs | 79.4% | 84.7% | 88.0% | 79.4% | 74.4% |
| Indirect Costs | 2.8% | 1.3% | 1.0% | 3.5% | 3.7% |
| Total Costs | 82.2% | 86.0% | 89.0% | 83.0% | 78.1% |
| Gross Profit | 17.8% | 14.0% | 11.0% | 17.0% | 21.9% |
| **SG&A Expenses** | | | | | |
| Base Payroll / Payroll Related (Exclusive of Owner Bonuses) | 5.8% | 3.9% | 3.6% | 4.9% | 7.8% |
| Professional Fees | 0.5% | 0.3% | 0.3% | 0.5% | 0.6% |
| Sales & Marketing Costs | 0.3% | 1.0% | 0.2% | 0.1% | 0.3% |
| Technology Costs | 0.3% | 0.2% | 0.2% | 0.2% | 0.3% |
| Administrative Bonuses | 0.7% | 0.4% | 0.5% | 0.7% | 0.8% |
| Other Expenses | 4.3% | 2.6% | 2.5% | 3.8% | 5.5% |
| Total SG&A Expenses | 11.8% | 8.3% | 7.3% | 10.2% | 15.3% |
| Income (Loss) from Operations | 6.0% | 5.7% | 3.7% | 6.8% | 6.6% |
| Interest income | 0.2% | 0.2% | 0.2% | 0.3% | 0.1% |
| Other investment income (loss) | 0.1% | 0.0% | 0.1% | 0.1% | 0.1% |
| Other income (expense) | 0.2% | 0.2% | 0.1% | 0.4% | 0.1% |
| Employee Retention Credits (ERC) | 0.2% | 0.0% | 0.1% | 0.1% | 0.4% |
| Interest expense | 0.3% | 0.1% | 0.1% | 0.4% | 0.4% |
| Total Other Income (Expense), net | 0.4% | 0.3% | 0.3% | 0.5% | 0.3% |
| Net Income (Loss) Before Income Taxes | 6.3% | 6.0% | 4.1% | 7.2% | 6.9% |
| Provision for Income tax expense (benefit) | 0.2% | 0.1% | 0.1% | 0.2% | 0.2% |
| Net Income (LOSS) | 6.2% | 5.9% | 3.9% | 7.1% | 6.7% |
| **BALANCE SHEET ($000s)** | | | | | |
| **Current Assets:** | | | | | |
| Cash and cash equivalents | $7,910 | $7,198 | $11,749 | $11,625 | $4,346 |
| Marketable securities and short-term investments | $1,648 | $1,557 | $2,183 | $2,238 | $1,028 |
| Contract Receivables currently due | $16,538 | $12,614 | $22,974 | $13,546 | $13,432 |
| Retainages on contracts | $1,756 | $1,036 | $2,922 | $1,492 | $1,279 |
| Unbilled work | $116 | $12 | $71 | $50 | $174 |
| Other receivables | $330 | $41 | $458 | $455 | $242 |
| (Less) Allowance for doubtful accounts | $65 | $16 | $17 | $107 | $84 |
| Total Accounts Receivable, Net | $18,675 | $13,687 | $26,408 | $15,437 | $15,043 |

## CFMA's ANNUAL FINANCIAL SURVEY - 2024 (continued)

| | All Companies | Residential<br>All Companies | Industrial & Non-Residential<br>All Companies | Heavy & Highway<br>All Companies | Specialty Trade<br>All Companies |
|---|---|---|---|---|---|
| **Contract Assets:** | | | | | |
| Costs and recognized earnings in excess of billings on uncompleted contracts | $2,407 | $1,278 | $2,355 | $2,651 | $2,184 |
| Retainage | $2,493 | $2,613 | $4,525 | $1,759 | $1,314 |
| Other | $105 | $0 | $122 | $116 | $82 |
| Total Contract Assets | $5,005 | $3,891 | $7,001 | $4,526 | $3,580 |
| Notes receivable, current | $102 | $300 | $165 | $111 | $39 |
| Inventories | $1,069 | $6,713 | $211 | $2,183 | $495 |
| Investments in and advances to construction joint ventures | $98 | $80 | $110 | $189 | $19 |
| Income taxes | $20 | $2 | $14 | $19 | $17 |
| Other current assets | $801 | $631 | $755 | $1,291 | $459 |
| Total Current Assets | $35,328 | $34,059 | $48,595 | $37,620 | $25,027 |
| **Noncurrent Assets:** | | | | | |
| Total Property Plant & Equipment | $14,396 | $2,864 | $6,555 | $38,697 | $9,033 |
| (Less) accumulated depreciation | $7,749 | $1,806 | $3,809 | $21,137 | $4,828 |
| Property, Plant and Equipment, Net | $6,646 | $1,058 | $2,746 | $17,560 | $4,205 |
| Finance Lease Right-of-Use Asset | $347 | $200 | $141 | $491 | $309 |
| (Less) Accumulated Amortization - Finance Lease Right-of-Use Asset | $56 | $56 | $30 | $77 | $25 |
| Finance Lease Right-of-Use Asset, Net | $290 | $144 | $111 | $413 | $284 |
| Operating Lease Right-of-Use Asset | $1,503 | $561 | $1,313 | $1,317 | $1,535 |
| Long-term investments | $198 | $8 | $231 | $569 | $103 |
| Notes receivable | $254 | $78 | $284 | $458 | $156 |
| Investments in and advances to construction joint ventures | $98 | $68 | $173 | $259 | $17 |
| Investments in unconsolidated affiliates | $35 | $0 | $37 | $37 | $17 |
| Deferred income taxes | $66 | $0 | $45 | $25 | $115 |
| Goodwill | $588 | $0 | $127 | $711 | $929 |
| Other Intangible assets | $272 | $3 | $28 | $223 | $345 |
| Other Noncurrent Assets | $408 | $676 | $407 | $590 | $297 |
| Total Other Noncurrent Assets | $1,268 | $679 | $562 | $1,524 | $1,571 |
| Total Noncurrent Assets | $10,360 | $2,596 | $5,502 | $22,161 | $8,001 |
| **Total Assets** | $45,688 | $36,655 | $54,096 | $59,781 | $33,028 |
| **Current Liabilities:** | | | | | |
| Trade, including currently due subcontractors | $10,590 | $12,073 | $20,899 | $7,419 | $5,353 |
| Subcontractors retainages | $2,452 | $4,142 | $7,305 | $1,048 | $296 |
| Other payables | $263 | $114 | $230 | $315 | $186 |
| Total Accounts Payable | $13,305 | $16,329 | $28,434 | $8,781 | $5,835 |
| Accrued expenses | $2,665 | $1,044 | $2,768 | $3,398 | $2,461 |

## CFMA's ANNUAL FINANCIAL SURVEY - 2024 (continued)

| | | Residential | Industrial & Non-Residential | Heavy & Highway | Specialty Trade |
|---|---|---|---|---|---|
| | All Companies | All Companies | All Companies | All Companies | All Companies |
| **Contract Liabilities:** | | | | | |
| Billings in excess of costs and recognized earnings on uncompleted contracts | $6,093 | $3,621 | $5,619 | $7,443 | $5,828 |
| Retainage | -$20 | -$12 | $142 | -$64 | -$126 |
| Other | $52 | $71 | $29 | $66 | $72 |
| Total contract liabilities | $6,124 | $3,680 | $5,790 | $7,445 | $5,774 |
| Income taxes Payable | $71 | $3 | $34 | $40 | $84 |
| Total Other Current Liabilities | $636 | $1,525 | $596 | $366 | $507 |
| Notes payable (current portion) and lines of credit | $722 | $2,419 | $207 | $1,023 | $703 |
| Finance Lease Liability (current portion) | $78 | $10 | $35 | $106 | $68 |
| Operating Lease Liability (current portion) | $341 | $151 | $287 | $420 | $315 |
| Current maturities of long-term debt | $498 | $522 | $161 | $1,156 | $345 |
| Total Current Liabilities | $24,439 | $25,684 | $38,312 | $22,737 | $16,092 |
| **Noncurrent Liabilities:** | | | | | |
| Long-term debt, excluding current maturities | $2,525 | $573 | $1,108 | $4,905 | $2,103 |
| Deferred income taxes | $215 | $6 | $42 | $433 | $109 |
| Finance Lease Liability (noncurrent portion) | $182 | $19 | $75 | $309 | $163 |
| Operating Lease Liability (noncurrent portion) | $1,215 | $428 | $1,078 | $948 | $1,277 |
| Other | $759 | $173 | $708 | $1,761 | $420 |
| Total Noncurrent Liabilities | $4,897 | $1,198 | $3,012 | $8,356 | $4,070 |
| Total Liabilities | $29,337 | $26,882 | $41,324 | $31,093 | $20,162 |
| **Equity:** | | | | | |
| Common stock, par value | $683 | $156 | $657 | $974 | $705 |
| Preferred stock, stated value | $20 | $0 | $26 | $7 | $28 |
| (Less) treasury stock | $524 | $135 | $386 | $1,195 | $497 |
| Additional paid-in capital | $1,405 | $592 | $870 | $3,028 | $1,329 |
| Retained earnings (accumulated deficit) | $12,866 | $6,165 | $10,228 | $21,571 | $10,275 |
| Net Corporate Stock | $14,450 | $6,778 | $11,396 | $24,386 | $11,840 |
| Partnership/LLC Capital | $1,843 | $2,520 | $1,736 | $3,702 | $964 |
| Noncontrolling Interests | $106 | $84 | $35 | $340 | $60 |
| Other equity | -$64 | $392 | -$395 | $260 | -$37 |
| Total Equity | $16,351 | $9,774 | $12,772 | $28,687 | $12,865 |
| Total Liabilities and Equity | $45,688 | $36,655 | $54,096 | $59,781 | $33,028 |
| **Statement of Operations ($000s)** | | | | | |
| Revenue | $103,329 | $105,902 | $156,398 | $101,897 | $70,338 |

## CFMA's ANNUAL FINANCIAL SURVEY - 2024 (continued)

|  | All Companies | Residential<br>All Companies | Industrial & Non-Residential<br>All Companies | Heavy & Highway<br>All Companies | Specialty Trade<br>All Companies |
|---|---|---|---|---|---|
| **Direct Costs** | | | | | |
| Direct Labor | $15,971 | $8,253 | $12,813 | $16,741 | $19,082 |
| Materials | $18,277 | $11,753 | $13,421 | $23,677 | $18,993 |
| Subcontracts | $43,724 | $69,121 | $112,472 | $23,770 | $10,038 |
| Equipment | $3,805 | $543 | $1,026 | $9,403 | $3,420 |
| Other Direct Costs | $6,688 | $5,645 | $4,918 | $10,861 | $4,361 |
| Total Direct Costs | $88,466 | $95,315 | $144,649 | $84,452 | $55,894 |
| Indirect Costs | $1,526 | $494 | $348 | $1,952 | $1,695 |
| Total Costs | $89,992 | $95,809 | $144,997 | $86,405 | $57,589 |
| Gross Profit | $13,336 | $10,093 | $11,401 | $15,493 | $12,749 |
| **SG&A Expenses** | | | | | |
| Base Payroll / Payroll Related (Exclusive of Owner Bonuses) | $4,029 | $2,072 | $3,679 | $3,784 | $4,433 |
| Professional Fees | $284 | $292 | $262 | $331 | $245 |
| Sales & Marketing Costs | $230 | $835 | $202 | $106 | $207 |
| Technology Costs | $289 | $115 | $313 | $302 | $297 |
| Administrative Bonuses | $786 | $534 | $785 | $1,124 | $805 |
| Other Expenses | $2,460 | $1,442 | $1,873 | $2,789 | $2,462 |
| Total SG&A Expenses | $8,079 | $5,290 | $7,115 | $8,435 | $8,449 |
| Income (Loss) from Operations | $5,258 | $4,803 | $4,287 | $7,057 | $4,300 |
| Interest income | $209 | $167 | $343 | $279 | $88 |
| Other investment income (loss) | $97 | $82 | $92 | $198 | $54 |
| Other income (expense) | $66 | $116 | $44 | $217 | $34 |
| Employee Retention Credits (ERC) | $44 | $25 | $31 | $23 | $62 |
| Interest expense | $251 | $38 | $127 | $501 | $214 |
| Total Other Income (Expense), net | $165 | $351 | $383 | $215 | $24 |
| Net Income (Loss) Before Income Taxes | $5,423 | $5,155 | $4,670 | $7,272 | $4,324 |
| Provision for Income tax expense (benefit) | $276 | $74 | $157 | $302 | $243 |
| Net Income (LOSS) | $5,146 | $5,080 | $4,513 | $6,971 | $4,081 |

# RMA'S CREDIT & LENDING DICTIONARY

# A

**Absentee Owner:** landlord who does not reside in his or her rental property.

**Abstract of Title:** condensed history of title to land and real property, consisting of ownership transfers and any conveyances or liens that may affect future ownership.

**Acceleration Clause:** provision in note or contract that allows holder to declare remaining balance due and payable immediately upon default in an obligation. Usual causes of default are failure to pay interest or principal installments in a timely manner, an adverse change in financing conditions, or failure to meet loan covenants.

**Acceptance:** drawee's signed agreement to honor draft as presented, which consists of signature alone, but will frequently be evidenced by drawee writing word "accepted," date it is payable, and signature. Sometimes called Trade Acceptance or Banker's Acceptance, depending upon function of acceptor.

**Accommodation:** 1. lending or extending credit to borrower. 2. loan or commitment to lend money.

**Accord and Satisfaction:** agreement between two or more persons or entities that satisfies or discharges obligation or settles claim or lawsuit. Generally involves disputed matter in which one party agrees to give and other party agrees to accept something in satisfaction different from, and usually less than, that originally asked for.

**Account:** 1. statement showing balance along with detailed explanation covering debits and credits. 2. right of payment for goods sold or leased or for services rendered on open account basis. 3. summarized record of financial transaction. 4. customer.

**Accountant:** person in charge of and skilled in the recording of financial transactions and maintenance of financial records.

**Accounting:** 1. theory and system of classifying, recording, summarizing, and auditing books of firm. 2. art of analyzing, interpreting, and reporting financial position and operating results of business.

**Account Manager:** 1. sometimes called Relationship Manager or Account Officer. 2. person responsible for overseeing all matters relating to a specific client or group of customers.

**Account Number:** unique identification number used to designate specific customer.

**Accounts Payable:** short-term liability representing amounts due trade creditors.

**Accounts Payable Department:** section of business office responsible for processing open account balances and paying amounts owed for goods and services purchased.

**Accounts Receivable:** money due to a business by its customers for goods sold or services performed on open account (or credit). Usually refers to short-term receivables.

**Accounts Receivable Aging Report:** report by customer that lists age of accounts receivable generally by 30-day intervals from invoice or due date. See also Aging of Accounts Receivable.

**Accounts Receivable Financing:** form of secured lending in which borrowings are typically limited to percentage of receivables pledged as collateral.

**Accrual Accounting:** basis of accounting in which expenses are recorded when incurred and revenues are recognized when earned, regardless of when cash is actually paid or received.

**Accrue:** 1. something gained, added, or accumulated, such as profit from a business transaction. 2. right to sue has become exercisable.

**Accrued Expenses:** short-term liabilities that represent expenses for goods used but not yet paid.

**Accrued Income:** income earned but not yet collected.

**Accrued Interest:** interest accumulated since last interest payment due date.

**Accrued Liabilities:** expenses or obligations for goods or services incurred but not yet paid.

**ACH:** see *Automated Clearinghouse*.

**Acid Test:** ratio between company's most liquid assets (generally, cash and accounts receivable) and current liabilities that represents the degree to which current liabilities can be paid with those assets.

**Acknowledgment:** 1. declaration making known receipt of something done or to be done; confirmation of receipt of order or of terms of contract. 2. statement of notary or other competent officer certifying that signature on document was personally signed by individual whose signature is affixed to instrument.

**Acquisition:** merger or taking over of controlling interest of one business by another.

**Acquisition and Development Loan:** loan made for the purpose of purchasing a property and completing all on-site improvements such as street layout, utility installation, and community area grading necessary to bring the site to a buildable state.

**Acquittal:** 1. release from obligation or contract. 2. to have accusation of crime dismissed by some formal legal procedure.

**Active Account:** 1. customer who makes frequent purchases. 2. bank account in which regular deposits or withdrawals are made.

**Activity Charge:** service charge imposed for check or deposit activity or any other maintenance charge.

**Act of God:** event that could not be prevented by reasonable foresight, is ca[used] exclusively by forces and violence of nature, and is uninfluenced by hu[man] power (storm, flood, earthquake, or lightning).

**Additional Dating:** means of extending credit beyond normal sales terms, gra[nted] to induce buyers to place orders in advance of season or for other specia[l rea]sons. See also Advance Dating and Dating.

**Adjudication:** judgment rendered by court, primarily used in bankruptcy proc[eed]ings.

**Adjustable Interest Rate:** interest rate on loan that may be adjusted up or d[own] at specific intervals. Index used in determining adjusted interest rate [and] potential frequency of adjustments must be stated in loan documents.

**Adjustable Rate Mortgage:** loan is pursuant to an agreement executed a[t] inception of the loan that permits creditor to adjust interest rate from ti[me to] time based on a specific interest rate index.

**Adjuster:** person who deals with insured party to settle amount of loss, clai[m or] debt.

**Adjustment:** 1. settlement of disputed account. 2. change or concession in p[rice] or terms. 3. determining amount one is to receive in settlement of claim. [4. in] accounting, entry made to correct or compensate for error or differenc[e in] account.

**Adjustment Bureau:** organization that supervises debt extensions and com[pro]mise arrangements or oversees orderly liquidation of troubled businesses [for the] benefit of creditors.

**Advance:** 1. payment made before it is due. 2. disbursement of loan proceeds.

**Advance Dating:** additional time granted customers to pay for goods rece[ived] and to earn available discounts. See also Additional Dating and Dating.

**Advancement of Costs:** prepayment of necessary legal expenses. Such char[ges,] set by law, may be for commencement of suit and vary in different courts [and] states. Some items for which prepaid costs may be requested are filing f[ees,] process serving, premiums on court bonds, trial fees, posting security [for] costs, entering judgment, recording abstract of judgment, issue execu[tion] and discovery actions after judgment.

**Advertising Allowance:** promotional discount in price or payment given c[us]tomers who share expense of advertising supplier's product.

**Affidavit:** voluntary written statement of facts pertaining to a transaction or ev[ent] signed under oath and witnessed by an authorized person.

**Affiliate:** business entity connected with another through common ownership [or] management, usually responsible for payment of its own obligations.

**After-Acquired Property:** security interest by which secured creditor autom[ati]cally obtains interest in assets that debtor acquires after lien had been filed.

**Agency:** legal relationship between two parties in which one is authorized to [act] for another.

**Agent:** person legally authorized to act for another.

**Agent Bank:** formal designation that applies to a bank responsible for negotiati[ng,] structuring, and overseeing a loan or commitment to a borrower in wh[ich] more than one bank is involved. See also Lead Bank.

**Aggregate Balances:** combined total of two or more demand deposit accou[nts,] money markets, or time certificates of deposit. Term can also be applied [to] credit facility totals.

**Aging of Accounts Receivable:** accounting record of customer's receivab[les] showing how long receivables have remained unpaid beyond regular terms [of] sale. Used as basis for advancing credit.

**Agreement:** a contract involving an offer and an acceptance between two or m[ore] parties, governing the terms of the contract and binding on the parties to [the] agreement (e.g., a loan agreement, security agreement, or guaranty).

**AKA:** see *Also Known As*.

**Alert Action:** a series of information services provided by credit reporting ag[en]cies; provides subscribers with listing of specific accounts on which unfav[or]able payment condition has recently been reported.

**Allegation:** statement of party to action, setting out what he or she intends [to] prove or contend.

**ALLL:** see *Allowance for Loan and Lease Losses*.

**Allocation:** sub-limit within a total credit facility that is to be used for a speci[fic] purpose.

**Allonge:** paper attached to a negotiable instrument for additional endorseme[nts] or other terms and conditions.

**Allowance:** accounting provision used to set aside amounts for depreciatio[n,] returns, or bad debts.

**Allowance for Bad Debts:** contra account against which uncollectible receivab[les] are charged. See also Bad Debt Reserve.

**Allowance for Loan and Lease Losses (ALLL):** contra account, generally fou[nd] on asset side of balance sheet as deduction from total loans outstandin[g;] amount is intended to cover future losses of loans currently in the financ[ial] institution's portfolio. The ALLL should be adjusted monthly, concurren[tly] with the generation of current financial statements.

**Also Known As (AKA):** sometimes used to designate a fictitious trade style [or] name.

**A Policy:** an extended coverage title insurance policy that protects the lender against losses resulting from any defects in the title or claims against the property. The policy's coverage includes encroachments, mechanic's liens, and other matters that a physical inspection or inquiry of the parties would disclose.

**Altered Check:** check on which original entries have been changed (date, payee, or amount); financial institutions generally refuse to honor or pay checks that have been altered.

**Amend:** to correct, add to, or alter legal document.

**Amicus Curiae:** friend of court; uninvolved third party who intervenes in lawsuit, with court's permission, to introduce information or arguments in respect to the issue or principle of law to be decided.

**Amortization:** 1. reduction of loan by periodic principal payments. 2. decline in the book value of an intangible asset over the period owned.

**Amortization Tables:** calculation charts showing amounts required periodically to discharge debts over various periods of time and at different interest rates.

**Amortize:** 1. to write off the value of an intangible asset over the period owned. 2. to reduce or pay off debt or obligation by making periodic payments of principal.

**Annual Percentage Rate (APR):** annual cost of credit expressed as percentage; creditors are required under Federal Truth in Lending Act to disclose true annual interest on consumer loans, as well as the total dollar cost and other terms of loan.

**Annual Report:** yearly report detailing a company's comparative financial and organizational conditions.

**Annuity:** series of fixed periodic payments made at regular intervals.

**Antecedent Credit Information:** historical record of significant business information concerning individuals who are involved in ownership or management of business enterprise.

**Anticipation:** bridge loan made to a municipal or government borrower to cover expenses until revenue or tax proceeds are collected.

**Appeal:** complaint made to higher court by either plaintiff or defendant for court's review, correction, or reversal of lower court's decision.

**Appearance:** coming into court formally as plaintiff or defendant in lawsuit.

**Appraisal:** opinion of current value of real or personal property based upon cost of replacement, market, income, or fair value analysis.

**Appreciation:** increase in value of asset over its cost due to economic and other conditions. Property that increases in value as result of improvements or additions is not considered to have appreciated.

**Appropriation:** sum of money designated for a special purpose only.

**APR:** See *Annual Percentage Rate.*

**Arbitration:** submission for settlement of disputed matter, by nonjudicial means, to one or more impartial or disinterested third persons selected by disputants.

**Arm's Length:** business transaction between two or more parties that is open, sincere, and without personal influence, favoritism, or close relations.

**Arrangement:** plan for corporate reorganization for rescheduling or extension of time for payment of unsecured debts, such as an arrangement under Chapter 11 or 13 of the U.S. Bankruptcy Code.

**Arrears:** total or partial debt amounts that remain unpaid and past due.

**Articles of Agreement:** any written statement or contract, terms to which all parties consent.

**Articles of Incorporation:** formal papers that set forth pertinent data for formation of corporation and are filed with appropriate state agency.

**Assess:** 1. to fix rate or amount. 2. to set value of real and personal property, as for tax purposes.

**Assessed Value:** in the case of real property, value set by government agency for purpose of levying taxes.

**Asset:** 1. anything owned having monetary value. 2. item listed on left-hand side of balance sheet representing cash, or property, real or personal, belonging to an individual or company and convertible to cash.

**Assigned Account:** 1. account receivable pledged by borrower to factor or lender as security. 2. past-due customer whose account has been placed with collection agency.

**Assigned Risk:** insurance plan that provides coverage for risks rejected by regular markets and in which all licensed insurers are made to participate by various state laws.

**Assignee:** person to whom some rights, authority, or property is assigned.

**Assignment:** 1. written contract for transfer of one's title, legal rights, or property from one person to another. 2. in some states, form used to transfer claim to agency that undertakes collection of account for benefit of assigning creditor.

**Assignment for the Benefit of Creditors:** A liquidation technique in which an insolvent debtor goes out of business and an assignee facilitates the transfer of the insolvent debtor's estate for administration and payment of debts. Property transferred to assignee places such assets beyond control of debtor or reach of creditors.

**Assignment of Claim:** claim assigned to third party for collection.

**Assignor:** 1. one who transfers claim, right, or property. 2. individual, partnership, or corporation making assignment.

**Assumed Liability:** acknowledgment of responsibility for payment of obligation by third party.

**At Sight:** words used in negotiable instrument directing that payment be made upon presentation or demand.

**Attached Account:** legally frozen account on which payments have been suspended; release or disbursement of funds can be made only after court order.

**Attachment:** 1. legal writ or process by which debtor's property (or any interest therein) is seized and placed in custody of law. 2. Supplemental data provided as clarifying information to a document.

**Attorney-in-Fact:** private attorney who has written authorization to act for another. This authority is given by an instrument called power of attorney.

**Attorney of Record:** lawyer whose name must appear in permanent court records as person acting on behalf of party in legal matter.

**Auction:** public sale of property that is sold to highest bidder.

**Audit:** to examine a firm's records, accounts, or procedures for purpose of substantiating or verifying individual transactions or to confirm if assets and liabilities are properly accounted for, including income and expense items.

**Audited Financial Statements:** financial statements that have been examined by an independent certified public accountant to determine if the financial statements present fairly the financial position, results of operations, and cash flows in conformity with generally accepted accounting principles.

**Auditor:** person who deals with examination and verification of financial accounts and with making financial reports.

**Auditor's Report:** part of complete set of financial statements that explains degree of responsibility that independent accountant assumed for expressing an opinion on management's financial statements and assurance that is provided by said opinion.

**Automated Cash Application:** computerized procedures enabling payments to be quickly and automatically applied to accounts receivable.

**Automated Clearinghouse (ACH):** computer-based clearing and settlement facility for interchange of electronic debits and credits among financial institutions. ACH entries can be substituted for checks in recurring payments such as mortgages or in direct deposit distribution of federal and corporate benefits payments. Federal Reserve Banks furnish data processing services for most ACHs, although some are privately operated. Final settlement, or net settlement, of ACH transfers is made against reserve accounts at Federal Reserve Banks.

**Available Balance:** checking account balance that the customer actually may use; that is, current balance less deposits not yet cleared through the account.

**Average Collected Balances:** average dollar amount on deposit in checking accounts defined as the difference between ledger balance and deposit float, or those deposits posted to the account but having not yet cleared the financial institution upon which they are drawn. See also Uncollected Funds.

**Average Collection Period:** average number of days required to convert accounts receivable to cash.

**Average Daily Balance:** average amount of money that depositor keeps on deposit when calculated on a daily basis.

## B

**Backdating:** predating document prior to date on which it was drawn.

**Backlog:** amount of revenue expected to be realized from work to be performed on uncompleted contracts, including new contractual agreements on which work has not begun.

**Bad Check Laws:** laws enacted in various states to encourage and facilitate lawful use of checks; statutes differ in various jurisdictions and are generally enforced according to state laws as well as local custom and usage.

**Bad Debt:** account receivable that proves uncollectible in normal course of business; full payment is doubtful.

**Bad Debt Ratio:** ratio of bad debt expense to sales, used as measure of quality of accounts receivable.

**Bad Debt Reserve:** reserve or provision for accounts receivables to be charged off company's books based on historical levels of bad debts or industry averages.

**Balance:** amount owed or unpaid on loan or credit transaction. Also called outstanding or unpaid balance.

**Balance Due:** total amount owed after applying debits and credits of account.

**Balance Sheet:** A financial statement listing the assets, liabilities, and owner's equity of a business entity or individual as of a specific date.

**Balloon Payment:** lump-sum payment of principal and sometimes accrued interest, usually due at end of term of installment loan in which periodic installments of principal and interest did not fully amortize loan.

**Bank:** financial institution chartered by state or federal government to transact financial business that includes receiving deposits, lending money, exchanging currencies, providing safekeeping, and investing money.

**Bank Draft:** sight or demand draft (order to pay) drawn by a bank (drawer) on its account at another bank (drawee).

**Banker's Acceptance:** draft or order to pay specified amount at specified time not to exceed 270 days, drawn on individuals, business firms, or financial institutions; draft becomes accepted when a financial institution formally acknowledges its obligation to honor such draft, usually by writing or stamping "Accepted" on face of instrument. When accepted in this manner, draft becomes liability of bank. See also *Draft* and *Time Draft*.

**Bank Overdraft:** check presented for collection for which there are not sufficient funds on deposit to make normal payment. Financial institution may honor such check, considering payment as loan to depositor for which the institution will usually collect interest or service charge.

**Bankrupt:** debtor who is unable to meet debt obligations as they become due or is insolvent and whose assets are administered for benefit of creditors.

**Bankruptcy:** Legal action taken under the U.S. Bankruptcy Code by or against an insolvent debtor who is unable to meet obligations as they become due. The bankrupt, if given discharge, is released from further liability of most debts listed as of the date of the bankruptcy filing.

- *Voluntary Bankruptcy:* any individual, partnership, corporation, estate, trust, or governmental unit may be afforded protection of debtor under U.S. Bankruptcy Code by filing petition. Exceptions: railroads, insurance or banking corporations, building and loan associations.
- *Involuntary Bankruptcy:* involuntary petition can be filed in bankruptcy court by three or more creditors or, if there are fewer than 12 creditors, by any one creditor. Petitioning creditors' claims must aggregate at least $5,000 in excess of value of any collateral of debtor. Involuntary cases may be filed against individuals, partnerships, or corporations other than farmers and nonprofit corporations and may be instituted under either Chapter 7 or Chapter 11 of the U.S. Bankruptcy Code. Involuntary petition must allege one of two grounds for relief: either that the debtor is generally not paying debts as they become due, or that the non-bankruptcy custodian, other than one appointed to enforce lien on less than substantially all of debtor's property, was appointed for, or took possession of, substantially all of debtor's property within 120 days of filing.
- *Chapter 7 Cases:* liquidation proceedings, formerly referred to as "straight bankruptcy," wherein nonexempt assets of debtor are converted to cash and proceeds distributed pro rata among creditors.
- *Chapter 9 Cases:* reorganization proceedings wherein municipality that is insolvent or unable to meet debts as they mature effects plan to adjust such debts.
- *Chapter 11 Cases:* reorganization proceedings available to all business enterprises; may be instituted either by debtor or creditor(s). For plan to be confirmed by court under Chapter 11, each class of creditors, as set forth in such plan, must accept plan or each class must receive at least that which it would receive on liquidation. Class of creditors has accepted plan when majority in number and two-thirds in dollar amount of those creditors actually voting approve it.
- *Chapter 12 Cases:* reorganization proceedings for agricultural concerns and small family-owned farms having debts under $1.5 million.
- *Chapter 13 Cases:* reorganization cases that may be instituted only by individuals with regular income who owe unsecured debts of less than $100,000 and secured debts of less than $350,000, other than stockbroker or commodity broker. For plan to be confirmed, it must provide for submission to trustee of all or any portion of debtor's future earnings as necessary for execution of plan, payment in full of all priority claims, and equal treatment of each member of class of creditors. While consent of unsecured creditors is not required, value of what they receive under plan may not be less than if debtor were liquidated.

**Bankruptcy Judge:** presiding judge of court in which bankruptcy cases are heard. (Formerly called Referee in Bankruptcy.) Duties of judge include supervising administrative details of bankrupt estates and ruling on all matters involving debtor-creditor problems.

**Basis:** 1. number of days used in calculating interest earned in investment or interest payable on bank loan. Also called accrual base. 2. original cost of asset plus capital improvements from which any taxable gains (or losses) are determined after deducting depreciation expenses.

**Basis Point:** 1/100th of a percent; 100 basis points equal 1%.

**Bearer:** negotiable item (check, note, bill, or draft) in which no payee is indicated or payee is shown as "cash" or "bearer." Item is payable to person in possession of it or to person who presents it for payment.

**Bearer Paper:** instrument that is made "payable to bearer." When negotiable instrument is endorsed in blank, it becomes bearer paper and can be transferred by delivery since it does not require endorsement.

**Beneficiary:** 1. person or organization named in will to inherit or receive property. 2. person or organization to whom insurance policy is payable. 3. person or organization for whose benefit trust is created.

**Bid Bond:** bond issued by surety on behalf of contractor that provides assurance to recipient of contractor's bid that if bid is accepted, contractor will execute contract and provide performance bond. Under bond, surety is obligated to pay recipient difference between contractor's bid and bid of next lowest responsible bidder if bid is accepted and contractor fails to execute cor or to provide performance bond.

**Billing Cycle:** number of days between payment due dates.

**Bill of Costs:** certified itemization of costs associated with lawsuit.

**Bill of Lading:** written instrument signed by common carrier or agent identi freight and representing both receipt and contract for shipment. It must s name of consignee, description of goods, terms of carrier's contract, directions for assigning to specific person at specific place. In form of n tiable instrument, it is evidence of holding title to goods being shipped.

**Bill of Sale:** written instrument evidencing transfer of title of specific per property to buyer.

**Binder:** 1. written agreement that provides temporary legal protection per issuance of final contract or policy. 2. temporary insurance contract; ma oral or written; also called cover note.

**Blank Endorsement:** endorser's writing on check, promissory note, or b exchange without indicating party to whom it is payable. Endorser m signs his or her name, making the instrument "payable to bearer." Also c endorsement in blank.

**Blanket Coverage:** property coverage applicable to group of exposures (b ings, inventory, equipment, etc., combined or individually, at one or locations), in single total amount of insurance; contrasts with Specific C age.

**Blanket Mortgage:** mortgage secured by two or more parcels of real prop frequently used by developers who acquire large tract of land for subdivi and resale to individual homeowners. Also called blanket trust deed.

**Bond:** contract issued by insurance or bonding company in support of princi obligation to obligee. See also *Fidelity Bond* and *Surety Bond*.

**Bonded Warehouse:** federally approved warehouse under bond for strict ob vance of revenue laws; used for storing goods until duties are paid or p erty is otherwise released. Bonded warehouse assures owner of property operators of warehouse are insured against loss by fraud and will keep pr inventory and accounting of goods in transit.

**Bonding Company:** company authorized to issue bid bonds, performance bo labor and materials bonds, or other types of surety bonds.

**Book Value:** 1. company's net worth calculated by adding total assets minus liabilities. 2. value of asset (cost plus additions, less depreciation) show books or financial report of an entity.

**Borrower's Certificate:** A document required under a loan or other agreeme be submitted by the borrower or another designated party to certify the v of collateral and compliance with the terms of the agreement.

**Bottom Line:** (colloq.) final price, net profit, or end results.

**Branch Banking:** multioffice banking. Branch is any banking facility away f bank's main office that accepts deposits or makes loans. State laws str control opening of new banking offices by state-chartered banks, nati banks, and thrift institutions.

**Breach of Contract:** failure to fulfill terms of contract, in part or whole.

**Breach of Warranty:** 1. failure to fully disclose information about condition property or insured party. 2. failure to perform as promised.

**Break-Even Analysis:** A method of determining the number of units that mus sold at a given price to recover all fixed and variable costs.

**Break-even Point:** 1. point at which total sales are equal to total expenses. be expressed in units or dollars. 2. amount received from sale that exa equals amount of expense or cost.

**Bridge Loan:** loan that provides liquidity until defined event occurs that will g erate cash, such as sale of noncurrent asset, replacement financing, or eq infusion.

**Bulk Sales Acts:** statutes designed to prevent defrauding of creditors thro secret sale in bulk of merchant's goods. Most states require notice of p posed sale to all creditors.

**Burden of Proof:** 1. duty of producing sufficient evidence to prove position ta in lawsuit. 2. necessity of proving fact or facts as to truth of claim.

**Business:** 1. commercial, industrial, or mercantile activity engaged in by indi ual, partnership, corporation, or other form of organization for purpos making, buying, or selling goods or services at profit. 2. occupation, pro sion, or trade.

**Business Failure:** 1. suspension of business resulting from insolvency or ba ruptcy. 2. inability to fulfill normal business obligations.

**Business Interruption Insurance:** property insurance written to cover loss profits and continuing expenses as result of shutdown by insured peril; sure is classified as consequential loss. Also called earnings insurance.

**Buyer's Market:** market condition in which supply exceeds demand, w causes prices to decline.

**Buy Out:** to purchase at least a controlling percentage of a company's stock take over its assets.

**Bylaws:** set of rules or regulations adopted to control internal affairs of organ tion.

## C

**…f Credit:** the "Five C's" of credit. A longstanding means of evaluating a customer by investigating Character, Collateral, Capacity, Conditions, and Capital.

**…ndar Year:** 12-month accounting period ending December 31.

**…ble Loan:** loan payable on demand.

**…eled Check:** check that has been paid by a financial institution and on which the financial institution has imprinted evidence of payment so that it cannot be presented again.

**…ellation Clause:** provision in contract or agreement allowing parties to rescind agreement under certain conditions.

**…city:** one of the "Five C's" of credit; a customer's ability to successfully absorb merchandise and to pay for the merchandise. Refers to customer's ability to produce sufficient cash so as to meet obligations when due.

**…tal:** 1. one of the "Five Cs" of credit; refers to financial resources the customer has at the time order is placed and those that he or she is likely to have when payment is due. 2. amount invested in business by owners or stockholders. 3. owner's equity in the business.

**…:** 1. money readily available for current expenditures; usually consists of cash on hand or money in a financial institution. 2. money equivalent, such as check, paid at time of purchase. 3. any medium of exchange that the financial institution will accept at face value upon deposit.

**…Basis Accounting:** basis of accounting in which revenues and expenses are reported in the income statement when cash is received or paid out for the time period in which the revenues and expenses occur.

**…Basis Loan:** loan on which interest payments are recorded when collected from borrower. This is a loan in which the borrower has fallen behind on interest payments and is classified as a nonaccrual asset.

**…Concentration and Disbursement (CCD):** corporate electronic payment used in business-to-business and intracompany transfers of funds. Funds are cleared on overnight basis through nationwide automated clearinghouse network.

**…Equivalents:** accounting term for actual cash on hand and total of bank deposits.

**…Flow:** is based on an activity format, which classifies cash inflows and outflows in terms of operating, investing, and financing activities.

**…ier's Check:** check drawn on financial institution's account, becoming direct obligation of the financial institution.

**…Management Account:** special type of deposit service that permits corporate customers to invest cash in demand deposit account until needed for operations.

**…Surrender Value:** in life insurance, amount payable under whole life policy when terminated by insured.

**…ualty Insurance:** coverage for automobile, liability, crime, boiler and machinery, health, bonds, aviation, workers' compensation, and other miscellaneous lines; contrasts with Property Insurance.

**…ificate of Insurance:** written statement issued by insurer indicating that insurance policy has been issued and showing details of coverage at time certificate was written; used as evidence of insurance.

**…ified Check:** depositor's check confirmed on its face as good by a financial institution and stamped "certified." It is then dated and signed by an authorized officer of the institution. Such check becomes an obligation of the financial institution, which guarantees that it is holding sufficient funds to cover payment of check on demand.

**…ified Copy of Policy:** document that provides evidence of insurance as of certain date; coverage may be terminated or changed after certification.

**…ified Public Accountant (CPA):** one who has been trained to do accounting and who has passed state test and received title of CPA; title certifies holder's qualification to practice accounting, audit, prepare reports, and analyze accounting information.

**…:** see *Comprehensive General Liability*.

**…racter:** one of the "Five Cs" of credit; refers to evaluating qualities that would impel debtor to meet his or her obligations. Generally identified as customer's reputation, responsibility, integrity, and honesty.

**…rge-Off:** portion of principal balance of a loan or account receivable that an entity considers uncollectible; this amount may be partially or fully recovered in future. Also called a *Write-Off*.

**…rt of Accounts:** listing of all financial accounts or categories (usually numbered) into which business transactions are classified and recorded.

**…ttel:** item of tangible personal property, animate or inanimate, as distinguished from real property.

**…ttel Mortgage:** instrument of sale in which debtor transfers title in property to creditor as security for debt. Failure by debtor to comply with terms of contract may cause creditor's title in property to become absolute.

**…ck:** order on a financial institution for payment of funds from depositor's account and payable on demand.

**…im:** 1. action to recover payment, reimbursement, or compensation from entity legally liable for damage or injury.

**…imant:** one who makes claim or asserts right.

**Cleanup:** period during which particular loan or entire borrowing has been paid off; out-of-debt period required under line of credit.

**Clearinghouse:** association of financial institutions or security dealers created to permit daily settlement and exchange of checks or delivery of stocks and other items between members in local geographic area.

**Closed-End Credit:** consumer installment loan made for predetermined amount, calling for periodic payments of principal and interest over specified period or term. Finance charge may be fixed or variable rate. Borrower does not have option of obtaining extra funds under original loan agreement. Contrasts with Open-End Credit.

**Cloud on Title:** outstanding claim or encumbrance on property that may impair owner's title.

**Cognovit Note:** form of promissory note or statement that allows creditor, in case of default by debtor, to enter judgment without trial. (Not recognized in all jurisdictions.)

**Collateral:** 1. one of the "Five C's" of credit; refers to real or personal property that may be available as security. 2. asset pledged by borrower in support of loan. See also *Secured Loan*.

**Collateral Note:** form of promissory note given for loan, pledging real or personal property as security for payment of debt.

**Collectible:** account capable of being collected.

**Collection Agency:** professional business service employed as agent to collect creditors' unpaid (past-due) accounts. Collection agency is usually compensated by receiving agreed upon contingent percentage of amount collected.

**Collection Agency Report:** report from collection agency that informs client of results of collection efforts, investigations, or recommendations.

**Collection Charges:** 1. fees charged by bank for collecting drafts, notes, coupons, or other instruments. 2. compensation paid to collection agency or attorney for collecting delinquent accounts.

**Collection Item:** 1. term for item received for collection that is to be credited to depositor's account after payment. Most financial institutions charge special (collection) fees for handling such items. 2. past due account assigned for collection.

**Collection Period:** number of days required for company's receivables to be collected and converted to cash.

**Comaker:** person who signs (and guarantees) note of another and by so doing promises to pay in full. See also *Cosigner*.

**Commensurate:** describes deposit balances that are in acceptable proportion to size of loan or commitment.

**Commercial Debt:** loan or obligation incurred for business purposes.

**Commercial Law League of America (C.L.L.A.):** national membership organization of commercial attorneys, commercial credit and collection agencies, credit insurance companies, and law list publishers. Objectives include setting standards for honorable dealings among members, improving the practice of commercial law, and promoting uniformity of legislation affecting commercial law.

**Commercial Paper:** short-term securities such as notes, drafts, bills of exchange, and other negotiable paper that arise out of commercial activity and become due on a definite maturity date.

**Commercial Property:** real estate used for business purposes or managed so as to produce income from rents and leases.

**Commitment:** agreement between a financial institution and borrower to make funds available under certain conditions for a specified period of time.

**Commitment Fee:** lender's charge for holding credit available, usually replaced with interest when funds are advanced, as in revolving credit. In business credit, a commitment fee is often charged for unused portion of line of credit.

**Commitment Letter:** letter from lender stating willingness to advance funds to named borrower, repayable at specified rate and time period, subject to escape clause(s) allowing lender to rescind agreement in event of materially adverse changes in borrower's financial condition.

**Committee Approval:** credit is approved by several people acting as group.

**Common Law:** body of law that was originated, developed, and administered in England.

**Community Property:** property shared by husband and wife, each having one-half interest in earnings of other; form of joint property ownership in some states.

**Community Reinvestment Act of 1977 (CRA):** federal law that requires mortgage lenders to demonstrate their commitment to home mortgage financing in economically disadvantaged areas. Prohibits redlining or credit allocation based on geographic region and requires lenders to file annual compliance statements.

**Compensating Balance:** demand deposit balance that must be maintained by borrower to compensate financial institution for loan accommodations and other services.

**Compound Interest:** interest calculated by adding accumulated interest to date to original principal. New balance becomes principal for additional interest calculations.

**Comprehensive General Liability (CGL):** policy form providing automatic coverage for all insured's business operations; may include auto exposures; newer form of CGL is called commercial general liability.

**Concession:** 1. granting of special privilege to digress from regular terms or previous conditions. 2. allowance or rebate from established price. 3. business enterprise operated under special permission.

**Conditional Sales Contract:** contract for sale of goods under which possession is delivered to buyer but title retained by seller until goods are paid for in full or until other conditions are met. In most states, conditional sales contracts have been replaced by security agreements having substantially the same definition under Uniform Commercial Code.

**Conditions:** one of the "Five C's" of credit; refers to general business environment and status of borrower's industry.

**Confession of Judgment Note:** note in which (after maturity) debtor permits attorney to appear in court and have judgment entered if payment is not made as agreed. Acceptance of note varies by state. See also *Cognovit Note*.

**Confirmation:** 1. supplier's written acknowledgment that he or she has accepted buyer's order. 2. customer's written verification of order previously placed. 3. proof verifying agreement or existence of assets and liabilities or claims against assets and liabilities.

**Consent Judgment:** judgment that debtor allows to be entered against him or her by motion filed with court.

**Consideration:** 1. element in contract without which contract is not binding. Contract is generally not valid without consideration. 2. reason for contracting parties to enter into contract. Act, promise, price, or motive for which agreement is entered into. 3. value given in exchange for benefit that is to be derived from contract. 4. compensation. Exchange of consideration is usually mutual, each party giving something up to other.

**Consign:** to send or forward goods to merchant, factor, or agent for sale with title retained by seller and with payment delayed, generally until sale is made.

**Consignee:** person or entity to which goods or property is consigned or shipped; ultimate recipient of shipment.

**Consignment:** arrangement under which consignor (seller) remains owner of property until such time as consignee (buyer) pays for goods; usually consignee pays consignor when goods are sold or holds proceeds of sale in trust for benefit of consignor.

**Consignor:** 1. one who delivers shipment or turns it over to carrier for transportation and delivery. 2. one who consigns goods to be sold without giving up title.

**Consolidated Financial Statement:** combined statement showing financial condition of parent corporation and its subsidiaries.

**Consolidating Financial Statement:** combined statement of subsidiary and parent companies that shows complete statement for each entity without netting intercompany transactions.

**Construction Loan:** interim financing for development and construction of real property, generally converted to long-term financing upon completion of construction.

**Consumer Credit:** debt incurred for personal, family, or household use.

**Consumer Credit Protection Act (Truth in Lending Act of 1968):** law that requires most lenders and those who extend consumer credit to disclose true credit costs. Act provides for limits on garnishment of wages, prohibits excessive interest, and makes available contents of consumer credit reports.

**Consumer Sale Disclosure Statement:** form required to be provided by creditor to customer, disclosing finance charge details as required under Consumer Credit Protection Act.

**Contingent Fee:** fee to be paid only in event of specific occurrence, usually successful results. Arrangement, for example, in which collection agency will receive stated percentage of any amounts recovered or in which lawyer will receive payment only if successful in prosecuting lawsuit.

**Contingent Liability:** liability in which a person(s) or business(es) is indirectly responsible for obligations of a third party. Such indirect liability is usually established by guaranty or endorsement, and the liability holder may turn to guarantors or endorsers for satisfaction of debt. See also Endorsement and Guaranty.

**Contra Account:** account that partially or wholly offsets another account or balance.

**Contract:** agreement between two or more entities or legally competent persons that creates, modifies, or destroys legal arrangement.

**Controlled Disbursement:** funds management technique in corporate cash management designed to maximize funds available for temporary investment in money market or for payment to trade creditors. Controls flow of checks through banking system to meet corporate investment and funds management requirements. Contrasts with delayed disbursement. See also *Federal Reserve Float* and *Treasury Workstation*.

**Controller:** person in business organization responsible for finances, internal auditing, and accounting systems in use in company's operations.

**Conversion:** process of consolidating or transferring data from one system to another.

**Conveyance:** 1. transfer of right, generally instrument transferring interest in estate in form of deed. 2. transfer of property ownership (sometimes includes leases and mortgages) from one person or organization to another.

**Copyright:** intangible right granted to author or originator by federal government to solely and exclusively reproduce or publish specific literary, musical, artistic work for certain number of years.

**Corporate Reorganization:** see *Bankruptcy*.

**Corporate Veil:** convention that corporate organization insulates organization owners from liability for corporate activities.

**Corporation:** artificial person or legal entity organized under and treated by laws, legally distinct from its shareholders and vested with capacity of continuous succession irrespective of changes in its ownership either in perpetuity or for limited term. It may be set up to contract, own, and discharge business within boundaries of powers granted it by its corporate charter.

**Correspondent:** organization or individual that carries on business relations acts as agent with others in different cities or countries.

**Cosigner:** one of joint signers of loan documents. One who signs note of another as support for credit of the principal maker.

**Cost of Funds:** dollar cost of interest paid or accrued on funds acquired from various sources within bank and borrowed funds acquired from other financial institutions, including time deposits, advances at Federal Reserve discount window, federal funds purchased, and Eurodollar deposits. Financial institution may use internal cost of funds in pricing loans it makes.

**Covenant:** written agreement, convention, or promise between parties to pledge to do or not to do certain things or that stipulates truth of certain facts.

**CPA:** see *Certified Public Accountant*.

**CRA:** see *Community Reinvestment Act of 1977*.

**Crash:** sudden sharp decrease in business activity that can negatively affect stock market volumes and prices.

**Credit:** 1. privilege of buying goods and services, or for borrowing money in return for promise of future payment. 2. in bookkeeping, entry on ledger signifying cash payment, merchandise returned, or allowance to reduce debt; accounting entry on right side of ledger sheet.

**Credit Advisory Board (CAB):** agency established by Financial Institutions Reform, Recovery, and Enforcement Act of 1989 "to monitor the credit standards and lending practices of insured depository institutions and the supervision of such standards and practices by the federal financial regulators as well as to "ensure that insured depository institutions can meet the demands of a modern and globally competitive world." This board was granted permanent authorization by the Federal Deposit Insurance Corporation Improvement Act of 1991. Formerly known as Credit Standards Advisory Committee (CSAC).

**Credit Analyst:** person who evaluates the financial history and financial statements of credit applicants to assess creditworthiness. Analysts are trained to evaluate applicant's financial strength and to opine on the probability of repayment, collateral adequacy, or whether a credit enhancement through cosigner or guarantor is needed.

**Credit Application:** form completed by potential borrower and used by creditor to determine applicant's creditworthiness.

**Credit Approval:** decision to extend credit.

**Credit Approval System:** internal methods by which credit decisions are made.

**Credit Bureau:** agency that gathers information and provides its subscribers with credit reports on consumers.

**Credit Checking:** examining and analyzing creditworthiness of customer by contacting references, reviewing credit reports, etc.

**Credit Department:** department within a financial institution that performs operations and credit support functions for underwriting activities. May include maintenance of credit files, credit investigations, financial statement analysis and spreading, customers' accounts receivable audits, lender training, portfolio reporting, facilitation of credit meetings, etc.

**Credit Enhancement:** enhancement to creditworthiness of loans underlying asset-backed security or municipal bond, generally to get investment-grade rating from bond rating agency and to improve marketability of debt securities to investors. There are two general classifications of credit enhancements:
- third-party enhancement, in which third party pledges its own creditworthiness and guarantees repayment in form of standby letter of credit or commercial letter of credit issued by a financial institution, surety bond from insurance company, or special reserve fund managed by financial guaranty firm in exchange for fee.
- self-enhancement, which is generally done by issuer through over-collateralization—that is, pledging loans with book value greater than face value of bonds offered for sale.

**Credit File:** creditor's file that compiles information about customer, including correspondence, credit memorandums and analyses, credit ratings, a credit history, payment patterns, and credit inquiries.

**Credit Granting:** approval and extension of credit to a customer.

**Credit Inquiry:** request made by a financial institution or trade creditor concerning the responding bank's own customer.

**it Insurance:** life and health insurance issued in conjunction with borrowing by individuals; covers payments or unpaid balance when borrower is disabled or dies; in business, covers loss of receivables when debtor becomes insolvent.

**it Interchange:** exchange of credit information between individuals or groups.

**it Interchange Bureau (CIB):** 1. local bureaus offering members or subscribers credit reports usually based on recent ledger experiences. Generally refers to organized system of cooperating bureaus operated by regional credit associations. 2. credit agency that may limit its reporting to a particular trade.

**it Investigation:** inquiry made by a financial institution or trade creditor concerning subject that is not the responding financial institution's customer.

**it Limit:** maximum amount of credit made available to customer by specific creditor.

**it Line:** commitment by a financial institution to lend funds to a borrower up to a given amount over a specified future period under certain pre-established conditions. Normally reviewed annually.

**it Management:** function of planning, organizing, implementing, and supervising credit policies of a company.

**itor:** 1. one to whom debt is owed by another as a result of a financial transaction. 2. one who extends credit and to whom money is due.

**itors' Committee:** voluntary representative group of creditors that may examine affairs of insolvent debtor. Group will usually advise as to continuation of business, study accountant's and appraiser's reports, act as watchdog over operating business, make recommendations to appropriate groups or legal body so that creditors will realize largest settlement possible, and advise as to acceptability of settlement.

**itors' Remedies:** legal rights enabling creditors to collect delinquent debts owed them.

**it Policy:** company's written procedures for making credit decisions. Used to aid company in meeting its overall risk management objectives.

**it Process Review:** assessment of entire credit-granting process concerning specific financial institution loan portfolio(s).

**it Rating:** appraisal made by a financial institution or credit agency as to creditworthiness of a person or company. Such a report will include background on owners, estimate of financial strength and ability to pay when due, and company's payment record.

**it Record:** written history of how well a customer has handled debt repayment.

**it Report:** 1. report to aid management in reaching credit, sales, and financial decisions. 2. confidential report containing information obtained by mercantile agency that has investigated a company's background, credit history, financial strength, and payment record.

**it Reporting Agency:** company or trade interchange group that confidentially supplies subscribers or members with credit information and other relevant data as to a company's ability or likelihood to pay for goods and services purchased on credit.

**it Research Foundation (CRF):** education and research affiliate of National Association of Credit Management.

**it Review:** follow-up monitoring of loan or extension of credit by credit review officer or department, senior loan committee, auditor, or regulatory agency intended to determine whether loan was made in accordance with lender's written credit standards and policies and in compliance with banking regulations. Errors, omissions, concentrations, etc., if detected by credit review process, can then be corrected by lending officers, thus preventing deterioration in credit quality and possible loan losses. Also called loan review.

**it Risk:** 1. evaluation of a customer's ability or willingness to pay debts on time. 2. risk that a financial institution assumes when it makes an irrevocable payment on behalf of its customer against insufficient funds.

**it Scoring:** statistical model used to predict the creditworthiness of credit applicants. Credit scoring estimates repayment probability based on information in credit application and credit bureau report. The two main types of credit scoring are application scoring for new accounts and behavior scoring for accounts that have been activated and are carrying balances.

**it Terms:** stated and agreed on terms for debt repayment.

**it Union:** nonprofit cooperative financial organization chartered by state or federal government to provide financial services such as deposit and loan activities to a specific and limited group of people.

**ditworthy:** term used to describe individual or entity deemed worthy of extension of credit.

**AC:** see *Credit Advisory Board*.

**rrent Assets:** short-term assets of company, including cash, accounts receivable, temporary investments, and goods and materials in inventory.

**rrent Liabilities:** short-term obligations due within one year, including current maturities of long-term debts.

**Current Open Account:** sale of goods or services for which customer does not pay for each purchase but rather is required to settle in full periodically or within specified time period after each transaction.

**Current Ratio:** total of current assets divided by total current liabilities; used as indication of a company's liquidity and ability to service current obligations.

## D

**D&B:** see *Dun & Bradstreet, Inc.*

**Dating (Terms):** extension of credit terms beyond normal terms because of industry's seasonality or unusual circumstance.

**Days Sales Outstanding (DSO):** a calculation that expresses the average time in days that receivables are outstanding.

**DBA:** see *Doing Business As*.

**DDA:** see *Demand Deposit Account*.

**Dealer Loan:** see *Floor Plan*.

**Debenture:** unsecured, long-term indebtedness or corporate obligation.

**Debit:** entry on left side of accounting ledger.

**Debit Card:** magnetized plastic card that permits customers to withdraw cash from automatic teller machines and make purchases with charges deducted from funds on deposit at a predesignated account.

**Debt:** 1. specified amount of money, goods, or services that is owed from one to another, including not only obligation of debtor to pay but also right of creditor to receive and enforce payment. 2. financial obligation of debtor.

**Debtor:** person or entity indebted to or owing money to another.

**Debtor in Possession (DIP):** In a Chapter 11 bankruptcy, a debtor may continue to maintain possession of its assets and use them in normal business operations.

**Debtor-in-Possession Financing:** credit facilities extended to borrower who is reorganizing under Chapter 11 bankruptcy.

**Debt Ratio:** measure of firm's leverage position derived by dividing total debts by equity.

**Debt Service:** total interest and scheduled principal payments on debt due within given time frame.

**Decision:** judgment, decree, or verdict pronounced by court in determination of case.

**Declarations Page:** policy form containing data regarding insured, policy term, premium, type and amount of coverage, designation of forms and endorsements incorporated at time policy is issued, name of insurer, and countersignature of agent.

**Deductible:** portion of loss that is not insured; may be stated amount deducted from loss or percentage of loss or of value of property at time of loss.

**Deduction:** partial amount of payment that is withheld.

**Deed:** legal, written document used to transfer ownership of real property from one party to another.

**Deed of Trust:** legal document used in some states in lieu of mortgage. Title to real property passes from seller to trustee, who holds mortgaged property until mortgage has been fully paid and then releases title to borrower. Trustee is authorized to sell property if borrower defaults, paying amount of mortgage loan to lender and any remaining balance to former owner.

**Defalcation:** misappropriation of funds held in trust for another.

**Defamation:** injury to person's or entity's character, reputation, or good name by false and malicious statements (includes both libel and slander).

**Default:** to fail to meet obligation or terms of loan agreement such as payment of principal or interest.

**Default Charge:** legally agreed upon charge or penalty added to account when payment of debt is late or another event of default occurs under a loan agreement.

**Defendant:** person or entity defending or denying claim; party against which suit or charge has been filed in court of law. See also Plaintiff.

**Defer:** to postpone or delay action.

**Deferred Payment Sale:** selling on installment plan with payments delayed or postponed until future date.

**Deficiency Judgment:** decree requiring debtor to pay amount remaining due under defaulted contract after secured property has been liquidated.

**Deficit:** difference between receipts and expenses when expenses are greater.

**Defraud:** to deprive person of property by fraud, deceit, or artifice.

**Defunct:** business that has ceased to exist and is without assets; concern that has failed.

**Delayed Disbursement:** practice in cash management whereby a firm pays vendors and other corporations by disbursing payments from a financial institution in a remote city. Also called remote disbursement. Contrasts with controlled disbursement. See also Federal Reserve Float.

**Delinquent:** 1. past-due obligation; overdue and unpaid account. 2. to be in arrears in payment of debts, loans, taxes. 3. to have failed in duty or responsibility.

**Demand Deposit Account (DDA):** funds on deposit in checking account that are payable by a financial institution upon demand of depositor. See also *Time Deposit*.

**Demand Draft:** written order directing that payment be made, on sight, to a third party.

**Demand Letter:** correspondence sent by creditor, collection agency, or lawyer to debtor requesting payment of obligation by specific date.

**Demand Loan:** loan with no fixed due date and payable on demand by maker of loan; loan that can be "called" by lender at any time.

**Demurrage:** charge that is fixed by contract and payable by recipient of goods for detaining freight car or ship longer than agreed in order to load or unload. Purpose is remuneration to owner of vessel for earnings he or she was improperly caused to lose.

**Deposit:** 1. amount of money given as down payment for goods or as consideration for contract. 2. funds retained in customer's bank account.

**Depreciation:** decline in value of fixed assets, allocating purchase cost of an asset plus additions to value over its useful economic life as outlined by the Federal Tax Code.

**Derivatives:** broad family of financial instruments with characteristics of forward or option contracts.

**Derogatory Account Information:** adverse information on customers who have not paid accounts with other creditors according to payment terms, as reported to a credit bureau.

**Directors and Officers Liability Insurance:** legal liability coverage for wrongful acts including breach of duty but not fraud or dishonesty. Often known as E & O, or Errors and Omissions Insurance.

**Disbursement:** full or partial advancement of funds.

**Discharge:** 1. to cancel or release obligation. 2. to release debtor from all or most debts in bankruptcy.

**Disclaimer Statement:** notice disclaiming responsibility for accuracy, completeness, or timeliness of credit information. Most disclaimer statements urge recipients of the information not to rely unduly on it and stress the confidential nature of information being disclosed.

**Discontinued Operations:** operations of a segment of a company, usually a subsidiary whose activities represent a separate line of business that, although still operating, is the subject of a formal plan of disposal approved by management.

**Discount:** 1. interest deducted from face amount of note at time loan is made. 2. trade term used for reduction of invoice amount when payment has been made within specified terms.

**Discounted Note:** 1. borrowing arrangement in which interest is deducted from face amount of note before proceeds are advanced (see also Note). 2. term used when customer endorses note received from another party and presents it to a financial institution to obtain funds.

**Dishonor:** to fail to make payment of negotiable instrument on its due date.

**Disintermediation:** withdrawal of funds from interest-bearing deposit accounts when rates on competing financial instruments, such as money market mutual funds, stocks, and bonds, offer better returns.

**Dismissal:** court order or judgment disposing action, suit, or motion without trial.

**Dispossess:** legal action taken by landlord to put individual or business tenant out of his or her property.

**Dissolution of Corporation:** termination of entity's existence by law, expiration of charter, loss of all members, or failure to meet statutory level of members.

**Distribution:** one or more payments made to creditors who have approved claims filed in a bankruptcy proceeding, assignment for the benefit of creditors, or receivership.

**Distributor:** business engaged in the distribution or marketing of manufacturer's goods to customers or dealers. See also Wholesaler.

**Dividend:** 1. periodic distribution of cash or property to shareholders of corporation as return on their investment.

**Document:** any written instrument that records letters with figures or marks that may be used as evidence.

**Documentary Evidence:** any written record or inanimate object, as distinguished from oral evidence.

**Documents of Title:** Include bill of lading, dock warrant, dock receipt, warehouse receipt, order for the delivery of goods, and any other document that in the regular course of business or financing is treated as adequately evidencing that the person in possession of it is entitled to receive, hold, and dispose of the document and the goods it covers. To be a document of title, a document must purport to be issued by, or addressed to, a bailee and purport to cover goods in the bailee's possession that are either identified or are fungible portions of an identified mass.

**Doing Business As (DBA):** reference term placed before trade name under which business operates. Sometimes used as fictitious trade style acknowledging that name is not part of corporation title or registered trademark.

**Domestic Corporation:** company doing business in state in which it is incorporated.

**Dormant Account:** inactive deposit account in which there have been no dep[osits] or withdrawals for a long period of time.

**Doubtful Assets:** assets that have all weaknesses inherent in substandard as[sets] with added characteristic that weaknesses make collection or liquidati[on] full, on basis of currently existing facts, conditions, and values, highly [ques]tionable and improbable. Possibility of loss is extremely high. Because of [cer]tain important and reasonably specific pending factors that may streng[then] assets, classification as estimated loss is deferred until more exact s[tatus] may be determined. Pending factors include proposed merger, acquisitio[n,] liquidation procedures, capital injection, perfecting liens on additional c[ollat]eral, and refinancing plans.

**Downgrading:** 1. lowering of assessment of customer's creditworthi[ness.] 2. worsening the internally assigned credit quality rating of a loan or rela[tion]ship in order to appropriately report risk.

**Down Payment:** up-front partial payment made to secure right to purc[hase] goods.

**Downstream Funding:** funds borrowed by holding company for a subsidi[ary's] use, generally to obtain more favorable rate; contrasts with Upstream F[und]ing.

**Draft:** written order by one party (drawer) directing second party (drawee) to [pay] sum of money to third party (payee). See also *Banker's Acceptance, Lett[er of] Credit, Sight Draft,* and *Time Draft.*

**Drawee:** person or entity that is expected to pay check or draft when instrum[ent] is presented for payment.

**Drawer:** party instructing drawee to pay someone else by writing or dra[wing] check or draft. Also called maker or writer.

**Drop Shipment:** shipment of goods delivered directly from manufacturer to [cus]tomer.

**DSO:** see *Days Sales Outstanding.*

**Dual Banking:** banking system in U.S., consisting of state banks, chartered [and] supervised by state banking departments, and national banks, chartered [and] regulated by Office of the Comptroller of the Currency.

**Due Date:** stated maturity date for debt obligation.

**Due Diligence:** 1. responsibility of an entity's directors and officers to act [in] prudent manner in evaluating credit applications; in essence, using sa[me] degree of care that an ordinary person would use in making same analysi[s. 2.] review that is made of a loan portfolio of a potential merger candidate b[y] acquiring institution.

**Due Process of Law:** law in its regular course of administration through court[s,] guaranteed by U.S. Constitution.

**Dun:** to repeatedly demand payment of debt; to be insistent in following de[btor] for payment.

**Dun & Bradstreet, Inc. (D&B):** international mercantile agency supplying in[for]mation and credit ratings on all types of businesses.

**Dun Letter:** letter or notice sent by creditor requesting payment of past-due de[bt.]

**D-U-N-S Number:** (Data Universal Numbering System) code developed by Du[n &] Bradstreet that identifies specific business name and location.

**Durable Goods:** goods that provide long-lasting qualities and continuing servi[ce.]

**Duress:** unlawful constraint that forces person to do what he or she would [not] have done by choice.

**Duty:** 1. legal, moral, or ethical obligation. 2. tax collected on import or expor[t of] goods.

## E

**Earnest Money:** money that one contracting party gives to another at the tim[e of] entering into the contract in order to bind the contract in good faith, a[nd] which will be forfeited if the purchaser fails to carry out the contract.

**Earnings Report:** 1. income statement showing a business's or individual's r[ev]enues and expenses for stated period of time.

**Easement:** right of owner of one parcel of land to use land of another for spe[cific] purpose. Usually easement rights pass with land when it is sold.

**Edge Act:** banking legislation, passed in 1919, that allows national banks to [con]duct foreign lending operations through federal or state-chartered s[ub]sidiaries called Edge Act corporations. Such corporations can be chartered [in] other states and are allowed to own banks in foreign countries and to inv[est] in foreign commercial and industrial firms.

**EFT:** see *Electronic Funds Transfer.*

**Electronic Funds Transfer (EFT):** computerized system enabling funds to [be] debited, credited, or transferred between financial institution accounts a[nd] vendors.

**Embezzlement:** fraudulent appropriation of one's property by person to whom [it] was entrusted.

**Encumbrance:** any right or interest in real or other property that diminishes [the] property's value and alters control of disposition.

**Endorsement:** 1. act of writing one's name on back of note, bill, check, or simi[lar] written instrument for payment of money; required on negotiable instrum[ent] to pass title properly to another. By signing such instrument, endor[ser]

becomes party to it and thereby liable, under certain conditions, for its payment. 2. change or addition to insurance policy, informally called rider.

**...repreneur:** person who plans, organizes, and runs operation of new business.

**...M Terms:** Shipments during a month are invoiced in a single statement dated as of the last day of that month or the first day of the following month.

**...al Credit Opportunity Act of 1974:** Federal Reserve Regulation B that prohibits creditors from discriminating against credit applicants on basis of age, race, color, religion, national origin, sex, marital status, age, or receipt of public assistance.

**...itable Subordination:** principles in section 510 (c) of U.S. Bankruptcy Code that permit bankruptcy court to subordinate, for purposes of distribution, all or part of creditor's claim against debtor's estate to claims of another creditor of that debtor after court has determined that first creditor has engaged in some form of wrongful conduct that has improved position relative to other creditors.

**...ity:** value of ownership, calculated by subtracting total liabilities from total assets.

**...cheat:** right of state to claim property or money if there is no legal claim made to it.

**...crow Account:** deposit account to which access is restricted or limited by terms of written agreement entered into by three parties, including a financial institution.

**...tate:** any right, title, or interest that a person may have in lands or other personal property.

**...timate:** amount of labor, materials, and other costs that a contractor anticipates for a project, as summarized in contractor's bid proposal for project.

**...ent of Default:** a breach of an agreement between parties to a contract; a violation of one or more of the loan covenants as set forth in either the loan agreement, commitment letter, or promissory note.

**...ergreen Revolving Credit:** commitment to lend money that remains in effect unless lender takes specific action to terminate agreement; agreement may provide that, in event of termination, any outstanding amount will convert to term loan.

**...change Rate:** value of one country's currency to that of another country at a particular point in time.

**...clusive Sales Agreement:** contractual arrangement, generally between a retailer and a manufacturer or wholesaler, giving retailer exclusive rights for sale of articles or services within a defined geographic area or through a defined distribution channel.

**...ecute:** to complete and give validity to a legal document by signing, sealing, and delivering it.

**...empt:** 1. to release, discharge, or waive from a liability to which others in the same general class are subject. 2. property not available for seizure.

**...emption:** 1. immunity from general burden, tax, or charge. 2. legal right of debtor to hold portion of property free from claims or judgments.

**...xpense:** cost or outlay of money used in business operating cycle.

**...port-Import Bank:** also called Ex-Im Bank. Provides guarantees of working capital loans for U.S. exporters; guarantees the repayment of loans or makes loans to foreign purchasers of U.S. goods and services. Ex-Im Bank also provides credit insurance that protects U.S. exporters against the risks of nonpayment by foreign buyers for political or commercial reasons. Ex-Im Bank does not compete with commercial lenders, but assumes the risks they cannot accept.

## F

**...ace Amount:** indicated value of a financial instrument, as shown on its front.

**...acility Fee:** lender's charge for making a line of credit or other credit facility available to borrower (for example, a commitment fee).

**...acsimile:** exact copy of an original.

**...actor:** entity that purchases borrower's accounts receivable and may extend funds to borrower prior to collection of receivables.

**...actoring:** short-term financing from nonrecourse sale of accounts receivable to third party or factor. Factor assumes full risk of collection, including credit losses. Factoring is most common in the garment industry, but has been used in other industries as well. There are two basic types of factoring:
- discount factoring, in which factor pays discounted price for receivables before maturity date.
- maturity factoring, in which factor pays the client purchase price of factored accounts at maturity.

**...air Credit Billing Act of 1974 (FCBA):** Federal Reserve Regulation Z details the provisions of this act by prescribing uniform methods of computing the cost of consumer credit, disclosure of credit terms, and procedures for resolving billing errors on certain kinds of credit accounts.

**...air Credit Reporting Act:** federal legislation that regulates consumer credit reporting activities and gives consumer right to learn contents of his or her credit bureau file.

**Fair Market Value:** price that property would sell for between willing buyer and willing seller, neither of whom is obligated to effect transaction.

**Fannie Mae:** see *Federal National Mortgage Association.*

**FASB:** see *Financial Accounting Standards Board.*

**FFB:** see *Federal Financing Bank.*

**FCBA:** see *Fair Credit Billing Act of 1974.*

**FDIC:** see *Federal Deposit Insurance Corporation.*

**FDICIA:** see *Federal Deposit Insurance Corporation Improvement Act of 1991.*

**Federal Deposit Insurance Corporation (FDIC):** 1. federal agency that insures bank accounts for up to $100,000 at both commercial banks and thrifts through Bank Insurance Fund and Savings Association Fund. 2. federal regulator for state-chartered banks that are not members of Federal Reserve System.

**Federal Deposit Insurance Corporation Improvement Act of 1991 (FDICIA):** legislation that provides for recapitalization of Bank Insurance Fund and restructuring of financial services industry through:
- emphasis on more capital.
- government standards for lending, operations, and asset growth.
- quicker government seizure of struggling institutions.
- reduced liquidity options for all but the strongest banks.
- incentives for uninsured depositors to use only the largest and strongest banks.
- sharply increased regulatory costs and fees.
- easier rules for acquiring banks and thrifts.

**Federal Financial Institutions Examination Council (FFIEC):** interagency group of federal banking regulators formed in 1979 to maintain uniform standards for federal examination and supervision of federally insured depository institutions, bank holding companies, and savings and loan holding companies. Also runs schools for examiners employed by banks, thrifts, and credit union agencies. Council produces Uniform Bank Performance Report.

**Federal Financing Bank (FFB):** agency in U.S. Treasury established by Congress in 1973 to centralize borrowing by federal agencies. Instead of selling securities directly to financial markets, all but largest federal agencies raise capital by borrowing from U.S. Treasury through FFB. FFB makes loans at favorable rates to agencies that do not have ready access to credit markets; its debt is direct obligation of U.S. Treasury.

**Federal Funds:** unsecured advances of immediately available funds from excess balances in reserve accounts held at Federal Reserve Banks. Technically, these funds are not borrowings but purchases of immediately available funds. Banks advancing federal funds sell excess reserves; banks receiving federal funds buy excess reserves from selling banks. Federal funds sold are credit transactions on account of selling banks. See also *Federal Funds Rate.*

**Federal Funds Rate:** rate charged in interbank market for purchases of excess reserve balances. Rate of interest is key money market interest rate and correlates with rates on other short-term credit arrangements. Because the federal funds rate re-prices with each transaction, it is the most sensitive of money market rates and is watched carefully by the Federal Reserve Board.

**Federal Home Loan Bank Board (FHLBB):** federal agency established by Federal Home Loan Bank Act of 1932 to supervise reserve credit system, Federal Home Loan Bank System, for savings institutions. Board also acted as chartering agency and primary regulator of federal savings and loan associations under Home Owners Loan Act of 1933. Financial Institutions Reform, Recovery, and Enforcement Act of 1989 abolished board, transferring its powers in examination and supervision of federally chartered savings institutions to new agency, Office of Thrift Supervision, bureau of U.S. Treasury Department. Regulatory oversight of district Home Loan Banks was transferred to the five-member Federal Housing Finance Board.

**Federal Home Loan Bank System:** system of 11 regional banks established by Federal Home Loan Bank Act of 1932, acting as central credit system for savings and loan institutions. District Home Loan Banks make short-term credit advances to savings institutions, much like Federal Reserve System acts as lender of last resort to commercial banks. Each Home Loan Bank operates independently and has its own board of directors.

**Federal Home Loan Mortgage Corporation (FHLMC):** corporation authorized by Congress in 1970 as secondary market conduit for residential mortgages. Corporation purchases loans from mortgage originators and sells its own obligations and mortgage-backed bonds issued by Government National Mortgage Association to private investors, namely financial institution trust funds, insurance companies, pension funds, and thrift institutions. Also called Freddie Mac.

**Federal Housing Administration (FHA):** federal agency that insures residential mortgages. Created by National Housing Act of 1934, FHA is now part of Department of Housing and Urban Development. Both FHA and Department of Veterans Affairs have single-family mortgage programs to assist homebuyers who are unable to obtain financing from conventional mortgage lenders (banks, savings and loans, and other financial institutions).

**Federal Housing Finance Board (FHFB):** independent federal agency regulating credit advance activities of 11 Federal Home Loan Banks. This board, estab-

lished by Financial Institutions Reform, Recovery, and Enforcement Act of 1989, has five members, including secretary of Housing and Urban Development, and four directors appointed by the President with Senate confirmation to serve seven-year terms. At least one director must represent the interests of community groups.

**Federal National Mortgage Association (FNMA):** federally chartered, stockholder-owned corporation that purchases residential mortgages insured or guaranteed by federal agencies, as well as conventional mortgages, in secondary mortgage market. Corporation raises capital to support its operations through collection of insurance and commitment fees, issuance of stock, and sale of debentures and notes. Also called Fannie Mae.

**Federal Open Market Committee (FOMC):** policy committee in Federal Reserve System that sets short-term monetary policy objectives for Fed. Committee is made up of seven governors of Federal Reserve Board, plus the presidents of six Federal Reserve Banks. President of Federal Reserve Bank of New York is permanent FOMC member. The other five slots are filled on rotating basis by presidents of other 11 Federal Reserve Banks. Committee carries out monetary objectives by instructing Open Market Desk at Federal Reserve Bank of New York to buy or sell government securities from special account, called open market account, at New York Fed.

**Federal Reserve Board (FRB):** U.S.'s central bank responsible for conduct of monetary policy; also oversees state-chartered banks that are members of Federal Reserve System, bank holding companies, and Edge Act corporations.

**Federal Reserve Float:** total amount of funds that Federal Reserve Banks, in their role as clearing agents, have credited to depositing institutions but have not charged to paying institutions.

**Federal Reserve System:** central bank of U.S. created by Federal Reserve Act of 1913. System consists of Board of Governors, made up of seven members, and a network of 12 Federal Reserve Banks and 25 branches throughout U.S. Board of Governors is responsible for setting monetary policy and reserve requirements. Board and banks share responsibility for setting the discount rate, the interest rate that depository institutions are charged for borrowing from Federal Reserve Banks.

**Federal Trade Commission (FTC):** federal regulatory agency that administers and enforces rules to prevent unfair business practices.

**Fee Simple:** estate in which owner is entitled to entire property and has unconditional power over its disposition.

**FFIEC:** see *Federal Financial Institutions Examination Council*.

**FHA:** see *Federal Housing Administration*.

**FHLBB:** see *Federal Home Loan Bank Board*.

**FHLMC:** see *Federal Home Loan Mortgage Corporation*.

**Fictitious Name:** pretend name used by firm in business transactions. Company is usually required to register this name with local authorities, along with true names and addresses of company's owners.

**Fidelity Bond:** contract issued by insurer to employer to cover loss caused by dishonest acts of employees; form of suretyship. Also called dishonesty insurance.

**Fiduciary:** person or entity acting in capacity of trustee for another.

**Field Warehousing:** method of using company's inventory to secure business loan. In leased and separate storage area of borrower's facility, goods act as security for loan and are released by custodian only upon lender's order.

**FIFO:** see *First-In First-Out*.

**File:** 1. organized folder containing accumulation of information and items retained for preservation or reference. 2. to deposit legal document with proper authority.

**File Revision:** routine gathering of credit information by credit grantor to update files on borrowers.

**Filing Claims:** 1. depositing of formal papers with proper public office and in manner and time frame prescribed by law in order to preserve creditor's rights. 2. method used to perfect security interest accomplished by recording in proper public office.

**Finance Charges:** total costs to an individual or business of obtaining credit, including interest and any fees.

**Financial Analysis:** evaluation by credit analyst of customer's financial situation to determine whether customer has ability to meet his or her obligations as they become due. Factors such as general condition of customer's industry, organizational structure, available collateral or guarantors, and past financial performance are considered.

**Financial Accounting Standards Board (FASB):** independent board responsible for establishing and interpreting generally accepted accounting principles, formed in 1973 to succeed and continue activities of Accounting Principles Board.

**Financial Institutions Reform, Recovery, and Enforcement Act of 1989 (FIRREA):** act signed into law on August 9, 1989, to provide funding and regulatory structure necessary to close several hundred insolvent savings associations and liquidate their assets, to consolidate federal insurance of banks and savings associations under direction of the Federal Deposit Insurance Corporation, to provide regulatory agencies with sweeping new enforcement pow-

ers, and to increase substantially civil and criminal penalties for violation federal banking statutes and regulations. Act substantially alters relation between savings institutions and regulators and imposes new requirem that must be observed in day-to-day operations of institutions.

**Financial Position:** standing of company, combining assets and liabilities entered on balance sheet.

**Financial Statements:** reports consisting of individual's or company's bal sheet, income statement, and statement of cash flows, footnotes, and supplemental schedules.

**Financing Statement:** form required to be completed by creditor and filed appropriate county and state authorities in order to perfect creditor's sec interest in collateral and to give public notice of such interest.

**FIRREA:** see *Financial Institutions Reform, Recovery, and Enforcement Ac 1989*.

**First Deed of Trust:** first recorded deed of trust that acts as first lien on prop it describes.

**First-In First-Out (FIFO):** method of valuing inventory in which the first go received are the first goods used or sold. Using this method, costs of in tory used to determine cost of goods sold are related to costs that v incurred first.

**First Mortgage:** mortgage on property that is superior to any others by fac having been filed first.

**Fiscal:** anything involving financial matters or issues.

**Fiscal Agent:** person or organization serving as another's financial agent or resentative.

**Fiscal Year:** fixed accounting year used as basis for annual financial reporting business or government.

**Five C's of Credit:** method of evaluating potential borrower's creditworthir based on five criteria: Capacity, Capital, Character, Collateral, and Conditior

**Fixed Assets:** property used in normal course of business that is of a long-t nature, such as land, machinery, fixtures, and equipment.

**Fixed-Rate Loan:** loan with interest rate that does not vary over term of loan.

**Fixture:** that which is permanently attached or affixed to real property.

**Flagging an Account:** temporarily identifying an account for specific purpos reason; may involve suspending activity.

**Float:** uncollected funds represented by checks deposited in one bank but not cleared through bank on which they are drawn.

**Floating Interest Rate:** loan interest rate that changes whenever the stated in rate, or base rate, changes.

**Floating Lien:** loan or credit facility secured by inventory or receivables. This t of security agreement gives lender interest in assets acquired by borro after agreement, as well as those owned when agreement was made. W agreement covers proceeds from sales, lender also has recourse against c collected from the payment of receivables.

**Floor Plan:** loan made to dealer for purchase of inventory acquired for resale secured by that inventory, such as automobiles or appliances.

**FNMA:** see *Federal National Mortgage Association*.

**FOB:** see *Free on Board*.

**FOB Point:** point at which responsibility for freight charges begins and passes. See also *Free on Board*.

**FOMC:** see *Federal Open Market Committee*.

**Forbearance:** Temporarily giving up the right to enforce a valid claim, in ret for a promise. It is sufficient consideration to make a promise binding ( example, protracted payment arrangements or interest rate reduction exchange for additional collateral or guarantors).

**Forced Sale:** 1. court-ordered sale of property, usually without owner's appro 2. voluntary sale of goods or property to raise cash or to reduce inventory.

**Foreclosure:** legal termination of all of debtor's rights in property secured mortgage after debtor has defaulted on obligation supported by such mo gage.

**Foreign Corporation:** corporation established under laws of a state other th that in which it is doing business.

**Foreign Exchange:** conversion of money of one country into its equivalent in c rency of another country.

**Foreign Item:** check drawn on any financial institution other than the financ institution where it is presented for payment. Also called transit item.

**Foreign Judgment:** judgment obtained in state or country other than the c where the debtor now lives, is doing business, or has assets.

**Forfeiture:** penalty resulting in automatic loss of cash, property, or rights for complying with legal terms of agreement.

**Forgery:** false making or material altering of any writing with intent to defraud.

**Form 8K:** report disclosing significant events potentially affecting corporatio financial condition or market value of its shares, required by Securities a Exchange Commission. Report is filed within 30 days after event (pendi merger, amendment to corporate charter, charge to earnings for credit losse took place and summarizes information that any reasonable investor wo want to know before buying or selling securities.

**10K:** annual financial report filed with Securities and Exchange Commission. Issuers of registered securities are required to file 10K, as are corporations with 500 or more shareholders or assets of $2 million and exchange-listed corporations. Report, which becomes public information once filed, summarizes key financial information, including sources and uses of funds by type of business, net pretax operating income, provision for income taxes and credit losses, plus comparative financial statements for past two fiscal years. Summary of 10K report is included in annual report to stockholders.

**10Q:** quarterly financial report filed by companies with listed securities and those corporations required to file annual 10K report with Securities and Exchange Commission. 10Q report, which does not have to be audited, summarizes key financial data on earnings and expenses and compares current financial information with data reported in same quarter of previous year.

**warding:** referral or placement of out-of-town claims with attorney who then acts on behalf of creditor. In collection process, when authorized, agency may forward account to attorney for collection or suit.

**nchise:** business agreement whereby one company allows another the right to conduct business under its name and/or distribute its products in exchange for royalties or another agreed upon method of payment.

**ud:** any act of deceit, omission, or commission used to deprive someone of right or property. Elements of fraud consist of intentional misrepresentation of fact, relied on by another to his or her detriment, that results in damages.

**udulent Conveyance:** a transfer of property by a debtor, for the intent and purpose of defrauding creditors. Such property may be reached by the creditors through appropriate legal proceedings.

**B:** see *Federal Reserve Board*.

**ddie Mac:** see *Federal Home Loan Mortgage Corporation*.

**e and Clear:** 1. property with an unencumbered title. 2. title that is free of defects.

**e and Clear Delivery Receipt:** delivery receipt signed by consignee completely absolving carrier from any claim for loss or damages.

**e Astray:** freight shipment that has been lost. If it is carrier's fault and shipment is located, it is carrier's obligation to make delivery to original destination at no additional cost to shipper or consignee.

**e Demand Letter Service:** pre-collection letter sent by collection agency to debtor, requesting that payment be made directly to creditor by given date. No charge is made for payments received within free demand period, but balances remaining unpaid are followed for collection by agency at its regular rates.

**e on Board (FOB):** term identifying shipping point from which buyer assumes all responsibilities and costs for transportation.

**e Port:** place where goods are imported or exported free of any duty.

**eight Forwarder:** business that receives goods for transportation; services include consolidation of small freight shipments of less than carload, truckload, or container lots assembled for lower shipping rates.

**ozen Account:** 1. account to which customer no longer has access. 2. account suspended by court order, violation of loan covenants, or checking account agreement, etc.

**ozen Assets:** any assets that cannot be used by owner because of pending legal action.

**C:** see *Federal Trade Commission*.

**nd:** cash or equivalents set aside for specific purpose.

**nd Accounting:** fiscal and accounting entity with self-balancing set of accounts recording cash and other financial resources, together with all related liabilities and residual equities or balances, and changes therein, which are segregated for purpose of carrying on specific activities or obtaining certain objectives in accordance with special regulations, restrictions, or limitations.

**nded Debt:** mortgages, bonds, debentures, notes, or other obligations with maturity of more than one year from statement date.

## G

**AAP:** see *Generally Accepted Accounting Principles*.

**arnishee:** 1. person or entity that has possession of money or property belonging to defendant and is served with writ of garnishment to hold money or property for payment of defendant's debt to plaintiff. 2. one against whom garnishment has been served.

**arnishment:** legal warning or procedure to one in possession of another's property not to allow owner access to such property as it will be used to satisfy judgment against owner.

**eneral Contractor:** contractor who enters into a contract with an owner for construction of a project and who takes full responsibility for its completion. Contractor may enter into subcontracts with various subcontractors for performance of specific parts or phases of project.

**eneral Ledger:** bookkeeping record comprising all assets, liabilities, proprietorship, revenue, and expense accounts. Entries for each account are posted, and balances are included for each entry.

**Generally Accepted Accounting Principles (GAAP):** conventions, rules, and procedures that define accepted accounting practices, including broad guidelines as well as detailed procedures. Financial Accounting Standards Board, an independent self-regulatory organization, is responsible for promulgating these principles.

**General Obligation Debt:** long-term debt or bond repaid from all otherwise unrestricted revenues, sales taxes, property taxes, license fees, property sales, rents, and so forth of municipality.

**General Partner:** participant in a business relationship who is personally liable, without limitation, for all partnership debts.

**Ginnie Mae:** see *Government National Mortgage Association*.

**GNMA:** see *Government National Mortgage Association*.

**Going Concern:** assumes that a business entity has a reasonable expectation of continuing in business and generating a profit for an indefinite period of time.

**Goods on Approval:** goods offered by seller to buyer with option of examining goods for specific period of time before deciding to purchase them.

**Goodwill:** 1. intangible assets of business consisting of its good reputation, valuable clientele, or desirable location that results in above normal earning power. 2. value or amount for which business could be sold above book value of its physical property and receivables.

**Government National Mortgage Association (GNMA):** corporation created by Congress that administers mortgage-backed securities program that channels new sources of funds into residential mortgages through sale of securities. Also called Ginnie Mae.

**Grace Period:** specified length of time beyond payment due date during which late fee will not be assessed.

**Grantee:** person to whom title in property is made.

**Grantor:** person who transfers title to property.

**Gross Margin:** gross profit as a percentage of sales.

**Gross Profit:** net sales less cost of sales.

**Gross Sales:** sales before returns and allowances; discounts are deducted to arrive at net sales.

**Guarantor:** person who agrees by execution of a contract to repay the debt of another if that person defaults.

**Guaranty:** separate agreement by which a party (or parties) other than debtor assumes responsibility for payment of obligation if principal debtor defaults or is subsequently unable to perform under the terms of the obligation.

**Guardian:** person who is legally responsible for the care and management of a minor or individual who is not mentally or legally competent (or of such person's property).

## H

**Hard Goods:** durable consumer goods, usually including such items as major appliances and furniture, with relatively long, useful lives.

**Heavy Industry:** industry involved in manufacturing basic products such as metals, machinery, or other equipment.

**Hidden Assets:** assets not easily identified and either intentionally not disclosed or publicly reported at lower value than their true worth.

**High Credit:** largest amount of credit used by borrower during specified period of time.

**Holder in Due Course:** person who has taken negotiable instrument (check or note) for value, in good faith, and on assurance that it is complete and regular, not overdue or dishonored, and has no defect in ownership on part of previous holder or endorser.

**Holding Company:** company organized to hold and control stock in other companies.

**Homestead Exemption:** state's law allowing householder or head of family to exempt residence from attachment by creditors.

**Housing and Urban Development, Department of:** cabinet-level federal agency, founded in 1965, that promotes housing development in U.S. through direct loans, mortgage insurance, and guaranties. It houses Federal Housing Administration and Government National Mortgage Association.

**HUD:** see *Housing and Urban Development, Department of*.

**Hypothecate:** to pledge or assign property owned by one entity as security or collateral for loan to second entity.

**Hypothecation:** 1. offer of stocks, bonds, or other assets owned by party other than borrower as collateral for loan, without transferring title. Borrower retains possession but gives lender right to sell property in event of default by borrower. 2. pledging of negotiable securities to collateralize broker's margin loan. If broker pledges same securities to bank as collateral for broker's loan, process is referred to as re-hypothecation.

## I

**Immunity:** condition of being exempt from duty that others are generally required to perform.

**Import Letter of Credit:** commercial letter of credit issued to finance import of goods.

**Import Duty:** government tax on imported items.

**Impound:** to seize or take into legal custody, usually at order of court. Cash, documents, or records may be impounded.

**Inactive Account:** account that has shown little or no activity over a substantial period of time.

**Inactive Files:** 1. accounts on which collection activity has been completed or suspended (claims either collected or found to be uncollectible) and on which no further work is being done. Also called closed or dead files. 2. stored records available for reference.

**In Arrears:** amounts due but not yet paid.

**Income Property:** real property acquired as investment and managed for profit.

**Income Statement:** summary of revenue and expenses covering a specified period.

**Income Tax:** tax levied by federal, state, or local governments on personal or business earnings.

**Incorporation:** formation of legal entity, with qualities of perpetual existence and succession.

**Incumbrance:** see *Encumbrance.*

**Indebtedness:** total amount of money or liabilities owed.

**In Default:** failing to abide by terms and conditions of note or loan agreement. This can include payments on interest or principal (or both) being past due.

**Indemnity:** 1. contract or assurance to reimburse another against anticipated loss, damage, or failure to fulfill obligation. 2. type of insurance that provides coverage for losses of this nature.

**Indirect Liability:** contingent liability such as a continuing guarantee.

**Individual Signature:** credit approved by one person on his or her own authority.

**Indorsement:** see *Endorsement.*

**Industrial Consumer:** purchaser who buys goods or services for business purposes.

**Inquiry:** request for credit information on a bank's customer.

**Insider Loans:** loans to directors and officers of bank, which must be reported to bank regulators under Financial Institutions Reform Act of 1978. Banking laws require that loans to insiders be made at substantially the same rate and credit terms as loans to other borrowers.

**Insolvency:** 1. inability to meet debts as they become due in ordinary course of business. 2. financial condition in which assets are not sufficient to satisfy liabilities.

**Installment Sale:** contract sale in which merchandise is purchased with down payment and balance is made in partial payments over agreed period of time.

**Instrument:** written formal or legal document.

**In-Substance Foreclosure Assets:** loans for which borrower is perceived to have little or no equity in the asset or project and the financial institution can reasonably anticipate proceeds for repayment only from the operation or sale of collateral.

**Insufficient Funds:** see *Non-sufficient Funds.*

**Insurable Interest:** interest such that loss or damage inflicts economic loss.

**Insurable Value:** maximum possible loss to which property is exposed; actual amount depends on basis of calculation per insurance policy.

**Intangible Assets:** nonmaterial assets of business that have no value in themselves but that represent value. Examples include trademarks, goodwill, patents, and copyrights.

**Interchange:** confidential exchange of credit information between individuals and trade groups.

**Interchange Bureau:** association organized to record and exchange or furnish confidential credit information about a member's payment experience and manner in which customers meet obligations.

**Interchange Group:** trade membership group within specific industry that meets regularly to exchange credit experiences and other confidential information.

**Interchange Report:** report usually obtained through credit interchange bureau showing recent credit experience as supplied by participating members.

**Inter-creditor Agreement:** document used when there is more than one lender involved in credit transaction to spell out each lender's rights and obligations.

**Interest:** 1. legally allowed or agreed upon compensation to lender for use of borrowed money. 2. any right in property but less than title to it.

**Interest Bearing:** term describing note or contract calling for payment of agreed interest.

**Interest Only:** loan term during which no principal repayments are made.

**Interest Rate:** cost of borrowing money expressed as an annualized percentage of the loan.

**Internal Guidance Line of Credit:** credit facility similar to a line of credit, but customer may or may not be advised of it; established for internal financial institution purposes, it provides financing for recurrent requests without referring each one to credit committee or other approval source.

**International Consumer Credit Association:** professional trade association of retail credit professionals. Association keeps members informed of latest developments in consumer credit and provides educational courses, seminars, textbooks, and other published material.

**Intestate:** dying without leaving valid will or any other specific instructions as disposition of property.

**Inventory:** current assets of business that represent goods for sale, including materials, work in process, and finished goods.

**Investigation:** 1. gathering of credit information on a person or entity. 2. systematic research for information necessary for a business decision.

**Investment:** use of money for purpose of earning profit or return.

**Investor:** person or entity that puts money to use for capital appreciation or to receive regular dividends.

**Invoice:** seller's descriptive, itemized billing for goods or services sold, show date, terms, cost, purchase order number, method of shipment, and other identifying information.

**Involuntary Bankruptcy:** see *Bankruptcy.*

**Itemized Statement:** detailed listing of activity on account for particular period time.

## J

**Jobber:** see *Wholesaler.*

**Joint Account:** financial institution account shared or owned in name of two more persons with full privileges available to each person.

**Joint and Several:** relative to liability, a term used when creditor has option pursuing one or more signers of an agreement individually or all signe together.

**Joint Tenancy with Rights of Survivorship:** interest in property held by two more persons that includes right of survivorship in which deceased person interest passes to survivors. See also *Tenancy by Entirety.*

**Joint Venture:** business or undertaking entered into on one-time basis by two more parties in which profits, losses, and control are shared.

**Journal:** account book of original entry in which all money receipts and expens are chronologically recorded.

**Judgment:** court's determination of rights of parties to claim.

**Judgment Creditor:** one who has obtained judgment against debtor and ca enforce it.

**Judgment Debtor:** one against whom judgment has been recovered but not sati fied.

**Judgment Note:** see *Cognovit Note.*

**Judgment Lien:** claim or encumbrance on property, allowed by law, usual against real estate of judgment debtor.

**Judgment-Proof:** term to describe judgment debtor from whom collection cann be obtained or person who has no money or assets or has concealed removed property subject to execution.

**Judicial Sale:** see *Forced Sale.*

**Junior Mortgage:** any mortgage filed after and subject to satisfaction of fir mortgage.

**Jurisdiction:** 1. legal authority, power, capacity, and right of court to act. 2. ge graphic area within which court or government agency exercises power.

## K

**Keyperson Life Insurance:** insurance policy written on owner or princip employee in which death benefits are payable to company.

**Key Ratios:** performance measures used to determine probable ability of bus ness to operate profitably. Results are expressed in percentages that are the weighed against average percentages in each industry.

## L

**Landlord's Waiver:** the relinquishment of a right(s) contained in a lease agree ment by a lessor.

**Last-In First-Out (LIFO):** method of valuating inventory in which last good received are the first ones sold. Using this method, inventory costs used t determine cost of goods sold are related to costs of inventory that wer incurred last.

**Late Charge:** special legally agreed upon fee, charged by creditor, on any pay ment that is not made when due.

**Lawful Money:** legal tender for payment of all debts.

**Law List:** compiled publication of names and addresses of those in legal profes sion, often including court calendars, private investigators, and other informa tion of interest to legal profession.

**Lawsuit:** suit, action, or cause instituted by one person against another in a cour of law.

**Lead Bank:** financial institution that has the primary deposit or lending relation ship in a multi-bank situation; usually in the context of shared credit and sometimes defined within an inter-creditor agreement. See also *Agent Bank.*

**Leaseback:** agreement by which one party sells property to another and, after completing sale, the first party rents it from second party.

**Lease Contract:** written agreement for which equipment or facilities can be obtained on rental payment basis for specified period of time.

**Leased Department:** section of department store not operated by store but by independent outside organization on contract or percentage-of-sales arrangement.

**Leasehold:** rights tenant holds in property as conferred by terms of lease.

**Leasehold Improvement:** permanent improvements made to rented property. Leasehold improvements are considered fixtures and depreciate over lease period.

**Leasehold Interest:** lessee's equity or ownership in leasehold improvements.

**Lease-Purchase Agreement:** contract providing for set amount of lease payments to be applied to purchase of property.

**Ledger:** in accounting, book of permanent records containing series of accounts to which debits and credits of transactions are posted from books of original entry.

**Ledger Experience:** trade experience reported by credit manager or interchange group. Such reports provide picture of account's paying habits, high credit, and terms of repayment.

**Legal and Sovereign Risk:** risk that government may intervene to affect bank's system or any participant of such system detrimentally.

**Legal Composition:** identification and description of lawful ownership or title to business entity.

**Legal Entity:** business organization that has capacity to make contract or agreement or assume obligation. Such organization may consist of individual proprietorship, partnership, corporation, or association.

**Legal Right:** natural right, right created by contract, and right created or recognized by law.

**Legal Tender:** any money that is recognized by law for payment of debt unless contract exists specifically calling for payment in another type of money.

**Legal Title:** document establishing right of ownership to property that is recognized and upheld by law.

**Lender:** one who extends funds to another with expectation of repayment with interest.

**Lender's Loss Payable Endorsement:** form attached to property insurance policies to cover lender's interest in what is insured; extends coverage to give lender protection beyond that in basic policy; language may be prescribed by banking industry, standard form prepared by insurance industry, or specified by lender. See also *Loss Payee Clause*.

**Lessee:** one to whom lease is given and therefore has right to use property in exchange for rental payments.

**Lessor:** owner who grants lease for use of property in return for rent.

**Letter of Agreement:** letter stating terms of agreement between addressor and addressee, usually prepared for signature by addressee as indication of acceptance of those terms as legally binding.

**Letter of Credit:** letter or document issued by bank on behalf of customer that is evidence of financial background of bank and ensures that payment will be made when proper documents confirm completion of related transaction. Such letters authorize drawing of sight or time drafts when certain terms and conditions are fulfilled. See also *Banker's Acceptance, Draft, Sight Draft, Standby Letter of Credit,* and *Time Draft*.

**Letter of Intent:** letter signifying intention to enter into formal agreement and usually setting forth general terms of such agreement.

**Liable:** duty or obligation enforceable by law.

**Liabilities:** indebtedness of an individual or entity.

**Libel:** written or published false and malicious statements about another that tend to defame or harm another's reputation.

**LIBOR:** see *London Interbank Offered Rate*.

**Lien:** legal right or encumbrance to secure payment performance on property pledged as collateral until the debt it secures is satisfied.

**LIFO:** see *Last-In First-Out*.

**Limited Liability Company:** legal entity that offers shareholders the same limitations on personal liability available to corporate shareholders. The owners of a limited liability company (LLC) have limited liability. They are not liable for the debts, liabilities, acts, or omissions of the company. Only their investment is at risk.

**Limited Liability:** legal exemption corporate stockholders or limited liability companies have from full financial responsibilities for debts of company.

**Limited Partnership:** partnership of one or more general partners who are personally, jointly, and separately responsible, with one or more special partners whose liabilities are limited to amount of investment.

**Line of Credit:** see *Credit Line*.

**Liquid Assets:** assets that can be readily converted into cash.

**Liquidate:** 1. to pay off or settle current obligation. 2. to sell off or convert assets into cash. 3. to dissolve business in order to raise cash for payment of debts.

**Liquidation:** process of dissolving a business, settling accounts, and paying off any claims or obligations; remaining cash is distributed to the owners of the business.

**Liquidation Value:** cash that can be realized from sale of assets in dissolving business, as distinct from its value as ongoing entity.

**Liquidity:** measure of quality and adequacy of current assets to meet current obligations as they come due.

**Liquidity Ratio:** company's most liquid assets (generally cash and accounts receivable) divided by current liabilities. Also called quick ratio.

**List Price:** generally advertised or posted price. Sometimes subject to trade or cash discounts.

**Litigation:** lawsuit brought to court for purpose of enforcing a right.

**LLC:** see *Limited Liability Company*.

**Loan:** money advanced to a borrower with agreement of repayment usually with interest within a specified period of time.

**Loan Agreement:** legal contract between a financial institution and a borrower that governs the terms and conditions for the life of a loan. Elements usually include description of loan, representations, and warranties reaffirming known facts about the borrower such as legal structure, affirmative and negative covenants, conditions that must be met before the loan is granted, delinquent payment penalties, and statement of remedies that the financial institution may take in event of default.

**Loan Participation:** sharing of loan(s) by a group of financial institutions that join together to make said loan(s), affording an opportunity to share the risk of a very large transaction. Arranged through correspondent banking networks in which smaller financial institutions buy a portion of an overall financing package. Participations are a convenient way for smaller financial institutions to book loans that would otherwise exceed their legal lending limits. Also called participation financing.

**Loan Policy:** principles that reflect a financial institution's credit culture, underwriting procedures, and overall approach to lending.

**Loans Past Due:** loans with interest or principal payments that are contractually past due a certain number of days.

**Loan-to-Value Ratio (LTV):** relationship, expressed as percent, between principal amount of loan and appraised value of the asset securing financing.

**Loan Value:** amount of money that can be borrowed against real or personal property.

**Lockbox:** regional financial institution depository used by corporations to obtain earlier receipt and collection of customer payments. Arrangement provides creditor with better control of accounts receivable and earlier availability of cash balances. Many large financial institutions offer lockbox processing as a cash management service to corporate customers. Lockboxes can be:
* retail, designed for remittance processing for consumer accounts.
* wholesale, in which payments from other entities are collected and submitted through depository transfer check or electronic debit into a concentration account for investment and disbursement as needed.

**London Interbank Offered Rate (LIBOR):** key rate index used in international lending. LIBOR is the rate at which major financial institutions in London are willing to lend Eurodollars to each other. This index is often used to determine interest rate charged to creditworthy borrowers.

**Long-Arm Statutes:** state statutes that allow state courts to exercise jurisdiction over nonresident persons or property outside their state's borders.

**Long-Term Capital Gain (Loss):** gain or loss realized from sale or exchange of capital asset held for longer than 12 months.

**Long-Term Liabilities:** all senior debt, including bonds, debentures, bank debt, mortgages, deferred portions of long term-debt, and capital lease obligations owed for longer than 12 months.

**Loss:** 1. circumstance in which expenses exceed revenues. 2. result if an asset is sold for less than its depreciated book value.

**Loss Assets:** assets considered uncollectible and of such little value that their continuance as realizable assets is not warranted.

**Loss Leader:** deliberate sale of product or service at or below cost in order to attract new customers.

**Loss Payee Clause:** provision in insurance policy or added by endorsement to cover lender/mortgagee's interest in property loss settlement. Provision is not as broad as lender's loss payable endorsement. Also called mortgagee clause and loss payable clause.

**LTV:** see *Loan-to-Value Ratio*.

**Lump-sum Settlement:** payment made in full with single, one-time payment.

## M

**Magnetic Ink Character Recognition (MICR):** description of numbers and symbols that are printed in magnetic ink on documents for automated processing. Fully inscribed MICR line of information may include item's serial number, routing and transit number, check digit, account number, process control number, and amount.

**Mail-Fraud Statute:** federal law against using mails to defraud creditors by mailing false financial statements. Prosecution under mail-fraud statute must prove beyond reasonable doubt that:
* statement is false.
* statement was made with intention it should be relied on.
* it was made for the purpose of securing money or property.

- statement was delivered by mail.
- money or property was obtained by means of false statement.

**Mailgram:** telegraphic message transmitted electronically by Western Union and delivered by U.S. Postal Service.

**Mail Teller:** employee of a financial institution who receives mail deposits, checks them for accuracy, and returns stamped receipts for deposits to customers.

**Majority Stockholder:** person or entity that owns more than 50% of voting stock of a corporation, thereby having controlling interest.

**Maker:** one who signs or executes negotiable instrument.

**Malpractice:** professional misconduct with negligence.

**Management:** persons responsible for administering and carrying out policy of business or other organization.

**Management Information System (MIS):** established flow of information developed to keep managers informed of what is happening within their organization and to do it within a time frame that permits effective reaction when required. Efficient MIS helps managers make better decisions.

**Management Report:** statement in unaudited financial statements that says financials are representations of firm's management.

**Manifest:** shipping document that lists freight's origin, contents, value, destination, carrier, and other pertinent information for use at terminals or custom house.

**Manufacturers Representative (Agent):** independent, commissioned sales agent who represents several noncompeting manufacturers for sale of their products to related businesses within agreed, exclusive sales territory.

**Marginal Account:** borderline credit risk that does not have sufficient operating capital and from which payment may be delayed.

**Markdown:** price reduction of goods below normal selling price.

**Market:** 1. customer base for a company's goods or services. 2. securities exchange and its associated institutions.

**Marketability:** ease and rapidity with which product, service, or other asset can be sold or converted to cash.

**Marketing:** 1. activities necessary to facilitate the sale of goods or services through planned research, manufacturing, promotion, advertising, and distribution. 2. business promotion devoted to getting the maximum purchases of products or services by consumers.

**Market Value:** price that goods or property would bring in current market of willing buyers and sellers.

**Markup:** amount or percentage added to cost of goods to arrive at selling price.

**Maturity Date:** date when financial obligation, note, draft, bond, or instrument becomes due for payment.

**Mechanic's Lien:** enforceable claim, permitted by law in most states, securing payment to contractors, subcontractors, and suppliers of materials for work performed in constructing or repairing buildings. Lien attaches to real property, plus buildings and improvements situated on land, and remains in effect until workers have been paid in full or, in event of liquidation, gives contractor priority of lien ahead of other creditors.

**Medium of Exchange:** money or commodity accepted in payment or settlement of debt.

**Memorandum (Consignment) Sale:** sale of goods for which seller is not paid until retailer has sold merchandise. Seller retains title to such goods until retailer has sold merchandise and payment is made to retailer.

**Mercantile Agency:** organization that compiles credit and financial information and supplies subscribers or members with reports on applicants for credit; can also perform other functions such as collection of accounts or compiling of statistical trade information.

**Merchandise Shortage:** goods purchased but not included in shipment.

**Merger:** combining of two or more businesses to form a single organization.

**Mezzanine Financing:** 1. in corporate finance, leveraged buyout or restructuring financed through subordinated debt, such as preferred stock or convertible debentures. Transaction is financed by expanding equity, as opposed to debt. 2. second- or third-level financing of companies financed by venture capital. Senior to venture capital but junior to financial institution financing, it adds creditworthiness to firm. Generally used as intermediate-stage financing, preceding a company's initial public offering, it is considered less risky than start-up financing.

**MICR:** see *Magnetic Ink Character Recognition.*

**Middle-of-Month (M.O.M.) Billing Term:** billing system in which all shipments are charged on one invoice issued twice a month. For first half of month, credit period runs to the 25th and, for the second half, to the tenth of the following month.

**MIS:** see *Management Information System.*

**Modified Accrual Accounting:** basis of accounting in which expenditures are recognized when liability is incurred. Revenues are recognized when measurable and available. Exception is in debt service funds in which expenditures are recorded only when due.

**M.O.M.:** see *Middle-of-Month Billing Term.*

**Money Judgment:** court decision that adjudges payment of money rather requiring act to be performed or property transferred.

**Monitoring:** service available through many credit reporting or interch bureaus enabling subscribers to request that certain listed accounts be matically monitored and reviewed and that updated reports be issued per cally.

**Moratorium:** 1. temporary extension or delay of normal period for payme account. 2. Formal postponement during which debtor is permitted to payment of obligations.

**Mortgage:** debt instrument giving conditional ownership of asset to borr secured by the asset being financed. The instrument by which real esta hypothecated as security for the repayment of a loan. Borrower gives len mortgage in exchange for the right to use property while mortgage is in e and agrees to make regular payments of principal and interest. Mortgage is lender's security interest and is recorded in title documents in public records. Lien is removed when debt is paid in full. Mortgage norr involves real estate and is considered long-term debt.

**Mortgagee:** lender who arranges mortgage financing, collects loan paym and takes security interest in property financed.

**Mortgagee Clause:** provision in property policy, or added by endorsement, extends protection, in limited manner, to mortgagee; not as broad as lenc loss payable endorsement.

**Mortgagee Waiver:** the relinquishment of right(s) contained in a mortgage mortgagee.

**Mortgage Verification:** request made by mortgagee to applicant's financial i tution for information on applicant's accounts, as part of mortgagee's c approval process.

**Mortgagor:** borrower in a mortgage contract who mortgages property exchange for a loan.

**Multinational Corporation:** corporation whose operations are conducted or international basis.

**Multiple Signature Credit Approval:** describes credit approval process in w credit is approved by two or more persons acting together.

**Mutual Account Revision:** routine exchange of credit information between tw more credit grantors that have extended credit to subject of inquiry.

## N

**NACM:** see *National Association of Credit Management.*

**National Association of Credit Management (NACM):** national business org zation of credit and financial professionals that promotes laws for so credit, protects businesses against fraudulent debtors, improves the in change of commercial credit information, develops credit practices, and p vides education and certification programs for its members.

**Negligence:** failure to use reasonable care that an ordinarily prudent pers would in like circumstances.

**Negotiable:** anything capable of being transferred by endorsement or delivery.

**Negotiable Instrument:** any written evidence of indebtedness, transferable endorsement and delivery or by delivery only, that contains uncondition promise to pay specified sum on demand or at some fixed date.

**Negotiate:** to discuss, bargain, or work out plan of settlement, terms, or comp mise in business transaction.

**Net:** amount left after necessary deductions have been made from gross amou

**Net Assets:** sum of individual's or entity's total assets less total liabilities.

**Net Earnings:** total sales, less total operating, administrative, and overhe expenses, but before other expenses and income such as interest and di dends.

**Net Income:** amount of income remaining after deducting all expenses from to revenues.

**Net Lease:** agreement in which tenant assumes payment of other prope expenses, such as taxes, maintenance, and insurance, in addition to rer payments.

**Net Price:** actual price paid after all discounts, allowances, and other authoriz deductions have been taken.

**Net Profit:** income earned by business over specific period of time. Profit fro transaction or sale, after deducting all costs, expenses, and miscellaneo reserves and adjustments from gross receipts.

**Net Sales:** total sales less returns, allowances, and discounts.

**Net Working Capital:** current assets less current liabilities; used as measure o company's liquidity and indicates its ability to finance current operations.

**Net Worth:** total assets less total liabilities; reflects owners' net interest in cor pany.

**No Account:** notation on rejected check when check writer does not have accou at the financial institution on which check is drawn.

**No Asset Case:** insolvent or bankrupt estate with no assets available for payme of creditors' claims.

**No Funds:** notation on rejected check when check writer has account but n funds to cover check.

**inal Balance:** an account balance of less than $100.

**inal Owner:** person whose name appears on title to asset, but who has no interest in it.

**accrual:** loan on which a financial institution does not accrue interest; also known as a nonperforming loan.

**borrowing Account:** banking relationship in which no extension of credit is involved.

**financial Information:** facts used to evaluate a customer's creditworthiness; focuses on background and history rather than financial measures.

**payment:** failure or neglect to pay or discharge debt in accordance with terms of agreement.

**performing Assets:** total of earning assets listed as nonaccrual; formerly, earning assets acquired in foreclosure and through in-substance foreclosures.

**performing Loans:** amount of loans not meeting original terms of agreement, including renegotiated, restructured, and nonaccrual loans. Loans included in this total vary according to bank policy and regulation.

**profit Corporation:** organization specifically classified by the IRS as generally tax exempt and whose primary purpose for existence is to provide services of a charitable, fraternal, religious, social, or civic nature.

**recourse:** inability of holder in due course to demand payment from endorser of debt instrument if party(ies) primarily liable fail to make payment.

**-sufficient Funds (NSF):** term used when collected demand deposit balances are less than the amount of the check being presented for payment and check is returned to payee's financial institution. See also Overdraft.

**Protest (N.P.):** instructions given by one financial institution to another not to protest check or note when presented for payment. N.P. is usually stamped on instrument to avoid protest fee.

**rth American Industrial Classification System (NAICS):** the Standard Industrial Classification (SIC) code is being replaced by the NAICS code. NAICS classifies establishments by their primary type of activity within a six-digit code. NAICS provides structural enhancements over SIC and identifies over 350 new industries. See also *SIC* and *Standard Industrial Classification*.

**ary Public:** public officer authorized to administer oaths, attest and certify certain types of documents, and to take acknowledgements of conveyances.

**te:** unconditional written promise by borrower to pay certain amount of money to lender on demand or at specified or determinable date. This instrument should meet all requirements of laws pertaining to negotiable instruments.

**tes Payable:** liabilities represented by promissory notes, excluding trade debts, that are payable in future.

**tes Receivable:** assets represented by promissory notes, excluding amounts due from customers for credit sales, to be collected in future.

**tice of Protest:** formal statement that a certain bill of exchange, check, or promissory note was presented for payment or acceptance and that such payment or acceptance was not made. Such notice will also state that because instrument has been dishonored, maker, endorsers, or other parties to document will be held responsible for payment.

**vation:** substitution of old contract for new one between same or different parties; substitution of new debtor or creditor for previous one, by mutual agreement.

**F:** see *Non-sufficient Funds*.

**lla Bona:** report made by sheriff when no assets are found within his or her jurisdiction on which to satisfy judgment against debtor.

## O

**ligation:** 1. law or duty binding parties to an agreement. 2. written promise to pay money or to do a specific thing.

**ligee:** person or entity to which payment is due.

**bligor:** person or entity required by contract to perform specific act.

**osolescence:** decline in perceived value of asset, frequently because of technological innovations, changes in an industry's processes, or changes required by law.

**CC:** see *Office of the Comptroller of the Currency*.

**ffer:** proposal to make contract, usually presented by one party to another for acceptance.

**fering Basis:** customer's loan requests considered individually on merits of each proposal.

**fice of the Comptroller of the Currency (OCC):** branch of the Treasury Department that regulates federally chartered banks.

**fice of Thrift Supervision (OTS):** branch of the Treasury Department that regulates state and federally chartered thrifts as well as those institutions in conservatorship.

**ffset:** amount allowed to be netted against another.

**n Account:** generally describes partial payment made toward settlement of unpaid balance.

**n Account Payment:** partial payment not intended as payment in full.

**n Demand:** debt instrument that is due and payable on presentation.

**Open (Book) Account:** credit extended without a formal written contract and represented on books and records of the seller as an unsecured account receivable for which payment is expected within a specified period after purchase.

**Open-End Credit:** consumer line of credit that may be added to, up to preset credit limit, or paid down at any time. Customer has option of paying off outstanding balance, without penalty, or making several installment payments. Contrasts with Closed-End Credit. Also called revolving credit or charge account credit.

**Open Terms:** selling on credit terms as opposed to having customer pay cash.

**Operating Performance Ratios:** financial measures designed to assist in evaluation of management performance.

**Operating Statement:** report of an individual's or entity's income and expenses for a specified period of time. See also Income Statement.

**Operational Risk:** risk concerning computer network failure due to system overload or other disruptions; also includes potential losses from fraud, malicious damage to data, and error.

**Oral Contract:** agreement that may or may not be written in whole or in part or signed but is legally enforceable.

**Order:** informal bill of exchange or letter or request identifying person to be paid.

**Order for Relief:** order issued by bankruptcy court judge upon filing of petition by debtor or filing of petition by creditors.

**Order to Order:** agreement for payment to be made for prior shipment before next delivery will be made.

**OREO:** see *Other Real Estate Owned*.

**Other Real Estate Owned:** real property usually taken as collateral and subsequently acquired through foreclosure, or by obtaining a deed in lieu of foreclosure, in satisfaction of the debts previously contracted. Real property formerly used as banking premises, or real property sold in a "covered transaction" as defined by banking regulations.

**OTS:** see *Office of Thrift Supervision*.

**Outlet Store:** retail operation where manufacturers' production overruns, discontinued merchandise, or irregular goods are sold at discount.

**Out-of-Court Settlement:** 1. settlement made by distressed debtor through direct negotiations with creditors or through creditors' committee; acceptance of such settlement is not obligatory to nonconsenting creditors. 2. agreement reached between opposing parties to settle pending lawsuit before matter has been decided by court.

**Out-of-Pocket Expense:** business expenses for which individual pays.

**Out-of-Trust:** an event occurring in floor plan financing where a borrower sells inventory securing the financial institution's loan and fails to promptly remit the proceeds to the financial institution in accordance with the loan agreement.

**Outstanding:** 1. amount of credit facility that is being used versus total amount made available. 2. unpaid or uncollected account.

**Overdraft:** negative account balance created when a check is paid when collected demand deposit balances are less than amount of check being presented for payment. See also Non-sufficient Funds.

**Overdue:** debt obligation on which payments are past due.

**Overhead:** selling and administrative business costs as contrasted with costs of goods sold.

**Oversold:** condition in which manufacturer or wholesaler finds itself after taking more orders than it can deliver within an agreed period of time.

**Owed:** debt that is due and payable.

**Own:** to have legal title to property.

**Owner:** person or entity that owns or has title to property.

**Owner's Equity:** mathematical difference between total assets and total liabilities that represents shareholders' equity or an individual's net worth.

**Ownership:** exclusive rights that one has to property, to exclusion of all others; having complete title to property.

**Owner's Risk:** term used in transportation contracts to exempt carrier from responsibility for loss or damage to goods.

## P

**Packing List:** detailed listing of information on shipment's contents (enclosed for inspection with package).

**Paid Direct:** payment made by debtor directly to original creditor instead of to collection agency or attorney handling account for collection.

**Paper Profit:** unrealized income or gain on asset.

**Paralegal:** trained aide to attorney who handles various legal tasks.

**Parent Company:** an entity that holds controlling majority interest in subsidiaries.

**Partial Payment:** payment not in full for amount owed.

**Participation:** purchase or sale of a loan or credit facility among two or more financial institutions in which the acquiring institution(s) has no formal or direct role in establishing the terms and conditions binding the borrower. Participants do not participate in the document negotiation between the originating financial institution and the borrower.

**Partnership:** business arrangement in which two or more persons agree to engage, upon terms of mutual participation, in profits and losses.
**Party:** person concerned or taking part in a transaction or proceeding.
**Past Due:** payment or account that remains outstanding and unpaid after its agreed-upon payment or maturity date.
**Pay:** to satisfy, or make partial payments on, a debt obligation.
**Payable:** obligation that is due now or in future.
**Payables:** liabilities owed to trade creditors for purchase of supplies. Also called accounts payable.
**Payee:** person or entity named on a negotiable instrument as the one to whom the obligation is due.
**Payer:** party responsible for making payment as shown on check, note, or other type of negotiable instrument; also called maker or writer.
**Payment:** discharge, in whole or in part, of debt or performance of agreement.
**Payment for Honor:** payment of past-due obligation by someone else to save credit or reputation of person responsible for payment.
**Payoff:** receipt of payment in full on an obligation.
**Penalty:** 1. legal fine, forfeiture, or payment imposed for defaulting or violating terms of contract. 2. interest charge imposed for late payments that is permissible by law and imposed with customer's prior agreement or knowledge of seller's terms of sale.
**Percentage Lease:** lease of real property in which rental payments are based on percentage of retailer's sales.
**Percentage of Completion:** method of accounting commonly used by contractors and developers in which costs are related to percentage of job completion.
**Perfection:** with respect to security interests in personal property under Article 9 of the UCC, the action required to give the secured party rights in the collateral as against third parties with competing claims. In general, a security interest is not perfected until a properly executed financing statement has been recorded or the secured party is in the possession of the collateral, whichever applies as to that specific collateral type.
**Performance:** fulfillment of promise or agreement according to terms of contract or obligation.
**Performance Bond:** guaranty to project owner that the contractor will perform the work called for by the contract in accordance with the plans and specifications. Customarily issued by bonding and insurance companies, although financial institution letters of credit may be used.
**Perjury:** willfully and knowingly giving false testimony under oath.
**Person:** individual (natural person) or incorporated enterprise (artificial person) having certain legal rights and responsibilities.
**Personal Check:** check drawn by individual on his or her own bank account.
**Personality:** legal term for personal property or possessions that are not real estate.
**Personally Liable:** individual's responsibility for payment of obligation, generally used to refer to owner's or guarantor's responsibility.
**Personal Property:** movable or chattel property of any kind.
Petition: written application, made in contradiction to motion. Also used in some states in place of complaint.
**Petition in Bankruptcy:** document filed in court to declare bankruptcy. Petition can be either voluntary (filed by debtor) or involuntary (filed by creditors), depending on bankruptcy chapter rules.
**Petty Cash:** cash on hand or in designated bank account that is available for small, miscellaneous purchases.
**Physical Inventory:** inventory verification obtained by visual observation of items and itemization of quantities of goods on hand.
**Piercing the Corporate Veil:** legal action taken by creditor, when fraud or unjust enrichment may be involved, to hold principals of corporation (or other entities) liable for debts of corporation.
**Plaintiff:** person or entity that initiates legal action against another.
**Plan of Arrangement:** procedure in bankruptcy under Chapter 11 for debtor to restructure debts or rehabilitate by arriving at arrangement with creditors. See also Bankruptcy, Chapter 11 Cases.
**Pledge:** promise of personal property as security for performance of act, payment of debt, or satisfaction of obligation.
**Points:** 1. percentage fee charged to obtain a mortgage loan. 2. in shares of stock, one point equals $1.00.
**Policy:** 1. written statement by management that explains an organization's philosophy and approach to doing business. 2. written contract of insurance between insured and the insurance company.
**Pooling Accounts:** arrangement by a debtor listing all his or her debts with a debt management or pro-rating service with the understanding that the service will receive, as its fee, a portion of debtor's payments to his or her creditors and proportionately distribute the balance of payments to each creditor on a scheduled basis. Activities of such services may be covered by individual state statutes.
**Postdated Check:** check written for payment, effective at future date.
**Power of Attorney:** written document that authorizes one person to act as another's agent.

**Preference:** 1. right of a creditor to be paid before other creditors by virtu[e of] having lien or collateral. 2. improperly paying or securing of one or [more] creditors, in whole or part, by an insolvent debtor to the exclusion of o[ther] creditors.
**Preference Period:** in bankruptcy, the 90-day period immediately prece[ding] debtor entering into bankruptcy. If a creditor files new or additional [liens] against a debtor during this time, such claims may be disallowed by b[ank]ruptcy court.
**Preferred Creditor:** creditor whose account takes legal preference for paym[ent] over claims of others.
**Prepaid Expenses:** payment for goods or services not yet received.
**Prepayment:** payment of loan or debt before it actually becomes due.
**Prime Contractor:** contractor who enters into contract with the owner of the [pro]ject for completion of all or portion of the project and takes full responsi[bility] for its completion. See also General Contractor.
**Prime Rate:** an index or base rate published or publicly announced by a finan[cial] institution from time to time as the rate it is generally willing to give its [most] creditworthy customers.
**Principal:** 1. amount of money loaned or borrowed. 2. key decision make[r in] management of entity.
**Priority:** legal preferences that secured creditors have over general creditor[s in] bankruptcy.
**Priority Lien:** lien recorded before other secured claims and payable ahea[d of] other liens if liquidation of pledged collateral occurs. First mortgage has pr[ior]ity over second and third mortgages, known as junior liens. Secured cred[itor] holding perfected security interest has priority over liens filed afterward.
**Private Enterprise:** business established to take economic risks for purpose [of] making profit.
**Privilege:** right that nature of debt gives to one debt holder over others.
**Proceeds:** actual amount of money given to or received from creditor after [all] deductions are made.
**Profit:** 1. amount of net income made by an entity in course of doing business [2.] increase in value of an asset over its depreciated book value at the time [of] sale.
**Profit and Loss Statement (P & L):** financial report of an individual's or enti[ty's] revenue and expenses for a given period of time. See also Income Statem[ent] and Operating Statement.
**Pro Forma:** projected financial statements.
**Progress Payments:** partial payments made on a long-term contract as it p[ro]gresses. Required when a manufacturer or contractor cannot afford, or do[es] not wish, to finance a project.
**Projection:** borrower's estimate of future performance over designated ti[me] period.
**Promissory Note:** written promise to make unconditional payment of specifi[c] amount on designated date, signed by maker.
**Proof of Claim:** creditor's formal document filed with court against estate [of] debtor if creditor is owed funds.
**Proof of Loss:** sworn statement filed by insured when making claim.
**Property:** something of value that is legally owned and in which person has excl[u]sive and unrestricted right or interest.
**Property Insurance:** coverage that applies to loss caused by physical damage [to] property (buildings, contents, earnings, etc.) owned by insured.
**Proposal:** oral or written offer that, if accepted, constitutes a contract.
**Proprietorship:** single and exclusive ownership of a business by one person.
**Pro Rata:** share calculated in proportion to total amount.
**Pro Rata Distribution:** payment proportionate to uniform percentage of oblig[a]tions to all creditors.
**Protest:** formal, written, notarized notice stating credit instrument has not be[en] honored and that makers or endorsers will be held responsible for payment.
**Prox.:** see Proximo.
**Proximo (Prox.):** sales term used in invoices to mean next month after month [of] invoice. This term is sometimes used instead of EOM terms.
**Proxy:** written statement or power of attorney, authorizing an individual to act [or] speak for another.
**Public Credit:** debt incurred by government, federal and local, for a use that me[ets] the needs of its citizens.
**Purchase Money Lien:** manufacturer's legal right to goods and products until th[e] buyer makes payment. Under the Uniform Commercial Code, manufacture[r's] rights can take priority over lender's lien rights if both claim interest in sam[e] inventory. Lender may receive such priority if funds were provided to pu[r]chase asset, provided liens are filed within 20 days of borrower taking pos[]session of collateral and noticing requirements have been met.
**Purchase Money Mortgage:** mortgage given by buyer to seller in lieu of cash, [as] partial payment on property.
**Purchasing Power:** value of money and its ability to buy goods and services in [a] given period.

## Q

**Qualified Acceptance:** agreement to terms of contract only if certain conditions are meet. This constitutes counteroffer and rejection of original offer.

**Qualified Endorsement:** transfer of debt instrument to endorsee without recourse or liability to endorser.

**Qualified Financial Statement:** audit report issued by independent accountants that indicates restrictions on scope of audit performed, uncertainties, or disagreements with management.

**Qualified Prospect:** potential customer whose background and credit have been checked and approved.

**Quantity Discount:** price reduction extended to purchaser of a large volume of goods.

**Quarterly Accounts Receivable Survey:** index, compiled by Credit Research Foundation in affiliation with the National Association of Credit Management and published quarterly, that shows average days' sales outstanding for manufacturers and wholesalers.

**Quick Assets:** current assets that can be readily converted into cash (generally, accounts receivable).

**Quick Assets Ratio:** cash and cash equivalents plus trade receivables (net) divided by total current liabilities; used as measure of liquidity.

**Quid Pro Quo:** 1. giving of one valuable thing for another. 2. mutual consideration between parties to contract.

**Quitclaim:** to release or relinquish claim or title.

## R

**Rack Jobber:** wholesale distributor who sells housewares and other convenience-type merchandise through retail stores and assumes responsibility for stocking and maintaining store's inventory.

**Rate of Exchange:** amount of one country's currency that can be bought with another country's currency at a particular point in time.

**Rate of Interest:** cost of borrowing money, usually expressed as annual percentage charge.

**Rating:** 1. assessment of borrower's financial strength and creditworthiness. 2. symbol used to denote borrower's creditworthiness.

**Ratios:** mathematical relationship between two or more things, used as indication of a company's financial strength relative to other companies of comparable size or in same industry.

**Real Property:** land and anything erected or growing on it or affixed to it.

**Receivables:** money due or collectible for goods sold, services performed, or money loaned. Also called accounts receivable.

**Receivables Turnover:** measurement of how effective a company is in collecting on its trade receivables.

**Receiver:** person appointed by the court to receive, take charge, and hold in trust a property in litigation or bankruptcy until a legal decision is made as to its disposition.

**Receivership:** 1. court action whereby money or property is placed under control, and administration of receiver is to be preserved for benefit of persons or creditors ultimately entitled to it. 2. procedure used to help a distressed debtor or to resolve a dispute.

**Reclamation:** 1. legal action by titleholder to recover property from another's possession. 2. process used to restore land to usable state.

**Record:** written account of act, transaction, or instrument drawn by proper legal authority that remains as permanent evidence.

**Recourse:** right of holder in due course to demand payment from anyone who endorsed instrument if original signer fails to pay.

**Recovery:** amount finally collected; amount of judgment.

**Reference Check:** contacting and interviewing business or professional associates of credit applicant to gain information about his or her creditworthiness.

**References:** names of trade suppliers or creditors provided by a customer to be used as a source of information about that customer.

**Refer to Maker:** term stamped by financial institution on a check to indicate its rejection.

**Refinance:** to reorganize existing debts by obtaining new debt that incorporates or pays off existing debts.

**Register:** book of factual public information, kept by a public official.

**Regulation 9:** regulation issued by the Comptroller of Currency allowing national banks to operate trust departments and act as fiduciaries. Under Regulation 9, a national bank is permitted to act as trustee, administrator, and registrar of stocks and bonds and engage in related activities, such as management of a collective investment fund, as long as these activities do not violate state legislation.

**Regulation A:** Federal Reserve Board regulation governing advances by Federal Reserve Banks to depository institutions at a Federal Reserve discount window. Credit advances are available to any bank or savings institution maintaining transaction accounts or non-personal time deposits. The Fed has two different programs for handling discount window borrowings:

- adjustment credit to meet temporary needs for funds when other sources are not available.
- extended credit, designed to assist financial institutions with longer-term needs for funds. This includes seasonal credit privileges extended to smaller financial institutions that do not have ready access to money market funds. Federal Reserve Banks may also extend emergency credit to financial institutions other than depository institutions in which failure to obtain credit would affect the economy adversely.

**Regulation B:** Federal Reserve regulation prohibiting discrimination against consumer credit applicants and establishing guidelines for collecting and evaluating credit information. Regulation B prohibits creditors from discriminating on the basis of age, sex, race, color, religion, national origin, marital status, or receipt of public assistance. Regulation B also requires creditors to give written notification of rejection, statement of applicant's rights under Equal Credit Opportunity Act of 1974, and statement listing reasons for rejection, or applicant has right to request reasons. If applicant is denied credit because of adverse information in credit bureau report, applicant is entitled to receive copy of bureau report at no cost. Creditors who furnish credit information when reporting information on married borrowers must report information in name of each spouse.

**Regulation C:** Federal Reserve regulation implementing Home Mortgage Disclosure Act of 1975, requiring depository institutions to make annual disclosure of location of certain residential loans to determine whether depository institutions are meeting credit needs of their local communities. Specifically exempted are institutions with assets of $10 million or less. Regulation C requires lenders of mortgages that are insured or guaranteed by a federal agency to disclose number and total dollar amount of mortgage loans originated or purchased in recent calendar year, itemized by census tract where property is located.

**Regulation D:** Federal Reserve regulation that sets uniform reserve requirements for depository financial institutions holding transaction accounts or non-personal time deposits. Reserves are maintained in form of vault cash or non-interest-bearing balance at a Federal Reserve Bank or at a correspondent bank.

**Regulation E:** Federal Reserve regulation that sets rules, liabilities, and procedures for electronic funds transfers (EFT) and establishes consumer protections using EFT systems. This regulation prescribes rules for solicitation and issuance of EFT debit cards, governs consumer liability for unauthorized transfers, and requires financial institutions to disclose annually terms and conditions of EFT services.

**Regulation F:** Federal Reserve regulation requiring state-chartered banks with 500 or more stockholders and at least $1 million in assets to file financial statements with the Board of Governors of the Federal Reserve System. In general, these state-chartered member banks must file registration statements, periodic financial statements, proxy statements, and various other disclosures of interest to investors. These regulations are substantially similar to those issued by Securities and Exchange Commission.

**Regulation G:** Federal Reserve regulation governing credit secured by margin securities extended or arranged by parties other than banks or broker/dealers. It requires lenders to register credit extensions of $200,000, secured by margin stock, or $500,000 in total credit, within 30 days after end of quarter.

**Regulation H:** Federal Reserve regulation defining membership requirements for state-chartered banks that become members of the Federal Reserve System. The regulation sets forth procedures as well as privileges and requirements for membership. The regulation also requires state-chartered banks acting as securities transfer agents to register with board.

**Regulation I:** Federal Reserve regulation requiring each member bank joining the Federal Reserve System to purchase stock in its Federal Reserve Bank equal to 6% of its capital and surplus. Federal Reserve Bank stock, which pays interest semiannually, is nontransferable and cannot be used as collateral. When bank increases or decreases its capital base, it must adjust its ownership of Federal Reserve stock accordingly.

**Regulation J:** Federal Reserve regulation providing legal framework for collection of checks and other cash items and net settlement of balances through Federal Reserve System. It specifies terms and conditions under which Federal Reserve Banks will receive checks for collection from depository institutions, presentment to paying banks, and return of unpaid items. It is supplemented by operating circulars issued by Federal Reserve Banks.

**Regulation K:** Federal Reserve regulation governing international banking operations by bank holding companies and foreign banks in the U.S. The regulation permits Edge Act corporations to engage in range of international banking and financial activities. It also permits U.S. banks to own up to 100% of non-financial companies located outside the U.S. Regulation K also imposes reserve requirements on Edge Act corporations, as specified in Regulation D, and limits interstate activities of foreign banks in the U.S.

**Regulation L:** Federal Reserve regulation prohibiting interlocking director arrangements in member banks or bank holding companies. Management official of state member bank or bank holding company may not act simulta-

neously as management official of another depository institution if both are not affiliated, are very large banks, or are located in same local area. Regulation L provides 10-year grandfather period for certain interlocks and allows some on exception basis, such as organizations owned by women or minority groups, newly chartered organizations, and in situations in which implementing regulation would endanger safety and soundness.

**Regulation M:** Federal Reserve regulation implementing consumer leasing provisions of Truth in Lending Act of 1968. It covers leases on personal property for more than four months for family, personal, or household use. It requires leasing companies to disclose in writing the cost of lease, including security deposit and monthly payments, taxes, and other payments, and in case of an open-end lease, whether a balloon payment may be applied. It also requires written disclosure of terms of lease, including insurance, guaranties, responsibility for servicing property, and whether lessor has an option to buy property at lease termination.

**Regulation N:** Federal Reserve regulation governing transactions among Federal Reserve Banks and transactions involving Federal Reserve Banks and foreign banks and governments. This regulation gives the board responsibility for approving in advance negotiations or agreements by Federal Reserve Banks and foreign banks, bankers, and governments. The Federal Reserve Bank may, under direction of the Federal Open Market Committee, undertake negotiations, agreements, or facilitate open market transactions. Reserve Banks must report quarterly to the Board of Governors on accounts they maintain with foreign banks.

**Regulation O:** Federal Reserve regulation limiting amount of credit member banks may extend to their own executive officers. Regulation O also implements reporting requirements of Financial Institutions Regulatory and Interest Rate Control Act of 1978 and Garn-St. Germain Depository Institutions Act of 1982.

**Regulation P:** Federal Reserve regulation that sets minimum standards for security devices, such as bank vaults and currency handling equipment, including automated teller machines. Member bank must appoint security officer to develop and administer program to deter thefts and file the annual compliance statement with its Federal Reserve Bank.

**Regulation Q:** Federal Reserve regulation requiring depository institutions to state clearly terms for depositing and renewing time deposits and certificates of deposit and also any penalties for early withdrawal of savings accounts.

**Regulation R:** Federal Reserve regulation prohibiting individuals who are engaged in securities underwriting, sale, and distribution from serving as directors, officers, or employees of member banks. Regulation R specifically exempts those involved in government securities trading and general obligations of states and municipalities.

**Regulation S:** Federal Reserve regulation implementing section of Right to Financial Privacy Act of 1978 requiring government authorities to pay reasonable fees to financial institutions for financial records of individuals and small partnerships available to federal agencies in connection with government loan programs or Internal Revenue Service summons.

**Regulation T:** Federal Reserve regulation governing credit extensions by securities brokers and dealers, including all members of national securities exchanges. Brokers/dealers may not extend credit to their customers unless such loans are secured by margin securities—securities listed and traded on national securities exchange, mutual funds, and over-the-counter stock designated by Securities and Exchange Commission as eligible for trading in national market system. Generally, brokers/dealers may not extend credit on margin securities in excess of percentage of current market value permitted by board.

**Regulation U:** Federal Reserve regulation governing extensions of credit by banks for purchasing and carrying margin securities. Whenever lender makes loan secured by margin securities, bank must have customer execute purpose statement regardless of use of loan.

**Regulation V:** Federal Reserve regulation dealing with financing of contractors, subcontractors, and others involved in national defense work. The regulation spells out the authority granted to Federal Reserve Banks under the Defense Production Act of 1950 to assist federal departments and agencies in making and administering loan guaranties to defense-related contractors and sets maximum interest rates, guaranty fees, and commitment fees.

**Regulation X:** Federal Reserve regulation extending provisions of other securities-related regulations—Regulations G, T, and U—to foreign persons or organizations who obtain credit outside U.S. for purchase of U.S. Treasury securities.

**Regulation Y:** Federal Reserve regulation governing banking and nonbanking activities of bank holding companies and divestiture of impermissible nonbank activities. Regulation Y spells out procedures for forming bank holding company and procedures to be followed by bank holding companies acquiring voting shares in bank or nonbank companies. Regulation Y also lists those nonbank activities that are deemed closely related to banking and therefore permissible for bank holding companies.

**Regulation Z:** Federal Reserve regulation implementing consumer credit provisions in the Truth in Lending Act of 1968. Major areas of regulation require lenders to:
- give borrowers written disclosure on essential credit terms, including c of credit expressed as finance charge and annual percentage rate.
- respond to consumer complaints of billing errors on certain credit accou within specified period.
- identify credit transactions on periodic statements of open-end cre accounts.
- provide certain rights regarding credit cards.
- inform customers of right of rescission in certain mortgage-related loa within specified period.
- comply with special requirements when advertising credit.

**Regulation AA:** Federal Reserve regulation establishing procedures for handli consumer complaints about alleged unfair or deceptive practices by a st member bank.

**Regulation BB:** Federal Reserve regulation implementing Community Reinve ment Act of 1977 (CRA). Banks are required to make available to publi statement indicating communities served, type of credit the lender is prepar to extend, and public comments to its CRA statement.

**Regulation CC:** Federal Reserve regulation implementing Expedited Funds Ava ability Act of 1987, setting endorsement standards on checks collected depository financial institutions. Endorsement standard is designed to fac tate identification of endorsing bank and prompt return of unpaid checks. T regulation specifies funds availability schedules that banks must comply w and procedures for returning dishonored checks.

**Release:** to discharge debt or give up claim against party from whom it is due party to whom it is due.

**Remedy:** legal means by which right is enforced or violation of right is prevent or compensated.

**Rent:** periodic payments made by tenant to owner in return for leasing lar building space, or equipment.

**Reorganization:** 1. voluntary or court-ordered change in capital structure of cc poration in which all assets of an old corporation are transferred to a new formed corporation. 2. restructuring of business entity, whether in or out bankruptcy.

**Replevin:** legal action taken to recover possession of property unlawfully taken.

**Repossess:** action taken by creditor in which he or she takes possession goods purchased under credit agreement or pledged as collateral if debt defaults on terms of contract.

**Rescind:** to void contract from its inception. Result is that parties are restored relative positions before contract was made.

**Rescission:** agreement by parties to contract that effects cancellation of contrac

**Reserve:** in accounting, funds set aside for specific purpose.

**Reserve for Bad Debts:** valuation account established for accounts receivab that may prove uncollectible.

**Residence:** place where person legally lives part or full time.

**Residual Value:** the estimated recoverable amount of a depreciable asset as the time of its removal from service.

**Resolution Trust Corporation (RTC):** federal agency established in 1989 to ove see the savings and loan bailout.

**Restraint of Trade:** any action, by agreement or by combination, that tends t eliminate competition, artificially sets up prices, or results in monopoly.

**Restrictive Endorsement:** endorsement on negotiable instrument that limits an further negotiability, for example, "for deposit only" written on back of check.

**Restructured Loan:** loan on which a bank, for economic or legal reasons relate to debtor's financial difficulties, grants concession to debtor that would not b considered otherwise.

**Retailer:** company that sells its product directly to end-user.

**Retained Earnings:** cumulative earnings and losses of company that remai undistributed to shareholders.

**Retentions:** amounts withheld by customer from total billings until contractor ha satisfactorily completed project.

**Retroactive:** 1. effective as of past date. 2. having reference to prior time.

**Return:** rate of profit or earnings on sales or investment.

**Return Items/Returned Checks:** checks, drafts, or notes returned unpaid to origi nating bank by drawee bank so that originator can correct any errors or irreg ularities and may present items for collection again.

**Revenue:** 1. income from sales, interest, or dividends. 2. income from invest ment or wages.

**Reviewed Financial Statements:** business financial statements that are reviewe by independent accountants through inquiries of management and perfor mance of analytical procedures on financials to provide limited assurance tha no material modifications are necessary for statements to conform to gener ally accepted accounting principles. Independent accountants do not express opinion on review statements.

Revolving Charge: credit type that allows borrower to become indebted up to an approved credit limit, with no fixed maturity date. Finance costs are assessed monthly on unpaid balance, and periodic payments are required.

Revolving Credit: commitment under which funds can be borrowed, repaid, and re-borrowed during life of credit. Such credits have stated maturity date at which time borrower may have option of converting outstanding balance into term loan. See also Evergreen Revolving Credit.

Rider: any schedule or amendment attached to a contract or document that becomes part of it.

Right of Rescission: consumer's right as prescribed by Truth in Lending Act of 1968 to rescind certain credit and mortgage contracts within three days without penalty.

Right of Setoff: right of financial institution to apply borrower's funds on deposit to debt owed to the financial institution in event that payment on the debt is not made as agreed.

Risk-Based Capital: level of capital that bank is required to maintain; level is determined by relating capital to risk by type of asset.

RMA: see Risk Management Association.

RMA General Figure Ranges: dollar amount ranges established by RMA to ensure accuracy and consistency when exchanging credit information. There are four ranges: low, 1-1.9; moderate, 2-3.9; medium, 4-6.9; and high, 7-9.9. Ranges can be applied to any figure category. Sample figure categories are: nominal = under $100; 3 figures = from $100 to $999; 4 figures = from $1,000 to $9,999; 5 figures = from $10,000 to $99,999;and 6 figures = from $100,000 to $999,999. Information is reported, using both range description and figure category; for example, "average balances are in medium 4-figure range."

Risk Management Association (RMA): association of lending, credit, and risk management professionals. Originally, RMA was founded to facilitate the exchange of credit information. Today, RMA works continuously to improve practices of the financial services industry and to provide members with networking opportunities, training, research publications, and seminars.

Robinson-Patman Act: federal legislation prohibiting firms engaged in interstate commerce from charging different buyers different prices for the same goods unless there is difference in costs or the price does not restrict competition.

R.O.G. Dating: payment term that uses date customer is in receipt of goods as effective sale date.

Royalty: compensation made to another for use of his or her work.

RTC: see Resolution Trust Corporation.

Rule of 72: method commonly used to approximate time required for sum of money to double at given rate of interest. Rule of 72 is computed by dividing interest rate by 72.

Rule of 78s: mathematical formula used in computing interest rebated when borrower pays off loan before maturity. Rule of 78s is applied mostly to consumer loans in which finance charges were computed using add-on interest or discounted interest method of interest calculation. Also called sum of digits method.

## S

Sale: agreement or contract that transfers title of goods or property from one person or entity to another for consideration.

Sale and Lease Back: arrangement whereby company sells goods with intent to lease those same goods from buyer.

Sale on Approval: purchase of goods conditioned on buyer approval of goods or retention of them beyond reasonable time.

Salvage Value: estimated worth of a depreciated asset at the end of its useful life.

Satisfaction: paying debt in full.

Satisfaction of Judgment: legal evidence that recorded judgment has been paid or settled and entered in court records.

Satisfaction Piece: legal evidence that debt has been paid in full or settled and that liens on collateral have been released.

SBA: see Small Business Administration.

Schedule: listing by account name or number of total sales, current sales, monies owing or paid, chargebacks, or credits. Also called aging schedule or trial balance.

Scheduled Liability: 1. in property insurance, listing of property—items or locations—covered. 2. in dishonesty insurance (fidelity bonding), listing of persons or positions covered.

Scheduled Payment: partial payments made at dates specified in credit agreement.

Schedules: in bankruptcy, lists showing debtor's property—location, quantity, and money value; names and addresses of creditors and their class; or names and addresses of stockholders of each class.

Scrap Value: worth of asset that is going to be destroyed or used for its components.

Seasonal Loans: loans used to finance cyclical buildup of current (working capital) assets until those assets can be converted to cash.

Second Lien: lien that can be honored only after first lien is satisfied.

Second Mortgage: mortgage secured by equity in property but one that cannot enforce payment until claims of first mortgage are satisfied.

Secret Partner: partner in business whose interest in partnership is not publicly known.

Secured Creditor: lender or other person whose claim is supported by taking collateral.

Secured Loan: loan supported by borrower's pledge of an asset such as marketable securities, accounts receivable, inventories, real estate, equipment, etc.

Secured Note: note that provides, upon default, certain pledged or mortgaged property that may be applied or sold in payment of debt.

Secured Party: 1. lender or other person to whom or in whose favor security interest has been given. Includes person to whom accounts or chattel paper have been sold. 2. trustee or agent representing holders of obligations issued under indenture of trust, equipment trust agreement, or the like.

Securities: 1. documents that evidence debt or property pledged in fulfillment of obligation. 2. evidence of indebtedness or right to participate in earnings and distribution of corporate, trust, and other property.

Security: guaranty or assets pledged that can be applied to loan or obligation.

Security Agreement: formally executed document that gives lender rights to property pledged by borrower in support of debt.

Security Interest: right that lender or lienholder obtains to debtor's goods as evidenced by security agreement.

Seller's Market: economic condition in which demand is greater than supply, and that typically causes prices to increase.

Sequestered Account: account that has been attached by court order with disbursements subject to court approval.

Service Business: firm that performs functions for its customers rather than sells goods.

Setoff: 1. defendant's counterdemand against plaintiff. 2. right of parties to contract to reduce debt owed to one party by netting it against amount owed by other. See also Right of Setoff.

Settle: 1. to mutually reach agreement for adjustment or liquidation of debt. 2. to negotiate payment of obligation or lawsuit for less than amount claimed.

Settlement: 1. adjustment or liquidation of accounts. 2. full and final payment of debt. See also Out-of-Court Settlement.

Shared National Credit (SNC): any loan originally $20 million or more that is shared at its inception by two or more financial institutions under a formal intercreditor or participation agreement or sold in part to one or more financial institutions with purchasing financial institution assuming its pro rata share of credit risk.

Shareholder: person or entity that legally owns stock in a corporation.

Sheriff's Sale: court-ordered sale of property to satisfy judgment, mortgage, lien, or other outstanding debt against debtor.

Sherman Antitrust Act: federal legislation aimed at prevention of business monopoly; act declares illegal every contract, combination, or conspiracy in restraint of normal trade.

Short-Term Liabilities: current debts that are due within one year.

Short-Term Loan: current debt obligation that matures within one year, evidenced by promissory note that spells out terms of agreement.

SIC: see Standard Industrial Classification.

Sight Draft: draft payable on demand when presented to drawee. See also Draft, Letter of Credit, and Time Draft.

Signal Action: notices that provide subscriber with list of accounts in which subscriber has interest and on which delinquent payments have been reported.

Signature Loan: unsecured loan backed only by borrower's signature on promissory note. No collateral is taken by lender. This loan is generally offered to individuals with good credit standing. Also called good faith loan or character loan.

Signature Verification: examination of signature on negotiable instrument to determine whether handwriting is genuine and whether person signing check is authorized to use account.

Simple Interest: interest calculated on outstanding principal amount of debt or investment only.

Single Proprietorship: ownership of company by one person.

Skip Tracing: process used to obtain information to locate debtor's whereabouts in order to collect payment on debts. Sources used include other creditors, friends, relatives, neighbors, directories, credit bureaus, court records, and other informants or references.

Slander: oral defamation of another's reputation.

Small Business Administration (SBA): federal agency whose function is to advise and assist small businesses; provides loan guaranties for small businesses, minorities, and veterans plus financial assistance to small businesses that have suffered catastrophes.

SNC: see Shared National Credit.

Soft Goods: nondurable consumer goods such as clothing and linen, having a short-term useful life.

**Soldier's and Sailor's Relief Act:** federal act, also passed by various states, under which right to legally enforce an obligation against a person is suspended during the period that person is in military service or for period thereafter.

**Sole Owner:** one with title to proprietorship.

**Solvency:** ability to pay one's debts in usual and ordinary course of business as they mature.

**Special Material:** made-to-order material or work done to customer's specifications that has no value to seller if order is canceled.

**Special Mention Assets:** as it relates to risk assessment of bank assets, assets that deserve management's close attention. If left uncorrected, these potential weaknesses may result in deterioration of repayment prospects for asset or in institution's credit position at some future date. Special mention assets are not adversely classified and do not expose institution to sufficient risk to warrant adverse classification.

**Specific Coverage:** property coverage on designated property or item. Contrasts with Blanket Coverage.

**Specific Performance:** court order directing party guilty of breach of contract to undertake complete performance of contractual obligation in instances in which damages would inadequately compensate injured party.

**Speculation:** investment made with hope of achieving large financial gain.

**Speculator:** one who makes risky investments for quick financial gain rather than long-term investment.

**Stale Check:** negotiable draft that has been held too long to be honored for payment; time varies from state to state.

**Standard Industrial Classification (SIC):** statistical classification standard underlying all establishment-based federal economic statistics classified by industry. SIC is used to promote comparability of establishment data describing various facets of the U.S. economy. Classification covers entire field of economic activities and defines industries in accordance with composition and structure of economy. It is revised periodically to reflect economy's changing industrial organization. See also *North American Industrial Classification System* and *NAICS*.

**Standby Letter of Credit:** type of letter of credit issued by bank that may be drawn on by payee only if party that makes letter of credit (drawer) defaults or does not perform according to terms of specific contract or agreement. See also Letter of Credit.

**Statement:** 1. itemized summary and accounting of charges, payments, and balance outstanding at close of billing period. 2. financial report.

**Statement of Cash Flows:** financial statement that shows cash receipts and disbursements for given period.

**Statement of Changes in Owner's Equity:** financial statement that reconciles changes in capital accounts (capital stock, paid in surplus, and retained earnings).

**Statute:** written law.

**Statute of Frauds:** law prohibiting filing of actions or suits against certain types of contracts unless the contracts are in writing.

**Statute of Limitations:** law that sets time frame for bringing action against another. Time frame varies according to nature of claim and jurisdiction.

**Stay:** act of arresting judicial proceeding by court order.

**Stipulation:** agreement between opposing attorneys in lawsuit, usually required to be in writing.

**Stock:** 1. merchandise or inventory on hand and available for sale. 2. certificate that indicates number of shares of ownership in corporation.

**Stock Power:** document executed in form of power of attorney by which owner of stock authorizes another party to sell or transfer stock.

**Stop Payment Order:** instructions given by depositor to a financial institution to dishonor, or not make payment on, a certain check.

**Subchapter S:** business concern chartered as corporation that is taxed as partnership. An S corporation has 35 or fewer shareholders and can use cash basis of accounting. Corporate gains (or losses) from operations are taxed to shareholders as individuals.

**Subcontract:** contract between prime contractor and another contractor or supplier to perform specified work or to supply specified materials in accordance with plans and specifications for project.

**Subject:** party on which credit information is requested.

**Sublimit:** specified, partial amount of credit facility that is designated for special use.

**Subordination:** 1. signed agreement acknowledging that one's claim or interest is inferior to another's. 2. act of agreeing to take secondary position.

**Subpoena:** process to demand person to appear in court and give testimony.

**Subrogation:** substitution of one creditor for another so that substituted creditor succeeds to rights, remedies, or proceeds of claim.

**Subsidiary:** business entity owned or controlled by another organization.

**Substandard Assets:** as it relates to risk assessment of bank assets, assets that are inadequately protected by current sound worth and paying capacity of obligor or of collateral pledged, if any. Assets so classified must have well-defined weakness or weaknesses that jeopardize liquidation of debt. They are characterized by distinct possibility that bank will sustain some loss if deficiencies are not corrected.

**Summons:** formal notice served on defendant stating that action has been instituted against him or her and requiring defendant to appear in court to answer it.

**Supplementary Proceedings:** statutory action requiring judgment debtor appear in court to discover property against which action can be taken creditor to enforce collection of judgment.

**Supplier:** business that sells goods, materials, or services to customers. A called vendor.

**Surety:** one who agrees to be primarily liable with another and to fulfill another obligations under terms of agreement.

**Surety Bond:** guaranty that payment or performance of some specific act will completed under penalty or forfeiture of bond usually issued by a bond company.

**Suretyship:** undertaking by person or entity to pay obligation of obligee in favor of principal when obligee defaults; such undertaking by individual is known personal suretyship and by insurance company as corporate suretyship.

**Suspense File:** group of accounts, records, or other items held temporarily until final disposition is determined.

**Swap:** A financial derivative contract between two parties to exchange fixed-rate interest payments for floating-rate interest payments, or floating-rate interest payments on different bases (e.g., prime rate versus LIBOR), calculated specific floating indices by reference to a notional principal amount for specified term.

**Sweep Account:** type of cash management tool in which, when prearrang amount of cash accumulates in account, amount is automatically invested.

**Swindle:** 1. to obtain money or property by deceitful misrepresentation. 2. cheat or fraudulently induce individual to give up his or her property willingly

**Swing Loan:** see *Bridge Loan*.

**Syndicate:** temporary association of persons or firms formed to carry out business venture or project of mutual interest.

**Syndication:** project financing whereby commercial or investment bankers agree to advance portion of funding. Syndicator acts as investment manager, collecting loan origination fee or commitment fee from borrower and arranging for sale to other banks in group. Typically, syndicator keeps only a small portion of total financing. A syndicated loan differs from loan participation because syndicate members are known at outset to borrower. Syndication also separates lead bank from group of financial institutions that ultimately fund obligation.

## T

**Takeover:** acquisition, seizure, control, or management of one business by another.

**Tangible Assets:** assets that can be weighed, measured, or counted, including cash, property, machinery, and buildings.

**Tax:** payments imposed by legislative authority for support of government and functions.

**Taxable Income:** portion of individual's or entity's income that is subject to taxation.

**Tax Avoidance:** act of using legal deductions, exemptions, and tax code provisions to reduce taxes payable.

**Tax Evasion:** failure to report taxable income to avoid proper payment of taxes.

**Tax Foreclosure:** legal seizure and sale of property by authorized public official satisfy unpaid taxes.

**Tax Levy:** legislative action by which tax is imposed.

**Tax Lien:** statutory claim by state or municipality against property of person owing taxes. Property may be sold to satisfy obligation or judgment filed against it.

**Tax Sale:** sale of property seized by governmental taxing body for nonpayment taxes.

**Tenancy by Entirety:** ownership in property by husband and wife in which each becomes whole owner of the entire estate upon the other's death. See also Joint Tenancy with Rights of Survivorship.

**Tenancy in Common:** two or more persons who hold title to land or other property in undivided ownership.

**Tender:** 1. unconditional offer of money or performance to satisfy claim. 2. offer to buy stock to take control of company.

**Term Loan:** fixed-term business loan with a maturity of more than one year and with defined periodic payments, providing borrower with working capital acquire assets or inventory or to finance plant and equipment.

**Terms:** conditions and requirements as set forth in sales proposal, contract, or promissory note.

**Terms of Sale:** mutually agreed upon conditions for transfer of title or ownership of goods or property.

**Testimony:** written or oral evidence given in court under oath.

**rd Party:** one who is not directly related to action between two parties but who may be affected by its outcome.

**rd-Party Claim:** demand made by person who is not party to action for delivery or possession of personal property, title to which is claimed by third party.

**ne Deposit:** 1. interest-bearing funds deposited in a financial institution for a specified period of time, such as certificates of deposit and savings accounts. 2. under Regulation D, deposit in which depositor is not permitted to make withdrawals within six days after date of deposit unless deposit is subject to early withdrawal penalty.

**ne Draft:** draft payable on fixed date or certain number of days after sight or date of draft. See also *Banker's Acceptance, Draft, Letter of Credit,* and *Sight Draft.*

**le:** document that evidences legal ownership and possession of property.

**le Company:** business that as contracted researches specific property's history through real estate records and issues policy to purchaser or lienholder guaranteeing that there are no known defects in title.

**le Insurance:** a guarantee by a title insurance company that it will indemnify the insured, in a specific amount, against losses resulting from defects in the title to a property. The insured may be the owner of the property, that person's heirs and devises, or the lender and future assignees.

**le Search:** to review history of property's ownership and any judgments or liens filed against it.

**lling the Statute:** act of debtor to freeze statute of limitations that extends period for creditor to legally enforce payment of account. Individual state laws and statutes apply.

**rt:** violation of legal duty that results in injury or damage to another.

**ade Acceptance:** draft, accepted by buyer, sent with shipment of goods, requiring customer to pay amount involved at specific date and place.

**ade Credit:** accounts payable; credit extended from one company to another.

**ade Debts:** liabilities due from one business to another for purchase of supplies, inventory, etc.

**ade-in:** property accepted by seller as partial down payment on purchase of new item.

**ade Information:** confidential exchange of payment history and credit information among suppliers.

**ademark:** distinctive identifying mark, word, or logo of product or service; protected when registered with U.S. Patent Office.

**ade Name:** name used by a company to identify itself in the course of business. Also known as Trade Style or Fictitious Name.

**ade Payment Record:** summary of performance of company in meeting terms of its credit obligations.

**ade References:** names of suppliers or business creditors with whom credit information on customer can be exchanged.

**easury Workstation:** microcomputer-based information management system that allows corporate treasurer to automate daily balance reporting of collected balances, to invest idle funds in short-term money market, and to disburse funds to trade creditors. Overall aim is improvement in productivity and eventual integration of funds management and corporate accounting systems, such as order entry and invoicing.

**ial Balance:** listing of all account balances from general ledger used in preparing financial statements.

**uck Jobber:** wholesale merchant who sells and delivers products from truck inventory at time of sale. Also called *Wagon Distributor.*

**ust:** right to real or personal property that is held by one for benefit of another.

**ust Company:** business that acts as fiduciary and agent, handling trusts, estates, and guardianships for individuals and businesses.

**ustee:** one who holds or is entrusted with management of property or funds for benefit of another.

**ustee in Bankruptcy:** person appointed by court or elected by creditors to manage bankrupt property and carry out responsibilities of trust in proceedings.

**ust Receipt:** trust agreement (in receipt form) between a financial institution and borrower. It is temporarily substituted for possessory collateral securing creditor's loan so that creditor may release instruments, documents, or other property without releasing title to property. Borrower agrees to keep property (collateral), as well as any funds received from its sale, separate and distinct from borrower's own property and subject to repossession by the financial institution in event that he or she fails to comply with conditions specified in trust agreement.

**uth in Lending Act of 1968:** See *Regulation Z.*

**rnkey:** something that is constructed, supplied, or installed and fully ready as intended.

## U

**CC:** see *Uniform Commercial Code.*

**tra Vires:** unauthorized acts taken by corporation beyond powers conferred on it by corporate charter.

**Umbrella Policy:** in liability insurance, policy that applies excess coverage to primary or underlying contract; provides large limits and broad coverage or may cover only primary basis risks not otherwise insured.

**Unaudited Financial Statement:** financial statement or report based on figures that have not been verified by a qualified accountant.

**Uncollected Funds:** deposits not yet collected by a financial institution, such as checks that have not yet cleared.

**Uncollectible Accounts:** receivables or debts not capable of being settled or recovered.

**Underwriter:** 1. person who reviews application for insurance and decides whether or not to accept risk. 2. one who agrees to purchase entire issue of bonds or securities at end of certain period.

**Undue Influence:** improper or illegal pressure used to wrongfully take advantage of person or to influence his or her actions or decisions.

**Unearned Discount:** A term used to reflect a reduced price (from the face value of an invoice) taken by a buyer without the consent of the seller.

**Unearned Income:** income received in advance of being earned.

**Unencumbered Property:** property that has no legal defects in its title; a property free and clear of any liens or debts.

**Unenforceable Claim:** debt on which all collection efforts have failed.

**Unfair Competition:** any fraudulent or dishonest practice intended to harm or unfairly attract competitor's customers.

**Uniform Commercial Code (UCC):** comprehensive set of statutes created to provide uniformity in business laws in all states, as approved by National Conference of Commissioners on Uniform State Laws. Statutes can vary from state to state.

**Unit Banking:** banking system in several states that prohibits branching or operation of more than one full-service banking office by state-chartered or national banks. Limited branching laws encourage chartering of large numbers of small, independently owned state banks and large multi-bank holding companies that own numerous unit banks.

**Unjust Enrichment:** doctrine whereby one is not allowed to profit inequitably at another's expense.

**Unsatisfied Judgment:** recorded judgment that has not been released or discharged.

**Unsecured Creditor:** one who grants credit without taking collateral in support of it.

**Unsecured Loan:** loan made on strength of borrower's general financial condition. Contrasts with Secured Loan.

**Upstream Funding:** funds borrowed by a subsidiary of a holding company for holding company's use. Contrasts with Downstream Funding.

**Usury:** The rate of interest that exceeds the legal limit allowed to be charged for the use of another's money. Legal limit of interest for different types of loan transactions is established by state law.

## V

**Valuable Consideration:** see *Consideration.*

**Valuation:** 1. the estimated or determined worth of something. 2. process of appraising or affixing value of something.

**Value Received:** phrase used in bill of exchange or promissory note to denote that lawful consideration has been given.

**Variable Interest Rate:** interest rate that fluctuates with changes in an identified base rate or index.

**Vendor:** trade supplier or service provider.

**Venture Capital:** capital invested or available for investment in the ownership element of a new enterprise.

**Verdict:** formal decision of judge or jury on matter submitted in trial.

**Verification:** 1. affidavit or statement under oath swearing to truth or accuracy of written document. 2. in accounting, confirmation of entries in books of account.

**Verification of Deposit (VOD):** formal request by creditor to debtor's bank for account balance information.

**Vest:** 1. to give immediate transfer of title to property. 2. to obtain absolute ownership.

**VOD:** see *Verification of Deposit.*

**Void:** having no legal force.

**Voidable Contract:** contract that is nullified as to party who committed invalid act but not with respect to other party, unless he or she agrees to treat it as such.

**Voluntary Bankruptcy:** bankruptcy initiated by debtor petitioning court to be declared bankrupt.

**Voucher:** 1. statement itemizing payment or receipt of money. 2. detachable portion of check that describes purpose for which check was issued.

## W

**Wage Assignment:** agreement by borrower that permits creditor to collect certain portion of borrower's wages from employer in the event of a default.

**Wage Garnishment:** court order requiring that percentage of debtor's earnings be withheld by employer and paid directly to creditor.

**Waiver:** intentional or voluntary relinquishing of known legal right.

**Warehouse Loans:** loans made against warehouse receipts that are evidence of collateral for material stored in public warehouse.

**Warehouse Receipt:** receipt issued by person engaged in business of storing goods for hire. It is document of title that gives evidence that person in possession of warehouse receipt is entitled to receive, hold, and dispose of document and goods it covers. Warehouse receipt in turn obligates warehouser to keep goods safely and to redeliver them upon surrender of receipt, properly endorsed, and payment of storage charges.

**Wholesaler:** company whose primary function is as intermediary between manufacturer of goods and retailer or other wholesalers.

**Will:** legal declaration by person making disposition of property, effective only after death.

**Windfall Profit:** large, unexpected return or income.

**Wire Fate:** instructions to financial institution requesting confirmation by wire that out-of-town check, sent for collection, has been paid.

**Without Exception:** see *Free and Clear*.

**Without Prejudice:** legal term used in offer, motion, or suit to indicate that parties' rights or privileges involved remain intact and to allow new suit to be brought on same cause of action.

**Without Recourse:** term used in endorsing negotiable instrument excluding endorser from responsibility should obligation not be paid.

**With Prejudice:** legal term used for dismissal of lawsuit that bars any future action and that, if prosecuted to final adjudication, would have been adverse to plaintiff.

**With Recourse:** endorsement of negotiable instrument on which endorser remains responsible should obligation not be paid.

**Working Capital:** 1. current assets less current liabilities, used as measure of firm's liquidity. 2. funds available to finance company's current operations.

**Working Papers:** information or schedules used by accountant in preparing financial reports.

**Work in Process (WIP):** goods in act of being manufactured, but not yet finished and ready for sale, representing a portion of inventory.

**Workout:** problem loan on which the financial institution is working closely with borrower for repayment, restructuring, or modification because of noncompliance with loan covenants.

**Wrap-Around Mortgage:** A second or junior mortgage with a face value of both the amount it secures and the balance due under the first mortgage. Covenant contained within second mortgage used to induce sellers of commercial properties to sell to buyer who has small down payment, normally when interest rates are high.

**Writ of Execution:** 1. writ issued by court ordering sheriff to attach debtor's property to enforce payment of judgment.

**Write-down:** partial reduction in book value of asset as result of obsolescence or depreciation.

**Write-off:** see *Charge-off*.

**Writ of Attachment:** court order directing sheriff to seize property of debtor held as security for satisfaction of judgment.

## Y

**Yield:** rate of return on investment.

## Z

**Zero Balance Account:** a checking account (subordinate account) used for disbursing or collecting funds in which no balances are maintained. At the end of the processing day, funds are transferred from a master account or concentration account to cover activity in the subordinate account.

**Zoning Ordinance:** municipal regulation dividing land into districts and prescribing structural, architectural, and nature of use of buildings within these districts.

# NOTES

# NOTES

# NOTES

# NOTES

# NOTES

# NOTES

# NOTES

# NOTES

# NOTES

# NOTES

# NOTES

# NOTES